the
AMERICANA ANNUAL

1973

AN ENCYCLOPEDIA OF THE EVENTS OF 1972
YEARBOOK OF THE ENCYCLOPEDIA AMERICANA

THE AMERICANA ANNUAL
EDITORIAL STAFF

contents

FEATURE ARTICLES OF THE YEAR

Contributors—**Martin E. Marty, Richard E. Wentz, James H. Smylie, Joe Hale,** and **Vinson Synan.** Five authorities report on the return of revivalism, with particular emphasis on young people. One section reviews the history of revivalism in America.

Contributors—**Sen. Edward M. Kennedy, Jerome F. Brazda, Dr. Charles A. Hoffman,** and **Brian Abel-Smith.** Both the administration and the Democrats have bills pending in Congress to provide some type of health-care protection, but they differ sharply in their basic approach to the problem. Senator Kennedy and the president of the AMA explain their views.

Contributors—**Bernard Gwertzman, Dr. David F. Musto,** and **Nelson G. Gross.** The deadly traffic in narcotics crisscrosses the globe. This report traces the major patterns of that traffic and discusses the steps that are being taken to choke it off.

Contributors—**Robert H. Lindsey, Lt. Gen. Benjamin O. Davis, Jr.,** and **Capt. John J. O'Donnell.** Skyjackers struck terror among airline passengers in increasing numbers in 1972. A new technique, the use of aerial hijacking for ransom, became more common. Included in this report are the views of the federal government and the airline pilots.

Contributor—**Larry Evans.** Chess captured headlines around the world in 1972, thanks to the world championship match between Bobby Fischer and Boris Spassky. In this report, an international chess grandmaster analyzes the match and explains what chess is all about.

SPECIAL REPORTS

classified listing of articles

Regular articles in this volume appear in alphabetical order in the Review of the Year, beginning on page 59. For the convenience of the reader, the articles listed below are grouped in broad subject categories. In addition, separate entries on the nations of the world, U. S. states and territories, and Canadian provinces will be found under their own alphabetically arranged headings.

BIOGRAPHIES

CITIES

CONTINENTS AND MAJOR REGIONS

classified listing (continued)

ECONOMICS, BUSINESS, AND INDUSTRY

EDUCATION

ENTERTAINMENT AND HOBBIES

GOVERNMENT, LAW, AND POLITICS

HUMAN WELFARE

HUMANITIES AND THE ARTS

MEDICINE AND HEALTH

MILITARY AFFAIRS

RELIGION

SCIENCE

SUPRANATIONAL ORGANIZATIONS

MISCELLANEOUS

preface

Although it may be premature to speak of the end of the Cold War, the year 1972 may well be identified by historians as the turning point in the struggle between East and West. Not since the end of World War II, in whose ruins the postwar conflict was spawned, have world leaders shown such a spirit of reconciliation and accord as they demonstrated in the year just concluded.

Running through the pages of this 51st edition of THE AMERICANA ANNUAL is the theme of bridge-building. Around the world, governments were reaching out to patch up old quarrels and to settle some of the differences that have polarized the world for more than a quarter century. Seemingly inspired by the example of President Nixon's two historic journeys to Peking and Moscow, the bastions of world communism, national leaders in Europe and Asia were moving to resolve conflicts that have kept the world in a state of tension and crisis since 1945.

Climaxing this trend toward accommodation were the two most significant arms-control agreements of the nuclear age, signed in Moscow in May. The treaty limiting antiballistic missiles and the interim agreement freezing offensive strategic missiles at current levels not only marked a milestone in themselves but gave rise to hopes that the world's two superpowers might at last be dampening the costly and dangerous arms race.

In Germany, which has served as the focal point for East-West confrontation during much of the history of the Cold War, the year saw the culmination of efforts to establish normal relations between the two parts of the divided country. The signing of a treaty by East and West Germany, in which each pledged to respect the other's independence and sovereignty, represented vast progress from the days when Soviet and American tanks faced each other in the heart of Berlin.

Similarly from Korea, which provided a major battleground in the early phase of the Cold War, came surprising and heartening news. Negotiations between North and South Korea had advanced to the point where they were even discussing reunification, and both sides took steps to implement that goal.

But perhaps no single event of 1972 so symbolized this new climate of peaceful coexistence as the meeting in February of President Nixon and Chairman Mao. The handclasp between Nixon, once the redoubtable Cold War warrior, and Mao, a virtual demigod of communism, may have ushered in a new era in international affairs. And in the months following, many nations, notably Japan, moved to recognize China, that vast land which such a short time ago had stood isolated from the community of nations.

As the year ended, however, the continuing stalemates in Vietnam and the Middle East—each in its own way a product of the Cold War—reminded us that the millennium had not yet arrived. But now, as a result of the initiatives mentioned above, mankind might hope that a new and more rational order in world affairs was being born.

S. J. FODERARO, *Executive Editor*

Comdr. Ronald Evans photographed the first view of earth's disk in total sunlight as Apollo 17 sped moonward after launch on December 7. African coast is clearly visible.

CHRONOLOGY 1972

FIRE RAZES LINER 'QUEEN ELIZABETH'

BANGLADESH LEADER RETURNS

TROOPS KILL 13 IN LONDONDERRY

JANUARY

S	M	T	W	T	F	S
						1
2	3	4	5	6	7	8
9	10	11	12	13	14	15
16	17	18	19	20	21	22
23	24	25	26	27	28	29
30	31					

JANUARY

1 Entertainer Maurice Chevalier dies in Paris at 83.

2 Mrs. Richard M. Nixon begins one-week goodwill tour of African republics.

4 Senator Edmund S. Muskie (D., Me.) formally declares his candidacy for presidential nomination.

5 Pay Board rejects first major contract settlement under Phase II of U. S. Economic Stabilization Program, ruling against a 12% wage increase in the aerospace industry.

7 President Nixon announces himself a candidate for reelection. ● Iberia Airlines jet crashes on Mediterranean island of Ibiza, killing 104.

9 Former luxury liner *Queen Elizabeth,* largest passenger ship ever built, burns in Hong Kong harbor.

10 Sheikh Mujib (Mujibur Rahman), long a prisoner in West Pakistan, arrives in Bangladesh to assume leadership of new nation. ● U. S. naval task force withdraws from Indian Ocean. ● Sen. Hubert H. Humphrey (D., Minn.) enters presidential race.

13 Gov. George Wallace of Alabama joins Democratic presidential race, entering Florida primary.

14 King Frederick IX of Denmark dies at 72 in Copenhagen and is succeeded by daughter Margrethe, the nation's first reigning queen.

15 Malta's prime minister, Dom Mintoff, cancels demand for British troop withdrawal after talks.

16 Dallas Cowboys defeat Miami Dolphins, 24–3, in professional football's Super Bowl game in New Orleans.

18 British and European Common Market negotiators reach agreement on terms for Britain's entry into the European Economic Community (EEC).

22 Ten nations sign pact to enlarge the 6-member European Economic Community by adding Britain, Norway, Denmark, and Ireland.

24 President Nixon projects budget deficit of $25.5 billion in fiscal 1973, as estimated deficit for 1972 is raised to $38.8 billion. ● USSR becomes first nation to recognize Bangladesh.

25 Nixon reveals that unsuccessful secret negotiations with the North Vietnamese to end Indochina War had been held in late 1971.

30 British troops kill 13 as new rioting erupts in Londonderry, Northern Ireland. ● Pakistan quits Commonwealth of Nations as other Commonwealth countries prepare to recognize Bangladesh.

31 King Mahendra of Nepal dies at 51 in Katmandu.

UPI

The end of the Queen Elizabeth *nears as smoke billows from the former transatlantic luxury liner. She was in Hong Kong being refitted as a floating university when she caught fire on January 9 and capsized.*

FEBRUARY

S	M	T	W	T	F	S
		1	2	3	4	5
6	7	8	9	10	11	12
13	14	15	16	17	18	19
20	21	22	23	24	25	26
27	28	29				

PRESIDENT NIXON IN CHINA
JAPAN HOST TO WINTER OLYMPICS
BRITISH OK MARKET ENTRY

FEBRUARY

4 United States and European Economic Community (EEC) reach provisional agreement on trade.

7 Discovery of smallest known virus reported by pathologist Theodor O. Diener of U. S. Department of Agriculture.

8 Author Clifford Irving, who prepared a biography of Howard Hughes based on alleged interviews with the billionaire recluse, refuses to testify before grand jury.

11 At Paris meeting, French President Georges Pompidou and German Chancellor Willy Brandt reach broad accord on Common Market policy. ● U. S. and USSR announce plan to pool research on cancer, heart disease, and environmental problems.

13 Eleventh Winter Olympics are concluded in Sapporo, Japan; USSR wins top honors with 8 gold medals.

14 President Nixon announces that he will take steps to offset federal court decisions requiring extensive school busing to achieve racial balance.

15 John Mitchell resigns as U. S. attorney general to direct Nixon reelection campaign. ● José María Velasco, five-time president of Ecuador, overthrown by a military junta.

16 Census Bureau reports steep decline in the U. S. birthrate between 1967 and 1971.

17 British House of Commons approves Britain's entry into EEC by narrow margin of 9 votes.

18 California Supreme Court declares capital punishment to be unconstitutional in that state. ● Christian Democrat Giulio Andreotti forms minority government in Italy.

21 At beginning of first visit to China by a U. S. chief executive, President Nixon confers with Chairman Mao Tse-tung in Peking.

23 Argentina devalues peso as national economic crisis reaches its peak.

24 President and Mrs. Nixon visit Ming Tombs and the Great Wall of China.

25 British coal miners vote to end 47-day strike that had crippled the nation's economy and caused electric power shortages throughout island.

26 Flash flood sweeps through a valley in Logan county, W. Va., taking 118 lives.

28 Presidential party returns to Washington after Nixon and Chinese Premier Chou En-lai announce agreement on widening of Chinese-U. S. contacts and gradual U. S. withdrawal from Taiwan.

UPI

Visiting mainland China, February 21–28, President Nixon looks somewhat apprehensive as his glass is filled with potent Mao-tai (above) and as Premier Chou En-lai serves a special delicacy (below).

KEYSTONE

3

MARCH

S	M	T	W	T	F	S
			1	2	3	4
5	6	7	8	9	10	11
12	13	14	15	16	17	18
19	20	21	22	23	24	25
26	27	28	29	30	31	

MARCH

UPI

AFL-CIO President George Meany, who quit as member of the Pay Board on March 22, testifies before the Price Commission.

Lobbyist Dita Beard testifies from her bed in a Denver hospital, March 26, before the Senate Judicial Subcommittee.

UPI

3 U. S. Senate Judiciary Committee begins hearings into charge that Justice Department settled an antitrust suit against International Telephone and Telegraph Co. (ITT) after firm offered to help finance 1972 Republican Convention.

7 Muskie wins 45% plurality in Democratic presidential primary in New Hampshire, while Nixon takes nearly 80% of the Republican vote.

8 Clifford Irving and wife are indicted for grand larceny in connection with book on Howard Hughes.

9 Former Attorney General Mitchell denies that he told ITT lobbyist Dita Beard that President Nixon had ordered him to settle ITT case.

12 India's Congress party, led by Prime Minister Indira Ghandi, wins 70% of Assembly seats in national election. ● First National Black Political Convention, meeting in Gary, Ind., votes to establish National Black Assembly in United States.

14 Governor Wallace, stressing the issue of busing, wins Democratic presidential primary in Florida.

16 President Nixon says that he favors legislative "moratorium" on court-ordered busing of schoolchildren. ● President's Commission on Population Growth and the American Future recommends that states liberalize abortion laws.

21 Chiang Kai-shek wins fifth 6-year term as president of Nationalist China in uncontested election. ● Premier George Papadopoulos of Greece dismisses Gen. George Zitakis and assumes office of regent.

22 AFL-CIO head George Meany and other labor members quit 15-member Pay Board, claiming that it is "unfair." ● Congress approves constitutional amendment guaranteeing equal rights for women.

23 U. S. suspends Paris peace talks. ● President Nixon reconstitutes Pay Board as a 7-member public group. ● British Prime Minister Edward Heath announces intention to suspend provincial government and Parliament of Northern Ireland and impose direct rule.

26 President Fidel Sanchez Hernandez of El Salvador announces restoration of order after an attempted coup in which more than 100 are killed.

30 Parliament in Britain adopts enabling bill on direct rule, as Northern Ireland's Prime Minister Bryan Falkner and his cabinet resign.

31 South Vietnamese outposts near demilitarized zone are abandoned as North Vietnam launches new offensive.

APRIL						
S	M	T	W	T	F	S
						1
2	3	4	5	6	7	8
9	10	11	12	13	14	15
16	17	18	19	20	21	22
23	24	25	26	27	28	29
30						

NORTH VIETNAM PRESSES ATTACK
5,000 DIE IN IRAN QUAKE
APOLLO 16 IN LUNAR MOUNTAINS

APRIL

1 North Vietnamese and Vietcong troops surge into South Vietnam in major push on several fronts.

3 Moviemaker Charles Chaplin greeted warmly in New York on first U. S. visit after 20-year absence.

4 George McGovern (D., S. Dak.) scores his first major primary victory in Wisconsin; President Nixon takes 97% of Republican primary vote.

5 North Vietnamese drive toward Hue, Quangtri City, and Saigon.

7 Syndicated crime figure Joseph Gallo is assassinated in New York City restaurant.

9 Communist offensive is blunted west of Quangtri.

10 Some 5,000 perish in Iran earthquake. ● UN treaty banning stockpiling of "germ warfare" weapons is signed by U. S., USSR, and 68 other nations.

13 Justice Department announces plan to file antitrust suits against the three major television broadcasting companies.

14 President Nixon arrives in Ottawa for 2-day Canadian visit; addresses Parliament.

15 U. S. bombers strike North Vietnamese port of Haiphong for first time since March 1968. ● Major league baseball season begins after delay due to 10-day players' strike.

20 Apollo 16 astronauts land in the Descartes area of the moon during first manned mission to the lunar mountains.

23 Lunar module blasts off from moon and reunites with command craft for 4-day return trip to earth.

25 Administration reveals that presidential adviser Henry A. Kissinger has returned from secret trip to Moscow. ● Humphrey takes Pennsylvania primary; McGovern wins in Massachusetts. ● President Nixon announces that he is withdrawing more U. S. troops from Vietnam despite continued enemy offensive.

27 Senator Muskie discontinues active campaigning for presidential nomination. ● Kwame Nkruma, 62, former president of Ghana, dies in Conakry, Guinea. ● U. S. returns to Paris peace table. ● U. S. Senate committee ends ITT hearings, votes to recommend confirmation of Richard Kleindienst as attorney general.

UPI

Injured man wanders through rubble of his house in which rest of family died in earthquake that struck Iran, April 10.

NASA

Apollo 16 astronaut Charles M. Duke, Jr., stands beside Lunar Rover during April 22 exploration of moon's surface.

U.S. MINES HAIPHONG HARBOR
WALLACE SHOT AT POLITICAL RALLY
NIXON SIGNS PACTS IN MOSCOW

MAY

S	M	T	W	T	F	S
	1	2	3	4	5	6
7	8	9	10	11	12	13
14	15	16	17	18	19	20
21	22	23	24	25	26	27
28	29	30	31			

MAY

UPI

Attempting to assassinate Alabama Gov. George Wallace during presidential campaign rally in Laurel, Md., on May 15, Arthur Bremer fires pistol (above). *Injured Wallace lies on pavement* (below).

UPI

2 FBI Director J. Edgar Hoover dies at 77. ● Ottawa reveals plans to curb foreign takeovers of Canadian firms. ● In Democratic primaries, Humphrey defeats McGovern in Ohio and Wallace in Indiana. ● Fire in Idaho silver mine kills 91.

4 U. S. again withdraws from Paris peace talks.

6 Crash of Alitalia DC-8 near Palermo, Italy, kills 115. ● Riva Ridge wins 98th Kentucky Derby.

7 Los Angeles Lakers win NBA professional basketball title, downing the New York Knicks, 4 games to 1.

8 President Nixon announces that U. S. is mining Haiphong harbor and has begun to bomb communications and military installations in North Vietnam to disrupt enemy offensive in the south.

11 Boston Bruins defeat New York Rangers to win professional hockey's Stanley Cup playoffs, 4 games to 2.

15 Governor George C. Wallace is shot and gravely wounded by a would-be assassin at political rally in Laurel, Md. ● Okinawa is returned to Japan by the United States.

16 Doctors say Wallace is out of danger, although his legs remain paralyzed due to a spinal wound; he wins expected victories in Michigan and Maryland primaries. ● John B. Connally, former Democratic governor of Texas, resigns as secretary of the treasury.

17 Nonaggression treaties with USSR and Poland are approved by West Germany's Bundestag (parliament).

21 Michelangelo's *Pieta,* in St. Peter's basilica in Rome, is damaged by deranged Hungarian refugee.

22 President Nixon arrives in Moscow for summit meetings with Soviet leaders.

24 Soviet Premier Aleksei Kosygin and President Nixon sign pact for joint U. S.-Soviet space venture.

26 Two agreements, limiting defensive and offensive missile systems, are signed by Nixon and Chairman Leonid Brezhnev, climaxing months of U. S.-Soviet negotiations at SALT meetings in Helsinki.

27 Mark Donahue wins Indianapolis 500 auto race.

28 Duke of Windsor, the former King Edward VIII of England, dies in Paris at 77.

30 Three Japanese gunmen hired by Palestinian commandos kill 28 persons at Lod Airport near Tel Aviv, Israel. ● President Nixon visits Iran.

JUNE

S	M	T	W.	T	F	S
				1	2	3
4	5	6	7	8	9	10
11	12	13	14	15	16	17
18	19	20	21	22	23	24
25	26	27	28	29	30	31

REPORT 100,000 DEAD IN BURUNDI
BRITAIN FLOATS THE POUND
'AGNES' DEVASTATES WIDE AREA

JUNE

1 Iraq and Syria expropriate assets of Iraq Petroleum Company, a major consortium of Western firms. ● President Nixon concludes 24-hour visit to Poland after receiving enthusiastic welcome in Warsaw.

3 Reports from Africa estimate that over 100,000 have been massacred in Burundi during 5 weeks of fighting between the Tutsi and Hutu peoples.

4 California jury acquits black activist Angela Davis of charges of murder, kidnapping, and criminal conspiracy arising from a courtroom abduction and shoot-out in San Rafael in 1970.

6 Senator McGovern defeats Senator Humphrey in California's "winner-take-all" primary and acquires a long lead over other Democratic contenders. ● Coal mine explosion in Rhodesia takes 426 lives.

9-10 Flash flood hits Rapid City area of South Dakota, killing 239 and leaving hundreds homeless.

12 Right of poor defendants to free legal counsel, previously applying only to felony cases, is extended by U. S. Supreme Court to misdemeanor actions; "stop and frisk" police authority is also enlarged. ● Over 75,000 young participants in the Jesus Movement gather in Dallas, Texas, for 6-day religious meeting.

14 Pesticide DDT banned for nearly all agricultural and other uses by U. S. government.

17 Five men with electronic surveillance devices are seized at Democratic National Headquarters in Watergate Building, Washington, D. C. ● *Fiddler on the Roof* becomes longest-running show in Broadway history, staging its 3,225th New York performance.

18 Soviet President Podgorny ends 4-day visit to Hanoi, predicts resumption of Vietnam peace talks. ● Jack Nicklaus wins his third U. S. Open golf title at Pebble Beach, Calif.

20 Senator McGovern wins New York Democratic primary.

23 Britain announces that it is freeing the pound sterling from its official rate of exchange and allowing it to float on international money markets. ● Nixon signs higher education aid bill, criticizing its anti-busing provisions as inadequate. ● Tropical storm Agnes subsides after inundating 5,000 square miles of land in seven Southern and Northeastern states, killing 118, and causing over $3 billion property damage (June 16–23).

27 President Nguyen Van Thieu of South Vietnam is voted authority to rule by decree for 6 months.

30 Congress approves 20% increase in Social Security benefits.

Tropical storm Agnes struck Pennsylvania on June 23. Harrisburg (below) and Wilkes-Barre sustained most flood damage.

KEYSTONE/LARRY DALTON

TANAKA NAMED IN JAPAN
DEMOCRATS PICK McGOVERN
EAGLETON LEAVES TICKET

			JULY			
S	M	T	W	T	F	S
						1
2	3	4	5	6	7	8
9	10	11	12	13	14	15
16	17	18	19	20	21	22
23	24	25	26	27	28	29
30	31					

JULY

1 Former Attorney General John N. Mitchell resigns as President Nixon's campaign manager.

3 Prime Minister Indira Ghandi of India and President Zulfikar Ali Bhutto of Pakistan sign wide-ranging agreement in Simla, India, ending diplomatic impasse caused by 1971 India-Pakistan War.

4 North and South Korean leaders announce agreement on plan for eventual reunification of Korea.

5 Ruling Liberal-Democratic party in Japan elects Kakuei Tanaka to succeed Eisaku Sato as premier. ● President Pompidou forces resignation of Jacques Chaban-Delmas and installs Pierre Messmer as premier of France.

7 Patriarch Athenagoras I, leader of 125 million Eastern Orthodox Christians, dies in Istanbul at 86.

8 Washington announces 3-year U.S.-Soviet trade agreement calling for sale of at least $750 million worth of grain to the USSR.

10 Democratic National Convention opens in Miami Beach.

13 Senator McGovern wins presidential nomination on the first ballot.

14 Democrats name McGovern's choice, Sen. Thomas F. Eagleton (D., Mo.), as their vice presidential nominee.

18 President Anwar el-Sadat of Egypt orders the withdrawal of Soviet military advisers and experts from his country.

19 AFL-CIO Executive Council votes to withhold its support from McGovern and urges a neutral stance for labor in 1972 presidential contest.

23 First unmanned Earth Resources Technology Satellite (ERTS-1) is launched to monitor global environment.

24 UN Secretary General Kurt Waldheim appeals to U.S. to halt bombing of dikes in North Vietnam.

25 Senator Eagleton reveals that he was hospitalized three times for "nervous exhaustion and depression" before 1966 and admits that he did not inform McGovern at time of his selection as vice presidential nominee.

31 Eagleton quits Democratic ticket after conferring with McGovern. ● Belgian statesman Paul-Henri Spaak, an architect of postwar European unity, dies in Brussels at 73.

Democratic presidential nominee Sen. George McGovern (right) and his original running mate, Sen. Thomas Eagleton, greet the convention on July 14.

AUGUST

S	M	T	W	T	F	S
		1	2	3	4	5
6	7	8	9	10	11	12
13	14	15	16	17	18	19
20	21	22	23	24	25	26
27	28	29	30	31		

BREMER GETS 63-YEAR TERM
ASIANS EXPELLED FROM UGANDA
GOP RENOMINATES NIXON

AUGUST

3 State of emergency declared in Britain due to dock strike. ● Senate approves U. S.-Soviet accord limiting each nation to two defensive missile sites.

4 Arthur H. Bremer is found guilty of shooting Governor Wallace and is sentenced to 63-year prison term.

5 McGovern selects R. Sargent Shriver, former director of Peace Corps, as new vice presidential running mate. ● Tens of thousands of Asian residents of Uganda are ordered to leave country within 3 months.

9 Senate votes to ban snub-nosed handguns of the type used in George Wallace and Robert Kennedy shootings.

12 Last U. S. ground combat troops leave South Vietnam.

14 Chief justice Warren E. Burger suggests abolition of 3-judge federal district courts. ● Crash of East German airliner in Berlin takes 156 lives; toll is second-largest in history of civil air disasters.

17 Morocco's minister of defense, Gen. Mohammed Oufkir, commits suicide after previous day's failure of military assassination attempt against King Hassan II. ● Under administration pressure, General Motors reduces proposed price increases on 1973 cars. ● First success in growing mature, fertile hybrid plants from artificially fused cells is announced in U. S.

18 House approves offensive missile pact with Soviets.

21 Republican National Convention convenes in Miami.

22 President Nixon renominated by GOP; delegates adopt 1976 convention rules favoring the smaller states.

26 General Accounting Office asks Justice Department investigation of possible violations of Election Campaign Act by Nixon campaign finance committee. ● Twentieth Summer Olympic Games begin in Munich with 7,000 athletes from 121 nations competing.

28 Nixon promises to end draft by July 1973 if Congress enacts a new military pay bill by that date.

After being renominated, President Nixon and Vice President Agnew share the platform of the Republican convention with their wives on August 23.

UPI

FISCHER WINS CHESS TITLE
11 ISRAELIS KILLED AT OLYMPICS
JAPAN, CHINA REACH ACCORD

SEPTEMBER

S	M	T	W	T	F	S
					1	2
3	4	5	6	7	8	9
10	11	12	13	14	15	16
17	18	19	20	21	22	23
24	25	26	27	28	29	30

SEPTEMBER

1 Bobby Fischer becomes first American chess champion of the world, defeating Boris Spassky of the USSR by 12½ points to 8½ in match at Reykjavík, Iceland. ● President Nixon and Premier Tanaka of Japan conclude 3-day meeting in Hawaii. ● Prime Minister Trudeau calls Canadian general election for October 30.

4 American swimmer Mark Spitz breaks all-time Olympic record by capturing a 7th gold medal. ● Kalevi Sorsa forms new 4-party coalition government in Finland.

5 Eleven members of Israel's Olympic team are killed in kidnap attempt by 8 Arab terrorists in Munich; 5 terrorists and a policeman also die in airport shoot-out.

8 Israeli planes bomb 10 Arab guerrilla bases in Syria and Lebanon in reprisal for Munich murders.

9 Secretary of Agriculture Earl L. Butz denies charge that administration leaks about U. S.-Soviet trade negotiations led to windfall profits for grain dealers.

11 Olympic Games end in Munich; Soviet athletes lead with 99 medals; U. S. is second.

12 Senate passes revenue-sharing measure calling for grants of $33.5 billion to state and local governments over 5-year period. ● Lieut. Gen. John D. Lavelle tells Senate Armed Services Committee that superiors had approved air raids on North Vietnam ordered in 1971.

14 Senate approves U. S.-Soviet offensive missile pact.

15 Seven men, including 2 former Nixon aides, are indicted on conspiracy charges in Watergate case.

17 Two-day Israeli ground invasion of Lebanon ends. ● Uganda reports invasion by 1,000 Tanzanian troops.

19 Israeli diplomat in London is killed by exploding envelope in bombs-by-mail terror campaign.

21 U. S. and Soviets agree to undertake 30 joint environmental projects in both countries.

23 President Ferdinand Marcos imposes martial law in the Philippines after a renewal of terrorism.

25 Kakuei Tanaka, first Japanese premier to visit Chinese mainland since World War II, flies to Peking.

26 Norwegian voters reject membership in European Economic Community. ● U. S. proposes broad reform of world monetary system, with more flexible exchange rates.

29 Premiers of Japan and China sign communiqué restoring diplomatic relations.

Memorial service for the 11 Israeli Olympic athletes murdered by Arab terrorists was held in the Olympic Stadium in Munich, September 6. Eighty thousand persons attended.

UPI

OCTOBER

S	M	T	W	T	F	S
1	2	3	4	5	6	7
8	9	10	11	12	13	14
15	16	17	18	19	20	21
22	23	24	25	26	27	28
29	30	31				

176 KILLED ON SOVIET PLANE

JACKIE ROBINSON DEAD AT 53

TRUDEAU SUFFERS ELECTION SETBACK

OCTOBER

2 Denmark approves entry into the European Economic Community in national referendum.

5 Train crash in Saltillo, Mexico, leaves at least 208 dead and 630 hurt.

12 U. S. presidential adviser Henry Kissinger returns from four days of private talks with North Vietnamese negotiator Le Duc Tho in Paris; hints that a settlement of the Indochina War is near.

13 Soviet Aeroflot Ilyushan-62 crashes in Moscow, killing all 176 persons aboard in the worst civil air disaster in history.

17 President Park Chung Hee proclaims martial law in South Korea; the U. S. voices disapproval.

18 U. S. and USSR sign agreement expected to bring trade to $1 billion annually by 1980; U. S. Senate threatens to block confirmation if Russians retain exit fees for Jews seeking to emigrate.

19 Nixon discloses plan to limit federal spending to $250 billion in 1972 despite refusal of Congress to set a spending ceiling.

20 U. S. Defense Department concedes U. S. bomb struck French mission in Hanoi on October 11.

21 North Vietnamese Premier Phan Van Dong says his government is ready to accept a cease-fire.

23 U. S. presidential adviser Henry Kissinger returns from South Vietnam after 5 days of secret talks with President Nguyen Van Thieu and other South Vietnamese and Cambodian officials.

24 Jackie Robinson, the first black baseball player in the major leagues, dies at 53. ● Thieu terms Paris peace proposals unacceptable. ● Chileans observe "day of silence" organized by anti-Marxist opposition to programs of President Salvador Allende.

26 Henry Kissinger confirms French and North Vietnamese reports that the U. S. and Hanoi had reached overall agreement on a 9-point plan to end the war; North Vietnam demands cease-fire by October 31.

27 President Nixon vetoes 9 social welfare, public works, and ecology bills as being too costly.

29 U. S. administration spokesmen say the Indochina peace accord will not be signed by October 31. ● Palestinian guerrillas hijack a German airliner and win release of three commandos accused of participation in slayings at the Munich Olympic Games.

30 Canadian Prime Minister Pierre Trudeau loses his parliamentary majority in general elections.

UPI

The body of baseball immortal Jackie Robinson is carried from the church after his funeral on October 27. The lead pallbearers are basketball star Bill Russell (left) and Don Newcombe (right), one of Robinson's teammates on the old Brooklyn Dodgers. Roy Campanella, another Dodger teammate, is in the wheelchair.

NOVEMBER

S	M	T	W	T	F	S
			1	2	3	4
5	6	7	8	9	10	11
12	13	14	15	16	17	18
19	20	21	22	23	24	25
26	27	28	29	30		

NOVEMBER

2 Prime Minister Trudeau of Canada refuses to resign despite election losses and says he will await session of Parliament to see if his government can stay in power.

3 Three weeks of strikes end in Chile following cabinet reshuffle and concessions by President Allende.

4 Bangladesh National Assembly approves new constitution to take effect on December 16; elections scheduled for March 1973. ● North and South Korea agree to end propaganda campaigns and sign accords in moves toward eventual reunification.

6 Prime Minister Heath announces a 90-day wage-price freeze to help stem tide of rampant inflation in Britain. ● East and West Germany complete negotiations on treaty to establish relations and clear way for their entry into UN.

7 President Nixon wins re-election in landslide victory, defeating George McGovern with 60.8% of the popular vote; Democrats retain control of House and Senate.

8 Several hundred American Indians leave Washington headquarters of Bureau of Indian Affairs, which they seized on November 2 to dramatize complaints over "broken treaties" and official neglect.

10 Maj. Gen. Alexander M. Haig, Henry Kissinger's deputy, arrives in Saigon for talks with Thieu.

14 Dow Jones industrial average closes above 1,000 for the first time in stock exchange history.

16 Hungary, Poland, Indonesia, and Canada agree to serve on Vietnam cease-fire unit.

17 Former dictator Juan D. Perón returns to Argentina after 17 years of exile.

20 Chancellor Willie Brandt's coalition government is re-elected in West Germany.

21 Heaviest fighting in two years breaks out between Israel and Syria in the Golan Heights.

25 Henry Kissinger and North Vietnamese representative Le Duc Tho recess Paris peace talks after 6 days.

27 U. S. Secretary of Housing and Urban Development George Romney and Secretary of Defense Melvin Laird resign in cabinet reshuffle.

28 Elliot L. Richardson nominated as secretary of defense; Casper W. Weinberger named to succeed him as secretary of health, education and welfare.

30 Peter J. Brennan, construction trade union leader, is nominated to be U. S. secretary of labor.

UPI

President and Mrs. Nixon and Vice President and Mrs. Agnew appear at a victory rally at Republican party election night headquarters in Washington, D. C., early on November 8. Tricia Nixon Cox applauds in background.

DECEMBER

S	M	T	W	T	F	S
					1	2
3	4	5	6	7	8	9
10	11	12	13	14	15	16
17	18	19	20	21	22	23
24	25	26	27	28	29	30
31						

WHITLAM WINS AUSTRALIAN VOTE
APOLLO 17 LANDS ON MOON
NICARAGUAN QUAKE KILLS 10,000

DECEMBER

1 Irish Parliament approves legislation to crack down on I. R. A. after Dublin bombing stirs public feeling.

2 Labor party, led by Edward Gough Whitlam, wins Australian elections, ousting coalition of Liberal and Country parties that ruled for 23 years.

4 Henry Kissinger and Le Duc Tho resume Paris talks.

5 James T. Lynn, undersecretary of commerce, is nominated as secretary of housing and urban development.

7 Apollo 17 blasts off for the moon with astronauts Eugene Cernan, Ronald Evans, and Harrison Schmitt aboard in last manned flight of Apollo series. ● Claude S. Brinegar, a California oil executive, is named secretary of transportation. ● Irish voters end favored status of Roman Catholic Church in Ireland.

9 Premier Tanaka's Liberal Democratic party gains victory in Japanese elections. ● Robert Strauss, Texas lawyer and businessman, elected Democratic national chairman, replacing Mrs. Jean Westwood.

10 Astronauts Cernan and Schmitt land on moon in valley near Taurus Mountains and begin 3 days of explorations and experiments.

13 Henry Kissinger and Le Duc Tho conclude round of talks on Vietnam truce without reaching accord.

14 Juan Perón leaves Argentina after 28-day return visit; refuses to accept nomination for presidency.

18 U. S. resumes heavy bombing of Haiphong and Hanoi.

19 Apollo 17 splashes down on target in the Pacific.

21 East and West Germany sign treaty opening new ties but stopping short of full diplomatic relations.

22 Australia and New Zealand announce establishment of diplomatic relations with China, breaking ties with Taiwan.

23 Earthquake destroys Managua, capital of Nicaragua, killing an estimated 10,000 persons.

26 Former President Harry S. Truman dies at age 88 in Independence, Mo.

30 Halt in bombing north of 20th parallel in Vietnam is announced by White House; Kissinger-Tho talks to resume January 8; loss of 15 B-52 bombers acknowledged.

31 Roberto Clemente, star outfielder for the Pittsburgh Pirates, dies in plane crash off Puerto Rico en route to Nicaragua with relief supplies.

Managua, Nicaragua, Christmas Day, 1972. Approximately 80% of the city was destroyed by a series of earthquakes on December 23, and thousands lost their lives.

GAMMA/BUREAU

UPI

UPI

"EXPLO '72," sponsored by the Campus Crusade for Christ International, was held in ` Dallas, Texas, in June. The events included a music festival, staged near downtown Dallas (top); a mass Bible reading (above); and a revival meeting (opposite page) whose high spirits the rain could not dampen.

UPI

That Old-Time Religion Again

By Martin E. Marty
Professor of Modern Church History,
University of Chicago

Revivalism is back in favor in America. Temporarily eclipsed in the war decade of the 1940's, it returned in genteel fashion during the Eisenhower era. Obscured in the 1960's by the excitement of the racial and peace movements, by radical dissent and the pop-mysticism of the Age of Aquarius—revivalism receives notice again in the 1970's. This time its appearance is not quite so genteel and routine, though before long the new-style evangelism may be settling down into predictable patterns. Observers of the American scene frequently are puzzled about how revivals come and go.

Background. By evangelism and revivalism most people mean the whole range of ways in which efforts are made to enlarge and vivify the circle of converts to Jesus Christ. These efforts are older than the nation itself. The First Great Awakening, for example, began in the late 1720's, and several other Great and many lesser Awakenings have since made their presence felt. The preachers and those who hit the sawdust

trail or gathered at the river with them were in the habit of expecting revival pendulums to swing. The fortunes of evangelism, they might say, may be low for a moment. But the faithful would be asked to wait: before long, hearts would again be warmed and lives would be made holy. God's Holy Spirit picks his season.

Ordinarily it was the outsider, the doubter, or the enemy of revivals who would predict their permanent demise when enthusiasm ebbed. However, in the 1960's a significant number of insiders, partisans of the Christian faith, claimed that never again would there be a season in which people would get emotional about Jesus and want their lives radically turned around in his name.

Re-create that moment, early in the 1960's. Not much revivalism was left. Billy Graham, the best-known leader of the 1950's kept attracting crowds, but he was characteristically dismissed as an exception. Who, it was asked, was Number Two? Who would be Graham's successor? In addition to the work of Graham, revivals were still practiced in depressed areas of the country, as in the hill country of Appalachia. Welfare programs and literacy, the skeptics surmised, would enlighten those ecstatic but mis-

15

The evangelical "Jesus Movement" that began in the 1960's continued in 1972. Here, "Jesus people" take part in a Christian Foundation service in Saugus, Calif.

guided folk. And cultural lag still operated in some Southern cities, where the less enlightened would pitch a tent and put up signs, attracting crowds for strident preachers of hellfire and damnation. But as education and affluence spread, that kind of scene would undoubtedly become extinct.

Christianity would not simply disappear, however. Some form of reference to the Bible, to Jesus Christ and the church, and probably—though many religious thinkers were less sure of this—to God, would survive. But these references would appear in a new setting. Enthusiasm would give way to reason; technology would be the new savior; the new city would be the substitute for the old church; the computer would liberate people. In place of personal piety, social action for the good of man would prevail.

The Youth Movement. Ten years after those prophecies of the early 1960's, the nation was two or three years into a new Christian revival of sorts. The mass media were fascinated—by the younger brothers and sisters of the very youth who 10 years earlier had seemed so serenely non-religious or who five years earlier were either feared as radicals or dismissed as pagan eccentrics. The television cameras focused on the junior element of the revival, "the Jesus Movement." Magazine reporters visited college campuses to find Roman Catholic counterparts in a movement called "neo-Pentecostalism." Instead of remaining regionally isolated in the south and

in the hills, the sound of evangelists' music, enhanced by a rock beat and high-decibel expressions of "soul," filled the air with *Amazing Grace*. Citified versions of the subject reached the stage in the form of *Jesus Christ Superstar* and *Godspell*.

The youth movement should not be regarded as the only sign of the spiritual awakening, but since it has attracted most attention it merits some analysis. The most noticed expressions occurred on the West Coast, particularly around the greater Los Angeles area. Evangelism had never really died out in that haven for disparate religious choices. But by 1970 it was attracting a surprising set of new people in a culture so often described as rootless, worldly, confused about values.

Before long, both in southern California and in the Bay area further north, word spread about the almost spontaneous combustion of revivalist groups. Some of them, retaining or adopting the external features of the "counter culture" or hippie world from which they had come, relished the name "Jesus freaks." They were known for eccentric apparel and hair styles; they chose to live in communes; they witnessed as "street people" to "straight people" in the cities. On campuses they confronted those who valued education. They turned their back on the churches.

Disguised behind this colorful screen are many less dramatic but possibly more durable

alternatives. The Campus Crusade for Christ International was able by the summer of 1972 to stage "Explo '72" in the Cotton Bowl in Dallas. There, about 80,000 young persons gathered to hear Billy Graham, to listen to rock music, and to engage in what looked like pep rallies. They also made ambitious plans to approach the nation and eventually the world with the word of Christ. The largely white gathering, which spoke very little about the physical needs of man and which virtually turned its back on the idea of social action in the name of Jesus, stressed conversion and the warmed heart.

The participants were not conventional outcasts of society. Instead, these were well-scrubbed, well-dressed, well-mannered sons and daughters of American suburbia. They were seeking an alternative to the cool Christianity of their parents' world and turning their backs on the congregations at home that seemed too highly organized, too impersonal, too unenthusiastic about Jesus.

Pentecostalism. Almost simultaneously with "Explo '72," about 12,000 Catholic neo-Pentecostalists gathered. They came not to an old Catholic ghetto, where what looked like superstition could be expected. Their locale was the campus of the University of Notre Dame in South Bend, Ind. Once again, the crowd was largely white and obviously middle class in makeup. Pentecostalists believe in the direct witness through them of God's Holy Spirit. Some of them have the "gift" of speaking ecstatically in unintelligible tongues (known as glossolalia). Others engage in prayerful healing activities. Nothing gets too far out of hand, but it is clear that these college-bred people expect deeper and warmer piety than their home parishes have often given them.

The Nature of the New Revivalism. Billy Graham crusades, Jesus freak communes, Explo-sized rallies, Catholic Pentecostal conferences—these are only a few of the many forms the new Christian revival is taking. The manifestations are colorful, obvious, easily and frequently reported on. More important are the questions about the reasons for the revival, concerns about its character and quality, its meaning and impact, its survival possibilities.

To some, the whole movement represented merely a breakdown of Western values. Instead of becoming ever more secular (simply preoccupied with this world) and rational, at times people cannot bear the strain of events and retreat into otherworldly religion and irrational ecstasy. Those who hold this opinion believe it is easy to see why the breakdown occurred. The assassinations of heroes, the frustrations of the civil rights movement, the morally pointless war in Vietnam, the infinitely complex moral and social issues of the day, the extremism of those who would change the world—all these shattered old dreams. A new generation had to start over.

Another set of observers never has believed that the human race is almost inevitably destined to become ever increasingly secular and rational. No, they say, man is by nature religious. That is, people have to make sense of a wonderful and terrifying universe. They have to deal with mystery and they have to seek meaning in order to function.

These observers, looking back, often say that they could have foreseen the Jesus revival in American Christianity. The Age of Aquarius has provided plenty of preparation for an outbreak of fervent spirituality. It must be remembered that when the secular-rational dream began to die in the mid-1960's, there had been an explosion of non-Christian religious energies. Magic was back, as were mysticism and metaphysics. People were attracted to the occult, and astrology was believed "religiously." In communes, on campuses, and in suburbs, Eastern religion was taken seriously. Many favored Zen Buddhism or yoga, or they followed Indian leaders into "transcendental meditation." American Indian awe for nature and tribalism served as models for others. High regard for African spirituality and American blacks' "soul" religion was not restricted to the black community, though it was that community which brought African modes of spirituality to the attention of non-blacks.

Eventually the quest turned back "home," to the American Protestant family album. On its pages were souvenirs of the Jesus-way, and people dusted them off and displayed them again. This school of thought would say that the revival is simply Western young peoples' way of reacting to a too-frantic and complex world, that it is a retreat into emotion.

Advocates of the movement do not resort to such confusing cultural explanations. Most of them are content to keep it simple: the revival in most of its forms is simply a supernatural intervention in history by God. His Holy Spirit picks the times and seasons for awakenings. Jesus Christ comes suddenly and spontaneously. To analyze the movement is to seek to explain it away in human terms.

Appeal of the Movement. One of the most obvious appeals of the movement is the fact that it provides what has been called "the immediate experience." If people wish to be religious at all in the 1970's, it is reasoned, they want to be able to feel religious. They are not content to hear the theologians interpret mysteries; they do not want bureaucrats to administer institutions

of piety. They are restless when they hear stories about the experiences of prophets or apostles or mystics only to be told that such experiences belong to the past. They want the experience themselves, and will not be denied. Almost every version of the Jesus revival includes emotion—stirring music, enthusiastic witness, fervency, and even ecstasy.

The movement, further, offers personal concern. The mass elements are there, but the test comes when people feel that they are important, that God singles them out and Jesus signals to them directly. They reinforce this by showing personal regard for each other. The "freaks" form communes, the Campus Crusade develops cells, the Pentecostalists favor prayer groups. Each person matters—an attractive feature in an often coldly impersonal world where people are numbered, programmed, computed, even in the name of God.

Some of the appeal lies in the simple philosophy of history that the revival offers. People often seem to need to know the meaning of history. Evangelistic Christianity in America for at least a century has favored "premillennial" views of history. They build on biblical texts which picture a thousand-year reign of Christ, and expect it to come after a period of great turmoil.

The talk about a "big bang" end to the world as it is now known is often called "apocalyptic." Apocalyptic thought tends to be simplistic; the world's problems will eventually be done away with. The parallel thought among many apocalypticists, then, runs like this: Why bother with efforts to do away with poverty and war? Of course, one should be personally moral and humane, but he or she should do this apart from politics. Human engineering will not bring progress or paradise. God will intervene and then all will be well. To the extent that this kind of thinking reaches into the revival, it has been criticized even by conservative Protestants who believe Christians have social responsibility.

Assessment. The most vehement critics of the movement connect this simplifying view of history with uglier themes. The Jesus people want to escape from freedom into authoritarianism. "Thus saith the Lord!" is used to justify every kind of prejudice and prejudgment. They are psychologically confused, misguided, and misled people who in the face of complexity have "short-circuited."

Anti-institutionalism is one of the features of the revival. Most devotees oppose routine religious organizations; the "freaks" are violently opposed to these institutions, and the straighter types are mildly uneasy about them.

What are the alternatives? The rational Christian prefers reasoned, thought-out faith. The developmental believer thinks it would be better to seek quiet nurture and personal growth in grace and not such a sudden emotional overload, one which can cause imbalance and eventual reaction. The social action-minded church member believes that Christ calls people into service in the world and is not so concerned with people's saying, "Lord, Lord!" The liberal Christian sees ties between the revival and old-style fundamentalism, and he regrets that as being obscurantist. Few of these critics have mounted a full-scale attack on the revival. They give evidence that they can tolerate it, believing that its worst features may well be ephemeral and will soon pass away. What is valuable may remain, may develop into spiritual energies that can be put to work in various ways.

Few except the most ardent believe that all the forms will survive. The extreme converts seem to disappear as fast as they come. Some of the more stand-offish give signs that, anti-institutional though they may be, they will organize institutions of their own. The best guess, if past examples are a guide, is that after the initial ferment has subsided the more durable effects will be felt in the existing denominations and congregations, which will be subtly transformed. Key 73, for example, the evangelistic campaign planned for 1973, will do what it can to channel the movement's energies into existing churches.

The least that can be said is that, whatever the reason for its appearance, the revival caught most people off guard and has meant much to its advocates. Both enemies and friends of the movement are making significant if not always subtle contributions to the debates over the nature of humans—their makeup and fears and dreams.

A SELECTION OF BOOKS ON REVIVALISM
General Works
McLoughlin, William G., Jr., Modern Revivalism, Charles Grandison Finney to Billy Graham (Ronald Press 1959).
Marty, Martin E., The New Shape of American Religion (Harper 1958).
Marty, Martin E., The Righteous Empire: The Protestant Experience in America (Dial Press 1971).
Sherrill, John L., They Speak With Other Tongues (Spire Books 1965).

For Specialized Study
Findlay, James F., Jr., Dwight L. Moody, American Evangelist, 1837–1899 (Univ. of Chicago Press 1969).
Heimert, Alan, and Miller, Perry, eds., The Great Awakening: Documents Illustrating the Crisis and Its Consequences (Bobbs–Merril 1967).
Hollenweger, Walter J., The Pentecostals (Augsburg Publishing House 1972).
O'Connor, Edward D., The Pentecostal Movement in the Catholic Church (Ave Maria Press 1971).
Smith, Timothy, Revivalism and Social Reform in Mid-Nineteenth Century America (Abingdon Press 1952).
Synan, H. Vinson, The Holiness-Pentecostalism Movement in the United States (William B. Erdmans Publishing Co. 1971).
Tyler, Alice Felt, Freedom's Ferment (University of Minnesota Press 1944).

Young people pray in the Joyful Noise, a "Christian coffee house" in the French Quarter of New Orleans, La., during the Mardi Gras festivities of 1972.

Jesus People,
'Freaks,' and Other Believers

By Richard E. Wentz

Associate Professor of Humanities and Coordinator of Religious Studies, Arizona State University

A gradual increase in the search for alternative life-styles has been observable in American society since World War II. That increase accounts not for a "counter-culture," as it has been sometimes called, but for a multicultural society. The ages of those who experiment and theorize are relative. While the search is basically a youthful enterprise, the scope of participation probably ranges at least to age 50. A large segment of the younger members of our society who were described as religiously indifferent in the 1960's has become involved in an odyssey of spiritual search in the 1970's.

Character of the Search. The great diversity of the search for alternative life-styles can be characterized as evangelical and revivalistic in the sense that most devotees of a particular style have been converted to a message that is good news to them. It is a message that seeks other converts and expresses itself in a manner that embraces the total affective and intellectual apparatus of the person.

All of these evangelical styles seem to share several characteristics. They are protestant, prophetic, proleptic, puerilistic, pragmatic, and pentecostal. They are *protestant* in their rejection of

established patterns of experience and social behaviors; and in their subsequent witness to a more adequate alternative. They are *prophetic* in their judgment of established society according to norms of humanization that are presumed to be universally held. They are also prophetic in their vision of an age that embodies those norms of humanization. They are *proleptic* in that they claim that the new age is already present in their search and its precepts. They are *puerilistic* in their romantic dedication to ideals to which their antecedents gave lip service, and in their innocent view of human nature which assumes that understanding and commitment guarantees performance. The *pragmatism* of the quest is discerned in the priority given to practice over theory. The searchers seem to be saying, "Show us what it can do for us, we are not interested in abstractions." They are *pentecostal* in a kind of "Mc-

TWO YOUNG DELEGATES to the giant "Explo '72" religious festival in Dallas wear Jesus Movement shirts, bearing the slogan "One Way." About 80,000 attended.

THE NEW YORK TIMES

Luhanesque" manner, an enjoyment of the spirit, the nonverbal, affective modes of existence.

Evangelism. The most observable pattern of these characteristics is the newly discovered Christian evangelical heritage. The United States has always been the setting for evangelical movements that have existed outside of, but sometimes in cooperation with, established institutional patterns. By far the most numerous representative of the evangelical heritage today is the so-called Jesus movement. In part, these new disciples are heir to the Student Christian Movement and YMCA-YWCA programs that have played such an important role in educational institutions in America. Taking its cue from successful campus evangelism and from the strategies of Billy Graham, this phase of the movement seeks to confront youth with a simple call of commitment to Christ. Such groups as Young Life in the high schools and Campus Crusade for Christ are highly programmed operations and use methods derived from the business and educational worlds. Theirs is usually a rather literal interpretation of the Bible, with primary emphasis on the peace and happiness that commitment to Jesus brings.

An entirely different phase of the Jesus movement is represented by those often referred to as "freaks." Many of these are youths, who have turned to a Jesus-commitment after disastrous encounters with drugs. They describe their conversion to Jesus as a means of experiencing more than they had ever anticipated from drug usage. While some of these devotees resemble the more traditional and biblicist evangelicals described above, they are usually distinguished by their imitation of a Jesus life-style. With them it is not so much an acceptance of the salvation wrought by Jesus as an emulation of his life and teachings. Many of the "freaks" could be called neo-Franciscan. Like St. Francis of Assisi, they attempt to abandon the established cultural values in favor of a life of simplicity and service to others.

Pentecostalism. There have always been those whose life-styles have been characterized by manifestations of fervor not experienced, or even approved, by the mainstream of society. Since Vatican II this pentecostalism has even been found in the Roman Catholic Church—beginning in the mid-1960's with an outbreak of Spirit testimony at Duquesne University in Pittsburgh and at the University of Notre Dame in South Bend, Ind.

These groups are often traditional and biblicist-evangelical in every other way. Within a given tradition there may be considerable controversy between those who witness to the gifts of the Spirit and those who do not. The most

The official symbol of Key 73, a U.S. and Canadian Christian evangelical movement that has designated 1973 as the year in which to realize the theme "Calling Our Continent to Christ."

Key 73: Major Campaign in U.S., Canada

BY JOE HALE
Member of the Executive Committee of Key 73

The birth of Key 73, a Christian evangelism movement in the United States and Canada focused on 1973, came about through a succession of informal consultations of Christian leaders. The first meeting, held on Sept. 28, 1967, was chaired by evangelist Billy Graham and Carl F. H. Henry, then editor of *Christianity Today.* A wide representation of Christian churches took part in the discussion, which centered on making a more profound witness and impact upon the American culture.

Influences in the early organizational meetings were varied. One group of participants advocated a united evangelistic witness. Another segment, moved by the significant unrest in society and within the church, spoke for a strong evangelical presence that would powerfully address persons both in their inward spiritual need and where they were being hurt by destructive social cross-currents.

The 1969 U. S. Congress on Evangelism in Minneapolis and a 1970 Canadian Congress in Ottawa further emphasized this total concern. These meetings bridged the disparate interests present in the early Key Bridge meetings and as the decade of the 1970's began, Key 73 evolved.

Objectives. In early 1970 five purposes of Key 73 were established:

• To share with every person in North America more fully and more forcefully the claims and message of the Gospel of Jesus Christ.

• To employ every means and method of communicating the Gospel in order to create the conditions in which men may more readily respond to the leading of the Holy Spirit.

• To apply the message and meaning of Jesus Christ to the issues shaping man and his society in order that they may be resolved.

• To develop new resources for effective evangelism for consideration, adoption, adaptation, or rejection by the participating churches or Christian groups.

• To assist the efforts of Christian congregations and organizations in becoming more effective redemptive centers and more aggressive witnesses of God's redeeming power in the world.

Schedule. A theme, "Calling Our Continent to Christ," was adopted and a calendar for the year 1973 was projected with six sequential periods which, to some degree, parallel the liturgical church year. Phase One, "Calling Our Continent to Repentance and Prayer," includes a Noon Prayer Call, a Faith-In-Action telecast, and a "launch Sunday" in all participating churches. Phase Two, "Calling Our Continent to the Word of God," includes the distribution and study of the Scriptures. Phase Three, "Calling Our Continent to the Resurrection," centers on laymen witnessing to their faith in the Risen Christ. In Phase Four, a call to "New Life," youth would share their faith through music, the arts, and drama in shopping centers, leisure areas, and fairs. Phase Five, "Calling Our Continent to the Proclamation," was planned to emphasize preaching evangelism. Phase Six, "Calling Our Continent to Commitment," will climax the Key 73 year and demonstrate the oneness Christians share in their response to the needs of the world.

Involvement. By the end of 1972 more than 140 denominations and groups, including both Protestants and Roman Catholics, had officially indicated participation in Key 73. Differences both in doctrine and method are recognized and respected. The bond of unity is a simple desire to proclaim Christ unitedly in North America.

Dr. T. A. Raedeke, a Lutheran churchman, serves as executive director of Key 73 in charge of United States coordination. Dr. Leslie Hunt, an Anglican, is chairman of the Canadian Central Committee. Dr. Thomas F. Zimmerman, general superintendent of the Assemblies of God Church, chairs the U. S. Committee.

common of these gifts is glossolalia—the gift of speaking in tongues, which varies from a kind of gibberish to the use of language foreign and unknown to the individual demonstrant. There is some evidence to suggest that pentecostalism is on the increase. It is not, of course, limited to youth, and there have always been sects and cults especially devoted to pentecostal gifts. It is a phenomenon which is also to be found in such orderly churches as the Presbyterian and Episcopal, beginning in the 1960's.

Antinomians and the Law of Love. The antinomians are individuals whose discovery of inner integrity and spiritual happiness means to them that they are no longer obligated to precepts and rules. They are above the law and therefore opposed to law. As pure children of God, their actions can no longer be measured by any code. What seems improper or immoral to others may be a pure and righteous act to the antinomian.

Closely related is the new love monism of those who believe that love is pervasive and easily demonstrable. Accordingly, any action that is motivated by love for another is a worthy act. Love is readily applicable to any situation; love is prior to any social structure or behavior pattern. For example, it is possible to find many evangelically committed youths whose sexual morality is defined solely by love and concern for others. This means that marriage is not necessarily monogamous or fundamental to full sexual relationships.

Communes. Another pattern of youthful religiosity is communalism. The longing for meaningful interpersonal and group relationships is itself a religious phenomenon. It is as prominent in the history of religions as is the evangelical heritage in the United States, and it is possible to trace the recurrent communitarian vision and experiment in Western history.

Communal living is one of the most prominent religious characteristics of today's youth. The process of gathering sociological data has only begun, and many of the existing communities are shy of visitors. There is mounting evidence to suggest that communal situations are so pervasive that the smallest town and city has its expression. Even those experiments that have been generated by theorists who are middle-aged and older seem to be populated primarily by youth. On the one hand there are those communes which adhere to the principles of some formal religious system—Christianity, Buddhism. On the other, there are those which are motivated by ideology, ecology, service, or ascetic rejected of the accepted social order. The religious antecedents may be traced in group marriage communes, open-land precincts, and the behavioralist compounds based on the thoughts of B. F. Skinner. Togetherness, love, protest, natural freedom, and disciplined community all represent part of the religious quest of modern youth.

Other Religious and Spiritual Influences. America has also become a ready market for traditional and more recent expressions of Far Eastern religions and spiritual techniques. Yoga and Zen Buddhist practices are very popular, and students have become serious readers of such books as the *I Ching,* a collection of propositions and explanations used in divination. More recently, the Divine Light Mission of Maharaj Ji and the more philosophical teachings of Sri Aurobindo have been receiving increased attention. Any college course in non-Western religion is likely to get very large enrollment. An offering using the term mysticism in the title guarantees the instructor a full classroom.

Forms of mysticism not derived from the Far East may also be due for a hearing. There is evidence of renewed interest in Islamic Sufism and Jewish Hasidism. The novels of Hermann Hesse, with their curious blend of eroticism and mystical ecstasy, have been popular for some time.

Much of the religious quest of modern youth began taking its cues from the Broadway musical *Hair* and its announcement of the zodiacal Age of Aquarius. There followed a rebirth of forms of religious life which numerous commentators thought had been left behind since man had "come of age" in the 20th century. Astrology, witchcraft, spiritualism (more properly dubbed spiritism), and chemical ecstasy are all part of the history of religions. And they have all been born again in the 1970's.

This fascination with more elementary religious forms can also be understood as related to the concern for a primitive and natural homology. It is therefore possible to interpret environmental convictions as a nostalgia for more primal relationship to the forces of the cosmos. In the Southwest, for example, the deeply religious foundations of Hopi and Zuñi cultures have become more than a subject of academic interest. Youth are asking, what do these people have to tell us about life and its commitments?

We are as yet too close and too involved in this period of our religious history to be able to critically evaluate it, and we must await the accumulation of further data before we may see clearly all that it entails. However, it is undeniable that the secular age heralded in the mid-1960's has been transformed into an age of spiritual celebration in the 1970's.

Great American evangelists have included Jonathan Edwards (above), who, in the 18th century, led the First Great Awakening; and Billy Graham (right), shown at "Explo '72" rally in Dallas.

UPI

History: From Edwards To Graham

By James H. Smylie
Professor of Church History,
Union Theological Seminary, Richmond, Va.

Although there have been manifestations of spiritual fervor throughout history, and although certain analogies can be drawn in the study of European and American life, revivalism is a modern and American phenomenon. It may be seen as an attempt of Christians to intensify religious commitment, to increase the membership of denominations, and to spread the influence of Christianity. In this sense it is one consequence of the breakdown in the 18th century of the Constantinian establishment of religion, in which one became Christian by following a ruler into the church, by the coercion of the sword, and by baptism into the church whose borders were coextensive with the state.

In America, despite some colonial establishments, Christians had to develop means of persuading people to commit and associate themselves voluntarily with Christianity, its organized forms, and its ethical convictions. Revivalism has also been associated with shifts in population—for example, the movements from Europe to America, east to west, rural to urban, urban to suburban—and with crises which have an impact on the churches, such as wars and depressions.

Intellectual challenges to Christianity, such as rationalism, evolution, and biblical criticism, have also occasioned revivals. During these times, revivalists have had a message about God, man, the world, which many Americans found persuasive.

The history of revivalism is a rich and complex affair, and it is not easy to generalize about the variety of experiences and strategies. One possible way of doing this is to identify the famous leaders who have had the greatest impact and helped to shape the major revivals—Jonathan Edwards (1703–1758), Charles G. Finney (1792–1875), Dwight L. Moody (1837–1899), Billy Sunday (1862–1935), and Billy Graham (1918–   ).

Jonathan Edwards. The First Great Awakening, with which Edwards is associated, came in reaction to 18th century religious formalism and rationalism. It was related to the movements known as Pietism on the Continent and the Evangelical Awakening led by John Wesley in the British Isles. It was an intercolonial movement which joined together Congregationalists, Dutch Reformed, and Presbyterians, and other dissenters from the Church of England. It was Calvinistic. Edwards took the lead in reempha-

sizing such doctrines as the sovereignty of God, man's total depravity, and God's grace.

Edwards maintained that the Awakening began in his community among young people who were sobered by the death of a friend, and by his preaching justification by faith alone. It produced religious "enthusiasm" (sometimes with abnormal physical manifestations); "censoriousness" (uncomplimentary warnings to those who had not been converted); "itineracy" (movement of pastors and people across parish lines for revival preaching); and divisiveness. George Whitefield, who traveled back and forth between England and the colonies, helped to give unity to the cause.

Charles G. Finney. While this first awakening seemed to lose its momentum, it was continued in some places by Presbyterians and especially by Baptists and Methodists, denominations which adapted revivalism as a means of growth in the 19th century. What is often called a Second Great Awakening began around 1800 and continued in various forms during the first half of the 19th century. Finney is a particularly good representative of this period. He started out as an ordained Presbyterian minister, but shifted in his theological attitudes to a modified Arminianism, a less stringent Calvinism, which became a dominant theological opinion of the century. Finney, trained as a lawyer, emphasized man's participation in the conversion experience. He introduced such techniques to revivalism as "protracted meetings," "camp meetings," and the "anxious bench."

Finney gathered around him young followers who became known as "Finney's band." Many of his converts involved themselves in the missionary, educational, and reforming enterprises typical of this period of optimism in American history. There was also strong reaction to the emerging revivalistic pattern among those who were disturbed about the trend in theology, the neglect of proper liturgy, and Christian nurture.

Dwight L. Moody. Revivalism continued with modifications after the Civil War, taking on some of the characteristics with which it is still marked. Moody was an uneducated businessman who became popular in the 1870's, first in the British Isles and then in America. While he was not a theologian, his ideas were generally more conservative than were Finney's, and under him revivalism developed more conservative attitudes toward social problems. Moody held many of his meetings in buildings other than churches, thus emphasizing the nondenominational character of his work and in order to accommodate larger crowds. He was the first to employ a professional singer at his services.

Observing that many of those converted by his preaching were adolescents, he gave more attention to young people in colleges and universities and at meetings of the Young Men's Christian Association and the Student Volunteer Movement. Moody's meetings usually took a great deal of preparation and financial backing, and he introduced business procedures into revivalism. More liberal "social gospel" contemporaries also thought of themselves as revivalists and believed that they were involved in a new great awakening of ethical responsibility and the social teachings of Jesus.

Billy Sunday and Billy Graham. Moody's methods were modified by Billy Sunday, who reached the peak of his influence in the 1920's, and Billy Graham, who came into prominence during the Eisenhower years, the 1950's, and has carried on since that time. Graham, a Baptist, came out of an organization known as Youth for Christ. He institutionalized his "crusades" in the Billy Graham Evangelistic Association and has continued to carry his message all over the world, skillfully utilizing the mass media. Graham's theology is a modified "fundamentalism," but his emphasis has been on the biblical call to repentance and a new life in Christ. While Graham is in the premillennialist tradition and is somewhat conservative in his social ethics, over the years he has deepened his concern for problems of an urban, technocratic, internationalized society. Graham has also shown the same inclination of other revivalists for a nondenominational approach to revivalism.

Conclusion. It would be erroneous and misleading to associate all revivals of religion in America with these men and their movements. Great religious interest has been stirred in a variety of ways, for example, through interest in liturgy, devotion to the Virgin Mary, study by college students of Reinhold Niebuhr, Paul Tillich, and Teilhard de Chardin, and involvement in the civil rights movement led by Martin Luther King, Jr. But revivalism, as associated with Edwards, Finney, Moody, Sunday, and Graham may be treated as a thread that runs through American religious history.

In assessing this past record for what may be expected during another wave of revivalism, we may look for broad cooperation, participation of the young, and an increase in the membership of churches. We can also expect continuous debate and dissension within the various Christian denominations over the nature of the Christian experience, the means of attracting adherents, and what may be expected of the convert in the way of an ethical response to the world's needs and its future.

BOB COMBS, FROM RAPHO GUILLUMETTE

The Pentecostals: In the Vanguard Of Revivalism

BY VINSON SYNAN
*Chairman of the Social Sciences Division
of Emmanuel College, Georgia*

The Pentecostal movement, which had been thought of as being on the fringe of American religious life, has caught on in many of the older and more traditional denominations in the United States. The movement is primarily derived from the Holiness movement, a descendant of 19th century Methodism. Some experts have called it the fastest growing movement in Christianity.

The central doctrine of the movement is belief in a postconversion spiritual experience called the "Baptism in the Holy Spirit," with the initial physical evidence of speaking in other tongues, or glossolalia—that is, speaking in supernatural languages that the recipient did not learn. Biblical passages that concern the power of the Spirit and speaking in tongues are cited in support of the practice; for example, Mark 16:17; Luke 11:13; Acts 2:4, 8:17, 19:44–46, and 19:6. Such charismatic gifts as prophecy, divine healing, and interpretation of tongues are also emphasized.

From its early 20th century origins, Pentecostalism has grown considerably and now encompasses a great variety of theological and ecclesiastical viewpoints. In the early 1960's it entered a new phase with the appearance of the "neo-Pentecostal movement" in the traditional Protestant churches. Beginning among Episcopalians and Presbyterians, the movement has grown until practically every Protestant denomination has a "charismatic renewal" group of ministers and laymen who are actively promoting the movement in their ranks.

By 1966 a Pentecostal-Catholic movement had begun which had its origins among the faculty and students of Duquesne University in Pittsburgh, Pa., and the University of Notre Dame in South Bend,

Ind. By 1972 some observers put the number of Pentecostal Catholics at 200,000 in the United States alone. Growth among Catholics was also seen in Europe and Latin America as the movement began a rapid expansion in worldwide Catholic circles.

Background. The Pentecostal movement in the United States consists of those churches influenced by an unusual revival in the Azusa Street Apostolic Faith Mission in Los Angeles, Calif., which began in 1906. Although Pentecostal doctrine had been formulated in 1901 by Charles Parham in Topeka, Kans., the movement received worldwide publicity under the leadership of William J. Seymour, a black, in the Azusa Street revival. From Los Angeles, Pentecostalism spread rapidly throughout the nation and around the world.

Leading figures in the development of the major American Pentecostal denominations were: A. J. Tomlinson, the Churches of God; J. H. King, the Pentecostal Holiness Church; C. H. Mason, the Church of God in Christ; E. N. Bell, the Assemblies of God; and Aimee Semple McPherson, the Church of the Foursquare Gospel. A later doctrinal variation produced the Pentecostal Unitarian or "Jesus Name" movement, which culminated in the United Pentecostal Church.

Worldwide Growth. Despite its relative newness Pentecostalism has crossed most national and cultural boundaries and now encompasses some 20 million adult members throughout the world. In Italy, Scandinavia, South Africa, Chile, and Brazil, the Pentecostals constitute the largest religious groups outside of the traditional Roman Catholic or Protestant "national" churches. In Latin America, Pentecostals number over 80 percent of all Protestants. Some local congregations in Chile and Brazil claim as many as 80,000 members.

In 1972 the Pentecostal movement showed new evidence of maturing into a nationally recognized religious force. The Pentecostal denominations continued to register membership gains while most of the older Protestant denominations experienced further decline. For example, the Assemblies of God grew from 645,000 in 1971 to 679,000 in 1972.

Public interest in the movement has been attested to by the burgeoning sales of books and magazines relating to Pentecostalism. Many books on glossolalia have appeared, with *Logos* and *Creation House* heading up the list of best sellers. The film *Marjoe*, which chronicled the life and hypocrisy of a Pentecostal child evangelist, was the source of some embarrassment. However, it has been pointed out that the subject of the film, Marjoe Gortner, was not a minister of a major Pentecostal body and that his chief appeal was to independent churches outside the mainstream of Pentecostalism.

Membership. The best statistics available for the Pentecostal movement in the United States show an adult membership of 2,357,514 in the major churches scattered among some 30,000 local congregations. With local store-front churches estimated to have an equal number of adherents, and 500,000 Pentecostals in mainline denominations, there are nearly 5 million Pentecostals in the United States. Along with the current evangelical revival the Pentecostal movement constitutes one of the most vibrant trends in religious life in the United States in the 1970's.

The Debate over National Health Care

DRAWING BY H. MARTIN © 1972 THE NEW YORKER MAGAZINE INC.

"Just press the buttons here corresponding to your ailment, and the printout will give us the diagnosis, suggested medications, tips for a speedy recovery, and my bill."

BY JEROME F. BRAZDA

Editor, "Washington Report on Medicine and Health"

National health insurance was expected to be a major issue in the 93d Congress that convened in January 1973. It was an important topic of discussion during the second session of the 92d Congress even though none of the many proposals languishing before appropriate committees ever made it to the floor of either House or Senate.

President Nixon, in a pre-election speech on health affairs (the only national address solely on the subject of health ever made by a President of the United States) urged adoption of the national health insurance plan he had proposed in a 1971 health message to Congress and which he again advocated in a similar message to Congress in 1972.

Need for a National Health Insurance Program. The cost of medical care rose again during 1972, although at a lesser rate than the previous year, apparently because of the Nixon administration's wage-price freeze program. The cost of hospital care increased by about 6% over the previous year; this was about half the rate by which hospital charges had been steadily gaining at the time the economic stabilization program went into effect. Physicians' fees and dental care costs rose even less during the year. According to the Social Security Administration, the total national expenditure for health care during the fiscal year ending June 30, 1972, was $83.4 billion, or about 7.6% of the gross national product. However, the growth rate for health expenditures—an increase over fiscal 1971 of only 10.3%—was the lowest since 1966 because of the economic stabilization program.

Of the total estimated expenditures for health care by Americans in fiscal 1972, $50.6 billion came from private sources and $32.9 billion from public sources. The per capita expenditure for health care during fiscal 1972 was $394.16, compared with $358 the previous fiscal year. Expenditures for hospital care during fiscal 1972 totaled $32.5 billion, for physicians' services $16.2 billion, and for dental care $5 billion.

The administration's Price Commission turned down some requests by hospitals for room rate increases and reduced some other requests. Most requests by health insurance companies for rate increases were granted, a circumstance explained by Price Commission officials as due to the fact that insurance rates are based on actuarial experience of paying claims.

Even those Americans who held health insurance policies, through group or individual plans, often found that the rising costs of health care

could far outstrip their insurance coverage in the event of illnesses such as kidney failure or severe mental illness that require frequent and expensive treatment—illnesses that economists term "catastrophic" in terms of costs.

Congressional Action. Organized labor, chiefly the AFL-CIO, placed national health insurance high on its list of "must" legislation for the 93d 'Congress. Sen. Edward M. Kennedy (D., Mass.), chief sponsor of labor's "Health Security" plan for national health insurance, stated that he intended to make enactment of the comprehensive plan a major personal goal during the 93d Congress.

Rep. Wilbur D. Mills (D., Ark.), chairman of the House Ways and Means Committee and a key figure in congressional consideration of national health insurance, had held hearings in late 1971 on numerous proposals by major political and professional organizations. But he never scheduled closed sessions of the committee to "mark up" a bill for floor consideration. Several tentative dates for executive sessions to vote on sending a bill to the floor were postponed until, finally, Mills said there was inadequate time for meaningful action on such a complicated measure during the 1972 session. Representative Mills, whose committee must initiate tax legislation, said at the end of the year that he considered national health insurance to be a high priority subject for his committee in the 93d Congress.

Shortly before the November elections, Representative Mills and Senator Kennedy appeared at a joint news conference at which they said they were attempting to agree on a Mills-Kennedy national health insurance bill. Such a proposal would be formidable because of the great political power of the two men.

Mills and Kennedy said they were attempting to agree on a method of financing a national health insurance program and of administering it. The Kennedy-labor Health Security bill would, as introduced in the 92d Congress, abolish the existing health insurance system. Mills indicated he would like to find a way to incorporate insurance companies, both commercial and nonprofit, into a national health insurance structure.

Catastrophic Health Insurance Plan. Frequent stories in the press about cases of catastrophic medical costs added to the growing public expectation of a national health insurance program. In recognition of this problem, Sen. Russell Long (D., La.), chairman of the Senate Finance Committee, sought to add a Catastrophic Health Insurance Plan to the social security amendments that were sent by his committee to

the Senate floor. The federally financed plan advanced by Senator Long would pay 80% of hospital care costs from the 61st day of hospitalization on and would pay 80% of medical costs above $2,000. Because of the press of time caused by the lateness in the 1972 session at which the huge package of amendments was sent to the Senate floor, Senator Long never put the proposal to a vote. But he said he would offer the plan again, possibly during the 93d Congress. Long, whose committee is similar in function to Rep. Mills' Ways and Means Committee, said he felt that a catastrophic plan would serve as a stopgap program until more extensive consideration could be given to a comprehensive national health insurance plan.

Senator Long did succeed, however, in adding to the social security amendments a plan for providing federal support for kidney patients requiring renal dialysis by artificial kidney machines. The plan, which was enacted into law, made anyone requiring kidney machine treatment eligible for Medicare coverage by defining such persons as disabled. The 1972 amendments added all disabled persons to Medicare coverage along with the aged.

Other Proposals. In a significant development related to national health insurance, attempts by both houses of Congress to enact a law providing federal assistance for development

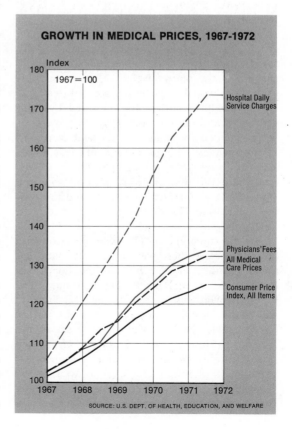

GROWTH IN MEDICAL PRICES, 1967-1972

Index
1967=100

Hospital Daily Service Charges

Physicians' Fees
All Medical Care Prices

Consumer Price Index, All Items

SOURCE: U.S. DEPT. OF HEALTH, EDUCATION, AND WELFARE

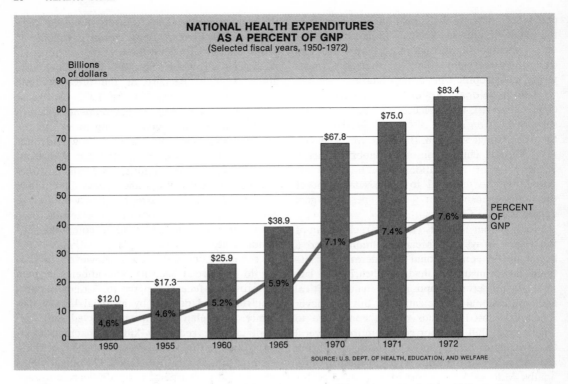

NATIONAL HEALTH EXPENDITURES AS A PERCENT OF GNP
(Selected fiscal years, 1950-1972)

SOURCE: U.S. DEPT. OF HEALTH, EDUCATION, AND WELFARE

of Health Maintenance Organizations (HMOs) ended in failure when Congress adjourned before action could be completed. Senator Kennedy, a major advocate of HMOs, blamed lobbying by the American Medical Association (AMA) for fatally stalling congressional action on the HMO legislation.

The AMA traditionally has opposed prepaid group practice plans in which physicians work for a salary. HMOs are a variation of prepaid group practice plans. Health Maintenance Organizations would be given preferential treatment by the Health Security bill sponsored by Kennedy on the supposition that they are a more efficient method of organizing medical care. An HMO provides a complete range of medical services to its subscribers. Examples of HMO currently in existence include the Health Insurance Plan (HIP) of Greater New York and the Kaiser Foundation Health Plans located mostly in California.

By the time the 1972 session of Congress drew to a close there were almost as many national health insurance bills in the hopper as there were national health organizations. The Fulton-Broyhill bill represents the "Medicredit" plan of the American Medical Association. Other plans include the "Ameriplan" proposal of the American Hospital Association (AHA), the "Healthcare" plan of the Health Insurance Association of America (HIAA), as well as the "Chronicare" plan of the American Nursing Home Association (ANHA). There was also a

proposal by New York Republican Sen. Jacob Javits, which was in addition to the Nixon administration and Kennedy-labor bills.

Except for the Kennedy-labor Health Security bill, all of the plans involved a variety of means to help Americans purchase health insurance from commercial or nonprofit companies. The AMA's Medicredit offers a plan of income tax credits to offset the cost of health insurance. The AHA's Ameriplan, on which a bill introduced by Rep. Al Ullman (D., Oreg.) was based, would establish health care corporations that would encourage those who can afford it to join them and would provide federal financial aid for families too poor to buy coverage. The Healthcare plan of the insurance industry would establish insurance pools for the poor and would encourage those who can afford it to buy health insurance.

The Chronicare plan advanced by the nursing home group would establish a plan for providing nursing home benefits for those requiring long-term care. The other plans offer little or no nursing home care for the aged or chronically ill. The plan offered by Senator Javits is based on an extension of the existing Medicare laws.

Nixon Administration National Health Insurance Plan. The national health insurance plan advanced by the Nixon administration was a combination of three elements—a National Health Insurance Standards Act (NHISA), a Family Health Insurance Plan (FHIP), and the existing Medicare program for the aged.

NHISA. The National Health Insurance Standards Act would require employers to provide adequate health insurance for their employees. Employers would pay at least 65% of the premium costs for the first two and one-half years of the program and a minimum of 75% after that. The insurance would be purchased from private companies. Pools would be established for risk-sharing among small employers, the self-employed, and people outside the labor force.

No federal financing of health insurance costs is involved in the NHISA proposal. Rather it would mandate minimum standards that health insurance must meet in order to be included in the employer-employee plans. Inherent in the proposal would be federal regulation of health insurance companies taking part to protect the interests of the consumer and to guard against underfinancing.

Deductibles of $100 per person up to three in a family would be paid by the family before coverage begins. Coinsurance to be paid by the beneficiary after the deductibles would be 25% of costs up to $5,000 per person.

Catastrophic coverage would begin after medical costs for an individual exceeded $5,000. All costs after that would be paid.

FHIP. The Family Health Insurance Plan would be designed to cover low-income families, replacing the present Medicaid program. It would be fully financed and administered by the federal government. Eligible families would be required to contribute toward the annual cost of their insurance on a scale determined by income and family size. The family of four earning less than $3,000 would pay nothing. A system of deductibles and coinsurance would vary with income and family size.

Medicaid would continue to cover the aged poor, the blind, the disabled, and some children. The 1972 social security amendments fully federalized these so-called "adult categories" of Medicaid, eliminating the need for contributions to their cost by the states.

In a test of the FHIP concept, the Department of Health, Education, and Welfare funded a number of largely rural "Family Health Centers" closely resembling the specifications for FHIP drafted by HEW.

Nixon's Position. In calling for congressional action on his national health insurance proposals, President Nixon emphasized that it would "build on the strengths of our present health insurance industry." The Nixon plan would, according to the President's statement, "reform and improve our present health care system."

Nixon characterized the Kennedy-labor bill, which was incorporated into the Democratic party platform, as a "medical system which is paid for by the taxpayers and controlled by the Federal government."

"Our plan would reform and improve our present health care system," the President said. "Our opponents' plan would tear that system apart. This is one of the clearest choices in this campaign." The particular intensity with which the President attacked the Kennedy plan was regarded as an indication of the increasingly controversial nature of the national health insurance issue.

Kennedy Explains His 'Health Security' Bill

BY SEN. EDWARD M. KENNEDY

I believe that in America today, health care should be a right for all, not just a privilege for the few. The basic goal of the Health Security program which I have sponsored is to make that right a continuing reality, not just the empty promise it is today. Just as the social security program of the decade of the 1930's brought hope and new faith to a nation mired in the social crisis of the great depression, so I believe that a Health Security program in the decade of the 1970's can guarantee high-quality health care to our people and lead us out of the current crisis of confidence in our health system.

WIDE WORLD

Sen. Edward M. Kennedy has long been interested in the problem of providing adequate health care for every American. In this article, he outlines his program for a comprehensive system of health care insurance. The Kennedy plan, known as Health Security, has received the endorsement of the AFL–CIO. Health Security aims not only at providing high-quality health care for all Americans but also at upgrading the organization and delivery of that care. The Massachusetts Democrat is the author of In Critical Condition: The Crisis in America's Health Care (1972).

The basic principle of the Health Security program is two-fold: (1) to establish a system of comprehensive national health insurance for the United States that is capable of bringing the same high-quality health care to every resident, and (2) to use the program to bring about major improvements in the organization and delivery of health care.

The Health Security program does not envisage a national health service, where the government owns the facilities and employs the personnel and manages all the finances of the health care system. On the contrary, the program proposes a working partnership between the public and private sectors in which there will be government financing and administration management, accompanied by private provision of health services through private practitioners, institutions, and other providers of services.

Eligibility. Every individual residing in the United States will be eligible to receive benefits. There will be no requirement of past individual contributions, nor will there be any test of income or other means.

Covered Services. The intent of the program is to provide comprehensive benefits for every eligible person. These benefits will encompass the entire range of personal health care services, including the prevention and early detection of disease, the care and treatment of illness, and medical rehabilitation. There are no cutoff dates, coinsurance, deductibles, or waiting periods. For example, the program provides full coverage for physicians' services, inpatient and outpatient hospital services, and home health services. It also provides full coverage for other professional and supporting services such as optometry services, podiatry services, eyeglasses, prosthetic devices, and hearing aids.

There are only four limitations of coverage, and these limitations are made necessary by inadequate resources. They deal with nursing home care, psychiatric care, dental care, and prescription drugs.

Skilled nursing home care is limited to 120 days per benefit period. The period may be extended, however, if the nursing home is owned or managed by a hospital.

Psychiatric hospitalization is limited to 45 days of active treatment during a benefit period. These limits do not apply, however, when care is provided through organized mental health systems or group practice programs.

Dental care is initially limited to children under age 15 with some emergency services available to adults. Coverage will gradually increase to the entire population.

Prescribed drugs are limited to those provided in a hospital, nursing home, or other institution and to those drugs required for treatment of long-term or chronic illness.

Financing the Program. The program will be financed through a Health Security Trust Fund similar to the Social Security Trust Fund. Income to the fund will come from four sources: 50% of the money will be from federal general revenues; 36% from a tax of 3.5% on employers' payrolls (most employers, of course, will discontinue purchase of any private insurance at a savings which largely offsets the tax); 12% from a tax of 1% on the first $15,000 of individual income from any source; and 2% from a tax of 2.5% on the first $15,000 of self-employment income. Employers may pay all or a part of their employees' Health Security taxes in accord with collective bargaining agreements.

Administration. The program will be administered by a five-member, full-time Health Security Board, appointed by the President and confirmed by the Senate. It will be assisted by a National Advisory Council with a majority of consumer members.

The administration will not, however, be highly centralized in Washington. The Health Security Board will administer the Trust Fund and establish national standards, but day-to-day decisions will be made at regional and local levels so that health policy and development of resources will be controlled by local people who have an understanding of local problems.

Payments to Providers. The essence of the Health Security's payment system and the central cost control feature of the program is that the health care system as a whole will be anchored to a budget established in advance. As in every area of our economic life, the health care system will be obliged to live within its budget. In this way we can end the unacceptable escalation of costs within our present system and the long financial binge in which health care has had a signed blank check on the whole economy of the nation.

Providers of health services will be paid directly by the Health Security program. Individuals will not be charged for services.

Hospitals and other institutional providers will be paid on the basis of annual negotiated budgets. Independent practitioners, including physicians, dentists, podiatrists, and optometrists may be paid by several methods: traditional fee-for-service, per capita payments, or in some cases by salary.

Resources Development Fund. An important feature of the program is the Resources Development Fund, which will come into operation two years before benefits are actually avail-

able. About $2 billion a year, or 5% of the Health Security Trust Fund, will eventually be earmarked exclusively for resource development. These funds will be used to support innovative health programs, particularly in areas such as manpower, education, training, group practice development, and other means to improve the delivery of health care. The Fund is a type of catalyst that will be used to accelerate reform of the nation's health care system.

Quality Control. Health Security will establish a Commission on the Quality of Health Care, and it will set national standards for participating professional and institutional providers. Independent practitioners such as physicians and dentists will be eligible to participate if they meet licensure and continuing education requirements. Specialty services, such as surgery, must be performed by a qualified practitioner.

Changing the System. Financial, professional, and other incentives are built into the program to move the health care delivery system toward organized arrangements for patient care and to encourage preventive care and the early diagnosis of disease.

In the area of health manpower, the program will supplement existing federal programs by providing special support for family physicians and other members of the family health care team. It will provide incentives to create Health Maintenance Organizations so that consumers will have a choice between a solo-practice physician and a group practice system.

The program provides funds for education and training programs, especially for members of minority groups and those disadvantaged by poverty. Finally, it will provide special support for the location of increased health personnel in urban and rural poverty areas.

Relation to Existing Programs. A number of federal health programs will be superseded in whole or in part by Health Security. Medicare and almost all of Medicaid will be absorbed, but the Department of Defense, the Veterans Administration, workmen's compensation, and temporary disability programs are not affected.

Program Costs. On the basis of data compiled by the Department of Health, Education, and Welfare, Americans will spend in excess of $90 billion for personal health services in 1974. If Health Security were operative in 1974, it would pay for approximately two-thirds of that amount and therefore cost $56.7 billion.

The cost of the Health Security program has been the source of enormous confusion and misunderstanding since the original version of the bill was introduced in 1970. The crucial point is that the $56.7 billion price tag for Health Se-

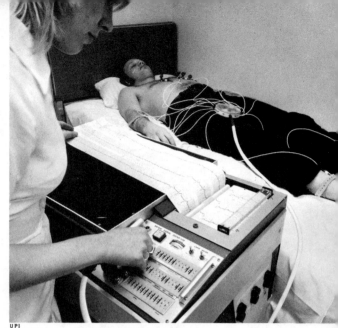

UPI

NEW KIND OF ELECTROCARDIOGRAPH records patient's heartbeat on magnetic tape, which is then sent by telephone to computer for instant diagnosis.

curity in 1974 in no way represents new expenditures. Rather, this is a portion of what Americans would pay anyway for care under the existing system.

Thus, the Health Security program is not a new layer of federal expenditures on top of existing public and private spending for health care. Instead, the Health Security program simply redistributes current expenditures.

Over the long run, by revitalizing the health care system and ending the excessive inflation in the cost of health services, Health Security will be far less expensive than the amount we will spend if we simply allow the present system to continue and even from the program's first day we will guarantee our citizens better value for their health dollar.

Summary. In summary, the Health Security program I have sponsored differs from all previous proposals for health care or national health insurance. It is not just another financing mechanism. It is not just another design for pouring more purchasing power into our already overburdened nonsystem. It is not just another proposal to generate more professional personnel or more hospitals and clinics without the means to guarantee their effective use.

Rather, it is a proposal to give America a national system of Health Security. Under this program, the funds we make available will finance and budget the essential costs of good health care for generations ahead. At the same time, these funds will be building a new capacity to bring adequate, efficient, and reliable health care to all families and individuals in the nation.

AMA Endorses the 'Medicredit' Proposal

By Dr. C. A. Hoffman
President, The American Medical Association

A pluralistic system of medicine has evolved in the United States to meet the needs of a diverse people living in a variety of communities spread across a continent. The American Medical Association (AMA) believes that this system can make health care of high quality available to all.

The system is not perfect. There are serious problems that must be worked out, but it is a viable, productive system that is flexible enough to provide for innovation, experimentation, and change. The AMA is developing a total program that will help remove barriers to improved care, while preserving the characteristics that have led to a high level of health and scientific accomplishment.

According to a survey in a new book, most Americans agree with this approach. In *U. S. Health Care: What's Wrong and What's Right*, Stephen P. Strickland evaluates a Gallup Poll and reports that most people have confidence in the U. S. health care system and do not believe current problems amount to a national crisis warranting a "radical overhaul of existing institutions." The poll in Strickland's book shows that 57% of the public favor some form of national health insurance, but that the public does not want the fundamental values of the current health care system violated.

Dr. Charles A. Hoffman, who was installed as president of the American Medical Association (AMA) in 1972, presents the health insurance system favored by this leading organization of the nation's physicians. Known as Medicredit, the plan would grant credits against personal income taxes to offset the premium cost of qualified private health insurance policies providing specified benefits. In 1972, Dr. Hoffman made an inspection tour of health care systems in the Soviet Union, Britain, Sweden, and West Germany.

Medicredit. One element in the AMA's program is just such a form of national health insurance. This proposal, called Medicredit, would remove the economic barriers that often block the poor from access to medical and health care. It would also protect all Americans from the devastating costs of catastrophic illness. Medicredit gained more support in 1972 than any other national health insurance bill. It was endorsed by 174 members of the 92d Congress, and it is widely supported by physicians.

Through a system of tax credits, Medicredit would make available to everyone under 65 a private program of comprehensive medical and health care protection. The federal government would pay for all or part of the basic coverage, depending on the financial condition of the family or individual as measured by federal income tax liability. The government would pay the premium for catastrophic coverage for everyone. There are deductibles and coinsurance in both the basic and catastrophic coverage, but deductibles incurred under basic coverage would apply to the one required under catastrophic coverage.

The protection under Medicredit would be in the form of a health insurance policy from a company, membership in a prepayment plan such as Blue Cross and Blue Shield, or membership in a prepaid group practice plan. The choice would be made by the insured, and all programs would be approved by the respective states to assure that benefits meet national standards.

Medicredit is capable of providing financial help to those who require it. At the same time it does not obligate the taxpayers to pay for the care of those who can afford to finance most of their medical care themselves. It stresses that the major contribution be made by the private sector of the economy, and it attempts to hold to a minimum the demands on an already burdened government.

Thus, Medicredit is responsive to a primary requirement for future national programs—fiscal responsibility. Brookings Institution stated that "the public is asking harder questions about federal programs, both old and new. It is asking whether they work." In the 1960's, the report said, "the idea persisted that if one could identify a problem and allocate some federal

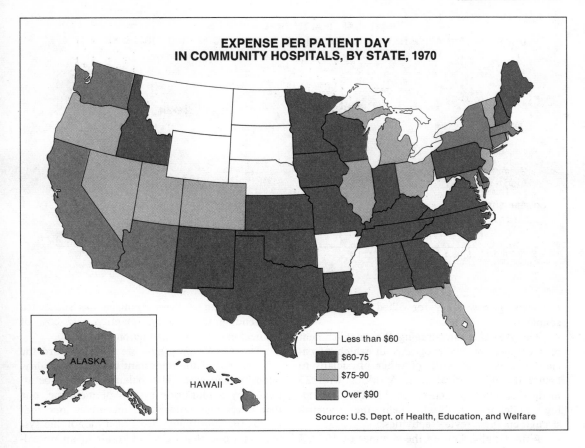

EXPENSE PER PATIENT DAY IN COMMUNITY HOSPITALS, BY STATE, 1970

ALASKA

HAWAII

Less than $60
$60-75
$75-90
Over $90

Source: U.S. Dept. of Health, Education, and Welfare

money to it, the problem would get solved." Now, the report points out, reductions in income coupled with government expansion call for a new approach to the setting of priorities.

Medicredit can be put into operation now. It would build upon the very real accomplishments of American medicine, augmenting a health care system that has already shown a capability of being the best in the world. The federal cost for Medicredit would be some $14 billion a year.

Other AMA Programs. The AMA's comprehensive program includes, in addition to the financing mechanism, emphasis on public education, professional education, manpower resources and distribution, health and medical facilities, and medical research. The United States has health-related problems that cannot be solved by medicine alone. Many Americans eat and drink too much, smoke cigarettes, and fail to exercise. Millions are injured on our highways. Inflation has driven up the cost of health care. These problems are social, cultural, and economic, and they require the efforts of everyone.

The AMA accepts its responsibility in these areas and is working with other organizations and with all levels of government to improve the quality of our national life. Last year the AMA launched a series of "quality of life" programs to stimulate action on such problems as drug abuse, housing, health education, infant and maternal care, alcoholism, cardiovascular conditions, aggressive behavior, air and water pollution, and physical fitness.

The AMA is supporting innovative health delivery projects in urban and rural areas. Through a program called Project USA, the AMA is recruiting physicians for volunteer duty in medically underserved communities where the government's National Health Service Corps program has been implemented. To the 92d Congress the AMA offered a draft bill that would help communities meet the need for emergency medical services. The AMA is also developing programs to improve health services in correctional institutions.

Medical education, both to produce more new physicians and to maintain the excellence of those in practice, is an important part of the AMA's activity. The association urged Congress to provide more funds for medical school construction and for the training of family physicians. It supported the Comprehensive Health Manpower Act and urged both houses of Congress to provide full funding. Other projects are designed to increase the nation's medical manpower by developing educational standards and

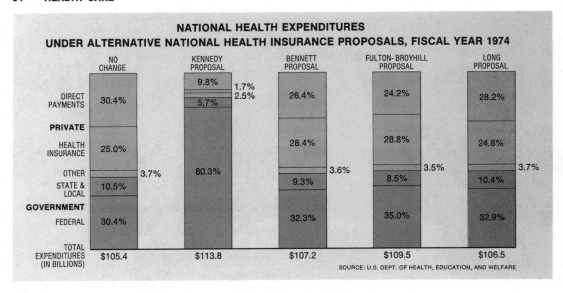

NATIONAL HEALTH EXPENDITURES
UNDER ALTERNATIVE NATIONAL HEALTH INSURANCE PROPOSALS, FISCAL YEAR 1974

	NO CHANGE	KENNEDY PROPOSAL	BENNETT PROPOSAL	FULTON-BROYHILL PROPOSAL	LONG PROPOSAL
DIRECT PAYMENTS	30.4%	9.8% 1.7% / 2.5% 5.7%	26.4%	24.2%	28.2%
PRIVATE					
HEALTH INSURANCE	25.0%		28.4%	28.8%	24.8%
OTHER	3.7%	80.3%	3.6%	3.5%	3.7%
STATE & LOCAL	10.5%		9.3%	8.5%	10.4%
GOVERNMENT					
FEDERAL	30.4%		32.3%	35.0%	32.9%
TOTAL EXPENDITURES (IN BILLIONS)	$105.4	$113.8	$107.2	$109.5	$106.5

SOURCE: U.S. DEPT. OF HEALTH, EDUCATION, AND WELFARE

by devising new roles for allied medical personnel.

The AMA is encouraging the establishment of local peer-review programs in which physicians evaluate the work of other physicians to assure quality medical care. Working with 23 medical specialty societies, the AMA is developing guidelines that will help the societies strengthen their review activities.

AMA Goals. During the summer of 1972, I toured in England, Sweden, West Germany, and the Soviet Union. I saw how we could profit by the examples of others to improve our system. I also saw that full access to health is a problem even in nations with fully socialized systems and that none of these countries has succeeded in blending the quality, quantity, and cost of medical care to the satisfaction of all.

The AMA's programs are aimed toward the achievement of the important balance of quality, quantity, and cost. This balance can best be attained by a pluralistic system of medicine, one that offers alternatives and incentives, one that avoids the stultifying effects of a monolithic system, and one that does not result in an unrealistic and costly administrative bureaucracy. The goal can be reached if our present health care system is strengthened and supported through the cooperative efforts of the public, the government, and the professions.

BECTON, DICKINSON AND COMPANY

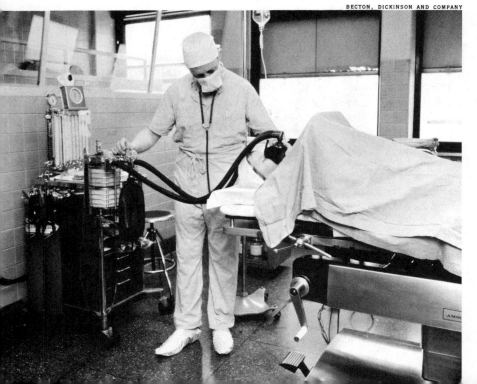

NEW LINE of hospital supplies sterilizes virtually every piece of anesthetic equipment that comes in direct contact with patients.

Health Plans at Work in Europe, Elsewhere

By Brian Abel-Smith

Professor of Social Administration, The London School of Economics and Political Science

In Europe, Australia, Japan, Canada, and Latin America, compulsory health insurance is widely developed. It is also considerably developed in the Middle East. The United States is almost the only developed country in the world that does not have compulsory health insurance or a government-financed health service for the bulk of the population.

All over the world there is concern about rising expenditures for health services. The proportion of national income devoted to health services, however, is lower in some countries that have compulsory health insurance covering the vast majority of the population than in the United States. Costs are held back mainly by limiting the daily payment made to hospitals and, in some countries, by controlling the extent of hospital construction to prevent excess provision and duplicated facilities.

Compulsory health insurance is the most common method of paying for health services in Western Europe. The system is financed by contributions deducted from payrolls—usually proportioned contributions up to a maximum and contributions levied on employers. Government subsidies to the system vary in different countries. In Britain, for example, the system is not insurance-based and is known as national health service.

Beginnings of Health Insurance in Europe. In Europe, compulsory health insurance began as an extension of voluntary health insurance that was started by groups of skilled manual workers and later covered unskilled workers during the 19th century. Local groups of workingmen joined together in Germany, Denmark, England, and other countries to form sick clubs that would provide cash benefits for members who were sick. Each member paid a regular subscription to obtain the right to treatment and cash benefit. Local physicians were contracted to certify sickness and to provide medical treatment. The cash benefit was usually at a standard rate per week, and the physicians were normally paid a cash sum per member of the club or society entitled to care. Paying the physician according to the number of subscribing members simplified accounting and made it relatively easy to ensure that the income from subscriptions was sufficient to meet the liabilities of the fund.

This system of health insurance was made compulsory for workers in the main industries of Germany in 1883 and for workers coming below a designated level of income in Britain in 1913. Compulsory health insurance came later to such countries as France, Sweden, and Norway. Gradually industries and occupations that were originally excluded were brought within the system. The rights of the worker were extended to his wife and children, and rights gained during working life were extended into retirement. The trend has therefore been for a higher and higher proportion of the population of Europe to be brought under compulsory health insurance.

Not only has coverage been extended but also the range of benefits provided has been increased to include dental, ophthalmic, and other services. The extent to which hospital care has been covered by health insurance has depended on the financing and ownership of hospitals. In Denmark and Sweden, the local government has long provided the bulk of the hospitals, and thus health insurance never needed to play much of a role in financing hospital care. In Britain voluntary nonprofit hospitals were extensively developed along with local government hospitals. Hospital care was never included in national health insurance in Britain since local government hospitals only charged patients who could afford to pay and the voluntary nonprofit hospitals were able to collect a sufficient income to provide a free service to the bulk of their users. In continental Europe, however, it became the common practice for compulsory health insurance to make payments per day of care for an uninsured person admitted to the hospital. Often separate payment is made to the specialist for his services, as is done in the United States. In Sweden and Denmark, however, physicians are normally paid salaries for their work in hospitals.

Payments to Patients. During this century, many countries that originally paid physicians per member entitled to service (capitation payment) have changed over to payment on a fee-for-service basis. This was largely a response to pressure from organizations of physicians. It was argued that capitation payments were too low, did not fairly reflect the work each physician was expected to undertake, and had resulted in closed panels of physicians servicing the members of particular sick clubs. The broad capitation system of payment is retained in Spain, the Netherlands, and in Britain. In Britain there have been no closed panels of physicians since compulsory health insurance was introduced in 1911. Every physician was and still is entitled to join the plan, and each patient can choose any doctor who has joined and is willing to accept

him—subject to a maximum number of patients on his list. The newer systems of compulsory health insurance, such as in France and Sweden, started with payment to physicians on a fee-for-service basis.

In some countries, such as France, physicians bill patients for their services and then claim reimbursement for the major part of the bill from the sickness insurance agency. In other countries, such as Germany, the physician bills the sick fund. For some services, no payment from the patient may be required; for other services the patient may be required to pay a share of the cost of a specified charge. In some countries the patient can go to any physician at any time and consult two physicians on the same illness, while in other countries the patient may be required to register with a particular physician for a stated period, such as three months, and access to a specialist may be only on the recommendation of his main physician. It is customary for doctors working in national health insurance also to have private patients. Thus patients are free to consult doctors on the traditional private basis if they wish to do so.

The operation of compulsory health insurance when doctors are paid on a fee-for-service basis normally involves negotiations with the profession to fix the rates to be paid for each type of service. Thus, over the years, very elaborate tariffs have been evolved listing all possible services and the value to be attributed to each for payment purposes. Moreover, safeguards have been developed to reduce the incentive for physicians to provide unnecessary services, and physicians believed to be abusing the system are investigated.

It is the general practice for agreement on scales of payment to be reached with the profession, and no physician can charge a patient more than is specified in the regulations. In Sweden, however, the insurance system pays a standard sum to the physician for seeing a patient, and the physician is free to charge the patient a further sum if he wishes to do so. Additional payments are usually requested in the urban areas. This relatively simple system appears to work well in Sweden, which is a small country where the physicians are a tightly knit group.

National Health Service. While the principle of insurance—benefit in return for contribution—has been stretched to extend coverage to dependents and retired people, there still remain small groups that are excluded, particularly those who have never been able to work and often those in the higher income groups who in many countries are left to make their own arrangements. To deal with the excluded groups, some countries have substituted national health services for national health insurance; for example, in Britain since 1948, the whole population became entitled to free health services. Since then modest charges have been introduced for pharmaceuticals, dentistry, and eyeglasses. Physicians still retain full clinical freedom. Physicians working out-of-hospital still contract to care for patients and are not employees of the national health service, and patients are still free to choose their physician.

Public Opinion. The negotiation of physicians' remuneration rates leads to occasional disputes that have in some countries resulted in strikes of physicians, though emergency services are usually maintained. Despite these perhaps inevitable disputes, European physicians have in general come to see more advantages than disadvantages in health insurance. The physician has no bad debts and is not influenced in the exercise of his clinical judgment by any consideration of what the patient can afford. While professional organizations press for relatively minor modifications in the working of health insurance, no national professional organization with long experience of compulsory health insurance now wants to have the system abolished.

The system has strong backing from trade union organizations and the support of the main political parties. Indeed, developments in health insurance are sponsored by diverse political parties. In the major countries of Europe, the question of whether there should or should not be compulsory health insurance has long since ceased to be a political issue.

It was the consumers who evolved voluntary health insurance. It was neither sponsored by the hospital organizations nor sold by commercial insurance companies. Government came in at a late stage to extend and develop the voluntary system.

The political support for health insurance is a reflection of public satisfaction. Illness is no longer a cause of major financial anxiety. People like to be able to visit their physician without worrying about the cost and to be able to receive expensive treatment without the stigma of public assistance. Health insurance has made health care into a right and not a privilege. By the conventional and albeit inadequate indicators, health standards in many countries of Western Europe are higher than in the United States. Whether this is due to national health insurance and health services or to differences in social conditions is an open question. But what is not in doubt is that there is no move in Western Europe to return to the private market in health services.

This Turkish cargo vessel, the Divanbakirli, *was seized in the port of Marseille, France, with 350 kilograms (772 pounds) of morphine.*

Narcotics Traffic:

The Deadly Web

By Bernard Gwertzman
"The New York Times"

Largely under the prodding of the U. S. government, many countries are making a more serious effort to stem the rising traffic in illicit drugs. Their principal target is the flow of opium and its main derivative, heroin, from poverty-stricken areas to Western Europe and the United States.

But an important U. S. government study concluded in August 1972 that despite the increased enforcement efforts the United States and other countries have been able to seize only "a small fraction" of the total illegal flow of heroin.

The U. S. report, known officially as "World Opium Survey 1972," was published by the Cabinet Committee on International Narcotics Control. It noted that enforcement efforts had led to an increase in the amount of heroin seized, and that the seizures were often accompanied by well-publicized accounts that another French or Latin "connection" had been cracked. The report said, however, that "the international heroin market almost certainly continues to have adequate supplies to meet the demand in consuming countries."

The problems are extremely grave. Authorities estimate that at least 200 tons of illicit production were available on the international market in 1972. This compares with the 21 tons seized in all of 1971. In the United States, the home of some 560,000 addicts, only six to ten tons a year are believed needed to keep them supplied.

Efforts to halt the flow have proved difficult, largely because the profits to the traffickers are

so incredible that they are willing not only to risk losing an occasional shipment but also arrest or violence from rival criminal syndicates. On an investment of at most $300,000 for 100 kilograms of heroin, the Corsicans who control the European market usually receive at least $1 million in New York on delivery. These same 100 kilograms, sold pure, bring in about $22 million in the United States. But the profits are even higher because the heroin is usually adulterated before being sold.

Even in the underdeveloped countries, such as Turkey, where growing opium became illegal in 1972, profits from illicit opium crops make it worthwhile for farmers to risk growing the white poppy. For instance a farmer in Turkey receives more than six times the income per acre for opium that he does for wheat or barley.

Success in improving international policing organizations has been slow, the U. S. report said, "largely because of widely varying national attitudes toward the drug problem." These differences "are regularly and skillfully exploited by the illicit international trafficker," it said. Efforts to curtail the growing of the poppy "are unlikely to be successful unless accompanied by serious changes in a number of longstanding social and economic traditions."

OPIUM PRODUCTION

Opium is produced from several varieties of the poppy, *papaver somniferum*. This annual grows three to four feet tall on a thin main stalk and produces several blossoms and egg-sized seed pods. It requires extensive labor at harvest time—usually in the spring. A white fluid oozes out of the pods and coagulates into a gum, from which the alkaloid morphine is extracted. It can grow in many different areas, but it does best in warm but not humid climates.

"The fact that the opium poppy can be cultivated in many regions of the world has serious implications for programs aimed at its elimination and complicates the task of estimating the amount of opium produced in the world," the U. S. government report said.

Harvesting the Poppy. The two greatest concentrations of the opium poppy are in India, where much of the production is legal, and in the so-called Golden Triangle of Burma, Thailand, and Laos. In 1971, India reported about 100,000 acres devoted to opium, and the amount in the Golden Triangle must be assumed to be about the same. Considerable amounts have also been grown in northwestern Pakistan, northeastern Afghanistan, Iran, Turkey, and in Eastern Europe, North Africa, Australia, Mexico, and South America.

The growing of opium is a difficult process because it requires considerable care. Pods must be lanced and the gum collected in a 24-hour period. Harvesting requires entire families. Sometimes other persons are hired for periods ranging from two weeks to two months. Because of the labor requirements, the poppy is most often grown in areas where there is cheap, surplus labor.

"The principal economic constraint on opium cultivation thus is the availability of cheap labor," according to the U. S. report. "In most parts of the world, opium can be produced profitably only if there is considerable underutilization of labor, and, in practice, most of the needed labor comes from within the cultivator's family. By the same token, opium is rarely produced where there exist sizable opportunities for wage employment."

At least 1,000 tons of illegal opium were produced in 1971, according to estimates. About 700 tons were grown in the hilly regions of the Golden Triangle, which represents the largest single area of production of illegal opium. About 220 tons were produced in India, Pakistan, and Afghanistan. Illegal Turkish opium was estimated at 35 tons.

Most of the world's illegal opium production is used by people in the areas in which it is grown and does not enter what is regarded as the "international market." For instance, Southeast Asians consume about 600 of the 700 tons produced in the Golden Triangle. China historically was known for its use of opium, but experts believe that China has not engaged in the opium traffic under Communist rule.

Just as the majority of the Golden Triangle's production remained in Southeast Asia, most of the opium grown in South Asia—India, Pakistan, and Afghanistan—was consumed in that region, principally in Iran where illegal imports may range from 100 to 300 tons a year.

Conversion into Heroin. "At present there are no means of estimating with any confidence how much of the total world illicit production of opium is available for, or is actually converted into, heroin for the international market," the U. S. government report states. "A rough approximation based on rather tenuous estimates of production and consumption in local markets is that a minimum of 200 tons of illicit production in 1971 probably was available for the international heroin market. In addition there were undoubtedly substantial illicit stocks available for the international markets. These include stocks of raw opium held by growers as well as stocks of processed opium, morphine base, and heroin held by processors and traffick-

ers. Indeed, chances are good that stocks in Southeast Asia rose in 1971 because little of the opium available in that region was converted to heroin after mid-year. However, most of the opium entering the international market from Turkey and Mexico was converted into heroin during 1971."

Making heroin from opium in so-called laboratories has been described as no more complex than the making of bootleg whiskey in the United States. The U. S. report explains:

"Neither high temperatures nor high pressures are involved in the process, the basic equipment used is simple, and only small amounts of common industrial chemicals are required. Electric power needs . . . are modest; ample, but not unusually large supplies of water are necessary. Processing does not require the services of a graduate chemist. For the most part, processing operations are run by so-called 'heroin chemists' who have learned the trade through apprenticeship to other heroin chemists. Aside from the chemist, only a few semi-skilled helpers are involved in processing."

THE INTERNATIONAL MARKETS

Opium and its derivatives reach the international marketplace through three major marketing complexes, intelligence agents believe.

The "primary complex," according to the American government, begins in Turkey and encompasses many countries in Western Europe and the Western Hemisphere before the product arrives in the United States. The second complex, based in Southeast Asia, provides only small amounts to the United States and Europe, but may increase in coming years. The third complex, comprising the countries in South Asia, also provides little opium to the United States. All three are studied intensely by enforcement officers, the first because it is the center of the heroin problem, and the second and third because of their potential for becoming dangerous.

The Long Journey Begins. The primary complex begins in the poppy fields of Turkey, includes international channels controlled by Turkish and French traffickers, and ends in systems operated by major American syndicates. According to the U. S. report:

"Each step in this process, including the illicit processing of Turkish opium and morphine base, the smuggling of narcotics from the Near and Middle East to Western Europe, the refining of the heroin in France, and the clandestine shipment of heroin to the United States, represents a separate and independent transaction handled by various groups brought together by the lure of high profits. There are no precise

answers to the questions of how much opium is produced in Turkey, how much morphine base enters Western Europe, or how much heroin enters the United States. It is known, however, that there is a constant demand for heroin in the United States and a constant effort to meet that demand by Turkish and French suppliers."

Once criminal agents purchase the illicit opium in Turkey, there are a few known variants for getting it to Europe. One involves narcotics that pass through the Middle East under the control of Syrian and Lebanese traffickers. Another variation includes the use of West Germany as a storage depot for Middle East middlemen who buy the Turkish opium and sell it to French heroin producers. Middlemen in Italy and other European countries help ship the goods to France.

"The methods a narcotics smuggler may use to transport opium or morphine base from Turkey to Lebanon to France are limited only by the scope of his imagination," the report said.

The most popular method uses specially built compartments—or "traps"—in cars, trucks, or buses. In addition, the narcotics are often hidden in trucks carrying bonded consignments. These trucks, operating under international customs agreements, will usually be allowed to cross frontiers with little or no inspection. And the great number of trucks entering Western Europe would seem to preclude any systematic inspection.

The most heavily traveled overland route used to bring Turkish opium to Europe runs through Bulgaria or Greece to Yugoslavia. From there, the goods are carried to West Germany via Austria or directly to France via Italy. The greatest change in recent years has been the emergence of West Germany as a major storage depot and staging area.

The French heroin traffic is dominated by a few gangs. For the most part, during the last 20 years, such gangs have been Corsican. "It is this ethnic group above all others that has controlled the heroin traffic in France. As these old leaders disappear from the business, however, they are being replaced by younger, and in many cases, non-Corsican French traffickers," the U. S. report said.

Making the Connection. To bring the heroin into the United States, three basic routes are followed: from Europe directly or via Canada; from Europe, via Mexico; and from Europe via various other countries in Latin America and the Caribbean. Since 1969, heroin seizures from Latin America accounted for about a third of the total, indicating the rising use of that par-

THE COUNTERATTACK

U. S. Official Tells of Government Efforts to Suppress Flow of Drugs

BY NELSON G. GROSS
*Senior Adviser and Coordinator
for International Narcotics Matters,
U. S. State Department*

Ten years ago, the use of marihuana was rare even on college campuses. Today, about 20 million persons in the United States have used marihuana. Reports show that one third of all high school and college students smoke marihuana.

Ten years ago, heroin addicts in the United States numbered about 40,000. Today, the U. S. heroin addict population exceeds 500,000. Heroin is moving into all types of communities, into all types of homes.

Marihuana and heroin represent only the two extremes of the drug scene. In between, the abuse of all drugs and narcotics, both natural and synthetic, has risen sharply.

The Domestic War on Drugs. Many explanations have been given for the phenomenal surge of drug abuse during the 1960's. No one can doubt that the availability of supply has been a major factor in the mushrooming of the drug subculture. Also, the abuse of harmful substances was ignored and tolerated too long; it could well be said that the nation was "asleep at the switch" when illicit drugs and narcotics began flooding our universities, high schools, and neighborhoods.

If America did sleep during the 1960's, it can also be said that it has now fully awakened to the problem. The federal government has made drug abuse control a top priority on both the domestic and international fronts. Although controls on all illicit materials are being reinforced, the principal target in the U. S. drug program is the elimination of illegal production and trafficking in opium, heroin, and the other opiates.

Federal expenditures on antidrug programs of all types increased from $65 million in 1969 to $729 million for the fiscal year 1972–73, more than a tenfold rise. The 1972–73 funds are allocated as follows: treatment and rehabilitation, $313 million; research, education, training, and prevention, $172.2 million; and law enforcement, $244.2 million.

The Comprehensive Drug Abuse Prevention and Control Act of 1970, a federal law that went into effect on May 1, 1971, is a basic tool in our attack on illicit drugs. Thus far, more than 40 states have passed laws or are framing drug control laws that parallel the federal legislation.

Through the efforts of two federal enforcement agencies, the Bureau of Narcotics and Dangerous Drugs and the Bureau of Customs, seizure of all forms of illicit drugs has increased. For example, in fiscal year 1971–72, 1,626 pounds of heroin were seized, compared with 1,163 pounds in the previous year.

To intensify the campaign against domestic supplies, President Nixon established the Office of Drug Abuse Law Enforcement in the U. S. Department of Justice on Jan. 28, 1972. Working with task forces in 38 target cities, the office uses special grand juries to gather information on drug traffickers for use by federal, state, and local law enforcement agencies. The Special Action Office for Drug Abuse Prevention, established under executive order by the President on June 17, 1971, and signed into law after congressional approval on March 21, 1972, coordinates the activities of 13 federal agencies in drug abuse prevention, education, treatment, rehabilitation, and research.

International Cooperation. While U. S. collective antidrug abuse efforts have moved ahead at home, we have also worked for worldwide cooperation. The U. S. government, acting through the Department of State as the primary U. S. agency for coordinating international narcotics controls, upgraded the drug problem to a high-priority foreign policy issue in mid-1971. Drug control officers at most U. S. missions abroad coordinate U. S. diplomatic efforts in foreign countries. Collaboration was strengthened among the appropriate federal agencies in Washington through the establishment of regional interagency task forces.

In September 1971, President Nixon established the Cabinet Committee on International Narcotics Control, designating Secretary of State William P. Rogers as chairman. Also serving on the committee are the heads of the departments of Justice, Defense, Treasury, Agriculture, and the Central Intelligence Agency, as well as the U. S. representative to the United Nations.

To systematize the bilateral approach to drug control, the Cabinet Committee has directed the preparation of narcotics control action plans for 59 countries considered to have a current or potential involvement in the production, processing, consumption, or transshipment of illicit hard drugs. Prepared by U. S. embassies abroad, the plans were reviewed in Washington in early 1972 and returned to Foreign Service posts to serve as a basis for opening discussions with host governments for the negotiation of bilateral narcotics control agreements or action programs. While U. S. cooperation is multifaceted, the thrust of our efforts abroad is to increase local enforcement capabilities and to gather and exchange intelligence with foreign governments with a view to curtailing supplies and interdicting the flow of illicit drugs.

The most heartening news in the battle against drug abuse was the decision announced by Turkey on June 30, 1971, to ban the cultivation of the opium poppy after the harvesting of the 1971–72 crop. In response, the U. S. government assured Turkey of financial assistance to offset foreign exchange losses from legitimate exports of opium gum and poppy products.

The action by Turkey is expected to remove a major source of opium for heroin marketed in the United States. But with the elimination of this Middle East source illegal traffickers will look elsewhere, and we are focusing on cooperative action plans with the governments in Southeast Asia to prevent that area from becoming a principal source for heroin in the streets of America.

Victory in the battle against illicit drugs will require a long, uphill struggle. However, through our bilateral approaches and our efforts to strengthen international drug treaties, we are off to a good start. Thanks to the steady efforts of our ambassadors abroad and other U. S. officials, the tragedy of the drug problem—particularly that of heroin —is now universally recognized.

ticular route. Almost all heroin, however, is brought to New York before being distributed elsewhere in the United States.

"The direct Europe-to-U. S. route is the oldest French heroin smuggling route and remains the most active," the American report asserted. "Direct shipments to the United States enable the French traffickers to avoid using foreign middlemen smugglers who might otherwise establish a closer relationship to the U. S. buyer. The French smugglers have the advantage of concealing their shipments within a huge volume of transatlantic commerce and need pass through only one customs check." Canada is used as an alternate route in the belief that Canadian customs and the U. S.-Canadian border customs are less vigilant than those on the U. S. East Coast.

Little has been known of the French–Latin American connection except that many of the leaders of the groups operating in South America are ethnic Corsicans and ethnic Italians with close ties to Europe. Many have been smuggling whiskey and cigarettes and have simply added heroin to their business. French heroin is believed to enter Latin America through Buenos Aires and Montevideo. From there it moves north, with much of the traffic through Panama. Sizable amounts have gone via Mexico, and the importance of this route may be increasing.

The distribution of opium products, including heroin, has been described by the report as "a big business in Southeast Asia." Supplies originate with the hill people who grow it in the tri-border area of Burma, Laos, and Thailand. Annual production of opium in the area runs to about 700 tons, with some 400 consumed by the hill people themselves. These 400 tons, however, are an important reserve supply, the American government estimates, "because growers can be induced to sell part of what they normally consume if offered an increase in price."

Before the large-scale involvement of U. S. servicemen in Southeast Asia, the 300 tons of opium not consumed by the hill people were sold and processed in Vientiane, Bangkok, and Hong Kong, where they were ultimately consumed by the opium and heroin communities of Asians who smoke the material. But the sudden emergence of a large American market in 1970 and 1971 led to a production boom for the high-quality No. 4 heroin, which can be injected. As American troops withdrew from the area, these sales began to drop. It is possible that if the traditional Turkish-French connection is blocked, the smuggling community might turn to the Asian market.

Opium and Morphine Base Movement from Turkey to Western Europe

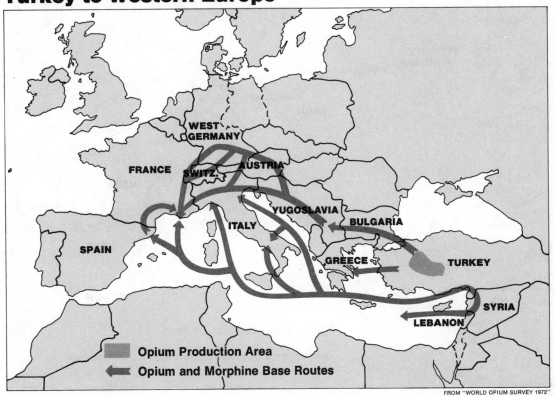

■ Opium Production Area

◀ Opium and Morphine Base Routes

FROM "WORLD OPIUM SURVEY 1972"

THE GEOGRAPHY OF OPIUM

In an appendix to their 1972 report, the U. S. analysts described the traffic by country. Countries discussed included the following:

Turkey. Turkey is the largest source of the raw material for the heroin sold on the American market. Turkish opium is preferred by heroin traffickers because the morphine content is one of the highest in the world, ranging from 9% to 14%. Legal prices for Turkey's opium exports far surpass those of other countries. The report noted Turkey's decision to ban the legal production of opium in the hope that this would also end illegal production. But the report said that "There will still be a need for vigorous law enforcement against smugglers if the flow of illegal opium is to be slowed after 1972, when production is banned. This is true because of the likelihood that illegal stocks . . . may be stored in Turkey."

"A large network exists in Turkey to collect and, in some cases, process and smuggle the opium out of the country," the report stated.

Afghanistan. Opium production in Afghanistan is all illegal, but about 100 tons is produced each year because the royal government "is simply unable to provide adequate enforcement." The report said that an effective enforcement program is blocked because in some areas opium is the only cash crop, and some tribes, like the Pathans, "enjoy special privileges, such as exemption from taxes and conscription. The King regards these tribes as an important pillar of support and will not wish to antagonize them."

Iran. Iran is a major customer for illegal Afghan opium exports for some 400,000 addicts. Iran's addict population declined from a peak of 1.5 million after a ban on opium was instituted in 1955, the report said, but Iran is still one of the world's leading consumers of narcotics.

Pakistan. The illegal opium production in Pakistan has ranged between 32 and 170 tons a year, all in the former Northwest Frontier province. Most of the opium is sold in Iran. The Pakistani government has expressed a willingness to combat the growing of illegal opium, but the U. S. report points out that "the new administration will be reluctant to risk antagonizing the tribal peoples with an opium eradication plan." The report notes that Pakistani officials consider

The Mid-East–South Asia Illicit Opium Network

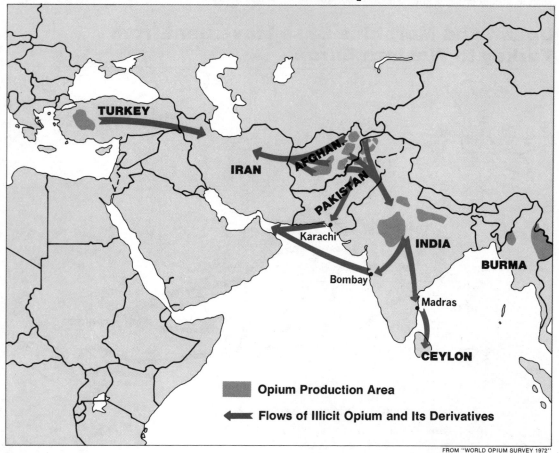

■ Opium Production Area

◀━━ Flows of Illicit Opium and Its Derivatives

FROM "WORLD OPIUM SURVEY 1972"

The Southeast Asia Illicit Opium Network

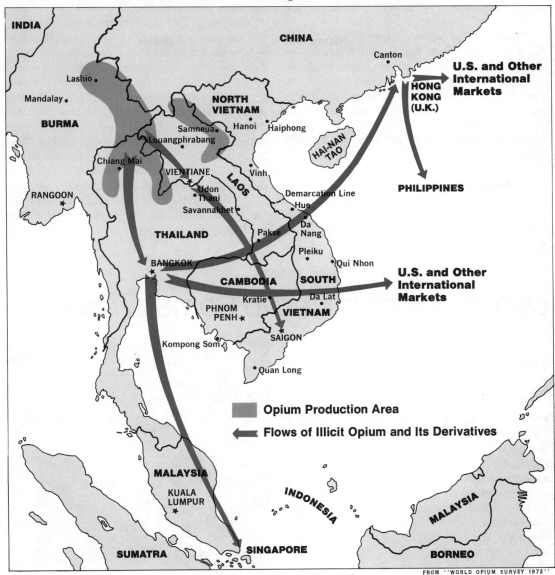

FROM "WORLD OPIUM SURVEY 1972"

opium consumption to be only a minor problem.

India. India is the world's largest producer of legal opium. With Turkey ending its production of legal opium, India has a virtual monopoly in this field. But the U. S. report also estimated that 100 tons a year enter the illegal market, although most of it is consumed in India itself.

Burma. Burma produces about 400 tons a year and is the largest single producer for overseas markets. The government does not regard the matter as serious, and refuses to participate in international control bodies. The Burmese traffic is controlled by Chinese, many of them former members of the Nationalist Chinese forces that retreated into Burma after the victory of the Communists in China in 1949. Most of the opium produced in northern Burma and northwest Thailand is processed in refineries

within an area of about 650 square miles at the junction of the borders of Burma, Thailand, and Laos.

China. Despite China's long association with the opium trade, the U. S. report found "no reliable evidence that China has either engaged in or sanctioned the illicit export of opium and its derivatives, nor are there any indications of government participation in the opium trade of Southeast Asia and adjacent markets."

France. France was praised in the report for increasing its attention to the drug problem after long believing that publicity would only contribute to the spread of drugs. Although addiction was less serious in France than in the United States, according to the report, heroin use had increased sharply. Despite the stepped-up enforcement, France was estimated to be the

secondary source of 80% of the heroin on the U. S. market.

Mexico. The report estimated that 25% of the heroin going into the United States moves through Mexico. An important heroin highway is Route 15, which runs northward along the western coast of Mexico. The heroin is brought across the border in cars, or sometimes in light planes or fishing boats. "The profits involved are so enormous—up to $50,000 for a single trip—that there is no shortage of entrepreneurs," the report said.

Panama. Panama was described as a long-time "staging area for contraband American cigarettes and other goods bound for Latin America." Because of the heavy ship traffic in the canal and the air traffic at its airport, control of smuggling "is a formidable task."

"Countless pilots have loaded their planes with contraband whiskey and cigarettes from Panama's free port areas and flown them to South America," the report said. "In the past the planes would usually return to Panama empty; now many return with cocaine from the Andean countries and with heroin that has been smuggled into Latin America from Europe. The drugs are flown to Miami or elsewhere in the United States, sometimes by way of Mexico. In recent years, some of the cocaine has been shipped from Panama to Europe in exchange for heroin which is ultimately smuggled into the United States."

Use of Opium Traced to Roman Times

By David F. Musto, M. D.
*Assistant Professor of History
and Psychiatry, Yale University*

The use of opium to lessen pain, induce sleep and create a feeling of dreamy pleasure was well known at least 2,000 years ago. The site of opium production in Greco-Roman times, a region stretching from Asia Minor to Persia, still exports opium. For most opium production, even the laborious process of scratching each poppy pod and scraping off the oozing juice has not changed over the centuries. The narcotic became a standard medical aid at least by the 1st century B. C.

Early Uses of Opium. The early applications of opium suggest that it was used mostly by the wealthy. Several of the best-known compounds that contained substantial amounts of opium allegedly protected the user against malicious poisoning. The first, introduced in the time of Julius Caesar, was named *mithradatium* after Mithradates VI, the king of Pontus, in Asia Minor. He was said to have protected himself against assassination by gradually increasing daily ingestion of various poisons until he was able to withstand doses that would have killed anyone else. Another popular poison antidote was *theriac,* a modification of mithradatium devised by Emperor Nero's personal physician. There is good reason to believe that a later emperor, Marcus Aurelius, became addicted to opium through daily administration of theriac. For more than 15 centuries both mithradatium and theriac remained popular.

BLACK STAR

The opium poppy harvest on the central Anatolian plateau of Turkey. Turkey has been the main source of raw material for the heroin sold on the U. S. market.

A third opium compound, *philonium,* was prepared in the 1st century after Christ as a remedy for an epidemic of dysentery in Rome. Such an application of opium would take advantage of one of its most powerful and characteristic effects, the slowing of intestinal action, which produces constipation in a healthy person but which moderates or stops diarrhea in someone ill of dysentery, cholera, or other intestinal ailments.

From the Middle East the cultivation of opium spread to India and eventually to China. Western travelers in the 16th and 17th centuries commented on the need of the user to continue daily ingestion of opium or suffer terrible pains or even death. Yet in Europe, perhaps because of the distance from opium production, there are few accounts of addiction. In the 16th century, however, an alcoholic extract of opium, laudanum, was introduced and became a favored remedy for almost any disease. It proved most useful in the treatment of dysentery, chronic pain, and anxiety. Concocted from crude opium, wine, and several spices, laudanum was as much like a cocktail as a medicine.

Several modern examples of multidrug opium preparations came into common use in the 18th century. Paregoric, which has soothed so many teething babies, appeared as a combination of opium and camphor. A powerful nonalcoholic form of opium, "blackdrop," avoided the alcoholic intoxication that would accompany repeated large doses of laudanum.

By the early 19th century opium's frequent use stimulated discussion on means of regulating its distribution. Such literary figures as Thomas De Quincey (who romanticized addiction in his *Confessions of an English Opium Eater,* 1821), Samuel Taylor Coleridge, and Wilkie Collins were among the victims of opiate addiction.

Opium and Modern Science. During the last 150 years scientific advances and engineering accomplishments have so altered opium preparations and their means of transportation and administration that the modern narcotic problem is profoundly different from earlier worries about laudanum and theriac. The first, and probably most significant, development was the isolation in 1804 of morphine, the chief active ingredient of crude opium. Thereafter, it was possible to obtain opium's effects, but with a drug of assured purity, of unvarying potency, and compact enough to transport cheaply and easily.

Within a few decades the extraction of morphine from opium became a simple commercial process, and the drug was welcomed as a boon to mankind. In 1853, Dr. Alexander Wood of Edinburgh began to report success in using morphine injections to treat patients with chronic pain. The hypodermic syringe became popular with physicians and patient alike. A curious belief grew that this means of administration avoided opium addiction.

By the late 19th century the danger of morphine, particularly when given hypodermically, was no longer doubted, but control of its generous use was not an easy matter. By 1900 in the United States, many state laws restricted access to large amounts of opium and morphine to physicians only. Yet the physicians, many of whom were poorly trained, could not all be trusted to exercise good judgment in the dispensing or prescribing of narcotics. And doctors and pharmacists did not completely control the availability of narcotics, for the drugs were also contained in patent medicines. The latter, often exempt from state laws, could be purchased by mail from suppliers in states with weak or nonexistent antinarcotic laws. The commercial introduction in 1898 of a new morphine derivative, heroin, further complicated control of addiction. Heroin was for a time thought to cure morphine addiction, but it was mostly sold as a cough suppressant.

International Control. In 1909 the United States convened in Shanghai the first international meeting to consider the opium traffic. In 1912, an International Opium Conference at The Hague endorsed a treaty to regulate the transportation and distribution of opium and of crude coca and its active ingredient, the stimulant cocaine.

Many subsequent international agreements were designed to bring dangerous narcotic drugs under control. To implement the Hague Convention, the United States passed the Harrison Antinarcotic Act (1914), which remained the basic antinarcotic law until the Comprehensive Drug Abuse Prevention and Control Act of 1970. As a result of the Harrison Act and its interpretation by the Supreme Court in 1919, the legal maintenance of addiction was ended, except in certain medical situations, until addiction maintenance through a synthetic narcotic, methadone, was legalized in the 1960's.

The effectiveness of international agreements in controlling narcotics traffic is still debated. Advances in communications and transportation have compounded the difficulty of preventing smuggling, just as the discovery and manufacture of purified narcotics is a by-product of scientific progress. Thus the greater medical benefits gained by research on opium and coca have been balanced by greater potential for social and individual harm.

SKYJACKING:
A New Tool Of Terrorists

On May 9, at Lod Airport, Tel Aviv, Israeli paratroopers disguised as airport maintenance crewmen storm a Belgian airliner hijacked by Arab guerrillas to rescue 90 passengers and 10 members of the crew. During an exchange of gunfire, two guerrillas were killed and two others captured by the attacking force.

UPI

By Robert H. Lindsey
Aviation Reporter, "The New York Times"

"The plane has been hijacked!" The world heard these words as never before in 1972, and often they carried new and deadly meanings. More than 50 commercial airliners from more than 10 countries were hijacked during the year. Air piracy—in the past predominately an avenue of protest and escape for malcontents and political militants—increasingly became a sinister tool of international extortion. Jet airliners, their crews, and passengers became pawns of terrorists and extortionists, who vowed to destroy them unless ransom was paid in the form of huge sums of money or the release of prisoners.

As hijackings increased in the United States, President Richard M. Nixon ordered tighter airport security measures. Civil Aeronautics Board Chairman Secor D. Browne and others urged the creation of a new federal airport police force. The Senate approved enabling legislation, but the House, bowing to administration displeasure over the potential cost, did not. The Nixon position was that airports and local police agencies should carry the major share of airport security responsibility, with costs passed on to the traveling public as higher fares.

Meanwhile, the United States and other countries looked for new tools of international law to discipline countries that harbor hijackers. Limited progress was made, but obstacles remained. Negotiations were to continue in 1973.

There was one diplomatic breakthrough: After a decade of aloofness on the subject, Cuba, the most popular haven for hijackers, offered to consider negotiating a treaty with the United States requiring extradition of persons who hijacked planes or ships. At year-end, some form of agreement seemed likely.

Background. Documents recorded by the U. S. Federal Aviation Administration (FAA) show instances of airliners being commandeered by sky pirates dating back to 1923. However, the problem was insignificant until after World War II, when there was a rash of hijackings by Eastern Europeans seeking refuge from communism. In the early 1960's the familiar pattern of the Havana-bound hijacker developed. This accelerated dramatically between 1968 and 1970, and more than 110 planes were commandeered to Havana during the decade. Hijackers also sought refuge in Algeria and other Middle Eastern countries.

Beginning in 1971 there emerged a new and perilous breed of extortionist-hijacker. Political extremists had used the tactic of hijacking for ransom before. The hijacking and subsequent destruction of four jetliners by Palestinian guerrillas seeking release of imprisoned terrorists in September 1970 was one of the grimmest episodes in aviation history.

But skyjacking for money was a new twist. Its antecedents were in the telephoned bomb threat. The first such incident occurred in May 1971, when a team of Australian criminals ex-

torted $500,000 from Qantas Airways after announcing that a bomb was aboard a Qantas jet. The United States experienced its first airline extortion the following August, when Western Airlines paid $25,000 to a telephone caller who made a bomb threat.

In November 1971, the skyjacking variant of the crime emerged: A passenger who identified himself as "D. B. Cooper" demanded and received $200,000 and four parachutes from Northwest Orient Airlines during a flight between Portland, Oreg., and Seattle. He had threatened to blow up the plane if the airline did not pay. Before the plane landed in Reno, Nev., "Cooper" had vanished; he apparently jumped out of a tail exit door of the Boeing 727. About a dozen persons attempted to use this technique in 1972.

Hijacking for Ransom. In all, the world's airlines paid more than $15 million to extortionists and hijackers in 1972, less than half of which was recovered subsequently. Political prisoners also were ransomed. The highest cash ransom, $5 million, was paid by Lufthansa German Airways to five Arab terrorists who hijacked a Boeing 747 on a New Delhi–Athens flight on February 21. The money probably went to finance the extremist Black September arm of the Palestinian liberation guerrilla army.

Several other notable hijackings and airline ransom cases occurred during the year. In January a man identified as Merlin St. George hijacked a Mohawk Airlines plane, demanding $200,000 and a parachute. He was killed by

FBI agents as he sought to escape at Poughkeepsie, N. Y. In March unknown persons placed bombs on two Trans World Airlines jetliners and demanded $2 million ransom or the planes would be blown up. One bomb severely damaged a Boeing 707 on the ground at Las Vegas. The extortionists failed to keep a prearranged rendezvous to collect the money.

In April a man identified as Richard F. McCoy, Jr., parachuted from a United Air Lines 727 over Utah after being paid $500,000. He was apprehended and sentenced to 45 years in jail. The money was recovered. In May, Frederick W. Hahneman hijacked an Eastern Airlines plane, was paid $303,000, and parachuted into the Honduran jungle. He was apprehended in June, but the money was not found. In Tel Aviv, Israeli agents stormed a Sabena Belgian Airlines jet that was held by four Arab guerrillas, who demanded the release of 317 Palestinian guerrillas imprisoned in Israel. Two of the hijackers were killed, and five passengers were injured during the shooting.

In June a man identified as William Holder, accompanied by a young woman, extorted $500,-000 from Western Airlines and ordered one of its planes to Algiers, where the couple joined a colony of expatriate Black Panthers. Algerian officials returned the ransom money. An unemployed Vietnam War veteran named Martin J. McNally obtained $502,000 from American Airlines, but was apprehended on the ground after

(*Continued on page 49*)

PILOTS and other airline employees demonstrate at the United Nations on September 19 as part of their campaign for tougher treatment of skyjackers.

Pilots Demand Quick Action To End Threat

BY CAPT. JOHN J. O'DONNELL
President, Air Line Pilots Association

To date, nearly 600 airline passengers, employees, and crew members had been murdered by aerial criminals. Over the past decade United States aircraft alone were subject to 159 hijacking assaults by 210 persons, 118 of whom remain fugitives from justice. Since 1967 one out of every 75 U. S. airline crew members has faced acid, knives, guns, bombs, or other weapons while on the job. In 1972, 1,888 U. S. airline passengers and crew members were endangered in 31 acts of air piracy.

The crime of hijacking has escalated to terror bombings, million-dollar holdups, and to tragic aerial and ground shoot-outs demonstrating how far fanatics will go to achieve their goals. We, the airlines' flight crews who bear major responsibility for the safety of air travelers, can no longer tolerate delay in seeking a solution to crimes involving aircraft.

Lack of Progress. It is incredible to us that airlines and governments have hesitated so long in implementing preflight screening. In the United States, the 92d Congress in 1972 was unable to pass a strong bill to combat hijacking, nor even to pass legislation needed to implement the Hague Convention of 1970 concerning sabotage on airliners. Little progress has been made in international control of hijacking through treaties, and none of the three treaties in effect calls for sanctions against countries that fail to prosecute or extradite hijackers.

Since 1968 the Air Line Pilots Association in the United States has been urging government and industry leaders to implement our recommenda-

tions for safety and security. We have established a top-priority flight security committee and initiated an international program, "T-plus," to promote ratification of treaties dealing with hijacking. In 1968 our executive board, in conjunction with the International Federation of Airline Pilots Associations, set machinery in motion to impose boycotts by pilots against nations that offer sanctuary to sky criminals. Frustrated by UN foot dragging, the U. S. and international airline pilots were forced to implement a one-day suspension of service, which we called an "SOS," on June 19, 1972.

Recommendations and Goals. We have no alternative other than to take the lead in this struggle against aerial terrorism. Our job should be to fly airplanes. We have no desire to be in the business of international diplomacy, and we will be pleased to be out of it as soon as the following defenses are taken.

International treaties must be implemented to eliminate all sanctuaries for hijackers and extortionists. We call for the prompt release of hijacked passengers, crew, and aircraft; the return of extortion money; the extradition of hijackers; and the imposition of minimum 20-year sentences for the crime.

A multimillion-dollar counteroffensive must be launched to detect and apprehend sky criminals before they board any U. S. or foreign aircraft at any of the 531 U. S. civil air terminals. All passengers must be screened, and those who meet the psychological profile must be searched and, if necessary, arrested. Airlines, domestic or foreign, must either refuse carry-on baggage or arrange for it to be electronically screened or hand-searched. Similar surveillance must be maintained over checked luggage in cargo compartments.

Cockpit sections of airliners must be protected by armored doors. Captains should have the option to be armed with nonlethal weapons and should retain final authority during attempts by law enforcement officers to thwart a hijacker aboard the aircraft, either in the air or on the ground. Fencing, lighting, and other equipment must be installed to create security envelopes separating public and operational areas at all civilian airports.

We are a long way from achieving these goals, partly because of the ineffective and duplicative efforts made by a wide range of government agencies, none of which has control of the total situation. We believe that the President of the United States should establish a single high-level agency with full responsibility for actions against hijackings. We further believe that the President should deny landing rights at U. S. airports to nations that will not cooperate in denying safe harbor to hijackers.

Crew Manifesto. We are not willing to live with the potential for mass murder aboard a large airliner or to hazard the senseless slaughter of fellow crew members. Should we lose an aircraft with passengers, or another crew member, we may find it necessary to deny our services to the airline industry until the government and airlines take the actions we demand to bring an end to this menace. Further, the U. S. and international airline pilots, the airline ground workers, and members of the maritime unions, alike, may be forced to refuse their services on the aircraft, at the airports, or at the shipping ports of any nation that offers haven to hijackers.

(*Continued from page 47*)
parachuting. Another parachutist-hijacker, Robb D. Heady, was captured after extorting $200,000 from United Air Lines at Reno, Nev.

In July a passenger on a Pacific Southwest Airlines jet was killed in San Francisco in an exchange of gunfire between FBI agents and two hijackers who had demanded $800,000 and charts for a flight to the Soviet Union. The hijackers also were killed. In Saigon, South Vietnam, Nguyen Thai Binh was shot to death by a passenger after hijacking a Pan American World Airways Boeing 747 and attempting to divert it to Hanoi, North Vietnam. Hijackers obtained $450,000 and $501,000, respectively, from Pacific Southwest and National Airlines, but were caught.

In August three men, two women, and three children, all from Detroit, hijacked a Delta Air Lines jet to Algiers, where they joined the Black Panthers. Their $1 million in ransom money was impounded by Algeria and returned. In Reno, Nev., F. M. Sibley, Jr., rode a bicycle past an unguarded airport gate. He demanded and received $1 million from United Airlines, but subsequently was shot by FBI agents.

In October, Palestinian guerrillas hijacked a Lufthansa Boeing 727 near Beirut, Lebanon, and threatened to kill 11 passengers unless the West German government freed the three Palestinian terrorists held in Munich for their part in the Olympic Games massacre in September. Securing the release of the three prisoners, the hijackers took the plane to Tripoli, Libya. In Houston, Texas, a U. S. Department of Commerce official, Charles H. Tuller, his two teen-aged sons, and a third youth hijacked an Eastern Airlines jet to Havana. The four hijackers, all of whom were wanted in connection with a double murder during an attempted bank robbery in Arlington, Va., killed an airline agent in Houston before boarding the jet.

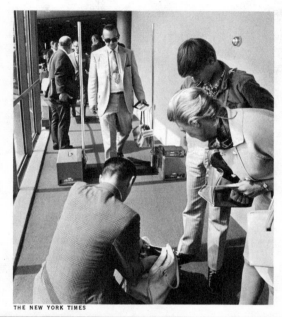

THE NEW YORK TIMES

AT AIRPORTS, devices such as magnetometers (right) *can detect metal objects in hand luggage or on the passenger.* (Below) *One of specially trained dogs used to sniff out hidden explosives.*

FAA, DEPARTMENT OF TRANSPORTATION

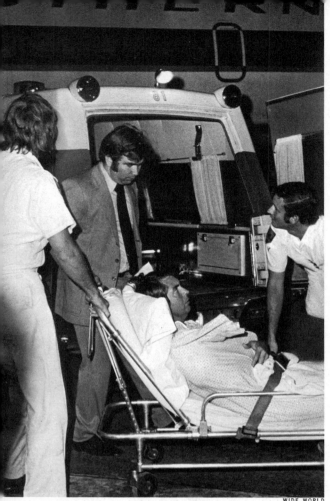

*WOUNDED COPILOT of hijacked South-
ern Airways plane that had landed at
six airports during its 29-hour ordeal in
November leaves ambulance in Miami.*

In November, three men commandeered a
Southern Airways DC-9, demanded $10 million,
and directed the plane on a 29-hour odyssey that
included landings at six airports, a threat to
crash the plane into the Oak Ridge nuclear
laboratory in Tennessee, the shooting of the co-
pilot, and an abortive FBI effort to ground the
plane by shooting its tires. Securing $2 million
in ransom, the hijackers sought refuge in Havana.

In December, seven hijackers (five men and
two women), believed to be members of the
Eritrean Liberation front, were killed in a mid-
air gun battle on a crowded Ethiopian airliner
over Addis Ababa.

Countermeasures. When hijacking became
a serious menace in 1968, the FAA developed a
two-part system to spot potential hijackers on the
ground. It consisted of a metal-sensing instrument for detecting weapons, called a magnetometer, used in conjunction with a behavioral
profile of characteristics believed common to hijackers. Passengers who met the profile (only
about 0.5% of the nation's 500,000 daily air

travelers did) would be subjected to questioning
and to search by the magnetometer.

After the outbreak of bomb threats and
parachute-ransom hijackings, President Nixon, in
March 1972, issued an emergency order requiring every U. S. airline immediately to implement
the profile-magnetometer screening programs,
which had been voluntary. He further ordered
airports to develop security plans to assure that
unauthorized persons do not have access to airliners. Later, foreign scheduled airlines operating
in the United States were required to develop
comparable passenger screening techniques. U. S.
airlines also were ordered to inspect all items
carried aboard by passengers on short flights.

A far more drastic presidential emergency
order in December, effective in January 1973, required U. S. airlines to screen all passengers electronically and to search all carry-on luggage.
Airports were to station armed local police
officers at boarding gates. The purchase of
weapon-detection devices would be federally
financed, with other costs to be borne by airlines
and airports.

Improved, more sensitive weapon-detectors
were developed, as were low-dose X-ray inspection devices that permitted airlines to look into
carry-on baggage without opening it. It was also
demonstrated that dogs trained as bomb sniffers
might be successfully utilized on planes. To
curb the widespread use of the Boeing 727 for
parachute-hijackings, the FAA ordered all airlines using this plane to install devices that
would prevent opening the rear door in flight.

FAA offices were flooded with unsolicited
advice on dealing with skyjacking, most of it im-
practical. Some suggested the installation of a
trap door in jetliner floors; others recommended
equipping aircraft with sleeping-gas dispensers or
hidden automatic guns.

Pilot Strike. On June 19, 1972, after many
months of complaints about the failure of nations to curb hijacking, the International Federation of Airline Pilots Associations called a global,
one-day strike to protest the diplomatic inaction.
In the United States, which has about 33,000 of
the 55,000 airline pilots in the non-Communist
world, the strike was only 10% effective because
many pilots opted not to participate, and airlines
won a court order barring other pilots from
joining. Elsewhere, however, in Rome, London,
Hong Kong, Madrid, Buenos Aires, and many
other cities, commercial air service was crippled
for the day. At year-end pilots were threatening
another—and perhaps longer—strike.

International Action. The pilot strike
prompted the UN Security Council, on June 20,
(Continued on page 52)

What the Government Is Doing

BY LT. GEN. BENJAMIN O. DAVIS, JR.
*Assistant Secretary for Safety and Consumer Affairs,
U. S. Department of Transportation*

On May 1, 1961, a lone Cuban boarded a National Airlines Convair at Marathon, Fla. Five minutes after takeoff for Key West, the man pulled out a gun and ordered the pilot to land in Havana instead. The first U. S. airliner had been hijacked.

Subsequent investigation showed that the Cuban had signed the passenger manifest as "El Pirata Cofresi." In Spanish, El Pirata means "the pirate." Cofresi was a notorious 18th century buccaneer. That touch of bravado stands alone in the annals of American air piracy. The successful hijackers who followed "Cofresi" made no such gesture, gave no hint as to their intentions. Until they struck, the air pirates were a faceless part of the half million people who daily travel by airliner in the United States. The volume and speed of modern civil aviation provided their cloak.

Government Action. In January 1969, when John A. Volpe became U. S. secretary of transportation, hijacking was approaching a crescendo. The criminal diversion of airliners to Cuba, sporadic through most of the 1960's, had taken a sharp rise in 1968 with 18 commercial flights commandeered. Volpe called for immediate action. One of his first directives set up a task force within the Federal Aviation Administration (FAA), the first concerted government counterattack on the air criminal. The task force began its work in what would prove to be the worst year in the chronology of hijackings in the United States. There were 40 incidents of air piracy in 1969, 34 of them successful. Given that impetus, Secretary Volpe's team created the FAA anti-hijack system, which utilized a security profile of hijackers' behavioral characteristics.

Experimental Program. In October 1969 the Department of Transportation (DOT) entered phase II of the anti-hijack campaign, inaugurating a program under which airlines voluntarily adopted security measures with government guidance and assistance. Eastern Air Lines was the first to volunteer—and with good reason: At that time, 50 percent of all domestic hijackings involved Eastern aircraft. Cooperating closely with the FAA, Eastern took just nine months to develop its deterrent system, using profiles, the weapon-detecting magnetometer, and law enforcement support. In less than a year, Eastern's share of skyjacking was down to 16%.

Prompted by the multiple hijackings by Palestinian guerrillas to the Jordanian desert, the Eastern experiment was augmented by the creation of a force of sky marshals in October 1970. The original job of the sky marshals could be termed "riding shotgun," for they served as armed guards aloft. However, it became increasingly clear that preventive concentration on the ground would be more effective. By 1972 most of the sky marshals had been diverted to supporting passenger screening at airport gates.

Regulatory Program. In March 1972, following three acts of bombing sabotage and extortion against domestic airliners, President Nixon made this strong statement: "We must not be intimidated by such lawlessness... rather we must and will meet this blackmail on the ground, as vigorously as we have met piracy in the air." The President had committed the government to its third phase, the regulatory program. The concept was to keep the potential hijacker or bomber off the plane in the first place, to intercept him before flight. That meant tougher regulations, more detectors, and tightened ground security. Above all, it mandated a sense of urgency.

In the first half of 1972, nearly 1,500 arrests of potential troublemakers were made at the nation's airports. A few who managed to get through boarding gates were arrested on the aircraft. Over 1,100 weapons were confiscated, and thousands of dollars worth of narcotics was seized.

In September 1972, Secretary Volpe announced that nearly $3 million had been allocated for new metal detection devices, both hand-held and walk-through, to be installed at the nation's airports. At the same time, the Department of Transportation exhorted the air carriers to carry out a policy of resistance to the air criminal. The DOT stressed three basic rules in resisting the hijacker: (1) all federal security regulations must be observed; (2) the payment or ransom or extortion money must be denied to the fullest extent possible, consistent with the safety of human beings; and (3) hijacked aircraft must be landed and kept on the ground, while the plane captain and the airline management cooperate with the FBI.

Following an upsurge of hijackings in the fall, President Nixon, on December 5, issued a stronger emergency order, requiring U. S. airlines to screen all passengers electronically and to search all carry-on luggage, effective Jan. 5, 1973. Effective February 5, all U. S. commercial airports must provide armed police officers to guard boarding gates before departures. Even these strengthened measures may prove fallible in a nation with a scheduled airline departure rate exceeding that of the rest of the non-Communist world combined.

Authority and Responsibility. A jurisdictional dispute hampered the passage of anti-skyjack legislation during 1972. As the 92d Congress ended, stringent legislation died in conference because of a Senate amendment providing for a federal force at the airports. The Nixon administration contends that security is the obligation of airlines and airports, backed by local law enforcement.

Because air piracy is a universal problem, the United States is leading the international movement toward eliminating hijack havens. All the while, differences over anti-hijack methods and authority are impeding the mandatory solution at home. Concerned voices are raised after each instance of air piracy and then, it seems, they subside. A continuity of purpose is imperative, for we confront the elements of great tragedy.

Major Skyjackings Around the World in 1972

Jan. 12—A lone hijacker seizes a jet en route from Houston to Kansas City, demanding $1 million for plane, crew, and 93 passengers and safe passage to South America. The hijacker, an ex-mental patient, surrenders to authorities at Dallas airport.

Jan. 27—The hijacker of a flight from New York City to Albany is killed by an FBI agent at Poughkeepsie, N. Y., after receiving $200,000 ransom.

Jan. 29—A hijacker of a Los Angeles–New York flight, who demanded a $300,000 ransom, is shot and arrested at Kennedy Airport by an FBI agent posing as a crewman.

Feb. 21-22—Three Arab guerrillas hijack German jet on flight from New Delhi to Athens and force it to land in Aden, Southern Yemen. The crew of 14 is held while 175 passengers are released; German government arranges $5 million ransom payment to Arab guerrilla organization in Lebanon.

April 11—A man who hijacked a jet en route from Albuquerque to Phoenix surrenders after being allowed two hours of radio and television time in which he decried injustices to the poor and minority groups.

May 3—Four Turkish guerrillas hijack a Turkish airliner in effort to win freedom of three condemned militants. Plane with 68 passengers is flown to Sofia, Bulgaria, where the four are granted political asylum after Turkey refuses to accede to demands.

May 5—Hijacker seizes jet on flight from Allentown, Pa., to Miami and bails out over Honduras with $303,000 after releasing passengers in Washington and New Orleans. The suspect, Frederick Hahnemann, surrendered to U.S. embassy officials in Honduras on June 2.

May 24-26—Two Lebanese men seize South African jet en route from Salisbury, Rhodesia, to Johannesburg with 58 passengers. After passengers disembark at Salisbury plane is flown to Malawi, where hijackers are arrested.

June 2-3—Jet is seized in Seattle by man and female companion who threaten to blow it up unless $500,000 ransom is paid. Couple are flown to Algeria and money is returned.

June 8—Ten Czechoslovaks force an airliner to divert from its course to Prague and land at Weiden, West Germany. Pilot is killed when he refuses to carry out request.

June 23-29—A man commandeers a flight from St. Louis to Tulsa, demanding $500,000 ransom and a parachute. Eighty of the 93 passengers are allowed off before flight is resumed to Fort Worth. Plane returns to St. Louis where ransom is collected. Hijacker bails out over Peru, Ind. The money was recovered by a farmer, and a suspect was arrested in Detroit.

July 5—Two hijackers are shot and killed by FBI agents at San Francisco airport while awaiting an $800,000 ransom and parachutes after they seized a flight to Los Angeles and killed a passenger.

July 12-13—Two men seize plane en route to New York from Philadelphia. After freeing 113 passengers and receiving $500,000 and $1,600 in Mexican pesos at Philadelphia, the plane flies on to Lake Jackson, Texas, where hijackers surrender after plane is damaged in landing.

July 12—Hijacker seizes jet en route to Dallas from Oklahoma City and demands $500,000. After receiving $200,000 of the ransom, he allows 51 passengers off and then surrenders.

July 31-Aug. 1—Three men and two women commandeer a Detroit-Miami flight, and after collecting a $1 million ransom are flown to Algeria.

Aug. 15—A band of 10 alleged terrorists seize a flight from Trelew, Argentina, to Santiago, Chile, where they surrender to police and ask for political asylum.

Sept. 15-16—Three Croatian extremists hijack airliner en route to Stockholm and force it to land at Malmo, Sweden, where six other Croatians imprisoned for the murder of the Yugoslav ambassador are turned over to them. They then fly to Madrid where they are taken into custody.

Oct. 29—Two Palestinian guerrillas commandeer a German airliner after takeoff from Beirut, Lebanon, and demand the release of three Arab commandos held in the slaying of 11 Israelis at the Munich Olympics. West German authorities arrange the turnover at Zagreb, Yugoslavia, and the plane is then flown to Tripoli, Libya.

Oct. 29—Four hijackers, including a father and two sons, seize a jet with 29 passengers at Houston, Texas, killing an airline ticket agent, before being flown to Havana where they are taken into custody by Cuban authorities.

Nov. 10-12—Three fugitives hijack jet with 27 passengers after takeoff from Birmingham, Ala. In 29 hours the plane travels 4,000 miles, landing in 6 different cities, and eventually arriving in Havana where trio are arrested. The hijackers demand $10 million and receive some $2 million; at one time they threaten to crash plane into the Oak Ridge atomic energy facilities. The co-pilot is wounded during the ordeal.

Dec. 8—Seven hijackers, two of them women, are killed by Ethiopian security guards after seizing a flight bound from Addis Ababa to Paris; five passengers, two security guards, and two stewardesses are wounded in the in-flight gun battle. An American passenger seizes a live grenade and tosses it into an unoccupied part of the plane where it blows a hole in the side of the aircraft, but the plane lands safely.

(*Continued from page 50*)

to deplore air piracy. Machinery was set in motion for a 15-nation conference held in Washington in September in an attempt to draft a new antihijacking treaty.

The three existing treaties pertaining to skyjacking are binding only on signatories, and hijackers can still find refuge in some countries. The Tokyo Convention of 1963 calls for contracting nations to permit the prompt return of hijacked planes, crews, and passengers. Under the Hague Convention of 1970, signatories agree either to extradite hijackers to the country of the plane's registry or to punish them under their own laws. The Montreal Convention of 1971 applies the same obligations in incidents endangering an aircraft in flight.

At the September 1972 conference, the United States and Canada jointly proposed a fourth treaty under which signatory countries would be obliged to suspend air service to any nation harboring a hijacker. Such joint international action would be imposed under the UN International Civil Aviation Organization (ICAO). The proposal was opposed by the Soviet Union, which argued that only the UN Security Council should have the right to impose joint international action. France, also opposed, claimed that the idea of disciplining a country for violating a treaty it had not signed would violate principles of international law.

The conference failed to reach agreement on a new treaty, but forwarded possible language for such a pact for consideration by the legal committee of the ICAO. The U. S.-Canada proposal will form the basis for discussions at an international diplomatic conference on hijacking scheduled for the summer of 1973.

Tournament chess demands intense concentration. Here, Bobby Fischer (left) meets Tigran Petrosian.

Chess: More Than Just a Game

By Larry Evans
International Chess Grandmaster

Chess is a game that illustrates the beauty of logic. For its enthusiasts it is a perennial fascination and pleasure, and the game's imagery and structure have entered literature and art. However, until 1972, chess competitions could hardly claim to have captured wide public attention—not until a 29-year-old Brooklyn man named Bobby Fischer won the world championship from Boris Spassky of the USSR. Fischer's extraordinary talent had already assured him of a prominent place in the annals of chess. What was more remarkable was the degree to which his intense, aggressive personality seized the public imagination, transforming the 1972 championship match into a big-money event and front-page news for two months.

THE HISTORY OF CHESS

The exact origin of chess is unknown. Legends have had it that Adam invented the game to console himself for the loss of his son Abel, or that a Buddhist priest sat down one day and devised it as a bloodless substitute for war. In fact the game probably grew—as music and poetry grew—from crude beginnings.

Early Chess. The earliest known form of the game dates from the 6th century A. D., when inhabitants of India played *chaturanga* (Sanskrit for army) on an uncheckered board of 64 squares on which four players arrayed eight pieces each in battle formation. The chariots were posted on the flanks, while the king and prime minister were in the protected center. The foot soldiers stood arrayed on the front line, as now, bearing the brunt of the battle, and the game was won by capturing the enemy king or stripping him of his forces. Originally dice throws determined which piece was to be moved, but as it became recognized that the element of skill involved in making such decisions would itself be a challenging feature of the game, the dice were used only to decide who moved first. Then they disappeared altogether.

From India the game spread to Persia, where it was called *shah,* or "the king," from which the

Castling.—Move involving king and either rook, permitted once to a player if pieces involved have not yet moved, if intervening squares are clear, and if pieces and squares involved are not under attack. King moves two squares toward either rook, and rook moves to square jumped over by king. Castling on king side is written 0–0; on queen side, 0–0–0.

Chain.—Formation in which each pawn is linked to another pawn, and anchored to a base pawn.

Check and checkmate.—See diagram caption.

Closed game.—Kind of position in which pawns are so blocked that most files cannot be opened.

Combination.—A forced series of moves, usually involving sacrifice, to improve one's position.

Development.—Early phase of game, requiring mobilization of pieces by posting them on good squares.

Discovered attack.—Attack on enemy piece by the moving away of an intervening man.

Double check.—A discovered attack, or check, on king, in which the man moved also checks the king.

Doubled pawns.—Two pawns of same color on a file.

En passant.—Special form of pawn capture, allowed only when a pawn moves two squares forward on first move to rest beside enemy pawn that has reached the fifth rank on an adjoining file. On next turn only, enemy may capture advanced pawn as if it had moved only one square forward, thus moving his own pawn diagonally forward to his sixth rank.

Endgame.—The final phase of a game, characterized by a sparsity of units, in which kings become active participants instead of hiding.

Fianchetto.—To post a bishop at QN2 or KN2.

Fork.—An attack on two or more pieces at once.

Gambit.—A risky offer of material in the opening game, to get an attack or a strong position.

Grandmaster.—The highest ranking in chess, awarded by the International Chess Federation.

Isolated pawn.—A pawn deprived of protection by pawns on adjacent files.

Major piece.—Rook or queen.

Middle game.—The phase following development, in which most of the complex action of a game occurs.

Minor piece.—Knight or bishop.

Open file.—File with no pawns on it.

Opening.—The first dozen or so moves in a game.

Passed pawn.—Pawn that cannot be opposed by an enemy pawn as it marches toward queening.

Perpetual check.—A method of drawing whereby one side must continue checking to avoid disadvantage.

Pin.—To fix an opponent's man by an attack that will capture more valuable piece if the man moves.

Queening.—Exchange of pawn for a queen, when the pawn has reached the eighth rank.

Sacrifice.—To abandon material for a purpose.

Stalemate.—A draw brought about when a player cannot make a legal move but his king is not in check.

Zugzwang.—Predicament of a player who must impair his position seriously when he moves.

Zwischenzug.—Move interpolated before necessary or expected move, presenting an unignorable threat.

---

present word "chess" derives. The Arabs took up the game and produced the first book on chess theory. The checkering of the board was a 13th century European innovation, introduced sometime after chess had spread to that continent. There, chessmen became replicas of European royal courts.

The chess piece now known as the queen was originally a male adviser to and defender of the king and was empowered to move only one square diagonally at a time. However, because of the phonetic similarity of the Arabic word *ferz,* or "counselor," and the French word *vierge,* or "maiden," the piece changed sex and, in the process, became the most powerful figure on the board—a development that English historian Robert Lambe, in his *History of Chess,* called "a ridiculous absurdity." In our own century, the apparent sexual symbolism in the game has not been overlooked by some psychoanalysts, although many others have disputed such interpretations. Kurt Adler, for example, maintains that "chess is a game of training in orientation for problem solving," saying that he would "dismiss completely the sexual symbolism."

Lure of the Game. Whatever the interpretations, chess has always exerted an enormous attraction on players, so intense at times as to seem diabolical. During the Middle Ages chess lent itself as a model for education, and the second book printed in English—by William Caxton in 1479—was a morality based on chess. The game was forbidden in times of stress, along with dice and cards. In 1689 an English minister likened chess to an addiction and foreswore the game, observing that "It hath not

done with me when I have done with it"—a sentiment echoed in the 20th century by Albert Einstein. Correspondence chess was played by noblemen in the 13th century, their moves being transmitted by troubadours. At times the game was restricted to royalty, and commoners caught playing were punished. Many a court had its own chess master, just as it had its jester and musicians, and some of the tenderest love poems employed the language of the game.

Reportedly more books have been written on chess than on all other games combined. Benjamin Franklin's *The Morals of Chess* (1779), the first such work in the New World, proposed that chess cultivated foresight, circumspection, caution, and perseverance. This might be disputed by one recent psychologist's conclusion that a considerable degree of chess skill is possible to one who is mentally deficient in almost any other line. Other current studies indicate that imagination and vision are more important than are memory and concentration.

In any case, it is a very satisfying game. As the psychiatrist Karl Menninger declared: "It seems to be necessary for some of us to have a hobby in which aggressiveness and destructiveness are given opportunity for expression, and since I long ago gave up hunting...I have found myself returning more and more to the most ancient of all games."

Past Masters. Modern chess dates from the first international tournament, held in London in 1851. It was organized by Howard Staunton, an eminent Shakespearean scholar recognized unofficially as the best player in the world. When the event was won by a German mathematics

professor, Adolf Anderssen, Staunton refused to relinquish his crown gracefully, and in fact showed the greatest jealousy of his rivals. An American player, Paul Morphy, crossed the Atlantic Ocean and decisively beat Anderssen and other chess masters in a series of matches in 1858, but Staunton pretended that he could not find time to accept Morphy's challenge. An embittered Morphy returned to New Orleans and eventually gave up chess, one story having it that he was deeply wounded by a woman who scorned to marry a "mere chess player." He refused to meet people, emerged from his mother's house only to take a walk or go to the opera, and in time became a victim of delusions of persecution. His chess game was characterized by accuracy of combination, rapid development of pieces, and a firm grasp of positional play.

Wilhelm Steinitz, a German born in Bohemia, was the first player to hold the official title of world chess champion, from 1866 to 1894. The game was the great passion of his life. Steinitz made no attempt to win games in their early stages because he was convinced that winning was possible only after an opponent made an error. He preferred to accumulate small advantages and patiently await his chance—a doctrine that was scorned in an age when playing to win from the very start was considered the only honorable course. In later years

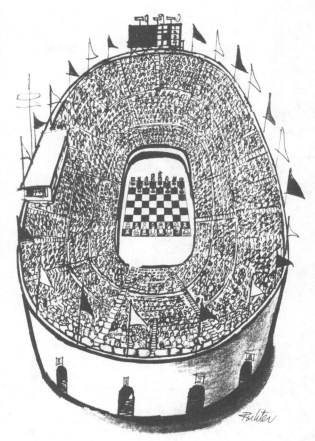

DRAWING BY RICHTER © 1972, THE NEW YORKER MAGAZINE INC.

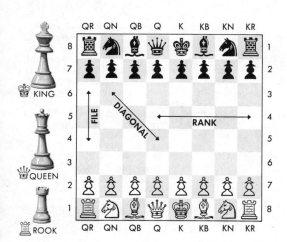

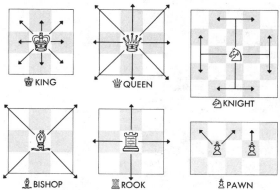

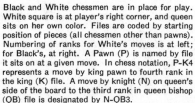

CHESSBOARD, MEN, AND NOTATION

Black and White chessmen are in place for play. White square is at player's right corner, and queen sits on her own color. Files are coded by starting position of pieces (all chessmen other than pawns). Numbering of ranks for White's moves is at left; for Black's, at right. A Pawn (P) is named by file it sits on at a given move. In chess notation, P-K4 represents a move by king pawn to fourth rank in the king (K) file. A move by knight (N) on queen's side of the board to the third rank in queen bishop (QB) file is designated by N-QB3.

The capture of a chessman is designated by the symbol x. Thus, KBxQR in chess notation designates the capture of the queen's side rook by the king's side bishop.

MOVES OF MEN AND OBJECT OF PLAY

The king (K) can move only to square next to one it is on. The queen (Q) moves any number of squares on a file, rank, or diagonal. A knight's move is two squares on a file or rank, then one square to either side (it is the only chessman that can jump over an intervening piece). A bishop (B) moves any number of squares on a diagonal, while the rook (R), or castle, moves any number of squares on a file or rank. A pawn moves either one or two squares forward in its file on first move, then one square at a time. A piece captures by moving onto a square occupied by an enemy chessman, removing him from the board. The capture is optional. A pawn captures by moving one square forward on a diagonal. A pawn reaching the 8th rank may be exchanged for any piece other than a king—usually the queen, a move called queening.

White moves first. The object is to capture opponent's king. Any move threatening capture of the king is called check and cannot be ignored; unavoidable capture is called checkmate and means victory for the other contestant. For the moves called castling and en passant, see glossary.

Bobby Fischer

Boris Spassky

BIOGRAPHICAL SKETCHES OF THE TITLE CONTESTANTS

Robert James Fischer was born in Chicago on March 9, 1943. His father, a physicist, and his mother, a registered nurse, were divorced when Fischer was a baby, and his mother eventually settled in Brooklyn with the boy and his older sister, Joan.

Fischer learned chess at the age of six, when his sister entertained him with a variety of games from a neighborhood candy store. He found an old chess book and from then on, recalls his mother, "he just didn't answer when you spoke." With fanatic dedication, Fischer turned the game into both a sword for conquest and an armor against the world.

Fischer's debut in the major ranks was inauspicious: a tie for 20th in a field of 26 at the U. S. Amateur Championship in 1955, then a first bid for the Junior Championship. He captured this title on his second try in 1956. His big year came in 1957 when he won the Junior, the Open, and the first of eight Closed Championships, enabling him to compete in the World Championship Interzonal at Portoroz, Yugoslavia, in 1958. He finished fourth and moved on to the Candidates in 1959, becoming a grandmaster at the age of 16.

Leaving high school to become a chess professional, Fischer in 1960 was the high scorer in the finals for the U. S. Olympic squad at Leipzig. In 1961 a wealthy chess patron put up an $8,000 purse for a match between him and Samuel Reshevsky. The match was even after 11 games, but Fischer then forfeited by refusing to show up for game 12 because of a scheduling dispute. He won the Interzonal at Stockholm in 1962 and again qualified for the Candidates in Curaçao, finishing fourth. At the Interzonal in Sousse, Tunisia, in 1967, Fischer walked out over a scheduling dispute although he was far in the lead at the halfway mark. He won two major tournaments in 1968. Then, embittered over what he still felt was Russian collusion, he retired from chess.

Fischer was lured out of self-exile in 1970 by a four-game match against Tigran Petrosian, in which he won two games and drew two. He swept the Interzonal at Palma, Spain, and in 1971 he shut out Mark Taimanov of the USSR and Bent Larsen of Denmark before taking Petrosian's measure, 6½ to 2½. In 1972 he defeated Boris Spassky for the world title. On the official Elo scale of the International Chess Federation, Fischer is the highest rated player in the game's history.
LARRY EVANS

Boris Spassky was born in Leningrad on Jan. 30, 1937. His parents were divorced when he was a child. Spassky learned chess during World War II when he was evacuated to a children's home in the Kirov Region. His sister Irena, who played checkers, later became the Soviet checker champion.

In 1949, Spassky won the Leningrad Junior Championship in chess. At his first international tournament, held in Bucharest in 1953, he tied for fourth place. After capturing the title of world junior chess champion in 1955, he tied for third place with world champion Mikhail Botvinnik in the 22d Soviet Championship, an achievement that qualified him for the Interzonal at Göteborg, Sweden. He then moved on to the Candidates Tournament in 1956 and was awarded the grandmaster title at the age of 19. Later that year he tied for first place in the 23d Soviet Championship.

At Mar del Plata, Argentina, in 1960, Spassky tied for first with Bobby Fischer, winning the first of their individual encounters. At the World Student Tournament in Leningrad that same year, however, he was beaten by William Lombardy of the United States.

In 1961, Spassky won the 28th Soviet Championship, and in 1964 he tied for first place at the Amsterdam Interzonal. In the Candidates Tournament the following year he defeated Paul Keres, Efim Geller, and Mikhail Tal, before losing the title match against Tigran Petrosian by one point. In 1966 he won the Piatigorsky Cup in Santa Monica, Calif., finishing ahead of Fischer and Petrosian. He again won the Candidates matches in 1968, defeating Geller, Bent Larsen, and Victor Korchnoi. "I have very strong nerves," said Spassky, "but such matches spoil the health of the players."

In 1969, Spassky captured the world championship by taking the return match against Petrosian, 12½ to 10½. Afterward he played infrequently and with indifferent results, finishing third at Göteborg in 1970 and tying for sixth place at Moscow in 1971. Spassky had also represented the USSR in the team Olympiads of 1962, 1964, 1966, 1968, and 1970, where he again defeated Fischer. In all, Spassky compiled a record of three wins and two draws against the young American before meeting him in the 1972 title match. After his defeat, Spassky told reporters, "Fischer is a man of art, but a rare human being in the everyday life of this century. I like him and I think that I understand him."
LARRY EVANS

Steinitz, too, suffered from delusions, believing that he could place a telephone call without wire or receiver and move chess pieces at will by emitting electrical currents. He died a charity patient in 1900.

Emanuel Lasker of Germany held the title for 27 years, from 1894 to 1921. His satisfactions from the game appear to have been entirely intellectual. He excelled in defense and took calculated risks to provoke his adversaries into attacking. "It is no easy matter," despaired a contemporary, "to meet Lasker's inferior moves." Lasker formulated a psychological approach to the chess struggle. Some of his victims also claimed that he stunned them with his foul-smelling cigars.

Cuba's José Capablanca held the world title from 1921 to 1927, abandoning an engineering career to become a chess giant and his country's hero. Capablanca's game was remorselessly accurate, and he also enjoyed competition in other fields such as tennis, bridge, and the pursuit of women. However, he came unprepared to his title match with Russian-born Alexander Alekhine, a naturalized French citizen, in 1927. Alekhine displayed greater stamina during the 10-week struggle and won by a margin of three points. He then refused to grant a return match, made impossible stipulations, and even balked at participating in tournaments if Capablanca was invited. Known as the "sadist of the chess world," Alekhine went through five marriages, participated in the Nazi campaign of anti-Semitism, and endured several bouts with dipsomania. The Netherlands' Max Euwe, a conventional paterfamilias and a mathematics professor with a cool passion for order on the chessboard, captured the world title in 1935. The first real amateur to win it, he sportingly agreed to a re-turn match. Alekhine regained the title in 1937 and held it until his death in 1946.

Recent Champions. A tournament to find a successor to Alekhine was organized in 1948, and rules were adopted that compelled the champion to defend his title every three years. Mikhail Botvinnik, a Russian electrical engineer, won the tournament. A man of iron will and painstaking thoroughness, he trained for matches with a radio blaring and an opponent blowing smoke in his eyes. By a supreme effort he retained his crown against a countryman, David Bronstein, in 1951 and in 1954, defended successfully against another Russian, Vassili Smyslov. In 1957, Smyslov finally took Botvinnik's measure, only to lose the return match in 1958. In the 1960's the Soviet firebrand Mikhail Tal demolished Botvinnik by four points, but lost the return match the following year by five points. In 1963, Botvinnik was deposed for the last time, by a Soviet Armenian, Tigran Petrosian, a player of consummate defensive skill. Denied the traditional right of a return match as a result of rule changes, Botvinnik turned his attention to the field of chess computers.

In 1966, Petrosian successfully defended his title against yet another Russian, Boris Spassky, but in 1969 Spassky scaled the heights. The postwar Soviet monopoly on the title was finally broken in 1972 by Robert Fischer of the United States. At Fischer's urging, the International Chess Federation (Fédération Internationale des Echecs, or FIDE) had changed the rules in 1971 to eliminate the possibility that the victor of the upcoming match could hold his title in subsequent matches simply by drawing. Thus, after 1972, the first player to score six victories was to be declared world champion, and draw games were not to count.

The Rumble at Reykjavík

Ground rules in the 1972 match called for a maximum of 24 games, with the champion needing only 12 points to retain his title. A win was worth one point, and a draw one-half point. After extensive haggling, it was determined that the match was to begin in Reykjavík, Iceland, on July 2. The players were to share equally in film and television revenues, and the $125,000 purse was to be divided 62½% to the winner and 37½% to the loser. (The preceding title purse had been only $5,000.) All seemed harmonious at last—until Fischer demanded that he receive 30% of the gate receipts. The organizers refused to budge, and a phone call from U. S. presidential aide Henry Kissinger failed to persuade Fischer to relent.

The American challenger failed to show up on schedule in Reykjavík. At that point an English financier, James Slater, doubled the purse, thus raising the winner's share to $156,-250. When Fischer finally responded to an ultimatum and arrived in Reykjavík on July 4, Spassky demanded a formal apology in writing and postponed the match until July 11. He did not, however, ask for a forfeit of the first game, despite a cable from Moscow urging him to do

so. The Soviet news agency Tass criticized Fischer's "disgusting spirit of gain," to which the head of the U. S. Chess Federation replied, "He is a chess professional in a country which does not provide governmental support for chess players"—unlike the Soviet Union—"and he should not be condemned for seeking the maximum private income for his endeavors." The controversy raged in headlines all over the world, and chess made the covers of several leading magazines. In New York, television coverage on the Public Broadcasting System equalled the ratings of the New York Mets baseball games.

The final score of 12½–8½ gives only a scant indication of the real dimension of the match. Setting aside the game that Fischer let go by forfeit and petulance, and the 11 games that were drawn, the match ended Fischer 7, Spassky 2. It was—after Fischer's initial temperamental flurry—no contest.

But there were two Boris Spasskys in this match: the one in the first lap, and the one in the stretch. To put the contest into perspective, Fischer's enormous lead of 6½ to 3½ points in

the first 10 games must be compared with his narrow 6-to-5 edge in the last 11. No one knew better than Spassky that he had failed to secure much of an advantage by playing white—and hence moving first—in the opening game, and that Fischer had beaten himself by trying to win what was clearly a draw. Nonetheless, Fischer's mistake encouraged the Russian team, which had counted on his impetuosity and overconfidence. Then, when Fischer did not show up at the second game because of a dispute over television cameras, no one thought that he could be persuaded to resume the match if the officials insisted on awarding the game to Spassky. The Russian later said that he was "dominated by a sense of unfair advantage" when the officials stood fast and upheld his forfeit.

Fischer showed up for the third game at the last minute, demanding that it be played in a back room. "Just this once. Never again," said Spassky—when, by remaining intransigent, he probably could have provoked another walkout and won the entire match by default. Gradually falling behind after Fischer played an unorthodox move early in the game, Spassky extended his hand in defeat on move 41. It was the first time he had ever lost to Bobby Fischer.

The champion was still leading 2 to 1, but he had lost an important psychological edge. He recovered strongly in game 4, and only the challenger's great resourcefulness under fire enabled him to stave off defeat and salvage a draw. But the fifth game proved to be an utter fiasco for Spaasky. On move 27 he committed one of the worst blunders of his career and lost outright.

In the next four games, Fischer's slashing onslaughts increased his lead to 3 points, but in game 11 he faltered (see insert). Game 12 was drawn, and Spassky threw away a draw in game 13 in the eighth hour of a marathon contest. Games 14 through 20 were draws, during which Spassky dipped into reservoirs of strength and pressed the initiative even as time was running out. Fischer later conceded that Spassky had him "under terrible pressure." However, Fischer then needed only one more point. In the 21st and final game, Spassky failed to make any headway with white, then desperately sacrificed material to force the issue. He sealed an inferior move and resigned by telephone the next day. On September 1, Fischer was champion.

SPASSKY-FISCHER: 11th MATCH GAME

White: Spassky   **Black: Fischer**

White	Black	White	Black
1 P–K4	P–QB4(a)	17 P–B4	N–B4
2 N–KB3	P–Q3	18 Q–Q3	P–R5
3 P–Q4	PxP	19 B–N4	N–Q3(f)
4 NxP	N–KB3	20 N/1–Q2	P–B4
5 N–QB3	P–QR3	21 P–QR3	Q–N3
6 B–KN5	P–K3	22 P–B5	Q–N4
7 P–B4	Q–N3	23 Q–QB3	PxB
8 Q–Q2	QxP	24 P–QR4	P–R6(g)
9 N–N3(b)	Q–R6	25 PxQ	PxPch
10 BxN	PxB	26 KxP	R–R6
11 B–K2	P–KR4	27 Q–B6	N–B4
12 O–O	N–B3	28 P–B6	B–B1
13 K–R1	B–Q2(c)	29 QPxP	BPxP
14 N–N1	Q–N5(d)	30 KR–K1	B–K2
15 Q–K3	P–Q4(e)	31 RxKP	Black
16 PxP	N–K2		Resigns

(a) This opening is called the Sicilian Defense. (b) This is known as the "Poison Pawn" variation. Black has plunged his queen perilously out of play to snatch a pawn deep in White's territory. The text—that is, the literature on this position—protects White's rook and threatens 10 P–QR3 and 11 R–R2, trapping Black's queen. The older move was 9 R–QN1, Q–R6, which Fischer had never before lost with Black in tournaments. (c) More accurate is 13 . . . N–R4, to avoid trouble. (d) An alternative is 14 . . . Q–R5 and 15 Q–K3, N–K2 to extricate the queen via QB3. After 14 . . . Q–N7 White can force a draw by repetition (15 N–B3, Q–R6 and 16 N–N1) or try for more with 15 P–QR4. (e) Black gives back a pawn for counterplay, but it is a violation of principle to open lines with the king still unsafe in the center. Necessary is 15 . . . N–K2 to vacate QB3 for the queen's escape (via R5). For if 16 P–QR4? P–B4! 17 N/1–Q2, PxP and 18 P–B3, N–Q4! is the saving resource. But simply 16 P–QB4 retains strong pressure. (f) A ragged retreat. But now he sees that 19 . . . N–N6ch 20 PxN, PxPch is refuted by 21 B–R3! (g) Desperation. But the queen is ambushed. If 24 . . . Q–K7, 25 QR–K1 traps her majesty. Black cannot get enough material compensation. Fischer could have resigned here instead of dragging it out. This was Spassky's finest—and last—win.

Bibliography

Davidson, Henry A., *A Short History of Chess* (McKay 1949).
Evans, Larry, *Chess: Beginner to Expert* (Lee 1967).
Evans, Larry, *Chess World Championships 1972: Fischer-Spassky* (Simon & Schuster 1972).
Fischer, Robert, *My Sixty Memorable Games* (Simon & Schuster 1969).
Sunnucks, Anne, *The Encyclopedia of Chess* (Robert Hale 1970).

UPI

Managua, the capital of Nicaragua, was virtually destroyed by a series of increasingly strong earthquakes that struck the city on December 23, killing thousands of persons.

1972
REVIEW
OF THE YEAR

UPI

KEYSTONE

(Above) *COLLISION of two trains near Seville, Spain, took 77 lives.* (Left) *Rescue workers search for some of the 100 dead after a train wreck in the Vierzy tunnel, France.* (Below) *Police check the tail section of an F-86 jet that had crashed into an ice cream parlor near the Sacramento (Calif.) Executive Airport, killing 22 persons.* (Opposite page, top) *In the worst air crash in British history, a British European Airways Trident jet plunged into a field minutes after taking off from London's Heathrow airport. All 118 aboard were killed.* (Opposite page, bottom) *The luxury liner Queen Elizabeth burns in Hong Kong harbor. The ship, which was being refurbished for use by college students, was a total loss.*

WIDE WORLD

KEYSTONE

LONDON DAILY EXPRESS

ACCIDENTS AND DISASTERS

In 1972 industries in the United States completed the first full year under the Williams-Steiger Occupational Safety and Health Act (OSHA), a monumental safety law covering nearly 60 million workers in more than 4 million places of employment. During fiscal 1972 the Department of Labor, under authority granted by the act, conducted 32,-701 inspections of 29,505 business establishments employing nearly 6 million people. Some 23,000 citations were issued to employers alleging more than 102,000 violations of standards. Penalties proposed for the violations totaled almost $2.3 million.

Vehicle Safety. Highway and vehicle safety efforts continued in 1972 with a growing trend towards the adoption of internationally used symbols and pictures in place of words on highway and street signs. The use of symbols and pictures is expected to result in faster and better communication with the driver.

Auto safety developments included the initial field-testing of passive restraints (air bags) for motor vehicles. The air bags inflate immediately from the dashboard during a crash, protecting the occupants. The proposed deadline for the installation of such devices in all new cars was Aug. 15, 1975, but this was delayed indefinitely.

─────── U. S. ACCIDENT FATALITY TOLL ───────

	1971	1970	Change
All Accidents[1]	115,000	115,000	0%
Motor-vehicle	54,700	54,800	−0.2%
Public non-motor-vehicle	22,500	22,500	0%
Home	27,500	27,000	+2%
Work	14,200	14,300	−1%

[1] The motor-vehicle totals include some deaths also included in the work and home totals. This duplication amounted to about 3,900 in 1971 and 3,600 in 1970. All figures are National Safety Council estimates.

MAJOR ACCIDENTS AND DISASTERS OF 1972

AVIATION

Jan. 8—Spanish airliner crashes on Mediterranean island of Ibiza, killing 104.

Jan. 26—Yugoslav airliner explodes in flight over northwestern Czechoslovakia, killing 27.

March 15—All 112 persons aboard a Danish airliner are killed in a crash east of Dubai on the Persian Gulf.

May 6—Italian airliner crashes into a mountain near Palermo, Italy, killing 115 persons.

June 14—Eighty-three persons aboard a Japanese airliner are killed when plane attempts to land near New Delhi, India.

June 15—British airliner crashes in the Central Highlands of South Vietnam, killing all 81 aboard.

June 18—All 118 aboard are killed when British jet airliner crashes shortly after takeoff from London Heathrow Airport.

Aug. 14—East German airliner crashes in suburb of East Berlin, killing all 156 persons aboard.

Sept. 24—Private jet crashes into an ice cream parlor in Sacramento, Calif., killing 22 persons.

Oct. 13—Russian airliner crashes near Moscow's Sheremetov airport, killing 176 persons; death toll is the greatest in civil aviation history.

Oct. 13—Plane crashes in the Andes Mountains of Chile on flight from Argentina. Twenty-nine die and 16 are rescued ten weeks later, after two of their number make their way to help.

Nov. 4—Bulgarian airliner crashes in the Rila Mountains in Bulgaria, killing all 34 persons aboard.

Nov. 28—A Japanese airliner crashes after takeoff from Moscow, killing 60; 16 survive.

Dec. 3—Spanish jet crashes after takeoff from Santa Cruz de Tenerife in the Canary Islands, killing all 155 aboard.

Dec. 8—Plane crashes on the Southwest Side of Chicago, killing at least 46 and injuring some 20 others.

Dec. 29—Jet on New York to Miami run crashes in the Everglades, near Miami, killing 99 and injuring 77.

FIRES AND EXPLOSIONS

Jan. 2—Explosion and fire destroy a grain storage building at the world's largest flour mill in Buffalo, N. Y., killing three persons.

Jan. 3—Explosion of a terrorist bomb in Belfast, Northern Ireland, injures 62.

May 2—Flash fire in a silver mine in Kellogg, Idaho, kills 91.

May 13—At least 115 persons are killed in a flash fire in a nightclub in Osaka, Japan.

June 6—Explosion in a coal mine in Wankie, Rhodesia, kills 426.

Sept. 1—Explosion and fire in a Montreal nightclub kills 37 persons.

Sept. 24—Fire in a restaurant on the Greek island of Rhodes kills 31 persons and injures 16 others.

Dec. 2—Fire in a theater in Seoul, Korea, kills 50 and injures 76.

Dec. 15—Explosion and fire at a coke plant near Weirton, W. Va., kills 21 and injures 20.

FLOODS, LANDSLIDES, AND AVALANCHES

Feb. 26—Flash flooding and the collapse of coal waste pile cause death of 118 near Man, W. Va.

March 3–25—Floods kill 36 and leave 150,000 homeless in Peru.

April 10—Avalanche on Mount Manaslu in the Himalayas in Nepal kills 15 mountain climbers.

June 9–10—Flash floods in Keystone, Sturgis, and Rapid City, S. Dak., kill 239 persons.

July 5—Landslide at Oimawashi Yama, Japan, kills at least 80 persons.

Aug. 14—Floods from heavy rains kill 300 persons in Seoul, South Korea, and leave 250,000 homeless.

LAND AND SEA TRANSPORTATION

Jan. 9—Luxury liner *Queen Elizabeth* burns and capsizes in Hong Kong harbor, where it was being refurbished as a floating campus for Chapman College in Orange, Calif.

Feb. 1—Tanker, the *V. A. Fogg*, carrying volatile chemicals, explodes and sinks 32 miles off Texas, killing 32.

Feb. 18—Bus plunges into Nile River canal 40 miles from Cairo, Egypt, killing at least 77 persons.

March 24—School bus collides with a freight train in Congers, N. Y., killing 5 high school students and injuring more than 40 others.

March 31—Passenger train plunges off a bridge near Potgietersrus, South Africa, killing 38 and injuring 174.

May 11—Collision of British cargo ship and a Liberian tanker in fog off Uruguay kills 83.

May 14—Collision of a bus and a tractor-trailer kills 14 near Bean Station, Tenn.

June 4—Passenger train collides with halted train, killing 76 and injuring at least 500 near Jessore, Bangladesh.

June 17—Express train is derailed by tunnel cave-in in Vierzy, France, killing at least 100.

July 21—Head-on collision of two trains near Seville, Spain, kills 77 and injures 103 others.

Aug. 6—At least 57 are killed and 100 injured when a train crashes into rear of another at Liaquatpur, Pakistan.

Oct. 5—Speeding train jumps tracks near Saltillo, Mexico, killing at least 208 and injuring 680 persons.

Oct. 30—A commuter train in Chicago backs into the front of an advancing train, killing at least 44 and injuring more than 320.

Nov. 5—Fire on an express train stalled in a tunnel near Fukui, Japan, kills at least 28 and injures over 500.

Dec. 26—Nineteen are killed and 10 injured when bus carrying church youth group collides with truck on narrow bridge near Fort Sumner, N. Mex.

EARTHQUAKES

Mar. 13—Earthquakes in the states of Amazonas and San Martín, Peru, leave several thousand homeless.

April 10—A series of five earthquakes hits area around Ghir, 600 miles south of Teheran, Iran, killing about 5,050.

Dec. 23—Earthquakes destroy Managua, the capital of Nicaragua, killing at least 10,000.

STORMS

Jan. 13—Tornado smashes into two trailer parks near Enterprise, Ala., killing 4.

Feb. 12—Blizzards and avalanches in remote areas of northwestern Iran are reported to have killed 180.

May 3—Severe thunderstorm causing flooding and avalanches in Mexico City results in 18 deaths and leaves 100,000 homeless.

June 16–23—Tropical storm Agnes leaves 118 dead and $3 billion damage in its wake in 7 Southern and Northeastern states. Hardest hit are Pennsylvania, Maryland, New York, and Virginia.

June 20—Heavy rains in Hong Kong cause landslides and the collapse of 3 apartment buildings, killing 100 persons.

July 2–Aug. 13—Six weeks of rain beginning with typhoon Rita flood island of Luzon in the Philippines, killing 427, leaving 800,000 homeless, and causing $300 million in damage.

MISCELLANEOUS

Dec. 23, 1971–Jan. 3, 1972—Ten-day heat wave in Buenos Aires kills an estimated 450.

May 7–21—Heat wave in India with temperatures of 123° F kills 247 persons.

May–August—Prolonged drought because of late monsoon rains in 13 of the 21 states of India results in starvation of many; at least 800 dead.

Sept. 16—Collapse of a wooden bridge at Naga in the Philippines kills 100 during religious procession.

Household Safety. Flammability standards for children's sleepwear went into effect on July 29, 1972. All garments not meeting the standards must be so labelled, and they must be removed from store shelves in one year.

Regulations requiring various types of safety closing devices on containers of potentially dangerous goods are already in effect for a number of items and will soon be extended to others. By the end of 1973, for example, three fourths of all prescription drugs will be covered by such laws.

A model bill requiring the use of safety glazing in hazardous locations in buildings had been adopted by 20 states by the end of 1972.

Recreational Safety. Escalating snowmobile fatalities led a number of states to initiate or implement snowmobile safety laws. The Federal Boat Safety Act now requires that U. S. Coast Guard-approved personal flotation devices be provided for anyone on board a water vessel.

HOWARD PYLE
President, National Safety Council

ADVERTISING

The volume of U. S. advertising in 1972 showed a strong increase over 1971, up 9.3%, for a total of more than $22.5 billion. Among the year's developments, the industry began to meet the challenge of consumerism and to establish closer relationships with both government and consumers.

Government Relations. The year began with a surge of activity by U. S. regulatory agencies, notably the Federal Trade Commission (FTC). Emphasizing substantiation of claims, the FTC relied on threats of enforced "corrective" advertising to stimulate advertisers to document assertions made in their ads. In self-policing efforts, the Association of National Advertisers adopted guidelines for advertising to children. Also, there was a strengthening of the industry's National Advertising Review Board, set up in 1971 to monitor truth and accuracy in advertising.

Creative. While pressure increased for believability and information in ads, messages had to establish rapport with consumers within a more crowded advertising environment. Increasingly, successful creative people relied on research into consumer needs, tastes, and attitudes to ensure that campaigns met the public's desires in tone and language as well as content. The search intensified for innovative, imaginative advertising, inspired by information rather than undocumented intuition. Many campaigns—from autos to supermarkets—promoted closer company-consumer relationships, stressing efforts to ameliorate grievances in such areas as service, prices, and product quality.

Relaxation of attitudes about sex, plus increasing toleration of frankness in theme and language, had a major impact in 1972. In line with the times, mass advertising—even on TV and radio—became franker in both content and treatment.

Advertising Practice. The trend toward do-it-yourself administration of advertising by some companies slowed considerably. Many advertisers who had subcontracted such functions as media buying and creative and research from independent suppliers returned to full-service agency operations.

Internationalization. Advertisers stepped up activity in world markets in 1972. Multinational companies, U. S. and foreign, accounted for 15% of the world's combined Gross National Product, or a total volume of $450 billion. Of the $5.7 billion in advertising billed by 15 top U. S. agencies having overseas operations, $2.7 billion came from abroad.

Media. Specialization, sports, and cable television (CATV) were the media highlights in the United States in 1972. Increasing segmentation of audiences spurred both print media and broadcasting to expand specialized editorial matter and programming. Ad content followed suit, pinpointing messages toward clearly defined targets. For example, FM radio was a growth medium, especially with young adults in major markets. Whatever the message, media successes in 1972 were those that catered to special interest segments with widely varying life-styles.

Sports on TV, once limited to weekends, boomed into successful—and sometimes sensational (as in the coverage of the Olympics)—prime-time fare. CATV systems spread, providing new or improved reception for millions of viewers.

On the negative side, concern about media clutter mounted as the public grew more and more dis-

POSITIVE IMAGE OF WOMEN AWARD of the National Organization for Women (NOW) went to Procter & Gamble for this advertisement for Pampers diapers.

contented with the volume of ad messages on television. The increase in commercial time (up 31% over 1960) and in the number of commercials led to the judgment that clutter is the industry's chief unsolved problem.

Expenditures. Stimulated by an improving economy, expenditures in all media rose to an estimated $22.5 billion. This was 9.3% over the $20.6 billion invested in 1971. TV's share led in national revenue, as network and spot advertising rose 11.1%, to more than $3 billion. Magazine advertising grew 5.4%, to about $1.5 billion, while newspapers enjoyed their best showing in recent years—up 10%, for $1.25 billion.

Increased outlays in network and spot moved radio off dead center, for a gain of 6.6%, to $485 million. Business publications, the only medium to decline, slipped 2.6%, to $701 million. Outdoor advertising, buoyed by tobacco dollars diverted from TV by the government ban, grew 9%, to $188 million. Investment in all other media—from direct mail to car cards—grew 6%, to about $5.5 billion. National ad spending totaled $12.6 billion, 7.2% ahead of 1971, while local advertising, spurred by growing retail use of broadcasting, jumped 12.2%. (The source for these data is *Advertising Age*.)

EDWARD H. MEYER
President and Chief Executive Officer
Grey Advertising Inc.

SPACE SHUTTLE, the controversial craft planned for testing in the late 1970's, was granted funds in May.

AEROSPACE INDUSTRY

The U. S. aerospace industry was relatively stable in 1972, in contrast to the three previous years in which sales, profits, and employment had declined sharply. The industry, which produces aircraft, missiles, rockets, spacecraft, and related products, includes 70 minor companies plus thousands of smaller firms that perform subcontract work.

There were no signs in 1972 that the industry would rebound to the booming status it enjoyed between 1964 and 1968, when the Apollo lunar landing project, the Vietnam War, strategic missile programs, and heavy outlays for airline jet aircraft brought the industry to a peak. However, an upswing was anticipated.

On the negative side, the industry complained that the government was spending too little on advanced research vital to future commercial projects. Also, the industry continued to have difficulty in applying its scientific and engineering talents to new nongovernmental markets. This left it dependent on the government and vulnerable to the boom-or-bust cycles that have hounded the industry.

Sales. Preliminary estimates indicated that sales totaled about $22.2 billion in 1972, about the same as in 1971 but far down from the peak year of 1968 when sales totaled $29 billion. The Department of Defense accounted for about 59% of the sales total in 1972; commercial airlines, 18%; the National Aeronautics and Space Administration, 12%; and nonaerospace products, 11%.

Employment. At the end of 1972, approximately 917,000 people were employed in the U. S. aerospace industry, 10,000 fewer than a year earlier. However, the industry's rate of decline in employment was slower than that during the 1969–1971 period. Total employment dropped 40% between the peak year of 1967 and the end of 1972. The work force included 150,000 scientists and engineers in 1972, down from the 1967 peak of 235,000.

Jetliner Market. The industry's export sales declined slightly from the record $4.3 billion set in 1971. Although much of the decline was attributable to the growing use of jumbo jets, some U. S. industry leaders said it represented the start of a long-term export decline. They cited the establishment within Europe of industrial-political consortiums to develop aircraft jointly and thereby provide competition for U. S.-made aircraft in world markets. The most prominent example is the 1,350-mile-per-hour British-French Concorde, due to enter service in 1974; but Italy, Germany, and other countries also are collaborating on the development of new planes.

Aerospace leaders have said that Congress' rejection of the program to develop a supersonic transport in 1971 would result in an export market loss to U. S. jetliner manufacturers. In 1972, however, the Boeing Company sold ten Boeing 707 jets to mainland China for $125 million, thereby becoming one of the first American companies to take advantage of the thaw in U. S.-Chinese relations.

Space Shuttle. To many in the industry, the most significant events of the year were the government's final go-ahead for development of the space shuttle and the victory of the North American Rockwell Company in a hard-fought battle for the development contract. The Downey, Calif., firm, prime contractor for the capsules used in the Apollo moon journeys, won the $2.6 billion contract in competition with Lockheed, McDonnell-Douglas, and Grumman. The company said it would subcontract about 50% of its work to other companies.

The space shuttle, a delta-wing vehicle about the size of a DC-9, will be launched vertically into an earth orbit by rockets. After returning from orbit to earth, the vehicle will land like an airplane. The space shuttle will be able to carry about 10 persons and will be usable for as many as 100 trips into orbit and back to earth.

Maiden Flights. Lockheed's L-1011 Tristar airliner made its first flight in 1972. The project was kept alive in 1971 only by an emergency federal loan guarantee. The F-15, which also made its maiden flight in 1972, is a highly maneuverable jet fighter developed for the Air Force by McDonnell-Douglas.

Trident Missile. The Department of Defense announced that a new submarine-launched missile called the Trident was to be developed. Trident missiles, which will be fitted in new submarines, will have a range of about 5,000 miles (8,000 km), about twice the range of the Poseidon missiles now carried by U. S. submarines.

See also AIR TRANSPORTATION; DEFENSE FORCES; SPACE EXPLORATION.

ROBERT H. LINDSEY
Aviation Reporter, "The New York Times"

AFGHANISTAN

The year 1972 was a difficult one for Afghanistan. Two consecutive years of drought and inadequate wheat distribution procedures caused the worst famine in the country's modern history. Legislative inactivity and executive stagnation continued to hinder the development of parliamentary democracy under a constitutional monarchy.

In a famine-stricken village of central Afghanistan a child, starving and ignored, lies in the street.

Famine. The severe famine, most serious in the relatively inaccessible central mountains, caused the deaths of thousands of persons and livestock. Heavy snows and rains brought bumper crops to some regions, but too late to help many disaster areas, and floods devastated some sections. Wheat gifts and purchases, mainly from the United States and the Soviet Union, made up some of the shortage. However, relief food distribution was started late and was inefficient, and there were widespread reports of corruption among local officials.

Political Development. Prime Minister Abdul Zahir tendered his resignation in September, but King Mohammed Zahir Shah asked him to reconsider. The lower house of the Shura, or parliament, seldom had a quorum and spent most of its session on a linguistic issue—whether civil servants should know both Pushtu and Dari (Persian), Afghanistan's two official languages. Arguments raged along ethno-linguistic lines, and no agreement was reached by adjournment in mid-August.

It was hoped that implementation of three pieces of legislation passed by parliament—the political parties law, provincial councils law, and municipal councils law—would give the 7-year-old movement to develop more democratic political processes a major boost. Although political parties were still not recognized legally, several groups of the left and center formed a United Front.

A 6-month student strike over administrative-academic reforms at Kabul University ended in April with the resignation of the rector. But new attempts to upgrade academic standards and expand extracurricular and social activities continued to meet opposition.

Foreign Affairs. More than in most recent years, Afghanistan was being drawn into regional problems in 1972. The creation of an independent Bangladesh and subsequent demands for regional autonomy by the Pushtun and Baluch of Pakistan revived the relatively quiescent "Pushtunistan" issue. At-tempts by Afghanistan and Iran to solve the century-old problem of the distribution of the waters of the Helmand River were inconclusive. The drug problem increased, and Afghanistan seemed to be getting entangled in an international drug net.

King Mohammed Zahir Shah visited the Soviet Union in March and Turkey and Italy in September–October. Foreign visitors to Afghanistan included President Zulfikar Ali Bhutto of Pakistan and former U. S. Treasury Secretary John Connally, who came as a special envoy of President Richard M. Nixon.

LOUIS AND NANCY HATCH DUPREE
American Universities Field Staff

——— **AFGHANISTAN • Information Highlights** ———

Official Name: Kingdom of Afghanistan.
Area: 250,000 square miles (647,497 sq km).
Population (1972 est.): 17,900,000. *Density,* 67 per square mile (26 per sq km). *Annual rate of increase,* 2.4%.
Chief Cities (1969 est.): Kabul, the capital, 299,800; Kandahar, 127,000.
Government: *Head of state,* Mohammed Zahir Shah, king (acceded Nov. 1933). *Head of government,* Abdul Zahir, prime minister (took office June 1971). *Legislature*—Shura: House of Elders, 84 members; House of the People, 215 members.
Languages: Pushtu and Dari (Persian), both official.
Education: *School enrollment* (1970)—primary, 540,687; secondary, 119,450; technical/vocational, 5,397; university/higher, 7,397.
Monetary Unit: Afghani (45 afghanis equal U. S.$1, July 1972).
Gross National Product (1970 est.): $1,500,000,000.
National Income per Person (1963): $57.
Agricultural Production Index (1971): 128 (1952–56=100).
Manufacturing (major products): Textiles, cement, processed fruits, refined sugar, carpets.
Major Agricultural Products: Wheat, corn, rice, barley, cotton, fruits and nuts, sheep.
Major Minerals: Natural gas, petroleum, coal, salt.
Foreign Trade (1970): *Exports,* $86,000,000 (chief exports—fruits and nuts; natural gas; karakul skins; raw cotton). *Imports,* $75,000,000 (chief imports, 1969—tea; sugar; machinery and transport equipment; textile yarn and thread; chemicals). *Chief trading partners* (1969)—USSR (took 38% of exports, supplied 33% of imports); India (19%—9%); United Kingdom (16%—4%); Japan; United States.
Tourism: Receipts (1970), $7,800,000.
Transportation: *Motor vehicles* (1969), 49,000 (automobiles, 30,800); *major national airline,* Ariana Afghan Airlines.
Communications: *Telephones* (1969), 10,833; *radios* (1969), 248,000; *newspapers* (1970), 18 (daily circulation, 101,000).

AFRICA

In general, 1972 was not a particularly successful year for Africa. There were too many coups or attempted coups. There was too much violence and social upheaval—not merely sporadic, but affecting large groups. Regrettably, some events showed clearly that ethnic hatreds were at work.

WORLD INTEREST IN AFRICA

In 1972 the world seemed to be taking a new interest in Africa and its problems. The reasons for this attention were perhaps to be found not so much in Africa itself as in outside events: the winding down of the war in Southeast Asia, the relative quiescence of the Middle East, and the détentes in great-power relations.

State Visits. Trips to Africa by the wife of the U. S. president and by the president of France were one sign that the continent was again becoming a center of world interest. Mrs. Nixon made a successful tour of Liberia, Ghana, and the Ivory Coast in early January. Later in the month President Pompidou followed up his 1971 trip to French-speaking Africa, this time visiting Niger and Chad.

UN Meeting in Ethiopia. The United Nations demonstrated its concern with Africa by holding a special session of the Security Council at Addis Ababa in January and February. This was the Council's first meeting in Africa and its first outside New York since 1952. The costly session drew some criticism, however, because of its burden on straitened UN finances.

The purpose of the meeting was to discuss "burning African issues." Its accomplishments, however, were limited. The Council passed resolutions condemning South Africa's policy in South West Africa (Namibia), the South African policy of apartheid, and Portugal's policies in its African territories. A resolution condemning the 1971 Anglo-Rhodesian agreement on the status of Rhodesia was vetoed by Britain.

Nairobi as a UN Headquarters. A further sign of Africa's growing weight in world affairs was the decision taken in November to locate the headquarters of the new UN international environment agency in Nairobi, Kenya. For the first time, a UN office or agency with a global mission was to be established outside North America and Western Europe, a decision reached over the objections of the United States and other Western countries.

AFRICAN INTERNATIONAL ORGANIZATIONS

OCAMM. The hitherto successful agency of the French-speaking African nations—the Afro-Malagasy and Mauritius Joint Organization (OCAMM) —had a difficult year. In February, President François Tombalbaye of Chad announced his country's withdrawal from Air Afrique, OCAMM's airline, because the company had refused to establish regional headquarters in Fort-Lamy. Tombalbaye also resigned as chairman of OCAMM, though Chad continued to be a member state. This development gave rise to much discussion of such topics as whether OCAMM was too explicitly linked with France, to what degree it was compatible with the more broadly based Organization of African Unity (OAU), and how to strengthen its activities.

OCAMM suffered another blow on April 19 when Zaïre—the former Belgian Congo—withdrew from the organization. The reason for this action was President Mobutu Sese Seko's resentment over West African criticism of his treatment of the archbishop of Kinshasa (see also ZAÏRE). On September 22 the Congo People's Republic withdrew from OCAMM, stating that OCAMM's policies were not in the prime interests of all members.

An OCAMM summit meeting was held in Lomé, Togo, on April 25–26. The closing speech by the new chairman, President Léopold Senghor of Senegal, called for the building of "economic communities" in West Africa. It was described by the distinguished Paris newspaper *Le Monde* as "a perfect example of skill and political realism."

In 1972, OCAMM began to move in the direction of establishing links with the English-speaking

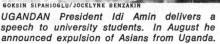
UGANDAN President Idi Amin delivers a speech to university students. In August he announced expulsion of Asians from Uganda.

states of West Africa, such as Ghana and Nigeria. But at the same time there was an increasing cleavage between West and Central African members.

Organization of African Unity (OAU). The Ministerial Council of OAU, the pan-African body, held its 18th session at Addis Ababa on February 14–18. The 19th session was held at Rabat, Morocco, on June 5–11, followed on June 12–15 by the 9th assembly of heads of state and government. The Council passed a number of resolutions concerning the Portuguese colonies, South West Africa, Rhodesia, and South Africa. The OAU summit conference was addressed by UN Secretary General Kurt Waldheim, who expressed complete sympathy for the aims of the various liberation movements.

MOVES TOWARD AFRICAN HARMONY

A number of steps were taken during the year to heal disputes between African states or between governments and rebels.

Algeria, Morocco, and Mauritania. The most notable event of the Rabat conference was the agreement on June 15 between King Hassan II of Morocco and President Houari Boumedienne of Algeria, ending the nine-year-old border conflict between their countries. The border delineation was not divulged, but it was stated that the most important resource of the disputed area, the Gara-Djebilet iron ore deposit, would be developed jointly.

Morocco, Algeria, and Mauritania began to act in concert in some matters and created a tripartite committee for this purpose. Their chief common interest was the future of Spanish Sahara with its large phosphate deposits. In January they called for the decolonization of the area.

Sudan. The civil war in southern Sudan, more or less continuous since 1956, was apparently ended by an agreement achieved in Addis Ababa in February. The pact provided for the disarming of the rebel forces and the creation of a partly autonomous Southern Sudan with a regional assembly. Though denounced by Gordon Mayen, a rebel leader in exile in Kinshasa, the agreement seemed to be working.

Chad and Libya. On April 12 it was announced from Niger that Chad and Libya had decided to restore diplomatic relations. Ties between them had been broken in August 1971, when Chad accused Libya of complicity in an attempted coup.

Guinea and Its Neighbors. Resolution of the discord between Guinea and Senegal dating from 1970 was the subject of strenuous efforts by a mediation committee of the OAU. A meeting took place on May 29 in Monrovia, Liberia, under the chairmanship of Ethiopian Emperor Haile Selassie. On May 31 an agreement was reached on normalizing Guinean-Senegalese relations, presumably on the basis of Guinea's giving up its demand for the return from Senegal of Guinean opponents of President Sékou Touré.

A meeting took place in Guinea on July 24 between Touré and President Félix Houphouët-Boigny of the Ivory Coast. This first conference of the two leaders since 1964 failed to produce any agreement.

Uganda and Tanzania. The foreign ministers of Uganda and Tanzania, meeting on October 4–5 in Mogadishu, Somalia, concluded an agreement ending the rather obscure hostilities that had broken out between the two states in September. The clashes were thought to have been caused by an invasion of Uganda by Tanzanian-based exiles opposed to President Idi Amin.

INTERNAL CONFLICTS

Offsetting the various hopeful moves toward African harmony were some alarming negative events. Of these, the most publicized was the wholesale expulsion of Asians from Uganda. Even more tragic were large-scale massacres in Burundi.

Uganda. Maj. Gen. Idi Amin, who took over as president of Uganda in 1971 from the leftist Milton Obote, was briefly thought of as a pragmatic and nonideological ruler. The image rapidly changed. Amin soon began ruling by decree and discovering enemies all around him. Hundreds in the army whose loyalty he suspected were shot. During 1972, Amin's course became still more capricious and unpredictable. In March, Israeli advisers were ordered

out of Uganda and Israel was denounced. Uganda also became a dangerous place for Europeans.

In August, Amin announced that he would give the Asians in Uganda who were entitled to British or South Asian passports three months to get out of the country. They were alleged to be "sabotaging the economy of the country and practicing corruption." Some 45,000 Asians left Uganda before the deadline, abandoning homes and businesses built up over generations. Most went to Britain, which accepted them reluctantly.

The only African state that offered haven to Uganda's Asians was Malawi. No refugees were allowed to enter neighboring Kenya or Tanzania, whose own anti-Asian policies differed only in degree from those of Uganda. Underlying the resentment toward the Asian minority in East Africa was its conspicuous success in business. Although expulsion may have done Uganda grave harm economically, it did the country no harm in African public opinion.

To any observer outside Africa, the actions of Amin seemed blatantly racist. But he encountered little criticism from other African states. When queried, most Africans seemed to believe he had done the right thing. Nor was he criticized in the OAU. Even Britain and the United States handled Amin cautiously.

Burundi. A second situation from which eyes were carefully averted was the bloody fighting in Burundi in the late spring. The ruling Tusi (Tutsi) group suppressed a rebellion led by the majority Hutu people, tens of thousands of whom were killed. Thousands of Tusi also lost their lives. This greatest African disaster since the Nigerian civil war was treated by the OAU as an "internal matter" and therefore not appropriate for OAU action.

Ghana. Prime Minister Kofi A. Busia was overthrown in Ghana on January 13 by a group of army officers who withdrew the constitution and afterward ruled by decree. It could be said that Busia had failed because of his virtues. His austerity measures to restore the economy that had been wrecked by deposed President Kwame Nkrumah were necessary but painful and unpopular.

The exiled Nkrumah—once the very symbol of independent Black Africa—died on April 27 in Rumania, where he was under treatment for cancer. Since his overthrow in 1966, he had been nominal co-president of Guinea. After a prolonged wrangle between Ghana and Guinea over custody of the body, Nkrumah was buried in Ghana on July 9.

Dahomey. In the fifth coup d'etat since Dahomey gained independence from France in 1960, the civilian government of President Justin Ahomadegbe was overthrown on October 26. The new government, a military junta, was led by Gen. Mathieu Kerekou.

Malagasy Republic. President Philibert Tsiranana, for 12 years virtually absolute ruler of the Malagasy Republic (Madagascar), but in grave difficulties for two years, yielded power on May 18 to Lt. Gen. Gabriel Ramanantsoa, chief of staff since 1960. The francophile, moderate, Western-oriented direction of Tsiranana had been arousing increasing hostility, especially among the young.

The new regime took a very different course. The policy of "dialogue" with South Africa was abandoned. The "Malagasation" of education, and much slacker ties with France and the pro-French states of OCAMM, became the new order.

The change of regime marked a considerable setback for the policies of South Africa, for Madagascar had been in a sense South Africa's bridgehead to Black Africa. Relations with Ramanantsoa's government were broken off on June 27.

Morocco. In August, King Hassan of Morocco again narrowly escaped assassination. The constitutional reforms introduced by him in February had evidently failed to end the threat to his rule.

SOUTHERN AFRICA

Southern Africa, as the largest area of the continent remaining under white control, continued to bulk larger than any other African question in the eyes of most African states. In 1972 there was little change in this region. The long-term threat to white supremacy was still posed by demographic and economic pressures, not by liberation movements of exaggerated significance and achievements.

Rhodesia. The big news of the year in Rhodesia was the collapse of the compromise agreement on the territory's political status, worked out in November 1971 by the British and white-minority Rhodesian governments. The agreement failed to be implemented because of a negative report by the British-sponsored Pearce Commission, which spent three months testing Rhodesian popular support for proposed constitutional changes that would have made independence from Britain legal. Issued in April, the report stated that "the people of Rhodesia as a whole" rejected the settlement.

In retrospect, the whole procedure smacked of naïveté or even fantasy. Who could have doubted that those who wanted more than a cautious, long-term compromise would fail to seize such an unparalleled opportunity to proclaim their discontent? On the other hand, it had been made easy for them to reject substance for shadow. The failure of the 1971 compromise did not bring the day of black democracy in Rhodesia nearer.

The Rhodesian government announced on July 12 plans for "provincialization," aimed at creating regional bodies within the country. It was not clear what the effect of these changes would be.

On January 25, the United States lifted its ban on the importation of Rhodesian chrome, an action in contravention of the theoretical UN ban on trade with Rhodesia.

South West Africa. The United Nations continued to press South Africa to relinquish its administration of South West Africa, which the world body had renamed Namibia. Secretary General Waldheim visited the territory in March, and in October he sent as his personal representative the retired Swiss diplomat Alfred Escher. Escher conferred with South African Prime Minister Balthazar Vorster, who indicated some willingness to compromise. The South African government had already been forced by a strike in South West Africa to modify its labor policy there. African opinion, insistent on the unity of the area, was particularly incensed by South Africa's policy of promoting separate regional development for different parts of South West Africa, beginning with Ovamboland in the north.

(See also articles on the individual African countries.)

ARTHUR CAMPBELL TURNER
University of California, Riverside

AGNEW, Spiro T. See BIOGRAPHY.

GRANT HEILMAN

A major trade agreement providing for the sale of $750 million of U. S. grain to the USSR was concluded in July. Here, wheat is harvested in Washington state.

agriculture

How agriculture fared in 1972—production trends, scientific developments, and other news—is reviewed in this article. It consists of the following sections: (1) World Agriculture; (2) U. S. Agriculture; (3) U. S. Agricultural Research; (4) Dairy Products; (5) Livestock and Poultry; (6) Grains; (7) Fruits; and (8) Vegetables.

World Agriculture

Adverse weather conditions in many places slowed world production of food and fiber in 1972. Preliminary figures seemed to indicate a small decline in total agricultural output from 1971, the first downturn since 1969. If this assumption turns out to be valid, world agricultural output for 1972 would be placed at an index number of 122 (1961–65 = 100), down from 124 in 1971 but still above 99 a decade earlier. This is based on estimates of 18 major countries that produce about two thirds of the world's farm production.

The winterkill of fall-sown grains, particularly of wheat, in the USSR and eastern Europe appears to have been extensive. It was followed by drought that damaged spring-planted crops. Floods in the Philippines and drought in India also cut the world food output. Meanwhile, more generous government subsidy programs aimed at reducing surplus farm output slowed production in the United States and in some other developed lands. However, there were indications of increased world output in some kinds of farm goods. World milk production, for example, rose in 1972, easing a scarcity that had driven the prices of dairy products to near-record levels.

World cotton production surpassed even the 1971 record high of 55 million bales in the marketing year ended July 31. It was estimated that 1972 output might reach about 57.5 million bales.

USDA Grain Report. Late in 1972, the U. S. Department of Agriculture issued a special report on the world grain situation. Grain production is the

single most important index of the world's agriculture situation. The department said that world grain production declined by about 42 million tons in 1972. However, at 1.06 billion tons, 1972 grain production was still the second largest on record.

The report placed the drop in the Soviet wheat crop alone at about 20 million tons, or a decrease of 25%. The Russians negotiated large wheat and corn purchases to offset their crop losses, with plans to buy at least 27 million tons of grain abroad (19 million tons of wheat and 8 million tons of feed grains) during the marketing year beginning July 1, 1972. Feed grains, usually corn, oats, barley, and rye, are essential for the maintenance of livestock which are the source of milk and meat. About two thirds of the Soviet grain purchases were to be made in the United States, with Canada, Australia, France, West Germany, Rumania, and Sweden also serving as major suppliers.

A long delay in the monsoon reduced India's 1972 fall grain crops. India expected to use its reserves in order to avoid an increase in imports.

In the People's Republic of China, the grain crop was about as large as that of 1971, the U. S. agency found. Quantities and timing of wheat purchases were normal compared with recent years, but the first sale in many years of U. S. wheat to China, amounting to some 400,000 tons, was arranged.

From something of a glut in 1971, a shortage of rice for export developed late in 1972. Heavy rains in the Philippines and military disruptions in Bangladesh, South Vietnam, and Cambodia increased immediate import needs. The Asian rice crop, usually harvested as late as December in several countries, was barely larger than that of the preceding year.

Effects of Subsidies. A major study covering 32 of the world's more developed countries, including the United States, concluded that the best way to solve continuing agricultural problems is to speed up commercialization of farming, which is already well under way in most parts of the world. The study was a co-operative effort by the FAO and the UN Economic Commission for Europe. The aim was to analyze the agricultural problems of developed lands and their impact on the development of poor nations. The study and its conclusions were presented at the eighth FAO Regional Conference for Europe in Munich on September 18–25.

One of the conference's most important findings was that farmers in developed lands have tended to produce too much food and fiber. Their governments have obligingly subsidized exports to get rid of the farm surplus. This has worked to the disadvantage of poorer nations which cannot compete with government subsidized exports. Dr. Addeke H. Boerma, FAO's director-general, reported that the developing exporting countries' share in world agricultural trade declined fairly steadily from 46% in 1955 to 34% in 1970. The study noted also that, even in developed lands, the majority of small farms benefited little if at all from subsidies, which seemed to be of help principally to larger farming enterprises.

Green Revolution. In early 1972, the U. S. Government reported that the "green revolution"—the development and widening use of higher-yielding wheat and rice varieties—was continuing to expand. The total acreage of the new wheat and rice strains planted in the 1970–71 harvest year was placed at about 50.5 million acres, up 24% in just one year. India and Pakistan continue to lead the developing world in using these improved varieties. The new kinds of wheat and rice first began making an impact on world farming in 1967 and are the basis for the sharp increase in food production in Asia, the Middle East, and North Africa. There were reports that the new seeds were being used also in Cuba, North Vietnam, and China.

1971 Production. Late in 1972, the FAO issued its annual preliminary report on world farm output in 1971. The data showed a continuation of the distressing trend of earlier years, which saw poor countries boosting production very little while richer lands increased output 6%.

The index of total world production of agricultural, fishery, and forest products in 1971 was placed at 124 (1961–65 average = 100), up from 119 in 1970, and from 111 in 1967. Although total world agricultural output in 1971 increased 3% over 1970, it was up only 1% in the developing countries. Production in Latin America was actually down from the preceding year. Per-capita farm output declined 4% in Latin America, 1% in the Far East (not including China), and remained about the same in the Middle East. The FAO was not as yet reporting on farm production in the People's Republic of China.

North America. In 1971, farm output in North America rose 8% (the largest increase in a single year since 1958) and probably reached the highest volume in history. "Many indices—trade volume and value, wheat, maize, barley, and feed-grain production—were at or near record levels, but net realized farm incomes stagnated," the FAO reported.

Much of the big increase was due to record wheat and corn and other feed-grain crops in the United States and generally higher yields throughout the region. Livestock production rose only slightly. The United States also harvested record crops of barley and sorghum. In Canada, barley production was higher by more than 50% as production continued to expand. The U. S. soybean crop set a record high, and Canada's output of rapeseed was up sharply.

Latin America. Despite considerable gains in several countries, reduced beef production in Argentina and lower sugar output in Cuba held down the region's farm production in 1971 to slightly less than that of 1970. Mexico failed to boost its farm output significantly, but large increases occurred in Costa Rica, Nicaragua, the Dominican Republic, and Jamaica.

Except for Argentina, Guyana, and Paraguay, South American countries showed agricultural production increases ranging from 1% in Ecuador and Uruguay to 6% in Chile.

Western Europe. Agricultural production and export earnings rose sharply in 20 European countries in 1971. Output was up 6%, a much greater gain than those of recent years. Production increases were most striking in Yugoslavia, where there was a 14% increase. Output rose 8% in Belgium and Spain and 7% in France and Sweden. It fell 1% in Italy and 3% in Portugal.

The most outstanding statistic was a 16% rise in the grain output of the 20 European countries, with production reaching a record 148 million tons. Wheat was up 19% and barley output achieved a record volume with an increase of 14%.

Eastern Europe. Bountiful cereal harvests, resulting largely from improved weather in 1971, pushed up farm output 7% above depressed 1970 levels in Eastern Europe. In the USSR, however, the total remained unchanged. Most Soviet crops

were below the previous year's levels, principally because of less favorable growing conditions due to bad weather. Soviet cereal production fell to 181 million tons, down from 187 million tons in 1970.

Rumania had the greatest expansion of farm output with an 18% gain, with Hungary next at 9%. Both countries had suffered heavy losses from excessive rains and floods in 1970. Output expanded faster in Poland and Czechoslovakia than in 1970. Albania's grain harvest was reported good. In East Germany, the weather was unfavorable, and the overall production target was not met.

Middle East. Good weather in most Middle Eastern lands in 1971 halted the decline in per-capita production apparent in the region since 1968. Afghanistan, Iran, and Iraq suffered severe drought that cut farm production as much as 12%.

In Turkey and Egypt, which together account for nearly half of the region's agricultural production, output increased by 3% and 4%, respectively. In Jordan, agricultural production rose 40%, and in the Libyan Arab Republic, it increased by 30%. Israel's output was up by about 4%.

Africa. While agricultural production rose by 4% in 1971 in Africa, population increases in many lands outpaced production gains. In 15 of the 39 developing African countries, the FAO reported, per-capita agricultural production was below the regional 1961–65 average. But farm development is being given more attention and is now the top development priority in many African countries.

Unlike most African nations, South Africa showed a sharp farm-output gain in 1971. Production was up 13% over that of 1969 and 1970, exceeding by 3% the 1967 record.

Far East. In this populous region, food and fiber production rose 2%, down from the 4% annual rise recorded in the previous two years. However, mainland China's production is not reflected in these figures since statistics are not available.

The slowdown was attributed to typhoons, floods, infestations, civil disturbances, and war in various lands. Per-capita output did increase significantly in Sabah and West Malaysia. There was slight improvement in Burma, Indonesia, and Ceylon and no increase in India and the Philippines. In other developing countries per-capita output declined.

Japan's agricultural production declined 2% in 1971, continuing a downward trend from the 1968 peak, mainly because the government moved to reduce rice production. Although livestock production continued to rise, the rate of increase (5%) was slower than that of the preceding two years.

China reported a farm production rise of about 10% for 1971. Grain production was said to have increased by 2.5%, to a record level of 246 million tons. Rice output was reported up by about 2%.

Oceania. Agricultural production in Australia increased by about 3% in 1971 and in New Zealand by about 1%. The Australian wheat harvest was up 5%, but remained 43% below the 1968 record harvest. Australian output of most feed grains, rice, and sugar also was above the 1970 level. Cotton production was down, but meat output continued to rise. In New Zealand, wheat and barley production recovered from the drought-depressed levels of 1970, and corn production continued upward; meat production was little changed, although pork rose again. In both countries, wool production was unchanged, and milk output fell.

JOE WESTERN, *Kominus Agri-Info Associates*

U. S. Agriculture

Record levels in production, realized net farm income, and farm export sales made U. S. agricultural news in 1972.

Production. Despite a decline in acreage planted for harvest, yields per acre rose to record levels, more than offsetting the smaller amount of tilled land. U. S. farm production of crops and livestock reached an index number of 113 (1967 = 100), up from the previous record in 1971 of 111, and up from 91 a decade earlier.

Plantings for harvest totaled 291 million acres, down 3% or 10 million acres from 1971. Yield per acre, however, rose to an index number of 113, 2 points more than the 1971 record. Nearly all of the increase in total crops and livestock production is due to the increase in crop production.

Production reached record highs for soybeans, hay, peanuts, and oranges. A 31% increase in cotton production and smaller increases in the output of rice, dry beans, tobacco, sugarcane and sugarbeets, and hops pushed production totals above those of 1971, but did not set any records. These increases offset declines in grain production.

Preliminary estimates showed livestock production at an index number of 109, up from 108 in 1971 and up from 92 a decade earlier.

Although there was a heavy consumer demand, red meat output ran behind 1971 totals by about 3%. Beef production was up 1%, but veal output was down 17%, pork down 8%, and lamb and mutton down 3%. Helping to offset this, milk production rose to about 120.5 billion pounds from 118.6 billion in 1971. Broiler chicken meat output reached a record high, nearly 10% more than in 1971. The turkey crop at 128 million birds was up 7% from 1971 and 1% from the 1967 record.

Exports. The most significant development of the year, however, was that U. S. farm exports began to increase sharply and rapidly in 1972. Final reports were expected to show a total of about $10 billion in farm exports in the marketing year ending June 30, 1973. This would be a $2 billion increase over the previous record, set in the same 12-month period a year earlier.

The U. S. Department of Agriculture reported that the continuing expansion in exports is due to several factors: a rising world demand for grains; the wheat crop failure in Russia; rapid improvement in economic conditions around the world; easing of trade restrictions with Russia and the People's Republic of China; the realignment of currencies making U. S. products cheaper abroad; the availability of huge U. S. supplies; and the capacity to move large quantities of grain.

Two thirds of the 1972 dollar increase in farm exports was due to larger volume shipped abroad (mainly of grains, soybeans, and cotton), and one-third was due to higher prices. The total volume of exported agricultural commodities in 1972 was estimated at 83 million metric tons.

The value of wheat exports was forecast to increase by about 90% to more than $2 billion, feed-grain exports by 36% to $1.6 billion, and soybeans and products by 13% to about $2.3 billion. Higher prices were also expected to boost livestock product exports by 32% to almost $1 billion. Slight increases were forecast for fruits and vegetables. Declines in value were expected only for dairy and poultry products (down 30%) and cotton (down

6%, even though cotton exports were expected to be up (5% in volume).

"The Soviet Union accounts for about half of the total increase forecast for U. S. agricultural exports this fiscal year," the U. S. Department of Agriculture reported late in 1972. Russian purchases were estimated at $1.2 billion, up from about $150 million a year earlier. Most of this huge expected increase would be in wheat, which may total around $660 million. Feed exports may total close to $400 million and soybeans $135 million.

Exports to western Europe were expected to reach about $3.2 billion, up slightly from a year earlier. Japan, the top single-country market for U. S. farm products, was expected to import a record $1.5 billion worth of such products in 1972. Exports to other Asian countries, including the Near East, were expected to show a substantial gain and total more than $2 billion. Late 1972 sales of linseed oil, wheat, and corn may bring exports to the People's Republic of China to about $50 million.

If reports of U. S. farm exports in the year ending June 30, 1973, show the expected increases, this country's share of total world agricultural trade would be substantially larger. The U. S. Department of Agriculture estimated the value of total world farm exports was $60.3 billion in 1970, the latest year for which statistics were available; this figure includes fish products as well as farm goods.

Even though the United States is a heavily industrialized country, it still is an agricultural supergiant in terms of production. It leads the world in exports and imports of farm commodities. In the year ended June 30, 1972, U. S. farm exports amounted to the equivalent of the output of one out of every five acres harvested, or 65 million acres of U. S. cropland, and represented about one seventh of farmers' cash receipts.

The export market took more than half of the U. S. output of rice and soybeans; two fifths of the wheat, cattle hides, and tallow; about one third of the tobacco and cotton; one fifth of the feed grains; and about one fourth of the dry beans, lemons, and dry milk.

Income. The enormously expanding export market, sharply rising prices, and mammoth production combined to make 1972 the most profitable farm year on record. Realized net farm income was placed at $18.6 billion, up from $16.1 billion in the previous year, and up from the previous high of $17.1 billion a quarter of a century ago in postwar 1947.

Gross sales of farm products in 1972 were estimated at $64.5 billion, up from about $60.1 billion in 1971. Production costs rose too, but more slowly than booming sales. Part of the reason for the increased sales was that the nation's economy improved. "Availability of manpower, credit, and most materials, coupled with strong public and private demand, point to further economic expansion," the U. S. Department of Agriculture reported.

Consumer demand for red meat and a decline in production kept prices well above 1971 levels. Livestock and product receipts were expected to rise about $3.5 billion above the $30.5 billion in 1971. Annual crop receipts were expected to be up, too, from 1971's total of $22.6 billion. In addition, a rise of about $1 billion (from the previous year's total of $3.1 billion) was anticipated in government payments to farmers. The record high for such payments was nearly $3.8 billion in 1969. Because the number of farms continued to decline and be-

cause income was up, net income per farm was also expected to surpass the record high of $5,757 in 1970.

Consumption. Per-capita food consumption declined slightly in the United States in 1972 to an index number of 103 (1967 = 100) from the record 103.5 in the previous year.

The consumption decline occurred mainly in red meat, fruit, vegetables, animal fats, eggs, and coffee. More than half the drop in red meat was offset by a large increase in poultry consumption. More fish also was eaten, along with slightly more sugar and sweeteners, dairy products, vegetable oils, and melons.

Unfavorable weather reduced expectations for crops of some noncitrus fruits and vegetables. Per-capita intake of both fresh and processed fruits was down 3% and the consumption of fresh vegetables was down 2%. However, consumption of canned and frozen vegetables rose sharply.

The average American consumed about 94 pounds (counting bones, gristle, and other waste), of red meat in the first half of 1972, down about a pound from a year earlier. Smaller pork consumption more than offset a small gain in beef and accounted for most of the decline. Use of veal, lamb, and mutton was also less than during January–June 1971. The same conditions continued in the last half of 1972, suggesting that the general rise in meat consumption in recent years lessened slightly in 1972.

Poultry meat consumption of both chicken and turkey was up. Per-capita consumption of chicken was as much as 4% more than the 41.4 pounds consumed in 1971. Turkey was up more than 5% over the 1971 figure of 8.5 pounds.

Consumers bought food in the second quarter of 1972 at an annual rate of $123.4 billion, up more than 5½% from a year earlier. It may be found that food expenditures for the entire year equalled the second quarter annual rate, with higher prices accounting for most of the increase.

Employment. Farm wages averaged $1.97 an hour in mid-October, up from $1.93 a year earlier, The farm labor force declined slightly from the average of 4,445,900 in 1971. The work force consisted of about 3 million farm operators and unpaid family members and 1 million hired workers.

Assets and Land Values. The market value of farm real estate on March 1, 1972, was up 8% from the same date a year earlier. This was a sharp increase over the 3% rise in 1971 and the equal of the 1968 increase. The sharp rate of gain partly reflected the expansion in the money supply during the last year and concurrent increase in the volume of funds available for real-estate purchases.

The index of farm real-estate values per acre reached 130 (1967 = 100), up from 121 in 1971. The increase in land values since 1967 ranged from 73% in Georgia to only 5% in Arizona.

JOE WESTERN
Kominus Agri-Info Associates

U. S. Agricultural Research

Research pursued by agricultural scientists has been instrumental in making U. S. agriculture the most productive in the world. The principal research agency of the federal government is the Agricultural Research Service (ARS) of the Department of Agriculture, whose activities extend from improving farm practices to human nutrition.

Animal and Plant Research. The second viroid, a newly discovered class of infectious particles, was isolated by ARS scientists in 1972. The newly identified viroid is the agent of chrysanthemum stunt disease, previously thought to be caused by a virus. Smaller than any known virus, the viroid is a fragment of ribonucleic acid (RNA). The first viroid, the agent of potato spindle tuber disease was isolated in 1971. Many other plant, animal, and human diseases may be caused by viroids.

For the first time there is hope of curing elm trees infected with Dutch elm disease fungus (DED). This hope is based on two developments that are being thoroughly tested: a pressure technique for injecting mature trees with liquids containing chemicals; and the development of a water-soluble form of the fungicide benomyl, which inhibits the disease without damage to the elm.

Corn genes with extra food potential have been recovered in studies of a primitive South American corn. Scientists discovered that the aleurone, the site of B-vitamins and high-quality protein just under the kernel hull, is two to five cells thicker in primitive Coroico corn than in U. S. commercial hybrids. Coroico may serve as parent stock to improve the nutritional value of U. S. hybrids.

Scientists continued to release new crop varieties, some of which included 290 plant collections gathered by plant explorers in the first botanical exploration of Siberia since the 1930's, new corn germ plasms, and eight new wheat, five new fruit, eight new cereal, two new spinach, and two new sorghum varieties.

Research presently underway is expected to result in a hybrid sunflower, which could become an important alternate cash crop in the South and a replacement for flax in the North. Scientists have already found a restorer gene, which returns fertility to male-sterile sunflower plants.

A major breakthrough in the freezing of boar semen promises to bring the full benefits of artificial insemination to the swine industry. Researchers developed a new additive and a special procedure for handling the semen before it is frozen.

Pollution Control. Treating agricultural wastes as a major resource rather than as a necessary evil may hasten the recycling of those materials as one way to help cleanse the environment. For example, ARS scientists have chemically treated barn wastes to increase digestibility, then blended them into rations for use as feed for sheep. They have also designed management systems to limit the handling of manure and of feedlot runoff, which pollutes nearby streams and ground water.

In addition, scientists have begun studies to find out if effluents from food processing plants can be used to irrigate fields used to feed cattle and sheep. Traditionally, fields sprayed with effluent are taken out of production.

Pest Management. ARS scientists have discovered and developed a number of synthetic sex attractants and are now studying the possible use of them as direct control agents, rather than as detection tools. Besides trapping insects, the materials may be released in sufficient quantity to permeate the insects' environment to disorient males in their efforts to find females. They may also prove useful in integrated pest-control programs.

Muscalure, a newly identified sex attractant for house flies, may reduce the amount of insecticide needed if it can efficiently attract flies to a small selected area that has been treated with insecticide. In another house fly experiment, genetic engineering has developed a male-producing strain of house flies that could reduce the cost and time required to separate flies by sex in a possible program aimed at controlling the breeding of flies through sexual sterilization.

A tiny parasitic wasp offers promise toward control of the bollworm, also known as corn earworm and tomato fruitworm. An experimental new lure—octyl butyrate—controls yellow jackets and related *Vespula* wasps without contributing to environmental pollution.

A major step toward integrating several control procedures for eradicating the boll weevil, a cotton pest, has been made with the discovery of a chemosterilant. Busulfan makes male boll weevils sexually sterile with little or no other damage to the weevil. Laboratory-sterilized male weevils were to be released for two years in a 25,000-acre test area of Mississippi, Alabama, and Louisiana to determine the feasibility of eradication.

Minnows that eat mosquito larvae may have sufficient potential as biological control agents to warrant their commercial production and distribution. The minnows cost less than half as much as insecticides while achieving good control.

In weed control research, ARS scientists have discovered that some aquatic weeds can be effectively killed with the herbicides diquat and paraquat, without harming fish. Uncontrolled aquatic weeds obstruct water flow, navigation, and drainage; they also cause large losses of water through transpiration and present health hazards. The discovery of an additive that enhances the efficiency of herbicides may lead to effective weed control with fewer applications and at lower herbicide rates per application.

Nutrition Research. Though milk is considered nature's best food, ARS scientists are trying to improve it for some people by increasing its content of unsaturated fats, which could significantly reduce saturated fat in the diet. Scientists found that when encapsulated safflower oil is fed to dairy cows, much of it reaches the milk in an unsaturated form.

Remote Sensing. The first of two Earth Resources Technology Satellites (ERTS) was launched July 23, 1972, to gather technology that will help agricultural scientists develop better management of plant, soil, and water resources. Four ARS experiments are included in the program—distinguishing among various kinds of vegetation, detecting insect infestations on a variety of crops, monitoring the effectiveness of wind erosion control, and using space data in watershed hydrology.

Marketing. ARS marketing specialists have proposed some solutions to the problems faced by small food store owners in the inner city. Suggested solutions include coordinated distribution systems and improved delivery and receiving methods. The program would result in a wider variety of more nutritious foods being made available to inner city residents.

Apples that currently end up as waste may now be salvaged by a mechanical pickup harvester. The recently developed harvester has rubber fingers that sweep the apples off the ground onto a retaining cloth and eventually deposits them in a pallet box mounted on the unit.

ROBERT B. RATHBONE
U. S. Agricultural Research Service

Dairy Products

The first per-capita rise since the mid-1950's in consumption of milk and dairy products in the United States occurred in 1972. Total U. S. and world production of dairy products also increased.

U. S. Production. Dairy farmers in the United States produced about 120.5 billion pounds of milk in 1972, up from the previous year's 118.6 billion pounds. Production has been steadily rising since 1970, following several years of decline from the record high of nearly 127 billion pounds in 1964.

Output per cow, which has been gaining annually since World War II, continued to increase in 1972. The average was estimated at 9,875 pounds, up from 9,607 in 1971. This increase, about 2.6%, was approximately the same gain as was made in 1971. In 1962, production per cow was estimated at only 7.496 pounds. Rising milk prices, a good supply of replacement heifers, and a slow decline in dairy-cow numbers helped push output upward.

The upturn in per-capita consumption of milk and dairy products amounted to about a 1% increase from 1971 levels. Contributing to this boost, the U. S. Department of Agriculture reported, were increasing disposable incomes, relatively small rises in retail dairy prices, higher meat prices, aggressive dairy promotions, the broadened food-stamp program, and returning veterans whose per-capita consumption is high.

In 1972, each American consumed about 562 pounds of milk in all dairy products, up 1% from that of the previous year.

Hard cheeses, whose sales generally have grown about 6% annually, were up more than 10% in 1972. Per-capita cheese consumption was about 13 pounds in 1972, up 9% from 1971. The per-capita consumption of frozen dessert rose, of butter and whole milk declined slightly, and of canned milk and of nonfat dry milk was down.

Numbers of milk cows on farms declined again in 1972, dropping to about 12.2 million from 12.4 million in the previous year. The downtrend had been under way since 1945. In 1972 the number of milk cows in the United States was at its lowest level since the late 1800's.

Milk and dairy product supplies in 1972 exceeded demand by a smaller amount than in 1971, resulting in smaller government purchases to support milk prices. The Commodity Credit Corporation (CCC) bought products equal to about 5.6 billion pounds of milk in 1972, down from the 7.3 billion in the previous year.

World Production. Milk output in the 36 lands that usually produce 85% of the world's milk was up to approximately 700 billion pounds from 680 billion in 1971. Much of the increase occurred in western Europe, Australia, and New Zealand.

JOE WESTERN
Kominus Agri-Info Associates

Livestock and Poultry

The number of cattle in the United States increased in 1972, but hogs, sheep, and lambs declined. Broiler production increased, as did the turkey crop. The world population of cattle and hogs increased, but the number of sheep decreased.

U. S. Livestock. The United States' cattle herd expanded at a faster rate in 1972 than in recent years, reaching about 121.9 million head on Jan. 1, 1973. The increase was greater than either the

JAMES ANDANSON—GAMMA

PROTESTING against the takeover of farmlands by the military, French farmers pasture their sheep beneath the Eiffel Tower.

3.5-million gain recorded during 1971 or the 2.25-million 1970 increase. Beef animals accounted for most of the gain in 1972.

Total red meat production in 1972 was slightly less than in the previous year, mainly because pork output was down. Per-capita red meat consumption averaged about 3 pounds less than the 192 pounds consumed in 1971. Beef consumption was up nearly 2 pounds per person, but pork intake declined by about 5 pounds. Veal consumption decreased again, but consumption of lamb and mutton was up slightly. While U. S. production of lamb and mutton was down, imports more than offset the decline.

The number of sheep in the United States declined about 750,000 head in 1972 to fewer than 18 million head.

U. S. Eggs and Poultry. Egg production in 1972 was down slightly from the record high of more than 71.6 billion eggs in the preceding year. Broiler production reached a record high in 1972, up nearly

10% over the 1971 total of nearly 3 billion chickens. The 1972 turkey crop also set a record at 128.4 million birds, 7% more than the 1971 figure.

World Livestock Populations. The number of cattle and buffalo in the world increased about 1% in 1972, reaching a record level of more than 1.2 billion head. The 1972 total was 14% more than the 1961–65 average. The larger number of cattle raised in the United States, the Soviet Union, and Australia accounted for most of the gain.

The world hog population rose for the eighth year, to nearly 634 million. The 1972 total was more than 3% above that of 1971.

The world total of sheep in 1972 declined about 1% to approximately one billion animals. In Australia, low wool prices led to a decline to 169 million head, 5% less than in 1971. The Russian flock rose slightly, to 138.5 million head.

JOE WESTERN
Kominus Agri-Info Associates

Grains

Grain crops generally declined in the United States in 1972. The greatest declines were in rye, oats, and barley. World production of wheat, rye, oats, and barley were also less than in 1971.

Wheat. The United States produced 1,558,996,-000 bushels of wheat in 1972. The crop was 5% smaller than the 1971 crop, but 14% larger than the 1970 crop. It was harvested from 47,839,000 acres, down 1% from 1971, but up 8% from 1970. The average yield per acre was 32.6 bushels, down 1.2 bushels from 1971, but up 1.6 bushels from 1970. Kansas led the states, producing 309,205,000 bushels of wheat. North Dakota was second, producing 218,044,000 bushels. Other leading states were Washington, 125,920,000 bushels; Montana, 97,100,-000 bushels; Nebraska, 94,646,000 bushels; and Oklahoma, 90,850,000 bushels.

Winter wheat production totaled 1,198,103,000 bushels, up 3% from 1971, and up 8% from 1970. The acreage harvested totaled 35,364,000 acres, about 7% more than in 1971, and up 6% from 1970. The yield averaged 33.9 bushels per acre. The 1972 yield was 1.3 bushels less than the 1971 yield, but 0.6 bushel over the 1970 yield. Kansas led the states in winter wheat production.

Production of spring wheat, other than durum, totaled 286,947,000 bushels, down 26% from 1971, but up 37% from 1970. The acreage harvested totaled 9,969,000 acres, down 21% from 1971, but up 13% from 1970. The yield per acre averaged 28.8 bushels, down 1.9 bushels from 1971, but up 5.1 bushels from 1970. North Dakota led the states in the production of spring wheat by producing 149,060,000 bushels. Minnesota was second, producing 45,540,000 bushels. The yield per acre averaged 29 bushels in North Dakota and 33 in Minnesota.

Durum wheat production totaled 73,946,000 bushels in 1972, down 16% from 1971, but up 46% from the 1970 crop. The durum crop was harvested from 2,506,000 acres, down 9% from 1971, but up 24% from the 1970 acreage. The yield per acre averaged 29.5 bushels, down 2.4 bushels from the 1971 crop, but up 4.5 bushels from 1970. North Dakota led the states in producing durum wheat with a crop of 66,552,000 bushels. The yield per acre in North Dakota averaged 29.5 bushels.

The world production of wheat was 300,489,000 metric tons of wheat in 1972, down from 323,188,-000 tons in 1971.

WORLD PRODUCTION OF GRAINS BY LEADING NATIONS

(In metric tons)

	Average 1966–70	1971	1972
Wheat			
USSR	74,543,000	81,900,000	62,300,000
United States	38,773,000	44,620,000	42,443,000
India	15,420,000	23,247,000	25,500,000
China (mainland)	22,320,000	24,000,000	24,000,000
France	13,590,000	15,360,000	16,042,000
Canada	16,797,000	14,412,000	13,811,000
Italy	9,585,000	10,070,000	9,455,000
Turkey	8,380,000	10,700,000	8,500,000
Australia	10,697,000	8,644,000	6,800,000
Argentina	6,249,000	5,440,000	6,500,000
Rye			
USSR	11,305,000	10,600,000	8,300,000
Poland	7,472,000	7,833,000	7,236,000
West Germany	2,967,000	3,093,000	2,985,000
East Germany	1,718,000	1,754,000	1,742,000
United States	740,000	1,294,000	795,000
Turkey	767,000	900,000	700,000
Austria	391,000	448,000	458,000
Czechoslovakia	678,000	610,000	433,000
Sweden	180,000	301,000	390,000
Argentina	296,000	256,000	350,000
Barley			
USSR	25,340,000	28,600,000	29,900,000
Canada	7,271,000	13,099,000	10,836,000
France	8,802,000	8,950,000	9,398,000
United States	8,806,000	10,069,000	9,104,000
United Kingdom	8,480,000	8,576,000	8,115,000
West Germany	4,551,000	5,601,000	5,849,000
Denmark	4,734,000	5,474,000	5,375,000
Spain	3,071,000	4,783,000	4,137,000
Turkey	3,560,000	4,100,000	3,200,000
India	2,674,000	2,865,000	3,000,000
Oats			
USSR	9,780,000	12,100,000	11,600,000
United States	12,740,000	12,712,000	10,607,000
Canada	5,492,000	5,606,000	4,515,000
West Germany	3,815,000	4,113,000	3,940,000
France	2,981,000	3,137,000	2,803,000
Poland	2,893,000	3,205,000	2,801,000
Sweden	1,390,000	1,867,000	1,920,000
Finland	1,071,000	1,424,000	1,425,000
Australia	1,446,000	1,277,000	...
United Kingdom	1,253,000	1,368,000	1,091,000
Corn			
United States	111,443,000	104,131,000	140,728,000
China (mainland)	23,277,000	26,426,000	25,340,000
Brazil	12,773,000	13,500,000	14,500,000
South Africa	6,149,000	8,582,000	10,270,000
Mexico	8,040,000	8,700,000	9,000,000
France	4,598,000	7,581,000	8,771,000
USSR	7,740,000	7,500,000	8,100,000
Romania	7,108,000	6,536,000	7,762,000
Yugoslavia	7,146,000	6,933,000	7,441,000
India	5,460,000	7,413,000	6,500,000
Rice			
China (mainland)	91,190,000	97,540,000	94,000,000
India	52,925,000	63,736,000	66,066,000
Indonesia	15,552,000	23,064,000	24,454,000
Pakistan	18,911,000	20,034,000	18,994,000
Japan	17,019,000	15,861,000	13,570,000
Thailand	11,935,000	13,270,000	13,400,000
Burma	7,694,000	8,128,000	8,250,000
South Korea	4,988,000	5,571,000	5,800,000
South Vietnam	4,665,000	5,700,000	5,800,000
Philippines	4,494,000	5,343,000	5,180,000

Source: Foreign Agricultural Service, U. S. Department of Agriculture.

Rye. Rye production in the United States totaled 31,315,000 bushels in 1972, a drop of 38% from 1971, and 19% under the 1970 crop. The crop was harvested from 1,153,000 acres, 36% fewer than in 1971, and 23% under 1970. The yield per acre averaged 27.2 bushels, down 0.8 bushel from 1971, but up 1.2 bushels from 1970.

World rye production totaled 25,442,000 metric tons in 1972, down 14% from 1971, and down 12% from the 1966–70 average.

Rice. Rice production in the United States totaled 85,057,000 bags (100 pound bags), up 1% from 1971, and up 2% from 1970. The yield per acre averaged a record 4,676 pounds, up 38 pounds from 1971, and up 61 pounds from 1970. The acreage harvested totaled 1,818,900 acres, about the same as in 1970 and 1971. Arkansas led the states in rice production by producing 22,050,000 bags. Texas ranked second, producing 21,870,000 bags.

SUNFLOWERS provide a new export crop on U. S. farms. Sunflower seed oil, high in polyunsaturates, is widely used for margarine in Europe.

GRANT HEILMAN

Corn. The nation's corn crop totaled 5,400,390,-000 bushels in 1972. The crop was down 25% from 1971, but was 32% greater than the 1970 crop. Yields of corn were a record 94.5 bushels per acre, up 7.7 bushels from 1971, and up 22.9 bushels from the 1970 crop. The acreage harvested totaled 57,-141,000 acres, down 10% from 1971, and down slightly from 1970. Iowa led the states in corn production by producing 1,201,750,000 bushels. Illinois, which produced 971,250,000 bushels, ranked second. Other leading states were: Nebraska, 530,-400,000 bushels; Indiana, 478,240,000 bushels; Minnesota, 460,750,000 bushels; Ohio, 273,064,000 bushels; and Missouri, 222,500,000 bushels.

Barley. The United States produced 418,165,000 bushels of barley in 1972, down 10% from 1971, but up 2% from 1970. The yield per acre averaged 43.4 bushels, down 2.2 bushels from 1971. Producers harvested the crop from 9,640,000 acres, down 5% from 1971. North Dakota led the states in barley production. The world barley production totaled 127,849,000 metric tons in 1972, down 2%.

Oats. Oat production totaled 730,762,000 bushels in the United States in 1972, a drop of 16% from 1971. The crop was harvested from 14,181,-000 acres, 10% fewer than in 1971. The average yield per acre was 51.5 bushels, down 4.2 bushels from 1971. Minnesota led the states in oat production by producing 132,500,000 bushels. World oat production totaled 49,123,000 metric tons, a drop of 10% from 1971.

Sorghum Grain. Production of sorghum grain totaled a record 895,595,000 bushels in 1972, up slightly from 1971, and up 28% from 1970. The crop was harvested from 13,975,000 acres, a drop of 16% from 1971. The crop yielded a record 64.1 bushels per acre, up 10.2 bushels from 1971. Texas led the states in production with 336,000,000 bushels.

NICHOLAS KOMINUS
Kominus Agri-Info Associates

Fruits

The citrus crop in the United States increased in 1971–72. However, the production of apples, pears, peaches, and other deciduous fruits declined.

Apples. The United States produced 5,956,100,-000 pounds of apples in 1972, a drop of 2% from 1971. The crop was up 7% in the Western states, but down 9% in the Eastern states, and down 2% in the central states.

Washington led the states in apple production, harvesting 1,450,000,000 pounds, an increase of 21% from a year earlier. New York ranked second, producing 850,000,000 pounds, a decline of 8% from the preceding crop. Michigan, which produced 720,000,000 pounds, ranked third. Other leaders were California, Virginia, Pennsylvania, North Carolina, and West Virginia, in that order.

Pears. Production of pears totaled 599,100 tons in 1972, a drop of 14% from 1971. California was the leading pear state, producing 296,000 tons, a decline of 4% from a year earlier.

Washington ranked second by producing 156,000 tons of pears, a drop of 6% from the preceding crop. Sixty-seven percent of Washington's production was Bartletts. Oregon ranked third by producing 93,000 tons, a drop of 47% from a year earlier.

Peaches. The United States produced 2,522,100 pounds of peaches in 1972, a drop of 13% from 1971. California led the states, producing 1,610,-000,000 pounds, or 64% of the total crop.

Cherries. The 1972 sweet cherry crop totaled 94,000 tons, a decline of 33% from 1971. Tart cherry production totaled 153,000 tons, up 10% from 1971.

Grapes. The nation produced 2,637,200 tons of grapes in 1972, 34% fewer than in 1971. Production in California, the leading state, totaled 2,320,-000 tons, a drop of 34% from a year earlier. California accounted for 88% of the grapes produced in the United States. Raisin varieties accounted for 62% of California production; wine varieties, 24%; and table varieties, 13%.

Plums and Prunes. Production of prunes and plums in 1972 in Michigan, Idaho, Washington, and Oregon totaled 42,000 tons, a drop of 34% from 1971. California produced 77,000 tons of prunes, 41% fewer than a year earlier.

Apricots. The 1972 apricot crop totaled 132,-000 tons, down 12% from a year earlier.

Nectarines. In 1972, nectarine production totaled 70,000 tons, up 1% from the preceding crop.

Cranberries. The 1972 cranberry crop totaled 2,025,000 barrels, up 23% from 1971. Production in Massachusetts and Wisconsin totaled 800,000 barrels.

Oranges. Florida produced 174,000,000 boxes of oranges in 1972–73, up 27% from 1971–72, and up 22% from 1970–71. Florida produced 82,000,-

U. S. PRODUCTION OF APPLES, PEACHES, AND PEARS, BY LEADING STATES
(In pounds)

	1970	1971	1972
Apples			
Washington	1,390,000,000	1,200,000,000	1,450,000,000
New York	945,000,000	925,000,000	850,000,000
Michigan	710,000,000	720,000,000	720,000,000
California	500,000,000	400,000,000	460,000,000
Virginia	463,000,000	480,000,000	450,000,000
Pennsylvania	510,000,000	505,000,000	400,000,000
North Carolina	223,000,000	185,000,000	250,000,000
West Virginia	242,000,000	275,000,000	210,000,000
Ohio	135,000,000	150,000,000	135,000,000
Illinois	94,100,000	103,000,000	100,000,000
Total U.S.	6,293,900,000	6,110,100,000	5,956,100,000
Peaches			
California	1,842,000,000	1,682,000,000	1,610,000,000
South Carolina	270,000,000	290,000,000	260,000,000
Georgia	160,000,000	120,000,000	190,000,000
Pennsylvania	84,000,000	105,000,000	80,000,000
Arkansas	40,000,000	43,000,000	42,000,000
Alabama	40,000,000	27,000,000	40,000,000
Washington	40,000,000	40,500,000	32,000,000
Texas	33,000,000	5,000,000	29,000,000
New Jersey	91,000,000	125,000,000	25,000,000
North Carolina	42,000,000	35,000,000	25,000,000
Total U.S.	3,016,000,000	2,888,900,000	2,522,100,000
Pears	(In tons)		
California	258,000	309,000	296,000
Washington	144,500	165,400	156,000
Oregon	90,000	174,000	93,000
Michigan	16,000	17,500	24,000
New York	13,500	19,000	20,500
Pennsylvania	3,400	2,600	3,500
Colorado	4,530	5,490	2,800
Connecticut	1,650	1,630	2,300
Idaho	1,200	2,300	800
Utah	4,300	4,200	200
Total U.S.	537,080	701,120	599,100

U. S. CITRUS PRODUCTION BY LEADING STATES[1]
(In number of boxes)[2]

	1970–71	1971–72	1972–73
Oranges			
California	37,500,000	43,300,000	...
Florida	142,300,000	137,000,000	174,000,000
Texas	6,200,000	5,800,000	6,800,000
Arizona	3,560,000	4,900,000	5,000,000
Total	189,560,000	191,000,000	...
Grapefruit			
Florida	42,900,000	47,000,000	45,000,000
Texas	10,100,000	9,200,000	10,400,000
Arizona	2,520,000	2,540,000	2,600,000
California	5,040,000	5,100,000	...
Total	60,560,000	63,840,000	...
Lemons			
California	13,300,000	13,600,000	17,000,000
Arizona	3,150,000	3,080,000	5,000,000
Total	16,450,000	16,680,000	22,000,000
Tangelos			
Florida	2,700,000	3,900,000	3,800,000
Tangerines			
Florida	3,700,000	3,200,000	2,600,000
Arizona	390,000	570,000	700,000
California	1,140,000	600,000	700,000
Total	5,230,000	4,370,000	4,000,000
Temples			
Florida	5,000,000	5,300,000	5,000,000

[1] The crop year begins with the bloom of the first year and ends with completion of harvest the following year. [2] Net content of box varies. Approximate averages are as follows: oranges—California and Arizona, 75 pounds; Florida and other states, 90 pounds; grapefruit—California desert valleys and Arizona, 64 pounds; other California areas, 67 pounds; Florida, 85 pounds; and Texas, 80 pounds; lemons—76 pounds; tangelos—90 pounds; tangerines—California and Arizona, 75 pounds; Florida, 95 pounds; and Temples—90 pounds. Source: Crop Reporting Board, U.S. Department of Agriculture.

000 boxes of valencias, an increase of 20% from 1971–72. Production of other varieties totaled 92,-000,000 boxes, up 34% from a year earlier. California production of varieties other than valencias totaled 27,000,000 boxes, up 21% from a year earlier. Texas produced 6,800,000 boxes, an increase of 17% from 1971–72. Production in Arizona totaled 5,000,000 boxes, an increase of 2% from a year earlier.

Grapefruit. The Florida grapefruit crop totaled 45,000,000 boxes in 1972–73, a drop of 2,000,000 boxes from a year earlier. Seedless varieties ac-

counted for 75% of the Florida crop. Pink varieties accounted for one quarter of the crop. Grapefruit production in Texas increased from 9,200,000 in 1971–72 to 10,400,000 boxes in 1972–73. Arizona production totaled 2,600,000 boxes, up 60,000 boxes from a year earlier. Production of desert valley grapefruit in California totaled 3,000,000 boxes, a drop of 200,000 boxes from a year earlier.

Lemons. The United States produced 22,000,000 boxes of lemons in 1972–73, up 32% from a year earlier. Production in California totaled 17,000,000 boxes, up 25% from 1971–72. Arizona produced 5,-000,000 boxes, 62% more than a year earlier.

Tangerines. Tangerine production totaled 4,-000,000 boxes in 1972–73, a drop of 8% from 1971–72, and a drop of 23% from 1970–71. Production increases in Arizona and California could not offset the decline in Florida.

Temples. Temple production totaled 5,000,000 boxes in 1972–73, a drop of 300,000 boxes from a year earlier.

Tangelos. Production of tangelos totaled 3,800,-000 boxes ·in 1971–72, down 100,000 boxes from 1971–72.

NICHOLAS KOMINUS
Kominus Agri-Info Associates

Vegetables

The United States produced more vegetables for the fresh market and for processing and more sweet potatoes in 1972 than in 1971, but fewer potatoes.

Vegetables and Melons. Production of the 19 major vegetable crops and 3 melon crops for the fresh market in 1972 totaled 235,415,000 hundredweight, up 1.2% from a year earlier. Vegetable production totaled 195,276,000 hundredweight, up 2.4%. Melon production totaled 40,139,000 hundredweight, a drop of 4.4%.

Large increases in broccoli, cauliflower, lettuce, green pepper, and tomato production offset declines in some of the other crops.

Production of winter and spring vegetables increased, but summer and fall vegetable production declined in 1972. Summer production accounted for 40.6% of the crop; spring production, 22.3%; fall production, 19.7%; and winter production, 17.3%.

About 1,645,000 acres were planted to the 1972 crops, an increase of 1% from a year earlier. Smaller acreages were planted to snap beans, cabbage, celery, sweet corn, onions, green peppers, and spinach in 1972. All other crop acreages were up.

Production of cantaloupes, honeydew melons, and watermelons declined. Watermelon acreage increased, but honeydew melon acreage remained unchanged, and cantaloupe acreage declined.

Vegetables for Processing. Producers increased the acreage planted in green lima beans, snap beans, beets, sweet corn, cucumbers, green peas, and spinach intended for processing in 1972. Fewer acres were, however, planted to tomatoes. Production increases were as follows: green lima beans, up 7%; sweet corn, up 6%; cucumbers, up 1%; spinach, up 5%; and tomatoes, up 6%. Decreases in production were: snap beans, down 1%; beets, down 1%; and green peas, down 2%.

Potatoes. The 1972 potato crop totaled 294,-498,000 hundredweight, a decline of 8% from the 319,554,000 hundredweight of 1971, and a decline of 10% from the 325,752,000 hundredweight of 1970. Potato acreage totaled 1,260,100, a drop of 9% from 1971, and 11% from 1970. The yield per

acre averaged 234 hundredweight, up from 230 hundredweight in 1971.

Idaho led the states by producing 78,795,000 hundredweight of potatoes. It was followed by Maine, which produced 33,280,000 hundredweight, and by Washington, which produced 29,160,000 hundredweight. Other leading potato producing states were California, North Dakota, Oregon, Minnesota, New York, Wisconsin, and Colorado. Idaho accounted for 27% of the potato crop. The yield per acre ranged from 65 hundredweight in Arkansas to 405 hundredweight in Washington.

Production declined in all seasonal groups— winter, early spring, late spring, early summer, late summer, and fall. Fall potato production totaled 294,498,000 hundredweight, a drop of 8% from 1971. The fall crop was harvested from 974,400 acres, down from 1,075,800 acres in 1971. The yield per acre was 241 hundredweight, up from 236 hundredweight in 1971.

Fall production accounted for 79.6% of the crop; winter production, 8%; early spring, 1.2%; late spring, 6%; early summer, 3.8%; and late summer, 8.5%. Yields per acre were: winter, 151 hundredweight; early spring, 138 hundredweight; late spring, 253 hundredweight; early summer, 157 hundredweight; and late summer, 244 hundredweight.

Sweet Potatoes. Sweet potato production totaled 12,605,000 hundredweight in 1972, up 8% from the 11,718,000 hundredweight produced in 1971. The crop was, however, 6% smaller than the 1970 crop. The crop was harvested from 116,000 acres. This was 2,400 acres more than in 1971, but 11,800 acres fewer than in 1970. The yield per acre averaged 109 hundredweight, up from 103 hundredweight in 1971.

North Carolina led the states by producing 3,840,000 hundredweight. It was followed by Louisiana, Virginia, Texas, California, and Mississippi. Yields ranged from 65 hundredweight per acre in Texas to 160 hundredweight in North Carolina.

NICHOLAS KOMINUS
Kominus Agri-Info Associates

AIR FORCE. See DEFENSE FORCES.

SIGN PROCLAIMING the results of the ban on DDT appears on a roadside stand in New Jersey. The development of effective substitutes for DDT has been slow.

JOHN PALUSZEK & ASSOCIATES

U. S. PRODUCTION OF VEGETABLES AND MELONS FOR THE FRESH MARKET
(Hundredweight)

	1970	1971	1972
Vegetables			
Artichokes	671,000	792,000	611,000
Asparagus	2,755,000	2,841,000	2,926,000
Beans, snap	3,109,000	3,120,000	3,041,000
Broccoli	3,104,000	3,157,000	3,674,000
Brussels sprouts	587,000	655,000	637,000
Cabbage	23,735,000	23,749,000	23,263,000
Carrots	18,190,000	19,146,000	18,056,000
Cauliflower	2,276,000	2,548,000	2,947,000
Celery	15,332,000	16,046,000	15,266,000
Corn, sweet	13,102,000	12,286,000	12,179,000
Cucumbers	4,440,000	4,369,000	4,387,000
Eggplant	467,000	501,000	521,000
Escarole	1,101,000	1,145,000	1,110,000
Garlic	728,000	481,000	663,000
Lettuce	46,272,000	47,177,000	54,699,000
Onions	30,493,000	29,863,000	27,724,000
Peppers, green	3,872,000	4,118,000	4,380,000
Spinach	589,000	674,000	643,000
Tomatoes	18,179,000	17,957,000	18,549,000
Total	189,002,000	190,625,000	195,276,000
Melons			
Cantaloupes	13,282,000	12,456,000	11,999,000
Honeydew melons	1,931,000	2,039,000	1,916,000
Watermelons	27,373,000	27,493,000	26,224,000
Total	42,586,000	41,988,000	40,139,000

Source: Crop Reporting Board, U. S. Department of Agriculture.

U. S. PRODUCTION OF VEGETABLES FOR PROCESSING
(Tons)

	1970	1971	1972
Asparagus	90,550	98,600	...
Beans, green, lima	78,750	80,650	86,150
Beans, snap	570,150	593,900	589,450
Beets	205,650	189,750	188,750
Cabbage, for kraut	266,100	234,950	
Corn, sweet	1,879,050	2,047,250	2,163,600
Cucumbers, for pickles	588,800	563,100	571,140
Peas, green	476,250	520,350	509,500
Spinach	151,050	160,050	167,450
Tomatoes	5,058,950	5,513,900	5,859,150
Total	9,365,300	10,002,500	10,135,190

Source: Crop Reporting Board, U. S. Department of Agriculture.

U. S. PRODUCTION OF FROZEN VEGETABLES
(Pounds)

	1970	1971
Asparagus	25,925,000	29,959,000
Beans, green, regular cut	119,099,000	127,675,000
Beans, green, French cut	75,817,000	74,741,000
Beans, green, whole	4,287,000	9,185,000
Beans, green, Italian	6,983,000	10,015,000
Beans, wax	6,176,000	7,147,000
Beans, baby lima	73,012,000	73,898,000
Beans, emerald lima	3,538,000	...
Beans, fordhook lima	36,844,000	40,690,000
Broccoli	185,157,000	189,600,000
Brussels sprouts	42,663,000	49,195,000
Butter beans	...	...
Butter beans, speckled	14,674,000	11,741,000
Carrots, diced	105,267,000	79,225,000
Carrots, sliced and crinkle cut	47,058,000	44,756,000
Carrots, chips, chunks, and julienne	20,729,000	19,700,000
Cauliflower	59,782,000	67,659,000
Celery	7,210,000	5,335,000
Collards	19,818,000	24,571,000
Corn, cut	216,097,000	226,835,000
Corn-on-cob	80,889,000	106,893,000
Kale	6,488,000	6,611,000
Mustard greens	15,597,000	13,011,000
Okra	44,168,000	32,234,000
Onions	52,205,000	75,882,000
Peas, black-eyed	30,084,000	33,027,000
Peas, green	344,520,000	348,418,000
Potatoes	2,404,389,000	2,565,118,000
Pumpkin and cooked squash	27,241,000	28,470,000
Rhubarb	7,950,000	11,033,000
Spinach	145,694,000	156,991,000
Squash, summer	18,953,000	26,882,000
Sweet potatoes and yams	10,913,000	7,391,000
Turnip greens	18,943,000	20,223,000
Turnips, turnip greens with turnips	23,415,000	26,940,000
Miscellaneous vegetables	15,146,000	23,310,000
Total	4,316,731,000	4,574,361,000

Source: American Frozen Food Institute.

The Dallas–Fort Worth Regional Airport, designed to allow for expansion as needs require and funds are available, is scheduled to open in 1973.

air transportation

The volume of traffic on the world's commercial airways reached record levels in 1972 after a three-year slump that had been caused largely by a troubled economy in the United States and other countries. While most other consumer commodities were continuing to rise in price, the cost of air travel remained relatively stable—and on some routes, declined—because of intense global competition among airlines for the traveler's business. Many airlines complained that the low fares were making it impossible for them to earn a profit, and there was wide confusion—and, in some cases, violation of the laws—as airline leaders sought to fill their jets and at the same time stay out of the red. Nevertheless, the prospect was for even better bargains in the future because in 1972 many governments began to loosen their regulations to permit more travelers to fly on low-cost charter flights.

Traffic. For the first time since 1968, U. S. domestic airlines experienced strong growth in passenger traffic. Preliminary estimates indicated that in 1972 they logged a total of 107.4 billion revenue passenger miles (one revenue passenger mile is one passenger flying one mile), 10% more than in 1971.

The average "load factor"—the percentage of seats occupied by paying passengers—increased on domestic flights from 60% in 1971 to 62% in 1972. On many international routes, traffic growth was even greater, increasing from 12% to 25%.

Fares. U. S. domestic air fares increased 2.7% in September 1972. The Civil Aeronautics Board (CAB) granted the raise in response to airline claims that it was needed to improve profits. At the same time, several airlines reduced fares on some routes in order to stimulate business and compete with the low-fare flights to Europe. For example, American, United, and Trans World Airlines introduced a special discount for the slow autumn months that included a $179 transcontinental round-trip, one of the lowest per-mile air fares in history.

Mergers. Two airline mergers were consummated in 1972 and a third was rejected by the CAB. Mohawk Airlines, which had been financially pressed, was absorbed into the healthier Allegheny Airlines, another short-haul regional carrier, to form the sixth-largest domestic carrier in the United States. In another marriage of weak and strong, Delta absorbed the troubled Northeast Airlines. This gave Delta, which is predominantly a southern carrier, access to New England and a chance to compete in the potentially lucrative New York–Miami route.

In disapproving the proposed merger of American and Western Airlines, the CAB said it would have offset competitive balances in the airline industry and would have given the merged airline an unacceptable competitive advantage.

Environmental Concerns. Opposition from environmental and community groups prevented the carrying out of airport construction projects in New

opposed such a move, arguing that it would cost more than $1 billion without producing a significant noise reduction. There were increasing demands from environmentalists to transfer governmental jurisdiction over airport noise from the FAA to the Environmental Protection Agency. FAA officials held that the best hope for reducing aircraft noise problems was the development of a new "quiet engine," and it predicted that government research would produce one within two to three years.

Other Problems. The resurgence of air travel in 1972 brought back some of the in-the-air and airport terminal congestion that had caused massive flight delays in 1968–69. FAA leaders predicted that by 1974 they would complete the installation of a computerized nationwide air traffic control system that would make it possible for the United States to absorb expected gains in air traffic.

More than two dozen cities in the United States imposed passenger departure "head taxes" (usually $1) following a Supreme Court ruling in the spring that such taxes were legal. Congress, after receiving vigorous complaints, voted to ban such taxes, but President Nixon vetoed the legislation.

Airline technical specialists were hounded by continuing mechanical problems with the Pratt & Whitney engines that power the 747 jetliner—the 44,000-pound thrust JT9D engines. Although the engines posed no serious safety hazard, airlines said that mechanical breakdowns of various elements in the engines had caused a large number of expensive special engine changes and repairs, which indirectly resulted in flight delays for many passengers.

Hijacking and other acts of air piracy posed major problems for world governments and airlines in 1972. (For a detailed report on the problem, see the special feature beginning on page 46.)

New Jetliner. Lockheed's L-1011 Tristar, the third member of the aviation world's new class of wide-body jets—the first two being the Boeing 747 and the McDonnell-Douglas DC 10—entered airline service in 1972. The 250-seat jet experienced initial problems with mechanical reliability that caused some flight delays, but after several months of operation airline leaders said they expected the problems to be worked out.

Supersonic Travel. Heralding the age of supersonic commercial travel, British Overseas Airways Corporation (BOAC) and Air France became the first airlines to place firm orders for the 1,400-mile-per-hour (2,250-km/hr) Concorde jetliner being developed jointly by Britain and France. The People's Republic of China and Iran also ordered the plane, but U. S. airlines—doubting that operating costs would enable them to fly the craft at a profit—withheld orders. Meanwhile, the Soviet Union made major technical modifications in its somewhat similar SST, the Tu-144, following flight tests, and predicted it would be carrying passengers sometime in late 1974—about the same time the Concorde is scheduled to haul its first paying passengers.

Future Prospects. All forecasts in 1972 were for a continuation of the increase in air travel. The FAA estimated that passenger enplanements in the United States would increase from 182.9 million in 1972 to 200 million in 1973, to 372 million by 1980, and to 524 million by 1984. It predicted that the number of private planes in use would increase from 133,000 in 1972 to 200,000 by 1980.

ROBERT H. LINDSEY
Aviation Reporter, "The New York Times"

CONCORDE, the Anglo-French supersonic jet passenger plane, arrives back in London after a world tour.

York, Los Angeles, Boston, Atlanta, Minneapolis, and other cities. Thus 1972 was the fourth consecutive year in which no major new U. S. airport construction was begun. The Federal Aviation Administration (FAA) warned that a continued suspension of airport construction would result in serious air traffic congestion in future years.

Environmentalists also accelerated their demands for night curfews at existing airports to reduce disruption of the sleep of nearby residents. Limited curfews were imposed in New York, Los Angeles, and Washington. One step that could ease the opposition, according to airport officials and anti-jetport forces, would be the installation of sound-absorbing muffling material around jet engines. But the airline industry, with strong support from the FAA,

YAK-40's, first Soviet passenger planes built for export, are ready for delivery to Afghanistan and Yugoslavia.

Non-Skeds Make New Inroads in Air Travel

Through the 1950's airlines served a clientele that was predominantly business-oriented. In 1958, the advent of the jet airliner, whose efficiency brought down the cost of air travel and whose speed made any place on earth only a few hours away, resulted in massive vacation travel by air. In 1972, with the public demanding even more low-cost leisure travel, there were signs of historic changes in the nature of air transportation from a system based on scheduled operations to one with a large proportion of non-scheduled charter flights.

Background. From its earliest days, commercial air travel was dominated by airplanes that operated, as the railroads had before them—according to a fixed timetable. This regularity was of great convenience to the traveler, but the costs of providing regular flights, whether all seats were sold or not, resulted in higher fares. In the early 1960's a second group of airlines, which chartered entire jets to groups, began to develop. Its growth was stimulated by the escalation of the war in Southeast Asia, since lucrative military airlift contracts permitted such secondary airlines to buy jets.

Because charter flights are not restricted by the low average load factors of scheduled flights, fares were about half as much. Consequently, by 1972 more than 70% of the flights on several routes between northern and southern Europe and more than 30% of those over the North Atlantic were charter flights.

Illegal By-products. In the United States and most European countries, only members of clubs, unions, professional or student groups, or comparable so-called "affinity groups" could legally take advantage of the charter flight bargains. However, the low prices of charter flights between the United States and Europe spawned a large, lucrative, underground travel industry in which travel agents chartered planes, concocted fictitious clubs, and then sold low-priced tickets to the public.

After three years of largely ineffective steps to deal with the practice, the Civil Aeronautics Board (CAB) in 1972 began requiring preflight screening of the passenger lists of some airlines. The move, coupled with a similar action in Britain, virtually eliminated the illegal flights, but the result was the stranding abroad of many travelers during the summer peak season. As many as 20,000 persons found that their return tickets were worthless because their illegal flights had been canceled during the crackdown. Most paid an extra fare and went home on regular flights.

The CAB launched a major investigation of another illegal by-product of the airlines' excess seating capacity over the North Atlantic. The agency claimed that several major scheduled airlines systematically sold tickets to certain travel agencies at less than the legal rates, apparently feeling that any income was better than none. CAB officials threatened stern action against future violators.

Change in Rules. In the face of increasing illegal practices and growing political and consumer pressures, the CAB promulgated rules in 1972 abolishing the affinity requirements for group fares. Henceforth, the board said, anybody—not just organization members—would be eligible for charter flight bargains, provided they meet certain restrictions, principally requiring passengers to sign up for the flight at least 90 days before departure and pay a 25% nonrefundable deposit. The British government promulgated a similar plan.

Although the U. S. scheduled airlines challenged the CAB's action as an unlawful effort to divert their passengers to charter airlines, it appeared that air transportation was on the threshold of a new revolution in lower-cost air travel. Some travel industry leaders forecast flights between the eastern United States and Europe for as little as $200 in the summer and $150 in the winter.

R.H.L.

ALABAMA

The assassination attempt against Gov. George C. Wallace was undoubtedly the event of greatest interest to Alabamians in 1972. In state politics, the Republican presidential candidate, President Richard Nixon, received 73% of Alabama's popular vote. At the same time, Democratic U. S. Sen. John J. Sparkman won reelection decisively over his Republican challenger, former U. S. Postmaster General Winton M. Blount.

Assault on Governor Wallace. Engaging in presidential politics again in 1972, Governor Wallace chose to launch a campaign for the Democratic nomination rather than follow the third-party route he had taken in 1968. During the spring, Governor Wallace entered preferential primaries in a number of states and showed surprising strength at the polls. But on May 15, while campaigning in Maryland, he suffered multiple gunshot wounds in an assassination attempt made as he mingled with the crowd following a speech at a shopping center in Laurel. He remained for some time in critical condition in a Silver Spring, Md., hospital, paralyzed in the lower part of his body by a bullet that had damaged his spine. A team of surgeons removed the bullet from Wallace's spinal column on June 18, but the paralysis continued.

On June 5, Lt. Gov. Jere Beasley became the acting governor under a provision of Alabama's constitution requiring that the lieutenant governor assume the duties of the office whenever the governor is out of the state for more than 20 days. His brief administration was of the caretaker variety, and Governor Wallace resumed office when he returned to Alabama on July 7 en route to the Democratic National Convention in Miami Beach, Fla. At the convention, his name was placed in nomination, he received approximately 380 delegate votes, and he was given the opportunity to address the convention in support of his views on the platform. After the convention, Governor Wallace underwent an extensive program of therapy in Alabama. By the end of the summer he was able to return to his office on a somewhat regular basis, although confined to a wheelchair. See also BIOGRAPHY—*Wallace.*

Elections. Since elections for state legislators and most executive officers are not scheduled until 1974, politics in Alabama in 1972 centered principally on presidential, congressional, and municipal contests. The most notable was the contest for the U. S. Senate seat held by the veteran John J. Sparkman, who won the Democratic primary in May. To oppose him, the Republican party—which held a primary election to nominate candidates instead of following that party's usual practice of utilizing a convention—chose former U. S. Postmaster General Winton M. Blount.

In the municipal elections, held in August and September, Negroes increased their representation on municipal governing bodies. Included among the offices won by black candidates were mayorships in Prichard (a suburb of Mobile) and Tuskegee.

In the November general election, Senator Sparkman was returned to the U. S. Senate, with 62% of the popular vote. Alabama's seven seats in the U. S. House of Representatives also were won by incumbents—four Democrats and three Republicans.

Court Decisions. At the end of 1971, decisions were still pending in several important cases in the federal courts. In one such suit, a temporary injunction against initiation of the Tennessee-Tombigbee Waterway was dismissed in August, clearing the way for the beginning of construction on the project.

Another decision, in April, ordered massive improvement in the state's mental health programs and facilities. Mental health remained a problem area, however. The department was beset with dissension, which culminated in a series of resignations and dismissals of highly placed executives, including the state commissioner of mental health. Sources of funding to implement the necessary improvements remained uncertain. But the governor indicated that surpluses remaining in the state treasury at the end of the fiscal year would help solve a number of problems not only in the mental health field but in education and other areas as well.

A decision, rendered in January, ordered a sweeping reapportionment of the state legislature. The court's plan reduced the membership of the House from 106 to 105. The number of senators (35) remained the same. Both senators and representatives would be elected from single-member districts. House districts were formed from census tracts, disregarding existing county boundaries, and were grouped into units of three to form Senate districts. The plan withstood review by the U. S. Supreme Court and will become effective in 1974 unless the legislature enacts an acceptable reapportionment in the meantime.

JAMES D. THOMAS
The University of Alabama

ALABAMA • Information Highlights

Area: 51,609 square miles (133,667 sq km).

Population (1970 census): 3,444,165. *Density:* 68 per sq mi.

Chief Cities (1970 census): Montgomery, the capital, 133,386; Birmingham, 300,910; Mobile, 190,026.

Government (1972): *Chief Officers*—governor, George C. Wallace (Democrat); lt. gov., Jere Beasley (D); secy. of state, Mrs. Mable Amos (D); atty. gen., William Baxley (D); treas., Mrs. Agnes Baggett (D); supt. of education, LeRoy Brown; chief justice, Howell T. Heflin. *Legislature*—Senate, 35 members (35 Democrats, 0 Republicans); House of Representatives, 106 members (104 D, 2 R).

Education (1971–72): *Enrollment*—public elementary schools, 427,696 pupils, 16,087 teachers; public secondary, 378,619 pupils, 17,085 teachers; nonpublic (1970–71), 54,776 pupils, 1,160 teachers; college and university, 105,000 students. *Public school expenditures,* $410,521,000 ($543 per pupil). *Average teacher's salary,* $7,887.

State Finances (fiscal year 1970): *Revenues,* $1,351,141,000 (4% general sales tax and gross receipts taxes, $212,-383,000; motor fuel tax, $116,760,000; federal funds, $409,-266,000). *Expenditures,* $1,369,773,000 (education, $582,-796,000; health, welfare, and safety, $230,680,000; highways, $291,383,000). *State debt,* $742,871,000.

Personal Income (1971): $10,610,000,000; *per capita,* $3,050.

Public Assistance (1971): $228,855,000. *Average monthly payments* (Dec. 1971)—old-age assistance, $67.42; aid to families with dependent children, $58.94.

Labor Force: *Nonagricultural wage and salary earners* (July 1972), 1,036,400. *Average annual employment* (1971)—manufacturing, 318,000; trade, 194,000; government, 214,-000; services, 135,000. *Insured unemployed* (Aug. 1972)—16,700 (2.3%).

Manufacturing (1970): *Value added by manufacture,* $4,370,-100,000. Primary metal industries, $729,200,000; chemicals and allied products, $489,400,000; paper and allied products, $422,500,000; food and kindred products, $366,800,-000; textile mill products, $354,900,000; apparel and other textile products, $329,500,000.

Agriculture (1970): *Cash farm income,* $832,582,000 (livestock, $534,904,000; crops, $218,215,000; government payments, $79,463,000). *Chief crops* (in order of value, 1971)—Cotton lint, peanuts (ranks 2d among the states), soybeans, corn.

Mining (1971): *Production value,* $291,491,000 (ranks 21st among the states). *Chief minerals*—Coal, $146,180,000; cement, $50,938,000; stone, $35,308,000; petroleum, $23,-496,000.

Fisheries (1971): *Commercial catch,* 36,727,000 pounds ($14,-141,000). *Leading species by value:* Shrimp, $11,449,000; croaker, $1,036,000; red snapper, $341,000.

Transportation: *Roads* (1971) 78,872 miles (126,929 km); *motor vehicles* (1971), 1,965,932; *railroads* (1972), 4,566 miles (7,348 km); *public airports* (1972), 90.

Communications: *Telephones* (1972), 1,650,000; *television stations* (1971), 16; *radio stations* (1971), 189; *newspapers* (1972), 23 (daily circulation, 726,000).

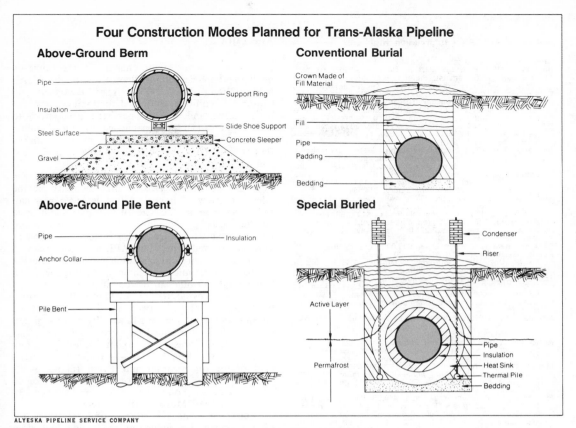

Four Construction Modes Planned for Trans-Alaska Pipeline

Above-Ground Berm

Pipe
Support Ring
Insulation
Slide Shoe Support
Steel Surface
Concrete Sleeper
Gravel

Conventional Burial

Crown Made of Fill Material
Fill
Pipe
Padding
Bedding

Above-Ground Pile Bent

Pipe
Insulation
Anchor Collar
Pile Bent

Special Buried

Condenser
Riser
Active Layer
Permafrost
Pipe
Insulation
Heat Sink
Thermal Pile
Bedding

ALYESKA PIPELINE SERVICE COMPANY

PIPELINE construction plans are geared to preventing environmental damage, but critics have forced further delay of project in the courts.

ALASKA

During 1972 Alaskans worked out terms of the Alaska Native Claims Settlement Act, selected state lands from the federal domain, and continued to enjoy a boom in construction.

Native Lands. The Native Claims Settlement Act of 1971 granted 40 million acres of land and $962.5 million to Eskimos, Aleuts, and Indians in Alaska. In 1972, the state legislature restructured Alaskan law to meet the needs of new regional native corporations mandated by the act and advanced them loans to facilitate their organization. By June, 45,000 of an estimated 75,000 eligible natives had enrolled to qualify for benefits under the act. The federal government set aside 99 million acres, from which the natives will select 40 million acres for villages and regional corporations.

State Land Selection. In January 1972, Gov. William Egan announced the state's selection of 77 million acres of federally controlled land, basing its claim on the Alaska Statehood Act. In March the U. S. Department of the Interior allotted the state 35 million acres of federal land, which was 42 million acres less than Alaska had selected in January. In September the state and the Interior Department made an out-of-court settlement in which the state dropped claims to about 30 million acres it had selected but won several valuable concessions in return.

Oil Pipeline. Early in 1972, the Interior Department released a final report on the environmental impact of the proposed trans-Alaska oil pipeline from Prudhoe Bay to the Pacific Coast port of Valdez. In May, Secretary of the Interior Rogers C. B. Morton announced his intention to issue a right-of-way permit for construction of the pipeline. In August, Federal District Judge George Hart, Jr,, decided that the Interior Department had met all legal requirements and dissolved a 1970 injunction against the project. Environmental groups appealed the decision, and it was predicted that 18 months might elapse before a final decision could be obtained from the U. S. Supreme Court.

Legislation. The 1972 legislative session was the longest on record, 161 hectic days in which controversy seethed over oil industry regulation, social legislation, and budgetary matters. Over the objections of oil lobbyists, the lawmakers enacted a package of oil legislation that included a cent-per-barrel oil severance tax, a pipeline right-of-way leasing act, an act regulating the pipeline, an oil spill liability act, a ban on oil leases in the Bristol Bay salmon fisheries area, and a local hire bill for the oil industry.

Social measures included a Medicaid Act to extend federally supported medical services through state channels to needy persons, creation of an Alaska Youth Conservation Corps, and creation of a new Department of Community and Regional Affairs. The legislature also initiated a policy of aiding private education by providing tuition aid for students attending Alaska Methodist University in Anchorage and by supplying busing aid to students attending private schools.

A state budget including $341 million in state funds and $198 million in federal grants was approved in 1972. The state's portion of the funds was slashed to $330.4 million when the governor vetoed certain funds.

——————— ALASKA • Information Highlights ———————

Area: 586,412 square miles (1,518,807 sq km).
Population (1970 census): 302,173. *Density,* 0.6 per sq mi.
Chief Cities (1970 census): Juneau, the capital, 6,050; Anchorage, 48,081; Fairbanks, 14,771; Ketchikan, 6,994.
Government (1972): *Chief Officers*—governor, William A. Egan (D); lt. gov., H. A. Boucher (D); atty. gen., John E. Havelock (D); treas., Eric E. Wohlforth; commissioner, dept. of education, Cliff Hartman; chief justice, George F. Boney (d. Aug. 30, 1972). *Legislature*—Senate, 20 members (10 Democrats, 10 Republicans); House of Representatives, 40 members (31 D, 9 R).
Education (1971–72): *Enrollment*—public elementary schools, 61,411 pupils, 2,591 teachers; public secondary, 22,387 pupils, 1,513 teachers; nonpublic schools (1970–71), 1,068 pupils, 130 teachers; college and university, 10,000 students. *Public school expenditures,* $113,632,000 ($1,432 per pupil). *Average teacher's salary,* $14,584.
State Finances (fiscal year 1970): *Revenues,* $1,211,648,000 (total sales and gross receipts taxes, $20,408,000; motor fuel tax, $10,372,000; federal funds, $103,453,000). *Expenditures,* $354,128,000 (education, $120,066,000; health, welfare, and safety, $23,279,000; highways, $98,255,000). *State debt,* $222,255,000 (June 30, 1970).
Personal Income (1971): $1,486,000,000; per capita, $4,749.
Public Assistance (1971): $18,729,000. *Average monthly payments* (Dec. 1971)—old-age assistance, $129.11; aid to families with dependent children, $215.83.
Labor Force: *Nonagricultural wage and salary earners* (July 1972), 111,600. *Average annual employment* (1971)—manufacturing, 8,000; trade, 16,000; government, 37,000; services, 10,000. *Insured unemployed* (Aug. 1972)—3,300 (5.7%).
Manufacturing (1970): *Value added by manufacture,* $174,000,-000. Food and kindred products, $65,500,000; lumber and wood products, $26,600,000.
Agriculture (1970): *Cash farm income,* $4,315,000 (livestock, $3,156,000; crops, $1,075,000; government payments, $84,-000). *Chief crops*—Hay, silage, potatoes, barley.
Mining (1971): *Production value,* $332,848,000 (ranks 20th among the states). *Chief minerals*—Petroleum, $257,562,-000; sand and gravel, $32,806,000; natural gas, $28,945,-000; coal, $5,710,000.
Fisheries (1971): *Commercial catch,* 449,089,000 pounds ($84,-504,000). *Leading species by value* (1971), salmon, $47,-006,150; halibut, $5,503,000; shrimp, $3,762,600.
Transportation: *Roads* (1971), 7,272 miles (11,703 km); *motor vehicles* (1971), 138,759; *railroads* (1971), 503 miles (809 km); *public airports* (1971), 537.
Communications: *Telephones* (1970), 85,000; *television stations* (1971), 7; *radio stations* (1971), 19; *newspapers* (1972), 6 (daily circulation, 74,000).

Elections. Alaska's three electoral votes went to President Nixon with 58% of the total vote, while George McGovern won 35% and John Schmitz 7%. U. S. Sen. Ted Stevens (R.) overwhelmed his Democratic opponent, Gene Guess, by winning reelection with 77% of the two-party vote.

The Democrats rallied to reelect their missing U. S. Representative Nick Begich, who got 56% of the vote over the opposition of Republican State Sen. Don Young. Begich disappeared on October 16 on a campaign flight from Anchorage to Juneau. In late December, a special election to fill his seat was scheduled for March 6, 1973.

The newly elected state legislature was closely divided, with the Republicans winning control of the Senate by 11 seats to 9, and the Democrats winning 20 House seats to 19 for the Republicans and 1 independent.

Voters also approved $124.5 million in state bonds for schools, airports, highways, flood control, and sewer and water facilities. They defeated a proposal for a constitutional convention.

Economy. New construction methods and equipment and increasing civilian building activity have extended the state's construction season to nearly 12 months per year. Construction awards were up almost 50% over their level in 1971, which had also been a good year.

The 1972 salmon catch was nearly the poorest since 1906, amounting to fewer than two million cases. Shellfish also were down, but the crab catch was far above 1971.

RONALD E. CHINN
University of Alaska

ALBANIA

There were no major changes in the domestic or foreign policies of the People's Republic of Albania (PRA) during 1972. The Ideological and Cultural Revolution continued to dominate the domestic scene, and the PRA persisted in its efforts to end its almost total dependence on the People's Republic of China by improving its ties with its Balkan neighbors, the countries of Western Europe, and the Afro-Asian nations.

The Ideological and Cultural Revolution. On February 26, Enver Hoxha, first secretary of the Albanian Party of Labor (APL), issued a new call for a decrease in the size of the party and state bureaucracies, greater involvement of party members in productive work, and a further reduction of bureaucratic red tape. The APL also continued to stress the women's emancipation movement and the campaign to eradicate remaining "bourgeois" and "revisionist" attitudes in the country.

Political Developments. In March, Prime Minister Mehmet Shehu underwent medical treatment for an undisclosed ailment in France. By early summer, however, he had resumed his normal schedule.

The 7th Congress of Albanian Trade Unions met on May 8–11. Rita Marko was reelected as president of the organization and Tonin Jakova as its secretary general. The 6th Congress of the Union of Albanian Labor Youth, which met on October 23–26, elected Rudi Monari First Secretary.

Economy. The official economic statistics for 1971 revealed that industrial production had risen by 11.5% during the year. This figure was substantially above the 7.5% rise foreseen by the plan. The agricultural sector, however, failed by a large margin to fulfill the planned 25.8% increase in output. At the second plenum of the APL Central Committee in June 1972, it was revealed that the agricultural failure was attributable to bad weather, poor management, low peasant morale, and the unsatisfactory use of modern farming techniques.

According to the economic plan for 1972, industrial production was to be 12.5% greater and agricultural production 9.2% higher than in 1971.

Foreign Relations. During 1972, Albania and Communist China differed over several foreign policy issues. The Albanians were unhappy about U. S. President Nixon's visit to mainland China in

——————— ALBANIA • Information Highlights ———————

Official Name: People's Republic of Albania.
Area: 11,100 square miles (28,748 sq km).
Population (1972 est.): 2,300,000. *Density,* 194 per square mile (75 per sq km). *Annual rate of increase,* 2.8%.
Chief Cities (1967 est.): Tiranë, the capital, 169,300; Durrës, 53,200; Vlorë, 50,400; Shkodër 49,800.
Government: *Head of state,* Haxhi Lleshi, president of the presidium (took office in 1953). *Head of government,* Maj. Gen. Mehmet Shehu, premier (took office in 1954). *First secretary of the Albanian Party of Labor,* Gen. Enver Hoxha (took office in 1946). *Legislature* (unicameral)—People's Assembly, 240 members (all members of the Albanian Party of Labor).
Language: Albanian (official).
Education: *School enrollment* (1969)—primary, 506,683; secondary, 58,900; university/higher, 23,180.
Monetary Unit: lek (4.61 leks equal U. S.$1, May 1972).
Industrial Production Index (1967), 145 (1963=100).
Manufacturing (major products): Processed foods, textiles, cement, tobacco products.
Major Agricultural Products: Corn, sugar beets, wheat, cottonseed, potatoes, tobacco.
Major Minerals: Petroleum, chromium ore, copper ore.
Foreign Trade (1964): *Exports,* $60,000,000. *Imports,* $98,-000,000. *Chief trading partners* (1964)—People's Rep. of China (took 40% of exports, supplied 63% of imports); Czechoslovakia (19%—10%).
Communications: *Television stations* (1971), 1; *newspapers* (1970), 3

UPI

In Tirana, Albania, members of the Women's Militia hold automatic weapons as they march in a May Day parade.

February. They were also distressed by China's diminishing interest in the anti-Soviet "Marxist-Leninist" movement as well as by Peking's support of moves for greater political and economic cooperation among the countries of Western Europe. Despite these differences, however, Sino-Albanian relations remained cordial. In April, China granted Albania a long-term, interest-free loan for the purchase of agricultural equipment.

Albania's hostility toward the Soviet Union showed no signs of abating. The Albanians denounced President Nixon's visit to Moscow in May as "further proof of the deepening conspiracy between the forces of U. S. imperialism and Soviet social-imperialism" to divide the world between them into two spheres of influence.

Albania established diplomatic relations with Luxembourg and Nepal and continued its efforts to expand commercial and cultural ties with Western Europe and the Afro-Asian countries. Although both the United States and Britain expressed interest in improving relations with them, the Albanians did not respond positively to these overtures.

NICHOLAS C. PANO
Western Illinois University

ALBERTA

In 1972 the people of Alberta were particularly interested in the workings of their new government and in the consequences of the spring rains.

Government. In its first full year, the new Progressive Conservative government instituted a variety of social programs designed to better the diagnosis and treatment of mental health, to improve the economic and living conditions of natives, and to preserve the ethnic and cultural heritage of the province. At the same time, new and heavier taxing arrangements were imposed on the oil and gas industry, and educational grants were tightened.

Education. All three provincial universities were experiencing decreasing enrollments in 1972, although registrations were increasing at other institutions of higher learning. The lower birthrates of the past decade began to affect public school systems, resulting in empty classrooms and serious financial problems as government grants declined.

The Rains. Cool, wet weather in the spring and

early summer minimized the outbreaks of forest fires in northern Alberta, but resulted in crop damage and the flooding of north-flowing rivers, which in turn virtually destroyed 37 miles (60 km) of the government-owned Alberta Resources Railway. However, the same conditions did much to restore the wetlands of the Peace-Athabasca delta, which had previously been affected by the Bennet Dam in British Columbia.

Agriculture and Industry. Farm production remained high in 1972 despite the crop damage, but unfavorable weather in the fall hampered harvesting

────── **ALBERTA • Information Highlights** ──────

Area: 255,285 square miles (661,189 sq km).
Population: 1,627,874 (1971 census).
Chief Cities (1971 census): Edmonton, the capital (438,152); Calgary (403,319); Lethbridge (41,217); Red Deer (27,674); Medicine Hat (26,518).
Government: *Chief Officers* (1972)—lt. gov., J. W. Grant McEwan; premier, Peter Loughead (Progressive Conservative); atty. gen. and prov. secy., C. Mervin Leitch (P. C.); prov. treas., Gordon T. W. Miniely (P. C.); min. of educ., Louis D. Hyndeman (P. C.); chief justice, Sidney Bruce Smith. *Legislature*—Legislative Assembly; 75 members (49 Progressive Conservative; 25 Social Credit; 1 New Democratic Party).
Education: *School enrollment* (1968–69)—public elementary and secondary, 385,972 pupils (17,492 teachers); private schools, 5,614 pupils (313 teachers); Indian (federal) schools, 3,668 pupils (179 teachers); college and university, 24,922 students. *Public school expenditures* (1971 est.)—$202,270,000; average teacher's salary (1968–69), $7,600.
Public Finance (fiscal year 1972 est.): *Revenues,* $1,174,600,-000 (sales tax, $97,300,000; income tax, $243,800,000; federal funds, $254,700,000). *Expenditures,* $1,297,800,000 (education, $408,300,000; health/social welfare, $446,200,-000; transport/communications, $105,700,000).
Personal Income (1969 est.): $4,550,000,000.
Social Welfare (fiscal 1972 est.): $90,500,000 (aged/blind, $4,100,000; dependents/unemployed, $62,600,000).
Manufacturing (1968): Value added by manufacture, $604,529,-000 (food and beverages, $155,712,000; fabricated metals, $55,670,000; primary metals, $41,025,000; transportation equipment, $16,258,000; nonelectrical machinery, $12,667,-000; electrical machinery, $10,105,000).
Agriculture (1971): *Cash farm income* (exclusive of government payments), $771,280,000 (livestock and products, $445,056,000; crops, $318,786,000). *Chief crops* (cash receipts)—wheat, $130,550,000 (ranks 2d among the provinces); barley, $77,152,000 (ranks 1st); rapeseed, $45,220,-000 (ranks 2d); flaxseed, $12,387,000.
Mining (1971 est.): *Production value,* $1,652,071,000. *Chief minerals*—crude petroleum, 377,368,000 bbls. (ranks 1st among the provinces); natural gas, 1,881,543,000,000 cubic feet (ranks 1st); sulphur, 2,963,000 tons (ranks 1st).
Transportation: *Roads* (1968), 97,151 miles (156,315 km); *motor vehicles* (1969), 735,729; *railroads* (1970 est.), 5,950 track miles (9,576 km); *licensed airports* (1971 est.) 56.
Communications: *Telephones* (1969), 696,098; *television stations* (1971), 38; *radio stations* (1971), 22; *daily newspapers* (1971) 7.
(All monetary figures given in Canadian dollars.)

and reduced the quality of the grain. Farmers were also plagued with problems of transporting their products because of dockers' strikes and a shortage of freight cars.

At the end of 1972, Alberta's unemployment rate was only 3%, the lowest in Canada. After several successive record-breaking years, urban construction was slightly down because of the halt in educational building.

JOHN W. CHALMERS, *University of Alberta*

ALGERIA

Algeria celebrated the 10th anniversary of its independence from France in 1972. The militantly left-wing, Arab-nationalist regime of President Houari Boumedienne continued to be one of the most stable governments in Africa.

Foreign Affairs. Algeria's improved relations with bordering states remained cordial during the year. Outstanding among various moves toward regional cooperation was the settlement of a long-standing border dispute with Morocco.

The agreement was signed in June by President Boumedienne and King Hassan of Morocco at the meeting of African heads of state and government in Rabat, the Moroccan capital. The demarcation of the frontier was not disclosed, but the two leaders announced that the disputed area's most valuable resource—the Gara-Djebilet iron ore deposits—would be developed jointly.

Earlier, Boumedienne and President Habib Bourguiba of Tunisia exchanged good-will visits, and President Mokhtar Ould Daddah of Mauritania visited Algiers. Algeria and Mauritania restated their desire, shared by Morocco, for a coordinated effort to bring about the withdrawal of Spain from Spanish Sahara. In July the Algerian foreign minister went to Madrid to urge a settlement of Spanish, Moroccan, and Mauritanian claims to the sparsely populated but phosphate-rich territory.

In May, Boumedienne conferred in Algiers with Presidents Anwar el-Sadat of Egypt and Muammar al-Qaddafi of Libya. He renewed his pledge to throw Algeria's full weight into a new war with Israel, which all three leaders considered inevitable.

In August the Algerian government returned $1 million extorted from a U. S. airline by hijackers who landed in Algiers. As in the past, however, the hijackers themselves were not turned over to U. S. authorities.

Political and Social Reform. Elections were held in September for neighborhood committees in Algerian towns. The committees, an innovation of the reform movement in the ruling National Liberation Front, were not given coercive powers but could draw the attention of municipal and prefectural authorities to local problems. Similar committees were to be set up in rural areas.

A long-delayed program of land redistribution, enacted into law in November 1971, got under way in June 1972. Several hundred acres of communal and government-held land were parceled out to former sharecroppers.

Economy. Algerian oil production, which had declined drastically in 1971, reached a record high of more than a million barrels a day in 1972. Since oil is the country's chief export, the resumption of full-scale production was considered vital to the government's top-priority programs of industrial and educational development.

The rise in oil output followed the settlement in December 1971 of a dispute with France over nationalization of French oil and gas interests in the Sahara. The agreement, which included compensation for the nationalized properties, ended a French boycott of Algerian oil and opened the way for large export contracts signed with U. S. companies. An additional boost to the economy resulted from final U. S. approval in June 1972 of liquefied natural gas imports from Algeria by American utilities.

The emergence of the United States as a significant Algerian customer raised the possibility of improved political relations between Washington and Algiers. In March, President Boumedienne conferred with Assistant Secretary of State David D. Newsom on economic matters. This was reported to be the first time Boumedienne had received a high-ranking U. S. official since the rupture of diplomatic relations with the United States in 1967.

Education. After ten years of independence, Algerians were cautiously optimistic about their progress toward educational goals. One fourth of the state's running budget was being spent on education. Over 2 million children were in school, compared with 850,000 in 1960 (when a large proportion of the students were Europeans). University enrollment was 22,000, as against 1,000 just after independence, and the Universities of Oran and Constantine had been brought up to the level of the University of Algiers. Algerian students were showing an increased interest in science and technology.

Full school attendance was still years away, however, and the attainment of this goal was jeopardized by rapid population growth. In 1972 about 60% of all Algerians were under 21 years old. Despite the training of more teachers, the use of foreign teachers, and the construction of new school facilities, the educational system was hard put to absorb the ever-mounting number of applicants at all levels of instruction.

RICHARD N. MOREHOUSE

─────── **ALGERIA • Information Highlights** ───────

Official Name: Democratic and Popular Republic of Algeria.
Area: 919,593 square miles (2,381,741 sq km).
Population (1972 est.): 15,000,000. *Density,* 16 per square mile (6 per sq km). *Annual rate of increase,* 3.3%.
Chief Cities (1966 census): Algiers, the capital, 943,142; Oran, 328,257; Constantine, 253,649; Annaba, 168,790.
Government: *Head of state* and *Head of government,* Houari Boumedienne, president (took office June 1965).
Languages: Arabic (official), French.
Education: *Expenditure* (1968), 17.6% of total public expenditure. *School enrollment* (1968)—primary, 1,585,682; secondary, 177,382; technical/vocational, 40,684; university/higher, 10,681.
Gross National Product (1971 est.): $4,300,000,000.
Monetary Unit: Dinar (4.547 dinars equal U. S.$1, Sept. 1972).
National Income per Person (1968): $251.
Economic Indexes: *Industrial production* (mining; 1970), 125 (1963=100); *agricultural production* (1971), 97 (1952–56=100); *consumer price index* (1967), 104 (1963=100).
Manufacturing (major products): Liquefied natural gas, processed foods, wine, cement.
Major Agricultural Products: Wheat, citrus fruits, grapes for wine, olives, dates, fish.
Major Minerals: Petroleum, natural gas, phosphate rock, iron ore, lead ore.
Foreign Trade (1970): *Exports,* $1,009,000,000 (chief exports, 1969—crude petroleum; alcoholic beverages; liquefied natural gas; fruits and nuts). *Imports,* $1,257,000,000 (chief imports, 1969—food; nonelectrical machinery; iron and steel; transport equipment). *Chief trading partners* (1969) —France (took 54% of exports, supplied 44% of imports); West Germany (15%—9%); USSR (6%—4%); Italy (3%—8%).
Transportation: *Motor vehicles* (1970), 243,200 (automobiles, 137,200); *railroads* (1970), 2,417 miles (3,889 km); *major national airline,* Air Algérie.
Communications: *Telephones* (1971), 184,063; *television stations* (1971), 6; *newspapers* (1968), 4 (daily circulation, 185,000).

AMBASSADORS AND ENVOYS

An important development on the diplomatic front in 1972 was the announcement by Chancellor Willy Brandt that West Germany would deal directly with East Germany. Brandt thus authorized the worldwide acceptance of a divided Germany, consisting of two virtually sovereign German states.

Among other significant developments, a U. S. Embassy was established on May 18 at Dacca in the new state of Bangladesh (formerly East Pakistan).

On December 5, 1972, President Nixon named Donald Rumsfeld, director of the Cost of Living Council, to be the next U. S. representative to the North Atlantic Treaty Organization (NATO).

The following is a list of ambassadors and envoys from and to the United States (as of Sept. 1, 1972, unless otherwise indicated). A designates ambassador extraordinary and plenipotentiary; CA, chargé d'affaires.

UPI

NEW AMBASSADOR TO JAPAN, Robert S. Ingersoll was chief executive officer of the Borg-Warner Corp.

LIST OF AMBASSADORS AND ENVOYS

Country	From U.S.	To U.S.
Afghanistan	Robert G. Neumann (A)	Abdullah Malikyar (A)
Argentina	John Davis Lodge (A)	Carlos Manuel Muñiz (A)
Australia	Walter L. Rice (A)	Sir James Plimsoll (A)
Austria	John P. Humes (A)	Arno Halusa (A)
Bahrain	William A. Stolzfus, Jr. (A)	....
Bangladesh	Herman F. Eilts (A)	S. K. Karim (CA)
Barbados	Eileen R. Donovan (A)	Valerie Theodore McComie (A)
Belgium	Robert Strausz-Hupé (A)	Walter Loridan (A)
Bolivia	Ernest V. Siracusa (A)	Edmundo Valencia-Ibáñez (A)
Botswana	Charles J. Nelson (A)	Amos M. Dambe (A)
Brazil	William M. Rountree (A)	João Augusto de Araujo Castro (A)
Bulgaria	Horace G. Torbert, Jr. (A)	Assen Yankov (CA)
Burma	Edwin W. Martin (A)	U Lwin (A)
Burundi	Robert L. Yost (A)	Nsanze Terence (A)
Cambodia	Emory C. Swank (A)	Sonn Voeunsai (A)
Cameroon	C. Robert Moore (A)	François-Xavier Tchoungui (A)
Canada	Adolph W. Schmidt (A)	Marcel Cadieux (A)
Central Afr. Rep.	....	Christophe Maidou (A)
Ceylon	Christopher Van Hollen (A)	Neville Kanakaratne (A)
Chad	Edward W. Mulcahy[1] (A)	Lazare Massibe (A)
Chile	Nathaniel Davis (A)	Orlando Letelier (A)
China (Taiwan)	Walter P. McConaughy (A)	James C. H. Shen (A)
Colombia	Leonard J. Saccio (A)	Douglas Botero-Boshell (A)
Costa Rica	Viron P. Vaky (A)	Rafael Alberto Zuñiga (A)
Cyprus	David H. Popper (A)	Zenon Rossides (A)
Czechoslovakia	Albert W. Sherer, Jr. (A)	Dusan Spacil (A)
Dahomey	Robert Anderson (A)	Wilfrid De Souza (A)
Denmark	....	Eyvind Bartels (A)
Dominican Republic	Francis E. Meloy, Jr. (A)	S. Salvador Ortiz (A)
Ecuador	Findley Burns, Jr. (A)	Carlos M. Ortega (A)
El Salvador	Henry E. Catto, Jr. (A)	Col. Julio A. Rivera (A)
Equatorial Guinea	C. Robert Moore[1] (A)	....
Ethiopia	E. Ross Adair (A)	Kifle Wodajo (A)
Fiji	Kenneth Franzheim, 2d (A)	S. K. Sikivou (A)
Finland	Val Peterson (A)	Leo Tuominen (A)
France	John N. Irwin, 2d[1] (A)	Jacques Kosciusko-Morizet (A)
Gabon	John A. McKesson, 3d (A)	Gaston R. Bouckat-Bou-Nziengui (A)

Country	From U.S.	To U.S.
Gambia	G. Edward Clark (A)	....
Germany	Martin J. Hillenbrand (A)	Rolf Pauls (A)
Ghana	Fred L. Hadsel (A)	Harry R. Amonoo (A)
Great Britain	Walter H. Annenberg (A)	The Earl of Cromer (A)
Greece	Henry J. Tasca (A)	Basil George Vitsaxis (A)
Guatemala	William G. Bowdler (A)	Julio Asensio-Wunderlich (A)
Guinea	Terence A. Todman (A)	Sadan Moussa Touré (A)
Guyana	Spencer M. King (A)	Rahman B. Gajraj (A)
Haiti	Clinton E. Knox (A)	René Chalmers (A)
Honduras	Hewson A. Ryan (A)	Roberto Galvez Barnes (A)

AT UNITED NATIONS, U. S. Ambassador George Bush casts second U. S. veto in UN history, September 10.

UPI

ED STATES

LIST OF AMBASSADORS AND ENVOYS (continued)

Country	From U. S.	To U. S.
Hungary	Alfred Puhan (A)	Karoly Szabó (A)
Iceland	Frederick Irving (A)	Gudmundur I. Gudmundsson (A)
India	Daniel Patrick Moynahan[1] (A)	Lakshmi Kant Jha (A)
Indonesia	Francis J. Galbraith (A)	Sjarif Thajeb (A)
Iran	Richard M. Helms[1] (A)	Amir-Aslan Afshar (A)
Ireland	John D. J. Moore (A)	William Warnock (A)
Israel	Walworth Barbour (A)	Lt. Gen. Yitzhak Rabin (A)
Italy	John A. Volpe[1] (A)	Egidio Ortona (A)
Ivory Coast	John F. Root (A)	Timothée N'Guetta Ahoua (A)
Jamaica	Vincent W. de Roulet (A)	Douglas V. Fletcher (A)
Japan	Robert S. Ingersoll (A)	Nobuhiko Ushiba (A)
Jordan	Lewis D. Brown (A)	Zuhayr Muftri (A)
Kenya	Robinson McIlvaine (A)	Leonard Oliver Kibinge (A)
Korea	Philip C. Habib (A)	Dong Jo Kim (A)
Kuwait	William A. Stoltzfus, Jr. (A)	Salem S. al-Sabah (A)
Laos	G. McMurtrie Godley (A)	Prince Khammao (A)
Lebanon	William B. Buffum (A)	Najati Kabbani (A)
Lesotho	Charles J. Nelson (A)	Mothusi T. Mashologu (A)
Liberia	Melvin L. Manfull[2] (A)	S. Edward Peal (A)
Libya	Joseph Palmer 2d (A)	Abdalla Suwesi (A)
Luxembourg	....	Jean Wagner (A)
Malagasy Republic	Joseph A. Mendenhall (A)	Henri Raharijaona[2] (A)
Malawi	William C. Burdett (A)	Nyemba Wales Mbekeani (A)
Malaysia	Jack W. Lydman (A)	Tan Sri Yoke Lin Ong (A)
Maldives	Christopher Van Hollen[2] (A)	....
Mali	Robert O. Blake (A)	Seydou Traoré (A)
Malta	John I. Getz (A)	Joseph Attard-Kingswell (A)
Mauritania	Richard W. Murphy (A)	Moulaye El Hassen (A)
Mauritius	William D. Brewer (A)	Pierre Guy Girald Balancy (A)
Mexico	Robert H. McBride (A)	José Juan de Olloqui (A)
Morocco	Stuart W. Rockwell (A)	Badreddine Senoussi (A)
Nepal	Carol C. Laise (A)	Kul Shekhar Sharma (A)
Netherlands	J. William Middendorf 2d (A)	Baron Rijnhard B. Van Lynden (A)
New Zealand	Kenneth Franzheim 2d (A)	Lloyd White[2] (A)
Nicaragua	Turner B. Shelton (A)	Guillermo Sevilla-Sacasa (A)
Niger	Roswell D. McClelland (A)	Abdoulaye Diallo[2] (A)
Nigeria	John E. Reinhardt (A)	John M. Garba (A)
Norway	Philip K. Crowe (A)	Arne Gunneng (A)
Pakistan	....	Sultan M. Khan (A)
Panama	Frank T. Bow (A)	José Antonio de la Ossa (A)
Paraguay	George W. Landau (A)	Roque J. Avila (A)
Peru	Taylor G. Belcher (A)	Fernando Berckemeyer (A)
Philippines	Henry A. Byroade (A)	Eduardo Z. Romualdez (A)
Poland	Richard T. Davies[2] (A)	Witold Trampczynski (A)
Portugal	Ridgway B. Knight (A)	Joao Hall Themido (A)
Qatar	William A. Stoltzfus, Jr. (A)	Abdullah S. Al-Mania (A)
Rumania	Leonard C. Meeker (A)	Corneliu Bogdan (A)
Rwanda	Robert F. Corrigan (A)	Fidèle Nkundabagenzi (A)
Saudi Arabia	Nicholas G. Thacher (A)	Ibrahim al-Sowayel (A)
Senegal	G. Edward Clark (A)	André Coulbary (A)
Sierra Leone	Clinton L. Olson (A)	Philip Jonathan Gbagu Palmer (A)
Singapore	Edwin M. Cronk (A)	Ernest S. Monteiro (A)
Somali	Matthew J. Looram, Jr. (A)	Abdullahi Ahmed Addou (A)
South Africa	John G. Hurd (A)	Johan S. F. Botha (A)
Spain	Adm. Horacio Rivero (A)	Angel Sagaz (A)
Sudan	Cleo A. Noel, Jr.[2] (A)	....
Swaziland	Charles J. Nelson (A)	S. T. Msindazwe Sukati (A)
Sweden	....	Hubert de Besche (A)
Switzerland	Shelby C. Davis (A)	Felix Schnyder (A)
Tanzania	W. Beverly Carter, Jr. (A)	Paul L. Bomani[2] (A)
Thailand	Leonard Unger (A)	Anand Panyarachun[2] (A)
Togo	Dwight Dickinson (A)	Epiphane Ayi Mawussi (A)
Tonga	Kenneth Franzheim 2d[2] (A)	....
Trinidad and Tobago	Anthony D. Marshall (A)	Ellis Emmanuel I. Clarke (A)
Tunisia	Talcott W. Seelye (A)	Slaheddine El Goulli (A)
Turkey	William J. Handley (A)	Melih Esenbel (A)
Uganda	Thomas P. Melady (A)	Mustapha Ramathan (A)
USSR	Jacob D. Beam (A)	Anatoli F. Dobrynin (A)
Upper Volta	Donald B. Easum (A)	Telesphore Yaguibou (A)
Uruguay	Charles W. Adair, Jr. (A)	Hector Luisi (A)
Venezuela	Robert McClintock (A)	Andres Aguilar (A)
Vietnam	Ellsworth Bunker (A)	Tran Kim Phuong (A)
Western Samoa	Kenneth Franzheim 2d (A)	....
Yemen Arab Republic	William R. Crawford, Jr.[2] (A)	Ahmad Ali Zabarah (CA)
Yugoslavia	Malcolm Toon (A)	Toma Granfil (A)
Zaïre	Sheldon B. Vance (A)	Lombo Lo Mangamanga[2] (A)
Zambia	Jean M. Wilkowski (A)	Unia G. Mwila (A)

[1] Nominated after Sept. 1, 1972. [2] Appointed after Sept. 1, 1972.

NEW NATO AMBASSADOR Donald Rumsfeld was moved from Cost of Living Council to replace David Kennedy.

THE WHITE HOUSE

AMERICAN INDIANS. See INDIANS, AMERICAN.
AMERICAN LITERATURE. See LITERATURE.
ANDERSON, Jack. See BIOGRAPHY.
ANDREOTTI, Giulio. See BIOGRAPHY.

———— ANGOLA • Information Highlights ————

Official Name: Overseas State of Angola.
Area: 481,351 square miles (1,246,700 sq km).
Population (1972 est.): 5,900,000. *Density,* 10 per square mile (4 per sq km). *Annual rate of increase,* 2.1%.
Chief City (1960 census): Luanda, the capital, 224,540.
Government: Local administration is headed by the governor general, appointed by the Portuguese government.
Languages: Portuguese (official), Bantu languages.
Education: *School enrollment* (1968)—primary, 333,767; secondary, 40,061; technical/vocational, 14,530; university/higher, 1,252.
Monetary Unit: Escudo (27.02 escudos equal U. S.$1, Aug. 1972).
Gross National Product (1970): $1,200,000,000.
Manufacturing (major products): Petroleum products, processed foods, processed fish products, sawnwood.
Major Agricultural Products: Coffee, sisal, cotton, tobacco, corn, fish.
Major Minerals: Diamonds (ranks 5th among world producers, 1970), petroleum, iron ore.
Foreign Trade (1971): *Exports,* $431,000,000. *Imports,* $423,-000,000. *Chief trading partners* (1969)—Portugal (took 37% of exports, supplied 37% of imports); United States (16% —11%); West Germany (8%—10%).
Communications: *Telephones* (1970), 25,315; *radios* (1970), 95,000; *newspapers* (1967), 5 (daily circulation, 50,000).

ANGOLA

Events in Angola in 1972 were again dominated by the war between Angolan nationalists and Portuguese forces. The conflict entered its 12th year with no signs of abating. Portugal remained unwilling to relinquish control of its African territories. In May, the Portuguese National Assembly passed legislation designating the overseas territories of Angola and Mozambique as "states," and giving them greater autonomy "without affecting the unity of the nation."

The War. The Movement for the Liberation of Angola (MPLA) announced in February that fighting had been extended to the southern part of Angola, near the Ovamboland area of South West Africa. The war previously had been restricted to the northern and eastern regions, and Portugal was concerned that fighting in the southern border area would hinder plans for the development of the Cunene River, which forms part of the border between Angola and South West Africa. The area was visited in early February by Angola's governor general, Camilo A. Rebocho Vaz.

The Nationalists. Rivalries among nationalist movements were limiting their effectiveness. On March 17–19, Zaïrese troops occupied an Angolan guerrilla training camp in Zaïre. The camp, run by the Angolan Liberation Army (ALNA), which had been under the direction of Holden Roberto's Angolan Revolutionary Government in Exile (GRAE), had rebelled against Roberto's leadership. However, some camp members attributed the revolt to infiltrators from the rival MPLA, based in Congo. It was announced in June that the presidents of Zaïre and Congo had mediated a settlement of the differences between the GRAE and MPLA.

Foreign Relations. The World Council of Churches decided at a meeting at The Hague in August that it would sell all its holdings in corporations that invest in or trade with white-ruled African territories, including Angola. It also decided to double its fund to aid nationalist movements in southern Africa.

On September 27 the UN Committee on Non-Self-Governing Territories voted to accept representatives of African liberation movements as observers.

Epidemic. A cholera epidemic erupted in late December 1971. By the end of January at least 27 persons had died from the disease.

JUDITH A. GLICKMAN

ANTARCTICA

Biological and geological research, including ambitious international projects, continued at the more than 40 installations scattered around the Antarctic continent. A few stations operated only during the 1971–72 summer season, but most remained active throughout the winter of 1972. Among the scientific and technical personnel were about 150 U. S. and 400 Soviet workers.

Biological Studies. The largest part of the National Science Foundation's research program was devoted to biological projects, including studies of adaptation and temperature regulation in Weddell seals. Investigations were also made into the capability of Antarctic fish to resist freezing temperatures, with possible application to the preserving of human tissues, blood, and vital organs.

At Cape Hallett, operated as a summer base by the United States and New Zealand, continuing projects included the study of the embryology and incubation behavior of Adélie penguins, the census taking and branding of Weddell seals, and investigations into the distribution and effects of chlorinated hydrocarbons such as DDT on the reproductive capacities of birds. Palmer Station's programs included studies of the behavior of Antarctic insects and spiders, the physiology and deep-diving activities of birds and seals, and the social behavior of penguins and their cardiovascular adjustments during exercise—including the way penguins keep their feet warm when walking on ice by contracting and expanding blood vessels to regulate the supply to their feet. The U. S. research ship *Eltanin* pursued its series of cruises in the ocean around Antarctica to study the marine ecosystem, while the Coast Guard cutter *Southwind* conducted a seal-population survey in which some 900,000 seals were found in the Bellingshausen and Amundsen Seas.

Concern over the dwindling numbers of certain species of Antarctic seals led to a meeting of the 12 nations of the 1959 Antarctic Treaty, in an attempt to set limits on seal hunting in waters lying beyond the areas covered by the treaty. In the interest of Antarctic ecology in general, the cleanup campaign was resumed. Thus at McMurdo Station and nearby Scott Base, a New Zealand installation, special incinerators designed to minimize pollution were completed, as was a concrete pad for a sewage treatment plant at McMurdo. Other clean-up programs took place at Hallett and Marble Point and at Cape Crozier, where the penguin rookery was to remain inviolate in the future.

International Geophysical Projects. The International Antarctic Glaciological Project (IAGP), a planned 10-year effort that involves Australia, France, the Soviet Union, and the United States, began intensive studies to determine the size, shape, and glaciological history of eastern Antarctica's entire ice sheet. A joint airborne survey by the United States and Britain, using radio echo-sounding techniques, revealed a mountain chain below the ice between Sovetskaya Station and the Pole of Inaccessibility, and a new maximum ice-cap thickness of 14,895 feet (4,540 meters) about 155 miles (250 km) northeast of Vostok Station. IAGP suffered a serious setback with the crash, on takeoff, of a U. S. Hercules 130 engaged in the resupply of a French traverse team in Wilkes Land. There were no injuries, but the plane's loss cut U. S. long-range airlift resources in Antarctica by one fourth. On

Deception Island, scientists from Argentina, Britain, Chile, the Soviet Union, and the United States studied the effects on glaciers of three recent volcanic eruptions that took place on the island.

Scientists from Japan, New Zealand, and the United States began another international program, the Dry Valley Drilling Project (DVDP), by flying a magnetic survey for the following season's deep-drilling sites in the dry valleys west of McMurdo Sound. The National Aeronautics and Space Administration also studied the dry valleys, since they bear resemblances to features observed in photographs of Mars. Other Victoria Land projects included the study of the geology of Precambrian and Paleozoic rocks and the Mawson Formation, a volcanic deposit of Jurassic age (135–180 million years old) that contains many invertebrate fossils.

Upper Atmosphere Studies. At Siple Station, a dipole antenna 13 miles (21 km) long and elevated 15 feet (4.5 meters) above the surface of the ice cap was completed. The antenna is used to monitor man-made, very low frequency signals called "whistlers," in conjunction with a similar installation at the point on the earth's surface directly opposite Siple—Roberval, Canada—since the signals travel along geomagnetic lines of force between such conjugate points. Such studies may lead to a static-free system of radio communication, unaffected by solar storms. In the winter of 1973, Siple becomes a year-round station for three years, devoted to atmospheric sciences and medical research.

Other Base and Personnel News. After 15 years of operation, Byrd Station was closed on Jan. 1, 1972, leaving the United States with three permanent, year-round stations. Several summer parties completed glaciological studies at Byrd, and a surface installation will be maintained as a plane refueling point between McMurdo and Siple.

At South Pole Station, a thermal probe into the ice cap ran into drilling difficulties and had to be postponed. Bad weather prevented completion of the geodesic dome to house a new station.

At McMurdo Station, a polar aurora radar system was placed in operation, an unmanned geophysical observatory achieved automatic performance, and the Elklund Biological Center was dedicated. The U. S. Coast Guard cutter *Staten Island* cracked her bow while ramming heavy ice in McMurdo Sound, and a March storm destroyed work on dock reinforcement at Elliott Quay.

Economy and reduced airlift capacity sharply curtailed Antarctica's visitor program. However, on the 60th anniversary of Roald Amundsen's attainment of the South Pole, explorer and geographer Finn Ronne and his wife, Edith, became the first husband-and-wife team to visit the pole.

Soviet Activities. The USSR selected a site for its seventh Antarctic station: Cape Burks on Hobbs Coast in western Antarctica's Marie Byrd Land. At the main Soviet base, Molodezhnava, a new medical laboratory studied microbiology, hygiene, and the acclimatization of man to Antarctic surroundings. In the Prince Charles Mountains, Soviet geologists discovered coal beds with petrified tree trunks and leaf imprints, attesting to the tropical environment in Antarctica 250 million years ago. The USSR also continued to emphasize meteorological studies. A University of California exchange scientist, Gregg A. Vane, spent the year at Novolazarevskaya operating a seismic station.

EDITH M. RONNE, *Antarctic Specialist*

ANTHROPOLOGY

Anthropologists in 1972 made studies of the cave-dwelling Tasaday tribe discovered on the Philippine island of Mindanao in June 1971. Several significant fossil finds were reported during the year, and a new anthropological society and two new journals came into being: The Society for Cross-Cultural Research, its journal, and *Urban Anthropology*. The 70th annual meeting of the American Anthropological Association (Nov. 18–21, 1971) attracted more than 4,000 persons, its largest attendance ever.

Cave-Dwelling Tribe. An expedition of anthropologists and journalists renewed contact in March with the jungle-dwelling Tasaday tribe on Mindanao. The friendly Tasadays, who apparently have been isolated for more than a thousand years, live in limestone caves and use stone tools. The culture of food-gatherers may resemble that of prehistoric men and is the first such discovery in modern times. Logging operations had been posing a threat to the territory of the tribe until the Philippine government proclaimed an area of some 50,000 acres as an exclusive Tasaday preserve.

Fossil Finds. New fossil discoveries are yielding more information on ancient hominids and man. Near Lake Rudolf in eastern Africa, an expedition led by Flynn Isaac and Richard Leakey, son of the late Louis S. B. Leakey, uncovered skull and lower leg fragments and thigh bones of what may be man's oldest immediate ancestor. About 2.6 million years old, the fragments indicate a manlike creature that walked upright and had a cranial volume of 800 cubic centimeters, a little more than half that of modern man. Previously discovered *Homo habilis*, which is about 1.75 million years old, had a smaller cranial volume, whereas *Homo erectus*, which is about 1 million years old, had a larger cranial volume but exhibited heavy brow ridges that are missing in the new fossil.

Phillip Tobias of the University of Witwatersrand announced the discovery in South Africa of a fossil skull estimated to be between 2 million and 2.5 million years old. The female skull was uncovered near the site where Robert Broom found the skull known as Sterkfontein 5, or Plesianthropus, in 1936. The significance of the new find lies in its estimated age, placing the "ape woman" in the lower Villafranchian of the Pleistocene Epoch.

Also reported in 1972 was the discovery of a fossil skull in the Sangiran area of central Java. The skull, found by a farmer in 1969, has been dated approximately to the Middle Pleistocene Epoch, about 550,000 years ago. It resembles the known Pithecanthropus type found in the same location in 1937. Classification of the new find will not be attempted until the whole skull has been removed from its matrix of sandstone.

In the United States an amateur archaeologist, Morlin Childers, found a human skeleton buried beneath a pile of rocks in the desert near El Centro, Calif. Preliminary dating of the remains by the carbon-14 process yielded a tentative age of 21,500 years. If substantiated, this would make them the oldest human bones found in the Americas.

Mathematical Analysis. Mathematical analysis is being applied increasingly to problems of fossil classification and identification. In the journal *Science*, U. S. anthropologist George P. Rightmire reported his use of "multivariate discriminant" analysis to compare fossil hand bones and the bones

FILIPINO CAVE DWELLERS, members of the Tasaday "lost tribe," were discovered in March 1972 in the rain forest of Cotabato province.

of living primate genera. He determined that the thumb of the fossil *Paranthropus* from South Africa may be functionally similar to that of the chimpanzee. The implication is that *Paranthropus* is closer to the line of evolutionary development of the great apes than to that of man.

Although the practice is decried by many anthropologists, mathematical analysis is also being applied with increasing frequency to various problems in social and cultural anthropology. For example, the journal *Science* published a typical article, by Alan Lomax, that describes the use of mathematics to establish evolutionary levels, while the journal *Ethnology* published an article by Harold E. Driver and others on the "Statistical Classification of North American Indian Ethnic Units." Similar efforts led to the publication, in 1971, of the results of a symposium on mathematical anthropology. The work is *Explorations in Mathematical Anthropology,* edited by Paul Kay.

Other Trends in Social and Cultural Anthropology. Most of the present developments in the fields of social and cultural anthropology are continuations of interests that have been in progress for the past several years. These include developments in ecological analysis, studies in urban anthropology, and a growing professional interest in oral literature. This interest in oral literature, as well as in other forms of folklore, together with a broad interest in the culture of the American Indian, is exemplified by the publication of *Shaking the Pumpkin* (1972). The work, which is edited by Jerome Rothenberg, is a collection of poems and stories from American Indian cultures. Another new work in 1972 is *African Folklore,* edited by Richard M. Dorson.

In addition, there has been an increase in interest in and use of ethnographic films for teaching, to the extent that a society for visual anthropology is about to be established.

New Interpretation of Cave Markings. In 1972 an amateur student of prehistory, Alexander Marshack, published *The Roots of Civilization.* In it he proposed that much of the "art" in Upper Paleolithic caves and the variety of scratches on Paleolithic artifacts are in reality time-related notations—observations of seasonal events, or lunar calendars—rather than ornamentations. This theory is more important to the field of anthropology than to archaeology alone, since it concerns the nature of human cognitive and symbolic comprehension, and it is already being widely debated.

Leakey and Steward. Two major figures in anthropology died in 1972: Louis S. B. Leakey, on October 1, and Julian H. Steward, on February 6. South African paleontologist Leakey and his wife, Mary, were the discoverers of the fossil hominids *Zinjanthropus* and *Homo habilis.* The discoveries served to validate the theory that man evolved in Africa rather than in Asia and that the evolution took place over a vast time scale. (See ARCHAEOLOGY.) Steward, a key U. S. anthropologist for over 30 years, taught at five major American universities, helped found the National Science Foundation, and prepared the six-volume *Handbook of South American Indians.* His major theoretical work was *Theory of Culture Change* (1955), in which he developed the idea of cultural ecology and multilinear cultural evolution.

HERMAN J. JAFFE
Brooklyn College
City University of New York

COFFIN in Chinese tomb discovered near Changsha dates back more than 2,100 years to the Han Dynasty. The third of the coffin's six nested units is shown.

ARCHAEOLOGY

There were new discoveries in all aspects of archaeology in 1972. Findings in classical and historical periods were particularly dramatic, and in the Western Hemisphere investigations of ancient Indian cultures continued.

Dr. Louis S. B. Leakey, the persevering British archaeologist whose sensational and revolutionary discoveries of fossil man contributed greatly to archaeology, died in London on Oct. 1, 1972.

EASTERN HEMISPHERE

Acid Test for Dating. A new method of dating fossils was developed by Jeffrey Bada, an organic chemist at the Scripps Institution of Oceanography in California. Working with an ancient (135,000-year-old) hominid bone provided by Dr. Leakey, Bada developed a technique based on the fact that polarized light passing through crystallized amino acids in modern living things rotates to the left while such light passing through amino acids in dead organisms rotates to the right. The age of fossils is calculated by measuring the ratio of left-rotating to right-rotating molecules in the common amino acid isoleucine. The technique works best on materials that have not been subject to any great temperature variations since their death.

Oldest Human Skull and Lower Paleolithic Footprints. Near Lake Rudolf in Kenya, Richard Leakey found the cranium and long bones of a fossil man with an estimated age of 2.6 million years, making it the oldest human fossil skull known. In the same region he also found a Lower Paleolithic boy's footprint preserved in ancient lacustrine silts. The Acheulean footprint is some 500,000 years old.

Korean Paleolithic. Late Pleistocene Stone Age industries have been uncovered in several localities in South Korea as part of an ongoing program led by the archaeologist Pow-Key Sohn. Artifacts feature large and small end scrapers, prismatic blades, chopping tools, and the wedge-shaped burin, a tool characteristic of the earliest known culture on both sides of the Bering Strait.

Preserved Mesolithic Cultures. North of the Arctic Circle near Utsjoki, Finland, the archaeologist Aarni Erae-Esko found a habitation site of the 10,000-year-old Komsa culture. The site includes wooden, leather, fibrous, and other normally perishable organic remains that have been preserved by a 10-centimeter layer of peat. He considers the find too good to excavate by present methods, and legal action is being taken to protect the site until advances in archaeological techniques have been made.

First Monumental Art. Excavations at the mysterious site of Lepenski Vir at the Iron Gates of the Danube in northern Yugoslavia have become more understandable. The upper layer belongs to the well-known Starcevo Stone Age farmers. The bottom level, however, represents a previously unknown group of hunters and fishermen who seem to have developed on the spot from a band-type organization to a bipartite tribal society (moiety system) and to have invented the first known village planning and the oldest monumental stone sculptures, usually appearing as piscine deities or human beings carved in relief on round boulders.

New Stone Age Town. The largest Neolithic settlement and nearly the largest prehistoric settlement ever found in Europe was unearthed 115 miles (185 km) south of Kiev in the Soviet Ukraine by N. M. Shmagli. Representing a late phase of the Tripolye culture prior to 3000 B.C., the town consisted of over 1,599 well-built houses covering an area of 700 acres (280 hectares) with an estimated population of 20,000. This would rank it in size with the city-states of contemporaneous Mesopotamia. The decline of this incipient urbanization in eastern Europe until the time of the Vikings raises questions about the decay of cities.

Bronze Age City. A team of Iranian and Italian archaeologists excavated what may be one of the world's best-preserved early cities. Situated in eastern Iran near the southwestern border of Afghanistan, the city was probably established 4,000 to 5,000 years ago. The excavators found a large number of artifacts probably produced by specialized craftsmen (such as weavers, potters, basketmakers, masons, and coppersmiths), together with evidence of cultivated plants, including wheat, barley, millet, cucumbers, melons, grapes, and poppies.

Phoenician Temple. At the ancient city of Sarepta, on coastal Lebanon, a temple has been unearthed by James Pritchard of the University of Pennsylvania. Dating from about 1200 B.C., the temple contains an altar, offering tables, and a treasury of religious objects and paraphernalia.

Royalty in the USSR. An unlooted Scythian grave, the first found in over 50 years, was discovered under an earthen tumulus near Ordzhonikidze, Ukraine. The tomb contained the skeletons of a prince, a princess, and an infant bedecked with gold ornaments, bracelets, and weapons. Several servants and six horses were also buried in the grave, and a "queen's chamber" contained servants and a warrior.

Findings from Ancient Greek Civilizations. The Mauseoleum of Halicarnassus, one of the seven wonders of the world in classical times, built by the Greek ruler Mausolus in what is now western Turkey, has been reinvestigated by Danish archaeologist-architect Kristian Jepperson. He not only has established more clearly the basic structure and colonnade of the monument but has also located the central tomb—believed to be that of Mausolus him-

self and his family—which still contained over 300 pieces of gold ornaments, earrings, and ivory pieces.

Two statuettes—a boy and a girl—still exhibiting traces of paint that decorated their surfaces and executed in the late Archaic style, have been found buried side by side by Greek archaeologist Efthymios Mastrokostas while excavating an ancient Greek cemetery in a field 25 miles (40 km) from Athens. The girl, crowned by a lotus blossom diadem (crown), fits perfectly into a base, found earlier, that bears the name "Phrasikleia" and the hallmark of Aristion, a master sculptor who lived on Paros in the 550's B. C.

Han Dynasty Relics. A 2,100-year-old Western Han tomb, distinguished by lavish interment and remarkable preservation, was discovered in China. Not only had the body survived well, but among the more than 1,000 articles in the grave were silk fabrics, bamboo, wooden utensils, bronzes, and pottery. One piece of silk exhibited a painting on it.

Celtic Iron Age Town. An international team of archaeologists, led by Gerard Thill of Luxembourg and H. L. Thomas and R. M. Rowlett of the United States, began excavations in earnest at the Titelberg, a Celtic Iron Age hill fort in southwestern Luxembourg. The fortified town was established by the Treveran tribe. The Romans allowed the tribe to continue living there after the conquest of Gaul. They also encouraged the development of the established craft industries in steel, pottery, and perhaps glass and coinage, and they introduced some technological refinements, especially in glass and ceramic works.

The 1972 summer excavations seem to have struck the mint for producing coins, an unusually frequent find on the Titelberg. This mint dates from the time of Augustus, when the Romans rearranged the layout of the town by imposing on it the Roman city blocks, or *insulae,* but the Roman urban renewal project had to be adapted to preexisting conditions at the old Celtic center.

Underneath the late prehistoric Iron Age remains are traces of a settlement of Stone Age farmers, with polished stone axes dating from about two millennia earlier.

Viking Church. The remains of a 10th century stave church have been found under a 13th century church that was being restored on the Swedish island of Gotland. At least 10 graves lay at the entry to the stave church, and more than 1,000 coins from the end of the Viking era (970–1025) date the church securely. The slaked lime floor was surprisingly sophisticated for the era.

RALPH M. ROWLETT
University of Missouri, Columbia

WESTERN HEMISPHERE

Investigations of ancient Indian cultures continued in 1972. Archaeologists were also concerned about contemporary problems, such as the demands of Indian activist groups that certain archaeological projects be curtailed because they are violating the heritage of Indian people. In addition, land development and building projects are destroying remains of prehistoric Indian cultures on a massive scale, while the reckless digging of "pothunters," or amateur archaeologists, poses a corresponding threat to the preservation of such sites.

Alabama. During the summer, researchers from the University of Alabama completed an archaeological survey in the Selma area, recording 60

┌───┐
│ **LOUIS S. B. LEAKEY (1903–1972)** │

Louis Seymour Bazett Leakey, the British archaeologist and anthropologist who spent most of his life in pursuit of fossil evidence of early man, died in London on Oct. 1, 1972. His discoveries moved back the date of man's emergence on earth by more than a million years and placed the origins of mankind in East Africa.

CAMERA PIX

The son of British missionaries, Leakey was born in the Kikuyu village of Kabete, near Nairobi, Kenya, on Aug. 7, 1903. After a boyhood in Kenya among Kikuyu youths, he went to England and eventually earned his Ph. D. degree at Cambridge University. In 1924, during his second year at Cambridge, he took part in a British Museum archaeological expedition to Tanganyika (now Tanzania). He became convinced that man's origins were to be found in Africa rather than in Asia, where scholars had been concentrating their efforts since the discovery of Java Man and Peking Man. For a number of years thereafter, Leakey divided his time between lecturing in England and leading expeditions to East Africa.

In 1931, Leakey began to explore Olduvai Gorge, where he discovered fossil remains of many species of extinct animal life, including some of the early forerunners of man. In 1959, his expedition found remnants of a skull of a human-like creature estimated to have lived some 1.75 million years ago. The hominid was named *Zinjanthropus.* Subsequent discoveries such as remnants of *Homo habilis,* an early toolmaking hominid, and *Kenyapithecus,* a link between ape and man, led Leakey to estimate in 1967 that the family of man is nearly 20 million years old. Some of his theories, including the view that man's evolution was contemporary with that of other related species, have provoked controversy.

During World War II, Leakey worked for British military intelligence, and from 1945 to 1961 he was chief curator of Nairobi's Coryndon Memorial Museum. He lectured at various institutions, and in his expeditions he was aided by his wife, Mary, and other members of his family. His works include *Adam's Ancestors* (1934), *Olduvai Gorge* (1951, 1965), and a grammar of the Kikuyu language.

HENRY SLOAN
└───┘

new sites of the Archaic and Woodland periods of Indian culture. Several of the newly found sites revealed villages of considerable extent.

Florida. Scientists from Florida State University continued to work in the region of the Apalachicola River, trying to develop a series of testable hypotheses about settlement and subsistence patterns in prehistoric Florida communities. Earlier investigations resulted in the extensive excavation of the Torreya site in Liberty county, yielding about 10,000 potsherds but little else. This finding presents a puzzle, since little evidence of food preparation has been found despite the volume of pottery. Thus the location is not refinable as a true habitation site. Possibly the location was used for gathering products instead.

Georgia. Archaeologists from the University of Georgia are focusing efforts on a platform temple mount on the Chattahoochee River in the north-

western part of the state. The imposing prehistoric religious center is 16 feet (4.9 meters) high and has an upper surface area of 60 by 100 feet (18.2 by 30.5 meters). It is constructed of at least ten superimposed mound levels that have been assigned tentatively to the Lamar phase of the Mississippian period of Indian culture. Although the scientists believe that the culture of the mound was locally derived, certain traits imply some affinity with the Etowah and Coastal mound cultures.

New York. Investigators from the Nassau County Museum identified the earliest evidence of human habitation on Long Island. The site, on the shore of Long Island Sound in Suffolk county, dates from 2600 B.C. It features the debris of many meals of shellfish. Tools such as projectile points, blades, antler points, bone awls, and scrapers have been recovered there, as well as a finely incised deer rib of unknown purpose.

Oregon. Smithsonian Institution-supported research into the prehistory of the northern Oregon coast has concentrated on two major village sites near the mouth of the Columbia River. The sites were occupied during the period 1000 B.C.–1000 A.D., but possessed distinctively different economic traditions and material cultures. In addition to some 4,600 stone, shell, and bone artifacts, nearly 70,000 food remains have been collected. Both of the sites contain definable stratigraphy and show evidence of semisubterranean dwellings.

Virginia. The first of ten planned years of investigation was begun at the Flowerdew Hundred site—named for Temperance Flowerdew, wife of Colonial Virginia's governor, Sir George Yeardley

SKULL that may be 2.6 million years old and represent man's earliest known immediate ancestor is held by Richard Leakey, a co-leader of the expedition that discovered the skull and other remains in East Africa.

BOB CAMPBELL © NATIONAL GEOGRAPHIC SOCIETY

—by archaeologists from William and Mary College. Dated at 1622, the site is considered to be the most important from the 17th century in North America. It has already produced what may be the earliest surviving stone house foundation from that time. A cache of arms recovered from the foundation area may refer to the perilous times in 1622 when the local Indian leader, Opechancano, sought to drive the colonists from the region. In addition, a fort site with some 4,000 feet (1,200 meters) of palisades, together with cannon, armor, household items, and numerous other artifacts, has been recovered.

Washington. Scientists from Washington State University, working in the Lind Coulee area near Warden, are excavating prehistoric camp features and associated faunal remains that they expect will provide further data concerning early cultures in the plateau region of eastern Washington state. The site is tentatively described as similar in culture to the Marmes Rock Shelter that, several years ago, produced the oldest human remains found thus far in the Western Hemisphere. Near Centralia, University of Washington archaeologists working in conjunction with the state's highways department have located a site believed to be one of the oldest yet found in the western part of the state. Early estimates place the antiquity of the artifacts there at 6,000 to 8,000 years.

British Columbia. Canadian archaeologists are now certain that cultures along the western coast of Canada have been relatively stable over the past 5,000 years, and evidence suggests that carving of totem poles has taken place over a period of at least 2,000 years. Although no very ancient totem poles are likely to be found, several examples of partially-preserved wood plank houses as much as 2,500 years old have been located in British Columbia and northwestern Washington. The craftsmanship needed to produce the houses would have been equally capable of producing the totem poles that—it is postulated—became necessary about 500 B.C. when coastal societies chose to define their property and territory clearly. Oddly enough, this striking custom did not spread rapidly beyond British Columbia.

Mexico. Eight projectile points of the concave-base type known as Clovis were recovered from a camp some 20 miles (35 km) north of Carbo, in Sonora state. The site can now be associated with the Paleo-Indian period of about 10,000 years ago, when big game hunters evidently were drawn there by the accessibility of suitable stone material near the location. Researchers anticipate that further studies at the site will reveal more Clovis materials in association with extinct faunal remains.

Brazil. A carbon-14 date of 10,820 B.C. was announced for an aggregation of nonprojectile stone implements in the state of Rio Grande do Sul. This represented the first evidence of human materials of such antiquity on the eastern coast of South America. Complexes of comparable antiquity in the southern part of the continent previously had been known only from Chile.

Peru. Near Lake Junín in the central highlands of Peru, archaeologists located a ceremonial site that dates from the ancient Chavin culture. The site lies significantly beyond the previously defined geographical limits for that culture, thus necessitating some reassessment of the range of Chavin influence in the Andes Mountains.

GEORGE E. PHEBUS, JR., *Smithsonian Institution*

The Weyerhaeuser Company's headquarters in Tacoma, Wash., was designed by Skidmore, Owings & Merrill to fit into a forested landscape.

architecture

Among the important events in architecture in 1972 were the development of Walt Disney World, the more economical construction of high-rise buildings, and a continuing concern for the relation of buildings to the environment.

Walt Disney World. The development of Walt Disney World in central Florida is significant less as architecture or a social statement than as a triumph of organizational autonomy, bypassing conventional bureaucracy, and as a testing ground for modern planning. On a 27,000-acre (10,900-hectare) site—an area twice the size of Manhattan—are not only fairgrounds but also hotels and residences. Technological ideas predominate. A highly integrated servicing system, located in a basement extending throughout the site, provides water and electricity and disposes of sewage. The basement also gives easy accessibility for maintenance and deliveries and serves as a backstage area for the costumed staff. A Swedish-designed vacuum system collects garbage from 15 locations. Through the combined design efforts of the Disney organization and Welton Becket & Associates, a factory was built close to the site for the construction of the prefabricated, room-sized, steel boxes, of which the Contemporary Hotel consists. The hotel is also the terminus of a monorail system.

High-Rise Structures. Technological and theoretical developments permitted the more economical construction of high-rise buildings. One such development is the tube-within-a-tube structural system. For example, the 110-story Sears Roebuck office building, being constructed in Chicago, was designed as a huge tube by its architects, Skidmore, Owings & Merrill, with the aid of Fazlur Kahn, an engineer recognized for his achievements in structural economy.

Another example of tube-within-a-tube structure is the 50-story building at One Shell Plaza in Houston, also by Skidmore, Owings, & Merrill with Kahn. Columns on the perimeter, 6 feet (1.8 meters) apart, are connected to form a rectangular, load-bearing tube. Below street level, three floors provide parking for 365 cars and a fourth floor—the uppermost—has retail stores. The main floor is 4 feet (1.2 meters) above street level. Above the main floor rise 42 office floors, and above them three floors containing a club, a restaurant, and an observation deck. The building, which occupies a full block, is lavishly finished with 27 tons of Italian travertine.

Structures Related to the Environment. In contrast to high-rise structures, the Weyerhaeuser headquarters in Tacoma, Wash., was conceived as an element in the forested landscape of Hylebus Creek Valley. Skidmore, Owings & Merrill designed the building, and Sasaki-Walker Associates landscaped it. The long, low structure, with its five floors of open office landscape, is placed between two hills so that it dams a lake, and its tapering ends merge into the landscape.

The headquarters of the Burroughs Wellcome Co. in Durham, N. C., designed by Paul Rudolph, echoes the Weyerhaeuser building in that its lineal distribution, which forms a giant "S," is easily accommodated into the landscape. However, its highly

KIMBELL ART MUSEUM

KIMBELL ART MUSEUM, Fort Worth, Texas, a series of cycloid vaults surrounding an entrance plaza, was designed by Louis I. Kahn of Philadelphia.

GALLERIES of the Kimbell Art Museum are illuminated by natural light from above. The absence of piers, columns, and windows gives the museum flexible exhibition areas.

THE NEW YORK TIMES

sculptural massing, like a flattened hexagon in cross section, is overly assertive in contrast to the land. Inside the Burroughs Wellcome building, slanted lines are repeated incessantly, creating a feeling of restlessness.

Government and Other Office Buildings. One of the largest, most expensive building projects to date is the new headquarters of the Federal Bureau of Investigation in Washington. The structure, which covers one block on Pennsylvania Avenue, has three stories underground and 11 above. The architects, C. F. Murphy Associates of Chicago, have dealt commendably with government bureaucracy and with the stylistic strictures imposed by the White House Advisory Commission. Unlike Murphy's ele-

gant works in Chicago inspired by Mies van der Rohe, the FBI building is heavily articulated in buff-colored, cast-in-place and pre-cast concrete.

In London, the firm of Spence and Webster won a competition for a building to include offices, recreational facilities, and television studios for members of Parliament. The bulky, rectangular structure will fill a block opposite the tower of Big Ben and adjacent to the River Thames. Four service towers will support an exposed steel truss roof, from which will hang floors enclosed with bronze-framed windows. An open plaza will run beneath the building.

In Toronto, the architectural firm of Diamond and Meyers designed new interiors for the Alcan Co. Emphasizing their client's product, they combined reflective aluminum sheets with neon tube lighting to produce spectacular, unconventional effects.

Cultural Buildings. The most outstanding art museum completed in 1972 was the small, one-story Kimbell Museum of Art in Fort Worth, Texas, designed by Louis I. Kahn. Exhibition areas unobstructed by columns or windows are provided by a beautifully executed series of 100-foot-long (30-meter), parallel, semicircular vaults. A unique system of slits in the tops of the vaults, combined with a cycloid baffle of reflective aluminum, deflects daylight into the interior. The natural light falling on the interior surfaces of travertine and oak imparts a warm quality.

The University of California at Berkeley completed the largest university art museum in the United States. The design—by Chiampi, Reiter, Jorasch & Wagner—was the winner of a national competition that attracted a total of 366 entries. The building presents a somewhat stark exterior of exposed concrete. The complex, more appealing interior is a boldly arranged series of five galleries radiating from a skylit court and connected by a series of ramps.

Architects Gio Ponti of Milan and James Sudler Associates of Denver designed Denver's first permanent art museum as part of a civic-center complex. In strong contrast to other Denver structures, the building has a facade covered with glass tile and exuberantly decorated with a random pattern of slit openings, behind which concealed neon strip lighting provides nighttime illumination. Entrance is through an enormous, open-ended, stainless-steel tube. Each of the seven floors contains two artificially lit galleries separated by a lobby.

Philip Johnson and the Architects Design Group completed an addition to the Boston Public Library, a 70-year-old, High Renaissance-style landmark by McKim, Mead & White. They achieved 480,000 square feet (146,300 square meters) of largely open space by hanging three floors from a top-floor grid consisting of interconnected trusses. The arcaded facades are faced in granite.

The new Harvard Graduate School of Design building in Cambridge, after many changes of personnel and views, was completed by the Toronto firm of John Andrews, Anderson, Baldwin in 1972. All graduate programs are united in a single studio space. Its four open levels are arranged as stepped-back terraces and are covered by a dramatically inclined roof of glass and tubular steel trusses. It is enclosed at the ends by high concrete wings of offices and seminar rooms. The uncompromising openness of the studio space perhaps oversimplifies the complexities of the school program.

ESTO

ONE SHELL PLAZA in Houston, Texas, designed by Skidmore, Owings & Merrill, stands 50 stories tall and is finished with 27 tons of travertine imported from Italy.

Aesthetically more successful is Finlandia Hall for concerts and congregations in Helsinki, completed in December 1971. Designed by Alvar Aalto, it has a well-proportioned exterior of marble and granite and an interior that uses Aalto-designed furnishings of wood, leather, and neutral-colored fabrics.

The facilities for the Olympic Games in Munich were designed by competition-winning architect Gunther Benisch of Stuttgart. His stadium seating 80,000, sports arena for 40,000, and swimming hall for 9,000, with the various sports areas below ground level, suggested the slope of ancient amphitheaters. He covered all these structures with a single 800,000-square-foot (243,840-square-meter) lattice of pre-stressed steel cables and acrylic panels suspended from pylons. Frei Paul Otto, famous for his work in suspended structures, was the engineer.

Preservation. In Chicago it was most discouraging to see the destruction of Louis Sullivan's decoratively detailed Stock Exchange (1890's), one of the last examples of the Chicago School, to make room for more profitable buildings. However, the Romanesque Glessner House (1886), H. H. Richardson's only remaining Chicago building, was saved and restored to its original condition by the Chicago School of Architecture Foundation. The foundation uses the magnificent granite and oak mansion as its headquarters. In Boston the Second Empire-style old City Hall, by Gridley Bryant and Arthur Gilman, was extensively renovated by the non-profit Architectural Heritage organization and Anderson, Notter Associates to hold law offices and a restaurant.

In Washington, the red brick, Second Empire-style Renwick Gallery (1861), occupied first by the Corcoran Collection and then by the U. S. Court of Claims, was saved from demolition. Architect John Carl Warnecke, with Universal Restorations, Inc., restored the exterior, and Hugh Newell Jacobsen sensitively refurbished the interior. The gallery will display American decorative arts and design.

Awards. The American Institute of Architects (AIA) Gold Medal went to Pietro Belluschi, the Italian-trained dean of the School of Architecture and Planning at M. I. T. He is noted for his Equitable Building (1948) in Portland, Oreg., the first multistory, curtain-wall building after World War II, and for his consultative work on St. Mary's Cathedral (1971) in San Francisco and the Boston Building (1972) in Boston.

AIA honor awards went to Marcel Breuer and Herbert Beckhard for the superbly constructed Koerfer house on Lake Maggiore, Switzerland, and to James Stewart Polshek and Associates for a design for the New York State Bar Center in Albany, which sensitively preserves a section of 19th century brownstone terrace housing. Awards also went to Edward Larrabee Barnes for the Walker Art Center in Minneapolis and to C. F. Murphy Associates for McCormick Place in Chicago. Winners of Bard Awards were the National Airlines Terminal at Kennedy Airport, New York, by I. M. Pei and Partners and the residential building at the Henry Ittleson Center for Child Research, Riverdale, N. Y., by Abraham W. Geller.

JOHN FOWLER, *Architect*

GRADUATE SCHOOL OF DESIGN at Harvard, by the Toronto architects John Andrews/Anderson/Baldwin, has studios arranged in terrace form.

ARCTIC REGIONS

The Arctic Ocean and the lands north of the Arctic Circle are still some of the least-known regions of the Northern Hemisphere. However, exploration is gradually reducing the unknowns. Discoveries of oil deposits spurred the exploration of little-known Arctic islands in 1972, and a scientific project promised to investigate the ice cover.

Oil. In February 1972 petroleum was discovered on Ellesmere Island, a part of Canada's Northwest Territories. It was the first oil strike to have been made in the Arctic islands. The oil was found to be a low-sulfur crude oil, which is less polluting to the atmosphere when burned. Other islands, where oil seepage has been seen on the surface, were to be explored for oil later. Meanwhile, the Soviets were drilling an exploratory well on Kolguyev Island, 375 miles (600 km) northeast of Archangel. They hoped to reach the supposedly huge petroleum resources under the continental shelf.

A major problem in Alaska was that of deciding on the means of transporting oil from the Prudhoe Bay area on the North Coast, where it had been discovered in 1968. The question was tentatively settled in 1972 in favor of a trans-Alaskan pipeline from Prudhoe Bay to Valdez. From Valdez the petroleum was to be shipped by tanker. The building of the pipeline had been stalled for more than two years, awaiting government approval. Conservationists had been trying to prevent its construction because they feared it would do damage to the tundra wildlife. On May 11, 1972, U. S. Secretary of the Interior Rogers C. B. Morton approved the pipeline. The conservationists accused him of bowing to oil interests. On August 15, federal Judge George L. Hart, Jr., dissolved a 1970 injunction against the pipeline, but the conservationists sought an appeal. The Alyeska Pipeline Service Company announced that it would not start work on the pipeline until the appeals court took action.

The Ice Cover. Investigation of the Arctic ice cover was continued in 1972 by the project AIDJEX (Arctic Ice Dynamics Joint Experiment). A thin veneer of pack ice about 10 feet (3 meters) thick covers the central Arctic Ocean throughout the year. The ice cover—which drifts with wind and ocean currents, continually breaking, ridging, and deforming—is believed by some to exert a controlling influence on the climate of the Northern Hemisphere. Some even believe that destruction of the pack ice by natural or artificial means would bring about another ice age. Pilot studies in the Beaufort Sea area of the Arctic Ocean, which had been started in 1971, continued. The shore base for the experiments was at Barrow, Alaska, in 1972, whereas the preceding year it had been at Tuktoyaktuk, Canada. The project was being carried out by researchers from Canada, Japan, and the United States. The 1972 project was visited by Soviet observers.

The main AIDJEX project, planned for 1975, was to have five manned camps on the ice, separated by distances of 60 miles (95 km). The drifts of the camps were to be tracked with satellite navigation systems to determine the deformation of the pack on a large scale. Winds, ocean currents, ocean tilt, and other measurements were to be made to determine the pattern of forces causing ice deformation.

KENNETH L. HUNKINS
Lamont-Doherty Geological Observatory of Columbia University

ARGENTINA

Former President Juan Domingo Perón returned to Argentina on Nov. 17, 1972, after 17 years of exile in Spain. But he left the country again on December 14, after a stay of only 28 days. The 77-year-old Perón had ruled Argentina from 1946 until he was overthrown by the military in 1955. The regime of Gen. Alejandro Lanusse had invited Perón to return in order to gain the support of his followers for elections scheduled for 1973.

The Return of Perón. The government limited the size of the public welcome for the returning exile. After agreeing with the regime on the need for "peace" and "national reconciliation," Perón moved to a house purchased by his supporters in the suburbs of Buenos Aires. Disqualified by the existing rules as a presidential candidate, Perón rejected the presidential nomination offered to him by the Justicialista party and a number of minor parties. He left the country on December 14, leaving his followers confused. Perón had endorsed his long-time supporter Héctor J. Cámpora for the presidency.

Argentina's major political problem continued to be the integration of the Peronists into the political system. Lanusse hopes to achieve a solution through a democratically elected government in which the military would continue to have some influence—a difficult concession for most civilian politicians.

Lanusse had opened direct negotiations with Perón in 1971. In January 1972, Perón's Justicialista party was recognized as a legitimate political organization, and a 1955 charge of treason against Perón was dismissed in April, removing the last legal obstacle to his return to Argentina. The former dictator was proclaimed the presidential candidate of the Justicialista party in June.

On July 7, Lanusse dared Perón to return to run for the presidency, guaranteeing that there would be no legal difficulties but declaring that all candidates would have to be in the country by August 25. Lanusse removed himself as a possible candidate and announced that any member of his regime who wished to run for office would have to resign by the same date. Perón rejected the ultimatum on July 22, demanding assurance of his safety in Argentina. On July 27, Lanusse charged that Perón was afraid to return to Argentina.

From Madrid, Perón directed attempts to achieve unity within the Peronist movement and to assure its return to power. But his continued absence from Argentina posed problems for the Peronist organization, including the question of his backing for the guerrilla groups. Perón tried publicly to disassociate himself from them. His 10-point plan for return to electoral politics, presented to the government in October, suggested a willingness to work with the regime until the March 1973 elections.

Other Political Developments. For the political parties, 1972 was the year of the Front. La Hora del Pueblo, founded in 1971 and dominated by the Unión Cívica Radical del Pueblo (UCRP), found competitors in the Peronist-organized Frente Cívico de Liberación Nacional (FRECILINA), and in the leftist Encuentro Nacional de los Argentinos. The Peronists were a part of La Hora and still remained within it, but to what degree was uncertain. Both groups wanted to retain their independence in the struggle for office and the spoils of victory, yet neither appeared to be in a position to return the

JUAN PERÓN RETURNS to Argentina after 17 years of exile in Spain. The former dictator, who arrived in Buenos Aires on November 17, smiles from a window of the house his followers had purchased for him in Vicente López, a Buenos Aires suburb.

UPI

country to civilian rule or to govern without the support of the other.

Meanwhile, the individual parties were organizing themselves nationally, setting strategy, and nominating candidates. The complexity and tension of these activities was evident in June when, at the UCRP's convention, which nominated Ricardo Balbin, a young man was shot and killed. At the Peronist party (Justicialista) meeting in the same month, two were wounded in a shoot-out, a scene repeated at Ezeira Airport in mid-August during a send-off of some Peronist leaders on a trip to Madrid.

Economy. The International Monetary Fund announced that Argentina's rate of inflation was the highest in the world. Wholesale prices increased over 55% during the first nine months of the year, and the parallel market rate of peso to U. S. dollar increased from about 10 to 1 to over 14 to 1 in

September. The unemployment rate continued high throughout the country.

Wheat production was estimated to be slightly higher than in 1971 (creating an increased exportable surplus), but the production and export of corn declined. Beef production remained constant and the sale of beef, the country's staple food, was banned on alternate weeks to spur exports and to take advantage of high world prices for beef and leather. The domestic meat industry was seriously depressed.

The failure of the Lanusse government to implement a consistent economic policy confused business circles. To pacify labor, Lanusse increased wages several times during the year but not enough to offset rising prices. Minister of Economy Cayetano Licciardo resigned on October 8, possibly in response to Lanusse's somewhat nationalist and populist policies.

In August the World Bank held up an $84 million loan to Argentina for refurbishing its railroads as leverage to force an increase in fares. Lanusse responded angrily that the bank could not dictate fare raises to Argentina. But some rates were increased several weeks later and it was announced in early September that the loan had gone through.

Domestic Unrest. Numerous disturbances erupted throughout the year in protest against rising prices and the government's economic policies. A 48-hour general strike was called by the powerful General Confederation of Labor (GCT) for February 29 and March 1. Some 5 million workers from 110 unions stayed away from their jobs, closing down an estimated 85% of the country's industry, commerce, and transportation.

The city of Mendoza was placed under a curfew on April 4 after violent clashes erupted between police and demonstrators protesting an 11% increase in electricity rates. The demonstrations coincided with a two-hour general strike that paralyzed the province of Mendoza. Conditions returned to normal only after President Lanusse went on television on April 7 to announce the suspension of electricity payments for January–April and the creation of a commission to overhaul the rate structure.

Protests against the government erupted into violence in several major cities in late June. In the provincial capital of Tucumán a strike by public employees, physicians, and teachers led to riots in which more than 100 persons were arrested. The

---

──────── **ARGENTINA • Information Highlights** ────────

Official Name: Argentine Republic.
Area: 1,072,158 square miles (2,776,889 sq km).
Population (1972 est.): 25,000,000. *Density,* 23 per square mile (9 per sq km). *Annual rate of increase,* 1.5%.
Chief Cities (1960 census): Buenos Aires, the capital, 2,972,-453 (1970 census); Rosario, 591,428; Córdoba, 586,015.
Government: *Head of state,* Alejandro Lanusse, president (took office March 1971). *Head of government,* Alejandro Lanusse. *Legislature*—National Congress (suspended 1966).
Language: Spanish (official).
Education: *Expenditure* (1969), 2% of gross national product. *School enrollment* (1969)—primary, 3,354,587; secondary, 924,806; technical/vocational, 519,079; university/higher, 271,496.
Monetary Unit: Peso (5 pesos equal U. S.$1, Sept. 1972).
Gross National Product (1971 est.): $26,100,000,000.
National Income per Person (1969): $914.
Economic Indexes: *Industrial production* (1971), 183 (1963 = 100); *agricultural production* (1971), 121 (1952–56 = 100); *consumer price index* (1971), 512 (1963 = 100).
Manufacturing (major products): Iron and steel, machinery, cement, meat, chemicals, petroleum products, motor vehicles.
Major Agricultural Products: Corn (ranks 3d among world producers, 1971), wheat, grapes, oats, barley, cattle, sheep.
Major Minerals: Petroleum, natural gas, coal, zinc ore, tungsten, manganese ore.
Foreign Trade (1971): *Exports,* $1,740,000,000 (chief exports, 1970—corn; wheat; hides and skins; meat). *Imports,* $1,869,000,000 (chief imports, 1969—nonelectrical machinery; iron and steel; chemicals; mineral fuels and lubricants). *Chief trading partners* (1969)—Italy (took 14% of exports, supplied 7% of imports); United Kingdom (10%—6%); United States (9%—22%); Brazil (8%—11%).
Tourism: *Receipts* (1970), $77,000,000.
Transportation: *Motor vehicles* (1969), 2,019,100 (automobiles, 1,304,000); *railroads* (1970), 24,742 miles (39,817 km); *merchant fleet* (1971), 1,312,000 gross registered tons; *major national airline,* Aerolineas Argentinas.
Communications: *Telephones* (1971), 1,746,015; *television stations* (1971), 31; *television sets* (1971), 3,300,000; *radios* (1970), 9,000,000; *newspapers* (1970), 179.

---

strikers were soon joined by the local CGT and university students. Troops were sent to the city to restore calm.

Troops occupied the town of General Roca in the province of Río Negro on July 4 after residents occupied the municipal government building. The population had virtually seceded from Argentina in protest against the provincial and national governments whose authorities it refused to recognize.

Guerrillas. Guerrilla activity was widespread throughout the country in 1972, spurred by economic recession and political confusion. Two apparent guerrilla objectives were to force the military to cancel the elections and to discourage foreign investment. On March 21 guerrillas kidnapped Oberdan Sallustro, president of the Italian-owned Fiat automotive industries. Lanusse refused to meet guerrilla ransom demands, and Sallustro was killed on April 10, after the police had discovered where he was being held. On the same day Gen. Juan Carlos Sánchez, commander of the Second Army Corps in Rosario, was assassinated in reprisal for his anti-guerrilla campaign.

Guerrillas raided an army-run maximum security prison in southern Argentina on August 16, freeing a group of political prisoners. Ten of the rebels hijacked a jet at nearby Trelew Airport and demanded to be flown to Santiago, Chile. There they released the passengers and crew and surrendered to the police, asking for political asylum. On August 25 they were granted safe conduct to Cuba over the objections of the Argentine government, which then recalled its ambassador and suspended sales of meat to Chile.

The government recaptured 19 prisoners on the day of the prison break, and 16 of them were killed on August 22 while allegedly trying to escape. The news weekly *Primera Plana* was raided by security police on August 28 after it disputed the official version of the deaths of the guerrillas, stating that they had been murdered.

Foreign Affairs. President Lanusse visited Ecuador, Colombia, and Venezuela in January and February. The most important event in foreign affairs was his meeting in March with Brazilian President Gen. Emilio Garrastazú Médici in Rio de Janeiro. Relations between the two nations were outwardly normal and friendly, but the meetings were described as tense. Argentina was alarmed at Brazil's commercial expansion in Latin America.

JAMES R. LEVY
University of New South Wales

ARIZONA

Arizona's voters continued their strong support for the Republican party in the 1972 elections and made important changes in the state constitution.

Elections. Since Arizona is the only state that has voted Republican in every presidential election since 1948, there was no surprise when President Nixon carried the state by an almost two-to-one margin over Senator McGovern. Major interest centered on the contest for Arizona's new 4th Congressional District seat, awarded to the state following the 1970 census. Four Democrats and three Republicans conducted hard-fought and often bitter primary contests. State Senator John Conlin won the Republican nomination on a strongly conservative platform, and went on to defeat Democrat Jack Brown in November.

As expected, the three incumbent congressmen were all reelected without difficulty; Republicans John Rhodes and Sam Steiger and Democrat Morris Udall all won after relatively routine campaigns. Neither of Arizona's U. S. senators, Barry Goldwater and Paul Fannin, was up for reelection in 1972.

Republicans also continued their control of both houses of the Arizona legislature. Despite reapportionment, there was no change in the 18–12 Republican margin in the state Senate. In the House only 2 of the 60 seats changed hands, with Republicans increasing their margin from 36–24 to 38–22.

Voters approved a constitutional amendment replacing legislative apportionment provisions which had been declared invalid by federal court decisions. Under the amendment, the legislature is required to divide the state into 30 legislative districts, each of which will elect one senator and two representatives. Such a plan had been ordered into effect as a "temporary" measure by the federal court in 1966. While authorizing the Legislature to reapportion itself, voters vetoed a proposed increase in legislative salaries from $6,000 per year to $10,000. The proposed change was the first recommended by a salary commission that had been created in 1970 through approval of an amendment removing specific salary amounts from the constitution.

Also approved was a popularly initiated law requiring the state to share income tax revenue with the cities.

Environmental Concerns. Threatened closures of some mining and smelting facilities were averted in 1972, at least temporarily, by a tentative agreement

─────── **ARIZONA · Information Highlights** ───────

Area: 113,909 square miles (295,024 sq km).
Population (1970 census): 1,772,482. *Density:* 16 per sq mi.
Chief Cities (1970 census): Phoenix, the capital, 581,562; Tucson, 262,933; Scottsdale, 67,823; Tempe, 63,550; Mesa, 62,853; Glendale, 36,228; Yuma, 29,007.
Government (1972): *Chief Officers*—governor, Jack Williams (R); secy. of state, Wesley Bolin (D); atty. gen., Gary K. Nelson (R); treas., Ernest Garfield (R); supt. of public instruction, Weldon P. Shoftstall (R); chief justice, Jack D. H. Hays. *Legislature*—Senate, 30 members (18 Republicans, 12 Democrats); House of Representatives, 60 members (34 R, 26 D).
Education (1971–72): *Enrollment*—public elementary schools, 316,498 pupils, 14,185 teachers; public secondary, 185,014 pupils, 5,971 teachers; nonpublic schools (1970–71), 29,841 pupils, 1,160 teachers; college and university, 102,000 students. *Public school expenditures,* $358,441,000 ($853 per pupil). *Average teacher's salary,* $10,050.
State Finances (fiscal year 1970): *Revenues,* $875,902,000 (3% general sales tax and gross receipts taxes, $173,739,000; motor fuel tax, $64,974,000; federal funds, $187,748,000). *Expenditures,* $779,322,000 (education, $374,768,000; health, welfare, and safety, $65,057,000; highways, $126,307,000). *State debt,* $90,929,000 (June 30, 1970).
Personal Income (1971): $7,157,000,000; per capita, $3,871.
Public Assistance (1971): $48,580,000. *Average monthly payments* (Dec. 1971)—old-age assistance, $72.50; aid to families with dependent children, $119.83.
Labor Force: *Nonagricultural wage and salary earners* (July 1972), 623,200. *Average annual employment* (1971)—manufacturing, 89,000; trade, 133,000; government, 129,000; services, 98,000. *Insured unemployed* (Aug. 1972)—8,700 (2.1%).
Manufacturing (1969): *Value added by manufacture,* $1,275,100,000. Electrical equipment and supplies, $303,700,000; nonelectrical machinery, $194,100,000; primary metal industries, $175,400,000; food and kindred products, $105,100,000; stone, clay, and glass products, $66,800,000.
Agriculture (1970): *Cash farm income,* $695,320,000 (livestock, $373,417,000; crops, $269,953,000; government payments, $51,950,000). *Chief crops* (in order of value, 1971)—Cotton lint, lettuce, hay, wheat.
Mining (1970): *Production value,* $1,166,767,000 (ranks 5th among the states). *Chief minerals*—Copper, $1,059,277,000; molybdenum, $26,700,000; sand and gravel, $19,804,000; cement, value not available.
Transportation: *Roads* (1971), 44,185 miles (68,667 km); *motor vehicles* (1971), 1,093,312; *railroads* (1971), 2,053 miles (3,304 km); *public airports* (1972), 104.
Communications: *Telephones* (1972), 1,055,300; *television stations* (1971), 12; *radio stations* (1971), 76; *newspapers* (1972), 12 (daily circulation, 457,000).

on air quality standards between the state and the mining industry. The stringent air pollution regulations previously adopted were temporarily relaxed somewhat, and the mining industry agreed to multi-million-dollar expenditures for control of smelter emissions. The problems, however, were far from solution.

As the rapid growth of the state's population continued, creating a demand for more roads, environmentalists moved to a new front. They strongly opposed planned extensions of the freeway system in the Phoenix metropolitan area.

Indian Affairs. Although in sharp contrast to the urban-metropolitan problems of the Phoenix area, the conflict between two of Arizona's Indian tribes over sparsely populated land was equally difficult. The Hopi tribe alleged that the much more numerous Navajos had virtually monopolized a large joint-use area between respective reservations of the two tribes. In 1972, Arizona Congressman Sam Steiger introduced a bill in Congress to divide the disputed land between the tribes, but it died in committee and the controversy remained unresolved.

JOHN P. WHITE
Arizona State University

ARKANSAS

The year 1972 was a calm one in Arkansas. Significant changes proposed in the past were implemented, but there were few startling new developments or unexpected programs for reform.

Elections. The number of potential voters increased in 1972. The residence period for registering to vote was reduced to 20 days after a federal court declared unconstitutional the one-year state and six-month county residence requirements. Additionally, 18-year-olds received the franchise. But the new voters did not change past voting patterns or cause much excitement in the humdrum election campaigns. Liberals were disappointed when incumbent Sen. John L. McClellan defeated David Pryor, a U. S. representative, for the senatorial nomination in a Democratic runoff primary. As expected, Democrats won all elected state administrative offices, and President Richard M. Nixon captured the state's electoral votes, the first Republican to do so since 1872.

The 1971 reapportionment created some metropolitan legislative districts composed predominantly of blacks, and, for the first time since the 1890's, four blacks were elected to the General Assembly—three to the House and one to the Senate.

Legislature. With little controversy in a 10-day special session, the legislature passed most of the measures proposed by Gov. Dale L. Bumpers. A rebuttal assumption clause, permitting a person with more than a specified quantity of a dangerous drug to be accused of intending to sell it, was added to the revised Controlled Substance Act. The Eagleton Institute of Politics in its study of the state legislature made several recommendations for reform, suggesting annual sessions, more pay for legislators, improved bill-drafting and editing services, and fewer legislative committees.

Governor. Dale Bumpers strengthened the fiscal position of his administration, ending the year with the largest revenue surplus in the state's history. The state also paid the last of a 1941 $136 million bond issue refinancing highway indebtedness incurred during the Depression. A state attorney

general's opinion interpreted the 1972 Administrative Reorganization Act so as to increase gubernatorial management, budget, and housekeeping controls over many state agencies.

Civil Rights. The Arkansas Supreme Court reversed a contempt citation levied against a Texarkana newspaper editor who defied a circuit court order by publishing the verdict made in open court in a rape trial. The court also negated an order barring an integrated law firm, which had clashed with a circuit judge while representing blacks involved in an Arkadelphia racial disturbance, from practicing law in the judicial district. Progress in promoting racial harmony was mixed. A black boycott of white businesses in Marianna ended. But there was friction between blacks and whites in a number of schools and at some college athletic events.

Ecology. The state Pollution Control and Ecology Commission prohibited Hot Springs from authorizing additional sewer tie-ins or septic-tank installations until the city expanded its sewer treatment systems. The Ecology Department began enforcing state laws requiring municipalities to establish solid waste management systems. A federal court suit initiated by environmentalists halted the almost completed Army Engineer's 230-mile Cache River Bayou DeView channelization project.

WILLIAM C. NOLAN
Southern State College

ARMS CONTROL. See DISARMAMENT.
ARMY, U. S. See DEFENSE FORCES.

art

Henry Moore stands amid a collection of his work shown in Florence, Italy, in the summer of 1972. A total of 289 sculptures, drawings, and prints made up the largest exhibition of Moore's work ever mounted.

In 1972 the art world was quieter than it had been for many years. Although social involvement continued, protest demonstrations subsided. In spite of developments in some avant-garde areas, emphasis shifted from novelty to rediscoveries.

REDISCOVERIES AND RESTATEMENTS

Traditional and Early Modern American Art. Many major exhibitions of American painting, especially of the 19th century, were held. At the Whitney Museum (New York) a large selection of 18th and 19th century paintings was on view, as well as genre scenes and portraits by Eastman Johnson and the panoramic landscapes of Albert Bierstadt. The Brooklyn Museum mounted a series of interesting exhibitions—19th and 20th century American drawings; watercolors, prints, and drawings by Winslow Homer and Sargent; a Norman Rockwell retrospective; and A Century of American Illustration. The Metropolitan Museum (New York) displayed work by Whistler and Homer. Many New York galleries showed American masters: Homer (Wildenstein), Martin Heade and William Richards (Periodot-Washburn), Frank Duveneck (Chapellier), Walt Kuhn (Kennedy), John Marin (Marlborough), and Charles Burchfield (Raydon).

The most impressive exhibits appeared outside New York. The National Collection of Fine Arts (Washington) mounted National Parks and the American Landscape. The University of Michigan (Ann Arbor) offered Art and the Excited Spirit in 19th Century America. The Los Angeles County Museum of Art presented The American West.

American folk art also was prominent. Four American Primitives (ACA Galleries, New York) showed many *Peaceable Kingdoms* by Edward Hicks and works by "Grandma" Moses, John Kane, and Horace Pippin. Masterpieces of American Folk Art (Dintenfass), from the collection of the late Edith G. Halpert, included portraits, weathervanes, and trade signs.

Decorative Arts. An exhibition of Soviet arts and crafts toured Washington, Los Angeles, Minneapolis, Chicago, Boston, and New York (Metropolitan). The 1,500 items, the largest group ever sent abroad by the Soviet government, ranged from ancient Scythian gold ornaments to modern Soviet embroidery, tapestry, and ceramics.

A striking display of abstract Navajo blankets appeared in Los Angeles; Brooklyn; Houston; Kansas City, Mo.; and Hamburg, West Germany. Two of the largest exhibitions of the Museum of Modern Art (New York) were devoted to decorative arts—Italy, the New Domestic Landscape, with elegant furniture and other objects and "environments," and a survey of African textiles and decorative arts. Italian furniture and accessories of the 17th and 18th centuries were seen at the Metropolitan.

Photography. The most challenging photography shows were documentary. One exhibit revealed the spectacular deterioration of Italy's art treasures and landscape (Metropolitan). Another, Executive Order 9066 (Whitney), was devoted to the internment of Japanese-Americans in World War II.

THE AVANT-GARDE AND ABSTRACTION

Avant-garde efforts were divided between anti-object, process, and conceptual artists on the one hand and new realists on the other. Neither group was able to dispel a growing skepticism about the future of art. Abstract art, however, flourished.

Anti-object, Process, and Conceptual Art. Unusually vulgar or wasteful events in the area of anti-object art contributed to the malaise. At the Venice Biennale, a retarded child was displayed as an "artistic" curiosity, and 10,000 butterflies were hatched only to die in their plastic incubator before they could fly away. At the O. K. Harris Gallery (New York) ants could either be preserved or killed for a dime. At Rifle Gap, Colo., the $700,000 orange parachute-cloth *Valley Curtain* by Christo was reported "torn to ribbons" by the wind.

VALLEY CURTAIN *by Christo spans Rifle Gap in Colorado. It cost $700,000 and weighed 6 tons.*

There was, of course, some more interesting work in New York. Robert Morris' most complex sculpture (Castelli) consisted of electrified, oversized metal furniture on an earth-covered platform accompanied by a three-hour taped review of the artist's intentions, aesthetic theories, linguistic analysis, and other sounds.

Among other experimental shows were Joel Shapiro's clay and metal processes (Cooper) and Harold Lehr's floating water-filtering mechanisms called "eco-structures" (Sonraed). Still others were Kenneth Sonnier's film and videotape event, Bruce Nauman's "sound sculpture" (both Castelli), and Scott Burton's tableaux vivants demonstrating body language and territoriality (Whitney).

New Realism and Pop Art. New, or sharp-focus, realists, along with older Pop artists, whose commonplace subjects, impersonal techniques, and "cool" point of view the new realists often share, have finally succeeded in reestablishing representation as a significant trend. In New York the new realists were well represented at the 40th Whitney Museum Annual, which included Philip Pearlstein, Alfred Leslie, and Richard Estes.

New realist works were also seen at the O. K. Harris Gallery, as for example, Kakagawa's large renditions of household items, John Fawcett's Mickey Mouse and McDonald hamburger themes, Richard Pettibone's collages of miniature facsimiles of paintings by Frank Stella and Andy Warhol, John de Andrea's nude couples cast from life, and Sig Rennel's rubber cars. Especially effective at O. K. Harris were paintings by Robert Bechtle and John Clem Clarke. Other new realists exhibited were Chuck Close (Bykert), Richard Estes (Stone), Philip Pearlstein (Frumkin), Don Eddy (French & Co.), and 28 painters and sculptors (Janis).

During 1972, Pop art was rarely exhibited in strength. There was, however, one exception—the James Rosenquist retrospective (Whitney), which displayed some of his largest and most powerful paintings, including the billboard-like 86-foot-long (26-meter) *F 111.*

Abstract Painting. New York exhibitions featuring relatively new materials and formats kept abstract painting in the public eye. At the Museum of Modern Art, Sam Gilliam presented color-stained canvases removed from the stretcher and draped like heavy curtains. Jo Baer used extremely deep stretchers around which she wrapped hard-edged color shapes (Lo Giudice). Larry Poons and Jules Olitski used gel additives to give rich textural effects to their stained and sprayed color fields (both at Rubin). Michael Balog treated layers of fiberglass and polyester resin with a sandblasting mechanism (Castelli), and Doug Sanderson painted on nylon previously bonded with latex to a wall (Cooper).

Masters of abstract expressionism were also shown in New York, notably Hans Hofmann (Metropolitan), Willem de Kooning (Janis), and Joan Mitchell (Jackson). American geometric abstractionists of the 1930's were surveyed at the Zabriskie Gallery. Other abstractionists shown were Milton Avery (Borgenicht), Gene Davis (Fischbach), Al Held (Emmerich), and Morris Louis (Emmerich). A Rothko restrospective was held at the National Museum of Modern Art in Paris.

Hilda Rebay, a former director of the Guggenheim Museum and a leading advocate of abstract painting, was honored indirectly by an exhibit of her favorite abstractionist, Rudolf Bauer (Hutton, New York), and directly in an "hommage" of 99 paintings by such masters as Kandinsky, Klee, Léger, and Moholy-Nagy (New Gallery, Bridgeport, Conn.).

Abstract and Other Avant-Garde Sculpture. Impressive New York exhibitions focused attention on the abstract sculpture of José de Rivera (Whitney), Eva Hesse, and John Chamberlain (both Guggenheim). Other significant exhibits included light sculpture by Stephen Antonakos (Fischbach), five steel pieces by Anthony Caro (Emmerich), glass boxes by Larry Bell (Pace), and cybernetic environments by Wen-Ying Tsai (Denise Rene). There were free-form shapes of "solid color" by Richard Van Buren (Cooper), kinetic pieces by Nicolas Schoffer (Denise Rene), and Kenneth Snelson's lightweight constructions of bamboo or brushed aluminum (Weber). Also on view were direct-welded pieces by Richard Stankiewicz (Zabriskie) and sheet-metal works by Edgar Negret (Bonino).

RETROSPECTIVES AND OTHER EXHIBITS

Old Masters. The first full retrospective was given to the 17th century French painter Georges de La Tour (Orangerie, Paris). Dutch Masterpieces from the 18th Century (Philadelphia, Minneapolis, and Toledo) surveyed a little-known period of Dutch art. Consistently outstanding were exhibitions at the Morgan Library (New York)—illuminated pages and color transparencies in French Painting in the Time of Jean de Berry, 1350–1450; English Drawings and Watercolors from the Mellon Collection; and Dutch Genre Drawings.

Modern European Masters. To celebrate the 90th birthday (Oct. 25, 1971) of the grand master of modern painting, Picasso, the Museum of Modern Art placed on view all its Picassos, resulting in one of the best exhibitions of 1972. The Guggenheim not only devoted a major exhibit to the paintings of the pioneer abstractionist Wassily Kandinsky, but gave his light-sound event of 1909, Yellow Sound, its American premier.

Picasso, Kandinsky, and other modern masters were also in an exhibit of 90 early modern works

SOVIET
EXHIBIT

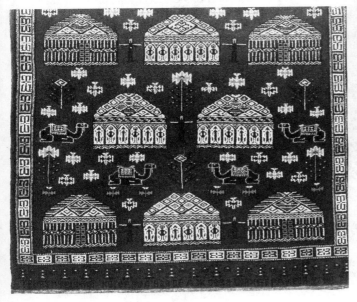

Soviet-sponsored art exhibit, on U. S. tour in 1972, included 17th century silver and enamel chalice (*top, left*); silver vase from the Armenian Republic (*top, right*); a 3000 B. C. silver bull (*center*); 18th century majolica jug (*above*); and modern carpet (*left*).

Living room of a 1915 Frank Lloyd Wright house in Wayzata, Minn., was set up in the Metropolitan Museum in 1972.

from the Philadelphia Museum of Art seen at the Museum of Modern Art. Modern Europeans seen elsewhere in New York were Giorgio de Chirico (New York Cultural Center), Max Ernst (Iolas), Emil Nolde (Sabarsky), Paula Modersohn-Becker (La Boetie), and Jean Dubuffet (Pace).

Modern European Sculptors. Four of the most important sculptors associated with early 20th century movements were exhibited: the German expressionist Wilhelm Lehmbruck (National Gallery, Washington), the Fauvist Henri Matisse (Museum of Modern Art), the abstractionist Jean Arp, and the cubist Jacques Lipchitz (both Metropolitan). The Lipchitz exhibit used new display techniques—videotape talks by the sculptor and computer-assisted question-and-answer sessions—to give the viewer greater insight into the creative process.

A major exhibition was that of Henry Moore. The huge, flowing forms of his sculptures showed to great advantage in the Fortezza di Belvedere, a 16th century former fortress overlooking Florence.

Universities. Exhibitions at university art museums have become important on the art scene. Among the best were American Art at Harvard (Fogg Art Museum), the American Landscape (Boston University Gallery), the first full survey of the 16th century engravings of Hendrik Goltzius (University of Connecticut), the photography of Edward Muybridge (Stanford University), and the graphic works of Mel Ramos (University of Utah).

Women's Art. Women's art exhibitions took their place next to black art shows as a new way to communicate social as well as aesthetic issues. Both coincided in Twenty Black Woman Artists at Mount Holyoke College. At Vassar College, the White Marmorean Flock presented a group of American woman neoclassical sculptors who worked in 19th century Rome. New York exhibitions demonstrated the work of woman abstractionists (Prince Street Gallery), the various roles of women in the arts (Com-

munity Church Gallery), and the wide-ranging stylistic and technical capabilities of women (Women's Interart Center). In Europe the work of 47 American women was shown at the Kunsthaus, Hamburg.

Non-Western Art. Fifty pages from a beautifully illuminated 16th century manuscript of the Persian Shah-nameh (Book of Kings) were displayed at the Metropolitan. Other Persian art treasures were shown at the New York Cultural Center. Buddhist sculptures and sketchily ink-brushed paintings by the scholar masters of the Japanese Nanga school were shown at Asia House (New York), and Chinese calligraphy was exhibited at the Metropolitan. For the Olympic Games in Munich, nearly 3,000 objects were displayed at the House of Art to document Asian, African, Oceanic, and pre-Columbian influence on European art.

MUSEUMS AND COLLECTIONS

New Museums and Additions. Several new museums in Texas were opened or enlarged: the Amarillo Art Center, new wings for the Houston Museum of Fine Arts and the Corpus Christi Art Museum, and the Kimbell Art Museum in Fort Worth. Mount Holyoke received a new building for its art collection, and the University of California (Los Angeles) will double the size of its museum.

Grants. The National Endowment for the Arts made 69 grants totaling $1.19 million to help museums with preservation. Among the recipients were the Joslyn Liberal Arts Society, Omaha ($272,156), and the Art Institute of Chicago ($112,430), both for air-conditioning and humidity control, and the California Palace of the Legion of Honor in San Francisco ($100,000) for a security system.

Acquisitions and Sales. The Metropolitan received Goya's $2–$3 million portrait of a boy as a gift from Mrs. Umberto de Martini. It purchased Frank Lloyd Wright's Francis W. Little House (Wayzata, Minn.), planning to install its 55-foot

(17-meter) living room with original furnishings. The National Gallery received a multimillion dollar gift of 22 paintings from the W. Averell Harriman Foundation. Included were works by Picasso, Cézanne, Monet, and Gauguin. Joseph H. Hirshhorn gave the uncompleted Hirshhorn Museum (Washington) 326 works, valued at $7 million, in addition to his original donation of art valued at more than $25 million.

Picasso gave the Museum of Modern Art a wire maquette (1928), which will be realized according to his original concept as a monumental steel construction at least 15 feet (4.5 meters) high. The Toledo Museum of Art bought Frank Stella's huge *Lac Laronge IV*. As a gift from the Joseph and Helen Regenstein Foundation, the Art Institute of Chicago acquired nine drawings of the 18th century Venetian painter G. B. Piazetta. The Metropolitan was criticized for selling privately four works by Van Gogh, Rousseau, Modigliani, and Gris.

Vandalism and Thefts. Museum officials were taking more precautions than ever before to protect masterworks from theft and vandalism. In an unusual act of vandalism, a deranged man swung a hammer at Michelangelo's marble *Pietà* in St. Peter's

GOYA PAINTING valued at between $2 million and $3 million was a gift to the Metropolitan Museum.

UPI

MICHELANGELO'S Pietà in St. Peter's Basilica, Rome, was badly damaged on May 21 when a fanatic attacked it with a hammer. The masterpiece has been restored.

Basilica. His blows knocked off the Madonna's nose, smashed her left eye, and severed her left arm. The masterpiece was repaired. At the Worcester Art Museum, thieves shot a guard and stole a Rembrandt, a Picasso, and two Gauguins. Guards were also injured at the Montreal Museum of Art when robbers stole 39 works, including paintings by Rembrandt, Bruegel, Courbet, and Delacroix. In Venice, police recovered 61 stolen paintings, among them 17 works from the Peggy Guggenheim Collection.

Auctions. In competition with Americans, Japanese were heavy buyers in 1972, especially of Oriental art. The prices of Japanese prints soared as a Japanese collector paid a record $37,000 for Utamaro's famous print of Ohisa. Sales from just three auctions of Oriental art at Parke-Bernet in New York totaled $1.57 million. Oriental art also set the record for work other than painting at Christie's in London—$573,300 for a rare 14th century Chinese wine jar. The record for sculpture by a living artist was set by Henry Moore's wood reclining figure ($260,000), and for Modigliani by a painting ($282,900) and a bust ($177,000). Ernst Barlach's wood *Schwertzieher* ($110,000) set a record for modern German sculpture.

AWARDS, HONORS, AND GRANTS

Guggenheim fellowships went to artists Mel Bochner, Robert Goodnough, Lester Johnson, Alex Katz, Dennis Oppenheim, and others. The American Academy and National Institute of Arts and Letters awarded Clyfford Still the Medal of Merit for painting. Elected to the Academy were Isabel Bishop and Isamu Noguchi, and to the Institute, Romare Bearden, Adolph Gottlieb, Philip Guston, and Richard Lindner. Altman prizes of $2,500 each were awarded by the National Academy of Design to John Hultberg and Gregorio Prestopino. The Art Dealers Association of America gave its first annual award for art history to Alfred H. Barr, Jr.

OBITUARIES

Among notables in the art world who died in 1972 were Franz Masereel (83), a Belgian printmaker and illustrator, and Francisco Javier Sánchez-Cantón (80), a leading Spanish art authority and former director of the Prado.

VICTOR H. MIESEL
University of Michigan

GOKSIN SIPAHIOGLU/JOCELYNE BENZAKIN

ASIA

South Vietnamese schoolchildren exhibit one of the many free flags distributed by Saigon officials in a government attempt to demonstrate national unity as it neared an eventual cease-fire with North Vietnam.

In 1972 there were several developments in Asia that were likely to alter the pattern of Asia's international structure for at least a generation: the birth of a more self-reliant Japan; negotiations aimed at the complete withdrawal of the United States from military engagement in Vietnam; and China's establishment of diplomatic and trade ties throughout the world. Other fundamental trends continued from the past: the birthrate was slightly reduced, but it nevertheless remained on a collision course with available resources; and the drive for economic development continued, more than ever guided by authoritarian and socialist principles.

A SHIFT IN THE POWER STRUCTURE

When Britain, France, and the Dutch withdrew from Asia after World War II, Asia fell under the dominance of the USSR and the United States. But in time China's military buildup modified this situation. A further modification began in 1971. Burdened with a highly unfavorable balance of trade with Japan, the U. S. government abruptly announced an important surcharge and then forced Japan, with others, to revalue its currency and limit its exports to the United States.

President Nixon's visit to China in February 1972 was planned without prior announcement to the Japanese. Japanese leaders began to wonder about the wisdom of trying to coordinate their policy with that of the United States. At mid-year Premier Eisaku Sato resigned, and instead of replacing him with his loyal aristocratic protégé, Takeo Fukuda, the Liberal Democratic party chose the aggressive,

independent Kukuei Tanaka as their new leader. In a month, Premier Tanaka announced his own trip to China without the usual prior consultation with the United States. That visit resulted in an agreement to establish diplomatic relations with China. Tanaka also drove a hard bargain at the Honolulu meeting with Nixon in September when, instead of agreeing to a major step to redress America's $3.9 billion trade deficit, he consented only to the quicker purchase of various goods valued at a little over $1 billion. The special relationship between these two Pacific powers had ended as Japan planned to spend twice as much on arms in the coming five years as it had in the past five.

Meanwhile, U. S. ability to influence Asian events by force appeared limited. Not even President Nixon's massive year-end bombing of North Vietnam was expected to produce a respectful or decisive victory in America's longest war. In the immediate future, it appeared that dominance in Asia could be achieved by the use of financial resources, and in this respect Japan presented itself as a powerful and independent competitor. Whether in terms of aid or trade, Japan matched the United States in providing financial rewards for other Asian nations. In 1970, Japan dispensed $1.8 billion in aid, mostly to other Asian nations. The United States gave $1.9 billion in that year. But Japan's contribution rose through 1972 whereas America's did not.

The Soviet Union consolidated its own influence in Asia by signing a treaty of friendship and cooperation with Iraq, a treaty similar to that signed with India the year before. Its position in the sub-

continent and in North Vietnam was as prestigious as ever.

In spite of the huge oil resources in West Asia, the people there were too divided to exert significant influence over the rest of the continent.

Pakistan had been divided the year before, and Indonesia was far too weak economically to exert significant influence on the actions of other Asians. India, one of the two population giants of the world, had a popular stable government and a slowly growing economy, but it was still too weak economically to play a strong role in Asia. Its trade was about 10% that of Japan, and its aid program was confined to its immediate neighbors, such as Bangladesh, Nepal, and Bhutan. In 1971 its army had defeated Pakistan, proving its capacity for effective regional action. But it possessed only a small navy, and no long-range air force or missiles.

On the other hand, China was on the brink of becoming a major military power. It had nuclear warheads, a few dozen short-range missiles, some missiles with a 2,500–3,500-mile (4,500–5,600-km) range, and over 4,000 planes. China's aid program was larger than that of the USSR, although over half of that was going to build the Zambia-Tanzania railway. Its previous military successes in Tibet and along its borders with the Soviet Union and India gave it an aura of invincibility.

However, China had a minuscule navy and much of its expensive army was tied down defending its border with the Soviet Union. Its trade with the rest of the world was only slightly larger than that of India—less than $5 billion worth of exports and imports as compared with Japan's $40 billion. And in spite of new trade prospects, China faced an imminent foreign currency shortage. Also, China had a history of governmental instability and erratic policy decisions. The Cultural Revolution damaged the governing apparatus to such a degree that the army had to govern much of the country. In 1972, Mao Tse-tung revealed that his protégé, Gen. Lin Piao, had actually tried to assassinate him before his fatal escape trip in September 1971.

Mao appeared to be ill and politically much weaker in 1972. At least 18 generals—professionals, not ideologues, who had put down the Red Guards —were reinstated during the year. So also were many civilian moderates who were close to Chou En-lai's position. Pragmatic politics may have returned, but respect for and confidence in China were lacking. Japan was more reliable and could provide more economically.

Two world powers—the United States and the Soviet Union—and two continental powers—Japan and China—dominated Asia. After the events of 1972 there was little reason to suppose that Japan would follow U. S. policy; highly skilled diplomacy might at best keep the estrangement from widening.

INCREASE IN AUTHORITARIANISM

There were few victories for democracy in Asia in 1972. Philippine democratic institutions were set aside after they had been tried for 27 years. Desperation over the corruption and ineffectiveness of the government was so great that by July an organization that wanted to exchange independence for U. S. statehood claimed the support of over 6 million people. In October, after a couple of suspiciously inept bombings and a strangely ineffective assassination attempt against a lesser government official, President Marcos declared martial law, claiming that Communist guerrillas, corruption, and a faulty governmental structure made the action necessary. He threw 40 opposition leaders in jail and closed all government offices and newspapers for a few days. Some felt that these actions stemmed from the fact that under the constitution he would have to relinquish the presidency in 1973. Following this, Marcos announced land and other reforms and promised eventually to present a new democratic structure.

At about the same time, Chung Hee Park of South Korea, whose term of office was also to end soon, imposed a tougher martial law than he had done the year before. The assembly was dissolved and all parties banned. In November he called for a vote on a new constitution that would prohibit all opposition and legitimize his authoritarian leadership. With the entire bureaucracy putting pressure on every village head, the vote was over 90% in favor.

The withdrawal of U. S. troops from South Vietnam encouraged President Thieu to tighten his hold over South Vietnam. In an unusual Special Senate session in June, with the speaker absent investigating the charge that opposition members were being barred from entering, the Senate passed a measure giving Thieu decree power in the fields of economy, defense, and security. A new press code ordered each

HONG KONG MUDSLIDE on June 19 swept over three Victoria Peak buildings and damaged an unoccupied fourth, taking a number of lives.

UPI

daily newspaper to deposit 20 million piasters, which would not be returned if "false" stories were written.

Authoritarianism was also maintained in many other Asian countries in 1972. In Thailand, Field Marshal Thanom Kittikachorn imprisoned three former members of Parliament for 10 years because they had lodged a suit of unconstitutionality in the courts against him for his dissolution of Parliament in 1971. He also had his term extended again, due to "Communist threats." Gen. Lon Nol proclaimed himself the first president of Cambodia as well as premier and commander in chief, after holding an election in which some of his biggest majorities strangely came from known Communist strongholds. In Nepal, newly crowned King Birendra had three former premiers and three assistant ministers jailed, while suspending others from Parliament. The powerful role of the military in Turkey was again demonstrated. After Dr. Nihat Erim's resignation, a cabinet led by Ferit Melen was selected by the Assembly, but only after reform-minded generals had rejected another premier.

Nor did free institutions fare well in many countries with liberal regimes. India held elections in most of its states, elections in which Indira Gandhi's Congress party generally won overwhelming victories. Yet the government imposed a 10-page limit on all dailies as a mild control over the influence of big business houses who published the most widely read newspapers. The Sri Lanka (Ceylon) Parliament passed a Press Council Bill that allowed the imposition of a 5,000 rupee fine or seven years in jail if a newspaper published without approval anything about a cabinet decision under consideration.

Sheikh Mujibur Rahman's government in Bangladesh imposed a ban on five "anti-Indian" weeklies, and jailed two editors. Zulfikar Ali Bhutto closed four more dailies in Pakistan for "abusive language," and jailed the editor of *Dawn,* the nation's top English newspaper.

SOCIALIST ECONOMIES

A trend toward the socialization of economic structures was particularly evident in South Asia in 1972, somewhat less evident in West Asia. The economic structures of East Asia changed relatively little. Through the Organization for Petroleum Exporting Countries, the oil-producing countries of West Asia not only secured higher payments from the West but also a greater degree of ownership for themselves. Bangladesh nationalized all domestically owned banks and insurance firms, as well as all jute, textile, and sugar mills. Pakistan nationalized all of its major industries in January. Burma nationalized 69 industries, and renamed the country: The Socialist Republic of Burma. Sri Lanka (Ceylon) also transformed itself into a "Democratic Socialist Republic," nationalized the graphite mines, and imposed an income ceiling of 2,000 rupees per month. Mild moves to the left took place in New Zealand and Australia, where their labor parties won electoral victories over more conservative parties. In Australia the Conservatives had been in power for 23 years; New Zealand's National party had held control for 12 years.

The socialist impetus seemed to be the strongest in the former British states, whose leaders had been impressed with Fabian Socialist ideology. The

CAMBODIA'S LON NOL (seated, center) *receives the acclaim of gathered officials on March 14 after ending parliamentary rule and swearing himself in as president, commander in chief, and president of Council of Ministers.*

UPI

former French, Dutch (Indonesia), and U. S. colonies (the Philippines) were content to leave most of their economies in private hands, as were the former British colonies where the Chinese controlled most of the private capital (Singapore and Malaysia).

ECONOMIC DEVELOPMENT

No overall figures for national growth were available for 1972, but many governments announced their 1971 growth during the year. The pattern was diverse. A few experienced phenomenal growth: Iran claimed a growth rate of 20% and to top it off discovered another major oil field during 1972. Singapore had a 14% increase in GNP in 1971, down a little from the previous year's 17% but equal to the growth rate since 1966. The Vietnam War may have hurt some of its growth, but significant capital was coming in from Hong Kong and Taiwan following the U. S.-Chinese détente. UN experts placed China's growth rate at 10%, a little above its average rate for the past decade. The Republic of China (Taiwan) and South Korea also announced growth rates of around 10%. Turkey, Saudi Arabia and Mongolia increased their production 9%. Japan and Indonesia experienced a respectable 7% increase, but Indonesia faced serious drought in 1972. Economic stagnation also followed a 6.5% increase in GNP in the Philippines in 1971.

Growth elsewhere was less impressive. India's growth rate fell to less than 5%, as the industrial sector declined. India experienced a poor monsoon in 1972 that cut its agricultural output by one third. The economies of Thailand, Sri Lanka, and Burma were stagnant, and the splitting of Pakistan produced particularly adverse economic consequences in Bangladesh.

Except for Israel, Lebanon, Turkey, and Cyprus, the West Asian economies again largely followed the fortunes of oil production. East Asia generally maintained its higher growth rates, but the opening of China troubled some countries who feared China's trade with the West in light consumer goods could undercut their own.

Such trade with the developed countries was becoming more important rather than less. At the 1972 meeting of ASEAN (the Association for South East Asian Nations, which includes Indonesia, the Philippines, Thailand, Malaysia, and Singapore) it was announced that although total trade with each other had increased from $1.7 billion to $2.1 billion between 1966 and 1970, the proportion of intra-organizational trade to the total trade of the countries had declined from 18% to 15%. And India announced a crash program by its Trade Development Authority to promote exports to the United States before China got the market. In the meantime, the economy of Asia was a little better off in 1972 than it had been before.

OUTLOOK FOR PEACE AND STABILITY

The year 1972 was not one of great international conflict, although some serious troubles persisted. Border skirmishes on the Israeli border with Syria and Lebanon continued for much of the year, as did terrorism toward Israelis—on international air flights, through the mails, and at the Olympics. The two Yemens came to a peaceful agreement after supporting insurgent activity in each other's territory.

In South Asia, India and Pakistan settled their borders, in dispute after the previous year's war, but little progress was made in exchanging prisoners or citizens between Pakistan and Bangladesh. China was still making things difficult for the Soviet Union. It abruptly broke off talks again over navigation on their disputed boundary rivers, and it prohibited Soviet ships from using their ports after the Haiphong harbor was mined—although other East European ships were allowed in. The Soviet Union added to its already extensive army along the border. Yet there were also signs of mellowing. China's new atlas, the first since the Cultural Revolution, no longer claimed for China 580,000 square miles (1.5 million sq km) of land taken by the czar, and in August China quietly signed a new trade agreement with the Soviet Union worth 240 million rubles—70% more than in the previous year's agreement.

Tension arose surprisingly in the Malacca Straits. Indonesia asked that warships going through the straits give prior notice, and Malaysia quickly agreed that they should not be treated as an international waterway. To avoid oil spills, it was suggested that very heavy oil tankers should go south of Java and Sumatra since the Malacca channel was dangerously shallow. With world prices for Malaysia's tin and rubber down, a Malaysian cabinet minister proposed a straits levy. China supported this idea, but the major maritime nations objected. Relations between Malaysia and Singapore became more cordial as Lee Kwan Yew made his first trip to Malaysia since their break five years before.

After engaging in the heaviest bombing of the war, the mining of North Vietnamese harbors, and helping to fight off a major offensive by Vietcong forces in the spring, the United States nearly completed its pull-out of American troops from Vietnam. Much of the Air Force was transferred to bases in Thailand, and President Thieu's government was supplied with enough planes to make South Vietnam's air force the fourth largest in the world. There was no certainty that the fighting would end if there were a cease-fire. The Vietcong seemed as angry about the proposed agreement as President Thieu. The political side of the proposal seemed most fragile—papering over differences rather than settling them. For millions of Vietnamese, 1972 had been another tragic year, and even if U. S. and North Vietnamese forces withdrew, they had reason to believe that the conflict would probably go on as a bloody, agonizing local conflict.

Each portion of the continent had different priorities in 1972. In much of West Asia the protection of Muslims was still a great concern. Several western Asian nations set up a delegation to promote better relations between their Muslim brothers in Pakistan and Bangladesh, but Bangladesh rejected the mission. Another delegation was sent to the distant Philippines to investigate reports of repression of Muslims in Mindanao. The Arab governments, save those of Jordan and Lebanon, continued to support the Palestinian liberation movement.

Egalitarian and populist values turned South Asian governments toward socialization. In East Asia, China and its neighbors spent considerable time normalizing relations with each other—usually at the expense of Taiwan. East Asia also generally exhibited the greatest concern for increasing overall economic production. However, 1972's most portentous trend seemed to be Japan's determination to free itself from subservience to the foreign policy of the United States.

RALPH C. MEYER
Fordham University at Lincoln Center

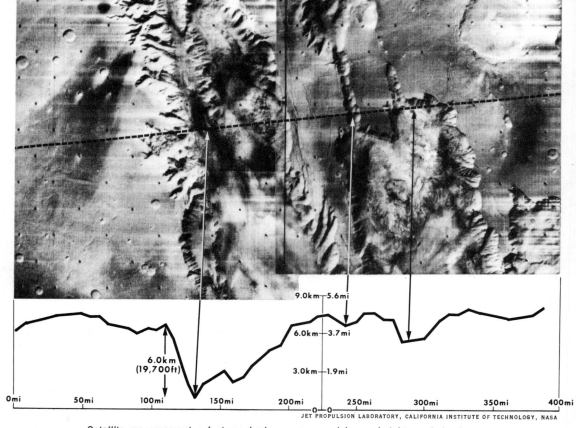

9.0km — 5.6mi
6.0km — 3.7mi
6.0km
(19,700ft)
3.0km — 1.9mi

0mi   50mi   100mi   150mi   200mi   250mi   300mi   350mi   400mi
0—0
JET PROPULSION LABORATORY, CALIFORNIA INSTITUTE OF TECHNOLOGY, NASA

Satellite measurements of atmospheric pressure and hence heights and depths on Mars revealed the great ruggedness of the surface, seen in profile at bottom.

astronomy

Significant new data were obtained in 1972 on the moon, the sun, other members of the solar system, distant celestial objects, and the interstellar medium. Some possible sites of "black holes" were suggested by astronomers. A large orbiting observatory was launched, and the Pioneer 10 space probe was sent toward the planet Jupiter.

Moon. The Apollo 16 and Apollo 17 flights in 1972 marked the end of that program of manned exploration of the moon. (See SPACE EXPLORATION.) Apollo flights have revealed a chemical difference between the lunar highlands and the maria, or "sea." The highlands are generally regarded as the original —although badly mauled—crust of the moon. Some maria are areas that were melted by the impact of very large bodies, while others were flooded by lava. Perhaps because of a kind of gravitational focusing produced by the earth, the bombardment that produced many maria was heavier on the earth-facing side of the moon, whereas the far side is almost exclusively highlands and is 1.2 to 2.4 miles (2–4 km) higher than the average lunar radius. The maria are rich in magnesium and have a low aluminum-silicon ratio, while the highlands consist primarily of a mineral called anorthosite. Rocks of a similar composition have been found in western Greenland and appear to be very ancient.

Sun. The solar eclipse of July 10 that passed over northern Canada was widely observed by many professional and amateur astronomers. The next total eclipse, on June 30, 1973, is over Africa.

Despite the fact that the sun was near the minimum of its cycle of activity in 1972, prominent flares occurred on August 2 and 7. The latter event produced copious amounts of X rays and radio waves, resulting in auroras and radio disturbances on earth.

Important information on the "solar wind" of particles streaming outward from the sun was secured by two space probes. At a distance of 71 million miles (114 million km), Pioneer 9 measured a solar wind velocity of 620 miles (998 km) per second, the highest recorded. However, the wind had slowed to 300 miles (483 km) per second by the time it had reached Pioneer 10, at a distance of 210 million miles (338 million km) from the sun. In the meantime, however, the temperature of the gas had risen from 100,000° K (180,000° F) to 2,000,000° K (3,600,000° F), and the magnetic field of the wind had increased by 100 times.

An experiment by Raymond Davis, Jr., of Brookhaven National Laboratory, in which he attempted to detect solar neutrinos by means of a tank of cleaning fluid placed deep in a South Dakota mine, revealed no neutrinos. The result cannot be accounted for by juggling theoretical models of the sun, and it may require the suggestion that neutrinos have a lifetime of less than the 500 seconds needed for them to reach the earth from the sun.

Venus. The Soviet probe Venera 8 landed on the sunward side of Venus on July 22 and relayed back data for about 50 minutes. It revealed that surface rocks at the landing site had a composition

resembling granite. The surface temperature was 470° C (878° F), and the pressure was 90 times that at sea level on earth. The atmosphere of Venus is 97% carbon dioxide, less than 1% water (in the cloud layers), 2% nitrogen, and less than 0.1% oxygen, with traces of other substances such as ammonia. Earth-based radar studies of the planet revealed a varied, rugged topography with mountainous regions 400 miles (640 km) long, including a peak about 2 miles (3.2 km) high.

Mars. Photographic and radar observations by the U. S. Mariner 9 probe that attained Martian orbit late in 1971 revealed the planet to be geologically dynamic. It is not quite like the moon, in spite of its craters, or like the earth. There appear to be several distinct geological areas representing different degrees of tectonic activity, wind erosion, and thermal action. These include ancient maria, heavily pocked with craters and somewhat similar to the lunar highlands; high, Tibetan-like plateaus; a region similar to an ocean basin, complete with volcanic structures similar to the Hawaiian chain on earth; narrow ravines simulating a water-eroded pattern, together with a great rift valley; and stratified polar regions that possibly were once glaciated. While some features resemble water-formed features on earth, water in liquid form does not exist on the surface of Mars.

Mariner 9 also investigated the Martian atmosphere and made infrared measurements of the surface of the planet. The polar caps were shown to be extremely thin layers of frozen carbon dioxide, possibly with some water content as well, and radio data suggested that permafrost may lie below the surface. Photographs of the Martian satellites, Deimos and Phobos, revealed them to be irregularly shaped, crater-pocked, evidently old objects locked in rotations synchronous with their revolution around Mars. The two Soviet probes that were also circling the planet indicated that Mars may have a weak magnetic field.

Outer Planets. New measurements of Jupiter's four largest satellites suggest lower densities than supposed, which indicates they may consist largely of snows. Titan has a much more extensive atmosphere than once thought, and it may have a snowy surface at a temperature as high as 150° K (−190° F), hidden under a cloud layer. Measurement of the infrared albedo of Uranus shows that it resembles that of Titan, Jupiter, and Saturn, which suggests that light is reflected from thin layers of methane crystals in the atmosphere of Uranus. The brightness temperatures of both Uranus and Neptune rise as radio waves penetrate deeper into their atmospheres, where the greenhouse effect is operative.

Stars. Two of the many interesting developments in stellar astronomy in 1972 are mentioned here. One concerns the S-type, or heavy-metal, stars that contain the unstable metal technetium, which has a half-life of about 200,000 years. Astronomers wondered what process could transport the metal from the interior to the surface of the star. It has now been suggested that protons from the hydrogen-rich interior can be swept outward to the region where the burning of helium has produced carbon 13, which in turn produces neutrons when it captures alpha particles. The neutrons are captured by iron atoms to form nuclei of elements of the zirconium group, particularly technetium. These heavy elements are then transported to the surface layers of the star by convection.

Another development was that several binary stars, including Algol and Beta Lyrae, were identified as radio stars by Robert M. Hjellming and C. M. Wade of the National Radio Astronomy Observatory. Material flows from one star to the other in these two-star systems, and in the process it presumably excites radio-frequency emissions.

Interstellar Matter. New molecules continue to be identified in interstellar space. The most recent discoveries are formaldimine (CH_2NH) and hydrogen sulfide (H_2S). The molecules are found in clouds that are enormously denser than the clouds of hydrogen found by 21-cm radiation, and they are always associated with grains of dust. The grains not only absorb ultraviolet radiation and preserve the molecules from dissociation, but also serve as catalysts in their production. It was shown experimentally how complex molecules can be formed in such clouds when the temperature of the gas is 100° K (−280° F) and that of the grains only 10° K (−441° F). The composition of the gas seems very similar to that of the solar system, suggesting that the interstellar medium has not changed greatly since the time when the solar system was formed.

It was once supposed that dust simply condensed from gas in interstellar space. Now there is much evidence that dust is formed in the outer envelopes of stars and blown into space. The ejected grains are probably silicates and various refractory substances that would condense first.

X-Ray Astronomy. The success of the Uhuru satellite in locating new X-ray sources since being launched on Dec. 12, 1970, has focused scientific attention on the processes that can generate X rays. These include thermal blackbody radiation; synchrotron radiation emitted by electrons moving in circular orbits in a magnetic field at speeds close to the velocity of light; the inverse Compton effect, when photons of non-X-ray wavelength collide with high-speed electrons and get shifted to the X-ray range; and thermal bremsstahlung, involving the acceleration of fast electrons in the electric fields of protons. Uhuru detected diffuse X-ray sources that lie in intergalactic space, extend for hundreds of thousands of light-years, and are about 100 billion times more luminous than the sun. Both the inverse Compton effect and thermal bremsstahlung have been invoked to explain these regions as hot gases, but this presents other problems.

Black Holes. It is theorized that very massive stars may eventually undergo complete gravitational collapse and become "black holes" in the universe, from which no radiation can escape. However, they would continue to have gravitational effects on other stars. Although no positive identifications are yet available, some serious candidates for black holes have been suggested in the past year or so. Included are the companions of binary stars such as Beta Lyrae or Epsilon Aurigae, various compact sources of high-energy radiation, and the center of the galactic system.

Problems in Cosmology. The large shift of lines toward the red in the spectra of faint galaxies has long been taken as a Doppler-effect indication of cosmological distances. However, two apparently normal galaxies may sometimes appear to be physically connected and yet have quite different red shifts. The objects known as quasars also remain a mystery. Are they really very luminous objects at great distances, or are they relatively close but endowed with some inexplicable source of red shift?

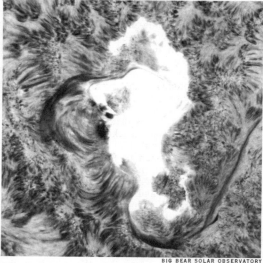

SOLAR FLARE, seen in detail in the lower picture, was one of several outbursts that occurred on the sun in August, affecting electrical transmissions on earth. The flares were unusual in that the sun is supposedly in a quieter phase of its cycle of magnetic activity.

French astronomers Jean-Claude Pecker and J. P. Vigier and the Australian A. P. Roberts have tried to explain anomalous red shifts as the result of frequency changes in low-temperature photons, the red shifts of the most remote objects then being explained as the result of the scattering of photons by the universal 3° K radiation.

Another major problem is that there does not seem to be enough mass in clusters of galaxies to keep them gravitationally bound. Furthermore, George Field of the University of California made a study indicating that there is not enough mass in the universe to keep it from expanding forever.

New Instruments. Pioneer 10, launched toward Jupiter on March 2, is studying the solar wind and magnetic fields en route and will make a detailed study of the atmosphere, temperature, spectrum, and charged-particle belts of the giant planet. The fourth and final Orbiting Astronomical Observatory,

called Copernicus, was launched on August 21. It carries an ultraviolet telescope, an X-ray detector, and a 32-inch (81.3-cm) reflecting telescope.

The Astronomy Committee of the National Academy of Sciences emphasized the importance of developing new observational techniques. Thus, while several enormous optical and radio telescopes are now under construction, the newer technique of aperture synthesis is represented by the hexagonal array of six 72-inch (183-cm) mirrors being erected in Arizona by the Smithsonian Astrophysical Observatory. The light from the six mirrors is brought to a detector at a single focus. As for telescope accessories, increasing emphasis is being placed on higher-sensitivity replacements for the photographic plate and improvements in image-tube systems.

LAWRENCE H. ALLER
University of California at Los Angeles

ATHENAGORAS I

Patriarch of Constantinople; b. Vassilikon, Epirus, Greece, March 25, 1886; d. Istanbul, Turkey, July 7, 1972.

The Eastern Orthodox Church has been virtually identified for most people in recent years with the person of Athenagoras I, Patriarch of Constantinople. The tall, bearded patriarch, who held the position of "first among equals" among bishops of the Orthodox faith, brought international attention to his church by his extensive ecumenical activities, which were climaxed by his historic meeting in Jerusalem with Pope Paul VI in 1964. It was the first such meeting in over 400 years between the leaders of the Orthodox and Roman Catholic churches, which have been officially separated since the 11th century.

Early Years. Athenagoras I was born in Vassilikon, Epirus, in northwestern Greece, the son of a physician, Matthew Spyrou, and was baptized with the name Aristocles. He graduated in 1910 from the theological school of the Patriarchate of Constantinople on the island of Halki, was ordained a deacon, and took Athenagoras as his ecclesiastical name. He served as archdeacon in the diocese of Pelagonia in Macedonia until 1918, when he transferred to the diocese of Athens.

Athenagoras was first secretary of the Holy Synod of the Church of Greece until 1922. In December of that year he was ordained a priest and one week later was consecrated a bishop and appointed Metropolitan of Corfu and Paxos.

Service in the New World. In 1931 the Holy Synod of the Patriarchate of Constantinople named Athenagoras archbishop of the Greek Orthodox Archdiocese of North and South America, an ecclesiastical jurisdiction assumed by the Church of Constantinople in 1922 following the breakdown of Orthodox Church unity in the New World because of the Russian Revolution. During his 18 years as archbishop of the Greek-American diocese, Athenagoras successfully unified the factious Greek Orthodox Church in America and created an efficient church organization with its own schools.

Patriarchate of Constantinople. Because of his pastoral, administrative, and diplomatic talents as well as such personal gifts as the ability to converse fluently in several languages, Athenagoras was the obvious choice of the Holy Synod of Constantinople in 1949 to assume the delicate and demanding post of archbishop of Constantinople and Ecumeni-

PARIS MATCH

ATHENAGORAS I (1886–1972)

cal Patriarch. The 21-year tenure of Athenagoras was marked by his struggle to preserve the prestige of the Church of Constantinople throughout the world and in the often hostile conditions of Turkey. He was successful largely because of his personal stature as a world leader in Christian ecumenism. Athenagoras favored his church's membership in the World Council of Churches and entered into direct relationship with all Christian churches. His ecumenical efforts were directed in particular to the Church of Rome. His personal meetings with Pope Paul VI in Jerusalem in 1964 and again in Istanbul and Rome in 1967 were symbolic of the hope for the eventual reconciliation of the two churches.

The ecumenical policies of Athenagoras were generally approved in his own church, but considerable dissent arose elsewhere, particularly in the Church of Greece, where some considered his actions to be contrary to the traditional Orthodox approach to Christian unity. Criticism was also leveled against the patriarch for his failure to bring about a council of the Orthodox Church that could confront the problems facing world Orthodoxy. Despite such controversy, Athenagoras was widely regarded as one of the most outstanding Orthodox leaders of the 20th century.

THOMAS HOPKO
St. Vladimir's Orthodox Theological Seminary

ATLANTA

A building boom highlighted the year 1972 in Atlanta. The city ended the year in the midst of a new school desegregation controversy and was awaiting the outcome of an attempt to rewrite the city charter for the first time since it was written in 1874.

Building Boom. Atlanta had experienced an unprecedented boom in construction in the 1960's, amid predictions of an even bigger boom in the 1970's. The new decade began quietly as Atlanta experienced in a mild form the inflation-recession economy of the rest of the nation, but in 1972 the boom arrived. The Henry Grady Hotel was torn down, and in its place construction began on what may be the world's largest hotel, a 70-story, $50 million structure being built by Portman Properties, Inc. Cousins Properties, Inc., began construction of a $65 million "multi-purpose megastructure" near its new $17 million, 16,000-seat sports emporium-coliseum. The latter is the home of the Atlanta Hawks professional basketball team and the Atlanta Flames, the professional hockey team that began play in 1972. The Hilton Hotel chain began construction on a $75 million hotel-office building-shopping area. And plans were completed for the $35 million World Congress Center, a world trade mart that will probably be financed through state taxes.

School Desegregation. Within a period of only a few weeks in 1972, the U. S. District Court in Atlanta declared Atlanta schools to be unitary and integrated, only to have the Circuit Court of Appeals in New Orleans overturn the ruling and order massive, total desegregation. The city was trying to work out an acceptable plan at year-end.

City Charter. Major components of a proposed new city charter include election of a portion of the city aldermen by districts rather than on a city-wide basis, and a total separation of the administrative and executive branches of city government. The City Charter Commission proposal was to be considered by the 1973 Georgia General Assembly.

Crime. On March 20, Atlantans got their first new chief of police in 25 years. John F. Inman was appointed to succeed the retiring Herbert T. Jenkins. Immediate changes included an internal "shakeup" and the formation of a "stake-out squad." Inman's chief rival for the chief's post, Clinton Chafin, was demoted from assistant chief to captain. The stake-out squad attempted to halt a rash of armed robberies. By year's end, four would-be robbers had been shot and killed by policemen hiding in back rooms of stores. Several others were injured and still others arrested without resistance.

During the Jenkins years, the chief and various mayors had held that vigilance on the part of police had kept the criminal syndicates out of Atlanta. Soon after taking office, Inman announced that there was evidence of organized crime in the city. Inman and Mayor Sam Massell charged that two brothers, Burton and Robert Wolcoff, who came to Atlanta from Chicago, had ties to organized crime. A grand jury found organized crime was seeking a foothold in Atlanta but so far had not made serious inroads.

Atlanta was named an "impact city" in 1972 and promised up to $20 million in federal funds to combat street crime. The money was to be used to reduce burglary and stranger-to-stranger crimes by 5% within two years and 20% within five years.

MARTA. The Metropolitan Atlanta Rapid Transit Authority (MARTA) continued planning to meet its 1980 deadline for a rapid transit system for Atlanta. MARTA took over the city's bus system in April, and reduced the fare from 40 to 15 cents.

GENE STEPHENS
Georgia State University

ATOMIC ENERGY. See ENERGY.

AUSTRALIA

Reflecting a major change in political mood, Australians voted the Australian Labor party into office in House of Representative elections on Dec. 2, 1972, ending the Liberal-Country party coalition's 23-year run of electoral successes. William McMahon, the prime minister since March 1971, resigned on December 5, turning the office over to 56-year-old Edward Gough Whitlam of the Labor party.

The election came at the close of a year of wage-price inflation and frequent industrial disputes, with slackness in the economy and higher unemployment—almost 2% at midyear. Labor played up the election slogan "It's time," and the new government immediately set about introducing changes in domestic and international policies.

Election Results. The Australian Labor party (ALP) won 67 of the 125 seats in the House, representing a solid majority for Whitlam, the first non-unionist to lead a Labor government in Australia's history. The ALP received 50% of the votes nationwide and was assisted by the Australia party's 2.3%, most of which flowed to the ALP as second-preference votes. The Liberal-Country parties polled 41.3%, and the Democratic Labor party (DLP) polled 5.1%. In the Senate, where elections were not held, the balance of power remained with the Democratic Labor party.

The change of government came after public opinion polls showed steady loss of support for the coalition led by Prime Minister McMahon. Feuds and dissension among Liberals contributed to the ineffectual performance, and McMahon failed in his efforts to bring the government back into favor.

The overall swing of 3% to the ALP showed that the electorate believed the handling of many pressing national problems called for more dynamic leadership. Whitlam promised positive action on unemployment, social welfare, education, and developmental and environmental issues and on blocking takeovers of Australian assets and resources by overseas companies. He also promised a more independent stance for Australia in international affairs. The Liberal-Country parties, on the other hand, pointed to their record of stability and stressed the value of traditional ties.

In reviewing the election result, a leading newspaper declared that the Liberals had been "too slow in adapting to changing trends in the community, particularly among young people." Election returns showed that the ALP made its principal gains—in some cases as much as 10% over 1969 figures—in Melbourne and Sydney suburban areas, where its policies clearly met the hopes and requirements of young homemakers.

Economy. It was a year of very slow economic improvement. Strong inflationary pressures and sluggish business activity dominated the first six months while the effect of the revaluation of the Australian dollar (in December 1971) was being absorbed. The budget, presented in August, provided some stimulus through income tax reductions and social security benefits. Retail sales picked up and building activity increased, but the improvement was spotty and automobile sales were slow.

─────── AUSTRALIA • Information Highlights ───────

Official Name: Commonwealth of Australia.
Area: 2,967,910 square miles (7,686,900 sq km).
Population (1972 est.): 13,000,000. *Density,* 5 per square mile (2 per sq km). *Annual rate of increase,* 1.9%.
Chief Cities (1971 census—metropolitan areas): Canberra, the capital, 156,334; Sydney, 2,717,069; Melbourne, 2,288,-941; Brisbane, 816,987; Adelaide, 809,466.
Government: *Head of state,* Elizabeth II, queen; represented by Sir Paul Hasluck, governor-general (took office April 1969). *Head of government,* Edward Gough Whitlam, prime minister (took office Dec. 1972). *Legislature*—Parliament: Senate, 60 members; House of Representatives, 125 members. *Major political parties*—Liberal party; Country party; Australian Labor party; Democratic Labor party.
Language: English (official).
Education: *Expenditure* (1967), 11.9% of total public expenditure. *School enrollment* (1968)—primary, 1,768,060; secondary, 1,080,524; technical/vocational, 189,985; university/higher, 164,528.
Monetary Unit: Australian dollar (0.8396 A. dollar equals U. S.$1, Sept. 1972).
Gross National Product (1971 est.): $34,400,000,000.
National Income per Person (1969): $2,434.
Economic Indexes: *Industrial production* (1970), 142 (1963=100); *agricultural production* (1971), 164 (1952–56=100); *consumer price index* (1971), 132 (1963=100).
Manufacturing (major products): Petroleum products, steel, meat, heavy machinery, chemicals, processed foods.
Major Agricultural Products: Wool (ranks 1st among world producers, 1971), barley, wheat, sheep, dairy products.
Major Minerals: Bauxite (ranks 2d among world producers, 1970), iron ore (world rank 4th, 1970), lead (world rank 3d, 1970), coal, petroleum, natural gas.
Foreign Trade (1971): *Exports,* $5,084,000,000 (chief exports—wool, wheat). *Imports,* $4,633,000,000 (chief imports, 1969—nonelectrical machinery, transport equipment, chemicals, textile yarn and fabrics). *Chief trading partners* (1969)—Japan (took 24% of exports, supplied 12% of imports); United States (14%—25%); United Kingdom (13%—22%).
Tourism: *Receipts* (1970), $105,000,000.
Transportation: *Motor vehicles* (1970), 4,870,000 (automobiles, 3,898,500); *railroads* (1970), 25,241 miles (40,620 km); *merchant fleet* (1971), 1,105,000 gross registered tons; *major national airline,* Qantas Airways.
Communications: *Telephones* (1971), 3,913,167; *television stations* (1971), 85; *newspapers* (1970), 58 (daily circulation, 4,028,000).

AUSTRALIA'S new prime minister, Gough Whitlam (right), at a nationally televised press conference in Canberra on December 5.

UPI

TENT CITY "embassy" was set up by young aborigines on the lawn of the Parliament building in Canberra to protest rejection of land claims.

Manufacturers were critical of the government's performance, and in spite of widespread prosperity, an air of caution prevailed. This attitude was translated into a record increase in savings in personal accounts.

In the fourth quarter the tempo of business improved, and investment plans were on the upturn. Interest rates eased, employment rose, and a slowing in the rate of price rises, combined with more buoyant sales, contributed to an improved outlook. By year-end, businessmen were confident of an early return to full employment and more efficient use of existing productive capacity. Stock exchange prices were up more than 25% over the year.

Returns from wool showed a strong rise during the year, with Japan the most active buyer. Other rural products sold well. Wheat stocks were cleared, and meat exports moved up sharply. Drought in some livestock raising areas was the only factor threatening immediate prospects.

Exports of minerals ran at a record rate, and as the international currency crisis subsided plans for further expansion went forward. A long-term agreement, signed with Japan, for supplying that country with uranium ore for peaceful uses was expected to result in large-scale exports in coming years. Meanwhile, Australia replaced the United States as the leading supplier of raw materials for Japan's iron and steel industry.

Australia's trading activities yielded a record surplus of over $1 billion in the fiscal year ending June 30. Imports remained close to the level of the preceding year, while exports were up strongly. Capital inflow was also running at record levels—some $2 billion for the year. The Whitlam government moved to halt take-overs of Australian companies by overseas interests as well as to change tariff procedures.

Defense and Foreign Affairs. Before the advent of the Labor government, foreign policy followed the establishment pattern of close identification with the ANZUS treaty nations (Australia, New Zealand, and the United States), SEATO (Southeast Asia Treaty Organization), and the ANZUK (Australia, New Zealand, and the United Kingdom) defense arrangement for Malaysia and Singapore.

In February, Indonesia's President Suharto visited Australia—the first Indonesia chief of state to do so. In June, Prime Minister McMahon visited Djakarta, where an economic aid program for Indonesia was signed, with Australia promising some $80 million over three years from mid-1973. The agreement followed a defense grant of about $20 million and a gift of aircraft and equipment to bolster Indonesia's air force.

In July a consultative committee on defense cooperation with New Zealand was set up. This was intended to be part of a review of the economic and defense objectives of the two nations.

Early in December, Prime Minister Whitlam began a reorientation of the country's international policies. Whitlam sought to move Australia toward "a more independent stance" and to lessen the emphasis on military pacts. By this time New Zealand also had elected a Labor government that had similar views.

Whitlam moved at once to establish normal diplomatic relations with China and gave Australia's support to the proposal within the United Nations for creation of a "peace zone" in the Indian Ocean. The ANZUS treaty remained basic to Australia's defense, and while underscoring its significance in this

RESCUING the injured after September 16 bomb explosion in a Sydney building housing a Yugoslav travel agency. Police sought link with Croatian nationalists.

context, Whitlam looked toward changes to maximize its importance as an instrument "for justice and peace and political, social, and economic advancement in the Pacific area."

Whitlam reaffirmed Australia's commitment to the granting of internal self-government to Papua New Guinea in 1973, full independence to follow when the government and the people seek it.

Aboriginal Rights. In January the government announced that it would not grant legal ownership of ancient tribal lands to Australia's aborigines because such a move "would lead to uncertainty and possible legal challenge to land titles throughout Australia." But to improve prospects for aborigines on reservations within the federally controlled Northern Territory, new land-tenure measures, including long-term leases, were introduced. A new type of general-purpose lease gave aborigines on reservations a 50-year title when it could be shown that reasonable economic and social use would be made of the land. In addition, the government declared its willingness to provide money to buy land outside reservations where aboriginal enterprises could be successfully established.

The Whitlam government went much further in support of aboriginal rights. By mid-December, in an action "demanded by the conscience of the Australian people," it had moved to give the aboriginal groups community title to tribal lands, as well as to mineral and timber rights.

The prime minister also announced reform of the white-administered aboriginal education system, with emphasis in the primary schools on instruction in the aboriginal tongue and in traditional arts and

skills so that the vanishing aboriginal culture may be preserved.

Major Public Works. Australia's biggest engineering project, the Snowy Mountains water conservation and hydroelectric undertaking in New South Wales, was completed in October, just 23 years after it began. The project is designed to store the water of swift coastal streams in the southeastern mountain knot and to turn it back through the ranges for use on the dry inland plains, while using the fall of the water to generate electricity. The total cost of the undertaking has been almost $1 billion, covering 16 large dams, 90 miles of tunnels, 50 miles of aqueducts, and 7 power stations.

The Ord River Dam, in Western Australia's rugged Carr Boyd Ranges, was completed in June. The high dam, located in the tropical northwestern part of the continent, holds back the largest man-made lake in Australia. The water is to be used for irrigating rich farmlands in the lower Ord Valley.

State Elections. A 6% swing to Labor in Tasmania's House of Assembly elections in April brought the party back to power with a 21–14 majority. Eric Reece, who was premier from 1958 to 1969, returned as premier. The Labor party now governs three states—Tasmania, Western Australia, and South Australia.

South Australia approved the vote for 18-year-olds, but a legal move to extend it to include voting in federal elections failed, the High Court holding that such a change could be made only by the federal parliament.

R. M. YOUNGER
Author, "Australia and the Australians"

AUSTRIA

For Austria, 1972 was a quiet year politically, following the elections of 1971.

Politics. With the clear Socialist majority gained in 1971, Chancellor Bruno Kreisky was able to steer a steady parliamentary course. In July an accord signed in 1971 with the Vatican went into effect. Under its terms the Austrian government agreed to pay 100% rather than 60% of the teachers' salaries in the country's nearly 100 Roman Catholic private schools. These schools account for about 10% of the Austrian education system.

A proposal to liberalize abortion aroused the opposition of the Catholic hierarchy. Nonetheless, the Socialist party congress overwhelmingly endorsed a resolution to legalize abortion, giving the pregnant woman the final decision, following consultation with medical and welfare experts.

The conservative People's party lost one of its stalwarts with the death, in July, of former Chancellor Alfons Gorbach (1961–64).

War Trials. In March, former SS officers Walter Dejaco and Karl Ertl were acquitted of murder and other criminal charges—the designing and building of gas chambers at Auschwitz—by a jury in a Vienna court. The verdict caused considerable unfavorable comment in the world press. Later, a jury also acquitted two other former SS officers, accused of torturing and murdering Jewish prisoners at Auschwitz. The further acquittal of former SS officer Johann Gogal, accused of torturing and murdering prisoners at the Nazi concentration camp at Mauthausen, led to demonstrations by the Jewish Defense League at the Austrian Embassy in Washington, D. C., in May. Former SS Capt. Franz

Novak, who had been Adolf Eichmann's chief transport officer, was sentenced to seven years' imprisonment by a Vienna court.

Economic Developments. Adjusted to account for inflation, the gross national product (GNP) rose 5% in 1971, a decline from the 7.8% increase of 1970. A severe drought cut agricultural production and also the generation of electricity. The first quarter of 1972 showed an annual GNP growth rate of 7.6% as compared with 6.5% for the same period in 1971. The main growth factor was domestic demand. In order to moderate the boom conditions, the Austrian National Bank increased its minimum reserve requirement by 1%.

Wages and salaries increased by 10.2% on the average in 1971, and the collective wage agreements largely concluded in April 1972 brought additional raises. In August 1971, total employment exceeded 2.5 million for the first time, and after a seasonal decline, this mark was reached again in June 1972. Foreign workers constituted 8.6% of those employed in industry at the end of 1971.

There were fewer strikes in 1971 than in any year since 1951 when the assembling of strike statistics began: 2,431 participants with a total loss of 29,614 hours. Consumer prices averaged 4.7% higher in 1971 than in 1970. Monthly trade figures for 1972 showed a slight increase over those of 1971, with imports expanding more than exports.

Foreign Affairs. In May, Peter Janowitsch, a veteran diplomat, presented his credentials as permanent representative of Austria to the United Na-

VISITING AUSTRIA en route to Moscow in May, U. S. President Nixon shakes hands with an Austrian child outside Klessheim Palace, near Salzburg.

UPI

tions. He succeeded Kurt Waldheim, who had become secretary general of the United Nations in January. Both Chancellor Kreisky and President Franz Jonas made official visits to various European capitals, primarily to seek support in the negotiation of an industrial free trade zone agreement with the European Economic Community (EEC) for Austria as well as three other neutrals—Switzerland, Sweden, and Finland. Austria is particularly concerned about favorable trade terms for paper, special steel, and ferrous alloys, and also some agricultural products. The attitude of the USSR toward such an agreement remains uncertain. There are some indications, however, that it has moderated its position on Austria's establishing trade ties with the EEC.

In May, a Czech emigré who had gone to the Austrian border to talk with his mother was shot by Czech guards, apparently on Austrian soil, and dragged into Czechoslovakia. The Austrian government announced that it would restrict its relations with Czechoslovakia to the absolute minimum, pending resolution of the incident.

In March, the United States, Britain, and France agreed to permit both Austrian Airlines and Scandinavian Airlines System to fly twice a week to and from Tegel air field in the French sector of West Berlin. This marks the first time since the end of World War II that non-Allied airlines have been allowed to land in West Berlin.

The Vienna Symphony Orchestra, led by Josef Krips, successfully toured the United States in February and March. In May, while en route to Moscow, President Nixon stopped in Salzburg, where he was entertained at luncheon by Chancellor Kreisky.

ERNST C. HELMREICH, *Bowdoin College*

AUTOMATION. See COMPUTERS.

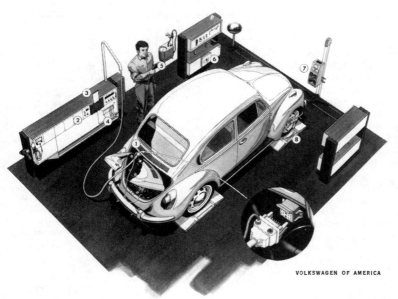

Computer Diagnosis, a new system built into all 1972 Volkswagens, cuts checkup times to about 20 minutes. The system plugs into a socket in the engine compartment, conducts a computerized program of more than 60 automatic and manual tests, and prints a diagnosis.

automobiles

United States automobile producers attained their third-highest production during the 1972 model year. A total of 8,589,049 cars was assembled, up 19% from the 1971 model year when a prolonged strike at General Motors held back volume. Only two previous model years were higher than 1972—1965 and 1966.

All of the Big Four auto makers posted production gains for the 1972 model year despite a host of government regulations. Prices and wages were under the control of federal agencies as a result of anti-inflation measures imposed by President Nixon in 1971. In addition, auto makers had to meet safety and exhaust-emission standards set by the government. For instance, a new seat belt and warning device had to be installed effective Jan. 1, 1972, and 1973 cars had to include new bumpers and flame-resistant interior fabrics, as required by the Department of Transportation. Also, 1973 cars were required to meet new exhaust-emission standards set by the Environmental Protection Agency.

1972 MODEL PRODUCTION

The 1972 model year saw the extension of a trend wherein standard-size and sports models lost ground not only to compacts and subcompacts but also to luxury models and medium-size cars.

General Motors (GM). GM surpassed its former record by producing 4,626,243 1972 cars, up 30% from 3,556,263 in strike-curtailed 1971 and 1.47% above GM's previous peak of 4,559,000 cars in 1965. GM raised its share of the overall production to 53.5%, compared with about 50% for 1971. Its Chevrolet Division regained the production lead over Ford's Ford Division in the 1972 model year, and its Cadillac and Oldsmobile divisions set new output records. Also, the subcompact Chevrolet Vega 1972 model set a production record for that car.

Ford Motor Company. Ford recorded its highest model-run total since 1966, partly because difficulty in meeting EPA engine-emission regulations for 1973 cars prompted Ford to extend its 1972 model production run by two weeks. The company increased its total production from 2,141,837 1971 cars to 2,366,988 1972 cars. More than 94,000 1972 Lincolns and Mark IV's were built, up 51% from 1971. The subcompact 1972 Ford Pinto set a production record for that car.

Chrysler Corporation. Chrysler's production of 1972 cars reached the highest level since its production of 1969 models. The company made a total of 1,331,193 1972 cars, compared with 1,256,259 1971 cars. Production of the Chrysler Imperial rose 30%, compared with production of 1971 Imperials.

American Motors Corporation (AMC). Production of 1972 cars by AMC was at the best level since its production of 1969 models. The company made a total of 259,125 1972 cars, compared with 244,758 in 1971. The subcompact AMC Gremlin 1972 model set a production record for that car.

Imported Cars. Increasing sales of domestic subcompacts slowed imported-car sales to 950,000 units in the first nine months of 1972, compared with 1,109,000 in the first nine months of 1971. On the nine-month comparison basis, Volkswagen sales totaled 355,000, off from 427,000; Toyota sales were 222,000, down from 232,000; and Datsun sales were 140,000, down from 147,000. Sales of the Japanese-made Mazda, which has a Wankel rotary engine, were up sharply to 38,000.

Imported-car sales accounted for about 15% of the total number of 1972 models in the United States. As of Jan. 1, 1972, about 8.2 million foreign-built cars were in operation on U. S. roads, up 1.2 million from Jan. 1, 1971.

THE 1973 MODELS

In the production of their 1973 models, auto makers had to meet new federal standards for front and rear bumpers, nitrogen oxide emissions, and fire-resistant fabrics. As a consequence they kept major styling changes to a minimum. Six inter-

mediate-size cars made by GM—Chevrolet Chevelle and Monte Carlo, Buick Century (renamed from Skylark), Oldsmobile Cutlass, and Pontiac LeMans and Grand Prix—were the only ones that were given an across-the-board redesign.

Bumpers. All front bumpers on 1973 cars were required to withstand impacts into immovable barriers at speeds up to 5 miles per hour without damage to safety-related components such as lights, brake fluid cylinders, and hood locks. Rear bumpers on 1973 cars were required to prevent damage to safety-related components in barrier impacts at speeds up to 2.5 miles per hour.

The car makers met these new "safety bumper" regulations in different ways. GM and AMC placed a hydraulic shock absorber between the front bumper and the car frame. In their designs, gas-filled and oil-filled bumper struts contract on impact and then return to normal position, not unlike the shock absorbers used in aircraft landing gear. Ford placed rubber blocks and steel bars between the bumper and the car body. With this design, the bumper moves back three or four inches on impact and then returns to its normal position. Chrysler used heavier steel for the bumper and the brackets holding it to the frame and added big rubber bumper guards. These new bumper designs may help the new-car owner reduce his collision insurance payments.

In the Chevrolet Monte Carlo and Pontiac Grand Am, damage from impacts is reduced in a novel way. In both of these cars the entire front end is made of a flexible molded urethane. When this plastic nose impacts at a speed of 5 miles per hour, the nose deforms and then returns to its original shape, much like a rubber ball.

Nitrogen Oxide Emissions. The Environmental Protection Agency (EPA) placed a limit of 1,800 parts per million for the allowable amount of nitrogen oxides emitted by an engine in a 1973 car. This kind of requirement to reduce air pollution

THE NEW YORK TIMES

WANKEL ENGINE (cutaway in foreground), the rotary engine that is simpler in design and smoother in performance than the piston engine, is incorporated in a new, Japanese-made automobile, the Mazda (rear).

U. S. PASSENGER CAR PRODUCTION

Company and make	1971 models	1972 models
AMERICAN MOTORS CORPORATION		
Ambassador	41,674	44,364
Hornet	74,685	71,055
Gremlin	53,480	61,717
Matador-Rebel	45,789	54,813
Javelin-AMX	29,130	27,176
Total AMC	244,758	259,125
CHRYSLER CORPORATION		
Valiant	231,559	256,431
Barracuda	18,690	18,450
Satellite-Belvedere	102,976	81,272
Fury	272,587	280,362
Subtotal Plymouth Division	625,812	636,515
Chrysler	174,291	204,764
Imperial	11,432	15,794
Dart	136,658	137,789
Coronet-Charger	165,387	159,758
Challenger	29,883	26,663
Polara	112,796	149,914
Subtotal Dodge Division	444,724	474,120
Total Chrysler Corporation	1,256,259	1,331,193
FORD MOTOR COMPANY		
Club Wagon	21,056	28,485
Torino-Fairlane	326,463	360,222
Ford	814,121	794,438
Mustang	149,678	125,093
Thunderbird	36,055	57,814
Maverick	145,371	136,925
Pinto	255,394	347,825
Subtotal Ford Division	1,748,138	1,850,802
Lincoln	35,551	45,969
Mark IV	27,091	48,591
Montego	57,094	135,092
Mercury	128,099	150,473

Company and make	1971 models	1972 models
Cougar	62,864	53,702
Comet	83,000	82,359
Subtotal Mercury Division	331,057	421,626
Total Ford Motor Company	2,141,837	2,366,988
GENERAL MOTORS CORPORATION		
Buick	333,303	420,847
Riviera	33,810	33,728
Skylark	184,075	225,346
Subtotal Buick Division	551,188	679,921
Cadillac	161,169	227,713
Eldorado	27,368	40,074
Subtotal Cadillac Division	188,537	267,787
Chevelle	327,159	357,820
Nova	197,361	367,999
Chevrolet	676,569	906,541
Corvette	21,806	27,004
Camaro	114,643	68,651
Monte Carlo	112,599	163,085
Vega	269,905	390,478
Subtotal Chevrolet Division	1,720,065	2,281,578
F-85	264,091	334,582
Oldsmobile	267,070	374,702
Toronado	29,265	48,900
Subtotal Oldsmobile Division	560,426	758,184
Pontiac	210,476	274,081
LeMans-Tempest	165,638	169,993
Firebird	53,124	29,951
Grand Prix	58,325	91,961
Ventura II	48,484	72,787
Subtotal Pontiac Division	536,047	638,773
Total General Motors Corporation	3,556,263	4,626,243
CHECKER MOTORS	4,650	5,500
Total U. S. production	7,203,767	8,589,049

Source: "Automotive News."

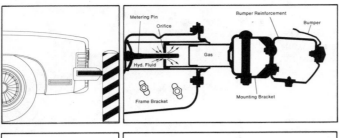

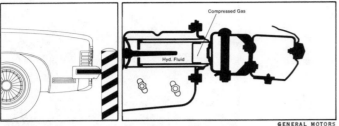

Car models in 1972 offered a variety of new shock-absorbing methods. The bumper at left incorporates a system of telescoping chambers. When impact occurs (*above*), the gas-filled front chamber is forced back so that a tapered metering pin enters an orifice in the chamber. Hydraulic fluid flows in from the rear chamber, compressing the gas in the front chamber by means of a floating cylinder (*below*). When the impact is ended, this compressed gas forces the fluid to return to its original chamber. More radical is the "soft nose" design offered by the Pontiac below. After a low-speed impact occurs the flexible urethane of the front end returns to its original shape like a rubber ball.

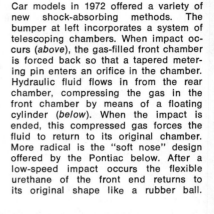

BETTER BUMPERS

was first imposed by California on 1972 cars sold in that state. In most domestic cars the new limit on nitrogen oxides in the exhaust was met by adding a pump that recirculates the exhaust gas. In this system the exhaust gas is recirculated and combined with the fuel-air mixture. This lowers the peak combustion temperature, reducing the formation of nitrogen oxides. Emissions of the two other major air pollutants in exhausts, carbon monoxide and gaseous hydrocarbons, were curbed by EPA regulations for several years prior to 1973.

Car manufacturers warned that emission controls not only increase gasoline consumption by 5% to 15% in 1973 cars but also make cars harder to start in cold weather because of the leaner mixture

of fuel and air in carburetors. Leaner fuel-air mixtures were introduced to reduce emissions of hydrocarbons and carbon monoxide.

Fire-Resistant Fabrics. The 1973 cars are the first ones whose interior fabrics must meet federal flammability standards. As a consequence, these cars are likely to have better fire-resistant interior fabrics than those in earlier models.

Design Trends. Auto producers increased the number of models offered for 1973 by four, as gains by GM offset moderate declines by Ford, Chrysler, and AMC. The model total rose from 297 to 301, which is 40 fewer than the 1971 total.

Only 9 convertibles were offered in the lineup of 1973 models, down from 17 in 1972. GM cut its soft-top group from 13 to 6, and Ford reduced its group from 4 to 3. Neither Chrysler nor AMC offered any convertibles. Safety factors and increasing use of air conditioning, vinyl roofs, and sunroofs have deflated the appeal of open cars.

In its 1973 intermediate-size cars, GM eliminated the hardtop design, in which there are no center pillars to support the roof. By reintroducing center pillars, the roof is stronger and less likely to crush if the car rolls over.

The hatchback rear end, in which both the trunk lid and the window lift up, was introduced in a number of 1973 cars, including the Oldsmobile Omega, a new compact. The hatchback previously had been introduced in the Chevrolet Vega and the Ford Pinto.

Prices. GM's and Ford's requests for price increases on 1973 cars were denied by the Price Commission, but Chrysler and American Motors were granted permission to boost their prices. Detroit contended that it needed price hikes to offset the costs of new safety and emission-control equipment. However, the long-standing federal excise tax on new-car sales was repealed in December 1971, and this contributed to the upward volume of 1973 cars.

MAYNARD M. GORDON
Editor, "Motor News Analysis"

WORLDWIDE MOTOR VEHICLE DATA

Country	1971 cars produced	1971 trucks produced	1971 vehicle registrations
Argentina	193,385	60,255	2,357,000
Australia	391,242	55,514	4,738,477
Austria	650	6,228	1,324,248
Belgium	278,687	17,077	2,350,719
Brazil	342,214	173,824	3,539,700
Canada	1,094,631	275,970	8,083,373
Czechoslovakia	149,016	27,846	992,000
Finland	...	1,500	822,994
France	2,693,989	316,305	14,404,750
Germany, East	132,000	26,000	1,405,400
Germany, West	3,696,779	285,943	15,604,890
Hungary	...	9,500	262,000
India	41,746	47,364	1,081,334
Italy	1,701,064	115,955	11,138,408
Japan	3,717,858	2,092,916	17,581,843
Mexico	153,598	57,242	1,791,868
Netherlands	78,087	13,225	2,837,500
Poland	86,200	59,500	771,700
Portugal	...	200	560,000
Rumania	8,000	27,000	330,000
Spain	452,921	79,437	3,130,500
Sweden	287,398	29,897	2,446,484
Switzerland	...	800	1,530,000
United Kingdom	1,741,940	456,206	13,702,500
United States	8,583,653	2,088,001	108,407,306[1]
USSR	518,000	612,000	6,250,000
Yugoslavia	114,477	17,891	852,923
World total	26,457,535	6,953,596	246,367,545[2]

[1] Excludes Puerto Rico, 525,000; Virgin Islands, 22,000, and Canal Zone, 19,511. [2] Includes all countries, of which others with more than 1,000,000 registrations are: Denmark, 1,329,023; New Zealand, 1,080,750; and South Africa, 2,115,000. These three countries and 17 others assemble cars and trucks but do not produce bodies and components for motor vehicles. Source: Motor Vehicle Manufacturers Association of United States, Inc.

BALTIMORE

Baltimoreans witnessed the best and the worst of urban living in 1972. On the positive side, they watched the continued development of the city's business district and inner harbor and participated in several community relations activities. But they were also subjected to increasing crime and violence, including a prison riot, and experienced a slight decrease in population.

Government. The year began with a new city hall administration. In November 1971 a wholly Democratic 18-seat city council had been elected, and Democrat William Donald Schaefer had been chosen 52d mayor of Baltimore to replace Thomas D'Alesandro, who retired in December 1971. During the first months of 1972, Mayor Schaefer focused his attention on economy moves and a restructuring of city departments.

Crime and Violence. In the incidence of violent crime, Baltimore ranked third among the nation's major urban centers. During the year it was disclosed that 1971 had been the most violent year in Baltimore's history, with a 12-month homicide toll of 253. This eclipsed the previous high for a single year of 236 homicides recorded in 1969. Incomplete statistics for 1972 indicated a continued rise in crime and violence in Baltimore.

In July 1972 part of the Maryland State Penitentiary adjacent to downtown Baltimore was seized by 75 inmates. The rioters set several fires in different parts of the building and captured four hostages. The fires, which grew into a four-alarm blaze, were put out, and a negotiating team headed by Maryland's governor, Marvin Mandel, entered the prison, while police massed outside. After two hours the negotiators convinced the prisoners to return to their cells and release the hostages. The riot had been sparked by long-standing grievances about living conditions. The governor promised that the rioters would suffer only "fair administrative action" as a result of the revolt. A few prison employees were injured during the uprising, but none seriously.

Redevelopment. The finishing touches were put on the city's Charles Center, an impressive complex of new office buildings, plazas, underground garages, hotels, apartment buildings, and a legitimate theater. Based on the success of this project the city immediately began the redevelopment of 240 acres surrounding the inner harbor. This massive project will cost more than $450 million, which will be supplied from both public and private sources.

Community Relations. In September more than 750,000 Baltimoreans participated in the third annual Baltimore City Fair, a three-day series of events involving various neighborhoods in the city. Several other community projects, such as concerts, art exhibits, and festivals, drew record crowds to the redeveloped central city during 1972.

Mass Transit. Baltimore's long-stalled rapid transit program began to stir with the approval in 1972 of Phase I, a 28-mile, $656 million line that was scheduled to serve the northwest and southern sectors of the metropolitan area by 1978.

Population. Baltimore's population was estimated to have been 900,500 at the beginning of 1972, a slight decrease from the 1970 census figure of 904,930. The loss was attributed to the continuing exodus to the suburbs.

WILLIAM F. AMELIA
The Equitable Trust Co., Baltimore

KEYSTONE

SHEIKH Mujib (right), prime minister of Bangladesh, is greeted by Soviet Premier Kosygin (left) in Moscow.

BANGLADESH

Bangladesh, formerly the eastern province of Pakistan, won its independence both by insurrection and Indian intervention late in 1971. The year 1972 was the first year of its independence. In addition to the usual adjustments and problems encountered by any new state, Bangladesh had to cope with the utter destruction resulting from the short-lived but intense war, the reconstruction of a viable economy, and the uncertainties of a continuing Indian embrace. Bangladesh was widely referred to as an "international basket case," and dire predictions were made about its future. But its government survived the year and remained independent of India, and its economy revived somewhat. Although its future is hardly bright, its collapse is no longer predicted with assurance.

Internal Politics. Sheikh Mujibur Rahman (Mujib) emerged as the leading political figure of East Pakistan. When the civil war and the Pakistan-India war ended in the defeat of the Pakistan government forces, it was natural that Mujib would head up the new government. On January 10, Sheikh Mujib returned from captivity in West Pakistan to assume the presidency, although he shortly took instead the position of prime minister. The government was patterned on the British parliamentary system, and a temporary constitution was declared.

─────── **BANGLADESH • Information Highlights** ───────

Official Name: People's Republic of Bangladesh.
Area: 55,126 square miles (142,776 sq km).
Population (1972 est.): 79,600,000. *Density,* 1,443 per square mile (558 per sq km).
Chief Cities (1961 census): Dacca, the capital, 362,006; Chittagong, 364,205; Narayanganj, 125,792; Khulna, 80,917.
Government: *Head of state,* Abu Sayeed Choudhury, president (took office Jan. 1972). *Head of government,* Mujibur Rahman, prime minister (took office Jan. 1972). *Major political party*—Awami League.
Language: Bengali (official).
Monetary Unit: Taka (7.25 takas equal U. S.$1, Oct. 1972).
Manufacturing (major products): Jute products, cotton textiles, sugar.
Major Agricultural Products: Jute (ranks 2d among world producers, 1971), tea, rice, potatoes, groundnuts, wheat, sugarcane, fish.
Major Mineral: Natural gas.
Foreign Trade: *Chief exports,* jute, tea, fish, paper. *Chief imports,* food, raw cotton, transport equipment, consumer goods.
Major National Airline: Bangladesh Biman.

(Above) Pregnant women, among the thousands who were raped by West Pakistani soldiers, wait at an abortion clinic in Dacca. Many rape victims were shunned by their families. (Below) Beggars scramble for food in Dacca. Severe food shortages were caused by the 1971 war.

Abu Sayeed Choudhury was named to the office of president.

An early problem was the disarming of the many guerrillas who roamed the countryside. Coupled with this were the need to restore internal order and the need for judicial handling of Pakistani prisoners of war and ethnic minorities that had supported West Pakistan in the war. There were new, if muted, scenes of violence as the Bengali government attempted to deal with non-Bengali segments whose loyalty was questioned.

By far the most critical problem was the devastation wrought by the war, estimated by one Bangladesh official as exceeding $3 billion. The relief distributions, always troublesome in Bengal, were less than perfect. By March, political repercussions had prompted Sheikh Mujib to order the police to "shoot down" troublemakers. Threatening to resign if the population did not respond to his efforts at reconstruction, Mujib continued to control a system possessing few resources for rebuilding.

By late April, government sources reported a mammoth crime wave, which they attributed to the large quantity of arms distributed during the war. An immediate problem was that of rebuilding police forces and a bureaucracy. Some police activities were performed by the Awami League Volunteer Corps. Awami League members, too, benefited in a variety of payoffs in the reconstruction, and there was public criticism of this. Among other acts, Mujib rescinded the ban on the Communist party in Bangladesh.

The students had become a political force once again by late spring. In student elections held in May the most radical of the groups proved victorious. By late 1972, their influence in Bengali politics was well established.

In April about 400 members of a constituent assembly met to frame a new constitution for Bangla-

SHEIKH MUJIB bids fare-
well to Prime Minister
Indira Gandhi of India at
the conclusion of two days
of talks in Dacca in March.
The two leaders signed a
25-year defense treaty.

UPI

desh. In early November the National Assembly voted to accept the new constitution. Immediately after it was approved, Sheikh Mujib said, "I am very happy because I have been able to give a constitution to my people. The dream of 75 million Bengalis has now come true."

The constitution became effective on Dec. 16, 1972, the first anniversary of the new nation. General elections were scheduled to be held on March 7, 1973.

An opposition party of sorts (extreme leftist) exists under the leadership of Maulana Bhashani. He generally has supported Mujib but has been critical of domestic policies and the new constitution. In particular, Bhashani had urged his followers to campaign against the new constitution because it did not make specific provisions for the establishment of a socialist society.

Foreign Affairs. Bangladesh achieved its independence largely as a result of the geographic division of Pakistan and the active assistance of India. Bangladesh in effect is a client state of India. In the war China and the United States supported Pakistan, while the USSR supported India. There was and remains a feeling of resentment in Bangladesh against official U. S. policy, although there is much evidence of popular goodwill. The United States recognized Bangladesh in April, whereas the Soviet Union had done so in January. Britain, West Germany, Sweden, Israel, Switzerland, and other countries extended recognition in February. Bangladesh's application for membership in the United Nations was vetoed by China in August, but in October, Bangladesh assumed the status of observer in the UN.

Indian forces left Bangladesh officially on March 12, but only days later they were reported to be still engaged in mopping-up exercises against anti-Bangladesh rebel forces. Understandably, India-Bangladesh relations have been very close, although the Indian presence has produced considerable resentment in Bangladesh. In February, Mujib met with Indira Gandhi, India's prime minister, and their joint statement made clear the desire of Bangladesh to be independent of India. In June the two countries formalized a broad agreement on eco-

nomic development and military assistance. By that time India had pledged $275 million in aid to Bangladesh.

In March, Sheikh Mujib traveled to the Soviet Union for talks with top Soviet leaders. He obtained pledges of economic and developmental aid from the Soviet Union.

Bangladesh remains a poor, unstable, and weak country in the subcontinent. Its creation and the dismemberment of Pakistan have resulted in a new power alignment, the implications of which are yet unclear. The nation's foreign affairs have been restricted to neighbors and to great powers that have assumed an interest in the subcontinent.

Economy. The economy of Bangladesh, often precarious in any case, was devastated by the 1971 conflicts in which large numbers of bridges and roads were destroyed. In March 1972 the government announced a nationalization of all the major industries. Further extreme moves seemed possible as the government continued to face the problem of national survival.

The agricultural economy, heavily dependent on good weather, was impeded by disruptions in communications and transportation. Other drawbacks were the general turbulence of the countryside and the political instability of the cities. Yet by the end of 1972, jute was again being exported, and some economic strides had been made.

Heavy infusions of disaster relief came from a number of sources. India was a heavy contributor. The Agency for International Development (AID) provided about $21 million in emergency foodstuffs in February. In May, AID announced that the most generous offer it had ever made was being given to Bangladesh. American aid for the fiscal year ending in 1973 is likely to be several times the $200-odd million committed by June 1972.

Distribution difficulties continued to plague what relief had been extended, with supplies piling up on the docks at Chittagong. In spite of all the difficulties a distinct economic improvement was seen by late spring, although by year-end much of the old confusion and chaos were still apparent.

CARL LEIDEN
University of Texas at Austin

USING A "BANK24" CARD, a customer of a Columbus, Ohio, bank can transact business 24 hours a day without entering the bank. The system offers patrons a wide range of banking services, including payment of utility bills.

BANKING

The U. S. economy expanded at a rapid rate during the first three quarters of 1972. Growth in real output rose from an annual rate of 5.6% in the first quarter to about 10% in the third. Unemployment continued to be a problem, however, having declined only to 5.5% by the end of the third quarter. Also, both wholesale and consumer prices continued an upward trend, despite the Price Commission "guidelines" which replaced 1971's 90-day price freeze.

International Aspects. The dollar was strengthened in international money markets by a rise in U. S. short-term interest rates relative to those abroad, and also by the enactment on April 3 of the Par Value Modification Act. This raised the official price of gold from $35 to $38 per fine ounce and effectively devalued the dollar in accordance with an international agreement (reached in December 1971) between the United States and nine other leading non-Communist trading nations. Trade deficits continued throughout the year, however, and although the balance of payments (on an official settlements basis) improved during the first six months of 1972, it deteriorated badly (to a $4.7 billion deficit position) in the third quarter.

Monetary Policy. In contrast to the anti-inflationary policy adopted in the latter part of 1971, the Federal Reserve System, during the first half of 1972, attempted to foster financial conditions conducive to sustainable real economic growth and increased employment. To this end, the discount rate was lowered to 4.5% in December 1971 and remained at that level throughout 1972.

By mid-year, the monetary authorities were concerned about international pressures on the dollar in the foreign exchange markets, following the decision of the British government to allow the pound sterling to "float." Consequently, from mid-year on, Federal Reserve open market operations shifted in the direction of maintaining somewhat higher short-term interest rates vis-à-vis those prevailing in European money markets. This was intended to prevent the outflow of the substantial volume of short-term dollar balances owned in this country by foreigners.

Bank Reserves and Money Supply. The principal monetary aggregates—bank deposits and reserves and the money supply—grew rapidly during the first half of 1972. Average money supply increased at an annual rate of 9.3% in the first quarter and 5.3% in the second.

The smaller rate of monetary expansion in the second quarter reflected the influence of two factors. First, there was an unusually large diversion of demand deposits into Treasury balances, as federal tax receipts were augmented by higher withholding rates. Second, in June, some shifting of funds abroad by foreign exchange speculators occurred.

The banking system possessed excess reserves during most of the first half of the year. These declined sharply, and bank borrowing from Federal Reserve banks rose substantially after mid-year as the Federal Reserve, in its open-market operations, "backed away" from the government securities market to permit short-term interest rates to rise.

Interest Rates, Loans, and Investments. Short-term interest rates, which had declined somewhat at the year's beginning, rose again late in the first

quarter, while bank deposits, and particularly time deposits, grew rapidly. Customer loan demand at the nation's commercial banks was strong in all categories; for example, business loans expanded during the quarter at an annual rate of 9.6%. In contrast, the annual rate of business loan increase during 1971 was only 4.2%.

The rise in short-term interest rates continued during the second quarter, as strong demands for housing credit and consumer credit led to continued rapid expansion of real estate and consumer loans. However, the rate of growth in business loans declined sharply during the second quarter (to an annual rate of but 4.3%). Most of the business loan decline occurred in June, and apparently reflected a temporary bunching of loan repayments coupled with, and resulting from, a sharp increase in sales of open-market commercial paper by nonfinancial corporations.

Overall loan demand, including business loan demand, expanded rapidly in the second half of the year. The annual rate of increase for September was 12%, for example. And as a reflection of this strong demand for credit, both long-term and short-term interest rates moved continuously upward throughout the second half of 1972.

Change in Prime Rate. The higher levels of loan demand and interest rates led to an increase in the prime rate (the lowest rate charged by large banks to their biggest and best short-term business borrowing customers) from 4¾% in March to 5¼% at the end of June. For the few banks which follow a policy of relating their prime rate to rates prevailing in the open market for commercial paper, the prime rate ranged from 4⅞% to 5¼% over the same period of time.

Bank Regulation. On June 21, the Board of Governors of the Federal Reserve System announced two regulatory changes intended to restructure reserve requirements of member banks and the check collection system. The changes, which were to be introduced on September 21, would (1) apply the same reserve requirements to member banks of like size regardless of a bank's location, in place of the former differentiation based on the reserve city-country bank classification; and (2) require all banks (including most nonmember banks) served by the Fed's check collection system to pay—in immediately collectable funds—for checks drawn on them the same day the Federal Reserve System presents the checks for payment. The new reserve requirements, which were based on net demand deposits, were 8% for the first $2 million, 10% for $2 million to $10 million, 13% for $10 million to $400 million, and 17.5% of amounts over $400 million. The old rate for amounts under $2 million, for example, had been 12.5%. The lesser rate was of particular import to smaller banks.

Representatives of nonmember banks, which would be required to make payments faster than before but without benefit of reduced reserve requirements, obtained a court restraining order barring introduction of the same-day payments rule in September; and because the rule changes were interrelated, the Federal Reserve postponed putting the new reserve requirements rule into effect as well. The court order was subsequently lifted, and both regulatory changes became effective with the reserve week beginning Nov. 9, 1972.

CLIFTON H. KREPS, JR.
University of North Carolina at Chapel Hill

BARBADOS

Economic issues were the dominant concern in 1972 in Barbados, which had a somewhat slower rate of economic growth than in 1971. Steps were taken toward greater economic independence by the Barbadian government, which also introduced measures designed to strengthen regional ties.

The Economy. While sugar production continued its decline of recent years and established a new low in total yearly production for the island, there were encouraging signs that the yield would soon increase. Island-wide planning for the introduction of an increasing number of cane cutting machines on the land most adaptable to such harvesting methods was undertaken. Greater diversity in crops was encouraged by the sale of carrots and onions to Guyana, Trinidad, and Jamaica, all of which are fellow members of the Caribbean Free Trade Association (CARIFTA). While the volume of trade with CARIFTA members increased, imports from member nations still exceeded exports from the island.

Tourism increased with respect both to the number of visitors and to the amount of money spent on the island, contributing to an economic growth rate of about 9%, down substantially from previous years. The island recently received its first long-term loan from the Inter-American Development Bank. It is to be used to increase smaller tourist facilities, aid industrial development, and improve the sewage-disposal system of Bridgetown, the capital. A loan was also received to aid in the modernization of Bridgetown's port facilities.

New Taxes. Increases in import duties on consumer products from non-CARIFTA nations were requested by Prime Minister Errol Barrow in an effort to deal with a budget deficit of EC$12.3 million (EC$1.84 = U. S. $1) and a noticeable trend toward inflation. The consumption duty on whiskey, brandy, gin, and vodka was also increased, as were license fees for motor vehicles. The prime minister hoped that reduced expenditures would erase the remaining amount of the deficit.

THOMAS G. MATHEWS
University of Puerto Rico

─────── **BARBADOS • Information Highlights** ───────

Official Name: Barbados.
Area: 166 square miles (430 sq km).
Population (1972 est.): 300,000. *Density,* 1,541 per square mile (595 per sq km). *Annual rate of increase,* 0.8%.
Chief City (1970 census): Bridgetown, the capital, 8,749.
Government: *Head of state,* Sir Winston Scott, governor-general (appointed May 1966). *Head of government,* Errol Walton Barrow, prime minister (took office for 3d 5-year term, Nov. 1971). *Legislature*—Parliament: Senate (appointed), 21 members; House of Assembly (elected), 24 members. *Major political parties*—Democratic Labour party; Barbados Labour party.
Language: English (official).
Education: *Expenditure* (1968), 21.3% of total public expenditure. *School enrollment* (1968)—primary, 39,328; secondary, 20,710; technical/vocational, 2,362; university/higher, 373.
Monetary Unit: East Caribbean dollar (1.84 EC dollars equal U. S.$1, May 1972).
Manufacturing (major products): Refined sugar, petroleum products, electrical goods.
Major Agricultural Products: Sugarcane, fish.
Major Minerals: Natural gas.
Foreign Trade (1970): *Exports,* $39,000,000. *Imports,* $118,-000,000. *Chief trading partners* (1969)—United States (took 23% of exports, supplied 23% of imports); United Kingdom (4%—29%); Canada (4%—11%).
Transportation: *Motor vehicles* (1970), 23,300 (automobiles, 19,300).
Communications: *Telephones* (1971), 29,014; *television stations* (1971), 1; *television sets* (1971), 17,500; *radios* (1970), 89,000; *newspapers* (1970), 1 (daily circulation, 23,000).

BELGIUM

A troubled economy, conflicting interests of political parties, and social unrest characterized Belgium during 1972.

Economy. Unemployment and inflation continued to plague Belgium in 1972. Although unemployment gradually decreased from February on, the number of people without work was greater in July than in the same month of 1971. Exports, which had declined sharply in the second half of 1971, increased notably in 1972.

The minister for economic affairs, Henri Simonet, presented new policies for economic expansion in February. They called for government assistance to businesses to help them penetrate foreign markets, as well as a number of measures to promote investment and private consumption.

Politics. The constitutional reforms of 1971, which federalized Belgium on a cultural basis and regionalized it on an economic basis, did not noticeably ease political tensions late in 1971 or in 1972. In the general election held on Nov. 7, 1971, the Social Christians and the Socialists—the two coalition government parties—retained the same total number of seats in the Chamber of Deputies, the Party of Liberty and Progress (Liberals) lost 13 seats, the Walloon Union gained 22, and the Flemish People's Union gained 1. The composition of the new chambers was: Social Christians, 67; Socialists, 61; Liberals, 34; Walloon Union, 34; Flemish People's Union, 21; and Communists, 5.

After the elections the two major parties had difficulties in reaching an agreement on a policy

------- **BELGIUM · Information Highlights** -------

Official Name: Kingdom of Belgium.
Area: 11,781 square miles (30,513 sq km).
Population (1972 est.): 9,800,000. *Density,* 821 per square mile (317 per sq km). *Annual rate of increase,* 0.2%.
Chief Cities (1969 est.): Brussels, the capital, 164,000; Antwerp, 230,200; Ghent, 151,160; Liège, 148,600.
Government: *Head of state,* Baudouin I, king (acceded July 1951). *Head of government,* Gaston Eyskens, prime minister (resigned November 1972). *Legislature*—Parliament: Senate, 178 members; Chamber of Deputies, 212 members. *Major political parties*—Social Christian; Socialist; Party of Liberty and Progress; Walloon Union; Flemish People's Union; Communist.
Languages: French, Flemish (both official).
Education: *Expenditure* (1968), 5% of gross national product. *School enrollment* (1968)—primary, 1,018,334; secondary, 847,605; technical/vocational, 518,709; university/higher, 64,779.
Monetary Unit: franc (44.18 francs equal U. S.$1, Sept. 1972).
Gross National Product (1971 est.): $26,600,000,000.
National Income per Person: (1970) $2,406.
Economic Indexes: *Industrial production* (1971), 140 (1963=100); *agricultural production* (Belgium-Luxembourg, 1971), 155 (1952–56=100); *consumer price index* (1971), 134 (1963=100).
Manufacturing (major products): Steel, pig iron and ferro alloys, textiles, cut diamonds, chemicals, glass, electronics.
Major Agricultural Products: sugar beets, potatoes, wheat, oats, barley, flax.
Major Minerals: Coal, iron ore.
Foreign Trade (including Luxembourg, 1971): *Exports,* $12,-391,000,000 (chief exports, 1969—iron and steel; transport equipment, nonferrous metals, textile yarn and fabrics). *Imports,* $12,856,000,000 (chief imports, 1969—food and live animals, motor vehicles, nonelectrical machinery, chemicals). *Chief trading partners* (1969)—West Germany (took 23% of exports, supplied 23% of imports); France (21%—16%); Netherlands (19%—14%); United States (7%—8%).
Tourism: *Receipts* (including Luxembourg, 1970), $348,000,-000.
Transportation: *Motor vehicles* (1970), 2,435,400 (automobiles, 2,059,600); *railroads* (1970), 2,649 miles (4,263 km); *merchant fleet* (1971), 1,883,000 gross registered tons; *major national airline,* SABENA.
Communications: *Telephones* (1971), 2,018,827; *television stations* (1971), 19; *television sets* (1971), 2,105,000; *radios* (1970), 3,604,000; *newspapers* (1968), 33 (daily circulation, 2,500,000).

program and in distributing the portfolios. The Socialists had not been happy about the constitutional reforms adopted by the previous Parliament, and the election indicated that there was considerable dissatisfaction with the reforms, especially among the Walloons.

Prime Minister Gaston Eyskens, leader of the Social Christians, was asked by King Baudouin to form a new government. After negotiations lasting more than a week he reached an agreement with the Socialists to continue the coalition. The Social Christians demanded that the two cultural councils, established by the constitutional reforms, be given responsibility for the educational budget, while the Socialists insisted that this function remain with the two educational ministers responsible to Parliament.

The compromise agreed upon was that Parliament would vote the overall amounts for education and promotion of culture, while the cultural councils would allocate specific funds to a strictly defined number of items. The financial subsidization of Catholic school construction was denied the cultural councils. However, it was agreed that a government commission would be set up to study this problem. Agreement could not be reached on the future status of Brussels and some nearby villages, educational policy, and economic policy.

The linguistic-cultural rivalry between the Dutch-speaking Flemish and the French-speaking Walloons also extended to the distribution of portfolios. The constitutional reforms provided for dividing the ministries, other than that of the prime minister, between the two linguistic communities on a parity basis. Since ministries are not of equal importance, some demanded that the principle of parity should also apply to the evaluation of the portfolios.

Agreement on the coalition program and the distribution of portfolios was reached on January 4, and the formation of a new government finally was announced on January 20. Of the 19 ministers and 10 secretaries of state in the cabinet, 9 ministers and 6 secretaries speak Flemish, and 9 ministers and 4 secretaries speak French. Prime Minister Eyskens is a Flemish-speaking Social Christian; the other ministers and secretaries were equally divided between the Social Christian and Socialist parties.

After 11 months in office, the coalition government led by Prime Minister Eyskens collapsed on Nov. 22, 1972. The key problem that brought down his government was the conflicting economic and political interests of the Flemish and French-speaking population groups. After telling Parliament that a solution to the problem was impossible to find, Eyskens submitted his resignation to King Baudouin.

Workers' Strike. On October 2–3, Belgium's cities were ghost towns as 700,000 shopkeepers and other independent workers struck. Practically all businesses were closed, and taxis ceased operation. The Common Front of Independent Workers had organized the action as a protest against a value-added tax, which it declared to be too complicated and costly to calculate. Other grievances included the rapid growth of chain stores and inequality with other groups in receiving social security benefits.

The movement, known as "Operation Deadtown," was declared by the organizers to have been a complete success. The Belgian cabinet appointed a committee to examine the complaints.

AMRY VANDENBOSCH
University of Kentucky

BERMUDA

Bermuda had a new prime minister and a new governor in 1972, and tourism there continued to increase.

Government. Sir Henry Tucker, Bermuda's prime minister, resigned on Dec. 28, 1971, and was succeeded by Sir Edward Trenton Richards, who was elected to the position by the ruling United Bermuda party (UBP). Richards, a former schoolteacher and lawyer, became the first black leader of the Bermuda government.

Elections held on June 7, 1972, occasioned a straight fight for seats between the UBP and the Progressive Labour party (PLP). It resulted in the UBP's retaining the 30 seats it had already held, and in the PBP's retaining 10 seats, thus producing no change in the party strengths in the legislature. A lack of interest in the election was reflected in the lower percentage of voters going to the polls, with a sharp drop from 90% in 1968 to only 77% in 1972.

Lord Martonmere, governor for the past eight years, retired in August. He was succeeded by Sir Richard Christopher Sharples, a former minister of state in Britain's Conservative government.

Economy. The estimated revenue for 1972–73 was $50.2 million, with taxes increasing by $4.5 million. Expenditures were estimated at $48.4 million. On July 31, 1972, following Britain's decision to float the pound sterling, the Bermuda dollar was pegged to the U. S. dollar instead of the pound, on a basis of parity.

Tourism figures for the first eight months of 1972, during which 342,160 visitors arrived in Bermuda, showed a 2.54% increase over the comparable period in 1971. Despite minor labor problems in the building industry, the new Southampton Princess Hotel opened on August 17.

RICHARD E. WEBB
Former Director, Reference and Library Division,
British Information Services, New York

BHUTAN

The major event of 1972 in Bhutan was the death of 45-year-old King Jigme Dorji Wangchuk on July 21 and the succession of his 17-year-old son, Jigme Singhi Wangchuk. The late king had ruled Bhutan since 1952 and was responsible for leading the tiny Himalayan country out of isolation. His son had studied in England, but had returned to Bhutan three years before his father's death to begin sharing some of the responsibilities of the monarchy. Although the Bhutanese constitution prescribes rule by a regency council until a crown prince reaches the age of 21, the royal advisory council decided to invest the young king with full powers immediately because of his intimate association with his father's reign.

International Relations. Bhutan became a member of the United Nations in 1971. Previously relying largely on India's guidance in foreign policy matters, it moved toward a more independent and active involvement in international affairs. Bhutan recognized neighboring Bangladesh in December 1971, and early in 1972 it established diplomatic relations with the new nation. Just before his death, the late king established a ministry of foreign affairs and appointed Lyonpo Dawa Shering as foreign minister. Nevertheless, Bhutan assured New

——————— **BHUTAN · Information Highlights** ———————

Official Name: Kingdom of Bhutan.
Area: 18,147 square miles (47,000 sq km).
Population (1972 est.): 900,000. *Density,* 496 per square mile (19 per sq km). *Annual rate of increase,* 2.2%.
Chief City: Thimbu, the capital.
Government: *Head of state,* Jigme Singye Wangchuk, king (acceded July 1972). *Head of government,* Jigme Singye Wangchuk. *Legislature* (unicameral)—National Assembly, 130 members.
Languages: Dzongka (official), Nepali.
Education: *School enrollment* (1968)—primary, 12,601; secondary, 2,774; technical/vocational, 153.
Monetary Unit: Indian rupee (7.279 rupees equal U. S.$1, May 1972).
Manufacturing: Weaving.
Major Agricultural Products: Rice, wheat, barley, fruits, forest products.
Major Mineral: Coal.
Foreign Trade: *Chief exports*—Timber, fruit. *Chief imports*—Textiles. *Chief trading partner*—India.

Delhi that it intended to remain aligned with India.

Economic Development. In 1972, Bhutan was in the second year of its third five-year plan (1971–76). Financed largely by India, the plan is concentrated primarily on road and air transport facilities, agriculture, education, and public health. In cooperation with the Bhutanese planning commission, the United Nations in 1972 agreed to undertake $5 million worth of projects, including the equipping of a cement plant, a sheep breeding station, and educational facilities.

FREDERICK H. GAIGE
Davidson College

BIOCHEMISTRY

In 1972 biochemists made great strides in the areas of gene function and protein synthesis as well as in the understanding of the process of aging and of the biochemistry of interferon and of hemoglobin.

DNA and RNA. Researchers continued to pursue the 1970 discovery of reverse transcriptase, the enzyme that can use a single-stranded ribonucleic acid, or RNA, of tumor viruses as a template for the synthesis of complementary stranded deoxyribose nucleic acid, or DNA. Much of the general interest in reverse transcriptase stems from the assumption that the infection and transformation of cells by RNA tumor viruses depends on the activity of reverse transcriptase.

Three investigators—R. C. Ting, S. S. Yang, and R. C. Gallo—prepared three derivatives of the antibiotic rifamycin—one that could inhibit the enzyme reverse transcriptase, one that could not inhibit it, and one that was intermediate in its inhibiting capacity—and determined how each affected the infection and transformation of cells by RNA tumor viruses. They found that those derivatives that inhibit the enzyme most potently blocked cell transformation by more than 95%, while those that have no effect on the enzyme blocked transformation by less than 25%, and those with moderate inhibitory capacity inhibited transformation by 50%. These results strongly suggest that reverse transcriptase activity is essential for infection of cells by RNA tumor viruses.

Reverse transcriptase has also become an important laboratory tool. It is theoretically possible that this enzyme could be used to synthesize DNA copies of mammalian messenger RNA. This, of course, would be tantamount to synthesizing mammalian genes in the test tube. In early work in this area, two laboratories have succeeded in incubating reverse transcriptase with RNA that contains the

message for the protein globin. Under appropriate conditions, reverse transcriptase catalyzes the polymerization of DNA, the DNA that is apparently the gene for the protein globin.

Progress has also been made in another aspect of gene research. Several enzymes are known that can polymerize DNA to extend a DNA chain that has already started, but no enzymes are known that can begin synthesis of a new chain. Recent evidence, however, indicates that RNA may be necessary for DNA synthesis.

Several molecular biologists have reported that the conversion of a single-stranded DNA to double helical DNA requires RNA synthesis in vitro. This is important since DNA synthesis appears to take place by a discontinuous mechanism in which new DNA is synthesized in short fragments, so-called Okazaki segments, which are later joined to a long DNA chain. Each segment must be initiated separately and cannot take place by continuous synthesis along the template. R. Okazaki and co-workers have recently suggested that each segment starts with a prime sequence of RNA. This RNA is incorporated into the fragments, although it is subsequently very rapidly removed from them after initiation of DNA synthesis.

Yet another intriguing discovery in 1972 was the observation of long sequences of polyadenylic acid in messenger RNA's. They have been found in a sufficiently large number of cells to suggest that strings of this acid are a universal characteristic of messenger RNA. There is also speculation that the poly-A sequences may play some part in the transport of RNA from the nucleus to the cytoplasm or that they may play some regulatory part in translation of the RNA.

Aging. Human fibroblast cells grown in tissue cultures have a limited life span that depends very largely on the age of the individual from whom the cells are derived. Two investigators—R. Holliday and G. M. Tarrant of the National Institute for Medical Research (NIMR) in London—suggested that the aging process in these cells is due to an accumulation of "errors" in protein synthesis. They used the drug 5-fluorouracil, which causes mistranslation of cellular proteins, to mimic the natural aging process in these cells and reported that aging could arise from accumulated mistranslation of RNA into protein.

Interferon. Searching for an explanation of how interferon inhibits the activity of viruses, two NIMR biochemists—D. H. Metz and M. Esteban—presented evidence that the primary action of interferon is at the level where viral RNA is translated into a viral protein. This has led to speculation on interferon's role in gene expression in normal cells.

Hemoglobin. Using crystallographic methods to study the detailed structure of human hemoglobin, Nobel laureate Max Perutz and co-workers have obtained important information on the binding of heme iron with the amino acids in the globin protein. Their observations provide a greater understanding of the peculiar properties of hemoglobin and the changes in hemoglobin structure that permit the all-important reversible binding of oxygen and the decreased ability of hemoglobin to bind oxygen in the presence of carbon dioxide.

STEPHEN N. KREITZMAN, *Emory University*

BIOLOGY. See BIOCHEMISTRY; BOTANY; GENETICS; MARINE BIOLOGY; MEDICINE; ZOOLOGY.
BIRTHRATES. See POPULATION.

GERALD EDELMAN, co-winner of the 1972 Nobel Prize for physiology or medicine, explains the structure and properties of an antibody molecule.

THE NEW YORK TIMES

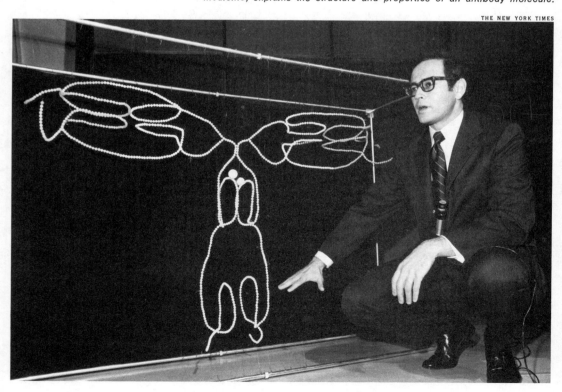

Biography

A selection of biographical sketches of persons prominent in the news during 1972 appears on this and the following pages. The subjects include men and women from many parts of the world, and representing a wide variety of pursuits. The list is confined to living persons; for biographical data on prominent people who died during the year, see the Classified Listing of Articles—Biographies (page v) and Necrology *(beginning on page 761). Unless otherwise indicated, all articles in this section are by Henry S. Sloan, Associate Editor, Current Biography.*

AGNEW, Spiro T.

Vice President Spiro T. Agnew was reelected to a second term in President Nixon's landslide victory of Nov. 7, 1972. He had approached the 1972 campaign in a relaxed and conciliatory manner that contrasted sharply with the forceful rhetoric that had become his trademark. Earlier in the year, Agnew had lashed into his favorite target, the liberal press, for "currying favor with a nest-fouling constituency of home-grown anti-Americans." He had denounced the presentation of a Pulitzer Prize to the New York Times for publishing the Pentagon Papers as "demeaning" to the award, and he had accused radical members of the academic community of "anti-intellectual yahooism." After his renomination at the Republican National Convention in August, Agnew admitted that he had not really enjoyed being the "cutting edge" of the Republican party, but had accepted the assignment from the President because he was a "team player."

The campaign took Agnew some 36,000 miles around the country. He concentrated on the issues, defending the President's Vietnam policy and economic program, ruling out amnesty for draft evaders, and assailing the foreign and domestic policies of George McGovern, the Democratic presidential candidate. Agnew showed more skill in dealing with hecklers, and his relations with the press improved. While Agnew's past pronouncements had won him a loyal following among right-wing Republicans, he denies that he is a doctrinaire conservative and defines his position as "centrist." Although he is noncommittal about running for President in 1976, he has described the office of vice president as having "two important functions: to serve the President and to learn from the President."

Background. Spiro Theodore Agnew, the son of a Greek immigrant, was born on Nov. 9, 1918, in Baltimore. He served as an Army officer in World War II, and after graduating from Baltimore Law School in 1947 he entered law practice and changed his political affiliation from Democrat to Republican. He was elected chief executive of Baltimore county in 1962 and was elected governor of Maryland in 1966. Although his early policies as governor earned him a reputation as a liberal on civil rights and social reform, he later adopted more conservative positions. Nominated as Nixon's running mate in 1968, Agnew took office as Vice President in January 1969.

ANDERSON, Jack

Jack Anderson, whose syndicated column, "Washington Merry-Go-Round," is published by over 700 newspapers and has a readership estimated at 67 million, was awarded the Pulitzer Prize for national reporting on May 1, 1972. He was cited for his January reports, based on secret government documents, indicating that contrary to public statements the Nixon administration had harbored a bias against India and was clearly partial to Pakistan during the India-Pakistan War of 1971.

Anderson scored another major coup in February with the publication of a secret memo suggesting that the Justice Department had settled antitrust actions in favor of the International Telephone and Telegraph Corporation (ITT) in return for a pledge of a $400,000 contribution toward the cost of the Republican National Convention. Other Anderson stories in 1972 dealt with such subjects as an alleged conspiracy by ITT to block the election in 1970 of leftist President Salvador Allende

(Below) *VICE PRESIDENT AGNEW and President Nixon share the applause of well-wishers at victory rally.* (Right) *Jack Anderson holds documents stamped "Secret/Sensitive."*

WIDE WORLD

UPI

131

in Chile; the involvement of Latin American and Southeast Asian governments in the narcotics trade; and the neglect of American Indians by the federal government.

In July, Anderson, who had usually taken great pains to ensure the accuracy of his reports, tarnished his own image when he failed to find proof to substantiate his charge that Sen. Thomas F. Eagleton, the Democratic vice presidential nominee, had been arrested in the past for drunken driving. He retracted this story and publicly apologized to Eagleton.

Background. The son of a postal clerk, Jackson Northman Anderson was born in Long Beach, Calif., on Oct. 19, 1922, and grew up near Salt Lake City, Utah. Interested in journalism from childhood, he began working for newspapers at the age of 12. He attended the University of Utah in 1940–41 and then served two years as a Mormon missionary in the South. After stints as a merchant marine cadet and a war correspondent in China, he was drafted into the Army in 1945. Back in civilian life, Anderson went to Washington, D. C., in 1947 and was hired as an assistant by columnist Drew Pearson, who soon made him his chief investigative reporter on his crusading "Washington Merry-Go-Round" column. Anderson inherited the column after Pearson's death in September 1969. He is the author of several books, including *Washington Exposé* (1967).

ANDREOTTI, Giulio

On June 26, 1972, Premier Giulio Andreotti of Italy —who had been heading a minority caretaker cabinet composed of Christian Democrats since February— formed a center coalition government of Christian Democrats, Social Democrats, and Liberals. This ended a five-month political crisis that had begun with the collapse of Premier Emilio Colombo's left-center coalition in January and had led to the premature election of a new parliament in May.

The new government, Italy's 34th since the fall of Fascism, was the first in a decade to exclude the Marxist Socialists. Its program called for economic and social reforms to meet immediate needs, a strong law-and-order policy to combat crime and politically inspired violence, measures to stem the growing tide of industrial unrest, improvements in health services, schools, and prisons, and continued support of Western European solidarity in cooperation with the United States.

A pragmatic party bureaucrat, lacking the flamboyance usually associated with Italian politicians, Andreotti was noted for his skill as an administrator, his ability to conciliate differences within the faction-ridden Christian Democratic party, and his sober, low-keyed approach to Italy's seemingly insurmountable problems. While maintaining a consistent anti-Communist position and openly endorsing U. S. involvement in Vietnam, Andreotti established a dialogue with Italy's labor and political leaders of the left. In October, after attending a summit conference of the European Economic Community in Paris, he became the first Italian head of government in over a decade to make an official visit to the Soviet Union. Andreotti's success in holding his fragile coalition together through the end of 1972 came as a surprise to most observers of the Italian political scene.

Background. Giulio Andreotti was born in Rome on Jan. 14, 1919. After working his way through the University of Rome, where he was a leader of the Roman Catholic student movement and earned a law degree, he became a protégé of Alcide de Gasperi, founder of the Christian Democratic party. De Gasperi placed him on the staff of *Il Popolo* and appointed him under-secretary in his government in 1947. From 1954 to 1968 Andreotti served in a succession of cabinet posts —as minister of the interior, of finance, of the treasury, of defense, and of commerce and industry. In 1968 he was elected chairman of the Christian Democratic party in the Chamber of Deputies. He served briefly as premier in 1970.

BÖLL, Heinrich

The West German author Heinrich Böll, once described as the "incorruptible conscience of his country," won the Nobel Prize for Literature on Dec. 10, 1972. He was the first German to be so honored since Thomas Mann received the award in 1929.

The senselessness of war and the victimization and dehumanization of the individual by powerful institutions are among the themes of Böll's works, which have been acclaimed both in the Soviet Union and in the United States. In announcing the Nobel award, Karl Gierow, secretary of the Swedish Academy, cited Böll for his work "which through its combination of a broad perspective on his time and a sensitive skill in characterization has contributed to a renewal of German literature."

Background. The son of a cabinetmaker, Heinrich Theodor Böll grew up in a liberal Roman Catholic environment in Cologne, where he was born on Dec. 21, 1917. After completing his secondary education and working as a bookseller's apprentice, he was drafted into the German army in 1939 and served until his capture by American forces in 1945. In Cologne, after the war, he began to devote himself to writing. With colorful realism and incisive irony, he depicted the effects of the war on its victims and survivors in such early novels as *Der Zug war pünktlich* (1949; *The Train Was on Time*, 1956), *Wo warst du, Adam?* (1951; *Adam, Where Art Thou?*, 1953), and *Und Sagte kein einziges Wort* (1953; *Acquainted With the Night*, 1954).

Böll's best-known work, the complex *Billiard um helbzehn* (1959; *Billiards at Half Past Nine*, 1962), chronicles the history of a German family for three generations. In the sardonic *Ansichten eines Clown* (1963; *The Clown*, 1965) he pits the "natural" individual against the artificiality of contemporary West German society and the Roman Catholic hierarchy. In *Ende einer Dienstfahrt* (1966; *End of a Mission*, 1968) he satirizes the West German military establishment. His works also include topical essays, an *Irish Journal* (1967), plays, short stories, and German translations of Shaw, Salinger, and other authors. His latest novel, *Gruppenbild mit Dame* (1971), was scheduled for U. S. publication in 1973 under the title *Group Portrait With Lady*. Böll became president of the international writers association, P. E. N., in 1971.

BRANDT, Willy

In the parliamentary elections of November 1972, Willy Brandt, federal chancellor and chairman of the German Social Democratic Party (SPD), won approval for his *Ostpolitik* ("Eastern policy") from 54% of the West German electorate, which constituted a substantial majority.

Ostpolitik aims at a rapprochement with East Germany and Eastern Europe at the price of accepting the political and territorial status quo in the East. In pursuit of this policy, Brandt obtained in June the ratification of friendship pacts with the USSR and Poland. He also concluded a traffic and travel pact with East Germany, facilitating visits of West Germans to East Germany and, on a limited basis, vice versa. A few days before the elections, a Basic Treaty (*Grundvertrag*) between the Federal Republic and the German Democratic Republic was completed. It affirmed the existence of two separate sovereign German states and pledged them to cooperation on all matters concerning practical and humanitarian problems.

Brandt's *Ostpolitik* did not imply a weakening of ties with the West. The chancellor remained anxious to see the U. S. military presence in Western Europe preserved at its present level. In appreciation of earlier American help, he announced the establishment of a $46.6 million German Marshall Plan Memorial on the plan's 25th anniversary. He also remained in close touch with Britain and France. While paying a visit to Britain, he was the personal guest of Queen Elizabeth

at Windsor Castle—an honor usually reserved for heads of state.

Domestic Politics. Preoccupied with foreign policy, Brandt made little progress in solving domestic problems. He was faced with mounting economic difficulties, with inflation at a record high of 6.4% per year. Long-promised reforms had to be curtailed or postponed altogether. His ministers were divided on many issues. Finance and Economics Minister Karl Schiller resigned and was replaced by the more flexible Helmut Schmidt. Defections over *Ostpolitik* deprived the chancellor of his majority in the parliament. In April he barely survived a no-confidence vote. To end the impasse, the Bundestag was dissolved.

Brandt's victory in the elections was a tribute not only to his foreign policy but also to his warm and sincere personality, so much more popular with West Germans than that of the opposition leader, Rainer Barzel.

Background. Willy Brandt was born in Lübeck on Dec. 18, 1913. He joined the SPD in 1930 at the age of 16, but soon switched to the more militant Socialist Workers party. Spending the Nazi era in exile in Norway and Sweden, he resumed his German citizenship in 1948 and rejoined the SPD.

Brandt was elected a member and later president of West Berlin's parliament and, in 1957, became mayor of West Berlin. After unsuccessful bids for the chancellorship in 1961 and 1965, he became foreign minister in a coalition government formed by the Christian Democratic Union and the SPD in 1966. When the coalition broke up after the 1969 elections, Brandt became chancellor of a government resting on a coalition of the SPD and the small Free Democratic party. In October 1971, Brandt was awarded the Nobel Peace Prize in recognition of his efforts to bring about a détente between East and West.

ANDREAS DORPALEN

BREMER, Arthur H.

An assassination attempt was made by 21-year-old Arthur Bremer on Alabama Gov. George C. Wallace at a campaign rally at Laurel, Md., on May 15, 1972. Bremer critically wounded Wallace with several shots from a .38-caliber revolver and injured three other persons, including a Secret Service agent. Arrested at the scene of the crime, Bremer was indicted by state and federal authorities on several charges. The shooting left the Alabama governor partly paralyzed and removed him as a candidate in the 1972 presidential election, a circumstance that probably contributed to President Nixon's landslide victory in November.

Investigation revealed Bremer to be a highly unbalanced individual with no clear political orientation but with an obsession about his own role in history. His 114-page diary, which indicated that he had previously plotted to assassinate President Nixon, contained such statements as: "I am as important as the start of World War I." On August 4, Bremer, who had pleaded insanity, was found legally sane by a jury of six men and six women and convicted on four charges of assault and five charges of weapons law violation. Sentenced to prison terms totaling 63 years, he was taken to Maryland State Penitentiary.

The son of a truck driver, Arthur Herman Bremer was born on Aug. 21, 1950, in Milwaukee, Wis., where he grew up in a poor working-class area and an unstable home environment. An uncommunicative loner with a passion for books, he was an average student with an I. Q. of 106. After graduating from high school he took a course in photography and worked at various jobs, including busboy, dishwasher, and janitor. In October 1971 he moved out of his family home, and a month later he was arrested on a concealed-weapons charge and fined. Among his possessions after the Wallace shooting were Black Panther newspapers, literature on the assassin Sirhan B. Sirhan, and a Confederate flag.

BREZHNEV, Leonid Ilich

Leonid Brezhnev, secretary general of the Soviet Communist party, chairman of the party Politburo, and member of the Presidium of the Supreme Soviet, received more publicity in 1972 than any other Soviet leader. The Soviet press praised his record as an army political officer during World War II, and noted that Stalin admired him. Volume 3 of Brezhnev's *Collected Works* was published and worshipfully reviewed. Yet he was still "first among equals" in the Soviet leadership rather than a supreme dictator like Stalin.

Brezhnev traveled abroad only twice in 1972, to Czechoslovakia for a meeting of Warsaw Pact allies and to Hungary on a goodwill visit. The economic difficulties caused by the poor Soviet harvest kept him extremely occupied in the USSR, where he delivered at least nine major speeches on agriculture, seven of them in Central Asia and Siberia during the harvest season. His agricultural speeches were not published, but in a public address to the Soviet congress of trade unions he demanded unequal pay (based on performance), iron labor discipline, and eradication of antisocial behavior.

Before President Nixon's May visit to Moscow, Brezhnev explained Soviet motives for befriending the United States in speeches to a conference of military political officers and to the Central Committee of the Soviet Communist party. During the visit he negotiated personally with the President, and on behalf of the USSR signed the two most important negotiated treaties: the pact limiting U. S. and Soviet antiballistic missile systems, and the agreement limiting each country's intercontinental nuclear missiles, submarine-based nuclear missiles, and missile-bearing nuclear submarines to those already constructed or being built.

Late in the year either a temporary illness or a medical operation kept Brezhnev absent from several official Soviet functions. When he resumed his duties, he appeared pale and thinner.

Background. Brezhnev was born in Dneprodzerzhinsk, the Ukraine, on Dec. 19, 1906. He has worked as a surveyor, agricultural administrator, metallurgical engineer, regional Communist party chief, high-ranking army political officer, and secretary of the party's central apparatus. From 1960 to 1964 he served as president of the USSR, a post he relinquished shortly before helping to oust Nikita Khrushchev from power.

ELLSWORTH RAYMOND

BROWN, Larry

Larry Brown, a running back for the Washington Redskins, gained 1,125 yards rushing in 1970, a total that seemed only half as important as the 1,216 that he gained in 1972. In the latter season his running was the key to the ground offense that helped the Redskins win the National Conference championship of the National Football League and a place in the Super Bowl. Brown, too, was a big factor in the passing game, catching 32 passes for 473 yards.

A slashing type of runner who employs both speed and power, Brown was named the league's most valuable player in more than one poll as well as being named to the all-pro team for the fourth straight year. He also gained a place in the record book alongside Jimmy Brown and Cookie Gilchrist as the only backs who gained more than 4,000 yards rushing in their first four seasons.

This is quite an achievement for a blocking back from Kansas State University who was almost overlooked in the pros' player draft. The Redskins selected him on the eighth round, the 191st player picked in 1969. He won a regular place as a runner that fall. The coach, Vince Lombardi, noting that Brown seemed to start slowly at the snap of the ball, had a hearing device installed in the player's helmet which overcame a slight problem and allowed him to hear the signals more clearly.

"Running the ball," Brown says, "is my job." And

WASHINGTON REDSKINS

LARRY BROWN, ace running back of the Washington Redskins, 1972 National Conference champions.

he ran for over 100 yards in each of six games in 1972, hitting a peak of 191 (a Redskin record) against the New York Giants. He was rested the last two games of the season and lost the rushing honors of the league by 35 yards to O. J. Simpson.

Brown, who was born in Clairton, Pa., on Sept. 19, 1947, is 5 feet 11 inches tall and weighs 195 pounds. As a youth, he lived in Pittsburgh and played on concrete fields in a deprived neighborhood.

The great defense men who have played against him are among his chief admirers. Larry Wilson of St. Louis said, "Larry Brown is the best since Gale Sayers. The key to his success is great desire."

BILL BRADDOCK

BURGER, Warren E.

The U. S. Supreme Court, under Chief Justice Warren E. Burger, experienced a shift to the right in 1972, with the addition of Nixon appointees Lewis F. Powell, Jr., and William H. Rehnquist in January, but its opinions were by no means mere echoes of administration policy. Its individual members maintained a high degree of flexibility. Although giving the President considerable support in such areas as law enforcement and criminal justice, the court differed with him in a number of instances, such as in its ruling against capital punishment as currently administered and in its ban on federal wiretapping without court authorization.

In 1972, Justice Burger himself continued to occupy a generally conservative position, casting his vote for decisions upholding a Massachusetts loyalty oath for state employees, surveillance of civilians by the Army, and curbs on pamphleteering in shopping center areas, among others. While adhering to a moderately liberal position on racial issues, he voted against the liberal majority in the case of *Wright* v. *City of Emporia,* drawing the distinction between desegregation, or the breaking down of racially separate school systems, which he acknowledges as the law of the land, and achievement of racial balance, involving the imposition of quotas, which in his view is not mandated by the

Constitution. Contrasting the Burger court with its liberal predecessor, columnist Max Lerner has observed that "the Warren philosophy had the court triggering crucial social changes while the Burger philosophy has it adjusting to them and trying to contain them."

Concerned about the increasing burdens facing the courts, Justice Burger called in May for the creation of a National Institute of Justice to help resolve federal and state judicial problems by conducting research, making grants available for private studies, and helping states and cities to improve their courts. A consistent advocate of prison reform, he also renewed his appeal for an improved penal system as the best means of combating crime.

Background. Of Swiss and German family background, Warren Earl Burger was born at St. Paul, Minn., on Sept. 17, 1907. He attended the University of Minnesota, and after obtaining his LL. B. with honors from St. Paul College of Law in 1931 he joined its faculty, combining teaching with law practice. As a delegate to the Republican National Convention in 1952 he helped Dwight D. Eisenhower win the presidential nomination. He served as assistant attorney general in charge of the civil rights division in the Justice Department from 1953 until 1956, when he was named judge of the Court of Appeals for the District of Columbia. As appeals court judge he pursued a firm law-and-order policy and maintained a fairly liberal position on civil rights, while advocating a number of judicial reforms. Nominated by President Nixon to succeed Earl Warren, Burger was sworn in as the 15th U. S. chief justice on June 24, 1969.

CHAPLIN, Charles

Charlie Chaplin, the "grand old man of comedy," made a triumphant return to the United States in April 1972, his first visit since he was barred in 1952 on political and moral grounds. The welcome he received indicated that his popularity as the tragicomic "little tramp" of Hollywood's golden age had remained intact. During his four-day stay in New York City, he was presented with the Handel Medallion, the city's highest award for achievement in the arts, by Mayor John V. Lindsay, and he was guest of honor at a "Salute to Charlie Chaplin," staged by the Film Society of Lincoln Center. The Academy Award ceremonies in Hollywood on April 10 were highlighted by the presentation to Chaplin of a special honorary "Oscar" for the "humor and humanity" he has brought to motion pictures.

The son of music hall performers, Charles Spencer Chaplin was born on April 16, 1889, in London, where he grew up amid poverty. He began as a boy to perform in London music halls, became a successful vaudeville trouper, and in 1910 went with the Fred Karno troupe on a tour in the United States. His per-

PETER L. GOULD

CHARLIE CHAPLIN was honored at the 1972 Academy Award ceremonies in April with special "Oscar" for his contribution to motion pictures.

formances there led to Hollywood film contracts, beginning with work for Mack Sennett's Keystone studios in 1913. During the next few years he appeared in scores of two-reel comedies, usually as the little vagabond who somehow manages to survive the adversities of life. After founding his own studio in 1918, he wrote, directed, produced, and acted in his own films, rarely deviating from his classic role.

Chaplin's full-length features include *The Kid* (1921), *The Gold Rush* (1925), *The Circus* (1928), and *City Lights* (1931). His last silent film was *Modern Times* (1936), a satire on industrial society, for which he composed the musical score. In his poignant lampoon of Nazism, *The Great Dictator* (1940), Chaplin appeared in a dual role—as Hynkel, the dictator of Tomania, and as a Jewish barber. He was seen as a debonair French Bluebeard with an antiwar message in *Monsieur Verdoux* (1947) and as an aging vaudevillian in *Limelight* (1952).

Meanwhile, Chaplin's personal and political life came increasingly under fire. Although he was acquitted of Mann Act charges in 1944, a court ruled against him in a paternity suit in 1945. Admittedly a "citizen of the world" and a "peacemonger," he became the target of congressional committees because of his identification with liberal causes in the midst of the Cold War. While on a trip abroad in 1952, Chaplin, who had remained a British subject, was notified that his reentry into the United States would be challenged. Thereafter he made his home in Switzerland with his fourth wife, the former Oona O'Neill, and their children. Chaplin starred in his production *A King in New York* (1957), a sharp satire on contemporary America, and wrote and directed *A Countess From Hongkong* (1967). He published *My Autobiography* in 1964.

CHOU EN-LAI

For Chinese Premier Chou En-lai, 1972 was a year of power, fame, and prodigious activity. Since the fall of Defense Minister Lin Piao in 1971, Chou had become the most powerful man after Mao Tse-tung. He was at the pinnacle of the state apparatus that administered the affairs of the country. While Mao remained head of the Chinese Communist party and laid down the general lines of policy, it was Chou who formulated specific policies and made crucial decisions in carrying out global strategy. An intellectual of pragmatic approach, he supplemented Mao the visionary.

One of the most experienced statesmen in modern diplomacy, Chou was the architect of China's "grand reconciliation" in 1972. He invited President Richard M. Nixon to China and together they brought an end to the 20-year hostility between China and the United States. Also in 1972, he conferred in Peking with Premier Kakuei Tanaka of Japan and secured Japan's recognition of Communist China. Chou bargained hard in the negotiations. His diplomatic skill and winning personality helped resolve difficulties on important issues.

Internally, Chou's major work in 1972 consisted in restoring political stability and furthering economic progress. He took steps to reorganize the military command shattered by the purge of Lin Piao and his military followers. His practical instinct called for appointments that would smooth out factional conflicts.

At 74, Chou was vigorous and energetic, with a remarkable memory and a firm grasp of details. But he was conscious of age. On more than one occasion he told his foreign guests that Communist China, because of historical factors, had too many elderly people in the government. He considered it highly essential that more younger men be elevated to the top leadership to ensure a smooth transition to a new line of successors.

Background. Chou En-lai was born in 1898 in Shaohing (Shaohsing), Chekiang. After graduating from Nankai Middle School in Tientsin in 1917, he studied first in Japan and then in France, where he joined the Chinese Communist party in 1922. Returning home in 1924, he quickly assumed a leading role in the party.

Chou became premier of the Communist government upon its establishment in 1949 and has held that position since. He displayed extraordinary administrative and diplomatic talents. Representing China at important conferences, including the Geneva Conference in 1954 and the Bandung Conference in 1955, he revealed diplomatic deftness.

During the Cultural Revolution (1966–69), Chou supported the Maoists but at the same time attempted to curb the militancy of the Red Guards. He emerged as a strong man toward the end of the Cultural Revolution, when China's return to political stability needed his moderation and flexibility.

CHESTER C. TAN

CONNALLY, John B.

Even after announcing on May 16 that he was resigning as secretary of the Treasury, John Connally stayed near the center of public affairs during 1972. He remained a major national figure with a possible future as a presidential candidate.

While still in the government, Connally served President Nixon in a variety of roles. Not only did he oversee the New Economic Policy and engage in international economic negotiations for the United States, he also carried out several purely diplomatic missions. He visited Asia and other areas as a fact finder for the President.

After resigning, Connally returned to Texas politics. He remained in the Democratic party in the face of many reports that he would join the GOP. He served as national chairman of "Democrats for Nixon" and brought many prominent national Democrats along with him. The landslide reelection victory for Nixon was, however, not entirely to Connally's advantage because the Texas senatorial race, in which he had supported the Democratic nominee, Barefoot Sanders, resulted in a victory for the Republican incumbent, John G. Tower. Nevertheless, Connally is often mentioned as a contender for the 1976 presidential nomination as a Democrat or as a Republican. As a middle-of-the-road Democrat he would present an alternative to the more liberal candidates who have dominated the party in the recent past. If he switches to the Republican party, he can run as a loyal servant of the administration. Many observers expected Connally to reenter the Nixon administration during the President's second term.

Background. John Bowden Connally, Jr., was born in Floresville, Texas, on Feb. 27, 1917. He earned an LL. B. at the University of Texas before joining the staff of Congressman Lyndon B. Johnson. He became President Kennedy's secretary of the Navy in 1961. He ran for governor of Texas in 1962, and was elected to three terms. In 1963, Connally was seriously wounded while riding in the car in which President Kennedy was assassinated, but he recovered fully. He has remained active in Texas politics, supporting the conservative faction in Democratic party affairs.

WALTER DARNELL JACOBS

DIMITRIOS I

On July 16, 1972, the 15-member Holy Synod in Istanbul elected Archbishop Dimitrios of Imroz and Tenedos, by a vote of 12 to 3, to be Archbishop of Constantinople and Ecumenical Patriarch of the Eastern Orthodox Church. He succeeded Athenagoras I, who died on July 7.

As Patriarch Dimitrios I, he became the spiritual leader of some 250 million Orthodox Christians throughout the world and *primus inter pares,* or "first among equals," of the bishops of the 15 autocephalous or independent Orthodox churches. The most junior of the bishops, Dimitrios had a reputation as a moderately liberal theologian, who remained aloof from church politics and concentrated on pastoral affairs. He became a candidate only after Archbishop Meliton of Chalcedon was barred from consideration by the Turkish government, which retains a veto power over patriarchal candidacies. Formally enthroned at St.

(Left) *DIMITRIOS I was elected Ecumenical Patriarch of the Eastern Orthodox Church and Archbishop of Constantinople in July.* (Above) *Jazz great Duke Ellington with the Rev. John Gensel, a Protestant clergyman.*

George's Church in Istanbul on July 18, Dimitrios declared: "We will follow the great way of our predecessor... towards Christian unity through the spirit of pan-Orthodox unity. And we will not ignore our duty of engaging in a dialogue with Islam and the other monotheistic religions."

Dimitrios, whose family name is Papadopoulos, was born in Istanbul about 1914 and received his early education at a Greek school in Therapia. He began his theological training at 17, at the island monastery and seminary of Halki, a leading educational center for Orthodox theologians. Ordained a deacon in 1937, he briefly served in a parish in Istanbul, then preached for two years in Greece before returning to Turkey in 1939. In 1942 he was ordained a priest for the Greek parish of Ferikoy, a middle-class suburb of Istanbul. He was consecrated a bishop in 1964, and on Feb. 15, 1972, was made Metropolitan (Archbishop) of Imroz and Tenedos, two Turkish islands in the Aegean Sea with a population of some 3,500.

EAGLETON, Thomas Francis

The Democratic vice presidential candidate for a brief period in 1972, Thomas F. Eagleton is a U. S. senator from Missouri. Elected to the Senate in 1968, he opposed the Vietnam War and Pentagon overspending and supported environmental and consumer protection. His youth, urban Roman Catholic background, and good labor record resulted in his selection as the vice presidential nominee.

After the convention closed in July, the Eagleton candidacy encountered difficulty. Anticipating media disclosure, Eagleton revealed on July 25 that he had been hospitalized three times between 1960 and 1966 for "nervous exhaustion and fatigue" and had undergone psychiatric treatment, including electric shock therapy, for "depression." George McGovern, the Democratic presidential candidate, supported Eagleton "1,000 percent," indicating that had he known the facts before the nomination it would have made no difference. However, pressure against Eagleton built up rapidly within the Democratic party, and influential newspapers called for a new vice presidential candi-

date. Eagleton wanted to stay on the ticket, but McGovern asked for his resignation and on July 31 the senator graciously withdrew.

The "Eagleton Affair" resulted in nationwide debate on mental illness and on the method of choosing vice presidential candidates. It delayed the Democratic campaign and undermined McGovern's public image. The mere selection of Eagleton made McGovern seem incompetent, though Eagleton could also be faulted for not telling McGovern of his past before accepting the nomination. McGovern's initial support for his running mate, followed by the "dumping" of Eagleton, suggested ruthlessness to many voters. Delay of nearly a week as McGovern offered one leading Democrat after another the second place on the ticket seemed to indicate indecisiveness.

Background. Son of a prominent St. Louis attorney, Thomas F. Eagleton was born on Sept. 4, 1929. A graduate of Amherst (1950) and Harvard Law School (1953), he moved up rapidly in Missouri politics, serving as circuit attorney (1957–60), attorney general (1961–65), lieutenant governor (1965–68), and as U. S. senator from 1969.

ORVILLE H. ZABEL

THOMAS EAGLETON, Missouri's junior senator, was the Democratic party's vice presidential candidate until he withdrew from the race after a controversy over his having been treated for a mental health problem.

ECHEVERRIA ALVAREZ, Luis

President Luis Echeverría Alvarez of Mexico concentrated his efforts in 1972 on making his country more self-sufficient and on raising the living standards of its population. He emerged as an important spokesman for Latin American interests. During a state visit to the United States in June, addressing a joint session of Congress, he sharply criticized American foreign policy for its neglect of small nations. Among the concessions he won from President Nixon was the assurance that the salinity of Colorado River waters, which had long been damaging Mexican farmlands, would be reduced.

Earlier in the year, Echeverría visited Japan to cement economic relations. His government also established diplomatic relations with the People's Republic of China and concluded a reciprocal trade agreement with Cuba. His domestic economic measures included land redistribution, nationalization of some banks and public utilities, a massive public works program, and restrictions on foreign investment in Mexican businesses. In his State of the Union message on September 1, Echeverría declared that the country was recovering from its recession and that inflation was being curbed.

Background. Luis Echeverría Alvarez, the son of a civil servant, was born in Mexico City on Jan. 17, 1922. He received a law degree from the National University of Mexico in 1945 and became a member of its law faculty two years later. After joining Mexico's dominant Institutional Revolutionary party in 1946, he served in a succession of administrative jobs with the party and sub-cabinet posts in the government. In 1964 he was appointed to the key cabinet position of minister of the interior. In that capacity he forcefully suppressed the student riots of 1968. He was elected to the presidency in July 1970 with only token opposition, and was inaugurated on December 1. During his first year in office he made conciliatory moves toward dissenters of the left and earned a reputation as a liberal reformer.

ELLINGTON, Duke

Composer, pianist, and band leader Duke Ellington, known as the "dean of black musicians" and acclaimed by jazz critic Ralph Gleason as "the greatest single talent... in the history of jazz," was honored in July 1972 by the proclamation of Duke Ellington Week in the state of Wisconsin. In October he presided over a convocation, at Yale University, of a "conservatory without walls" that launched the $1 million Duke Ellington Fellowship Program, a special division of the Yale School of Music. The program seeks to preserve the Afro-American musical heritage through scholarships, teaching fellowships, and other projects. The fundraising event was highlighted by an Ellington concert and presentations of the new Duke Ellington Medal. Earlier it was announced that Ellington would present his collection of original letters and manuscripts of 19th and 20th century black writers and composers, including his own compositions and arrangements, to Yale University's James Weldon Johnson Collection of Negro Arts and Letters.

Ellington's more than 900 compositions, spanning over half a century, include sacred works, background music for plays and motion pictures, compositions for ballet and musical comedy, and such popular hit tunes as "Mood Indigo," "In My Solitude," and "Sophisticated Lady." Among his more ambitious orchestral works are *Liberian Suite* (1947), written for the government of Liberia; *Harlem Suite* (1950), commissioned by Arturo Toscanini; and *Far East Suite,* inspired by his 1963 State Department tour of the Orient. In 1965 he conducted the first of a series of sacred concerts.

A pioneer in the use of new musical techniques and arrangements, Ellington won numerous Grammy awards for his recordings. On his 70th birthday he received the Presidential Medal of Freedom from President Nixon at a White House ceremony, and in 1970 he was elected to the National Institute of Arts and Letters.

Background. The son of a government employee, Edward Kennedy Ellington—who acquired the nickname "Duke" as a child—was born on April 29, 1899, in Washington, D. C. He began to play the piano at the age of 7 and created his first composition at 16. In the 1920's he built up his own orchestra, which won national recognition during its engagement at Harlem's Cotton Club from 1927 to 1932. Since then, this unusual orchestra, whose gradually shifting personnel always included several outstanding solo instrumentalists, has been heard in major concert halls throughout the world.

ELLSBERG, Daniel

Daniel Ellsberg, a former government military strategist, whose release in 1971 of the Pentagon Papers made him a hero among many critics of the Vietnam War, went on trial in the summer of 1972 for his role in making the material available to the news media. The papers, a classified report dealing with the history of the U. S. involvement in Indochina from 1945 to 1967, were held by the Rand Corporation, where Ellsberg had been employed.

The 12-count indictment brought against him on Dec. 30, 1971, charged him with conspiracy, espionage, and theft of government property, making him subject to a possible maximum penalty of 115 years imprisonment and a $120,000 fine. On Dec. 12, 1972, after several months of delay, a mistrial was declared and the jurors were dismissed on the ground that they might have become prejudiced during the long waiting period. Ellsberg and his co-defendant, Anthony J. Russo Jr., had tried unsuccessfully to obtain a Supreme Court hearing on an appeal, charging that they had been subjected to illegal wiretapping by the government.

After the defendants waived double jeopardy protection, selection of a new jury was begun in January 1973. During 1972, Ellsberg made a number of public appearances around the country, addressing antiwar rallies and promoting his new book, *Papers on the War.*

Background. The son of an engineer, Daniel Ellsberg was born in Chicago on April 7, 1931, and was educated in private schools in Detroit. After graduating from Harvard in 1952 and studying at Cambridge, England, he served with the U. S. Marines in the Middle East from 1954 to 1957. Upon receiving his Ph. D. from Harvard in 1959 he joined the Rand Corporation as a specialist in nuclear strategy. In 1964 he joined the Defense Department as a special assistant for international security affairs, and in 1965 he went to Vietnam to work on the pacification program. He returned to the Rand Corporation in 1967. Increasingly disillusioned with the Vietnam War, he decided to make the Pentagon Papers, which he had helped to prepare, available to the public. They began to appear in the New York *Times* in June 1971.

FONDA, Jane

Film star Jane Fonda, whose sensitive portrayal of a call girl in the detective thriller *Klute* won her the best actress award of 1971 from the Academy of Motion Picture Arts and Sciences, also made headlines during 1972 in her real-life role as a militant antiwar activist. Early in the year she toured U. S. military bases in the Philippines, Japan, and Okinawa with her satirical antiwar revue *F. T. A.* ("Free the Army"). The show, which had previously toured the United States and won an Obie Award as an Off-Broadway production, was also seen in 1972 as a motion picture. During a "fact-finding tour" of North Vietnam in July, she broadcast, on Hanoi Radio, an appeal to U. S. pilots to stop their bombing raids. This action brought her censure from the State Department and from members of Congress.

In December, Jane Fonda announced that she planned to marry the antiwar activist Tom Hayden after her divorce from the French film director Roger Vadim became final. Her most recent motion picture appearance was in Jean-Luc Godard's *Tout Va Bien.*

Background. Jane Seymour Fonda, the daughter of the veteran motion picture star Henry Fonda, was born in New York City on Dec. 21, 1937. She was educated in private schools and at Vassar College. She enrolled in the Actors Studio in 1958 and financed her studies there by working as a photographer's model. Her Broadway stage debut in Joshua Logan's production of *There Was a Little Girl* (1959) brought her favorable notices. She then embarked on a successful motion picture career, appearing in such films as *Period of Adjustment* (1962), *Sunday in New York* (1964), *Cat Ballou* (1965), *Any Wednesday* (1966), *Barefoot in the Park* (1967), *Barbarella* (1968), and *They Shoot Horses, Don't They?* (1969). Since the late 1960's, she has devoted a major part of her time to social causes.

GANDHI, Indira

Prime Minister Indira Gandhi's dominant position in the Indian political scene was further consolidated in 1972. In State Assembly elections held in March in 16 states and 2 union territories, Mrs. Gandhi's ruling Congress party won over 70% of all the contested assembly seats and a clear majority in all but two small states and one union territory. After the elections she reorganized her cabinet and was influential in the formation of new Congress governments in many states and in the reorganization of the Congress party at state and local levels. She had less success on the economic front, especially in trying to implement her election pledge to abolish poverty.

In early February, after two days of talks in Calcutta, Mrs. Gandhi and Sheikh Mujibur Rahman, prime minister of the new state of Bangladesh, agreed that Indian troops would be withdrawn from Bangladesh by March 25. In mid-March Mrs. Gandhi visited Dacca, where she and Sheikh Mujib signed a treaty of friendship, cooperation, and peace.

In late June and early July Mrs. Gandhi and Pakistan's President Zulfikar Ali Bhutto held a summit meeting in Simla. In the Simla Agreement they pledged to resolve their disputes by peaceful means, to resume communications, trade, and other contacts, and to withdraw their troops to "their side of the border."

On June 14, Mrs. Gandhi made a major address to the UN Conference on the Human Environment, meeting in Stockholm. Immediately afterward she paid state visits to Czechoslovakia and Hungary.

Background. The only daughter of the late Prime Minister Jawaharlal Nehru, Indira Gandhi was born in Allahabad on Nov. 19, 1917. She was educated in India, Switzerland, and at Oxford. On her return to India she became active in the independence movement and was imprisoned by the British in 1942–43.

When her father became the first prime minister of the Republic of India in 1947, Mrs. Gandhi served as his official hostess. She was president of the Congress party in 1959–60 and minister of information and broadcasting in 1964–66. She became prime minister in January 1966. The Congress party was split by ideological differences, and Mrs. Gandhi's wing was given a decisive majority in the Lok Sabha (the lower house) in the 1971 general elections. She won further support by her firm leadership in the crisis with Pakistan in 1971.

NORMAN D. PALMER

GENEEN, Harold S.

In March 1972, Harold S. Geneen, the president, chairman, and chief executive officer of the International Telephone and Telegraph Corporation, defended himself and his company against damaging statements reported by syndicated columnist Jack Anderson. In late February, Anderson published the so-called Dita Beard memorandum that linked an ITT pledge of $400,000 for the 1972 Republican National Convention at San Diego with an out-of-court settlement of three antitrust actions against ITT, agreed to by the U. S. Department of Justice and ITT in July 1971. In an appearance before the Senate Judiciary Committee on March 15, 1972, Geneen testified that "there was absolutely no connection" between ITT's pledge and the antitrust settlement with the government and that the pledge was for $100,000 in cash and another $100,000 if needed. He also testified that he knew nothing about the Beard memo until he read about it in the press.

In compliance with the antitrust settlement, Geneen took steps in 1972 to divest ITT of four of its subsidiaries to enable it to retain its largest and most profitable subsidiary, the Hartford Fire Insurance Company.

Background. Harold Sydney Geneen was born in Bournemouth, England, on Jan. 22, 1910, and was brought to the United States at the age of one. After graduating from New York University in 1934, he held a succession of jobs as an accountant and then served in executive positions with the Bell & Howell Company, Jones & Laughlin Steel Corporation, and Raytheon Manufacturing Company. Taking charge of ITT in 1959, he reorganized it almost singlehandedly and greatly expanded its holdings around the world. Under his direction, its sales climbed from $765 million in 1959 to about $7.3 billion in 1971, making ITT not only the ninth-largest industrial concern in the United States but also the largest conglomerate in the nation.

GRAY, L. Patrick, 3d

Assistant Attorney General L. Patrick Gray, 3d was named by President Nixon as acting director of the Federal Bureau of Investigation on May 3, 1972, following the death of J. Edgar Hoover. Shortly after taking charge of the Bureau, Gray announced widespread changes, including plans to hire women and more minority group members as special agents, relax standards of dress and grooming for FBI agents, allow greater public scrutiny of the Bureau's activities, and intensify its campaign against organized crime and drug traffic. Over the next few months he instituted major personnel changes in many of the FBI's top offices throughout the nation. Gray's innovations have been widely praised.

Background. Louis Patrick Gray 3d was born in St. Louis, Mo., on July 18, 1916, and grew up in Houston, Texas. A 1940 graduate of the U. S. Naval Academy and a law graduate of George Washington University, he served on submarines during World War II and the Korean War, rising to the rank of captain. Gray was military assistant to the chairman of the Joint Chiefs of Staff from 1958 until 1960, when he resigned from the Navy to join Nixon's presidential campaign staff. After several years in private law practice, he became executive assistant to Nixon's secretary of health, education, and welfare Robert Finch in 1969 and assistant attorney general in charge of the Justice Department's Civil Rights Division in 1970. Senate confirmation of his nomination as deputy attorney general was pending at the time of his appointment as acting FBI director.

GRAYSON, C. Jackson, Jr.

C. Jackson Grayson, Jr., chairman of the seven-member Federal Price Commission created in October 1971, continued his efforts to hold the line on inflationary price increases in 1972. Early in the year the commission suspended all pending rate increases requested by telephone companies and gas and electric utilities. It also ruled that the costs of wage increases exceeding the 5.5% guideline could not be passed on to the consumer. While exempting small business from price controls, the commission tightened its reins on larger firms and in April began to order price rollbacks for companies whose profits exceeded allowable margins.

Concerned about rising food prices, Grayson warned that raw agricultural products would be placed under controls if the food price rise continued. In May,

(Above, left) *L. PATRICK GRAY III, acting director of the FBI.* (Above) *Film actress Jane Fonda, speaking after her return from North Vietnam.* (Left) *Harold S. Geneen, president of ITT, at March 16 meeting of Senate Judiciary Committee.*

he created a "food watch unit" to examine inflationary trends. In June, he persuaded President Nixon to remove all quota restrictions on meat imports and to bring raw seafood, fresh fruit, vegetables, and eggs under price controls. Although the Price Commission failed to attain its goal of holding the price increase rate down to the 2.5% guideline during its first year, leading economists credited it with helping to stem the tide of inflation. At a congressional hearing in November, Grayson said that while the actual price increase rate for the preceding year was 3.2%, it would have been as much as 5.2% without controls.

The son of a farmer, Charles Jackson Grayson, Jr. was born at Fort Necessity, La., on Oct. 8, 1923. He attended Tulane University and the University of Pennsylvania's Wharton School, and he received a doctorate from the Harvard graduate school of business administration in 1959. After World War II service in the Navy he was successively an instructor at Tulane, a newspaper reporter, an FBI agent, manager of the family farm, and a partner in an import-export firm. He returned to the Tulane faculty in 1953 and became dean of its business school in 1963. Appointed dean of the school of business administration at Southern Methodist University in 1968, he instituted major reforms in its curriculum. He took a leave of absence from SMU in 1971 when he became chairman of the Price Commission.

HEATH, Edward

British Prime Minister Edward Heath received his reward for 10 years' effort to bring Britain into the European Economic Community (EEC), or Common Market, when Britain signed the Treaty of Rome in Brussels on Jan. 22, 1972. Membership followed on Jan. 1, 1973. The fact that the Labour party had opposed entry on the terms negotiated and that British opinion was divided on the question of EEC membership was brought home by an incident at the time of the signing when Heath was splashed with ink by a woman opposed to Britain's membership.

Despite some opposition from within Heath's own party, the government's European Communities Bill passed its second reading in the House of Commons in February. With a number of Labour votes to assist him, Heath succeeded by a majority of eight. In June, the Commons passed, also by eight votes, the most controversial feature of the bill—the absorption of EEC law into British law. The bill became law in October. The Labour party pledged, if returned to power, to renegotiate the terms of the entry and then to consult the British electorate.

Heath continued his late 1971 retreat from the commitment to reduce governmental intervention in the economy. Shipbuilding was heavily subsidized by the government during the course of the year, as was the computer industry. The expansion of the money supply was facilitated by the June decision to "float" sterling. But Heath's determination to stand firm against union pay demands, especially in the nationalized industries, was ineffective. In February the miners won large pay increases as a result of strike action, and in March the railwaymen followed suit. Neither a compulsory "cooling-off" period nor a compulsory strike ballot, required by the Industrial Relations Act, prevented the railwaymen from winning more from the Railways Board than it was initially willing to give. In November, after his failure to get a voluntary system of incomes restraint, Heath imposed a 90-day

EDWARD HEATH, British prime minister, talks about the economy at a press conference on September 26.

wage, price, and dividend freeze, thus reversing his 1970 pledge not to consider a statutory incomes policy.

In Northern Ireland, direct rule was imposed by the British government in March. A period of conciliation and relaxation was followed, in July, by more drastic army action against extremist groups.

Heath reshuffled his government in April, July, and November, but relatively few of his existing ministerial team left the government altogether. Through the year, by-election results recorded significant anti-government swings. The local government elections showed heavy Conservative losses, and in December the government lost a seat to the Liberals. The opinion polls showed that Heath was not significantly less popular than Labour's Harold Wilson, and toward the end of the year the popularity of both Heath and his party increased slightly.

Background. Edward Richard George Heath was born in Broadstairs, Kent, on July 9, 1916, and was educated at Balliol College, Oxford. After military service during World War II, he entered the civil service as an administrator of civil aviation. Since 1950 he has represented Bexley, a London suburb, as a Conservative in Parliament. Successively party whip, minister of labor, and lord privy seal, he was elected Conservative party leader in 1965 and became prime minister after the Conservative victory in the 1970 election.

A. J. BEATTIE

IRVING, Clifford

One of the most imaginative literary hoaxes ever perpetrated was unfolded during January and February 1972, when a much-heralded "as-told-to" autobiography of the recluse tycoon Howard Hughes—scheduled for serialization in *Life* magazine and for publication by McGraw-Hill—was revealed to have been a complete fabrication, concocted by author Clifford Irving. Having convinced the McGraw-Hill staff, by means of forged documents, that the manuscript submitted to them was based on actual interviews with Hughes, Irving was paid $750,000, of which $650,000 was to have gone to

Hughes. The details of the affair gradually came to light after the revelation that the checks, made out to "H. R. Hughes" at Irving's request, were deposited in Swiss bank accounts under the name Helga R. Hughes, and that the depositor was, in fact, Irving's wife, Edith.

In a "book about the book," *What Really Happened*, published in the fall of 1972 and co-authored with Richard R. Suskind, his collaborator in the plot, Irving revealed that he had constructed the "autobiography" from material taken from the Library of Congress and the files of Time, Inc., among other sources. Found guilty of fraud and sentenced to two and one-half years in prison and a $10,000 fine, Irving entered the Allenwood, Pa., federal prison in August. Edith Irving, released after serving two months of a two-year sentence, faced forgery and bank fraud charges in Switzerland. Suskind, convicted of conspiracy and grand larceny, served five months in a New York state prison.

Background. Clifford Michael Irving, the son of cartoonist Jay Irving, was born in New York City on Nov. 5, 1930. He studied creative writing at Cornell University, earning his B. A. in 1951, and later taught at the University of California at Los Angeles. His writings include the novels *On a Darkling Plain* (1956), *The Losers* (1957), *The Valley* (1961), and *The 38th Floor* (1967). On the strength of *Fake!* (1969), a book about the art forger Elmyr de Hory, Irving received an advance of $100,000 from McGraw-Hill for his next four books. A resident of the Spanish island of Ibiza since 1962, Irving was married to German–born Edith Sommer, his fourth wife, in 1967; they have two sons.

KISSINGER, Henry A.

In 1972, Henry A. Kissinger continued to serve as President Nixon's principal adviser on foreign policy during a period of startling developments in international affairs. As assistant to the President for national security affairs, Kissinger has traveled to the People's Republic of China, the Soviet Union, Vietnam, France, and other countries. Each trip preceded dramatic events. Kissinger's secret visit to China in 1971 prepared the way for Nixon's historic journey in February 1972 and a basic change in American policy toward the Maoist leadership. In May, Kissinger accompanied the President to Moscow where the SALT agreements on limitation of offensive missiles and defensive systems were signed.

Kissinger commuted to Paris and Saigon and even to Hanoi in an effort to work out a cease-fire in Vietnam. After protracted negotiations, he announced on October 26 that peace in Vietnam was "at hand." But on December 16 he had a gloomier report, and blamed Hanoi for a deadlock and failure to achieve an agreement that Nixon regarded as "just and fair."

Kissinger left his imprint on American foreign relations and on the nature of international politics. Adhering to a balance of forces theory, he urged a reassessment of a new world situation in which China and the USSR would play a major part. He argued for U. S. acceptance of objective reality and for the discarding of old assumptions. Demonstrated skills and limitless energy made Kissinger, in the view of some, the "one indispensable person" in the administration. In almost daily contact with the President, he serves as executive secretary of the National Security Council, chairman of the Council on International Economic Policy, chairman of the Defense Programs Review Board, and on other bodies. He has not always been popular throughout the Executive Department but is widely respected. His authority conflicts somewhat with that of Secretary of State William Rogers, but no evidence of friction exists.

Early Career. Henry Alfred Kissinger was born in Fürth, Germany, on May 27, 1923. His family went to New York City in 1938. He served in the U. S. Army during World War II. At Harvard, he earned a B. A. in 1950 *summa cum laude* and a Ph. D. in 1954. He served with the Council on Foreign Relations, and in 1957 published *Nuclear Weapons and Foreign Policy*. Kissinger advised various governmental agencies and

headed the Rockefeller Brothers Fund special studies project. He directed Harvard's Defense Studies Program from 1959 to 1969, when he went to Washington with a leave of absence from Harvard. Kissinger, who is divorced, has two children.

WALTER DARNELL JACOBS

KLEINDIENST, Richard G.

On July 12, 1972, Richard G. Kleindienst was sworn in as U. S. attorney general. A strong advocate of "law and order" with a moderately liberal record on civil rights, Kleindienst had been serving as deputy attorney general under John N. Mitchell. Although he had been nominated by President Nixon on February 15, following Mitchell's resignation, his confirmation by the Senate was delayed because of allegations linking a favorable settlement of three antitrust actions against the International Telephone and Telegraph Corporation (ITT) with a pledge of some $400,000 made by the corporation to help finance the 1972 Republican National Convention. Though Kleindienst had been involved in the settlement of these actions, six weeks of Senate Judiciary Committee hearings failed to uncover any clear evidence of wrongdoing on his part. On June 8 he was confirmed by a Senate vote of 64 to 19.

On taking office, Kleindienst pledged himself to the firm enforcement of civil rights and antitrust laws, a vigorous campaign against organized crime and the drug traffic, and prison reform. On December 8, President Nixon announced that he would retain Kleindienst as attorney general during his second term, to ensure "continuity of firm leadership" in the Justice Department.

The son of a railway brakeman, Richard Gordon Kleindienst was born on Aug. 5, 1923, in Winslow, Ariz. He attended the University of Arizona, served in the Army Air Force in World War II, and entered law practice after graduating from Harvard Law School in 1950. After serving in the Arizona House of Representatives in 1953–54, he became state Republican chairman. In 1964 he was pre-convention campaign manager for Republican presidential candidate Barry Goldwater and, in the same year, made an unsuccessful bid for the Arizona governorship. A key campaign aide to Nixon in 1968, Kleindienst was appointed deputy attorney general in January 1969.

KOSYGIN, Aleksei Nikolayevich

Despite some Western predictions that he might retire in 1972, Soviet Premier Aleksei Kosygin continued to be head of the government and second in rank in the Soviet leadership only to Leonid Brezhnev, the first secretary of the Communist party. However, Kosygin seemed to become increasingly secondary, making only one major speech during the year compared with more than a dozen by Brezhnev.

Only two trips abroad were made by Kosygin during 1972, the first being to Czechoslovakia for a meeting of the Warsaw Pact leaders. The second, in April, was to Iraq, where he negotiated and signed the trail-blazing Soviet-Iraqi 15-year treaty of friendship and cooperation, by which Iraq was promised Soviet armament, technical aid, and cooperation in the joint struggle against "Zionism."

In May, Kosygin took part in the Soviet negotiations with President Nixon, when the latter visited Moscow. The premier and President signed the U. S.-Soviet treaty for cooperation in the exploration and use of outer space. But Brezhnev signed the more important agreements limiting Soviet-American strategic armament.

Kosygin's sole major public speech in 1972 was on September 30 to the Soviet State Planning Committee. Admitting that the harvest slump had caused difficulties for Soviet industry, he demanded that the 1973 economic plan force factories to work three daily shifts instead of the present two, improve present factories rather than build new ones, and stop the costly im-

PRESIDENTIAL AIDE Henry Kissinger became a world figure through his many diplomatic journeys in 1972.

portation of industrial goods which the USSR can produce at home.

Background. Kosygin was born in St. Petersburg (now Leningrad) on Feb. 20, 1904. He is a skilled economist and since 1939 has held such high posts as chairman of the State Planning Committee, vice premier of the USSR, premier of the Russian Soviet republic, and head of the ministries for the textile industry, light industry, the consumer goods industry, and finance. He was a Politburo member from 1946 to 1952, and from 1957 on. Following the ouster of Nikita Khrushchev as premier in 1964, Kosygin succeeded him. One of the more popular leaders, he is considered less Stalinist than Brezhnev.

ELLSWORTH RAYMOND

LAIRD, Melvin R.

After four years as U. S. secretary of defense, Melvin R. Laird resigned in January 1973. He had endeavored to leave a defense establishment modeled to his concept of "a national security strategy of realistic deterrence." While Laird held office, the U. S. ground combat role in the Indochina War was virtually ended, but American air and sea power was still heavily committed.

In turning to "realistic deterrence," Laird abandoned the "flexible response" strategy geared to the needs of Vietnam-type wars. Realistic deterrence rested on strategic sufficiency, technological superiority, improved readiness and modernization, strong National Guard and reserve forces, assistance to friendly countries, and total utilization of resources. None of these concepts is without controversy, but Laird established his overall defense concept by combining them logically.

Within budget limitations, Laird laid the groundwork for the new all-volunteer Army, and he sought to meet demands for improved conditions of life in the military services. He urged modernization of the strategic forces to include development of the B-1 bomber and the Trident submarine, noting that neither weapon is

POLAROID LAND

WIDE WORLD

(Left) *EDWIN H. LAND is founder, president, and research director of Polaroid Corporation.* (Right) *Henry Lewis, music director of New Jersey Symphony, became first black conductor at Metropolitan Opera, New York.*

prohibited by the strategic-arms limitations agreement with the Soviet Union.

As Laird left office, critics of the Pentagon still found the department rife with inefficiency. They cited cost overruns on new weapons and questioned the effectiveness of some weapons. Increases in drug addiction and racial unrest and scattered breakdowns in discipline also caused concern. As a result, Laird's goal of restoring public respect for the armed forces was not fully realized.

Background. Melvin Robert Laird was born in Omaha, Nebr., on Sept. 1, 1922, and grew up in Marshfield, Wis. He graduated from Carleton College and served in the Navy in World War II. He was a member of the U. S. House from 1953 to 1969.

WALTER DARNELL JACOBS

LAND, Edwin H.

Edwin H. Land, the developer of practical one-step photography and the founder, president, and research director of the Polaroid Corporation, demonstrated his revolutionary new pocket-sized SX-70 Polaroid color-film camera on April 25, 1972.

The SX-70, which weighs 26 ounces and measures about 1 inch by 4 inches by 7 inches when folded flat, is the product of seven years of research and an investment of nearly $250 million. It is a single-lens reflex camera that ejects a 3⅛-inch by 3⅛-inch bluish-green sheet about 1.2 seconds after exposure. A recognizable image appears before one's eyes within one minute, and a completely finished brilliant color photograph forms within 4 to 10 minutes. The camera is loaded with a 10-picture film pack, and a wafer-thin battery is built into each pack. The battery powers a transistorized exposure control system and a miniature electric motor. Film advancement is done automatically, and there are no chemical-laden negatives to throw away after picture-taking. In Land's view, the SX-70 heralds "a system that will be a partner in perception, enabling us to see the objects in the world around us more vividly." (See also PHOTOGRAPHY.)

Edwin Herbert Land was born in Bridgeport, Conn., on May 7, 1909. He graduated from Norwich Academy in 1926 and began to experiment on ways to polarize light while a student at Harvard University in 1928. Leaving the university without graduating, Land carried on his research independently and in 1934 obtained his first patents on polarizing sheets, which eliminate much of the glare from light. In 1937 he founded the Polaroid Corporation, which at first worked on the development of polarizers for automobile headlights but later was more successful in producing sunglasses, industrial goggles, World War II military equipment, filters for cameras, and viewing glasses for 3-D motion pictures.

In 1943, Land conceived of the idea of "instant" photography, and five years later he began marketing the first "snap it, see it" black-and-white Polaroid camera, which brought the company $5 million worth of sales within a year. The development of one-step color photography was announced by Land in 1959, and the first Polaroid camera using that process was marketed in 1963. Under Land, the fast-growing Polaroid Corporation became the chief competitor of the Eastman Kodak Company. An estimated 30 million Land cameras were in use in 1972.

LEWIS, Henry

In October 1972, Henry Lewis, music director of the New Jersey Symphony, became the first black conductor at the Metropolitan Opera of New York. His engagement was one of a series of moves by the Metropolitan's late general manager Goeran Gentele to revitalize the company. Conducting *La Bohème,* with Anna Moffo and Richard Tucker, for his Met debut, Lewis was praised by critics for his "robust energy" and his "fresh" and "vigorous" approach to that often-performed opera.

Henry Lewis was born on Oct. 16, 1932, in Los Angeles, Calif. A musical prodigy, he learned to play stringed instruments and the piano in his early childhood. At 16, having mastered the double bass, but unable to obtain an audition, Lewis gave a series of private recitals and was hired by the Los Angeles Philharmonic as a double bassist, becoming its first black musician and its youngest member. While serving in Europe with the U. S. Army from 1955 to 1959, Lewis played the double bass with the Seventh Army Symphony and also served for a time as its music director, conducting concerts in Germany and the Netherlands.

Returning to the Los Angeles Philharmonic after his discharge, he founded the Los Angeles Chamber Orchestra, and toured Europe with it in 1963 under the sponsorship of the U. S. State Department. From 1965 to 1968 he was music director of the Los Angeles Opera Company. During the 1960's he also made appearances as a guest conductor with the San Francisco Opera, La Scala in Milan, and the Boston and Chicago symphonies. Appointed music director and conductor of the New Jersey Symphony in Newark in 1968, Lewis became the first black director of a statewide orchestral organization, and during his first years in that post he greatly enhanced its stature. In 1960 Lewis married the mezzo-soprano Marilyn Horne, a star with the Metropolitan Opera.

McGOVERN, George Stanley

On Nov. 7, 1972, American voters overwhelmingly rejected the presidential candidacy of Sen. George S. McGovern of South Dakota. Running against President Nixon, he won only 17 electoral votes, from Massachusetts and the District of Columbia. He gained about 38% of the popular vote in one of the worst defeats ever suffered by a Democratic candidate. McGovern ascribed his defeat to the "Eagleton matter," the neutrality of George Wallace, and the ability of his opponents to label him a radical.

In winning the Democratic party nomination, McGovern had relied on youth, minorities, and other disaffected groups. He utilized new party rules, which opened party affairs to greater public participation, to dominate the primaries and state conventions. He won the presidential nomination on the first ballot at the convention in Miami Beach on July 13. Winning the convention in this fashion, he alienated a number of old party bosses and functionaries and offended some elements of the labor movement. His national campaign began with a party so divided that the former Democratic coalition of city machines, blacks, the South, and labor unions no longer existed. McGovern planned to substitute a new coalition of young people and liberals.

Hopes for such a coalition were almost immediately dashed. McGovern chose Sen. Thomas F. Eagleton of Missouri as his vice presidential candidate. When it was learned that Eagleton had undergone electric shock treatment for depression, McGovern said that he was behind him "one thousand percent." A week later, he removed Eagleton from the ticket and replaced him with R. Sargent Shriver. Some voters interpreted the Eagleton matter as showing that McGovern was "just another politician" and not the new man of integrity after all.

The Wallace problem arose for the McGovern candidacy during the primaries when Gov. George C. Wallace of Alabama seemed to be attracting many voters who might otherwise go to McGovern. McGovern turned back the Wallace challenge in the party, but most of the potential Wallace voters went to Nixon in the general election and not to McGovern.

McGovern was identified by many as the candidate of the left. He attempted to overcome that impression and to present himself as a reasonable and thoughtful candidate of all the people. His supposed positions on amnesty for draft dodgers, legalization of marihuana, abortion, tax refom, welfare assistance, defense cuts, and Israel contributed to his "radical" image, although he attempted repeatedly to clarify his views on these questions. His strongest issue, opposition to the war in Vietnam, was undercut by reports of progress in the peace negotiations.

McGovern said he will not run for president again. His term as senator from South Dakota expires in 1974, and he is expected to seek reelection. He has resisted charges by some Democratic leaders that the party is in a "shambles," and has indicated that he will work to restore party unity. In December, McGovern gave some positive evidence of this by accepting with good grace the selection of a new Democratic National Committee chairman who had been opposed by his own faction.

Background. George Stanley McGovern was born in Avon, S. Dak., on July 19, 1922, the son of a Methodist minister. He graduated from Dakota Wesleyan University and earned M. A. and Ph. D. degrees from Northwestern University. In World War II, he served as a pilot on a B-24 in 35 combat missions over Europe. He taught political science at Dakota Wesleyan. McGovern served in the U. S. House of Representatives from 1957 to 1961, as director of the Food for Peace Program in 1961–62, and was elected to the Senate in 1962 and 1968. McGovern is married to the former Eleanor Stegeberg and has five children and three grandchildren.

WALTER DARNELL JACOBS

SEN. GEORGE McGOVERN, Democratic presidential nominee, with Mrs. McGovern and their grandson.

MARCOS, Ferdinand E.

President Ferdinand E. Marcos of the Philippines imposed martial law on Sept. 21, 1972, for an indefinite period. He declared that he was doing so to save the country from Communist revolution and to enable him to institute thorough reforms in the economy and the government.

During the year, Philippine troops were sporadically engaged in combat with Muslim dissidents in the south and with guerrillas of the Maoist New People's Army. In August, Marcos declared a state of emergency in Luzon, following massive floods described as the worst natural calamity in the nation's history. His proclamation of martial law in September came after a month-long wave of violence.

Ruling by decree, Marcos jailed hundreds, began weeding out corruption in government by dismissing thousands of civil servants, enforced a strict prohibition of firearms, and inaugurated a land distribution program. He promised educational and judicial reforms, measures to stimulate foreign investment and tourism, and a revised tax structure to extract more revenue

FERDINAND MARCOS, president of the Philippines, declared a state of martial law in late September after the nation had undergone a month of violence.

from the wealthy. His actions won wide acceptance among Filipinos. Marcos eased restrictions on public debate toward the end of the year to permit discussion of a new constitution to be voted on in a referendum. The country was shaken on December 7 by the wounding of its popular first lady, Mrs. Imelda Marcos, in an alleged right-wing plot against the president and his family.

Background. The son of a prominent educator and politician, Ferdinand Edralin Marcos was born on Sept. 11, 1917, in Sarrat, Luzon. He studied law at the University of the Philippines and fought in the anti-Japanese resistance in World War II. A member of the Liberal party, he was elected to the House of Representatives in 1949 and to the Senate in 1959, becoming Senate president in 1963. After joining the opposition Nationalist party, Marcos was elected president in 1965 and reelected in 1969.

MEIR, Golda

In 1972, Premier Golda Meir of Israel renewed her efforts to obtain support for her goal of a lasting peace settlement for the Middle East that would give Israel secure and recognized frontiers. She went to Rumania in May at the invitation of its government, becoming the first Israeli premier to visit a Communist country. To take advantage of an apparent rift between the Soviet Union and Egypt that led to the expulsion of Soviet military advisers from Egypt in July, Mrs. Meir tried, without success, to initiate peace talks with Egyptian President Anwar el-Sadat.

In response to the massacre of 11 members of the Israeli Olympic team by Arab terrorists at Munich in September, she pledged swift retaliation against all acts of terror. Subsequent massive Israeli air strikes against Palestinian guerrilla bases in Syria and Lebanon led to the condemnation of Israel in the United Nations. In response Mrs. Meir declared that the Israeli government had "no choice but to do what is necessary for the Jewish state."

Background. A native of Kiev, Russia, Golda Meir (Mrs. Morris Myerson) was born Golda Mabovitch on May 3, 1898. She came to the United States at the age of eight. In Milwaukee, Wis., where she spent her formative years, she studied at a teachers college and became interested in socialism and Zionism. In 1921 she emigrated to Palestine, where she worked on a kibbutz and later helped organize the labor confederation Histadruth. From 1946 to 1948 she served in its executive branch and headed the political department of the Jewish Agency. She was a signer of Israel's declaration of independence in 1948. She served as minister to the Soviet Union (1948–49), as minister of labor (1949–56), as foreign minister (1956–66), and as secretary general of the Mapai party (1966–68). On March 17, 1969, she became Israel's fourth premier, succeeding Levi Eshkol.

MESSMER, Pierre

Pierre Messmer, noted for his loyalty to the late Gen. Charles de Gaulle, was named by President Georges Pompidou on July 5, 1972, as premier of France. He succeeded the liberal Gaullist Jacques Chaban-Delmas, whose government had been shaken by financial scandals earlier in the year. Messmer's appointment was seen as a move by Pompidou to consolidate his Gaullist party, the Union for the Defense of the Republic, for the forthcoming elections, scheduled for March 1973, against a new "left union" of Communists and Socialists.

In September, Messmer introduced a social reform program. The following month he outlined a program to bring greater efficiency to the government. Leftist spokesmen in parliament, dissatisfied with Messmer's reforms, tried unsuccessfully in October to obtain a censure motion against his government. A public opinion poll released in December, showing the leftist coalition ahead of the Gaullists, seemed to signal a move away from Messmer's orthodox policies for the election campaign.

Background. Of Alsatian parentage, Pierre Auguste Joseph Messmer was born in Vincennes on March 20, 1916. After obtaining a degree in Oriental languages and a law doctorate from the Sorbonne, he studied at the École Coloniale to prepare for a career in the colonial service, which he entered in 1938. During World War II he fought with General de Gaulle's Free French forces in North Africa and Europe, and after the war he served as an administrator in Indochina. In the 1950's he was governor or high commissioner of several of France's African colonies. As minister of the armed forces from 1960 to 1969, Messmer modernized and revitalized the French army, restored some degree of loyalty to its demoralized officer corps, and created the nuclear strike force demanded by de Gaulle. After a brief absence, he returned to the government in 1971 as minister in charge of colonies.

NICKLAUS, Jack

After he had beaten Jack Nicklaus by a stroke for the 1972 British Open championship, Lee Trevino said, "I'm glad that I was able to beat Jack because he's still the greatest golfer there is. Nobody's in his class." At the end of the year, the Golf Writers Association of America confirmed what Trevino and most golf fans thought by naming Nicklaus among the top five golfers who ever played the game. The others were Bobby Jones, Walter Hagen, Ben Hogan, and Arnold Palmer for his play in the 1960's.

Nicklaus' loss in the British Open ended his effort to win the four major pro titles in one year—the Masters, the U. S. Open, the British Open, and the Professional Golfers' Association championship. However, he remains the only golfer to have won all of the titles more than once. He has taken the Masters four times (1963, 1965, 1966, 1972), the U. S. Open three times (1962, 1967, 1972), the British Open twice (1966, 1970), and the PGA twice (1963, 1971). He also won the U. S. Amateur championship in 1959 and 1961, giving him a total of 13 major titles, a record he shares with Bobby Jones.

It was his early success as a pro that marked Nicklaus as a great golfer. The big blond (he was just under 6 feet and weighed 215 pounds at the time) won three events in his first year on the pro tour, including the U. S. Open. In the following season he began a string of 10 consecutive years in which he won over $100,000, as he challenged Palmer for the top honors of the game.

JACK NICKLAUS, golf's leading money winner and the PGA's Golfer of the Year in 1972, receives trophy after winning the Walt Disney Open tournament.

WIDE WORLD

At one point, the "Golden Bear" reduced his weight to 185, renewed his enthusiasm, and attacked the game with more fervor. By 1972, at the age of 30, he had become the leading career money winner, raising his record earnings to $320,000 for a season. He was also named PGA Golfer of the year for the second time.

However, in December, when he received a $30,000 check for winning the last tourney of the year, he said that the money was not as important as the crowd's reactions. Nicklaus was admired for his booming drives, his precision with his irons, and his excellent putting (though criticized for the slowness of his game), but he never enjoyed crowd support comparable to that given to Palmer by "Arnie's Army" or to the late Tony Lema by "Lema's Legions." But at the end of 1972 he was elated that people were now following him on the course. "The galleries," he said, "have been fantastic." Most of those in the galleries said the same of Nicklaus.

BILL BRADDOCK

NIXON, Richard M.

The last year of Richard M. Nixon's first term was dominated by his continuing efforts to end the Vietnam War, personal visits to Communist China and the Soviet Union, and implementation of revenue sharing—a potentially far-reaching change in the federal-state relationship. The President's year was climaxed when he won reelection to a second term in a landslide.

Foreign Affairs. By the end of 1972, prospects for a ceasefire in Vietnam were uncertain. President Nixon had withdrawn virtually all American ground troops but the war continued unabated in the air. Dr. Henry Kissinger, the President's foreign affairs adviser, met repeatedly with North Vietnamese representatives in Paris, but he reported on December 16 that a "just and fair agreement" had not been achieved.

Major foreign policy initiatives were undertaken through President Nixon's visits to the People's Republic of China in February and to the Soviet Union in May. The trip to China ended more than 20 years of official U. S. hostility toward the Communist government of that country. The President met with Premier Chou En-lai and party chairman Mao Tse-tung. Nixon agreed to broaden contacts between the two nations and to recognize Peking's contention that Taiwan is a part of mainland China.

The meetings with the Soviet leaders resulted in the signing of agreements on joint space missions, technology, the environment, trade, medical research, incidents at sea, and the limitation of strategic arms. The last agreement overshadowed the others by limiting the deployment of antiballistic missiles and by placing a freeze on offensive weaponry.

Domestic Affairs. President Nixon and his advisers claimed credit for a general upturn in the economy, but critics suggested that the upswing might be temporary or a response to other economic stimuli. Whatever reason, unemployment was down, the stock market averages broke records, and inflation showed some signs of decline through stabilization of prices and wages.

The President made major changes in his cabinet. Attorney General John N. Mitchell resigned to direct the reelection campaign, a position from which he later also resigned to return to private law practice. Secretary of the Treasury John Connally resigned in May, but later headed a campaign group called Democrats for Nixon. Secretary of Commerce Maurice Stans resigned to head the campaign finance drive. The three were replaced by Richard G. Kleindienst at Justice; George P. Shultz at Treasury; and Peter G. Peterson at Commerce. After the President's reelection he announced that Kleindienst and Shultz would retain their posts, but Peterson was replaced by Frederick B. Dent. (For a complete list of the President's cabinet, see UNITED STATES.)

Probably the most far-reaching domestic legislation to come out of the Congress as a response to Presi-

PRESIDENT RICHARD NIXON relaxes at Camp David, Md., during his campaign for reelection in 1972.

dent Nixon's initiative was the State and Local Fiscal Assistance Act of 1972, more commonly known as revenue sharing. Under the act much-needed funds for state and local governments are provided through direct payment from the federal treasury and may be used for any legal expenditure except to "match" federal grants. The payments are allocated according to a formula that takes into account population, general tax effort, percent of urban population, per capita income, and state income tax collection. It is expected that most state and local governments will use the money to provide new services, improve old ones, or reduce taxes.

Election. President Nixon was reelected on November 7 by a landslide 60.7% of the popular vote, losing only Massachusetts and the District of Columbia to Sen. George McGovern. But Nixon provided little coattail assistance to other Republican candidates. The party lost two additional seats in the U. S. Senate and one governorship, and gained 12 seats in the House of Representatives, the smallest gain for an incumbent president in many years. Because he campaigned very little for others on the ticket, the President was criticized by some members of his party.

Background. Nixon was born in Yorba Linda, Calif., on Jan. 9, 1913. After serving in the Navy during World War II he was elected to the U. S. House from California in 1946 and 1948 and to the Senate in 1950. He served as vice president during both terms of President Dwight D. Eisenhower and received the Republican nomination for President in 1960. After being narrowly defeated by John F. Kennedy he returned to California, where in 1962 he ran for governor and lost. He then joined a Wall Street law firm in New York City but maintained his interest in Republican party affairs. He was nominated and elected President of the United States in 1968 after one of the most striking comebacks in American political history.

ROBERT J. HUCKSHORN

UPI

POPE PAUL VI speaks to a little girl during a Lenten visit to St. Mary of the Visions Church, Rome.

PAUL VI, Pope

During 1972 the efforts of Pope Paul VI were chiefly devoted to the promotion of justice and peace in the world and the preservation of unity within the Catholic Church.

On September 26 the pope celebrated his 75th birthday. There had been considerable speculation on the possibility of his resignation on reaching 75, the age he had set for the retirement of bishops. The day, however, passed routinely with no announcement beyond an assurance of the pope's continued good health. There were no trips abroad, comparable to the famous papal journeys undertaken in other years of Paul's pontificate. In September the Pope did travel to Venice to visit the 17th Italian Eucharistic Congress being held there.

In February, Pope Paul received a delegation of four leaders from the Russian Orthodox Patriarchate of Moscow. He welcomed them warmly and spoke of the common faith that united Catholics and Orthodox. The pope's denial of the request to establish a Ukrainian Catholic Patriarchate was interpreted as a reluctance to injure the cordial relations developing with Moscow, where the Ukrainian Catholic Church is outlawed. Concern for the 5 million Ukrainian Catholics presently within the Soviet Union was also thought to be a factor.

The pope denied in a January address that there had been any loss of vitality in the ecumenical movement and suggested that Catholic disunity was a great obstacle to Christian unity. He expressed sadness in an address later in the year at the divisions and rivalries within the Church and warned against an exaggerated pluralism that threatened the unity of the Church. In October he met with Cardinal Bernard Alfrink to review the entire situation of the Church in the Netherlands, where several disputes in the course of the year had revealed a viewpoint considerably different from the Vatican's. (See RELIGION—*Roman Catholicism*.)

A note of caution was evident in the weekly allocutions of the pope throughout the year. He spoke on several occasions of the true meaning of conscience and the role of authority in its formation, apparently concerned with what some have viewed as a growing subjectivism in Catholic morals. He praised, however, the youth of the day for their search for deeper satisfactions than mere material prosperity.

In his New Year's Day address the pope called for justice and peace in the world. In the spring he addressed a special message to the participants in the Paris peace talks on the Indochina War, and again in July made a particularly dramatic plea for an end to the bloodshed there. U. S. Secretary of State William Rogers visited the Vatican to thank the pope for his efforts toward an exchange of prisoners. In August, along with other world leaders, the pontiff condemned the killings at the Munich Olympic Games by Arab terrorists. At the same time he cautioned against equally violent reprisals. The tragic conflict in Northern Ireland, where Catholic and Protestant extremists engaged in wanton terrorism, was also a cause of serious concern and anxiety. In October, Prime Minister Heath of Britain visited the Vatican to discuss the Northern Ireland conflict with the pope.

JOSEPH A. O'HARE, S. J.

PERÓN, Juan D.

Former Argentine dictator Juan D. Perón, who has continued to command a greater popular following among his countrymen than any other public figure, returned to Argentina on Nov. 17, 1972, after 17 years of exile, to embark on what he termed a mission of "peace and conciliation." Although he had been barred by previous governments, the military regime headed by Gen. Alejandro Lanusse invited him to return. Lanusse hoped that Perón would reintegrate his followers into the political life of the nation and help pave the way for national elections scheduled for March 1973.

But Perón's visit failed to create the impact his supporters had hoped or his opponents had feared. He managed to organize a loose coalition around his Justicialista party, but it disintegrated within a few days. Nominated twice by his supporters for the presidency—despite a government-imposed residency requirement that made him ineligible—he refused the nomination and pledged merely to help find solutions "that will permit the end of the military dictatorship." He left Argentina on December 14, after a stay of only 28 days.

Background. Juan Domingo Perón Sosa was born on Oct. 8, 1895, in Lobos, Buenos Aires Province. After attending the National Military College he was commissioned an infantry sublieutenant at the age of 18. He became an admirer of Benito Mussolini during an assignment in Italy, and joined with other pro-Axis officers in 1943 to overthrow Argentina's civilian government. By 1944 he was vice president and minister of war and labor, and won the loyalty of millions of workers by introducing important reforms.

Elected president in 1946 and reelected in 1952, Perón built Argentina into a strong welfare state combining populism, state socialism, and nationalism, with the help of his wife, Eva, who shared his popularity. His regime, which transformed Argentina from a rural into an industrial nation, was also notorious for political arrests, corruption, persecution, and the denial of civil liberties. Perón was overthrown by a military coup in 1955, and during the next few years he lived in several Latin American countries before settling in Spain in 1960.

POMPIDOU, Georges

Nearly midway through his seven-year term as president of France, Georges Pompidou met with such opposition at home and abroad as to suggest that the political and diplomatic achievements of Gaullism might be of limited duration. Nevertheless, his hold on the nation seemed unshaken. The National Assembly dutifully accepted his dismissal of the premier, to whom it had just given a strong vote of confidence. His Com-

mon Market partners finally compromised to give him the substance of what he sought.

His position in the dominant party, the Union of Democrats for the Republic, was unchallenged. Despite the relative popularity of Premier Jacques Chaban-Delmas, his replacement by the more disciplined, less well-known Pierre Messmer occasioned no outcry against the president. In style and comportment, Pompidou had something of de Gaulle's distant air, though his goals were less grandiose and the means chosen, principally that of rapid industrialization, were less sensational.

In 1973, Pompidou would have to face challenges from a new Socialist-Communist coalition, from a new Reformist Movement (the Radical party and the Democratic Center), and even from the Independent Republicans within the ruling majority. Fearing all this, he had wished to hold the elections to the National Assembly before its term expired. But a testing of opinion on April 23, disguised as a referendum on enlarging the Common Market, revealed less than overwhelming support. He drew back to re-examine the home situation, regroup his ministers, and prepare more carefully.

During the year he was host for four state visits: by President Franz Jonas of Austria, March 21–24; by Britain's Queen Elizabeth, May 15–19; by Queen Juliana of the Netherlands, June 19–22; and by party chief Edward Gierek of Poland, October 1–6. He himself visited the republics of Niger and Chad in January and visited Germany in September.

Background. Pompidou was born in Montboudif in central France on July 5, 1911. Formerly a schoolmaster, he joined General de Gaulle's staff shortly after the Liberation in 1944 and remained with de Gaulle even after he left office in 1946. In 1951 Pompidou joined the Rothschilds' banking firm. Though not associated with the wartime resistance, he continued to serve General de Gaulle, and after the latter's return to power in 1958, he resumed full-time work with him. In 1959, however, he returned as director general to the house of Rothschild until summoned in April 1962 to be premier. In this capacity he dealt with the strikes and disorders that almost toppled de Gaulle in 1968. He was then sacked for his ambition and success. Boldly presenting himself as a candidate, even before the general's miscalculation on the referendum and subsequent resignation in 1969, Pompidou was easily elected that year to the presidency by 58% of the vote.

JOHN C. CAIRNS

POTTER, Philip Alford

The Rev. Philip A. Potter, a Methodist minister from the British West Indies, was elected on Aug. 16, 1972, to succeed the Rev. Eugene Carson Blake as general secretary of the World Council of Churches (WCC) by unanimous vote of its 120-member central committee. Taking office on October 1, for a five-year term, Potter became the third man to head the WCC since its founding in 1948 and the first representing the underdeveloped "third world."

As general secretary, Potter is the chief spokesman of the world's foremost ecumenical organization, representing about 400 million Christians belonging to some 250 Protestant, Anglican, and Orthodox churches. A distinguished theologian as well as a skilled administrator, Potter had been associated with the WCC for a number of years. In his acceptance speech he reaffirmed his "passion for Christian unity" and for "the unity of mankind," and pledged to carry on his predecessor's fight against racism.

Of African, French, and Irish ancestry, Philip Alford Potter was born on Aug. 19, 1921, to an estate-owning family on the island of Dominica, in the British West Indies. Although his father was a Roman Catholic, Potter was baptized in his mother's Methodist faith. He was educated at the Canewood Theological College in Kingston, Jamaica, and at the University of London, where he obtained his bachelor of divinity and master of theology degrees.

UPI   WIDE WORLD

THE REV. PHILIP POTTER (left) and Elliot Richardson (right) have taken on new jobs.

In 1948, Potter was a youth delegate to the first WCC assembly. His career includes four years' service as a Methodist pastor in Haiti, four years as a member of the WCC's youth division, and seven years as field secretary for Africa and the West Indies with the British Methodist Missionary Society. At the time of his election as general secretary, Potter had been serving since 1967 in Geneva as director of the WCC's Commission on World Mission and Evangelism. He has also served as chairman of the council's Section for Faith and Testimony.

Inspired by the theological works of Karl Barth, Potter describes his own theology as "biblical, not systematic or dogmatic." He also credits the writings of Reinhold Niebuhr and Paul Tillich with influencing his thought.

RICHARDSON, Elliot L.

Secretary of Health, Education and Welfare (HEW) Elliot L. Richardson was nominated by President Nixon on Nov. 28, 1972, to succeed Melvin R. Laird as secretary of defense, effective January 1973. The appointment of Richardson, a moderate Republican, to the top civilian post in the Pentagon was believed to reflect an administration decision to streamline the defense establishment and bring its budget under control. As secretary of HEW, Richardson proved himself an effective administrator, bringing a measure of order and efficiency to the department's vast bureaucratic apparatus. He was fairly successful in balancing liberal demands for expanded welfare programs against efforts by conservatives to curtail such expensive programs, and in promoting such policies as school desegregation and welfare reform within the limitations imposed by the Nixon administration.

Background. A member of a socially prominent family, Elliot Lee Richardson was born in Boston on July 20, 1920. After World War II military service, he obtained his LL. B. degree *cum laude* in 1947 from Harvard Law School, where he was editor of the *Harvard Law Review*. He served as law clerk to Judge Learned Hand and to Supreme Court Justice Felix Frankfurter before entering private practice in 1949. During 1953–54 Richardson worked as an aide to Sen. Leverett Saltonstall of Massachusetts. In 1958 he served briefly as acting head of HEW, and from 1958 to 1961 he was U. S. attorney for Massachusetts. He served as lieutenant governor of Massachusetts (1964–67), as the state's attorney general (1967–69), and as undersecretary of state from 1969 until June 1970, when he became secretary of HEW.

ROGERS, William P.

Amid reports that he would leave office in 1973, Secretary of State William P. Rogers reviewed the changes that had taken place during his four years in

President Nixon's cabinet. He said that "rapid and profound" changes had occurred in international relations and that progress had been made toward substituting "negotiation for confrontation."

Among the changes, Rogers cited the President's visit to China in 1972 as guest of a government with which the United States had no diplomatic relations, the first visit of an American president to the Soviet Union (also in 1972), the Strategic Arms Limitation Agreements with the USSR, agreements among the Big Four powers on the status of Berlin, continuation of the Middle East cease-fire initiated by the United States in 1970, and steps to make the international economic system "more equitable." Rogers also praised the maintenance of a strong national defense. He noted the "more equal" partnership with U. S. allies and friends in Europe.

While the accomplishments of the Department of State during the Rogers administration were considerable (and included activities toward a European Security Conference, mutual and balanced force reductions, international cooperation to improve the environment, and Vietnam negotiations), his relations with Dr. Henry A. Kissinger continued to dominate public evaluation of his stewardship. Rogers insisted that his relations with Kissinger, who had become the President's principal adviser on foreign affairs, were friendly and cooperative. Rogers said that "the success of our foreign policy" is the important thing, not personal rivalries.

Background. William Pierce Rogers was born in Norfolk, N. Y., on June 23, 1913. He obtained a B. A. from Colgate University and an LL. B. from Cornell Law School. After serving as assistant district attorney to Thomas E. Dewey he entered the Navy during World War II. He met Richard Nixon after the war while acting as counsel to U. S. Senate committees dealing with government expenditures. He was deputy attorney general (1953–57) and attorney general (1957–61). He practiced law until he became secretary of state in Nixon's cabinet in 1969.

WALTER DARNELL JACOBS

SADAT, Anwar el-

Anwar el-Sadat completed his second year as president of Egypt in 1972. Although beset by domestic pressures from student demonstrations in January and from reported Army restiveness in the fall, he remained in firm control.

The president was in Moscow in February and April seeking more arms in order to fight the Israelis. Dissatisfied with the extent of Soviet aid, he ordered the nearly 20,000 Russian advisers out of Egypt in July. This step was popular, but by the year's end Sadat had improved relations with the USSR somewhat, and Egypt was again receiving some Soviet military aid.

Although the expulsion of the Russians had made peace with Israel a bit more likely, little was accomplished toward that end. Rejecting the appeal of Israeli Prime Minister Golda Meir to meet with her for "a joint supreme effort" at peace, Sadat said that Egypt would never admit defeat, nor would he negotiate while Israelis occupied Egyptian soil.

In August, Sadat and President Muammar al-Qaddafi of Libya agreed to merge their countries in a close federation, with Cairo as the capital and Sadat as president. Egypt, Libya, and Syria had formed a loose federation in 1971.

Sadat continued his popular policy of gradually abolishing controls instituted by his predecessor, Gamal Abdel Nasser. In October 1972 the government abandoned its practice of confiscating private property by administrative action.

Background. Sadat was born on Dec. 25, 1918, in a village in the Nile Delta. In 1938 he and Gamal Abdel Nasser formed a secret group with other army officers to work for the liberation of Egypt from its feudal monarchy and British influence. This group was the nucleus of the officers' committee that overthrew King Faruk in 1952.

Though influential, Sadat did not hold prominent office until 1969, when he was appointed vice president. He was elected to the presidency on Oct. 15, 1970, after the death of President Nasser.

CARL LEIDEN

SHRIVER, R(obert) Sargent, Jr.

R. Sargent Shriver, Jr., former director of the Peace Corps and of the Office of Economic Opportunity and former ambassador to France, replaced Thomas F. Eagleton as the Democratic vice presidential nominee in August 1972.

As a result of the "Eagleton Affair," Democratic presidential candidate George McGovern, after being refused by six other party leaders, offered Shriver second place on the ticket. Shriver accepted and was approved by the Democratic National Committee on August 8. An articulate, attractive, personable man, Shriver's liberal and antiwar views, governmental experience, identification with the Kennedy family, Roman Catholicism, and long association with minority groups were expected to add strength to the ticket. He campaigned enthusiastically, trying to heal wounds and build support among reluctant party regulars.

Attacking Nixon's record, Shriver charged that the President "blew" a chance for a negotiated Vietnam peace in 1969. Later in the campaign Shriver made major policy speeches on justice, the Kennedy family, and the State Department. Although he traveled 80,000 miles and delivered 500 speeches, there was evidence that the public considered Shriver more of a supersalesman than a serious candidate. The ticket received only about 38% of the vote. Under the peculiar circumstances of 1972, perhaps Shriver's first campaign for election to public office was not a fair test of his potential.

Background. A descendant of an old Maryland family, Shriver was born on Nov. 9, 1915. He attended Canterbury School and graduated from Yale (1938) and Yale Law School (1941). After experience as a lawyer, World War II naval officer, and journalist, he was employed by Joseph P. Kennedy as manager of Chicago's Merchandise Mart. In 1953 he married Kennedy's daughter Eunice. A civic leader, he served five years as president of the Chicago board of education. He participated in John Kennedy's 1960 presidential campaign, and in 1961 was chosen by his brother-in-law to be first director of the Peace Corps, one of the most successful achievements of the Kennedy administration. He continued as director under President Johnson, and in 1964 also became head of the Office of Economic Opportunity to direct the "war on poverty." In 1968, Johnson appointed him ambassador to France, a position he retained under President Nixon until 1970.

ORVILLE H. ZABEL

SHULTZ, George P.

George P. Shultz, who succeeded John B. Connally as secretary of the treasury on June 12, 1972, was appointed by President Nixon on December 1 to the additional post of presidential assistant in charge of a new cabinet-level council on economic policy. The appointment, part of the President's reorganization plan to improve the formulation and execution of policy during his second term, placed Shultz in the position of "overall coordinator of the entire economic-policy decision-making process, both domestically and internationally."

As an advocate of a free-market economy, former budget director Shultz had expressed misgivings about Nixon's new economic policy of wage and price controls, but he loyally helped to implement the President's program. In an interview on Dec. 31, 1972, he said that controls have "given us a little extra strength in the fight against inflation" but added that rising food prices must be curbed. He expected 1973 to be "a good year for the American economy..., a year with rising output, rising employment, and general prosperity."

Born in New York City on Dec. 13, 1920, George Pratt Shultz grew up in Englewood, N. J., and graduated *cum laude* from Princeton in 1942. After World War II service as a Marine Corps officer, he earned his Ph. D. degree in industrial economics at Massachusetts Institute of Technology in 1949 and then joined its faculty. In 1957 he became a professor at the University of Chicago graduate school of business, and from 1962 to 1968 he served as its dean. Concurrently with his academic duties, he worked as senior staff economist with the President's Council of Economic Advisers in 1955–56 and as a consultant to government agencies and arbitrator of industrial disputes in the 1960's. As President Nixon's first secretary of labor in 1969–70, he promoted equal opportunities for minority groups. Named by the President in June 1970 as chairman of the new Office of Management and Budget, he remained in that post until he became the treasury secretary.

SMITH, Gerard C.

Gerard C. Smith resigned as director of the Arms Control and Disarmament Agency and as head of the U. S. delegation to the strategic arms limitation talks (SALT) at the end of 1972. His painstaking and often frustrating bargaining with Soviet negotiators culminated in an agreement to limit strategic nuclear weapons signed by President Nixon and Soviet Communist party chief Leonid I. Brezhnev on May 26, 1972, during the president's visit to Moscow.

The arms pact, which was hailed by both sides as a major breakthrough, marking the first step toward limiting the spiraling armaments race between the world's two major powers, was worked out by Smith and Soviet Deputy Foreign Minister Vladimir S. Semyonov in SALT talks begun in November 1969 and carried on in some 130 separate sessions in Helsinki and Vienna. The agreement limited each country to two defensive anti-ballistic sites with a maximum of 100 missiles at each site. It also included a 5-year pact on offensive weapons that froze the number of missile launchers. Smith and Semyonov embarked on a new round of SALT talks in Geneva on November 21 to make the interim agreement on offensive weapons permanent and more comprehensive.

Background. The son of a lawyer and business executive, Gerard C. Smith was born in New York City on May 4, 1914. He graduated from Yale Law School in 1938 and entered law practice after World War II service in the U. S. Navy. He was appointed a special assistant to the Atomic Energy Commission in 1950 and became an adviser on atomic affairs with the State Department in 1954. He served as assistant secretary of state for policy planning from 1957 to 1961 and was a consultant to the Washington Center of Foreign Policy Research from 1961 to 1969. Noted for his diplomatic skill and his ability to assess the realities of power politics, Smith was appointed by President Nixon as director of the U. S. Arms Control and Disarmament Agency on Jan. 29, 1969.

SOLZHENITSYN, Aleksandr I.

Soviet novelist Aleksandr I. Solzhenitsyn, acclaimed as one of the world's greatest living writers, continued in 1972 to stand courageously against the official ostracism to which he has been subjected in his own country. In his long-awaited Nobel lecture, published in August in the Nobel Foundation's yearbook, he condemned official persecution of writers as "a danger to the whole of mankind" and deplored the growing acceptance of violence throughout the world, but expressed some hope in the unfettered pursuit of truth by the international community of artists and writers.

Solzhenitsyn had won the 1970 Nobel Prize for Literature but did not travel to Sweden to accept the award, fearing that to do so would result in his permanent exile. An effort by the Swedish Academy to present him with the prize at a private ceremony in

SARGENT SHRIVER (above) replaced Sen. Thomas Eagleton as the 1972 Democratic vice presidential candidate. (Right) George Shultz became secretary of the treasury on June 12.

Moscow in April 1972 was blocked by Soviet authorities. His latest work, *August 1914* (1971), the first part of a projected World War I trilogy, was banned in the Soviet Union, although it was hailed in the West as an epic on a Tolstoyan scale.

Background. Aleksandr Isayevich Solzhenitsyn was born in Kislovodsk, in the Caucasus, on Dec. 11, 1918. After graduation from the University of Rostov in 1941, he served as an artillery officer in World War II. He was arrested in 1945 for making a derogatory comment about Stalin and spent the next eight years in prison, but was officially rehabilitated in 1957. Later he settled in Ryazan, where he taught school and wrote. His first novel, *One Day in the Life of Ivan Denisovich* (1962), based on his prison camp experiences, was published with official sanction during Premier Khrushchev's de-Stalinization campaign, but his subsequent novels, *The Cancer Ward* and *The First Circle,* were banned in the Soviet Union. Their appearance in the West in English translation in 1968 established his reputation as a writer of international importance.

SPITZ, Mark

Mark Spitz showed during the 1972 Olympic Games at Munich that he had listened well to his father's admonition that winning, not just swimming well, was the important thing. Mark had begun to swim competitively in Sacramento, Calif., in 1958 when he was eight years old, and he culminated 14 years of grueling

UPI

MARK SPITZ won seven gold medals for the United States at the 1972 Summer Olympic Games in Munich.

work with the greatest individual performance in Olympic history. Spitz won four championships and aided the United States in the winning of three relays. His total of seven gold medals for first-place finishes was two more than any Olympic athlete had ever attained.

Mark Andrew Spitz was born in Modesto, Calif., on Feb. 10, 1950. His parents made many moves to get the best possible training for their son to make him a winner. First he was at the Arden Hills Swim Club under Sherman Chavoor, then at Santa Clara under George Haines. In 1966 the 16-year-old won his first AAU indoor title while in high school at Santa Clara. The following season he took both AAU butterfly events in record American times and won five gold medals in the Pan-American Games (three in relays), setting world records in the butterfly events. He bettered each of the marks a fortnight later in the AAU meet, then broke them again in Europe and added a world record in the 110-yard butterfly. He wound up 1967 by being voted the male swimmer of the year. But by the end of 1968 he was the world's most frustrated swimmer.

Spitz was considered likely to win five or six gold medals in the 1968 Olympics in Mexico City. He was also considered by many as brash and overly cocky. He had a bad meet, winning only two gold medals in the relays, a second place in one event, and a third in another.

In 1969, Spitz entered Indiana University, where, under the guidance of Jimmy Counsilman, he again became a first-class competitor. He gained maturity and achieved better rapport with his teammates. In four years he won eight NCAA titles and continued to shatter world records. In 1971 he was voted the Sullivan Award as the top amateur athlete. Fully prepared now, he set world records in four individual events in the Olympics. He had expected to win only one.

BILL BRADDOCK

STANFIELD, Robert L.

On Oct. 30, 1972, Robert L. Stanfield, the mild-mannered leader of Canada's opposition Progressive Conservative party, scored a near upset over the colorful and charismatic Prime Minister Pierre Elliott Trudeau in the closest federal election in Canadian history.

During the eight-week election campaign, Stanfield concentrated on "bread and butter" issues, criticizing Trudeau's Liberal government for permitting unemployment to rise to 7.1% while failing to stem the tide of inflation, and calling attention to high taxes and rising costs of unemployment insurance and welfare benefits. He indicated that he would proceed more gradually than Trudeau in implementing the bilingualism program opposed by many English-speaking Canadians.

Emerging from the election in a virtual tie, neither Trudeau's Liberal party nor Stanfield's Progressive

Conservatives was in a position to command a majority in the 264-member House of Commons. Declaring his readiness to form a Conservative minority government, Stanfield called on Trudeau to resign, contending that he had "lost the confidence of the people," but the prime minister decided to remain in office and leave the fate of his government up to the new Parliament.

Background. Robert Lorne Stanfield, the son of a Nova Scotia lieutenant governor, was born in Truro, Nova Scotia, on April 11, 1914. He attended Dalhousie University in Halifax and graduated from Harvard Law School in 1939. He became leader of the Progressive Conservative party in his home province in 1948. From 1956 to 1967 he was premier of Nova Scotia, serving also as minister of education from 1960 to 1967. Following his election to the Canadian House of Commons in 1967, Stanfield became leader of the opposition Progressive Conservative party in the Parliament, where he earned a reputation as a skilled conciliator and negotiator.

STEIN, Herbert

On Jan. 1, 1972, Herbert Stein succeeded Paul W. McCracken as chairman of President Nixon's Council of Economic Advisers. Stein, who had been the chief architect of the economic controls established in 1971 under Phase II of the President's new economic policy, became the government's leading spokesman in behalf of that policy during 1972.

At hearings of the congressional Joint Economic Committee in February he asserted that the administration had initiated "the strongest program to reduce unemployment that there ever has been in this country." In April he told the committee that wage and price controls had "dramatically reduced the anxiety in the country" and had a significant impact on inflation. He reassured businessmen in May that despite recent price rollbacks ordered by the Price Commission companies would be permitted to make reasonable profits. While conceding that food prices had risen, he noted in September that the situation was "not critical" and that the average worker's capacity to buy food had increased substantially within the past year. Stein said in late October that wage and price controls would be gradually reduced rather than completely eliminated in 1973 and that unemployment would drop to the 4%–5% range.

Background. Herbert Stein, the son of a machinist, was born in Detroit on Aug. 27, 1916. He graduated from Williams College in 1935 and received a Ph. D. in economics in 1958 from the University of Chicago. In 1938 he began his government career with the Federal Deposit Insurance Corporation. During World War II he worked for several federal wartime agencies before entering the naval reserve. In 1945 he joined the staff of the privately supported Committee for Economic Development, and he remained with that organization until he became a senior fellow at the Brookings Institution in 1967. He joined the Nixon administration as a member of the Council of Economic Advisers in 1969. Originally opposed to government controls of the economy, he became convinced in 1971 of the need for drastic measures to deal with inflation.

STOKOWSKI, Leopold

Long recognized as one of the world's greatest orchestral conductors, Leopold Stokowski appeared to be in full command of his artistic faculties as he reached the age of 90 on April 18, 1972. Honored at a gala birthday celebration in the grand ballroom of the Plaza Hotel in New York City, he was presented with the Mayor's Award by New York City Mayor John V. Lindsay. Earlier that day, he had conducted a three-hour rehearsal of the American Symphony Orchestra, which he founded in 1962. In June, as a guest conductor of the London Symphony, he won unanimous acclaim from British music critics.

Stokowski, who was born in London on April 18, 1882, to a Polish father and an Irish mother, gave evidence of exceptional musical talent in early childhood, when he learned to play the piano and violin. He graduated from Queen's College, Oxford, and studied at London's Royal College of Music and in France and Germany. After beginning his professional career at 18 as an organist in London, he served from 1905 to 1908 as organist and choirmaster of St. Bartholomew's Church in New York City and from 1909 to 1912 as conductor of the Cincinnati Symphony. He became an American citizen in 1915.

In 1912, Stokowski was named conductor of the Philadelphia Orchestra, which he built into one of the world's top-ranking ensembles. His practice of regularly including in his concerts works by major modern composers, including Mahler, Stravinsky, Prokofiev, Shostakovich, Schoenberg, and Varèse, provoked opposition from members of the orchestra's board of directors, and Stokowski resigned as musical director in 1938. Under his baton, Alban Berg's opera *Wozzeck* had its American premiere in 1931.

Stokowski organized the All-American Youth Orchestra in 1940 and toured with it through North and South America for two years. In 1942–43 he was associate conductor, with Arturo Toscanini, of the NBC Symphony, and in 1944–45 he led the New York City Symphony, which he helped to organize. He was conductor of the Hollywood Bowl Orchestra from 1945 to 1947 and co-conductor of the New York Philharmonic in 1949–50. From 1955 to 1960 he directed the Houston Symphony.

Stokowski is credited with introducing new techniques into sound recording and radio broadcasting, and his orchestral transcriptions of Bach organ works, while provoking some controversy among purists, became highly popular. He appeared in the motion pictures *The Big Broadcast of 1937* (1936), *One Hundred Men and a Girl* (1937), and *Carnegie Hall* (1947), and he collaborated with Walt Disney on the animated musical feature *Fantasia* (1940). Among his compositions are *Dithyrambe* for flute, cello, and harp (1917) and works for organ.

Stokowski was married (and divorced) three times—to the pianist Olga Samaroff, to Evangeline B. Johnson, and to heiress Gloria Vanderbilt. His book *Music for Us All* was published in 1943.

STRAUSS, Robert

Robert Strauss was elected chairman of the Democratic National Committee on Dec. 9, 1972. A millionaire lawyer and businessman from Texas and a former party treasurer, his election followed an intra-party fight that led to the resignation of Jean Westwood, who had served as chairman since Sen. George McGovern's nomination at the Democratic national convention in July. Strauss' first task was the restoration of the Democratic party to a position of strength following McGovern's landslide defeat in the November presidential election.

Strauss had long been identified with the conservative wing of the Texas Democratic organization and had the backing of party leaders opposed to the sweeping reforms introduced by the liberal McGovern forces. But he indicated that he was not beholden to any faction and that he would seek to restore unity to the badly splintered party. He asserted that some of the McGovern reforms, such as the increased participation of blacks and women on the committee, would be retained. Strauss also stated that those who had refused to support the McGovern ticket—including his close friend former Texas governor and U. S. treasury secretary John Connally—should be denied titular office in the party.

Background. Robert Schwarz Strauss was born on Oct. 19, 1918 in Hamlin, Texas, where his father owned a dry-goods store. After graduating from the University of Texas Law School in 1941 he worked as a special agent with the Federal Bureau of Investigation. In 1945 he opened a Dallas law firm which became one of the most prominent in the city. He began his active involvement in politics as principal fund raiser for John Connally's first gubernatorial campaign in 1962. Connally appointed him to the state banking board and in 1968 named him to the Democratic National Committee. As the party's treasurer from 1970 to July 1972, Strauss reduced its debts substantially.

SUHARTO

President Suharto remained firmly in control of Indonesia in 1972. There were signs of restiveness among the intellectuals, who with the military have been the main support of his government, but there was no serious threat to his regime.

President Suharto made a number of important state visits during the year. In Australia, New Zealand, and the Philippines in February, he stressed Indonesia's need for economic development and its desire for private foreign investment. Suharto and President Ferdinand Marcos of the Philippines agreed to intensify their efforts to make the Association of Southeast Asian Nations a more effective instrument of peace, progress, and stability in the region.

While Suharto was in Japan in May, it was announced that Indonesia would supply Japan with 58 million kiloliters of low-sulfur oil over a 10-year period. Japan granted Indonesia a $200 million loan for the development of its oil sector.

Background. Suharto was born on June 8, 1921, near Djokjakarta, in central Java. His military career began with service in the Netherlands Indies army before World War II. He served in the local defense corps during the Japanese occupation, and after the war he took part in Indonesia's struggle for independence from the Netherlands. He rose steadily in the ranks of the army of the Republic of Indonesia.

In 1965, Suharto crushed an attempted Communist coup, and soon after was named army chief of staff. As President Sukarno's complicity in the coup became increasingly clear he was forced to hand over most of his powers to Suharto. In March 1966, Sukarno transferred all executive power to Suharto. The next year the People's Consultative Congress named Suharto acting president and in March 1968 unanimously elected him president for a 5-year term.

AMRY VANDENBOSCH

TANAKA, Kakuei

Kakuei Tanaka, minister of international trade and industry, succeeded Eisaku Sato as prime minister of Japan on July 6, 1972. Elected president of the ruling Liberal Democratic party (LDP) at a special caucus on July 5, Tanaka's election as premier by the Diet was automatic.

The 54-year-old Tanaka is Japan's youngest prime minister since the end of World War II. Known as "Kaku-san" by friends and the press, he is a maverick among the leadership of the moderate, business-backed LDP. With no university education, no well-placed connections, and little experience in the lower bureaucracy, he is an articulate spokesman and moves through all strata of Japanese society. He is called a "computerized bulldozer."

Policy. Tanaka has described U. S.-Japanese relations as like air and water, saying that "Without them, we cannot live." He met President Richard Nixon in Hawaii in late August and reaffirmed the 25-year U. S.-Japanese alliance. Tanaka visited the People's Republic of China in September and signed a joint statement with Premier Chou En-lai reestablishing diplomatic relations between their countries.

Domestically, although he supports Japan's mixed capitalist system, Tanaka has pointed to internal problems, including housing, the environment, and the need for redevelopment of the cities. His party was returned to power in nation-wide elections held on December 10, but with a reduced majority in the House of Representatives (the lower house of the Japanese Diet).

Early Career. Kakuei Tanaka was born on May 4, 1918, in the village of Nishiyama, in Niigata prefecture, the only boy among seven children in a poor family. He finished six years of primary school and then at age 15 became a construction worker. While attending a secondary technological school in Tokyo at night, he set up his own small construction firm. He was drafted when he was 20 and served two years in Manchuria. Discharged for health reasons, he returned to the construction business, and by 1945 his firm had become one of the top 50 construction companies in Japan.

Tanaka was elected to the House of Representatives in 1947 and has since been reelected 10 consecutive times. He was named deputy minister of justice in 1949, but soon after was jailed briefly on charges of accepting bribes in a coal-mining scandal. He was acquitted several years later.

Tanaka became minister of communications in 1957 and later served as finance minister in three cabinets. Between cabinet posts he served five terms as secretary general of the LDP. He was appointed minister of international trade and industry by Premier Sato in 1971. Tanaka has amazed colleagues by accurately storing in his mind data on every one of Japan's 123 electoral districts.

ARDATH W. BURKS

THIEU, Nguyen Van

President Nguyen Van Thieu of South Vietnam directed his efforts in 1972 toward increasing his authority and blocking any Indochina settlement negotiated by the United States and North Vietnam that might leave his own regime at a disadvantage. After the North Vietnamese launched a new spring offensive against the south, Thieu imposed martial law. Over the next few months he instituted a number of repressive measures, including the closing down of most opposition newspapers and the suspension of elections of village officials.

After U. S. presidential adviser Henry Kissinger went to Saigon in October to present a tentative draft peace agreement he had worked out with the North Vietnamese, Thieu called the accord a "surrender to the Communists," objecting in particular to its failure to require the removal of all North Vietnamese troops from the south and its imposition of a tripartite coalition government with Communist participation. By year's end, discussions between Thieu and U. S. officials had failed to yield a solution acceptable to both the North and South Vietnamese.

In November, Thieu launched a new political organization, the Democracy party, designed to be strong enough to compete with the Communists in the event of a political settlement. On December 27 he signed a measure banning virtually all other political parties.

Background. Nguyen Van Thieu, the son of a small landowner and fisherman, was born on April 5, 1923, in a village in Annam, French Indochina. After World War II he became a cadet at the French military academy at Dalat, from which he graduated with a commission in 1948. Rising rapidly through the ranks of the army after the creation of the Republic of Vietnam in 1954, he took part in the coup that overthrew Ngo Dinh Diem in 1963 and was made nominal chief of state in 1965. Two years later, in the first election under a new constitution, he was chosen president over ten other candidates. He was inaugurated for a second term on Oct. 31, 1971, after an election in which he ran unopposed.

TRUDEAU, Pierre Elliott

The government of Canadian Prime Minister Pierre Trudeau stood on shaky ground at the end of 1972. In the federal election held on October 30, the prime minister's Liberal party lost its majority in the House of Commons. In the face of Progressive Conservative demands that he resign, Trudeau decided to remain in office and present a legislative program to Parliament, which was scheduled to convene in January 1973. The success of this move depended on the cooperation of the New Democratic party, which had to vote with the Liberals if Trudeau's minority government were to survive an early defeat in the House of Commons.

Activities in 1972. On the diplomatic front, two events highlighted Trudeau's year. First, President Nixon paid a state visit to Canada that culminated in Trudeau and the President signing the Great Lakes Quality Agreement on April 15. Second, in August, during a visit to China by External Affairs Minister Mitchell Sharp, it was announced that Trudeau would visit China "in the near future." Accomplishment of this visit, however, hung on the outcome of political developments.

Indeed, internal politics preoccupied Trudeau during most of 1972. Throughout his political activity, Trudeau has advocated a strong federal government for Canada —a policy aimed at countering the Quebec drive for independence. With Quebec as his main concern, Trudeau, despite his cross-country appearances during the year, did not seem to recognize the emergence of similar antifederalist feelings in other parts of the country. As regionalism developed in the western and midwestern provinces, it found expression in attacks on the prime minister's bilingual and regional development policies and on his strong federalist stance. Thus, his good work in defusing the Quebec separatist movement was countered by a flurry of misunderstanding regarding the western regions of the country.

In the election campaign that began on October 30, Trudeau drew the desired response from Quebec, which elected a healthy majority of Liberals. But elsewhere in Canada voters did not understand or were unimpressed by his view that the election was a challenge to "nothing less than the integrity of Canada." Instead, they voted against unemployment, a liberal immigration policy, and a welfare policy that appeared to some to subsidize indigence. The result was a setback for Trudeau and his party. (See CANADA.)

Background. Trudeau, a lawyer, was born in Montreal on Oct. 18, 1919. He was elected to Parliament in 1965 and joined the Liberal government of Lester Pearson in 1967 as minister of justice and attorney general. When Pearson retired as party leader in 1968, Trudeau succeeded him. In the election that followed, the Liberals increased their representation in Parliament, and a two-year era of "Trudeaumania" began.

W. A. MCKAY

WALDHEIM, Kurt

Kurt Waldheim, who succeeded U Thant as secretary general of the United Nations on Jan. 1, 1972, proved to be much more of an activist secretary general than his predecessor. His conception of his office, as he said in an interview in September, was that he was charged with protecting the interests of the world community through the exercise of the moral authority of the United Nations.

Waldheim acted on his own initiative on a number of occasions during 1972: in Cyprus, where he intervened to reduce tension over reported arms shipments to the government in February; in a border dispute between the two Yemens; and in connection with the talks between India and Pakistan. His overtures to both sides to allow him to mediate the Vietnam War in April, however, failed, as did his exploration of the prospects of constructive action on Vietnam by the Security Council in May.

Waldheim's outspoken comments on a number of topics have provoked sharp reactions from the governments concerned—the United States, for example, quickly challenging his statement at the end of July that U. S. bombing had intentionally damaged the dikes in North Vietnam. His feeling about terrorism, expressed both after the Munich killings on September 5 and at a news conference on September 12, led to his placing the issue on the General Assembly's agenda.

Traveling more than his predecessors, he put his visits overseas to good purpose. This was illustrated by his success in South Africa in March, when

some progress appeared to have been made in solving the problem of Namibia (South West Africa). Equally constructive was his visit to Paris in April, when he persuaded France to pay its annual contribution to the United Nations in advance. He also visited China and South America.

One of Waldheim's outstanding achievements was to reduce administrative costs, and he was able to report to the administrative and budgetary committee on September 29 that there would be no deficit in the 1972 budget. The freezing of 300 job vacancies in the secretariat and the decrease in the paper output by 15% saved $6 million.

Background. Born on Dec. 12, 1918, the son of a government official, Kurt Waldheim was educated at the Consular Academy at Vienna and the University of Vienna. He joined the foreign service in 1945, serving in a number of posts before leading Austria's observer mission to the United Nations in 1955–56. In 1958 he headed Austria's first delegation to the United Nations, and in 1964 became Austria's permanent representative, serving until 1968 when he became minister for foreign affairs. He returned to the United Nations again as permanent representative in 1970. In 1971, he ran unsuccessfully for the presidency of Austria. Waldheim was elected UN secretary general by the General Assembly on Dec. 22, 1971.

RICHARD E. WEBB

WALLACE, George C.

As he was shaking hands with supporters after a campaign rally on May 15, 1972, in Laurel, Md., Gov. George C. Wallace of Alabama was shot by a would-be assassin, Arthur Bremer. The shots left Wallace paralyzed below the waist, and his campaign for the presidential nomination of the Democratic party was dramatically interrupted.

By the time of the assassination attempt, Wallace had won primaries in Florida, Tennessee, and North Carolina, and had run well in Wisconsin, Pennsylvania, and Indiana. Even after the assault, Wallace won the Maryland and Michigan primaries on May 16. His supporters continued the Wallace campaign, and at the convention in Miami Beach in July he had recovered sufficiently to appear in the hall in a wheel chair and to address the delegates.

Wallace's supporters had rallied under the slogan "Send Them a Message." The main points of the message were as follows: end the busing of school children to achieve racial balance in the public schools; strengthen law and order; clean up the "welfare mess;" reduce taxes; improve national defense; and end foreign aid. Wallace received 385.7 of the 3,016 votes at the convention, finishing third in the contest for the nomination.

In 1972, Wallace did not head a third-party ticket as he had done in 1968 for the American Independent party. Nor did he support the Democratic nominee, Sen. George McGovern of South Dakota. Wallace returned to his duties as governor of Alabama and appeared to be planning for a possible attempt to gain the Democratic nomination in 1976. The likelihood that he would not achieve a complete recovery from the shooting clouded his prospects.

Background. George Corley Wallace was born in Clio, Ala., on Aug. 25, 1919. He attended the University of Alabama and earned the LL. B. in 1942. During World War II he served in the Air Force in the Pacific. After the war, Wallace served two terms in the state legislature and as judge of the Third Judicial Circuit from 1953 until 1959. In 1962 he was elected governor of Alabama.

Wallace's first term as governor was marked by racial conflict. He took office with a pledge to preserve segregation. Finally, President John Kennedy federalized the Alabama National Guard to force the integration of the University of Alabama.

Ineligible to succeed himself in 1966, Wallace supported his wife, Lurleen, who was elected governor.

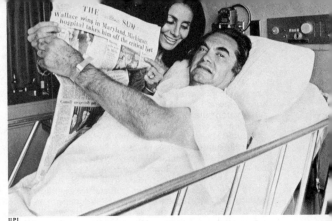

UPI

GOV. GEORGE C. WALLACE of Alabama and his wife, Cornelia, hold newspaper announcing his victories in two state primaries the day after he was shot.

Wallace was reelected in 1970 and was expected to run again in 1974, the state constitution having been changed to permit him to do so. After the death of his first wife in 1968, Wallace married Cornelia Snively in 1971.

WALTER DARNELL JACOBS

WANKEL, Felix

The German research engineer Felix Wankel is the inventor of the rotary internal-combustion engine, which is now used in Japanese-made Mazda automobiles. In August 1972, General Motors announced that it would offer the Wankel rotary engine as optional equipment in its Chevrolet Vega in about two years.

The engine, refined since its development by Wankel in the 1950's, has one or two triangular rotors that revolve in a nearly elliptical chamber and transmit power to an eccentric shaft. About one-half the size of a conventional piston-cylinder reciprocating engine, it is also lighter, smoother running, quieter, and has fewer moving parts. The gasoline-burning Wankel engine is not inherently pollution-free, but it permits easy installation of pollution-control equipment. While the Wankel rotary engine gained popularity in the automobile field in 1972, its inventor continued to work on the development of a rotary diesel engine and a combination automobile-boat that would be capable of crossing an ocean.

The son of a forestry official, Felix Wankel was born in Lahr, Germany, on Aug. 13, 1902. After dropping out of secondary school, Wankel became an apprentice with a book publishing firm in Heidelberg in 1921. While with that firm in 1924, he made his first technical drawing of a rotary engine. Having demonstrated an early aptitude as a draftsman and mechanic, he became a partner in an engineering firm in 1927.

Wankel worked on rotary engine development while employed by the Bavarian Motor Works (BMW) in the mid-1930's, and he did research and development work for the German air ministry during World War II. From 1951 to 1960, Wankel was with NSU, a small German auto company. In conjunction with NSU, Wankel built the first operating rotary engine in 1957. NSU's rotary-engine car failed to make money, and the company was merged with a Volkswagen subsidiary in 1969. In 1971, Wankel and Ernest Hutzenlaub sold their partnership, Wankel G. m. b. H., to a British firm for about $30 million.

WEINBERGER, Caspar W.

Caspar W. Weinberger, director of the Office of Management and Budget (OMB), was nominated on Nov. 28, 1972, to succeed Elliot L. Richardson as secretary of health, education, and welfare (HEW), a move that was part of President Nixon's cabinet reorganization for his second term. Weinberger is a fiscal con-

servative who habitually trimmed the departmental spending requests and thereby earned the nickname "Cap the Knife." He was expected to assume a hard line in administering the department of HEW, which has a staff of more than 110,000 persons for the operation of more than 250 social programs. Based on this expectation, his nomination apparently underscored the President's determination to keep federal spending, particularly for social programs, under control. ·

Background. Born in San Francisco, Calif., on Aug. 18, 1917, Caspar Willard Weinberger graduated from Harvard Law School with an LL. B. degree in 1941. He served for four years in the U. S. Army during World War II and rose from private to captain. After working as law clerk for a federal judge from 1945 to 1947, he entered private law practice. He was a member of the California state legislature from 1952 to 1958, chairman of the California state Republican central committee from 1962 to 1964, chairman of the California commission on government organization and economy in 1967–68, and state director of finance in 1968–69. Weinberger joined the Nixon administration in January 1970 as chairman of the Federal Trade Commission, and he was credited for a revitalization of the agency during his six months in that office. He became deputy director of the newly established OMB in June 1970 and succeeded George P. Shultz as its director two years later.

WHITELAW, William

On March 24, 1972, British Prime Minister Edward Heath named House of Commons majority leader William Whitelaw as secretary of state for Northern Ireland, placing the province under the direct rule of the British crown with a view toward ending years of fratricidal strife between its Protestant majority and Roman Catholic minority. Authorized to assume legislative and executive powers in Ulster, Whitelaw adopted a policy of conciliation and persuasion, freeing hundreds of Catholics who had been interned without trial, while seeking to isolate extremist elements from the community. In late June he managed to persuade leaders of the militant provisional wing of the Irish Republican Army to agree to a truce, which brought a temporary easing of the conflict. But the truce collapsed in renewed violence two weeks later. In September he announced suspension of the policy of internment without trial.

On October 30, Whitelaw set forth his tentative plans for Ulster in a "green paper" entitled *The Future of Northern Ireland,* which called for an administration "completely even-handed both in law and fact." In place of the old Protestant-dominated parliament, the new plan would provide for a legislative body in which Catholics would be equitably represented. Although Ulster would "remain part of the United Kingdom as long as that is the wish of the people," Whitelaw's plan for the first time recognized common interests between Northern Ireland and the Republic of Ireland and left the door open for an eventual united Ireland.

Background. A member of a wealthy land-owning family, William Stephen Ian Whitelaw was born in Monkland, Nairn, Scotland, on June 28, 1918. He was educated at Winchester College and at Trinity College, Cambridge, and he served as an officer in the Scots Guards from 1939 to 1947. Elected to Parliament in 1955, he served in several parliamentary posts and was named chief opposition whip in 1964. When the Conservatives returned to power in 1970 he became leader of the House of Commons. As spokesman for the liberal wing of the Tories, he helped persuade Heath to establish direct rule over Northern Ireland.

WHITLAM, Gough

Labor party leader Gough Whitlam became prime minister of Australia on Dec. 5, 1972, succeeding William McMahon, whose Liberal-Country party coalition had ruled Australia for 23 years. Campaigning on the slogan "It's Time," and promising increased social and economic benefits and a revitalization of the nation's federal system, as well as a more independent and flexible foreign policy, Whitlam led his Labor party to a victory in the national elections of December 2 that brought it 67 seats in the 125-member House of Representatives. His 27-member cabinet, in which he retained the portfolio of foreign affairs, was sworn in on December 19.

Shortly after taking office, Whitlam suspended military conscription, freed imprisoned draft resisters, relaxed censorship regulations, and took steps to give Australia's aborigines freehold rights over their traditional lands. He announced the immediate withdrawal of Australia's remaining military forces in Vietnam, formally established diplomatic relations with Communist China, and registered opposition to the white supremacist policies of Rhodesia and South Africa.

Background. The son of a lawyer who served as Commonwealth solicitor general, Edward Gough Whitlam was born in Kew, Victoria, on July 11, 1916. Educated in private schools and at the University of Sydney, where he obtained degrees in law and the arts, he entered law practice in a Sydney suburb after World War II service in the Royal Australian Air Force. After unsuccessful bids for local and state office, he was elected in 1952 as a Labor party candidate to the national House of Representatives. From 1956 to 1959 he served on the joint parliamentary committee on constitutional review. After becoming parliamentary leader of the Labor party in 1967, Whitlam transformed it from a doctrinaire socialist party into a more moderate and reformist organization. He is the author of several books, including *Beyond Vietnam: Australia's Regional Responsibility* (1968).

WHITMAN, Marina von Neumann

On Jan. 29, 1972, Marina von Neumann Whitman, a professor of economics at the University of Pittsburgh and a member of the Price Commission, was nominated by President Nixon to the Council of Economic Advisers. Upon her confirmation on February 18, Mrs. Whitman became the first woman to serve on the three-member council. An authority on foreign trade and investment, her responsibilities include international monetary and trade problems and liaison between the council and the Pay Board and the Price Commission.

Before becoming a member of the council, Mrs. Whitman had been a senior staff economist for the council in 1970–71 and had served on the seven-member Price Commission from October 1971 to February 1972. According to one colleague, Mrs. Whitman had showed an "incredible ability to cut through all the words and statistics to get to the heart of the problem."

In April 1972, Mrs. Whitman said that there was clear evidence of "progress toward the President's goal of bringing down the rate of inflation." Addressing a meeting of the American Insurance Association in May, she predicted a "healthy expansion" of corporate profits and a "strong economic recovery" during 1972 despite existing limitations on profit margins. She pointed out that companies could expand sales and reduce costs rather than increase prices.

Marina von Neumann was born in New York City on March 6, 1935, the daughter of John von Neumann, a distinguished mathematician and pioneer in computers. After graduating from Radcliffe College in 1956 at the head of her class, she undertook graduate studies at Columbia University. In 1962 she joined the faculty of the University of Pittsburgh as a lecturer in economics. She was appointed assistant professor in 1964, associate professor in 1966, and professor in 1971. She married Robert F. Whitman in 1956 and became the mother of two children. Her husband is now the head of the English department at the University of Pittsburgh.

BOATING

Long-awaited standards for controlling pollution were set for U. S. boats in 1972. In racing, history was made when a non-American boat won the Bermuda race for the first time and when Ohioan Sandy Satullo won the Hennessy Grand Prix for the fourth time in a row.

Regulations. Fulfilling provisions of the Federal Boat Safety Act of 1971, the Environmental Protection Agency announced pollution standards for U. S. boats. The standards affect all of the nation's 600,000 marine vessels, including 550,000 recreational boats equipped with marine toilets. Essentially, the government has adopted a "no discharge" policy, which requires that pollutants be retained in holding tanks aboard the ship until it reaches land, where they can be pumped out to facilities ashore and presumably can be treated by local municipal sewage systems. At present, most marine toilet wastes are emptied into the surrounding waters. The new standards will go into effect for new boats in 1975 and for older boats in 1978.

Other rulings and modifications under the Boat Safety Act were made in four significant categories:

(1) All boats, no matter how small, must carry a life-saving device of some type, approved by the Coast Guard, for every person on board.

(2) The so-called "unsafe condition" law, in which Coast Guard boarding officers could order boats back to port if they deemed conditions unsafe, was modified to include only those conditions that could actually be observed on the boat. This ruled out anticipation of dangers or value judgments by the officers, such as assessments of a boat's ability to withstand predicted bad weather.

(3) Boat manufacturers are required to notify dealers, distributors, and purchasers of any defect in their product that creates a substantial risk of personal injury.

(4) For all boats of under 20 feet (6 meters) that are not sailboats, canoes, kayaks, or inflatable boats, manufacturers must list the maximum safe load, maximum safe horsepower, amount of flotation, and a hull identification number.

Racing. The Bermuda race, held in June 1972, was won by the British sloop *Noryema*. It was the first time that the winner was not an American-owned boat, although yachts from many countries had usually participated. The boat fleet was the largest ever, including 178 vessels. The racers had to confront a storm of near-hurricane intensity, and it was a tribute to the ability of modern racing craft and their crews that although several boats were dismasted at no time was any of them in serious danger. The amazingly good safety record of the Bermuda race series was thus maintained.

The powerboat ocean race for the Hennessy Grand Prix, which drew 250,000 spectators on shore and 4,000 spectator boats, was won for a record-setting fourth consecutive time by Cleveland restaurant-owner Sandy Satullo in his 36-foot (11-meter) *Copper Kettle*. His average speed over the 181.3-mile (291-meter) course in smooth seas along the mid-Atlantic U. S. coast was 72 mph (116 km/hr).

Statistics. The number of reported boat accidents has been rising in the United States. Some of the increase is thought to be due to more accurate reporting, but much of it can be accounted for by the increase in the number of registered boats in the water. A record 5,510,092 boats were registered in early 1972, a rise of about 400,000 in one year. Fatalities resulting from boat accidents totaled 1,058 in 1969, 1,418 in 1970, and 1,518 in 1971.

Sales figures revealed that interest in boating was increasing in 1972, after a lull of about a year. The Boating Industry Association estimated that retail boat sales for 1971 totaled more than $3.6 billion, an increase of $170 million over 1970. An estimated 45 million persons boated more than twice during the year in a nationwide fleet of some 9 million registered and unregistered craft.

ZACK TAYLOR
Boating Editor, "Sports Afield"

BOLIVIA

Serious economic and political problems plagued the military government of Gen. Hugo Banzer Suárez in Bolivia in 1972. But at year's end there appeared to be no serious threat to his continuing in office. Banzer had ousted the leftist president, Juan José Torres, in a coup in August 1971.

Political Affairs. Government officials stated in February that hundreds of Bolivian exiles were being trained as guerrilla fighters in Chile by the Cuban government. No official charges were made against the Chilean government, but there were allegations that it was extending protection to the Cubans and Bolivian exiles.

A major problem of the Banzer regime was the need to retain the support of the professional and business population, which had helped overthrow the leftist government in 1971. At the same time, Banzer had to avoid hostility from the militant tin miners' union and the large Indian population that had favored the Torres regime but had remained relatively passive during the 1971 coup.

Several crushing blows were dealt to the guerrilla movement that had been organized by Ernesto "Che" Guevara in the Bolivian countryside in the

--------- BOLIVIA · Information Highlights ---------

Official Name: Republic of Bolivia.
Area: 424,163 square miles (1,098,581 sq km).
Population (1972 est.): 4,900,000. *Density,* 10 per square mile (4 per sq km). *Annual rate of increase,* 2.4%.
Chief Cities (1969 est.): Sucre, the legal capital, 48,000; La Paz, the actual capital, 525,000; Cochabamba, 157,000.
Government: *Head of state,* Hugo Banzer Suárez, president (took office Aug. 1971). *Head of government,* Hugo Banzer Suárez. *Legislature*—Congress (suspended Sept. 1969): Senate, 27 members; Chamber of Deputies, 102 members.
Languages: Spanish (official), Quechua, Aymará.
Education: *Expenditure* (1969), 26.2% of total public expenditure. *School enrollment* (1969)—primary, 663,829; secondary, 76,244; technical/vocational, 9,692; university/higher, 27,352.
Monetary Unit: peso boliviano (11.88 bolivianos equal U. S.$1, Aug. 1972).
Gross National Product (1971 est.): $970,000,000.
National Income per Person (1969): $180.
Economic Indexes: *Industrial production* (manufacturing, 1966), 139 (1963=100); *agricultural production* (1971), 217 (1952–56=100); *consumer price index* (1970), 151 (1963=100).
Manufacturing (major products): Processed foods, textiles, leather goods, cement, glass ceramics.
Major Agricultural Products: Coffee, corn, sugar, wheat, rice, potatoes, almonds, chestnuts.
Major Minerals: Tin (ranks 2d among world producers, 1970), antimony (world rank 3d in 1970), tungsten, gold, silver.
Foreign Trade (1969): *Exports,* $182,000,000 (chief exports—tin; petroleum; tungsten; antimony). *Imports* $165,000,000 (chief imports—commercial and passenger motor vehicles; wheat flour; iron tubes and pipes; food). *Chief trading partners* (1969)—United Kingdom (took 46% of exports, supplied 5% of imports); United States (31%—31%).
Transportation: *Motor vehicles* (1970), 49,000 (automobiles, 19,200); *railroads* (1970), 2,236 miles (3,599 km); *major national airline,* Lloyd Aereo Boliviano.
Communications: *Telephones* (1970), 37,551; *television stations* (1971), 1; *television sets* (1971), 8,000; *radios* (1969), 1,350,000; *newspapers* (1970), 21.

mid-1960's. This militant organization, defeated in rural areas, had moved into the major urban areas of the country. The government carried out heavy raids against the guerrillas in La Paz in 1972, killing or capturing many of the movement's leaders and seizing stocks of arms and ammunition. The ministry of the interior claimed that the movement had been crushed, but occasional sabotage continued throughout the year.

Economic Affairs. Bolivia's economy showed little improvement in 1972. The growth rate of the Gross National Product continued at about 4%. Income from the country's exports rose slightly to about $180 million, one third of which went into retirement of the national debt. Fear of popular disapproval prevented the government from devaluating the currency from the official rate of 11.88 bolivianos to the U. S. dollar, although the black market was twice as high.

Petroleum production increased somewhat in 1972, and the completion of a gas pipeline from Santa Cruz to Argentina will add an estimated $25 million a year to the national budget. The tin mines showed little profit, discouraging foreign investment and U. S. technical and economic aid.

Foreign Affairs. The official leanings of the Banzer government were rightist. But domestic political splits and a bankrupt treasury forced the regime to implement agreements with both Communist and non-Communist governments offering economic and other forms of assistance.

In spite of continued Soviet economic and technical assistance, relations between Bolivia and the Soviet Union deteriorated after the ouster of the Torres government. On March 29 the Bolivian government ordered an estimated 119 "members of the Soviet embassy staff" to leave the country. The Soviet ambassador protested that his embassy had a staff of only 40 attachés.

In April, President Banzer met with Brazil's President Emilio Garrastazú Médici in Corumbá, Brazil, where they signed agreements that gave formal shape to Brazil's growing program of economic and military aid to its smaller neighbors. The agreement called for Brazil to help Bolivia with road construction and the purchase of road-building equipment.

Former U. S. Treasury Secretary John Connally visited Bolivia in June as part of a 6-nation Latin American tour as a special emissary for President Nixon. Connally conferred with Banzer in La Paz, reportedly promising U. S. aid for Bolivian development programs.

OLEN E. LEONARD, *University of Arizona*

BONDS. See STOCKS AND BONDS.
BOOK PUBLISHING. See PUBLISHING.

BOSTON

The year 1972 was a busy one for Bostonians. It was filled with major events, social and political, happy and saddening. For example, the renowned Boston Symphony Orchestra announced the appointment of a new music director. Seiji Ozawa will replace William Steinberg, who retired in April. Ozawa will not officially assume his duties until the fall of 1973, so the orchestra spent the 1972–73 season under the batons of several guest conductors. In baseball, the Boston Red Sox finished a close second in the American League Eastern Division. The Bos-

ton Bruins won hockey's Stanley Cup for the second time in three years. In a tragedy that the whole city mourned for weeks, nine Boston firemen were killed when a section of a 100-year-old hotel collapsed in a fire on June 17. It was the worst accident in the history of the department.

Conflicts with State Government. Political controversy was especially widespread. Two such conflicts involved the city and state governments. The Boston Redevelopment Authority was stymied in its attempt to win state approval for a large downtown urban renewal plan, the "Park Plaza" project. State officials accused the B. R. A. of poor planning. Some saw in the refusal, however, another chapter in the continuing battle between Boston's Democratic mayor, Kevin H. White, and the Republican governor, Francis W. Sargent.

In another conflict with the state, a number of Boston-area mayors, led by White, attempted to force the state to take over financing of the Massachusetts Bay Transportation Authority (MBTA), which provides area-wide transportation services. The mayors withheld their approval from the MBTA budget for many weeks. This conflict again pitted Mayor White against Governor Sargent. The MBTA financial crisis was finally resolved in favor of the state when the legislature acted. It was predicted, however, that White and Sargent would lock horns again, perhaps as a prelude to a repeat of their 1970 fight for the governor's chair.

Elections. For a time during the summer, Sen. George McGovern, the Democratic presidential nominee, considered asking Mayor White to be his running mate. In November, McGovern carried Boston handily. The Boston congressional contests included the defeat of Rep. Louise Day Hicks, known for her opposition to the busing of schoolchildren to achieve racial integration, by John J. Moakley, a Democrat running as an independent.

Summer Unrest. The oppressive heat of late July helped spark several nights of violence and property damage in Boston's South End, which in recent years has become the city's chief Puerto Rican neighborhood. The disturbances were the first in several years in Boston and were quickly brought under control by local authorities.

Newspaper Folds. On Sunday, June 18, Boston ceased to have three daily newspapers as the Boston *Herald Traveler* published its last edition. Mounting labor and production costs plus a federal decision forcing the paper to give up its ownership of a television station were the factors that caused the paper's demise. The *Herald*'s name and modern plant were purchased by the Hearst Corporation's *Record-American*, which began publishing as the *Record-American Herald Traveler*.

HARVEY BOULAY, *Boston University*

BOTANY

Interactions among plants, animals, and the environment were stressed in botanical research in 1972. A new theory was proposed on how sap rises in trees; a technique was suggested for studying fossils of ancient plants; and for the first time plants were grown from artificially fused cells.

Plants and Pollinators. U. S. scientists Bernd Heinrich and Peter H. Raven indicated that the energy budgets of insects and other pollinators—that is, the balance between the energy expended in obtaining plant food and the caloric reward of that

Biologists examine a hybrid tobacco plant, the first plant grown from fused cells of different species.

food—have played an important role in the evolution of flowering plants. Important factors include flowering time, number of flowers, and distances between individual plants and flowers. Thus pollinators and flowers have evolved together with respect to the expenditure of energy on the part of the animals and the amount of cross-pollination on the part of the plants.

The bases of the petals of various species of flowers have color markings, designated as "nectar guides," that lead pollinating insects to food. It has been found that these markings possess ultraviolet-absorbing pigments that are discernible only to certain insects. The suggestion is again made that there has been a coevolution of flowers containing ultraviolet-absorbing pigments and insects sensitive to ultraviolet light.

Plants and Ecology. The role of plants in the removal of pollutants has been of increasing concern to biologists and environmentalists. A U.S. biologist, William H. Smith, determined the amounts of lead and mercury concentrated in the leaves and twigs of woody plants in a city of 137,000 persons, as compared to concentrations in plants in a suburban area. The contamination in six species of city trees was very high, which means that these trees play an important role in the cycling of heavy metals in the environment and may be significant for certain kinds of pollution control.

The environmental role of plant ecosystems, such as tropical rain forests, continues to be studied. The opinion that such forests will never disappear was challenged by three Mexican botanists, who presented evidence that, if present trends continue, forests are in danger of mass extinction. To preserve these gigantic pools of genetic diversity, they urged massive international action through the establishment of new national parks, arboretums, botanical gardens, and genetic stock centers.

Sap Transport in Trees. Two U.S. chemists, Robert C. Plumb and William B. Bridgman, advanced a new model to explain the rise of sap in trees, a phenomenon long of interest to botanists.

Whereas the most accepted explanation has been in terms of gradients of hydrostatic pressure in trees, the two men proposed a "gel structure" hypothesis instead. They suggested that the synthesis of cellulose fibrils in cell walls leaves behind a filamentous, gel-like structure that is able to support columns of sap without any need for pressure gradients. Measurements of the concentration of this "gel" in the conducting tissues of trees can help to determine whether this proposed model of sap transport should be preferred.

Fossil Plant Study. The question of the oldest life to be found in fossil form is reinvestigated every two or three years. The organisms most frequently described from the oldest fossil-bearing rocks are the filamentous blue-green algae, and a new technique for interpreting such fossils was published in December 1971 by two U.S. scientists, John H. Oehler and H. William Schopf. Their technique is to subject microscopic algae in crystalline silica to elevated temperatures and pressures, thus simulating geochemical processes that take many millions of years. They reported that the artificially produced fossils were comparable to natural ones and thus could provide a basis for interpreting the morphology and chemistry of preserved microorganisms. The technique may also provide valuable information concerning the changes that take place during the process of fossilization.

Plants from Fused Cells. At Brookhaven National Laboratory, biologists Peter S. Carlson, Harold H. Smith, and Rosemarie D. Dearing grew mature and fertile hybrid tobacco plants from artificially fused leaf cells of two wild tobacco species. Although cells had previously been fused artificially, it was the first time that an entire higher organism had been produced from such cells. The new technique, called parasexual hybridization, avoids many of the natural barriers to reproduction between different species. While the method requires further development, it offers the potential for new kinds of crop plants.

DAVID E. FAIRBROTHERS, *Rutgers University*

——— BOTSWANA • Information Highlights ———

Official Name: Republic of Botswana.
Area: 231,804 square miles (600,372 sq km).
Population (1972 est.): 700,000. *Density,* 2.6 per square mile (1 per sq km). *Annual rate of increase,* 2.2%.
Chief Cities (1964): Gaborone, the capital, 17,698 (1971); Serowe, 34,182; Kanye, 34,045; Molepolole, 29,625.
Government: *Head of state,* Sir Seretse Khama, president (took office Sept. 1966). *Head of government,* Sir Seretse Khama. *Legislature*—Parliament: National Assembly, 36 members; House of Chiefs (a consultative body), 15 members. *Major political parties*—Democratic party; People's party; National Front.
Languages: English (official), Tswana.
Education: *Expenditure* (1969), 12.9% of total public expenditure. *School enrollment* (1969)—primary, 82,214; secondary, 4,228; technical/vocational, 876.
Monetary Unit: South African rand (0.7617 rand equals U. S. $1, June 1972).
Gross National Product (1970 est.): $66,000,000.
National Income per Person (1967): $97.
Manufacturing (major products): Processed foods, skins.
Major Agricultural Products: Cotton, peanuts, sorghum.
Major Minerals: Manganese ore, diamonds, nickel, copper.
Foreign Trade: *Chief exports*—Cattle carcasses, hides and skins, manganese ore. *Chief imports*—Food and live animals; machinery and transportation equipment. *Chief trading partners*—South Africa; Rhodesia.
Transportation: *Motor vehicles* (1970), 5,000 (automobiles, 1,900); *railroads* (1970), 399 miles (642 km); *major national airline,* Botswana Airways.
Communications: *Telephones* (1971), 3,981; *radios* (1970), 8,500; *newspapers* (1970), 2 (daily circulation, 13,000).

BOTSWANA

Increased foreign loans to develop mineral potential enabled Botswana in 1972 to balance its national budget without British subsidy for the first time since independence in 1966.

Orapa Diamond Mine. Botswana's president, Sir Seretse Khama, officially opened the De Beers diamond mine at Orapa in the Central District on May 26. He stressed the need to spread mining benefits to rural areas, where 90% of the people live on subsistence agriculture, in order to bridge the gap between urban and rural living standards.

Economic Development. Besides the Orapa diamond mine, Botswana's leaders and foreign investors plan to exploit known reserves of 37 million tons of copper and nickel at Selebi-Pikwe. More than 40 development agreements were signed in 1971 and 1972 in Gaborone, the capital, with the World Bank and several countries, including the United States, West Germany, Britain, and Canada.

Botswana's National Development Plan for 1970–75 allocated 78% of appropriated funds for roads and other improvements to support mining, 14% for agriculture and water resources, and 8% for education and medical services. A dam on the Shashi River will bring electrical power and irrigation.

United States Aid. On September 9, U. S. Ambassador Charles J. Nelson signed an agreement providing for a $12.6 million loan from the United States to help build a road linking Botswana and Zambia. The road will enable Botswana to bypass white-ruled southern Africa for direct trade with black African countries. Paradoxically, while the Nixon administration cut aid to many other developing countries, it increased aid to Botswana in order to prove, according to one source, the viability of multiracial states in southern Africa.

Religion. In July the Anglican Church in Botswana discontinued its association with that of Rhodesia, becoming a separate diocese with its own bishop. The Rt. Rev. Charles Mallory, an American on the staff of Makerere University in Kampala, Uganda, was named Botswana's first bishop.

FRANKLIN PARKER, *West Virginia University*

BRANDT, Willy. See BIOGRAPHY.

BRAZIL

The economic boom that has led some to call Brazil the "Japan of Latin America" showed no signs of abating in 1972. But there was growing criticism of the fact that the economic benefits were unevenly distributed, with the poor getting poorer as the rich got richer. The military dictatorship, in power since 1964, remained unwilling to indicate when it would sanction the return of democratic government.

Political Affairs. President Emilio Garrastazú Médici, head of the military regime, was firmly in control. In a move to end even the limited opposition that had been tolerated theretofore, the president had published a decree in December 1971 giving him authority to issue decrees whose contents need not be made public and whose existence would be known only from their titles as published in the *Diario Oficial.* On April 3, 1972, the government sent to Congress a constitutional amendment postponing the 1974 state gubernatorial elections.

In early February the government arrested over 200 "suspected subversives" in Rio de Janeiro. Reports of torture as a method of interrogation were widespread despite continued government denials. On June 10 the National Conference of Bishops charged that torture and illegal arrests were continuing and condemned the use of torture during the interrogation of suspects.

Reports in the government-censored press on September 25 said that Brazil's armed forces were fighting rebels in the remote Amazon jungle region. But the government quickly denied all reports of a military operation, claiming there was no guerrilla warfare in the country.

Censorship. On May 8 the Brazilian government ordered that all television programs be recorded and submitted to official censorship before being broadcast. In June the country's major newspapers published, against the wishes of the government, a study by the Superior War College advocating freedom of the press. The study asserted that Brazil's widespread press censorship violated the people's right of free expression and might lead to tyranny. In response, President Médici announced on July 4 that the existing curbs on civil liberties would be retained.

150th Anniversary. On September 7, Brazil celebrated the 150th anniversary of its independence from Portugal with festivities led by President Médici and Portuguese Premier Marcello Caetano. The occasion was marked by the removal from Portugal to Brazil of the remains of Dom Pedro I, father of Brazilian independence, who, on Sept. 7, 1822, had uttered the famous Cry of Ipiranga—"Independence or death!"

Treatment of Indians. One of Brazil's leading Indian specialists, Antonio Cotrim, resigned from the National Indian Foundation in protest over government policies. He charged that the rights of Indians in Brazil's forests were being violated by land development companies and were not being protected by the Indian Foundation.

Foreign Relations. The government denied having imperialistic aspirations for Brazil. Foreign Minister Mario Gibson Barbosa declared that the nation's development was tied to that of the other Latin American countries, but insisted that Brazil had no ambition to direct or orient the others' economies.

President Médici met with the presidents of two neighboring states, Argentina and Bolivia. At a meeting in Brasília in March with President Alejandro Lanusse of Argentina, the problems of economic relations between the two countries were discussed. A meeting in Corumbá in April with Bolivian President Hugo Banzer Suárez resulted in a pact providing for a Brazilian loan and technical assistance to Bolivia for highway and railroad construction. Brazil also agreed to buy Bolivian petroleum.

On April 22 a Brazilian-Portuguese treaty went into effect providing mutual rights of citizenship for Portuguese and Brazilian citizens.

In an agreement signed on May 9 the United States recognized the right of Brazil to regulate shrimp fishing within the 200-mile (320-km) offshore limit claimed by Brazil. However, the United States denied that the agreement indicated recognition of the 200-mile offshore sovereignty rights claimed by a number of Latin American countries.

Brazil was one of six Latin American countries visited in June by former U. S. Secretary of the Treasury John Connally as a special emissary for President Richard M. Nixon. Connally discussed economic and financial matters with President Médici in Brasília and declared himself impressed by Brazil's economic boom "due in part to the favorable investment climate which has attracted private U. S. capital."

Brasília and Amazonia. September 7 was the deadline for the removal of all diplomatic missions from Rio de Janeiro to Brasília, marking the final establishment of the newly founded city as the federal capital of Brazil. Designed to turn Brazilian eyes toward the interior, Brasília has not only opened up the sparsely settled central plateau for migration and development but has also focused national attention on the vast potentials of Amazonia. The Trans-Amazon Highway, which is to extend from Recife to the Peruvian border, is the key to the development of the Amazon River basin. Nearly half of the projected 5,000-mile (8,000-km) road network has been completed.

An unprecedented national enthusiasm, called "Amazon fever," has focused on the superlative possibilities supposed to exist in the vast river basin. The National Colonization and Agrarian Reform Institute has been implementing a homesteading program that provides for the settlement of 100,000 families, most of them from the overpopulated and impoverished northeast. The plan calls for the distribution of farm villages along the new roads, and for the establishment of larger communities at intervals of about 25 miles (40 km). Each settler is to be granted long-term loans for a house, land, tools, seed, and animals. The new arrivals are to be paid a small salary for the first six months and are to receive title to the land after two years. Some 10,000 settlers had been relocated by mid-1972.

Economic Affairs. The economic surge maintained the growth rate of the gross national product at over 9%. Coffee continued to be the principal agricultural product, accounting for 29% of total exports, but sugar production was rising under the stimulus of agricultural diversification. Brazilian sugar agreements were concluded with the Soviet Union and Communist China, although sales to the latter were canceled in April because of a shipping delay. Wheat production had also staged a spectacular increase, due to the development of miracle

---

BRAZIL • Information Highlights

Official Name: Federative Republic of Brazil.
Area: 3,286,478 square miles (8,511,965 sq km).
Population (1972 est.): 98,400,000. *Density,* 28 per square mile (11 per sq km). *Annual rate of increase,* 2.8%.
Chief Cities (1970 census): Brasília, the capital, 525,000 (metropolitan area); São Paulo, 5,978,977; Rio de Janeiro, 4,296,800; Belo Horizonte, 1,255,415.
Government: *Head of state,* Emílio Garrastazú Médici, president (took office Oct. 1969). *Head of government,* Emílio Garrastazú Médici. *Legislature*—National Congress: Chamber of Deputies, 310 members; Federal Senate, 66 members. *Major political parties*—Aliança Renovadora Nacional (ARENA); Movimento Democrático Brasiliero (MDB).
Languages: Portuguese (official).
Education: *Expenditure* (1969), 17.5% of total public expenditure. *School enrollment* (1969)—primary, 12,294,343; secondary, 3,629,375; technical/vocational, 337,917; university/higher, 346,824.
Monetary Unit: Cruzeiro (5.915 cruzeiros equal U. S.$1, June 1972).
Gross National Product (1971 est.): $38,500,000,000.
National Income per Person (1970): $341.
Economic Indexes: *Industrial production* (1967), 117 (1963=100); *agricultural production* (1971), 188 (1952–56=100); *consumer price index* (1971), 1,268 (1963=100).
Manufacturing (major products): Processed foods, chemicals, textiles, metals, transportation equipment, petroleum products.
Major Agricultural Products: Coffee (ranks 1st among world producers, 1971), bananas (world rank 1st, 1970), cassava (world rank 1st, 1970), cacao, corn (world rank 2d, 1971), sugarcane (world rank 1st, 1971), rice, natural rubber, livestock, forest products.
Major Minerals: Manganese ore (ranks 3d among world producers, 1970), iron ore, bauxite, coal, petroleum, natural gas, gold.
Foreign Trade (1971): *Exports,* $2,771,000,000 (chief exports, 1970—coffee, iron ore, cotton, cacao). *Imports,* $3,370,-000,000 (chief imports, 1969—nonelectrical machinery, chemicals, food, petroleum, crude and partly refined). *Chief trading partners* (1969)—United States (took 26% of exports, supplied 30% of imports); West Germany (10%—13%); Argentina (7%—7%); Japan (5%—5%).
Tourism: *Receipts* (1970), $30,100,000.
Transportation: *Motor vehicles* (1969), 2,658,700 (automobiles, 2,002,600); *railroads* (1970), 19,894 miles (32,015 km); *merchant fleet* (1971), 1,731,000 gross registered tons; *major national airlines,* VARIG (Viacao Aerea Rio-Grandense); VASP (Viacao Aerea São Paulo).
Communications: *Telephones* (1971), 2,000,726; *television stations* (1971), 50; *television sets* (1971), 6,500,000; *radios* (1970), 5,700,000; *newspapers* (1969), 257 (daily circulation, 3,393,000).

---

wheat strains. Long a big importer of wheat, Brazil hoped to become self-sufficient within a few years.

Agriculture minister Luis Cirne Lima announced on August 5 that the government's land reform program would begin in the three northeastern states of Paraíba, Pernambuco, and Ceará. These are agricultural areas with serious problems stemming from unequal land distribution. For the first time the government also applied agrarian reform to lands in the wealthy south central part of the country.

Brazil's steel industry embarked on a $1.25 billion expansion program, financed by both domestic and foreign sources. On February 11, Finance Minister Antônio Delfim Netto announced that Brazil would borrow $64.5 million from the World Bank to build up its steel capacity. The developing steel industry has enabled Brazil to utilize more of its almost unlimited resources of high-grade iron ore. But Brazil has a serious petroleum deficiency. Oil imports have been a drain on Brazilian exchange and have therefore stimulated oil prospecting.

The U. S. Export-Import Bank announced on February 1 that it would provide a $138 million loan to help Brazil construct a nuclear power plant near Rio de Janeiro. The loan was to support the purchase of equipment in the United States. The Soviet Union supplied Brazil with generators for a major power station in the state of São Paulo.

Brazil's auto plants, using domestically made parts, have greatly expanded their output, producing 500,000 cars annually. A number of major auto companies, including Volkswagen, Toyota, General Motors, Ford, and Chrysler, have made sizable in-

vestments in Brazilian plants for the manufacture of small cars.

Foreign capital has contributed greatly to the industrial expansion of Brazil, but the government has ruled that the majority investment in each corporation must be Brazilian. The government itself has played a major role in business, with 45 of the 100 biggest companies being government-owned or operated. The sectors in which the government is especially active include petroleum, power, communications, steel, and public utilities.

Brazil's industrialization program aimed not only at supplying the domestic market but at exports as well. The sale of manufactured goods abroad contributed to a record rise in total exports in 1972. Finance Minister Netto declared that Brazil would fight for free trade and oppose economic barriers to ensure markets for its goods. The United States was strongly urged not to set up artificial barriers against imports from Brazil.

Education. There has been a sudden blooming of interest in education in Brazil. Industrial expansion has accentuated the importance of literacy and education in achieving higher living standards. A national literacy drive called *Mobral,* inaugurated in 1970 and aimed at Brazil's 16 to 20 million illiterates over the age of 15, has taught over 2 million persons to read and write. All levels of government sponsor *Mobral,* which is basically community-oriented and makes each small town responsible for setting up classes to teach reading and writing. Funds for the program come from both public and private sources.

The number of students in primary schools was about 15 million in 1972, more than double the 1962 total. But about 35% of school-age children were still not attending classes. The rush for education has caused a severe shortage of teachers and classrooms. The teacher shortage has been eased somewhat by allowing high school graduates to teach primary classes.

Higher education has become increasingly popular in Brazil as a result of the increasing demand for college-trained personnel. Some 600,000 students took college entrance examinations in January. But the country's colleges had room for only about one third of the applicants.

J. LLOYD MECHAM, *University of Texas*

BREMER, Arthur H. See BIOGRAPHY.
BREZHNEV, Leonid I. See BIOGRAPHY.

BRIDGES

Bridge builders were active in many countries in 1972, constructing or completing numerous highway bridges to reduce driving time or relieve traffic congestion. In the United States much of the bridge building involved the completion of links in the Interstate Highway System, a 42,500-mile (68,400-km) network of modern multilane expressways nearing completion under a 20-year program.

The Federal Highway Administration reported in 1972 that 89,000 highway bridges needed to be repaired or replaced, including 24,000 bridges in the federal-aid highway system. It also said that there were about 563,500 highway bridges in the nation and that more than 400,000 of them had been built before 1935. The agency concluded that a national bridge replacement program was vital to the cause of highway safety.

Houston Ship Channel Bridge. The first bridge over the Houston Ship Channel was completed in 1972. It has ten Interstate 610 traffic lanes, two outside parking lanes, and a 17-foot (5-meter) median strip. The $18 million structure, Texas' largest bridge, has an overwater portion 1,230 feet (375 meters) long. Each of the three-section suspended center spans is 290 feet (88 meters) long. The bridge has a horizontal clearance of 600 feet (183 meters) and a vertical clearance of 135 feet (41 meters).

Mississippi River Bridges. A 4,200-foot (1,280-meter) bridge over the Mississippi River at Vicksburg, Miss., was completed in 1972. It is a three-span steel cantilever structure with an 870-foot (265-meter) main span and two 423-foot (129-meter) anchor arms. The bridge is part of the east-west Interstate 20. It supplements an old road and railway bridge that remains in service for local traffic.

Another bridge under construction across the Mississippi River will carry Interstate 155 between Pemiscot County, Mo., and Dyer County, Tenn. The 3,590-foot (1,094-meter) crossing is about 120 miles (193 km) north of Memphis. The 12-span steel structure has ten girder spans and a two-span through-truss cantilever unit consisting of a 520-foot (159 meter) anchor arm span and a 920-foot (280-meter) channel span. Maximum horizontal and vertical clearances will be 901 feet (275 meters) and 52 feet (16 meters), respectively. Carrying four traffic lanes, the new bridge will eliminate several ferry crossings. It will help motorists because the nearest bridge is about 100 miles (161 km) upstream.

Whiskey Bay Bridge. The Whiskey Bay Bridge, spanning the Atchafalaya River as part of Interstate 10 between Lafayette and Baton Rouge, La., was completed in 1972. The 2,700-foot (823-meter) bridge, costing $13 million, has its four central piers resting on massive concrete caissons 155 feet (47 meters) below water level.

Tennessee River Bridge. Alabama is scheduled to complete its longest plate girder bridge in 1973. It crosses the Tennessee River, carrying Interstate 65 near Decatur. Twin structures for north- and south-bound traffic are about 9,900 feet (3,018 meters) long, including approaches. The center portion of each structure includes plate girder spans of 300, 375, 375, and 300 feet (91, 114, 114, and 91 meters).

Uffington Bridge. The 1,549-foot (472-meter) Uffington Bridge across the Monongahela River at Morgantown, W. Va., is scheduled for completion in 1973. The $6.3 million continuous-deck truss bridge will carry Interstate 79 between Pittsburgh, Pa., and Charleston, W. Va.

Wade Bridge. The 5,193-foot (1,583-meter) long George N. Wade Bridge over the Susquehanna River north of Harrisburg, Pa., is scheduled for completion in 1973. The steel girder bridge, which will rise to a height of 55 feet (17 meters) above the stream bed, will carry six lanes of Interstate 81.

Thames River Bridge. Connecticut's longest bridge, 6,300 feet (1,920 meters) long, is scheduled to open in 1973. Its gold-painted steel superstructure is a twin to the Gold Star Memorial Bridge, which will be widened when the new one opens. Each bridge will carry five one-way traffic lanes, plus two 10-foot (3-meter) shoulder lanes. The new bridge was built to help relieve congestion on Interstate 95 at New London. Its four main truss spans,

CHESAPEAKE BAY BRIDGE-TUNNEL was forced to close after a tug and barge, abandoned in high seas and gale winds, crashed into it in September.

each about 350 feet (107 meters) long, soar 130 feet (39.6 meters) above the Thames River.

Dent Bridge. The first vehicular suspension bridge in Idaho was completed in 1972. It carries traffic formerly carried by a road that was inundated by the formation of a reservoir at Dworshak Dam. The $8 million Dent Bridge, 1,550 feet (472 meters) long, includes a 1,050-foot (320-meter) main span and two 250-foot (76-meter) side spans. It crosses a gorge 600 feet (183 meters) deep. When the gorge is filled with water, the bridge will have a 30-foot (9-meter) clearance above the maximum water level of the reservoir.

Paraná River Bridge. Argentina completed a suspension bridge over the Paraná River in 1972, connecting the provinces of Corrientes and Chaco. Total length of the bridge and elevated access roads is 5,469 feet (1,667 meters), with a roadway 27 feet (8.3 meters) wide for two-lane traffic. The designers chose a precast prestressed concrete structure to obtain large span openings with light, simple, and fast construction.

Danube River Bridge. Czechoslovakia finished construction of a unique bridge across the Danube River at Bratislava in 1972. The two-level, cable-stayed girder structure has a total length of 1,391 feet (424 meters) and is 69 feet (21 meters) wide. Its main span is 994 feet (303 meters) long. The dominant feature of the bridge is an A-shaped, 279-foot (85-meter) steel pylon leaning back from the right bank of the river. Anchored to the pylon are three clusters of suspension cables supporting the weight of the bridge, thus eliminating the need for piers in the river. On the pylon, 272 feet (83 meters) above the embankment, is a restaurant for 120 people. An elevator within the pylon provides access to the restaurant.

Algyoi Bridge. The Algyoi Bridge, a steel and concrete structure crossing the Tisza River, was under construction near Szeged, Hungary, in 1972. The structure, which has a total length of 1,608 feet (490 meters), includes three main spans. The 335-foot (102-meter) center span is flanked by two 189-foot (58-meter) side spans. For this bridge, the designers used prefabricated steel girders and precast concrete beams, which were chosen for economy and speedy erection. When completed in 1974, the bridge will carry two lanes of traffic.

Martigues Bridge. France completed the $8-million, 2,867-foot (874-meter) Martigues Bridge in 1972. It carries the A55 motorway at Martigues, which is about 20 miles (32 km) northwest of Marseille. To meet navigation requirements on the river channel between the Mediterranean and the inland port basin, the 984-foot (300-meter) box girder central span was raised 150 feet (46 meters) above the river and placed in position on the piers.

Hooghly River Bridge. The world's longest cable-stayed girder bridge was being built over the Hooghly River at Calcutta, India, in 1972. It has a 1,500-foot (457-meter) main span flanked by 300-foot (91-meter) side spans. The box girder steel span will carry six lanes of traffic on its 113-foot (34-meter) deck. The concrete and steel deck is supported by 15 clusters of cables, which are suspended from two 340-foot (104-meter) towers.

Urato Bay Bridge. In 1972, Japan completed its longest concrete box girder bridge. It crosses Urato Bay at Kochi. The 755-foot (230-meter) main span is flanked by 427-foot (130-meter) side spans. The overall length of the structure is 3,000 feet (91 meters). It carries two lanes of traffic.

WILLIAM H. QUIRK
"Contractors & Engineers" Magazine

—— BRITISH COLUMBIA · Information Highlights ——

Area: 366,255 square miles (948,597 sq km).
Population (1972 est.): 2,247,000.
Chief Cities (1971 census): Metro Victoria, the capital (193,-512); Metro Vancouver (1,071,081).
Government: *Chief Officers*—lt. gov., John R. Nicholson; premier, David Barrett (New Democratic party); atty. gen., Alex Macdonald (NDP); prov. secy., Ernest Hall (NDP); min. of educ., Eileen Dailly (NDP); min. of labor, William King; chief justice (vacant). *Legislature:* Legislative Assembly (convened October 17, 1972); 55 members (38 New Democrat, 10 Social Credit, 5 Liberal, 2 Progressive Conservative).
Education: *School enrollment* (June 1972)—public elementary and secondary, 534,523 pupils; private schools, 22,400 pupils; Indian (federal) schools, 3,079 pupils; college and university, 40,189 students. *Public school expenditures* (1971–72), $393,592,000; median teacher's salary (1971–72), $10,332.
Public Finance (fiscal year 1972–73 est.): *Revenues,* $1,453,-436,000 (sales and fuel taxes, $362,000,000; income and inheritance taxes, $396,500,000; natural resources taxes, $223,030,000). *Expenditures,* $1,451,963,000 (education, $448,671,000; health and social services, $548,988,000).
Personal Income (1971): $8,125,000; average annual income per person, $3,719.
Social Welfare (fiscal year 1972 est.): $136,200,000 (aged and blind, $12,200,000; dependents and unemployed, $99,-200,000).
Manufacturing (1971 est.): $4,012,600,000 (wood industries, $1,205,500,000; paper and allied industries, $624,000,000; food and beverages, $665,000,000).
Agriculture (1971): *Total cash receipts,* $221,060,000 (livestock, $138,675,000; crops, $68,567,000). *Chief Products* (cash receipts): dairy products, $50,665,000; cattle and calves, $35,825,000; fruit, $29,014,000; eggs, $22,602,000.
Mining (1971): *Production value,* $526,812,000. *Chief minerals:* copper, 278,508,000 lbs.; crude oil, 25,154,000 bbl.; zinc, 305,451,000 lbs.; coal, 4,565,000 tons; lead, 247,928,000 lbs.; molybdenum, 21,885,000 lbs.
Forest Products (1971): Lumber, 8,970,400,000 board feet; pulp, 4,767,000 tons; paper and paper board, 1,910,000 tons.
Fisheries (1971): *Total fish landings,* 228,752,000 pounds ($58,588,000). *Leading species:* salmon, 132,367,000 pounds ($44,476,000).
Transportation: *Roads* (1971), 27,988 miles; *motor vehicles* (1971), 1,084,000; *railroads* (1971 est.), 4,550 miles (7,325 km) of 1st main track.
Communications (1971): *Telephones,* 1,099,791; *television stations,* 8; *radio stations,* 54; *daily newspapers,* 19.
(All monetary figures given in Canadian dollars.)

BRITISH COLUMBIA

In British Columbia, 1972 marked the end of 20 years of government by the Social Credit party, headed by W. A. C. Bennett. On August 30 the people of British Columbia elected members of the New Democratic party to fill 38 seats in the 55-seat Provincial Legislature, and on September 4, David Barrett was sworn in as premier of British Columbia.

New Program. The new government proposed a wide range of legislation for consideration at future sessions of the provincial legislature. Chief among these proposals were a guaranteed minimum monthly income of $200 for senior citizens, a government automobile insurance plan, the establishment of an industrial development corporation (to assist in the expansion of employment while maintaining environmental quality), the extension of collective bargaining rights to all employees in the province, and heavier royalties on raw materials being exported from the province.

Economic Developments. A high level of investment continued to sustain the province's rapid economic growth, with capital and repair expenditures estimated at more than $3.7 billion in 1972. Production began at new mines in the Highland Valley and at Fording River, Princeton, McLeese Lake, and Babine Lake. The most substantial growth in new investment occurred in trade, finance, and commercial services, with this expansion highlighted by a number of major office complexes in the city of Vancouver.

The province's economy continued to show evidence of a sustained recovery from the slowdown of 1970 and early 1971. While the rate of unemployment remained undesirably high, the renewed strength of the economy was clearly demonstrated by record levels of consumer spending, with 1972 retail sales in the province more than 10% above 1971 levels.

Transportation and Construction. Further expansion of British Columbia's infrastructure included progress on the 420-mile extension of the British Columbia Railway from Fort St. James to Dease Lake in the northwest corner of the province, the announcement of major port facility expansion in the Vancouver area and at Squamish, and the completion of the $136-million Mica Dam north of Revelstoke. In order to keep pace with the demands of the rapidly growing population, public investment in British Columbia remained at a high level, with the construction of new hospital and education facilities continuing to dominate such investment.

J. R. MEREDITH
Director, B. C. Bureau of Economics and Statistics

BUDDHISM. See RELIGION—*Oriental Religions.*
BUILDING AND CONSTRUCTION. See ECONOMY; HOUSING.

BULGARIA

Bulgaria's Communist party leaders attempted in 1972 to enforce greater domestic ideological unity on the population, at the same time strengthening economic and political ties with the country's Communist neighbors. Several important changes were made in top government posts.

Political Changes. On April 27, 1972, Vladimir Bonev, a member of the Politburo and of the Party secretariat, was elected chairman of the National Assembly. The former chairman, Georgi Traikov,

———— BULGARIA · Information Highlights ————

Official Name: People's Republic of Bulgaria.
Area: 42,823 square miles (110,912 sq km).
Population (1972 est.): 8,700,000. *Density,* 199 per square mile (77 per sq km). *Annual rate of increase,* 0.7%.
Chief Cities (1968 est.): Sofia, the capital, 840,100; Plovdiv, 234,500; Varna, 200,800.
Government: *Head of state,* Todor Zhivkov, president and first secretary of the Communist party (took office July 1971). *Head of government,* Stanko Todorov, premier (took office July 1971). *Legislature* (unicameral)—National Assembly, 416 members (all members of the Fatherland Front).
Language: Bulgarian (official).
Education: *Expenditure* (1969), 4.7% of gross national product. *School enrollment* (1969)—primary, 1,064,200; secondary, 377,788; technical/vocational, 274,836; university/higher, 95,706.
Monetary Unit: Lev (1.08 leva equal U. S.$1, May 1972).
Gross National Product (1970 est.): $11,100,000,000.
National Income per Person (1970): $1,300.
Economic Indexes: *Industrial production* (1971), 238 (1963 = 100; *agricultural production* (1970), 158 (1957–59 = 100); *consumer price index* (1969), 104 (1963 = 100).
Manufacturing (major products): Processed foods, machinery and equipment, chemicals, steel, tobacco products, clothing.
Major Agricultural Products: Wheat, corn, barley, sugar beets, fruits, tobacco.
Major Minerals: Lignite, iron ore, coal, zinc ore, copper ore, lead ore.
Foreign Trade (1971): *Exports,* $2,182,000,000 (chief exports, 1969—tobacco and tobacco products; alcoholic beverages; clothing; agricultural machinery). *Imports,* $2,119,000,-000 (chief imports, 1969—ferrous metals; petroleum and petroleum products; coal and coke; agricultural machinery). *Chief trading partners* (1969)—USSR (took 55% of exports, supplied 56% of imports); East Germany (8%—9%); Czechoslovakia (6%—5%); Poland (4%—5%).
Tourism: *Receipts* (1970), $85,000,000.
Transportation: *Railroads* (1970), 3,952 miles (6,360 km); *merchant fleet* (1971), 704,000 gross registered tons; *major national airline,* Bulgarian Airlines "BALKAN."
Communications: *Telephones* (1971), 473,047; *television stations* (1971), 7; *television sets* (1971), 1,030,000; *radios* (1970), 2,291,000; *newspapers* (1970), 12 (daily circulation, 1,642,000).

was appointed first deputy chairman of the State Council and chairman of the National Council of the Fatherland Front, a mass political organization.

On Dec. 13, 1971, foreign minister Ivan Bashev died in a skiing accident. The National Assembly elected Petar Miladenov as his successor. Born in 1936, Miladenov thus became the youngest foreign minister in Europe. An alumnus of the Moscow Institute for International Relations, he was also a deputy to the National Assembly, a member of the Central Committee of the Communist party, and a secretary of the Komsomol (the Young Communist League) in the Vidin district.

Ideological Uniformity. On numerous occasions party officials attacked literary and university groups for deviating from "socialist realism." Those demanding more freedom of expression and increased contacts with the West were officially rebuked. Party organs charged with ideological matters drew attention to inadequacies in ideological education and propaganda. They also called upon the relevant institutions to profit by Soviet experience and achievements in those fields.

In May the Komsomol held its 12th congress. To meet the charges that it was failing to indoctrinate the youth properly, it called for reforms and some change in leadership.

On June 8, 1972, almost the entire administrative council of the Bulgarian Writers' Union was changed. The union's president, Georgi Dzhagarov, was replaced by Panteley Zarev. The new leadership committed itself to raise the level of literature to new "socialist heights."

Legislation. In August the Council of Ministers issued a decree aimed at ending the continuing shortage of teachers. Out of 140,000 who had graduated from teacher-training programs since 1944, over 35% had failed to follow careers in teaching. As a result, some 10,000 teaching positions remained to be filled.

On June 17, the state council decreed that all private medical practice would be prohibited after Oct. 1, 1972.

Economy. A massive campaign was launched to encourage the fulfillment of the country's sixth 5-year plan, which had been formally inaugurated by the National Assembly in December 1971. Emphasis was placed on equalling "international standards" of labor productivity and quality.

The agro-industrial complexes, which had begun operations on an experimental basis in 1969, were favorably commented on by the press in 1972. New plans were announced for improving the vertical integration of the production process from the basic agricultural and animal raw materials to their processing and marketing. In June, a series of government decrees accorded the complexes still greater organizational autonomy and technical as well as financial benefits.

In August the Dobruja substation of the power line transmitting electric power from the USSR to Bulgaria was put in operation. The new power imported will be 4 billion kw-hr annually, representing an addition of 20% to Budgaria's own electric power output.

New economic agreements with Italy, West Germany, France, and Britain, who are Bulgaria's most important western European partners, provided for increased trade. Trade with these countries had decreased in recent years from 13.9% of Bulgaria's entire foreign exchange in 1966 to 9.5% in 1971.

Foreign Affairs. Relations with Yugoslavia continued to improve. Several high government officials of the two countries exchanged visits, which were accompanied by mutually friendly articles in the press. In the second half of April, Erich Honecker, leader of East Germany's Communist party, visited Sofia. The joint communique, issued at the end of the visit, pledged further efforts to achieve economic integration of eastern Europe within the structure of Comecon, the economic alliance of several Communist countries. In the middle of May Czechoslovakia's foreign minister, Bohuslav Chnoupek, visited Bulgaria, and soon after Fidel Castro, Cuba's premier, toured the country for ten days.

In July, the Polish foreign minister, Stefan Olszowski, visited Bulgaria, followed in August by the Polish premier, Piotr Jaroszewicz, and the first secretary of the Polish United Workers' party, Edward Gierek. A joint communique emphasized their agreement on economic and scientific-technological cooperation between the two countries and expressed "full unanimity of views" on the projected European security conference.

Religious Developments. In May, Rumania's Patriarch Pimen was ceremoniously received by church, party, and state officials. In June, Arthur Michael Ramsey, archbishop of Canterbury, paid an official visit. He advocated bridge-building between the East and West as well as unity within Christendom. He also formally invited Bulgaria's Patriarch Maxim to visit Britain. Upon his return to London, Dr. Ramsey mildly criticized the lack of religious freedom and inadequate religious education in Bulgaria.

JAN KARSKI
Georgetown University

BURGER, Warren E. See BIOGRAPHY.

BURMA

In 1972, Burma began its second decade under the leadership of strong-man Ne Win with several major changes in its political and administrative systems and indications of further alterations of even greater magnitude. The Burmese economy, however, continued to stagnate, and there were no signs of any early improvement.

Politics. General Ne Win, Burma's soldier-ruler for 10 years, resigned his military rank in April, symbolically indicating his stated hope that the country's government might become a civilian one in the future. Twenty military subordinates followed his lead, but these did not include Brigadier San Yu, who was elevated to the rank of general. San Yu, recognized as Ne Win's heir-apparent, was deputy premier and secretary of the Socialist Program party, Burma's only legal political party.

Ne Win also announced in April that the first draft of a constitution for the country was ready. It was expected to take effect in 1973. The new constitution, which is modelled after those of the East European Communist states, provides for a single-chamber elected parliament and one political party. Elections for the legislature were tentatively set for 1974.

Earlier, in March, the Burmese leader announced major administrative changes in the way the country was to be governed. The administrative system of district officers, a carry-over from British colonial days, was abolished. Each district had been pre-

sided over by a district officer who had filled a number of disparate roles. Enlarged security and administrative committees, consisting of civilians and soldiers, succeeded to most of the old district officer's duties. On the national level, the "Secretariat," the central administrative apparatus since British times, was also abolished and its functions assigned to various ministries.

Insurgent Groups. One of the purposes of the new political institutions that were to be created by the Communist-style constitution was the reduction of divisiveness, Burma's principal domestic political problem since independence. Militarily, the government scored further successes against the various insurgent groups in 1972. While a quarter of the land remained in rebel hands, the pacification of central and lower Burma was completed and no significant threat remained in that part of the country.

Although the National Unity Liberation Front made a daring leaflet air-raid over Rangoon in April, its fortunes faded during the year. Based in eastern Burma the rebel group lost its leading political figure, ex-Premier U Nu who had been ousted by Ne Win in 1962. Nu had refused to support his allies' espousal of the right of secession.

The strongest remaining insurrectionary presence was that of the Communists in northern Burma, along the border with China. The Chinese continued to arm and otherwise aid these insurgents.

Foreign Relations. Burma began 1972 with an altogether new foreign policy problem—how to avoid involvement in the tripartite rivalry among the Soviet Union, China, and India over the newly-created state of Bangladesh. The Ne Win government served as go-between for China and Bangladesh and evacuated Chinese diplomats and those of other nations from the new state.

Although China opposed Bangladesh and refused either to recognize the new state or support its admission to the United Nations, Burma did establish diplomatic ties with the Dacca government, largely because the two nations shared a common frontier.

Economy. There was no improvement in Burma's stagnant and mismanaged economy during 1972. Government statistics on the first ten years of the "Burmese Way to Socialism," released in March, were modestly impressive. However, various goods, including many necessary items of food and cloth-

ing, remained scarce, while agricultural and mining output increased only marginally, inflation continued, and black marketeering and smuggling reached unprecedented proportions. Japan and West Germany, the two major sources of aid, increased their assistance, while two U. S. oil companies were permitted to explore offshore deposits on a fixed-fee contract basis.

RICHARD BUTWELL
State University of New York at Brockport

────── **BURUNDI • Information Highlights** ──────

Official Name: Republic of Burundi.
Area: 10,747 square miles (27,834 sq km).
Population (1972 est.): 3,800,000. *Density,* 329 per square mile (127 per sq km). *Annual rate of increase,* 2.3%.
Chief City (1965 est.): Bujumbura, the capital, 71,000.
Government: *Head of state,* Michel Micombero, president (took office Nov. 1966). *Head of government,* Albin Nyamoya, premier (took office July 1972). *Legislature—* Parliament (dissolved Oct. 1965). *Major political party—* National Unity and Progress party (UPRONA).
Languages: Kirundi, French (both official).
Education: *Expenditure* (1969), 29.1% of total public expenditure. *School enrollment* (1969)—primary, 182,444; secondary, 8,857; technical/vocational, 2,264; higher, 397.
Monetary Unit: Franc (87.5 francs equal U. S.$1, Aug. 1972).
Gross National Product (1970 est.): $230,000,000.
Manufacturing (major products): Processed agricultural products.
Major Agricultural Products: Coffee, cotton, tea, bananas, sweet potatoes and yams, cassava.
Foreign Trade (1971): *Exports,* $19,000,000. *Imports,* $30,-000,000. *Chief trading partners*—United States, Belgium-Luxembourg.

BURUNDI

The year 1972 will undoubtedly be remembered as the most tragic episode in Burundi's history. An abortive uprising by the Hutu population in April led to massive retaliation by the ruling Tusi (or Tutsi) minority that took tens of thousands of lives.

Rebellion and Retaliation. Two major currents of opposition to the regime of President Michel Micombero were evident as the year opened. Dissident Tusi in the north objected to the overwhelming influence of southerners in the government. More ominous was the anti-government feeling stemming from the underlying conflict between the Hutu and Tusi peoples.

The situation was further complicated by the return in March of former King Ntare V, who had lived in West Germany since he was deposed in 1966. Although he had received assurances of personal safety, he was immediately arrested on charges of trying to invade the country. The government feared that Ntare's presence might unite opposition forces.

Hoping to pacify the country, President Micombero dismissed his cabinet on April 29, but on the following day the Hutu population rose against the government in the southern provinces and, to a lesser extent, in the capital. In the northern town of Gitega, an attempt to liberate Ntare led to his execution. Thousands of Tusi were massacred in the south by the insurgent Hutu before the uprising was contained.

The Tusi reaction was merciless. In many villages, the entire Hutu population was exterminated. Many Tusi set about the task of liquidating every educated Hutu. By the end of May, the number of victims was conservatively estimated at 100,000. Some 40,000 refugees fled the country. Burundi's ailing economy faced impending disaster as hundreds of thousands of peasant homesteads were destroyed.

EDOUARD BUSTIN, *Boston University*

────── **BURMA • Information Highlights** ──────

Official Name: Union of Burma.
Area: 261,789 square miles (678,033 sq km).
Population (1972 est.): 29,100,000. *Density,* 106 per square miles (41 per sq km). *Annual rate of increase,* 2.3%.
Chief Cities (1958 est.): Rangoon, the capital, 1,718,000 (1968 est.); Mandalay, 195,000; Moulmein, 108,000.
Government: *Head of state,* Gen. Ne Win, chairman of the Revolutionary Council (took office March 1962). *Head of government,* Gen. Ne Win, premier. *Legislature—*Parliament (dissolved March 1962).
Languages: Burmese, English (both official).
Education: *Expenditure* (1967), 16.8% of total public expenditure. *School enrollment* (1969)—primary, 3,328,000; secondary, 699,615; technical/vocational, 4,080; university/higher, 45,876.
Monetary Unit: kyat (5.456 kyats equal U. S.$1, July 1972).
Gross National Product (1970 est.): $2,080,000,000.
Manufacturing (major products): Processed foods, textiles, tobacco products, wood, petroleum products.
Major Agricultural Products: Rice, sugarcane, groundnuts, sesame seeds, tobacco, millet, cotton, forest products.
Major Minerals: Petroleum, lead ore, zinc ore, salt.
Foreign Trade (1971): *Exports,* $124,000,000. *Imports,* $94,-000,000. *Chief trading partners* (1968)—India (took 17% of exports, supplied 7% of imports); Japan (9%—22%); United Kingdom (7%—11%); Netherlands (3%—8%).
Communications: *Telephones* (1970), 24,654; *radios* (1970), 400,000; *newspapers* (1969), 28.

CABINET, U. S. See UNITED STATES.

CALIFORNIA

The 1972 elections in California brought few surprises, but they were unusual in the number of propositions on which the voters were asked to pass judgment. The year was one of relative calm in such previously troubled areas as the educational systems and labor-management relations. Dramatic changes were evident chiefly in the results of a population study, which showed a sharp drop in California's traditionally high rate of growth.

Elections. The June primary carried with it some drama because it represented the culmination of the contest for the Democratic presidential nomination between Senators Hubert H. Humphrey and George McGovern. Although McGovern won by only 5 percentage points, he received all of California's delegate votes and thus was in a position to gain the party nomination on the first ballot.

President Richard M. Nixon was an easy winner in California's Republican presidential primary. In November he received 56% of the popular vote.

State legislative and congressional elections were held under a reapportionment plan adopted by the legislature and designed to maintain the fairly even division between the two major parties that had prevailed previously. In devising the plan, the legislature had the task of adding five new congressional districts to provide for the increase (from 38 to 43) in California's congressional delegation under the 1970 census. Despite Gov. Ronald Reagan's veto of the plan, the California supreme court ordered that it be used for the elections but instructed the legislature to continue to work on a plan that could be enacted into law. In November the plan worked as intended, with the result that the Democrats elected 23 members to the U. S. House of Representatives, and the Republicans, 20. The state Senate also maintained a balance between the two parties, with 19 Democrats and 19 Republicans (2 vacancies), but the Assembly was a surprise: 51 Democrats, 29 Republicans.

Of the 22 propositions on the November ballot, 13 were referendum items, submitted by the legislature. Most of them were noncontroversial, and all but one passed. The other 9 propositions, involving the initiative procedure, were placed on the ballot by petition. Because several dealt with questions of nationwide concern, the results were of unusual interest. Most of the electorate (63%) voted to set aside the state law calling for the busing of schoolchildren to achieve racial balance. Two thirds of the voters opposed an initiative that would have legalized the possession (but not the sale) of marihuana.

Earlier in 1972 the California supreme court had ruled that the state's death penalty provides for "cruel and unusual" punishment. But by popular initiative in November, 68% of the voters chose to set this ruling aside. Although the death penalty was restored, its validity—in light of U. S. Supreme Court decisions—was in doubt.

An omnibus proposal drastically restricting most activities that pollute the environment was defeated in the June primaries. But in November, California voters approved a moderate proposal calling for a moratorium on land-use changes along the coast until state and regional master plans have been developed.

Legislation. The major piece of legislation, enacted on December 2, was a compromise tax-reform

plan, which raises the property-tax exemption on homes, gives relief to renters through an income tax credit, and increases the state sales tax as well as taxes on bank and corporation profits. The plan includes increased aid to public schools under a formula providing more aid to poorer districts. This provision is of special interest in light of a 1971 California supreme court decision which held that the local property tax as a chief means of school support is discriminatory against poor districts and therefore unconstitutional. In November, the voters had defeated a proposal calling for sharp reduction in all local property taxes.

The Economy. Unemployment, which had been above the national average since 1967, declined in 1972 to a point near the national average. The construction industry experienced a small upturn.

Fruit and vegetable growers who use a considerable amount of "stoop" labor placed on the November ballot an initiative proposal designed to regulate agricultural labor-management relations. It would have prohibited strikes during the harvest season and provided for a secret ballot on the question of establishing a labor union as the official negotiator on behalf of the workers. The initiative proposal was opposed by Chicano activists, as well as by much of organized labor and other groups, and was defeated.

Population. For decades California experienced a rate of population growth at least twice the national average, and in 1970 it displaced New York

as the most populous state. But a Census Bureau study has revealed that since the 1970 census the annual rate of growth in California has dropped to about the national average (slightly more than 1%). Both Los Angeles and San Francisco counties have lost population, the former for the first time in its history. The largest increases have occurred in suburbs of Los Angeles in Orange county and in San Diego county.

Education. Although absolute increases occurred in public college and university enrollments in 1972, the rate of increase slowed dramatically from previous years, and the projected increase for 1973 was revised to less than half of earlier estimates. A change in young people's preferences and social expectations has invalidated enrollment projections based on the time-honored assumption that the percentage of high school students going on to college would continue to rise.

In the public school system, segregation appeared to be on the rise. For example, between 1970 and 1971 the number of schools with minority enrollments of 50% or more increased from 1,105 to 1,215.

CHARLES R. ADRIAN
University of California, Riverside

CAMBODIA (Khmer Republic)

Cambodia, or the Khmer Republic, became a veritable "second Vietnam" in 1972. Much of its countryside lay in ruins—small towns largely destroyed, farms deserted, and large sections of major roads controlled by Communist insurgents. Two thirds of the land was in the hands of the foreign Communist Vietnamese or their increasingly effective Khmer Rouge (Red Cambodian) indigenous allies. Only the capital of Phnompenh, other large towns, and the rice-rich western province of Battambang were under effective rule of the government of President (and Marshal) Lon Nol.

The War. The war went badly for Cambodia in 1972—partly by default. Government forces had suffered a major and humiliating defeat at the hands of the Communists in December 1971 and, as a result, initiated no military action against the enemy during 1972. Instead, the armed forces waited for the foe to attack and engaged him only in defensive action. Two years of American training and $340 million in U. S. military aid had failed to transform the 150,000-man Khmer army into an effective fighting force.

The Khmer Rouge improved steadily, and with increasing speed, after the Indochina War came to Cambodia in earnest in March–April 1970. From an ineffective force of about 3,000 men in March 1970, the indigenous Communists grew in strength to a menacing fighting arm of at least 30,000 guerrillas in late 1972. Communist Vietnamese soldiers in the country declined from 50,000 to about 12,000 men during the same period.

At the beginning of 1972, the Communists (Vietnamese and Cambodian combined) controlled somewhat more than half the national territory and approximately one third of the population. By the end of the year, the invaders and indigenous insurgents had extended their domination from the lightly settled northeast and north to the more populated southern part, controlling two thirds of the country and nearly one half of its population.

Peace Settlement. There was visible relief in the government-controlled parts of the country in

PRESIDENT LON NOL of Cambodia, during a ceremony in March, assumed complete power as president, head of state, and commander of the nation's armed forces.

late October 1972, when it was revealed that Hanoi and Washington had reached general agreement on peace terms for Indochina. U. S. presidential adviser Henry Kissinger visited Phnompenh to confer with Marshal Lon Nol in mid-October, but Cambodia itself clearly played no part in the peace talks. It was generally believed that the Communists would not be dislodged by any settlement from the territory they already held.

The Cambodian government sought its own negotiations with the Khmer Rouge, with strong Soviet and less obvious American encouragement, but to no avail. North Vietnam was opposed to a coalition settlement for Cambodia—although it sought such a solution in South Vietnam—because it might stabilize the country and ultimately require the Vietnamese Communists to evacuate the eastern part of Cambodia, which it held and desired to keep.

Political Affairs. Marshal Lon Nol, still partly paralyzed from his 1971 stroke, proclaimed himself president in March, replacing chief of state Cheng Heng, and named civilian adviser Son Ngoc Thank as prime minister (who was replaced in October by Hang Thun Hak). In June, 54% of the electorate voted for the 59-year-old Khmer soldier-leader as president, thus legitimatizing the March take-over in which the constitution had been abandoned and the ineffective National Assembly dissolved.

Highly controlled voting in separate elections for the National Assembly and Senate in September

——— CAMBODIA • Information Highlights ———

Official Name: Khmer Republic.
Area: 69,898 square miles (181,035 sq km).
Population (1972 est.): 7,600,000. *Density,* 115 per square mile (45 per sq km). *Annual rate of increase,* 3.0%.
Chief Cities (1962 census): Phnompenh, the capital, 393,995; Battambang, 38,780; Kompong Cham, 28,532.
Government: *Head of state,* Gen. Lon Nol, president (took office March 1972). *Head of government,* Hang Thun Hak, premier (took office Oct. 1972). *Legislature*—Parliament: Senate, 24 members; National Assembly, 82 members.
Languages: Khmer, also called Cambodian (official), French.
Education: *Expenditure* (1967), 21.6% of total public expenditure. *School enrollment* (1968)—primary, 1,024,456; general secondary, 104,227; technical/vocational (1967), 5,787; university/higher, 11,094.
Monetary Unit: Riel (120 riels equal U. S.$1, May 1972).
Gross National Product (1970 est.): $760,000,000.
National Income per Person (1963): $117.
Consumer Price Index (1971): 227 (1963=100).
Manufacturing (major products): Textiles, tobacco products, paper, sawnwood.
Major Agricultural Products: Rice, corn, natural rubber, sweet potatoes, fruits, fish, forest products, cattle.
Major Minerals: Coal, phosphate, iron ore.
Foreign Trade (1971): *Exports,* $15,000,000 (chief exports, 1969—natural rubber and rubberlike gums; rice, corn, cattle). *Imports,* $79,000,000 (chief imports, 1968—chemicals; transport equipment; nonelectrical machinery; textile yarn and fabrics). *Chief trading partners* (1969)—France (took 16% of exports, supplied 26% of imports); Hong Kong (14%—6%); Japan (5%—24%); China (2%—7%).
Transportation: *Motor vehicles* (1970), 38,700 (automobiles, 27,500); *railroads* (1970), 403 miles (649 km); *major national airline,* Air Cambodge.
Communications: *Telephones* (1971), 8,139; *television stations* (1971), 2; *television sets* (1971), 18,000; *radios* (1969), 1,000,000; *newspapers* (1968), 26 (daily circulation, 145,000).

resulted in Lon Nol's Social Republican party capturing all the seats in both chambers. Lon Non, the influential and ambitious brother of Lon Nol, emerged as a cabinet minister for the first time in the new government formed after the balloting.

Sihanouk's Maneuvers. Prince Norodom Sihanouk, ousted as chief of state by Lon Nol in 1970, sought to keep alive his political future by pressing China to champion his leadership of the antigovernment Cambodian United National Front against North Vietnam's partiality to the Communist Khmer Rouge (dominant element in the Front). A visit to Hanoi in mid-February and early March seemed to reinforce Sihanouk's nominal leadership.

Sihanouk, from his exile in Peking, claimed that even the United States was willing to accept his return to power in Phnompenh. Whether or not this was so, it was apparent that growing numbers of politicians, bureaucrats, and intellectuals—including many who had once opposed Sihanouk—were beginning to regard the years of the prince's former leadership with increasing approval.

Economy. An acute rice shortage caused by Communist control of a key highway into the capital, resulted in two days of rioting and looting in Phnompenh in September. Cambodia, which exported 180,000 tons of rice worth $16 million as recently as 1969, imported a record 100,000 tons in 1972. The country's rice harvest, badly hit by drought as well as war, was only half its normal yield. The tripling of rice prices late in the year testified to the economic problems caused by the war.

Foreign Affairs. The great powers continued their contest for influence in Cambodia in 1972. The United States maintained its support of Lon Nol, Peking backed Sihanouk, and the USSR pushed for a negotiated coalition government with the Khmer Rouge. Cambodia itself sought more U. S. aid, encouraged Soviet diplomatic efforts, and signaled to Hanoi its willingness to resume Sihanouk's policy of tolerating a Vietnamese Communist presence.

RICHARD BUTWELL
State University of New York at Brockport

CAMEROON

Cameroon became a unitary state in 1972 and was renamed the United Republic of Cameroon. The country had been a federal state since its formation in 1961 by the merger of the former British and French trust territories of Cameroon.

New Constitution. On May 6, President Ahmadou Ahidjo announced details of a draft constitution to end the federal structure and create a unitary state. Submitted to a referendum on May 21, all but 0.03% of those voting favored the new constitution.

The new constitution abolished the regional assemblies and provided instead for a single National Assembly of 120 members. In July, Ahidjo announced the first cabinet under the new government structure and created a number of new departments to be headed by appointees of ministerial rank. The president established a Supreme Court on August 31 to deal with political crimes under the new constitution.

A major reason for the abandonment of the federal system was the fiscal weakness of West Cameroon, which, in spite of large subsidies from the federal government, had shown budget deficits for many years. President Ahidjo and other leaders stressed that the objects of unification were greater efficiency and social justice. Both French and English remained official languages.

Foreign Relations. Cameroon and Nigeria signed an agreement in March providing for cultural and technical cooperation. However, relations between the two countries were marred during the year by a dispute over territorial waters. Nigeria wanted a limit of 30 nautical miles (50 km) to be imposed, but Cameroon claimed that such a law, if enforced, would shut its fishermen out of their most profitable trawling areas.

The controlling council of the École Supérieure Internationale de Journalisme de Yaoundé met in the Cameroon capital on July 13–14. The school, designed to improve the quality of African journalism, was formed in April 1970 by Cameroon, Gabon, the Central African Republic, and Chad.

The 8th African soccer championship was held in Cameroon from February 23 to March 5. The competing teams were from Cameroon, Congo, Kenya, Mali, Morocco, Sudan, Togo, and Zaïre.

GRAHAM W. IRWIN, *Columbia University*

———CAMEROON • Information Highlights ———

Official Name: United Republic of Cameroon.
Area: 183,569 square miles (475,442 sq km).
Population (1972 est.): 6,000,000. *Density,* 31 per square mile (12 per sq km). *Annual rate of increase,* 2.0%.
Chief Cities (1965 est.): Yaoundé, the capital, 101,000; Douala, 200,000.
Government: *Head of state,* Ahmadou Ahidjo, president (re-elected for 3d 5-year term March 1970). *Head of government,* Ahmadou Ahidjo. *Legislature* (unicameral)—National Assembly, 120 members. *Major political party*—Cameroon National Union.
Languages: French, English (both official).
Education: *Expenditure* (1969), 19.1% of total public expenditure. *School enrollment* (1969)—primary, 888,435; secondary, 67,765; technical/vocational, 15,782; university/higher, 2,030.
Monetary Unit: CFA franc (255.79 CFA francs equal U. S.$1, Aug. 1972).
Gross National Product (1970 est.): $990,000,000.
Manufacturing (major products): Aluminum, processed foods.
Major Agricultural Products: Coffee, cacao, cotton, peanuts, fish, bananas, natural rubber, palm oil and kernels, forest products.
Major Minerals: Bauxite, iron ore.
Foreign Trade (1971): *Exports,* $206,000,000. *Imports,* $249,000,000. *Chief trading partner* (1969)—France (took 33% of exports, supplied 50% of imports); Netherlands (26%—3%); West Germany (10%—10%); United States (6%—6%).

UPI

Rivals in the campaign of 1972: Liberal Prime Minister Pierre Trudeau (above), shown with his wife, Margaret, at a rally; and the leader of the Progressive Conservatives Robert Stanfield (right), with his family. The results of the general election on October 30 were so close as to be almost a deadlock.

CANADA

UPI

Both Canada and the United States were preoccupied with general elections in 1972, although President Nixon did find time in April for a visit to Canada. While relations between the United States and Canada remained relatively stable during the year, Canada and China noticeably increased their ties, particularly economic ones.

After the election in October, Prime Minister Pierre Elliott Trudeau's Liberal government remained in power, but the voters eliminated his party's majority in the House of Commons. The election took place while the economy was buoyant and employment was at or near an all-time high. But unemployment also continued to be very high and was a major concern of the government.

FOREIGN AFFAIRS

Canadian-American Relations. President Nixon arrived in Ottawa on a state visit on April 13, and the following day he addressed a joint session of the Senate and the House of Commons. In his speech, the President called for an end to "sentimental rhetoric" about the American and Canadian partnership. Instead, he looked for a new approach based on the recognition of the "separate identities" of the two partners and the "significant differences" between them.

On April 15, Prime Minister Trudeau and President Nixon signed the Great Lakes Water Quality Agreement. This pact called for a joint effort to

clean up the Great Lakes, all five of which have been polluted in varying amounts. Canada was to spend about $450 million over a five-year period, while government and private sources in the United States were to spend about $3 billion.

In June, a 14-mile oil spill from a Cherry Point, Wash., refinery polluted beaches in British Columbia. This mishap cooled Canadian-American relations a little, as had the May announcement that the United States probably would issue a permit for the construction of the Alaskan pipeline. Because of the elections in both Canada and the United States, trade talks were not resumed in 1972.

Vietnam Peace-Keeping Force. Canadians continued to caution the government against the kind of involvement in Vietnamese peace-keeping operations that would see Canada embroiled in a Southeast Asia conflict. Mitchell Sharp, minister of external affairs, offered Canadian services for an attempt to keep the peace in Vietnam, but he insisted that peace arrangements satisfactory to the belligerents must be made before any "peace-keeping" force could be effective. Canada and three other nations have been chosen to provide peace-keeping forces after the Vietnam War comes to an end.

Canadian-Chinese Relations. During the 94th Canadian National Exhibition, in Toronto in August, the Chinese government mounted the largest exhibition of Chinese industrial and cultural products ever held outside mainland China. Also in August, Mitchell Sharp opened the largest exhibition that Canada has ever staged abroad. It was held in Peking, where more than 200 Canadian companies participated in a trade fair.

While in China, Sharp and Chinese officials reached an agreement on a wide range of cultural, scientific, and other exchanges involving students, teachers, doctors, scientists, agricultural experts, and sports teams. Also, Sharp said that Premier Chou En-lai had pledged that Canada could count on China as a long-term wheat customer. Over a 10-year period, Chinese purchases of Canadian wheat have amounted to more than $1 billion.

Canadian-Russian Relations. In July, Canada and the USSR signed an agreement that provided for cultural and scientific exchanges. The agreement was considered to be particularly important in that it placed emphasis on cooperation in the development of Arctic regions.

Canadian-Iranian Relations. In January, Canada and Iran signed an agreement to cooperate in promoting peaceful uses of atomic energy. It was hoped that the agreement eventually would pave the way for the sale of a $90 million Canadian-built nuclear power reactor to Iran.

FEDERAL ELECTION

Prime Minister Trudeau, the leader of the Liberal party that has held majority rule since 1968, asked for a dissolution of Parliament on September 1 and announced a general election for October 30. In doing so he said, "The challenge is nothing less than the integrity of Canada—the homeland of persons so dedicated to the social advantages of tolerance and moderation, so convinced of the value of a single strong economic unit, so proud of our accomplishments and our image that we are committed to Canada."

The Election Campaign. In reality, the election campaign had begun for the opposition parties in midsummer. Robert Stanfield, leader of the Pro-

WIDE WORLD

DURING A STATE VISIT to Canada in April, U.S. President Nixon receives a standing ovation after addressing a joint session of Parliament in Ottawa.

gressive Conservative (PC) party, took the theme "A Job for Canadians" as a slogan sure to appeal to a majority of the voters. Stanfield had difficulty in fielding candidates in Quebec, which traditionally has been neglected by the Progressive Conservatives except on election years. However, he persuaded Claude Wagner, a former Liberal minister of justice, to be a PC candidate and thus serve as a rallying point for the PC party in Quebec.

David Lewis, the leader of the New Democratic party (NDP) since 1971, prepared for his first federal campaign as party leader by stressing economic issues. Lewis used the theme "Corporate Welfare Bums" as his election slogan. In a 118-page paperback entitled *Louder Voices—The Corporate Welfare Bums,* Lewis listed 115 corporations that he felt got undeserved tax breaks, and in some cases paid no corporation tax at all, because of what he called the Liberal government's penchant for taxing the poor and exempting the rich. The New Democratic party, like the Conservatives and Liberals, had candidates across the country. One reason that the NDP did not win more seats in Quebec is that its policy on Quebec separatism has not won wide acceptance in the province.

Réal Caouette, leader of the Social Credit party (SC), made a cross-Canada campaign, even in many areas where he was unable to field a local SC candidate. His election theme was a guaranteed annual income. Under his plan, the government would provide $1,200 a year for every Canadian over 18 years of age, $2,400 a year for married couples plus $250 per child per year, and $2,400 a year for every

LESTER B. PEARSON (1897–1972)

UPI

Lester Bowles Pearson, Canada's former prime minister (1963–68), who battled valiantly for Canadian solidarity and world peace, died in Rockcliffe Park, a suburb of Ottawa, on Dec. 27, 1972, at age 75. He devoted 40 years of service to his government and steered Canada into prominence in world affairs. In recognition of his negotiation of a compromise to the Suez crisis of 1956, he was awarded the Nobel Peace Prize in 1957.

Pearson was president of the UN General Assembly in 1952–53 and was twice nominated for UN secretary general. Retiring as prime minister of Canada in 1968, he occupied himself during his last years in such "retirement" positions as chancellor of Carleton University in Ottawa and chairman of the World Bank Commission on International Aid and Development.

Pearson was born in Toronto on April 13, 1897. He entered the University of Toronto at the age of 16, but left to serve as a corporal and a flight lieutenant in the Canadian forces in World War I. He received his B. A. degree in history from Toronto in 1919 and B. A. and M. A. degrees from Oxford in 1923 and 1925.

Pearson entered government service in 1928 as a first secretary with the Department of External Affairs, a post he held until 1935. He then served in diplomatic posts in London (1935–41) and in Washington (1942–46). He was Canada's representative at the 1944 Dumbarton Oaks Conference, which drew plans to establish the United Nations, and he played a leading role in formulating the UN charter at San Francisco in 1945. In 1945–46 he was Canada's ambassador to the United States.

Recalled to Ottawa in 1946 as undersecretary of state for external affairs, Pearson became a Liberal party member of Commons and, in 1948, secretary of state for external affairs. He retained these positions until 1957, while also heading the Canadian delegation to the UN General Assembly (1946–57). Pearson signed the North Atlantic Treaty for Canada in 1949, played a major role in the Korean truce of 1953, and was primarily responsible for arranging the Suez truce. He became Liberal leader in Commons in 1958 and prime minister of Canada on April 22, 1963.

Canadian over 60. Caouette estimated the cost of this guaranteed annual income plan at $18 billion per year.

The election campaign was marked by the low-key philosophical-discursive approach of Prime Minister Trudeau, who appeared on a number of open-line radio shows; by the increasing attention the media paid to David Lewis' daily revelations of "corporate welfare bums"; and by Stanfield's consistent attacks on the government, particularly its inflation and unemployment record.

Election Results. The results staggered the Liberal party and annoyed the Progressive Conservatives, while the voting was so close that five or six seats changed hands as a result of recounts. Alberta elected 19 Progressive Conservatives. Quebec elected 56 Liberals, and only Claude Wagner and one other PC candidate, while the Social Credit party won 15 Quebec seats. After all tallies were in, the standings in the 264-member House of Commons were: Liberals, 109; Progressive Conservatives, 107; New Democratic party, 31; Social Credit, 15; and independent, 2. Before the election the standings were as follows: Liberals, 147; Conservatives, 73; NDP, 25; Social Credit, 13; and independent, 2. Thus, a main result of the election was that Trudeau's Liberal government lost its majority in the House of Commons.

Post-Election Moves. After the blow delivered by the voters, the Progressive Conservatives demanded the resignation of Prime Minister Trudeau. He decided, as was his constitutional right, to continue in office and to present a program of legislation to the new Parliament, which was slated to meet in January 1973. Meanwhile, he reconstructed his 30-member cabinet since a number of ministers had not been reelected. Overall, he made 18 changes in his cabinet, including the appointments of eight newcomers. One of them, Jeanne Sauve, is the first woman to serve in a Trudeau cabinet.

PROVINCIAL AFFAIRS

Two long-time provincial premiers went down to defeat in 1972.

Smallwood's Defeat. Joseph R. Smallwood, Liberal premier of Newfoundland since its entry into Confederation in 1948, came out of the October 1971 election without a majority, the result being Liberals, 21; Progressive Conservatives, 20; and New Labrador party, 1. Thomas Burgess, the New Labrador party winner, initially threw his support to Frank Moores of the Progressive Conservatives, and Moores took over from Smallwood on January 18. On March 24 a new election was held, resulting in a Progressive Conservative victory for Moores.

Bennett's Defeat. In British Columbia, Premier W. A. C. Bennett's Social Credit party lost its 20-year hold on the province when David Barrett, a former social worker, led the New Democratic party to a sweeping victory over the old-guard Social Creditors on August 30. In the elections in British Columbia and Newfoundland what issues there were seemed to be overshadowed by the age and length of tenure of the leaders.

Mineral Rights. In June the five eastern provinces—Newfoundland, Nova Scotia, Prince Edward Island, New Brunswick, and Quebec—agreed to present a united front to the federal government on the ownership of offshore mineral rights, saying that the federal offer to divide royalties on a 50–50 basis was unacceptable. The premiers of the five provinces announced that they were asserting ownership of the minerals on the continental shelf. By August an agreement had been worked out, as Prime Minister Trudeau announced that the federal government did not insist on a 50% share of the royalties but expected a constant exchange of information.

McKeough's Resignation. In Ontario, provincial treasurer Darcy McKeough and Dalton Bales, attorney general of Ontario, were accused of a "conflict of interest" in connection with land development near Toronto. McKeough resigned as treasurer and was succeeded by Charles McNaughton, but Bales did not resign.

Federal Election Activities. During the federal election all three NDP provincial premiers—Allan Blakeney of Saskatchewan, Edward Schreyer of Manitoba, and David Barrett of British Columbia—pledged support for David Lewis' New Democratic party candidates, while Premier William

Davis of Ontario put his "Big Blue Machine" at the disposal of Robert Stanfield's Progressive Conservative campaign. This was the first time that Ontario had taken such an active part in a federal election.

Quebec separatist leader René Lévesque advised his followers to take no part in the federal election. According to his thinking, the election involved a federal government that his party was determined to ignore.

Both Lewis and Caouette stated that they would not oppose Quebec separation if the decision to separate was made clearly and democratically in a referendum or a plebiscite. On the other hand, Stanfield declared that Quebec by itself did not have the right to decide whether to separate from Canada.

Prime Minister Trudeau said his government would not accept the separation of Quebec if a separatist government were elected in Quebec. In fact, separatism did not become an issue outside Quebec.

(See also ALBERTA; BRITISH COLUMBIA; MANITOBA; NEW BRUNSWICK; NEWFOUNDLAND; NORTHWEST TERRITORIES; NOVA SCOTIA; ONTARIO; PRINCE EDWARD ISLAND; QUEBEC; SASKATCHEWAN; YUKON TERRITORY.)

PROGRESS IN THE ECONOMY

Employment continued at an all-time high level in Canada in 1972, although unemployment rose from 6.2% of the labor force in June to 7.1% in September. The latter figure was the worst unemployment situation in Canada since 1961. Despite high unemployment, damaging strikes, and inflation, the economy remained buoyant during 1972.

Federal Government Programs. The federal government, shifting its attack from inflation to unemployment, put another $20 million into its Opportunities for Youth program, provided $50 million for Local Initiatives programs, and allocated $3 million for various cultural programs. The Opportunities for Youth program provided summer employment for students, and the Local Initiatives program provided winter work for poor unemployed persons. Nevertheless, the government was unable to make a significant impact on the unemployment problem. In the March budget, the government introduced special new features, including faster write-offs for new industrial machinery and tax incentives. These measures may have an effect over a long period, but they made little difference in the economy during the first few months they were in effect.

The government also revealed details of the Canada-Newfoundland Development Corporation, which was to be funded by $20 million of federal money and $2 million of Newfoundland money. These funds were to be used by the corporation to provide loans, counseling services, and assistance to develop resources in Newfoundland.

Wheat. Sales of wheat to the USSR, China, and Brazil amounted to more than 400 million bushels in 1972, while prices rose to the highest level in 50 years. At year-end the Canadian Wheat Board had called for a wheat census of every bushel held on farms and in elevators so that farmers and grain dealers would not oversell abroad. It appeared that Canada's wheat surplus was about to disappear.

Oil and Gas. Panarctic Oils Ltd., a consortium of private companies and the federal government, announced the discovery of crude oil on Ellesmere Island in February 1972. The company previously had made gas discoveries on Melville Island, King

Christian Island, and Ellef Ringnes Island in the high Arctic. In October additional gas and oil discoveries were announced at Sable Island off the Nova Scotia coast, Melville Island in the Arctic, and the Grand Banks off Newfoundland. By year-end the estimated gas reserves of the Arctic islands had reached about 15 trillion cubic feet (tfc), about 10 tfc short of the amount needed to make a pipeline to eastern Canada practicable.

Hydroelectric Power. In June, Prime Minister Trudeau opened the Churchill Falls power plant, a $950 million hydroelectric project 700 miles northeast of Montreal. The new plant will have a capacity of 5.2 million kilowatts and will produce about 34.5 billion kilowatt-hours a year, which is more than 22% of all the hydroelectric energy produced in Canada in 1969.

Domestic Communications Satellite. Canada's first domestic communications satellite, Anik 1, was launched from Cape Kennedy on November 9. From its position 22,300 miles above the equator at a point off the coast of Mexico, Anik 1 will provide television, radio, telephone, and data services to nearly all northern communities. The Canadian Broadcasting Corporation has leased three satellite channels; one will be used for French-language TV programs originating in Montreal, and the other two will be used for English-language programs. The satellite, which was produced by Telesat Canada, was expected to begin providing services in January 1973 and to have a lifetime of seven years.

LABOR RELATIONS

During 1972 the number of man-hours lost due to strikes was greater than in 1971, although there were fewer strikes and lockouts.

ANIK I, Canada's new communications satellite, was launched into synchronous orbit from Cape Kennedy, Fla., on November 9. It is designed to provide television, radio, telephone, and data services throughout Canada.

HUGHES AIRCRAFT COMPANY

TEAM CANADA scores its sixth and winning goal in the final hockey match of the 8-games series played between the Canadian and Russian teams in September. The first four games were played in Canadian cities and the last four in Moscow. The Canadian team won the series four games to three, with one game ending in a tie.

CBC Strikes. On January 21 technicians of the Canadian Broadcasting Corporation (CBC) began a series of rotating strikes that effectively disorganized live broadcasting across Canada until the dispute over salaries and job security was settled in June.

Air Traffic Controllers Strike. An 11-day air traffic controllers strike tied up almost all commercial air traffic in January. The dispute over salaries and hours of work cost Air Canada alone $1.3 million per day in gross revenue.

Longshoremen's Strikes. Dock workers at the St. Lawrence River ports of Quebec City, Trois-Rivières, and Montreal went on strike on May 9, returned to work briefly, and then walked out again on May 16. In July, Parliament went into an overtime session to pass special legislation ordering the dock workers back to work. They returned on July 10, three days after Parliament adjourned.

Longshoremen shut down the port of Vancouver on August 9 and then shut down all west coast ports on August 23 after negotiations between the Maritime Employer's Association and the International Longshoremen's and Warehousemen's Union had broken down. As a result, about 40 unloaded deep-sea freighters swung at anchor in Vancouver harbor while about 4,800 railway grain cars were stacked up in British Columbia and Alberta. Prime Minister Trudeau recalled Parliament on August 31, and special federal legislation was passed. It ordered the shipping companies and longshoremen to resume work at once and to resume negotiations at once, and it extended the old contract to Dec. 31, 1972.

Utility Workers Strike. In Ontario, about 11,400 workers for the government-operated Ontario Hydro-Electric Power Commission were on strike in July, mainly over issues of wages and job classifications. About 1,200 supervisory personnel were able to maintain electric power service to the public until the strike was finally settled in October by submission to arbitration.

Snow Removal and Garbage Strikes. In Montreal snow removal crews struck February 18–24 during a blizzard that immobilized 300,000 cars. In the summer, citizens in Montreal, Toronto, and Vancouver were subjected to annoying garbage strikes as civic employees attempted to bring their take-home pay into line with that of industrial workers.

Common Front Strike. In April, Quebec province was hit by a "common front" strike of 200,000 workers belonging to the Confederation of National Trades Unions (CNTU), the Quebec Teacher's Corporation, and the Quebec Federation of Labour. The strike, which disrupted hospitals, schools, and other public services, was ended after 14 days by tough legislation passed by the Quebec government.

Strike leaders Louis Laberge, Marcel Pepin, and Yvon Charbonneau were given one-year sentences for urging workers to ignore the back-to-work order. Their arrest was followed by sporadic strikes at Thetford Mines, St. Jerome, Sept-Iles, and other points. On May 23 the three leaders were freed on a performance bond to continue negotiations on civil service contracts.

Trade Unions. On June 9 representatives of 150 Quebec labor unions voted to found a new labor organization, the Centrale des Syndicats Democratiques. It was formed under the leadership of Paul-Emilien Dalpé, Jacques Dion, and Amédée Daigle, former CNTU officials who had said that the CNTU was becoming too involved in politics. The new organization represented about 57,500 workers.

When the CNTU met on June 17, it reelected Marcel Pepin as president. In his acceptance speech, Pepin called for more political action by the CNTU, specifically the defeat of the Liberal Quebec government led by Premier Robert Bourassa.

On August 14 the 30,000-member civil servants' union left the CNTU common front alliance, thereby reducing the common front to less than 180,000 members. On October 11 the common front reached an agreement with the Quebec government after having won a minimum wage of $100 per week for almost all workers in the common front.

THE ENVIRONMENT

Jack Davis, minister of the environment, committed Canada to support the whole United Nations antipollution program at a probable cost to Canada of about $100 million a year. The new UN program was to include measures enabling Canada to protect its coastal waters from pollution by disabled foreign vessels. (See also ENVIRONMENT.)

James Bay Hydroelectric Project. A federal-provincial task force recommended an extensive study of the effects of the proposed $7 billion James Bay hydroelectric project, which includes plans for

dams on five rivers that flow into James Bay. The task force called for studies of the effect on 5,400 Indians in the area as well as studies of the effect on the environment. Construction would change river courses and estuaries, flood timberlands, and threaten the wildlife of the region. The project, launched by Premier Robert Bourassa of Quebec in 1971, is designed to produce enough electrical energy so that there will be a substantial portion for export to the United States. At the end of 1972, a $5.8 billion portion of the project was scheduled for completion in 1983.

NAMES AND EVENTS IN THE NEWS

Sports. The sports highlight of the year was the eight-game ice hockey series between Canada and the Soviet Union. Team Canada lost the first game, 7–3, in Montreal, won the next, 4–1, in Toronto, tied the third, 4–4, in Winnipeg, and lost the fourth, 5–3, in Vancouver. In the second part of the series in Moscow, Team Canada lost the first game and then won three straight. As a result of its thrilling finish, Team Canada won the series from the USSR by four games to three with one game tied.

The biennial Arctic Winter Games, staged in 1972 at Whitehorse in the Yukon Territory, attracted more than 1,000 participants from the North American Arctic region. Teams represented at the Winter Games, the largest event ever staged in the Yukon, included Alaska, Arctic Quebec, the Northwest Territories, and the Yukon. On opening day, March 6, the temperature was 27° below zero.

People. Col. Robert Samuel McLaughlin, an Ontario farm boy who became president of General Motors of Canada, died on January 6 at the age

---

THE CANADIAN MINISTRY
(As of December 1972)

Pierre Elliott Trudeau, Prime Minister
Paul Martin, Leader of the Government in the Senate
Mitchell Sharp, Secretary of State for External Affairs
Otto Lang, Minister of Justice and Attorney General
John Turner, Minister of Finance
Allan MacEachen, President of the Privy Council
Charles Drury, President of the Treasury Board
Jean Chrétien, Minister of Indian Affairs and Northern Development
Donald Macdonald, Minister of Energy, Mines, and Resources
Jack Davis, Minister of the Environment
Jean-Eudes Dubé, Minister of Public Works
Ronald Basford, Minister of State for Urban Affairs
Warren Allemand, Solicitor General
Hugh Faulkner, Secretary of State
Stanley Haidasz, Minister of State
Marc Lalonde, Minister of Health and Welfare
Dan MacDonald, Minister of Veterans' Affairs
André Ouellet, Postmaster General
Jeanne Sauvé, Minister of State for Science and Technology
Eugene Whelan, Minister of Agriculture
Robert Andras, Minister of Industry, Trade, and Commerce
Jean-Pierre Goyer, Minister of Supply and Services
Herbert Gray, Minister of Consumer and Corporate Affairs
Donald Jamieson, Minister of Regional Economic Expansion
Jean Marchand, Minister of Transport
John Munro, Minister of Labour
Gérard Pelletier, Minister of Communications
James Richardson, Minister of National Defence
Robert Stanbury, Minister of National Revenue

---

of 100 years. Colonel McLaughlin, the last of the old-time auto makers, was a friend of the Durants and the Chevrolet brothers. At his death, the plant in Oshawa, Ontario, was producing 300,000 motor vehicles a year and employing 30,000 people.

Bobby Hull, the Golden Jet of the Chicago Black Hawks for more than a decade, joined the Winnipeg Jets of the newly formed World Hockey Association. The 33-year-old star leftwinger received a check for $1 million, and the Jets will pay him $1.75 million more over the next 10 years.

George Maxwell Bell, wealthy Alberta racehorse breeder and owner of eight Canadian daily papers, including *The Globe and Mail* in Toronto and the *Winnipeg Free Press*, died on July 19 at 59.

Canada lost one of her old-time entertainers, Charlie Chamberlain, radio and TV singer with the Don Messer Jubilee since the 1930's. He once claimed times were so bad in the 1930's that he earned only 35 cents for an evening show. Chamberlain died on July 11.

The Rev. Bruce McLeod of Toronto was elected as moderator of Canada's largest Protestant denomination, the United Church of Canada, in August. He took office at a time when desire for union between the United and Anglican churches, originally scheduled for 1974, seemed to have cooled.

Restored Cathedral. St. Boniface Cathedral, in the first Roman Catholic parish west of the Great Lakes, was rededicated at Winnipeg in July 1972 after having burned in July 1968. The original cathedral was established on the same site in 1818 by Bishop Norbert Provencher.

Sailors' Rum Ration. A ritual going back to 1667 ended for sailors of the Canadian Navy when the traditional tot of rum to splice the main brace was issued for the last time on March 30, 1972.

W. A. McKay
Scarborough College, University of Toronto

CANADA • Information Highlights

Official Name: Canada.
Area: 3,851,809 square miles (9,976,185 sq km).
Population (1972 est.): 22,200,000. *Density,* 5 per square mile (2 per sq km). *Annual rate of increase,* 1.7%.
Chief Cities (1971 census): Ottawa, the capital, 302,341; Montreal, 1,214,352; Toronto, 712,786; Edmonton, 438,152; Vancouver, 426,256.
Government: *Head of state,* Elizabeth II, queen (represented by Roland Michener, governor general: took office April 1967). *Head of government,* Pierre Elliott Trudeau, prime minister (took office April 1968). *Legislature*—Parliament: Senate, 102 members; House of Commons, 264 members. *Major political parties*—Liberal; Progressive Conservative; New Democratic; Social Credit.
Languages: French, English (both official).
Education: *Expenditure* (1969) 8.9% of gross national product. *School enrollment* (1969)—primary, 3,841,040; secondary, 1,752,073; technical/vocational, 246,502; university/higher, 562,648.
Monetary Unit: Canadian dollar (0.9831 dollar equals U.S.$1, Aug. 1972).
Gross National Product (1971 est.): $84,700,000,000.
National Income per Person (1970): $3,214.
Economic Indexes: *Industrial production* (1971), 154 (1963= 100); *agricultural production* (1971), 149 (1952–56=100); *consumer price index* (1971), 130 (1963=100).
Manufacturing (major products): Pulp and paper, petroleum products, motor vehicles, aluminum, iron and steel.
Major Agricultural Products: Barley (ranks 2d among world producers, 1971), oats (world rank 3d, 1971), wheat, rye, potatoes, fish, forest products, livestock, furs.
Major Minerals: Iron ore (ranks 5th among world producers, 1970), asbestos (world rank 1st in 1970), nickel (world rank 1st, 1970), zinc, gold (world rank 3d, 1970), silver (world rank 2d, 1970), petroleum, natural gas.
Foreign Trade (1971): *Exports,* $17,573,000,000 (chief exports—manufactured goods, newsprint, wood, wheat). *Imports,* $15,457,000,000 (chief imports, 1969—transport equipment, nonelectrical machinery, food, electrical machinery). *Chief trading partners* (1969)—United States (took 71% of exports, supplied 73% of imports); United Kingdom (7%—6%); Japan (4%—3%); West Germany (2%—2%).
Tourism: *Receipts* (1970), $1,192,000,000.
Transportation: *Motor vehicles* (1970), 8,338,200 (automobiles, 6,602,200); *railroads* (1970), 43,613 miles (70,189 km); *merchant fleet* (1971), 2,366,000 gross registered tons; *major national airlines,* Air Canada; CP Air.
Communications: *Telephones* (1971), 9,752,537; *television stations* (1971), 378; *television sets* (1971), 7,700,000; *radios* (1970), 15,890,000; *newspapers* (1970), 118.

CANADIAN LITERATURE. See LITERATURE.

CANALS

In many parts of the world major canals and waterways were being planned or built in 1972.

California Water Project. Canals are the key components in conveying surplus water nearly 700 miles (1,125 km) from northern California to water-short central and southern California. The California Water Project, the largest public works scheme ever undertaken in one state, is costing $2.3 billion. Most of its facilities were to be operational in late 1973 after 12 years of construction. Stored water from 22 dams was to be carried by tunnels, pipelines, and canals. The canals will total 474 miles (763 km) in length.

Cross-Florida Barge Canal. Conservation and environmental groups stopped the U. S. Corps of Engineers from completing the 107-mile (172-km) Cross-Florida Barge Canal, which would have connected the Atlantic Ocean with the Gulf of Mexico. Some $54 million had already been spent on the $185 million project when President Nixon ordered a halt to construction on Jan. 19, 1971. An alternate route was under consideration in 1972 in the hope that it would not be opposed by ecologists.

McClusky Canal. A multipurpose waterway is being dug for the U. S. Bureau of Reclamation in North Dakota. The 20-mile (32-km) McClusky Canal, part of the Pick-Sloan Missouri Basin program, will be used for irrigation, municipal and industrial water, conservation of fish and wildlife, and recreation. It will be 23 feet (7 meters) deep and will have a bottom width of 25 feet (7.6 meters). The project was to take three years to complete and to cost nearly $6 million.

Welland Canal. Part of the 27.5-mile (44-km) Welland Canal between Lake Erie and Lake Ontario is being relocated. A new 8.3-mile (13-km) bypass section will replace a narrow and winding section that runs through Welland, Ontario. The bypass is being dug 3 miles (5 km) east of the city. The relocated channel will be 350 feet (107 meters) wide, 30 feet (9 meters) deep, and will be unobstructed by bridges over the waterway. The $188 million job, which includes the excavation of 65 million cubic yards (50 million cu meters) of material, was to be completed in 1973. The new channel will cut 30 minutes off the time oceangoing ships must take to pass through the canal. It will also relieve traffic congestion that was caused by lift bridges.

Kootenay Canal. Under construction in British Columbia, Canada, is a 3-mile (5-km) concrete-lined canal that will draw water from the Kootenay River to a 500-megawatt powerhouse. Excavation for the channel includes 6 million cubic yards (4.5 million cu meters) of material, one third of which is rock. The cost is expected to be $33 million.

Ruse-Varna Canal. Bulgaria is planning a 100-mile (161-km) long canal between Ruse on the Danube River and Varna on the Black Sea. The proposed waterway, entirely within Bulgaria, would cut 115 miles (185 km) from the present route that follows the Danube between Bulgaria and Rumania to its confluence with the Black Sea.

Europa Canal. Another section of the trans-European Europa Canal was completed in Germany in 1972. The 45-mile (72-km) section completed between Bamberg and Nuremburg is part of the link between the Main and Danube rivers. The remaining 80-mile (129-km) canal link from Nuremburg to Regensburg is scheduled to be completed by 1981. When completed the trans-European river and canal system will link the North Sea and the Black Sea via the Rhine, Main, and Danube rivers and connecting canals.

The Europa waterway is 180 feet (55 meters) wide, 13 feet (4 meters) deep, and can accommodate ships up to a 1,500-ton capacity. Vessel speed is limited to 7 miles (11 km) per hour because higher speeds produce a wave action that would erode the canal banks. When completed, the Europa Canal will cut the 5,000-mile (8,050-km) journey via the Atlantic Ocean, the Strait of Gibraltar, and the Mediterranean Sea by 3,000 miles (4,830 km).

Charlemagne tried unsuccessfully in 793 to link the Main and the Danube with a canal. In 1846, however, King Ludwig I of Bavaria built a waterway over part of what will be an international route.

Kra Isthmus Canal. Thailand's National Executive Council has approved plans for digging a 100-mile (161-km) canal across the Kra Isthmus about 350 miles (560 km) south of Bangkok. It would connect the Indian Ocean and the South China Sea. The proposed $450 million waterway would accommodate 100,000-ton oil tankers and would take nine years to construct. It would cut about 1,000 miles (1,600 km) from the passage through the Strait of Malacca between Malaya and Sumatra.

WILLIAM H. QUIRK
"Contractors & Engineers" Magazine

CARIBBEAN

The agricultural production of the Caribbean region continued to decline in 1972, while industrial development increased. For the first time the region was beginning to recognize the dangers of environmental pollution, with particular reference to the damage that might be done to the natural resources of the Caribbean Sea. Political activity monopolized attention on some of the islands where changes in government occurred.

Agriculture. In contrast to the previous year, when the Caribbean saw a record number of tropical storms, 1972 was notable for the absence of any storm of hurricane strength. For the most part, the northern and eastern rim of the area experienced a lower level of rainfall than normal, while the southern Caribbean and Guiana coast had above average rainfall.

The region's sugar production continued to decline, placing a severe strain on the economies of the small islands such as St. Kitts, which have no alternative source of income. The government of St. Kitts took over the sugar industry and planned to administer it through a 10-member central management committee under the permanent secretary in the ministry of agriculture. Falling prices for bananas on the world market and strikes affecting shipping caused some losses to Caribbean growers. But a long-sought Caribbean association of banana producers was formed when Jamaica joined the previously existing Windward Island group.

Tourism. With skyjacking to Cuba less frequent and local unrest no longer capturing the headlines, tourism returned in strength to the Caribbean in 1972. Particularly notable was the increase in tourist ships visiting the many island ports of the Caribbean. Among the major ports of call, only Port of Spain on the island of Trinidad noted a decline, this being due to a polio epidemic on Trinidad in early 1972.

Industry. Industrial development, particularly in the larger islands, continued to increase, but at a somewhat slower pace, as the local governments became more cautious of possible environmental damage from industrial activities. In the Dominican Republic, a large $200 million Canadian plant designed to produce 33,000 tons of ferronickel annually began operation in June. However, in Puerto Rico, a 12-month delay was ordered in plans for the construction of a nuclear power plant that had been judged necessary to supply power to the growing industrial complexes on the southern coast of the island. The delay was motivated by growing concern for the effect such a plant might have on the marine and land environment.

Environmental Protection. During 1972, governments as well as private citizens within the Caribbean community demonstrated an active concern for protecting the marine resources in the region. Puerto Rico and the Virgin Islands, stimulated by the U. S. Department of Interior, prepared extensive reports studying the effects on the sea around the islands of such activities as tourism, industrial development in coastal zones, the use of port facilities and marine transportation, and the disposal of wastes. A series of proposals based on the studies called for government remedial and protective action.

The Jamaican government, in conjunction with the International Oceanographic Institute of the University of Malta and the Center for the Study of Democratic Institutions, sponsored an international conference focusing on the Caribbean Sea, its use and misuse. The government of the Netherlands Antilles took under consideration a series of laws designed to protect the surrounding reefs, which are the natural habitat of the marine life of the Caribbean Sea. In addition, international conferences were held in Cuba under UNESCO sponsorship and in the Dominican Republic under the sponsorship of the Organization of American States (OAS) to study the common uses of, and benefits to mankind from, the world's seas, with particular emphasis on the Caribbean.

Elections. The year began with a particularly vigorous political campaign in Jamaica where, on February 29, the opposition People's National party, led by Michael Manley, turned out the government of Hugh Shearer, leader of the Jamaican Labour party. At about the same time, in the Windward Island of Grenada, the incumbent premier, Eric Gairy, had no trouble returning his party to office with 13 of the 15 seats in the legislature. With such an endorsement, Gairy promised to move his island rapidly toward full independence from Britain.

The island of St. Vincent held an election in April that produced a unique result. The vote for two major parties was so equally divided that neither gained a majority in the island's parliament. An independent, James F. Mitchell, was asked to become premier of the island and to form a government with the help of the People's Political party.

In September, Prime Minister Lynden O. Pindling of the Bahamas led his party into another term of office by capturing three fourths of the assembly seats. Pindling had campaigned on a program promising prompt independence from Britain. His victory led to predictions that the Bahamas would be independent by mid-1973.

Elections were held in November in both the Virgin Islands and Puerto Rico. In the former the election of the legislature overshadowed a lackluster support for the referendum on the first constitution for the U. S. Virgin Islands.

In a particularly hard-fought election in Puerto Rico, the Popular Democratic party (PDP) staged a comeback, defeating the incumbent governor, Luis Ferré. The new governor, 36-year-old Hernandez Colon, was the youngest person elected to that post. The election was seen by many as an endorsement of the PDP's commitment to perpetuating the island's Commonwealth status rather than seeking statehood or independence.

Regional Cooperation. In March, UN Secretary General Kurt Waldheim urged that the OAS readmit Cuba. The prime minister of the four sovereign members of the Commonwealth of Nations in the Caribbean—Barbados, Guyana, Jamaica, and Trinidad and Tobago—met in Trinidad in October and voted unanimously to seek diplomatic relations with Cuba.

The prime ministers of the member states and the associated states of the British Caribbean agreed to establish a Caribbean Common Market by May 1, 1973. This historic agreement by the leaders of the states forming the Caribbean Free Trade Association (CARIFTA) followed a recommendation by William Demas, the secretary general of CARIFTA. Earlier in the year, Demas had also recommended a coordinated foreign policy and cooperation in various other areas.

A declaration entitled "Toward an Eastern Caribbean Federation" was signed by 14 distinguished West Indians, including Sir Arthur Lewis, president of the Caribbean Development Bank, and Sir Hugh Wooding, chancellor of the University of the West Indies. The document put forth the arguments that only a united federal voice could protect the interests of the states in the light of Britain's entry into the European Common Market, could create a sense of nationhood, could foment and institute the necessary action toward economic integration, and could establish safeguards for individual civil liberties.

On a smaller scale, definite steps toward integration in the Caribbean were taken when the premiers of the Windward Islands of St. Lucia, St. Vincent, and Grenada met in June on the island of Petit St. Vincent to draft an agreement known as the Petit St. Vincent Initiative. The pact, which went into effect in August, established freedom of movement between the three islands, eliminated work permits formerly required for immigrant workers, and abolished landholding restrictions for those from the three islands. The steps were to be reviewed at a later date to measure their success and to see whether further unification or cooperation could continue.

Another move toward cooperation and eventual integration of the region was the incorporation of Colombia and Venezuela as full-fledged members of the Caribbean Development Bank. In December some 30 presidents and chancellors of the universities in and around the Caribbean region met in Montego Bay, Jamaica, for the third biennial meeting of the Association of Caribbean Universities and Research Institutes. The association, which is funded in part by private foundations, planned for cooperative research and teaching projects to further the regional approach toward higher education within the Caribbean.

THOMAS G. MATHEWS
University of Puerto Rico

CENSORSHIP

Echoes of the Pentagon Papers censorship crisis lingered on in the United States in 1972. The Justice Department commenced investigation of the Unitarian Universalist Church's Beacon Press for publishing the version of the Pentagon Papers supplied by Sen. Mike Gravel (D-Alaska), whose plea of senatorial immunity was denied by the U. S. Supreme Court. The Association of American Publishers called the action "a huge threat to book publishing in the United States."

In 1971 the New York *Times* and other newspapers had been temporarily restrained from publishing this material, gleaned from classified documents concerned with the Indochina War, but the Supreme Court ruled against the government and allowed publication to resume. Legal irregularities caused delay of the trial of Daniel Ellsberg and Anthony Russo, Jr., whom the Justice Department sought to prosecute under the Espionage Act for their role in disclosing these documents to the press.

A 1972 case involving a projected publication by a former CIA agent presented similarities to the Pentagon Papers case. The CIA secured a permanent injunction stipulating agency consent before publication, and an appeals panel held that the secrecy agreement the author had signed with his former employer did not violate the First Amendment.

In other actions, courts upheld the constitutionality of a law barring subscription to magazines published by "hostile nations," the right of a school board to remove offending books from school libraries, and the right of shopping center owners to bar political handbills from their premises. Left standing, however, was a California Supreme Court decision declaring illegal an anti-littering ordinance outlawing distribution of "shopper's newspapers." A statute banning the mailing of ads relating to abortion was found unconstitutional, as was denial of official recognition of a student political organization by a state-supported college because the administration found the organization's philosophy abhorrent.

Faced with mounting criticism of the Federal Election Campaign Act, a special three-judge panel ruled that in certain of its restrictions on political advertising, the act presented "substantial questions of constitutionality." It ordered the Justice Department not to enforce key sections of the law, among them a requirement that the publisher obtain written permission from any candidate named in an advertisement. The action stemmed from a case wherein the New York *Times* refused to publish, out of fear of government prosecution, an ad of the American Civil Liberties Union urging voter support of 102 congressmen whose individual written permissions neither the ACLU nor the *Times* had secured.

Judicial Censorship. Censorship at the trial court level accelerated during 1972. Power of the judiciary to control the release of information previously restricted largely to the courtroom spread to cover pre-trial and post-verdict periods, as courts ordered judicial and police officers and even reporters to be silent on criminal cases. Where these orders were challenged, appellate courts regularly held that the trial courts exceeded their authority. However, a U. S. court of appeals ruled that the press should obey prior restraints while seeking further legal determination.

Censorship for Morality. Belief that alleged obscenity can be countered by "nuisance laws"—those designed to combat anything deemed detrimental to the well-being of the community—was buttressed by Supreme Court acceptance for the 1972–73 term of cases involving such laws and by their successful employment by citizens' groups in several states. Librarians in California were contesting an attorney general's opinion that they are liable for prosecution under the state's "harmful matter statute."

Nationwide, localities enacted a flurry of ordinances calculated to bar young people from the alleged harmful effects of obscenity. Many of these ordinances were intended to keep minors under 18 from "adult" bookstores and movies. A New York statute made the wholesaling of pornography a felony, punishable by upwards of seven years in prison. If it sustains court review, the law is expected to serve as a model for other states.

Censorship at the Source. An investigation by a congressional committee concluded that the Freedom of Information (FoI) Act of 1967 had failed in its purpose of freeing information from bureaucratic censorship due mainly to the inadequacy of the law's language. Nevertheless, the press continued to rely on the law. Despite pleas based on the FoI Act, courts in 1972 upheld the government in its decision not to release information on the assassination of President John F. Kennedy, nor to open certain Security Exchange Commission files. The Defense Department refused a newspaper request for results of a poll of attitudes of broadcast stations to an array of advertising campaigns.

Under court order to produce documents relating to an underground nuclear test sought by 33 members of Congress, the executive branch asked the Supreme Court to overrule the lower court's decision on the argument that the FoI Act does not permit judges to inspect classified information. Such actions have served to exacerbate congressional condemnation of the secrecy practices of the executive branch. Rep. William S. Moorhead (D-Pa.) introduced a bill that would establish a nine-member classification review commission controlled by Congress. President Nixon issued a directive requiring a "more progressive" system of classification of government-held papers. The declassification process was accelerated, but six years remained the shortest time in which a document could be declassified.

There were some victories in 1972 in the effort to free government-held information. The Department of Agriculture was forced to open meat plant inspection records and to disclose a Farmers Home Administration study of charges of discrimination against Negro borrowers. The Department of Defense was pressured to release secret portions of an Army study of the Mylai massacre in Vietnam. Courts ordered officials of the Department of Health, Education, and Welfare to provide for the release of Medicare inspection reports on nursing homes and other facilities. The Internal Revenue Service was ordered to make available manuals it employs in tax settlement cases.

Censorship by the Media. Under attack by the movie industry, but supported by the courts, was the spreading practice by newspapers of denying advertising space to movies rated X (adults only). Meanwhile, the movie rating program, administered by the Motion Picture Association of America, drew fire from a wide array of critics who said it was, at best, an industry effort to reduce public pressure and,

at worst, a full-scale system of prior restraint of expression.

Winding up hearings on the condition of press freedom in the United States, the Senate Subcommittee on Constitutional Rights heard television writers charge that networks frequently censored scripts and sometimes required approval by outside professional associations before broadcasting.

Censorship: World View. In its 1972 annual report on worldwide conditions of press freedom, the International Press Institute said, "Slowly, the independence of the press is being eroded on the nibble system. The powers nibble here, and nibble there. . . . These . . . erosions can be detected in varying degrees in the countries with a tradition of press freedom. . . ." The institute found the trend at its worst in developing countries.

The Associated Press and the Inter-American Press Association reported increasing censorship in Latin America. Press censorship was incorporated into law in Argentina, while Chile notably increased official pressure on newsmen. In Brazil, the press was forbidden to discuss presidential succession. The Peruvian government ruled that broadcast programs must be "socially useful."

Martial law was declared in the Philippines, Turkey, and South Korea. The Philippines government commenced censorship of news dispatches and dissolved a number of newspapers and radio stations. A government-authorized daily was established, staffed by "respectable" journalists. Turkey also closed several newspapers and periodicals, and South Korea issued a series of guidelines to the press.

The South Vietnamese government virtually silenced the opposition press by closing 14 daily newspapers and 15 other periodicals that had failed to post large bonds as guarantees against possible fines for violation of a strict press code.

The UN General Assembly faced, but did not resolve, questions concerning control of international communications by satellite transmission. A UNESCO draft declaration proclaimed the people's right to know, but recognized, as a matter of international law, the right of any government to cut off its people from direct satellite television broadcasts.

PAUL FISHER
Director, Freedom of Information Center
University of Missouri

CENTRAL AFRICAN REPUBLIC

Events in the Central African Republic (CAR) in 1972 were dominated by President Jean Bedel Bokassa, who continued to concentrate power in his own hands.

Domestic Affairs. On February 22 a congress of the country's single political party, the Mouvement pour l'Évolution Sociale de l'Afrique Noire (MESAN), was summoned for the first time since Bokassa had seized power in a military coup in 1966. The congress appointed Bokassa president for life of the CAR and life secretary general of MESAN.

Concerned by a rising crime rate, Bokassa decided in July to make an example of the worst offenders. He ordered soldiers to beat dozens of prisoners, most of them convicted thieves. Several of the victims were whipped to death, and their bodies were put on public display in Bangui.

Foreign Relations. Relations between the CAR and France remained cool in 1972. A major cause of friction was Bokassa's concern about his country's lack of economic freedom as a member of the franc zone. In particular, he wanted the CAR to have more control over the earning and disposal of its foreign exchange. Early in the year he seemed about to withdraw from the franc zone, but later stated that he would be content if some of the services provided by the zone's central bank were shifted from Paris to Bangui.

CONVICTED THIEVES are beaten in the Central African Republic on orders of President Bokassa (left). Several prisoners died of injuries.

CENTRAL AFRICAN REPUBLIC • Information Highlights

Official Name: Central African Republic.
Area: 240,535 square miles (622,984 sq km).
Population (1972 est.): 1,600,000. *Density,* 8 per square mile (3 per sq km). *Annual rate of increase,* 2.1%.
Chief City (1966 est.): Bangui, the capital, 150,000.
Government: *Head of state,* Jean Bedel Bokassa, president (seized office Jan. 1966, in a military coup). *Head of government,* Jean Bedel Bokassa. *Political party*—Mouvement pour l'Évolution Sociale de l'Afrique Noire.
Languages: French (official), Sango.
Education: *Expenditure* (1969), 15.4% of total public expenditure. *School enrollment* (1969)—primary, 170,048; secondary, 8,682; technical/vocational, 1,202.
Monetary Unit: CFA franc (255.79 CFA francs equal U. S.$1, Aug. 1972).
Gross National Product (1970 est.): $200,000,000.
Manufacturing (major products): Textiles, soap, processed agricultural products.
Major Agricultural Products: Cotton, coffee, groundnuts, forest products, livestock.
Major Minerals: Diamonds, uranium.
Foreign Trade (1970): *Exports,* $31,000,000. *Imports,* $34,000,000. *Chief trading partners* (1969)—France (took 51% of exports, supplied 55% of imports); United States.
Communications: *Telephones* (1969), 2,800; *radios* (1970), 46,000; *newspapers* (1967), 2 (daily circulation, 800).

Bokassa was also unhappy with a French refusal to finance construction of a railroad from Bangui to the Atlantic coast, and turned to Eastern Europe and the Middle East for aid. He visited Iraq, Lebanon, and Greece. The CAR later signed a 20-year friendship treaty with Iraq and an economic cooperation treaty with Kuwait. Relations between the CAR and France improved after Bokassa's visit to France in June.

Economy. A land-locked state, the CAR continued in 1972 to seek better transportation outlets for its products. A step of great potential significance was taken on Dec. 31, 1971, when the CAR and Sudan signed an agreement providing for the construction of a railroad to connect the two states.

GRAHAM W. IRWIN
Columbia University

CENTRAL AMERICA. See LATIN AMERICA and the articles on Central American countries.

CEYLON (Sri Lanka)

In 1972, Ceylon adopted a new constitution, became a republic, and changed its name to Sri Lanka (the island's ancient Sinhalese name). Mrs. Sirimavo Bandaranaike's United Front government remained in power despite growing criticism, reverses in by-elections, deteriorating law and order, and a continuing grim economic condition.

The New Constitution. A draft constitution—presented to the Constituent Assembly on Dec. 29, 1971—was adopted in final form on May 22, 1972. It declared the Republic of Sri Lanka to be a "free and sovereign republic pledged to realize the objectives of a socialist democracy." It was to be a unitary state with a president nominated by the prime minister and with a National Assembly as "the supreme instrument of state power," exercising "the legislative, executive, and judicial power of the people." The validity of the acts of the Assembly were not to be questioned in ordinary courts of law, but only by a constitutional court appointed by the president for the duration of each National Assembly. The Assembly was to be chosen at six-year intervals in free, direct elections by citizens over the age of 18. Members of the first Assembly were to be the members of the Constituent Assembly, which had been chosen in the elections of May 1970.

The new constitution's chapter on fundamental rights and freedoms contains no provision for property rights. Two chapters were controversial—one that names Sinhalese as the official language (though providing for translations into Tamil) and one giving Buddhism the "foremost place" while also granting complete freedom to other religions.

In the new republic, Mrs. Bandaranaike, prime minister of Ceylon at the time of the change, became the first premier of Sri Lanka, and William Gopallawa, the last governor-general of Ceylon, was sworn in as the first president. Sri Lanka retained membership in the Commonwealth of Nations.

Political Events. There were only minor changes in the government during 1972. A swing from the United Front seemed to be indicated by the loss of two assembly seats in four by-elections on October 9—the first ones held since the general election of May 1970.

The government was alarmed by the rising crime rate in areas where the insurgency of 1971 had been strongest. It announced that some 5,000 of the approximately 15,000 young insurgents in custody would be released, but 8,000 others were to be tried on charges of "criminal complicity."

The Economy. Sri Lanka continued to be plagued by a host of economic ills, including high budget deficits, reductions in real income and in external assets, shortages of consumer goods, and high prices. The National Assembly enacted laws for ceilings on land ownership and incomes, more stringent price controls, and land reform.

Foreign Relations. In February the rice-rubber agreement with China was renewed. As a result, Ceylon purchased 200,000 tons of rice and supplied China with 39,000 tons of rubber. There was also trade in other commodities. On June 25–July 5, Mrs. Bandaranaike made an official visit to China, where she signed agreements for economic and technical cooperation and for the construction by China of a cotton mill in Sri Lanka. The government officially recognized the new state of Bangladesh.

NORMAN D. PALMER, *University of Pennsylvania*

CEYLON • Information Highlights

Official Name: Republic of Sri Lanka.
Area: 25,332 square miles (65,610 sq km).
Population (1972 est.): 13,200,000. *Density,* 495 per square mile (191 per sq km). *Annual rate of increase,* 2.3%.
Chief City (1967 est.): Colombo, the capital, 551,200.
Government: *Head of state,* William Gopallawa, president (took office May 1972). *Head of government,* Mrs. Sirimavo Bandaranaike, premier (prime minister until May 1972, took office May 1970). *Legislature* (unicameral)—National Assembly, 157 members. *Major political parties*—Sri Lanka Freedom party; Lanka Sama Samaj party; United National party; Communist party.
Languages: Sinhalese (official), Tamil (semiofficial), English.
Education: *Expenditure* (1967), 4.4% of gross national product. *School enrollment* (1969)—primary, 2,298,120; secondary, 355,665; technical/vocational, 7,565; university/higher, 14,400.
Monetary Unit: Rupee (6.388 rupees equal U. S.$1, July 1972).
Gross National Product (1971 est.): $2,140,000,000.
National Income per Person (1969): $150.
Economic Indexes: *Industrial production* (1966), 115 (1963=100); *agricultural production* (1971), 157 (1952–56=100); *consumer price index* (1971), 130 (1963=100).
Manufacturing (major products): Milled rice, chemicals, cement, petroleum products.
Major Agricultural Products: Tea (ranks 2d among world producers, 1971), natural rubber (world rank 4th, 1971).
Major Minerals: Graphite, ilmenite, salt, gemstones.
Foreign Trade (1971): *Exports,* $327,000,000 (chief exports—tea, rubber, coconut products). *Imports,* $334,000,000 (chief imports, 1969—cereals and preparations, nonelectrical machinery, transport equipment, chemicals). *Chief trading partners* (1969)—United Kingdom (took 20% of exports, supplied 17% of imports); China (13%—11%).
Tourism: *Receipts* (1970), $3,600,000.
Transportation: *Motor vehicles* (1970), 132,600 (automobiles, 87,700); *railroads* (1970), 965 miles (1,553 km); *major national airline,* Air Ceylon.
Communications: *Telephones* (1971), 62,954; *radios* (1969), 500,000; *newspapers* (1970), 17.

CHAD

The rebellion in Chad, which has long plagued the government of President François Tombalbaye, showed no sure signs of ending in 1972.

Domestic Affairs. Opposition to the central government continued to be led by the Chad Liberation Front (FROLINAT), headed by Dr. Abba Siddick and based in Libya. Government forces were supported in the field by French contingents supplied under the Franco-Chadian defense agreement. It was announced in January that 600 French officers and noncommissioned officers were serving with the Chad army and police, together with 600 French army and 700 French air force personnel under independent command. In the same month the totals of casualties reportedly suffered by both sides since April 1969 were made public: killed—French, 36; Chadians, 164; rebels, 2,869; wounded—French, 98; Chadians, 211; rebels, 1,032.

In June, FROLINAT claimed that during the first 3 months of 1972 its forces had destroyed 4 helicopters, 2 transport aircraft, and 3 army trucks. In September, French Gen. Edouard Cortadellas resigned as commander of Franco-Chadian forces, claiming the rebellion had been checked.

Foreign Relations. The president of France, Georges Pompidou, paid an official visit to Chad in January. In his speeches he made it clear that France would continue to supply Chad with the "exceptional and temporary aid" guaranteed under the defense agreement and would continue to help in the economic development of the country.

Diplomatic relations between Chad and Libya, which had been broken in August 1971, were restored on April 12 through the mediation of President Hamani Diori of Niger.

Economy. The burden of combating the rebellion began to weaken Chad's finances in 1972. President Tombalbaye admitted in June that Chad owed private firms more than $10 million.

The heads of state of Cameroon, Chad, Niger, and Nigeria—the founding states of the Chad Basin Commission, established in 1964—met at Fort-Lamy on July 5–6. They agreed to establish a development fund and to create specialized agencies to solve the various agricultural problems of the Chad Basin area.

GRAHAM W. IRWIN
Columbia University

——————— **CHAD · Information Highlights** ———————

Official Name: Republic of Chad.
Area: 495,754 square miles (1,284,000 sq km).
Population (1972 est.): 3,900,000. *Density,* 8 per square mile (3 per sq km). *Annual rate of increase,* 2.3%.
Chief City (1968 census): Fort-Lamy, the capital, 132,500.
Government: *Head of state,* François Tombalbaye, president (took office Aug. 1960). *Head of government,* François Tombalbaye. *Legislature* (unicameral)—National Assembly, 75 members. *Political party*—Chadian Progressive party.
Languages: French (official), Arabic, African languages.
Education: *Expenditure* (1966), 14.3% of total public expenditure. *School enrollment* (1969)—primary, 162,333; secondary, 9,911; technical/vocational, 903.
Monetary Unit: CFA franc (255.79 CFA francs equal U. S.$1, Aug. 1972).
Gross National Product (1970 est.): $259,000,000.
Manufacturing (major product): Processed cotton.
Major Agricultural Products: Cotton, groundnuts, millet, sorghum, rice, cattle.
Foreign Trade (1970): *Exports,* $30,000,000. *Imports,* $61,000,-000. *Chief trading partner* (1969)—France (took 83% of exports, supplied 35% of imports).
Communications: *Telephones* (1971), 4,690; *radios* (1970), 60,000; *newspapers* (1969), 1 (daily circulation, 1,000).

CHAPLIN, Charles. See BIOGRAPHY.

CHEMISTRY

About 364 billion pounds of chemicals were produced for use as industrial raw materials in 1972. The growth of certain areas of the chemical industry was indicated by the fact that in 1958 the capacity of a typical ethylene plant was 15,000–20,000 tons and by 1972, 500,000-ton plants were built. Nevertheless, basic research and development in the chemical industry was sluggish in 1972. The industry's emphasis shifted to products that needed little research (and could thus yield quick profits) and to cost-saving measures, process improvement, and market research.

Hydrogen Fuel. With impending shortages of natural gas and increased consumption of electricity, the term "energy crisis" became almost a household word. (See ENERGY.) According to one estimate, the supply of fossil fuels (coal, oil, and fuel gas) would be adequate for only 100 years, even if chemical technology is used to process oil shales and produce gas from coal. When these fossil-fuel reserves are exhausted, hydrogen produced by nuclear power may become an important fuel. The hydrogen could be produced, for example, by electrolysis of seawater, with oxygen as a saleable by-product. Because the main combustion product of hydrogen is water, with only traces of nitrogen oxides derived from the atmosphere, many pollution problems would be solved. But other pollution problems might be created by nuclear power plants generating the vast amounts of electricity needed for large-scale electrolysis of seawater.

Plastics and the Environment. Technology for recycling plastics continued to expand. The Ford Motor Company had in pilot-plant stage a process for decomposing flexible polyurethane foams and then re-using the decomposition products to make polyurethane, and the Upjohn Company worked on a process for recovering polyols from rigid polyurethanes. Gewain announced plans to build a plant in Pennsylvania, with a capacity of about 10 million pounds per year, to convert polyethylene plastics into resins suitable for making molded plastic products. The company planned to handle polyester rejects from textile mills and photographic film from which silver had been removed. But in the case of municipal wastes, which contain mixtures of various types of plastics, it was still not economical to sort out plastics for recycling.

The Federal Trade Commission began a probe of fire hazards caused by use of polyurethanes and polystyrene for construction and for home and office furnishings. During fires, smoldering of these plastics produces toxic fumes and large quantities of smoke, causing death from inhalation of these materials. One expert said that burning polyurethane can produce nitrogen oxides and hydrogen cyanide, a deadly gas. Fires in nursing homes were a particular problem. It was estimated that over 1 billion pounds of these two plastics were sold in 1971 and that by 1980 the figure would reach 4 billion pounds.

Biodegradable plastic products were used on a substantial scale in the United States for the first time. Seven and a half million lids for carry-out cold drink cups were made for a restaurant chain having 250 outlets, mainly in the Western states. Oxidation of the lids was said to be triggered by exposure to sunlight or ultraviolet light. The lids disintegrate in 30 to 90 days and disappear in about

12 months. It was said that indoor lighting has no effect on the lids during their shelf life. Once disintegration is triggered, however, it continues even in the dark, provided oxygen is present.

Another development that may reduce environmental pollution by plastics was a bottle made largely from water-soluble hydroxycellulose, a chemical commonly used as a food stabilizer. The hydroxycellulose is sandwiched between two thin layers, an outer layer of polystyrene and an inner layer of a polymer whose composition depends on the contents of the bottle. When the bottle is immersed in water, the middle layer—which makes up 90% of the bottle's weight—dissolves, leaving only the polymer layers as solid waste.

Artificial Sweeteners. The search continued for artificial sweeteners to replace cyclamates, which were banned in 1970, and possibly to replace saccharin, about which serious questions were raised in 1972. In one experiment cancers were found in rats fed on saccharin. However, in several other feeding experiments the findings were negative. One possible sugar substitute is aspartylphenylalanine, expected to be marketed under the name Aspartame. But for four years the company developing the sweetener had said that it would be available within two years. One problem was that it breaks down in acid solution, and many beverages contain acid. Unlike cyclamates and saccharin, which are synthetic chemicals foreign to the body, this new sweetener is based on natural substances, a combination of the amino acids phenylalanine and aspartic acid, which are among the building blocks of proteins.

Another sweetener in development, expected to be marketed in 1974, is produced from the berry of an African tree. Unlike Aspartame, this sweetener is activated by acid. If allowed to coat the tongue before meals, it causes even a lemon to taste sweet, while foods such as steak and potatoes merely taste better. Of particular interest to dieters is the fact that test subjects were unable to finish a 575-calorie meal of steak, potatoes, vegetables, and dessert, because accentuation of their taste sensations caused the subjects to feel as though they had eaten a much larger meal. This sweetener was being developed by a privately owned company, whose stockholders included Reynolds Metals and the Prudential Insurance Company. The berries were being grown in five countries, with the largest plantation (about 100,000 trees) in Jamaica.

Other Food Additives. At least 2,500 to 3,000 chemical additives were being used to flavor, color, preserve, and improve the texture and appearance of food. Of these, 1,100 to 1,400 were flavoring substances. By 1972, the World Health Organization had evaluated more than 140 artificial colors and declared some unsafe. Also, the U. S. Food and Drug Administration (FDA) decided to re-evaluate the 600 additives on its GRAS (Generally Recognized As Safe) list to prove or disprove their safety.

Questions were raised regarding the safety of nordihydroguaiaretic acid, a chemical prepared from the leaves and stems of the creosote bush and used to prevent rancidity in food. According to reports, the chemical has been shown to interfere with the metabolism of rat liver cells and of dog hearts. Some believe that this interference also applies to human cells.

Questions were also raised about the nitrites used in cured meats to impart a red color and prevent growth of the bacteria causing botulism. In the intestinal tract, nitrites can combine with secondary amines to form nitrosoamines, which have been shown to cause cancer in rats. In February, the U. S. Department of Agriculture reported that samples of cooked bacon had yielded up to 110 parts per billion of nitrosopyrrolidene, a nitrosoamine, and that bacon drippings had yielded 200 parts per billion. Ralph Nader and some of his associates petitioned the department to ban immediately nitrites in bacon and baby food, to determine the amount needed to inhibit growth of botulism organisms in other food products, and to limit the nitrite content to that level. Norway had already banned the use of nitrites for food coloring after 1972.

Hexachlorophene. Late in 1971, evidence showed that hexachlorophene, used as a germicide in products such as drugs, soap, and cosmetics, might be a nerve poison, and the FDA recommended that hospitals stop the routine bathing of infants in a 3% solution of hexachlorophene. This action was criticized by some because of subsequent staphylococcus outbreaks in some hospitals.

In August 1972 the deaths of about 40 babies in France were associated with hexachlorophene. The infants had been dusted with talcum powder containing 6% of the chemical. Autopsies revealed lesions in their brains identical to those caused by hexachlorophene in experimental animals. Subsequently, in September, the FDA imposed a virtual ban on the chemical. No product, excepting prescription items, could contain more than 0.1% and all items containing more than 0.75% had to be either recalled or sold on prescription. Prior to the imposition of restrictions on its sale, the use of hexachlorophene by the U. S. drug and cosmetic industry had reached some 4 million pounds per week.

Origin of Life. In search of an answer to the question of what caused amino acids on the primitive earth to combine into the proteins of the first living organisms, a Russian scientist subjected a mixture of such acids to blast waves from an explosion and found that protein-like substances were formed. He suggested that blast waves on the primitive earth, caused by meteoritic impact or terrestrial upheaval, may have created similar substances.

The Russian scientist said also that experiments have shown that blast waves can be used to make rubber in only one one-hundred-thousandth of a second per batch, compared with the hour and a half required for vulcanization. Tires made from this rubber, he said, would last 10% longer than ordinary rubber tires, because—unlike vulcanized rubber—the blast-formed rubber would contain no sulfur, which shortens tire life. He conjectured that rubber might be put into molds, placed in an armored chamber, and blasted into high-quality tires.

Life on the Moon. Analysis of lunar soil samples brought back by Apollo missions produced no evidence that life exists or has existed on the moon. However, precursors of amino acids were found. On hydrolysis these precursors yielded up to 70 parts per billion of amino acids. The most abundant were the simplest known—particularly glycine, with alanine and glutamic acid present in smaller amounts. It was speculated that solar winds, meteorites, or interstellar dust are involved in formation of these precursors and that lack of water in the lunar environment blocked their evolution into amino acids.

Rescue workers try to free victims from the wreckage of two commuter trains that crashed in Chicago on October 30.

Venus. According to data returned by Venus 8, the Soviet probe that landed on the daylight side of Venus in July, temperatures reached 500° C, which is above the melting point of lead, and atmospheric pressures were 100 times more than those on the earth's surface. After landing, instruments in the probe functioned for 50 minutes.

The atmosphere, which is 97% carbon dioxide, was calm at the surface, but above an altitude of 15 to 20 kilometers hurricane winds raged. Ammonia was detected in the ionosphere and cloud layer. Radio waves reflected from the surface showed that the soil was loose, with a density of 1.5 grams per cubic centimeter, and gamma-ray spectroscopy indicated that the chemical composition of the soil is similar to that of granites on earth. A Soviet geochemist who analyzed the data said that earth and Venus are probably made of the same materials, and he noted that this finding supports the theory that all planets were formed by the same process.

EUGENIA KELLER
Managing Editor, "Chemistry" Magazine

CHESS. See special feature beginning on page 53.

CHICAGO

The year 1972 in Chicago was marked by a mounting challenge to the political power of Mayor Richard J. Daley's local Democratic machine; by a continuing financial crisis in the city's schools; and by initial steps on the part of the city government to reorganize its powers and functions under the city's new home rule powers granted by the 1970 Illinois constitution.

Politics. Mayor Daley's Democratic organization suffered major reversals in the March primary election and in the November general election. Incumbent Democratic State's Attorney Edward Hanrahan, who had been indicted for conspiring to obstruct justice in a police raid on a Black Panther headquarters in which two Panther leaders were killed, was dumped as the Democratic candidate for state's attorney in favor of Municipal Court Judge Raymond K. Berg. Hanrahan, however, defeated Berg and the organization in the primary after being acquitted in his trial, and thus became the party's candidate for state's attorney.

Democratic Lt. Gov. Paul Simon, the organization's candidate for the Democratic gubernatorial nomination, was defeated in the same primary by Daniel Walker, an anti-organization reform-oriented attorney. Walker was the author of the *Walker Report,* which criticized the conduct of the Chicago police during the Democratic National Convention in 1968. He had criticized Mayor Daley as a machine boss.

In the November elections, Hanrahan was defeated for Cook county's state's attorney by Republican Bernard Carey, a former FBI agent, and the Democratic organization lost control of one of the most important county offices. Walker's victory over incumbent Republican Gov. Richard B. Ogilvie gave control of the most important state office to an anti-organization reform Democrat.

At the national level, the Daley organization also suffered a major blow. The Democratic convention in Miami Beach refused to seat Mayor Daley and 58 other delegates from Illinois who had been elected with the support of the Daley organization. The convention ruled that the Daley delegates were not elected in accordance with the McGovern Commission's guidelines, and seated an anti-Daley slate of delegates led by reform Alderman William Singer and the Rev. Jesse Jackson, head of the organization PUSH (People United to Save Humanity). PUSH had replaced the Southern Christian Leadership Conference's Chicago division as the most important local black organization.

In the Chicago city council, the Daley organization's dominance was repeatedly, although unsuc-

cessfully, challenged by a reform coalition of independents, dissident Democrats, and Republicans. Although the Daley forces continued to control the council, a group of Democratic organization aldermen, seeking to gain greater influence, moved to challenge the leadership of Mayor Daley and Alderman Thomas Keane, Daley's floor leader.

Another revolt against Mayor Daley's leadership was led by black Congressman Ralph Metcalfe, a former Democratic organization stalwart, who assumed the leadership of the black community's protest against police practices in Chicago.

It was becoming increasingly clear that the jockeying for position for the succession to the mayoralty, if Daley retired in 1975, was beginning.

Education. The financial crisis which plagued Chicago's schools continued. The board of education borrowed approximately $30 million from funds set aside for new school construction to meet its current budgetary needs. But barring a massive increase in either state or federal subsidies, neither of which seemed likely, it appeared that the financial crisis confronting Chicago's schools would continue and probably deepen in the years to come.

Other Events. Mayor Daley took cognizance of the election returns and the conservative political trend in the country by holding the line on expenditures in the forthcoming city budget, and by promising to reduce property taxes in the city by approximately 15%.

The Chicago Home Rule Commission, headed by Chairman Patrick O'Malley, made a series of recommendations to the city council for governmental reorganization, revenue overhaul, expanded

CHICAGO's Mayor Daley applauds Senator McGovern, Democratic presidential candidate, at Chicago rally.

WIDE WORLD

health and housing programs, and a broad expansion of the city's powers under its new home rule capabilities.

Mayor Daley's plan to build the Crosstown Expressway, a north-south thoroughfare on the far western end of the city, was tentatively halted by opposition from the Citizen's Action Program (CAP), a civic reform group.

MILTON RAKOVE
University of Illinois at Chicago Circle

CHILD WELFARE. See SOCIAL WELFARE.
CHILDREN'S LITERATURE. See LITERATURE.

CHILE

Life in Chile during 1972 was turbulent. Inflation continued, and shortages of consumer products produced widespread dissatisfaction and a black market. Strikes, demonstrations, and violence were common. A strike by 50,000 truck drivers in October and November triggered a confrontation between the Marxist president, Salvador Allende, and his political opponents that brought the country to the verge of civil war.

Push to Revolutionize Chile. Pressing for government domination of the economy, the Allende regime took over major food distributors, 22 cattle auction markets, several factories, the Bank of Chile, a large distributor of agricultural and industrial equipment, and control of the sale of all airplane tickets.

The president introduced a constitutional amendment to replace the bicameral congress with a unicameral body, but Congress turned this down. A congressional measure to limit the president's power to take over businesses was vetoed by Allende. Disputes arose within the president's multiparty coalition, and several cabinet changes were made during the year.

Relations between the president and the congressional majority worsened when the legislators, on Jan. 6, 1972, voted censure of the minister of the interior for not protecting the rights of some 15,000 women whose protest demonstration had been suppressed by force. The women had paraded through the streets of Santiago noisily banging on pots and pans to protest against food shortages and high prices, and many had been arrested. Required by the constitution to remove the censured minister from office, Allende immediately appointed him minister of defense, thereby defying the spirit of the law.

Strike. As Allende approached the end of his second year in office, a strike by truck drivers, commencing on Oct. 11, 1972, touched off the most serious crisis of his administration. When the president refused to grant the truckers' demands, bank clerks, engineers, airline pilots, students, sailors in the merchant marine, bus drivers and owners, physicians, dentists, and about 200,000 small farmers joined the strike, and most retail businesses closed.

President Allende reacted by placing 22 provinces under a state of emergency. Thousands were jailed, and a nightly curfew was imposed in the major cities. Demonstrators continuously clashed with the police, some sabotage took place, a few bombs went off, and a few people were killed. The strike was never pushed to its limit, however, as food stores and pharmacies stayed open, and some food continued to reach the cities.

CHILE · Information Highlights

Official Name: Republic of Chile.
Area: 292,257 square miles (756,945 sq km).
Population (1972 est.): 10,200,000. *Density,* 349 per square mile (13.5 per sq km). *Annual rate of increase,* 1.9%.
Chief Cities: Santiago, the capital, 2,900,000 (1970 census-metropolitan area); Valparaiso (1969 est.), 289,000.
Government: *Head of state,* Salvador Allende Gossens, president (took office Nov. 1970). *Head of government,* Salvador Allende Gossens. *Legislature*—Congress: Senate, 50 members; Chamber of Deputies, 150 members. *Major political parties*—Christian Democratic party; Socialist party; National party; Communist party.
Language: Spanish (official).
Education: *Expenditure* (1969), 10.6% of total public expenditure. *School enrollment* (1969)—primary, 1,980,815; secondary, 267,769; technical/vocational, 85,987; university/higher, 73,025.
Monetary Unit: Escudo (15.80 escudos equal U. S.$1, June 1972).
Gross National Product (1971 est.): $8,090,000,000.
National Income per Person (1970): $613.
Economic Indexes: *Industrial production* (mining, 1970), 112 (1963=100); *agricultural production* (1971), 139 (1952–56=100); *consumer price index* (1971), 718 (1963=100).
Manufacturing (major products): Iron and steel, petroleum products, pulp and paper, chemicals, metal products.
Major Agricultural Products: Wheat, sugar beets, potatoes, corn.
Major Minerals: Copper (ranks 2d among world producers, 1970), nitrates, iron ore, coal, gold, potash.
Foreign Trade (1970): *Exports,* $1,247,000,000 (chief exports—copper; iron ore; nitrates). *Imports,* $931,000,000 (chief imports, 1969—nonelectrical machinery; food and live animals; transport equipment; chemicals). *Chief trading partners* (1969)—United States (took 17% of exports, supplied 39% of imports); United Kingdom (14%—5%); West Germany (9%—10%); Argentina (6%—10%).
Transportation: *Motor vehicles* (1970), 326,500 (automobiles, 176,700); *railroads* (1970), 6,041 miles (9,721 km); *merchant fleet* (1971), 388,000 gross registered tons; *major national airline,* LAN-CHILE (Linea Aerea Nacional).
Communications: *Telephones* (1971), 369,198; *television stations* (1971), 3; *television sets* (1971), 400,000; *radios* (1970), 1,400,000; *newspapers* (1968), 122 (daily circulation, 818,000).

The strike was settled on November 6, after Allende had named army chief Gen. Carlos Prats as minister of the interior. Both sides claimed victory and turned their energies to preparing for the congressional elections scheduled in March 1973, which were expected to decide the fate of the Allende government. The three-week strike cost the country about $200 million.

Elections and Politics. The president's supporters lost elections to fill two congressional vacancies in January, but won one in July. In April the government's candidate for rector of the University of Chile lost to a Christian Democrat. Most upsetting to the Allende forces was the strong showing made by the Christian Democrats in the May election for leaders of the United Confederation of Labor.

In preparation for the 1973 congressional elections, the Christian Democrats and other opposition factions formed a confederated party, while the Allende supporters also joined forces. With only two candidates competing for each seat, the election promised to become a clear referendum on the Allende program.

Economy. Much of the economic difficulty Chile faced in 1972 originated in the lack of foreign exchange to pay for imports. The World Bank refused to lend additional funds to Chile, which already owed it $134 million, but a group of U. S. banks lent Chile $160 million to refinance its debts until 1974, and banks and governments in China, Mexico, Brazil, the Soviet Union, Bulgaria, Peru, Colombia, and Hungary granted extensive credits and loans. Meanwhile, an agreement negotiating debts between Chile and 14 creditor nations was signed in Paris on April 20, 1972.

To slow the outflow of foreign exchange, about 75% of Chile's imports required a 10,000% prior deposit in cash. This severely limited the volume and total value of imports. It also stimulated shortages, smuggling, and the black market.

During the first nine months of 1972 the cost of living increased 99.8%. A 100% salary increase for all workers on October 1 helped alleviate the pinch, but inflation continued. As the year drew to a close, the escudo, selling at 42 to the U. S. dollar at the official rate, was selling at 150 to 180 to the U. S. dollar on the black market. A drastic decrease in tourism further deteriorated Chile's foreign exchange position.

International Relations. During 1972, Chile established diplomatic relations with North Korea, North Vietnam, Bangladesh, and the People's Republic of the Congo. In November and December, Allende made official visits to Cuba, Mexico, and the Soviet Union. Addressing the United Nations, he accused the United States of suffocating Chile financially. He also charged that the International Telephone and Telegraph Corporation (ITT) had attempted to incite civil war.

In April 1972, Chile played host to delegates from most of the world's nations attending the United Nations Conference on Trade and Development (UNCTAD).

HARRY KANTOR
Marquette University

CHILEAN WOMEN marched in January to demonstrate to the government their anger over food shortages.

CHINA

Snow removal in Peking. Men, women, and children wield shovels and brooms to clear the snow during visit of U.S. President Nixon.

China is the most populous nation in the world. Two opposing regimes lay claim to both China and Taiwan—the People's Republic of China, situated on the mainland, and the Republic of China on the island of Taiwan.

THE PEOPLE'S REPUBLIC OF CHINA

The People's Republic of China continued its stabilization efforts after the purge of Lin Piao. Chairman Mao Tse-tung remained the supreme leader, but Premier Chou En-lai assumed an increasingly important role in reorganizing the political and military establishments. Economic development was pushed forward with an emphasis on heavy industry and air transport.

Chinese foreign policy in 1972 was directed toward ending China's isolation and strengthening its position in order to deal with the Soviet threat on the northern border. President Nixon's visit to China and Japan's recognition of China paved the way for more nations to establish diplomatic relations with Peking. China championed the cause of the countries of the "third world" in their struggle against the domination of the superpowers. In these underdeveloped countries, trade became the instrument of Chinese diplomacy.

The Fate of Lin Piao. After almost a year of silence, Peking saw fit to discuss the fate of Lin Piao, former defense minister and designated political successor to Chairman Mao Tse-tung. According to Chinese statements in July, Lin Piao was killed in an air crash deep in Mongolia on Sept. 12, 1971, while fleeing from China after plotting to assassinate Mao Tse-tung and to establish a military dictatorship. Lin was now described as two-faced, a man who was in reality opposed to the revolutionary line of Mao Tse-tung and who planned to take over power by usurping the leadership of the party and the army. He was also condemned for opposing

Mao's foreign policy and attempting to flee to the Soviet Union.

Mao had used Lin Piao and his military backing to purge Liu Shao-ch'i, head of state, during the Cultural Revolution of 1966–69. But the rapid rise of Lin in both the party and the army was regarded as a threat to the power of Chairman Mao. According to Chou En-lai, Lin soon realized that he could not become Mao's successor, and so he engaged in conspiracy. Chou gave no details of Lin's plot and made no mention of the fate of Lin's wife, Yeh Ch'un, and his son Li-kuo, who were believed to have fled China with Lin in the same plane. Nor did he comment on Huang Yung-sheng, chief of staff of the Chinese armed forces; Li Tso-p'eng, political commissioner of the navy; and Ch'iu Hui-tso, head of general logistics—the three military leaders who had disappeared at the same time as Lin Piao.

Peking's statements on Lin's death were made to foreign countries; inside China there were no public announcements, although a secret document had been circulating among Communist officials in March, charging him with plotting against Mao and attempting to obtain Soviet military and diplomatic support. The fact that Peking finally broke its silence on the incident seemed to indicate that it felt the political situation was sufficiently under control.

Military Reorganization. Peking made extensive efforts to purge military leaders who had been closely associated with Lin Piao. At least 40 such persons were dismissed from the army and the government. Among the more important were Liu Hsing-yuan, chairman of the ruling Revolutionary Committee of Kwangtung Province; Lan Yi-nung, chief of Kweichow Province; and Wen Yu-ch'eng, commander of the Peking garrison.

On the other hand, Peking moved cautiously in making military replacements at the top level. While

Yeh Chien-ying, a 73-year-old former marshall, seemed to exercise general supervision over the defense ministry, no new appointments were made for the posts left vacant by Huang Yung-sheng, Li Tso-p'eng, and Ch'iu Hui-tso. Yet military men still dominated as key political figures in many provinces. And in the central government 8 of the 12 ministers had military backgrounds. Factional rivalries within the military forces remained sufficiently powerful to preclude drastic shifts in personnel.

The Leadership. With the elimination of Lin Piao, Mao Tse-tung remained the unquestioned leader of China. Chou En-lai rose to a position of power second only to Mao, gaining steadily in prestige and popularity as the country's chief administrator. But the party apparatus was badly dislocated. Of the 25 full and alternate members of the Politburo, 12 had disappeared from the political scene. In 1969 the Standing Committee of the Politburo had consisted of five members: Chairman Mao, Lin Piao, Chou En-lai, Ch'en Po-ta, and K'ang Sheng. Now only Mao and Chou were left to exercise the supreme power of issuing directives in the name of the party.

The Chinese leadership survived the crisis created by the struggle with Lin Piao, but whether the situation had been stabilized was far from certain. One of the disconcerting questions confronting the Communist party was that of the succession to Chairman Mao, who turned 79 in December 1972. No successor had been named. Presumably Chou En-lai could take over after Mao's death, but at 74, he, too, could not be expected to remain at the helm for long. Chou himself seemed to be greatly concerned over the future leadership. In an interview with American newspaper editors in October, he mentioned Yao Wen-yuan, a Shanghai party leader, as belonging to the "desired younger age bracket" for successors. But the statement was intended more as a declaration of the need for younger leaders than as a specific suggestion of who should succeed Mao. As it was, the uncertainty of succession contributed much to covert rivalry among factions that were maneuvering for the eventual struggle.

Defense Strategy. The purge of Lin Piao and his followers had no serious effects on the morale and effectiveness of China's armed forces. There was, however, a shift in defense strategy, as more emphasis was now placed on modern weapons and professionalism in the army. The Chinese were believed to have deployed 15 to 30 medium-range missiles (up to 600 miles, or 960 km) and 5 to 15 intermediate-range missiles (up to 2,000 miles, or 3,200 km). Their intercontinental missiles with a range of 3,000 miles (4,825 km) were expected to be ready for deployment by 1975.

China's defense strategy was largely designed to cope with the threat of the Soviet Union, which had concentrated over 45 ground divisions and large nuclear-war forces along the Chinese border. For some time China had deployed militia and paramilitary units along the border, hoping to draw the Soviet army deep into Chinese territory where it would be attacked by regular Chinese forces. The new policy, however, sought an immediate challenge to the Soviet army at any early stage to prevent it from penetrating into China's industrial centers. Two nuclear tests held in northwest China in 1972, in the range of 20–200 kilotons, were aimed at developing tactical weapons to be used against the Russian concentrations along the Chinese border.

Economic Development. China reported substantial economic growth in 1971 with a gain of 10% in industrial and agricultural output. Primacy was given to the development of basic industry, especially the iron and steel industry, which furnished raw material for the manufacture of much-needed machinery.

In spite of impressive advances made in nuclear and rocket technologies, Chinese industry in general remained backward in comparison with the West. China was short of capital and machinery and had to rely to a great extent on manual labor. For example, large numbers of laborers were mobilized for vast projects of irrigation and road-building that in the West would be accomplished by an extensive use of machinery.

Peking aimed at broad economic gains in 1972, the second year of its fourth five-year plan. It began to move away from the wage-equality concept and to abandon its stand against "economism"—a term formerly used to stigmatize the idea of material incentive. In the factories wages were raised for lower-paid workers to encourage better performance. Determining how much a worker should be paid now depended less on political loyalty and more on work-points accumulated.

Despite droughts reported in some areas, grain output in 1972 was expected to fall no more than

DRINKING TOASTS with visiting heads of state, Chinese Premier Chou En-lai raises his glass to U.S. President Nixon (top) and his cup of sake to Japan's Prime Minister Tanaka at banquets in Peking.

UPI

UPI

4%. A vigorous campaign was launched for greater efforts in spring plowing and sowing. Peasants were urged to organize themselves for the best use of fertilizers and production techniques so as to achieve maximum increase in agricultural output.

Somewhat to the surprise of Western demographers, Peking announced in a new atlas that China's population in 1970 was 697,260,000. Western estimates usually placed it above 800 million. The slow population growth, if true, would probably alleviate the food situation, which in the past had frequently become a serious problem.

President Nixon's Visit. On Feb. 17, 1972, President Nixon began his historic journey to the Chinese mainland. He was the first American president to visit China since its opening to the West in

---
COMMUNIST CHINA • Information Highlights

Official Name: People's Republic of China.

Area: 3,691,512 square miles (9,561,000 sq km).

Population (1970 est.): 697,260,000. *Density*, 205 per square mile (79 per sq km). *Annual rate of increase*, 1.7%.

Chief Cities (1971 est.): Peking, the capital, 7,000,000; Shanghai, 10,000,000; Tientsin, 4,000,000; Canton, 3,000,-000; Shenyang, 3,000,000.

Government: *Head of state*, Mao Tse-tung, chairman of the Chinese Communist party (took office 1935). *Head of government*, Chou En-lai, premier (took office 1949). *Legislature* (unicameral)—National People's Congress, 3,040 members. *Major political party*—Chinese Communist party.

Language: Mandarin Chinese (official).

Education: *School enrollment*—primary (1959), 90,000,000; secondary (1958), 9,990,000; technical/vocational (1958), 850,000; university/higher (1962), 820,000.

Monetary Unit: Renminbi (2.267 renminbis equal U. S.$1, June 1972).

Gross National Product (1970 est.): $119,500,000,000.

National Income per Person (1970): $145.

Economic Indexes: *Industrial production est.* (1971), 243 (1957=100).

Manufacturing (major products): Steel, trucks, cotton cloth, iron and steel, machinery, petroleum products, armaments.

Major Agricultural Products: Rice (ranks 1st among world producers, 1971), sweet potatoes and yams (world rank 1st, 1971), soybeans (world rank 2d, 1971), sorghum and millet, groundnuts (world rank 2d, 1971), tea (world rank 3d, 1971), cotton (world rank 2d, 1971), oilseeds.

Major Minerals: Coal (ranks 3d among world producers, 1970); iron ore, tungsten (world rank 1st, 1971); antimony (world rank 2d, 1970), salt, magnesite.

Foreign Trade: *Chief exports*—Agricultural products, raw materials, textiles. *Chief imports*—Food grains, chemical fertilizers and pesticides, machinery and equipment, raw materials. *Chief trading partners*—Japan, Hong Kong, West Germany, United Kingdom.

Transportation: *Railroads* (1970 est.), 21,751 miles (35,003 km); *merchant fleet* (1971), 1,022,000 gross registered tons; *major national airline*, Civil Aviation Administration.

Communications: *Television stations* (1971), 30; *television sets* (1971), 300,000; *radios* (1965), 11,500,000.

the 19th century. He was also the first president to visit a nation that had no diplomatic relations with the United States. He called his mission "a journey for peace." Though he had no illusions about resolving all differences between the two countries, he believed that peace in Asia, and in the world, depended on the ability of the great powers to live together on the same planet despite their various differences.

On the Chinese side, it was recognized that reconciliation with the United States was essential to China's global policy. The "liberation" of Taiwan, the prevention of Japan's developing into a military power, the maintenance of China's influence in Southeast Asia—all these would require some sort of understanding with the United States. Furthermore, friendship with the United States would strengthen Peking's position in countering the mounting Soviet threat on the northern border. And a presidential visit would undoubtedly enhance China's prestige not only in the eyes of its own people but also before the world.

President Nixon arrived in Peking on February 21. He was accompanied by Mrs. Nixon, Secretary of State William P. Rogers, national security adviser Henry A. Kissinger, who had arranged the visit with the Chinese, and 11 policy and administrative aides. The total American contingent numbered over 300, of whom 87 represented the press. The extensive television coverage of the journey, transmitted through satellites, gave Americans at home a most colorful presentation that at once kindled enormous American interest in China.

President Nixon was given a courteous but minimal welcome at the airport, in a manner considered proper for a chief of a state that had no diplomatic relations with the People's Republic of China. He was greeted by Premier Chou En-lai, a large number of high Chinese officials, and a 500-man military honor guard. There were no large crowds lining the streets for the welcome.

The President was, however, immediately received by Chairman Mao Tse-tung in his private study. The meeting of the two leaders was described as "frank and serious." Mao's friendly greetings, which were televised and widely broadcast, left no doubt of China's good will. Indeed, a genuinely

HISTORIC MEETING: On February 21, the day President Nixon arrived in Peking, he met with Chairman Mao at Mao's residence. On hand were (left to right) Chou En-lai; an interpreter; Chairman Mao; President Nixon; and Henry Kissinger, President Nixon's foreign affairs adviser, who had played a key role in the preparations for the presidential visit.

warm atmosphere prevailed in the magnificent banquet given by Premier Chou to the American visitors the same day. There 800 Chinese and American guests mingled, roaming from table to table to drink to the health of each other.

In his toast at the banquet, Premier Chou described the President's journey as a "positive move" opening the gates to friendly contact between the two nations. He recognized the fundamental differences between the social systems of China and the United States, but he said that these differences should not hinder the normalization of relations between them.

In response, Nixon urged that the two countries start "a long march together," not in lock step, but on different roads leading to the same goal: the goal of building a world structure of peace and justice in which all nations would determine their own form of government without outside interference or foreign domination.

The Joint Communiqué. On February 27, after a series of hard-bargaining conferences, a joint communiqué was issued by Chou and Nixon in Shanghai. It summed up their divergent views on a wide range of issues. On the Taiwan question, Peking reaffirmed its position that the People's Republic of China was the sole legal government of China, that Taiwan was a province of China, and that the "liberation" of Taiwan was an internal concern of China and that it would brook no outside interference. The United States agreed that Taiwan was part of China, but reaffirmed its interest in a peaceful settlement of the Taiwan question by the Chinese themselves. It declared that its ultimate objective was to withdraw all U. S. forces from the islands. In the meantime it would progressively reduce its forces "as the tension in the area diminishes."

On the subject of Indochina, China expressed firm support for the peoples of Vietnam, Laos, and Cambodia in their struggles there, while the United States stressed self-determination for each country in the area and envisaged the ultimate withdrawal of the U. S. forces. For Korea, China stressed unification, while the United States emphasized efforts to seek a relaxation of tension in the peninsula. China was opposed to the revival and outward expansion of "Japanese militarism," while the United

States placed the highest value on friendly relations with Tokyo.

After listing these differences, the communiqué came to the mutual agreements. The two sides agreed to broaden their contacts in the fields of science, technology, culture, sports, and journalism. They also agreed to facilitate the progressive development of trade between the two countries.

In spite of a tight schedule for official talks, President Nixon accepted Chinese invitations to a number of entertainments and sight-seeing tours. Before leaving he expressed deep appreciation for the "boundless hospitality" extended to the American visitors by the Chinese. On February 28 the presidential party left Shanghai to return to the United States.

IN THE IMPERIAL PALACE, in Peking's Forbidden City, an elderly visitor gazes through a window at some of the treasures that had belonged to China's emperors.

The Nixon journey did not result in the recognition of the Peking regime, which the Chinese leadership had desired. But it is not to be denied that the summit meeting opened up new prospects for the normalization of relations between the two countries.

Trade and Cultural Exchanges. The first large trade transaction subsequent to the Nixon visit was China's purchase in September of 10 Boeing 707 airplanes at the cost of $150 million. This was followed by purchases of American grains totalling over $50 million. The transactions at once moved U.S.-China trade to a high level, although it was too early to forecast a rapid growth of trade in the near future.

Progress was also made in cultural and scientific exchanges when in July an agreement was reached to arrange for a visit to the Chinese mainland by 22 American newspaper editors. In October, 11 Chinese medical doctors visited the United States. They were the first scientific delegation from Communist China since the Revolution of 1949.

Sino-Soviet Relations. Relations between China and the Soviet Union showed little improvement in 1972. The Kremlin displayed concern over Nixon's trip to China, for a Sino-American alignment could conceivably strengthen the Chinese position in world politics. The United States' mining of the ports of North Vietnam in May made it necessary for Soviet war supplies to Hanoi to be shipped through China. But hopes that the crisis would lead to close collaboration between the two Communist countries were not fulfilled. Peking agreed to provide massive rail facilities for shipments from the Soviet Union but refused to open China's ports to Soviet freighters.

In August the two countries renewed their polemics against each other. On the Chinese border, the Soviets added three mechanized divisions to their force, bringing it to 49 divisions. In response, Peking mustered 40 divisions along the border, in

The pictures on these pages and the lower one on page 187 are NBC News photos by Audrey Topping, shot during the filming of the NBC television documentary The Forbidden City, *produced by Lucy Jarvis. Aspects of Peking life include a fruit market* (top), *card players* (above), *and a mother and her daughter enjoying a summer stroll* (opposite page).

addition to large forces in areas not far from the frontier.

The border talks in Peking were resumed upon the return of the Soviet delegation to the Chinese capital in March, but no progress was reported. The two countries, however, signed a new trade agreement on July 3, increasing the turnover from 139 million rubles in 1971 to 232 million rubles.

Japan's Recognition of Peking. With the resignation of Premier Eisaku Sato, who had hesitated to offend Taiwan by drawing closer to Peking, Japan set about normalizing its relations with China. On September 25, Kakuei Tanaka, the new Japanese

premier, visited Peking to negotiate the establishment of diplomatic relations. A joint communiqué issued by Chou En-lai and Tanaka on September 29 outlined their agreements: Japan recognized the government of the People's Republic of China; it respected the Chinese stand that Taiwan was an inalienable part of Chinese territory; China renounced its demand for World War II indemnities from Japan. Returning to Tokyo, Tanaka said he had obtained Premier Chou's understanding that Japan would maintain trade relations with Taiwan.

Vietnam. To allay North Vietnam's misgivings concerning Nixon's visit to China, Peking reaffirmed its full support of Hanoi in the struggle against the United States. Communist China denounced the United States' mining of North Vietnamese ports and its intensive bombing near the Chinese border.

When President Nixon passed the deadline of October 31 for signing the truce agreement drafted by the United States and North Vietnam, Peking accused the U. S. government of "going back on its own words." Though China was not always in agreement with North Vietnam over tactical questions, it found it necessary to align itself with Hanoi's stand on the war.

Other Countries. Parallel with its accommodation with the United States, Peking made extensive efforts to normalize its relations with other Western nations. On March 13, China and Britain agreed to establish full diplomatic relations. Britain acknowledged that Taiwan was a province of China and closed its consular offices on Taiwan. China established diplomatic relations with Greece on June 5 and with West Germany on October 11. Australia's newly elected Labor government announced on December 5 the beginning of negotiations with China aimed at diplomatic recognition. Western foreign ministers visiting Peking during the year included France's Maurice Schumann, Canada's Mitchell F. Sharp, and Britain's Sir Alec Douglas-Home.

China's support of Pakistan was reaffirmed when President Zulfikar Ali Bhutto visited Peking in February. China agreed to turn $110 million in previous loans into grants and ship large quantities of military equipment to Pakistan.

In the Middle East, China was looking for a chance to extend its influence at the expense of the Soviet Union. It was jubilant when President Anwar el-Sadat of Egypt in August decided to expel Soviet military advisers. During the year, delegations from Syria, Yemen, Iraq, and Sudan were welcomed to Peking and were promised loans and other economic assistance.

China resumed active diplomacy in Africa during 1972. It expanded economic relations with Algeria, Ethiopia, Tanzania, and Zambia and granted loans to Burundi and Rwanda. Chinese interest in Latin America was evidenced by $100 million loan to Chile and the establishment of diplomatic relations with Peru and Argentina.

REPUBLIC OF CHINA

The new ministry under Premier Chiang Ching-kuo took drastic steps to improve administrative efficiency and to broaden the representative basis of the government. Taiwan's international status deteriorated as more and more nations recognized Peking, but steady economic progress encouraged hopes of survival.

Domestic Politics. The National Assembly, the highest legislature of Nationalist China, was convened on February 20. Its first important task was to revise the constitution so as to create new seats in the legislative bodies, whose memberships had remained unchanged since the Nationalist government moved to Taiwan in 1949. The broadening of the representative basis was deemed necessary to alleviate dissatisfaction among young people and native Taiwanese who felt they had been denied an opportunity to take part in the government.

The National Assembly voted on March 17 to add new legislators with fixed terms, while incumbents were to retain their seats indefinitely. In pursuance of this amendment, President Chiang Kai-shek decreed on June 29 that in the new election to be held in late December, 53 seats were to be added to the National Assembly and 51 seats to the Legislative Yüan, the state organ that enacts laws and approves the budget.

On March 21 the National Assembly reelected Chiang Kai-shek to his fifth six-year term as president of Nationalist China. Chiang Ching-kuo, the eldest son of Chiang Kai-shek, was appointed premier to replace C. K. Yen, who continued as vice president. To his cabinet of 18, Premier Chiang appointed 10 new ministers, of whom six were native Taiwanese. The move was viewed as a significant effort to forward cooperation between Taiwanese and mainlanders.

Foreign Relations. Taiwan expressed grave concern over U. S. efforts to improve relations with Peking. The United States had been Nationalist China's ally since the mutual security treaty of 1954; its new move was viewed by the Nationalists as a serious threat to their international position. When the Chou-Nixon communiqué was issued in February, the Nationalist press was bitter in its denunciation. In a statement of February 28, the Nationalist government declared that it would consider "null and void" any agreement involving the rights and interests of the Republic of China. In asserting that the Taiwan question could be settled only when the Nationalists recovered the mainland, Taipei practically rejected the U. S. proposal that the question be peacefully settled "by the Chinese themselves." Though the United States gave repeated assurance that it would continue to honor its defense commitments, its conception of "ultimate" withdrawal of American forces from the island cast a dark shadow on the future status of Taiwan.

Taiwan reacted angrily against Japan's recognition of the Peking regime as the sole legal government of China. In a statement of September 29, the Nationalist government denounced the Japanese move as "a perfidious action." It declared "null and void" Japan's abrogation of the 1952 peace treaty and any action that damaged Nationalist China's rights and interests.

Although strong action against Japan was urged in some quarters, the Nationalist government was cautious. It had to consider the effects on the economy, which depended so much on trade with Japan. The Nationalist government rejected retaliation and launched no boycott of Japanese products. The Nationalist embassy in Tokyo and the Japanese embassy in Taipei remained open pending arrangements for the establishment of liason offices in each country for trade and non-diplomatic purposes.

To reduce dependence on Japanese products, Taiwan took steps to divert purchases of material from Japan, which had accounted for 38% of Taiwan's total imports. The Nationalist government recommended that companies buy from American or European sources on orders exceeding $20,000. At the same time, it sought to establish contacts with Communist nations that were not "puppets" of Communist China. Taiwan began to relax restrictions on imports from Eastern Europe.

Nationalist China found it difficult to rally countries in the Asia-Pacific region to its policy of isolating Communist China. Not only did Japan recognize Peking, but such staunch anti-Communist countries as South Korea and Thailand began to adopt an "open-minded" attitude toward mainland China. Seoul spoke of maintaining a world order through dialogue rather than ideological confrontation. Thailand sent a table-tennis team to Peking. The Philippines and Malaysia were adjusting to the new situation created by the rapprochement policies of the United States and Japan. On December 22 the new governments of Australia and New Zealand extended diplomatic recognition to Peking, thus ending their ties with Nationalist China.

The Economy. It was clear that Taiwan's survival would depend on its economic development. Continued prosperity was essential not only to politica¹ unity but social stability as well. The Nationalist government therefore called for acceleration of industrial development, especially in steel, shipbuilding, machinery, and electronic industries. Attention was also given to the increase of agricultural output. Under a new agricultural program farmers were assisted to improve their productive technology, and special loans were offered by the government for the mechanization of agriculture.

Taiwan reported substantial economic progress in 1972. For the first half of the year industrial production registered a growth of 27%. Agricultural production, however, declined about 1% owing to bad weather.

Foreign trade in the first 10 months of 1972 reached $4,908 million, up 47% over the same period a year earlier, with a favorable balance of $191 million. Foreign reserves were expected to exceed $1.3 billion by the end of the year. Through hard work and self-reliance Taiwan was striving toward self-sufficiency.

CHESTER C. TAN, *New York University*

—— NATIONALIST CHINA • Information Highlights ——

Official Name: Republic of China.
Area: 13,885 square miles (35,961 sq km).
Population (1972 est.): 14,700,000. *Density,* 1,010 per square mile (390 per sq km). *Annual rate of increase,* 2.3%.
Chief Cities (1969 est.): Taipei, the capital, 1,712,100; Kaohsiung, 785,500; Tainan, 388,000.
Government: *Head of state,* Chiang Kai-shek, president (reelected for 5th 6-year term March 1972). *Head of government,* Chiang Ching-kuo, premier (took office May 1972). *Legislature* (unicameral)—Legislative Yüan, 493 members.
Languages: Mandarin Chinese (official).
Education: *Expenditure* (1969), 16.5% of total public expenditure. *School enrollment* (1969)—primary, 2,428,041; secondary, 1,028,752; technical/vocational, 155,947; university/higher, 184,215.
Monetary Unit: new Taiwan dollar (40.10 NT dollars equal U. S.$1, Sept. 1972).
Gross National Product (1971 est.): $6,080,000,000.
National Income per Person (1970): $364.
Economic Indexes: *Industrial production* (1970), 312 (1963=100); *agricultural production* (1971), 193 (1952–56=100); *consumer price index* (1971), 127 (1963=100).
Manufacturing (major products): Processed foods, electrical goods, fertilizer, petrochemicals, wood products, clothing.
Major Agricultural Products: Sweet potatoes and yams (ranks 3d among world producers, 1971), bananas, mushrooms, vegetables, tea, sugar, rice, fish.
Major Minerals: Coal, natural gas.
Foreign Trade (1971): *Exports,* $1,997,700,000 (chief exports, 1969—fruits and vegetables; textile yarn and fabrics; clothing; electrical machinery and apparatus). *Imports,* $1,844,000,000 (chief imports, 1969—nonelectrical machinery; electrical machinery, apparatus, appliances; transport equipment; cereals and preparations). *Chief trading partners* (1969)—United State (took 38% of exports, supplied 24% of imports); Japan (15%—44%); West Germany (5%—4%); Thailand (3%—2%).
Transportation: *Motor vehicles* (1970), 98,500 (automobiles, 49,500; *railroads* (1970), 629 miles (999 km); *merchant fleet* (1971), 1,322,000 gross registered tons; *major national airline,* China Airlines Limited.
Communications: *Telephones* (1971), 403,348; *television stations* (1971), 4; *television sets,* 420,000; *radios* (1969), 1,428,000.

CHOU EN-LAI. See BIOGRAPHY.

Stamford, Conn., made progress in its downtown renewal project when three 17-story residential towers (right) were completed in 1972. A model is shown above. The $200 million complex may be completed in five years.

cities and urban affairs

Both progress and reversals were recorded in the continuing fight to save U. S. cities in 1972. The prospects for improvement of urban life were enhanced by such developments as the enactment of revenue sharing and the increasing role of cable television. On the other hand, such massive urban problems as high taxes, poor housing and education, welfare, crime, congestion, and pollution still confronted city dwellers and policymakers.

Quality of Urban Life. About 67% of all Americans lived in urban areas in 1972, and many of them apparently have become increasingly restless about the quality of urban life. A year-end Gallup poll showed that only 13% of all Americans would choose to live in a city, about 33% would choose to live in a small town, 31% would prefer a suburb, and 23% would choose to live on a farm.

During 1972, local elected officials seemingly were in agreement with citizens on the problems of urban life. Almost to a man, the mayors of the major cities insisted that these cities were heading toward disaster—a decline in the quality or quantity of services, increased crime and pollution, substandard housing and education, and municipal bankruptcy. The officials contended that the only immediate solution was revenue sharing, a controversial 14-year-old plan for distributing a portion of federal income tax receipts to state and local governments, with minimal restrictions on how they spend the money.

BOSTON GOVERNMENT CENTER, nearly completed in 1972, was a successful venture in city planning. Children play in a pool, with City Hall in the background.

Revenue Sharing. In October 1972, the 92d Congress passed and President Nixon signed into law a major revenue-sharing proposal allocating $30.2 billion over a five-year period to states and localities. One third of the funds is to go to state governments, and two thirds to local governments. The major factors in determining the distribution of funds are population, poverty, and tax effort, which is the amount of taxes an individual state or local jurisdiction raised in relation to the income level of its citizens. This formula was devised not only to distribute a greater proportion of the revenue-sharing funds to low-income states and localities, but also to ensure that nearly all 50 states, 38,000 local governments, and the District of Columbia benefit from the program.

The state governments may spend the revenue-sharing funds as they wish, but Congress limited local governments to expenditures for "high-priority" purposes only. In the legislation, high-priority items are defined as law enforcement, public safety, environmental protection, public transportation, health, recreation, libraries and social services, and major capital items such as city halls, fire trucks, and school buildings.

Although the enactment of revenue sharing was a landmark for the cities, further federal action still was needed to stem the urban crisis.

Federal Welfare Reform. Perhaps one of the major disappointments of the 92d Congress, which adjourned in October 1972, was its failure to reform the federal welfare program. Such diverse groups as the Nixon administration, the Congress, state and city officials, social workers, and welfare recipients saw that the existing national welfare program was neither rational nor effective. Major reform was required so that thousands of Americans, particularly those in urban areas, would not continue to suffer under the poorly designed program.

The major issues in the welfare controversy in Congress were the amount of financial aid that a family should receive and the stipulation that all able recipients must seek work. Thus, while there was general agreement that the existing system did not work, there was little agreement on how it should be changed. At year-end the prospects for reform in the immediate future were not good.

Housing and Community Development. The Omnibus Housing and Community Development bill was another issue that the 92d Congress did not resolve. The legislation would have provided community development grants, consolidation and reform of federal housing programs, and funds to aid urban mass transit. Many experts regarded this program as essential to orderly urban development.

Water Pollution Control. While the welfare reform and the omnibus housing and community development bills languished in the 92d Congress, another extremely important program did pass. The Federal Water Pollution Control Act of 1972 authorized $18 billion for cities to construct waste treatment facilities. By 1977, all municipalities must have "secondary treatment" facilities that significantly reduce the pollution in sewage discharges into America's waters. In addition, Congress set a goal of eliminating all polluted discharges by municipal sewage treatment plants and by industry by 1985.

After Congress had set these goals, President Nixon said they would have to be delayed somewhat because the massive spending necessary to curb water pollution conflicted with his program of limiting federal expenditures to $250 billion for the fiscal year ending June 30, 1973, and that a tax increase would be required if expenditures were not held within that limit. Consequently, he would release only about 50% of the amount that Congress authorized for spending in this period.

Model Cities and Public Employment Programs. The President's action to limit expenditures will undoubtedly affect other urban programs. Two programs that have been particularly important in aiding the urban poor are the model cities and the public employment programs.

The model cities effort infused substantial federal funds into the poor sections of cities to aid the citizens of those areas. It has created jobs, supplemented education programs, upgraded housing, and accelerated community development. The public employment program was designed to alleviate unemployment, particularly in urban areas where the unemployment rate exceeded 5%. Under its provisions, the federal government has provided assistance to cities and counties to hire the unemployed and put them to work on public projects. The public employment program and the model cities program will both terminate in 1973 unless Congress extends them and the President signs the necessary legislation.

Crime. Crime continued to plague cities in 1972, and the fight against it became more controversial. Much debate was concentrated on the analysis of crime data and the validity of how the data were interpreted. Citizens were presented with reports that crime in some larger cities had decreased substantially in 1971 and that subsequent periods in 1972 showed similar trends. Also, serious crime, as defined by the Federal Bureau of Investigation, continued to rise nationally, but at a much slower rate than in the late 1960's. However, these encouraging reports gave little comfort to the residents of the cities, who were still living with the gnawing fear of crime that had grown during the previous decade. Regardless of the statistics, most Americans did not feel any safer in 1972.

For its part, the Nixon administration extensively supported crime reduction in the District of Columbia and continued funding for the Law Enforcement Assistance Administration (LEAA) in the Department of Justice. By channeling grants-in-aid funds through the states, LEAA has disseminated about $1.5 billion to local officials in charge of elements of the criminal justice system. Although some projects funded by the agency have been criticized, much of the money has gone toward the upgrading of law enforcement and criminal justice agencies.

During 1972 debates continued to rage about what can be effective in checking crime in the streets. Some authorities argued that few attempts have been made to deal with the root causes of crime. Nonetheless, measures dealing with acts of crime probably will continue to take much of the effort of those charged with the responsibility of making the cities safer places to live. See also CRIME.

The Wired City. In the spring of 1972, a "communication revolution" that may have a great impact on urban areas was given an official go-ahead. After a five-year freeze on the expansion of cable television (CATV) in the 100 largest TV markets, the Federal Communications Commission (FCC) put into effect a set of regulations that will allow CATV "to develop and demonstrate whether it really is the wave of the future," according to FCC Chairman Dean Burch. Cable television proponents predicted that CATV will revolutionize communications and related aspects of urban life because its multichannel capacity and two-way communications capability give it the ability to provide incoming and outgoing message services as well as entertainment. (See also COMPUTERS.)

Because CATV can provide families with as many as 40 TV channels, it is uniquely suited to specialized, community-oriented programming in which educational or public-service television is directed to small audiences with particular needs and interests. This programming, which is locally originated, is called cablecasting. Well over half of all CATV systems have such capabilities.

During 1972 some possible new uses of cable TV were demonstrated by several innovations:

• In Connecticut, Peter Goldmark, former head of CBS Laboratories and a prolific inventor, initiated an experiment designed to bring cultural and other big-city amenities to rural "new towns" via cable TV and thus demonstrate that population redistribution is possible from an education, social, and business point of view.

• Candidates in presidential primaries, who had found the cost of broadcast TV time prohibitive, appeared on local cable TV systems in several areas to address local voters about issues of particular importance to them.

• Cost-free public-access channels in New York City and several other cities were used effectively by educators, local theater groups, and public service organizations who hoped to improve ghetto healthcare practices and citizen and community-oriented organizations.

Although the cable TV industry has been allowed to proceed, many internal and external issues must be resolved before the revolution is realized. At the end of 1972, the most pressing problems were legal and political rather than technical.

RICHARD E. THOMPSON
President, Revenue Sharing Advisory Service, Inc.

CIVIL LIBERTIES AND CIVIL RIGHTS

In 1972 civil liberties issues were injected into the political debates of a presidential election year as Congress considered legislation concerning school busing, school prayer, and the death penalty. Army surveillance of civilians, limitations on federal habeas corpus, newsmen's testimonial privilege, and women's rights also were considered. While the congressional debates continued, with most issues remaining unresolved, the Supreme Court decided a series of controversial cases, many of which tested major Justice Department policies.

The Supreme Court's decisions failed to reflect the expected solidification of a conservative majority on the court because Justices Powell and Rehnquist joined the court too late to hear many cases. Nevertheless, the number of decisions in which the court upheld appeals based on the Bill of Rights continued to diminish. The court also decided several major cases on statutory or jurisdictional grounds, thus avoiding the necessity of ruling on a series of novel constitutional challenges. One of the most important was the decision not to rule on the allocation of the war-making power between Congress and the President. This ruling was the latest in an unbroken pattern going back to the earliest challenges to the Vietnam War.

Freedom of the Press. The judicial debate over the First Amendment rights of the press continued in 1972. The Supreme Court ruled that a newsman does not have a First Amendment privilege to refuse to answer grand jury questions relating to his confidential sources. A number of bills designed to give newsmen a statutory privilege were introduced in the House of Representatives, but no final action was taken. At the same time, an attempt to cite the Columbia Broadcasting System for contempt of Congress for refusing to reveal its source materials for the documentary *The Selling of the Pentagon* failed.

Army Surveillance. Both the court and the Congress turned their attention to Army surveillance of civilians, a practice which was claimed to inhibit the free exercise of the First Amendment rights. In Congress, Sen. Sam Ervin of North Carolina introduced legislation designed to curb this practice. The Supreme Court, meanwhile, refused to decide the constitutionality of such surveillance, ruling that the parties who had brought the case before the court had not shown sufficient personal injury to justify a ruling on their claim.

Free Expression. The Supreme Court also ruled that the attorney general's action in refusing to waive a noted foreign Marxist's ineligibility to enter the United States was valid. It held that so long as his refusal was supported by a "facially legitimate" reason, the court would not balance the interests of the government with the interests of those who wished to speak to and listen to the Marxist.

In other free-expression cases, the Supreme Court upheld Massachusetts' loyalty oath for public employees. It also ruled that procedures for recognizing campus groups at state colleges must comply with First Amendment requirements, and once again refused to rule on the validity of hair length regulations in schools.

Religion. The Supreme Court held that a Wisconsin law requiring parents to send their children to public schools until the age of 16, and penalizing the parents for any failure to do so, infringed

the religious freedom of Amish parents. Meanwhile, the candidates of both major political parties endorsed the concept of a tax credit for parents who send their children to religious schools. A proposed constitutional amendment which would permit non-denominational prayers in public schools failed to pass the Congress.

Voting Rights. In a series of cases, the Supreme Court considered challenges to state election procedures. The court held that Tennessee's one-year residency requirement for voter registration and Texas' system of filing fees for placement on the ballot in primary elections were invalid. It approved, however, an Ohio statute prohibiting a person who votes as a member of one party from becoming the candidate of another party for a 4-year period. The court also ruled that the Senate's power to judge the qualifications of its members does not preclude state recounts of election returns. Finally, by granting a stay (suspension) of the ruling of a lower court, the Supreme Court guaranteed that the challenges to the California and Illinois delegations to the Democratic National Convention would be resolved by the convention and not the courts.

Death Penalty. In a decision in which each justice rendered an opinion, the Supreme Court, by a 5–4 majority, held that the death penalty, as presently imposed, violates the Eighth and Fourteenth Amendments. A majority of the opinions indicated, however, that the court would uphold the death penalty if administered without discrimination in carefully delineated circumstances. In the House of Representatives, legislation was passed imposing the death penalty for hijacking.

Rights of Criminal Suspects. The Supreme Court also considered a series of cases dealing with the rights of criminal suspects. In two of these cases, the court ruled that neither the due process clause nor the Sixth Amendment requires unanimous decisions of juries in state non-capital criminal cases. The court also held that the right to counsel does not extend to a pre-indictment line-up.

On the other hand, the right to counsel at trial was extended to include all cases involving the possibility of imprisonment. In a case that marked a retreat from the approach of the Warren court, the Supreme Court held that for a confession to be admissible it need not be found voluntary beyond a reasonable doubt. The court also ruled that the due process clause guarantees a parolee the right to a hearing before his parole can be revoked.

Busing and Desegregation. School busing became a volatile issue both in the election campaign and on the floor of Congress. The House of Representatives passed a bill that would prohibit courts from ordering long-distance busing to desegregate schools. A filibuster in the Senate blocked further action on the bill in this congressional session although temporary legislation was passed delaying the implementation of busing orders by lower courts until appeals were exhausted. Legislation was enacted to provide federal aid to help school districts desegregate and to strengthen the enforcement power of the Equal Employment Opportunity Commission by providing for judicial enforcement of its orders. (See also EDUCATION.)

On the judicial side, the Supreme Court ruled that a city that had been part of a segregated county school system could not establish its own school system if the effect would be to impede the county's dismantling of its segregated system. However, the court held that racial discrimination by a private club with a state liquor license did not violate the Fourteenth Amendment. The court once again refused to hear claims challenging de facto segregation.

Rights of Women. The Equal Rights Amendment, which would ban all state and federal discrimination on the basis of sex, was passed by the Senate and sent to the states for ratification. Twenty-one states have already ratified the amendment, with the approval of 38 states necessary for final adoption. Congress also extended the jurisdiction of the Civil Rights Commission to include cases of sex discrimination.

Right to Privacy. In decisions that overrode Justice Department policies, the Supreme Court placed strict limits on government wiretapping. It rejected the government's contention that the executive branch has the authority to order electronic surveillance of domestic subversives and held that the President does not have a statutory or constitutional right to order such surveillance without a court order. The Supreme Court also ruled that a grand jury witness has a statutory right to refuse to answer questions based on unlawful electronic surveillance. Finally, the court extended the concept of a constitutional right to privacy, holding that a Massachusetts statute forbidding the distribution of contraceptives to unmarried persons was an invalid infringement of that right.

Rights of the Poor. In a major case involving the Aid to Families with Dependent Children (AFDC) program, the court held that Texas' method of reducing the family need level by a fixed percentage was valid even though the percentage figure was lower for AFDC than for other programs. In another case, the court ruled that a parent's absence from home because of military service was a "continued absence" which satisfied AFDC requirements.

In Congress, the "Workfare" program was passed and became effective on July 1. The new program requires physically fit AFDC recipients to register for work with state employment agencies. Failure to do so, or failure to accept an offered job, results in suspension of benefits.

Rights of Other Groups. In a case involving the rights of illegitimate children, the Supreme Court ruled invalid a Louisiana workmen's compensation statute allowing unacknowledged illegitimate children to be awarded damages for injuries to a parent only after legitimate and acknowledged illegitimate children had received theirs.

In a series of cases involving state procedures for the commitment to mental institutions of convicted criminals and persons mentally incapable of standing trial, the Supreme Court held that where such commitments were, in fact, for an indefinite period, the procedures could not differ from those used in indefinite civil commitments.

The court also dealt with academic freedom. It held that a nontenured teacher does not have the right to a hearing on the nonrenewal of his contract unless the teacher can show that the nonrenewal deprives him in some way of personal liberty or a property right.

(See also LAW.)

NORMAN DORSEN
New York University School of Law

CLEMENTE, Roberto. See SPORTS—*Baseball.*

CLEVELAND

Emerging from a quasi-somnolent business state in 1972, Cleveland, Ohio's largest city, appeared ready to burgeon in 1973. By October 1972 this major steelmaker and producer of machine tools, heavy equipment, and automobile parts saw its unemployment rate drop to a level 3.7% below the national rate. Employment in the standard metropolitan four-county area climbed to 845,100, up 5% over the previous year.

Construction. Municipal officials foresaw new building worth $500 million in the succeeding few years, much of it in the downtown area. During 1972 several large office buildings either opened or neared completion in the downtown Erieview renewal section, including Penton Plaza, the Diamond Shamrock Building, and Bond Court. Also in Erieview, Park Centre, with 1,000 apartment units and numerous shops, was scheduled to open in 1973. At the western end of Erieview, a $16 million, 550-room hotel was contracted for. Scheduled for occupancy in 1974, it was expected to be a convention hotel, adjacent to Convention Center.

Other Major construction projects underway downtown were the $91 million Cuyahoga County-Cleveland City Justice Center (encompassing courts, a jail, and a central police station), northwest of Public Square, and a long-range $75 million expansion program at Cleveland State University on Euclid Avenue at East 22nd Street. A proposed $1 billion jetport in Cleveland harbor, joined to the mainland, was to be the subject of a feasibility study in 1973. Opposition already had developed on economic and ecological grounds.

Municipal Problems. Though it appeared that some of Cleveland's troubles of the past several years were moderating, blots remained in 1972. The deficit in the municipal operating budget, listed at more than $20 million at the end of 1971, was being reduced through economies, increasing income tax revenues, and a $9.6 million loan.

Republican Mayor Ralph J. Perk, elected in 1971, created headlines in October 1972 when he criticized police performance and ordered Police Chief Gerald J. Rademaker to shake up the force. Murder flourished in Cuyahoga county at a record rate of more than one homicide a day.

The May 2 primary elections brought embarrassment to the Cuyahoga County Board of Elections as 608 voting machines proved not to be ready for use. A federal court order kept precinct polling places open an additional 5½ hours. Thirty-four precincts that had been unable to accommodate all would-be voters on May 2 were ordered opened on May 9. The board director resigned after the fiasco.

Changes. Three prominent Clevelanders left the city during 1972: Harold J. Enarson, president of Cleveland State University from its founding in 1964, was appointed head of the Ohio State University, in Columbus. Succeeding him was Walter B. Waetjen, a vice president of the University of Maryland and a former professional footballer. William E. Scheele, for 23 years director of the Cleveland Natural History Museum, went to Washington as director of the U. S. World Wildlife Foundation. Carl B. Stokes, the first black mayor of Cleveland (1967–1971), moved to New York City to become a television newscaster.

Stokes' brother, Congressman Louis Stokes, a Democrat representing Ohio's 21st district, became embroiled in dissension with other officials of the "21st District Caucus," a movement formed in 1968 in an effort to unify black political power locally and possibly nationally. Stokes split with a faction headed by Arnold Pinkney, who had been backed by the Stokes brothers in an unsuccessful mayoralty campaign in 1971.

Sports. Nick Mileti, owner of the Cleveland Cavaliers professional basketball team and the Barons hockey team, in 1972 acquired the Indians' American League baseball franchise and a new World Hockey Association team named the Crusaders.

JOHN F. HUTH, JR.
"The Plain Dealer," Cleveland

COAST GUARD

The U. S. Coast Guard, an agency of the Department of Transportation, continued in 1972 to promote maritime safety, enforce marine law, combat pollution, and further oceanographic research.

Vietnam. The Coast Guard finished withdrawing its cutters from Vietnam, turning over two high-endurance cutters to the South Vietnamese, but its merchant marine detail in Saigon continued to enforce safety laws concerning U. S. flag vessels.

Search and Rescue. The Coast Guard responded to more than 55,000 calls for assistance, saving 2,500 lives while aiding over 117,000 persons. About $1.5 billion in property was saved.

Law Enforcement. The Coast Guard continued to enforce laws governing U. S. territorial waters and international fishing agreements and worked to prevent fishing disputes involving U. S. vessels. The service continued stepped-up activity in enforcing oil pollution laws and directed improvements of design and construction for ships carrying oil and other hazardous cargoes. The Ports and Waterways Safety Act of 1972 gave the Coast Guard broad authority to protect the environment and to establish vessel traffic systems.

AIR CUSHION VEHICLES, designed for speeds of 70 knots, get a test run by the U. S. Coast Guard.

OFFICIAL U. S. COAST GUARD PHOTO

Aids to Navigation and Safety. The Coast Guard maintained over 46,000 navigation aids, including about 200 light stations, 5 lightships, 5 large navigational buoys (LNB) replacing lightships, and 65 LORAN stations.

More than 45 million people operated over 5.5 million boats in 1972. The Coast Guard sets boat construction standards and enforces boating safety laws. The Coast Guard Auxiliary's 34,000 volunteer members instructed 530,000 persons in safe boating and saved 396 lives. (See also BOATING.)

Marine Science. Oceanic, ice, and weather research was continued by the Coast Guard's International Ice Patrol, 7 polar icebreakers, and 5 Atlantic and 1 Pacific ocean stations. The Coast Guard was building a 400-foot (120-meter), 60,000 hp icebreaker, to be the world's most powerful.

Budget and Strength. The Coast Guard budget for fiscal 1972 was $727,439,000. There were 38,766 military and 6,096 civilian personnel. The Coast Guard had 283 cutters and 165 aircraft.

CHESTER R. BENDER, *Admiral, USCG*
Commandant, U. S. Coast Guard

COIN COLLECTING

A strong market in 1972 saw many coin prices rise to new highs, and several pieces reached the $100,000 level. An error at the Philadelphia mint sent collectors searching for 1972 "Double Die" Lincoln cents. Gold coins, increasingly popular with collectors in recent years, continued their activity. The same was true for world coins, with the release of many new proof sets and other issues, and with price records being set for older pieces.

New Issues. In January 1972 the U. S. Mint announced that 1,655 proof sets minted in San Francisco in 1971 inadvertently lacked the usual *S* mintmark on the nickel. Inasmuch as 3,224,138 regular proof sets with the *S* mintmark on all coins were minted in 1971, the *S*-less nickel sets are very rare by comparison. By the end of 1972 these were trading for $500 to $600 per set, compared with about $5 for a regular 1971 set.

Eisenhower dollars were produced at the Denver, Philadelphia, and San Francisco mints in 1972, but the demand and mintage were less than they had been for 1971, the first year of this design. In 1971, 4,252,279 Eisenhower dollars in silver, as opposed to the regular issues in clad metal, were minted in proof at San Francisco for collectors. Collectors complained that the $10 issue price for each coin was too high. The coins fell in value from the issue price and became available for less than $10 each. Consequently, orders for 1972 proof dollars fell off, and less than half the 1971 total was minted.

The 1972 "Double Die" cent, with sharply doubled letters on the obverse, was discovered in July. In August the Philadelphia mint estimated that 20,000 to 100,000 of these error coins had been minted. The price of this cent rose to nearly $100 but by year's end subsided to about $70 per coin.

Controversy surrounded plans for the bicentennial of the American Revolution in 1976, with various arguments heard for and against issuing commemorative coins, medals, and other numismatic items. In September the Bicentennial Commission announced that 940,000 philatelic-numismatic covers —specially-stamped envelopes containing medals with themes relating to the American Revolution— had been sold.

LONDON DAILY EXPRESS

COINS SALVAGED from wreck of 18th century Dutch ship include Spanish dollar (top) and piece of eight.

The 25th wedding anniversary of Queen Elizabeth II and Prince Philip was commemorated in England by a crown (dollar-size coin) and by other coins in some other Commonwealth countries.

Old Issues. In November the General Services Administration began accepting bids, with a minimum of $30 per coin, on hundreds of thousands of 1882-CC, 1883-CC, and 1884-CC silver dollars minted in Carson City, Nev., and subsequently stored in Treasury vaults. The original government prospectus noted that these dollars were a "sound investment," but failed to disclose that their current market values—in the $30 to $40 range per coin— would be affected by the tremendous number to be sold by the government, nor was the extent of the government holding revealed to the general public in the offering. This caused much criticism.

The market for rare coins was strong, and at least three U. S. coins with price tags of $100,000 each found new buyers. These were a 1913 Liberty nickel and an 1804 silver dollar offered by a dealer, A. Kosoff, and purchased by World Wide Numismatics, Inc., and a specimen of the 1907 Extremely High Relief $20 gold piece, sold by Bowers and Ruddy Galleries, Inc., to a private collector. Auction and private sale records for other items set new highs in many series.

The market for world coins was strong, reflecting the growth of the hobby in Germany, Japan, and elsewhere. In November an auction in Zürich, Switzerland, featured coins sold by New York's Metropolitan Museum of Art as part of the disposition of its numismatic holdings over the next several years. The coins, all of the ancient gold series, realized record prices.

Q. DAVID BOWERS
Author of "Coins and Collectors"

COLLEGES. See EDUCATION; UNIVERSITIES.

COLOMBIA

The Liberal and Conservative parties remained the dominant political forces in Colombia in 1972. But the year marked the beginning of the end for the National Front arrangement, under which Liberals and Conservatives have alternated in the presidential office every four years since 1958. The April elections for municipal councils and departmental (state) assemblies were the first elections in 14 years in which voters were free to choose between Liberals and Conservatives without regard to the compromise formulas that had previously governed the operation of the Colombian political system.

Political Affairs. The April 16 elections were, in fact, another test of strength between the National Front coalition (Liberals and Conservatives) and the National Popular Alliance (ANAPO), the party of former dictator Gustavo Rojas Pinilla. Rojas, running on a populist platform, had been narrowly defeated for the presidency in 1970 by the coalition. In the 1972 elections the National Front won a resounding victory over ANAPO, regaining control of practically all of the municipal councils and departmental assemblies.

Detracting from what otherwise might be regarded as a decisive victory for the coalition was the fact that less than 30% of those Colombians eligible to vote actually voted. Those who voted favored the forces of the National Front. The combined vote for Liberal and Conservative candidates was about 1,500,000, compared to only 400,000 for ANAPO. The Liberal party showed that it was the majority party within the National Front, with about a 240,000-vote edge over the Conservatives.

Both the Liberals and Conservatives suffered early in the year from splits within their ranks, but these were papered over in time to present a united front for the elections. It is probable that such divisions, often due to personality clashes, will reappear for the 1974 presidential election.

On the Liberal side, the split was between those who adhered to the leadership of Julio César Turbay Ayala and those who proclaimed the dual leadership of former President Carlos Lleras Restrepo and Alfonso López Michelsen. An interesting aspect of Liberal politics in 1972 was the return to the political arena of Alberto Lleras Camargo, the first president under the National Front formula. Lleras Camargo is still widely popular in Colombia and is regarded as something of an elder statesman. On the Conservative side, the two major candidates to emerge were Alvaro Gómez Hurtado and Belisario Betancur.

Many believed that if the two old-line parties cannot maintain a united front in the 1974 elections, ANAPO will have a good chance to capture the presidency. At the end of 1972 the united front put together for the April elections still existed, and Carlos Lleras Restrepo appeared to be emerging as the strongest contender for the presidency in 1974.

Economy. The difficult task that Colombian policy-makers faced in 1972 was that of returning to higher growth levels and at the same time dampening inflation and maintaining balance-of-payments strength. Growth rates in 1971 had experienced a downturn compared with 1968–70 levels, and although 1972 showed some increase in growth, performance was still below the earlier levels. Inflationary pressures continued strong during the year, but Colombia improved its balance of trade.

─────── COLOMBIA · Information Highlights ───────

Official Name: Republic of Colombia.
Area: 439,736 square miles (1,138,914 sq km).
Population (1972 est.): 22,900,000. *Density,* 49 per square mile (19 per sq km). *Annual rate of increase,* 3.4%.
Chief Cities (1968 est.): Bogotá, the capital, 2,148,000; Medellín, 913,000; Cali, 772,000; Barranquilla, 590,300.
Government: *Head of state,* Misael Pastrana Borrero, president (took office Aug. 1970). *Head of government,* Misael Pastrana Borrero. *Legislature*—Congress: Senate, 118 members; House of Representatives, 210 members. *Major political parties*—Conservative party; Liberal party; National Popular Alliance (ANAPO).
Language: Spanish (official).
Education: *Expenditure* (1969), 12.7% of total public expenditure. *School enrollment* (1968)—primary, 2,733,432; secondary, 654,066; technical/vocational, 191,573; university/higher, 61,359.
Monetary Unit: Peso (21.98 pesos equal U. S.$1, June 1972).
Gross National Product (1971 est.): $6,975,000,000.
National Income per Person (1970): $358.
Economic Indexes: *Industrial production* (1969), 139 (1963=100); *agricultural production* (1971), 172 (1952–56=100); *consumer price index* (1971), 214 (1963=100).
Manufacturing (major products): Textiles, beverages, iron and steel, petroleum products, cement, processed foods.
Major Agricultural Products: Coffee (ranks 2d among world producers, 1971), bananas, cotton, sugar, tobacco, rice.
Major Minerals: Petroleum, iron ore, gold, coal.
Foreign Trade (1970): *Exports,* $724,000,000 (chief exports—coffee; petroleum). *Imports,* $844,000,000 (chief imports, 1968—nonelectrical machinery; chemicals, transport equipment; electrical machinery, apparatus, appliances). *Chief trading partners* (1969)—United States (took 42% of exports, supplied 50% of imports); West Germany (13%–9%); Spain (4%–6%); Britain (4%–5%).
Tourism: *Receipts* (1970), $33,900,000.
Transportation: *Motor vehicles* (1969), 285,500 (automobiles, 150,500); *railroads* (1970), 2,125 miles (3,420 km); *merchant fleet* (1971), 209,000 gross registered tons; *major national airline,* AVIANCA (Aerovías Nacionales de Colombia).
Communications: *Telephones* (1971), 974,415; *television stations* (1971), 14; *television sets* (1971), 600,000; *newspapers* (1967), 25 (daily circulation, 1,021,000).

The Consultative Group on Colombia, sponsored by the World Bank, announced during the year that it was making available over $400 million in new official assistance to the country. This strong expression of international support for Colombia contributed to a healthy balance of payments for 1972. A modest increase in the price of coffee, Colombia's major export, coupled with a substantial rise in other exports, also considerably aided Colombia's international financial position.

Foreign Affairs. Colombian Foreign Minister Alfredo Vasquez Carrizosa formally proposed a solution to the problem of territorial sea limits, which has been vexing relations between the United States and several Latin American nations. According to the Colombian formula, a 12-mile (19-km) limit to the territorial sea would be established, with nations having certain additional rights up to a limit of 200 miles (320 km). Other Latin American nations reacted favorably to the proposal, but none immediately adopted the Colombian formula.

ERNEST A. DUFF
Randolph-Macon Woman's College

COLORADO

A desire to control or limit the state's booming growth of the past two decades emerged during 1972 as a potent force in Colorado. It was evident in an anti-Olympics movement, in politics, and in the state legislature.

Legislation. The 1972 General Assembly spent more time in session (152 days) and appropriated more money ($1.2 billion) than any previous legislature in the state's history. Despite strong lobbying efforts by land developers, it passed laws giving the state new authority to deny drilling permits for small household wells and requiring counties

to consider the developers' plans for providing water and sewage disposal before approving new subdivisions.

The list of legislative accomplishments was shortened by an overriding concern with reapportionment of legislative and congressional districts. The state constitution requires redistricting every 10 years, and population increases shown by the 1970 census required the state to add a fifth congressional district.

Politics. Two congressional veterans were defeated by Colorado voters. U. S. Rep. Wayne Aspinall, chairman of the House Interior Committee and a 24-year veteran, lost in the Democratic primary. Republican Gordon Allott, a U. S. senator for 18 years, lost to Democrat Floyd Haskell in the general election. In each case opposition from environmentalists was judged to be a factor.

The Colorado Labor Council was the first state federation to defy the national AFL-CIO's demand for neutrality in the 1972 presidential race. George Meany, national AFL-CIO president, tried to remove its officers and charter after the Colorado group refused to rescind its endorsement of Sen. George McGovern. However, a federal district court order prevented Meany's attempted take-over.

In the November elections a relative unknown, Floyd E. Haskell, scored a surprising victory over Republican Sen. Gordon Allott, a three-term incumbent, in the U. S. Senate race. Haskell, a former Republican state representative, had switched to the Democratic party two years earlier. President Nixon carried the state easily with 63% of the vote.

--------- **COLORADO · Information Highlights** ---------

Area: 104,247 square miles (270,000 sq km).
Population (1970 census): 2,207,259. *Density:* 22 per sq mi.
Chief Cities (1970 census): Denver, the capital, 514,678; Colorado Springs, 135,060; Pueblo, 97,453; Lakewood, 92,787; Aurora, 74,974; Boulder, 66,870; Arvada, 46,814.
Government (1972): *Chief Officers*—governor, John A. Lore (R); lt. gov., John D. Vanderhoof (R); secy. of state, Byron A. Anderson (R); atty. gen., Duke W. Dunbar (R); treas., Palmer Burch (R); chief justice, Edward E. Pringle. *General Assembly*—Senate, 35 members (21 Republicans, 14 Democrats); House of Representatives, 65 members (38 R, 27 D).
Education (1971–72): *Enrollment*—public elementary schools, 309,602 pupils; 12,016 teachers; public secondary, 254,900 pupils; 12,458 teachers; nonpublic schools (1970–71), 35,568 pupils; 1,850 teachers; college and university, 122,-000 students. *Public school expenditures,* $469,599,000 ($905 per pupil). *Average teacher's salary,* $9,655.
State Finances (fiscal year 1970): *Revenues,* $956,014,000 (3% general sales tax and gross receipts taxes, $137,768,000; motor fuel tax, $71,801,000; federal funds, $244,505,000). *Expenditures,* $885,423,000 (education, $391,339,000; health, welfare, and safety, $66,548,000; highways, $139,-482,000). *State debt,* $124,352,000 (June 30, 1970).
Personal Income (1971): $9,263,000,000; per capita, $4,057.
Public Assistance (1971): $174,990,000. *Average monthly payments* (Dec. 1971)—old-age assistance, $75.06; aid to families with dependent children, $177.17.
Labor Force: *Nonagricultural wage and salary earners* (July 1972), 810,900. *Average annual employment* (1971)—manufacturing, 118,000; trade, 181,000; government, 187,000; services, 135,000. *Insured unemployed* (Aug. 1971)—5,700.
Manufacturing (1969): *Value added by manufacture,* $1,880,-400,000. Food and kindred products, $394,800,000; nonelectrical machinery, $233,300,000; printing and publishing, $142,600,000; rubber and plastic products, $133,500,-000; electrical equipment and supplies, $115,100,000; stone, clay, and glass products, $93,100,000.
Agriculture (1970): *Cash farm income,* $1,282,593,000 (livestock, $951,278,000; crops, $263,280,000; government payments, $68,035,000). *Chief crops* (in order of value, 1971) —Hay, wheat, corn, sugar beets (ranks 3d among the states).
Mining (1970): *Production value,* $401,750,000 (ranks 18th among the states). *Chief minerals*—Molybdenum, $118,-286,000; petroleum, $81,441,000; coal, $33,800,000.
Transportation: *Roads* (1971), 82,315 miles (132,470 km); *motor vehicles* (1971), 1,442,478; *railroads* (1971), 3,576 miles (5,755 km); *public airports* (1972), 74.
Communications: *Telephones* (1971), 1,468,400; *television stations* (1971), 11; *radio stations* (1971), 94; *newspapers* (1972), 26 (daily circulation, 727,000).

Environment. Denver's selection as the host city for the 1976 Winter Olympic Games stirred up an anti-Olympics movement among Coloradans who feared the unwanted growth and the environmental damage that the event might cause. In the November elections, voters approved amendments on the Denver and state ballots to prohibit the use of tax revenues for the Games.

Denver voters in July defeated a $200 million revenue bond issue to develop new water sources in western Colorado to serve Denver. Since only newcomers would have to pay for the new water, the vote was interpreted as antigrowth sentiment.

Improvements. Despite their rejection of the water bonds, Denverites were not opposed to spending tax money for civic improvements. They approved $87.6 million in general obligation bonds for projects ranging from sewer improvements and city shops to a sports arena and performing arts center.

The Johns-Manville Corp. moved its headquarters from Manhattan to a ranch south of Denver. Its sales, in excess of $600 million a year, made it the largest corporation in the state.

Transportation. The first of the twin bores of the nation's longest tunnel (8,941 feet)—Straight Creek Tunnel on Interstate Highway 70—was holed through in July, 11,000 feet up in the Rockies. The first bore was expected to be ready for traffic by the spring of 1973.

FRED BROWN, *The Denver "Post"*

COMMONWEALTH OF NATIONS

In 1972 the Commonwealth had two changes in membership and was concerned with international monetary reform and other economic matters.

Commonwealth Membership. Two changes in membership in the Commonwealth in 1972 resulted from the creation of the new nation of Bangladesh (formerly East Pakistan). Because Britain, Australia, and New Zealand intended to recognize Bangladesh, Pakistan announced, on January 30, that it would leave the Commonwealth. Bangladesh, whose independence was recognized by Britain on February 4 and by the United States on April 4, joined the Commonwealth April 18, with the agreement of the other members.

A new republican constitution for Ceylon, which took the name "Sri Lanka," went into effect May 22. The same day, Arnold Smith, Commonwealth secretary-general, on behalf of the other Commonwealth governments, welcomed Sri Lanka's continued membership in the Commonwealth.

Aid to Commonwealth Territories. Under the Colombo Plan, total expenditure for technical assistance during 1970 was $154.6 million. The cumulative total from the inception of the plan in 1951 to 1970 was $1,523.6 million. The number of new places for students and trainees arranged in 1970 was 7,033, of which 2,976 were provided by the United States. The total since 1951 was 72,577.

New investments in 1971 of the Commonwealth Development Corporation (financed by Britain) totaled £29.05 million, an increase of 54% over £18.87 million reported for 1970. Total investment commitments by the end of 1971 were £190.2 million, of which £151 million was already invested. Of the total, 40% was in Africa. In 1971, 28 new projects were started, making a total of 210.

By March 31, 1972, investments of the Commonwealth Development Finance Company (a pri-

COMMONWEALTH OF NATIONS

Component	Area (sq mi)	Pop. (mid-1971 estimate)	Status
EUROPE			
Great Britain & islands of British seas[1]	94,528	55,900,000	Sovereign state
Gibraltar	2	27,000	Dependent territory
Malta	122	325,000	Sovereign state
Total in Europe	94,652	56,252,000	
AFRICA			
Botswana	231,804	668,000	Sovereign state
British Indian Ocean Territory	30	2,000	Dependent territory
Gambia	4,361	375,000	Sovereign state
Ghana	92,099	8,858,000	Sovereign state
Kenya	224,959	11,694,000	Sovereign state
Lesotho	11,720	935,000	Sovereign state
Malawi	45,747	4,549,000	Sovereign state
Mauritius (and dependencies)	809	836,000	Sovereign state
Nigeria	356,668	56,510,000	Sovereign state
Rhodesia	150,803	5,500,000	Internally self-governing colony[2]
St. Helena	47	5,000	Dependent territory
Ascension	34	1,000	
Tristan da Cunha	40	1,000	
Other islands	41	......	
Seychelles	145	53,000	Dependent territory
Sierra Leone	27,700	2,600,000	Sovereign state
Swaziland	6,704	421,000	Sovereign state
Tanzania	364,899	13,634,000	Sovereign state
Uganda	91,134	10,127,000	Sovereign state
Zambia	290,585	4,275,000	Sovereign state
Total in Africa	1,900,329	121,044,000	
AMERICA			
Antigua	171	60,000	West Indies Associated state
Bahamas	5,380	185,000	Dependent territory
Barbados	166	239,000	Sovereign state
Bermuda	20	54,000	Dependent territory
British Honduras (Belize)	8,867	124,000	Dependent territory
British Virgin Islands	59	11,000	Dependent territory
Canada	3,851,809	21,786,000	Sovereign state
Cayman Islands	100	10,000	Dependent territory
Dominica	290	72,000	West Indies Associated state
Falkland Islands (and dependencies)	6,198	3,000	Dependent territory
Grenada	133	96,000	West Indies Associated state
Guyana	83,000	736,000	Sovereign state
Jamaica	4,232	1,897,000	Sovereign state
Montserrat	38	12,000	Dependent territory
St. Kitts-Nevis-Anguilla	138	62,000	West Indies Associated state
St. Lucia	238	103,000	West Indies Associated state
St. Vincent	150	90,000	West Indies Associated state
Trinidad and Tobago	1,980	1,030,000	Sovereign state
Turks and Caicos	166	6,000	Dependent territory
Total in America	3,963,135	26,576,000	
ASIA			
Bangladesh	55,126	79,000,000	Sovereign state
Brunei	2,226	135,000	Internally self-governing sultanate
Ceylon (Sri Lanka)	25,332	12,669,000	Sovereign state
Cyprus	3,572	639,000	Sovereign state
Hong Kong	399	4,045,000	Dependent territory
India	1,261,813	550,400,000	Sovereign state
Malaysia	128,430	12,324,000	Sovereign state
Singapore	224	2,110,000	Sovereign state
Total in Asia	1,477,122	661,322,000	
OCEANIA			
Australia	2,967,910	12,728,000	Sovereign state
Christmas Island	52	3,000	External territory
Cocos Island	5	1,000	External territory
New Guinea Territory	92,160	1,790,000	Trusteeship
Norfolk Island	14	2,000	External territory
Papua	86,100	691,000	External territory
Fiji	7,055	531,000	Sovereign state
Nauru[3]	8	7,000	Sovereign state
New Hebrides	5,700	84,000	Anglo-French condominium
New Zealand	103,736	2,853,000	Sovereign state
Niue Island	100	5,000	Dependency
Tokelau Islands	4	2,000	Dependency
Pitcairn Island	2	82	British dependent territory
Tonga	270	90,000	Sovereign state
Western Pacific Islands: British Solomon Islands Protectorate	11,500	166,000	Dependent territory
Gilbert and Ellice Islands	342	57,000	Dependent territory
Western Samoa	1,097	143,000	Sovereign state
Total in Oceania	3,276,055	19,153,000	
Grand Total	10,711,293	884,347,000	

[1] Includes Northern Ireland, Channel Islands, and Isle of Man.
[2] Rhodesia declared its independence Nov. 11, 1965, but technically retains Commonwealth status. [3] Nauru is a special member.

UPI

ON COMMONWEALTH TOUR in early 1972, Queen Elizabeth II, Prince Philip, and Princess Anne ride with sultan of Brunei in gilded chariot drawn by soldiers.

vate corporation owned by businesses based in the Commonwealth) amounted to £30.1 million. New 1972 commitments totaled £5.7 million in 15 countries. The company's loss (1971–72) was £170,008.

Meetings. At a meeting of Commonwealth finance ministers in London on September 21 and 22, the dominating theme was international monetary reform. Also discussed were problems arising from the devaluation of the dollar, the floating of the pound sterling, and the phasing out of the pound as a reserve currency.

Representatives of Commonwealth governments discussed relations with the European Economic Community in April and July. The second Commonwealth conference on human ecology met at Singapore (April 25–28). A Commonwealth press union conference met in London (May 31–June 1), as did the 25th congress of the federation of Commonwealth chambers of commerce (June 6–9).

Visits. Queen Elizabeth and the Duke of Edinburgh toured Thailand, Singapore, Malaysia, Brunei, the Maldive Islands, the Seychelles, and Mauritius (February 8–March 26). Princess Margaret visited the British Virgin Islands (March 7–9) in connection with their celebration of the tercentenary of British rule. Sir Alec Douglas-Home, foreign and Commonwealth secretary, visited India (February 5–7), Hong Kong (February 13–15), and Bangladesh, Australia, and New Zealand (beginning June 22).

RICHARD E. WEBB
Former Director, Reference and Library Division
British Information Services, New York

COMMUNICATIONS. See POSTAL SERVICE; TELECOMMUNICATIONS; TELEVISION AND RADIO.

Soviet participants in a Warsaw Treaty committee meeting in Prague were (seated, from left) Konstantin Katushev, Leonid Brezhnev, and Aleksei Kosygin.

COMMUNISM

The world Communist movement continued to be deeply divided during 1972. The 14-year-old Sino-Soviet dispute presented Communist parties everywhere with the problem of which side to support. Of the 89 known Communist parties, only 35 supported the Soviet Union while a mere six backed Communist China. As many as 34 parties had split into pro-Moscow and pro-Peking factions, some of which had developed into separate political organizations. At least 11 parties remained neutral in the controversy, with the number of neutrals increasing. Clearly neither the USSR nor China controlled the fragmented international Communist movement.

Despite all this dissension, world Communist party membership by 1972 had increased by about 500,000 over 1971, to a total of 47 million. Of this total, 94% resided in Communist-ruled countries, in which most of the increase occurred. Smaller gains were recorded in Europe, Asia, and Latin America. African membership declined.

USSR and China. The Soviet Union and Communist China in 1972 continued to wage their war of words, each accusing the other of being un-Marxist, un-Leninist, imperialist, fascist, militaristic, racist, expansionist, and brutal toward national minorities. The Soviet press also alleged that China tried to incite colored nations against white nations,

opposed nuclear and world disarmament, illegally exported opium to the United States, and was sacrificing southeast Asia for the sake of U. S.-Chinese friendship. China retorted that the Soviet government was restoring capitalism within the USSR, betraying Communist world revolution, and threatening the Chinese with nuclear weapons, and that it was illegally occupying 575,000 square miles (1,500,000 sq km) of former Chinese territory. China also charged that the USSR was striving for naval domination of the Indian and west Pacific oceans, and that it was seeking world hegemony jointly with the United States.

Neither China nor the USSR reported any skirmishes along their 2,000-mile (3,200-km) common border during 1972, but negotiations to delimit the frontier more precisely were bogged down throughout the year. China also refused a Soviet offer to conclude a Sino-Soviet nonaggression pact.

Eastern Europe. Total Communist party membership in the Communist-ruled countries of Eastern Europe in 1972 increased by about 200,000, principally as a result of a large expansion of the Rumanian party. As before, these countries remained divided in their attitude toward the Sino-Soviet dispute. Bulgaria, Czechoslovakia, East Germany, Hungary, and Poland supported the USSR, while

Albania backed Communist China, and Rumania and Yugoslavia stayed neutral.

From February through September, Soviet troops conducted joint maneuvers with forces from other Warsaw Pact countries (Bulgaria, Czechoslovakia, East Germany, Hungary, Poland, and Rumania) in Bulgaria, Czechoslovakia, East Germany, and Poland. Rumania refused to permit Warsaw Pact joint maneuvers on its territory, but sent troops to participate in the war games on Bulgarian soil and allowed Rumanian ships to take part in Black Sea joint naval exercises.

On February 24 the Hungarian-Rumanian military alliance was renewed for another 20 years, and on May 12 the East German-Rumanian alliance was extended for a similar period.

CMEA (the Council for Mutual Economic Assistance), which is the Communist common market consisting of Bulgaria, Cuba, Czechoslovakia, East Germany, Hungary, Poland, Rumania, Mongolia, and the USSR, was more active in 1972 than the year before. CMEA's International Investment Bank had issued development loans to various East European members, the main recipients being Czechoslovakia, Hungary, and Rumania. These loans were largely for railway modernization and for increased production of trucks, buses, and railway cars in order to improve communications among East European countries.

In 1972 CMEA also sponsored a Soviet-Rumanian agreement for Rumania to help mine iron, asbestos, and other minerals in the USSR, with Rumania receiving part of the mineral production. At a CMEA meeting in July, it was decided that Bulgaria, Hungary, East Germany, Poland, and Rumania would aid the construction of pulp mills in the USSR, with the pulp production to be divided among all six countries. Despite these multinational projects, the Polish press complained that most CMEA activity consists of bilateral trade and services between pairs of CMEA member countries.

In 1972 the highest Soviet decoration, the Order of Lenin, was bestowed on Yugoslav President Tito on his 80th birthday and on Hungarian first party secretary Janos Kadar and East German first party secretary Erich Honecker on their 60th birthdays.

On February 3 the Soviet newspaper *Pravda* made an unusual criticism of the Hungarian people, accusing them of "anti-communism, anti-Sovietism, and nationalism." As if in confirmation, on March 15, thousands of Hungarian students in Budapest held a nationalistic demonstration, which was stopped only by the arrest of several hundred demonstrators. Later that month, Hungarian Premier Jeno Fock complained in a press interview that the USSR had refused to commit itself to long-term deliveries of Soviet raw materials in the amounts needed by Hungarian industry.

Western Europe. The largest aggregation of Communist party members outside of the Communist-controlled nations was to be found in non-Communist Europe in 1972. Here resided some 2 million Communists, three fourths of whom were concentrated in Italy and one seventh in France.

Only seven Communist parties in non-Communist Europe firmly supported the USSR in the Sino-Soviet dispute. Eleven others (in Austria, Belgium, Finland, France, West Germany, Greece, Italy, Portugal, Spain, Sweden, and Switzerland) were divided into pro-Moscow and pro-Peking factions, while the Dutch and Norwegian parties were neutral.

WORLD COMMUNIST MEMBERSHIP, 1972

Country	Membership	Country	Membership
Africa		**Hungary**	693,000
Algeria*	400	Iceland	1,500
Morocco*	300	Ireland	300
Nigeria*	1,000	Italy	1,521,000
Réunion	500	Luxembourg	500
South Africa*	100	Malta	100
Sudan*	4,800	Netherlands	10,000
Tunisia*	100	Norway	2,250
Asia and Oceania		Poland	2,270,000
Afghanistan	400	Portugal*	2,000
Australia	3,900	Rumania	2,175,000
Ceylon	4,000	Spain*	5,000
China, Communist	17,000,000	Sweden	17,000
India	162,000	Switzerland	3,500
Iran*	500	United Kingdom	29,000
Iraq*	2,000	Yugoslavia	1,049,000
Israel	2,000	**North America**	
Japan	300,000	Canada	2,000
Jordan*	500	Costa Rica*	1,000
Korea, North	1,600,000	Cuba	125,000
Laos	13,000	Dominican Republic*	1,400
Lebanon	1,500	El Salvador*	100
Malaysia*	2,000	Guadeloupe	2,000
Mongolia	58,000	Guatemala*	750
Nepal*	10,000	Honduras*	300
New Zealand	300	Martinique	1,000
Pakistan*	1,750	Mexico	5,000
Philippines*	1,850	Nicaragua*	100
Singapore*	200	Panama*	250
Syria*	3,000	United States	16,500
Thailand*	1,000	**South America**	
Turkey*	1,250	Argentina*	60,000
Vietnam, North	1,100,000	Bolivia*	2,800
Europe		Brazil*	13,000
Albania	87,000	Chile	90,000
Austria	25,000	Colombia	11,000
Belgium	12,500	Ecuador*	1,200
Bulgaria	700,000	Guyana	100
Cyprus	13,000	Paraguay*	4,500
Czechoslovakia	1,200,000	Peru	3,200
Denmark	5,000	Uruguay	20,000
Finland	50,000	Venezuela	8,000
France	275,000	**USSR**	
Germany, East	1,909,800	USSR	14,500,000
Germany, West*	39,400		
Greece*	28,000		

* Countries in which the Communist party is illegal. (Source: U.S. Department of State.)

In the Italian parliamentary elections in May, the Italian Communist party won 27.4% of the total popular vote, but was still unable to obtain any ministerial posts in the governmental cabinet. In June the French Communist and Socialist parties formed a united front by adopting a common election program for future elections.

Regardless of their attitudes toward the Sino-Soviet dispute, all of the West European Communist parties propagandized for withdrawal of all U. S. forces from Europe, as well as for the dissolution of NATO and of the European Common Market. They also advocated foreign diplomatic recognition of East Germany, independence of Cyprus from Greece, annexation of Ulster by Ireland, and the overthrow of the Greek, Spanish, and Portuguese dictatorial governments.

Far East. Membership in the Communist parties of non-Communist Asia in 1972 totaled about 551,000, of whom more than half belonged to the large Japanese party and almost one third to the three Communist parties of India. Communist party membership in free Asia increased slightly in 1972, with most of the gain occurring in India.

In the Sino-Soviet controversy during 1972, the USSR was solidly supported by only four Asian Communist parties, those of Afghanistan, Iran, Mongolia, and Turkey. China was fully backed by only five of the other Asian parties, those of Burma, Cambodia, Malaysia, Singapore, and Thailand. In the last three, most of the members were the descendants of Chinese immigrants. Maintaining neutrality toward the Sino-Soviet dispute were the Communist parties of Japan, Laos, North Korea, and

North Vietnam. All of the remaining parties in Asia were badly split over the question, as was also the case with the parties of Australia and New Zealand.

The Indian Communist movement in 1972 was divided into three separate parties: the pro-Soviet Communist party of India (CPI), the pro-Chinese Commuist party of India—Marxist (CPI–M), and the terrorist Communist party of India—Marxist Leninist (CPI–ML), which was also pro-Peking. In the elections to India's state legislatures, held in March, the CPI won only 4% of the legislative seats and the CPI–M obtained only 1%, while the CPI–ML did not participate.

In April, Premier Kim Il Sung of North Korea was awarded the Order of Lenin by the USSR in honor of his 60th birthday.

In Indochina in 1972 the Communist-led troops and guerrillas of North Vietnam, the Vietcong, and Pathet Lao were still stalemated in their attempts to conquer all of Cambodia, Laos, and South Vietnam. Aided by arms from China, Communist-led guerrillas were also fighting against the legal governments in remote areas of Burma, Thailand, and the Philippines, with the guerrillas achieving little success. During the summer the Indonesian government arrested several army officers and about 150 civilians for allegedly being underground Communist agents.

Despite varying attitudes toward the Sino-Soviet dispute, all Far Eastern Communist parties in 1972 again demanded the withdrawal of United States military forces from southeast Asia, cessation of United States support for Indochinese non-Communist governments, and the dissolution of the Southeast Asian Treaty Organization (SEATO). They also pressed for the freeing of New Guinea from Australian rule, for an end to U. S. arms aid to Taiwan, and for abolition of U. S. military bases in Japan, South Korea, Taiwan, the Philippines, South Vietnam, and Thailand.

Middle East. The propaganda of Middle Eastern Communist parties in 1972 supported Arab unity, the Palestine guerrilla movement, Arab friendship with the USSR and Communist East Europe, and nationalization of Western-owned oil fields, pipelines, and refineries in Arab territories. The parties also opposed Western arming of Israel, the United States naval buildup in the Indian Ocean, and Israeli occupation of Arab territories.

In March a Syrian "Progressive National Front" was formed, consisting of the Syrian Communist party and several socialist political organizations. The front was headed by the president of Syria. Ironically, the Communist party remained an illegal organization in Syria, though it had become a part of the ruling coalition.

Africa. In most African countries in 1972 there were no Communist parties as such, only individual Communists, whose Marxism was less popular than the widespread ideologies of African socialism and African nationalism. There were thought to be less than 9,000 Communists in all of Africa (including Egypt) in 1972. The decline in membership was thought to have been caused by the heavy governmental suppression of the large Sudanese party, which had attempted to seize power in 1971.

Of the few African Communist parties existing in 1972, those of Algeria, Nigeria, South Africa, the Sudan, and Tunisia supported the USSR in the Sino-Soviet dispute, while the parties of Morocco and Réunion stayed neutral.

African Communists agitated mainly for the independence of the Portuguese colonies in Africa, and for a black take-over of the South African and Rhodesian governments. They also advocated the nationalization of the African properties of Western oil companies and the ending of Western political and economic influence over African nations.

Latin America. The total number of Communist party members in Latin America in 1972 increased by 50,000 to about 350,000, of whom more than one third resided in Cuba, more than one fourth in Chile, and about one sixth in Argentina. The fastest-growing Communist party was that of Chile, which doubled in membership in one year, presumably because Communists participated in the ruling government coalition.

With regard to the Sino-Soviet dispute, 11 parties, including the Chilean and Argentine, supported the USSR. The Communist parties of Bolivia, Brazil, Colombia, Ecuador, Paraguay, Peru, and Venezuela in South America, and of the Dominican Republic, Honduras, and Mexico to the north, were divided over the issue. Cuba remained neutral, though it receives a great deal more material aid from the USSR than from Communist China.

In the summer, Cuban Premier Fidel Castro visited the Soviet Union, where he was awarded the Order of Lenin. In July, Cuba became a member of CMEA.

Apparently inspired by the partial success of the Chilean Communists, there was a tendency of Communist parties in other Latin American countries to form united fronts with non-Communist left-wing groups in an attempt to win power through parliamentary elections. In 1972 such united fronts were operating in Colombia, Uruguay, and Venezuela, and one was formed in Ecuador in February.

Latin American Communists advocated nationalization of U. S. business properties in Latin America and abolition of U. S. military bases in the Caribbean area. They also propagandized for the transfer of the Panama Canal to Panamanian control, overthrow of local military dictatorships, and independence for British Honduras and Puerto Rico.

Canada. The small Canadian Communist party, concentrated mostly in urban Ontario, was pro-USSR in the Sino-Soviet dispute. Canadian Communists sought Canada's withdrawal from NATO and a reduction of U. S. influence over Canada's economy.

United States. The small U. S. Communist party was anti-Zionist, anti-Israel, and anti-Chinese, and opposed U. S. economic, military, and political involvement in Indochinese affairs. In February the party held a national convention in New York City, nominating the party's general secretary, Gus Hall, as its candidate for the U. S. presidency and a black Communist youth leader, Jarvis Tyner, as its candidate for vice president. Both candidates were listed on only a few state ballots and obtained only a handful of votes in the 1972 national elections.

After being acquitted of charges of murder, black militant Angela Davis, a member of the Central Committee of the U. S. Communist party, toured the USSR during the fall of 1972. While there, she received a Soviet decoration, an honorary professorship at Moscow University, and an honorary doctorate from the University of Tashkent.

(See also separate articles on the Communist countries.)

ELLSWORTH RAYMOND
New York University

COMPUTERS

The computer industry experienced an upturn in 1972 after two depressing years marked by company failures and substantial losses. Two interrelated trends emerged from the disillusionment of 1970 and 1971. One was that commercial and industrial users became increasingly skeptical about any computer application not demonstrably cost-effective. The other was that computer vendors increasingly emphasized the development of hardware and software for solving everyday problems rather than for exploring new state-of-the-art activities. Thus practicality, rather than sophistication for its own sake, was the dominant theme in 1972.

Minicomputers. Minicomputers, typically priced at about $10,000, continued to post the industry's highest growth rate. Worldwide shipments of these small machines in 1972 were estimated at 22,000, thus raising the total number of installed minicomputers from 32,000 to 54,000 in one year. About 92% of the minicomputers currently in use were manufactured by 10 firms, but by the end of 1972 there were nearly 50 minicomputer manufacturers.

Approximately 40% of all minicomputers sold in 1972 were used in industrial control applications, another 40% were divided equally between laboratory instrumentation and data communications, and the remainder had scientific and engineering problem-solving, educational, or other applications.

Data Communications. Data communications includes all applications involving the transmission of encoded information between geographically dispersed computers or computer terminals. This broad and dynamic field accounted for some of the most impressive and far-reaching uses of computers in 1972. Notable data communications achievements in 1972 included construction of nationwide message-carrying systems to compete with services previously provided only by American Telephone and Telegraph Co. and Western Union; expansion of the U. S. Air Force's military command and control system, which now interconnects high-speed, large-scale computers at more than a hundred locations around the world; growth of a national computer network developed by the Advanced Research Projects Agency for data related to scientific research projects; development of systems for linking the computers of all member firms of the New York and American stock exchanges; and the first experimental use of a microwave technique ("Data-Under-

SUNDSTRAND

DIRECT NUMERICAL CONTROL (DNC), or on-line, computer-controlled automation of a manufacturing process, is used in making tools in Roanoke, Va.

Voice") developed by the Bell System for transmitting high-speed data together with voice signals of telephone calls.

Data communications could soon significantly alter everyday life. For instance, in 1972 a program was initiated in South Orange, N. J., to make that municipality the first to have two-way data communications via cable television. In the proposed system, a home television set is given the capabilities of a computer terminal. According to its developer, Video Information Systems, be-

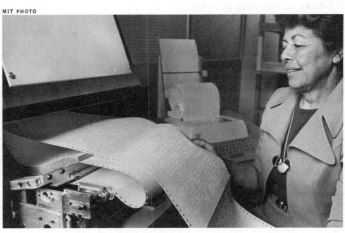

MIT PHOTO

COMPUTERIZED BRAILLE SYSTEM developed at Massachusetts Institute of Technology translates English type into braille. A telephone line links a teletypewriter and the braille embossing machine with a computer, which is programmed to do the difficult task of translation almost instantaneously.

tween 2,000 and 4,000 TV viewers in South Orange will soon be able to shop, vote, receive stock quotations or other specialized data, and report emergencies simply by pressing buttons on a device attached to the TV set, which is connected by cable to a central computer.

IBM Antitrust Case. A Justice Department suit calling for the divestiture of the International Business Machines Corporation into several independent companies neared trial late in 1972. At issue was whether giant IBM dominates the industry by sheer size. IBM had revenues of more than $7 billion in the first nine months of 1972, and its stock had a market value of almost $45 billion.

IBM argued that its share of the computer market declined from about 70% in 1952 to 50% in 1972, a contention largely based on data collected from more than 1,700 companies engaged in providing or using computer products and services. IBM obtained this data in connection with other antitrust suits brought against IBM by rival firms. The Justice Department disagreed with IBM's interpretation of the data. Altogether more than 27 million documents have been submitted to the government for study in the case, which is already the largest and most protracted antitrust investigation ever undertaken.

Computer Technology. In mid-1972, IBM announced that its System/370 series of computers would be supplied with "virtual storage" software. This technique, first demonstrated in the 1960's, had never been available on an optional basis for a complete series of general-purpose computers. With the new software, System/370 computers automatically and rapidly transfer temporarily unused portions ("pages") of internally stored programs to less-expensive external memory devices. Then just before the pages are required for processing, they are reloaded into main memory. Since all such transfers occur without delaying the computer's programmed sequence of operations, they make the computer's main memory appear to be much larger than it actually is. This difference between appearance and actuality explains why the technique is called "virtual storage."

Largest Computer. Burroughs Corporation installed ILLIAC IV, the world's largest and most powerful computer, at NASA's Ames Research Center in Mountain View, Calif.

ALAN R. KAPLAN
Editor, "Modern Data" Magazine

CONGO, Democratic Republic of. See ZAÏRE.

CONGO, People's Republic of the

Congo's president, Marien Ngouabi, initiated a gradual return to more moderate positions in 1972 after several years of increasing movement to the left. His actions followed in the wake of an unsuccessful coup led by elements of the radical left.

Political Affairs. An infantry battalion attempted to seize control of the government on February 21. Led by Lt. Ange Diawara, one of five members of the political bureau of the ruling Congolese Worker's party (PTC), the coup was quickly suppressed by army units loyal to the government.

President Ngouabi then embarked on a systematic purge of what he called the "left adventurists." Among those arrested were former Premier Ambroise Noumazalay, former Vice President Alfred

---

CONGO • Information Highlights

Official Name: People's Republic of the Congo.
Area: 132,047 square miles (342,000 sq km).
Population (1972 est.): 1,000,000. *Density,* 8 per square mile (3 per sq km). *Annual rate of increase,* 2.1%.
Chief Cities (1962 census): Brazzaville, the capital, 136,200; Pointe-Noire, 79,500.
Government: *Head of state,* Marien Ngouabi, chairman of the Council of State (took office Jan. 1969). *Head of government,* Marien Ngouabi. *Executive Body*—Council of State. *Political party*—Congolese Workers' party.
Language: French (official), African languages.
Education: *Expenditure* (1969), 24.2% of total public expenditure. *School enrollment* (1969)—primary, 228,578; secondary, 28,405; technical/vocational, 2,594; university/higher, 1,786.
Monetary Unit: CFA franc (255.79 CFA francs equal U. S.$1, Aug. 1972).
Gross National Product (1970 est.): $233,000,000.
National Income per Person (1963): $180.
Consumer Price Index (1971): 124 (1963 = 100).
Manufacturing (major products): Processed foods; veneer and plywood.
Major Agricultural Products: Coffee, cacao, groundnuts, sugar, bananas, sweet potatoes and yams, forest products.
Major Minerals: Industrial diamonds, lead, tin, gold.
Foreign Trade (1970): *Exports,* $31,000,000 (chief exports—wood, diamonds). *Imports,* $57,000,000 (chief imports, 1969—transport equipment; nonelectrical machinery; food; chemicals). *Chief trading partners* (1969)—France (took 14% of exports, supplied 57% of imports); West Germany (17%—8%); Netherlands (14%—4%); United States (2%—7%).
Transportation: *Major national airline,* Linacongo.
Communications: *Telephones* (1971), 10,042; *television stations* (1971), 1; *television sets* (1971), 2,000; *radios* (1970), 65,000; *newspapers* (1969), 1 (circulation, 600).

Raoul, and Ndala Graille, a former first secretary of the PTC. A military court was convened to try the 169 persons indicted for their alleged parts in the coup, and its verdicts were announced on March 7. The court sentenced 125 persons to prison terms ranging from 2 to 20 years, 30 persons to life imprisonment, and 13 persons to death (although these sentences were later commuted). Diawara remained at large, however.

In an address to the first congress of the PTC in April, Ngouabi reaffirmed his regime's continued adherence to the principles of "scientific socialism." But observers noted that he appeared to be following a more moderate course. When 55-year-old Fulbert Youlou, the anti-Marxist former president of Congo who was deposed in 1963, died in Madrid on May 6 the government decided to allow his body to be repatriated for burial. Its action was interpreted as a bid for reconciliation with the alienated followers of the former president.

Foreign Affairs. In March, Ngouabi made an official visit to Paris, his first since becoming president in 1969. In June, Ngouabi and President Mobutu Sese Seko of Zaïre mediated a reconciliation between the two major Angolan nationalist movements, based respectively in Brazzaville and Kinshasa. Ngouabi and Mobutu also agreed in August to normalize relations between their countries.

EDOUARD BUSTIN, *Boston University*

CONNALLY, John B. See BIOGRAPHY.

CONNECTICUT

During its 1972 session the Connecticut legislature adopted a large budget in response to a plea from the state's governor and passed a no-fault automobile insurance law. Two abortion laws and a reapportionment plan were declared unconstitutional.

Legislation. The 1972 session of the Connecticut General Assembly was limited to budget and emergency matters. A budget of $1.17 billion was adopted in consideration of Gov. Thomas J. Meskill's call for a 10% increase in state expenditures

and for payment, over a ten-year period, of the state deficit of $244 million. The additional spending was to be financed by an increase in sales tax to 7%. The new budget provided for pensions for the legislators for the first time in Connecticut's history, and also included provisions for salary raises for legislators, judges, and top elective officials. The governor was to receive in 1975 a salary increase from $35,000 to $42,000 annually.

A no-fault automobile insurance law was passed, and went into effect on Jan. 1, 1973. It provides for up to $5,000 for bodily injury and limited damage suits. The age of majority was lowered from 21 to 18, effective Oct. 1, 1972. The General Assembly rejected the proposed 27th amendment to the U. S. Constitution, which would assure women equal rights, but authorized a voter referendum in 1974 on a state constitutional amendment prohibiting discrimination because of sex.

In April 1972 a three-judge federal court decision struck down Connecticut's 112-year-old abortion statute as unconstitutional. The legislature quickly passed a new and stricter law at a special session called by Governor Meskill in May. This law was also declared unconstitutional.

To avert the discontinuance of bus service in Connecticut's towns and cities, Governor Meskill called another special session of the General Assembly in September. The legislators passed an act directing transportation commissioner A. Earl Wood to use available funds to subsidize bus companies

THE NEW YORK TIMES

GOVERNOR MESKILL signs new abortion law in May. A federal court declared measure unconstitutional.

in the large cities and distributing $3 million in surplus highway funds to the cities and towns. The governor line-vetoed the first section of the act and left untouched the section authorizing distribution of the $3 million. In October he authorized Commissioner Wood to offer local transit authorities up to 25% of their operating losses.

Reapportionment. On March 30 a U. S. District three-judge panel ruled the Connecticut General Assembly's reapportionment (Saden) plan unconstitutional. State Superior Court Judge Walter J. Sidor ruled that elections would be held on November 7 for the General Assembly in accord with a revised Saden plan. In July, revised congressional districts were ordered by the federal court, and these went into effect for the November 7 election.

Environment. On August 4, Governor Meskill and the New England River Basins Commission appointed a joint committee to study preservation and development of Long Island Sound. Sen. Abraham Ribicoff's bill creating a historic riverway from the sound to Haddam, including 46,300 acres in a national park, received U. S. Senate approval, but some of the eight towns affected opposed provision of recreational facilities. A 1972 law authorized the regulation of dredging, filling, and building in inland wetlands.

Prisons. A legislative committee studying Somers State Prison recommended more money for rehabilitation and vocational training and for hiring and training guards. In May the 900 inmates had been locked in their cells for two weeks after attacking guards with baseball bats. In September, Carl Robinson was appointed the first black warden.

State Song. Governor Meskill issued an executive order in 1972 naming Jesse Greer's *The Hills of My Connecticut* as the official state song. Previously, Yale University's song *Boola Boola* had been used unofficially as the state song. Governor Meskill is a graduate of Trinity College and of the University of Connecticut Law School.

GEORGE ADAMS
Connecticut State Library

———— CONNECTICUT • Information Highlights ————

Area: 5,009 square miles (12,973 sq km).

Population (1970 census): 3,032,217. *Density:* 633 per sq mi.

Chief Cities (1970 census): Hartford, the capital, 158,017; Bridgeport, 156,542; New Haven, 137,707; Stamford, 108,- 798; Waterbury, 108,033; New Britain, 83,441.

Government (1972): *Chief Officers*—governor, Thomas J. Meskill (R); lt. gov., T. Clark Hull, Jr. (R); secy. of state, Mrs. Gloria Schaffer (D); att. gen., Robert K. Killian (D); treas., Robert I. Berdon (R); commissioner, dept. of education, William J. Sanders; chief justice, Charles S. House. *General Assembly*—Senate, 36 members (19 Democrats, 17 Republicans); House of Representatives, 177 members (99 D, 78 R).

Education (1971–72): *Enrollment*—public elementary schools, 483,836 pupils, 19,689 teachers; public secondary, 183,- 031 pupils, 14,220 teachers; nonpublic (1970–71), 107,939 pupils; 5,880 teachers; college and university, 126,000 students. *Public school expenditures*, $694,349,000 ($1,130 per pupil). *Average teacher's salary*, $10,800.

State Finances (fiscal year 1970): *Revenues*, $1,236,950,000 (6.5% general sales tax and gross receipts taxes, $258,- 659,000; motor fuel tax, $99,191,000; federal funds, $215,- 672,000). *Expenditures*, $1,347,675,000 (education, $420,- 394,000; health, welfare, and safety, $215,832,000; highways, $169,902,000). *State debt*, $1,919,455,000 (1970).

Personal Income (1971): $15,503,000,000; per capita, $5,032.

Public Assistance (1971): $228,271,000. *Average monthly payments* (Dec. 1971)—old-age assistance, $102.47; aid to families with dependent children, $244.82.

Labor Force: Nonagricultural wage and salary earners (July 1972), 1,173,600. *Average annual employment* (1971)— manufacturing, 401,000; trade, 226,000; government, 161,- 000; services, 193,000. *Insured unemployed* (Aug. 1972) —50,300 (4.7%).

Manufacturing (1970): *Value added by manufacture*, $6,580,- 000,000. Transportation equipment, $1,411,600,000; nonelectrical machinery, $891,600,000; electrical equipment and supplies, $665,400,000; fabricated metal products, $661,100,000; primary metal industries, $427,700,000.

Agriculture (1970): *Cash farm income*, $167,182,000 (livestock, $102,691,000; crops, $63,718,000; government payments, $773,000). *Chief crops* (in order of value)—Tobacco, hay, apples, potatoes.

Mining (1971): *Production value*, $27,961,000 (ranks 45th among the states). *Chief minerals*—Stone, $15,649,000; sand and gravel, $10,262,000.

Fisheries (1971): *Commercial catch*, 7,261,000 pounds ($1,- 775,000). *Leading species by value* (1971): Lobsters, $715,000; clams, $270,000; oysters, $228,000.

Transportation: *Roads* (1971), 18,407 miles (29,622 km); *motor vehicles* (1971), 1,732,609; *railroads* (1971), 664 miles (1,069 km); *public airports* (1972), 14.

Communications: *Telephones* (1972), 2,122,600; *television stations* (1971), 5; *radio stations* (1971), 58; *newspapers* (1972), 27 (daily circulation, 952,000).

CONSERVATION

The year 1972 was notable neither for accomplishments nor for new directions in conservation, but rather for the continuation of earlier efforts, and new frustrations and conflicts. Public values and attitudes continued to evolve toward the crusade for conservation of environmental quality, and the traditional questions were still being asked, as evidenced by articulation of the so-called "energy crisis." (See ENERGY.)

World Conference. Conservationists were involved in the United Nations World Conference on the Human Environment which convened in Stockholm, June 5, 1972, with 112 nations represented. Although some observers were disturbed by occasional political activity, the conference did help focus world-scale attention on the need to conserve wildlife, plant resources, and quality of environment for human living. It advocated the establishment of a United Nations organization, to be funded with about $100 million a year, to coordinate activities designed to conserve environmental quality and protect natural resources. (See also ENVIRONMENT.)

Endangered Species. Concern for protection of endangered wildlife increased, especially on the international level. In the United States the list of endangered foreign wildlife was expanded by adding cheetahs, leopards, tigers, snow leopards, jaguars, ocelots, margays, and tiger cats.

The whaling and sealing industries came under international pressure for conservation. While the International Whaling Commission defeated a United States proposal for a 10-year ban on all whaling, the commission did reduce the allowable harvest of whales to 34,000, down from 40,000 in 1972. It also extended the ban on blue and humpback whales and added right and gray whales to the protected list. Japan and the USSR, two nations which together account for about 85% of the total whale harvest, agreed to inspection of whaling vessels on the high seas. A Canadian commission urged an end to Atlantic seal hunting by 1974 and at least a 6-year moratorium. During the year a 12-nation convention prohibiting hunting of Antarctic seals was signed.

Land Conservation Projects. Planning and regulation of land use received major attention during the year. Florida initiated a significant approach to conservation of natural areas as voters approved a $240 million bond issue to provide funds for purchase and preservation of natural areas of marshes and beaches endangered by the spread of urban populations. In addition, state voters approved a constitutional amendment allowing the sale of revenue bonds for purchase of recreational lands and park improvements.

Responsibility for conservational management of coastal zone areas received attention in a controversial report by the President's National Advisory Committee on Oceans and Atmosphere. The committee recommended that management of coastal zones should be the responsibility of the National Oceanic and Atmospheric Administration (NOAA) of the Commerce Department. However, administration spokesmen have generally favored considering coastal zone management as part of the nation's responsibility under the Interior Department.

The Tennessee Tombigbee Waterway Project was revitalized in 1972 when the suit to halt construction was dismissed by the court. The project, authorized in 1946 to connect the Tennessee River with the Gulf of Mexico, was opposed on the grounds that it would damage fragile riverine environment and wildlife habitat.

The $400 million Tocks Island Dam, involving creation of a 72,000-acre parkland and major reservoir on the Delaware River of New York, New Jersey, and Pennsylvania, was strongly opposed on the grounds that it would damage an unspoiled sector of the river. Significantly, Gov. William Cahill of New Jersey criticized the project plan to provide for 10 million visitors annually and proposed reevaluation to provide for only 4 million. As a result, federal funds were authorized only for land acquisition, and the project was delayed.

Alaskan Pipeline. The proposed 789-mile (1,270-km) Alaska oil pipeline, which is to run from the Arctic slope fields near Prudhoe Bay to Valdez on the south coast, continued to be vigorously opposed by wildlife and wilderness groups. They expressed fears of the potential degrading of fragile Arctic environment and pollution of coastal waters from potential oil spills. The U. S. Interior Department during the year issued a statement on the pipeline's environmental impact, together with an economic analysis which concluded that the pipeline is essential to national security. The 1970 injunction against the project was lifted in August 1972, but the Department of the Interior continued to withhold the necessary construction permit. The Alyeska Pipeline Company indicated there would be no construction until legal questions were settled.

New Parklands. President Nixon signed into law two measures which created the first national recreation areas in high density urban environs. One is the Gateway National Recreation Area in New York–New Jersey, to include up to 26,250 acres of oceanfront and bayside at the entrance to New York harbor. The other is the Golden Gate Recreation Area authorized with $61.6 million for land acquisition to preserve areas on both sides of San Francisco's Golden Gate. Among other additions are the Cumberland Island National Seashore, authorized to include up to 40,500 acres of Georgia's coast; Glen Canyon National Recreation Area; Fossil Butte National Monument, in Wyoming; and the Hohokam National Monument, in Arizona.

President Nixon signed a bill authorizing preservation of 72,420 acres of wilderness along the Menam River in northeastern Oregon.

Use of Wilderness and Park Areas. Wilderness advocates led by the California-based Sierra Club won a restraining order barring logging and roadbuilding in some 52 million acres of Forest Service lands proposed for wilderness consideration but not yet classified for preservation. The suit contended that Forest Service reviews were inadequate and that environmental impact studies had not been made.

In 1972 the National Park Service undertook to reexamine its role and especially the increasing problems resulting from greater public use, which threaten to endanger the natural grandeur for which the parks were established. At the request of the Park Service, the Conservation Foundation made an in-depth appraisal of the National Park Service.

The Forest Service issued regulations banning clear-cutting (the complete removal of mature timber in given areas) on National Forest lands where regeneration could not reasonably be expected within five years or where clear-cutting might result in environmental damage.

J. GRANVILLE JENSEN, *Oregon State University*

In 1972, as part of Phase 2 of the price freeze, the government required retail stores to make basic price lists available to consumers.

consumerism

Consumerism has now become the more commonly used term for what over the years has been variously referred to as the consumer movement, consumer affairs, and consumer education. Mrs. Virginia Knauer, President Nixon's special assistant for consumer affairs, stated, "Consumerism is nothing more and nothing less than a challenge to business to live up to its full potential—to give consumers what is promised, to be honest, to give people a product that will work, and that is reasonably safe, to respond effectively to legitimate complaints, to provide information concerning the relevant quality characteristics of a product, to take into consideration the ecological and environmental ramifications of a company decision, and to return to the basic principle upon which so much of our nation's business was structured—'satisfaction guaranteed, or your money back.'"

Consumerism has now become a force which must be acknowledged and reckoned with by both government and the business community. Government and business have reacted in both positive and negative ways to "consumerism." At one extreme, some business leaders have been predicting the demise of the free enterprise system as we know it. They claim that the overzealousness of consumer groups in seeking passage of legislation which is ostensibly intended to protect the consumer, actually places such restrictions on free enterprise that the latter is being eroded away. Other business leaders have stated that if the free enterprise system, as we know it, survives, it will be primarily due to the consumer advocates who have been working diligently to see that the business community serves the consumer in the way it should. Without consumer pressure these business leaders have predicted that the free enterprise system might well have collapsed from within, before business realized that it was not serving the consumer in the way that he had a right to be served.

Congressional Failure. During 1972 consumer interests were well represented in Congress by the number of consumer bills that were introduced into the Senate and House, ranging not quite from A to Z, but from Advertising to Warranties. However, the few bills that were actually enacted into law failed to deal adequately with consumer problems.

The bill thought to be the most significant by many consumer advocates never came to a vote. The proposed bill would have established a strong independent consumer agency, empowered to act as a watchdog over the federal government's entire consumer activities. Such an agency would have become a participant in the day-to-day decisions of the government that affect consumers. Three times the Senate voted against cloture, which would have cut off a filibuster and brought the measure to a vote. On the third attempt the vote was 52 to 30, failing by only 3 votes to reach the necessary two-thirds majority.

Consumer Product Safety Act. The most significant consumer law enacted by Congress in 1972 was the Consumer Product Safety Act, which was signed into law by President Nixon on October 28.

This act creates a new independent regulatory agency to be headed by five commissioners appointed by the President with confirmation by the Senate. It will have the authority to set standards for judging potentially hazardous products and to initiate court action to ban those that cannot be controlled by safety standards. Its responsibilities include the testing and regulating of safety aspects of product performance, construction, design, labeling, warnings, and instructions for use. The Food and Drug Administration's (FDA) regulation of hazardous chemicals used in the home and of toys and substances that can accidentally poison children was transferred to the new agency. The FDA's Bureau of Product Safety was also transferred. Companies or individuals violating the commission's standards are liable to criminal or civil penalties. Products already under the supervision of other agencies and not transferred to the new commission or regulated by other laws—such as automobiles, pesticides, tobacco, alcoholic beverages, medical devices, and cosmetics—are not under the commission's authority. The Federal Trade Commission's responsibilities over flammable fabrics have also been transferred to the new commission.

The need for the establishment of such an agency was shown by FDA experts, who stated that the greatest causes of personal injuries are windows and glass doors, which cause 150,000 mishaps a year; faulty power mowers, causing 140,000 accidents annually; and inadequately insulated gas floor furnaces, responsible for 30,000 mishaps a year. The National Commission on Product Safety estimated that 30,000 Americans are killed annually and 110,000 permanently disabled by accidents connected with products in and around the home. The objective of the new agency is to set performance standards to assure the safety of products and let manufacturers decide how to meet them. The law stipulates that hazardous products cannot be banned from the marketplace without court action. In signing the bill President Nixon called it "the most significant consumer protection legislation passed by the 92d Congress."

Another consumer bill enacted by Congress was the Motor Vehicle Information and Cost Saving Act. It includes a provision that prohibits resetting the mileage on automobile odometers and carries a maximum penalty of $1,500. The act also authorizes the secretary of transportation to require bumpers on passenger cars to provide the "maximum feasible" protection against damage.

No-Fault Automobile Insurance. Congressional legislation mandating the establishment by states of uniform no-fault automobile insurance was bottled up in the Senate Judiciary Committee, while bills introduced to establish a national no-fault insurance program did not even get to the hearings stage.

Advertising Substantiation. The Federal Trade Commission (FTC) continued to ask various companies to submit substantiation for the various claims that were being made for their products in advertisements. Requests have been made for substantiation of ads for such diverse products as automobiles, detergents, air conditioners, and electric shavers. The follow-up has been difficult, but what this move seems to have accomplished is to make advertisers a little more hesitant in making outlandish, exaggerated, and exorbitant claims.

Corrective Ads. The FTC has moved in to force negotiated settlements for companies whose ads have been ruled to be false. The companies must spend up to 25% of their ad budgets for these products, correcting the misinformation which the previous ads gave to the consumer. This FTC action created consternation among the advertisers.

Door-To-Door Sales. On Oct. 18, 1972, the FTC promulgated a rule that will give the consumer additional defense when dealing with door-to-door salesmen when it goes into effect. The rule stipulates that on any purchase of $25 or more from a door-to-door salesman, the buyer has the right to cancel the transaction, without any penalty or obligation, within three business days from the date of purchase. The buyer is to be informed in writing of these rights by the seller at the time the transaction takes place.

Care Labeling. An FTC ruling became effective on July 3 which requires that articles of wearing apparel bear permanent labels clearly indicating instructions for their care and maintenance.

Food and Drug Administration. Opinions about the effectiveness of the FDA in dealing with consumer welfare during 1972 ranged from very effective to so ineffective that its responsibilities should have been transferred to the newly created Product Safety Commission—a proposal defeated in Congress. There is little doubt in the minds of most consumer advocates that the FDA in the last few years has grown much stronger and has taken on a greater concern for the consumer's rights. Its actions in 1972 included a massive and unprecedented review program to ensure that the many thousands of non-prescription drugs are safe and effective for self-treatment of minor, symptomatic conditions. It also banned the use of hexachlorophene in all products, except on a prescription basis.

Phase 2—Price Controls. The magnitude of inflation has been slowed down for the consumer by the actions of the Price Commission. Inflation, which had reached almost 6% per year by the end of 1970, was about 4.3% in 1971, and in the 12 months following the enactment of price controls increased slightly under 3%. There is little that the consumer has been able to do to control the prices of specific goods, since the controls are based more on the level of profits of a firm than on the price of any individual product. For most Americans wages and salaries have been going up more than enough to offset inflation, so that the economic well-being of the average family improved in 1972.

The Consumer and the States. As was true with Congress, considerable consumer legislation was introduced in many state legislatures, but the number of bills passed and their importance were minimal. Connecticut and New Jersey passed no-fault automobile legislation, while in 30 other states such legislation was defeated. The more significant bills passed by various legislatures included: (1) the creation of a state consumer protection division in Oregon; (2) a bill that stipulates that meat advertised, sold, or offered for sale in New York must be labeled with its "true name" instead of fanciful and meaningless names such as "His and Her Steaks," "California Roast," and "Chicken Steak"; (3) bills that eliminate the holder-in-due-course doctrine in credit sales in New Jersey and Maine; and (4) a bill which reduces the maximum rate allowable for revolving charge accounts in stores in Connecticut from 18% to 12%.

The Business Community Responds. The business community has been made well and sometimes

painfully aware of the growing agitation for consumer rights. More and more response has been coming from business. One of the key questions being asked by consumers is how much of the response is merely tokenism to stem the uproar, and how much of the response is generated by the business community's realization that it must assume a greater degree of corporate responsibility in its relations with customers. More companies are writing clearer warranties and guarantees. More companies are creating high-level positions on their staffs for persons responsible for the business' relation to the consumer. A number of businesses have introduced a "hot line"—a toll-free telephone number that a consumer may call to get information or register a complaint. Some companies are gradually coming to the realization that they can do a much better job in putting additional needed information on their labels. In commercially packaged foods, for example, the consumer is seeing more packages listing ingredients, some even listing ingredients by percentages. More information about the nutritional value of the product is also being put on the label. This remains an area where much still needs to be done if the consumer is to have, at the point-of-purchase, adequate information to make a judgment about which product best meets his needs.

Adequate self-regulation in the business community still is lacking. Little progress has been made, although the national Council of Better Business Bureaus has encouraged businesses to increase their responsiveness to consumer demands as well as various environmental concerns.

The National Elections. Both the Democrats and Republicans were long on promises and short on fulfillment for the consumer during the election year. President Nixon did not press for any significant consumer legislation, and the Democratic-controlled Congress did very little to render legislative assistance to the consumer. The consumer issue was not a major issue during the presidential campaign, and 1972 will certainly not go down as a significant year for the consumer.

STEWART M. LEE, *Geneva College*

COSTA RICA

Costa Rica had a good year in 1972 with the economy expanding despite minor inflation. The nation's tax system was revised, and bananas replaced coffee as the leading export in value. On the diplomatic front, relations between Costa Rica and the Soviet Union were begun.

Domestic Affairs. A surge in imports in 1970 led to a $120 million balance-of-trade deficit in 1971. This forced the introduction of a system of dual exchange rates, which provoked Guatemala, El Salvador, and Nicaragua into closing their borders to Costa Rican goods in September 1972. The effect was to practically destroy the Central American Common Market. Costa Rica, as the most prosperous Market member, had always bought more from the other states than it sold to them.

In March 1972 the Costa Rican assembly passed a law extensively revising the tax system. New taxes ranging from 10% to 50% were levied on less essential imports. The progressive income tax was raised to 5% on the first 5,000 colones of taxable income and to 50% on taxable income over 350,000 colones. An interesting feature of the new law is that it lists the amounts that physicians and other

———— **COSTA RICA · Information Highlights** ————

Official Name: Republic of Costa Rica.
Area: 19,575 square miles (50,700 sq km).
Population (1972 est.): 1,900,000. *Density,* 97 per square mile (37 per sq km). *Annual rate of increase,* 2.7%.
Chief Cities (1970 est.): San José, the capital, 205,700; Alajuela, 29,200; Limón, 24,500; Heredia, 24,000; Puntarenas, 23,500.
Government: *Head of state,* José Figueres Ferrer, president (took office May 1970). *Head of government,* José Figueres Ferrer. *Legislature* (unicameral)—Legislative Assembly, 57 members. *Major political parties*—Party of National Liberation; Party of National Unification; National Republican party.
Language: Spanish (official).
Education: *Expenditure* (1969), 35% of total public expenditure. *School enrollment* (1968)—primary, 322,683; secondary, 62,256; technical/vocational, 6,524; university/higher, 11,449.
Monetary Unit: Colon (6.62 colones equal U. S.$1, Aug. 1972).
Gross National Product (1971 est.): $967,000,000.
Manufacturing (major products): Pharmaceutical products, fertilizers, paints, furniture, clothing, wood.
Major Agricultural Products: Coffee, cacao, bananas, sugarcane, vegetables, cattle, forest products.
Major Minerals: Salt, gold.
Foreign Trade (1971): *Exports,* $226,000,000. *Imports,* $344,000,000. *Chief trading partners* (1969)—United States (took 48% of exports, supplied 35% of imports); West Germany (7%—8%); Nicaragua (7%—6%); El Salvador (5%—6%).
Communications: *Telephones* (1971), 61,268; *television stations* (1971), 4; *television sets* (1971), 120,200; *radios* (1970), 125,000; *newspapers* (1970), 8 (daily circulation, 177,000).

professionals will be assumed to have earned in one year, unless they can prove otherwise.

The most ambitious project begun by the Costa Rican government involved the International Bank, the USSR, and the Alcoa Company in a feasibility study for a $400 million, 500,000-kilowatt hydroelectric plant in Guanacaste to supply power for an aluminum smelter in San Isidro de General. This project would make Costa Rica a major aluminum exporting nation while also serving to control floods and irrigate new farmlands.

During 1972 foreign loans were obtained from the International Development Bank, the West German government, the Central American Economic Integration Bank, and private United States banks. Favorable trade contracts were signed with several Japanese firms, which agreed to buy 30,000 bags of coffee, a year, and with the USSR, which was to buy 6,000 tons of coffee annually for 5 years.

Violence, unusual for Costa Rica, occurred on Dec. 12, 1971, when a group of Nicaraguans landed a hijacked commercial airliner at San José's El Coco airport and demanded fuel. José Figueres, Costa Rica's president, brandishing a machine gun, led the police in attacking the hijackers and recapturing the plane. One of the hijackers was killed.

International Affairs. In May 1972, Costa Rica's foreign minister, Gonzalo Facio, announced that henceforth Costa Rica would claim exclusive fishing rights within 200 miles (320 km) of its coasts. All foreign vessels would need permission from the Costa Rican government to fish within this limit.

During most of the year a dispute raged over establishing diplomatic ties with the Soviet Union. Despite demonstrations and polemics, President José Figueres defended his policy as contributing to ending the cold war and stimulating sales to the USSR. He received the Soviet ambassador on Feb. 2, 1972. Further controversy arose when two Russians were expelled from the country for "agitating" workers in the banana region.

José Luis Molina, the Costa Rican delegate to the United Nations, was elected a vice president of the UN General Assembly for 1972.

HARRY KANTOR, *Marquette University*

UPI

Umberto's Clam House in New
York City's "Little Italy" was the
scene of the gangland slaying of
Joseph "Crazy Joe" Gallo (right).
The reputed mobster was one of
several men killed in gangland
war in New York in early April.

CRIME

UPI

Crime continued to be a political issue of considerable proportions in the United States during the election year of 1972, and candidates for office generally felt obligated to take a public position on measures they deemed essential in reducing muggings, rapes, homicides, and other so-called "street crimes." Incumbents, understandably, generally maintained that their efforts have made a significant impact on the amount of crime, while those seeking office insisted that they would do better than what is being done to protect the public more adequately from criminal depradations.

The voter, meanwhile, has increasingly seen himself as a potential crime victim. A Gallup poll found that the number of people who fear walking alone in their neighborhood at night has risen sharply, particularly in smaller cities. Nearly 60% of the women interviewed said they were afraid to go out at night, an increase of 14% from 1968.

A typical response in rural areas in regard to crime was reported from Perry, Iowa, a town of 6,500 residents. In the past the rural population generally left the front doors of their homes unlocked day and night and extended hospitality to any stranger happening by. In 1972, solid bolts on the doors, cynical inspection of strangers through a peephole, floodlit areas surrounding the house, and similar precautionary measures were reported to be in common use.

The mood of residents of metropolitan areas was aptly captured by Richard R. Lingeman, a writer who had gone for a stroll in New York City late on a hot August night. Lingeman was slugged from behind and stomped. Later, he wrote poignantly:

"I, once a lover of the New York night ... will be more hesitant next time about venturing into it. I will look back from time to time to see if there

is that silent angry [person] stalking me. I, who have listened to the hum of the city in the late hours, to the sound of cars on rainy pavements like crushing tissue paper, who have walked the lonely streets and stared up into windows empty and black like the eye socket of a skull—no, I shall never walk these streets again without caution... call it fear."

THE CRIME ISSUE IN THE 1972 CAMPAIGN

Both President Nixon and Senator George McGovern, responding to the public concern about crime, devoted considerable time to the subject during the 1972 presidential campaign.

Nixon's Position. In a major address in mid-October President Nixon insisted that he had brought the "frightening trend of crime and anarchy" to a virtual standstill during his term of office and thus had clearly fulfilled his 1968 pledge to restore respect for law, order, and justice in the United States. In making his case, the President used statistics from the Federal Bureau of Investigation's *Uniform Crime Reports.* The President cited FBI figures that indicated that serious criminal behavior had risen only 1% during the first six months of 1972, the slowest rate of increase in several decades. Nixon contrasted this increase to that for the eight years prior to his assuming office, during which time serious crime had increased 122%.

The President further pointed to a drop of 50% in the amount of crime in the District of Columbia during his term in office, as reported by D. C. officials. The District of Columbia had been called the "crime capital of the world" by Nixon in 1968. The President said he had made the D. C. resident "more secure" through an increase in the number of policemen and by appointing judges who interpreted the Constitution strictly. He also said that domestic actions and diplomacy initiated by his administration had "stemmed the raging heroin epidemic." In the same address the President pledged that he would "work unceasingly to halt the erosion of moral fiber in American life, and the denial of individual accountability for individual action."

Kleindienst's Support. Support for the President's position was offered by Attorney General Richard Kleindienst who, among other things, cited the following items:

(1) A total of 72 of the nation's major cities recorded a decrease in serious crime during the first six months of 1972, compared with 53 cities showing decreases in the same period in 1971 and 34 in 1970.

(2) Suburban areas reported a 5% increase in serious crime in the first half of 1972, compared with a 10% increase during the first half of 1971.

(3) There were 1,600 fewer robberies in the first half of 1972 than in the first half of 1971.

Kleindienst attributed the slowdown in the rapidly rising crime rate of the 1960's to an underlying change in public support of law enforcement and the effects of massive government spending for crime control under President Nixon. He maintained that the previous Democratic administration had confused the public by "fiction and fancy, fable and fairy tale" about such phenomena as organized crime. According to Kleindienst, the Democrats had said that organized crime was relatively harmless and that if it were let alone it would disappear as gangsters killed one another off. "The truth is," the

UPI

NO MORE CAPITAL PUNISHMENT: Death row inmate and Tennessee State Prison's electric chair after the Supreme Court ruled the death penalty unconstitutional.

attorney general declared, "that organized crime takes billions of dollars out of the pockets of Americans every year in illegal bookmaking, loan sharking, theft of securities, cargo hijacking, extortion, and illicit drugs." Kleindienst said that the Nixon administration had gotten 1,600 indictments against organized criminals by using court-authorized wiretaps, with "no complaints that an innocent party's privacy had been invaded."

McGovern's Position. Senator McGovern's campaign approach to crime issues took two lines. First, he insisted that President Nixon distorted the crime picture in the United States in order to make his own efforts to combat crime look much better than they were in actuality. Second, he said that the President was defining the concept of "crime" so narrowly that very serious matters of honesty and integrity were being ignored by the administration. McGovern maintained that many of these latter matters related to the presidential campaign itself, most notably to the Watergate affair in which it was claimed that illegal efforts were made by Republicans close to the White House to burglarize and bug Democratic election headquarters.

Senator McGovern promised to make eradication of crime and drug abuse "the number one domestic issue" if he were elected. He said he would increase the number of foot patrolmen and inaugurate a "crackdown on exploitative commercial advertising which suggests that everyday problems can be cured by swallowing some kind of drug." Mc-

HOLD-UP MAN AND HOSTAGE: *This 19-year-old gunman, who held up a Brooklyn check-cashing agency and took a woman hostage, was killed while trying to escape.*

Govern also called for strict control of handguns and for streamlining the country's judicial apparatus so that not more than 60 days would elapse between the arrest and the trial of an accused criminal. Improved job training and job development for prisoners also were part of the McGovern platform.

Attacking the statistics used by the President, Senator McGovern insisted that the period of the Nixon administration had been "the worst crime years in the nation's history." McGovern pointed out that during the first three years of the Nixon regime there had been a 30% increase in serious crime, the highest for such a time span since statistics were first recorded. McGovern also charged that much of the $1.5 billion made available to the Law Enforcement Assistance Administration had gone for meaningless and wasteful programs.

Senator McGovern also attacked the claim that the crime rate in the District of Columbia had declined. He alleged that the police had merely begun to put lesser values on stolen items, thereby keeping a large number of larcenies and burglaries out of the category of "serious crimes." McGovern observed that "the falsification of D. C. crime statistics has been extensively documented," and his aides said that it had become the practice of D. C. policemen not to record those crimes they doubted they could solve.

Support for the position of Senator McGovern on the Watergate affair came from Tom Wicker, a columnist for the New York *Times,* who charged that the Nixon administration in its reelection campaign had "tolerated" the services of paid agents who had been hired "to eavesdrop, forge, fake, lie, and harass."

ANALYSIS OF CRIME STATISTICS

The use of crime statistics for political purposes brought forth cautionary statements from law professors and social scientists who maintained that rhetoric founded on crime statistics hid as much as it revealed.

Effect of Age Structure. In a May 1972 article in the *Oklahoma Law Review,* Yale Kamisar, professor of law at the University of Michigan, noted that a sizeable segment of the increase in reported crime can be traced to changes in the age structure in the United States. Persons in the 15-to-24-year-old category have always been the most crime-prone group in the country. Because of the postwar baby boom, the size of this age group increased four times more rapidly than the entire population.

Kamisar also pointed out that both crime and the fear of it are a function of the closeness of people, so that the growing urbanization of the United States has been instrumental in creating both conditions. Norval Morris, a law professor at the University of Chicago, characterized the situation this way: "If you live your life in a room with 10 people with a given crime rate and then increase the number of people in that room to 20, it is obvious that the fear will increase as you move about the room in relation to crime without any change in the rate of crime."

CAPITAL PUNISHMENT

Since 1967 no person in the United States has been executed for a crime. The United States will have joined most nations of the Western world in outlawing capital punishment unless a 1972 decision by the Supreme Court is overturned by legislative, judicial, or referendum votes in the future.

State Court Rulings. In January, the New Jersey Supreme Court declared that the death penalty was unconstitutional in that state because it coerced defendants into pleading guilty to escape the risk of ending up in the electric chair if they chose to stand trial on first-degree murder charges.

In February, the California Supreme Court ruled that capital punishment violated the state's constitutional privilege against "cruel or unusual" punishment.

U. S. Supreme Court Ruling. In June, the United States Supreme Court ruled that death penalties imposed by judges or juries who had to decide between this punishment or life imprisonment were "cruel and unusual" and thus violated the Eighth Amendment's prohibition of "cruel and unusual punishments." Justice Potter Stewart, writing with the 5–4 majority, concluded that capital punishment had been imposed "wantonly and freakishly" in that the death penalty fell unevenly on blacks, the poor, and other relatively powerless persons. Death sentences in the United States, Justice Stewart maintained, were "cruel and unusual" in the same manner that "being struck by lightning is cruel and unusual."

The dissenters pointed out that capital punishment has been regarded as a useful response to certain kinds of crime for 191 years. One dissenter, Justice Lewis F. Powell, said that the decision violated fundamental principles of "federalism, judicial restraint, and most importantly, separation of powers."

By year-end, some erosion had already occurred in the court's stand against capital punishment through state action. A referendum vote in California found almost 70% of the voters supporting the death penalty for a limited number of offenses. Then, in December, the Florida Legislature enacted a law allowing capital punishment at the discretion of the courts. There was some doubt, however, whether the legislation would be upheld by the Supreme Court.

GILBERT GEIS
University of California, Irvine

CUBA

Despite another disappointing sugar harvest, Cubans were cheered in 1972 by the appearance of a few more consumer goods on the shelves of their state-owned stores and by the news of Cuba's admission to full membership in the Soviet-bloc economic community. Cuba's economic ties to Eastern Europe and its sympathy with the "emerging nations" of Africa were underscored in 1972 by Premier Fidel Castro's lengthy visits to those continents. Peru became the second country in South America to reestablish diplomatic relations with Cuba.

Economic Developments. Unfavorable weather conditions and a continuing labor shortage were partly responsible for one of Cuba's smallest sugar harvests in years—less than 5 million tons. Worker apathy and absenteeism, as well as the deterioration of mill and transport machinery, continued to plague the sugar industry in 1972. A shortage of chemical weed-killer was also cited as a factor in the low yield. In order to meet its export commitments, the government reduced the domestic sugar ration by one third.

Other foods were somewhat more plentiful as the government relied increasingly on material incentives to coax more production from the island's workers. Monetary wages acquired real value as more food and consumer goods became available for purchase. Pork production remained low because of an epidemic of swine fever, but more fish was available, although most of the nation's catch was destined for export. Under Soviet tutelage the Cuban fishing industry has become at least the fifth largest in Latin America.

Admission to Comecon. By not announcing a national goal for the 1972 sugar harvest, Castro confirmed that the "heroic era" of battles of production was definitely a thing of the past. He was not even in the country during the last two months of the harvest. The new economic orientation became clear on July 11, when Cuba was formally admitted as the ninth member nation of the Council for Mutual Economic Assistance (CMEA, or Comecon), joining the USSR, the six other Warsaw Pact allies, and the People's Republic of Mongolia in the Soviet-led trading bloc.

Cuba's new status as a full member of Comecon —it was previously accredited as an observer—formally extended the economic alliance into the Western Hemisphere and assured Cuba of more aid from the USSR's European partners. The arrangement thus relieved the USSR of the full burden of supporting Cuba. By 1972 the Soviets were providing military and economic aid to Cuba at the rate of more than $750 million a year. Cuba's Comecon membership put the economic portion of this aid on a more permanent, multilateral basis, and virtually guaranteed that the Havana regime would not become a casualty of a Moscow-Washington détente.

Western observers assumed that Cuba's admission to Comecon was contingent on Castro's abandoning two projects that were cherished by the late Ernesto "Che" Guevara: the economic reconstruction of Cuba through the use of "moral incentives" and promoting the spread of revolution to the rest of Latin America by guerrilla warfare. It was also believed that Castro promised to entrust centralized economic planning to qualified, Moscow-approved technicians and to refrain from imposing his own on-the-spot improvisations to their plans. Castro's

UPI

CUBAN PREMIER CASTRO receives bouquet during visit to Poland in June. On hand for the welcoming ceremony is Communist party leader Edward Gierek.

month-long visit to Chile late in 1971 and his two-month tour of Africa and Eastern Europe in 1972 demonstrated that he was no longer involved in the day-to-day operations of his government.

Foreign Affairs. After a speech likening the Cuban revolution to "a rock of immovable granite," Castro took off from Havana on May 3 for visits to Guinea, Sierra Leone, Algeria, Bulgaria, Rumania, Hungary, Poland, East Germany, Czechoslovakia, and the Soviet Union. He was well received at every stop, and several trade agreements were signed en route. Cuba's entrance into Comecon had been negotiated by Cuban Communist Party Secretary Carlos Rafael Rodríguez, who preceded the premier to Moscow and had an agreement ready for Castro's approval when he arrived in the Soviet capital on June 26. All three top Soviet leaders—Party Secretary Leonid Brezhnev, President Nicolai Podgorny, and Premier Alexei Kosygin—turned out to welcome the Cuban leader to Moscow, making his public reception warmer than that given U. S. President Richard Nixon a month earlier.

There was a slight improvement in Cuban-U. S. relations toward the end of 1972. Tension between Havana and Washington had mounted earlier in the year when U. S. naval patrols were authorized to fire on Cuban warships menacing vessels of other countries—provided the U. S. commander on the scene had "no knowledge" that a threatened vessel

─────────── CUBA • Information Highlights ───────────

Official Name: Republic of Cuba.
Area: 44,218 square miles (114,524 sq km).
Population (1972 est.): 8,700,000. *Density,* 189 per square mile (73 per sq km). *Annual rate of increase,* 1.9%.
Chief Cities (1970 census): Havana, the capital, 1,755,400; Santiago de Cuba, 276,000; Camagüey, 196,900.
Government: *Head of state,* Osvaldo Dorticos Torrado, president (took office July 1959). *Head of government,* Fidel Castro Ruz, premier (took office Feb. 1959).
Language: Spanish (official).
Education: *Expenditure* (1966), 16.1% of total public expenditure. *School enrollment* (1969)—primary, 1,427,607; secondary, 266,651; technical/vocational, 60,332; university/higher, 30,708.
Monetary Unit: Peso (0.92 peso equals U. S.$1, June 1972).
Gross National Product (1970 est.): $3,300,000,000.
Per Capita Gross National Product (1970): $388.
Economic Indexes: *Industrial production* (1966), 116 (1963= 100); *agricultural production* (1971), 122 (1952–56=100).
Manufacturing (major products): sugar products, tobacco products.
Major Agricultural Products: Sugarcane, tobacco, rice, oranges, tangerines, sweet potatoes and yams.
Major Minerals: Nickel, manganese ore, salt, chromium ore.
Foreign Trade (1970): *Exports,* $1,043,000,000 (chief exports, 1968—sugar; nickel ore and concentrates; tobacco products). *Imports,* $1,300,000,000 (chief imports, 1968—food; nonelectrical machinery; chemicals; petroleum, crude and partly refined). *Chief trading partners* (1968)—USSR (took 45% of exports, supplied 61% of imports); Czechoslovakia (6%—4%); East Germany (6%—4%); France (2%—6%).
Transportation: *Motor vehicles* (1969), 102,000 (automobiles, 71,000); *railroads* (1970), 3,281 miles (5,280 km); *merchant fleet* (1971), 385,000 gross registered tons; *major national airline,* CUBANA (Empresa Consolidada Cubana Aviación).
Communications: *Telephones* (1971), 291,264; *television stations* (1971), 25; *television sets* (1971), 555,000; *radios* (1970), 1,330,000; *newspapers* (1969), 11.

had been engaged in hostilities against Cuba. In a speech to the Organization of American States (OAS), U. S. Secretary of State William Rogers denounced Cuba for "interventionist behavior" in the hemisphere and for receiving arms shipments from the USSR. In November, however, U. S. officials had nothing bad to say about the Castro regime, with whom they began negotiating through the Swiss embassy in Havana for an agreement to combat airplane hijacking.

The OAS defeated, in April, a Peruvian resolution which stated that, in view of the changed world situation, member nations were free to reconsider individually their economic and diplomatic relationships with Cuba. In July, Peru joined Mexico and Chile in defying the OAS boycott by establishing full diplomatic relations with Havana. Later in the year, OAS members Jamaica, Barbados, and Trinidad and Tobago followed suit.

NEILL MACAULAY
University of Florida

CYPRUS

In 1972, Cyprus went through a crisis in its relations with Greece and again tried to devise a system of government that would be acceptable to both the Greek Cypriot majority and the Turkish Cypriot minority.

Crisis with Greece. In February the Greek government demanded that a shipment of Czech arms, secretly purchased by Archbishop Makarios, president of Cyprus, and delivered in January, be given over to the control of the United Nations peacekeeping force stationed on the island since 1964. The Greeks also insisted that Makarios reform his ministry to include men more favorable to union (*enosis*) with Greece. A main source of contention was the activities of Gen. George Grivas, a comrade of the archbishop in the struggle for independence from Britain, reported to be organizing underground forces to foment trouble against Makarios.

Makarios eventually turned over control of the Czech arms to the United Nations peacekeeping force. He also met with Grivas, who otherwise kept in hiding. Spyros Kyprianou, who had been foreign minister of Cyprus since 1960, resigned in May. He was one of those in the ministry to whom Greece particularly objected. In June, Makarios changed his cabinet, retaining only three of his former ministers. After these actions, relations with Greece seemed to improve. In August, Greece sent a new ambassador to Cyprus to fill a post that had been vacant for six months.

The Bishops' Stand. Three bishops, Metropolitan Anthemos of Kitium, Metropolitan Kyprianos of Kyrenia, and Metropolitan Gennadios of Paphos, who together with Makarios form the island's Holy Synod, called for his resignation from the presidency. Citing canon law, they said that it was improper for him to be both president of Cyprus and archbishop, despite the fact that he had held the presidential post for 12 years without previous challenge. However, there are ample precedents for the involvement of Greek hierarchs in political matters. The feeling that the Greek government was behind the bishops' move was reinforced when Metropolitan Anthemos was received in Athens by the Greek premier George Papadopoulos. Makarios refused to bow to the bishops' pressure.

Intercommunal Talks. Negotiations between the Greek Cypriot and the Turkish Cypriot communities entered their fifth year. This time the Cypriots were joined by two constitutional consultants, one from Greece and one from Turkey, as well as by a special representative of the secretary general of the United Nations, Kurt Waldheim. At year-end it was rumored that a basis for agreement was finally being worked out.

GEORGE J. MARCOPOULOS
Tufts University

─────────── CYPRUS • Information Highlights ───────────

Official Name: Republic of Cyprus.
Area: 3,572 square miles (9,251 sq km).
Population (1972 est.): 600,000. *Density,* 176 per square mile (68 per sq km). *Annual rate of increase,* 0.9%.
Chief Cities (1970 est.): Nicosia, the capital, 115,000 (metropolitan area); Limassol, 51,500; Famagusta, 42,500.
Government: *Head of state,* Archbishop Makarios III, president (reelected to a 5-year term, Feb. 1967). *Head of government,* Archbishop Makarios III. *Legislature* (unicameral) —House of Representatives, 50 members. *Major political parties*—Greek Cypriots; Turkish Cypriots.
Languages: Greek, Turkish, English (official).
Education: *Expenditure* (1969), 14.8% of total public expenditure. *School enrollment* (1969)—primary, 71,236; secondary, 39,221; technical/vocational, 4,218; university/higher, 580.
Monetary Unit: pound (0.3838 pound equals U. S.$1, Sept. 1972).
Gross National Product (1971 est.): $585,000,000.
National Income per Person (1970): $802.
Economic Indexes: *Industrial production* (mining; 1971), 112 (1963=100); *agricultural production* (1971), 247 (1952–56=100); *consumer price index* (1971), 113 (1967=100).
Manufacturing (major products): Cement, cigarettes, wine and spirits.
Major Agricultural Products: Citrus fruits, olives, grapes, potatoes, carrots, barley.
Major Minerals: Copper, asbestos, chromium ore, iron pyrites, sulfur.
Foreign Trade (1971): *Exports,* $115,000,000 (chief exports— citrus fruits; copper; potatoes; iron pyrites.) *Imports,* $263,000,000 (chief imports, 1969—food; nonelectrical machinery; transport equipment; textile yarn and fabrics.) *Chief trading partners* (1969)—United Kingdom (took 40% of exports, supplied 31% of imports); West Germany (18% —8%); Italy (7%—10%).
Tourism: *Receipts* (1970), $20,400,000.
Transportation: *Motor vehicles* (1970), 69,200 (automobiles, 55,500); *merchant fleet* (1971), 1,498,000 gross registered tons; *major national airline,* Cyprus Airways.
Communications: *Telephones* (1971), 40,744; *television stations* (1971), 2; *television sets* (1971), 42,000; *radios* (1970), 167,000; *newspapers* (1970), 10 (daily circulation, 68,000).

CZECHOSLOVAKIA

The pursuit of Marxist-Leninist orthodoxy continued unabated in Czechoslovakia throughout 1972. A number of "regenerated" associations, purged of all undesirables, held their congresses. And stiff penalties for alleged subversive activities were meted out to several groups of persons who had once played an important role in the "Czechoslovak spring," the liberalization movement of 1968.

The Year of the Congresses. After having put the finishing touches to the "consolidation" of the Communist party at the long-delayed 14th Party Congress in 1971, Communist leaders of Czechoslovakia turned their attention in 1972 to professional and cultural organizations designed to serve as the party's "transmission belts." In quick succession the unions of cooperative farmers, trade associations, Czechoslovak-Soviet friendship, journalists, writers, and dramatic artists convened their congresses during the period April–June. In every instance, the newly chosen functionaries turned out to be men handpicked by the party leadership, and the congressional resolutions echoed the prescribed party line.

Political and Cultural Repression. In the summer of 1972, Czechoslovakia gained worldwide attention for a series of political trials in which 46 persons, most of them prominent participants in the 1968 liberalization movement, were sentenced to long imprisonment for distribution of leaflets reminding people of their constitutional rights. Even a number of prominent West European Communists protested the harsh treatment of the dissidents.

"Normalization" continued to be pressed home also on the cultural front. Twelve liberal-minded members of Prague's prestigious National Theater were forced into retirement. The renowned Prague avant-garde theater known as the Theater Behind the Gate was closed, and eight actors and actresses of the Waterloo Theater in the mining city of Ostrava were sent to jail for alleged provocative distortion of a Soviet play. The number of titles on the index of prohibited books reached 250. The class-political criterion in admissions to institutions of higher learning was reemphasized, textbooks continued to be expunged, and obligatory political-ideological courses were further expanded.

Religion. The regime also escalated in 1972 its campaign against religion in general and the Roman Catholic Church in particular. While being waged largely with the help of propaganda in the Czech lands, the campaign acquired at times an outright persecutory character in Slovakia.

Government and Politics. Following the general elections of November 1971, a reshuffling took place in December 1971 in the composition of the highest state organs. The veteran pro-Soviet hardliner, Alois Indra, became the new chairman of the Federal Assembly. Another orthodox Communist, Václav David, former minister of foreign affairs and a close associate of former President Antonín Novotný (deposed in 1968), was chosen as chairman of the Federal Assembly's Chamber of the People. His predecessor, Dalibor Haneš, took over the chairmanship of the Chamber of Nations. Lubomír Štrougal was reappointed as chairman of the federal Council of Ministers. No significant charges occurred in the new cabinet, except that the foreign affairs portfolio was assigned to Bohuslav Chňoupek, former ambassador to the Soviet Union. One other change

——— CZECHOSLOVAKIA • Information Highlights ———

Official Name: Czechoslovak Socialist Republic.
Area: 49,370 square miles (127,869 sq km).
Population (1972 est.): 14,900,000. *Density,* 293 per square mile (113 per sq km). *Annual rate of increase,* 0.5%.
Chief Cities (1969 est.): Prague, the capital, 1,103,350; Brno, 339,227; Bratislava, 291,124; Ostrava, 279,771.
Government: *Head of state,* Ludvík Svoboda, president (took office March 1968). *Head of government,* Lubomír Štrougal, premier (took office Jan. 1970). *Communist party secretary general,* Gustáv Husák (took office April 1969). *Legislature*—Federal Assembly: Chamber of the People, 200 members; Chamber of Nations, 150 members.
Languages: Czech and Slovak (both official), Hungarian, German, Russian.
Education: *Expenditure* (1969), 7.5% of total public expenditure. *School enrollment* (1969)—primary, 2,002,053; secondary, 390,057; technical/vocational, 274,178; university/higher, 133,524.
Monetary Unit: Koruna (6.63 koruny equal U. S.$1, June 1972).
Gross National Product (1970 est.): $30,900,000,000.
Per Capita Gross National Product (1970): $2,244.
Economic Indexes: *Industrial production* (1970), 156 (1963=100); *agricultural production* (1970), 113 (1957–59=100); *consumer price index* (1971), 101 (1969=100).
Manufacturing (major products): Chemicals, petroleum products, glass and ceramics, textiles, iron and steel, footwear, automobiles, processed foods, beverages.
Major Agricultural Products: Sugar beets, rye, oats, wheat, potatoes, hops.
Major Minerals: Lignite, coal, magnesite, iron ore, antimony.
Foreign Trade (1971): *Exports,* $4,180,000,000 (chief exports, 1969—nonelectrical machinery; transport equipment; iron and steel; electrical machinery and appliances; chemicals). *Imports,* $4,010,000,000 (chief imports 1969—nonelectrical machinery; food; mineral fuels and lubricants; chemicals). *Chief trading partners* (1969)—USSR (took 34% of exports, supplied 34% of imports); East Germany (11%—13%); Poland (7%—8%); West Germany (5%—4%).
Tourism: *Receipts* (1970), $46,100,000.
Transportation: *Motor vehicles* (1970), 1,024,400 (automobiles, 825,800); *railroads* (1970), 8,275 miles (13,317 km); *merchant fleet* (1971), 83,000 gross registered tons; *major national airline,* Ceskoslovenske Aerolinie.
Communications: *Telephones* (1971), 2,003,421; *television stations* (1971), 28; *television sets* (1971), 2,997,000; *radios* (1970), 3,858,000; *newspapers* (1970), 28 (daily circulation, 3,641,000).

worthy of notice was the removal of Bohuslav Kučera, chairman of the Czechoslovak Socialist party, from his post of minister without portfolio. As a result, for the first time since the Communist take-over in 1948, the Council of Ministers was staffed exclusively by Communists.

A new federal law in June brought about a reorganization of the administration of agriculture. With an avowed purpose of strengthening further the influence of the state on agricultural production, the regional and district agricultural associations were replaced by regional and district agricultural administrations headed by directors appointed jointly by the ministers of agriculture and of food.

Economy. On the whole, economic results attained in the first half of 1972 were favorable. Compared to the same period of 1971, industrial production increased by 7.3%, with especially high rates of growth in rubber and plastic processing, chemicals, and oil refining. Construction rose by 12.5%, largely as a result of heavy concentration on Czechoslovakia's "building project of the century"—the pipeline being constructed from the Soviet border across Czechoslovakia and designed to provide transit for Soviet petroleum to be sold to the West. Labor productivity in industry climbed by 6.6% and in construction by 9.3%. The income of the population increased by 5.8%, and retail trade rose by 5.7%.

Nonetheless, some 15% of industrial plants and more than 30% of building enterprises failed to meet their midyear quotas. As a result, less than 40% of dwellings planned for 1972 were completed in the first half of 1972, and only a mere 18% of apartments scheduled to be constructed in Prague in 1972 were ready for occupancy by July.

The outlook for agricultural production was said to be only moderately good.

Artist's rendering of Dallas' new City Hall complex, scheduled to be completed in 1975.

Foreign Affairs. The fifth round of the protracted West German–Czechoslovak talks on the normalization of relations was held in Prague in June. Once again, however, the negotiations remained deadlocked because of the West German refusal to yield to Czechoslovakia's demand that West Germany declare the Munich Agreement of 1938 (which resulted in the dismemberment of Czechoslovakia) as having been invalid from its inception.

A further cooling in Czechoslovak-Austrian relations occurred in May as a result of a new border incident in which Czechoslovak border guards abducted from Austrian territory a naturalized South African citizen of Czech descent.

EDWARD TABORSKY
University of Texas at Austin

DAHOMEY

Rapid changes of government and a weak economy continued to plague Dahomey during 1972.

Domestic Politics. Dahomey's unique three-man Presidential Council underwent its first leadership transition on May 7 when Justin Ahomadégbé became president, succeeding Hubert Maga who had filled the office since 1970. The armed forces, actively involved in Dahomean politics since 1963, did not interfere with the transition. However, a military coup in Cotonou on October 26 ousted the new president, and an 11-man military government was named the following day. Maj. Mathieu Kerekou, who reportedly led the coup, was named head of state and defense minister, and Maj. Michel Alabaye

was named foreign minister. Dahomey now has had 11 changes in government, including five successful military coups, since it gained independence in 1960.

In February an abortive attempt to assassinate Col. Paul Émile de Souza, the army chief of staff, led to the arrest and trial of 22 soldiers. Lieut. Col. Maurice Kouandete and five others were condemned to death, while five were given life sentences; all were pardoned after the October coup.

International Politics. Maga visited Washington in December 1971 for talks with President Nixon. In January Dahomey was admitted to the Afro-Asian Peoples' Solidarity Organization. Maga agreed, in a meeting with President Eyadema of Togo, to reduce frontier restrictions to an "absolute minimum."

Economic Development. France continued to pour support into the Dahomean economy. A grant of $877,000 in December 1971 and a loan of $1.8 million went directly to various projects. The International Development Association provided a credit of $1.6 million for cotton production, while the United States loaned $7.5 million for renovation of the main road in northern Dahomey.

Social Unrest. High schools were rocked in December 1971 by strikes, leading the government to close all schools and to dissolve the students' union.

CLAUDE E. WELCH, JR.
State University of New York at Buffalo

DAIRY PRODUCTS. See AGRICULTURE.

DALLAS

Dallas, the second-largest city in Texas and the eighth-largest in the United States, continued to grow in 1972. The city's population was estimated to have been 858,350 in July 1972, an increase of nearly 14,000 over the 1970 census. Approval of major improvement programs and the tremendous amount of construction underway in 1972 seemed to promise considerable further expansion.

Improvements and Construction. In June, Dallas voters approved the second-largest capital improvements program in the city's history. Among the items included in the $172 million program were $23 million for improvements to parks and recreation facilities, funds for the design and construction of three additional branch libraries, and an appropriation for the design of a new central library. Funds were also appropriated for a site for a centralized multimodal transportation facility that

---

——— **DAHOMEY · Information Highlights** ———

Official Name: Republic of Dahomey.
Area: 43,483 square miles (112,622 sq km).
Population (1972 est.): 2,800,000. *Density,* 62 per square mile (24 per sq km). *Annual rate of increase,* 2.6%.
Chief Cities (1965 est.): Cotonou, the capital, 111,100; Porto-Novo, 74,500.
Government: *Head of government,* Maj. Mathieu Kerekou (took power October 1972), head of 11-member military government.
Languages: French (official), numerous tribal languages.
Education: *School enrollment* (1968)—primary, 148,625; secondary, 15,772; technical/vocational, 717; higher, 174.
Monetary Unit: CFA franc (255.79 CFA francs equal U. S.$1, Aug. 1972).
Gross National Product (1970 est.): $235,000,000.
Manufacturing (major products): Palm oil products.
Major Agricultural Products: Coffee, palm oil and kernels, cotton, cassava, sweet potatoes and yams.
Foreign Trade (1971): *Exports,* $42,000,000. *Imports,* $76,-000,000. *Chief trading partners* (1969)—France (took 36% of exports, supplied 39% of imports); Netherlands (13%—7%); United States (10%—6%).
Communications: *Telephones* (1971), 6,424; *radios* (1970), 85,000; *newspapers* (1970), 2 (daily circulation, 2,000).

would be capable of accommodating rapid transit, ground transportation service to airport terminals, rail transportation, and intercity buses.

In August, ground was broken for the new City Hall complex, scheduled for completion in January 1975. I. M. Pei and Partners designed the $35.5 million structure. It was to be fronted by a 6.5-acre park plaza and was to have three levels of underground parking facilities. Tunnel walkways were to connect the complex with the Dallas Memorial Auditorium–Convention Center. Expansion of the Convention Center itself was completed in 1972, increasing available convention space in the city by 1.4 million square feet.

Some 4 million square feet of office space were added in the Dallas area during 1972. Among the buildings under construction during the year were the First International Building, a 58-story structure of silver-mirror glass, which will be Dallas' tallest building; the 2001 Bryan Tower, a 41-story mirror-glass building; and Main Tower, a 28-story opaque-glass building. The Dallas–Fort Worth International Airport was ahead of its construction schedule in 1972. Four of a planned 13 loop-shaped terminals were expected to open by mid-1973. These four terminals alone were to provide more than 60 gates for eight major airlines.

Education. The Dallas County Junior College System marked the beginning of the 1972–73 academic year with the opening of its third suburban facility, the Richmond Campus. Located in north Dallas between the suburbs of Garland and Richardson, it enrolled an initial 3,500 students. Its anticipated maximum enrollment was 5,000. Underscoring both the need for and the self-supporting nature of the Junior College System, Dallas voters, in the first such referendum since 1965, approved $85 million in bonds for the system. New moneys were to be directed toward expanding existing facilities and constructing three additional campuses.

Entertainment. The State Fair Music Hall, located on the grounds of the 200-acre Fair Park, underwent major renovation in 1972 at a cost of $5.5 million. It reopened in October during the annual State Fair of Texas. The Music Hall is a center for many of the city's cultural activities, including the Dallas Summer Musicals, opera, ballet, concerts, and special events.

The Dallas Symphony Orchestra, under conductor Anshel Brusilow, carried out an international good-will tour in September 1972. Dallas' mayor, Wes Wise, accompanied the orchestra on its visits to El Salvador, Colombia, Panama, and Nicaragua.

SALLY CALDWELL
North Texas State University

DAMS

Dam failures and resultant flood damages in 1972 resulted in congressional action on a nationwide dam-inspection safety program. The inspection by the U. S. Army Corps of Engineers will include all artificial barriers and accessory works that impound water and are at least 25 feet (7.6 meters) high. Estimates indicate that there are 30,000 water-impounding structures and that 3,500 of them are more than 50 feet (15 meters) high. Dams that impound less than 15 acre-feet of water are excluded from the inspection.

Throughout the world, dams are being planned and constructed for many purposes—water storage, flood control, irrigation, navigation, electric power development, and recreational activities in reservoirs or along their shores.

Cochiti Dam. Cochiti Dam, on the Rio Grande between Albuquerque and Santa Fe, N. Mex., will be one of the country's largest earthfill dams. Its embankment, containing 63 million cubic yards (48 million cu meters) of earth, will rise 251 feet (77 meters) above the river. It will extend 5.1 miles

The 988-foot (300-meter) Nurek Dam on the Vakhsh River in Tadzhikistan, USSR, was completed in 1972.

NOVOSTI, FROM SOVFOTO

(8.2 km) across two adjacent watersheds as well as the river. This irrigation project by the U. S. Corps of Engineers is scheduled for completion in 1975 at a cost of $63 million.

Chatfield Dam. Another Corps of Engineers project is Chatfield Dam, an $83.5-million earth barrier being built primarily to protect the Denver, Colo., area from flooding by the South Platte River. It also has irrigation and recreational functions. The finished structure will be 13,070 feet (3,984 meters) long and will rise 150 feet (46 meters) above the riverbed. Its reservoir, which will provide 10 miles (16 km) of shoreline, will have a capacity of 20,000 acre-feet.

Wynoochee Dam. On Washington State's Olympic Peninsula, the Corps of Engineers is constructing Wynoochee Dam, a concrete gravity structure 672 feet (205 meters) long that rises 177 feet (54 meters) above the Wynoochee River. It contains 82,000 cubic yards (63,000 cu meters) of concrete. This section is flanked by earth dikes that extend the barrier to a length of 2,050 feet (625 meters). The reservoir being formed will be 4.4 miles (7 km) long, with a capacity of 70,000 acre-feet. The $13.3-million multipurpose project will enlarge the water supply of the city of Aberdeen and other communities in the area, improve the water supply for industry and agriculture, and aid in flood control.

Castaic Dam. Castaic Dam is a dual-purpose project of the California Water System. The earth-fill embankment has a mile-long (1.6-km) crest length and a height of 335 feet (102 meters). The dam, which slopes out to a maximum base width of 2,200 feet (670 meters), contains more than 44 million cubic yards (33.6 million cu meters) of material. It cost $53-million to construct. Castaic Lake, formed by the dam, is 40 miles (64 km) north of Los Angeles. It provides water for domestic use and also serves as a reservoir for a type of hydroelectric power plant called a pumped-storage plant.

Pyramid Dam. Another California Aqueduct project is Pyramid Dam, which is scheduled for completion in 1973. Costing $22 million, the rock-filled embankment will be 381 feet (116 meters) high and 1,000 feet (305 meters) long and will contain 6.7 million cubic yards (5.1 million cu meters) of material. The dam will create a 179,000 acre-foot reservoir, storing water for consumption, irrigation, and a pumped-storage generating plant.

Lost Creek Dam. The Corps of Engineers is building a rock and earthfill structure on the Rogue River near Medford, Oreg. Lost Creek Dam, for flood control and power development, will be 3,700 feet (1,128 meters) long and 227 feet (69 meters) high. Its two generators will produce 49,000 kw of electric power. The embankment will contain over 10 million cubic yards (7.6 million cu meters) of material. It will cost about $50 million.

Cassatot Dam. Cassatot Dam, a rockfill barrier for flood control and water supply, is under construction at Gillham Lake on the Cassatot River, Ark. Containing over 1.5 million cubic yards (1.1 million cu meters) of material, the 1,750-foot (533-meter) long dam will be 160 feet (49 meters) high. It will cost about $3.5 million and will be completed by 1976.

Tachien Dam. In Taiwan, Italian and Japanese contractors are building Tachien Dam to develop the hydroelectric potential of the Tachia River basin. Scheduled for completion in 1974, the double-curvature concrete-arch dam rises 590 feet (180 meters) and has a crest length of 935 feet (285 meters). It ranges in thickness from 15 to 66 feet (4.5 to 20 meters), with a concrete volume of 549,000 cubic yards (430,000 cu meters). The reservoir will have a storage capacity of 230 million cubic yards (175 million cu meters). An underground powerhouse will have three turbine generators developing 234,000 kw. The stored water also will be used for irrigating agricultural lands.

Sirikit Dam. In Thailand, Italian contractors, a crew of 1,500 Thai workers, and American earth-moving machines completed Sirikit Dam in 1972. The rolled-earth dam is located on the Nan River near Uttaradit, about 280 miles (450 km) north of Bangkok. The dam and its power plant not only will provide irrigation and electric power but also will aid flood control, salinity control, and navigation on the lower reaches of the Chao Phraya, Thailand's principal river. Built at a cost of $28.4 million, the dam has a crest length of 2,559 feet (780 meters) and a height of 338 feet (103 meters). Originally called Phansom Dam, the structure was renamed in honor of Thailand's Queen Sirikit.

Chivor Dam. In Colombia, an Italian contracting firm is building rockfill Chivor Dam, a hydroelectric project on the Bata River. The 771-foot (235-meter) structure will rank among the ten highest dams in the world. In the powerhouse, four turbine-generator sets will develop 1 million kw of power when placed in operation in 1975.

Mrantinje Dam. The Mrantinje Dam, under construction on the Piva River, is about 60 miles (97 km) from Titograd, Yugoslavia. The double-curvature concrete-arch dam is 722 feet (220 meters) high, 73 feet (22 meters) thick at the crest, and 130 feet (40 meters) thick at the base. It will rank among the 15 highest in the world when completed and will contain 970,000 cubic yards (742,000 cu meters) of concrete. The hydroelectric power project will develop 360,000 kw in an underground powerhouse scheduled for completion in 1973.

Reza Shah Kabir Dam. When completed, the Reza Shah Kabir Dam will be Iran's highest. Located in a rocky gorge on the Karoun River near the Persian Gulf, the concrete-arch structure will have a height of 656 feet (200 meters), a crest length of 1,250 feet (381 meters), and a base thickness of 93 feet (28 meters). It will contain 1.6 million cubic yards (1.3 million cu meters) of concrete. The multipurpose dam will create a reservoir of about 21 square miles (54 sq km), providing about 2.35 million acre-feet of storage for irrigation and power development. The powerhouse will have four 250,-000 kw generating units; two units were to be installed by May 1974, with the third and fourth units following at one-year intervals. Named in honor of the father of the present Shah, the project will cost approximately $120 million.

Ragun Dam. The USSR is planning to build a 1,040-foot (317-meter) high dam at Ragun, on the Vakhsh River in southern Tadzhikistan. The earth and rockfill embankments will contain 73 million cubic yards (56 million cu meters) of material, have a crest length of 2,624 feet (800 meters), and measure 4,920 feet (1,500 meters) toe-to-toe through the base. When completed, Ragun Dam will be the highest one in the world, topping the record 988-foot (300-meter) Nurek Dam, on the Vakhsh River, which was inaugurated in November 1972.

WILLIAM H. QUIRK
"Contractors & Engineers" Magazine

dance

New York City Center staged a benefit performance on January 12 to save the New York Public Library's dance collection. Among the many illustrious participants in the gala were (front row, second and third from left) Agnes de Mille and Margot Fonteyn.

Statistics published in 1972 indicate that attendance at ballet or modern dance events in the United States has increased 500% since 1965 and that in the same period the number of dance performances has increased 600%. The dance audience, which was formerly limited to New York and one or two other large cities, has shifted, with the result that 73% of the audience is now outside New York. Although the larger audience includes people of all ages, the young are especially prominent, and a survey conducted by the Association of College and University Concert Managers showed that on the 140 campuses covered by the study more ballet performances were sold out than rock concerts.

A major event that showed the variety and fertility of dance in America took place in New York at the City Center on January 24, a gala performance to benefit the Dance Collection of the New York Public Library. The program, directed by Donald Saddler, consisted of excerpts, short works, and solos in wide-ranging styles from American modern dance and classic ballet. Outstanding modern selections were a pas de deux danced by Merce Cunningham and Carolyn Brown; Judith Jamison in *Cry,* a solo choreographed by Alvin Ailey; and the New York premiere of *Tragic Celebration,* a solo choreographed by John Butler and danced by Lawrence Rhodes. Even more impressive were the classical works performed by such dancers as Melissa Hayden, Peter Martins, Natalia Makarova, Carla Fracci, Violette Verdy, Eleanor D'Antuono, Patricia McBride, Dame Margot Fonteyn (partnered by Attilio Labis of the Paris Opera), and many others. Gelsey Kirkland and Helgi Tomasson of the New York City Ballet danced a spectacular *Don Quixote Pas de Deux,* and the American Ballet Theatre presented a revival of Antony Tudor's *Judgment of Paris,* with Agnes de

Mille, Lucia Chase, Maria Karnilova, Hugh Laing, and John Kriza. Miss Chase and Miss Karnilova still perform character roles, but the others had retired years ago. Laing and Miss de Mille were performing roles they had created in 1938.

There have been other gala benefit programs, but it is doubtful that any have assembled on one stage such a large collection of the world's most important dancers as on this historic occasion. The Dance Collection was in danger of being closed because of financial deficit, and the purpose of the benefit was to raise $63,679 to cover it. The dancers and musicians all contributed their services, and the gross for the evening was more than $105,000.

Ballet in America. In January the Danish dancer Erik Bruhn suddenly announced his retirement as a performer at the age of 43 because of illness (a peptic ulcer). Trained at the Royal Danish Ballet and since 1950 associated with the American Ballet Theatre (ABT), Bruhn was considered by many authorities the greatest classical dancer of his generation. He was a remarkable technician even in his early youth, and in his maturity he developed interpretive abilities that made him a great dancing actor. Bruhn had partnered both of ABT's principal ballerinas, Carla Fracci and Natalia Makarova. Niels Kehlet, also a Dane, was imported to fill a number of Bruhn's scheduled engagements. He made a fine impression as Miss Fracci's partner in *Coppélia,* showing the same impeccable line and technique that had distinguished Bruhn as a young dancer.

Later in the season, ABT engaged Paolo Bortoluzzi, formerly of Maurice Béjart's Ballet of the 20th Century. His first performances in *Giselle* and *Spectre of the Rose* were marred by stylistic excesses. However, he soon adjusted to ABT's style and gave more than creditable performances in

several ballets, especially in *La Sylphide* (partnering Miss Makarova).

Ivan Nagy, already a promising soloist with the American Ballet Theatre, was frequently paired with Miss Makarova and improved considerably when challenged by the task of partnering this famous defector from the Soviet Union. As the year progressed they developed a warm rapport and gave exciting performances in such works as *Giselle, Swan Lake,* and *La Fille mal gardée.*

Of the ballets added to ABT's repertoire during 1972, Eliot Feld's *Intermezzo* was the most successful. Like Balanchine's *Liebeslieder Walzer,* it is danced to a piano score by Brahms, and some critics noted Balanchine's influence on Feld's choreography, but the work has bravura qualities and touches of humor that are uniquely Feld's.

America's other great classical company, the New York City Ballet (NYCB) produced a controversial work in Jerome Robbins' *Watermill,* set to a score by the Japanese composer Teiji Ito. It concerns a man contemplating his entire life, and Edward Villella had a great success as the central character. The ballet, however, is a difficult one for audiences because of its innovativeness. Clive Barnes, dance and drama critic of the New York *Times,* commented on Robbins' development of "the idea of time as a space rather than as an entity." Subtleties of this kind were lost on many in the audience at the world premiere (February 3), and there were boos among the cheers at the end of the performance. Barnes championed the work in several articles, and he wrote that although he admitted that *Watermill* would probably never become popular, it is "a ballet that will be talked about as long as people talk about ballet or indeed talk about art."

Ballet history was made in June when the New York City Ballet staged a monumental festival in honor of the late Igor Stravinsky, with whom George Balanchine, NYCB's ballet master and principal choreographer, had collaborated many times. The festival, which took place at the New York State Theater at Lincoln Center June 18–25, consisted of seven performances devoted entirely to works set to music by Stravinsky. There were revivals of such ballets as Balanchine's *Firebird, Apollo, Agon,* and *Orpheus,* along with 20 world premieres of works choreographed by Balanchine, Jerome Robbins, John Taras, Todd Bolender, and others. Although the new works were not of uniform excellence, the festival, which is without precedent, was a major artistic triumph. Balanchine's *Violin Concerto* and Robbins' *Dumbarton Oaks* were especially well received, as was *Pulcinella,* on which Balanchine and Robbins collaborated and in which they performed small roles. Later in the summer the company danced a number of the new Stravinsky works at Saratoga Springs, N. Y., where NYCB appears annually, and in the fall 14 of the new ballets entered the regular NYCB repertoire. In August, the company danced in Munich, West Germany, as part of the cultural program that was an adjunct to the Olympic Games, and in September and October they made a tour of Poland and the Soviet Union.

New works presented by the City Center Joffrey Ballet included Gerald Arpino's *Sacred Grove on Mount Tamalpais* and *Chabriesque.* Neither was judged to be up to the level of Arpino's best work, but *Chabriesque* was more successful when revised for the fall season. *Double Exposure* by Joe Layton, a ballet inspired by Oscar Wilde's *Picture of Dorian Gray,* was a failure dramatically and choreographically. The company had better luck with revivals of Leonide Massine's *Le Beau Danube* and Jerome Robbins' *Interplay,* both of which were welcomed by critics and public alike.

Although New York remains the dance capital of the nation, companies resident in other cities are growing in strength. The Pennsylvania Ballet, from Philadelphia, and the National Ballet, from Washington, D. C., came up for reappraisal in 1972, presenting short seasons in New York. The National Ballet, which stresses the classics, appeared at the City Center in February in a repertoire that included two of their full-length works. They were *The Sleeping Beauty* (Tchaikovsky) and *Cinderella* (Prokofiev), staged by Ben Stevenson, who co-directs the company with Frederick Franklin. Both works were regarded as major achievements, and the company's level of dancing has improved considerably.

Most New York critics noted a similar improvement in the work of the Pennsylvania Ballet in their appearances at the City Center in April. The company's male contingent, led by Lawrence Rhodes and Keith Martin, is particularly strong. However, aside from the works by Balanchine and John Butler, the repertoire seemed weak.

JUDITH JAMISON, acclaimed in 1972 both as a member of the Alvin Ailey American Dance Theater and on her own as a solo performer, is seen below in Cry.

ROSEMARY WINCKLEY

The Boston Ballet, one of the most prominent companies outside New York, has failed to improve at the same rate as the National and Pennsylvania companies. Both Clive Barnes and Walter Terry, dance critic of *Saturday Review,* reported disappointment in the work of the company's resident choreographer Samuel Kurkjian (they were reviewing his *Leopardi Fragments* to a score by Peter Maxwell Davies) and in the quality of the company's dancing. However, the Boston Ballet presented the American debut of an important Italian dancer, Liliana Cosi. Miss Cosi, prima ballerina at La Scala in Milan, was partnered by Richard Cragun (of the Stuttgart Ballet) in *Les Sylphides* and the pas de deux from Act I of John Cranko's *Romeo and Juliet.*

Modern Dance in America. Many modern American choreographers and such companies as those of Paul Taylor and Alwin Nikolais receive greater acclaim in Europe, where they seem exotic or advanced, than they do in the United States, where they are taken somewhat for granted and where they dance for comparatively small audiences. The Alvin Ailey City Center Dance Theater, however, is an exception, and when it opened its spring season, the City Center management announced that Ailey's company had had a larger advance sale of tickets than any other event in the history of that theater. New works in the spring season were Ailey's *The Lark Ascending* (to music by Vaughan Williams) and *A Song for You* (with music by Leon Russell). There was also a new production of Donald McKayle's *Rainbow Round My Shoulder.*

The Ailey Company, predominantly black, has many virtues that attract its enthusiastic audiences, but a part of the troupe's popularity must be credited to the emergence of Judith Jamison, the company's leading female soloist, as a major star, whose appeal reaches beyond the usual audience for modern dance. In May, Miss Jamison received the Dance Magazine Award, given for significant contributions in the field of dance.

A unique panorama of modern dance was presented in New York at the ANTA Theater by the City Center American Dance Marathon, a six-week festival that began October 2, including 20 companies (or soloists). In style the works featured at the marathon ranged from that of older established choreographers, such as Anna Sokolow and José Limón (who died in December), to the avant garde as represented by Twyla Tharpe and others. Several major choreographers such as Martha Graham, Paul Taylor, Merce Cunningham, and Alwin Nikolais did not appear, but the marathon gave a broad survey of the current state of modern dance. The participating companies included those of Donald McKayle, Bella Lewitzky, Gloria Newman, Paul Sanasardo, Lotte Goslar, Cliff Keuter, Elizabeth Keen, Erick Hawkins, and Viola Farber; Pauline Koner and Carmen de Lavallade were among the soloists. The marathon was a frank bid to build for modern dance the kind of audience that currently supports ballet companies.

Visitors from Abroad. Among the foreign companies that appeared in the United States was Britain's Royal Ballet, which in April made its first visit to New York since choreographer Kenneth MacMillan became director of the company. The dancers were in spendid form in the classics, but the repertoire included many weak contemporary ballets such as Macmillan's *Triad, The Invitation,* and *Anas-*

AMERICAN BALLET THEATER

NATALIA MAKAROVA AND IVAN NAGY became a bright new dance team (above, in Giselle) for the American Ballet Theater after her previous partner retired.

tasia. The Vienna State Opera Ballet made a transcontinental tour, but did not appear in New York. Their reception was generally poor despite the presence of guest star Dame Margot Fonteyn. The Netherlands Dance Theater, a modern dance company that performed at the Brooklyn Academy of Music, created a small sensation with its nude ballet, *Mutations,* choreographed by Glen Tetley.

Maurice Béjart's Ballet of the 20th Century gave 19 performances of Béjart's *Nijinsky—Clown of God* at the Felt Forum in New York. Billed as a "super spectacle too large for any theater," it had passionate defenders and detractors. In the New York *Times* it was defended by Baird Searles as an eye-opening theater piece and damned by Clive Barnes as a monumental bore.

On the whole, the visitors who did best were folk or ethnic companies such as the Dukla Ukrainian Dance Company, and if a new trend was discernible in the bookings for the 1972–73 season, it was toward the exotic, typified by the Brooklyn Academy's Afro-Asian Festival, which presented the Dancers of Mali, dervish dances performed by a religious brotherhood from Turkey, and the Darpana Dance Company of India.

José Limón. One of the giants of modern dance, José Limón, died in Flemington, N. J., on December 2. Limón had headed his own dance troupe since the late 1940's and was probably best known for his interpretation of the Othello story in *The Moor's Pavane* (1949), which he choreographed and in which he danced the Moor. See also NECROLOGY.

WILLIAM LIVINGSTONE
Managing Editor, "Stereo Review"

DEATH RATES. See POPULATION.

DEFENSE FORCES

The year 1972 marked the first time in the 25-year-old Cold War that the defense forces of the two superpowers, the Soviet Union and the United States, were limited in size by agreements arrived at between the two nations. The size constraints were set forth in two documents signed by President Nixon and Communist Secretary Leonid I. Brezhnev during their May summit meeting in Moscow. Several years of hard bargaining between representatives of the two nations at the Strategic Arms Limitation Talks (SALT) preceded the acceptance of the arms restrictions by the two leaders.

The rationale for finally making a start on arms control by the world's two most powerful nations is suggested in a third document agreed to in Moscow in May. This document, entitled *Basic Principles of Relations Between the United States of America and the Union of Soviet Socialist Republics,* includes the statement: "They will proceed from the common determination that in the nuclear age there is no alternative to conducting their mutual relations on the basis of peaceful coexistence. Differences in ideology and in the social systems of the United States and the USSR are not obstacles to the bilateral development of normal relations based on the principles of sovereignty, equality, noninterference in internal affairs and mutual advantage."

The SALT accords were not comprehensive in their coverage, and they call for no limitations at all on the quality of weapons developed and deployed by the two superpowers. The accord does specify quantitative limitations only on intercontinental ballistic missiles (ICBM's), submarine-launched ballistic missiles (SLBM's), and antiballistic missiles (ABM's). No limitations were placed on the number of bombers nor on the number of nuclear warheads for missiles or bombs for aircraft.

United States

The major event in U. S. defense policy in 1972 was the signing of the SALT agreements in May. The administration's defense budget and spending were also important issues.

SALT. The SALT accords generally were well received in the United States and won approval by wide margins in the Congress, but some influential spokesmen for conservative and military interests expressed concern over parts of the agreements.

The section of the SALT accord most enthusiastically received in the United States was the one titled *Treaty Between the United States of America and the Union of the Soviet Socialist Republics on the Limitations of Anti-Ballistic Missile Systems.* By this agreement, which is a permanent treaty, the antiballistic missiles, or ABM's, of each nation are limited in number to 200. The treaty stipulates that no more than 100 ABM's be placed around each nation's capital, with the second 100 located around an intercontinental ballistic missile (ICBM) installation. Such deployment allows each nation

J. P. LAFFONT, GAMMA

Bombs stacked in Guam are for use in Vietnam. Since 1965, the United States has dropped in Indochina about 3½ times the explosives used in World War II.

Soviets actually possessed approximately 740 SLBM's to the American total of 656. The difference in current numbers of SLBM's relative to the maximum number permissible is explained by the fact that each side may "trade in" a certain number of old ICBM's in order to receive the option of building the same number of new SLBM's.

The *Interim Agreement* provided the United States with a greater number of missile warheads (5,700 to 2,500) and many more long-range bombers (approximately 500, compared with 140) than the Soviet Union. The difference in numbers of missile warheads was accounted for by the fact that the United States had started to place multiple independently targeted reentry vehicles (MIRV's) on many of its ICBM's and SLBM's, whereas the Soviets still lagged in such development.

The MIRV is a package of warheads instead of the normal single warhead carried by each missile. In the case of U.S. ICBM's there are at least three warheads in every MIRV package, and for SLBM's there may be as many as ten warheads in each MIRV package. The greater number of long-range bombers allowed the United States reflects the fact that the United States has always enjoyed a marked superiority in such aircraft since the Cold War began in the late 1940's.

Those concerned about the greater number of missiles permitted the Soviet Union by the *Interim Agreement* were also worried by the fact that the Soviets are expected to perfect and deploy MIRV's in the near future and because some of the Soviet ICBM's are much larger and can carry more payload than American ICBM's. Thus the Soviets could conceivably possess within the next five years —the life of the *Interim Agreement*—a substantially greater number of both missiles and warheads than the United States. Some view this circumstance as dangerous, for it might provide the Soviets with the capability of launching a "first strike"—that is, a strike designed to destroy U.S. land-based retaliatory forces before they can be launched. Such a "first strike" would be dangerous for the Soviet Union unless it was also able to destroy the U.S. SLBM's, either before or after their launching.

Administration Counterattack. The Nixon administration countered the criticism of the *Interim Agreement* in two ways. First, it accepted the advice of the so-called "hardliners" that in the second round of SALT negotiations, which began in late 1972, the American negotiators be instructed to seek further agreements that would provide for U.S.-Soviet strategic nuclear forces to be relatively equal in numbers. Should this be accomplished the general expectation is that the *Interim Agreement* would then be replaced by a permanent treaty embodying a rough parity relationship between the two superpowers. Further, the Nixon administration holds what it claims are important bargaining chips for use in either pressuring the Soviets to accept a treaty based on weapons equality, or if such a treaty is not obtained and the Soviets move for superiority, that it has the infrastructure to compete with the Soviets in weapons acquisitions.

The bargaining chips, or infrastructure, to race the Soviets in weapons acquisitions is represented by two major new strategic nuclear weapon systems now being researched and developed by the United States—one called Trident, the other, the B-1 bomber. Trident, formerly termed underseas long-range missile system, or ULMS, is perhaps the most

to protect its capital from accidental small firings of missiles by the other side and from Chinese attack until such time as China develops large numbers of sophisticated missiles. Further, the treaty permits the superpowers to build and test their ABM systems in case they need to expand them in response to the Chinese threat. There are no qualitative restrictions in the ABM treaty.

Interim Agreement on Offensive Arms—Pros and Cons. Most of the objections to the SALT accords were directed at the agreement titled *Interim Agreement Between the United States of America and the Union of Soviet Socialist Republics on Certain Measures with Respect to the Limitation of Strategic Offensive Arms*, which became known as the *Interim Agreement on Offensive Arms.* Sen. Henry M. Jackson (D, Wash.), Sen. James L. Buckley (C, N.Y.), and others pointed out that this agreement permitted the Soviet Union higher numbers of ICBM's and SLBM's than were permitted U.S. forces. For example, the Soviet Union is permitted 1,618 ICBM's, the number of missiles operational or under construction at the time of the agreement signing, while the number permitted the United States is 1,054. The number of SLBM's permitted the Soviet Union is a maximum of 950 carried on no more than 62 nuclear-powered submarines. The number for the United States is 710 SLBM's aboard no more than 44 similar submarines. At the time the agreement was signed the

THE F-5E, the Air Force's new twin-jet supersonic fighter, made its maiden test flight in August 1972.

impressive of the systems. It would be composed of new, larger, harder-to-detect nuclear-powered submarines that would carry a new missile with a 5,000-mile range, considerably greater than the currently deployed SLBM's.

The threat to deploy the Trident is not only a ploy in pressuring the Russians to make further SALT agreements but it also serves as a hedge in case the Soviets add large numbers of MIRV's to their larger number of missiles, thus endangering the U. S. land-based bombers and ICBM's. Should that happen, the clear intent of the United States is to move its retaliatory forces to the sea with Trident. Besides increasing the survivability of the U. S. forces, the Trident system, if deployed, would greatly increase the difficulty of the Soviets in their efforts to blunt an American retaliatory strike. Not only would the Trident submarines be harder to discover than the current SLBM submarines but their missiles can be launched from all points of the compass toward targets in the Soviet Union. These facts greatly increase the difficulty of the Soviet's defense task. At the present time, because of their relatively short range, American SLBM's can be fired at the Soviet Union only from certain areas in the oceans, which means the Soviets can calculate the direction of an attack and concentrate their defensive efforts accordingly.

The second and possibly weaker bargaining chip, or part of the infrastructure, involves the development of the new strategic bomber called the B-1, formerly termed the advanced manned strategic aircraft, or AMSA. This plane is being designed to penetrate the extensive radar and defensive missile facilities operated by the Soviets. Although the U. S. Air Force disagrees, many contend that the B-1 is less desirable than the Trident because of its vulnerability to attack before takeoff by Soviet SLBM's fired from off the U. S. coast, thus cutting warning time substantially.

Administration Defense Spending and Force Levels. In something of a contradiction, the budget approved for fiscal 1973 for the Department of Defense was approximately $74.5 billion, the largest defense spending sum since World War II. There were two reasons for this high figure at a time when many believed the United States was reducing its military forces due to SALT and the reduction of participation in the war in Southeast Asia. First, increases in pay and fringe benefits were sought to enable the armed services to retain qualified personnel and to prepare for an all-volunteer Army, which by 1973 must rely on financial inducements rather than the draft. Second, there were increases in the budget for research and development and for other facets of the Strategic Offensive and Strategic Defensive Forces.

The Strategic Offensive Forces consists of the ICBM's and long-range bombers of the Strategic Air Command and the SLBM's of the Navy. Their mission is to deter attack on the United States and possibly Western Europe by threatening the "assured destruction" of the attacking nation in retaliation. The major spending in regard to offensive forces was for continued development of the Trident system and the B-1 bomber, for modernization of the ICBM and SLBM systems, and to add MIRV's to both types of missiles. Funds were also allocated to maintain the effectiveness of the bomber fleet. Such expenditures included the addition of the SRAM (short-range attack missile) to the bombers to enable them to attack enemy targets without flying so close as to drop bombs; the development of the SCAD (subsonic cruise armed decoy) for later deployment with the bombers as a device to confuse enemy anti-bomber defenses by simulating the radar reflection of a bomber; and the development of "satellite bomber bases" which would provide alternative basing for the dispersal of bombers in response to the threat of a Soviet SLBM attack.

The Strategic Defensive Forces is charged with providing warning of an attack on the United States and with providing "damage limitations" should an attack occur. These tasks are to be accomplished with a combination of fighter interceptors, ABM's, warning radars, communication arrangements of various kinds, and the Civil Defense program. The major spending areas in regard to the Strategic Defensive Forces were for AWACS (airborne warning and control system), which will involve the use of large jet aircraft to carry aloft radars for the early detection of bomber attack; and AABNCP

DIRECTORY OF MAJOR U. S. MISSILES

Missile	Status[1]	Service	Range[2] (nautical miles)	Propulsion
Surface-to-Surface				
Asroc[3]	O	Navy	...	Solid
Dragon[4]	O	Army	...	Solid
Lance	D	Army	...	Storable liquid
Honest John	O	Army	20	Solid
Minuteman I, II	O	AF	6300 and 7000	Solid
Minuteman III	O	AF	...	Solid
Pershing IA	O	Army	400	Solid
Polaris A-2, A-3[5]	O	Navy	1500 and 2500	Solid
Poseidon[5]	O	Navy	2500	Solid
Sergeant	O	Army	...	Solid
Shillelagh	O	Army	short	Solid
STAM[3]	S	Navy	...	...
Subroc[3]	O	Navy	10+	Solid
Titan II	O	AF	6300+	Storable liquid
Tow[4]	O	Army	...	Solid
ULMS and SLMS	D	Navy	5000+	Solid
Surface-to-Air				
APDMS	S	Navy	...	...
Bomarc B	N	AF	400	Solid or ramjet
Chaparral	O	Army	...	Solid
Hawk	O	Army	22	Solid
Improved Hawk	P	Army	...	Solid
Nike Hercules	O	Army	75	Solid
Redeye	O	Army	...	Solid
Sam-D	D	Army	...	Solid
Sea Sparrow	O	Navy	...	Solid
Sea Sparrow, NATO	D	Navy, NATO	...	Solid
Spartan	P	Army	Several hundred	Solid
Sprint	P	Army	25	Solid
Standard	O	Navy	10–30+	Solid
Stinger	D	Army	...	Solid
Talos	O	Navy	65+	Solid or ramjet
Tartar	O	Navy	10+	Solid
Terrier	O	Navy	20+	Solid
Air-to-Air				
Agile	D	Navy	...	...
Falcon	O	AF	2+	Solid
Genie	O	AF	6+	Solid
Phoenix	D	Navy	...	Solid
Sidewinder	O	AF–Navy	2+	Solid
Sparrow	O	AF–Navy	12	Solid
Sparrow III (Advanced)	D	AF–Navy	...	Solid
Air-to-Surface				
Bullpup	O	AF	5+	Liquid
Condor	D	Navy	...	Solid
Hound Dog	O	AF	600+	Turbojet
Maverick	P	AF	...	Solid
SCAD	S	AF	1000	Turbojet
Shrike	O	AF–Navy	...	Solid
SRAM	D	AF	50+	Solid
Standard ARM	O	AF–Navy	...	Solid
Walleye	O	AF–Navy	20+	None
Zuni	O	Navy	5	Solid
Air-to-Surface/Surface-to-Surface				
Harpoon	D	Navy	30+	Solid

[1] Status code: D, under development; N, nonoperational; O, operational; P, production; S, study. [2] One nautical mile equals 1.15 statute miles or 1.85 km. [3] Antisubmarine missile. [4] Antitank missile. [5] Subsurface to surface.

THE F-15, an air superiority fighter, was unveiled by the Air Force in 1972. It is expected to outperform any other aircraft in long-range or close combat.

(advanced airborne national command post), which involves the procurement of up to seven Boeing 747 jet transports that will be used to provide at all times an airborne command post presumably more secure from attack than are those on the ground. Related to maintaining the effectiveness of both the Strategic Offensive and Strategic Defensive Forces during a massive Soviet nuclear attack was funding to counter the possibility that an ominous phenomenon could be generated by large nuclear explosions. What was feared is called EMP (electromagnetic pulse), which, if the Soviets can induce it, would produce surges of energy that might seriously disrupt the communications and firing arrangements of U. S. Strategic Offensive and Defensive Forces.

The third combat component, the General Purpose Forces, whose mission is to deter or fight wars from below the thermonuclear level down to counterinsurgency actions, received slightly less funding in 1972 than in 1971. This despite procurement of several hundred new tanks; a new fighter plane for the Air Force, the F-15; and additional F-14's for the Navy. The reduction in the General Purpose Forces funding was obtained by decreases in Army and Air Force manpower made possible by the reduction of U. S. participation in Vietnam.

Presidential Election Politics. The defense force proposals of defeated Democratic candidate George McGovern to reduce the budget by some $20 billion to $30 billion in the next several years contrasted vividly with President Nixon's proposition of maintaining the defense budget in the current range or higher, until such time as substantially greater SALT-type agreements can be reached.

U. S. Air Force

In 1972 about half of all Air Force sorties in support of ground operations in Vietnam were taken over by the Air Force of South Vietnam. However, massive enlargement of bombing and other kinds of sorties over North Vietnam resulted in a substantial net increase in U. S. Air Force operations. In September the United States had about 950 combat aircraft in Southeast Asia—200 B-52 bombers in Thailand and Guam, four aircraft carriers with some 260 Navy fighters in the South China Sea, and 415 Air Force and 75 Marine warplanes based in Vietnam and Thailand.

Bombing Controversy. In the presidential election year, the people of the United States were given conflicting information and data as to Air Force operations. Many Air Force officers were claiming that air bombing was being severely restricted, at the very time when Congress was investigating

MCDONNELL DOUGLAS CORPORATION

alleged unauthorized bombing. One Air Force commander said, "We have a much greater capacity for destruction, but we are not going to inflict untold suffering on civilians. We are grinding the North Vietnamese forces up and sooner or later Hanoi will have to throw in the towel."

On the other hand, Gen. John D. Lavelle was dismissed in March and demoted for allegedly ordering unauthorized bombing of North Vietnam. General Lavelle had been severely criticized in December 1971 by the Joint Chiefs of Staff for not being sufficiently aggressive. In 1972, he allegedly ordered his men at least 20 times to bomb preplanned targets without first waiting to be fired upon —a violation of the "protective reaction" rules of engagement laid down by higher authority.

The case became even more serious when it was charged that 200 pilots and senior officers had faked classified reports to cover up what had been done, and that the unauthorized raids—which occurred over a period of some five months—had been known to Adm. Thomas H. Moorer, chairman of the Joint Chiefs of Staff, and to Gen. Creighton W. Abrams, nominee for Army chief of staff, who was the overall commander in Vietnam at the time. Both generals heatedly denied the charges. Senators John C. Stennis of Mississippi and Harold E. Hughes of Iowa made public their distress over the conflicting testimony and held that it would be equally disturbing whether the bombing was covered up at high levels or unknown to those higher echelons. The senators led an investigation by the Senate

MISSILE SYSTEMS DIVISION, NORTH AMERICAN ROCKWELL

"SMART BOMB," guided to pinpoint accuracy by television, was widely used in Vietnam in 1972.

Armed Services Committee. In October the committee exonerated Moorer and Abrams, but further reduced Lavelle's rank to that of major general.

Forces and Weapons Systems. Strategic arms limitations agreements signed in 1972 will have a direct and continuing effect on Air Force strategy and weapons systems. A congressional conference committee killed important efforts by the Air Force to upgrade the quality and effectiveness of nuclear warheads for ICBM's on the grounds that such steps may connote a U. S. move toward a "first strike" posture.

Congress approved $445 million for the Air Force–North American Rockwell B-1 bomber program and $561 million to complete the site, authorized under the 1972 arms limitation treaty, to protect Minuteman missiles at Grand Forks, N. Dak. The B-1 bomber was undergoing tests by its builders in 1972 and was set for an Air Force critical design review in March 1973.

Recruiting. With a reenlistment rate of 36% the Air Force met its recruiting objectives for fiscal 1972 (which ended June 30) and reversed a downward trend in the quality of recruits. The recruiting goal for fiscal 1973 was set at 100,000, to be obtained with a budget of $60.4 million.

During the year the Air Force noted a change in attitude of high school youth toward vocational education and emphasized its trade school advantages—95% of those who leave the Air Force go back to civilian life with a salable skill, and the Air Force retains the remaining 5% in a usable skill upon discharge. The Air Force refused to relax its discipline and training standards, easing its standards back to the level held before a slight slippage occurred at the height of the Indochina War.

Personnel. Gen. John W. Vogt, commander of the Seventh Air Force in Vietnam, was named to succeed Army Gen. Frederick C. Weyand as deputy commander of all forces in Vietnam, while continuing to serve as commander of the Seventh Air Force. This naming of General Vogt to a post formerly held by an Army general reflected the shift from ground warfare to heavy air activities.

Maj. Gen. Robert A. Patterson succeeded Lieut. Gen. Alonzo A. Towner as Air Force surgeon general. General Patterson is a pilot-physician and has been nominated for promotion, which is normal for his new duties.

WILLIAM J. McCONNELL
Colonel, USA, Retired; Colorado State University

U. S. Army

Reduction of the U. S. Army's manpower base continued in 1972. The total reduction for 1971–72 was the largest since the demobilization that followed World War II. In August the last Army ground combat unit was withdrawn from Vietnam. With the presidential election receiving so much attention during the year, there seemed to be a notable reduction in the amount of public interest in Army matters, and the almost complete lack of domestic upheaval within the United States contributed to this "low profile" for the Army in 1972.

Forces. The Army was committed to becoming a volunteer force by June 1973. Public statements by Secretary of Defense Melvin Laird indicated that there was small probability of anyone being drafted after Jan. 1, 1973. Recruiter strength was doubled in 1972 to 6,000, specifically to work toward the all-volunteer Army. Rewards to all ranks were sweetened by an Army regulation that grants furlough time for finding acceptable applicants for Army service.

Scandals, such as senior noncommissioned officers misusing recreational funds, hurt the Army's image, making the job of recruiters more difficult. There was a trend in 1972 away from "promising too much too soon" in terms of revitalizing the Army and making it more attractive to young Americans. There was even some consideration by Congress of eliminating funds for civilian KP's on the claim that such work is character-building.

The early release program, designed in part to help keep National Guard and Reserve units up to authorized strength, fluctuated rather wildly during the year. A liberalized program, initiated in December 1971, allowed those electing to do so to join an Army Reserve or National Guard unit in exchange for a 180-day early release. It was so successful that it was terminated on Feb. 21, 1972,

because continuation would have created some critical shortages among certain skills in Army units. More than 5,000 volunteers had taken advantage of the program during the period of about 80 days of its operation. Provisions for a 60-day early release remained in effect.

ROTC. Beginning in the fall of 1972, women were allowed to enroll in college-level ROTC (Reserve Officers Training Corps). The test program was initiated in ten colleges that offer ROTC on a full-time basis. Previously, a few women had broken the all-male barrier, but the latest step was seen as necessary to meet future officer personnel needs—in particular, to serve as a base for rapid expansion of the Women's Army Corps.

More funds and more scholarships became available to college students in ROTC as Public Laws 92-166 and 92-177 went into effect. The number of Army ROTC scholarships was increased by 1,000 to a new total of 6,500. The allowance was doubled to $100 per month for 10 months of the academic year, and this applied to all advance course students whether on scholarship or not.

The Army also announced an expansion of its civilian schooling program. Goals called for all commissioned officers to have achieved the baccalaureate degree and for 20% of all career commissioned officers to have graduate degrees.

Logistics. Redeye, the now-famous, heat-seeking rocket used for defense against low-flying aircraft, will be replaced by a newer missile that has improved characteristics. The new missile will be known as Stinger. Earlier, Stinger, was referred to as Redeye II. A $47.7 million engineering development contract for Stinger was given in June to General Dynamics Corporation, which has been constructing the Redeye.

Drug Problem. Illegal drug use continued to be a major problem for the Army in 1972, particularly at overseas bases. Enormous efforts were made to stop its spread. A major program to reduce drug traffic in Korea, launched by the Eighth Army, was aimed at the pushers instead of the users.

Command. In June, President Nixon nominated Gen. Creighton W. Abrams as Army chief of staff, replacing Gen. William C. Westmoreland, who retired. General Abrams had been commander of American forces in Vietnam since 1968. Congressional investigation of alleged unauthorized bombing raids on North Vietnam at an earlier and possibly critical time, however, delayed Senate approval, which was finally given.

General of the Army Omar Nelson Bradley was honored at a Pentagon ceremony and at a star-studded dinner on June 14, 1972, the Army's 197th birthday.

WILLIAM J. MCCONNELL
Colonel, USA, Retired; Colorado State University

U. S. Navy

The U. S. Navy in 1972 was faced with declining capabilities in an aging fleet and with the spiraling costs of weaponry and warships. With national policy entering a period of retrenchment it was reasonable to assume that the Navy would play a larger proportionate role in U. S. defense, but despite increased maritime emphasis, the 1973 defense budget slipped to the lowest percentage of the gross national product (GNP) in 22 years. The Navy in 1972 was reduced to fewer than 600 ships, less than two thirds the number that made up the fleet in 1965, when the United States enlarged its role in the Southeast Asia war. There were also 20% fewer aircraft, and the number of uniformed personnel declined by 10%.

All of this happened at a time when modern Soviet warships were becoming increasingly prominent on the seas. Great momentum in shipbuilding by the Soviets since the early 1960's was producing qualitative as well as quantitative improvement. It was estimated that the USSR spends more per year building *Yankee*-class ballistic missile submarines than the amount of the entire shipbuilding budget of the U. S. Navy. Consequently, supremacy on the seas may be passing to the USSR, ending a 27-year domination by the United States.

Operations. U. S. Naval operations markedly increased throughout 1972. At the height of the India-Pakistan war, Task Force 74 of the U. S. Seventh Fleet, led by the attack carrier *Enterprise*, sailed into the Indian Ocean and the Bay of Bengal. Its mission was to evacuate Americans from East Bengal if necessary and to aid in stabilizing a chaotic political situation, complicated somewhat by the presence of a Soviet task force built around a cruiser and three submarines.

The early spring offensive by the North Vietnamese brought strong U. S. counteraction, with the Navy in the key role. President Richard M. Nixon, in a televised address on May 8, announced that planes operating from U. S. Navy carriers were mining Haiphong and other North Vietnamese harbors and that U. S. aircraft were bombing enemy rail and supply lines from Communist China. Twenty-eight vessels, mostly Soviet, were trapped at Haiphong. The minefield and maritime blockade were subsequently declared 100% effective. Heavily increased air action—aided considerably in effectiveness by the new TV or laser-guided "smart bombs"—soon brought U. S. naval strength to its greatest since the Korean War. There was a threefold increase of strength in the South China Sea, with six carriers on station. At one time in early June all nine of the Pacific fleet aircraft carriers were at sea.

Reorganization. Plans neared completion in 1972 for a sweeping reorganization of the Navy, placing all ships and aircraft into three major commands—one each for forces on the sea, under the sea, and in the skies. The three commands, with branches in the Atlantic and Pacific fleets, were to be the Surface Force, Submarine Force, and Air Force. The major change was to be in the Surface Force, which would absorb the Cruiser-Destroyer, Amphibious, and Service forces. The consolidation drastically cuts staff functions, providing more efficient management at a lower cost.

Personnel. The Chief of Naval Operations, Adm. Elmo R. Zumwalt, announced a historic program in 1972. Women were to be accorded "rights and opportunities equal to their male counterparts in all areas of the Navy." The far-reaching program authorized the limited entry of women into all enlisted ratings and staff corps, all ROTC programs, joint Staff Colleges, and—in a pilot program—to sea duty aboard the hospital ship *USS Sanctuary*.

Another idea being tested was the "Mod Squad," a new elite force in Destroyer Squadron 26 in the Mediterranean. All commanding officers, executive officers, and departments heads of the seven ships were a rank lower and several years younger than normal for such key billets. Designed to give promising officers earlier opportunities at command, the

program exceeded expectations, resulting in improved readiness and greater stability in personnel.

Protests. Toward the end of 1972 a series of sit-down demonstrations, largely by black crewmen, occurred at sea aboard the aircraft carriers *Constellation* and *Kitty Hawk* and the oiler *Hassayampa*. There were fights between black sailors and white, sabotage, and other forms of protest. A congressional investigation was begun in San Diego.

Command. Secretary of the Navy John H. Chafee resigned and was succeeded by John W. Warner on May 9, 1972. On September 1, Adm. John S. McCain, Jr., commander in chief, Pacific, retired and was relieved by Adm. Noel A. M. Gayler. On November 1, Adm. Charles K. Duncan, commander in chief, Atlantic, retired and was relieved by Adm. Ralph W. Cousins.

PAUL R. SCHRATZ, *Captain, USN, Retired*
University of Missouri

U. S. Marine Corps

Reflecting a year in which major international tensions were eased, the U. S. Marine Corps was quiescent in 1972. While a part of the Marine air arm continued to be active in Southeast Asia, it played a relatively minor part in the conflict, not conducive to the glamour usually associated with the role of the elite Corps.

Strength. Marine Corps strength was slightly reduced in 1972, to 198,000. This figure, which is expected to be relatively permanent, continued to support the traditional three divisions and three aircraft wings, plus one division and one air wing in reserve. But even this small reduction caused a problem of rank in the top grades. The Corps has the highest ratio of troops to senior generals of any of the branches of service. But the law that gave the Marines a second four-star billet (for the assistant commandant) specified that whenever the Corps' strength falls below 200,000 men, the second four-star slot would be lost when its current holder left office. This caused an apparent inequity between the other branches of the defense forces, which have a ratio of one four-star billet for every 66,000 men, and the Marine Corps, which would be left with four stars for the commandant only, a ratio of one such billet for 198,000 men.

Personnel. The 1972 theme of Marine recruiting—"The Marines are looking for a few good men" —was carried over into the fiscal year 1973, which began July 1, 1972. Some 2,950 Marine recruiters made strenuous efforts to get rid of the "rifle-toting grunt" image as they stressed the Marine Air Wings and the technical skills needed in the Corps.

Although the Marine Corps does not need the numbers the Army does, it faced many of the same personnel problems as all branches of the service prepared to receive only volunteer recruits by mid-1973, when the draft was expected to end. The Marines hoped to recruit 56,800 men in fiscal 1973, at a cost of $42.4 million. Although only one out of every 20 men who volunteer for the Corps is found qualified, the Marines reported that they had no intention of lowering their mental or physical standards in recruiting an all-volunteer Corps or of easing the rigors of basic training. Even so, Secretary of Defense Melvin Laird reported to President Nixon that the Marine Corps could be expected to maintain its authorized strength.

Officer Education. A Marine Corps Command and Staff College Extension Course was established as part of the Continuous Officer Personnel Education Program. Majors and lieutenant colonels with 15 or more years of service may be required to take this course, which in 1972 was available through Senior Officer Seminars or individual study programs.

WILLIAM J. McCONNELL
Colonel, USA, Retired; Colorado State University

National Guard

In contrast to recent years, when state governors called on National Guard units to cope with domestic disturbances, the Guard's primary duty in 1972 was to do battle against the ravages of floodwaters. More than 12,000 Army and Air National Guardsmen were called to duty in June in the flood area extending from Florida to New York. In the aftermath of hurricane Agnes, eight states called out their militia to provide essential services, including property protection, water purification, inoculation against disease, and traffic management.

Revitalization Policy. The major policy shift introduced in the fiscal year 1972, calling for "increased reliance on National Guard and Reserve forces," was continued in fiscal year 1973. In a report to the President in August 1972, Secretary of Defense Laird stated that "the credibility and overall effectiveness of the Guard and Reserve suffered badly during the build-up of the active forces in Vietnam prior to 1969. The Guard and Reserve had a questionable combat role, since their mission was ill-defined and their units seldom called to duty . . . their equipment was diverted to the Active Forces . . . [and] their units included many who joined them to avoid the draft and the war in Vietnam." He went on to say that "these conditions are being corrected and there is highly encouraging evidence of revitalization within the Guard . . . ."

Actions in 1972 to effect this "revitalization" were: (1) a decision at the highest levels of government that Guard and Reserve components shall be relied upon as the initial and primary augmentation for the active forces; (2) replenishment of equipment inventories of the Army Guard and Army Reserve at an annual rate approaching $1 billion; (3) supplying the Air Guard and Air Force Reserve with more modern aircraft; and (4) increasing the Guard and Reserve portion of the defense budget from $2.1 billion in fiscal year 1969 to $4.1 billion in fiscal 1973.

Manpower. Wide fluctuations in manpower marked the National Guard in 1972. Early in the year the Army suddenly terminated a special early release program that was designed to help keep National Guard units at authorized strength. (More than 5,000 volunteers had taken advantage of this liberal program during its 80 days of operation.) In fiscal year 1972, during which recruiting varied widely from month to month, the Army Guard missed by 12,461 men its year-end goal of 400,000 members. According to Guard officials, this situation dramatized the need for recruiting incentives, the most effective of which are probably enlistment and reenlistment bonuses. On the other hand, the Air Guard ended the fiscal year with 250 members above its goal of 88,986.

Minority Recruitment. Minority representation in the Guard, which had lagged in fiscal year 1971, improved in fiscal 1972. While its total strength dropped by 14,500 men, the Army Guard increased its black membership from 4,961 to 7,680, for a total black strength of 2%.

Draft Rulings. The selective service system, in a reversal of long-standing rules, announced in June 1972 that men scheduled for induction after July 1 would be permitted to enlist in or be appointed to the National Guard after receiving their induction orders. This was another in a series of unusual moves to increase the flow of men—in this case non-prior-service men—into the Guard. However, with the draft expected virtually to end by January 1973, the effect on recruitment may be temporary.

Public Relations. In a program aimed at gaining public support, particularly from the business and industrial community, the Defense Department appointed James M. Roche, retired board chairman and chief executive of General Motors, as chairman of the National Committee for Employer Support of the National Guard and Reserve Forces. An imposing group of American business leaders was named to serve in the executive committee under Roche.

Command. Maj. Gen. Francis S. Greenlief, appointed in 1971, continued as chief of the National Guard Bureau in 1972.

WILLIAM J. McCONNELL
Colonel, USA, Retired; Colorado State University

North Atlantic Treaty Organization

During the last few years, with so much concern centered on the struggle in Southeast Asia, NATO received proportionately less attention from its member nations. In 1972, with the increasing likelihood that the Vietnam War was drawing to a close, NATO's most powerful member, the United States, supported several initiatives that would prepare the alliance to meet the changing times.

Mutual Balanced Force Reductions. Perhaps the most interesting possibility for change was the suggested reduction of armed forces in both NATO and the Warsaw Pact counteralliance. Discussions of such reductions are not new. In fact, they extend back to the mid-1950's, when the Polish Foreign Minister Adam Rapacki proposed that a demilitarized and denuclearized zone be created in central Europe along the line separating the nations of the two alliances. The plan was rejected by the United States and other allies on the grounds that it was a trick to ease American troops out of Europe so that the Soviet Union could incorporate the rest of Europe in its sphere of influence.

That times have changed for NATO is indicated by the growing discussion with the Warsaw Pact as to how Mutual Balanced Force Reductions (MBFR) could be commenced for eastern and western Europe. Several altered conditions accounted for the interest in MBFR from the NATO point of view. First, there was the era of apparent détente between the United States and the USSR. Second, there was the spirit of détente between West Germany on the one hand and East Germany and the USSR on the other. Third, the continued economic growth of the NATO partners meant that there was less need to rely on U. S. assistance. Fourth, considerable pressure was generated in the United States to reduce the number of Americans stationed in Europe. Fifth, it was thought in many quarters that the Soviet threat that had been judged to justify NATO's military preparedness had now subsided, partly because of the USSR's need to be concerned with events on its border with China. Those holding this point of view argued that the USSR was legitimately looking for ways to ease tensions in Europe.

CENTRAL PRESS

BRITISH ARMY unveiled its new 105-mm towed light gun, which has a maximum range of more than 10 miles.

U. S. Actions. Despite this talk about reducing military forces, the United States in particular took special care in 1972 to build up areas of weakness in NATO's defenses. Presumably these precautions were taken so that negotiations with the Communist alliance could be made from a position of strength, and so as to provide a strong military posture in case the negotiations failed and a serious military confrontation arose instead. For its part, the United States built units back to nearly full strength that had been reduced in personnel and equipment by the Vietnam War. In addition, it withdrew older F-100 fighter-bombers from European assignment and replaced them with F-111's and F-4's. And, in an effort to provide greater protection for its aircraft in case of a surprise air attack, the United States built some 400 aircraft shelters in Europe. It also constructed small landing strips, known as dispersal fields, where planes could be stationed during a tense period in order to make it more

difficult for an attacker to destroy all the American planes. This sheltering and dispersal program was in part a response to the fact that the nations of the Warsaw Pact possess large numbers of attack aircraft and missiles, capable of blanketing western Europe. With respect to ground forces, the United States improved its fighting capability by introducing a new tank and several new kinds of antitank missiles into its units in Europe.

European Actions. For their part, the European members of NATO spent approximately $1 billion more in 1972 than in the previous year on modernization of certain aspects of their defense structures. This activity was part of an agreed-upon 5-year modernization effort called the European Defense Improvement Program (EDIP). The French continued their drive to establish a modest nuclear capacity with their Mirage bombers, two recently acquired intermediate ballistic missile squadrons, and the expected completion of four submarines capable of launching ballistic missiles. In addition, France operates two aircraft carriers whose fighter-bombers presumably carry tactical nuclear weapons. The British continued to operate their four SLBM submarines but scrapped the aircraft carrier *Eagle,* which left only HMS *Ark Royal* in service with the Royal Navy. The West Germans remained the largest contributor to NATO in terms of conventional forces, with 12 divisions. Although West Germany does not possess its own nuclear weapons, the United States would provide it with such weapons under some circumstances.

Relations between some NATO nations and Greece remained strained because of the nondemocratic nature of the Greek government. Nevertheless the United States discussed the possibility of using the Greek port of Piraeus as home base for the carrier task force of the Sixth Fleet.

Soviet Union

Despite the Strategic Arms Limitation Talks (SALT) accords and various other agreements with the United States, the Soviet Union continued to make impressive strides in overall defense procurement and deployment. For the Pentagon, one of the most worrisome facets of the Soviet defense establishment was what Defense Secretary Melvin Laird termed the Soviet challenge to American "technological superiority." By this Laird meant that existing forces constitute only a part of a nation's total military capacity. The other part is found in the research and development activities that can be turned into new weapons. Regarding such research effort, Laird noted that apparently the USSR increased its spending for research by 9% in 1972.

Naval Forces. In terms of specific improvements in military posture, the USSR appeared to be making rapid strides in the growth of its naval forces. There was considerable speculation that a large ship reported under construction would be the nation's first regular aircraft carrier. Previously the Soviet Union had launched two small helicopter carriers, the *Moskva* and the *Leningrad.* As for concrete additions to the Soviet fleet observed during the year, there was an impressive new kind of ship to which NATO has given the code name "Nanuchka." Some 10 or 12 such ships have been built thus far. They are important in having the size and range to challenge American naval forces operating in the Barents, Mediterranean, and Nor-

wegian seas—areas where the numerous but short-range Komar and Osa-class patrol boats cannot operate with great effectiveness. It is presumed that the new Soviet craft are equipped with a new ship-to-ship missile. Such missiles as the Styx, which is carried aboard patrol boats and has a range of 25 miles (40 km), and the Shaddock, which is found on destroyers and cruisers and has a range of 450 miles (725 km), constitute an advanced type of naval armament unmatched by anything possessed by the U. S. Navy.

Despite the continued growth in the Soviet Navy, Secretary Laird was careful to point out that there remain basic deficiencies in the forces, as well as constraints upon the manner in which Soviet naval units can be used. The most important problems for the USSR in this respect are that they have to maintain their operations with very few all-weather ports, they lack air cover for their forces when they operate far from Soviet-controlled coasts, and they lack vessels with which to resupply the combat ships on high seas. Thus, while the Soviet forces with their ship-to-ship missiles pose a formidable threat to American units that operate close to the Soviet coasts, the Russian Navy is still no match for the American fleet in the Atlantic, Pacific, and Indian Oceans. Nor is the Soviet fleet any match in terms of the number of surface ships. The USSR operates approximately 9 cruisers, 10 destroyers, 10 intermediate Nanuchkas, and about 125 patrol boats. In comparison, the U. S. Navy has 207 surface combat ships, including 16 aircraft carriers. Only in submarines does the Soviet Union hold a numerical lead, with 295 submarines of all types, as compared with the U. S. Navy's 99.

Air and Ground Forces. The significant numbers of Soviet ICBM's and SLBM's were mentioned earlier. In addition, the Soviet Air Force possesses many more jet fighters than does the United States. Perhaps the most impressive addition to the Soviet Union's air strength in 1972 was a new, swing-wing —that is, a variable-geometry wing—jet bomber that NATO has given the code name "Backfire." The new aircraft is twice as heavy as the U. S. FB-111, the newest American bomber. According to Secretary Laird, the Backfire probably has an in-flight refueling capability that brings most targets inside the United States within its range. In addition, the USSR appears to be developing replacements for its jet fighter Foxbat (MIG-23), which in its own right is still a first-class craft.

There were no significant changes in Soviet ground forces during the year. However, they continue to receive new weapons.

Warsaw Pact Nations

The military counteralliance to NATO is the Warsaw Pact, which was organized by the USSR in 1955. The group consists of the Communist nations of eastern Europe, except for Yugoslavia, which never joined, and Albania, which has sided with the People's Republic of China in its dispute with the Soviet Union and hence does not participate. The Warsaw Pact military forces are patterned after those of the Soviet Union, and the USSR supplies some of the heavy equipment used by these forces. It is believed in the Western world that the USSR has not supplied nuclear weapons to the other members of the alliance, however.

In 1972 there was no substantial change in the configuration of the Warsaw Pact forces, except

CHINESE Army honor guard welcomed U. S. President Richard Nixon on his arrival in Peking in February.

UPI

that the general quality of equipment and training was thought by the NATO nations to be improving. In spite of the fact that the Soviet Union kept first-line divisions on its border with China, it also maintained some of its best troops in the Warsaw Pact area that faces NATO nations.

People's Republic of China

Contrary to what some observers had anticipated, the Chinese did not demonstrate a full-scale test of an ICBM in 1972. However, according to Defense Secretary Laird, China may have conducted a reduced-range test of an intercontinental missile, and a full-scale firing could still come at any time.

The growth of the Chinese military establishment has been impressive. For example, since its first nuclear detonation in 1964, China has conducted at least 12 nuclear tests, both of atomic and thermonuclear bombs. Within the last two years the nation has launched two earth satellites by means of multistage rockets. Secretary Laird expressed his belief that the Chinese could begin the deployment of an ICBM with a thermonuclear warhead and a range of 3,000 miles (4,800 km) by 1975. Such a missile could enable China to strike at almost all of the Soviet Union. However, the United States would be out of range except for the state of Alaska.

It was thought in the Pentagon that by the end of 1972 the Chinese had deployed some medium-range and/or intermediate-range ballistic missiles that could be fired over distances of up to 2,000 miles (3,200 km). Such a capability would place most cities in India, Pakistan, Southeast Asia, the Philippines, Japan, and a substantial portion of the Soviet Union within range of a Chinese attack. Furthermore, the Chinese are reported to be building medium-range jet bombers copied after an earlier model produced in the USSR. These aircraft can reach targets 1,700 miles (2,700 km) away on unrefueled flights and can carry nuclear bombs.

The Chinese People's Liberation Army consists of some 2.5 million men with 150 combat divisions. These troops are constantly being supplied with more modern arms from the nation's manufacturing plants. The tactical air force and naval air arm, which supports the army, operates some 3,000 jet fighter-bombers—an increase of several hundred aircraft over 1971. The navy's primary offensive force consists of about 40 non-nuclear submarines equipped with conventional torpedoes. There is some evidence that the Chinese are working on the development of a nuclear-powered submarine that launches ballistic missiles.

The primary deficiencies of the Chinese military establishment continue to lie in the area of logistic support. China does not possess either the merchant ships and naval escorts or the heavy jet transport planes that would permit it to operate and resupply large armies far from its borders. China also lacks as yet a nuclear capacity sufficient to destroy the Soviet Union or hurt the United States. According to Secretary Laird, the United States is impressed with the progress shown by the People's Republic of China in its military acquisitions, but generally believes that the purpose of the Chinese military establishment is to deter a Soviet or American attack rather than to attack either superpower.

India

It perhaps comes as somewhat of a surprise to many persons to learn that the Indian Army is now the fourth largest in the world, exceeded in size only by the armies of the Soviet Union, the People's Republic of China, and the United States. Supporting the large Indian army is a small but modern air force that is now being supplied with MIG-21 jet fighters of Indian manufacture on Soviet license. The Indian Navy is small and consists of patrol boats and a few frigates of British design.

The Indian government continues to state that it sees no need to develop nuclear weapons. However, it is keeping this option open by refusing to sign the nuclear nonproliferation treaty and by building a civilian nuclear and space program that could well serve as the basis for a nuclear missile effort in the late 1970's or the early 1980's, should the government feel that the international situation required it.

ROBERT M. LAWRENCE
Colorado State University

231

——————— DELAWARE · Information Highlights ———————

Area: 2,057 square miles (5,328 sq km).
Population (1970 census): 548,104. *Density*, 281 per sq mi.
Chief Cities (1970 census): Dover, the capital, 17,488; Wilmington, 80,386; Newark, 21,078; Elsmere, 8,415; Seaford, 5,537; Milford, 5,314; Smyrna, 4,243.
Government (1972): *Chief Officers*—governor, Russell W. Peterson (R); lt. gov., Eugene D. Bookhammer (R); secy. of state, Walton H. Simpson (R); atty. gen., W. Laird Stabler, Jr. (R); treas., Emily W. Womach (D); supt. of public instruction, Kenneth C. Madden; chief justice, Daniel F. Wolcott. *General Assembly*—Senate, 19 members (13 Republicans, 6 Democrats); House of Representatives, 39 members (23 R, 16 D).
Education (1971–72): *Enrollment*—public elementary schools, 73,887 pupils, 3,110 teachers; public secondary, 61,126 pupils, 3,140 teachers; nonpublic schools (1970–71), 18,-608 pupils, 770 teachers; college and university, 24,000 students. *Public school expenditures*, $136,900,000 ($1,097 per pupil). *Average teacher's salary*, $10,664.
State Finances (fiscal year 1970): *Revenues*, $293,376,000 (total sales and gross receipts taxes, $42,798,000; motor fuel tax, $18,252,000; federal funds, $42,006,000). *Expenditures*, $326,251,000 (education, $142,115,000; health, welfare, and safety, $39,451,000; highways, $70,661,000). *State debt*, $420,919,000 (June 30, 1970).
Personal Income (1971): $2,550,000,000; per capita, $4,557.
Public Assistance (1971): $28,968,000. *Average monthly payments* (Dec. 1971)—old-age assistance, $92.00; aid to families with dependent children, $123.31.
Labor Force: *Nonagricultural wage and salary earners* (July 1972), 216,200. *Average annual employment* (1971)—manufacturing, 69,000; trade, 44,000; government, 33,000; services, 32,000. *Insured unemployed* (Aug. 1972)—3,300 (1.9%).
Manufacturing: *Value added by manufacture*, $1,072,300,000; Food and kindred products, $200,600,000; rubber and plastic products, $72,500,000; nonelectrical machinery, $28,400,000; primary metal industries, $28,400,000; fabricated metal products, $24,900,000.
Agriculture (1970): *Cash farm income*, $147,841,000 (livestock, $97,697,000; crops, $48,492,000; government payments, $1,652,000). *Chief crops* (in order of value, 1971)—Corn, soybeans, potatoes, hay.
Mining (1971): *Production value*, $2,241,000 (ranks 50th among the states). *Chief minerals*—Sand and gravel, $2,231,000; clays, $8,000; gem stones, $2,000.
Fisheries (1971): *Commercial catch*, 9,031,000 pounds ($1,-490,000). *Leading species by value* (1971), Clams, $1,079,-000; oysters $191,000; crabs, $112,000.
Transportation: *Roads* (1971), 4,892 miles (7,873 km); *motor vehicles* (1971), 312,342; *railroads* (1971), 287 miles (462 km); *public airports* (1972), 2.
Communications: *Telephones* (1972), 387,400; *radio stations* (1971), 15; *newspapers* (1972), 3; (daily circulation, 157,-000).

DELAWARE

Politics and elections dominated the news in Delaware in 1972. Although President Richard Nixon won 60% of the presidential vote, the Republicans lost the governorship and one U. S. Senate seat. The November election was notable for the large turnout of voters, especially among the young.

Elections. The period between May and late August was marked by conflict within the Republican party over the gubernatorial nomination. As a result of a bruising struggle at the party convention in July, incumbent Gov. Russell W. Peterson was forced into a primary election battle against David P. Buckson, a former state attorney general. Governor Peterson won the primary but at the cost of a serious party split, which resulted in his defeat in November by the Democratic challenger, state Rep. Sherman W. Tribbitt. At the same time, Joseph R. Biden, Jr., a 29-year-old Democratic New Castle county councilman, won a narrow victory over incumbent Republican U. S. Sen. J. Caleb Boggs. When he takes the oath of office in January 1973, Biden—who turned 30 on November 20—will become the youngest popularly elected U. S. senator ever seated at the beginning of a new Congress. Pierre S. du Pont 4th, a Republican, was reelected to Delaware's only seat in the U. S. House.

The Republicans retained control of both houses of the General Assembly by narrow margins. The Democrats won several state offices and county offices in New Castle, Kent, and Sussex counties.

Legislation. As a result of fiscal difficulties experienced by the Peterson administration in 1971, the 1972 legislature levied several new taxes. It also approved a "piggyback" form of income tax, which permits at the state level most of the exemptions and deductions allowed at the federal level. The purpose of this was to facilitate the filing of returns and promote efficiency in auditing.

On urging from law-enforcement officials, the legislature enacted a wire-tapping bill, which provides for surveillance of suspected persons by listening to telephone conversations. Authority to tap must be obtained by the attorney general through application to a state Superior Court judge. The bill was opposed by many of the liberal elements in Delaware.

Economy. Delaware's economy showed a slight improvement over the previous year. The unemployment rate declined by about 0.5% during 1972, and none of the larger industries of the state experienced strikes of any significance.

PAUL DOLAN, *University of Delaware*

DEMOCRATIC PARTY. See ELECTIONS; POLITICAL PARTIES.

DENMARK

The death of a king, the accession of a new queen, debate and a positive vote on entry into the Common Market, and the resignation of Jens Otto Krag as prime minister brought Denmark into the world spotlight in 1972. Issues in foreign policy, economic crises, and educational reforms received national attention.

Succession of Margrethe II. The Danes mourned the late King Frederick IX, who died on January 14, but greeted their new 31-year-old sovereign warmly. She is the first woman to rule Denmark since Margrethe of the 14th century Nordic union.

The Common Market. Debates on the issue of Denmark's entry into the European Economic Community (EEC) started in November 1971 and continued until the plebiscite on Oct. 2, 1972. The arguments grew increasingly heated despite three favorable votes in the Folketing by 2-to-1 margins. Fears of the loss of Danish independence, submersion in a great Europe, and economic uncertainties fed negative views. Nonetheless, those opposing entry into the Common Market were soundly defeated by a margin of 63.5% to 36.5%, with nearly 90% of those eligible voting. However, membership requires legislative changes. These were outlined for the Folketing at its opening session on October 3. On the same day the traditional speech, given by Prime Minister Krag, ended dramatically with his announcement of his immediate resignation.

New Prime Minister. Without delay, the Social Democrats voted to select Anker Jørgensen as head of the government, with no other changes in personnel. A leader in the labor movement without previous cabinet experience, Jørgensen brought his popularity, in both party and unions, as support for a government in crisis.

Cabinet Troubles. Jørgensen had much to resolve. His party remained in power only with the cooperation of the Socialist Peoples' party and two votes from Greenland representatives. The former pledged its support, even though defeated on the Common Market issue, because its members refused the alternative of a bourgeois government. The

———— **DENMARK** • **Information Highlights** ————

Official Name: Kingdom of Denmark.
Area: 16,629 square miles (43,069 sq km).
Population (1972 est.): 5,000,000. *Density,* 295 per square mile (114 per sq km). *Annual rate of increase,* 0.5%.
Chief Cities (1970 est.): Copenhagen, the capital, 627,800; Aarhus, 236,129; Odense, 164,679.
Government: *Head of state,* Margrethe II, queen (acceded Jan. 1972). *Head of government,* Anker Jørgensen, premier (took office Oct. 1972). *Legislature* (unicameral)—Folketing, 179 members. *Major political parties*—Social Democratic party; Conservative People's party; Agrarian party; Radical Liberal party; Socialist People's party.
Languages: Danish (official).
Education: *Expenditure* (1969), 17.7% of total public expenditure. *School enrollment* (1969)—primary, 534,000; general secondary, 215,890; technical/vocational (1968), 171,629; university/higher, 70,062.
Monetary Unit: Krone (6.894 kroner equal U. S.$1, Aug. 1972).
Gross National Product (1971 est.): $16,000,000,000.
National Income per Person (1970): $2,875.
Economic Indexes: *Industrial production* (1970), 157 (1963= 100); *agricultural production* (1971), 123 (1952–56=100); *consumer price index* (1971), 154 (1964=100).
Manufacturing (major products): Beverages, processed foods, machinery, ships, chemicals, furniture, textiles.
Major Agricultural Products: Barley, sugar beets, dairy products, cattle, hogs, fish.
Major Minerals: Peat, lignite, salt, kaolin.
Foreign Trade (1971): *Exports,* $3,685,000,000 (chief exports, 1969—nonelectrical machinery; bacon and ham; chemicals; electrical machinery and appliances). *Imports,* $4,615,000,000 (chief imports, 1969—nonelectrical machinery; transport equipment; chemicals; petroleum and petroleum products). *Chief trading partners* (1969)—United Kingdom (took 19% of exports, supplied 14% of imports); Sweden (16%—16%); West Germany (13%—19%); United States.
Tourism: *Receipts* (1970), $314,300,000.
Transportation: *Motor vehicles* (1970), 1,332,600 (automobiles, 1,076,100); *railroads* (1970), 1,578 miles (2,540 km); *merchant fleet* (1971), 3,520,000 gross registered tons; *major national airline,* Scandinavian Airlines System (with Norway and Sweden).
Communications: *Telephones* (1971), 1,696,765; *television stations* (1971), 30; *television sets* (1971), 1,510,000; *radios* (1970), 1,597,000; *newspapers* (1970), 58 (daily circulation, 1,790,000).

party also approved retention of price and wage regulations, but opposed budget cuts.

The Socialist Peoples' party reserved its special criticism for the drastic cuts in expenditures from current appropriations, made earlier in the year by Budget-Finance Minister Per Haekkerup. These and other measures had failed to prevent a money crisis in mid-April which forced the national bank to purchase bonds in the open market. Later in the year, one week before the vote on entry into the Common Market, the government had to close money exchanges because of the weakness of the krone. In addition, a large import surplus and decreases in returns on foreign trade created havoc in fiscal balances. On the favorable side, however, the government could look at an increase in industrial and agricultural production, a slight advance in the gross national product, and reasonable figures for unemployment.

Foreign Policy. An exceptionally strong resolution condemned American bombing of North Vietnam, but the Folketing reaffirmed continued support of NATO. The Danes sent a representative to Peking for trade agreements and considered recognition of the East German Republic.

Educational and Environmental Reforms. Legislation extended compulsory school attendance to nine years (or the 17th birthday), provided state support for all music conservatories, and created a national research council to coordinate grants and policies. The Folketing also passed stringent anti-pollution laws and approved purchase of recreation, historic site, and development properties to block non-Danish acquisition in the "land rush" expected with Danish entry into the Common Market.

RAYMOND E. LINDGREN
California State University, Long Beach

DETROIT

Court orders designed to end racial segregation in Detroit schools aroused controversy that attracted national attention to the city in 1972.

Schools. On June 14, 1972, Federal District Judge Stephen J. Roth ordered Detroit and 52 suburban school districts to put into effect a busing program to end racial segregation in the public schools. He demanded that desegregation, which was to be supervised by an 11-member panel, be complete for all grades by September 1973. The program could involve 350,000 of the 780,000 school children in the area. Roth also ordered that at least 10% of the faculty of each school district be black. On July 10 he ordered the state of Michigan to pay $3 million for 295 buses to start a partial busing program by September 1972. But on July 20 the U. S. sixth circuit court of appeals ordered delays in carrying out Judge Roth's orders, pending hearings on appeals of his findings of deliberate segregation.

On December 8 the appeals court ruled that cross-district busing is legal, and it returned the case to the federal district court in Detroit for further hearings, which must include testimony from suburban school districts. Lawyers for suburban districts planned further appeals.

Detroit public schools also faced financial collapse, closing the 1971–72 fiscal year with a deficit of $38 million. The deficit threatened to grow to $80 million by the end of 1972–73. It was ruled that the 1972–73 school year would be shortened from 180 to 117 days and that 1,548 teachers would be laid off, but as part of his desegregation order Judge Roth had prohibited the moves, ruling that Detroit must offer an educational program that is comparable to that of the suburban school districts.

Detroit voters rejected tax proposals for schools on May 16, August 8, and again on November 7. Voters throughout the state rejected a proposal on November 7 to remove the local property tax as a means of supporting public schools, with the state legislature replacing the money from other sources.

City Charter. A proposed new city charter was rejected by Detroit voters on November 7. Mayor Roman S. Gribbs had opposed the recommendations of the elected charter commission, which had worked on the document for almost two years. The previous city charter had been adopted in 1918.

Construction and Industry. Plans to build a $126 million domed sports stadium on the Detroit riverfront were halted by the state supreme court, which ruled on June 16 that the public had not been properly informed that tax money could be used to cover stadium deficits. The Wayne State County Stadium Authority, which was planning the facility, estimated that the court's action would delay construction at least a year.

Ground was broken November 1 for a 27-story federal office building on an urban renewal site in downtown Detroit. Its estimated cost was $49 million. Auto plants in the Detroit area produced 7,265,957 cars in the first 10 months of 1972, up slightly from 7,195,045 produced in the same period of 1971.

CHARLES W. THEISEN
The Detroit "News"

DIMITRIOS I. See BIOGRAPHY.

UPI

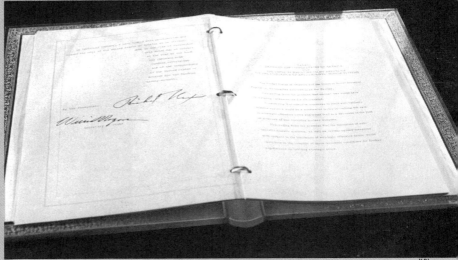

UPI

UPI

The strategic arms limitation treaty between the United States and the Soviet Union is signed (top photo) by President Nixon and party chief Brezhnev in Moscow on May 26. (Above) A close-up of the historic document, showing the signatures. (Left) The two leaders exchange signed copies of the treaty.

Disarmament and Arms Control

On May 26, 1972, in Moscow, President Richard M. Nixon of the United States and Leonid I. Brezhnev, general secretary of the Communist party of the Soviet Union, signed the two most important arms control accords of the nuclear era. The agreements were reached after months of bargaining in the Strategic Arms Limitation Talks (SALT).

Virtually all observers saw the U. S.-USSR achievement as a giant step toward limiting the costs and dangers of strategic nuclear arms. The agreements were the most dramatic manifestation of a deeper understanding reached by the two nuclear superpowers and expressed in a joint Nixon-Brezhnev statement of principles signed in Moscow three days later.

The first arms control accord was a treaty limiting antiballistic missile (ABM) systems of both powers, and the second was an interim agreement freezing offensive strategic missiles at current levels for up to five years. Both subsequently were approved by Soviet and U. S. legislative bodies, and ratification instruments were exchanged between the two governments in early October.

Following ratification, the second stage of SALT, known as SALT 2, commenced in November in Geneva, Switzerland. The United States and the Soviet Union abandoned the cumbersome system of rotating sessions in Vienna, Austria, and Helsinki, Finland, and agreed on "permanent" headquarters in Geneva, which was also the site of the ongoing United Nations-sponsored, 25-nation Geneva disarmament conference. France is a member but does not participate.

ABM Treaty. The Treaty of the Limitation of Anti-Ballistic Missile Systems must be seen against the backdrop of the present policy of Washington and Moscow to maintain a posture of mutual deterrence by denying to each a comprehensive defense against nuclear retaliation. The function of an ABM system is to destroy incoming missiles before they reach their targets. If either country had an effective nationwide ABM system, it theoretically could launch an effective first strike against the other without fear that the retaliatory attack would cause unacceptable damage.

Under certain political conditions the country with comprehensive ABM protection might be tempted to initiate nuclear war. Further, even if one side had a partial ABM system, the other would have to deploy more offensive weapons to offset it, which in turn would stimulate an increase of ABM defenses on both sides. This would trigger an action-reaction cycle that would fuel the nuclear arms race and destabilize the existing strategic balance.

The ABM treaty was designed to prevent this situation by limiting the United States and the Soviet Union to two ABM sites each, thus denying either a nationwide system. At the time of signing, the USSR already had deployed an ABM network with 64 missile-interceptor launchers around Moscow. In the United States the construction of two ABM complexes was underway: one at Grand Forks Air Force Base in North Dakota was nearing completion, and the other at Malmstrom Air Force Base in Montana had just been started.

Terms. The ABM pact permits each side only two ABM sites, one around the national capital (Washington and Moscow), and one located at least 800 miles (1,300 km) away. Each site was limited to 100 ABM launchers and 100 interceptor missiles. Radar deployment at each location was also specifically limited. For the future, each country agreed not to develop, test, or deploy sea, air, space, or mobile land-based ABM systems; multiple launchers or warheads; or automatic reloading systems. Further, the deployment of exotic ABM systems, such as those involving lasers, is prohibited, even at the two permitted sites.

The treaty does not provide for independent, international, or on-site inspection in either country, but will rely on each government to monitor the behavior of the other by nonintrusive means, primarily photo-reconnaissance satellites. In a unique provision, each side agreed not to interfere with these means of verification by deliberate concealment or in other ways.

The duration of the treaty is unlimited, but either party may withdraw on six-months' notice if it decides that extraordinary events related to ABM weapons have jeopardized its national interests.

Agreement on Offensive Missiles. The Interim Agreement on Certain Measures with respect to the Limitation of Strategic Offensive Arms and its associated protocol also were signed on May 26 by Nixon and Brezhnev. The agreement limits the number of deployed strategic offensive missile launchers to approximately current levels for up to five years. This applies to intercontinental ballistic missiles (ICBM), submarine-launched ballistic missiles (SLBM), and modern ballistic missile submarines.

This agreement was expected to slow the strategic arms race by braking the momentum of the Soviet missile buildup, which was at its peak in 1972. The United States had reached its current level of offensive missiles in 1967, with 1,054 ICBMs and 656 SLBMs on 41 missile submarines; thereafter it concentrated on improving its offensive strategic arms rather than on increasing its missile inventory. But the Soviet Union accelerated its construction of missiles in the late 1960's, and by 1970 it was deploying each year about 250 ICBMs, and 128 SLBMs on eight new submarines.

Terms. The 1972 agreement on offensive missiles froze at approximately current levels the total inventory of ICBMs and SLBMs deployed and under construction on each side. Neither country was permitted to exceed the number of fixed ICBM launchers operational or under active construction as of July 1, 1972. At that time the USSR had in place or under construction an estimated 1,618 ICBMs, compared with 1,054 for the United States. Each side also was prevented from increasing the number of launchers for modern heavy missiles.

Both sides are limited to the number of SLBMs operational or under construction as of May 26, 1972. This permits the United States 656 and the Soviet Union 740, with increases to 710 and 950, respectively, if the new missiles replace an equal number of older land-based ICBM launchers. The agreement allows the United States 44 modern nuclear submarines and the Soviet Union 62. Each side is permitted to modernize its launchers or submarines on a one-to-one replacement basis.

The agreement does not limit any current U. S. offensive arms programs, such as MIRV (Multiple Independently Targeted Reentry Vehicle) deployment. Nor does it limit the number of nuclear war-

heads. The current United States lead over the Soviet Union of 2.5 to 1 in numbers of warheads was expected to increase within the next five years.

As in the ABM treaty, this agreement did not provide for international on-site inspection, but will rely on each side to monitor the other's compliance, neither side being permitted to interfere with the other's verification efforts. Either party may withdraw from the agreement on six-months' notice if it believes its supreme national interests are jeopardized by extraordinary events.

Response of the U. S. Congress. The ABM treaty and the interim agreement on offensive missiles immediately received widespread expressions of approval in the United States, the Soviet Union, and throughout the world.

The ABM treaty encountered little difficulty in the U. S. Senate, where it was approved by a vote of 88 to 2 on August 3. In explaining his negative vote, Sen. James L. Buckley, Republican of New York, said he had "strong misgivings as to both the prudence and the ultimate morality of denying ourselves for all time—or denying the Russians for that matter—the right to protect our civilian populations from nuclear devastation."

In contrast, the interim agreement to freeze offensive missiles provoked a six-week debate, principally in the Senate. Not being a formal treaty, it did not require congressional sanction, but President Nixon requested a joint resolution approving it to give him a mandate to negotiate a full-fledged treaty. Sen. Henry F. Jackson, Democrat of Washington, was the most influential critic of the agreement. He spoke for those critical of U. S. acquiescence to numerical superiority in strategic missiles for the Soviet Union. While acknowledging that the United States enjoyed a considerable advantage in deployed nuclear warheads because of its strategic bombers and its superior technology in multiple warheads, Jackson argued that Washington should insist on the principle of "equality" in missiles in any future treaty and introduced an amendment to this effect. His view was supported by the administration apparently because the President believed that a clear congressional expression on this point would strengthen the U. S. position in follow-on SALT negotiations.

The House of Representatives approved the interim agreement on August 18 by a vote of 329 to 7, without any reservations. It was not approved by the Senate until September 14, and then only with the Jackson amendment, which was co-sponsored by 43 other senators. The vote was 88 to 2. The amendment "urges and requests the President" to seek a future treaty that "would not limit the United States to levels of intercontinental strategic forces inferior to the limits provided for the Soviet Union." This means, said Jackson, that we should insist on "equality" in numbers of ICBMs, SLBMs, and long-range bombers in any future treaty. The Senate amendment, which is not binding on the President, was approved by the House on September 25.

When signing the weapons freeze agreement on September 30, President Nixon said that it did not guarantee there "will be no war," but that it was "the beginning of a process that is enormously important, that will limit now, and we hope, later reduce the burden of arms."

Limited Impact. U. S. defense experts were quick to point out that the ABM treaty and the interim agreement taken together would not lead to an early reduction of strategic inventories in either country. The treaty permits the Soviet Union to construct a new ABM site in addition to its Moscow installation. It prohibits the completion of the Montana ABM installation, but permits the construction of a new one to protect Washington, D. C.

The offensive weapons agreement freezes missiles at approximately 1,710 for the United States and 2,358 for the Soviet Union. This means that both sides can go on producing more nuclear warheads, perfecting guidance systems, or making other qualitative improvements in offensive arms. Hence, in the short term, the SALT agreements could lead to an actual increase in defense spending. There were pressures in both countries to proceed rapidly with strategic systems not banned by the agreement as a hedge against significant escalation in permitted arms by the other and to establish a better bargaining position for SALT 2.

SALT 2. At year-end, both powers exhibited a wait-and-see attitude, pending the outcome of the second phase of SALT, which resumed in Geneva on November 21. The purpose of these negotiations, which were expected to go on for years, is to achieve a comprehensive and permanent agreement to limit, and hopefully reduce, the number of strategic offensive weapons. One major problem and goal is to include in any new treaty the weapons systems not covered in the interim agreement, such as heavy bombers. Another is to impose limits on qualitative improvements as well as numbers. A long-term treaty embracing these elements could save each side billions of dollars and still keep the present strategic balance intact. President Nixon warned that the new negotiations were "more complex and more difficult" than those of the first phase.

When the Geneva SALT session recessed on December 21, the United States and the Soviet Union announced the ·creation of a joint four-man consultative commission to meet at least twice a year in Geneva to supervise the interim strategic arms agreement, the ABM treaty, and the agreement on measures to reduce the risk of nuclear war negotiated by SALT in 1971. Its task was to ensure that the provisions are working effectively and to provide a forum for airing any doubts about compliance. This was the modest goal of this short session, the eighth since SALT began three years before. The next session was scheduled to open in March 1973.

Geneva Disarmament Conference. The dramatic SALT achievements overshadowed other arms control developments. The Geneva Conference of the Committee on Disarmament (CCD), the principal forum for negotiating more limited multilateral pacts since 1962, continued its work during 1972 but arrived at no new agreements. France, though formally a CCD member, continued not to participate. The People's Republic of China was not a participant in the CCD or any other regular arms-control forum, except for the United Nations itself. Both Washington and Moscow have indicated their willingness for Peking to join the CCD negotiations.

The Convention on the Prohibition of the Development, Production, and Stockpiling of Bacteriological (Biological) and Toxin Weapons and on Their Destruction, negotiated by the CCD and endorsed by the UN in December 1971, was opened for signature in Washington, London, and Moscow on April 10, 1972. Signed by the United States, Britain, the Soviet Union, and 86 other states, it was the first arms control agreement since the end of

World War II to provide for the actual destruction of an existing class of weapons.

On May 18, 1972, the Seabed Arms Control Treaty entered into force when the United States, the Soviet Union, and Britain formally signed this pact banning nuclear weapons and other weapons of mass destruction from the seabed outside a 12-mile (29-km) coastal zone. Opened for signature in February 1971, the treaty has been signed by 86 countries and ratified by 33.

A Soviet-proposed convention barring chemical warfare, which was presented to CCD in March 1972, was expected to make little progress because of the long-standing deadlock between Moscow and Washington on verification of compliance.

Other Developments. On Nov. 22, 1972, the preparatory session of the Conference on Security and Cooperation in Europe opened in Helsinki. While not an arms control effort, this conference of more than 30 NATO, Warsaw Pact, and neutral European countries sought to consider the feasibility of balanced troop reduction in Europe.

The idea of a worldwide disarmament conference was discussed again at the United Nations, though none of the nuclear powers, with the possible exception of the Soviet Union, was enthusiastic about the prospect. Nevertheless, on November 25, the UN Political Committee voted 105 to 0 to create a study committee to examine the feasibility of such a conference. In spite of various reservations, China, the Soviet Union, Britain, and France supported the resolution, largely because it was considered harmless and was sponsored by 59 small and medium-size countries. The United States abstained, contending that a conference of 136 countries would be unwieldly and costly and would be unlikely to accomplish the solid results of more limited forums such as CCD and SALT.

ERNEST W. LEFEVER
The Brookings Institution

DISASTERS. See ACCIDENTS AND DISASTERS.
DISTRICT OF COLUMBIA. See WASHINGTON, D. C.

DOMINICAN REPUBLIC

The Dominican Republic experienced considerable political violence in 1972, but there were the beginnings of what may be a major program of economic and social reform. One event of international significance was the Caribbean Conference on the Sea, held in Santo Domingo in June, which passed a resolution asserting the participants' claims to 200-mile (320-km) offshore limits.

Political Violence. The first major outbreak of violence took place on January 12, arising from a search for a gang that held up the Royal Bank of Canada in November 1971 for $60,000. Eight policemen and four guerrillas were killed in a shoot-out near the capital, but the principal objects of the search—Plinio Matos Moquete, a Communist lawyer accused of leading the band, and Harry Jimenez Castillo, an associate—eluded capture. The clash was followed by Santo Domingo University student demonstrations in support of the guerrillas.

Students were again involved when police alleged that Tacito Perdomo Robles, a leader of the Maoist Popular Democratic Movement, was hiding in the Catholic University of Santiago, and made an armed attack on the campus on April 3 without finding their man. The next day there was a student protest march, and schools were also closed in Santo Domingo. Later a number of police were arrested for stealing property during the raid, and President Joaquín Balaguer condemned the police for brutality while also chastising the university authorities.

Late in April the mayor of Santo Domingo, Manuel Jimenez Rodriguez—a member of Balaguer's Reformist party—was removed from office on the charge of conspiring with "leftists" to overthrow the regime. He took refuge in the Mexican Embassy and later left the country. Retired Gen. Rafel Valdez Hilario had denounced the alleged plot, saying that he had been contacted by the plotters.

Early in June there were further clashes between police and guerrillas. One policeman was killed and four wounded, and a weapons cache was found.

Reform Bills. In April, President Balaguer submitted 14 bills providing for agrarian and tax reforms. The bills were quickly passed. Among other things, they provided that all rice lands using public irrigation be turned over to the Agrarian Institute to be granted by the Institute to small farmers. Parcels of land less than 80 acres (32.4 hectares) in extent were exempted. Also to be divided among small farmers were 200,000 acres (80,940 hectares) nominally in the hands of the Institute. The latter act would drastically affect military officers who had built homes on and taken de facto possession of part of the land, which had belonged to the late General Trujillo.

Economy. Economically the year was better than average. In June a Canadian-owned nickel refinery opened at Banao—the fourth-largest such plant in the world. Two U. S.-based firms were granted concessions for prospecting and exploiting gold and silver mines, under a new law providing that the Dominican government should take a flat 40% of the resulting income and 18% of the profits. The firms were given tax concessions on imports.

ROBERT J. ALEXANDER, *Rutgers University*

— DOMINICAN REPUBLIC · Information Highlights —

Official Name: Dominican Republic.
Area: 18,816 square miles (48,734 sq km).
Population (1972 est.): 4,600,000. *Density,* 231 per square mile (89 per sq km). *Annual rate of increase,* 3.4%.
Chief Cities (1970 census): Santo Domingo, the capital, 671,-400; Santiago de los Caballeros, 155,200.
Government: *Head of state,* Joaquín Balaguer, president (took office July 1966). *Head of government,* Joaquín Balaguer. *Legislature*—National Congress: Senate, 27 members; Chamber of Deputies, 74 members. *Major political parties* —Reformist party; Dominican Revolutionary party; Popular Democratic Movement.
Language: Spanish (official).
Education: *Expenditure* (1969), 16% of total public expenditure. *School enrollment* (1969)—primary, 726,398; secondary, 102,707; technical/vocational, 4,636; university/higher, 18,817.
Monetary Unit: Peso (1 peso equals U. S.$1, Sept. 1972).
Gross National Product (1971 est.): $1,490,000,000.
National Income per Person (1968): $272.
Economic Indexes: *Industrial production* (manufacturing, 1967), 103 (1963=100); *agricultural production* (1971), 155 (1952–56=100); *consumer price index* (1971), 108 (1963=100).
Manufacturing (major products): Refined sugar, processed foods.
Major Agricultural Products: Sugarcane, bananas, rice, coffee.
Major Minerals: Bauxite, salt.
Foreign Trade (1971): *Exports,* $243,000,000 (chief exports—sugar, coffee, cacao, bauxite, tobacco). *Imports,* $311,-000,000 (chief imports, 1968—chemicals and pharmaceuticals; nonelectrical machinery; electrical machinery, apparatuses, appliances; food). *Chief trading partners* (1969)—United States (took 82% of exports, supplied 55% of imports); West Germany (2%—7%); Japan; Netherlands.
Transportation: *Motor vehicles* (1970), 60,900 (automobiles, 39,300); *major national airline,* Dominicana de Aviación.
Communications: *Telephones* (1971), 47,400; *television stations* (1971), 6; *television sets* (1971), 77,000; *radios* (1970), 164,000; *newspapers* (1969), 6.

HEROIN ADDICTS receive their doses of methadone at Beth Israel Hospital in New York City—one controversial solution to a deadly problem.

DRUG ADDICTION AND ABUSE

In 1972 there was a continued increase in drug addiction and abuse, countered in part by a strong effort by federal, state, and local governments to deal with drug problems. Federal activities were highlighted by the creation of the Special Action Office for Drug Abuse Prevention, designed to coordinate federal antidrug programs.

Barbiturates. The year 1972 may come to be known as the year of the "downer." The increase in the use of sleeping pills as a means of becoming intoxicated rose sharply, especially in metropolitan centers. "Reds" (secobarbital) were used by too many young and old people, alone or in combination with other drugs, to produce a drunken state. Because of the threat of overdose when they are used with alcohol and the seriousness of withdrawal symptoms, "downers" are more dangerous than any other class of drugs.

Heroin. Heroin addiction continued to increase, despite a major effort by the federal government to control supplies and provide treatment for addicts. The latest official federal estimate was that there were 550,000 heroin addicts in the United States. About 65,000 of them were under treatment in methadone maintenance programs. Since methadone programs involve substituting one narcotic drug for another, considerable controversy over its use has developed. Some people have even suggested that a form of heroin maintenance be instituted because there is evidence that only half of a community's addicts will apply for methadone maintenance. Others condemn methadone maintenance because it keeps people enslaved to narcotics.

Heroin maintenance proponents want to supply free heroin to those addicts who have failed in other treatment programs. This, they claim, would decrease crime and eliminate the drug syndicates. It would also improve the health of the addict by providing him with clean materials. Those who object to heroin maintenance say that it will increase supplies of "street" heroin (heroin available for illegal sale), produce large numbers of new addicts, and compound the problem. They ask why addicts would ever try to become abstinent if heroin maintenance were readily available.

Methadone. It now appears that methadone maintenance, when combined with counseling and employment services, will keep about half of those who enter such programs heroin free. Numerous problems remain, particularly those related to the diversion of methadone onto the black market. More and more, the directors of such programs are coming to the opinion that methadone maintenance serves as a tool to hold the patient in treatment. When he has learned more about himself and has undergone a change in his life style—a steady job, schooling, and new friends—he should be considered for discontinuance from methadone maintenance.

Methadone detoxification should not be confused with methadone maintenance. The latter procedure keeps the patient on a daily oral dose of methadone, sufficient to decrease heroin craving and to produce a cross tolerance to heroin-induced euphoria. Maintenance may go on for months, years, or, as some investigators feel, for a lifetime. Methadone detoxification is the use of decreasing doses of the drug in order to avoid the withdrawal symptoms and produce a drug-free state in 3 to 21 days. Less than 10% of those undergoing detoxification will remain abstinent. Nevertheless, it is a worthwhile procedure to achieve freedom from heroin for a short period of time, to decrease the cost of a heroin "habit," or to prepare a patient to enter a drug-free type of program such as a therapeutic community.

Narcotic Antagonists. A major effort to find and develop a long-acting, safe narcotic antagonist was launched in 1972. The antagonists are drugs that resemble the narcotics chemically but exert an

opposite effect. This is accomplished by preempting the binding site on the nerve cell that heroin would normally occupy. Nalorphine (Nalline) is a narcotic antagonist that is used in California as a test of recent heroin use. An injection of nalorphine will displace heroin from the nerve cells and produce withdrawal symptoms. Other antagonists such as naloxone (Narcan) have been used with small numbers of patients. When sufficient naloxone is in the body, an injection of heroin will not produce the "high" associated with the drug.

Drug Seizures. Statistics released by the Justice Department's Bureau of Narcotics and Dangerous Drugs indicate that federal seizures of illegal drugs are rapidly increasing. In 1971 over 1,500 pounds (680 kg) of heroin was seized by federal authorities, over three times as much as in 1970. Although the effort to control supplies has been marked by increasing success, it cannot be hoped that illicit drugs can be completely interdicted. Controls are necessary, but other techniques must be used to solve the drug abuse problems.

Federal Activities. There were major reorganizations of the federal antidrug effort in 1972. A law signed on March 21 formally created the Special Action Office for Drug Abuse Prevention, with $1 billion in funds. This agency operates out of the Executive Office of the President. It has broad policy-making and supervisory authority over federal drug abuse training, research, and treatment programs. To coordinate the law enforcement and control aspects, President Nixon established an Office of Drug Abuse Law Enforcement, in which the activities of the Bureau of Narcotics and Dangerous Drugs were to be integrated with those of the Customs Bureau and the Internal Revenue Service. One of its first acts was to establish a heroin hot line that was to receive information about narcotics pushers.

In an effort to reduce the use of stimulants, the government announced in February that it was cutting the allowable production of amphetamines by about 82% from the production of 1971. Large amounts of these drugs were being manufactured in the United States and sent to Mexico, from which they were sent back illegally to the United States.

The President's National Commission on Marihuana and Drug Abuse released its first report on March 22, 1972. It recommended decriminalization of private use of marihuana and of casual, not-for-profit sales. Heavy penalties would remain for cultivation, trafficking, and possession with intent to sell. President Nixon, however, said that he still opposed any legalization of marihuana. A final commission report was expected in 1973.

It appeared unlikely that the possessor of small amounts of marihuana would soon be reclassified out of the criminal category. Bills to such effect were introduced in Congress, but early favorable action was not expected. Most states now provide misdemeanor penalties for possession of marihuana.

In November, California voters rejected, by a two-to-one majority, a referendum that would have constituted a qualified legalization of marihuana. The proposal would have permitted persons over 18 to cultivate the plant and to smoke it, but would have retained the legal prohibition against the commercial cultivation and sale of marihuana.

The armed services have instituted a number of operations in response to a growing heroin addiction problem, particularly in Vietnam. Units are periodically subject to a "drug screen," an unannounced urine examination for narcotics and other drugs. An amnesty program has been instituted for military personnel who have become addicted. If they come forward for treatment, punitive measures are set aside. Programs of education and treatment for the serviceman have been started, and liaison with Veterans Administration hospitals has been effected in order to assure continuity of care following discharge.

Drug Abuse Education. If controlling supplies can be only partially successful and if treatment of the abuser is difficult and not uniformly rewarding, then prevention should be a more definitive community response to the problem. Unfortunately, reliable techniques of persuading people, especially young people, to avoid or abandon dangerous drug usage are not at hand. In fact, certain efforts at educating may have made drug misuse seem a seductive or manly activity with results exactly opposite to those desired. One hopeful approach to education is to provide worthwhile alternatives to drug taking. Family and community must assist young people to discover nondrug "highs" that are more rewarding and sustaining than a chemically induced euphoria.

Professional and Paraprofessional Training. In a rapidly expanding prevention and treatment effort, one of the critical shortages is the lack of experienced, trained personnel. Doctors, nurses, and other professionals receive little instruction in the dependency disorders during their formal schooling. Paraprofessionals, including ex-addicts who want to begin a career of rescuing others from addiction, require considerable background information in order to make them more effective.

A national training center was established in 1972 in Washington, D. C. The course offered at the training center plus that of regional training centers should create a core of more knowledgeable personnel. In addition, a number of universities are including special courses in drug abuse for their medical psychology and social welfare students.

(See also the special feature on narcotics traffic beginning on page 37.)

SIDNEY COHEN, M. D.
Executive Director, Council on Drug & Alcohol Abuse, University of California, Los Angeles

EAGLETON, Thomas F. See BIOGRAPHY.

EARTHQUAKES

Earthquake activity in 1972 was much less than usual, and there were comparatively few casualties except for disastrous quakes in Iran and Nicaragua. Seismologists have been seeking a way to predict earthquakes so that people can flee an area before a quake strikes. During the year their hopes were raised by the development of a new method of prediction. Another highlight of the year was the assumption by the National Oceanic and Atmospheric Administration of responsibility for all seismic information in the United States.

Earthquake Activity. In the early morning hours of April 10, a quake of magnitude 7 struck southern Iran, about 560 miles (900 km) south of Teheran. About 5,050 persons were killed, thousands more were injured or homeless, and the village of Qir was completely destroyed. The damaged area covered about 400 square miles (1,000 sq km). On the same day there were nine aftershocks with magnitudes between 4 and 5 on the Richter scale. From

April 12 to April 16 about six more aftershocks occurred. (See also IRAN.)

On December 23 a quake of magnitude 6.25 devastated Managua, Nicaragua, the capital and largest city of the country. At least 10,000 persons were killed, more than 10,000 were injured, and thousands were homeless. (See also NICARAGUA.)

On March 20 a quake of magnitude 6.9 hit northern Peru. Seven persons were killed, and there was property damage in the Juanjui area. Taiwan was hit by a quake of magnitude 7.2 on April 24; four persons were killed, 11 were injured, and there was moderate property damage. On April 25 a quake of magnitude 7.3 struck the Philippine Islands; there was some damage in the Manila area, but no casualties were reported. On June 24 a quake of magnitude 6 struck the Hindu Kush region in Afghanistan, killing 11 persons near Ishkamish.

Earthquake Prediction. Probably the most important research under way in seismology in 1972 was an investigation of the possibility of earthquake prediction. A slight ray of hope broke through on this subject early in the year when Soviet and Japanese scientists reported that the ratio of the speeds of the two main earthquake waves, called P waves and S waves, ceased to be constant when the waves were traveling in the area of a developing earthquake.

Previously, seismologists had known that at relatively moderate depths below the earth's surface, P waves (primary waves) travel at about 5 miles per second, and S waves (secondary waves) travel at about 3 miles per second. They also had established that these speeds increase with depth in the earth's mantle but that the ratio of the speeds was always constant, this ratio being 1.73 to 1. The Soviet and Japanese scientists found some evidence that the ratio is not constant in the area of a developing quake. This suggested that the variation in the ratio might be used to predict the occurrence of earthquakes. However, much more research was needed before the correlation could be definitely established and its significance evaluated.

Seismologists can be proud of how they have increased man's knowledge of earthquakes in a short span of time. It was only about 80 years ago that Rebeur Paschwitz first discovered that an earthquake sends out waves that enable the quake to be detected from a distance. While experimenting with a pendulum in Potsdam, Germany, Paschwitz accidently recorded a violent earthquake in Japan, 5,500 miles (8,850 km) away. He was not interested in earthquakes but had set up his pendulum to try to detect disturbances of gravity caused by the moon.

Seismic Information Center. As of June 15, 1972, the National Oceanic and Atmospheric Administration (NOAA), at Boulder, Colo., became the government agency responsible for all seismic information in the United States, a responsibility previously held by the U. S. Coast and Geodetic Survey. From that date forward, all requests for official seismic information were to be sent to Seismological Investigations Group, NOAA/ERL/ESL/RB3, East University Campus, Boulder, Colo. 80302.

In May 1972, NOAA released a report on the 5-megaton nuclear blast set off on Amchitka Island on Nov. 6, 1971. Its report stated that the blast, which had a magnitude of 7 on the Richter scale, did not trigger "any natural earthquake-causing processes." The blast did give rise to about 22 aftershocks, the largest of these registering 3.5 on the Richter scale. However, the report said these aftershocks were merely "minor structural adjustments in the earth's crust" following the nuclear blast.

J. JOSEPH LYNCH, S. J.
Director, Fordham University Seismic Observatory

ECHEVERRÍA, Luís. See BIOGRAPHY.
ECOLOGY. See CONSERVATION; ENVIRONMENT.

A child, carried by her grieving father, was one of thousands of victims of a quake that struck Iran in April.

UPI

SAME OLD THING EVERY SHOPPING DAY!!

Economy of the U.S.

Economic activities in the United States in 1972 are examined in this article under the following headings: (1) Economic Review; (2) National Income and Product; (3) Industrial Production; (4) Retail Sales; and (5) Wholesale Sales.

Other related developments are reviewed in AUTOMOBILES; BANKING; ENERGY; HOUSING; INTERNATIONAL FINANCE; INTERNATIONAL TRADE; LABOR; MINING; STEEL; STOCKS AND BONDS; TAXATION; and UNITED STATES.

ECONOMIC REVIEW

The U. S. economy underwent a broad-based expansion in 1972, with gains registered in all sectors. The economy got off to a strong start as a result of the momentum generated in the last quarter of 1971, and economic advances spread and picked up additional force as the year progressed. Industrial output, which had stood still for two years at a high level, finally began rising strongly as the year proceeded. This rise was accompanied by additional increases in consumer spending, which reflected greater consumer confidence in the economy.

Progress in the continuing battle against price inflation was by no means decisive, but the debilitating psychological force of price rises at least appeared to be blunted. Government activity continued to be an economic stimulus, but the U. S. position in foreign trade continued to worsen. Nevertheless, the economic strength generated during the year, mirrored in rising business spending for new plant, increasing consumer outlays for durable goods, and the rising levels of stock prices, promised to carry well into 1973.

Gross National Product. The U. S. gross national product (GNP) increased sharply in 1972. The gain primarily reflected an improvement in real output rather than a predominance of price increases, which had characterized changes in the GNP over the previous three years. The total output of the economy in 1972 increased by more than $100 billion as measured in current prices, representing a gain of around 9.5%. In terms of real output, measured in constant prices, the gain was well over 6%, compared with gains of 2.5% and 2.7% in 1969 and 1971 and a decline of 0.7% in 1970.

Two components of the GNP—private domestic investment outlays and government purchases of goods and services—led the gains in national products over more than the first half of the year, but consumer expenditures rose to contribute markedly to the increases as the year advanced. Geographically and industrially, the gains were widely distributed. In the net total of GNP gain, only foreign trade was a drag as net imports continued to rise through the first three quarters of the year.

Prices. Accompanying the gains in economic output were slowdowns in the rate of price advances, which showed there was some progress in the battle against inflation. The broadest measure of price change is the GNP price deflator, which is a weighted average of component price indexes. On the basis of this measure, prices rose by more than 5% in the first quarter of the year and by only slightly over 2% in the second quarter. However, this measure may have unduly reflected the post-freeze clustering of price increases and federal pay raises in the first quarter. By midyear all prices appeared to be gaining at a rate of about 3.2%, a marked deceleration from the 3.9% rate that had prevailed earlier although the progress was not even.

An adjusted average of all prices, including industrial components, was an abstraction to the consumer in 1972 because he was periodically startled during the year by jumps in food prices and other living costs. By year-end consumer prices, as measured by the Consumer Price Index, were 27% above the 1967 level, and the wholesale price index continued to show erratic but occasionally sharp uptrends. "Inflation," commented the chairman of the President's Council of Economic Advisors, "remains a national problem."

241

PRESIDENT NIXON is flanked by retiring Secretary of the Treasury John Connally (right) and George Shultz, who succeeded Connally.

UPI

Industrial Sector. Basic to the strength of the economic revival in 1972 was the marked gain in industrial output, which had been lagging since 1969. As measured by the Federal Reserve Board's Index of Industrial Production (1967 = 100), total industrial output rose to a preliminary average of 112.7 for 1972, compared with an average of 106.8 for 1971, 106.7 for 1970, and 110.7 for 1969. Most notable was the gain in the manufacture of durable goods, a basic sector that had shown no improvement for several years. Output by utilities, nondurable goods producers, and mining concerns also contributed to the rise in the total industrial output.

Joining in the upsurge in industrial output were the steel and automobile industries. Steel output maintained strength throughout 1972, avoiding the precipitate midyear dropoff and failure to recover that had made 1971 the worst year in a decade. With steady high-level demand throughout 1972, steel output returned to more nearly normal levels and was running close to 10% ahead of the preceding year. Automobile assemblies also responded to strong basic demand, and output was well ahead of that in 1971.

Business Sector. Adding to the expansionary forces in the economy was the solid strength in the business sector. Corporate profits probed new high ground in 1972, and the business community also was cheered by strong sales. In addition, the inventory-to-sales ratio continued its decline from a high 1.90 average in 1970 to a 1.65 seasonally adjusted annual rate after midyear 1972. By this time it appeared that inventories had been worked down to the point that the long-awaited inventory buildup would commence.

As a result of the general improvement, businessmen showed increasing willingness to expand capital plant, and expenditures for new plant and equipment showed continued strong rises throughout 1972. In contrast, this sector had shown virtually no gain in 1970 and only a moderate gain in 1971. On top of the sizable increases in 1972, there were anticipations of continued gains at near the 10% level for several quarters in 1973.

Government Sector. Government spending for goods and services increased by about 10% in 1972, and the spending was pushed up by all levels of government. Although defense spending by the federal government was below the high levels of recent years, there was an increase over 1971. Also, the total outlay by the federal government in 1972 was running ahead of the previous year by even larger amounts. State and local governments continued to increase their spending in 1972 at a rate well ahead of the average for the economy as a whole.

The most significant stimulus to spending was the continued impact of the federal government's deficit. For both fiscal year 1971 and fiscal year 1972, the federal deficit was approximately $23.0 billion, and it was estimated that the deficit would increase to $25.0 billion in fiscal year 1973 (July 1972 to June 1973). Some observers questioned the economic reasonableness of increased deficits at a time of rising economic activity and troublesome inflation, but others pointed out that tax reform and a tighter federal revenue structure could reduce the size of the projected deficit. Additionally, the administration served notice that it intended to cut federal expenditures by significant amounts.

Consumer Sector. Buoyed by rising personal income and declining unemployment, consumers came into the market in 1972 and registered the largest gain in consumer spending in recent years. Whereas personal consumption expenditures had increased in 1971 by $48 billion over the preceding year, the seasonally adjusted annual rate in the third quarter of 1972 was $58 billion ahead of last year. Most significant was the increased willingness to purchase consumer durable goods, whose sales were running nearly 12% ahead of sales in 1971. In addition, consumer purchases of nondurable goods and services were running well ahead of those in 1971. Backing up these figures were those registered by retail merchants, whose retail sales were nearly 13% ahead of sales in 1971.

The mood of the consumer is well measured by his willingness to purchase new automobiles. Declines in auto purchases correlate closely with general business downturns, whereas rises in auto purchases closely accompany broad general business upturns. Significantly, in the fourth quarter of 1972 consumers anticipated purchasing a million more new cars than at the same time in 1971.

One impetus behind the consumer's willingness to spend was his rapidly rising level of personal income. Gains in recent years have bulked large in dollar terms, as rises of roundly $59.6 billion were shown for 1968 over 1967, $62 billion for 1969, $56 billion for 1970, and $55 billion for 1971. Toward

the end of 1972, however, personal income was more than $93 billion ahead of that in 1971, a strong rise measuring nearly 10.5%.

Another significant development was a shift in consumer savings patterns. In terms of savings as a percentage of disposable personal income, the consumer savings level was 6.4% in mid-1972, dropping from the average high level of 8.2% in 1971. The declining percentage probably reflected both the rapidly rising level of income and the lessening of caution as economic conditions improved.

The unemployment problem has proved to be among the most intractable in recent years. Toward the end of 1972 unemployment declined to a 5.2% rate, the lowest level recorded since August 1970. The persistent hovering around the 6.0% level over the past two years had been the cause of considerable concern, so the slight improvement was welcomed.

One of the major sources of strength in the economy in recent years has been housing construction. Housing starts totaled 1.4 million units in 1970, and a surge to 2.05 million units in 1971 was thought by many to make up for a lag in earlier years. However, housing starts rose to new record highs in 1972 and stood at a seasonally adjusted annual rate of 2.4 million units toward year-end.

Overview of the Economy in 1972. Virtually all sectors of the economy participated in the gains registered in 1972. State and local governments improved their revenue positions, and as the year progressed many of them were considering surplus positions instead of being concerned with deficits. Many corporations improved their cash flow and liquidity positions and were able to shift capital financing in part to internally generated funds or to stock flotations and away from the bond market. The stock market celebrated all this by pushing closely watched averages to new all-time highs. In particular, the Dow-Jones Industrial Average rose above the 1,000 mark for the first time in its history and stayed there until the year closed. On top of all this, the year finished with the economic indicators pointed up and the leading-indicator index forecasting continued upward movement on a broad-based scale.

Outlook. On these grounds and out of the ebullience generated by the overall performance of the economy in 1972, many forecasters saw another bright year in 1973. The consensus forecast called for another gain of more than $100 billion in the GNP in 1973, with about 6% of the increase in real output and the remainder of around 3.5% showing up as price increases. The economy was expected to surge forward for about six months on momentum alone. Some developments, such as the federal refund of overwithheld income taxes in 1972, were expected to stimulate the economy further in the first half, particularly if, as some estimates have it, more than $5 billion is handed back to consumers who were overwithheld. On the other hand unpredictable developments, such as how the war in Vietnam is settled, underlie all assumptions about the future of the economy.

JACKSON PHILLIPS
Vice President, Moody's Investors Service

NATIONAL INCOME AND PRODUCT

The national income of the United States totaled $934.9 billion in 1972, up sharply from $855.7 billion in 1971. National income—the income earned by U. S. residents from production—expanded at

FOOD PRICE POLICY is defended in September by Herbert Stein, chairman of the Council of Economic Advisers, who holds roast whose price he said went down.

9.3% rate in 1972, a substantially faster pace than it had in 1971 when it rose 7.2%.

The expansion in national income was the result of a sharp rise in the volume of production, which increased 6.5% in 1972, as contrasted with a gain of only 2.7% in 1971. The rate of price inflation slowed sharply as measured by the implicit price deflator, which was up only 3.0% in 1972 compared with a 4.7% increase in 1971. The implicit price deflator is the ratio of the gross national product (GNP) in current dollars to the GNP in constant dollars.

National Income. The upward change in the rate of growth of the national income was particularly marked in two components, wages and salaries and farm proprietors' income. Wages and salaries increased 9.2% in 1972, whereas they had risen only 5.8% in 1971. Farm proprietors' income scored a sharp 13.3% gain in 1972, as contrasted with a rise of only 3.0% in the previous year.

The rate of increase in nonfarm proprietors' income in 1972 was little changed from that in 1971. Their income rose 5.7% in 1972 and 5.4% in 1971.

Somewhat smaller gains were reported in 1972 than in 1971 for supplements to wages and salaries, rental income of persons, corporate profits, and net interest. Supplements to wages and salaries were up 11.3% in 1972, whereas they had risen 14.2% in 1971. The rental income of persons increased 4.5% in 1972, whereas this component had risen 5.2% in the previous year. Corporate profits increased 11.6% in 1972, whereas they had risen 12.4% in 1971. Net interest was up only 7.3% in 1972, whereas it had increased 10.6% in the prior year.

Personal Income. Personal income—the income received by persons from all sources—rose 8.6% in 1972, as contrasted with an increase of 6.8% in 1971. The change of 1.8 percentage points in the rate of increase in personal income was substantially less than the 2.1 percentage point change in the rate of gain in national income.

GROSS NATIONAL PRODUCT OR EXPENDITURES

(Billions of dollars)[1]

	1969	1970	1971	1972
Gross national product.............	930.3	976.4	1,050.4	1,152.1
Personal consumption				
expenditures.................	579.5	616.8	664.9	721.1
Durable goods................	90.8	90.5	103.5	116.3
Nondurable goods.............	245.9	264.4	278.1	299.5
Services......................	242.7	261.8	283.3	305.4
Gross private domestic investment.	139.0	137.1	152.0	180.2
Fixed investment..............	131.1	132.2	148.3	174.3
Nonresidential..............	98.5	100.9	105.8	120.4
Structures...............	34.2	36.0	38.4	42.2
Producers' durable				
equipment............	64.3	64.9	67.4	78.2
Residential structures........	32.7	31.2	42.6	53.9
Change in business inventories..	7.8	4.9	3.6	5.8
Net exports of goods and services..	1.9	3.6	.7	−4.1
Exports......................	55.5	62.9	66.1	73.7
Imports.....................	53.6	59.3	65.4	77.8
Government purchases of goods				
and services................	210.0	219.0	232.8	254.9
Federal....................	98.8	96.5	97.8	105.9
State and local................	111.2	122.5	135.0	148.9

[1] Detail may not add to total because of rounding. Source: Bureau of Economic Analysis, U. S. Department of Commerce.

NATIONAL INCOME BY TYPE OF INCOME

(Billions of dollars)[1]

	1969	1970	1971	1972
National income......................	766.0	798.6	855.7	934.9
Compensation of employees...........	566.0	603.8	644.1	705.2
Wages and salaries................	509.7	541.9	573.5	626.4
Private.......................	405.6	426.8	449.7	491.9
Government.................	104.1	115.1	123.8	134.6
Supplements to wages and salaries..	56.3	61.9	70.7	78.7
Proprietors' income..................	67.2	66.8	70.0	75.2
Business and professional..........	50.5	49.9	52.6	55.6
Farm.........................	16.7	16.8	17.3	19.6
Rental income of persons.............	22.6	23.3	24.5	25.6
Corporate profits and inventory valu-				
ation adjustment.................	79.8	69.9	78.6	87.7
Profits before tax..................	84.9	74.3	83.3	93.7
Inventory valuation adjustment.....	−5.1	−4.4	−4.7	−6.0
Net interest........................	30.5	34.8	38.5	41.3

[1] Detail may not add to total because of rounding. Source: Bureau of Economic Analysis, U. S. Department of Commerce.

The smaller change in the rate of gain in personal income principally reflected a marked slowing in the growth of transfer payments, which are included in personal income but are not included in national income. Government transfer payments to persons increased 11.1% in 1972, while in 1971 such payments had risen 18.4%.

Personal tax payments showed a large spurt of 19.8% in 1972; in the previous year personal taxes had risen only 0.3%. This marked surge in taxes was largely due to the introduction of new withholding tax schedules, which led to a substantial volume of overwithholding on 1972 tax liabilities.

With personal taxes rising so sharply, the advance in personal income did not carry through to disposable personal income—the income available to persons for spending or saving. In 1972, disposable personal income increased by 6.8%, while it had increased 8.0% in the previous year.

Although the growth of disposable personal income slowed in 1972, consumer spending accelerated moderately as the rate of increase in consumer spending rose from about 7.8% in 1971 to 8.5% in 1972. Because the growth in disposable personal income was slowing and the growth in consumer spending was rising, there was a sharp drop in personal saving. Personal saving fell 10.2% in 1972, whereas in 1971 personal saving had risen 10.9%. The drop in saving brought the personal saving rate down to 6.9% in 1972, as compared with an annual peak rate of 8.2% in 1971.

Gross National Product. The gross national product is the current market value of all the goods and services produced by a nation's economy during a year. As shown by the breakdown in the accompanying table, the GNP provides a detailed picture of the major market developments underlying the movement in aggregate production.

The rate of growth of the gross national product rose from 7.6% in 1971 to 9.7% in 1972. Thus, the upward change in the rate of increase of the GNP was 2.1%. Such an upward change in the rate of increase of some quantity is called an acceleration. The acceleration in the growth of the GNP in 1972 reflected marked increases in the markets for nonresidential fixed investment, inventories, consumer nondurable goods, and federal government purchases. Nonresidential fixed investment rose 13.8% in 1972, up sharply from the 4.9% gain in 1971. Business inventories rose at a 61.1% rate in 1972, whereas in 1971 the growth of inventories had slowed down. Federal government purchases of goods and services rose 8.3% in 1972, while in 1971 such outlays had increased at a rate of only 1.3%. Consumer purchases of nondurable goods increased 7.7% in 1972, as contrasted with a gain of 5.2% in 1971.

Accelerations in the markets just reviewed were partially offset by slowdowns in the rate of growth of personal consumption expenditures for durable goods and for services, a slowdown in the growth rate of residential construction, and slowdowns in state and local government purchases. Consumer purchases of durable goods rose 12.4% in 1972, while in 1971 they had increased 14.4%. Consumer purchases of services increased 7.8% in 1972, whereas in the previous year they had risen 8.2%. While the gain in residential structures in 1972 was quite large at 26.5%, it was considerably below the increase of 36.5% scored in 1971. State and local government purchases increased at a rate of 10.3% in 1972, a rate not significantly below the 10.2% gain scored in 1971.

Net exports of goods and services turned negative in 1972 as an 19% rise in imports outpaced an 11.5% gain in exports.

JOHN A. GORMAN
Bureau of Economic Analysis
U. S. Department of Commerce

INDUSTRIAL PRODUCTION

U. S. industrial production gained 6.5% in 1972, according to preliminary estimates. Revised data showed a negligible increase of 0.1% for 1971 instead of the 0.3% decline reported on the basis of preliminary estimates.

Industrial production remained relatively free of labor strife during 1972 as few contracts were up for renegotiation, but production was affected somewhat by the floods that followed tropical storm Agnes in mid-June. Environmental protection efforts closely related to industrial production costs were felt more sharply than in previous years. A new water-pollution law was passed, and enforcement actions were stepped up under the Refuse Act of 1899 and the new standards set by the 1970 Clean Air Act.

Industrial Production Index. The industrial production index, prepared by the Board of Governors of the Federal Reserve System, measures the physical volume of production by U. S. factories, mines, and utilities. It covers about 40% of the nation's total output of goods and services and reflects current trends in the economy. The index underwent

THE U.S. ECONOMY IN 1972—PICTURE OF A RECOVERY

GROSS NATIONAL PRODUCT

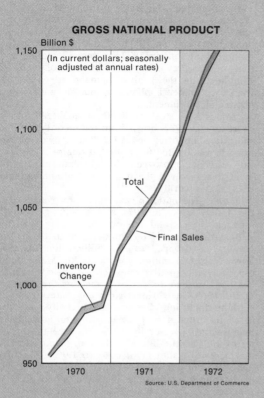

Billion $

(In current dollars; seasonally adjusted at annual rates)

Total

Final Sales

Inventory Change

Source: U.S. Department of Commerce

UNEMPLOYMENT RATE

Percent

(Seasonally adjusted)

Total

Married Men

Source: U.S. Department of Commerce

INDUSTRIAL PRODUCTION

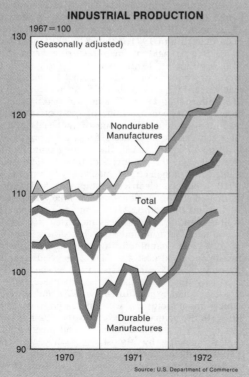

1967 = 100

(Seasonally adjusted)

Nondurable Manufactures

Total

Durable Manufactures

Source: U.S. Department of Commerce

PERSONAL INCOME

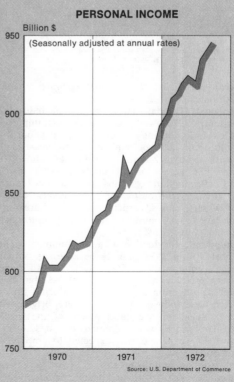

Billion $

(Seasonally adjusted at annual rates)

Source: U.S. Department of Commerce

U. S. INDUSTRIAL PRODUCTION INDEX
(1967 = 100)

	1971	1972[1]
Industrial production, total	106.8	112.7
Major industry groupings		
Manufacturing, durable and nondurable	105.2	111.6
Mining	107.0	108.1
Utilities	133.9	140.9
Major market groupings		
Consumer goods	115.7	121.5
Equipment, including defense	89.4	92.8
Materials	107.4	114.8

[1] Preliminary data.   Source: Board of Governors of the Federal Reserve System.

ANNUAL SURVEY OF MANUFACTURES, 1971

	Number of employees	Payroll (millions of dollars)	Value added by manufacture (millions of dollars)
All manufacturing establishments, including administrative and auxiliary units, total[1]	18,408,900	156,569	313,684
Operating manufacturing establishments	17,421,900	144,105	313,684
Nondurable goods			
Foods and kindred products	1,582,400	12,241	34,151
Tobacco manufactures	67,600	471	2,561
Textile mill products	907,600	5,330	10,096
Apparel and other textile products	1,315,300	6,455	12,444
Paper and allied products	634,600	5,540	11,713
Printing and publishing	1,050,000	8,963	18,152
Chemicals and allied products	844,600	8,201	29,050
Petroleum and coal products	141,700	1,565	5,691
Rubber and plastics products	540,300	4,257	9,388
Leather and leather products	274,200	1,506	2,756
Durable goods			
Lumber and wood products	528,000	2,767	6,798
Furniture and fixtures	434,200	2,807	5,232
Stone, clay, and glass products	588,400	4,865	10,842
Primary metal industries	1,168,600	11,175	21,053
Fabricated metal products	1,273,400	10,968	21,942
Machinery, except electrical	1,751,300	16,272	31,158
Electrical equipment and supplies	1,648,500	14,317	27,651
Transportation equipment	1,621,300	16,778	34,562
Instruments and related products	382,200	3,357	8,415
Miscellaneous manufacturing industries	410,000	2,731	5,707
Ordnance and accessories	257,700	2,858	4,641

[1] Warehouses, power plants, repair shops, and similar facilities that serve the manufacturing establishments of a company rather than the general public were reported separately. Source: U. S. Department of Commerce, Bureau of the Census.

a general revision in 1971, producing more reliable final estimates.

Consumer Goods. The recovery in industrial production in 1972 owed a great deal to an unprecedented boom in housing. A record high of about 2.4 million housing starts was made during the year, compared with just over 2 million housing starts in 1971.

Consumer goods of all kinds were in brisk demand. Production of consumer durables rose 8% in 1972, as the output of home goods—appliances, TV sets, radios, carpeting, and furniture—increased 10%. The output of nondurable consumer goods rose close to 6%.

Equipment. Production of new equipment went up almost 5% in 1972, mainly because the output of business equipment rose 6%. Defense and space equipment production increased about 2%, but this reversed a production decline of 25% during 1969–71. Aerospace industry prospects were brightened by the go-ahead on the development of the space shuttle. This project was estimated to cost $2.6 billion over six years and was expected to employ a peak of 500,000 workers.

Automobiles and Trucks. The year 1972 was the busiest ever for auto and truck manufacturers and assemblers. Total assemblies reached a record

11.25 million, topping the previous high of 11.1 million set in 1965. Truck production set an all-time record of nearly 2.5 million in 1972, almost 20% higher than the previous production peak in 1971. About 8.8 million passenger cars were built in 1972, compared with nearly 8.6 million in 1971.

Steel. Steelmakers poured 133 million short tons of raw steel in 1972, compared with 120 million short tons in 1971. Shipments reached 92 million short tons in 1972, against 87 million short tons in the previous year. The use of steel was stimulated by the healthy demand for autos and trucks, consumer appliances, housing, and business plant and equipment.

Imports of steel declined to about 17 million short tons in 1972, down from the record 18 million short tons imported in 1971. The growth of steel imports was limited to an annual rate of 2.5% in an extended and improved voluntary restraint arrangement that involved the major steel-producing countries of the world.

Coal. The nation's coal mines, recovering from the 45-day strike in 1971 and benefiting from the shortage of gas and oil, produced more than 583 million short tons of bituminous coal in 1972. Coal output had dropped to 552 million tons in 1971, down from 603 million tons in 1970. Many mines, especially the smaller ones, closed their operations because they had difficulties in meeting the standards of the 1969 Coal Mine Health and Safety Act.

Manufacturing Sector. Productivity, as measured in terms of output per man-hour, rose in the manufacturing sector by 4.2% from the third quarter of 1971 to the like 1972 period, helping to keep the increase in unit labor costs to 1.9%. Manufacturing profits jumped more than 15% in 1972, and plant capacity utilization inched close to 80% by year-end, up from about 75% in 1971.

According to the Annual Survey of Manufactures issued by the Bureau of the Census in September 1972, about 18.5 million workers were employed in manufacturing in 1971, about 830,000 fewer than in 1970. Wages paid by manufacturing firms totaled $156.6 billion in 1971, about $4 billion more than in the preceding year. Value added by manufacture reached $313.7 billion in 1971, an increase of over $15 billion over 1970. (Value added represents the difference between the value of products shipped by manufacturers and the value of materials and supplies sent to manufacturers for use in production.) In terms of value added, the leading manufacturing groups include the producers of transportation equipment, food, nonelectrical machinery, chemicals and allied products, electrical equipment and supplies, fabricated metal products, and primary metals.

Capital Spending. After a sluggish year in 1971, capital spending by business increased 9% in 1972 as nonmanufacturing industries hiked new investment by 12% and manufacturing industries raised their investment by almost 4%. Durable goods manufacturers increased capital spending by nearly 10%, paced by the stone-clay-glass producers, who increased capital expenditures by 37%, and the motor vehicle manufacturers, who increased spending by 19%. In the primary metals industry new investment was up 1.5% as blast furnaces and steelworks cut capital spending by almost 8%, while nonferrous metals producers increased new investment by 13%.

AGO AMBRE, *Current Business Analysis Division*
Bureau of Economic Analysis
U. S. Department of Commerce

RETAIL SALES

Retail sales advanced sharply in the first half of 1972, climbing 9% after a three-year period when growth was attributable largely to price inflation. For the first six months of 1972, sales totaled a record $209.9 billion, or 9% higher than a year earlier. Prices accounted for about one third of the advance, with a higher physical volume of goods accounting for the remainder. Larger consumer demand led to a fall in personal savings from an unusually high 8% of disposable personal income in both 1970 and 1971 to just under 7% in the first half of 1972.

Inventories. Stocks of retail stores at the end of June 1972 reached $51.9 billion, up $2.3 billion from the corresponding period of 1971. This rise was smaller than the sales advance so that the stock-sales ratio fell from 1.46 in mid-1971 to 1.41 in mid-1972. Virtually the entire decline in this ratio occurred at durable goods stores.

Sales Trends. The advance in sales was pervasive, and, as is usual in periods of cyclical recovery, the increases in durable goods far outpaced those in nondurables. Durable goods sales were 14% higher. Reflecting the very sharp rise in construction, sales by lumber, building, and hardware dealers and by furniture and house-furnishing stores increased 16% and 15%, respectively. Automotive dealers' deliveries rose 13%—a particularly noteworthy performance since 1971 sales were swollen by the recovery from the 1970 General Motor's strike and included excise taxes that were removed in 1972.

Nondurable goods stores reported a sales increase of 7%. Above average advances were reported by general merchandise stores (up 10%) and eating and drinking places (up 9%). Sales of gasoline stations rose 7%, food and drugs stores 5% each, and apparel stores 4%.

Sales by firms operating 11 or more stores totaled $62.1 billion in the first six months of 1972, an increase of 8% over the previous year. While this increase was slightly lower than that for smaller retail organizations, the former group does not handle a significant amount of autos or other durable goods.

By geographic division, sales rose at a below-average rate in the heavily weighted Middle Atlantic and East North Central divisions (5% and 7% respectively), sharply in the New England and Mountain divisions (over 15%), and from 10% to 12% in all other divisions.

SALES OF RETAIL STORES, 1970–72
(millions of dollars)

	1971	1970	1972[1]	1971
	Full year		First six months	
All retail stores	408,850	375,527	209,894	192,099
Durable goods stores[2]	131,814	114,288	71,037	62,358
Automotive group	78,916	64,966	43,336	38,428
Furniture and appliance group	18,560	17,778	9,832	8,528
Lumber, building, hardware group	17,378	15,346	9,013	7,754
Nondurable goods stores[2]	277,036	261,239	138,857	129,741
Apparel group	20,804	19,810	9,650	9,284
Drug and proprietary stores	13,736	13,352	6,933	6,632
Eating and drinking places	31,131	29,689	16,140	14,823
Food group	89,239	86,114	45,766	43,584
Gasoline service stations	29,163	27,994	14,812	13,899
General merchandise group, with nonstores	68,134	61,320	32,121	29,084
Department stores	42,027	37,295	19,474	17,726

[1] Preliminary.   [2] Includes estimates for other kinds of business not shown separately.   Source: U.S. Department of Commerce.

MERCHANT WHOLESALERS' SALES, 1970–72
(millions of dollars)

	1971	1970	1972[1]	1971
	Full year		First six months	
Merchant wholesalers total	267,357	246,643	142,515	128,627
Durable goods[2]	122,420	111,778	66,292	58,553
Motor vehicles, automotive equipment	24,506	20,203	13,522	11,696
Electrical goods	16,800	15,809	8,752	7,820
Furniture, home furnishings	6,096	5,343	2,957	2,847
Hardware, plumbing, heating equipment, supplies	11,813	10,634	6,377	5,591
Lumber, construction materials	13,003	10,836	7,265	5,841
Machinery, equipment, supplies	31,044	28,515	17,044	15,006
Metals, metalwork (except scrap)	12,353	12,625	6,855	6,253
Scrap, waste material	4,882	5,986	2,567	2,661
Nondurable goods[2]	144,937	134,865	76,223	70,074
Groceries and related products	53,610	50,430	28,220	25,876
Beer, wine, distilled alcoholic beverages	14,071	12,862	7,057	6,421
Drugs, chemicals, allied products	10,397	9,619	5,664	5,000
Tobacco, tobacco products	6,498	6,118	3,356	3,130
Dry goods	11,799	10,391	6,169	5,579
Paper, paper products (excluding wallpaper)	7,600	7,317	3,995	3,731
Farm products (raw materials)	15,741	14,336	8,407	7,826
Other nondurable goods	25,222	23,792	13,355	12,511

[1] Preliminary.   [2] Includes estimates for other kinds of business not shown separately.   Source: U.S. Department of Commerce.

WHOLESALE SALES

Sales by merchant wholesalers totaled $142.5 billion in the first six months of 1972—up 10.8% from the corresponding period of 1971. The increase reflected both higher selling prices—up 4% —and the economic recovery underway. After allowance for the price rise, the physical volume of sales rose about 6.5%.

Inventories. Merchant wholesalers held $29.6 billion of inventories at the end of June 1972—an increase of almost $2.3 billion over the June 1971 total. This increase was greater than that in sales, and the stock-sales ratio rose about 2% during this period.

Sales Trends. Wholesale establishments dealing in durable goods reported a 13% gain in sales between the first half of 1971 and the first half of 1972. Sales by lumber and construction materials dealers rose 24%—just about matching the increase in the number of new housing units started. Sales of hardware, plumbing, and heating equipment supplies advanced 14%, also reflecting the large increase in construction. Motor vehicles and machinery-equipment dealers' sales showed above average increases. Moderate increases were shown by metal and metalwork dealers and by the furniture-home furnishings group.

Sales by wholesalers of nondurable goods totaled $76.2 billion in the first half of 1972—an advance of 9% from the similar period of 1971. Sales of groceries and allied products also rose 9%. Within the group, meats, poultry, and fresh friuts and vegetables sales rose 10% to 14%, while all groceries increased by 8%. Drugs, chemicals, and allied products increased 13%, while sales of apparel and dry goods and of beer, wine, and alcoholic beverages each advanced about 10%. Dry goods outpaced apparel, while beer sales rose more than those of other beverages. Sales of tobacco and tobacco products all rose 7%.

LAWRENCE BRIDGE
Bureau of Economic Analysis
U. S. Department of Commerce

ECUADOR

Political uncertainties that had plagued Ecuador for three years ended on Feb. 16, 1972, when the armed forces overthrew 5th-term President José María Velasco Ibarra in a bloodless coup. General elections were canceled, and a "nationalist revolutionary government" was established.

Political Developments. Velasco had seized dictatorial power from his own government in June 1970. From then on he ruled by decree. Increasingly, however, it became clear that his military backers held much of the real power. The President promised improvements in the country's moral and administrative climate and claimed that his freedom to rule without congressional or party interference would allow efficient government. Much optimism was expressed in Ecuador over the imminent completion of major petroleum production and export facilities by a Texaco-Gulf consortium.

Velasco seemed determined to interfere with preparations for the 1972 elections, despite pledges to the contrary. Assad Bucaram Elmhalim, the obvious popular favorite, received permission to return from exile only in January, and Velasco's bitter personal antagonism toward him continued. With 13 parties running candidates, meddling by the President seemed likely. Finally, as Bucaram was about to return to the capital, Velasco commanded military leaders to prevent his doing so. When they refused, and Velasco sought personally to invoke public support against them, they arrested him and forced him into exile.

Other events contributed to Velasco's downfall. The President had displeased many conservatives by his overt friendliness to Fidel Castro during the Cuban leader's visit to Ecuador in December 1971. Velasco's detainment and fining of 59 U. S.-owned ships for fishing in waters claimed by Ecuador was a generally popular nationalist act, but it caused the U. S. Congress to block further American aid and

------------ ECUADOR • Information Highlights ------------

Official Name: Republic of Ecuador.
Area: 109,483 square miles (283,561 sq km).
Population (1972 est.): 6,500,000. *Density,* 54 per square mile (21 per sq km). *Annual rate of increase,* 3.4%.
Chief Cities (1969 est.): Quito, the capital, 496,410; Guayaquil, 738,600.
Government: *Head of state,* Gen. Guillermo Rodríguez Lara, president (took office Feb. 1972). *Head of government,* Gen. Guillermo Rodríguez Lara. *Legislature*—Congress (suspended June 1970).
Language: Spanish (official).
Education: *Expenditure* (1969), 25% of total public expenditure. *School enrollment* (1968)—primary, 928,687; secondary, 173,614; technical/vocational, 50,998; university/higher, 22,637.
Monetary Unit: Sucre (25.25 sucres equal U. S.$1, Aug. 1972).
Gross National Product (1971 est.): $1,682,000,000.
National Income per Person (1970): $247.
Economic Indexes: *Industrial production* (manufacturing, 1968), 180 (1963 = 100); *agricultural production* (1971), 232 (1952–56 = 100); *consumer price index* (1971), 137 (1965 = 100).
Manufacturing (major products): Processed foods.
Major Agricultural Products: Bananas (ranks 3d among world producers, 1970), coffee, cacao, rice, sugar, fish.
Major Minerals: Petroleum, silver, gold.
Foreign Trade (1971): *Exports,* $238,000,000 (chief exports—bananas and plantains; coffee; cacao). *Imports,* $303,-000,000 (chief imports, 1969—machinery and transport equipment; chemicals; mineral fuels and lubricants; food). *Chief trading partners* (1969)—United States (took 41% of exports, supplied 32% of imports); West Germany (12% —13%); Japan (11%—9%).
Transportation: *Motor vehicles* (1970), 90,800 (automobiles, 39,600); *railroads* (1970), 661 miles (1,064 km); *major national airline,* Compañía Ecuatoriana de Aviación.
Communications: *Telephones* (1970), 94,300; *television stations* (1969), 11; *television sets* (1969), 110,000; *radios* (1970), 1,700,000; *newspapers* (1970), 25 (daily circulation, 250,000).

arms sales to Ecuador in December 1971. Budget deficits rose steadily during the President's last months in office, and the 1972 projected budget, with many items concealed or clouded, would have contained a deficit of 3 billion sucres ($125 million), or 40% of the total. Last, there was nervousness in Ecuador over the renegotiation of the oil industry's status, required by the Petroleum Law of 1971.

A three-man military junta, representing the Army, Navy, and Air Force, lasted a week after Velasco's overthrow. When the Navy was given several vital cabinet posts, the Army commander, Gen. Guillermo Rodríguez Lara, seized executive power. In May 1972, Navy influence was reduced further.

Initial statements by the new government sounded very leftist and nationalist, especially in regard to matters affecting "the oligarchy" of landowners, bankers, and industrialists. However, the details of internal policy suggested that, apart from nationalist treatment of oil, the goals of the regime would be largely social-democratic and concerned with national economic growth. On the whole, the military government was very well received.

Economic Affairs. Ecuador's national policy in recent years had been strongly import-substitution oriented. Three official institutions funneled funds generated by internal taxation, foreign borrowing, and internal credit operations into industry. A projected $192 million investment in the period 1972–1982 was expected to more than double electrical production. Gross domestic product rose 8.7% in 1970 and 7.0% in 1971, but the 1973–1978 economic plan of the military government called for an increase of 10% a year.

These policies had caused severe budget overspending and overseas borrowing. About 21% of the final 1972 budget was earmarked for servicing of the public debt. On Dec. 31, 1971, monetary reserves of the Central Bank were $17.4 million, only 42% of the trade deficit for the year. Thus, income from petroleum exports, which began on Aug. 15, 1972, was very welcome. Texaco estimated that oil exports would yield the government about $120 million a year from the end of 1972.

The new Petroleum Law established rules for control of all aspects of the industry by the Ecuadorian State Petroleum Corporation (CEPE). An implementing decree of June 30, 1972, required renegotiation of all aspects of producing concessions by the end of 1972, on terms much less favorable to the companies than before. Areas were limited to 160,000 hectares (395,000 acres), all concessions were to expire after 20 years of production, and no compensation was to be paid for surface investments by the companies. The government was expected soon to receive up to 80% of all the revenues.

Foreign Relations. Ecuador continued to press its claim to waters within 200 miles (320 km) of its shores, despite U. S. pressure. The "tuna war" calmed somewhat in early 1972 when 35 U. S.-owned boats bought Ecuadorian fishing licenses for the first time, but it also was shown that over 50% of the domestic fishing industry was U. S.-owned.

Ecuador declared its support for Cuba's readmission to the Organization of American States, though, in light of Cuba's lack of interest, it did not push the matter. Active trading relations with the USSR began, but the military government also expelled several Soviet diplomats for alleged interference in labor disputes.

PHILIP B. TAYLOR, JR., *University of Houston*

education

School busing to achieve racial integration aroused widespread opposition. (Above) A school bus is buried in Memphis. (Below) Antibusing mothers from Michigan marched to Washington, D. C.

The busing of children to schools out of their neighborhoods as a means of improving the racial balance in individual schools overshadowed all other education issues in the United States in 1972. Members of Congress were able to agree only on a measure delaying court-imposed busing orders until the end of 1973. This measure was added to the highly significant Education Amendments of 1972—an act concerned mainly with higher education but authorizing federal programs at all levels.

School and college enrollments in the fall of 1972 increased less than 1%—the smallest increase in 28 years—but educational expenditures for the 1972–73 school year were expected to rise by more than 6%. Questions of finance continued to plague both public and nonpublic institutions and to raise questions of constitutionality.

THE BUSING CONTROVERSY

In March, President Richard Nixon formally asked Congress, in an 8,000-word special message, to call a temporary halt to all further court-ordered busing until July 1, 1973, or until broader legislation to control busing could be enacted. He proposed that Congress use the authority given it under the 14th Amendment to "clear up the confusion which contradictory court orders have created and to establish reasonable national standards." The 14th Amendment guarantees all citizens "the equal protection of the laws" and empowers Congress to carry out this and other provisions by "appropriate legislation."

Legislation. Throughout the summer the battle over busing was waged in Congress. President Nixon's proposal prohibiting all new busing became mired in committee hearings and discussions. Meanwhile, Senate and House conferees sought to iron out differences over various busing amendments that had been added to the "higher education bill" (officially, the Education Amendments of 1972), then under consideration. Finally, it was agreed to prohibit the implementation of federal court orders

249

for busing to achieve racial balance until all appeals have been exhausted or until the time for such appeals has expired. That provision is effective only until Dec. 31, 1973. In June, President Nixon signed the bill reluctantly, for he felt that it did not go far enough in its restriction of busing.

In August, the House of Representatives passed a strong antibusing bill by a vote of 282 to 102. It would have prohibited busing except as a last resort for desegregation. Even then, no child could have been bused farther than the second-closest school to his home that provided the proper grade level. The bill also would have permitted the reopening of desegregation suits already settled by the courts to ensure that they conform with the provisions of the legislation.

Supporters of the bill insisted that there was nationwide opposition to the use of busing to achieve school integration. Opponents argued that the bill would roll back progress made toward desegregation over the last two decades.

During the week of October 9, Senate sponsors of the House-approved bill made three attempts to end debate and force a vote on the antibusing measure. The bill had the support of a majority of senators and the Nixon administration, but opponents were able to muster enough votes to forestall the required two-thirds majority necessary to invoke cloture. The final vote—49 to 38 in favor of cloture—was 9 votes short of the required two thirds. The Senate then voted to set the measure aside for the remainder of the year.

Court Decisions. Throughout the South many school districts were simply continuing court-ordered large-scale busing. The Charlotte and Mecklenburg county schools in North Carolina bused 43,600 pupils to school daily during the 1971–72 session without incident. Other Southern cities under court-ordered plans to achieve racial balance through massive busing have adjusted to the arrangement, often reluctantly.

In Richmond, Va., the Fourth U. S. Circuit Court of Appeals on June 6 overruled a U. S. district court order that would have required the merger of the Richmond city school system (70% black) with the two suburban counties of Henrico and Chesterfield (each more than 90% white) and would have resulted in massive busing between inner city and suburban schools. The case has been appealed to the U. S. Supreme Court.

In Detroit, the Sixth Circuit Court of Appeals was asked to review a U. S. district court order, issued on June 14, that would join Detroit with 52 suburban school districts in a desegregation plan involving 780,000 public school pupils. Massive movement of pupils between the city and the suburbs would be necessary to attain in each school the 75% white and 25% black enrollment that the plan stipulates should be sought.

Both the Richmond and the Detroit cases have enormous national implications. If the district court rulings should be sustained by the U. S. Supreme Court, the entire framework of school divisions based on political units of government would be challenged. The issue is charged with emotion. Advocates of busing insist that it is the only way to achieve quality education for all. Opponents question the benefits of massive busing to achieve racial balance in individual schools. Educators differ in their opinion of its effects on the pupil.

THE EDUCATION AMENDMENTS OF 1972

After months of bickering, bargaining, and compromising, Congress finally passed Public Law 92-318, officially entitled the Education Amendments of 1972 but referred to generally as the "higher education bill." It was signed into law by President Nixon on June 23, 1972.

Significance. Differences between the House and Senate versions of the bill took nine weeks to negotiate, culminating in an all-night conference session that produced a $21.6 billion compromise measure extending over a 3-year period ending June 30, 1975. As has been noted, the busing controversy, which loomed large in both houses during the months of consideration, was finally resolved by the adoption of an amendment to this bill delaying court-imposed busing orders.

The Education Amendments of 1972 is an amazing document, running to 146 closely printed pages. Even more striking are the scope and character of the programs it authorizes. Sidney P. Marland, Jr., the U. S. commissioner of education, described the act as "the most significant educational legislation of our times."

Major Provisions. More than two thirds of the legislation concerns higher education, although programs at all levels are authorized. A few of the highlights can be summarized briefly.

The act expands student assistance programs by adding Basic Educational Opportunity Grants, under which every college student in good standing would be eligible for federal financial aid up to $1,400 a year. The actual amount would be determined on the basis of family income and the cost of attending the particular institution. The cost of this program, if fully funded by Congress, is estimated at $892 million.

The act also sets up a new government-sponsored private corporation called the Student Loan Marketing Association. The association would buy existing student loans from banks and other lending institutions, thus providing lenders with capital for new loans under the present Guaranteed Student Loans program.

A $1 billion a year program of general aid to institutions of post-secondary education is authorized. Grants may be used for any purpose, including instruction. These "cost of education" payments are geared chiefly to the number of students receiving federally supported financial assistance.

The act creates a National Institute of Education (NIE), consisting of a director and a 15-member National Council on Educational Research. The purposes of NIE, which will replace the present research unit in the U. S. Office of Education, are to conduct educational research, collect and disseminate information, and train researchers.

The new law establishes interlocking programs of support for community colleges and the promotion of occupational education at all levels. The states are encouraged through federal grants to upgrade the status of occupational education, with special emphasis on the expansion of vocational and technical course offerings in 2-year colleges.

There is a $2 billion authorization of federal assistance to local school districts for three purposes: (1) to meet special needs incident to desegregation, either voluntary or court-ordered; (2) to encourage voluntary elimination, reduction, or prevention of racial isolation; and (3) to aid school

children in overcoming the educational disadvantages of minority group isolation. The authorizations are $1 billion for each of the fiscal years 1973 and 1974.

These are only a few of the far-reaching provisions of the new law. Its final impact on education at all levels will be determined by the actual appropriations made by Congress to fund the various programs that are authorized.

BACK-TO-SCHOOL FIGURES

Fall enrollments in U. S. schools and colleges in 1972 rose only 0.5% over enrollments in 1971, according to data supplied in September by the U. S. Office of Education's National Center for Educational Research. This was the smallest increase in 28 years. But total educational expenditures for the 1972–73 school year were expected to reach a record $90.5 billion—a 6.3% increase over 1971–72.

Enrollments. Although the total enrollment in 1972–73 will rise to 60.4 million persons, most of the increase is occurring at the higher education level. The number of degree-credit students in colleges and universities is expected to reach 9 million —a gain of 6% over the 1971 fall enrollment of 8.5 million. The largest increase continues to take place in public community colleges.

The total enrollment in elementary and secondary schools is expected to decline by approximately 200,000 in 1972–73. A gain of 300,000 at the secondary level is more than offset by a decline of 500,000 in elementary school enrollment. The decline in birthrate is beginning to be felt more keenly as the number of children in the elementary grades continues to drop.

Public schools expected a fall 1972 enrollment of about 46.2 million, with 32.1 million in the elementary schools and 14.1 million in high schools. The enrollment in nonpublic schools is estimated at 5.2 million.

The high school graduating class of 1973 is expected to exceed 3.1 million—the largest such class in history. Predictions are that for persons today in the 16–17 age group, more than three fourths, or 78%, will graduate from high school; 48% will enter a college or university; 25% will earn a bachelor's degree; 8%, a master's degree; and 1.5%, a doctorate.

Costs. Expenditures and interest for education on all levels, public and private, in 1972–73 are expected to increase nearly $5 billion over 1971–72, totaling $79.2 billion for the current session. Capital outlay will add $11.3 billion, bringing the total cost of education to $90.5 billion.

Federal grants for education are continuing to increase. They have risen from $3.4 billion in 1965 to $11.6 billion in 1972 and are expected to total $12.8 billion for the fiscal year ending June 30, 1973.

The Plight of the Catholic Schools. Figures from the U. S. Office of Education covering the 10 school years 1961–70 show that Catholic elementary and secondary schools, which accounted for 91.5% of the total nonpublic school enrollment in 1961, accounted for only 80.6% in 1970. Within the Catholic schools, enrollments declined 17% during this period, while the number of pupils attending other nonpublic schools increased 66%.

A report by the National Catholic Education Association, issued in August 1972, indicated that
(Continued on page 254)

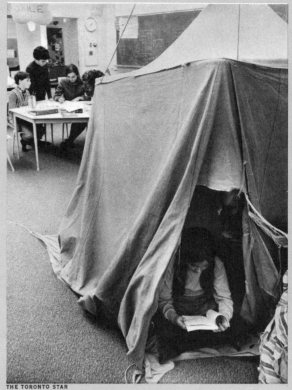

THE TORONTO STAR

A child seeking privacy studies in a tent in one of Ontario's "open area" schools. Many Canadians have questioned the effectiveness of these schools.

LEARNING HOW TO LEARN
The Open Classroom

The open classroom is a term used to describe an educational program, usually at the elementary level, in which room interiors have been changed to give pupils freedom to choose and direct their own activities. It is an aspect of what is known as "open education," a philosophy of learning that emphasizes a new, more flexible approach to teaching as an alternative to the traditional public school program.

The philosophy underlying the open classroom is one that recognizes both the shared and the unique capabilities of children. Innately curious, children are eager to know more about the world in which they live. They possess a potential for creativity and natural learning that can be nurtured and developed. An atmosphere of mutual trust and respect produces the best possible learning situation, and a rich classroom environment stimulates and facilitates learning. Children learn and develop not only at their own rate but in their own style and thus should be active participants in the learning process.

Development of the Open Classroom in Britain. The restructuring of the traditional classroom began in the British infant schools (for children 5–7) prior to World War II. It was sparked by a group of educators who sought to reform both the learning environment and the classroom teaching practices that prevailed in this setting.

ONE-ROOM elementary school in Greece, N.Y., allows a class to watch a film while other groups do their regular activities. The film equipment is mobile.

When British education was disrupted during World War II, teaching in informal situations often became necessary. The release from stereotyped classroom procedures proved to be an effective learning stimulus. Children took a new interest in schooling that considered them as individuals, recognized their varying abilities to learn, and provided an atmosphere of freedom rather than of repression. Children's interests received new recognition, and the response was enthusiastic. The freedom to learn produced results that surprised many parents who were dubious about the soundness of the new permissiveness.

The idea took hold and spread with increasing rapidity. As the zest for learning was given increasingly free play, it became evident that happy children learn more and that they learn more easily. Within 30 years, some 70% of the British public infant schools and nearly half of the junior schools (for children up to age 12) were reorganized to permit greater freedom in the classroom and to make possible individual patterns of learning. Thus informal schooling had begun to dominate British early education. In 1967, it received high official sanction when a parliamentary commission strongly urged adoption of the innovative techniques.

Emergence in the United States. In the 1960's a growing disillusionment with the methods and results of U.S. education found expression in a number of highly critical books and magazine articles. The Carnegie Corporation commissioned a 3-year study of the problems of U.S. education by Charles E. Silberman, whose report, *Crisis in the Classroom,* appeared in 1970. Silberman described the typical U.S. school as a "grim, joyless place," where children's spirits are repressed, their sense-of-self sacrificed, spontaneity mutilated, and the joy of learning and creating lost. Both slum and suburban schools housed "joyless classrooms" where teaching was unimaginative, and "education for docility" flourished.

In contrast, Silberman described with enthusiasm his visits to the new informal British primary schools. He was convinced that schools "can be genuinely concerned with gaiety and joy and individual growth and fulfillment without sacrificing concern for intellectual discipline and development."

In the United States, Silberman's book drew national attention to the British concept, which had been advocated by a few pioneer U.S. colleges of education since the mid-1960's. Schools employing the philosophy and technique of the open classroom developed in widely scattered areas—the Watts section of Los Angeles; the urban cores of New York and Atlanta; upper-middle-class towns such as Andover, Mass., and Culver City, Calif.; and in the rural villages of North Dakota, where it has been officially adopted for the public school system of the state.

Characteristics of Open Classrooms. Open classrooms in the British infant schools, as well as their U.S. counterparts, have certain characteristics in common. They bear little resemblance to the traditional classroom of either country, and can be best described perhaps, as workshops for carrying on learning activities.

Each classroom is decentralized, with separate areas for various subjects. There is a reading corner that contains a collection of books of varying difficulty. The science area provides a variety of living things—plants, rabbits, fish, turtles—that the children care for and whose growth they watch. A museum furnishes opportunity to exhibit rocks, minerals, shells, mounted insects, and various other items of interest in the environment—collected and labeled by the pupils. The mathematics area is stocked with numerous devices employing numbers and computation, ranging from measuring sticks to mathematical puzzles.

The art area contains easels, drawing boards, modeling clay, finger paint, poster paper, and other materials for creative expression. Walls are decorated with freehand drawings, paintings, and friezes created by pupils. Bulletin board space is utilized for posting poems, essays, and other examples of creative work in language.

The classroom atmosphere is decidedly informal. At first it seems completely disorganized. Children are free to move as they wish throughout the classroom, to work independently or to join with others in a cooperative endeavor, and, perhaps most striking, to choose their own activities.

The apparent disorder is actually a working atmosphere in which pupils are occupied with tasks that engage their interest. The movement and conversation around them are not distracting because of the degree of concentration they give to a purposeful activity.

Role of the Teacher. Such a learning situation places special demands upon the teacher. In the absence of the traditional course of study, with development of certain skills, understandings, and abilities specified for each grade, the teacher is free to plan and organize a program tailored to the needs and interests of his pupils. Pupil participation in planning is characteristic of the open classroom both on a daily and long-term basis. The role of the teacher is to provide a stimulating and appropriate learning environment and to see that a wide variety of learning materials is available.

The teacher works mostly with individuals or small groups, while the rest of the children proceed at their own pace. The role of the teacher in the open classroom has been described as that of "a facilitator or guide to learning." In creating the learning environment, he must be familiar with the interests of children and be able to utilize their interests to bring about desirable learning progress. His job is essentially to help pupils "learn how to learn," which is the central theme of "open education."

Under the guidance of a capable teacher, pupils become increasingly self-directive, both in what and how they learn. While the atmosphere is permissive, responsible behavior is expected. Ground rules are agreed upon by pupils and teacher. Antisocial behavior that interferes with other children's work is not tolerated by the teacher or, more importantly, by the rest of the group.

Mutual respect is the keynote. The teacher respects the child's personality and assumes that he wants to learn. The emphasis is on freedom and responsibility rather than conformity and following directions. "Joyful classrooms" in which real learning takes place are the goal.

Criticisms. There have been some misgivings about the open classroom. It has been called an expensive fad introduced hastily to teachers, pupils, and parents without sufficient preparation or understanding.

The effectiveness of the learning-through-joy idea has been questioned, especially in terms of achievement in fundamental subjects. Comparative testing under the conventional and the informal systems is difficult, for such testing is geared to the traditional curriculum and fails to take into account the important intangible results in pupil attitudes toward learning.

The teacher is the key person in the success of the program. At present, the number of teachers with the preparation and personality to be effective is limited. An understanding of the philosophy underlying the plan and of the techniques to be used is essential. However, institutions such as the University of Pittsburgh are now offering specific courses in the open classroom. There are also in-service training programs.

It is difficult to judge the effects of the plan upon pupil adjustment and progress in subsequent secondary and higher education, for the concept is still relatively new. However, interest in the open classroom continues to mount. The National Education Association and the National Federation of Teachers have endorsed it. The newer school buildings are designed to accommodate the features of the open classroom.

The pupils themselves are the best evidence of the success of the open classroom plan. Their enthusiasm for school and their interest in learning have amazed doubting parents. The open classroom seems to be here to stay.

EDWARD ALVEY, JR.

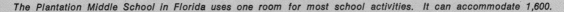

The Plantation Middle School in Florida uses one room for most school activities. It can accommodate 1,600.

UPI

(Continued from page 251)
enrollments dropped from 5,573,810 in 1965–66 to 4,027,183 in 1971–72—a decline of 28%. The number of Catholic elementary and secondary schools declined from 13,292 to 10,829 during the same period. The 1971–72 school year opened with 513 fewer schools in operation than in 1970–71.

Numerous factors contribute to the declining enrollments. Fewer nuns are entering teaching orders, necessitating the employment of many more lay teachers at salaries competitive with those paid by the public schools. Parents are hard pressed to pay the increased tuition that results, and pupils are withdrawn to attend public schools.

Courts have repeatedly ruled state aid to parochial schools to be unconstitutional. In October the U. S. Supreme Court struck down a 1971 Ohio law allowing direct tuition grants to parents of children attending parochial and other private schools. The 8–1 decision indicates the improbability of obtaining court approval of financial aid of this kind. Meanwhile, Congress considered legislation to allow limited federal income tax credit for parents and others paying tuition to private elementary and secondary schools.

Teachers. The number of elementary and secondary teachers employed in 1972–73 is estimated at 2,320,000—about 20,000 more than in 1971–72. Of these, about 2,100,000 are in public schools, and 220,000 in nonpublic schools.

The leveling off of school enrollments had its effects on job openings for teachers. Graduates of 1972 with preparation for teaching in the elementary grades and most academic subjects in high school found jobs to be scarce. Yet the National Education Association's Research Division challenges the existence of a teacher surplus if a "quality criterion" is applied—if overcrowded classes are reduced, special instructional services provided, and teachers with substandard preparation replaced.

The National Education Association released highlights from its latest periodic survey (1970–71) of the status of the U. S. public school teacher. The report affords some interesting comparisons with a similar survey in 1960–61.

The typical teacher in 1971 was younger (35 years of age, compared with 41 a decade earlier), had slightly less teaching experience (8 years, compared with 11 years), was better educated (only 3% lacked at least a bachelor's degree, compared with 15% in 1961), and earned a substantially higher salary ($9,300, compared with less than $5,300). The proportion of male teachers had grown from 31% in 1961 to 34% in 1971.

HIGHER EDUCATION

As colleges opened in the fall of 1972, officials in many institutions were concerned over an unprecedented shortage of students. Throughout the nation, costs were a major concern. Community colleges continued to increase their enrollments, and the trend toward coeducation accelerated.

Vacancies. A survey by the National Association of College Admissions Counselors in July indicated that about 1,500 colleges still had room for 175,000 students in their freshman classes and 125,000 transfer students in upper classes. Admissions officers cited a number of factors contributing to the decline in enrollments. Among these were the rising costs of a college education, which fall most heavily on middle-income families; changes in the draft law, which no longer make it necessary for young men to attend college to avoid military service; and a smaller pool of 18-year-olds, from which the entering classes would usually be drawn. Also cited were growing doubts about the value of a liberal arts college degree, compared with shorter, less expensive specialized training, and the new practice among young people of postponing college entrance for a year in order to travel or obtain work experience. Also, many upperclassmen are leaving college temporarily to break what they have called the "attendance lockstep."

Most hard hit by declining enrollments are the smaller independent or church-related institutions. The prestigious colleges and universities and the great state universities have more applications than they can handle. Many 4-year colleges, both public and private, have lost students to the 2-year community colleges, which offer an inexpensive education within commuting distance.

Student Costs. College charges for tuition, fees, and room and board increased again in 1972–73, although the rise was not so sharp as it had been during the previous three or four years. Among the Ivy League institutions the average reported increase was $292. This seemed to be about the typical increase nationally. Some colleges, however, have kept charges at the present level for the first time in several years. The disparity between the cost of attending public and private institutions remains great, even with the scholarship aid that many of the more affluent private universities have available.

Carnegie Commission Recommendations. To meet the financial crisis in higher education, the Carnegie Commission on Higher Education—headed by Clark Kerr, the former president of the University of California—proposed several steps that might be taken. A commission report issued early in the year called for increased federal and state aid. A second report, issued in June, urged colleges to make more effective use of existing resources. It suggested that costs could be cut by "cautiously" increasing faculty-student ratios, having faculty members teach more course hours, curtailing the introduction of new doctoral programs and new courses, and adopting better management techniques.

The commission commended the trend toward offering 3-year bachelor's degree programs by allowing course credit through examination, offering year-round programs of study, and making other provisions for acceleration. It urged colleges to weed out "reluctant attenders," directing them toward jobs or vocational programs, and recommended the expansion of off-campus study opportunities through educational television, correspondence courses, and the like. It also suggested more cooperative ventures among institutions. If steps such as these were taken, the commission believes that by 1980 the institutions might be able to cut their yearly costs by 20%.

Career Education. Education for careers has become an important concern of the 2-year public colleges, which now enroll a large proportion of the nation's youth. Pasadena (Calif.) City College now offers 64 career-oriented courses, in which about half of its 14,000 students are enrolled. New York City Community College offers its 15,000 students a choice of 34 different career education and college transfer courses, with about 80% of the student

body enrolled. Central Piedmont Community College, in Charlotte, N. C., offers an around-the-clock instructional program in 34 occupations for its 8,000 students.

Counseling and placement services are a vital part of the career education program. Students may enter a program at any time, accomplish their objectives at their own rates, and terminate attendance when they can meet the requirements of the jobs in which they are interested. Cooperative arrangements with local firms provide on-the-job experience before programs are completed.

Trend Toward Coeducation. Approximately three fourths of all U. S. colleges and universities are now coeducational. The trend that began a decade ago has gained momentum until in 1972 only about 2% of all college students were attending single-sex institutions. Both men's and women's colleges have been affected, especially the latter. In a single 2-year period, 1968–1970, the number of colleges admitting women only dropped from 248 to 150. The majority of the surviving women's colleges are small and church-related, mainly Roman Catholic. Fewer than 10% of all female students are enrolled in colleges exclusively for women.

OTHER DEVELOPMENTS

Public school systems continued to confront rising costs of salaries and new construction. Efforts to aid non-English-speaking children benefited from federally sponsored projects.

School Financing. In October the U. S. Supreme Court began hearings on the constitutionality of the local property tax as the chief means of financing public schools. It is maintained that inequalities in educational opportunity result from the property tax revenues available in poor school districts as compared with wealthy districts. Nationwide, localities support somewhat more than half of school costs. If the local property tax system is ruled unconstitutional, a restructuring of support will be necessary in many instances.

Bond issues for new school construction continued to face difficulties. According to the U. S. Office of Education, the percentage of such issues approved by voters during fiscal 1971 reached a record low of 46.7%—only 507 out of 1,086. In Fairfax county, Va., voters rejected a $54.9 million school bond issue in 1972, marking the first time since 1950 that such funds have been defeated in this rapidly growing area adjacent to Washington, D. C.

Teachers' Strikes and Contracts. Salaries continued to be the chief issue in strikes that delayed the opening of schools in numerous communities, but other factors entered into negotiations. In Philadelphia, Pa., both wages and working hours were involved. The 13,000 teachers there sought a 34% across-the-board wage increase. The school board, already $52 million in debt, offered a 5% salary increase and demanded a 40-minute increase in the length of the workday in high schools and the elimination of 485 teaching positions. Striking teachers agreed to return to classrooms on September 27, pending negotiation of a new contract.

In Washington, D. C., schools were disrupted for two weeks as striking teachers demanded a 17% pay increase. The strike ended on October 3, when the school board offered an immediate 7% pay increase, with an additional 5% next year, and agreed to hire 182 new teachers (to reduce class size) and to provide $350,000 for needed school supplies.

THE NEW YORK TIMES/ NANCY MORAN

NEW PRESIDENT of Bennington College is 29-year-old Gail Parker. Her husband, Thomas, is vice president.

In New York City, a strike was avoided and schools opened smoothly after a new 3-year contract was negotiated. It made experienced teachers among the best paid in the nation. In the third year of the contract, teachers with advanced degrees and 7½ years of experience would earn $20,350.

Bilingual Programs. In an effort to aid an estimated 5 million youngsters with limited or no command of English, the federal government is spending about $35 million a year to develop bilingual programs in public schools. The U. S. Office of Education is sponsoring 213 bilingual projects in about 30 states. Involved are some 100,000 children speaking 19 languages other than English.

The majority are Spanish-speaking—children of the heavy concentration of native speakers of that language in Florida, California, and Texas, as well as urban centers elsewhere. The Spanish Curriculum Center in Miami, Fla., is developing a complete bilingual program for grades one through three. The child is taught first in Spanish and then gradually introduced to English in his reading, arithmetic, and science classes. Bilingual programs for Mexican-Americans are being emphasized in California and Texas. New York City has a number of programs in operation, but as yet they are reaching only a small proportion of the estimated 135,000 children, mainly Puerto Rican, with limited facility in English. Teachers are sought who are bicultural as well as bilingual, so that the pupils' pride in their native heritage can be maintained.

EDWARD ALVEY, JR., *Mary Washington College*

EGYPT'S war minister, General Sadek (left), and Soviet party leader Brezhnev (center) in Moscow in June. Sadek was later dismissed from his post.

EGYPT

The major event in Egypt during 1972 was President Anwar el-Sadat's expulsion of nearly 20,000 Russian military advisers in July. Peace with Israel, however, did not come about. In fact, the President continued to insist that another war with Israel was necessary and inevitable.

In the summer it was announced that Libya and Egypt would merge. The Egyptian economy remained relatively static throughout the year.

Domestic Affairs. In July, Egyptians celebrated the 20th anniversary of the military revolt that swept away the regime of King Farouk. President Sadat seemed firmly in control, although unconfirmed reports later in the year suggested a restlessness in the armed forces.

In January 1972 police clashed with Cairo University students, who were demanding that the government pursue a more militant policy toward Israel. Perhaps 1,000 students were arrested. Sadat stated that "outside forces"—later called Israeli agents—had galvanized the students in their protests. The National Congress of the Arab Socialist Union—Egypt's only political party—met in February to give Sadat its warm support on the issues involved.

Aziz Sidky was named prime minister in January before the student demonstration began, and it was conceded that the new cabinet was a more militant one. Late in the year Gen. Mohammed Sadek was dropped as war minister and army commander, probably as a gesture to the Russians.

In October the Egyptian government abolished the procedure through which considerable private property had been seized by administrative rather than court action. This was a continuation of Sadat's efforts to deemphasize many of the controls imposed by his predecessor, Gamal Abdel Nasser.

Relations with the USSR. President Sadat flew to the Soviet Union in early February and received what was termed "a quiet welcome." He sought more and better arms to fight the "inevitable war" with Israel. The trip was unproductive. In late April, Sadat was back in the Soviet capital, once

again asking for arms. Continued military assistance was promised him on this occasion.

In March, a conference of Russians, Egyptians, and other Arabs was held in Cairo to discuss mutual differences. It was disclosed then that Soviet military assistance to Egypt had amounted to $5 billion.

On July 18, in a surprise move, Sadat ordered Soviet "military advisers and experts" to leave Egypt immediately and to surrender their equipment and facilities to Egyptian forces. Sadat stated that he had expected certain arms deliveries from the Soviet Union to enable Egypt to fight the "decisive" battle with Israel in 1971 but that these deliveries had not been made. It was apparent, he said, that Russia had no intention of supporting Egypt in the all-out war with Israel that he deemed necessary. The Soviet Union immediately began to remove its personnel, but ultimately a few hundred remained. Both sides attempted to minimize the importance of the action and to maintain ties.

After the ouster of the Russians it was revealed that Sadat had been under considerable domestic pressure to reduce the Soviet influence in Egypt. His action proved very popular at the time.

In August the Soviet Union warned the Egyptians of Israel's nuclear weapons capabilities and cautioned Arabs not to depend on the friendship of the United States. Although the Soviet exit from Egypt had changed the strategic balance in the Middle East and made war by Egypt against Israel much less likely, Israel did not, publicly at least, respond with any gesture calculated to ease tensions. Nor did the United States, in a presidential election year, put much pressure on the Israelis.

By October the Egyptians began to have second thoughts about their relations with the Soviet Union. A rapprochement was urged and facilitated by President Hafez al-Assad of Syria. On October 16, Egyptian Prime Minister Sidky flew to Moscow to explore the possibility of establishing some sort of new relationship with the USSR. Although at the time no reference was made to continued Soviet assistance, by early November reports of shipments of advanced Soviet missiles were in the press.

On October 15, President Sadat had insisted that the stresses and strains of Egypt's tie with Russia would be overcome. One apparent gesture was made on October 26. This was the removal of General Sadek, who reportedly had been a key factor in the expulsion of the Russians in July. At year's end relations between Egypt and the Soviet Union were warming once more.

The Struggle with Israel. All Egyptian political developments in 1972 were colored by the unsettled issues with Israel. Very little progress was made in settling these issues. Israel continued to control the Sinai and Gaza. The Suez Canal remained closed. What little possibility of negotiations existed seemed to have been diminished by the slayings of Israeli athletes by Arab terrorists during the summer Olympic Games in Munich.

A U.S. agreement in 1972 to give more military assistance to Israel drew an angry reaction in Egypt. One result was that various U.S. plans for achieving peace—among which was Secretary of State William P. Rogers' suggestion of an interim agreement on reopening the Suez Canal—were no longer taken seriously in Cairo. Diplomatic relations between the United States and Egypt remained broken, although many commercial activities continued normal.

In June and July brief flare-ups of air warfare occurred over the Mediterranean and Sinai. Generally, however, the year was quiet. Egypt greeted Israeli military actions against Lebanon and Syria with invective but did nothing to intervene. The year ended with the situation much the same as it had been the year before, except for the departure of the Russians.

Relations with the Arab World. In 1971, Egypt, Lybia, and Syria had formed a loose federation. In August 1972, Egypt and Libya agreed to a merger of their two countries, with "unified political leadership" and Cairo as the capital. The merger was to take practical effect before September 1973, but there was doubt that it would be completely consummated.

In March, King Hussein of Jordan proposed a federation of Jordanians and Palestinians. The proposal was denounced by Cairo, and Egypt broke diplomatic relations with Jordan in April.

——— **EGYPT · Information Highlights** ———

Official Name: Arab Republic of Egypt.
Area: 386,660 square miles (1,001,449 sq km).
Population (1972 est.): 35,900,000. *Density,* 85 per square mile (33 per sq km). *Annual rate of increase,* 2.8%.
Chief Cities (1966 census): Cairo, the capital, 4,219,853; Alexandria, 1,801,056; Port Said, 282,977.
Government: *Head of state,* Anwar el-Sadat, president (took office Oct. 1970). *Chief minister,* Aziz Sidky, premier (took office Jan. 1972). *Legislature* (unicameral)—National Assembly, 360 members. *Major political party*—Arab Socialist Union.
Languages: Arabic (official), English, French.
Education: *Expenditure* (1969), 21% of total public expenditure. *School enrollment* (1969)—primary, 3,618,750; secondary, 1,357,972; technical/vocational, 245,862; university/higher, 197,055.
Monetary Unit: Pound (0.4348 pound equals U.S.$1, Sept. 1972).
Gross National Product (1970 est.): $6,580,000,000.
National Income per Person (1969): $203.
Economic Indexes: *Industrial production* (1969), 136 (1963= 100); *agricultural production* (1971), 176 (1952–56=100); *consumer price index* (1970), 112 (1967=100).
Manufacturing (major products): Textiles, fertilizers, iron and steel, petroleum products.
Major Agricultural Products: Cotton, rice, wheat, corn, dates (ranks 1st among world producers, 1971).
Major Minerals: Petroleum, phosphate rock, iron ore.
Foreign Trade (1971): *Exports,* $789,000,000 (chief exports —cotton, rice). *Imports,* $890,000,000 (chief imports, 1969—food, chemicals, nonelectrical machinery, transport equipment). *Chief trading partners* (1969)—USSR (took 33% of exports, supplied 14% of imports); India (5%—6%); West Germany (4%—7%); France (2%—10%).
Tourism: *Receipts* (1969), $65,600,000.
Transportation: *Motor vehicles* (1970), 160,800 (automobiles, 130,700); *railroads* (1970), 3,036 miles (4,885 km); *merchant fleet* (1971), 241,000 gross registered tons; *major national airline,* Egyptair.
Communications: *Telephones* (1968), 365,000; *television stations* (1971), 23; *television sets* (1971), 500,000; *radios* (1970), 4,400,000; *newspapers* (1968), 15 (daily circulation, 722,000).

Cairo continued its cautious association with the various Palestinian guerrilla groups, including the Black September organization, which was responsible for the Olympics massacre. On the other hand, President Sadat's proposal in September that the guerrilla groups set up a government in exile met with very little enthusiasm from the Palestinian leaders.

In May a conflict arose with the Sudanese government over its new ideological directions (see also SUDAN). As a result Egypt asked in October that Sudan withdraw its contingent of troops from the Suez Canal Zone. Matters improved by the end of the year, however.

CARL LEIDEN
University of Texas at Austin

PRESIDENT Sadat (right) confers with other Egyptian government officials on July 18 before announcing the withdrawal of Soviet advisers from Egypt.

UPI

UPI

UPI

(Above) *President Nixon, campaigning for reelection, greets supporters during motorcade through northeastern Ohio in October.* (Left) *The Nixons greet the Agnews at Republican election-night headquarters following their victory over McGovern and Shriver.*

elections

Richard M. Nixon swept to victory in the U. S. presidential election of Nov. 7, 1972, winning a second term in one of the greatest landslides in American history. The president carried 49 states and received 520 electoral votes, losing only the 17 votes of Massachusetts and the District of Columbia to the Democratic nominee, Sen. George McGovern of South Dakota. The President received 47,168,963, or 60.7% of the votes cast. McGovern got 29,169,342, or 38.0%. John G. Schmitz, candidate of the American party, received 1,080,541, or 1.0%.

Presidential voting represented not party strength or allegiance but, more accurately, voter approval or disapproval of the two major candidates. Although the total popular vote for President was the

largest in the nation's history, only 55% of the eligible voters participated in the election. The proportion of voters going to the polls was the lowest since 1948. A decline of voter interest noticeable in the past three elections was steeper in 1972, in part because the voting rolls were opened to 18-year-olds for the first time. Moreover, in many polling places, the vote for President was below that for other offices.

Democratic candidates for state and congressional offices fared better in general than their nominee for President. Only in a few states did the President's coattails clearly make the difference in local elections.

THE PRESIDENTIAL RACE

From the outset the Democratic party, despite its marked advantage in registered voters, faced a difficult struggle for the presidency. Opinion polls regularly reported President Nixon well in the lead. A long series of presidential primaries drained resources from Democratic candidates, as did controversies over party organization and over procedures in the nominating convention, creating a residue of dissension hard to overcome in the campaign. Senator McGovern was not the first choice of many Democratic voters and workers. The South, historically an important bastion of Democratic strength but increasingly hostile to federal programs supported by liberals, was particularly cool.

(See POLITICAL PARTIES for a discussion of the party primaries and national conventions.)

The Campaign. After his nomination at the Democratic convention in July, McGovern encountered a number of setbacks in his attempts to unify the party and win voter support. A month set aside for organizing the campaign was lost while McGovern replaced the vice presidential nominee, Sen. Thomas F. Eagleton, with R. Sargent Shriver. A man of great personal compassion, McGovern at first supported Eagleton after the latter revealed his history of electric shock treatments for depression. McGovern then wavered as the issue began to dominate the campaign, and seemed indecisive to many voters.

The AFL-CIO council voted, 27–3, not to endorse any candidate for President, supporting its president, George Meany, and withholding—notwithstanding some union defections—its customary Democratic support. Staff dissension dogged the early days of the campaign. Lawrence F. O'Brien, former Democratic chairman and one of several campaign managers, said on August 31 that "everything needs tightening up" or the campaign "is going to drift."

On August 29, McGovern proposed a new welfare plan, to replace a much-criticized one in which he had suggested a grant of $1,000 a year for every American. He had conceded that the precise terms of his original proposal "may have been a mistake." The new plan would shift welfare for the aged to social security, create public service jobs for employables, and ensure a minimum income. It would be financed by taxing capital gains as ordinary income and reducing the military budget by $10 billion. Elliot L. Richardson, secretary of Health, Education, and Welfare, called the proposal "costly and scatterbrained."

McGovern pledged a "total end to our involvement in the Indochina War" and gave assurances that captured American prisoners would quickly be returned. In foreign policy he promised a "new internationalism" based on free and open cooperation with all nations and help to developing ones.

McGovern crisscrossed the country tirelessly for rallies and engaged extensively in local telethons to answer questions. A steady flow of money by mail left the campaign almost free of debt. Shortly before the election, McGovern attacked the Nixon administration as the "most corrupt in history." He charged it with espionage in such episodes as the surveillance of the Democratic headquarters in the Watergate office building in Washington, D. C., by persons connected with the Republican campaign, and he accused it of granting favors in return for financial contributions. The President commented that he would not respond "in kind." The greatest deception, McGovern contended, was a report in late October that peace in Vietnam was "at hand." The President, he said, had "no respect" for "personal freedom" and would not "hesitate to wiretap . . . even your home."

By comparison, President Nixon's campaign was olympian. Busy with the duties of office, he was content with a few well-organized trips, sometimes heckled by dissidents, and with a final spate of televised appearances. He ruled out debate with his opponent on grounds of the national interest, saying that a President "makes policy every time that he opens his mouth." He announced that the draft of servicemen would end by July 1973. He banned formal quotas for minority employment in federal programs and opposed busing of school pupils exclusively for racial balance. He declared a goal of

VICE PRESIDENT AGNEW, renominated by acclamation, adopted a more restrained style of campaigning in 1972.

AL SATTERWHITE/CAMERA 5

STATE GOVERNORS ELECTED IN 1972	
Ark......D. Bumpers (D)	N. C....J. Holshouser, Jr. (R)
Del......S. W. Tribbitt (D)	N. Dak. A. A. Link (D)
Ill.......D. Walker (D)	R. I.....P. W. Noel (D)
Ind......O. R. Bowen (R)	S. Dak..R. F. Kneip (D)
Iowa.....R. D. Ray (R)	Texas...D. Briscoe (D)
Kans....R. B. Docking (D)	Utah....C. L. Rampton (D)
La........E. W. Edwards (D)	Vt......T. Salmon (D)
Mo......C. S. Bond (R)	Wash...D. J. Evans (R)
Mont....T. L. Judge (D)	W. Va...A. A. Moore, Jr. (R)
N. H.....M. Thomson, Jr. (R)	

no new taxes in a second term. He had said of his opponents in his acceptance of renomination, "Theirs is the politics of paternalism where master planners in Washington make decisions for people. Ours is the politics of people—where people make decisions for themselves." In his final addresses, Nixon called for a philosophy of individualism, self-reliance, and hard work. He spoke for a strong America committed to peace and a fully responsible role in international cooperation.

A major part of the Republican campaign was conducted by "surrogates," high officials of the administration speaking extensively throughout the country. In measured tones, Vice President Spiro T. Agnew defended the administration and denounced charges of the opposition as "reckless."

John Connally, former governor of Texas and former secretary of the treasury in the Nixon administration, headed a group called Democrats for Nixon. The Finance Committee to Re-elect the President mounted organizational and fund-raising programs.

Voting Patterns. Election returns lent new credence to the doctrine that middle America, with its traditional values, is the source of political power. Many Democratic candidates in state and local contests, except in the most liberal constituencies,

"Cliffhanger"

BRUCE SHANKS/BUFFALO EVENING NEWS

avoided close identification with McGovern. McGovern, in a campaign of almost evangelistic fervor, became labeled as an advocate of rapid and perhaps unpredictable social change. The election demonstrated that in an age of mass communication the image of national candidates is at times a stronger force than party allegiance.

Estimates of voting results gave Nixon 54% to 59% of the blue-collar vote; 53% to 59% of the Catholic vote, the first modern Republican presidential candidate to carry it; 39% of the Jewish vote, more than twice the 1968 figure; 45% to 47% of unemployed workers' votes; 63% and 68%, respectively, of middle and upper income votes in suburbs; 54% of the votes in low-income areas; and 67% in small towns and rural areas. Independents and former voters for George Wallace went heavily for the President. Voters under 30 were almost evenly divided. However, voters 18 to 24 years of age gave McGovern 52% to Nixon's 46%. In the age group from 25 to 29, the President received 54% to McGovern's 44%. Black voters supported McGovern overwhelmingly. Persons from labor union families gave McGovern 50% of their votes to 48% for Nixon.

In the 49 states carried by Nixon, his vote varied from 78% in Mississippi to 52% in Minnesota. McGovern carried Massachusetts with 55% of the vote and the District of Columbia, which had the lowest voter turnout in the nation (27% of those eligible by age) with 79%.

CONGRESS

Democrats retained control of both houses of Congress, by an increased margin of two in the Senate (57–43) but by a lead diminished by 12 in the House (242–192). Voter independence of party lines, in state after state, was remarkable in the face of the landslide for President Nixon. Observers expected the Senate to remain liberal and the House to continue a more conservative outlook.

The Senate. Thirty-three Senate seats were open. Twenty incumbent senators, 12 Republicans and 8 Democrats, were reelected. Five incumbents were defeated in November, four of them Republicans. From five retirements, three of them Republicans, no net change in party resulted. One Democratic incumbent died and was replaced by another Democrat.

Two Democratic senators were defeated in primaries. They were B. Everett Jordan (North Carolina) and David H. Gambrell (Georgia). The latter had been appointed to succeed the late Richard B. Russell. Georgia easily elected Democratic state legislator Sam Nunn to the Senate, but North Carolina voters rejected liberal Democratic nominee Nick Galifianakis to elect conservative Republican Jesse Helms, a television commentator.

Prominent Republican senators reelected included Charles H. Percy (Illinois), who ran even more strongly than the President did in the state; Edward W. Brooke (Massachusetts); Robert P. Griffin (Michigan); Carl T. Curtis (Nebraska); Clifford P. Case (New Jersey); Strom Thurmond (South Carolina); and John G. Tower (Texas). Sen. Mark O. Hatfield (Oregon), running against former Democratic Sen. Wayne Morse, won.

Successful Democratic incumbents included John J. Sparkman (Alabama), who defeated former Postmaster General Winton Blount; John L. McClellan (Arkansas), who had been forced into a close run-

RESULTS OF THE 1972 PRESIDENTIAL ELECTION, BY STATES

	Electoral vote	Popular vote[1]			Electoral vote			Percentage of popular vote		
		Nixon	McGovern	Schmitz	Nixon	Mc-Govern	Schmitz	Nixon	Mc-Govern	Schmitz
Alabama	9	728,701	256,923[2]	11,918	9			73	26	1
Alaska	3	55,349	32,967	6,903	...[3]			58	35	7
Arizona	6	402,812	198,540	21,208	6			65	32	3
Arkansas	6	448,541	199,892	2,887	6			69	31	...
California	45	4,602,096	3,475,847	232,554	45			55	42	3
Colorado	7	597,189	329,980	17,268	7			63	35	2
Connecticut	8	810,763	555,498	17,239	8			59	40	1
Delaware	3	140,357	92,283	2,638	3			60	39	1
Dist. Columbia	3	35,214	127,628	815		3		22	78	...
Florida	17	1,857,759	718,117	...	17			72	28	
Georgia	12	881,490	289,529	815	12			75	25	...
Hawaii	4	168,865	101,409	...	4			62	38	...
Idaho	4	119,384	80,827	28,869	4			65	26	9
Illinois	26	2,788,179	1,913,472	2,471	26			59	41	...
Indiana	13	1,405,154	708,568	...	13			68	32	...
Iowa	8	706,207	496,206	22,056	8			58	41	1
Kansas	7	619,812	270,287	21,808	7			68	30	2
Kentucky	9	676,446	371,159	17,627	9			64	35	1
Louisiana	10	686,852	298,142	52,099	10			66	29	5
Maine	4	256,458	160,594	...	4			61	39	...
Maryland	10	829,305	505,781	18,726	10			61	37	1
Massachusetts	14	1,112,078	1,332,540	2,877		14		45	54	...
Michigan	21	1,961,721	1,459,435	63,321	21			56	42	2
Minnesota	10	897,569	802,346	31,407	10			52	46	2
Mississippi	7	505,125	126,782	11,598	7			78	20	2
Missouri	12	1,154,050	698,531	3,110	12			62	38	0
Montana	4	183,976	120,197	13,430	4			58	38	4
Nebraska	5	406,298	169,991	...	5			71	29	...
Nevada	3	115,750	66,016	...	3			64	36	...
New Hampshire	4	213,724	116,435	3,386	4			64	35	1
New Jersey	17	1,845,502	1,102,211	34,378	17			62	37	1
New Mexico	4	235,606	141,084	8,767	4			61	37	2
New York	41	4,192,778	2,951,084	...	41			59	41	...
North Carolina	13	1,054,889	438,705	9,039	13			70	30	...
North Dakota	3	174,109	100,384	5,646	3			62	36	2
Ohio	25	2,441,827	1,558,889	80,067	25			60	38	2
Oklahoma	8	759,025	247,147	23,728	8			72	24	2
Oregon	6	486,686	392,760	42,211	6			53	42	5
Pennsylvania	27	2,714,521	1,796,951	70,593	27			59	39	2
Rhode Island	4	220,383	194,645	...	4			53	47	...
South Carolina	8	477,044	184,559	10,075	8			71	27	1
South Dakota	4	166,476	139,945	...	4			54	46	...
Tennessee	10	813,147	357,293	30,373	10			68	30	2
Texas	26	2,298,468	1,154,109	...	26			67	33	...
Utah	4	323,643	126,304	28,549	4			68	26	6
Vermont	3	117,149	68,174	...	3			63	37	...
Virginia	12	988,493	438,887	19,721	11[3]			68	30	1
Washington	9	837,135	568,334	58,906	9			57	39	4
West Virginia	6	484,964	277,435	...	6			64	36	...
Wisconsin	11	989,430	810,174	47,525	11			54	44	2
Wyoming	3	100,464	44,358	748	3			69	30	1
Totals	538	47,168,963	29,169,342	1,080,541	520	17	0	60.7	38	1

Others, 264,963; total vote, 77,460,056.

[1] Total votes for minor party candidates: Dr. Benjamin Spock, People's party, 78,801; Linda Jenness or Evelyn Reed, Socialist Workers, 65,290; Louis Fischer, Socialist Labor, 53,614; Gus Hall, Communist party, 25,222; Earle H. Munn, Prohibition party, 13,444; John Hospers, Libertarian, 2,691; John Mahalchik, America First, 1,743; Gabriel Green, Universal party, 199; others, 23,959. [2] Includes 219,108 votes on the regular Democratic ticket and 37,815 votes under the listing of the National Democratic party of Alabama. [3] Nixon's apparent electoral vote total of 521 was reduced when a Republican elector from Virginia cast his vote for Theodora Mathan, Hospers' running mate on the Libertarian ticket.

off primary; Walter F. Mondale (Minnesota); James O. Eastland (Mississippi); and Claiborne Pell (Rhode Island), who defeated former governor and secretary of the navy John H. Chaffee.

Defeat of Republican Sen. Margaret Chase Smith (Maine), by U. S. Rep. William V. Hathaway, left the Senate without a female member. Age, health, and a minimal campaign contributed to her loss. The defeats of conservative Republican Gordon Allott (Colorado) and Republican Jack Miller (Iowa) were unexpected. Republican Sen. J. Caleb Boggs (Delaware) and Democratic Sen. William B. Spong (Virginia) lost close races. Joseph R. Biden, 29, a liberal attorney, won in Delaware, and U. S. Rep. William L. Scott in Virginia.

Other new senators included former Republican Gov. Dewey F. Bartlett (Oklahoma), Republican Peter Domenici (New Mexico), and Democrat Walter Huddleston (Kentucky). Louisiana chose former state legislator J. Bennett Johnston, Democrat, to replace the late Sen. Allen J. Ellender, who died in July while campaigning for renomination.

The House. While Democrats easily held control of the House of Representatives, the number of first-term members elected to the new 93d Congress was unusually large. Reapportionment and redis-

tricting resulting from the census of 1970, primary election defeats, and retirements under a liberal pension plan were contributing factors prior to the elections held for all House members on November 7. Thirteen incumbents, eight Democrats and five Republicans, were defeated in November. Redistricting was a factor in 10 cases.

Several prominent Democratic committee chairmen met defeat in the primaries. Emanuel Celler (New York), dean of the House and chairman of Judiciary, was defeated by Elizabeth Holtzman. Wayne N. Aspinall (Colorado), chairman of Interior and Insular Affairs, and John L. McMillan (South Carolina), chairman, District of Columbia, also lost bids for renomination.

In the elections, Republicans gained eight new Southern seats, two in Mississippi and one each in Florida, Louisiana, South Carolina, Tennessee, Texas, and Virginia. Election of David C. Treen in Louisiana gave the state its first Republican in the House since Reconstruction. The South also elected two black members for the first time in the century: Andrew Young, Jr. (Georgia) and state senator Barbara Jordan, Texas, both Democrats. Their election and that of Yvonne Brathwaite Burke (California), a Democrat, increased the number of black members in the house to 16. The number of women in the House increased to 14. Louise Day Hicks (Massachusetts), was the only woman incumbent to go down to defeat.

Shifts in apportionment gave the largest delegation, 43, to California, followed by New York, 39. For the first time the Virgin Islands and Guam receive nonvoting delegates in the House, joining the delegate from the District of Columbia and the resident commissioner from Puerto Rico.

THE DEMOCRATIC TICKET was made up of vice presidential candidate Sargent Shriver (top, center), shown with two dock workers in Houston, Texas; and presidential candidate George McGovern, photographed at Mt. Rushmore in his home state of South Dakota.

House majority leader Hale Boggs (Louisiana) and Rep. Nicholas J. Begich (Alaska), both Democrats, were reelected though missing in an Alaska plane crash and later presumed dead.

GOVERNORS

Democrats increased from 30 to 31 the number of governorships they held. On November 7, helped by voters' extensive ticket-splitting, they won 11 of 18 races.

All incumbent Democrats running for reelection won easily: Dale Bumpers (Arkansas), Robert Docking (Kansas), Richard F. Kneip (South Dakota), and Calvin L. Rampton (Utah). Democrats also retained governorships in Montana, North Dakota, Rhode Island, and Texas. On February 1 they had been successful in Louisiana.

Two Republican incumbents were defeated. In Delaware, Republican Gov. Russell W. Peterson, plagued by rising taxes, lost to state legislator Sherman W. Tribbitt, and in Illinois Dan Walker, a reform-minded attorney, narrowly defeated Republican Gov. Richard B. Ogilvie. In Vermont, liberal Democrat Thomas P. Salmon swamped a candidate supported by the retiring governor.

Republicans picked up two governorships. In Missouri, Christopher Bond won handily to become the first Republican governor of the state in 32 years and, at 33, the youngest in the nation. North Carolina voters, in a surprise, elected James E. Holshouser. Three Republican incumbents were reelected: Robert D. Ray (Iowa), Daniel J. Evans (Washington), and Arch A. Moore, Jr. (West Virginia). Moore defeated John D. (Jay) Rockefeller IV. Republicans also kept governorships in Indiana and New Hampshire.

In Puerto Rico, Rafael Hernandez Colon, who ran on a platform advocating continued commonwealth status for the island, won the governorship and carried his Popular Democratic party to victory in the legislature.

(Below) *SENATOR McGOVERN with his original running mate, Sen. Thomas Eagleton of Missouri. Eagleton later left the ticket after disclosing that he had undergone shock therapy for depression. (Bottom) Senator and Mrs. McGovern campaign in West Virginia.*

UPI

MICHAEL LLOYD CARLEBACH, FROM NANCY PALMER

DRAWING BY DONALD REILLY © 1972 THE NEW YORKER MAGAZINE, INC.

OTHER VOTING

Referenda on the ballots brought mixed results. New York voters approved by 2 to 1 a $1.15 billion state bonding program for cleaner air and water. California and Washington approved plans for shoreline development and control. Massachusetts and North Carolina adopted measures for environmental protection. Florida authorized loans of $240 million to buy recreational land. South Dakota banned the hunting of mourning doves.

School finance proposals to add other revenue sources for relief of property taxpayers met defeat in California, Colorado, Michigan, and Oregon, but Ohio voters preferred the new state income tax to higher property levies. Massachusetts rejected graduated state income taxes; Washington approved a statewide ceiling on property taxes but gave more latitude to communities for school taxes. Maryland rejected tuition grants to students attending nonpublic schools.

Californians voted 2 to 1 to restore the death penalty for some crimes and opposed removing state penalties for using marihuana. They rejected proposals for strict control of pornography and of farm workers' unions. Voters in Michigan and North Dakota defeated liberalized abortion laws. Proposals permitting lotteries won in Maryland, Iowa, and Washington but lost in Colorado. Voters in Colorado also banned use of state funds for the 1976 Winter Olympics.

(See also STATE GOVERNMENT.)

FRANKLIN L. BURDETTE
University of Maryland

NEW VOTER learns how it is done. An election official in Ann Arbor, Mich., instructs a young voter in the use of the voting machine.

THE NEW YORK TIMES

COMPARISON OF PARTY STRENGTH IN CONGRESS BEFORE AND AFTER 1972 ELECTIONS, BY STATES

(D = Democrat; R = Republican)

	Senate				House			
	Before		After		Before[1]		After[2]	
	D	R	D	R	D	R	D	R
Ala.	2	0	2	0	5	3	4	3
Alaska	1	1	1	1	1	0	1	0
Ariz.	0	2	0	2	1	2	1	3
Ark.	2	0	2	0	3	1	3	1
Calif.	2	0	2	0	20	18	23	20
Colo.	0	2	1	1	2	2	2	3
Conn.	1	1	1	1	4	2	3	3
Del.	0	2	1	1	0	1	0	1
Fla.	1	1	1	1	9	3	11	4
Ga.	2	0	2	0	8	2	9	1
Hawaii	1	1	1	1	2	0	2	0
Idaho	1	1	1	1	0	2	0	2
Ill.	1	1	1	1	12	11	10	14
Ind.	2	0	2	0	5	6	4	7
Iowa	1	1	2	0	2	5	3	3
Kans.	0	2	0	2	1	4	1	4
Ky.	0	2	1	1	5	2	5	2
La.	2	0	2	0	8	0	7	1
Me.	1	1	2	0	2	0	1	1
Md.	0	2	0	2	5	3	4	4
Mass.	1	1	1	1	8	4	8	3
Mich.	1	1	1	1	7	12	7	12
Minn.	2	0	2	0	4	4	4	4
Miss.	2	0	2	0	5	0	3	2
Mo.	2	0	2	0	9	1	9	1
Mont.	2	0	2	0	1	1	1	1
Nebr.	0	2	0	2	0	3	0	3
Nev.	2	0	2	0	1	0	0	1
N. H.	1	1	1	1	0	2	0	2
N. J.	1	1	1	1	9	6	8	7
N. Mex.	2	0	2	0	1	1	1	1
N. Y.	0	2[3]	0	2[3]	24	17	22	17
N. C.	2	0	1	1	7	4	7	4
N. Dak.	1	1	1	1	1	1	0	1
Ohio	0	2	0	2	7	17	7	16
Okla.	1	1	0	2	4	2	5	1
Oreg.	0	2	0	2	2	2	2	2
Pa.	0	2	0	2	14	12	13	12
R. I.	2	0	2	0	2	0	2	0
S. C.	1	1	1	1	5	1	4	2
S. Dak.	1	1	2	0	2	0	1	1
Tenn.	0	2	0	2	5	4	3	5
Texas	1	1	1	1	20	3	20	4
Utah	1	1	1	1	1	0	2	0
Vt.	0	2	0	2	0	1	0	1
Va.	2[4]	0	1[5]	1	4	6	4	7
Wash.	2	0	2	0	6	1	6	1
W. Va.	2	0	2	0	5	0	4	0
Wis.	2	0	2	0	5	5	5	4
Wyo.	1	1	1	1	1	0	1	0
Totals	55	45	57	43	255	177	242	192

[1] As of Jan. 1972; total does not add to 435 because of 3 vacancies. [2] Total does not add to 435 because Massachusetts delegation of 12 members includes one independent. [3] Includes one elected as a Conservative-Republican. [4] Includes one elected as an independent. [5] Elected as an independent.

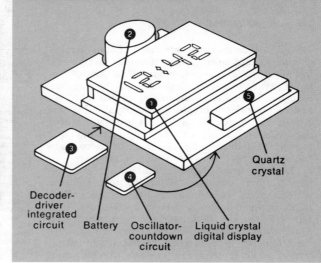

LIQUID CRYSTAL WATCH is representative of a trend toward consumer devices that use electronics to produce lighted displays of numbers or letters. It has five replaceable parts (right).

WALTHAM WATCH COMPANY

Decoder-driver integrated circuit Battery Oscillator-countdown circuit Liquid crystal digital display Quartz crystal

ELECTRONICS

The U. S. electronics industry regained much of its vigor during 1972, recovering from a 2-year slump that was one of the worst in the industry's history. Shipments of electronic products reached about $31 billion, up about $2.8 billion from shipments in 1971, and setting a new industry record. Much of the industry's resurgence came from the development of new markets for its products and a generally improved economic climate.

The Nixon administration's new economic policies, introduced in 1971, had a profound effect on the industry in 1972. The industry was forced to alter corporate marketing plans, take a stronger stand on imports, cut back on inventories, and produce longer term and more accurate market forecasts.

For the consumer, developments in the industry foreshadowed increasing everyday contact with various electronic products, including minicalculators, electronic ignition systems for automobiles, and electronic controls in cameras.

Minicalculators. One of the most exciting developments in the industry during 1972 was the sudden emergence of low-priced minicalculators for personal use. A minicalculator is small enough to be carried about in a clothes pocket or purse, and it weighs less than a pound. A typical minicalculator will add, subtract, multiply, or divide, giving an eight-digit answer with a floating decimal point. Already, some students have used minicalculators to do their schoolwork computations, and some businessmen have found them useful in computing costs while away from the office and its bigger office calculators.

Although only about 500,000 minicalculators had been sold by the end of 1972, the market for them was growing about as fast as their price was dropping. The average retail price of a minicalculator dropped from about $240 in early 1971 to less than $100 by the end of 1972, and it may well be less than $50 within the next two or three years. Calculator manufacturers estimate that worldwide sales will total at least 1.5 million units by 1974.

Government Spending. Although the electronics industry still depends on the Department of Defense (DOD) and the National Aeronautics and Space Administration (NASA) for almost half of its total revenue, it can expect little in the way of increased spending for electronics hardware from these sources in the next few years. As a result,

many of the industry's aerospace and defense-oriented companies began to direct their talents toward a variety of new programs that are aimed at selling to the government's "civilian" agencies, such as the Federal Aviation Administration.

Economic Forecast to 1985. One of the highlights of 1972 was an extraordinary conference called Electronics 1985—A Look Into The Future, which was sponsored by the Electronics Industries Association (EIA). About 45 of the industry's leading executives attended the conference along with top economists. Based on their discussions, the EIA produced a 300-page economic forecast. Some of the report's major predictions were:

(1) The world market for electronic products, which was $56.7 billion in 1970, will rise to $91.3 billion in 1975, climb to $137.3 by 1980, and reach nearly $205 billion in 1985.

(2) The rate of growth of the world market will average 10% annually through 1975, slow after 1975, and average about 8.3% between 1980 and 1985.

(3) Worldwide sales of industrial electronic products will account for most of the growth in the world market between 1972 and 1985, with volume reaching $121.1 billion as compared with about $24.2 billion in 1970.

(4) Worldwide sales of consumer electronic products will reach $35.6 billion in 1985, up about $26 billion from the 1970 total.

(5) Sales of electronic products to U. S. and other governments will rise to $48 billion in 1985, up about $27.2 billion from the total in 1970.

(6) The world market for electronic components will reach $45.6 billion by 1985, compared with about $14.8 billion in 1970.

New Electronic Applications. Much of the growth in the sales of electronic components is expected to come from a variety of relatively new applications, such as electronics for automobiles. During 1972 several U. S. semiconductor manufacturers, in anticipation of a large market for their products in the automotive field, set up departments exclusively devoted to developing and selling semiconductor devices for this market. Auto manufacturers expect that each U. S.-made car will have about $800 worth of electronic equipment in the not too distant future. This equipment would include light-emitting digital displays on the instrument panel; an electronic ignition system; temperature, pressure, and other sensor systems; and even a diagnostic system that monitors car performance.

As another example, integrated circuits are beginning to take over various functions in cameras, including shutter control, motor drive control, internal synchronization, and through-the-lens exposure metering. Also, the joining of two relatively new technologies—complementary metal oxide silicon (a control circuit) and liquid crystals (readout display)—is creating a truly all-electronic watch that is expected to displace a major share of the mechanical watches on the market within a few years.

Imports from Japan. American electronics manufacturers continued to charge that Japanese manufacturers were dumping many of their electronic products—that is, pricing them at less than fair value in the U. S. market. In a meeting in Washington in September 1972, Japanese government representatives accused the Nixon administration of unfair protectionism in its antidumping policies and bitterly assailed the proposed new dumping rules being developed by the Treasury Department. The U. S. Treasury Department insisted the tougher approach to dumping was not protectionism. The U. S. view has been that strict interpretation of the nation's antidumping laws kills off demands for protectionist legislation in Congress. At the end of 1972, the Treasury Department's Tariff Commission was still hearing cases of alleged dumping by Japanese firms, particularly color TV picture tubes.

Sales to Eastern Bloc Countries. In late 1972 the United States and its North American Treaty Organization (NATO) allies agreed to lift the export embargo on the shipment of many electronic products to Eastern Bloc countries. The United States, through its Export Control Board in the Commerce Department, will bring most of its export curbs into line with the liberalized NATO coordinating committee list. Previously, the United States had barred shipment of as many as 600 products that U. S. allies were free to ship to the Eastern Bloc under the more liberal NATO regulations.

RONALD A. SCHNEIDERMAN, *"Electronics News"*

EL SALVADOR

National concern in El Salvador in 1972 centered on a presidential election in February and an unsuccessful coup d'etat in March.

Election. The two major candidates for president were Col. Arturo Armanda Molina, nominee of the incumbent National Conciliation party (PCN), which was controlled by large landowners and the military, and José Napoleón Duarte, three-term mayor of San Salvador and head of the left-wing National Opposition Union. Both men ran on moderate platforms emphasizing agrarian reform. Molina presented himself as a middle-of-the-road alternative between the "leftist" Duarte and two "rightest" minor party candidates, Gen. José Alberto Medrano of the Independent Democratic United Front and Dr. Antonio Rodríguez Port of the Salvadorean Popular party. Duarte attempted to build a coalition based on the Christian Democratic party and two left-of-center parties—the Movement for National Revolution and the National Democratic Union—united in the new National Opposition Union.

The campaign, begun in October 1971, was marred by numerous charges and countercharges of electoral manipulation and fraud. After balloting on February 20, the official vote tally (March 1) showed Molina, with 314,748 votes, the winner by a slight plurality. Duarte received 292,621 votes;

─────── **EL SALVADOR · Information Highlights** ───────

Official Name: Republic of El Salvador.
Area: 8,260 square miles (21,393 sq km).
Population (1972 est.): 3,700,000. *Density,* 427 per square mile (165 per sq km). *Annual rate of increase,* 3.0%.
Chief Cities (1969 est.): San Salvador, the capital, 349,700; Santa Ana, 102,300; San Miguel, 50,700.
Government: *Head of state,* Arturo Armando Molina, president (took office July 1972). *Head of government,* Arturo Armando Molina. *Legislature*—Legislative Assembly (unicameral), 52 members. *Major political parties*—Party of National Conciliation; Christian Democratic party.
Language: Spanish (official).
Education: *Expenditure* (1967), 25.4% of total public expenditure. *School enrollment* (1969)—primary, 516,875; secondary, 84,783; technical/vocational, 27,250; university/higher, 8,151.
Monetary Unit: Colon (2.50 colones equal U. S.$1, Aug. 1972).
Gross National Product (1971 est.): $1,043,000,000.
Manufacturing (major products): Processed foods, textiles, petroleum products, furniture, pharmaceuticals.
Major Agricultural Products: Sugarcane, coffee, cotton, rice.
Major Minerals: Quartz, kaolin, gypsum, limestone, salt.
Foreign Trade (1971): *Exports,* $228,000,000. *Imports,* $249,000,000. *Chief trading partners* (1969)—United States (took 21% of exports, supplied 29% of imports); West Germany (22%—7%); Guatemala (18%—18%); Japan (10%—9%).
Communications: *Telephones* (1971), 39,020; *television stations* (1971), 4; *television sets* (1971), 100,000; *radios* (1970), 405,000; *newspapers* (1970), 13.

Medrano, 47,748; and Rodríguez Porth, 10,686. The Salvadorean constitution requires that if a presidential candidate receives less than 50% of the vote, the Legislative Assembly is to act as an electoral college and decide between the top two candidates. In this instance, however, PNC domination of the Legislative Assembly made this procedure a mere formality, and Molina was inaugurated on July 1.

Elections for the Assembly and municipal offices were held on March 12, with the PCN winning an overwhelming majority of 38 of 52 seats in the Assembly and 206 of 261 municipal mayoralties.

Coup d'Etat. In the wake of the elections, on March 25, dissident elements of the National Guard, to which Medrano belonged, attempted to overthrow incumbent President Fidel Sánchez Hernández, who had supported Molina. One of the leaders, Col. Antonio Núñez, arrested President Sánchez and his 17-year-old daughter, confining them to a military barracks. A three-man junta assumed power. It consisted of the leader of the coup, Col. Benjamín Mejía, former commander of the Presidential Guard, with Col. Manuel Reyes Alvarado and Maj. Pedro Guardado. Defeated presidential candidate Duarte broadcast an appeal for popular support of the rebels.

The bulk of the army and air force remained loyal to the president, however, and the revolt was put down within 24 hours. An estimated 100 or more soldiers and civilians, but no prominent politicians, were killed, and some 200 persons were severely injured. The leaders of the coup were forced into exile or imprisoned. On April 4, the Assembly unanimously declared a month-long state of siege.

The unsuccessful revolt produced at least one significant international repercussion. Duarte was arrested by Salvadoran authorities in the home of the first secretary of the Venezuelan embassy, where he had sought refuge. The Venezuelan ambassador protested this action as a violation of the right of asylum. A committee consisting of a U. S. official, an Italian, and a Brazilian attempted negotiation of the dispute. Ultimately, Salvadoran authorities allowed Duarte to obtain asylum in Caracas.

ROBERT L. PETERSON
University of Texas at El Paso

ELLINGTON, Duke. See BIOGRAPHY.
ELLSBURG, Daniel. See BIOGRAPHY.
ENGLISH LITERATURE. See LITERATURE.

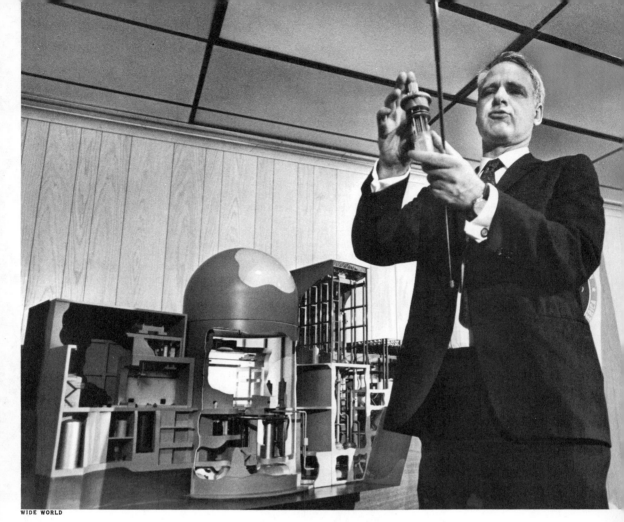

energy

James R. Schlesinger, chairman of the Atomic Energy Commission, holds up core of a model of a fast-breeder reactor to be built near Oak Ridge, Tenn.

In 1972 the United States continued to make increasing demands on the shrinking supply of natural resources, worsening a situation that has come to be known as the energy crisis. The nation consumed some 70 quadrillion British thermal units of energy, and the National Petroleum Council estimated that by 1980 the nation would have increased its consumption of energy by 50%.

Nuclear Energy. Despite delays due to construction difficulties and protests by environmentalist groups, there were some advances made in building nuclear power plants in several countries. The United States announced plans to build the nation's first commercial type of fast-breeder nuclear reactor power plant, which creates, or "breeds," more fuel than it consumes. The plant, to be built near Oak Ridge, Tenn., will cost $500 million, about half of which will be paid by private utility companies. Construction was not expected to begin before 1974 at the earliest.

The Soviet Union announced completion of its first large breeder, which is about the same size as the future Oak Ridge project. In Toronto, Canadians dedicated their first commercial power plant fueled by an atomic reactor. Construction difficulties delayed the start-up of Britain's first breeder reactor, which is in Scotland, until mid-1973.

Electricity. In the United States there were several developments in the field of electricity. The Atomic Energy Commission (AEC) began research to shift away from the gasoline-powered automobile engine and to the use of electric batteries in cars. The project was undertaken because of the increasing shortage of gasoline and the pollution created by the gasoline engine.

General Electric announced a breakthrough in the underground transmission of electricity at cryogenic (extremely low) temperatures. This could eventually help solve electric power supply shortages in major cities. Scientists at the AEC laboratory in Los Alamos, N. Mex., explored a way to expand the nation's usable source of geothermal energy by drilling into the molten rock and circulating hot water, thus creating steam that can drive large electric generators.

Environmentalism was having an increasing impact on the supply of energy in 1972. The Federal Power Commission (FPC) predicted that the price of electric power would more than double by 1990, and singled out environmentalism as a major cause of an impending power shortage. A study of utilities by the Council on Economic Priorities reported that private power companies had been lagging in installing available pollution-abatement equipment.

Gas. According to the FPC, the shortage of gas production that had developed in the United States in 1971 would grow worse. Accordingly, the government permitted higher gas prices and new imports of gas. For the first time, the FPC authorized a company to begin long-term importation of liquefied natural gas. The imports—to come from Algeria over a period of 20 years—represented what could become a major new source of imported energy, albeit a more expensive one. The FPC also adopted a new natural gas pricing policy that allowed domestic producers to raise their prices on new supplies. This was done in hopes that the prospect of larger profits would lead to more exploration.

Natural gas exploration efforts were stepped up in several areas of North America—including Texas, Oklahoma, and Nova Scotia—and in the Soviet Union, where production began on a gigantic Siberian gas field. Gas resources there are so great that, possibly in the 1980's, they could help heat and fuel homes and industry in the eastern United States.

Petroleum. In 1972, the U. S. government announced that it would go ahead with the laying of the controversial Alaskan oil pipeline, but at year-end the project still lacked final approval and work on it had not yet begun. (See ALASKA.) Meanwhile, President Nixon sharply increased the flow of oil imports, raising the quota for all petroleum products east of the Rocky Mountains from 1.7 million to about 2.3 million barrels a day.

Coal. Another new source for gas was found in coal, which is more plentiful than any other fossil fuel but is of only limited use because it pollutes the air so badly when burned. In 1972 the American Gas Association reported that gas had been made from coal in a large-scale experimental plant that could ultimately produce 1.5 million cubic feet of gas daily.

In areas of the world where environmentalism has aroused less concern, coal continued to be heavily used. The Soviet Union approved a gigantic power-generating project, in its sparsely-populated Asian region, that will supply European Russia with badly needed electricity by the end of the 1970's.

SANDRA SALMANS
Associate Editor, "Newsweek" Magazine

Nuclear Energy

Two conflicting trends emerged more clearly in 1972. On the one hand, there was a greater urgency for nuclear energy developments because observers in government, industry, and the universities foresaw an impending world energy crisis. On the other hand, public concern over safety and environmental issues slowed the speed of these developments.

NUCLEAR POWER PLANTS

Continuing debates over radiation standards and nuclear reactor safety served to focus more public attention on nuclear power plants.

Advantages. In contrast to a coal-fueled or oil-fueled electric power plant, a nuclear power plant does not pollute the atmosphere by emitting particulate matter, sulfur dioxide, or other combustion by-products. The nuclear fuel is compact, and it can be put to use with less mining and transportation, less land disruption, and fewer mining injuries than are encountered in using coal and oil. Also, the use of nuclear fuel results in the conservation of coal and oil, which will have important chemical uses in future technologies.

Disadvantages. To balance these advantages, the following facts should be considered. Light-water nuclear reactors have low thermodynamic efficiencies of about 32%, whereas a fossil-fueled plant has an efficiency close to 40%. Thus in producing a given amount of electricity by means of a light-water reactor, considerably more heat must be absorbed by the environment, an unwanted result that is called thermal pollution. Also, the accumulation of fission products in spent fuel elements makes it necessary to provide transportation and permanent storage of these radioactive waste elements. Perhaps most importantly, reactor safety and radiation leakage problems have continued to be major items of public concern.

Safety. During 1972 the safety of nuclear power plants continued to be an issue of major public concern. Under pressure from the public and environmentalists, the industry moved ahead in developing more acceptable locations for power plants.

The offshore nuclear power plant, designed for minimal environmental disturbance, neared reality in 1972 when the first contract for an offshore facility was signed in September by a New Jersey utility. In this project, two 1.15 million kilowatt units are to be moored behind a massive breakwater 12 miles (19 km) northeast of Atlantic City. The billion-dollar facility, a joint venture of Tenneco and Westinghouse, is slated for completion by 1981. The pact was described as the largest equipment contract in the history of the electric utility industry.

Emergency Core Cooling Systems. A new issue of public concern over the safety of nuclear power plants surfaced in 1972. This issue was the effectiveness of emergency core cooling systems (ECCS) in nuclear plants. In the event of a disruption of the flow of coolant through a reactor core, a backup system must provide sufficient cooling to prevent a melting of fuel elements due to their internal heat production. The problem is especially severe in pressurized-water reactors, which normally use pressurized water as the coolant. Recent tests of the standard backup cooling systems in current use have indicated they may not function as expected.

Under the direction of the U. S. Atomic Energy Commission (AEC), hearings on interim standards for emergency core cooling systems were held throughout 1972. To lessen the risk associated with operating a plant with a less-than-certain backup cooling system, the AEC suggested new standards that would reduce the maximum allowable temperature of the fuel-rod cladding from 2300° F to 2000° F (1260° C to 1205° C) in the event of a loss-of-coolant accident. Although these standards would result in power reduction ranging up to 20% in some of the 26 nuclear power plants in operation in 1972, they would lessen the danger stemming from a disruption of the normal flow of coolant.

Radioactive Waste Disposal. The disposal of nuclear wastes from the growing nuclear power industry also was under consideration in 1972. After the AEC temporarily suspended its plans to create a depository for radioactive materials in an underground salt formation near Lyons, Kans., it began a search for alternative schemes of waste disposal.

Both underground and surface storage are to be studied for 10 years before a final choice is made. The AEC has been considering the use of man-made storage vaults at or near the earth's surface as an alternative to underground storage in salt formations or other natural geologic containers.

A NUCLEAR FIRST FOR CANADA, the generating station that was dedicated on February 25 at Pickering, a suburb of Toronto, became the country's first full-scale commercial nuclear power plant.

Fuel-Rod Design. The problem of damage to nuclear fuel rods also received much attention. There were reports of fuel-rod damage at several nuclear power plants in the United States and Europe, and this caused some concern about the safe operation of nuclear power plants in the United States. For instance, a detailed examination of the fuel rods in the Rochester Gas and Electric Company's Ginna plant showed damage in up to 10% of the plant's 21,000 fuel rods. The damage apparently was caused by shrinkage of the uranium-oxide pellets, which are contained in metal rods. Such shrinkage created voids in a rod, which subsequently deformed under pressure in the reactor core. It is expected that the problem will be eliminated by the future use of pressurized fuel elements.

Nuclear Power Leaders. According to figures released in mid-1972, the United States has overtaken the United Kingdom in the cumulative production of electricity by means of nuclear fission. By the end of 1972 the United States had produced a cumulative total of 39.5 billion kilowatt-hours of electrical energy from nuclear fission power plants, a figure 50% greater than the cumulative total produced in the United Kingdom, which had been the leader until 1971. The U. S. total in 1971 represented a 67.5% increase over its total in 1970.

Other sharp increases in 1971 were registered by Canada (306%), Japan (109%), Spain (173%), Sweden (60.7%), and France (63.5%). The Commission of European Communities predicted that western Europe, excluding England, would have a nuclear generating capacity of more than 100 million kilowatts by 1985.

In the United States as of June 30, 1972, 26 nuclear power plants with a total electric power capacity of 11.8 million kilowatts were in operation; 51 power stations with a total capacity of 44 million kilowatts were under construction; and 66 plants with a total capacity of 65.9 million kilowatts were ordered. Thus, the total number of nuclear plants operating, under construction, or ordered was 143, and their total capacity was 121.7 million kilowatts. Also by the end of the first six months of 1972, electric utilities had made known plans for 12 new

nuclear power stations with a total electric power capacity of 19.4 million kilowatts. Total U. S. electrical generating capacity from all sources was about 396 million kilowatts as of July 1, 1972.

Environmental Protection. The cost of protecting the environment from fossil-fueled and nuclear-fueled electric power plant operations was expected to reach $10.7 billion by 1976. One result would be that the cost of electricity for the average household would increase at rates up to $17.50 per year.

NUCLEAR REACTOR RESEARCH AND DEVELOPMENT

Two possible alternatives to present commercial nuclear-fission power reactors are the breeder reactor and the thermonuclear reactor. The breeder reactor, a special kind of nuclear-fission reactor, was in the late development stage in 1972. The thermonuclear reactor, which makes use of nuclear fusion rather than fission, was in the research stage.

Breeder Reactor. The development of the first liquid-metal-cooled fast breeder reactor (LMFBR) for producing electricity for industrial and commercial users in the United States was undertaken jointly by the AEC, the Tennessee Valley Authority (TVA), and the Commonwealth Edison Company in 1972. They are cooperating in building a demonstration LMFBR on the Clinch River in eastern Tennessee. Two corporations, the Breeder Reactor Corporation and the Project Management Corporation, have been specifically created for the project, which is scheduled to be completed by 1980. The Westinghouse Electric Corporation was selected as the lead reactor manufacturer for the project.

In the breeder reactor, nonfissile uranium-238 (U-238) is converted to the fissionable isotope plutonium-239 (Pu-239), which is produced as a by-product of the fission reaction. Since a successful breeder reactor would use U-238, man could then make use of 50% to 80% of the world's known uranium resources. In contrast, present commercial reactors can only make use of the U-235 isotope, which accounts for only 0.7% of the uranium found in nature. Because of this difference, breeder reactors would be able to supply the world's electrical needs for at least several hundred years.

Some environmental opposition to the fast breeder reactor already has been expressed, much of it based on the fact that considerable quantities of plutonium will be produced in its operation.

Thermonuclear Reactor. Most fusion research is aimed at the development of a thermonuclear reactor. In the past, these research efforts generally have been directed toward containing the fusion reaction within a sort of magnetic "bottle" that is produced by magnetic forces.

A new approach to achieving a controlled fusion reaction was first introduced by Russian researchers who showed in 1968 that a laser beam could initiate a fusion reaction. In 1972 the AEC revealed a new method of producing the high-power laser beams that are required for this purpose. The method involves heating a gas pellet of deuterium and tritium with many separate laser beams, which converge in a manner so as to compress the pellet. As a result of this compression, the pellet is very rapidly heated to a temperature of 100 million degrees Celsius (or centigrade). Under these extreme density and temperature conditions, the fusion reaction can occur.

A major advance, using the more conventional approach, was also announced in December 1972 at the Adiabatic Toroidal Compressor at AEC's Princeton Plasma Physics Laboratory. This device—a version of the "tokomak" concept—achieved for the first time a plasma density in the range in which a fusion reactor must operate. By compressing the plasma with a pulsed magnetic field, electron temperatures of 25 million degrees (C) and densities of several hundred trillion particles per cubic centimeter have been achieved.

NEW USES FOR NUCLEAR ENERGY

Significant developments in the use of nuclear energy occurred in a variety of fields in 1972, especially in medicine.

Nuclear-Powered Heart Pacemaker. The first implants of nuclear-power heart pacemakers in U. S. citizens were made in July 1972 in Buffalo, N. Y. The pacemakers are powered by plutonium-238 in a power unit designed by a French company. The AEC budgeted $1 million for further development of nuclear-powered pacemakers in fiscal 1973.

Nuclear-Powered Artificial Heart. A nuclear-powered artificial heart moved closer to reality in 1972 when the National Institutes of Health announced that an experimental unit had passed preliminary tests. The unit consisted of a plutonium-238 heat source, a miniature steam engine, and a pump. The unit was successively implanted in 75 calves for periods ranging from 2 to 10 days. The heat source and steam engine, which weigh six pounds, were placed in the abdomen of a calf, and the pump was placed near the animal's natural heart. Heat from the plutonium-238 converted water in the engine to steam, and the steam engine drove the pump, which substituted for heart action.

Neutron Cancer Therapy. Irradiation by neutrons has been coming into common use for treatment of cancerous tumors. For instance, Texas A & M University's cyclotron was to be used by the M. D. Anderson Hospital and Tumor Clinic in the first large-scale test of fast-neutron cancer therapy in the United States. The program, sponsored by the National Cancer Institute, is patterned after the successful use of fast neutrons at the Hammersmith Hospital, London.

New Isotopes for Medicine. A high-power proton accelerator at the AEC's Brookhaven National Laboratory has been producing new isotopes for medicine. So far, cesium-127 and cesium-129 have been used to evaluate damage from heart attacks, and iron-52 as a tracer in studies of anemia.

Californium-252. In June 1972 the AEC announced the establishment of a californium-252 demonstration center at the Gulf Radiation Technology laboratory near San Diego. About 100 milligrams of Cf-252, a spontaneous fissioning source that emits neutrons, were to be made available to the laboratory. A similar center was opened earlier in 1972 at Louisiana State University.

Californium-252, a man-made isotope, can be used to assay nuclear materials, detect heavy metals in lake and river sediments, irradiate cancerous tissues, and serve as a source for neutron activation analysis. The small and portable californium-252 sources are more convenient for such applications than are reactors or accelerators.

Civilian Uses for Nuclear Explosives. The Plowshare program to develop civilian uses for nuclear explosives continued in low key during 1972. Research continued on the use of underground nuclear explosions to stimulate the recovery of natural gas, and the AEC hoped to test a sequential firing device called Yadit at the Nevada Test Site in 1973.

Some experts believe that underground nuclear explosions, such as those in the Plowshare program, could be used to develop geothermal power sources in the western United States and elsewhere in the world. Geothermal power sources use the natural heat of the earth's interior to heat circulating water, from which power may be extracted. In 1972, about 200 megawatts of electric power were derived from geothermal sources throughout the world.

MILITARY AND SPACE APPLICATIONS

Nuclear Weapons Tests. The major nuclear powers continued bomb testing and weapons development during 1972. By treaty, the United States and the USSR may conduct only underground nuclear tests. China and France continued to stage atmospheric bomb tests, with France using the Polynesian area of the Pacific Ocean. A major underground detonation was set off by the USSR in November 1972. It had an explosive force of 1 megaton, equivalent to the force of 1 million tons of TNT.

Reactors for U. S. Naval Vessels. The U. S. Navy's program for nuclear-powered vessels moved forward on three fronts in 1972. Advanced nuclear reactors were developed for attack submarines, an improved reactor was developed for the undersea long-range missile system (ULMS) submarine, and work continued on a high-power nuclear reactor for aircraft carriers.

Nuclear Rocket. Nuclear rocket development slowed almost to a halt in 1972, even though about $1.4 billion had been spent on the program since 1955. The AEC request for nuclear rocket development in the fiscal year 1973 declined to $5 million. The program will concentrate on developing a nuclear rocket with a thrust of 15,000 to 20,000 pounds, which is small compared with the old goal of a rocket with a 75,000-pound thrust.

Nuclear Power on Interplanetary Spacecraft. Pioneer 10, launched in March 1972, is scheduled to explore the vicinity of the planet Jupiter in December 1973. The spacecraft is equipped with four SNAP-19 (Space Nuclear Auxiliary Power) gen-

SUPERCONDUCTING generator (above) *produces alternating current of 5 million watts. Special wire in rotor* (right) *is maintained at a temperature of* —452.2° F (—269° C).

erators—the first use of nuclear power on an interplanetary spacecraft. Fueled by plutonium-238, each of its four generators produces 37 watts of electricity, which primarily is used by scientific data-collecting instruments and communications equipment. For the Jupiter fly-by mission, nuclear-electric power is much preferable to solar-electric power provided by solar cells because of the low solar intensity at such a great distance from the sun. The SNAP-19 generators will enable Pioneer 10 to communicate with earth stations for up to six years after launch. (See also SPACE EXPLORATION.)

Waste Treatment on Manned Spacecraft. A human-waste recycling system powered by plutonium-238 has been developed for manned spacecraft. It is capable of recycling an astronaut's waste materials to usable water and disposable ash. The ash volume is less than 1% of the original material's.

U. S. ATOMIC ENERGY COMMISSION

Budget. The AEC budget request for the fiscal year 1973 was $2.123 billion for operating expenses and $440 million for plant and capital equipment. The operating budget includes $878.5 million for weapons; $485.2 million for reactor development; $426.6 million for nuclear materials; $282.8 million for physical research; $94.5 million for biology and medicine; $12.4 million for training, education, and information; $6.8 million for civilian applications of nuclear explosives; and $5.9 million for isotopes development. The highlights of the AEC program

include $132 million for fast-breeder development and $53.3 million for safety programs for breeder and light-water reactors.

New Commissioner. In July, President Nixon announced the appointment of Dixy Lee Ray of Tacoma, Wash., as an AEC commissioner, replacing Wilfrid E. Johnson. Dr. Ray, an expert in marine biology, is the second woman to serve on the AEC. Previously, she served as director of the Pacific Science Center and as associate professor of zoology at the University of Washington. In December, AEC Chairman James R. Schlesinger was named head of the Central Intelligence Agency (CIA).

ROBERT E. CHRIEN
Brookhaven National Laboratory

Electricity

The electric utility industry in the United States reached record highs in 1972 in production of electricity, generating capacity, sales, and revenues. Also, electrical manufacturers shipped an estimated $52.2 billion worth of electrical products in 1972, according to the National Electrical Manufacturers Association. This was a record high and an increase of 9.9% over the 1971 total.

Power Supply. To keep pace with rising demand, utilities spent a record $13.2 billion on new plants and equipment in 1972. This was 14.3% of the new construction expenditures by all U. S. industry.

Utilities were operating 20 nuclear power plants as of Oct. 1, 1972, and 118 nuclear plants were under construction or ordered. The Edison Electric Institute expected that nuclear plants would increase their share of the nation's electric power capacity from 2.3% in 1971 to about 50% in 2000.

Electric utilities produced 1.744 trillion kilowatt-hours (kw-hrs) of electric energy in 1972, an increase of 8.1% over the 1971 output.

At year-end, all generating facilities had an estimated total capacity of 406.5 million kw, a 10.4% increase over the 1971 total of 368.1 million kw. Electric utilities had 78% of this capacity, and government agencies and rural electric cooperatives provided the rest. The margin of reserve was estimated at 20.5% above the 1972 peak demand.

Sales. An estimated 1.576 trillion kw-hrs of electric energy were sold in 1972, up 7.5% from the 1971 total of 1.466 trillion kw-hrs. Average annual use of electric energy in the American home was a record 7,685 kw-hrs in 1972, up 305 kw-hrs.

WORLDWIDE PRODUCTION OF ELECTRIC ENERGY

Country	1969	1970
	(millions of kilowatt-hours)	
United States	1,552,757	1,638,010
USSR	689,050	740,400
Japan	316,261	359,490
United Kingdom	238,534	248,588
West Germany	221,199	237,209
Canada	190,320	203,702
France	131,516	140,708
Italy	110,447	117,423
East Germany	65,463	67,650
Poland	60,053	64,531
Sweden	58,084	60,645
India	56,312	59,975
Norway	57,021	57,606
Spain	52,124	55,901
Australia	48,901	53,826

Source: 1971 UN Statistical Yearbook.

By adding about 1.8 million new customers in 1972, the industry raised its total to 76.1 million. Almost 90% of the new customers were residential customers. Gross revenues of the utilities totaled $24.1 billion in 1972, a 13.3% annual gain.

Rates. In 1972 the average price for residential electric service was 2.30 cents per kw-hr, compared with 2.19 cents per kw-hr in 1971.

Environment. The Edison Electric Institute reported that electric utilities spent more than $2.1 billion in 1972 to enhance environmental quality, a 36% increase over 1971.

SANDRA SALMANS
Associate Editor, "Newsweek" Magazine

Gas

The U. S. gas industry set records in sales, revenues, and number of customers in 1972, and the rate of increase of overall sales recovered from a record slump in 1971. The Federal Power Commission (FPC) estimated that the nation's shortage of natural gas in the winter of 1972–73 would be the worst on record and almost twice as great as in the previous winter. The FPC said the seriousness of the shortage would depend on the weather.

Business Volume. Preliminary year-end estimates by the American Gas Association (AGA) showed that total sales reached 17,030 trillion Btu in 1972, up 2.1% from 16,680 trillion Btu in 1971. Revenues from gas sales climbed to $12.3 billion, an 8.0% increase over the $11.4 billion revenues in 1971. About 736,000 new customers were added during 1972, bringing the total to 43 million.

Business Outlook. Projections by the AGA showed sales reaching 25,075 trillion Btu by 1980, assuming a 4.6% annual growth rate during the

LNG TANKERS are helping to meet U. S. natural gas needs. Tankers carry liquefied gas at −258° F (−161° C) in aluminum vessels, one of which may be seen in cutaway section. Gas is shipped as a liquid to save space.

ALCOA

WORLDWIDE PRODUCTION OF NATURAL GAS

Country	1969	1970
	(millions of cubic meters[1])	
United States	586,112	620,727
USSR	181,121	197,945
Canada	56,009	64,465
Netherlands	21,848	31,617
Rumania	23,873	24,790
Mexico	17,218	17,832
Italy	11,960	13,171
West Germany	8,799	12,455
Iran	2,781	11,223
United Kingdom	5,060	11,100
Venezuela	7,980	8,990
France	6,506	6,880
Argentina	5,327	6,015
Poland	3,672	4,975
Kuwait	3,728	4,041

[1] One cubic meter equals 35.31 cubic feet. Source: 1971 UN Statistical Yearbook.

1970's. By 1995, sales are expected to increase to 45,083 trillion Btu—nearly triple the figure for 1972. AGA projections also indicated that the total number of customers will be more than 67 million by 1995.

Gas Supply. According to the AGA, proved reserves of gas totaled 278.8 trillion cubic feet (tfc) at the end of 1971, compared with 290.7 tfc a year earlier. The record reserve figure was set in 1967. At 1971 consumption rates, the proved reserves of gas amount to about 13 years' supply, and potential reserves amount to an additional 50 years' supply. Meanwhile, wildcat drilling has declined steadily, dropping by 49% between 1956 and 1971.

Steps to bring new supplies of gas to market included government-approved price hikes for gas sold in interstate commerce and the first large-scale importation of liquefied natural gas from overseas.

Gas Distribution Network. The vast underground network of pipelines and distribution mains for transporting gas from wells to customers was increased by about 19,000 miles in 1972, raising the total to 954,000 miles. The AGA expects a growth to nearly 2 million miles by 1995.

SANDRA SALMANS, *"Newsweek" Magazine*

Petroleum

In 1972 the much-talked-about energy crisis was brought home to the general public, not so much as signifying a fuel shortage but more as the end of the age of cheap energy. This was one result of the long-term price and ownership agreements made between the large Middle East crude-producing countries and the major international oil companies. Another result was an increase of oil from the North Sea, North Africa, and the Far East.

Production. Crude oil was produced worldwide at a rate of 49,921,000 barrels per day (b/d) in 1972, or 3.6% above 1971. This moderate increase reflected an actual 0.5% decline in the United States, to 9,481,000 b/d, and a 1.2% decrease for the entire Western Hemisphere. There also was an unusually small gain, about 8%, in the Middle East, although that region remained the world's largest supplier, with 36% of the 1972 world total.

Exploration. Drilling showed a strong 7% increase in 1972, the result of the rising need for more new oil fields. The non-Communist world had an estimated 36,507 wells, compared with 34,083 in 1971. Gains were recorded throughout the world, with the United States increasing 6.8% to 28,015 wells, and western Europe going up 8.3%.

WORLD CRUDE OIL PRODUCTION

(Thousands of barrels daily)

	1969[1]	1970[1]	1971[2]	1972[2]
North America				
Canada	1,124.0	1,200.0	1,322.6	1,490.4
Mexico	410.6	428.8	427.1	444.2
United States	9,238.0	9,637.0	9,529.0	9,481.3
Totals	10,772.6	11,265.8	11,278.7	11,415.9
South America and West Indies				
Argentina	356.4	393.0	423.2	427.0
Bolivia	40.4	24.0	36.2	41.7
Brazil	156.2	164.0	174.3	166.6
Chile	36.7	34.0	35.3	32.9
Colombia	211.3	222.0	228.1	219.8
Ecuador	4.4	4.0	4.4	32.5
Peru	73.0	72.0	61.9	67.5
Trinidad and Tobago	157.3	140.0	129.9	143.9
Venezuela	3,594.1	3,703.0	3,578.8	3,207.3
Totals[3]	4,629.8	4,761.0	4,672.1	4,339.2
Totals, Western Hemisphere	15,402.4	16,026.8	15,950.8	15,755.1
Europe (excluding USSR and other Communist countries)				
Austria	51.3	52.0	46.8	46.1
Denmark	0	0	0	2.7
France	50.2	47.0	37.4	31.2
Germany, West	158.2	146.2	148.4	139.1
Italy	29.0	28.1	25.8	20.8
Netherlands	37.8	36.0	32.1	31.2
Norway	0	0	4.3	35.1
Spain	8.5	3.0	2.5	2.5
United Kingdom	1.6	1.8	2.7	1.5
Yugoslavia	52.9	55.0	60.9	59.0
Totals	389.5	369.1	360.9	369.2
USSR and other Communist countries				
Albania	26.0	28.0	27.0	30.0
Bulgaria	7.2	7.0	6.1	5.6
Czechoslovakia	3.7	4.0	4.0	4.0
Germany, East	5.8	6.0	2.0	1.2
Hungary	36.7	39.0	41.0	40.0
Poland	11.2	12.0	8.0	8.0
Rumania	268.7	270.0	280.0	280.0
USSR	6,545.4	7,060.0	7,521.0	7,812.0
Totals[4]	6,904.7	7,426.0	7,889.1	8,180.8

	1969[1]	1970[1]	1971[2]	1972[2]
Africa				
Algeria	959.1	1,022.0	793.5	1,061.8
Angola	10.1	14.0	14.2	11.7
Cabinda	37.3	89.0	94.3	123.0
Gabon[5]	99.9	108.8	114.6	124.3
Libya	3,109.1	3,318.0	2,760.8	2,228.4
Morocco	1.2	0.9	0.5	0.5
Nigeria	541.7	1,085.0	1,523.5	1,794.9
Tunisia	77.0	88.3	87.3	81.4
Totals	4,835.4	5,726.0	5,388.7	5,426.0
Middle East				
Abu Dhabi[6]	611.5	694.0	356.8	417.4
Bahrain	76.1	77.0	75.3	71.8
Dubai[6]	0	85.8	125.5	132.0
Iran	3,374.9	3,829.0	4,513.6	4,879.6
Iraq	1,512.3	1,536.0	1,691.7	1,396.2
Israel	52.5	70.0	130.7	120.0
Kuwait	2,575.5	2,735.0	2,894.5	2,987.3
Murban[6]	0	0	542.5	605.3
Neutral Zone	452.0	503.0	550.3	538.3
Oman	327.0	332.0	290.4	282.5
Qatar	355.5	363.0	428.5	459.5
Saudi Arabia	3,216.6	3,799.0	4,455.6	5,529.0
Syria	62.0	83.0	110.0	118.3
Turkey	70.2	69.0	65.0	65.0
United Arab Republic	242.0	326.7	293.9	220.0
Totals	12,928.1	14,502.5	16,524.3	17,822.2
Far East and Oceania				
Australia	43.3	178.0	309.3	307.8
Brunei & Sarawak	136.4	160.0	192.4	266.7
Burma	18.0	18.0	19.0	18.0
Communist China	220.0	420.0	510.0	580.0
India	134.0	135.0	143.9	151.1
Indonesia	742.4	853.6	892.3	1,027.2
Japan	15.1	16.0	16.4	14.9
Pakistan	7.6	9.2	8.2	9.0
Taiwan	0	0.5	0.5	2.0
Totals	1,316.7	1,790.3	2,092.0	2,367.7
Totals, Eastern Hemisphere	26,374.4	29,813.9	32,255.0	34,165.9
World totals	41,776.8	45,840.7	48,205.8	49,921.0

[1] Final. [2] Preliminary (Sources: U.S. Bureau of Mines and World Petroleum). [3] Cuba omitted from totals, as current reports indicate production is almost nil. [4] Because of the several sources of data for the USSR and its satellites, figures given for individual countries do not always add up to total shown for the group. [5] Congo (Brazzaville) is included with Gabon. [6] Abu Dhabi includes Dubai until 1970 and Murban until 1971.

Reserves. Estimates of proved crude oil reserves in the world at the end of 1971 amounted to 569.5 billion barrels, 4.8% above the level at the end of 1970. The Middle East alone accounted for 346.8 billion barrels, or 61%, and the United States for 38 billion barrels, or 6.7%. Natural gas showed an even bigger growth, 8.1%, to a 1971 total of 1,755 trillion cubic feet (tcf), of which the Soviet Union had 636 tcf (36%) and the United States 279 tcf (16%).

Consumption. The strong growth in demand for crude oil and liquid hydrocarbons derived from natural gas continued in 1972. Data on the non-Communist world showed an average of 44.7 million b/d, or 6.6% above 1971. The largest single consuming nation, the United States, reached 16 million b/d, or 4.5% above the year before.

Transportation. As of the middle of 1972, there were 3,336 oil tankers of 10,000 deadweight tons (dwt) or greater in operation, 132 more ships than in mid-1971. They totaled 179,180,119 dwt, 13.2% higher than a year earlier. In 1972 there were 572 tankers being built, totaling 95,945,900 dwt.

Refining. World total crude distillation capacity was 56,227,400 b/d in mid-1972, an 8.3% gain over 1971. The United States, with 13,087,000 b/d, had 23.2% of the total. The United States, Japan, Italy, France, West Germany, and Britain—each with 2 million b/d or more—together accounted for 60% of the non-Communist world total capacity.

Refineries continued to favor the use of hydrogenation processes because they are effective in reducing atmospheric pollution. The 1972 increase in hydrogen processing capacity was 11.7%, reaching a worldwide rate of 13,823,000 b/d. The other two important processes used in making finished petroleum products are catalytic cracking, which rose 4.8% to 7,288,000 b/d, and catalytic reforming, which rose 7.3% to 6,759,000 b/d.

Petrochemicals. There were 1,637 petrochemical plants in operation in the non-Communist world in 1972, 12.6% more than in 1971. Major sales products of these materials included synthetic textiles, synthetic rubbers, plastics, and fertilizers.

WILLIAM C. UHL
Editorial Director, "World Petroleum"

Coal

During 1971 the United States burned more than 550 million tons of bituminous coal and lignite, which represented 17.6% of the nation's total energy consumption. Electric utilities used more than 326 million tons to generate 44.3% of the nation's electricity. The steel industry took 88 million tons, other industries used 11 million tons, and exports accounted for 56 million tons.

Production of bituminous coal and lignite for 1972 was an estimated 590 million tons, up nearly 7% from 1971 output. Production from underground mines in 1971 was down 63 million tons from 1970, but the output from strip mines increased by 15 million tons. From January through October 1972 production from strip and underground mines totaled more than 491 million tons, up 4.6% from 1971.

Cleaner-Burning Fuel. Research programs emphasized reducing pollutants that are produced when coal is burned. As part of these efforts, a pilot plant was being built in Tacoma, Wash., in 1972. This plant is designed to produce an ash-free, low-sulfur fuel that is refined from all grades of coal.

Coal Gasification. Other research efforts were directed at the transformation of coal to gas so that the product can be used interchangeably with natural gas. Gas from coal could be transported through the nation's existing pipeline network or burned at the conversion site. Production of clean gas from coal appeared promising, and it received impetus through government and industry research funding. A pilot plant in Rapid City, S. Dak., and another in Chicago were in operation in 1972, and ground for a third pilot plant was broken in Homer City, Pa. Commercially usable quantities of gas from coal are expected by the early 1980's.

BETSY KRAFT, *National Coal Association*

COAL GASIFICATION PLANT in Chicago is being tested by the Institute of Gas Technology. Plant converts abundant bituminous coal into clean-energy gas.

INSTITUTE OF GAS TECHNOLOGY

U. S. BITUMINOUS COAL AND LIGNITE PRODUCTION, 1971

State	Output (thousands of short tons)
Alabama	17,945
Colorado	5,337
Illinois	58,402
Indiana	21,396
Kentucky	119,389
Missouri	4,036
Montana	7,064
New Mexico	8,175
North Dakota	6,075[1]
Ohio	51,431
Oklahoma	2,234
Pennsylvania	72,835
Tennessee	9,271
Utah	4,626
Virginia	30,628
West Virginia	118,258
Wyoming	8,052
Other	7,038
Total	552,192

[1] Lignite. (Source: U. S. Bureau of Mines.)

One day's garbage from New York City, piled at a Staten Island landfill, made a striking display of the size of the environmental problem of waste disposal. The pile weighed 30,000 tons, yet represented only solid wastes.

environment

In 1972 the nations of the world, spurred in recent years by alarms of damage to the natural conditions that sustain life on earth, began the practical task of organizing protective measures. Acting on the recommendations of a unique Conference on the Human Environment in Stockholm in June, the UN General Assembly voted in December to establish a new Environment Secretariat with a five-year $100 million Environmental Fund and a 109-point action plan. In a surprise move Nairobi, Kenya, was designated as the site for the Environment Secretariat.

There were also a number of important bilateral and regional governmental agreements and projects during the year, including a landmark agreement between the United States and Canada to protect the Great Lakes and an agreement between the United States and the Soviet Union for joint action projects and research.

Contrary to some forecasts that environmental concerns would prove to be a fad, a worldwide debate was stirred by the "Limits to Growth" report, based on computerized studies at the Massachusetts Institute of Technology. The report, sponsored by the Club of Rome, a private group of businessmen, scientists, and economists, asserted that if present trends continued in the growth of population, in-

dustrialization, and pollution of the oceans and atmosphere and in the consumption of food and other resources, then a sudden and uncontrollable collapse would occur within the next century—in population growth because it could no longer be sustained in the degraded environment and in industrialization because of resource depletion.

UN CONFERENCE ON THE HUMAN ENVIRONMENT

The very convening of the United Nations Conference on the Human Environment in Stockholm, June 5–13, was hailed in advance as a major accomplishment in environmental protection. The 113 government delegations at the Conference produced a surprisingly meaningful 26-point Declaration on the Human Environment, a 109-point action plan, and a proposal for new UN administrative machinery. The UN General Assembly, which met in October, was not called on to adopt either the Stockholm Declaration or the action plan but only to acknowledge them and to pass them along to projected permanent environmental institutions.

New Environmental Institutions. Among the United Nations' projected institutions is a powerful Environment Secretariat headed by an executive director. (Maurice Strong of Canada, who had been secretary general of the Conference, was elected

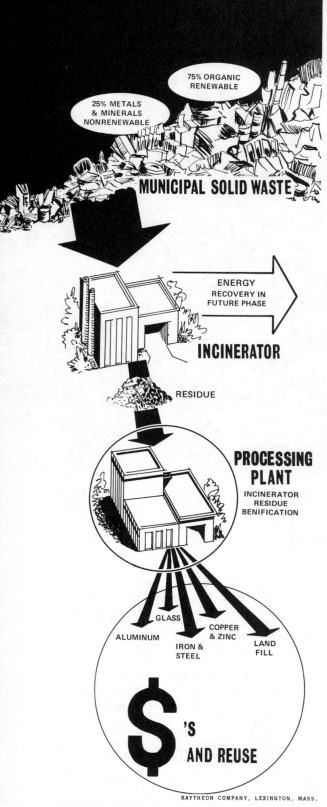

MUNICIPAL SOLID WASTE

75% ORGANIC RENEWABLE

25% METALS & MINERALS NONRENEWABLE

ENERGY RECOVERY IN FUTURE PHASE

INCINERATOR

RESIDUE

PROCESSING PLANT

INCINERATOR RESIDUE BENIFICATION

GLASS

ALUMINUM

COPPER & ZINC

IRON & STEEL

LAND FILL

$'s AND REUSE

RAYTHEON COMPANY, LEXINGTON, MASS.

WASTE RECOVERY PLANT at Lowell, Mass., will be the nation's first full-scale plant to recover reuseable metals and minerals from solid waste. At the initial operating level of 65,000 tons per year, the plant will subject incinerator residue to screening, size reduction, magnetic separation, flotation, and other processes to separate it into salable fractions of various metals, glass, and sand, with only about a 5% remainder of unreclaimed material for landfill.

by the General Assembly on the nomination of the secretary general). The Secretariat will coordinate and devise international environmental activities under the policy supervision of an international Governing Council, which will report to the General Assembly through the Economic and Social Council. The Stockholm Conference had recommended a 54-nation Governing Council but this was expanded to 58 nations.

An Environmental Coordinating Board was also established. It includes representatives of other UN agencies, but has the Environment Secretariat's executive director as chairman, in order to avoid conflict, duplication, and overlap with existing UN programs.

Declaration of Stockholm. Among the Declaration's proclamations was one that: "Governments have the right to exploit their own resources and develop their own environment policies but they also have the responsibility to ensure that activities within their national jurisdiction do not cause damage to the environments of other countries or areas." This was widely regarded as a possible first step toward ultimate international law that, as one expert put it, whereas unknowing degradation of a neighbor's environment or pollution of "the common," such as the oceans, can have been excused in the past, because of ignorance, knowingly doing harm to a neighbor's environment or to "the common" is tantamount to aggression.

The Declaration also stated that: "National environmental policies should enhance and not adversely affect the development potential of poor nations or hamper the attainment of better living conditions for their citizens." This was seen as an assurance to the less developed countries—one of many similar assurances throughout the conference —that the poor countries' need for improved economic conditions would not be sacrificed to less pressing expenditures for environmental protection.

The significance of the text of the Declaration as something more than rhetoric was underscored when a vote on one of its principles was deferred at Stockholm. The principle in question concerned the nations' responsibility simply to inform one another of developments that might affect them. The deferment stemmed from a river-water dispute between Brazil and Argentina. The issue was not resolved until the New York session when Brazil introduced a resolution, with the co-sponsorship of 42 other states, including Argentina. The resolution said that (1) states in the development of their resources must not produce harmful effects outside their jurisdiction; (2) cooperation between states will be met if official and public knowledge is provided with technical data relating to the work to be carried out; and (3) this cooperation should not be construed as enabling a state to delay or impede a project.

Action Plan. Some of the most important recommendations in the 109-point action plan approved in October were: to establish an "earthwatch program"—a worldwide surveillance network including at least 110 monitoring stations, under the auspices of the World Meteorological Organization—to keep track of changes in the world's atmosphere that might lead to climate and weather modification; to establish safety limits for common air and water contaminants and to establish guidelines to help governments control significant sources of marine pollution; to adopt a global convention to restrict

SOVIET CARTOON view of water pollution shows much the same grim humor as cartoons in the United States and other industrial nations, a reflection on the worldwide scope of the problem. Man on shore asks, "What's the matter, can't they swim?" Woman on raft replies, "They're afraid of getting dirty."

SOVFOTO

ocean dumping and shore-generated wastes; to adopt an international registry of chemicals in the environment; to sponsor research and pilot projects in new techniques for housing construction, alternative methods of urban transportation, understanding the physical and mental stresses caused by living in cities, and training specialists for environmental and city planning and community development; to increase family planning assistance by the UN to countries that request it; to take steps to preserve the world's natural and cultural resources through international conventions; to preserve the world's wetlands and cultural and natural resources of international significance such as the Grand Canyon and the Pyramids by means of a World Heritage Trust; to preserve the world's genetic resources by setting up gene pools for endangered plant and animal species; and to take international action to protect wildlife, develop fisheries, improve forestry and agriculture, and insure the development of water, mineral, and energy resources without adverse environmental effects.

The action plan also advocated steps to expand education for a better environment through the issuance by the UN of periodic reports on the state of the world's environment, a computerized international referral service to facilitate exchange of information and know-how on tried and workable solutions to environmental problems, a new UN program of international environmental education to be directed mainly toward the average citizen, and the training of a corps of environmental specialists and technicians by international agencies.

Although the Soviet Union and some of its Communist satellite governments did not attend the Stockholm Conference, for reasons not related to the objectives of the conference, Moscow had played a major role in the preparatory work, and the Soviet Union did not stand in the way of the adoption of the Conference's central recommendations when they came before the General Assembly. Similarly Communist China, which had been rebuffed on certain issues at the Conference, did not oppose the majority at Stockholm or in the Assembly.

SETBACK ON WHALING AGREEMENT

At Stockholm, the UN Conference voted 53–0 to recommend a 10-year moratorium on commercial whaling. This proved a short-lived victory for conservationists, however. When the conference recommendation came before the 14-member International Whaling Commission in London two weeks later, it was badly defeated. Only the United States, Mexico, Britain, and Argentina voted for the ban; opposed were Iceland, Japan, Norway, Panama, South Africa, and the Soviet Union, while Australia, Canada, Denmark, and France abstained. The Japanese argued that the United States, Norway, and other nations curtailed whaling only when it became unprofitable, whereas for Japan it not only was lucrative but necessary. High-protein whale meat accounts for 10% of all meat eaten in Japan.

OTHER INTERNATIONAL AGREEMENTS AND MEETINGS

Convention on the Dumping of Wastes at Sea. On November 13, in a follow-up to the Stockholm Conference, 91 governments, including all of the world's major maritime nations, agreed on a global convention to prohibit the dumping at sea of high-level radioactive waste, biological and chemical warfare agents, crude oil, and certain pesticides and durable plastics, but to allow the discharge, with special permits, of relatively less harmful substances such as arsenic, lead, copper, scrap metal, and fluorides.

The Convention was hailed by Russell Train, chairman of President Nixon's Council on Environmental Quality, who headed the U.S. delegation. The Convention was to take effect as soon as ratified by the legislatures of 15 signatory countries. However, an effort to establish a so-called "pollution zone" of territorial coasts was shelved.

U.S.–Canada Great Lakes Agreement. On April 15, President Nixon and Premier Trudeau signed in Ottawa the U.S.-Canadian Great Lakes Water Quality Agreement, establishing as mutual ob-

jectives the so-called "five freedoms"—freedom from toxic substances; freedom from nutrients in quantities that stimulate growth of unsightly weeds and algae (accelerated eutrophication); freedom from oil, floating debris, scum, and other floating materials; freedom from material producing odor, color, or other nuisance conditions; and freedom from objectionable sludge deposits.

The agreement prescribed maximum ambient concentrations for specific pollutants and maximum loadings for phosphorus. U. S. and Canadian water quality standards must conform to these objectives, which in some cases are stricter than existing U. S. federal and state water quality standards.

The International Joint Commission, originally established in a 1909 treaty, was charged with monitoring progress in fulfilling goals. The United States was made responsible for funds to construct municipal waste treatment plants and to help finance water pollution control programs.

U. S.–Soviet Agreement. On May 23, President Nixon and USSR President Podgorny signed in Moscow a five-year U. S.–Soviet agreement to work together in 11 problem areas ranging from air and water pollution and urbanization to the influence of environmental change on climate, earthquake prediction, and arctic and subarctic ecological systems. The agreement, going far beyond past U. S.–Soviet exchange agreements, called for explicit joint action programs.

REPORTS FROM AROUND THE WORLD

Throughout the world, in national and regional programs, the emphasis shifted from warnings and assessments to action plans and legislation.

United States. The United States clearly ranked among the world's leading environmentally minded countries. Environmental consciousness was demonstrated not the least by the November decision of the voters of Colorado to forego the 1976 Winter Olympics on grounds not only of economy but fear of untoward environmental impact. Earlier the same fear had led Colorado citizens to reject a $200 million bond authorization to expand the state's water system.

Congressional Actions and Elections. In Congress, 10 major environmental laws were enacted, including a water pollution control measure passed over President Nixon's economy-grounded veto. This law authorized $24.6 billion over three years to clean up lakes and rivers and of which the federal government would provide $18 billion to help cities build sewage-treatment plants. The goal is "no discharge" by 1985. Later, President Nixon ordered that this sum be reduced substantially.

A Product Safety Act, Marine Protection Research and Sanctuaries Act, and Federal Environmental Pesticide Control Act were among the laws passed. However, five major measures, including a bill to ban strip mining on certain coal slopes and a variety of multiple-purpose bills on land use died in committees.

Environmental protection proved to be an election factor in some state campaigns. The "environmentalist vote" resulted in state laws calling for an expenditure of $1.5 billion for various environmental improvements.

EPA Actions. The Environmental Protection Agency (EPA), under William D. Ruckelshaus, proved tough. In May, the EPA administrator denied a one-year extension of the legal requirement for 1975 automobile emission standards, requested by five automobile manufacturers. In June the EPA banned—as of December 31—the general use of DDT, the controversial pesticide, concluding that its benefits to agriculture were outweighed by its potential danger. The EPA order, facing court adjudication, did not affect possible public health use of DDT, exports of DDT, nor its use for three minor crops. However, if the ban is upheld in the courts, the general agricultural use of DDT in the United States will soon end.

Western Europe. On May 26 the Council of the Organization for Economic Cooperation and Development (OECD) adopted a set of environmental principles that were specially significant because they included a "polluter pays" approach to financing environmental controls and for minimizing handicaps to trade that may result from environmental protection action. The Council recognized that the "polluter pays" principle might not be enforceable in the transitional stage, and it noted that while harmonization of anti-pollution protection standards was desirable there might be good reasons, based on geography and other natural conditions, for differences in standards.

As a means of coping with automobile traffic, no less than 35 European cities were reported planning underground railways, 28 German cities introduced auto-free zones, and Florence, Italy, banned automobiles from a 40-block area. The French government helped finance development of five kinds of electric vehicles for urban use—although it, along with Communist China, continued to defy world appeals for ending nuclear testing in the environment. In Germany, the constitution was changed to enable the setting of federal standards for solid waste disposal, with severe penalties for those who breached them.

The USSR and Eastern Europe. In March the Soviet Union announced a $1 billion program for 421 new industrial waste treatment plants and stricter enforcement of pollution control measures in the Volga and Ural river valleys. The program, the biggest thus far made public in the Soviet Union, reflected the government's increasing loss of self-consciousness over the issue. It also became known that delays had been encountered in efforts to install a more effective water filtration system at Lake Baikal, polluted by the effluents of paper mills and other industries on the lake shores.

COMECON, the East European equivalent of the OECD, devoted several sessions during the year to research and survey programs as a basis of subsequent cooperative environmental action. Yugoslavia and Rumania underscored their interest in environmental problems by attending the Stockholm Conference, despite the Soviet boycott.

In April the Polish government set up a special Ministry for Regional Planning and Environmental Protection and gave it a $773 million budget over five years. Poland also banned the use of DDT and announced a $2 million water pollution control program sponsored by the EPA and financed by American funds held in Poland.

China, Japan, and the Far East. Communist China's active participation in the Stockholm Conference drew attention to its domestic environmental efforts. Visitors noticed that Chinese cities are remarkably clean and reported seeing throughout the country posters with ideographs representing "Three

(Continued on page 280)

Emblem of UN Conference on Human Environment.

STOCKHOLM CONFERENCE

First UN Parley on the Environment, an 'Ecological Happening,' Adopts an Ambitious Program to Save the Earth

The first United Nations Conference on the Human Environment was held in Stockholm on June 5–16, 1972. Some 1,200 delegates representing 113 countries took part in the official attempt to come up with recommendations for a global effort to correct ecological abuses and enhance the quality of life on earth. Several thousand environment activists, scientists, academicians, businessmen, and "ecofreaks," representing organizations or themselves, were also present.

In unseasonably warm, sunny weather the atmosphere was one of highjinks as well as high purpose. Leading officials, besides participating in solemn deliberations, were photographed riding bicycles as a gesture against auto pollution, although many more jammed Stockholm's streets with fleets of long, black limousines. Antiwar protestors sought to block traffic but were quickly removed by reinforced police units. Some hippies doffed their clothes in Kings Park. Nobody seemed to mind or notice. There were free concerts and stage plays dedicated to "the environment." And there were many nongovernmental seminars, discussions, and lectures, along with the protests and put-ons, music and manifestos.

Some called it "Woodstockholm," an "ecological happening." But when the conference was over, the consensus was that it had been an outstanding success, whether or not the UN General Assembly ultimately adopts its recommendations.

An "Action Program." The purpose, as set forth in a 1968 resolution of the General Assembly, had been to focus the attention of governments and public opinion on "the importance of urgency" of the problem of environmental degradation and to determine what could be done through international cooperation. However, by the time the delegates convened in the modernistic Folkets Hus, the preparations themselves, including detailed national reports, had served to educate governments and alert public opinion. With the world's attention already captured, Maurice Strong, the Canadian secretary general of the Conference, insisted upon an "action program." The delegates found before them several hundred proposals and only two weeks to deal with them. "We have come together today to affirm our common responsibility for the environmental problems of an earth whose vulnerability we all share," Strong admonished the delegates. "The task is enormous. But its very size must not daunt us."

To make sure that the work was completed, committee meetings were scheduled concurrently with the plenary debate. Often, as in any parliament, the plenary hall was nearly empty as speakers harangued the microphones for the record and the press. But scattered throughout the city, committees hammered out agreements in lengthy sessions that interfered with cocktail receptions and forced dinner cancellations.

Politics Enter In. Not surprisingly, politics of all kinds intruded on the deliberations, since this was, after all, a meeting of delegates from various governments. The Soviet Union, which was among the leaders in preparing for the Conference, boycotted it because East Germany was not eligible for voting rights. Under the rules only members of the United Nations or its agencies could vote. West Germany, as a member of The World Health Organization, was eligible. Communist China, a new UN member, ostentatiously sought to establish leadership with the "third world" but ran into trouble when it insisted, along with France, on its right to pollute the atmosphere with nuclear tests. Olaf Palme, the Swedish prime minister, irritated the U. S. delegation by attacking the Vietnam War.

Prominent Speakers. A number of world leaders addressed the conference and its auxiliary programs, including Indira Gandhi of India and Abba Eban of Israel. Shirley Temple Black of the United States gave a spirited talk in the Hall and then joined in a "women's lib" protest against the male-dominated proceedings. René Dubos, Barbara Ward, Margaret Mead, Thor Heyerdahl, and Gunnar Myrdal spoke for the protection of "Only One Earth," the conference slogan.

Recommendations. The delegates adopted a declaration with a carefully enumerated 7-point introduction and 26 high sounding principles, albeit couched in some of the most wooden language ever employed to inspire anyone, let alone all mankind. An "action plan" with 109 recommendations was approved, covering virtually every known environmental ailment, as well as resolutions for a new UN Environment Secretariat, operating under a 54-member governing council and responsible for a voluntarily subscribed environmental fund. Proposals to celebrate every June 5 as World Environment Day and to hold a second conference, presumably in four years, were also adopted.

While the language was uninspired, the commitments—especially one that national governments were responsible for environmental damage they knowingly caused other countries or "the common" (such as the atmosphere and the oceans)—were hearteningly ambitious. While it remained for the General Assembly to act on the recommendations, the Stockholm Conference was an event of historic proportions.

JACK RAYMOND

SMOG hangs over a freeway near downtown Los Angeles during the evening rush hour. Despite pioneering efforts in pollution control, the city is still beset by environmental problems.

(Continued from page 278)
Wastes, Three Benefits." These alluded to land, air, and water and were part of a nationwide exhortation to recycle wastes. The *Peking Review* reported in April that a complex of factories in Shanghai had recovered more than 20 tons of raw materials through sorting solid wastes and more than 1.4 million tons of chemicals from liquid wastes.

The Japanese courts proved tough in behalf of environmental protection, ruling that plaintiffs need submit only statistical medical evidence that their ailments are caused by air pollution, and that the burden of proof rests on the polluter. Japanese courts awarded damages to plaintiffs suffering from asthma and other respiratory diseases.

NONGOVERNMENTAL ACTIVITIES

In support of the UN's environmental program the International Institute for Environmental Affairs conducted two briefings by Canada's Maurice Strong for world business leaders, one in cooperation with the International Chamber of Commerce (ICC) in Paris in February, and a second in cooperation with the Conference Board in New York in May. Subsequently the ICC resolved to establish a formal link with whatever environmental machinery the UN created, and in November announced plans for establishment of an international industrial environment center.

Many nongovernmental organizations under the leadership of Barbara Ward (Lady Jackson) and Margaret Mead formulated an initial program to establish a relationship between their organizations and the UN Secretariat.

JACK RAYMOND, *President*
International Institute for Environmental Affairs

EQUATORIAL GUINEA

The most dramatic event in Equatorial Guinea's foreign affairs in 1972 was its appeal to the United Nations Security Council to investigate a charge that the country's islands near Gabon had been invaded. On the domestic front, President Francisco Macias Nguema, who had ruled the country since its independence in 1968, was appointed life president by the ruling National Union party on July 14.

Invasion Charge. On September 12, Equatorial Guinea's permanent representative to the United Nations, Primo José Escono Mica, charged that neighboring Gabon had invaded his country's coastal islands. The charge was made in a letter from Escono Mica to the president of the UN Security Council. In his letter, Escono Mica enclosed a cablegram from his country's foreign minister charging that Gabon, "after extending its territorial waters to 170 miles (270 km) on August 23, invaded all of the islands of Equatorial Guinea: Elobey Grande, Elobey Chico, Corisco, and the islands adjacent to its province of Río Muni."

Gabon is located to the south and east of Equatorial Guinea's mainland district of Río Muni. Relations between the two nations had been normal, in spite of the fact that Gabon had become a haven for Spanish nationals forced to leave Equatorial Guinea after that country achieved independence from Spain in October 1968.

The Organization of African Unity established a four-nation commission to determine whether Gabon or Equatorial Guinea owns two unhabited islands in the Bay of Corisco. See also GABON.

FRANKLIN PARKER, *West Virginia University*

—— EQUATORIAL GUINEA • Information Highlights ——

Official Name: Republic of Equatorial Guinea.
Area: 10,831 square miles (28,051 sq km).
Population (1972 est.): 300,000. *Density,* 26 per square mile (10 per sq km). *Annual rate of increase,* 1.4%.
Chief City (1960 census): Santa Isabel, the capital, 37,237.
Government: *Head of state,* Francisco Macias Nguema, president (took office Oct. 1968). *Head of government,* Francisco Macias Nguema. *Legislature* (unicameral)—National Assembly, 35 members.
Languages: Spanish (official), various African languages.
Education: *Expenditure* (1964), 2.4% of total public expenditure. *School enrollment* (1966)—primary, 38,395; secondary, 2,473; technical/vocational, 130.
Monetary Unit: Guinea peseta (63.56 = U. S.$1, July 1972).
Gross National Product (1970 est.): $76,000,000.
Major Agricultural Products: Cacao, coffee, bananas, forest products, palm oil.

ETHIOPIA

In 1972, a large number of international loans were secured by Ethiopia for economic and health resource development. Violent student rioting continued throughout the country. Emperor Haile Selassie successfully mediated a conclusion to the civil war in Sudan.

Foreign Assistance. In June the Ethiopian government announced that the United States Agency for International Development (AID) would provide a $34.5 million loan to finance agricultural development activities during 1972 and 1973. The loan is to be repaid over 40 years at 3% interest. At the same time AID announced it would loan $21.3 million to aid in the construction and asphalting of three primary roads in Ethiopia. One hundred and thirty-five Peace Corps volunteers from the United States went to Ethiopia in 1972 to aid in education, health, and agricultural development.

As part of a 1971 economic and technical assistance agreement, the People's Republic of China sent 19 experts to Ethiopia to survey the nation's interior for the installation of electric power facilities and to assist in feasibility studies for the development of small-scale industries. China also agreed to the annual purchase of large amounts of Ethiopian coffee. In July, civil aviation agreements were signed which would eventually establish air routes between Addis Ababa and China.

The International Development Association (IDA) announced loans of $39.1 million for road construction, $24.9 million to establish 100 coffee cleaning centers, and $21.8 million to finance industrial and agricultural development projects. The Soviet Union agreed to finance the construction of and provide equipment and staff for a laboratory to study plant diseases. Britain loaned Ethiopia $1 million for the purchase of airline landing equipment.

Italy announced that it would provide financial assistance for an antitrachoma and communicable eye disease project in Ethiopia. An agreement for a cultural exchange program, which was to include teachers, scientific researchers, and theatrical groups was negotiated between Ethiopia and Nigeria.

Domestic Affairs. Disturbances involving high school and college students continued in 1972. After attempting to secure reforms in high schools and colleges, more than half of the 5,000 university students at Haile Selassie I University were expelled in February and a large number were temporarily arrested. Government troops stormed the main university campus in Addis Ababa, beating students and indiscriminately arresting them. A number of European lecturers at the university were asked to leave the country.

Fighting between the Muslim separatist Eritrean Liberation Movement and the Ethiopian government continued, although the number and intensity of the clashes declined in 1972. Calm continued to prevail in Gojam province, the scene of severe fighting between government troops and antitax rebels in 1968–70.

Three major land reform bills, before Parliament since 1968, remained tabled despite pressure from Haile Selassie. Designed to equalize landlord-tenant relations, the bills have unified traditional opposition forces. Most of Ethiopia's farming is governed by an almost feudal system, with farmers tilling small plots of land and being required to give as much as 50% of their crops to landowners. The system provides little incentive to farmers to increase production and arouses great resistance to change on the part of landowners.

Amid jubilation throughout the country, Haile Selassie celebrated his 80th birthday on July 23. Representatives and diplomats from numerous African countries attended the various ceremonies. Despite the apparent joy, many young people privately expressed the hope that the emperor would use the occasion to step down. Haile Selassie had been emperor for 42 years.

Communications Satellite Station. Ethiopia plans to begin construction of an earth-satellite station by 1974. The hook-up with the communications satellite system is expected to provide a more efficient means of contact with the outside world at considerably less cost than conventional communications systems.

International Relations. Through the good offices of Haile Selassie, an agreement ending 16 years of civil war in Sudan was reached in Addis Ababa on February 26. The war between the Anyanya rebels of the south and the Khartoum government had affected Ethiopia since the movement of refugees from Sudan had sparked numerous border disputes between the two countries.

The UN Security Council held a special session in Addis Ababa from Jan. 28 to Feb. 4, 1972. It was the Council's first session outside New York in 20 years and also the first ever in an African country. The opening meeting was addressed by the emperor, who welcomed the delegates to his country.

In 1972, Haile Selassie continued his world travels, visiting Sierra Leone, Sudan, Morocco, Yugoslavia, England, and France, and holding talks with government leaders. In Yugoslavia, the emperor was made an honorary citizen, the first time a head of state had been accorded that privilege by the Yugoslavs.

PETER SCHWAB
State University of New York at Purchase

--- **ETHIOPIA · Information Highlights** ---

Official Name: Empire of Ethiopia.
Area: 471,777 square miles (1,221,900 sq km).
Population (1972 est.): 26,200,000. *Density,* 52 per square mile (20 per sq km). *Annual rate of increase,* 2.1%.
Chief Cities (1968 census): Addis Ababa, the capital, 644,100; Asmara, 190,500.
Government: *Head of state,* Haile Selassie I, emperor (proclaimed emperor April 2, 1930). *Head of government,* Tsafi Tizaz Akilu Habte-wold, prime minister (took office April 17, 1961). *Legislature*—Parliament: Senate, 125 members (appointed); Chamber of Deputies, 250 members (elected).
Languages: Amharic (official), English.
Education: *School Enrollment* (1969)—primary, 590,445; secondary, 114,443; technical/vocational, 6,168; university/higher, 5,831.
Monetary Unit: Ethiopian dollar (2.303 E. dollars equal U. S. $1, July 1972).
Gross National Product (1971 est.): $1,810,000,000.
National Income per Person (1963): $44.
Economic Indexes: *Agricultural production* (1971), 158 (1952–56=100); *consumer price index* (1971), 143 (1963=100).
Manufacturing (major products): Textiles, cement, processed foods, leather.
Major Agricultural Products: Coffee, cotton, sugar, corn, millet and sorghum, oilseeds, pulses, cattle and sheep.
Major Minerals: Salt, gold.
Foreign Trade (1971): *Exports,* $126,000,000 (chief exports—coffee; oilseeds; hides and skins; cereals). *Imports,* $189,000,000 (chief imports, 1969—nonelectrical machinery; transport equipment; chemicals; electrical machinery, apparatus, appliances). *Chief trading partners* (1969), United States (took 42% of exports, supplied 10% of imports); West Germany (10%—14%); Italy (7%—15%); Japan (5%—11%).
Transportation: *Motor vehicles* (1970), 57,500 (automobiles, 47,200); *railroads* (1970), 675 miles (1,087 km); *major national airline,* Ethiopian Air Lines.
Communications: *Telephones* (1971), 45,937; *television stations* (1971), 1; *television sets* (1971), 6,500; *radios* (1970), 160,000; *newspapers* (1970), 8.

PUERTO RICANS in New York. (Above) Members of the militant "Young Lords" march in Puerto Rico Day parade. (Left) Children's art is exhibited in a Puerto Rican day-care center.

ETHNIC GROUPS

Two major issues in 1972 generally affected minority groups in the United States: the busing of children to achieve racial integration in schools, and the use of quota schemes specifying percentages of minority groups to be included in industry, the professions, and politics. Ethnic groups themselves were working on goals and timetables, as at the first National Black Political Convention and the first national convention of the Mexican-American party, La Raza Unida.

Ethnic problems in other parts of the world included the plight of Soviet Jews seeking to emigrate to Israel, the strife between Hutus and Tutsis in Burundi, and the expulsion of Asian nationals from Uganda.

Busing. In January, U. S. District Court Judge Robert Merhige, Jr., in the first court directive requiring the merger of city and suburban schools, ordered Virginia state authorities to consolidate the schools of Richmond with two suburban counties. In July, District Court Judge Stephen Roth ordered a similar busing effort to integrate Detroit with suburban schools. The latter was the most extensive such order issued by a federal court, involving 300,-000 out of 780,000 students in 54 school districts. However, neither order was to stand. Roth's decision was stayed by a higher court, and in June a circuit court of appeals overturned Merhige's decision in a five-to-one ruling.

These actions may have been influenced by a concurrent wave of opposition to busing. For example, the Florida electorate voted overwhelmingly in March to support a straw ballot proposing an antibusing constitutional amendment. Two days later President Nixon proposed legislation to deny courts the power to order busing of elementary school children to achieve racial integration. He said that the courts had created "confusion and contradiction in the law" and "anger, fear, and turmoil in local communities." The President called instead for more federal aid to poorer school districts.

Congressmen immediately attached to an education bill already in conference an amendment that would delay the implementation of court-ordered school busing until Jan. 1, 1974, or until all new judicial busing orders had been appealed. This bill

became law in June. Later the House passed another bill that barred court-ordered busing across school district boundaries and permitted the reconsideration of an estimated 100 court-settled desegregation suits—most of them in the South—to determine whether the court rulings conformed with the new legislation. However, the bill permitted the continued pairing of schools in which selected grades of white schools were combined with those of nearby black schools. Reactions among liberal politicians and minority-group leaders were mixed. Some charged that 18 years of desegregation progress had been betrayed, but most black leaders followed the trend emphasizing ethnic self-determination and supported the antibusing measures.

The constitutionality of such legislative action came into question almost immediately, but this did not affect most existing busing directives. Roth's decision was stayed because a higher court decided to hear arguments on the constitutionality and applicability of the busing moratorium law. In a split decision, a circuit court of appeals ordered the board of education in Memphis, Tenn., to begin busing some 12,000 students in January 1973. The court charged the board with failing to prove that its conduct was not responsible for the de facto segregation of Memphis schools, while the dissenting judges argued that the court had not observed the "constitutional rights of black and white children who do not want to be bused away from their neighborhood schools." In another court decision, the Atlanta, Ga., school system was ordered to devise an integration plan that would pay special attention to 20 unsegregated, all-white schools.

Quotas. Quota schemes for minority groups became an election issue in 1972, when the Democratic party adopted new reform rules requiring proportional representation of non-white minorities, women, and young people in its national convention. As a result of this measure, 14% of the delegates were black. In contrast, the Republican party strongly opposed adoption of any quota system, although its convention platform expressed a desire for the broad participation of all "minority and heritage groups" in party affairs. At the GOP convention, 4.1% of the delegates were black—an increase from 1.9% in 1968.

President Nixon led the attack against the Democratic quota scheme, calling it a "dangerous detour away from the traditional value of measuring a person on the basis of ability." The Democratic nominee, Senator McGovern, while promising jobs to blacks in his administration in proportion to their number in the population, denied that he had any intention of setting quotas. The President ordered all government agencies to expunge any trace of a strict quota system from federal programs. This led to a review of all programs potentially involving quotas, including the much-emulated "Philadelphia Plan" under which contractors in government construction projects were obliged to set goals for minority-group hiring. Since the president's order caused confusion for agencies that had been following exactly contrary orders, officials issued statements insisting that quotas should be ruled out but that "goals and timetables" should be set.

Whether in the form of "quotas" or of "goals and timetables," changes were brought about by pressure from various agencies. The Justice Department employed provisions of the Equal Employment Opportunity Act for the first time and filed suits against local government agencies in Montgomery, Ala., and Los Angeles, charging them with racial discrimination in hiring for public jobs. A district court judge issued an order that in effect required the Philadelphia police department to hire one black man for each white hired, for an indefinite time period. Pressure from the Office of Civil Rights of the Department of Health, Education, and Welfare obliged the City University of New York to agree to supply an accounting of the race and sex of all employees. Most significant of all was the announcement by American Telephone and Telegraph that it would hire and promote thousands of minority group members over a 15-month period. Criticism of the plan as inadequate led the Depart-

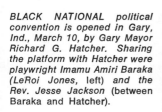

BLACK NATIONAL political convention is opened in Gary, Ind., March 10, by Gary Mayor Richard G. Hatcher. Sharing the platform with Hatcher were playwright Imamu Amiri Baraka (LeRoi Jones, left) *and the Rev. Jesse Jackson* (between Baraka and Hatcher).

ment of Labor's Office of Federal Contract Compliance to announce it would assume jurisdiction and probably require a more extensive agreement.

Ethnic Group Activities. National meetings of ethnic groups provided arenas for the struggles between those persons who desired integration and those who desired ethnic self-determination in order to maintain power potential as a bloc. As to means, there were those who sought to bring about change within the establishment, and those who would seek to overturn the establishment instead.

In March, the first National Black Political Convention brought all kinds of viewpoints together. More than 3,000 delegates from 43 states met in Gary, Ind., in order to shape "a concrete and specific means of gaining political power for black people." While the leaders called for black unity, the delegates disagreed over political cooperation with whites, school integration, and the presidential candidacy of Shirley Chisholm, eventually refusing to endorse any candidate in the presidential election. Nevertheless they joined hands in several important matters, establishing a permanent National Black Assembly empowered to "endorse candidates, run national voter education and registration drives, lobby for black issues, assess black progress," and to "be a chief brokerage operation for dealing with the white power political institutions." A 51-member steering committee was to select representatives from all regions and ideologies.

The National Black Political Agenda adopted at the close of the meeting called for a black development agency and a constitutional amendment guaranteeing black congressional representation in proportion to population. The agenda was ratified in May. Some black leaders, including those of the National Association for the Advancement of Colored People, condemned it as having a "separatist and nationalist intent."

Moderates predominated at the first national convention of La Raza Unida (The United People), the independent party of Chicanos (Mexican Americans), which was held in El Paso, Texas, in September. The convention voted not to endorse a presidential candidate and to concentrate on elections in Texas and other southwestern states. It ratified a platform calling for instruction in Spanish in all American schools, restoration of Spanish and Mexican land grant rights, free legal service for Mexican Americans, and national economic and social reforms. Because of "strong conditions" imposed on the subject matter of his speech, Chicano leader Cesar Chavez refused an invitation to attend and address the convention, and delegates on the last day refused to allow activists to address them.

The impact of these conventions in the November elections was unclear, since Chicano candidates and causes in general faired poorly, and the black vote of 89% against Nixon was buried under the presidential landslide. However, blacks exerted their greatest influence ever in other elections. Edward Brooke of Massachusetts defended his Senate seat, black representatives retained theirs, and three more black House members were added—two of them the first since Reconstruction days to be elected from the deep South. A black congressman became chairman of the House District Committee, and black voters showed great strength in many local elections.

Plight of Soviet Minorities. In August, a Soviet measure that awakened international interest was the imposition of a high emigration tax on educated and professional persons seeking to leave that country—a measure that primarily affected Jews who wished to go to Israel. Pressure by Jewish spokesmen in the United States stimulated a move in Congress to stop a proposed trade agreement between the United States and the USSR and probably resulted in the release of some Soviet Jews without the tax, but Jewish leaders in Moscow estimated that the number of persons still needing permits approached half a million. After staging a protest in Moscow, about 30 Jews were arrested. Some were released in a few days, some were kept longer, and two were believed to be interned in mental hospitals.

Russian is the native tongue of only about 60% of the Soviet population, and ethnic nationalism intensified in 1972. Early in the year, 17,000 Lithuanian Catholics signed a letter to the United Nations secretary general, complaining of religious repression. Two young Lithuanian men burned themselves alive in separate protests, and riots broke out in the wake of each death. A Soviet court sentenced several youths to prison for their part in the riots.

In the Ukraine, news of resistance was spread through underground publications and the public trial of some Ukrainian leaders.

African Developments. In Burundi, the strife between the ruling Tutsis and the rebelling Hutus, who make up 80% of the population, may have claimed more than 100,000 lives. In Uganda, President Idi Amin ordered all Asians out of his country, including 25,000 Ugandan citizens. (For accounts of these two major developments, see BURUNDI; UGANDA.)

In Rhodesia, soon after the arrival of the Pearce Commission—a British study group assigned to determine whether the accord reached with the Rhodesian government in 1971 was acceptable to the population as a whole—rioting broke out in three cities as blacks demonstrated their opposition to the agreement. A number of prominent Rhodesians were imprisoned in the wake of the riots.

More heartening was the Sudanese announcement that the poorly reported civil war between Negro tribesmen and their Muslim Arab leaders had ended, and that relief efforts to the stricken tribesmen were being undertaken.

Other Ethnic Clashes. An acute rice shortage precipitated riots and looting of Chinese-owned stores in Pnompenh, Cambodia, in September. The shortage resulted partly from Communist closure of most key roads, but also allegedly from speculation by merchants, most of whom were Chinese. In West Pakistan, tribal and regional groups pressed claims for increased autonomy, most notably Pathan groups said to be preparing for all-out hostilities and Sind groups that demanded national recognition of Sindi script. In India, the government resumed military operations against rebel Naga tribesmen for the first time since 1966, announcing that members of rebel organizations would be prosecuted.

In Europe in October, conflicts took place between Basque separatists and Spanish police in which several Basques and one policeman were killed, followed by the detention of about 100 Basques. In the Netherlands, where there had been an influx of 150,000 foreign laborers in recent years, violence erupted between Dutch youths and Turkish workers. Skirmishes continued for five days as gangs of youths smashed windows of Turkish-owned buildings.

ROBERT L. CANFIELD
Washington University, St. Louis

EUROPE

EEC delegates include (from left) Brandt of West Germany, Biesheuvel of the Netherlands, Pompidou of France, Heath of England, Andreotti of Italy.

Dramatic changes in the relationship of the great world powers—the Soviet Union, China, and the United States—produced important repercussions in Europe in 1972. An atmosphere of détente between the Communist and non-Communist blocs was established, which resulted in the signing of a general treaty normalizing relations between East and West Germany and the convening of a preparatory conference to lay the groundwork for an all-European security conference in 1973. In Western Europe, the relaxation of tension in the Cold War made political union appear not only unattainable but unnecessary; and, as a result, debate within the European Community and with nations seeking membership concentrated on the capacity of the Community to guarantee the economic well-being of its members.

Inflation and unemployment caused unrest in many countries of Western Europe, bringing about the fall of the Italian government and the imposition of a wage-price freeze in Britain. In Eastern Europe, by contrast, new leaders found it essential to seek popular support by re-allocating resources to make more consumer goods available.

The most dramatic and pervasive influence in 1972 in Europe was, however, the widespread eruption of terrorism—through individual skyjackings and bombings for political or monetary goals, in the conflict of Protestant and Catholic in Northern Ireland, and in the spillover to Europe of the violence of the Arab-Israeli conflict.

Europe in a Changed World System. Since World War II, Europe had been divided between a non-Communist bloc aligned with the United States and a Communist bloc led by the Soviet Union.

During the 1960's, Europe had ceased to be the center of confrontation in the Cold War; in 1972, there were signs that Europe might become the area where a genuine accommodation between the blocs could be achieved.

The key lay in Russia's re-evaluation of its policy toward Europe. In part, this changed attitude was due to desire for greater trade and technological assistance from the West, in part to the re-emergence of the People's Republic of China as an active participant in world politics, which was dramatized by the visit of President Nixon to Peking in February. Soviet rivalry with China, which remained an ideological battle for leadership of world communism and a national confrontation along disputed borders in Asia, had led the Soviet government to station 44 divisions, one fourth of its military strength, along the Chinese frontier.

It appeared imperative to the USSR, therefore, to prevent too close a rapprochement between the United States and China, and to reduce its own military commitment in Europe. This reduction would be possible only when relations between East and West Germany were normalized, when the United States agreed to mutual reduction of troops in Europe, and when the European states agreed to the summoning of a security conference.

For these reasons, the Soviet government invited President Nixon to visit Moscow after his visit to China, and joined with him, during his visit in May, in signing twin agreements on arms limitation—the one permitting each nation two antiballistic missile systems only and the other freezing the number of intercontinental ballistic missile launchers and sub-

marines. At the same time, an agreement on principles "took note of favorable developments in the relaxation of tensions in Europe," and called for multilateral consultations for preparation of a European security conference and talks on "reciprocal reduction of armed forces and armaments."

In December, ambassadors and mission heads of 32 European countries and the United States and Canada, met in Helsinki to prepare for a Conference on European Security and Cooperation, to be held in the spring of 1973. It was also agreed to hold a meeting of NATO and Warsaw Pact powers in January to discuss mutual reduction of forces.

Normalization of Relations Between East and West Germany. The détente between the two blocs in Europe was facilitated by the ratification in May by the West German parliament of non-aggression treaties with the Soviet Union and Poland and by the conclusion in November of a general treaty between East and West Germany.

The Social-Democratic chancellor of West Germany, Willy Brandt, had based his foreign policy since taking office in 1969 upon a search for better relations with the Communist states of Eastern Europe, an *Ostpolitik*. In the spring, this policy seemed threatened by the opposition of the Christian Democrats and by erosion of his own majority. Nevertheless, the Bundestag ratified the non-aggression treaties, which renounced the use of force for settlement of dispute among the signatories and recognized the cession of the formerly German Oder-Neisse territories to Poland. The Christian Democrats abstained, however.

In view of his shaky majority, Brandt called new elections for the fall to gain popular approval of his foreign policy. During the campaign, he climaxed this policy by signing a general treaty with the East German government on November 8. The two states were to establish formal relations through the exchange of officials with the duties, though not the rank, of ambassadors, and to cooperate in such areas as the economy, science and technology, transport, and public health. Two weeks later, a massive turnout of voters, 91.2% of the electorate, gave Brandt's coalition of Social Democrats and Free Democrats a majority of 48 seats. The general treaty was signed in East Berlin in December, and Brandt promised to negotiate a similar normalization of relations with Czechoslovakia.

Expansion of the European Community. The atmosphere of détente also affected the process of European integration. In the late 1940's and 1950's, many European statesmen had felt that the nation-state was an anachronism, which should be replaced by a supranational union of the West European states that could safeguard their interests in the Cold War. Political and military unification was regarded as the probable result of the economic unification undertaken by the Six (France, West Germany, Italy, Belgium, the Netherlands, Luxembourg) when they created the European Coal and Steel Community in 1952 and the European Economic Community (EEC, or Common Market) and Euratom in 1958. However, in the 1960's, attempts by the executives of these communities, known collectively since 1968 as the European Community, to gain independent financing and status were blocked by French President Charles de Gaulle; and, in the 1970's, the European Community had become primarily an economic union whose administrators were largely restricted to technical, bureaucratic

implementation of policies determined by the national governments. As a result, most West Europeans had come to regard the Community institutions with apathy, if not antipathy.

In 1972, all efforts to revive the process of political integration in Western Europe failed. The Dutch remained the primary proponents of increased political integration. But, in the summit meeting in Paris, in October, of the heads of government of the Six and of Britain, Norway, and Ireland, who were to become members in January 1973, French President Pompidou refused the Dutch demand that the European Parliament be given increased powers and that its members be elected directly and not by national parliaments. The Community Commission and the European Parliament were merely directed to prepare a report on possible political integration within three years. Suspicion of French desire for hegemony in Western Europe felt by the smaller countries compelled Pompidou to drop his proposal that the EEC create a political secretariat in Paris.

The summit conference did take several concrete steps to meet the economic demands of both new and old members. To keep fluctuations of currencies of the members within a 2.25% margin, a European monetary cooperation fund was to be created in April 1973, with resources of $1.4 billion that could be used to stabilize endangered currencies and thus prepare for eventual establishment of a common currency. Another fund was to be created by the end of 1973 to aid the underdeveloped regions of the Community, especially the south of Italy. Aid to developing nations was to be increased. And, perhaps most important of all in the short run, the finance ministers were to adopt short-term measures for dealing with inflation. They produced a non-binding program to reduce inflation from 6% to 4% annually by holding price increases to 4%, restricting growth in money supplies to equal the rate of growth of the gross national product plus 4%, and to hold down government spending.

Economic Difficulties and Political Repercussions in Western Europe. A report on October 13 by the European Commission showed that the anti-inflation program was overdue. Inflation in the Community was running at 6%, and was likely to grow worse, since wage increases of 13.3% in Belgium, 11.2% in France, and 9.2% in Germany had been granted. In Britain, the situation was worse. In February, after a strike of angry coal miners had brought on a nationwide electricity shortage and put one fifth of the labor force out of work, pay raises of 11%–24% were granted. During the summer, labor unions refused voluntary wage restraints, and on November 6, Prime Minister Heath was compelled to slap a 90-day freeze on wages and most prices, rents, and dividends, to be followed by more lasting controls.

In Germany, where inflation was running at 6.4% at election time, Brandt was fortunate that the popularity of his foreign policy and the poor campaign of the Christian Democrats diverted attention from economic issues. In Italy, which had achieved the highest growth rate in the Community during the first decade of operation of the Common Market, excessive wage demands brought on a major recession, in which unemployment reached 5%. The government of Christian Democrat Emilio Colombo was deserted by his Republican partners, who accused him of inflationary economic policies. In new elections, called in May a year ahead of schedule,

the wide economic discontent was seen in increased votes for the Communists and neo-Fascists. The formation of a more conservative government under Christian Democrat Giulio Andreotti gave little promise of restoration of political stability or economic prosperity.

The economic difficulties of the Common Market countries raised doubts about the viability of their economic union. The Norwegian government, like the governments of Britain, Ireland, and Denmark, had signed the Treaty of Accession in January. But after a heated referendum campaign, in which opponents emphasized the danger of competition within the Community to Norwegian farmers and fishermen, the Norwegians voted in October against membership in EEC by 53.9% to 46.1%

In Britain, fear of the impact of membership upon unionized labor and upon those living on fixed incomes was so great that the Conservative government refused to put the issue to the public in a referendum. The bill authorizing entry into EEC passed the House of Commons on July 13 by a vote of only 301 to 284. Fear of loss of their markets in Britain, if they did not join EEC when Britain did, persuaded the voters in Ireland and Denmark to give overwhelming endorsements to membership in EEC.

The Consumer in Eastern Europe. In the countries of the Communist bloc, newly established leaders found it essential for their own political survival to make important adjustments in the allocation of the state's economic resources to permit higher living standards for the workers. The pattern had been set as early as 1963–66 by Hungary's János Kádár, who had been put in power by the Russian armed forces after the 1956 uprising. Kádár promised material incentives through the New Economic Mechanism. By this program, which was still continuing in 1972, loans were provided for purchase of homes and even of vacation cabins, and for automobiles, and a wide range of consumer goods was produced.

Party Secretary Gustav Husák, who had been similarly installed in power in Czechoslovakia after Russian troops had overthrown the popular regime of Alexander Dubček in 1968, followed Kádár's example. With 60,000 Russian troops stationed in Czechoslovakia and the trials of Dubček liberals increasing in number, Husák used the $1 billion aid received from the USSR to increase the amount of consumer goods available, including luxuries imported from the Communist bloc and from the West. He revamped the economic plan to permit more construction of apartments and greater allocation of raw materials to consumer industries.

In Poland, where riots in 1970 had swept Edward Gierek to power in place of Władysław Gomułka, even greater concessions were needed to win back the support of the workers who were outraged at the inept economic policy and political repression of Gomułka. Gierek revised the five-year plan to provide more consumer goods, kept down prices, raised pensions, and permitted greater market freedom to the farmers. He promised that by 1975 average income would rise 18%, one million apartments built, and 600,000 automobiles made.

In East Germany as well, party secretary Erich Honecker, who had replaced the repressive Walter Ulbricht in May 1971, found it wise to seek some degree of popularity. He reversed course completely in relations with West Germany, showed goodwill in the negotiations that culminated in the general treaty, and made the major concession of recognizing the separate status of West Berlin. The five-year plan provided for construction of a half million new apartments and more consumer goods. Freedom of tourism for East Germans within the bloc was increased by conclusion of separate travel agreements with Poland and Czechoslovakia.

Even in the USSR, the leaders gave in to the "automobile mania," reallocating steel and rubber from defense industries to permit the new Italian-built factory at Togliatti (Tolyatti) to begin turning out 1,000 medium-sized cars a day. And to avoid food shortages brought on by disastrous harvests in 1971 and 1972, the Soviet government negotiated large contracts for purchase of cereals in the United States and Canada.

Minority Problems in East and West Europe. Over 140,000 Jews sought exit visas to emigrate from the Soviet Union to Israel. While 40,000 were expected to emigrate in 1972, severe difficulties were imposed by the government's decision in September to collect very large sums from emigrants as payment for the free education they had received. Ethnic Germans, on the other hand, were permitted to emigrate to West Germany from Poland as a result of the nonaggression treaty. Croatian separatists, who felt their province was discriminated against in favor of Serbia in the Yugoslav federation, were purged from the Communist party by Marshal Tito following widespread demonstrations in Zagreb in December 1971.

Civil strife mounted in Northern Ireland in 1972. In 1968, the half million Catholics had begun to demonstrate for equal rights in housing, education, and jobs with the one million Protestants. In 1970, the Irish Republican Army, especially its violent "Provisional" wing, had begun terrorist attacks on Protestants and British troops that were sent to enforce peace on both sides. On Jan. 30, 1972, British troops fired on an illegal Catholic demonstration in Londonderry, killing 13 people. Violence escalated, with both Protestant and Catholic groups forming well-armed civilian guerrilla groups. The British government suspended the Protestant-dominated government of Northern Ireland in March and imposed direct rule. In November, it declared that it would hold a referendum to permit the citizens of Northern Ireland to decide whether they wished to unite with Southern Ireland.

The Scourge of Terrorism. Terrorists struck in many parts of Europe with relative impunity. Ultra-left groups in Italy bombed offices of American companies. In West Germany a revolutionary left-wing gang was finally captured in June. But the most pervasive terrorist activity grew out of the Arab-Israeli conflict.

In September, Palestinian terrorists of the Black September group seized hostages from the Israeli team at the Olympic Games in Munich and killed them during a shootout with the German police. Letter bombs mailed to Israelis killed one diplomat in London and injured others; a month later an Arab propagandist was murdered in Rome. The ease of travel within Western Europe and especially the vulnerability of airliners to hijacking at Europe's overcrowded airports gave little hope that the increased security precautions would be effective.

F. ROY WILLIS
University of California, Davis

EYE DISEASES. See MEDICINE.

Fashion

Ease was the key fashion word in 1972. A universal fashion truth was hit upon by Ken Scott, a U. S. designer doing business in Italy, when he said, "Today, fashion is a constant reevaluation. It must be simple to last."

Suits worn with sweaters, shirt dresses for day and night, and coats wrapped like bathrobes, were typical of 1972 styles. Classics continued to be the important clothes, with accent on personality. The emphasis was once more where it belonged, on becomingness and comfort. Styles that looked new were usually revivals, staging a comeback because of some simple rule of appeal, wearability, or proportion.

Coats. The short coat, which had its first success in the rumble seats of the 1930's, was renamed the "topper" and came in style again in 1972 because its proportion was right for pants and it had the young "zingy" look that women love. The new silhouette was flaring. One important fur designer made "swingers" in fur because "they are a way of life," good for travel, sports, or evening.

Big coats, tent and kimono shapes with deep armholes, were liked because they are comfortable over suits. Fur-lined coats were popular because of their cozy warmth. Long fox boas returned because nothing is more flattering or has more dash. Cloth coats had big collars, which were worn turned up (as in the late 1940's and 1950's), making a glamorous frame for smoothly coiffed or turban-wrapped heads. The vogue for white coats harked back to the 1950's, when they were the standard summer vacation garment, even for little girls. Now they were used year-round. Again, the reason was becomingness and the go-with-everything concept.

The most prophetic coat silhouette was Yves St. Laurent's fit and flare shape, predicting tight-to-the-body lines. This coat had a fitted top moving into a wide swirl. Made in bright red wool, it was midcalf length. Emanuel Ungaro also came out with midcalf styles for fall, but most coat lengths were just below the knees.

Dresses. The dress with a tight top was sponsored by Marc Bohan and Pierre Cardin in Paris. The chemise had a revival, and America's Donald Brooks made it look different with deep pleated pockets, a big collar, and long sleeves. The smock chemise was another variation in flannel or jersey, satin or chiffon.

The typical shirt dress of 1972 was often in a print pattern, worn with a long sweater. Evening shirt dresses with pleated skirts also paired off with sweaters, some in brilliant stripes, with matching cardigans. One of the most successful knitted dresses had a wide ribbed midriff, recalling a best seller of the 1930's. The tiered dress made a pretty silhouette for evening. Hemlines and necklines that were outlined with roses were both frivolous and delightful.

Bare backs made sensational news in evening dresses, long daytime cottons, beach fashions, and tops for pants. The halter, revived from the 1940's, left the back naked, day or night. Some evening dresses were strapless as in the 1950's; other bared one shoulder or both. Strapless stretch bandeau-bras were worn for beach or evening, with skirts or pants.

THE BARE BACK was a 1972 fashion highlight. This camellia-accented taffeta is by Bill Blass.

Suits. Suit jackets were long or short, the long ones often fur collared. One of the most important suits made news by combining its long, pocketed, safari-style jacket of wool jersey with a crepe de chine pleated skirt. St. Laurent did it in navy blue with a red blouse. Short dinner suits came in satin, trimmed with fur. Waist-length suit jackets, liked by many women who are small or of average height, were introduced again by Adele Simpson. On the classic side, gray flannel was used for both skirts and pantsuits.

Pants. Two things brought the 1972 pants fashion picture into focus. The smock top caught the eye first. Whether on the streets of Paris, London, New York, or San Francisco or in any suburb, whether worn with jeans or sleek Italian knit pants, girls and young women paraded across two continents in sheer white lawn or voile peasant-type smocks. This innocent-looking little garment was part of the maternity-look craze that reached a farcical level when two New Yorkers invented the "Pregnancy Puff," a pillow to wear under dresses to make a woman look pregnant and guarantee her a seat on a bus.

The second aspect of pants fashion was Palazzo pants, which became popular for all ages in 1972. These wide-legged fashions, usually for evening wear, looked more like skirts than pants. Pleated, gathered like a dirndl, or bias-cut and flared, combined with jackets, halters, or strapless tops, they were made in satin, velvet, or crepe for winter and in cottons for resort wear. The shirt-jackets and pleats gave Palazzo pants a new look, but they were derived from the "hostess pajamas" of the 1940's.

International Trends. The Chinese influence on fashion was not as far-reaching as expected, possibly because trade agreements were in the early stages. A firm in Portland, Oreg., imported "the real thing" in Mao jackets and pants through Hong Kong, and flurries of American adaptations appeared here and there. The lovely classical fabric pongee (raw silk) became available and was a favorite with leading designers. Chinese food, both the authentic kind and American versions, surged into great popularity, with Chinese restaurants mushrooming in cities and villages throughout the country, especially in college communities. Caftans, inspired by Moroccan originals, were worn at night at home and to outside parties.

The Fashion Group, whose organizations blanket American cities, staged U. S. embassy-sponsored exchange fashion shows in Paris and Athens. A Japanese department store chain was said to be wooing U. S. designer Bill Blass to export his menswear. Blass was quoted as saying, "It's now necessary to move toward an international basis."

Color and Fabric. A rush for white and cream shades in 1972 saw women in white coats, men in white pants. White-ground prints had infallible appeal. White mohair and white flannel were the year's glamour fabrics. Bright red was a summer color; burgundy, eggplant, and lacquer yellow were shades chosen for fall; shrimp and apricot tones were the news for resort wear.

Reversible wools, reminiscent of the 1950's, made beautiful coats. New reversibles were brushed wools and flannels. Real silk shantung, real linen, and cotton organdy could be found again. Jersey, satin, and sheer organzas were widely used. Spangles returned for evening, and there were pantsuits made entirely of black sequins.

BURLINGTON DOMESTICS

SPRING MILLS, INC.

BLACK SHIELD, PRINCESS FLOWERS BY SIMMONS

Fashion designers entered the lucrative market of domestic furnishings. Among the favorite designs were sheets and pillowcases by Vera (*top left*) and Bill Blass (*above*) and a bed and matching curtains by Oscar de la Renta (*left*). Rudi Gernreich lounges with his boldly patterned quilts.

For Bed and Bath

Big-Name Fashion Designers Turn Their Talents to Creating Household Items

KNOLL INTERNATIONAL

No art form makes a pigeonhole for itself. Fashion designers have proved this, and 1972 saw an increasing number of U. S. designers entering areas other than wearing apparel. A few had pioneered a year or two before, but now a strong trend was emerging, especially among the best-known high-fashion creators.

Designers Branch Out. Fashion designers have become involved in the creation of perfumes and the design of luggage, watches, lamps, needlepoint, wallpaper, china, candy boxes, shopping bags, and wigs. But the principal direction has been toward bed and bath. Coty award winners, who for years had been dictating changes of shape and color to the "best dressed," turned their talents to keeping step with the millions who were rushing to buy no-iron sheets and pillowcases and luxurious bathroom appointments. Why?

First, a matter of economics. In a period of fashion uncertainty and increasingly high production costs, the need for a new source of profit was pressing. Coco Chanel, a genuine pragmatist, had shown the way years ago by creating her world-famous perfume, Chanel No. 5, which made a fortune for her. Most European designers followed

suit. In the United States, Norman Norell and Adele Simpson were among those to enter this tremendous field, Norell with his scent called simply "Norell" and Adele Simpson with "Collage," which she describes as "the essence of everything beautiful."

Second, realizing that fashion pervades the contemporary scene and that in the hearts of many women home decor comes next to clothes, designers took the logical step. Checking sales records, they found beautiful sheets and towels high on shopping lists. Therefore they offered their ideas to gigantic mills, which in turn were eager to snap up names to make news.

Designs for the Home. Bill Blass, three-time Coty award winner (which makes him a fashion "immortal"), provides an excellent example. A great colorist and fabric expert, sensitive to the winds of change and to the wishes of women and men, he turned to bed and bath with humor and enthusiasm, contending that today "we are bringing back to our private lives the luxuries of the Roman baths." Beginning with sheets, he designed "Summer Sky," clouds on a field of blue, with the novel idea of three pillowcases. Other Blass designs were "Country Flowers," which he combined with a trellis pattern, and "Paisley," inspired by old cashmere shawls from India, translated into bright modern shades. Towels and quilted throw bedspreads came in the same patterns. He also designed evening and at-home dresses of the sheeting, urging women to buy extra sheets and "make their own." Blass has designed watches and luggage as well.

Rudi Gernreich was inspired by his own fall 1972 fashions to make pillows and throws for his home. An international company bought them on sight. No nostalgia or folk art here; his designs were strictly contemporary geometric patterns made in quilted double-knit wool.

Designer Oscar de la Renta, head of his own manufacturing company for five aspects of fashion, designed mattress and drapery motifs for one of the big mills. His designs for mattresses, headboards, and draperies included "Eastern Clouds," inspired by a Japanese painting; "American Art," derived from folk art forms; and "Princess Flowers." They were cleverly promoted.

Vera, U. S. designer who made the first "signature scarves," reproduced from her own signed paintings, expanded her print fashions to shirts, shifts, and pants. In 1970 she started a series of sheets, blankets, bedspreads, and towels. The 1972 collection, called "The Presidential," featured colorful, magnified patterns, including "Long Stems," a geometric called "Crescent," and "Silhouette," massive African violets and butterflies in white, dramatic on a black background. Screen-printed shower curtains and laminated hampers, wastebaskets, and tissue holders came in the same patterns.

Giorgio di Sant'Angelo, an architect turned fashion designer, widely acclaimed for his theatrical gypsy costumes, has designed wallpaper, pillows, and draperies. His ornamental lights in the form of pyramids on mirror bases, designed for Christmas, were also used in other seasons. In 1972, sensing the trend for needlepoint, he designed needlepoint kits, which were excellent vehicles for his special flare.

RUTH MARY (PACKARD) DUBOIS

Accessories. Platform and wedge-soled shoes took over. Unlike originals worn in the 1940's, 1972 versions of platform soles came in satin for evening as well as casual styles. Heels were higher and bulkier.

Gradually, a few more women were taking to hats, but the milliners' struggle was uphill. The favorite hat was St. Laurent's knitted roller with a fat, tirelike brim. The wrapped head (do it yourself with a scarf) was easy and well liked. A few of the courageous adopted garden-pretty brimmed straws trimmed with flowers.

Jewelry was oversized in 1972. Beads were as large as marbles, and mammoth pendants hung from heavy chains. Ivory, wood, bone, horn, tortoiseshell, amber, agate, seeds, and leather were made into bracelets and necklaces. Big shoulder bags persisted because of their practical qualities. Reversing the economy-size trend, skinny belts looked newer than wide ones.

NORMAN NORELL (1900–1972)

Norman Norell, the American designer responsible for putting the United States in the running with Paris as a fountainhead of fashion, died in New York on Oct. 25, 1972, at the age of 72.

Norell was a creative designer who concentrated on clothes that women could wear for years, simple and virtually timeless but with unmistakable identity. Scrupu-

WIDE WORLD

lous about quality and workmanship, he took charge of production himself, hiring skilled workers, paying them well, and insisting that the person who started a garment complete it.

Norell brought recognition to Seventh Avenue by making clothes considered to be on a par with those from Paris. Seventh Avenue began to take on its world role in 1941 when Norell presented a successful collection for the firm of Traina-Norell. Cut off from Paris by World War II, other U. S. designers were thereafter encouraged to do original work. He became head of his own firm in 1960.

He was born Norman Levinson in Noblesville, Ind., on April 20, 1900. He went to New York at the age of 18 and studied fashion illustration at the Parsons School of Design and Pratt Institute. Stage-struck from childhood, he haunted the theaters and soon was designing for Paramount Pictures and for stars in silent films. He then went to work for the Brooks Costume Company, where he designed costumes for burlesque and vaudeville, beginning his lifelong loyalty to feathers and sequins for evening wear. During this time he changed his name to Norell.

A meeting with American designer Hattie Carnegie in the 1920's led to a job in her workrooms. Norell stayed there until 1940, studying the construction of Paris dresses, increasing his instinctive flair for style and elegance, and learning to be a designer in his own right. Norell collections, for most of his years, were black-tie events at 9 P. M. in his showroom at 550 Seventh Avenue.

Leading a simple life, Norell avoided the fashion crowd's luncheon spots and cocktail parties, preferring his models for companions and friends. Asked what he believed was his major contribution to fashion, Norell answered "the simple, round neckline . . . it did change the look of clothes."

RUTH MARY (PACKARD) DUBOIS

Youth Fashions. One of the Fashion Group bulletins announced that youth fashions were "an international language." Blue jeans became the universal uniform—"the youth status symbol of the world," Rosemary McMurtry, vice president of McCall Patterns, told a fashion audience. France began to manufacture jeans, copied from those in America, studded, and embroidered. The newest fad was to appliqué the face of a loved one on the back of a jean jacket. Blue denim enjoyed such prestige that a new sports car, American Motors' "Levi Gremlin," had its bucket seats covered with the fabric.

In addition to jeans, youth fashions included smocks and pinafores, sweaters, especially bulky ones, blanket plaids, and long cotton skirts. India prints and scarves had a summer vogue in London, where many of the youth fashions originate.

Cosmetics. The organic food habits of the dungaree crowd were transferred by an interesting sleight of hand into the cosmetic industry. Cucumber lotions, herbal cleansers, vitamin E lipsticks, avocado creams, protein shampoos, and honey and almond soaps sold briskly in stores as well as from door to door. Spokesmen for most of the big cosmetic companies contended that natural ingredients had been used in their products for years, but most agreed that interest in organic foods and gardening had made the public more aware and eager to buy. Compounding this awareness was the fact that today's women are said to be more health conscious than in previous years.

The second noticeable trend was for musk perfume and all its derivatives. The young crowd was drenching itself in scents from musk to old-fashioned lavender.

Children's Fashions. Both boys and girls joined in a chorus "not to be duded up" in fancy clothes. Work clothes—jeans, sweaters, and T-shirts—were copied from the teens. Little girls did dress up, however, in long skirts and dresses, usually in gingham checks, possibly because their big sisters were doing so. Body shirts, borrowed from adult styles, were worn with shorts or pants. Knits, being rugged, were universal. Sleepwear manufacturers made headlines by complying with U. S. Department of Commerce standards of flammability.

Men's Fashions. Double-knits, relatively new in 1971, came to the mass market in 1972 in suits and separate jackets and pants. Pleats and cuffs were seen again on pants. "Ice cream" (off-white) pants came from the 1920's. A strong trend for rugged, stormy-weather styles brought in short wool or leather pile-lined coats with big collars, heavy wools in lumberjack plaids, and that old favorite, the white Hudson Bay Blanket coat.

Checks and tartans were the rule for sports jackets in 1972. Sweaters became part of the total look, and were color coordinated with shirts and jackets. The British policeman's coat in navy blue melton with silver buttons and a whistle on a chain was made in the United States for both men and women, a nod in the unisex direction.

RUTH MARY (PACKARD) DUBOIS
Freelance Fashion Writer, Lecturer, and Columnist

CRISTÓBAL BALENCIAGA (1895–1972)

WIDE WORLD

Known to the press as the "King of Fashion" and to fellow couturiers as "The Master," Cristóbal Balenciaga died on March 24, 1972, in Valencia, Spain, at the age of 77. He was buried in Guetaria, the Basque village where he was born on Jan. 21, 1895.

Engrossed in fashion from an early age, he attained world fame in Paris in his middle years. His revolutionary suit of 1952, with a loose jacket, low hipband, and no waistline, was the shape that turned the corner into the era of contemporary "easy" clothes as opposed to waistline-conscious silhouettes. He was also the father of the chemise, first ridiculed but later the most ubiquitous dress of the generation.

In the 1950's and 1960's, Balenciaga was copied by practically every designer in the world. Hubert de Givenchy was his disciple, his adopted son, and, finally, his rival. Christian Dior called Balenciaga "our master." In her book *In My Fashion*, Bettina Ballard of Vogue said that in reviewing slides of French imports over the years, "the only clothes that stand up as timeless are Balenciaga's and Chanel's."

Aloof, preoccupied, and absorbed in his work, Balenciaga had simple tastes and a few devoted friends. He cut his own toiles, and could sew and embroider. His workroom was conducted with the dedication of a monastery, his workers known as the "little monks." He hated publicity, good or bad, and was the first to ban the press from the showings of his collections. He consistently refused to lend his name to any ready-made label. His prestigious clientele included Queen Victoria Eugenia of Spain, Queen Fabiola of Belgium, Elizabeth Taylor, and the Duchess of Windsor.

When "crazy" clothes took over in the late 1960's, Balenciaga closed his doors, coming out of seclusion in 1972 only to design the wedding dress of the granddaughter of Generalissimo Franco. It was his last creation.

"Today, with the pendulum swinging away from outré and back to so-called normal clothes," commented Gloria Emerson of the New York *Times*, "Balenciaga's kind of clothes are again in the limelight." There is no better epitaph.

RUTH MARY (PACKARD) DUBOIS

FASHION FAVORITES were comfortable, and the look was one of relaxed elegance. (Opposite page) The shirtwaist dress was revived, but now was topped with a knit tank sweater. The Halston evening dress, sexy yet casual, was one of the year's favorites. (Left) Dior's white coat with raglan shoulders and dolman sleeves made coat news. One of the most popular pantsuits (right) was a casual-looking plaid topper and checked pants, designed by Irene Galitzine.

MANING

FEDERATION OF ARAB REPUBLICS

Formed on Sept. 1, 1971, the Federation of Arab Republics is a merger of Egypt, Syria, and Libya. A similar union, called the United Arab Republic, was formed between Egypt and Syria in 1958, but Syria withdrew in 1961. See EGYPT; LIBYA; SYRIA.

--------- FIJI · Information Highlights ---------

Official Name: Fiji.
Area: 7,055 square miles (18,272 sq km).
Population (1972 est.): 600,000. *Density,* 72 per square mile (28 per sq km). *Annual rate of increase,* 1.8%.
Chief City (1966 census): Suva, the capital, 54,157.
Government: *Head of state,* Elizabeth II, queen; represented by Sir Robert Foster, governor-general (took office 1970). *Head of government,* Ratu Sir Kamisese Mara, prime minister (took office Oct. 1970). *Legislature*—Parliament: Senate, 22 members; House of Representatives, 52 members.
Language: English (official).
Monetary Unit: Fiji dollar (0.8548 F. dollar equals U. S.$1, 1972).
Gross National Product (1969 est.): $179,500,000.
Manufacturing (major products): Sugar, coconut oil.
Major Agricultural Products: Sugar, coconuts, fish.
Major Minerals: Gold, copper, bauxite, manganese ore.

FIJI

A national election and continued economic growth were the highlights of 1972 in Fiji.

Election. The first general election since independence in 1970 was held in April. Ratu Sir Kamisese Mara retained the office of prime minister. After the election he made several cabinet changes and increased the number of members from 12 to 14.

Economy. The Fijian government is promoting an extensive pine planting program that United Nations advisers believe may bring timber export revenues up to the level of sugar exports by the 1980's. The government has projected a pine forest area of 210 square miles (545 sq km).

Pacific Hotels and Developments Ltd. has completed a tourist hotel as part of its Pacific Harbour project at Deuba on the island of Viti Levu. The company has also purchased Wakaya Island in the central Fijis for private residence development.

The sugarcane land worked by more than 6,000 tenant farmers was to be transferred from the Australian-owned Colonial Sugar Refining Company to the Fijian government in April 1973 under an agreement reached in 1970, prior to Fijian independence.

University Graduation. The first class of 43 students graduated from the University of the South Pacific at Laucala Bay near Suva on Dec. 3, 1971. It was addressed by King Taufa'ahau Tupou IV of Tonga, chancellor of the university.

HOWARD J. CRITCHFIELD
Western Washington State College

FINLAND

Both parliamentary and local elections were held in Finland during 1972, and a possible fourth term for President Urho Kaleva Kekkonen was the subject of much discussion. Relations with the Soviet Union remained good, and Finland persevered in its efforts to normalize diplomatic ties with the two German states. A tentative agreement with the European Economic Community (EEC) was reached, but a final arrangement awaited further study and parliamentary consideration. There was mounting interest in exploring opportunities for greater cooperation with the Soviet bloc's economic entity, the Council for Mutual Economic Assistance (CMEA).

Elections. In the parliamentary elections on January 2–3, modest gains were made by the Social Democrats and the Communist-controlled People's Democrats. The 200 seats in the Eduskunta (parliament) were divided between 108 non-Socialists and 92 leftists.

Although many Finns preferred a majority government, a one-party minority Socialist government, headed by the veteran Rafael Paasio, took office on Feb. 23, 1972. Political realities and presidential intervention forced the formation of a majority government. Paasio resigned on July 19, stating that such a government was essential for ratifying the EEC arrangements. On September 4, a four-party government, led by the Social Democrat Kalevi Sorsa, assumed control. Of 16 cabinet posts, 7 went to the Social Democratic party, 5 to the Center party, 2 to the Swedish People's party, one to the Liberal party, and one to an unaffiliated administrator.

The local elections, held Oct. 1–2, 1972, were marked by gains for the Social Democratic party, the People's Democratic League, and the Conservatives, and by losses for the Center party and the farmers' parties. Of nearly 11,000 seats at stake, the proportion held by non-Socialists fell to 55% from 56.2% in 1968.

The Presidency. Early in 1972 it was suggested that special provisions be made for extending the term of President Kekkonen beyond 1974 on the grounds that a bitterly fought campaign "might jeopardize Finland's prestige abroad and even injure the solution of domestic matters." Reactions were mixed. The 71-year-old incumbent himself was coy. "If a majority of the populace deems it best that I conduct the presidential office beyond March 1, 1974," he said on February 18, "then I shall be compelled to continue my service. I cannot predict how this is to be done, but that is not my concern."

--------- FINLAND · Information Highlights ---------

Official Name: Republic of Finland.
Area: 130,120 square miles (337,009 sq km).
Population (1972 est.): 4,800,000. *Density,* 36 per square mile (14 per sq km). *Annual rate of increase,* 0.4%.
Chief Cities (1971 est.): Helsinki, the capital, 528,800; Tempere, 157,810; Turku, 156,882.
Government: *Head of state,* Urho Kaleva Kekkonen, president (took office March 1968 for 3d 6-year term). *Head of government,* Kalevi Sorsa, premier (took office Sept. 1972). *Legislature* (unicameral)—Eduskunta, 200 members. *Major political parties*—Social Democratic party; National Coalition party; Center party; People's Democratic League (Communist); Swedish People's party; Liberal party; Christian party; Rural party.
Languages: Finnish, Swedish (both official).
Education: *Expenditure* (1969), 23.9% of total public expenditure. *School enrollment* (1969)—primary, 393,942; secondary, 497,535; technical/vocational, 99,808; university/higher, 58,444.
Monetary Unit: Markka (4.14 markkas equal U. S.$1, May 1972).
Gross National Product (1971 est.): $10,300,000,000.
National Income per Person (1970): $1,933.
Economic Indexes: *Industrial production* (1971), 164 (1963=100); *agricultural production* (1971), 151 (1952–56=100); *consumer price index* (1971), 122 (1967=100).
Manufacturing (major products): Wood and paper products, machinery, chemicals, cement, textiles, metals.
Major Agricultural Products: Oats, potatoes, sugar beets.
Major Minerals: Iron ore, copper, zinc, nickel, vanadium.
Foreign Trade (1971): *Exports,* $2,357,000,000 (chief exports —paper; wood; wood pulp). *Imports,* $2,795,000,000 (chief imports, 1969—nonelectrical machinery; transport equipment). *Chief trading partners* (1969)—United Kingdom (took 18% of exports, supplied 13% of imports); USSR (14%—13%); Sweden (13%—15%); West Germany (10%—16%).
Tourism: *Receipts* (1970), $120,000,000.
Transportation: *Motor vehicles* (1970), 823,000 (automobiles, 712,000); *railroads* (1970), 3,320 miles (5,343 km); *merchant fleet* (1971), 1,471,000 gross registered tons; *major national airline,* Finnair.
Communications: *Telephones* (1971), 1,180,785; *television stations* (1971), 65; *television sets* (1971), 1,061,300; *radios* (1970), 1,759,000; *newspapers* (1970), 67.

Foreign Relations. Relations with the USSR remained good. Important joint mining and forestry projects were under way within the Soviet Union.

On July 10 the Finnish government sent notes to both East and West Germany, reiterating its earlier view that "the time was ripe to begin efforts for establishing relations with both Germanies." The response of East Germany was positive, and preliminary agreements were reached September 6. From West Germany, however, came word that the timing was not propitious, and that "the quarrels between the Germans ought not to be extended to third parties."

Economic Affairs. After prolonged negotiations, a draft agreement covering Finland's association with EEC was made public July 23. While hailed by many Finns as a good compromise, it aroused strenuous opposition and considerable questioning, especially by the Communists. Norway's decision in October not to enter the Common Market encouraged the opposition forces in Finland, and hopes for eventual Nordic economic integration took a brighter turn.

There was, concurrently, growing interest in the CMEA. President Kekkonen appointed a high-level delegation to meet with CMEA officials in the fall. Opinion was again deeply divided, although many favored trade both with the Common Market and Eastern bloc.

Moderate gains were made in Finland's economy during 1972, after a disappointing year in 1971. But inflation, although less than in 1971, was severe, and living costs jumped some 6%. There was growing awareness of the necessity of diversifying the country's exports, so long dependent on wood, pulp, and paper products.

JOHN I. KOLEHMAINEN
Heidelberg College, Ohio

FIRES

Fires in the United States in 1972 killed 11,900 persons and caused $2.9 billion in property losses, according to preliminary estimates of the National Fire Protection Association (NFPA).

Continued headway against the nation's fire problem is reflected in NFPA studies. During the years 1960–71, the number of fire deaths per million persons declined steadily, from 69.5 to 57.2 a year. The number of fires per million persons rose only slightly, despite the great increase in the amount of property subject to burning. However, largely due to inflation, the per capita cost of fire rose from $8.61 in 1960 to $13.25 in 1971.

Worst Fires. The greatest loss of life from fire during the first half of 1972 occurred in the May 2 silver mine disaster at Kellogg, Idaho, where 91 men died after a blaze broke out 3,700 feet underground. In Tyrone, Pa., on January 16, 12 hotel residents died when trapped in their rooms by flames. Three fires in housing for the sick and elderly each claimed 10 lives: in Lincoln Heights, Ohio, on January 26; in Rosecrans, Wis., on April 4; and in Springfield, Ill., on May 6.

In dollar cost, the most serious fire during the first half of 1972 was at a shopping plaza in Tifton, Ga., on June 14. This $5 million fire started when an employee placed a cigarette on a display rug. An explosion in a department store in Butte, Mont., on Feb. 28, cost $4 million. Losses of $3 million each resulted from three fires: on January 2, when an

UPI

BOSTON FIREFIGHTERS carry an injured comrade over a mountain of rubble. Nine firemen lost their lives fighting the blaze in an old Back Bay hotel.

explosion ripped through a flour mill in Buffalo, N. Y.; on March 6, at a television station in Las Vegas, Nev.; and on June 12, when fire bombs caused destruction of a furniture store during a period of community unrest in Alton, Ill.

1971 Losses. Final NFPA estimates for 1971 show that 2,728,200 fires claimed 11,850 lives and destroyed property valued at $2,743,260,000. Significantly, the number of lives lost was 3% lower than that during the preceding year.

LARGE-LOSS FIRES IN THE UNITED STATES, 1971
(Individual loss of $250,000 or more)

Classification	Number	Loss
Stores and offices	114	$ 63,712,000
Manufacturing	103	62,925,000
Warehouses and other storage	95	63,117,000
Schools and institutions	32	14,343,000
Restaurants	27	9,156,000
Basic industries	21	21,740,000
Churches	19	11,666,000
Hotels and motels	15	3,967,000
Miscellaneous	73	67,234,000
Total	499	$307,860,000

Building fires numbered 996,600 (up 0.5%) and cost $2,266,000,000 (up 2.6%). These included 639,000 fires in homes and apartments, resulting in 6,550 deaths and $760 million in property losses. Fires in places other than buildings numbered 1,731,600 (up 11.1%).

CHARLES S. MORGAN
National Fire Protection Association

FISCHER, Bobby. See special feature on chess beginning on page 53.

ARTHUR LAVINE, CHASE MANHATTAN BANK

Peru's vital fishing industry was seriously threatened by a change in ocean currents that drove fish away.

FISHERIES

The world's fish catch continued to increase in 1972, but anxieties also intensified. Concern increased about over-fishing, pollution, and, above all, territorial fishing claims. Locally, Peru suffered a major drop in its catch due to a shift in the pattern of ocean currents. (See PERU.)

Problems of U. S. Fishing Industry. Virtually all of New England's historically important species suffer from over-fishing. In addition, the New England fleet is generally obsolete and therefore has difficulty competing with the modern, efficient vessels of foreign countries, which also fish its traditional grounds. The most dramatic illustration of these points is Georges Bank haddock. In the 1955–60 period U. S. landings averaged more than 40,000 metric tons a year, but foreign catches rose to over 80,000 tons a year in the late 1960s. Since 1969 the U. S. annual catch has been in the neighborhood of only 13,000 tons.

Perhaps most endangered, but primarily from domestic rather than foreign exploitation, is the lobster fishery. The need for conservation is so pressing that in August 1972 Secretary of Commerce Peter G. Peterson called on the Atlantic states from Maine to North Carolina to join with the National Marine Fisheries Service to develop a

long-range program to avoid depletion of the resource.

Shrimping. For all the problems facing the historical fisheries which have aroused so much concern about the downfall of· the United States as a fishing power, there are two notable exceptions— the shrimp and tuna fisheries.

The shrimp fishery, economically the nation's most important, is booming. Boatyards along the South Atlantic and Gulf of Mexico are turning out shrimp trawlers as fast as they can to meet increased demand.

Although shrimping is thriving some problems have arisen. The tendency of many countries to extend their claims over territorial waters up to as much as 200 miles (320 km) has interfered with U. S. shrimp boats, which have fished in foreign waters for many years. In mid-1971 Brazil, for example, began enforcing its claims to a 200-mile limit and some U. S. boats left the area. In May 1972 an agreement was concluded between the United States and Brazil that established a shrimp conservation zone in which U. S. boats can fish under regulations. The new rules are not expected to seriously inhibit fishing activity.

Tuna Fishing. The U. S. tuna fleet, whose large, highly sophisticated million-dollar vessels roam the world, has also apparently overcome its major crisis in regard to disputed waters. While the United States has not changed its position opposing the 200-mile fishing limit claims of Peru and Ecuador it has apparently modified it on economic grounds. The U. S. State Department is now advising U. S. fishermen to buy licenses "under protest" to work within the 200-mile limit, rather than pay the enormous fines that have been levied in the last few years.

Law of the Sea Conference. Decisions on the fishing limit claims are the primary concern of the

LEADING FISHING COUNTRIES
(In billions of pounds, live weight)

Country	1968	1969	1970
Peru	23.2	20.2	27.8
Japan	19.1	19.1	20.5
USSR	13.4	16.2	16.0
China (mainland)	12.8	12.8	12.8
United States	5.4	5.6	6.0
Norway	6.2	4.9	6.6
6-nation total	80.1	78.8	89.7
Other countries	61.0	58.2	63.1
World catch	141.1	137.0	152.8

U. S. commercial fishing industry at the 1973 Law of the Sea Conference. Many observers in the fishing industry are pessimistic about its outcome. In effect the conference has already begun in a series of preliminary meetings. There is some agitation for the conference to be postponed, although the United States would like to see it held on schedule.

U. S. and World Catch. The total U. S. fisheries catch for 1971 was valued at $643.2 million, a record high. Shrimp accounted for $166.6 million of this, a figure that also set a record. Menhaden, the low-cost industrial fish that accounts for the largest volume in the U. S. fisheries, also set a record at 1.6 billion pounds.

The total world catch for 1970, the last year for which figures were available, amounted to 152.8 billion pounds for a value of $11.7 billion, up from 1969's 138.7 billion pounds worth $10.5 billion.

WILLIAM A. SARRATT
Editor, "The Fish Boat," New Orleans

FLORIDA

Political events of national significance and a mushrooming economy focused national attention on Florida during 1972.

Politics. Florida's increasing national importance was demonstrated when all the Democratic presidential candidates campaigned in the state's first presidential primary. Busing proved to be the major political issue, and the legislature decided to include a straw vote on busing on the March 14 ballot. Governor Ruben Askew announced his opposition to attempts to prohibit busing because this would deny some students the opportunity of securing a quality education. The legislature agreed to include on the ballot a straw vote on "quality education." In the balloting 74% of the voters opposed busing, while 79% approved quality education for all. Although Askew's stand on busing was rejected by the voters, his popularity was hardly diminished. George Wallace won a clear victory in the primary with his stand against busing.

Florida again became the focal point of national politics during the summer when both Democrats and Republicans held their conventions in Miami Beach. Determined to prevent any repetition of the violence of the 1968 Democratic convention in Chicago, Miami Beach secured substantial federal and state aid in planning security measures. These measures, combined with a smaller turnout of protesters than anticipated, resulted in orderly conventions and the protection of legal dissent.

At the state level, the 1972 legislature demonstrated the same progressive spirit that had characterized the 1971 session. Major legislation included a $192 million revenue-sharing program to aid cities and counties, increases in workmen's and unemployment compensation, increased aid to dependent children, a therapeutic abortion law, prison reforms, creation of a consumer adviser position in the governor's office, and several environmental laws. In a special session it reimposed capital punishment. True to his pledge, Governor Askew worked to prevent corporations, especially utility corporations, from passing the cost of new corporate taxes on to the consumer.

Environment. During 1972 there was a growing commitment to the belief that the long-term prosperity of Florida depends on sensible environmental planning. Low rainfall over much of the state

---

————— **FLORIDA** • Information Highlights —————

Area: 58,560 square miles (151,670 sq km).
Population (1970 census): 6,789,443. *Density:* 130 per sq mi.
Chief Cities (1970 census): Tallahassee, the capital, 72,586; Jacksonville, 528,865; Miami, 334,859; Tampa, 277,767; Saint Petersburg, 216,232; Fort Lauderdale, 139,590; Hollywood, 106,873.
Government (1972): *Chief Officers*—governor, Reubin O'D. Askew (D); lt. gov., Tom Adams (D); secy. of state, Richard Stone (D); atty. gen., Robert L. Shevin (D); treas., Thomas D. O'Malley (D); commissioner, dept. of education, Floyd T. Christian (D); chief justice, B. K. Roberts. *Legislature*—Senate, 48 members (33 Democrats, 15 Republicans); House of Representatives, 119 members (81 D, 38 R).
Education (1971–72): *Enrollment*—public elementary schools, 780,189 pupils, 33,148 teachers; public secondary, 649,763 pupils, 31,002 teachers; nonpublic schools (1970–71), 124,-571 pupils, 5,010 teachers; college and university, 222,000 students. *Public school expenditures,* $1,153,614,000 ($850 per pupil). *Average teacher's salary,* $9,500.
State Finances (fiscal year 1970): *Revenues,* $2,226,037,000 (4% general sales tax and gross receipts taxes, $658,197,-000; motor fuel tax, $225,399,000; federal funds, $385,-525,000). *Expenditures,* $2,116,316,000 (education, $1,075,-701,000; health, welfare, and safety, $259,306,000; highways, $416,998,000). *State debt,* $891,039,000 (June 30, 1970).
Personal Income (1971): $27,091,000; per capita, $3,848.
Public Assistance (1971): $237,855,000. *Average monthly payments* (Dec. 1971)—old-age assistance, $58.46; aid to families with dependent children, $91.91.
Labor Force: *Nonagricultural wage and salary earners* (July 1972), 2,244,600. *Average annual employment* (1971)—manufacturing, 316,000; trade, 584,000; government, 416,-000; services, 416,000. *Insured unemployed* (Aug. 1972)—34,200 (2.1%).
Manufacturing (1970): *Value added by manufacture,* $4,523,-000,000. Food and kindred products, $845,400,000; chemicals and allied products, $427,000,000; nonelectrical machinery, $401,100,000; electrical equipment and supplies, $364,800,000; fabricated metal products, $322,400,000; printing and publishing, $313,300,000.
Agriculture (1970): *Cash farm income,* $1,302,714,000 (livestock, $395,544,000; crops, $888,680,000; government payments, $18,490,000). *Chief crops* (in order of value, 1971)—Oranges (ranks 1st among the states), grapefruit (ranks 1st), tomatoes, sugarcane for sugar and seed (ranks 3d).
Mining (1971): *Production value,* $343,731,000 (ranks 23d among the states). *Chief minerals*—Phosphate rock, value not available; stone, $64,332,000; cement, $53,847,000; sand and gravel, $18,836,000.
Fisheries (1971): *Commercial catch,* 173,904,000 pounds ($45,-154,000). *Leading species by value:* Shrimp, $16,287,000; lobster, $7,057,000; crabs, $2,649,000; red snapper, $2,-505,000.
Transportation: *Roads* (1971), 89,499 miles (144,031 km); *motor vehicles* (1971), 4,120,363; *railroads* (1971), 4,274 miles (6,878 km); *public airports* (1972), 114.
Communications: *Telephones* (1972), 4,546,100; *television stations* (1971), 25; *radio stations* (1971), 289; *newspapers* (1972), 51 (daily circulation, 2,132,000).

---

forced some urban areas to impose voluntary restrictions on water use for brief periods, serving as a reminder that water is the most vital resource. Clearly the underground water supply, the river systems, and the natural basins must be protected from pollution. The only effective way to protect these water areas, such as the Green Swamp in central Florida, is through purchase by the state or national government. Additional funds for the purchase of endangered lands were made available when the voters in November approved a $240 million bond issue.

The 1972 Legislature was labeled the "environmental session" because of its interest in ecology. Its Environmental Land and Water Management Act was cited by President Nixon as the type of commitment that other states should emulate. New restrictions were imposed on oil-well drilling, dredging and landfill projects, and on construction in areas along beaches.

Education. The early months of 1972 were marked by the controversy over busing, and no major changes were made in the public school system. It was widely recognized that new methods of financing are needed, and changes may come in 1973 after Governor Askew's Citizen's Committee on Education makes its report.

TRAILER PARK near Key West was demolished by a water spout that struck in July. About 20 trailers were completely destroyed.

Economy. A record year of tourism, a rapidly growing population, and a record year for the citrus industry made Florida's economy one of the brightest in the nation. In central Florida, Walt Disney World attracted 10.7 million visitors in its first year, stimulating the hotel-restaurant industry and other related service industries throughout the state. Sales-and-use tax collections for the 1972 fiscal year were 22.5% above 1971, and a $66 million surplus was left in the state's general fund.

Unemployment at midyear was more than 2% below the national average; however, per capita income lagged further behind the national average. According to Census Bureau reports, Florida ranked 28th in per capita income in 1971, compared with 24th in 1969. One explanation for this drop is that thousands of Floridians are employed in agriculture or agriculture-related industry, which is seasonal and pays relatively low wages. The percentage of nonagricultural workers is increasing.

J. LARRY DURRENCE, *Florida Southern College*

FONDA, Jane. See BIOGRAPHY.

FOOD

World food production declined slightly in 1972. The major drop occurred in cereal production, due primarily to the failure of the wheat crop in the Soviet Union. Declines were also registered in the potato and peanut crops and in some noncitrus fruits. Small increases occurred in meats and dairy products and in sugar, citrus fruit, and oilseed production. In the United States interest centered on consumer demands, new government regulations, and attempts by the food processing industry at self-regulation.

WORLD FOOD SUPPLY

World food production per person declined in 1972. Production of cereals fell about 4% short of the record level of 1971. Output of sugar, citrus fruit, and most important oilseeds was up but not enough to offset the reduced crops of grain, potatoes, peanuts, and several noncitrus fruits. Incomplete statistics on world production of meat and milk show small increases from 1971 over all, but probably no grains per capita.

Decreased Grain Harvest. The most far-reaching agricultural event of 1972 was the failure of the grain crop in the USSR. Against a target of 190 million tons, the harvest was no more than 160 million, compared with 181 million in 1971. The greatest shortfall was in wheat. Unusually severe weather and inadequate snow cover led to winterkill on around 30% of the winter wheat area. Hot dry weather during the early summer reduced the yield in the surviving area, resulting in a winter wheat crop of about half of what had been planned. Production of spring wheat, although relatively better, fell short of the harvests of 1970 and 1971.

Much of the winterkilled area was replanted to spring grains for feed. The consequent increase in area over 1971 more than offset a decline in yields, so total production of feed grains (barley, oats, rye and corn), in the Soviet Union was slightly higher in 1972 than in 1971.

Grain production also fell in the United States, Canada, Australia, Brazil, Mexico, Turkey, India, Indonesia, and the "rice bowl" countries of Southeast Asia (Burma, Thailand, Cambodia, and Vietnam). In all countries but the United States the decreases were unintentional, due to weather or war. For the United States a reduction of 8% in

area planted was planned, and production fell 6%. India harvested a record crop of wheat early in 1972, but the summer monsoon rains were late and below average. Yields of corn, millet, sorghum, and rice were substantially less than in 1971. The 1972 grain crop in western Europe was slightly above the record 1971 crop. France and Sweden showed big gains, while Spain, Italy, and Austria had smaller harvests. Outside Europe, Argentina was the only big gainer.

Soviet Grain Purchases. With rising goals for output of animal products and record numbers of grain-consuming animals, the USSR reacted to the shortfall of the wheat crop by purchasing grain in unprecedented volume. In previous periods of stringency the adjustment in the USSR had been made by accelerating the slaughter of livestock, to reduce requirements for grain, rather than by importing grain to augment the supply. By late October the Soviet Union had bought about 27 million tons of grain, about two thirds from the United States and the balance from Canada, Australia, France, West Germany, Rumania, and Sweden. About 5 million tons were believed to be for delivery to countries to which the Soviet Union normally exports grain. Three fourths of the grain for delivery to the USSR is wheat.

World Grain Trade. Largely because of extraordinary imports by the Soviet Union, world trade in grain in the marketing year that began July 1, 1972, was expected to set a new record, one sixth above the 1971–72 season. The record 1971 grain harvest left very large stocks in the United States on June 30, 1972. These stocks and the 1972 harvests give the United States abundant, although far from record-breaking, supplies for domestic uses and exports. U. S. exports of wheat and flour in the marketing year beginning July 1, 1972, were expected to exceed 30 million metric tons (1,125 million bushels), at least 6 million tons above the previous record in 1965–66, and more than three fourths as much as the 1972 harvest. U. S. exports of feed grains will also break the 1965–66 record.

Grain Use. Three fourths of the grain bought by the USSR was wheat for making bread, but less than half of the grain consumed in the USSR is for food. Livestock feed, seed, harvesting and marketing waste, and industrial uses account for more than half of total grain consumption. The quantities used for livestock feed have been rising in the Soviet Union, as in other industrialized countries, as the demand for meat, eggs, and milk has grown. The United States, Canada, and both western and eastern Europe used much more grain for feed than for food in 1964–66, the latest period for which complete data have been published by the Food and Agriculture Organization (FAO) of the United Nations. At the other extreme, most countries in Africa and the Far East use very small quantities of grain for feed.

Grain prices in international markets rose rapidly in the summer of 1972 in response to the large Russian purchases. Except where restrained by governments, these higher prices will be reflected in higher prices for bread and livestock products. Since the price of wheat has risen more than prices of feed grains, the feeding of wheat to livestock will be discouraged.

The end uses of cereals in economically developed countries differ greatly from the uses in the poor countries. The highest levels of consumption

UPI

SEEKING A HALT in rising food prices, consumers in New Hampshire staged a three-week beef boycott.

of grains for food are in the middle-income countries. In richer countries the people eat less bread and relatively more meat and fats; in the poor countries people eat less, on the average, than in the middle- and high-income countries and often substitute cheap root crops, such as cassava or yams, for grain.

By using large quantities of cereals, per person, for livestock feed the economically developed countries produce much greater quantities of livestock products for food per person than the less developed countries. One reason they are able to do this is that their cows, hens, and pigs have been carefully bred for decades to respond to heavy feeding of grain with profitable outputs of milk, eggs, and meat. Livestock in the less developed countries would produce more if fed more, but they could not match the output per animal of the rich countries, since they have been selected primarily to survive and reproduce in harsh environments with minimal feed.

CHARLES A. GIBBONS
U. S. Department of Agriculture

U. S. FOOD INDUSTRY

In 1972 the food industry in the United States marshalled its resources in order to meet challenges posed by changing consumer concerns and an increased emphasis on government regulations and requirements.

Consumer Outlook. A major concern of consumers has been the increase in food costs. Cost cutting, affecting all segments of the food industry, has been widely instituted to combat this rise. In the retail area, profits have suffered, while processor competition has increased greatly. There is evidence that food costs have altered consumer food habits, especially in the protein food area. In 1972, U. S. consumers spent approximately 16% of their disposable income on food.

Many consumers use prepared and convenience foods, but others are hesitant to buy them because

of the supposed overprocessing and increased use of additives and formulated ingredients, which they feel is a trend away from natural foods. However, the president of a large food company recently predicted that approximately 100,000 new products will be introduced in the 1970's, most of them foods. While some consumer critics condemn new or processed foods, many knowledgeable food experts are expressing concern over the rise in food fads among the consumer population.

Food "faddists" can be separated into three broad categories: the organic or natural food group, the special diet group, and the component or specific nutrient group. They feel that commercial foods are low in nutrition, contain excess additives and/or pesticides, and do not promote good health.

Health foods may be divided into grain products, fruits and vegetables, sweeteners, meats, and specialty type foods. Surveys forecast a rapid increase in the dollar value of, and the number of outlets for, health foods. To date few regulations governing this market have been forthcoming, despite the fact that conventional food processors are being closely scrutinized and the nutritional well-being of the population has been a major concern.

Recent botulism scares, product recalls, doubts about food additive safety, questions on nutritive value of foods, and others have led to a skeptical attitude on the part of consumers about the U. S. food supply. Concerted informational efforts by government and industry plus consumer education will be needed to overcome this credibility gap.

Government Surveillance and Regulation. Governmental agencies such as the Food and Drug Administration (FDA), the Department of Agriculture (USDA), the U.S. Department of the Interior (USDI), the Federal Trade Commission (FTC), the U. S. Public Health Service (USPHS) and others either regulate or affect food industry actions. Numerous programs to improve the food supply or to assist the industry with problems are under way. Increased pressure from consumer groups, congressmen, and others has resulted in new proposals plus increased emphasis on existing programs.

One law whose impact is currently being felt in the food industry is the Williams-Steiger Occupational Safety and Health Act of 1970, or OSHA. The act applies to all industries and businesses that affect commerce—in other words, practically every employer in the country. Its purpose is to provide for safe and healthful working conditions for the 60 million workers covered under the act. Administered by the Department of Labor, OSHA is a comprehensive act, containing a penalty system to insure correction of conditions discovered during inspections. While the emphasis is on safety, OSHA will have a strong effect on the handling, processing, storage, and marketing of all foods, since sanitation also falls within its scope.

FDA published proposed guidelines for nutritional labeling in March. The aim of the proposal was to provide consumer information on the nutrient quality of food. The proposal and its labeling requirements have been discussed by many industry and government groups. To date no agreement on the precise form of labeling or nutritive terms has been reached, although several large firms have instituted voluntary labeling programs for selected foods.

In 1972, the FDA announced an intensified regulatory program designed to eliminate unsanitary conditions in food plants. While microbiological contamination problems such as salmonella and botulism will continue to receive priority, new emphasis will be placed on good housekeeping operations, including cleanliness of personnel, equipment, and premises. The expected 1973 budget will provide for up to 300 additional food plant inspectors to complement current programs and give priority to conditions under which foods are processed, packed, shipped, and stored, while continuing the level of inspection of the finished food product. Concurrently, FDA, the National Canners Association, container companies, and other associations are combining with universities to institute a certification program for retort operators (canners) and can seam inspectors.

In another action, FDA added a new dimension to the review of GRAS (Generally Recognized As Safe) additives, by contracting with FASEB (Federation of American Societies of Experimental Biology) and its expert panel to judge and report on selected additives and their safety. Although other expert groups are evaluating simultaneously, FASEB will have access to the most recent data. The ultimate aim is to report whether or not there is any indication of harm from the use of additives.

Other Industry Activities. The food industry in 1972 was also involved at a policy level with matters having to do with nutritional labeling, new product development, product recall procedures, food fortification, and consumer education. Of these the newest, most innovative, and perhaps most important were the formation of the Expert Panel on Food Safety and Nutrition and the Committee on Public Information (CPI), both created by the Institute of Food Technologists (IFT).

Nine prominent non-industry scientists make up the Expert Panel, whose task is to define areas of significant current and potential interest related to food safety and nutrition, and to prepare summaries and interpretations in these areas. Once the scientific status summaries are developed, CPI revises them into a format for all media. After reapproval by the panel, summary reports and releases are made available to all media and groups. At this point, official IFT local representatives known to the news and broadcast media are available for contact and interview. The aim is to provide accurate, up-to-date, and unbiased information to the public.

KIRBY M. HAYES, *University of Massachusetts*

U. S. FOOD INDUSTRY

Group	Employees[1] (1,000)		Value added by manufacture (billions)		Value of shipments (billions)	
	1970	1971	1970	1971	1970	1971
Meat and poultry products..........	317.3	313.1	$4.4	$5.0	$25.0	$26.0
Dairy products........	204.4	191.3	3.7	3.9	13.7	14.6
Canned, cured, frozen foods........	267.8	265.4	4.3	4.7	11.0	12.1
Grain mill products....	112.7	106.6	3.3	3.4	10.8	11.1
Bakery products......	255.1	243.1	4.0	4.2	7.2	7.4
Sugar (raw and refined)............	30.8	29.4	0.8	0.9	2.7	2.8
Confectionery and related products.....	84.7	79.7	1.6	1.6	3.3	3.4
Beverages, alcoholic and nonalcoholic....	229.6	217.7	5.9	6.5	12.2	13.2
Miscellaneous food products[2]..........	136.8	136.2	3.9	4.0	11.9	12.6
Total[3]............1,639.2		1,582.4	$31.9	$34.2	$97.6	$103.3

[1] Excludes employees at central administrative offices, distribution warehouses, and other auxiliary establishments. [2] Includes animal and vegetable oils and fats, roasted coffee, macaroni, potato chips, etc. [3] Details may not add to totals because of rounding. Source: Annual Survey of Manufacturers, U. S. Bureau of the Census.

NUTRITION

The impetus given to nutritional programs in the United States by the 1969 White House Conference on Food, Nutrition, and Health remained evident in 1972. The conference had heard the charge that many Americans were not eating well enough to sustain health. Since that time a number of programs and educational efforts to improve nutrition in the nation have been introduced or expanded.

National Surveys. Since 1936, the U. S. Department of Agriculture (USDA) has conducted five nationwide surveys evaluating the quantity, money value, and nutritive content of diets. Recent results from the 1965–66 survey show surprising changes. In 1955, 60% of the surveyed households met or exceeded USDA's good diet definition, while in 1965 only 50% had the same rating. Families with poor diets increased 6% to a total of 21%. Diets were measured against the Recommended Dietary Allowances (RDA) of the Food and Nutrition Board-National Research Council for seven nutrients—protein, calcium, iron, vitamin A value, thiamin, riboflavin, and ascorbic acid (vitamin C).

Food Assistance Programs. The USDA, the U. S. Department of Health, Education, and Welfare (HEW), the American Medical Association (AMA), the Red Cross, and other organizations have created many programs to combat and correct nutritional deficiencies. Of these, the USDA has the broadest and most comprehensive series of programs. The school lunch program provides federal funds to states to reimburse a participating public or nonprofit private school of high school grade or under. To receive aid, schools must agree to serve nutritious lunches that meet the requirements of a Type A lunch as established by the secretary of agriculture. The lunch must contain milk, meat or alternate, vegetables and/or fruits, and bread and butter, and must provide one third of the daily RDA for children. The School Breakfast Program ensures that needy pupils and children bused to school from some distance away receive a nutritious breakfast produced from locally purchased or USDA-donated foods.

Other programs include the special milk program designed to encourage schools, camps, and child-care centers to serve milk, or to pay for milk served to needy children. The Special Food Service Program for Children offers to help states and communities provide food services for preschool and school-age children in public and nonprofit private institutions such as day-care centers and summer day camps. There are also programs that fund the purchase of food service equipment or aid in funding the administrative costs of school lunch programs.

On May 6, 1972, President Nixon proposed a three-part program to expand and improve efforts to provide food for needy children. These were (1) a comprehensive school nutrition bill to revise school lunch and breakfast programs so that the more pupils served, the more assistance a state receives, with children from families below the poverty line receiving free lunches; (2) an additional $25 million to feed needy children in cities in 1972; and (3) another $19.5 million to extend the school breakfast program to some 3,000 more schools.

Family Food Assistance. An important effort of the USDA is the improvement of nutrition for the needy, the low income family, and the elderly. The Food Distribution Program (Commodity Distribution) assists participating families through direct food donations. Although it has been in existence for a number of years, its impact has been slight. The Food Stamp Act (1964) has proved to be of greater value, and while adjusted periodically to changing conditions, it is highly acceptable to users and will probably eventually replace the commodity program. In Commodity Distribution, families pick up available foods at specified locations, whereas the food stamp user exchanges food money for coupons of higher worth to buy food in retail stores, with the United States paying the difference.

A third and new program is FIND. It seeks to locate and inform elderly persons about food assistance programs and to assist them to participate.

Education. The nutritional surveys and food programs have shown that nutrition education is a vital part of nutrition programs. Currently, educational programs are aimed at mothers with preschool children, school-age children, families using food assistance programs, and the elderly. Program evaluations indicate progress, but change will be slow and expensive.

Formulated Foods. The Food and Nutrition Service (FNS) of the USDA is evaluating new or formulated foods and their role in improving the nutritional impact of FNS programs, or to help extend its programs to nonparticipating eligible citizens. While fortification and enrichment of foods is not new, FNS criteria are based on factors of improved nutrition, lower cost, greater preparation convenience, higher acceptability, and improved stability. Foods must be generally accepted, and not be intended solely for government programs.

Present Status. It is difficult to judge the present level of nutrition in the United States or to measure the full impact of the nutrition programs. The Ten-State National Nutrition Survey indicated that a significant proportion of the surveyed population was malnourished or risked developing nutritional problems. However, malnutrition in certain segments varied in severity and in the specific nutrients involved. Prevalence of nutritional inadequacies was higher in low-income groups and most common among blacks, less among Spanish-Americans, and least among whites, but other social, cultural, and geographic difference factors were also found. The 10–16 year olds and the over 60 group both showed undesirable nutritive status. The evidence indicated that many people were making poor food choices that led to inadequate diets and poor use of money for food.

Available statistics show impressive gains in a three-year period. Participation in family assistance programs rose from 6.9 million in 1969 to 14.9 million in mid-1972, of which 11.8 million were participating in the food stamp program. While there were 440 counties and cities without family food programs in 1969, only a few rural counties were without such programs in 1972. Free or reduced-price meals in schools were provided for 8.1 million children, over double the 1969 figure. The school lunch program fed about 25 million in 1972, the breakfast program had tripled to one million, and the summer feeding activity was up to two million participants, 20 times the 1969 total. Some 64% of the affiliated families in the active program were nonwhite.

KIRBY M. HAYES, *University of Massachusetts*

FOREIGN AID

Developed nations and international organizations expanded their economic assistance to less-developed nations in 1971. Although the economies of the less-developed nations also expanded during 1971, there were shortcomings both in the contribution and use of economic-assistance funds. Early data indicated that these trends continued in 1972.

Governmental and Private Aid from Individual Nations. Sixteen industrialized nations accounted for nearly all of the economic aid provided by non-Communist nations in 1971. According to the Development Assistance Committee (DAC), the net flow of their financial resources to developing countries was $18.1 billion in 1971, which was $2.2 billion above 1970, or a 7% increase in real terms taking into account changes in monetary rates and price rises.

Official development assistance, the most important portion of the foreign-aid flow, rose 5% in real terms to $7.7 billion in 1971, its second-largest increase in a decade. Private investment and export credits reached a new high of $8.2 billion in 1971, up from $7 billion in 1970. Measured in terms of gross domestic product (GDP), the developing countries' economies grew an estimated 6.9% in 1971, an increase averaging 4.2% per capita.

According to the DAC, economic aid from the United States government totaled $3.32 billion in 1971, an increase from $3.05 billion in 1970 after three years of decline. Twelve of the other 15 nations increased their governmental assistance in 1971, while Australia, Austria, Canada, and Switzerland did not. According to the DAC, the rises were particularly substantial for Denmark (up from $59 million in 1970 to $74 million in 1971), West Germany (up from $559 million to $744 million), Portugal (up from $39 million to $52 million), and Britain (up from $447 million to $561 million).

The United Nations target for official economic development assistance from the advanced nations is 0.70% of their GNP by 1975. Unfortunately, this goal was only half achieved in 1971, and World Bank projections indicated that only a little further progress could be expected by 1975. Another problem was that the developing countries' debt repayment expenses climbed by one fifth in 1971 and were headed higher. Also, their population growth cut heavily into the living-standard improvement, and their economic gains were unevenly distributed among their peoples.

Aid from International Organizations. International organizations continued to increase their economic assistance to the less-developed countries. The World Bank group—the International Bank for Reconstruction and Development, the International Development Association, and the International Finance Corporation—listed a record $3.1 billion in new loans, investments, and credits in fiscal 1972, up from $2.3 billion in the previous year. World Bank President Robert S. McNamara reported that the group will surpass its goal of doubling its 1964–68 operations in 1969–73. For the following five years, 1974–78, McNamara proposed a further expansion in aid commitments of about 11% a year. He also set forth a policy of applying aid in ways to help the poorest 40% of the population in developing countries, instead of merely enriching the rich.

Contributions to the United Nations Development Program (UNDP) increased from $240.6 million in 1971 to $268.8 million in 1972. Its projected economic aid programs for 1972 totaled $311 million, a rise from $245 million the year before. Rudolph A. Peterson succeeded Paul G. Hoffman as head of the UNDP in January 1972.

U. S. Aid. American overseas-assistance programs again suffered from uncertainty on long-range aims and from struggles in Congress. For fiscal 1973 (starting July 1, 1972), President Nixon asked Congress for a total of $3.65 billion in military and economic aid, exceeding the fiscal 1972 appropriation by $1.02 billion. The House and Senate passed differing measures, and they were unable to agree on a final version before adjourning in October. Instead, Congress adopted a stopgap resolution temporarily continuing the aid programs at a rate of $2.63 billion a year, including about $1 billion a year for economic aid, through Feb. 28, 1973. The regular aid legislation for fiscal 1973 died with adjournment, forcing its reintroduction after the opening of the new Congress in January 1973.

Aid from Communist Nations. According to the U. S. State Department, economic credits and grants from Communist nations to less-developed countries totaled $1.7 billion in 1971, up from $1.1 billion in 1970. The Soviet Union accounted for $862 million of the 1971 total, with major commitments to Egypt, Pakistan, Iraq, and Algeria. Chinese commitments of $410 million went mainly to African nations, including Somalia, Ethiopia, Algeria, Sudan, and Mauritania. East European aid of $421 million was divided among African, Latin American, and Middle Eastern and South Asian countries.

LEWIS GULICK
Diplomatic Affairs Reporter, Associated Press

TOTAL FLOW OF FINANCIAL RESOURCES FROM DAC COUNTRIES TO DEVELOPING COUNTRIES AND MULTILATERAL AGENCIES, 1966-71

Grants by voluntary agencies
Other official flows
Private investment
Official development assistance
Private export credits

Source: Development Assistance Committee

FORESTRY AND LUMBERING

The question of clear cutting in national forest timber stands continued to be a major forestry issue in the United States in 1972. The year was also highlighted by congressional authorization for a large-scale reforestation program and for expanded public aid to private timberland owners.

Clear Cutting. The U.S. Forest Service announced a new plan for "National Forest Management in a Quality Environment." The plan called for a more sensitive approach to the use of clear cutting (the practice of completely removing mature timber stands in given areas). Where environmental impacts from clear cutting might be judged unacceptable, the areas were to be withdrawn from the base used in allowable cut calculations. Harvests were to be deferred on tracts where there was no assurance that a suitable stand of new trees could be established within five years.

Cooperative Forestry. The U.S. Congress approved amendments to the Cooperative Forest Management Act of 1950 which expanded the types of technical services to be provided by public service foresters. Henceforth, these were to include the establishment and protection of trees in urban areas. Fund authorization for federal participation in cooperative forest management was raised from $5 million to $20 million, of which $5 million was earmarked for urban forestry.

Reforestation. The Congress enacted legislation to channel receipts from duties on imports of timber into reforestation of national forest lands. Some 5 million acres in the national forests were in need of reforestation. Timber import duties amount to about $60 million annually.

Acreage planted to trees by all agencies in 1971 totaled 1,692,939 acres, according to Forest Service reports. This was an increase of 93,120 acres over 1970 planting. Of the total, over 1.3 million acres represented plantings by private landowners, principally on industry-owned land.

Forest Practice. A new Forest Practice Act for Oregon was passed by the legislature of that state. The measure called for rules governing five major classes of forest activity: timber harvesting, reforestation, road construction, application of chemicals, and slash disposal. In California, state courts declared portions of a similar forest practice act unconstitutional, but members of the California Forest Protective Association, who owned some 4 million acres of commercial timberland, pledged to continue observing the state forest practice rules despite the court decisions.

Wilderness. President Nixon directed the secretaries of agriculture and the interior to accelerate the identification of areas in the eastern United States that have wilderness potential. According to the Forest Service, almost no lands remain in the East that would qualify for wilderness status under terms of the 1964 Wilderness Act. A bill was introduced in Congress proposing the establishment of a system of "primitive-type" areas in Eastern states.

The West fared better. Congress approved the designation of a 19,500-acre Pine Mountain Wilderness in the Prescott and Tonto national forests in Arizona, and a 46,000-acre tract in Arizona's Coconino, Kaibab, and Prescott national forests, to be called the Sycamore Canyon Wilderness.

Fire. Favorable weather helped to hold forest fire losses in the United States to moderate levels during the first half of 1972, but midsummer saw the outbreak of one of California's most disastrous conflagrations in the Big Sur area. In 1971, New Mexico experienced one of its worst fire seasons, with more fires recorded and more acres burned than ever before in a single year. Florida also suffered in 1971, with the smoke from fires in the Everglades and Big Cypress Swamp areas causing Miami and Fort Lauderdale airports to be closed on several occasions. In most other parts of the country the fire situation in 1971 was no worse than usual.

For the United States as a whole, the Forest Service reported a total of 108,398 fires in 1971. They burned a total of 4,278,472 acres. Of the more than 1.3 billion acres of forest and other wild lands classed as needing fire protection, about 7%, mostly in the Southern states, still lacked organized protection services. Some 17% of the burned area in 1971 was on these unprotected lands.

U.S. Forest Service. For the fiscal year 1973, President Nixon's budget requested a total of $522,148,000 for the Forest Service of the U.S. Department of Agriculture. This was an increase of about $12 million over 1972. The 1973 total included $217,816,000 for national forest management, $158,840,000 for forest roads and trails, $55,085,000 for forest research, and $27,598,000 for federal cooperation with the states and with private owners of forest lands.

The Forest Service in 1972 was administering 182,340,000 acres of national forests, 3,802,000 acres of national grasslands, 149,000 acres of land utilization projects, and 121,880 acres of research and experimental areas. Forest research was being carried on at eight regional experiment stations, as well as at the Forest Products Laboratory in Madison, Wis., and the Institute of Tropical Forestry in Puerto Rico.

Lumber. Production of lumber in the United States in 1971 was estimated by the National Forest Products Association at 36,639,000,000 board feet, an increase of nearly 2.2 billion over 1970. Lumber output in the first five months of 1972 was running at a seasonally adjusted rate of about 8% above that recorded in 1971.

In Canada, lumber production in 1969 totaled 11,574,000,000 board feet, an increase of about 4½% over the preceding year. More than 95% of the total was softwood lumber.

Estimated world production of sawnwood in 1969, according to the UN, was 408.5 million cubic meters, a 7.5 million increase over 1968. (One cubic meter equals 424 board feet.) The 1969 increase was almost wholly in softwood production. The Soviet Union ranked first in lumber production, followed by the United States, Japan, and Canada.

CHARLES E. RANDALL
"Journal of Forestry"

U.S. LUMBER PRODUCTION, 1970–71

(In million board feet)

Producing Regions	1970	1971
Southern pine region	7,295	8,432
Douglas fir region	7,475	8,247
Western pine region	9,227	10,082
California redwood region	2,374	2,341
Other softwoods	1,068	1,181
Total softwoods	27,439	30,283
Southern hardwoods	3,684	3,351
Appalachian hardwoods	1,174	1,045
Other hardwoods	2,165	1,960
Total hardwoods	7,023	6,356

The International Conference Center in Paris was the scene of the October meeting of the representatives of the European Common Market.

FRANCE

The limits of French authority in Europe became more clearly defined in 1972. At home, political strife foreshadowed possible trouble for the Republic in the near future. President Pompidou's ambition to have France assume the moral leadership of the European Community seemed at least temporarily blocked. A series of government and parliamentary scandals may have weakened the foundations of the system he inherited from General de Gaulle. But despite political unrest and strikes, the regime remained largely unchanged.

DOMESTIC AFFAIRS

Politics. In early 1973 the country was to go to the polls to elect a new National Assembly, and much of 1972 was concerned with political maneuvering preparatory to the election. Troubled by continued divisions within the ruling Union of Democrats for the Republic (UDR), Pompidou suddenly announced a referendum, to be held April 23, on the entry into the Common Market of Britain, Denmark, Ireland, and Norway. He hoped that massive support on this issue could be turned to his domestic advantage. The Socialists had just approved British entry; thus it would be difficult for them to vote against it on merely political grounds. The Communists were bound to vote against it. The center parties of Jean-Jacques Servan-Schreiber and Jean Lecanuet, favorable to British entry, would find it difficult to vote against it. Massive popular support in the referendum would strengthen the president against die-hard Gaullists, within and without the government, still hostile to anything remotely approaching a supranational community.

The outcome of this political gimmick was at best ambiguous, if not a defeat. The Socialists decided to abstain; the Communists voted No; the center groups declared they must vote Yes. But it was by no means clear that this split between the Socialists and Communists reduced the chance of the long-sought agreement between them. Pompidou carefully avoided staking his prestige on the referendum. Yet he counted on the outcome as strengthening the position of France in Europe. He and his cabinet toured the provinces, speaking on the theme of a strong France in a "new Europe." The immediate result was that the Socialists and Communists divided as he had hoped, and the Center was embarrassed by being forced to explain that its "Yes" meant support for an enlarged Common Market, not support for the government. The public seemed generally uninterested.

Despite last-minute TV appeals, the outcome was disappointing for the administration. Some 40% of the electorate stayed home, whereas the normal rate of voting abstention had been 15 to 20%. Less than 68% of the voters voted for the proposal, nearly 32% voted against. The Socialist abstention campaign had evidently paid off. Many votes in favor reflected the purely "European" responses of the Radicals and Democratic Center. Equally, the Communists could feel no comfort in the negative vote, since it was below their usual percentage of the electorate. And many votes against the proposition came from extreme nationalists, intransigent Gaullists, and the perpetually discontented small shopkeepers and artisans.

Pompidou's strategem had miscarried; only the Socialists had clearly profited. Their secretary general, François Mitterrand, remarked, "If I'm not saying who won, I know very well who lost." And however it might be interpreted, the referendum cast

a pall of uncertainty over the regime and the political process for the rest of the year. The rumored prospect of early national elections now vanished.

Not until the summer vacation period did Pompidou respond. Then on July 5 he demanded the resignation of Premier Jacques Chaban-Delmas, on whom fell the blame for the weak turnout. This move was the more surprising in that Chaban-Delmas had obtained a 368 to 96 vote of confidence in the overwhelming Gaullist Assembly in May.

Pompidou's action in part stemmed from Chaban-Delmas' difficulties in explaining his tax situation. In addition, Chaban-Delmas had been identified with a certain liberal attitude in domestic politics, the creation of a "New Society" skeptically viewed by the Right and condemned as inadequate by those suffering from unemployment and inflation.

He was succeeded by Pierre Messmer, an old-time Gaullist who had been defense minister and had kept the trust of General de Gaulle to the end. Despite this shift to the Right, the major ministers were confirmed in their posts, while ex-Premier Edgar Faure was brought in as minister of social affairs (a gesture toward the Center) and Hubert Germain as minister of post and telecommunications (a gesture toward intransigent Gaullists).

Messmer's statement to the National Assembly on October 3 was mildly progressive: equal salaries for men and women, increased representation for consumers on the Economic and Social Council, help for the lowest paid and the unemployed, a commission to represent youth interests, and an ombudsman to mediate between the people and the state. Significantly, however, Messmer did not bother presenting his cabinet for formal Assembly approval. As Pompidou said at his March 16 press conference, "If in the future at any given moment there was no other choice than between return to the Assembly system or the presidential system, I, for my part, would prefer the presidential system."

Somewhat surprisingly, the Socialist party congress on March 11–12 approved the existing semi-presidential system. This represented a victory for Secretary-General Mitterrand over his predecessor, Guy Mollet, who continued support for a more strictly parliamentary form of government. Backed by this approval, as well as by the Socialists' relative success in the April 23 referendum, Mitterrand finally achieved the elusive political accord with the Communist party on June 27. The lengthy document he signed with Georges Marchais, deputy leader of the Communists, was more far-reaching than the 1967 accord. The two parties agreed that they would govern together, with whatever help they could get from the Center. They would nationalize 15 major industries, including the banks; abandon the nuclear force; improve labor conditions; and modify relations with the EEC and NATO. Conceived as propaganda to demonstrate the possibility of an alternative to the Gaullist regime, the program was ratified by both parties on July 9.

Undoubtedly the Socialists would have preferred to be part of a great Left-Center coalition. The last thing they wished was to see Communists gain control of key ministries, let alone the state. The Communists had the greatest suspicion of Mitterrand, as of all reform socialists, but the accord was their sole way out of the political ghetto in which the almost fixed percentage of their national support held them. Unquestionably the accord meant that a serious challenge to the Gaullists had come

KEYSTONE

ELIZABETH II of England and French President Pompidou, with Mme. Pompidou and Prince Philip, at the Palace of Versailles in May.

into being. But few expected the Left would triumph at the polls in 1973. Such a situation would bring about the decisive crisis of the Republic, possibly forcing Pompidou to submit or to suspend the regular procedures of government, with incalculable results. At the least, this Socialist-Communist alliance would bring in a more effective parliamentary opposition, limited as its function might be. At most, Mitterrand, or some other Socialist, might possibly capture the presidency in 1976.

This accord was almost the sole lively element in French politics. It did something to polarize politics. It did nothing to vitalize the independent Center. It pointed up again the authoritarian nature of the regime, the essential futility of the parliament as it now existed—save insofar as its members mediated between constituents and the administration. Pompidou's press conferences and speeches underlined his rigid adoption of de Gaulle's style in domestic affairs, while in European affairs the hoped-for leadership of France seemed to slip farther from reach. Every party showed signs of strain and cleavages. No one expected an upset in 1973, but colliding ambitions and troubles among the Gaullists and the opposition parties suggested political problems of some magnitude in the future.

Scandals. The Fifth Republic has had as many scandals as its predecessors. On February 15, Premier Chaban-Delmas discussed on television his financial operations in the wake of publication of his 1966–69 tax returns. It turned out that he had merely, if unwisely, taken advantage of loopholes in the law. Nevertheless, the image of his office was somewhat tarnished. It was not greatly enhanced by Pompidou's remark on March 16 that anyone who was purer could cast the first stone. It was also

MEMORIAL to Charles de Gaulle towers over his home town of Colombey-les-deux-Églises. Huge monument is in the form of the Cross of Lorraine, a symbol associated with the late general.

revealed that Chaban-Delmas, when he was president of the Assembly, had tried to obtain a drastic reduction of a meat-broker's fine for financial malpractice. These exposures underlined the extent to which the "New Society" had failed to improve upon the old.

A scandal broke in the state-controlled radio and television organization when it was revealed on April 26 that officials were receiving payoffs for arranging free advertising of various goods and services. The effect of the charge was to tighten the government's control of radio and television, where the political hand was already heavy.

The UDR itself suffered by the attempt of its secretary-general, René Tomasini, to dismiss these affairs as the machinations of Communists and fellow-travellers; and by his own implication in a television payoff deal. He resigned on August 24 and was replaced by Alain Peyrefitte. The involvement of a Gaullist deputy in a Lyon prostitution case was similarly unhelpful to the UDR.

Similarly stifled were the revelations in September of a civil servant, Gabriel Aranda of the Public Works ministry, who had photocopied documents showing ministers, deputies, and party leaders using their influence on behalf of private interests. Premier Messmer immediately denounced Aranda's immorality. Pompidou at his September 21 press conference angrily condemned Aranda for acting against "the most elementary rules of morality and individual dignity," which, he noted, could damage not only the government but parliament. The transparent cynicism of these responses only provided fuel for the still small fires of the opposition.

Civil Unrest. At his March 16 press conference, the president recited the many social gains France had achieved during his 10-year tenure, when he was first premier, then president. Characteristically, he began with the number of kilometers of superhighway laid down, the doubling of kindergartens, the tripling of swimming pools, while skirting inadequate hospital and housing facilities. He wound up with the statement that the number of automobiles on the roads had doubled during this period. This legerdemain did nothing to end the usual round of strikes in a country where the cost of living was generally high and a large part of the labor force made less than $200 a month. Unrest simmered in the university and secondary school systems, with demonstrations and arrests.

Breton separatists continued to dynamite public and private property to dramatize the cause of autonomy. They wanted a separate legislature with some control of local taxes and use of the Breton tongue. Of the 11 tried before the National Security Court in October, some were acquitted, some received suspended sentences, after a trial in which order was restored only after gendarmes with submachine guns were brought in. All but one of the defendants admitted guilt. An overt attempt at appeasement, the verdict was politically inspired. It did little for the cause of justice in a country where ordinary offenders were severely treated and where a government commission suggested in January that all 180 prisons in France urgently required reforms.

GOKSIN SIPAHIOGLU/JOCELYNE BANZAKIN

A five-mile funeral procession passed through Paris on March 4 to protest the shooting by a factory guard of Pierre Orvernay, a recently dismissed young worker, as he distributed leaflets outside the Renault auto works. The man had been a Maoist. Leaders of 12 extreme left-wing movements turned out for the protest, and such sympathizers as Jean-Paul Sartre, Simone de Beauvoir, and Jane Fonda participated. In retaliation for this killing, members of an extremist group, the New People's Resistance, kidnapped Renault executive Robert Nogrette on March 8, demanding release of those arrested during the protests and reinstatement of fired workers. Nogrette was released unharmed after 48 hours. President Pompidou denied having been more upset by the Nogrette kidnapping than by the Overnay murder, but suspicion remained, here as elsewhere, that the regime favored the rich and powerful over the less well-to-do.

Economy. If France had one particular economic trouble, it was that of overambitious growth goals. Pompidou had persistently set a doubling of industrial capacity within the decade as his highest priority. It was the equivalent, perhaps, of his predecessor's search for international prestige. Though Finance Minister Valéry Giscard d'Estaing said balanced foreign trade and full employment were the highest priorities, the annual growth rate, which he set at 5.6% on October 24, appeared to have absolute priority. A consequence was inflation with wages rising faster than in neighboring countries. The anti-inflationary measures he announced in early September (limited bank credit, price-freezing on goods and services of state-run firms until March 31, enforcement of price agreements between manufacturers and the Ministry of Finance, and an attempt to obtain Common Market measures against inflation) were unpopular with unions.

With elections looming in 1973, the Messmer cabinet was caught between union demands for higher wages, pensions, and family allowances and industry's opposition to higher wages and social benefits, which raise prices and lower profit margins. To check inflation, the government announced on December 7 cuts in the value-added tax and the floating of a $1 billion state loan. If the savings from the tax cut were passed on to the consumer in lower prices, it could provide a check on inflation. The loan was partly intended to soak up surplus money, also anti-inflationary in its immediate effect.

Defense. Defense policy did not change. Another series of nuclear tests occurred over Mururoa atoll during the summer, conducted in secrecy, accompanied by the familiar and futile international protests. "The way things are going," commented *le Monde*, "the political ravages caused by the Pacific tests will have gone well beyond the supposed advantages of rising to the rank of a thermonuclear power." Like China, France continued to oppose total test banning. Although the Messmer cabinet denied it contemplated tests in 1973, already charges of this intent and protests against further explosions were rising as 1972 drew to an end.

FOREIGN AFFAIRS

With enlargement of the European Community certain, the French appeared both convinced of its advantages and bored by discussion of its prospects. A poll conducted in late March showed that 60% believed a European government should be established to handle major common interests, leaving

--------- FRANCE • Information Highlights ---------

Official Name: French Republic.
Area: 211,207 square miles (547,026 sq km).
Population (1972 est.): 51,900,000. *Density,* 241 per square mile (93 per sq km). *Annual rate of increase,* 0.7%.
Chief Cities (1971 est.): Paris, the capital, 2,488,600; Marseille, 889,029; Lyon, 527,800.
Government: *Head of state,* Georges Pompidou, president (took office June 1969). *Chief minister,* Pierre Messmer, premier (took office July 1972). *Legislature*—Parliament: National Assembly, 487 members; Senate, 283 members. *Major political parties*—Union of Democrats for the Republic; Independent Republican party; Socialist party; Communist party; Center for Progress and Modern Democracy.
Language: French (official).
Education: *Expenditure* (1969), 22.3% of total public expenditure. *School enrollment* (1969)—primary, 5,019,837; secondary, 4,106,647; technical/vocational, 953,609; university/higher, 615,326.
Monetary Unit: Franc (5.012 francs equal U. S.$1, Sept. 1972).
Gross National Product (1971 est.): $155,300,000,000.
National Income per Person (1970): $2,606.
Economic Indexes: *Industrial production* (1971), 160 (1963= 100); *agricultural production* (1971), 166 (1952—56=100); *consumer price index* (1971), 138 (1963=100).
Manufacturing (major products): Steel, machinery, automobiles, metals, chemicals, airplanes, processed foods, clothing, beverages.
Major Agricultural Products: Barley (ranks 4th among world producers, 1971), grapes (world rank 2d, 1971), wheat, oats, sugar beets, apples, vegetables, cattle, fish.
Major Minerals: Iron ore (ranks 3d among world producers, 1970), coal, bauxite, potash, lead, natural gas, sulfur.
Foreign Trade (1971): *Exports,* $20,327,000,000 (chief exports, 1969—food; nonelectrical machinery; transport equipment; chemicals). *Imports,* $21,006,000,000 (chief imports, 1969—nonelectrical machinery; food, petroleum, crude and partly refined; chemicals). *Chief trading partners* (1969)—West Germany (took 21% of exports, supplied 22% of imports); Belgium-Luxembourg (11%—11%); Italy (10%—10%); United States (5%—9%).
Tourism: *Receipts* (1970), $1,191,500,000.
Transportation: *Motor vehicles* (1970), 15,704,100 (automobiles, 12,800,000); *railroads* (1970), 22,706 miles (36,540 km); *merchant fleet* (1971), 7,011,000 gross registered tons; *major national airline,* Air France.
Communications: *Telephones* (1971), 8,774,261; *television stations* (1971), 106; *television sets* (1971), 10,200,000; *radios* (1969), 15,796,000; *newspapers* (1969), 106 (daily circulation, 11,957,000).

national governments to deal with local issues; 62% favored a directly elected European parliament; 58% thought unification had not gone far enough; 53% favored a European currency; but only 39% favored creation of a European army.

The president was evidently disgruntled by the lackluster vote in the April 23 referendum on the desirability of expanding membership in the Common Market. During welcoming remarks to Premier Gaston Eyskens of Belgium on June 2, Pompidou threatened to call off the scheduled 10-nation Community summit meeting for October. He warned against "vague declarations of intent," clearly showing a determination to force progress on economic and financial accords before discussing creation of supranational institutions.

The president was caught between the urging of Belgium and Holland for rapid creation of supranational institutions and the hostility of much of his own party to them. Moreover, the referendum had failed to give him the firm base he wanted from which to deal with such demands and to impose the primacy of France within the Community. Specifically, he wanted the political secretariat to be situated in Paris. The five (and presumably the new entrants also) favored Brussels, where existing Market institutions were located. Their attitude appeared to be that Pompidou was bluffing; they were ready to call him on it. Two days of talks with the Italian government in late July seemed to ease the situation. Italy would back him on his economic and financial priorities; he, in turn, seemed more willing to contemplate the political questions.

Through August the president blew hot and cold on the summit conference. After much high-level

discussion, the two-day meeting was held in Paris, October 19–20. The nine nations (Norway having voted against joining the Market) agreed to establish a "European Union" by 1980. This vaguely defined compromise between what the Low Countries wished and what the French would grant marked a partial success for Pompidou. It was made possible by ratification of monetary and economic measures agreed to beforehand. The conference communiqué was drafted before the meeting even took place. Pompidou told the Council of Ministers on October 25 that union would come after practical steps had been taken, and not as "a prefabricated and rigid framework." But, as he remarked at his September 21 press conference, "perhaps the French people could have shown a little more enthusiasm for Europe."

Britain's entry into the Community was opposed by only 12% of those polled in March; 66% were in favor, 22% had no opinion. British-French relations were generally good. In talks with Prime Minister Edward Heath at Chequers on March 22, Pompidou failed to move him on the location of the political secretariat, although accord on other matters was reached. An unprecedented second state visit to France by Queen Elizabeth and the Duke of Edinburgh, May 15–19, led the *Canard Enchaîné* to comment that there were larger crowds for the queen than for the referendum. On August 16 the two governments announced agreement on the next phase of studies on the Channel Tunnel, an enterprise repeatedly considered and rejected since the century began. No final decision was to be made until late 1973. Much firmer were the dozen orders

THE EIFFEL TOWER is still the tallest structure in Paris, but its loftiness seems to be diminished by the many new skyscrapers going up all around it.

UPI

placed for the Anglo-French Concorde supersonic aircraft in the two countries.

Relations with Italy were cordial. On February 23 the two nations agreed on the Fréjus tunnel project. Regarding Spain, Pompidou said publicly, September 21, that he favored its entry into the Community "as soon as possible," though acknowledging both economic and political difficulties. Apparently he would welcome support from the Mediterranean countries, especially against the industrial colossus of Germany, by whose economic might France measured its own strength. Relations with the West Germans were fair, marked by the usual exchange of top-level visits: in Paris, February 10–11; in Munich, September 9. Farm policy problems were again resolved by a provisional agreement, March 22.

With eastern Europe, relations were good, bolstered by technical and economic accords. Cooperation with the Soviet Union, Pompidou said, September 21, was "better today than ever." However, Soviet press attacks on French politicians indicated annoyance with French criticism of the situation of Russian Jews and with Gaullist electioneering tactics against the French Communist party in preparation for the 1973 elections. Mitterrand was sharply criticized for cancelling a trip to Moscow after he accused the Soviet government of discriminatory practices. Nonetheless, relations were generally fair, and on April 4 the Soviets put a French satellite into orbit. They had no wish, moreover, to spoil the prospects of the European security conference, which opened in November. Another indication of closer relations with the Soviet sphere was the state visit to France by Polish Communist party leader Edward Gierek, October 1–6, when a friendship and cooperation pact was signed.

With the United States there were problems about monetary reform, the drug traffic, aerial highjacking, and the apparently endless war in Vietnam. The fact that U. S. aircraft bombed the French mission in Hanoi, October 11, killing Pierre Susini, the ranking diplomat there, had no outward consequences. Pompidou met with Henry Kissinger in mid-September and again in December, during the Vietnam peace negotiations. "France knows Indochina too well not to have ideas in this domain," he remarked, "but we also believe before all else that as things now stand, we must let the negotiations continue."

In the Middle East and Africa no policy changes were apparent. France continued to take a middle way between Israel and the Arab states, urging peace, but, as Pompidou said on March 16, "We are compelled to recognize the fact that for the time being we are talking to a blank wall." On February 15, France agreed to buy back the 50 Mirage jets sold to the Israelis in 1967 but never delivered, paying 7% interest per annum on the total sum. France also agreed to look again at the arms deals with Libya if the Libyan merger with Egypt should extend to their armed forces. French interest in and control over Africa continued to be guaranteed by economic, financial, military, and cultural accords. In Senegal and the Ivory Coast, French business concerns remained predominant. In some ways the French position in Africa was, in other than political affairs, much what it had been before African independence.

JOHN C. CAIRNS, *University of Toronto*

FRENCH LITERATURE. See LITERATURE.

GABON

The Gabonese government, assisted by the continued economic prosperity of the country, enjoyed another year of stability in 1972.

Political Affairs. On January 22, President Albert-Bernard Bongo announced the conditional release from prison of Lt. Jean Essone, leader of the 1964 attempted coup against Bongo's predecessor, Léon Mba. President Bongo reshuffled his cabinet in February, adding the portfolio of territorial organization to his numerous other duties. Paul Moukambi, who had played a major part in the negotiations for the financing of the proposed trans-Gabon railroad, was appointed minister of finance and budgeting.

In spite of the continued predominance of French capital and personnel, a slight trend toward Africanization was perceptible. Following President Bongo's visit to Senegal in February, it was announced that Gabon may recruit Senegalese technicians, teachers, and doctors to fill some of the positions still held by Europeans because of the shortage of trained Gabonese nationals. In August, the government decreed that foreign corporations operating in Gabon would be required to offer 10% of their holdings for sale to the republic.

Foreign Relations. Gabon remained unwaveringly pro-French. Bongo attended the annual summit meeting of the Afro-Malagasy and Mauritius Joint Organization (OCAMM), the organization of French-speaking African states, in Lomé, Togo, in April. At the conclusion of the conference Bongo announced that he had been reconciled with Nigerian head of state Yakubu Gowon. Of the four African states that had recognized Biafra, Gabon was the last to normalize relations with Nigeria.

The governments of Gabon and Equatorial Guinea accused one another in September of having invaded offshore islands claimed by each country. A commission with representatives from Gabon, Equatorial Guinea, Zaïre, and Congo was established to determine which nation owns the uninhabited islands of Mbane and Cocobeach in the Bay of Corisco.

Economy. Mining production continued to increase. The output of manganese reached 1.8 million tons in 1971, and the production of oil and okoume timber also set new records.

EDOUARD BUSTIN, *Boston University*

--------- GABON • Information Highlights ---------

Official Name: Gabonese Republic.
Area: 103,346 square miles (267,667 sq km).
Population (1972 est.): 500,000. *Density,* 5 per square mile (2 per sq km). *Annual rate of increase,* 0.8%.
Chief City (1967 est.): Libreville, the capital, 57,000.
Government: *Head of state,* Albert-Bernard Bongo, president (took office Dec. 1967). *Head of government,* Albert-Bernard Bongo. *Legislature* (unicameral)—National Assembly, 47 members. *Major political party*—Parti Démocratique Gabonais.
Languages: French (official), Fang, Bantu languages.
Education: *Expenditure* (1969), 17.7% of total public expenditure. *School enrollment* (1969)—primary, 94,914; secondary, 8,255; technical/vocational, 1,273; higher, 58.
Monetary Unit: CFA franc (255.79 CFA francs equal U.S.$1, Aug. 1972).
Gross National Product (1970 est.): $309,000,000.
Manufacturing (major products): Petroleum products, wood.
Major Agricultural Products: Coffee, cacao, bananas, palm oil, cassava, forest products.
Major Minerals: Petroleum, manganese ore, uranium, iron ore, gold, natural gas.
Foreign Trade (1970): *Exports,* $121,000,000. *Imports,* $80,000,000. *Chief trading partners* (1969)—France (took 35% of exports, supplied 58% of imports); United States.
Transportation: *Motor vehicles* (1969), 10,000 (automobiles, 5,200); *major national airlines,* Air Gabon; Transgabon.
Communications: *Telephones* (1971), 6,895; *television stations* (1971), 2.

--------- GAMBIA • Information Highlights ---------

Official Name: The Gambia.
Area: 4,361 square miles (11,295 sq km).
Population (1972 est.): 400,000. *Density,* 83 per square mile (32 per sq km). *Annual rate of increase,* 1.9%.
Chief City (1967 est.): Bathurst, the capital, 31,800.
Government: *Head of state,* Sir Dauda Jawara, president (took office as president April 1970). *Head of government,* Sir Dauda Jawara. *Legislature* (unicameral)—House of Representatives, 32 members. *Major political parties*—People's Progressive party; United party; People's Progressive Alliance.
Languages: English (official), Mandinka, Wolof.
Education: *School enrollment* (1969)—primary, 17,140; secondary, 5,468; technical/vocational, 141.
Monetary Unit: Dalasi (1.9188 dalasis equal U.S.$1, Aug. 1972).
Gross National Product (1970 est.): $46,000,000.
National Income per Person (1963): $79.
Manufacturing (major product): Groundnut oil.
Major Agricultural Products: Groundnuts, palm oil and kernels, rice, millet, and sorghum.
Foreign Trade (1971): *Exports,* $13,000,000. *Imports,* $24,000,000. *Chief trading partners* (1969)—United Kingdom (took 38% of exports, supplied 31% of imports); Japan; France; China.
Communications: *Telephones* (1971), 1,625; *radios* (1970), 50,000.

GAMBIA

Gambia displayed moderation in politics during 1972, and the nation moved further toward economic self-sufficiency.

Political Developments. On the eve of Gambia's 7th anniversary of independence, President Sir Dauda Jawara called for elections to the House of Representatives. Held in March, they did not alter the People's Progressive party's control of the legislature. The PPP retained its 28 seats, while the United party (UP) won only 3 seats, and one Independent was returned.

The UP, once a strong rival of the PPP, lacked campaign issues and contested only 14 seats. Despite their failure to propose alternative policies, the opposition candidates received 37% of the popular vote and thus showed that Gambia is not yet ready for one-party government. The moderate nature of PPP policies was apparent in that the 2-month campaign produced no violence.

Economic Development. Gambia's economic health was shown by the increase of 10 dalasis ($5) per ton paid to peanut farmers. Finance Minister S. M. Dibba's 1972–73 budget was a restatement of Gambia's modest economic goals and its dedication to living within its income. The major development goals were to improve the quality of peanuts and increase the amount of land devoted to rice production. The tourist industry continued to prosper, as was shown by the opening of the Fajara Hotel to help accommodate an expected 100% increase in tourists. The World Bank announced it would finance harbor improvements and Yundum Airport's modernization. It also underwrote a 50-year, $3.25 million loan for rice development, while UNICEF pledged $400,000 for upgrading education.

Britain's projected entry into the European Economic Community (EEC) caused great concern because 30% of Gambia's peanut oil and cake is exported to Europe. The loss of Commonwealth preference combined with a 10% EEC tariff on these items would undoubtedly hurt Gambia's economy. In order to counter this, Gambia became the first English-speaking African state to seek associate status with the Common Market.

HARRY A. GAILEY
California State University, San Jose

GANDHI, Indira. See BIOGRAPHY.

GARDEN FOR THE BLIND, its plants chosen for their odor or texture, was installed at the Jewish Braille Institute in New York City.

GARDENING AND HORTICULTURE

Continuing increases in labor costs and growing pressure from environmentalists and ecologists for a ban on the use of pesticides were major concerns among commercial horticulturalists in 1972. The sentiment favoring elimination of the use of DDT and other pesticides has also spurred research in the development of feasible alternatives. Among prizes awarded, three hybrid tea roses took top honors at the All-America Rose Selections.

Pesticides and Research. Agriculturalists were briefly encouraged when, at the conclusion of federal hearings on the possibility of banning the use of DDT, the examiner stated that seven months of testimony had failed to prove allegations that DDT causes severe environmental damage and recommended that the government refrain from banning its use. On June 14, however, the administrator of the Environmental Protection Agency, William D. Ruckelshaus, issued an order outlawing all agricultural uses of DDT except for green peppers, onions, and sweet potatoes in storage. The ban was to become effective Dec. 31, 1972.

Other persistent pesticides currently undergoing extensive review by the Environmental Protection Agency to determine if they are endangering the environment are lindane, benzene hexachloride, and endrin. It was feared that if more stringent restric-

tions were to be placed on the use of pesticides for production of food crops, consumer prices would skyrocket.

Because of the restrictions already placed on the use of pesticides in the production of horticultural crops, there was increased emphasis on research to develop plants that are resistant to diseases and insects. Research aimed at developing alternative methods of controlling disease and insects has also been increased. Results of this research have created some exciting possibilities for the control of certain plant pests. Scientists at Louisiana State University, for example, found that the sex attractant taken from one virgin female sweet potato weevil was sufficient to attract 1,200 male weevils to a single trap in an 8-hour period. These findings may lead to the ultimate eradication of this particular pest.

Rising Labor Costs. Competition from foreign production continued to grow in 1972. It is believed that competition will continue to increase because the higher minimum wage authorized by Congress in 1972 will result in higher labor costs, placing American growers in an even less advantageous position. Increased labor costs can also be expected to lead to higher food prices for the consumer.

Winning Roses. Hybrid tea roses captured the limelight in the All-America Rose Selections trials in 1972, with three beautiful cultivars—Electron, Gypsy, and Medallion—making a clean sweep of the awards. The three winners were to be featured in the 112 All America Rose Selections-accredited Public Rose Gardens scattered throughout the United States. Plants of the three winners became available in the fall of 1972 at leading nurseries and garden centers and by mail from the major mail-order rose specialists.

Electron is an Irish rose that, under the name Mullard Jubilee, had already won nine awards in Europe. It is a bright rose-pink hybrid tea that produces large quantities of fragrant blossoms. The long, pointed buds open to high-centered, well-formed blooms of exhibition quality and are produced on stems of medium length. When cut, the open blossoms are long lasting and hold their color well. Electron should prove to be the most decora-

GYPSY MOTH infestation was particularly heavy in the northeastern United States in the summer of 1971.

tive garden variety because of the shapeliness of the plant and its ability to produce numerous high-quality blossoms throughout the flowering season.

Gypsy is an outstanding rose with long sturdy branches that hold aloft, like orange-red torches, their large, 5-inch, fully double blossoms. Typical of the hybrid tea, the husky bush grows with a vigor that gives an abundance of blossoms for garden display, house, and exhibition use. A mantle of leathery, rich green foliage covers the entire plant and adds to its rugged beauty.

Medallion is a distinctive variety having probably the largest blossoms of any All-America Award winner. The huge 7- to 8-inch blossoms are formed by up to 35 broad petals of apricot pink. The light green oval-shaped foliage covers the vigorous plant and has good disease resistance.

New Books. Several interesting and useful books on horticulture were published in 1972. *Gardening Indoors Under Lights* by Frederick and Jacqueline Kranz is an updated edition of a book first published in 1957. Details are given on how to grow crops under artificial light, with special attention to the cultivation of orchids, African violets, begonias, poinsettias, cinerarias, cyclamens, and Easter lilies. The book also contains up-to-date information on the indoor culture of ornamental plants and vegetables.

Propagating House Plants by Arno and Irene Nehrling is designed for the amateur, and contains information primarily on plants grown indoors. It offers a discussion of some of the concepts of propagation, and describes such specific aids and techniques as hormones, mist propagation, and light. Growing facilities, such as greenhouses and window boxes, are treated. The book contains a dictionary of plants in which the propagation procedures and directions for the growing and handling of various plants are discussed. Also included in a section that outlines projects for children.

Two other books are worthy of note. *Water Gardens—Pools, Fountains and Plants* by Jack Kramer deals with formal and informal pools and fountains, dishes and bowls for pools, and plants to use in water gardens. *Popular Orchids* by Brian and Wilma Ritterhousen should be of interest to both the experienced and beginning orchid grower.

DONALD W. NEWSOM
Louisiana State University

GENEEN, Harold S. See BIOGRAPHY.

GENETICS

Advances in genetics during 1972 included the production of hybrid plants by a nonsexual fusion technique, the development of a biochemical method of joining genes together, and the discovery that DNA synthesis is initiated on short molecules of RNA.

Hybrid Plants. Hybrid plants have been produced for thousands of years by the mating of interfertile closely related species. In 1972, Peter S. Carlson, Harold H. Smith, and Rosemarie D. Dearing of Brookhaven National Laboratory developed a nonsexual method of producing hybrid plants that is thought to be independent of the interfertility of the two species being hybridized. Free mesophyll cells of young leaves of the two species were stripped of their walls by treatment with an enzyme that decomposes cellulose, a constituent of the cell wall, producing wall-less protoplasts. The protoplasts were then stimulated to fuse by treatment with sodium nitrate. Only fused hybrid protoplasts regenerated their walls, multiplied in culture, and, when placed in a special culture medium, grew into shoots. These shoots were then grafted onto young plants of one of the parental species to complete the growth of hybrid leaves. Flowers and fertile seed capsules were subsequently obtained from the hybrids.

The efficiency of the fusion method of hybridization was very low: only 33 hybrid plants were obtained from a mixture of more than 10 million protoplasts of each species. For their initial experiment, Dr. Carlson and his co-workers chose two species of tobacco plant that had previously been hybridized by sexual mating and the properties of whose hybrids had been studied. This experimental system was chosen because cells of this hybrid can grow in the special culture medium but parental cells cannot. Further experiments are in progress for obtaining more general methods for preferentially recovering hybrids formed by protoplast fusion and for trying to extend the method to species that are not interfertile.

Biochemical Joining of Genes. One goal of contemporary genetics is the development of methods by which known genes can be incorporated into mammalian cells. An important first step in this direction has been made by David A. Jackson, Robert H. Symons, and Paul Berg of Stanford University. They have fused the deoxyribonucleic acid, or DNA, of the bacterial virus lambda dvgal, which includes the genes that control the metabolism of the sugar galactose, to the DNA of SV40 virus, which is able to enter into a stable, heritable association with chromosomes of some mammalian cells and can cause tumors. By a specific enzymatic reaction, the circular DNA of SV40 was cleaved to form a linear molecule. A "tail" of A residues was then added to one end of each strand by a second enzyme-catalyzed reaction. Similarly, a "tail" of T residues was added to one end of each strand of lambda dvgal DNA. When the two DNA preparations were mixed, the polyA tails formed double stranded regions by bonding to the polyT tails. Further biochemical reactions were used to fill the gaps and close the DNA into a complete double stranded circle. Experiments are in progress to determine whether this hybrid DNA can integrate into mammalian chromosomes.

DNA Synthesis. The replication of DNA proceeds by using the existing strands of DNA as templates for the assembly of their complementary strands from the four types of deoxynucleotide precursors. A molecule of bacterial DNA is over 3 million base pairs long. Early experiments suggested that replication begins at one end of the molecule and proceeds in a continuous manner to the other end.

In 1966, however, Reiji Okazaki and his colleagues discovered that bacterial DNA is not replicated in this way but by a discontinuous mechanism involving synthesis and joining of short DNA units about 1,500 nucleotides long. In 1972, Okazaki, Akio Sugino, and Susumu Hirose, working at Nagoya University in Japan, found that each of these short DNA units is initiated by first assembling a short stretch (50–100) of ribonucleotides onto which deoxynucleotides are then assembled. Thus the short DNA unit first synthesized is in fact a hybrid of RNA and DNA. The ribonucleotides do not, however, become incorporated into the final long strands

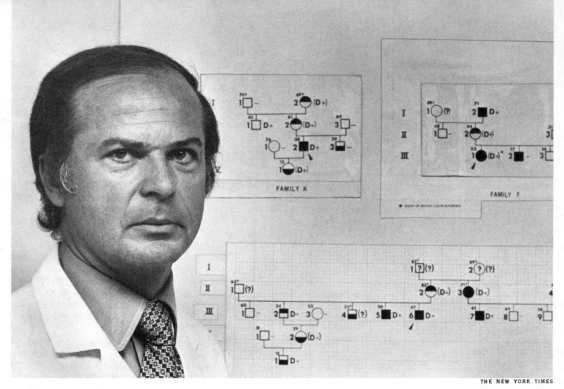

RONALD R. FIEVE headed a team of scientists at Columbia University in determining that some cases of manic-depressive illness might be transmitted from generation to generation as the result of an X chromosomal defect.

of DNA, but are digested away prior to the joining step. Similar results have been obtained by Arthur Kornberg and his colleagues at Stanford University for replication of bacteriophage DNA. These findings are expected to lead to an understanding of the special sites at which DNA synthesis is initiated.

FRANK G. ROTHMAN
Brown University

GEOGRAPHY

Geographical research and education in 1972 emphasized problems of the environment, cities, and minority groups. In July, the launching of ERTS-1, the first Earth Resources Technology Satellite, heralded an era when geographers' skills in interpreting man's impact on the environment would be put to use as never before, especially when combined with concurrent developments in computer mapping. In August, Canadian geographers hosted the 22nd International Geographical Congress (IGC) at the University of Montreal, with about 2,500 members from 74 countries attending. In the latter half of the year, a commercial U. S. aerial reconnaissance group undertook the first thorough mapping of the Amazon River basin of eastern Peru.

Environmental Quality. Sessions at the annual meeting of the Association of American Geographers (AAG) in April focused on such environmental themes as visual blight, concentration of toxic substances, waste disposal and material recycling, and the energy crisis. The National Geographical Society continued to support research projects on worldwide environmental and ecological themes, and at the IGC meeting there were discussions of the international dimension of environmental problems. The heightened interest in such studies marks a return to geography's tradition of research into the interactions of man and environment. However, contemporary studies emphasize varying human perceptions toward environmental situations, especially within varying cultural contexts, rather than the deterministic influence of the physical environment on man.

Urban Problems. Geographers also continued research into and analyses of urban and social problems. Grants from the National Science Foundation to the AAG support two such projects. One will study the progress made in meeting public policy goals in urban employment and poverty, recreation and open space, land use and transportation, modification of the physical environment, and other areas. Over 20 metropolitan vignettes and an Atlas of Urban America will summarize the results of the project. The other grant will support investigations of suburban black enclave towns in several large metropolitan areas. The enclave towns will be studied as ports of entry for black inner-city migrants, as sites for enhanced economic opportunities, as alternative residential areas, and as potential models for integrated communities.

Minority Groups. More than a dozen black geographers are engaged in the above urban research, and the AAG Commission on Geography and Afro-America continued its efforts toward incorporating minority groups into American geographical studies. Thus over 60 blacks have participated in its graduate fellowship programs, and several hundred secondary school and college teachers attended workshops and leadership conferences on environmental problems, the black community, and urban and social analysis. The *Southeastern Geographer* (November 1971) and *Economic Geography* (January 1972) produced special numbers on "Contributions to an Understanding of Black America" and "Geographic Aspects of Black America," respectively.

Geography in Education. Enrollments in college geography courses continued to increase. In 1972 more than 750,000 students were enrolled in such

courses, as compared to 530,000 in 1966. The number of colleges offering major programs in geography increased from 296 to 395 in the same time period, and the number of B. A. or first professional degrees in geography almost doubled. This rate of increase was nearly twice that in other social sciences. Similarly, job opportunities in geography continued to increase, particularly in applied areas such as retail and wholesale location analysis, planning, and the fields of environmental impact and planning. Current projections indicate a stabilization in the job market for geographers, but the outlook is favorable.

J. WARREN NYSTROM
Association of American Geographers

GEOLOGY

Wide-ranging explorations of ocean basins and shallow seas continued in 1972, and problems associated with continental drift and plate tectonics were again focal points of interest. Advances were made in astrogeology as the moon was again explored by man, Mars was extensively photographed, and a spacecraft studied the surface of Venus.

JOIDES. The Deep Sea Drilling Project of the Joint Oceanographic Institutions for Deep Earth Sampling (JOIDES), begun in 1965 under a grant from the National Science Foundation, completed six more "legs" of its mission. It was granted funds for 19 more cruises through August 1975.

Leg 20 concentrated on the sea floor southeast of Japan and east of the Marianas Trench, where rocks date from the Late Jurassic Period or earlier. Although the ocean there is mostly deeper than 20,000 feet (6,000 meters), 13 holes were drilled by the *Glomar Challenger*. An unusual thickness of chalk was found, which geologists interpreted as having accumulated 55 million years ago when that region of the sea floor lay at the equator, about 930 miles (1,500 km) southeast of its present location, since such sediments are produced most abundantly at equatorial latitudes. Thus the plate of the earth's crust underlying the drilled region is apparently moving northwestward toward the Asian coast at about 4 inches (10 cm) per year. Where it meets the coast it is being destroyed by downbending and subsequent melting.

Leg 21 was spent in the area between Australia and New Guinea, on the one side, and Tonga, the Kermadec Islands, and New Zealand, on the other. The records obtained from eight sites drilled there indicate some geological unrest in Early Tertiary times, about 50 million years ago. There was a general lack of deposition of sediment from the Late Eocene to the Middle Oligocene epochs, which may have coincided with the active movement of the Australian plate away from Antarctica. After this separation, the ocean gradually deepened.

Eight holes were drilled on Leg 22 in the eastern Indian Ocean. The plate of which India is a part has been shown to have moved northward rapidly in Cretaceous times, about 100 million years ago, but to have moved very little in the Early Tertiary. Calcite-rich sediments regarded as of warm-water origin and dating from the Late Cretaceous to the Miocene, about 20 million years ago, were found to be widely distributed in the area.

Leg 23 accomplished the drilling of six sites in the Arabian Sea and six in the Red Sea. The eastern Arabian Sea has been receiving calcite-rich sediment since at least Paleocene times, about 60 million years ago. Sediments beneath the Red Sea were especially rich in copper, zinc, and vanadium, and they may be the source of the metals previously found in hot brines near that sea bottom.

Leg 24 began in the Gulf of Aden near Djibouti and continued around the Horn of Africa, ending at Mauritius with 12 holes drilled.

Seabed Assessment. JOIDES and other projects are contributing to the International Decade of Ocean Exploration, which began in 1970 and in which more than 30 nations are taking part. The most interesting of these other projects to geologists is Seabed Assessment, an investigation of continental margins, midoceanic ridges, and deep-sea mineral resources. The U. S. Geological Survey completed a seven-month voyage of 26,500 miles (42,700 km) to learn more about the geology of the Gulf of Mexico and the Caribbean Sea. No drilling was done, but profiles were obtained of the sea floor to depths of several thousand feet by means of seismic reflection techniques. Five areas in particular were studied: the Bay of Campeche, the eastern coast of the Yucatán peninsula, a large area adjacent to Puerto Rico and the Lesser Antilles, the continental margin between Venezuela and the Caribbean Sea, and across the Atlantic Ocean off the coast of Liberia. The last study was aimed at finding geological links between the two continental areas.

Study of the Moon. About 245 pounds (110 kg) of material were returned by the Apollo 16 lunar mission in April. Most of the many different kinds of moon rocks were rich in aluminum and calcium and closely approached pure anorthosite. Individual specimens showed a remnant magnetism, as did instruments left on the moon. Such magnetism is acquired as molten rocks cool and "lock in" a magnetism proportional to the prevailing magnetism at the time of cooling, so the evidence indicates that the moon has a magnetic history even though its present field is very weak. It appears to have been exposed to a rather strong field for at least one billion years early in its history. Three explanations have been offered: first, that the moon may have been near enough to the earth at one time to be magnetized by the earth's field; second, that the source may have been a stronger solar magnetism in the past; and third, that the moon generated its own field when it possessed an electrically conductive, mobile core. Each of these explanations, however, presents certain difficulties.

By great good luck a large meteoroid—estimated at about 20 feet (6 meters) in diameter—struck the moon on May 13, when four seismic stations were in operation on the lunar surface. The resulting seismic records confirmed the existence of a lunar mantle and crust some 40 miles (65 km) thick and hinted at the presence of a core beginning about 620 miles (1,000 km) below the surface.

Martian Geology. The U. S. Mariner 9 spacecraft reached the vicinity of Mars in November 1971 and returned several thousand photographs of the surface in the months that followed. The pictures revealed an amazing variety of features besides the cratered terrain previously observed. There are old lava flows and inactive volcanoes up to 5 miles (8 km) high and 310 miles (500 km) wide at their bases. One plateau region shows numerous parallel faults and sunken rifts as deep as 2.8 miles (4.5 km). Peculiar curved ridges in the polar regions may be moraines of once-large ice caps, and there

are large dunes and other wind-formed features. Most intriguing of all are what appear to be water-carved canyons with complex tributary systems. These may be formed by subsurface movements or wind action, but some scientists think that enough water may lie frozen in the ice caps or in near-surface materials to provide streams.

Surface of Venus. On July 22 the USSR's Venus 8 landed on Venus and relayed back radio data for nearly an hour. The probe indicated that surface materials at the landing site may have a composition like granite and be of volcanic origin.

ERTS. The first Earth Resources Technology Satellite (ERTS-1) was orbited in July. It will provide information on oceans, minerals, erosion effects, and climate changes of importance to geologists.

(See also ASTRONOMY; SPACE EXPLORATION.)

WILLIAM LEE STOKES, *University of Utah*

GEORGIA

The first reorganization of state government in Georgia in four decades was instituted in 1972. The year also saw a continuing feud between Gov. Jimmy Carter and Lt. Gov. Lester Maddox, a battle for the U. S. Senate, purchase of the banks along a four-mile stretch of the Chattahoochee River for a wild river park, and an upturn in the fortunes of the state's largest employer, Lockheed-Georgia Co.

Reorganization. Georgia's state government was last reorganized in 1931. But in 1972, Governor Carter, assisted by the General Assembly, streamlined state government by grouping together scattered functions and eliminating many duplicating efforts. The legislature passed 90% of the reorganization measures submitted by the governor.

Major features included creation or revamping of 22 major operating agencies of the Executive Branch of the government. The major new divisions created were the departments of Human Resources, Natural Resources, and Offender Rehabilitation. Human Resources consolidated health, welfare, vocational rehabilitation, and several other functions affecting the personal welfare of Georgians. Natural Resources was given responsibility for protecting Georgia's air, land, water, minerals, and wildlife, and for providing parks and recreational facilities. Thirty-three separately budgeted agencies or functions of agencies were merged into this department or assigned to it for administrative purposes. Offender Rehabilitation merged the old departments of Corrections and Probation and the administrative functions of the Board of Pardons and Paroles so that a unified effort could be made to rehabilitate the public offender through institutions, probation, parole, or community-based services.

As in any massive undertaking of this type, there were conflicts. State Labor Commissioner Sam Caldwell and State Treasurer William Burson clashed with the governor. Caldwell charged Carter with a "power grab" attempt, but by the end of the year Caldwell was under investigation for alleged use of pressure tactics in collecting campaign funds. Burson went to court to keep his office from being abolished by a constitutional amendment included in the reorganization plan.

Feud. The feud between Governor Carter and Lieutenant Governor Maddox continued, and at year's end Maddox charged that Carter was behind an attempt to strip his office of its powers to appoint state Senate chairmen. Carter denied the charge.

GEORGIA · Information Highlights

Area: 58,876 square miles (152,489 sq km).
Population (1970 census): 4,589,575. *Density:* 80 per sq mi.
Chief Cities (1970 census): Atlanta, the capital, 497,421; Columbus, 155,028; Macon, 122,423; Savannah, 118,349; Albany, 72,623; Augusta, 59,864; Athens, 44,342.
Government (1972): *Chief Officers*—governor, Jimmy Carter (D); lt. gov., Lester G. Maddox (D); secy. of state, Ben W. Fortson, Jr. (D); atty. gen., Arthur K. Bolton (D); treas., William H. Burson (D); supt. of schools, Jack P. Nix (D); chief justice, Bond Almand. *General Assembly*—Senate, 56 members (50 Democrats, 6 Republicans); House of Representatives, 195 members (173 D, 22 R).
Education (1971–72): *Enrollment*—public elementary schools, 701,000 pupils; 29,301 teachers; public secondary, 393,-000 pupils; 19,627 teachers; nonpublic schools (1970–71), 32,678 pupils; 1,620 teachers; college and university, 132,000 students. *Public school expenditures*, $789,377,-000 ($788 per pupil). *Average teacher's salary,* $8,226.
State Finances (fiscal year 1970): *Revenues,* $1,631,621,000 (3% general sales tax and gross receipts taxes, $335,-807,000; motor fuel tax, $154,699,000; federal funds, $408,-746,000). *Expenditures,* $1,576,441,000 (education, $725,-588,000; health, welfare, and safety, $261,192,000; highways, $208,498,000). *State debt,* $870,190,000 (June 30, 1970).
Personal Income (1971): $16,545,000,000; per capita, $3,547.
Public Assistance (1971): $319,641,000. *Average monthly payments* (Dec. 1971)—old-age assistance, $56.42; aid to families with dependent children, $101.88.
Labor Force: *Nonagricultural wage and salary earners* (July 1972), 1,612,100. *Average annual employment* (1971)—manufacturing, 309,000; services, 198,000. *Insured unemployed* (Aug. 1972)—20,500 (1.8%).
Manufacturing (1970): *Value added by manufacture,* $5,439,-700,000. Textile mill products, $1,091,500,000; food and kindred products, $710,300,000; transportation equipment, $551,400,000; apparel and other textile products, $538,-100,000; paper and allied products, $499,200,000; chemicals and allied products, $399,200,000.
Agriculture (1970): *Cash farm income,* $1,272,312,000 (livestock, $712,957,000; crops, $475,734,000; government payments, $83,621,000). *Chief crops* (in order of value, 1971)—Peanuts (ranks 1st among the states), corn, tobacco, cotton lint.
Mining (1971): *Production value,* $229,533,000 (ranks 29th among the states). *Chief minerals*—Clays, $119,096,000; stone, $69,897,000; cement, $23,940,000; sand and gravel, $5,310,000.
Fisheries (1971): *Commercial catch,* 18,409,000 pounds ($7,-478,000). *Leading species by value:* Shrimp, $6,466,000; crabs, $680,000; shad, $133,000.
Transportation: *Roads* (1971), 99,995 miles (160,922 km); *motor vehicles* (1971), 2,584,042; *railroads* (1971), 5,435 miles (8,747 km); *public airports* (1972), 107.
Communications: *Telephones* (1972), 2,586,800; *television stations* (1971), 16; *radio stations* (1971), 228; *newspapers* (1972), 33 (daily circulation, 1,007,000).

Elections. U. S. Sen. David Gambrell, the Atlanta attorney appointed by Governor Carter to complete the unexpired term of the late Richard B. Russell, lost in the Democratic primary to State Rep. Sam Nunn of Perry. In the general election, Nunn defeated the Republican candidate, U. S. Rep. Fletcher Thompson of Atlanta. President Nixon easily won Georgia's 12 electoral votes, but the Democrats retained their large majorities in the General Assembly.

River Park. A $4 million grant from the U. S. Bureau of Outdoor Recreation helped Georgia acquire 377 acres along the banks of a 4.1-mile stretch of the Chattahoochee River in the metropolitan Atlanta area for the Chattahoochee Palisades State Park. The unpolluted stretch of wild river, part of a 48.1-mile segment that may eventually become parkland, is unique in urban America.

Lockheed. The Lockheed-Georgia Co., on the verge of bankruptcy in 1971 because of cost overruns in production of the world's largest airplane, the C-5A, tightened its belt in 1972, selling or abandoning use of some 1 million square feet of space and cutting employment from 15,000 to 12,000. Officials said the firm was operating at a profit as 1972 ended.

GENE STEPHENS
Georgia State University

GERMAN LITERATURE. See LITERATURE.

East and West German negotiators meet in Bonn on November 9 to initial a treaty that pledges cooperation and a mutual recognition of sovereignty.

GERMANY

Germany is divided into two separate states. The Federal Republic of Germany (West Germany) is a democratic, parliamentary republic and a member of such Western organizations as the North Atlantic Treaty Organization (NATO), the European Coal and Steel Community, and the European Economic Community (Common Market). The German Democratic Republic (East Germany, also known as the DDR from the initials of its name in German) is, in effect, a Communist one-party state. It is affiliated with the Warsaw Pact and the Council for Mutual Economic Assistance (COMECON), the Eastern counterparts of NATO and the EEC.

Between these two states, West Berlin, a Western outpost within East Germany, maintains its precarious existence. Economically, it is integrated into the Federal Republic, but politically and militarily it has a separate status.

EAST-WEST GERMAN RELATIONS

Throughout 1972 relations between the Federal Republic and the DDR continued to improve. The initialing of a Basic Treaty (*Grundvertrag*) on November 9 settled the terms for a more permanent relationship between the two states. Leading up to the treaty, agreements were signed concerning better postal and telephone services and transit traffic between West Germany and West Berlin, the latter agreement a complement to the Big Four accord of 1971 on Berlin.

A traffic pact eased travel restrictions; supplementary statements of the East Berlin government allowed for more frequent and longer visits of West Germans and West Berliners to the DDR and also permitted East Germans of all ages, not just the elderly, to visit West Germany in "pressing family matters." A general amnesty including political prisoners, among them many West Germans, was also viewed as a goodwill gesture on the part of the DDR. Similarly a law, passed by the People's Chamber, released from their DDR citizenship all those who had escaped from East Germany before Jan. 1, 1972. It also exempted them from prosecution for their escape, thus allowing them to return as visitors to East Germany.

The Basic Treaty. The treaty provided for the good-neighborly, peaceful coexistence of the two German states. It pledged both countries to respect each other's independence and sovereignty and to cooperate in practical and humanitarian matters. Both states were to exchange permanent "representative missions"; in dealings with third countries, neither would speak for the other. Supplementary notes acknowledged the rights and responsibilities of the United States, the USSR, Britain, and France in Berlin and in Germany as a whole. Correspondingly, the Big Four reaffirmed the continuation of their prerogatives in the event that the two Germanys should join the United Nations in 1973—a move the Big Four would support.

Clearly a compromise, the Basic Treaty satisfied the demands of the DDR for recognition as a separate sovereign state by the Federal Republic. At the same time it took into account the West German refusal to treat East Germany as a foreign country by providing for the appointment of "representative

missions" instead of ambassadors in the two capitals. Beyond this its effectiveness would depend on its implementation.

From the Western viewpoint, the first effects of the rapprochement were beneficial. Travel to and from East Germany became easier, traffic between West Berlin and West Germany moved smoothly, and families separated for years were reunited. West Germans amnestied under the recent law were being returned to the Federal Republic. During the year several million West Germans and West Berliners visited the DDR.

But there were clear limits to the détente. While the Basic Treaty did not expressly abrogate the concept of an overall German nation, the DDR made it clear that its Marxist concept of a nation differs sharply from the "bourgeois" concept of a "class-torn" nation. The DDR thus considered itself closer to other socialist nations than to the "monopoly-capitalist, imperialist" West Germans. Moreover, both the East German government and the (Communist) Socialist Unity party (SED) were carefully guarding against any political and security problems that closer contacts between East and West Germany might create. Nonetheless, early ratification of the treaty by both West Germany and East Germany was assured after the West German electorate expressed its approval in the parliamentary elections of November 19.

West Berlin. The city became more accessible due to the new travel and transit accords. The improvements were reflected in decreasing air travel and increasing automobile trips to and from West Berlin (60,000 fewer flights and 121,000 more car trips in July 1972 as compared with July 1971). Air freight, too, decreased. The greater feeling of security also accounted for the above-average rise of West Berlin stocks. Similarly, real estate values almost doubled in the more affluent parts of the city. The amount of industrial investments, on the other hand, did not increase, since lack of space and a shortage of manpower barred any further expansion at the time.

FEDERAL REPUBLIC OF GERMANY
(West Germany)

The issue of Bonn's rapprochement with East Germany and Eastern Europe was one of the predominant themes of West German politics throughout the year 1972. On November 19 the West Germans endorsed the *Ostpolitik* ("Eastern policy") of Chancellor Willy Brandt by giving his Social Democratic party (SPD) and its partner, the Free Democratic party (FDP), a small party of old-line liberals and entrepreneurs headed by Foreign Minister Walter Scheel, a substantial majority of votes in the elections for a new Bundestag.

The elections were called because, due to defections over Brandt's *Ostpolitik,* his government had lost its slim majority in the Bundestag. Both the government and the opposition, consisting of the Christian Democratic Union (CDU) and its Bavarian offshoot, the Christian Social Union (CSU), were supported by exactly one half of the deputies. While CDU and CSU had earlier helped to ratify other "Eastern" treaties through mass voting abstentions and might even have allowed ratification of the Basic Treaty in the same way, it was unlikely they would support government-sponsored internal reforms. Moreover, a series of state elections in which the government parties invariably suffered setbacks had led to a further stiffening of their position. The expected stalemate could be resolved only by new elections.

The election campaign centered as much on economic problems as it did on the Basic Treaty, which both the CDU and the CSU denounced as a surrender to the East Germans. West Germany was plagued by inflation, at a record rate of 6.4% per year, urban and environmental problems, and a deepening educational crisis.

In the election campaign, the CDU, headed by Deputy Rainer Barzel, and the CSU, led by ex-Finance Minister Franz-Josef Strauss, predicted financial chaos if the SPD/FDP coalition were returned to office. Their joint 9-point program called for a reorganization of government finances and full employment, in a "humane society based on individual accomplishments." The SPD, in turn, promised to improve the "quality of life" by improving public services and widening the opportunities of individual self-realization beyond the domain of material consumption. It, too, pledged itself to maintain full employment. The FDP, determined to continue its coalition with the SPD, emphasized its role as a check on SPD social reform plans.

The SPD won 45.9% of the vote and 230 Bundestag seats, a gain of 6 seats. For the first time in the West German Republic's existence, it emerged as the largest party. The FDP received 8.4% and 42 seats, while CDU and CSU got 44.8% and 224 seats. The remaining votes went to the German Communist party and the neo-Nazi National Democrats. Neither won any seat. West Berlin was to send 22 deputies to Bonn (12 Social Democrats, 1 Free Democrat, 9 Christian Democrats) who, however, could vote only on certain matters. An impressive 91.2% of the electorate cast its vote.

The new government again was headed by Willy Brandt as federal chancellor (inaugurated on December 14), with Walter Scheel as before serving as vice chancellor and foreign minister. The Bundestag elected a woman, Annemarie Renger-Loncarevic (SPD), as its president—a first in German parliamentary history.

Economic Policy. The spreading inflation forced the government to decide whether to continue its deficit spending, in order to deal with pressing reforms, or to increase taxes but also reduce expenditures and abandon many of these reforms. Finance and Economics Minister Karl Schiller called for the latter course; other ministers insisted on the former. When the cabinet accepted foreign-exchange controls to stem the influx of foreign capital, Schiller, increasingly isolated, resigned in protest against what he considered unwise tampering with the free-market economy.

He was succeeded by Helmut Schmidt (SPD), until then minister of defense. Schmidt, who was as much concerned with the distribution as with the size of the social product, favored an enlarged social reform program. His proposed budget for 1973 provided for a 10.5% increase of expenditures to be covered by higher taxes.

While West Germany still enjoyed full employment, the growth of the economy had slowed down. Whether "stagflation" could be overcome depended, however, not only on what measures the West German government would take. Such was the integration of West Germany with other Common Market countries that its economic problems could not be solved solely on the national level.

Cultural Life. For the first time since the 1920's, a German novelist, Heinrich Böll, won the Nobel Prize for literature (see BIOGRAPHY). Böll, a writer whose deceptively simple style conceals a highly skilled literary craftsman, had made a name for himself as a social critic and satirist and a bitter opponent of nationalism. Because of his leftist views, some conservative newspapers felt called upon to denounce the award as an interference in the election campaign, meant to help Willy Brandt and the SPD.

Educational problems continued to dominate the cultural scene. Both high schools and universities lacked the facilities to meet the rising demand for secondary and higher education. Rapid expansion and inadequate facilities led to an alarming decline in the quality of students and teachers. Student discontent was less activist, but continued. Moreover, while West Germany's student body had been increasing rapidly, complaints were widespread that study stipends were insufficient to allow working-class youths to attend a university. Both SPD and FDP promised to remedy this situation. To make this possible financially and in terms of facilities, much stricter academic admission standards would have to be introduced.

The educational crisis was aggravated by the fact that the federal government had no jurisdiction over education, which was a state matter. In 1972 five of the states were governed by the CDU or CSU. More conservative than the SPD/FDP coalition in Bonn, these governments were reluctant to cooperate on the educational reforms proposed by the federal government.

The Olympics. In late summer West Germany was host to the XXth Olympiad. The games, held in Munich, set new records in various fields. West Germany won fourth place in its overall performance; East Germany was third. East German

WILLY BRANDT and his wife vote in the November 18 election that kept his coalition government in power.

GOKSIN SIPAHIOGLU/JOCELYNE BENZAKIN

WEST GERMANY • Information Highlights

Official Name: Federal Republic of Germany.
Area: 95,743 square miles (247,973 sq km). West Berlin, 186 square miles (481 sq km).
Population (1972 est.): 59,200,000. *Density,* 622 per square mile (240 per sq km). *Annual rate of increase,* 0.2%.
Chief Cities (1969 est.): Bonn, the capital, 300,400; Hamburg, 1,818,600; Munich, 1,302,600; Cologne, 860,800.
Government: *Head of state,* Gustav Heinemann, president (took office July 1969). *Head of government,* Willy Brandt, federal chancellor (took office Oct. 1969). *Legislature—* Parliament: Bundestag, 496 members; Bundesrat, 45 members. *Major political parties*—Christian Democratic Union; Social Democratic party; Free Democratic party.
Language: German (official).
Education: *Expenditure* (1969), 11.2% of total public expenditure. *School enrollment* (1969)—primary, 6,098,425; secondary, 4,280,996; technical/vocational, 2,086,194; university/higher, 440,647.
Monetary Unit: Deutsche mark (3.202 D. marks equals U. S. $1, Sept. 1972).
Gross National Product (1971 est.): $192,200,000,000.
National Income per Person (1970): $2,698.
Economic Indexes: *Industrial production* (1971), 161 (1963= 100); *agricultural production* (1971), 152 (1952–56=100); *consumer price index* (1971), 127 (1963=100).
Manufacturing (major products): Iron and steel, chemicals, machinery and equipment, automobiles, textiles, electrical equipment, processed foods.
Major Agricultural Products: Rye (ranks 3d among world producers, 1970), oats (world rank 4th, 1970), wheat, potatoes, sugar beets, barley, hops, forest products.
Major Minerals: Coal (ranks 5th among world producers, 1970), lignite (world rank 2d, 1970), iron ore, lead ore, potash, petroleum, natural gas.
Foreign Trade (1971): *Exports,* $39,034,000,000 (chief exports, 1969—nonelectrical machinery; transport equipment; chemicals; electrical machinery, apparatus, iron and steel). *Imports,* $34,341,000,000 (chief imports, 1969— food and live animals; mineral fuels and lubricants; nonelectrical machinery; nonferrous metals). *Chief trading partners* (1969)—France (took 13% of exports, supplied 13% of imports); Netherlands (10%—12%); United States (9%—11%).
Tourism: Receipts (1970), $1,021,300,000.
Transportation: *Motor vehicles* (1970), 14,515,600 (automobiles, 13,513,600); *railroads* (1970), 18,448 miles (29,687 km); *merchant fleet* (1971), 8,679,000 gross registered tons; *major national airline,* Deutsche Lufthansa.
Communications: *Telephones* (1971), 13,834,827; *television stations* (1971), 171; *television sets* (1971), 16,800,000; *radios* (1970), 19,622,000; *newspapers* (1970), 1,093.

---

achievements were readily acknowledged by the warm applause of the West German audience.

These accomplishments were overshadowed, however, by the assassination of 11 members of the Israeli team by Arab terrorists. To Bonn's distress there were rumors that the Munich police had been laggard in its rescue attempts because of anti-Semitism. The charges could be quickly refuted since all moves made against the Arabs were made in consultation with Israel's chief of internal security, who had been rushed to the scene. The Bonn government granted the families of the slain men indemnities of $1 million each as a token of its condolence. (See OLYMPIC GAMES.)

Terrorism. The killings in Munich intensified Bonn's concern about its own terrorists. West Germany had long been plagued by arson, bomb explosions, and bank robberies, attributed to anarchistic extremists who thus expressed their defiance of the political system. The best known of these roving bands was the "Red Army Faction," or Baader-Meinhof group, named after its leaders, Andreas Baader, a student, and Ulrike Meinhof, a journalist. In May the Baader-Meinhof group assumed responsibility for the bombing of a U. S. Army installation in which four American servicemen were killed. In June, after a nationwide search of many months, both Baader and Meinhof were arrested.

The question of antiterrorist countermeasures touched off a debate as to how to reconcile the requirements of internal security with the civil rights of an open society. Twice during the year persons suspected of subversive activities had been shot by police without justification. Again, in a trial in the summer, an alleged member of the Baader-Meinhof

ARAB TERRORIST, one of a group holding Israeli athletes captive at Munich Olympic Village, appears at a window to talk with German officials on September 5.

immediate consequence was East Germany's admission to the UN Educational, Scientific, and Cultural Organization (UNESCO). But in June, Bonn continued to block East Germany's admission to the World Health Organization. The DDR was accorded the right to have a permanent observer at the United Nations. It seemed likely it would be admitted to full UN membership in 1973, along with West Germany. It also had unofficial contacts with Washington about mutual diplomatic recognition.

Even without the Basic Treaty, the DDR was gaining increased recognition. Among the countries establishing diplomatic ties with East Germany was Finland, the first non-Communist country in Europe to do so. France and other Western countries that had withheld recognition only from consideration for West Germany were expected to follow the example of Finland.

Domestic Politics. At home the DDR presented a mixed picture of self-assurance and diffidence. Its amnesty of thousands of political prisoners on the 23d anniversary of its founding conveyed an impression of confidence in its internal consolidation. So did its willingness to allow escapees to

EAST GERMAN woman greets a grandson she had never met as the Berlin Wall, closed for six years, is opened to West Germans for an eight-day period at Easter.

group had been convicted on what some observers considered inconclusive evidence. In July a series of legal reforms designed to improve law enforcement caused some concern about the increase of state power. The events at the Olympics and the subsequent hijacking of a Lufthansa airliner by two Palestinians revived the debate. However, law and order did not become a major election issue.

Foreign Policy. West Germany's friendship treaties with the USSR and Poland, negotiated in 1970, were ratified after long delays in June 1972. In October the Federal Republic and the People's Republic of China established diplomatic relations.

At the same time Bonn stressed its close relationship with the West. On the 25th anniversary of the Marshall Plan, Chancellor Brandt announced the creation of a $46.6 million German Marshall Plan Memorial for the study of U. S.-European problems. On a visit to the United States, Brandt obtained President Nixon's assurance that no American troops would be withdrawn from Europe for the time being. The chancellor also remained in close touch with London and Paris.

In 1973 the Federal Republic expected to be admitted as a full-fledged member to the United Nations, to which it is presently accredited as a permanent observer without voting rights.

GERMAN DEMOCRATIC REPUBLIC
(East Germany)

Foreign Relations. For the DDR the conclusion of the Basic Treaty with West Germany constituted the most important event of 1972. After years of procrastination the Federal Republic had accepted the East German claim to separate sovereignty. The

return for visits. On the other hand, East Germany's border fortifications were reinforced with new types of automatic signal and firing devices lest the rapprochement with West Germany encourage a new wave of escapes.

More important, the Central Committee of the SED issued a 15-point declaration calling upon all party members to practice "close vigilance" and intensify party work in order to counteract the ideological dangers resulting from increased contacts between peoples of different social systems.

Another directive forbade top officials in government and public administration, parties, mass organizations, and major enterprises as well as high-ranking officers in police and the armed forces to receive visitors, even relatives, from the West in their homes or meet with them elsewhere without special permission. People in these categories were also asked to refrain from visits to the West. Similarly lower officials, workers in plants, and other groups were urged to sign pledges not to receive Western visitors or take trips to the West.

Whether these were simply precautionary measures to ward off any objectionable influences or whether such influences had made themselves felt already as a result of the increased contacts with West Germans, it was impossible to say. Whatever the reason, as Erich Honecker, the first secretary of the SED put it, peaceful coexistence of the two German states was not to lead to any "ideological mishmash."

Economic Conditions. In the summer socialization of the economy was completed. The remaining private and partly private, partly state-owned businesses had to be sold to the state.

The change affected some 100,000 craftsmen and some 3,500 private and 5,000 semiprivate firms. At the time of the take-over their combined output, mostly consumer goods, amounted to 14% of total production. The size of the compensation was not made public; it was to be paid in strictly limited installments.

This later provision was in keeping with an overall redistribution of income that drastically cut large salaries. Beginning in July, top pay was not to exceed 2,000 marks a month (about $660). At the same time, pensions and other social benefits were raised.

In a further move to aid the low-income groups, imports of Western-made goods, especially clothing, were increased and were sold without major markups. This could be done without an undue drain on East Germany's Western currency reserves since the DDR, by way of its special relationship with West Germany, was treated like a member of the EEC and has done a good deal of business with it.

Unexpectedly, new shortages in textiles and shoes developed when visa requirements were dropped between East Germany, Poland, and Czechoslovakia. Literally millions of Polish and Czech tourists flocked to the DDR and bought large amounts of clothing available at lower prices or of better quality than in their homelands. They also put a heavy strain on the limited number of hotels, cafés, and restaurants in East Germany. This latter problem was further aggravated by the huge influx of West German tourists, following the easing of travel restrictions for them. Some alleviation of these difficulties was expected when the Polish government limited to $50 the amount of zlotys that could be taken into East Germany.

Conversely, East German tourists bought in Poland and Czechoslovakia such items as electrical appliances, foodstuffs, tires, and gasoline that were either unobtainable at home or more expensive. Less could be taken back from Czechoslovakia, however, after the Prague government prohibited the export of many items without a permit.

Social Conditions. In March the People's Chamber passed a law providing for abortions on demand within 12 weeks after conception. When first published, the proposal was widely debated in the press and in other media. It ran into opposition, not only from the churches, but also from party members who predicted the collapse of "socialist morality." The bill was passed with 14 deputies voting against it and 8 abstaining—possibly the first law not enacted unanimously by the Chamber. At the same time 16-year-olds were given the right to request birth control pills. Both measures were taken to put a stop to illegal abortions.

However, with an almost stagnant, overaged population the state did not discourage childbearing, even though women constituted a substantial part of the work force. Child allowances were increased and newlyweds were given financial aid to establish homes. The work week was reduced from 45 to 40 hours for working mothers, and their annual vacations were extended to a minimum of 21 days. Illegitimacy bore no stigma; unmarried mothers were the heroines of a number of recent novels.

The Olympics. East Germany won third place in the Olympic Games, right after the USSR and the United States. Even granting the fact that its team had undergone especially concentrated and gen-

---

EAST GERMANY · Information Highlights

Official Name: German Democratic Republic.
Area: 41,766 square miles (108,174 sq km).
Population (1972 est.): 17,400,000. *Density,* 389 per square mile (150 per sq km). *Annual rate of increase,* 0.0%.
Chief Cities (1971 census): East Berlin, the capital, 1,084,-866; Leipzig, 583,311; Dresden, 500,051; Karl-Marx-Stadt, 298,335.
Government: *Head of state,* Walter Ulbricht, chairman of the Council of State (took office Sept. 1960). *Head of government,* Willi Stoph, minister-president (took office Sept. 1964). *First Secretary of the Socialist Unity (Communist) party,* Erich Honecker (took office May 1971). *Legislature* (unicameral)—Volkskammer (People's Chamber), 500 members. *Major political party*—Socialist Unity party.
Language: German (official).
Education: *Expenditure* (1969), 8.3% of total public expenditure. *School enrollment* (1969)—primary, 2,485,367; secondary, 659,536; technical/vocational, 582,380; university/higher, 91,947.
Monetary Unit: DDR mark (2.047 DDR marks equal U. S.$1, June 1972).
Gross National Product (1969 est.): $34,000,000,000.
National Income per Person (1969): $2,000.
Economic Indexes: *Industrial production* (1971), 160 (1963 = 100); *agricultural production* (1970), 119 (1957–59 = 100); *consumer price index* (1969), 116 (1963 = 100).
Manufacturing (major products): Iron and steel, machinery, chemicals, transport equipment, electronic equipment, precision and optical instruments, fertilizers, synthetic rubber and fibers.
Major Agricultural Products: Rye (ranks 4th among world producers, 1970), potatoes, sugar beets, wheat, oats, barley.
Major Minerals: Lignite (ranks 1st among world producers, 1970), coal, potash, iron ore, copper ore, salt.
Foreign Trade (1971): *Exports,* $5,076,000,000 (chief exports, 1969—nonelectrical machinery; transport equipment; electrical machinery, apparatus, appliances). *Imports,* $4,960,-000,000 (chief imports, 1969—motor vehicles; crude petroleum). *Chief trading partners* (1969)—USSR (took 40% of exports, supplied 42% of imports); Czechoslovakia (10%—9%); Poland (8%—6%); West Germany (7%—10%).
Transportation: *Motor vehicles* (1970), 1,556,400 (automobiles, 1,159,800); *railroads* (1970), 9,108 miles (14,657 km); *merchant fleet* (1971), 1,016,000 gross registered tons; *major national airline,* Interflug.
Communications: *Telephones* (1971), 2,089,216; *television stations* (1971), 25; *television sets* (1971), 5,310,000; *radios* (1970), 5,985,000; *newspapers* (1968), 40 (daily circulation, 7,608,000).

erously funded training, this was an impressive feat, considering the limited human resources the DDR had to draw upon.

Cultural Trends. Artistic work was given more scope, with the emphasis on variety and colorfulness. Playwrights, painters, sculptors, and movie producers began experimenting with new themes and styles. The novels of Christa Wolf and Hermann Kant, whose implied criticisms had made them objectionable, were being reprinted. The work of Wolf Biermann, a dissident poet and folk singer long in disgrace, was the subject of a serious public discussion. These changes were intended to arouse greater interest in art and help it fulfill its function of assisting in the development of "socialist personalities." Obviously, as party chief Honecker pointed out, such changes could take place only within the Marxist-Leninist framework.

Ideology was brought to bear on other activities as well. Economic planners were admonished not to lose sight of the Marxist goals over their computerized systems analyses. Social scientists, in turn, were called upon to explore the DDR's ties with other socialist nations—in accordance with its "national" dissociation from West Germany.

ANDREAS DORPALEN, *The Ohio State University*

GHANA

The government of Prime Minister Kofi A. Busia, which had ruled Ghana since 1969, was overthrown on Jan. 13, 1972, while he was in London for medical treatment. The bloodless military coup was led by Col. Ignatius Acheampong, who became chairman of the newly established National Redemption Council (NRC). The constitution was suspended, Parliament was dissolved, and political parties were banned.

During the year the military regime consolidated its position and attempted to solve the intractable economic problems that had doomed the government of Kofi Busia. In July the body of former President Kwame Nkrumah was returned to Ghana for burial.

Domestic Affairs. The new government received early promises of support from trade unionists and other working groups, and there were signs of public goodwill toward the military rulers. An advisory committee of distinguished civilians was appointed in February, but it was suspended after press complaints that it consisted of "tired old men." By May the situation appeared sufficiently relaxed for 323 supporters of the banned Progress party to be released from detention.

However, the government announced on July 16 that it had foiled a plot to restore former Prime Minister Busia to power. Two days later the NRC issued a decree imposing rigorous penalties for subversion, and announced that the decree had gone into effect on January 13. Four civilians and five soldiers were brought to trial in August for their part in the alleged coup.

Economic Developments. Statements by members of the NRC made it clear that a return to civilian government would be subordinated to the establishment of firm social and economic foundations. The new economic policy was designed to place priority on agriculture (especially on food production), to "use state power to capture the commanding heights of the economy" and ensure that economic development would benefit all Ghanaians, and to end dependence on foreign markets.

One of the first measures of the NRC was to repudiate debts to four British companies totalling some $94 million and dating from the administration of Kwame Nkrumah. The government also suspended payments on other short- and medium-term debts pending attempts to renegotiate better terms.

In one of its most popular steps, the regime cancelled Busia's 44% devaluation of the cedi, raising its official value from U. S.$0.55 to U. S.$0.78. The revaluation was combined with attempts to exercise more rigorous price and import controls and to repress smuggling and tax evasions, and with various austerity measures.

Death of Nkrumah. Former President Kwame Nkrumah died in Rumania on July 27. The 62-year-old Nkrumah, who led Ghana to independence in 1957, had lived in exile in Guinea since his overthrow in 1966. News of his death stimulated discussion of his contribution to Ghanaian development, and many opponents of the former president paid warm tributes to his achievements.

Plans to return Nkrumah's body to Ghana were at first barred by Guinea's President Sékou Touré, but agreement was arranged at a summit meeting of the Organization of African Unity in Rabat. The body was brought to Accra on July 7 and lay in state before being taken to Nkrumah's home town of Nkroful for burial on July 9.

Foreign Affairs. The change of regime ended the talk of "dialogue" with South Africa, and the NRC seemed anxious to recover Ghana's former eminence in pan-African affairs. Foreign Affairs Commissioner Nathaniel A. Aferi announced in October that Ghana and Guinea had agreed to resume diplomatic relations at the ambassadorial level.

J. D. HARGREAVES
University of Aberdeen

――――――― **GHANA • Information Highlights** ―――――――

Official Name: Republic of Ghana.
Area: 92,099 square miles (238,537 sq km).
Population (1972 est.): 9,600,000. *Density,* 98 per square mile (38 per sq km). *Annual rate of increase,* 2.9%.
Chief Cities (1970 census): Accra, the capital, 633,880; Kumasi, 342,986; Sekondi-Takoradi, 161,071.
Government: *Head of state,* Col. Ignatius K. Acheampong, chairman of National Redemption Council (took office Jan. 1972). *Legislature*—National Assembly (dissolved Jan. 1972).
Languages: English (official), 50 tribal languages and dialects.
Education: *Expenditure* (1969), 20.3% of total public expenditure. *School enrollment* (1968)—primary, 1,281,003; secondary, 211,195; technical/vocational, 8,932; university/higher, 5,699.
Monetary Unit: New cedi (1.2821 new cedis equal U. S.$1, Sept. 1972).
Gross National Product (1971 est.): $2,540,000,000.
National Income per Person (1968): $222.
Economic Indexes: *Industrial production* (1970), 149 (1963= 100); *consumer price index* (1970), 172 (1963=100).
Manufacturing (major products): Processed agricultural product, wood, cement.
Major Agricultural Products: Cacao (ranks 1st among world producers, 1970), groundnuts, cassava, corn, sweet potatoes and yams, forest products, fish, livestock.
Major Minerals: Diamonds (ranks 4th among world producers, 1970); gold, manganese ore, bauxite.
Foreign Trade (1970): *Exports,* $433,000,000 (chief exports— cacao, wood, diamonds, manganese). *Imports,* $411,000,-000 (chief imports, 1969—food and live animals; chemicals; nonelectrical machinery; textile yarn and fabrics). *Chief trading partners* (1969)—United Kingdom (took 37% of exports, supplied 27% of imports); United States (15% —18%); West Germany (11%—11%); Japan (9%—6%).
Transportation: *Motor vehicles* (1970), 63,500 (automobiles, 36,500); *railroads* (1970), 592 miles (953 km); *merchant fleet* (1971), 166,000 gross registered tons; *major national airline,* Ghana Airways.
Communications: *Telephones* (1971), 61,183; *television stations* (1971), 4; *television sets* (1971), 15,000; *radios* (1970), 703,000; *newspapers* (1970), 7.

GRAY, L. Patrick, 3d. See BIOGRAPHY.
GRAYSON, C. Jackson. See BIOGRAPHY.

The Duke of Windsor lies in state in St. George's Chapel at Windsor Castle (above). Queen Elizabeth and the Duchess of Windsor leave the chapel after the funeral (left).

GREAT BRITAIN

Public preoccupations in Britain in 1972 were, in large measure, the same as they were in 1971. Beset with continued economic problems—inflation and unemployment, and attendant labor unrest—the Conservative government of Prime Minister Edward Heath still suffered widespread unpopularity. And although the government took measures to quell the strife in Northern Ireland, the tragic conflict there was unabated by year's end (see pages 324–325).

Britain's entry into the European Economic Community (EEC, or Common Market) having been successfully negotiated in 1971, it was perhaps no longer the chief issue in foreign relations—although it still was a matter of partisan debate. The 1971 agreement by which Britain would recognize the independence of Rhodesia, its former colony, apparently came unstuck when a governmental commission reported that Rhodesia's majority black population did not support it. A new problem did arise in 1972 when President Idi Amin of Uganda expelled resident Asians, assigning to Britain the responsibility for those with British passports.

GOVERNMENT AND POLITICS

Throughout 1972 the Labour opposition emphasized the Conservative government's failure to cure inflation and limit unemployment. Labour believed that trade-union militancy was the government's fault, and that such militancy stemmed from high

321

unemployment, the industrial relations act, rising prices and rents, and the "undemocratic" decision to join the EEC. The government contended that its image arose from the usual "midterm" discontent. The Conservatives were confident that their policies would command widespread support in the long term.

Party Politics. The Common Market issue and Britain's continued economic difficulties dominated party politics in 1972.

On February 17 the House of Commons approved the general principles of the European Communities Bill by the narrow margin of 8 votes. Although pro-EEC Labour members of Parliament (MPs) tended to take less part in Parliamentary proceedings than in 1971, enough of them supported the government in February to get the principles accepted.

A number of front-bench Labour MPs, including the deputy Labour leader, Roy Jenkins, continued to speak in favor of the EEC. In April, Jenkins resigned as deputy leader, and six other Labour MPs left the shadow cabinet with him. Although the strongest opposition to British membership in the EEC came from the Labour party's "left wing," this section had limited control over other Labour MPs.

In April, Edward Short replaced Jenkins as deputy leader in an election in which Short defeated the left-wing candidate. In October, elections to the shadow cabinet revealed this same pattern, and a significant number of pro-EEC Labourites were elected. Labour's leader, Harold Wilson, tried to steer a cautious course between outright opposition to EEC membership and the party disunity that too favorable a view would provoke. In the end, the Labour party inside and outside Parliament adopted the view that British membership in the Common Market had been decided upon without consulting the electorate. Therefore they determined that any future Labour government would so consult and, if necessary, renegotiate the terms of entry or withdraw from the EEC. Only the Trades Union Congress, in September, opposed EEC entry in principle; the majority of the Labour party resisted this extreme view.

Throughout the year, opinion polls and by-election results recorded the unpopularity of the government. Labour led the Conservatives in the polls by a margin of about 10%, and in local government elections the Labour party made significant gains. Both major parties received shocks late in the year. In October the Liberals won the Rochdale seat from Labour with a swing of more than 11%. In December the Conservatives lost Sutton to the Liberals on a 32% swing. Also in December, the Conservatives retained the Uxbridge seat, keeping the swing to Labour down to 2.2%. The government believed that this represented a revival of Conservative fortunes and showed the popularity of its more interventionist economic policy.

Ministerial Changes. Prime Minister Heath maintained his reputation as a man reluctant to make frequent changes in his ministerial team. Only three sets of significant changes occurred in 1972.

In April, 11 new ministers were appointed, and five were dropped. At cabinet level, Robert Carr replaced William Whitelaw as leader of the House of Commons, following the latter's appointment as secretary of state for Northern Ireland. Maurice Macmillan replaced Carr as employment secretary; Christopher Chataway became minister of industrial development, a newly established post.

In July, Reginald Maudling resigned as home secretary, following the bankruptcy hearings of John Poulson, an architect with whom Maudling had been associated. Maudling stated that since a police investigation of various matters related to the case was to be undertaken it would be improper for him, as minister responsible for such activities, to remain in office during this investigation. Robert Carr replaced Maudling as home secretary.

In November, James Prior replaced Carr as

UPI

ROYAL ANNIVERSARY: Queen Elizabeth and Prince Philip in their silver wedding (25th) anniversary photograph (left), and as they looked when they were honeymooners in 1947 (below).

KEYSTONE

lord president and leader of the House. Joseph Godber replaced Prior at agriculture. Geoffrey Rippon replaced Peter Walker at the department of the environment; Walker replaced John Davies at the department of trade and industry; and Davies moved to take special responsibilities for EEC questions. Sir Geoffrey Howe became minister for trade and consumer affairs.

Royal Family. Queen Elizabeth and Prince Philip, accompanied by Princess Anne, undertook a state visit to Southeast Asia in November. This trip included stops in the cities of Bangkok, Singapore, and Kuala Lumpur.

In April, Queen Juliana and Prince Bernhard of the Netherlands traveled to London on a state visit.

In mid-May, the queen and Prince Philip visited France, where the queen saw her uncle, the duke of Windsor. The duke died on May 28, at the age of 77, and lay in state at St. George's Chapel, Windsor Castle, on June 2. More than 40,000 people visited the chapel on this occasion.

Prince William of Gloucester, a first cousin of the queen, was killed on August 28 while participating in an air race. He was 30 years old.

On November 20 the queen and Prince Philip celebrated their silver wedding anniversary.

ECONOMY

Britain's economic ills continued to attract a great deal of attention during 1972. Debate about the economic situation revolved around the alleged reversal of policy undertaken by the government in the course of the year. In 1970 and early 1971 the government stressed its determination to rely on reduced governmental intervention and on market forces to foster growth and competitiveness. It expected to cure inflation by increasing efficiency and productivity, as well as by limiting what it called the monopoly bargaining power of the unions. By mid-1971 the high level of unemployment had led the government to adopt a more interventionist policy. In 1972 the combination of mounting inflation, high unemployment, and industrial unrest continued.

Government Economic Policies. By January 1972 unemployment had risen over the million mark for the first time since 1947, and the rate of price increases had not abated. At first, the government stuck to its policy of standing up to the unions and eschewing statutory controls of prices and incomes. At the same time it was trying to stimulate expansion by boosting the money supply.

There were fairly immediate signs that the government had already abandoned its earlier intention not to subsidize ailing industries. In February 1972 the government announced subsidies of £35 million for shipbuilding on the Upper Clyde River. In the following month John Davies, secretary for trade and industry, set up an industrial development executive to facilitate expansion and development in depressed areas. Funds of £800 million were to be made available for this purpose. In April the government gave £3 million to the shipbuilding firm of Cammell Laird, and gave £45, in May, to Harland & Wolff, the Belfast shipbuilders. In July, more than £14 million was made available to International Computers.

Not all of the government's actions were departures from its previous course. In May the government applied its policy of "hiving off" the more profitable parts of the nationalized industries to the

UPI

PROTESTING the jailing of five dock workers for contempt of industrial relations court, trade unionists marched in London on July 25.

extent of selling the Thomas Cook travel agency to a private consortium for £22 million.

As the expansion of credit continued, and as its relations with the unions worsened, the government became concerned about the effect of inflation on the balance of payments. The budget presented by Chancellor of the Exchequer Anthony Barber in March revealed that the government remained determined to stimulate expansion of employment by fiscal and monetary means: the budget reduced net revenue by £1,200 million. Income tax allowances, surtax levels, purchase tax, and estate duty were all relaxed, and old-age pensions were to be increased.

To insulate the trade balance from this stimulation policy, Barber announced on June 23 that the pound sterling would be freed from its parity rate and would float temporarily. The Bank of England imposed temporary controls on capital movements between Britain and other countries in the sterling area. Recognizing that a floating rate would cause difficulties within the EEC, the government announced that it would peg the rate before Jan. 1, 1973. By the end of the year, the pound had been devalued, in effect, by 10%.

In an attempt to tackle the domestic problems of

ABBAS, FROM JOCELYNE BENZAKIN

In one of many such incidents in Northern Ireland in 1972, firemen and paratroopers come to the aid of a bomb victim in Belfast.

NORTHERN IRELAND

A Year of Growing Violence

Terrorism continued in Northern Ireland in 1972. Determined to end the partition of Ireland and to purge Ulster of British influence, the extremists of the Irish Republican Army (I. R. A.) intensified their guerrilla warfare. Snipers fired on British soldiers, land mines blew up military vehicles, rockets shattered police stations, and gunmen murdered members of the Ulster Defense Regiment. The most damaging tactic, however, was the use of gelignite bombs to create panic in public places and disrupt business.

Jittery British soldiers often reacted to I. R. A. tactics by opening fire before asking questions. Men suspected of belonging to the I. R. A. were interned and interrogated. Every "innocent" Catholic killed or injured by soldiers added new recruits to the I. R. A. The result of this escalation in violence was starkly reflected in the number of deaths in 1972. The toll for the year soared to about 470, as against 173 in 1971, for a total of more than 675 since 1969.

Londonderry March. The year began with Ulster Premier Brian Faulkner's decision to extend the ban on all marches and demonstrations. In protest against this decree, the leaders of the Catholic community in Londonderry (Derry) organized an illegal protest march for Sunday, January 30. Stones were thrown at soldiers who blocked the marchers' route. Several shots were fired (each side later accused the other of firing first), and the

troops were ordered to disperse the crowds. Some 200 paratroopers then stormed into the Bogside district in pursuit of suspected snipers. Firing at will, they killed 13 civilians.

The "Derry massacre" provoked a violent reaction by Catholics in the North. Mass protests also were held in Dublin, where the British embassy was burned (see IRELAND), and in London and New York. British Prime Minister Edward Heath's government survived a motion of no-confidence in the House of Commons on February 1 by 304 to 266. In retaliation for the Derry shootings, the "official" wing of the I. R. A. detonated a bomb on February 22 outside an officers' mess at Aldershot army camp, near London, killing seven.

Direct Rule. Bernadette Devlin, the controversial member of the British Parliament for Mid-Ulster, warned the House of Commons on February 1 that the Derry massacre might "doom the last vestige of British rule" in the North.

The first vestige to go was the Unionist regime in Ulster. After the I. R. A. stepped up its bombing campaign in crowded urban areas, and after these explosions had touched off an ominous Protestant backlash, Prime Minister Heath's cabinet decided that only direct rule from London could avert civil war or anarchy. Accordingly, on March 30, 1972, the provincial government of Northern Ireland was officially suspended, and Faulkner's Unionist ministry resigned.

The burden of direct rule fell to William Whitelaw, the Conservative leader of the House of Commons, who became secretary of state for Northern Ireland. In protest against this historic change, Unionist and Orange leaders called a two-day strike in March and held a mass rally of over 50,000 Protestants.

Internee Releases and Cease-Fire. Following a short lull in the fighting during the Easter holidays, Whitelaw released 97 of the 801 men held in internment camps and prisons on political charges. On April 27 he also ordered amnesty for 283 persons, including Bernadette Devlin, who had been convicted a week earlier for taking part in illegal political rallies. During May, militant Protestants, led by gangs of young vigilantes, attacked Catholics intermittently. The shooting in Derry on May 21 of a young Catholic soldier home on leave from army service in Germany prompted a number of Catholic women to denounce the I. R. A.'s tactics.

On May 29 the "official" I. R. A. responded to the mounting pressure of Catholic moderates by announcing a cease-fire. The "provisionals" immediately repudiated this act of "surrender." But dissension within their own ranks soon moved them to negotiate a truce with Whitelaw and the army on June 26. Hailed by all responsible Irishmen as a breakthrough, this truce lasted only two weeks. During that interval at least 10 people died at the hands of unknown assailants, the latest victims in a series of "motiveless" murders apparently carried out by sectarian gangs.

End of Cease-Fire. The "provisional" cease-fire came to an abrupt and violent end on July 9, when fighting broke out between soldiers and Catholic militants in Belfast. During July the "provisionals" began to use Soviet-built rocket launchers in their ambushes. A wave of 20 coordinated bombings in central Belfast on July 21, known as "Bloody Friday," left 9 dead and 130 injured.

These bombs also left Whitelaw's policy of reconciliation in ruins. The army responded by invading areas known to be strongholds of the I. R. A. With British troop strength at an all-time high of 21,000, the army carried out successful raids on I. R. A. arms caches in Belfast and Derry on July 30–31. I. R. A. units had pulled out of the Bogside, having prudently decided not to engage in a "shoot-out" with the British army.

The campaign of bombs and bullets continued throughout the autumn. Whitelaw reduced the number of internees to 243 and made other concessions to SDLP demands, but he refused to set free all the "hard-core" political prisoners. Only three of Northern Ireland's various political parties joined Whitelaw in the "all-party" conference at Darlington, England, on September 25–27. Both the SDLP and the extreme Protestant groups boycotted these talks on Northern Ireland's future, and the participants disagreed on fundamental issues. As the death toll edged ever higher, Whitelaw promised plebiscites and more concessions to Catholics in 1973. But these promises altered none of the realities of social and political conflict.

L. PERRY CURTIS, JR.
University of California, Berkeley

inflation, the government in November edged nearer to intervention in wages and prices by calling for talks between unions, employers, and the government. Prime Minister Heath proposed that, in return for a government commitment to a 5% annual growth rate and special treatment for lower-paid workers, the Confederation of British Industry (CBI) and the Trades Union Congress (TUC) voluntarily limit increases in wages, prices, and dividends. Heath pointed out that since 1970, although prices had increased by an average of 8% annually, average earnings had risen by about 12% annually, resulting in a real earnings increase of 4%.

The CBI was willing to accept Heath's proposals, but the TUC was not. On November 6, Heath announced that, voluntary means having failed, the government would introduce an immediate freeze on pay, prices, and dividends. The freeze was to last 90 days, and could be extended a further 60 days. During that time the government would be empowered to veto all increases and to penalize workers or employers who broke the law. The government hoped that the freeze would break the vicious circle caused by large wage demands put forward by unions that expected inflation to continue. The government would use the freeze period to plan a more flexible (and, it hoped, a more consultative) Phase II.

Industrial Relations. Much of the government's change of heart on the question of a statutory incomes policy arose from its earlier failure to reach an understanding with the unions. This, in turn, was linked to the Conservatives' industrial relations policy.

Between January 9 and February 28, Britain had a national mines strike. The miners demanded a

UGANDAN refugees arrive in London, the first of many Asians holding British passports ousted by order of Ugandan President Idi Amin.

47% pay increase, and they picketed power stations and related industries. Power cuts occurred with increasing frequency, and on February 10 employment secretary Robert Carr announced the creation of an independent inquiry under Lord Wilberface. The inquiry report, which was published on February 18, recommended granting most of the miners' demands, which was done.

This major breach in the government's policy of "holding the line" in the nationalized industries was followed in March by the railwaymen's demand for a 16% increase. The railways board offered 11%. An independent "referee" recommended a 12% offer, which the board accepted but the unions refused. On March 17 the rail unions began to "work to rule," and two days later the National Industrial Relations Court upheld a government plea that the railwaymen were in breach of contract and ordered a 14-day "cooling-off" period. Disagreement between the unions and the board continued, and on May 11 the court granted a government application to force the unions to hold a ballot on the question of further strike action. The members voted in favor of striking by 129,500 to 23,000. On June 12 the board agreed to a pay rise of a fraction over 13%.

The government's difficulties in attempting to use legal framework in dealing with problems in industrial relations were further demonstrated on the docks. Here, the problem of containerization, provoking fears of unemployment among dockers, created much union militancy. In March, the industrial relations court found the Transport and General Workers Union in contempt of its ruling against the "blacking," or refusal to handle, of containers at Liverpool docks and imposed a £5,000 fine. In April the court imposed a fine of £50,000 for con-

tinuing contempt, and the Liverpool dockers concerned refused to accept official union advice to drop the picketing. In May the union agreed to pay the fine and succeeded in getting the TUC to contribute, on the grounds that the union was representing official TUC policy of total opposition to the Industrial Relations Act, which had created the court. In June the Court of Appeals quashed the fines on the grounds that the union was not responsible for the actions of its members. This verdict was reversed by the House of Lords in July.

In June the industrial court arrested three London dockers for contempt of its orders to cease picketing container depots. The official solicitor intervened to secure their release after 35,000 dockers went on strike in protest. The court jailed five dockers in July for a similar contempt, but it later freed them in the light of the Lords' decision with regard to union liability.

On July 25, the Aldington-Jones report tried to settle the long-term question of dock employment, but a national dock strike (July 28–August 16) occurred. Agreement on the question of dockers' employment was eventually reached between dock authorities and unions.

Forecast. By the end of the year a number of economists were pessimistic about the trend of the British economy. During 1972 more than 20 million working days had been lost through strike action, and the government's ability to face up to the unions with any hope of success had been questioned. In 1971 Britain had a surplus of £1,042 on the balance of payments current account. At the end of 1972 this statistic had dropped to a deficit of £40 million. Inflation had only slowly dropped from the previous rate of about 8% annually, and unemployment was still near the million mark. The slow growth of productivity and the extent to which increased consumer credit had increased imports with little compensating increase in investment or exports caused disquiet.

OTHER DOMESTIC ISSUES

Although few issues engendered as much public discussion as did the state of the economy, other domestic matters merited—and received—attention.

Criminal Law Revision. In June the Criminal Law Revision Committee published its report. The committee recommended the abolition of a number of existing rights currently guaranteed to accused persons, including the right to refuse to answer questions asked by the police without such refusal being put forward, in court proceedings, as evidence of guilt. The committee argued that the balance between prosecution and defense had in recent times become too heavily weighted against the prosecution. Committee members contended that curtailing certain rights of the accused would be more than offset by other safeguards.

Report on Privacy. The Special Committte on Personal Privacy, a governmental committee chaired by Sir Kenneth Younger, a former Labour minister, reported in July. While rejecting the idea of a general law to safeguard the individual from intrusions against privacy, the committee made a large number of specific recommendations for improving protection of privacy in computer operations, banking, the press, and other areas. It also recommended changes in the rules and laws relating to breaches of state security through the publication of classified information.

Housing Finance Act. In July the Housing Finance Act became law. The act was in part an attempt to change the emphasis in state housing policy from statutory limits on rents of unfurnished dwellings to letting rents find a free market level, with the incomes of those most adversely affecting being supplemented. A number of local councils refused to comply with the new act. Such resistance was overcome only by the central government's threatening legal and financial sanctions.

Speech from the Throne. The queen's speech to Parliament in October revealed future government priorities. These included the restoration of a fixed parity for sterling, tax reforms, regional development, consumer protection, the reorganization of water supplies to conserve the environment, and increased compensation for those adversely affected by public works projects. Also mentioned was the appointment of an "ombudsman" to investigate complaints against local authorities.

EXTERNAL AFFAIRS

British entry into the Common Market having been settled in 1971, the matter was no longer the main focus of foreign policy discussion in 1972—although it certainly was still a debated issue.

Common Market. Britain signed the accession treaty to the EEC in January 1972. This provided for Britain's entry in January 1973. In October, Sir Christopher Soames, British ambassador to France, and George Thomson, a former Labour minister, were appointed Britain's members on the EEC commission.

Report on Rhodesia Accord. In May the report of the commission, headed by Lord Pearce, that investigated Rhodesians' reaction to the constitutional and racial settlement reached by the two governments in November 1971 was published. The report stated the view that the agreement negotiated by British Foreign Secretary Sir Alec Douglas-Home and Rhodesian Prime Minister Ian D. Smith on the terms for Rhodesian independence and internal majority rule had not received the support of the majority of the Rhodesian people, who are black.

The British government had stated that the 1971 agreement was conditional upon acceptance by the blacks. Now, Sir Alec announced that the government accepted the view of the Pearce commission and would maintain economic sanctions against the Smith government. The Rhodesian leaders refused to accept the report as a reliable account of black opinion. Sir Alec reiterated his willingness to continue the search for a settlement acceptable to all sections of the Rhodesian population.

Malta Base Accord. Britain and Malta signed an agreement in March ensuring Britain's continued use of military facilities in Malta for seven years. Britain agreed to pay £5,250,000 a year for use of naval base facilities, and other members of the North Atlantic Treaty Organization (NATO) were to provide a further £8,750,000 annually. By November, Prime Minister Dom Mintoff of Malta was intimating that the effective devaluation of the pound had presented his country with new problems, but the British government stated that it was not considering any revision of the agreement.

Ugandan Expulsion. President Idi Amin of Uganda (a former British protectorate) announced on August 5 that all Ugandan Asians with British passports would have to leave the country within three months. He said that those Asians would be the responsibility of the British government. Despite allegations from some quarters that Britain had no legal or moral responsibility, the British government (although strongly deprecating President Amin's actions) set up a resettlement board to welcome and assist deported Asians with British passports. When the deadline arrived, 27,200 Ugandan Asians had gone to Britain.

Relations with China. Britain and Communist China agreed to establish full ambassadorial relations in March, and in May the first Communist Chinese ambassador to London was appointed. In October, Sir Alec Douglas-Home became the first British foreign secretary to visit China. Topics he discussed included the war in Indochina and the future of the British colony of Hong Kong.

Conflict with Iceland. Relations between Britain and Iceland were increasingly strained because of a conflict over fishing rights. In 1971 the Icelandic government extended its territorial offshore waters from 12 to 50 nautical miles. After its protests were rejected, the British government appealed to the International Court of Justice (World Court), which recommended that Iceland revert to the former limits, pending further discussions. Iceland refused and announced that British trawlers fishing within the new limits would be seized.

The British sent naval escorts with their trawlers, and by autumn a number of minor incidents within the 50-mile limit had been reported. Iceland refused to enter into talks with Britain until naval intervention was terminated.

Heath in Japan. In September, Prime Minister Heath met Japanese Premier Kakuei Tanaka in Tokyo. They discussed, among other things, the Japanese trade surplus with Britain and how Japanese exports could be limited.

A. J. BEATTIE
*The London School of Economics
and Political Science*

BRITAIN ENTERS THE COMMON MARKET: Prime Minister Heath signs the 10-nation agreement in Brussels on January 22.
KEYSTONE

——————— GREECE • Information Highlights ———————

Official Name: Kingdom of Greece.
Area: 50,944 square miles (131,944 sq km).
Population (1972 est.): 9,000,000. *Density,* 173 per square mile (67 per square km). *Annual rate of increase,* 0.8%.
Chief Cities (1971 census): Athens, the capital, 862,133; Salonika, 339,496; Piraeus, 186,223; Patras, 110,632.
Government: *Head of state,* Constantine II, king (acceded March 1964; in self-exile since Dec. 1967)—*Head of government and regent,* George Papadopoulos, premier (took office Dec. 1967). *Legislature*—Parliament (dissolved in 1967).
Languages: Greek (official), English, French.
Education: *Expenditure* (1969), 10.7% of total public expenditure. *School enrollment* (1968)—primary, 960,812; secondary, 498,426; technical/vocational, 95,432; university/higher, 74,962.
Monetary Unit: Drachma (30 drachmas equal U. S.$1, 1972).
Gross National Product (1971 est.): $10,450,000,000.
National Income per Person (1969): $891.
Economic Indexes: *Industrial production* (1971), 222 (1963= 100); *agricultural production* (1971), 195 (1952–56=100); *consumer price Index* (1971), 121 (1963=100).
Manufacturing (major products): Textiles, chemicals, metals, construction materials, petroleum products, ships.
Major Agricultural Products: Olives (ranks 3d among world producers, 1971), tobacco, cotton, wheat, grapes.
Major Minerals: Bauxite, lignite, magnesite, iron ore.
Foreign Trade (1971): *Exports,* $662,000,000 (chief exports— tobacco; currants, raisins, and grapes). *Imports,* $2,098,- 000,000 (chief imports, 1969—transport equipment; non-electrical machinery; food and live animals; chemicals). *Chief trading partners* (1969)—West Germany (took 19% of exports, supplied 19% of imports); United States (10%–10%); Italy (10%—9%); United Kingdom.
Tourism: *Receipts* (1970), $193,600,000.
Transportation: *Motor vehicles* (1970), 343,700 (automobiles, 226,500); *railroads* (1970), 1,598 miles (2,571 km); *merchant fleet* (1971), 13,066,000 gross registered tons; *major national airline,* Olympic Airways.
Communications: *Telephones* (1971), 1,044,777; *television stations* (1971), 4; *newspapers* (1970), 110 (daily circulation, 705,000).

GREECE

The premier of Greece, George Papadopoulos, tightened his grip on the government in 1972, as rumors circulated that he might not favor a return of the king to Greece. As a member of NATO, Greece was assured of continuing American support with the reelection of President Nixon, who, unlike his opponent George McGovern, favored friendly relatious with the present Greek administration.

Internal Changes. On March 21, Gen. George Zoitakis was replaced as regent by Premier Papadopoulos, who had first come to power as the result of a military coup on April 21, 1967. Papadopoulos reformed his cabinet in January, and again in July when he promoted his brother, Constantine Papadopoulos, from the position of undersecretary to that of minister to the premier in matters of planning and governmental policy.

George Papadopoulos' control over the Greek governmental structure seemed by the end of 1972 to be stronger than ever before. He was not only regent and premier, but also minister of foreign affairs, minister of defense, and minister of planning and governmental policy. On December 16 he announced that representative government would not be restored to Greece in the near future.

Economy. As in years past, the Papadopoulos regime attempted to increase the country's industrial potential. A concession to build a third oil refinery in Greece was granted by the government to private interests. It was announced that a 15-year economic and social development plan had been prepared for the government.

Relations with the United States. The Greek government reached an agreement with the United States whereby the U. S. 6th Fleet would have home-port facilities in Greece for service personnel and dependents. Some critics in the U. S. Congress attacked this arrangement as an unwarranted strengthening of the Papadopoulos regime, while in Greece there was evidence of public dissatisfaction with the judicial immunity granted under specific conditions to U. S. servicemen. The friendly relations between Greece and the United States were underscored when William P. Rogers, U. S. secretary of state, visited Athens in July.

In campaigning for the presidency, Sen. George S. McGovern announced that if elected he would cut off all aid to the current Greek regime and review the home-port agreement. President Nixon took the stand that aid to Greece was as important now as it had been during Harry S. Truman's term of office.

Truman's death in December brought on many expressions of sympathy in Greece, where he was recalled as the country's savior from communism in the late 1940's.

Cyprus. Early in the year the Greek government attempted to force Archbishop Makarios, president of Cyprus, to accept more direct Greek control over his government. He resisted the pressure but made some concessions that allowed Greece to take up, at least publicly, a more correct attitude toward him. Clearly, the Papadopoulos regime was hoping to find a settlement on Cyprus that would remove a source of friction between the Greek and Turkish governments. See also CYPRUS.

The Question of the Monarchy. Although King Constantine II continued to be recognized by the Greek government as the rightful king of the Hellenes, he and his family remained outside Greece, as they had since December 1967 when he had unsuccessfully attempted to oust the regime that had staged the April 21 coup. The king made a number of trips during 1972 from his residence in Rome. In January he and his wife, Queen Anne-Marie, attended in Copenhagen the funeral of her father, Denmark's King Frederick IX. In July, Constantine and Anne-Marie visited Iran as guests of the shah. Attending the Olympic Games at Munich during the summer, Constantine and Anne-Marie appeared publicly at Olympic Stadium with Constantine Aslanides, an undersecretary in the Greek cabinet. Although denying that the king had spoken to him about going back home, Aslanides did say that according to the grand duke of Luxembourg, Constantine very much wished to return to Greece.

The question of Constantine's return to Greece led to much speculation. Papadopoulos' assumption of the regency on March 21 was followed by rumors that he planned to end the monarchical system in Greece. The king's mother, Queen Frederika, who had been a controversial figure in Greek politics, was rumored to have assured her son that she would not return to take up residence in Greece if that would smooth his way.

Speaking at the University of Verona in the fall, Constantine indicated that on his return to Greece he would not seek nor would he want the power to force his wishes on anyone. His speech was taken as a sign that he would accept the 1968 constitution, which the Papadopoulos regime had fostered but which had not yet been fully implemented in Greece. However, the revelation in November that Constantine had sold 390 acres (158 hectares) of the royal estate at Tatoi for $5,200,000 brought on speculation that the king really saw little chance for a return to his throne.

Religion. During the autumn, Patriarch Pimen of Moscow visited Greece and met with Premier Papadopoulos. Archbishop Ieronymos of Athens,

primate of Greece, was present at the funeral of Ecumenical Patriarch Athenagoras I at Istanbul in July.

Queen Frederika, mother of Constantine II, was cleared by the Holy Synod of Greece of charges brought by the Metropolitan of Florina that her memoirs, published in 1971, contained concepts contrary to the teachings of the Greek Orthodox Church.

Death of Princess Aspasia. Princess Aspasia of Greece, widow of King Alexander I (reigned 1917–1920), died at the age of 75 in Venice on August 7. When she was the beautiful commoner, Aspasia Manos, her romance with Alexander had brought about political complications that resulted in a morganatic marriage in 1918 and the denial to her of the title of queen. Their only child, Alexandra, became the wife of King Peter II of Yugoslavia.

GEORGE J. MARCOPOULOS
Tufts University

GUATEMALA

A smoldering, century-old dispute with Britain over Belize (British Honduras) flared anew in 1972, temporarily diverting national attention in Guatemala from the seemingly endless urban terrorism and guerrilla warfare that began in the early 1960's. A unique agrarian plan for bettering rural life through increased production was instituted.

Struggle Over Belize. A rumor that Belize was about to receive its independence from Britain caused a buildup of Guatemalan troops along the Belizean border. Defenseless Belize feared an invasion at any moment and requested assistance from Britain. Claiming that military maneuvers in Belize had been announced previously, Britain airlifted 1,000 troops and rushed three warships and an aircraft carrier to the disputed area. Guatemala reacted by placing all its armed forces on alert.

The impasse was broken when Britain responded to pressure from the Organization of American States (OAS) by agreeing to withdraw its troops and accept OAS mediation of the dispute. For his part, Prime Minister George Price of Belize stated that Guatemalan actions underscored the need for a big power guarantee of Belizean independence, a guarantee that neither the United States nor Britain has been willing to give.

Guerrilla and Terrorist Activity. Guerrilla operations resumed in rural Guatemala, with an outbreak of activity in the northern region known as the Peten. Government forces weakened the movement in May by killing guerrilla leader Augusto Flores Rodríguez. Urban terrorism diminished but did not die out. Olivero Castañeda Paiz, vice president of the Chamber of Deputies, was shot to death on June 25 in a downtown Guatemala City restaurant. Castañeda had been a leftist before going over to a rightist terror group, *La Mano Blanca* (White Hand), which leftists held responsible for the deaths of scores of their followers in 1972. In the manhunt occasioned by the murder of Castañeda, one guerrilla and two policemen were killed. In mid-July four members of the Movimiento de Liberación Nacional, one of the parties in the ruling coalition, were slain.

Rural Development. In April the administration of President Carlos Arana Osorio instituted a land-use plan as part of its rural development program. It promised to facilitate peasants' participation in the economy by increasing and diversifying agricultural production and guaranteeing fair prices.

── **GUATEMALA · Information Highlights** ──

Official Name: Republic of Guatemala.
Area: 42,042 square miles (108,889 sq km).
Population (1972 est.): 5,400,000. *Density,* 124 per square mile (48 per sq km). *Annual rate of increase,* 2.6%.
Chief City (1964 census): Guatemala City, the capital, 635,-000 (metropolitan area).
Government: *Head of state,* Carlos Arana Osorio, president (took office July 1970). *Head of government,* Carlos Arana Osorio. *Legislature* (unicameral)—National Congress, 55 members. *Major political parties*—Institutional Democratic party; National Liberation Movement; Revolutionary party.
Languages: Spanish (official), Indian dialects.
Education: *Expenditure* (1969), 18.6% of total public expenditure. *School enrollment* (1969)—primary, 489,565; secondary, 60,645; technical/vocational, 11,784; university/higher, 14,151.
Monetary Unit: Quetzal (1 quetzal equals U. S.$1, Aug. 1972).
Gross National Product (1971 est.): $1,932,000,000.
National Income per Person (1970): $338.
Economic Indexes: *Industrial production* (1970), 145 (1963=100); *agricultural production* (1971), 216 (1952–56=100); *consumer price index* (1971), 107 (1963=100).
Manufacturing (major products): Textiles, petroleum products, chemicals, pharmaceuticals, leather goods.
Major Agricultural Products: Coffee, cotton, sugar, bananas, corn, beans, rice, forest products.
Major Minerals: Lead, zinc, nickel, silver.
Foreign Trade (1971): *Exports,* $288,000,000 (chief exports—coffee; cotton; bananas; sugar). *Imports,* $297,000,000 (chief imports, 1968—chemicals; nonelectrical machinery; textile yarn and fabrics; transport equipment). *Chief trading partners* (1969)—United States (took 28% of exports, supplied 34% of imports); El Salvador (14%—13%); West Germany (10%—10%); Japan (8%—10%).
Transportation: *Motor vehicles* (1970), 67,000 (automobiles, 42,600); *railroads* (1970), 510 miles (821 km); *major national airline,* Avieteca.
Communications: *Telephones* (1971), 39,510; *televison stations* (1971), 2; *television sets* (1971), 119,000; *radios* (1969), 559,000; *newspapers* (1967), 9.

Financed by both the Guatemalan and the U. S. governments, as well as by the Inter-American Development Bank, the $145 million plan envisioned massive capital investment in and technical assistance to small farmers. An agency was set up to buy farm produce at guaranteed prices. The immediate goal was an end to the seasonal migration of peasants from the highlands to the coastal areas at harvest time. As a long-range goal, the government set a threefold increase in the income of small farmers. The program was soon receiving criticism from both the political left and right. However, the program staff reported that their main difficulty was the apathy, suspicion, and despair among the peasants.

Simultaneously, a comprehensive rural health program was launched in 325 communities, benefiting 750,000 persons. The $6 million project covered the construction and equipment of health facilities and the training of a corps of health technicians. An Agency for International Development loan of $2.5 million was obtained for the program.

Favorable Economic Indicators. Economic growth of more than 6% was forecast for 1972. Exports were expected to surpass those of 1971, valued at nearly $300 million, and world market prices for coffee, cotton, and sugar remained high. Additional earnings were anticipated from greater exports of beef to the United States.

Deciding against confiscation, Guatemala, in May, acquired the biggest power and light utility in the country through outright purchase. A spokesman for Boise Cascade Corporation, a U. S.-based firm that owned 96% of the company's shares, said that the company was treated "fairly and equitably."

Guatemala obtained a $16 million loan from the World Bank for the improvement of telecommunications. The loan was to cover foreign exchange costs of a five-year program to improve and expand services.

LARRY L. PIPPIN
Elbert Covell College, University of the Pacific

———— GUINEA • Information Highlights ————

Official Name: Republic of Guinea.
Area: 94,926 square miles (245,857 sq km).
Population (1972 est.): 4,100,000. Density, 43 per square mile (16.7 per sq km). Annual rate of increase, 2.3%.
Chief City (1967 census): Conakry, the capital, 197,267.
Government: Head of state, Sékou Touré, president (took office for 2d term 1968). Head of government, Lansana Beavogui, premier (took office April 1972). Legislature (unicameral)—National Assembly, 75 members. Major political party—Democratic Party of Guinea.
Languages: French (official), local languages, English.
Education: Expenditure (1965), 19.4% of total public expenditure. School enrollment (1968)—primary, 167,340; secondary, 41,736; technical/vocational, 5,334; university/higher, 942.
Monetary Unit: Sily (227.36 silys equal U. S.$1, June 1972).
Gross National Product (1970 est.): $315,000,000.
Manufacturing (major products): Alumina and aluminum products, processed foods, soap.
Major Agricultural Products: Coffee, palm oil and kernels, pineapples, rice, cassava.
Major Minerals: Bauxite (ranks 7th among world producers, 1970), iron ore, diamonds.
Foreign Trade: Chief exports—Alumina; bananas; palm oil and kernels; bauxite; iron ore. Chief imports—Textiles; rice; motor vehicles; machinery; petroleum products. Chief trading partners—United States; Common Market.
Communications: Telephones (1968), 6,600; radios (1970), 91,-000; newspapers (1970), 1 (daily circulation, 5,000).

GUINEA

Two interconnected themes dominated the politics of Guinea during 1972. One was the attempt by President Sékou Touré and his associates to continue the Revolution and make more effective the control of the Parti Démocratique de Guinée (PDG). The other was the fear of fifth column activity and foreign intervention that might threaten the Revolution. Guinea resumed tentative moves to end its isolation in West Africa.

Political Developments. The party leadership was formally reviewed at the ninth party congress held in April, and the structure of government was altered to give the bulk of executive power to a 7-man ministry chosen from the party's Central Committee. For the first time a premier was selected who would supervise the activities of this executive group. Named to this post was Lansana Beavogui, the economics minister and a strong supporter of the president. Although President Touré relinquished three portfolios to the new ministry, his position as head of state was never questioned, and he was reelected secretary-general of the party.

In September the National Revolutionary Council decreed that public officials should be able to read and write all the Guinean dialects and set 1977 as a target date for this. Throughout 1972, Radio Conakry poured out a steady stream of warnings concerning impending sabotage of the Revolution and potential invasions. Over 70 of those arrested earlier for "fifth column activities" were released, but in May the National Assembly ratified the death penalty for 13 former ministers convicted of anti-state activities.

Foreign Affairs. During 1972 the heads of state of Cameroon, Cuba, Liberia, Nigeria, and Zaïre visited Conakry. Most unexpected was the July meeting in Faranah, Guinea, between Touré and President Houphoüet-Boigny of the Ivory Coast, a state Touré once characterized as a willing tool of neocolonialism. Contact was established in April with the military regime in Ghana, and discussions opened on ways of normalizing diplomatic relations, which had been suspended after Ghana's overthrow of Kwame Nkrumah and his exile in Guinea. Nkrumah's death in April removed a stumbling block to reconciliation.

Guinea's most serious diplomatic problem was its feud with Senegal, which arose over President Senghor's refusal to return alleged political criminals to Guinea. This rupture had been responsible for the breakup of the Organization of Senegal River States (OERS) in 1971. The Organization of African Unity (OAU) created a 7-member reconciliation committee chaired by Emperor Haile Selassie of Ethiopia, and in May, Touré and Senghor signed a 7-point agreement restoring relations between the two states to the level existing prior to the Portuguese invasion of Guinea in November 1970.

Economic Developments. Cooperation continued with European firms on the expansion of the giant bauxite reduction complexes at Boké, Fria, and Tougué. In July 1972, Guinea and Algeria signed a trade agreement, and a new direct air route between Algiers and Conakry was promised. A Guinean delegation was sent to Zaïre, following President Mobutu's state visit, to explore areas of greater economic cooperation.

HARRY A. GAILEY
California State University, San Jose

GUYANA

Efforts to stimulate the sluggish economy, political reshuffling, and two international gatherings marked the year 1972 in Guyana.

Economy. It was announced in July that Guyana's growth rate was averaging only about 3% annually. The government continued to seek an expansion of the national economy, particularly an increase and diversification of exports. A trade mission from the People's Republic of China opened offices in Georgetown in March.

Guyana received a loan of $1,111,500 from the U. S. Export-Import Bank in March for the purchase of equipment for a coastal drainage program. In September, the country received a $3 million loan from the Agency for International Development for improvement of streets in New Amsterdam.

Political Affairs. Prime Minister Forbes Burnham reshuffled his cabinet and expanded it to 18 ministers in August. Only one member, Minister of Information Edwin McDavid, was replaced, but seven others shifted portfolios. Burham relinquished

———— GUYANA • Information Highlights ————

Official Name: Republic of Guyana.
Area: 83,000 square miles (214,970 sq km).
Population (1972 est.): 800,000. Density, 10 per square mile (4 per sq km). Annual rate of increase, 2.8%.
Chief City (1970 census): Georgetown, the capital, 190,000 (metropolitan area).
Government: Head of state, Arthur Chung, president (took office March 1970). Head of government, Forbes Burnham, prime minister (took office Dec. 1964). Legislature (unicameral)—National Assembly, 53 members. Major political parties—People's National Congress; People's Progressive party.
Languages: English (official), various East Indian dialects.
Education: Expenditure (1969), 13.1% of total public expenditure. School enrollment (1968)—primary, 130,836; secondary, 53,078; technical/vocational, 1,938; university/higher, 816.
Monetary Unit: Guyana dollar (2.15 G. dollars equal U. S.$1, Sept. 1972).
Gross National Product (1970 est.): $252,000,000.
Manufacturing (major products): Processed foods, alumina, beverages.
Major Agricultural Products: Sugarcane, rice, coffee, livestock.
Major Minerals: Bauxite (ranks 5th among world producers, 1970), gold, diamonds.
Foreign Trade (1971): Exports, $135,000,000. Imports, $133,-000,000. Chief trading partners (1969)—United States (took 25% of exports, supplied 21% of imports); United Kingdom (24%—31%); Canada (19%—8%); Trinidad and Tobago (7%—12%).
Communications: Telephones (1971), 14,665; television sets (1971), 3,500; radios (1970), 80,000; newspapers (1970), 3 (daily circulation, 44,000).

several cabinet positions but remained minister of defense as well as prime minister.

The major opposition party, the People's Progressive party (PPP), continued to have internal problems. In September, the leader of the PPP, former Prime Minister Cheddi Jagan, announced the expulsion from the party of two of its members of parliament, Edgar Ambrose and Lillian Brance. Both members refused PPP demands that they withdraw from the legislature, continuing to sit as independents.

Foreign Affairs. The capital city of Georgetown was the site of two important international events in 1972. The foreign ministers of 60 nonaligned nations met there on August 8–12. From August 25 to September 15 the city was the scene of the "Carifesta," a cultural and entertainment festival of Caribbean and Latin American countries.

Full diplomatic relations were established with China and Poland. Venezuela ended its policy of trying to exclude Guyana from Caribbean affairs, but controversy arose in August following Venezuelan press reports that Guyanese troops had crossed the Venezuelan border.

ROBERT J. ALEXANDER, *Rutgers University*

HAITI

Power plays in the ruling group surrounding President Jean-Claude Duvalier dominated the political news in Haiti in 1972. Tourism and light industry that affect perhaps 1% of the population continued to improve, but agriculture, the mainstay of the Haitian people, stagnated. In foreign affairs, the government concentrated its efforts on seeking loans from the United States and from international lending agencies.

Political Situation. As the young Duvalier settled into his role of president-for-life, the battle for the real power in Haiti came to the fore. For most of the year it seemed as if Luckner Cambronne, minister of interior and defense, had successfully routed all opposition. On January 2, Max Dominique, husband of Jean-Claude's strong-willed sister Marie-Denise, was dismissed as ambassador to France. In February two cabinet officers who opposed a foreign oil deal in which Cambronne was interested were fired. However, Cambronne was becoming an embarrassment to Haitian businessmen and foreign investors. Critics accused him of amassing a personal fortune through his political position. He was said to control the main tourist agency, the airline, and the "quickie" divorce trade.

Marie-Denise Dominique returned to Haiti in September after several months of exile. On November 16, Cambronne was ousted from his position by presidential decree. He took refuge in the Colombian embassy and was expected to go into exile in Colombia. His fall was expected to help in efforts of the Haitian government to improve its image.

The Economy. Tourism and light industry continued to grow during 1972, and short-term financial prospects remained good. Foreign exchange holdings reached a new high of $17.3 million in February, and U. S. investments, now totaling over $50 million, continued to enter the country. In addition, the government continued negotiations with foreign financiers to develop the Île de la Tortue and to build "jet-set" residential estates. Wendell Phillips Co. received a lucrative, 35-year oil concession over 33,340 square miles (86,317 sq km) of land and sea. The company was given the right not only

———————— HAITI • Information Highlights ————————

Official Name: Republic of Haiti.
Area: 10,714 square miles (27,750 sq km).
Population (1972 est.): 5,500,000. *Density,* 453 per square mile (175 per sq km). *Annual rate of increase,* 2.4%.
Chief Cities (1960 est.): Port-au-Prince, the capital, 240,000.
Government: *Head of state,* Jean-Claude Duvalier, president for life (took office April 1971). *Head of government,* Jean-Claude Duvalier. *Legislature* (unicameral)—National Assembly, 58 members. *Major political party*—Parti Unique de l'Action Revolutionnaire et Gouvernementale
Languages: French (official), Creole patois.
Education: *School enrollment* (1968)—primary, 291,000; secondary, 34,230; technical/vocational, 6,400; university/higher (1966) 1,527.
Monetary Unit: Gourde (5 gourdes equal U. S.$1, July 1972).
Gross National Product (1970 est.): $440,000,000.
Manufacturing (major products): Processed foods, sugar.
Major Agricultural products: Sugarcane, bananas, sisal, coffee, cacao, corn.
Major Minerals: Bauxite, copper.
Foreign Trade (1971): *Exports,* $47,000,000. *Imports,* $59,000,000. *Chief trading partner*—United States.
Communications: *Television stations* (1971), 1; *television sets* (1971), 10,500; *radios* (1970), 83,000; *newspapers* (1969), 6.

to explore and drill but also to exploit, refine, transport, and market whatever petroleum and gas it discovered.

The second turbine at Peligre Dam began operation in February, and work continued on installation of a third. West Germany contributed some new irrigation equipment as part of a $2 million technical aid program. None of this has yet produced results in agriculture. Coffee production and exports continued their downward trend, offset, however, by a modest increase in sugar production in a year of high prices. Cocoa bean production remained stagnant, while sisal exports dropped drastically as a result of low 1971 production.

One of the government's primary goals was the opening of new lines of credit, but most lenders remained cautious. The Inter-American Development Bank made public in January its approval of $1.8 million in loans for industrial and agricultural development, and in September it announced a new $10 million loan for port improvements in the capital. Early in the year the U. S. government reported that the Overseas Private Investment Corporation had agreed to underwrite a $100,000 hotel investment, the first since 1966, and had 16 others under consideration.

The United States announced that it had resumed licensing of the sale of arms to Haiti through Aerotrade of Miami. Aerotrade, a minority stockholder of Air Haiti, sold trucks, jeeps, and M-16 rifles and supplied instructors both for the new equipment and for Haiti's 250-man air force. The United States refused a request for military credits, but Haiti reportedly was purchasing six patrol boats from private dealers and several jets from the U. S. government.

Diplomatic Efforts. Haiti also tried to improve its relations with its Caribbean neighbors. President Anastasio Somoza of Nicaragua visited Haiti in March, and a Haitian trade mission visited Jamaica in February.

Talks continued with the neighboring Dominican Republic, but little progress was made in settling differences. The border remained closed, and the Dominican government remained cool about permitting Haitians to enter the country as farm laborers. Relations further soured in the summer, when the Haitians sought to justify their need for arms by citing not only the Haitian exile and Communist threats but also the Dominican danger.

KARL M. SCHMITT
The University of Texas at Austin

───────── HAWAII • Information Highlights ─────────

Area: 6,450 square miles (16,706 sq km).
Population (1970 census): 769,913. *Density:* 123 per sq mi.
Chief Cities (1970 census): Honolulu, the capital, 324,871; Kailua, 33,783; Kaneohe, 29,903; Hilo, 26,353; Waipahu, 24,150; Pearl City, 19,552; Wahiawa, 17,598.
Government (1972): *Chief Officers*—governor, John A. Burns (D); lt. gov., George A. Ariyoshi (D); atty. gen., George T. H. Pai (D); supt., dept. of education, Shiro Amioka; chief justice, William S. Richardson. *Legislature*—Senate, 25 members (17 Democrats, 8 Republicans); House of Representatives, 51 members (33 D, 17 R, 1 vacancy).
Education (1971–72): *Enrollment*—public elementary schools, 102,106 pupils, 4,774 teachers; public secondary, 80,357 pupils, 3,339 teachers; nonpublic schools (1970–71), 21,776 pupils, 1,240 teachers; college and university, 33,000 students. *Public school expenditures,* $174,243,000 ($1,039 per pupil). *Average teacher's salary,* $10,898.
State Finances (fiscal year 1970): *Revenues,* $608,494,000 (4% general sales tax and gross receipts taxes, $162,689,000; motor fuel tax, $17,723,000; federal funds $138,585,000). *Expenditures,* $684,595,000 (education, $263,009,000; health, welfare, and safety, $60,137,000; highways, $63,621,000). *State debt,* $528,175,000 (June 30, 1970).
Personal Income (1971): $3,732,000,000; per capita, $4,797.
Public Assistance (1971): $2,301,000. *Average monthly payments* (Dec. 1971)—old-age assistance, $101.51; aid to families with dependent children, $71,564,000.
Labor Force: *Nonagricultural wage and salary earners* (July 1972), 315,000. *Average annual employment* (1971)—manufacturing, 25,000; trade, 72,000; government, 78,000; services, 61,000. *Insured unemployed* (Aug. 1972)—9,700 (3.6%).
Manufacturing (1970): *Value added by manufacture,* $398,000,000. Food and kindred products, $219,800,000; printing and publishing, $43,000,000; stone, clay, and glass products, $29,700,000; apparel and other textile products, $21,600,000; fabricated metal products, $17,300,000; lumber and wood products, $5,000,000.
Agriculture (1970): *Cash farm income,* $224,234,000 (livestock, $42,041,000; crops, $171,078,000; government payments, $11,115,000). *Chief crops*—Pineapples, sugarcane for sugar and seed, papayas, macadamia nuts.
Mining (1971): *Production value,* $28,108,000 (ranks 44th among the states). *Chief minerals*—Stone, $14,441,000; cement, $10,196,000; sand and gravel, $1,967,000; pumice, $779,000.
Fisheries (1971): *Commercial catch,* 17,177,000 pounds ($5,159,000). *Leading species by value,* Aku (skipjack), $2,752,710; ahi (bigeye and yellowfin), $1,085,214; akule, $227,470; striped marlin, $122,507.
Transportation: *Roads* (1971), 3,529 miles (5,679 km); *motor vehicles* (1971), 405,441; *public airports* (1972), 23.
Communications: *Telephones* (1971), 457,307; *television stations* (1971), 10; *radio stations* (1971), 29; *newspapers* (1972), 5 (daily circulation, 238,000).

HAWAII

A revision of the penal code and continuing problems related to the economy and the environment were of major concern in Hawaii in 1972.

Penal Legislation. Law officers voiced alarm over the fact that the legislature's revision of the state's century-old penal code would in effect legalize social gambling. The U. S. district attorney predicted that when the new law becomes effective in January 1973, mainland crime syndicates would infiltrate not only local gambling but also the tourist industry. He linked several gunshot killings in Honolulu to the incipient struggle for power among criminal groups. Legislative leaders replied that adequate law enforcement would keep organized gambling out of the state, which still prohibits horse and dog racing but tolerates cockfighting.

Economy. The state's economic expansion, which had faltered in 1971, resumed in 1972. Tourism grew by about one third, with continued increases in the number of visitors from Japan.

In some economic areas, however, difficulties loomed. Unemployment persisted, averaging 5% to 6%. Plantation agriculture, formerly the major sector of Hawaii's economy, shrank further. A large sugar plantation on the island of Hawaii closed, and the Dole Company, which had come to derive most of its pineapple crop from the Philippines, announced that its plantation on Molokai would close in 1975.

A two-day dock strike in Honolulu in mid-October was the first to take, place there in 23 years. Later in October, masters, mates, and pilots struck Hawaiian and West Coast ports over the issue of automation. Also in October, public school teachers throughout the state left their classrooms for a day to protest the failure of the Department of Education to provide additional teachers and meet other conditions of the teachers' first collective bargaining agreement. However, under court injunction, their union called off a full-fledged strike. Other government employee groups were negotiating initial contracts late in the year.

Antiwar Feeling. Although the leaders of several labor unions switched their allegiance to President Nixon in the presidential election, Democrats Patsy Mink and Spark Matsunaga, who opposed Nixon's war policies, were returned to Congress. Direction from Honolulu of air and naval operations against North Vietnam stimulated more antiwar protest. Three men entered command headquarters at Hickam Air Base and spilled on the files what they said was human blood. Two were fined by a federal judge, and one was acquitted when the armed forces refused to allow the files to be used as evidence.

Ecology. Environmental problems remained prominent. A court order stayed, at least temporarily, construction of a major highway across hitherto unimproved Moanalua Valley in central Oahu. Conservation groups generally backed a Honolulu plan to construct a fixed-wheel, rapid-transit system across Oahu's congested southern coastal plain. The Oceanic Institute reported that the waters of the Ala Wai Canal, bordering Waikiki, were on the verge of "environmental collapse" and would kill the fish and pollute adjacent tourist and residential areas. A measure was passed authorizing the state to renovate this and other areas.

ROBERT M. KAMINS, *University of Hawaii*

HEALTH CARE. See special feature beginning on page 26.
HEART DISEASE. See MEDICINE.
HEATH, Edward. See BIOGRAPHY.
HIGHWAYS. See TRANSPORTATION.
HIJACKING, Aerial. See special feature beginning on page 46.

HONDURAS

Gen. Oswaldo López Arellano overthrew the coalition government of President Ramón E. Cruz in a bloodless coup on Dec. 4, 1972. Protracted negotiations in 1972 between Honduras and El Salvador failed to produce a peace treaty officially ending their 1969 border war. Honduras did reach an economic understanding with Nicaragua.

Negotiations with El Salvador. An aura of optimism pervaded efforts by Honduras and El Salvador in early 1972 to resolve unsettled matters resulting from the so-called "Soccer War" of 1969. Politicians talked of a "new era of goodwill," and Honduran soldiers along the disputed boundary were photographed shaking hands with their adversaries. Pressure for a settlement came from Guatemala and Nicaragua, whose presidents, in a joint communiqué on March 8, called for reestablishment of diplomatic relations between the former belligerents and expressed approval of efforts made in that direction.

Progress toward a rapprochement was set back somewhat because a new administration was installed

------- **HONDURAS • Information Highlights** -------

Official Name: Republic of Honduras.
Area: 43,277 square miles (112,088 sq km).
Population (1972 est.): 2,900,000. *Density,* 67 per square mile (25.9 per sq km). *Annual rate of increase,* 3.2%.
Chief City (1968 est.): Tegucigalpa, the capital, 205,000.
Government: *Head of state,* Ramón Ernesto Cruz, president (took office June 1971). *Head of government,* Ramón Ernesto Cruz. *Legislature* (unicameral)—National Congress, 64 members. *Major political parties*—National party; Liberal party.
Languages: Spanish (official), English.
Education: *Expenditure* (1969), 19.5% of total public expenditure. *School enrollment* (1968)—primary, 376,966; secondary, 34,794; technical/vocational, 4,923; university/higher, 3,459.
Monetary Unit: Lempira (2 lempiras equal U. S.$1, Aug. 1972).
Gross National Product (1971 est.): $714,000,000.
National Income per Person (1969): $249.
Economic Indexes: *Industrial production* (manufacturing; 1966), 151 (1963=100); *agricultural production* (1971), 200 (1952–56=100); *consumer price index* (1971), 110 (1966=100).
Manufacturing (major products): Processed foods, vegetable oils, sugar, beverages, tobacco products, cement.
Major Agricultural Products: Bananas, coffee, corn, sugarcane, cotton, tobacco, forest products.
Major Minerals: Gold, silver, lead, zinc.
Foreign Trade (1971): *Exports,* $184,000,000 (chief exports—bananas, coffee, wood, silver). *Imports,* $194,000,000 (chief imports, 1969—nonelectrical machinery, chemicals, transport equipment, food). *Chief trading partners* (1969)—United States (took 47% of exports, supplied 43% of imports); West Germany (12%—6%); Guatemala (4%—10%); El Salvador (4%—7%).
Transportation: *Motor vehicles* (1970), 35,700 (automobiles, 18,800); *railroads* (1970), 632 miles (1,017 km); *merchant fleet* (1971), 70,000 gross registered tons; *major national airline,* SAHSA (Servicio Aerea de Honduras SA).
Communications: *Telephones* (1971), 13,567; *television stations* (1971), 5; *television sets* (1971), 45,000; *radios* (1970), 147,000; *newspapers* (1967), 7.

in El Salvador on July 1. However, just seven weeks later, Honduran Foreign Minister Andrés Alvarado Puerto met his Salvadorean counterpart, Mauricio Borgonovo, in Guatemala City. That confrontation was the first since 1969 between foreign ministers of the belligerent nations. Between mid-1969 and mid-1972, Honduras had spent an estimated $13 million on military hardware, obviously unwilling to rely entirely on the promise of a negotiated settlement of the quarrel.

Honduras-Nicaragua Pact. In April the Honduran government signed a bilateral treaty with Nicaragua, the first negotiated by Honduras since withdrawing from the Central American Common Market (CACM) in 1971. It was to serve as a basis for free trade and an electric-power interconnection between the two countries. The pact was signed during a state visit to Nicaragua by Honduran President Ramón E. Cruz. On his return, Cruz was accompanied by Nicaraguan cotton technicians, who were to help revitalize that industry, which was devastated by the "Soccer War." Negotiations leading to a similar pact with Costa Rica were suspended after Costa Rica revealed a serious foreign-trade deficit.

Power Plant. Funded by the World Bank and its affiliates, Honduras is building the largest power plant in Central America. In 1972, Honduras obtained a loan of $12.3 million, in addition to the $33 million already provided. The project is one step in a coordinated development program of the Honduran and Nicaraguan power sectors.

Skyjacking. On June 3, after a month in hiding, Frederick W. Hahnemann turned himself over to U. S. authorities in Tegucigalpa, ending a multinational search for the skyjacker of an American jetliner. Hahnemann, a U. S. citizen born in Honduras, had been protected by several influential families before being flushed out by agents of the Honduran National Investigation Department. Hahnemann was a cousin of Roberto Martínez Ordóñez, the Honduran ambassador to the United States.

Coup d'Etat. In a communiqué justifying his December take-over of the government, General López accused President Cruz of economic irresponsibility and termed his two-party coalition a "shameful spectacle." Hoping to avoid a possible intervention by the military, the minority Liberal faction of the ruling coalition had called on their partners, the Nationalists, to adhere to the 1971 unity pact and its amendments. The Nationalists called a special convention on October 25, but they were unable to placate the Liberal dissidents.

LARRY L. PIPPIN
Elbert Covell College
University of the Pacific

HONG KONG

Hong Kong sustained its strong economic momentum during 1972, as it maintained its stability, prosperity, and progress throughout the year.

Economy. The first six months of 1972 showed increases of 9.7% for domestic exports, 2.4% for imports, and 14.7% for reexports, compared with the same period in 1971.

Hong Kong's stock market has risen about 116% in the past two years, whereas London gained 18%, Tokyo 15%, and New York only 5%. The boom was attributed to the growth of company profits, general liquidity of the local economy, and the influx of cash from overseas investors. Hong Kong is emerging as a major financial center in Asia.

The first industrial census in Hong Kong showed a total of 24,149 manufacturing establishments employing 671,000 persons in August 1971. Total sales and work done were valued at more than $3.2 billion, of which 65% were exported.

A loans for small industry scheme came into operation in July 1972. It provides loans for factories employing less than 200 workers.

The 1-mile (1.6-km) cross-harbor tunnel linking Kowloon and Hong Kong Island was opened in August 1972. Two new tunnels were being constructed to link Kowloon with two new towns, Kwun Tong and Sha Tin.

In July, the government approved a mass transit system for Hong Kong and invited firms to submit proposals for an underground railway that will cost more than $1 billion.

------- **HONG KONG • Information Highlights** -------

Official Name: Hong Kong.
Area: 398 square miles (1,034 sq km).
Population (1972 est.): 4,400,000. *Density,* 10,347 per sq mi (3,955 per sq km). *Annual rate of increase,* 2.4%.
Chief City (1966 est.): Victoria, the capital, 585,000.
Government: *Head of state,* Elizabeth II, queen (acceded Feb. 1952). *Head of government,* Sir Murray MacLehose, governor (took office 1971). *Major political parties*—Democratic Self-Government party; Labor party of Hong Kong; Socialist Democratic party.
Languages (official): English, Cantonese Chinese.
Education: *Expenditure* (1969), 22.1% of total public expenditure. *School enrollment* (1969)—primary, 746,429; secondary, 254,617; technical/vocational, 13,383; university/higher, 19,874.
Monetary Unit: Hong Kong dollar (5.65 H. K. dollars equal U. S.$1, July 1972).
Gross National Product (1970 est.): $3,620,000,000.
Manufacturing (major products): Textiles, clothing, furniture, jewelry, plastic articles, electronic components, household utensils, toys.
Major Agricultural Products: Rice, vegetables, fish.
Foreign Trade (1971): *Exports,* $2,871,000,000. *Imports,* $3,-387,000,000. *Chief trading partners* (1969)—United States (took 35% of exports, supplied 13% of imports); United Kingdom (12%—8%); Japan (6%—23%); China (0.3%—18%).
Communications: *Telephones* (1971), 583,222; *television stations* (1971), 3; *television sets* (1971), 429,000; *newspapers* (1969), 74 (daily circulation, 1,936,000).

In Hong Kong, a landslide caused by heavy mid-June rains demolished several buildings on this mountainside.

Education. Government expenditures on education were about $90 million in 1971, or twice that in 1967. Compulsory primary education was introduced in September 1971, and free primary schooling was to be extended to free secondary education in 1976. In 1972 the school population was nearly 1.3 million, including about 1.2 million in pre-primary, primary, and secondary education; about 73,000 in postsecondary and adult education; and nearly 3,000 in special education for handicapped children.

Environmental Conservation. Growing awareness of the need for conservation of the environment resulted in the establishment of an advisory committee on environmental pollution on land and water, the introduction of a clean air ordinance, and the allocation of $214,000 to finance a "Keep Hong Kong Clean" campaign. Also, $5.9 million was set aside to develop parks, picnic areas, and hiking facilities throughout the colony.

The marine department set up a pollution control unit to safeguard Hong Kong waters, and the public works department began a pollution study in April 1972. In November the urban services department began a street-by-street cleaning program throughout urban areas.

The Shell Company of Hong Kong applied for construction a $250 million oil refinery on Lamma Island. The move will not be approved if marine life or recreational facilities are endangered.

Government. Membership of the Legislative Council was increased from 26 to 28 in June 1972. A policy of bilingualism was being implemented, and Chinese was made an official language.

Relations with China improved greatly during 1972. In February a regular telephone link opened between Peking and Hong Kong. In April and May about 46,000 Chinese in Hong Kong were permitted to attend the Canton Trade Fair. The Chinese government also agreed to supply 3 billion gallons of water to Hong Kong in July and August in addition to its annual provision of 15 billion gallons.

DAVID CHUEN-YAN LAI
University of Victoria

HOOVER, J. Edgar

Director of the Federal Bureau of Investigation (FBI): b. Washington, D. C., Jan. 1, 1895; d. Washington, D. C., May 2, 1972.

For nearly half a century, J. Edgar Hoover, director of the Federal Bureau of Investigation (known until 1935 as the Bureau of Investigation of the U. S. Department of Justice), stood in the vanguard of the battle against crime in the United States. After taking over in 1924 as head of what was then a small, politics-ridden organization, he built it into a tough, efficient, and incorruptible force that became known as one of the world's foremost law enforcement agencies. Through its success in apprehending spies, saboteurs, and foreign agents, the FBI under Hoover's direction earned a reputation as an effective guardian of the national security.

Early Life and Career. John Edgar Hoover, a native and lifelong resident of the nation's capital, was born on New Year's Day, 1895. He was the son of an official of the U. S. Coast and Geodetic Survey. After working his way through George Washington University law school as a messenger in the Library of Congress, he received his LL. B. degree in 1916 and a master's degree the following year.

In 1919, in the midst of the post-World War I "Red scare," Hoover joined the Department of Justice as a special assistant to Attorney General A. Palmer Mitchell and was assigned responsibility for the rounding up and deportation of suspected alien radicals. In 1921 he was appointed assistant director of the Bureau of Investigation, then under the direction of William J. Burns. Named by Attorney General Harlan Fiske Stone to succeed as director in 1924, Hoover accepted on condition that the bureau would be entirely free from outside political control.

Achievements as FBI Director. On taking over as director of the Bureau of Investigation, Hoover immediately began to overhaul it completely. He instituted improved methods of recruiting and training, establishing new standards of professionalism by hiring lawyers and public accountants as special agents, and he pioneered in the application of modern methods of science and technology to the detection of crime. Under his administration, a centralized fingerprint bureau was established as part of a new Identification Division in 1925; the compilation and publication of nationwide crime statistics was begun in 1930; and a crime laboratory was created in 1932. The FBI Academy, established in 1935, has trained selected police officers from every part of the United States and from foreign countries in the most effective methods of law enforcement.

The FBI's relentless campaign against gangsterism, and in particular, against the wave of kidnapping and bank robberies during the 1930's, led to the smashing of crime syndicates, the solution of such major crimes as the Lindbergh kidnapping, and the apprehension of such notorious criminals as John Dillinger and Alvin Karpis. In keeping with Hoover's admonition—"If there is going to be publicity, let it be on the side of law and order"—the FBI's exploits captured the imagination of the American public, which accepted the "G-man" as a national hero.

In 1939 the FBI was directed by President Franklin D. Roosevelt to coordinate all matters relating to

J. EDGAR HOOVER (1895–1972)

UPI

the national security. During World War II it rounded up thousands of enemy aliens, and through effective methods of intelligence and counterespionage it apprehended Axis agents, spies, and saboteurs. With the beginning of the Cold War era and the atomic age at the end of World War II the FBI was charged with gathering information on suspected Soviet espionage agents. In 1947 it began the assignment of checking the loyalty of all federal employees. For the remainder of Hoover's life, the pursuit of suspected subversives of the left occupied the major part of the FBI's activities. In 1967 the FBI's highly efficient National Crime Information Center began operations.

Evaluation. Although he was confirmed in his post by every president from Calvin Coolidge to Richard Nixon, and was permitted to remain in office well beyond the mandatory retirement age of 70, Hoover was nonetheless a highly controversial figure. Critics charged him with exercising virtually uncontrolled power and with violating civil liberties through the use of such means of surveillance as wiretapping. While proceeding with great vigor against student radicals, antiwar demonstrators, and other dissenters of the left, he was, in the view of many observers, derelict in the safeguarding of the civil rights of minorities. Other criticisms centered around his alleged intolerance and lack of objectivity, and the rigid standards of personal behavior that Hoover imposed on his subordinates. Even his staunchest critics, however, recognized his basic integrity and his contributions to the battle against crime.

HENRY SLOAN

HORTICULTURE. See GARDENING AND HORTICULTURE.

HOSPITALS. See MEDICINE.

HOTELS AND MOTELS. See TOURISM.

Another building in St. Louis' ill-fated Pruitt-Igoe public housing complex is dynamited on April 21. The demolition was ordered because some of the buildings in the project were in such poor condition.

HOUSING

In housing, 1972 seemed to be in most respects an extension of 1971. Construction costs continued to rise; there was more experimentation with industrial housing; massive subsidy contracts were made, and torrents of savings were still available for mortgages; high interest rates remained stabilized; and there was a continuation of temporizing with community subsidies, pending new legislation, which was postponed to 1973. But most important of all, there was a further extension of the record number of housing starts set in 1971. During 1971–72, housing construction led the way in the recovery from the recession of 1970, just as it had done in 1949–50, 1954–55, and 1959. The housing industry —often castigated as archaic, disorganized, and inefficient—rose again in 1972 to peak production under the stimulus of available funds—both short-term funds for building and long-term funds for marketing.

Record Production. Residential starts in 1972 totaled about 2.4 million units, surpassing the 1971 record by 250,000 units. A companion record of more than 500,000 mobile home shipments brought the total to more than 2.9 million new units— clearly exceeding the controversial annual rate of 2.6 million units required for the 1969–78 national housing goal, which was enunciated in the Housing Act of 1968. The principal laurels for the record belonged to that classical energizer of capitalism— the chance of making a profit. The counterbalancing risk of loss had been substantially muted for the important classes of entrepreneurs. High-ratio home loans assured immediate payments to producers, depending only on modest down payments by purchasers. For institutional lenders, 7%–8% interest for 30-year terms on insured investments assured necessary capital from near-record deposit gains.

Multifamily Units. The most impressive increase was in the building of multifamily units, including elevator buildings, walk-up apartments, low-rent public housing, and in some areas condominium town houses. Some 1 million such units were begun in 1972, whereas prior to 1970 such production was not even dreamed of—in the booming 1920's construction rates remained at about 250,000 such units per year, and the rate during most of the 1960's was only about 500,000 annually. Reasons for the 1970's apartment explosion were complex but surely involved such factors as new money, new tax rules, new markets, new products, and new subsidies.

The immensity of the inflow of savings deposits in 1971–72 and official encouragement to diversification in lending resulted in new financing for multifamily structures. Real estate investment trusts and new forms of guaranteed bonds brought to apartments both equity and debt financing from broader parts of the money system.

New tax rules in 1969 gave extra preference to moderate income rental housing in depreciation write-off of housing investments. In combination with avoidance of investment trust tax by quick distribution of earnings from real estate trusts, these depreciation allowances were providing those who pay high income taxes with attractive incentives to invest in apartment houses.

A new market was created by the unprecedented number of young couples disposed toward apartment living. Because of their common disposition toward a zero population growth, these couples tended to plan small families, and prolonged apartment-occupancy was frequently the result. The number of unmarried adults also grew, increasing the demand for bachelor apartments. In addition, more of the elderly maintained apartments. This reflected improved health and greater longevity in the nation, as well as rising pensions and savings and the greater conveniences offered in modern accommodations. It also reflected a response to the needs of the younger generation for mobility freedom from the older folks.

A growing number of buildings with swimming pools, sauna baths, security systems, and central

air conditioning made apartment dwelling vastly different from anything offered to previous generations. Condominium tenure also gained popularity in 1972. This relatively new feature offered home ownership in apartments, with attendant tax and gain potentials, without requiring the owners to dedicate themselves to the lawn and household chores required of those living in single-family houses.

Aside from the subsidies camouflaged in the income tax regulations, overt subsidies for multifamily housing had been tremendously expanded under the national housing goals enunciated in 1968. Inspired by opportunities directed toward builders, investors, and lenders on behalf of low- and moderate-income families, Congress authorized subsidy contracts—through programs of the Federal Housing Administration (FHA) and "Turnkey" programs of public housing—that would be ample for 500,000 units a year, weighted somewhat toward multifamily construction. This compared with the recurring figure of 35,000 units of public housing yearly that had been authorized during much of the 1950's.

The Ten-Year Goal. The 1968 Housing Act had boldly set forth a housing production goal of 26 million units in a ten-year period—give or take some for rehabilitation of existing housing. The average number of units needed annually to reach this goal was first met in 1971 and 1972 with 2.6 million and 2.9 million units under construction (including mobile homes), following a decade in which production had been below needs. The meeting of the annual goals in 1971–72 moved the nation closer to answers to the questions of how realistic the assumptions of growth, replacement, and vacancy behind the proposed production rate had been.

Clearly, growth and demolition in periods of prosperity warrant housing production well above the annual levels of from 1.2 million to 1.5 million (excluding mobile homes) that persisted during the 1960's. Clearly also, help in the form of subsidies to families unable to obtain acceptable housing is essential to community health and to the absorption of marginal high-volume housing production.

As deliveries of housing approached the annual rates of 2.6 million to 2.8 million (completions lag 6–12 months behind starts), the behavior of vacancies began to be critically important. Vacancies modestly above the 1970–71 low points of 1% for owner housing and 5% for rental housing assure both choice and reasonable mobility. Some growth in this direction was evident by mid-1972.

If added vacancies are from depreciated units that are filtering out of the effective supply, then absorption of high volume production will not weaken the market. But if acceptable, marketable vacant units exceed market needs—as appeared to be happening in late 1972 in isolated markets—then the rate of 2.5 million to 2.8 million units per year would seem less justified. Perhaps reduced production or, alternatively, larger subsidies to households in inadequate housing may be in order.

Home Financing. In home financing, new Federal Home Loan Bank regulations in 1972 authorized member associations to make 95% conventional loans if suitably insured, thus approaching the best terms in nonsubsidized FHA-insured loans.

Also during 1972, national systems of secondary markets were instituted for conventional mortgages —one in the Federal National Mortgage Association and one within the Federal Home Loan Bank System. Together these may lead to the uniformity and marketability of conventional mortgages needed for a truly national market, such as has long existed for FHA and VA (Veterans Administration) mortgages.

Federal Home Loan Bank pronouncements in 1972 encouraged variable interest rate provisions, permitting rate adjustments for future mortgages as money market yields vary during the life of the mortgages. Past use of such terms in U. S. mortgage lending has been limited by borrower resistance to what has seemed to mean continual upward adjustments.

Discrimination in Housing. In 1972 several new federal measures challenged housing discrimination. For rental and sales projects requiring subsidy, new criteria for project selection were put into effect to maximize project dispersion and minority opportunities for housing outside segregated neighborhoods. Affirmative advertising was required to inform minority families of new subsidized units for rent or for sale outside areas of minority concentrations. Also, court actions were initiated in some suburban communities to prevent the use of "snob zoning" to exclude low-income families.

Housing Scandals. The FHA insures mortgages for families with marginal credit ratings, often to buy marginal quality homes in neighborhoods of doubtful stability. These new standards for properties and borrowers evidently provided as fertile opportunities for "fast-buck artists" as for disadvantaged families. During 1972 in Detroit, Philadelphia, New York, and elsewhere, press and congressional investigations, often followed by criminal indictments, revealed widespread speculator purchases of dilapidated houses in declining neighborhoods, "cosmetic" repair by painting and superficial modernization, and sale at inflated prices to unwary home buyers. Too often, overly generous property appraisals by FHA appraisers occurred, sometimes reflecting appraiser inexperience, but sometimes also reflecting the influence of bribes or other scandals. There was concern that the necessary tightening of procedures after these scandals might, due to overreaction, unduly restrict the program's intended opportunities for benefits to deserving families.

Investigations by the Department of Housing and Urban Development (HUD) in 1972 also revealed land sales irregularities by less scrupulous promoters —both interstate and intrastate—through high - pressure tactics and misrepresentation or concealment

GEORGE ROMNEY is target of criticism by a flood victim in Wilkes-Barre, Pa., who charged federal inaction.

UPI

AT HOUSTON, American and Soviet space officials met in July to discuss the joint venture in space that their countries have planned for 1975. The model they hold (left) is of a Soviet Soyuz docked with an American Apollo spacecraft by means of a third unit to be produced by the United States. The Soviet officials are at left.

UPI

of important facts. Some of these cases also attracted attention from grand juries as well as administrators.

Congressional Inaction. The U.S. Senate and House of Representatives were unable to agree on new housing legislation in 1972. In March, the Senate passed a bill consolidating FHA programs and providing revenue-sharing block grants for urban community development. An alternate bill from the House Committee in September was killed by the House Rules Committee. Accordingly, existing authorities were extended for several months pending new action early in 1973. Nonpartisan studies in 1972 that claimed that the housing subsidy programs were filled with inequities were behind the House decision to postpone legislation. There was speculation that a new bill in 1973 might attempt to reform the present system.

HUD Secretary George Romney emphasized that housing measures alone do not and will not solve all of the social ills associated with poor housing. Perhaps improved remedial programs can grow from this deepening understanding.

ALLAN F. THORNTON
Federal Housing Administration

HOUSTON

Houston, the nation's sixth-largest city in population and fifth-largest in land area, increased its area in 1972 to 506.7 square miles by annexing 53.7 square miles of adjacent land containing approximately 35,000 residents. Otherwise, the year was one of moderate growth.

Economy. An economic boom continued into 1972, but the effects of a sluggish national economy were felt locally. Unemployment edged up from 2.9% in October 1971 to 3.0% in October 1972, but remained well below the national average of 5.5%. Construction expanded, with building permits for the first 10 months of the year valued at $532.6 million.

Transportation. Faced with growing traffic congestion, Houston began serious consideration of mass transit proposals. A study by Alan M. Voorhees and Associates recommended a $1.45 billion system of both fixed guideway transport and buses, which would take 15 years to complete. Initial

hurdles include the obtaining of enabling legislation from the state legislature, the establishment of jurisdictional boundaries, and passage of a proposal for a bond issue to secure funds for construction.

The Port of Houston Authority undertook a $19 million expansion at its Bayport Division to accommodate containerized ocean-going shipping. The U.S.-Soviet wheat deal was expected to boost port tonnage in 1973.

Medical Projects. The Texas Medical Center continued the rapid expansion of facilities begun in 1971, when almost $26 million was spent on capital improvements. During 1972, multi-million dollar projects were announced in more than half of the 23 constituent institutions. The largest of these projects was a $30 million expansion of the University of Texas M. D Anderson Hospital and Tumor Institute, which will make this facility the largest cancer treatment and research center in the world.

In September a proposal for a "high school of medical careers" to be operated in conjunction with Baylor College of Medicine was adopted by the local school district. This program, the first of its kind in the nation, is designed for students planning to go into medical fields. All classes are to be held at Baylor.

Government and Politics. Reapportionment following the 1970 census resulted in significant increases in representation for Houston at both the state and federal levels. Harris county's state legislative delegation increased from 19 assemblymen and 3 senators to 24 assemblymen and 5 senators. Harris county's U.S. congressional delegation increased from 3 members to 5. Houstonians Bill Hobby and John Hill were elected as the state's lieutenant governor and attorney general, respectively. They were the first Houstonians to hold statewide office since 1935.

With her election to Congress, Barbara Jordan of Houston became the first black woman to represent a Southern congressional district and the first black member of the Texas congressional delegation since Reconstruction. The establishment of single-member state legislative districts resulted in an increase in the number of black state legislators from Harris county from one to four.

VICTOR L. EMANUEL, *Rice University*

HUNGARY

Efforts to narrow the gap that still exists between the government and the population of Hungary continued in 1972. There were fewer burdensome political mass meetings and demonstrations, and emphasis was put on a higher economic and cultural standard of living. The party organs called for revision of some ineffective university courses in Marxism-Leninism, recommending the elimination of "indigestible material which bears no relation to reality," the avoidance of "dogmatism," and greater consideration for those ideas related to current domestic and international problems.

Domestic Politics. After long preparation and many public debates, the National Assembly unanimously approved a new constitution on April 19, 1972. The basic structure of the state remained unchanged. The new constitution recognized the Hungarian Workers' Party as "the leading force in society," singled out the People's Patriotic Front together with trade unions as the most valuable "social organizations," and gave primacy in the national economy to nationalized and socialized productive forces. However, the constitution "recognized" small-scale individual producers, provided "private property and private initiative do not violate public interest."

In April, the Roman Catholic weekly *Uj Ember* published data indicating a growing shortage of priests. Out of approximately 4,000 priests, 31% were over 50 years old. The six existing seminaries had only 300 students. Further, no more than 40 to 50 yearly ordinations had been processed since the mid-1950's.

In no small measure, the crisis was due to official policy, which continued to obstruct the training of priests. Not all of the dioceses were permitted to have their own seminaries, and admissions of candidates were strictly rationed. The applicants had to undergo military service, and each candidate for ordination was subject to government veto.

According to the most recent statistics, there were 24,000 practicing physicians in Hungary in 1972—one doctor for every 400 inhabitants. Still, there were some 2,000 unfilled medical positions, and the party press called on the government to take action.

Economy. The budget for 1972 provided for 74,500 new apartments. Expenditures for culture, health, and care of the aged increased 20% over those of the preceding year.

In May, special bonuses were granted to those members of the collective farms who distinguished themselves by long and "loyal" service. A campaign to recruit more young farmers intensified. Over 25% of Hungary's farmers were over 55 years old; young persons seemed to prefer city life.

By the end of 1971 there were some 260,000 private automobiles in Hungary. Although about 60,000 cars were imported in 1972, there were still over 116,000 applications for the purchase of new vehicles outstanding at the end of the year.

In the second part of the year, the press revealed new plans concerning the development of areas near Hungary's borders in cooperation with neighboring countries. Individual projects, enterprises, and various fields of cooperation with Yugoslavia, Austria, and Rumania received special attention.

Foreign Policy. In foreign affairs, Hungary continued to follow Soviet policies closely. The Chinese leadership was criticized in official party organs for anti-Marxism as well as anti-Sovietism, and the Chinese were urged to travel the road of Socialist solidarity.

However, there were also signs that Hungary's domestic reforms aroused some apprehension in Moscow. There, the press, although ostentatiously praising Budapest, also frequently referred to "Zionist intrigues," cosmopolitanism, "worship of the West," and growth of the *petite bourgeoisie* in Hungary. The Czechoslovak party press was even more explicit in criticizing what it called Budapest's "antisocial orientation."

ON A STATE VISIT TO HUNGARY in May, Cuban Premier Fidel Castro stands beside János Kádár, Hungary's Communist party chief, to wave to crowds during a motorcade through Budapest.

KEYSTONE

——— HUNGARY • Information Highlights ———

Official Name: Hungarian People's Republic.
Area: 35,919 square miles (93,030 sq km).
Population (1972 est.): 10,400,000. *Density,* 287 per square mile (111 per sq km). *Annual rate of increase,* 0.3%.
Chief Cities (1970 census): Budapest, the capital, 1,940,000; Miskolc, 173,000; Debrecen, 155,000.
Government: *Head of state,* Pál Losonczi, chairman of the Presidential Council (took office April 1967). *Head of government,* Jenö Fock, premier (took office April 1967). *First secretary of the Hungarian Socialist Workers'* (Communist), János Kádár (took office Oct. 25, 1956). *Legislature* (unicameral)—National Assembly, 352 members.
Language: Hungarian (official).
Education: *Expenditure* (1969), 7.3% of total public expenditure. *School enrollment* (1969)—primary, 1,177,887; secondary, 454,552; technical/vocational, 330,332; university/higher, 53,237.
Monetary Unit: Forint (10.81 forint = U. S.$1, June 1972).
Gross National Product (1968 est.): $13,200,000,000.
National Income per Person (1968): $1,280.
Economic Indexes: *Industrial production* (1971), 151 (1963 = 100); *agricultural production* (1970), 118 (1957–59 = 100); *consumer price index* (1970), 102 (1967 = 100).
Manufacturing (major products): Machinery, machine tools, commercial vehicles, chemicals, pharmaceuticals, aluminum.
Major Agricultural Products: Corn, wheat, potatoes.
Major Minerals: Bauxite, coal, petroleum, natural gas.
Foreign Trade (1971): *Exports,* $2,500,000,000 (chief exports, 1969—food and live animals; machinery). *Imports,* $2,-990,000,000 (chief imports, 1969—nonelectrical machinery; chemicals; mineral fuel and lubricants; food and live animals). *Chief trading partners* (1969)—USSR (took 35% of exports, supplied 37% of imports); East Germany (11%—10%); Czechoslovakia (9%—7%).
Tourism: *Receipts* (1970) $72,400,000.
Transportation: *Automobiles* (1970), 242,700; *railroads* (1970), 5,090 miles (8,191 km); *major national airline,* Malev-Hungarian Airlines.
Communications: *Telephones* (1971), 823,600; *television stations* (1971), 11; *newspapers* (1970), 27 (daily circulation, 2,207,000).

On June 5, 1972, Hungary signed a two-year agreement on educational and cultural cooperation with Yugoslavia. June also marked the occasion of a visit to Budapest by Cuban Premier Fidel Castro. The visit was widely publicized, and cooperation between the two countries was agreed upon.

Hungarian-American relations improved in 1972. In May, Hungary and the United States concluded an agreement providing for the construction of their first joint industrial-commercial enterprise. Known as the Euroamerican Technocorporation, it will produce and market the Hungarian biochemical invention "fibrinbioplast," a human tissue substitute, usable in 30 different kinds of surgical operations.

On July 6, U. S. Secretary of State William Rogers visited Budapest. Rogers was the first member of a U. S. cabinet to be received by János Kádár, the first secretary of the Communist party. Later, a joint communiqué, mentioned "frank talks" and closer U. S.–Hungarian relations.

Foreign Trade. Foreign economic exchange improved. Although there was still a deficit in the balance of trade with non-Communist countries, it was reduced by 50% in comparison with the deficit of the preceding year. The trade with Socialist countries showed a slight surplus.

Criticism of Peking's foreign policy notwithstanding, Hungary's trade with China progressed. Exports increased 96% over the previous year, amounting to 194,000,000 foreign exchange forint. Imports increased by 11%, amounting to 164,000,-000 forint. In August, an exhibition of the Hungarian machine industry was mounted in Tientsin.

In May, the traditional International Fair opened its gates in Budapest. Some 41 countries as well as 2,900 individual exhibitors displayed their wares. China also participated for the first time in six years. The International Fair marked a record success in trade contracts.

JAN KARSKI, *Georgetown University*

ICELAND

Iceland elected a president, passed a major tax and governmental reform, established a 50-mile (80-km) sea boundary, started a "codfish war," and played host to a highly publicized chess match in 1972. In the vote on June 25, Kristján Eldjárn was reelected president without serious opposition.

Legislation and Reforms. A broad tax revision increased income, property, auto, and other taxes and removed governmental responsibilities and rights to taxation from local political units. Police functions went to the national government, and health and pension taxes ceased after Jan. 1, 1972; the expenditures for both are now taken from general funds. Health services were reorganized, and the number of medical districts, hospitals, and services was increased.

NATO and Keflavík Airport. Despite some opposition Iceland continued membership in NATO and that body's use of Keflavík airport. Its runways were to be extended, with the assistance of an American loan, to accommodate larger aircraft.

The "Codfish War." The Althing's unanimous approval of a 50-mile sea boundary, effective September 1, started an international conflict. Iceland responded to British, West German, and other protests in a note of August 11 setting forth conditions for fishing within the 50-mile limits, while disregarding an adverse judgment of the International Court. On September 1 and later, British and West German trawlers fished within the limits set by Iceland, and there were some incidents, such as the cutting of nets and near collisions. Negotiations between Britain and Iceland continued. An international study proved Iceland's claim of North Atlantic fish depletion.

Chess Match. Many visitors were drawn to Reykjavík for the world championship chess match between the defending champion, Boris Spassky of Russia, and the American challenger, Bobby Fischer, who won. The match, postponed several times, was played from July 11 to September 1. (See the special feature on chess beginning on page 53.)

Economy. Iceland's fish catch for 1971–72 exceeded averages of recent years. An arbitration court decision provided for retroactive pay increases for civil service personnel. A new 40-hour week went into effect on Jan. 1, 1972.

RAYMOND E. LINDGREN
California State University, Long Beach

——— ICELAND • Information Highlights ———

Official Name: Republic of Iceland.
Area: 39,768 square miles (103,000 sq km).
Population (1972 est.): 200,000. *Density,* 5 per square mile (2 per sq km). *Annual rate of increase,* 1.2%.
Chief City (1970 est.): Reykjavik, the capital, 81,600.
Government: *Head of state,* Kristján Eldjárn, president (took office June 1968). *Head of government,* Olafur Johannesson, prime minister (took office July 1971). *Legislature*—Althing: Upper House, 20 members; Lower House, 40 members. *Major political parties*—Independence; Progressive; People's Alliance; Social Democratic.
Language: Icelandic (official).
Education: *Expenditure* (1968), 12.7% of total public expenditure. *School enrollment* (1968)—primary, 27,356; secondary, 21,584; technical/vocational, 5,000; university/higher, 1,302.
Monetary Unit: króna (87.42 krónur equal U. S.$1, Aug. 1972).
Gross National Product (1971 est.): $500,000,000.
Manufacturing (major products): Fish products, clothing, shoes, chemicals, fertilizer.
Major Agricultural Products: Potatoes, hay, dairy products.
Major Minerals: Shell sand, perlite, pumice, peat.
Foreign Trade (1971): *Exports,* $150,000,000. *Imports,* $210,-000,000. *Chief trading partners* (1969)—United States (took 28% of exports, supplied 9% of imports); United Kingdom (14%—13%); West Germany (9%—17%).

UPI

DISASTER struck the Sunshine Mine, Kellogg, Idaho, in May when an underground fire killed 91 miners. Two survivors (above) were brought to the surface after being trapped for a week.

UPI

IDAHO

The November elections and a mine disaster figured prominently among Idaho events of 1972.

Politics. Republicans did well in the November elections. President Nixon won handily. U. S. Rep. James A. McClure took the U. S. Senate seat vacated by Len Jordan, and Steven D. Symms won the seat vacated by McClure. In addition, Republicans gained four Senate seats in the state legislature, giving them a 23–12 margin, and ten House seats for a 51–19 majority.

Sen. Len Jordan's announcement that he was retiring created great interest. Four Republicans, including former Gov. Robert E. Smylie, and four Democrats contested. Republican James A. McClure and Democrat William E. (Bud) Davis, Idaho State University president, won the primaries. For the House seat vacated by McClure, Republican Steven D. Symms beat out Democrat E. V. Williams, who resigned as Gov. Cecil D. Andrus' administrative assistant. In the southern district, incumbent Orval Hansen defeated Democrat Willis Ludlow.

Disaster. A fire that started on May 2 in the Sunshine Mine killed 91 miners. Over 100 escaped just after the fire started. Eight days later two were rescued. They had survived in an air pocket and subsisted on lunches belonging to their dead comrades. On the tenth day the rest of the men were found dead. Charges that reflected on Sunshine's safety practices were made, but the investigation that followed did not develop any clear proof of company negligence. The mine remained closed.

Legislature. The Legislature reduced to 18 the age at which males might contract and marry (female age of majority has long been 18). The age for jury duty for both sexes was reduced to 18, and the age for consumption of all alcoholic beverages, to 19. The legislature also repealed a new 1971 criminal code, which had been six years in development, because prosecuting attorneys claimed it was too easy on criminals.

Nine constitutional amendments were proposed, but only four passed, including one that will force the Legislature to reduce the 268 state agencies to 20 and one allowing passage of revenue bond issues with a simple majority instead of the present two thirds. Amendments to allow busing of children to parochial schools, to require the governor and lieutenant governor to be from the same party, and to provide a practical way to set legislative salaries failed by wide margins.

Environment. The U. S. Congress created the Sawtooth Recreation Area to give protection to the White Cloud peaks at the headwaters of the Salmon River. These had been a center of controversy with mining interests for five years. The 10-year moratorium bill to protect the Middle Snake from dams did not pass. Sen. Frank Church (D) requested a $4-million appropriation to buy lands along the Snake that are likely to be sought by land developers.

Finance. Legislative appropriations rose from $126.4 million to $137.3 million. The amount allotted to public schools went from $44 million to $47.8 million, while that going to higher education rose from $27.7 million to $29.5 million.

CLIFFORD DOBLER
University of Idaho

─────── **IDAHO • Information Highlights** ───────

Area: 83,557 square miles (216,413 sq km).
Population (1970 census): 713,008. *Density,* 9 per sq mi.
Chief Cities (1970 census): Boise, the capital, 74,990; Pocatello, 40,036; Idaho Falls, 35,776.
Government (1972): *Chief Officers*—governor, Cecil D. Andrus (D); lt. gov., Jack M. Murphy (R); secy. of state, Pete T. Cenarrusa (R); atty. gen., W. Anthony Park (D); treas., Marjorie Ruth Moon (D); supt. of public instruction, Delmer F. Engelking (D); chief justice, Henry F. McQuade. *Legislature*—Senate, 35 members (19 Republicans, 16 Democrats); House of Representatives, 70 (41 R, 29 D).
Education (1971–72): *Enrollment*—public elementary schools, 93,148 pupils; 3,777 teachers; public secondary, 91,966; pupils; 4,232 teachers; nonpublic schools (1970–71), 6,171 pupils; 320 teachers; college and university, 34,000 students. *Public school expenditures,* $129,182,000 ($732 per pupil). *Average teacher's salary,* $7,621.
State Finances (fiscal year 1970): *Revenues,* $315,434,000 (3% general sales tax and gross receipts taxes, $41,679,000; motor fuel tax, $25,330,000; federal funds, $78,261,000). *Expenditures,* $316,366,000 (education, $106,694,000; health, welfare, and safety, $33,806,000; highways, $62,267,000). *State debt,* $33,102,000 (June 30, 1970).
Personal Income (1971): $2,490,000,000; per capita, $3,402.
Public Assistance (1971): $28,970,000. *Average monthly payments* (Dec. 1971)—old-age assistance, $76.66; aid to families with dependent children, $204.69.
Labor Force: *Nonagricultural wage and salary earners* (July 1972), 230,000. *Average annual employment* (1971)—manufacturing, 41,000; trade, 51,000; government, 51,000; services, 34,000. *Insured unemployed* (Aug. 1972)—6,600.
Manufacturing (1969): *Value added by manufacture,* $577,200,000. Food and kindred products, $168,600,000; lumber and wood products, $150,000,000; chemicals and allied products, $108,000,000; printing and publishing, $22,600,000; fabricated metal products, $11,100,000.
Agriculture (1970): *Cash farm income,* $715,135,000 (livestock, $304,163,000; crops, $363,020,000; government payments, $47,952,000). *Chief crops* (in order of value, 1971)—Potatoes (ranks 1st among the states), hay, wheat.
Mining (1971): *Production value,* $107,167,000 (ranks 32d among the states). *Chief minerals*—Silver, $28,593,000; phosphate rock, value not available; lead, $17,647,000.
Transportation: *Roads* (1971), 56,049 miles (90,200 km); *motor vehicles* (1971), 473,873; *railroads* (1971), 2,668 miles (4,294 km); *public airports* (1972), 122.
Communications: *Telephones* (1972), 380,400; *television stations* (1970), 7; *radio stations* (1971), 50; *newspapers* (1972), 15 (daily circulation, 185,000).

ILLINOIS

Politics and taxes were the dominant concerns in Illinois in 1972, with considerable shifts of power occurring within both state party organizations.

Elections. A major political upset was pulled off by Daniel Walker, an independent Democratic, reform-oriented attorney, who was voted in as governor. In the primaries, Walker challenged Chicago Mayor Richard J. Daley's powerful Democratic organization by announcing that he would run for the Democratic nomination for governor without the Cook County machine's support. The Daley candidate was the popular, liberal lieutenant governor of Illinois, Paul Simon, who had achieved an unprecedented victory in 1968, winning his office at the same time that the voters were electing a Republican governor, Richard B. Ogilvie.

Walker began his primary campaign as a decided underdog with a walk across Illinois, stopping in lunchrooms and bowling alleys, and staying in private homes as he traversed the state. His walk made him a household name in downstate Illinois, which Democrats normally lose to Republicans by 250,000 votes. His opponent made a major political blunder by telling a press conference that he might raise state income taxes if he were elected governor. Two weeks before the primary election, a federal district court ruled that the Illinois primary law requiring a 23-month interval before voters could switch into another party's primary was unconstitutional. This made possible a massive crossover into the Democratic primary by Republicans who preferred Walker, and he defeated Simon.

Walker then defeated the incumbent Republican governor, Richard B. Ogilvie, by 77,494 votes in a close election. Despite recognition as one of the nation's most capable governors, and almost universal newspaper endorsement across the state, Ogilvie was an underdog in the race against Walker. Most political analysts attributed Ogilvie's defeat primarily to the fact that he pushed through the state's first income tax in 1969.

In the other state races, Neil Hartigan, a rising young Democratic politician from Chicago, was elected lieutenant governor at age 34. One other Democrat, State Auditor Michael Howlett, was elected secretary of state by a plurality of 172,783 over Republican Edmund Kucharski. Two Republican state officials were elected. Incumbent Attorney General William J. Scott defeated his Democratic opponent, Thomas Lyons, by a 1,285,095-vote landslide, leading the Republican ticket. Republican George Lindberg was elected to the newly created office of state comptroller over Democrat Dean Barringer by 122,642 votes. In the state legislature the Republicans emerged with a one-vote plurality in each house. This gave the Republicans the power to elect the presiding officers in both houses, but the narrow plurality made a two-party stalemate on most matters of public policy almost inevitable.

At the national level, President Richard Nixon carried Illinois over Sen. George McGovern by over 600,000 votes. Incumbent Republican Sen. Charles Percy defeated his Democratic opponent, Congressman Roman Pucinski, by 1,146,047 votes, running far ahead of President Nixon and slightly behind Attorney General Scott. By his massive electoral victory, Percy established himself as a potential candidate for the Republican presidential nomination in 1976. Under the new congressional district lines drawn by one house of the Republican state legislature and approved by a federal court, the Republicans elected 14 congressmen while the Democrats elected only 10, thus altering the normal 12–12 distribution between Republicans and Democrats in the Illinois congressional delegation.

Politics. Ogilvie's defeat and Walker's election created a new and fluid political situation in Illinois. The Republican organization built by Ogilvie was in the process of being dismantled, and Attorney General Scott and Senator Percy were emerging as the dominant Republican figures in the state. It seemed almost certain that Scott would run for governor in 1976, and he was expected to dominate the state party organization. Since Percy's ambitions appeared to be aimed at the presidency in 1976, the interest of the two men were not necessarily in conflict.

In the Democratic party, it seemed possible that Governor Walker might build a powerful enough organization in Springfield to challenge Mayor Daley of Chicago for the leadership of the Democratic party in Illinois. It appeared, however, that Walker might be handicapped as governor by the fact that the Republicans in the state legislature would not be interested in helping him build a record and that the bulk of the Democratic legislators were Cook County Democrats, with strong ties to the Daley organization, or downstaters who worked with the Daley Democrats.

——— ILLINOIS • Information Highlights ———

Area: 56,400 square miles (146,076 sq km).

Population (1970 census): 11,113,976. *Density,* 200 per sq mi.

Chief Cities (1970 census): Springfield, the capital, 91,753; Chicago, 3,369,359; Rockford, 147,370; Peoria, 126,963; Decatur, 90,397; Evanston, 79,808; Joliet, 78,887.

Government (1972): *Chief Officers*—governor, Richard B. Ogilvie (R); lt. gov., Paul Simon (D); secy. of state, John W. Lewis (R); atty. gen., William J. Scott (R); treas., Alan J. Dixon (D); supt. of public instruction, Michael J. Bakalis; chief justice, Robert C. Underwood. *General Assembly*—Senate, 58 members (29 Democrats, 29 Republicans); House of Representatives, 177 members (87 D, 90 R).

Education (1971–72): *Enrollment*—public elementary schools, 1,489,500 pupils; 67,050 teachers; public secondary, 878,-000 pupils; 45,440 teachers; nonpublic schools (1970–71), 446,243 pupils; 17,450 teachers; college and university, 434,000 students. *Public school expenditures,* $2,179,444,-000 ($1,032 per pupil). *Average teacher's salary,* $10,961.

State Finances (fiscal year 1970): *Revenues,* $4,347,716,000 (4% general sales tax and gross receipts taxes, $1,008,-182,000; motor fuel tax, $311,313,000; federal funds, $863,758,000). *Expenditures,* $4,069,153,000 (education, $1,564,302,000; health, welfare, and safety, $615,188,000; highways, $574,292,000). *State debt,* $1,305,942,000 (June 30, 1970).

Personal Income (1971): $53,422,000,000; per capita, $4,772.

Public Assistance (1971): $1,056,726,000. *Average monthly payments* (Dec. 1971)—old-age assistance, $67.61; aid to families with dependent children, $238.32.

Labor Force: *Nonagricultural wage and salary earners* (July 1972), 4,328,200. *Average annual employment* (1971)—manufacturing, 1,266,000; trade, 944,000; government, 648,000; services, 688,000. *Insured unemployed* (Aug. 1972)—72,400 (2.3%).

Manufacturing (1970): *Value added by manufacture,* $22,166,-200,000. Nonelectrical machinery, $3,564,500,000; food and kindred products, $2,981,100,000; electrical equipment and supplies, $2,688,000,000; fabricated metal products, $2,162,200,000; chemicals and allied products, $1,928,900,-000; printing and publishing, $1,812,300,000.

Agriculture (1970): *Cash farm income,* $2,919,761,000 (livestock, $1,292,205,000; crops, $1,460,912,000; government payments, $166,644,000). *Chief crops* (in order of value, 1971)—Corn, soybeans (ranks 1st among the states), hay, wheat.

Mining (1971): *Production value,* $700,819,000 (ranks 11th among the states). *Chief minerals*—Coal, $318,878,000; petroleum, $135,621,000; stone, $106,084,000; sand and gravel, $59,397,000.

Transportation: *Roads* (1971), 129,942 miles (209,116 km); *motor vehicles* (1971), 5,237,876; *railroads* (1971), 10,831 miles (17,430 km); *public airports* (1972), 82.

Communications: *Telephones* (1972), 7,342,800; *television stations* (1971), 24; *radio stations* (1971), 222; *newspapers* (1972), 91 (daily circulation, 3,973,000).

Public Policy. The results of the election and the massive ticket splitting in Illinois were clear indications of the temper of the voters and of the probable course of public policy in the state for the following four years. Political leaders and elected officials in both parties would probably oppose raising taxes and would attempt to reduce the state's involvement in programs of welfare, education, mental health, transportation, prison reform, and in any other programs that might require raising taxes. It was hoped that there would be more federal help through revenue sharing. In any case, politicians would try not to offend the tax-paying voters in the next few years.

MILTON RAKOVE
University of Illinois at Chicago Circle

IMMIGRATION

A total of 384,685 aliens became permanent U. S. residents during fiscal year 1972. Of these, 295,504 obtained visas abroad, and 89,181 were in the United States and adjusted their status to that of permanent residence. Under the 1965 Immigration and Nationality Act, Eastern Hemisphere countries are allotted 170,000 immigrant visa numbers annually, with no more than 20,000 numbers available to any one country. Preference is given to close relatives of U. S. citizens and resident aliens, aliens whose skills are needed, and refugees. As of July 1, 1968, an annual limitation of 120,000, available on a first-come, first-served basis, has been placed on Western Hemisphere immigration to the United States. In both hemispheres the parents, spouses, and children of U. S. citizens are exempt from numerical restriction.

Table 1—IMMIGRANT ALIENS ADMITTED TO THE UNITED STATES, BY COUNTRY OF BIRTH
(Year ended June 30, 1972)

Country of birth	Total admitted	Immigrants subject to numerical limitations	Immigrants exempt from numerical limitations
All countries	384,685	283,666	101,019
Europe	89,993	66,828	23,165
Czechoslovakia	1,783	1,529	254
France	1,966	1,210	756
Germany	6,848	2,224	4,624
Greece	11,021	8,763	2,258
Hungary	1,698	1,342	356
Ireland	1,780	1,331	449
Italy	21,427	17,620	3,807
Netherlands	988	501	487
Poland	4,784	3,781	1,003
Portugal	10,343	9,385	958
Rumania	1,329	1,096	233
Spain	4,386	3,254	1,132
Sweden	603	323	280
Switzerland	695	469	226
USSR (Europe and Asia)	902	639	263
United Kingdom	10,078	5,996	4,082
Yugoslavia	5,922	5,325	597
Other Europe	3,440	2,040	1,400
North America	144,375	107,358	37,017
Canada	10,776	5,891	4,885
Mexico	64,040	41,707	22,333
Cuba	20,045	19,170	875
Other West Indies	41,327	35,438	5,889
Central America	8,110	5,113	2,997
Other North America	77	39	38
South America	19,359	14,923	4,436
Asia	121,058	87,466	33,592
China	17,339	14,503	2,836
India	16,926	16,197	729
Japan	4,757	1,957	2,800
Korea	18,876	12,907	5,969
Philippines	29,376	19,209	10,167
Turkey	1,986	1,489	497
Other Asia	31,798	21,204	10,594
Africa	6,612	5,119	1,493
Oceania	3,286	1,971	1,315
Australia	1,551	808	743
New Zealand	497	268	229
Other Oceania	1,238	895	343
Other countries	2	1	1

Table 2—PRINCIPAL COUNTRIES OF FORMER ALLEGIANCE OF PERSONS NATURALIZED IN THE UNITED STATES
(Years ended 1969–1972)

Country or region of former allegiance	1969	1970	1971	1972
All countries	98,709	110,399	108,407	116,215
Europe	51,403	48,348	45,065	44,934
Austria	688	679	627	588
Czechoslovakia	340	506	629	655
France	1,416	1,398	1,328	1,083
Germany	10,618	10,067	8,455	6,953
Greece	3,029	2,906	2,614	4,243
Hungary	1,725	1,599	1,438	1,474
Ireland	2,620	2,249	2,144	1,751
Italy	8,773	7,892	7,637	8,375
Netherlands	1,930	1,795	1,428	1,101
Poland	3,643	3,426	3,318	3,147
Portugal	1,543	1,374	1,306	2,035
Rumania	434	670	936	831
Spain	721	791	776	826
Switzerland	514	495	508	445
USSR	767	677	850	795
United Kingdom	7,979	7,549	6,983	6,819
Yugoslavia	1,808	1,725	1,694	1,787
Other Europe	2,855	2,550	2,394	2,026
Asia	15,806	16,896	17,839	28,097
China and Taiwan	3,399	3,099	2,880	9,434
Iran	346	416	501	569
Israel	1,836	1,516	1,628	1,413
Japan	2,067	1,828	1,716	1,676
Jordan	397	429	544	756
Korea	1,646	1,687	2,083	2,933
Philippines	3,877	5,469	5,488	7,001
Other Asia	2,238	2,452	2,999	4,315
North America	24,831	37,693	36,941	34,451
Canada	6,387	6,340	5,915	4,835
Mexico	5,111	6,195	6,361	5,850
Cuba	9,654	20,888	19,754	18,397
Dominican Republic	522	538	752	930
Haiti	282	433	554	812
Honduras	343	448	560	473
Jamaica	481	479	500	606
Panama	848	1,035	989	873
Other North America	1,203	1,337	1,556	1,675
South America	3,758	4,679	5,713	5,837
Argentina	1,014	1,226	1,459	1,315
Colombia	742	970	1,182	1,290
Ecuador	444	558	737	752
Peru	365	432	537	634
Other South America	1,193	1,493	1,798	1,846
Africa	671	767	795	921
Oceania	384	391	466	382
U. S. possessions	285	347	353	352
Stateless	1,571	1,288	1,235	1,241

Source: Immigration and Naturalization Service, U. S. Department of Justice.

Nonimmigrants. Aliens admitted into the United States for temporary periods are classified as nonimmigrants. During 1972 there were 5,171,460 such nonimmigrants. This number included tourists, visitors for business, aliens in transit, students and their spouses and children, foreign government officials and NATO representatives, temporary workers and trainees and their spouses and children, exchange visitors and their spouses and children, representatives to international organizations or foreign information media, treaty traders and investors and their spouses and children, returning resident aliens, fiancés or fiancées of U. S. citizens and their children, and intracompany transferees and their spouses and children.

Deportable Aliens. Deportable aliens located during 1972 totalled 505,949. Of these, 398,290, mostly Mexican nationals, had entered without inspection. A total of 16,266 aliens were deported, and another 450,927 were required to depart without formal proceedings.

Naturalization. During 1972, a total of 116,215 permanent resident aliens became U. S. citizens through naturalization. Certificates of citizenship were awarded to 14,457 children born overseas to U. S. citizens and to 15,804 persons who acquired citizenship through the naturalization of parents or through marriage.

RAYMOND F. FARRELL
Commissioner of Immigration and Naturalization
U. S. Department of Justice

INDIA

Rural Indians worship a cobra caught by a snake "charmer" in one of the village houses. The snake will be fed and released into the jungle.

India celebrated the 25th anniversary of its independence on Aug. 15, 1972. A mood of national self-confidence, resulting from greater political stability and the victory over Pakistan in December 1971, was tempered by a sober realization of continuing economic and social problems.

The March 1972 elections for most of the state legislatures reaffirmed the overwhelming popular mandate that Prime Minister Indira Gandhi had received in the fifth general elections the year before. In foreign affairs, with a more dominant position in South Asia since the war of 1971, India devoted most of its attention to its new relations with Pakistan and Bangladesh.

DOMESTIC AFFAIRS

On January 21, Mrs. Gandhi formally inaugurated the three new states of Manipur, Tripura, and Meghalaya and the two new union territories of Arunachal Pradesh and Mizoram. Manipur and Tripura had been union territories; Meghalaya, an autonomous state within the state of Assam; Arunachal Pradesh, the North East Frontier Agency; and Mizoram, the Mizo Hills district of Assam.

Political Developments. In the first 10 weeks of 1972, political developments centered on preparations for the election of members of legislative assemblies of 16 states and 2 union territories. The voting took place from March 2 to 12. Determined to give a new and more radical look to the Congress party, Mrs. Gandhi insisted on the nomination of many new and often inexperienced candidates. As in the March 1971 general elections, she dominated the campaign, and again the "Indira wave" proved to be irresistible. The Congress party won 48% of the total votes and over 70% of the

seats (1,926). The next largest number of seats (112) and the next highest percentage of votes (4.12%) were won by the Communist party of India (CPI), mainly in states where it had an electoral arrangement with the Congress.

Most of the opposition parties retained only nominal representation in only a few states. For example, the opposition Congress—or Congress (O)—won only 88 seats, 82 of them in four states. The Communist party of India (Marxist)—or CPI (M)—got 30 of its 34 seats in Tripura and West Bengal; but in the West Bengal assembly, where it had held more seats than the Congress, its strength was so greatly reduced as to change the whole political complexion of India's most volatile state. In Delhi, a union territory, the strength of the Jana Sangh in the 56-seat municipal council declined from a majority to only 5 seats, whereas the Congress got 44. The Swatantra party, with only 16 seats—mainly in Rajasthan—was virtually wiped out as a national political force.

The Congress won a clear majority in all of the assemblies for which elections were held, except those of the smaller states of Manipur and Meghalaya and the union territory of Goa, where local parties were strong. On March 11 it also won an important by-election in an assembly contest in the union territory of Pondicherry, where its candidate, also supported by the Congress (O), defeated the candidate of the Dravida Munnetra Kazhagam, the regional party that controlled the government of Tamil Nadu and that until shortly before the elections had been cooperating with the Congress.

Immediately after the assembly elections new Congress governments, mostly under new chief ministers, were formed in the 14 states and the union

territory (Delhi) where the Congress had won a majority. In three states—Bihar, Gujarat, and Mysore—Mrs. Gandhi herself, at the request of the state Congress leaders, selected the new chief ministers. With the formation of new governments, president's rule (temporary direct rule by the central government) was revoked in Bihar, Gujarat, Manipur, Mysore, Punjab, Tripura, and West Bengal, and many changes were made in the leadership of state and local Congress committees.

On March 31, April 1, and April 8, elections were held for 73 of the 243 seats in the Rajya Sabha, the upper house of the Indian Parliament. The Congress won 49 seats, increasing its strength in the Rajya Sabha to 119, four short of an absolute majority. On April 18, elections took place in the union territory of Mizoram. The Mizo Union, a local party, defeated the Congress candidate for Mizoram's one seat in the Lok Sabha, the lower house of the Indian Parliament, and won a majority in the territorial assembly. The Congress did not contest September municipal elections held in Srinagar, the capital of the state of Jammu and Kashmir. A sweeping victory went to the united front that had been forged by Sheikh Abdullah (the "Lion of Kashmir") and Maulvi Farooq.

On May 11, Shankar Dayal Sharma, who had served as one of the three general secretaries of the Congress, was chosen as president of the Congress, succeeding Damodaram Sanjivayya, who had died on May 7. In late July, Mrs. Gandhi reorganized her cabinet. She appointed Durga Prasad Dhar, who had been chairman of the Policy Planning Committee in the Ministry of External Affairs, as minister of planning and deputy chairman of the Planning Commission. She moved C. Subramaniam from these posts to the Ministry of Industrial Development, Science and Technology. Tonse Ananth Pai, who had been chairman of the Life Insurance Corporation of India, became minister of railways.

Economy. On the economic front the two dominant themes of 1972 were *Garibi Hatao* ("abolish poverty") and *Arthik Swaraj* ("economic independence"). Limited progress was made toward each goal, but the general economic outlook remained rather grim. A great deal of attention was given to the government's programs of land ceilings and land reform. Almost all states had passed land ceiling legislation, but most of these acts were not strictly enforced, and most had many loopholes. Sweeping land reforms remained an objective, rather than a significant reality.

India had attained virtual self-sufficiency in food, accumulating a food-grain stockpile of some 9 million tons; but because of a serious drought and other adverse circumstances, food-grain production in 1972 fell short of the target of 112 million tons by nearly 12 million tons, and the stockpile was reduced to about 5 million tons. The growth rate of industrial production, which had been less than 3% in 1971, rose to approximately 7%. The wholesale price index rose by 6.8%. India was still plagued by an inflationary spiral, a widening budgetary gap, and an extensive black market.

The economic survey for 1971–72, presented to Parliament on March 13, pictured the period as one of the most difficult since independence. The country's reserves were greatly strained by the expenditures involved in the relief of nearly 10 million refugees from former East Pakistan (now Bangladesh), in disaster relief necessitated by many natural calamities, in meeting the costs of the December 1971 war with Pakistan, and by the adverse

KEYSTONE

DURING THE DROUGHT of the summer of 1972, water was a precious commodity that was either sold (below) or doled out (right).

UPI

REFRIGERATED COLD WATER
3 PAISA PER GLASS
मशीन का ठंडा पानी
३ नया पैसा ए

effects of international monetary and political developments. Although the foreign exchange reserves actually increased, there was a growing strain on the country's external assets because of a sharp rise in imports, debt repayments, and debt servicing and a sharp decrease in external assistance.

The annual plan for 1972–73, presented to Parliament on April 4, called for an outlay of approximately $5.3 billion, an increase of more than 25% over the expenditures for 1971–72. Shortly afterward, the midterm appraisal of the fourth five-year plan (1969–74) called for increased expenditures for schemes intended to promote social justice. A preliminary report on the fifth five-year plan (1974–79), released in 1972, indicated an estimated expenditure of approximately $49 billion in the public sector and $28 billion in the private sector during the course of the plan, and an increased emphasis on the removal of poverty, economic self-reliance, the reduction of dependence on external assistance, and "distributive justice."

In various international conferences and organizations—notably in the third session of the United Nations Conference on Trade and Development, held in Santiago, Chile, from April 13 to May 23—India's representatives called for more enlightened policies on the part of the developed countries to help the developing countries.

As one major program to commemorate the silver jubilee of its independence, India hosted the Third Asian International Trade Fair in Delhi, from No-

INDIRA GANDHI, India's prime minister, with Pakistani President Bhutto in Simla (top, left); being congratulated on election victory (top, right); and lowering time capsule containing materials associated with Jawaharlal Nehru.

vember 3 to December 17. Nearly 50 nations participated, including West Germany, France, Japan, and the Soviet Union, but not Britain or the United States.

The magnitude of the economic tasks still ahead for India was suggested by Mrs. Gandhi in her message to the nation on the occasion of the 25th anniversary of Indian independence, on August 15. "Democracy," she stated, "has come to stay and has proved itself. But economic freedom in the shape of the economic self-reliance of the nation and also improvement in the daily lives of our common people has yet to be achieved."

Deaths. Several prominent Indians died in 1972. Lt. Gen. B. M. Kaul was a controversial high-ranking military officer who had been chief of the Army General Staff and commander of the Indian forces in the North East Frontier Agency during the border war with China in late 1962. Damodaram Sanjivayya was a Harijan, or "untouchable," who had been chief minister of Andhra Pradesh and president of the Congress party. Professor P. C. Mahalanobis was a famous economist and statistician who had been a member of the Planning Commission. Bakshi Ghulam Mohammed was chief minister of Jammu and Kashmir from 1953 to 1963. Charu Mazumdar was a top leader and chief ideologist of the Maoist Naxalite movement. Sant Fateh Singh was a famous leader of the Akali Dal and the Sikh community in Punjab.

FOREIGN AFFAIRS

Relations with Bangladesh. By the end of February 1972, most of the refugees from what had been East Pakistan had returned to Bangladesh, and shortly thereafter the last of the nearly 150,000 Indian troops in Bangladesh were withdrawn. The withdrawal was completed about two weeks before the deadline of March 25 agreed upon by Mrs. Gandhi and Sheikh Mujibur Rahman, the prime minister of Bangladesh, in a meeting in Calcutta on February 7–8. On March 19, at the conclusion of a three-day visit to Dacca, Mrs. Gandhi joined Sheikh Mujib in signing a joint declaration and a treaty of friendship, cooperation, and peace. India continued its extensive assistance to Bangladesh, and relations between the two countries remained cordial in spite of some anti-Indian feeling in Bangladesh.

Relations with Pakistan. Both Mrs. Gandhi and President Zulfikar Ali Bhutto of Pakistan insisted in 1972 that they wanted to put Indo-Pakistan relations on a new and more peaceful basis. At a summit meeting in Simla, India, in late June and early July, following a meeting of top-level officials of the two countries in Murree and Rawalpindi, Pakistan, in late April, the heads of government signed a significant agreement. The Simla agreement stated that "the two countries are resolved to settle their differences by peaceful means through bilateral negotiations or by any other peaceful means mutually agreed upon between them"; that "they will refrain from the threat or use of force against the territorial integrity or political independence of each other"; that "steps will be taken to resume communications" and to "promote travel facilities for the nationals of the other country"; that "trade and cooperation in economic and agreed fields will be resumed as far as possible"; that "Indian and Pakistani forces shall be withdrawn to their side of the international border"; that "in Jammu and Kashmir the line of control resulting from the cease fire of Dec. 17, 1971, shall be respected by both sides"; and that troop

withdrawals "shall commence upon the entry into force of this Agreement and shall be completed within a period of 30 days thereafter."

In May a serious clash between Indian and Pakistani troops occurred in the Tithwal sector of Kashmir. Mrs. Gandhi accused Pakistan of deliberately stalling in the implementation of the Simla agreement. President Bhutto accused India of violating the Geneva Convention by refusing to return 93,000 Pakistani prisoners of war, military and civilian. Apparently India was insisting that Pakistan recognize Bangladesh before prisoners of war would be returned. In December, after long delays, Indian and Pakistani military commanders completed demarcation of the line of control in Kashmir, and the agreed-upon troop withdrawals were made.

Relations with the United States. Indo-American relations, which had reached a new low in 1971, continued to deteriorate in 1972. Mrs. Gandhi, President Nixon, and other Indian and American spokesmen repeatedly stated that they wished to enter into a "serious dialogue" and to place relations between the two countries on a more satisfactory basis. But no such dialogue occurred, and many new frictions arose. President Nixon continued a policy of neglect, which India interpreted as anything but "benign," and India took a number of actions that seemed designed to reduce contacts with the United States at both official and unofficial levels.

In October the president of the Congress party, Shankar Dayal Sharma, in a press conference in Calcutta, made sweeping charges of U. S. Central Intelligence Agency (CIA) machinations in India. Shortly afterward, Mrs. Gandhi said that it was not up to India to prove the charges against the CIA,

---
INDIA • Information Highlights

Official Name: Republic of India.
Area: 1,261,813 square miles (3,268,090 sq km).
Population (1972 est.): 584,800,000. *Density*, 435 per square mile (168 per sq km). *Annual rate of increase*, 2.5%.
Chief Cities (1971 census): New Delhi, the capital, 292,857; Bombay, 5,931,989; Delhi, 3,695,000; Calcutta, 3,000,000.
Government: *Head of state*, V. V. Giri, president (took office Aug. 1969). *Head of government*, Mrs. Indira Gandhi, prime minister (took office Jan. 1966). *Legislature*—Parliament: Rajya Sabha (Council of States), 240 members; Lok Sabha (House of the People), 521 members. *Major political parties*—Congress (Ruling); Communist party; Dravida Munnetra Kazhagam; Jana Sangh; Congress (Opposition).
Languages: Hindi (official), English, 14 national languages.
Education: *Expenditure* (1966), 17.8% of total public expenditure. *School enrollment* (1965)—primary, 49,499,000; secondary, 7,650,102; technical/vocational, 450,101; university/higher, 1,054,273.
Monetary Unit: Rupee (7.279 rupees equal U. S.$1, May 1972).
Gross National Product (1971 est.): $55,160,000,000.
National Income per Person (1969): $88.
Economic Indexes: *Industrial production* (1970), 139 (1963= 100); *agricultural production* (1971), 154 (1952–56=100); *consumer price index* (1971), 190 (1960=100).
Manufacturing (major products): Iron and steel, industrial machinery and equipment, chemicals, fertilizer, cotton and jute textiles.
Major Agricultural Products: Rice (ranks 2d among world producers, 1971), groundnuts (world rank 1st, 1971), wheat (world rank 4th, 1970), cotton (world rank 3d, 1971), jute (world rank 1st, 1971), tea (world rank 1st, 1971).
Major Minerals: Coal, iron ore, manganese ore, bauxite, chromium ore, mica.
Foreign Trade (1971): *Exports*, $2,108,000,000 (chief exports, 1970—jute fabrics; black tea). *Imports*, $2,433,000,000 (chief imports, 1969—food; nonelectrical machinery; chemicals; petroleum, crude and partly refined). *Chief trading partners* (1969)—United States (took 17% of exports, supplied 29% of imports); USSR (13%—11%); United Kingdom (12%—6%); Japan (13%—4%).
Tourism: Receipts (1970), $50,800,000.
Transportation: *Motor vehicles* (1970), 1,113,600 (automobiles, 606,100); *railroads* (1970), 37,006 miles (59,553 km); *merchant fleet* (1971), 2,478,000 gross registered tons; *major national airlines*, Indian Airlines; Air India.
Communications: *Telephones* (1971), 1,245,352; *television stations* (1971), 1; *television sets* (1971), 21,000; *radios* (1970), 11,837,000; *newspapers* (1969), 650.

and that it was instead the responsibility of the CIA to prove that it was not guilty of intrigues in India. Mrs. Gandhi and other Indian spokesmen stepped up their criticism of U. S. policy in Vietnam. In December signs of a "thaw" in U. S.–Indian relations were finally apparent. President Giri of India, Prime Minister Gandhi, and Foreign Minister Swaran Singh all publicly expressed a desire for better relations with the United States, and President Nixon and Secretary of State William Rogers cordially reciprocated this sentiment. The appointment in December of Daniel Patrick Moynihan, a Harvard University professor, as the new American ambassador to India was well received in India.

Diplomatic Visits Abroad. On June 14, in Stockholm, Mrs. Gandhi delivered a widely applauded address at a plenary session of the UN Conference on the Human Environment. "Poverty and need," she stated, "are the greatest polluters." Immediately thereafter she made state visits tò Czechoslovakia and Hungary.

NORMAN D. PALMER
University of Pennsylvania

INDIANA

The legislative session, presidential primary, and November elections kept politics in the fore in Indiana in 1972. Partisan lines were blurred by a prevailing conservative mood and much ticket splitting. But with this conservatism, there was a trend toward social, economic, and constitutional change.

Legislation. Despite Republican majorities in both legislative branches, the 1972 session produced little important legislation. Once again, an unsuccessful attempt was made to revise the state revenue system by reducing levies on property and raising them principally on sales and income taxes. The effort to extend voting and other rights normally given those 21 or over to 18-year-olds was also unsuccessful. Legislative seats were reapportioned into exclusively single-member districts. Congressional districts were also reapportioned.

Constitutional Revision. Four out of five proposed constitutional amendments were accepted by the voters in November. These four authorized the legislature to specify how the state superintendent of public instruction should be selected, extended the time in which a governor may veto laws, allowed the legislature to determine how vacant Assembly seats should be filled, and made the governor eligible to serve two successive terms.

The Economy. Indiana's diversified economy showed some advance and much stability. A simmering conflict continued over state banking policy, with lines drawn for and against legislation to allow banks to engage in statewide operations and also to establish multibank holding companies. An outbreak of hog cholera in various counties in the fall and early winter hurt hog farmers. The edging upward of the economy, coupled with stringent economy moves, made possible a state budget surplus.

Education. The new Commission on Higher Education took steps toward coordination of state university budgets and curricula. Strikes of public school teachers at Gary and Indianapolis pointed up the need for legislation to resolve teacher and school board disputes. They also reflected the need for increased economy in public school operations and a more equitable tax base for support of education rather than heavy reliance on property taxes.

Operas performed at the new, nationally acclaimed Musical Arts Center at Indiana University, Bloomington, and plays offered by the new Indianapolis Repertory Theater received a good response from both critics and audiences.

Politics. In the May presidential preference primary, Hubert Humphrey eked out a plurality victory on the Democratic ticket, followed closely by George Wallace. Richard Nixon won the Republican presidential preference vote without formal opposition. In November, Nixon crushed his Democratic rival, George McGovern, winning 67% of the popular vote to only 33% for McGovern.

The race for governor, which had attracted most attention because it was expected to be close, gave four-time House speaker Otis Bowen 57% of the vote against 33% for Matthew Welsh, a former governor. All six incumbent Republican congressmen were reelected, as were four Democratic holdovers. However, one Democratic incumbent fell to a Republican aspirant. The Republicans won lopsided majorities in both houses of the General Assembly and also won most of the numerous county offices.

Blacks. Theodore Wilson, an Indianapolis lawyer, received the Democratic nomination for attorney general, making him the first black to win nomination for a major position on the state ticket for a major party. He lost in November by about the same margin as did the balance of his ticket.

DONALD F. CARMONY, *Indiana University*
Editor, "Indiana Magazine of History"

─────────── **INDIANA • Information Highlights** ───────────

Area: 36,291 square miles (93,994 sq km).
Population (1970 census): 5,193,669. *Density:* 146 per sq mi.
Chief Cities (1970 census): Indianapolis, the capital, 744,743; Fort Wayne, 178,021; Gary, 175,415; Evansville, 138,764; South Bend, 125,580; Hammond, 107,888; Anderson, 70,787.
Government (1972): *Chief Officers*—governor, Edgar D. Whitcomb (R); lt. gov., Richard E. Folz (R); secy. of state, Larry A. Conrad (D); atty. gen., Theodore L. Sendak (R); treas., Jack L. New (D); chief justice, Norman F. Arterburn. *General Assembly*—Senate, 50 members (21 Democrats, 29 Republicans); House of Representatives, 100 members (46 D, 54 R).
Education (1971–72): *Enrollment*—public elementary schools, 672,447 pupils, 26,501 teachers; public secondary, 558,343 pupils, 25,781 teachers; nonpublic schools (1970–71), 107,849 pupils, 4,800 teachers; college and university, 201,000 students. *Public school expenditures*, $930,606,000 ($837 per pupil). *Average teacher's salary*, $10,300.
State Finances (fiscal year 1970): *Revenues*, $1,714,889,000 (2% general sales tax and gross receipts taxes, $380,739,-000; motor fuel tax, $192,795,000; federal funds, $316,974,-000). *Expenditures*, $1,600,681,000 (education, $809,576,000; health, welfare, and safety, $69,712,000; highways, $257,-978,000). *State debt*, $583,823,000 (June 30, 1970).
Personal Income (1971): $20,952,000,000; per capita, $3,973.
Public Assistance (1971): $185,569,000. *Average monthly payments* (Dec. 1971)—old-age assistance, $57.10; aid to families with dependent children, $147.71.
Labor Force: *Nonagricultural wage and salary earners* (July 1972), 1,878,300. *Average annual employment* (1970)—manufacturing, 679,000; trade, 368,000; government, 296,000; services, 226,000. *Insured unemployed* (Aug. 1972)—22,100 (1.6%).
Manufacturing (1970): *Value added by manufacture*, $11,447,-800,000. Primary metal industries, $1,844,600,000; electrical equipment and supplies, $1,644,500,000; transportation equipment, $1,467,400,000; nonelectrical machinery, $1,207,-700,000; chemicals and allied products, $1,049,100,000; food and kindred products, $912,800,000.
Agriculture (1970): *Cash farm income*, $1,629,800,000 (livestock, $830,051,000; crops, $688,703,000; government payments, $111,046,000). *Chief crops* (in order of value, 1971)—Corn (ranks 2d among the states), soybeans (ranks 3d), hay, wheat.
Mining (1971): *Production value*, $281,569,000 (ranks 25th among the states). *Chief minerals*—Coal, $110,796,000; cement (value not available); stone, $48,218,000; sand and gravel, $29,094,000.
Transportation: *Roads* (1971), 91,011 miles (146,464 km); *motor vehicles* (1971), 2,815,388; *railroads* (1971), 6,416 miles (10,325 km); *public airports* (1972), 65.
Communications: *Telephones* (1972), 3,044,600; *television stations* (1971), 17; *radio stations* (1971), 159; *newspapers* (1972), 80 (daily circulation, 1,677,000).

INDIANS, AMERICAN

For the American Indian, 1972 was a year of progress and confusion. The progress stemmed from the steady course of the Nixon administration in encouraging Indian self-determination without ending federal support. The confusion stemmed from the internal divisions and struggles among those claiming to speak for the Indian.

Yakima Indian Lands. About 21,000 acres (8,-500 hectares) in the state of Washington, incorporated within the Mount Rainier Forest Reserve in 1908 on the mistaken belief that it was public land, were returned to the Yakima Indian Tribe. The Yakima's right to the land, recognized by treaty in 1855, had been upheld by the Indian Claims Commission in 1966. Since awards by the commission are payable only in monetary form, the return of the lands wrongfully taken had to be achieved by an executive order of the President, dated May 20, 1972. The area returned has religious significance.

Crisis in Indian Leadership. The careful cultivation of the Indian point of view by the Nixon administration bore fruit in 1972. Although Indian groups are traditionally Democratic, a number of them supported the President's successful bid for reelection. The Indian point of view, however, was not always easy to determine. Indian leadership remained uncertain and confused.

Pan-Indian organizations continued to have trouble representing their constituent members, who were often hostile toward or suspicious of one another. The existence of competing pan-Indian groups heightened the confusion. The tribal chairmen's group, formed in 1971, assumed an increasingly important position in 1972 relative to competing leadership groups such as the National Congress of American Indians and the American Indian Movement (AIM). As the tribal chairmen's group developed a close relationship with the BIA, which actively sought its advice on policy matters, it generated criticism from some Indians who felt that the embrace of the bureau was too warm. Vine Deloria, Jr., the leading contemporary Indian political writer, charged that, like sheep being led to the slaughter, Indians had created "an Indian organization for the BIA: the tribal chairmen's group, which is carefully nurtured and fed by certain Area Directors who always wanted to enter Indian politics but were afraid to ask."

Late in the year the tribal chairmen's group was abruptly challenged by AIM, a group contemptuous of traditional elected tribal leadership, dedicated to the cause of the nonreservation urban Indian, and more militant but less responsible than its rivals. AIM leaders organized a "Trail of Broken Treaties" march on Washington. About 500 Indians occupied the Bureau of Indian Affairs Building during the first week of November to draw attention to a list of varied demands. The organizers made a point of invoking the support of Stokely Carmichael and the Black Panthers. Furniture in the building was broken, and files were pilfered and scattered.

Through the protest, AIM leaders sought to seize leadership of the already existing movement for Indian reform while discrediting conventional leadership groups and the BIA. The occupation of the BIA Building attained extensive media coverage, enhanced the importance of AIM, and diminished that of the tribal chairmen's group.

On December 2, Secretary of the Interior Rogers C. B. Morton relieved three department officials of their authority over Indian affairs. They were Assistant Secretary Harrison E. Loesch, Indian Commissioner Louis R. Bruce, and Deputy Commissioner John O. Crow. Authority for control of all Indian affairs in the immediate future was placed in the hands of Richard S. Bodman, assistant secretary of the interior.

The trashing of the BIA provided the occasion for a thorough reconsideration of U. S. Indian policy. Although congressional bitterness was evident in hearings conducted in early December by the Indian Affairs subcommittee of the House Interior and Insular Affairs Committee, executive branch reaction was more muted. Indications pointed to a continuation and acceleration of the policy of encouraging tribal governments to assume greater responsibility for reservation administration.

Potawatomi Nation. The knotty problem of the nature of Indian political organization was considered by the Indian Claims Commission in a case

LEAVING the Bureau of Indian Affairs building in Washington, D. C., on Nov. 8, after occupying it for a week, Indian protesters carry a load of supplies. They claimed they had previously removed three truckloads of documents.

NAVAJO BLANKETS that were exhibited in museums across the United States in 1972. The top two are in "Chief Pattern," the bottom one in "Banded Style."

brought by the Citizen Band of Potawatomi Indians and others. The commission found on March 28 that the Potawatomi Nation was an entity rather than several independent tribal groups. "That the Indians themselves may not have entertained the same notions of political unity as the United States imputed to them," the majority noted, "is not significant if the Indians generally acted as a single political entity in their treaty relations with the Government."

Sales of Artifacts. Indians protested during the year the sale of artifacts of their native heritage,

such as wampum belts and masks, and forced the withdrawal of such items from a scheduled auction at the Sotheby Parke-Bernet galleries in October. Emboldened by a decision of the New York state legislature in 1971 to return five belts held by the state museum to the Onondaga Indians, Indian activists continued to object to the trafficking in such objects even when no evidence of fraud in their acquistion by whites existed.

Eastern Indian Conference. A conference bringing together leaders of Eastern Indians met in Washington, D. C., December 7–9, hosted by the Native American Rights Fund. Organized by concerned lawyers—Indian and white—the conference marked the beginning of a drive to obtain federal recognition and increased benefits for the descendants of the once-powerful tribes of the East.

Authority of the Indian Commissioner. The discretionary authority of the secretary of the interior with regard to Indian affairs was restricted as a result of two suits successfully maintained against Secretary Rogers Morton. In a suit brought by the Pyramid Lake Paiute tribe, the U. S. district court for the District of Columbia ruled that the secretary's earlier decision allocating water resources of Pyramid Lake, Nev., to various Indian and non-Indian users, while done in good faith, failed to meet his fiduciary duty to the Paiute. In an action brought by Ramon and Anita Ruiz, members of the Papago tribe living off the Papago Reservation, the U. S. court of appeals for the ninth circuit ruled that the appellants could not be excluded from certain welfare benefits previously restricted by administrative regulations of the BIA to Indians living on the reservation.

Books on the Indians. The strong public interest in the Indian, exemplified by the continued heavy sales of Dee Brown's best seller, *Bury My Heart at Wounded Knee* (1971), encouraged publishers to seek manuscripts not only about Indians, but by Indians. McGraw-Hill, Inc., was faced during the year with the embarrassing revelation that *The Memoirs of Chief Red Fox* (1971), reputedly the recollections of a 101-year-old Sioux chief, was plagiarized in large part from a book published in 1940 by James H. McGregor, former superintendent of the Pine Ridge Sioux Reservation.

Indian Arts. Respect for Indian achievement in the arts continued to grow. Chad Walsh, in reviewing two books of Indian and Eskimo poetry, remarked that "Eskimo poetry sounds like Emily Dickinson and North American Indian poetry like Walt Whitman." As the white man grappled with problems of pollution and overpopulation, the ecological sense of the native Americans—expressed simply and directly in their poetry—seemed both sensible and beautiful.

The Brooklyn Museum hosted a show of "Native North American Art" by eight contemporary American Indians, and the National Collection of Fine Arts of the Smithsonian Institution in Washington, D. C., showed the work of two American Indians, Fritz Scholder and his pupil T. C. Cannon. The American Indian Theatre Ensemble Company, the first all-Indian theater troupe in the United States, staged impressive performances of Indian-written and Indian-directed theater pieces at New York City's La Mama Experimental Theatre. Particularly powerful was Hanay Geiogamah's play *Body Indian.*

WILCOMB E. WASHBURN, *Smithsonian Institution*

KEN WAGNER. UPI

Members of the last U. S. ground-combat unit in Vietnam board copter in August after their final mission. They were replaced by South Vietnamese.

INDOCHINA WAR

Two of the major parties in the Indochina War, the United States and North Vietnam, seemed about to reach a military settlement in October 1972, but by mid-December full-scale bombing of North Vietnam had been resumed by the United States.

The original breakthrough in peace talks between Washington and Hanoi came in the wake of a major North Vietnamese offensive that had been largely checked. It may have reflected the Vietnamese Communists' realization that a military victory was not possible at that time. It also unquestionably resulted from pressure on the Communists from both Peking and Moscow to reach an agreement with the Americans. North Vietnam resented such pressures as reflecting its allies' greater concern with big-power relations, but it did respond to them.

The Vietnamese Communists had increased, though not substantially, the extent of their territorial control in South Vietnam as a result of the offensive that began March 30. In Laos and Cambodia, on the other hand, the Communists did significantly expand the area under their domination, as the governments of both these lands failed to distinguish themselves militarily during the year.

THE FIGHTING

More than 100,000 persons were killed as a result of the formidable military offensive launched by North Vietnam on March 30, but that offensive failed to fulfill Hanoi's hopes of achieving lasting victories against troops of the Saigon government.

By mid-year the back of the Communist offensive push had been broken, and the war lapsed into one of the periodic lulls that seemed inevitably to follow major efforts in the drawn-out Vietnam War.

North Vietnam's dramatic announcement on October 26 of its agreement with the United States in principle on a nine-point peace plan was not, however, followed by a significant drop in combat activity. Indeed, the Indochina War—on all of its fronts—subsequently continued much as it had before the breakthrough in the negotiations. On the day of the North Vietnamese announcement, the Communists launched more attacks in the south than in any 24-hour period since the 1968 Tet offensive.

The Communists' attacks toward the year's end seemed to be aimed primarily at expanding the territory under their control in the event of an early settlement. They did not alter, however, the seeming military draw between the two sides.

The "Easter Offensive." The North Vietnamese offensive that began Easter weekend (March 30) was apparently designed to secure a major military victory and possibly even to induce the collapse of the Saigon government. Initially, the well-planned Communist thrust scored impressive gains as some South Vietnamese units literally broke ranks—partly because of the absence of good leadership. There were fears in Washington and Saigon of a major, perhaps decisive, rout, discrediting altogether the much publicized "Vietnamization" of the non-Communist military forces.

Backed by unprecedented American bombing, the South Vietnamese armed forces dug in, however, and halted the Communist offensive. Their performance in the field ultimately was impressive, and Hanoi presumably realized that a military victory was not possible at this time. Saigon troops had assumed the initiative by mid-year, as they retook Quang Tri, recaptured Binh Dinh in the northeast, and made impressive stands at Kontum and An Loc.

The Communists' 1972 thrust was costly to both sides. In the first six months of the offensive, South Vietnam's armed forces suffered 14,000 dead, 50,000 wounded, and 5,000 missing, while 70,000 Communists were reported to have died in action. North Vietnam also was forced to face resumed intensive U. S. air bombing of its major cities, while the American decision in May to mine Haiphong and other harbors interrupted Hanoi's receipt of vitally needed war supplies.

The War in Laos. There were no dramatic developments in the war in Laos in 1972, but the Communists did expand the amount of territory under their control. Fighting was not particularly intensive until the later months of the year, when the prospects of a peace settlement probably encouraged both sides to try to make new gains in anticipation of an in-place cease-fire. Bitter conflict took place, accordingly, near the much fought-over Plain of Jars in the north and for control of key towns in the southern part of the land.

Attempts by U. S. CIA-supported Meo tribesmen (led by Gen. Vang Pao) to retake the Plain of Jars were successfully repulsed. Assuming the initiative again near the year's end, the Communists launched a major rocket attack against the airport at the royal capital of Luang Prabang in mid-November.

The Cambodian Conflict. Despite receipt of $340 million in U. S. military aid and intensive American training activity, the rapidly expanded Khmer armed forces proved no match for either intruding North Vietnamese elements or the allied Khmer Rouge ("Red Cambodian") insurgents. The Cambodian front was the one on which the Communists registered their greatest gains in 1972.

Two thirds of the country was in enemy hands by the year's end. Only the major population cen-

ters remained in the government's hands, and all but one of the main highways leading to the capital had been closed by the Communists.

North Vietnamese troops in the country dropped from 50,000 to 12,000 during the year, as the well-armed and increasingly troublesome Khmer Rouge insurgents assumed main responsibility for military action against the government. The once small and ineffective Khmer Rouge, numbering 40,000 in 1972, had shown extraordinary improvement in fighting capability since the Indochina War expanded dramatically to include Cambodia in 1970.

Role of the United States. The U. S. role in the Vietnam ground war came to an end in 1972, as the last combat infantryman left in August and the huge Longbinh army headquarters was turned over to the South Vietnamese in November. U. S. army personnel remaining in Vietnam comprised advisers, helicopter crewmen, and supply and staff personnel.

But the American air-war role became increasingly important during the year. Bombs dropped by U. S. aircraft during the first three-quarters of the year topped the total for all of 1971 (763,160 tons); according to the Defense Department, more than 800,000 tons of "air ammunition" were released over North and South Vietnam, Laos, and Cambodia through September. American officials attributed the increase to support of South Vietnamese troops who were responding to the Communists' Easter offensive and to the related resumption in May of heavy and systematic bombing of North Vietnam. But in the first two months of 1972, American aircraft bombed five times as many targets as in the same period in 1971.

As peace talks in Paris reached a disappointing juncture in December, the U. S. staged its heaviest B-52 air assault of the war against targets in North Vietnam on December 14. Four days later, Defense Secretary Melvin Laird announced resumption of systematic large-scale bombing and mining of North Vietnam. The administration stated that these raids "will continue until such time as a settlement is arrived at."

Casualties. The cost of the Indochina War continued to grow in 1972. The major Vietnam theater of the conflict, which cost the United States alone

North Vietnamese made use of tanks in their major thrust across the demilitarized zone on March 30.

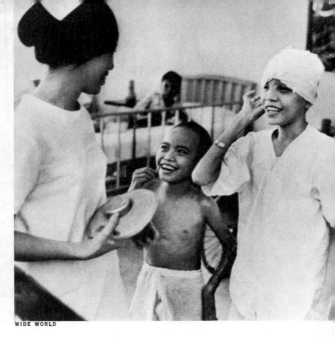

INNOCENT VICTIMS of an accidental napalm attack included 9-year-old Phan Thi Kim Phuc, who runs down the road after ripping off her burning clothes. Two months later she (center) is shown recovering in a Saigon hospital.

more than an officially acknowledged $105 billion through mid-1972, took, according to the U. S. government, a combat toll of 1.3 million lives in the period Jan. 1, 1961–Oct. 21, 1972. The lives of 45,884 U. S. servicemen were lost in combat in this nearly 11-year period. Another 10,281 American military personnel died in Vietnam from other causes.

During the same period, 182,494 South Vietnamese servicemen and 205,000 civilians died in the fighting, according to the same U. S. government figures, which were lower than earlier casualty statistics released by Sen. Edward M. Kennedy's subcommittee on refugees. The lives of 904,000 North Vietnamese combatants were also reportedly lost.

In the first six months of the Communists' 1972 offensive, 14,000 South Vietnamese servicemen were killed in combat, the highest figure for a comparable period in the whole war.

American military personnel missing (or captured) from January through early November totaled 1,809, according to U. S. military sources. These included 543 men known to have been captured in North or South Vietnam or Laos.

NEGOTIATIONS AND LAND DISENGAGEMENT

North Vietnam dramatically and surprisingly announced on October 26, just prior to the U. S. presidential election, that Washington and Hanoi had reached agreement in principle on a nine-point military settlement during secret talks in Paris. Involved in the talks were American presidential adviser Henry Kissinger and North Vietnamese diplomats Le Duc Tho and Xuan Thuy. According to Hanoi, the United States had agreed to sign such a pact by October 31 and was reneging on its promise. Washington denied the charge. The would-be agreement called for an in-place cease-fire and withdrawal of American military forces from Vietnam within 60 days of a settlement. Prisoners of war would be released within the same period.

The Kissinger Negotiations. Responding to the North Vietnamese October 26 announcement, Kissinger stated that "peace" was "at hand" and that a final agreement could be completed in one additional round of negotiations "lasting not more than three or four days." These talks began between Kissinger and Le Duc Tho on November 20, recessed

November 25, resumed December 4, and recessed again December 13—without an agreement.

There were reports before the second recess of a hardening of the U. S. position in the negotiations, partly in response to the objections of South Vietnamese President Nguyen Van Thieu. Some suggested there were differences between Kissinger and President Nixon over the concessions Washington should make. In a December 16 press briefing, however, Kissinger laid the blame for the lack of early success in the renewed talks on the North Vietnamese. Hanoi, he said, raised new objections or took new positions every time agreement seemed at hand, often going back on points already agreed upon. Nonetheless, according to the U. S. negotiator, a military settlement was "99%" agreed upon.

The original breakthrough in the negotiations followed an October 8 initiative by Hanoi in the earlier secret peace talks. But both sides made genuine concessions on key questions. The U. S. agreed to an in-place cease-fire, abandoning its prior demand that all North Vietnamese troops quit South Vietnam as part of a settlement. Hanoi, for its part, accepted a military settlement without a prior political agreement and gave up its insistence that President Thieu resign as a condition of such a settlement and that a coalition government be immediately established in Saigon.

The U. S. Position. President Nixon stated on November 2 that no agreement would be signed by the U. S. government until all the remaining issues were resolved. Washington was willing to settle for less politically in 1972 than earlier, but it wanted to make sure that any agreement reached would be kept. Post-agreement inspection and supervision, accordingly, was one major question in U. S. eyes.

Regarding this matter, Hanoi wished to limit supervision personnel to not more than 250, while Washington wanted "several thousand" according to Kissinger. The difference was fundamental to the strategies of the two sides. Hanoi continued to claim that there was only one Vietnam, and consequently it had a strong interest in limiting future inspection of cease-fire violations. The United States still hoped for a separate South Vietnam and wished to use international inspection as a means of preventing resumption of the war.

Guns of the U. S. S. Newport News *fire at North Vietnam. A blast aboard the cruiser in October took 20 lives.*

The United States may also have sought some modification of the agreement in principle, reported on October 26, in order to satisfy South Vietnamese President Thieu, who opposed a cease-fire without the removal of Hanoi's troops.

The Communist Strategy. There were conflicting reports of how the North Vietnamese behaved in the Paris negotiations between Kissinger and Le Duc Tho that were resumed on November 20. It was claimed, for example, that Hanoi was willing to withdraw as many as 110,000 troops from South Vietnam if the Saigon government would reduce its armed forces by the same number. Whether or not this was so, there was a major difference between Washington's and Saigon's perceptions of the size of North Vietnamese forces in the south. Some Washington estimates placed the figure as low as 110,000, while President Thieu claimed that the number was 300,000. Both figures were in addition to about 35,000 Vietcong insurgents.

According to Kissinger's December 16 press briefing, however, there was evidence that the North Vietnamese were preparing for a massive attack even before a cease-fire took effect. This, Kissinger implied, raised questions about Hanoi's sincerity— as did North Vietnam's alleged general attitude from early December on, when, according to Kissinger, the Communists began raising new questions on which agreement had previously been reached.

The diplomatic stalemate between the two sides may have been rooted in genuine misunderstandings, changed positions on either side (or both sides), or the fundamental difference in their respective objectives concerning the future political control of the southern portion of the divided Vietnamese nation. Ultimately, the last factor was the one above all others that really divided Washington and Hanoi in Paris in the late months of 1972.

Thieu's Objections. The tentative agreement in principle prematurely announced by North Vietnam on October 26 was strongly opposed by South Vietnamese President Thieu. Thieu at first opposed any settlement that did not require the withdrawal of all North Vietnamese troops from South Vietnam. But he subsequently relented to the extent of demanding only that any peace pact acknowledge the legal right of the Saigon government to rule all the territory it controlled at the war's start and that any North Vietnamese troops remaining in the country be considered as being there illegally. Neither position was acceptable to Hanoi, but the change indicated that Thieu's attitude could alter.

The United States made a major effort to effect still further changes in Thieu's political posture. Subsequent to the October 26 announcement, a major and much accelerated delivery of American military equipment to Saigon took place. The number of aircraft in the South Vietnamese air force increased from 1,450 to 2,100. The helicopter component of that service was especially expanded. Other war supplies also flowed in greater quantity to Saigon. In his December 16 briefing, however, Kissinger stated flatly that the United States would not be deterred from signing a military settlement with Hanoi even if Saigon objected.

Besides seeking North Vietnamese troop withdrawal from the south, Thieu also had major reservations about the tripartite National Council of Reconciliation and Concord, on which Washington and Hanoi agreed in October. This body was to organize and supervise new elections in the south and negotiate the future structure of government there. Without Saigon's concurrence, however, it was difficult to see how this part of a bilateral U. S.-North Vietnamese pact could be implemented.

De Facto U. S. Withdrawal. American military personnel in Vietnam totaled 24,800 by mid-December, somewhat below the target figure of 27,000 which President Nixon announced on August 29 for December 1. Of the 24,800 servicemen, 14,000 were soldiers, 8,000 airmen, 1,500 sailors, 1,200 marines, and 100 coast guardsmen. Another 100,000 U. S. military were on ships of the Seventh Fleet, in Thailand, and on Guam. In April 1969, there had been 549,400 American servicemen in Vietnam.

According to a Pentagon announcement in December, U. S. troop withdrawals from Vietnam were to continue on a limited basis but there would be no more prior announcements. The expectation in Washington, however, was that few additional American servicemen would be withdrawn from Vietnam prior to final military agreement with Hanoi.

RICHARD BUTWELL
State University of New York at Brockport

Indonesian President Suharto (left) chats with U. S. Secretary of State Rogers during latter's visit in July.

INDONESIA

The Indonesian economy made slow but steady progress in 1972. In the political field some mild dissension became apparent.

Economy. Production in Indonesia was rising in nearly all sectors. The 1971 rice crop was excellent, about 6% higher than that of the previous year, and prospects for attaining the desired goal of self-sufficiency in 1973–74 seemed very good. Oil production increased and export prices improved, thus helping Indonesia's foreign exchange position considerably. Industrial production increased and investment activity, both domestic and foreign, expanded. In spite of an increase in the volume of exports, Indonesia's balance of payments remained under some pressure. Ordinary government revenues and routine expenditures were brought into approximate balance. The rupiah was devalued by 8.9%.

The Intergovernmental Group on Indonesia (Indonesia's 12 chief creditors) met in Amsterdam in April to consider economic developments in the country as well as to review Indonesia's request for $670 million in aid for 1972–73. The request was approved. However, the Group, while expressing satisfaction at the progress reported, noted that improvement in aid utilization and project execution was desirable.

Because of the harshness of the Japanese occupation in World War II, as well as the fear of economic domination, Indonesia was long reluctant to accept extensive aid and investments from Japan, the strongest industrial country in Asia. Yet, Japan has gradually extended her economic interests in Indonesia, and in the current year it is giving economic aid in the amount of $145 million. As of March 31, 1972, Japanese private investments in Indonesia totalled $246,806,000.

Politics. The year was relatively quiet politically. The Suharto regime continued to hold the support of the generals, the industrialists, and the intellectuals. Sekber Golkar, the improvised party which won the national elections in 1971, had not yet developed into a dynamic party with a purposeful program to enable it to give the country political stability.

Strain between various factions became visible during the year. Major General Amir Machmud,

the minister of internal affairs, branded as subversive a number of organizations, among them the World Assembly of Youth (WAY), the Family Planning Association, the Lions Club, and even the distributors of Coca Cola. The daily newspaper, *Kami,* published the reactions of the various branded groups. The minister of education, the chairman of the Senate of the University, and others took issue with Machmud's accusations. Maj. Gen. Amir Martono accused the intellectuals of planning a gradual takeover of power. The apparent division at the top government levels left the public puzzled.

Malacca Strait Conflict. The Indonesian and Malaysian governments caused grave concern among a number of powers with their declaration that the Malacca Strait lies in the territorial waters of the

---

INDONESIA • Information Highlights

Official Name: Republic of Indonesia.
Area: 735,269 square miles (1,904,345 sq km).
Population (1972 est.): 128,700,000. *Density,* 210 per square mile (81 per sq km). *Annual rate of increase,* 2.9%.
Chief Cities (1961 census): Djakarta, the capital, 2,973,052; Surabaja, 1,007,945; Bandung, 972,566.
Government: *Head of state,* Suharto, president (took office March 1968). *Head of government,* Suharto. *Legislature—* People's Consultative Assembly, about 920 members; House of the People, 460 members. *Major political parties—*Sekber Golkar, Muslim Scholars' party, Parmusi, Indonesian Nationalist party.
Languages: Bahasa Indonesia (official), Javanese Madurese, other Malayo-Polynesian languages, English.
Education: *School enrollment* (1969)—primary, 12,802,415; secondary, 1,637,375; technical/vocational, 385,833; university/higher, 192,416.
Monetary Unit: Rupiah (374 rupiahs equal U. S.$1, July 1972).
Gross National Product (1970 est.): $12,600,000,000.
National Income per Person (1970): $107.
Economic Indexes: *Agricultural production* (1971), 143 (1952–56=100); *consumer price index* (1971), 71,740 (1963=100).
Manufacturing (major products): Processed foods, petroleum products, mineral products.
Major Agricultural Products: Rice (ranks 3d among world producers, 1971), natural rubber (world rank 2d, 1971), sweet potatoes and yams, coffee, tea, corn, cassava (world rank 2d, 1970), copra, palm oil.
Major Minerals: Petroleum, tin, bauxite, nickel, coal.
Foreign Trade (1970): *Exports,* $1,009,000,000 (chief exports—crude petroleum and products; rubber; coffee; tin ore and concentrates). *Imports,* $893,000,000 (chief imports, 1969—chemicals; textile yarn and fabrics; food; nonelectrical machinery). *Chief trading partners* (1969)—Japan (took 31% of exports, supplied 29% of imports); United States (15%—20%); Singapore (18%—5%).
Tourism: *Receipts* (1970), $16,200,000.
Transportation: *Motor vehicles* (1970), 363,200 (automobiles, 238,600); *railroads* (1970), 4,926 miles (7,928 km); *merchant fleet* (1971), 619,000 gross registered tons; *major national airline,* Garuda Indonesia Airways.
Communications: *Telephones* (1971), 200,514; *television stations* (1971), 4; *newspapers* (1965), 85.

THE SUHARTOS at home in Djakarta. President Suharto visited the United States on May 26–June 2.

two countries and that passage through it is subject to their regulation. This declaration raised a formidable question of international law.

Over 27,000 ships pass annually through the 600-mile (965-km)-long strait, one of the most important seaways of the world. For more than a third of its length the strait is less than 24 miles (39 km) wide. Moreover it is rather shallow—only 25 feet (8 meters) deep in some places. In 1969 the Indonesian and Malaysian governments announced that they had instituted a territorial belt of 12 miles (19 km) around their coasts. The boundary line in Malacca Strait was fixed in a treaty concluded in 1970. In November 1971, the two governments declared that the strait was not an international waterway and that henceforth it would be open only to "innocent passage." Use of the strait for the passage of foreign naval vessels would require the consent of the two governments. Moreover, in the interest of maritime safety and the prevention of pollution, foreign oil tankers of more than 200,000 deadweight tons were prohibited passage through the strait.

The declaration of sovereignty over this vital international seaway by Indonesia and Malaysia was highly disturbing to the leading maritime countries, especially to Japan, the world's third-largest industrial nation, which consumes enormous quantities of oil. About 90% of Japan's petroleum imports come from the Persian Gulf region by way of the Malacca Strait in giant oil tankers. In this service, Japan in 1972 was using some 35 oil tankers of more than 200,000 deadweight tons. It already had one of 372,000 deadweight tons in use and one of 477,000 deadweight tons under construction. An alternate course would add many miles to the oil tanker route.

Japan rejected the claim of a 12-mile territorial belt and the legal right of Indonesia and Malaysia to exercise sovereignty over the strait. Tokyo was supported in this position by the Soviet Union, which has displayed an interest in the Indian Ocean in recent years. It was reported that a conference between a Russian diplomat and Indonesian Foreign Minister Adam Malik was abortive. Britain and the United States issued no official statements but it was assumed that they informed Djakarta of their opposition to the move to restrict passage through the Malacca Strait.

Japan indicated that it would raise the question of the legal status of the strait at the third conference on the law of the sea to be held at Geneva in 1973. Previous conferences were unable to agree on the width of the sea belt over which a state may exercise national sovereignty.

Foreign Relations. In 1972, Indonesia continued to pursue its policy of active, "positive" neutrality. It favored the seating of Communist China in the United Nations, but moved very cautiously on the issue of renewing relations with Peking. One of the conditions set by the Indonesian government for reestablishing diplomatic relations with China was that Peking stop beaming Communist propaganda to Indonesia. In July, Foreign Minister Malik said that no consultations on the matter were taking place between the two governments.

Although Indonesia is a leading member of the Association of Southeast Asian States, it has not joined the Asian and Pacific Council. However, Indonesia was represented by an observer at the Council's annual ministerial meeting held at Seoul, Korea, in June.

In 1972, President Suharto made state visits to Australia, New Zealand, the Philippines, and Japan. U. S. Secretary of State William Rogers was in Djakarta on June 30, and British Foreign Secretary Sir Alec Douglas-Home was there on July 4.

The exchange of visits between President Suharto and Prime Minister William McMahon of Australia had special significance. The Indonesian president visited Australia on February 6–10 and the Australian prime minister's visit took place June 5–8. Although Indonesia is Australia's nearest neighbor, Suharto's visit was the first by an Indonesian head of state. Both Suharto and McMahon "reaffirmed that both governments will continue efforts to strengthen national and regional resilience."

Spelling Reform. Indonesia's many ethnic groups, each with its own language, have impeded the development of national unity in the country. On Java alone there are three distinct languages. Under Netherlands rule there were two official languages, Dutch and Malay. The Malays, who originated in Sumatra and crossed the strait to the Malay peninsula, were a seafaring people. They carried their language to the ports of the region and thus Malay became widely used as the language of the market place. When Indonesia became independent it adopted "Indonesian" as the official national language. Its base was Malay, which was hurriedly expanded to serve as the medium of national communication.

The British in Malaya followed a less complicated spelling system than the Dutch. To bring about greater uniformity in the written language of the two countries, the Indonesian government decided to adopt the simpler English spelling. Beginning in August 1972, the changes were to be put into effect over a period of five years. One of the chief changes was in the common *dj* combination. The *d* was to be dropped and thus, for example, Djakarta, Indonesia's capital, was to be spelled Jakarta. In other changes *sj* was to become *sy; nj, ny;* and *tj* simply *c.* The combination *oe* was to be changed to *u.* It was also decided to add five new letters to the alphabet: *f, v, z, q,* and *x.*

AMRY VANDENBOSCH, *University of Kentucky*

INDUSTRIAL PRODUCTION. See ECONOMY OF THE U. S.

INSURANCE

The insurance business in the United States continued in 1972 to adjust to a changing social and economic environment. Automobile insurance continued in the spotlight, and "no-fault" legislative activity increased.

PROPERTY AND LIABILITY INSURANCE

A significant improvement in underwriting results produced a net underwriting gain of approximately $450 million for the property-liability insurance business in 1971, according to the Insurance Information Institute. The results contrasted with substantial underwriting losses, after policyholder dividends, over a 15-year period ending in 1970. Improved underwriting results were attributed in part to such factors as lower-than-usual losses from major hurricanes and other catastrophies in 1971, although Hurricane Agnes caused privately insured losses of more than $500 million in June 1972. A turndown in the national economy and the large number of substantial rate increases obtained in 1970 also contributed to better 1971 results.

Automobile Insurance. Most state legislatures, as well as Congress, displayed a mounting interest in proposals for a change from the traditional third-party liability system of automobile insurance to one based to some degree on the first-party system under which a person who suffers a loss is compensated by his own insurance company. The reported success of a Massachusetts "no-fault" auto insurance law (effective since Jan. 1, 1971) was seen as one of the factors that in 1971 had led to adoption by the legislatures of Delaware, Florida, Illinois, and Oregon of laws embodying, to some extent, the first-party concept. In 1972 such laws also were enacted in Connecticut and New Jersey, effective Jan. 1, 1973. Meanwhile, the 1971 Illinois law was struck down as unconstitutional.

Economic losses from auto accidents increased in 1971 to an all-time high of $16.9 billion. Although traffic deaths dropped slightly—to 54,700 from the 1970 total of 54,800—increases were recorded in the numbers of auto accidents and traffic injuries. In an effort to cut the costs of accidents on the highway, insurers stepped up their studies of the damageability and repairability of autos and increased their support of state legislation that would establish minimal requirements for more crash-resistant bumpers. Some insurers began to grant premium discounts for bumpers that meet such standards.

Statistics. The Federal Bureau of Investigation reported increases in 1971 of 6.1% in losses resulting from robberies, 10% from burglaries, and 11.3% from larcenies ($50 and over). Other sources in 1972 estimated the dollar cost of crime to business alone at almost $16 billion.

Final figures showed that fire losses in the United States totaled $2,245,835,000 in 1971, exceeding $2 billion for the second time in history but nevertheless slightly lower than the record figure for 1970. The most costly catastrophe of 1971 was the Los Angeles earthquake of February 9, which caused an estimated insured loss of $31.6 million.

The number of communities eligible for low-cost flood insurance under a government-industry program administered by the National Flood Insurers Association continued to grow. By May 31, 1972, it had reached 1,201 in 50 states and Puerto Rico.

LIFE INSURANCE

The average insured U. S. family had $25,700 worth of life insurance at the start of 1972. This amounted to only slightly more than two years of that family's disposable personal income.

Purchases and Payments. New life insurance purchases amounted to $189 billion in 1971. Of this sum, $140 billion represented individually purchased ordinary and industrial life insurance. New purchases of group life insurance totaled $49 billion. During 1971, life insurance companies paid more than $17 billion in benefits to policyholders and annuitants and in payments to beneficiaries.

Investments. Assets of the 1,805 legal reserve life insurance companies totaled $222 billion on Jan. 1, 1972. Corporate securities accounted for 44.9% and mortgages for 34.0% of these investment holdings. In a time when banks and other lenders were charging high interest rates, loans to policyholders reached 7.7% of the total assets of insurance companies. The net pretax earning rate on life insurance company investments in 1971 was 5.4%, the highest in 51 years.

Urban Program. The special Life Insurance Urban Investment Program, a large-scale effort by the industry to help people living in inner-city neighborhoods, neared completion in 1972. Of the $2 billion pledged, $1.8 billion (90%) had been allocated by Jan. 1, 1972, to finance housing, job-creating enterprises, and medical and community facilities for slum and ghetto residents.

Corporate Social Responsibility. In 1972, the life insurance business began a systematic assessment of its efforts in other phases of social responsibility—including health, environment, employment, contributions, and community involvement. A permanent Committee on Corporate Social Responsibility was established during the year. In addition, a clearinghouse was set up to facilitate the exchange of information on programs and projects among member companies in their individual efforts and to provide liaison between companies and interested segments of the public.

Equity Products. In the past several years, a number of life insurance companies have made equity products available to their policyholders. A tabulation showed that in 1971 about 280 life insurance companies had affiliated mutual funds, and some 110 companies offered variable annuities. Several insurance companies proposed variable life insurance, another equity-based product, but this type of insurance could not be made available for purchase until regulatory machinery was established.

HEALTH INSURANCE

A record 180 million persons had health insurance through private organizations in the United States at the start of 1972. Private health insurance policyholders received $19 billion in benefit payments in 1971. The coverage was provided by insurance companies, Blue Cross–Blue Shield organizations, other plans approved by medical societies, and independent plans.

Since life insurance companies provide much of the nation's health insurance, they were freely involved in the growing debate about various national health care proposals. (For a discussion of these proposals, see the special feature beginning on page 26.)

KENNETH BLACK, JR., *Georgia State University*

LIVE PLANTINGS add to the decor of the Weyerhaeuser Company offices in Tacoma, Wash. (above), which also feature a tapestry of a forest scene, and (right) Union Carbide's Linde Laboratory in Tarrytown, N.Y.

INTERIOR DESIGN

A particularly prominent element in the early 1970's in the interior design of public spaces or private dwellings is the living plant. According to Everett Conklin, a leading horticulturist involved in contract installations of plants, the reason is "... a new understanding of the fact that people are unhappy without plants and flowers around them. Conscious or unconscious, there is the desire for an oasis of living green as an escape from the pollution of the urban atmosphere and the sterility of glass, metal, and concrete." The last phrase somewhat echoes architect Jacob Kahn's statement that plants give "direct but restrained contrasts [to man-made environments] comparable to the tensions that occur between components of lineal structures and natural objects."

Whatever the reason, plant growers have expanded within recent years to represent a sizable economic industry of over $200 million annually in sales. Hardly a new bank, office, airport, or hospital does not reflect that industry's effort to influence interior design.

Offices. Plants play an important part in the open office-landscape concept (*Bürolandschaft*), which developed in Germany and has become widely influential. As an example, the October issue of *Interior Design* magazine discussed the new offices planned for the Port Authority on 14 floors of the World Trade Center in New York City. On the fifth floor the open office-landscape features lavish use of tree-sized plants to provide serenity, divide space, and absorb sound. A library-like calm and quiet is achieved in large part by the foliage, which, in addition to its sound-absorbent qualities, produces a faint, fresh scent. There is also a woodland sound of trickling water. This comes from a fountain surrounded by plants. If the fifth-floor experiment is successful, eventually all 14 floors will create similar open, plant-filled designs.

One of the most spectacular symbiotic relationships between nature and architecture, completed in 1972, is the headquarters of the Weyerhaeuser Company in Tacoma, Wash. The architects Skidmore, Owings, and Merrill and space planner Sydney Roberts set the building in an area of extreme natural beauty and developed a joyful interior plan. The

open office-landscape enriches large open areas with a profusion of plantings formally set in rows of uniform terra-cotta pots. There are hundreds of plants on each floor. Included in the 27 varieties chosen are fig trees, rubber plants, ferns, palms, lemon trees, and conifers. Since large windows on each floor look out on a setback, landscaped terrace formed by the roof of the floor below, each interior attains continuity with the countryside surrounding the building.

Nature as a decorative theme is even more spectacularly represented by two tapestries designed by Helen Hernmarck, which hang at either end of the 150-foot (46-meter) open, central expanse of the Weyerhaeuser executive floor. The weaver worked from giant color photographs of a forest blown up to scale, matching each piece of yarn to a color dot on the photograph. The remarkably three-dimensional *trompe l'oeil* forest that resulted is a restful backdrop to a conversational group of seating pieces upholstered in natural-colored suede. The realism of the two tapestries is by no means reduced by live trees grouped nearby nor by the forest outside the adjacent windows.

Banks. In his designs for the Philadelphia National Bank, space planner Marvin Affrime used flowering plants and trees not just for their humanizing effect in an otherwise austerely elegant bank, but also, through placement, to create a delightful, offbeat surprise. His flowers are set in clusters, consisting of three pots each, in the huge, barren, central area of the bank. Trees, which bow gently

UNION CARBIDE CORPORATION

over the heads of the tellers, stand behind the long, severe, rectilinear divider between the many teller stations and the public. The surprise effect is heightened by ceiling-hung downlights sparkling down on the filigree formed by myriads of small leaves. Other trees hover protectively over seating groups in the reception area.

Parkin Architects used a curvilinear motif to "create an ambience of calm and confidence" in the office of the Bank of Nova Scotia in San Francisco. The actual space is not large, and each functional area, delineated by the independent curve into which it fits, remains part of the whole. In place of structural dividers, plants are used as visual dividers. Indeed, the function of the plants set adjacent to the street entrance, in white circular planters of varying heights from knee-level to eye-level, is twofold. The first is gracefully to screen a small reception area from the street, and the second is to unwind the curvilinear motif, which follows throughout the interior plan.

Technical Centers. The Union Carbide Corporation's new technical center in Tarrytown, N. Y., is not set deep in a country valley or wooded glade but is on the edge of a main highway. Yet within the building, Vincent Kling and Partners created a country feeling. The central court, the ground floor of which serves as a reception area, springs up three floors—the height of the building—and is topped by a large skylight. Tall trees randomly placed about the court give it an air of relaxing charm. As in nature, light filters through the leaves casting broken shadows, thus reducing the glare from the skylight. For purely decorative purposes, the court also features low planters holding flowers at the base of wide columns.

Residences. Virginia Frankel, interior designer and author, used plants to transform the standard, box-shaped living room of her New York apartment. Spartan in its lack of rugs and curtains and its paucity of furniture, the room has only two large sofas, a spacious coffee table, and a long, wall-hung shelf, which supports a collection of sculpture and acts as a base for a grouping of paintings and graphics. Despite its severity, the room is relaxing and friendly because large and small trees and a profusion of plants artfully arranged lend it an invitingly warm personality.

In a totally different design statement, architect Richard Henderson created a sophisticated, cool country living room for playwright Loring Mandel and his wife. The room focuses on a fireplace—a dark square hole punctuating a perfectly plain wall. The chief objects in the room are a plain, square sofa and chairs covered in an off-white textured fabric and a collection of metal-frame chairs designed by Marcel Breuer surrounding a round, glass-topped table. The only relaxed, humanizing object in this intellectual setting is a large potted plant, whose assymetrical form acts as a foil to the otherwise rigid lines and dictated placement of the furniture.

French designers such as Georges Gumpel and Jacques Bédat also use plants in domestic interiors. Examples are the indoor jungle effect against old wood and damask in the home of writer Lise Deharme and the lush clusters of foliage with stainless steel and leather furniture in the salon of the Paris decorator François Catroux.

JEANNE G. WEEKS
Kirk-Brummel Associates, Inc.

At the annual meeting of the International Monetary Fund and the World Bank, President Nixon pledged U.S. leadership in efforts to reform the international monetary system.

international finance

The Smithsonian Agreement, signed by the major industrial nations in Washington on Dec. 18, 1971, removed a crisis atmosphere that had prevailed for three months. The agreement established a new pattern of exchange rates along the lines that President Nixon had said the United States wanted when on Aug. 15, 1971, he suspended the U. S. policy of converting into gold all dollars presented to the U. S. Treasury by foreign governments.

At the Smithsonian meeting the United States agreed to devalue the dollar by raising the official price of gold from $35 to $38 an ounce, but it did not promise to resume the conversion of dollars into gold. The official devaluation took place in May 1972 following appropriate congressional action, and the dollar demained inconvertible to gold throughout the year.

Three major questions had been left unresolved at the close of 1971. Would the realignment of exchange rates be sufficient to restore equilibrium to the U. S. balance of payments? Would the patchwork international monetary system hold together long enough for experts to devise, and the nations of the world to agree upon, a better system? And what would be the major characteristics of a reformed international monetary system? None of these questions was resolved during 1972. There were some hopeful signs, but there were also some setbacks and disappointments.

U. S. BALANCE OF PAYMENTS

The Trade Balance. In 1971 the United States had a trade deficit of $2.7 billion—its first since 1893. Through October 1972 there was a deficit of $5.3 billion, in contrast to a deficit of only $1.4 billion for the first ten months of 1971. The U. S. dollar had been devalued by around 10% vis-à-vis the other major currencies by the Smithsonian Agreement, but the effects of the devaluation were slow in appearing.

The dollar's devaluation was expected in the long run to raise the price of imports, to reduce import demand, and to reduce the value of imports. In the short run, however, there was a tendency for foreign suppliers to maintain the dollar prices of their exports to the United States and absorb the devaluation in reduced profits. Moreover, U. S. consumers could be slow in responding to any price increases that might occur. In any case, the rapid expansion of the U. S. economy in 1972 added to the demand for imports. On the export side, the dollar's devaluation was expected in the long run to lower the foreign currency prices of U. S. exports and to increase their volume and value. But in the short run these effects might not be observed. In 1972 demand abroad was sluggish, except for U. S. agricultural exports.

At the end of the year it was too early to tell whether the devaluation of the dollar would be sufficient to restore the traditional surplus to the U. S. balance of trade or how large any surplus might be. But along with the delayed impact of the devaluation there was another factor suggesting a favorable prognosis. The rate of increase of prices in the United States was reduced from more than 4% in 1971 to about 3% in 1972, while inflation in the rest of the world was continuing at over 5%.

The Basic Balance. Despite the deterioration of the U. S. trade balance, the U. S. basic balance—all current-account and long-term capital transactions—changed little in 1972. For all of 1971 the deficit was $9.4 billion; for the first half of 1972 it was $5.5 billion. Given the severe trade balance deterioration, there was marked improvement in other elements of the basic balance. This came from reduced government and U. S. direct investment outflows and from increased foreign purchases of U. S. securities.

The U. S. target for improving the basic balance was an eventual $8 billion turnaround as a result

of the dollar's devaluation. This target had been scaled down from an initial one of $13 billion. After 1972, two questions remained. Would the devaluation achieve the expected improvement? And would this improvement, if it occurred, be sufficient to achieve a basic balance of about zero?

The Official Reserve Transactions Balance. In 1971 the increase in dollars held by foreign governments plus the decrease in U. S. reserve assets amounted to an official reserve transactions deficit of $30 billion. For the first three quarters of 1972 the deficit was just under $9 billion. This improvement reflected a reduced outflow of short-term capital in 1972. But the expected massive backflow of the dollars that had poured out of the United States in 1971 failed to occur, partly because the easy-money policy fueling the U. S. expansion continued to keep domestic interest rates relatively low.

NEW STRAINS IN THE MONETARY SYSTEM

Japan. The continued trade and balance of payments deficits in the United States in 1972 were matched in large part by continued surpluses in Japan. Following the yen's revaluation of almost 17% versus the dollar and by a smaller amount versus every other major currency in late 1971, the Japanese trade balance surplus increased from $7.8 billion in 1971 to around $9 billion in 1972. For the first ten months of 1972 Japan reported a $2.4 billion increase in its reserves. It was generally known, however, that the actual increase was closer to $8 billion, bringing Japan's reserves to over $23 billion, larger than any other country's. The difference between Japan's actual and reported reserves was due to special transactions designed to mask the reserve increase and reduce international pressure on Japan to appreciate the yen further. Japan was also trying to reduce its balance of payments surplus by relaxing tariffs and quotas on imports, by trying to restrict exports, and by expanding domestic demand.

Europe. One of the more interesting developments in 1972 was the implementation by the six members of the European Economic Community (EEC) of a plan to restrict the margins within which each member's currency could fluctuate in relation to other members' currencies. As part of the Smithsonian Agreement, the band within which each country's exchange rate was allowed to fluctuate without requiring government intervention had been widened from 1% to 2¼% around a country's central rate. Thus, the exchange rate of any two EEC countries could be as far as 4½% from the rate implied by their central values. As of April 24, 1972, the EEC countries agreed to intervene in their exchange markets to cut the maximum deviation among member currencies to 2¼%. This gave rise to the analogy of the EEC currencies being a "snake" within the wider "tunnel" of the Smithsonian margins. The prospective new members of the EEC—Britain, Norway, Ireland, and Denmark—joined the snake on May 1. On September 25, however, the voters of Norway defeated a referendum on Norwegian membership in the EEC.

In late June the British pound sterling came under sharp attack, and the United Kingdom lost $2.5 billion trying to maintain its new central rate of $2.60 per pound and to stay within the EEC snake. The speculative attack resulted from Britain's deteriorating trade position and continued rapid wage and price inflation. Consumer prices were increasing at between 8% and 10% a year. On June 23, Britain withdrew from the EEC snake and also abandoned its central value, allowing the pound to float. The pound sterling immediately dropped almost to its pre-Smithsonian par value of $2.40, and in late October it declined to about $2.35.

On July 23 a free trade agreement was signed between the EEC and the six members of the original European Free Trade Association that were not then planning to become full members of the EEC.

PAR VALUES OF CURRENCIES OF MEMBER COUNTRIES OF THE INTERNATIONAL MONETARY FUND

Member	Currency unit	U. S. cents per unit December, 1972	Member	Currency unit	U. S. cents per unit December, 1972
Australia	Dollar	121.6	Libyan Arab Republic	Dinar	304.
Austria	Schilling	4.2918	Luxembourg	Franc	2.2313
Barbados	E. Caribbean Dollar	...[1]	Malawi	Kwacha	...[1]
Belgium	Franc	2.2313	Malaysia	Dollar	35.4666
Botswana	S. African Rand	...[1]	Malta	Pound	...[3]
Burma	Kyat	18.6961	Mexico	Peso	8.
Canada	Dollar	...[2]	Morocco	Dirham	21.4547
Cyprus	Pound	260.571	Netherlands	Guilder	30.8195
Denmark	Krone	14.3266	New Zealand	Dollar	121.6
Dominican Republic	Peso	100.	Nicaragua	Cordoba	14.2857
Ethiopia	Dollar	43.4285	Nigeria	Pound	304.
Finland	Markka	23.8097[1]	Norway	Krone	15.048
France	Franc	19.5477	Panama	Balboa	100.
Gambia	Dalasi	...[1]	Portugal	Escudo	3.6697
Germany, West	Deutsche Mark	31.0318	Rwanda	Franc	1.0857
Ghana	New Cedi	78.	Saudi Arabia	Riyal	24.1269
Greece	Drachma	3.3333	Sierra Leone	Leone	...[1]
Guyana	Dollar	...[1]	Singapore	Dollar	35.4666
Haiti	Gourde	20.	Somalia	Shilling	14.4400
Honduras	Lempira	50.	South Africa	Rand	127.7312[4]
Iceland	Króna	1.1363	Spain	Peseta	1.5510
India	Rupee	...[1]	Swaziland	S. African Rand	...[1]
Iraq	Dinar	304.	Sweden	Krona	20.7775
Ireland	Pound	...[1]	Tanzania	Shilling	14.
Israel	Pound	23.8095	Tunisia	Dinar	206.803
Italy	Lira	.1720	Turkey	Lira	7.1429
Jamaica	Dollar	...[1]	Uganda	Shilling	14.
Japan	Yen	.3247	United Kingdom	Pound	...[3]
Jordan	Dinar	280.	United States	Dollar	100.
Kenya	Shilling	14.	Yugoslavia	Dinar	5.8823
Kuwait	Dinar	304.	Zaïre	Zaïre	200.
Lesotho	S. African Rand	...[1]	Zambia	Kwacha	140.

[1] Floating with the British pound. [2] Floating as of June 1, 1970. [3] Floating as of June 23, 1972. [4] As of Oct. 24, 1972. Countries for which a par value has not been established with the IMF: Algeria, Cameroon, Central African Republic, Chad, People's Republic of the Congo, Dahomey, Equatorial Guinea, Fiji, Gabon, Guinea, Indonesia, Ivory Coast, Khmer Republic (formerly Cambodia), Korea, Laos, Malagasy Republic, Mali, Mauritania, Mauritius, Niger, Senegal, Togo, Upper Volta, Vietnam, Yemen Arab Republic; Yemen, People's Democratic Republic of (formerly Southern Yemen).

FLOATING OF POUND, a surprise move taken by Britain in June to ease its currency crisis, reflected the continuing unsettled conditions in the financial world.

Gold. Along with the sterling crisis, the private or free market price of gold rose in June to a new high of over $65 an ounce. On August 2, the price rose to an all-time high of $70 an ounce, before falling back to around $60 toward the end of the year.

REFORM OF THE INTERNATIONAL MONETARY SYSTEM

IMF Report. On Sept. 5, 1972, the International Monetary Fund (IMF) issued a report, "Reform of the International Monetary System," that had been authorized at its 1971 annual meeting. The IMF's mandate had been essentially superseded by the Smithsonian Agreement and subsequent events, but the report presented most of the issues and alternatives that would have to be included in any discussion of international monetary reform. It did not advance any specific proposals.

U. S. Initiative. On September 25, President Nixon addressed the opening session of the IMF annual meeting in Washington. He indicated that the United States was prepared to be constructive on the question of international monetary reform.

The next day Secretary of the Treasury George P. Shultz outlined the U. S. position on some major reform issues. (1) The United States wanted an improved balance-of-payments adjustment system utilizing exchange-rate changes more extensively than in the past, with pressures and sanctions applied to both surplus and deficit countries according to objective criteria based on reserves. (2) The United States wanted the dollar's exchange rate to be treated symmetrically with that of other countries under a system of wide bands around par values, with every country permitted to alter its exchange rate when appropriate. (3) The United States foresaw an increased role for the international money known as Special Drawing Rights (SDR's) issued by the IMF and a gradually reduced role for gold, with the role of reserve currencies, particularly the dollar, ambiguous. (4) The United States saw the need for a stronger and expanded IMF administering rules of conduct covering a broad range of international economic policies—the use of trade and capital controls, for example, as well as other balance-of-payments policies. Although the U. S. positions were not immediately seconded by other countries, they were accepted as a useful basis of discussion.

The Committee of 20 (C-20). The IMF's Committee of the Board of Governors of the Fund on Reform of the International Monetary System and Related Issues met for the first time in September. Its 20 committeemen represented all 124 IMF members, either directly or through groupings of countries, and each of the 20 could appoint two associates and two deputies. At the meeting Ali Wardhana, minister of finance of Indonesia, was elected chairman of the C-20. Subsequently C. Jeremy Morse, an executive director of the Bank of England, was chosen as chairman of the deputies who would do the hard bargaining concerning a reformed international monetary system. The C-20 hoped to have a report prepared for the IMF meetings set for Nairobi, Kenya, in September 1973.

EDWIN M. TRUMAN
Yale University
Board of Governors, Federal Reserve System

INTERNATIONAL LAW. See LAW.

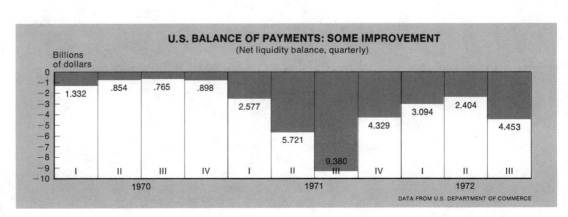

U.S. BALANCE OF PAYMENTS: SOME IMPROVEMENT
(Net liquidity balance, quarterly)

Billions of dollars

1970 — I: 1.332, II: .854, III: .765, IV: .898
1971 — I: 2.577, II: 5.721, III: 9.380, IV: 4.329
1972 — I: 3.094, II: 2.404, III: 4.453

DATA FROM U.S. DEPARTMENT OF COMMERCE

international trade

U. S. Secretary of Commerce Peter Peterson (left foreground) was in Moscow in August for talks with Soviet trade officials. The two nations had previously completed bilateral grain agreements.

TASS, FROM SOVFOTO

The value trade of the non-Communist world showed exceptional growth in 1972, boosted by higher average exchange rates and substantial inflation in many industrial and developing countries. The U. S. trade balance registered further serious deterioration as the perverse effect of the currency realignments at the end of 1971 were felt through higher prices before a change in volume. Developments for the year are discussed in the following sections: (1) Trade Trends; and (2) Tariffs and Trade Restrictions.

TRADE TRENDS

Measured in U. S. dollars, free-world exports in 1972 showed the largest advance since the early 1950's. Soaring by 18% in the first six months to $356 billion at an annual rate, world exports were likely to total $375 billion for the year as a whole. Close to half of the increase was attributable to the upward revaluation of world currencies vis-a-vis the U. S. dollar in December 1971. Inflation, especially in key West European countries and in many developing nations, also contributed to the exceptional advance in value. Further, prices for certain primary products—notably wheat, coffee, sugar, and wool—climbed strongly as demand exceeded supply. The actual increase in the volume of goods exchanged was probably no more than 9%.

With the completion of the first Kennedy Round of tariff reductions on Jan. 1, 1973, the major trading nations agreed to undertake new negotiations for liberalizing trade. At the General Agreement on Tariffs and Trade (GATT) meeting in Geneva, Switzerland, in November 1972, they discussed basic goals and a timetable for the second Kennedy round.

In April and May the third UN Conference on Trade and Development was held in Santiago, Chile. There, 135 nations discussed the trade problems of the developing nations, particularly their desire for greater participation in the decision-making process on world trade issues.

In referendums regarding accession to the European Economic Community (EEC or Common Market) carried out in the autumn, the people of Denmark voted to join, while those of Norway rejected their government's bid. Thus, as of Jan. 1, 1973, the six-member EEC (France, West Germany, Italy, Belgium, the Netherlands, and Luxembourg) was to be enlarged by three (Britain, Denmark, and Ireland).

In the course of the year, President Richard Nixon, Secretary of Commerce Peter Peterson, and other U. S. government officials met with representatives of the USSR, Poland, and the People's Republic of China and opened the way for an eventual sizable expansion of U. S. trade with these Communist countries. A comprehensive series of agreements between the United States and the Soviet Union was signed on October 18. These covered, among other items, trade matters and reciprocal credits. The U. S. agreed to make available Export-Import Bank credits to the USSR, and the Soviets gave reciprocal assurances that Soviet credit facilities would be available to American importers.

The trade agreement provided for (1) reduction of tariff levels to those generally applicable to other countries (MFN or "most-favored-nation" treatment); (2) protection against market disruptions; (3) availability of business facilities in the USSR to Americans; (4) establishment of a U. S. commercial office in Moscow and a Soviet trade representative in Washington, D. C.; and (5) encouragement of third-country supervised arbitration for commercial disputes. MFN treatment requires action by the U. S. Congress, and the agreement will not go into force until enabling legislation is enacted. It is anticipated that the total two-way trade between the two countries will be at least triple the 1969–71 value of $500 million in the three-year period of the agreement (1972–1974). This estimate excludes the unusual Soviet grain purchases made in 1972.

United States. U. S. foreign trade worsened drastically in 1972 as imports exceeded exports by a wide margin. At seasonally adjusted annual rates through September, the deficit was $6.5 billion, with exports valued at $47.8 billion and imports at $54.3 billion. This level of deficit was more than three

PRINCIPAL U.S. TRADING PARTNERS
(First nine months of 1972, in millions of dollars)

- U.S. Exports
- U.S. Imports

	Canada	Japan	West Germany	Britain
U.S. Exports	9,059	3,501	2,031	1,927
U.S. Imports	10,778	6,657	3,146	2,130

U.S. TRADING PARTNERS, 1971–1972
(Millions of dollars)

Country	Exports and reexports		General imports	
	1971	Jan.-Sept. 1972	1971	Jan.-Sept. 1972
Total	44,137	35,949	45,602	40,564
Australia	1,004	635	620	581
Belgium-Luxembourg	1,078	823	845	694
Brazil	966	902	762	707
Canada	10,366	9,059	12,762	10,778
Colombia	378	231	239	207
France	1,380	1,148	1,088	1,006
Germany, West	2,832	2,031	3,651	3,146
Hong Kong	424	350	991	916
India*	648	276	329	336
Israel	707	397	173	169
Italy	1,314	1,062	1,406	1,327
Japan	4,055	3,501	7,261	6,657
Korea, South	681	544	462	499
Mexico	1,622	1,401	1,262	1,210
Netherlands	1,785	1,271	534	462
Netherlands Antilles	119	88	386	300
Philippines	340	275	496	351
South Africa	622	428	286	241
Spain	627	699	458	442
Sweden	470	342	455	439
Switzerland	627	480	493	444
Taiwan	510	462	817	948
United Kingdom	2,374	1,927	2,459	2,130
Venezuela	787	679	1,216	952
Other countries and undisclosed shipments	8,421	6,938	6,151	5,622

* Exports exclude "special category" shipments for which information is withheld for security reasons. Source: U.S. Department of Commerce.

mand falls off because of higher prices, while exports should rise in response to lower prices.

U. S. Imports. Consumer goods continued to dominate the import surge with an increase of close to $3 billion in the first nine months of 1972. There were strong advances in arrivals of electronic products—radios, TV sets, tape recorders—and in clothing, footwear, motorcycles, and bicycles. Cars from countries other than Canada dropped in number by 9%, but their value was up by 12%.

Increases of nearly $2 billion in supplies imported for industry and of $1.2 billion in capital goods were registered in January–September over the same period of 1971. Greater quantities of lumber and petroleum, both at higher prices, and of nonferrous metals accounted for the major part of the growth in industrial supplies. Capital goods imports increased greatly in transportation products, such as aircraft parts from Canada, jet engines from Britain, and lightweight trucks from Japan. Meat and fish at higher prices accounted for most of the 5% advance in food imports in the first nine months.

U. S. Exports. Almost 30% of the $2 billion increase in exports was due to growing sales of agricultural products. Such sales benefited not only from large make-up shipments early in the year following the 1971 strikes at U. S. ports, but also from strong demand from the USSR and Western Europe. Early in July, the United States and the Soviet Union signed an agreement whereby the Russians would take at least $750 million of U. S. grain over a three-year period. It appeared, however, that close to $1 billion was already purchased in the summer months. By the end of September little of this new purchase had moved to the USSR, but sizable amounts of corn and other grains had been shipped against a 1971 contract.

Nonagricultural products advanced by $1.4 billion, or 5%, over 1971, with machinery sales in the forefront. A steep increase, mostly to Canada, was recorded in agricultural machinery and air conditioning equipment. Greater spending by U. S. petroleum companies in the Near East caused expansion in shipments of mining and well-drilling equipment. Exports of cars, trucks, and automotive parts to Canada rose substantially. In contrast, aircraft deliveries dropped, with declines largely concentrated in small passenger planes and military aircraft.

U. S. Balance of Payments. The basic balance of U. S. international transactions (made up of current account and long-term capital balances), which had deteriorated in the second half of 1971, worsened further in the first half of 1972. From a deficit of $4.3 billion in January–June 1971, this balance registered a minus $5 billion in July–December 1971 and a minus $6.5 billion in January–June 1972. The official reserve transactions balance, however, improved from 1971's record deficit of $29.8 billion to only $4.1 billion through June 1972.

The more commonly used measure of current trends, the basic balance, deteriorated because of the growing deficit in the trade account and a declining surplus in earnings from services. The drop in the latter stemmed from lower net investment income as payments on investments in the United States rose, higher net military expenditures, and a small rise in the travel and transportation deficit. Improvement was shown in the long-term capital accounts, both government and private, but it was not enough to offset the decline in both goods and services.

The great improvement in the official balance

times the imbalance of 1971 when the first deficit in the 20th century was recorded. A major part of the deterioration stemmed from the strong growth in the U. S. economy, which caused imports to rise in value by 19%, the fastest rate of gain since 1968. At the same time, demand for U. S. exports was limited by the sluggish economic activity in many key markets.

A second negative factor was the initial effect on U. S. trade of the Smithsonian Agreement by which the par values of world currencies were readjusted. With the revaluation of most foreign currencies, U. S. imports became more expensive. This, coupled with inflation in other countries, brought about a 6% increase in prices of imports through August. In the long run, the devaluation of the dollar should cause imports to be reduced as de-

generally reflected favorable shifts in expectations regarding the U. S. dollar in international markets. Private capital shifted from the huge outflows of 1971 to a net inflow in the first half of 1972.

Export-Import Bank. In the fiscal year ended June 30, the Eximbank sharply expanded its business and improved its programs to meet changing conditions in international trade. The bank increased by 38% its authorizations in support of export sales to a total of $9.5 billion. An estimated $3 billion was contributed to the balance of payments from repayments and interest on Eximbank loans and on export credits guaranteed or insured. New authorizations of loans, guarantees, and insurance advanced to $7.2 billion, one third over fiscal 1971.

The Export Expansion Finance Act of 1971, passed in August 1971, granted the bank substantially increased commitment authority, enabling it to establish a short-term discount loan program and to upgrade its medium-term loan program in 1972. Further, it removed the prohibition on Eximbank assistance to East European nations for transactions determined by the President to be in the national interest. Such a decision was made regarding credit for the large Soviet grain purchase.

Canada. Canada, like the United States, reported a boom in imports and relatively sluggish exports in the first nine months of 1972. Imports, up by one fifth, reached $13.5 billion (Canadian), while exports rose by only 8% to a total of C$14.1 billion. This left Canadian trade still in surplus by C$600 million, but it was below the positive balance of C$1,800 million for the same period in 1971.

About one fourth of the import expansion consisted of larger arrivals of automotive products— mainly from the United States, but also from Japan at a sharply increased rate. Other buoyant imports in 1972 were industrial machinery, communications equipment, petroleum, and food.

The United States and Japan were the major markets that took increased amounts of Canadian exports. Through September, sales to the United States were up by 14% and the U. S. share of total Canadian exports exceeded 70%. Exports to EEC and Commonwealth markets were weak, well below comparable 1971 levels.

The Canadian balance of payments on current account was in deficit in the first half of 1972 by C$342 million, in sharp contrast to C$500 million surplus for the same period of 1971. The positive trade balance deteriorated, and the deficit on non-merchandise transactions deepened. Net capital movements shifted by C$1.1 billion—from an outflow of over C$200 million in January–June 1971 to an inflow in 1972 of C$925 million. Canada's official monetary assets totaled U.S.$6,218 million as of June 30, 1972, with a part of the rise resulting from the revaluation of Canada's gold-based assets.

Western Europe. Exports of the West European countries moved strongly upward in the first half of 1972 over both halves of the preceding year, when measured in U. S. dollars. A significant part of the 20% rise above January–June 1971 and the 10% gain over July–December 1971, however, represented about a 10% average rise in the value of European currencies as a result of currency realignments rather than a real expansion in trade. Inflation, running at around 6% in Western Europe, also contributed to the increased value of exports. The rise in the volume of goods traded was significantly less than indicated by dollar figures.

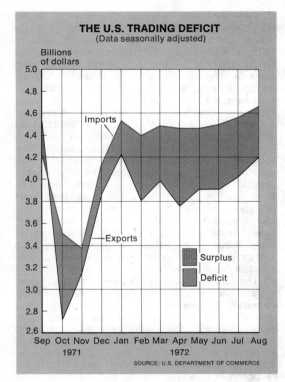

THE U.S. TRADING DEFICIT
(Data seasonally adjusted)

Billions of dollars

Imports
Exports
Surplus
Deficit

Sep Oct Nov Dec Jan Feb Mar Apr May Jun Jul Aug
1971   1972

SOURCE: U.S. DEPARTMENT OF COMMERCE

The balance of trade of the original six Common Market members, which had moved into surplus in the second half of 1971, continued strongly positive as all countries showed improvement in their trade position. In Belgium-Luxembourg, vigorous export growth brought a shift from a deficit to a surplus position. The French negative balance was reduced, and both the Dutch and Italian accounts, heavily in deficit in 1971, neared balance in 1972.

The Federal Republic of Germany, whose trade is far and away the largest in Europe, recorded a 7.4% increase in the Deutsche mark (DM) value of exports and a 5.7% rise in imports in the first half, resulting in a further increase in the already large surplus to DM8.4 billion. Since the 13.6% revaluation of the mark had reduced the cost of imports and raised that of exports, the expansion in the quantity of imports was considerably greater than that for exports.

Inflation continued to plague the German economy and to affect demand for German products. Nevertheless, new export orders were strong, and increased economic activity among Germany's trading partners in Europe was expected to improve shipments still further in the second half of 1972.

Through September, British exports were identical in value to those of the previous year, but imports were over 10% higher. Thus, from a surplus of £225 million in the first 9 months of 1971, British trade shifted to a deficit of about £500 million in the same months of 1972. The dramatic deterioration was due in part to disputes on the docks during the summer, which adversely affected exports more than imports. Some of the shortfall in exports was expected to be made up in the final quarter. An even stronger reason behind the stagnation in exports was the exceptionally fast rate of inflation in Britain, which served to price many British goods out of the market.

Latin America. With the strengthening of demand and prices for some key products of the region, Latin American exports rose in value in 1972. The growth for the area as a whole could not be characterized as strong, however, despite good gains in shipments from three of the leading exporters, Mexico, Brazil, and Argentina, which were each expected to have record sales in 1972. Venezuela, the other major Latin American exporter, did not appear to be benefiting from the higher prices and larger export volumes for petroleum.

A dramatic turnaround in Mexico's export sales occurred in the first five months of 1972. These grew by 25% over the same period of 1971, as agricultural shipments, notably of cotton, recovered. Even more important was a nearly one-third jump in exports of manufactures. Imports into Mexico also expanded. Nevertheless, on the basis of improved trade and tourist earnings, the current account deficit of the balance of payments for 1972 was expected to be lower than the already sharply reduced deficit of 1971.

The booming Brazilian economy allowed about a 20% rise in foreign purchases, with machinery, chemicals, and petroleum imported at much higher quantities and values. Exports were soaring at an even faster rate. Sugar sales benefited from world shortages and higher prices, and coffee exports garnered windfall profits because of a freeze that reduced production. As in Mexico, manufactured exports received fiscal incentives, and exports of those products rose by 39% in the first half of the year. It was possible that manufactured exports would exceed the value of Brazil's traditional principal export product, coffee.

The Argentine economy continued to be plagued by inflation. Imports were rising despite increasing restrictions, as stockbuilding added to the normal need for raw materials, intermediate products, and capital goods. Argentine exports also advanced sharply, since higher prices brought larger returns from sales of meat, corn, and wheat. Meat sales in the first quarter of 1972 were three times their value a year earlier.

TARIFFS AND TRADE RESTRICTIONS

Over 500 bills relating to international trade were introduced in the United States during the 92d Congress (1970–72). About one third of these either contained specific quota restrictions on imports into the United States or general orderly marketing provisions, applicable when imports surpassed stated levels of domestic consumption.

The most important and wide-ranging of these was the Foreign Trade and Investment Act of 1972, the so-called Hartke-Burke bill named for Sen. Vance Hartke of Indiana and Rep. James Burke of Massachusetts, who introduced it on Sept. 28, 1971. This bill, which was strongly supported by the AFL-CIO and widely discussed in business, labor, and government circles, did not come to a vote in 1972, but is expected to be reintroduced into the 93d Congress opening in January 1973. Its major provision was that most items imported into the country be restricted by quotas at the 1965–69 level and be increased only as population increases. Secretary of Commerce Peterson termed the bill "a national disaster for the United States and an international disaster for the world in which we live."

The 10% surcharge imposed on many U. S. imports by President Nixon on Aug. 15, 1971, was lifted on Dec. 20, 1971, after agreement had been reached in Washington on currency realignments among the Group of Ten major industrial countries. The Revenue Act of 1971, signed by the President on December 10 of that year, included provisions for the establishment of Domestic International Sales Corporations (DISC's) whereby companies were given tax deferrals on earnings from export sales. Over 3,000 U. S. export firms established DISC's during 1972.

New voluntary restraint arrangements were announced by the White House on May 6 under which Japan, the six-nation EEC, and the United Kingdom undertook to continue for three years, 1972–74, their control of exports of steel-mill products to the United States, which had been in effect since 1969. These eight countries, which accounted for about 85% of U. S. steel imports in 1971, agreed to specified tonnages for 1972 and an average annual growth in 1973 and 1974 of no more than 2.5% a year.

With the EEC scheduled for enlargement to nine members on Jan. 1, 1973, the seven countries formerly associated with Britain and Denmark in the European Free Trade Association (EFTA) pressed for new trading agreements with the EEC. As a result, an accord was signed in Brussels in July, under which Belgium established a 16-nation free-trade area for trade in industrial goods. Membership included the nine EEC members and the seven non-candidate members of EFTA. The dismantling of tariffs on such products was to begin on April 1, 1973, and completed by July 1, 1977. The new EEC members formerly in EFTA—Britain and Denmark—were to continue duty-free trade in these goods with the remaining EFTA members.

FRANCES L. HALL
Director, International Trade Analysis Division
U. S. Department of Commerce

NON-COMMUNIST WORLD TRADE, BY REGIONS, 1971–1972

(Billions of dollars; quarterly figures expressed as annual rates[1])

Area	1971 1st Quarter	1971 2d Quarter	1971 3d Quarter	1971 4th Quarter	1972 1st Quarter	1972 2d Quarter[2]
Total exports, f.o.b.[3]	291.0	311.9	311.4	333.8	343.7	368.0
Developed areas						
U. S. and Canada	61.8	65.3	62.2	60.5	66.4	71.1
Western Europe	144.4	154.2	154.3	175.1	177.8	192.1
Japan	20.3	23.4	25.3	27.2	24.7	26.2
Australia, New Zealand, South Africa	7.8	9.0	9.3	9.0	9.8	10.8
Developing areas						
Latin America	13.4	15.3	14.7	14.9	15.0	15.4
Other Western Hemisphere	2.4	2.5	2.6	2.8	3.0	3.1
Middle East	12.7	12.7	13.0	14.0	15.5	16.5
Other Asia	14.8	15.7	17.0	17.1	18.0	19.0
Africa	12.4	13.0	12.2	12.2	13.0	13.3
Other countries	1.0	0.8	0.8	1.0	0.5	0.5
Total imports, c.i.f.[4]	309.6	332.2	323.3	347.9	363.9	382.0
Developed areas						
U. S. and Canada	59.6	68.8	66.4	66.7	74.9	79.9
Western Europe	160.1	169.1	163.4	184.9	191.5	202.8
Japan	19.5	20.0	18.7	20.7	21.7	22.1
Australia, New Zealand, South Africa	10.7	10.9	11.4	11.2	10.8	10.4
Developing areas						
Latin America	14.6	15.0	16.0	15.8	16.5	16.8
Other Western Hemisphere	4.0	4.1	4.2	5.0	4.7	4.8
Middle East	9.0	9.5	8.5	9.5	9.8	10.0
Other Asia	20.1	21.3	21.5	22.2	21.0	22.0
Africa	11.8	12.1	12.6	11.9	12.0	12.2
Other countries	0.2	1.4	0.6	..	1.0	1.0

[1] Figures do not add because of rounding. [2] Second quarter 1972 values partly estimated. [3] Free on board. [4] Cost, insurance, and freight. Source: U. S. Department of Commerce.

—————— IOWA • Information Highlights ——————

Area: 56,290 square miles (145,791 sq km).
Population (1970 census): 2,825,041. *Density:* 51 per sq mi.
Chief Cities (1970 census): Des Moines, the capital, 201,404; Cedar Rapids, 110,642; Davenport, 98,469; Sioux City, 85,925; Waterloo, 75,533; Dubuque, 62,309; Council Bluffs, 60,348.
Government (1972): *Chief Officers*—governor, Robert D. Ray (R); lt. gov., Roger W. Jepsen (R); secy. of state, Melvin D. Synhorst (R); atty. gen., Richard C. Turner (R); treas., Maurice E. Baringer (R); chief justice, C. Edwin Moore. *General Assembly*—Senate, 50 members (13 Democrats, 37 Republicans); House of Representatives, 100 members (37 D, 63 R).
Education (1971–72): *Enrollment*—public elementary schools, 465,122 pupils, 17,223 teachers; public secondary, 195,301 pupils, 15,905 teachers; nonpublic schools (1970–71), 71,-404 pupils, 3,590 teachers; college and university, 109,000 students. *Public school expenditures*, $606,034,000 ($965 per pupil). *Average teacher's salary*, $9,933.
State Finances (fiscal year 1970): *Revenues*, $1,173,618,000 (3% general sales tax and gross receipts taxes, $223,464,-000; motor fuel tax, $100,831,000; federal funds, $234,109,-000). *Expenditures*, $1,173,652,000 (education, $475,722,000; health, welfare, and safety, $134,240,000; highways, $189,-486,000). *State debt*, $97,999,000 (June 1970).
Personal Income (1971): $11,053,000,000; per capita, $3,876.
Public Assistance (1971): $118,538,000. *Average monthly payments* (Dec. 1971)—old-age assistance, $127.34; aid to families with dependent children, $194.02.
Labor Force: *Nonagricultural wage and salary earners* (July 1972), 904,700. *Average annual employment* (1971)—manufacturing, 207,000; trade, 212,000; government, 178,000; services, 152,000. *Insured unemployed* (Aug. 1972)—8,600 (1.5%).
Manufacturing (1970): *Value added by manufacture*, $3,814,-600,000. Food and kindred products, $983,300,000; non-electrical machinery, $826,500,000; electrical equipment and supplies, $390,800,000; chemicals and allied products, $317,200,000; printing and publishing, $234,800,000; fabricated metal products, $206,200,000.
Agriculture (1970): *Cash farm income*, $4,351,808,000 (livestock, $2,841,407,000; crops, $1,274,586,000; government payments, $235,815,000). *Chief crops* (in order of value, 1971)—Corn (ranks 1st among the states), soybeans (ranks 2d), hay, oats.
Mining (1971): *Production value*, $127,817,000 (ranks 31st among the states). *Chief minerals*—Cement, $49,644,000; stone, $45,209,000; sand and gravel, $20,530,000; coal, $4,609,000.
Transportation: *Roads* (1971), 112,119 miles (180,433 km); *motor vehicles* (1971), 1,790,061; *railroads* (1971), 8,058 miles (12,968 km); *public airports* (1971), 109.
Communications: *Telephones* (1972), 1,685,500; *television stations* (1971), 13; *radio stations* (1971), 110; *newspapers* (1972), 42 (daily circulation, 977,000).

IOWA

A very productive legislative session, redistricting, and the November elections dominated Iowa news in 1972.

Legislation. The second session of the Iowa 64th General Assembly lasted only 75 days, one of the shortest in this century and one of the most productive. Major statutes enacted included unification of the state court system, replacing lower courts with magistrates; establishment of a new department of environmental quality; lowering of the adult rights age from 21 to 19; providing low-rent housing without a public vote; establishment of a uniform state building code; enactment of a municipal code to implement constitutional home rule; establishment of a uniform fiscal year of July 1 to June 30 for all political subdivisions; establishment of an office of citizens' aide (ombudsman); and appropriation of money for a private college of osteopathic medicine to buy lands and buildings.

The Assembly passed for the second time three constitutional amendments: (1) repealing the anti-lottery section of the constitution; (2) authorizing the state Supreme Court to remove judges from office with just cause; and (3) extending to four years the terms of the governor, lieutenant governor, secretary of state, state treasurer, state auditor, and attorney general. The amendments were submitted to the electorate on November 7, and all passed.

Elections. In the primary elections, which were held for the first and probably only time on August

1, the Republican party nominated incumbent Gov. Robert Ray for reelection. State Sen. Arthur Neu defeated Speaker of the House William Harbor for the Republican nomination for lieutenant governor. The Democrats chose Paul Franzenberg over state Sen. John Tapscott, while former minority house leader Bill Gannon was unopposed for lieutenant governor.

Because of the total legislative reapportionment required by the courts, all 100 House seats and all 50 Senate seats were up for election. Because of redistricting, many incumbents were tossed into the same districts. As a result, several long-time legislators were defeated in the primary elections.

In the 1972 general elections, Iowans supported President Richard Nixon over Sen. George McGovern by a margin of more than 250,000 votes. U. S. Sen. Jack Miller was defeated for a third six-year term by Democrat Richard Clark. Republican incumbents reelected to the U. S. House of Representatives were H. R. Gross, William Scherle, and Wiley Mayne; Democratic incumbents reelected were John C. Culver and Neal Smith. Edward Mizvensky, Democrat, defeated incumbent Fred Schwengel. Gov. Robert Ray was reelected to a third two-year term, and other Republican candidates who won state offices included Arthur Neu, lieutenant governor; Melvin D. Synhorst, secretary of state; Maurice E. Baringer, state treasurer; Lloyd R. Smith, state auditor; Attorney General Richard C. Turner, and Robert L. Lounsberry, secretary of agriculture.

The Republicans elected 55 members to the House, and 45 seats were captured by the Democrats; 28 Republicans and 22 Democrats were elected to the Senate.

Economy. Unemployment in Iowa in September was at a low point of only 2.7% of the total work force, while the national average still was above 5.5%. Iowa's corn and soybean crops for 1972 were expected to reach an all-time high average of bushels harvested per acre.

RUSSELL M. ROSS
University of Iowa

IRAN

Iran, though facing some serious problems, continued to prosper and to increase in importance in 1972 under the rule of Shah Mohammed Reza Pahlavi, a man of great political skill, and under the administration of Premier Amir Abbas Hoveida.

Economic Development. The current pace of economic development remained remarkably fast. Indeed, an article in the prestigious *Economist* of London (July 8) speculated that Iran may be "the next Japan." In the Iranian year ending March 20, 1972, gross national product increased 13% in real terms, whereas the increase in population was only 3.2%. A similar level of increase in GNP was maintained in 1972–73. Oil income, over $2.1 billion in 1971–72, was expected to rise to $2.7 billion for 1972–73. The ongoing negotiations between the Middle East oil-producing countries and the oil companies could only result in further increases in Iranian oil revenues.

Iran was involved in a wide range of development projects, most of which seemed practicable and well-chosen—by no means always the case in developing countries. Iran Aircraft Industries was expanding its activities with a view to undertaking engine overhaul. Iran National Airlines placed an

order for three of the Anglo-French Concordes, for possible delivery in 1975–76. On February 10 the International Finance Corporation announced a $14.2 million loan for an integrated pulp and paper mill, to cost $62 million in all. The Iranian Central Bank on March 15 obtained a $70 million Euro-dollar development loan raised in London. One fifth of this loan was to come from Japan, which, as a heavy user of Iranian oil, had a stake in the country's progress. Other large projects either announced or under way in 1972 involved petrochemicals, metals, pipelines, power stations, and the extensive copper mining undertaking at Sar-Cheshmeh.

On the debit side, it has to be noted that much of the development was being financed by foreign loans, and debt service was making up 17% of Iranian exports. Prices were rising at an annual rate of 7% or 8%. More serious was the social fact that, with development, the rural poor were moving to the cities and becoming the urban poor, a dangerous phenomenon politically. This process was accelerated by two years of disastrous drought.

Guerrilla Violence. There were dissident elements in Iran, as was evidenced by the sporadic eruption of violence, attributed to Communist guerrillas. This was being countered by the government by methods unlikely to win the endorsement of the American Civil Liberties Union.

A series of trials from January to March led to death sentences or long terms of imprisonment for an undetermined number of guerrillas accused of crimes of violence. Access by journalists or other observers to these trials was restricted, so specific information was lacking. It was known, however, that on April 19 an Iranian army firing squad executed four men convicted by a military court of attempting to overthrow the government and of being members of the banned Communist party. A fifth man's sentence was commuted by the shah to

life imprisonment. On July 29 the police killed four guerrillas during a raid on a house in Teheran. This was estimated to have brought to more than 60 the number of Iranian rebels slain or executed over a two-year period. Domestic reactions to these events included several bomb explosions and a student strike at the University of Teheran. There was, however, no incident comparable in importance to the terrorist murder in 1971 of General Farsiou, chief of the Iranian military court.

Earthquake. A major temblor on April 10, centered 600 miles (965 km) south of Teheran, killed some 5,000 people and devastated scores of villages.

Enhanced International Stature of Iran. Since the British withdrawal from the Persian Gulf in 1971, Iran has been the strongest power in the gulf region, a role the shah is consciously developing. The enmity toward Iran by neighboring Iraq, also a gulf state, arises from the bitterness felt by the weaker toward the stronger and by a regime oriented to the left toward a monarchic state.

On January 4, Fereydun Hoveyda, Iran's chief delegate to the United Nations, filed a protest with UN Secretary-General Waldheim over the deportation by Iraq, under circumstances of the greatest brutality, of some 60,000 Iranians from the border cities of Najaf and Karbala. The Iraqi chief delegate responded that his government had ejected only those who had entered the country illegally and who presented a security risk. Iraqi-Iranian relations continued to be hostile throughout the year.

A scheduled visit to the United States by Premier Hoveida was cancelled in January because of tension with Iraq. However, the rising international prestige of Iran was evidenced by a series of visits paid to Teheran by foreign statesmen in 1972. President Nixon, in his first stop after leaving Russia, visited Iran on May 30–31. In a full military welcome at the airport, the shah spoke of the "sincere understanding" between the two countries. On the visit the President conferred on various issues, including those of the Middle East. He pledged that he would not allow his diplomatic overtures to Russia and China to damage bonds between old friends. Former Treasury Secretary John Connally also visited Iran, July 7–9, in the course of a Pacific and Asian tour to 11 countries.

West Germany's Chancellor Willy Brandt made an official visit to Iran March 5–8, conferring in Teheran with the shah and the premier. The visit was concerned in part with the West German government's desire to create a reserve of 10 million tons of crude oil.

Foreign Policy. The foreign policy of Iran, a Muslim but non-Arab country, tends to be cautious and pragmatic. Iran supplies Israel with oil, but in an interview in January the shah declined the role of mediator in the Middle East conflict, condemning Israeli retention of Arab lands. The shah at the same time in effect warned the Arab states that the Persian Gulf area was not available as a place in which they might compensate themselves for frustrations in their dealing with Israel.

Iran was enjoying normal trade and diplomatic relations with the USSR, but the Soviet-Iranian border had been an area of conflict as recently as the late 1940's, and there could be little doubt that the Iraqi-Soviet friendship treaty of April was a disquieting event for Iran.

ARTHUR CAMPBELL TURNER
University of California, Riverside

———— IRAN • Information Highlights ————

Official Name: Empire of Iran.
Area: 636,294 square miles (1,648,000 sq km).
Population (1972 est.): 30,200,000. *Density,* 44 per square mile (17 per sq km). *Annual rate of increase,* 2.8%.
Chief Cities (1966 census): Teheran, the capital, 2,719,730; Isfahan, 424,045; Meshed, 409,616; Tabriz, 403,413.
Government: *Head of state,* Mohammed Reza Pahlavi, shah (acceded Sept. 1941; crowned Oct. 1967). *Chief minister,* Amir Abbas Hoveida, premier (took office Jan. 1965). *Legislature*—Parliament: Senate, 60 members; Majlis (lower house), 219 members. *Major political parties*—Iran Novin party; Mardom party.
Languages: Persian (official), Turki.
Education: *Expenditure* (1969), 6.8% of total public expenditure. *School enrollment* (1969)—primary, 2,916,266; secondary, 930,053; technical/vocational, 23,335; university/higher, 67,268.
Monetary Unit: Rial (75.75 rials equal U. S.$1, Aug. 1972).
Gross National Product (1971 est.): $11,500,000,000.
National Income per Person (1970): $341.
Economic Indexes: *Industrial production* (1971), 299 (1963= 100); *agricultural production* (1971), 170 (1952–56=100); *consumer price index* (1971), 119 (1963=100).
Manufacturing (major products): Petroleum products, iron and steel, textiles, processed foods, rubber tires.
Major Agricultural Products: Wheat, rice, barley, cotton, tobacco, fruits.
Major Minerals: Petroleum (ranks 3d among world producers, 1970), coal, iron, copper, chromium ore, lead, natural gas.
Foreign Trade (1971): *Exports,* $2,642,000,000 (chief exports—petroleum, cotton). *Imports,* $1,879,000,000 (chief imports, 1969—iron and steel, nonelectrical machinery, chemicals, motor vehicles). *Chief trading partners* (1969)—Japan (took 28% of exports, supplied 7% of imports); United Kingdom (22%—12%); United States (4%—19%); West Germany (3%—22%).
Tourism: *Receipts* (1970), $42,200,000.
Transportation: *Motor vehicles* (1970), 351,700 (automobiles, 278,200); *railroads* (1970), 3,052 miles (4,911 km); *major national airline,* Iran National Airlines.
Communications: *Telephones* (1971), 307,500; *television stations* (1971), 8; *television sets* (1971), 250,000; *radios* (1968), 2,500,000; *newspapers* (1970), 33.

IRAQ

Three principal themes dominated political developments in Iraq in 1972: a rapprochement with the Soviet Union, accompanied by a rehabilitation of the Communist party of Iraq; an all-out attack on Western oil interests; and overt hostility to Iran. Reckless as these policies might appear, Iraq enjoyed considerable success in its pursuit of them, except possibly of the last.

Relations with the USSR. Closer relations with the Soviet Union were certainly the year's most important development. Very early in the year it became clear that the Iraqi Communist party was drawing closer to the radical front on which the Baathist party government depends for support.

Sidan Hussein Takriti, vice president and reputed "strong man" of the government's Revolutionary Command Council, made a week-long visit (February 11–18) with a delegation to Moscow. The visit produced Russian promises of military and economic aid, and in particular of assistance in developing a national oil industry. It was clear that the USSR was aiming at a friendship treaty with Iraq along the lines of those signed with Egypt and India in 1971.

This objective was attained during the state visit to Iraq—on April 6–10, 1972—of Soviet Premier Kosygin. On April 9, Iraq and the Soviet Union signed a 15-year treaty of friendship and cooperation. The 14-article treaty, among other things, provided for military assistance from the Soviet Union. In return, Iraq offered Basra as a port for Soviet warships.

The new treaty and the new orientation of Iraqi foreign policy that it crystallized may be of very considerable significance. Diplomats believed it was part of a Soviet design of de-emphasizing relations with Egypt and of strengthening ties with the more radical Arab states of Syria, Iraq, and Libya. Iraq, an ally of the West prior to 1958 and later a left-leaning neutral, had come over definitely to the side of the Soviet Union.

The pact may well bring Iraq under the control, direct or indirect, of Russia, and thereby give the latter a footing in the Persian Gulf. It was noted that the USSR sent a naval squadron to the Iraqi gulf port of Umm Qasr on April 11—the day after Kosygin left Iraq.

On June 8 an economic accord was concluded between Iraq and the Soviet Union, but its terms were not revealed.

Cabinet Changes. In a cabinet reshuffle on May 14, two leaders of the Iraqi Communist Party were given places in the government. The new cabinet included five Kurds, a sign of the regime's desire for continuing cooperation with the Kurdish Democratic Party of General Barzani. The problem of Kurdish separatism in Iraq has diminished, but certainly has not disappeared: a clash on January 15 and 16 was reported in which 10 Kurdish guerrillas and 36 Iraqi soldiers lost their lives.

Seizure of IPC. On June 1, Iraq seized the Iraq Petroleum Company (IPC), a consortium of U. S., British, Dutch, and French firms that produced about 10% of all Middle East oil. Syria followed suit the same day. Negotiations had been going on for some time over two main issues: the slowdown in IPC production, which had reduced Iraqi royalties seriously and which the government claimed was unnecessary; and the 10-year-old question of compensation to IPC for the 1961 Iraqi seizure of the North Rumaila oilfield. A final compromise proposal by IPC had been rejected on May 31.

The British government attempted to organize affected countries to demand fair compensation for the IPC seizure, but the French government gave a friendly reception to Vice President Takriti in Paris, June 14–18. A new agreement assuring French oil supplies was followed by similar agreements between Iraq and Italy, India, and Brazil. The Organization of Arab Petroleum-Exporting Countries (OAPEC) supported the Iraqi and Syrian actions and on June 19 promised them a loan.

Relations with Iran. Relations between Iraq and its larger neighbor Iran had been bad in 1971, when diplomatic relations were severed in November; they were worse in 1972. On January 3, Iran filed a complaint with the United Nations that in the previous three months Iraq had deported 60,000 Iranians long resident in Iraq. Many of the expelled Iranians were said to have been beaten and tortured. The same day, six Iranians were said to have been killed in Iraq. Border clashes between the two countries took place from April 11 to 14. Iraq resented the seizure by Iran of certain Persian Gulf islands in 1971, and in general contested conservative, monarchical Iran's emerging role of regional leadership in the Gulf area. However, it is difficult to believe that this policy can achieve much against the much greater power of Iran.

Relations with the United States. The World Bank approved a $13.4 million education loan to Iraq on June 22 over U. S. opposition. On the other hand, the United States was seeking to achieve friendlier relations with Iraq, with whom diplomatic ties had been severed since the 1967 war. On July 27 it was announced that the United States was opening an "interest section," to be staffed by two Foreign Service officers, in Baghdad, with the express hope that this would be a first step toward the re-establishment of diplomatic relations.

ARTHUR CAMPBELL TURNER
University of California, Riverside

--------- **IRAQ • Information Highlights** ---------

Official Name: Republic of Iraq.
Area: 167,925 square miles (434,924 sq km).
Population (1972 est.): 10,400,000. *Density,* 57 per square mile (22 per sq km). *Annual rate of increase,* 3.4%.
Chief City (1968 est.): Baghdad, the capital, 1,949,500 (metropolitan area).
Government: *Head of state,* Ahmad Hassan al-Bakr, president (took office July 1968). *Head of government,* Ahmad Hassan al-Bakr. *Legislature*—Legislative power is exercised by the Revolutionary Command Council. *Major political party*—Baath party.
Language: Arabic (official).
Education: *Expenditure* (1968), 5.5% of gross national product. *School enrollment* (1969)—primary, 1,040,968; secondary, 316,230; technical/vocational, 9,994; university/higher, 36,736.
Monetary Unit: Dinar (0.3289 dinar equals U. S.$1, Sept. 1972).
Gross National Product (1970 est.): $2,830,000,000.
National Income per Person (1969): $274.
Economic Indexes: *Agricultural production* (1971), 139 (1952–56=100); *consumer price index* (1971), 121 (1963=100).
Manufacturing (major products): Petroleum products, textiles, cigarettes, processed foods, cement.
Major Agricultural Products: Barley, wheat, dates (ranks 2d among world producers, 1971), rice, cotton, tobacco.
Major Minerals: Petroleum, sulfur, salt.
Foreign Trade (1971): *Exports,* $1,538,000,000 (chief export—petroleum). *Imports,* $694,000,000 (chief imports, 1969—sugar, tea, and maté; iron and steel shapes; internal combustion engines; motor vehicles and parts). *Chief trading partners* (1969)—Italy (took 24% of exports, supplied 8% of imports); France (20%—5%); Netherlands (9%—2%); United Kingdom (5%—12%).
Transportation: *Motor vehicles* (1970), 109,400 (automobiles, 67,400); *railroads* (1970), 1,395 miles (2,245 km); *major national airline,* Iraq Airways.
Communications: *Telephones* (1971), 119,650; *television stations* (1971), 4; *newspapers* (1968), 5.

IRELAND

The continuing bloody violence that beset Northern Ireland in 1972 was deeply felt in the Irish republic, affecting both its national and international life. The conflict in the North resulted in increased tension between Britain and Ireland and a mounting threat to the latter's internal security. (For a discussion of events in Northern Ireland, see GREAT BRITAIN.)

Irish-British Relations. The death of 13 civilian protesters shot by British troops in Londonderry on January 30 severely strained relations between Ireland and Britain. The day after the shooting, the Irish government recalled Dr. Donal O'Sullivan, its ambassador to London, and on February 2, at a news conference at the United Nations in New York, Dr. Patrick J. Hillery, the external affairs minister, called on friendly nations to persuade Britain to abandon its "lunatic policies" in the North.

The widespread protests in the Republic culminated in the burning of the British embassy in Dublin on the night of February 2. Addressing Parliament the next day, Prime Minister Jack Lynch deplored the burning and promised to compensate Britain for the damage.

Relations improved somewhat after Britain imposed direct rule on Northern Ireland on March 24. Prime Minister Lynch called the move a "step forward in seeking a lasting solution," and Ambassador O'Sullivan returned to London. The solution, according to an article Lynch wrote for *Foreign Affairs* (July 1972), is "an Ireland united by agreement, in independence," with constitutional guarantees for the rights of religious minorities.

The I. R. A. The outlawed Irish Republican Army

----------IRELAND • Information Highlights----------

Official Name: Republic of Ireland (Éire).
Area: 27,136 square miles (70,283 sq km).
Population (1972 est.): 3,000,000. *Density,* 109 per square mile (42 per sq km). *Annual rate of increase,* 0.7%.
Chief Cities (1971 census): Dublin, the capital, 566,034; Cork, 128,235.
Government: *Head of state,* Éamon de Valéra, president (took office for 2d 7-year term, June 1966). *Head of government,* John (Jack) Lynch, prime minister (Taoiseach) (took office Nov. 1966). *Legislature*—Parliament: House of Representatives (Dáil Éireann), 144 members; Senate (Seanad Éireann), 60 members. *Major political parties*—Fianna Fáil; Fine Gael; Labour party.
Languages: Irish (official), English (major).
Education: *Expenditure* (1968), 11.2% of total public expenditure. *School enrollment* (1968)—primary, 521,546; secondary, 185,216; technical/vocational, 46,513; university/higher, 25,660.
Monetary Unit: Pound (0.4084 pound=U. S.$1, Sept. 1972).
Gross National Product (1971 est.): $4,200,000,000.
National Income per Person (1970): $1,248.
Economic Indexes: *Industrial production* (1971), 160 (1963= 100); *agricultural production* (1971), 145 (1952–56=100); *consumer price index* (1971), 158 (1963=100).
Manufacturing (major products): Processed foods, clothing, textiles.
Major Agricultural Products: Potatoes, wheat, sugar beets, barley, oats, dairy products, cattle.
Major Minerals: Lead, gypsum, limestone, slate, clay, peat.
Foreign Trade (1971): *Exports,* $1,308,000,000 (chief exports, 1969—meat, fresh, chilled, or frozen; live animals; dairy products and eggs; metalliferrous ores and metal scrap). *Imports,* $1,835,000,000 (chief imports, 1969—nonelectrical machinery; food and live animals; chemicals; textile yarn and fabrics). *Chief trading partners* (1969)—United Kingdom (took 66% of exports, supplied 53% of imports); United States (11%—9%); France (4%—3%); West Germany (3%—7%).
Tourism: *Receipts* (1970), $185,800,000.
Transportation: *Motor vehicles* (1970), 446,300 (automobiles, 393,500); *railroads* (1970), 1,333 miles (2,145 km); *merchant fleet* (1971), 174,000 gross registered tons; *major national airlines,* Aer Lingus Teoranta; Aerlinte Éirann.
Communications: *Telephones* (1971), 307,497; *television stations* (1971), 22; *television sets* (1971), 522,000; *radios* (1970), 630,000; *newspapers* (1970), 7 (daily circulation, 686,000).

(I. R. A.), which has been using the Republic as a staging ground and sanctuary for operations in the North, was somewhat harnessed in 1972, as it became more obviously a threat to the stability of the Irish government. The first effort to crack down on the I. R. A came on May 26 with the establishment of a special three-judge court for trying suspected I. R. A. members without a jury. (Juries had refused to hand down convictions.) In June and July the court sentenced more than 20 suspects. On May 18, some 30 political prisoners had incited a riot in Dublin's Mountjoy Prison, partly in protest against the holding of I. R. A. suspects for up to four months without a trial. It had taken 200 soldiers and 100 police using tear gas to quell the riot.

At the end of October, during the annual conference of the Sinn Fein, the political wing of the I. R. A., incendiary devices started small fires in three Dublin hotels, and a bomb was found in one of the city's major railway stations. Many persons attributed such acts of terrorism to Protestant extremists from the North, who had vowed to counter I. R. A. activity in Northern Ireland with retaliatory action in the Republic. Government efforts to discourage I. R. A. terrorism resulted in the arrest on November 19 of Sean MacStiofain, chief of staff of the I. R. A. "provisionals" in the south. Finally, on December 1, after three explosions in the center of Dublin killed at least two persons and injured more than 70, the Irish Parliament quickly passed a bill cracking down on the I. R. A. The bill was hailed by many, but some saw the change in the rules of evidence—giving more weight to the word of a senior policeman—as a shift of the burden of proof from the prosecution to the defense.

Voters' Referenda. Two important referenda were approved by Irish voters in 1972. In the first, on May 10, 83% of the voters supported Ireland's entry into the European Economic Community (EEC, or Common Market). The vote, in effect, represented a show of confidence in the Lynch government. In another referendum, on December 7, 85% of the voters agreed to abolish the "special position" of the Roman Catholic Church in the Irish constitution.

L. PERRY CURTIS, JR.
University of California, Berkeley

IRVING, Clifford. See BIOGRAPHY.
ISLAM. See RELIGION.

ISRAEL

The year 1972 was one of peace for Israel in the limited sense that full-scale war was again averted. But the absence of war did not imply any real tranquility. A wide spectrum of anti-Israel terrorist activities underlined the fact that Israel maintains itself against the continued hostility of its Arab neighbors. There were, however, indications that a diplomatic détente or possibly even some formal stabilization of the existing situation might be forthcoming.

Domestic Affairs. The diminution of the external threat to Israel's existence was accompanied by a perceptible deterioration in the internal consensus. Some pessimistic observers have even questioned Israel's ability to survive peace. More realistically, Israel becomes, with each year of survival, more like other states, with their internal pressures and dissensions.

FALLEN ATHLETES: At Lod Airport near Tel Aviv, mourners surround the coffins of the Israeli athletes slain by Palestinian guerrillas at the Summer Olympic Games in Munich.

The most obvious sign of internal tension was the rising crime rate. There were 53 murders committed in the first half of 1972, compared with 31 in all of 1971. Burglaries, bank robberies, assaults, and vandalism were all increasing sharply. Another indication of the surfacing of internal problems was the incessant strikes, which hit all areas of Israel's economy.

A record $4.03 billion budget was approved by the cabinet on January 17 for the fiscal 1972–73 year. The overall level of expenditure was 15% higher than the previous year, with greater priority given to the needs of social welfare for the poor and the new immigrants. The $1.2 billion included for defense represented a compromise between Defense Minister Moshe Dayan, who had sought $1.5 billion, and Finance Minister Pinhas Sapir. The cuts in military spending were made possible by a slight easing of the military threat, which was also reflected in Chief of Staff Lt. Gen. David Elazar's statement that the period of compulsory military service might be shortened.

The immigration question was one of the major issues of the year. Some 13,000 Soviet Jews had emigrated to Israel in 1971. But their emigration was hampered in 1972 by the Soviet Union's decree requiring that all educated persons wishing to leave the country pay an exit tax graduated according to their level of education and going up to some $25,-000 for a holder of a doctorate. The exit tax was protested by Prime Minister Golda Meir in a speech before the Knesset on August 23.

The election in October of two liberal theologians as chief rabbis was significant and something of a relief to the government. The official rabbinate controls a number of areas of law including marriage, and the prohibition of civil marriage had been increasingly unpopular. (See RELIGION—*Judaism.*)

Arab Populations. Scheduled elections were held for town leaders in the Israeli-occupied West Bank of the Jordan River on March 28 and on May 2. The Arab inhabitants had been leaning to a boycott

until it emerged that King Hussein of Jordan was not seriously opposed to the elections. Despite threats of terrorism, the voter turnout was higher than the percentage of the electorate that had voted in the last election, under Jordanian rule.

Israeli policy, combining firmness with some concessions, seemed to be paying off. New Israeli settlements were being established in the former Arab-held territories, but travel restrictions for all West Bank residents were greatly eased in January. Arabs living in the West Bank were allowed to move freely within Israel and were permitted to go abroad for up to a year. In a gesture of confidence on the part of the Israeli authorities, residents of Arab countries were permitted to visit their relatives and friends in the West Bank.

Travel restrictions were also eased in the Gaza Strip, and the government continued to break up the giant refugee camps, a festering sore for 24 years. Families were being resettled, and prosperity rose as thousands of workers commuted daily to earn higher wages in Israel.

Controversy erupted over the cabinet decision on July 23 to bar the return home of the exiled villagers of Barem and Ikrit. Christian Arabs, they had been evicted in 1948 from their lands near the Lebanese border "for security reasons." A protest demonstration involving both Arabs and Jews was held in Jerusalem on August 23.

Terrorist Attacks. Israel was the target to an increasing extent in 1972 of activity by Arab terrorists, particularly the extreme Black September group, allegedly part of a worldwide network. A Belgian plane with 100 persons aboard was hijacked by Palestinian guerrillas en route from Vienna to Tel Aviv on May 8. The crew and passengers were rescued at Lod airport, near Tel Aviv, on May 9 by Israel paratroopers, who killed two of the four terrorists.

ISRAEL • Information Highlights

Official Name: State of Israel.
Area: 7,992 square miles (20,700 sq km).
Population (1972 est.): 3,000,000. *Density,* 363 per square mile (140 per sq km). *Annual rate of increase,* 2.4%.
Chief Cities (1969 est.): Jerusalem, the capital, 283,100; Tel Aviv-Jaffa, 382,900; Haifa, 214,500.
Government: *Head of state,* Zalman Shazar, president (took office May 1963, reelected March 1968). *Head of government,* Golda Meir, prime minister (took office March 1969). *Legislature* (unicameral)—Knesset, 120 members. *Major political parties*—Labour-Mapam Alignment; Gahal; National Religious.
Languages: Hebrew and Arabic (both official), English.
Education: *Expenditure* (1967), 7.6% of gross national product. *School enrollment* (1969)—primary, 456,079; secondary, 134,528; technical/vocational, 58,469; university/higher, 49,076.
Monetary Unit: Pound (4.20 pounds equal U. S.$1, Sept. 1972).
Gross National Product (1971 est.): $4,700,000,000.
National Income per Person (1970), $1,636.
Economic Indexes: *Industrial production* (1971), 228 (1963 = 100); *agricultural production* (1971), 342 (1952–56 = 100); *consumer price index* (1971), 155 (1963 = 100).
Manufacturing (major products): Foods and beverages, textiles, polished diamonds, chemicals, petroleum products, electric and electronic equipment, machinery.
Major Agricultural Products: Citrus fruits, vegetables, cotton, eggs.
Major Minerals: Potash, phosphate rock, clay, copper, glass.
Foreign Trade (1971): *Exports,* $919,000,000 (chief exports—polished diamonds; citrus fruits). *Imports,* $1,764,000,000 (chief imports, 1969—diamonds, nonelectrical machinery; electrical machinery, apparatus, appliances; iron and steel). *Chief trading partners* (1969)—United States (took 19% of exports, supplied 23% of imports); United Kingdom (10%–19%); West Germany (9%–12%).
Tourism: *Receipts* (1970) $103,500,000.
Transportation: *Motor vehicles* (1970), 221,900 (automobiles, 151,200); *railroads* (1970), 490 miles (789 km); *merchant fleet* (1971), 646,000 gross registered tons; *major national airline,* El Al Israel Airlines.
Communications: *Telephones* (1971), 510,550; *television stations* (1971), 12; *television sets* (1971), 340,000; *newspapers* (1970), 24 (daily circulation, 600,000).

Two events later stood out as among the most appalling terrorist acts so far committed, those at Lod airport on May 30 and at the Munich Olympics on September 5. The first was an indiscriminate attack on a crowd at the airport by three Japanese gunmen, hired by an Arab terrorist organization, which left 28 dead and dozens wounded. Two of the terrorists were killed and one was captured and later sentenced to life imprisonment. In the Munich tragedy 11 members of the Israeli Olympic team were killed by Arab terrorists in a 23-hour drama that began at dawn in the Olympic Village. Five of the terrorists and a German policeman were also killed in a gun battle at an airport near Munich. Three of the Arabs were taken prisoner. (See OLYMPIC GAMES.)

The reaction in Israel to these events was one of fury, compounded by what Israelis saw as the incompetence and reluctance with which the West Germans in particular and other states in general faced the problem of Arab terrorism. Their anger increased in November, when the three surviving Munich terrorists were released by West Germany in exchange for a hijacked plane.

Military Activity. Despite increasing demands by Israelis that terror be met by terror, the country confined its retaliation to its now fairly customary massive strikes against states that harbor terrorists. But the government announced in October that Israel would choose its own moment to fight rather than continue to strike only in retaliation for a specific terrorist act.

The Israeli army raided guerrilla bases in Lebanon a number of times during the year, and the air force shelled guerrilla targets in Lebanon and Syria. There was an air battle between Israeli and Egyptian planes over the Mediterranean in June. This was the first such confrontation since the cease-fire of August 1970. The heaviest fighting in over two years along the cease-fire line between Israel and Syria erupted in the Israeli-occupied Golan Heights on November 21.

Diplomatic Activity. Israel's foreign relations seemed to be going through a period of marking time in 1972. The year passed in an atmosphere of expectancy. Some diplomatic breakthrough, some ingenious formula, some new method of opening Arab-Israeli negotiations was momentarily expected, but was never quite found.

The United States tried to promote "indirect" talks between Israel and Egypt, but the terrorist activity hardened Israel's positions. It was reported that direct, secret negotiations had been about to be held at the time of the Munich massacre. Many believed that the atrocities were planned by Arab terrorists precisely to abort these negotiations.

Foreign Minister Abba Eban spoke optimistically of the prospects of increasing tranquillity in the Middle East after Egypt expelled 20,000 Soviet military advisers at the end of July, but the dove of peace seemed to be permanently circling in a holding pattern. The Israeli government, assured in January of a continuing supply of U. S.-built warplanes, seemed confident that it could wait out indefinitely a diplomatic situation that was interpreted as gradually shifting in its favor.

(See also MIDDLE EAST.)

ARTHUR CAMPBELL TURNER
University of California, Riverside

ITALIAN LITERATURE. See LITERATURE.

Italy's endangered monuments include the Milan Cathedral (right) and the Colosseum in Rome (bottom). Scaffolding covers parts of both structures, and barricades keep people away from dangerous areas. Automobile traffic will not be allowed near the cathedral because auto fumes have contributed to blackening the building and destroying its statues.

ITALY

Italy was bedeviled in 1972 by increasing inflation and continued unemployment, strikes, violence, and ecological difficulties. By year-end, despite the temporary political stability offered by a new government, these problems remained unsolved.

GOVERNMENT

The most important political event in 1972 was the parliamentary election in May and the formation of a new Center-Right government after a long period of caretaking cabinets.

Failures to Form a Government. On January 15 the government of Premier Emilio Colombo resigned because of strains within the Center-Left coalition (Christian Democrats, Social Democrats, Republicans, and Socialists) on which it was based. It had held power for 17 months—considerably longer than the 10-month average for Italian governments since the advent of the republic.

On January 21, President Giovanni Leone asked Colombo to organize another Center-Left government. Colombo faced almost insoluble disagreements over economic policies, social reforms, and especially the controversial divorce law of 1970. Although only 15,000 Italians were granted divorces (50,000 more were pending), militant Catholics, neo-Fascists, and other conservatives wanted a referendum to repeal the law. The Socialists and Republicans stoutly opposed such a referendum, fearing that it might not only rescind the law but push the country toward the neo-Fascist right. Their price for staying in a new Center-Left government was a revised divorce law that would avoid a referendum. After two weeks of vain negotiations, Colombo gave up the attempt to form a government.

On February 18, President Leone turned to Giulio Andreotti, leader of the right wing of the Christian

Democrats. Rejecting a Center-Left coalition, Andreotti formed a cabinet exclusively of Christian Democrats. Nine days later the Senate refused him a vote of confidence (158–151). Concluding that no viable government could then be established, Leone dissolved parliament 14 months before the end of its 5-year term and called for new elections on May 7. Dissolution also postponed the referendum on divorce. Pending the elections, Andreotti continued to head a one-party, caretaker government.

Factions. Many observers regarded the Italian elections as one of the most crucial in a quarter century. The contest was essentially three-cornered among centrist, Communist, and neo-Fascist forces. The two largest parties—Christian Democrats and Communists—entered the fray in flabby condition. The Christian Democrats seemed in worse shape because of weak leadership and neo-Fascist inroads. The Roman Catholic hierarchy indicated it would strongly back the Christian Democrats, a stand representing a swing back toward the church's deep political involvement after World War II.

The neo-Fascist Italian Social Movement (MSI), in alliance with the Monarchists, began to campaign earlier and more vigorously than the other parties. It was speculated that a "law and order" backlash against crime would work to its advantage.

The Communist party faced unwelcome competition from a Maoist faction, Il Manifesto, with its own slate of candidates. This new, ultra-leftist party took its name from a three-year-old publication that had a circulation of 70,000.

On March 13 the Communist party opened its national congress in Milan. It elected Enrico Berlinguer party secretary replacing Luigi Longo, who became party president. Berlinguer denounced Il Manifesto, reiterated the desire of his party to enter the government as a partner of the Socialists and Christian Democrats, and affirmed that his party was prepared to assume its "responsibilities."

Violence. Violence punctuated the campaign. On March 11 about 1,000 left-wing extremists in Milan, who were demonstrating against a meeting of some 3,000 neo-Fascists, turned the central city into a battlefield, overturning cars, attacking a newspaper office, and fighting hundreds of police. At least 80 persons were injured.

Attention was diverted from both the Communist congress and the national campaign when police reported on March 16 that Giangiacomo Feltrinelli, a left-wing millionaire publisher, had been found dead in a field near Milan, apparently the victim of an explosive charge he presumably was planting under a power-line pylon. Extreme leftists charged, however, that Feltrinelli was murdered by a rightist conspiracy to provoke a "law and order" backlash. His death created a sensation throughout the country. Despite an inquiry and numerous arrests, mystery continued to shroud the case.

Attacks on Christian Democrats. The Christian Democratic government, stung by neo-Fascist charges that parliamentary democracy had fostered crime and worried by prospects of a backlash vote, issued statistics to show that the rate of killings per 100,-000 had, in fact, declined from 4.9 in 1930 in the Fascist era to 2.1 in 1970.

In April the Christian Democrats were embarrassed by further attacks. One of their founders, Rev. Giuseppe Dossetti, announced that he was going to live among the Arabs in Israel because there was "nothing to be done" in Italy any more. He accused his party of having become conservative and uninterested in social reforms. Similarly the Christian Association of Italian Workers, a left-wing Catholic movement of perhaps 500,000 partly founded by Pope Paul, proclaimed independence of the church hierarchy. It condemned the Christian Democratic party as a machine dominated by conservatives and dedicated to capitalism. It organized a slate of candidates under the banner of the Catholic Workers Political Movement.

AFTER ATTACKING Michelangelo's Pietá with a hammer on May 21, Laszlo Toth is subdued and captured by other visitors to St. Peter's Basilica in Rome.

UPI

--- **ITALY · Information Highlights** ---

Official Name: Italian Republic.
Area: 116,303 square miles (301,225 sq km).
Population (1972 est.): 54,500,000. *Density,* 461 per square mile (178 per sq km). *Annual rate of increase,* 0.7%.
Chief Cities (1969 est.): Rome, the capital, 2,731,400; Milan, 1,701,600; Naples, 1,276,800.
Government: *Head of state,* Giovanni Leone, president (took office Dec. 1971). *Head of government,* Giulio Andreotti, premier (took office Feb. 1972). *Legislature*—Parliament: Chamber of Deputies, 630 members; Senate, 322 members. *Major political parties*—Christian Democrats, Communists, Socialists, Liberals.
Language: Italian (official).
Education: *Expenditure* (1969), 19.2% of total public expenditure. *School enrollment* (1969)—primary, 4,728,075; secondary, 3,640,274; technical/vocational, 917,337; university/higher, 420,417.
Monetary Unit: lira (581.88 liras equal U. S.$1, Sept. 1972).
Gross National Product (1971 est.): $94,100,000,000.
National Income per Person (1970): $1,587.
Economic Indexes: *Industrial production* (1971), 146 (1963=100); *agricultural production* (1971), 145 (1952–56=100); *consumer price index* (1971), 134 (1963=100).
Manufacturing (major products): Automobiles, petroleum products, textiles, machinery, chemicals.
Major Agricultural Products: Grapes (ranks 1st among world producers, 1971), olives (world rank 1st, 1971), tomatoes, citrus fruits, rice, wheat.
Major Minerals: Mercury (ranks 3d among world producers, 1970), antimony, lead ore, lignite, manganese ore.
Foreign Trade (1971): *Exports,* $15,111,000,000 (chief exports, 1969—nonelectrical machinery, motor vehicles, food, textile yarn and fabrics). *Imports,* $15,968,000,000 (chief imports—food and live animals; petroleum, crude and partly refined; nonelectrical machinery; chemicals). *Chief trading partners* (1969)—West Germany (took 20% of exports, supplied 19% of imports); France (14%—12%); United States (11%—11%); Netherlands (4%—4%).
Tourism: *Receipts* (1970), $1,638,600,000.
Transportation: *Motor vehicles* (1970), 11,232,600 (automobiles, 10,209,000); *railroads* (1970), 10,078 miles (16,218 km); *merchant fleet* (1971), 8,139,000 gross registered tons; *major national airline,* ALITALIA.
Communications: *Telephones* (1971), 9,368,732; *television stations* (1971), 68; *television sets* (1971), 9,100,000; *newspapers* (1968), 70 (daily circulation, 6,768,000).

Elections. At last, on May 7, some 37 million voters (93.1% of the electorate) went to the polls. When the votes were counted it was clear that 61% of the voters had rejected totalitarian models on both the extreme right and left. However, the neo-Fascists doubled their seats in the Chamber of Deputies (from 24 to 51) to about 10% of the whole—mostly at the expense of the Liberals (from 31 to 21), a party identified with conservative big business. The most impressive neo-Fascist gains were in Rome and the deep south. After the election the neo-Fascists and their Monarchist allies fused.

The Christian Democrats (from 266 seats to 267) and Communists (from 177 to 179) both gained slightly in the Chamber. The Socialists (from 62 to 61) and most of the smaller parties, with the exception of the Republicans, suffered losses. On the whole, the extreme left lost ground because the Proletarian Socialist party, which had collaborated with the Communists since its advent in 1964, lost all its 23 seats. After the election the Proletarian Socialists merged their party with the Communists. Neither Il Manifesto nor the Catholic Workers Political Movement won any seats. In sum, the elections revealed that Italy's national mood had edged slightly to the right after a decade of increasing disillusionment with Center-Left governments.

Renewal of Violence. Before a new cabinet could be formed, further acts of violence occurred. On May 17, an unidentified gunman shot the chief police investigator of the Feltrinelli case. Soon afterwards, police raided the offices of *Corriere delle Sera,* Milan's major newspaper, charging that one of its reporters had divulged restricted information about the Feltrinelli case. Protesting this raid, newsmen staged work stoppages on May 26. The following week four bombs exploded in American-owned companies in the Milan area but caused no injuries.

Center-Right Government. As soon as the newly elected parliament convened in late May, President Leone asked Premier Andreotti to succeed himself by forming a new government. On June 26, Andreotti reported success, thereby ending five months of political crisis. The new government, instead of collaborating with the Socialists, welcomed the conservative Liberal party, which for many years had been excluded from power. Christian Democrats dominated the new government with 17 ministries, including the posts of foreign affairs (Giuseppe Medici) and interior (Mariano Rumor). The Social Democrats were given 5 ministries, the Liberals 4. The Republican party refused to enter the government because of the exclusion of the Socialists.

On July 7, Premier Andreotti won a vote of confidence in the Chamber (329–288), and on the 13th in the Senate (163–155). The coalition government was not expected to last long, however, as it rested on slender majorities and was further weakened by infighting within Andreotti's own party.

The platform priorities announced by Andreotti's Center-Right government included economic reforms, crime control, a national health service, and prison, education, and labor reforms. The divorce issue, which had been kept out of the campaign as if by "gentlemen's agreement," was revived in September. The Communists, clearly anxious to avoid a showdown with the church and fearing that a referendum might reject divorce altogether, favored an accord with the Christian Democrats to enact a new law making divorce more difficult.

FARM WORKERS march down Via Cavour in Rome in October to demonstrate for better working conditions.

ECONOMY

Italy's economy in 1972 continued to be plagued by a serious recession that dated from the "long hot autumn" of wage negotiations in 1969. The recession was aggravated by the lack of a government strong enough to take steps to stimulate the economy. More than 1 million were unemployed at the start of the year—at least 4% of the labor force. In contrast, West Germany's unemployment was only 1%. Italy's net growth rate in 1971, adjusted for inflation, was only 1.4%, the lowest in the postwar era. Few expected it to improve in 1972.

Labor. At the start of the year, plans were underway to bring about a merger by January 1973 of the three biggest labor unions—the 3.4 million Communist-Socialist Italian General Confederation of Labor (GGIL), the 2.4 million Christian Democratic Italian Confederation of Labor Syndicates (CISL), and the 1.5 million Social Democratic Italian Union of Labor (UIL)—into a United Trade

NEW PREMIER, Giulio Andreotti, on June 26 formed a coalition government composed chiefly of moderates and ended an Italian political crisis that had lasted for five months.

Union Front. But in February UIL announced that such a fusion would be "premature." Meanwhile, a neo-Fascist Italian Confederation of National Workers Syndicates increased its strength in the south and among white-collar workers.

Strike-prone Italian workers, including millions of alienated laborers from the deep south, continued to be filled with anger over the persistent chasm between rich and poor, inefficient health services, ramshackle schools, inadequate housing, and poor commuter transportation. In view of their dissatisfaction, Italy seemed certain to win again in 1972 the world's title for labor strikes. During each of the past three years Italy had an average of 1,230 days of strikes per 1,000 wage-earners, compared with 410 days in Britain, 140 in France, and 20 in West Germany. The autumn 1972 round of renegotiations of three-year wage contracts affecting 4 million workers accelerated the wave of strikes in such areas as construction, chemicals, medicine, agriculture, airlines, teaching, telephone communication, and the merchant marine.

Management contended that union demands would raise wage costs from 25% to 50%. Italian wage costs per unit of output already have been rising at the fastest rate in the European Economic Community (EEC). In 1971 the Italian increase was 14.5%, compared with Belgium's 9%, West Germany's 8%, and France's 6%. In 1972 striking Italian seamen won a contract that gave them the world's highest pay after that of the Americans.

Inflation. In September, when the government sought to freeze the retail price of food, resistance from merchants forced it to fall back on a system of voluntary restraints. In October the cost-of-living index made its biggest monthly jump (1.25%) since World War II. That same month the announcement by the Andreotti government that it would double the salaries of cabinet members and top civil servants aroused a storm of criticism.

Pollution. Water and air pollution problems remained serious. Fewer than 150 of the 8,000 cities and towns had sewage-treatment plants. Industrial fumes and traffic continued to damage ancient buildings and works of art, such as Milan Cathedral and the doors of the Baptistery in Florence. Heavy autumn rains weakened the Colosseum walls and monuments in the Roman Forum, forcing authorities to close many of them to tourists. Politics delayed the use of available sums in a loan fund to save Venice from sinking. Such problems did not deter the flood of foreign tourists coming to Italy in 1972. They were expected to exceed 1971's record-breaking figure of 33 million.

INTERNATIONAL RELATIONS

Italy lost face in the European Economic Community but maintained good relations with the United States, France, and the Soviet Union.

EEC Relations. Italy's prestige in EEC declined somewhat in the spring when a Dutchman, Sicco L. Mansholt, rather than an Italian, was chosen to fill the unexpired term of Franco Maria Malfatti as president of the Common Market's executive authority. Malfatti resigned to run for the Italian parliament. EEC members also expressed irritation at Italy's delay in imposing a value-added tax, as they had. Italy in turn was annoyed that West Germany hired non-EEC workers instead of Italian unemployed.

U. S. Relations. As soon as Andreotti's Center-Right government was formed in July, U. S. Secretary of State William Rogers arrived in Rome to brief the government on President Nixon's policies and to convey the President's good wishes. Andreotti, a staunch supporter of NATO and U. S. foreign policies in general, granted the U. S. Navy a home port for nuclear-powered submarines on La Maddalena island off Sardinia.

Arab Relations. In July, Andreotti's new government called for cordial relations with all of the Arab countries and with Israel and advocated a conference on security in the Mediterranean as soon as possible.

In August, Palestinian guerrillas, asserting that their "revolutionary policy" was to attack the interests of Israel's "friends and allies," sabotaged the Trieste oil pipeline terminal, which carries crude oil to Italy, Austria, and West Germany.

French and Soviet Relations. In July in Lucca, President Georges Pompidou of France, President Leone, and Premier Andreotti reached agreement on some of the economic items on the agenda for the October meeting in Paris of the nine heads of government in the expanded Common Market. Italy promised neither to float nor devalue the lira before that meeting.

In August the government announced that experimental color programs on television would be broadcast, using both the French SECAM and the West German PAL systems. This decision came after discussion whether Italy could afford color television and protests that adoption of the French system would tend to isolate Italy from the West and tie it to the Soviet bloc, which had already adopted the French system.

In late October, Premier Andreotti visited Moscow, where it was announced that Italy and the USSR had agreed to hold regular consultations twice a year at the level of foreign ministers or their deputies. They also agreed to improve shipping arrangements between Italian and Soviet seaports.

CHARLES F. DELZELL
Vanderbilt University

—————— IVORY COAST • Information Highlights ——————

Official Name: Republic of the Ivory Coast.
Area: 124,503 square miles (322,463 sq km).
Population (1972 est.): 4,500,000. *Density,* 34 per square mile (13 per sq km). *Annual rate of increase,* 2.4%.
Chief Cities (1963 est.): Abidjan, the capital, 285,000; Bouake, 53,000.
Government: *Head of state,* Felix Houphouët-Boigny, president (reelected to 3d 5-year term, Nov. 1970). *Head of government,* Felix Houphouët-Boigny. *Legislature* (unicameral)—National Assembly, 100 members. *Major political party*—Democratic party of the Ivory Coast.
Languages: French (official), tribal languages.
Education: *Expenditure* (1968), 27.7% of total public expenditure. *School enrollment* (1969)—primary, 464,817; secondary, 59,676; technical/vocational, 4,794; university/higher, 2,943.
Monetary Unit: CFA franc (255.79 CFA francs equal U. S.$1, Aug. 1972).
Gross National Product (1970 est.): $1,424,000,000.
National Income per Person (1970): $309.
Consumer Price Index (1971): 131 (1963 = 100).
Manufacturing (major products): Processed foods, textiles, beverages, building materials, furniture, sawnwood.
Major Agricultural Products: Coffee (ranks 3d among world producers, 1971), cacao, bananas, cassava, pineapples, sweet potatoes, palm oil, cotton, forest products, fish.
Major Minerals: Diamonds, manganese ore.
Foreign Trade (1971): *Exports,* $456,000,000 (chief exports—coffee; wood; cocoa). *Imports,* $399,000,000 (chief imports, 1969—transport equipment; nonelectrical machinery; food; textile yarn and fabrics). *Chief trading partners* (1969)—France (took 31% of exports, supplied 46% of imports); United States (14%—8%); West Germany (10%—9%); Italy (11%—5%).
Transportation: *Motor vehicles* (1970), 96,500 (automobiles, 56,400); *railroads* (1970), 743 miles (1,196 km); *major national airline,* Air Afrique.
Communications: *Television stations* (1971), 4; *television sets* (1971), 11,000; *radios* (1970), 75,000; *newspapers* (1970), 3 (daily circulation, 44,000).

IVORY COAST

Concern over economic problems caused austerity programs to be initiated in the Ivory Coast in 1972. Other problems included the continuing heavy dependence of the economy upon agriculture and the dropout rate in public education.

Domestic Politics. Warning of "dark days ahead" and of the need for austerity, President Felix Houphouët-Boigny announced strictures on government employees in January, including expense account limitations. The total number of civil servants had soared from 22,000 in 1967 to nearly 38,000 in 1971. The measures did not occasion any public outcry, as the country remained calm and stable under Houphouët-Boigny's firm control.

International Relations. During the year, Houphouët-Boigny moved closer to two former rivals for leadership in French-speaking Africa. An 11-day visit in December 1971 by Senegal's President Léopold Senghor led to treaties of friendship and cooperation and agreements on trade and cultural exchange. Despite what was described as a "frank and brotherly atmosphere," a secret meeting with Guinea's President Sekou Touré failed to produce a formal agreement.

Economic Development. A declining rate of economic growth caused concern about over-dependence upon agriculture. Cocoa, coffee, and timber account for about 85% of export earnings of the Ivory Coast. A new state enterprise, Agripac, was to construct storage facilities. During the year, the Ivory Coast surpassed Somalia to become the largest African exporter of bananas.

The $38 million port of San Pedro entered full-scale operation, handling an annual export traffic of 650,000 tons. The African Development Bank loaned $3 million to the Ivory Coast for railroad equipment.

Social Change. In July secondary school teachers indicated the need for reforms in the educational system, including a national curriculum. It was pointed out that almost four fifths of the nation's students were dropping out before reaching secondary school, and that only a tenth of secondary school teachers were Ivory Coast citizens. Meanwhile, the Association of African Universities decided to build a center for French studies in Abidjan.

CLAUDE E. WELCH, JR.
State University of New York at Buffalo

JAMAICA

General elections, resulting in a change of government, constituted the most important event in Jamaica during 1972. The fight against unemployment also received a great deal of attention.

Elections. On February 29 the ruling Jamaica Labor party (JLP) was displaced by the People's National party (PNP), and Michael Manley succeeded Hugh Shearer as prime minister. The PNP won 36 of the 53 seats in Parliament, marking an end to the ten-year period of rule by the JLP.

Economy. One major problem facing the new government was the 20%–40% of the work force that is unemployed or underemployed. Soon after taking office, the Manley government launched an emergency public works program to employ some of those without work. Among the economic and social proposals in the governor-general's speech opening Parliament were a drive to make literate 500,000 more people in three years, establishment of farms on government lands to grow food staples, the building of access roads to the more remote agricultural areas, a housing program to construct 2,450 homes in 1972, and drawing up of a "massive program of slum clearance." The regime also promised effective planning machinery to seek to mobilize the most efficient use of the country's resources.

One sizable loan for economic development was received. The Export-Import Bank provided $11,-835,000 to the Jamaica Public Service Co. to finance the expansion of electrical facilities. Some $15.5 million more was received from other sources for the same project.

ROBERT J. ALEXANDER
Rutgers University

—————— JAMAICA • Information Highlights ——————

Official Name: Jamaica.
Area: 4,232 square miles (10,962 sq km).
Population (1972 est.): 2,100,000. *Density,* 471 per square mile (182 per sq km). *Annual rate of increase,* 2.1%.
Chief City (1970 census): Kingston, the capital, 550,100.
Government: *Head of state,* Elizabeth II, queen; represented by Sir Clifford Campbell, governor-general (took office Dec. 1962). *Head of government,* Michael N. Manley, prime minister (took office March 1972). *Legislature*—Parliament: House of Representatives, 53 members; Senate, 21 members. *Major political parties*—Jamaica Labour party; People's National party.
Language: English (official).
Education: *Expenditure* (1969), 18.5% of total public expenditure. *School enrollment* (1968)—primary, 353,997; secondary, 45,089; technical/vocational, 4,127; university/higher (1967), 2,234.
Monetary Unit: Jamaican dollar (0.8264 J. dollar equals U. S. $1, Sept. 1972).
Gross National Product (1970 est.): $1,178,000,000.
Manufacturing (major products): Alumina, processed foods, petroleum products, beverages.
Major Agricultural Products: Sugarcane, bananas, coffee, cacao.
Major Minerals: Bauxite (ranks 1st among world producers, 1970).
Foreign Trade (1970): *Exports,* $343,000,000. *Imports,* $522,-000,000. *Chief trading partners* (1969)—United States (took 38% of exports, supplied 42% of imports); United Kingdom (20%—21%); Canada (17%—9%).
Communications: *Telephones* (1971), 71,823; *television stations* (1971), 9; *television sets* (1971), 70,000; *radios* (1969), 450,000; *newspapers* (1969), 2 (daily circulation, 128,000).

JAPAN

In the opening ceremonies of the 11th Olympic Winter Games, held in Sapporo, Japan, the torchbearer, Hideki Takada, runs up the steps of the stadium carrying the Olympic torch.

During 1972 the Japanese people showed signs of responding directly to changes in what they recognized as a complex, multipolar, international system. Buffeted by the "Nixon shocks" of 1971 and the resultant rather sharp business recession, they had time—after a decade of headlong growth—to think about goals for the 1970's and to reorder national priorities.

On June 6, speaking at the UN Conference on the Human Environment, held in Stockholm, Director Buichi Oishi of the Environment Agency voiced Japanese concern over the costs of growth. Obsession with gross national product (GNP) also brought pollution. The Japanese were seriously reconsidering for whom and for what purpose economic development had been pursued in years past, he said, and as a result the government had switched its top priority to respect for human life.

In July, after a record 2,797 days (7 years, 8 months) of tenure by Premier Eisaku Sato, Japan turned to new leadership. Kakuei Tanaka was elected the 40th premier of Japan, at age 54 the youngest premier since World War II. He promptly announced a desire to normalize relations with the People's Republic of China, and at home, a determination to take bold steps to try to solve pressing problems of the environment and of the quality of Japanese life. After a series of dramatic shifts of posture abroad and changes of emphasis domestically, Tanaka dissolved the House of Representatives in November, and a new election was called. On December 10 the premier's Liberal-Democratic party was returned to power, but with a loss of about 10 seats in the House. At the same time, the Socialists and Communists each made important gains.

INTERNATIONAL AFFAIRS

The long-awaited reversion of Okinawa to Japanese jurisdiction itself represented a subtle shift in the very special relationship between Japan and the United States, a further movement "from dependence to independence." Meanwhile, the foreign ministry, in its summary of 1972 diplomacy, identified normalization of Sino-Japanese relations as the new government's most pressing issue. The intricate interrelationships among Japan, the United States, China, and the USSR provided the background for talks between Tokyo and Moscow about a long-delayed peace treaty.

Reversion of Okinawa. After two years of complex negotiations, Japan and the United States agreed on January 7 that Okinawa would return to Japanese administration on May 15. Premier Sato obtained agreement from President Nixon in summit talks held in San Clemente, Calif. Their joint communiqué called attention to Article VII of the reversion treaty, which promised the return of Okinawa "in a manner consistent with the policy of the government of Japan." This was an indirect way of stating that, although the American presence in the form of bases would continue on the island by agreement, Okinawa would revert to Japanese administration without nuclear weapons. On March 15, just prior to his reassignment, U. S. Ambassador Armin Meyer exchanged ratifications of the Okinawa agreement with Foreign Minister Takeo Fukuda. Robert S. Ingersoll, the new ambassador, arrived in Tokyo early in April. In his first statements, he promised that the United States was prepared to discuss "prior consultation" clauses regarding military

bases in the Japanese security treaty; these clauses were about to be extended to Okinawa.

The official Okinawa reversion ceremony was held in Tokyo on May 15. Vice President Spiro Agnew and Gen. James B. Lampert, high commissioner for the Ryukyus, represented the United States; the emperor and Premier Sato represented Japan. Tokyo officials and newly elected Gov. Chobyo Yara of Okinawa attended a simultaneous ceremony in Naha.

Meanwhile, the Japanese government was embarrassed when a secretary in the foreign ministry, Kikuko Hasumi, leaked to a reporter on *Mainichi Shimbun* top-secret cables regarding the Okinawa reversion. The writer in turn released the cables to opposition Socialists, who charged that Japan had promised to assume the debt of $4 million owed by the United States to Okinawan landowners whose property had been damaged during the U. S. occupation. A trial of the two involved in the leak, in which limits on the freedom of the press were contested for the first time, began on October 14.

The Japan-China-U. S. Triangle. Reduction of tension between the United States and the People's Republic of China was clearly revealed in the Sato-Nixon communiqué of January. No mention was made of an earlier statement to the effect that Okinawa was tied to the maintenance of security in the Taiwan Straits between mainland China and Taiwan. The pressure on Premier Sato to follow in American footsteps toward mainland China steadily increased as the Japanese public watched the arrival of the American president in Peking on February 21.

Presidential adviser Henry Kissinger made what was called an unofficial visit to Japan in June, after a long delay caused by the spring offensive in Vietnam. As though to appease the Japanese for the "Nixon shocks" in 1971, he carried an invitation to the emperor to tour the United States in 1973, to be followed by a presidential visit to Japan. With one eye on China, Kissinger announced that the United States was not interested in a greater Japanese military presence in East Asia. Nevertheless, Peking made it quite plain that only a successor to Premier Sato would be welcomed to China. Sato represented pro-Taiwan "hawks" in the majority Liberal Democratic party (LDP).

Beginning in August, after Tanaka was elected premier, Japan's transport ministry began survey flights preparatory to establishing an air link to mainland China. In summit meetings held first with Dr. Kissinger on August 18–19 in Tokyo, and then with President Nixon on August 31–September 1 in Hawaii, Premier Tanaka gave assurances that normalization of Tokyo-Peking ties should not interfere with close Japan-U. S. relations; he reaffirmed the intention of Japan to maintain the U. S. security treaty; and he informed the Americans about his forthcoming visit to Peking. Later, the new foreign minister, Masayoshi Ohira, admitted that establishment of relations with the People's Republic would automatically void the 1952 peace treaty with the Republic of China on Taiwan. Some Diet representatives, however, continued to hope that trade and investment ties with Taiwan could be maintained. By mid-September, Tanaka had been able to build up a consensus within the LDP sufficient to allow him to go to Peking.

Color television relayed from Japanese equipment temporarily established on the mainland carried to millions of Japanese the return of Tanaka to China on September 25. (The premier had been assigned as a serviceman to Manchuria during the war.) After five days of intensive talks, Premier Tanaka and Premier Chou En-lai agreed to the restoration of diplomatic relations effective September 29. Ambassadors were soon to be exchanged, and rumors in Tokyo had it that Japan's first envoy would be Heishiro Ogawa of the Foreign Service Institute, a veteran in Chinese affairs who had helped draft Japan's position in the negotiations. Premier Tanaka voiced a widespread Japanese sentiment, if indirectly, by assuming "Japan's responsibility" for "enormous damages" done to the Chinese in the war. The People's Republic in turn waived any war reparations. Japan recognized the People's Republic as "the sole legal government" of China. Peking reaffirmed that Taiwan is "an inalienable part" of one China.

In October, Deputy Premier Takeo Miki prepared for a tour of other Asian countries to explain the historic China-Japan normalization agreement. He observed that "the pendulum is swinging back from the right to the middle course." Japan's domestic and foreign policies must be dedicated to peace and aimed toward nonaggression pacts with the United States, the USSR, and China.

Relations with the USSR. In 1956, Japan and the USSR had by joint declaration reestablished diplomatic relations. A peace treaty, however, awaited settlement of what Japan called the "northern territories" issue. After the sudden U. S. approach to China, which in 1971 had caught Tokyo by surprise, opposition members of the Diet returning from Moscow reported that the USSR might consider reversion of the southern Soviet-occupied Kurile islands within a peace treaty, if Japan were to abrogate the U. S. security treaty.

WORLD WAR II HOLDOUT Shoichi Yokio, a sergeant in the Japanese Imperial Army who lived in the jungles of Guam for 28 years, visits family grave in Nagoya.

UPI

─────── **JAPAN • Information Highlights** ───────

Official Name: Japan.
Area: 143,659 square miles (372,077 sq km).
Population (1972 est.): 106,000,000. *Density,* 725 per square
  mile (280 per sq km). *Annual rate of increase,* 1.2%.
Chief Cities (1970 census): Tokyo, the capital, 8,840,942;
  Osaka, 2,980,487; Yokahama, 2,238,264; Nagoya, 2,036,053.
Government: *Head of state,* Hirohito, emperor (acceded Dec.
  1926). *Head of government,* Kakuei Tanaka, premier (took
  office July 1972). *Legislature*—Diet: House of Representa-
  tives, 491 members; House of Councillors, 252 members.
  Major political parties—Liberal Democratic party; Japan
  Socialist party; Komeito; Japan Democratic Socialist party;
  Japan Communist party.
Language: Japanese (official).
Education: *Expenditure* (1969), 20.4% of total public expendi-
  ture. *School enrollment* (1969)—primary, 9,403,193; sec-
  ondary, 9,233,147; technical/vocational, 1,833,786; univer-
  sity/higher, 1,631,319.
Monetary Unit: yen (308 yen equal U. S.$1).
Gross National Product (1971 est.): $209,000,000,000.
National Income per Person (1970): $1,658.
Economic Indexes: *Industrial production* (1971), 270 (1963=
  100); *agricultural production* (1971), 159 (1952–56=100);
  consumer price index (1971), 153 (1963=100).
Manufacturing (major products): Ships, automobiles, electronic components, textiles, iron and steel, petrochemicals, machinery, electrical appliances, processed foods.
Major Agricultural Products: Rice, wheat, barley, vegetables,
  fruits, tea, fish (ranks 2d among world producers, 1970).
Major Minerals: Coal, iron pyrites, copper, lead, manganese.
Foreign Trade (1971): *Exports,* $24,090,000,000 (chief exports,
  1969—transport equipment; iron and steel; electrical
  equipment, apparatus, appliances; textile yarn and fabrics). *Imports,* $19,667,000,000 (chief imports, 1969—
  petroleum and petroleum products; food; wood, rough and
  roughly shaped; iron ore and concentrates.) *Chief trading
  partners* (1969)—United States (took 31% of exports, supplied 27% of imports); Australia (3%—8%); Canada (3%—
  4%); Philippines (3%—3%).
Tourism: *Receipts* (1970), $232,000,000.
Transportation: *Motor vehicles* (1970), 17,485,000 (automobiles,
  8,779,000); *railroads* (1970), 16,954 miles (27,283 km); *merchant fleet* (1971), 30,509,000 gross registered tons; *major
  national airlines,* Japan Airlines; All Nippon Airways.
Communications: *Telephones* (1971), 26,233,360; *television
  stations* (1971), 186; *television sets* (1971), 24,150,000;
  radios (1969), 25,742,000; *newspapers* (1970), 168 (daily
  circulation, 53,023,000).

In Tokyo on January 24, Soviet Foreign Minister Andrei Gromyko announced that Japan and the USSR had agreed to study preconditions for conclusion of a peace treaty. Settlement of outstanding disputes over salmon and crab fishing in territorial waters was effected, and an exchange agreement was signed whereby Japan was to extend scientific and technological aid to the USSR. Gromyko expressed Soviet interest in Japanese participation in development of continental shelf and Tyumen oil-field resources. Significantly, for the first time he set no preconditions concerning the Kurile islands issue.

On October 23 in Moscow, foreign ministers Ohira and Gromyko began formal negotiations toward conclusion of a peace treaty. Ohira explained that the Sino-Japanese joint communiqué had explicitly stated that normalization was not designed to impair the interests of third countries. Gromyko replied that Soviet apprehensions had been removed. The two countries agreed to hold ministerial consultation every year alternately in Japan and in the USSR.

Relations with Asian States. In several other ways during 1972, Japan showed an increasing tendency to pursue independent diplomatic initiatives, while continuing close ties with the United States. On February 16, Japan recognized the new nation of Bangladesh. In 1961, Japan in fact recognized the Mongolian People's Republic, when that nation entered the United Nations, but embassies had not been established by the two nations. On February 19 a joint communiqué was released simultaneously in Tokyo and in Ulan Bator, formally establishing diplomatic relations between Japan and Mongolia.

In its relations with another continental neighbor, the peninsula of Korea, Japan found it "difficult" to normalize relations. Speaking to the Diet in November, Premier Tanaka stated that his government could not maintain an "equal distance" between the Republic of (South) Korea and the Democratic People's Republic of (North) Korea. This was because Japan had signed a Treaty of Basic Relations with South Korea in 1965. Nonetheless, Japanese watched with interest the evolving Seoul-Pyongyang dialogue toward peaceful reunification, amidst the reduction of tension in East Asia.

On January 23, Japan signed its first private five-year trade agreement with North Korea. Thereafter two-way trade steadily expanded and was expected to exceed $100 million in 1972 (about $40 million more than the volume in 1971). In November, the justice ministry approved for the first time the entry of 12 North Korean engineers, who were studying the possible export of Japanese industrial plants. On September 12 in Seoul, after an intensive two-day ministerial conference, South Korea and Japan expressed hope for "peaceful unification" of Korea "in the near future." The Japanese side pledged $170 million in aid for 1972–73.

PRIME MINISTER Tanaka of Japan met in September with Chairman Mao of China in Peking and with U. S. President Nixon in Honolulu.

EMPEROR HIROHITO (extreme right) *leads banzai cheers during ceremonies in Tokyo marking the formal reversion of Okinawa to Japan. U. S. Vice President Spiro Agnew is second from left.*

Incident in Israel. Shocked upon receiving a communication from its embassy in Israel that three Japanese terrorists had killed and wounded innocent people at Lod International Airport, the Japanese government moved promptly to express its "apologies and condolences" for the incident. On June 1, Tokyo dispatched Kenji Fukunaga, a member of the Diet, as special ambassador to Israel to offer regrets and sympathy. In an unprecedented action, Japan entrusted to the Japanese Red Cross $1,500,000 for aid to the families affected. On June 9, Consul General Masao Sawaki of New York arrived in San Juan to express condolences to 16 Puerto Rican families, whose members had been on a pilgrimage in Israel and were among the victims at Lod Airport.

Japan's International Economic Status. As part of an agreement on currency rates reached in Washington in December 1971, the yen was revalued upward (for the first time since its establishment in 1871) by 16.9% to 308 yen to the dollar. Despite this shift, Japan's overall balance of payments' surplus continued to climb: by August 1 foreign exchange reserves reached $15.9 billion; by October 1 they totaled $16.5 billion; and by November 1 they topped $17.7 billion. Finance ministry officials predicted that, if the trend continued, there would be pressure toward another revaluation.

In his first speech in the Diet on October 27, Premier Tanaka promised that the government would take effective measures to limit the balance of payments surplus to less than 1% of the GNP. He described the measures as "the most urgent question facing Japan at this moment."

Especially urgent was the huge surplus in U. S.-Japan trade in the latter's favor, expected to exceed $4 billion in 1972. Thus whereas the Japanese business community welcomed the reelection of Richard Nixon as U. S. president, since presumably he was acquainted with Japan's leaders, some (like Yoshizane Iwasa of Fuji Bank) were wary in view of protectionist bills that could be expected to be introduced in the Congress of the United States in 1973.

DOMESTIC AFFAIRS

On the domestic front, Japan continued to feel the impact of yen revaluation in 1971, a phenomenon that was paralleled by a persistent recession in 1972.

Economic Developments. In the 'fiscal year ending March 31, 1972, Japan's GNP fell off to $182.4 billion (60.9 trillion yen as compared with 72.7 trillion yen in fiscal 1970–71). Early in November, the Economic Planning Agency (EPA) revised its official economic forecast for 1972–73, putting the GNP at 93.2 trillion yen ($302.6 billion). This would represent a growth rate of 14.8% in nominal terms and 9.5% in real terms.

Inflation accounted for the gap between apparent and real growth. On January 12 the government approved an expansive 11.5 trillion yen budget for fiscal 1972–73. This marked a 22% expenditures increase, designed to stimulate the economy by investment in social infrastructure. By June 1972, there were indeed signs of recovery but also the specter of inflation. At midyear the national consumer price index was a full 10% over the level of 1970 (Tokyo's index was up 11%). According to an announcement by the Bank of Japan, the balance of note issues at the end of October was 6,185 trillion yen, an increase of almost 21% over the previous year.

Parties, Politics, and Elections. Despite the fact the ruling Liberal Democratic party (LDP) continued to hold a comfortable majority of seats in both houses of the Diet, its share of popular support steadily declined. Premier Sato and his faction of the LDP represented a policy of status quo in the face of sweeping, worldwide changes in diplomacy. Having set a record for tenure in the premiership, Sato nonetheless saw his greatest triumph—the reversion of Okinawa—marred by irregularities. In April, he was forced to take responsibility for the widely publicized "secret cables" case concerned with Japan's assumption of U. S. debts to Okinawan landlords. In an emotion-packed appearance on June 24, from which he barred

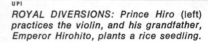

ROYAL DIVERSIONS: Prince Hiro (left)
practices the violin, and his grandfather,
Emperor Hirohito, plants a rice seedling.

newspaper reporters, Sato announced that he would not again stand for election to the presidency of the LDP. In effect, the retirement constituted an end to his premiership as well.

On July 5, in a special caucus of all LDP members of the Diet plus 47 party delegates from the prefectures, the party chose Kakuei Tanaka to be party president in a run-off ballot. His closest rival was Sato's foreign minister, Takeo Fukuda. Tanaka was formally elected by the Diet and confirmed as premier by Emperor Hirohito on July 6. His adviser on diplomatic affairs, Masayoshi Ohira, entered the new cabinet as foreign minister; Takeo Miki, as deputy premier; and Yasuhiro Nakasone, important faction leader and potential future premier, minister of international trade and industry. The new premier promised (and later effected) a normalization of diplomatic relations with the People's Republic of China.

In his bold plan for improving the quality of Japanese life at home, Premier Tanaka fared less well through the rest of the year. When he was industry minister, Tanaka had written a general plan, "Remodeling the Japanese Archipelago," which after he assumed national leadership promptly became a best-seller. Opposition leaders argued that this blueprint, involving the decentralization of urban settlement and industry, would spread "gross national pollution" evenly across Japan.

Meanwhile, Japanese were demonstrating their political restiveness on the prefectural level in local elections. Before Tanaka's election, Okinawans in June returned incumbent Chobyo Yara to the elected governorship of the Ryukyus. Yara represented the island residents' dissatisfaction with the reversion agreement (especially the continuing "American presence"), their concern for the possible revival of Japan's historic neglect of the prefecture, and their frustration over disruption of Okinawa's welfare under U. S. military administration. Yara was the fourth Socialist to be elected governor, joining successful opposition candidates in Tokyo (Gov.

Ryokichi Minobe), Kyoto, and Osaka. On July 3, Yawara Hata, a lawyer supported by an opposition coalition, defeated a LDP candidate for the governorship of Saitama prefecture. His victory ended three decades of conservative rule. Finally, late in October, Shiro Nagano was elected the first reformist governor of Okayama prefecture.

Nonetheless Premier Tanaka believed by November that he had piled up enough national support to test his new government in a general election. After a special Diet session convened October 27, passed the supplemental budget, the government on November 13 dissolved the lower House of Representatives and scheduled Japan's 12th postwar election for December 10. On that date, Premier Tanaka's government was confirmed in power with the victory of the LDP, with the Socialists and Communists both making impressive gains at the expense of the Democratic Socialist party and the Komeito. The victory, however, fell short of what the LDP had hoped for. Though its popular vote declined less than 1% from the previous election, it suffered a loss of 17 seats in the lower house.

Other Developments. One feature of Premier Tanaka's plan for resettling the Japanese islands was to expand high-speed rail links already established in the Tokyo-Osaka megalopolitan corridor. The longest underwater tunnel in the world, the 33.6-mile (55-km) Seikan tube linking Honshu and Hokkaido, was under construction and scheduled for completion in 1979. To the south, the new superexpress Sanyo rail line extended Tokyo-Osaka "bullet" train service as far as Okayama, beginning March 15.

The first winter Olympic Games ever held in Asia opened on February 3 in Sapporo on Hokkaido (see OLYMPIC GAMES). Ten days later Japan's northern metropolis, with over 1 million population, inherited government-built expressways, huge apartment complexes, and the first subway built north of Tokyo.

ARDATH W. BURKS, *Rutgers University*

JAPANESE LITERATURE. See LITERATURE.

JORDAN

Jordan's King Hussein found himself alienated diplomatically and economically from many of the neighboring Arab states due to the military actions he had taken against Palestinian guerrillas in July 1971. In 1972, the rift was deepened further by the controversial Middle East plan that he announced in March and by his unwillingness to allow the commandos to return to Jordan. In fact, most of the activities of the Jordanian government in 1972 were intimately involved with the king's plans to reestablish stability both in his country and the Middle East.

Diplomatic Isolation. Jordan's diplomatic isolation in the Arab world was a principal concern for King Hussein in 1972. However, national concerns, rather than the goal of Arab solidarity, dominated his diplomatic initiatives. On March 15, Hussein revealed a comprehensive plan for peace between Israel and Jordan. He proposed the establishment of a United Arab Kingdom, which would be a federated state made up of two autonomous regions: the Israeli-occupied West Bank and the present national territory east of the Jordan River. He also suggested that Jerusalem be the capital of the West Bank region.

Although the proposal complicated Jordan's relations with the Arab world, the major question was how the Israelis would react. Response was slow. By November, the Israeli government had said only that the plan was "courageous" but that any peace in the Middle East would have to include the enlargement of Israel's national territory and that under no circumstances would Jerusalem be given up. Since Hussein's plan involved only minor territorial adjustments and the return of the section of Jerusalem formerly held by Jordan, substantive negotiations did not begin.

The reaction of the Arab states to Hussein's plan was severe. On April 6, Egypt broke off relations with Jordan, as had the two other members of the Federation of Arab Republics—Libya and Syria—in the previous two years. Even though Kuwait had granted Jordan a substantial loan on March 14, the oil-rich state refused, after a trip there by Jordanian Premier Ahmed al-Lawzi in the last week of April, to resume the $40 million annual subsidy that had been cut off since July 1971.

Hussein was also accused of working with Israel and the United States, especially after his April 28 talks with President Nixon. As a result, Hussein was forced to seek support for his plan in other regions of the Middle East, such as the Persian Gulf and Iran.

Domestic Politics. The major developments in domestic affairs were the formation of a new cabinet on February 9, and the successes of the Arab National Union, a state-supported national political party that had been proclaimed in September of the previous year.

The new cabinet was expected to help Jordan out of its isolation, improve relations with Israel, and ensure the resumption of the Kuwaiti subsidy. As for the Arab National Union (ANU), its charter had important ramifications, since its salient principle was the territorial and demographic integrity of pre-1967 Jordan. In addition, the charter reflected the king's determination to reassert his position as spokesman of the Palestinians, in defiance of the leadership claims of the commandos, and his

---

JORDAN · Information Highlights

Official Name: Hashemite Kingdom of Jordan.
Area: 37,738 square miles (97,740 sq km).
Population (1972 est.): 2,500,000. *Density,* 62 per square mile (24 per sq km). *Annual rate of increase,* 3.3%.
Chief Cities (1969 census): Amman, the capital, 330,220; Zarqa, 121,303.
Government: *Head of state,* Hussein Ibn Talal, king (acceded Aug. 1952). *Head of government,* Ahmed al-Lawzi, premier (took office Nov. 1971). *Legislature*—National Assembly: House of Representatives, 60 members; Senate, 30 members.
Language: Arabic (official).
Education: *Expenditure* (1969), 9.6% of total public expenditure. *School enrollment* (1969)—primary, 259,388; secondary, 88,090; technical/vocational, 2,801; university/higher, 4,463.
Monetary Unit: Dinar (0.3571 dinar equals U. S.$1, Sept. 1972).
Gross National Product (1967 est.): $575,000,000.
National Income per Person (1969): $280.
Consumer Price Index (1971): 120 (1967=100).
Manufacturing (major products): Cement, petroleum products, cigarettes, vegetable oil.
Major Agricultural Products: Wheat, tomatoes, barley, fruits, olives, grapes, vegetables, tobacco.
Major Minerals: Phosphate rock, salt, potash.
Foreign Trade (1971): *Exports,* $32,000,000 (chief exports—phosphates; tomatoes). *Imports,* $215,000,000 (chief imports, 1967—food and live animals; textile yarn and fabrics; motor vehicles; iron and steel). *Chief trading partners* (1969)—United Kingdom (supplied 14% of imports); United States (9%); West Germany (8%).
Tourism: *Receipts* (1970), $11,800,000.
Transportation: *Motor vehicles* (1970), 21,300 (automobiles, 15,400); *railroads* (1970), 298 miles (480 km); *major national airline,* ALIA—The Royal Jordanian Airline.
Communications: *Telephones* (1971), 31,104; *television stations* (1971), 1; *television sets* (1971), 50,000; *radios* (1970), 150,000; *newspapers* (1970), 5 (daily circulation, 56,000).

---

opposition to any peace settlement with Israel that would not return the West Bank to his sovereignty.

During 1972, the Jordanian government made strenuous but quiet efforts to find allies among the peoples of the West Bank and the Gaza Strip. These efforts were successful to the extent that the ANU established roots in the occupied territories and mustered support for the proposed United Arab Kingdom. It also increased cooperation between the people of the occupied lands and the people of East Jordan, especially by providing trade facilities for the people of the West Bank, as well as passports and financial aid for the people of the Gaza Strip.

Economic Problems. In 1972, Jordan continued to suffer from the economic consequences of the loss of the occupied territories and Hussein's liquidation of the Palestinian guerrilla movement. Cut off from valuable subsidies and its primary agricultural sectors, and relying on what was essentially a one-commodity economy—phosphates—Jordan reeled under the impact of a 240% increase in its balance of payments deficit and an export figure that formed only 11.9% of the value of imports.

The economic picture began to improve by midyear, however, as agricultural production increased and the effects of the Syrian government's February 24 relaxation of border obstructions to Jordanian phosphate traffic began to be felt. Although the record budget announced on May 18 envisioned a $36 million deficit, Jordan's economic planners were sufficiently confident of the future to announce late in 1972 a three-year development plan that would cost $540 million.

It was expected that the United States and Saudi Arabia would continue their substantial aid programs to Jordan. Jordan received $15 million in January from the United States and $10.6 million in February from the Saudi government.

F. NICHOLAS WILLARD
Georgetown University

JUDAISM. See RELIGION.

KANSAS

In 1972, Kansas had another banner crop year, gave a large plurality to President Richard Nixon, reelected Gov. Robert B. Docking to an unprecedented fourth term, and returned most other state officials to office.

Agriculture. The 1972 Kansas wheat crop, estimated at 314 million bushels, was the state's largest of record. The projected production as of October 1 of 24 million bushels of soybeans and 5.6 million tons of hay were new record highs.

The prospective harvest of corn and sorghum grain was also near record on October 1, but the wet fields or snow cover that prevailed in the following weeks caused lagging fall harvests and some field losses. The preliminary crop production index for Kansas in 1972, however, was 153% of the 1957–59 base and would equal the previous year's record high production if harvesting losses proved minor.

Elections. On November 7, Kansans voted for President Nixon by a 68%-to-30% margin over Democratic challenger Sen. George McGovern. Republican incumbent U. S. Sen. James Pearson was given a convincing 73% of the vote over Arch Tetzlaff.

The state's four Republican incumbent U. S. House members, Keith G. Sebelius, Larry Winn, Jr., Garner E. Shriver, and Joe Skubitz, all won handily, while the state's lone Democratic congressman, Wil-

--------------KANSAS • Information Highlights --------------

Area: 82,264 square miles (213,064 sq km).
Population (1970 census): 2,249,071. *Density,* 28 per sq mi.
Chief Cities (1970 census): Topeka, the capital, 125,011; Wichita, 276,554; Kansas City, 168,213; Overland Park, 79,034; Lawrence, 45,698; Salina, 37,714; Hutchinson, 36,885.
Government (1972): *Chief Officers*—governor, Robert Docking (D); lt. gov., Reynolds Shultz (R); secy. of state, Mrs. Elwill M. Shanahan (R); atty. gen., Vern Miller (D); treas., Walter H. Peery (R); commissioner, dept. of education, C. Taylor Whittier; chief justice, Harold R. Fatzer. *Legislature*—Senate, 40 members (32 Republicans, 8 Democrats); House of Representatives, 125 members (84 R, 41 D).
Education (1971–72): *Enrollment*—public elementary schools, 291,455 pupils, 13,066 teachers; public secondary, 214,179 pupils, 12,818 teachers; nonpublic schools (1970–71), 35,150 pupils, 1,950 teachers; college and university, 107,000 students. *Public school expenditures,* $391,665,000 ($854 per pupil). *Average teacher's salary,* $8,580.
State Finances (fiscal year 1970): *Revenues,* $794,678,000 (3% general sales tax and gross receipts taxes, $145,-371,000; motor fuel tax, $81,402,000; federal funds, $197,-406,000). *Expenditures,* $792,242,000 (education, $330,-545,000; health, welfare, and safety, $24,232,000; highways, $144,533,000). *State debt,* $223,590,000 (June 30, 1970).
Personal Income (1971): $9,234,000,000; per capita, $4,090.
Public Assistance (1971): $140,731,000. *Average monthly payments* (Dec. 1971)—old-age assistance, $52.29; aid to families with dependent children, $167.66.
Labor Force: *Nonagricultural wage and salary earners* (July 1972), 686,000. *Average annual employment* (1971)—manufacturing, 129,000; trade, 159,000; government, 156,000; services, 104,000. *Insured unemployed* (Aug. 1972)—8,800 (2.0%).
Manufacturing (1970): *Value added by manufacture,* $2,263,-800,000. Transportation equipment, $481,500,000; food and kindred products, $318,200,000; chemicals and allied products, $281,400,000; nonelectrical machinery, $218,800,000; printing and publishing, $167,000,000; petroleum and coal products, $140,900,000.
Agriculture (1970): *Cash farm income,* $2,214,622,000 (livestock, $1,265,930,000; crops, $721,053,000; government payments, $227,639,000). *Chief crops* (in order of value, 1971)—Wheat (ranks 1st among the states), sorghum grain (ranks 2d), corn, hay.
Mining (1970): *Production value,* $601,454,000 (ranks 16th among the states). *Chief minerals*—Petroleum, $273,975,-000; natural gas, $131,176,000; natural gas liquids, $59,-257,000; helium, $40,831,000.
Transportation: *Roads* (1971), 133,987 miles (215,625 km); *motor vehicles* (1971), 1,547,643; *railroads* (1971), 7,779 miles (12,519 km); *public airports* (1972), 119.
Communications: *Telephones* (1972), 1,347,500; *television stations* (1971), 12; *radio stations* (1971), 83; *newspapers* (1972), 50 (daily circulation, 651,000).

liam R. Roy, scored a comfortable victory over Charles McAtee in Topeka.

Kansans gave an unprecedented fourth term to Democratic Gov. Robert B. Docking, electing him by 63% to 37% over Republican Morris Kay. Democrats also retained the office of attorney general through Vern Miller's 68%–32% win over Robert Hoffman.

Although Republicans lost five seats in the state Senate, they still maintained a two-thirds majority by winning 27 seats to 13 for the Democrats. There were to be 80 Republicans and 45 Democrats in the new House, a switch of four seats from the Republican to the Democratic side.

Three supreme court justices up for affirmation, John F. Fontron, Robert H. Kaul, and Perry Owsley, won handily. The constitutional amendments, two of which related to a unified court system and executive reorganization, were passed. The latter was a repeat submission, since a similar proposal, approved by the electorate in 1970, was nullified on a technicality by the state Supreme Court in 1971.

Legislation. The 1972 session of the Kansas Legislature approved a total state budget approximating one billion dollars. Major acts included a new corporation code, provisions for penal reform, the broadening of the homestead property tax exemption, and the organization of groundwater management districts.

An "age of majority" law was passed, giving persons aged 18–20 the rights and obligations of those aged 21 and older, except for the purchasing and consuming of alcoholic beverages. The Legislature ratified an amendment to the U. S. Constitution guaranteeing equal rights to women.

Highway legislation provided for issuance of a maximum of $320 million in highway revenue bonds, over an eight-year period, to accelerate the construction of superhighways; for a feasibility study of a turnpike from Hutchinson, through Wichita, to a point on the Kansas-Oklahoma border near Arkansas City; and for better billboard controls.

The 1970 Property Tax Lid Act was extended to May 31, 1973. The session's major tax increase bill disallows the deduction of federal income tax payments from state returns by corporations and financial institutions.

NYLE H. MILLER
Kansas State Historical Society

KENTUCKY

Among noteworthy developments in Kentucky in 1972 were productive legislative sessions, good crops, a generally healthy business climate, and an unusual amount of ticket-splitting in the fall elections.

Legislation. Early in the year, Democratic Gov. Wendell Ford presented the General Assembly with a record-breaking budget of $3.525 billion for the next biennium and a program of progressive legislation. The budget was approved, and laws passed included modifications of the state's Sunday-closing law, pay raises for teachers, more funds for mental health, a strong consumer fraud bill, expanded home rule for cities and counties, a wild-rivers bill, a no-fault divorce law, and a generic drug bill. Other new laws removed the sales tax on food, increased the corporate income tax, imposed a severance tax on coal, raised the levy on gasoline, permitted an increase in the rate of interest charged by industrial

loan companies, and increased salaries of legislators and certain other state officials.

During a brief special session in June, the General Assembly liberalized voting laws, redrew legislative and congressional district lines, and conferred strong powers on an Environmental Quality Commission. It also approved the proposed equal-rights-for-women amendment to the U. S. Constitution—the 19th state to do so.

Education. As the fall school term approached, three counties—Christian, Fayette, and Jefferson—faced federal court action in regard to their desegregation plans. A threatened boycott of Fayette schools failed to materialize, and in November a federal judge approved that county's integration program.

Kentucky State College, once an all-Negro school, became Kentucky State University. The recently founded Northern Kentucky State College expanded its curriculum by absorbing the Chase Law School, which formerly had been located in Cincinnati, Ohio.

Elections. In spite of President Nixon's landslide, Kentucky voters chose Democrat Walter D. Huddleston over former Republican Gov. Louie B. Nunn to succeed the retiring Republican U. S. Sen. John Sherman Cooper. Huddleston thus became the first Kentucky Democrat in 16 years to be elected to the national Senate. Except in the 6th Congressional District, where the Democratic incumbent was not a candidate and where Democrat John B. Breck-

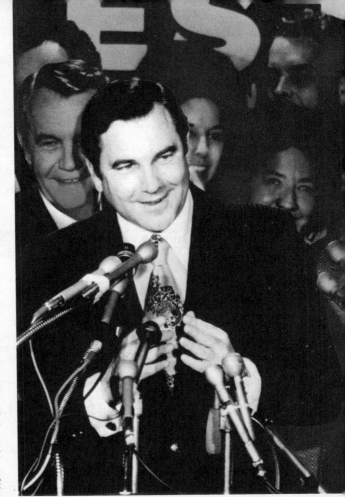

WIDE WORLD

KENTUCKY'S new U.S. senator, Walter (Dee) Huddleston, is the first Democrat in 16 years to win Senate election from the state.

--------- **KENTUCKY · Information Highlights** ---------

Area: 40,395 square miles (104,623 sq km).
Population (1970 census): 3,219,311. *Density,* 82 per sq mi.
Chief Cities (1970 census): Frankfort, the capital, 21,902; Louisville, 361,958; Lexington, 108,137; Covington, 52,535; Owensboro, 50,329; Bowling Green, 36,253; Paducah, 31,627.
Government (1972): *Chief Officers*—governor, Wendell H. Ford (D); lt. gov., Julian M. Caroll (D); secy. of state, Mrs. Thelma L. Stovall (D); atty. gen., Ed Hancock (D); treas., Drexell Davis (D); supt. of public instruction, Wendell Butler; chief justice, Samuel S. Steinfeld. *General Assembly*—Senate, 38 members (23 Democrats, 15 Republicans). House of Representatives, 100 members (72 D, 28 R).
Education (1971–72): *Enrollment*—public elementary schools, 455,000 pupils; 18,168 teachers; public secondary, 263,900 pupils; 11,725 teachers; nonpublic schools (1970–71), 63,023 pupils; 3,340 teachers; college and university, 102,000 students. *Public school expenditures,* $434,000,000 ($650 per pupil). *Average teacher's salary,* $7,817.
State Finances (fiscal year 1970): *Revenues,* $1,263,556,000 (5% general sales tax and gross receipts taxes, $267,-688,000; motor fuel tax, $104,615,000; federal funds, $337,-319,000). *Expenditures,* $1,290,838,000 (education, $511,-693,000; health, welfare, and safety, $208,029,000; highways, $302,360,000). *State debt,* $1,224,078,000 (June 30, 1970).
Personal Income (1971): $10,792,000,000; per capita, $3,288.
Public Assistance (1971): $184,063,000. *Average monthly payments* (Dec. 1971)—old-age assistance, $59.28; aid to families with dependent children, $118.80.
Labor Force: *Nonagricultural wage and salary earners* (July 1972), 952,100. *Average annual employment* (1971)—manufacturing, 248,000; trade, 185,000; government, 180,000; services, 139,000. *Insured unemployed* (Aug. 1972)—13,700 (2.1%).
Manufacturing (1970): *Value added by manufacture,* $4,496,-100,000. Food and kindred products, $629,800,000; electrical equipment and supplies, $593,000,000; nonelectrical machinery, $590,700,000; tobacco manufactures, $430,300,-000; chemicals and allied products, $414,200,000; transportation equipment, $244,900,000.
Agriculture (1970): *Cash farm income,* $972,556,000 (livestock, $517,277,000; crops, $409,479,000; government payments, $45,800,000). *Chief crops* (in order of value, 1971)—Tobacco (ranks 2d among the states), hay, corn, soybeans.
Mining (1971): *Production value,* $925,884,000 (ranks 9th among the states). *Chief minerals*—Coal, $774,734,000; stone, $52,446,000; petroleum, $35,925,000; natural gas, $18,253,000.
Transportation: *Roads* (1971), 69,071 miles (111,156 km); *motor vehicles* (1971), 1,762,517; *railroads* (1971), 3,513 miles (5,653 km); *public airports* (1972), 47.
Communications: *Telephones* (1972), 1,518,300; *television stations* (1971), 10; *radio stations* (1971), 164; *newspapers* (1972), 27 (daily circulation, 769,000).

inridge was the winner, all congressmen were re-elected. One referendum viewed with interest by several communities in the state was the overwhelming approval by voters of Fayette county and Lexington, the county seat, to merge their county and city governments.

Agriculture. Sales of the 1971 tobacco crop continued to bring high prices in the first months of 1972, during which year the crop was expected to be larger, again with satisfactory prices. Evidence of a change in Kentucky's agricultural patterns was given by the state's 1971 cattle sales, which, for the first time, earned higher revenues than those derived from tobacco. An outbreak of hog cholera in August resulted in an estimated loss of about $1 million.

The Economy. Excluding the mining industry, which was troubled by a market slump and criticism of stripping practices, Kentucky's economic outlook seemed bright in 1972. Reports in July showed that state revenues for the preceding fiscal year exceeded estimates by 1.7% and surpassed the preceding year's income by 13.8%. Economists at the University of Kentucky were optimistic, forecasting rising personal income and, except in specific areas, such as mining and agriculture, higher employment as well.

JAMES F. HOPKINS
University of Kentucky

─────── KENYA • Information Highlights ───────

Official Name: Republic of Kenya.
Area: 224,959 square miles (582,644 sq km).
Population (1972 est.): 11,600,000. *Density,* 49 per square
   mile (19 per sq km). *Annual rate of increase,* 3.0%.
Chief Cities (1969 census): Nairobi, the capital, 472,914;
   Mombasa, 235,308.
Government: *Head of state,* Jomo Kenyatta, president (took
   office Dec. 1964). *Head of government,* Jomo Kenyatta.
   Legislature (unicameral)—National Assembly, 158 elected
   members; 12 appointed members. *Major political party—*
   Kenya African National Union (KANU).
Languages: English (official), Swahili (official).
Education: *Expenditure* (1968), 4.8% of gross national prod-
   uct. *School enrollment* (1970)—primary, 1,427,589; sec-
   ondary, 137,008; technical/vocational, 2,136; university/
   higher (1968), 4,967.
Monetary Unit: Kenya shilling (7.143 shillings equal U. S.$1,
   Sept. 1972).
Gross National Product (1971 est.): $1,660,000,000.
National Income per Person (1970): $130.
Economic Indexes: *Industrial production* (manufacturing,
   1968), 143 (1963=100); *consumer price index* (1970), 113
   (1963=100).
Manufacturing (major products): Construction materials, processed agricultural products, petroleum products.
Major Agricultural Products: Coffee, tea, sisal, corn, cassava,
   livestock.
Major Mineral: Salt.
Foreign Trade (1971): *Exports,* $219,000,000 (chief exports—
   coffee; tea; sisal). *Imports,* $516,000,000 (chief imports,
   1969—petroleum and petroleum products; chemicals, motor
   vehicles, iron and steel). *Chief trading partners* (1969)—
   United Kingdom (took 23% of exports, supplied 31% of
   imports); West Germany (12%—8%); United States
   (7%—7%).
Tourism: *Receipts* (1970), $51,710,000.
Transportation: *Motor vehicles* (1970), 119,400 (automobiles,
   100,500); *railroads* (regional total with Tanzania and
   Uganda, 1970), 3,676 miles (5,915 km); *major national airline,* East African Airways (with Tanzania and Uganda).
Communications: *Telephones* (1971), 77,475; *television stations*
   (1971), 3; *television sets* (1971), 20,000; *radios* (1969), 500,-
   000; *newspapers* (1970), 4 (daily circulation, 155,000).

KENYA

Kenya continued on a stable, almost placid, course in 1972. President Jomo Kenyatta, 82 years of age, completed his eighth year as Kenya's first president.

Decline of KANU. Although Kenya's only political party, the Kenya African National Union (KANU), continued to absorb its former opponents in 1972, it had become virtually defunct as a political organization. The party, constantly plagued by factionalism and inconsistency of purpose, had never played the active role in national development that many observers had expected it to play after independence. The decline of the KANU organization became even more apparent after the assassination of its secretary general, Tom Mboya, in 1969. Three years after Mboya's death, no permanent successor had been named to fill his KANU post.

Party elections were scheduled for March 1972 in order to rejuvenate the party machinery. Because of intense competition for party posts, however, the elections were pushed back to May 1 and later postponed indefinitely. On May 12, Vice President Daniel Arap Moi said the elections would not be held until a majority of the people in Kenya became registered as KANU members. With only 338,000 members enrolled at the time of Moi's statement, his announcement seemed to foreclose quick rescheduling of party elections. The acting secretary general of KANU, Robert Matano, charged on July 4 that "tribalism, nepotism, and utter selfishness" within KANU were responsible for delaying its reorganization, and that the party had become nonexistent.

The party machinery is particularly important in Kenya because its smooth operation is generally considered to be essential to an orderly succession in the event of the death of the aged president.

Law and Order. Faced with serious problems of crime, major officials issued several tough statements on law and order during the year. Vice President Moi condemned drug abuse and increasing violence in schools and laid the blame on "volunteer teachers from overseas" and "itinerant tourists, commonly known as hippies." In a speech on the eighth anniversary of independence President Kenyatta focused his attacks on "illicit dealers in ... skins and trophies" and threatened to deport poachers in order to protect wildlife.

In January, after a strong speech against criminals by Attorney General Charles Njonjo, the National Assembly approved a bill providing for the death penalty for armed robbery with violence. Njonjo had previously taken a position in the assembly against such measures.

Economic Development. The 1970–1974 Kenya Development plan placed priority on agricultural development. Agricultural products have provided virtually all of Kenya's foreign exchange not produced by tourism. In mid-1969 a growth rate in the gross national product of 6%–7% had been predicted for 1972. In February, however, Minister for Finance and Economic Planning Mwai Kibaki announced that droughts in late 1971 and early 1972 and unfavorable prices on the world market would probably lower anticipated agricultural production and the rate of economic growth.

On January 12, Kibaki announced a total ban on some imports and widespread restrictions on the availability of foreign exchange for other items. One goal of the import restrictions was the protection of local industries by banning foreign competition. In this connection, the importation of clothing, dairy products, meat, and foodstuffs was reduced. A second goal of the new measures was the conservation of Kenya's scarce foreign exchange through limitation of expensive imports.

The International Development Association announced on January 6 that it would lend Kenya $22 million for a highway project being built in cooperation with Sweden. In April in Nairobi, 37 of the 41 member states of the Organization of African Unity participated in the first All-African Trade Fair.

The Position of Asians. The expulsion of Asians from neighboring Uganda in 1972 raised questions in Kenya about the future of its Asian residents, who constituted about 2% of the population. Kenya's policy has been to protect the rights of non-African citizens, while gradually Africanizing posts held by noncitizens.

The regulations on noncitizen executives and directors of companies were tightened in 1972. The government resisted some political pressure to adopt anti-Asian measures similar to those of Uganda. But in an August 23 speech at Mombasa, President Kenyatta warned all non-African residents to identify themselves with the aspirations of the African people or go back to their own countries.

Foreign Affairs. The key international event affecting Kenya was the continued fighting between its partners in the East African Community—Uganda and Tanzania. As in 1971, Kenya attempted to mediate the dispute by taking a neutral stance.

JAY E. HAKES
Louisiana State University in New Orleans

KHMER REPUBLIC. See CAMBODIA.
KISSINGER, Henry. See BIOGRAPHY.
KLEINDIENST, Richard G. See BIOGRAPHY.

UPI

NORTH KOREANS honor visiting president of Somalia, Mohammed Siad Barre, by holding a mass demonstration in Pyongyang Stadium.

KOREA

The year 1972 saw the first results of the negotiations that South Korea and North Korea began in 1971. Their aspiration for Korean nationhood and national identity led them to a discussion of reunification for the first time since 1948. The two ideological opponents agreed to establish normal relations, even undertaking to rewrite their constitutions. South Korea had its third coup since 1960, this one called the "October restoration."

The year 1972 was the first of the ambitious third 5-year economic plan in South Korea and the second of the 6-year economic plan in North Korea. Both Koreas are looking toward 1976, the last year of their current economic plans, in anticipation of brilliant economic achievements.

SOUTH KOREA

South Korea made conciliatory moves toward North Korea for the first time since its establishment as a separate political entity in 1948.

Under the protective umbrella of the "national emergency decree" of December 1971, and in the absence of the National Assembly, which met on July 3 for the first time in 1972, South Korea conducted secret negotiations with the North.

Exchange Visits. On July 4 an astounding joint communiqué was announced simultaneously by Lee Hu Rak, director of the Central Intelligence Agency of South Korea, and Kim Yong-ju, director of the Organization and Guidance Department of the Korean Workers' party in the North and a younger brother of Premier Kim Il Sung. The communiqué, which became a milestone in the North-South dialogue, stated that Lee visited Pyongyang May 2–5 and met high officials of the North including Premier Kim, and in return Pak Sung Chul, the second vice premier of the North, visited Seoul May 29–June 1 on behalf of Kim Yong-ju and met President Park. The communiqué further noted that the two archenemies agreed to end hostilities and work toward peaceful reunification by transcending differences in ideologies and social systems and by pro-

moting first of all the idea of one nation. The agreement, which consisted of seven articles, established a joint coordinating committee and also pledged both parties to refrain from conducting acrimonious propaganda campaigns against each other.

One of the difficult tasks confronting the two sides was how to eradicate mutual misunderstanding and mistrust. To solve it, at a meeting on October 12 in Panmunjom, both sides agreed to refrain from criticizing each other and to form the Joint Coordinating Committee to implement the accord of the joint communiqué. Consequently the two sides met again in Pyongyang on November 2 and agreed to establish a 10-member Coordinating Committee, which will hold plenary meetings every two to three months besides its monthly administrative meeting. They also agreed to set up a permanent joint secretariat at Panmunjom as well as political, military, diplomatic, economic, and social subcommittees and to discontinue propaganda radio broadcasting from November 11.

All this was groundwork for a "political talk" between the two governments, which alone can bring about the unification scheme. To this effect Tae Wan-son, the vice premier of South Korea, revealed in a press conference on October 22 that political talks will be held in 1973.

Coup. The most dramatic event of 1972 in South Korea was a "coup in office" staged by President Park. Asserting that political parties could not be trusted to push unification talks with the North, he proclaimed martial law on October 17, dissolved the National Assembly, suspended certain articles of the 1962 constitution as well as political activities, imposed domestic press censorship, and temporarily closed all colleges and universities. Except for the National Assembly, all restrictions imposed, including martial law, were lifted by the middle of December. A new draft constitution was announced on October 27, and, in a national referendum held on November 21, the voters accepted it.

The new constitution, which consists of a preamble and 126 articles, plus 11 articles on supple-

A FIRST STEP toward unification of the two Koreas may have been taken when Red Cross delegates from North and South Korea began a series of talks. At left, the delegates meet briefly in Panmunjom.

UPI

mentary provisions, was promulgated on December 27 when President Park was inaugurated as the eighth president of the republic. It is intended to facilitate progress toward impending multilateral initiatives for unification of Korea by establishing a National Conference for Unification, a representative body composed of 2,359 members, who were elected on December 15. Although the National Assembly is to be formed by March 1973 as a legislative branch of the government, the Conference is charged with legal responsibility for eventual Korean unification.

The first Conference was convened on December 23 and elected President Park for an unlimited number of 6-year terms. Park, who had promised only last year to seek no additional terms, was the sole candidate for this new term. Popular criticism of this undisguised dictatorship has not surfaced, perhaps because unification seems to be worth almost any price.

------- SOUTH KOREA • Information Highlights -------

Official Name: Republic of Korea.
Area: 38,022 square miles (98,477 sq km).
Population (1972 est.): 33,700,000. *Density,* 837 per square mile (323 per sq km). *Annual rate of increase,* 2.0%.
Chief Cities (1970 census): Seoul, the capital, 5,536,377; Pusan, 1,880,710; Taegu, 1,082,750; Inchon, 646,013.
Government: *Head of state,* Park Chung Hee, president (took office Dec. 1963). *Head of government,* Kim Jong Pil, premier (took office June 1971). *Legislature* (unicameral)— National Assembly, 175 members. *Major political parties*— Democratic Republican party; New Democratic party.
Language: Korean (official).
Education: *Expenditure* (1969), 21% of total public expenditure. *School enrollment* (1969)—primary, 5,622,816; secondary, 1,701,301; technical/vocational, 259,601; university/higher, 186,675.
Monetary Unit: Won (399 wons equal U. S.$1, Aug. 1972).
Gross National Product (1971 est.): $9,047,000,000.
National Income per Person (1970): $241.
Economic Indexes: *Industrial production* (1971), 432 (1963= 100); *agricultural production* (1971), 199 (1952–53=100); *consumer price index* (1971), 205 (1965=100).
Manufacturing (major products): Textiles, petrochemicals, clothing, processed food, plywood, hair products.
Major Agricultural Products: Rice, barley, wheat, soybeans.
Major Minerals: Coal, tungsten, iron ore, lead, kaolin.
Foreign Trade (1971): *Exports,* $1,068,000,000 (chief exports, 1969—clothing, plywood, textile yarn and fabrics). *Imports,* $2,394,000,000 (chief imports, 1969—nonelectrical machinery, cereal and preparations, transport equipment); Japan (21%—41%).
Chief trading partners (1969)—United States (took 50% of exports, supplied 29% of imports); Japan (21%—41%).
Transportation: *Motor vehicles* (1970), 125,400 (automobiles, 60,700); *railroads* (1970), 2,489 miles (4,006 km); *merchant fleet* (1971), 940,000 gross registered tons; *major national airline,* Korean Air Lines.
Communications: *Telephones* (1971), 633,818; *newspapers* (1969), 43 (daily circulation, 2,060,000).

Red Cross Talks. The immediate practical effect of the agreement was to expedite already deadlocked South Korea–North Korea Red Cross preliminary meetings, which had been conducted since August 1971. At the 24th preliminary meeting at Panmunjom on August 11 the two Red Cross delegations finally reached an accord to hold full-dress talks on August 30 in Pyongyang and on September 13 in Seoul to work out ways of uniting separated families. These first-round meetings, which were conducted by missions composed of 54 members each, were merely ceremonial, with the delegates expressing hope that talks would succeed. It was during the second-round talks, held on October 24 in Pyongyang and on November 22 in Seoul, that both sides agreed to create a joint agency and liaison office at the truce village of Panmunjom to carry out agreements reached to trace 10 million Koreans separated from their families for over 20 years.

NORTH KOREA

North Korea had a relatively tranquil 1972. The year was marked by improvements in foreign relations, especially with South Korea and Japan, and to a limited extent with the United States. North Korea's continuous efforts to seek confederation with the South since November 1960 through "political talk" made headway in 1972; and American representatives visited the North for the first time since the Korean armistice in 1953.

Japanese Exchanges. The Japanese were the most frequent foreign visitors to North Korea. Representatives of most of the large Tokyo newspapers visited North Korea. The English edition of the *Asahi Shimbun,* called the *Asahi Evening News,* on Sept. 28, 1972, reported that Premier Kim Il Sung "outlined a plan under which Korea after unification would not sign military alliances . . . and would aim to become a so-called 'neutral type' country."

It was reported that the ruling Japanese Liberal Democratic party plans to dispatch a high-level mission to Pyongyang in early 1973 for talks aimed at normalizing bilateral relations between Tokyo and Pyongyang. The first North Korean economic delegation to visit Japan arrived in Tokyo on October 21 for a three-week session aimed at expanding trade between the two countries. These movements caused some strain between Japan and South Korea.

——— NORTH KOREA • Information Highlights ———

Official Name: Democratic People's Republic of Korea.
Area: 46,540 square miles (120,538 sq km).
Population (1972 est.): 14,700,000. *Density,* 298 per square mile (115 per sq km). *Annual rate of increase,* 2.8%.
Chief City (1967 est.): Pyongyang, the capital, 840,000.
Government: *Head of state,* Choi Yong Kun, chairman of the Presidium of the Supreme People's Assembly (took office 1957). *Head of government,* Kim Il Sung, premier (took office 1948). *Legislature*—Supreme People's Assembly, 383 members.
Language: Korean (official).
Monetary Unit: Won (1.11 wons equal U. S.$1, June 1972).
Industrial Production Index (1968): 267 (1963=100).
Manufacturing (major products): Steel, metallurgical coke, pig iron and ferroalloys, textiles, cement.
Major Agricultural Products: Rice, soybeans, sweet potatoes.
Major Minerals: Graphite (ranks 1st among world producers, 1970), coal, lignite, iron ore, lead, manganese, nickel.
Foreign Trade: *Chief exports*—Metals, farm products. *Chief imports*—Machinery. *Chief trading partners*—USSR; China.

Education. Beginning with the fall 1972 semester, North Korea increased the length of compulsory education from nine to ten years, a measure adopted during the July plenary conference of the Korean Workers' party. Under this new system, a 6-year-old will get four years of elementary school, four years of junior high, two years of senior high school, graduating at 16.

Constitution. As though to coincide with the changes in the South Korean constitution, North Korea also announced it was rewriting its constitution "with a view to consolidating by law the successes registered in the socialist revolution and socialist construction, and lay down by the law the principles in the political, economic and cultural life and in the military field under the socialist system."

The official North Korean press agency reported that "the draft of a new North Korean constitution had been completed to prepare for the reunification of the divided peninsula." The North Korean government claimed jurisdiction only over the northern part of the peninsula, rather than the entire country, implying that North Korea recognized South Korea's jurisdiction over its part of the country. It appeared from the content and the timing of the two constitutional revisions that there had been at least tacit agreement by the leaders of the two Koreas to recognize each other's authority and to define a political basis for negotiations. The draft constitution was submitted for approval to the first session of the Fifth Supreme People's Assembly, which was convened in Pyongyang on December 25. Elections for both deputies to the Fifth Assembly and members of various levels of local people's assemblies were completed on December 12.

During the first session of the Fifth Assembly, Premier Kim was elected president of North Korea under the new constitution, which also calls Pyongyang the capital and drops the contention in the old charter that Seoul is the true capital.

KEY P. YANG
Korean Area Specialist, The Library of Congress

KOSYGIN, Aleksei N. See BIOGRAPHY.

KUWAIT

The principal concerns of Kuwait during 1972 were centered on the ownership of its oil industry and resources and on the general economic and financial future of the country. World diplomatic changes, especially in regard to Israel, were carefully watched, as were political developments in neighboring Persian Gulf countries and Yemen.

Petroleum. Working through the Organization of Petroleum Exporting Countries (OPEC), Kuwait and four other Persian Gulf states were able to increase the internationally agreed upon average posted price per barrel of crude oil from $2.23 to $2.42.

Total oil production in Kuwait in 1971 rose to 1,068 million barrels, and it was estimated that Kuwaiti oil reserves totaled 78 billion barrels, over 13% of the world's total. Nevertheless, it was rumored that the reserve was considerably less, and moves were taken to limit production. The government set 1 billion barrels as the ceiling for 1972. Aside from the need to conserve resources, this decision reflected Kuwait's belief that oil appreciates in value more surely when left in the ground than when converted into bank balances abroad subject to inflation and currency devaluation.

Also through OPEC, Kuwait joined in demanding joint ownership and participation with the oil companies in lieu of nationalization. On Oct. 5, 1972, in New York, OPEC and the oil companies agreed on a plan for the producing countries to obtain 20% ownership immediately and to control 51% by 1980.

Economics. In May 1972 an Arab Tanker Company based in Kuwait was formed with a capital of $500 million, 51% from the members of the Organization of Arab Petroleum Exporting Countries (OAPEC), and 49% open to public participation. In April the World Bank sold 20 million of Kuwaiti dinar bonds in Kuwait. The Kuwaiti budget for the year 1972–73 was approved at about $1,210 million, and the income from oil was about $1,560 million.

Arab Affairs. Concerned about the success of the newly established United Arab Emirates (UAE), Kuwait was vocal in protesting Iran's occupation of three islands in the Persian Gulf area. Kuwait also formed diplomatic training seminars for personnel from the UAE, as well as from Oman and Yemen. Kuwait participated in mediation of the dispute between the two Yemens, and the Kuwait Fund for Arab Economic Development loaned $3.7 million to Yemen for salt production.

World Interests. Relations with the Soviet Union improved steadily, and high-level visits between Moscow and Kuwait multiplied in 1972. Kuwait contracted for four Soviet-built vessels. In July a delegation from the Kuwait National Assembly visited mainland China.

SYDNEY NETTLETON FISHER
The Ohio State University

——— KUWAIT • Information Highlights ———

Official Name: State of Kuwait.
Area: 6,178 square miles (16,000 sq km).
Population (1972 est.): 800,000. *Density,* 129 per square mile (50 per sq km). *Annual rate of increase* (including immigration gains), 8.2%.
Chief City (1965 census): Kuwait, the capital, 99,609.
Government: *Head of state,* Sabah al-Salim al-Sabah, amir (acceded Nov. 1965). *Head of government,* Jabir al-Ahmad al-Jabir, prime minister (took office Nov. 1965). *Legislature* (unicameral)—National Assembly, 50 members. *Major political parties*—Bedouin party; Merchants party; Arab Nationalist Movement (ANM).
Language: Arabic (official).
Education: *Expenditure* (1969), 11.3% of total public expenditure. *School enrollment* (1969)—primary, 54,418; secondary, 60,985; technical/vocational, 1,733; higher, 1,713.
Monetary Unit: Dinar (0.3289 dinar equals U. S.$1, Aug. 1972).
Gross National Product (1970 est.): $2,750,000,000.
Manufacturing (major products): Petroleum products, fertilizers, chemicals, distilled water.
Major Minerals: Petroleum, natural gas.
Foreign Trade (1970): *Exports,* $1,654,000,000. *Imports,* $625,000,000. *Chief trading partners* (1969)—United States; Japan; United Kingdom; West Germany.
Communications: *Telephones* (1971), 66,551; *television stations* (1971), 2; *newspapers* (1970), 5.

THE NEW YORK TIMES

VOLVO

Boredom is a basic problem of assembly line work. (Above) Workers at General Motors' fast assembly line at Lordstown, Ohio, disrupted production several times, protesting that the rapid pace affected their performance. (Left) At Volvo's plant in Göteborg, Sweden, employees may volunteer to move from job to job, as indicated by the diagram.

LABOR

Employment rose in 1972 but not as fast as desired, while unemployment fell but not as far as hoped. Still 1972 was a year of healthy recovery from the economic retardation of 1970–71.

Everything workers like to see go up went up, including real earnings, productivity, the average work week, and pay. Also, consumer prices cooled off notably after the sharp rises during 1968–70. Only the international trade picture worsened as total imports continued to increase more rapidly than total exports. The persistent trade imbalance ultimately might lead to policies that would adversely affect domestic employment.

In the anti-inflation program, the Pay Board drew responsibility for driving down the size of wage settlements. It began the year as a 15-member panel with equal representation for labor, management, and the public. Within 3 months, labor withdrew. The blowup came on the heels of a West Coast stevedoring settlement in which public and

employer members lined up 8–5 to outvote the labor members and cut back the settlement. George Meany, president of the American Federation of Labor and Congress of Industrial Organizations (AFL-CIO), denounced the board and walked off, accompanied by three other labor members. President Nixon then reduced the Pay Board to a seven-member public unit having five members from the public and one each from labor and management. Frank Fitzsimmons, president of the Teamsters union, remained on the board as the lone labor member. He indicated that he could best serve labor and teamster interests by doing so.

STRIKES AND LOCKOUTS

The Pay Board's standard called for average increases of 5.5%. According to the Bureau of Labor Statistics (BLS), wage increases in major contracts moved downward toward that figure in 1972. The wage increases in contracts covering at least 1,000 workers averaged about 6.6% over the life of the contract in 1972, compared with 8.1% in 1971. First-year settlements, which take account of workers' desires to catch up with inflation, averaged about 7.2%, which was a deep dip from the 11.6% posted in 1971. Construction wage settlements, which had led the parade during the inflationary period, came down even more.

The unions sought shorter contracts in anticipation of an eventual end of the wage control program. BLS data indicated that the life of contracts signed in 1972 averaged a little more than 24 months compared with about 28 months in the same contracts in the previous bargaining cycle.

Collective bargaining in 1972 was light compared with the other two years of the typical three-year bargaining cycle. Union negotiators bargained for about 2.8 million workers under major contracts in 1972, in contrast to almost 5 million in both 1970 and 1971.

Man-days lost because of strikes and lockouts reflect both the fullness of the collective bargaining schedule and the number and size of the deadlocks. In 1972, the bargaining schedule was relatively empty, the number of deadlocks was fewer, and the size of the deadlocks was smaller than in 1970–71. Roughly 21 million man-days were lost in the first three quarters of 1972, compared with 34 million in the same period in 1971 and 44 million in the same period in 1970.

Aerospace. One of the biggest settlements, which covered about 120,000 aerospace workers, actually was concluded in late 1971. The Machinists Union, the United Automobile Workers, and five aerospace companies agreed to contracts that called for average 51-cents-an-hour (about 12%) increases in the first year and 3% increases in each of the next two years.

A Pay Board majority balked at the size of the first-year settlement, as the public and employer members lined up against the labor members. The board directed the bargainers to conclude a new first-year settlement in which the wage increase did not exceed 8.3%. In July, a Federal district court, in response to suits filed by the two unions, accepted the union argument that 34 cents of the first-year increase was actually money due under the previous contract. The federal government appealed the district court decision for the Pay Board. An appeals court verdict was not in as the year closed.

Longshoremen. For the first time in the nation's history, both the East and West coasts were shut down by bargaining deadlocks between shipowners and longshoremen in 1971. The West Coast dock strike, which began in July 1971, was deadlocked over pay and royalties on packing containers and remained that way despite mediation services and a brief intervention by President Nixon in September. In October the Nixon administration reluctantly asked for its first 80-day Taft-Hartley injunction to halt temporarily the West Coast walkout. The injunction became effective Oct. 6, 1971.

In January 1972 the Western dockers resumed their strike. They finally settled with the Pacific shippers in February, following a month of bargaining without either contract or injunction in effect. Before the settlement, President Nixon had received a bill mandating compulsory arbitration of the dispute after the disputants had 40 days to settle it themselves. Faced with this threat, the longshoremen and shippers agreed to a contract that called for 72 cents in the first year, about a 15% increase. This raise was rejected by the Pay Board, which cut it by one fourth. After an attempt to have the severed portion placed in escrow and an abortive court suit, the West Coast longshoremen and the Pacific shippers accepted the board's decision.

The East Coast dock strike began on Sept. 30, 1971. Late in October, the administration was forced to get an injunction to send the East Coast longshoremen back to the docks. The injunction was granted as a 10-day back-to-work order, to which was added 70 more days after hearing. It was the eighth consecutive injunction applied in East and Gulf coast deadlocks.

First settlements on the East Coast were reached in January 1972, before the expiration of the Taft-Hartley injunction. They provided about $1.50 an hour in wage increases over 3 years, with a 70-cent increase in the first year. Another deadlocked point, a guaranteed annual income provision, was resolved by giving shippers more freedom in job assignments. The Pay Board trimmed back the East Coast settlement from 70 cents to 55 cents, and it rejected a request for reconsideration. In June, the union and the East Coast shippers acquiesced in the board's decision.

Construction. Settlements in the building industry, which led the large wage increases of the past two or three years, averaged 6.6% in 1972, down sharply from 10.8% in 1971. First-year increases dropped to an average of 7.1%, compared with 12.6% in 1971.

Unemployment was higher in construction than nationwide in all industries in 1972, and nonunion labor at lower wages was encroaching on available jobs. As a result, a number of local unions agreed to extend their contracts with little or no change in wage rates. Such settlements occurred in Columbus, Ohio; Washtenaw County, Mich.; Mobile, Ala.; Rochester, N. Y.; and in the state of Maine.

Railroads. A bitter 35-year-old dispute between the United Transportation Union (UTU) and the nation's railroads was resolved. The key issue was the job of fireman on diesel locomotives. Since the shoveling of coal was no longer necessary, the UTU emphasized a fireman's contribution to safety by being another pair of eyes and hands on a fast-moving train. Railway officials reasoned that if firemen were not needed for safety purposes on coal-burning locomotives, they were not needed on diesels. Finally in July 1972, the railroads and the

AFL-CIO executive council decided not to endorse any presidential candidate in 1972. AFL-CIO leader George Meany (left) and United Steelworkers president I. W. Abel (center) supported the move, while Jerry Wurf (right), president of the American Federation of State, County, and Municipal Employees, cast his vote against it.

UTU agreed to eliminate the job of fireman on diesel freight locomotives but to retain the job on diesel passenger locomotives. About a fourth of the firemen work on passenger trains. The settlement affects about 18,000 firemen. They were to be dropped from the rolls as they died, retired, or quit. The agreement called for all to retire at age 65.

Automobiles. The United Automobile Workers (UAW) staged a series of hit-and-quit strikes at plants across the country in 1972 in an effort to force General Motors (GM) to change production standards that the union and workers opposed. One of the strikes was a 174-day stoppage at the ultra-modern plant at Norwood, Ohio. General Motors argued that its reductions in the number of men on the assembly line and its pacing of the line's speed served efficiency. While seeking to force GM to alter the standards, the union had to avoid a prolonged drain on the strike fund because the regular round of bargaining in automobile manufacturing is scheduled for 1973.

Airlines. A long dispute between the Machinists Union and National Airlines culminated in a $6 million award of back pay to 947 mechanics and ground-service employees in February 1972. The company and the union bargained the final settlement, which union officials estimated as averaging $6,000 per worker with a range from $500 to almost $10,000.

The dispute began in 1969 when the company tried to reduce the number of workers in taxiing crews, and the union struck. In 1970, a federal appeals court ruled that the workers had been improperly locked out. The U. S. Supreme Court refused to review this ruling.

In June, some members of the Airline Pilots Association struck for one day in an effort to pressure nations to take stern action against aerial hijackers. The stoppage did not yield an immediate dividend. In fact, two of the most hair-raising hijackings occurred in October and November.

Communications. A prolonged strike by the New York unit of the Communications Workers of America (CWA) against the New York Telephone Company ended in February 1972. Telephone installers and repairmen in the local unit made an agreement that slightly exceeded the nationwide agreement reached by other CWA units in July

1971. The pact for the New York area provided $30 a week in wage increases and a union shop, instead of $29 a week and a modified union shop as in the national agreement.

Teachers. Teachers in Washington, D. C., Philadelphia, and other communities struck to enforce their demands in 1972. In Washington, the school board agreed to restore some cut positions, and Congress passed a 12% pay raise. Teachers in Philadelphia returned to work without a contract until the end of 1972 to permit union negotiators to bridge a wide gap between union demands and school board offers. New York City teachers got much of what they asked, thus averting a strike.

Baseball Players. In April, baseball players struck both major leagues for the first time in the history of the sport. The strike was called just before the season opened to build maximum pressure on the owners. It ended in compromise two weeks after it began, a result that eliminated some games from the schedule. The owners compromised over the players' demands for an additional $1.1 million payment into the pension fund by agreeing to finance the medical part of the pension plan and to increase pension payments by using a half million dollars of the increase in pension fund earnings.

TRADE UNIONS

After the Pay Board was created in November 1971, organized labor held a Damocles sword of noncooperation over it. When the Pay Board reduced the West Coast dock settlement in March 1972, the sword fell but the board lived on. Organized labor more or less adjusted to it. The continuing unemployment situation and the subsidence of inflation contributed to the unions' acquiescence.

Frank Fitzsimmons, president of the International Brotherhood of Teamsters, stayed on the Pay Board. George Meany, president of the AFL-CIO, did not endorse a presidential candidate in 1972, although several of its major affiliates did. The labor federation struggled in court with some of its state bodies that wanted to take an active political role. When a federal district court ruled that the Colorado AFL-CIO could participate in the election, the federation asked a federal appeals court to uphold its constitution's provision binding local bodies to executive council decisions.

United Mine Workers. It was a relatively quiet year for labor in 1972 after the early flareup over the dock settlement and the federation's decision to sit out the presidential election. But it was not a quiet year for the United Mine Workers (UMW), as a string of legal disasters shook the union leadership.

On March 31, UMW President W. A. (Tony) Boyle was convicted in federal district court of misusing union funds for political purposes. On June 27, the court sentenced him to 5 years in prison and fined him $130,000. While his sentence was being appealed, he was freed on $179,000 bond.

In another action in June, a federal district court set aside the union's 1969 election in which Boyle was reelected. The judge ordered a new election, which was conducted by secret ballot at local union meetings in December 1972. While the 196,-000-member union was technically without elected leadership, the court appointed the U. S. Department of Labor to oversee financial and other activities of the union carried on by the caretaker leadership. In a long order, the judge closely circumscribed what the union could do. He also laid down ground rules to promote fairness in the new election. The Boyle slate was defeated by a slate led by 50-year-old Arnold Miller, a former president of a UMW local in West Virginia and a former campaign manager for Joseph A. Yablonski, who was killed soon after he lost the 1969 union election to Boyle. Miller's slate took 55% of the vote.

A separate order required payment of $11.5 million in damages to 70,000 beneficiaries of the mine workers welfare and retirement fund because two of the union fund trustees and a bank owned by the union placed pension and welfare funds in non-interest-bearing accounts of the bank.

Mergers. Unions continued to merge and to talk about mergers in 1972. In April, the New York State Teachers Association, an affiliate of the National Education Association, and the United Teachers of New York State coalesced into a new 200,000-member organization. In another merger, a new 130,000-member Graphic Arts International Union was formed from the Lithographers and Photoengravers Union and the Bookbinders Union. The United Papermakers and Paperworkers Union and the International Brotherhood of Pulp, Sulphite, and Paper Mill Workers united in a new 350,000-member United Paperworkers International Union.

Negotiations for possible mergers were conducted by a number of unions. Among them were the American Postal Workers Union (300,000 members), the National Association of Letter Carriers (220,000), and the Communications Workers of America (550,000); the United Steelworkers of America (1,100,000) and District 50, Allied and Technical Workers (165,000); and the Teamsters (2,000,000) and the International Longshoremen's and Warehousemen's Union (65,000).

Unions undertake mergers for many reasons: to avoid jurisdictional disputes; to provide a haven for the members of a union with little potential for growth; to increase financial and organizational power; to accommodate technological changes; and to augment bargaining strength.

Alliance for Labor Action. The Alliance for Labor Action (ALA), created by the Teamsters and the United Automobile Workers, broke up as 1972 began. In 1971, the Alliance's lone convert, the Chemical Workers Union, gave up and returned to the AFL-CIO. The United Automobile Workers stopped making its monthly payment to the Alliance in July 1971 because of a financial crisis brought on by the financial drain of the big 1970 General Motors strike and by the cost of the union's Black Lake recreational and training center for members and their families. The Teamsters stopped making their $100,000-a-month payment until the UAW could resume its contribution. But new year 1972 brought the end of the Alliance.

FEDERAL LEGISLATION

The year 1972 was marked by important labor legislation that did not quite become law.

Presidential Powers. Legislation to give President Nixon new powers to handle strikes and lockouts in the railway, airline, trucking, shipping, and stevedoring industries was shelved at midyear. Spokesmen indicated the legislation would be resubmitted in the next Congress after labor and management had new opportunities to make suggestions.

Wages and Pensions. A bill to raise the federal minimum wage from $1.60 an hour to $2.00 an hour reached the threshold of enactment and then failed to pass when the House and Senate could not resolve differences over a special subminimum rate for young people. Another bill to give workers vested interests in private pensions after a specified number of years of service did not go anywhere.

Exports and Imports. A bill (Burke-Hartke) to reduce the export of U. S. technology and capital and retard the inflow of imports failed despite heavy support from organized labor.

Occupational Safety. The Occupational Safety and Health Act, passed in 1971 to protect the employee in the workplace, became embroiled in an enforcement controversy in 1972. The act, which covers more than 57 million workers in more than

NONFARM PAYROLL EMPLOYMENT IN THE UNITED STATES

Industry	Annual average 1971	October 1972
Total	70,699,000	74,064,000
Mining	601,000	605,000
Contract construction	3,259,000	3,760,000
Manufacturing	18,610,000	19,283,000
Durable goods	10,590,000	11,104,000
Ordnance and accessories	193,000	196,800
Lumber and wood products	579,800	622,300
Furniture and fixtures	459,000	512,700
Stone, clay, and glass products	628,500	676,700
Primary metal industries	1,224,600	1,255,500
Fabricated metal products	1,331,900	1,394,900
Machinery, except electrical	1,791,000	1,885,000
Electrical equipment	1,787,800	1,863,600
Transportation equipment	1,751,400	1,778,800
Instruments and related products	432,000	467,900
Miscellaneous manufacturing	410,600	449,900
Nondurable goods	8,020,000	8,179,000
Food and kindred products	1,753,500	1,817,000
Tobacco manufactures	73,600	76,300
Textile mill products	961,700	1,002,800
Apparel and other textile products	1,361,500	1,351,300
Paper and allied products	687,500	705,100
Printing and publishing	1,087,700	1,086,400
Chemicals and allied products	1,014,800	1,004,500
Petroleum and coal products	189,800	189,600
Rubber and plastic products	582,000	645,500
Leather and leather products	307,900	300,300
Transportation and public utilities	4,481,000	4,520,000
Wholesale and retail trade	15,174,000	15,901,000
Wholesale trade	3,855,000	3,983,000
Retail trade	11,319,000	11,918,000
Finance, insurance, and real estate	3,800,000	3,952,000
Services	11,917,000	12,448,000
Government	12,858,000	13,595,000
Federal government	2,664,000	2,633,000
State and local government	10,194,000	10,962,000

Source: Bureau of Labor Statistics, U. S. Department of Labor.

4 million places of employment, calls for workplace inspections to ensure compliance with the law. Organized employers sought to have smaller firms excluded from the law, whereas organized labor opposed any exclusions. An amendment exempting firms with three or fewer employees was included in the labor-HEW bill voted on economy grounds by the President late in the year.

Job Discrimination. One important labor bill that did pass Congress was the Equal Employment Opportunity Act of 1972. This bill, which survived much debate and maneuvering, granted the Equal Employment Opportunity Commission power to go to court with complaints of discrimination on the basis of race, religion, or sex that it could not resolve through mediation and conciliation. In an important step, state and local government employment, prolific sources of new jobs, were brought under federal equal employment opportunity standards. Cases against states and localities would be brought by the U. S. Department of Justice.

COURT DECISIONS

When a new owner takes over a unionized firm, must he deal with the union and abide by the inherited contract? The National Labor Relations Board (NLRB) answered both questions in the affirmative. A federal appeals court said "yes" to dealing with the union but "no" to abiding by the inherited contract. In *NLRB* v. *Scrivener,* the U. S. Supreme Court agreed with the appeals court. The court reasoned that since the bargaining unit was still largely intact, the union was largely intact. It also reasoned that the provisions of the contract had not been agreed to by the new owner, and hence he need not be bound by them.

If a worker passes information to the NLRB to assist one of its investigations of unfair labor practices, can that worker be fired? In *NLRB* v. *Burns International Security Services,* the Supreme Court ruled that the worker could not. A worker who helps an investigation along is as immune from discharge or other discipline as one who testifies to the NLRB or lodges charges with the board that bring on the investigation. The decision harmonized with the court's predilection for putting the broadest interpretation on specific provisions of the Labor Management Relations Act.

EMPLOYMENT

The economy spawned 2.3 million more jobs by October 1972 than there were a year earlier. The new jobs appeared mainly in state and local government, wholesale and retail trade, services, and manufacturing. These sectors normally pace employment gains. During the height of the Vietnam War, manufacturing posted unusually strong employment gains. With the war winding down, gains in that sector have returned to more normal levels. Although more than 500,000 jobs were created in manufacturing in the year ending in October 1972, this was less than a third of the total jobs lost in that sector during the 1970–71 recession.

More than 87 million men, women, and teenagers were in the labor force in October 1972, and 82.5 million of them were working. The unemployment rate dropped from just under 6% to 5.5% from June to November when it fell to 5.2%.

During the early stages of the 1970–71 setbacks, unemployment among men increased more, relatively, than among women or teenagers. This happened

EMPLOYMENT STATUS OF THE U. S. POPULATION

	Annual average 1971	October 1972
Total labor force	86,929,000	89,591,000
Civilian labor force	84,113,000	87,176,000
Employed persons	79,119,000	82,707,000
Agricultural employment	3,387,000	3,721,000
Nonagricultural employment	75,732,000	78,986,000
Unemployed persons	4,994,000	4,470,000

mainly because men predominated in the hard-goods industries hit first by the slowdown. Conversely, the improved economy put men back to work and absorbed men entering the labor force more swiftly.

Unemployment rates for men averaged 3.9% in the third quarter of 1972, compared with 4.4% a year earlier. Women's unemployment rates were 6% in the third quarter 1972, compared with 5.7% a year earlier. The 16.1% jobless rate averaged by teenagers in the third quarter of 1972 was slightly below the 16.8% posted a year earlier.

Blacks. Black joblessness rose more slowly than white joblessness in the early stages of the 1970–71 recession, causing the relative unemployment of blacks to move a little closer to that of whites. Since the Korean War, black unemployment has been roughly twice as great, proportionately, as white unemployment. During the 1970–71 recession, it was less than twice as great. With recovery, white unemployment fell from 5.5% in the third quarter of 1971 to 5% in the same quarter of 1972. Black joblessness remained about the same—10.1% in the third quarter of 1971 and 9.9% a year later. So the roughly 2-to-1 pattern reestablished itself.

Veterans. Veterans in their twenties who have come out of the service during the Vietnam War have experienced higher unemployment than their nonveteran counterparts. The situation improved in 1972, but veterans' unemployment still remained slightly higher—7.2% in the third quarter compared with 6.3% for nonveterans. Black veterans had the worst employment trouble among veterans—1 in 7 was out of work compared with 1 in 14 among white veterans.

Earnings. After almost no movement in the period from 1965 to 1970, real weekly earnings of workers rose 3.7% in the year ending in September 1972. The improvement resulted from a continued though slower rise in gross earnings and a subsidence in inflation. Though subsiding, inflation remained a fact of life. For instance, a worker who earned $137 in September 1972 could buy no more with it than one who earned about $109 in 1967.

Construction workers continued to lead other rank-and-file workers in gross average weekly earnings, even though they suffered higher relative unemployment than workers in most other industries. In September 1972, construction workers on average grossed $235 a week. They were followed by workers in mining ($193), transportation and public utilities ($191), manufacturing ($157), financial, insurance, and real estate institutions ($128), services ($110), and wholesale and retail trade ($107). In September 1972, the weekly earnings of rank-and-file workers in the private, nonfarm sector— male and female, full-time and part-time, married and single—averaged $139.

ROBERT W. FISHER
Bureau of Labor Statistics
U. S. Department of Labor

LAIRD, Melvin R. See BIOGRAPHY.
LAND, Edwin H. See BIOGRAPHY.

LAOS

In 1972, negotiations between Washington and Hanoi to end the Vietnam War were paralleled in Laos by direct discussions between the Laotian government and the Communist Pathet Lao, the two chief combatants in the satellite war there. However, the possibility of peace served only to increase armed clashes in Laos, as both the government and the Communists sought to capture control of as much territory as possible from each other before the fighting stopped.

The War. The military struggle between the forces of the U. S.-allied regime of Premier Souvanna Phouma and those of the North Vietnamese and their indigenous partner, the Communist Pathet Lao, continued to go badly for the government in 1972. The Communists mounted a sizable offensive against the besieged Souvanna administration late in the year, seeking to extend control to an area approximating four fifths of the national territory.

The challenge to the government occurred on three fronts—the Plain of Jars, in the southern part of Laos near the regional center of Saravane, and in the vicinity of the royal capital of Luang Prabang. The most serious situation was on the Plain of Jars, north of the administrative capital, Vientiane. In early October, the Souvanna regime began a drive to recapture the key plain from the Communists only to have to abandon it a few weeks later. The government offensive met very strong resistance from Communist forces made up primarily of North Vietnamese. Meo General Vang Pao, aided by the CIA and the Thai government, was unable to prevail despite unusually heavy U. S. air support.

The fighting around Saravane was also heavy. As the rainy season ended in October, government forces here, too, vainly attempted to recapture a town largely held by the Communists since mid-1970. The situation near Luang Prabang, residence of the king, deteriorated so much in late 1972 that a dawn-to-dusk curfew had to be enforced. Fighting occurred within 10 miles of the city.

The morale of the government forces lowered visibly during the year. The Communists seemed to fight with greater determination than their adversary as peace appeared to be near at hand.

Prospects for Peace. Neither side in the war in Laos played any role in the negotiations between the United States and North Vietnam in 1972, even though these were the main two external patrons of the rival factions in the fighting. Souvanna Phouma visited Washington in October for talks with President Nixon, but the Laotian leader was informed only of the state of negotiations between Hanoi and the Americans. The apparent tentative agreement reached between the two parties provided that all foreign forces should leave Laos. However, North Vietnam had never admitted that it had military personnel in Laos, and the United States greatly minimized its combat role there.

In mid-October, negotiations were also resumed between the government and the Pathet Lao in Vientiane. At month's end, Souvanna Phouma himself became a participant. Souvanna sought a new Geneva conference—on the model of the one that brought peace to Laos in the early 1960's—as a means of structuring a coalition government and obtaining international guarantees for it. The Laotian leader also called for the departure of North Vietnamese troops. The Pathet Lao primarily sought an end to the U. S. military presence in Laos, including a cessation of American bombing. However, the Pathet Lao did not make a bombing halt a precondition for resumed talks as it once did.

Politics. The complex political situation in Laos was closely related not only to the war and the peace talks but also to economic difficulties in the country. At midyear an unsuccessful attempt was made to force the resignation of the administration of Souvanna Phouma, with onetime rightist minister Phoui Sananikone taking the lead in forming a large bloc of National Assembly members called the "Group for the Protection of the Constitution." Phoui sought to topple the Souvanna government, which includes unfilled seats that have been reserved for a decade for absent and insurgent Pathet Lao representatives. The opposition claimed that Souvanna had acted unconstitutionally when, following National Assembly elections in January, he did not resign and form a new government. A Phoui victory would have created an even greater political polarization of left and right in Laos.

In an unprecedented action in June, the National Assembly voted unanimously to censure Finance Minister Tiao Srisuk na Champassak for his alleged inability to cope with Laos' economic problems.

Economy. The Laotian economy experienced its share of difficulties in 1972. A number of shops in Vientiane closed down—some declaring bankruptcy. Part of the reason for the business decline was the government's increase in the exchange rate between the Laotian kip and the U. S. dollar by 240 kips. Previously, at the old rate of 600 kips to the dollar, currency exchanges could take place on the free market. After the rate change only the Bank of Laos was allowed to exchange currencies.

In May, merchants and students sought to join in a demonstration against the government for its inability to cope with the deteriorating economy. However, they were stopped by the armed forces.

Foreign Policy. Laotian dependence on the United States and American influence in the country continued to be apparent in 1972. U. S. funds from the Food for Peace program and the Agency for International Development were used to support paramilitary elements. American threats to halt aid caused the government to ban opium production and sales. Thai mercenaries, numbering 5,000 early in 1972, nearly doubled during the year. Nonetheless, fear existed that the United States and other allies would abandon Laos to achieve peace in Vietnam.

RICHARD BUTWELL
State University of New York at Brockport

LAOS · Information Highlights

Official Name: Kingdom of Laos.
Area: 91,429 square miles (236,800 sq km).
Population (1972 est.): 3,100,000. *Density,* 34 per square mile (13 per sq km). *Annual rate of increase,* 2.5%.
Chief City (1966 census): Vientiane, the capital, 132,253.
Government: *Head of state,* Savang Vatthana, king (acceded November 1959). *Head of government,* Prince Souvanna Phouma, premier (took office June 1966). *Legislature* (unicameral), National Assembly, 59 members.
Languages: Lao, French (both official).
Education: *Expenditure* (1969), 10.7% of total public expenditure. *School enrollment* (1969)—primary, 216,577; secondary, 13,105; technical/vocational, 1,625; higher, 559.
Monetary Unit: Kip (600 kips equal U. S.$1, June 1972).
Gross National Product (1970): $216,000,000.
Consumer Price Index (1971): 302 (1963=100).
Manufacturing (major products): Cigarettes, textiles.
Major Agricultural Products: Rice, corn, coffee, cotton.
Major Mineral: Tin.
Foreign Trade: *Chief exports*—Tin; timber; coffee. *Chief imports*—Mineral products; food; chemicals; machinery; transport equipment. *Chief trading partners*—United States; Japan; Thailand; France.

GAMA

GAMA

(Above) Supporters of former Argentine President Juan Perón, just returned from exile, gather outside his home, November 18. (Left) Perón, with wife, waves to the crowd.

LATIN AMERICA

The general tendencies in Latin America in 1972 were toward political stability and sustained economic growth. There were only two successful military coups (in Ecuador and Honduras), both bloodless, in a year that saw a marked decline in revolutionary violence. The few terrorist movements that managed to sputter along were deprived of their former support from Cuba, which embarked on a new "good neighbor" course and even began negotiating with the United States for an agreement to curtail airplane hijacking.

While strikes and other symptoms of social and political unrest continued to plague many parts of the hemisphere, governments were seldom shaken by them. Even the reemergence of charismatic former dictators, such as Argentina's Juan Perón, did not greatly disturb the established order. Nationalism remained in vogue throughout the region, and there was no letup on criticism of the United States' Latin American policy, or lack of one.

The economic underpinnings of Latin America's new political stability were reflected in figures released in May 1972 by the Inter-American Development Bank (IADB). The region's economy, according to the IADB, had grown 6.6% during the previous year. While huge Brazil's extraordinary economic

growth rate of 11.5% was a big factor in the regional average, a majority of the 23 Latin and Caribbean nations surveyed showed increases of at least 5%. The highest gains were registered in industrial production, electric power, construction, transportation, and communications. Agricultural production, however, lagged, barely keeping pace with the region's 2.8% rate of population growth, the highest in the world. Nevertheless, Latins had reason to hope that continued expansion of the nonagricultural sectors would provide jobs for many of the region's unemployed, currently more than 25% of the labor force, and better lives for future generations. Only the government of Trinidad and Tobago openly advocated birth control.

Role of the United States. President Richard Nixon announced in January 1972 that no more U. S. aid would go to countries that expropriated American property without prompt and adequate compensation. The move was viewed as a response to actions by the Marxist government of President Salvador Allende of Chile. Except in matters of expropriation, Washington appeared little concerned with Latin America. With no high-level Latin American specialist in the Nixon administration, the U. S. attitude seemed to be shaped by officials considered less than *simpático* by the Latins.

Former U. S. Treasury Secretary John Connally, a Texan associated with the oil industry, was sent on a quick swing through six Latin American countries in June, ostensibly to report on President Nixon's visits to Peking and Moscow. The Latins had not forgotten the Texan's role in the formulation of the new U. S. monetary policy, which they felt had treated them unfairly, nor his statement that the United States could afford to take a tough stand on Latin America "since we don't have any friends left there anyway." On the trip Connally, who speaks enough Spanish to get by, explained the U. S. monetary policy to Latin leaders. He expressed regret that the devaluation of the dollar had cut into their currency reserves and that the current political atmosphere in the United States made it impossible to enact preferential tariffs for Latin American products.

While U. S. aid to Latin America generally declined during 1972, Washington continued to provide 95% of the capital of the Inter-American Development Bank. At a meeting of the IADB Board of Governors in May, U. S. Assistant Secretary of the Treasury John M. Hennessy declared that the United States had come to the "new realization" that economic interests should supercede political, ideological, and security concerns. That declaration came little more than a year after Hennessy's boss, John Connally, had been influential in the removal of Chile's Felipe Herrera as president of the IADB. Herrera had been replaced as bank president by Antonio Ortiz Mena of Mexico and, early in 1972, Henry J. Constanzo, an American, took over as executive vice president, the man really in charge. Constanzo presided over a sweeping reorganization of the IADB, making it more responsive to U. S. demands, including President Nixon's directive that all lending institutions supported predominantly by U. S. funds withhold loans from any nation that unfairly seized American property.

Organization of American States. Latin delegates to the General Assembly of the Organization of American States (OAS), meeting in Washington in April, were clearly unhappy with the stiffening U. S. attitude. OAS Secretary General Galo Plaza

asked the United States for a "concrete definition" of its new policy toward Latin America, noting that many observers were saying that Washington had no policy at all. President Nixon responded by suggesting that the United States preferred to deal with Latin America on a country-by-country basis.

Nevertheless, U. S. Secretary of State William Rogers appealed to hemispheric solidarity in seeking votes to maintain the OAS boycott of Cuba and to defeat a resolution freeing member nations to determine individually their economic and diplomatic relationships with Fidel Castro's regime. The resolution failed, but Peru, Jamaica, Barbados, and Trinidad and Tobago later established diplomatic ties with Cuba anyway.

The absence of U. S. diplomatic representation in Cuba did not prevent Washington from beginning discussions with the Castro regime in November, through the Swiss Embassy in Havana, on an agreement to combat airplane hijackings. At the end of the year it was speculated that U. S. insistence on ostracizing Cuba would soon be abandoned.

While the OAS General Assembly was meeting in Washington, Chile was host to the Third United Nations Conference on Trade and Development (UNCTAD). The conference was dominated by representatives of Latin America and other underdeveloped regions, who denounced the manipulation of international commerce by the Western industrialized nations, the "Group of Ten" that set the policies of the International Monetary Fund (IMF). Later in the year the Group of Ten was expanded by the addition of 10 less developed nations, including Argentina, Mexico, and Brazil.

Brazil and Mexico. Although the purchase of 16 French jet fighters by Brazil in 1972 caused some concern among its neighbors, that nation's burgeoning economic power, stimulated by U. S. investment, was far more disturbing to many Latin Americans. In 1972 the U. S. Export-Import Bank lent Brazil $139 million to build nuclear power plants and $323 million to expand steel production.

During the year the Brazilian government petroleum enterprise, Petrobras, unveiled plans for its first refinery on foreign soil at Dina, Colombia, to be completed by 1976. In the meantime, Petrobras technicians were advising Tennecol, a U. S.-Colombian company, on the possibility of constructing a 270-mile (435-km) oil pipeline from Yara, Colombia, to the Brazilian city of Manaus. Brazil also signed agreements with Bolivia to provide much of the technical and financial aid that the Bolivians formerly received from the United States. An accord between Brazil and Paraguay to develop the hydroelectric potential of the Seven Falls of the Paraná River was protested by Argentina, which feared a drop in the water level of its Río de la Plata estuary.

Brazil's rightwing military government did not let ideology stand in the way of profitable arrangements with Chile or the Soviet Union. Brazilian imports in Chile were up 500% in the first half of 1972, and about one half of Soviet trade with Latin America, excluding Cuba, was with Brazil.

Brazil's closest rival for economic leadership of Latin America has been Mexico, the world's largest Spanish-speaking country. In 1972, Mexico's energetic President Luis Echeverría continued to offer his country as both a model and a source of support for economic developments in Latin America. Mexico, long admired in the region for its political

stability and avoidance of military rule, pleased nationalistic Latin Americans with its firm support for Chile's expropriation of U. S. copper interests. Mexico's government-owned Diesel Nacional signed an agreement in 1972 with the government of Chile to manage two automobile factories in that country. Elsewhere, Mexicans outmaneuvered Brazilians in winning a contract to process lead and copper ores in Peru.

Fishing Controversy. Brazil and Mexico stood together in supporting the claims of most coastal Latin American nations to sovereignty over marine life up to 200 miles (320 km) from their shores. The United States, hitherto adamantly opposed to any exercise of sovereignty beyond a 12-mile (19-km) limit of fishing control, began to soften its stand in 1972. For the first time the U. S. government advised American fishermen to buy licenses, albeit "under protest," from Ecuador and Peru to work within 200 miles of their coasts.

Also during 1972 the United States signed an agreement with Brazil to restrict the number of American fishing vessels, mostly shrimp boats, within 200 miles of the Brazilian coast. No Brazilian licenses were required, however, and the agreement was worded so that there was no explicit U. S. recognition of the 200-mile limit. In November, President Nixon reaffirmed his government's adherence to the 12-mile principle in signing a law that would automatically cut off U. S. aid to any nation that illegally seized American fishing boats.

Ecuador, which was quick to publicize a suspension of U. S. military and economic aid following its seizure of some American fishing boats, was joined by Peru, the world's foremost fishing nation, in vigorously denouncing the United States for clinging to the 12-mile concept. Peru and Ecuador gave conservation arguments to support their stand on the 200-mile limit, citing a need to curb indiscriminate fishing. Both nations strictly control the licensing of their own fishing vessels in order to maintain the delicate ecological balance in the Humboldt Current.

In September and October 1972, in a quirk of nature, the normally frigid Humboldt Current warmed, making the waters off Peru less attractive to anchovies, the mainstay of that country's fishing industry. The government placed a ban on anchovy fishing, to extend perhaps to March 1973, with resulting hardship for Peruvian fishermen. The decline of the anchovy caused Peru to give more attention to the tuna, the fish sought by the American vessels off its shores.

Despite their insistence on recognition of the 200-mile principle, Peru and Ecuador, it was felt, would be willing to accept an agreement with the United States similar to the one Brazil received. With the United States' own domestic fishing industry up in arms over Soviet trawlers sweeping the coastal waters of North America, Washington's resolve to defend the 12-mile concept was clearly weakening.

In the meantime, official representatives of 13 Caribbean countries, meeting in Santo Domingo, Dominican Republic, in June 1972, issued a declaration endorsing a 200-mile limit. They called for an international agreement, preferably on a world scale, to define the lateral boundaries of each nation's "territorial sea," extending 12 miles from the coast, and "patrimonial sea," reaching 200 miles into the ocean.

Subregional Groups. Some progress toward economic integration was made by subregional groups in 1972. The prospects of the Caribbean Free Trade Association (CARIFTA) were bright enough to prompt nonmembers Colombia, Venezuela, Peru, and the Dominican Republic to seek closer ties with countries in the group. The member nations of CARIFTA agreed in 1972 to establish a Caribbean Common Market by May 1973.

The much older Central American Common Market (CACM), however, continued to travel a rocky road. Originally composed of five members, the CACM was reduced to three with the withdrawal of Costa Rica in 1972; Honduras had quit the market in 1970. Costa Rica withdrew in a dispute over exchange rates in September, but the next month made preferential tariff arrangements with each of the remaining members—Guatemala, Nicaragua, and El Salvador—on a bilateral basis. Honduras refused to rejoin the group, but maintained special trading relationships with all of its former associates except El Salvador. Honduras, which is building the largest power plant in Central America, agreed to furnish electricity to Nicaragua, while Nicaragua, one of the world's most efficient cotton producers, sent cotton technicians to Honduras. Costa Rica, the only Central American republic that has diplomatic relations with the USSR, agreed to trade coffee for industrial machinery.

The Andean Group continued to impress observers as the most successful of the Latin American subregional organizations. Trade among its five members—Colombia, Ecuador, Peru, Bolivia, and Chile—has increased 170% since the group was launched in 1969. In 1972 the group announced a timetable for the elimination of foreign control over subregional industries. Under the terms of the agreement foreign-owned enterprises in Chile, Peru, and Colombia must sell 51% of their shares to national interests within 15 years. Outside investors have 20 years to dispose of their majority holdings in Ecuador and Bolivia. Each government, however, will be allowed to make certain exceptions.

The five nations agreed in August 1972 to pool technical personnel and capital for the production of industrial machinery. Also planned is an Andean Court of Justice, which would carry subregional cooperation a step beyond economic integration. In 1972 the United States made a $15 million loan to the Andean Development Corporation, the group's lending institution, to be used to bolster the private sector of the Andean economy.

The Andean nations moved to exploit some important new oil fields in 1972. A rich strike in eastern Peru yielded a high-lubricating, low-sulfur fuel that is ideally suited for the U. S. and Japanese markets. Discoveries in Ecuador have led experts to speculate that a vast pool of petroleum lies beneath the Amazonian wilderness of Ecuador, Peru, and Colombia, and perhaps extends into Brazil. Ecuador has allowed a Texaco-Gulf combine to exploit this field, and has publicly acknowledged that it would be absurd to nationalize an industry that yields $150,000 a day to the government, which is making no investment and taking no risks. Half of Ecuador's royalties have been earmarked for hydroelectric power development, with the other half going to defense.

Relations with the USSR and China. The USSR put Fidel Castro's regime on a tight rein in 1972 and showed increasing interest in South America,

where it maintains diplomatic relations with every nation except Paraguay. A disastrously low sugar harvest in Cuba gave Moscow the opportunity to impose managerial reforms on the Cuban economy. Cuban-supported subversive activity all but ceased in South America, as both Havana and Moscow sought friendly ties with existing governments on that continent.

The USSR granted Peru a $30 million low-interest loan to develop its fishing industry and also sent 50 Soviet technicians. Bolivia accepted a $27 million Soviet loan for modernizing tin and zinc production. President Salvador Allende secured $183 million in Soviet credits for Chile when he visited Moscow in December 1972.

However, Soviet relations with Latin America were not trouble free: both Bolivia and Colombia expelled Soviet citizens for espionage or other "improper activities." Moscow's rival in the Communist world, the People's Republic of China, pledged loans to Chile and Guyana ($70 million and $26 million respectively) and established diplomatic relations with Argentina and Mexico.

Political Developments. The political scene in Latin America was relatively quiet in 1972. The year's most dramatic event was the return of former dictator Juan Perón to Argentina after a 17-year exile. Expressing a desire to "contribute to a solution of the problems that trouble my country," the 77-year-old Perón flew to Buenos Aires from Europe in November on a chartered Italian jetliner. The trip had the blessings of the incumbent Argentine strongman, Gen. Alejandro Lanusse, who hoped that Perón and his followers, estimated to be about a third of the nation's population, would participate peacefully in the presidential elections scheduled for 1973. The Peronists were assured that they could enter a candidate in the presidential race; but they could not run Perón, who did not meet a special "residency requirement" decreed by the government. The Peronists were unable to persuade the government to drop this restriction on *El Viejo* and Perón left Argentina on December 14.

Another former dictator from the 1950's, Marcos Pérez Jiménez, faced a similar obstacle in Venezuela. The country's two major political parties joined forces in the Congress to approve a constitutional amendment which, if ratified by the states, would deny the presidency to anyone convicted of "economic crimes" (Pérez Jiménez has served time in prison for misappropriating government funds). Equally dim were the election prospects of Colombia's former dictator, Gustavo Rojas Pinilla, whose political party fell into disarray after making a dismal showing in local elections in 1972. One dictator from the 1950's appeared certain to win his country's next presidential election: Paraguay's Alfredo Stroessner, in power continuously since 1954, planned to run for reelection again in 1973.

There were elements of the "old politics" in Latin America's two successful military coups in 1972. In February, President José María Velasco Ibarra was forcibly ejected from the presidency of Ecuador for the fourth time. In December, Col. Oswaldo López Arellano assumed power in Honduras for the third time.

Political terrorism declined in Uruguay after President Juan María Bordaberry declared a state of internal war in March and committed his country's army to the struggle against the Tupamaros. This urban guerrilla organization, one of the most effective ever to operate in Latin America, was virtually destroyed by the end of the year. Across the Río de la Plata in Argentina, terrorism reached the peak with the kidnapping and murder of the Italian industrialist Oberdan Sallustro in April 1972. The rate of political violence in Argentina fell off toward the end of the year, as prospects improved for free elections in 1973.

Strikes, demonstrations, and protests plagued the government of Chile in 1972. President Salvador Allende's severest test was a transportation strike that began on October 10 and virtually paralyzed Chile for 26 days. The owner-drivers of trucks, fearing nationalization of their industry, halted operations and were supported by small businessmen and others who feared the consequences of what they considered a headlong rush into socialism. The strike ended on November 5, after the government suspended its plans for a state-owned trucking company and made other concessions to the protesters. The settlement was arranged through the mediation of Chile's army commander, Gen. Carlos Prats, who was appointed by Allende to the post of interior minister during the crisis. On November 30, Allende felt secure enough to depart on a two-week trip to Mexico, Cuba, the USSR, and the United Nations in New York, leaving General Prats in charge of Chile.

Bolivia was also plagued by economic unrest. Workers in La Paz went on strike on November 22 to protest a sudden jump in the cost of living, caused by a 60% devaluation of the Bolivian peso, and to demand corresponding wage increases. The military government of Col. Hugo Banzer responded the next day by putting the city under virtual martial law and forcing many of the workers to return to their jobs. In the countryside, Banzer's army dealt successfully with an attempt by the clandestine ELN (the "National Liberation Army" founded by "Che" Guevara) and militant elements among the Catholic clergy to launch a new guerrilla campaign.

There was lingering guerrilla activity in other Latin American countries, including Colombia and Guatemala. In each case the government appeared to have the situation well in hand.

Even the government of 21-year-old President Jean-Claude Duvalier of Haiti displayed amazing strength in 1972. "Baby Doc" confounded prognosticators by firing his powerful interior minister, Luckner Cambronne, with no dire consequences for his regime. Political order was maintained as Haiti's economy, fueled by U. S. investment, continued to make impressive gains.

Latin Americans paid a high price in freedom for their political stability. In 1972 most Latins lived under authoritarian governments that had little regard for civil liberties. At the Inter-American Press Association (IAPA) meeting in Miami in September it was noted that never had enemies of press freedom in the hemisphere been "so open and blatant and in so many places at the same time." The chairman of the IAPA Committee on Freedom of the Press, Germán Ornés, described the situation in Cuba, Haiti, Paraguay, and Panama as "hopeless." Some press freedom remained in Brazil and Peru, but was fast disappearing under government pressure. According to Ornés, the press was under duress, but still "free," in Chile and Uruguay.

NEILL MACAULAY, *University of Florida*

LATIN AMERICAN LITERATURE. See LITERATURE.

Law

The Supreme Court of the United States, as of April 20, 1972, consisted of (left to right), *front row:* Associate Justices Stewart and Douglas; Chief Justice Burger; and Associate Justices Brennan and White; *back row:* Associate Justices Powell, Marshall, Blackmun, and Rehnquist.

UPI

Major developments of 1972 in the chief areas of law, in the United States and among nations, are surveyed under the headings (1) Supreme Court; (2) U. S. Legislation and Case Law; and (3) International Law.

Other legal developments are reviewed in CENSORSHIP; CIVIL LIBERTIES AND CIVIL RIGHTS; CRIME; DISARMAMENT; POLICE; PRISONS; UNITED NATIONS; and UNITED STATES.

Supreme Court

The 1971–72 term of the U. S. Supreme Court saw the appointment of two more Nixon justices and the apparent beginning of a historic shift away from the liberalism of the Warren Court toward a harder line in criminal prosecutions and a lessened concern for First Amendment rights.

In 1971 Justices Hugo Black and John M. Harlan, the court's two intellectual leaders, had retired for reasons of health, and both had died by the end of the year. President Nixon, two of whose previous nominees had been rejected by the Senate, sent six names to the American Bar Association (ABA) Committee on the Judiciary for clearance. However, the two for whom he indicated a preference, one of whom was a woman, were rejected as unqualified.

Nixon avoided another clash with the Senate by quickly switching to two men of undoubted ability. The first, Lewis F. Powell, Jr., a noted Richmond attorney and former president of the ABA, was confirmed by the Senate with only one dissenting vote. The second, William H. Rehnquist, a Goldwater Republican and assistant attorney general in the Department of Justice, was opposed by Senate liberals but was confirmed, 68 to 26.

The four Nixon appointees, Chief Justice Warren E. Burger and Justices Harry A. Blackmun, Powell, and Rehnquist, all held conservative views and tended to vote as a unit, outnumbering the three liberal holdovers from the Warren Court: William O. Douglas, William J. Brennan, and Thurgood Marshall. This left Potter Stewart and Byron R. White holding the balance of power on the court. White was more likely than Stewart to join the conservatives and so was regarded as "swing man" on the court.

The court handed down 129 signed opinions and two major per curiam opinions on capital punishment and on delegate disputes at the Democratic convention. Only 42 (32%) of these decisions were unanimous. Nineteen 5-to-4 decisions were handed down during the half-term when the court was at full strength. In five, the Nixon appointees dissented; in eight, the dissenters were the three liberals plus Stewart. Douglas cast 66 dissenting votes, Brennan 40, Marshall 36, Burger 31, Blackmun 24, Stewart 17, Rehnquist 16, Powell 14, and White 12.

CRIMINAL PROSECUTIONS

President Nixon's chief criticism of the Warren Court was that it gave too much protection to defendants in criminal cases, handicapping the "peace forces" in society. During the 1971–72 term the court appeared to respond to this charge by several decisions that made the task of prosecution and conviction somewhat easier. The abandonment by Louisiana and Oregon of the unanimous vote requirement for jury convictions in criminal cases was approved (5–4) in *Johnson* v. *Louisiana.*

In other 5-to-4 divisions the court held in *Kirby* v. *Illinois* that a suspect who had been arrested but not charged was not entitled to counsel at a police showup; and, in *Milton* v. *Wainwright,* that an unconstitutionally obtained confession did not invalidate a conviction where there was so much other evidence of guilt that the error was harmless. The court ruled (6–3) in *Adams* v. *Williams* that the police may "stop and frisk" a person on an anonymous tip that the suspect was carrying a loaded pistol. In two 5-to-2 decisions, *Kastigar* v. *United States* and *Zicarelli* v. *New Jersey State Commission of Investigation,* the court held that a grant of immunity under which persons are compelled to testify before grand juries protects them only against subsequent use of their testimony in a criminal proceeding; it does not give them protection from prosecution for any crime mentioned in their testimony.

However, other decisions of the Supreme Court were strongly supportive of the constitutional claims of criminal defendants. The major case was *Furman* v. *Georgia,* where Stewart and White joined the three liberals to hold that the death penalty, as presently imposed, is cruel and unusual punishment in violation of the Eighth Amendment. There was no opinion for the court, each of the five majority justices filing a separate opinion. Neither Stewart nor White argued that the death penalty was un-

constitutional per se but contended that it was cruel and unusual under present practices, because the penalty is capriciously imposed on a "random handful" of convicted persons while many others guilty of crimes equally serious escape with lesser punishment.

In a major defeat for the Nixon administration, the court held unanimously that there is no inherent executive power to wiretap alleged subversives. By a 5-to-4 vote the court ruled in *Gelbard* v. *U. S.* that a witness may refuse to testify before a grand jury unless the government demonstrates that the evidence that prompted the witness to be called was not obtained by illegal wiretapping.

The court held in *Peters* v. *Kiff* (6–3) that a white man may challenge his conviction on the ground that Negroes were systematically excluded from the grand jury that indicted him, and in *Alexander* v. *Louisiana* (9–0) it required state officials to assume the burden of showing that their selection of grand jurors was not racially discriminatory. In *Argersinger* v. *Hamlin* the court was also unanimous in holding that counsel, already required to be furnished by the state to indigent defendants in serious criminal cases, must also be provided even for petty crimes if any period of imprisonment is involved; and in *Morrissey* v. *Brewer* that a hearing must be held when parole is revoked.

FIRST AMENDMENT RIGHTS

In three important decisions, the court denied First Amendment claims by 5-to-4 votes; the majority in each instance was composed of the Nixon appointees plus White. *Branzburg* v. *Hayes* held that the First Amendment does not entitle newsmen to refuse to testify before a grand jury concerning information secured in confidence. Press spokesmen bitterly complained that this violates press freedom and that the ruling makes reporters investigative arms of the government. The same lineup of justices held in *Lloyd Corp.* v. *Tanner* that a large shopping center may bar the distribution of pamphlets on public issues within its limits.

A third 5-to-4 ruling (*Laird* v. *Tatum*) dismissed a suit seeking to enjoin the Army from carrying on surveillance of civilian political activities. The fact that the military was maintaining files and collecting information on many prominent American officials and other politically active citizens, on the apparent theory that such data would help in dealing with possible civil disorders, had caused great concern when it was revealed in 1971. But the court majority held that there was no justiciable controversy since there was no showing of past or future harm to any specific individual.

Other decisions were more favorable to First Amendment claims. The court held unanimously in *Healy* v. *James* that a state college may not deny campus recognition and privileges to students wishing to form a local chapter of Students for a Democratic Society (SDS) without some evidence that they intend to engage in disruptive activities.

The obscenity front was quiet, as three major cases were postponed until the following term. The court did hold in *Rabe* v. *Washington* that there was no statutory basis for punishing the owner of a drive-in theater showing X-rated movies that could be seen from outside the fence by passing motorists and neighborhood children. The conviction of a lecturer on contraception, who in the course of his lecture gave away samples of contraceptive materials, was reversed in what some justices regarded as a First Amendment case but which the court treated as an equal protection case because the statute treated the rights of married and unmarried persons differently (*Eisenstadt* v. *Baird*).

The court entered a new field—academic tenure —with two decisions. *Perry* v. *Sindermann* held unanimously that nonrenewal of the contract of a professor employed for ten years in a state college system, if based on his criticism of the college administration, was a denial of his freedom of speech and that, even in the absence of a tenure system, he was entitled to a hearing if he could show that reemployment was the common practice in the college. *Board of Regents* v. *Roth,* involving failure to reemploy after a one-year probationary college appointment, held there was no property interest in employment and no hearing requirement.

EQUAL PROTECTION

The court held (6–3) that the Harrisburg, Pa., Moose Lodge, which bars Negro members, as a private club was also free to bar Negroes from food and beverage service as guests, and that the state was not a party to this discrimination by reason of having granted a liquor license to the club. One month later the Pennsylvania supreme court ruled that since the club permitted white nonmembers to use its facilities, it was no longer a private club and so could not discriminate against blacks.

In spite of President Nixon's strong opposition to school busing to achieve racial balance, the court generally declined to interfere with court-ordered desegregation plans. In two cases, *Wright* v. *Emporia* and *U. S.* v. *Scotland Neck Board of Education,* it struck down efforts by predominantly white Southern cities to secede from largely black county school systems. The vote in the Emporia, Va., case was 5 to 4—the first school segregation case in which the court was not unanimous. The court let stand a lower court decision declaring unconstitutional the sale of an unused school building in Alabama to an all-white private academy, and affirmed a lower court holding that private schools may be denied tax exemption if they exclude blacks.

Although the Equal Rights Amendment had not yet been ratified, the court began to apply the equal protection clause against discrimination based on sex. In *Reed* v. *Reed* an Idaho law giving preference to males in the appointment of administrators of estates was voided, and in *Drewrys Ltd.* v. *Bartmess* a corporation was told its compulsory retirement age for women could not be lower than that for men. But the ban on discrimination cut both ways, because the court held in *Stanley* v. *Illinois* that an unwed mother could not be given preference over an unwed father in the custody of children, and, in *Pan American World Airways* v. *Diaz,* that airlines were forbidden to impose a "women only" qualification for the job of flight steward. On the other hand, the court ruled that a male homosexual's rights were not violated when he was denied a promised job as librarian in a state university after he applied for a license to marry another man.

The court, in *Weber* v. *Aetna Casualty and Surety Co.,* continued its recent interest in equal protection for illegitimate children, declaring unconstitutional (8–1) a Louisiana law that permitted legitimate but not illegitimate children to receive full workmen's compensation benefits because of the work-connected death of their parents.

Welfare provisions that had been attacked as discriminatory were upheld, 5 to 4, in *Jefferson* v. *Hackney.* The case concerned persons in the aid to dependent children program in Texas, 87% of whom were blacks or Chicanos. These recipients were paid at the rate of 75% of their actual need, whereas the other Social Security assistance programs in the state (for the aged, disabled, and blind), whose beneficiaries were predominantly white, were funded at rates of 95% and 100% of recognized need.

ELECTIONS AND VOTING

In an unusual special session on July 7, 1972, the court declined (6–3) to get involved in disputes over seating of delegates to the Democratic national convention on the ground that the convention itself should decide these issues. The court took a similar hands-off position in refusing to invalidate the loyalty oath required by Ohio for minority parties to get on the ballot or to invalidate the 1971 state legislative elections in Mississippi because at-large elections in urban counties had prevented black voters from electing black legislators.

The Supreme Court did intervene in the elections process in two important cases. In *Bullock* v. *Carter* a Texas law requiring candidates in primary elections to pay filing fees as high as $8,900 was unanimously voided as a denial of equal protection. In *Dunn* v. *Blumstein* the Tennessee voting eligibility requirement of residence in the state for one year and in the county for three months was held unconstitutional, over a dissent by the chief justice. The court considered 30 days ample time for the administrative tasks of registering new voters.

RELIGION

The court held that official action had denied free exercise of religion in several cases. Members of the Amish religious sect have had trouble in several states for refusing to send their children to public schools past the eighth grade. They contend that further education is unnecessary for the rural life they lead in their self-contained communities and that it would place the children in a worldly environment hostile to Amish religious beliefs. Wisconsin's effort to compel school attendance was declared unconstitutional in *Wisconsin* v. *Yoder.*

The court, in *West Morris Regional Board of Education* v. *Sills,* upheld a New Jersey law requiring local school boards to provide bus transportation for pupils to private and parochial schools, but, in *Brusca* v. *State Board of Education,* also approved the refusal of Missouri to spend public funds for church-related schools. In the latter case it had been argued that the refusal of the state to assist sectarian schools violated the religious freedom of parents who wished to send their children to such schools.

LEGISLATIVE IMMUNITY

In two controversial cases the court limited congressional immunity from legal proceedings, in spite of the constitutional provision that for "any speech or debate" congressmen "shall not be questioned in any other place." The first case involved the action of Sen. Mike Gravel of Alaska in reading portions of the secret "Pentagon Papers" into the record at a Senate committee meeting and then arranging for their publication by a Boston firm. A grand jury subpoenaed one of the senator's aides and questioned him about how the papers had been obtained. By a 5-to-4 vote the court ruled that, although congressional immunity covered the legislative activities of a congressional aide, neither the senator nor his aide could claim immunity from testifying about the arrangements for publication of the papers, which was not considered a necessary part of the legislative function.

The second case concerned the conviction of Daniel B. Brewster, then senator from Maryland, for accepting money to influence his vote on some legislative proposals. A 6-to-3 decision held that congressional immunity did not protect against criminal prosecution for bribery.

BUSINESS REGULATION

In *Flood* v. *Kuhn* the court reaffirmed (5–3) its 1922 ruling that professional baseball is exempt from the antitrust laws. The exemption admittedly is irrational, but the court majority thought it should be ended by congressional, rather than judicial, action. In *Laird* v. *Nelms,* the Federal Tort Claims Act was held not to authorize suits against the government for damages caused by sonic booms of jet aircraft.

Environmentalists lost several cases. The Sierra Club was held (4–3) to lack legal standing to protest the proposed Disney development in Mineral King Valley, Calif., in the absence of a showing that its members would be directly affected. Appeals to block construction of the pumped storage electric plant at Storm King Mountain on the Hudson River were rejected, 8 to 1. In *Minnesota* v. *Northern States Power Co.,* the states were forbidden (7–2) to establish stricter radiation-control standards for nuclear power plants than those set by the Atomic Energy Commission.

C. HERMAN PRITCHETT
University of California, Santa Barbara

U. S. Legislation and Case Law

Consumer product safety, civil rights, "no-fault" automobile insurance, and a startling phase of copyright were involved in important legislative and case law developments in 1972.

Federal Legislation. Reflecting a rising public concern, a new federal Consumer Product Safety Act created an independent regulatory commission with authority to establish and enforce standards for potentially hazardous products that are used by consumers in households or schools, in recreation, or "otherwise." The commission can ban the sale of products that are not "reasonably safe." In a sense, this is a companion to another law authorizing the secretary of transportation to ensure that passenger car bumpers be so constructed as to provide "maximum feasible" protection.

A similar concern about "noise pollution" resulted in the Environmental Protection Agency being authorized by law to establish limits on noise from interstate trucks, buses, and trains, and on irritating noise devices such as jackhammers, compressors, and motorcycles. It was directed to study the feasibility of regulating airplane and airport noises.

The Civil Rights Act of 1964 forbade discrimination in employment on grounds of race, color, religion, sex, or national origin. In March 1972 the act was amended to include educational institutions. The Equal Pay Act of 1963 was amended in June 1972 to include professional and administrative employees as well.

The spiraling costs of campaigning for public office, especially via television, radio, and newspapers, have been characterized as a dangerous barrier to informing the voters. To halt this spiral, Congress had enacted (1971), and the president approved (1972) the Federal Election Campaign Act. This statute, which includes criminal penalties for violation, limits the amounts these media may charge qualified candidates for public office, and also limits ($50,000 for president, $35,000 for senators, and $25,000 for representatives) the expenditures of candidates for federal office from their own personal or immediate family funds.

No-Fault Legislation. The U. S. Congress in 1972 had a number of "no-fault" automobile insurance bills in committee: for example, the prescribing of minimum standards for state "no-fault" laws, and the establishing of a deadline beyond which a federal "no-fault" law would automatically take effect if the state has failed to pass one.

Of the 43 state legislatures that convened during 1972, "no-fault" measures were considered in 37 of these bodies. However, only the states of Connecticut and New Jersey adopted such laws, thus joining Puerto Rico, Massachusetts, Illinois, Delaware, Florida, and Oregon, all of which have statutory "no-fault" plans.

Case Law. A decision filed Feb. 16, 1972, by Commissioner James F. Davis in the U. S. Court of Claims, in *Williams & Wilkins Company* v. *The United States* marks what may be a significant turning point in how the courts will respond to the new technological developments in photocopying, particularly in libraries. The import of the decision is that a library that makes a photocopy of a copyrighted work in its collection for scientific or scholarly purposes is liable in damages for copyright infringement. Under Title 17 of the U. S. Code, in cases of copyright infringement the minimum statutory damages will be at least $250 for each infringement.

The commissioner actually held that the publisher could recover "reasonable and entire" compensation. The decision aroused the research and academic communities, for it will have a serious adverse impact on library service. The U. S. Justice Department is appealing to the full seven-member Court of Claims for a reversal of the decision, and it appears that if the court affirms the commissioner's decision, the U. S. Supreme Court will be petitioned to review it. (See also LIBRARIES.)

May an aggrieved party bring a civil action for damages against federal officers for violation of his Fourth Amendment rights? The U. S. Court of Appeals for the Second Circuit believes so. Hence, federal officers unconstitutionally arresting and searching alleged violators of narcotics laws are not immune from damage suits, although they may establish the defense that they acted in the matter in good faith and with reasonable belief in the validity of their action. (*Bivens* v. *Six Unknown Named Agents of the Federal Bureau of Narcotics.*)

In *Plumley* v. *Klein,* the Michigan supreme court for the first time permitted a child to maintain a negligence action against his or her parent. The court added: "Like our sister states, . . . , we note two exceptions to this new rule of law (1) where the alleged negligent act involves an exercise of reasonable parental authority over the child, and (2) where the alleged negligent act involves an exercise of reasonable parental discretion with respect to the provision of food, clothing, housing, medical and dental services, and other cases."

In *Brooks* v. *Robinson,* Indiana similarly overruled its established rule and abolished interspousal tort immunity.

The right of indigents to counsel was considered by the courts with varying results. In a child neglect proceeding, *In re Ella R. B.,* the New York Court of Appeals ruled that an indigent parent was entitled to legal assistance, especially as the parent could not only be faced with a criminal charge later, but also risked losing the child. But a North Carolina statute prohibiting indigents from waiving their right to counsel was ruled unconstitutional by the state supreme court because it did not equally apply the prohibition to affluent defendants (*State* v. *Mems*).

The constitutionality of New York's abortion law was upheld by the New York Court of Appeals on the theory that an embryo is not a legal person, entitled to a right to life under the constitutions of New York and the United States (*Byrn* v. *N. Y. C. Health & Hospitals Corp.*).

Courts. The 1972 Qualification for Jury Service Act changed the minimum age qualification from 21 years to 18 years. A six-member jury was upheld on March 6 by the U. S. Court of Appeals for the Ninth Circuit in *Colgrove* v. *Battin.* The court held that a six-member jury was not violative of the Seventh Amendment, and sustained a local court rule announced by the U. S. District Court for the District of Montana, following similar action by some 34 other district courts. In this context, the Judicial Conference of the United States, meeting in April, voted to approve legislation then pending in Congress for reduction in sizes of juries from 12 to 6 in federal civil cases.

JULIUS J. MARKE
New York University

ANGELA DAVIS, tried in California for complicity in the murder of a San Rafael judge, was acquitted.

International Law

The major developments in international law in 1972 occurred at the World Court, in arms control, and in negotiations on hijacking and terrorism.

World Court. One case was decided by the International Court of Justice during 1972, and three new cases were filed. This left the court with more pending business than it usually has at year's end.

On August 18 the court decided a case brought in 1971 by India against Pakistan arising out of the hijacking of an Indian commercial aircraft and its destruction in Pakistan. India had banned overflights of its territory by Pakistani aircraft after the hijacking. Pakistan had then brought the matter to the Council of the International Civil Aviation Organization (ICAO), charging that the Indian overflight ban violated treaties in force between the two states. India objected to the jurisdiction of the ICAO Council and sought to appeal the council's decision upholding its jurisdiction.

The court held, first, that it had jurisdiction to hear India's appeal, and, second, that the ICAO Council had jurisdiction to decide the overflight dispute. On both points, the court strongly affirmed that the party contesting the jurisdiction of an international organ to hear a dispute that is brought to it under the jurisdictional clause of a treaty cannot avoid review by alleging that the treaty had been suspended or terminated. The court considered that otherwise the parties "would be in a position themselves to control that competence, which would be inadmissible." The overflight dispute was accordingly returned to the ICAO Council for consideration on the merits.

Two of the new cases filed in 1972 challenged the extension by Iceland of its exclusive fisheries jurisdiction from 12 to 50 nautical miles, effective Sept. 1, 1972. In both cases at the request of the applicant states, the United Kingdom and the Federal Republic of Germany, respectively, the court issued temporary orders on August 17 restraining Iceland from enforcing its new rules against vessels of the applicant states pending final decision of the cases. Iceland denied the court's jurisdiction and did not appear at the preliminary hearings on the ground that the agreements relied upon by the applicants had terminated.

Iceland has since put the 50-mile limit into force and has interfered in some respects with British fishing operations. Iceland has not made clear its intentions as to the next phase in the cases, which is limited by order of the court to the question of the court's jurisdiction to hear the disputes. But in view of the court's holding on the treaty termination questions raised in the *India* v. *Pakistan* case reported above, Iceland's failure to appear would not block a decision on the court's jurisdiction, and thus Iceland could be expected to participate in this phase of the case.

The third case filed in 1972 sought the review through a special General Assembly committee of a judgment of the UN Administrative Tribunal on a claim brought against the United Nations by a former official of the UN Development Programme.

Arms Control. Important links were added to the treaty structure of international arms control agreements during 1972. The Biological Weapons Treaty, which totally bans the development, production, acquisition, and retention of biological agents and toxins and the means of delivery, was signed on April 10 by more than 70 nations at Washington, London, and Moscow. The 1971 Seabed Weapons Treaty, which banned nuclear weapons from the seabed and the ocean floor, entered into force on May 18. Finally, on May 26, the United States and the Soviet Union signed two agreements resulting from the bilateral Strategic Arms Limitation Talks (SALT); the Treaty on the Limitation of Anti-Ballistic Missile (ABM) Systems; and an Interim Agreement on the Limitation of Strategic Offensive Arms. The agreements entered into force on October 3.

The ABM Treaty was a permanent arrangement intended to put an end to development and deployment of ABM systems. It limited such systems to two widely separated deployment areas in each country, one for the defense of the national capital, the other for the defense of ICBMs. The overall limit was 200 ABM launchers and 200 ABM missiles for each party, to be verified by national technical means consistent with international law.

The Interim Agreement was a temporary freeze on strategic offensive weapons systems designed to hold the line while SALT continued. It was intended to last for five years, unless replaced earlier by a more complete limit on strategic offensive arms.

Both agreements contained the standard withdrawal clause in arms control agreements. Each party may withdraw on six months notice "if it decides that extraordinary events related to the subject matter [of the agreement] have jeopardized its supreme interests." For the first time, however, each party has undertaken not to interfere with the other's verification efforts and not to use concealment measures to impede verification.

Hijacking and Terrorism. Attacks on diplomats, seizures of airline passengers as hostages, the kidnapping and murder of 11 Israeli Olympic Athletes and coaches at Munich, and indiscriminate terrorist attacks on civilians led to strong pressure during 1972 for action against hijacking and terrorism.

The UN International Law Commission completed work on a draft treaty under which states would agree to prosecute or to extradite all persons who attack or kidnap diplomats. In this respect the treaty paralleled the 1970 ICAO hijacking and the 1971 ICAO aircraft sabotage conventions. Under all three treaties, the wrongful act was termed an offense of international significance such that all states ought to have jurisdiction to prosecute, and no state ought to provide a safe haven.

Considering that not all states have been willing to accept the prosecute-or-extradite obligations of the ICAO conventions, proposals made in 1972 called for joint action against states that aid, encourage, or give sanctuary to hijackers or saboteurs. Draft articles were strongly pressed at ICAO legal meetings, aiming to establish a process that could lead to collective suspension of all international air services to and from a state that failed to take effective action against hijackers and saboteurs. Finally the United States proposed a new treaty applying the prosecute-or-extradite principle to persons who kill, seriously injure, or kidnap civilians in a foreign state with the aim of harming, or forcing concessions from a state or an international organization. Discussions of this proposal were expected to produce a treaty on international terrorism in 1973. (See special feature on Skyjacking beginning on page 46.)

DANIEL G. PARTAN, *Boston University*

LEBANON

The continuing growth of the economy in 1972, the general elections for the Chamber of Deputies in April, the protracted cabinet crisis, and the government's failure to remedy student dissatisfaction were the dominant domestic factors in President Suleiman Franjieh's second year in office. However, domestic politics were overshadowed by the consequences of Lebanon's position as the Palestinian guerrillas' primary base of operations for attacks against Israel.

Guerrillas and Israel. The effectiveness of Israeli reprisal raids against Lebanese-based guerrillas resulted in a January 1972 agreement between Lebanese Premier Saeb Salam and Palestine Liberation Organization leader Yasir Arafat. The guerrillas agreed to consult with the Lebanese government on future operations, giving the government the authority to veto those operations if it felt that they would provoke Israel. The settlement reflected the guerrillas' need to avoid a showdown with the Lebanese government, since Lebanon was the last country in which the Palestinians enjoyed a semblance of autonomy of action against Israel. Although these agreements reduced the number of violations of Israeli territory originating in Lebanon, they did not do anything to curb the activities of more extremist Palestinian groups that continued to operate, with grave implications, out of the Lebanese capital.

Tel Aviv and Munich. Two attacks on Israel perpetrated by Palestinian extremist groups with headquarters in Beirut served to provide the major crises for Lebanon and the Middle East in 1972. On May 30, three Japanese gunmen, sent by the leftist Popular Front for the Liberation of Palestine, opened fire on civilians at Tel Aviv's Lod Airport, killing 26 and wounding 76. An international crisis followed. Israel held Lebanon responsible for the attack, called unsuccessfully for an international boycott of the Beirut airport, and launched reprisals into southern Lebanon that killed as many Lebanese civilians as guerrillas.

In the aftermath, Salam and Arafat were compelled to conclude new agreements on the terms governing the commandos' presence in Lebanon. The June agreements called for the cessation of attacks against Israel from Lebanese territory. The major question facing both the Palestinians and the Lebanese was whether or not the settlement could be enforced. Their doubts were substantiated on Sept. 5, when members of the underground "Black September" group captured 11 members of the Israeli Olympic team in Munich and held them hostage, demanding the release of Israeli-held guerrillas. The ensuing death of the 11 Israelis placed Lebanon's security in jeopardy as Israel again held President Franjieh's administration responsible. On September 8 and 16, Israel launched massive air and land strikes against southern Lebanon. The latter attack resulted in a temporary occupation of Lebanese territory and a confrontation with the Lebanese army. Sweeping through 15 villages and 130 square miles (337 sq km) of Lebanon, the Israeli attack compelled President Franjieh to declare a state of national emergency, which lasted until October 4.

Diplomatically, Lebanon's relations with the West were compromised as European governments began a crackdown on Arab residents and the United

——————— LEBANON • Information Highlights ———————

Official Name: Republic of Lebanon.
Area: 4,015 square miles (10,400 sq km).
Population (1972 est.): 3,000,000. *Density,* 694 per square mile (268 per sq km). *Annual rate of increase,* 2.9%.
Chief Cities (1964 est.): Beirut, the capital, 893,000 (metropolitan area); Tripoli, 127,600.
Government: *Head of state,* Suleiman Franjieh, president (took office Sept. 1970). *Head of government,* Saeb Salam. *Legislature* (unicameral)—Chamber of Deputies, 99 members. *Major political groups*—Maronite Christians; Sunnite Muslims; Shiite Muslims; Greek Orthodox.
Languages: Arabic (official), French, English.
Education: *School enrollment* (1968)—primary, 425,840; secondary, 134,724; technical/vocational, 2,103; university/higher, 33,587.
Monetary Unit: Lebanese pound (3.01 pounds equal U. S.$1, Sept. 1972).
Gross National Product (1970 est.): $1,525,000,000.
National Income per Person (1968): $487.
Consumer Price Index (1971): 109 (1966=100).
Manufacturing (major products): Processed foods, textiles, petroleum products, tobacco products, cement.
Major Agricultural Products: Fruits, vegetables, tobacco, wheat.
Major Mineral: Salt.
Foreign Trade: *Exports* (chief exports, 1969—fruits and vegetables, chemicals, transport equipment, nonmetallic mineral manufactures). *Imports* (chief imports, 1969—food and live animals, chemicals, textile yarn and fabrics, nonelectrical machinery). *Chief trading partners* (1969)—Saudi Arabia (took 20% of exports, supplied 2% of imports); Syria (9%—5%); United States (4%—10%); United Kingdom (4%—7%).
Tourism: *Receipts* (1970) $131,500,000.
Transportation: *Motor vehicles* (1970), 152,600 (automobiles, 136,000); *railroads* (1970), 259 miles (417 km); *merchant fleet* (1971), 127,000 gross registered tons; *major national airline,* Middle East Airlines/Airliban.
Communications: *Telephones* (1971), 192,000; *television stations* (1971), 9; *television sets* (1971), 250,000; *radios* (1970), 600,000; *newspapers* (1970), 52.

States vetoed a UN Security Council resolution calling for cessation of Israeli attacks. The remainder of the year was spent in an attempt by the Lebanese government to repair its relations with the West and to redefine its relationship with the Palestinian resistance movement.

Domestic Developments. The three-stage elections held April 16, 23, and 30 for the 99 parliamentary seats were the first under Suleiman Franjieh's presidency. The seats were hotly contested—there were 79 candidates for Beirut's 20 seats—with candidates representing the Lebanese political spectrum from the new generation left to the traditional right. The results were somewhat surprising. Many administration-backed men failed, and a number of young leftists won. Combining with the traditional left, led by Kamal Jumblat, these younger deputies gave added support to traditional anti-Salam forces.

Opposition to Premier Salam's cabinet centered on several issues, including a government proposal to give the administration greater control over the organization and activities of political parties, and on Salam's October 2 dismissal of Henri Edde, the minister of education. Edde's dismissal accentuated the year-long dissatisfaction with the government's education policy. Following teachers' strikes in January and massive street demonstrations and violence in April, Salam had agreed to the students' demands, but by the end of the year had not implemented the desired reforms.

In the economic sphere, Lebanon looked to another year of progress. Realizing a $3 million annual increase in its balance of payments, Lebanon announced a $2.4 billion, six-year economic and social development plan in January. Losses caused by the closure of the Jordanian border to goods shipped from Lebanon across Syria and on to Arab markets were offset by increased trade with the Soviet Union and western Europe.

F. NICHOLAS WILLARD
Georgetown University

————— LESOTHO • Information Highlights —————

Official Name: Kingdom of Lesotho.
Area: 11,720 square miles (30,355 sq km).
Population (1972 est.): 1,100,000. *Density,* 88 per square mile (34 per sq km). *Annual rate of increase,* 1.8%.
Chief City (1966 census): Maseru, the capital, 19,000.
Government: *Head of state,* Moshoeshoe II, king (acceded March 1960). *Head of government,* Chief Leabua Jonathan, prime minister (took office April 1965); suspended the constitution on Jan. 30, 1970.
Languages: English, Lesotho (both official).
Education: *Expenditure* (1967), 21.6% of total public expenditure. *School enrollment* (1967)—primary, 167,803; secondary, 4,298; technical/vocational, 472; university/higher, 379.
Monetary Unit: South African rand (0.7616 rand equals U. S. $1, June 1972).
Gross National Product (1970): $94,000,000.
Manufacturing (major products): Candles, carpets, retreaded tires.
Major Agricultural Products: Corn, wheat, peas, barley, livestock, wool.
Major Mineral: Diamonds.
Foreign Trade: *Chief exports*—Livestock; wheat; diamonds; wool and mohair. *Chief imports*—Food; manufactured goods; machinery and transportation equipment; mineral fuels and lubricants. *Chief trading partner*—South Africa.
Communications: *Telephones* (1971), 2,332; *radios* (1970), 5,000.

LESOTHO

In 1972, in order to retain his political power, Lesotho's prime minister, Chief Leabua Jonathan, changed from a cooperative friend to a critic of the white-ruled Republic of South Africa, which physically surrounds and economically dominates independent black Lesotho.

Internal Reconciliation. Strong internal opposition to Prime Minister Jonathan's pro-South Africa stand had led him to suspend the constitution in 1970 and to jail opposition leaders under a state of emergency that remained in force in 1972. The last 50 detainees were released on Jan. 3, 1972. In April, Jonathan dismissed Commissioner of Police Fred Roach, the man who had enabled him to seize power. These moves were viewed as the prime minister's attempt at reconciliation with opponents who deplore South Africa's racial policy of apartheid.

Resisting South Africa. Prime Minister Jonathan took steps to hinder South Africa's attempts to establish trade and a diplomatic dialogue with black Africa. First, he sent an envoy to persuade the Ivory Coast's president not to go too far in his friendly exchanges with South African representatives. Then, in March, he asked the few black states that favored negotiation with South Africa to postpone action pending approval by the Organization of African Unity. In South Africa, irritated government officials called his acts "ill-advised."

The prime minister's criticism of apartheid and his caution in regard to a dialogue with South Africa may have helped embolden hitherto timid black leaders within South Africa's Bantustans to speak out. In July, Lesotho's representative to the United Nations charged that South Africa was retaliating against the prime minister by harassing UN technicians who must pass through South Africa to enter Lesotho.

FRANKLIN PARKER
West Virginia University

LIBERIA

The major event of 1972 in Liberia was the inauguration of William R. Tolbert as president. Liberia continued its efforts to increase its contact with the outside world and to expand its economy.

Domestic Affairs. The inauguration of President Tolbert took place on January 3. As vice president,

he succeeded to the presidency on July 23, 1971, on the death of William S. Tubman.

A new cabinet was announced on January 10. Mai Padmore, the first woman in Liberian history to hold cabinet rank, became minister of health and welfare. Rochefort L. Weeks replaced Joseph R. Grimes as secretary of state.

President Tolbert followed his predecessor's policy of gradual modernization. The voting age was reduced from 21 to 18, the security and civil services were being streamlined, and Liberian clocks, for many years "behind" those of neighboring countries by 45 minutes, were set on Greenwich Mean Time.

In June, in an untypical display of militancy, students of the University of Liberia petitioned Tolbert for a redress of grievances against the university administration, supporting their demands with a strike and a march to the Executive Mansion.

Foreign Affairs. In July the Liberian government decided to exchange ambassadors with the USSR and, throughout the year, it sought closer cooperation with Sierra Leone, Guinea, and the Ivory Coast. The country's traditional links with the United States were maintained. A $2 million long-term U. S. loan for the purchase of military equipment was negotiated in July.

Economy. Liberia's remarkable economic development rate was maintained during 1972, and foreign capital continued to flow in. Credits of $7.2 million in April and $1.2 million in May were made available for education and agriculture by the World Bank. The large-scale foreign investment in Liberia since 1945, however, has not yet significantly raised the standard of living of the people. A number of strikes, in the rubber, timber, and brewing industries, indicated increasing worker militancy. In March pressure from Liberian shopkeepers led to measures designed to curb the activities of foreigners, mainly Lebanese, operating retail businesses.

A "crusade for development" was launched in August 1972. Its announced goal was a grand total of $10 million, the whole to be subscribed by Liberian citizens. The funds obtained were to be used for improvements in education and agriculture, and for public transport, health programs, and building construction.

GRAHAM W. IRWIN
Columbia University

————— LIBERIA • Information Highlights —————

Official Name: Republic of Liberia.
Area: 43,000 square miles (111,370 sq km).
Population (1972 est.): 1,200,000. *Density,* 28 per square mile (11 per sq km). *Annual rate of increase,* 2.7%.
Chief City (1962 census): Monrovia, the capital, 80,922.
Government: *Head of state,* William R. Tolbert, president (took office July 1971). *Head of government,* William R. Tolbert. *Legislature*—Congress: House of Representatives, 52 members; Senate, 18 members. *Major political party*—True Whig party.
Languages: English (official), tribal dialects.
Education: *Expenditure* (1968), 2% of gross national product. *School enrollment* (1970)—primary, 120,245; secondary, 16,770; technical/vocational, 887; university/higher, 1,109.
Monetary Unit: Liberian dollar (1 L. dollar equals U. S.$1, July 1972).
Gross National Product (1970 est.): $352,000,000.
Manufacturing (major products): Cement, construction materials, petroleum products, textiles, aluminum.
Major Agricultural Products: Natural rubber, cassava, rice, bananas, coffee, cacao, forest products, fish.
Major Minerals: Iron ore, diamonds, bauxite, manganese.
Foreign Trade (1971): *Exports,* $222,000,000. *Imports,* $157,000,000. *Chief trading partners* (1969)—United States (took 28% of exports, supplied 34% of imports); West Germany (13%—14%); Netherlands (19%—4%); Japan (6%—9%).
Communications: *Telephones* (1970), 6,051; *television stations* (1971), 1; *television sets* (1971), 6,500; *radios* (1970), 155,000; *newspapers* (1970), 2 (daily circulation, 7,000).

The Ohio Historical Center Library-Archives in Columbus received a 1972 honor award for being a "bold, imaginative, almost startling structure."

libraries

Unemployment and reductions in service were the specters haunting American libraries and librarians in 1972. A sharp decline in governmental support for libraries meant that the era of abundance, which began in the early 1960's, had ended. Librarians no longer enjoyed the luxury of a sellers' market for their services, and libraries in major metropolitan areas reduced hours and closed branches. The New York Public Library, with a debt of more than $1 million at the end of the fiscal year 1972, faced the possibility of closing its privately endowed Science and Technology Division and its collections at the Lincoln Center for the Performing Arts. Only a $500,000 grant from the National Endowment for the Humanities and a $700,000 fund-raising effort of its own enabled the library to keep its privately maintained research facilities in operation.

Regional meetings during 1972 of the newly created National Commission on Libraries and Information Science gave citizens an opportunity to express their views about present and future needs. The year brought intensified efforts to increase the number of unionized librarians, as well as further controversy over alleged infringement of copyright arising from photocopying. Around the world, 1972 was observed as International Book Year.

Unionization. Efforts to increase the number of unionized librarians around the country involved a variety of issues. At the University of Chicago the question concerned the composition of the bargaining unit. A group of library staff members there had asked the university to recognize a local of the National Council of Distributive Workers of America for the purpose of collective bargaining. In hearings before the National Labor Relations Board, representatives of the union sought to enlarge the number of those eligible for membership while the university sought to restrict the number.

In another development, the Board of Trustees of the New York Library made an "agency shop" agreement, effective Jan. 1, 1972, with a local of the American Federation of State, County, and Municipal Employees (AFL-CIO). The contract required librarians either to join the union or to pay an equivalent "contract consideration fee." It specified further that staff members who did not choose one of the options could not remain in the employ

of the library. When the agreement took effect, about 40% of the eligible members had not joined the union. Some librarians, opposed to agency-shop status, questioned its validity in a petition to the Public Employees Relations Board of New York.

The petitioners contended that the library is a city agency, or public employer, subject to New York's Taylor Act, which prohibits an agency shop for public employees. In support of this contention they cited the fact that nearly 90% of the library's operating funds come from public sources. The library trustees argued that under its charter the library is a private corporation. The legality of the agency-shop agreement therefore depended on whether the library was determined to be a public or a private employer.

In the spring a hearing officer of the Public Employees Relations Board upheld the library's status as a private corporation. This decision was appealed to the full board, which subsequently ruled that the library and the city are joint employers of the library staff and that the New York Office of Collective Bargaining, which deals exclusively with public agencies, has jurisdiction over the case. As a result of this ruling, it seemed likely that the agency-shop agreement would be rescinded unless the Office of Collective Bargaining disclaimed jurisdiction. In that event, the dispute would revert to the Public Employees Relations Board—and possibly entail court action.

Copyright Questions. The incongruity between advances in photocopying technology and an outdated copyright law continued to plague the nation's libraries during 1972. Of particular significance were developments in the case of *Williams & Wilkins Co.* v. *The United States* (1968). Williams & Wilkins Co., a Baltimore publisher of medical materials, filed suit in 1968 against the federal government, alleging infringement of copyright by the National Library of Medicine and the National Institutes of Health. The publisher, joined by the Association of American Publishers and the Authors League, contended that the government agencies violated copyright by making available to researchers copies of legally protected medical works. The government, in concert with the American Library Association and the Association of Research Libraries, argued that photocopying alone is insufficient grounds on which to prove transgression of copyright. In its action, Williams & Wilkins observed that photoduplication of periodical articles by library users was reducing subscriptions to its medical journals. In its defense the government cited the 1935 "gentlemen's agreement," or single-copy doctrine, between the National Association of Book Publishers and the American Council of Learned Societies, which authorizes a library to make a single copy of copyrighted material for legitimate scholarly purposes.

The commissioner of the U. S. Court of Claims gave his opinion in this case on Feb. 16, 1972, ruling that the publisher is "entitled to recover reasonable and entire compensation for infringement of copyright arising from photocopying." According to the commissioner, technological progress has nullified the gentlemen's agreement, and although government agencies make only a single copy for each request, there may be many individual requests for the same article. A final decision must await the judgment of the full Court of Claims and the result of any appeals.

PROVIDENCE COLLEGE NEWS BUREAU

PROVIDENCE COLLEGE LIBRARY in Providence, R. I., another honor award winner, was cited for the "interplay of spaces within" (above). The building's exterior is shown on the opposite page.

In midsummer, Williams & Wilkins announced magazine rates for its library subscribers averaging 12.5% above rates for individual subscribers, prohibited libraries from making copies for interlibrary loan, and set a royalty fee of 5 cents a page, per copy, on multiple copies of a single work. But when the National Library of Medicine rejected the idea that the increased rates conferred a license for photocopying (where none was needed, in the opinion of the library), the company disclaimed any connection between the rates and such a license and withdrew the proposed interlibrary loan fee pending court decisions on its appeals in the case.

National Planning and Federal Library Activity. The National Commission on Libraries and Information Science, which became operative in 1971, held regional meetings during 1972 in Chicago and San Francisco. At these hearings citizens presented their views regarding present and future requirements for library and information services. At a meeting in February the commission emphasized that its interest in the very broad problem of information transmission did not preclude a concern with the development of libraries. Court decisions of 1971 in California and other states, which found the

local property tax an improper base for the funding of public education, prompted the commission to resolve that "if the current method of funding public schools is changed, library funding must change, too."

It became evident during the year that cable communication will be integral to any national plan for library and information service. In February the Federal Communications Commission issued its long-awaited rules, effective March 31, 1972, governing the carrying of broadcast signals by cable television systems. Under the rules two channels have been made available for noncommercial use during a 5-year trial period. Librarians, unhappy with that decision, tried to convince Congress and

the White House Office of Telecommunications Policy that a minimum of 20% of system capacity should be allocated to governmental, educational, and library use. During the summer it was announced that librarians will be presented on the Federal-State/Local Advisory Committee of the Federal Communications Commission—a panel that will make recommendations regarding the procedural aspects of cable franchising and regulation by federal, state, and local authorities.

During the year a joint panel of the Committee on Scientific and Technical Information and the Federal Library Committee explored the possibility of connecting all federal libraries and information services within a network that would enable each

PROVIDENCE COLLEGE NEWS BUREAU

one to serve others. The further integration of federal library and information services received a boost in late spring, when the Library of Congress and the directors of the National Library of Medicine and the National Agricultural Library jointly announced that the U. S. National Libraries Task Force on Automation and Other Cooperative Services will cooperate directly with the more broadly based Federal Library Committee. Under this arrangement the executive secretary of the Federal Library Committee will also serve as chairman of the U. S. National Libraries Task Force.

In the fall, work was completed on the first phase—excavation and foundation work—of the James Madison Memorial Building of the Library of Congress. The new building, planned for completion about mid-1975, will make use of compact shelving that is expected to increase the library's total stack area by 80%.

During 1972, Congress reacted more favorably than President Nixon to the ongoing requirements of established libraries. In general, the administration developed a philosophy that stressed support for impoverished libraries and minority librarians while reducing aid to libraries that need operating funds but are not in need of remedial assistance. Total appropriations for library programs in the fiscal year 1973 amounted to some $140.5 million, compared with $164.5 million for fiscal 1972.

Other Events Around the Nation. Libraries were among the casualties of tropical storm Agnes, which in late June devastated large areas in several Eastern states. All libraries with flood losses were asked to report to the American Library Association's Ad Hoc Committee on Flood Damaged Libraries, which sought to gather information and to help coordinate efforts to rebuild collections and restore services.

Verner W. Clapp died on June 15, 1972, at the age of 71. His distinguished library career included service as chief assistant Librarian of Congress and president of the Council on Library Resources. At the time of his death he had become a giant of 20th century American librarianship.

National Library Week. The themes of National Library Week, April 16–22, 1972, were "Reading Makes the World Go Round" and "You've Got a Right to Read." This annual event (the 15th) was again sponsored by the American Library Association and the National Book Committee. Librarians expressed dismay, as they have with considerable force over the past few years, that the themes disregarded the presence of nonprint media in libraries. The sponsoring committee explained that the themes were related to the Right to Read Program of the U. S. Office of Education and to the UNESCO-sponsored International Book Year, 1972.

Library Education. The number of graduate library schools accredited by the American Library Association increased to 57 in 1972 with the approval of master's degree programs offered by the School of Information and Library Studies of the State University of New York at Buffalo and by the Division of Library Science of Southern Connecticut State College at New Haven.

A report published in June revealed that the average salaries received by the 1971 graduates of accredited library schools were only 2.6% better than those received by the 1970 graduates and that this rate was only about half the rate of gain between 1969 and 1970. The average beginning salary for all 1971 graduates was $8,846. The proportion of graduates finding jobs in the different kinds of libraries remained much the same as in 1970. About 59% found positions in college, university, or public libraries; 26% entered school libraries; and 15% found other kinds of library work.

Awards. The 1972 Beta Phi Mu Award for distinguished service to education for librarianship went to Margaret E. Monroe, professor and former director of the Library School at the University of Wisconsin. The Melvil Dewey Award for recent creative professional achievement—particularly in the fields of library management, library training, cataloging and classification, and the tools and techniques of librarianship—was given to Jerold Orne, university librarian at the University of North Carolina. The Joseph W. Lippincott Award for distinguished service in the library profession was received by Guy R. Lyle, director of libraries at Emory University.

Edmond I. Applebaum, assistant director for acquisitions and overseas operations in the processing department of the Library of Congress, was awarded the Margaret Mann Citation for outstanding professional contribution in cataloging and classification. Carol A. Nemeyer, senior associate, education and library services of the Association of American Publishers, received the Esther J. Piercy Award for contributions to librarianship in the field of technical services by younger members of the profession. The Isadore Gilbert Mudge Citation for distinguished contributions to reference librarianship was given to Thomas John Galvin, associate professor of library science at Simmons College. Ronald W. McCracken, librarian at the Keswick, Ontario, public school, received the Grolier Award for achievement in guiding and stimulating the reading of children and young people. (For other awards, see *American Library Association,* below.)

International Library Activities. The theme of International Book Year, 1972, sponsored by UNESCO, was "Books for All." Article X of "The Charter of the Book," prepared in connection with this worldwide event, read, in part: " 'Since wars begin in the minds of men,' the UNESCO Constitution states, 'it is in the minds of men that the defences of peace must be constructed.' Books constitute one of the major defences of peace because of their enormous influence in creating an intellectual climate of friendship and mutual understanding."

During the International Book Year, the French ministry of education gave five books to each couple marrying in France. This program was inspired by a study indicating that 57% of adult Frenchmen have not read a book since childhood.

While libraries burned in the warfare in Northern Ireland and in the conflict between India and Pakistan, UNESCO censured the International Federation of Library Associations during 1972 for its failure to rebuke those of its member countries—including South Africa, Rhodesia, and Angola—that practice racial discrimination. Suspended from "consultative status" by UNESCO, the federation decided to sever relations with the South African Library Association if that organization refused to satisfy UNESCO's criteria on race relations. The South African association refused to accede and withdrew from the federation. It was anticipated that the federation would then meet UNESCO's standards for membership and financial support.

DAN BERGEN, *University of Rhode Island*

AMERICAN LIBRARY ASSOCIATION

Robert Wedgeworth took office on Aug. 15, 1972, as executive director of the American Library Association (ALA). He succeeded David H. Clift, who retired after 20 years to become executive director emeritus.

Conferences and Projects. The newly organized ALA Council, which functions as the association's governing body, met for the first time at the 91st annual conference of the ALA, which was held in Chicago on June 25–July 1, 1972. The reconstituted council consists of 100 members at large and 54 chapter representatives, who took office following the annual conference.

The major actions of the ALA Council in 1972 were the establishing of a Round Table on Government Documents, a Federal Librarians Round Table, and an Ad Hoc Joint Committee of the American Association of School Librarians and the National Council of Teachers of Mathematics in connection with the proposed change to the metric system. Other council actions included the approval of the merger of the Adult Services Division and the Reference Services Division and the adoption of the new *Standards for Accreditation*.

At the end of the annual conference, Katherine Laich of the University of Southern California's School of Library Science became president of the ALA. Jean E. Lowrie of Western Michigan University's Department of Librarianship became president-elect and first vice president.

ALA participated in the UNESCO-sponsored International Book Year, 1972, in several ways. It endorsed three projects—a Bookmobile of the Americas, a Black Caucus to provide cultural exchange between American and African libraries, and an exchange between the libraries of Fisk and Howard universities and counterpart libraries in Botswana and Malawi. *Children's Books of International Interest* was published, and the board of directors of the Library Administration Division (LAD) approved a 5-year program to assist foreign library schools to acquire LAD materials.

ALA opposed the sharply increased postal rates for book and library mailings set by the U. S. Postal Service. The general copyright revision bill will be reintroduced in Congress in 1973, and ALA has worked vigorously to guard the right of photocopying for interlibrary loan and the right of fair use for library patrons. ALA filed a Brief of Exceptions for the U. S. Court of Claims in the Williams & Wilkins case that was being tried before it, involving alleged violation of copyright in connection with photocopying.

Publications. The following are among ALA publications of special interest to librarians, issued in 1972: *Administrative Patterns for Service; American Theatrical Arts; The Changing Environment of Libraries; Interlibrary Communications and Information Networks; Job Dimensions and Educational Needs in Librarianship; Moving from Ideas to Action; A Multi-Media Approach to Children's Literature: A Selective List of Films, Filmstrips, and Recordings Based on Children's Books; New Directions in Staff Development: Moving from Ideas to Action; Print, Image, and Sound: Essays on Media; Public Libraries in Cooperative Systems: Administrative Patterns for Service; State Library Policy: Its Legislative and Environmental Contexts; A Strategy for Public Library Change.*

PHILLIPS EXETER ACADEMY LIBRARY, Exeter, N. H., was designed by Louis I. Kahn. Its interior uses vast amounts of poured concrete.

Awards. Numerous awards were made in 1972, in addition to those cited above under *Awards*.

The J. Morris Jones–World Book Encyclopedia–ALA Goals Award was divided between two ALA committees. The Intellectual Freedom Committee received $14,000 for a prototype educational workshop; and the Committee on Accreditation, $10,000 for a seminar to prepare evaluators of graduate programs of library education under the new *Standards for Accreditation*.

The Newbery Medal for the most distinguished children's book was awarded to Robert C. O'Brien for his *Mrs. Frisby and the Rats of NIMH*. The Caldecott Medal for the most distinguished picture book went to Nonny Hogrogian for *One Fine Day*. The Mildred L. Batchelder Award for the most outstanding book originally published in a foreign language and in a foreign country went to Holt, Rinehart & Winston for its 1970 publication of Hans Peter Richter's *Friedrich*, translated from the German by Edite Kroll.

The Herbert Putnam Honor Fund Award was given to Michael H. Harris, of the University of Kentucky's College of Library Science; and the Hammond Incorporated Library Award, to the Patterson Library, Westfield, N. Y. The Francis Joseph Campbell Citation was shared by Frederick A. Thorpe, publisher of Ulverscroft Large Print Books, and Keith Jennison, publisher of Keith Jennison Large Print Books.

CURTIS E. SWANSON
American Library Association

LIBYA

Col. Muammar el-Qaddafi, Libya's young head of state, continued in 1972 to face the questions of how to unify the Arab world in its fight against Israel and how to lead his oil-rich country through a social revolution within the framework of strict Muslim law and morality. Both at home and abroad Qaddafi was frustrated by forces not in harmony with his revolutionary purposes.

Relations with Arab States. In his attempt to radicalize the Arab world, President Qaddafi continued his support of revolutionary movements to overthrow feudal Arab governments. On Wednesdays and Saturdays the Libyan government was waging a propaganda war by radio against King Hassan II of Morocco. The hour-long diatribes openly condoned the attempted assassinations of the king, one of which occurred on August 16.

Though the Federation of Arab Republics, linking Libya, Syria, and Egypt, still existed on paper, the fact that Egypt and Libya proposed on August 2 to form one state suggested that Syria was not interested in the federation. The union was to be completed before September 1973. The first step was taken on Sept. 18, 1972, when Cairo was chosen as the future capital, and it was agreed that there would be one popularly elected president and one political party.

Relations with non-Arab States. A Libyan delegation, headed by Majors Abdul-Salam Jallud and Mustafa el-Kharubit, travelled to the Soviet Union at the end of February for a conference with Soviet leaders. On March 4, Libya and the USSR concluded an agreement jointly to develop and refine Libyan oil, and to work out an arms arrangement in which Libya would buy such Soviet weapons as the MIG-23 bombers and ground-to-ground missiles. Some of these would probably find their way to Egypt, which was too poor to pay for such arms in cash. The agreements slightly improved Libyan-Soviet relations, which had foundered on Qaddafi's disappointment with the USSR in its refusal to support more aggressive policies toward Israel and on the expansion of Soviet naval power in the eastern Mediterranean. The agreement also helped to ease the strain brought about by Qaddafi's support for the Sudanese government when Sudanese Communists had tried to overthrow it in 1971.

Libya's reaction to the death of the Israeli athletes at the Munich Olympics on September 5 was to hail the Palestinian terrorists who were responsible. On September 12 a heroes' funeral was held in Libya for five Palestinian guerrillas who had been killed when they tried to escape with the Israeli hostages.

Domestic Reform. Frustrated by the attitudes of more conservative Arab leaders, President Qaddafi assumed an increasingly radical posture. He has seen himself as the only true advocate of Arab nationalism, the kind of nationalism once represented by Egypt's Gamal Abdel Nasser when the latter aimed at the leadership of the Arab world. He was deeply impressed when Nasser once said to him, "You remind me of my youth."

In an attempt to exorcise the hateful memory of imperialism and the decades in which Italy ruled Libya as one of its colonies, the president had the bodies of Italian soldiers who had been buried in Libya exhumed and sent to Italy, where they were re-interred at Bari on June 5. Qaddafi has even gone so far as to threaten to "fight Great Britain and the United States on their own land."

To radicalize the young of Libya, he called for Spartan simplicity in their way of life and has threatened to have their hair trimmed if it is grown in the Western style. He has demanded that the youth adopt a more sober style of dress. Those who do not conform with his wishes in clothing and behavior are threatened with induction into the army for "training in popular resistance." The campaign President Qaddafi has been carrying out was designed to eliminate traditions of foreign origin and to reeducate the Libyans spiritually and morally.

Government Changes. A new cabinet was formed on July 16, whether at the request or against the wishes of Qaddafi was not known. Civilians replaced the military in all but two positions, the premiership, held by Abdul-Salam Jallud, and the ministry of the interior. The portfolio of defense, formerly held by Qaddafi, was not filled, though Qaddafi remained head of state.

Oil. At a conference in October of the oil-producing states and the foreign concession holders, Libya's petroleum minister announced that Libya had secured a 50% share of the concession held in Libya by ENI, the Italian state oil company.

JAMES D. L. BYRNES
Edinboro State College, Pennsylvania

———— LIBYA • Information Highlights ————

Official Name: Libyan Arab Republic.
Area: 679,360 square miles (1,759,540 sq km).
Population (1972 est.): 2,000,000. *Density,* 3 per square mile (1 per sq km). *Annual rate of increase,* 3.1%.
Chief Cities: Tripoli, joint capital, 247,400 (1968 est.); Benghazi, joint capital, 137,295 (1964 census).
Government: *Head of state,* Col. Muammar el-Qaddafi, president of the Revolutionary Command Council (took office Sept. 1969). *Head of government,* Maj. Abdul-Salam Jallud, premier (took office July 1972). *Chief organ*—Revolutionary Command Council, 12 members. *Major political party,* Libyan Arab Socialist Union.
Language: Arabic (official).
Education: *Expenditure* (1967), 11.6% of total public expenditure. *School enrollment* (1969)—primary, 310,846; secondary, 50,779; technical/vocational, 1,457; higher, 2,215.
Monetary Unit: Dinar (0.3289 dinar equals U. S.$1, Sept. 1972).
Gross National Product (1970 est.): $3,140,000,000.
National Income per Person (1968): $1,305.
Economic Indexes: *Agricultural production* (1971), 233 (1952–56 = 100); *consumer price index* (1971), 97 (1970 = 100).
Manufacturing (major products): Petroleum products, processed foods.
Major Agricultural Products: Wheat, barley, tomatoes, dates, olives.
Major Minerals: Petroleum (ranks 6th among world producers, 1970), gypsum, salt, limestone.
Foreign Trade (1970): *Exports,* $2,366,000,000 (chief exports—crude petroleum). *Imports,* $554,000,000 (chief imports, 1969—nonelectrical machinery; food and live animals; motor vehicles; electrical machinery, apparatus, and appliances). *Chief trading partners* (1969)—Italy (took 23% of exports, supplied 23% of imports); West Germany (22%—9%); United Kingdom (14%—12%); France (12%—5%).
Tourism: *Receipts* (1970), $11,200,000.
Transportation: *Motor vehicles* (1970), 145,500 (automobiles, 100,100); *major national airline,* Libyan Arab Airlines.
Communications: *Telephones* (1971), 41,495; *television stations* (1971), 2; *television sets* (1971), 200,000; *radios* (1970), 85,000; *newspapers* (1967), 7 (daily circulation, 35,000).

Literature

Developments in world literature during 1972 are reviewed in this article under the following headings: (1) AMERICAN LITERATURE; (2) CHILDREN'S LITERATURE; (3) CANADIAN LITERATURE; (4) ENGLISH LITERATURE; (5) FRENCH LITERATURE; (6) GERMAN LITERATURE; (7) ITALIAN LITERATURE; (8) JAPANESE LITERATURE; (9) LATIN AMERICAN LITERATURE; (10) SOVIET LITERATURE; (11) SPANISH LITERATURE.

German novelist Heinrich Böll was awarded the 1972 Nobel Prize for literature. (See also BIOGRAPHY—*Böll, Heinrich*.) With the death in November of Ezra Pound, the English-speaking world lost one of its literary giants. (See also POUND, EZRA.)

American Literature

Despite the growing economic crisis in American publishing, the year 1972 saw the publication of a number of distinguished books, including several significant first novels. Some writers of established reputation produced major novels as well. The short story continued to decline, and there seemed a continued reluctance to publish anyone but a proven winner. A conservative impulse was also felt in poetry. Though several collections by established poets saw publication, fewer works by younger poets were in evidence. At the same time, nonfiction attracted a wider audience than usual.

In the National Book Awards, the poetry prize was shared by Frank O'Hara's *Collected Poems* and Howard Moss' *Selected Poems*. *Flannery O'Connor: the Complete Stories* won the fiction award. The history prize was awarded to volumes VII and VIII of Allan Nevins' series, *Ordeal of the Union*, and Joseph P. Lash took the prize in biography for *Eleanor and Franklin*. The Arts and Letters prize went to Charles Rosen for *The Classical Style: Haydn, Mozart, Beethoven*.

Winners of the Pulitzer Prizes for literature included James Wright for *Collected Poems* in poetry, Wallace Stegner for *Angle of Repose* in fiction, Carl M. Degler for *Neither Black Nor White* in history, Joseph P. Lash for *Eleanor and Franklin* in biography, and Barbara Tuchman for *Stilwell and the American Experience in China, 1911–1945* in general nonfiction. (See also PRIZES AND AWARDS.)

Novels. John Barth published *Chimera*, a three-part narrative which retells the ancient stories of Scheherazade, Perseus, and Bellerophon. The hero, a writer, appears among his characters—talking, imagining, and complicating an essentially simple tale into elaborate patterns of metaphor, symbol, and allegory. Essentially a novel of self-discovery, *Chimera* reflects Barth's continuing fascination with the mythical dimension in modern life.

All My Friends Are Going To Be Strangers, by Larry McMurtry, is about a writer, a naive young man who makes a year-long trip from Texas to California and back. On the way, he marries and breaks up with one woman and falls in love with another who is unable to love him. There are a number of memorable minor characters in this energetic novel by a promising young talent.

Enemies: A Love Story is Isaac Bashevis Singer's first novel about America and his first with a contemporary setting. Jewish refugees from the Europe of the 1940's live scattered in lonely rooms in New York City. One of them, the central character, constructs a complex web of lies to separate the three women who complicate his life and, through his fantasies, perpetuates for himself the terror of the holocaust. The characters are victims, not only of the Nazis, but also of their own desperation and inability to escape the past and build new lives. The book is perhaps Singer's most pessimistic.

Chaim Potok's third novel, *My Name Is Asher Lev*, deals with another kind of transition from an old Jewish order to a new. Asher Lev, son of a Hasidic family, finds his compulsion to paint and his genius for it in tragic confrontation with his father's role in the movement to rescue Soviet Jews. Both son and father suffer from the misunderstandings that arise as a result of Asher's devotion to art and his father's anger and disappointment at his son's choice of the secular life.

A similar conflict of values lies at the heart of *The Optimist's Daughter*, a sensitive and absorbing novel by Eudora Welty, perhaps her finest to date. Miss Welty's ear for dialect and her unsurpassed talent for comedy reach their controlled peak in the novel. By contrast, *The Ewings*, a posthumously published novel by John O'Hara, lacks the force and discipline that mark so much of his earlier work. George P. Elliott's *Muriel* was a disappointing book by a fine writer.

Other contributions by older, established writers included John Hersey's *The Conspiracy*, Frederic Prokosch's *America, My Wilderness*, and Herman Wouk's *The Winds of War*. Hollis Summers' *The Garden* and Hortense Calisher's *Standard Dreaming* were well received; James Purdy was adjudged less successful in *I Am Elijah Thrush*.

Among younger writers, Page Stegner came under fire for *Hawks and Harriers* and Richard Elman was adversely criticized for *Fredi and Shirl and the Kids*, a curious hybrid of fiction and autobiography. More successful entries included Harry Crews' *Car*, John A. Williams' *Captain Blackman*, Ishmael Reed's *Mumbo-Jumbo*, Lois Gould's *Necessary Objects*, and D. Keith Mano's *The Proselytizer*.

An unusually great number of first novels were published in 1972. Among the most distinguished were James Whitehead's *Joiner*, Alan Friedman's *Hermaphrodeity: the Autobiography of a Poet*, and Barry Hannah's *Geronimo Rex*. Marilyn Durham's *The Man Who Loved Cat Dancing* enjoyed great popularity, as did Cynthia Buchanan's *Maiden*. Other noteworthy first novels included Jon Appleby's *Skate*, Cyrus Colter's *The Rivers of Eros*, Gerald Rosen's *Blues for a Dying Nation*, and Steven Millhauser's *Edwin Mullhouse*.

Short Fiction. The appearance in one volume of Ernest Hemingway's *The Nick Adams Stories* was a welcome event, particularly since the collection included eight previously unpublished tales. Similarly, John O'Hara's *The Time Element and Other Stories* brought together 34 uncollected stories, 14 of them published for the first time.

John Updike's *Museums and Women and Other Stories* demonstrated this gifted writer's acknowledged mastery of style and form. Another talented craftsman, Joyce Carol Oates, contributed *Marriages and Infidelities*, an uneven collection.

The stories in Donald Barthelme's *Sadness* offer strong confirmation of his growing stature as one of our finest writers of short fiction. His inventiveness

MARIANNE MOORE (1887–1972

Marianne Moore, winner of the 1952 Pulitzer Prize for poetry for her *Collected Poems* (1951), died at her home in New York City on Feb. 5, 1972. Often referred to as the "first lady of poetry," she was noted for her precisely crafted rhythms, for the wit and subtlety of her imagery, and for her ability to describe feelings, events, and things as though she were experiencing them for the first time. A wry but gentle moralist, she criticized human foibles indirectly, frequently using plants and animals, rather than humans, as the subjects of her poetry. Such loves of her life as baseball, the New York subways, and tricorn hats are humorously reflected in much of her verse.

WIDE WORLD

While she was not the product of any particular school, Miss Moore's work seems to reflect influences of such prose stylists as Edmund Burke and Samuel Johnson. She used a syllabic form of versification often found in French but uncommon in English. Robert Lowell described her as "the best woman poet in English."

Marianne Craig Moore was born in Kirkwood, Mo., on Nov. 15, 1887. While attending Bryn Mawr College, where she received her B. A. degree in 1909, she published her first poems in the student magazine. In 1915, after working for some years as a teacher, she had several of her poems published in the *Egoist,* a London periodical specializing in Imagist verse. In the same year, Harriet Monroe published some of her work in *Poetry* magazine in Chicago. When a collection of Miss Moore's verse, *Observations* (1924), won the Dial Award in 1925, she became acting editor of *Dial,* a leading literary journal. She edited it until its demise in 1929.

Among Miss Moore's other verse collections are *Pangolin, and Other Verse* (1936); *What Are Years?* (1941); *Nevertheless* (1944); *Like a Bulwark* (1956); and *The Arctic Ox* (1964). *The Complete Poems of Marianne Moore* appeared in 1967. She also translated *The Fables of La Fontaine* from the French (1954), and published a volume of essays, *Predilections* (1955). Among her many literary awards were the National Book Award for Poetry and the National Medal for Literature of the National Book Committee.

HENRY S. SLOAN

and fresh approach to experimentation are everywhere in evidence in this book. Richard Brautigan, another experimenter, produced *Revenge of the Lawn: Stories 1962–1970,* which, though not up to the level of his earlier achievement in *Trout Fishing in America,* conveyed his imaginative power.

Two short novels of considerable merit appeared in 1972. Philip Roth's *The Breast* is a strangely compelling fable of a man who turns into a female breast. In *Transparent Things,* the distinguished novelist Vladimir Nabokov recounted the complicated adventures of Hugh Person, Nabokov's penchant for word-play working to great effect.

Other notable collections of short stories include *Gorilla, My Love* by the talented young black writer Toni Cade Bambara, Sallie Bingham's *The Way It Is Now,* Norma Klein's *Love and Other Euphemisms,* and Sol Yurick's *Someone Just Like You.* Ann Birstein's group of novellae, *Summer*

Situations, also deserved attention. Richard Bach's *Jonathan Livingston Seagull* enjoyed widespread popularity despite its limited literary significance.

Poetry. The year 1972 was notable for a number of important collections by individual poets. Foremost among these was A. R. Ammons' *Collected Poems: 1951–1971.* A nature poet with a decidedly contemporary point of view, Ammons is among the most skillful practitioners of the form, and this book should help to establish his reputation as a major American poet.

Archibald MacLeish's *The Human Season* brings together that remarkably durable poet's best work, written over the space of nearly 50 years. The distinguished classical scholar Richmond Lattimore presented a substantial collection in *Poems from Three Decades.* When considered next to his lively translations of the classical poets, however, the poems too often seem ponderous and pedantic.

Stanley Burnshaw's *In the Terrified Radiance* exhibits that gifted poet's great imaginative power and erudition. *The World of Gwendolyn Brooks* brings together four volumes of her poetry, along with a novel, *Maud Martha.* Miss Brooks' reputation has grown steadily in recent years.

Three books by distinguished poets appeared posthumously. In *Straw for the Fire: From the Notebooks of Theodore Roethke 1942–1963,* David Wagoner has selected and arranged some revealing material. The book is a fascinating and useful addition to the Roethke canon and tells us much about the poet's fertile imagination. John Berryman's *Delusions, Etc.* is, on the whole, a disappointing book. A collection of miscellaneous poetry, most of it painful and exacerbated, the book appeared not long after the poet's suicide on Jan. 7, 1972. There is a terrifyingly prophetic quality to these poems, despite their somber religiosity. *Winter Trees* is Sylvia Plath's last collection of poems, some of them unfinished. Like Berryman's, hers is a poetry of death and despondency, but no less powerful and enchanting for all that.

Several other notable volumes appeared in 1972. W. H. Auden's *Epistle to a Godson* came as something of a disappointment to many who look to Auden as the reigning monarch of modern poetry. Eleanor Ross Taylor's *Welcome Eumenides,* on the other hand, was a solid entry, displaying her deftness and skill at every turn. James Merrill's *Braving the Elements* is a distinguished collection.

The war still provided the subject for much poetry. The most impressive volume in this category was Michael Casey's *Obscenities,* which won the Yale Series of Younger Poets Award. Perhaps the best poetry anthology of 1972 was Jerome Rothenberg's *Shaking the Pumpkin: Traditional Poetry of the Indian North Americas.* Other important verse collections included Clayton Eshleman's *Altars,* John Ashbery's *Three Poems,* Jay Wright's *The Homecoming Singer,* Philip Levine's *They Feed They Lion,* and Mary Oliver's *The River Styx, Ohio, and Other Poems.*

Literary History and Criticism. Critical attention continued as usual to focus largely on modern literature. The major exceptions to this trend included Charles H. Brown's *William Cullen Bryant,* the first full-length biography in nearly 100 years. The book is an impeccable work of scholarship on an early and important American poet and journalist. Daniel Hoffman's *Poe Poe Poe Poe Poe Poe Poe,* though in many ways a fascinating interpretation of

that enigmatic American romantic, is marred by a pervasive whimsicality.

In *Henry James: The Master, 1901–1916,* Leon Edel concluded his definitive five-volume biography of the novelist. Perhaps the longest literary biography on record, it is itself a major work of art and seems destined to become a classic.

Four important modern poets were the subjects of significant studies. *T. S. Eliot's Intellectual Development, 1922–1939,* by John D. Margolis, and *T. S. Eliot's Social Criticism,* by Roger Kojecky, are major treatments of important issues. Russell Kirk's *Eliot and His Age: T. S. Eliot's Moral Imagination in the Twentieth Century,* despite its author's conservative bias, is an original and challenging work. Hugh Kenner's *The Pound Era* is sensitive and erudite and should take its place as the definitive treatment of a complex artist who died in November 1972. (See POUND, EZRA.) A. Walton Litz's *Introspective Voyager: the Poetic Development of Wallace Stevens* provides a lucid and rewarding examination of another difficult poet. *The Poetry of Randall Jarrell,* by Suzanne Ferguson, is a perspective study of this major poet.

The F. Scott Fitzgerald industry continued to thrive. Students of his life and work will be grateful for *Dear Scott/Dear Max: the Fitzgerald-Perkins Correspondence,* edited by John Kuehl and Jackson Bryer, a collection of the letters that passed between the writer and his editor, Maxwell Perkins. Matthew J. Bruccoli's *As Ever, Scott Fitz* brings together for the first time Fitzgerald's correspondence with his agent, Harold Ober. Another fiction writer was the subject of a strong critical study: *Flannery O'Connor: Voice of the Peacock,* by Sister Kathleen Feeley, S. S. N. D.

In a sense, the most impressive criticism of the year came in the form of collected essays by a number of eminent writers and critics. Three novelists offered astute critical perceptions: Reynolds Price, in *Things Themselves: Essays and Scenes;* Joyce Carol Oates, in *The Edge of Impossibility: Tragic Forms in Literature;* and George P. Elliott, in *Conversions: Literature and the Modernist Tradition.* Other important collections included the late Paul Goodman's *Speaking and Language: Defense of Poetry* and Philip Young's *Three Bags Full: Essays in American Literature and Culture, 1951–1971.* Two specialized studies also merited mention: Harold Kaplan's *Democratic Humanism and American Literature,* and Nathan Irvin Huggins' *Harlem Renaissance.*

History and Biography. The venerable dean of American naval historians, Samuel Eliot Morison, contributed two important volumes on early American history. *Samuel de Champlain: Father of New France* is an absorbing biography of the early explorer and might have gained more attention had it not been overshadowed by *The European Discovery of America: the Southern Voyages,* the companion to Morison's *Northern Voyages,* published in 1971.

Students of American military history welcomed several important books. *North America Divided: the Mexican War, 1846–1848,* by Seymour V. Connor and Odie B. Faulk, traces the complicated story of what many historians feel is one of the most disgraceful episodes in U. S. history. In *The Children of Pride: a True Story of Georgia and the Civil War,* Robert Manson Myers presented some 1,200 letters written by a Georgia minister and his family and friends between 1854 and 1868. It is a

MARK VAN DOREN (1894–1972)

COLUMBIA UNIVERSITY

Mark Van Doren, American man of letters, died in Torrington, Conn., on Dec. 10, 1972. Throughout a long career that began in the 1920's, Van Doren was regarded as an inspired teacher, an astute critic, and, most importantly, an accomplished poet, whose verse, at once lyrical and intellectual, gently celebrated both humanistic values and the truth, warmth, and beauty of nature. Immersed in American traditions, he traced his literary lineage to Emerson and Thoreau, through Emily Dickinson, Edwin Arlington Robinson, and Robert Frost. In 1940 he received a Pulitzer Prize for *Collected Poems.*

Van Doren was born in Hope, Ill., on June 13, 1894. His family moved to Urbana in 1900, where Mark graduated from the University of Illinois (B. A., 1914; M. A., 1915). He then went to New York City to attend Columbia University, from which, after serving in the Army in World War I, he received his Ph. D. in 1920. That year he began to teach English at Columbia, retiring in 1959. One of his students, the writer Thomas Merton, wrote that he used his gifts "to make people admire and understand poetry and good writing and truth."

As a critic, Van Doren was particularly interested in American literature, although he produced important books on Dryden (1920; rev. ed., 1931), Shakespeare (1939), and the English metaphysical poets (with Theodore Spencer, 1939). His works on American literature included studies of Thoreau (1916), E. A. Robinson (1927), and Hawthorne (1949). He also was the editor of several anthologies of poetry and the author of literary surveys, plays, novels, and short stories.

Van Doren's first book of poems, *Spring Thunder,* was published in 1924. Titles of volumes that followed indicate his themes and preoccupations: *A Winter Diary* (1935), *The Country Year* (1946), *Spring Birth* (1953), and *Morning Worship* (1960). His last-published volume of new poems, *That Shining Place,* appeared in 1969.

Van Doren wrote an autobiography (1958), and his wife, Dorothy, also an author and editor, published amusing accounts of life with her husband, including *The Professor and I* (1959).

NATHAN H. PLETCHER

moving and intimate story. E. B. Long's *The Civil War Day by Day* is an almanac which should prove of great use to Civil War buffs. Steven Jantzen wrote of another war in *Hooray for Peace, Hurrah for War: the United States During World War I.*

The 20th century continued to attract the attention of specialists. Among the more significant studies of special topics were Paul L. Murphy's *The Constitution in Crisis Times, 1918–1969* and two other "crisis" books: Joyce and Gabriel Kolko's *The World and United States Foreign Policy, 1945–1954* and Joseph R. Starobin's *American Communism in Crisis: 1943–1957.* David S. Broder's *The Party's Over: the Failure of Politics in America* is about a more recent crisis.

Several biographies were among the most impressive entries of the year. In *The Randolphs of Virginia: "America's Foremost Family,"* Jonathan Daniels presented a thoroughgoing account of an

influential dynasty. David Freeman Hawke took up the life of *Benjamin Rush: Revolutionary Gadfly,* concentrating upon Rush's early career as a leading cultural reformer during the early years of the republic. Two black Americans were the subjects of biographies. Emma Lou Thornbrough's *T. Thomas Fortune: Militant Journalist* recovers the life and times of a black liberationist who lived from 1855 to 1928 and became one of the country's leading journalists. Silvio A. Bedini's *Life of Benjamin Banneker* is a fascinating account of the brilliant scientist and inventor who flourished in 18th century Maryland.

Three other biographies dealt with significant figures of the 19th century. Jonathan Messerli's *Horace Mann: a Biography* takes up the varied careers of a man who is perhaps best known today for his pioneering work in the field of education. Justin G. Turner and Linda Levitt Turner wrote *Mary Todd Lincoln: Her Life and Letters,* a work which should help to dispel the myths that continue to surround this enigmatic and tragic woman. And in Alexander B. Adams, the almost legendary *Geronimo* found a competent biographer.

The most significant biography of the year was unquestionably Joseph P. Lash's *Eleanor: the Years Alone,* which takes up Mrs. Roosevelt's life after the death of the President—the years which mark the major phase of her career. Margaret Truman's affectionate biography of her father, *Harry S. Truman,* is surprisingly informative and candid and manages to avoid the excessive sentimentality that characterizes so many personal portraits. Herbert S. Parmet published *Eisenhower and the American Crusades;* W. A. Swanberg wrote a massive and ponderous biography of publishing mogul Henry Luce, *Luce and His Empire;* and the distinguished historian and diplomat George F. Kennan produced a second autobiographical volume, *Memoirs, 1950–1963.*

Other related books published during 1972 include Sidney Lens' *The Forging of the American Empire,* a history of American imperialism; Alexander De Conde's *Half Bitter, Half Sweet: an Excursion into Italian-American History;* Nathan G. Hale, Jr.'s *Freud and the Americans;* and Morton White's *Science and Sentiment in America: Philosophical Thought from Jonathan Edwards to John Dewey.*

Other Nonfiction. Among the many notable works of nonfiction published during 1972, two were especially significant. Frances FitzGerald's *Fire on the Lake: the Vietnamese and the Americans in Vietnam* is a moving, often shocking, account of American involvement in Vietnam. Based upon her own six-year experience there, the book analyzes American policy and shows how it contributed to the destruction of Vietnamese culture.

A. Alvarez's *The Savage God: A Study in Suicide* should prove equally valuable. Alvarez concentrated upon literary suicides, devoting considerable attention to his close friend, the poet Sylvia Plath, who committed suicide in 1963. In investigating the relationship between the poet's subjects and her tendency towards self-destruction, Alvarez invites us to extend the pattern into our violence-prone culture, which so often seems bent on destroying itself.

Another kind of destruction, that of the land, was the subject of several thoughtful books. In *A Continuous Harmony: Essays Cultural and Agricultural,* Kentucky poet and novelist Wendell Berry offers a compelling argument against strip mining, a practice that also comes under attack in two other books on Appalachia: Harry M. Caudill's *My Land Is Dying,* and Bill Peterson's *Coal Town Revisited: an Appalachian Notebook.* Burton Bernstein's *The Sticks* provides an absorbing profile of the region and people of Essex County, New York.

Three books treated the current crisis in American education. Jonathan Kozol's *Free Schools,* a sequel to his award-winning *Death at an Early Age,* describes the founding of a ghetto school in West Roxbury, Mass. Pat Conroy wrote of another kind of ghetto in *The Water Is Wide,* an account of the year he spent teaching 18 illiterate black children on Yamacraw Island off the coast of South Carolina. Donald Barr speaks from yet a different perspective in *Who Pushed Humpty Dumpty?: Dilemmas in American Education Today.* Two fathers of disturbed children contributed moving and courageous books: Robin White wrote *Be Not Afraid* and Josh Greenfeld wrote *A Child Called Noah: a Family Journey.*

The field of politics and political theory was ably represented by Herbert Marcuse's *Counterrevolution and Revolt,* Hannah Arendt's *Crisis of the Republic,* and former Chief Justice Earl Warren's *A Republic, If You Can Keep It.* Vastly different in many respects, all three are worthy of attention by students of contemporary politics. Less significant are the random pieces gathered together in Dean Acheson's *Grapes from Thorns,* a posthumous collection by the former secretary of state.

Several prominent literary figures published collections of miscellaneous essays. Norman Mailer's *Existential Errands* brings together 26 pieces on such topics as movies, books, the theater, boxing, bullfighting, politics, and the making of his film *Maidstone.* Politics also comes under Mailer's biting wit in *St. George and the Godfather,* which covers the 1972 political conventions and is a kind of follow-up to *Miami and the Siege of Chicago.* The Southern poet and novelist James Dickey contributed an interesting collection: *Sorties: Journals and New Essays.* Also noteworthy were Jonathan Bishop's *Something Else,* James Baldwin's *No Name in the Street,* and essays by the gifted young black poet Nikki Giovanni, *Gemini.*

Amid a plethora of books on sex, marriage, and the role of women, two stood out: Juliet Mitchell's *Woman's Estate,* and *Open Marriage,* by Dr. George O'Neill and Nena O'Neill. Among other miscellaneous works of note were Daniel Ellsberg's *Papers on the War;* Julian Bond's *A Time to Speak, A Time to Act;* the incomparable R. Buckminster Fuller's *Intuition;* and Eliot Wigginton's fascinating compilation *The Foxfire Book.*

DANIEL R. BARNES
The Ohio State University

Children's Literature

Hard-cover children's books published in 1972 numbered some 2,000 individual titles, approximately the same as in the previous year. Paperbacks continued to increase in quantity and quality, with virtually all major publishers putting increased emphasis on reprinting backlist juvenile titles and, in some cases, new works. High production costs and buyer resistance caused several publishers to experiment with the simultaneous publication of a hard-cover edition for schools and libraries and a paperback edition for the general trade.

1972 NEWBERY MEDAL for the most distinguished children's book went to Mrs. Frisby and the Rats of NIMH, *which was written by Robert C. O'Brien and illustrated by Zena Bernstein. The book's title page (left) is shown with several characteristic illustrations.*

Overall, the quality of books published in the United States during the year was not impressive. Adult interests and concerns were reflected in the hundreds of books dealing with ecological themes, Indians in fact and fiction, arts and crafts, women's liberation, and black power. Picture books, which totaled nearly a quarter of the year's output, were not distinguished, nor did teen-age novels achieve any new level of aggressiveness or creativity. However, several novels originally published in England and exported to the United States were hailed for their originality and power.

Awards. The major awards presented in 1972 for children's books published in 1971 were as follows: The American Library Association's John Newbery Medal for the most distinguished contribution to American literature for children went to Robert C. O'Brien for *Mrs. Frisby and the Rats of NIMH,* a story for the 10–14 age group about escaped laboratory rats made wise and inventive from scientific injections. The ALA's Randolph Caldecott Medal for the most distinguished picture book was given to Nonny Hogrogian for *One Fine Day,* a retelling of an Armenian folktale.

Lillie D. Chaffin received the 30th annual award of the Child Study Association of America for dealing honestly and realistically with the world in which young people are growing up, in *John Henry McCoy,* the story of an uprooted Appalachian family. The Hans Christian Andersen Award, a biennial international prize for the greatest contribution to the literature of the children of the world, went to Scott O'Dell. The National Book Award for children's books was won by Donald Barthelme for an unconventional picture book, *The Slightly Irregular Fire Engine or the Hithering Thithering Djinn* —a choice that provoked great displeasure among traditional librarians and critics.

Fiction. Among the books published during the year, the most outstanding was *Snow-White and the Seven Dwarfs,* a tale from the Brothers Grimm, translated by Randall Jarrell and exquisitely illustrated by Nancy Ekholm Burkert. Other important picture books for the 4–7 age group were *I Saw a Ship A-sailing,* the familiar rhyme made noteworthy by Janina Domanska's swirling graphics; a bright and busy catalog of things and the sounds they make in *Crash! Bang! Boom!* by Peter Spier; *George*

and Martha, five brief farces about two hippopotamuses, and *What's the Matter with Carruthers?* featuring a bear in need of hibernation—both written and illustrated by James Marshall; *The Funny Little Woman,* a tale set in Old Japan, told by Arlene Mosel and illustrated by Blair Lent; and Robert Kraus' *Milton the Early Riser,* with bold, colorful pictures of pandas and jungle creatures by José and Ariane Aruego.

Outstanding in the age 6–9 category were two books of whimsical short stories written and illustrated by Arnold Lobel—*Frog and Toad Together* and *Mouse Tales.* Also important were *Soldier and Tsar in the Forest,* a Russian tale of punishment and reward translated by Richard Lourie and illustrated by Uri Shulevitz, and *D'Aulaires' Trolls,* an entertaining survey of the creatures of Norwegian mythology by Ingri and Edgar Parin d'Aulaire.

The best books for readers of age 9–12 were Charlotte Baker's *Cockleburr Quarters* about a 10-year-old boy caring for a half-blind dog and her eight pups; Zilpha Keatley Snyder's *The Witches of Worm,* in which a lonely, angry girl thinks she is bewitched by her cat; Betsy Byars' *The House of Wings,* a story of a boy and his grandfather caring for a blind crane; William Steig's *Dominic,* a fantasy about the adventures of a congenial hound; Norma Klein's *Mom, the Wolf Man and Me,* a mildly daring novel about an 11-year-old girl and her unmarried mother; and *The Fairy Tale Treasury,* 32 tales selected by Virginia Haviland and illustrated in rich detail by Raymond Briggs.

Among teen-age novels the best were Gail Graham's poignant and tragic portrayal of an American soldier and four Vietnamese children in *Cross-Fire;* Jill Paton Walsh's account of a girl's last summer of childhood in *Goldengrove;* Mollie Hunter's powerful evocation of a girl's grief and poverty in rural Scotland after World War I in *A Sound of Chariots;* two books touching on themes of homosexuality—Isabelle Holland's *The Man Without a Face* and Lynn Hall's *Sticks and Stones;* Sharon Bell Mathis' tale of love, loyalty, and tragedy among three young black brothers in the inner city, in *Teacup Full of Roses;* and two taut thrillers—Robb White's *Deathwatch* and George Woods' *Catch a Killer.*

Nonfiction. The most distinguished nonfiction books of the year were *The Upstairs Room* by Johanna Reiss, the author's account of hiding out in Nazi-occupied Holland during her childhood; *Death Is a Noun* by John Langone, a medical journalist's examination of aspects of the end of life; *Standing Up for the People,* a biography of Estes Kefauver by Harvey Swados; *A Twister of Twists, a Tangler of Tongues,*—tongue twisters collected by Alvin Schwartz; and *The Impossible People: A History Natural and Unnatural of Beings Terrible and Wonderful* by Georgess McHargue, a scholarly, graceful survey of creatures of folktale, myth, and superstition—giants, fairies, dwarfs, pixies, devils, centaurs, mermaids, and the like.

GEORGE A. WOODS
Editor, Children's Books, "The New York Times"

Canadian Literature

A growing concern for Canada—its politics, its past, and its prospects—marked Canadian publishing in 1972. There were many books on public affairs and history, and some fiction and poetry dealt with the problems and rewards of being a Canadian.

Public Affairs. Prime Minister Pierre Elliott Trudeau's *Conversations with Canadians* is a compilation by Ivan Head of Trudeau's pronouncements on many topics. To no one's surprise, the volume was called "political." In *The Trudeau Question,* journalist W. A. Wilson looks at the great political events in which Trudeau took part during his first four years in office. Bruce Thordarson's *Trudeau and Foreign Policy* examines an area in which Trudeau has been particularly active.

One Country or Two, edited by R. M. Burns of Queen's University, is a scholarly look at the strength and weakness of Canadian nationality. Richard Simeon's *Federal-Provincial Diplomacy* predicts a decentralization of the federal-provincial structure and forecasts important future federal-provincial decisions. *The Shouting Signpainters,* which is about the young Quebec writers who started the leftist movement in Quebec, was written by Malcolm Reid, a former Canadian Press newsman. Reid, who is well acquainted with the literary and political figures in Quebec's revolutionary nationalism, concludes: "The young people I am speaking of will not stop shouting until the walls come down."

Pierre Vallières' *L'Urgence de Choisir* was translated from the French by Penelope Williams as *Choose!* In it Vallières renounces the revolutionary Front de Libération du Québec and urges the Québécois to unite and create their own socialist state. He now supports the separatist Parti Québécois.

Dr. Patrick McGeer's *Politics in Paradise* is a sometimes amusing, often indignant book about British Columbian politics, in which the author played a leading role while he was Liberal leader in the legislature. Robert Perry's *Galt, U.S.A.,* about Galt, Ontario, is subtitled *The American Presence in a Canadian City.* It details how Canadians fail to secure independence from U. S. capital.

Biography and Autobiography. *Devil in Deerskins* is a biography of Grey Owl, the naturalist and writer of the 1930's. It was written by Anahareo, the Mohawk Indian woman who married him. Ella Pipping's *Soldier of Fortune,* translated from the Swedish, tells of the Finnish adventurer Gustaf von Schoultz, whose exciting life ended in Canada in 1838, when he was hanged for insurrection. In *Recollections of an Assiniboine Chief,* 100-year-old Dan Kennedy (Ochankugahe) looks back on the efforts of the Assiniboines to adjust to the ways of the white man.

History. Aloysius Balyder's *Canadian-Soviet Relations Between the World Wars* is a very thorough examination of its subject. Volume 2 of *The Gunners of Canada,* by Col. G. W. L. Nicholson, takes Canada's artillerymen from 1919, where the first volume had concluded, to the present. Martin Robin's *The Rush for Spoils: The Company Province, 1871–1933,* the first in a series on the history of British Columbia, is marred by some inaccuracies.

Poetry. *Two Seasons* is a comprehensive selection of works written by the leading poet Dorothy Livesay since 1928. Alden Nowlan's *Between Tears and Laughter* adds to the reputation of a mature poet. Nowlan's experiences on a New Brunswick newspaper are put to good use in *The Night Editor's Poem,* a restrained and powerful statement about the death of Martin Luther King, Jr.

The prolific George Bowering published *Genève,* a handsome volume on the theme of tarot cards and their images. Raymond Souster's *The Years* is in

three parts, devoted to the 1960's, 1950's, and 1940's, respectively. Souster writes directly and well on a variety of themes, touching them all with poetry. Al Purdy drew praise for his *Selected Poems,* which appeared 28 years after the publication of his first volume. Gwendolyn MacEwan looks at the heart of darkness within each of us in *The Armies of the Moon.* In *Nobody Owns th Earth,* bill bisset, who prefers his name uncapitalized, breaks the rules of grammar and spelling, sometimes with successful results. In his poems, as in the title, "the" is spelled "th."

Fiction. Harry J. Boyle departs from the humorous writing of his previous books in *The Great Canadian Novel.* This work details the problems of a 50-year-old advertising man who is trying to compose a masterpiece of Canadian fiction. As always, Boyle writes well. Descriptions of the hero's youth in Saskatchewan ring clear and true, and there are meaningful passages that examine what is involved in being a Canadian.

In *Scann,* Robert Harlow's third novel and his best to date, the protagonist writes local history and discovers that history is what he makes of it. Arved Viirlaid's *Graves Without Crosses* is a big, angry novel about the Russian and German invasions of Estonia during World War II. E. G. Perraut's *The Twelfth Mile,* a suspense story of espionage at sea, achieved considerable popularity. Sylvia Fraser's *Pandora* is an honest first novel about the experience of childhood. Another first novel, David Morell's violent *First Blood* is skillfully written, and Margaret Atwood's *Surfacing* is a story of a woman's search for identity.

Miscellaneous. *Toward the Discovery of Canada,* by historian Donald Creighton, is a collection of essays that reflect concern about the pressures that threaten Canada's survival. In *Science and Politics in Canada,* G. Bruce Doern deals with the use of science to solve public problems. Paul Duval's *Four Decades: The Canadian Group of Painters and Their Contemporaries* is beautifully illustrated and authoritative.

In *A Whale for the Killing,* Farley Mowat records the dying days of a fin whale trapped in a salt-water lagoon near Burgeo, Newfoundland. While Mowat tried to save the whale, others shot hundreds of rounds of ammunition into it. This story of 20th century greed pleads for an end to commercial whaling. *The Devil's Butler,* by the Vancouver *Sun* writer Simma Holt, is a well-documented account of how a young transient was held captive by members of the Satan's Angels motorcycle club and of the subsequent trial and conviction of the abductors.

Don Bell's *Saturday Night at the Bagel Factory* is a collection of stories and sketches describing Montreal's odd characters. *The Lace Ghetto,* by Maxine and Deanna White, documents the realities of being female. Tom and Christie Harris' *Mule Lib* is a humorous tale of a man and a mule in World War I.

The West Coast Trial and Nitinat Lakes by John Twigg and Ken Farquharson was published by the Sierra Club of British Columbia. It is a hiker's guide to the fascinating 50-mile trail between Port Renfrew and Bamfield on Vancouver Island.

Conservationist James Woodford's *Violated Vision: The Rape of Canada's North,* paints an alarming picture and suggests what actions are needed. Woodford sees the federal government's development of the north as being, in too many cases, short-sighted and exploitative. He pleads for an Arctic federal parks program. *The Pollution Guide,* by Tiny Bennett and Wade Rowland, avoids hysteria, presents facts, and demonstrates the differences between "quality of life" and "standard of living."

Also appearing in 1972 was *Read Canadian: A Book About Canadian Books,* edited by Robert Fulford, David Godfrey, and Abraham Rotstein. It is made up of essays, with accompanying lists of books, by 30 experts in different areas of Canadian writing.

DAVID SAVAGE, *Simon Fraser University*

FRENCH CANADIAN LITERATURE

The area of French literature showing the most vitality in Canada during 1972 was the theater. Plays were popular both in performance and in print. In particular, the plays of Michel Tremblay—from *Trois petits tours* to *À toi, pour toujours, ta Marie-Lou*—were gaining such influence that there was great demand for them both on the stage and in the bookstore.

Poetry. The year did not produce any remarkably new or exciting poetry. The most notable poetry publications were one-volume editions of the major works of Paul-Marie Lapointe and of Fernand Oullette, which hold up well on rereading. The poems of Gilbert Langevin were finally collected in a volume entitled *Origine,* which offers the reader many surprises. In *Paysage,* the poet Michel Beaulieu continued his search for a poetic language with both immediacy and sensual resonance.

Fiction. A new edition of the tales of the 19th century Canadian author Louis Honoré Fréchette was published in 1972, and his *Les Originaux et détraqués* remained as popular as the almanac. Victor-Lévy Beaulieu published two works of fiction during the year—*Un Rêve québécois,* in which he uses monologue as much as possible and creates an atmosphere of a sado-masochistic nightmare, and *Les Grand-pères,* without a doubt his best book.

The Acadian novelist Antonine Maillet wrote with great relish and verve in *Pointes-aux-coques* and even more so in *Don l'Original.* In *Le Loup* the talented Marie-Claire Blais describes the intimate love affair of a somewhat unreal hero. The work, however, lacks adequate psychological consistency.

Jacques Garneau's first novel, *Mémoires de l'oeil,* is astonishing in its degree of introspection, going against current literary trends, but it offers a new treatment of voyeurism. Motion picture producer Jacques Godbout's fourth novel, *D'Amour, P. Q.,* published in Paris, is an ambiguous work that calls into question the traditional narrative forms and opens the way for a new popular art form.

Nonfiction. The most heralded essay of the year was *L'Urgence de choisir,* in which the militant Pierre Vallières broke with his former policy of political violence in favor of more peaceful means of action. This declaration of his stance seemed to herald the end of terrorism in Canada.

In addition to his new fiction, Victor-Lévy Beaulieu published a notable essay on Jack Kerouac and unexpectedly indulged himself in autobiography in *Pour saluer Victor Hugo.* The discussion of the type of French that should be spoken in Quebec continued in 1972, and in *Éloge du français québécois,* Henri Bélanger denounced traditional purism in favor of the language spoken by the Québécois.

ANDRÉ MAJOR, *Literary Critic, Montreal*

PETER NICHOLAS LESSING

DORIS LESSING treats man's struggle for a life of dignity in The Story of a Non-Marrying Man.

English Literature

The year 1972 was a particularly harsh one in English political and social life, with continual bloodshed in Northern Ireland and fierce disputes between the government and labor at home. Much of the year's best literature reflected these astringent facts of life in ways that again demonstrate the permanent value of art as a faithful mirror of man's world.

Fiction. In many respects, the weightiest novel of the year was Margaret Drabble's *The Needle's Eye,* the study of a wealthy woman who gives away her fortune in an effort to live a righteous life. Miss Drabble's story of the eccentric heiress Rose Vassilou is reminiscent of a morality play, a work in which virtue sometimes appears to be only "a dim reflex of the voracious self," but in which it can also shine through as incandescent and genuinely self-disregarding. Austere in its narrative line, true to the unglamorous difficulties of the moral life, *The Needle's Eye* has the unusual quality of somber beauty.

Striking in many of the same ways was Doris Lessing's fine novella, *The Temptation of Jack Orkney,* one of several pieces collected in *The Story of a Non-Marrying Man.* Like Miss Drabble, Mrs. Lessing is fascinated by man's efforts to lead a life of dignity and moral adventurousness in a dark, destructive time. Her hero, Jack Orkney, is a journalist, social critic, and political organizer shown in confrontation with his public and private ghosts. The climactic moment comes when this rational man experiences a religious temptation to which he almost submits. He does not, however, confirming instead his belief in a "skeptical, obdurate" kind of contemporary stoicism. Telling his story, Mrs. Les-

sing displays her strong gifts for social observation. Only Mrs. Lessing's most devoted admirers would want to read all the stories in the volume, but *The Temptation of Jack Orkney* has a universal appeal. In the U. S. edition of the book, the story was properly given pride of place as the title work of the collection.

Several novels were praised for their handling of contemporary social and personal problems. C. P. Snow's *The Malcontents* deals with the conflict between young radicals and the Establishment in an English university city. *The Holiday Friend* by Snow's wife, Pamela Hansford Johnson, explores the tension experienced by an art professor caught in the opposing currents of his desire for sexual promiscuity and the obligations of family life. The campus in Thomas Hinde's *Generally a Virgin* is located in the United States, but many Englishmen found his novel to be witty and pertinent to their lives. Auberon Waugh's way of exploring contemporary self-divisions was to write a playful, modern-dress version of *As You Like It* in novel form. His *A Bed of Flowers* describes the efforts of a disaffected industrialist to live in a commune in Somerset. For some reviewers, however, the basic idea of the novel was more interesting than anything that Waugh was able to embody in his narrative.

Several of the year's most distinctive novels did not deal with contemporary problems but explored the past in vigorous departures from conventional realism. John Berger's *G,* for example, retells the Don Juan legend against the background of late 19th and early 20th century political violence. The form of *G* is entirely discontinuous, for in Berger's view "the writer's desire to finish is fatal to the truth. The End unifies. Unity must be established in another way." Many readers delighted in Berger's experimental audacity. However, some complained that his solemnly inconclusive meditations on politics and sexual relations were tedious and unilluminating.

Thomas Keneally also mixed history, intrigue, and psychological rumination in *The Chant of Jimmy Blacksmith,* a novel set in the Australian back country at the turn of the century. Another work of considerable originality was Susan Hill's *The Bird of Night,* cast in the form of an old scholar's memoir of his dead friend, the mad poet Francis Croft.

No chronicle of experimental fiction can neglect the latest contribution of Samuel Beckett. *The Lost Ones,* a timeless, elegant, desperate fable about the extinction of life on earth, was first written in French and then translated by the author into English. Paradoxically, the Irish-born Beckett is now proudly claimed for the literature of France as well as that of England.

Other outstanding novels of 1972 included George Mackay Brown's *Greenvoe;* David Storey's *Pasmore;* Edna O'Brien's *Night;* C. J. Driver's *Death of Fathers;* Lennox Cook's *A Feeling of Disquiet;* Arthur Koestler's *The Call Girls;* John Braine's *The Queen of a Distant Country;* Elizabeth Jane Howard's *Odd Girl Out;* Len Deighton's *Close-up;* and Andrew Sinclair's *Magog.*

Much of the year's most interesting work in short fiction appeared in traditional realistic forms. William Trevor wrote melancholy comedies of the insulted and injured in *The Ballroom of Romance.* Elizabeth Taylor's *The Devastating Boys* offered unostentatious but authoritative studies of human loneliness. Nadine Gordimer told urgent tales of

African racial stress and politics in *Livingstone's Companions*. One modern master, Graham Greene, brought all his short fiction together in *Collected Stories*. It was a pleasure for many readers to encounter again such skillfully told stories as *The Basement Room* and *The End of the Party*. Another modern master was poorly represented. E. M. Forster's *The Life to Come* is a posthumous collection of previously uncollected tales that might better have been left ungathered.

Nonfiction. The most widely discussed nonfiction work to appear in 1972 was Quentin Bell's two-volume biography of his aunt, *Virginia Woolf*. In the first volume, published early in the year, Bell recreated the famous Bloomsbury environment of "maximum pressure," which, in Angus Wilson's words, "nurtured both her genius and her future insanities." Volume one was filled with revelations about Leslie Stephen's startling daughter, Virginia: how as a child she was the unwilling, confused victim of an older half-brother's sexual advances; how she flirted with Clive Bell, nearly married Lytton Strachey, and finally did marry Leonard Woolf. Volume two, which appeared in October, completed the account with emphasis on Mrs. Woolf's intense, complicated relationships with other women, notably Victoria Sackville-West. Although many people read the biography with eager fascination, some complained that Bell virtually ignored the one thing that, in fact, makes Mrs. Woolf important, her books. In this view, the biography is more interesting as a revelation of a complex, neurotic woman than as an account of a great creative artist.

Two other figures of Mrs. Woolf's generation were also subjects of important scholarly works. Bernard Shaw's letters were collected by Dan H. Lawrence, and the correspondence of Roger Fry, English painter and art critic, was gathered by Denys Sutton. The Shaw volume covers the period from 1898 to 1910, when the Irish genius became firmly established as a playwright. Valuable not only as a revelation of Shaw's fantastic wit and energy, the collection is also a matchless record of theatrical life at the turn of the century. The two volumes of Fry's letters show how he helped shape modern taste through his advocacy of the post-Impressionists and through his strongly expressed ideas regarding form as the essential in art.

Two very different but imposing figures of a later generation were subjects of absorbing biographies. A. J. P. Taylor explored the life and influence of Lord Beaverbrook, the powerful newspaper magnate, who counseled British statesmen and was the influential minister of aircraft production in the early years of World War II. Peter Stansky and William Abrahams examined the early life of Eric Blair at Eton, in Burma, and in London, before he became the legendary George Orwell. Their volume, *The Unknown Orwell*, kindled a warm controversy about an enigmatic man of letters.

Again, as in 1971, personal memoirs were a popular literary form. That ancient gadfly, Malcolm Muggeridge, claimed attention with *The Green Stick*, the first volume in a projected autobiography called *Chronicles of Wasted Time*. One acidulous reader suggested that a more suitable title might have been *Advertisements for Myself*. Photographer and designer Cecil Beaton entertained the public with the third volume of his recollections, *The Happy Years: 1944–1948*, even though his much publicized relationship with the actress Greta Garbo was perhaps too dryly handled. Three important figures in English political life told of their participation in the turbulent events of the last 30 years. *Pointing the Way*, the fifth volume of Harold Macmillan's memoirs, covers a crucial period of his premiership, 1959–61. *Ten Year Stint* is Lord Robens' account of his chairmanship of the national coal board. Lord Gladwyn's *Memoirs* described his years as ambassador to the United Nations and to France.

Four collections of literary and philosophical essays were noteworthy. George Steiner pleased his admirers and irritated his detractors with his controversial *Extraterritorial: Papers on Literature and the Language of Revolution*. In *Nor Shall My Sword*, F. R. Leavis collected recent pieces on education, culture, and society, but his shrill repetitive tone made the collection a set of sermons for the already converted. Conor Cruise O'Brien meditated on the relationship between art and politics in *The Suspecting Glance*. The philosopher Stuart Hampshire combined lucidity with suggestiveness in *Freedom of Mind and Other Essays*.

Perhaps in a class by themselves were two books that do not exactly qualify as literature, but which were widely discussed in literary circles. *Pornography: the Longford Report* generated more talk than action. The publication of the first volume of the Supplement to the *Oxford English Dictionary* (A-G) provided a field day for wordmongers.

Poetry. Sir John Betjeman, author of such volumes of poetry as *Ghastly Good Taste, Old Bats in New Belfries*, and *A Few Late Crysanthemums*, as well as the verse autobiography *Summoned by Bells*, was named Poet Laureate on October 10. Sir John, who was knighted in 1969, is one of the most widely read living poets in England. He succeeded Cecil Day-Lewis, who died on May 22.

Although no one single volume of verse created a stir in English literature in 1972, the year's work in poetry was varied and interesting. The older generation of poets was represented by W. H. Auden, Stephen Spender, Stevie Smith, and W. R. Rodgers. Auden's *Epistle to a Godson* may well have been the most widely read new book of poetry, although opinion divided between those who delighted in his skill and wisdom and those who complained of his seeming casualness of concern. Spender, whose son was the recipient of Auden's epistle, published *The Generous Days*, an affecting sample of recent work. The two other noteworthy volumes were posthumous. One was *The Collected Poems* of the Ulster poet W. R. Rodgers, who died in 1969. The other was *Scorpion*, the last book of unnerving comic poems by the unique Miss Smith, who died in 1971.

In the middle generation were Charles Tomlinson with *Written on Water*, D. J. Enright with *Daughters of Earth*, and Peter Porter with two volumes, *After Martial* and *Preaching to the Converted*. The best books by younger poets were John Fuller's *Cannibals and Missionaries*; Derek Mahon's *Lives*; Seamus Heaney's *Wintering Out*; Douglas Dunn's *The Happier Life*; Brian Patten's *The Irrelevant Song*; and Molly Holden's *Air and Chill Earth*.

One book certain to influence literary taste for many years to come was Helen Gardner's anthology, *The New Oxford Book of English Verse*. Its predecessor, *The Oxford Book of English Verse*, compiled by Sir Arthur Quiller-Couch, has sold nearly one million copies since its publication in 1900.

LAWRENCE GRAVER, *Williams College*

JULES ROMAINS (1885–1972)

Jules Romains, one of France's most distinguished men of letters, died in Paris on Aug. 14, 1972. During his lifetime he wrote over 90 books, including novels, plays, poetry, short stories, and philosophical essays. His philosophy of *unanimisme,* which maintains that man can attain fulfillment only as a member of a community and that "the adventure of humanity is

THE NEW YORK TIMES

essentially an adventure of groups," is the central theme of his monumental 27-volume novel *Les Hommes de bonne volonté* (1932–47; *Men of Good Will*). It is a pageant of French and western European history from 1908 to 1933, written in a pessimistic and antiromantic vein. As a playwright, he was best known for his *Knock ou la triomphe de la médecine* (1923; *Dr. Knock*).

The son of a schoolteacher, Jules Romains was born Louis Farigoule at Saint-Julien Chapteuil on Aug. 26, 1885. He spent his early years in Paris and graduated from the École Normale Supérieure in 1909 with a degree in philosophy and science. His first book of verse, *La Vie unanime* (1908), in which he expounded his unanimist philosophy, was followed in 1911 by the play *L'Armée dans la ville* and the novel *Mort de quelqu'un* (*Death of a Nobody*). Among his other works of that period are the novels *Les Copains* (1913) and *Sur les Quais de La Villette* (1914; *On the Wharves of La Villette*). He also published a number of philosophically oriented poems, including the antiwar *Europe* (1916), as well as purely lyrical verse.

In 1919, after teaching philosophy for a decade, Romains decided to devote himself entirely to writing and travel. In 1928 he published the volume of verse *Chants des dix années 1914–1924*. Several works for the theatre followed, including the drama *Le Dictateur* (1926) and the comedies *Monsieur le Trouhadec* (1923) and *Donogoo* (1930). In *Donogoo* he satirized the foibles of mankind in a manner that has been compared with Molière. The writing of his major work *Les Hommes de bonne volonté* occupied him for the next 15 years. In *A Visit to the Americans* (1936) and *Salsette Discovers America* (1942), Romains praised American democracy. *The Seven Mysteries of Europe* (1940) describes his own diplomatic work.

Romains spent World War II in the United States and Mexico, where he worked tirelessly in behalf of the Free French cause and the Allied war effort. After the war he returned to France, where he resumed his literary activities and began writing a regular column for the newspaper *L'Aurore.* His later works include *Napoléon par lui-même* (1963) and *Marc-Aurèle, ou l'Empereur de bonne volonté* (1968). He held the rank of grand officer in the French Legion of Honor and was elected to the Académie Française in 1946.

HENRY SLOAN

French Literature

In 1972 the French literary world was saddened by the death of Jules Romains in Paris at the age of 86. A member of the Académie Française, Romains, whose real name was Louis Farigoule, made his mark as a poet, playwright, and novelist. He was also a founder of the French movement known as *unanimisme,* which stressed the value of the group in society. He was famous as the author of the stage hit *Knock ou le triomphe de la médecine* and of *Les Hommes de bonne volonté* (1932–1947), a 27-volume novel on French society between 1908 and 1933.

In 1972, Julian Green, who had been elected to the Académie Française in 1971, published *Ce qui reste de jour.* This was the ninth part of his multivolume *Journal,* one of his most important works.

Fiction. Numerous novels were published in France in 1972. Among the most popular works in the traditional style were *Trois sucettes à la menthe* by Robert Sabatier, a nostalgic evocation of Paris in the 1930's; *Les Bons Enfants* by Lucie Faure, in which the author looks upon the generation gap in today's world; *Des bleus à l'âme* by Françoise Sagan, a light-handed, poetic "essay-novel"; Benoîte Groult's *La Part des choses,* and her sister Flora's *Maxime ou la dechirure,* both interesting but conventional books. Romain Gary wrote *Europa,* a half-realistic, half-surrealistic novel based on the problems and definition of the European idea of art, literature, and customs. In *Malevil* by Robert Merle, the seven survivors of an atomic war reorganize their lives in the Languedoc region of France. Robert Cesbron's *Voici le temps des imposteurs* is a thesis novel denouncing the deception wrought by a certain type of journalism. *L'Accusée* by Michel de Saint Pierre is a generous novel about the trial of a woman accused of having committed murder in order to keep her children. The main themes of the novel are women's rights and the imperfections of an outdated, overburdened legal system.

Avant-garde literature was represented by Hélène Cixous' *Neutre,* which the author describes as a "chaos-mos," a combination of *chaos* and *cosmos,* and considers a "system of metaphors in which the conscious, the subconscious, and chance work each in its own way." Philippe Sollers, a revolutionary with Maoist leanings, wrote *Lois,* in which he used a so-called "terrorist" technique, a style full of new words coined to shock "bourgeois" readers. He is by turns irritating, puerile, threatening, and deeply original. The "nouveau roman" was represented by Robert Pinget's *Fable.* Nathalie Sarraute, a fine author whose work borders on the "nouveau roman," wrote *Vous les entendez,* a subtle, poignant work about the conflict between the generations.

Nonfiction. One of the major nonfiction works of 1972 was volume three of *L'Idiot de la famille,* Jean-Paul Sartre's monumental study of Gustave Flaubert. In this volume, Sartre analyzes the psychosociological climate in France between the years 1840 and 1850. He presents the thesis that Flaubert was "programmed" by the forces which give a certain predictable direction to the way in which French society evolves and which he sees as deriving from the traditionally French spirit of objectivity. Sartre, considering Flaubert a neurotic bourgeois author writing for a neurotic bourgeois society, says that Flaubert experienced ahead of his time the *"crise de conscience"* of the bourgeoisie that erupted in the years between 1848 and 1852 and continued into the years of the Second Empire.

In *Tout compte fait,* the renowned Simone de Beauvoir contemplates with "familiarity and detachment" that "strange object," her life. Jean-Louis Curtis' *La Chine m'inquiète,* is a collection of delightful literary pastiches composed around the general theme of the revolution and the "events" of May 1968. Other outstanding works of nonfiction included the remarkable biography of Pierre-Augustin Caron de Beaumarchais, *Figaro ou la vie*

de Beaumarchais by the duke of Castries, and Jacques Scherer's searching essay on Diderot, *Le Cardinal et l'Orang-Outang.*

Poetry. A major poetic work of 1972 was *L'Arrière-pays* by Yves Bonnefoy. The "back country" to which the author alludes in the title cannot be located geographically. Bonnefoy undertakes to try to reach another world, another life, and to penetrate into a surreal land of the imagination.

Also worthy of mention were the love poems of Michel Alves collected in *Des Lois-naturelles,* as well as the volumes *La Peau et les mots* by Bertrand Noel, *La Main de bronze* by Pierre Gabriel, and *Sol absolu,* by Laurand Gaspar. Most of these poets express their thoughts in tightly knit, singing lines that strive to set off sparks. Their principal themes are physical love and the description of various natural phenomena. Pierre Seghers published *Anthologie des poètes maudits,* containing works of the "accursed poets of today," among them, André de Richaud and Antonin Artaud.

Theater. Almost all the hit plays in 1972 were revivals, or productions of foreign works. One notable exception was Eugène Ionesco's *Macbett,* an entertaining, powerful, gory farce with surrealistic overtones, based on the theme of Shakespeare's tragedy.

PIERRE BRODIN
Lycée Français de New York

German Literature

A conservative trend in German literary life, which was discernible in 1971, became more pronounced in 1972. The explanation for its development lay not in the languishing economic situation but in the greater willingness of progressive writers to utilize traditional style elements in their search for popular acceptance.

A German, Heinrich Böll, received the Nobel Prize for Literature in 1972. (See BIOGRAPHY.)

Poetry. The new emphasis was foreshadowed by the appreciation shown, posthumously, to the Franconian poet Ludwig Friedrich Barthel (died 1963), whose autobiographical verse, *Stücke des Lebens,* has now been completely published. Among younger poets a terse realism seemed to be in vogue. This was illustrated by three new collections: Günter Eich's selected verse, *Lesebuch;* Rolf Bongs' engaging poems *A bis plus minus Zett;* and Wolfram Dahl's *Zwischen Eins und 2000.* Günter Radke's *Davon kommst du nicht los* should also be mentioned.

Prose. Critics accustomed to Peter Handke's ravings against the laggard public found his new novel, *Der kurze Brief zum langen Abschied,* something of a surprise. Its theme is a conventional one—a pilgrimage through the United States in search of an elusive girl friend. In its style it unabashedly adopts late 19th century literary devices. On the other hand, Gabriele Wohmann retains her pessimistic view of contemporary society in her new prose works, *Selbstverteidigung* and *Gegenangriff.* A less distanced, more committed stance is displayed by Alfred Andersch in *Norden Südan rechts und links,* and by Rudolf Hagelstange in his published conversation with the graphic artist H. A. P. Grieshaber about the policy of defoliation in Vietnam, *Ein Gespräch über Bäume.*

Max Frisch, whose works continue to rank among the best sellers in Germany, published *Tagebuch 1966–1971.* Only superficially autobio-

MCGRAW-HILL

HEINRICH BÖLL, a leading postwar German novelist and playwright, was the winner of the 1972 Nobel Prize in literature. The award is worth about $100,000.

graphical, it has as its main concern the discrepancy between the rival claims of the political systems of our time and the disappointing results of their application in real life, as observed from the melancholy viewpoint of an aging poet. The prominent East German author Hermann Kant finally succeeded in overcoming his publisher's objections against the publication of his new novel *Impressum,* which criticizes the glorification of Stalin.

Entertaining novels of all categories, including science fiction, were brought out by a number of publishers. The most ambitious stories were Peter Kuhn's *Siam-Siam,* Horst Eckert's *Cholonek oder Der liebe Gott aus Lehm* (published under the pen name "Janosch"), and Wolfgang Georg Fisher's *Möblierte Zimmer,* which is a refugee chronicle. German translations of English novels by Dee Brown, Eric Malpass, and Frederic Forsyth found their way onto the best-seller list. In the genre of "black humor" was Ben Witter's *Argernisse.*

Finally, in a somewhat autobiographical novel, *Aus dem Tagebuch einer Schnecke,* Günter Grass reminisces about adolescence and examines his commitment to socialism with humor and objectivity.

Theater. Thomas Bernhard's thoroughly modern play *Der Ignorant und der Wahnsinnige* was a rousing success at its Salzburg premiere. In his pitiless exposure of the reality behind the operatic illusions of Mozart's *Magic Flute,* Bernhard reveals a debt to Ionesco, but the exercise ends in a manly acceptance of life's contradictions rather than in bottomless despair. The same spirit pervaded Tankred Dorst's successful stage version of Hans Fallada's novel *Kleiner Mann—was nun?* and his dramatization of Knut Hamsun's last years, *Das*

lange Leben. Social dramas by Rolf Hochhuth and by the young Bavarian playwright Franz Xaver Kroetz also found sympathetic audiences, while the revolutionary message of Peter Weiss' *Hoelderlin* was less well received.

Nonfiction. The vogue of scholarly, yet well-written historical accounts for the general public continued in 1972. It had begun before Christmas of 1971 with the publication of Golo Mann's definitive, lengthy *Wallenstein* and Peter Haage's witty biography of Egon Friedell, *Der Partylöwe, der nur Bücher frass.* Alexander Lernet-Holenia's controversial *Die Geheimnisse des Hauses, Österreich, Roman einer Dynastie* borders on fiction. More significant is Norbert Muehlen's criticism of the stereotyped image of the "ugly American" in his *Amerika —im Gegenteil.* A correspondent on U. S. affairs for the weekly *Deutsche Zeitung,* Muehlen was able to achieve an independent German parallel to Arnold Beichman's *Nine Lies about America.* Another book about America is C. W. Ceram's *Der erste Amerikaner.* Kurt W. Marek, who wrote under the pen name of C. W. Ceram, died in April before its appearance.

Obituaries. Gertrud von Le Fort, Ludwig Marcusse, György Lukacs, and Bertolt Brecht's wife, Helene Weigel, died in 1971. The year 1972 saw the death of three less famous figures: Ludwig Tügel, author of *Pferdemusik;* Georg Rendl, who wrote *Bienernroman;* Hugo Hartung, author of *Piroschka;* and Ernst von Solomon, author of *Der Fragebogen.*

ERNST ROSE
Author of "A History of German Literature"

Italian Literature

Italian literature fared quite well in 1972. It was a strong year for fiction and a number of best sellers aroused considerable interest.

Fiction Awards. The Strega Prize was won by Giuseppe Dessi for *Paese d'ombra.* A highly successful work, the novel had sold some 125,000 copies before it was honored with the prize. In a realistic, almost Flaubertian manner, Dessi tells the story of Angelo Uras, a strong and honest man of humble origin, who rises from poverty to wealth and social prominence, partly through chance and partly through his own conscious efforts and clear intelligence. Uras' life is closely linked to his homeland, Sardinia, to its history and customs during the second half of the 19th century. The descriptions of the island form an organic part of the author's simple but rich and fluent narrative, written in the best tradition of Italian regional literature.

The Viareggio Prize was given to Carlo Laurenzi for *Quell' antico amore.* A well-known poet, Laurenzi made his debut as a novelist with this work. The novel, which sold over 30,000 copies within two months of publication, was acclaimed for its elegant style and for its fusion of humor, emotion, irony, and melancholy lyricism. The work is divided into four parts, with its young hero, Carlo, serving as the connecting link. Carlo describes his two fathers, one natural and the other legal. After some probing, he discovers the fascinating distant relatives after whom he was named—a 19th century cardinal and the Duke of Parma, who was possessed by a secret passion for a Florentine girl.

Other Fiction. A popular favorite in 1972 was Romano Bilenchi's *Il Bottone di Stalingrad,* regarded by some critics as the best Italian novel of the post-war period. It marked a return to fiction for Bilenchi, a talented Tuscan journalist, after 30 years of voluntary silence. Bilenchi portrays the experiences of Marco, a young Communist, describing his difficult life before, during, and after the Fascist era in Italy and during the days of the anti-German resistance. Marco's fiancée is killed by police fire during a strikers' demonstration, but he has enough courage and strength to overcome even this tragedy, which seems to complete a political, moral, and emotional education forged through battle, blood, and tears. Marco's destiny, woven into the larger tapestry of historical events, is unfolded masterfully, in a sober, incisive way which combines emotional restraint with dramatic suspense.

Carlo Castellaneta's *La Paloma* also has social overtones, but is written in a completely different style. Its hero, a combination of saint, poet, and utopian, is an anarchist split between political passions and family affections, between dreams of universal transformation and the realities of daily existence. In *La Città di Miriam* by Fulvio Tomizza, the hero, Stefano, a half-Slavic, half-Italian native of Trieste, marries Miriam, who belongs to the Jewish bourgeois society of the Adriatic port. He acquires a real education in marriage through his tormented erotic and sentimental relations with his wife, a vividly and skillfully drawn figure. Another work of psychological realism was Giovanni Arpino's *Randagio e l'eroe,* about a restless and rebellious man who abandons his passionate mistress in his desire for self-assertion and inner freedom.

Mention should also be made of *La Putina Greca,* another of Neri Pozza's collections of tales about Venetian artists of the Renaissance, such as Titian, Giorgione, Bellini, and Palladio. Pozza, a sculptor and engraver as well as a writer, combines a romantic imagination with scrupulous historical documentation. In *Memorie di una ladra,* Dacia Maraini, the wife of novelist Alberto Moravia, describes the colorful adventures of a female professional thief, a kind of Italian Moll Flanders, rendered attractive by her vitality and naïveté.

Several experimental novels were written in 1972. In *La Bella di Lodi,* Alberto Arbasino builds a complex structure of linguistic experiments around a deceptively simple plot. He describes the love affair of a rich Lombardian girl and a penniless mechanic. The hero is interested primarily in the heroine's money, while she is conquered by his virility. The eroticism is much stronger in Alfredo Todisco's *Il Corpo,* which depicts the love of an aging man for a young girl of 20 and abounds in pessimistic maxims on the lure of sex, in a style reminiscent of Schopenhauer. Two extraordinary narratives were Libero Bigiaretti's *Dalla Donna alla luna,* a sharp satire of modern society, and Luigi Bongiorno's *La Selva oscura,* a Dantesque, symbolic vision of contemporary urban civilization.

Nonfiction. The death in 1972 of Dino Buzzati, the master of fantastic tales, prompted the publication in leading periodicals of many essays analyzing this type of literature.

The year also saw the publication of the first two volumes of the monumental six-volume *Storia d'Italia.* The project has enlisted the services of a large group of Italian and foreign historians, and the appearance of the first volumes was hailed as a great publishing event.

MARC SLONIM
Sarah Lawrence College Foreign Studies

Japanese Literature

In 1972, the younger generation of writers, those born since 1926, during the reign of Emperor Hirohito, made their presence strongly felt. The dwindling ranks of their older colleagues, born during the Meiji and Taisho periods, were reduced even further by the suicide, in April, of the famous novelist, Yasunari Kawabata. His death reminded Japan and the world of the ritual suicide of his celebrated protégé, Yukio Mishima, in November 1970.

Non-Fiction. Works on the national character of Japan and on the country's future were more popular in 1972 than in the previous year. Thus, *Nihon Retto Kaizoron* (*Remodeling the Japanese Islands*), an outline of a master plan for the social and economic transformation of Japan, by Kakuei Tanaka, the energetic new prime minister, was widely read.

In *Yonaoshi-no Rinri to Ronri* (*Ethics and Logic for Revolution*), Makoto Oda, a New Leftist, asserts that *tada-no hito* (the common man) should become *sukatantaisho* (a man of action) through his own personal revolution. Another book expressing dissatisfaction with the status quo was Yasuji Hanamori's *Issengorin-no Hata* (*A One-and-a-Half Cent Flag*), in which he indicts what he regards as the dangerous aspects of modern Japan.

Two of the most interesting books on Japanese culture were Kazuko Tsurumi's *Kokishin to Nihonjin* (*Curiosity and the Japanese*) and *Nihonjin to Nihonbunka* (*The Japanese and Japanese Culture*) by Ryotaro Shiba and Donald Keene. Shiba and Keene point out that the most important quality of Japanese culture is *taoyameburi* (maidenliness). Literary criticism was represented by Shigeki Senuma's *Nihon Bundanshi* (*The History of Japanese Literary Circles*).

Numerous memorial issues were published on the death of Kawabata. The American scholar Edward Seidensticker, translator of Kawabata's *Snow Country* and other works, noted that Kawabata's death marked the end of an era.

Fiction. Many younger fiction writers were active in 1972. Among the most successful were Kaisei Ri, a Korean, and Mineo Higashi, Akio Miyahara, and Hiroshi Hatayama—all of whom received the Akutagawa Prize. In *Kinuta-o Utsu Onna* (*A Woman Beating the Fulling Block*), Ri offers a memorable portrait of a Korean mother living in Japan. Higashi's *Okinawa-no Shonen* (*A Boy in Okinawa*), is a study of adolescence in occupied Okinawa. *Dareka-ga Sawatta* (*Somebody Touched*) by Miyahara, deals with relationships between teachers and pupils in an isolated leper colony school. In *Itsuka Kiteki-o Narashite* (*Someday Blowing a Whistle*), Hatayama analyzes the suffering endured by his harelipped hero.

One of the most talked about books of 1972 was Sawako Ariyoshi's *Kokotsu-no Hito* (*The Ecstatic One*). In this work the author realistically and compassionately studies the way of life of aged people, examining the "spiritual rapture" of childishness brought on by mental deterioration. Other outstanding novels included Taijun Takeda's *Fuji* (*Mt. Fuji*); Yasushi Inoue's *Goshirakawain* (*The Retired Emperor Goshirakawa*); Saiichi Maruya's *Tatta Hitorino Hanran* (*One Man's Rebellion*); and Morio Kita's *Yoidore Bune* (*A Drunken Boat*).

Biography. *Tsuda Sokichi-no Shisoshiteki-kenkyu* (*Sokichi Tsuda in the History of Thought*) by Saburo Ienaga marked the first serious research on the late, great thinker. Daizo Kusayanagi published *Tokko-no Shiso* (*The Thought of the Special Corps*), about Adm. Takijiro Onishi, the fanatic advocate of Kamikaze suicide attacks. Other biographies included Takaaki Yoshimoto's *Minamoto-no Sanetomo,* about the medieval *tanka* poet, and Kenichi Matsumoto's *Kita Ikki Ron* (*Essay on Ikki Kita*), about the late ultranationalist.

Poetry. In 1972, as in 1971, some fine *tanka* verse was written. Outstanding works were *Hekigan* (*Blue Rocks*) by Tetsuhisa Tsubono and *Irekae* (*Switching*) by Kakuji Toyama. Other fine poets who produced *tanka* included Shizue Hatsui, Taeko Kuzuhara, and Yukitsuna Sasaki. The field of *haiku* was also well represented. *Santoka Zenshu* (*The Complete Works of Santoka*) by the late poet Santoka Taneda was extremely popular. Another important work was *Saikin Haiku Saijiki* (*Anthology of Recent Haiku Classified by Seasons*) by Kenkichi Yamamoto.

Drama. Numerous plays were published and staged in 1972. Chief among them were Masakazu Yamazaki's *O, Eroizu* (*Oh, Heloise*); Chikao Tanaka's *Jikan-to-yu Kisha* (*A Train Named Time*); Mitsuo Nakamura's *Katei-no Kofuku?* (*Happiness at Home?*); Seicho Matsumoto's *Kokkakaizohoan* (*Plan for the Reorganization of Japan*); Tadasu Iizawa's *Chinshi-no Fujin* (*The Lady of Mr. Shen*); and Juro Kara's *Nitomonogatari* (*A Tale of Two Cities*).

SHINJI TAKUWA
Kyushu University, Fukuoka, Japan

Latin American Literature

In 1972 there was continued activity in all areas of Latin American literature. Brazil celebrated the 50th anniversary of its famous Semana da Arte Moderna, the official beginning of the Modernist movement in 1922.

Fiction. Several Latin American writers won important prizes. The prestigious Premio Barral of Spain was awarded to the Argentinian author Haroldo Conti for *En Vida,* a bitter narrative in which the characters desperately seek to escape the routine of daily life. Bryce Echenique and Manuel Scorza, both Peruvians, were finalists for Spain's influential Premio de la Crítica.

The Cuban Premio Casa de las Américas was won by Fernando Medina Ferrada of Bolivia for his novel *Los muertos están cada día más indóciles.* Colombia's Gabriel García Márquez, author of the best-seller of a few years ago, *Cien años de soledad,* won Venezuela's Premio Rómulo Gallegos. In 1972 he published a controversial collection of short stories, *La increíble y triste historia de la cándida Eréndida y de su abuela desalmada.*

Two Cuban novelists published major works. Alejo Carpentier wrote *El derecho de asilo* and Severo Sarduy wrote *Cobra.* Argentinians were very active in 1972. Eduardo Mallea's *Gabriel Andaral* offered a protagonist who unfolds through reflections on every possible topic and metaphysical subject. In *Los monstruos sagrados,* Silvina Bullrich portrayed the career of a writer who struggles amid praise and criticism. Beatrice Guido published *El ojo de la ballena,* a collection of short stories and plays written between 1947 and 1970. The Uruguayan Mario Benedetti's *Cuentos completos,* which include three previously published volumes, deal with his country's middle class. Juan José Arreola of Mexico wrote two new books, *La feria* and *Cuen-*

tos, varia invención. In Brazil, Otávio de Faria was elected to the Academia Brasileira de Letras, and Ariano Suassuna, a noted dramatist, published his first novel, *A pedra e o reino.*

Poetry. Pablo Neruda, of Chile, who won the 1971 Nobel Prize for literature, published 28 poems under the title *Aún.* Humberto Díaz Casanueva, who introduced philosophical poetry in Chile, won his country's Premio Nacional de Literatura. The Premio Casa de las Américas was awarded to the Bolivian poet Pedro Shimose for his book *Quiero escribir, pero me sale espuma.* Venezuela's Premio Nacional de Letras went to Ida Gramcko, one of Latin America's leading women poets. Brazil's Premio Nacional de Poesia was won by Cassiano Ricardo for *Os sobreviventes.* The well-known novelist Julio Cortázar of Argentina published *Pameos y meopas.* In Mexico the Premio Nacional de Poesía was awarded to Oscar Oliva for *Estado de sitio.* Mexico's leading poet, Octavio Paz, published *Renga* in collaboration with three other poets. His countryman José Gorostiza published *Poesía.*

Theater. There were several major drama festivals in 1972. At the Festival Latino-Americano de Teatro Universitario, held in Manizales, Colombia, the first prize was given to the Colombian Carlos José Reyes for his play *Soldados.* At the Second Latin American Theater Festival, which took place in Mexico, the highest honors were shared by Jorge Díaz of Chile and Virgilio Piñera of Cuba. Mexico continued to be the scene of experimental and innovative theater. Two interesting and successful plays were *Las monjas,* a highly anarchic and symbolic revolutionary piece by the Cuban Eduardo Manet, and *El juicio,* on the theme of the Mexican Revolution, by Vicente Leñero. *Milagro en el mercado viejo* by the Argentinian Osvaldo Dragún, dealing with criminal elements and low life, also had a very successful run.

The government of Brazil passed a law to encourage productions of national plays. Some 60% of government appropriations must be allotted to the theater for productions of works by Brazilians.

Nonfiction. Several well-known novelists published valuable essays. Ernesto Sábato's *Claves políticas* is a compilation of interviews and discussions dealing with his political ideas. The Mexican Carlos Fuentes put down his thoughts in *Tiempo mexicano.* Venezuela's Arturo Uslar Pietri analyzed major contemporary problems in *Vista desde un punto.* Eduardo Mallea published *Triste piel del universo.* The Peruvian Mario Vargas Llosa analyzed a fellow artist's creative powers in *Gabriel García Márquez, Historia de un deicidio.* In the imaginative book, *El estudiante de la mesa redonda,* Germán Arciniegas of Colombia allowed fictitious students from the beginnings of history to discuss their times.

Other important essays and studies included Octavio Paz' *Los signos en rotación y otros ensayos,* a collection of 20 essays on poetry, art, and history; Mario Ferrero's *Escritores a trasluz,* about 13 leading Chilean authors of the last 25 years; Julio Ortega's *Imagen de la literatura peruana actual;* and Joseph Sommers' *Yáñez, Rulfo, Fuentes: la novela mexicana moderna.*

Obituaries. In 1972 three prominent literary figures died: the Mexican poet Rosario Sansores, the Uruguayan poet and historian Angel Falcó, and the Brazilian dramatist Oduvaldo Vianna, Sr.

MARÍA A. SALGADO
University of North Carolina

Soviet Literature

Literary events of 1972 in the USSR included an international congress of translators, numerous exhibits in libraries and museums, and many round table discussions on the present and future of the printed word in connection with the UNESCO International Book Year. The authorities continued to stress the high place of the Soviet Union in world book production. In recent years over 72,000 titles were produced annually, many of them new works. Yet, the quantity of much of Soviet literature exceeds its quality.

Fiction. Only a few novels published in 1972 were noteworthy. One of the most interesting and controversial of the year was Bulat Okudzhava's satirical narrative, *Merçi, or Shipov's Adventures.* Okudzhava, a poet and novelist, was recently expelled from the Communist party because of his unorthodox views and independent behavior. The narrative is based on a historical fact—a house search, ordered by czarist authorities at Yasnaya Polyana, the estate of Leo Tolstoy, during its owner's absence in 1862. This perquisition, which Tolstoy bitterly denounced in a personal letter to the czar, was the consequence of a fantastic report by Shipov, a secret agent and police informer. Okudzhava portrays Shipov as a liar, drunkard, and scoundrel and depicts his revels and fabrications in a grotesquely exaggerated style reminiscent of Nikolai Gogol and Andrei Bely. Many passages of this amusing picaresque tale contain unmistakable allusions to the modern Soviet scene.

The Contemporaries, a prolix and dull novel by Semyon Babayevsky, deals with the petty struggles between party functionaries in the south of Russia. Vera Ketlinskaya's *Evening, Window and People* traces the tragic destiny of a woman wounded during the siege of Leningrad in World War II. Several other works of Soviet fiction were devoted to problems of morality and of family life, including *Red Light* by Nora Adamian, *The Recovery* by Ruth Zernova, and *Here is the Giant* by Konstantin Vorobiev.

Several political thrillers were published in 1972. In his *A Bomb for the Chairman,* Yulian Semenov describes the kidnapping of a Bulgarian scientist by German neo-Nazis. In a more realistic vein is *Under the Code Name of Dora* by Shandor Daro, a Soviet secret agent of Hungarian origin, who was active in Europe during World War II. Daniil Kraminov, a journalist and editor of the influential Communist monthly *October,* wrote *Twilight at Noon,* about political intrigues among European diplomats in the period 1938–39.

Nonfiction. Memoirs are a very popular literary form in the Soviet Union. One of the finest in 1972 was *A Broken Life, or Oberon's Magic Horn* by the distinguished writer Valentin Katayev. In it he subtly and humorously evokes his own childhood and adolescence in the colorful port of Odessa, one of the liveliest cities of the Ukraine.

Recollections was a best-selling work by Anastasia Cvetayeva, sister to Marina Cvetayeva, the famous poet who committed suicide in 1941. The book vividly describes life in Moscow between 1900 and 1920. Another well-known woman writer, Marietta Shaginian, wrote *Man and Time* in which she depicted her school-days and her travels in Europe in the early 1900's. Also successful was a well-edited reprint of *Memoirs* by Anna Dostoyevsky, the novelist's widow.

Marshall Nikolay Krylov's *The Bastion of Fire,* on the defense of Sebastopol in 1942, was edited and carefully trimmed before publication, in a manner typical of Soviet official reports about World War II. Altogether banned from publication in the USSR was the second volume of *Memoirs* by Nadezhda Mandelstam, widow of Osip Mandelstam, the great Russian poet who died in a concentration camp in 1938. The first volume, *Hope Against Hope,* had appeared in the West in 1971 in the Russian original and numerous translations. Its sequel, the second volume of *Memoirs,* contains a great deal of philosophical speculation as well as acute judgments of historical persons and events. It appeared in the West in 1972.

Poetry and Drama. Collections of old and new poetry by Andrei Voznesensky, Leonid Martynov, Viktor Sosnora, and Vadim Shefner attracted many readers in 1972. Plays, such as Aleksei Arbuzov's *The Tale of the Old Arbat,* Viktor Rozov's *From Midnight to Midday,* and Michael Rostchin's *Valentin and Valentina,* drew large audiences.

The 150th anniversary of the birth of Nikolai Nekrasov was the occasion for numerous essays on the work of this great civic poet.

Obituary. The novelist Mikhail Slonimsky died at the age of 75. He wrote the trilogy *Engineers, Friends,* and *Born with the Century* (1950–59).

MARC SLONIM
Sarah Lawrence College Foreign Studies

Spanish Literature

The literary year 1972, positive by any standard, offered evidence of Spain's progressive development and liberalization. The variety and quality of works produced reflected the vitality of Spain's great literary tradition and provided a fair sample of the creativity that might blossom under more amenable political conditions.

Fiction. Among significant prize-winning novels were José María Requena's *El cuajarón* (Nadal Prize), which dealt with the bulfighting milieu; Angel Palomino's *Torremolinos, gran hotel* (National Prize), which touched on Spain's burgeoning tourist industry; and Juan Pla's *Maremagnum* (Aguilas Prize), which portrayed the world of newspapermen. J. Leyva's *La circuncisión del señor solo* won the Biblioteca Breve Prize.

Several established novelists published well-received works. With *Guerra civil,* Ignacio Agustí ended his long study of modern Catalonia—*La ceniza fue árbol.* Juan Benet added *Un viaje de invierno* to a growing list of well-written hermetic novels, and José María Gironella published *Condenados a vivir.* Among the other significant novels published in 1972 were Manuel Barrio's *Epitafio para un señorito,* Alfonso Martínez-Mena's *Introito a la esperanza,* Santiago Lorens' *V.I.P.,* Raúl Guerra Garrido's *Ay,* and José María Carrascal's *El capitán que nunca mandó un barco.*

Short fiction was especially important. Two major novelists combined essays and short stories in innovative collections: Francisco Ayala's *El jardín de las delicias,* which received the Critic's Award, and Camilo José Cela's *El bonito crimen del carabinero.* Another important novelist, Rodrigo Rubio, was awarded the Felguera Prize for *Penúltimo invierno.* Other noteworthy short-story collections that appeared during 1972 included Fernando Díaz-Plaja's *Cuentos crueles* and Jorge Ferrer-Vidal's *Sábado, esperanza....*

Nonfiction. Important scholarly works published in 1972 included Luis Felipe Vivanco's *Moratín y la ilustración mágica,* a fresh view of the 18th century Enlightenment in Spain. José Siles Artes contributed *El arte en la novela pastoril;* Alberto Porqueras Mayo, *Temas y formas de la literatura española;* George O. Schanzer, *La literatura rusa en el mundo hispánico;* Francisco Flores Arroyuelo, *Pío Baroja y la historia;* Martín Alonso, *Sequndo estilo de Bécquer;* Joan Corominas, *Tópica hespérica* (a valuable contribution to Iberian dialectology); Joaquín Marco, *Nueva literatura en España y América;* and Antonio Prieto, *Ensayo semiológico de sistemas literarios.*

Among collections of essays were Francisco Umbral's *Memorias de un niño de derechas* and *Amar en Madrid,* featuring the past and present of Spain's lovely capital; Miguel Delibes' year-long diary, *Un año de mi vida;* philosopher José Ferrater Mora's *Las palabras y los hombres;* and Julio Carabias' humorous *Habladurías.*

Poetry. Major prizes for poetry during the year were awarded to José Infante (Adonais Prize) for *Elegía y no,* José Luis Rodríguez Argenta (Boscán Prize) for *La nada que me une,* and Victoriano Cremer (Barcelona Prize) for *Lejos de esta lluvia amarga.* The Leopoldo Panero Prize was won by Francisca Aguirre, whose *Itaca* distilled poetry from everyday life. The novelist Aquilino Duque received the Fastenrath Prize for *De palabra a palabra.*

Especially significant in 1972 was the publication of volumes by such exceptional young poets as Jorge G. Aranguren (*Largo regreso a Itaca y otros poemas*), Juan Mena Coello (*Tierra escondida*), José Luis García Martín (*Marineros perdidos en los puertos*), Arturo del Villar (*Su exilio está en la noche*), Anibal Núñez (*Fábulas domésticas*), and José María Bermejo (*Epidemia de nieve*). Bermejo, whose verse projects the haunting lyricism of youthful sadness, was a runner-up for the Adonais Prize.

Two important anthologies of poetry also appeared. Aguilar brought out the *Obras completas* of Miguel Labordeta, an exceptional Aragonese poet of the 1940's and 1950's, and Luis Jiménez Martos published *La generación poética del 36,* an indispensable compilation of work by the mature contemporary generation of Spanish poets.

Theater. The Lope de Vega Prize was awarded to Manuel Alonso Alcalde, a relative newcomer, for *Solos en esta tierra,* and the Valladolid Prize went to José María Pemán, patriarch of the Spanish theater, for *Tres testigos.* But the real highlights of the theatrical season were works by established names. These included Antonio Buero Vallejo's *Llegada de los dioses,* a pertinent study of authenticity in contemporary life; Jaime Salom's *La noche de los cien pájaros;* José López Rubio's *El corazón en la mano,* containing the playwright's usual lively and humorous dialogue; and the first commercial success by vanguard dramatist José María Bellido, *Milagro en Londres.*

Translations. Among recent translations of Spanish works into English are Damaso Alonso's *Children of Wrath,* by Elias L. Rivers; Saint John of the Cross' *Living Flame of Love,* by E. Allison Peers; Américo Castro's *The Spaniards,* by Willard F. King and Selma Margaretten; and Julián Marías' *Metaphysical Anthropology,* by Frances M. López-Morillas.

ALFRED RODRIGUEZ
University of New Mexico

LOS ANGELES

Events of 1972 in Los Angeles, California's largest city and county, tended to be undramatic, except in collegiate and professional basketball.

Government and Politics. For the first time in nearly 25 years, a majority on the Los Angeles County Board of Supervisors were freshmen. Two former members of the state Assembly, Republicans James A. Hayes and Peter Schabarum, were elected to fill vacancies created by deaths. In addition, Baxter Ward, a former television newscaster, unseated the veteran incumbent Warren Dorn.

During the year the Los Angeles City Council argued the question of reapportioning its districts to increase the chances of Mexican-American representation (no Mexican-American has held a council seat since 1962). There seemed to be agreement that a district should be carved out on the east side of the city. But each plan met opposition either from incumbents or from Mexican-American leaders, and at year-end the issue was unresolved.

Budgets. Both the city and the county adopted record budgets for the 1972–73 fiscal year. Mayor Samuel Yorty and the city council differed over details, as usual, and the mayor vetoed appropriations totaling $6.5 million. But the council overruled him concerning 75 citywide street-and-highway improvement projects. The final budget of $622.7 million was out of balance by at least $18 million.

Education. The Los Angeles Board of Education, also in financial difficulties, benefited from a $10.5 million increase in state aid and, more important, a windfall of about $130 million. The latter came about when Los Angeles teachers voted to join the state retirement system and the legislature allowed the board to retain the city teacher retirement funds, subject to certain limitations. As a result, the board was able to avoid proposed program cutbacks and to provide teachers with a 5.5% salary increase.

In September, the board began a voluntary program of busing minority pupils from older schools that are not earthquake resistant to safer schools, primarily in the San Fernando Valley and in West Los Angeles. About 2,400 pupils were involved, in addition to another 2,100 who were being bused voluntarily from overcrowded schools in black and Mexican American areas.

Antipoverty Programs. The year brought many charges of inefficiency and incompetence in the city's antipoverty programs, and experts agreed that the five "model neighborhoods" had had a negligible impact on residents of the area. Considerable money was spent on nonproductive enterprises such as the cleaning of vacant lots and an ineffective rat-eradication program, as well as on salaries of administrators who, it was charged, frequently lacked preparation for the duties assigned them. Finally, in October, the city council voted to dismiss the administrator of the Model Cities program.

A similar controversy centered on the Economic and Youth Opportunity Agency (EYOA), where there were charges of ineffective programs, administrative inefficiency, and friction between the EYOA and the U.S. Office of Economic Opportunity (OEO), from which it receives most of its funds. In additon, there were complaints from Mexican Americans that the executive director of EYOA discriminated against their groups and in favor of blacks. Late in the year, the city council and county board were proceeding to comply with the regional OEO director's request that they replace the EYOA with a new coordinating agency to administer antipoverty programs.

Sports. It was a great year for Los Angeles area basketball fans. The University of California at Los Angeles (UCLA) won its sixth national title in a row. It has been the national collegiate champion for eight of the last nine years. The team won 30 games and lost none during the 1971–72 season.

The professional Los Angeles Lakers had an even more spectacular year. By Dec. 12, 1971, they had set an all-time National Basketball Association (NBA) record by winning 21 games in a row. They kept on winning until their victory streak reached 33 games, an all-time record for consecutive victories by any professional sports team. During the regular season, the Lakers won 69 games, also a record. In May, they won the NBA championship by defeating New York, 4 games to 1.

In the fall, the undefeated University of Southern California football team was named the national champion and went on to win in the Rose Bowl.

CHARLES R. ADRIAN
University of California, Riverside

LOUISIANA

In 1972, Louisiana's representation in Congress was altered not only by the November national election but by the death of Sen. Allen Ellender and the disappearance in Alaska of Rep. Hale Boggs. Within the state, work was planned for a new state constitution at the request of Gov. Edwin Edwards, who had been elected to the gubernatorial office in February. Two major racial confrontations brought death in their wake.

Congressional Changes. Sen. Allen Ellender, chairman of the Senate Appropriations Committee, a product of the Huey Long political machine and a veteran of 36 years in office, died in July in the midst of a re-election campaign. Three months later, a private plane carrying Rep. Hale Boggs of Louisiana and Alaska's Rep. Nick Begich disappeared during a Begich campaign swing in Alaska. Boggs, in Congress for 26 years and unopposed for reelection, was House majority leader.

Ellender's sudden death changed the complexion of the U.S. Senate race as Republicans quickly shifted to a stronger candidate, and former Gov. John McKeithen entered the race as an independent. The winner, however, was J. Bennett Johnston, a Shreveport attorney who a year earlier had lost to Edwin Edwards in the Democratic primary for the governor's office.

In the November elections, David Treen, a Metairie Republican and a former election opponent of Hale Boggs, captured a congressional seat after being reapportioned into another district. Treen became the first Republican from Louisiana in Congress since Reconstruction days.

Legislation and Administration. The new Edwards administration won legislative approval for a start on governmental reorganization, for a constitutional convention to revise the state's basic document during 1973, and for a one-cent increase in the natural gas tax to finance health, education, and prison improvements. Also passed was Edwards' plan to simplify state aid to local governments, replacing a complicated system of property

TWO BLACK STUDENTS were killed at Southern University in Baton Rouge in a clash with police, November 16, following protests against the school administration.

UPI

tax reimbursements with direct revenue sharing.

In the November elections, voters picked 105 delegates to the constitutional convention and Governor Edwards appointed 27. It was to start preliminary work in January 1973, and get down to the core work in July.

The changing of the guard in the state government created some turmoil. Commissioner of Insurance Sherman Bernard attempted to investigate insurance rates, but was blocked by the Edwards-appointed insurance commission, which met without him.

Civil Disturbance. In January, Black Muslims and their supporters barricaded a Baton Rouge thoroughfare. The resultant confrontation with law enforcement officers erupted into a gun battle. It ended with two officers and two Muslims dead.

In November police were summoned to Baton Rouge's all-black Southern University as students protested unfavorable conditions there. As the protesters were being routed from the administration building, two fleeing students were fatally wounded. A state investigation reported that the fatal shots had been fired by a sheriff's deputy.

LOUISIANA • Information Highlights

Area: 48,523 square miles (125,675 sq km).
Population (1970 census): 3,643,180. *Density,* 82 per sq mi.
Chief Cities (1970 census): Baton Rouge, the capital, 165,963; New Orleans, 593,471; Shreveport, 182,064; Lake Charles, 77,998; Lafayette, 68,908; Monroe, 56,374.
Government (1972): *Chief Officers*—governor, Edwin W. Edwards (D); lt. gov., James E. Fitzmorris, Jr. (D); secy. of state, Wade O. Martin, Jr. (D); atty. gen., William J. Guste, Jr. (D); supt. of education, Louis J. Michot; chief justice, E. Howard McCaleb. *Legislature*—Senate, 39 members (38 Democrats, 1 Republican); House of Representatives, 105 members (103 D, 1 R, 1 vacancy).
Education (1971–72): *Enrollment*—public elementary schools, 517,821 pupils; 21,884 teachers; public secondary, 339,497 pupils; 17,496 teachers; nonpublic schools (1970–71), 142,-745 pupils; 5,390 teachers; college and university, 126,000 students. *Public school expenditures,* $681,280,000 ($867 per pupil). *Average teacher's salary,* $9,113.
State Finances (1970): *Revenues,* $1,660,273,000 (3% general sales tax and gross receipts taxes, $166,485,000; motor fuel tax, $119,841,000; federal funds, $410,793,000). *Expenditures,* $1,593,669,000 (education, $587,273,000; health, welfare, and safety, $275,904,000; highways, $275,323,000). *State debt,* $864,987,000 (June 1970).
Personal Income (1971): $11,957,000,000; per capita, $3,248.
Public Assistance (1971): $253,959,000. *Average monthly payments* (Dec. 1971)—old-age assistance, $73.91; aid to families with dependent children, $88.12.

Labor Force: *Nonagricultural wage and salary earners* (July 1972), 1,078,100. *Average annual employment* (1971)—manufacturing, 173,000; trade, 236,000; government, 215,-000; services, 158,000. *Insured unemployed* (Aug. 1972)—22,100 (3.0%).
Manufacturing (1970): *Value added by manufacture,* $3,358,-100,000. Chemicals and allied products, $956,000,000; food and kindred products, $549,900,000; petroleum and coal products, $458,100,000; paper and allied products, $332,200,000; transportation equipment, $193,800,000.
Agriculture (1970): *Cash farm income,* $705,474,000 (livestock, $278,148,000; crops, $372,221,000; government payments, $55,105,000). *Chief crops* (in order of value, 1971)—Soybeans, rice (ranks 3d among the states), cotton lint, sugarcane for sugar and seed (ranks 2d).
Mining (1970): *Production value,* $5,117,365,000 (ranks 2d among the states). *Chief minerals*—Petroleum, $3,038,-031,000; natural gas, $1,549,399,000; natural gas liquids, $329,169,000; sulfur, $67,212,000.
Fisheries (1971): *Commercial catch,* 1,396,214,000 pounds ($72,630,000). *Leading species by value* (1971): Shrimp, $43,288,000; menhaden, $19,927,000; oysters, $4,207,000.
Transportation: *Roads* (1971), 52,845 miles (85,043 km); *motor vehicles* (1971), 1,742,351; *railroads* (1971), 3,752 miles (6,038 km); *public airports* (1972), 70.
Communications: *Telephones* (1972), 1,857,500; *television stations* (1971), 15; *radio stations* (1971), 133; *newspapers* (1972), 25 (daily circulation, 804,000).

Economy. In 1972, Louisiana led Texas and Mississippi in the race for a superport on the Gulf coast. Plans were under way for a private corporation, organized by major oil companies, to build the deep-water facility.

Federal off-shore leasing for oil and gas resumed in 1972, but natural gas production was falling below the state's industrial needs. Near the year's end, Governor Edwards announced possible construction of a synthetic gas manufacturing plant near Baton Rouge to help fill the energy supply gaps.

EDWIN W. PRICE, JR., *Managing Editor*
"The Morning Advocate," Baton Rouge

LUMBER. See FORESTRY AND LUMBERING.

--------- **LUXEMBOURG · Information Highlights** ---------

Official Name: Grand Duchy of Luxembourg.
Area: 999 square miles (2,586 sq km).
Population (1972 est.): 400,000. *Density,* 339 per square mile (131 per sq km). *Annual rate of increase,* 0.4%.
Chief Cities (1970 census): Luxembourg, the capital, 76,143; Esch-sur-Alzette, 27,575.
Government: *Head of state,* Jean, grand duke (acceded Nov. 1964). *Head of government,* Pierre Werner, premier (took office Feb. 1959). *Legislature* (unicameral)—Chamber of Deputies, 56 members. *Major political parties*—Christian Social party; Socialist party; Democratic party; Communist party; Social Democratic party.
Languages: French (official), German, Letzeburgesch.
Education: *Expenditure* (1969), 15.2% of total public expenditure. *School enrollment* (1969)—primary, 36,035; secondary, 18,036; technical/vocational, 9,347; higher, 422.
Monetary Unit: Franc (44.18 francs equal U.S.$1, Sept. 1972).
Gross National Product (1971 est.): $1,000,000,000.
Manufacturing (major products): Iron and steel, chemicals.
Major Agricultural Products: Barley, wheat, oats, grapes.
Major Minerals: Iron ore, slate.
Foreign Trade, including Belgium (1971): *Exports,* $12,391,-000,000. *Imports,* $12,856,000,000. *Chief trading partners* (1969)—West Germany; France; Netherlands.
Transportation: *Motor vehicles* (1970), 103,800; *major national airline,* Luxair (Luxembourg Airlines).

LUXEMBOURG

Iron and steel prices were depressed and inflation continued to be a problem in Luxembourg during 1972. Steel accounts for 45% of exports and 25% of the gross national product and employs nearly half the labor force. The industry operates with coal from the Ruhr and ore from Lorraine.

By continuing to encourage foreign investments, the government has tried to free Luxembourg from its heavy dependence on the steel industry. Since the mid-1960's, the government has been successful in inducing large American corporations to open factories in Luxembourg. The Goodyear Rubber Company, which began with a small factory not many years ago, was in the process of enlarging its operation in 1972. When the expansion program is completed, Goodyear is expected to be the second largest employer in Luxembourg, with an investment of $10 million.

Foreign Affairs. One of the year's more significant developments was the establishment of diplomatic relations between Luxembourg and Albania.

President Georges Pompidou of France, accompanied by Madame Pompidou, made a state visit to Luxembourg on May 3 and 4. At a press conference, he stated that he and Luxembourg Prime Minister Pierre Werner attached great importance to developing the European Economic Community into an economic and monetary union with a common foreign policy.

AMRY VANDENBOSCH, *University of Kentucky*

McGOVERN, George S. See BIOGRAPHY.
MAGAZINES. See PUBLISHING.

MAINE

The most important event in Maine in 1972 was the defeat of Republican Margaret Chase Smith in her bid for reelection to the U.S. Senate. Mrs. Smith, who was 74, lost to William D. Hathaway, a 48-year-old Democratic congressman from Auburn.

Legislation. In a special session beginning on January 24, the legislature approved bills to effect the state's 1971 executive reorganization plan. Under the plan, various departments and agencies will be consolidated under umbrella departments, including agriculture, manpower affairs, environmental protection, public safety, education and cultural services, finance and administration, commerce and industry, transportation, secretary of state, and military, civil, and veterans affairs. Departments not approved were human services, natural resources, and business regulation. The legislature also extended land use regulations to cover residential subdivision, municipal, and educational areas and granted full adult rights to 18-year-olds.

Elections. In addition to Sen. Margaret Chase Smith, another prominent Maine political leader suffered defeat in 1972. Sen. Edmund Muskie, long considered the front-runner for the Democratic presidential nomination, was defeated by South Dakota Sen. George McGovern at the party's convention in July. In state contests, Democratic Congressman Peter N. Kyros retained his seat, while Republican William S. Cohen of Bangor was elected to fill the seat vacated by Senator-elect William Hathaway. Republicans kept control of both houses of the state legislature. Maine voters gave President Nixon a decisive margin in the presidential balloting. In referendums, they approved an $8 million bond issue for the University of Maine and a $10 million bond issue for highway construction.

"Red Tide." In September an infestation of the "red tide," a poisonous algae, closed clam-digging operations along the Maine coast. The ban on digging was lifted later in the fall, but not before clam

NEW MAINE SENATOR, William D. Hathaway, scored an upset victory over Margaret Chase Smith on November 7.

UPI

──────── MAINE • Information Highlights ────────

Area: 33,215 square miles (86,027 sq km).
Population (1970 census): 993,663. *Density:* 32 per sq mi.
Chief Cities (1970 census): Augusta, the capital, 21,945; Portland, 65,116; Lewiston, 41,779; Bangor, 33,168; Auburn, 24,151; South Portland, 23,267; Biddeford, 19,983.
Government (1972): *Chief Officers*—governor, Kenneth M. Curtis (D); secy. of state, Joseph T. Edgar (R); atty. gen., James S. Erwin (R); treas., Norman K. Ferguson (R); commissioner, dept. of education, Carroll R. McGary; chief justice, Armand A. Dufresne, Jr. *Legislature*—Senate, 32 members (18 Republicans, 14 Democrats); House of Representatives, 151 members (80 R, 71 D).
Education (1971–72): *Enrollment*—public elementary schools, 178,500 pupils; 7,369 teachers; public secondary, 69,200 pupils; 3,962 teachers; nonpublic schools (1970–71), 19,514 pupils; 1,390 teachers; college and university, 35,000 students. *Public school expenditures,* $185,567,000 ($803 per pupil). *Average teacher's salary,* $9,051.
State Finances (fiscal year 1970): *Revenues,* $420,181,000 (5% general sales tax and gross receipts taxes, $83,240,000; motor fuel tax, $36,557,000; federal funds, $90,708,000). *Expenditures,* $433,326,000 (education $142,458,000; health, welfare, and safety, $71,485,000; highways, $95,444,000). *State debt,* $232,322,000 (June 30, 1970).
Personal Income (1971): $3,429,000,000; per capita, $3,419.
Public Assistance (1971): $73,860,000. *Average monthly payments* (Dec. 1971)—old-age assistance, $63.81; aid to families with dependent children, $146.74.
Labor Force: *Nonagricultural wage & salary earners* (July 1972), 340,500. *Average annual employment* (1971)—manufacturing, 103,000; trade, 68,000; government, 69,000; services, 44,000. *Insured unemployed* (Aug. 1972)—9,500 (4.3%).
Manufacturing (1970): *Value added by manufacture,* $1,227,200,000. Paper and allied products, $347,600,000; leather and leather products, $205,400,000; food and kindred products, $151,200,000; lumber and wood products, $105,100,000.
Agriculture (1970): *Cash farm income,* $256,240,000 (livestock, $162,309,000; crops, $92,264,000; government payments, $1,667,000). *Chief crops* (in order of value, 1971)—Potatoes (ranks 2d among the states), hay, apples.
Mining (1971): *Production value,* $21,898,000 (ranks 47th among the states). *Chief minerals*—Cement, value not available; sand and gravel, $5,881,000; stone, $2,913,000; copper, $2,610,000.
Fisheries (1971): *Commercial catch,* 142,619,000 pounds ($31,068,000). *Leading species by value:* Lobsters, $17,481,000; shrimp, $3,671,000; clams, $2,702,000; ocean perch, $2,347,000.
Transportation: *Roads* (1971), 21,356 miles (34,368 km); *motor vehicles* (1971), 515,492; *railroads* (1971), 1,678 miles (2,700 km); *public airports* (1972), 42.
Communications: *Telephones* (1972), 520,900; *television stations* (1971), 7; *radio stations* (1971), 50; *newspapers* (1972), 9 (daily circulation, 266,000).

harvesters faced economic hardship. In response, President Nixon declared a state of emergency that provided assistance to distressed areas.

General Economy. Maine's economic picture remained cloudy in 1972. The tourist industry suffered because of poor weather in June, and manufacturing experienced little, if any, growth. However, the price of potatoes, Maine's major agricultural crop, exceeded $5 a barrel, giving growers their first "good" year in nearly a decade.

Property Values. Land and property values in Maine, particularly in coastal towns, have been rising at an extraordinary rate, apparently as a result of demand by buyers from outside the state. Maine citizens are expressing concern over the emerging disparity between their income level and the rising value of real estate.

Piscataqua River Bridge. A new bridge over the Piscataqua River, connecting Kittery, Me., and Portsmouth, N. H., was opened in October.

RONALD F. BANKS, *University of Maine*

MALAGASY REPUBLIC

Civil disorder erupted in the Malagasy Republic in 1972 as a student strike touched off larger demonstrations by discontented workers and civil servants. Clashes with police resulted in 34 deaths, a state of emergency, military rule, and the resignation in October of the president.

Riots. On March 5 striking students from Belefatanana medical college demanded the same degree as will be awarded by the new medical faculty in Tananarive. They also demanded reform of the traditional French curriculum. Secondary school students joined the strike, and on May 13 students clashed with police in Tananarive and burned public buildings. President Philibert Tsiranana declared a state of emergency.

On May 15 some 100,000 workers, civil servants, and students demonstrated outside Tsiranana's residence, demanding educational reform and release of those arrested. Two days later some 400 imprisoned students were freed. Tsiranana dissolved his government on May 18. Retaining the presidency, he handed over power to Army Chief of Staff Gen. Gabriel Ramanatsoa as prime minister.

Background. Behind the turmoil were years of low wages, rising prices, and shortages. In April 1971 a violent revolt against the aging and autocratic president had erupted in the south. On Jan. 30, 1972, Tsiranana was reelected, unopposed, to a third 7-year term in an allegedly controlled election. Among reasons for the unrest were the depressed economy, opposition to dominant French economic and military influence, Tsiranana's unpopular dialogue with South Africa, and differences between the coastal people and the Merinas of the plateau.

Aftermath. The new military government released the 2,000 people arrested in April 1971. The dialogue with South Africa was discontinued. On October 8, Prime Minister Ramanantsoa was endorsed in a referendum that granted him the power to rule without parliament for five years. President Tsiranana resigned on October 11.

The government declared a state of siege in and near Tamatave on December 14 after two days of rioting over plans to give education a more national character. Coastal students accused the Merinas of instigating the changes.

FRANKLIN PARKER, *West Virginia University*

──── MALAGASY REPUBLIC • Information Highlights ────

Official Name: Malagasy Republic.
Area: 226,657 square miles (587,041 sq km).
Population (1972 est.): 7,300,000. *Density,* 32.2 per square mile (12.4 per sq km). *Annual rate of increase,* 2.1%.
Chief Cities (1969 est.): Tananarive, the capital, 334,800; Tamatave, 54,700.
Government: *Head of government,* Gen. Gabriel Ramanantsoa, prime minister (took office May 1972). *Legislature*—Parliament (suspended Oct. 1972): National Assembly, 107 members; Senate, 54 members. *Major political parties*—Parti Social Démocrate; Parti du Congrès de l'Indépendance.
Languages: Malagasy, French (both official).
Education: *Expenditure* (1967), 20% of total public expenditure. *School enrollment* (1968)—primary, 815,307; secondary, 103,107; technical/vocational, 6,376; university/higher, 3,429.
Monetary Unit: Franc (255.79 francs = U. S.$1, Aug. 1972).
Gross National Product (1970 est.): $878,000,000.
National Income per Person (1970): $124.
Consumer Price Index (1971): 123 (1963 = 100).
Manufacturing (major products): Beer, petroleum products, cigarettes, cement.
Major Agricultural Products: Vanilla bean (ranks 1st among world producers, 1970), rice, sisal, sugarcane, cassava, sweet potatoes, livestock.
Major Minerals: Graphite, mica, chromium ore.
Foreign Trade (1971): *Exports,* $147,000,000 (chief exports—coffee; vanilla; rice; sugar; sisal). *Imports,* $213,000,000 (chief imports, 1969—nonelectrical machinery; transport equipment; chemicals; food). *Chief trading partners* (1969)—France (took 36% of exports, supplied 51% of imports); United States (24%—8%); West Germany (4%—9%).
Transportation: *Motor vehicles* (1970), 87,800 (automobiles, 45,500); *railroads* (1970), 549 miles (884 km); *major national airline,* Air Madagascar.
Communications: *Telephones* (1971), 26,799; *television stations* (1971), 1; *television sets* (1971), 1,000; *radios* (1970), 540,000; *newspapers* (1970), 13.

─────── MALAWI • Information Highlights ───────

Official Name: Republic of Malawi.
Area: 45,747 square miles (118,484 sq km).
Population (1972 est.): 4,700,000. *Density,* 98 per square mile (38 per sq km). *Annual rate of increase,* 2.5%.
Chief City (1966 census): Zomba, the capital, 19,666.
Government: *Head of state,* Hastings K. Banda, president (took office July 1966). *Head of government,* Hastings K. Banda. *Legislature* (unicameral)—National Assembly, 65 members. *Political party*—Malawi Congress party.
Languages: English (official), Bantu languages.
Education: *Expenditure* (1967), 4.1% of gross national product. *School enrollment* (1968)—primary, 333,876; secondary, 10,904; technical/vocational, 536; university/higher, 788.
Monetary Unit: Kwacha (0.8197 kwacha=U. S.$1, Aug. 1972).
Gross National Product (1971 est.): $350,000,000.
Manufacturing (major products): Processed agricultural products, cement, cotton textiles, sawnwood.
Major Agricultural Products: Tea, tobacco, groundnuts, cotton, corn, forest products.
Major Mineral: Limestone.
Foreign Trade (1971): *Exports,* $72,000,000. *Imports,* $109,000,000. *Chief trading partners* (1969)—United Kingdom (took 46% of exports, supplied 30% of imports); Rhodesia (6%—17%); South Africa (3%—15%).
Communications: *Telephones* (1971), 12,519; *radios,* 90,000.

MALAWI

Cabinet changes, constitutional amendments, and an unprecedented visit by South Africa's president were Malawi's outstanding events in 1972. Malawi was also the scene of the denouement of an exciting airline hijacking.

Cabinet Changes. In a series of reshuffles on February 28, April 4, and June 26 several new cabinet ministers were named: Watson Deleza, labor; John Gwengwe, transport and communications; John Msonthi, education; Aleke Banda, trade, industry, and tourism; Richard Matenja, finance; Aaron Gadama, community development and social welfare; and President Hastings K. Banda, agriculture and natural resources.

Constitution. Constitutional amendments approved by parliament in February reduced the qualifying age for the presidency from 45 to 40 and changed the way that a presidential council is to be constituted in the absence of the head of state. The moves were seen as President Banda's preparation for the succession of Aleke Banda, who was 33 years old in 1972. No relation of the president, the younger Banda was known as his "political son." Aleke Banda faced difficulties in that he was a northerner from the Tonga tribe and remained unpopular with Malawians of the more populated center and south.

Foreign Affairs. In the first such visit to an independent black state, the Republic of South Africa's president, J. J. Fouché, visited Malawi from March 17 to 24. With him were South Africa's minister of foreign affairs, Hilgard Muller; secretary for foreign affairs, B. G. Fourie; minister of water affairs and forestry, S. P. Botha, and others.

While openly condemning South African apartheid, Hastings Banda said that trade and diplomatic exchanges were more likely to change South Africa's racial attitudes than were war, isolation, or boycotts. He repeated this theme on July 6 at an independence day banquet for South African Bantustan chiefs. Calling on them not to fight South Africa, he declared, "If there was a war every single African government would topple."

Banda was, in 1972, independent black Africa's chief advocate of dialogue with South Africa. Recent changes of governments and attitudes had cooled the ardor of other countries previously interested in trade and diplomatic relations with South Africa, namely the Malagasy Republic, Ghana, Lesotho, and the Ivory Coast. In this new context, Banda's friendly position was in danger of becoming isolated. Anti-white guerrillas were reportedly working to unseat Banda.

Airline Hijacking. Malawi troops captured two Lebanese hijackers of a Boeing 727 jetliner on May 26. As the plane approached Johannesburg, South Africa, from Salisbury, Rhodesia, the hijackers threatened to blow it up with 58 passengers aboard. Demanding to be taken to the Seychelles, they made the pilot change course. The hijackers reportedly hoped to extort money from Harry Oppenheimer, chairman of South Africa's Anglo-American Mining Co., one of the world's largest diamond concerns. The pilot persuaded the hijackers to refuel at Salisbury, where all but five hostages were released, and to stop at Blantyre, Malawi. There, while the hijackers were counting the ransom money brought on board for them, they were attacked and captured by Malawi soldiers.

FRANKLIN PARKER, *West Virginia University*

MALAYSIA

The year 1972 in Malaysia was marked by a perceptible slowdown in economic activity, a government campaign to win support for its proposed neutralization of Southeast Asia, and fresh efforts to curb Communist guerrillas in East and West Malaysia.

Economy. In his January budget speech, Finance Minister Tun Tan Siew Sin cited adverse economic effects of lower export earnings in 1971 as a result of depressed prices for key exports of rubber, tin, and timber. He noted that the economic growth rate was reduced to 5% and unemployment was 7.6%. He foresaw greater diversification through increased exports of palm oil and petroleum. Stimulated by government loans, small manufacturing increased by 9%. A new 5% sales tax on manufactured goods and certain imports but excluding foodstuffs and industrial raw materials was introduced to increase revenue. Every adult citizen in the state of Sabah received a share of the Sabah Foundation, a government-run lumbering and shipping enterprise.

Foreign Relations. The government sought support for the Kuala Lumpur Declaration, made by the Association of Southeast Asian Nations (ASEAN) in 1971, which called for a regional neutral zone. In May the declaration was endorsed by the Preparatory Committee of Non-Aligned Nations meeting in Kuala Lumpur. The ASEAN foreign ministers, meeting in Manila in July, reiterated their support.

In Rangoon in February, the chairman of the Burmese Revolutionary Council, Gen. Ne Win, gave Malaysian Prime Minister Tun Abdul Razak a qualified approval of the neutralization proposal but indicated that Burma would join a regional grouping only if the other members were "genuinely" neutral. The declaration was also endorsed by the French secretary of state for foreign affairs, Jean de Lipkowsky, in March. Indonesian President Suharto, however, stressed to visiting Malaysian Deputy Prime Minister Tun Ismail the prior importance of each country's strengthening its own defenses rather than relying primarily on a guarantee by outside great powers.

Further evidence of the government's new emphasis on nonalignment was Razak's visit to the Soviet Union and Poland in September to solicit technical assistance for Malaysia's development plan. In

addition, during the June visit of Australian Prime Minister William McMahon, Kuala Lumpur showed mild support for its defense arrangement with Australia, New Zealand, Britain, and Singapore.

Guerrilla Campaigns. The Malaysian government was increasingly troubled by two groups of insurgent Communist guerrillas, one in the west on the Thai border and one in the east in Sarawak on Borneo. Each group was largely composed of ethnic Chinese and, after years of preparation in Thailand and Indonesia respectively, had been steadily gaining strength in Malaysia. Their tactics included the recruitment of tribal villagers, by means of self-help and medical-aid programs, for military training and indoctrination at Communist bases.

A Malaysian-Thai Border Committee was not conspicuously successful in suppressing Communist activities in the west. In the east the government launched Operation Ngayau, which used the same aid tactics as the Communists, as well as military force. The government later claimed to have overrun 60 Communist camps, capturing 700 Communist supporters and many weapons.

In April the Malaysian and Indonesian governments formalized a new security arrangement for their contiguous Bornean territories to deal with Communist operations. A new border committee, to be manned by senior military personnel from the two countries and alternately chaired by Tun Ismail and the Indonesian defense minister, General Maraden, will meet semiannually to plan military actions against the Communists in Borneo.

Territorial-Waters Dispute. A minor controversy followed the joint Malaysian-Indonesian declaration in November 1971 that the highly strategic Straits of Malacca, narrowly dividing the two countries,

came within the 12-mile (20-km) limits of their territorial waters and hence was not an international waterway. The Soviet Union promptly rejected this claim and was supported by Japan, whose ships were its heaviest users. Peking charged Soviet-Japanese "collusion." The dispute was exacerbated when the chairman of the Malaysian state economic corporation called in March for a levy on all Malacca Straits shipping. Meanwhile, Singapore called for "free access" for all ships in the Straits.

Internal Politics. The governing Alliance party moved to strengthen its position in the various Malaysian states. In February the Alliance formed a coalition government in Penang with the ruling Gerakan party, which had been weakened by the departure of three leaders to form a new party. Gerakan was also to support the Alliance in the national parliament and other state legislatures.

In May the Alliance formed a coalition in Perak with the People's Progressive party (PPP). The coalition extended to the Ipoh Municipal Council, controlled by the PPP, which is mainly Chinese. Some members of the Alliance's Chinese affiliate, the Malaysian Chinese Association, expressed intense opposition to the new Perak coalition, prompting the MCA president to expel two senior party officials and force several others in the Perak branch to retire. Meanwhile the Alliance was negotiating with the militant Pan-Malayan Islamic party for a similar coalition, which would complete Alliance control of all 13 Malaysian states.

Partly offsetting these gains was a severe factional conflict in the Alliance's Malaysian Indian Congress between its president and his deputy. The Alliance's leading opposition, the Democratic Action party (DAP), suffered a serious setback in June with the abrupt departure of its founder and vice president, Goh Hock Guan, and three other DAP members of Parliament.

C. PAUL BRADLEY
University of Michigan—Flint

————— **MALAYSIA · Information Highlights** —————

Official Name: Malaysia.
Area: 128,430 square miles (332,633 sq km).
Population (1972 est.): 11,400,000. Annual increase, 2.8%.
Chief Cities (1960 census): Kuala Lumpur, the capital, 316,-230; Kuching, 50,579; Kota Kinabalu (Jesselton), 21,719.
Government: *Head of state,* Sultan Abdul Halim Muadzam, supreme sovereign (took office Feb. 1971). *Head of government,* Tun Abdul Razak, prime minister (took office Sept. 1970). *Legislature*—Parliament: Dewan Ra'ayat (House of Representatives), 144 members; Dewan Negara (Senate), 58 members. *Major political parties*—Alliance; Pan-Malayan Islamic party; Democratic Action party; Sarawak National party; Gerakan Rakyat Malaysia (Malaysian People's Movement).
Languages: Malay (official), English, Chinese.
Education (West Malaysia): *Expenditure* (1969), 14.6% of total public expenditure. *School enrollment* (1969)—primary, 1,369,376; secondary, 524,844; technical/vocational, 12,632; university/higher, 13,045.
Monetary Unit: Malaysian dollar (2.86 M. dollars equal U. S.$1, June 1972).
Gross National Product (1971 est.): $4,021,000,000.
National Income per Person (1967): $302.
Economic Indexes (West Malaysia): *Agricultural production* (1971), 226 (1952–56=100); *consumer price index* (1971), 107 (1963=100).
Manufacturing (major products): Petroleum products, refined sugar, steel, fertilizers, sawn wood.
Major Agricultural Products: Natural rubber (ranks 1st among world producers, 1971), palm oil (world rank 1st, 1971), rice, tea, pepper, coconuts, fruits, forest products.
Major Minerals: Tin (ranks 1st among world producers, 1970), bauxite, petroleum, iron ore.
Foreign Trade (1971): *Exports,* $1,722,000,000 (chief exports—rubber, tin, timber, iron ore). *Imports,* $1,527,000,000 (chief imports, West Malaysia, 1969—food and live animals, motor vehicles, chemicals, nonelectrical machinery). *Chief trading partners* (West Malaysia, 1969)—Singapore (took 20% of exports, supplied 7% of imports); United States (18%—6%); Japan (13%—17%); United Kingdom (6%—14%).
Tourism: *Receipts* (1970), $9,200,000.
Transportation: *Motor vehicles* (1970), 352,000 (automobiles, 279,400); *railroads* (1970), 1,132 miles (1,822 km).
Communications: *Telephones* (1971), West Malaysia, 153,395; Sarawak, 13,675; *television stations* (1971), 12; *television sets* (1971), 180,000; *radios* (1969), 423,000; *newspapers* (1969), 37 (daily circulation, 781,000).

MALDIVES

Britain's Queen Elizabeth II visited the Republic of Maldives in 1972, becoming the first foreign head of state to do so. The Maldives had been a British protected state before attaining independence in 1965. Soon after the royal visit, Amir Ibrahim Nasir, president of the republic, announced that the islands were encouraging tourism for the first time. A manager was imported from Sri Lanka (Ceylon) to run the nation's only hotel, an eight-room unit that had been converted from a warehouse. Travelers who enjoy a quiet out-of-the-way place with warm, humid weather and who do not require modern conveniences were encouraged to visit the tiny nation.

Background. The Maldives consist of a group of about 2,000 low-lying coral islands, occupying an area of 115 square miles (298 sq km), about 400 miles (645 km) southwest of Sri Lanka. A fleet of more than 30 ships carries 2–3 million tons of tramp cargo per year. The chief export is dried bonita, a type of tuna. The population of the 215 inhabited islands is about 110,000 (1970 census). Malé, the capital, has a population of about 12,000. Most of the islanders are Muslim and live by a strict Muslim code. The official language is Divehi, a dialect of Sinhalese. The republic's legislature is a 54-member body called the Majlis.

──────── MALI · Information Highlights ────────

Official Name: Republic of Mali.
Area: 478,765 square miles (1,240,000 sq km).
Population (1972 est.): 5,300,000. *Density,* 10 per square mile
  (4 per sq km). *Annual rate of increase,* 2.3%.
Chief Cities (1968 est.): Bamako, the capital, 182,000; Mopti,
  33,000; Ségou, 31,000; Kayes, 29,000.
Government: *Head of state,* Col. Moussa Traoré, president
  (assumed office Sept. 1969). *Head of government,* Col.
  Moussa Traoré.
Language: French (official), tribal languages.
Education: *Expenditure* (1969), 24.5% of total public expendi-
  ture. *School enrollment* (1969)—primary, 218,416; secon-
  dary, 7,181; technical/vocational, 2,889 higher, 392.
Monetary Unit: Mali franc (511.57 francs equal U. S.$1, Sept.
  1972).
Gross National Product (1970 est.): $510,000,000.
Manufacturing (major products): Processed foods.
Major Agricultural Products: Groundnuts, cotton, rice, millet
  and sorghum, fish.
Major Mineral: Salt.
Foreign Trade (1971): *Exports,* $35,000,000. *Imports,* $55,-
  000,000. *Chief trading partners* (1969)—Ivory Coast (took
  39% of exports, supplied 9% of imports); France (16%—
  39%); USSR (2%—10%); Senegal (5%—8%).
Communications: *Telephones* (1968), 7,800; *radios* (1970),
  60,000; *newspapers* (1968), 3 (daily circulation, 3,000).

MALI

Events in Mali in 1972 continued to be influ-enced by domestic tensions. Ruled since 1968 by the Military Committee on National Liberation (MCNL), the country's instability has resulted from a chronic distrust among the military officers and between officers and civil servants. Younger officers, who have accused their elders of "immobilism," may make common cause with influential civil servants for more rapid progress toward modernization.

Domestic Affairs. The MCNL, headed by Col. Moussa Traoré, was concerned with retaining its power. The extent of its concern was evident in the severe sentences given those who had been charged with attempting to overthrow the government in March 1971. On July 31, 1972, the state security court sentenced three former military officers, in-cluding Yoro Diakité, former president of the MCNL, and Malik Diallo, who had been commis-sioner for education, to life imprisonment at hard labor. Observers were surprised at the severity of Diakité's sentence because President Traoré had been his assistant at the Kabi military school. An-other plot against the government was allegedly dis-covered shortly before the trial.

A convention was signed between the govern-ment and the Catholic Church on August 8 incorpo-rating private Catholic schools into Mali's national education system.

In November the government announced the creation of a committee to draft a constitution to be approved by the MCNL and submitted to the people.

Economy. Mali's economic prospects were im-proving in spite of some acute shortcomings. Partly because of better weather conditions, the production of cotton, rice, and peanuts was increased. But rice continued to be imported to meet consumer de-mands in urban centers.

One of the country's most pressing economic problems has been the lack of an adequate transpor-tation network. Railroads carry only 60% of Mali's merchandise, and the shortage of transportation of-ten prevents exports and imported consumer goods from reaching their destination.

The 1972 budget was unbalanced. The largest category was defense, with appropriations almost equal to the combined expenditures for education, youth, and production.

Foreign Affairs. President Traoré paid his first official visit to France in April. The French agreed to increase their assistance to Mali for training plan-ning specialists, and for expanding railroad, electrifi-cation, and social infrastructure projects.

A treaty establishing the West African Economic Community was signed in Bamako on June 3 by seven French-speaking African states—Mali, Ivory Coast, Dahomey, Upper Volta, Mauritania, Niger, and Senegal. Mali continued its diplomatic support for African liberation movements and called for a pan-African military force against colonial repres-sion.

W. A. E. SKURNIK, *University of Colorado*

MALTA

Maltese affairs during the early part of 1972 were dominated by the dispute with Britain and the North Atlantic Treaty Organization (NATO) coun-tries over the renewal of Malta's defense agreement. A crisis had been reached in December 1971, when Malta rejected British offers, and Prime Minister Dom Mintoff threatened to expel British forces by Jan. 1, 1972. The deadline was extended to January 15, as Britain began withdrawing its troops, and was dropped following discussions in Rome on January 14–15 with Lord Carrington, the British defense minister, and Dr. Joseph Luns, NATO secretary general. Negotiations continued in the weeks that followed, aided by the mediation of the archbishop of Malta and the Italian government.

Agreement with Britain and NATO. Talks on the defense issue in London on March 17–24 were suc-cessful, and an agreement was signed by Mintoff and Carrington in London on March 26. Under this agreement, which will run until March 31, 1979, Malta will receive £14 million annually from NATO countries, the British share of the sum being £5.25 million. NATO countries also agreed to provide a further £7 million in aid over the 7-year period, and the Italian government agreed to make an additional payment of £2.5 million.

Relations with China. Diplomatic relations were established between Malta and mainland China com-mencing Jan. 31, 1972, and Prime Minister Mintoff visited China on April 2–8. An agreement on a long-term, interest-free loan of 100 million yuan was signed on April 8.

RICHARD E. WEBB
*Former Director, Reference and Library Division
British Information Services, New York*

──────── MALTA · Information Highlights ────────

Official Name: Malta.
Area: 122 square miles (316 sq km).
Population (1972 est.): 300,000. *Density,* 2,459 per square
  mile (949 per sq km). *Annual rate of increase,* 0.7%.
Chief Cities: Valletta, the capital, 15,400 (1968 est.); Sliema,
  21,000 (1967 census).
Government: *Head of state,* Elizabeth II, queen; represented
  by Sir Anthony Mamo, governor-general (took office June
  1971). *Head of government,* Dom Mintoff, prime minister
  (took office June 1971). *Legislature* (unicameral)—House
  of Representatives, 55 members. *Major political parties*—
  Labour party; Nationalist party.
Languages: Maltese, English (both official), Italian.
Education: *Expenditure* (1968), 18.6% of total public expenditure. *School enrollment* (1967)—primary, 52,585; secondary, 12,305; technical/vocational, 2,359; university/higher,
  1,449.
Monetary Unit: Pound (0.3744 pound equals U. S.$1, June
  1972).
Gross National Product (1970 est.): $229,000,000.
Manufacturing (major products): Processed foods, beverages,
  textiles, clothing, chemicals.
Major Agricultural Products: Potatoes, onions, grapes, barley.
Major Mineral: Salt.
Foreign Trade (1971): *Exports,* $45,000,000. *Imports,* $156,-
  000,000. *Chief trading partners* (1969)—United Kingdom
  (took 34% of exports, supplied 42% of imports); Italy
  (11%—16%).

——————— MANITOBA • Information Highlights ———————

Area: 246,512 square miles (638,466 sq km).
Population: 988,247 (1971 census).
Chief Cities (1971 census): Winnipeg, the capital (246,246); St. James-Assiniboia (71,431); St. Boniface (46,714).
Government: *Chief Officers* (1972)—lt. gov., William J. McKeag; premier, Edward R. Schreyer (New Democratic party); atty. gen., Alvin H. Mackling (N. D.); min. of finance, Saul M. Cherniack (N. D.); min. of educ., Ben Hanuschak (N. D.); chief justice, Samuel Freedman. *Legislature*—Legislative Assembly: 57 members (31 New Democratic party; 21 Progressive Conservatives; 3 Social Credit; 1 Liberal; 1 Independent).
Education: *School enrollment* (1968–69)—public elementary and secondary, 231,650 pupils (9,926 teachers); private schools, 9,708 pupils (583 teachers); Indian (federal) schools, 6,225 pupils (254 teachers); college and university, 15,099 students. *Public school expenditures* (1971 est.)—$86,600,000; *average teacher's salary* (1968–69), $7,125.
Public Finance (fiscal year 1972 est.): *Revenues,* $625,800,000 (sales tax, $131,000,000; income tax, $152,700,000; federal funds, $200,500,000). *Expenditures,* $644,900,000 (education, $180,600,000; health and social welfare, $269,500,000; transport and communications, $49,600,000).
Personal Income (1969 est.): $2,785,000,000.
Social Welfare (fiscal year 1972 est.): $68,500,000 (aged and blind, $100,000; dependents and unemployed, $43,400,000).
Manufacturing (1968): Value added by manufacture, $443,002,-000 (food and beverages, $111,649,000; printing and publishing, $39,694,000; clothing, $33,659,000; primary metals, $29,333,000; transportation equipment, $27,520,000; non-electrical machinery, $25,172,000).
Agriculture (1971): *Cash farm income* (exclusive of government payments), $366,986,000 (livestock and products, $197,135,000; crops, $166,103,000. *Chief crops* (cash receipts)—wheat, $70,133,000; barley, $30,145,000; flaxseed, $14,699,000 (ranks 2d); rapeseed, $13,613,000).
Mining (1971 est.): *Production value,* $319,959,000. *Chief minerals* (tons)—nickel, 74,151 (ranks 2d among the provinces); copper, 56,463; crude petroleum, 5,648,000 bbl; cement, 516,000 tons.
Transportation: *Roads* (1968), 44,770 miles (72,400 km); *motor vehicles* (1969), 394,975; *railroads* (1970 est.), 4,750 track miles (7,640 km); *licensed airports,* 19.
Communications: *Telephones* (1969), 417,575; *television stations* (1971), 18; *radio stations* (1971), 12; *daily newspapers* (1971), 7.
All monetary figures given in Canadian dollars.

MANITOBA

The year 1972 was a relatively quiet one of consolidation for Manitoba. The New Democratic party (NDP) government introduced little innovative legislation. The economy continued to expand slowly, unemployment remained comparatively low, and the provincial budget was balanced.

Politics. Of considerable potential significance was the hard-fought Wolseley by-election won by Liberal party leader I. H. "Izzy" Asper. This election gave the Liberals a leader in the Legislative Assembly and enough members to be once again considered an official party. The Progressive Conservative party, the official opposition, decided at its November convention that it was opposed to coalition with the Liberals before the expected 1973 general election, but it endorsed cooperation at the constituency level.

The NDP government found its small majority in the Assembly reduced by a number of defections. On April 7, Jean Allard, objecting to the growth of unspecified radical and socialist influences in the party, left the government caucus to sit as an independent. On June 26 maverick Joe Borowski, opposed to the replacement of the film censor board by a classification system and to liberalization of abortion laws, left to sit as an Independent New Democrat. These defections give the government a majority of one over the combined opposition ranks.

School Question. The long-controversial issue of state support for denominational schools broke out again in 1972. At the beginning of the session of the Legislative Assembly, Premier E. R. Schreyer announced a personal initiative to extend financial aid to private and parochial schools. On March 2 mines

minister Sidney Green resigned from the cabinet in opposition to the premier's objectives. After an all-night debate on July 20 a free vote resulted in the defeat of the Schreyer resolution. Twelve NDP members, including four cabinet ministers, voted against the change, while 16 supported it. Opposition parties also divided. On July 21, Green was reappointed mines and resources minister and minister of urban affairs. Internal party wounds were patched up, and the province seemed ready to forget for a while this chronically divisive issue.

Federal Election. In the federal general election held on October 30, Manitoba showed disillusionment with the Trudeau government and elected to the House of Commons 8 Progressive Conservatives, 3 New Democrats, and 2 Liberals.

JOHN A. BOVEY
Provincial Archivist of Manitoba

MANUFACTURING. See ECONOMY OF THE U. S.
MARCOS, Ferdinand. See BIOGRAPHY.

MARINE BIOLOGY

There were several significant developments in marine biology in 1972, two of them involving natural disasters.

Effects of Hurricane Agnes. Hurricane Agnes resulted in severe flooding of the numerous rivers that flow into Chesapeake Bay, the nation's most complex estuary. The salinities were drastically reduced, thousands of tons of silt and debris were deposited in the bay, and many sandbars and mud flats were eroded. The total effect of reduced salinity, siltation, and erosion is not yet known, but marine biologists now believe that many of the estuarine populations of oysters, clams, and other shellfish were eradicated, resulting in a significant loss to shell fishermen.

Studies designed to measure the long-term effects of the flood have been implemented. They will enable biologists to measure the rate at which highly disturbed marine communities return to their original state and the extent to which freshwater was moved to the sea.

"Red Tides" and Toxic Marine Plants. The second catastrophe in marine biology in 1972 was the sudden outbreak of paralytic shellfish poisoning in New England coastal waters. This phenomenon, often erroneously called a "red tide," results when a single-celled, plantlike organism grows in abnormal numbers. This organism contains a substance highly toxic to humans and other warm-blooded animals but not to clams, mussels, and other bivalves. The shellfish feed on the single-celled plants, concentrating toxins in their tissues. When a man eats such shellfish that have fed on toxic organisms, he may be severely poisoned. Marine biologists are not yet certain what ecological conditions account for the sudden blossoms of these toxic organisms. Extensive sections of the west coast of North America have annual blooms of these organisms, and shell fishermen generally cease to harvest clams during these periods, but it is the unexpected blooms that are potentially dangerous and of particular interest.

Similar species of marine toxic plants are, however, known to be toxic to marine life itself. In Japan dense populations of these toxic organisms were carried into ponds in which marine finfish were being reared, resulting in the death of the fish and the possible loss of as much as $23 million.

Vertical Migration of Plankton. The recent development of complex plankton nets that can be opened and closed by electronic signals now permits biologists to sample accurately the amount of plankton at different depths throughout the day. Scientists at the National Institute of Oceanography in Surrey, England, reported considerable diurnal movements of plankton with numerous species living at depths of 1,000 meters (3,280 feet). Vertical migrations are extremely important to the Navy because they may interfere with underwater sound transmission and the detection of submarines.

Marine biologists at Plymouth Marine Biological Laboratory in England investigated the significance of squid, whale, and other animal remains found in the stomachs of bottom-dwelling deep-sea sharks and found evidence that many squid live at the bottom of very deep waters and that whales might be attacked during deep feeding dives. The presence of certain parasitic worms common to whales in the digestive tracts of sharks suggested that the parasites may be carried downward from surface waters.

Waste Disposal in Oceans. Recognizing that man is polluting deep oceanic waters and, in fact, may soon start using the deeper coastal waters as a repository for solid wastes, several marine microbiologists are investigating the effect of deep waters on the bacteria that normally degrade sewage, paper, and other wastes. Preliminary results indicate that microbial degradation of organic substances is either terminated completely or markedly slowed at depths of up to 2,000 meters (6,560 feet), probably because of the low temperatures and great pressure. This research clearly questions the consequences of placing large amounts of organic wastes in abyssal depths.

Mariculture. National prominence has been given to experiments in which wastes are used to enrich waters used in mariculture. One program uses sewage as a nutrient source for phytoplankton growth. The plankton is harvested and fed to clams and other shellfish, and the solid waste produced by the clams is in turn consumed by shrimp, a second valuable "crop."

JOHN B. PEARCE, *Ecosystems Investigations*
Sandy Hook Laboratory, N. J.

MARINE CORPS. See DEFENSE FORCES.

MARYLAND

In the 1972 general election, Maryland voters gave President Richard M. Nixon a landslide victory over Sen. George S. McGovern in their race for the presidency. For the first time since 1956, Maryland supported the Republican presidential candidate.

Other Elections. Voters also reelected incumbent Congressmen William O. Mills (R) over John Hargreaves (D) in the 1st district; Clarence D. Long (D) over state Sen. John J. Bishop, Jr. (R), in the 2d; Paul S. Sarbanes (D) over Robert D. Morrow (R), in the 3d; Lawrence J. Hogan (R) over state Sen. Edward T. Conroy (D), in the 5th; Goodloe E. Byron (D) over state Sen. Edward J. Mason (R), in the 6th; Parren J. Mitchell (D) over Verdell Adair (R), in the 7th; and Gilbert Gude (R) over Joseph Anastasi (D), in the 8th. In the newly created 4th district, where there was no incumbent, voters elected Marjorie S. Holt (R) over Werner Fornos (D). With Mrs. Holt's victory, Republicans gained one seat, giving the state a congressional delegation split 4–4.

Also voted on and approved were 17 constitutional amendments, including a controversial plan for a state lottery for the first time since 1851; an equal rights amendment prohibiting discrimination on the basis of sex; and a reapportionment plan for the General Assembly.

In a referendum, voters rejected a law authorizing state aid to private and parochial schools. The law had been passed by the legislature in 1971 after a bitter fight and was appealed to referendum by opponents, who promised a court challenge if the referendum passed.

Legislative Session. In an unusual act of independence the legislature overrode three gubernatorial vetoes in the opening days of the 1972 session. These bills concerned consumer protection in financial loans, hiring of public employees, and the transfer of racing days. Other legislative actions included passage of an austere $2.1 billion operating budget; establishment of a state auto insurance fund

AFTER ATTEMPT on the life of Gov. George Wallace of Alabama on May 15, Arthur H. Bremer is taken into custody by police and FBI agents. Bremer, who shot the Democratic presidential candidate while the latter was giving a primary-campaign speech in Laurel, Md., was later convicted of shooting Wallace and three others and sentenced to 63 years in prison.

DURING PRISON DISTURBANCE in July, some inmates of the Maryland House of Correction wear towels over their heads to prevent identification as they mill around the yard.

for poor-risk drivers; and handgun control and stop-and-frisk laws. The legislature also imposed a partial ban on strip mining in western Maryland by 1973.

Also passed were raises in state alcohol taxes; increases in state gas taxes to provide funds for a state transportation system and for rapid transit; and a higher assessment on farmlands rezoned for more intensive use. New state departments of agriculture and mental retardation were created. The Maryland legislature ratified the proposed U. S. constitutional amendment guaranteeing women equal rights.

Education. The legislature approved $300 million for school construction, twice the 1971 figure, but a plan to abolish the senatorial scholarship program in favor of a program based on student need was defeated. Under the present system, each state senator can award about $14,500 almost without restriction. The program came under attack in 1971 when reports revealed that several scholarships had gone to political workers and to relatives of political incumbents.

Campus Unrest. In mid-April antiwar demonstrations took place at the University of Maryland, leading to clashes between police and students. After three days of confusion and violence, the governor sent in the National Guard to restore order and maintain a curfew. The National Guard was also called in to put down new disturbances in the early part of May.

JEAN E. SPENCER
University of Maryland

--- **MARYLAND · Information Highlights** ---

Area: 10,577 square miles (27,394 sq km).
Population (1970 census): 3,922,399. *Density*, 404 per sq mi.
Chief Cities (1970 census): Annapolis, the capital, 30,095; Baltimore, 905,759; Dundalk, 85,377; Towson, 77,799; Silver Spring, 77,496; Bethesda, 71,621; Wheaton, 66,247.
Government (1972): *Chief Officers*—governor, Marvin Mandel (D); lt. gov., Blair Lee, III (D); secy. of state, Fred L. Wineland (D); atty. gen., Francis B. Burch (D); treas., John A. Luetkemeyer (D); supt., dept. of education, James A. Sensenbaugh; chief justice, Hall Hammond. *General Assembly*—Senate, 43 members (33 Democrats, 10 Republicans); House of Delegates, 142 members (121 D, 21 R).
Education (1971–72): *Enrollment*—public elementary schools, 529,060 pupils, 21,903 teachers; public secondary, 401,930 pupils, 20,647 teachers; nonpublic schools (1970–71), 116,614 pupils, 5,610 teachers; college and university, 154,000 students. *Public school expenditures,* $907,719,000 ($1,071 per pupil). *Average teacher's salary,* $11,128.
State Finances (fiscal year 1970): *Revenues,* $1,670,011,000 (4% general sales tax and gross receipts taxes, $236,843,-000; motor fuel tax, $111,326,000; federal funds, $283,931,-000). *Expenditures,* $1,541,010,000 (education, $511,778,000; health, welfare, and safety, $176,761,000; highways, $286,-246,000). *State debt,* $1,145,879,000.
Personal Income (1971): $18,055,000,000; per capita, $4,514.
Public Assistance (1971): $279,936,000. *Average monthly payments* (Dec. 1971)—old-age assistance, $66.14; aid to families with dependent children, $160.58.
Labor Force: *Nonagricultural wage and salary earners* (July 1972), 1,359,600. *Average annual employment* (1971)—manufacturing, 253,000; trade, 316,000; government, 256,000; services, 245,000. *Insured unemployed* (Aug. 1971)—28,000 (2.9%).
Manufacturing (1970): *Value added by manufacture,* $4,046,-300,000. Food and kindred products, $662,700,000; primary metal industries, $616,600,000; electrical equipment and supplies, $446,300,000; chemicals and allied products, $438,700,000; transportation equipment, $333,400,000; printing and publishing, $265,800,000.
Agriculture (1970): *Cash farm income,* $401,510,000 (livestock, $266,211,000; crops, $127,313,000; government payments, $7,986,000). *Chief crops* (in order of value, 1971)—Corn, hay, tobacco, soybeans.
Mining (1971): *Production value,* $90,235,000 (ranks 37th among the states). *Chief minerals*—Stone, $31,472,000; cement, value not available; sand and gravel, $21,251,000; coal, $8,767,000.
Fisheries (1971): *Commercial catch,* 72,680,000 pounds ($18,-441,000). *Leading species by value:* Oysters, $9,969,000; clams, $3,530,000; crabs, $3,201,000.
Transportation: *Roads* (1971), 26,309 miles (42,339 km); *motor vehicles* (1971), 1,871,834; *railroads* (1971), 1,110 miles (1,786 km); *public airports* (1972), 20.
Communications: *Telephones* (1972), 2,591,100; *television stations* (1971), 6; *radio stations* (1971), 85; *newspapers* (1972), 12 (daily circulation, 720,000).

437

AT HARVARD, West German Chancellor Willy Brandt presents former Secretary of Treasury C. Douglas Dillon with deed to $47 million fund for an educational foundation specializing in European problems. The June 5 ceremony marked the 25th anniversary of George C. Marshall's address to Harvard alumni, outlining his aid plan for war-torn Europe. The fund is named the German Marshall Fund.

UPI

MASSACHUSETTS

Election politics—presidential and other—dominated the news in Massachusetts throughout 1972. For many years the state has been a center of Democratic party strength, but never before had its key role in politics been so sharply defined.

Elections. The political year in Massachusetts began in earnest with Sen. George McGovern's impressive victory in the March presidential primary. The win locked up the state's Democratic convention delegates for McGovern and contributed to the building of momentum for the South Dakota senator's drive for the nomination. Few predicted how unique his support in the state would be. In the November election, Senator McGovern carried only Massachusetts and the District of Columbia. He carried Boston by more than 2 to 1 and won more than 80% of the urban areas of the state. The intensity of feeling among McGovern partisans in Massachusetts was typified by a citizen living near the New Hampshire border who erected a sign on the highway near his home with the message, "You are leaving the United States."

In view of the strong Democratic vote, the vic-

tory of Edward W. Brooke, a Republican seeking reelection to a second term in the U. S. Senate, was an impressive one. Brooke won easily over his Democratic opponent, Middlesex county District Attorney John Droney, by a vote of 1,505,932 to 823,278. Brooke's highly visible win strengthened his position as a national Republican leader. He remains the only black U. S. senator.

Races for Massachusetts' 12 seats in the U. S. House of Representatives resulted in the election of 8 Democrats, 3 Republicans, and 1 independent. Four of the contests were widely viewed as significant. In the 9th district, Rep. Louise Day Hicks was defeated by John J. Moakley in her quest for reelection. Democrat Moakley ran as an independent after the popular Boston incumbent won the Democratic primary. Several suburban Boston communities had been included in Representative Hicks' district by reapportionment, and Moakley's strongest support was in these suburbs.

In the 5th district, John Kerry, a Vietnam War veteran and an outspoken critic of the war, was defeated by his Republican opponent, Paul W. Cronin. Kerry's defeat surprised many political observers who had thought that his chances of becom-

---

MASSACHUSETTS • Information Highlights

Area: 8,257 square miles (21,386 sq km).

Population (1970 census): 5,689,170. *Density:* 735 per sq mi.

Chief Cities (1970 census): Boston, the capital, 641,071; Worcester, 176,572; Springfield, 163,905; New Bedford, 101,777; Cambridge, 100,361; Fall River, 96,898; Lowell, 94,239.

Government (1972): *Chief Officers*—governor, Francis W. Sargent (R); lt. gov., Donald R. Dwight (R); secy. of the commonwealth, John F. X. Davoren (D); atty. gen., Robert H. Quinn (D); commissioner, dept. of education, Neil Sullivan; chief justice, G. Joseph Tauro. *General Court*—Senate, 40 members (27 Democrats, 13 Republicans); House of Representatives, 240 members (177 D, 62 R, 1 vacancy).

Education (1971–72): *Enrollment*—public elementary schools, 685,000 pupils, 26,959 teachers; public secondary, 490,000 pupils, 25,465 teachers; nonpublic schools (1970–71), 199,186 pupils, 9,620 teachers; college and university, 306,000 students. *Public school expenditures,* $961,059,-000 ($907 per pupil). *Average teacher's salary,* $10,590.

State Finances (fiscal year 1970): *Revenues,* $2,369,416,000 (3% general sales tax and gross receipts taxes, $168,443,-000; motor fuel tax, $135,816,000; federal funds, $512,-904,000). *Expenditures,* $2,448,437,000 (education, $527,-286,000; health, welfare, and safety, $729,051,000; highways, $329,580,000). *State debt,* $1,861,766,000.

Personal Income (1971): $26,404,000,000; per capita, $4,586.

Public Assistance (1971): $799,896,000. *Average monthly payments* (Dec. 1971)—old-age assistance, $108.49; aid to families with dependent children, $251.83.

Labor Force: *Nonagricultural wage and salary earners* (July 1972), 2,256,800. *Average annual employment* (1971)—manufacturing, 604,000; trade, 499,000; government, 331,-000; services, 474,000. *Insured unemployed* (Aug. 1972)—77,700 (4.6%).

Manufacturing (1970): *Value added by manufacture,* $9,582,-300,000; Electrical equipment and supplies, $1,435,100,000; nonelectrical equipment, $1,363,100,000; printing and publishing, $696,100,000; instruments and related products, $692,000,000; fabricated metal products, $639,600,000.

Agriculture (1970): *Cash farm income,* $164,358,000 (livestock, $85,626,000; crops, $78,113,000; government payments, $619,000). *Chief crops* (in order of value, 1971)—Cranberries (ranks 1st among the states), hay, tobacco, apples.

Mining (1971): *Production value,* $50,199,000 (ranks 43d among the states). *Chief minerals*—Stone, $23,582,000; sand and gravel, $23,058,000; lime, value not available; clays, $377,000.

Fisheries (1971): *Commercial catch,* 273,064,000 pounds ($45,-970,000). *Leading species by value,* Flounders, $11,520,-000; scallops, $5,965,000; cod, $5,551,000; haddock, $5,-320,000.

Transportation: *Roads* (1971), 29,074 miles (46,789 km); *motor vehicles* (1971), 2,574,838; *railroads* (1971), 1,441 miles (2,319 km); *public airports* (1972), 26.

Communications: *Telephones* (1972), 3,638,200; *television stations* (1971), 11; *radio stations* (1971), 103; *newspapers* (1972), 46 (daily circulation, 2,231,000).

ing the first Vietnam veteran in Congress were quite good. In the 4th district, Robert F. Drinan, a Jesuit priest and the incumbent Democratic representative, narrowly defeated Martin A. Linsky, a liberal Republican. The battle between the two popular liberals was a bitter one. In the 12th district, Democrat Gerry E. Studds won a surprising victory over Republican William D. Weeks. This district has long been regarded as Republican territory.

Contests for state legislative seats resulted in continued strong dominance by Democrats—33 to 7 in the Senate, and 186 to 52 in the House. In the November election, the voters defeated—for the third time in a decade—a proposed constitutional amendment that would have replaced the state's present 5% flat-rate income tax with a graduated tax. They overwhelmingly approved an amendment requiring judges to retire on reaching the age of 70. Passage of the latter affected 38 Massachusetts judges who were at or over this age limit.

Other Developments. The Massachusetts shellfish industry was severely hit in late summer, when a so-called "red tide" of marine organisms caused contamination of major shellfishing areas. All sales of shellfish were banned by the state for a period of several weeks.

The state commissioner of education, Neil Sullivan, resigned in 1972 after almost 10 years on the job. Sullivan had become a controversial figure in state politics because of his strong enforcement of the state's racial imbalance law, which forbids de facto segregation in the public schools. Continuing unrest in Massachusetts' prisons made the state corrections commissioner, John O. Boone, a target of continued criticism.

A restudy of the future transportation needs of the Bay State, conducted while a moratorium on all highway construction was in effect, led Gov. Francis W. Sargent to cancel several pending highway projects and to announce plans to substitute mass transit for new roads in the greater Boston metropolitan area. The governor's decision ended a decade of protest by opponents of highways.

In March, Massachusetts became one of a growing number of states with state-operated lotteries (see STATE GOVERNMENT).

HARVEY BOULAY, *Boston University*

MATERIALS

There were no significant breakthroughs in developing new materials in 1972, but new applications were found for old materials.

Ceramics. Silicon nitride (Si_3N_4) received attention in 1972 because it reached a stage in development where extremely high strengths are possible. A bending strength of 130,000 pounds per square inch (psi) is now possible, and a strength of 150,000 psi may soon be achieved. This material has possibilities for aerospace applications.

Sales of traditional ceramics looked good in 1972. A volume of $1,026 million was predicted for whiteware, $1,936 million for heavy clay products, $769 million for porcelain enamel, $4,878 million for glass, and $350 million for abrasives.

U. S. production of porcelain-enameled steel reached 1.4 billion square feet in 1971, a rise of 3.3% over 1970. Kitchen ranges and heating equipment remained the major users, but home laundry appliances accounted for 242 million square feet and refrigerators for 220 million square feet.

Glass. One company announced production of the largest flat-glass panels ever made. These panels, which are 11 feet wide, 40 feet long, and 0.75 inch thick, are for use in commercial structures.

An experimental glass-asphalt pavement using more than 90,000 reclaimed bottles and jars was installed on a heavily traveled road at New York's John F. Kennedy International Airport in 1972. The test road strip is highly visible at night because it reflects light from automobile headlights.

Very fine glass-fiber bundles are being used experimentally to carry visible-light signals generated by laser diodes. This technique has great promise in communications, even though loss of light through pores in the glass makes it necessary to provide signal amplification every few miles along the length of a fiber bundle.

Several years ago scientists learned to temper glass by chemical treatment. Now, eyeglass lenses can be produced that are nearly 20 times stronger than the minimum federal requirement.

Metals. Strong, lightweight aluminum continues to find more and more use as a structural metal. For instance, one cab-over-engine truck tractor consists of 610 pounds of aluminum, 45 pounds of steel for framing, 80 pounds of steel for doors, and 41 pounds of fiberglass for the hood.

After a 30-year search for better alloys for gas turbines, it was found that the addition of ultrafine thoria (ThO_2) strengthens cobalt base alloys. These strengthened alloys can be extruded to form air foils, which are used as the first-stage stator blades in jet engines. Also, thoria dispersed in nickel alloys causes the alloy to exhibit superior high-temperature strength and thermal conductivity not usually found in nickel alloys. However, the presence of thoria makes forming difficult.

Molybdenum-hafnium-carbon alloys having a highly superior hot strength because of the precipitation of hafnium carbide have been developed, with strengths of more than 100,000 psi at 2700° F.

Plastics. The Society of the Plastics Industry estimated that nearly 20 million pounds of plastics were produced in 1971, a 6% gain over 1970. In 1971, plastic pipe production was up 25% over 1970; vinyl pipe was the leader.

NEW WIRE of superconducting niobium-titanium alloy carries as much electricity as the thick bar of copper.

Urethane-foam filters may someday replace the wire-mesh type of air cleaners in cars. Tests show that a urethane-foam filter is 98% efficient, making dust penetration into carburetors and cylinders almost nonexistent. Injection-molded rubber has been used to make automobile bumpers and other large parts. One experimental bumper that weighed only 16 pounds was developed; it consisted of 8 pounds of rubber and 8 pounds of steel.

Composites. Composites are materials made by combining dissimilar materials, such as glass fibers in a plastic material. In 1971, reinforced plastics consumption in the United States increased to 978 million pounds, up 23% from 1970. Engineers found 250 different uses for glass-fiber reinforced plastics in 1972 automobiles.

JAMES R. TINKLEPAUGH, *Alfred University*

MAURITANIA

The social and political climate in Mauritania worsened in 1972, the result of long-standing tensions occasionally breaking the surface. But events continued to be dominated by President Mokhtar Ould Daddah and the ruling political party.

Domestic Affairs. The government has wanted to gain control of the trade unions, which have served as an outlet for discontent. Dissidents organized a protest demonstration on May Day, but the police quickly reestablished order. The Political Bureau of the PPM announced on July 24 that it had decided to merge the Mauritanian Workers Union, the country's only central trade union, with the PPM within six months.

In May a trial of persons charged with conspiracy to overthrow the government yielded comparatively mild results. All the accused were exonerated of complicity charges, and several important leaders were given suspended sentences for other offenses, but with stiff fines.

Economy. Mauritania's economic prospects were very poor in the agricultural sector. A succession of droughts caused severe crop losses, and the government feared that famine would result unless relief measures were taken. As part of its policy of economic diversification, the government awarded a contract to Italy's Agip-Mineraria for oil drilling in the eastern desert.

Foreign Affairs. President Daddah paid an official visit to Senegal in January and signed an agreement with President Léopold Senghor to step up aid between the two countries. In June, Mauritania joined with six other French-speaking states to establish the West African Economic Community.

Mauritania continued to call for the coordination of African pressures to help liberate Spanish Sahara. During a visit to Mauritania in February, Libyan President Muammar al-Qaddafi declared his nation's readiness to wage war with Mauritania to liberate Spanish Sahara.

The People's Republic of China began to implement a November 1971 agreement to build a port in Mauritania. Several hundred Chinese technicians were reportedly at work.

W. A. E. SKURNIK, *University of Colorado*

———— MAURITANIA • Information Highlights ————

Official Name: Islamic Republic of Mauritania.
Area: 397,954 square miles (1,030,700 sq km).
Population (1972 est.): 1,200,000. *Density,* 3 per square mile (1 per sq km). *Annual rate of increase,* 2.1%.
Chief City (1966 est.): Nouakchott, the capital, 16,000.
Government: *Head of state,* Mokhtar Ould Daddah, president (took office Aug. 1971 for 3d 5-year term). *Head of government,* Mokhtar Ould Daddah. *Legislature* (unicameral) —National Assembly, 50 members. *Political party*—Parti du Peuple Mauritanien.
Languages: French (official), Arabic (national).
Education: *Expenditure* (1964), 16% of total public expenditure. *School enrollment* (1968)—primary, 26,200; secondary, 3,186; technical/vocational, 159.
Monetary Unit: CFA franc (255.79 CFA francs equal U. S.$1, Sept. 1972).
Gross National Product (1970 est.): $180,000,000.
Major Agricultural Products: Gum arabic, millet, corn, sweet potatoes, rice, groundnuts, dates, fish.
Major Mineral: Iron ore.
Foreign Trade (1970): *Exports,* $79,000,000. *Imports,* $48,-000,000. *Chief trading partners* (1969)—United Kingdom (took 24% of exports, supplied 10% of imports); France (20%—38%); Belgium-Luxembourg; West Germany.

———— MAURITIUS • Information Highlights ————

Official Name: Mauritius.
Area: 720 square miles (1,865 sq km): dependencies, 69 square miles (180 sq km).
Population (1972): 900,000. *Density,* 1,060 per square mile (409 per sq km). *Annual rate of increase,* 1.9%.
Chief City (1967 est.): Port Louis, the capital, 134,900.
Government: *Head of state,* Elizabeth II, queen; represented by Sir Leonard Williams, governor-general (took office Sept. 1968; died Dec. 1972). *Head of government,* Sir Seewoosagur Ramegoolam, prime minister (took office Sept. 1967). *Legislature* (unicameral)—Legislative Assembly, 71 members. *Major political parties*—Independence party; Social Democrats.
Languages: English (official), French, Creole, Hindi.
Education: *Expenditure* (1969), 11.7% of total public expenditure. *School enrollment* (1969)—primary, 146,490; general secondary, 42,444; technical/vocational (1968), 603; university/higher, 668.
Monetary Unit: Rupee (5.46 rupees equal U. S.$1, Aug. 1972).
Gross National Product (1970 est.): $189,000,000.
Manufacturing (major products): Processed sugar, tea.
Major Agricultural Products: Sugarcane, tea, potatoes, groundnuts, corn, cassava, fish.
Foreign Trade (1971): *Exports,* $65,000,000. *Imports,* $83,-000,000. *Chief trading partner* (1969)—United Kingdom.
Communications: *Telephones* (1971), 18,038; *television stations* (1971), 1; *newspapers* (1969), 9.

MAURITIUS

The continuing search for means to stimulate the economy and provide more jobs was the chief concern in Mauritius in 1972. The governor general, Sir Leonard Williams, died on December 27.

The Economy. The government of Mauritius set up an Export Processing Zone similar to the free zones which exist in Taiwan, Hong Kong, and Singapore. Under this scheme, manufacturers were to be allowed to import machinery and raw materials into the island duty free and received such incentives as 10- to 20-year tax abatements.

Domestic Affairs. A state of emergency was declared in December 1971, following disturbances caused by a dock, transport, municipal, and electric workers' strike. Leaders of the left-wing Mouvement Militant Mauricien were arrested.

Though overpopulation remained the island's gravest problem, there was some indication of a drop in the birthrate from 3% in 1968 to just over 2% in 1971. Emigration had also increased.

Foreign Affairs. In May, Mauritius became a party to the Yaoundé Convention, associating 18 African nations with the European Common Market. Common Market tariffs were to be lifted for nearly all Mauritian exports except sugar, which was to be subject to negotiations in 1974. The Common Market was to provide $5 million in aid through 1974. Britain was committed to provide $25 million in interest-free loans in 1973–76.

BURTON BENEDICT
University of California, Berkeley

MEDICARE. See SOCIAL WELFARE and special feature beginning on page 26.

In Moscow, Presidents Nixon and Podgorny sign agreement pledging their countries to joint action against cancer and heart disease.

UPI

medicine

During 1972 physicians continued to search for the causes and cures of many common and serious diseases, to study possible new avenues of treatment —such as prostaglandins therapy and methods traditionally employed by the Chinese—and to focus increasing attention on some mental health problems. In the United States research switched to a targeted approach with concentrated biological and medical research on cancer.

Cancer. In 1972 the Nixon administration supported a new program against cancer—the largest program the government has ever mounted against a single disease. The program, which will involve over 5,000 persons, calls for the expenditure of some $430 million in the fiscal year ending in 1973. The amount is expected to go to $600 million in 1975 and to $1 billion in 1976.

As part of the new all-out campaign, the National Cancer Institute will not only plan research into the causes of cancer but will also treat cancer victims. Direct support of patient care by the federal government has never been done before, at least not on such a large scale. Fifteen patient care centers are being set up in the United States. It is hoped that as newer methods of managing the disease are developed in the laboratory, they will be applied to sick people more rapidly and more widely than has been done previously.

Dr. Frank Rauscher was appointed head of the new attack on cancer in May. Dr. Rauscher is a specialist on tumor viruses and discovered the virus —known as the Rauscher virus—that produces leukemia in mice. Dr. Rauscher believes in the systems management approach to handling scientific research. In this approach, the myriad steps involved in designing and producing a specific article are carefully broken down and programmed ahead so that the finished article is completed on schedule. Dr. Rauscher thinks that this type of planning is the only way to control his truly gargantuan program. However, some scientists have criticized the idea on the grounds that there seems to be no place in such a system for unexpected findings that might open up different avenues of research.

A study of the use of the antituberculosis vaccine known as the bacillus of Calmette and Guerin, or BCG vaccine, in treating cancer made national headlines in 1972. The use of BCG in treating cancer is part of the recent development of immunology in treating disease. A vaccine stimulates the body's production of protective agents against a specific disease, and now it is being discovered that triggering the body's own defense mechanism may enable it to remove cancer cells. BCG is one of the agents that have been tried on leukemia patients for this purpose. The work was done at Oak Ridge National Laboratory by Dr. Michael Hanna. The BCG vaccine worked only on one type of experimental animal tumor and only on guinea pigs. Unfortunately, however, local newspaper reports misled the public into thinking that a cure for cancer was at hand. As a result, scientists have become more careful about discussing their research.

Dr. Sol Roy Rosenthal, director of the University of Illinois' Institute for Tuberculosis Research, made a study of leukemia mortality rates among children under six who had been vaccinated with BCG at birth in Chicago's Cook County Hospital.

CONTENTS

Their mortality rates were compared with non-vaccinated children, and the results were significant: there was only one death in the BCG group, a rate of 0.31 per 100,000 per year, while among the unvaccinated children the rate was 2.02, or nearly seven times higher. And the only child to die in the vaccinated group was a five-year-old who had not been brought in for any follow-up. However, Dr. Rosenthal pointed out that "this is a retrospective study" and so no firm conclusions can be drawn. Nevertheless, the results suggest that BCG may be considered as a vaccine against acute leukemia.

Sickle Cell Anemia. Another disease that received a great deal of attention in 1972 was sickle cell anemia. This disease affects one in every ten black Americans to varying degrees and occasionally hits whites, mostly those of Mediterranean origin. In those afflicted with sickle cell anemia, the red blood cells are sickle-shaped and cannot transport oxygen throughout the body as normal red blood cells can. Sickle cells are often destroyed more quickly than they are replaced, so patients suffer crises of acute pain if they are in some stressful situation that calls for more oxygen than their cells can transport.

Early in 1972 a research group at the Rockefeller University in New York reported that it had been treating sickle cell anemia victims with a drug called cyanate. This drug seems to prevent the red blood cells from developing the sickle shape and possibly increases the number of red blood cells. The National Institutes of Health is also guiding a number of studies of urea, a chemical producer of cyanate. There are also mass screening programs underway that will try to identify the carriers of the sickle cell trait and warn carriers of possible hazards should they have children.

Hepatitis. In San Antonio, Texas, an Air Force sergeant who was dying of liver coma brought on by hepatitis was given a radically new treatment that saved his life and gave promise of saving many other lives. According to Dr. Gerald Klebanoff, who worked out the details in a long series of animal studies, the new treatment is a total body washout and consists of flushing out the blood and keeping the patient completely bloodless for a short period of time. The patient made such a dramatic recovery that the researchers recommend the treatment be tried on hepatic coma cases that do not respond to more conventional therapy and who might otherwise die.

Prostaglandins. Prostaglandins, hormonelike chemicals in the body, have been described by Dr. Elias J. Corey, professor of chemistry at Harvard University, as "messenger chemicals that control the reactions of the cell." Although they were identified some 35 years ago, their use in therapy is still in its infancy. However, in 1972 a group at Harvard, under Dr. Corey, synthesized five members of the prostaglandins family, thus opening up a whole new area of possible hormone research.

Prostaglandins are found in many animals and in a wide range of tissues. About 16 kinds are known, and they have been seen in the brain, lungs, pancreas, thymus, and eyes and in male and female reproductive systems. Even infinitesimal amounts seem to have a great effect when added or taken from the body and appear to regulate the various organs of the body. For example, it is known that one type of prostaglandins found in the kidney can keep down blood pressure, while another type can raise it through narrowing the blood vessels. "These chemicals are ubiquitous and will probably be found in all cells," according to Dr. Corey. They may become valuable therapeutic agents in the treatment of many disorders.

Isolation of a Flu Virus. In 1972 scientists succeeded in capturing the virus of one of man's commonest ailments—short-duration intestinal flu. This uncomfortable "bug," whose symptoms are diarrhea, nausea, cramps, and sickness, some fever, and often a severe headache, is now called the "Norwalk agent" because its virus was first collected from specimens taken from victims of an outbreak in Norwalk, Ohio. Dr. Raphael Dolin and a group at the National Institutes of Health report that it is a tiny naked virus peculiar to humans. It upsets the digestive system for periods of as long as one week, after which it disappears, apparently conferring immunity for about 4½ months. It does not, however, protect against other species of intestinal viruses, and researchers warn that there may be as many different intestinal viruses as there are respiratory ones so that the prospect of an overall vaccine may be as remote as one against the "common cold."

Multiple Sclerosis Linked to a Virus. In 1972 three independent groups of researchers—American, German, and British—found virus particles in the brains of patients afflicted with multiple sclerosis. The virus may not cause the disease but may simply be an invader into body systems already weakened by multiple sclerosis. However, epidemiologists have noticed that multiple sclerosis seems prevalent only in temperate climate zones, and though it can appear in more than one member of a family no hereditary pattern has been established for it. It seems more likely to come from some shared environment that might involve a shared virus, though not an infectious one.

The virus found in the brains of patients afflicted with multiple sclerosis was one of a group known as myxoviruses and appears to be related to the group of parainfluenza type I virus that is distantly related to those causing respiratory illnesses. The research involved an exchange of material from patients between the University of Göttingen in West Germany and the Wistar Institute in Philadelphia, with confirmation from a Newcastle, England, hospital and an Australian researcher.

Warning About Unnecessary Surgery. In July 1972 Herbert S. Denenberg, Pennsylvania insurance commissioner, brought out a "Shopper's Guide to Surgery," listing 14 points for consumers to think about when considering surgery. Denenberg estimates that there are over 2 million unnecessary operations performed annually on Americans, the commonest being tonsillectomies, hemorrhoidectomies, and hysterectomies. The guide recommends that people consult a trusted family physician who may refer them to a reliable surgeon, and that if this specialist suggests an operation they should ask for an independent consultation with a second authority who has no prospect of financial gain and so is presumably unbiased. The guide also recommends that the surgeon be a fellow of the American College of Surgeons or the American College of Osteopathic Surgeons, and that surgery be performed in a hospital accredited by the American Hospital Association and preferably one that allows staff privileges both to the surgeon and the family physician. All costs should be discussed frankly, and the patient should be told of possible complications.

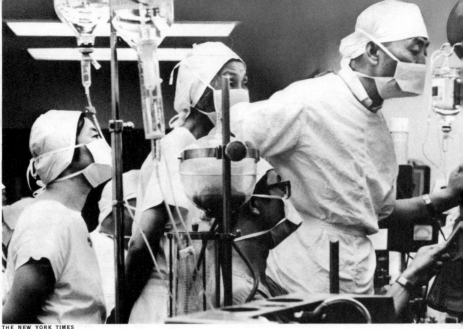

CHINESE DOCTORS watch open-heart surgery in a hospital in New York City. Eleven Chinese physicians made a three-week tour of the United States in October and November.

Untreated Syphilis Patients. The American public was shocked to learn that for 40 years, 443 black men with syphilis from around Tuskegee, Ala., were part of a U. S. Public Health study that deliberately left their disease untreated in order to determine at autopsy the effects of the disease. The victims were not aware that they were being used as human guinea pigs. Penicillin was found to be effective against syphilis ten years after the study began, but no attempt to administer it to the group was made. A citizens committee appointed by the Department of Health, Education, and Welfare urged that the research be abandoned and the 72 known survivors, now all over 65 years of age, be treated. Ironically, the study became public just as Americans were warned that venereal disease was on the increase—indeed, was out of control.

Decrease in Childhood Diseases. During the first nine months of 1972, the number of cases of measles dropped 61% and of rubella, or German measles, 44%, as a result of an intensified campaign by the U. S. Public Health Service to vaccinate children. The Public Health Service hopes to have inoculated all children, even those in scattered rural areas and ghettoes that have so far escaped mass vaccination programs, by the end of 1973.

Declining Birthrate. For the first time in history, the birthrate in the United States dropped below the recognized "replacement level" of 2.1 children to a family. This was true even though there are more women of childbearing age in the population. A National Fertility Study made at Princeton University attributes the drop in births to increased acceptance of the contraceptive pill, sterilization procedures, and use of the intrauterine device (IUD). There were an estimated 5 million vasectomies in the United States in 1972—a great increase over the estimated one million in 1971.

Blood Banks. In August 1972 the U. S. Food and Drug Administration (FDA) began to establish a nationwide system of blood collection to bring some 5,000 blood banks and 200 blood-processing centers in the country under some government control. Until now, only 530 blood banks that shipped blood across state lines were subject to federal regulation, but these handle over 75% of the eight million pints taken annually. The blood banks were given 60 days to conform to the federal regulations and were also screened a second time three months later —something new in government-managed proficiency testing programs. The screening was designed to eliminate hepatitis virus-infected blood, which causes between 1,500 and 3,000 deaths annually.

Interest in Chinese Medicine. Interest in acupuncture, spurred by President Nixon's early 1972 trip to China, continued throughout the year. A number of acupuncturists were found practicing in the United States, but some who lacked recognized medical certification were forced to stop practicing. Meanwhile, for the first time in 23 years, a group of Chinese medical scientists visited United States health centers in a whirlwind tour of the country. The exchange of ideas was stimulating and some interesting differences in national health problems were recognized; for example, in China cancer outranks coronary disease as a cause of death, while in the United States the reverse is true.

Depression as a Common Illness. The publicity concerning Sen. Thomas F. Eagleton's admission that he had undergone electroshock therapy for acute mental depression focused attention on the very rapidly increasing incidence of depression among many Americans. The development led many Americans to rethink their attitude toward mental illnesses and those who suffer or have suffered from them. Also raised was the issue of physical and mental fitness in those running for high government office.

Judging Physicians. In late 1972 the New York *Times* published a lengthy article on Dr. Max Jacobson, a New York physician with many prominent patients whose therapy often involved the use of amphetamines, otherwise known as "speed." The story raised the question of why, when other doctors knew of his methods, he was allowed to continue to practice. Even the conservative American Medical Association is now urging doctors to break their traditional "conspiracy of silence" if they know of a colleague who drinks too much, takes drugs, or has severe psychiatric problems, and to urge them to seek help. It has also accepted the writing of a "peer review" provision into the Social Security Act.

CHARLES S. MARWICK
Senior Writer, "Medical World News"

Posters warning against the misuse of alcohol are part of a campaign by the National Institute on Alcohol Abuse and Alcoholism, an agency of HEW.

ALCOHOLISM: 'The Worst Drug Problem'

Alcoholism is the worst drug problem in the United States—worse by far than the narcotic and drug abuse problem that has received a great deal of attention in recent years. Over 9 million Americans suffer from physical, psychological, or social difficulties caused by excessive drinking. Such people are unable to control their drinking and get into trouble of one kind or another—on the job, at home, on the highway—because of their drinking. In these ways, alcoholic people are a burden to themselves, their families, and society, adversely affecting the lives of tens of millions of their relatives and associates and draining the economy of $15 billion a year.

Less than 5% of alcoholic people and problem drinkers are public inebriates or skid row derelicts. Most alcoholics—75% are men—live with their families in respectable neighborhoods, hold jobs, or are full-time homemakers. Alcoholics are represented in all income brackets, in all races, and in all religions, but in minority groups that have experienced exceptional deprivation, the incidence of alcoholism is now at epidemic levels, and among American Indians the rate is 10%, or twice as high as the national average.

Alcohol plays a major role in half of the highway deaths in the United States; the proportion is even higher among youths aged 16 to 24. Public intoxication alone accounts for one-third of all arrests reported annually. Alcoholism is also related to one-third of the suicides and one-half of the homicides that occur annually.

Early Countermeasures. In the U. S. only in recent years has alcoholism been recognized as an illness—not a moral or criminal offense—and as a major health problem demanding a national program of treatment, rehabilitation, and prevention. Before that, no such national program existed, and the battle against alcoholism was ineffective.

Simple answers to the complex disorder were sought and fostered by medical-social-environmental factors. Legislation banning the manufacture and sale of alcoholic beverages (Prohibition), campaigns aimed at shaming or scaring alcoholic people into sobriety, and scientific research that attempted to understand and break the chain of biochemical events that characterize alcohol addiction—these and other approaches all proved failures, leading many to throw up their hands and declare the battle hopeless. After the repeal of Prohibition in 1933, each state was left to its own devices, and the ensuing patchwork of local laws (a "dry" county here, a "wet" county there) served only to reflect the conflicting attitudes of diverse groups toward the use of alcohol.

Fortunately, many determined persons continued the uphill struggle. Forming a variety of activist groups, such as Alcoholics Anonymous, the National Council on Alcoholism, and the Alcohol and Drug Problems Association of North America, and working together with state and local agencies created to foster alcoholism programs, they sought to gain recognition of the problem of alcoholism from the public, the health professions, and the government.

Beginnings of Change. Due to the combined concerted efforts of dedicated individuals, there was gradually a major shift in public attitudes

toward the tragedies inflicted by alcoholism. The first major indication of change came in 1966 when District of Columbia courts held that an alcoholic person cannot be criminally punished for intoxication. This decision was based on a new definition which describes alcoholism as an illness with the alcoholic person drinking involuntarily as a result of his disease.

With the historic and unanimous passage by both Houses of Congress of the "Comprehensive Alcohol Abuse and Alcoholism Prevention, Treatment and Rehabilitation Act of 1970," alcoholism was recognized as a major public health problem. Under the provisions of the law, which enlisted the support of such diverse interests as mental health, general health, alcoholism groups, and the liquor industry, the National Institute on Alcohol Abuse and Alcoholism was established within the U. S. Department of Health, Education, and Welfare.

As the primary focal point for developing national alcoholism prevention and control programs, the National Institute on Alcohol Abuse and Alcoholism (NIAAA) has responsibility for formulating and recommending national policies and goals with respect to alcohol problems. It is also responsible for executing programs in this health area for the support of research, training, development of treatment and rehabilitation services, and prevention through education.

NIAAA Goals and Programs. The planning and program structure in each of NIAAA's program areas is aimed at meeting three paramount goals: (1) to mobilize, strengthen, and expand all existing resources for the treatment and rehabilitation of alcoholic persons at the community level; (2) to develop the most effective methods of preventing alcoholism and problem drinking; and (3) to launch intensive investigations of alcohol metabolism and the development of mechanisms for eliminating or reducing the physiological damage that alcohol can cause.

These goals of treatment and prevention are being implemented by NIAAA funding of a nationwide network of comprehensive alcoholism programs that are based within local communities. Only those programs that provide a wide spectrum of services—ranging from emergency care services through outpatient care and school programs—that are flexible enough to meet individual needs and broad enough to meet the total needs of alcoholics and their families, are being supported.

Through its program of research grants, NIAAA supports investigations into the etiology, diagnosis, treatment, and prevention of alcoholism.

Since one of the main hindrances in implementing alcoholism programs in the U. S. has been the severe shortage of expert and knowledgeable people working in this specialized field, NIAAA is supporting programs to train physicians, psychiatrists, nurses, social workers, and other alcoholism therapists. To meet the severe alcoholism problems of special population groups, NIAAA is conducting collaborative programs with other federal, state, and local agencies and with private volunteer organizations, targeted at the drinking driver, the public inebriate, the employee whose drinking gets him into trouble on the job, the American Indian, and other disadvantaged groups. The results from helping these people secure treatment and rehabilitation services are gratifying. While figures indicating the degree of "success" attained in some of these areas not yet available, industries that have established programs to help alcoholic employees and problem drinkers report a recovery rate of over 50%.

Since no disease is eliminated by treating only the victims, NIAAA places a top priority on prevention and supports programs of public information and education aimed at developing public and professional awareness of all aspects of the problem and recognition of alcoholism as an illness for which the afflicted person needs help and can be helped. These programs include campaigns on television and radio, in the press, magazines and other public media, and educational programs in schools and in parent and community organizations. NIAAA's recently established National Clearinghouse on Alcohol Information develops and distributes information on all aspects of the use and abuse of alcohol.

The centuries-old struggle against alcoholism is still far from won, but the dramatic progress that has been made in the past few years is most encouraging. Within the first year of its existence, NIAAA's aim to decrease the incidence of this public health problem was deemed so vital and its early accomplishments so promising that its budget was increased sixfold.

Uniform Laws. The establishment of NIAAA launched a major national effort to encourage the enactment of a consistent pattern of state and local alcoholism legislation throughout the country. The most significant development occurred with the adoption, in August 1971, of a Uniform Alcoholism and Intoxication Treatment Act. The NIAAA is encouraging each state to introduce the Uniform Act in its legislature and to press for early enactment. Basically, the Uniform Act states that alcoholic persons and intoxicated persons may not be subjected to criminal prosecution because of their consumption of alcoholic beverages but rather should be afforded a continuum of treatment so that they may lead productive lives.

MORRIS E. CHAFETZ, M. D.
*Director, National Institute
on Alcohol Abuse and Alcoholism*

APPARENT CONSUMPTION OF ABSOLUTE ALCOHOL IN THE UNITED STATES, 1970

gallons per person *

Region	distilled spirits	wine	beer	gallons per person *
Pacific	43%	19%	38%	3.06
New England	50%	10	40%	3.00
Middle Atlantic	44%	12	44%	2.84
Mountain	43%	10	47%	2.72
East North Central	42%	8	50%	2.61
South Atlantic	51%	9	40%	2.56
West North Central	41%	6	53%	2.46
West South Central	37%	9	54%	2.19
East South Central	44%	5	51%	1.63

*In the drinking age population, 15 and over.

The regions are the standard regions of the U.S. Census Bureau. Amounts calculated according to tax-paid withdrawals.

Allergies

Progress in 1972 was made in clinical and laboratory areas. New allergens and allergic reactions were recognized; new testing techniques were reported; new treatments were tried; and new facts about the nature of allergy were disclosed.

Diagnostic Advances. Attention was called to hypersensitivity pneumonitis, a condition that may occur in 15% of the allergic population after repeated exposure to mold protein. Although its symptoms include wheezing, this disease is associated with circulating antibodies rather than tissue-fixed ones. On the other hand, a new entity, variant asthma, was described in which patients have a cough rather than wheezing as the chief problem of their allergic chest disease. It was also recognized that pre-school children often wheeze with acute viral infections, especially with those caused by respiratory syncitial virus, and that many of these children later develop typical allergic asthma.

Allergens and Allergic Reactions. Among the substances recognized as possible causes of allergic reactions was tartrazine, a food coloring, that was shown to cause hives and asthma, particularly in aspirin-sensitive patients. Tetanus toxoid was described as a very potent antigen which, after repeated dosages, can produce severe local reactions and sometimes systematic ones, including kidney disease in many people. This report emphasized the potential hazard of too-frequent tetanus boosters. On the other hand, it was shown that egg-intolerance is not in itself reason to defer vaccination with such egg-based vaccines as those against measles, German measles, mumps, influenza, and rabies, but that skin testing with the individual vaccine is the best way to determine sensitivity.

Testing Aid. A new liquid crystal tape—a preparation of liquid cholesterol crystals in a plastic tape—used to grade changes in skin temperature and thereby skin reactivity to substances being skin-tested was reported during the year.

Treatment. Two new drugs, beclomethasone, a steroid, and salbutanol, a sympathomimetic, for use by spray, were investigated during the year. Both seemed effective and safe but needed further study. Scientists in India also reported the oral use of the leaf of the plant *Tylophora indica* in the treatment of asthma. A completely new field in allergy treatment was opened by the use of the immunological dialyzer. This technique, which uses an artificial kidney to remove specific blood proteins, promises to provide immediate, though temporary, relief for patients with life-threatening allergic and immunological diseases.

Biochemical Investigations. New basic information was disclosed about the biochemical nature of allergic disease. Interest was shown in the immune complement system, in the mediator substances of allergic disease, and in autonomic responses. On the cellular level, adenosine monophosphate from leukocytes was found to have an important place in producing the symptoms of allergic disease. The enzyme adenyl cyclase, known to inactivate adenosine monophosphate, was therefore offered as a possible means of preventing the symptoms of allergy. Prostaglandins have been found to stimulate the production of adenyl cyclase in vitro and were held a possible future treatment for allergic diseases.

IRWIN J. POLK, M. D.
St. Luke's Hospital, New York City

Cancer

Cancer research in 1972 was concentrated on the link between cancer and viruses, on the tumor angiogenesis factor, and on the role of hormonal treatment in certain types of cancer.

Cancer and Viruses. The attempt to identify a link between cancer and viruses in man has been hampered by negative results and a lack of tests sensitive enough to provide a meaningful result. Since known viral-induced cancers often do not themselves produce virus, emphasis has centered on detecting small quantities of viral-specific proteins in human tumors or cell lines cultured from them. In 1972 the search was extended to viral nucleic acids (either RNA or DNA) themselves. Single-stranded RNA or DNA molecules containing complementary sequences can combine spontaneously under a technique known as molecular hybridization. Purified radioactive nucleic acids complementary to the nucleic acids of many known or suspect cancer viruses are newly available. This makes it now possible to seek matching and therefore possibly viral nucleic acids in cell extracts.

Maurice Green of the St. Louis University School of Medicine has estimated that as few as 1,000 viral nucleic acid molecules may be detected in this manner, a degree of sensitivity not previously approached. By this technique, Green and his co-workers have analyzed over 200 cancers of 19 different varieties, searching for nucleic acids of specific human and feline viruses. All these tests gave negative results, but a group led by Sol Spiegelman of Columbia University found successful hybridization between DNA made from mouse mammary tumor virus and RNA extracts of 19 out of 29 human breast cancers. Benign breast tissue, leukemic cells, and human sarcomas gave negative results. The same technique has established similarities between the nucleic acids of the mouse mammary tumor virus and those of the particles found in milk of 10 of 20 women with a strong family history of breast cancer. These observations add significantly to the evidence in favor of a human viral cause for breast cancer in man. Spiegelman's group has also observed hybridization between labelled DNA complementary to the RNA of the murine Rauscher leukemia-sarcoma virus (MSV) and RNA extracts of 18 of 25 human sarcomas. Green's group obtained a similar result in studies with MSV and human ovarian cancer, but also noted hybridization in lesser degree with normal human ovaries.

Tumor Angiogenesis. It has been known for decades that transplanted tumors in animals can stimulate the formation of blood vessels, thereby acquiring the nutrients necessary for further growth. In 1971 and 1972, Judah Folkman and co-workers at the Children's Hospital Center in Boston reported the isolation of a tumor factor responsible for angiogenesis, or the formation of new blood vessels. This tumor-angiogenesis factor (TAF) has been demonstrated in extracts of tumor from the rat, mouse, and man and from human placenta. TAF appears to be a large complex molecule containing carbohydrate, ribonucleic acid, protein, and lipid.

Folkman proposes that TAF diffuses from the tumor and stimulates the lining cells and the surrounding connective tissue cells of nearby blood vessels to proliferate. If the mechanisms by which TAF elicits its effect can be established and blocked,

it might provide a new avenue for anticancer therapy.

Hormone Receptors. Cancer of the breast in female rats, mice, and in many humans is at least partly dependent on estrogenic hormones. Hormonal manipulations that result in a decrease in the level of circulating estrogens produce clinical improvement with regression of cancer in 30% to 40% of appropriately selected patients. Heretofore, the selection of patients for hormonal manipulations has been empiric, based on such factors as age and menstrual status, but recent work on hormone receptors, pioneered by Elwood V. Jensen of the University of Chicago, may permit a more rational patient selection procedure.

The investigations of a number of laboratories have demonstrated that the initial steps in steroid hormone action involve binding of the hormone to a specific receptor in the cell's cytoplasm. The hormone-receptor complex then becomes tightly bound to the cell's chromatin (hereditary material in the nucleus) and influences its genetic expressions by altering the synthesis of nucleic acids and new proteins. In pre-treatment studies on biopsy specimens of breast cancer patients who subsequently underwent hormone manipulations, Jensen and co-workers found that only 1 out of 29 patients responded when the tumor failed to show a hormone receptor. In contrast, 10 out of 13 estrogen-binding tumors responded. If these studies are confirmed and the assay can be widely applied many women can be spared a nonproductive operation.

CHARLES W. YOUNG, M. D.
Sloan-Kettering Institute for Cancer Research

Dentistry

The dominant theme in every phase of dentistry has become prevention of dental disease. In the dental office, prevention includes regular dental prophylaxis, patient education in correct dental hygiene measures and diet, and use of special fluoride techniques and sealants. Preventive dentistry, however, cannot be confined to the dental office, and the profession is concerned with involving individuals and the community in prevention programs.

Committee on Preventive Dentistry. A coordinating committee was created to review prevention activities and to promote prevention to the profession and the public. Committee members represent the fields of dental practice, dental education, dental research, public health, health-care programs, public information, and legislation. Interest was stimulated by an annual program of awards.

Dental Health Measures. A joint statement by members of the dental profession and the Public Health Service called for the following measures to help prevent decay and dental disease: daily plaque removal; limited intake of sweets, especially sweet snacks; use of a fluoride toothpaste; and fluoridation of all community water supplies. Dentistry continued to press for a national fluoridation program and it also registered opposition to a bill permitting snack machines in schools.

Research. Meanwhile, research projects went forward in the biology of plaque, in various aspects of the problem of preventing periodontal disease by chemical and mechanical means, and in the effect of periodontal disease on general health. Research indicates that bone destruction in dental disease may be connected with certain leukocytes which, when stimulated with material from plaque, release a substance that triggers bone resorption. Prostaglandins (hormonelike chemicals) produced by some bacteria are also under suspicion.

Two research projects focused on means of caries prevention in nonfluoridated areas of the country. One study indicated the value of regular mouth-rinsing with a fluoride solution. The other, a 12-year study of a rural school population in a region where only the school water supply was fluoridated, showed that there were 39% fewer decayed, missing, and filled teeth in the children who attended school regularly as compared with the control group.

Dental Auxiliaries. The report of an inter-agency committee on dental auxiliaries aroused great interest among those concerned with dental health. The report's basic philosophy included these points: (1) every effort should be made toward maximum utilization of existing dental auxiliaries in expanded functions; (2) the auxiliary education system must be developed at local and national levels to provide the qualified personnel needed; and (3) the dentist should continue to have legal, ethical, and moral responsibility for supervision of auxiliaries within the existing framework of state law.

The committee also developed guidelines for the education of dental auxiliaries, covering course content and performance goals for formal education programs, on-the-job training, and continuing education programs in 15 expanded-duty functions.

A Minnesota study showed that assistants were capable of performing delegated procedures within acceptable time limits and that dental students' attitudes toward the delegation of duties was favorable. In an Alabama study, therapists compared well with senior dental students in performance of dental prophylaxis.

Education. Major efforts were made to recruit members of minority groups to dental schools. More women and more blacks and other ethnic groups were represented in enrollments. Full dental school scholarships were awarded to 74 students who were black or were members of other minority groups. To accelerate the training of dentists, a flexible curriculum that permits variation in the rate at which students complete their work has been introduced at several schools.

Two museum exhibits of dental significance opened. One, in the California Museum of Science and Industry, is jointly sponsored by the state dental society and the museum. It stresses preventive dentistry to the public, especially children, and stimulates students to consider careers in dentistry. The other, the first major public exhibit devoted to showing the potential of the scanning electron microscope, opened in Chicago's Field Museum. Jointly sponsored by the museum and the dental profession, the exhibit explores tooth structure and feeding mechanisms in small vertebrate and invertebrate animals.

Political Action. Committees have been formed in nearly half the states to communicate the dental profession's point of view to public officials and national leaders, and thus to influence legislation that affects dental health care. The inclusion of dental benefits in some national health insurance plan is one of the goals of the committees.

New Techniques. A collimating device that limits the X-ray beam and a monitoring device for control of the beam were reported effective in reducing radiation exposure during dental radiographic examinations. High-frequency oscillation

was explored as a fast and painless means of moving and extracting teeth. Preliminary studies were reported in the potential role of laser energy in prevention of caries. Acupuncture for oral anesthesia was proposed and will be investigated. A simple method of detecting lead poisoning in children by atomic absorption spectrometer analysis of shed deciduous teeth was initiated in Cleveland schools.

LELAND C. HENDERSHOT, D. D. S.
Editor, American Dental Association

Eye Diseases

During 1972 there were several advances in the diagnosis and treatment of eye diseases.

Surgical Advances. Combined cataract and corneal transplantation operations have been improved, and the technique for anti-glaucoma operations combined with cataract extraction has been made more effective. During the past few years a method for the removal of cataracts by ultrasound emulsification and aspiration has been developed, but this procedure is usually only possible in large eye surgical institutions because of the high cost of the emulsifier that liquifies the lens. It was found that intralenticular foreign bodies forming a cataract are best removed by using a cryoprobe to remove the cataractous lens. Cancer of the eyelids was also treated with cryosurgery.

Lamellar corneal transplantation has been improved with the use of the binocular operating microscope, the binocular ophthalmometer, and the microtome. Until recently loss of the vitreous in intraocular surgery was disastrous, but now preserved vitreous and normal saline solutions have been developed and used to replace lost vitreous or aspirated hemorrhagic vitreous, with better techniques and results. Ultrasound techniques for the production of chorioretinal adhesions to press retinal detachments back into place and to liquify vitreous have also been used with increasingly fruitful results. Among other surgical advances was the development of new and more rapid operative techniques for the correction of trichiasis, or ingrowing eyelashes, and entropion, or inward turning of the edge of the eyelid.

Advances in Diagnosis, Prevention, and Nonsurgical Treatment. During the year there were extensive investigations of the causes of certain eye diseases and significant contributions to our knowledge of the pathogenesis and treatment of diseases of the uvea (term for the iris, ciliary body, and choroid). A number of eye conditions that may be due to immunoglobulin disorders and the structure of many immunoglobulins and their importance in tears have also been studied. Tears have been found to be a source of greater antibody production against disease antigens than formerly suspected. The eye, because of the avascularity (lack of blood flow) of some of its parts, is one of the organs most vulnerable to disease organisms of low virulence. When antibody formation in a patient's tears does not keep pace with antigen formation, there can be rapid spread of some eye conditions and increased morbidity.

Earlier recognition of histoplasmosis has been accomplished by noting a smaller and earlier granuloma formation, with angiography a helpful diagnostic aid. The preferred treatment is corticosteroids, but photocoagulation may be effective

COUNT, a basenji, has lived five years since being fitted with a therapeutic pacemaker. Owner Karl Ross (left) *and veterinarian James Buchanan celebrate event.*

in some cases. Ultrasonic scanning has been used in differential diagnosis of unilateral exophthalmos. Among other advances was the development of a vaccine against trachoma and the finding that the antibiotic gentamycin, which has a wide spectrum of antibacterial activity, enters the anterior chamber of the eye when injected subconjunctivally.

ROLAND I. PRITIKIN, M. D.
Author of "Essentials of Ophthalmology"
M. L. DUCHON, M. D.
Consultant in Ophthalmology

Heart and Vascular Disease

Heart disease is the leading cause of death in the United States. About 675,000 Americans die each year of heart attacks, and more than 27 million have some form of cardiovascular disease. In 1972 there were advances in cardiovascular surgery and studies of the relationship of cardiovascular disease to oral contraceptives, blood fats, alcohol, and smoking, as well as work in pediatric cardiology and drug therapy.

Cardiovascular Surgery. The use of saphenous vein grafts—that is, grafts from large veins in the leg—to bypass coronary artery narrowing has proceeded at a rapid pace. Many cardiac surgeons advise this procedure for patients with angina pectoris who have significant narrowing of one or more of the coronary arteries; but others advise a critical selection of patients and controlled efficacy studies. Many cardiac surgeons claim graft patency in 80% to 85% of patients studied up to 2 or 3 years after surgery, but less enthusiastic observers had noted graft failure in 10% to 40% within one year. Long-term data are not yet available. The use of coronary artery bypass surgery on an emergency basis in patients with an impending heart attack is even more controversial.

The intraaortic balloon pump has emerged as the most widely used temporary mechanical assist device. By employing this technique with emergency revascularization of the heart muscle, Charles Sanders and associates at the Massachusetts General Hospital have been able to save nearly 50% of patients with cardiogenic shock, a condition that had previously been almost 100% lethal.

Dr. Brian Barratt-Boyes of New Zealand has employed a technique of deep hypothermia combined with cardiac perfusion to operate on newborns and infants and totally correct serious congenital cardiac lesions. This new technique has been hailed by many cardiac surgeons as a significant advance.

Oral Contraceptives, Estrogen, and Cardiovascular Disease. It is now clearly established that there is a definite cardiovascular risk associated with the use of oral contraceptives. There is a marked increase in the risk of thrombophlebitis and pulmonary embolism in young women taking the drug as compared to nonpregnant women of the same age. There is also a small but definite increased incidence of high blood pressure, migraine headaches, strokes, and heart attacks. Estrogen therapy in menopausal women and as a prophylactic drug in the prevention of coronary artery disease in men is now being seriously questioned because it has been observed that estrogen, especially in higher dosages, may cause an increase in thromboembolic disease and produce in susceptible individuals a striking increase in levels of blood triglyceride (one of the blood fats).

Studies of Increased Blood Fat Levels. There have been several studies of the role of hyperlipidemia, or increased blood fats, in the pathogenesis of vascular disease. Recent studies have added to the understanding of the inheritance of certain forms of hyperlipidemia, and the ability to diagnose high levels of cholesterol in the blood taken from the umbilical cords of infants now permits the initiation of preventive therapy. The National Heart and Lung Institute has now established 12 lipid research centers for the long-term study of the role of diet and medication in the reduction of blood fat levels and its effect on reducting cardiovascular complications.

Alcohol and Heart Disease. Alcohol is emerging as a significant factor in some forms of heart disease. It can increase blood triglycerides, which are thought to be a risk factor in causing heart attacks, and it also has a direct deleterious effect on heart muscle. In some susceptible individuals alcohol can cause serious and even fatal heart muscle disease.

Smoking and Heart Disease. Cigarette smoking has been established as a definite risk factor in producing heart attacks. A man who smokes more than one pack per day has a threefold increase in risk of heart attack and especially of sudden death. Stopping smoking, however, quickly reduces the risk.

Pediatric Cardiology. The seriousness of patent ductus in premature infants with respiratory distress syndrome and the urgency for early surgical correction have been recently emphasized. The importance of preventing intrauterine rubella (German measles), and the attendant congenital cardiac abnormalities, by appropriate vaccination of susceptible children and young women has also been demonstrated.

Drug Therapy. The use of drugs—such as urokinase and streptokinase that lyse clots and aspirin and other agents that alter platelet function by preventing clumping or agglutination—in the treatment of certain thrombotic disease is under investigation, but the data are inconclusive.

RALPH C. SCOTT
Cardiac Laboratory
University of Cincinnati Medical Center

LONG-DISTANCE CONSULTATION is made possible by miniature device that the heart patient holds on his chest. System allows him to relay his electrocardiogram directly to a doctor at a remote location by telephone.

UPI

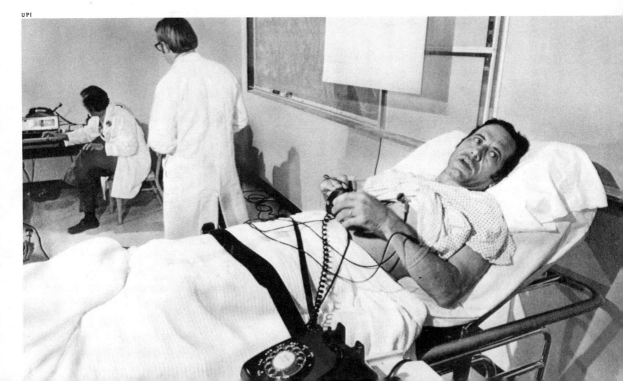

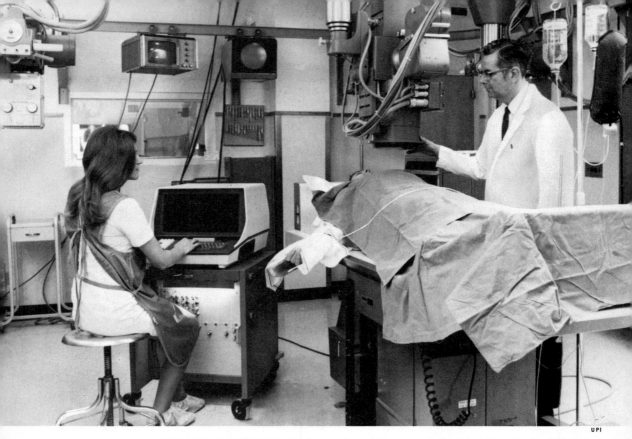

COMPUTERIZED HEART STUDY is simulated in a Denver hospital. As catheter is inserted, instruments display and analyze cardiological data. At left is the communications link with small computer.

Hospitals

Public and government pressure on hospitals to hold down the rising cost of medical care intensified during 1972 with some apparent success. At the same time, demands increased that hospitals guard against inadequate or substandard patient care.

Nixon administration officials were joined by leaders of the American Hospital Association (AHA) in announcing late in 1972 that the federal government's Economic Stabilization Program had been successful in slowing down the rapid spiral of monthly increases in the consumer price index that had caused alarm the year before. Consumer advocate organizations and congressional health leaders increased their demands for improved guarantees of good care in hospitals. One example of such pressure was the iconoclastic Pennsylvania state insurance commissioner Herbert Dannenberg's book *Shopper's Guide to Philadelphia Hospitals,* which alleged wide disparities in charges and care quality between hospitals. Most groups agreed on some form of peer review where panels of physicians judge the work of other physicians.

Congress approved the Social Security amendments of 1972, the final form of which, signed into law by President Nixon in early November, contained a feature related to the regulation of hospital care. This amendment requires the Department of Health, Education, and Welfare to establish Professional Standards Review Organizations in each locality to supervise use of Medicare and Medicaid programs. Its chief intent is to guard against overuse of the two tax-supported health care programs, but assurance of quality of care also was included.

AHA Plans. Responding to the demands for guarantees of improved care, the AHA, which represents most of the nation's nonprofit hospitals, developed a proposed Quality Assurance Program (QAP) that calls for the creation of a committee of a hospital's medical staff with two major subcommittees in charge of utilization review and medical audit. Continuing education would be recommended for physicians whose uses of hospital facilities for their patients have been found to set a pattern of either overutilization or underutilization.

The AHA also named a new, full-time executive officer, J. Alexander McMahon, who announced his intention to move the organization more vigorously than before into a leadership role in public health policy.

Increased Emphasis on Social Issues and Outpatient Care. A developing trend in hospital care during 1972 was an increasing emphasis on social issues such as involvement in alcoholism and drug abuse programs in the community. Under agitation from consumer groups, the federal government issued regulations setting guidelines for the amount of charity care that must be given by hospitals built with the aid of funds from the federal Hill-Burton program.

A trend toward development of more outpatient or ambulatory care services by hospitals was also evident in 1972. A noteworthy development was the emergence of "surgicenters" where minor surgery can be performed on an outpatient basis. The objective is to reduce more expensive inpatient use of hospitals wherever possible.

JEROME F. BRAZDA
Editor, "Washington Report on Medicine & Health"

Mental Health

There were several significant developments in the field of mental health during 1972, including changes in the role of mental hospitals and community services and increased attention focused on the mental health of children and minority groups and on such problems as depression, crime and antisocial behavior, drug abuse, and alcohol abuse.

There was also major emphasis on the relationship of mental health and physiological functioning. Exciting projects are in progress in the field of biofeedback and visceral conditioning. Investigators have found increasingly strong evidence that human beings can be taught to alter physiological processes such as blood pressure, heart rate, and muscle tension by biofeedback techniques, and this has broad implications for the treatment of psychophysiological problems. See also PSYCHOLOGY.

Mental Hospitals. As of June 1971, the latest year for which statistics are available, there were 308,024 people in state and county mental hospitals, 9% fewer than in the preceding year, thus continuing the sharp drop in the number of resident patients that has been apparent during the past few years. Even so, one third of all hospital beds are occupied by mental patients. Many factors have contributed to this decline, among them new methods of treatment, psychoactive drugs, and the availability of community mental health centers. The programs of the mental hospitals themselves encouraged the drop, by a continued change from custodial care to providing for treatment, rehabilitation, and prevention.

Community Mental Health Services and Centers. In 1970, the number of persons receiving care at community mental health centers was 518,000, and many more were reached through indirect services such as consultation to schools and other community groups and agencies. The community-based services are supported by federal, state, and local funds. At present, 325 centers are operational and serving in urban, rural, and suburban areas.

By July 1, 1972, federal grants for construction and/or staffing had been made to 493 centers in all 50 states, Puerto Rico, Guam, and the District of Columbia. When fully operational the centers must provide five essential services: partial hospitalization, 24-hour-a-day emergency care, inpatient service, outpatient service, and consultation and education. Many centers provide or affiliate in developing children's programs, drug abuse prevention programs, and services for alcohol abuse.

Child Mental Health. The gravity of the mental health problems of children in the United States, is shown by these 1969 figures: approximately 466,000 children were in outpatient psychiatric clinics; 42,000 were mental hospital patients; 21,000 were in residential treatment centers; 8,800 in day/night services; and 81,000 in community mental health services. There were 37,000 treated in general hospital inpatient psychiatric units.

Mental Health of Minorities. For the first time on a national scale, efforts are being made to meet the mental health needs of minority groups—black, Spanish-speaking, Indian, Chicano, and others. Research is under way to develop increased knowledge of the stresses of minority life, the impact of the larger community and its activities upon minority groups, how to measure the effects of various actions upon the minority communities, and regional or local problems that affect minority populations.

Depression. There was increased national interest in research and services for persons suffering from depressive illness, a common affliction that affects millions of Americans from all walks of life and every socioeconomic level. Depression is frequently curable, and statistics indicate that of some 250,000 patients hospitalized for depression each year the majority recover completely, through the use of psychotherapeutic means that may include electroshock or antidepressant drugs.

Crime and Antisocial Behavior. Behavioral scientists sought to find new ways to deal with the problems of crime and antisocial behavior. Attention was paid to resolving conflicts in urban environments through better identification of root causes and finding new coping techniques. The mental health aspects of "safe streets"—as a goal of all elements of society—continued to attract the attention of many agencies in the mental health field and with the cooperation of the criminal justice system. Studies were encouraged to find ways to improve the criminal justice system, the treatment of offenders in institutions, and the training of personnel, and to establish innovative programs for mentally ill offenders.

Drug Abuse. Drug abuse prevention, treatment and rehabilitation, research, and training continued to make strides against the totality of the drug problem. The Special Action Office for Drug Abuse Prevention established by the President continued its national efforts to attack narcotic and drug abuse problems. By the end of the year, 139 community-level drug abuse treatment and rehabilitation service programs had been funded through the National Institute of Mental Health (NIMH), with 88 of these fully operational and serving 23,000 heroin addicts and other drug abusers. There was also a strong drive, led by the Bureau of Narcotics and Dangerous Drugs, to prevent the importation of hard drugs into the country, and the search to find chemical substances that will block the effects of heroin in the body was intensified. (See also DRUG ADDICTION AND ABUSE and the special feature on Narcotics beginning on page 37.)

Alcohol Abuse and Alcoholism. Alcoholism, or problem drinking, afflicts an estimated 9 million persons in the United States, and affects an additional large number of people—the families, friends, employers, and other close associates of the alcoholics. For the first time in recent years, alcohol abuse and alcoholism have been recognized as massive public health problems.

The National Institute on Alcohol Abuse and Alcoholism has established two major deals: (1) to help make the best treatment and rehabilitation services available at the community level, and (2) to develop effective prevention programs. A wide range of research is under way to get at the complex interaction of biological, psychological, and social factors involved and to better understand the causes, natural history, and treatment of alcoholism. Basic and applied research is conducted at universities, medical schools, and other institutions, and demonstration projects are supported to develop and evaluate new techniques, approaches, and treatment and prevention methods. High priority has been given to public education and to training adequate personnel to cope with the problem. (See also MEDICINE—*Alcoholism*.)

BERTRAM S. BROWN, M. D.
Director, National Institute of Mental Health

Nursing

Among the trends in nursing in the United States in 1972 were a continued expansion of the role of registered nurses in health services, an increase in the number of male nurses, and the birth of new programs of specialized nursing care for the aged.

Expanded Role. The role of registered nurses continued to expand in many specialty areas. The new "nurse practitioner" functioned in an expanded nursing role in pediatrics, psychiatry, obstetrics and gynecology, medical-surgical services, and other specialty areas. The report of the Committee to Study Extended Roles for Nurses, appointed by the secretary of Health, Education and Welfare in May, stated that "the knowledge and skills of nurses need to be broadened" so that nurses can "assume broader responsibility in primary care, acute care, and long-term care."

Men in Nursing. A male nursing boom began to develop in 1972. This occurred because of "the unlikely combination of military nursing education programs and the women's lib movement," according to a spokesman of Marquette University. Male nursing students who are on active military duty are studying at universities through Army and Navy educational programs. Returning military medical corpsmen have enrolled in nursing schools. The military programs have helped to dispel the Florence Nightingale image of the nurse, and the women's liberation movement has indirectly contributed to the breakdown of nursing's feminine image by forcing the people to rethink the belief that some jobs are only for men, while others are only for women.

While the number of men attending nursing schools is still small, males constitute a rapidly increasing minority. Most schools of nursing have experienced a significant increase in the number of male applicants. Approximately 1% of all registered nurses in the United States in 1972 were men.

Better Care for the Aged. In an effort to improve the care of the elderly in nursing homes in the United States, the American Nurses' Association (ANA) undertook to update and improve the knowledge and skills of 3,000 registered nurses practicing in nursing homes. The program was made possible by a contract awarded by the Department of Health, Education and Welfare. The ANA project included a prototype seminar held in July at Duke University. This was to serve as a working model for 40 state and regional seminars scheduled through 1973.

Nurse Population. The number of practicing registered nurses increased from 723,000 in 1971 to 748,000 in 1972. Approximately 524,000 were employed full time and 224,000 part-time. The ratio of nurses to population increased slightly over 1971, from 353 to 361 per 100,000. Despite the increase, the need for registered nurses continued. The problem was further complicated by the maldistribution of existing nursing personnel.

Education. During the 1970–71 academic year, graduations from schools of nursing numbered 47,-001, up from 43,639 in 1969–70. Enrollments totaled 187,551, a gain of 14%. Associate-degree two-year programs in community colleges numbered 491, while there were 285 four-year baccalaureate programs and 587 hospital-based diploma programs. More registered nurses were also obtaining advanced degrees. In 1972, 785 held doctoral degrees.

ANNE R. WARNER
American Nurses' Association, Inc.

Pediatrics

During 1972 work in pediatrics centered on a growing awareness of atherosclerosis as a problem in children, on pica, and on the routine use of smallpox vaccination and hexachlorophene.

Atherosclerosis. Since the process of atherosclerosis—the accumulation of fats in the wall of the arteries that is a primary cause of coronary artery disease—often begins in infancy, pediatricians are becoming increasingly interested in detecting high risk children and in finding ways to minimize the rate of fat deposition. Numerous studies have suggested that the dietary intake of cholesterol and fat is associated with elevated blood levels of these substances. Recently the role of genetic factors has been investigated, and it has been shown that the tendency to high blood cholesterol and fat levels may be inherited. Consideration is being given to screening infants, particularly those born of parents or grandparents who had evidence of coronary artery disease in middle life, to detect those with elevated levels of cholesterol and fats in their blood.

It is currently recommended that children with one of the known genetic forms of hyperlipidemia (elevated blood levels of certain fats) be placed on an appropriate diet. However, there is no evidence at the present time that a low fat diet in infancy or childhood will benefit the vast majority of children, but as more is learned of the role of heredity and diet in the prevention of coronary heart disease, infant screening and dietary recommendations may change.

Pica. Approximately 50% of children between the age of 1 and 3 ingest non-food substances, a habit termed pica. If these substances include chips of paint, plaster, or putty containing lead, lead poisoning can result. Hundreds of children with elevated blood levels of lead are seen each year, many with obvious poisoning. The hazard is greatest among children living in old and poorly maintained houses, and surveys performed in low-income areas indicate that lead-based paint is found in 40% to 80% of old houses and that elevated blood levels are present in as many as 40% of the children living in them. In March 1972 the U.S. Food and Drug Administration (FDA) published regulations, to become effective Dec. 31, 1973, prohibiting the interstate shipment of paint containing hazardous concentrations of lead.

Smallpox Vaccination. The continued need for universal vaccination against smallpox has come into question. This is because smallpox has not been reported in the United States since 1949, and because smallpox vaccination sometimes, though rarely, causes serious complications, including generalized rash and inflammation of the central nervous system, resulting in seven or eight deaths a year. Many physicians believe that the risks now exceed the possible benefits for the usual child.

The American Academy of Pediatrics and the Committee on Immunization Practices of the Public Health Service recommended in 1972 that route immunization should be discontinued and vaccination be required only for individuals at a special risk—that is, travelers to and from areas where smallpox remains endemic. They further recommend careful surveillance of travellers entering the United States and active support of smallpox surveillance and eradication programs throughout the world.

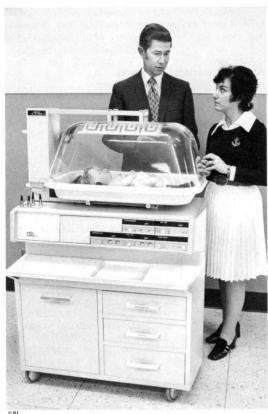

UPI
NEW INCUBATOR, the "Infa-Care," was developed by Paul Byrne (left) of Cardinal Glennon Memorial Hospital for Children, in St. Louis. Unit monitors a baby and controls its environment while allowing easy access.

Use of Hexachlorophene. Hexachlorophene, which is absorbed through the skin, has been widely used in newborn nurseries for skin care since it effectively reduces skin infections, particularly those caused by certain strains of staphylococcus that periodically occur in epidemic proportions in newborn nurseries. The FDA published an initial warning in October 1971, and subsequent studies that included the finding that infant monkeys bathed daily for 90 days with a 3% hexachlorophene solution developed brain lesions persuaded the Academy of Pediatrics to recommend in January 1972 that the routine use of hexachlorophene be discontinued. In September 1972 several deaths of newborn infants in France were attributed to hexachlorophene poisoning. Subsequently, the FDA ordered all products containing potentially toxic amounts of hexachlorophene removed from the market.

WILLIAM E. SEGAR, M. D.
University of Wisconsin

Pharmacology

There were several significant developments in pharmacology during 1972, including an important court decision and a new plan for implementing earlier recommendations on over-the-counter drugs.

Court Decision. Federal Judge William Bryant issued a decision setting up a timetable for the Food and Drug Administration (FDA) to follow in discharging its obligations concerning the implementation of the drug efficacy study. The agency was given a series of deadlines to meet in putting its judgments into effect, with the length of time varying according to whether the drug had been judged "probably effective," "possibly effective," or lacking in evidence of effectiveness. The decision was handed down after the American Health Association and the National Council of Senior Citizens filed suit, charging that the FDA had been so remiss in implementation as to pose a threat to public health by allowing drugs whose effectiveness had not been proved to remain on the market.

O-T-C Review. Relatively few nonprescription, or over-the-counter, drugs in any given therapeutic category were rated in the efficacy review. The FDA decided that the best way to ensure uniformity would be to set up a system that would produce standards applying to all drugs in a given classification. The drugs are divided by category—antacids, analgesics, and so forth. An independent panel of scientists, working with FDA personnel, reviews the data and makes recommendations on the efficacy of ingredients and the claims manufacturers should be allowed to make for the products. All drugs must conform to these standards or be removed from the market, according to the misbranding section of the Food, Drug, and Cosmetic Act.

Hexachlorophene. Another major decision that confronted the FDA in 1972 involved the safety and efficacy of hexachlorophene, a substance that had become a common ingredient in many soaps, toiletries, and cosmetics. After some investigators found nearly toxic levels of hexachlorophene in the blood of some infants, the FDA, along with the American Academy of Pediatrics, warned against using hexachlorophene in total body washing of infants. Later data further alarmed FDA scientists, and the agency decided to permit the sale of hexachlorophene on a prescription-only basis and to order its immediate removal from over-the-counter products.

Biologicals. In 1972 the FDA was given authority over the regulation of biologicals (a term used to include such substances as globulins, serums, vaccines, and antitoxins), a function formerly executed by the Division of Biologics Standards in the National Institutes of Health. DBS had fallen under severe criticism from consumer groups and from Sen. Abraham Ribicoff (D, Conn.) whose executive reorganization subcommittee held hearings on the division's operations. DBS was accused of being too closely intertwined with the companies that it regulated and inclined to favor established firms in the vaccine field as against newcomers—charges it vigorously denied. It is generally assumed that the new Bureau of Biologicals in the FDA will take a tougher regulatory stance than did the DBS.

Drug Control Remains in HEW. The main legislative activity involving drugs centred on a bill introduced by Sen. Warren Magnuson (D, Wash.) that would have transferred authority for drug regulation out of the FDA to a new, independent agency. Impetus for the move came from the belief among some senators and congressmen that the agency as is functions poorly and not always in the public interest. The Department of Health, Education, and Welfare (HEW), of which the FDA is a part, fought the projected change. The Magnuson bill failed, and in its place a product safety law was passed. FDA lost jurisdiction only over poison prevention packaging, which was ceded to a new agency.

JEANNE F. ANDERSON
Editor, "Washington Drug & Device Letter"

Public Health

In the public health area, significant actions were taken during 1972 to combat the problems of emergency medical care, venereal disease, sickle cell anemia, and alcoholism.

Emergency Medical Care. To reduce the large and increasing numbers of unnecessary deaths of Americans from sudden illnesses and injuries, the Emergency Medical Service Special Projects Office was organized in February 1972. Demonstration projects were funded in Arkansas, Illinois, Florida, Ohio, and California as focal points for the development of comprehensive emergency medical care systems. Thirty-six regional medical programs responded to this priority with $8.4 million for 28 projects.

VD Epidemic. The first nationwide attack on gonorrhea was launched to combat an all-time high in the incidence of the disease. Grants totaling $22.3 million were awarded to strengthen state and local venereal disease control programs.

Sickle Cell Anemia. To attack the ravages of sickle cell anemia, a disease that affects mostly blacks, a Sickle Cell Disease Office was established to provide education, information, counseling, and screening. Nineteen screening and education clinics were funded to serve some 400,000 persons.

Alcoholism. A National Clearinghouse for Alcohol Information was organized to collect and disseminate professional, technical, and public information and data on alcohol, alcohol use and abuse, and alcoholism. Meanwhile, a nationwide educational campaign to inform the public of the uses and abuses of alcohol was under way.

Health Services. The first National Health Service Corps delivery team, organized to provide federal health service workers to areas where personnel and services are inadequate, was fielded in 1972, less than six months after the corps received its first appropriation. By year-end, 185 professionals were working in 100 communities in 40 states. They included 153 physicians, 14 dentists, 15 nurses, and 3 allied health professionals. The program is not meant to deal with the problem of the overall shortage of physicians and other health personnel in the nation. Rather, it is aimed at alleviating some problems with the intent of learning more about the use of this device as a possible national strategy for addressing the problem of manpower shortage.

Drug Abuse. A total of 139 community programs for treating and rehabilitating drug addicts were funded in 1972. Of these, 88 were fully operational, serving an estimated 23,000 drug abusers.

Nursing Homes. President Nixon's call for a program of short-term courses for personnel that would provide services to nursing home patients was implemented with the training of some 41,000 nursing home personnel during the year.

Lead Poisoning. Surveys were conducted in 27 large northeastern cities to determine the number of small children afflicted with lead poisoning from eating the peeling flakes of lead-based paint. Screening by blood tests revealed elevated lead levels in 9.1% of the children tested.

Coal Miners Examined. The first round of medical examinations of coal miners, required by the Federal Coal Mine Safety Act of 1969, was completed in 1972. A national coal workers' autopsy study also was developed to aid survivors in establishing claims of black lung benefits under the act.

Smallpox in Yugoslavia. During March-April 1972, Yugoslavia experienced an outbreak of smallpox involving 174 cases and 35 deaths. At the request of the Yugoslavian government the U.S. Center for Disease Control sent a medical team, a supply of vaccine, and several jet injectors to provide assistance against the epidemic.

VERNON E. WILSON, M.D.
*Administrator, Health Services
and Mental Health Administration*

Respiratory Diseases

Work in respiratory diseases in 1972 centered on continued study of influenza and a search for ways to prevent respiratory illnesses.

Influenza. Unlike 1971, epidemic influenza was prevalent throughout the United States in early 1972. Cases were first reported in December 1971, and the peak of reported cases occurred at the end of January 1972. The epidemic appeared to be short-lived, however, for by the end of February there was no evidence of significant influenza activity occurring in the United States.

Because most of the influenza viruses isolated from patients during the epidemic were closely related to the original Hong Kong strain, and since influenza epidemics of this type usually occur in two- or three-year cycles, the U.S. Public Health Service did not anticipate an epidemic occurring in 1973. However, one disturbing fact became evident during 1972: that influenza isolates obtained from patients ill with influenza in England presented significant differences from the original Hong Kong strain isolated in 1968. Although no predictions concerning the relative importance of the new strains could be made at the time, some specialists thought there was a possibility that the change in virus type was significant enough to raise the possibility of further epidemic influenza in 1973. This anticipation may be justified, for outbreaks of influenza, characterized by the type of virus isolated in England, occurred in Korea, Malaysia, and Singapore in the spring of 1972, and in September a closely related type of epidemic influenza was reported in Australia, Hong Kong, and Thailand.

Prevention of Respiratory Diseases. There has been little overall progress in finding a means to prevent respiratory disease. If respiratory diseases were due to a single virus, a single vaccine that might prevent all respiratory diseases could be produced. However, since respiratory diseases have hundreds of viral and bacterial causes, the approach to their prevention must combine both vaccines and antiviral agents.

Progress in developing any respiratory disease vaccines has been very slow. It does appear, however, that we are getting closer to a vaccine, which uses a mutated virus, that prevents severe lower respiratory tract diseases in children. However, even there no large-scale field trials are contemplated during the year.

Even less progress has been made in the development of antiviral agents. Work continues on the production of substances designed to stimulate the production of interferon, an antiviral substance naturally produced by the body in response to viral infections. Although several chemicals are being tested in animals and in tissue cultures, there have been no significant breakthroughs.

BERNARD PORTNOY, M.D.
University of Southern California

Surgery

Surgery witnessed no particularly new or exciting developments in 1972. Enthusiasm for organ transplants, excepting those of the kidney, waned perceptibly, and only Dr. Norman Shumway of Pasadena, California, continued in transplanting hearts —with continually improving long-term survivals. Coronary revascularization operations designed to bring more blood to the vessels of the heart were increasingly performed. Hyperalimentation to provide sufficient calories, vitamins, minerals, and other essential substances to certain surgical patients became much more widely accepted. But with its increased use came a rising incidence of complications, particularly infections, and there was a concentrated effort to provide hyperalimentation solutions with the precise ingredients needed and as few foreign proteins and sources of contamination or unfavorable reactions as possible. Other significant work in surgery focused on intestinal bypass surgery and the replacement of heart valves.

Intestinal Bypass—*For Obesity.* In the past several years surgeons have been asked to alter the intestinal tract of patients with life-threatening obesity, nearly all of whom suffer from eating too much rather than from a metabolic or hormonal imbalance. Because the calories contained in food must be absorbed primarily in the 25-foot-long small intestine in order ultimately to be metabolized and burned, it occurred to physicians that it might be possible to reduce obesity by removing much of the intestine. In 1959, Dr. J. Howard Payne of Los Angeles began excluding the ileum, the entire distal half of the intestine, in a number of patients. These patients, who were otherwise unable to lose weight, were able after the operation to lose weight rapidly, even though they ate everything they wanted. At present, Dr. Payne and his group are performing what they call the "14-4 operation" in which the surgeon connects the first 14 inches of the small intestine to the last 4 inches and excludes the intervening 23½ feet. Ingested foods are therefore exposed to only about 6% of normal absorbing intestinal surface. Dr. Payne recently reported the results of this operation in 80 patients and found that nearly all—even on an unlimited diet—lost about 11 pounds per month for six months and about seven pounds per month for the next year or two, after which the weight leveled off; some patients have lost as much as 200 pounds. Because certain vitamins (A, B_{12}, D, and K) and two important elements—calcium and potassium—are inadequately absorbed after this operation, patients must receive them regularly. Diarrhea is a problem for the first three to six months, but later becomes minimal.

ACUPUNCTURE: Too Much Yin or Yang

One of the most dramatic and widely discussed subjects in medicine in 1972 was acupuncture. The excitement generated by the TV coverage of operations filmed by Americans during their visit to mainland China was nearly unprecedented. Millions of people in the West became interested in this technique and many demanded to be treated by it. At present, one of the greatest problems related to acupuncture in America concerns who will be permitted to practice it—only formally licensed medical doctors or others trained just in acupuncture.

Medicine in ancient China was a well-respected profession and included both herbalists and acupuncturists. Both forms of medical practice have continued since ancient times. In China today, acupuncturists still outnumber Western-type physicians by 20 to 1.

According to traditional acupuncture theory, there are two opposing expressions of Chi, the spirit of life, in the body. These expressions, Yin and Yang, pulsate through the body along a system of channels called meridians. There are twelve meridians, ten named for the major organs of the body and two for organs unknown to anatomists: the "triple warmer" and the "circulatory-sex organ." Diseases are a reflection of too much Yin or Yang and can be treated by tapping the proper meridian with needles to add more of the opposing force. Usually, the needle in place is twisted nearly continuously, or in recent times can be attached to a small electrical source that delivers a periodic charge.

Although the application of standard acupuncture theory to its use as anesthesia is hard to comprehend, there seems to be real evidence that acupuncture can provide total anesthesia for a wide variety of operations, including dental extractions, removal of a lung, cesarean section, and tonsillectomy. Outstanding American doctors have observed and can testify to the effectiveness of acupuncture anesthesia in mainland China, where surgeons have performed more than 400,-000 operations since 1968. In addition, millions of Chinese patients have been treated for a whole spectrum of medical illnesses. In such European countries as France, Germany, Italy, England, and in many South American countries, acupuncture is an accepted therapeutic modality and is quite popular in the treatment of many diseases and disorders.

Acupuncture as anesthesia would have great advantages over modern Western anesthesia because it would obviate the use of strong anesthetic agents and drugs, all of which have potential toxicity and powerful side effects.

Although no one knows how acupuncture anesthesia works, the "gate" theory of Professor Ronald Melzack at Montreal's McGill University is the one currently championed. According to Professor Melzack, there are in the central nervous system two systems of "gates" which allow only a certain quota of impulses to reach the brain and to be registered as stimuli. One "gate" is in the spinal cord and the other is in the thalamic portion of the brain. By inserting and twirling needles near peripheral nerves, one sends many impulses to the spinal cord on their way to the brain, but there they flood the gates, which then close. When the painful stimuli from the surgical incision then reach the closed gates, they cannot pass on to the cerebral cortex to be registered as pain.

Many Western doctors, however, remain dubious of the claims by the Chinese about acupuncture, particularly about its use to cure deafness, blindness, complete paralysis, and poliomyelitis. Indeed, one prominent American doctor labelled acupuncture "a medley of philosophy, religion, superstition, magic, sorcery, alchemy, astrology and quackery," and there are many American doctors who agree. In spite of this negativism, a number of top-rank anesthesiologists and other scientists are planning serious, scientifically valid experiments to test the validity of this ancient technique, so that its use can either be expanded or curtailed in the United States.

IRVING F. ENQUIST

Dr. H. William Scott of Nashville, Tenn., and Dr. Peter Salmon of Alberta, Canada, have extensive experience with operations of this type, and have reported similar results.

For Hypercholesterolemia. A similar intestinal bypass operation has been performed for patients with hypercholesterolemia, or high blood cholesterol level. In most instances, a patient with a high blood cholesterol can reduce the level by a strict diet, but in some severe cases other control measures are needed.

Because ingested cholesterol is absorbed primarily in the ileum. Drs. Henry Buchwald and Richard Varco of the University of Minnesota decided to treat appropriate patients by an operation in which the food (and cholesterol) is not exposed to the ileum. Their operation consists of bypassing the terminal 6½ feet of ileum. In one series of patients they found that stringent reduction of cholesterol intake for three months resulted in a mean drop of 10% in the blood cholesterol level. However, within three months after the bypass operation, with continuation of the diet, the average drop in blood cholesterol was 40%. Exclusion of one third of the small intestine did not result in any weight loss, and children with the operation grew and developed normally.

Heart Valves. Inflammation of the heart valves, which is caused by rheumatic fever or other diseases, leads to a thickening and scarring of the valves to the point where they cannot function perfectly. With intracardiac surgery now feasible, surgeons are trying to repair or replace scarred and inefficient valves. Many valves, constructed of non-reactive plastics and stainless steel, have been placed in appropriate patients, and thousands are walking around comfortably with one, two, or three in place, some for as long as six or seven years. Unfortunately, all of the prosthetic valves are associated with certain risks: they may break loose; their repeated clicking with each heart beat may damage red blood cells; the plastic or metal may break; and as foreign material they serve as possible sites of clotting that may result in free fragments (emboli) that float away and plug important arteries.

Because of these serious complications, surgeons tried using biological valves, taking valves from pigs, cattle, and human cadavers, sterilizing them, and using them to replace pathologic valves in patients. Most of these valves function well for several months or a year, but later degenerate, probably due to a very slow immune reaction (rejection), and must be replaced, so that now the use of such grafts has been largely abandoned.

As early as 1965, Dr. Ake Senning of Zurich began to replace defective valves by valves made from the patient's own tissue, specifically from the fascia lata, a strong band of thick white tissue in the thigh. These valves can function well—opening widely during contraction of the heart and closing to prevent leakage during relaxation. Drs. Donald Ross and Marian Ionescu in London, Dr. Harris Shumacker in Indianapolis, and Dr. Frank Gerbode in San Francisco have joined with Senning in testing this type of autograft. To date, more than 800 such grafts have been fashioned and implanted, and the early results have been good—particularly in the aortic valve position. These valves give rise to no red cell destruction and no clotting problem.

IRVING F. ENQUIST
Director of Surgery, Methodist Hospital of Brooklyn

Venereal Disease

Gonorrhea currently ranks first among all nationally reportable communicable diseases. During the year ending June 30, 1972, there were 718,401 cases reported in the United States, an increase of 15.1% over the number reported in 1971 and almost double the annual number reported five years ago. Increases were reported in all age groups among both males and females and in both urban and rural areas. When unreported and undetected cases are considered, the actual incidence of gonorrhea is estimated at 2.5 million infections per year.

The number of cases of primary and secondary syphilis—the infectious stages of syphilis—has increased steadily in 1970, 1971, and 1972. In the year ending June 30, 1972, there were 24,000 cases reported, an increase of 28% over the number reported in 1969 but only a 2.8% increase over the number reported in 1971. It is estimated that there are about 85,000 new cases of syphilis occurring each year. Reported cases of congenital syphilis among infants under 1 year of age numbered 422 in fiscal 1972, an increase of 5.5% over the number reported the previous year. Overall syphilis in all stages numbered 95,076 cases in 1972. The reservoir of cases needing treatment, most of which are in the latent stages of disease and are detectable only by means of blood tests, is currently estimated to number between 500,000 and 550,000.

Control Programs. In special gonorrhea culture screening programs, more than 293,600 women were tested, with the average positivity rate being 5.8%. Federal assistance to states for gonorrhea control included the extension of diagnostic and treatment services, culture screening programs to identify and treat those infected, and patient interviewing and contact tracing activities for case detection and case prevention purposes.

Syphilis control activities included the follow-up of positive tests for syphilis to detect cases of untreated syphilis. During 1972, 38 million blood specimens were examined, and follow-up investigations carried out on positive blood tests resulted in some 11,000 case reports of primary and secondary syphilis and 55,000 case reports of syphilis in other stages. Epidemiology (the interview-contact tracing procedure) included the interview of 96% of all infectious cases. These contact-tracing activities led to the diagnosis and treatment of an additional 7,800 cases of syphilis, including 4,000 infectious cases. In addition, some 18,500 contacts exposed to infectious syphilis but who showed no clinical or laboratory evidence were treated prophylactically.

Education and Research. Programs of venereal disease education, using all forms of news media and instruction materials in elementary and high schools, were intensified throughout the United States.

Research efforts centered on a continuing search for an effective blood test for gonorrhea, an improved medium for transporting gonorrhea culture specimens from doctors' offices to laboratories, an improved blood test for syphilis, and the development of a vaccine for syphilis and gonorrhea.

JOSEPH H. BLOUNT
Venereal Disease Branch, U.S. Public Health Service

MEIR, Golda. See BIOGRAPHY.
MERCHANT MARINE. See TRANSPORTATION.
MESSMER, Pierre. See BIOGRAPHY.

Volunteers race from flooding Susquehanna River near Wilkes-Barre, Pa. (above), *as dike bursts* (right).

meteorology

Better methods of weather prediction continued to be developed in 1972, using a wide variety of earth-based and satellite-borne instruments. Cloud-seeding and fog-clearing experiments were successful, and important studies were made of ozone and particulate matter in the atmosphere. The 1972 United Nations Conference on the Environment assigned the task of continuous atmospheric monitoring to the World Meteorological Organization.

Weather Prediction. Present mathematical models for weather prediction perform about as well as do highly experienced weather forecasters. They are usually too conservative in their predictions of amounts of precipitation, and their present reasonable forecasting limit is 72 hours. These limits are due to the inadequate simulation of nature by the models and to inadequate global observations. Thus new methods are being developed for representing the heretofore neglected cumulative effects of smaller-scale factors such as surface friction, cloud dynamics, smaller radiative processes, and the turbulent transfer of energy. For example, progress has been made in calculating the considerable drag exerted by mountain chains on air currents and thereby on jet streams—an important factor, since about 15% of the Northern Hemisphere is occupied by mountains.

The continuing effort to discover early signs and symptoms of storms is another aspect of meteorological research related to weather prediction. The fact that tornadoes are usually spawned in severe electrical storms has led to a number of techniques for detecting intense electrical fields at a distance, and the search is on for electrical signals that will identify tornado-spawning storms. In Oklahoma, Missouri, Kansas, and several other

states frequented by tornadoes, a series of instruments was set up that was tuned to three megahertz —a frequency not observed in weaker storms—and in one year the instruments identified four out of five tornado-spawning storms correctly. Another characteristic of severe storms that may be useful for advance warnings is that a front of severe gusts usually precedes such storms, usually at a distance of 2 to 4 miles (3–6 km). Even the rumbling of thunder tells a story. An analysis of the sound reveals that the deeper rumbles are caused by cloud-to-cloud lightning with a peak frequency of 28 hertz, whereas cloud-to-ground lightning is acoustically three times as energetic and has a peak frequency of 50 hertz.

The use of historical data on the characteristics of hurricanes and the tracks that they follow has led to the development of a computerized analog

TROPICAL STORM AGNES, accompanied by torrential rains, caused record flooding in the East in June. Much of Wilkes-Barre (above) had to be evacuated. President Nixon surveys the flood damage at Harrisburg, Pa. (right).

technique for forecasting their motions. If the initial position of a hurricane is established precisely, the technique permits 12-hour forecasts of the location of the storm's center to within about 30 nautical miles (55 km), and 24-hour forecasts to within about 80 nautical miles (150 km).

Remote Sensors and Satellites. Increasing information for weather prediction is being made available by many earth-based monitors. For example, a remote television camera at Stampede Pass, east of Seattle, Wash., yields visual information from that rugged terrain. Another remote sensor is the new, 100-ton weather buoy stationed 225 miles (360 km) off the coast of the Gulf of Mexico to give early warnings of tropical storms. At Oklahoma's National Severe Storms Laboratory, a new Doppler radar enables scientists to observe circulation patterns within storms. Such patterns can be useful in storm prediction. For example, a counterclockwise flow presages a tornado.

Satellite-installed infrared spectrometers and radiometers also continue to yield data for weather studies. The instruments map nocturnal cloud covers and furnish information on vertical temperature and moisture distribution in the atmosphere. The data are invaluable for areas with sparse surface observation, such as the oceans, so that 94 countries have installed a total of 500 stations to receive such information. Satellites also track hurricanes and other tropical disturbances, thus throwing new light on the origin of the storms. One fourth of the about 100 tropical disturbances discovered during the so-called storm season (June 1–November 30) develop the closed circulation typical of tropical depressions, and one out of three depressions intensifies to become a named storm with gale or hurricane winds. More than half the disturbances start over Africa. Their primary cause remains obscure.

Weather Modification. A new U.S. public law (92-205) requires that all nonfederal weather modification projects and activities be reported to the National Oceanographic and Atmospheric Agency before they are begun, and that a detailed account of the results be given upon their completion. Violators of these rules are subject to fine.

Experiments made during the year included the dropping of flares into potential hail clouds to disperse silver iodide. Conducted over Canadian prairies, the tests indicated that hailstones falling from seeded clouds are smaller than those from nonseeded ones, thus potentially reducing the crop-damaging effects of such storms. Several fog-clearing experiments entered the operational stage at airports, where below-freezing fogs are now routinely thinned out by dispensing liquid propane from the edges of runways. It has also been proposed that artificially cooled and dried air be injected into fogs at above-ground level to force partial evaporation and downward motion of the fog. Some success with warm fogs has been achieved with a spray of ammonium nitrate, urea, and water.

Further analysis of the 1971 Florida experiments to alleviate a severe drought by cloud seeding showed that an estimated 7.84 billion cubic feet (220 million cubic meters) of rain were produced over a target area of 4,800 square miles (13,430 square km). The seeding probably doubled the rainfall that would have occurred naturally. Such estimates are possible because of the availability of a reliable physical model, which also permits selection of suitable clouds for the operations.

Atmosphere Studies. In order to gauge whether man interferes with the natural shield of stratospheric ozone that protects life on earth from the full strength of the sun's ultraviolet radiation, the Nimbus 3 meteorological satellite observed ozone concentrations at some 2,000 to 3,000 points around the globe. Nimbus observed a great deal of fine structure in the ozone layer, with high and low concentrations in close juxtaposition. These structures seem to be related to intense storms in the lower atmosphere and near jet streams, with low values usually noted over tropical storms and to the right of jet streams in the Northern Hemisphere. The greatest contrast over the shortest distances occurred in the jet streams that flow above the Japanese Islands.

Regional data collected in the United States show that the pall of suspended particulates over vast areas is increasing. Even rural areas, if they are near urbanized or industrialized regions, now have ten times as many suspended particles as do remote sites, and over some metropolitan areas the palls cover as much as 100,000 square miles (260,000 square km). Pilots complain about the increased haziness, and even in medium-sized communities the hours of good visibility have decreased by as much as 20% in five years. The bulk of the suspended particles resides in the lowest mile of the atmosphere. Rocket soundings have demonstrated that at a height of 5 miles (8 km) there are only 30 to 45 particles per cubic inch (50–75 per cubic cm), and at 10 to 13 miles (16–20 km) only about 12 per cubic inch (20 per cubic cm).

H. E. LANDSBERG, *University of Maryland*

The devastating storm dumped almost a foot of water on the Washington, D. C., area. This is Manassas, Va.

UPI

THE WEATHER IN 1972

The Year of the Floods

In weather annals, 1972 must undoubtedly go down as the year of the floods. A summary of these floods and other weather highlights is given below.

December 1971–February 1972. Winter in the Northern Hemisphere was severe in many areas. In the United States, gales hit the Carolina coast just before Christmas, while in the second week of January a storm with winds of 150 miles (240 km) per hour struck the Pacific Northwest. Moving eastward, the storm still packed winds of 90 miles (145 km) per hour in Denver, Colo., causing injuries and about $1 million in damages there. The Seattle-Tacoma region had a devastating snowstorm toward the end of January, and at the same time gales were plaguing New York, Buffalo, and Chicago. A cold spell in Siberia early in February forced the closing of Yakutsk schools as temperatures dropped to a 45-year low of −72° F (−58° C) and a thick ice fog settled on the city. Cold snaps brought casualties in Iran that same month, with severe avalanches in Azerbaijan Province, and blizzards in Gilan Province that killed 180 persons and trapped 4,000 travellers. In neighboring Turkey, snow and cold caused scores of deaths. Jerusalem had its worst snowfall in decades, with an accumulation of 8 inches (20 cm).

Floods caused havoc in many localities around the world. Twice in January they hit the island of Java, driving 200,000 persons from their homes. That same month, excessive rains in Brazil's Rio de Janeiro State left many homeless; flash floods wiped out the town of La Cabuya, Colombia, and killed 60; and 10,000 Peruvians were isolated by floods near the border of Ecuador. On St. Valentine's Day in Venice, ancient St. Mark's Square lay under 3 feet (1 meter) of floodwater. Four days later, the heaviest rainfall ever recorded in Melbourne, Australia, created chaos in that city. Tropical storms also caused devastation in Queensland and the New Hebrides.

Summer in the Southern Hemisphere brought a heat wave to Buenos Aires in early January. An estimated 450 deaths resulted from the hot spell.

March–May 1972. Spring in the Northern Hemisphere had a very wintry beginning in some regions. Quebec was hit early in March by an ice storm that broke transmission lines and blacked out Montreal for 10 hours. The St. Lawrence Seaway did not open until April 12, 11 days behind schedule, and in May the North Atlantic sea lanes were threatened by as many as 600 icebergs south of latitude 48° N—the highest number to be seen there in that month since 1959.

Floods and high winds continued to bring misery in many places. Early in March, 75 persons were killed in Iran by floodwaters, while flooded rivers along the coast of Peru caused 36 deaths and 200 injuries and left 150,000 persons homeless. On March 18, rains produced floods 12 feet (3.7 meters) deep in several Philippine provinces, driving thousands of persons from their homes and causing millions of dollars in damage to crops and livestock. At the end of March, 118 persons were killed by floods in the Afghanistan province of Herat. Early in April, a tornado in India killed 150 Bengalis, while in Vancouver, Wash., a windstorm killed 6 and injured 250. Toward the end of the month, a 24-hour downpour ended Austria's driest winter of the century, and the ensuing floods in the province of Styria killed 4 persons and caused $4 million damage. Even the Sahara in northern Algeria had a rare rainfall—about 0.5 inch (1.2 cm).

Early in May, a major flood in Mexico City caused 18 deaths. From May 4 to 9, Chile's heaviest rainfall in 12 years deluged the region from Santiago down to Aysen Province, killing 7 persons, disrupting roads, and leaving 15,000 homeless. A heavy rain in Texas on the 11th caused flash floods that required the evacuation of thousands in the New Braunfels-Seguin-San Marcos area. In the middle of May, monsoons and gale winds in Ceylon killed 28 persons and left 2,000 homeless. At the end of the month, Alaska's Kuskokwin River had its worst flood in history, forcing 200 persons to be evacuated from Napaiskak Village.

June–August. The most extensive flood disaster in United States history occurred in June. The troublemaker was a tropical storm spawned on June 14 over the Yucatán Peninsula. The storm briefly reached hurricane strength over the Gulf of Mexico, where it gained the name Agnes, and finally blew itself out in western Pennsylvania on June 23. The toll of the storm was 129 confirmed deaths, including 7 in Cuba, with damages totalling $3.5 billion, and 120,000 persons had to be evacuated along its path. The hardest-hit states were Maryland, New York, Pennsylvania, and Virginia, where many localities had 6 to 14 inches (15–35 cm) of rain within 24 hours. The total rainfall in the eastern United States amounted to 25 cubic miles (100 cubic km), or about one fourth the volume of Lake Erie. The Susquehanna River discharged water at its highest rate in two centuries.

Precipitation was excessive elsewhere in the United States, as well. Cloudbursts hit the Black Hills of South Dakota on June 9 and 10, causing floods in Keystone, Sturgis, and Rapid City. There were 213 confirmed fatalities, and damages came to more than $100 million. Most bridges and many miles of roads and railroads in the vicinity were destroyed.

The Far East suffered several major disasters. In India, a delay of the monsoon season caused a heat wave in 14 states that took 800 lives. In Hong Kong, three days of torrential rain in mid-June led to the collapse of three apartment buildings, killing 100 persons and injuring many more. July typhoons caused floods on the Japanese islands of Kyushu, Shikoku, and Honshu, killing 287, injuring 814, and causing great damage. When the Philippine Islands had 23 days of heavy rain during the month, the death toll reached 427; 800,000 were left homeless, and damage amounted to $300 million. In August, a heavy rainfall in Seoul, South Korea, killed 300 persons and left 250,000 homeless.

September–November. Fall was cool over most of the contiguous United States. October and November were particularly cold in the area from the Mississippi River to the California coast, except along the Canadian border. An early snow cover developed from the Great Lakes westward and in the western Great Plains, reinforcing the tendency for cold conditions. Only Florida and the coastal plain from Georgia to North Carolina were generally warmer than average.

Precipitation was heavy all along the East Coast. Many stations broke long-term seasonal records, and many annual records for precipitation were surpassed —for example, in New York and Philadelphia.

East Coast storms in North America were unusually frequent. In October rampaging floodwaters inundated Virginia for the second time in 1972. Major damage centered in Petersburg, Va., where the Appomattox River hit record heights. In early November, New York and New Jersey were struck. On November 8, metropolitan New York had a record 5 inches (12.7 cm) of rain in 15 hours. Gales on the Great Lakes on November 15 caused waves that killed 20 persons on Lake Erie and forced evacuation of coastal areas.

Noteworthy elsewhere were the violent storms in Spain and Italy from September 5 to 8, with flash floods that caused landslides and halted trains. On September 15, typhoon Helen cut a swath of destruction through Honshu, causing 150 deaths. On October 23 and 24, hurricane Bebe lashed islands in the South Pacific, passing over the Gilbert and Ellice and Fiji groups with winds up to 182 miles (293 km) per hour and devastating Funafuti, where 50-foot (15-meter) waves rolled over the flat atoll.

H. E. LANDSBERG

FRIENDLY NEIGHBORS

President Luís Echeverría Álvarez of Mexico visited the United States in June 1972. In welcoming ceremonies on the south lawn of the White House (*above*), President Nixon and President Echeverría review honor guard. After the formal ceremonies the two leaders exchanged a friendly embrace.

MEXICO

The year 1972 was one of economic expansion, political and economic reform, and relative public peace for the administration of President Luís Echeverría. Perhaps the most significant political action of the year was a short-lived conflict between church and state.

Church-State Conflict. In early 1972, criticism leveled against the government by the archbishop of Chihuahua, the bishop of Ciudad Juárez, Chihuahua, and the Mexican Jesuit provincial father threatened to reopen the old church-state conflict. The priests blamed the government for the recent increases in public violence, claiming it allowed institutionalized violence to exist by not ending social injustice and because it was undemocratic and used violence to repress dissenters. While condemning violence in general, the churchmen believed that it was understandable in this context because there were no other available means to protest the conditions they deplored.

In response, government spokesmen attacked the church for breaking the law by commenting on politics (forbidden by the constitution), for being undemocratic itself, and for being wealthy. When the churchmen were forcefully reminded that the church had lost all prior conflicts with the state, the controversy quickly died.

Political Reform. President Echeverría in 1972 sought to broaden the base of political participation by facilitating the creation of new political parties and ensuring that they would have some congressional representation. In specific legislation by congress, the number of national deputies elected by majority vote to the national Chamber of Deputies was increased to 195 (one for every 250,000 inhabitants or fraction over 125,000). Minority parties now need only 1.5% (instead of 2.5%) of the national vote to obtain congressional seats. The maximum number of seats allotted under this system was increased to 25. All political parties were given votes in electoral organisms and in the formation of the federal voter registration lists. Further, all parties were guaranteed franking privileges and free access to the communications media. Finally, in an effort to appease young Mexicans, the minimum ages for federal deputies and senators were reduced to 21 and 30, respectively. Critics of the government interpreted these moves as meaningless tokenism that would not alter the one-party monopoly of Mexican government.

The guerrilla activity and student unrest that plagued Mexico in 1971 were substantially reduced in 1972, apparently as a result of concerted governmental efforts to raise the standard of living, of

——————— **MEXICO • Information Highlights** ———————

Official Name: United Mexican States.
Area: 761,602 square miles (1,972,546 sq km).
Population (1972 est.): 54,300,000. *Density,* 67 per square mile (26 per sq km). *Annual rate of increase,* 3.3%.
Chief Cities (1970 census): Mexico City, the capital, 2,902,-969; Guadalajara, 1,194,646; Monterrey, 858,107; Ciudad Juarez, 407,000.
Government: *Head of state,* Luís Echeverría Álvarez, president (took office Dec. 1970). *Head of government,* Luís Eche-verría Álvarez. *Legislature*—Congress; Chamber of Deputies, 213 members; Senate, 60 members.
Language: Spanish (official).
Education: *Expenditure* (1969), 13.5% of total public expenditure. *School enrollment* (1969)—primary, 8,539,462; secondary, 1,483,856; technical/vocational, 361,167; university/higher, 188,011.
Monetary Unit: Peso (12.49 pesos equal U. S.$1, Sept. 1972).
Gross National Product (1971 est.): $34,670,000,000.
National Income per Person (1970): $632.
Economic Indexes: *Industrial production* (1970), 182 (1962= 100); *agricultural production* (1971), 196 (1952–56=100); *consumer price index* (1971), 130 (1963=100).
Manufacturing (major products): Petroleum products, iron and steel, chemicals, transportation equipment, aluminum, cement, petrochemicals.
Major Agricultural Products: Corn (ranks 4th among world producers, 1970), cotton, sugarcane, coffee, vegetables, fish, livestock.
Major Minerals: Silver (ranks 3d among world producers, 1970), iron ore, petroleum, sulfur, lead, zinc, graphite, mercury, gold, manganese.
Foreign Trade (1971): *Exports,* $1,471,000,000 (chief exports—cotton; sugar; coffee; shrimp; zinc; lead; copper). *Imports,* $2,407,000,000 (chief imports, 1969—nonelectrical machinery, transport equipment; chemicals; electric machinery, apparatus, appliances). *Chief trading partners* (1969)—United States (took 57% of exports, supplied 62% of imports); Japan (7%–5%); West Germany (3%–8%).
Tourism: *Receipts* (1970), $575,000,000.
Transportation: *Motor vehicles* (1970), 1,791,800 (automobiles, 1,233,800); *railroads* (1970), 14,988 miles (24,120 km); *merchant fleet* (1971), 401,000 gross registered tons; *major national airlines,* Aeronaves de México; Mexicana de Aviación.
Communications: *Telephones* (1971), 1,507,363; *television stations* (1971), 62; *television sets* (1971), 2,675,000; *radios* (1970), 14,005,000; *newspapers* (1970), 200.

political reforms, and of the election of a government party president, Jesus Reyes Heroles, who was committed to opening up the political system. Most important, however, was the fact that President Echeverría seemed to be a genuine political reformer who was rekindling the social reform impulse of the Mexican Revolution.

Education. The government made expansion and reorientation of the public educational system one of its major concerns during the year. The education budget was increased by $840 million, a 23% jump over 1971. The federal program of school construction planned to spend 1.77 million pesos to increase the number of elementary schools.

Technical and vocational education received the most attention during the year. An increased number of free textbooks were either technical or technically oriented. Enrollment in the National Polytechnical Institute was increased 14%, and the institute was also being decentralized to provide access for a greater number of students. More technical-vocational schools were being built.

Economy. During 1972 the government sought to accelerate economic expansion while holding the inflation rate to a minimum. Governmental expenditures in the first seven months were increased 24.1% over the same period in 1971. Federal public investment was expected to be 37.8 billion pesos, up 30% over 1971. One third of total investment was directed toward industrial development, while about 10 billion pesos went to social benefit programs.

In the first half of the year economic activity increased 15.6% as opposed to 2.7% for the same period of 1971. Manufacturing industry production increased 6.5% in the first eight months. Production advances in the first six months included: automobiles (4.9%), stoves (5.9%), washing machines (12%), refrigerators (13%), television sets (5.5%), iron and steel (14%), and construction (13%). The gross national product was expected to be about 6% higher than that of 1971, a rate of growth not much below the average annual increase since 1950. In addition, wholesale prices rose only 2.1% in the first half of the year, while the inflation rates for the year had moderated to 4%, one of the lower rates in the world and about the average for the decade.

On the foreign trade front, exports in the first six months of 1972 were 22% higher than in the same period in 1971, with manufactured articles showing the greatest increase (29.4%). Agricultural exports continued to provide the bulk of the nation's export earnings, but manufactured exports had come to represent 43% of all exports. Imports during this period increased 11.5%.

The customary trade deficit in commodity exports was made up by profits to Mexico from border and tourist transactions. Mexico's drive to increase tourism was paying off as tourism increased 28% during the first seven months.

The government took steps to increase internally generated revenue and to decrease dependence upon foreign loans. Income tax rates were made more progressive, and collection procedures were improved. The government borrowed $80 million from 34 private Mexican banks to finance development programs—the largest loan ever made by private banks to the government. Foreign indebtedness increased only 2.5%, which was a lower growth rate than previously.

Government Planning. The administration of President Echeverría took numerous important steps to improve the socioeconomic conditions of rural areas and to make the government more effective. An Intersectorial Commission for Ejidal Colonization was created to establish regional plans for new population centers. Related to this activity was the formation of a National Program of Farmer Investment and Development to extend credit and technical aid to small and communal farmers. Social security benefits were extended to more farmers than ever before, and the *ejidatarios* (collective or communal farmers) of Yucatán were brought entirely into the social security program for the first time in history.

Industrial development also received stimulus, particularly to encourage the relocation of industry in depressed rural zones. The government began financing ten major industrial parks in different parts of the country at an estimated cost of $204 million while continuing to aid 40 other industrial parks and cities throughout Mexico. Industries locating in these areas were also to be given tax breaks. A special fund has been created to aid import-substitution and export industries to modernize their plants. Finally, industries are allowed the duty-free import of devices that reduce environmental contamination.

The living conditions of workers received special attention in 1972. Minimum wages rose throughout the country. A National Public Employment Service, with offices in Mexico City and ten states, has been instituted to attack unemployment by establishing better communication between potential employees and employers. The newly created National Workers' Housing Institute (INFONAVIT) was to provide low-interest, 20-year mortgages to workers and expected to construct 100,000 houses

annually. Also created was a national housing fund for members of the armed forces.

The Mexican government has taken several steps to ensure that the communications system serves the national interest. The government acquired majority interest in the National Telephone Company and has been expanding its service. On another front, the government has bought control of a major television network and converted it into an educational public broadcasting system, and it has purchased other television and radio stations. The government promised a closer watch on radio and television broadcasts to ensure that they will serve the people.

International Relations. During the first half of the year, President Echeverría traveled abroad extensively to expand Mexican markets and to assert Mexican leadership in the Third World. In March, Echeverría traveled to Japan in his efforts to expand Mexican markets in that country and to encourage further Japanese investment in Mexico. In April, the president went to Chile to address the third United Nations Conference for Commerce and Development, where, as a spokesman for Latin America, he attacked the leading industrial nations of the world for ignoring the problems of the Third World. While there he conferred with Chilean President Salvador Allende, praising him for his nationalistic and social reform policies, which the Mexican president saw as consistent with the Mexican Revolution.

In June, President Echeverría visited the United States, where he addressed a joint session of Congress and conferred with President Nixon. He complained that U. S. trade policies since August 1971 were attempts to shift the solution of U. S. problems to other countries, that the pacts signed between the great powers ignore the problems of the Third World, and that U. S. import restrictions were damaging Mexico, one of the United States' best customers.

DONALD J. MABRY
Mississippi State University

MICHIGAN

Major issues in Michigan during 1972 were the busing of students to integrate public schools and a proposed relaxation of the state's abortion laws. Voters rejected proposals to reform state tax laws. A lottery to raise state funds began operation, and the state adopted no-fault insurance.

Busing. Controversial programs of busing students to desegregate public schools were carried out under court orders in Kalamazoo and Grand Rapids and by action of boards of education in Lansing and Jackson. A massive desegregation plan involving Detroit and 52 of its suburbs was ordered by a federal judge in July but delayed pending appeals. (See DETROIT.) Although their action had no legal effect, more than 200,000 voters registered objections to busing in advisory votes held in several Michigan communities. In Macomb county, which borders Detroit, 94% of those voting on May 16 opposed busing. Leaders of a Pontiac-based antibusing group, the National Action Group, conducted a "walk to Washington" to publicize their support for national antibusing legislation.

Pontiac schools had been integrated by federal court order in 1971. Bitter opposition to busing was cited as the reason Alabama Gov. George C. Wallace won 51% of the vote on May 16 when Mich-

igan held its first presidential primary in 44 years. Antibusing sentiment also was seen as a major factor working for President Richard M. Nixon, who won by a 400,000-plus vote margin in the November 7 election in the normally Democratic state. Republican incumbent U. S. Sen. Robert Griffin, a strong busing foe, won reelection by defeating Atty. Gen. Frank J. Kelley in the most hotly contested state race.

Abortion. By a margin of 9 to 5, Michigan voters rejected in the November 7 election a proposal to allow abortions through the 20th week of pregnancy. The proposal, which was placed on the ballot after a statewide petition drive calling for relaxation of the state's abortion law, aroused vigorous support and opposition. Despite the vote, pressure for reform of the abortion law, which now allows abortions only to save the life of the mother, continued in the courts. A Wayne county circuit court judge found the state's abortion law unconstitutional in an October ruling and directed local law-enforcement officials not to enforce the law, but the state supreme court set aside the order and assumed jurisdiction over four pending abortion prosecutions.

Lottery. Michigan held its first lottery drawing on November 24. On May 16 voters had approved a constitutional amendment giving the Legislature authority to write a lottery law. Supporters of a lottery argued that it would raise $25 million to

——— **MICHIGAN • Information Highlights** ———

Area: 58,216 square miles (150,779 sq km).
Population (1970 census): 8,875,083. *Density:* 158 per square mile.
Chief Cities (1970 census): Lansing, the capital, 131,546; Detroit, 1,513,601; Grand Rapids, 197,649; Flint, 193,317; Warren, 179,260; Dearborn, 104,199; Livonia, 110,109.
Government (1972): *Chief Officers*—governor, William G. Milliken (R); lt. gov., James H. Brickley (R); secy. of state, Richard H. Austin (D); atty. gen., Frank J. Kelley (D); treas., Allison Green; supt. of public instruction, John W. Porter; chief justice, Thomas M. Kavanagh. *Legislature*—Senate, 38 members (19 Democrats, 19 Republicans); House of Representatives, 110 members (58 D, 52 R).
Education (1971–72): *Enrollment*—public elementary schools, 1,199,257 pupils, 41,200 teachers; public secondary, 1,099,852 pupils, 55,270 teachers; nonpublic schools (1970–71), 285,248 pupils, 9,230 teachers; college and university, 362,000 students. *Public school expenditures,* $2,303,628,000 ($1,148 per pupil). *Average teacher's salary,* $12,092.
State Finances (fiscal year 1970): *Revenues,* $4,131,546,000 (4% general sales tax and gross receipts taxes, $828,491,-000; motor fuel tax, $237,735,000; federal funds, $718,-611,000). *Expenditures,* $3,932,246,000 (education, $1,592,-488,000; health, welfare, and safety, $601,252,000; highways, $357,414,000). *State debt,* $958,461,000 (June 30; 1970).
Personal Income (1971): $38,841,000,000; per capita, $4,317.
Public Assistance (1971): $812,587,000. *Average monthly payments* (Dec. 1971)—old-age assistance, $80.10; aid to families with dependent children, $228.33.
Labor Force: Nonagricultural wage and salary earners (July 1972), 2,914,900. *Average annual employment* (1971)—manufacturing, 1,049,000; trade, 596,000; government, 516,000; services, 426,000. *Insured unemployed* (Aug. 1972)—171,400 (4.7%).
Manufacturing (1970): *Value added by manufacture,* $17,512,-000,000. Transportation equipment, $5,333,100,000; nonelectrical machinery, $2,789,700,000; fabricated metal products, $2,133,500,000; primary metal industries, $1,679,-800,000; food and kindred products, $1,139,300,000; chemicals and allied products, $991,900,000.
Agriculture (1970): *Cash farm income,* $962,503,000 (livestock, $484,644,000; crops, $412,161,000; government payments, $65,698,000). *Chief crops* (in order of value, 1971)—Corn, hay, dry beans (ranks 1st among the states), soybeans.
Mining (1971): *Production value,* $640,723,000 (ranks 12th among the states). *Chief minerals*—Iron ore, $159,854,000; cement, $110,625,000; sand and gravel, $62,898,000; copper, $58,245,000.
Fisheries (1971): *Commercial catch,* 19,137,000 pounds ($2,671,000). *Leading species by value,* Whitefish, $1,463,-000; chubs, $568,000; yellow perch, $168,000.
Transportation: *Roads* (1971), 114,729 miles (184,633 km); *motor vehicles* (1971), 4,569,319; *railroads* (1971), 6,183 miles (9,950 km); *public airports* (1972), 129.
Communications: *Telephones* (1972), 5,344,600; *television stations* (1971), 20; *radio stations* (1971), 203; *newspapers* (1972), 55 (daily circulation, 2,447,000).

help pay state expenses in its first nine months and $60 million a year after it was established. A top prize of $1 million is to be awarded after 30 million 50-cent lottery tickets are sold, with lesser prizes offered at shorter intervals.

Taxes. Two proposals—both placed on the ballot after petition drives organized by the Michigan Education Association, a teachers' professional organization—to change Michigan tax procedures were rejected by voters on November 7. One proposal would have eliminated the local property tax as the principal means of financing public school education, directing the Legislature to provide other means of support. Defeat of the proposal was analyzed as a rebuff to Gov. William Milliken, who campaigned vigorously for it. Voters also rejected a proposal to allow the state to levy a graduated income tax. The state constitution allows the Legislature to impose only a flat-rate income tax.

A "temporary" 50% increase in the state's income tax, approved in 1971, was extended indefinitely before its expiration on August 1. Leaders said expiration would have cost the state $250 million a year and forced many spending cutbacks.

No-fault Insurance. The state adopted compulsory no-fault insurance legislation, to take effect Oct. 1, 1973. The law provides that an accident victim's own insurance company must pay his claims regardless of who may be at fault in the accident.

Other Developments. Great Lakes navigation was hindered throughout the summer by the sinking on June 5 of a freighter in the St. Clair River off Port Huron. During a mid-November storm, unseasonably high Great Lakes water levels were blamed for flooding that caused millions of dollars of damage along the state's eastern shoreline.

Voters returned Michigan to daylight saving time in the November 7 election, overturning legislative action that had exempted the state from the 1967 federal Uniform Time Act. The state will go on daylight time in 1973.

CHARLES W. THEISEN, *The Detroit "News"*

MICROBIOLOGY

Several important developments in various fields of microbiology were reported in 1972.

Agricultural Microbiology. In agricultural microbiology important progress was made in converting some of the 600 million tons of agricultural wastes that accumulate each year into usable animal feed and fuel gas (methane). Microorganisms and enzymes in the cellulose-containing manure convert the mixture into sugars, acids, alcohols, carbon dioxide, and hydrogen gas. These substances are then converted to microbial proteins, amino acids, and methane. The resulting proteins are more than four times that contained in the original material and can be dried and used to supplement animal feeds, while the methane is used for fuel. Other advances included determining the role of microorganisms in soil fertility and progress in the use of bacteria and viruses as bioinsecticide agents to help control certain plant diseases.

Food Microbiology. Dates, prunes, and figs are spoiled largely by yeasts. Now a new preservative technique has been discovered. It consists of dipping the fruits in potassium sorbate solution and then injecting methyl bromide into sealed packages. In another development, the microorganisms responsible for the sweet taste and alcoholic flavor of ragi

and tape, two important fermented rice or cassava tuber foods in Southeast Asia, were isolated and a modern industrial process was established.

Microbial Diseases. A plant disease known as "lethal yellowing" that threatens palm trees in the United States and elsewhere was shown to be caused by a little-understood microorganism that seems to be neither a bacterium nor a virus. The animal diseases hog cholera and rabies both increased in 1972, and a national emergency was declared in certain poultry-raising areas of the United States because of a severe epidemic of Newcastle disease. (See VETERINARY MEDICINE.)

There were also important discoveries relating to meningitis and influenza vaccines, and new relationships between viruses and cancer were established. In leukemia research, blood from human leukemia patients was inoculated into primates and the virus later isolated. This work holds strong promise for a better understanding of leukemia.

Dental Microbiology. Bacteria are considered the cause of tooth decay, or caries, but until 1972 attempts to prepare vaccines that influence the development of caries were unsuccessful. In 1972 the enzyme glucosyltransferase, considered responsible for some of the bacterial plaque on tooth enamel and which stimulates antibody production, was isolated from streptococci. Further research may bring advances in the prevention of tooth decay.

Immunology. There were several important discoveries in this branch of microbiology, which deals with the mechanics by which the body defends itself against infectious diseases and resists tissue or organ transplants. The 1972 Nobel Prize in physiology or medicine was awarded to two immunologists—the Englishman Rodney R. Porter and the American G. M. Edelman—for their work on the chemical structure of antibodies, the blood proteins that play a crucial role in the body's fight against infection. The discovery that the BCG (bacillus Calmette-Guérin) vaccine, long used in the prevention of tuberculosis, is, when injected into some animals, effective against certain tumors may lead to a better understanding and treatment of some kinds of cancer.

Other Developments. Among other advances were some in the field of genetics. A notable finding was that when bacteria are starved, their messenger RNA is degraded rapidly, while their transfer RNA and ribosomes are only very slightly affected. (See GENETICS.)

Other advances included the finding of a unique nitrogen-fixing bacterium growing in association with molds that may be responsible for the destruction of large quantities of potential lumber each year. Various fungi growing on tobacco were identified as potential sources of carcinogenic (cancer-producing) compounds in tobacco. Also identified were microorganisms that degrade parts of some plant sterol molecules and that may be useful in the manufacture of certain medicinal steroids.

UN Conference on the Human Environment. Several recommendations concerning microbiology were made at the UN Conference in Stockholm in 1972. Among them were the suggestions that genetic stocks of microorganisms be properly catalogued and preserved and that studies be made on the role of microorganisms in waste disposal and recycling, in controlling diseases and pests, in food technology, and nutrition, and in soil fertility. (See also ENVIRONMENT.)

J. R. PORTER, *University of Iowa*

Israel unveiled a U. S.-made, self-propelled 175mm gun, called the M-107, during military exercises in the Sinai desert in 1972.

MIDDLE EAST

In the complex arena of the Middle East, some significant and novel events took place in 1972, particularly in regard to Egypt's relations with its Arab neighbors and with the Soviet Union. On the other hand, there was little movement on the question that it had been customary to regard as the issue of overriding importance in the region: that is, the relations between Israel and the Arab states. During 1972, Israel continued to exist, and to exist within the boundaries it had enjoyed since June 1967; and the Suez Canal remained closed. Arab hostility to Israel, varying very much in intensity from state to state, also persisted.

ARAB-ISRAELI RELATIONS

Military Activity. The U. S.-sponsored cease-fire of August 1970 remained in effect throughout 1972. There was some military activity from time to time, mainly on Israel's borders with Lebanon and Syria. An air clash between Egyptian and Israeli planes took place on June 14, the first since 1970, but there was no ground fighting along the canal. The governments of Israel and Jordan permitted Arab civilians to move more or less freely across the de facto Israeli-Jordan border in either direction.

Israeli moves against Lebanon and Syria were in accord with Israel's long-term policy of striking against guerrilla hideouts and making it uncomfortable for states that harbored them. Among the more notable actions of the kind were Israeli raids into Lebanon in June and September, the latter lasting three days, and an air strike against Lebanon in October. In the latter half of the year Syria, emboldened by the receipt of Russian military equipment, became the chief protagonist in challenging Israel. There was fairly severe fighting, initiated by Syria, in the Golan Heights in November, and again at the end of the year. Syria shelled Israeli settle-

ments in the Golan Heights several times, December 28–30, and Israel retaliated with two air strikes on Syria, one on an army camp at Nebk, north of Damascus and well inside the border.

New Forms of Guerrilla Activity. The formerly prominent activities of Al-Fatah, the Palestine Liberation Front, and other border-raiding Arab terrorist groups were diminishing. They seemed in 1972 of less importance than they did in the summer of 1970, when the Arab guerrilla fighters achieved world prominence with their hijacking of airliners to the Jordanian desert and with their presence in Cairo at the funeral of President Nasser. These events of 1970 were not a prelude to further successes; they formed the high-water mark of their importance. The crucial event in diminishing their power was the ruthless and successful attack on guerrilla-held areas in Jordan that had been launched in September 1970 by King Hussein and his faithful bedouin army. The guerrilla groups lost their standing in Jordan, and were restricted in their activities in Lebanon. They were generally regarded with some reserve by most Arab leaders. Early in November 1972, battles in Lebanon between rival Arab guerrilla factions, said to be over the possession of funds donated by President Qaddafi of Libya, led to some 30 deaths.

The extremist Black September group dominated anti-Israeli terrorist activity in 1972, and under its direction it assumed a markedly different form. Apart from the massacre at Lod airport on May 30, which was carried out by Japanese hirelings, most actions took place outside the borders of Israel, in such varied places as London, Munich, and Bangkok. A letter-bomb—one of many that were mailed in 1972—killed an Israeli diplomat in the London embassy. Eleven members of the Israeli Olympic team were murdered by Arab terrorists. Near the end of

December, Arab terrorists for a time held Israeli diplomats hostage in the Bangkok embassy.

Since Israel, unlike Western governments, has a fixed national policy of not yielding to terrorist blackmail, whatever the cost to individuals may be, no specific gains could or did result from such criminal actions, which were reminiscent of 19th century anarchism rather than examples of serious political activity.

Quiet on the Diplomatic Front. The tone and mood of the Mideast situation altered subtly in 1972. There was some hope that peace might eventually be achieved. Chaim Hertzog, a distinguished correspondent, wrote in the London *Times* (February 28) that the Middle East was now bent on a "quest for formulas," and that there was "a growing tendency towards coexistence between Israel and the Arab peoples." Yet the acceptable formula proved elusive, and there was very little diplomatic activity of any consequence in 1972. One reason, no doubt, was that the United States was preoccupied by Southeast Asia, and also was unwilling to embark on serious diplomacy regarding Israel in an election year. However, more fundamental reasons for inactivity were to be found in the attitudes of the states chiefly involved, Egypt and Israel.

Ever since the 1967 war, Egypt had been trying to get Israel to give up its conquered territory, not by war or by direct negotiation, but by securing the support of third powers which would put pressure on Israel. Israel, however, having once obliged third parties in 1956 in return for guarantees that turned out to be worthless, was not eager to make the same error twice.

Israel did not lay formal claim to all the 1967 occupied territories; the only non-negotiable areas appeared to be the Golan Heights and the whole of Jerusalem. The Israelis merely said that they would not surrender anything without a settlement, one made in direct negotiation with Egypt and other interested Arab states. Assured it would receive sufficient U.S. arms, and also apparently again receiving some arms from British sources, Israel intended to sit out the crisis until Egypt finally gave up its strategy of avoiding a directly negotiated settlement.

Dr. Gunnar Jarring, the UN negotiator, made visits to the Middle East capitals in January and February, but these proved unproductive. In March, King Hussein of Jordan unveiled his plan for a semi-autonomous Palestinian area comprising the West Bank and the Gaza Strip. The plan aroused great interest except in Israel and Egypt. The immediate consequence was that Egypt broke off relations with Jordan. Jordan again showed a conciliatory attitude when on September 9 the new foreign minister, Salah Abu Zaid, said that the return of East Jerusalem to Jordanian sovereignty was not a necessary precondition to a separate peace between Jordan and Israel.

The Munich massacre of Israeli athletes set back the cause of a possible general Israeli-Arab peace, and may indeed have been committed with that aim in view.

The Arab states scored a nominal success in the United Nations when on December 8 the General Assembly passed, 86 to 7, a resolution urging member governments to withhold "'aid which would constitute recognition" of Israel's territorial gains of 1967. The United States announced that U.S. aid to Israel would be unaffected.

THE USSR AND THE MIDDLE EAST

Expulsion from Egypt. In one of the most surprising developments of the year, Soviet military personnel, experts, and advisers were expelled from Egypt, beginning July 17. Thus the growing Soviet military presence in Egypt, a significant and ominous feature of the preceding five years, was all but terminated. It was a considerable blow to Soviet policy in the eastern Mediterranean.

The event, which the Soviet Union accepted calmly, had to some extent been foreshadowed by friction between the Soviet leaders and Sadat. The latter had been disappointed by the Soviet Union's lack of all-out support for Egypt's Israeli policy. Sadat's third visit to Moscow (February 2–4) as Egypt's president was not a success. In March it was reported that Egypt was objecting to the presence in Egypt of 500 members of the KGB (secret police).

If Sadat expected that the Soviet departure would be followed by warm overtures from the United States, he was mistaken. In the late fall, Sadat was to be found again making approaches to the USSR, and it seemed that Soviet advisers, in limited numbers, would be readmitted.

The personal position of the Egyptian leader was repeatedly reported in 1972 to be shaky, but these

GOKSIN SIPAHIOGLU/JOCELYNE BENZAKIN

ARAB guerrillas are seated at press conference in Tripoli. They hijacked West German jetliner on October 29 and won release of Arab commandos involved in murder of Israeli Olympic athletes.

reports were exaggerated. Egypt had not been a country subject to frequent coups; there had been none since 1952. The January reconstruction of the cabinet strengthened Sadat's hand. He handled the student riots firmly and adroitly. There was no evidence of widespread popular feeling against him, nor was there much reason for it. Life in Egypt was less grim and puritanical than under Nasser, and there was less press censorship.

Soviet Union and the Radical Arab States. Even before the enforced Soviet retreat from Egypt, there was evidence that the Soviet leaders were modifying their Mideast policy. They were beginning

COFFINS of two of the Arab terrorists slain in the Munich Olympic Games incident are carried by supporters at their funeral in Libya.

to court Arab countries other than Egypt, especially the radical Arab states. The outstanding example was the alliance formed with Iraq in a 15-year treaty of cooperation, signed April 9 during a state visit by Premier Kosygin to Baghdad. The USSR was also drawing closer to radical Syria and supplying it with arms. Even in regard to Libya, whose fervent Arab nationalist president Qaddafi had hitherto looked askance at the Soviet Union, there were signs of a rapprochement.

The Soviet-Iraqi treaty had an obvious bearing on developments in the oil-rich Persian Gulf area, which some observers thought might, in the power vacuum left by the 1971 British withdrawal, become the next area of Great-Power confrontation. The Iraqi treaty gave the USSR naval facilities on the Gulf. Iraq in itself was clearly no match for Iran, the most important local power; but Iraq plus the Soviet Union was another matter. Soviet relations with Iran, however, remained friendly.

USSR and Israel. There were repeated reports in 1972 that the Soviet Union was exploring through third parties the possibility of restoring diplomatic relations with Israel. In any event, it was fairly clear that the USSR no longer—if it had ever truly done so—viewed the destruction of Israel as a desirable objective.

MOVES TOWARD ARAB UNITY

The quest for Arab unity, long pursued in vain, had led to a number of unions or alleged unions in which the constant nucleus was Egypt. The recurring problem had been to decide whether these projects were to be taken more seriously than, or perhaps not as seriously as, the short-lived Egypt-Syrian union of 1958–61. On the whole, a good deal of skepticism seemed in order.

Egypt-Libya Union. A decision to bring about a "full political union" between Egypt and Libya by Sept. 1, 1973, was announced by presidents Sadat and Qaddafi on August 2, at the end of three days of talks in Libya. The statement spoke of setting up a joint political command, which would shape the definite plan for the union. All measures were to be completed by Sept. 1, 1973.

The union was urged upon Sadat by Qaddafi in February, but Sadat had asked for five months to consider it. Since Libya was one of the oil-rich countries whose subsidies had enabled Egypt to survive financially, to refuse the proposal would presumably have been awkward. Other elements in Libya were reported to be much less interested in the proposal than Qaddafi.

One of the many oddities about the announcement was that no mention was made of the three-nation "Federation of Arab Republics," comprising Egypt, Libya, and Syria, announced on April 17, 1971, and approved in referenda in the three states on Sept. 1, 1971.

According to some observers, Syrian belligerence toward Israel in the latter part of 1972 was primarily intended as a Syrian test of Qaddafi's sincerity. The London *Economist*, in its issue of November 25, argued that in fighting Israel, Syrian leaders were in fact challenging the Libyan leader either to join in the war against Israel or else to give up his pretensions to a major position among the anti-Israeli powers.

For the moment the French government was continuing to supply Mirage aircraft to Libya, discounting the possibility that they might, as a result of the union with Egypt, be used against Israel. About 40 of a contracted 100 planes had been delivered by the end of 1972.

WRIGHT/THE MIAMI NEWS

OTHER MIDEAST DEVELOPMENTS

Yemen. In October peace was achieved between North and South Yemen as a result of the intervention of other Arab countries and steps were taken to unify the two states.

Oil. Lengthy negotiations resulted in 1972 in major concessions by the oil companies to the advantage of the oil-producing states. In addition to higher prices, most of these states were demanding increasing "participation," that is, step-by-step nationalization. The Iraq Petroleum Company was nationalized outright by Iraq and Syria on June 1. The Persian Gulf States, however, were more interested in stable and increasing returns, safeguarded against the effects of currency fluctuations.

ARTHUR CAMPBELL TURNER
University of California, Riverside

MILWAUKEE

A start on the biggest building in Wisconsin and a halt in freeway construction were among the principal news events of 1972 in Milwaukee.

Urban Development. The $50 million First Wisconsin Center rose in downtown Milwaukee, near Lake Michigan. The completed building, 601 feet high and covering 1,300,000 square feet, will be the tallest and largest building in Wisconsin. It will contain offices, stores, and parking areas. The Center is part of $100 million in construction projects that also include a $15 million convention hall.

The city began to reorganize the Department of City Development, its renewal, housing, and planning agency. The department head, Kenneth E. Fry, resigned before the reorganization was completed.

Transportation. Mounting opposition virtually halted additions to the county's freeways and put the future of the freeway system in question. Critics of the freeway said that the concrete ribbons destroyed too much housing—more than 6,300 units in 10 years—and were harming the environment.

Milwaukee's privately owned bus system also announced that it was in trouble, as it increased rates for the second time in two years. A blue ribbon committee formed by Gov. Patrick J. Lucey proposed a publicly owned system, rather than a private or subsidized system. The Milwaukee County Board began discussing a takeover of the firm, but progress has been slow.

Politics. Democratic Mayor Henry W. Maier was re-elected to his fourth four-year term, winning 67% of the vote over a little-known college professor, Bernard E. Novak. Pro-Maier candidates also won the offices of city attorney and comptroller and a majority of seats on the common council, solidifying Maier's control of city government. Most of his campaigning consisted of attacks on the Milwaukee *Journal,* which endorsed him nonetheless.

In the presidential race, Maier nominally supported Sen. George McGovern for president, but Maier's wife, Mary Ann, broke with the Democratic party. In a late evening telephone call to the Milwaukee *Sentinel* she said she was annoyed over the treatment she and Maier had received at the Democratic National Convention. Later at the Republican Convention, Mrs. Maier seconded the nomination of President Nixon.

The circuit court ordered a grand-jury investigation into the affairs of County Board Chairman Richard C. Nowakowski. The investigation grew out of a series of stories in the *Sentinel.*

Economy. Milwaukee's port was closed for two and one-half months, cutting sharply into overseas cargo tonnages. Terminal operators refused to open the port because longshoremen had not agreed to a new contract. Settlement was reached in June.

Despite the port lockout, the economy of Milwaukee was on the upswing. By September, employment had risen 1% over 1971. The unadjusted unemployment rate in August was 4.5%, compared with 4.7% a year earlier. The number of permits for constructing new dwelling units increased 23.2% over 1971.

LAWRENCE C. LOHMANN, *The Milwaukee "Journal"*

MINING

Activities and trends in mining are reviewed in this article under the headings of World Mineral Production and U. S. Mining Technology. (See also the separate article ENERGY—*Petroleum*.)

WORLD MINERAL PRODUCTION

The general economic recession that began in 1970 had its inevitable impact on the mineral industries, an impact that may well prove to have reached its peak in 1972 while continuing on into the year beyond. Signs of what was to come could be seen in 1971. Of 73 mineral commodities for which relatively comprehensive international production statistics are obtainable, the 1971 output of 42 of them increased an average of only 6.8% as compared to an average 8.4% increase for 53 minerals the previous year, while the output of 31 decreased an average 8.6% in 1971 compared with 3.8% for 17 in 1970. It seems probable that 1972 mineral production will have declined generally, in response to lessened demand.

Effects of Recession. The effects of the recession are various and complex. Predictably, prices have declined along with mineral production. This has had more or less serious consequences for many developing countries whose economies are heavily dependent upon mineral production, such as Chile, Peru, Zambia, or the Philippines. The loss of expected income makes it necessary to curtail many social and economic programs, which in turn further stirs up restless populations. A common result for the governments of such countries is to seek immediate—albeit usually only short-term—benefits by nationalizing mines, controlling mineral production and sales, or taking similar actions.

Another obvious consequence is the postponement of planned mineral projects, with a resultant loss of revenue and jobs for the country concerned. In 1972 this was particularly noticeable in Australia, where four to seven large new iron mines, a large aluminum project, and one or possibly two new nickel projects were all delayed by two to four years, pending better economic conditions. In addition, by means of negotiations the Japanese reduced 1972 deliveries from the West Australian iron ore producers by an amount exceeding the full 10% annual variance permitted under contracts. This move will cost Australian producers between $90 million and $92 million in 1972–73.

Much the same happened with producers of other minerals for Japanese use, such as British Columbia copper mines. However, in order to minimize adverse effects on producers while reducing the amount of their own capital tied up in temporary unwanted inventory, Japanese firms have been encouraging their government to establish a stockpile that could be used to stabilize some of the more volatile or sensitive commodity trades such as copper, lead, and zinc concentrates.

Exploration and Development. Mineral exploration continued, for the most part, despite the recession, fundamentally because the long-term upward trend in world demand for minerals is recognized. Moreover, a characteristic of many mineral industries that is usually overlooked is that if the unit cost of production of the mineral from a new mine is sufficiently low, the mine will be brought into production. For example, several new copper mines were developed in British Columbia during the year

even though at least half a dozen copper mines in the area closed at the same time.

In 1972 Australia and the Indonesian Archipelago were centers of intensive activity in the continuing search for new mineral deposits. The Philippine Islands should also have been such a center, but political conditions prevented this. Activity was strong in South Africa but intermittent throughout the rest of the African continent. Most significant exploration has ceased in Latin America, except for Mexico and Brazil. In North America, nationalism and other factors have lately tended to curtail mineral exploration, most recently and perhaps unexpectedly in western Canada.

Nationalism. The various manifestations of nationalism continue to affect mineral development in countries such as Australia, Canada, and Ireland, each of which has recently undergone a major mining boom of great economic importance to the country, and each of which can be classified as an economically developed nation. The basic effect with respect to mining is a general concern with the extent of foreign control of the industry. This concern is expressed on the national level and, more strongly, on the state or provincial level, and in each country some action has been taken to curb the foreign influence. In Canada the situation was compounded in 1972 by provincial elections that returned new, socialist-oriented parties to the western provinces of British Columbia and Saskatchewan, both of which are important mineral producers. Each of the three new governors outlined a program of mineral rights allocation that, together with fiscal policies, has already caused two major companies to terminate exploration programs in the area.

Production and Prices. Except for the Soviet Union and associated nations that are to some degree isolated from economic conditions in the rest of the world, the general rate of increase in mineral production—where increases actually occurred —tended to be lower in 1972 than in previous years. During the early part of the year, prices tended to fall. Later, in response to growing economic activity, mineral prices showed new strength and some actually rose. In general, however, the tenor was one of uncertainty rather than clearcut trends.

Precious Metals and Minerals. The output of gold, silver, and platinum declined in 1971. Platinum fell in direct response to lowered demand, whereas gold and silver declined at least partially as a result of decreased byproduct recoveries in the United States due to a prolonged copper strike. In 1972 the price of all three metals rose. The London gold price exceeded $50 per troy ounce in May and reached a record high of $72.25 on August 2, remaining at around $60 for the rest of the year. The New York silver price rose steadily from $1.47 per ounce in January to about $1.80 by the year's end. Platinum stood at $110 per ounce in February, then rose to $130 in August as a result of the three-year contract of the Ford Motor Company to purchase the metal for use in catalytic control of auto-exhaust emissions. Other automobile manufacturers followed suit, and platinum producers announced plans to increase their output.

Ferrous Metals and Alloys. World output of iron ore, pig iron, and steel declined in 1971 and probably in 1972 as well. Nevertheless, the worldwide economic recovery had gathered sufficient momentum by the latter part of the year to foster

(*Continued on page 472*)

WORLD PRODUCTION OF MAJOR MINERALS[1]

Aluminum (Thousands of metric tons)

	1970	1971
United States	3,607.0	3,561.0
USSR[2]	1,100.0	1,180.0
Canada	972.0	1,002.0
Japan	733.0	893.0
Norway	529.8	529.0
West Germany	309.0	428.0
France	381.0	384.0
Australia	204.1	223.0
India	161.5	178.0
China	130.0	140.0·
Spain	115.2	127.0
Italy	146.0	120.0
Netherlands	75.0	117.0
Greece	87.1	116.0
Ghana	113.4	111.0
Rumania	101.6	[2]110.0
Poland	98.9	100.0
Switzerland	91.6	94.0
Austria	89.8	91.0
Sweden	66.2	76.0
Hungary	66.2	67.0
Surinam	55.0	60.0
Cameroon	52.0	51.0
Total (est.)	9,645.0	10,250.0

Antimony (Metric tons)

	1970	1971
South Africa	17,370	14,246
China[2]	12,000	12,000
Bolivia	11,766	11,667
USSR[2]	6,700	6,900
Mexico	4,468	[2]3,200
Turkey	2,770	[2]2,800
Yugoslavia	2,900	[2]2,600
Thailand	2,357	2,294
Morocco	1,973	1,920
Italy	1,299	1,275
Australia	909	1,149
United States	1,025	930
Peru	599	[2]600
Czechoslovakia[2]	600	600
Austria	610	467
Total (est.)	68,841	63,747

Asbestos (Thousands of metric tons)

	1970	1971
Canada	1,507.4	1,482.9
USSR[2]	1,065.0	1,150.0
South Africa	287.4	319.3
China[2]	170.0	160.0
Italy	118.5	119.5
United States	113.7	118.7
Rhodesia[2]	80.0	80.0
Total (est.)	3,486.0	3,581.1

Barite (Thousands of metric tons)

	1970	1971
United States	774.9	748.4
West Germany	412.6	408.9
USSR[2]	284.9	299.4
Mexico	319.1	279.7
Italy	217.3	201.5
Ireland	[2]160.6	[2]160.6
China[2]	150.0	139.7
Peru	130.0	[2]129.7
Canada	133.6	124.3
North Korea[2]	120.0	120.0
Rumania[2]	116.5	116.1
France	105.0	[2]105.2
Greece	54.2	98.9
Spain	84.6	85.3
Morocco	84.8	84.5
Yugoslavia	79.7	79.9
India	71.9	61.6
Iran	60.2	[2]59.9
Japan	66.0	57.9
Poland[2]	50.0	55.3
Total (est.)	3,750.3	3,767.2

Bauxite (Thousands of metric tons)

	1970	1971
Jamaica	12,009.7	12,766.7
Australia	9,387.3	12,541.1
Surinam	5,341.4	[2]6,260.9
USSR[2]	4,267.4	4,470.6
Guyana[2]	4,144.5	3,817.3
France	3,051.2	3,115.2
Greece	2,278.0	3,087.8
Guinea	[2]2,641.7	[2]2,641.7
Hungary	2,021.9	2,090.0
United States	2,115.4	2,019.9
Yugoslavia	2,099.2	1,958.9
India	1,359.5	1,436.7
Dominican Rep.	1,066.9	1,311.7
Indonesia	1,229.4	1,237.5
Malaysia	1,139.0	977.4
Haiti	631.0	643.2
Sierra Leone	439.9	590.3
China[2]	497.9	548.7
Brazil	499.9	[2]499.9
Ghana	350.0	329.2
Total (est.)	57,163.0	62,975.8

Cement (Millions of metric tons)

	1970	1971
USSR[2]	95.20	100.30
United States	69.05	72.86

Cement (cont'd) (Millions of metric tons)

	1970	1971
Japan	57.19	53.75
West Germany	38.32	32.69
Italy	33.12	31.73
France	28.52	28.95
United Kingdom	17.05	17.90
Spain	16.54	16.99
India	13.54	14.89
Poland	12.18	13.08
China[2]	10.00	12.01
Brazil	9.00	9.80
Canada	7.21	8.65
Rumania	8.13	8.23
East Germany	7.99	[2]8.00
Turkey	6.37	7.54
Mexico	7.27	7.36
Czechoslovakia	7.40	7.27
Belgium	6.73	6.93
South Korea	5.82	6.87
South Africa	5.75	5.86
Total (est.)	571.96	590.22

Chromite (Thousands of metric tons)

	1970	1971
USSR[2]	1,750.0	1,800.0
South Africa	1,427.3	1,644.2
Turkey[2]	518.8	603.4
Albania	468.0	[2]600.0
Philippines	566.4	432.2
Rhodesia[2]	360.0	360.0
India	270.9	261.1
Iran[2]	200.0	200.0
Malagasy Rep.	[3]130.3	[2]140.0
Finland	120.5	112.0
Cyprus	33.3	40.6
Yugoslavia	40.6	34.3
Japan	33.0	31.6
Sudan	47.1	21.1
Total (est.)	6,049.0	6,357.4

Coal (Millions of metric tons)

	1970	1971
USSR	616.3	[2]633.9
United States	555.8	508.8
China[2]	382.8	410.0
East Germany	261.9	[2]266.1
West Germany	219.7	215.3
Poland	172.9	180.0
United Kingdom	138.2	[2]146.6
Czechoslovakia	109.8	113.0
India	77.2	72.8
Australia	73.4	72.3
South Africa	54.5	58.6
France	40.1	[2]35.0
Japan	39.7	33.6
Yugoslavia	28.4	30.9
North Korea	27.5	30.5
Hungary	27.8	27.4
Bulgaria	29.3	27.0
Total (est.)	2,809.4	2,821.7

Copper (mine) (Thousands of metric tons)

	1970	1971
United States	1,560.0	1,381.0
Chile	710.7	718.0
Canada	610.3	653.1
Zambia	684.1	652.0
USSR[2,4]	570.0	620.0
Zaïre	385.7	407.0
Peru	220.2	213.0
Philippines	160.3	208.3
Australia	157.8	177.0
South Africa	149.2	157.5
Japan	119.5	121.0
China[2]	100.0	100.0
Yugoslavia	90.8	94.4
Poland[2]	72.0	90.0
Mexico	61.0	63.2
Bulgaria	43.1	45.0
S. West Africa	31.4	32.0
Rhodesia	26.5	29.3
Finland	30.9	28.5
Sweden	26.3	27.5
Norway	19.9	22.5
Turkey	27.2	19.4
Cyprus	18.2	18.6
Uganda	19.2	17.1
Total (est.)	6,017.7	6,049.6

Diamonds (Thousands of carats)

	1970	1971
Zaïre	14,087	[2]13,700
USSR[2]	7,850	8,800
South Africa	8,112	7,031
Ghana	2,550	2,562
Angola	2,396	[2]2,167
Sierra Leone	1,955	1,935
S. West Africa	1,865	[2]1,900
Tanzania	708	[3]803
Liberia[3]	[3]812	739
Venezuela[2]	500	[2]500
Central African Republic	482	467
Total (est.)	42,586	42,189

Fluorspar (Thousands of metric tons)

	1970	1971
Mexico	978.5	1,181.0
Thailand	318.2	427.3
USSR[2]	408.2	417.3
Spain	341.7	399.9
France	290.3	299.4
Italy	289.3	291.0
China[2]	272.2	254.0
United States	244.2	247.0
United Kingdom	193.3	244.9
South Africa	173.0	239.0
Canada	124.1	72.6
Total (est.)	4,170.3	4,638.0

Gas (natural) (Billions of cubic feet)

	1970	1971
United States	23,786.5	24,104.0
USSR[2]	7,520.0	7,900.0
Canada	2,624.2	2,825.3
Venezuela	1,710.2	1,680.3
Netherlands	1,118.4	1,546.7
Iran	1,094.2	1,305.2
Rumania	875.4	935.3
Saudi Arabia	710.9	[2]915.0
Mexico	665.0	633.4
Libya	683.9	556.5
Total (est.)	46,454.5	49,014.3

Gold (Millions of troy ounces)

	1970	1971
South Africa	32.16	31.39
USSR[2]	6.50	6.70
Canada	2.40	2.24
United States	1.74	1.50
Ghana	0.70	0.70
Australia	0.62	0.67
Philippines	0.60	0.64
Rhodesia[2]	0.50	0.50
Japan	0.26	0.25
Colombia	0.22	0.19
Zaïre	0.18	0.18
Brazil	0.18	0.16
Mexico	0.20	0.15
Total (est.)	47.53	46.51

Graphite (Thousands of metric tons)

	1970	1971
USSR[2]	75.3	79.8
North Korea[2]	75.3	75.3
South Korea	59.5	72.5
Mexico	55.6	50.9
China[2]	30.0	30.0
Austria	27.7	21.4
Malagasy	19.9	20.1
West Germany	16.4	[2]17.2
Norway	10.4	8.3
Total (est.)	386.8	389.3

Gypsum (Thousands of metric tons)

	1970	1971
United States	8,560.2	9,448.3
Canada	5,723.1	6,168.9
France	6,088.2	5,111.5
USSR	[2]4,717.4	[2]4,717.4
Spain	4,228.0	[2]4,200.3
United Kingdom	4,275.5	4,173.0
Italy[2]	3,300.0	[2]3,501.7
Iran	2,100.0	[2]2,250.0
West Germany	1,473.0	1,593.3
Mexico	1,290.9	1,298.2
India	920.5	1,070.0
Australia	845.4	[2]919.8
Poland[2]	850.0	850.0
Austria	629.8	593.7
China[2]	550.0	550.0
Japan	538.8	535.9
Total (est.)	51,930.9	53,125.5

Iron Ore (Millions of metric tons)

	1970	1971
USSR	194.2	203.0
United States	91.2	82.1
Australia	51.2	62.1
France	56.8	55.9
China[2]	43.7	54.9
Canada	47.5	44.0
Brazil[2]	40.2	42.7
Sweden	31.8	33.3
India	31.4	32.3
Total (est.)	766.6	785.8

Iron (pig) excluding ferroalloys (Millions of metric tons)

	1970	1971
USSR	84.81	[2]88.30
United States	83.65	73.83
Japan	68.05	72.75
West Germany[5]	33.38	29.78
China[6]	22.00	27.00
France	18.74	17.90
United Kingdom	17.51	15.26
Belgium	10.84	10.40
Italy	8.33	8.54
Czechoslovakia[7]	7.55	7.96
Canada	8.24	7.88
Poland	6.85	[2]7.30
India	7.03	6.56
Australia	6.15	[2]6.13
Spain	4.17	4.83
Brazil	4.20	4.74

WORLD PRODUCTION OF MAJOR MINERALS[1] (Continued)

Iron (pig) (cont'd) (Millions of metric tons)

	1970	1971
Luxembourg	4.81	4.59
Rumania	4.21	4.38
South Africa	3.92	[2]4.01
Netherlands	3.59	3.76
Austria	2.96	2.85
Sweden	2.79	2.76
North Korea[2],[6]	2.40	2.50
Mexico	2.26	2.36
East Germany	1.99	2.03
Total (est.)	431.81	430.12

Lead (smelter) (Thousands of metric tons)

	1970	1971
United States	604.8	589.7
USSR[2]	440.0	450.0
Australia	352.6	323.6
Japan	209.0	215.1
Canada	185.6	156.6
Mexico	150.3	136.1
France	119.9	108.3
Bulgaria	98.6	[2]99.8
China[2]	99.8	99.8
Yugoslavia	97.4	99.1
West Germany	112.4	94.9
Belgium	89.4	80.2
Spain	68.7	72.1
Peru	72.0	67.1
North Korea[2]	54.4	63.5
Poland	54.5	60.2
S. West Africa	70.1	58.8
Italy	54.3	48.4
Argentina	38.1	43.5
United Kingdom	43.8	38.6
Rumania[2]	36.3	36.3
Sweden	40.6	32.2
Zambia	27.3	27.7
East Germany[2]	24.5	23.6
Morocco	24.9	18.7
Total (est.)	3,286.1	3,168.1

Magnesium (Thousands of metric tons)

	1970	1971
United States	101.61	112.02
USSR[2]	49.90	51.71
Norway	35.34	36.46
Japan	10.34	9.69
Italy	7.58	[2]7.98
Canada	9.39	6.58
France	4.64	[2]4.72
Total (est.)	222.56	232.97

Manganese Ore (Thousands of metric tons)

	1970	1971
USSR[2]	6,841.1	6,985.3
South Africa	2,679.5	3,236.5
Brazil	1,878.8	2,601.8
Gabon	1,453.0	1,868.6
India	1,651.0	1,779.0
Australia	751.1	1,075.9
China[2]	997.9	997.9
Ghana	405.4	598.6
Zaïre	346.9	387.4
Japan	270.4	285.0
Mexico	273.9	266.9
Hungary	168.8	169.6
Rumania[2]	127.0	127.0
Morocco	112.4	101.5
Italy	50.1	30.6
Total (est.)	18,219.9	20,692.0

Mercury (Thousands of flasks)

	1970	1971
Spain	45.54	67.53
USSR[2]	48.00	50.00
Italy	44.38	42.67
Mexico	30.27	35.39
China[2]	20.00	20.00
Canada	24.40	[2]18.00
United States	27.30	17.63
Yugoslavia	15.46	15.56
Turkey	8.59	[2]9.50
Japan	5.17	[2]5.70
Philippines	4.65	5.02
Peru	3.13	[2]1.80
Total (est.)	283.82	305.72

Molybdenum (Thousands of metric tons)

	1970	1971
United States	50.5	49.7
Canada	15.3	12.8
USSR[2]	7.7	8.0
Chile	5.7	6.3
China[2]	1.5	[8]N.A.
Total (est.)	80.7	78.5

Nickel (Thousands of metric tons)

	1970	1971
Canada	277.5	266.7
USSR[2]	108.9	117.9
New Caledonia	105.4	102.3
Cuba[2]	35.2	36.3

Nickel (cont'd) (Thousands of metric tons)

	1970	1971
Australia	28.9	[2]30.8
Indonesia	18.0	27.0
United States	14.1	14.2
South Africa	11.6	12.8
Total (est.)	629.7	640.5

Petroleum, Crude (Millions of barrels)

	1970	1971
United States	3,517.5	3,453.9
USSR	2,594.6	2,778.3
Saudi Arabia	1,387.3	1,741.5
Iran	1,397.5	1,661.9
Venezuela	1,353.4	1,295.4
Kuwait	1,090.0	1,166.9
Libya	1,209.3	1,007.7
Iraq	569.7	624.3
Nigeria	395.8	558.4
Canada	461.2	495.7
Trucial States	283.5	386.7
Indonesia	311.6	325.7
Algeria	371.8	279.6
China[2]	146.0	186.2
Qatar	132.5	156.9
Mexico	156.5	155.9
Argentina	143.4	154.5
Oman	121.2	107.4
Total (est.)	16,689.6	17,563.2

Phosphate (Thousands of metric tons)

	1970	1971
United States	35,143	35,277
USSR (all forms)	20,808	21,650
Morocco	11,400	12,008
Tunisia	3,016	3,162
Nauru Island[3]	2,114	[2]2,087
South Africa	1,685	1,729
Togo	1,508	1,715
Senegal	1,129	1,545
China[2]	1,179	1,179
North Vietnam (all forms)[2]	1,048	1,143
Christmas Island[3]	1,072	1,089
Israel	1,161	765
UAR	584	[2]744
Jordan	1,200	650
Total (est.)	85,709	87,514

Potash[9] (Thousands of metric tons)

	1970	1971
USSR[2]	4,450	5,350
Canada	3,103	3,513
West Germany	2,645	2,915
East Germany	2,419	[2]2,449
United States	2,476	2,346
France	1,904	[2]1,905
Total (est.)	18,521	20,066

Pyrite[10] (Thousands of metric tons)

	1970	1971
USSR[2]	4,000	2,464
Spain	2,736	2,429
Japan	2,641	2,363
China[2]	2,000	2,000
Italy	1,568	1,518
Finland	963	861
Rumania[2]	807	840
Cyprus	930	781
Norway	747	781
South Africa	868	750
Sweden	575	663
West Germany	554	[2]554
North Korea[2]	500	500
Total (est.)	22,225	19,918

Salt (Millions of metric tons)

	1970	1971
United States	41.60	39.99
China[2]	15.97	14.97
USSR[2]	12.97	12.97
United Kingdom	9.19	[2]9.25
West Germany	10.45	8.41
France	5.48	6.55
India	5.59	5.79
Canada	4.86	4.84
Italy	4.37	[2]4.45
Mexico	4.15	4.36
Netherlands	2.87	3.17
Australia	3.07	[2]3.08
Poland	2.90	2.96
Rumania	2.26	[2]2.27
East Germany	2.18	[2]2.18
Total (est.)	145.50	142.67

Silver (Millions of troy ounces)

	1970	1971
Canada	44.25	45.95
United States	45.01	41.56
USSR[2]	38.00	39.00
Peru	39.84	38.40
Mexico	42.84	36.66
Australia	25.99	21.62
Japan	10.80	11.54
Bolivia	6.82	[2]6.80
Chile	2.39	5.36

Silver (cont'd) (Millions of troy ounces)

	1970	1971
East Germany[2]	4.80	5.00
Sweden	6.11	4.82
Honduras	3.82	3.64
South Africa	3.53	3.38
Yugoslavia	3.42	3.35
Ireland	2.17	[2]2.20
Argentina	2.05	[2]2.05
France	2.28	[2]2.00
Philippines	1.70	1.94
West Germany	1.77	1.80
Zaïre	1.71	1.80
Spain[2]	1.64	1.64
Total (est.)	303.90	294.71

Sulfur (elemental) (Millions of metric tons)

	1970	1971
United States (all forms)	8.67	8.75
Canada (recovered)	4.41	4.89
Poland (Frasch, ore)[2]	2.71	2.82
France (recovered)	1.73	1.81
USSR (all forms)[2]	1.60	1.70
Mexico (all forms)	1.38	1.27
Total (all forms) (est.)	22.10	22.88

Tin (mine) (Thousands of long tons)

	1970	1971
Malaysia	72.6	74.2
USSR[2]	27.0	28.0
Bolivia	28.9	27.4
Thailand	21.4	21.3
China[2]	20.0	20.0
Indonesia	18.8	19.4
Australia	9.4	9.4
Nigeria	7.8	7.0
Zaïre	6.3	[2]6.4
Total (est.)	229.4	229.5

Titanium (ilmenite) (Thousands of metric tons)

	1970	1971
Australia	889.9	814.8
Canada	766.3	775.3
Norway	579.0	641.6
United States	787.4	619.6
Malaysia[3]	192.5	156.0
Finland	151.0	139.5
Total (est.)	3,588.6	3,375.6

(rutile)

	1970	1971
Australia	368.1	366.7
Sierra Leone	44.1	5.2
Total (est.)	417.2	377.8

Tungsten[11] (Metric tons)

	1970	1971
China[2]	7,983	7,983
USSR[2]	6,713	6,985
United States	3,676	3,130
Thailand	711	2,508
North Korea[2]	2,140	2,140
South Korea	2,070	2,059
Bolivia	1,845	1,850
Canada	1,387	1,802
Australia	1,265	1,547
Brazil	1,156	1,398
Portugal	1,425	1,386
Peru	804	770
Japan	677	730
Total (est.)	33,581	36,618

Uranium Oxide (Metric tons)

	1970	1971
United States	11,583	11,709
South Africa	3,737	3,800
Canada	3,723	3,638
France	1,582	1,521
Gabon	377	545
Niger	38	506
Australia[2]	299	272
Total (est.)[12]	21,644	22,300

Zinc (smelter) (Thousands of metric tons)

	1970	1971
United States	796.3	695.3
USSR[2]	610.0	650.5
Japan	676.2	601.1
Canada	417.9	372.0
Australia	260.6	258.7
Poland	209.0	220.0
France	223.7	218.7
Belgium	241.2	206.8
Italy	142.1	138.9
West Germany	150.2	126.4
United Kingdom	146.6	116.5
China[2]	99.8	99.8
North Korea[2]	89.8	99.8
Spain	89.2	89.3
Mexico	80.7	77.9
Bulgaria	76.1	76.0
Total (est.)	4,879.5	4,611.0

[1] Output of countries not individually listed and estimates for other countries are included in world totals. [2] Estimated. [3] Exports. [4] Smelter production. [5] Includes blast furnace ferroalloys except ferromanganese and spiegeleisen. [6] Includes ferroalloys. [7] Includes blast furnace ferroalloys. [8] Not available. [9] Marketable in equivalent K₂O. [10] Gross weight. [11] Contained tungsten (W basis). [12] Excludes all socialist bloc countries.

(*Continued from page 469*)
expectations that several large new iron mines would commence development in Australia and possibly in Africa by early 1974.

The abnormally high chromite prices of recent years were relieved in 1972 when the United States resumed imports from Rhodesia despite sanctions by the United Nations. Most Rhodesian output had been reaching the world market by devious routes anyway. The price of chromite went from $72 to $55 per ton. Molybdenum output fell in 1971, and the low price and low demand in 1972 resulted in the closing of a number of marginal mines.

Nickel production increased in 1971 and probably in 1972. Little of the Canadian capacity that had been idled in 1970 was reactivated, but new lateritic production from the Pacific Basin area and the Dominican Republic entered the market in 1972. The price rose from $1.33 to $1.53 per pound by the middle of the year.

Nonferrous Metals. Aluminum output continued to grow in 1971, but prices remained weak through 1972. In May the list price of the metal was reduced from $0.27 to $0.25 per pound, but actual sales were at $0.22. Several planned new projects were postponed for a year or so, but by the end of 1972, much North American capacity that had been idled in 1970–71 was back at work, and output was at 90% of capacity. The move toward use of minerals other than bauxite as ores of aluminum gained momentum in Mexico and the United States, where development of alunite deposits was under way.

The New York price for copper remained weak in 1972, fluctuating around the level of $0.50 per pound throughout the year. The big new mine on Bougainville Island in the Solomons came into production, and plans to develop new mines in Panama, Iran, Peru, and Zaïre proceeded apace. Property in Zaïre contains upward of 20 million tons of ore averaging over 6% copper. In contrast, the average grade of U. S. copper ore is only 0.5%

Lead remained in the doldrums, in part because of its uncertain future use in gasoline. The price strengthened briefly in mid-1972, but then fell back to $0.15 per pound. Zinc was in somewhat short supply because of the closure of seven zinc smelters in the United States since 1970 for environmental reasons. The price of the metal rose one cent to $0.18 in May, but a number of sales involved premiums of two to three cents per pound.

Other Metals and Minerals. The fertilizer industry remained uncertain in 1972. Sulfur prices continued to be low, and several Frasch producers ceased operations because of the increasing output of cheap sulfur recovered from sour-gas and antipollution programs. The Saskatchewan government's prorationing program for potash production maintained prices and output during the year, but the basic condition of surplus capacity will last out the decade. The phosphate market strengthened, and one or two new projects were announced.

The demand for, and hence the price of, uranium for nuclear power plants is increasing, and a number of new mines are approaching development. A large, high-grade uranium area has been discovered in northwestern Australia and, possibly, another in central Africa. Several lower-grade deposits are under development in the United States and Canada.

FRANK H. SKELDING
Director of Corporate Planning
Fluor Utah, Inc.

U. S. MINING TECHNOLOGY

Mining research in the United States in 1972 was strongly influenced by the psychological impact of the death of more than 90 miners in Idaho's Sunshine silver mine. (See IDAHO.) Other influences were the nagging uncertainty caused by the continued withdrawal of federal lands from mineral privileges, the pyramiding costs generated by public and legislative demands for environmental protection and for new restrictions on strip and open-pit mining, and the resulting decline in economically recoverable domestic mineral and fuel reserves. The net effect was that most available industrial research and development money went to cover mine safety and environmental protection costs.

New Devices for Miners. Many devices for improving the health, working conditions, and safety of miners were evaluated by mining and related companies. Thus mufflers were adapted to pneumatic equipment to reduce noise, and electronic "ear muffs" and individual audio dosimeters, devices for measuring and subduing noise, were developed. Many kinds of one-man oxygen supply packs of lunchbox size for emergency use were tested, as were miniature radio transmitters and sound generators that would permit trapped miners to send signals through several feet of rock. Other developments included glare-reduction systems using polarized light, personal air shields for protection against mine dust, self-advancing roof supports, and fully lined tunnels and shafts for unstable ground. Fire control systems—generally of the water-spray type—became standard on most underground equipment, and in an effort to reduce the possibility of spontaneous combustion in coal mines, renewed interest was shown in the technique of growing microorganisms on rock surfaces in the mines.

Environmental Problems. One major concern for clean-air regulations in 1972 was the removal of sulfur dioxide and other gases formed during the smelting of sulfide ores or the combustion of sulfur-rich coal and petroleum. Installation of million-dollar prototype sulfuric acid and liquid sulfur dioxide plants began at several facilities, and the feasibility of obtaining elemental sulfur from stack emissions through a citrate reaction process was actively investigated. The question remains as to whether these corrective measures will meet government regulations, and there is the further question as to whether an overabundance of recovered sulfur products will create new disposal problems.

Concern for environmental protection was also pursued with the development of improved ways for disposing of mine and mill rock wastes underground, renovating mine waste water, and selectively revegetating and fertilizing areas disturbed by strip and open-pit mines and other facilities. However, dams that had been built in West Virginia out of mined materials in order to let wastes settle out of mine wash water came under attack when one dam collapsed on February 26, killing 118 persons.

Rock Stabilization Techniques. The U. S. Bureau of Mines developed several improved methods for stabilizing rock faces. These included bolts secured in place by quick-setting polymers, hollow bolts swelled in place by explosives, bolts composed entirely of polymers and fiberglass threads and formed right in the drill holes, and nonrupturing bolts that stretch like wire. Tunnel and shaft stabilization is being improved by "shotcrete" liners—that

is, concrete impregnated with fiber glass or other fibrous materials and sprayed on rock surfaces. The Bureau also found better methods for recognizing potential rock failures, such as the forcing of air into selected drill holes so that the air passes along rock fractures and is recovered and measured in adjoining holes. The monitoring device notes any changes in rate of air flow if the rock fractures start to open, thus providing an advance warning of impending rockfalls. Also tested was a rock-bolt mount that senses the early movement of rock masses held by the bolt.

Education. The Federal Mine Health and Safety Academy was opened in Beckley, W. Va., in July, as a step toward helping the mining industry to conform to government regulations. The two-year institution will train 600 mine inspectors annually.

JOHN G. BOND, *Senior Geologist*
Idaho Bureau of Mines and Geology

MINNESOTA

Minnesota voters on Nov. 7, 1972, gave a new look to the Legislature, traditionally all-white, male, and dominated by the Conservative faction. During the year the Twin Cities lost one subject of controversy when flamboyant "supermayor" Charles McCarty was defeated in his bid for reelection in St. Paul, and it gained another with the completion of the 57-story Investors Diversified Services tower, which dramatically changed the Minneapolis skyline.

Elections. For the first time in the state's history, Liberal (Democratic-oriented) majorities were elected to both houses of the Legislature. The first black ever and the first woman in modern times won seats in the Senate, and six women and one black were elected to the House. The legislators, almost 40% of whom will be serving first terms, ran in districts that a judicial panel had reapportioned to reflect population shifts in the 1960's. The panel at first had drastically reduced the number of legislators. When that plan was overturned by the U. S. Supreme Court on April 29, district lines were redrawn with only one house seat eliminated. Voters approved a constitutional amendment permitting the Legislature to hold annual sessions.

Minnesota followed the national trend in giving its 10 electoral votes to President Nixon (897,569 popular votes to 802,346 for Senator McGovern), but it reelected Democratic Sen. Walter F. Mondale by a wide margin. All incumbent congressmen, 4 Democrats and 4 Republicans, were also reelected.

On April 25, Democrat-Farmer-Laborite Lawrence Cohen was elected mayor of St. Paul, the first to serve under a new "strong-mayor" charter.

Floods. Duluth and communities on the Mississippi, Minnesota, and Red rivers suffered an estimated $134 million in flood damage during the year. Heavy spring rains inundated 1½ million acres of cropland in 23 western counties. In July flash floods struck 11 counties in central Minnesota, while in August and again in September torrential rains fell on Duluth.

Economy. It was predicted that the income of Minnesota farmers would reach an all-time high in 1972, although still only about 81% of nonfarm income. High livestock and soybean prices were an important factor. A record harvest of soybeans (86.2 million bushels) was forecast, but yields for other crops—many hard hit by the floods—were down from 1971.

Two bitter strikes marked the labor scene. A strike-lockout that began on June 12 in the basic trades idled more than 100,000 workers for 40 days at 'the height of the construction season. A pilots' strike severely curtailed Northwest Airlines flights from June 30 to October 2.

Education. Two new medical schools opened their doors in 1972, joining one established in 1888 at the University of Minnesota in Minneapolis: the Mayo Medical School at Rochester and the School of Medicine on the Duluth campus of the university. Plans were under way to implement an Area Health Education Center at St. Cloud, funded by a $3.4 million federal grant. In St. Paul the publicly supported Minnesota Metropolitan State College inaugurated its experimental program with approximately 250 students.

Prehistory. University of Minnesota scientists announced on July 9 a preliminary investigation of human bones and artifacts discovered in the Boundary Waters Canoe Area that could be among the oldest ever found in North America.

Indian Relations. Tension in Minnesota's resort area between whites and Indians came to a climax in May during the convention of the American Indian Movement at Cass Lake, but violence was avoided. On June 20 settlement of a three-year legal dispute between the state and the Leech Lake Indian Reservation gave the Indians greater control over ricing, fishing, and hunting rights.

JEANNE SINNEN
University of Minnesota Press

——————— **MISSISSIPPI · Information Highlights** ———————

Area: 47,716 square miles (123,584 sq km).
Population (1970 census): 2,216,912. *Density,* 47 per sq mi.
Chief Cities (1970 census): Jackson, the capital, 153,968; Biloxi, 48,486; Meridian, 45,083; Gulfport, 40,791; Greenville, 39,648; Hattiesburg, 38,277; Pascagoula, 27,264.
Government (1972): *Chief Officers*—governor, William L. Waller (D); lt. gov., William Winter (D); secy. of state, Heber A. Ladner (D); atty. gen., A. F. Summer (D); treas., Brad Dye (D); supt. of public education, Garvin Johnston; chief justice, Robert G. Gillespie. *Legislature*—Senate, 52 members (50 Democrats, 2 Republicans); House of Representatives, 122 members (119 D, 2 R, 1 independent).
Education (1971–72): *Enrollment*—public elementary schools, 307,631 pupils, 12,612 teachers; public secondary, 221,735 pupils, 10,237 teachers; nonpublic schools (1970–71), 67,327 pupils, 1,040 teachers; college and university, 74,000 students. *Public school expenditures,* $312,464,000 ($634 per pupil). *Average teacher's salary,* $6,716.
State Finances (fiscal year 1970): *Revenues,* $935,458,000 (5% general sales tax and gross receipts taxes, $227,930,000; motor fuel tax, $88,502,000; federal funds, $265,995,000). *Expenditures,* $928,083,000 (education, $345,217,000; health, welfare, and safety, $123,275,000; highways, $143,821,000). *State debt,* $455,186,000 (June 30, 1970).
Personal Income (1971): $6,157,000,000; per capita, $2,766.
Public Assistance (1971): $140,233,000. *Average monthly payments* (Dec. 1971)—old-age assistance, $58.48; aid to families with dependent children, $55.48.
Labor Force: *Nonagricultural wage and salary earners* (July 1972), 609,500. *Average annual employment* (1971)—manufacturing, 188,000; trade, 109,000; government, 133,000; services, 71,000. *Insured unemployed* (Aug. 1972)—5,200 (1.3%).
Manufacturing (1970): *Value added by manufacture,* $2,061,300,000. Lumber and wood products, $233,000,000; apparel and other textile products, $224,300,000; food and kindred products, $200,300,000; electrical equipment and supplies, $172,000,000; transportation equipment, $167,200,000; chemicals and allied products, $166,700,000.
Agriculture (1970): *Cash farm income,* $1,037,857,000 (livestock, $513,237,000; crops, $378,120,000; government payments, $146,500,000). *Chief crops* (in order of value, 1971) —Cotton lint (ranks 2d among the states), soybeans, cottonseed (ranks 1st), hay.
Mining (1970): *Production value,* $247,598,000 (ranks 26th among the states). *Chief minerals*—Petroleum, $193,402,000; natural gas, $23,139,000; sand and gravel, $11,141,000; clays, $8,055,000.
Fisheries (1971): *Commercial catch,* 397,605,000 pounds ($13,380,000). *Leading species by value:* Menhaden, $4,823,000; shrimp, $4,233,000; red snapper, $886,000; oysters, $472,000.
Transportation: *Roads* (1971), 66,782 miles (107,472 km); *motor vehicles* (1971), 1,117,311; *railroads* (1971), 3,653 miles (5,879 km); *public airports* (1972), 71.
Communications: *Telephones* (1972), 955,200; *television stations* (1971), 10; *radio stations* (1971), 138; *newspapers* (1972), 21 (daily circulation, 338,000).

MISSISSIPPI

Of particular interest in Mississippi in 1972 were the election of two Republican congressmen and the attempt of the newly inaugurated Democratic governor, William L. Waller, to effect a compromise between the two factions of his party. As usual, the Legislature commanded much attention.

Legislature. With two fifths of its members serving for the first time, the 1972 Legislature proved to be particularly hardworking. Its chief accomplishment was approval of a $600 million highway-construction program to be financed by increased taxes on cigarettes, gasoline, and trucks. The program is the largest public works project ever authorized by the state.

Other significant actions included realigning the state's congressional districts to conform with the 1970 census, liberalizing voting provisions to permit absentee balloting by students and other persons, liberalizing existing drug-control statutes, and authorizing the state college board to establish degree-granting branches of colleges and universities. Major reorganization of the executive department failed to win legislative approval, as did proposals for "no-fault" automobile insurance and public kindergartens.

Preelection Politics. Governor Waller's efforts to fashion a unified Democratic party within the state in the election year of 1972 met with failure. Both the "regular" Democrats, who controlled the state party machinery, and the "loyalist" Democrats, who had the recognition of the national party, chose delegates to the Democratic National Convention. Although the regulars lost their bid for seats, they nonetheless certified a slate of electors pledged to the national ticket. The governor and the regular party organization, however, did not campaign for their election. State Republicans sent a strong Nixon delegation to the Republican National Convention.

Elections. In the November presidential election, Mississippi voted Republican for only the second time since Reconstruction; and, for the first time since 1944, the state was on the side of the winning candidate. President Nixon received 78% of the nearly 650,000 votes cast, while his Democratic opponent, Sen. George McGovern, received 20% and carried only 3 of the state's 82 counties. The remaining vote went primarily to American party nominee John Schmitz.

Democratic incumbent Sen. James O. Eastland won reelection to an unprecedented 6th term in the U. S. Senate by defeating Gil Carmichael, the first Mississippi Republican to be nominated in a statewide primary election. In capturing 58% of the vote, the recently named president *pro tempore* of the Senate did less well than expected against a political newcomer who had campaigned without the active support of the Nixon administration. Two independents also entered the race but received only 3% of the vote.

Republicans demonstrated surprising strength in congressional contests as first-time candidates. Thad Cochran and Trent Lott, in the 4th and 5th districts, won two of the three seats that had been vacated by veteran Democrats. Democrat David Bowen, who also was seeking office for the first time, won in the 2d district. In the 1st and 3d districts Democrats Jamie Whitten and G. V. Montgomery were reelected without opposition.

Funding Dispute. Charging payment of excessive salaries, Governor Waller in June and August vetoed Office of Economic Opportunity grants totaling nearly $8 million for two programs providing health care services primarily to black indigents in the Mound Bayou and Jackson areas. However, the governor's vetoes later were overridden by federal officials.

Other Events. In January, the 1971 legislative reapportionment plan that had been authored by a three-judge federal panel was rejected by the U. S. Supreme Court insofar as future elections are concerned.

On October 16, U. S. District Judge William C. Keady ordered the governor and state penitentiary board to formulate a long-range plan for ending unconstitutional practices and bad conditions at Parchman, the state's 21,000-acre prison farm. Needed reforms include better housing and food and an end to corporal punishment and to the use of "trusty" inmates as guards.

Environmentalists in Mississippi continued to lose rounds in their legal battle to prevent construction of the Tennessee-Tombigbee Waterway, a portion of which is to flow through northeastern Mississippi.

In 1972, for the first time in Mississippi's history, the governor appointed blacks to several state policy-making boards.

DANA B. BRAMMER
University of Mississippi

——————— MISSOURI • Information Highlights ———————

Area: 69,686 square miles (180,487 sq km).
Population (1970 census): 4,677,399. *Density:* 69 per sq mi.
Chief Cities (1970 census): Jefferson City, the capital, 32,407; St. Louis, 622,236; Kansas City, 507,330; Springfield, 120,096; Independence, 111,630.
Government (1972): *Chief Officers*—governor, Warren E. Hearnes (D); lt. gov., William S. Morris (D); secy. of state, James C. Kirkpatrick (D); atty. gen., John C. Danforth (R); treas., William E. Robinson (D); commissioner, board of education, Arthur L. Mallory; chief justice, James A. Finch, Jr. *General Assembly*—Senate, 34 members (25 Democrats, 9 Republicans); House of Representatives, 163 members (112 D, 51 R).
Education (1971–72): *Enrollment*—public elementary schools, 778,184 pupils; 30,491 teachers; public secondary, 300,015 pupils; 15,007 teachers; nonpublic schools (1970–71), 141,567 pupils; 6,700 teachers; college and university, 187,000 students. *Public school expenditures,* $745,000,000 ($812 per pupil). *Average teacher's salary,* $9,156.
State Finances (fiscal year 1970): *Revenues,* $1,480,279,000 (3% general sales tax and gross receipts taxes, $344,799,000; motor fuel tax, $115,359,000; federal funds, $407,292,000). *Expenditures,* $1,502,620,000 (education, $573,467,000; health, welfare, and safety, $291,136,000; highways, $313,464,000). *State debt,* $141,922,000 (June 30, 1970).
Personal Income (1971): $18,413,000,000; per capita, $3,877.
Public Assistance (1971): $257,534,000. *Average monthly payments* (Dec. 1971)—old-age assistance, $75.85; aid to families with dependent children, $109.54.
Labor Force: *Nonagricultural wage and salary earners* (July 1972), 1,621,600. *Average annual employment* (1971)—manufacturing, 424,000; trade, 371,000; government, 292,000; services, 262,000. *Insured unemployed* (Aug. 1972)—39,000 (3.3%).
Manufacturing (1970): *Value added by manufacture,* $6,747,100,000. Transportation equipment, $1,334,100,000; food and kindred products, $939,700,000; chemicals and allied products, $581,400,000; printing and publishing, $555,800,000; electrical equipment and supplies, $479,600,000; fabricated metal products, $443,400,000.
Agriculture (1970): *Cash farm income,* $1,727,164,000 (livestock, $1,138,831,000; crops, $434,414,000; government payments, $153,919,000). *Chief crops* (in order of value, 1971)—Corn, soybeans, hay, cotton lint.
Mining (1970): *Production value,* $395,387,000 (ranks 17th among the states). *Chief minerals*—Lead, $137,064,000; cement, $73,297,000; stone, $59,456,000; iron ore, $36,238,000.
Transportation: *Roads* (1971), 115,261 miles (185,490 km); *motor vehicles* (1971) 2,407,687; *railroads* (1971), 6,351 miles (10,220 km); *public airports* (1972), 102.
Communications: *Telephones* (1972), 2,857,100; *television stations* (1971), 23; *radio stations* (1971), 49; *newspapers* (1972), 54 (daily circulation, 1,789,000).

MISSOURI

The election of the first Republican governor in 32 years highlighted news events in Missouri during 1972. Voters also approved an extensive reorganization of the state government and a tax relief package.

Elections. Republican State Auditor Christopher S. (Kit) Bond, capitalizing on audits showing inefficiency in various state departments, was elected governor in a hard-fought contest with Democrat Edward L. Dowd, a former circuit attorney of St. Louis. Bond, who at age 33 became the state's youngest governor, easily won the Republican primary in August and then defeated Dowd by nearly 190,000 votes. He promised to eliminate the spoils system for hiring state employees and in selecting banks for state deposits. Dowd had been nominated in a close four-man primary fight that left its scars for the general election. Bond, a native of Mexico, Mo., is a former assistant attorney general.

Republicans won two other state offices and Democrats retained two. State Rep. William C. Phelps of Kansas City rode Bond's coattails to a narrow victory over Democratic State Rep. Jack Schramm of University City. Attorney General John C. Danforth, a Republican, was the highest vote getter in winning reelection. He was ineligible to run for governor because he failed to meet the state's 10-year residency requirement. Bond, who practiced law in Georgia and Washington, D. C., in the 1960s, was challenged on the same grounds, but withstood a state supreme court test. Secretary of

State James C. Kirkpatrick won reelection, and former state Rep. James I. Spainhower was elected treasurer to give the Democrats two state officers.

Eight Democratic incumbents were joined by Jerry Litton of Chillicothe, a Democrat, and Gene Taylor of Sarcoxie, a Republican, in the U. S. House. Litton and Taylor replace W. R. Hull (Dem.) and Durwood Hall (Rep.), who retired.

In the presidential balloting, Richard Nixon won 63% of the vote in defeating the Democratic candidate, Sen. George McGovern. The latter's campaign in the state was damaged when Sen. Thomas Eagleton of Missouri was dropped as the vice presidential candidate. He had revealed a history of electric shock treatments for depression. See POLITICAL PARTIES.

State Government. A constitutional amendment on governmental reorganization received bipartisan support and was easily approved in August. The amendment calls for reducing 87 state agencies to 14 cabinet-like departments. Petition drives for four other proposed constitutional amendments failed when it was ruled that none had sufficient signatures to place them on the ballot.

Legislation. A statewide public defender system and a state fair housing law were two of the legislature's most notable achievements. It also increased junior college aid and established a scholarship program for college students. A two-cent increase in the gasoline tax was approved and earmarked for highway purposes.

Tax Reform. A constitutional amendment on tax reform was the most popular issue on the November ballot. Although its passage will cost the state nearly $60 million a year in lost revenue, it will do away with two very unpopular nuisance taxes—those on household goods and bank deposits —and will allow the legislature to grant tax relief to the elderly.

Death of Former President. Missourians mourned the death on Dec. 26, 1972, of Harry S. Truman, 33d President of the United States. (See TRUMAN.)
RONALD D. WILLNOW
The St. Louis "Post-Dispatch"

MONGOLIA

In 1972, as before, Mongolia remained a loyal ally of the USSR and was rewarded by the highest per capita economic aid that the Soviet Union has ever granted to any nation. Largely because of this aid, Mongolian industrial output increased 8.6% over the 1971 level, while industrial wages registered an 11% gain. During the year, Mongolian relations with Communist China remained hostile.

Domestic Affairs. President Zhamsarangin Sambu died in May. In June the Great People's Khural (national legislature) appointed Vice Premier Sonomyn Lubsan as acting president. He was head of the Mongolian-Soviet Friendship Association and had served as ambassador to both Communist China and the USSR.

In June the Central Committee of the Mongolian People's Revolutionary (Communist) party abolished all party control commissions (party courts) and placed all control work under a governmental committee with ministerial rank.

Foreign Affairs. In February, Mongolia and Japan established diplomatic relations. Mongolian Premier Yumzhagiyn Tsedenbal attended a meeting of Soviet and East European Communist leaders in

─────── MONGOLIA · Information Highlights ───────

Official Name: Mongolian People's Republic.
Area: 604,248 square miles (1,565,000 sq km).
Population (1972 est.): 1,400,000. *Density,* 2.6 per square mile (1 per sq km). *Annual rate of increase,* 3.1%.
Chief Cities: Ulan Bator, the capital, 250,000 (1967 est.); Darkhan, 25,000 (1968 est.).
Government: *Head of state,* Sonomyn Lubsan, acting president (appointed June 1972). *Head of government,* Yumzhagiyn Tsedenbal, premier and first secretary of the Communist party (took office Jan. 1952). *Legislature* (unicameral)—Great People's Khural, 287 members.
Language: Khalkha Mongolian (official).
Education: *School enrollment* (1969)—primary, 137,420; secondary, 84,837; technical/vocational, 8,254; university/higher, 7,226.
Monetary Unit: Tugrik (3.68 tugriks equal U. S.$1, June 1972).
Manufacturing (major products): Processed foods, leather goods.
Major Agricultural Products: Wheat, barley, vegetables, livestock (sheep, horses, camels, cattle, goats, yaks).
Major Minerals: Lignite, coal, salt.
Foreign Trade: *Chief exports*—Live animals; hides, skins, and furs; meat; butter; wool and hair. *Chief imports*—Machinery; petroleum; cloth; building materials. *Chief trading partner*—USSR.
Transportation: *Railroads* (1970), 868 miles (1,397 km); *major national airline,* Air Mongol.
Communications: *Telephones* (1971), 19,547; *television stations* (1971), 1; *television sets* (1971), 600; *radios* (1970), 166,-000; *newspapers* (1970), 2 (daily circulation, 133,000).

the Crimea in July, and in September he conferred in Moscow with Chairman Leonid Brezhnev on "close coordination" of Soviet and Mongolian foreign policies.

Delegations from 56 countries attending a conference of Asian and African women, in Ulan Bator on August 14–18, approved the 1972 detente between the United States and the USSR. Mongolia is the headquarters for the Asian Buddhist Congress for Promotion of Peace, which met in Ceylon in April and condemned U. S. intervention in Vietnam and alleged Israeli aggression against the Arabs.

ELLSWORTH RAYMOND
New York University

MONTANA

A new constitution, reorganization of state government, continuity of Democratic party control, several economic shocks, increased strip mining, and a productive agricultural season highlighted events in Montana in 1972.

New Constitution. A constitutional convention wrote a 12,000-word document to replace the 1889 constitution and submitted it in the primary election on June 6. A multiple ballot first asked for approval of the constitution generally, which resulted in 116,415 votes for and 113,883 against. Three alternate choices within the constitution were also listed. First, the voters favored a bicameral form of legislature over a unicameral one. Second, the voters changed the former ban on any gambling by allowing the people or the legislature to authorize gambling. Third, the voters approved a continuation of the death penalty, with 147,023 for it and 77,749 against.

Since 237,600 persons voted on the various issues and only 116,414 voted for the main document, opponents alleged that it did not receive the required majority of those voting. Several groups brought suit to declare the constitution defeated. By a 3-to-2 vote, the supreme court held the constitution was approved. In an appeal, the court sustained its decision.

Government Reorganization. Retiring Gov. Forrest H. Anderson said his chief accomplishment was the reorganization of the executive branch of government. Under the Executive Reorganization Act of 1971, he had combined over 100 agencies into 19 departments, each operating under the general supervision of the governor.

Elections. In the November election, the state's electoral votes went to President Nixon. However, for the first time since 1938 the Democrats won control of both executive and legislative branches. Governor-elect Thomas L. Judge, a Democrat, will work with a Senate that is Democratic by 27–23 and a House that has a 54–46 Democratic margin. Sen. Lee Metcalf, Democrat, won reelection, as did Democrat John Melcher from the eastern 2d district. In the 1st district, Richard Shoup, Republican, also was returned.

Economy. Melvin Laird, secretary of defense, halted construction of a large antiballistic missile installation near Conrad on May 27. This move, which immediately followed the U. S.-Soviet agreement to limit antimissile systems, depressed the economy of the entire region. A strike on Northwest Airlines halted operations for 95 days after June 30, reducing travel drastically during the tourist season. The Public Service Commission granted the Montana Power Company an 11% increase in electric rates and a 19% increase in natural gas rates. A near-record wheat crop commanded increased prices following an agreement with the USSR to purchase American wheat. Strip mining of eastern Montana coal surged as companies mined enormous amounts of coal for Midwestern consumption.

MERRILL G. BURLINGAME
Montana State University

─────── MONTANA · Information Highlights ───────

Area: 147,138 square miles (381,087 sq km).
Population (1970 census): 694,409. *Density:* 5 per sq ml.
Chief Cities (1970 census): Helena, the capital, 22,730; Billings, 61,581; Great Falls, 60,091; Missoula, 29,497; Butte, 23,368; Bozeman, 18,670; Havre, 10,558; Kalispell, 10,526.
Government (1972): *Chief Officers*—governor, Forrest H. Anderson (D); lt. gov., Thomas L. Judge (D); secy. of state, Frank Murray (D); atty. gen., Robert L. Woodahl (R); treas., Alex B. Stephenson (R); supt. of public instruction, Dolores Colburg (D); chief justice, James T. Harrison. *Legislative Assembly*—Senate, 55 members (30 Democrats, 25 Republicans); House of Representatives, 104 members (50 D, 54 R).
Education (1971–72): *Enrollment*—public elementary schools, 105,711 pupils; 5,362 teachers; public secondary, 68,046 pupils; 3,604 teachers; nonpublic schools (1970–71), 11,422 pupils; 620 teachers; college and university, 31,000 students. *Public school expenditures,* $147,918,000 ($904 per pupil). *Average teacher's salary,* $8,931.
State Finances (fiscal year 1970): *Revenues,* $350,354,000 (total sales and gross receipts taxes, $48,211,000; motor fuel tax, $28,766,000; federal funds, $115,711,000). *Expenditures,* $343,105,000 (education, $101,892,000; health, welfare, and safety, $34,564,000; highways, $110,498,000). *State debt,* $81,786,000 (June 30, 1970).
Personal Income (1971): $2,463,000,000; per capita, $3,479.
Public Assistance (1971): $33,960,000. *Average monthly payments* (Dec. 1971)—old-age assistance, $63.92; aid to families with dependent children, $153.39.
Labor Force: *Nonagricultural wage and salary earners* (July 1972), 215,300. *Average annual employment* (1971)—manufacturing, 24,000; trade, 49,000; government, 54,000. *Insured unemployed* (Aug. 1972)—3,800 (2.9%).
Manufacturing (1969): *Value added by manufacture,* $359,-100,000. Lumber and wood products, $105,400,000; food and kindred products, $60,200,000; petroleum and coal products, $39,600,000; printing and publishing, $19,500,000; stone, clay, and glass products, $11,500,000.
Agriculture (1970): *Cash farm income,* $685,207,000 (livestock, $355,887,000; crops, $243,959,000; government payments, $85,361,000). *Chief crops* (in order of value, 1971)—Wheat (ranks 4th among the states), hay, barley (ranks 2d), sugar beets.
Mining (1971): *Production value,* $285,073,000 (ranks 22d among the states). *Chief minerals*—Petroleum, $104,128,-000; copper, $92,125,000; sand and gravel, $25,207,000.
Transportation: *Roads* (1971), 78,209 miles (125,970 km); *motor vehicles* (1971), 484,990; *railroads* (1971), 5,030 miles (8,095 km); *public airports* (1972), 117.
Communications: *Telephones* (1972), 376,100; *television stations* (1971), 12; *radio stations* (1971), 48; *newspapers* (1972), 14 (daily circulation, 191,000).

PAVILION is opened by Communist China at Montreal's annual Man and His World Exposition. The building, featuring China's cultural heritage, was formerly occupied by Nationalist China.

CANADIAN CONSULATE GENERAL, NEW YORK

MONTREAL

The government of the Montreal Urban Community (MUC), which is composed of delegates from the 29 municipalities on Montreal Island, had problems in 1972 in integrating its public services and approving its budget. The city of Montreal, which because of its large size has a majority representation in the MUC's executive committee, dominated the government, much to the distress of many of the smaller member communities. There were also problems of language which affected city restructuring and education, and there was much talk about the Summer Olympic Games of 1976.

Community Government. Lawrence Hanigan, backed by Mayor Jean Drapeau of Montreal, was elected executive chairman of the executive committee of the MUC on Feb. 16, 1972. Yves Ryan, mayor of Montreal North, became vice chairman. The election was held after the resignation of the first chairman, Lucien Saulnier, who had been appointed by the provincial government in 1970.

The newly elected government was confronted with numerous conflicts between the constituent communities. The budget was one of the principal sources of irritation. Estimates for the 1973 budget allowed for increases totaling $16 million, of which $13 million was earmarked for the police. This elicited vigorous opposition from several of the MUC mayors, who felt they would have to raise taxes to meet the higher costs. Police expenses would constitute two thirds of the total budget. Since the MUC police forces perform a certain number of functions that are more properly the responsibility of the province (such as the fight against terrorism), some members of the MUC demanded that the government of Quebec assume half the costs. At the end of October the smaller communities of the MUC joined in a battle against a plan to combine the island's police forces. They also opposed a united fire department.

The 29 municipalities that make up the actual territory of the MUC were to be regrouped into three or four cities. Members of the Hanigan committee, which is responsible for the restructuring, were grappling with the linguistic problem. The Quebec government wished to avoid at all costs the creation of linguistic blocs. As the total population of Montreal Island is about 70% French-speaking and 30% English-speaking, the future municipalities should follow those proportions approximately.

Education. Language was also a problem in the field of education. Due to a drop in enrollment, several French-language schools were forced to close in 1972, despite the protestations of the French-speaking citizens. The fall in enrollment was probably due to the exodus of French Canadians to the suburbs, a decline in the birthrate, and the anglicization of immigrants, encouraged by a 1969 school bill that has been a source of tension. Faced with the urgency of restructuring the educational system, the provincial government prepared a revised school bill to be presented to the Parliament in January 1973. If passed, as expected, the bill would regroup the existing 33 school boards into seven—five Catholic and two Protestant. A coordinating Council of Education to be created for Montreal Island would have the power to levy taxes and apportion revenues, and all commissioners would be elected.

Plans for Olympics. Plans to hold the Summer Olympic Games of 1976 in Montreal aroused great interest in 1972. In March, Roger Rousseau was named commissioner general of the Games. The fact that voters in Denver, Colo., defeated a referendum supporting the holding of the Winter Olympic Games of 1976 in that city made Montrealers realize that a similar referendum would have to be passed by the suburban communities around Montreal to authorize the financing of their Summer Olympics. The communities involved did not wish to be called upon at the last moment to come to Montreal's aid, as had happened with the metro (subway) and with Expo '67.

In anticipation of having the Olympics in Montreal, work on an extension of the city's transit system accelerated. A referendum was approved by the voters of the MUC to double the size of the metro. The extension of the central line alone was to add 9.3 miles to the already existing 13.7 miles.

Population. Twenty-five of Montreal's 38 districts suffered a decline in population between the national censuses of 1966 and 1971, and the city as a whole decreased from 1,222,255 inhabitants in 1966 to 1,214,352 in 1971. The population of the metropolitan area increased from 2,436,817 to 2,743,208, passing metropolitan Toronto which reached only 2,628,043 in 1971. There was, however, some reapportionment of area in Montreal between the two censuses.

ROBERT COMEAU
Université du Québec à Montréal

MOORE, Marianne. See LITERATURE.

MOROCCO

In August 1972 opposition to the regime of King Hassan II, ruler of Morocco since 1961, reached its second violent climax in 13 months. As in 1971, the king narrowly escaped an attempt by elements of the armed forces to overthrow him.

Unsuccessful Coup. On August 16, as Hassan was flying back to Rabat from a trip to France and Spain, his plane was attacked and damaged by Moroccan air force jets. The king was not injured. After he landed at Rabat, the airport was strafed by jets, but again Hassan escaped without injury. The following day it was announced that Defense Minister Mohamed Oufkir had committed suicide. On the 18th he was accused of having planned the assassination attempt.

In November, 11 air force officers were sentenced to death for complicity in the plot, after a trial that lasted several weeks. Another 32 defendants received prison terms, but 177 men were acquitted. The verdicts were similar to those handed down in January 1972, ending trials of more than 1,000 officers and men charged with involvement in the previous year's attempted coup. In that instance all but 73 of the accused were acquitted.

Constitutional Reform. A new constitution proposed by the king on February 17 was approved by Moroccan voters on March 1. Hassan stated that the purpose of the constitutional change was to bring about administrative reforms, a redistribution of wealth "compatible with the spirit of socialism in Islam," and "impartial justice." Two thirds of the members of the Chamber of Deputies were to be elected by universal direct suffrage, and the remainder by local political and economic groups—roughly the reverse of the existing proportions. The king was to retain broad powers. He could name the entire cabinet, dismiss the Chamber of Deputies,

and rule by decree in periods of national emergency.

Premier Mohamed Karim Lamrani, who resigned after the referendum, formed a new, transitional cabinet on April 12. Most of its members had served in the previous cabinet. After the August attempt on the king's life, Hassan took measures to tighten his control of the government. On the 19th he abolished the posts of defense minister and army chief of staff, which had been held by the coup's alleged leader, and assumed command of the armed forces himself. On November 2 he appointed a new premier, Ahmed Osman, his brother-in-law.

Thus the king's constitutional reform seemed to have failed even before elections could be held for the new Chamber of Deputies. The two leading opposition parties—the traditionalist Istiqlal and the leftist National Union of Popular Forces (UNFP)—refused to join a coalition cabinet, and the August assassination attempt showed that the king did not have the full confidence of the armed forces. Public opponents of Hassan's policies pressed for broader changes, including more representative and efficient government, a swing away from close ties with the United States, the strengthening of relations with more militant Arab states, and a faster pace of economic development.

Foreign Relations. Morocco hosted the 1972 summit conference of the Organization of African Unity (OAU), which was held in Rabat from June 12 to 15. King Hassan was named chairman of the OAU until the 1973 summit meeting.

One of the most important results of the conference was the signing on June 15 of an agreement between Morocco and Algeria ending their longstanding border dispute. The boundary agreed on was not made public, but Hassan and Algerian President Houari Boumedienne announced that the disputed area's chief natural resource—the Gara-Djebilet iron ore deposits—would be developed jointly by their two countries.

At the conference, the king called for the liberation of African territories still under foreign control. One of these was Spanish Sahara, adjoining Morocco, Mauritania, and Algeria. The three Islamic states had agreed on the need for a cooperative effort to bring about Spain's withdrawal from the territory, claimed by both Morocco and Mauritania.

Hassan expressed his regret that Libya's leader, Col. Muammar al-Qaddafi, did not attend the Rabat conference. The king said he had hoped for a settlement of differences between Morocco and Libya at the meeting. Relations with Libya had been suspended in 1971 because of Qaddafi's publicly stated sympathy with leaders of that year's attempted coup. Afterward the Libyan government had launched a radio propaganda campaign against Hassan, urging Moroccans to overthrow him.

Economy. The World Bank and its affiliate, the International Development Association, agreed in October to advance $34 million to Morocco to help finance an agricultural project. The three-year development scheme included loans to 8,000 farmers.

The U. S. Export-Import Bank was helping to finance a $20 million project to restore Morocco's declining iron ore production. The object of the investment was to tap lower-grade deposits at the Nador mines, near the Mediterranean coast. The closeness of these mines to European markets would partly offset competition from African countries with high-grade ores.

RICHARD MOREHOUSE

MOROCCO · Information Highlights

Official Name: Kingdom of Morocco.
Area: 172,413 square miles (446,550 sq km).
Population (1972 est.): 16,800,000. *Density,* 91 per square mile (35 per sq km). *Annual rate of increase,* 3.4%.
Chief Cities (1969 est.): Rabat, the capital, 320,000; Casablanca, 1,320,000; Marrakesh, 295,000; Fez, 280,000.
Government: *Head of state,* Hassan II, king (acceded Feb. 1961). *Head of government,* Ahmed Osman, prime minister (took office Nov. 1972). *Legislature* (unicameral)—Chamber of Deputies, 240 members. *Major political parties*—Istiqlal; Union Nationale des Forces Populaires.
Languages: Arabic (official), Berber, French.
Education: *Expenditure* (1969), 16.3% of total public expenditure. *School enrollment* (1969)—primary, 1,142,810; secondary, 295,434; technical/vocational, 8,021; university/higher, 12,770.
Monetary Unit: Dirham (4.56 dirhams equal U. S.$1, July 1972).
Gross National Product (1971 est.): $3,515,000,000.
National Income per Person (1969): $186.
Economic Indexes: *Industrial production* (mining; 1970), 113 (1963=100); *agricultural production* (1971), 165 (1952–56=100); *consumer price index* (1971), 111 (1963=100).
Manufacturing (major products): Processed foods, metals, textiles, cement, wine.
Major Agricultural Products: Barley, wheat, citrus fruits, vegetables, grapes, sheep, wool.
Major Minerals: Phosphate rock (ranks 3d among world producers, 1970); iron ore, coal, manganese, antimony.
Foreign Trade (1971): *Exports,* $498,000,000 (chief exports—citrus fruits; phosphates; tomatoes; preserved fish; manganese). *Imports,* $691,000,000 (chief imports, 1969—nonelectrical machinery; food; chemicals; transport equipment). *Chief trading partners* (1969)—France (took 35% of exports; supplied 30% of imports); West Germany 9%—10%).
Tourism: *Receipts* (1970), $136,400,000.
Transportation: *Motor vehicles* (1970), 304,200 (automobiles, 220,800); *railroads* (1970), 1,104 miles (1,777 km); *merchant fleet* (1971), 56,000 gross registered tons; *major national airline,* Royal Air Maroc.
Communications: *Telephones* (1971), 169,614; *television stations* (1971), 8; *television sets* (1971), 145,000; *radios* (1970), 935,000; *newspapers* (1966), 9 (daily circulation, 197,000).

Motion Pictures

In 1972, trend-spotters for the motion picture industry had no difficulty discerning the dominant trend at the box-office—violence and more violence. The runaway moneymaker of the year was the Francis Ford Coppola–Mario Puzo work, *The Godfather,* a film that threatened to eclipse the all-time box-office records set by *Gone with the Wind, The Sound of Music,* and *Love Story.* Film-makers discovered to their delight that violence was less censorable in the eyes of the hypocritical ratings board than the most innocuous nudity, and the United States' double standard as a violent but prudish society was once again confirmed. At year-end, a New York judge and jury were deliberating over the alleged obscenity of a trivial porno film entitled *Deep Throat,* while audiences around the country were gurgling with pleasure over the garrotings in *The Godfather.*

Crime and Violence. The nation's love affair with the family secrets of the Mafia caused some furrowing of brows among high-minded editorialists, and there was even speculation that the public's extraordinary tolerance of the ITT and other political scandals could be attributed, at least in part, to the cynicism engendered by *The Godfather.* Thus was revived the old chicken-and-egg controversy about whether films actually create or merely reflect social attitudes. Either way, motion picture producers were overjoyed to discover a film genre that was almost guaranteed to return a profit.

The Godfather, *based on Mario Puzo's novel of life and love in the crime syndicates, reaped huge box-office rewards in 1972. Marlon Brando (above)* was widely acclaimed in the title role.

ALLIED ARTISTS

LIZA MINNELLI scored a critical success as Sally Bowles in Cabaret, yet another reworking of Christopher Isherwood's short stories about characters adrift in Berlin during the 1930's.

Curiously, Mafia films of the past, such as *Johnny Cool* and *The Brotherhood*, had been singularly unsuccessful at the box office. Now, however, production plans for a flood of gangster pictures of all types were set well into 1973 and 1974. Even in 1972, a distributor of foreign films retitled Jean-Pierre Melville's stylish French gangster picture of some years back, from *Le Samourai* to *The Godson*. Other backfires from *The Godfather* included Michael Ritchie's *Prime Cut*, Michael Winner's *The Mechanic*, Terence Young's *The Valachi Papers*, and Sam Peckinpah's *The Getaway*. An offshoot from 1971's *The French Connection* was Richard Fleischer's *The New Centurions*, with its lurid law-and-order point of view. The year's stab at *Dirty Harry* was Philipe Labro's *Without Apparent Motive*, and 1972's approximation of *Bonnie and Clyde* was Martin Scorsese's *Boxcar Bertha*.

Much of the rhetoric on film violence merely repeated in 1972 what had been uttered back in the 1930's in the wake of such crime classics as Howard Hawks' *Scarface*, William Wellman's *Public Enemy*,

and Mervyn Leroy's *Little Caesar*. Some films of 1972, however, in which violence functioned metaphorically or allegorically or even metaphysically, eluded simplistic classification. Among these were Alfred Hitchcock's *Frenzy*, Blake Edward's *The Carey Treatment*, Lamont Johnson's *The Groundstar Conspiracy*, John Boorman's *Deliverance*, and Sam Peckinpah's *Straw Dogs*.

Attempts to mingle violence and humor met with relatively little success. The public registered marked disinterest in such spoofs and absurdities as Stephen Frears' *Gumshoe*, Richard A. Colla's *Fuzz*, Peter Yates' *The Hot Rock*, and Cy Howard's *Every Little Crook and Nanny*.

Black Films. Among the most popular pictures of 1972 were the more than two dozen black genre films produced in 1972. Among the most notable of these were Gordon Parks, Jr.'s *Super Fly;* Sidney Poitier's *Buck and the Preacher;* Mark Warren's *Come Back, Charleston Blue;* Barry Shear's *Across 110th Street;* Gordon Parks' *Shaft's Big Score;* William Crain's *Blacula;* Hugh A. Robertson's *Melinda;* and Sidney J. Furie's *Lady Sings the Blues.* There were also films on Malcolm X and Angela Davis. In a year glutted with white rodeo pictures, such as Cliff Robertson's *J. W. Coop*, Sam Peckinpah's *Junior Bonner*, Steve Ihnat's *The Honkers*, and Stuart Miller's *When the Legends Die*, there was also, almost inevitably, Jeff Kanew's *Black Rodeo*.

By the end of 1972, a strong reaction against black fantasy and violence had been registered by various spokesmen for the black community. Martin Ritt's saccharine film *Sounder* was boosted as an uplifting alternative to all the black forms of violence.

Foreign Films. Foreign films continued to provide varied forms of virtuosity. An outstanding contribution was Luis Buñuel's surprisingly buoyant and bubbly surrealist dream, *The Discreet Charm of the Bourgeoisie.* Also notable were François Truffaut's *Two English Girls;* Claude Jutra's *Mon Oncle Antoine;* Kenji Mizoguchi's *Utamaro and His Five Women;* Alain Tanner's *La Salamandre* and *Charles, Dead or Alive;* Yasujiro Ozu's *Tokyo Story* and *Late Spring;* Alain Resnais' *Je t'aime, Je t'aime;* Robert Bresson's *Four Nights of a Dreamer;* Eric Rohmer's *Chloe in the Afternoon;* and Ingmar Bergman's *Cries and Whispers* (voted the year's best film by the New York Film Critics). Other notable foreign films were Jacques Tati's *Traffic;* Claude Sautet's *Cesar and Rosalie;* Federico Fellini's *Fellini's Roma;* Jan Troell's *The Emigrants;* Mai Zetterling's *The Girls;* Jacques Rivette's *Mad Love;* Uwe Brandner's *I Love You, I Kill You;* Carlos Saura's *The Honeycomb;* Woiciek J. Has' *Saragossa Manuscript;* Claude Lelouch's *Smic, Smac, Smoc;* Claude Chabrol's *Ten Days Wonder;* Andre Cayatte's *To Die of Love;* Andre Mikhaikov-Konchalovsky's *Uncle Vanya;* Abram Room's *Belated Flowers;* Susan Sontag's *Brother Carl;* Lina Wertmuller's *The Lizards;* and Nanni Loy's *Why.*

Westerns. Westerns enjoyed an extraordinary resurgence in 1972, proving once again the almost infinite adaptability of this popular genre. Among the Westerns seen during the year were Robert Aldrich's *Ulzana's Raid;* Sergio Leone's *Duck, You Sucker;* Robert Benton's *Bad Company;* Burt Kennedy's *Hannie Caulder;* Mark Rydell's *The Cowboys;* John Huston's *The Life and Times of Judge Roy Bean;* Sydney Pollack's *Jeremiah Johnson;* and John Sturges' *Joe Kidd.*

Comedies. George Cukor's *Travels With My*

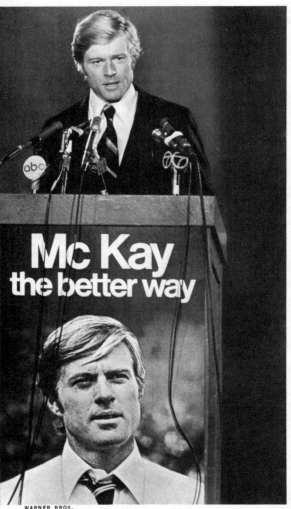

ROBERT REDFORD in The Candidate *portrayed an idealistic presidential contender who becomes the pawn of his own campaign efforts.*

Aunt, Billy Wilder's *Avanti!*, Elaine May's *The Heartbreak Kid*, and the Herbert Ross–Woody Allen film *Play It Again, Sam* led the comedy carnival of 1972. Others were Edward Dmytryk's *Bluebeard*; Milton Katselas' *Butterflies Are Free*; Gene Saks' *Last of the Red Hot Lovers*; Martin Ritt's *Pete 'n' Tillie*; Peter Medak's *The Ruling Class*; Melville Shavelson's *The War Between Men and Women*; Peter Bogdanovich's *What's Up, Doc?*; and Ian Macnaughton's *And Now for Something Completely Different*.

Documentaries. Marcel Ophuls, son of the late, great Max Ophuls, was clearly the documentarian of the year for his searing, yet compassionate contemplations in *The Sorrow and the Pity*, about occupied France in World War II, and *A Sense of Loss*, about the travail of Northern Ireland. Other documentaries of note were Budd Boetticher's *Arruza*, Louis Malle's *Phantom India*, and Howard Smith and Sarah Kernochan's *Marjoe*.

Political Subjects and Women's Lib. There were more than the usual number of narrative films with explicitly political content in 1972. Chief among these were Joseph Losey's *The Assassination*

of *Trotsky;* Joseph Sargent's *The Man;* Michael Ritchie's *The Candidate;* Luis Sergio Person's *The Case of the Naves Brothers;* George Roy Hill's *Slaughterhouse-Five;* Bernard Girard's *Happiness Cage;* and George C. Scott's *Rage*.

The Women's Lib Movement was represented by only the most token gestures in such faltering works as Irvin Kershner's *Up the Sandbox*, Mel Stuart's *One Is a Lonely Number*, and Jackie Cooper's *Stand Up and Be Counted*. Molly Haskell, in her lucidly articulated book *From Reverence to Rape: The Treatment of Women in Film*, made the observation that the motion pictures of the 1960's and 1970's, while freeing women from the wholesome, bloodless stereotype of earlier decades, had created a new stereotype by presenting them as the very sex objects that censors formerly prohibited. Hence the supposed sexual revolution on the screen has become for women a new form of sexual submission. In this respect, the dominant female role of Susannah York in Robert Altman's *Images* and the co-equal role of Janet Suzman (with Alan Bates) in Peter Medak's *A Day in the Death of Joe Egg* were far more the exception than the rule in 1972.

From Stage to Screen. It was a dreadfully derivative year for musicals. Only Bob Fosse's *Cabaret*, Peter Hunt's *1776*, and Arthur Hiller's *The Man From La Mancha* ever tried to carry a tune on the screen.

All in all, it was not a triumphant year for theatrical adaptations despite such strenuous attempts as Joseph L. Mankiewicz's *Sleuth*, Sidney Lumet's *Child's Play*, and Paul Newman's *The Effect of Gamma Rays on Man-in-the-Moon Marigolds*, which introduced his daughter Nell Potts.

BLACK BOYHOOD in the South of the 1930's was the subject of Sounder, *the story of the trials of a Louisiana sharecropper's family.*

NOTABLE MOTION PICTURES OF 1972

The following list of films released in the United States in 1972 presents a cross-section of the most popular, most typical, or most widely discussed motion pictures of the year.

Across 110th Street. Director, Barry Shear; screenplay, Luther Davis from novel by Wally Ferris. With Anthony Quinn, Yaphet Kotto, Paul Benjamin, Ed Bernard, Richard Ward, Norma Donaldson, Antonio Fargas, Anthony Franciosa.

Arruza. Director, Budd Boetticher; narration written by Boetticher and Ken W. Purdy; narration read by Anthony Quinn.

The Assassination of Trotsky. Director, Joseph Losey; screenplay, Nicholas Mosley. With Richard Burton, Alain Delon, Romy Schneider, Valentina Cortese.

Avanti! Director, Billy Wilder; screenplay, Wilder and I. A. L. Diamond from play by Samuel Taylor. With Jack Lemmon, Juliet Mills, Clive Revill, Edward Andrews.

Bad Company. Director, Robert Benton; screenplay, David Newman and Benton. With Jeff Bridges, Barry Brown, Jim Davis, David Huddleston.

Bartleby. Director, Anthony Friedman; screenplay, Friedman and Rodney Carr-Smith from story by Herman Melville. With Paul Scofield, John McEnery.

Belated Flowers. Director, Abram Room; adapted by Room from novella by Anton Chekhov. With Olga Zhizneva, Irina Lavrntyeva, Alexander Lazarev, Valeri Zolotukhin.

Blacula. Director, William Crain; screenplay, Joan Torres and Raymond Koenig. With William Marshall, Vonetta McGee, Denise Nicholas, Elisha Cook.

Bluebeard. Director, Edward Dmytryk; screenplay, Ennio Di Concini, Dmytruk, and Maria Pia Fusco. With Richard Burton, Raquel Welch, Joey Heatherton, Virna Lisi, Nathalie Delon, Manilu Tolo.

Boxcar Bertha. Director, Martin Scorsese, screenplay, Joyce H. Corrington and John William Corrington from the autobiography of Boxcar Bertha Thompson. With Barbara Hershey, David Carradine, Barry Primus, Bernie Casey, John Carradine.

Buck and the Preacher. Director, Sidney Poitier; screenplay, Ernest Kinoy from story by Kinoy and Drake Walker. With Sidney Poitier, Harry Belafonte, Ruby Dee, Cameron Mitchell.

Butterflies Are Free. Director, Milton Katselas; screenplay, Leonard Gershe from his stage play. With Goldie Hawn, Eileen Heckart, Edward Albert.

Cabaret. Director, Bob Fosse; screenplay, Jay Allen from play by John Van Druten and the *Berlin Stories* by Christopher Isherwood. With Liza Minnelli, Michael York, Helmut Griem, Joel Grey.

The Candidate. Director, Michael Ritchie; screenplay, Jeremy Larner. With Robert Redford, Melvyn Douglas, Peter Boyle, Allen Garfield.

The Carey Treatment. Director, Blake Edwards; screenplay, James P. Bonner from novel *A Case of Need* by Jeffrey Hudson. With James Coburn, Jennifer O'Neill, Pat Hingle, Skye Aubrey, Elizabeth Allen, Alex Dreier, Dan O'Herlihy.

Cesar and Rosalie. Director, Claude Sautet; screenplay, Jean-Loup Dabadie and Sautet. With Yves Montand, Romy Schneider, Sami Frey.

Child's Play. Director, Sidney Lumet; screenplay, Leon Prochnik from play by Robert Marasco. With James Mason, Robert Preston, Beau Bridges.

Chloe in the Afternoon. Director, Eric Rohmer; screenplay, Rohmer. With Bernard Verley, Zouzou, Françoise Verley.

The Cowboys. Director, Mark Rydell; screenplay, Irving Ravetch, Harriet Frank Jr., and William Dale Jennings from novel by Jennings. With John Wayne, Roscoe Lee Browne, Colleen Dewhurst, Bruce Dern, Slim Pickens.

Cries and Whispers. Director-scenarist, Ingmar Bergman. With Harriet Andersson, Ingrid Thulin, Cari Sylwan, Liv Ullmann.

A Day in the Death of Joe Egg. Director, Peter Medak; screenplay, Peter Nichols from his play. With Alan Bates, Janet Suzman, Peter Bowles, Sheila Gish.

Deliverance. Director, John Boorman; screenplay, James Dickey from his novel. With Jon Voight, Burt Reynolds, Ned Beaty, Ronny Cox.

The Discreet Charm of the Bourgeoisie. Director, Luis Buñuel; screenplay, Jean-Claude Carriere. With Fernando Rey, Jean-Pierre Cassel, Delphine Seyrig, Stephane Audran, Bulle Ogier.

Dulcima. Director, Frank Nesbitt; screenplay, Nesbitt from story by H. E. Bates. With Carol White, John Mills, Stuart Wilson, Bernard Lee.

The Effect of Gamma Rays on Man-in-the-Moon-Marigolds. Director, Paul Newman; screenplay, Alvin Sargent from play by Paul Zindel. With Joanne Woodward, Nell Potts, Roberta Wallach, Judith Lowry.

The Emigrants. Director, Jan Troell; screenplay, Troell and Bengt Forsund from novels by Vilhelm Moberg. With Max von Sydow, Liv Ullman, Eddie Axberg, Svenolof Bern.

Fat City. Director, John Huston; screenplay, Leonard Gardner from his novel. With Stacy Keach, Jeff Bridges, Susan Tyrrell, Candy Clark, Nicholas Colasanto, Art Aragon, Curtis Cokes.

Fellini's Roma. Director, Federico Fellini; screenplay, Bernardino Zapponi and Fellini. With Anna Magnani, Gore Vidal, Fellini.

Four Nights of a Dreamer. Director-scenarist, Robert Bresson; from Dostoyevsky's *White Nights.* With Isabel Weingarten, Guillaume des Forets, Jean Maurice Monnoyer.

Frenzy. Director, Alfred Hitchcock; screenplay, Anthony Shaffer from novel by Arthur La Bern. With Jon Finch, Barry Foster, Barbara Leigh-Hunt, Anna Massey, Alec McCowen, Vivien Merchant.

Fritz the Cat. Director-scenarist, Ralph Bakshi; from the character created by Robert Crumb.

The Getaway. Director, Sam Peckinpah; screenplay, Walter Hill from novel by Jim Thompson. With Steve McQueen, Ali MacGraw, Ben Johnson, Al Lettieri, Sally Struthers.

The Girls. Director, Mai Zetterling; screenplay, Miss Zetterling and David Hughes. With Bibi Andersson, Harriet Andersson, Gunnel Lindblom, Gunnar Björnstrand, Erland Josephson.

The Godfather. Director, Francis Ford Coppola; screenplay, Mario Puzo from his novel. With Marlon Brando, Al Pacino, James Caan, Richard Castellano, Robert Duvall, Diane Keaton.

The Godson. Director-scenarist, Jean-Pierre Melville. With Alain Delon, Nathalie Delon, François Perier, Cathy Rosier.

Gumshoe. Director, Stephen Frears; screenplay, Neville Smith. With Albert Finney, Billie Whitelaw, Frank Finlay, Janice Rule.

The Heartbreak Kid. Director, Elaine May; screenplay, Neil Simon from story by Bruce Jay Friedman. With Charles Grodin, Cybill Shepherd, Jeannie Berlin, Eddie Albert, Audra Lindley.

Heat. Director-scenarist, Paul Morrissey; from original idea by John Hollowell. With Joe Dallesandro, Sylvia Miles, Andrea Feldman, Pat Ast.

The Hot Rock. Director, Peter Yates; screenplay, William Goldman from novel by Donald E. Westlake. With Robert Redford, George Segal, Ron Leibman, Zero Mostel, Paul Sand, Moses Gunn, Topo Swope.

Images. Director-scenarist, Robert Altman. With Susannah York, René Auberjonois, Marcel Bozzuffi, Hugh Millais, Cathryn Harrison.

J. W. Coop. Director, Cliff Robertson; screenplay, Robertson, Carey Cartwright and Edwin Shrake. With Robertson, Geraldine Page, Christina Ferrare, R. G. Armstrong, R. L. Armstrong.

Jeremiah Johnson. Director, Sydney Pollack; screenplay, John Milius and Edward Anhalt from *Mountain Man* by Vardis Fisher and *Crow Killer* by Raymond W. Thorp and Robert Bunker. With Robert Redford, Will Geer, Allyn Ann McLerie, Stefan Gierasch, Delle Bolton.

Joe Kidd. Director, John Sturges, screenplay, Elmore Leonard. With Clint Eastwood, Robert Duvall, John Saxon, Don Stroud, Stella Garcia.

Junior Bonner. Director, Sam Peckinpah; screenplay, Jeb Rosebrook. With Steve McQueen, Robert Preston, Ida Lupino, Ben Johnson, Joe Don Baker, Barbara Leigh.

Kansas City Bomber. Director, Jerrold Freedman; screenplay, Thomas Rickman and Calvin Clements from a story by Barry Sandler. With Raquel Welch, Kevin McCarthy, Helena Kallianiotes, Norman Alden, Jeanne Cooper, Mary Kay Pass.

The King of Marvin Gardens. Director, Bob Rafelson; screenplay, Jacob Brackman and Rafelson. With Jack Nicholson, Bruce Dern, Ellen Burstyn, Julia Anne Robinson, Benjamin Crothers, Charles Lavine.

Lady Sings the Blues. Director, Sidney J. Furie; screenplay, Terence McCloy, Chris Clark, and Suzanne de Passe from the book by Billie Holliday and William Dufty. With Diana Ross, Billy Dee Williams, Richard Pryor, James Calahan, Paul Hampton, Sid Melton, Virginia Capers, Yvonne Fair, Benjamin Crothers.

Last of the Red Hot Lovers. Director, Gene Saks; screenplay, Neil Simon, adapted from his Broadway play. With Alan Arkin, Sally Kellerman, Paula Prentiss, Renee Taylor.

Late Spring. Director, Yasujiro Ozu; screenplay, Ozu and Kogo Noda. With Chisu Ryu, Setsuko Hara, Haruko Sugimura, Jun Osami.

The Life and Times of Judge Roy Bean. Director, John Huston, screenplay, John Milius. With Paul Newman, Jacqueline Bissett, Tab Hunter, John Huston, Stacy Keach, Roddy McDowall, Anthony Perkins, Ava Gardner.

Malcolm X. Adapted by Arnold Perl from *The Autobiography of Malcolm X* with the assistance of Alex Haley; Narration, James Earl Jones; Eulogy, Ossie Davis.

The Man. Director, Joseph Sargent; screenplay, Rod Serling from novel by Irving Wallace. With James Earl Jones, Martin Balsam, Burgess Meredith, Lew Ayres, William Windom, Barbara Rush.

Man of La Mancha. Director, Arthur Hiller; screenplay, Dale Wasserman from his Broadway musical play. With Peter O'Toole, Sophia Loren, James Coco, Harry Andrews, Ian Richardson.

Marjoe. Directed by Howard Smith and Sarah Kernochan. With Marjoe Gortner.

Melinda. Director, Hugh A. Robertson; screenplay, Lonne Elder 3d from story by Raymond Cistheri. With Calvin Lockhart, Rosalind Cash, Paul Stevens, Rockne Tarkington, Vonetta McGee, Lonne Elder.

My Uncle Antoine. Director, Claude Jutra; screenplay, Clement Perron and Jutra. With Jean Duceppe, Olivette Thibault, Jutra, Jacques Cagnon, Lyne Champagne, Lionel Villeneuve, Helene Loiselle.

The New Centurions. Director, Richard Fleischer; screenplay, Stirling Silliphant from novel by Joseph Wambaugh. With George C. Scott, Stacy Keach, Jane Alexander, Scott Wilson, Rosalind Cash.

The Other. Director, Robert Mulligan; screenplay, Tom Tryon, from his novel. With Uta Hagen, Diana Muldaur, Chris Udvarnoky, Martin Udvarnoky, Norma Connelly, Loretta Leversee, Victor French.

Outback. Director, Ted Kotcheff; screenplay, Evan Jones from novel by Kenneth Cook. With Gary Bond, Donald Pleasence, Sylvia Kaye, Al Thomas, Chips Rafferty, Jack Thompson.

Pete 'n' Tillie. Director, Martin Ritt; screenplay, Julius J. Epstein from novella *Witch's Milk* by Peter DeVries. With Walter Matthau, Carol Burnett, Geraldine Page, Barry Nelson, René Auberjonois.

Phantom India. Director, Louis Malle.

The Pied Piper. Director, Jacques Demy; screenplay, Andrew Birkin, Demy and Mark Peploe. With Donovan, Donald Pleasence, Jack Wild, John Hurt, Cathryn Harrison, Michael Hordern, Roy Kinnear, Diana Dors.

Play It Again, Sam. Director, Herbert Ross; screenplay, Woody Allen, from his play. With Woody Allen, Diane Keaton, Tony Roberts, Jerry Lacy, Susan Anspach, Jennifer Salt, Joy Bang, Viva.

Play It As It Lays. Director, Frank Perry; screenplay, Joan Didion and John Gregory Dunne from novel by Miss Didion. With Tuesday Weld, Anthony Perkins, Tammy Grimes, Adam Roarke, Ruth Ford, Severn Darden, Arthur Knight, Albert Johnson.

Portnoy's Complaint. Director, Ernest Lehman; screenplay, Lehman from novel by Philip Roth. With Richard Benjamin, Karen Black, Lee Grant, Jack Somack, Jill Clayburgh, Jeannie Berlin.

Poseidon Adventure. Director, Ronald Neame; screenplay, Stirling Silliphant and Wendell Mayes from novel by Paul Gallico. With Gene Hackman, Ernest Borgnine, Red Buttons, Carol Lynley, Roddy McDowall, Stella Stevens, Shelley Winters, Jack Albertson, Pamela Sue Martin, Arthur O'Connell, Eric Shea, Leslie Nielsen.

Rage. Director, George C. Scott; screenplay, Philip Friedman and Dan Kleinman. With George C. Scott, Richard Basehart, Martin Sheen, Barnard Hughes.

The Ruling Class. Director, Peter Medak; screenplay by Peter Barnes from his play. With Peter O'Toole, Alastair Sim, Arthur Lowe, Harry Andrews, Coral Browne, Michael Bryant, Nigel Green.

La Salamandre. Director, Alain Tanner; screenplay, Tanner and John Berger. With Bulle Ogier, Jean-Luc Bideau, Jacques Denis.

A Sense of Loss. Director, Marcel Ophuls.

A Separate Peace. Director, Larry Pearce; screenplay, Fred Segal from novel by John Knowles. With John Heyl, Parker Stevenson, Peter Brush, Victor Bevine, Scott Bradbury, John E. A. Mackenzie.

1776. Director, Peter Hunt; screenplay, Peter Stone from his Broadway musical play. With William Daniels, Howard DaSilva, Ken Howard, Donald Madden, Blythe Danner.

Shaft's Big Score. Director, Gordon Parks; screenplay, Ernest Tidyman. With Richard Roundtree, Moses Gunn, Drew Bundini Brown, Joseph Mascolo, Kathy Imrie, Julius W. Harris.

Slaughterhouse-Five. Director, George Roy Hill; screenplay, Stephen Geller from novel by Kurt Vonnegut, Jr. With Michael Sacks, Ron Leibman, Eugene Roche, Sharon Gans, Valerie Perrine.

Sleuth. Director, Joseph L. Mankiewicz; screenplay, Anthony Shaffer from his stage play. With Laurence Olivier, Michael Caine.

The Sorrow and the Pity. Director, Marcel Ophuls.

Sounder. Director, Martin Ritt; screenplay, Lonne Elder 3d, from novel by William H. Armstrong. With Cicely Tyson, Paul Winfield, Kevin Hooks, Carmen Matthews, James Best, Janet MacLachlan.

Straw Dogs. Director, Sam Peckinpah; screenplay, Peckinpah and David Z. Goodman from Gordon Williams's novel *Siege at Trencher's Farm*. With Dustin Hoffman, Susan George, Peter Vaughan, T. P. McKenna, Del Henney, Ken Hutchinson, Colin Welland, Jim Norton, Sally Thomset, David Warner.

Super Fly. Director, Gordon Parks, Jr., screenplay, Phillip Feny. With Ron O'Neal, Carl Lee, Sheila Frazier, Julius W. Harris, Charles McGregor.

To Die of Love. Director, André Cayatte; screenplay, Cayatte and Albert Naud; adaptation and dialogue, Pierre Dumayet. With Annie Girardot, Bruno Pradal, François Simon, Monique Melinand.

Tokyo Story. Director, Yasujiro Ozu; screenplay, Kogo Noda and Ozu. With Chishu Ruy, Chiyeto Higashiyama, So Yamamura, Hruko Sugimura, Setsuko Hara, Kyoto Kagawa, Shiro Osaka.

Traffic. Director, Jacques Tati; screenplay, Tati with the creative collaboration of Jacques LaGrange. With Jacques Tati, Maria Kimberly, Marcel Fraval, H. Bostel, Tony Kneppers.

Travels with My Aunt. Director, George Cukor; screenplay, Jay Presson Allen and Hugh Wheeler from novel by Graham Greene. With Maggie Smith, Alec McCowen, Lou Gossett, Robert Stephens, Cindy Williams.

Two English Girls. Director, François Truffaut; screenplay, Truffaut and Jean Gruault from novel by Henry-Pierre Roché. With Jean-Pierre Leaud, Kika Markham, Sylvia Marriott, Marie Mansart.

Ulzana's Raid. Director, Robert Aldrich; screenplay, Alan Sharp. With Burt Lancaster, Bruce Davison, Jorge Luke, Richard Jaeckel, Joaquin Martinez, Lloyd Bochner.

Uncle Vanya. Director-scenarist, Andrei Mikhaikov-Konchalovsky from play by Anton Chekhov. With Innokenty Smoktunovsky, Sergi Bondarchuk, Vladimir Zedin, Irina Kupchenko, Irina Miroschnichenko.

Up the Sandbox. Director, Irvin Kershner; screenplay, Paul Zindel from novel by Anne Richardson Roiphe. With Barbra Streisand, David Selby.

Utamaro and His Five Women. Director, Kenji Mizoguchi; screenplay, Yoshikata Yoda from novel by Kanji Kunieda. With Minnosuke Bando, Kinuyo Tanaka, Kotaro Bando, Hiroko Kowasaki, Kinnosuke Takamatsu, Toshiko Izuka, Masso Hori.

What's Up, Doc? Director, Peter Bogdanovich; screenplay, Buck Henry, David Newman, Robert Benton from story by Bogdanovich. With Barbra Streisand, Ryan O'Neal, Kenneth Mars, Madeline Kahn, Austin Pendleton, Sorrel Booke, Stefan Geirach.

When the Legends Die. Director, Stuart Millar; screenplay, Robert Dozier from novel by Hal Borland. With Richard Widmark, Frederic Forrest, Luana Anders.

Why. Director, Nanni Loy; screenplay, Sergio Amidei and Emilio Sanna. With Alberto Sordi, Elga Andersen.

Without Apparent Motive. Director, Philippe Labro; screenplay, Labro and Jacques Lanzmann from the novel *Ten Plus One* by Ed McBain. With Jean-Louis Trintignant, Dominique Sanda, Sacha Distel, Carla Gravina, Laura Antonelli, Jean-Pierre Marielle, Erich Segal.

Women in Revolt. Director, Andy Warhol and Paul Morrissey. With Candy Darling, Jackie Curtis, Holly Woodlawn.

Young Winston. Director, Richard Attenborough; screenplay, Carl Foreman from *My Early Life: A Roving Commission* by Sir Winston Churchill. With Simon Ward, Anne Bancroft, Robert Shaw, John Mills, Laurence Naismith, Colin Blakely.

Chloe in the Afternoon (left), a study of a platonic love affair, was last in a six-film cycle by French director Eric Rohmer that included My Night at Maud's and Claire's Knee.

(Right) *Liv Ullmann in* Cries and Whispers, *Ingmar Bergman's study of a dying woman and her sisters, voted best film by New York film critics.*

Woody Allen starred in the film of his Broadway comedy, Play It Again, Sam, *as an unheroic soul with a profound admiration for old Bogart films.*

Other Films. Out of a full complement of horror and fantasy films only Robert Mulligan's *The Other* (based on the novel by the film actor Thomas Tryon, who also wrote the screenplay), Waris Hussein's *Possession of Joel Delaney,* and Douglas Trumbull's *Silent Running* revealed higher than catchpenny aspirations. Straight old-fashioned action melodrama still proved an audience-pleasing experience for patrons of Ronald Neame's *The Poseidon Adventure*—which centers on the capsizing of a large passenger liner by a tidal wave—and, to a much lesser degree, John Guillermin's *Skyjacked.*

That realism was not entirely dead as a tradition was confirmed by the success of John Huston's *Fat City.* Prep school students found cinematic reflections in Larry Pearce's *A Separate Peace.* Generally, however, it was not a banner year for the "Now" pictures, among the most prominent of which were Bob Rafelson's *The King of Marvin Gardens;* Paul Newman's *Sometimes a Great Notion;* Paul Williams' *Dealing: Or the Berkeley-to-Boston Forty-Brick Lost-Bag Blues;* Frank Perry's *Play It As It Lays;* Stuart Rosenberg's *Pocket Money;* and Bill L. Norton's *Cisco Pike.*

As always, there were the dedicated literary adaptations. Anthony Friedman's *Bartleby,* based on Herman Melville's *Bartleby the Scrivener,* was considerably more inspired than Joseph Anthony's *Tomorrow,* based on a work by William Faulkner. And as always, there were the runaway stylists on the rampage in Curtis Harrington's *Who Slew Auntie Roo* and Ken Russell's *The Savage Messiah.* There was also the annual waxworks biography in *Young Winston,* and the annual December–May romance and tragedy in Frank Nesbitt's *Dulcima.*

Awards. The National Society of Film Critics chose Luis Buñuel's *The Discreet Charm of the Bourgeoisie* as the best film of 1972. The group, which comprises critics from 23 magazines and newspapers also named Buñuel as the year's best director. Ingmar Bergman was voted best scenarist and Sven Nykvist best cinematographer for *Cries and Whispers.* Al Pacino was selected best actor for *The Godfather,* and Cicely Tyson best actress for *Sounder.* Top honors for supporting actor were shared by Eddie Albert in *The Heartbreak Kid* and Joel Grey in *Cabaret.* Jeannie Berlin was honored as best supporting actress for her performance in *The Heartbreak Kid.*

One of the two first annual Rosenthal Foundation awards of $2,000 for insufficiently appreciated film achievements went to Claude Jutra for *My Uncle Antoine.* The other award was split between Ivan Passer for *Born to Win* and Robert Kaylor for *Derby,* these films having been released in 1971.

The New York Film Critics selected Ingmar Bergman's *Cries and Whispers* as best picture of the year and Bergman as best director and best screenwriter. Liv Ullmann was voted best actress for her performance in *Cries and Whispers.* Laurence Olivier was chosen as best actor for his performance in *Sleuth.* Robert Duvall was named best supporting actor (*The Godfather*) and Jeannie Berlin best supporting actress (*The Heartbreak Kid*). Marcel Ophuls' *The Sorrow and the Pity* received a special award from the New York Film Critics, thus matching the special award it had received in 1971 from The National Society of Film Critics. (See also PRIZES AND AWARDS.)

ANDREW SARRIS
Columbia University

MOZAMBIQUE

Events in Mozambique in 1972 were again dominated by the war between Mozambique nationalists and Portuguese forces. Portugal remained determined to retain control of its African territories. The Portuguese Assembly in May designated the overseas territories of Mozambique and Angola as "states" and gave them greater autonomy "without affecting the unity of the nation."

The War. The major activities of the Mozambique Liberation Front (FRELIMO) in 1972 were centered in the Tete district in western Mozambique, where the Portuguese were building the Cabora Bassa Dam on the Zambezi River. The vast hydroelectric project has been opposed by FRELIMO, which charged that it would be used by Portugal to strengthen its hold on Mozambique. Throughout the year guerrillas harassed trucks and trains carrying supplies to the project. The most serious attack occurred in February when guerrillas blew up a truck near the dam site, killing nine persons and wounding five. Portuguese vehicles were forced to move in convoys, each led by a mine-sweeping unit. But the government reported that work on the dam was proceeding on schedule.

Portuguese security forces announced in April that rebel casualties in 1971 had been 1,041 killed or seriously wounded. During the same month the vice president of FRELIMO, Marcelino dos Santos, told the UN decolonization committee that 2,900 Portuguese soldiers had been killed in 1971 and that guerrillas controlled about one quarter of Mozambique, an area with a population of about 1 million.

Foreign Relations. Portuguese official sources claimed in April that Tanzania had shot down a border patrol aircraft in Mozambique. But Tanzanian authorities accused the Portuguese of having attacked a Tanzanian village with 13 aircraft.

The World Council of Churches decided at a meeting at The Hague in August that it would sell all its holdings in corporations either investing in or trading with white-ruled territories in Africa, including Mozambique and Angola, and to double funds for liberation movements in southern Africa.

The UN Committee on Non-Self-Governing Territories voted on September 27 to accept representatives of African liberation movements as observers. Portugal voted against the resolution.

JUDITH A. GLICKMAN

───── **MOZAMBIQUE • Information Highlights** ─────

Official Name: Overseas State of Mozambique.
Area: 302,329 square miles (783,030 sq km).
Population (1972 est.): 8,100,000. *Density,* 26 per square mile (10 per sq km). *Annual rate of increase,* 2.1%.
Chief City (1967 est.): Lourenço Marques, the capital, 250,000 (metropolitan area).
Government: Local administration headed by Governor General Manuel Pimental dos Santos, appointed Oct. 1971 by the Portuguese government in Lisbon.
Languages: Portuguese (official), Bantu languages.
Education: *School enrollment* (1967)—primary, 485,045; general secondary (1966), 10,092; technical/vocational, 15,346; university/higher, 904.
Monetary Unit: Escudo (27.02 escudos = U. S.$1, Aug. 1972).
Gross National Product (1970): $1,200,000,000.
Manufacturing (major products): Processed foods and agricultural products, tobacco, textiles, petroleum products.
Major Agricultural Products: Cashew nuts (ranks 1st among world producers, 1970), cotton, tea, sisal, corn, wheat, potatoes, sugar.
Major Mineral: Coal.
Foreign Trade (1970): *Exports,* $156,000,000. *Imports,* $326,-000,000. *Chief trading partners* (1969)—Portugal (took 41% of exports, supplied 31% of imports); South Africa (11%—15%); United States (10%—7%).
Communications: *Telephones* (1971), 27,488; *radios* (1970), 90,000; *newspapers* (1970), 6.

Leopold Stokowski leads American Symphony Orchestra in New York City's St. Bartholomew's Church on April 16, two days before reaching 90. His first American position, in 1905, had been as the church organist at St. Bartholomew's.

Music

The year 1972 saw many changes and new appointments at leading musical institutions all over the world. Most of the changes seemed to have little immediate impact on the institutions involved. Perhaps the most dramatic change came about through the tragic death of Goeran Gentele, only weeks after he had assumed the post of the Metropolitan Opera's general manager. Gentele's assistant, Schuyler Chapin, was elevated to the post.

A major event in U. S. musical life took place well outside of the musical "Establishment." This was the world premiere of a 60-year-old opera, *Treemonisha,* by the American composer Scott Joplin, who a few years ago was almost totally forgotten.

CLASSICAL MUSIC

New Posts. After Goeran Gentele died in an automobile accident on the island of Sardinia, Italy, in July 1972, less than a month after succeeding Sir Rudolf Bing as general manager, the Metropolitan Opera's board named Assistant Manager Schuyler Chapin as acting general manager for an indefinite period. Earlier in the year Gentele and Rafael Kubelik, who is slated to become music director in 1973, had announced the selection of James Levine as principal conductor of the company, effective with the 1973–74 season. Later Levine was tapped to head Chicago's Ravinia Festival as well.

Two major American orchestras announced conductorial appointments. The Boston Symphony chose Seiji Ozawa as music director beginning in 1973–74. The Detroit Symphony named Aldo Ceccato principal conductor for the period 1973–75. In the fall of 1972, James De Preist became associate conductor of the National Symphony Orchestra of Washington.

In Vienna, Rudolf Gamsjäger, secretary-general of the Society of Friends of Music, became the new general manager of the Vienna State Opera, starting in September 1972. As the fall season opened, La Scala had a new team: Paolo Grassi, superintendent; Massimo Bogianckino, artistic director; and Claudio Abbado, permanent music director. Romolo Valli was named artistic director of the Spoleto (Italy) Festival of Two Worlds.

New Facilities. In October, the Maurice Gusman Philharmonic Hall, the new home of the Miami Philharmonic Orchestra, was inaugurated in Miami, Fla. The building, formerly the Olympia Theater, was refurbished with $4 million donated by Gusman. The opening was celebrated with a performance of Beethoven's Ninth Symphony under Alain Lombard, the orchestra's music director. In Rochester, N. Y., the Eastman Theatre, part of the complex that includes the Eastman School of Music, was extensively renovated and restored, at a cost of $2.3 million, and reopened in January as part of the celebration of the Eastman School's 50th anniversary festival. An acoustical shell will make the hall adaptable for all types of concerts.

In Virginia, the Norfolk Symphony Orchestra moved into a new auditorium, Chrysler Hall. It

was inaugurated in April with an all-American program under the baton of Russell Stanger. Also in April, the $5 million Arnold Bernhard Arts-Humanities Center opened on the campus of the University of Bridgeport in Connecticut. The building, which houses the music, theater, and art departments of the college, also has a 900-seat theater. A month of concerts to celebrate the Center's opening was climaxed by a new opera on the Don Juan theme, *Again, D. J.,* commissioned from Neil Slater and Nick Rossi of the university's music department.

In April, Indiana University in Bloomington inaugurated its new $11.3 million Musical Arts Center with *Heracles,* an opera by John Eaton of the Indiana School of Music faculty. In addition to its 1,460-seat auditorium, the structure houses classrooms, studios, and a ballet center.

In Paris, the French Ministry of Culture announced that the Opéra-Comique will become a graduate school of operatic art. To be called L'Opéra-Studio de Paris, the school will train singers, stage directors, designers, and conductors after they have graduated from the Conservatoire.

Concert Life. The works of two disparate composers seemed especially prominent in New York's concert life in 1972: George Crumb and Stefan Wolpe, who died in New York in April. In February, Pierre Boulez, as part of his New York Philharmonic series called "Prospective Encounters," presented Crumb's *Ancient Voices of Children,* a song cycle with texts by García Lorca, at New York University's Loeb Student Center. In April, in the "New and Newer Music" series at Alice Tully Hall, Dennis Russell Davies gave the New York premiere of Crumb's *Songs, Drones, and Refrains of Death.* And in October, the Aeolian Chamber Players played Crumb's *Vox Balaenae* ("Voice of the Whale") for the first time in New York. Richmond, Va., was the scene in January, of the world premiere of Crumb's *Lux Aeternae* for five masked musicians. It was presented at the Virginia Museum Theater by the Philadelphia Composers' Forum.

At a February concert of the Performer's Committee for Twentieth-Century Music, in Columbia University's McMillin Theater, a retrospective devoted to Stefan Wolpe included performances of his works written from 1924 to 1969. In April, the planned tribute to Wolpe of the International Society of Contemporary Music became a memorial instead. Five chamber works were performed. At Alice Tully Hall in May, Speculum Musicae played a program devoted to Stravinsky, Wolpe, and others.

Boulez continued his "Prospective Encounters" and "Informal Evenings" with the New York Philharmonic at locations other than Philharmonic Hall. The orchestra's 1972–73 prospectus included two "retrospective series" devoted to the works of Haydn and Stravinsky. A highlight of the New York concert season was the appearance of the distinguished American black conductor Dean Dixon with the New York Philharmonic in March. Conductor Lukas Foss provided Brooklyn Philharmonia audiences with "musical marathons" at the Brooklyn Academy of Music, these being lengthy programs on the American composer, modern classics, and other themes.

On October 16 pianists gathered in Carnegie Hall for a "monster concert" that included Czerny's *Overture to Rossini's Semiramide* arranged for 16 pianists with 8 pianos and an arrangement of Sousa's *Stars and Stripes Forever* for 10 pianists. In November the Bach Aria Group began its 25th season with a Tully Hall program of cantata arias under its conductor William H. Scheide.

Other events in New York included the appearance of two Canadian ensembles. Karel Ancerl led the Toronto Symphony in the New York premiere of Oscar Morawetz's *From the Diary of Anne Frank,* for soprano and orchestra. In February the National Arts Center Orchestra of Canada, under Mario Bernardi, made its New York debut in Tully Hall, performing works of Tippett, Ravel, Beethoven, and the contemporary Canadian composer Harry Somers. The group returned to Tully Hall in November to offer, among other things, *Tableau,* by another Canadian, Harry Freedman.

At the Washington, D. C., Kennedy Center in October, Antal Dorati led the National Symphony Orchestra and soloists in the world premiere of John La Montaine's *Wilderness Journal,* for baritone, organ, and orchestra, commissioned by Katherine Filene Shouse. Paul Callaway was the organist and Donald Gramm the baritone soloist in the piece, the texts for which were drawn from the essays and journals of Henry Thoreau. Earlier, the Concert Hall was the scene of 31 concerts in a 12-day series called "The Old and the New," whose programming ranged from the Italian Baroque to contemporary works. Participating were I Virtuosi di Roma and the Rome Piccolo Opera, the Contemporary Chamber Ensemble under Arthur Weisberg, the Theatre Chamber Players of Baltimore led by Leon Fleisher, and the National Symphony under Bruno Maderna and Michael Gielen.

In March, Washington heard the American premiere of Olivier Messiaen's *La Transfiguration de Notre Seigneur, Jésus-Christ,* a vast work for orchestra, chorus, and soloists. Dorati led the National Symphony Orchestra and the Westminster Chorale in the performance, and a few days later repeated it in Carnegie Hall in New York.

Several important world premieres highlighted the Chicago Symphony's spring and fall schedules. In March, Maderna led the premieres of Jacob Druckman's *Windows,* which garnered the composer the 1972 Pulitzer Prize, and of his own work, *Aura.* The fall season opened in September with the premiere of Goffredo Petrassi's *Ottavo Concerto,* led by Carlo Maria Giulini, principal guest conductor. In mid-November, Georg Solti, the orchestra's musical director, gave the first performance of Hans Werner Henze's *Heliogabalus Imperator.* In December, Solti brought to New York a concert version of Berlioz's *La damnation de Faust,* earlier heard in Chicago, with soloists Josephine Veasey, Stuart Burrows, and Roger Soyer, and Margaret Hillis' Chicago Symphony Chorus. Late in December, Solti premiered Alan Stout's *Lieder of Stefan George,* for baritone soloist and orchestra.

In May the Jacksonville Symphony Orchestra under Willis Page brought to New York two works, which were composed for the Florida city's sesquicentennial and had their world premieres there: Duke Ellington's *Celebration* and Carlisle Floyd's monodrama for soprano soloist and orchestra, *Flower and Hawk.*

Opera. At the Metropolitan Opera in New York, Verdi's *Otello,* the final new production of the 22-year regime of Sir Rudolf Bing, was unveiled in March. The lavish staging was by Franco Zeffirelli. Teresa Zylis-Gara, James McCracken, and Sherrill Milnes had the leading roles. Karl Böhm conducted.

The Metropolitan's fall season began with a new production of *Carmen* that was to have been directed by the late Goeran Gentele. Stage director Bodo Igesz executed Gentele's conception based upon conversations and written notes; Marilyn Horne was Carmen, James McCracken, Don José, and Tom Krause, Escamillo. Leonard Bernstein conducted. The production was based on the *"opéra-comique"* version, with spoken dialogue rather than the traditional recitatives composed by Ernest Guiraud after Bizet's death. The result was unconventional and uneven, but many critics thought it brilliant and, on the whole, successful.

There was also a new production of Wagner's *Siegfried,* the third of the series based upon the Salzburg Easter Festival versions of Herbert von Karajan. In 1972, also, the American black conductor Henry Lewis made his debut with the Metropolitan Opera (see BIOGRAPHY).

The operatic highlight of the year was *Treemonisha,* written between 1907 and 1911 by "the father of ragtime," Scott Joplin. The world premiere was held in January at Atlanta's Memorial Arts Center as the climax of an Afro-American Music Workshop sponsored by Morehouse College in that city. Since Joplin's own orchestration has been lost, T. J. Anderson scored the work and Robert Shaw conducted instrumentalists from the Atlanta Symphony. Katherine Dunham choreographed and directed the production. The singers included soprano Alpha Floyd in the title role, tenor Seth McCoy, and bass Simon Estes. The production, this time orchestrated by William Bolcom, was repeated in August at the Filene Center in Wolf Trap Farm Park in Vienna, Va., with the orchestra under Paul Hill.

In March the Seattle Opera offered the world premiere of Thomas Pasatieri's *Black Widow.* Its two main female roles were written for Evelyn Mandac and Joanna Simon, who were praised highly for their respective interpretations. Henry Holt conducted. Another first for Pasatieri was the world premiere, on television in February, of his opera *The Trial of Mary Lincoln,* with a libretto by Anne Howard Bailey. It was especially commissioned by the National Educational Television Opera Theater. Elaine Bonazzi starred in the title role.

Boston became the first U. S. city to see a fully staged performance of Berlioz' two-part Virgilian opera *Les Troyens* in February. Sarah Caldwell's Opera Company of Boston produced the work in the Aquarius Theater, first doing the two parts—*La prise de Troie* and *Les Troyens à Carthage*—on separate evenings and then together on one day. Among the leading singers were Régine Crespin, Maralin Niska, and Louis Quilico. Miss Caldwell conducted.

The San Francisco Opera, celebrating its 50th season, offered the American premiere of Gottfried von Einem's *The Visit* on its fall program. Regina Resnick sang the central role and film director Francis Ford Coppola directed. Also on the docket were three full cycles of Wagner's *Der Ring des Nibelungen.* Paul Hager was stage director for the series, which featured conductor Otmar Suitner and singers Jess Thomas, Birgit Nilsson, and Thomas Stewart. The Chicago Lyric Opera opened its fall season with Verdi's *I due Foscari,* starring Franco Tagliavini and Katia Ricciarelli, and continued with Wagner's *Die Walküre,* Berg's *Wozzeck,* and Debussy's *Pelléas et Mélisande.*

NEWPORT JAZZ FESTIVAL had a peaceful 19th annual meeting in New York City after 1971 disorders in Rhode Island forced its ban there. Among musicians were (from left) Bob Wilbur, Bud Freeman, and Yank Lawson.

SCOTT JOPLIN OPERA Treemonisha, *not performed since it was published by the black pianist in 1911, was given a belated and ambitious staging in 1972 at Atlanta's Memorial Art Center by a workshop from Morehouse College.*

ARTHUR "BUD" SMITH

The Opera Society of Washington, D. C., presented the U. S. premiere of Frederick Delius' *A Village Romeo and Juliet* in April, in an excellent production by Frank Corsaro. The Cincinnati Summer Opera moved from its former home at the city zoo to a newly renovated Music Hall, and opened in June with Boito's *Mefistofele*. Santa Fe was the locale of the American premiere of Aribert Reimann's opera *Melusine* in August.

Abroad, the Paris Opéra, in February, offered the Paris premiere of *Sud,* by the American composer Kenton Coe based on a play by the Paris-born American author Julien Green. London's Covent Garden was the scene, in July, of the world premiere of Peter Maxwell Davies' *Taverner,* loosely based on the life of the 16th century English composer John Taverner.

Festivals. Perhaps the most impressive array of talent at any festival in 1972 was seen at the Munich Festival in Munich, Germany. Two operas had world premieres—Isang Yun's *Sim Tjong,* and Rafael Kubelik's *Cornelia Faroli.* Performing groups included the Sadler's Wells Opera, La Scala, the NHK Symphony of Tokyo, the Moscow Philharmonic (with David Oistrakh), and the Hamburg State Opera.

In nearby Bayreuth, the usually serene atmosphere of the Wagner festival at the Festspielhaus was ruffled by the East German stage director Götz Friedrich's conception of *Tannhäuser,* which some saw as a Communist attack on the bourgeois West German establishment.

At Tanglewood, in August, the Berkshire Music Center's Festival of Contemporary Music celebrated the 20th anniversary of its sponsor, the Fromm Music Foundation. The opening concert included a Fromm commission, Charles Wuorinen's *Concerto for Amplified Violin and Orchestra,* with violinist Paul Zukofsky and the Boston Symphony under Michael Tilson Thomas. Later in the month the Berkshire Music Center Chamber Ensemble under Maderna and Gunther Schuller offered works by Berio, Carter, Maderna, and Schuller—all Fromm commissions. The Schuller and Maderna pieces were world premieres.

POPULAR MUSIC

Just about any moral desired could be read into the kaleidoscopic events on the popular-music scene in 1972. Spurred by the extraordinary interest in Scott Joplin, the ragtime revival continued apace, and Eubie Blake, the ragtime pianist and composer who is nearly 90, became something of a folk hero, giving concerts on the East and West coasts, Canada, St. Louis, and elsewhere.

Meanwhile, the Broadway musical was demonstrating its staying power. *Fiddler on the Roof,* chalking up its 3,225th performance, became Broadway's longest-running show. New York's Vivian Beaumont Theater presented a successful revival of *Man of La Mancha.* The same work opened in Moscow to acclaim a few months later. Meredith Willson's *The Music Man* created a stir in Warsaw, Poland.

In August, the 11th annual Philadelphia Folk Festival had another triumph at the Old Pool Farm. Participants included John Hartford, Bonnie Raitt, Loudon Wainwright III, Don McLean, and Mother Scott, an 80-year-old singer and guitarist who once sang with Leadbelly.

Rock partisans had reason to rejoice as well, though the much-publicized three-day Mar y Sol pop festival in Vega Baja, Puerto Rico, in April proved disappointing in spite of the appearances of B. B. King, the Allman Brothers Band, the Mahavishnu Orchestra, and Rod Stewart and Faces. In July, at Long Pond, Pa., about 200,000 young people congregated at the Pocono International Raceway for the successful Concert 10, at which the standout groups where the J. Geils Band, Humble Pie, Emerson Lake and Palmer, and Three Dog Night. Later in the month the Rolling Stones capped an 18-week, 30-city tour of North America, their first since 1969. Another highlight of 1972 was Elvis Presley's appearance in New York in four summer concerts.

But jazz fans perhaps had the most to cheer about. George Wein moved his Newport Jazz Festival to New York City for nine days in July, and Philharmonic Hall and Carnegie Hall, among other locations, resounded with the sounds of Charlie Byrd, Dizzy Gillespie, Lee Wiley, Ornette Coleman, Stan Getz, Mary Lou Williams, Max Roach, Duke Ellington, and others. Later in July, Ellington and his orchestra appeared at a Duke Ellington Festival in Madison, Wis.; Gov. Patrick Lucey welcomed the group by proclaiming a "Duke Ellington Week" in the state. (See BIOGRAPHY—*Ellington.*)

ROBERT S. CLARK
Contributing Editor, "Stereo Review"

NARCOTICS. See DRUG ADDICTION and special feature beginning on page 37.

——————— NAURU · Information Highlights ———————

Official Name: Republic of Nauru.
Area: 8 square miles (21 sq km).
Population (1970 est.): 7,000. *Density,* 862 per square mile (333 per sq km). *Annual rate of increase,* 5.5%.
Government: *Head of state,* Hammer DeRoburt, president (took office May 1968). *Head of government,* Hammer De-Roburt. *Legislature* (unicameral)—Legislative Assembly, 18 members.
Languages: Nauruan, English (official).
Education: *School enrollment* (1969)—primary, 1,347; secondary, 371.
Monetary Unit: Australian dollar (0.8396 A. dollar equals U.S.$1, July 1972).
Gross National Product (1970): $25,000,000,000.
Major Mineral: Phosphate rock (ranks 5th among world producers, 1970).
Communications: *Telephones* (1971), 525; *radios* (1969), 1,400.

NAURU

Financial and commercial development continued to dominate the affairs of the Republic of Nauru during 1972.

Elections. All nine members of the Nauru Local Government Council were returned to office as the result of elections held on March 11. The council supervises Nauru's commercial enterprises, including aviation, ocean shipping, and tourism.

Foreign Investments. Early in the year President Hammer DeRoburt expressed his government's intention to broaden investments of surplus funds in order to ensure a sustained income when the island's diminishing phosphate deposits are exhausted. In the past most of the phosphate revenues have been invested in Australia. One area of potential investment is the Trust Territory of the Pacific Islands. An offer by Nauru to purchase shares in the trust territory's Transpac ocean cargo line was declined in June, but in September the Nauru Pacific Line was granted cargo shipping rights through the port of Majuro.

Cruise Service. Nauru Pacific, the Nauru-owned shipping line, converted one of its vessels from combined cargo and passenger service to first-class luxury cruising. The ship, the *Enna G,* accommodates 100 passengers. Its cruise schedule in the South Pacific and Coral Sea operates from Sydney, Australia.

HOWARD J. CRITCHFIELD
Western Washington State College

NAVY, U. S. See DEFENSE FORCES.

NEBRASKA

A controversial legislative session, numerous constitutional amendments, a Republican election sweep, increased taxes, new educational leadership, excellent crops, and continued football fever characterized Nebraska in 1972.

Legislature and Government. The Legislature approved a budget of over one-half billion dollars for the year beginning July 1. Gov. J. James Exon vetoed 13 bills, including the two most controversial measures of the session—a $160 million state school aid bill and a business-farm personal property tax exemption measure. The latter veto was overridden by the legislators. New laws also approved "no-fault" divorces, judicial reform, natural resources districts, lowering the age of majority to 19, and increasing homestead tax exemptions for the elderly.

Nebraskans voted on 32 amendments to the state constitution. Most of them were proposed by the Constitution Revision Commission to update the document and were not controversial. All 16 voted

on in the May primary were approved, as were the other 16 in November.

The November election saw Republicans sweep the state. President Nixon defeated George McGovern by 406,298 to 169,991. Republican Congressmen Martin, McCollister, and Thone were reelected, as was U. S. Sen. Carl T. Curtis.

Taxes. The State Board of Equalization raised the personal state income tax rate for 1972 from 10% of federal liability to 15%. The state sales tax remained at 2.5%.

Education. All three University of Nebraska campuses received new chancellors during 1972: James Zumberge at Lincoln, Ronald Roskens at Omaha, and Robert Sparks at the Medical Center. Total enrollment in Nebraska colleges declined for the second year; the four state colleges were hardest hit, with a drop of 13%.

Financing for public elementary and secondary education, now based largely on real estate taxes, was a major concern. Governor Exon vetoed the state aid bill, and when the Legislature refused to repeal a 1965 law requiring the sale of 1.5 million acres of state school land the governor aided in initiating a federal suit that was designed to block the sale.

Church and State. Church-state relations in Nebraska were affected by an amendment to the state constitution that allowed public schools to provide federally financed services for students in parochial or private schools. The arrangement was approved by a 7–2 ruling of the U. S. Supreme Court in October. Also, the 1972 Legislature authorized

——————— NEBRASKA · Information Highlights ———————

Area: 77,227 square miles (200,018 sq km).
Population (1970 census): 1,483,791. *Density,* 19 per sq mi.
Chief Cities (1970 census): Lincoln, the capital, 149,518; Omaha, 346,929; Grand Island, 31,269; Hastings, 23,580; Fremont, 22,962; Bellevue, 21,953; North Platte, 19,447.
Government (1972): *Chief Officers*—governor, J. James Exon (D); lt. gov., Frank Marsh (R); secy. of state, Allen J. Beermann (R); atty. gen., Clarence A. H. Meyer (R); treas., Wayne R. Swanson (R); commissioner of education, Cecil E. Stanley; chief justice, Paul W. White. *Legislature* (unicameral)—49 members (nonpartisan).
Education (1971–72): *Enrollment*—public elementary schools, 188,500 pupils, 8,935 teachers; public secondary, 142,500 pupils, 7,950 teachers; nonpublic schools (1970–71), 44,665 pupils, 2,030 teachers; college and university, 71,000 students. *Public school expenditures,* $224,500,000 ($713 per pupil). *Average teacher's salary,* $8,746.
State Finances (fiscal year 1970): *Revenues,* $486,473,000 (2.5% general sales tax and gross receipts taxes, $74,-883,000; motor fuel tax, $67,781,000; federal funds, $113,-629,000). *Expenditures,* $452,301,000 (education, $174,054,-000; health, welfare, and safety, $12,771,000; highways, $107,183,000). *State debt,* $73,535,000 (June 30, 1970).
Personal Income (1971): $6,045,000,000; per capita, $3,998.
Public Assistance (1971): $75,099,000. *Average monthly payments* (Dec. 1971)—old-age assistance, $58.83; aid to families with dependent children, $152.03.
Labor Force: *Nonagricultural wage and salary earners* (July 1972), 503,300. *Average annual employment* (1971)—manufacturing, 83,000; trade, 122,000; government, 105,000; services, 85,000. *Insured unemployed* (Aug. 1972)—4,100 (1.3%).
Manufacturing (1970): *Value added by manufacture,* $1,471,-000,000. Food and kindred products, $493,300,000; non-electrical machinery, $168,600,000; electrical equipment and supplies, $124,000,000; fabricated metal products, $112,000,000; primary metal industries, $98,400,000; transportation equipment, $75,000,000.
Agriculture (1970): *Cash farm income,* $2,330,017,000 (livestock, $1,446,323,000; crops, $680,687,000; government payments, $203,007,000). *Chief crops* (in order of value, 1971)—Corn, hay, wheat, sorghum grain.
Mining (1970): *Production value,* $74,641,000 (ranks 39th among the states). *Chief minerals*—Petroleum, $35,343,-000; copper, value not available; sand and gravel, $13,-000,000; stone, $8,963,000.
Transportation: *Roads* (1971), 100,445 miles (161,646 km); *motor vehicles* (1971), 974,158; *railroads* (1971), 5,498 miles (8,848 km); *public airports* (1972), 90.
Communications: *Telephones* (1972), 926,400; *television stations* (1971), 14; *radio stations* (1971), 63; *newspapers* (1972), 19 (daily circulation, 487,000).

tuition aid from public funds for students in private colleges in the state.

Agriculture and Industry. Nebraska produced bumper grain crops in 1972 although the harvest was hampered by fall storms. Both total and per-acre yields of corn exceeded previous records. Grain prices were somewhat improved over 1971, especially for wheat, and high livestock prices also stimulated the economy. Construction continued on the Fort Calhoun and Brownville nuclear power plants, both of which were scheduled to be operational in 1973.

Football. Rated Number 1 nationally in football in both 1970 and 1971, the University of Nebraska Cornhuskers retained its position in 1972 as one of the top-rated teams in the nation. Statewide interest in and support of Coach Bob Devaney and the "Big Red" were overwhelming.

ORVILLE H. ZABEL, *Creighton University*

NEPAL

The most important event in Nepal during 1972 was the death of King Mahendra on January 31 and the assumption of power by his 27-year-old son Birendra. King Mahendra had ruled Nepal since 1955. In foreign relations, his adroit handling of Nepal's dealings with neighboring India and China assured the nation's independence. Domestically, his policies did not produce the impetus for economic development that he had sought.

Internal Politics. King Birendra was educated at Eton and later studied for short periods at Harvard and in Israel and Japan. As soon as he ascended the throne, he made it clear that he would follow his father's foreign policy of nonalignment. But throughout most of 1972 he appeared uncertain about his position regarding Nepal's chief domestic problems: slow economic growth and increasing demands for political liberalization. During this period of King Birendra's seeming uncertainty, opponents of the monarchy-dominated panchayat (village and district council) system of government grew continually more outspoken.

In August, this opposition culminated in an unsuccessful attempt by members of the generally passive national legislature to pass a no-confidence motion against the Council of Ministers. At that time, a number of antigovernment members were jailed and others prohibited from attending the remainder of the summer legislative session.

──────── **NEPAL • Information Highlights** ────────

Official Name: Kingdom of Nepal.
Area: 54,362 square miles (140,797 sq km).
Population (1972 est.): 11,800,000. *Density,* 210 per square mile (80 per sq km). *Annual rate of increase,* 2.2%.
Chief City (1961 census): Katmandu, the capital, 175,000 (metropolitan area).
Government: *Head of state,* Birendra Bir Bikram Shah Deva, king (acceded Jan. 1972). *Chief minister,* Kirtinidhi Bista, prime minister (took office April 1971). *Legislature*—National Council, 125 members.
Language: Nepali (official).
Education: *Expenditure* (1967), 6.5% of total public expenditure. *School enrollment* (1969)—primary, 449,141; secondary, 103,069; technical/vocational, 6,000; university/higher, 17,025.
Monetary Unit: Rupee (10.125 rupees equal U. S.$1, Sept. 1972).
Gross National Product (1970): $885,000,000.
Manufacturing (major products): Tobacco products, wood products, textiles.
Major Agricultural Products: Rice, jute, wheat, corn, oilseeds, tobacco, medicinal herbs, forest products.
Foreign Trade: *Chief exports*—Rice, jute and jute products, oilseeds, timber, corn, herbs. *Imports*—Textiles, food, petroleum products, machinery and equipment, iron and steel. *Chief trading partner*—India.
Communications: *Telephones* (1971), 6,200; *radios* (1970), 55,000; *newspapers* (1970), 16.

Also in August, student discontent with a new educational plan crystallized into a boycott of classes and spread to most of the colleges and many of the high schools. There were large-scale arrests of outspoken critics and of student strike leaders, and, in October, the king stated clearly his opposition to the political changes being demanded. These included freedom of the press, sessions of the national legislature open to the public, direct elections to the legislature, and election of the Council of Ministers by the legislature.

The king had reshuffled the Council of Ministers in April, retaining most of his father's appointees, including Prime Minister Kirtinidhi Bista. In October, he selected former Prime Minister Tulsi Giri, an advocate of the political status quo, as his political adviser. Both actions confirmed the king's decision not to alter the form of government.

The Economy. King Birendra's commitment to a revitalization of the economy was underscored by his reorganization of the government's economic planning machinery. He appointed a new six-member National Planning Commission, charged with the responsibility for formulating long-range as well as short-term plans and for biannual evaluation of progress in reaching plan targets. Three of the members were young Ph. D.'s with publicly known progressive views about planning.

FREDERICK H. GAIGE, *Davidson College*

NETHERLANDS

The year 1972 in the Netherlands was marked by a political crisis and continued economic problems. In July, the 13th ministry since World War II fell after one year in office. Elections were held on November 29. The economy, which had been in trouble in 1971 and through the first half of 1972, showed some signs of improving in the second half of the year.

Economy. Through the early months of 1972 both unemployment and the price index continued to rise, though at declining rates. The gross national product, which rose by 5.5% in 1970 and 4% in 1971, was expected to increase by only 2% in 1972. In the summer and fall, however, the economic situation began to appear more promising. The Dutch position with respect to foreign trade had improved, and the volume of exports was increasing more rapidly than that of imports.

Political Crisis. Economic difficulties brought about the fall, on July 20, of the ministry of Barend W. Biesheuvel. Formed in mid-1971, with great difficulty after much political maneuvering, Biesheuvel's coalition ministry proved unable to draft a unanimously approved budget to ease the country's severe inflation, which was running at a rate of about 8% annually. The crisis was precipitated by two ministers belonging to the Democratic Socialists-70 party—Willem Drees of Transport and Waterways and Maurits L. de Brauw of Science and Higher Education. They refused to accept the reductions that were proposed for their two ministries, urging instead a cut in defense spending. They also demanded a sharp and immediate increase in university tuition fees and the freezing of wages and prices. The cabinet rejected their proposals, and the two resigned. With the departure of these ministers, parliamentary support for the cabinet was reduced to 74, one less than half of the members of the Second Chamber.

THE NETHERLANDS' most serious traffic disaster occurred in August on the fog-shrouded Breda-Rotterdam Motorway. Some 20 persons were killed in the pile-up.

UPI

elected. The system used in the Netherlands is proportional representation in very nearly its purest form. While guaranteeing wide representation, it encourages party fragmentation and results in extreme political instability. In the election held in April 1971, 28 parties ran candidates for the Second Chamber, and 14 parties won seats. Reform will require either creation of a new small or single-member district system or the denial of representation to parties unless they obtain a substantial percentage of the total votes. The three major religious parties held discussions about presenting a single group of candidates in the November 29 election, but the idea was abandoned.

Trouble with Turkish Workers. Although the Dutch successfully absorbed some 200,000 refugees from Indonesia after World War II, they occasionally have had trouble assimilating smaller groups of guest workers since that time. Violence against Turkish laborers broke out in Rotterdam on August 8 and raged for several days. The mayor of Rotterdam, seeking to calm the crowds, had to be rescued by the police. The Rotterdam municipal council sought to restrict the number of foreign inhabitants in any city district, but it suspended its new ruling when the central and provincial authorities objected to it.

Nazi Prisoners. Demonstrations and heated debates followed the cabinet's announcement, in February, of its plan to release, on humanitarian grounds, three aged German Nazis imprisoned for serious offenses. The Second Chamber rejected the ministry's proposal by a vote of 81 to 65. In response, the cabinet instituted a commission to examine individual petitions from the prisoners.

AMRY VANDENBOSCH
University of Kentucky

After Biesheuvel failed in his attempt to restore the coalition and then to forge a new ministry, Queen Juliana called for a parliamentary election to be held on November 29. She asked the Biesheuvel ministry, minus the two Social Democrats, to continue in office until a new cabinet could be formed following the election.

Election Results. Over 80% of the electorate participated in the election. Some 750,000 new voters, added to the rolls by the lowering of the voting age from 21 to 18 appeared to show a preference for the extremes of left and right. The Labor party, the largest in Parliament, gained 4 seats, but with a total of 43 seats it still had less than a third of the total membership of the Second Chamber. The Liberals, actually a conservative party, increased their representation from 16 to 22 seats. The Christian Democratic bloc, which constituted the core of the Biesheuvel ministry, was reduced from 58 to 48 seats. The Catholic People's party, the largest party in the Christian Democratic bloc, lost 8 seats and had only 27 in the new Chamber. The so-called Left Wing Alliance, headed by Joop Den Uyl, leader of the Labor party, could be expected to muster only 56 votes in the new Chamber. As a result of the election, the only ministry possible seemed to be an unstable coalition.

Need for Political Reform. The Dutch were deeply concerned about the repeated ministerial crises of the past and considered modifying the system by which the members of parliament are

───── **NETHERLANDS • Information Highlights** ─────

Official Name: Kingdom of the Netherlands.
Area: 15,770 square miles (40,844 sq km).
Population (1972 est.): 13,300,000. *Density*, 826 per square mile (319 per sq km). *Annual rate of increase*, 1.0%.
Chief Cities (1971 est.): Amsterdam, the capital, 820,406; Rotterdam, 679,032; The Hague, 537,643.
Government: *Head of state*, Juliana, queen (acceded Sept. 1948). *Head of government*, Barend W. Biesheuvel (took office July 1971). *Legislature*—Staten-Generaal; First Chamber, 75 members; Second Chamber, 150 members. *Major political parties*—Catholic People's; Labor; Democratic Socialists—70; Christian Historical Union; Freedom and Democracy; Anti-Revolutionary.
Language: Dutch (official).
Education: *Expenditure* (1968), 25.1% of total public expenditure. *School enrollment* (1969)—primary, 1,450,647; secondary, 1,117,020; technical/vocational, 536,460; university/higher, 211,513.
Monetary Unit: guilder (3.236 guilders equal U. S.$1, Sept. 1972).
Gross National Product (1971 est.): $32,600,000,000.
National Income per Person (1970): $2,156.
Economic Indexes: *Industrial production* (1971), 188 (1963 = 100); *agricultural production* (1971), 160 (1952–56 = 100); *consumer price index* (1971), 152 (1963 = 100).
Manufacturing (major products): Metals, processed foods, petroleum products, chemicals, textiles, machinery and equipment, electrical appliances.
Major Agricultural Products: Sugar beets, potatoes, wheat, barley, dairy products.
Major Minerals: Natural gas, petroleum, coal, salt.
Foreign Trade (1971): *Exports*, $13,971,000,000 (chief exports, 1969—food; chemicals; electrical machinery, apparatus, appliances; textile yarn and fabrics). *Imports*, $15,570,-000,000 (chief imports, 1969—food; nonelectrical machinery; mineral fuels and lubricants; chemicals). *Chief trading partners* (1969)—West Germany (took 30% of exports, supplied 27% of imports); Belgium-Luxembourg (14%—18%); France (12%—8%); United States (4%—10%).
Transportation: *Motor vehicles* (1970), 2,826,000 (automobiles, 2,500,000); *railroads* (1970), 1,956 miles (3,148 km); *merchant fleet* (1971), 5,269,000 gross registered tons; *major national airline*, KLM Royal Dutch Airlines.
Communications: *Telephones* (1971), 3,409,842; *television stations* (1971), 13; *television sets* (1971), 3,150,000; *radios* (1969), 4,036,000; *newspapers* (1968), 94 (daily circulation, 3,907,000).

NEVADA · Information Highlights

Area: 110,540 square miles (286,299 sq km).
Population (1970 census): 488,738. *Density:* 4.6 per sq mi.
Chief Cities (1970): Carson City, the capital, 15,468; Las Vegas, 125,787; Reno, 72,863; North Las Vegas, 36,216; Sparks, 24,187; Henderson, 16,395.
Government (1972): *Chief Officers*—governor, Mike O'Callaghan (D); lt. gov., Harry M. Reid (D); secy. of state, John Koontz (D); atty. gen., Robert List (R); treas., Michael Mirabelli (D); supt. of public instruction, Burnell Larsen; chief justice, David Zenoff. *Legislature*—Senate, 20 members (13 Democrats, 7 Republicans); Assembly, 40 members (18 D, 22 R).
Education (1971–72): *Enrollment*—public elementary schools, 75,920 pupils; 2,875 teachers; public secondary, 55,475 pupils; 2.450 teachers; nonpublic schools (1970–71), 4,449 pupils; 190 teachers; college and university, 14,000 students. *Public school expenditures*, $110,100,000 ($910 per pupil). *Average teacher's salary*, $10,600.
State Finances (fiscal year 1970): *Revenues*, $287,822,000 (3% general sales tax and gross receipts taxes, $54,710,000; motor fuel tax, $24,054,000; federal funds, $66,233,000). *Expenditures*, $266,500,000 (education, $90,279,000; health, welfare, and safety, $26,226,000; highways, $54,060,000). *State debt*, $34,111,000 (June 30, 1970).
Personal Income (1971): $2,482,000,000; per capita, $4,895.
Public Assistance (1971): $17,619,000. *Average monthly payments* (Dec. 1971)—old-age assistance, $73.16; aid to families with dependent children, $110.39.
Labor Force: *Nonagricultural wage and salary earners* (July 1972), 221,700. *Average annual employment* (1971)—manufacturing, 8,000; trade, 40,000; government, 38,000; services, 83,000. *Insured unemployed* (Aug. 1972)—6,600 (4.0%).
Manufacturing (1969): *Value added by manufacture*, $161,800,-000. Chemicals and allied products, $31,800,000; printing and publishing, $23,700,000; stone, clay, and glass products, $20,700,000.
Agriculture (1970): *Cash farm income*, $85,403,000 (livestock, $69,192,000; crops, $14,131,000; government payments, $2,080,000). *Chief crops* (in order of value, 1971)—Hay, alfalfa seed, barley, wheat.
Mining (1971): *Production value*, $164,774,000 (ranks 30th among the states). *Chief minerals*—Copper, $100,806,000; gold, $15,464,000; sand and gravel, $12,225,000.
Transportation: *Roads* (1971), 49,704 miles (79,989 km); *motor vehicles* (1971), 354,590; *railroads* (1971), 1,574 miles (2,533 km); *public airports* (1972), 52.
Communications: *Telephones* (1972), 362,400; *television stations* (1971), 7; *radio stations* (1971), 29; *newspapers* (1972), 7 (daily circulation, 148,000).

NEVADA

Although the unemployment rate continued at a high 6.7% level during 1972, tourism and gaming were on the upswing, and the state of Nevada continued to prosper economically.

Elections. A big political upset was pulled by James Bilbray, a 34-year-old Las Vegas attorney, in defeating 10-term conservative Congressman Walter Baring in the Democratic primary. However, Bilbray was in turn upset by the Republican candidate, Minden realtor David Towell, who was elected to Congress in his first try for public office. Towell received 53% of the vote cast and was helped considerably by Baring's endorsement and President Nixon's coattails.

Economy. Despite the closing of a large hotel-casino at north Lake Tahoe, the gaming industry continued to thrive during the year. Nevada casinos had gross revenues of $657.7 million during the 1971–72 fiscal year, an increase of 12% over the previous year. Revenue from gambling taxes increased substantially due to congressional action in late 1971 that returns 90% of the federal slot-machine tax to the state for educational purposes.

A number of Las Vegas gaming operators were indicted by a federal grand jury for falsifying the amounts of winnings at certain hotel-casinos, but the first defendants, tried by jury in the fall, were acquitted, and the others were still awaiting trial at the end of the year.

Education. The Las Vegas schools were two weeks late in opening in September 1972 because of a dispute over federal Judge Bruce Thompson's order to use extensive busing for integration. The

state supreme court dissolved the stay order issued by a state district judge and ultimately ruled that the state judge did not have the authority to intervene in the case. The busing plan was then put into effect with little interference from parents.

The University of Nevada, Reno, had an 8% decrease in enrollment for the fall semester, 1972, whereas the University of Nevada, Las Vegas, had a slight increase, and the two new community colleges in Las Vegas and Carson City enrolled more students than had been expected.

Legislature. A special three-judge federal panel upheld the reapportionment plan passed by the 1971 Legislature. The 1973 Nevada Legislature was to be controlled by the Democrats, with a 25–15 margin in the Assembly and a 14–6 majority in the Senate.

DON W. DRIGGS, *University of Nevada*

NEW BRUNSWICK

In 1972 the twin problems of unemployment and regional economic stagnation were dominant public issues in New Brunswick. In the political sphere, the axe fell on one of the most flamboyant members of Premier Richard Hatfield's Conservative cabinet. In the October 30 federal elections, the Conservatives and Liberals each won five parliamentary seats —exactly as in 1968.

Among the 80 bills passed by the legislature were a massive community planning bill allowing the government to create seven regional districts for planning purposes; a measure to lower the age of

NEW BRUNSWICK · Information Highlights

Area: 27,985 square miles (72,481 sq km).
Population: 634,557 (1971 census).
Chief Cities (1971 census): Fredericton, the capital (24,254); St. John (89,039); Moncton (47,891).
Government: *Chief Officers* (1972)—lt. gov., Hedard J. Robichaud; premier, Richard B. Hatfield (Progressive Conservative); prov. secy., Rodman E. Logan; min. of justice, John B. M. Baxter (P. C.); min. of finance, Jean-Maurice Simard (P. C.); min. of educ., J. Lorne McGuigan (P. C.); chief justice, G. F. G. Bridges. *Legislature*—Legislative Assembly, 58 members (33 Progressive Conservative, 25 Liberal).
Education: *School enrollment* (1968–69)—public elementary and secondary, 169,703 pupils (7,252 teachers); private, 468 pupils (60 teachers); Indian (federal) schools, 682 pupils (28 teachers); college and university, 8,961 students. *Public school expenditures* (1971 est.)—$107,830,-000; average teacher's salary (1968–69), $5,520.
Public Finance (fiscal year 1972 est.): *Revenues*, $466,100,000 (sales tax, $96,100,000; income tax, $56,100,000; federal funds, $216,900,000). *Expenditures*, $499,200,000 (education, $150,200,000; health and social welfare, $150,300,000; transport and communications, $70,400,000).
Personal Income (1969 est.): $1,302,000,000.
Social Welfare (fiscal year 1972 est.): $44,300,000 (aged and blind, $14,200,000; dependents and unemployed, $20,-300,000).
Manufacturing (1968): Value added by manufacture, $240,753,-000 (food and beverages, $76,097,000; paper and allied industries, $57,433,000; wood industries, $19,737,000; transportation equipment, $14,918,000; electrical products, $14,653,000; fabricated metals, $10,189,000).
Agriculture (1971): *Cash farm income*, $51,599,000 (livestock and products, $31,364,000; crops, $18,397,000). *Chief crops* (cash receipts)—potatoes, $13,549,000 (ranks 2d among the provinces); fruits, $1,719,000; vegetables, $1,648,000.
Mining (1971 est.): *Production value*, $107,361,000. *Chief minerals* (tons)—zinc, 159,567; lead, 1,298,883; copper, 9,959; silver, 5,011,000 troy ounces; coal, 510,000 tons.
Fisheries (1971): *Commercial catch*, sea fish. (Statistics of freshwater fish are confidential)—370,054,000 pounds ($16,-245,000). *Leading species*—lobster, 5,866,000 pounds ($4,765,000); herring, 241,949,000 pounds ($3,685,000); tuna, 6,699,000 pounds ($1,456,000); redfish, 31,093,000 pounds ($1,014,000).
Transportation: *Roads* (1968), 13,330 miles (21,450 km); *motor vehicles* (1969), 199,980; *licensed airports* (1971 est.), 13.
Communications: *Telephones* (1969), 215,533; *television stations* (1971), 11; *radio stations* (1971), 13; *daily newspapers* (1971), 6.
(All monetary figures given in Canadian dollars.)

majority from 21 to 19; and another to boost the remuneration of members of the Legislative Assembly from $5,000 to $8,000 a session, as well as to raise their expense accounts.

The Economy. On January 13, Premier Hatfield and the federal minister of regional economic expansion, Jean Marchand, jointly announced a stopgap, $10 million spending program to create 3,000 jobs in the depressed northeastern part of the province. In February the unemployment situation was dramatized nationally when militant jobless took over the Bathurst office of the Unemployment Insurance Commission for two days in a widely publicized protest against delays in the issuance of insurance checks.

Politics. Hatfield announced on August 16 that he had asked for the resignation of his controversial, outspoken tourism minister, Charles Van Horne, because of work orders issued by Van Horne without competitive bids. Hatfield subsequently appointed a two-man inquiry board to investigate "unapproved and unauthorized financial commitments" by the tourism department. The board's report, made public December 20, found that Van Horne had followed "wasteful and inefficient practices."

Francophone Culture. At Fredericton, on May 20–22, the first general conference of Acadians took place. Delegates agreed to establish a provincial Francophone association to defend Acadian interests. Demands for extended French-language services from the provincial government were prominent among 150 resolutions considered.

Premier Hatfield paid a "very, very successful" visit to France in November and had talks with Premier Pierre Messmer, Foreign Minister Maurice Schumann, and other senior cabinet members. On November 17 in Paris he said that he expected the journey would result in an increased flow of French experts to his province to assist in government and in educational and industrial development.

JOHN BEST
Foreign Affairs Editor, The Canadian Press, Ottawa

NEW HAMPSHIRE

New Hampshire was dominated by national and state politics in the election year of 1972.

Special Session of the Legislature. Gov. Walter Peterson called the legislature into special session in February and March. The leading concern was "tax reform," long the dominant political issue in New Hampshire, the only state in the union without either a general sales tax or a general income tax. The special session was urged to pass a combination income-sales tax to provide more than the $200 million plus state biennial budget. Much of these new revenues was promised to cities and towns to alleviate the rising level of property taxes, almost the sole source of income for local government. But the special session refused tax "reform."

The special legislative session also refused to pass a no-fault auto insurance plan, refused to reform the abortion law, and did little to implement recent voter approval of "open-space" requirements aimed at holding land away from developers and thus saving the natural beauty of the state.

Presidential Primary. New Hampshire's "first in the nation" primary had three candidates in the Republican contest: President Nixon, Congressman John Ashbrook (R-Ohio), and Congressman Paul (Pete) McCloskey (R-Calif.). The seven candidates in the Democratic primary included Senators George McGovern (D-S. Dak.), Edmund Muskie (D-Me.), and Mayor Sam Yorty of Los Angeles.

The challenges to President Nixon were from McCloskey on a strong anti-Vietnam War theme and from Ashbrook on more conservative grounds. President Nixon received an overwhelming endorsement (70%).

Senator McGovern gathered 37% of the Democratic vote, showing more strength than many had supposed. Senator Muskie's total fell below the expected 50% level (he actually got 47%), inviting speculation that there was a weakness in the man from Maine. The opposition of the Manchester *Union-Leader* cost Senator Muskie his "magic number" since only in the city of Manchester did the newspaper-backed candidate (Yorty) gain any support among Democrats. Yet, others would blame Senator Muskie's disappointing total on his emotional confrontation with the *Union-Leader*.

State Election. The gubernatorial contest was won by Republican Meldrim Thomson, a well-known opponent of taxes, who received 42% of the vote. Democrat Roger J. Crowley won 39%, and independent Malcolm McLane, a liberal Republican, received 19%. Incumbent Governor Peterson had been defeated by Thomson in the primaries.

National Election. President Nixon received a heavy vote in the presidential election, winning 64% of the vote to Senator McGovern's 35%. Sen. Thomas McIntyre, a Democrat, was reelected to the U. S. Senate. He bucked the Republican tide by defeating former Gov. Wesley Powell. Both Republican congressmen, Louis C. Wyman and James C. Cleveland, were easily reelected to their offices.

ROBERT E. CRAIG, *University of New Hampshire*

------- **NEW HAMPSHIRE • Information Highlights** -------

Area: 9,304 square miles (24,097 sq km).
Population (1970 census): 737,681. *Density:* 84 per sq mi.
Chief Cities (1970 census): Concord, the capital, 30,022; Manchester, 87,754; Nashua, 55,820; Portsmouth, 25,717.
Government (1972): *Chief Officers*—governor, Walter Peterson (R); secy. of state, Robert L. Stark (R); atty. gen., Warren R. Rudman (R); treas., Robert W. Flanders; commissioner of education, Newell J. Paire; chief justice, Frank R. Kenison. *General Court*—Senate, 24 members (15 Republicans, 9 Democrats); House of Representatives, 400 members (249 R, 149 D, 2 vacancies).
Education (1971–72): *Enrollment*—public elementary schools, 97,345 pupils; 4,097 teachers; public secondary, 66,757 pupils; 3,353 teachers; nonpublic schools (1970–71), 27,578 pupils; 1,600 teachers; college and university, 30,000 students. *Public school expenditures,* $127,962,000 ($847 per pupil). *Average teacher's salary,* $9,039.
State Finances (fiscal year 1970): *Revenues,* $281,268,000 (total sales and gross receipts taxes, $62,778,000; motor fuel tax, $23,865,000; federal funds, $56,114,000). *Expenditures,* $273,445,000 (education, $71,583,000; health, welfare, and safety, $29,127,000; highways, $71,440,000). *State debt,* $157,949,000 (June 30, 1970).
Personal Income (1971): $2,826,000,000; per capita, $3,708.
Public Assistance (1971): $32,881,000. *Average monthly payments* (Dec. 1971)—old-age assistance, $168.24; aid to families with dependent children, $216.50.
Labor Force: *Nonagricultural wage and salary earners* (July 1972), 277,700. *Average annual employment* (1971)—manufacturing, 85,000; trade, 51,000; government, 39,000; services, 47,000. *Insured unemployed* (Aug. 1972)—3,400 (1.8%).
Manufacturing (1970): *Value added by manufacture,* $1,048,300,000. Electrical equipment and supplies, $213,600,000; nonelectrical machinery, $138,200,000; leather products, $124,500,000; paper and allied products, $101,300,000.
Agriculture (1970): *Cash farm income,* $55,150,000 (livestock, $41,354,000; crops, $13,248,000; government payments, $548,000). *Chief crops* (in order of value, 1971)—Hay, apples, sweet corn, potatoes.
Mining (1971): *Production value,* $10,284,000 (ranks 48th among the states). Chief minerals—Sand and gravel, $6,777,000; stone, $3,433,000; clays, $34,000.
Transportation (1971): *Roads,* 14,823 miles (23,855 km); *motor vehicles,* 361,711; *public airports* (1972), 16.
Communications: *Telephones* (1972), 452,300; *television stations* (1971), 3; *radio stations* (1971), 39; *newspapers* (1972), 9 (daily circulation, 169,000).

NEW JERSEY

In 1972 there was an unsuccessful attempt to reform the state's tax structure and continued evidence of corruption at all levels of government.

President Nixon easily carried the state in the November elections, and Republican Sen. Clifford P. Case won a fourth term by defeating Paul Krebs.

Tax Reform. The long-awaited recommendations of Gov. William T. Cahill's Tax Policy Commission came in late January. They contained proposals for an income tax, a statewide property tax, an expanded sales tax, and higher business and corporation taxes. The chief objective was to ease local property taxes and thus provide greater financial flexibility for major urban areas. Under the new program, local property taxes would have a ceiling of $3 for every $100 of assessed valuation with an additional statewide tax of $1 for every $100 assessment. The most controversial feature of the proposals was the income tax, which called for a graduated 1% to 7% tax on all income earned in New Jersey up to $23,000 and a top rate of 14% for incomes over $500,000.

Legislative reaction to the program was hostile, although many felt there was no alternative in view of the order of the state supreme court to find a substitute for local property taxes as a means of financing public education. Governor Cahill supported the plan, as did the New Jersey Tenants Organization, which was attracted by the income deduction allowed to renters. Opposition mounted during the spring of 1972, stemming largely from the state AFL-CIO, the wealthy suburbs that resented a program they thought was designed to benefit the cities at their expense, and many lower-middle-class workers who were against new taxation on principle. The whole tax program was defeated at a special session of the legislature in early July, but Governor Cahill vowed to make tax reform a major issue in his 1973 reelection campaign.

Politics. In January the Republicans gained control of the Assembly—even though they were outnumbered—by persuading Assemblyman David Friedland, a Hudson County Democrat, to vote for Republican Thomas Kean for speaker. Some viewed this as a scandal, while others felt it was a political deal to secure Republican support for the tax program. The Republicans also gained in congressional

"PEACE NAVY," consisting of antiwar demonstrators in canoes, attempt to delay loading of munitions on a cargo ship at the Earle Naval Ammunition Depot, off Leonardo, N. J.

NEW JERSEY • Information Highlights

Area: 7,836 square miles (20,295 sq km).
Population (1970 census): 7,168,164. *Density,* 969 per sq mi.
Chief Cities (1970 census): Trenton, the capital, 104,638; Newark, 382,288; Jersey City, 260,545; Paterson, 144,824; Elizabeth, 112,654; Camden, 102,551; Clifton, 82,437; Bayonne, 72,743.
Government (1972): *Chief Officers*—governor, William T. Cahill (R); secy. of state, Paul J. Sherwin (R); atty. gen., George F. Kugler, Jr. (R); treas., Joseph M. McCrane, Jr.; commissioner, dept. of education, Carl L. Marburger; chief justice, Joseph Weintraub. *Legislature*—Senate, 40 members (24 Republicans, 16 Democrats); General Assembly, 80 members (39 R, 40 D, 1 Independent).
Education (1971–72): *Enrollment*—public elementary schools, 1,003,556 pupils, 44,560 teachers; public secondary, 516,-983 pupils, 30,331 teachers; nonpublic schools (1970–71), 263,106 pupils, 11,700 teachers; college and university, 217,000 students. *Public school expenditures,* $1,735,000,-000 ($1,289 per pupil). *Average teacher's salary,* $11,350.
State Finances (fiscal year 1970): *Revenues,* $2,624,852,000 (5% general sales tax and gross receipts taxes, $355,-613,000; motor fuel tax, $200,318,000; federal funds, $458,611,000). *Expenditures,* $2,539,755,000 (education, $705,264,000; health, welfare, and safety, $159,504,000; highways, $572,626,000). *State debt,* $1,762,768,000 (June 30, 1970).
Personal Income (1971): $35,271,000,000; per capita, $4,832.
Public Assistance (1971): $585,122,000. *Average monthly payments* (Dec. 1971)—old-age assistance, $75.55; aid to families with dependent children, $255.57.
Labor Force: *Nonagricultural wage and salary earners* (July 1972), 2,644,100. *Average annual employment* (1971)—manufacturing, 816,000; trade, 558,000; government, 385,-000; services, 420,000. *Insured unemployed* (Aug. 1972)—97,500 (4.8%).
Manufacturing (1970): *Value added by manufacture,* $14,296,-600,000. Chemicals and allied products, $3,473,900,000; electrical equipment and supplies, $1,663,700,000; food and kindred products, $1,407,300,000; nonelectrical machinery, $1,171,100,000; fabricated metal products, $1,018,-700,000; transportation equipment, $707,700,000; stone, clay, and glass products, $589,700,000.
Agriculture (1970): *Cash farm income,* $246,918,000 (livestock, $96,464,000; crops, $146,162,000; government payments, $4,292,000). *Chief crops* (in order of value, 1971)—Tomatoes, hay, peaches, potatoes.
Mining (1971): *Production value,* $93,575,000 (ranks 36th among the states). *Chief minerals*—Sand and gravel, $38,279,000; stone, $36,157,000; zinc, $9,653,000; magnesium compounds, value not available.
Fisheries (1971): *Commercial catch,* 114,416,000 pounds ($12,-025,000). *Leading species by value:* Clams, $5,559,000; lobsters, $1,425,000; menhaden, $1,023,000; oysters, $675,-000.
Transportation: *Roads* (1971), 32,059 miles (51,593 km); *motor vehicles* (1971), 3,585,637; *railroads* (1971), 1,764 miles (2,839 km); *public airports* (1972), 27.
Communications: *Telephones* (1972), 4,971,600; *television stations* (1971), 4; *radio stations* (1971), 61; *newspapers* (1972), 30 (daily circulation, 1,851,000).

reapportionment. On April 12 a federal court ordered a redistricting so as to eliminate one Hudson County Democratic seat (that of Cornelius Gallagher) and to create two new districts: the first in the rural northwest and the second in an all-black district of Newark.

Corruption. The year witnessed a further stage in the collapse of the Hudson County political machine of John V. Kenny. In the spring, Kenny was found to be in good enough health to stand trial for filing false income tax returns and extorting kickbacks from contractors doing business in the county. He pleaded guilty in federal court and was fined $30,000 and sentenced to a possible 18 years in jail, depending on his health. He is now in the federal prison hospital in St. Louis. An important step for reformers, known as the "Mayors Coalition," was achieved in June when they defeated the organization slate in Hudson County elections.

As in past years there were a number of indictments concerning corruption in office. The most important was against Secretary of State Paul Sherwin, the second most important man in the Cahill administration. He was charged with accepting a $10,000 bribe from the president of a construction company for a $300,000 contract to construct a portion of Route 46 in Warren County. In November, Sherwin was sentenced to from one to two years in prison.

Hackensack Meadows. After a two-year controversy between conservationists and developers, a compromise concerning the Hackensack Meadows was reached. Plans had called for the creation of a city of 150,000 and a major sports complex, but influential conservationist groups pointed out that a major wildlife preserve would thus be destroyed. The compromise called for maintaining at least one third of the Meadows in their natural state and reducing the size of the planned city to 120,000.

HERMANN K. PLATT
St. Peter's College, Jersey City

NEW MEXICO

In 1972, New Mexicans wrestled with problems of crime, drug abuse, and environmental preservation, while commemorating 60 years of statehood.

Political Activity. In the November elections, Congressmen Manuel Lujan, Jr., Republican, and Harold Runnels, Democrat, won reelection. Republican Pete V. Domenici took the U. S. Senate seat vacated by Democrat Clinton P. Anderson.

Education. State educational facilities responded to growing public demands for new programs in bilingual (English-Spanish) instruction. The state Department of Education made plans for opening a third bilingual teacher-training center in Roswell to supplement centers already functioning in Silver City and Las Vegas.

Manuel Reyes Mazón, a native of Gallup, was named director of the Institute of Cultural Pluralism at the University of New Mexico. Funded by the U. S. Office of Education, this institute, the only one of its kind, will provide technical assistance to Teacher Corps projects throughout the nation.

Health and Drug Abuse. In May, Gov. Bruce King disbanded his interagency Drug Abuse Task Force, established in mid-1971, and transferred its responsibilities to the more comprehensive Health Care Task Force. The latter body now formulates policy for alcoholism, drug abuse, and the commu-

nity health care programs, which the Department of Hospitals and Institutions administers and monitors.

Crime. Growing lawlessness aroused consternation among New Mexicans. On August 29, the FBI released a report showing that Albuquerque, the state's largest city, had the highest crime rate in the nation. It had 5,926 serious crimes per 100,000 population, a figure higher than that for Miami, Los Angeles, or New York City. Early in the same month, Governor King issued an emergency proclamation enjoining state police to concentrate all efforts upon breaking a criminal ring believed responsible for the theft of priceless Spanish colonial religious art taken from 15 churches over the past two years.

Environment. Public concern over the unregulated activities of large land subdividers, who were chopping up huge rural tracts, led to the introduction of seven different subdivision bills during the 60-day session of the 30th Legislature. All measures died, however, owing mainly to the lawmakers' reluctance to address the controversial problem of land-use controls.

The state Evironmental Improvement Agency fought a proposal by Tucson Gas and Electric Company to construct a more than 250-mile-long transmission line along the western New Mexico border from the new San Juan Power Plant near Farmington to Tucson, Ariz., but the state Public Service Commission declared in favor of the project.

MARC SIMMONS
Author and Historian

——— **NEW MEXICO · Information Highlights** ———

Area: 121,666 square miles (315,115 sq km).
Population (1970 census): 1,016,000. *Density,* 8.5 per sq mi.
Chief Cities (1970): Santa Fe, the capital, 41,167; Albuquerque, 243,751; Las Cruces, 37,857; Roswell, 33,908; Clovis, 28,495; Hobbs, 26,025.
Government (1972): *Chief Officers*—governor, Bruce King (D); lt. gov., Robert A. Mondragon (D); secy. of state, Mrs. Betty Fiorina (D); atty. gen., David L. Norvell (D); treas., Jesse D. Kornegay (D); supt. of public instruction, Leonard LeLayo; chief justice, J. C. Compton. *Legislature*—Senate, 42 members (28 Democrats, 14 Republicans); House of Representatives, 70 members (48 D, 22 R).
Education (1971–72): *Enrollment*—public elementary schools, 154,295 pupils, 6,110 teachers; public secondary, 131,379 pupils, 5,750 teachers; nonpublic schools (1970–71), 13,-837 pupils, 810 teachers; college and university. 46,000 students. *Public school expenditures,* $208,079,000 ($807 per pupil). *Average teacher's salary,* $8,450.
State Finances (fiscal year 1970): *Revenues,* $604,901,000 (4% general sales tax and gross receipts taxes, $85,-709,000; motor fuel tax, $42,516,000; federal funds, $178,-066,000). *Expenditures,* $544,301,000 (education, $266,-805,000; health, welfare, and safety, $75,092,000; highways, $107,059,000). *State debt,* $120,694,000 (June 30, 1970).
Personal Income (1971): $3,495,000,000; per capita, $3,394.
Public Assistance (1971): $55,074,000. *Average monthly payments* (Dec. 1971)—old-age assistance, $54.40; aid to families with dependent children, $115.57.
Labor Force: *Nonagricultural wage and salary earners* (July 1972), 323,000. *Average annual employment* (1971)—manufacturing, 21,000; trade, 64,000; government, 92,000; services, 54,000. *Insured unemployed* (Aug. 1972)—6,600 (3.4%).
Manufacturing (1969): *Value added by manufacture,* $207,-200,000. Food and kindred products, $42,600,000; printing and publishing, $19,400,000; stone, clay, and glass products, $19,100,000; electrical equipment and supplies, $10,900,000.
Agriculture (1970): *Cash farm income,* $509,872,000 (livestock, $372,276,000; crops, $94,505,000; government payments, $43,091,000). *Chief crops* (in order of value, 1971)—Hay, sorghum grain, cotton lint, lettuce.
Mining (1970): *Production value,* $1,073,589,000 (ranks 8th among the states). *Chief minerals*—Petroleum, $419,-566,000 copper, $193,916,000; natural gas, $161,926,000; potassium salts, $84,343,000.
Transportation: *Roads* (1971), 67,326 miles (108,348 km); *motor vehicles* (1971), 637,371; *railroads* (1971), 2,120 miles (3,412 km); *public airports* (1972), 65.
Communications: *Telephones* (1972), 530,600; *television stations* (1971), 7; *radio stations* (1971), 73; *newspapers* (1972), 20 (daily circulation, 224,000).

G. E. ARNOLD

The New Orleans Theater for the Performing Arts, scheduled to open in early 1973.

NEW ORLEANS

Construction in New Orleans continued at a record-breaking pace in 1972. Other highlights included the continued war on crime and the near completion of the first building of a new cultural center.

Construction. On the drawing boards were $447 million worth of office buildings, hotels, and retail outlets within the central business district, and Mayor Moon Landrieu announced a plan to refurbish the area. Businessmen were to be brought into the planning, and a special taxing district was to be created. Plans for a "new town" project in the eastern area of New Orleans would allow the city to contract with federal agencies and private enterprise to develop a new residential section. Office building construction was led by the opening of One Shell Square, a $50 million, 51-story structure, the tallest in the state. Plans were also announced for a $1 million renovation project that would turn the area around St. Louis Cathedral into a "people place," which would include new malls and landscaping, with a sweeping view of the Mississippi River.

Construction of the 28-story, $150 million Louisiana Superdome, which will seat 75,185 spectators, was one-third complete in 1972. Opening was set for mid-1974. The massive building, believed to be the largest indoor arena in the world, was one of the highlights of the largest building boom in the 254-year history of New Orleans.

Cultural Center. After more than a decade of planning and building and several decades of dreaming, a cultural center in New Orleans became a reality. The New Orleans Theater for the Performing Arts was nearly completed in 1972. Its opening, which had been set for November 1972, was delayed until sometime in 1973. The 2,316-seat theater, which will be the home of the New Orleans Philharmonic Symphony Orchestra and the New Orleans Opera House Association, promised to be only the first of a group of theaters that will make up a cultural center at some time in the future. New Orleans, which was a leader in the nation's cultural life in the 19th and early 20th centuries, has long been without a suitable concert hall, and operas have not been performed in a suitable house since the burning of the old French Opera House in 1919.

Port of New Orleans. The port, the city's largest industry, continued its $40 million expansion program in 1972. The first of nine containerized cargo terminals was leased, while work was progressing on the second. Port tonnage for 1972 decreased 7%, but grain exports increased 20%, making New Orleans first in the world in grain export.

War on Crime. The police took a bold step in 1972, when Superintendent Clarence Giarrusso announced the formation of a felony action squad—a volunteer group of policemen ordered to shoot and kill any felon who was armed with a weapon and refused to heed the police. Chief Giarrusso also changed police policy and began identifying certain juvenile offenders. Meanwhile, a Parish (County) Prison report cited the need of a new jail, pointing out the health and security hazards in the present antiquated prison.

Politics. New Orleans was able for the first time to elect two of its own residents to high-ranking state offices. They were Lt. Gov. James E. Fitzmorris, Jr., and Attorney General William Guste.

On October 16, a light plane carrying U. S. Rep. Hale Boggs of New Orleans and three other men disappeared on a flight from Anchorage to Juneau, Alaska. Boggs was House majority leader.

Other News. The Federal Environmental Protection Agency threatened to cut off federal funds to New Orleans unless the city stopped dumping raw sewage into the Mississippi River. A period of grace was allowed in which to correct the situation.

The city, amid some controversy, continued its policy of detouring vehicles and thus converting Bourbon and Royal streets—the main streets of the French Quarter, or Vieux Carré—into pedestrian malls during peak traffic hours.

VINCENT P. RANDAZZO, JR.
"The Times-Picayune," New Orleans

NEW YORK

Deteriorating state-city relations, state finances, and a disastrous flood in western New York were among the major concerns of New Yorkers in 1972. In a presidential election year, most of the political excitement in the state was generated by a few congressional races.

Elections. President Richard M. Nixon easily carried the state in the presidential election. The Democratic congressional primary in June attracted much attention, especially in New York City, where redistricting on the basis of the 1970 census had eliminated two U. S. House of Representatives seats and had thrown two pairs of incumbent Democrats into competition with each other. In these races, Jonathan B. Bingham defeated James H. Scheuer in the newly drawn 22d district, and William F. Ryan defeated Bella S. Abzug in the 20th district. After Ryan's death on September 17, the Democrats nominated Mrs. Abzug to run in his place. Ryan's widow, Priscilla M. Ryan, who had sought the Democratic nomination, received the Liberal party nomination.

In a surprising Democratic primary vote in another New York City district, newcomer Elizabeth Holtzman, a 30-year-old lawyer, defeated 84-year-old Rep. Emanuel Celler, who had served in Congress for 50 years and was chairman of the House Judiciary Committee. In the November election, Bingham, Abzug, and Holtzman were easy victors. And New York's congressional delegation of 39 members (reduced from 41 as a result of the census) remained largely as before, with 22 Democrats and 17 Republicans.

In contests for seats in the newly apportioned state legislature, Republicans gained 5 seats in the Senate (for a total of 37, to 23 for the Democrats) and 4 seats in the Assembly (for a total of 83 to 67). A $1.15 billion environmental bond issue on the November ballot received the overwhelming approval of New York voters.

Legislation. The year opened with Gov. Nelson Rockefeller's attempt to close an anticipated 15-month budget gap of $1.5 billion. Because the fate of New York City's transit fare was linked to the state's fiscal problems, the governor had called a special legislative session late in December 1971. An impasse, created by sharp divisions along both party and regional lines, was broken on January 4, when the legislators compromised on a $407 million tax increase package, which included a 2.5% surcharge on the state income tax for 5 years, and then passed legislation limiting the New York City transit fare increase to 5 cents, for a 35-cent fare.

When the regular session convened on January 5, the governor submitted a "no growth" budget of $7.87 billion for the fiscal year 1972–73. New York City Democrats joined with Republicans in passing this budget in which school, welfare, narcotics education, and revenue-sharing aid was held at the previous year's level and the City University of New York was kept tuition free. Among other major bills passed by the legislature and signed by the

NEW WATER POLLUTION control system (left, foreground) cleans industrial wastewater entering Hudson River from paper mill near Corinth, N. Y.

UPI

──────── **NEW YORK** • **Information Highlights** ────────

Area: 49,576 square miles (128,402 sq km).
Population (1970 census): 18,241,266. *Density:* 384 per sq mi.
Chief Cities (1970 census): Albany, the capital, 115,781; New York, 7,895,563; Buffalo, 462,768; Rochester, 296,233; Yonkers, 204,297; Syracuse, 197,297.
Government (1972): *Chief Officers*—governor, Nelson A. Rockefeller (R); lt. gov., Malcolm Wilson (R); secy. of state, John P. Lomenzo (R); atty. gen., Louis J. Lefkowitz (R); commissioner of education, Ewald B. Nyquist; chief judge, Stanley H. Fuld. *Legislature*—Senate, 57 members (32 Republicans, 25 Democrats); Assembly, 150 members (79 R, 71 D).
Education (1971–72): *Enrollment*—public elementary schools, 1,921,000 pupils, 92,600 teachers; public secondary, 1,-596,000 pupils, 94,900 teachers; nonpublic schools (1970–71), 747,049 pupils, 31,250 teachers; college and university, 849,000 students. *Public school expenditures,* $4,645,405,-000 ($1,468 per pupil). *Average teacher's salary,* $12,100.
State Finances (fiscal year 1970): *Revenues,* $10,350,729,000 (4% general sales tax and gross receipts taxes, $1,012,-036,000; motor fuel tax, $374,821,000; federal funds, $1,-977,504,000). *Expenditures,* $9,894,498,000 (education, $3,-362,209,000; health, welfare, and safety, $394,599,000; highways, $1,092,574,000). *State debt,* $7,387,836,000 (March 31, 1970).
Personal Income (1971): $92,335,000,000; per capital, $5,021.
Public Assistance (1971): $3,539,980,000. *Average monthly payments* (Dec. 1971)—old-age assistance, $102.36; aid to families with dependent children, $287.68.
Labor Force: *Nonagricultural wage and salary earners* (July 1972), 6,935,900. *Average annual employment* (1971)—manufacturing, 1,635,000; trade, 1,422,000; government, 1,-238,000; services, 1,360,000. *Insured unemployed* (Aug. 1972)—216,300 (3.7%).
Manufacturing (1970): *Value added by manufacture,* $28,426,-800,000. Printing and publishing, $3,928,300,000; electrical equipment and supplies, $3,038,700,000; apparel and other textile products, $2,987,400,000; instruments and related products, $2,916,100,000; nonelectrical machinery, $2,555,-500,000.
Agriculture (1970): *Cash farm income,* $1,133,289,000 (livestock, $810,588,000; crops, $300,692,000; government payments, $22,009,000). *Chief crops* (in order of value, 1971) —Hay, potatoes, grapes, apples (ranks 2d among the states).
Mining (1971): *Production value,* $298,836,000 (ranks 24th among the states). *Chief minerals*—Stone, $73,418,000; salt, $43,601,000; sand and gravel, $28,328,000.
Fisheries (1971): *Commercial catch,* 36,617,000 pounds ($18,-676,000). *Leading species by value:* Clams, $11,254,000; lobsters, $2,054,000; oysters, $1,682,000; flounder, $945,268.
Transportation: *Roads* (1971), 105,753 miles (170,188 km); *motor vehicles* (1971), 6,718,026; *railroads* (1971), 5,624 miles (9,051 km); *public airports* (1972), 68.
Communications: *Telephones* (1972), 12,341,800; *television stations* (1971), 29; *radio stations* (1971), 254; *newspapers* (1972), 80 (daily circulation, 7,405,000).

governor was one creating a state board to settle controversies regarding the location of new electric power plants. The lawmakers also passed a proposed constitutional amendment permitting the legislature to legalize any form of gambling. But to take effect, the amendment must be passed by the next legislature and then approved by the voters.

Among measures vetoed by the governor was a bill repealing the state's liberalized abortion law passed in 1970. Subsequently, in July, the New York court of appeals upheld the constitutionality of the liberalized law. This decision is on appeal to the U. S. Supreme Court. The governor also vetoed a bill, passed by wide margins in the legislature, that would have imposed a moratorium on the compulsory assignment of school children to achieve racial balance. The veto message cited the fact that a similar antibusing law, passed in 1969, had been declared unconstitutional by federal courts in 1970.

A "no fault" automobile accident insurance bill was buried in the Assembly, despite the governor's support. The governor also suffered a major defeat in the legislature's rejection of proposed constitutional amendments to reform the courts by creating a unified, state-run court system.

Education. After a 2-year study, the State Commission on the Quality, Cost, and Financing of Elementary and Secondary Education—popularly known as the Fleischmann Commission—issued a series of

reports during 1972. Among other measures, the commission recommended busing and consolidation of school districts to overcome racial imbalances and urged the state to assume responsibility for raising and distributing all nonfederal funds for public schools. It suggested a fundamental reorganization of secondary schools to eliminate "general" programs, which leave graduates unprepared for college and without marketable skills, and at the elementary level to strengthen reading and mathematics programs through improved preparation of teachers.

Population Trends. A breakdown of 1970 census figures showed that during the decade 1960–70, New York had a greater net outward migration of its white population (638,000, or 4.2%) than any other state. In central cities of metropolitan areas the loss was one of every 10. New York also outdistanced all other states in attracting new black residents, with a net in-migration of 396,000. The total increase in nonwhite population during the decade was 905,000, or nearly two thirds of the entire population gain of 1.4 million. However, the white population still accounted for about 87% of the state's 18 million residents.

Floods. Three days of torrential rains in late June caused rivers in western New York to rise over their banks, devastating areas in 16 counties. Hardest hit were the cities of Elmira and Corning. Twenty-three deaths were reported. The number of homeless was estimated in the hundreds of thousands and the amount of property damage in untold millions. At year-end, restoration of public facilities, homes, and businesses was still under way.

LEO HERSHKOWITZ
Queens College, City University of New York

NEW YORK CITY

Plans for new construction, especially multiple-use complexes, and renewed attempts to combat crime and improve essential services for its rapidly changing population characterized New York City and gave evidence of its viability during 1972. Politically the year was marked by Mayor John V. Lindsay's unsuccessful bid for the Democratic presidential nomination, continued conflict between Mayor Lindsay and Republican Gov. Nelson Rockefeller, and the fact that New York City remained Democratic in the presidential election, although by a smaller margin than in the past.

Elections. In effect, Mayor Lindsay began his quest of the Democratic presidential nomination in August 1971, when he switched from the Republican to the Democratic party. He withdrew from the race early in April, after failing to attract any sizable constituency in the Florida and Wisconsin primaries. In the November presidential election, Sen. George McGovern carried New York City, but by a margin of fewer than 100,000 votes. In other contests the Democratic party showed its usual strength. Democrats were elected in all but one of the 18 congressional districts wholly or partly in the city. Among the winners were incumbents Shirley Chisholm, Bella Abzug, and Herman Badillo.

The Budget and Politics. At the beginning of the year Mayor Lindsay proposed a capital budget of $1.8 billion, with the largest shares going to environmental protection (29%), transportation (22%), and education (20%). A controversial "bare bones" operating budget of almost $10 billion also was submitted by the mayor and hotly debated. Proposed

UPI

The scribbling of graffiti on subway cars and station walls reached epidemic proportions in New York City in 1972.

new taxes of $141 million and additional state aid were key issues of the debate, in which party rivalries (intensified by the upcoming mayoral election in 1973) led the mayor and members of the Democratically controlled City Council and Board of Estimate frequently to accuse one another of "double-crossing." Finally, in June, a $9.4 billion budget was adopted for the fiscal year beginning July 1. At an increase of only 9.3% over the 1971–72 figure, this budget represented the smallest percentage increase for many years. New taxes were averted, but the mayor warned of the need for job freezes and some layoffs in city departments.

Conflict between the traditionally Democratic city and the Republican-dominated state government was particularly evident at public hearings held early in the year. During February a panel known as the New York State Commission to Make a Study of the Governmental Operation of New York City heard testimony condemning the city administration as bureaucratic and unresponsive to residents' needs. At about the same time the City Commission on State-City Relations heard witnesses charge the state with apathy and lack of initiative, especially in obtaining federal subsidies for local social services.

Population Changes. Although New York City experienced only a 1% net gain in population during the decade 1960–70, it underwent population changes that altered racial balances and profoundly affected the city's ability to provide housing and other services adequate to the needs. According to a special analysis of census figures, the city gained 1 million black and Puerto Rican residents during the decade and lost approximately the same number of white residents (exclusive of Puerto Ricans). By 1970, blacks, Puerto Ricans, and "others" (mainly Orientals) made up 35% of the city's total population of about 7.9 million. These minorities represented the fastest growing components of the population as well as those with the lowest median age levels.

One result of the changes in population has been the growth of segregated residential patterns. Although there are some integrated areas in all five boroughs of the city, the main trend has been toward expansion of the areas—most of them officially designated as poverty areas—where minorities were already established.

Housing and Other Construction. The shortage of low- and middle-income housing remained critical, although Mayor Lindsay announced early in the year that a record number of 30,000 city-assisted housing units were under construction. An attempt to build a low-income housing project (three 24-story buildings with 840 apartments) in a predominantly Jewish middle-class area of Forest Hills, in the borough of Queens, brought such strong opposition from residents that by midsummer Mayor Lindsay suggested a compromise (three 12-story buildings with 432 units). But the compromise was rejected by militant whites and blacks, and at year-end the issues remained unresolved.

In January, the City Council voted the first funds for construction of a $100 million convention center on the Hudson River shore in mid-Manhattan. In April, the mayor and David Rockefeller, chairman of the Chase Manhattan Bank, announced a joint effort to assemble government loans and private financing for the development of apartments and offices on platforms above the East River, bordering the financial district of Lower Manhattan. Plans were also announced during the year for a commercial and residential development, known as Battery Park City, to be built on filled land off the western tip of Lower Manhattan.

A threat to remove the Yankees baseball team was stayed when the city announced plans to buy and renovate Yankee Stadium. In return, the Yankees agreed to remain in the Bronx for 30 years.

Education. A threatened teachers' strike in the city's public schools was averted by agreement on a three-year contract shortly before the schools opened on September 11. But a strike threat by the City University faculty remained at year-end.

Harvey B. Scribner, who took office in 1970 as the first chancellor of the newly decentralized city school system, announced in December his intention to leave the post at the expiration of his contract in June 1973. His reason was the "gap of confidence" between the board of education and himself.

Crime and Corruption. In September, Governor Rockefeller—acting on a recommendation of the Knapp Commission, which had been appointed by the mayor in 1970 to investigate corruption in New York City—named Maurice H. Nadjari as a special deputy attorney general to take over from the city's five district attorneys all cases of corruption involving policemen, prosecutors, and judges. The disclosure in mid-December that some 80 pounds of heroin seized 10 years ago in the case dramatized in the film *The French Connection* had been stolen from city police department vaults—together with the discovery that large amounts of other confiscated narcotics also were missing—emphasized the need for further action in this area.

LEO HERSHKOWITZ
Queens College, City University of New York

NEW ZEALAND

The major political event in New Zealand in 1972 was the victory of the Labour party in the November general election. On the economic front the government continued its struggle against inflation. Protests against nuclear testing in the Pacific dominated foreign affairs.

National Election. In the November general election, the National party, which had held office for the previous 12 years, was ousted. After a campaign that featured such domestic issues as housing, health, and the cost of living, the Labour party, led by Norman Kirk, captured 55 of the 87 seats in Parliament. Only 32 National party candidates survived the landslide.

Kirk became both prime minister and foreign minister in the new government. Matiu Rata, a Maori, became minister for Maori affairs.

Earlier in the year, in February, Sir Keith Holyoake, who had been the National party prime minister for 12 years, stepped down in favor of his longtime deputy, John Marshall. However, Holyoake retained the portfolio of foreign affairs. A major cabinet reshuffle followed, in which the minister of finance, Robert Muldoon, became deputy prime minister.

Prior to the November elections, public opinion polls put Labour marginally ahead of the National party in popularity, leaving the Social Credit party, which was racked by internal dissension, reduced to 3% support.

Economy. During 1972, much of the government's attention was devoted to the management of inflation. The year opened with the adoption of measures designed temporarily to freeze both prices and wages and certain government charges. In June a budget was presented that was described by some as "all carrot but no stick." Among its most notable features were a 10% across-the-board reduction in income tax, sizable increases in many social welfare benefits, and a 16½% rise in government spending. If the intention was to stimulate a sluggish economy, the budget certainly raised the morale of the business community. Subsequently, neither shifts in unemployment figures nor movement in the cost-of-living index were considered excessive.

Domestic Affairs. In September, a controversial report urged the early adoption of a rapid rail network for metropolitan Auckland. Utilizing the existing track, the five radiating arms and central loop were scheduled for completion by the year 2002, at a projected cost of 213 million New Zealand dollars. However, the government was not disposed to meet certain costs, and the issue was unresolved.

To promote the vending of the nation's wool clip, a bill providing for the establishment of a wool marketing commission was introduced. Following resistance by groups of producers, the clauses of the bill giving the commission compulsory powers of acquisition were watered down.

In July, Dr. C. P. McMeekan, New Zealand's most eminent agricultural scientist and a senior adviser to the World Bank, was drowned in a boating accident in Waitemata Harbour, Auckland.

Referenda were held by five Protestant churches actively considering union. By margins ranging from 8% to 69%, all voted in favor of union. However, the vote was not considered decisive enough to constitute a mandate for early implementation.

Foreign Affairs. New Zealand was in the vanguard of those protesting nuclear weapons testing by the French in the Pacific. A motion sponsored by New Zealand condemning such tests, especially those conducted in the atmosphere, was carried at the Stockholm environment conference.

When the prime minister visited Australia in June, both he and the Australian prime minister agreed on the desirability of ending the French tests. Other matters reviewed were defense cooperation and agreements on trade.

GRAHAM BUSH, *University of Aukland*

─────── **NEW ZEALAND • Information Highlights** ───────

Official Name: New Zealand.
Area: 103,736 square miles (268,675 sq km).
Population (1972 est.): 3,000,000. *Density,* 26 per square mile (10 per sq km). *Annual rate of increase,* 1.7%.
Chief Cities (1971 census): Wellington, the capital, 135,515; Christ Church, 165,198; Auckland, 151,567.
Government: *Head of state,* Elizabeth II, queen; represented by Sir Denis Blundell, governor-general (took office Sept. 1972). *Head of government,* Norman Kirk (took office Dec. 1972). *Legislature* (unicameral)—House of Representatives, 87 members. *Major political parties*—National party; Labour party.
Language: English (official).
Education: *Expenditure* (1969), 4.4% of gross national product. *School enrollment* (1969)—primary, 514,774; secondary, 184,301; university/higher, 56,353.
Monetary Unit: New Zealand dollar (0.8367 N. Z. dollar equals U. S.$1, Aug. 1972).
Gross National Product (1971 est.): $6,300,000,000.
National Income per Person (1970), $2,004.
Economic Indexes: *Industrial production* (1969), 142 (1963=100); *agricultural production* (1971), 159 (1952–56=100); *consumer price index* (1971), 150 (1963=100).
Manufacturing (major products): Processed foods, meat products, fertilizers, petroleum products, automobiles.
Major Agricultural Products: Wheat, potatoes, dairy products, sheep, wool, forest products.
Major Minerals: Coal, petroleum, natural gas, mineral sands.
Foreign Trade (1971): *Exports,* $1,359,000,000 (chief exports—wool; lamb and mutton). *Imports,* $1,346,000,000 (chief imports, 1969—nonelectrical machinery, transport equipment; chemicals; textile yarn and fabrics). *Chief trading partners* (1969)—United Kingdom (took 39% of exports, supplied 30% of imports); United States (16%—12%).
Tourism: *Receipts* (1970), $33,600,000.
Transportation: *Motor vehicles* (1970), 1,072,900 (automobiles, 891,200); *merchant fleet* (1971), 181,000 gross registered tons; *major national airline,* Air New Zealand.
Communications: *Telephones* (1971), 1,262,427; *television stations* (1971), 20; *newspapers* (1970), 40 (daily circulation, 1,058,000).

——— NEWFOUNDLAND • Information Highlights ———

Area: 156,185 square miles (404,520 sq km).
Population (1971 census): 522,104.
Chief Cities (1971 census): St. John's, the capital (88,102); Corner Brook (26,309).
Government: *Chief Officers* (March 1972)—lt. gov., Ewart J. A. Harnum; premier, Frank Duff Moores (Progressive Conservative); min. of provincial affairs, Anthony J. Murphy (P. C.); min. of justice, T. Alex Hickman (P. C.); min. of finance, John C. Crosbie (P. C.); min. of educ., John A. Carter (P. C.); chief justice, Robert S. Furlong. *Legislature*—Legislative Assembly; 42 members (33 Progressive Conservative, 8 Liberal, 1 New Labrador).
Education: *School enrollment* (1968–69)—public elementary and secondary, 151,976 pupils (5,855 teachers); private schools, 230 pupils (26 teachers); college and university, 4,782 students. *Public school expenditures* (1971 est.)—$56,199,000; average teacher's salary (1968–69), $5,600.
Public Finance (fiscal year 1972 est.): *Revenues,* $410,100,000 (sales tax, $77,300,000; income tax, $35,000,000; federal funds, $242,200,000). *Expenditures,* $500,000,000 (education, $124,700,000; health and social welfare, $131,700,000; transport and communications, $52,900,000).
Personal Income (1969 est.): $829,000,000.
Social Welfare (fiscal year 1972 est.): $48,100,000 (aged and blind, $4,200,000; dependents and unemployed, $38,400,000).
Manufacturing (1968): *Value added by manufacture,* $88,386,000 (food and beverages, $34,606,000; nonmetallic mineral products industries, $4,509,000; printing and publishing industries, $3,692,000; fabricated metals, $3,638,000).
Mining (1971 est.): *Production value,* $336,715,000. *Chief minerals* (tons)—iron ore, 22,600,000 (ranks 1st among the provinces); asbestos, 77,000; copper, 12,875; zinc, 15,106; lead, 9,768.
Fisheries (1971): *Commercial catch,* sea fish (statistics on freshwater fish are confidential), 871,849,000 pounds ($35,815,000). *Leading species*—cod, 256,774,000 pounds ($13,557,000); flounder and sole, 190,151,000 pounds ($9,205,000); herring, 303,956,000 pounds ($4,121,000); lobster, 3,042,000 pounds ($2,440,000); redfish, 60,059,000 pounds ($2,075,000).
Transportation: *Roads* (1968), 6,234 miles (10,018 km); *motor vehicles* (1969), 112,027; *railroads* (1970 est.), 943 track miles (1,517 km); *airports* (1971 est.), 8.
Communications: *Telephones* (1969), 127,190; *television stations* (1971), 24; *radio stations* (1971), 16; *daily newspapers* (1971), 3.
(All figures given in Canadian dollars.)

NEWFOUNDLAND

Politics dominated Newfoundland in 1972, as both provincial and federal elections were held. Liberal Joseph R. Smallwood, premier of Newfoundland since it joined Canada in 1949, was defeated. Progressive Conservative Frank D. Moores became the new premier.

Provincial Elections. The ending of the career of Premier Smallwood took two elections. In the first, in October 1971, his Liberal party won 20 seats in the Newfoundland Legislative Assembly, while the Progressive Conservatives won 21 and the New Labrador party took one. In the second, "runoff," election, which took place on March 24, 1972, the Progressive Conservatives won 33 seats under their leader Frank Moores, and the Liberals won 9 under a new leader, 31-year-old Edward Roberts.

The courts of Newfoundland intervened twice in controversial election results. In November 1971 a judicial recount in a district won by the Conservatives by only 8 votes was halted when a court discovered that the ballots in the small community of Sally's Cove had been burned on election night. In January 1972 the supreme court decided that a by-election was not necessary, and the Conservative candidate had indeed won. This was enough to convince Premier Smallwood that he had to resign, and the new government took over on January 18. In June 1972 the courts intervened again to declare the Liberal victory in Labrador South, won by one vote in March, invalid on the grounds of voting irregularities. A subsequent by-election in August finally settled the distribution in the House of Assembly at 33 Conservatives, 8 Liberals, and 1 New Labrador party.

The New Government. Under Premier Moores, the new Progressive Conservative government quickly took over two major industrial enterprises on behalf of the province. One was a fish plant in Burgeo, and the other was a linerboard mill at Stephenville. The new minister of finance, John Crosbie, brought down his budget in May and revealed that between 1966 and 1971 the debt of the province had increased by 200%. The 1971 debt stood at $1.1 billion, and loans guaranteed by the province added another $391 million. Crosbie also revealed that money spent without direct approval by the House of Assembly had totaled $256 million between 1966 and 1972. In July, a Royal Commission alleged that former Premier Smallwood and one of his deputy ministers were personally involved in irregularities connected with the leasing of rental property to the Newfoundland Liquor Commission. Smallwood, who since retirement has spent his time writing his autobiography, denied the charges.

Federal Election. Although Canada elected more Conservatives in nationwide elections in October, Newfoundland elected two more Liberals to bring its total in the House of Commons to three Liberals and four Progressive Conservatives.

SUSAN MCCORQUODALE
Memorial University of Newfoundland

NEWSPAPERS. See PUBLISHING.

NICARAGUA

In Nicaragua, a year that was otherwise dominated by political maneuvers on behalf of President Anastasio Somoza came to a disastrous end when an earthquake leveled Managua on Dec. 23, 1972.

Political Developments. A complicated formula was devised to enable President Somoza to retain power in effect while giving it up in appearance to satisfy a constitutional prohibition against consecutive presidential terms. An agreement was worked out between Somoza's National Liberal party and the opposition Conservative party, headed by Fernando Agüero Rocha, whereby the Nicaraguan Congress was dissolved in September 1971, to make way for a Constitutional Assembly. The Assembly, elected on Feb. 6, 1972, was to draft a new constitution prior to the holding of new elections in 1974.

Although the 1972 Assembly election results gave the Conservative party only 174,897 votes to the National Liberal party's 534,171, the Conservatives, by prior agreement, received 40 on the 100 Assembly seats and the Liberals, 60.

As part of the same agreement President Somoza resigned from the presidency on May 1, turning over power to a three-man junta selected by the Constitutional Assembly on April 15. The junta, which is to govern Nicaragua until the 1974 elections, consists of Roberto Martinez Lacayo and Alfonso Lobo Cordero, both members of the Liberal party, and the Conservative Fernando Agüero.

Although Somoza formally resigned as president, he retained real power through his leadership of the powerful Liberal party and his control of the armed forces, of which he was named the head immediately after resigning the presidency. On May 1, it was announced that Somoza was to be a candidate for president in 1974.

Opposition. These maneuvers evoked several types of response. The conservative archbishop of Managua, Miguel Obando y Bravo, condemned the

——————— NICARAGUA · Information Highlights ———————

Official Name: Republic of Nicaragua.
Area: 50,193 square miles (130,000 sq km).
Population (1972 est.): 2,200,000. *Density,* 39 per square mile (15 per sq km). *Annual rate of increase,* 2.9%.
Chief Cities (1967 est.): Managua, the capital, 296,000; León, 58,900; Granada, 35,900.
Government: *Head of state,* Governing Council: Roberto Martinez Lacayo, Alfonso Lovo Cordero, Fernando Agüero Rocha (took office May 1972). *Head of government,* Governing Council. *Legislature—*Congress: Senate, 16 members; Chamber of Deputies, 42 members. *Major political parties—*National Liberal party; Conservative party.
Language: Spanish (official).
Education: *Expenditure* (1968), 19% of total public expenditure. *School enrollment* (1969)—primary, 266,346; secondary, 45,624; technical/vocational, 4,221; university/higher, 7,682.
Monetary Unit: Cordoba (7.00 cordobas equal U. S.$1, Aug. 1972).
Gross National Product (1971 est.): $873,000,000.
National Income per Person (1970): $387.
Economic Indexes: *Industrial production* (manufacturing, 1965), 119 (1963 = 100); *consumer price index* (1969), 117 (1963 = 100).
Manufacturing (major products): Chemicals, paper products, petroleum products, electrical appliances, processed foods.
Major Agricultural Products: Cotton, coffee, corn, beans, rice, sugarcane, cattle, forest products.
Major Minerals: Copper, silver, gold, salt.
Foreign Trade (1971): *Exports,* $183,000,000 (chief exports—cotton; coffee; meat; sugar; sesame). *Imports,* $210,000,-000 (chief imports, 1969—chemicals; nonelectrical machinery; food; electric machinery and appliances). *Chief trading partners* (1969)—United States (took 33% of exports, supplied 38% of imports); Japan (19%—7%); West Germany (11%—7%); Costa Rica (9%—7%).
Transportation: *Motor vehicles* (1970), 53,300 (automobiles, 34,400); *railroads* (1970), 216 miles (348 km); *major national airline,* LANICA (Linea Aereas de Nicaragua).
Communications: *Telephones* (1971), 25,922; *television stations* (1971), 2; *television sets* (1971), 55,000; *radios* (1970), 109,000; *newspapers* (1967), 7.

Liberal-Conservative agreement in January and publicly refused to register to vote.

Various dissident political groups requested voters to boycott the February 6 elections. Their efforts were apparently successful since one third of the electorate failed to vote.

In the spring the government threatened to nationalize *La Prensa,* the only opposition newspaper in Nicaragua. *La Prensa*'s publisher, Pedro J. Chamorro, immediately protested the administration's action to the Inter-American Press Association.

Small guerrilla bands were reported operating in the countryside in a more violent form of opposition, but these scattered groups were not regarded as a significant threat to the government.

Government reaction to the opposition included censorship of reading materials and a tightening of control over educational institutions. There were also reports that a number of opposition union leaders had been killed in the northern mountains.

Economic Affairs. The production of raw materials continued to increase in 1972. Nicaragua attained the distinction of growing more cotton per acre than any other region in the world. In April a pact was concluded with Honduras providing for an enterchange of electric power.

Earthquake. A series of increasingly severe earthquakes virtually destroyed the capital city of Managua on December 23. The government estimated that more than 10,000 persons were killed and more than 10,000 seriously injured. The government proclaimed martial law and, fearing an epidemic, ordered the total evacuation of the city.

The disaster could be expected to severely retard Nicaragua's economic growth. Most of Managua's buildings were destroyed or declared unsafe. The city will have to be completely rebuilt.

ROBERT L. PETERSON
University of Texas at El Paso

NIGER

The year 1972 was a relatively quiet one in Niger. The government of President Hamani Diori remained firmly in control.

Domestic Affairs. Opposition to the visit of French President Georges Pompidou in January led to strikes and the closing of several secondary schools. The schools were reopened in March after 31 students had been expelled and 41 suspended. A resolution in the National Assembly supported the government's handling of the strike and criticized the educational system as a "resounding failure."

President Diori substantially reshuffled his administration in August. Six of the country's seven prefects were shifted, as were more than half of the heads of the 35 districts.

Foreign Relations. Normally cordial relations with France cooled markedly after Pompidou's visit. President Diori pressed for the creation of an economic council composed of the heads of state of the African nations in the franc zone. He also suggested higher pensions for Africans who had served in the French army and urged accelerated French investment in the Akohan uranium mine.

French economic and technical aid was frozen in June after the Niger government asked for the replacement of the French ambassador. But the crisis was resolved by the mediation of President Félix Houphouët-Boigny of the Ivory Coast. Renegotiation of Niger's agreements with France began in October.

The Liptako-Gourma regional commission, consisting of Niger, Mali, and Upper Volta, met on several occasions in 1972. Among the proposed projects were a rail line between Ouagadougou, the capital of Upper Volta, and the Niger River, and the regulation of the river's flow between Timbuctoo and Niamey. Niger also agreed with the Ivory Coast, Togo, and Upper Volta to hold a joint international lottery, to be known as Entente 73.

Economic Development. The Arlit uranium mine was officially opened in January. It was to produce 750 tons of uranium annually. The European Development Fund awarded Niger $22 million to reconstruct the Niamey-Zinder road, and Canada agreed to help build electric transmission lines from the dam at Kainji.

CLAUDE E. WELCH, JR.
State University of New York at Buffalo

——————— NIGER · Information Highlights ———————

Official Name: Republic of the Niger.
Area: 489,190 square miles (1,267,000 sq km).
Population (1972 est.): 4,100,000. *Density,* 8 per square mile (3 per sq km). *Annual rate of increase,* 2.9%.
Chief City (1967 est.): Niamey, the capital, 60,000.
Government: *Head of state,* Hamani Diori, president (elected to 3d 5-year term Oct. 1970). *Head of government,* Hamani Diori. *Legislature* (unicameral)—National Assembly, 50 members. *Political party—*Parti Progressiste Nigérien.
Languages: French (official), Hausa and other African languages.
Education: *Expenditure* (1969), 12.4% of total public expenditure. *School enrollment* (1969)—primary, 84,248; secondary, 6,272; technical/vocational, 137.
Monetary Unit: CFA franc (255.79 CFA francs equal U. S.$1, Aug. 1972).
Gross National Product (1970 est.): $315,000,000.
Manufacturing (major products): Processed agricultural products, soft drinks.
Major Agricultural Products: Millet, sorghum, beans, groundnuts, cotton, cassava, livestock.
Major Minerals: Tin, uranium, cassiterite.
Foreign Trade (1970): *Exports,* $32,000,000. *Imports,* $58,-000,000. *Chief trading partners* (1969)—France (took 63% of exports, supplied 49% of imports); Nigeria (16%—2%).
Communications: *Telephones* (1970), 3,298; *television stations* (1971), 1; *television sets* (1971), 100; *radios* (1970), 100,000; *newspapers* (1969), 1 (daily circulation, 2,000).

──────── **NIGERIA** • **Information Highlights** ────────

Official Name: Federal Republic of Nigeria.
Area: 356,668 square miles (923,768 sq km).
Population (1972 est.): 58,000,000. *Density,* 155 per square mile (60 per sq km). *Annual rate of increase,* 2.6%.
Chief Cities (1963 census): Lagos, the capital, 665,246; Ibadan, 627,379; Ogbomosho, 319,881; Kano, 295,432.
Government: *Head of state,* Gen. Yakubu Gowon, president (assumed power Aug. 1966). *Head of government,* Gen. Yakubu Gowon.
Languages: English (official), Hausa (official in the north), Ibo, Yoruba, other tribal languages.
Education: *Expenditure* (1965), 2.3% of gross national product. *School enrollment* (1968)—primary, 1,791,309; secondary, 200,378; technical/vocational, 19,428; university/higher, 9,775.
Monetary Unit: Pound (0.3289 pound equals U. S.$1, Sept. 1972). (After Jan. 1, 1973 the monetary unit will be the naira, 0.6578 naira=U. S.$1.)
Gross National Product (1970 est.): $5,800,000,000.
National Income per Person (1963): $71.
Consumer Price Index (1971): 159 (1963=100).
Manufacturing (major products): Processed foods, cotton textiles, petroleum products.
Major Agricultural Products: Cacao (ranks 2d among world producers, 1970), groundnuts (world rank 4th, 1971), palm kernels (world rank 1st, 1971), cotton, sweet potatoes and yams (world rank 2d, 1971), natural rubber, forest products, fish.
Major Minerals: Petroleum, tin, coal, limestone.
Foreign Trade (1971): *Exports,* $1,811,000,000 (chief exports—crude petroleum, cocoa, groundnuts and oil, palmnuts and oil, tin). *Imports,* $1,510,000,000 (chief imports, 1969—nonelectrical machinery, chemicals, textile yarn and fabrics, motor vehicles). *Chief trading partners* (1969)—United Kingdom (took 27% of exports, supplied 35% of imports); United States (13%—12%); Netherlands (13%—5%); France (10%—3%).
Transportation: *Motor vehicles* (1969), 63,000 (automobiles, 39,300); *railroads* (1970), 2,178 miles (3,505 km); *merchant fleet* (1971), 96,000 gross registered tons; *major national airline,* Nigeria Airways.
Communications: *Telephones* (1971), 79,828; *television stations* (1971), 8; *television sets* (1971), 53,000; *radios* (1970), 1,275,000; *newspapers* (1966), 24.

NIGERIA

In 1972 an ever-expanding petroleum industry remained the key to Nigeria's rapid recovery from its devastating civil war of the 1960's. There was, however, a drop in the prices of agricultural exports, while inflation and unemployment continued.

Economic Development. The economic situation in Nigeria was hopeful, owing to the continued increase in petroleum production in the delta and east coast areas. Delta Oil, a Nigerian-owned company, joined foreign firms in oil exploration. Construction began on new pipelines to old terminals at Bonny and Brass and on a new 21-tanker terminal at the mouth of the Qua Iboe River. Petroleum exports in 1971 earned more than £N350 million, or 73% of all Nigeria's foreign earnings.

The petroleum boom allowed the government to make its deferred payments, control runaway expenditures, maintain an army of a quarter-million men, and repair some of the devastation of war. The government also applied considerable capital to the second four-year plan (1970–73), and the Central Bank had no difficulty raising the initial sum of the £N30 million loan for the plan. A new bridge over the Sokoto River was planned, and final appropriations for restoring the Niger Bridge were made. Federal, state, and private capital contributed to major improvements in the ports of Bonny, Brass, Warri, and Sapele. In addition, coal production in 1972–1973 was expected to double that of the preceding year. In the north, large expenditures were planned for communications, stock breeding, and crop experiments.

Capital from oil also allowed the government to begin a policy of "indigenization" to prevent control of the economy by foreign investors. In February it issued the Nigerian Enterprises Promotion Decree, which barred aliens, after March 31, 1974, from entering or owning 55 categories of business. Other foreign-owned companies must allow Nigerians to purchase at least 40% of their shares and to participate in management.

Economic Problems. There was a darker side to Nigeria's economy. The value of its traditional exports of peanuts from the north and cocoa and oil palm products from the south continued to decline because of low prices and decreasing production. As a result, the Western state had to curtail some development plans, causing unrest among workers, teachers, and students in 1971 and early 1972.

In addition, despite the Price Control Decree of 1970 and government bans on strikes and lockouts, inflation and consequent labor unrest continued. Hospital workers in Ibadan demanded more pay, 100 doctors in Lagos state threatened to resign, and the government rushed police to the Abeokuta area to protect earth satellite installations from restive workers. A mass resignation of teachers was narrowly averted by the government's agreeing to consider large salary increases.

Unemployment was high. It was estimated at 2 million in the cities in 1970. While it was hoped that the four-year plan would generate 1 million new jobs, unemployment was expected to increase to 2½ million by late 1973.

Inflation and unemployment were part of the reason for widespread smuggling, which continued to disturb the government. Troops and customs officials were stationed in 12 villages on the northern border to block the illegal diversion to Niger of an estimated £N2 million worth of goods. The governor of the Western state suggested the death penalty for smugglers crossing the border into Dahomey. Pitched battles with smugglers did not stop complex, two-way, illicit traffic across the Cameroon border.

Reconstruction. Although many scars of the civil war remained, the economies of the Rivers and South-East states were stronger than before the war. The East-Central state, which was the hardest hit, made a remarkable recovery, with brewing and cement-making at prewar levels and textile, furniture, pottery, and shoe factories all in operation. Enugu, the capital, had more business than in 1967. Nevertheless, the East-Central state still faced grave problems. Unemployment was extremely high, even though a few Ibo had migrated to other states. Capital was scarce, and the budget of £N31 million for 1972–73 depended on federal grants.

Internal Stresses. Many elements contributed to internal friction. Nigeria's cities were still growing, mostly without planning. Lagos, with an estimated population of 1.7 million in 1972, could have more than 5 million in the 1980's. Unchecked growth created almost insoluble problems—mainly severe shortages of jobs, transportation, housing, and water.

Another element creating stress was the question of what form of government would replace the military regime in 1976. The State of Emergency Decree (1966) was still in force but did not prevent criticism of the military, as evidenced in underground protest in Kwara state and the Nigerian Bar Association's criticism of the government's tendency to interfere in juridical matters.

Nigerians also continued to be disturbed by widespread armed robbery. Special robbery tribunals were maintained and public executions were held, including one mass execution of 14 men in Port Harcourt. In addition, there was a wave of kid-

nappings of children, with some suspected kidnappers being lynched or beaten.

Education. In the civil-war-damaged eastern areas more than 700 schools were rebuilt since 1970, largely with the help of UNICEF. In 1972 the World Bank loaned the East-Central state £N17 million for the repair and extension of 23 secondary schools and 7 primary-teacher-training colleges. School enrollment there had risen to the 70% average of all school-age children that prevailed in the southern states. Despite continuing allocation of large sums to the northern areas, however, they lagged far behind in facilities and enrolment, and there was an acute shortage of teachers.

The University of Nigeria at Nsukka planned to expand to 24 colleges. In order to ensure a supply of trained Nigerians, the government took direct control of the four state universities in addition to the two others that it already controlled.

Foreign Affairs. The head of state, Gen. Yakubu Gowon, appeared willing to assume the role of a major spokesman for all Africa, as evidenced by his numerous state visits in 1971–72 to Senegal, Niger, Guinea, Cameroon, Mali, Togo, and Dahomey. Nigeria pressed for the start of a West African economic union.

Without extremism Nigeria opposed all vestiges of European colonialism, particularly with reference to Rhodesia. Nigeria's foreign minister in late January even threatened to reexamine Nigeria's position in the Commonwealth if Britain did not take a more active role in opposing the Rhodesian government.

Nigeria joined other African states in putting pressure on the Olympic Committee to withdraw its invitation to Rhodesia. Nigeria remained cool to the United States partly because of large-scale U. S. trade with South Africa, Rhodesia, and the Portuguese territories. In March, Nigeria exchanged ambassadors with the People's Republic of China.

HARRY A. GAILEY
California State University, San José

NIXON, Richard M. See BIOGRAPHY.
NOBEL PRIZES. See PRIZES AND AWARDS.

NORTH CAROLINA

The Republican party scored at least two notable victories in North Carolina in the general elections in 1972.

Elections. In November the state elected a Republican governor, James Holshouser, and a Republican senator, Jesse Helms. Holshouser, the first Republican governor of the state since 1901, defeated Hargrove Bowles, Jr., a former state senator. Helms beat Nick Galifianikis, who had vacated his congressional seat.

Voters also approved five amendments to the state constitution. These (1) require the General Assembly to set maximum age limits for judges; (2) authorize the Assembly to set procedures for censure and removal of judges; (3) permit the Assembly to conserve the state's natural resources; (4) forbid the incorporation of new towns in close proximity to already existing towns; and (5) raise the minimum age for holding public office from 18 to 21.

Ecology. In May the voters overwhelmingly approved a $150 million bond issue for clean-water projects. As a result, local governments will be

----- NORTH CAROLINA • Information Highlights -----

Area: 52,586 square miles (136,198 sq km).
Population (1970 census): 5,082,059. *Density:* 105 per sq mi.
Chief Cities (1970 census): Raleigh, the capital, 123,793; Charlotte, 241,178; Greensboro, 144,076; Winston-Salem, 134,676; Durham, 95,438; High Point, 63,259.
Government (1972): *Chief Officers*—governor, Robert W. Scott (D); lt. gov., H. Pat Taylor, Jr. (D); secy. of state, Thad Eure (D); atty. gen., Robert B. Morgan (D); treas., Edwin Gill (D); supt. of public instruction, Craig Phillips (D); chief justice, William H. Bobbitt. *General Assembly*—Senate, 50 members (43 Democrats, 7 Republicans); House of Representatives, 120 members (97 D, 23 R).
Education (1971–72): *Enrollment*—public elementary schools, 821,511 pupils, 32,726 teachers; public secondary, 358,473 pupils, 16,321 teachers; nonpublic schools (1970–71), 28,679 pupils, 1,050 teachers; college and university, 151,000 students. *Public school expenditures,* $758,009,000 ($695 per pupil). *Average teacher's salary,* $8,345.
State Finances (fiscal year 1970): *Revenues,* $1,944,505,000 (3% general sales tax and gross receipts taxes, $264,461,000; motor fuel tax, $213,709,000; federal funds, $372,638,000). *Expenditures,* $1,829,648,000 (education, $899,550,000; health, welfare, and safety, $84,265,000; highways, $383,864,000). *State debt,* $541,551,000 (June 30, 1970).
Personal Income (1971): $17,427,000,000; per capita, $3,387.
Public Assistance (1971): $226,273,000. *Average monthly payments* (Dec. 1971)—old-age assistance, $72.68; aid to families with dependent children, $117.58.
Labor Force: *Nonagricultural wage and salary earners* (July 1972), 1,839,500. *Average annual employment* (1971)—manufacturing, 709,000; trade, 323,000; government, 273,000; services, 215,000. *Insured unemployed* (Aug. 1972)—16,400 (1.2%).
Manufacturing (1970): *Value added by manufacture,* $8,983,000,000. Textile mill products, $2,558,300,000; tobacco manufactures, $1,183,100,000; chemicals and allied products, $865,000,000; furniture and fixtures, $641,400,000; electrical equipment and supplies, $586,600,000; food and kindred products, $549,900,000.
Agriculture (1970): *Cash farm income,* $1,585,419,000 (livestock, $624,076,000; crops, $901,661,000; government payments, $59,682,000). *Chief crops* (in order of value, 1971) —Tobacco (ranks 1st among the states), corn, soybeans, peanuts.
Mining (1971): *Production value,* $112,451,000 (ranks 33d among the states). *Chief minerals*—Stone, $58,026,000; sand and gravel, $14,690,000.
Fisheries (1971): *Commercial catch,* 143,475,000 pounds ($11,227,000). *Leading species by value:* Shrimp, $4,765,000; menhaden, $1,192,000; crabs, $1,153,000.
Transportation: *Roads* (1971), 86,019 miles (138,430 km); *motor vehicles* (1971), 2,825,801; *railroads* (1971), 4,154 miles (6,685 km); *public airports* (1972), 61.
Communications: *Telephones* (1972), 2,528,000; *television stations* (1971), 19; *radio stations* (1971), 273; *newspapers* (1972), 48 (daily circulation, 1,281,000).

able to meet the growing costs of developing water supplies and controlling pollution.

Court action was successfully brought against the U. S. Soil Conservation Service to prevent channelization of streams in the state, a procedure that would have destroyed wildlife habitats and increased the risk of downstream flooding.

The National Environmental Research Center, a $25 million facility in the Research Triangle Park, reached full operation in 1972. Its purpose is to determine how pollution affects human and animal organisms and the plants from which they derive their food.

Education. All 152 public school districts in the state were declared to be in compliance with the Civil Rights Act of 1964. Unitary school systems as defined by federal law now exist throughout the state, and all are eligible for full federal assistance. A task force was appointed to study the question of career education in public schools.

In July ten public institutions of higher education merged with six previous members of the Consolidated University of North Carolina. William C. Friday was continued as president of the 16-campus university, whose enrollment of 87,631 students makes it the fifth-largest educational system in the nation. A budget of $571.6 million was recommended for the next two years. In 1972 North Carolina ranked ninth in the amount of state funds spent per student in the public four-year colleges.

Cultural Activities. The Carolina Repertory Company, a newly organized professional touring theater, opened its first season in April and made a 10-week tour of the state. The company, which has its headquarters in the Research Triangle Park, receives support from the North Carolina Arts Council and from foundations in the state.

In May voters approved a $2 million bond issue for building a state zoo on 1,371 acres near Asheboro. The zoo is scheduled to open in 1975.

At Southern Pines ground was broken for the construction of a $2 million World Golf Hall of Fame, which is expected to be completed in midsummer 1974. The facility will have a research library and will feature exhibits relating to the history of the game and individual golfers of note.

WILLIAM S. POWELL
University of North Carolina

NORTH DAKOTA

North Dakotans in 1972 rejected a new constitution and an attempt to liberalize abortion laws. They elected a new governor for the first time in 12 years. The state's second-largest wheat harvest was reaped during an upsurge in grain prices, and a new oil field was discovered. A controversy raged over exploitation versus protection of coal and water resources.

Politics. A proposed constitution to replace the 1889 document was adopted by a constitutional convention, after more than a year's work, only to be turned down by the voters, 105,059 to 63,645, on

------- **NORTH DAKOTA · Information Highlights** -------

Area: 70,665 square miles (183,022 sq km).
Population (1970 census): 617,761. *Density,* 8.7 per sq mi.
Chief Cities (1970 census): Bismarck, the capital, 34,703; Fargo, 53,365; Grand Forks, 39,008; Minot, 32,290; Jamestown, 15,385; Dickinson, 12,405.
Government (1972): *Chief Officers*—governor, William L. Guy (D); lit. gov., Richard F. Larsen (R); secy. of state, Ben Meier (R); atty. gen., Helgi Johanneson (R); treas., Bernice Asbridge (R); supt. of public instruction, M. F. Peterson; chief justice, Alvin C. Strutz. *Legislative Assembly*—Senate, 49 members (37 Republicans, 12 Democrats); House of Representatives, 98 members (58 R, 39 D, 1 vacancy).
Education (1971–72): *Enrollment*—public elementary schools, 97,557 pupils, 4,430 teachers; public secondary, 46,862 pupils, 2,645 teachers; nonpublic schools (1970–71), 11,972 pupils, 690 teachers; college and university, 30,000 students. *Public school expenditures,* $102,800,000 ($740 per pupil). *Average teacher's salary,* $7,620.
State Finances (fiscal year 1970): *Revenues,* $288,536,000 (4% general sales tax and gross receipts taxes, $42,926,000; motor fuel tax, $19,819,000; federal funds, $71,058,000). *Expenditures,* $280,977,000 (education, $110,494,000; health, welfare, and safety, $29,234,000; highways, $46,247,000). *State debt,* $37,324,000 (June 30, 1970).
Personal Income (1971): $2,115,000,000; per capita, $3,383.
Public Assistance (1971): $31,000,000. *Average monthly payments* (Dec. 1971)—old-age assistance, $92.26; aid to families with dependent children, $205.91.
Labor Force: *Nonagricultural wage and salary earners* (July 1972), 171,300. *Average annual employment* (1971)—manufacturing, 10,000; trade, 45,000; government, 50,000; services, 29,000. *Insured unemployed* (Aug. 1972)—1,600 (1.8%).
Manufacturing (1970): *Value added by manufacture,* $244,800,000. Printing and publishing, $87,700,000; food and kindred products, $62,200,000; nonelectrical machinery, $25,300,000; fabricated metal products, $14,800,000.
Agriculture (1970): *Cash farm income,* $935,713,000 (livestock, $264,656,000; crops, $503,818,000; government payments, $167,239,000). *Chief crops* (in order of value, 1971)—Wheat (ranks 2d among the states), barley (ranks 1st), hay, oats (ranks 3d).
Mining (1970): *Production value,* $95,213,000 (ranks 34th among the states). Chief minerals—Petroleum, $63,800,000; coal, $9,500,000; sand and gravel, $9,300,000; natural gas, $6,051,000.
Transportation: *Roads* (1971), 106,897 miles (172,029 km); *motor vehicles* (1971), 428,081; *railroads* (1971), 5,098 (8,204 km); *public airports* (1972), 90.
Communications: *Telephones* (1972), 336,500; *television stations* (1971), 12; *radio stations* (1971), 37; *newspapers* (1972), 10 (daily circulation, 191,000).

April 28. Gov. William L. Guy, a Democrat who had served since 1960, declined to seek reelection, and voters in November chose another Democrat, Rep. Arthur A. Link, to succeed him. North Dakota's one seat in the U. S. House of Representatives was retained by Republican Mark Andrews. A campaign based on resistance to "abortion on demand" helped defeat a liberalized abortion law.

A three-judge federal court panel voided the state's redistricting law. It ordered the Senate increased by one seat and the House by four seats, while reducing the number of legislative districts by one.

For the first time blacks and Indians were members of the state delegation to the Democratic National Convention. There were numerous women candidates for legislative seats and other public offices.

Agriculture. Wheat farmers, who had planted 17% less acreage than in 1971, faced the prospect of lower prices and another buildup in carry-over stocks. The U. S.-USSR grain deal changed that situation. Wheat from the 1971 record crop and from storage in previous years was shipped in August, and the 1972 bumper crop went into bins carrying price tags worth an additional $100 million to North Dakota.

Sugar-beet growers organized three new cooperatives to operate refineries.

Mining. Plans for additional electric generating plants and for new coal gasification plants prompted speculation in lignite coal mining and brought 1.5 million acres under lease. Discovery of a new oil field in the Badlands triggered the greatest interest in oil in 21 years. A $10 million deal was negotiated for a piece of the action in the new field, and oil leases worth over $1.5 million were signed.

Environment. The increased activity in the coal fields brought protests over strip-mining practices and threats of legal or legislative action. More serious was a controversy involving environmentalists and farmers against the federal bureaucracy over the taking of farmland for a canal right-of-way as part of an irrigation project.

STAN CANN
"The Forum," Fargo

NORTHERN IRELAND. See GREAT BRITAIN.

NORTHWEST TERRITORIES

Development of the Northwest Territories and other northern Canadian regions became a national endeavor in 1972, as the Ottawa government turned its attention toward that largely undeveloped land.

National Plans. In March the Canadian government outlined its northern objectives, priorities, and strategies for the remainder of the 1970's. The people's needs were to be considered more important than the natural resources, and the maintenance of ecological balance was to be essential.

Prime Minister Pierre Trudeau announced in April that his government would build a transportation and communications corridor along the Mackenzie River Valley, beginning immediately with a 1,050-mile, all-weather highway from the northern border of Alberta to Tuktoyaktuk on the Arctic Ocean. Pipelines and communications lines would be included in the project. Other developments included the creation of two national parks in the Northwest Territories—the 1,840-square-mile South

NORTHWEST TERRITORIES • Information Highlights

Area: 1,304,903 square miles (3,379,699 sq km).
Population: 34,807 (1971 census).
Chief Town (1971 census): Yellowknife, the capital (6,122).
Government: *Chief Officers* (1972)—commissioner, Stuart M. Hodgson; deputy commissioner, John H. Parker; territorial treas., C. McCurdy; director of educ., B. C. Gillie; judge of the Territorial Court, W. G. Morrow. *Legislature*—Territorial Council, 14 members (10 elected, 4 appointed).
Education: *School enrollment* (September 1972)—elementary and secondary, 11,390 pupils, including 4,111 Eskimos, 1,994 Indians, 5,285 others (611 teachers). *Public school expenditures* (1971–72)—$28,031,700.
Public Finance (fiscal year 1970–71): *Revenues,* $61,848,970 (liquor profits, $2,400,792). *Expenditures,* $72,237,464 (education, $13,363,609; social development, $4,848,947; local government, $4,760,908; industrial development, $3,598,124; health, $3,891,588; capital projects, $13,939,101).
Mining (1971 est.): *Production value,* $124,004,060. *Chief minerals* (tons)—Zinc, 225,000; lead, 110,000; gold, 319,560 (troy ounces); silver, 2,525,000 (troy ounces).
Fur Production (1970–71 est.): $1,112,576 value.
Forest Products (1970): 3,873,000 board feet.
Fisheries (1971): *Commercial catch,* 3,791,171 pounds ($1,003,881).
Transportation: *Roads* (1971 est.): 916 miles (1,475 km); *motor vehicles,* 8,474; *licensed airports,* 15.
Communications (1971): *Telephones,* 7,200; *television stations,* 4; *radio stations,* 4; *newspapers,* 5.
(All figures given in Canadian dollars.)

Nahanni National Park and the 8,200-square-mile Baffin Island National Park—and the launching of the first satellite for the Telecast Canada Corporation, facilitating television broadcasts and telephone communication to northern Canada.

Local Government. An amendment to the municipal ordinance provided a framework for orderly progression toward municipal status for places in the Northwest Territories. Although some 20 centers of population still lacked any administrative control from Yellowknife in 1972, the Territories could boast of having one city (Yellowknife, the capital), three towns (Inuvik, Fort Smith, and Hay River), nine hamlets (including Carol Harbour, Pangnirtung, Fort Franklin, and Pelly Bay—all created in 1972), 33 organized settlements (although unincorporated), and 14 unorganized settlements.

C. CECIL LINGARD
Former Editor, "The Canada Yearbook"

NORWAY

The question of Norway's future relationship with the European Economic Community continued to dominate Norwegian political life in 1972. A referendum held in late September rejected Norwegian membership in the EEC, and Prime Minister Trygve Bratteli resigned. Economic activity continued at a high level in 1972, though growth was moderate.

Political Events. In January, the minority Labor government, which strongly favored full EEC membership for Norway, reached agreement with Community officials on the terms of entry. These did not include the special, permanent concessions for agriculture and fisheries that Norway's farmers and fishermen had demanded, and their organizations came out strongly against membership.

The anti-market cause won support from many other sources. Many idealistic young people opposed joining because they regarded the EEC as a "rich nations' club" which would widen the economic gap between Europe and the developing countries. Sociologists and environmentalists felt that the EEC was overly concerned with economic growth, regardless of its probable costs in terms of increased pollution, centralization, and urbanization. Devout Lutherans feared an influx of Catholic workers from the south. The far left was against anything that would strengthen Norway's ties to

the West, and many voters of all parties disliked the idea of ceding part of their national sovereignty to the "Brussels bureaucrats."

Early in March, Bratteli announced that a consultative referendum would be held in late September. The following six months saw a bitter and divisive political debate that disregarded traditional party lines. Supporters of Common Market membership formed a non-party organization, "Yes to EEC." A corresponding organization, composed of those opposed, the "Popular Movement Against the EEC," had been active since mid-1970. Both groups campaigned vigorously and feelings ran much higher than in a normal election.

In August, with opinion polls still predicting a "no" verdict, Bratteli staked his government's future on the referendum result. The outcome was that 53.5% of the total poll was against membership and Bratteli honored his pledge to resign. His government was followed, in mid-October, by a coalition of the three "middle" parties in the Storting, or parliament. These were the Center Party (farmers), the Christian People's Party, and the Liberal Party, with Christian People's Party leader Lars Korvald as prime minister. The new government, formed with the main purpose of negotiating a trade agreement with the EEC, had a precarious parliamentary basis. In the Storting, pro-market representatives of various parties outnumbered the anti-market forces by more than two to one. However, the pro-market groups promised the new government "passive cooperation" in its task of securing a satisfactory trade pact with the Common Market, provided it followed a moderate course on other issues.

The Economy. The demand for such traditional Norwegian exports as paper and pulp and aluminum increased in 1972, as a result of the general inter-

NORWAY • Information Highlights

Official Name: Kingdom of Norway.
Area: 125,181 square miles (324,219 sq km).
Population (1972 est.): 4,000,000. *Density,* 31 per square mile (12 per sq km). *Annual rate of increase,* 0.7%.
Chief Cities (1971 est.): Oslo, the capital, 481,204; Trondheim, 127,699; Bergen, 113,489.
Government: *Head of state,* Olav V, king (acceded Sept. 1957). *Head of government,* Lars Korvald, prime minister (took office Oct. 1972). *Legislature*—Storting: Lagting, 38 members; Oldelsting, 112 members. *Major political parties* —Conservatives; Liberals; Christian People's party; Center party.
Language: Norwegian (official).
Education: *Expenditure* (1969), 16.9% of total public expenditure. *School enrollment* (1969)—primary, 390,046; secondary, 300,324; technical/vocational, 65,875; university/higher, 46,715.
Monetary Unit: Krone (6.54 kroner equal U. S.$1, July 1972).
Gross National Product (1971 est.): $12,000,000,000.
National Income per Person (1970): $2,550.
Economic Indexes: *Industrial production* (1971), 150 (1963 = 100); *agricultural production* (1971), 116 (1952–56 = 100); *consumer price index* (1971), 149 (1963 = 100).
Manufacturing (major products): Metals, ships, pulp and paper, chemicals, fish products, processed foods, machinery.
Major Agricultural Products: Potatoes, barley, dairy products, livestock, forest products, fish.
Major Minerals: Iron ore, copper, coal, sulfur.
Foreign Trade (1971): *Exports,* $2,563,000,000 (chief exports— ships; aluminum; fish; paper; wood pulp). *Imports,* $4,083,-000,000 (chief imports, 1969—transport equipment; nonelectrical machinery; chemicals; mineral fuels and lubricants). *Chief trading partners* (1969)—Sweden (took 16% of exports, supplied 19% of imports); West Germany (15%—15%); United Kingdom (17%—13%); United States 7%—8%).
Tourism: *Receipts* (1970), $156,200,000.
Transportation: *Motor vehicles* (1970), 899,400 (automobiles, 747,200); *railroads* (1970), 2,668 miles (4,294 km); *merchant fleet* (1971), 21,720,000 gross registered tons; *major national airline,* Scandinavian Airlines System (with Denmark and Sweden).
Communications: *Telephones* (1971), 1,144,795; *television stations* (1971), 64; *television sets* (1971), 853,000; *radios* (1970), 1,191,000; *newspapers* (1970), 81 (daily circulation, 1,487,000).

national economic revival. Norway's large merchant fleet also benefitted from the improved international economic situation. Freight rates rose, and many ships that were laid up early in the year were put back into service.

Rising prices and costs continued to be a problem for businessmen and industrialists, and many firms found it difficult to operate at a reasonable profit. Wage awards to large groups of workers in the spring gave another twist to the inflationary spiral, and in September the Labor government declared a price freeze. It came less than a year after the end of the previous freeze, which had lasted for 10 months and was ordered by the old four-party coalition.

North Sea Oil. Norway received its first production royalties from North Sea oil—for the 8.2 million barrels of oil produced by the Phillips consortium on its Ekofisk field in Norwegian waters during the year ended June 1972. Production at the field continued at a limited rate, pending a decision by the Norwegian government concerning the route and destination of a pipeline from Ekofisk. The Phillips group wanted a line to take oil to Teesside, England. However, many Norwegian politicians of all parties felt that the oil should be landed in Norway if this was technically possible. Oil companies operating in Norway's sector of the North Sea feared that the change of government, following Bratteli's resignation, might delay still further a decision on the pipeline issue and the allocation of new oil search concessions in Norwegian waters.

Norway's new state oil company was founded in the autumn. It will operate from headquarters in Stavanger, on the west coast.

THOR GJESTER
"Norwegian Journal of Commerce and Shipping," Oslo

NOVA SCOTIA

Public interest in Nova Scotia in 1972 centered on cabinet changes, new tax legislation, and government purchase of a large, private power utility.

Cabinet. In August, Liberal Premier Gerald Regan announced an extensive reshuffling of his cabinet. The changes included shifting the colorful and controversial minister of highways and tourism, A. Garnet Brown, to provincial secretary; transferring the education portfolio from Peter Nicholson, who continued as finance minister, to Allan E. Sullivan; and transferring J. William Gillis from agriculture and marketing to public welfare.

Legislation. The 1972 legislature, which prorogued on May 15 after 77 days (the longest session since 1914), passed 131 of 154 bills. The most controversial measures were acts dealing with income taxes, gift taxes, and succession duties. Other significant legislation included the Environmental Protection Act, which, among other things, enabled establishment of a department of the environment, and the Labour Standards Code, which increased the minimum wage to $1.55 an hour and improved wage recovery provisions. Also important was the Trade Union Act, which took into account recommendations by the Nova Scotia Joint Labour-Management Study Committee and which contains important changes with respect to unfair labor practices and successor rights.

Economy. In 1972 the economy improved in some areas and deteriorated in others. Residential building, and consequently lumber production, rose

——— NOVA SCOTIA • Information Highlights ———

Area: 21,068 square miles (54,566 sq km).
Population: 788,960 (1971 census).
Chief Cities (1971 census): Halifax, the capital (122,035); Dartmouth (64,770); Sydney (33,230).
Government: *Chief Officers* (1972)—lt. gov., Victor de B. Oland; premier, Gerald A. Regan (Liberal); atty. gen., Leonard L. Pace (L); min. of finance, Peter M. Nicholson (L); min. of educ., Allan E. Sullivan; chief justice, Alexander H. MacKinnon. *Legislature*—Legislative Assembly, 46 members (24 Liberal; 20 Progressive Conservative; 2 New Democratic party).
Education: *School enrollment* (1968–69)—public elementary and secondary, 204,607 pupils (8,487 teachers); private schools, 3,255 pupils (199 teachers); Indian (federal) schools, 649 pupils (24 teachers); college and university, 11,905 students. *Public school expenditures* (1971 est.)—$58,520,000; average teacher's salary (1968–69)—$6,296.
Public Finance (fiscal year 1972 est.): *Revenues,* $496,800,-000 (sales tax, $118,100,000; income tax, $63,900,000; federal funds, $217,100,000). *Expenditures,* $587,300,000 (education, $156,500,000; health and social welfare, $253,-800,000; transport and communications, $39,000,000).
Personal Income (1969 est.): $1,760,000,000.
Social Welfare (fiscal year 1972 est.): $55,000,000 (aged and blind, $900,000; dependents and unemployed, $42,300,000).
Manufacturing (1968): Value added by manufacture, $261,-044,000 (food and beverages, $73,004,000; transportation equipment, $35,313,000; paper and allied industries, $34,-233,000; wood industries, $14,057,000.
Agriculture (1971): *Cash farm income,* $62,572,000 (livestock and products, $49,736,000; crops, $11,399,000. *Chief crops* (cash receipts)—fruits, $4,478,000; vegetables, $1,529,000; potatoes, $936,000.
Mining (1971 est.): *Production value,* $59,536,000. *Chief minerals* (tons)—coal, 1,946,000; gypsum, 4,932,000 (ranks 1st among the provinces); salt, 850,000 (ranks 2d); sand and gravel, 7,700,000.
Fisheries (1971): *Commercial catch,* sea fish (statistics on freshwater fish are confidential), 656,726,000 pounds ($57,-540,000). *Leading species*—lobster, 18,437,000 pounds ($18,112,000); scallops, 9,590,000 pounds ($11,237,000); cod, 109,910,000 pounds ($7,247,000); haddock, 49,637,000 pounds ($5,647,000).
Transportation: *Roads* (1968), 15,638 miles (25,162 km); *motor vehicles* (1969), 314,550; *railroads* (1970 est.), 1,301 track miles (2,093 km); *licensed airports* (1971 est.), 7.
Communications: *Telephones* (1969), 272,735; *television stations* (1971), 12; *radio stations* (1971), 16; *daily newspapers* (1971), 6.
(All monetary figures given in Canadian dollars.)

sharply. The value of manufacturing shipments, farm cash income, and construction also increased. Income from fishing declined chiefly because of smaller catches of groundfish. Pulpwood production was down as inventories decreased and foreign sales declined. The unemployment rate rose despite increased employment.

On January 7 the provincial power authority, the Nova Scotia Power Commission, won its bid to purchase the Nova Scotia Light and Power Company, Ltd. (NSLP), the largest privately owned power utility in eastern Canada. The government offered $13 for each NSLP share, which sold at slightly more than $10 when the bid was made.

In spite of major public support for denturists, on April 24 the provincial legislature voted 21–20 against legislation that would have granted them the right, which they hold in three provinces, to fit dentures for the public. After defeat of the bill the dental society financed raids by private investigators on denturists' offices to get evidence to take the denturists to court to prevent their practicing, since they continued to offer their services while trying to gain legal recognition.

A plan for a national park along the eastern shore of Nova Scotia was announced in August. The cost of the land was to be shared equally by the provincial and federal governments.

ANDREW S. HARVEY, *Dalhousie University*

NUCLEAR ENERGY. See ENERGY.
NUMISMATICS. See COIN COLLECTING.
NURSING. See MEDICINE.
OBITUARIES. For a list of prominent persons who died in 1972, see pages 761–772.

Artist's rendering of undersea project FLARE of the National Oceanic and Atmospheric Administration. Scientists housed in mobile Edalhab II on the ocean floor will conduct research in geology, marine life, and the effects of currents and water pollution. The support vessel, at top, is a catamaran.

oceanography

Ocean research in 1972 was characterized by a growing concern with the planetary environment. Accordingly, major projects of the International Decade of Ocean Exploration (IDOE) were continued in the areas of environmental quality, environmental forecasting, and seabed assessment. More than 30 nations participated in this comprehensive program for the 1970's, which is planned, managed, and largely funded by the National Science Foundation. Concern was also expressed during the year over the dwindling number of whales. See also GEOLOGY.

Environmental Quality. The aim of the IDOE is to determine the state of environmental quality of the oceans, evaluate the impact of human activity, and establish a scientific basis for actions necessary to preserve or improve the quality of the oceans. Samples were taken along selected base lines in the Atlantic and Pacific oceans, the Gulf of Mexico, and the Caribbean Sea, and analyzed for their content of potentially harmful compounds such as heavy metals, pesticides, herbicides, and petroleum residues. Evidence was found that additions of lead

to the marine environment by man exceed those that result from natural weathering processes. Also found were anomalously high concentrations of mercury, cadmium, copper, zinc, arsenic, and antimony; they occurred in marine organisms in certain coastal areas especially near to known sources of pollution input.

Investigation of the almost exclusively man-made halogenated hydrocarbons was concerned mainly with DDT and its derivatives and with PCB, or polychlorinated biphenyl, used by industry as an insulator and heat-transfer medium and in paints and pesticides. These compounds have been found to be ubiquitous in the Atlantic and Pacific oceans, the Gulf of Mexico, and continental seas. The highest values in plankton samples are from areas known to be locally polluted.

Petroleum is also being recognized as a serious contaminant in parts of the world's oceans. It was found to have entered the marine food chain at locations both in coastal waters and in the open ocean. The fate of crude oil that is introduced into the ocean is not fully understood, and the fundamental interactions of petroleum and its components with living organisms are essentially unknown. These and other preliminary results serve to focus future research on the determination of kinds, amounts, and pathways of global fluxes of pollutants.

Environmental research on a more fundamental level was carried out by a second base-line study, which seeks to establish present concentrations of trace elements, nutrients, and compounds that may be useful in testing oceanic circulation models and geochemical pathways in the sea. The study also aims to serve as a base for future work on changes in the quality of ocean water. The Geochemical Ocean Sections Study (GEOSECS) program includes the sampling of ocean waters in the Atlantic and Pacific oceans by the research vessels *Knorr, Melville,* and *Glacier,* with associated work by the French, German, and Japanese ships *Jean Charcot, Meteor,* and *Hakuho Maru.* Data were collected on salinity, temperature, oxygen, carbonates, optical scattering, nutrients, and noble gases, and samples were taken for isotope studies on various elements.

Environmental Forecasting. An understanding of long-term weather patterns is important in estimating dispersal of pollutants, predicting the success of fishing efforts, selecting shipping routes, and calculating water renewal rates in the deep ocean, among other reasons. The IDOE environmental forecasting program consists of a few long-term, major projects designed to increase this understanding.

One project is the Coastal Upwelling Experiment (CUE), in which scientists use moored arrays, research vessels, and aircraft to monitor changes in the ocean waters along the Oregon coast. The systems provide the detailed information needed to generate models that will allow the prediction of upwelling. Other nations have similar programs. There is considerable economic interest in these investigations, since upwelling of deep, cold, nutrient-rich waters characterizes regions where 50% of the world's fish catch occurs.

Another project, the Mid Ocean Dynamics Experiment (MODE), is designed to provide data for formulating numerical models of medium-scale dynamic processes such as geostrophic eddies, or eddies related to the effect of the Coriolis force. The models help oceanographers to understand the roles that these processes play in ocean circulation and global climate. The first phase of the project, MODE-I, is concerned with the description of the movement of medium-scale eddies in an area south of Bermuda. The vessels participating in MODE-I are *Chain, Discoverer, Discovery,* and *Trident.*

Data records on past conditions of the open ocean could be used to evaluate climatic changes through geological time. Such records are virtually nonexistent except for about the past 30 years, but the sediments of the ocean contain them. Thus a study of deep-sea cores makes it possible to relate chemical and biological analyses of the layers of sediments to prehistoric oceanic and climatic conditions.

At present the IDOE program in this field is concerned with describing climatic changes that occurred throughout the ice ages. The goal is to increase man's understanding of the mechanisms responsible for these changes, so that the knowledge can be applied to an assessment of the impact of human civilization on climate.

Seabed Assessment. The present revolution in geological understanding that grew out of geological oceanography—and that is characterized by the concepts of sea-floor spreading, subsidence, and subduction, continental separation, and the theory of plate tectonics—continues to dominate research in marine geology. With a view toward long-term economic interests such as petroleum, sulfur, and ore deposits, the IDOE seabed assessment program emphasizes the large-scale structure of and sediment distribution on the continental shelves, geophysical reconnaissance of the ocean floor, and study of mid-ocean rift valleys and deep ocean trenches. Field studies for a four-year project involving geophysical study of the continental margin of the eastern Atlantic Ocean began in 1972, using the research vessel *Atlantis II.* Processes and motions in oceanic rifts and trenches are the subject of a major study by the vessels *Yaquina* and *Kana Keoki* of the Nasca lithospheric plate between South America and the East Pacific Rise. Several foreign nations are undertaking research along similar lines, in part within the framework of IDOE and in part independently.

The highly successful Deep Sea Drilling Project (DSDP) also continues to add fundamentally to man's knowledge of the ocean floor. The project is managed by Scripps Institution of Oceanography, and it is conducted with scientific guidance from the Joint Oceanographic Institutions for Deep Earth Sampling (JOIDES). The latter includes Lamont-Doherty Geological Observatory, Rosenstiel School of Marine and Atmospheric Sciences, Scripps Institution of Oceanography, Woods Hole Oceanographic Institution, and the University of Washington. In 1972, geologists from several countries joined in the cruises of the DSDP drilling vessel, *Glomar Challenger.* (For a description of these cruises, see GEOLOGY.)

Arctic Research. Pilot studies are under way on a large-scale experiment planned in the Arctic Ocean, called the Arctic Ice Dynamics Joint Experiment. The project is designed to provide an understanding of the dynamics and thermal balance of the pack ice of the Arctic Ocean. This understanding is important as a basis for forecasting worldwide weather patterns and climatic trends. In the Bering Sea, studies made of the physiology of diving in seals and their temperature regulation were made by the research vessel *Alpha Helix.*

Antarctic Research. The circumpolar waters of the Antarctic Ocean strongly influence deep-sea circulation and the global climate in general. In 1972, the research vessel *Eltanin* continued its detailed circumantarctic survey of the area north and south of the Antarctic Polar Front. It investigated the energy flow in the Antarctic marine ecosystem, the physical oceanography, and the geophysics and sediment patterns in the region. Operations of ships working within areas covered by sea ice are now greatly facilitated by Antarctic sea-ice forecasting, using satellite imagery.

Ocean Engineering. Basic technology is evolving in the survey and selection of sites for sea-floor facilities, analysis of sea-floor soil properties with relation to foundations for such facilities, construction of deep-submersible fixed installations and vehicles, and development of test facilities and equipment. These technological advances are of special interest to the Navy and will undoubtedly prove useful both for scientific research and commercial applications.

Fishing and Whaling. As demands on the ocean's resources rise, long-range scientific research into stocks of marine life is needed if heavily exploited fisheries are to be conserved as a continuing source of much-needed protein. As a sign of international concern, a resolution by the United Nations Conference on the Human Environment, held in Stockholm, called for a complete ban on all whaling for 10 years. While it rejected the ban, the International Whaling Commission did make considerable cuts in catch quotas. It also announced provisions for monitoring compliance by whaling stations.

WOLFGANG H. BERGER
Scripps Institution of Oceanography

OHIO

Although Republican President Richard M. Nixon swept Ohio in the November election, Democrats won control of the state House of Representatives and came close to gaining control of the state Senate. These successes, together with the voters' rejection of a proposal to repeal Ohio's newly enacted state income tax law, seemed to reflect favorably on the programs of Democratic Gov. John J. Gilligan. Highlights of the 1972 legislative session included enactment of one of the nation's strongest measures for control of strip-mining and establishment of a new state environmental protection agency.

Elections. The presidential primaries held in Ohio in May gave Sen. Hubert H. Humphrey of Minnesota a very slim margin over Sen. George McGovern of South Dakota in the battle for delegates to the Democratic National Convention. President Nixon was virtually unopposed for Ohio's delegates to the Republican National Convention. U. S. Rep. John M. Ashbrook, Republican of Ohio, entered Republican primaries in a number of states as a Conservative challenger to President Nixon, but his support turned out to be meager.

In the November election, President Nixon won 60% of the Ohio popular vote to 39% for Senator McGovern, and Republicans retained their large majority in Ohio's delegation to the U. S. House of Representatives. Ohio Republicans lost one seat by redistricting. Voters elected 16 Republicans, all but two of them incumbents, and 7 Democrats, all incumbents. But in the state legislative contests

the Democrats gained 13 seats and took control of that body, 58 to 41. In the Senate, Democrats gained 3 seats, for a total of 16, but Republicans, with 17 seats, retained dominance there.

Legislation. The 1972 legislative session (a second-year nonbudgetary session) dealt with a variety of issues, many of them controversial. Governor Gilligan and friends of reclamation battled lobbyists for strip-mining companies for some time before the legislature enacted measures to establish stronger strip-mining rules and govern the granting of licenses. Under the new law, applications for licenses must be accompanied by detailed plans for reclamation, supposedly ensuring restoration of the land to its most valuable uses without erosion or pollution. The new state environmental protection agency was set up to absorb all pollution-control activities previously embraced in the departments of health and natural resources.

In March, after bitter controversy, the legislature sanctioned a proposal, to be submitted to the voters in the May primary, for repeal of a constitutional provision that prohibits lotteries in Ohio. In late April the Ohio supreme court ruled this proposal off the ballot because the legislature had not taken action, as the law requires, 75 days before the election. The court also ruled off the ballot a package proposal calling for 14 changes in state government, including the election of the governor and lieutenant governor as a team. The court held that the package plan did not provide for clear-cut approval or rejection of the separate items. A lack of en-

——————— OHIO • **Information Highlights** ———————

Area: 41,222 square miles (106,765 sq km).
Population (1970 census): 10,652,017. *Density:* 263 per sq mi.
Chief Cities (1970 census): Columbus, the capital, 540,025; Cleveland, 750,879; Cincinnati, 452,524; Toledo, 383,818; Akron, 275,425; Dayton, 243,601; Youngstown, 140,909.
Government (1972): *Chief Officers*—governor, John J. Gilligan (D); lt. gov., John W. Brown (R); secy. of state, Ted W. Brown (R); atty. gen., William J. Brown (D); treas., Gertrude W. Donahey (D); supt., dept. of education, Martin W. Essex; chief justice, C. William O'Neill. *General Assembly*—Senate, 33 members (20 Republicans, 13 Democrats); House of Representatives, 99 members (54 R, •45 D).
Education (1971–72): *Enrollment*—public elementary schools, 1,686,650 pupils, 55,480 teachers; public secondary, 736,-400 pupils, 49,820 teachers; nonpublic schools (1970–71), 321,651 pupils, 12,780 teachers; college and university, 377,000 students. *Public school expenditures*, $1,948,-655,000 ($871 per pupil). *Average teacher's salary*, $9,509.
State Finances (fiscal year 1970): *Revenues*, $3,876,193,000 (4% general sales tax and gross receipts taxes, $658,759,-000; motor fuel tax, $320,166,000; federal funds, $657,672,-000). *Expenditures*, $3,477,696,000 (education, $1,044,111,-000; health, welfare, and safety, $381,697,000; highways, $647,842,000). *State debt*, $1,631,898,000 (June 30, 1970).
Personal Income (1971): $44,775,000,000; per capita, $4,154.
Public Assistance (1971): $536,408,000. *Average monthly payments* (Dec. 1971)—old-age assistance, $61.91; aid to families with dependent children, $160.66.
Labor Force: *Nonagricultural wage and salary earners* (July 1972), 3,860,800. *Average annual employment* (1971)—manufacturing, 1,329,000; trade, 780,000; government, 578,000; services, 588,000. *Insured unemployed* (Aug. 1972)—44,400 (1.6%).
Manufacturing (1970): *Value added by manufacture*, $23,133,-400,000. Nonelectrical machinery, $3,363,100,000; transportation equipment, $2,937,200,000; primary metal industries, $2,919,000,000; electric equipment and supplies, $2,449,800,000; fabricated metal products, $2,409,000,000; chemicals and allied products, $1,752,400,000.
Agriculture (1970): *Cash farm income*, $1,441,432,000 (livestock, $773,466,000; crops, $578,353,000; government payments, $89,613,000). *Chief crops* (in order of value, 1971) —Corn (ranks 3d among the states), soybeans, hay, wheat.
Mining (1971): *Production value*, $593,421,000 (ranks 14th among the states). *Chief minerals*—Coal, $229,918,000; stone, $78,246,000; lime, $62,829,000; sand and gravel, $59,801,000.
Fisheries (1971): *Commercial catch*, 9,045,000 pounds ($1,225,000).
Transportation: *Roads* (1971), 108,926 miles (175,295 km); *motor vehicles* (1971), 5,975,256; *railroads* (1971), 7,845 miles (12,625 km); *public airports* (1972), 102.
Communications: *Telephones* (1972), 6,378,300; *television stations* (1971), 27; *radio stations* (1971), 226; *newspapers* (1972), 95 (daily circulation, 3,494,000).

thusiasm for these changes kept them off the November ballot.

Spirited demands developed, however, for the repeal of Ohio's first state income tax—a graduated personal and corporate tax that had been enacted in December 1971 after months of controversy. The proposal for repeal, as it appeared on the ballot, provided that any state income tax must be at a fixed rate and must also have voter approval. The proposal was soundly rejected, 70% to 30%.

Federal Court Decisions. In May the U. S. Supreme Court dismissed a challenge to Ohio's requirement that a political party must execute a loyalty oath to get on the Ohio ballot. The court held that the Socialist Labor party, which brought the suit, had demonstrated no injury and presumably had executed an affidavit when it appeared on the ballot.

The state budget passed in December 1971 had sought to avoid constitutional objections to assistance to parochial schools by authorizing a subsidy of $90 a year to parents of nonpublic school children. In April a three-judge federal panel declared the subsidy unconstitutional. Later—in October—the U. S. Supreme Court affirmed the panel's decision. Meanwhile, the legislature approved state income tax credits for parents of nonpublic school children, but opponents again carried the case to the federal courts.

FRANCIS P. WEISENBURGER
The Ohio State University

OIL. See ENERGY—*Petroleum.*

OKLAHOMA

The year 1972 revealed new trends in Oklahoma politics, urban affairs, and education. Disaffection with government administration was evident among segments of the state's Indian population.

Elections. The people of Oklahoma voted overwhelmingly for President Nixon's reelection in November. So strong was the pull of the President that it helped carry former Republican Gov. Dewey F. Bartlett to victory over veteran Democratic congressman Ed Edmonson in the contest for the U. S. Senate seat vacated by Democrat Fred Harris. For the first time since the 1920's the state will be represented in the Senate by two Republicans.

Democrats won most state offices, and Speaker of the House Carl Albert was returned to Congress along with four other Democrats and one Republican.

Government. Already on the defensive due to his tax policy, Gov. David Hall received a stinging rebuke in March, when voters defeated his proposed "Freeway 77," a $250 million road bond issue.

The Oklahoma House rejected ratification of the women's equal rights amendment to the U. S. Constitution. A proposal to liberalize the state's abortion laws was killed in committee.

Urban Affairs. Discontent with their voting power in the Association of Central Oklahoma Governments, Oklahoma City and Oklahoma county withdrew in August, thereby crippling that regional planning organization, which serves also as a clearinghouse for federal funds. But two months later Oklahoma City rejoined the association.

Education. School systems in the state's two largest cities, Oklahoma City and Tulsa, reeled under the impact of busing to implement integration.

Desegregation, which began under federal court order in the fall of 1969, progressed to the elementary schools in 1972. Boycotts cut enrollments in Oklahoma City. In Tulsa further integration occurred with court-ordered pairing of five all-black *de jure* schools with four all-white schools. The federal court refused to require integration of four all black *de facto* schools.

Indian Affairs. When the school boards of Pawnee and Marland refused to allow Indian youths to attend public schools unless they cut their long hair, the Indians refused to comply. The dropout rate of Indians in Oklahoma schools, already the highest in the nation, increased. Militant Indians charged misuse of Johnson-O'Malley federal funds intended for the improvement of Indian education. As a result, the federal Bureau of Indian Affairs suspended a regional official and conducted hearings on the charges.

Liquor Raid. In the continuing controversy over liquor sold by the drink, state officers in July raided the Amtrak train as it passed through Oklahoma and arrested the bartender for running an open saloon. However, the federal government won an injunction against the state. In November, voters rejected a liquor-sold-by-the-drink provision.

Agriculture. Federal aid was allocated to farmers and ranchers in southwestern Oklahoma, who suffered $250 million in losses from the spring drought, the worst since the Dust Bowl days of the 1930's. Much of the wheat crop was lost.

C. B. CLARK
University of Oklahoma

OLDER POPULATION

For the older population, 1972 was a promising year as a result of the interest generated by the 1971 White House Conference on Aging and by the national election, with the increased participation of older people.

Conference Impact. Activity across the country associated with the White House Conference on Aging involved thousands of people and numerous groups, organizations, and government agencies. The momentum for increased action to improve circumstances for present and future generations of older people accelerated during 1972. Conference chairman Arthur S. Flemming was appointed as special consultant to the President to stimulate implementation of recommendations at all levels of government and to encourage voluntary action. From The White House, the Domestic Council's Committee on Aging directed department and agency heads to assess conference recommendations, implement what they could, and suggest new legislation. A post-conference citizen planning board evaluated the government's responses and proposed implementation strategies.

One effect of the conference was an increase in the appropriation for the Administration on Aging (AoA), the focal point in the federal government for advocacy and program leadership. Most of the additional funds were allotted to the states to expand community services. Other agencies, such as the Department of Housing and Urban Development (HUD) and the Public Health Service, earmarked more of their resources to complement AoA's community effort.

Improving Benefits for Older People. Numerous conference recommendations urged higher incomes for older people, 50% of whom are poor. In June, Congress enacted legislation to increase social security benefits by 20% and to provide for automatic cost-of-living adjustments. Also, the administration launched project FIND. A notice was enclosed with the August social security checks regarding the availability to older people of food stamps and surplus foods. Nearly 1.5 million responded, and 330,000 proved eligible under the food programs.

In October, Congress enacted a modification of an administration bill (H.R.1) which increases social security benefits for 3.8 million widows and widowers, improves benefits for men aged 62 to 64, raises the amount retirees may earn without loss of benefits, provides for a 1% bonus for each year a worker delays retirement beyond age 65, and establishes a minimum monthly benefit of $170 for all beneficiaries who worked 30 years. A landmark provision of the legislation calls for the federal government to assume welfare responsibility for the aged, blind, and disabled in 1974, with a minimum federal payment of $130 per month to a single person without income and $195 to a couple. (See also SOCIAL WELFARE—*Social Security*.)

Nutrition and Health. The most significant measure for improving the health of the older population was the passage of the Nutrition Program for the Elderly Act. The act provides for serving 400,-000 hot meals 5 days per week to low-income, isolated older people in such facilities as senior centers, schools, and churches. Each center will have a social program, and transportation will be provided to the center if necessary.

Efforts to improve the quality of long-term care for the aged, launched in 1971 on the initiative of the President, were accelerated. Trained personnel in all states inspected nearly 7,000 homes for the elderly to ensure that they complied with fire, safety, and sanitary regulations.

Social security legislation under H.R.1 permits persons eligible for Medicare to enroll in prepaid group health maintenance organizations with the government paying the premiums. Further, doctor "peer review" groups were established to monitor work of doctors paid from federal funds, in the hope of reducing such wasteful practices as unneeded operations.

Housing. Acting on a recommendation of the White House Conference, HUD appointed a special assistant to the secretary for Programs for the Elderly and Handicapped. Assistants were placed in regional and area offices to work with state and community agencies to increase the supply of retirement housing and services available to residents. HUD estimated that 82,000 new units for the elderly would be provided in 1972. The department financed the creation of a National Center for Housing Management to train managers for federally assisted housing to reduce financial failures. The center is giving special attention to retirement housing.

Participation by Older People. The White House Conference recommended that education be provided older people so that they may learn how to advocate on their own behalf. It also recommended that they be included in policy and program decision making and that more of them be employed in community service activities. A continuing flow of studies indicates that such proposals are compatible with the desires of many retired persons. Supplemental appropriations following the conference expanded opportunities for low-income older persons to engage in paid, voluntary service.

Concern with public affairs appears to increase in the middle and later years, and organizations of older people now include from 6 to 8 million members, more than at any time since the Townsend Movement of the 1930's. Participation in elections reaches a peak at ages 45–64 and declines only slowly thereafter. Both political parties bid strongly for this vote in 1972.

Research and Training. The White House Conference urged increased support of gerontological training and research. Additional funds for these purposes were made available to the AoA within two weeks after the conference adjourned. In October, Congress passed legislation to establish a National Institute on Aging, to support research and training in mental health and aging, and to establish university centers of gerontology. The legislation was vetoed by the President, however.

Conferences. The Institute of Gerontology of the University of Michigan and Wayne State University held its 25th annual Conference on Aging. It announced the establishment of the Wilma T. Donahue Gerontology Library, in recognition of the pioneer work of the institute's long-time director.

The 9th International Congress of Gerontology was held in Kiev, USSR, with 3,000 participants from 50 countries. The 10th Congress will be held in Israel in 1975. The International Center for Social Gerontology announced plans for a world conference on gerontological training in Oslo in May 1973 and a conference on housing for older adults in Washington, D. C., in October.

CLARK TIBBITTS, *Administration on Aging*
U. S. Department of Health, Education, and Welfare

Olympic Games

THE GAMES OF THE XXth OLYMPIAD, billed as the "Happy Olympics," came to a tragic halt with the murder of 11 Israelis by Arab terrorists on September 5. (Opposite) A memorial service for the slain Israelis, with Olympic and national flags at half staff, was held the next morning at the main stadium, after which the Games were resumed. (Above) An Arab guerrilla spokesman negotiates with West German and Olympic officials for release of 200 Arab terrorists held in Israel in exchange for the Israeli hostages. The Israelis later were killed at airport outside Munich during abortive rescue attempt by West German police. Among the slain Israelis were three weight lifters (right), whose coach (wearing jacket) managed to escape.

In an effort to offset the bad taste left by the Hitler-controlled Olympics of 1936, the West German government spent $265 million to create the locale for the Games of the XXth Olympiad. The contests at Munich, Aug. 26–Sept. 11, 1972, were planned as the "Happy Olympics." But by the conclusion of the Games, a nightmarish gloom pervaded Olympic Village. Some political leaders believed that the Olympics should be abolished. Various athletic councils held that the Games should be restructured, with the element of nationalism de-emphasized or eliminated.

Though many Olympic problems were not new, they received greater emphasis in 1972. Uppermost was the question of professionalism. It had been a point of dissension at the 1968 Winter Olympics; it was given stress that summer at Mexico City with the distribution of cash to track athletes by shoe manufacturers; and it caused a major uproar at the 1972 Winter Olympics with the disqualification of an Austrian skier. If it were less an issue at Munich, it was only because it was overshadowed.

Less than a week before the scheduled start of the Games, with over 8,000 athletes gathered from 123 nations and spectators flowing into the Bavarian city, several African countries threatened to withdraw if Rhodesia were allowed to participate. Their objection was to the racial policies of Rhodesia. Actually, the Rhodesian athletes (blacks among them) were to compete under the British flag as a colony. But as the tension mounted, including the possibility that black American athletes would go home, the International Olympic Committee banned Rhodesia, while deploring the political pressure.

The Tragedy. The Olympic flame was lit on schedule in a festive opening on August 26, and 5,000 doves of peace were released over Munich. Within 12 days Olympic Village was engulfed in a disaster that cost the lives of 17 persons, ruptured diplomatic relations, and almost ended the competition. The event had no connection with the Olympics. It was caused by Palestinians of the Black September group. Before dawn on September 5, eight terrorists swept into the Israeli housing unit and killed two men. The terrorists held nine Israeli athletes as hostages, demanding that 200 Arab guerrillas imprisoned in Israel be released. West German police swarmed into the area, and the day's athletic events were halted.

After intense maneuvering and discussions with Israel, the terrorists and their hostages were flown in helicopters to a nearby airport, where an attempt to free the Israelis led to slaughter. All nine Israelis and a German policeman were massacred. Five terrorists were killed, and the remaining three captured. The world reeled in horror. Despite widespread demands that the Games be discontinued, top Olympic officials ruled for resuming the Games, to which Israel agreed. On the morning of September 6, a memorial service for the slain Israelis was held in the main stadium, and the Games continued amid much controversy.

UPI

FINAL MEDAL STANDING
Summer Games
(Munich, West Germany, Aug. 26–Sept. 11, 1972)
(Gold for 1st place, silver for 2d, and bronze for 3d)

Nation	Gold	Silver	Bronze	Total
Soviet Union	50	27	22	99
United States	33	30*	30	93
East Germany	20	23	23	66
West Germany	13	11	16	40
Hungary	6	13	16	35
Japan	13	8	8	29
Bulgaria	6	10	5	21
Poland	7	5	9	21
Italy	5	3	10	18
Britain	4	5	9	18
Australia	8	7	2	17
Sweden	4	6	6	16
Rumania	3	6	7	16
France	2	4	7	13
Kenya	2	3	4	9
Cuba	3	1	4	8
Finland	3	1	4	8
Czechoslovakia	2	4	2	8
Netherlands	3	1	1	5
North Korea	1	1	3	5
Yugoslavia	2	1	2	5
Canada	0	2	3	5
Norway	2	1	1	4
New Zealand	1	1	1	3
Austria	0	1	2	3
Colombia	0	1	2	3
Switzerland	0	3	0	3
Iran	0	2	1	3
Uganda	1	1	0	2
Belgium	0	2	0	2
Greece	0	2	0	2
Mongolia	0	2	0	2
Brazil	0	0	2	2
Ethiopia	0	0	2	2
Spain	0	0	2	2
Denmark	1	0	0	1
Argentina	0	1	0	1
Lebanon	0	1	0	1
Mexico	0	1	0	1
Pakistan	0	1	0	1
South Korea	0	1	0	1
Tunisia	0	1	0	1
Turkey	0	1	0	1
Ghana	0	0	1	1
India	0	0	1	1
Jamaica	0	0	1	1
Nigeria	0	0	1	1
Niger	0	0	1	1

* The U. S. basketball team refused the silver medal in protest against officiating in game against the USSR.

26

UPI

516

SCENES FROM SUMMER OLYM-PICS: (Opposite, top) Canoeist guides kayak through turbulent waters of artificial slalom course at Augsburg, West Germany, on August 29. (Opposite, bottom) John Williams of the U.S.A. shows peerless form in capturing men's archery title. (Right) Prince Philip of England congratulates winning West German team in Grand Prix jumping on September 11, the last event of the Olympic Games. (Below) Soviet basket-ball players rejoice after 51–50 upset of U. S. team in final game marred by questionable officiating in closing seconds.

Swimming. When the terrorist action erupted, the track-and-field program was at its midpoint, but the swimmers had just completed a series of sensational performances in which world records were bettered in 23 of the 29 events. The most outstanding performer was Mark Spitz of Carmichael, Calif., who won seven gold medals.

Spitz, a graduate of Indiana University, was not new to Olympic competition. He had been heralded in 1968 as possibly the world's finest swimmer, but he failed to do well at Mexico City. Better prepared mentally for Munich, he achieved more than any individual athlete in one session of the Olympics. He set four world records in the individual events he won and helped the United States win all three men's relays, in world-record times. His individual triumphs were in the 100-meter and 200-meter free-style and in the 100-meter and 200-meter butterfly.

But Spitz was not allowed to enjoy the remainder of the Games as their finest athlete. Following the attack on the Israelis, security officials fearing that other Jewish athletes might be included in the terrorists' plans whisked Spitz out of Germany to England and then back to California.

In addition to Spitz, seven other American swimmers—two men and five women—won gold medals, some setting world records. There had been a third man, Rick DeMont, winner of the 400-meter free-

SUMMER GAMES

Archery
Men—John Williams, Cranesville, Pa. (2,528 pts)
Women—Doreen Wilber, Jefferson, Iowa (2,424 pts)

Basketball
Soviet Union (defeated United States, 51–50, in final)

Boxing
Light Flyweight—Gyoergy Gedo, Hungary
Flyweight—Gheorghi Kostadinov, Bulgaria
Bantamweight—Orlando Martínez, Cuba
Featherweight—Boris Kousnetsov, USSR
Lightweight—Jan Szczepanski, Poland
Light Welterweight—Ray Seales, Tacoma, Wash.
Welterweight—Emilio Correa, Cuba
Light Middleweight—Dieter Kottysch, West Germany
Middleweight—Viatschesiav Lemechev, USSR
Light Heavyweight—Mate Parlov, Yugoslavia
Heavyweight—Teofilo Stevenson, Cuba

Canoeing
Men's Kayak
Slalom—Siegbert Horn, East Germany (268.56 pts)
Singles—Aleksandr Shaparenko, USSR (3:48.06)
Pairs—Nikolai Gorbachev and Viktor Kratassyuk, USSR (3:31.23)
Fours—USSR (3:14.02)

Men's Canadian
Slalom—Reinhard Eiben, East Germany (315.84 pts)
Singles—Ivan Patzaichin, Rumania (4:08.94)
Pairs—Vladas Chessyunas and Yuri Lobanov, USSR (3:52.60)
2-Man Slalom—Walter Hofmann and Rolf-Dieter Amend, East Germany (310.68 pts)

Women's Kayak
Slalom—Angelika Bahmann, East Germany (364.50 pts)
Singles—Yulia Ryabchinskaya, USSR (2:03.17)
Pairs—Ludmila Pinaeva and Ekaterina Kuryshko, USSR (1:53.50)

Cycling
Individual Pursuit—Knut Knudsen, Norway (4:45.74)
Team Pursuit—West Germany (4:22.14)
Road Race, Individual—Hennie Kuiper, Netherlands (4:14:37)
Road Race, Team—Soviet Union (2:11:17.8)
1,000-Meters—Niels Fredborg, Denmark (1:06.44)
Tandem—Vladimir Semenets and Igor Tselovalnikov, USSR
Sprint—Daniel Morelon, France

Equestrian
Dressage—Liselott Linsenhoff, West Germany (1,229 pts); team: USSR (5,059)
Three-Day—Richard Meade, Britain (57.73 pts); team: Britain (95.53)
Jumping—Graziano Mancinelli, Italy (8); team: West Germany (32 faults)

Fencing
Men's Foil—Witold Woyda, Poland; team: USSR
Men's Épée—Dr. Csaba Fenyvesi, Hungary; team: Hungary
Men's Saber—Viktor Sidiak, USSR; team: Italy
Women's Foil—Antonella Ragno Lonzi, Italy; team: USSR

Field Hockey
West Germany (defeated Pakistan, 1–0, in final)

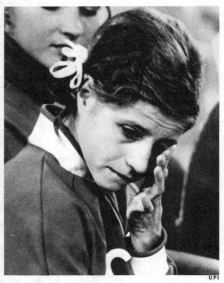

USSR's OLGA KORBUT, who won first in balance beam and floor exercises, cries after slip on parallel bars denied her third gold medal.

Gymnastics
Men
Individual All-Around—Sawao Kato, Japan (114.650)
Floor Exercises—Nikolai Andrianov, USSR (19.175)
Long Horse—Klaus Koeste, East Germany (18.850)
Side Horse—Viktor Klimenko, USSR (19.125)
Horizontal Bar—Mitsuo Tsukahara, Japan (19.725)
Parallel Bars—Sawao Kato (19.475)
Rings—Akinori Nakayama, Japan (19.350)
Team—Japan (571.25)

Women
Individual All-Around—Ludmila Turischeva, USSR (77.025)
Floor Exercises—Olga Korbut, USSR (19.575)
Parallel Bars—Karin Janz, East Germany (19.675)
Balance Beam—Olga Korbut, USSR (19.400)
Side Horse—Karin Janz, East Germany (19.525)
Team—USSR (380.50)

Handball, Team
Yugoslavia (defeated Czechoslovakia, 21–16, in final)

Judo
Lightweight—Takao Kawaguchi, Japan
Middleweight—Shinobu Sekine, Japan
Welterweight—Toyokazu Nomura, Japan
Light Heavyweight—Shota Chochoshvily, USSR
Heavyweight—Wim Ruska, Netherlands
Open—Wim Ruska, Netherlands

Modern Pentathlon
Individual—Andras Balczo, Hungary (5,412)
Team—USSR (15,968)

Rowing
(All races 2,000 meters)
Single Sculls—Yuri Malishev, USSR (7:10.12)
Double Sculls—Aleksandr Timoshinin and Gennadi Korshikov, USSR (7:01.77)
Pairs with Coxswain—Wolfgang Gunkel and Joerg Lucke; Klaus-Dieter Neubert, coxswain, East Germany (7:17.25)
Pairs without Coxswain—Siegfried Brietzke and Wolfgang Mager, East Germany (6:53.16)
Fours with Coxswain—West Germany (6:31.85)
Fours without Coxswain—East Germany (6:24.27)
Eights with Coxswain—New Zealand (6:08.94)

Shooting
Free Pistol—Ragnar Skanaker, Sweden (567 pts)
Rapid Fire Pistol—Jozef Zapedski, Poland (595)
Free Rifle—Lones Wigger, Columbus, Ga. (1,155)
Small Bore Rifle (3-position)—John Writer, Clarendon Hills, Ill. (1,166; world record)
Small Bore Rifle (prone position)—Ho Jun Li, North Korea (599; world record)
Moving Target—Iakov Zhelezniak, USSR (569; world record)
Skeetshooting—Konrad Wirnhier, West Germany (195)
Trapshooting—Angelo Scalzone, Italy (199; world record)

Soccer
Poland (defeated Hungary, 2–1, in final)

style. But he was disqualified after tests revealed traces of ephedrine in his system. Ephedrine, one of the drugs banned by Olympic rules, had been taken by DeMont since childhood as a medication for asthma, but this fact did not affect the ruling. He had to surrender his gold medal, which was then given to Australia's Brad Cooper, who had finished second in the race.

The only other double winner among the Americans was Melissa Belote, who took both backstroke races, setting a world record in the 200-meter event. The other women gold medalists were Keena Rothhammer, Cathy Carr, and Karen Moe—all three in world-record time—and Sandy Neilson. The American women also won both relay events, bettering the world record. The other gold medalists among the men were Mike Burton and John Hencken.

The biggest individual winner aside from Spitz was Shane Gould, a 15-year-old Australian girl, who had shattered virtually all of the women's free-style records during the preceding winter (Australian summer). She won gold medals in the 200- and 400-meter freestyle and the 200-meter individual medley, lowering the record in each one. In the 100-meter freestyle, she was beaten by Sandy Neilson and another American, Shirley Babashoff. Two other Australian girls excelled. Gail Neall set a world mark in the 400-meter medley, and Beverly Whitfield took the 200-meter backstroke, giving Australia second place among the gold-medal winners.

The men's competition had two other double winners. Roland Matthes of East Germany, acclaimed the best backstroke swimmer in the world, won both events without trouble. Gunnar Larsson of Sweden, who had attended college in the United States and had swum for a California club, took the two individual medley events, bettering the world mark in the 200-meter race.

The other championships—one women's and one men's—went to Japan's Mayumi Aoki (100-meter butterfly) and Nobutaka Tagushi (100-meter breaststroke), each in world-record time.

Swimming

Men

100-Meter Freestyle—Mark Spitz, Carmichael, Calif. (0:51.22; world record)

200-Meter Freestyle—Mark Spitz (1:52.78; world record)

400-Meter Freestyle—Brad Cooper, Australia (4:00.27; Rick DeMont won event but was disqualified for using unauthorized medication)

1,500-Meter Freestyle—Mike Burton, Carmichael, Calif. (15:52.58; world record)

100-Meter Backstroke—Roland Matthes, East Germany (0:56.58)

200-Meter Backstroke—Roland Matthes (2:02.82; equals world record)

100-Meter Breaststroke—Nobutaka Taguchi, Japan (1:04.94; world record)

200-Meter Breaststroke—John Hencken, Cupertino, Calif. (2:21.55; world record)

100-Meter Butterfly—Mark Spitz (0:54.27; world record)

200-Meter Butterfly—Mark Spitz (2:00.70; world record)

200-Meter Individual Medley—Gunnar Larsson, Sweden (2:07.17; world record)

400-Meter Individual Medley—Gunnar Larsson (4:31.98)

400-Meter Freestyle Relay—U.S. (Dave Edgar, Knoxville, Tenn.; John Murphy, Hinsdale, Ill.; Jerry Heidenreich, Dallas; Mark Spitz; 3:26.42; world record)

400-Meter Medley Relay—U.S. (Mike Stamm, San Diego; Tom Bruce, Sunnyvale, Calif.; Mark Spitz; Jerry Heidenreich; 3:48.16; world record)

800-Meter Freestyle Relay—U.S. (John Kinsella, Hinsdale, Ill.; Fred Tyler, Winter Park, Fla.; Steve Genter, Lakewood, Calif.; Mark Spitz; 7:35.78; world record)

Springboard Diving—Vladimir Vasin, USSR (594.09 pts)

Platform Diving—Klaus Dibiasi, Italy (504.12 pts)

Women

100-Meter Freestyle—Sandy Neilson, El Monte, Calif. (0:58.59)

200-Meter Freestyle—Shane Gould, Australia (2:03.56; world record)

400-Meter Freestyle—Shane Gould (4:19.04; world record)

800-Meter Freestyle—Keena Rothhammer, Santa Clara, Calif. (8:53.68; world record)

100-Meter Backstroke—Melissa Belote, Springfield, Va. (1:05.78)

200-Meter Backstroke—Melissa Belote (2:19.19; world record)

100-Meter Breaststroke—Cathie Carr, Albuquerque, N. Mex. (1:13.58; world record)

200-Meter Breaststroke—Beverly Whitfield, Australia (2:41.71)

100-Meter Butterfly—Mayumi Aoki, Japan (1:03.34; world record)

200-Meter Butterfly—Karen Moe, Santa Clara, Calif. (2:15.57; world record)

200-Meter Individual Medley—Shane Gould, Australia (2:23.07; world record)

400-Meter Individual Medley—Gail Neall, Australia (5:02.97; world record)

400-Meter Freestyle Relay—U.S. (Sandy Neilson, El Monte, Calif.; Jennifer Kemp, Cincinnati; Jane Barkman, Wayne, Pa.; Shirley Babashoff, Mountain Valley, Calif.; 3:55.19; world record)

400-Meter Medley Relay—U.S. (Melissa Belote, Springfield, Va.; Sandy Neilson; Cathy Carr, Albuquerque, N. Mex.; Deena Deardruff, Cincinnati; 4:20.75; world record)

Springboard Diving—Micki King, Hermosa Beach, Calif. (450.03 pts)

Platform Diving—Ulrika Knape, Sweden (390 pts)

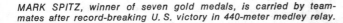

MARK SPITZ, winner of seven gold medals, is carried by teammates after record-breaking U.S. victory in 440-meter medley relay.

MAMMOTH CHRIS TAYLOR applies leg hold in easy win over Bulgarian opponent in early super heavyweight event. U. S. wrestler lost in final match to Alexandr Medved of the USSR in an unpopular decision.

Track and Field

Men

100-Meter Dash—Valery Borzov, USSR (0:10.14)
200-Meter Dash—Valery Borzov (0:20.00)
400-Meter Dash—Vince Matthews, Brooklyn, N. Y. (0:44.66)
800-Meter Run—Dave Wottle, Canton, Ohio (1:45.9)
1,500-Meter Run—Pekka Vasala, Finland (3:36.3)
5,000-Meter Run—Lasse Viren, Finland (13:26.4)
10,000-Meter Run—Lasse Viren, Finland (27:38.4; world record)
3,000-Meter Steeplechase—Kipchoge Keino, Kenya (8:23.6)
Marathon—Frank Shorter, Ranchos de Taos, N. Mex. (2:12:19.8)
110-Meter Hurdles—Rod Milburn, Opelousas, La. (0:13.24; equals world record)
400-Meter Hurdles—John Akii-bua, Uganda (0:47.82; world record)
20-Kilometer Walk—Peter Frenkel, East Germany (1:26:42.4)
50-Kilometer Walk—Bern Kannernberg, West Germany (3:56:11.6)
400-Meter Relay—U. S. (Larry Black, Miami, Fla.; Robert Taylor, Houston, Texas; Gerald Tinker, Miami; Eddie Hart, Pittsburg, Calif.; 0:38.19; equals world record)
1,600-Meter Relay—Kenya (Charles Asati, Hezahiah Nyamau, Robert Ouko, Julius Sang; 2:59.8)
Long Jump—Randy Williams, Compton, Calif. (27 ft ¾ in)
High Jump—Yuri Tarmak, USSR (7 ft 3¾ in)
Triple Jump—Victor Saneev, USSR (56 ft 11 in)
Pole Vault—Wolfgang Nordwig, East Germany (18 ft ½ in)
Hammer Throw—Anatoli Bondarchuk, USSR (247 ft 8½ in)
Discus—Ludvik Danek, Czechoslovakia (211 ft 3 in)
Shot Put—Wladyslaw Komar, Poland (69 ft 6 in)
Javelin—Klaus Wolfermann, West Germany (296 ft 10 in)
Decathlon—Nikolai Avilov, USSR (8,454 pts; world record)

Women

100-Meter Dash—Renate Stecher, East Germany (0:11.07)
200-Meter Dash—Renate Stecher (0:22.40; equals world record)
400-Meter Dash—Monika Zehrt, East Germany (0:51.08)
800-Meter Run—Hildegard Falck, West Germany (1:58.6)
1,500-Meter Run—Ludmila Bragina, USSR (4:01.4; world record)
100-Meter Hurdles—Annelie Ehrhardt, East Germany (0:12.59)
400-Meter Relay—West Germany (0:42.81; equals world record)
1,600-Meter Relay—East Germany (3:23; world record)
Discus—Faina Melnik, USSR (218 ft 7 in)
Javelin—Ruth Fuchs, East Germany (209 ft 7 in)
Shot Put—Nadezhda Chizova, USSR (69 ft; world record)
Long Jump—Heidemarie Rosendahl, West Germany (22 ft 3 in)

Track and Field. The track athletes were far less successful in bettering world marks, partly because of the disruption caused by the terrorists and partly because U. S. athletes failed to achieve their best. The Americans won only six gold medals in the men's competition and none in the women's.

The failures came in the pole vault, as Bob Seagren, the world record holder, finished second to Wolfgang Nordwig of East Germany; the shot put, in which George Woods was second to Wladyslaw Komar of Poland; and the high jump, in which Dwight Stones could get only a third place behind Yuri Tarmak of the USSR and Stefan Junge of East Germany.

One surprise victory was Frank Shorter's in the marathon, which no American had won since 1908. The short sprints went to a Russian, Valery Borzov, but Vince Matthews of Brooklyn won the 400-meter dash, with Wayne Collett of Santa Monica, Calif., second. Dave Wottle of Canton, Ohio, captured the 800-meter run. Rod Milburn of Opelousas, La., tied the world mark in winning the 110-meter hurdles, but in the 400-meter hurdles Ralph Mann of Provo, Utah, ran second to John Akii-Bua of Uganda. The winner's time of 47.8 seconds bettered the world record of David Hemery of Britain, who finished third. Randy Williams, of Compton, Calif., won the long jump.

Team Medals. Athletes from the Soviet Union and East Germany were consistent in their performances in track as well as minor sports, and the Russians led the overall medal winners with 99, of which 50 were gold. The U. S. total, second best, was 93, of which 33 were gold, 30 silver for second place (basketball medal was refused) and 30 bronze for third. East Germany came next with a total of 66, beating West Germany by 26 in total medals. The East Germans had 20 gold medals, and the West Germans 13.

Troubles for Americans. Frustrations for the U. S. team began before the Games got under way and continued through the final day, culminating in

Volleyball

Men—Japan (defeated East Germany, 3–1, in final)
Women—USSR (defeated Japan, 3–2, in final)

Water Polo

USSR (awarded championship on basis of total points scored against points allowed, 22–16, in all final-round games)

Weight Lifting

Flyweight—Zygmunt Smalcerz, Poland (744 lbs total)
Bantamweight—Imre Foldi, Hungary (832 lbs; world record)
Featherweight—Norair Nourikian, Bulgaria (887 lbs; equals world record)
Lightweight—Mukharbi Kirzhinov, USSR (1,104 lbs; world record)
Middleweight—Yordan Bikov, Bulgaria (1,069 lbs; world record)
Light Heavyweight—Leif Jenssen, Norway (1,118 lbs)
Middle Heavyweight—Andon Nikolov, Bulgaria (1,157 lbs)
Heavyweight—Yan Talts, USSR (1,278 lbs)
Super Heavyweight—Vassili Alexeev, USSR (1,411 lbs)

Wrestling

Freestyle

Paperweight—Roman Dmitriev, USSR
Flyweight—Kiyomi Kato, Japan
Bantamweight—Hideaki Yanagida, Japan
Featherweight—Zagalav Abdulbekov, USSR
Lightweight—Dan Gable, Waterloo, Iowa
Welterweight—Wayne Wells, Norman, Okla.
Middleweight—Levan Tediashili, USSR
Light Heavyweight—Ben Peterson, Comstock, Wis.
Heavyweight—Ivan Yarygin, USSR
Super Heavyweight—Alexandr Medved, USSR

Greco-Roman

Paperweight—Gheorghe Berceanu, Rumania
Flyweight—Peter Kirov, Bulgaria
Bantamweight—Rustem Kazakov, USSR
Featherweight—Gheorghi Markov, Bulgaria
Lightweight—Shamil Khisamutdinov, USSR
Welterweight—Vitezslav Macha, Czechoslovakia
Middleweight—Csaba Hegedus, Hungary
Light Heavyweight—Valery Rezantsev, USSR
Heavyweight—Nicolae Martinescu, Rumania
Super Heavyweight—Anatoly Roshin, USSR

Yachting

Dragon—Australia (John Cuneo, helmsman)
Finn—France (Serge Maury)
Flying Dutchman—Britain (Rodney Pattison)
Soling—U. S. (Harry Melges, Zenda, Wis.)
Star—Australia (David Forbes)
Tempest—USSR (Valentin Mankin)

a strange basketball game that was still under protest when the Olympic flame was snuffed out. First there was a protest, lodged by the East Germans, against Bob Seagren's vaulting pole. The protest was upheld, and Seagren had to start getting accustomed to another pole. Then Chris Taylor, an American super-heavyweight wrestler, was considered to have gotten such bad decisions from the referee in losing to Alexandr Medved, the Soviet champion, that the referee was banned for the rest of the Games. A young boxer, Reggie Jones of Newark, N. J., whacked his Soviet opponent thoroughly, especially in the final round, and was ahead in points, but the judges awarded the decision to the Soviet boxer, causing a near-riot among the spectators and the banning of the judges. The decision against DeMont in swimming kept him out of the 1,500-meter event in addition to the loss of his championship. Mike Burton won the event for the United States and bettered DeMont's world-record time.

Two crack American sprinters, Eddie Hart of Pittsburg, Calif., and Rey Robinson of Lakeland, Fla., advised incorrectly of the time of the race, missed the final of the 100-meter dash.

Because Matthews and Collett did not stand at attention during the playing of the national anthem at the medal presentation ceremony, they were adjudged guilty of demeaning the Olympic code and were banned from further participation. This eliminated them from the U. S. 1,600-meter relay team, and the IOC barred substitutes.

However, the final near-fiasco in basketball put the cap on American frustration. With the game apparently over and the Americans victorious, officials three times gave the ball to the Russians, turning back the clock three seconds after the second one, and the USSR finally won, 51–50. It was the first U. S. basketball loss in the Olympics after 63 wins.

Winter Olympics. The Winter Games at Sapporo, Japan, on February 3–13, also beautifully staged, began under a cloud of dissension, too. Avery Brundage, IOC president, had long inveighed against the professionalism of leading skiers, and their exclusion from the Olympics was a matter of much discussion. However, the only one barred was Karl Schranz of Austria. He told his teammates to stay and compete, although fans at home agitated for withdrawal. The Austrians and the strong French team did not do well in Alpine skiing. Favored Anna Marie Proell finished second to Marie Thérèse Nadig of Switzerland in the downhill and giant slalom, and Barbara Cochran of Richmond, Vt., captured the slalom. Sue Corrock of Seattle won the bronze medal in the downhill.

American speed skaters from Northbrook, Ill., took two of the gold medals in women's races. Anne Henning won at 500 meters, and Dianne Holum at 1,500. Miss Henning was third in the 1,000-meter event, and Miss Holum took second in the 3,000. The outstanding skater was Ard Schenk of the Netherlands, who won three events.

The Soviet Union won the hockey championship, as the Americans took third place. Janet Lynn, another Illinois girl, took the bronze medal in figure skating. Japanese ski jumpers swept the medal places in the 70-meter jump, with Yukio Kasaya first. There were 1,130 athletes from 37 countries at the Winter Games.

Brundage, the 84-year-old defender of simon-pure amateur athletics, was succeeded as IOC president at the end of the Munich Games by Lord Killanin of Ireland. One of his first pronouncements concerned the need to reexamine the rules governing amateurism.

BILL BRADDOCK
"The New York Times"

FINAL MEDAL STANDING
Winter Games
(Sapporo, Japan, Feb. 3–13, 1972)

Nation	Gold	Silver	Bronze	Total
Soviet Union	8	5	3	16
East Germany	4	3	7	14
Norway	2	5	5	12
Switzerland	4	3	3	10
Netherlands	4	3	2	9
United States	3	2	3	8
Italy	2	2	1	5
Austria	1	2	2	5
West Germany	3	1	1	5
Finland	0	4	1	5
Sweden	1	1	2	4
Czechoslovakia	1	0	2	3
Japan	1	1	1	3
France	0	1	2	3
Poland	1	0	0	1
Spain	1	0	0	1
Canada	0	1	0	1

BARBARA COCHRAN is carried by brother Bob (left) and Rick Chaffee after winning slalom race in Alpine skiing competition at the Winter Olympics. Hers was the only U.S. gold medal in skiing.

UPI

WINTER GAMES
(Sapporo, Japan, Feb. 3–13, 1972)

Biathlon

Individual—Magnar Solberg, Norway (1:15:55.50)
Relay—USSR (1:41:44.92)

Bobsledding

2-Man—Wolfgang Zimmerer and Peter Utzschneider, West Germany (4:57.07)
4-Man—Switzerland (Jean Wicki, Edy Hubacher, Hans Leutenegger, Werner Carmichel; 4:43.07)

Hockey

USSR (4 victories, 0 losses, 1 tie)

Luge

Men's Singles—Wolfgang Scheidel, East Germany (3:27.58)
Men's Doubles—Tie between Paul Hildgartner and Walter Plaikner, Italy, and Horst Hornlein and Reinhard Bredow, East Germany (1:28.35)
Women's Singles—Anna Marie Muller, East Germany (2:59.18)

Skating, Figure

Men—Ondrej Nepela, Czechoslovakia (2,739.1 pts)
Women—Beatrix Schuba, Austria (2,751.5)
Pairs—Irina Rodnina and Alexei Ulanov, USSR (420.4)

Skating, Speed
Men

500 Meters—Erhard Keller, West Germany (0:39.44)
1,500 Meters—Ard Schenk, Netherlands (2:02.96)
5,000 Meters—Ard Schenk (7:23.61)
10,000 Meters—Ard Schenk (15:01.35)

Women

500 Meters—Anne Henning, Northbrook, Ill. (0:43.33)
1,000 Meters—Monika Pflug, West Germany (1:31.40)

1,500 Meters—Dianne Holum, Northbrook, Ill. (2:20.85)
3,000 Meters—Stien Baas-Kaiser, Netherlands (4:52.14)

Skiing, Alpine
Men

Downhill—Bernhard Russi, Switzerland (1:51.43)
Slalom—Francisco Ochoa, Spain (1:49.27)
Giant Slalom—Gustavo Thoeni, Italy (3:09.62)

Women

Downhill—Marie Thérèse Nadig, Switzerland (1:36.68)
Slalom—Barbara Cochran, Richmond, Vt. (1:31.24)
Giant Slalom—Marie Thérèse Nadig (1:29.90)

Skiing, Nordic
Men

70-Meter Jump—Yukio Kasaya, Japan (244.2 pts)
90-Meter Jump—Wojciech Fortuna, Poland (219.9)
Nordic Combined—Ulrich Wehling, East Germany (3d in cross-country, 4th in jumping; 413.34 pts)
15-Kilometer Cross Country—Sven-Ake Lundback, Sweden (45:28.24)
30-Kilometer Cross Country—Vyacheslav Vedenin, USSR (1:36:31)
50-Kilometer Cross Country—Paal Tyldum, Norway (2:43:14.75)
40-Kilometer Relay—USSR (2:04:47.94)

Women

5-Kilometer Cross Country—Galina Koulacova, USSR (17:00.50)
10-Kilometer Cross Country—Galina Koulacova (34:17.82)
15-Kilometer Relay—USSR (48:46.15)

Touring northern Ontario in February, Canada's Prime Minister Trudeau operates a drill in the Falconbridge Mine.

OMAN

Early in January 1972, Sultan Qabus Ibn Said forced his uncle, Prime Minister Tariq Ibn Taymur, to resign and took all power into his own hands.

Internal Affairs. On Jan. 31, 1972, Sultan Qabus signed an agreement with Petroleum Development (Oman) Ltd., owned 85% by Shell, 10% by Compagnie Française des Pétroles, and 5% by Gulbenkian. Though not a member of the Organization of Petroleum Exporting Countries, Oman nevertheless followed the lead of OPEC and raised the posted price of oil by 8.49% because of the devaluation of the dollar. This action raised the price of crude oil at Mina al Fahal from $2.310 a barrel to $2.506 a barrel.

In 1972 most of the Arab hill tribesmen in Oman gave their allegiance to Sultan Qabus and turned against rebels in Dhofar Province, near the Yemen border. The rebels supported the Popular Front for the Liberation of the Arabian Gulf. In May, Oman requested that the Arab League place observers at the Oman-Yemen border and offered to pay the cost itself.

Foreign Affairs. Late in 1971, Oman became a member of the World Bank and also of the International Monetary Fund with an assigned quota of $7,000,000. Relations between Oman and the other Arab states improved in 1972. King Faisal of Saudi Arabia promised Sultan Qabus an undisclosed sum of money to aid in his struggle in Dhofar.

SYDNEY NETTLETON FISHER
The Ohio State University

――――――― **OMAN · Information Highlights** ―――――――

Official Name: Sultanate of Oman.
Area: 82,030 square miles (212,457 sq km).
Population (1972 est.): 700,000. *Density,* 8 per square mile (3 per sq km). *Annual rate of increase,* 3.1%.
Chief Cities (1962 est.): Muscat, the capital, 6,000; Matrah, 14,000.
Government: *Head of state,* Qabus Ibn Said, sultan (acceded July 1970). *Head of government,* Qabus Ibn Said.
Language: Arabic (official).
Monetary Unit: Saidi rial (0.3744 rial equals U.S.$1, June 1972).

ONTARIO

Major themes in Ontario public affairs in 1972 included reorganization of the cabinet, divestiture rules for the cabinet, and financial reforms.

Government Reorganization. Early in the year Premier William Davis created five new "super ministers" to coordinate provincial government policy. The secretary for justice was Allan F. Lawrence, who, after his resignation to enter federal politics, was succeeded by George Kerr. The secretary for finance and intergovernmental affairs was Darcy McKeough, followed, after his resignation, by Charles S. MacNaughton. The secretaries for social development and resource development were Robert Welch and A. B. R. Lawrence, respectively. The chairman of the management board was Charles S. MacNaughton, who was later succeeded by Eric Winkler.

New Divestiture Rules. On September 14, Davis set new rules governing the financial holdings of cabinet members. These rules required ministers to disclose their (and their immediate family's) landholdings and to divest themselves of, or put into a "blind trust," all shares in public corporations. Ministers and their families were also forbidden to purchase land or interest in land development companies or engage in day-to-day business.

These rules resulted from the disclosure in August that Attorney-General Dalton Bales held land near a proposed new international airport and that Secretary for Finance Darcy McKeough, while minister of municipal affairs, had a financial interest in a company owning land whose subdivision had been approved by the department of municipal affairs. McKeough resigned on September 6.

Provincial Budget. On March 28 a record budget of $5.051 billion was introduced. A forecast deficit of $597 million, less than that of 1971 ($683 million), represented a rise of only 4.5% in provincial spending compared with a 15% increase in 1971. The highest priority was given to health, the only area in which spending was permitted to rise significantly, to $1.28 billion. The budget allotted

——————— ONTARIO • Information Highlights ———————

Area: 412,582 square miles (1,068,589 sq km).

Population: 7,703,106 (1971 census).

Chief Cities (1971 census): Toronto, the provincial capital (712,786); Hamilton (309,173); Ottawa, the federal capital (302,341); London (223,222); Windsor (203,300).

Government: *Chief Officers* (Oct. 1972)—lt. gov., W. Ross MacDonald; premier, William G. Davis (Progressive Conservative); prov. secy., John Yaremko (P. C.); prov. secy. for justice, George Kerr; prov. secy. for financial and intergovernmental affairs, Charles S. MacNaughton; chairman of management, Eric Winkler; chief justice, George A. Gale. *Legislature*—Legislative Assembly: 117 members (78 Progressive Conservative; 20 Liberal; 19 New Democratic party).

Education: *School enrollment* (1968–69)—public elementary and secondary, 1,868,788 pupils (79,300 teachers); private schools, 42,986 pupils (3,365 teachers); Indian (federal) schools, 6,752 pupils (278 teachers); college and university, 92,589 students. *Public school expenditures* (1971 est.)—$845,321,000; median teacher's salary (1967–68 est.), $6,900.

Public Finance (fiscal year 1972 est.): *Revenues,* $5,277,300,-000 (sales tax, $1,300,800,000; income tax, $1,330,700,000; federal funds, $985,800,000). *Expenditures,* $5,705,400,000 (education, $1,751,200,000; health and social welfare, $1,916,500,000; transport and communications, $550,600,-000).

Personal Income (1969 est.): $25,104,000,000.

Social Welfare (fiscal year 1972 est.): $358,300,000 (aged and blind, $31,000,000; dependents and unemployed, $236,-700,000).

Manufacturing (1968): Value added by manufacture, $9,714,-889,000 (transportation equipment, $1,489,821,000; food and beverages, $1,165,291,000; primary metals, $937,076,000; fabricated metals, $892,972,000; electrical products, $775,-268,000; chemical and chemical products industries, $766,-087,000; nonelectrical machinery, $549,190,000.

Agriculture (1971): *Cash farm income,* $1,385,447,000 (livestock and products, $929,942,000; crops, $419,355,000. *Chief crops* (cash receipts)—tobacco, $127,304,000 (ranks 1st among the provinces); corn, $58,948,000 (ranks 1st); vegetables, $57,189,000 (ranks 1st); fruits, $40,580,000 (ranks 1st); soybeans, $27,898,000 (ranks 1st); wheat, $21,161,000; potatoes, $20,330 (ranks 1st).

Mining (1971 est.): *Production value,* $1,562,646,000. *Chief minerals* (tons)—nickel, 224,254,505 (ranks 1st among the provinces); copper, 295,092,446 (ranks 1st); zinc, 340,242,-033 (ranks 1st); cement, 3,683,000 (ranks 1st); sand and gravel, 84,500,000 (ranks 1st); stone, 27,500,000 (ranks 2d).

Transportation: *Roads* (1968), 80,076 miles (128,842 km); *motor vehicles* (1969), 2,953,790; *railroads* (1970 est.), 10,045 track miles (16,162 km); *licensed airports* (1971 est.), 93.

Communications: *Telephones* (1969), 3,668,630: *television stations* (1971), 44; *radio stations* (1971), 83; *daily newspapers* (1971), 49.

(All monetary figures given in Canadian dollars.)

$26.6 million to be spent on the environment. To hold down the deficit, taxes on tobacco, alcoholic beverages, and gasoline were raised. Fees for motor vehicle licenses and university tuition were also increased, and fees were introduced at teachers' colleges and nursing schools.

Local Government. Alarmed by the increasing costs of local government and the unequal burden of property taxes, the provincial government made provision for $1.386 billion in basic grants, together with $585 million in "reform" grants, to local authorities.

To ease the burden of property taxes on low-income groups, the standard shelter allowance of $70 was replaced with a sliding property-tax credit based on personal income. To facilitate planning, implement land-use policies, and equalize local taxation, the policy of amalgamating smaller municipalities was continued. Two new regional governments, in Sudbury and Waterloo, were introduced. To prevent conflict of interest, it was made illegal to hold simultaneously elective offices at the provincial and municipal levels.

The Environment. The development of municipal mass transit systems was encouraged by the doubling of provincial grants to $12 million. The proposal to build a second international airport for Toronto in Pickering township generated much opposition, as voiced during the federal election by national Progressive Conservative leader Robert Stanfield. There was also objection to the route proposed by

the Ontario Hydro Commission for a new transmission line through the Niagara area to Toronto.

Economic Nationalism. Dissatisfaction with the federal government's apparent laissez-faire policy toward foreign investment in the Canadian economy led Ontario, the industrial center of Canada, to introduce laws requiring the majority of the directors of Ontario corporations, including foreign-owned subsidiaries, to be Canadian citizens ordinarily resident in Canada. Corporation business could be conducted only in meetings "at which a majority of the directors present are resident Canadians."

Education. Ceilings were maintained on spending by local boards of education, indicating that education had declined in priority. The continued failure of enrollment to meet predictions caused financial difficulties for Ontario universities. Student leaders and university officials have blamed the failure on tuition increases. The system of university financing based on enrollment was being questioned, since expansion seemed over.

PETER J. KING, *Carleton University*

OREGON

President Nixon carried Oregon in November 1972 by a margin of 52.5% to 42.5%. Sen. Mark Hatfield won reelection over former Sen. Wayne Morse, and Democrats captured control of the legislature.

Presidential Primary. Imitated by other states, Oregon's presidential primary attracted less attention than formerly. A distinctive feature was the inclusion of Sen. Edward Kennedy's name, despite protestations of noncandidacy, but the decisive element was not Kennedy charisma but McGovern organization. McGovern won a clear majority over his 10 rivals.

Senatorial Race. Former Sen. Wayne Morse lost his bid to unseat Republican Sen. Mark O. Hatfield. In the Democratic primary, Morse's principal challenge, as in 1968, came from former Congressman Robert Duncan. Few issues separated Hatfield and Morse, the latter's age (72) being a major factor in his defeat. The most serious threat to Hatfield, in fact, was the near-candidacy of Gov. Tom McCall, who was disturbed by the other candidates' long-standing opposition to the Vietnam War. Threatening even after the primary to run as an independent, McCall did not finally declare himself out of the race until mid-August.

Other Elections. All four U. S. congressmen were reelected by safe margins, Democrat Al Ullman running unopposed. Secretary of State Clay Myers and Attorney General Lee Johnson, Republicans, easily won reelection also. The office of state treasurer remained in Democratic hands, former legislator James Redden turning back political newcomer Craig Berkman. Redden had not been the original Democratic candidate, but was named by the state central committee to replace Alice Corbett, who won in the primary but was ruled ineligible because of a previous election-law violation.

Democrats won control of both houses of the legislature, taking 33 of 60 seats in the House and 18 of 30 in the Senate. For the first time in Oregon history, "regular" Democrats, rather than conservatives in coalition with Republicans, gained control of the Senate.

"Youth power" was evident in the election of ten House members still in their 20's, the median

Area: 96,981 square miles (251,181 sq km).
Population (1970 census): 2,091,385. *Density:* 22 per sq mi.
Chief Cities (1970 census): Salem, the capital, 68,856; Portland, 380,555; Eugene, 78,389; Corvallis, 35,056; Medford, 28,454; Springfield, 27,220.
Government (1972): *Chief Officers*—governor, Tom McCall (R); secy. of state, Clay Myers (R); atty. gen., Lee Johnson (R); treas., Robert W. Straub (D); supt. of public instruction, Dale Parnell; chief justice, Kenneth J. O'Connell. *Legislative Assembly*—Senate, 30 members (16 Democrats, 14 Republicans); House of Representatives, 60 members (26 D, 34 R).
Education (1971–72): *Enrollment*—public elementary schools, 278,685 pupils, 11,870 teachers; public secondary, 201,805 pupils, 9,988 teachers; nonpublic schools (1970–71), 25,906 pupils, 1,480 teachers; college and university, 104,000 students. *Public school expenditures* $431,312,000 ($979 per pupil). *Average teacher's salary,* $9,857.
State Finances (fiscal year 1970): *Revenues,* $1,035,308,000 (total sales and gross receipts taxes, $90,089,000; motor fuel tax, $64,485,000; federal funds, $242,561,000). *Expenditures,* $1,018,526,000 (education, $338,867,000; health, welfare, and safety, $131,312,000; highways, $154,304,000). *State debt,* $689,680,000 (June 30, 1970).
Personal Income (1971): $8,460,000,000; per capita, $3,920.
Public Assistance (1971): $108,218,000. *Average monthly payments* (Dec. 1971)—old-age assistance, $60.92; aid to families with dependent children, $173.65.
Labor Force: *Nonagricultural wage and salary earners* (July 1972), 776,900. *Average annual employment* (1971)—manufacturing, 174,000; trade, 166,000; government, 152,000; services, 117,000. *Insured unemployed* (Aug. 1972)—18,100 (3.2%).
Manufacturing (1970): *Value added by manufacture,* $2,521,400,000. Lumber and wood products, $877,800,000; food and kindred products, $363,300,000; paper and allied products, $238,900,000; nonelectrical machinery, $176,100,000; electrical equipment and supplies, $127,200,000; transportation equipment, $100,000,000.
Agriculture (1970): *Cash farm income,* $601,488,000 (livestock, $267,920,000; crops, $310,456,000; government payments, $23,112,000). *Chief crops* (in order of value, 1971)—Hay, wheat, potatoes, barley.
Mining (1971): *Production value,* $77,885,000 (ranks 40th among the states). *Chief minerals*—Sand and gravel, $28,707,000; stone, $26,708,000; cement, value not available; nickel, value not available.
Fisheries (1971): *Commercial catch,* 75,770,000 pounds ($16,226,000). *Leading species by value* (1971): Salmon, $6,066,000; tuna, $3,665,000; crabs, $3,450,000; shrimp, $1,210,000.
Transportation: *Roads* (1971), 95,063 miles (152,985 km); *motor vehicles* (1971), 1,369,233; *railroads* (1971), 3,070 miles (4,941 km); *public airports* (1972), 98.
Communications: *Telephones* (1972), 1,260,000; *television stations* (1971), 13; *radio stations* (1971), 100; *newspapers* (1972), 22 (daily circulation, 663,000).

age being 39. Earlier, Portlanders had elected Neil Goldschmidt, 31, the youngest metropolitan mayor in the nation.

Taxes. One-party control of the legislature was expected to facilitate changes in the tax system, clearly the foremost public concern. In a special election on January 18, voters narrowly approved an increase in the cigarette tax from four cents a pack to nine. Far more significant was an initiative measure, placed on the November ballot by the Farm Bureau Federation, to prohibit the use of property taxes for schools and community colleges. Opposed by business, labor, and other farm groups, the measure was defeated by a 3-to-2 margin, but only after the governor and legislators pledged to reduce the property tax burden. The measure would have forced the state to provide $400 million a year from other sources.

Pollution. In a unique display of cooperation, the state Department of Environmental Quality (DEQ) and the federal Environmental Protection Agency agreed to a joint waste discharge permit system. Cities and industries will be subject to combined federal-state review of water pollution activities.

SAMUEL K. ANDERSON
Oregon College of Education

ORGANIZATIONS. See SOCIETIES AND ORGANIZATIONS.

ORTHODOX EASTERN CHURCH. See RELIGION.

OTTAWA

In 1972, the Ottawa region underwent a marked change in its political scene when Mayor Kenneth Fogarty resigned on April 4 to become a provincial court judge. Fogarty was succeeded as mayor of Canada's capital and fourth largest metropolitan area (1972 metropolitan population, 602,500) by Controller Pierre Benoit. Benoit's seat on the board of control was taken by Alderman Garry Guzzo. Mayor Benoit was reelected in December.

Serious problems were anticipated for the Regional Municipality, whose levies are apportioned on an assessment basis, because of a provincial court decision that required a lowering of assessment on apartments and multiple-family dwellings in Nepean Township, the second-largest municipality in the region. This decision, upheld by the Ontario Municipal Board, was appealed by the regional government to the Ontario Court of Appeal.

Municipal Finance. The city of Ottawa estimated a total expenditure in 1972 of $54.7 million, a net increase of nearly 17% over 1971. The Ottawa board of education estimated an expenditure of $68.7 million. The largest item projected by the Regional municipality was for social welfare, $17 million, or an increase of $853,000.

The Ottawa region also proposed capital expenditures during the year of $32 million, mainly on roads, pollution control equipment, and hospitals. The snow removal budget was expected to be some $400,000 less than the high 1971 figure of $3.7 million, which resulted from two very severe winters.

Education. The 1971 trend of falling school enrollment within the city, in contrast to a rapidly expanding number of students in the suburban areas, continued into 1972. September enrollment in Ottawa was divided as follows: public elementary, nearly 24,000; public secondary, 27,000 (more than two thirds of it in the English section); Catholic schools, 26,500 (about equally divided between English and French). Under the Carleton board of education, public elementary enrollment was about 23,000, public secondary, 11,500, and Catholic schools 14,000, in a ratio of about four English to three French.

Under a historic agreement between the Ottawa board of education and the city's three Catholic high schools, some 900 Catholic students in grades 11, 12, and 13 were to be phased into the public school system, beginning in September 1973. This would relieve mounting financial pressure on the Catholic high schools, which do not receive provincial grants for students beyond grade 10. Ottawa high school teachers, unable to reach a contract agreement, were working by the rule-book and refused to supervise extracurricular activities.

The Federal Government. The federal government announced a plan to buy 44 acres of land (for $29.5 million) and to dismantle, over a 10-year period, the E. B. Eddy Company's pulp and paper plant. This 121-year-old enterprise, straddling the Ottawa River near Parliament Hill, had long been thought an aesthetic and environmental liability.

The government planned to spend over $100 million on public works in the Ottawa area during 1972, including new departmental buildings, completion of the new Airport Parkway, and continuation of construction on the controversial Portage Bridge over the Ottawa River.

PETER J. KING, *Carleton University*

PACIFIC ISLANDS

The South Pacific Forum held its second meeting at Canberra, Australia, on Feb. 23–25, 1972, to consider matters of trade, immigration, civil aviation, education, and regional cooperation. The Cook Islands, Fiji, Nauru, Tonga, Western Samoa, Australia, and New Zealand sent representatives to the Forum, which was founded in 1971. Delegates agreed to establish a South Pacific Bureau for Economic Cooperation, with headquarters in Suva, Fiji. A third meeting was held in Suva in September.

The Pacific Islands Producers' Association met at Rarotonga, Cook Islands, in June to discuss the problems of banana marketing and fertilizer purchases. The association voted to extend its activities for three more years, although its functions might be assumed eventually by the newly formed South Pacific Bureau for Economic Cooperation.

A South Pacific Festival of Arts staged in Suva, Fiji, May 6–20, was sponsored by the South Pacific Commission. The program included music, dance, drama, and exhibitions of Pacific islands art.

Micronesia. A series of conferences in 1972 between the Congress of Micronesia and representatives of the U. S. government dealt with the future political status of the American-administered UN trust territory of Micronesia, officially known as the Trust Territory of the Pacific Islands. At the conclusion of the sixth round of talks, held in September and October, it was apparent that the Mariana Islands would be granted separate status under trust administration. The Marianas were expected eventually to merge with Guam, an unincorporated U. S. territory whose people are culturally similar, thus strengthening U. S. defenses off the east coast of Asia. The remainder of the Micronesian islands continued to press for local autonomy and independence at an early date. Further details of the changing political status of Micronesia were to be discussed at a seventh meeting in December.

The United States in May announced plans to return Eniwetok Atoll to the Trust Territory at the end of 1973. Since 1946, Eniwetok had been under military control for the purpose of defense research and development. Its people had been resettled on other islands in the Marshalls group. Prior to their return, the islands of the atoll were to be restored to a habitable condition under a project similar to that which rehabilitated Bikini. The United States reaffirmed its intention to continue use of Kwajalein

Atoll for defense research activities for an indefinite period.

Gilbert and Ellice Islands. The British administration of Gilbert and Ellice Islands Colony was transferred from the Western Pacific High Commission to the Foreign and Commonwealth Office in London on Jan. 1, 1972. At the same time the colony added five uninhabited atolls in the Line Islands to its jurisdiction. Sir John Field, who had been resident commissioner, became the first governor of the colony. As a result of the new status of the colony only the British Solomon Islands and the British interests in the Anglo-French New Hebrides condominium remained under the jurisdiction of the Western Pacific High Commission. The High Court of the Western Pacific was to continue to have judicial authority in the Gilbert and Ellice Islands.

Republic of Minerva. Members of an international group named the Ocean Life Research Foundation landed on Minerva Reefs about 250 miles (400 km) southwest of Tonga in January to found the "Republic of Minerva." The group of scientists, doctors, scholars, and businessmen announced plans to create land by dredging and to establish a sea city. The reefs are largely an undersea formation. Radar beacons and a lighthouse stand on its two mounds of sand and coral.

Tonga was among the first states to protest the development, raising the question of ownership at the South Pacific Forum at Canberra in February. On June 26, King Taufa'ahau visited the reefs and proclaimed Tongan sovereignty.

American Samoa. The U. S. Department of Commerce made a grant of $980,000 to American Samoa for the development of an industrial park at Tafuna near the international airport. One of the first factories to occupy the site was to manufacture suits for the U. S. market. In response to increasing tourism, work was begun during the year on extensions to the Intercontinental Hotel at Pago Pago.

French Polynesia. French scientists completed another series of nuclear tests at Mururoa Atoll in August under unusually tight secrecy. The number and nature of explosions were not revealed. Protest groups staged demonstrations in several South Pacific countries, and Australian and New Zealand waterside unions imposed a ban on shipping to French Polynesia during the testing period.

New Caledonia. A causeway joining the Isle of Nou to Nouméa on the mainland of New Caledonia was opened to traffic in April. Its construction was part of a program of harbor developments to provide additional shipping berths for Nouméa.

Niue and the Tokelau Islands. The UN General Assembly passed a resolution on Dec. 20, 1971, calling upon New Zealand to expedite plans for self-government in Niue and the Tokelau Islands. New Zealand subsequently invited a UN mission to visit Niue in 1972 to survey local economic and social conditions.

Ryukyu Islands. Okinawa and 72 smaller islands in the Ryukyu chain were transferred from U. S. to Japanese jurisdiction on May 15, 1972. The United States was to continue operating military bases on Okinawa, but under the limitations imposed by terms of its mutual security treaty with Japan. See also JAPAN.

HOWARD J. CRITCHFIELD
Western Washington State College

PACIFIC ISLANDS OF THE UNITED STATES

Island or Group	Area (sq mi)	(km)	Population (1970 Census)	Capital (1970 Census)
American Samoa[1]	76	197	27,159	Pago Pago (2,491)
Baker[2]	1	2.6	...	...
Canton and Enderbury[3]	27	70	...	...
Guam[1]	212	549	84,996	Agana (2,131)
Howland[2]	0.6	1.6	...	...
Jarvis[2]	2.2	5.7	...	...
Johnston and Sand Islands[5]	...[5]	...	1,007	...
Kingman Reef[4]	...[5]	...	...	...
Midway[4]	2	5	2,220	...
Palmyra[2]	4	10	...	...
Ryukyu Islands[6]	848	2,196	982,000[7]	Naha (284,000)[8]
Trust Territory of the Pacific Islands (including Carolines, Marianas, Marshalls)[2]	687	1,779	90,940[8]	Saipan (9,590)[7]
Wake[2]	3	8	1,647	...

[1] Unincorporated U. S. territory. [2] Administered by U. S. Department of the Interior. [3] Jointly administered by United Kingdom and United States. [4] Under U. S. Navy control. [5] Less than ½ square mile. [6] Under U. S. military government until May 15, 1972, when they reverted to Japan. [7] 1969 est. [8] 1968 est.

PAINTING AND SCULPTURE. See ART.

PAKISTAN

Formerly consisting of two provinces, East and West Pakistan, Pakistan had been divided by bitter civil war in 1971 as well as by Indian intervention. East Pakistan broke away to form an independent state, Bangladesh. The former western province now retains the name of Pakistan.

The year 1972 was the first of going it alone for the former western province. It suffered severely from the effects of the war. Its previous military elite was discredited. Many thousands of its soldiers remained in prison camps in India. Its new president, Zulfikar Ali Bhutto, kept the system together, however, and pursued a foreign policy that generated some support for Pakistan, now in a subcontinent in which the balance of political power has substantially shifted.

Domestic Affairs. The military government of General Yahya Khan collapsed in late 1971, and the chief civilian critic of the government, Zulfikar Ali Bhutto, became president on Dec. 20, 1971. He immediately dismissed many of the senior officers in the armed forces; in March he dismissed an air marshal and an army lieutenant-general (even though they had supported his own accession to power in December 1971). On the other hand, Lt. Gen. Tikka Khan was made army chief of staff, with the rank of general, in March; he had been chiefly responsible for the repressive military regime in East Pakistan (Bangladesh) the preceding year.

The collapse of Yahya's government encouraged the emergence of political opposition groups, and Bhutto encountered much difficulty with them throughout the year. His government was attacked in the early months for maintaining martial law, which had been in effect off and on for years. In late April, Bhutto ended martial law but kept the "state of emergency" that gave his government strong and broad powers. In April, a resurrected National Assembly approved an interim constitution and reaffirmed Bhutto as president. Press censorship had been ended in January, although a month later newspaper editors were still being arrested.

In early March, Bhutto announced a major land reform scheme that would, he said, destroy "the curse of feudalism" in Pakistan. The government had already in January taken over a number of major industries. By year's end, however, the reforms had not been fully implemented.

By far the major threat to the regime and, indeed, to the viability of the state itself was the spectre of separatism within truncated Pakistan. It rose to a peak in the spring, then subsided somewhat, though it remained very much alive. The breakaway of Bangladesh had been an act of separatism, and the example spurred other minorities in the western province to reconsider their goals.

In the Northwest Frontier Province, Khan Abdul-Wali Khan, the leader of the Pathans, has proved to be the major opponent of Bhutto and his policies. The son of the legendary Khan Abdul-Ghaffar Khan (known as "the frontier Gandhi") and the leader of the National Awami party, Wali Khan has pursued a left-wing course combined with Pathan nationalism. Bhutto responded to Wali Khan's political attacks by making a number of political concessions as well as attempting to secure strong army support against the Pathans.

In Sind, the provincial assembly in July made Sindhi the only official language in the province, in

—————— PAKISTAN • Information Highlights ——————

Official Name: Islamic Republic of Pakistan.
Area: 310,403 square miles (803,941 sq km).
Population (1972 est.): 66,900,000. *Density,* 212 per square mile (82 per sq km).
Chief Cities (1961 census): Islamabad, the capital, 50,000 (1967 est.); Karachi, 1,447,419; Lahore, 1,227,996.
Government: *Head of state,* Zulfikar Ali Bhutto, president (took office Dec. 1971). *Head of government,* Zulfikar Ali Bhutto. *Legislature*—National Assembly. *Major political party*—Pakistan People's party.
Languages: Urdu (official), English.
Monetary Unit: Rupee (11 rupees equal U. S.$1, July 1972).
Manufacturing (major products): Textiles, processed foods, cement, petroleum products, chemicals, metals.
Major Agricultural Products: Wheat, cotton, rice, wool, livestock.
Major Mineral: Natural gas.
Foreign Trade: *Chief exports,* textile yarn and thread, woven cotton fabrics, raw cotton, rice, leather, floor coverings and tapestries. *Chief imports,* nonelectrical machinery, fertilizers, road motor vehicles, aircraft, petroleum, vegetable oils, iron and steel products. *Chief trading partners* —United States, United Kingdom, Japan.

spite of the fact that 45% of the people there speak Urdu. Repeated clashes and demonstrations in Karachi and other Sindhi towns followed, in which at least 47 people were killed. A later compromise giving Urdu speakers 12 years to learn Sindhi reduced the violence but almost certainly contained the seeds for future difficulties.

Pakistan had refugee problems of its own that had not been resolved by the end of 1972. At least a half-million people had become refugees as a result of the Indian-Pakistani border fighting in the West the year before. These can be expected to be reduced as the Simla accord with India (July 3) becomes fully implemented. There were also some thousands of refugee Biharis, who had fled from East Pakistan, in Karachi; unwanted in Pakistan, they had bleak prospects.

PAKISTANI President Ali Bhutto (right) talks with Gen. Tikka Khan, who became army chief of staff in March.

PRESIDENT BHUTTO shakes hands with Chairman Mao Tse-tung. The two leaders met during Ali Bhutto's visit to mainland China in February.

Then in November, Pakistan announced that it would permit the 10,000 Bengali women and children still living in Pakistan to return to Bangladesh. India responded by agreeing to return to Pakistan about 6,000 Pakistani women and children. As for the military prisoners, Pakistan took the first step on November 27 when it freed the 617 Indian prisoners of war it was holding in camps in Pakistan. President Bhutto asked the Indians to reciprocate by releasing the approximately 84,000 Pakistanis still interned in India. India's Foreign Minister Swaran Singh told parliament on the same day that India had offered to release the 540 Pakistanis captured on the western front. But without the approval of Bangladesh, India could not release those captured in East Pakistan.

There were a number of strikes during the year, even among police and civil servants.

Foreign Affairs. Both Pakistan's domestic and foreign affairs were dominated by the crushing defeat Pakistan had suffered at India's hands and by the separation of Bangladesh. One of Bhutto's first moves in January was the release of Sheikh Mujibur Rahman, who returned to become the first president of Bangladesh. Bhutto was adamant at first that Bangladesh remain associated somehow with Pakistan. But by year's end it had become probable that Pakistan would recognize Bangladesh as independent.

In late June, after much preliminary uncertainty, Bhutto journeyed to Simla, India, to confer with Indian Prime Minister Indira Gandhi over some kind of settlement of their dispute. Prime among the issues was the fate of nearly 100,000 Pakistani prisoners of war. On July 3, the Simla accord was announced. India and Pakistan agreed to withdraw their troops to their respective borders; their positions in Kashmir were temporarily frozen pending further negotiations (in September these negotiations failed to secure agreement); and they agreed that some "step-by-step" solution of their mutual difficulties would be undertaken. The prisoner of war question was not resolved at that time. In the months following Simla, however, both Pakistan and India made many small agreements on such matters as communications and tourist exchanges.

The Soviet Union had supported India in the 1971 war. In March, Bhutto journeyed to Moscow to mend relations. A communiqué indicated that trade relations and aid agreements would be resumed.

In January, Bhutto warned nations recognizing Bangladesh that Pakistan would probably break relations with them. In the same month Pakistan withdrew from the Commonwealth when Bangladesh was recognized by Britain, Australia, and New Zealand. But Pakistan quickly abandoned the threat to sever relations with those recognizing Bangladesh.

In February, Bhutto visited Peking. China had been a supporter of Pakistan in the war with India. By June it was apparent that substantial military and economic aid, about $300 million, had been granted Pakistan by China.

The United States continued a modest supporting role of Pakistan, although there was strong antagonism in Congress toward the possible resumption of arms shipments. Full resumption of foreign aid, except military aid, to Pakistan from the United States was announced in June.

Major foreign policy realignment was announced in November. On November 8, Pakistan withdrew from the Southeast Asia Treaty Organization (SEATO); Bhutto also announced his intention to withdraw from the Central Treaty Organization (CENTO). He also recognized North Vietnam and North Korea and indicated that recognition would also be extended to East Germany.

Economy. Although affected by the war less seriously than Bangladesh, Pakistan suffered enormous economic setbacks from the conflict. The cost of refurbishing its armed forces, even with Chinese help, has been great. In June the government announced a budget in which a record 60% of federal revenues was earmarked for defense.

During the year the rupee was devalued. Although several nationalization decrees were put into effect in 1972, and socialism as an ideology was extolled, the changes have not yet been profound. Many announced social reform programs seem impossible to effect because of severe budget readjustments.

Economic progress was not great during the year, but the government did survive with an economy that is proving surprisingly resilient.

CARL LEIDEN
University of Texas at Austin

PALEONTOLOGY

During 1972 there were several significant advances in knowledge of vertebrate and invertebrate paleontology.

Vertebrate Paleontology. The year's most interesting find was made by a former Antarctic explorer, James A. Jensen of Utah University, who excavated at Delta, Colo., the remains of the largest Brachiosaurid (sauropod dinosaur) so far known. The animal had probably been some 100 feet (30 meters) long, in which case it must have weighed about 80 tons (72 metric tons).

An intriguing discovery of fossil amphibia was made by N. Wakefield of Monash University. Found in Devonian deposits (approximately 380 million years old) in Victoria, Australia, the fossil, which shows five-toed and webbed hind feet and perhaps three-toed front feet, is thought to be the oldest set of amphibian footprints yet discovered, and it raises many important questions about primitive amphibian terrestrial movement. Another contribution to amphibian paleontology was P. P. Vaughn's description of an interesting new Microsaur from upper Pennsylvanian deposits (about 275 million years old) of central Colorado.

E. C. Olsen of the University of California made two important contributions: a classification of the radiation of highly terrestrial Permian amphibians (approximately 250 million years old) and a theory of the cause of dinosaur extinction based on climate and floral changes, a thesis supported by L. van Allen of Chicago University and R. E. Sloan of Minnesota University in their biogeographical studies of the Upper Cretaceous-Paleocene (about 65-million-year-old) boundary of Montana. The ostrich dinosaurs (ornithomimids) of western Canada were further studied by Dale Russell of Ottawa. In another advance, Cherrie Bramwell of Reading University in England used a computer to unravel the flying or gliding behavior of the American pterosaur (*Pteranodon*) and found that it probably had a lift-drag ratio similar to that of gliding birds.

In England, A. D. Walker of Newcastle University did further archosaur research on the South African *Spherosuchus* that suggested to him that crocodiles and birds represent one basal stock. The discovery of 12-million-year-old ostrich and Aepyornithoid eggshells in calcareous sediments in the Canary Islands suggests to two German paleontologists—Franz Sauer and P. Rothe—that there were once more land connections available to these flightless birds. Knowledge of fossil mammals was advanced by A. E. Wood's description of the earliest hystriognathous rodent from the Eocene (approximately 45 million years ago) of Texas.

D. Dineley of Bristol University suggested that the early development of jawless and early jawed fishes took place in wide, shallow, sedimentary basins adjacent to Atlantis and other continental areas, especially those with carbonate platforms like those of Siluro-Devonian times in Canada.

Invertebrate Paleontology. Erle Kauffman of the Smithsonian Institution elaborated on the evolutionary rates and patterns of Cretaceous mollusks. Other finds included the discovery of some impressions of medusoids clear enough to show the details of their internal structure.

WILLIAM E. SWINTON
Massey College, University of Toronto

PANAMA

The regime led by Brig. Gen. Omar Torrijos Herrera, head of the 8,000-man National Guard, continued to dominate Panama in 1972. The country's constitution was extensively rewritten to institutionalize the power of the regime, which had seized control in a military coup in 1968. Relations with the United States remained strained.

Political Developments. Panama's first elections since the 1968 coup were held in August. Some 94% of the country's eligible voters turned out to elect 505 members of the new Assembly of Community Representatives, which served as a constituent assembly. Meeting in September and October, it substantially rewrote the 1946 constitution, which had been suspended in 1968, and created a unique constitutional dictatorship in which Torrijos retained all executive, legislative, and judicial powers. The assembly also elected Demetrio B. Lakas to the titular presidency, a post he had held provisionally since 1969.

The changes were drafted by a commission under the chairmanship of Torrijos' brother-in-law, Marcelino Jaen. The revamped charter reserved all top-level management positions in both private and public enterprises for Panamanians. It also decreed that all prelates of the Roman Catholic Church must have been born in Panama.

Panama Canal Conflict. Negotiations between the United States and Panama on a new canal treaty reached an impasse in 1972, with the United States refusing Panamanian demands for complete sovereignty over the Canal Zone. A resolution approved by the assembly in September charged that the Canal Zone had been arbitrarily occupied since 1903 as a result of the United States' unilateral interpretation and application of the Hay-Bunau-Varilla Treaty. The resolution called on General Torrijos to reject the $1.93 million annuity paid by the United States.

--------- **PANAMA · Information Highlights** ---------

Official Name: Republic of Panama.
Area: 29,209 square miles (75,650 sq km).
Population (1972 est.): 1,600,000. *Density,* 49 per square mile (19 per sq km). *Annual rate of increase,* 2.9%.
Chief City (1970 census): Panama, the capital, 412,000.
Government: *Military junta,* led by Brig. Gen. Omar Torrijos Herrara (took power Oct. 1968). *Head of state,* Demetrio B. Lakas, president. *Legislature* (unicameral)—Assembly of Community Representatives, 505 members.
Languages: Spanish (official), English.
Education: *Expenditure* (1969), 34.6% of total public expenditure. *School enrollment* (1969)—primary, 238,593; secondary, 73,371; technical/vocational, 25,449; university/higher, 7,252.
Monetary Unit: Balboa (1 balboa equals U. S.$1, Sept. 1972).
Gross National Product (1971 est.): $1,090,000,000.
National Income per Person (1970): $629.
Economic Indexes: *Industrial production* (manufacturing, 1968), 149 (1963=100); *agricultural production* (1971), 210 (1952–56=100); *consumer price index* (1971), 113 (1963=100).
Manufacturing (major products): Processed foods, petroleum products, textiles, wood products, clothing, pharmaceuticals.
Major Agricultural Products: Bananas, vegetables, fish, rice, forest products.
Major Minerals: Copper, molybdenum.
Foreign Trade (1971): *Exports,* $120,000,000 (chief exports—bananas; refined petroleum; shrimp). *Imports,* $391,000,-000 (chief imports, 1969—petroleum, crude or partly refined; chemicals; food; nonelectrical machinery). *Chief trading partners* (1969)—United States (took 65% of exports, supplied 37% of imports); West Germany (14%—3%); Venezuela (supplied 21%); Japan (supplied 6%).
Tourism: *Receipts* (1970), $42,000,000.
Transportation: *Motor vehicles* (1970), 62,800 (automobiles, 48,300); *railroads* (1970), 152 miles (245 km); *merchant fleet* (1971), 6,262,000 gross registered tons; *major national airline,* COPA (Compañía Panamena de Aviación).
Communications: *Television stations* (1971), 11; *newspapers* (1970), 13.

Drug Traffic. Another problem area in relations with the United States involved Panama's unwillingness to cooperate in the suppression of narcotics traffic through the Canal Zone en route to the United States. In March, U. S. Rep. John Murphy charged that the Panamanian government either condoned or was actually involved in the drug-running operation. Panama's government retaliated by ousting three U. S. narcotics agents, who had implicated such high-ranking officials as Foreign Minister Juan Antonio Tack and Ambassador to Spain Moisés Torrijos, brother of the junta leader.

Power Utility Nationalized. In June the government took over the Panama Power and Light Company, owned primarily by the American Boise Cascade Corporation. The company was threatened with expropriation within 30 days unless it reestablished a suspended $50 million five-year investment program, settled a $2 million bill with its oil suppliers, and returned $5 million to users, in the form of rebates. The Panamanian government announced in September that it had reached an agreement with the utility to buy its properties. The purchase price was reported to have been $22.5 million, although the owners had placed a value of $73.6 million on the utility.

Budget Deficit. A $9.8 million standby loan was extended by the International Monetary Fund in June, reflecting Panama's fiscal difficulties in 1972. The budget deficit for the year was estimated at $40 million. Tax increases on gasoline, tobacco, and whiskey were expected to cover half the deficit.

LARRY L. PIPPIN
Elbert Covell College
University of the Pacific

PARAGUAY

Paraguay in 1972 remained firmly under the control of President Alfredo Stroessner, who has ruled for 18 years. In spite of a repressive political atmosphere, some progress took place in the area of economic development.

Domestic Affairs. In September, Stroessner was nominated by his governing Colorado party to run for his fifth five-year term in the 1973 presidential elections. The Paraguayan army showed its support for Stroessner by sending 30 generals to the nominating convention.

Conflict continued between the regime and the Roman Catholic Church. The Paraguayan Episcopal Conference in May accused the government of carrying out a "systematic persecution" of the church. The charge followed the expulsion from Paraguay of eight Catholic priests. The country's bishops have vowed to continue the "long struggle for social and economic justice" for all Paraguayans.

Students and leaders of the opposition forces attending a "day of reflection" at the Catholic university in September were beaten and driven from the building by persons alleged to be Colorado party terrorists.

Economic Developments. The 1972 budget's proposed expenditures were 24% higher than those of 1971, and a $6 million deficit was expected during the fiscal year. But soaring world and domestic prices for beef brought considerable improvement in the export market and helped to strengthen the country's economy. Exports of logs and sawnwood were also strong, and accounted for 16% of the 1971 total. Tourist revenues increased slightly in

─────── **PARAGUAY** • **Information Highlights** ───────

Official Name: Republic of Paraguay.
Area: 157,047 square miles (406,752 sq km).
Population (1972 est.): 2,600,000. *Density,* 16 per square mile (6 per sq km). *Annual rate of increase,* 3.4%.
Chief City (1969 est.): Asunción, the capital, 375,000.
Government: *Head of state,* Gen. Alfredo Stroessner, president (took office Aug. 1954). *Head of government,* Gen. Alfredo Stroessner. *Legislature*—Congress: Chamber of Deputies, 60 members; Senate, 30 members. *Major political party*—Colorado party.
Languages: Spanish (official), Guaraní.
Education: *Expenditure* (1969) 2.6% of gross national product. *School enrollment* (1969)—primary, 408,524; general secondary, 44,514; technical/vocational (1968), 2,507; university/higher, 7,266.
Monetary Unit: Guaraní (126 guaranís equal U. S.$1, Sept. 1972).
Gross National Product (1971 est.): $605,000,000.
National Income per Person (1970): $230.
Economic Indexes: *Industrial production* (1969), 137 (1963=100); *agricultural production* (1971), 151 (1952–56=100); *consumer price index* (1971), 116 (1964=100).
Manufacturing (major products): Meats, leather, wood products, quebracho extract, vegetable oil.
Major Agricultural Products: Cassava, bananas, tobacco, citrus fruits, cattle, forest products.
Major Minerals: Limestone, salt.
Foreign Trade (1971): *Exports,* $65,000,000 (chief exports—meat; timber; oilseeds; tobacco; quebracho extract). *Imports,* $70,000,000 (chief imports, 1969—machinery; beverages and tobacco; food). *Chief trading partners* (1969)—Argentina (took 29% of exports, supplied 18% of imports); United States (21%—26%); West Germany (5%—14%).
Transportation: *Motor vehicles* (1970), 28,300 (automobiles, 15,300); *railroads* (1970), 308 miles (496 km); *major national airline,* LAP (Lineas Aereas Paraguayas).
Communications: *Telephones* (1971), 23,649; *television stations* (1971), 1; *newspapers* (1970), 11.

1971 and early 1972.

Some taxes were increased in 1972 to cover the budget deficit, but little was done about a long overdue restructuring of the tax system. The government moved to encourage investment in agriculture and light industry by offering equal tax incentives to domestic and foreign enterprises.

After years of negotiation and disagreement over the matter of a site, Paraguay and Argentina agreed to build a $700 million dam across the Paraná River, which forms part of the boundary between the two states. The dam was to be started in 1976 and was expected to produce 3.3 million kilowatts annually by 1980.

Paraguay and Argentina also agreed to expand their transportation links and, with Brazil, to begin studying the hydroelectrical potentials of sites on the Paraná River.

Foreign Relations. President Stroessner paid a three-day visit to Argentina in August. At the conclusion of his visit he signed a number of mutual aid pacts with Argentine President Alejandro Lanusse.

In September, the government extradited Auguste Joseph Ricord to the United States for trial on charges of heading a world heroin-smuggling ring. Ricord, a French-born Argentine citizen, had been in custody in Paraguay since March 1971. The Paraguayan government had originally refused to extradite him on the grounds that narcotics traffic was not illegal in Paraguay and was not a subject of the extradition treaty with the United States. Before the Paraguayan government reversed its decision in September, the United States had cut off $5 million of credit and broken a 111-year-old tradition of holding a July 4th celebration for Paraguayan officials at the U. S. embassy in Asunción.

LEO B. LOTT
University of Montana

PAUL VI, Pope. See BIOGRAPHY.
PEARSON, Lester. See CANADA.
PEDIATRICS. See MEDICINE.

FLOODS triggered by tropical storm Agnes resulted in devastation over much of Pennsylvania. This was the scene at Harrisburg.

PENNSYLVANIA

In 1972, Pennsylvania experienced a major natural disaster—tropical storm Agnes. Also noteworthy during the year was a focus on some consumer-oriented legislative action.

Tropical Storm Agnes. Five days of rains and floods, spawned by tropical storm Agnes, washed over Pennsylvania in late June and left the state reeling from its worst flood disaster. The toll: 50 dead, $2.5 billion property damage; 250,000 homeless; 3,000 small businesses destroyed or damaged; 52,000 jobless; 370 miles of highways closed; and 175 bridges washed out.

Nearly all sections of Pennsylvania reported flood damage, but the central portion of the state was the hardest hit. The Susquehanna River, swollen by more than 11 inches of rain, raged through the state's industrial and rural heartland. Wilkes-Barre and Harrisburg were among the 33 communities suffering serious flood damage. In Harrisburg, water covered the first floors of the governor's mansion, city hall, the main police station, the railroad station, and a number of factories.

Some 100 communities were temporarily without safe drinking water, and pollution problems continued after the flood abated. Sludge waste stored in lagoons was swept into the Schuylkill River, resulting in a 16-mile oil slick between Pottstown and Philadelphia. Environmentalists predicted it may take years to clean up the river.

Pennsylvania's legislature responded to the disaster by passing four bills designed to aid flood victims and appropriating $150 million for flood relief. In November voters approved amending the state's constitution to permit direct state aid to victims of Agnes.

Elections. In the November election Republicans gained control of the state House of Representatives. Of the 203 House seats contested, Republicans gained 16, giving them 106, while the Democrats lost 16 seats, leaving them with a 97-member minority. Democrats retained control of the state Senate by a 26-to-24 margin. Democrats were also returned to the offices of auditor general and state treasurer and, in congressional races, retained their 13-to-12 edge. In the presidential contest, President Nixon won 59% of the state's total vote against 39% for Senator McGovern.

Major Legislation. Gov. Shapp asked legislators to help him make 1972 "The Year of the Consumer." As the legislature prepared to adjourn for the year the governor was still pressing for enactment of major consumer-oriented bills locked in committees. These included a no-fault insurance plan, free public transit for the elderly, proposed elimination of retail milk price fixing, expansion of property tax assistance to the elderly, a measure to control construction costs of school buildings, and allocation of the state's share of federal revenue sharing to aid communities in holding the line on property taxes.

No-fault insurance, the most controversial of the proposed consumer bills, would have accident victims receive benefits automatically from their own insurance companies regardless of who was at fault. Supporters of the proposal claimed it would eliminate costly, time-consuming court cases and thus reduce insurance premiums. Opponents of no-fault, including the Pennsylvania Trial Lawyers Association, contended the plan would deny accident victims their right to sue for pain and suffering.

A Commonwealth Compensation Commission recommended a 62% pay hike for legislators and

——————PENNSYLVANIA • Information Highlights ——————

Area: 45,333 square miles (117,412 sq km).
Population (1970 census): 11,793,909. *Density,* 264 per sq mi.
Chief Cities (1970 census): Harrisburg, the capital, 68,061; Philadelphia, 1,950,098; Pittsburgh, 520,117; Erie, 129,231; Allentown, 109,527; Scranton, 103,564; Reading, 87,643.
Government (1972): *Chief Officers*—governor, Milton J. Shapp (D); lt. gov., Ernest P. Kline (D); secy. of state, Mrs. De-Lores Tucker (D); atty. gen., J. Shane Creamer (D); treas., Mrs. Grace M. Sloan (D); secy., dept. of education, David H. Kurtzman; chief justice, Robert N. C. Nix, Jr. *General Assembly*—Senate, 50 members (26 Democrats, 24 Republicans); House of Representatives, 203 members (113 D, 90 R).
Education (1971–72): *Enrollment*—public elementary schools, 1,244,400 pupils, 56,300 teachers; public secondary, 1,128,-100 pupils, 53,600 teachers; nonpublic schools (1970–71), 500,723 pupils, 20,470 teachers; college and university, 409,000 students. *Public school expenditures,* $2,372,690,-000 ($1,073 per pupil). *Average teacher's salary,* $10,300.
State Finances (fiscal year 1970): *Revenues,* $4,914,691,000 (6% general sales tax and gross receipts taxes, $948,357,-000; motor fuel tax, $344,966,000; federal funds, $883,059,000). *Expenditures,* $5,113,744,000 (education, $1,777,542,000; health, welfare, and safety, $838,430,000; highways, $1,002,799,000). *State debt,* $3,220,438,000 (June 30, 1970).
Personal Income (1971): $49,025,000,000; per capita, $4,127.
Public Assistance (1971): $1,056,635,000. *Average monthly payments* (Dec. 1971)—old-age assistance, $97.80; aid to families with dependent children, $239.26.
Labor Force: *Nonagricultural wage and salary earners* (July 1972), 4,304,600. *Average annual employment* (1971)—manufacturing, 1,430,000; trade, 840,000; government, 628,000; services, 699,000. *Insured unemployed* (Aug. 1972)—126,800 (3.8%).
Manufacturing (1970): *Value added by manufacture,* $21,408,-900,000. Primary metal industries, $3,644,700,000; non-electrical machinery, $2,201,500,000; electrical equipment and supplies, $2,063,700,000; food and kindred products, $1,864,400,000; fabricated metal products, $1,640,700,000; chemicals and allied products, $1,637,900,000.
Agriculture (1970): *Cash farm income,* $1,071,968,000 (livestock, $784,210,000; crops, $262,599,000; government payments, $25,159,000). *Chief crops* (in order of value, 1971) —Hay, corn, potatoes, apples.
Mining (1971): *Production value,* $1,047,561,000 (ranks 7th among the states). *Chief minerals*—Coal, $633,154,000; cement, $140,656,000; stone, $115,380,000; sand and gravel, $35,272,000.
Transportation: *Roads* (1971), 115,167 miles (185,338 km); *motor vehicles* (1971), 5,818,553; *railroads* (1971), 8,371 miles (13,471 km); *public airports* (1972), 68.
Communications: *Telephones* (1972), 7,715,400; *television stations* (1971), 23; *radio stations* (1971), 284; *newspapers* (1972), 107 (daily circulation, 4,067,000).

30% to 40% pay raises for judges and cabinet officers. This would have raised legislators' salaries and expense allowances from $15,600 to 25,000 a year. Responding to what legislators termed "press inspired" public criticism, the lawmakers approved an across-the-board hike of $2,500 for legislators, judges, and top executive officials, including the governor.

After twice rejecting proposals to cut the size of the General Assembly, the House of Representatives approved a proposed constitutional amendment that would reduce its membership from 203 to 161 and cut the number of Senate seats from 50 to 40. Following Senate concurrence, the proposal, to become law, must be passed by the next legislature and submitted to voters in a referendum. It would take effect in 1976.

Gov. Shapp's resolute opposition to a really tough anti-abortion bill was upheld when the House of Representatives refused to override his veto. In other action, the General Assembly became the 21st state legislature to ratify a proposed 27th Amendment to the U. S. Constitution, an amendment that would, if adopted, forbid discrimination on the basis of sex.

Gov. Shapp signed laws giving 18-year-olds rights that they previously had to wait until age 21 to receive. The rights include signing contracts, marrying without parental consent, and holding public office at the local level. Additional responsibilities for 18-year-olds include paying local taxes and serving on juries.

Administrative Actions. Pennsylvania's insurance commissioner, Robert S. Denenberg, clashed with lawyers over a proposed no-fault insurance plan and with the medical profession over Blue Shield reforms. The Pennsylvania Trial Lawyers Association and the trustees of the Pennsylvania Medical Society called on the governor to fire Denenberg for what they regarded as intemperate remarks.

Employment. In January 1972, Pennsylvania's unemployment rate was 5.9%, the highest for any January in eight years.

WILLIAM L. DULANEY
Pennsylvania State University

PERSIAN GULF STATES

In addition to Iran, Iraq, and Saudi Arabia, there are four smaller independent Persian Gulf states: Kuwait (see KUWAIT), Bahrain, Qatar, and the United Arab Emirates. The emirates of Abu Dhabi, Dubai, Sharja, Ajman, Fujaira, and Umm al-Qaiwain formed the United Arab Emirates on Dec. 2, 1971, and Ras al-Khaima became the seventh member on Feb. 11, 1972.

United Arab Emirates (U. A. E.). By its constitution, drafted on July 18, 1971, the U. A. E. recognizes some local independence for each of the seven states, each of which will continue to have its own flag and control its affairs locally. The U. A. E.'s 40-member council met for the first time on Feb. 12, 1972. Abu Dhabi and Dubai each have eight members, Sharja and Ras al-Khaima each have six, and the others have four members each. Sheikh Zaid Ibn Sultan, emir of Abu Dhabi, was chosen as the first president, to serve five years. Sheikh Rashid Ibn Said of Dubai is vice president, and his son, Emir Maktum Ibn Rashid, is prime minister.

Prior to the meeting of the council, the U. A. E. became a member of the Arab League on Dec. 6, 1971, and a member of the United Nations on December 8. On December 9, an 18-member cabinet was announced, which on December 20 assumed control of the 1,700-man force organized in 1952 by the British. On Feb. 15, 1972, full diplomatic relations were established with the USSR.

On Jan. 24, 1972, Emir Sheikh Khalid Ibn Muhammad al-Qasimi of Sharja was killed in an unsuccessful coup by a former emir, his cousin Sheikh Saqr Ibn Sultan al-Qasimi. However, the latter was seized by Khalid's brother Sheikh Saqr Ibn Muhammad al-Qasimi, who became the new emir. Aid from the U. A. E. was instrumental in winning the day for Sheikh Saqr Ibn Muhammad and for gaining the adherence of Ras al-Khaima to the U. A. E.

Oil production in Abu Dhabi in 1971 reached 934,000 barrels per day, and it was estimated that it would exceed one million in 1972. Dubai was producing over 150,000 barrels per day in 1972.

Bahrain. On Dec. 23, 1971, Bahrain and the United States signed an agreement whereby the latter assumed responsibility for the naval base in Bahrain being vacated by Britain. No military or political commitments were involved. Bahrain refused to exchange ambassadors with the USSR.

There is one large oil field in Bahrain. Its average production for several years has been 75,000 barrels per day.

Qatar. The emirate of Qatar declined to join the United Arab Emirates. It became a member of the United Nations on Sept. 21, 1971. On Feb. 22, 1972, the emir of Qatar, Sheikh Ahmad Ibn Ali al-

Thani, was deposed in a bloodless coup by his cousin, Sheikh Khalifa Ibn Hamad al-Thani. The new emir dismissed the two British commanders of the army and police and pledged to modernize the administration, to cut consumer prices, and to raise civilian and military salaries by 20%.

Oil production in Qatar rose in 1971 to an average of 430,000 barrels per day and reserves were estimated at 6 billion barrels. Oil revenues stood at $200 million in 1971 and were expected to reach about $300 million in 1972.

SYDNEY NETTLETON FISHER
The Ohio State University

PERU

The year 1972 was a comparatively tranquil one for Peru. The Revolutionary Government of the Armed Forces continued its efforts to reorganize the country; the Aprista party remained the center of opposition; and new deposits of oil were discovered in the Amazon lowlands. But the country's economy was gravely affected by a mysterious ecological problem that caused the disappearance of anchovies along the coast.

The National Revolution. The military regime of Gen. Juan Velasco Alvarado continued to try to remake Peruvian society. It began to institutionalize the "nationalistic revolution" by creating a mass base. The National System to Support Social Mobilization (SINAMOS) was established to carry through the government's commitment to change. Headed by a general, SINAMOS aimed to teach the people how to organize themselves.

The only important step toward democratic participation took place in April, when elections were held on the northern coast sugar plantations to select administrative councils to supervise the cooperatives that were created after the government instituted its agrarian reform program. The cooperatives had previously been supervised by the military. Union leaders loyal to the American Popular Revolutionary Alliance (Aprista) won the posts on all but one of the plantations. Meanwhile, the Aprista party continued to call for general elections.

General Velasco and the military junta continued to issue new laws to further the revolution they envisioned. In March the government decreed a sweeping educational reform to create "New Peruvians," who would live in a new society of "justice, liberty, and solidarity." The most important section of the new law provided for bilingual education for the more than 40% of the population that speaks Indian languages and does not know Spanish.

In May the government decreed new standards to restrict television and radio programming and advertising. Under the new regulation all programs must reflect "human values" and be "socially useful." Whenever possible the context and themes of programs must be "Peruvian."

Economy. The government decreed an indefinite halt to all exports of fish meal and fish oil beginning October 1, thus officially recognizing the worst fishing crisis in the country's history. Ecological changes caused by a mysterious shift in the pattern of ocean currents caused anchovies and related species to vanish from coastal waters. Anchovies are used to make fish meal and fish oil, of which Peru is the world's largest supplier. The fishing crisis had a damaging effect on the country's entire economy.

PERU • Information Highlights

Official Name: Republic of Peru.
Area: 496,223 square miles (1,285,216 sq km).
Population (1972 est.): 14,500,000. *Density,* 28 per square mile (11 per sq km). *Annual rate of increase,* 3.1%.
Chief Cities (1961 census): Lima, the capital, 1,800,000 (metropolitan area); Callao, 155,953; Arequipa, 135,358; Trujillo, 100,130.
Government: *Head of state,* Gen. Juan Velasco Alvarado, president (took office Oct. 1968). *Head of government,* Juan Velasco Alvarado. *Legislature*—National Congress (suspended Oct. 1968).
Languages: Spanish (official), Quechua, Aymara.
Education: *Expenditure* (1969), 19.4% of total public expenditure. *School enrollment* (1968)—primary, 2,334,982; secondary, 563,698; technical/vocational, 93,034; university/higher, 101,099.
Monetary Unit: Sol (38.70 sols equal U. S.$1, Sept. 1972).
Gross National Product (1971 est.): $6,250,000,000.
National Income per Person (1970): $363.
Economic Indexes: *Industrial production* (manufacturing; 1969), 148 (1963=100); *agricultural production* (1971), 157 (1952–56=100); *consumer price index* (1971), 156 (1966=100).
Manufacturing (major products): Processed foods, textiles, household wares, chemicals, metal products, assembled automobiles.
Major Agricultural Products: Cotton, sugarcane, rice, potatoes, coffee, sheep, fish (ranks 1st among world producers, 1970).
Major Minerals: Silver (ranks 4th among world producers, 1970), copper, iron ore, lead, tungsten, zinc, gold.
Foreign Trade (1971): *Exports,* $891,000,000 (chief exports—fish meal; copper; sugar; iron ore; silver; zinc). *Imports,* $743,000,000 (chief imports, 1968—nonelectrical machinery; food; dyeing, tanning and coloring materials). *Chief trading partners* (1969)—United States (took 35% of exports, supplied 31% of imports); Japan (16%—7%); West Germany (12%—11%); Argentina (2%—10%).
Transportation: *Motor vehicles* (1970), 347,900 (automobiles, 230,400); *railroads* (1970), 1,353 miles (2,177 km); *merchant fleet* (1971), 421,000 gross registered tons; *major national airline,* Faucett-Companie de Aviacion.
Communications: *Telephones* (1971), 222,776; *television stations* (1971), 18; *newspapers* (1970), 85.

Inflation and beef shortages continued to plague Peru. The government issued a decree in April prohibiting the sale of beef in the province of Lima during the first 15 days of each month and on Mondays and Tuesdays in nine other provinces.

Peru's international financial position remained critical, but 16 private U. S. banks agreed in February to refinance $535 million in Peruvian debts. During the year various European, Asian, and U. S. banks and governments gave Peru loans for developmental purposes.

The bright spot in Peru's economic future was the discovery of new petroleum deposits in the Amazon region. The government reported that it would take about $400 million to develop the new fields, and various international oil companies competed to supply the necessary funds and to help produce and transport the oil.

Soviet engineers continued to work on the development of a fish-processing plant in northern Peru. Contracts were signed with Japanese firms to build a $31.2 million copper refinery and to investigate the prospects for building a $4.25 million textile plant. Other economic agreements were signed with Mexico and Rumania.

International Relations. Communist China's first ambassador to Peru presented his credentials to General Velasco on February 9. Peru reestablished diplomatic relations with Cuba in July and sent a high-level delegation to visit that country.

Heavy Rains. An estimated 30 persons were killed and 150,000 injured in March from floods and avalanches along the Pacific coast after exceptionally heavy rains in the Andes.

HARRY KANTOR, *Marquette University*

PETROLEUM. See ENERGY.
PHARMACOLOGY. See MEDICINE.

PHILADELPHIA

Of concern to Philadelphia in 1972 were a budget deficit that led to a 22-day teachers' strike, plans for a bicentennial exposition, and charges of police and official corruption.

Budget and Taxes. The city council adopted a record operating budget of $694,123,000 for the fiscal year 1972–73. Mayor Frank Rizzo, needing $113 million in federal and state aid to balance the budget, acknowledged that the city's financial needs were acute. A controversial source of revenue was the $3 head tax on outgoing air travelers at Philadelphia International Airport, initiated July 1. It was strongly opposed by airlines and passengers, but after President Nixon vetoed a bill abolishing such levies the city vowed rigorously to enforce it. It was expected to yield between $6 million and $7 million by the end of the fiscal year. To help finance school and city construction projects, voters approved four bond issues totaling $223 million.

Teachers' Strike. Plagued by a $52 million deficit, the Philadelphia school board sought to cut costs by extending a five-hour teaching day by 40 minutes and by increasing class sizes. These measures would have eliminated 385 teaching jobs in addition to 187 nonteaching jobs the board sought to abolish. In response to the teachers' demand for a 34% salary increase, the board offered a nominal $300 increase only to teachers at the top of the salary scale. The result was a 22-day strike.

Although negotiations between the board of education and the Philadelphia Federation of Teachers were still going on, classes finally opened on September 29, when teachers agreed to return to classrooms under their old contract until December 31. Initial plans called for a full 187-day year, making up for lost days by eliminating vacations and extending the year by one week till June 27. The deficit, however, forced the board to adopt a calendar that would end classes April 13, 48 days short of the state requirement.

Bicentennial Exposition. Philadelphia spent $3 million in the course of selecting and planning a suitable site for an international exposition to celebrate the nation's bicentennial in 1976. Several sites were discarded because of high cost or community opposition before a site near the airport was chosen. In May the American Revolution Bicentennial Commission recommended that President Nixon reject the Philadelphia proposal on the grounds of expense to the federal government and lack of time. President Nixon did so, urging instead that Philadelphia be a "focal point" of a national celebration. It was too late for another city to plan an exposition in Philadelphia's place.

Law Enforcement. State and city law enforcement officials clashed over alleged police corruption. A state crime commission report asserted that police corruption in Philadelphia was "citywide." The city's district attorney criticized the report and accused the commission of using unlawful means to gather evidence.

A Philadelphia special grand jury, investigating for a year the sale of substandard housing to low-income families, returned 24 indictments against 78 defendants. Realtors, contractors, and former high-ranking FHA officials were charged with bribery, fraud, and tax evasion.

The unemployment rate of 7.2% in June 1972, an increase of 0.2% over June 1971, was a factor in the crime rate. Many of the jobless were Negro youths, who contributed to much of the gang violence that continued to disturb the city. Police were strictly enforcing laws against concealed weapons and unregistered weapons in public.

National Elections. Mayor Rizzo, a Republican-turned-Democrat, strongly endorsed Republican President Nixon in the 1972 presidential campaign. Rizzo was credited with helping cut Democratic candidate McGovern's lead in Philadelphia to 89,244 votes, the lowest for a Democratic presidential candidate since 1948.

WILLIAM L. DULANEY
Pennsylvania State University

PHILANTHROPY

In 1972 the financial base for private giving in the United States was expanding, reflecting the continuing recovery of the nation's economy from the recession of 1970. The pace of the recovery was moderate, however, and this may have led to caution in the giving plans of contributors. Nonetheless the available data indicated a continuation of the upward trend of private philanthropy. At least $20 billion in private gifts supported the 1972 operations of philanthropic agencies.

Donors. The Internal Revenue Service reported that charitable bequests on estate tax returns had amounted to $2.13 billion in 1969, up from $1.31 billion in 1966. By 1971 the total had probably grown to more than $3 billion, the rise including $1 billion in Johnson and Johnson stock, received by the Robert Wood Johnson Foundation.

The American Association of Fund-Raising Counsel reported that in 1971 nine of the 20 largest bequests were used to endow foundations and the other 11 went to colleges and universities. The growth in bequests since 1961 reflected both a doubling in the number of estates large enough to require an estate tax return and a rise in philanthropy's share of those estates.

Total giving by living individuals and families reached a level between $15 billion and $16 billion in 1972. Internal Revenue Service data for 1970 listed 35.5 million personal income tax returns itemizing $12.9 billion in deductions for gifts, a total not including gifts by taxpayers taking the standard deduction or not required to file a return. Deductions for contributions, however, did not grow as rapidly as those for taxes and interest.

Recipients. Reports from agencies receiving philanthropic support reflected the shifting directions of giving. The United Way of America, Inc., reported that it had raised $865 million in 1971 in 2,230 local campaigns, up 3% from 1970. Contributions to 21 national health agencies rose from $312 million in 1970 to $335 million in 1971, up 7.5%. Corporate giving to the arts in 1970 reached $56 million, up from $45 million in 1968 and $22 million in 1965.

The dollar value of giving to religious institutions continued to rise in 1972, but questions were raised about the future. Surveys indicated little or no growth in church membership, a drop in church attendance, and a decline in religious organizations' share of the family's philanthropic dollar.

Giving to colleges and universities, which had fallen to $1.78 billion in the 1969–70 academic year, rose to $1.86 billion in 1970–71, a record high according to the Council on Financial Aid to Edu-

cation. On the other hand, a Ford Foundation-sponsored study of the income and total growth performances of 36 college and university endowments over a 10-year period revealed that the common stock portfolios for 32 of the 36 had done less well than the stock market as a whole and that only four had outperformed the market.

RALPH L. NELSON
Queens College, City University of New York

PHILATELY. See STAMP COLLECTING.

PHILIPPINES

In September 1972, President Ferdinand E. Marcos of the Philippines proclaimed martial law and assumed strong-man rule in the face of growing lawlessness and corruption, raging inflation, and alleged Communist subversion. Meanwhile, the constitutional convention, deliberating upon reforms in the officially democratic government, completed a new draft charter to be submitted to a national plebiscite on Jan. 15, 1973.

On Dec. 7, 1972, Mrs. Imelda R. Marcos, wife of the president, was stabbed in an apparent assassination attempt while presiding at a ceremony. Her assailant was killed.

Martial Law. On Sept. 21, 1972, President Marcos placed the entire country under martial law. He said he was prompted to take this action because of "widespread lawlessness and anarchy, consequences of the activities of groups of men engaged in criminal conspiracy to take over the government by force and violence." Martial law was needed to "save the country and to form a new society."

Utilizing his extraordinary emergency powers, the president issued orders and decrees not only to restore tranquility and stability, but also to bring about needed social, political, and economic reforms in Philippine society. On September 23 he banned the carrying of firearms by private individuals. The

next day, by presidential decrees, he put into effect the Integrated Reorganization Plan that Congress had failed to enact, extended the land reform act to the entire country, and put into force a law pending in Congress that was to appropriate funds for the rehabilitation and reconstruction of flood-damaged projects. The reorganization plan, the president explained, was needed to effect the desired changes and reforms demanded by the New Society. The land reform measure was intended to ensure a "dignified existence for small farmers free from pernicious restraint and practices which have not only retarded the agricultural development of the country but also produced widespread discontent and unrest among our farmers."

In October presidential decrees were issued to accelerate the country's economic growth. Various fees imposed on the livestock industry were abolished. The bill long pending in Congress on oil exploration and promotion of the oil industry was enacted into law. Taxes on profits from real estate sales were suspended, and those on stock exchange deals were reduced.

Constitutional Convention. The convention, which began its sessions on June 1, 1971, moved slowly due to protracted deliberations on constitutional proposals and to controversies over supposed pressures being brought to bear on delegates. By July 27, 1972, the last day of plenary session, the convention had produced 50 draft articles, of which 15 had been approved. Sessions were resumed on August 3. On November 28 the convention approved the final working draft of the proposed new charter. Included was an article providing for an orderly transition from the presidential to the parliamentary form of government. It allowed President Marcos to hold power for the duration of the emergency that had given rise to martial law and confirmed the decrees, orders, and directives which the president had promulgated under martial law, giving them sanction as the law of the land. The

Children play in the waters covering a Manila thoroughfare as the worst flood in 26 years hit the Philippines in July.

new charter was presented officially to Marcos by Diosdado Macapagal, constitutional convention president, on December 1.

Floods. Heavy rains generated by successive tropical storms that battered the country in July caused the flooding of extensive areas in Luzon, including the Greater Manila area. The disaster, the worst within the memory of most Filipinos, severely damaged the country's economy. Roads, bridges, irrigation works, dikes, and communication lines were swept away. Many lives were lost, thousands of people were left homeless and destitute, and immense quantities of food crops were destroyed. The country faced formidable problems of relief, reconstruction, and rehabilitation.

Foreign Affairs. The decision taken in 1971 to maintain relations with Socialist and Communist countries was implemented on March 10, 1972, when diplomatic ties were established with Yugoslavia and Rumania. On February 13, President Suharto of Indonesia arrived for a three-day state visit. On February 24 the Philippine government extended formal recognition to Bangladesh.

A major controversy in Philippine–U. S. relations was resolved when the Supreme Court of the Philippines, on August 19, ruled that land rights acquired by U. S. citizens under the parity provision of the Philippine constitution would end on July 3, 1974. President Marcos resolved to give "just and fair" compensation to Americans who would be required to surrender their land holdings.

Commemorative Ceremony. The first centenary of the execution of Burgos, Gomez, and Zamora, three Filipino priests who had fought for justice and racial equality for the Filipino clergy, was observed on Feb. 17, 1972. In commemorative ceremonies, a monument to the three priests was unveiled at the plaza in front of the Manila cathedral. President and Mrs. Marcos were the principal guests of honor.

NICOLAS ZAFRA
University of the Philippines

PHILIPPINES • Information Highlights

Official Name: Republic of the Philippines.
Area: 115,830 square miles (300,000 sq km).
Population (1972 est.): 40,800,000. *Density,* 352 per square mile (136 per sq km). *Annual rate of increase,* 3.3%.
Chief Cities (1968 est.): Quezon City, the capital, 545,500; Manila, 1,499,000; Cebu, 332,100; Iloilo, 201,000.
Government: *Head of state,* Ferdinand E. Marcos, president (took office for 2d term Dec. 1969). *Head of government,* Ferdinand E. Marcos. *Legislature*—Congress: House of Representatives, 104 members; Senate, 24 members. *Major political parties*—Nationalist party; Liberal party.
Languages: Pilipino (official), English, Spanish.
Education: *Expenditure* (1968), 3.1% of gross national product. *School enrollment* (1967)—primary, 6,406,826; secondary, 1,363,129; technical/vocational, 90,009; university/higher, 600,787.
Monetary Unit: Peso (3.90 pesos equal U. S.$1, Aug. 1972).
Gross National Product (1971 est.): $10,890,000,000.
National Income per Person (1970): $342.
Economic Indexes: *Industrial production* (1970), 150 (1963= 100); *agricultural production* (1971), 173 (1952–56=100); *consumer price index* (1971), 156 (1971=100).
Manufacturing (major products): Petroleum products, processed foods.
Major Agricultural Products: Rice, corn, copra, sugar, abaca, sweet potatoes and yams, forest products.
Major Minerals: Chromium ore (ranks 3d among world producers, 1970), gold, nickel, copper, iron ore, mercury.
Foreign Trade (1971): *Exports,* $1,122,000,000 (chief exports—Coconut products; sugar; wood; copper; hemp). *Imports,* $1,330,000,000 (chief imports, 1969—nonelectrical machinery; transport equipment; food; chemicals). *Chief trading partners* (1969)—United States (took 42% of exports, supplied 28% of imports); Japan (38%—30%).
Tourism: *Receipts* (1970), $32,100,000.
Transportation: *Motor vehicles* (1970), 458,600 (automobiles, 279,900); *merchant fleet* (1971), 946,000 gross registered tons; *major national airline,* Philippine Airlines.
Communications: *Telephones* (1971), 309,922; *television stations* (1971), 24; *newspapers* (1966), 23 (daily circulation, 906,000).

PHILOSOPHY

Social philosophy was the fastest-growing field in philosophy in 1972. There was also much interest in the views of such 20th century philosophers as Merleau-Ponty, Quine, Strawson, and Searle.

Social Philosophy and Related Fields. Within the diverse and far-ranging field of social philosophy, ecology, alienation, war, revolution, and law received particular attention. The study of ecological problems suggests that progress in improving our environment will depend largely on social values replacing more selfish ones.

Many discussions emphasize the importance of considering alienation and point up Karl Marx's failure to do so. Marx's view that revolutions are justified has led philosophers to consider the relative merits of revolution and evolution as instruments of social change. The morality of war, and especially the morality of the "rules of war" and of conscription, also came under critical analysis.

Underlying these and many other problems in social philosophy is the question of the role of law in society. The relation of legal reasoning to judicial decision-making received special attention. The growing interest in social philosophy is illustrated by the names of some of the societies that met in 1972, such as The Society for Social Philosophy, The Society for Women in Philosophy, and The Society for Philosophy and Public Affairs.

20th Century Philosophy. The period that received the most increased study was 20th century philosophy. This was largely due to continuing growth of interest in phenomenology and analysis. In phenomenology, Martin Heidegger and Jean-Paul Sartre were given less consideration than in 1971. However, the doctrines of Maurice Merleau-Ponty received increasing attention, especially his views on the primacy of perception and the relation of man to his world. Another indication of the growing importance of phenomenology was the appearance of a new journal, *Research in Phenomenology*.

In contemporary analysis the problem of meaning, and, more specifically, the problem of referring, has received increased coverage. The views of Willard V. O. Quine, Peter F. Strawson, and especially John Searle have been given the greatest consideration. The basic problem is one of determining how the predicates and descriptive terms of ordinary language refer to the real things that constitute the universe. In other words, how does our articulated discourse refer to unarticulated reality? Searle and others argue that referring is an intentional act—that is, by performing a "speech act" we commit ourselves. Two related questions being discussed are: (1) How do singular terms refer? and (2) Can terms refer to nonexistent entities?

History of Philosophy. During 1972 interest in ancient philosophy remained constant, but the consideration given to medieval philosophy increased greatly, and that given to modern philosophy declined significantly. In medieval philosophy more articles were devoted to Augustine, Boethius, Abelard, Averroës, and Henry of Ghent. However, no additional coverage was given to Aquinas or Anselm.

In modern philosophy more attention was given to Spinoza. The probable reason is that his theory of man and his emotions is relevant to many discussions in the philosophy of mind.

RICHARD H. LINEBACK
Bowling Green State University

photography

New Polaroid SX-70 Land camera, a single lens reflex, ejects exposed film unit 1.5 seconds after picture is taken. The dry film develops (above) for several minutes outside the camera.

POLAROID

POLAROID

There were substantial advances in the technology of photography in 1972. This was a Photokina year in Cologne, Germany, and a total of 770 firms displayed a variety of new products to an estimated 250,000 people during the eight days that photography's biennial world fair was open to the public.

High development and production costs have continued to change the structure of the industry. A trend towards internationalization noted last year was best exemplified in 1972 by the signing of a technical cooperation agreement between E. Leitz of Wetzlar, Germany, makers of Leica cameras, and the Minolta Camera Company, Ltd., of Osaka, Japan. Initially the agreement calls for standardizing some special use lenses so they can be used with either Leitz or Minolta products. Only items that can be standardized with a minimum of technical problems will be involved at first. In the near future, the firms have indicated that certain more common lens mounts will be standardized to allow their use on products of both manufacturers. The policy will be to gradually broaden standardization to avoid costly repetitive research and development programs. The two firms also plan to exchange information regarding their measuring and calibration methods, with the aim of establishing joint standards. It is highly likely that cooperative agreements of this type will become increasingly common.

STILL CAMERAS

Pocket Instamatic Cameras. The Eastman Kodak Company of Rochester, N. Y., began marketing the Kodak pocket Instamatic camera line of true pocket cameras this year. Ranging in weight and length from 5.6 ounces and 5⅛ inches for the Instamatic 20 to 9 ounces and 5¾ inches for the Instamatic 60, these are the smallest cameras produced by the Eastman Kodak Company. All models are less than 1 inch thick. While not strictly subminiature in size, they are nevertheless true pocket cameras. With the exception of the inexpensive model 20 all pocket Instamatic cameras are equipped with electronic shutters. The film for the camera is contained in a plastic instant-load cassette, similar to but much smaller than the cassette used for the large Instamatic that the Eastman Kodak Company has been marketing for the past decade. The 16mm film is supplied in both 12 and 20 exposure loads. The image size is 13 x 17mm.

An improved color negative film, Kodacolor II, was introduced concurrently with the new small camera. Superior in resolving power to Kodacolor X, the new film makes it possible to produce 3½″ x 4½″ prints that are nearly equal in quality to prints of identical dimensions made from the much larger negatives of the standard size instamatic cassette. Cameras to produce subminiature negatives have been on the market for many years. They have had a relatively slight impact on the total market because of the shortage of special processing facilities needed for subminiature negatives and because of the lack of films with sufficiently high resolution to permit reasonable enlargement. The great success of the new line of Instamatics can be attributed to a substantial degree to the new film as well as to the existence of a large network of laboratories equipped with special processing machines needed to develop and print the new subminiature film.

New Polaroid System. A radically new instant color camera was announced in 1972 by the Polaroid Corporation of Cambridge, Mass. Called the SX-70, the new camera is one of the most sophisticated instruments ever produced for the amateur market. The photographer, after composing and focusing through a single-lens reflex viewer, presses the shutter release. In less than 2 seconds a picture 3⅛″ x 3⅛″ with a white border emerges. At first the picture is a uniform pale green. Within 1 minute the image begins to appear. It takes just under 10 minutes for the photo to take its final form. The

(*Continued on page 540*)

© DAVID DOUGLAS DUNCAN, WHITNEY MUSEUM OF AMERICAN ART

David Douglas Duncan

THE NEW YORK TIMES

Famed photographer David Douglas Duncan (*opposite page*) was honored in New York City in June–August 1972 by the first photographic exhibition ever held at the Whitney Museum of American Art. Among his war pictures, courtesy of the museum, are views of a helicopter evacuating bodies of U. S. marines killed in Vietnam (*opposite page*); marines —themselves later killed—running past a dead North Korean soldier (*above*); and faces of marines in Vietnam, peering out from beneath their decorated helmets (*right*).

(Continued from page 537)
manufacturer feels that the high quality of the final photo combined with a simplified picture-taking procedure and an absence of chemical residue more than compensate for the fact that development time is longer than with the regular Polaroid color film.

The camera is radical in appearance as well as in operation. When folded it is a completely enclosed flat pack 1" x 4" x 7". A complex electronic exposure control system using integrated circuitry employs the equivalent of 300 transistors. The camera body itself does not contain a battery. Every new film pack, each with material for 10 exposures, contains a fresh battery to power both the exposure control system and the electric motor that ejects the picture from the camera after exposure.

The film for the new system utilizes a different chemistry than the previous Polaroid color process. Before exposure the individual film sheet consists of 17 different layers. The front or top layer is a relatively thick transparent sheet followed by a number of control and color-sensitive silver-halide layers. The final coatings are metalized-dye developers. All the layers are coated on a heavy opaque support. The developing process is initiated when the contents of a small pod containing the activating agents are spread on the emulsion by rollers as the film is ejected from the camera after exposure. The presence of a chemical light shield allows the developing process to take place in bright sunlight.

In addition to such standard attachments as closeup lenses and a microscope adapter, a special linear array of 10 flashbulbs will be available for the new camera. The control circuit in the camera automatically selects the next good bulb. The flash system was designed by the General Electric Company. Marketing of the new camera began in Florida in November, and distribution throughout the rest of the country is anticipated in early 1973.

Double-Magazine Camera. One of the most unusual instruments to be presented at Photokina was the Domnick 2 Cassette camera, to be made in Weisbaden, Germany. It is claimed by the manufacturer to be the first camera in the world that can be loaded simultaneously with two different cartridges of film, enabling the user to choose between emulsions without changing film backs. In use two separate magazines, each loaded with a roll of standard 120 or 220 film, are fitted to opposite ends of the camera. An electric motor on command from the operator advances either film. After each exposure the film is wound back onto the original reel. A total of 4 electric motors are employed in the film-drive mechanism. The camera is equipped with rangefinder focusing and interchangeable Zeiss lenses. It is expected to be available in 1973.

MOVIE CAMERAS

Panaflex. Panavision, Inc., manufacturers of equipment for the professional moviemaker, introduced a new highly versatile 35mm reflex movie camera. Called the Panaflex, the new unit is both a studio and hand camera. According to the manufacturer it can be converted from a complete sound stage camera to a hand-holdable field unit in less than 60 seconds. In its hand-held mode it weighs less than 25 pounds. In operation it has a noise level of about 27 decibels. It is said to be so silent that none of the special sound-damping devices

EASTMAN KODAK COMPANY

POCKET-SIZED Instamatic designed by Kodak is an inexpensive and convenient camera for snapshot takers.

routinely used with studio sound cameras need be employed. Electronic digital display is used for the footage counter and motor tachometer.

Leicina. For the amateur moviemaker E. Leitz of Wetzlar, Germany, will market the new Leicina Special Super Eight. It is equipped with an Opti-Varon f/1.8 6-66mm zoom lens. The zoom ratio of 11 to 1 is one of the highest available to amateur moviemakers. A unique feature is a macro zoom range that allows the user to focus down to 3 inches for extreme closeup work. To further increase the versatility of this camera, it has been so designed that the lens mount will accept most bayonet-mount regular Leica lenses.

LENSES AND SHUTTERS

Multilayer Lens Coatings. Single-layer lens coatings to reduce transmission of non-image-forming light have been used for more than 30 years, and came into widespread use by 1950. In 1972 a number of manufacturers started to use multilayer coatings to further reduce the transmission of unwanted light. A single-layer coating reduces such transmission from 5% to 1%. With multilayer coatings the figure drops to ¼%. Coatings of this type have been in use for some years in a number of scientific applications; however, this is the first time they are being used routinely in regular photographic equipment. For certain specialized situations multilayer coatings may offer a significant improvement in image quality.

Mirror Telephoto Lens. The Minolta Camera Co., Ltd., of Osaka, Japan, will shortly market a new 1,600mm catadioptric-mirror telephoto lens. About 12 inches long, the new lens is intended for use with Minolta single lens reflex cameras, but with

adapters can be used with most cameras of this type. A mirror lens employs a system of internal mirrors in combination with conventional refractive lens elements to fold the light path, thus reducing the length of long-focus optical systems. The physical length of this lens is about 1/5th of its focal length. Maximum aperture is f/11, and aperture control is by means of a series of neutral density filters, which come with the lens.

Electronic Focal-Plane Shutter. Minolta also announced a particularly versatile electronic focal plane shutter to be used on its new XM series single lens reflex camera. The shutter is capable of speeds from 16 seconds to 1/2,000 of a second. Between 1 and 16 seconds speed changes are by steps. From 1 second to 1/2,000 of a second speed changes are continuously variable.

SPECIAL APPLICATIONS

Timing Camera. Photography was utilized as a tool at the 1972 Olympic Games to an unprecedented degree. Very advanced finish-line time cameras replaced standard timing devices. Built by Junghans, the watch manufacturer, and Linhof, the West German camera firm, the timing cameras employ a clock with a quartz-crystal oscillator for extreme accuracy. Electronic digital printers register times down to 1/1,000 second on the bottom margin of the film. Although such timing accuracy is rarely required, it is occasionally needed. In one of the swimming events at Munich, the difference between the winner and second place was in the 1/100-second range. According to the manufacturer no other device permits such a high degree of accuracy in recording a sporting event while simultaneously meeting all other athletic requirements.

Photogrammetry. The construction of the roof of the main Olympic stadium in Munich was aided by photography in a somewhat unusual manner. A bat-

ELECTRONIC FLASH is an integral feature of Keystone's new 60-Second Everflash instant picture camera.

KEYSTONE

tery of 18 Linhof cameras was used to record photogrammetric stress tests on models before construction of the complex structure.

Several years ago, the firm of Victor Hasselblad of Göteborg, Sweden, manufactured a special model of its 500 EL electric-drive camera for the National Aeronautics and Space Administration (NASA). These cameras were used by U. S. astronauts on all of the Apollo missions. One version of this camera is now being marketed for photogrammetry. Designated the Hasselblad MK 70, it is equipped with a graticule plate in the image plane. Such a plate was responsible for the regular pattern of fine crosses seen on all space and moon photographs taken with Hasselblad cameras. The plate has a dual function. It ensures optimum film flatness and permits exact measurements of image dimensions in the film plane. Used with a selection of Hasselblad lenses including a special minimum-distortion 60mm f/5.6 Biogon which had been designated for NASA, the MK 70 has most of the features of the moon cameras, including large controls and extra-capacity film magazines.

Electrophotographic Color Printer. The Japanese firm of Toshiba and Sakata has announced an electrophotographic color printer for commercial photofinishing. The printer produces postcard-size prints from 35mm color transparencies in less than one minute. Working on the same general principle as an electrostatic office copier, it employs an aluminum-foil-covered paper coated with a zinc compound to provide the necessary white base. The paper is first charged and then exposed sequentially to red, blue, and green images produced by the use of filters in the light path from the color transparency. Colored toners are added after each partial exposure. The result is a full-color pigment image that is very stable.

Xeroradiography. Xerography, the widely used non-silver-halide imaging system, is being used to record X-ray images. In xerography the picture is formed by the discharge of a static electric charge on a selenium plate when an optical image is projected on it. The charged area becomes visible when an electrostatically charged powder is applied to this surface and subsequently transferred to a piece of paper or other support material. The principle of Xeroradiography is essentially the same, except that X rays take the place of visible light rays. The image obtained is far more detailed than radiographic images produced on conventional photographic plates. The Xerox Corporation has developed a Xeroradiographic unit which is now being used for routine breast X rays. Aside from greater detail, another advantage of this system is virtually instant processing, with the picture being available in one minute. The system is particularly applicable for mass examinations.

LITERATURE

The Focal Press of London and New York has reprinted E. J. Wall's classic *History of Three-Color Photography.* First published in 1925, it covers the history of color photography from Clerk Maxwell through the year of publication. It is exhaustive in detail, the author having referred to 12,000 articles and patents while compiling material for the book, and it has an extensive bibliography.

PHILIP L. CONDAX
Curator, Equipment Archives, International Museum of Photography at George Eastman House

An accelerator that produces a proton beam at energies of 800 million electron volts was tested in June at the Clinton P. Anderson Meson Physics Facility at Los Alamos, N. Mex. The machine will probe interactions in atomic nuclei. After leaving the generator (*right*), protons attain their highest energies in the final wavelength unit (*above*).

Probing the Heart of Matter

PHYSICS

The year 1972 was an exciting one in physics. A U. S. particle accelerator became the most powerful one in the world; experimental results seemed to confirm parts of Einstein's general theory of relativity; increased emphasis was placed on controlled thermonuclear fusion; and the role of physics in the United States was examined in a wide-ranging report. On the negative side, the manpower surplus in the field of physics continued.

Particle Accelerators. The giant proton accelerator at the National Accelerator Laboratory (NAL) near Batavia, Ill., reached its design energy of 200 GeV (billion electron volts) in the spring of 1972, far surpassing the USSR's 76-GeV machine, which had been the most powerful accelerator in the world. In July 1972 the NAL's machine broke its own record by accelerating protons to an energy of 300 GeV. Moreover, it was expected that the machine will accelerate protons at energies up to 500 GeV.

Before the successes in 1972, a major problem was condensation of moisture caused by high humidity in the tunnel of the accelerator's main ring, which has a diameter of about 1.25 miles (2 km). The moisture caused breakdowns in many of the more than 1,000 magnets that guide and control the proton beam. This problem was solved. Although other problems remain before the accelerator is fully operational, actual experiments have begun.

Los Alamos Accelerator. A lower-energy but ultrahigh-intensity accelerator at the Clinton P. Anderson Meson Physics Facility in Los Alamos,

N. Mex., was successfully tested at its full design energy of 800 MeV (million electron volts) in June 1972. This 0.5-mile-long accelerator was designed for medium-energy physics research, complementing the NAL's accelerator, which was designed for high-energy physics research.

The Los Alamos facility is called a meson factory because the 800-MeV protons can strike targets and thereby produce a very large number of mesons. One exciting possibility is the use of π mesons (pions) in treating cancers.

Superheavy Elements. Scientists have created the elements having atomic numbers from 93 to 105. Since production of these man-made elements has been increasingly difficult, it might appear that the creation of transuranium elements has neared the end of the line. However, calculations based on the shell model of the nucleus indicate there are some mass numbers, called "magic numbers," that correspond to nuclei of great stability. The next nucleus of great stability beyond element 105 is an isotope of element 114 that would have a mass number of 298. Calculations indicate that one isotope of element 114 may last for many millions of years.

As yet there is no firm experimental evidence for the existence of any superheavy element. Nevertheless, theorists have been speculating about "islands" of stability for nuclei that have mass numbers much greater than those of nuclei so far found in nature. Meanwhile, the search for superheavy elements in nature is continuing.

A combination of two cyclotrons at Dubna, USSR, has accelerated heavy xenon ions to nearly 1 GeV.

Also, the Princeton Particle Accelerator and the bevatron at the Lawrence Radiation Laboratory in Berkeley have been used to accelerate nitrogen ions to many GeV. Besides applications in various areas of physics and chemistry, there are many possible medical applications. One of the findings is that heavy ions passing through the retina of the eye create flashes of light, which presumably explains the flashes reported by the Apollo astronauts.

Gravity Waves. In the past few years, Joseph Weber of the University of Maryland has reported observations of gravity waves. According to Einstein's general theory of relativity, gravity waves should occur whenever gravitational mass is accelerated. However, these waves have such extremely low energy that detection of the waves is very difficult. Due to this difficulty, there is still skepticism over the reported identification of gravity waves.

An Israeli scientist, Dror Sadeh, reported that gravity waves were emitted by pulsating stars (pulsars). He used a seismograph to measure vibrations in the earth. According to Sadeh, the measured vibrations apparently were caused by gravity waves from the pulsar nearest to earth. Other experiments in the United States, England, Germany, and Italy were in preparation. Thus, a clear-cut determination of gravity waves may be forthcoming in a few years.

Some preliminary theoretical interpretations of Weber's results indicate that the entire Milky Way would have to have burned out in order to account for the amount of gravitational radiation that Weber observed. One way out of this difficulty is to assume that gravitational radiation from the center of the Milky Way is somehow beamed in the plane of the galaxy instead of radiating uniformly in all directions. This would save Weber's results because the earth is very nearly in the plane of the galaxy.

Clocks in Flight. Another prediction of Einstein's theory of relativity is that time kept by a moving clock runs slower than time kept by a stationary clock. A test of this part of Einstein's theory was made in late 1971.

Joseph C. Hafele of Washington University and Richard E. Keating of the U. S. Naval Observatory traveled around the world twice, once in each direction, on commercial jet airliners that carried four very precise cesium-beam clocks (atomic clocks). As compared with clocks at the Naval Observatory, they observed a gain of about 275 billionths of a second when traveling westward against the earth's rotation and a loss of about 60 billionths of a second when traveling eastward with the earth's rotation. After taking account of the effects of the earth's rotation and the earth's gravitational field, they concluded that Einstein's predicted time difference between a traveling clock and a fixed clock is now an established experimental fact.

Controlled Thermonuclear Fusion. One fundamental problem facing the world is the development of energy sources. Present-day fission reactors provide a first step toward a solution, and research is continuing on breeder reactors, which produce more useful fissionable isotopes than are consumed. The primary alternative to fission processes is controlled thermonuclear fusion.

Uncontrolled fusion of light elements, as in hydrogen weapons, has been established for 20 years. Major advances in controlled fusion have been made in the past few years, but the practical problems are monumental. The basic nuclear reaction is fairly simple; for instance, the fusion of deuterium with tritium releases energy. The problem is to heat the materials so that the fusion reaction will occur and to control the process. The temperatures involved are in the range from 10 million to 100 million degrees Kelvin. At such extremely high temperatures the fusion materials have little resemblance to ordinary matter; instead, they form a plasma (ionized gas). The most difficult problem appears to be the containment of the plasma long enough to prevent cooling below the ignition temperature. No solid wall material can contain the plasma at the required temperatures, so researchers have tried to use external electric or magnetic fields that serve as a container for the plasma.

The USSR has placed great emphasis on controlled fusion research, and the U. S. Atomic Energy Commission is increasing its efforts in this area. In the past year or so, both countries apparently have emphasized a new approach—the possibility of triggering the fusion with high-powered lasers. The present consensus appears to be that fusion reactors should be available by 2000, and possibly much earlier if an all-out effort is made. See also ENERGY—*Nuclear Energy.*

Physics Survey Report. A distinguished group of 21 physicists released a 1,088-page report in 1972 on the role of physics in the United States. The report, made for the National Academy of Sciences, emphasized where physics stands now, what the priorities should be for the future, and how to attain these goals.

The physicists, headed by D. Allan Bromley of Yale University, made a striking case for the value of physics in maintaining and improving the competitive position of U. S. industry and in correcting problems arising from the misuse of existing technologies. The group not only emphasized the need for increased support of all areas of physics but also presented a list of priorities.

According to the study, the top 15 areas in which adequate financial support was likely to produce dramatic results were: (1) lasers and masers; (2) National Accelerator Laboratory; (3) quantum optics; (4) university group studies of elementary particle physics; (5) Stanford Linear Accelerator Center; (6) nuclear dynamics; (7) studies of elementary particle physics at major accelerator facilities and improvement of alternating-gradient synchrotrons; (8) Brookhaven National Laboratory, alternating-gradient synchrotron; (9) nuclear excitations; (10) heavy-ion interactions; (11) higher energy nuclear physics; (12) nuclear astrophysics; (13) theoretical relativistic astrophysics; (14) neutron physics; and (15) nuclear theory.

Manpower. Employment difficulties for physicists continued in 1972, mainly because of reductions in federal research spending, the general economic slowdown, and cutbacks in areas such as the aerospace industry. Almost all predictions on the number of Ph. D. physicists and the number of jobs indicated a continuing short-term oversupply of physicists. However, many of these predictions also indicated a shortage of physicists in the not too distant future. The problem is that science funding and the science student population appear to be locked in boom-or-bust cycles. Almost all scientists continued to plead for long-term scientific budgetary and manpower planning.

GARY MITCHELL
North Carolina State University at Raleigh

PITTSBURGH

A rapid transit fight, a battle over the city zoo, severe flood damage, and confessions in the Yablonski murder case were highlights in Pittsburgh in 1972.

Rapid Transit Plan. A proposed rapid transit system for Pittsburgh and its suburbs was to be built by the county government's Port Authority Transit. Pittsburghers and other residents of Allegheny county nicknamed the project for its best-known feature, the Skybus—a rubber-tired, computer-operated vehicle that runs on a concrete pad.

On January 10, Mayor Peter F. Flaherty, county commissioner William R. Hunt, and the mayors of a dozen suburban communities filed suit in Allegheny county common pleas court, asking for an injunction to halt spending on the $228.5 million transit plan. They claimed, among other things, that the Port Authority acted arbitrarily and capriciously in planning and funding the program. On November 6, Judge Anne X. Alpern enjoined the authority from further spending until several requirements were met. Among them were the development of a sound financial plan, obtaining an independent engineer's opinion, and getting approval from municipalities along the route. The case was appealed to the state supreme court. There was no immediate halt of the program pending legal maneuvering, but little construction had begun.

In addition to the Skybus through the South Hills suburbs, the program involves development of two bus-only roads to the south and east and upgrading of existing trolley lines.

City Zoo Battle. On January 29 it was revealed that Mayor Flaherty had canceled agreements under which the private Pittsburgh Zoological Society operates large portions of the city zoo. The mayor said he wanted more control over zoo operations, thus firing the first shot in a widely debated issue. Edward J. Magee, society president, took the case to court and won. On March 16 a court injunction prohibited Flaherty from canceling the agreements, and the issue died.

Flood Damage. In June the rains of Hurricane Agnes swelled the Allegheny, Monongahela, and Ohio rivers, punishing the city with its third worst flood. The U. S. Army Corps of Engineers estimated the damage at $45 million. Water crept up the tip of the Golden Triangle—Pittsburgh's downtown—covering Point State Park and coming within a few feet of the hotel-office complex known as Gateway Center. Sections of the city's North Side and communities down the Ohio River also were flooded, as well as parts of the area's main expressway.

Yablonski Murder Case. In nearby Washington, Pa., the courtroom epic of the Yablonski murder trials reached a climax. So far, seven people have been charged in the Dec. 31, 1969, shooting deaths of former United Mine Workers (UMW) official Joseph A. "Jock" Yablonski, his wife, Margaret, and their daughter, Charlotte, in their Clarksville, Pa., home. On April 13 a statement by one of those charged, Mrs. Annette Gilley, was read in court, spelling out details of the whole affair. Her statement said that she was told the murder had the approval of the "big man." "To me," she said, "that meant Tony Boyle, president, UMW." So far, two suspects have been convicted, with the juries returning death verdicts; three have confessed and await sentencing; and two others await trial.

Parking-Lot Shutdown. On August 4, commuters got the feel of what it would be like with rapid transit as they took to the buses during a three-day strike by parking-lot attendants. Most downtown lots and garages remained closed until the Teamster members received pay increases. Then the city returned to its normal traffic-jammed condition.

DAVID Y. WARNER
News Correspondent

PLASTICS. See MATERIALS.

Pittsburgh was inundated by floodwaters of the Allegheny River when Hurricane Agnes struck the area in June.

UPI

POLAND

Political events of 1972 were highlighted by the March election, which brought the greatest turnover in the national parliament since 1956. The economy benefitted from substantially increased productivity in both agriculture and industry. In foreign affairs, a main event was the establishment of full-fledged diplomatic relations with West Germany.

Election and Politics. The national election took place one year ahead of schedule, reflecting the urgency with which the PZPR (Communist party) leader, Edward Gierek, sought to stabilize and legitimize his new regime. About 22 million persons (97.9% of the electorate) reportedly cast ballots. The outcome was no different from the 1969 election in terms of aggregate party representation in the Sejm (parliament). Out of 460 seats, 255 went to the ruling PZPR; 117 to the Peasants' party and 39 to the Democratic party—both adjuncts of the dominant PZPR; and 49 to several Catholic groups. But the turnover was so great that some 300 incumbents were not returned. Preelection meetings served as outlets for popular criticism of the regime, and the unusually large number of official candidates on the ballots encouraged voters to cross out the names of the most objectionable.

One of the first actions of the new Sejm was approval of Gierek's five-year (1971–75) economic plan, calling for greater diversification of the Polish economy, more investment in research and technology, more productivity-related incentives, and managerial decentralization. The new parliament removed Józef Cyrankiewicz (an associate of Gierek's predecessor, Władysław Gomułka, from the presidency of the Council of State. Henryk Jabłoński, former minister, was elected president on March 28 to replace him.

Political changes of potentially great importance came in October with the establishment of a new system of local governments. The country was divided administratively into some 2,400 areas, each with its own locally elected council and a leader named by the central government. The leader was endowed with great autonomy in local decision-making, particularly with respect to economic matters. The impact of the new organization—promising the Polish people some easement from a long chain of bureaucratic red tape—was still unclear in 1972.

Economy. The Gierek regime realized a number of significant improvements for Polish consumers since the hard winter of 1970–71. Meat shortages were eased; many farm products were supplied in 1972 at a rate not anticipated by the plan until 1975. The wages of the lowest paid workers were increased, some prices were cut, and worker bonuses were augmented. The volume of Polish exports rose nearly one fourth over that of 1971. Tourism from and into the country was expanded. Still barely affected by Gierek's policies were Poland's massive and chronic housing shortages and, for the most part, low and stagnant worker incomes.

Cultural Affairs. The regime moved toward somewhat more liberal policies in cultural affairs. At a February meeting in Warsaw, the Polish Writers' Union reelected a moderate, Jarosław Iwaszkiewicz, as president over a liberal, Igor Newerly. The executive board was balanced among liberal, conservative, and moderate factions. A new literary weekly, *Literatura,* appeared in Warsaw in March, beginning a more tolerant and open cover-

POLAND · Information Highlights

Official Name: Polish People's Republic.
Area: 120,724 square miles (312,677 sq km).
Population (1972 est.): 33,700,000. *Density,* 272 per square mile (105 per sq km). *Annual rate of increase,* 0.9%.
Chief Cities (1970 census): Warsaw, the capital, 1,308,100; Łódź, 761,700; Crakow, 583,400; Wrocław, 523,300; Poznań, 469,000.
Government: *President of the Council of State,* Henryk Jabłoński (took office March 1972). *Premier,* Piotr Jaroszewicz (took office Dec. 1970). *First secretary, United Workers' party,* Edward Gierek (took office Dec. 1970). *Legislature* (unicameral)—Sejm, 460 members. *Major political parties*—United Workers' party; United Peasants' party; Democratic party.
Language: Polish (official).
Education: *Expenditure* (1969), 5.2% of gross national product. *School enrollment* (1969)—primary, 5,443,132; secondary, 1,254,757; technical/vocational, 905,781; university/higher, 322,464.
Monetary Unit: Zloty (3.68 zlotys equal U. S.$1, June 1972).
Gross National Product (1971 est.): $48,600,000,000.
National Income per Person (1971): $1,000.
Economic Indexes: *Industrial production* (1971), 192 (1963= 100); *agricultural production* (1970), 125 (1957–59=100); *consumer price index* (1971), 100 (1970=100).
Manufacturing (major products): Petroleum products, transportation equipment, chemicals, machinery, metal products, processed foods.
Major Agricultural Products: Potatoes (ranks 2d among world producers, 1971), rye (world rank 2d, 1970), oats, sugar beets, wheat, livestock.
Major Minerals: Coal, lignite, zinc, lead, iron ore, sulfur, copper.
Foreign Trade (1971): *Exports,* $3,872,000,000 (chief exports, 1969—coal; meat and meat products; ships and boats; rolled products, including pipes). *Imports,* $4,038,000,000 (chief imports, 1969—food; petroleum and petroleum products; rolled products, including pipes; cotton). *Chief trading partners* (1969)—USSR (took 36% of exports, supplied 37% of imports); East Germany (9%—10%); Czechoslovakia (9%—8%).
Tourism: *Receipts* (1970), $30,000,000.
Transportation: *Motor vehicles* (1970), 739,300 (automobiles, 479,400); *railroads* (1970), 16,506 miles (26,563 km); *merchant fleet* (1971), 1,760,000 gross registered tons; *major national airline,* LOT-Polish Airlines.
Communications: *Telephones* (1971), 1,867,086; *television stations* (1971), 24; *television sets* (1971), 4,023,000; *radios* (1970), 5,658,000; *newspapers* (1970), 43 (daily circulation, 6,832,000).

age of contemporary issues than had been allowed since the mid-1960's. There was an increase in book publication in 1972, with some titles on subjects that had previously been taboo.

Religion. Early in the year the government eased its policy on financial record-keeping required of the Roman Catholic Church. This long has been regarded as a form of harassment by the Polish episcopate. Following the ratification of the Polish–West German nonagression treaty in June, the Vatican transferred a number of formerly German territories to the jurisdiction of Polish bishoprics. There was renewed speculation that Pope Paul VI would visit Poland sometime in 1973. Despite these developments, church-state frictions in Poland continued, chiefly with respect to the regime's severe restrictions on building permits for new churches.

Foreign Affairs. The establishment of diplomatic relations with West Germany in June ended more than 20 years of mutual political hostility and brought indications of greatly increased trade and personal exchanges. The June visit by President Tito of Yugoslavia was expected to further trade with countries outside the Warsaw Pact orbit.

U. S. President Richard Nixon visited Warsaw on May 31 on his return from the Moscow summit. Among the immediate results of his visit were the establishment of a joint Polish-American trade commission, the announcement of a consular treaty, and an agreement to expand scientific, cultural, and technological contacts. In November, President Nixon announced that Export-Import Bank credits would be made available to Poland.

ALEXANDER J. GROTH
University of California, Davis

UPI   THE NEW YORK TIMES

THE DISTAFF SIDE OF LAW AND ORDER

Policewomen now do work once reserved for men. Mary Almasov (*left*) became the first woman on Yale's campus police force. The first female cadets (*top right*) enter Pennsylvania State Police Academy. Sgt. Margaret Powers (*bottom right*) of New York City's 24th Precinct is the first woman supervisor of a police station. In Ann Arbor, Mich., policewomen (*opposite page*) deal efficiently with a female suspect.

POLICE

Methods for improving the relationship between the police and the public dominated law enforcement planning efforts during 1972. Among the more notable efforts of the year were those focusing on the employment of greater numbers of men from minority groups and women, improving training standards, reorganizing selection procedures, and inaugurating programs to bring community members and law enforcement officers into closer contact. Invitations to high school and college students to ride along with patrol car officers—so that they might see for themselves the kinds of problems faced by the officer, the risks he takes, and the manner in which he operates—are becoming increasingly common police practice throughout the United States.

"Policeman's Syndrome." The continuing psychological toll of police work was underlined in a 1972 study, which maintained that increasing numbers of law enforcement officers were suffering from what was labelled the "policeman's syndrome." Symptoms were said to include accelerated heart beat, sweating, and lightheadedness, which are brought on by the aggravated tensions and anxieties of the police role. The study's author, Martin G. Binder, a San Francisco psychiatrist, claimed the condition was a result of the "abrupt change in the policeman's role." Formerly, the job of policing, Binder noted, was a "straightforward one of politi-

UPI

cally approved and heroic opponent of evil." Today, however, policemen find themselves acting as buffers between "ill-defined but powerful social forces" in a new role that is "unfamiliar, complex, ambiguous and politically charged." Formerly, the police used to deal only with the criminal element, Binder observed. Recently, however, they have been faced with protests from segments of the society that they used to believe they had been sworn to protect. "Policeman's syndrome" was said to be a consequence of the confusion and dismay of police officers at the hostility directed against them.

British Views. Four British police constables who paid a working visit to the police force in Winston-Salem, N. C., during the year pointed up the contrast between their jobs and those of their U. S. counterparts. Respect in Britain for the bobby, they said, was partly a function of high standards of training and conduct for police recruits. Public respect for the British police, they thought, grew out of confidence and not out of fear or patterns of obedience. In large measure, the British public trusted their police because constables performed their work without the use of weapons. "If I started to wear a firearm, I'd lose the respect of my public," Constable Ian Munro of Essex claimed. But the constable also thought that crime was too severe and dangerous now in the United States for officers to forego guns. "How do you tell millions of Americans to rid themselves of sidearms?" a British officer asked. One of their number summed up the comparative position of British and American law enforcement workers by saying, "I'd love to be a policeman here. But I'm not brave enough."

Other British commentators have pointed out that the last British political assassination in their country occurred in 1812—160 years ago—when Prime Minister Spencer Percival was shot dead in the lobby of the House of Commons. In 1971, there were only 29 homicides involving guns in all of England and Wales, which have a total population of 50 million, compared with 965 gun slayings in New York City, which has fewer than 8 million residents. Absence of police firearms is believed to contribute to the relatively passive and nonaggressive nature of English crime, though the homogeneous nature of the people and the relatively static character of the class structure (the people are not striving frantically to "better themselves") are also believed to relate to the low rate of homicide as a consequence of lower rates of frustration.

Hiring of Minorities. Some progress along the road to an improved public image for the police was noted by James Vorenberg, former director of the President's Commission on Law Enforcement and Administration of Justice, in an article published in the May 1972 issue of the *Atlantic Monthly*. Vorenberg cited Oakland and New York as cities in which police chiefs "have made it clear that decent treatment of citizens is a top priority and will be given weight in promotion and assignment of officers." But Vorenberg thought that the general record of the nation's police in adding minority group officers was, at best, mixed. The five largest cities in the United States had shown an increase of 23% in the number of black policemen between 1967 and 1972, but some departments, such as those in Cleveland and Philadelphia, had fewer blacks in 1972 than they did in 1967. Alabama and Mississippi continued to bar Negroes from their state police.

Policewomen. Although resistance to a greater use of women in police work remained strong in some police departments, there was a notable increase in the number of policewomen in 1972. The increase was prompted primarily by the fact that women tend to be less threatening than men and therefore to arouse less hostile reactions from the public. A survey indicated that women were being assigned to more dangerous undercover police work than they had been in the past. In New York, about 10 women were working with the drug detail, where their job was to purchase narcotics and then arrest the supplier. One woman, a grade three detective earning $17,500 annually, described the job in the following colorful terms: "It's the easiest thing in the world to buy dope. The hardest thing is to stay alive." But the women were proving notably effective, since they were less apt than men to arouse the suspicions of drug dealers.

Police Recruiting. Research completed during the year indicated that improvement might be made in the caliber of police officers as a result of screening procedures for recruits. The study, conducted by the Rand Institute, involved examination of the records of 2,000 New York policemen and found that of 600 men who received at least one unsatisfactory mark during their 6-month probation period, 35% were later convicted at a department trial for corruption or some other serious infraction. The rate proved to be 50% higher than for men with no unsatisfactory ratings. The study also found, rather surprisingly, that men with criminal records for minor offenses were apt to make better policemen in some important respects. "Men who had been arrested for nonviolent crimes prior to joining the police force," it was noted, "were less likely than other officers to be later charged with such things as false arrest and illegal search and seizure. Seemingly, their own personal experience tempered their relations with crime suspects."

GILBERT GEIS
University of California, Irvine

Delegates to the 1972 Republican Convention greet the Nixon family (above) at opening session and cheer renominated Vice President Agnew and President Nixon (opposite page) at close.

political parties

President Richard M. Nixon, assured of being the Republican nominee for reelection, announced his candidacy on Jan. 7, 1972, when he disclosed he would enter the New Hampshire primary. He said that he would not campaign for office until after the nominating convention.

In early 1972, Sen. Edmund S. Muskie of Maine, the 1968 Democratic nominee for vice president, seemed to be his party's leading candidate. However, the decline in his support, the eclipse of Sen. Hubert H. Humphrey of Minnesota—the 1968 presidential candidate—and the gradual rise of Sen. George McGovern of South Dakota to become the overwhelming Democratic convention choice marked the year for the Democrats.

The liberal and welfare-oriented People's party nominated Dr. Benjamin Spock for president at a convention in St. Louis on July 29. The American party, hoping to nominate Alabama Gov. George C. Wallace until he firmly refused to run, chose Rep. John G. Schmitz, a conservative California Republican, as its candidate.

DEMOCRATIC PARTY

Muskie's early strength brought him 38% of the Arizona delegates on January 29, but Mayor John V. Lindsay of New York received a surprising 24% and McGovern, 20%. In the first preference primary, in New Hampshire on March 7, Muskie felt the first blow to his prestige as he won only 46% of the vote, while McGovern took 37%. Muskie had campaigned in general terms, while McGovern had attacked the Vietnam War and had advocated programs to aid minorities and the poor and to make the tax structure more equitable. In Florida a week later, Governor Wallace, opposing school busing for

This article covers the presidential primaries and national conventions. For the campaigns and results of the November voting, see ELECTIONS.

racial balance and costly federal programs, ran first with 42% of the vote, with Humphrey a distant second. April brought McGovern leads in Wisconsin and—by a majority—in the Kennedy stronghold of Massachusetts.

Sen. Edward M. Kennedy steadfastly insisted that he would not be a candidate. Labor support for Humphrey brought him victories in Pennsylvania and Ohio. Muskie, failing to show strength in the primaries, announced on April 27 that he would remain a candidate but that he did not have sufficient funds to continue in the primaries.

Wallace in May carried Tennessee and North Carolina by majorities but was defeated by Humphrey in West Virginia. On May 15, Wallace received paralyzing gunshot wounds in an attempted assassination as he campaigned in Maryland, but the next day he carried Michigan by a majority and Maryland by a plurality over Humphrey, McGovern, and Muskie. Unacceptable to Northern liberals, Wallace received strong support from white workers.

Thereafter, McGovern led in all primaries—in Oregon, Rhode Island, California, New Mexico, and New York. California's winner-take-all primary on June 6 gave him 271 delegate votes from a plurality of 44% and made him the unquestioned leader for the nomination. Other candidates included black liberal Rep. Shirley Chisholm (N. Y.); Sen. Henry M. Jackson (Wash.); and former North Carolina Gov. Terry Sanford.

Convention and Platform. Reform of the party's rules gave the national convention, which opened in Miami Beach on July 10, a younger, less affluent, and less experienced attendance. Rule changes had required the selection of delegates on the basis of racial, ethnic, and sexual balance. Of the delegates, 40% were women, 21% were under 30, and 25% were black. Many old-line politicians felt excluded, and there was talk of a divided party.

McGovern won the nomination on the first ballot with 1,715.35 votes—before switches for the final tabulation—well above the 1,509 required. A last-minute stop-McGovern movement that centered on an effort to distribute 151 of his California votes to delegates representing other primary candidates failed. Senator Jackson, to whom some labor delegates turned, received 534 votes; Wallace, 385.7; Chisholm, 151.95; Sanford, 77.5; and a scattering for others. Humphrey and Muskie had withdrawn.

After refusals from Kennedy, Sen. Abraham Ribicoff, and Gov. Reubin Askew of Florida—McGovern selected Sen. Thomas F. Eagleton, a Missouri liberal with close ties to labor, for vice presi-

DEMOCRATIC National Committee headquarters, Washington, D.C., scene of controversial Watergate affair.

dent. By July 25, however, Eagleton had revealed that he had on three occasions sought psychiatric treatment and that he had not informed McGovern of this before the nomination. After insisting that he would remain on the ticket and after various declarations of support by McGovern, Eagleton appeared with McGovern in Washington to resign the nomination. At McGovern's suggestion, the national committee on August 8 nominated R. Sargent Shriver, former ambassador to France and a brother-in-law of Senator Kennedy, to replace Eagleton.

The Democratic platform set a note for "new directions, '72–76." It pledged "immediate total withdrawal of all Americans from Southeast Asia" to end the war; reduced military spending; a commitment to provide Israel with equipment for deterrent strength; and return "to Congress, and to the people, a meaningful role in decision on peace and war." The platform also committed Democrats to full employment, reform of tax preferences, direct election of the president, firm law enforcement, and numerous social reforms. It supported "equalization in spending among school districts" and "the goal of desegregation as a means to achieve equal access to quality education," with transportation (busing) of students "another tool to accomplish desegregation."

Despite a dramatic appearance in a wheelchair by Wallace, the convention refused to support a platform plank against school busing for racial balance and planks advocating voluntary school prayers, the right to bear arms, a strong military defense, and remaining in Vietnam until prisoners of war were released. It also rejected liberal proposals for freedom of choice in abortion and for a guaranteed minimum income of $6,500 for a family of four.

Convention delegates adopted a plan to more than double the size of the national committee, which was authorized to call a conference in 1974 to consider proposals for party reorganization that would have to be approved by the 1976 convention. The committee accepted McGovern's choice of Mrs. Jean Westwood of Utah as its chairman, the first woman to head a major party. In December, after resisting attempts to oust her, she resigned and was replaced by Robert Strauss of Texas.

REPUBLICAN PARTY

The Nixon presidency brought remarkable activity in foreign policy. The reduction of American military personnel in Vietnam helped ease domestic tensions, and visits to Communist China and the USSR enhanced his popularity. In domestic policy President Nixon pressed for enlarged programs in social and environmental improvement, employment, housing, inflation control, and increased opportunity for minorities and women.

Preconvention Campaign. Partly to bring pressure on the President to move toward their views, some liberal and conservative Republicans supported token presidential candidates. Republican Congressman Paul McCloskey of California, advocating withdrawal from Vietnam and emphasis on domestic social legislation, and conservative Representative John M. Ashbrook of Ohio entered several primaries but received little support. McCloskey made his best showing on March 7 in New Hampshire, receiving 20% of the vote. He withdrew from the campaign on March 10.

Convention and Platform. As expected, controversy was minimal at the Republican national convention, which opened in Miami Beach on August 21. The President had announced in June that he wanted Spiro T. Agnew to continue as vice president. To maximize television interest in the absence of suspense, there were filmed tributes to Mrs. Nixon, the late President Eisenhower, and Nixon himself.

Opinion polls through the year reported the President well ahead of Democratic opposition, but party leaders warned against complacency and called for a vigorous campaign. Of the 1,348 delegates to the convention, 30% were women (up from 17% in 1968), 8% were under 30, and 4% were black.

At the opening session Gov. Ronald Reagan of California declared that McGovern's nomination for president "disenfranchised millions of Democrats." In an expansion of the traditional keynote address, the convention heard a trio of speakers, including Sen. Edward W. Brooke of Massachusetts. Brooke, refraining from attacking McGovern, said that Nixon has "done more to establish a lasting peace than any president . . . in our lifetime."

GEORGE WALLACE, victim of a would-be assassin's bullets, addresses Democratic convention from wheelchair.

DEMOCRATIC presidential nominee George McGovern poses (above) with his rivals in the primaries and his vice presidential choice Thomas Eagleton, at far left; and (left) with Sargent Shriver, who replaced Eagleton.

The only floor dispute in the convention arose over proposals from large states and urban areas that more delegates in 1976 be assigned in proportion to the number of Republican votes cast. The convention voted to continue to give bonus delegates to states that cast Republican majorities. Smaller states thereby retained an advantage in the number of their possible delegates.

New York's Gov. Nelson Rockefeller placed President Nixon's name in nomination and was followed by 11 brief seconding speeches designed to show a cross-section of support. Delegates renominated the president on August 22 by 1,347 votes to 1 for McCloskey and renominated Agnew the following night. In his acceptance speech, the President asked for "a new American majority bound together by our common ideals" and emphasized his belief in the American system. He said that "one of the clearest choices of this campaign" was the difference in the philosophy of the opponents. Demonstrators in the streets were unable to disrupt the last night of the convention; 1,129 of them were arrested by local police.

The Republican platform, styled to the President's policies, added fuel to the campaign by unusually strong language. The choice, it declared, "is between moderate goals . . . and far-out goals of the far left." It stated that "the national Democratic Party has been seized by a radical clique which scorns our nation's past and would blight her future." The "New Democratic Left would undercut our defenses" and "retreat into virtual isolation." The party supported a volunteer army, mutual arms limitation, and full employment. It pledged "to spread the tax burden equitably" and supported basic medical care through insurance "financed by employers, employees, and the federal government," but it opposed a "nationalized compulsory" approach. Pledging equitable financing of quality education and "ending *de jure* school segregation," it opposed "busing for racial balance."

The platform supported law enforcement with justice for everyone, rehabilitation of offenders, and control of drug abuse. It promised "fair prices" for farmers, urban development, low and moderate income housing, and the preservation of natural resources. The party also pledged to support equal rights for women and improved opportunities for children, older citizens, veterans, and minorities.

In foreign policy, the platform emphasized "a full generation of peace" with "a strategy of national strength" and "a new sense of international partnership." It pledged to seek a Vietnam War settlement that would permit Southeast Asians to live under governments "of their own choosing," but insisted that U. S. prisoners be returned before complete withdrawal of forces.

In December, Sen. Robert Dole resigned as national chairman, and George Bush, U. S. ambassador to the United Nations, was named to replace him.

FRANKLIN L. BURDETTE, *University of Maryland*

POMPIDOU, Georges. See BIOGRAPHY.

(Left) *John D. Rockefeller 3d, chairman, reports findings of the President's Commission on Population.* (Above) *Emblem for United Nations' World Population Year 1974.*

WIDE WORLD

POPULATION

The population of the world, estimated at almost 3.8 billion in mid-1972, continued to increase at about 2.0% per year. As before, the rate of increase was typically high in underdeveloped nations and much lower in those with developed economies, ranging from a high of 3.4% in Morocco and Rhodesia down to 1.0% in the United States and fractions of 1% in most of the countries of Europe. Since mortality is relatively low throughout the world, differences in rates of population growth depend mainly on fertility.

BIRTHS PER 1,000 POPULATION, SELECTED COUNTRIES, 1960–1972

	1960–64[2]	1965–69[2]	1970	1971	1972[3]
Eastern Europe					
USSR	22.4	17.6	17.5	17.0	17.4
Bulgaria	16.9	15.8	16.3	17.0	16.3
Czechoslovakia	16.3	15.5	15.8	15.5	15.8
East Germany	17.4	15.1	13.9	14.0	13.9
Hungary	13.6	14.3	14.7	15.0	14.7
Poland	20.1	16.6	16.8	16.3	16.8
Western Europe					
Austria	18.5	17.3	15.2	16.5	15.2
Belgium	17.1	15.4	14.7	14.6	14.7
England and Wales	17.9	17.2	16.0	17.1[4]	16.2[4]
France	18.0	17.2	16.7	16.7	16.7
West Germany	18.3	16.8	13.3	15.0	13.3
Ireland	21.8	21.5	21.8	21.5	21.8
Netherlands	20.9	19.2	18.3	19.2	18.4
Sweden	14.5	15.0	13.6	13.5	13.7
Switzerland	18.5	17.7	15.8	16.5	15.8
Other Developed Economies					
United States	22.4	18.2	18.2	18.2	17.3
Canada	25.2	18.8	17.4	17.6	17.5
Australia	21.9	19.7	20.5	20.0	20.5
New Zealand	25.9	22.6	22.1	22.5	22.1
Japan	17.2	17.8	18.8	18.0	19.0
Underdeveloped Economies					
Ceylon	35.2	32.1	29.4	32.0	31.0
Thailand[1]	36.9	34.6	46.0	42.0	43.0
Egypt[1]	42.6	39.3	34.9	44.0	44.0
Colombia[1]	39.2	34.7	45.0	44.0	44.0
Ecuador[1]	46.2	40.6	45.0	45.0	45.0
Peru[1]	36.3	38.2	42.0	43.0	42.0
Venezuela[1]	44.3	41.6	38.1	41.0	41.0
El Salvador	48.7	44.4	40.0	47.0	40.0
Guatemala	47.7	43.9	39.0	42.0	43.0
Mexico	44.4	43.4	41.3	42.0	43.0

[1] Based on incomplete registrations. [2] Averages of annual rates.
[3] Preliminary figures. [4] United Kingdom.

TREND IN WORLD BIRTHRATES

The generally downward movement of birthrates throughout the world is indicated in the accompanying table, which gives the number of births per 1,000 population in selected countries, 1960–72. In the socialist countries of eastern Europe, the figure fell to between 15 and 17 in 1972, with significantly lower rates only for East Germany and the Russian population of the USSR. In the capitalist or social-welfare nations of Western Europe, the overall rate is now at about the same level. As in the past, Ireland and the Netherlands have somewhat higher rates and Sweden somewhat lower. The remarkable characteristic, however, is not such relatively small differences but rather the consistency over a wide range of social-economic environments in all of Europe.

Similarly the trend in other developed economies was downward, although generally to rates somewhat higher than the European norm. Except for Japan, these countries have much lower population densities, so that continued population growth does not pose an obvious and immediate problem.

Trends in the underdeveloped countries are more difficult to determine. Some of the largest—such as Communist China, India, or Indonesia—lack adequate statistics, and data in many of the others are only marginally acceptable. To the degree that they can be determined from the available statistics, the trends are ambiguous. In a few small and politically stable areas—among them, Hong Kong, Singapore, South Korea, Taiwan, and Puerto Rico—fertility has fallen significantly. In other countries it apparently rose, although in some cases the rise may have been the consequence only of the improved registration of births. In the main countries of the underdeveloped world, fertility has apparently been more or less stable at rates about double those for the developed nations.

Population growth is thus a world problem, not merely because of the resulting ecological imbalances but because the centers of industrial civilization are being overwhelmed by the far more rapid increase of population in underdeveloped areas.

CONTINUED DOWNSWING IN U. S. BIRTHS

The average number of children in the American family dropped from 2.39 in 1971 to 2.08 in 1972. An average family size of 2.1 children would be required eventually to keep the population static,

VITAL STATISTICS OF SELECTED COUNTRIES

	Estimated population mid-1971[1]	Birthrate per 1,000 population[2]	Death rate per 1,000 population[2]	Current population growth (percent)	Number of years to double population[3]	Population under 15 years (percent)[4]	Population projections to 1985 (millions)[1]	Per capita gross national product (U. S. $)[5]
World...............	3,782,000,000	33	13	2.0	35	37	4,933	...
North America								
Canada...............	22,200,000	17.5	7.3	1.7	41	30	27.3	2,650
Cuba.................	8,700,000	27	8	1.9	37	31	11.0	280
Dominican Republic.....	4,600,000	49	15	3.4	21	47	7.3	280
El Salvador...........	3,700,000	40	10	3.0	23	45	5.9	290
Guatemala.............	5,400,000	43	17	2.6	27	46	7.9	350
Haiti.................	5,500,000	44	20	2.4	29	38	7.9	...[6]
Honduras.............	2,900,000	49	17	3.2	22	47	4.6	260
Mexico...............	54,300,000	43	10	3.3	21	46	84.4	580
Nicaragua.............	2,200,000	46	17	2.9	24	48	3.3	380
Puerto Rico...........	2,900,000	25	7	1.4	50	37	3.4	1,410
United States..........	209,200,000	17.3	9.3	1.0	70	29	246.3	4,240
South America								
Argentina.............	25,000,000	22	9	1.5	47	30	29.6	1,060
Bolivia...............	4,900,000	44	19	2.4	29	42	6.8	160
Brazil................	98,400,000	38	10	2.8	25	43	142.6	270
Chile.................	10,200,000	28	9	1.9	37	39	13.6	510
Colombia.............	22,900,000	44	11	3.4	21	47	35.6	290
Ecuador..............	6,500,000	45	11	3.4	21	48	10.1	240
Paraguay.............	2,600,000	45	11	3.4	21	46	4.1	240
Peru.................	14,500,000	42	11	3.1	23	45	21.6	330
Uruguay..............	3,000,000	21	9	1.2	58	28	3.4	560
Venezuela.............	11,500,000	41	8	3.4	21	47	17.4	1,000
Europe								
Austria...............	7,500,000	15.2	13.4	0.2	347	24	8.0	1,470
Belgium...............	9,800,000	14.7	12.3	0.2	347	24	10.4	2,010
Bulgaria..............	8,700,000	16.3	9.1	0.7	99	23	9.4	860
Czechoslovakia.........	14,900,000	15.8	11.4	0.5	139	24	16.2	1,370
Denmark..............	5,000,000	14.4	9.8	0.5	139	24	5.5	2,310
Finland...............	4,800,000	13.7	9.5	0.4	174	26	5.0	1,980
France................	51,900,000	16.7	10.6	0.7	99	25	57.6	2,460
Germany, East.........	16,300,000	13.9	14.1	0.0	...	15	16.9	1,570
Germany, West........	59,200,000	13.3	11.7	0.2	347	25	62.3	2,190
Greece...............	9,000,000	16.3	8.3	0.8	87	25	9.7	840
Hungary..............	10,400,000	14.7	11.7	0.3	231	21	11.0	1,110
Ireland...............	3,000,000	21.8	11.5	0.7	99	31	3.5	1,110
Italy.................	54,500,000	16.8	9.7	0.7	99	24	60.0	1,400
Netherlands...........	13,300,000	18.4	8.4	1.0	70	27	15.3	1,760
Norway...............	4,000,000	16.6	9.8	0.7	99	25	4.5	2,160
Poland................	33,700,000	16.8	8.2	0.9	77	28	38.2	940
Portugal..............	9,700,000	18.0	9.7	0.8	87	29	10.7	510
Rumania..............	20,800,000	21.2	9.5	1.2	58	26	23.3	860
Spain.................	33,900,000	19.6	8.5	1.0	70	28	38.1	820
Sweden...............	8,200,000	13.7	9.9	0.4	174	21	8.8	2,920
Switzerland...........	6,400,000	15.8	9.1	1.0	70	23	7.4	2,700
United Kingdom........	56,600,000	16.2	11.7	0.5	139	24	61.8	1,890
USSR.................	248,000,000	17.4	8.2	0.9	77	28	286.9	1,200
Yugoslavia............	21,000,000	17.8	9.0	0.9	77	28	23.8	580
Africa								
Algeria...............	15,000,000	50	17	3.3	21	47	23.9	260
Congo (Zaïre)..........	18,300,000	44	23	2.1	33	42	25.8	...[6]
Egypt................	35,900,000	44	16	2.8	25	43	52.3	160
Ethiopia..............	26,200,000	46	25	2.1	33	44	35.7	...[6]
Kenya................	11,600,000	48	18	3.0	23	46	17.9	130
Morocco..............	16,800,000	50	16	3.4	21	46	26.2	190
Nigeria...............	58,000,000	50	25	2.6	27	43	84.7	...[6]
South Africa...........	21,100,000	41	17	2.4	29	40	29.7	710
Sudan................	16,800,000	49	18	3.1	23	47	26.0	110
Tanzania.............	14,000,000	47	22	2.6	27	44	20.3	...[6]
Asia								
Afghanistan...........	17,900,000	51	27	2.4	29	...	25.0	...[6]
Burma................	29,100,000	40	17	2.3	30	40	39.2	...[6]
Ceylon...............	13,200,000	31	8	2.3	30	41	17.7	190
China (Mainland).......	786,100,000	30	13	1.7	41	...	964.6	...[6]
China (Taiwan)........	14,700,000	28	5	2.3	30	43	19.4	300
India.................	584,800,000	42	17	2.5	28	42	807.6	110
Indonesia.............	128,700,000	47	19	2.9	24	44	183.8	100
Iran.................	30,200,000	45	17	2.8	25	46	45.0	350
Japan................	106,000,000	19	7	1.2	58	24	121.3	1,430
Korea, North..........	14,700,000	39	11	2.8	25	...	20.7	280
Korea, South..........	33,700,000	31	11	2.0	35	40	45.9	210
Malaysia..............	14,100,000	37	8	2.8	25	44	16.4	340
Nepal................	11,800,000	45	23	2.2	32	40	15.8	...[6]
Pakistan (and Bangladesh)	146,600,000	51	18	3.3	21	45	224.2	110
Philippines............	40,800,000	45	12	3.3	21	47	64.0	210
Thailand..............	38,600,000	43	10	3.3	21	43	57.7	160
Turkey................	37,600,000	40	15	2.5	28	42	52.8	350
Vietnam, North........	22,000,000	...	...	...	...	...	28.2	...[6]
Vietnam, South........	18,700,000	...	...	...	...	...	23.9	140
Oceania								
Australia..............	13,000,000	20.5	9.0	1.9	37	29	17.0	2,300
New Zealand...........	3,000,000	22.1	8.8	1.7	41	32	3.8	2,230

[1] Estimates from United Nations. [2] Latest available year. North American rates computed by Population Reference Bureau; others from United Nations, adjusted for deficient registration in some countries. [3] Assuming continued growth at current annual rate. [4] Latest available year. Derived from United Nations. [5] 1969 data from International Bank for Reconstruction and Development. [6] Less than U. S. $100.
Source: Population Reference Bureau, Washington, D. C.

but this figure does not yet apply because of the high proportion of persons of childbearing age in the current population—the "boom babies" born in the late 1940's and early 1950's.

It was generally anticipated that the birthrate would rise as members of this exceptionally large cohort began to marry and have children, for even if the size of each family remained the same, the number of families would rise considerably. Indeed, this upswing began in the fall of 1968 but was soon reversed.

The number of births registered in the United States in 1968—some 3.5 million—increased to 3.7 million in 1970 but then dropped, by 4.8%, to fewer than 3.6 million in 1971. Every geographic division except the Mountain states, where there was no change, registered fewer births in 1971 than in the year before. In New York state, birth registrations declined by over 10%, and in New York City, by 11.6%. In contrast to the national trend, ten states —especially Arizona, Utah, West Virginia, and New Mexico—registered more births in 1971 than in the preceding year. But during the first half of 1972 the decline became nationwide. On the basis of the number of births registered during the first six months, there would be an 8.6% decrease in 1972, to a total of about 3.3 million—about a quarter of a million fewer births than were registered the year before.

Reasons for the Decline. Undoubtedly a number of factors contributed to the fall in the birthrate, but two can be taken as the most important —the sluggish economy and the readier access to contraceptive services. The economic recession of 1969–70, allowing for a suitable time lag, corresponded precisely with the falling off in fertility. Because the economy has been recovering its momentum since some time in 1970, an upturn in birthrate might be expected to follow—especially in view of the large number of persons of childbearing age. If that should happen, the number of births per year might increase by about 40% by the end of the 1980's. But any such projection can be only an indication of possibilities, with no assurance that so large an upturn will indeed take place. Any forecast should be based on the demographers' new dictum, "We must expect to be surprised."

Abortions. The reasons for postponing childbearing, whether economic or other, were probably less significant than the radical change in attitudes and laws concerning contraception and, particularly, abortion. According to a Gallup poll in June 1972, 64% of the general public (including 56% of the Catholic respondents) believed that the decision about whether or not to have an abortion should be made exclusively by the patient and her physician. In a similar poll in 1968, only 15% of the respondents had favored such a policy. It would be hard to cite a public issue of comparable importance on which there has been so rapid and so radical a change of public opinion.

In many jurisdictions where only a few years ago abortions were a felony, they are now legal. And in some places there is even a move to have abortions performed at public expense. In 1971 the social service commissioner of New York State issued an order denying any Medicaid payment for an abortion unless it was necessary to maintain the woman's health. This ban, upheld by the New York Court of Appeals, was reversed in August 1972 by a federal court, which held that it was unconstitutional to deny Medicaid payment for any abortion, since this would "deny indigent women the equal protection of the laws."

This decision follows the earlier trend with respect to birth control, which had moved quickly from illegality to a government-funded activity. In the 1972 amendments to various social security programs, federal contributions to family planning were substantially increased. Moreover, if a state failed to provide family-planning services "promptly" to all applicants for Aid to Families with Dependent Children (AFDC), the federal contribution to this welfare program would be cut by 1%. Since the federal government provides 90% of AFDC funds under the current matching formula, such an action would increase the state's cost by almost 10%.

"Natural" Family Planning. The active campaign against "feticide," as opponents term abortion, has been supplemented by organized attempts to improve and popularize the rhythm method of contraception. In the United States this effort to promote what its proponents term "natural" family planning is centered in the Human Life Foundation, founded in 1968 with a grant from the National Conference of Catholic Bishops and based in Washington, D. C. Similar groups exist also in Canada, England, France, Australia, Taiwan, and the Philippines (as well as Mauritius, which is of interest because of the island's especially rapid population increase). Plans are under way to organize these groups into an international association, which could represent the Catholic point of view to world agencies.

Early in 1972 the Human Life Foundation held a three-day conference jointly with the National Institute of Child Health and Human Development, the principal federal agency for funding population research. According to participants, periodic abstinence (the rhythm method) using the best techniques has shown improved results, although it remains less effective than oral or mechanical-chemical contraceptives. In fiscal 1972 the foundation provided more than $70,000 to four research projects on the human menstrual cycle. Their findings might further improve the present efficacy of the rhythm method as a means of family planning.

POPULATION COMMISSION REPORT

The Commission on Population Growth and the American Future, a presidential commission chaired by John D. Rockefeller 3d, issued in 1972 a volume entitled *Population and the American Future*. This report was greeted with considerable fanfare, but its recommendations were in large part obsolete or irrelevant. The commission defined its "immediate goal" as "to encourage the American people to make population choices, both in the individual family and society at large, on the basis of greater rationality rather than tradition or custom, ignorance or chance." "The time has come," the statement continued, "to challenge the tradition that population growth is desirable." The language reflects the mood generated by the high fertility of the post-1945 decade rather than the subsequent unanticipated decline to its present nadir. Though we do not know in detail the reasons for this decline, we can assert with full assurance that a greater dependence on rational family planning has already replaced "tradition or custom, ignorance or chance."

WILLIAM PETERSEN
The Ohio State University

PORTUGAL

Premier Marcello Caetano steered Portugal in an increasingly conservative direction in 1972. Although he had seemed to favor liberalizing trends when he succeeded the conservative António de Oliveira Salazar in 1968, fear of pressure from growing liberal sentiment had evidently altered his views. Consequently the wars in Portuguese Africa continued to strain the budget, and the unreformed economy continued to founder.

The Election. Caetano maintained control of the National Popular Action, the only legal party in Portugal, which, as the National Union party, had supported Salazar. Caetano's friends had urged him to arrange for his own election or that of a close associate as president, thus virtually combining the premiership and the presidency, but the military reportedly would have proposed its own candidate rather than accept a civilian as commander. Caetano finally decided to support for a third term the 77-year-old incumbent, Adm. Américo Thomaz, who represented the military and banking establishments created by Salazar, and with whom Caetano had worked well. On July 25 a special electoral college chose Thomaz with no opposition.

Liberal circles viewed the election pessimistically, regarding it as Caetano's coming to terms with the forces that had supported Salazar. Some more violent dissidents caused the explosion of 18 time bombs on August 8, the day of Thomaz' inauguration, resulting in the disruption of electricity in Lisbon and other centers. There was speculation that the sabotage was the work of Communists or of right-wing activists who wanted to force Caetano to take more repressive measures against the opposition or possibly to prepare for a military coup. Thomaz, in his inaugural address, sanctioned by Caetano, gave a rather pessimistic picture of Portugal's situation, domestic and overseas.

Church and Press. Antonio Ferreira Gomes, Bishop of Oporto and Portugal's leading liberal churchman, in a New Year's Day address, denounced war in general but obviously referred to his country's military action in Angola, Mozambique, and Portuguese Guinea. The bishop's speech was considered near heresy in Portugal, which has not permitted criticism of the armed forces, and censors delayed its publication by more than a week. Ferreira Gomes—once banished by Salazar, but reinstated by Caetano—received spirited replies from the chief chaplain of the armed forces, Bishop Antonio dos Rios Rodrigues, and from Armando Reborado e Silva, former navy chief of staff. The latter, speaking in the National Assembly on March 8, with the approval of Caetano, called Ferreira Gomes anti-Portuguese and denounced him for having "unjustly and wrongly treated" Portugal's armed forces. Liberal Catholics interpreted the attack as part of Caetano's shift from more liberal views.

As another example of Caetano's growing conservatism, the National Assembly, which he dominated, declared a "state of subversion." On May 5 it decreed rigid new controls of the press.

Education. Before 1972, Portugal had announced ambitious new education programs. In the spring of 1972 the government doubled the educational budget, although the expenditure would still amount to only 3% of the gross national product, the lowest percentage in western Europe. This increase was reckoned sufficient, however, to raise the years of compulsory education from six to eight and to begin work on three new universities. The plan included creation of a system of technical schools to convert peasants into skilled industrial workers. But because of the slow-moving Portuguese bureaucracy, it was doubtful that the program could be carried out on schedule.

Economics. There had also been plans for ambitious economic reforms and development. To put them into effect, Caetano had brought into his cabinet several vigorous young economists and technocrats. Involved were an easing of price controls, a weakening of monopolies, construction of a large new port at Sines and a shipyard at Setúbal, and expansion of the steel and petrochemical industries and the already large tourist industry. But as the year progressed, the program was described as moving at only a "glacial pace." Caetano removed from office several men who had been expected to carry it out.

Chief causes of the slowdown were obstruction by the military and the 11-year-old colonial wars, which were devouring 42% of the national budget and tying down 150,000 men. Also important was the continued emigration of young men to escape depressed conditions and four years of compulsory military service. Their loss was seriously reducing the labor supply and raising production costs.

Foreign Relations. On Dec. 10, 1971, Portugal signed an executive agreement with the United States extending American base rights in the Azores. The agreement was not in the form of a treaty, and details were not made public. In June 1972, the U. S. Senate Foreign Relations Committee slashed $550 million from an administration request for military aid, partly because the President had not submitted certain documents on the agreement to the Senate.

CHARLES E. NOWELL, *University of Illinois*

PORTUGAL · Information Highlights

Official Name: Portuguese Republic.
Area: 35,553 square miles (92,082 sq km).
Population (1972 est.): 9,700,000. *Density,* 272 per square mile (105 per sq km). *Annual rate of increase,* 0.8%.
Chief Cities (1968 est.): Lisbon, the capital, 828,000; Oporto, 324,400.
Government: *Head of state,* Américo Thomaz, president (took office June 1958). *Head of government,* Marcello Caetano, premier (took office Sept. 1968). *Legislature*—National Assembly (unicameral), 130 members. *Official political party*—Acção Nacional Popular.
Language: Portuguese (official).
Education: *Expenditure* (1967), 7.9% of total public expenditure. *School enrollment* (1968)—primary, 961,546; secondary, 378,277; technical/vocational, 151,572; university/higher, 42,560.
Monetary Unit: Escudo (27.02 escudos equal U. S.$1, Aug. 1972).
Gross National Product (1971 est.): $6,500,000,000.
National Income per Person (1970): $610.
Economic Indexes: *Industrial production* (1970), 172 (1963= 100); *agricultural production* (1971), 125 (1952–56=100); *consumer price index* (1971), 163 (1963=100).
Manufacturing (major products): Processed foods, canned fish, wine, electronics, textiles, ships, cork.
Major Agricultural Products: Grapes, potatoes, wheat, figs (ranks 1st among world producers, 1970), olives, forest products, fish.
Major Minerals: Coal, iron ore, wolframite, beryl, copper.
Foreign Trade (1971): *Exports,* $1,034,000 (chief exports—wine, cork, fish). *Imports,* $1,770,000,000 (chief imports, 1969—nonelectrical machinery, food, chemicals, transport equipment). *Chief trading partners* (1969)—United Kingdom (took 21% of exports, supplied 14% of imports); Angola (13%—9%); West Germany (6%—16%); United States (9%—5%).
Tourism: *Receipts* (1970), $222,000,000.
Transportation: *Motor vehicles* (1970), 668,100 (automobiles, 581,000); *railroads* (1970), 2,238 miles (3,602 km); *merchant fleet* (1971), 926,000 gross registered tons; *major national airline,* TAP (Transportes Aereos Portugueses).
Communications: *Telephones* (1971), 749,963; *television stations* (1971), 8; *television sets* (1971), 360,000; *radios* (1969), 1,406,000; *newspapers* (1967), 29 (daily circulation, 674,000).

SPEEDING THE MAIL

Automated processing of bulk mail began in this Kearny, N. J., mail distribution plant in June 1972. The flow of mail is monitored by closed-circuit television (*above*). Packages on conveyor belts (*left*) are punched with ZIP codes that tell the system where to drop them.

POSTAL SERVICE

The first complete year of the new U. S. Postal Service was not an unqualified success. Some gains were made in the areas of fiscal responsibility but often at the expense of the quality of service. Public complaints increased at a rapid rate. On the other hand, Postmaster General Elmer T. Klassen cited personnel administration improvement, the development of delivery standards, the introduction of new methods of handling mail, and the reduction of the work force. Other supporters, notably congressmen, suggested that one year was too short a time for a fair evaluation of a system that had replaced one created in Benjamin Franklin's day.

Rates. In June 1972, the Postal Rate Commission recommended and the service accepted that the 8-cent cost for first-class mail and the 11-cent rate for air mail, put into effect in May 1971, be made permanent. The commission also recommended an increase in the second-class rate paid for newspapers and magazines, but at a figure less than requested, and the maintenance of the 6-cent rate for postcards. In addition the commission proposed the immediate application to third-class mail of the highest rate of what had been a proposed five-year plan of escalating rates.

In August 1972, the postmaster general announced that there would be no request for new increases in fiscal 1973. However, he warned that collective bargaining negotiations for new contracts to take effect in July 1973 might force the system to request increases for fiscal 1974. He explained that no increases were needed in fiscal 1973 because of the reduction of Postal Service personnel by 33,000 employees through attrition and early retirement, saving $375 million per year. In fiscal 1972, the Postal Service showed a gross income of $9.4 billion while it spent $9.5 billion in the same period. Some 87.2 billion pieces of mail were delivered from 37,722 U. S. post offices.

Competition. The Postal Service in 1972 showed an increasing concern about the competition from private delivery firms. Some utility companies were hand-delivering bills. Other large mailers were experimenting with other methods, such as the use of milk companies to deliver the mail at the same time as milk. The private United Parcel Service for the first time delivered more parcels than did the Postal Service, provided better service, and showed a profit of $30 million.

In order to compete successfully, the mail unions suggested a second delivery attempt when the customer is not at home, parcel pickups at business establishments sending large numbers of packages, and late shifts at the post office.

Service. Length of time for delivery is still the most frequent complaint despite the Postal Service's contention that 95% of the mail was delivered on time.

The cutback of mail pickup, the reduction of many deliveries to business and residential areas, the failure of the ZIP code system to live up to its promise, and the introduction of a complicated new system of mailbox pickup contributed to the disenchantment of the customer. In addition, while the concentration of mail sorting in centralized locations may have increased the overall efficiency of the Postal Service, the public was not convinced. This points up that most of the changes made were not adequately explained to the public.

Labor Relations. Labor-management relations were exacerbated by the reduction of the work force and the change in work practices. The tendency of local postmasters to pass along personnel and work practice problems to top management, as well as a quickly developing backlog of unsettled grievances, were characteristic of the new employee relations system. Also coming into play was the use for the first time of the services of the National Labor Relations Board by federal employees and arbitration as the final step in the grievance procedure. Procedures for agreeing to local level memorandums of understanding were not successful. The right-to-strike was being advocated by postal unions in order to make collective bargaining more effective. At the end of the year, merger discussions were under way among the letter carriers, the postal workers, and the communications workers.

The postal unions were using the strike ban as a reason for continuing agitation for legislative action, much to the chagrin of members of Congress who thought that collective bargaining had eliminated personnel administration problems as a legislative concern. The unions campaigned for modification of the Hatch Act so as to allow greater participation in the political process.

Progress. Not all the developments in the new postal system were discouraging. The Postal Service had technically balanced its profit-loss statement, standards were being developed for delivery, and customers were beginning to get the idea that their cooperation was needed.

Through the bargaining process unions highlighted the problem areas of morale and service. The unsettled issues carried over from the pioneer contract negotiations of 1971 were resolved in January. Management training was increased, and management promotion was being made more frequently on merit and from the ranks. Over 800 post offices were modernized and made safer and more efficient. Plans to upgrade 10,000 existing post offices and build 2,000 new buildings at a cost of $1 billion were announced. In order to compete with private parcel delivery systems, a $250 million capital bond issue was floated to finance the construction of 21 bulk mail facilities.

In 1973, new negotiations for union contracts were to take place that would undoubtedly raise new problems of finance and administration. In the 1970 legislation, Congress retained the right to oversee the new system, and it conducted hearings in 1972. Similar hearings in 1973 could be longer and more significant if promised improvements do not come about and if the customer continues to believe that he is "paying more for less."

HARVEY L. FRIEDMAN
University of Massachusetts

POTTER, Philip A. See BIOGRAPHY.
POVERTY. See SOCIAL WELFARE.

POUND, Ezra

American poet: b. Hailey, Idaho, Oct. 30, 1885; d. Venice, Italy, Nov. 1, 1972.

Ezra Pound remains the most controversial of the literary giants of this century. From the beginning of his short-lived professional career as a teacher of romance philology at Wabash College (a post from which he was fired, after only a few months, on suspicion of moral turpitude) to his incarceration 40 years later for allegedly treasonous activity, Pound found himself continually embroiled in controversy. Even during his 13-year confinement in St. Elizabeth's Hospital for the criminally insane, Washington, D. C., he continued to be the subject of heated controversy.

In 1949, Pound was awarded the Bollingen Prize for poetry, an act which caused an outcry of indignation matched only by that of his supporters when, a few months before his death, he was denied the Emerson-Thoreau Medal of the American Academy of Arts and Sciences by reason of his anti-Semitism and fascism. Even though 23 years had passed, the issue and the man were as controversial as ever.

Even apart from his eccentric, if not treasonous, ideologies, Pound's poetry and poetics, though admired and emulated by many, continue to be roundly condemned by others as willfully obscure. There seems little question, however, that as well as being the most controversial, Ezra Pound is the single most influential figure in modern literature.

Life and Works. While yet a teenager, Pound resolved that by the time he reached 30 he would know more about poetry than any man living, that he would know "what was accounted poetry everywhere, what part of poetry was 'indestructible,' what part could not be lost by translation . . . what effects were obtainable in one language only and were utterly incapable of being translated." Accordingly, he prepared at the University of Pennsylvania and Hamilton College for a teaching career in romance languages. But in 1907, after his brief, unhappy encounter with teaching at Wabash College, Pound journeyed to Europe, where he was to spend most of the rest of his life. His first book of verse, *A Lume Spento,* was published in Venice in 1908. In that same year he settled in London.

Pound remained in London from 1908 to 1920, publishing translations of Italian and Provençal poetry and adaptations from Chinese poems. He also published *Homage to Sextus Propertius* (1917) and *Hugh Selwyn Mauberley* (1920), two of his most important poems. It was during this time that he served as London representative for *Poetry* magazine and, later, *The Little Review,* posts which enabled him to promote the work of his fellow writers.

It was during the London years that Pound began to write *The Cantos,* sections of which have been published at intervals since 1925 and which remained unfinished at his death. This long, discursive poem deals with subjects ranging from aesthetics to economics and evokes civilizations and traditions from the ancient Chinese to modern American.

In 1920, Pound moved to Paris, where he became acquainted with Joyce and Hemingway, among others. Five years later he settled in Rapallo, Italy, which was to be his home for the next 20 years and where he continued to work on *The Cantos.* He became increasingly interested in eco-

EZRA POUND (1885–1972)

"... the single most influential figure in modern literature."

nomic questions and openly condemned governments he felt were supporting systems of usury. This position, concerning which he became progressively more outspoken, led to charges of anti-Semitism and fascism. His pro-Fascist radio broadcasts from Italy, after the U.S. declaration of war against that country, led to his indictment for treason. He was confined to a detention center at Pisa in 1945, from which he was subsequently transferred to St. Elizabeth's Hospital in Washington, D.C., in 1946. When he was finally released in 1958, through the efforts of a number of prominent literary friends, he returned to Italy, where he remained until his death.

In addition to his poetry and translations, Pound is noted for his *Guide to Kulchur* (1938), *Literary Essays* (1954), and *Impact* (1960), a collection of essays on history and money. His interest in Confucius, developing over a period of years, resulted in his translation of the Confucian canon during his period of confinement, and he published three volumes of Confucian works in the 1950's.

Significance. Pound's influence on the course of literature in the 20th century has been profound. He, more than anyone else, defined and determined the direction it was to take, largely through the force of his own personality. There is scarcely a significant literary movement in the century that did not feel his effect, from Imagism to Vorticism and beyond, and there was scarcely a major writer he did not befriend and encourage when few others would. He went to great lengths to assure the health and safety of Joyce's family and the promotion of Joyce's work and took an active part in the shaping of Eliot's great poem *The Waste Land*.

Pound's early encouragement of Frost, Hemingway, Eliot, and Joyce is a matter of record; no less so is his influence on the elder figures of his day, notably Ford Madox Ford and Yeats. But one suspects that his true legacy lies—however ironic it may

seem in the light of his stormy life—in the pervasive and positive effect he had upon his country's culture. Pound exiled himself from his country the better to see it for what it was, its strengths as well as its weaknesses. His vision, however faulty or impaired it may have been at times, described for us the era in which we now find ourselves.

DANIEL R. BARNES
The Ohio State University

PRINCE EDWARD ISLAND

During 1972, the economy of Prince Edward Island weakened following a decline in income from agriculture and fishing. Employment remained steady, influenced by increased government spending on residential and institutional construction. The provincial budget rose 14% to a record $112 million, with capital expenditures 13% higher than in 1971.

Industrial Development. Industrial Enterprises Inc., a crown corporation for financing new industries, extended its operations to research, promotion, and management assistance. The change reflected new policies in the island's department of industry following a revision of the Federal-Provincial Island Development Plan, which called for more emphasis on industry to absorb workers released because of the reorganization of labor in agriculture and fishing.

Legislation. The 1972 legislature passed a new education act, completing the Foundation Program to consolidate the school system and equalize the treatment given to urban and rural students. The age of majority was lowered from 21 to 18. The minimum wage for women was raised to $1.10 per hour compared with $1.50 for men.

Farming and Fishing. The government initiated a plan for capital grants to family farms undertaking expansion. Improvement of port facilities under a federal-provincial agreement continued in 1972. These capital expenditures offset the effects of a further decline in potato prices, crop failures caused by a severe late spring frost, and ice damage to inshore shellfish and fishing equipment.

R. F. NEILL, *Carleton University*

—PRINCE EDWARD ISLAND · Information Highlights—

Area: 2,184 square miles (5,656 sq km).
Population: 111,641 (1971 census)
Chief Cities (1971 census): Charlottetown, the capital (19,-133); Summerside (9,439).
Government: *Chief officers* (1972)—lt. gov., J. George McKay; premier, Alexander B. Campbell (Liberal); prov. secy. and min. of finance, T. Earle Hickey (L); atty. gen. and min. of educ., Gordon L. Bennett (L); chief justice, C. St. Clair Trainor. *Legislature*—Legislative Assembly, 32 members (27 Liberal, 5 Progressive–Conservative).
Education: *School enrollment* (1968–69)—public elementary and secondary, 29,217 pupils (1,397 teachers); Indian (federal) schools, 53 pupils (2 teachers); college, 1,555 students. *Public school expenditures* (1971 est.)—$8,-282,000; average teacher's salary (1968–69) $5,000.
Public Finance (fiscal year 1972 est.): *Revenues,* $90,000,000 (sales tax, $17,700,000; income tax, $6,000,000; federal funds, $52,100,000). *Expenditures,* $95,300,000 (education, $26,400,000; health and social welfare, $27,300,000.
Personal Income (1969 est.): $200,000,000.
Social Welfare (fiscal 1972 est.): $8,800,000 (aged and blind, $2,600,000; dependents and unemployed, $4,900,000).
Manufacturing (1968): Value added by manufacture, $16,-569,000 (food and beverages, $11,370,000).
Agriculture (1971): *Cash farm income,* $39,104,000 (livestock and products, $23,757,000; crops, $13,775,000). *Chief crop* (cash receipts)—potatoes, $10,208,000.
Fisheries (1971): *Commercial catch* (salt water fish), 97,-501,000 pounds ($9,425,000). *Leading species*—lobster, 8,195,000 pounds ($5,861,000); redfish, 18,354,000 pounds ($679,000).
Transportation: *Roads* (1968), 3,280 miles (5,278 km); *motor vehicles* (1969), 38,812; *licensed airports* (1970), 2.
Communications: *Telephones* (1969), 32,357; *television stations* (1971), 1; *daily newspapers* (1971), 3.
(All figures given in Canadian dollars.)

PRISONS

U. S. prisons continued to be troubled in 1972. Strikes, riots, demonstrations, or violence occurred in jails and prisons in Arizona, California, Connecticut, Kentucky, Maryland, Massachusetts, Minnesota, New Jersey, New York, Ohio, and Washington, D. C. Institutions of all kinds, including some in the Federal Prison System, were involved.

Court Rulings. Federal District Judge Robert R. Merhige, Jr., ordered Virginia prison officials to put an end to a number of unusually harsh prison practices used in that state, such as bread and water diets and direct corporal punishment. Judge Merhige ruled that such practices violated "the most common notions of due process and humane treatment."

A three-judge panel characterized the entire Philadelphia prison system as a failure. The panel claimed that the system violated the constitutional rights of the prisoners to protection from cruel and unusual punishment, due process of law, freedom of speech, and the assistance of counsel.

San Quentin. Living conditions were by no means eased at San Quentin prison in California during 1972, following the violence of the preceding year. In August 1971, a number of inmates and employees of the prison had been killed in a riot that erupted over the alleged escape attempt of one of the prisoners. In December 1972, the New York *Times* reported that since the killings, prisoners in San Quentin had come under tighter control, guards had become more militant, and "the polarization of all races is almost complete."

A single incident in the prison could easily produce racial warfare, according to Associate Warden James Park. He said, "When we have a hit (assault), the first thing we try to find out now is not who did it, but if the color of the man running was the same as the man who is down. If the man down is black and the man running is black we're all right. But if the man down is black and the one running is white, then we know we're in for trouble. We know that we'll have a killing before the day is over. That's how it is now."

Park called attention to the existence of a "new type of prisoner" at San Quentin. According to Park, "It used to be that when we got a man he recognized that he had done something wrong and he accepted coming here as punishment. But its not that way anymore. Now we get what they call political prisoners. They say that its society's fault that they are here. It doesn't make any difference whether they were caught robbing or stealing or assaulting someone or what.... They say they are political prisoners and they have this revolutionary ethic. Some of them would just as soon kill a guard if he turned his back on them." Warden Park added, "Most of those who consider themselves political prisoners are non-white."

Gov. Ronald Reagan announced plans to close San Quentin, which was built in 1852, and to transfer the most troublesome inmates to two 400-man maximum security facilities. Opposition to the construction of these new "super maximum" security prisons soon developed. Some held that these prisons would be extremely costly and, with the state's prison population dropping, space could be found in existing institutions. Others insisted that the new prisons would amount to "concentration camps" for black and Chicano prisoners.

THE NEW YORK TIMES

INMATE chats with his son during the first father-son picnic at Green Haven prison, New York State's largest maximum-security facility.

Attica. In late 1972, the New York State Special Commission on Attica, chaired by Robert McKay, dean of the New York University School of Law, reported on its investigation of the September 1971 Attica prison revolt, during which 30 prisoners and 10 hostages were killed, making it the most violent prison revolt in U. S. history. Among the commission's conclusions were the following:

Contrary to popular views, the Attica uprising was neither a long-planned revolutionary plot nor a proletarian revolution against the capitalist system.

Rather than being revolutionary conspirators bent only on destruction, the Attica rebels were part of a new breed of younger, more aware inmates, largely black, who came to prison full of deep feelings of alienation and hostility against the established institutions of law and government, enhanced self-esteem, racial pride, and political awareness, and an unwillingness to accept the petty humiliations and racism that characterize prison life.

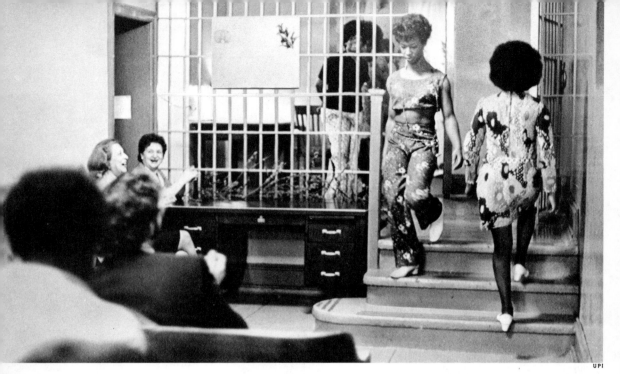

FASHION SHOW is put on in a New Jersey jail by women inmates who sewed the clothes they are modeling before correction officers and their wives.

Like the urban ghetto disturbances of the 1960's, the Attica uprising was the product of frustrated hopes and unfulfilled expectations, after efforts to bring about meaningful change had failed.

The uprising began as a spontaneous burst of violent anger and was not planned or organized in advance; the relative ease with which the inmates took control of large areas of the prison was due not to a preconceived plan but to a combination of fortuitous circumstances. . . .

More fundamentally, if future Atticas are to be avoided, correction personnel must stop looking for individual scapegoats and concentrate on major efforts to train officers to understand and deal with the new breed of inmates, to eliminate the petty harassments and root out the racist attitudes which these inmates will never tolerate, and accelerate programs to make prisons—as long as they must exist—more humane environments for men to live in.

Many of the men who were at Attica at the time of the riot were transferred to other prisons, and the prison population was reduced from 2,250 to 1,200 by mid-summer 1972. In July, 900 of these men held a three-day work-hunger strike. A state of emergency was declared but there was no violence by inmates or staff. The inmates were allowed to present a list of 11 "demands" that included the reopening of the prison commissary, which had been destroyed in the September riot; a review of parole board practices; and the establishment of a liaison between the new superintendent and the prisoners committee. The inmates also wanted to ascertain the validity of a constitution they had drawn up after the September riot. Corrections Commissioner Russell G. Oswald had announced earlier that although he had signed an agreement to implement 26 of the original demands of the Attica prisoners, he did not consider himself bound by that agreement since the inmates had not released the hostages unharmed.

Two Attica inmates who were allowed to testify in February 1972 before the Select Committee on Crime of the U. S. House of Representatives complained of continuing harassment and brutality by guards against alleged participants in the 1971 riot. Inmate Frank Lott testified, "The only change is

we've been getting two spoons of sugar at each meal. Everything else is worse."

In March 1972, Commissioner Oswald reported that while budgetary requests to have more guards and to provide them with special equipment had been approved, his department's budget had been cut $22 million by the state legislature. Most of the funds eliminated were earmarked for inmate "rehabilitation programs."

Commissioner Oswald also reported during 1972 that selection of the site for a new "maximum program, maximum security" prison had been narrowed to two choices; that 339 new guards had been recruited, largely "because of the militant tendency of some inmates"; that "thousands of gas masks have been distributed to the institutions of this department"; and that bidding had begun for "new diversified metal detectors." Improvements for inmates, said Mr. Oswald, were "better nutritional standards, an increase in the number of showers allowed prisoners, the establishment of inmate liaison committees, an expanded clothing issue, and a better provision of toilet tissue."

Reform Efforts. In a number of states, complaints were brought to federal courts in an effort to provide constitutional rights to prisoners in such procedures as prison disciplinary and parole-board hearings.

Expanded use of probation and local correction facilities continued to reduce the population of some state prisons. In Massachusetts, Dr. Jerome G. Miller, commissioner of youth services, succeeded in closing all prisons for juveniles and redistributing the institutional population to community corrections facilities. Only about 30 youths, considered dangerous juvenile offenders, remained in close confinement. Penologists around the country were studying the results of this effort at real prison reform.

DAVID A. WARD
University of Minnesota

PRIZES AND AWARDS

Several new prizes announced in 1972 were expected to take their places among the world's most coveted awards. The Institute of Life Prize, a $50,000 award for outstanding contributions to the life sciences, funded by a donation from the French electricity system, was won by René Dubos, retired microbiologist of Rockefeller University. Recipients of other new awards included Alfred Lunt and Lynn Fontanne, who jointly won the National Artist Award of the American National Theater and Academy, and Chancellor Willy Brandt of West Germany, 1971's Nobel Peace Prize recipient, who won the Reinhold Niebuhr Award of the Reinhold Niebuhr Fund for achievement in the areas of social justice, public life, or world affairs.

A selected list of the most important and newsworthy prizes and awards announced in 1972 follows.

NOBEL PRIZES

Nobel Prizes were awarded in 1972 in literature, chemistry, physics, physiology or medicine, and economics, but no peace prize was given. The awards, each worth about $100,-000, were presented on Dec. 10, 1972, by Crown Prince Carl Gustaf of Sweden, standing in for the ailing King Gustaf VI. Heinrich Böll, West German novelist and playwright, was awarded the literature prize for his contributions to "a renewal of German literature." (For a separate article on Böll, see BIOGRAPHY.)

Chemistry. The 1972 Nobel Prize in chemistry was shared by three Americans, who were cited for their fundamental contributions to enzyme chemistry: 56-year-old Christian Boehmer Anfinsen of the National Institutes of Health at Bethesda, Md.; 59-year-old Stanford Moore of Rockefeller University in New York City; and 61-year-old William Howard Stein, also of Rockefeller University. Working with the enzyme ribonuclease, Anfinsen, Moore, and Stein "illuminated some of the most important principles describing the relation between the chemical structure and the catalytic activity of an enzyme."

Physics. The 1972 Nobel Prize in physics also was shared by three Americans: 64-year-old John Bardeen of the University of Illinois in Urbana, who was the first man to win two Nobel Prizes in the same field; 42-year-old Leon N. Cooper of Brown University; and 41-year-old John Robert Schrieffer of the University of Pennsylvania. The three scientists were cited for their jointly developed theory of superconductivity, known as the BCS theory, which explains why certain metals and alloys lose all resistance to an electric current when chilled to extremely low temperatures.

Physiology or Medicine. The 1972 Nobel Prize in physiology or medicine was shared by Gerald M. Edelman, a 43-year-old molecular biologist at Rockefeller University, and Rodney Robert Porter, a 55-year-old professor of biochemistry at Oxford University, for their separate research on the chemical structure of antibodies. In granting the award, the Nobel Committee stated that their work "incited a fervent research activity . . . in all fields of immunologic science."

Economics. The 1972 Nobel Prize in economics also was shared by an American and a Briton. Kenneth J. Arrow, a 51-year-old professor of economics at Harvard, and John Richard Hicks, a 68-year-old retired Oxford economist, were cited for their "pioneering contributions to general economic equilibrium theory and welfare theory." Additionally, Professor Hicks was cited for his contributions to monetary and business cycle theory and Professor Arrow for his work on growth theory and decision theory.

PULITZER PRIZES

Winners of the Pulitzer Prizes were announced by the president of Columbia University on May 1, 1972. Each prize was worth $1,000 except the public service gold medal. No award was given for drama.

Journalism. Local general reporting—Richard Cooper and John Machacek of the Rochester, N. Y., *Times-Union,* for coverage of the Attica prison riot in September 1971. Local special reporting—Timothy Leland, Gerard M. O'Neill, Stephen A. Kurkjian, and Ann DeSantis of the Boston *Globe,* for exposure of corruption in Somerville, Mass. Editorial writing—John Strohmeyer of the Bethlehem, Pa., *Globe-Times,* for a campaign to reduce racial tensions in a situation of hostility encountered by Puerto Ricans. Editorial cartooning—Jeffrey K. MacNelly of the Richmond, Va., *News Leader.* International reporting—Jack Anderson, syndicated columnist, for his disclosures of administration policymaking

during the India-Pakistan war. Spot news photography—Horst Faas and Michel Laurent of The Associated Press, for a series depicting Bangladesh vengeance against Pakistanis. Feature photography—Dave Kennerly of United Press International, for photographs showing the desolation of the Indochina War. Commentary—Mike Royko, columnist of the Chicago *Daily News.* Criticism—Frank Peters, Jr., music critic of the St. Louis *Post-Dispatch.* Meritorious public service—the New York *Times,* for publication of the Pentagon Papers, the U. S. Defense Department's secret study of the Indochina War.

Letters. History—Carl N. Degler, for *Neither Black Nor White.* Biography—Joseph P. Lash, for *Eleanor and Franklin.* Poetry—James Wright, for *Collected Poems.* General nonfiction—Barbara W. Tuchman, for *Stilwell and the American Experience in China, 1911–1945.* Fiction—Wallace Stegner, for *Angle of Repose.*

Music. Jacob Druckman, for *Windows,* an orchestral piece.

ARTS

American Composers Alliance, Laurel Leaf Award for "distinguished service to contemporary music"—Leopold Stokowski.

American Institute of Architects awards: gold medal—Pietro Belluschi, former dean of the School of Architecture and Planning at the Massachusetts Institute of Technology; critics' medal—Wolf Von Eckardt, architecture critic of the Washington *Post.*

American Institute of Graphic Arts Gold Medal—Milton Glaser.

American Society of Composers, Authors, and Publishers, Deems Taylor Award ($1,000) for an outstanding book on music—Lee Eliot Berk for *Legal Protection for the Creative Musician.*

Brandeis University, Creative Arts Awards ($1,000 each): fiction—Katherine Anne Porter; architecture—Louis I. Kahn; dance—Merce Cunningham; theater—Alfred Lunt and Lynn Fontanne.

Dance Magazine Awards—Judith Jamison of the Alvin Ailey American Dance Theater and Anthony Dowell of the Royal Ballet.

Metropolitan Opera National Council Awards ($2,000 each)—Christine M. Weidinger, Jan Redick, and Roger Patterson.

National Academy of Recording Arts and Sciences, Grammy Awards for excellence in phonograph records: album—*Tapestry,* sung by Carole King; record of the year—*It's Too Late* by Carole King; song of the year—*You've Got A Friend* by Carole King; new artist—Carly Simon; instrumental arrangement—Isaac Hayes and Johnny Allen for *Theme from Shaft;* contemporary male vocal performance—James Taylor for *You've Got A Friend;* contemporary female vocal performance—Carole King for *Tapestry;* contemporary vocal performance by a group—the Carpenters for *The Carpenters;* female rhythm and blues vocal performance—Aretha Franklin for *Bridge Over Troubled Water;* male rhythm and blues vocal performance—Lou Rawls for *A Natural Man;* rhythm and blues song—*Ain't No Sunshine* by Bill Withers; male country vocal performance—Jerry Reed for *When You're Hot, You're Hot;* female country vocal performance—Sammi Smith for *Help Me Make It Through the Night;* instrumental composition—Michel Legrand for *Theme from the Summer of '42;* original score written for a motion picture or television—*Theme from Shaft* by Isaac Hayes; score from an original cast show—*Godspell* by Stephen Schwartz; comedy recording—Lily Tomlin for *This Is a Recording;* classical album of the year—*Horowitz Plays Rachmaninoff;* opera recording—Verdi's *Aida* performed by the London Symphony Orchestra; spoken word recording—*Desiderata* by Les Crane.

National Artist Award of the American National Theater and Academy—Alfred Hunt and Lynn Fontanne.

National Institute of Arts and Letters awards: art ($3,000)—Richard Aarke, Varujan Boghosian, Lowry Burgess, Mary Frank, Maud Gatewood, Herman Rose, and Anton Van Dalen; music ($3,000)—Earle Brown, John Eaton, John Harbison, and William O. Smith; award of merit medal for painting—Clyfford Still; Arnold W. Brunner Memorial Prize in Architecture ($1,000)—Richard Meier; Marjorie Peabody Waite Award ($1,500)—Vittorio Rieti; Richard and Hinda Rosenthal Foundation Awards ($2,000)—Barkley L. Hendricks and Thomas McGuane; Charles E. Ives Award ($10,000)—Harold Faberman.

JOURNALISM

American Newspaper Guild, Heywood Broun Memorial Award ($1,000)—Aaron Latham of *Esquire* magazine.

Maria Moors Cabot Gold Medals for "distinguished journalistic contributions to the advancement of inter-American understanding ($1,000)—Tom Streithorst of NBC News; Arturo Uslar Pietri, editor of *El Nacional,* Caracas, Venezuela; Pedro G. Beltan, former editor and publisher of *La Prensa,* Lima, Peru.

Long Island University, George Polk Memorial Awards: foreign reporting—Sydney H. Schanberg of the New York

CROWN PRINCE Carl Gustaf of Sweden (left) applauds American Nobel Prize winners for 1972 (l. to r.) Leon Cooper and John Schrieffer, physics, and William Stein (in wheelchair) and Christian Anfinsen, chemistry.

Times; national reporting—the New York Times; metropolitan reporting—Donald L. Bartlett and James B. Steele of the Philadelphia Inquirer; education reporting—Joseph Lelyveld of the New York Times; public service—Frances Cerra of Newsday; magazine reporting—Ross Terrill of the Atlantic; television documentary—Peter Davis, Perry Wolff, and Roger Mudd of CBS News; news photography—Michel Laurent and Horst Faas of the Associated Press; criticism—Richard Harwood of the Washington Post; book—Erik Barnouw for A History of Broadcasting in the United States.

New York Press Photographers Association, Freedom of the Press awards—Frank Stanton of CBS and Arthur Ochs Sulzberger of the New York Times.

Overseas Press Club awards: George Polk Memorial Award for the best reporting requiring exceptional courage and enterprise abroad ($500)—Nicholas W. Stroh of the Washington Post; Robert Capa Gold Medal for still photography—Larry Burrows of Life magazine; news reporting from abroad in any medium—Leonard S. Silk of the New York Times; Asia Magazine Award—John Rich of NBC Radio; Vision Magazine Ed Stout Award for reporting on Latin America—Jonathan Kapstein of Business Week magazine; book on foreign affairs—Anthony Austin for The President's War; magazine reporting from abroad—Arnaud de Borchgrave of Newsweek magazine; magazine interpretation of foreign affairs—Gordon L. Williams and John L. Cobbs of Business Week magazine; television interpretation of foreign affairs—John Hart and CBS news team; television documentary on foreign affairs—George Watson and Ernest Pendrell of ABC; radio reporting from abroad—CBS News; radio documentary—NBC News; radio interpretation of foreign affairs—NBC News; cartoon on foreign affairs—Don Wright of the Miami, Fla., News; photographic reporting from abroad in a magazine or book—Frank Fischbeck of Life magazine; daily newspaper or wire service reporting on foreign affairs—Sydney H. Schanberg of the New York Times; newspaper or wire service photographic reporting from abroad—the New York Times; daily newspaper or wire service interpretation of foreign events—Robert S. Elegant of the Los Angeles Times; special award—Neil Sheehan and the New York Times for coverage of the Pentagon Papers.

Drew Pearson Prize for excellence in investigative reporting ($6,000)—Carl Bernstein, Robert Woodward, and Barry Sussman of the Washington Post, for their series on political sabotage and espionage relating to the break-in

at Democratic party headquarters in June 1972.

White House Correspondents Association awards: Raymond Clapper Memorial Award for "exceptionally meritorious Washington correspondence" ($1,000)—James R. Polk of the Washington Evening Star; Worth Bingham Prize ($1,000)—Frank Wright of the Minneapolis, Minn., Tribune; Merriman Smith Memorial Fund award—Carroll Kilpatrick of the Washington Post.

John Peter Zenger Award of the University of Arizona—the New York Times for its publication of the Pentagon Papers.

LITERATURE

Academy of American Poets Fellowship Award ($10,000)—James Wright.

American Library Association Awards: Newbery Medal—Robert C. O'Brien for Mrs. Frisby and the Rats of NIMH; Caldecott Medal—Nonny Hobrigian, illustrator, for One Fine Day; Grolier Award ($1,000)—Ronald W. McCracken, librarian at Keswick Public School, Keswick, Ont.; Beta Phi Mu Award ($50)—Margaret W. Monroe, professor and former director of the University of Wisconsin Library School; Melvil Dewey Award—Jerrold Orne, librarian of the University of North Carolina; Joseph W. Lippincott Award—Guy Lyle, director of libraries at Emory University; Margaret Mann Citation—Edmond L. Applebaum of the Library of Congress; Clarence Day Award—Robert Cromie, newspaper columnist and television host.

Bancroft Prizes of Columbia University for distinguished writing in U. S. history and international relations ($4,000 each)—Carl N. Degler for Neither Black Nor White; Slavery and Race Relations in Brazil and the United States; Robert Middlekauff for The Mathers: Three Generations of Puritan Intellectuals, 1596–1728; Samuel Eliot Morison for The European Discovery of America: The Northern Voyages.

Books Abroad Prize for literature ($10,000)—Gabriel García Marquez.

Carey-Thomas Award for a distinguished project of creative book publishing—Oxford University Press for The Compact Edition of the Oxford English Dictionary: The Complete Text Reproduced Micrographically.

Goncourt Prize in literature—Jean Carrière for L'Epervier de Maheux.

Governor General's Awards (Canadian): English fiction—Mordecai Richler for St. Urban's Horseman; English non-

fiction—Pierre Berton for *The Last Spike;* English poetry and drama—John Glassco for *Selected Poems;* French fiction—Gerard Bessette for *Le cycle;* French nonfiction—Gerard Fortin for *La Fin d'un règne;* French poetry and drama—Paul-Marie LaPointe for *Le réel absolu.*

Mystery Writers of America, Edgar Allan Poe ("Edgar") Awards: mystery novel—Frederick Forsyth for *Day of the Jackal;* first mystery novel—A. H. Z. Carr for *Finding Maubee;* true-crime book—Sandor Frankel for *Beyond a Reasonable Doubt;* mystery short story—Robert L. Fish for *Moonlight Gardener;* mystery screenplay—Ernest Tidyman for *The French Connection.*

National Book Awards ($1,000 each): fiction—Flannery O'Connor for *Flannery O'Connor: The Complete Stories;* arts and letters—Charles Rosen for *The Classical Style: Haydn, Mozart, Beethoven;* philosophy and religion—Martin E. Marty for *Righteous Empire: The Protestant Experience in America;* science—George L. Small for *The Blue Whale;* poetry—Frank O'Hara for his *Collected Poems* and Howard Moss for *Selected Poems;* translation—Austryn Wainhouse for his translation from the French of Jacques Monod's *Chance and Necessity: An Essay on the Natural Philosophy of Modern Biology;* biography—Joseph P. Lash for *Eleanor and Franklin;* history—Allan Nevins for *The Ordeal of the Union Series,* volumes 7 and 8; contemporary affairs—Steward Brand for *The Last Whole Earth Catalog;* children's book—Donald Barthelme for *The Slightly Irregular Fire Engine or the Hither-Thithering Djinn.*

National Book Committee, National Medal for Literature ($5,000)—Lewis Mumford.

National Institute of Arts and Letters awards in literature ($3,000): Harry Crews, Peter Davison, Paula Fox, Penelope Gilliatt, Pauline Hanson, Michael S. Harper, Israel Horovitz, Walter Kerr, Gilbert Rogin, and Ann Stanford; gold medal for the novel—Eudora Welty; gold medal for history—Henry Steele Commager; E. M. Forster Award ($5,000)—Frank Tuohy; Loines Award for Poetry ($2,500)—William Jay Smith; Morton Dauwen Zabel Award ($2,500)—Donald Barthelme.

P. E. N. American Center, Translation Award ($1,000)—Richard and Clara Winston for their English translation of *The Letters of Thomas Mann.*

Poetry Society of America Awards: Gold Medal of Achievement—John Hall Wheelock; Alice Fay di Castagnola Award for a work in progress ($3,500 shared)—Erica Jong and Myra Sklarew; Shelley Memorial Award ($1,800)—Galway Kinnell; Melville Cane Award ($500)—James Wright.

Nebula Awards of the Science Fiction Writers of America: novel—Robert Silverberg for *A Time of Changes;* short story—Robert Silverberg for *Good News from the Vatican;* novella—Katherine MacLean for *The Missing Man;* novelette—Paul Anderson for *The Queen of Air and Darkness.*

PUBLIC SERVICE

American Friends of the Hebrew University, Scopus Award—Diane and Arthur Belfer.

Anisfield-Wolf Award for the best scholarly work concerned with the problem of intergroup understanding ($750)—Noboth Mokgatle for *The Autobiography of an Unknown South African.*

Browning Achievement Awards for accomplishment in religious, moral, social, economic, and intellectual endeavors, sponsored by the New York Community Trust ($5,000 each)—Paul Bigelow Sears, Orville Alvin Vogel, E. Cuyler Hammond, Nathan Browne Eddy, and Manoel de Mello.

Ralphe Bunche Award, sponsored by the Alumni Association of the University of California at Los Angeles—U Thant.

Samuel C. and Minna Dretzin Prize of Brandeis University for constructive educational impact ($5,000)—Earl Warren.

Four Freedoms Foundation, Franklin D. Roosevelt Award—Frank E. Fitzsimmons, president of the International Brotherhood of Teamsters.

Freedom of Speech Award of the Americans for Democratic Action—Daniel Ellsberg.

Freedoms Foundation awards for contributions toward a better understanding and greater appreciation of the American way of life: George Washington Award ($5,000)—Omar N. Bradley; special awards—Clare Boothe Luce, Henry Viscardi, W. Clement Stone, George C. Roche, Alfred J. Barran, Albert Ettenger, Denise Evers, and Walter Trohan.

National Association for the Advancement of Colored People (NAACP) Spingarn Medal for the "highest achievement of an American Negro"—Leon Howard Sullivan, clergyman and activist.

National Conference of Christians and Jews, Human Relations Award—Mr. and Mrs. W. C. Truehaft.

National Institute of Social Sciences Gold Medals for "distinguished service to humanity"—Henry A. Kissinger, Mrs. Laurance Rockefeller, George Bush, and Archbishop Fulton J. Sheen.

New York Civil Liberties Union, Florina Lasker Civil Liberties Award ($1,000)—Helen Buttenweiser.

Reinhold Niebuhr Award for excellence in social justice,

public life, or world affairs ($5,000 each)—Willy Brandt, chancellor of West Germany, and Theodore M. Hesburgh, president of the University of Notre Dame.

Presidential Medal of Freedom for significant contributions to the "quality of American life"—Lila and DeWitt Wallace, founders of the *Readers' Digest,* and John Paul Van, U. S. adviser in the Indochina War.

Margaret Sanger Award for "courageous leadership"—Alan F. Guttmacher.

Woodrow Wilson Award of Princeton University—Ralph Nader.

SCIENCE AND TECHNOLOGY

American Cancer Society awards: national award—Henry S. Kaplan of Stanford University; distinguished service award—Murray M. Copeland of the University of Texas.

American Chemical Society awards: Priestley Medal—George Kistiakowsky; Arthur C. Cope Award in organic chemistry ($40,000)—Robert B. Woodward and Roald Hoffmann; Irving Langmuir Award in chemical physics ($5,000)—Harden M. McConnell; ACS Award for Nuclear Applications in Chemistry ($2,000)—Anthony Turkevich; Peter Debye Award in Physical Chemistry ($2,000)—Clyde A. Hutchison, Jr.; James T. Grady Award for interpreting chemistry for the public ($2,000)—Dan Q. Posin; ACS Award in Pure Chemistry ($2,000)—Roy Gerald Gordon; Garvan Medal ($2,000)—Jean'ne M. Shreeve.

American Geographical Society, David Livingstone Centenary Medal—Akin L. Mabogunje; George Davidson Medal—F. Raymond Fosberg.

American Heart Association, Research Achievement Award—Eugene Braunwald of Harvard Medical School.

American Institute of Aeronautics and Astronautics awards: AIAA Aircraft Design Award—Ben R. Rich; Octave Chanute Award ($500)—Donald Segner.

American Physical Society awards: Tom W. Bonner Prize in nuclear physics ($1,000)—John D. Anderson and Donald Robson; Davisson-Germer Prize ($2,500)—Erwin W. Mueller; Oliver E. Buckley Solid-State Physics Prize ($1,000)—James C. Phillips; High-Polymer Physics Prize ($1,000)—Anton Peterlin.

American Society of Mechanical Engineers, Hoover Medal—Luis A. Ferre, engineer and governor of Puerto Rico.

Atomic Energy Commission (AEC) awards: Enrico Fermi Award ($25,000)—Manson Benedict of the Massachusetts Institute of Technology; Ernest Orlando Lawrence Awards ($5,000 each)—Charles C. Cremer, Sidney D. Drell, Paul F. Zweifel, Marvin Goldman, and David A. Shirley.

Cottrell Award for achievement in improving the environment or controlling pollution, administered by Research-Cottrell, Inc. ($5,000)—Arie J. Haagen-Smit of the California Institute of Technology.

Egleston Medal for contributions in civil engineering, sponsored by the Columbia University Alumni Association—Jewell M. Garrelts.

Albert Einstein Award for outstanding contributions to the physical sciences ($5,000)—Eugene Paul Wigner of Princeton University.

Franklin Institute, Franklin Medal—Hannes Alfvén of the University of California at San Diego.

Louisa Gross Horowitz Prize for outstanding research in biology ($25,000)—Stephen W. Kuffler of Harvard Medical School.

Institute of Life Prize ($50,000)—René Dubos of Rockefeller University, for work on environmental problems.

Albert Lasker Medical Research Awards for cancer chemotherapy ($2,000 each)—Emil Frei, 3d, Emil Freireich, James F. Holland, Donald Pinkel, Paul Carbone, Vincent T. DeVita, Jr., Min Chiu Li, Roy Hertz, Edmund Klein, Eugene J. Van Schott, Denis Burkitt, Joseph H. Burchenal, John L. Ziegler, V. Anomah Ngu, and Isaac Djerassi; special award ($5,000)—C. Gordon Zubrod.

Mental Health Association Award for achievement in research ($10,000)—Seymour Kety of Harvard University.

National Academy of Engineering, Founders Medal—Edwin H. Land of the Polaroid Corporation.

National Academy of Sciences awards: Hartley Public Service Medal—Leonard Carmichael of the National Geographic Society; Arthur L. Day Prize ($10,000)—Hatten S. Yoder, Jr. of the Geophysical Laboratory of the Carnegie Institution; Agassiz Medal ($1,000)—Seiya Uyeda of the University of Tokyo; Henryk Artowski Medal ($5,000)—Francis S. Johnson of the University of Texas; James Craig Watson Medal ($2,000)—André Depit of the National Aeronautics and Space Administration; U. S. Steel Foundation Award in Molecular Biology ($5,000)—Howard M. Temin of the University of Wisconsin.

National Aeronautics Association, Robert J. Collier Trophy—David R. Scott, James B. Irwin, Alfred M. Worden, and Robert Gilruth.

J. Robert Oppenheimer Prize in theoretical physics ($1,000)—Robert Serber of Columbia University.

THE DICK CAVETT SHOW *won an "Emmy" award in 1972 as the best talk-show series. Cavett* (right), *shown with Robert Mitchum, was later cut to one week per month.*

Bradford Washington Award of the Boston Museum of Science for contributions toward "public understanding of science" ($5,000)—Walter S. Sullivan of the New York *Times.*

World Health Organization, Léon Bernard Prize for contributions to social medicine and international public health —George Godber of Britain's Department of Health and Social Security.

TELEVISION AND RADIO

Academy of Television Arts and Sciences ("Emmy") Awards: best program—*Brian's Song* (ABC); best variety series—*The Carol Burnett Show* (CBS); variety series-talk—*The Dick Cavett Show* (ABC); dramatic series—*Elizabeth R* (PBS); comedy series—*All in the Family* (CBS); single performance in a drama—Glenda Jackson in *Elizabeth R* and Keith Michell in *Elizabeth R*; leading actor in a dramatic series—Peter Falk in *NBC Mystery Movie* (NBC); leading actress in a dramatic series—Glenda Jackson in *Elizabeth R*; leading actor in a comedy series—Carroll O'Connor in *All in the Family* (CBS); leading actress in a comedy series—Jean Stapleton in *All in the Family* (CBS); supporting dramatic actor—Jack Warden in *Brian's Song* (ABC); supporting dramatic actress—Jenny Agutter in *The Snow Goose* (NBC); supporting actor in a comedy series—Edward Asner in *The Mary Tyler Moore Show* (CBS); supporting actress in a comedy series—Valerie Harper in *The Mary Tyler Moore Show* (CBS) and Sally Struthers in *All in the Family* (CBS); performer in music or variety—Harvey Korman in *The Carol Burnett Show* (CBS); writing achievement in dramatic adaptation—William Blinn for *Brian's Song* (ABC); writing achievement in comedy, variety, or music special—Anne Howard Bailey for *The Trial of Mary Lincoln* (PBS); writing achievement in drama—Allan Sloane for *To All My Friends on Shore* (CBS); directorial achievement in comedy, variety, or music—Walter C. Miller for *Jack Lemmon in 'S Wonderful, 'S Marvellous, 'S Gershwin* (NBC); directorial achievement in drama—Tom Gries for *The Glass House* (CBS); sports—Roone Arledge, executive producer, for *ABC's Wide World of Sports* (ABC); news documentary—*The Search for the Nile* (NBC); general news program—*The Pentagon Papers* (PBS); regularly scheduled news program—Bob Scheiffer, Phil Jones, Don Webster, and Bill Plante for *The CBS Evening News* (CBS); writing achievement in a news program—Michael Hastings and Derek Marlow for *The Search for the Nile* (NBC); special awards for achievement in news coverage—Frank Stanton, retiring president of CBS, for his "defense of our industry under attack," and posthumously to William H. Lawrence of ABC News.

George Foster Peabody Awards for distinguished achievement in television and radio: television dramatic programs—*Brian's Song* (ABC), *The Price* (NBC), *Jane Eyre* (NBC), and *The Snow Goose* (NBC); television documentary—*This Child Is Rated X* (NBC); television entertainment—*The American Revolution, 1770–1783: A Conversation with Lord North* (CBS); television children's program—*To Make a Wish* (ABC); television educational program—*The Turned On Crisis* (WQED-TV, Pittsburgh); broadcast news—John Rich and NBC Radio and Television; radio public service—*Second Sunday* (NBC); radio educational programming—WHA, Madison, Wis.; radio children's program—*Junior Town Meeting of the Air* (WWVA, Wheeling, W. Va.); television special awards—George

Heinemann (NBC) and Frank Stanton (CBS); radio special awards—Arthur Godfrey (CBS) and WCCO Radio, Minneapolis, Minn.

THEATER AND MOTION PICTURES

Academy of Motion Picture Arts and Sciences ("Oscar") Awards for 1972: best film—*The French Connection;* best foreign-language film—*The Garden of the Finzi-Continis* (Italian); best actor—Gene Hackman in *The French Connection;* best actress—Jane Fonda in *Klute;* supporting actor—Ben Johnson in *The Last Picture Show;* supporting actress—Cloris Leachman in *The Last Picture Show;* director—William Friedkin for *The French Connection;* screenplay based on material from another medium—Ernest Tidyman for *The French Connection;* original screenplay—Paddy Chayefsky for *The Hospital;* nonmusical score—Michel Legrand for *The Summer of '42;* musical score—John Williams for *Fiddler on the Roof;* original song—*Theme from Shaft* by Isaac Hayes; art direction—John Box, Ernest Archer, Jack Maxsted, and Gil Parrando for *Nicholas and Alexandra;* set decoration—Vernon Dixon for *Nicholas and Alexandra;* editing—Jerry Greenberg for *The French Connection;* cinematography—Oswald Morris for *Fiddler on the Roof;* special visual effects—Danny Lee, Eustace Lycett, and Alan Maley for *Bedknobs and Broomsticks;* costume design—Yvonne Blake and Antonio Castillo for *Nicholas and Alexandra;* sound—Gordon K. McCallum and David Hildyard for *Fiddler on the Roof;* short subject (live action)—Producciones Concord for *Sentinels of Silence;* short subject (cartoon)—Maxwell-Petok Productions for *The Crunch Bird;* documentary feature film—David L. Wolper Productions for *The Hellstrom Chronicle;* special award—Charles Chaplin.

American Theater Wing, Antoinette Perry ("Tony") Awards: best drama—*Sticks and Bones* by David Rabe; best musical—*Two Gentlemen of Verona,* adapted by John Guare and Mel Shapiro; best actor (musical)—Phil Silvers in *A Funny Thing Happened on the Way to the Forum;* best actor (drama)—Cliff Gorman in *Lenny;* best actress (musical)—Alexis Smith in *Follies;* best actress (drama)—Sada Thompson in *Twigs;* dramatic supporting actor—Vincent Gardenia in *The Prisoner of Second Avenue;* dramatic supporting actress—Elizabeth Wilson in *Sticks and Bones;* musical supporting actor—Larry Blyden in *A Funny Thing Happened on the Way to the Forum;* musical supporting actress—Linda Hopkins in *Inner City;* director (drama)—Mike Nichols for *The Prisoner of Second Avenue;* director (musical)—Hal Prince for *Follies;* costume design—Florence Klotz for *Follies;* lighting—Tharon Musser for *Follies;* choreography—Michael Bennett for *Follies;* scenic design—Boris Aronson for *Follies;* score—Stephen Sondheim for *Follies;* special awards—Ethel Merman, Richard Rogers, and *Fiddler on the Roof.*

Cannes International Film Festival Awards: Gold Palm Grand Prix—*Il Caso Mattei* (Italian) and *La Classe Operaia Va in Paradiso* (Italian); special jury prize—*Solaris* (USSR); jury prize—*Slaughterhouse—Five* (American); actor—Jean Yanne for *Nous ne Viellirons pas Ensemble* (French); actress—Susannah York for *Images* (Irish); director—Miklos Jancso for *Meg Ker a Nep* (Hungarian).

Drama Desk-Vernon Rice Awards for outstanding achievements in the off-Broadway theater: most promising playwrights—Jason Miller, Michael Weller, David Wiltse, J. E. Franklin, Richard Wesley, Philip Hayes Dean, J. E. Gaines; directors—Dan Sullivan and Gilbert Moses; scenic designer—Video Free America; costume designer—Carrie F. Robbins; composer—Andrew Lloyd Webber; writer—Melvin Van Peebles.

New York Drama Critics' Circle Theatre Awards: drama—*That Championship Season;* musical—*Two Gentlemen of Verona;* foreign drama—*The Screens.*

New York Film Critics' Awards: best film—*Cries and Whispers;* actor—Laurence Olivier in *Sleuth;* actress—Liv Ullmann in *Cries and Whispers;* director—Ingmar Bergman for *Cries and Whispers.*

PROTESTANTISM. See Religion.

PSYCHOLOGY

In 1972 there was widespread interest in learning technique, particularly as it is applied to visceral responses in what is known as "biofeedback."

Biofeedback Experiments. After more than 35 years of studying how animals learn, Dr. Neal E. Miller, now of Rockefeller University and for many years professor of psychology at Yale University, has concluded that the differences between learning skeletal responses (such as turning left or pushing a lever) and the mechanisms for learning visceral re-

sponses (such as shifting the level of blood pressure or changing the rate of stomach contractions) have been greatly exaggerated. Prior to his work, it had been generally assumed that visceral responses were beyond willful control and thus could not be changed by training. By presenting appropriate rewards, Miller has now been able to teach rats to speed up or slow down their heart beat, or to raise or lower their blood pressure, or to increase or decrease intestinal contractions.

Most psychologists, including Miller, have insisted that basic to any learning is the tendency of the organisms to repeat those responses that are instrumental in gaining rewards or avoiding punishment. Psychologists, however, did not believe that visceral responses could be trained. The internal organs of the body are extremely well insulated from direct training experiences. Miller began to investigate visceral learning in 1958 and by 1969 tried his procedures on his first human subjects.

The learning technique is called "biofeedback training" because it is necessary to give the individual some artificial feedback through a monitoring device so that he can become aware of visceral reactions such as blood pressure, stomach contractions, or heart beat. For example, in training humans to alter their blood pressure on cue, Miller uses an inflatable pressure cuff around the arm, the amplified sound of blood moving through an artery, and an oscilloscope.

APA Awards. In September 1972 the American Psychological Association (APA) held its 80th annual convention in Honolulu and honored Dr. Carl Rogers as the first recipient of the association's Distinguished Professional Contribution Award. The APA also presented its annual Distinguished Scientific Contribution awards to Dr. Edwin E. Ghiselli of the University of California for his research in industrial psychology, to Dr. Patrick Suppes of Stanford University, a specialist in mathematical models applied to learning and perception, and to Dr. Dorothea Jameson and Dr. Leo Hurvich, a husband-and-wife research team known primarily for their technical investigations of color vision.

AUSTIN E. GRIGG, *University of Richmond*

PUBLIC HEALTH. See MEDICINE and special feature beginning on page 26.

PUBLIC OPINION RESEARCH

Although opinion surveys in 1972 continued to report on many aspects of the public's knowledge, attitudes, and behavior, their major attention was focused on the presidential election campaign.

Political Surveys. The Gallup Poll and the Harris Survey continued to chart American political attitudes during 1972 when traditional party preference and voting behavior were undergoing marked change. Their task was further complicated by the introduction of the 18–20 age group into the ranks of eligible voters.

Both polls documented the lack of Democratic consensus on a presidential candidate. In late May, about 25% of the Democratic voters favored Sen. Hubert H. Humphrey, 25% favored Sen. George McGovern, 25% favored Gov. George Wallace, and the remainder favored other candidates or had no opinion. Meanwhile, the measured public approval of President Nixon's performance in office climbed steadily after his visits to China and the Soviet Union. A Gallup Poll report in August first noticed that the McGovern effort to register young voters might prove counterproductive, as a majority of the under-30 group expressed a preference for Nixon.

McGovern's high point in the polls came after his victory in the Wisconsin primary in April, when a Gallup Poll showed 49% for Nixon, 39% for McGovern, and 12% undecided. A similar survey following the Democratic convention showed 56% for Nixon, 37% for McGovern, and 7% undecided.

The dropping of Sen. Thomas A. Eagleton as vice presidential candidate shifted many McGovern supporters into the undecided group. In early August, 57% declared for Nixon, 32% for McGovern, and 11% were undecided. After the Republican convention later that month, most of these undecided voters turned to Nixon, as Gallup showed the President with 64% of the vote, McGovern with 30%, and 6% undecided. By mid-October the President still commanded 59% of the vote, and an announcement of impending peace in Vietnam raised this to 61%. The President's actual share of the vote was 60.83%.

Confidence Surveys. Despite Nixon's overwhelming reelection, public opinion surveys continued to reflect declining confidence in American institutions. In response to the question, "In general, would you say you are satisfied or dissatisfied with the direction in which the nation is going?," only 35% told Gallup interviewers in August that they were satisfied, while 58% expressed dissatisfaction. A Harris Survey in October asked people whether they had "a great deal of confidence, only some confidence, or hardly any confidence at all" in 16 institutions ranging from the military through science and education to Congress and the Supreme Court. For none of the 16 did as many as half the population express a great deal of confidence. Medicine, finance, science, and the military ranked in the top four in public confidence, while the press, television, labor, and advertising were at the bottom of the list. These findings contrasted sharply with answers given to the same question in 1966. Whereas 62% had a great deal of confidence in the military in 1966, only 35% did in 1972. Confidence in Congress declined from 42% to 21%, and confidence in education dropped from 61% to 33%. In fact, every institution inquired about suffered a significant loss in public confidence.

Truth-in-Polling Bill. Hearings were held in the fall on Congressman Lucien Nedzi's (D-Mich.) truth-in-polling bill. The bill would require polltakers who conduct surveys for publication to file with the Library of Congress within 72 hours of publication information on the sponsor, sampling method, sample size, time and method of interviewing, questions asked, number of nonrespondents, and results. The bill's intent is to provide fuller disclosure of survey methodology.

Social Science Data Survey. The National Opinion Research Center began its national data program for the social sciences in 1972, with funding provided by the National Science Foundation and the Russell Sage Foundation. Under this program, national surveys were to be conducted annually from 1972 through 1976, with data made available to any interested student or professional for the cost of reproduction and shipping.

PAUL B. SHEATSLEY
National Opinion Research Center
University of Chicago

PUBLISHING

The publishing world and its 1972 activities are reviewed in this article under three headings— Books, Magazines, and Newspapers.

Books

In 1972 there was a moderate upturn in sales of books for general readers; paperback and book club sales were especially strong. Schoolbook sales income was up slightly from 1971. A survey of college teachers showed that they considered textbooks to have declining though still major importance.

Published official industry estimates of 1971 sales revealed a total of $3,082,000,000 received by publishers for books of all kinds. Modest growth was seen for 1972 sales with an estimated total on the order of $3,250,000,000. Price rises accounted for a good part of the increases in receipts. However, book price rises in 1971 were shown to be lower than the increases in the Consumer Price Index.

Book title output continued steadily in 1971 and 1972, at an annual rate of more than 35,000 recorded by book industry bibliographers. About 25,-000 of these titles were new.

Exports of books, including thousands of small shipments not officially reported by the government, were estimated at $300 million. Imports of books were estimated at about $110 million.

Best Sellers. *Jonathan Livingston Seagull* was the year's surprise hardcover, runaway best seller, with more than 1,375,000 copies reported sold up to the Christmas season. Other books, including several that sold well into six figures, were far behind. The following lists, arranged alphabetically, represent a composite chosen from monthly lists compiled by the *Publishers Weekly:*

FICTION

August 1914, Aleksandr Solzhenitsyn
Captains and the Kings, Taylor Caldwell
The Exorcist, William P. Blatty
Jonathan Livingston Seagull, Richard Bach
My Name Is Asher Lev, Chaim Potok
The Odessa File, Frederick Forsyth
On the Night of the Seventh Moon, Victoria Holt
To Serve Them All My Days, Ronald F. Delderfield
The Winds of War, Herman Wouk
The Word, Irving Wallace

NONFICTION

The Best and the Brightest, David Halberstam
Dr. Atkins' Diet Revolution, Robert C. Atkins
Eleanor: The Years Alone, Joseph P. Lash
The Game of the Foxes, Ladislas Farago
I'm O.K., You're O.K., Thomas Harris
O Jerusalem, Larry Collins and Dominique Lapierre
Open Marriage, Nena and George O'Neill
The Peter Prescription, Laurence J. Peter
Supermoney, "Adam Smith"
A World Beyond, Ruth Montgomery

Organizations. The basic good health of the retail bookselling industry was dramatized by the unprecedented total attendance of 6,000 persons at the American Booksellers Association annual convention and trade fair in Washington, D. C., in 1972. The Association of American Publishers solidified its structure in 1972 and expanded its services, especially in the mail order and paperback book fields. It stepped up its statistical reporting and was increasingly active in the areas of legislation and defense against censorship. However, it had to curtail most of its financial support for the non-profit association, the National Book Committee. A new industry group, the American Association of Book Wholesalers, was formed. The Association of American University Presses discussed ways to meet the financial pressures that were affecting many of its members. Many of these presses received some aid in specific publishing areas from the Ford and Mellon foundations.

International Book Year. American publishers, librarians, educators, and others used the International Book Year proclaimed by UNESCO, in 1972, to dramatize book and reading programs. Library and functional literary activities were expanded, with support from the federal Right to Read program. Several U. S. publishers joined in forming an International Association of Scholarly Presses under partial UNESCO sponsorship. The Book Manufacturers' Institute, the Information Industry Association, and other groups studied the accelerating use of computerized composition, layout, and editing techniques, and of the continuous belt press, among other recently developed devices.

Book Industry Issues. The sensation of the year in book publishing was the hoax perpetrated by Clifford Irving in writing his biography of Howard Hughes, based on alleged interviews with the eccentric multi-millionaire. The exposure and conviction of Irving, his wife, and an associate, Richard Suskind, for their parts in this deception, including the acceptance of payment from McGraw-Hill under false pretenses, raised serious questions about judgment in publishing.

Symptomatic of a much deeper problem was an increasing amount of grumbling about the difficulties of publishing within extremely large, diversified corporations, which make demands that are not necessarily compatible with publishing aims and operations.

Increased federal funds for health and education, including book and library programs, were vetoed in 1972 by President Nixon. Book and library groups challenged, in Federal courts, an estimated 14% rise in book postage rates. The Federal Trade Commission continued attempts to regulate encyclopedia sales practices.

Enactment of a domestic copyright law was again deferred, and existing provisions were again extended. The Senate ratified the Paris amendment to the Universal Copyright Convention, a measure that should ease the use of copyrighted materials by developing countries.

In the continuing conflict over alleged unfair use of copying machines, Williams & Wilkins Co. of Baltimore, Md., won a round in a claim against government libraries. However, broad issues in this area remained unreconciled. (See also LIBRARIES.)

CHANDLER B. GRANNIS
Editor-at-Large, "Publishers Weekly"

Magazines

An issue that had arisen repeatedly since the early days of the Republic emerged again in 1972 as magazine publishers sought to save their preferential mailing rates. The threat they faced was an apparent retreat by the Nixon administration from the historic policy of encouraging the diffusion of knowledge through below-cost second-class rates for periodicals. The Postal Service imposed increases tentatively in 1971, and these were confirmed in 1972 by the appeals body, the Postal Rate Commission.

THE GREAT HOAX

Author of the spurious Howard Hughes "biography," Clifford Irving and wife, Edith, are shown on way to federal court for sentencing (*right*). Harold W. McGraw, Jr. (*below*), president of publishing company that bought book, holds facsimiles of checks paid to Hughes and endorsed "H. R. Hughes." Nina Van Pallandt (*below, right*) denied Irving could have met Hughes in Mexico. (*Bottom*) Mrs. Irving is released from prison after serving 2 months.

General-interest magazines protested each phase of the step-ups, which were scheduled to continue until 1976, with a total increase in rates of 127%. Many magazines devoted editorial space to pleading their case, insisting that the new schedules would entirely absorb potential profits. Smaller publications organized a Committee for Diversity of the Press, which argued that higher rates could destroy many unprofitable political and cultural magazines. In response, Postmaster General E. T. Klassen maintained that the increases would still leave second-class rates at low levels—at 5.8 cents, for example, for an 8-ounce magazine as opposed to 8 cents for a single ounce of first-class mail. He also argued that second-class mail constituted 25% of the total weight delivered, but only 5% of the revenues. Nonetheless, he deferred the increase set for Jan. 1, 1973. In Congress, the small publishers received support from Sen. Gaylord Nelson of Wisconsin, who introduced a bill that would freeze rates for the first 250,000 copies of a magazine.

The End of *Life*. The increase in postal rates was a major factor in the closing down of *Life* magazine. After having lost more than $30 million in four years, *Life* ceased publication with its issue of Dec. 29, 1972. The magazine had been popular since its first issue—that of Nov. 23, 1936—and had remained the leader of photojournalistic publications throughout its 36 years. The excellence of *Life*'s photography was widely acknowledged, but rising costs of postage and publishing and loss of advertising income and interest to television ended *Life* just as it had the other major general interest magazines—*Look, Collier's,* and the weekly *Saturday Evening Post.* The end of *Life* marked the end of the era of large photo magazines.

Advertising. Most other magazines appeared to be enjoying a stable year financially. The Publishers Information Bureau reported that final 1971 figures showed a 6% rise in advertising revenue for general and farm magazines, to $1.3 billion. The Magazine Publishers Association claimed the first gain in 25 years in magazines' share of the advertising market. Total revenues for the first seven months of 1972 showed a continued rise, at a rate of 9% over 1971. The American Business Press, however, tabulated a slight decrease in 1971 revenue figures, from $836.1 million in 1970 to $813.8 million.

Editorial-Publishing. *Saturday Review,* under the new management that had bought the weekly in 1971, moved its offices from New York to San Francisco and underwent sharp changes. In a novel marketing scheme, the publication was broken into four monthly magazines, one each dealing with science, the arts, education, and society. Subscriptions, at greatly increased rates, could be purchased for any number of the four monthlies. The magazine underwent a severe financial crisis at the time of the changeover, but ultimately survived it.

Look magazine, closed by Cowles Communications late in 1971, left considerable unfinished business. Owing $30 million in unused subscriptions, the company worked through the year to induce subscribers to accept other magazines, books, or art prints. Two libel suits against *Look* were in court. One, filed by Johnson City, Tenn., for $48 million —because *Look* had called it a "fascist state"—was dismissed by the state supreme court. The other, filed for $12.5 million by Mayor Joseph L. Alioto of San Francisco over allegations of underworld connections, ended twice in mistrials.

The National Magazine Awards, sponsored by Columbia University, went to *Philadelphia,* which received the public-service prize, *Architectural Record, Esquire, Mademoiselle,* and *Atlantic Monthly.*

New Ventures. The following were among the periodicals that began publication in 1972:

Money, a monthly devoted to personal finances. It was the first major magazine initiated by Time Inc. since *Sports Illustrated* in 1954.

Oui, a monthly for men of 18 to 30 years, founded by Hugh Hefner of *Playboy.*

World, "a review of ideas, creative arts, and the human condition," published weekly under the editorship of Norman Cousins, former editor of *Saturday Review. World* uses many former *Saturday Review* writers.

Encore, a monthly news magazine for the black community, edited and published by Ida Lewis.

Folio, a quarterly magazine devoted to the magazine industry.

JAMES BOYLAN, *Columbia University*

Newspapers

A triple paradox on the 1972 newspaper scene, despite booming prosperity for the press as a whole, involved the decline and fall of three honored dailies, the Boston *Herald Traveler,* the Washington *News,* and the Newark *News.* The year's event of major significance was the 5-to-4 Supreme Court decision which held that the constitutional guarantees of free speech and free press were not abridged by requiring newsmen to testify before grand juries.

Demise of Three Newspapers. The trio of Boston, Washington, and Newark papers all went out of business within six months. At the same time, total advertising revenues were running at a $6.7 billion rate, up about 14% over 1971, and many news organizations reported record earnings.

In Boston, it had been a long struggle. The *Herald Traveler,* a 192,000-circulation daily with roots going back 125 years, and its sister broadcasting channel, WHDH-TV, were profitable properties. In 1970 they had made $2 million. But after a licensing challenge involving WHDH-TV, the corporation lost the channel, its richest money maker. After unsuccessfully fighting the challenge through commissions and courts, the *Herald Traveler* yielded its license on March 19 to Boston Broadcasters, Inc., a citizens' group. The corporation lost $600,000 and in May sold out to the Hearst Corporation's Boston *Record-American.* The papers merged.

In 1921, Scripps-Howard Newspapers planted the *News* in Washington to give that aggressive chain a voice in the nation's capital. Despite a circulation that eventually reached 209,000, the *News* never made much money. On July 13 it was merged with the Washington *Evening Star,* and the District of Columbia was reduced to a two-newspaper area.

The Newark *News,* which had achieved through the years a reputation as New Jersey's leading daily, came to an untimely end on August 31, just one day short of its 89th birthday. Indifferent management and an 11-month strike were believed to be the causes. In 1970 the *News,* always a family property, was sold to Media General, Inc., a prosperous Richmond, Va., group. In May 1971, the *News* workers went on strike and stayed out until April 1972. Meanwhile, Media General sold the *News'* physical plant and abandoned its Sunday edition. When the paper resumed publication, it lacked the strength to survive.

ANOTHER NEWSPAPER DIES: A pressman pulls from the presses the last edition of the Washington Daily News. *It ceased publication after purchase by another Washington paper.*

Indexes of Prosperity. Elsewhere, proof of prosperity appeared in two ways: reports on earnings and an unusual spurt in changes of ownership. Earnings, down during the economic slump of two years before, had begun to move up as the year began. Ads were back in the papers, particularly lucrative classified advertisements. Some newspapers were posting profit increases in the 20% to 30% range. Record years were reported by Knight Newspapers, the Los Angeles *Times Mirror Co.,* the Booth chain in Michigan, Gannett Newspapers, and others.

The rush to acquire new properties began early and lasted late. Gannett added its 53d newspaper when it bought the Nashville *Banner* in January for $14 million. Later in the year Gannett added the El Paso *Times.* The Green Bay (Wis.) *Press-Gazette* bought the Sturgis (Mich.) *Journal.* The New York *Times* added four more Florida papers to its holdings. United Feature Syndicate, Inc., took over the Bell-McClure Syndicate and North American Newspaper Alliance, Inc., including the Jack Anderson column. Howard Publications of California bought the Corning (N. Y.) *Leader.* Harry R. Horvitz, publisher of four Ohio newspapers, bought the Troy (N. Y.) *Record.* The Ottaway subsidiary of Dow Jones added the Traverse City (Mich.) *Record-Eagle.* The Texas-based group Harte-Hanks, in a year of aggressive buying, acquired the Anderson (S. C.) *Independent & Mail,* the Woodbury (N. J.) *Times,* the Yakima (Wash.) *Herald-Republic,* and eight San Diego area weeklies.

A new development was the emergence as buyers of comparative newcomers, not only publishers but banking and insurance investors. The Carmage Walls Newspaper Group, based in Alabama, moved into Liberal, Kan., Monett, Mo., Lubbock and Amarillo, Texas. The Morris Newspaper Corporation (Georgia) bought the Great Bend (Kan.) *Tribune.* In all, group ownership operated 883 dailies in 155 groups.

There were 1,749 U. S. daily newspapers in 1972, a gain of one over 1971. Audited circulation was up slightly, to 62,231,258. New dailies included the Aroostock, Me., *County Times* and *Brooklyn Today. Newsday* on Long Island entered the Sunday field.

Supreme Court Ruling. The major decision by the Supreme Court, on June 29, requiring newsmen to testify before grand juries grew out of the subpoena cases of Earl Caldwell of the New York *Times,* Paul Branzburg of the Louisville *Courier-Journal,* and Paul Pappas of station WTEV-TV in New Bedford, Mass. The government sought information respectively on the Black Panthers and on drug traffic. In the Caldwell case the decision overturned a ruling of a lower court. Justice Byron R. White wrote the majority opinion, concurred in by Chief Justice Warren E. Burger and Justices Harry A. Blackmun, Lewis F. Powell, Jr., and William H. Rehnquist, all Nixon appointees. Two dissents were written by Potter Stewart and William O. Douglas, with Justices William J. Brennan and Thurgood Marshall concurring in the Stewart dissent. In October, a reporter for the defunct Newark *News,* Peter J. Bridge, went to jail for 21 days because he refused to answer grand jury questions about alleged housing corruption.

Other Developments. Besides Newark, other cities had newspaper labor difficulties during the year. *La Presse,* Montreal, returned in February after a 3-month strike. The workers at *El Mundo,* San Juan, struck on February 10. The paper tried to continue publishing, but violence stopped that. Publication resumed the third week in September.

Another prominent development in 1972 was a growing wave of systematized self-criticism, as well as public criticism of the press. In some cases newspapers hired ombudsmen to improve community relations. A larger number of locally edited journalism reviews appeared.

Women were gaining new and deserved recognition in newsrooms, clubs, societies, and offices. Sigma Delta Chi, journalistic society, opened its membership to women. Only the San Francisco Press Club voted to close its doors to women.

Counteradvertising appeared as an increasing threat, an effort to gain the right of access to the media for ads that dispute the claims of other ads. This and other concerns of the "new" journalism, such as advocacy, activism, and democracy in the newsroom, were the agenda for the A. J. Liebling Counter Convention of 1,500 journalists and writers in April at the time of the American Newspaper Publishers Association convention in New York.

The gold medal of the Pulitzer Prizes went to the New York *Times* in 1972 for its role in publishing the Pentagon Papers.

RICHARD T. BAKER, *Columbia University*

PUERTO RICO

The Popular Democratic party was the victor in the 1972 election in Puerto Rico. A United Nations subcommittee took the island's "colonial status" under study. Several Puerto Rican travelers were killed by terrorists in a Tel Aviv airport.

Election Results. Puerto Rico's first elected governor, Luis Muñoz Marín, who raised the island to commonwealth status in 1952, returned on October 7 to campaign for his Popular Democratic party in the 1972 election. A record turnout of about 85% of the registered voters gave the Popular Democrats a 51% majority, with the result that in January 1973, Rafael Hernandez Colon, the president of the Senate, was slated to become Puerto Rico's fourth elected governor—and, at 36 years old, the youngest.

Incumbent governor Luis Ferre and his New Progressive party got 44% of the vote, while the other four participating parties garnered 5% or less. Whereas Ferre's party is for statehood for Puerto Rico, Hernandez Colon has stated that one of his first acts as governor will be to deal with the United States with the aim of strengthening, perfecting, and possibly perpetuating the commonwealth status that his party originated. Ferre's followers reacted angrily to their defeat, demanding a recount.

UN Study. On August 28, the United Nations Committee on Colonialism voted to appoint a nine-member group to examine the status of Puerto Rico and report in 1973 on whether it should still be regarded as a U. S. colony. The action was requested by interests favoring Puerto Rican independence, since designation as a colony would bring the matter to the UN General Assembly under the 1960 resolution supporting independence for such territories.

——— **PUERTO RICO • Information Highlights** ———

Area: 3,435 square miles (8,897 sq km).
Population (1970 census): 2,712,033. *Density,* 790 per sq mi.
Chief Cities (1970 census): San Juan, the capital, 452,749; Bayamon, 147,552; Ponce, 128,233; Carolina, 94,271; Mayaguez, 68,872; Caguas, 63,215; Guaynabo, 55,310.
Government (1972): *Chief Officers*—governor, Luis A. Ferré (New Progressive party); secy. of state, Fernando Chardón (NPP); atty. gen., Wallace González-Oliver (NPP); secy., dept. of education, Ramón Mellado; chief justice, Luis Negrón-Fernández. *Legislature*—Senate, 27 members (12 New Progressive party, 15 Popular Democratic party); House of Representatives, 51 members (27 NPP, 24 PDP).
Education (1970–71): *Enrollment*—public elementary schools, 464,199 pupils; public intermediate, 167,494 pupils; public high schools, 104,292 pupils, 21,750 teachers; nonpublic schools, 88,609 pupils; college and university (fall 1971), 64,000 students. *Public school expenditures* (1970–71), $298,898,057 ($432 per pupil).
Commonwealth Finance (fiscal year 1969–70): *Revenues,* $823,327,000 (excise taxes, $213,000,000; motor fuel tax, $19,719,000; federal funds, $306,000,000). *Expenditures,* $1,081,200,000 (education, $339,100,000; health, welfare, and safety, $231,900,000; highways, $115,700,000).
Personal Income (1969–70): $3,817,100,000; per capita, $1,427.
Public Assistance (1971): $93,877,000. *Average monthly payments* (Dec. 1971)—old-age assistance, $18.24; aid to families with dependent children, $45.95.
Labor Force: *Nonagricultural wage and salary earners* (1970), 827,000. *Average annual employment* (1970)—manufacturing, 738,000; trade, 138,000; government, 113,000; services, 123,000. *Insured unemployed* (Aug. 1972)—62,600.
Manufacturing (1970): *Value added by manufacture,* $952,700,000. Machinery and metal products, $175,000,000; clothing, $169,000,000; foods, $162,500,000; chemicals, $108,400,000; stone and glass products, $48,600,000.
Agriculture (1970): *Cash farm income,* $271,098,000 (livestock, $135,070,000; crops, $114,540,000; government payments, $21,488,000). *Chief crops*—sugarcane, coffee.
Mining (1971): *Production value,* $67,040,000. *Chief minerals* —Cement, $27,753,000; sand and gravel, $23,319,000.
Transportation: *Highways under maintenance* (1970), 3,684 miles (5,940 km); *motor vehicles* (1970), 614,000; *public airports* (1970), 5.
Communications: *Telephones* (1971), 333,738; *television stations* (1970), 8; *radio stations* (1970), 64; *newspapers* (1971), 4 (daily circulation, 277,871).

Tel Aviv Massacre. On May 30 at Lod Airport near Tel Aviv, 68 Puerto Ricans on a pilgrimage to the Holy Land were subjected to a terrorist act by three Japanese working for the Arab Popular Front for the Liberation of Palestine. About two thirds of the 28 persons killed were Puerto Rican, and nearly 30 other Puerto Ricans were wounded.

Rock Festival. Early April saw the onset of a rock festival near the town of Vega Baja. Some 30,000 persons attended, nearly all from mainland United States. Many Puerto Ricans objected that the festival had nothing to do with the island's culture. Hundreds of participants ran out of money and had to be helped home, one youth was killed by stabbing, and three persons were drowned at sea.

Roberto Clemente. Puerto Ricans were saddened by the death of baseball superstar Roberto Clemente in a plane crash on December 31 while on a relief mission to earthquake victims in Nicaragua. A three-day mourning period was observed in his honor.

EARL PARKER HANSON
Former Consultant, Department of State
Commonwealth of Puerto Rico

PULITZER PRIZES. See PRIZES AND AWARDS.

QUEBEC

Quebec was plagued by labor problems in 1972. Federal-provincial relations were strained over social welfare issues, and the national elections were greatly affected by Quebec's votes.

Labor Problems. The liberal government of Robert Bourassa was confronted in 1972 with the demands of the 210,000 members of the Common Front, a confederation of public service employees, which is divided—according to salaries and functions—into three principal unions: the Confederation of National Trade Unions (CNTU), the Quebec Federation of Labor (QFL), and the Quebec Teachers Corporation (QTC). After an initial 24-hour strike on March 28 and the breakdown of negotiations on April 5, some 200,000 workers called a general strike of unlimited duration. Government injunctions were ignored, and in the weeks that followed there was an increasing number of planned and spontaneous demonstrations.

On April 21, the provincial parliament passed a law suspending the right to strike, ordering an immediate return to work, and threatening severe reprisals for refusal to do so. On May 8 the presidents of the three unions were each sentenced to a year in prison, triggering explosive reactions from the workers. Government threats and police reinforcements soon put an end to the strike, which had been the most important walkout in the history of the Quebec labor movement. Negotiations proceeded sporadically until an agreement was signed on October 13. Some issues were ironed out later.

An anti-union reaction followed conclusion of the agreement. The CNTU, which showed strong socialistic leanings in 1972, was badly shaken. Nearly 60,000 of its members, of which about half were employees of the province, disaffiliated themselves from the union and formed a new union, the Centrale des Syndicats Démocratiques. The new union rejected all forms of political action.

Federal-Provincial Relations. When Minister of Finance John Turner announced the federal budget on May 8, he initiated a veritable constitutional crisis in Quebec. The national budget scuttled Que-

bec's social security proposal for family allowances, worked out by Claude Castonguay, Quebec's minister of social affairs. Castonguay threatened to resign from the provincial cabinet, accusing the Trudeau government of hindering social politics in Quebec. He asked Premier Bourassa to adopt a stronger policy with Ottawa in matters touching social affairs, labor, and agriculture. On May 10, with the province still virtually paralyzed by the Common Front strike, Bourassa dissuaded Castonguay from adding to the crisis by resigning.

Elections. In the federal elections held in October, Quebec again voted in favor of Trudeau's Liberal government. All 56 seats were retained by the Liberals in Quebec. The votes of the French-speaking citizens of the province prevented the establishment of a Progressive Conservative government for Canada, which the nation's English-speaking population seemed to prefer.

Robert Bourassa's Liberal party led a hard battle against the separatist Parti Québécois (PQ), which constituted virtually the entire opposition in Quebec. This party, which nominated candidates only for the provincial parliament, was very active during the federal election campaign, increasing its attacks against the Trudeau regime. During the year former Under Secretary of Intergovernmental Affairs Claude Morin joined the PQ and the party's president, René Lévesque, made a trip to Europe. These incidents assured the party of a lot of publicity, and it became the prime target of the heads of the four federal parties.

Provincial Affairs. The Bourassa government remained powerless in preventing the stagnation of investments and the continuation of a high rate of

UPI

POWER BLACKOUT in March forced these Quebec telephone switchboard operators to work by candlelight.

QUEBEC • Information Highlights

Area: 594,860 square miles (1,540,669 sq km).
Population (1971 census): 6,027,764.
Chief Cities (1971 census): Quebec, the capital (186,088); Montreal (1,214,352); Laval (228,010); Verdun (74,718).
Government: *Chief Officers* (1972)—lt. gov., Hugues Lapointe; premier, Robert Bourassa (Liberal); min. of justice, Jerome Choquette (L); min. of finance, Raymond Garneau (L); min. of educ., François Cloutier (L); min. of social affairs, Claude Castonguay. *Legislature*—National Assembly: 108 members (72 Liberal, 17 Unité-Québec, 12 Créditistes, 7 Parti Québécois).
Education: *School enrollment* (1968–69)—public elementary and secondary, 1,460,000 pupils (73,000 teachers); private schools, 95,375 pupils (6,350 teachers); Indian (federal) schools, 3,625 pupils (155 teachers); college and university, 64,401 students. *Public school expenditures* (1971 est.)—$786,110,000.
Public Finance (fiscal year 1972 est.): *Revenues*, $4,353,-700,000 (sales tax, $1,060,800,000; income tax, $1,365,-000,000; federal funds, $1,165,300,000); *Expenditures*, $4,793,300,000 (education, $1,350,900,000; health and social welfare, $2,346,200,000; transport and communications, $494,200,000).
Personal Income (1969 est.): $15,718,000,000.
Social Welfare (1972 est.): $680,000,000 (aged and blind, $45,000,000; dependents and unemployed, $332,200,000).
Manufacturing (1968): Value added by manufacture, $5,215,-464,000 (food and beverages, $731,478,000; paper and allied industries, $512,531,000; transportation equipment, $405,829,000; fabricated metals, $371,900,000; primary metals, $351,450,000; electrical machinery, $324,317,000.
Agriculture (1971): *Cash farm income*, $692,266,000 (livestock and products, $569,218,000; crops, $61,044,000. *Chief crops* (cash receipts)—vegetables $19,706,000 (ranks 2d among the provinces); potatoes, $12,407,000 (ranks 2d).
Mining (1971 est.): *Production value*, $770,008,000. *Chief minerals* (tons)—copper, 187,062 (ranks 2d among the provinces); asbestos, 1,333,000 (ranks 1st); iron ore, 12,-661,000; zinc, 190,059 (ranks 2d); cement, 47,277,000.
Fisheries (1971): *Commercial catch*, sea fish, 238,739,000 pounds ($10,243,000). *Leading species*—cod, 55,188,000 pounds ($2,890,000); redfish, 67,424,000 pounds ($2,297,-000); lobster, 2,443,000 pounds ($1,870,000).
Transportation: *Roads* (1968), 56,548 miles (90,986 km); *motor vehicles* (1969), 1,998,001; *railroads* (1970 est.), 5,329 track miles (8,570 km); *licensed airports* (1971 est.), 73.
Communications: *Telephones* (1969), 2,510,229; *television stations* (1971), 51; *daily newspapers* (1971), 16.
(All monetary figures given in Canadian dollars.)

---

unemployment, which remained between 8.0% and 8.7% throughout 1972. In spite of the fact that new jobs had been created, unemployment continued to rise.

Economic problems, however, received less attention in 1972 than did linguistic ones. Montreal's powerful English-speaking minority had long delayed the adoption of provincial legislation concerning the use of French on the job and in other situations. Meanwhile, the proportion of Canadians whose mother tongue is French declined from 28% in 1961 to 26% in 1971. The matter was viewed as especially important in Quebec, four fifths of whose residents are French-speaking people. These people made up over 80% of all the French-speaking population of the nation.

James Bay Project. The multibillion-dollar program to develop the energy resources of the James Bay area in northern Quebec proceeded in 1972 with the selection of the first hydroelectric site, Grand Rivière. This first project, which was expected to cost $6 billion, was the subject of much criticism, centering on the fact that the task of managing the development was assigned to a subsidiary of a foreign firm (Bechtel Corp. of San Francisco) rather than kept under the full control of Hydro Quebec. The Indians of northern Quebec, who saw the project as a menace to their survival, also voiced protests.

ROBERT COMEAU
Université du Québec à Montréal

RADIO. See TELEVISION AND RADIO.
RAILROADS. See TRANSPORTATION.

Colin Davis (above) *conducted performances of two of 1972's most impressive classical releases—Berlioz'* Benvenuto Cellini *and Mozart's* Le Nozze di Figaro *—both with the BBC Symphony Orchestra, of which he is chief guest conductor.*

recordings

The recording industry, though in a state of some confusion, showed signs of strength in 1972. Sales were up, with the industry attempting to meet changes in taste and listenership. In all recording areas—classical, popular, and jazz—there was a sense of excitement that had been missing for a number of years. In the technical field, the development of four-channel equipment continued to occupy the attention of manufacturers, despite the emergence of several competing systems.

CLASSICAL RECORDS

The pessimism that has pervaded the classical recording community over the past five years showed signs of lifting during 1972. Virtually every manufacturer could point to increased sales, and dealers in three U.S. cities—New York, Chicago, and San Francisco—reported a marked rise in consumer interest. One Chicago store, in fact, boasted that over 50% of its turnover was in the classical line.

Youth Market. Significantly, there is a growing number of young people between the ages of 20 and 30 who are beginning to investigate classical records of all sorts, from baroque to avant-garde. One explanation is the current trend to use classical music as the basis of film scores. Such popular films as *2001* (with music by both Richard and Johann Strauss), *Elvira Madigan* (Mozart), and *A Clockwork Orange* (Beethoven) have exposed a great many youthful filmgoers to classical music for the first time. (The easy availability of classical composers' "Greatest Hits" series by RCA and Columbia has also clearly contributed to the expanding market, although the rather lazy appeal of these albums probably is aimed at the more casual older buyer.)

An even more likely explanation for the younger generation's sudden discovery of the classics may be traced, oddly enough, to their earlier rock-and-roll teenage years. The recordings of the Beatles, the Rolling Stones, Simon and Garfunkel, the Mothers, and other groups of the 1960's, unlike the easy-listening trivia of the 1950's, prepared youngsters for an active exploration of the richer, more demanding listening experiences offered by classical music. At any rate, in all college communities there is an increased demand for this kind of music.

A SELECTION OF NOTABLE CLASSICAL RELEASES IN 1972

BACH, *Cantatas* (Vols. 1, 2, 3): Concentus Musicus and the Leonhardt Consort; Nikolaus Harnoncourt and Gustav Leonhardt, conductors (Telefunken, 6 discs)

BERLIOZ, *Benvenuto Cellini:* Nicolai Gedda and other singers; BBC Symphony Orchestra, Colin Davis, conductor (Philips, 4 discs)

BERNSTEIN, *Mass:* Alan Titus, baritone; chorus and orchestra, Leonard Bernstein, conductor (Columbia, 2 discs)

BRAHMS, *Die schöne Magelone:* Dietrich Fischer-Dieskau, baritone; Sviatoslav Richter, piano (Angel)

CRUMB, *Black Angels:* New York String Quartet (CRI)

DELIUS, *A Mass of Life:* Heather Harper, Benjamin Luxon, and other singers; London Philharmonic Choir and Orchestra, Charles Groves, conductor (Angel, 2 discs)

FOSTER, *Songs:* Jan DeGaetani, mezzo; Leslie Guinn, baritone; Gilbert Kalish, piano (Nonesuch)

JANÁČEK, *Works for Piano and Orchestra:* Rudolf Firkusny, piano; Orchestra of the Bavarian Radio, Rafael Kubelik, conductor (Deutsche Grammophon, 2 discs)

LISZT, *Operatic Paraphrases:* Jorge Bolet, piano (RCA)

LISZT, *Tone Poems* (complete): Concertgebouw Orchestra, Bernard Haitink, conductor (Philips, 5 discs)

MAHLER, *Symphony No. 8:* Soloists and chorus; Chicago Symphony Orchestra, Georg Solti, conductor (London, 2 discs)

MONTEVERDI, *Madrigals* (Books 8, 9, and 10): Soloists, Glyndebourne Opera Chorus, and the Ambrosian Singers; English Chamber Orchestra, Raymond Leppard, conductor (Philips, 5 discs)

MOZART, *The Marriage of Figaro:* Jessye Norman, Mirella Freni, and other singers; BBC Symphony Orchestra, Colin Davis, conductor (Philips, 4 discs)

OFFENBACH, *The Tales of Hoffman:* Joan Sutherland, Placido Domingo, and other singers; L'Orchestre de la Suisse Romande, Richard Bonynge, conductor (London, 3 discs)

ROSSINI, *La Cenerentola:* Teresa Berganza, Luigi Alva, and other singers; London Symphony Orchestra, Claudio Abbado, conductor (Deutsche Grammophon, 3 discs)

SCHOENBERG/BERG/WEBERN, *String Quartets* (complete): LaSalle Quartet (Deutsche Grammophon, 5 discs)

STRAUSS, *Capriccio:* Gundula Janowitz, Hermann Prey, and other singers; Bavarian Radio Orchestra, Karl Böhm, conductor (Deutsche Grammaphon, 3 discs)

WAGNER, *Ring of the Nibelungs:* Martha Mödl, Wolfgang Windgassen, and other singers; Chorus and Orchestra of RAI, Rome, Wilhelm Furtwangler, conductor (Seraphim, 19 discs)

Distribution. The perennial problem of distribution remains serious. Many prospective classical collectors in smaller cities find themselves thwarted simply because local record stores cannot afford to keep a comprehensive stock of available discs. How to reach this market is one of the industry's main dilemmas, and the mail order system now offered by large dealers in metropolitan areas is only a stopgap solution at best.

European Imports. Europe, Britain in particular, still provides the source of almost all classical discs marketed in the United States, largely as a result of the high fees demanded by American unions and the unwillingness of Columbia and RCA to expand their catalogs. In addition to discs by the major European firms, a dizzying assortment of records by smaller firms are being imported, usually by record stores themselves. This development provides another indication that classical record sales are showing healthy growth in the United States.

PETER G. DAVIS
Music Editor
"High Fidelity" Magazine

POPULAR RECORDS

The popular music field in 1972 was continually teased (badgered?) with the promise (threat?) that rock and roll was making a comeback. It didn't happen, but all the talk seemed to have an effect.

Changing Tastes. Such groups as the J. Giels Band, which concentrated on making music loud and danceable rather than stylish, had their best season in years, and the Rolling Stones, the world's premier rock group, timed the release of *Exile on Main Street,* an oddly muddy-sounding, unprogressive album, to coincide with their massively publicized American tour. The album was an enormous commercial success, but no one seemed certain whether that was because of the tour, because any Stones album would sell, or because people actually did want music to boogie to.

Folk and Rock. Modernized folk singers still commanded attention. The first months of the year saw practically everyone humming Don McLean's *American Pie,* so far the most popular song of the 1970's. *American Pie,* the culmination of McLean's many years of hard work in small clubs, described "the day the music died" and purported to chronicle the decline and fall of the "rock culture" of the 1960's.

Other important folkies, such as Steve Goodman, John Prine, and Jackson Browne, emerged from obscurity during the year. Goodman's *City of New Orleans* was included in John Denver's critically successful but uncommercial *Aerie* album, then earned heavy radio play for Arlo Guthrie. Prine and Browne had songs recorded by several well-known performers, in addition to cutting albums themselves. Denver's *Goodbye Again* became popular at year's end, despite its similarities to his famous *Leaving on a Jet Plane.*

Tom Paxton returned to the biting satire of his early career in an excellent album, *Peace Will Come.* Randy Newman was funnier, more ironic, and less categorizeable than ever in his *Sail Away*

SELECTED POPULAR RELEASES IN 1972

DAVID ACKLES: *American Gothic,* Elektra EKS-75032
JACKSON BROWNE, *Jackson Browne,* Asylum SD 5051
ERIC CLAPTON: *History of Eric Clapton,* Atco SD 2-803
JUDY COLLINS: *Living,* Elektra EKS-75014
DELANEY AND BONNIE: *D & B Together,* Columbia KC 31377
JOHN DENVER: *Aerie,* RCA LSP-4607
FAIRPORT CONVENTION: *"Baddacombe" Lee,* A & M SP 4333
ARETHA FRANKLIN: *Amazing Grace,* Atlantic SD 2-906
DAN HICKS AND HIS HOT LICKS: *Striking It Rich,* Blue Thumb BTS36
JETHRO TULL: *Thick as a Brick,* Reprise MS 2072
DR. JOHN: *Gumbo,* Atco 7006
ELTON JOHN: *Honky Chateau,* Uni 93135
PAUL KANTNER AND GRACE SLICK: *Sunfighter,* Grunt FTR-1002
THE KINKS: *Everybody's in Show-Biz,* RCA VPS-6065; *Muswell Hillbillies,* RCA LSP-4644
GORDON LIGHTFOOT: *Don Quixote,* Reprise MS 2056
VAN MORRISON: *Saint Dominic's Preview,* Warner Bros. BS 2633
RANDY NEWMAN: *Sail Away,* Reprise MS 2064
TOM PAXTON: *Peace Will Come,* Reprise 2096
SEALS AND CROFTS: *Year of Sunday,* Warner Bros. BS-2568
PAUL SIMON, *Paul Simon,* Columbia KC 30750
ROD STEWART: *Never a Dull Moment,* Mercury SRM 1646
JIMMY WEBB: *Letters,* Reprise MS 2055
NEIL YOUNG: *Harvest,* Reprise MS 2032

Three Dog Night made a hugely successful tour of the United States. In the process it was learned that all seven of the group's albums had been certified as "gold"—that is, each had sales of more than $1 million.

Hard Rock. In the realm of hard rock, Jethro Tull produced the enigmatic *Thick as a Brick,* a one-song album encased in a 12-page satirical "newspaper" jacket. The Kinks had two excellent theme albums, *Muswell Hillbillies,* describing the alienation of the workingman, and *Everybody's in Show-Biz,* dealing with the joys and sorrows of the struggle for recognition. Rod Stewart, who seems always to come up with something big for the opening of school each fall, had the song *You Wear it Well* on most radios. It sounded a bit like his 1971 entry, *Maggie May.* Elton John's *Honky Chateau* album, particularly its *Rocket Man* cut, drew public and critical praise.

NOEL COPPAGE
Contributing Editor, "Stereo Review"

JAZZ RECORDS

There were stirrings in 1972 that suggested the jazz world was about to move out of the doubt and doldrums through which it fumbled in the 1960's. The most vivid—if somewhat localized—evidence of this change was the interest aroused by the Newport Jazz Festival, which moved from Rhode Island to New York City in July. For nine days the festival sent out tremors of excitement—because it was held in New York and because it was the celebrated Newport event.

Recording Activity. Reflecting the change, the recording industry showed a new sense of involvement in jazz. It demonstrated its interest by issuing discs that represented both the new and the old. In the first category was *The Inner Mounting Flame* (Columbia KC 31067) by John McLaughlin's Mahavishnu Orchestra, whose combination of jazz and electronic rock made this group one of the most popular concert attractions of 1972. In the second was *Skies of America* (Columbia KC 31562), the debut performance of Ornette Coleman's composition for symphony orchestra and jazz group. Appearances by McLaughlin and Coleman were among the most widely heralded events at the Newport festival.

The year saw the return to recording activity of two giants of an earlier era. Tenor saxophonist Sonny Rollins, who drew fascinated young audiences that knew him only as a figure of legend when he made his return appearance in the spring of 1972, brought out *Next Album* (Milestone 9042). Charles Mingus' new 20-piece orchestra, which played brilliantly in jazz clubs but had not yet completely found itself, established a reputation with *Let My Children Hear Music* (Columbia KC 31309).

New Labels. Several new jazz labels expanded the flow of jazz releases. Cobblestone served as a showcase for a wide variety of new, young jazz musicians, most notably the saxophonist Eric Kloss (Cobblestone 9006) and the polished young guitarist Pat Martino (Cobblestone 9015). MPS released a flood of European recordings by such internationally famous jazz stars as Oscar Peterson, Ella Fitzgerald, Stuff Smith, Buddy Tate, and Earl Hines. Chiaroscuro, a small label, concentrated on pianists such as Don Ewell (Chiaroscuro 106) and Mary Lou Williams (Chiaroscuro 103), but it also put out one of the best recorded examples of cornetist

MICK JAGGER, lead singer of the Rolling Stones, the world's most popular rock group. The Stones timed the release of their enormously successful new album, Exile on Main Street, to coincide with their 1972 American tour.

album. Neil Young's *Harvest* was his simplest and most successful album, with *Old Man* and *Heart of Gold* ranking with the year's most popular hits. Before *Harvest* appeared, a trio of young Americans living in Britain—and calling themselves "America"—wrote and tried to sound as much like Young as possible, scoring with *Horse With No Name,* the year's second big single.

Bobby Hackett's work, *Live at the Roosevelt Grill* (Chiaroscuro 105).

Reissues. Two outstanding reissue series were introduced during 1972. Prestige began organizing some classic jazz performances of the 1950's in two-disc albums by the Modern Jazz Quartet, Charlie Parker, Miles Davis, John Coltrane, Thelonious Monk, Charles Mingus, Sonny Rollins, and others. Capitol, through the initiative of EMI, its Netherlands affiliate, was represented by 15 collections of recordings made in the late 1940's and early 1950's by Miles Davis, Art Tatum, Lennie Tristano, Duke Ellington, Billie Holiday, Stan Kenton, Gerry Mulligan, and many more.

One particularly notable reissue development was an arrangement between Biograph Records, a small reissue label, and Columbia whereby Biograph gained access to recordings that Columbia was not planning to reissue under its own label. This unprecedented arrangement resulted in the release of long-unavailable collections by early 1930's groups featuring Benny Goodman (Biograph C-1) and Jack Teagarden (Biograph C-2) and by the pioneering Boswell Sisters (Biograph C-3).

Other Releases. Other jazz releases of special interest in 1972 included Harold Ashby, *Born to Swing* (Master Jazz Recordings 8112); Count Basie, *Super Chief* (Columbia G 31224); Gary Burton, *Alone at Last* (Atlantic SD 1598); Charlie Christian, *Solo Flight* (Columbia G 30779); Dizzy Gillespie–Bobby Hackett–Mary Lou Williams, *Giants* (Perception 19); Billie Holiday, *Gallant Lady* (Monmouth–Evergreen 7046); JPJ Quartet, *Montreux '71* (Master Jazz Recordings 8111); Stan Kenton, *Today* (London 44179-80); Lee Konitz, *Spirits* (Milestone 9038); *Spirituals to Swing, 1967* (Columbia G 30776); and Dick Wellstood, *From Ragtime On* (Chiaroscuro 109).

JOHN S. WILSON, *"The New York Times" and "High Fidelity" Magazine*

AUDIO EQUIPMENT AND TECHNIQUES

As it has for the past several years, four-channel technology absorbed much of the thought and activity of audio manufacturers in 1972. With the tape cassette sidelined for the moment because of restrictions imposed by Philips, its developer and licenser, the four-channel recording media remain limited to open-reel tape, eight-track tape cartridge, and, most importantly, phonograph records. This year as last, the greatest attention was focussed on the several competing systems for four-channel disc recording, and particularly on the CBS (Columbia)-SQ and RCA-JVC (Japan Victor Corporation) systems.

CBS-SQ Progress. For the CBS-SQ system, which is presently the leader among the so-called matrix systems for four-channel recording and reproduction because of its initiative in the market, 1972 was a year of building and consolidation. Much of this effort was directed toward acquiring new licensees for the system, which now number approximately 52, and enlarging the repertoire of SQ-processed LP's available to the consumer. Early in the year CBS and Electro-Voice agreed to coordinate their development efforts to ensure reasonable compatibility between their two systems. Electro-Voice controls a basic patent on matrixing through its association with matrix pioneer Peter Scheiber. A direct result of their joint efforts was the "new" Electro-Voice matrix system, which shares characteristics of both the SQ system and the original Electro-Voice matrix. The new Electro-Voice decoding parameters may serve as a model for SQ circuits in relatively inexpensive applications of the near future.

In autumn of 1972 the Sony Corporation of America, the original SQ licensee, introduced the SQD-2000 decoder ($299.50) containing so-called "full-logic" or "wave-matching" SQ decoding. Lafayette also brought out the LR-4000 four-channel receiver with the same facility. Although full-logic SQ decoding was used in the first demonstrations of the SQ system, it was previously unavailable to the consumer. Full-logic is able to identify the signals intended to go to each of the speakers in a four-channel array after they are decoded, and virtually "turn off" any speaker not supposed to be playing at a particular moment. This prevents that speaker from reproducing "leakage" information from other channels. However, in its present form, full-logic decoding cannot prevent inter-channel leakage (loss of stereo separation) between speakers that have simultaneous signals assigned them by the matrix.

RCA-JVC Progress. Throughout most of 1972 the developers of the JVC "discrete" disc system maintained a low profile while they dealt with a number of practical problems. Among these were the recording on a disc of a subcarrier of so high a frequency as to be beyond audibility, which prevents the user's reproducing stylus from obliterating the high frequencies through record wear; and fitting the additional subcarrier information on the disc without reducing the loudness level of the recording or its playing time per side. RCA's efforts bore fruit in early autumn with Hugo Montenegro's *Love Theme from The Godfather,* the first American-made CD-4 release. It was molded from a hardened vinyl compound for resistance to record wear. Soon after, with *The Fantastic Philadelphians, Volume 2,* a playing time of 25 minutes per side was achieved—which approaches the figure considered a reasonable maximum for conventional LP records.

Although demodulators (decoders) for the JVC CD-4 (Compatible-Discrete Four Channel) system have been available for some time in Japan, their introduction in the U. S. has been delayed. Late in 1972 component demodulators were still not being advertised, although samples had been distributed to the press. However, RCA has announced that the bulk of its new material will be released in CD-4 form—at standard LP prices—to emphasize the stereo compatibility of the system.

Sansui QS System. At the New York convention of the Audio Engineering Society in September, Sansui demonstrated a new development in its QS matrix system, called "Vario-Matrix" decoding. It consists of a matrix decoder with continuously varying parameters that works to enhance the localization of the strongest signals being processed at any given moment. The theoretical basis for the system is a psychoacoustical phenomenon of the human hearing mechanism by which a sound source enjoying a 10-decibel loudness advantage over one or more competing sources "masks" the locations (directionality) of the others. The Vario-Matrix decoder demonstrated was a professional unit and as yet no plans for a consumer version have been announced.

RALPH W. HODGES
Associate Technical Editor, "Stereo Review"

REFUGEES

The world refugee population was estimated to be nearly 16 million at the end of October 1972. During the 12-month period ending on Oct. 31, 1972, a record number of new refugees entered the company of the homeless.

Asia. In South Vietnam the increased tempo of the fighting in 1972 resulted in 500,000 new refugees, raising this country's total number of refugees to more than 4 million. In Cambodia there were more than one-half million war refugees, many of whom had left their homes because of the bombing.

More than 10 million people fled East Pakistan during the fighting there and returned six months later to the new country of Bangladesh. About 32 million people in Bangladesh, including the 10 million returnees, need emergency housing, medical aid, and educational facilities. As a result, the largest international emergency relief operation in history has been undertaken. The U. S. government and private agencies have committed nearly $270 million to this task.

The crown colony of Hong Kong received more than 14,000 refugees from China in 1972, the largest number since the great exodus of May 1962. Most of these refugees were under 25.

Middle East. Palestinian refugees, numbering 1.6 million, continued their restless wait for a political settlement that would offer a solution to their problem. Refugees since 1948, they have waited longer than any other group in the world.

Africa. After 17 years of fighting, peace was reached by Sudan in 1972. More than 200,000 refugees are expected to return from surrounding asylum countries during the next few years. The Sudanese refugees were resettled in the Central African Republic, Uganda, and the Congo by the UN high commissioner for refugees, and the high commissioner's office has been supervising their repatriation. Sudan is the most underdeveloped country in Africa, and a strong international effort is under way to build the basic educational, medical, and vocational facilities needed by its people.

In Burundi an intertribal bloodletting resulted in the death of more than 100,000 members of the Hutu tribe. About 108,000 Hutu escaped to Uganda, Tanzania, and the Congo.

In Zambia there were 10,000 new refugees from Malawi. They were members of the Jehovah's Witnesses who fled the country after they had had violent clashes with members of the youth wing of the Malawi Congress party.

Uganda, whose government has given asylum to many thousands of refugees over the years, created a refugee problem of its own in 1972 by forcing the repatriation of at least 55,000 Asians, most of whom had lived in East Africa for a generation or more. Many African countries have expelled noncitizens on the ground that all available employment should go to their own nationals. The Ugandan action was unique only in the number of victims and the haste with which their expulsion was accomplished. The United States agreed to take 1,000 of these refugees. About 20,000 holding British passports were to go to England, and the remainder were to go to other countries in the West, as well as to India and Pakistan.

R. NORRIS WILSON
United States Committee for Refugees

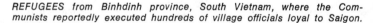
REFUGEES *from Binhdinh province, South Vietnam, where the Communists reportedly executed hundreds of village officials loyal to Saigon.*

RELIGION

Participants in January ecumenical service in St. Patrick's Cathedral (from left): the Most Rev. Michael Ramsey, Archbishop of Canterbury; Terence Cardinal Cooke, Archbishop of New York; Greek Orthodox Archbishop Iakovos.

Developments in the major religions of the world in 1972, including trends, meetings, and principal events, are covered under the following headings: (1) General Survey; (2) Protestantism; (3) Roman Catholicism; (4) Judaism; (5) Eastern Orthodox Church; (6) Islam; and (7) Oriental Religions. A statistical table giving the membership of U. S. denominations is included. (See also a special feature on Religion beginning on page 14.)

General Survey

In 1972 there was intensified, and at times dramatic, disagreement among members of religious groups and scholars of religion regarding the distinctive role of religion in an era of rapid social change. Some pointed to the significant numerical expansion of religious bodies that offer clearly defined total interpretations of life and demand extensive commitment of time and money as evidence for the essentially personal and devotional character of religion, in contrast with the declining memberships of established liberal groups. Others hailed the continued free exploration of new formulations of traditional faiths and more radical involvement of religious groups in political and social action as expressions of the most authentic, if not the most popular, functions of religion.

Evangelical and Conservative Growth. The most rapidly growing religious groups in the United States are evangelical and conservative. The Church of Jesus Christ of Latter-day Saints (Mormon),

which in October elected Harold Bingham Lee as president, has grown by 50% in the United States and 250% outside the United States in the past 12 years. The Southern Baptist Convention, which now has a national constituency, has rapidly expanded to become one of the largest Protestant groups in the United States. Pentecostal and evangelistic bodies are experiencing unprecedented growth. "Jesus movements," which stress emotional satisfaction and conservative theology, are attracting increasing numbers of students and other young people. In Japan, the militant Nichiren Shoshu sect of Buddhism (Soka Gokkai) has grown from 3,000 members in 1945 to 8 million in 1972, including at least 100,000 in the United States.

Protestantism. Older and more established Christian bodies, which have been more extensively involved in social action and are more permissive in theological and ethical formulations, continued to decline in numbers and financial support. In August the World Council of Churches (WCC) elected Dr. Philip Potter, a Methodist from the West Indies, as its first non-Caucasian secretary general. At the same time the WCC came under increased criticism for its support of some militant political groups in Africa, and financial difficulties caused curtailment of some programs.

Roman Catholicism. Similar conflict of definition and aim continued in Roman Catholicism. In May the Vatican announced wider episcopal participation and some consultation with lower clergy and

U.S. CHURCH MEMBERSHIP

Religious Body	Members	Religious Body	Members
Adventists, Seventh-day	420,419	Friends United Meeting	67,785
American Carpatho-Russian Orthodox		Greek Orthodox Archdiocese of	
Greek Catholic Church	106,900	North and South America	1,950,000
Apostolic Overcoming Holy Church of God	75,000[1]	Independent Fundamental Churches	
Armenian Apostolic Church of America	125,000	of America	111,611
Armenian Church of North America,		Int'l Church of the Foursquare Gospel	89,215[11]
Diocese of the	300,000	Jehovah's Witnesses	388,920
Assemblies of God	1,064,631	Jewish Congregations	5,780,000
Baptist Association, American	790,000	Latter-day Saints, Church of Jesus Christ of	2,073,146
Baptist Association of America, Conservative	300,000	Latter-day Saints, Reorganized Church	
Baptist Church, United Free Will	100,000[2]	of Jesus Christ of	152,670
Baptist Churches, General Association		Lutheran Church, The American	2,543,293
of Regular	210,000	Lutheran Church in America	3,106,844
Baptist Convention, American	1,472,478	Lutheran Church—Missouri Synod	2,788,536
Baptist Convention, Inc., National Primitive	1,523,000	Lutheran Synod, Wisconsin Evangelical	381,321
Baptist Convention, Inc.,		Mennonite Church	88,522
Progressive National	521,692[3]	Methodist Church, The United	10,671,774
Baptist Convention of America, National	2,668,799[1]	Methodist Church of North America, Free	64,901
Baptist Convention, Southern	11,628,032	Methodist Episcopal Church, African	1,166,301[5]
Baptist Convention, U.S.A., Inc., National	5,500,000[4]	Methodist Episcopal Church, Christian	466,718[12]
Baptist Evangelical Life and Soul Saving		Methodist Episcopal Zion Church, African	940,000
Assembly of U.S.A., National	57,674[5]	Moravian Church in* America,	
Baptist General Conference	103,955	Southern Province, The	36,449
Baptist General Conference,		North American Old Roman Catholic Church	59,121
North American	54,997	Orthodox Church in America (Russian Orthodox	
Baptist Missionary Association of America	187,246	Greek Catholic Church of America)	1,000,000
Baptists, Free Will	186,136	Pentecostal Church, Inc., United	250,000
Baptists, General Ass'n of General	65,000	Pentecostal Church of God of America, Inc.	115,000[13]
Baptists, Primitive	72,000[6]	Pentecostal Holiness Church, Inc.	67,778
Baptists, United	63,641[7]	Polish National Catholic Church of America	282,411[14]
Brethren, Church of the	186,136	Presbyterian Church, Cumberland	92,025
Buddhist Churches of America	100,000	Presbyterian Church in the U.S.A.,	
Bulgarian Eastern Orthodox Church	86,000[8]	The United	3,087,213
Christian and Missionary Alliance, The	112,519	Reformed Church, Christian	285,628
Christian Church (Disciples of Christ)	1,424,479	Reformed Church in America	367,606
Christian Reformed Church	285,628	Roman Catholic Church, The	48,214,729
Church of Christ, Scientist	268,915[9]	Rumanian Orthodox Episcopate of America	50,000
Church of God, The	75,890	Russian Orthodox Church Outside Russia	55,000[7]
Church of God (Anderson, Ind.)	150,198	Serbian Eastern Orthodox Diocese	
Church of God (Cleveland, Tenn.)	272,276	for the U.S.A. and Canada	65,000[3]
Church of the Nazarene	383,284	Spiritualists, International General	
Churches of Christ	2,400,000[10]	Assembly of	164,072[1]
Congregational Christian Churches,		Unitarian Universalist Association	265,408[15]
National Association of	85,000	United Church of Christ	1,960,608
Episcopal Church, The	3,285,826	Wesleyan Church, The	84,499
Evangelical Covenant Church of America	67,441		
Evangelical Free Church of America, The	70,490		

Figures are mainly for the years 1970 and 1971. [1] 1956. [2] 1952. [3] 1967. [4] 1958. [5] 1951. [6] 1950. [7] 1955. [8] 1962. [9] Data not reported; figure given here from U.S. Census of Religious Bodies, 1936. [10] 1962. [11] 1963. [12] 1965. [13] 1967. [14] 1960. [15] 1969. (Source: National Council of Churches of Christ in the U.S.A., Yearbook of American Churches for 1971.

laymen in the nomination and appointment of bishops. Fresh forms of liturgical expression and more vigorous social action were also encouraged. On the matter of clerical celibacy and the exclusion of women from clerical functions, however, Pope Paul VI rigorously reaffirmed a conservative traditional position. Theologians who were deemed to be going too far in their criticisms of traditional doctrines, including that of papal infallibility, were rebuked, and Dutch Catholics were warned against the use of a new liberal catechism.

Other Religious Groups. Jews in the United States and abroad vigorously protested a tax on Jews seeking emigration from the Soviet Union, and leaders of many religious groups joined Jews in expressions of outrage at the use of terrorist tactics by militant Arab Palestinians, including massacres at the Tel Aviv airport and in Munich at the Olympic Games.

Demetrios I was elected to succeed Athenagoras I as ecumenical patriarch of Eastern Orthodox Christians in July. There were calls for new vitality and unity among the 250 million members of that communion, and for greater independence for the patriarchate in Turkey.

Muslims continued to debate the extent of reform of traditional teaching required and permitted for the process of modernization. Arab Muslim rights in Palestine continued to dominate political concerns, but there were varying views of appropriate political action.

In August the major societies of scholars for the study of religion met in an international congress in Los Angeles. The theme was "Religion and the Humanization of Man." It was noted that religious studies are flourishing in colleges and universities, but also that political conflicts have curtailed the free movement of scholars between the continents.

J. A. MARTIN, JR.
Columbia University

Protestantism

The Protestant scene in 1972 could perhaps be best characterized as ambivalent. On the one hand, the denigration of the institutional church and organized religion in general lost its strident tone. Many of the larger Protestant bodies, heeding those critics who deplored the rise of bureaucracies, have drastically cut their staff, in part because of loss of contributions but also to give local or regional bodies a chance to express their own creativity. On the other hand, the rise of spontaneous, evangelical movements characterized by mass rallies—such as Explo 72—have added a new vitality to the institutional church. No new structures have been added to the churches, but the uninstitutionalized Christianity expressed by these movements has strengthened the institutional church. Furthermore, there also was evidence of a lessening of the social activism of the 1960's and greater concern for the deepening of the personal spiritual life.

The Jesus People and the Charismatics. Two major movements within Protestantism in 1972, one neo-Evangelical and the other neo-Pentecostal, have had a significant impact. Both of the movements stress prayer and a strong Biblical orientation. The neo-Evangelicals emphasize the ministry of preaching; the neo-Pentecostals focus more on the baptism and gifts of the Holy Spirit, such as healing and speaking in tongues.

The most dramatic indication of the strength of the neo-evangelical movement was Explo 72, a gathering of some 80,000 young people in Dallas, Texas, in June. The gigantic week-long rally was intended to prepare them to take the message of Christ to the world. (See special feature on Religion beginning on page 14.)

Ecumenism. Protestantism in the United States was shocked when the United Presbyterian Church in the U. S. A., a 3-million-member body, voted at its annual convention to withdraw from the Consultation on Church Union (COCU). COCU is a church unity effort to merge nine Protestant denominations into one church of 25 million members. Although leaders for union in the remaining eight church bodies expressed the hope that the unity talks would proceed, the general feeling was that the merger movement would either fade away or possibly take some different form.

In Britain, the Scheme for Union of the Methodist Church and the Anglican Church failed despite the fact that the reunion of the two churches had been studied and discussed for some years. In Canada, the proposed union of the United Church of Canada, the Anglican Church in Canada, and the Disciples was also declared virtually dead, although a joint committee from the three bodies was continuing its studies.

One church union did occur in October when the Assemblies of Congregationalists and English Presbyterians merged to form the United Reformed Church.

The rather dismal outcome of the many church union efforts drew a variety of reactions from theological observers. There was overall agreement that many church members and their leaders hesitated to give up traditional beliefs or practices for the sake of a larger church body which might also develop an even more formidable central bureaucracy. Likewise within many of the church bodies there remained a large group of conservative members who believed that a merger might mean a watering down of theological principles.

Although there was a reluctance to unify churches into one body, there were many instances during the year of denominations achieving better theological understanding of each other's confessions. Such understanding, while not as dramatic as the merger of denominations, could eventually lead to structural unification. Lutheran and Roman Catholic theologians, for example, issued a report that declared, "It is possible for both loyal Lutherans and loyal Catholics to envision new possibilities of concord." Earlier the theologians had declared there was common agreement on the Apostles and Nicene Creeds and on the meaning of the Holy Communion or Mass. The group also declared that the issue of the pope's first rank position in the Catholic Church was open to discussion. In addition, Lutherans declared that the Pope's office could be a unifying force in Christendom.

A joint Lutheran-Episcopal dialogue group also reported that sufficient theological agreement existed between the two confessions to permit intercommunion in parishes where there are good ecumenical relations.

Internal Disharmony. The Lutheran Church-Missouri Synod, a 3-million-member body, became involved in a bitter intramural battle between theological conservatives and liberals in 1972. The genesis of the quarrel was a report issued by the synodical president, Jacob A. Preus, which accused the faculty of Concordia Seminary in St. Louis of holding a "view of Scriptures which in practice erodes the authority of the Bible." The seminary faculty countered with a report denying the charges of heretical beliefs. The issues will probably not be resolved until 1973 when the synod meets for its biennial convention.

The Southern Presbyterians (Presbyterian Church in the U. S.) are engaged in a similar battle between liberals and conservatives, with the latter group maintaining that the church has abandoned many fundamental theological beliefs in favor of social activism. While the majority of the congregations have not left the church, a small group, which has come to be known as the "Vanguard Presbytery," organized itself into a "Provisional Presbytery for Southern Presbyterians and Reformed Churches Uniting."

Church Gains and Losses. The Gallup Poll on U. S. churchgoing, released in January 1972, showed a continuing downward trend starting in 1958, with 40% of adults of all faiths attending their place of worship in a typical week. The decline was most pronounced among Roman Catholics, while churchgoing among Protestants remained at 37%.

On the other hand, the 1972 Yearbook of American Churches reported a slight increase in overall church membership of 63.2%, as contrasted with 62.4% in the previous yearbook. Some of the mainline Protestant denominations reported losses, notably the United Methodist church, down about 200,000 to 10,671,774.

While some denominations reported gains in contributions, there was a general downward trend. Religion received 40.7% of the charitable dollar, even though giving to religion had increased by $300 million. Inflation, competition for the dollar, and declining church attendance were contributory factors.

Transition. World Protestantism mourned the death of Lord Geoffrey Francis Fisher, Archbishop of Canterbury from 1945 to 1961, who died on September 14 at 85. (See NECROLOGY.)

The Rev. Dr. Philip A. Potter, a 51-year-old West Indian Methodist, was elected secretary general of the World Council of Churches, succeeding Dr. Eugene Carson Blake, who retired on October 31. (See BIOGRAPHY—*Potter.*)

ALFRED P. KLAUSLER
Executive Director, Associated Church Press

Roman Catholicism

During 1972 the Roman Catholic Church continued the process of reform that had been encouraged by the second Vatican Council (1962–66). The process was marked by some uncertainty and conflict, particularly as an emerging pluralism within the church encountered resistance among those who saw a need for stricter orthodoxy and tighter unity. The main focus of the church's external apostolic effort was that defined by the 1971 Synod of Bishops —justice in the world.

Pluralism and Unity. The tension between those who called for greater decentralization in order that the church might more effectively adapt to particular peoples and cultures, and those who feared a loss of identity and authority through fragmentation, was most clearly evident in a series of controversies. They involved Vatican congregations, officials, and the pope himself on the one hand, and the bishops, people, and clergy of the Catholic Church in the Netherlands, on the other.

Three incidents in particular brought the different viewpoints of Rome and the Netherlands before the public eye. Early in the year Pope Paul appointed a conservative churchman, Jan. M. Gijsen, to the diocese of Roermond. The new bishop was known to be unsympathetic to the liberal views of many in the diocese and had not been recommended by those consulted. He soon encountered difficulties even with his own staff, although he was later vindicated by a Vatican investigation. A Dutch national pastoral council, scheduled to meet in October, was cancelled because of Vatican objections that the authority of the hierarchy would be challenged by such a meeting. The Dutch bishops themselves disagreed. Finally, after two years of study, two Roman congregations ordered that an experimental catechism used in secondary schools be withdrawn from the schools.

Selection of Bishops. The problems of the Dutch church reflected a widely felt need in the church for new structures that would allow for greater participation in the life of the church and the kind of shared responsibility for all the faithful that seemed to be the vision of Vatican II's ecclesiology of the "people of God." Although new norms for the selection of bishops were published in the spring that made some provision for the consultation of the people of a diocese, there was widespread criticism that the norms had not gone nearly far enough. The Canon Law Society of America, in its October meeting, proposed a different procedure and urged the American bishops to press for revision of the previously published norms. The new proposal would allow for collective consultation on the diocesan level by priests' senates and pastoral councils. There was also discussion of possible changes in the method of electing the pope. Some modifications seemed to be in preparation, but Vatican sources said that the suggestion that local bishops participate in the election had been rejected.

Role of Women in the Ministry. In August two *motu proprios* (documents in the Pope's "own hand") were published revising what had been called minor orders in the church's ministries. The offices of exorcist, porter, and subdeacon were eliminated, and the offices of lector and acolyte were to be called ministries and would involve a formal investiture by the bishop. These would be necessary stages for those wishing to be ordained deacons and priests, but would also be open to qualified laymen. Tonsure, the rite of clipping the hair in the shape of a cross or the shaving of the crown of the head as a sign of the clerical life, was also eliminated. A new rite to symbolize entry into the clerical state was to be developed.

Although the changes were relatively minor, the documents evoked severe criticism since they explicitly excluded women from any of the ministries. The exclusion did not seem to represent the results of the study on women and the ministry commissioned by the 1971 Synod, and surely did not express any definitive position of the church. The incident underscored the increasingly important role of women, both religious and lay, in the church. It also pointed up that the question of their admission to the ministry would have to be confronted more seriously in the near future.

Marriage and Divorce. There was considerable discussion during 1972 of changes, actual and possible, in the church's laws governing marriage. Marriage courts, which decide on petitions for annulment (declarations that no valid marriage exists), have been allowed to make more decisions on the local level as procedures were simplified and authority decentralized. While most canonists praised such efforts and urged that the system be made as efficient and humane as possible, some challenged the very existence of the tribunal. In deciding annulments greater importance was being given to psychological factors in determining whether individuals were capable of realizing a valid marriage either absolutely or relative to a particular partner. There was some speculation on the part of individual theologians on the legitimacy of divorce, but the normal discipline of the church continued to forbid this.

A very sensitive issue was the question of whether divorced and remarried Catholics should be allowed to participate in the sacramental life of the church. Several dioceses in the United States adopted what was called the "good conscience" procedure which allowed individuals to judge themselves whether they were truly bound by a former marriage, even when they could not establish grounds for annulment. Although the practice was suspended pending further study by the Vatican, a committee of the Catholic Theological Society of America urged a more liberal approach to the problem.

Justice in the World. In his message to the United Nations Conference on Trade and Development (UNCTAD) in Santiago, Chile, in April, Pope Paul VI pointed out that justice demands that the poor nations of the world be given a voice in decisions affecting their economic life. Representatives of the Pontifical Justice and Peace Commission told the same conference that structural changes were necessary to correct the imbalance of economic and political powers that created such inequities between rich and poor nations, as well as inequities between classes within nations.

This distinctively new emphasis on the objective evil of unjust structures and systems was reflected in the various Latin American theologies of liberation. One of the most striking examples of these groups was the Christians for Socialism in Chile, who met in Santiago at the same time as the UNCTAD meeting. Although the Archbishop of Santiago disapproved of the group, the bishop of Cuernavaca, Mexico, accepted an invitation to participate. Elsewhere in Latin America the church came in conflict with repressive military regimes. The most notable conflicts were in Brazil, where there were repeated protests against government torture of political prisoners, and in Bolivia and Paraguay, where priests were accused of fostering guerrilla movements among the peasants.

During 1972 the church made available extensive relief to victims of the India-Pakistan War and to flood victims in the Philippines.

JOSEPH A. O'HARE, S. J.
Associate Editor, "America"

Judaism

The problem of the persecution of Jews in Russia and Eastern Europe and continued Arab-Israeli conflict were of importance in world Judaism in 1972. Other events of interest included the election of two new chief rabbis in Israel, the ordination of the first woman rabbi in the United States, organizational changes, and some new Jewish publications.

Russia and Eastern Europe. In the Soviet Union the harassment of Jews who wished to emigrate to Israel continued. While Jews from Soviet Georgia and other areas near the Turkish and Iranian border were allowed to emigrate, great obstacles were put in the way of would-be Jewish emigrants from other parts of Russia. An exorbitant "diploma tax" for exit visas was imposed on Russian Jewish academicians. This resulted in worldwide Jewish and non-Jewish protests. The Soviets then waived the visa fees in several dozen cases.

Arab-Israeli Conflict. The Arab or Arab-instigated terrorist attacks at Lod Airport in Israel, the Munich Olympic Village, and other places shocked both Jews and non-Jews throughout the world.

New Chief Rabbis in Israel. In October two new chief rabbis, one for Ashkenazi and the other for Sephardic Jews in Israel, were elected by a 150-member electoral college in Tel Aviv. The election was unusual in that incumbents are traditionally automatically re-elected, serving until death. Rabbis Ovadia Yosef, 51, of the Sephardic group, and Shlomo Goren, 55, of the Ashkenazim, one-time chief military rabbi, were also considerably younger than their predecessors. The Supreme Rabbinical Council which they head is empowered under Israeli law to judge all questions of marriage and divorce in Israel. Many of the more secular Jews in Israel have been unhappy with the conservative interpretations of rabbinic law handed down in the past, and they are hopeful that the comparative youth and broader backgrounds of the new chief rabbis will lead to more liberal interpretations of the law.

First Woman Rabbi. The first woman rabbi in the United States was ordained in June. Sally J. Priesland, 25, a graduate of Hebrew Union College, will serve a Reform congregation in New York City. The only other known woman rabbi, Regina Jonas, was ordained in Germany in the 1930's by a rabbi in Offenbach after the rabbinical school she attended refused to ordain her. She was arrested in 1940 by the Nazis and died in a concentration camp. Reform Judaism, the most liberal in its interpretation of Jewish tradition of the three major Jewish groups in the United States, is the only group that has moved to ordain women. Three other women were studying in Reform seminaries in the United States in 1972.

Organizations. The Council of Jewish Federations and Welfare Funds created a new central instrument, the Joint Cultural Appeal, for more adequate funding of major Jewish cultural, historical, and educational organizations. The Conference of Presidents of Major Jewish Organizations, whose member organizations increased to 30, provided a unified platform for the leadership of practically the entire Jewish community in the United States to pursue cooperative actions and ensure the security of the Jewish people in Israel and the world over.

Publications. The first complete Jewish encyclopedia to be published in 65 years was issued in 1972. Written in English, the 16-volume *Encyclopedia Judaica* was published in Israel. It was compiled by experts from 39 countries and was completed in five years.

A new prayer book, or mahzor, for the High Holy Days was issued for Conservative Jews. Published by the Rabbinical Assembly, it attempts to incorporate more contemporary elements into Jewish public worship and includes exerpts from contemporary Jewish authors.

Education. More public high schools in several U. S. cities introduced Hebrew language classes in 1972, and the number of students enrolled in them increased by 20%. An increased number of colleges also planned to offer Jewish studies courses, in response to increasing demand. The number of Jewish "day" schools in the United States and Canada increased to a total of 498.

RAPHAEL PATAI
Fairleigh Dickinson University

Eastern Orthodox Church

In 1972 the Eastern Orthodox Church had a major change in leadership with the death of Athenagoras I, patriarch of Constantinople, and the election of his successor. The Orthodox Church in the Soviet Union continued its struggle for a viable existence, and several other changes in leadership and organization took place.

Patriarchate of Constantinople. On July 16, Dimitrios Papadopoulos, metropolitan of Imbros and Tenedos in Turkey, was elected patriarch of Constantinople, succeeding Athenagoras I, who died on July 6. (See ATHENAGORAS I.) The new patriarch, who now holds the see of honorary primacy in Orthodoxy, was chosen by the synod of the church of Constantinople by a vote of 12 to 3 (see also BIOGRAPHY—*Dimitrios I*). The election was hastily conducted because of pressure from the Turkish government, and several leading contenders for the see were barred from candidacy by the Turkish authorities.

Because of the pressures on the Constantinopolitan see from the Turkish government, spokesmen from several Orthodox churches have called for the relocation of the patriarchate outside Turkey, and the establishment of an international center of Orthodoxy with representatives from all of the self-governing Orthodox churches. Opponents of this position, particularly from the church of Constantinople, see this as a betrayal of the church's Byzantine heritage and the opening of the question of Constantinople's right to primacy among the Orthodox.

Orthodoxy in the Soviet Union. The Orthodox Church in the Soviet Union continued in its difficult task of preserving the faith in a country whose laws forbid the public promotion of religion. The Nobel Prize-winning writer Alexandr Solzhenitsyn, an Orthodox communicant, raised a storm of controversy by publishing an "open letter" to Patriarch Pimen of Moscow. He accused the hierarchy of the church of weakness and servility before the demands of the Soviet state.

In April and May, Patriarch Pimen visited Orthodox churches in Egypt, Israel, and Syria, and in October he visited Yugoslavia, Rumania, and Greece. These were his first major trips outside his country since his election in 1970.

North America. In the United States, Theodosius Lazor, the 39-year-old missionary bishop of Sitka, Alaska, was elected bishop of Pittsburgh and was

installed on June 25. The "Iglesia Ortodoxa Catolica" of Mexico formally became part of the Orthodox Church in America as a missionary exarchate. The 20,000-diocese is headed by Bishop José Ortes y Olmos, who was consecrated in New York in April.

Japanese Orthodoxy. The metropolitan of Tokyo of the Orthodox Church of Japan, Vladimir Nagosky, an American, resigned. Theodosius Nagashima replaced him as primate of the Japanese Church. He is the first native Japanese to hold the position.

Pan-Orthodox Council. Plans for a "great council" of all Orthodox Churches continued, but the session of the Pan-Orthodox Commission to prepare the council was cancelled. Political pressures on most of the churches make the convening of the council unlikely in the near future.

THOMAS HOPKO
St. Vladimir's Orthodox Theological Seminary

Islam

The emergence of the new nation of Bangladesh was the major event of 1972 in the Islamic world. The Arab-Israeli conflict and flagging efforts at Muslim-Arab unity were also of major significance, as were questions about Islamic law in several Muslim countries.

Bangladesh. The new state of Bangladesh, with a Muslim population of 65 million, is second only to Indonesia in the number of its Muslim citizens. Bangladesh was born out of the Pakistani civil war and the India-Pakistan War of 1971. Hopes for reunification were ended by the quick diplomatic recognition afforded the new state by a number of larger nations. The dissolution of East-West Pakistan, which was founded on the principle that Muslims have a basis of unity in their common religion which can overcome cultural and linguistic differences, and the extensive suffering and disaster that followed upon that dissolution, are bound to have long-term effects upon the Muslim population of the Indian subcontinent. Many Muslims found themselves fighting at the side of Hindu Indians against their fellow Muslims in the 1971 war.

Middle East. The Arab-Israeli conflict intensified with the recurrence of Arab guerrilla attacks in Israel and Israeli retaliatory raids against Lebanon and Syria. The Lod airport massacre, the tragedy at the Munich Olympics, and the Israeli reprisal action against southern Lebanon were key events that made peace in the Middle East less likely without having any noticeable effect on the cause of Muslim-Arab unity. King Hussein's peace proposal for the region was found acceptable neither by the Israelis nor by his Arab allies, and Egypt broke diplomatic relations with Jordan as a result. (See MIDDLE EAST.)

In a year of conflict, war, and disunity among many Muslim countries, one proposed accord to further Arab-Muslim unity was significant. Egypt and Libya decided to bring about a political union of the two countries by September 1973. If the proposed union is actually realized, the new country will be the largest in Africa.

Islamic Law. In Libya, Col. Muammar al-Qaddafi, head of the Libyan Revolutionary Command Council, decided to reintroduce the Islamic Penal Code into the civil courts of his country. The trend in most Muslim countries over the last hundred years or so has been to modify the Islamic legal system (*shari'ah*) along Western lines.

In Egypt, Muslim authorities have decided to allow women to pray in mosques during the Friday services. However, the women will have to stand in a line behind the men who are gathered there for prayer.

DAVID EDE
Western Michigan University

Oriental Religions

There was a paucity of public news during 1972 concerning the existence of either internal religious stress or open confrontation between adherents of Oriental faiths and other groups. This is a sign that the present period is one of quiet review, reorientation, and renewal. The prospect of achieving greater world peace, with its promise of lessening interference by great and small powers in each other's internal affairs, has raised the hope of a return to much-desired religious autonomy and stability.

Hinduism. The somewhat precarious position of Hindus in East Pakistan before the Bangladesh rebellion became critical during the attempts of the West Pakistani forces to put down the revolt. Hundreds of thousands of East Pakistanis, Hindus, and others fled to India, although many others were killed. However, the aid given by India to the rebels, which led to their triumph, resulted in the easing of the lot not only of Hindus in Bangladesh loyal to the new regime, but also of the refugees returning from India. So long as resident Hindus are not suspected of disloyalty to the new state, the Muslim majority is tolerating their religious beliefs.

Within India itself, the talks at Simla in June between Indian Prime Minister Indira Gandhi and Pakistani President Zulfikar Ali Bhutto, preparing the way for peaceful settlement of the two countries' disputes, has resulted in a diminution of rioting among Muslims and Hindus in India. However, when the Indian parliament passed a law in May opening Aligarh University, hitherto restricted to Muslims, to teachers and students of all faiths, groups of Muslims marched in protest in the cities of Uttar Pradesh, and clashes between them and Hindu spectators resulted in scores of deaths and injuries.

Buddhism. In May, Ceylon changed its name to reflect a new political outlook, becoming the independent Socialist Republic of Sri Lanka ("great beautiful island"). It was anticipated that changes will also bring greater peace between the Buddhist majority and Hindu and Christian minorities.

In South Vietnam, Buddhists are finding that the Catholics are willing to make a coalition with them in opposing President Thieu's drift toward dictatorial rule. The Buddhists have also received an invitation from the World Council of Churches to join in discussions.

In Japan, a hundred-million-dollar shrine at the foot of Mt. Fuji was completed by Soka Gakkai, a Buddhist sect. It is claimed to be the largest religious structure in the world, and is also earthquake-proof. The new shrine symbolizes the rapid growth of this denomination, which in 1945 numbered but a few thousand adherents and now approaches a membership of 10 million.

JOHN B. NOSS
Author of "Man's Religions"

REPUBLICAN PARTY. See ELECTIONS; POLITICAL PARTIES.
RESPIRATORY DISEASES. See MEDICINE.

RHODE ISLAND

Politics took center stage in Rhode Island during 1972.

Political Affairs. By late winter the Democratic party leaders had lined up solidly in favor of Sen. Edmund Muskie as candidate for the presidency. However, by the time Rhode Island's newly established presidential primary was held on May 23, Muskie had withdrawn and Sen. George McGovern had gained momentum. McGovern won the candidate-preference part of the contest.

Following a dispute over which delegates should go to the Democratic National Convention in Miami, an almost completely McGovern slate was chosen, made up of relative political newcomers and virtually no party leaders. This—and general unhappiness with the national slate—prompted most leading Democrats to concentrate on state races. Gov. Frank Licht did support McGovern, and Sen. John O. Pastore headed his local campaign.

State contests offered an array of sharp confrontations. Former three-term Republican Gov. John H. Chafee resigned his post as secretary of the Navy and returned to challenge incumbent Democratic Sen. Claiborne Pell. Both are extremely popular as well as proven vote-getters (though both are Yankee Protestants in a two-thirds Catholic state). Pell was apparently well behind at the start, in part no doubt because the Democratic party had enacted the state's first income tax in 1971. After a hard-fought campaign, however, Pell won with a comfortable 54% of the vote.

The Democratic candidate for governor, Mayor Philip W. Noel of Warwick, seemingly would bear the main brunt of the antitax sentiment. Governor Licht was apparently dissuaded from running on the ground that as proposer of the income tax, he faced almost certain defeat. The Republican candidate, Herbert F. DeSimone, a former state attorney general, had been narrowly defeated by Licht in 1970.

Again the Democrat gradually caught up with his opponent and, by election day, was able to win with 53% of the vote. Thus the state's GOP saw its two strongest candidates in many years go down to defeat. The party did make slight gains in the General Assembly and managed to retain the attorney general's office, but the dominance of the Democratic party seemed to have been reasserted.

Other Developments. During 1972 the newly established and unique Coastal Resources Management Council got into full operation. Its job is to plan the development of the state's shoreline.

A separate Department of Corrections—to focus attention on prisoner rehabilitation and prison reform—was set up, and a bond issue to build a new prison was approved by the voters.

In education, racial difficulties continued in the Providence high schools, with white parent groups calling for the end of crosstown busing. In the spring, Brown University announced that it would expand its medical program and thus establish the first full medical school in the state.

ELMER E. CORNWELL, JR., *Brown University*

————— RHODE ISLAND • Information Highlights —————

Area: 1,214 square miles (3,144 sq km).
Population (1970 census): 949,723. *Density,* 915 per sq mi.
Chief Cities (1970 census): Providence, the capital, 179,-116; Warwick, 83,694; Pawtucket, 76,984; Cranston, 74,-287; East Providence, 48,207; Woonsocket, 46,820.
Government (1972): *Chief Officers*—governor, Frank Licht (D); lt. gov., J. Joseph Garrahy (D); secy. of state, August P. LaFrance (D); atty. gen., Richard J. Israel (R); treas., Raymond H. Hawksley (D); commissioner, dept. of education, Fred G. Burke; chief justice, Thomas H. Roberts. *General Assembly*—Senate, 50 members (41 Democrats, 9 Republicans); House of Representatives, 100 members (75 D, 24 R, 1 independent).
Education (1971–72): *Enrollment*—public elementary schools, 106,914 pupils, 4,668 teachers; public secondary, 83,782 pupils, 4,558 teachers; nonpublic schools (1970–71), 37,-067 pupils, 1,940 teachers; college and university, 47,000 students. *Public school expenditures,* $180,670,000 ($1,-006 per pupil). *Average teacher's salary,* $10,268.
State Finances (fiscal year 1970): *Revenues,* $438,738,000 (5% general sales tax and gross receipts taxes, $78,324,-000; motor fuel tax, $27,699,000; federal funds, $100,-679,000). *Expenditures,* $444,604,000 (education, $135,223,-000; health, welfare, and safety, $94,400,000; highways, $53,863,000). *State debt,* $373,200,000 (June 30, 1970).
Personal Income (1971): $3,914,000,000; per capita, $4,077.
Public Assistance (1971): $98,550,000. *Average monthly payments* (Dec. 1971)—old-age assistance, $60.07; aid to families with dependent children, $229.28.
Labor Force: *Nonagricultural wage and salary earners* (July 1972), 340,200. *Average annual employment* (1971)—manufacturing, 114,000; trade, 71,000; government, 53,000; services, 56,000. *Insured unemployed* (Aug. 1972)—13,800 (5.0%).
Manufacturing (1970): *Value added by manufacture,* $1,404,-300,000. Primary metal industries, $160,400,000; textile mill products, $152,200,000; nonelectrical machinery, $130,000,000; jewelry, silverware, plated ware, $119,900,-000.
Agriculture (1970): *Cash farm income,* $20,933,000 (livestock, $10,527,000; crops, $10,334,000; government payments, $72,000). *Chief crops* (in order of value, 1971)—Potatoes, hay, apples, peaches.
Mining (1971): *Production value,* $4,299,000 (ranks 49th among the states). *Chief minerals*—Sand and gravel, stone, gem stones.
Fisheries (1971): *Commercial catch,* 84,553,000 pounds ($12,-398,000). *Leading species by value:* Flounder, $2,591,000; scup, $776,000; cod, $295,000.
Transportation: *Roads* (1971), 5,342 miles (8,597 km); *motor vehicles* (1971), 488,277; *railroads* (1971), 146 miles (235 km); *public airports* (1972), 7.
Communications: *Telephones* (1972), 552,400; *television stations* (1971), 2; *radio stations* (1971), 22; *newspapers* (1972), 7 (daily circulation, 312,000).

RHODESIA

The report of a British-appointed commission to determine the acceptance among Rhodesians of a proposed Anglo-Rhodesian settlement on the status of Rhodesia ended all hopes for such an agreement in 1972. In other developments, Rhodesia was cheered by the United States' purchase of its chrome despite UN sanctions.

Pearce Commission. From January through March the Commission on Rhodesian Opinion, headed by Lord Edward H. Pearce, tested the support among black and white Rhodesians for an agreement on constitutional changes worked out in November 1971 by Rhodesian Prime Minister Ian D. Smith and British Foreign Secretary Sir Alec Douglas-Home, which would have ended the illegality of Rhodesia's 1965 unilateral break with Britain. The commission met a resounding "no" from the African majority on the proposals that set education and income voting qualifications as a condition for majority rule. Critics claimed that few Africans could meet such qualifications in the foreseeable future.

Riots accompanied the commission activities, with 14 deaths and 1,505 arrests reported by February 16, including the detention of former Prime Minister Garfield Todd and his daughter Judith, both later released. Officials charged intimidation of Africans, mainly by the African National Council (ANC), formed on Dec. 16, 1971, headed by Methodist Bishop Abel Muzorewa. On a visit to Britain and the United States, Muzorewa denied ANC involvement in the riots. On March 27 the Rhodesian government barred the ANC from selling membership cards to raise funds, and on June 6 from receiving foreign funds as a political party.

─────── **RHODESIA • Information Highlights** ───────

Official Name: Republic of Rhodesia (by unilateral declaration).
Area: 150,803 square miles (390,580 sq km).
Population (1972 est.): 5,400,000. *Density,* 35.8 per square miles (13.8 per sq km). *Annual rate of increase,* 3.4%.
Chief Cities (1969 census): Salisbury, the capital, 385,530; Bulawayo, 245,590.
Government: *Head of state,* Clifford Dupont, president (took office April 1970). *Head of government,* Ian D. Smith, prime minister (took office April 1964). *Legislature*—Parliament: Senate, 23 members; House of Assembly, 66 members. *Major political parties*—Rhodesian Front; Centre.
Languages: English (official), Bantu languages.
Education: *Expenditure* (1967) 16.9% of total public expenditure. *School enrollment* (1965)—primary, 627,806; secondary, 15,146; technical/vocational, 832; university/higher, 1,064.
Monetary Unit: Rhodesian dollar (0.7142 R. dollar equals U. S.$1, 1972).
Gross National Product (1970 est.): $1,427,000,000.
National Income per Person (1970): $252.
Economic Indexes: *Industrial production* (1970), 167 (1963= 100); *consumer price index* (1971), 122 (1963=100).
Manufacturing (major products): Metals and metal products, processed foods, textiles, chemicals, beverages, tobacco products, clothing and footwear.
Major Agricultural Products: Tobacco, sugarcane, tea, groundnuts, cotton, corn, millet and sorghum.
Major Minerals: Asbestos, chromium ore, coal, copper, iron ore, tin, gold.
Foreign Trade (1971): *Exports,* $388,000,000 (chief exports, 1965—tobacco, unmanufactured; food; asbestos; copper; chromium ore). *Imports,* $395,000,000 (chief imports, 1965—transport equipment; nonelectrical machinery; chemicals; textile yarn and fabrics). *Chief trading partner*—South Africa.
Transportation: *Motor vehicles* (1969), 178,600 (automobiles, 126,600); *railroads* (1970), 1,616 miles (2,600 km); *major national airline,* Air Rhodesia.
Communications: *Telephones* (1971), 131,572; *television stations* (1971), 2; *newspapers* (1970), 4 (daily circulation, 83,000).

The Pearce Commission's report, released in Britain on May 23, stated that while some intimidation had occurred and while most Rhodesian whites, Asians, and coloreds (persons of mixed race) had favored the proposals, massive African opposition made it clear that "the people . . . as a whole do not regard the proposals as acceptable as a basis for independence." Britain was committed to continuing UN trade sanctions against Rhodesia.

U. S. Chrome Purchases. A 1971 amendment to the military procurement bill by Sen. Harry F. Byrd (D, Va.) permitted the purchase of Rhodesian chrome—in violation of UN sanctions. On May 31, 1972, the Senate affirmed this policy in a 40–36 vote against a provision in a State Department budget bill that would have repealed the Byrd amendment. Sen. Gale W. McGee (D, Wyo.), who led the unsuccessful Senate fight, blamed President Richard Nixon for lack of support. Proponents of the chrome purchase claimed that the United States was paying twice the Rhodesian price for Soviet chrome and that the United States should not depend on the USSR for a strategic material. Opponents said the United States was oversupplied with chrome and could not justify breaking UN sanctions.

Moderation. Prime Minister Smith overcame right-wing extremists at his ruling Rhodesian Front party congress on September 21–23. Two arguments reportedly helped him move delegates to a more moderate racial policy: (1) nationalist guerrillas in and out of Rhodesia cannot be contained unless the African majority supports the government, and (2) the economy is stagnant in the face of mounting African unemployment and alienation.

Mine Disaster. On June 6 explosions of unknown origin at the Wankie coal mine trapped and killed 426 miners—390 African and 36 white. This was the second worst mine disaster in African history. The temporarily reduced coal output hurt Rhodesia's already depressed economy.

Barred from Olympics. Bowing to mounting international pressure from African and U. S. athletes and from UN spokesmen, the International Olympics Committee barred the Rhodesian team from competing in the 1972 Olympics in Munich, Germany. Critics called the 7 blacks on the 44-member team "window dressing" and said that sports are segregated inside Rhodesia. Rhodesia had been barred from the 1968 games, but was invited to compete again as British-ruled "Southern Rhodesia."

FRANKLIN PARKER, *West Virginia University*

ROBINSON, Jackie

American baseball player: b. Cairo, Ga., Jan. 31, 1919; d. Stamford, Conn., Oct. 24, 1972.

Jackie Robinson was the first black man to play in the major leagues. His signing with the Brooklyn Dodgers in 1947 broke major league baseball's color barrier, which had been in effect since 1876.

In 10 seasons with the Dodgers, his timely hitting, daring base running, and aggressive play helped the team win six pennants and one world series. His lifetime batting average was .311. In his peak season (1949), he led the National League in batting (.342) and in stolen bases (37) and was voted its most valuable player. A right-handed batter who held his bat high in a closed stance, he was feared both as a slugger and a bunter. As a base runner, he was a constant threat to steal or take an extra base. Though primarily a second baseman, he filled in at first and third and played left field.

Robinson quit baseball after the 1956 season when he was about to be traded to the New York Giants. He became personnel director for a chain of coffee shops and served in various capacities in business, banking, and civil rights organizations. In 1962 he was elected to the Baseball Hall of Fame. He died on Oct. 24, 1972, shortly after being honored at a World Series game in Cincinnati.

Early Years. Jack Roosevelt Robinson was one of four children, and after the death of his father in 1920, his mother moved the family to Pasadena, Calif. Jackie became proficient at many sports, and at Pasadena Junior College he reached one of his athletic goals. In the long jump he leaped 25 feet 6⅓ inches, bettering the junior college mark set by his brother Mack, a sprinter on the 1936 U. S. Olympic team.

Robinson moved on to the University of California at Los Angeles where he starred in three sports. In football in 1938, he led the nation in punt returns with an average of 21 yards. In basketball in 1940, he led the Southern Division of the Pacific Coast Conference in scoring. At the NCAA track meet in 1940, he won the long jump with a leap of 24 feet 10¼ inches.

In 1942, Robinson entered the Army, went to officer candidate school, and was commissioned in 1943. He was discharged in 1944 and in the following year joined the Kansas City Monarchs, a black baseball team, as a shortstop.

Baseball Career. On Oct. 23, 1945, in a move that shattered precedent, Robinson was signed to a contract with the Montreal Royals, a Dodger farm club in the International League. Branch Rickey, president of the Dodger organization, had first outlined to Robinson his plan to break the color barrier. Robinson, a fiercely competitive athlete, was made to understand the difficulty of the task that

UPI

JACKIE ROBINSON (1919–1972)
"When Jackie took the field, something reminded us of our birthright to be free."
—*The Rev. Jesse L. Jackson, delivering the eulogy.*

lay before him. Rickey impressed upon him, especially, the importance of enduring attacks by bigots and racists without fighting back. Robinson accepted the challenge and passed the first test at the Royals' Florida training camp early in 1946. His white teammates soon accepted him, especially when they discovered how well he could play.

Assigned to second base, Robinson drew instant acclaim for his hitting and base running in his first appearance in the North. On opening day in Jersey City, before 53,000 fans, he got four hits, including a home run. He went on to spark the Royals to the championship, leading the league in batting and stolen bases and in fielding among second basemen. His play was outstanding as the Royals defeated Louisville in the Little World Series.

The next step was the move up to the major leagues. Rickey was more determined than ever, and Robinson, buoyed by his minor-league success, was ready to continue the battle. On April 10, 1947, during an exhibition game between Montreal and Brooklyn, the Dodgers announced the signing of Robinson. A surprise also was Rickey's assignment of Robinson to play first base, a position that he had not played before.

Robinson was equal to the challenges that faced him in the heat of major league competition. Holding his temper, he brushed off the taunts and insults of intolerant players and fans and began to demonstrate his capabilities as a major-league ballplayer. The first jibes came from some members of the Dodgers, but this trouble was handled firmly by Rickey. Robinson survived a brush with the Philadelphia manager and then was given backing from many sources when St. Louis players tried to incite a league strike against him. Ford Frick, the president of the National League, ordered the suspension of any player who refused to play against a black.

This ended any organized resistance, and Robinson fended off, with utmost tact, all other efforts to involve him in an incident that might militate against his acceptance by players and fans. In time he was able to assert his competitive instincts to the fullest extent. For his role in Brooklyn's pennant-winning drive of 1947, he was voted rookie of the year. By 1950 several other outstanding black players had moved into the major leagues, and the door was open for blacks in all professional sports.

BILL BRADDOCK, *"The New York Times"*

ROGERS, William P. See BIOGRAPHY.
ROMAINS, Jules. See LITERATURE—*French Literature*.
ROMAN CATHOLIC CHURCH. See RELIGION.

RUMANIA

In 1972, the Rumanian leader Nicolae Ceauşescu tightened his regime and tried to improve relations with the Soviet Union.

Internal Reforms. In Bucharest in February, authorities discovered a mysterious treason case involving the general commanding the military garrison. His apparent execution, allegedly as a Soviet spy, marked the initiation of Ceauşescu's removal of "unreliables" from the Communist party hierarchy. Rumania's failure in Western-oriented economic experiments, combined with Moscow's continued displeasure over Ceauşescu's independent line, contributed to the removal of five top-ranking party officials in April. Among those assigned "to other posts" was leading party theorist Paul Niculescu-Mizil. All party secretaries except Ceauşescu have been removed since 1968. Private citizens were required henceforth to report conversations with foreigners on "matters of state." A party plenum in April started a new ideological drive to ostracize dissidents and introduce a hard-line policy in cultural activities.

After three months, Ceauşescu secured a vote of confidence from a party conference in July. At that time he spoke warmly of the USSR—an indication of a return to former close ties with Moscow. He claimed the distinction of encouraging U. S. President Nixon's friendly policies toward Moscow and Peking, cities visited by Nixon in 1972. Ceauşescu revealed that Rumania's basic problems were economic and that an economic "recession" in Western nations required Rumania to utilize more effectively existing plant capacities by harder work rather than by increased investment. Failure to gain admittance to the European Economic Community may also have contributed to this change in Rumanian economic policy.

Also at the conference the party's Central Committee was increased from 165 to 185 members (including Ceauşescu's wife, Elena) to admit younger cadres. Among other promises Ceauşescu made were higher wages, a shorter work week, more consumer goods, and increased pensions. Democratic government was increased to the extent that more than one candidate was to be permitted to stand for each seat in the national legislature. It was announced that a drive would begin against idlers and young people who shirked industrial work. This drive presaged an educational reform stressing technical training.

In October, Ceauşescu removed from office Corneliu Manescu, foreign minister since 1961 and for-

mer president of the UN General Assembly (1967–68), who was a spokesman for friendlier relations with the West. All these measures contributed to the indisputable formation of a personality cult around Ceauşescu.

Relations with the USSR. In January, Ceauşescu met with Soviet leaders Brezhnev and Kosygin in Prague, where Communist bloc leaders approved of Rumania's appeal for general disarmament and demilitarization of Central and Eastern Europe. This move was designed to encourage talks with NATO about military disengagement throughout Europe. Ceauşescu and Brezhnev next met in August in the USSR—their first personal session since 1968. A warm reception for Rumania's new envoy to Moscow and Rumania's active participation in the annual COMECON (Warsaw Pact) meeting indicated an accommodation and reconciliation between these formerly antagonistic Communist bloc states.

Relations with the United States. Economic and cultural relations with the United States increased in 1972. U. S. importers were ready to buy a small, Jeep-like, four-wheel-drive Rumanian automobile. Washington permitted the Export-Import Bank to extend credits for the sale of American goods in Rumania. Rumania accepted private U. S. investments and a loan from the Export-Import Bank to help finance offshore oil drilling in the Black Sea. Secretary of State William Rogers signed a consular agreement in Bucharest.

A Rumanian library was opened in New York, and a 5,000-volume U. S. counterpart was established in Bucharest. The Ion Creanga Children's Theater and the Jewish State Theater performed in the United States during the summer. In Bucharest, the U. S. tennis team defeated Rumanian stars Ilie Nastase and Ion Tiriac in the Davis Cup finals.

Relations with Other Countries. Ceauşescu continued friendly relations with Yugoslavia by meeting twice with Marshal Tito. The Rumanian leader

toured eight African capitals in March, visited Belgium in October, signed a 20-year friendship treaty with Hungary, and agreed to establish Communist China's first European air link. He also negotiated for improved relations with the Vatican and received Premier Golda Meir of Israel for a four-day visit in May. She was the first Israeli premier to visit a Communist state. While in Bucharest, Mrs. Meir attended Jewish Sabbath services in Bucharest's historic Choral Synagogue amid a joyous welcome by some of Rumania's surviving 100,000 Jews.

On the other hand, Ceauşescu's plans to visit Japan and West Germany in 1972 were shelved for undisclosed reasons.

SHERMAN D. SPECTOR
Russell Sage College

RWANDA · Information Highlights

Official Name: Republic of Rwanda.
Area: 10,169 square miles (26,338 sq km).
Population (1972 est.): 3,800,000. *Density*, 354 per square mile (136 per sq km). *Annual rate of increase*, 2.9%.
Chief City (1970 est.): Kigali, the capital, 17,000.
Government: *Head of state*, Grégoire Kayibanda, president (took office for a 3d term Sept. 1969). *Head of government*, Grégoire Kayibanda. *Legislature* (unicameral)—National Assembly, 47 members. *Major political party*—Democratic Republican Movement (Parmehutu).
Languages: French, Kinyarwanda (both official).
Education: *Expenditure* (1968), 27.3% of total public expenditure. *School enrollment* (1967)—primary, 372,184; secondary, 8,842; technical/vocational, 912; university/higher (1969), 287.
Monetary Unit: Franc (92.1 francs equal U. S.$1, Oct. 1972).
Gross National Product (1970 est.): $195,000,000.
Manufacturing (major products): Processed foods, handicrafts, textiles.
Major Agricultural Products: Coffee, cassava, sweet potatoes, tea, cotton, bananas, pyrethrum.
Major Minerals: Tin concentrates, beryl.
Foreign Trade (1971): *Exports*, $17,000,000. *Imports*, $23,-000,000. *Chief trading partners* (1969)—Belgium-Luxembourg (took 30% of exports, supplied 15% of imports); Uganda (8%—12%).
Communications: *Telephones* (1970), 1,433; *radios* (1970), 30,000.

RWANDA

Rwanda's major political problems in 1972 were caused by developments outside its boundaries. Although the current Rwandan government emerged from a Hutu uprising against the Tusi aristocracy, it felt powerless to stop the massacre of over 100,000 Hutu in neighboring Burundi, and the flow of refugees added to Rwanda's strained resources.

In August, tension suddenly mounted between Rwanda and Uganda, which controls Rwanda's main export route and in 1971 blocked vital coffee exports for nearly a month. Uganda's President Idi Amin accused Rwanda of harboring Israeli agents and of allowing its territory to be used by forces hostile to his government. Amin threatened to unleash some 20,000 Tusi exiles living in Uganda. The charges were denied in Kigali, but Amin persisted in his accusations, and the threat of economic blockade hung over Rwanda until the outbreak of hostility between Uganda and Tanzania diverted Amin.

By contrast, Rwanda and Zaïre continued their joint interest in the projected exploitation of the methane gas deposits of Lake Kivu and, with Uganda, in the development of tourism in their border areas. A conference among the three countries on these and other matters, scheduled for late October, was jeopardized by Amin's announcement that he would boycott it. The conference did take place, but only Zaïre and Rwanda attended.

EDOUARD BUSTIN, *Boston University*

RUMANIA · Information Highlights

Official Name: Socialist Republic of Rumania.
Area: 91,700 square miles (237,500 sq km).
Population (1972 est.): 20,800,000. *Density*, 220 per square mile (85 per sq km). *Annual rate of increase*, 1.2%.
Chief Cities (1968 est.): Bucharest, the capital, 1,432,000; Cluj, 193,400; Timisoara, 184,800; Brasov, 175,300.
Government: *Head of state*, Nicolae Ceauşescu, president of the State Council and secretary general of the Communist party (took office July 1965). *Head of government*, Nicolae Ceauşescu. *Legislature*—Grand National Assembly, 465 members. *Political party*—Communist party.
Languages: Rumanian (official), Hungarian.
Education: *School enrollment* (1969)—primary, 2,886,855; secondary, 650,482; technical/vocational, 366,239; university/higher, 151,705.
Monetary Unit: Leu (5.53 lei equal U. S.$1, June 1972).
Gross National Product (1969 est.): $21,100,000,000.
National Income per Person (1969): $700.
Economic Indexes: *Industrial production* (1970), 229 (1963= 100); *agricultural production* (1970), 135 (1957–59=100); *consumer price index* (1969), 102 (1966=100).
Manufacturing (major products): Machinery, processed foods, metal products, chemicals, construction materials.
Major Agricultural Products: Corn, sugar beets, potatoes, rye, wheat, sunflower seeds.
Major Minerals: Petroleum, lignite, coal, iron ore.
Foreign Trade (1970): *Exports*, $1,851,000,000 (chief exports, 1969—machinery and equipment; fuels, minerals, and metals; food). *Imports*, $1,960,000,000 (chief imports, 1969—machinery and equipment; fuels, minerals, and metals). *Chief trading partners* (1969)—USSR (took 28% of exports, supplied 27% of imports); Czechoslovakia (9%—6%); West Germany (7%—10%); Italy (6%—5%).
Tourism: *Receipts* (1970), $59,800,000.
Transportation: *Commercial motor vehicles* (1970), 45,100; *railroads* (1970), 6,907 miles (11,115 km); *merchant fleet* (1971), 364,000 gross registered tons; *major national airline*, TAROM (Transporturie Aeriene Române).
Communications: *Telephones* (1969), 639,000; *television stations* (1971), 17; *newspapers* (1970), 55 (daily circulation, 3,422,000).

SAINT LOUIS

In the two most debated issues of 1972, St. Louis voters approved a downtown convention center and supported a plan for new airport facilities in Missouri rather than Illinois.

Downtown Development. Stagnant downtown St. Louis was stirred by two development proposals. The Mercantile Trust Co. announced plans to start a $150 million development, including a 35-story office building, near its bank. Voters, by a 3-to-1 margin, approved a bond issue for a $25 million convention center, which they had defeated in 1971, because the new-issue bonds would be partly paid off in business rather than property taxes.

Hopes were also raised by proposals to develop a new gaslight square as an entertainment district, to reopen the bankrupt Spanish Pavilion as an aquacenter, and to convert the vacant Old Post Office into an arcade of shops, restaurants, and a hotel. Financing, however, was not immediately available.

Airport Development. Debate raged over where or whether to build a new airport. Although Mayor Alfonso J. Cervantes teamed with Illinois Gov. Richard B. Ogilvie in promoting a site across the Mississippi in Illinois, nearly all other Missouri political and business leaders fought for an airport in Missouri, either Lambert Field or a new one. While the Federal Aviation Administration studied plans for the Illinois site, the Missouri legislature created a regional airport authority, which produced a $370 million plan to expand and update Lambert Field. Since a straw vote found local Missouri residents favoring Lambert Field by 10 to 1, Cervantes asked the FAA to delay a decision to allow study of the Lambert plan.

City Government. Four minor scandals resulted in grand jury indictments. In the city's police courts, allegations of ticket-fixing led to the indictment of Municipal Judge Nathan B. Young and three others and elicited promises of court reform from the mayor. Nine persons, including five election board employees, were indicted for mail fraud in the use of absentee ballots in the primary elections, apparently to control votes. Eight persons were indicted in connection with the alleged forging of signatures of petitions to place a transportation bond issue on the state ballot. A construction-firm officer was indicted for obtaining money under false pretenses for allegedly soliciting a bribe in connection with bids on a new municipal parking garage.

In the November election there was another scandal when hundreds of persons were disenfranchised by overzealous canvassers. A federal judge ordered the polls to remain open until all persons reinstated by circuit judges, more than 700, had voted.

Housing. The much-maligned, federally built Pruitt-Igoe housing project gained new notoriety when demolition experts razed several of its buildings. The 18-year-old project, which once housed 10,000 persons and was considered a model for public housing, held only about 2,000 in 1972. Many residents were unhappy with poor maintenance, high crime, and other bad conditions. Meanwhile the city's housing authority threatened to close down all public housing projects if the federal government did not provide additional money for upkeep.

Other Events. The city's first heart transplant patient, Vincent Dobelmann, received a new heart in February and survived until rejection of the new organ caused his death December 19. A union boss and a labor racketeer were murdered in gangland style. A strike of ironworkers shut down most construction for two months. Two real estate dealers were indicted in a continuing investigation of arson-for-profit. A new project designed to reduce air pollution and the cost of trash disposal burned household trash with coal.

RONALD D. WILLNOW
The St. Louis "Post-Dispatch"

SAMOA. See PACIFIC ISLANDS; WESTERN SAMOA.

SAN FRANCISCO

The year 1972 in San Francisco was marked by the inclusion of numerous parcels of city-owned land in the newly created Golden Gate National Recreation Area, a continued building boom, and widespread dissension over the running of the public school system.

Recreation Area. In mid-October, Congress approved establishment of the Golden Gate National Recreation Area. Some 34,000 acres of public and privately owned land in San Francisco and Marin counties were permanently set aside for recreational uses, to be administered by the Interior Department. Included in the project were city, state, and federal properties on both sides of the Golden Gate, among them such famous San Francisco landmarks as the Marina Green, Sutro Heights, and part of the city's historic military post the Presidio, as well as the bay islands, Alcatraz and Angel. The legislation authorized $51.6 million for the purchase of privately owned land needed to round out the property, which will bind together a strip of shoreline extending from Fort Funston to the tip of Point Reyes, some 38 miles to the north.

Building Boom. Nearing completion at year's end were several large hotels in the retail shopping district, and the lofty, pyramid-shaped Transamerica Building at Montgomery and Jackson. Three office buildings, 40 stories or more in height, were simultaneously under way on Market Street.

The Yerba Buena Center, a $385 million project designed to provide the city with an adequate auditorium, exhibit halls, and other needed convention facilities, together with a sports arena, airline terminal, and merchandise mart, moved closer to realization. The building of the Center, intended to occupy a six-block area of rundown buildings south of Market Street, had been delayed until suitable housing could be provided for residents now on the site. In September city funds, supplemented by two federal grants, were made available to house residents about to be displaced, and work on the Center got actively under way.

As the year ended, the $1.4 billion Bay Area Rapid Transit System (BART), under construction since 1965, neared completion. In mid-September, trains began operating over the 28-mile section linking Oakland with the southern Alameda County town of Fremont. Two other sections, connecting Oakland with Richmond to the north and Concord to the east, are scheduled to open in January and April 1973, respectively. The final section, which will join San Francisco with the east bay communities by means of a tunnel beneath the bay, will open in the fall of 1973, marking the completion of the first all-new transportation system to be built in the United States in more than 50 years.

TRANSAMERICA PYRAMID, a 48-story office building, nears completion in San Francisco financial district.

Election. In the November 7 election, San Francisco, traditionally a Democratic city, gave Sen. George McGovern a lead of some 45,000 votes over President Nixon. Both incumbent congressmen, William Mailliard (Rep.) and Phillip Burton (Dem.), were reelected, as were state Sen. Milton Marks (Rep.) and the four local assemblymen. The voters also approved two bond issues—one of $39 million to finance improvements in the municipal water system, and one of $25 million for flood control and the rebuilding of sewers.

OSCAR LEWIS
Author, "San Francisco: Mission to Metropolis"

SASKATCHEWAN

Saskatchewan enjoyed a steady, unspectacular year in 1972, despite initial fears about the grain crop and some apprehension about landholding legislation introduced by the year-old New Democratic government of Premier Allan Blakeney. A further but slight decline in population was reported.

Legislation. The Assembly passed a record 158 bills in 1972, many of a housekeeping nature. The major piece of legislation established a government land bank, enabling the government to buy land from farmers with uneconomic holdings or those wishing to retire. The land would be rented for a minimum of five years to young farmers or others needing to expand. By October, some 1,600 landowners had offered to sell. More controversial was a bill intended to limit the ownership of farmland by nonresidents of Saskatchewan. A special committee toured the province soliciting citizen opinion, which was generally unfavorable. The premier then announced that the bill would be referred to a special legislative committee for public hearings.

———— SASKATCHEWAN • Information Highlights ————

Area: 251,700 square miles (651,904 sq km).
Population: 926,242 (1971 census).
Chief Cities (1971 census): Regina, the capital (139,469); Saskatoon (126,449); Moose Jaw (31,854).
Government: *Chief Officers* (1972)—lt. gov., Stephen Worobetz; premier, Allan E. Blakeney (New Democratic party); prov. secy., Ed Tchorzewski (NDP); atty. gen., Roy Romanow (NDP); min. of educ., Gordon MacMurchy (NDP); chief justice, E. M. Culliton. *Legislature*—Legislative Assembly, 60 members (45 New Democratic party, 15 Liberal).
Education: *School enrollment* (1968–69)—public elementary and secondary, 245,526 pupils (11,109 teachers); private schools, 1,987 pupils (159 teachers); Indian (federal) schools, 5,025 pupils (225 teachers); college and university, 13,884 students. *Public school expenditures* (1971 est.)—$98,660,000. *Average teacher's salary* (1968–69), $6,848.
Public Finance (fiscal year 1972 est.): *Revenues,* $602,400,000 (sales tax, $131,200,000; income tax, $84,200,000; federal funds, $179,500,000). *Expenditures,* $624,200,000 (education, $170,700,000; health and social welfare, $220,100,000; transport and communications, $82,700,000).
Personal Income (1969 est.): $2,413,000,000.
Social Welfare (fiscal year 1972 est.): $49,800,000 (aged and blind, $1,400,000; dependents and unemployed, $36,600,-000).
Manufacturing (1968): *Value added by manufacture,* $170,002,-000 (food and beverages, $62,568,000; petroleum and coal products, $20,213,000; nonmetallic mineral products, $16,-666,000; printing and publishing, $15,028,000).
Agriculture (1971): *Cash farm income* (exclusive of government payments), $904,818,000 (livestock and products, $277,753,000; crops, $624,181,000). *Chief crops* (cash receipts)—wheat, $422,288,000 (ranks 1st among the provinces); barley, $75,558,000 (ranks 2d); rapeseed, $72,080,-000 (ranks 1st); flaxseed, $29,611,000 (ranks 1st).
Mining (1971 est.): *Production value,* $381,826,000. *Chief minerals*—crude petroleum, 90,000,000 bbl. (ranks 2d among the provinces); potash, 3,872,000 tons (ranks 1st).
Transportation: *Roads* (1968), 127,490 miles (205,186 km); *motor vehicles* (1969), 472,360; *railroads* (1970 est.), 8,570 track miles (13,790 km); *licensed airports* (1971 est.), 34.
Communications: *Telephones* (1969), 358,881; *television stations* (1971), 22; *radio stations* (1971), 19; *daily newspapers* (1971), 4.
(All monetary figures given in Canadian dollars.)

Education. In August, Thomas A. Shaheen, superintendent of the Unified School District for just over two years, resigned his post. The reason for his resignation was a series of irreconcilable differences with a majority of the seven-member board of education over certain policies he had introduced into the local school system. He was succeeded by Steven Morena, a former executive of the San Francisco Community College District.

Economy. Farmers—dismayed by dock strikes in Montreal and Vancouver that had threatened grain shipments and beset by bad weather—were cheered by increased grain prices and huge sales to China and Russia. A general upturn in the economy reflected the improved farm situation. But there was considerable labor unrest, resulting in strikes in the printing and construction industries.

Other Events. Woodrow S. Lloyd, former premier (1961–64) of Saskatchewan, died on April 8 at the age of 58 in Seoul, Korea, while on a United Nations assignment.

A nationwide controversy erupted when Jack Ramsay, a former Royal Canadian Mounted Police corporal and a resident of Regina, criticized the force in an article in the July issue of *Maclean's* magazine. He charged that morale was low, discipline harsh, and justice uncertain. Although they refuted the charges, administrative officers later announced that for the first time rank-and-file members could have direct access to the commissioner's office in Ottawa. Ramsay expressed satisfaction with this move toward a grievance procedure, and talk about a Mounties' union subsided.

HELEN A. McKAY, *Regina Public Library*

SAUDI ARABIA

Saudi Arabia enjoyed substantial gains as an oil-producing country in 1972, reflected in increased budgetary outlays for 1972–73. By the end of the year, Saudi Arabia's brilliant minister for petroleum and mineral affairs, Sheikh Ahmed Zaki Yamani, had secured the agreement of foreign concession holders in Saudi Arabia's oil fields that Saudi Arabia, and other oil-producing states for which it spoke, would gain majority control of the concessions within a decade.

Oil Production and Concession Ownership. More than 90% of Saudi Arabia's 1972 national revenue increase of $600 million came from greater production of oil and from its higher price. The 8.49% increase in the posted price for oil had been achieved in January by the Persian Gulf producers.

Following this increase in price, Sheikh Yamani began negotiations with the foreign concession holders for participation in the ownership of these concessions. In cooperation with Kuwait, Iraq, Qatar, and Abu Dhabi, Sheikh Yamani reached an agreement in principle on October 5 (confirmed on October 27) with the foreign oil companies that the producing countries should achieve 51% ownership by 1983. It was also agreed that the producing countries should make an immediate purchase of 25% control of foreign concessions. Prior to the oil companies' approval of the principle of participation, Saudi Arabia had contemplated limiting oil production to a level where income to the producing state would not exceed immediate needs; devaluations of Western currencies and inflation had greatly dampened Saudi interest in amassing large cash balances in foreign banks.

Sheikh Yamani also proposed that Saudi Arabia would guarantee to supply U. S. petroleum needs in the future, even up to 12 million barrels a day by 1980, if Saudi Arabia could enter the field of refining and marketing petroleum products in the United States.

Oil revenues for the fiscal year of Aug. 10, 1972, to July 30, 1973, were estimated at $2.95 billion. Oil production increased from 4,770,000

——— SAUDI ARABIA • Information Highlights ———

Official Name: Kingdom of Saudi Arabia.
Area: 830,000 square miles (2,149,690 sq km).
Population (1972 est.): 8,200,000. *Density,* 10 per square mile (4 per sq km). *Annual rate of increase,* 2.8%.
Chief Cities (1965 est.): Riyadh, the capital, 225,000; Jidda, 194,000; Mecca, 185,000.
Government: *Head of state,* Faisal Ibn Abdul-Aziz, king (acceded Nov. 1964). *Head of government,* Faisal Ibn Abdul-Aziz.
Language: Arabic (official).
Education: *Expenditure* (1969), 10% of total public expenditure. *School enrollment* (1969)—primary, 397,153; secondary, 79,469; technical/vocational, 1,777; university/higher, 6,942.
Monetary Unit: Riyal (4.14 riyals equal U. S.$1, Sept. 1972).
Gross National Product (1970 est.): $3,140,000,000.
National Income per Person (1969): $350.
Manufacturing (major products): Petroleum products, cement, fertilizers, iron and steel.
Major Agricultural Product: Dates.
Major Mineral: Petroleum (4th among world producers, 1970).
Foreign Trade (1970): *Exports,* $2,423,000,000 (chief exports —crude petroleum and petroleum products). *Imports,* $692,000,000 (chief imports, 1969—food, motor vehicles, iron and steel, electrical machinery, apparatus, appliances). *Chief trading partners* (1969)—Japan (took 25% of exports, supplied 10% of imports); United Kingdom (9%—9%); Netherlands (8%—8%); United States (3%—19%).
Transportation: *Motor vehicles* (1970), 115,300 (automobiles, 64,900); *railroads* (1970), 376 miles (605 km); *major national airline,* Saudi Arabian Airlines.
Communications: *Telephones* (1968), 44,250; *television stations* (1971), 8; *television sets* (1971), 300,000; *radios* (1970), 85,000; *newspapers* (1970), 5 (daily circulation, 60,000).

barrels per day in 1971 to nearly 6 million barrels per day in 1972. At the end of 1971, known oil reserves were set at 157.3 billion barrels. In 1972 several new strikes were made, one at Mazalij that has been estimated to equal the Ghawar field, the largest field known in the world.

Budget Outlays. On August 10, King Faisal announced the budget for the new fiscal year, revealing the new directions to be followed in developing the state. Total revenues were estimated at $3.18 billion. The largest single item in the budget is for defense, which was increased by 51% to $855 million. New military bases are being created, such as the one in southwestern Arabia at Khamis Musheit, which is equipped with jet fighters, tanks, heavy artillery, helicopters, and missiles. Naval expansion is contemplated in an outlay of $180 million. These expenditures are to strengthen the state's position in the Persian Gulf and along the Red Sea and Arabian Sea. A direct appropriation of $160 million is provided for assistance in Arab affairs, including aid to Egypt, Jordan, and Palestinian refugees.

The second-largest single budget item is $260 million for roads and ports. Telephone and telegraph are assigned $87 million. Explorations are under way for uranium and other radioactive minerals, and Sheikh Yamani is pushing exploration and development of many other minerals, including gold, copper, zinc, tungsten, and iron.

Over 12% of the budget is appropriated for education, a sizable part of which will go for the education of girls. In June, the first class was graduated from the College of Petroleum and Minerals at Dhahran. It was opened in 1965 and is Saudi Arabia's third advanced educational institution.

Large sums have been set aside for health and public services. Irrigation projects are under way, and in 1972 the government distributed 865,000 acres of land in its program of settling nomads.

SYDNEY NETTLETON FISHER
The Ohio State University

SHULTZ, George. See BIOGRAPHY.
SEISMOLOGY. See EARTHQUAKES.

DRAFT LOTTERY is held in February to determine the order of call-ups for 1973. The order was fixed by picking a capsule with a date of the year from the left drum and pairing it with a numbered capsule from the right drum.

SELECTIVE SERVICE

The year 1972 could be characterized as one in which the "winding down" of Selective Service was begun. In the previous year the Nixon administration had been forced to fight desperately to get a renewal of the draft law. But as 1972 began, the administration wasted no time in proving that it considered the draft a stopgap measure on the way to an all-volunteer armed forces. Secretary of Defense Melvin Laird announced plans to reduce induction drastically and to call no one in the first three months. He also indicated that over a million men who had become eligible for induction in 1971 but had not been called would not be called even though they were still vulnerable for the first three months of 1972.

Ending the Draft. In March, the administration indicated it would end the draft by July 1973 and not exceed 50,000 inductions during 1972. This figure, the lowest since 1949, was down from a peak of 364,000 in 1966 and from 96,000 in 1971. In May it was also announced that the drafting of medical doctors would end because decreased demands and new pay incentives could provide sufficient volunteers. President Nixon may have been trying to keep inductions as low as possible in an election year as well as to keep draftees out of Vietnam and casualty lists. In June he announced that no more draftees would receive a Vietnam assignment unless they requested it.

Ending the draft was difficult to achieve, however, in the face of the general military manpower situation. Congress had instructed the Army to reduce from 1,123,000 men in July 1971 to 850,000 by July 1972. As a result, the Army had to take a

number of steps to cut its existing forces while simultaneously taking in enough men to assure the future force level. Even though substantial pay increases had been granted in the previous year, the Army, when faced with strictures on drafting men and declining draft pressure on registrants, had to take such unprecedented steps as seeking still higher pay, offering greater reenlistment bonuses, increasing the number of women in service, and instituting an innovative and expensive recruitment campaign. The Army even tried its first enlistment bonus since the Civil War. Between January and August it offered $1,500 to enlistees in the combat branches that normally contain 96% conscripts. Opinions of manpower experts differed as to the feasibility and final cost of these efforts, but by August the president and the Department of Defense were predicting that there would be sufficient enlistments to end the draft in July 1973 if Congress would pass the Uniform Services Special Pay Act of 1972, as it finally did.

A serious problem remained, however, in the dwindling number of enlistments in the National Guard and Reserves caused by the decrease in draft pressure. In recent years these service branches had a waiting list of well over 100,000 men wanting to join to avoid being drafted. But as draft quotas declined, the waiting lists disappeared.

Reform. Even as the Selective Service System was "winding down," the two-year program of gradually reforming its procedures was nearing its end. Director Curtis Tarr asserted that the system had moved from a state and local focus to President Nixon's goal of a national system. He ended the three-month freeze on appeals and personal appearances that had backlogged thousands of cases.

Tarr also announced the following changes: (1) Those whose call-ups had been postponed for a long period of time could request their cases be reopened and submit new evidence. (2) Personal appearances before appeals' boards were to be permitted for the first time on 15-day notice. (3) Registrants were to be permitted to have witnesses at their discretion, rather than at that of the local board. (4) Local boards were required to have a quorum present for all decisions. (5) Each registrant was guaranteed 15 minutes for a presentation. (6) Boards were required to give the registrants written reason for denial of requests for reclassification. (7) Registrants were permitted to wait until completion of their personal appearance before their boards before filing an appeal, and no longer be required to do both simultaneously.

The lottery that would decide which men would be drafted in 1973 was also held earlier than usual in order to permit young men to make plans as soon as possible, and it was carried out under new procedures called the "fairness system." Under this procedure, for example, boards throughout the nation would be required to call up all men with the numbers between 1 and 15, rather than have national headquarters set a "ceiling number" such as 25 and let boards reach whatever number under 25 they needed to fill their quota. The latter procedure increased uncertainty for the registrants, and questions of fairness had been raised.

Draft Protesters. The violence and protest that had rocked the system in recent years subsided somewhat and seemed more diffusely aimed at armed forces recruiters, ROTC, and other manifestations of military presence. Three prominent figures associated with past violence against the system were again in the news. The Rev. Daniel J. Berrigan, who was sentenced to three year's imprisonment for destroying draft records, was given a medical parole from federal prison. His brother, the Rev. Philip Berrigan, and Sister Elizabeth McAlister were convicted of smuggling letters into federal prison and each sentenced to a year. The government, however, dropped the charges that they had conspired to kidnap the presidential adviser on national security, Henry Kissinger, and to plant bombs in Washington. Philip Berrigan was already serving a

sentence for destroying draft records. His new sentences could be served concurrently, and thus he and Sister Elizabeth were eligible for immediate parole. Their supporters contended that these final results proved that the government case had never been more than political persecution and harassment because the Berrigans had embarrassed the FBI in evading capture for so long.

Amnesty. Inevitably, the question of amnesty for the estimated 50,000 to 70,000 exiled draft evaders and deserters came to the forefront as the war and draft receded as issues. It became an issue of some salience in the presidential campaign. Though both the President and Senator McGovern agreed that amnesty must await the end of hostilities and the return of prisoners in Vietnam, detractors of Senator McGovern portrayed him as "soft" on the amnesty question. Late in the campaign, the President spoke out more strongly against granting amnesty.

Sen. Edward Kennedy made statements indicating that he leaned toward immediate unconditional amnesty, to be accomplished by administrative means rather than by congressional legislation. He contended that administrative means had been utilized after World War II. But after holding hearings on the subject he appeared to shift ground and back away from unconditional amnesty because of the potentially harmful effects on discipline and morale of the armed forces.

Bills were introduced in Congress to provide amnesty for those who would return and accept civilian service in lieu of induction, but no bill seemed likely to succeed until the Vietnam fighting was ended and prisoners of war were returned. Other proposals included a special commission to review and pass on each case.

Clearly there were a number of subtle and complex aspects of the question. Evaders presented a variety of types, each of which presumably would require different handling if justice were to prevail. There were those who (1) had refused to register and fled; (2) had registered, sought conscientious objection, and failing to get it, fled; and (3) had been inducted and deserted. It also seemed likely that registrants with less education and intelligence and lower socioeconomic status more often chose to flee or desert as a solution to their dilemma than to appeal the case on grounds of abstract civil rights. The course of action chosen, however, seemed more an outgrowth of life-style than a measure of lack of respect for the law. If amnesty were granted it would also seem necessary to review the sentences of those currently in prison for evasion.

The Future. While such aftermath questions were not settled in 1972, it was clear that the Selective Service, in the form in which it had existed since 1918, was nearing an end. The lottery held in 1972 may have been the last one that would result in actual inductions. Secretary Laird said that the Selective Service System would continue to exist for emergencies, but clearly he was referring to a record-keeping mode of operation like the ones seen briefly by the system in 1948. Proof of the pending change is seen in the quiet resignation in April of Director Curtis Tarr and his assumption of a new position in the Department of State. One newspaper account described his departure as "a move to a more secure position."

GARY L. WAMSLEY
University of Kansas

DEFENSE Secretary Laird tells a news conference of the need for legislation to permit an end to the draft.

WIDE WORLD

DRAFT CALLS

299,000 289,900

163,500

98,

1970 197

──────── SENEGAL • Information Highlights ────────

Official Name: Republic of Senegal.
Area: 75,750 square miles (196,192 sq km).
Population (1972 est.): 4,100,000. *Density,* 52 per square mile (20 per sq km). *Annual rate of increase,* 2.4%.
Chief City (1969 est.): Dakar, the capital, 581,000.
Government: *Head of state,* Léopold Sédar Senghor, president (took office Sept. 1960). *Chief minister,* Abdou Diouf, premier (took office Feb. 1970). *Legislature* (unicameral) —National Assembly, 100 members. *Major political party* —Senegalese Progressive Union.
Languages: French (official), Wolof, Fulani, Mandingo.
Education: *Expenditure* (1965), 14.7% of total public expenditure. *School enrollment* (1968)—primary, 255,493; general secondary, 42,228; technical/vocational (1967), 10,-608; university/higher, 2,965.
Monetary Unit: CFA franc (255.79 CFA francs equal U. S.$1, Sept. 1972).
Gross National Product (1970 est.): $700,000,000.
Manufacturing (major products): Peanut oil, cement, processed foods, textiles, leather, shoes, chemicals.
Major Agricultural Products: Groundnuts, cotton, millet and sorghum, rice, cassava.
Major Minerals: Phosphate rock, limestone, iron ore.
Foreign Trade (1971): *Exports,* $125,000,000. *Imports,* $218,-000,000. *Chief trading partners* (1969)—France (took 60% of exports, supplied 41% of imports); West Germany (2%—11%); Netherlands (5%—3%); Ivory Coast (3%—5%).
Communications: *Telephones* (1970), 28,000; *television stations* (1971), 1; *television sets* (1971), 1,500; *radios* (1970), 268,000; *newspapers* (1970), 1 (daily circulation, 20,000).

SENEGAL

The most positive developments in Senegal in 1972 were the revival of its economy and an improvement in its relations with Guinea. A troubling note was the continuation of violent clashes with Portuguese forces along the Casamance border with Portuguese Guinea.

Economic Affairs. Rains, after four years of severe drought, brought a great increase in peanut production. Disastrous drought conditions had seriously damaged the harvest of Senegal's main crops. Tonnage of peanuts produced had fallen from over 1 million metric tons in 1967 to only 554,000 in 1970. Sorghum production was off by almost 50% during the same period. But nearly normal conditions prevailed in 1971 and 1972, and Senegal's general economy paralleled the improvement in the crop yields.

Reports of mining explorations were satisfactory, particularly at La Falémé, where there is an estimated 1.2 billion tons of high-grade iron ore. A team of Russian mining engineers reported that the traces of gold previously discovered in eastern Senegal were indicative of much larger deposits.

Internal Affairs. The improvement in the economic sector helped produce a calmer political atmosphere. On National Day, President Léopold Senghor reduced the sentences of a number of persons convicted of crimes against the state. Among those affected was former Premier Mamadou Dia, whose sentence was reduced from life to 20 years. The national congress of the ruling Senegalese Progressive Union confirmed Senghor's control of the party and state by recommending that he be reconfirmed as secretary general of the party and nominating him as the sole candidate for president in the January 1973 election.

The chiefs of staff of the armed services and police were reshuffled in June, and a new armed forces ministry was created to function directly under the control of Premier Abdou Diouf. In July, the size of the National Assembly was increased from 80 to 100 deputies to reflect the considerable growth in population.

Foreign Affairs. Animosity between Portugal and Senegal erupted in violence in May. Senegal charged that over 200 Portuguese troops had crossed the border of Portuguese Guinea and attacked the village of Santiaba-Manjak in southern Senegal (the Casamance), resulting in the death of six Senegalese soldiers. The Portuguese claimed that none of their troops were involved and that the action was in an area known to shelter Guinean nationalist guerrillas. But Portugal was censured by the UN Security Council, and a special mission was sent to investigate the continuing border difficulties.

The persistent antipathy between Senegal and Guinea was the cause of the breakup of the Organization of Senegal River States in March. But a special nine-man committee of the Organization of African Unity, headed by Emperor Haile Selassie of Ethiopia, mediated the differences between the two states, and President Senghor and Guinea's President Sékou Touré signed an agreement in May.

In April, Senegal became one of the founding states of the West African Economic Community, consisting also of six other French-speaking states— Ivory Coast, Dahomey, Upper Volta, Mali, Mauritania, and Niger. Despite the ill feelings in Senegal caused by the deportation of over 700 Senegalese from Zaïre, the two governments concluded long-term trade agreements.

HARRY A. GAILEY
California State University, San Jose

SHIPPING. See TRANSPORTATION.
SHRIVER, R. Sargent. See BIOGRAPHY.

SIERRA LEONE

The year 1972 was a relatively quiet one in Sierra Leone. The government of President Siaka Stevens, which had been threatened by an attempted coup in 1971, remained firmly in control in spite of continued economic difficulties and signs of dissatisfaction in some quarters. Government spokesmen frequently claimed that sufficient national consensus existed to justify introducing a one-party state.

Political Affairs. The state of emergency was lifted in Kailahun district in September to allow the first 3 of 12 pending by-elections to take place. But the Sierra Leone People's party (SLPP) was unable to nominate candidates. On September 6, its leader Salia Jusu-Sheriff, and nine other party leaders

──────── SIERRA LEONE • Information Highlights ────────

Official Name: Republic of Sierra Leone.
Area: 27,700 square miles (71,740 sq km).
Population (1972 est.): 2,800,000. *Density,* 98 per square mile (38 per sq km). *Annual rate of increase,* 2.3%.
Chief City (1969 est.): Freetown, the capital, 170,600.
Government: *Head of state,* Siaka P. Stevens, president (took office April 1971). *Head of government,* S. I. Koroma, prime minister (took office April 1971). *Legislature* (unicameral)—House of Representatives, 78 members. *Major political parties*—All People's Congress; Sierra Leone People's party.
Languages: English (official), Creole.
Education: *Expenditure* (1969), 17.9% of total public expenditure. *School enrollment* (1968)—primary, 154,898; secondary, 30,797; technical/vocational, 860; university/higher, 1,119.
Monetary Unit: Leone (0.8264 leone equals U. S.$1, Sept. 1972).
Gross National Product (1970 est.): $425,000,000.
Manufacturing (major products): Processed foods, soap.
Major Agricultural Products: Rice, palm oil and kernels, cacao, coffee, kola nuts, ginger.
Major Minerals: Diamonds, iron ore, bauxite.
Foreign Trade (1971): *Exports,* $97,000,000. *Imports,* $113,-000,000. *Chief trading partners* (1969)—United Kingdom (took 75% of exports, supplied 31% of imports); Netherlands (9%—4%); Japan (4%—10%); United States (5%—8%).
Communications: *Telephones* (1970), 9,000; *television stations* (1971), 1; *newspapers* (1969), 5 (daily circulation, 40,000).

were arrested and charged with the murder of a government supporter who had allegedly been killed by an SLPP vehicle. Seven of the accused were later released, not including Jusu-Sheriff. The SLPP felt unable to contest any of the remaining by-elections, thus guaranteeing victory to the governing All People's Congress. It appeared that a decisive step might have been taken towards a one-party state, but President Stevens declared that this question would be not settled until after the general election due in 1973.

In January, the government announced the suspension of the system of local government through elected district councils, which were condemned as wasteful and ineffective.

Economy. In February, the governor of the Bank of Sierra Leone, S. L. Bangura, used the word "stagflation" to describe the state of the economy in 1971, when economic stagnation and declining exports had been combined with severe inflation. The country's basic economic position did not improve in 1972, although Finance Minister C. Kamara-Taylor claimed in July that the gross domestic product was increasing at an annual rate of 5% in real terms. External trade remained essentially dependent on the export of minerals, primarily diamonds.

The government initiated negotiations to secure a controlling interest in the Sierra Leone Development Company, and it continued its efforts to reduce losses resulting from diamond smuggling by introducing new measures against "strangers" in the digging areas. The third-largest diamond ever found —969.8 carats—was discovered in Sierra Leone in February. It was named the "Star of Sierra Leone" by President Stevens.

Recognizing the difficulty of controlling export prices, the president emphasized the need "to make maximum financial benefits accrue to the country from our internal economic activities." Priority was given to encouraging production of rice, the staple food, in order to reduce imports.

Foreign Affairs. The detachment of Guinean troops sent to Sierra Leone at President Steven's request during the crisis following the unsuccessful coup in 1971 remained in the country, although inconspicuously.

Ethiopia's Emperor Haile Selassie visited the country in January, and Prime Minister Fidel Castro of Cuba was there in May.

J. D. HARGREAVES
University of Aberdeen

SINGAPORE

Parliamentary elections, the continuing economic boom, and Prime Minister Lee's visit to Malaysia made news in 1972.

Singapore's ruling People's Action party (PAP), led by Prime Minister Lee Kuan Yew, easily won reelection in September, winning all seats in the enlarged parliament of 65 members. But five small opposition parties gained an impressive 30.9% of the vote for the 57 contested seats, in sharp contrast to the token opposition that PAP faced in the 1968 elections.

Visibly disappointed by the unexpected increase in the opposition vote, Prime Minister Lee interpreted it as an antigovernment protest vote, which he attributed mainly to dislocations necessitated by Singapore's rapid industrialization and urban renewal. The opposition parties proved unable to

---

——— SINGAPORE • **Information Highlights** ———

Official Name: Republic of Singapore.
Area: 224 square miles (581 sq km).
Population (1972 est.): 2,200,000. *Density,* 9,138 per square mile (3,528 per sq km). *Annual rate of increase,* 2.2%.
Chief City (1970 census): Singapore, the capital, 2,122,466.
Government: *Head of state,* Benjamin Henry Sheares, president (took office Dec. 1971). *Head of government,* Lee Kuan Yew, prime minister (took office May 1959). *Legislature* (unicameral)—Parliament, 58 members. *Major political party*—People's Action party.
Languages: Malay (official), English, Chinese, Tamil.
Education: *Expenditure* (1969), 15.2% of total public expenditure. *School enrollment* (1969)—primary, 366,881; secondary, 152,110; technical/vocational, 20,635; university/higher, 12,659.
Monetary Unit: Singapore dollar (2.86 S. dollar equal U. S.$1, June 1972).
Gross National Product (1970 est.): $1,970,000,000.
Manufacturing (major products): Petroleum products, steel, textiles, tires, wood products, processed foods, electronic components, ships, assembled automobiles.
Foreign Trade (1971): *Exports,* $1,755,000,000. *Imports,* $2,828,000,000. *Chief trading partners* (1969)—Malaysia (took 16% of exports, supplied 17% of imports); United States (11%—8%); Japan (7%—16%); United Kingdom (6%—7%).
Communications: *Telephones* (1971), 161,310; *television stations* (1971), 2; *television sets* (1971), 149,000; *radios* (1970), 101,000; *newspapers* (1970), 12 (daily circulation, 412,000).

---

form a united front against PAP, and the leftist Barisan Sosialis divided on electoral participation.

Economy. The Singapore economic boom continued. In March, Finance Minister Hon Sui Sen stated that the economic growth rate in 1971 was 14%, slightly lower than the previous year but still the second-highest in Asia after Japan. In the rapidly expanding manufacturing sector increases in output of petroleum refining, shipbuilding, and manufacture of electrical machinery were noteworthy, averaging well over 30%.

The anticipated adverse effects of the withdrawal of British bases had been minimized, with the number of jobless kept at a level of 38,000 persons. More than 70,000 workers were in fact imported from outside Singapore, mainly from Malaysia, to service certain labor-intensive industries. While European and American investors provided most new industrial investment, the Japanese had invested heavily in 30 enterprises in shipbuilding and repairing, tire manufacturing, electrical appliances, and precision instruments.

Foreign Affairs. In foreign affairs an important development was Prime Minister Lee's visit to Kuala Lumpur in March, the first since Singapore's separation from the Federation of Malaysia in 1965. A surprising cordiality marked Lee's conversations with Malaysian Prime Minister Tun Abdul Razak. They agreed on distributing the residual assets of the Malaya British Borneo Currency Board, with Malaysia receiving 74%, Singapore 18%, and Brunei the remaining 8%. Singapore had previously claimed 35.5%. The two states also agreed on reciprocal guarantees for approved new investments by nationals of one country in the other.

In April, Singapore was host to the fifth annual ministerial meeting of the Association of Southeast Asian Nations (ASEAN). The conference initiated an overall review of ASEAN procedures, with a view to setting up a central secretariat, and approved a special coordinating committee to conduct future discussions with the European Economic Community.

C. PAUL BRADLEY
University of Michigan-Flint

SMITH, Gerald C. See BIOGRAPHY.
SOCIAL SECURITY. See SOCIAL WELFARE.

Elderly people sit in the sun in St. Petersburg, Fla. Older Americans began receiving 20% higher social security benefits in September.

social welfare

In 1972, social welfare developments included attempts by the federal government to take increased responsibility for welfare programs, a rise in social security benefits, and the imposition of limitations to the revenue-sharing law.

Legislative activity, new or revised programs, and other news developments in the field of social welfare during 1972 are reviewed in this article under the following headings: (1) General Survey; (2) Social Security; and (3) Child Welfare.

General Survey

The piecemeal enactment of hotly contested long-range policy changes in a flurry of end-of-session congressional and executive activity posed many readjustment problems for social welfare organizations at the close of 1972. Important aspects of new legislation received scant attention in the news compared with "the welfare mess," "revenue sharing," and "defeat for Nixon welfare reform." The complex political maneuvering meant that only those in daily contact with Congress could hope to be well informed.

Revenue sharing and welfare reform, proposed in 1969, came up for final passage only as Congress sought to adjourn in 1972. Agreement could not be reached on some important proposals, and they were dropped. The legislation thus left some programs intact, while others will be drastically changed by 1974. In the states, social service projects face uncertain futures, dependent on the local impact of the revenue-sharing act.

The media focused on the irreconcilable differences that developed over "welfare reform," as

represented by President Nixon's proposed Family Assistance Plan (FAP). When Congress dropped the proposal, the largest federal-state public assistance program, Aid to Families with Dependent Children (AFDC), with its 11 million recipients in 3 million families, was left essentially unchanged even though almost nobody was satisfied.

The media, on the other hand, almost ignored the passage of the part of the president's proposals that does away with other federal-state assistance programs and drastically alters the arrangements for financing social services by the states. For those who are involved in the administration of any of these programs, 1973 will be a year of transitional uncertainty.

Behind these shifts and proposed shifts lie some fundamental facts and dilemmas in the life of the United States. Among them are:

(1) The population explosion has increased the number of children and elderly ("unproductive") persons to be provided for by those who are currently producing.

(2) Traditional agrarian expectations of individual self-sufficiency stand in the way of collective action to provide for personal contingencies.

(3) Allocation of federal and state responsibilities in this field remains contested. The federal government has been involved since 1935, but "states' rights" sentiment is still potent. Federal insurance programs generally have worked better than state insurance and assistance programs, which have been extremely uneven, causing irritation and bickering among recipients, taxpayers, and state and federal officials.

(4) Fear that somebody may "get something for nothing" results in assistance programs encumbered by a multitude of work and other requirements that are often little related to the facts of present need or employment opportunities.

(5) The idea of a minimum income, widely recognized as essential, is frustrated legislatively by argument over the level at which it should be set.

Congressional Action. During 1972 each of these points was evident in the struggles over the president's proposals, embodied in a House-passed bill, HR 1. The Senate Finance Committee studied it from April 1971 until September 1972. Sen. Russell B. Long, the committee chairman, openly disagreed with some of the proposals. Impatient senators secured separate passage of one item, providing increased social security benefits, but the bill as finally passed was still one of the longest pieces of legislation in U. S. history.

These points also underlay related areas of congressional controversy: two presidential vetoes of appropriation bills for the Department of Labor and the Department of Health, Education, and Welfare; rapidly escalating demands by the states for matching funds for social services; and the president's recommendation that federal revenues be shared with the states.

The abandoned FAP proposal would have assured minimum incomes to all families with children, whether the parents were employed or not. Assistance to employed or employable persons seemed to many to be excessively generous and a disincentive to work, while to others the proposed levels of guaranteed income (originally $1,600 per year for a family of four, increased to $2,400 in HR 1) seemed so low as to make the plan worthless. Fear that incentive to work would be lost led Senator Long to demand a work-related program, which was attacked as both primitive and undercutting of minimum wage standards. The Finance Committee finally recommended retaining the present AFDC, excluding from it all employables, who would go into work programs; and work bonuses and wage supplements for low-income workers.

The Senate divided into three groups: supporters of the Finance Committee, of the administration, and of a moderately liberal proposal advanced by Sen. Abraham Ribicoff ($2,800 for a family of four, a far cry from the $6,500 demanded by the National Welfare Rights Organization). Another possibility —a uniform payment of perhaps $1,000 a year to each person without regard to need—was mentioned by Sen. George McGovern in his presidential primary campaign, but it never received consideration in Congress. There compromise proved impossible, FAP died, and AFDC remained.

HR 1 provisions for radical changes in other federal-state assistance programs did not encounter similar difficulties. Effective in 1974, Old Age Assistance, Aid to the Blind, and Aid to the Disabled will be consolidated under federal administration, with recipients guaranteed a minimum monthly income of $130 (or $195 for a couple) and permitted to retain portions of social security and earnings in addition. While states may supplement the federal grants, in most cases this will not be necessary for recipients to experience greater comfort and spending power. In nearly all states millions of dollars of state or local funds will be freed for other uses. States might improve AFDC grants, which are far smaller than in the other categories.

Revenue Sharing. Another change of major significance to federal-state welfare relations was written into the revenue-sharing law. Retroactive to July 1, 1972, previously unlimited 75% federal matching grants for state social services under the Social Security Act were limited to $2.5 billion a year, with no state receiving more than its share on a population basis. This means that some states that had been rapidly expanding these programs must refinance or sharply curtail some of them.

Social Security Benefits. Of greater immediate importance to the average person is the 20% increase in social security benefits and the tax adjustments to finance them. The benefits increase, together with the new guaranteed levels in public assistance, will bring nearly all aged and disabled persons up to the so-called "poverty level," and persons in the higher earning brackets can look forward to higher retirement benefits. To pay for this, previously authorized tax increases will be extended to earnings in the $10,200 to $12,000 range.

Role of the Federal Government. The federal government is thus assuming responsibility, formerly shared with the states, for assuring minimum adequate income to the elderly and disabled. In the poorer states the effect on standards of living is likely to be considerable. Similar action has not yet been taken with respect to able-bodied adults or families with children, but this discussion has been opened, and in the next few years the federal government may well assume virtually complete responsibility for income maintenance, leaving the states with no more responsibility for it than private philanthropy now has.

Time will be required to resolve the ideological differences over FAP. This will provide opportunity for the states, still suffering from severe fiscal crises, to adjust their budgets to the transfer of adult assistance programs to the federal government, the influx of federal revenue-sharing funds, and new rules on federal financing of social service programs. A federal take-over of all income maintenance functions could then occur in an orderly step-by-step process, rather than in a single convulsive episode with the states neither administratively nor psychologically prepared to take the best advantage of their new fiscal freedom.

Meantime there are conflicting elements in the present situation. Inadequate provision for children in need seems related to efforts to enforce a "work ethic" on their parents. Even some thoughtful, nonemotional journalists attribute these efforts to "racism." If this is indeed the case, it is ironic that the great majority of the children who are and will be deprived are white, despite all the publicity that has emphasized the high incidence of poverty among blacks. In the face of widespread complaints about breakdowns in family life there are strong pressures to force women whose children have reached the age of six, or even only three, to get jobs. After urging Congress to pass employment and day-care measures President Nixon vetoed such bills as inflationary.

Other Action. While Congress delayed decisions on these matters, states took a wide variety of steps to ease their budget problems. The flood of social service projects involving federal financing was one. Legislative efforts to circumvent Supreme Court decisions against residency requirements were negated in the courts. "Experimental" administrative projects to require recipients to pick up their checks at

"It's nice to know that every four years we regain our importance to society."

central locations turned out to be harassment tactics rather than screening devices. Projects to require recipients to work out the value of their checks, but no more, were fought in the courts on grounds of peonage and as a method of avoiding appropriate budgeting for staff needs.

These court tests emphasized developing aspects of the welfare scene. "Maximum feasible participation of the poor" under the "war on poverty" resulted in an unprecedented amount of community organizational activity in economically deprived areas, both urban and rural. The National Welfare Rights Organization (NWRO), a nationwide network of local organizations of public assistance recipients—by lobbying, demonstrations, and legal action—has challenged the status quo in welfare and has fought administrative or legislative rules that appeared detrimental to the interests of its members. It has received notable assistance from OEO legal-aid services, which have often successfully defended the NWRO position in state and federal courts and in the Supreme Court.

Pressure from this group probably had much to do with the inconclusive outcome of the FAP portion of HR 1. Its legal success in fighting state governmental structures is undoubtedly one reason for President Nixon's refusal to permit the legal-aid system to be set up under an independent board of directors.

Conclusions. In sum, the effect of the many changes introduced into the social welfare system cannot yet be measured. The states will have more responsibility for social service programs and the federal government for basic income needs. The demands of recipients will be heard. All of these point to increasing acceptance of the idea that in our present-day complex society the individual has only limited control over his own destiny.

This trend, frightening as it is to some, is worldwide. At an International Council on Social Welfare meeting at The Hague in August the problems of urbanization, aging, income gaps, and provision of appropriate services were similar, no matter what the political outlook of the country or the de-

gree of its economic development. To some observers from highly developed countries, the United States appeared laggard in the amount and quality of thought being directed to the solution of its versions of these worldwide problems.

RALPH E. PUMPHREY
Washington University, St. Louis

Social Security

Significant and far-reaching improvements were made in social security in 1972, and a new program of supplementary security income for needy, aged, blind, and disabled persons was enacted.

Amendments. Social security benefits were raised by 20%, to rise automatically with the cost of living, and the maximum amount of a worker's annual earnings that may be counted in figuring benefits was increased. Amendments raised from $1,680 to $2,100 in 1973—and then automatically as average wages rise—the amount of yearly earnings a person may have without any withholding of benefits, and assured that a beneficiary who works will always have more total income than if he does not. A special minimum benefit was provided for those who have worked many years at low earnings under social security coverage. The cash benefits contribution rate for both employers and employees was set at 4.85% for 1973–77 and 4.8% for 1978 and succeeding years until well into the next century.

Medicare protection was extended to social security disability insurance beneficiaries now and in the future after they have gotten such benefits for at least two years, and to most others under 65 who need hemodialysis treatment or require a kidney transplant. The Medicare hospital insurance program was put back on a sound financial basis through contribution rates of 1% for 1973–77, rising in steps to 1.45% in 1993 and thereafter.

Financing. In 1972 employers and employees each paid contributions of 5.2% on the first $9,000 of the worker's earnings. The rate for the self-employed was 7.5%. For all, 0.6% was earmarked for hospital insurance. The corresponding 1973–77 rates will be 5.85%, 8.0%, and 1.0%, respectively, and

will apply to earnings up to $10,800 for 1973, rising to $12,000 for 1974 and after as wages rise. The monthly premium for the supplementary medical insurance part of Medicare, matched by the federal government, was $5.60 through June and $5.80 thereafter. Under 1972 amendments this premium will be raised only when there is a general cash benefit increase, and by a corresponding percentage.

Operations. In the year ending June 30, monthly cash benefits totaled $38,265,000,000. Lump-sum death payments came to $322,300,000. In the Medicare program, approved hospital insurance claims totaled 7,200,000. The average amount reimbursed was $823 per hospital claim, $89 per home health claim, and $393 per extended-care claim. About 48,200,000 medical insurance claims were recorded for fiscal 1972. Allowed charges totaled $2.9 billion, of which $2.1 billion was reimbursed.

Supplementary Security Income. Administered by the Social Security Administration but financed out of the general revenues of the federal government, this new program goes into effect in January 1974, replacing state-administered separate programs of old-age assistance and aid to the blind and the permanently and totally disabled. It will establish a minimum income for about 5 million persons and is also designed to encourage states to supplement federal payments in order to maintain existing payment levels, where these are higher. It will provide for monthly payments to assure a minimum monthly income of $130 for an individual and $195 for a couple, if both are eligible. The amount will be less if there is other countable income, but $20 per month of any income and $65 of earned income plus one half of the rest of earnings will not be considered countable. Resource limitations of $1,500 for an individual and $2,250 for a couple will apply uniformly throughout the nation. Ownership of a home, household goods, personal effects, and an automobile generally will not affect eligibility.

ROBERT M. BALL
Commissioner of Social Security

Child Welfare

In 1972 a number of significant developments in services to children and their parents were initiated or supported by the Federal Office of Child Development. These included the launching of a major effort to create a new profession, Child Development Associates, in order to meet the increasing need for trained personnel. Credentials are based on demonstrated skill in working with young children, rather than on academic credits.

Home Start. A three-year demonstration program was inaugurated to help disadvantaged parents provide child development services in their own homes. Called Home Start, it was designed to enable these parents to succeed as primary educators of their own children. Fifteen such programs were conducted in varied geographic, cultural, and ethnic settings as part of ongoing Head Start programs.

Education for Parenthood. A joint program was set up by the Office of Child Development and the Office of Education to show teenagers how to become good parents. The program, at first involving some 500,000 students (1973), aimed to increase awareness by young people of the social, emotional, and health needs of children. A curriculum for use in secondary schools combined classroom instruction and experience in working with children at day-care and Head Start centers and kindergartens.

An Important Partnership. In a coordinated program, Head Start and Community Mental Health Centers strove to improve the quality of mental health care as to preventive, diagnostic, and treatment services for Head Start children and their families. Dr. Edward F. Zigler, then director of the Office of Child Development, called the effort "a first—one important step forward in integrating all existing HEW resources for the sake of emotionally disturbed, mentally retarded and physically handicapped Head Start children and their families."

First Parent Participation at National Level. The National Head Start Advisory Committee, established in July 1972, was the first national committee to advise on Head Start plans and operations and assist the director in evaluating the programs' effectiveness. The committee is composed of parents of Head Start children, parents of former Head Start children, and staff of local Head Start programs.

Dr. Zigler, first director of the Office of Child Development, who resigned July 31, gave creative leadership in establishing that agency as the national advocate for children. Dr. Saul Rosoff, deputy director of OCD, became acting director.

UNICEF. The United Nations' Children's Fund, as always, played an important part in the UN's program of assistance in emergency needs arising in various nations. Among the nations receiving emergency relief in 1972 were Afghanistan, Bangladesh, Pakistan, and the Philippines.

For Afghanistan, which had suffered more than two years of drought, UNICEF's Executive Board approved $1.25 million for a rural water supply program to provide drinking water in areas of greatest need. The executive director authorized $200,000 from the emergency reserve to provide drugs, medicines, and high-protein food mixtures for children and mothers, as well as blankets and clothing.

Bangladesh was a major emergency area, with $30 million budgeted for 1972 through June 1973, the largest emergency program in UNICEF's history. The government's first request of UNICEF was to resume the child feeding program, which serves over 2 million children. Another high priority area was safe drinking water. UNICEF allotted two thirds of an estimated $9 million budget for sinking 100,000 new tubewells, rehabilitation of 60,000 old wells, and cleaning and repair of others. UNICEF sponsored training courses in agriculture, food production, and nutrition for in-service primary school teachers. There was a $6 million budget for hospital equipment, emergency drugs, vaccines, diet supplements, equipment for rural health centers, and vehicles for transporting health personnel.

In 1972 the government of Pakistan requested aid from UNICEF for programs for women and children. The executive director authorized $160,-000 for drugs, medical supplies, quilts, blankets, clothing, cooking utensils, and reed matting.

In the Philippines month-long heavy rains caused flooding and serious damage to crops. The executive director of UNICEF authorized $100,000 to help mothers and children affected by the flood. An assessment of the most immediate needs revealed a priority requirement for drugs and medical supplies, and UNICEF arranged for immediate release of 2,500 sets of drugs and diet supplements.

ISABELLA J. JONES
Executive Vice President
National Association of Consultants
for Children and Youth

SOCIETIES AND ORGANIZATIONS

This article lists a selection of some of the most noteworthy associations, societies, foundations, and trusts of the United States and ·Canada. The information for each listing has been furnished by the organization concerned, and includes membership figures, dates of annual meetings, officers, and headquarters location or address.

Alcoholics Anonymous (The General Service Board of A. A., Inc.). Membership: over 600,000 in more than 18,000 affiliated groups. Annual conference: New York, N. Y., April 24–29, 1973. Chairman, John L. Norris, M. D. Headquarters: 468 Park Avenue S., New York, N. Y. Mailing Address: Box 459, Grand Central Station, New York, N. Y. 10017.

American Academy of Arts and Letters. Membership: 50. Annual ceremonial: New York, N. Y., May 1973. President, Aaron Copland; secretary, John Hersey. Headquarters: 633 West 155th St., New York, N. Y. 10032.

American Academy of Arts and Sciences. Membership: approx. 2,600. Annual meeting: Boston, Mass., May 9, 1973. President, Harvey Brooks; secretary, Denis Robinson. Headquarters: 280 Newton St., Brookline Station, Boston, Mass. 02146.

American Academy of Political and Social Science. Membership: 23,500, including 7,000 libraries. Annual meeting: Philadelphia, Pa., April 13–14, 1973. President, Marvin E. Wolfgang; business mgr., Ingeborg Hessler. Headquarters: 3937 Chestnut St., Philadelphia, Pa. 19104.

American Anthropological Association. Membership: 7,900. Annual meeting: New Orleans, La., Nov. 28–Dec. 2, 1973. President, Joseph B. Casagrande; exec. director, Edward J. Lehman. Headquarters: 1703 New Hampshire Ave. NW, Washington, D. C. 20009.

American Association for the Advancement of Science. Membership: 127,000 and 289 affiliated groups. Meeting: San Francisco, Calif., Feb. 25–March 2, 1974. President, Leonard M. Rieser; exec. officer, William Bevan. Headquarters: 1515 Massachusetts Ave. NW, Washington, D. C. 20005.

American Association of University Professors. Membership: 91,000. Annual meeting: St. Louis, Mo., April 27–28, 1973. President, Walter Adams; general secretary, Bertram H. Davis. Headquarters: One Dupont Circle, NW, Washington, D. C. 20036.

American Association of University Women. Membership: 173,000. President, Anne Campbell; general director, Alice L. Beeman. Headquarters: 2401 Virginia Ave. NW, Washington, D. C. 20037.

American Astronomical Society. Membership: 2,800. Meetings, 1973: Las Cruces, N. Mex., Jan. 9–12; Columbus, Ohio, June 25–28; Tucson, Ariz., Dec. 2–6. President, Bart J. Bok; secretary, L. W. Fredrick; exec. officer, H. M. Gurin. Address: 211 FitzRandolph Rd., Princeton, N. J. 08540.

American Automobile Association. Membership: 15 million in 868 affiliated groups. Annual meeting: Vancouver, Canada, Sept. 17–19, 1973. President, Charles J. Gallagher; secretary, Knox Farrand. Headquarters: 1712 G St. NW, Washington, D. C. 20006.

American Bankers Association. Membership: 18,307 banks and branches. Annual meeting: Chicago, Ill., Oct. 6–10, 1973. President, Eugene H. Adams; secretary, George H. Gustafson. Headquarters: 1120 Connecticut Ave. NW, Washington, D. C. 20036.

American Bar Association. Membership: 162,000. Meeting: Washington, D. C., Aug. 11–15, 1973. President, Robert W. Meserve; secretary, Kenneth J. Burns, Jr.; exec. director, Bert H. Early. Headquarters: 1155 East 60th St., Chicago, Ill. 60637.

American Bible Society. 1971 Scripture distribution: 124,933,653 copies. Annual meeting: New York, N. Y., May 10, 1973. President, Edmund F. Wagner; general secretary, Laton E. Holmgren; treas., Charles W. Baas. Headquarters: 1865 Broadway, New York, N. Y. 10023.

American Booksellers Association, Inc. Membership: 4,000. National convention: Los Angeles, Calif., June 10–13, 1973. President, Eliot Leonard; exec. director, G. Roysce Smith. Headquarters: 800 Second Ave., New York, N. Y. 10017.

American Cancer Society, Inc. Membership: 190 voting members; 57 chartered divisions. Annual meeting: New York, N. Y., Nov. 7–9, 1973. President, Arthur G. James, M. D.; secretary, Samuel M. Seegal. Headquarters: 219 East 42d St., New York, N. Y. 10017.

American Chemical Society. Membership: 112,000. National meetings, 1973: Dallas, Texas, April 8–13; Chicago,

Ill., Aug. 26–31. President, Alan C. Nixon; exec. director, R. W. Cairns. Headquarters: 1155 16th St. NW, Washington, D. C. 20036.

American Civil Liberties Union. Membership: 180,000. Exec. director, Aryeh Neier; board chairman, Edward J. Ennis. Headquarters: 22 East 40th St., New York, N. Y. 10016.

American College of Physicians. Membership: 21,200. Annual meeting: Chicago, Ill., April 8–13, 1973. President, William A. Sodeman, M. D.; exec. vice president, Edward C. Rosenow, Jr., M. D. Headquarters: 4200 Pine St., Philadelphia, Pa. 19104.

American College of Surgeons. Membership: 33,000. Annual meeting: Chicago, Ill., Oct. 15–19, 1973. President, William P. Longmire, Jr., M. D.; director, C. Rollins Hanlon, M. D. Headquarters: 55 East Erie St., Chicago, Ill. 60611.

American Council of Learned Societies. Membership: 35 professional societies concerned with the humanities and the humanistic aspects of the social sciences. Annual meeting: Philadelphia, Pa., Jan. 18–19, 1973. President, Frederick Burkhardt; admin. secretary, Charlotte Bowman. Headquarters: 345 East 46th St., New York, N. Y. 10017.

American Council on Education. Membership: 1,389 colleges and universities, 134 associated organizations, 60 affiliates, and 68 constituent organizations. Annual meeting: Washington, D. C., Oct. 10–12, 1973. President, Roger W. Heyns; exec. secretary, Charles G. Dobbins. Headquarters: One Dupont Circle, NW, Washington, D. C. 20036.

American Dental Association. Membership: 117,000. Annual session: Houston, Texas, Oct. 28–Nov. 1, 1973. President, Louis A. Suporito, D. D. S.; exec. director, C. Gordon Watson, D. D. S. Headquarters: 211 E. Chicago Ave., Chicago, Ill. 60611.

American Economic Association. Membership: 17,500 and 7,650 subscribers. Annual meeting: New York, N. Y., Dec. 28–30, 1973. President, Kenneth Arrow; secretary-treasurer, Rendigs Fels. Headquarters: 1313 21st Ave. S., Nashville, Tenn. 37212.

American Farm Bureau Federation. Membership: 2,175,-780 families. Annual meeting: January of each year. President, William J. Kuhfuss; secretary-treasurer, Roger Fleming. Headquarters: 225 Touhy Ave., Park Ridge, Ill. 60068.

American Geographical Society. Membership: 3,000. Annual dinner: New York, N. Y., Nov. 1973. President, William A. Hance; director, Burton W. Adkinson. Headquarters: Broadway at 156th St., New York, N. Y. 10032.

American Geophysical Union. Membership: 11,085 individuals and 43 organizations. Meetings, 1973: Washington, D. C., April 16–20 and San Francisco, Calif., Dec. 10–14. President, Philip H. Abelson; gen. secretary, Charles A. Whitten; exec. director, A. F. Spilhaus, Jr. Headquarters: 1707 L St. NW, Washington, D. C. 20036.

American Heart Association. Membership: 91,500 in 55 affiliates, 127 chapters, and about 1,000 local subdivisions. Annual meeting: Atlantic City, N. J., Nov. 8–13, 1973. President, Paul N. Yu, M. D.; secretary, Elwood Ennis. Headquarters: 44 East 23d St., New York, N. Y. 10010.

American Historical Association. Membership: 17,500. Annual meeting: San Francisco, Calif., Dec. 28–30, 1973. President, Lynn White; exec. secretary, Paul L. Ward. Headquarters: 400 A St. SE, Washington, D. C. 20003

American Horticultural Society. Membership: 16,000 individual; 250 organizational, institutional, and commercial. National congress: New Orleans, La., Oct. 3–7, 1973. President, Dr. David G. Leach; exec. director, O. Keister Evans. Headquarters: 901 N. Washington St., Alexandria, Va. 22314.

American Hospital Association. Membership: 17,000 personal; 7,500 institutional. Annual meeting: Washington, D. C., Feb. 5–8, 1973; Annual convention: Chicago, Ill., Aug. 20–23, 1973. Chairman of the board, John W. Kauffman; president, John Alexander McMahon; secretary, James E. Hague. Headquarters: 840 North Lake Shore Drive, Chicago, Ill. 60611.

American Institute of Aeronautics and Astronautics. Membership: 24,000 plus 4,000 student members. Exec. secretary, James J. Harford. Headquarters: 1290 Avenue of the Americas, New York, N. Y. 10019.

American Institute of Architects. Membership: 23,150. National convention: San Francisco, Calif., May 7–10, 1973. President, S. Scott Ferebee, Jr.; first vice pres., Archibald C. Rogers; secretary, Hilliard T. Smith, Jr. Headquarters: 1735 New York Ave. NW, Washington, D. C. 20006.

American Institute of Biological Sciences. Membership: 13,675, with 39 adherent societies and 11 industrial member groups. Annual meeting: Amherst, Mass., June 17–22, 1973. President, Robert W. Krauss; vice pres., George Sprugel, Jr.; secretary-treasurer, Richard Gruelich; director, John R. Olive. Headquarters: 3900 Wisconsin Ave. NW, Washington, D. C. 20016.

American Institute of Certified Public Accountants. Membership: 92,000. Annual meeting: Atlanta, Ga., Oct. 14–17, 1973. President, LeRoy Layton; exec. vice pres., Wallace E. Olson; admin. vice pres. and secy., John Lawler. Headquarters: 666 Fifth Ave., New York, N. Y. 10019.

American Institute of Chemical Engineers. Membership: 38,812. Annual meeting: Philadelphia, Pa., Nov. 11–15, 1973. President, T. Weaver; secretary, F. J. Van Antwerpen. Headquarters: 345 East 47th St., New York, N. Y. 10017.

American Institute of Graphic Arts. Membership: 1,800. Annual meeting: New York, N. Y., May, 1973. President, Robert O. Bach; exec. director, Edward Gottschall. Headquarters: 1059 Third Ave., New York, N. Y. 10021.

American Institute of Mining, Metallurgical, and Petroleum Engineers, Inc. Membership: 50,564. Annual meeting: Chicago, Ill., Feb. 25–March 1, 1973. President, James B. Austin; exec. director, Joe B. Alford. Headquarters: 345 East 47th St., New York, N. Y. 10017.

American Legion, The. Membership: 2,700,000. National convention: Chicago, Ill., Aug. 18–24, 1972. National commander, Joe L. Matthews; national adjutant, William F. Hauck. Headquarters: 700 N. Pennsylvania St., Indianapolis, Ind. 46206.

American Management Associations. Membership: 55,000. Annual meeting: Sept. 19, 1973. Chairman of the board, Lawrence A. Appley; president and chief exec. officer, James L. Hayes. Headquarters: 135 West 50th St., New York, N. Y. 10020.

American Mathematical Society. Membership: 14,500. Annual meeting: Dallas, Texas, Jan. 25–29, 1973. President, Saunders MacLane; secretary, Everett Pitcher. Headquarters: P. O. Box 6248, Providence, R. I. 02904.

American Medical Association. Membership: 204,000. Annual meeting: New York, N. Y., June 24–28, 1973. President, C. A. Hoffman, M. D.; secretary-treasurer, Richard E. Palmer, M. D.; exec. vice pres., Ernest B. Howard, M. D. Headquarters: 535 N. Dearborn St., Chicago, Ill. 60610.

American Meteorological Society. Membership: 9,000 including 130 corporate members. President, William W. Kellogg; exec. director, Dr. Kenneth C. Spengler; secretary-treasurer, David F. Landrigan. Headquarters: 45 Beacon St., Boston, Mass. 02108.

American National Red Cross. Adult membership: 36,423,804 in 3,190 chapters. National convention: New Orleans, La., June 3–6, 1973. Chairman, E. Roland Harriman; president, George M. Elsey. Headquarters: 17th and D Sts. NW, Washington, D. C. 20006.

American Newspaper Publishers Association. Membership: 1,084. Annual convention: April 23–26, 1973. Chairman, Davis Taylor; president and gen. manager, Stanford Smith. Headquarters: 11600 Sunrise Valley Drive, Reston, Va. 22070. Mail Address: P. O. Box 17407, Dulles International Airport, Washington, D. C. 20041.

American Nurses Association. Membership: 200,000 in 53 states and territorial associations. National convention: San Francisco, Calif., June 10–14, 1974. President, Rosamond C. Gabrielson; exec. director, Eileen M. Jacobi. Headquarters: 2420 Pershing Road, Kansas City, Mo. 64108.

American Philological Association. Membership: 2,800. Annual meeting: Atlanta, Ga., Dec. 28–30, 1973. President, Agnes K. L. Michels; secretary-treasurer, John J. Bateman. Headquarters: University of Illinois, Foreign Languages Building, Urbana, Ill. 61801.

American Physical Society. Membership: 29,000 American and foreign. Annual meeting: New York, N. Y. Jan. 29–Feb. 1, 1973. President, Dr. Joseph E. Mayer; exec. secretary, Dr. W. W. Havens, Jr. Headquarters: 335 East 45th St., New York, N. Y. 10017.

American Psychiatric Association. Membership: 19,800; 65 district branches. Annual meeting: Honolulu, Hawaii, May 7–11, 1973. President, Perry C. Talkington, M. D.; secretary, Robert W. Gibson, M. D.; medical director, Walter E. Barton, M. D. Headquarters: 1700 18th St. NW, Washington, D. C. 20009.

American Psychological Association. Membership: 32,000. Annual meeting: Montreal, Canada, Aug. 27–31, 1972. President, Leona Tyler; exec. officer, Kenneth B. Little. Headquarters: 1200 17th St. NW, Washington, D. C. 20036.

American Society of Civil Engineers. Membership: 67,000. Annual meeting: New York, N. Y., Oct. 29–Nov. 2, 1973. President, John E. Rinne; exec. director, Eugene Zwoyer. Headquarters: 345 East 47th St., New York, N. Y. 10017.

American Society of Composers, Authors, and Publishers. Membership: 15,200 composers and authors; 5,100 publishers. Annual meeting: New York, N. Y., March, 1972. President, Stanley Adams; secretary, Morton Gould. Headquarters: One Lincoln Plaza, New York, N. Y. 10023.

American Society of Mechanical Engineers. Membership: 65,190. President, Richard G. Folsom; exec. director and secretary, Rogers B. Finch. Headquarters: 345 East 47th St., New York, N. Y. 10017.

American Society of Newspaper Editors. Membership: 785. National convention: Washington, D. C., May 1–4, 1973. President, J. Edward Murray; secretary, Howard H. (Tim) Hays. Headquarters: Box 551, 1350 Sullivan Trail, Easton, Pa. 18042.

American Sociological Association. Membership: 15,000. Annual meeting: New York, N. Y., Aug. 27–30, 1973. President, Minna Komanorsky, secretary, J. Milton Yinger. Headquarters: 1722 N St. NW, Washington, D. C. 20036.

American Statistical Association. Membership: 10,500. Annual meeting: New York, N. Y., Dec. 27–30, 1973. President, Clifford Hildreth; secretary, Fred C. Leone. Headquarters: 806 15th St. NW, Washington, D. C. 20005.

American Youth Hostels, Inc. Membership: 74,000; 29 Councils in the United States. Annual meeting: Minneapolis, Minn., December, 1973. President, Lyman Moore; exec. director, Frank D. Cosgrove. Headquarters: National Campus, Delaplane, Virginia 22025.

Archaeological Institute of America. Membership: 6,000; subscribers, 12,000. President, James B. Pritchard; exec. director, Charles C. Dold; general secretary, Elizabeth A. Whitehead. Headquarters: 260 West Broadway, New York, N. Y. 10013.

Arthritis Foundation, The. Membership: 76 chapters. Annual meeting: Los Angeles, Calif., June 9, 1973. Chairman of the board, Charles B. Harding; secretary, Robert H. French. Headquarters: 1212 Ave. of the Americas, New York, N. Y. 10036.

Association of American Publishers. Membership: approx. 225. Annual meeting: Florida, May 1973. Chairman of the board, Robert L. Bernstein; president, Edward M. Korry; vice president, Austin J. McCaffrey. Addresses: One Park Ave., New York, N. Y. 10016 and 1826 Jefferson Place, NW, Washington, D. C. 20036.

Association of Junior Leagues, Inc. Membership: 222 member Leagues in U. S., Canada, and Mexico. Annual conference: San Francisco, Calif., May 13–17, 1973. President, Mrs. Rufus C. Barkley, Jr. Headquarters: 825 Third Ave., New York, N. Y. 10022.

Benevolent and Protective Order of Elks. Membership: 1,531,912 in 2,175 Lodges. National convention: Chicago, Ill., July 15–19, 1973. Grand exalted ruler, Francis M. Smith; grand secretary, Homer Huhn, Jr. Headquarters: 2750 Lake View Ave., Chicago, Ill. 60614.

B'nai B'rith. Membership: 510,000 in 4,000 local men's, women's, and youth units. President, David M. Blumberg; exec. vice president, Rabbi Benjamin M. Kahn. Headquarters: 1640 Rhode Island Ave. NW, Washington, D. C. 20036.

Boy Scouts of America. Membership: 6,427,026 boys and leaders in 485 Boy Scout councils. Annual meeting: Minneapolis, Minn., May 16–18, 1973. President, Norton Clapp; Chief scout executive, Alden G. Barber. Headquarters: North Brunswick, N. J. 08902.

Boys' Clubs of America. Membership: 1,000,000 in 1,014 clubs. National convention: Denver, Colo., May 27–31, 1973. President, John L. Burns; national director, William R. Bricker. Headquarters: 771 First Ave., New York, N. Y. 10017.

Camp Fire Girls, Inc. Membership: 600,000 in over 9,000 communities. National council meeting: Detroit, Mich., Nov. 1–4, 1973. President, Mrs. Albert E. Bollengier; national exec. dir., Dr. Hester Turner. Headquarters: 1740 Broadway, New York, N. Y. 10019.

Canadian Library Association. Membership: 3,100 persons and 900 organizations. Annual conference: Sackville, New Brunswick, June 16–22, 1973. President, H. H. Easton. Headquarters: 151 Sparks St., Ottawa, Ont. K1P 5E3.

Canadian Medical Association. Membership: 23,350. Annual meeting: Vancouver, British Columbia, June 17–23, 1973. President, Gustave Gingras, M. D.; gen. secretary, J. D. Wallace, M. D. Headquarters: 1867 Alta Vista Drive, Ottawa, Ont. K1G OG8.

Catholic Library Association. Membership: 3,308. National convention: Denver, Colo., April 23–26, 1973. President, Reverend Joseph P. Browne, C. S. C.; exec. dir., Matthew R. Wilt. Headquarters: 461 W. Lancaster Ave., Haverford, Pa. 19041.

Chamber of Commerce of the United States of America. Membership: about 4,000 trade associations and local chambers, more than 39,000 business members, and nearly 5,000,000 underlying membership. Annual meeting: Washington, D. C., April 29–May 1, 1973. President, William S. Lowe; exec. vice president, Arch N. Booth. Headquarters: 1615 H St. NW, Washington, D. C. 20006.

Council on Foreign Relations, Inc. Membership: 1,600. Annual meeting: New York, N. Y., Oct. 11, 1972. President, Bayless Manning. Headquarters: 58 East 68th St., New York, N. Y. 10021.

Daughters of the American Revolution (National Society). Membership: 193,345 in 2,929 chapters. Continental congress: Washington, D. C., April 17–21, 1972. President general, Mrs. Donald Spicer. Headquarters: 1776 D St. NW, Washington, D. C. 20006.

Freemasonry, Ancient Accepted Scottish Rite of (Northern Masonic Jurisdiction): Supreme Council, 33°. Membership: 509,842 in 380 affiliated groups. Annual meeting: Detroit, Mich., Sept. 25–27, 1973. Sovereign grand commander, George A. Newbury; grand secy. gen., Laurence E. Eaton; exec. secy., Stanley F. Maxwell. Headquarters: 39 Marrett Road, Lexington, Mass. 02173.

Freemasonry, Ancient and Accepted Scottish Rite of (Southern Jurisdiction): Supreme Council, 33°. Membership: 610,000 in 216 affiliated groups. National convention: Washington, D. C., Oct. 15–18, 1973. Sovereign grand commander, Henry C. Clausen; grand secretary gen., C. Fred Kleinknecht. Headquarters: 1733 16th St. NW, Washington, D. C. 20009.

Future Farmers of America. Membership: 432,288 in 50 state associations. National convention: Kansas City, Mo., Oct. 16–19, 1973. National advisor, H. N. Hunsicker; exec. secretary, W. P. Gray. Headquarters: Box 15160 Alexandria, Va. 22309.

Garden Club of America, The. Membership: approx. 12,700 in 178 member clubs. Annual meeting: Lake Placid, New York. May 22–24, 1973. President, Mrs. Frederick C. Tanner; secretary, Mrs. Peter Van S. Rice. Headquarters: 598 Madison Ave., New York, N. Y. 10022.

General Federation of Women's Clubs. Membership: 10,000,000 in 14,000 U. S. organizations and 36 abroad. National convention: Baltimore, Md., June 3–7, 1973. President, Mrs. Kermit V. Haugan; exec. secretary, Mrs. Wilson Y. Christian. Headquarters: 1734 N St. NW, Washington, D. C. 20036.

Geological Society of America. Membership: 9,400. Annual meeting: Dallas, Texas, Nov. 12–14, 1973. President, John Maxwell; exec. secretary, Edwin B. Eckel. Headquarters: 3300 Penrose Place, Boulder, Colo. 80301.

Girl Scouts of the U. S. A. Membership: 3,904,000. National president, Mrs. William McLeod Ittmann; exec. director, Dr. Cecily C. Selby. Headquarters: 830 Third Ave., New York, N. Y. 10022.

Holy Name, Confraternity of the. Membership: 600,000 active in 19,000 affiliated groups. National director, Brendan Larnen. Headquarters: 141 East 65th St., New York, N. Y. 10021.

Institute of Electrical and Electronics Engineers, Inc. Membership: 160,000. International convention: New York, N. Y., March 26–30, 1973. President, Harold Chestnut; general manager, Donald G. Fink. Headquarters: 345 East 47th St., New York, N. Y. 10017.

Jewish War Veterans of the U. S. A. Membership: 100,000 in 750 units. National commander, Norman D. Tilles; national exec. director, Felix M. Putterman. Headquarters: 1712 New Hampshire Ave. NW, Washington, D. C. 20009.

Kiwanis International. Membership: 270,000 in 6,000 clubs in U. S. and abroad. Annual convention: Montreal, Canada, June 24–27, 1973. President, Lorin J. Badskey; secretary, R. P. Merridew. Headquarters: 101 East Erie St., Chicago, Ill. 60611.

Knights of Columbus. Membership: 1,200,000. Annual meeting: Seattle, Wash., Aug. 21–23, 1973. Supreme knight, John W. McDevitt; supreme secretary, Virgil C. Dechant. Headquarters: Columbus Plaza, New Haven, Conn. 06507.

Knights of Pythias, Supreme Lodge. Membership: 175,-862 in 1,695 subordinate lodges. Biennial meeting: Baltimore, Md., Aug. 11–14, 1974. Supreme chancellor, Andrew A. Oden; supreme secretary, Jule O. Pritchard. Office: 47 N. Grant St., Stockton, Calif. 95202.

League of Women Voters of the United States. Membership: 160,000. National convention: San Francisco, Calif., May 6–10, 1974. President, Mrs. Bruce B. Benson; first vice pres., Mrs. David G. Bradley. Headquarters: 1730 M St. NW, Washington, D. C. 20036.

Lions International. Membership: 992,065 in 25,867 clubs in 148 countries and geographic areas. President (1973–74), Tris Coffin. Headquarters: York and Cermak Roads, Oak Brook, Ill. 60521.

Loyal Order of Moose. Membership: 1,229,789 in 3,956 units. National convention: Chicago, Ill., May 27–31, 1973. Director general, Paul P. Schmitz; supreme secy., Carl A. Weis. Headquarters: Mooseheart, Ill. 60539.

Modern Language Association of America. Membership: 30,000. Annual convention: Chicago, Ill., Dec. 27–30, 1973. President, John H. Fisher; exec. secretary, William D. Schaefer. Headquarters: 62 Fifth Ave., New York, N. Y.

National Academy of Sciences. Membership: approx. 950. Annual meeting: Washington, D. C., April 23–25, 1973. President, Philip Handler; exec. officer, John S. Coleman. Headquarters: 2101 Constitution Ave. NW, Washington, D. C. 20418.

National Association for Mental Health, Inc. Membership: 1,000 state and local organizations. Annual meeting: Atlanta, Ga., Nov. 14–17, 1973. President, Mrs. J. Skelly Wright; exec. director, Brian O'Connell. Headquarters: 1800 North Kent St., Rosslyn Station, Arlington, Va. 22209.

National Association for the Advancement of Colored People. Membership: 400,000 in 1,500 units. National convention: Indianapolis, Ind., July 2–6, 1973. President, Kivie Kaplan; board chairman, Bishop Stephen G. Spottswood; exec. director, Roy Wilkins. Headquarters: 1790 Broadway, New York, N. Y. 10019.

National Association of Manufacturers. Membership: 13,000. Annual meeting: New York, N. Y., Dec. 6–7, 1973. President, E. Douglas Kenna; secretary, John McGraw. Headquarters: 277 Park Ave., New York, N. Y. 10017.

National Audubon Society. Membership: over 218,000. Annual convention: Denver, Colo., June 7–11, 1973. President, Dr. Elvis J. Stahr; exec. vice pres., Charles H. Callison. Headquarters: 950 Third Ave., New York, N. Y. 10022.

National Conference of Christians and Jews, Inc. Membership: 75 regional offices. Annual meeting: New York, N. Y., Nov. 19–20, 1972. President, Dr. Sterling W. Brown; exec. vice president, Dr. David Hyatt; secretary, Oscar M. Lazrus. Headquarters: 43 West 57th St., New York, N. Y. 10019.

National Congress of Parents and Teachers. Membership: 8,590,622 in 38,359 PTA's. National convention: St. Louis, Mo., May 20–23, 1973. President, Mrs. John M. Mallory; secretary, Mrs. W. Hamilton Crockford III. Headquarters: 700 North Rush Street, Chicago, Ill. 60611.

National Council of the Churches of Christ in the U. S. A. Membership: 33 Protestant, Anglican, and Orthodox denominations. President, Rev. W. Sterling Carey; general secretary, Dr. R. H. Edwin Espy. Headquarters: 475 Riverside Dr., New York, N. Y. 10027.

National Council of the Young Men's Christian Associations. Membership: 5,407,712 in 1,820 organizations. National board chairman, Richard C. Kautz; exec. director, Robert W. Harlan. Headquarters: 291 Broadway, New York, N. Y. 10007.

National Easter Seal Society for Crippled Children and Adults. Membership: 52 state and territorial societies. National convention: Washington, D. C., Nov. 27–Dec. 1, 1973. President, Thomas C. Teas; exec. director, Jayne Shover. Headquarters: 2023 W. Ogden Ave., Chicago, Ill. 60612.

National Education Association of the U. S. Membership: 1,166,203, with units in every state, and 9,369 local affiliates. Annual meeting: Portland, Ore., June 29–July 6, 1973. President, Catharine Barrett; acting exec. secretary, Allan West. Headquarters: 1201 16th St. NW, Washington, D. C. 20036.

National Federation of Business and Professional Women's Clubs, Inc. Membership: 170,000 in 3,800 clubs. National convention: Miami Beach, Fla., July 8–12, 1973. President, Mrs. Jeanne C. Squire; fed. director, Mrs. Lucille H. Shriver. Headquarters: 2012 Massachusetts Ave. NW, Washington, D. C. 20036.

National Federation of Music Clubs. Membership: 600,000 in 4,300 clubs and 13 national affiliates. Annual meeting: Green Bay, Wis., Aug. 16–19, 1973; biennial convention, Atlantic City, N. J., April 5–9, 1973. President, Dr. Merle Montgomery; office manager, Mrs. John McDonald. Headquarters: 600 S. Michigan Ave., Chicago, Ill. 60605.

National Foundation—March of Dimes, The. Membership: 3,000 chapters. President, Joseph F. Nee; senior vice president, Charles L. Massey. Headquarters: 1275 Mamaroneck Ave., White Plains, N. Y. 10605.

National Recreation and Park Association. Membership includes professional park and recreation administrators and citizens concerned with conservation of human and natural resources. Annual congress: Washington, D. C., Sept. 29–Oct. 4, 1973. Executive director, Dwight F. Rettie. Headquarters: 1601 North Kent St., Arlington, Va. 22209.

National Research Council of Canada. Membership: council, 21; laboratory staff, 3,375. Annual meeting: Ottawa, Ont., March 1973. President, Dr. W. G. Schneider; secretary, B. D. Leddy. Headquarters: Montreal Rd., Ottawa, Ont.

National Safety Council. Membership: 15,000. National Safety Congress and Exposition: Chicago, Ill., Oct. 29–Nov. 1, 1973. President, Howard Pyle; secretary-treasurer, H. W. Champlin. Headquarters: 425 N. Michigan Ave., Chicago, Ill. 60611.

National Tuberculosis and Respiratory Disease Association. Membership: 282 affiliated groups. Annual meeting: New York, N. Y., May 20–23, 1973. President, John C.

Harrison; managing dir., Robert J. Anderson, M. D. Headquarters: 1740 Broadway, New York, N. Y. 10019.

National Urban League, Inc. President, James A. Linen; secretary, Mrs. Helen Mervis; exec. director, Vernon E. Jordan, Jr. Headquarters: 55 East 52d St., New York, N. Y. 10022.

National Woman's Christian Temperance Union. Membership: 250,000 in 6,000 local unions. National convention: St. Paul, Minn., Aug. 29–Sept. 5, 1973. President, Mrs. Fred J. Tooze; secretary, Mrs. Herman Stanley. Headquarters: 1730 Chicago Ave., Evanston, Ill. 60201.

Planned Parenthood Federation of America, Inc. (Planned Parenthood–World Population). Membership: 188 affiliates throughout U. S. Annual meeting: New York, N. Y., Oct. 25–28, 1973. President, Alan F. Guttmacher, M. D.; chairman of the board, Alan Sweezy, Ph. D.; secretary, Mrs. William D. Gregory II. Headquarters: 810 Seventh Ave., New York, N. Y. 10019.

Rotary International. Membership: 725,000 in 15,482 clubs functioning in 149 countries. International convention: Lausanne, Switzerland, May 13–17, 1973. President, Roy D. Hickman; general secretary, Harry A. Stewart. Headquarters: 1600 Ridge Ave., Evanston, Ill. 60201.

Special Libraries Association. Membership: 7,500. Annual conference: Pittsburgh, Pa., June 9–13, 1973. President, Edward G. Strable; president-elect, Gilles Frappier; exec. director, F. E. McKenna. Headquarters: 235 Park Ave. S, New York, N. Y. 10003.

United States Jaycees, The. Membership: 325,000 in 6,400 affiliated groups. Annual meeting: Minneapolis, Minn., June 25–29, 1973. President, Samuel D. Winer; exec. vice pres., Ray Roper. Headquarters: Box 7, Tulsa, Okla. 74102.

United Way of America (formerly **United Community Funds and Councils of America, Inc.**). Membership: United Funds, Community Chests, and Community Health and Welfare Councils in 2,240 North American communities. Chairman of the Board of Governors, James R. Kerr; national executive, William Aramony. Headquarters: 801 North Fairfax St., Alexandria, Va. 22314.

Veterans of Foreign Wars of the United States. Membership, V. F. W. and Auxiliary: 2,287,000. National convention: New Orleans, La., Aug. 17–24, 1973. Commander-in-chief, Patrick E. Carr; Adj. general, Julian Dickenson. Headquarters: V. F. W. Building, Broadway at 34th St., Kansas City, Mo. 64111.

World Council of Churches (United States Conference). Membership: 27 churches or denominations in U. S. Annual meeting: Madison, Wis., April 30–May 1, 1973. Chairman, John Coventry Smith; exec. secretary, Eugene L. Smith. Headquarters: 475 Riverside Dr., New York, N. Y. 10027.

Young Women's Christian Association of the U. S. A. Members and participants: approx. 2,400,000. President, Mrs. Robert W. Claytor; exec. director, Edith M. Lerrigo. Headquarters: 600 Lexington Ave., New York, N. Y. 10022.

Zionist Organization of America. Membership: 110,000 in 600 districts. 76th National convention: Houston, Texas, Aug. 30–Sept. 2, 1973. President, Herman L. Weisman; national secy. and exec. director, Leon Ilutovich. Headquarters: 145 East 32d St., New York, N. Y. 10016.

SOCIOLOGY

In 1972, developments in sociology ranged from studies of local and regional problems to consideration of space age problems.

Suburbs vs. Cities. The latest population data analyzed by sociologists indicate that the white population in most of the large American cities is moving in significant numbers to the suburbs. At the same time the social statistics indicate that the percentage of the black population in these cities is approaching 50 to 55%. The population of the large cities is also being augmented by recent immigrants, and the economically poor whites continue to struggle with the problems of earning a daily livelihood. The urban renewal movement of recent years has not succeeded in halting the "downward trend of societary conditions" in large cities. Housing conditions, unemployment, and the crime rate are all more serious problems in the cities than they are in the suburbs.

Reaction to Violence. In the June 1972 issue of the *American Sociological Review,* M. Edward Ransford reported on a research study in which he found "moderate support" for the widely held thesis that "white working class people are highly antagonistic toward students and blacks who demand massive social changes." Further, it appears that this antagonism is "a rational response to tangible strains" as much as to "personal bigotry." These adverse reactions were found to be noticeable on the part of both white and black workers when they were experiencing a sense of "social powerlessness."

Simulation of Games. There is an increasing emphasis on introducing college students to the study of sociology through "games simulations," (Donald W. Ball, "The Scaling of Games," *Pacific Sociological Review,* July 1972). As "recreational events," games may be viewed as reflecting important characteristics of social life. They replicate significant "dimensions of social and cultural life," and they may function as "socialization mechanisms." As guides to an understanding of social life, games function through chance, skill, and strategy.

Space Age Sociology. With the rise of macrosociology, the sociologist is beginning the study of new social problems arising out of the currently developing space age. The sociologist's ultimate frame of reference is no longer a crowded urban area, but the diverse human activities that are already developing within the rapidly enlarging boundaries of outer space. Sociologists are beginning to study the social problems that are being raised by the advance of the physical sciences into outer space and raising questions as to what social body or bodies on earth shall exercise control over whole areas of outer space and who shall be the chief recipients of any possible benefits of space age projects.

Annual Meeting of the American Sociological Association. The 67th session of the American Sociological Association was held in New Orleans in August 1972. William J. Goode of New York University gave the presidential address on "Force and Force-Threat in Human Society." The meeting also offered short "refresher courses" on different aspects of sociology and chose Mirra Komarovsky of Barnard College as president for 1973.

Anniversary of "Social Forces." In June 1972 *Social Forces,* a leading sociological journal in the United States, celebrated the 50th anniversary of its founding. The founder, the late Howard W. Odum of the University of North Carolina, had discussed several goals in the first issue, including advancing the cause of social theory, linking theory to empirical facts, improving the techniques of quantitative measurement, solving the problems of race relations, analyzing the problems of the cities, defining the role of religion in the modern world, and the readjustment of life and labor as functioning between man and woman.

Regional Sociological Societies. The growth of interest in sociology in the United States in recent years is indicated by the expansion of what are generally known as regional sociological societies. Regional societies offer at least three major advantages: convenience in traveling to a city in one's own geographic area; an opportunity for a greater number of sociologists to appear on a program; and an opportunity for sociologists who are interested in the same regional social problems to meet each other.

EMORY S. BOGARDUS
University of Southern California

SOMALIA

The major developments in Somalia in 1972 concerned foreign aid programs, the implementation of socialism, and the strengthening of ties with African states.

Domestic Affairs. President Mohammed Siad Barre initiated a campaign on February 1 to implement "scientific socialism" in Somalia. Prior to the opening of the campaign, the state had taken over transport and medical facilities and the film industry. In April, President Siad stated that "the national army is the vanguard of the socialist revolution in Somalia." Two former members of the Supreme Revolutionary Council (SRC), which governs Somalia, were sentenced to death in May for plotting to overthrow the state. Six other alleged conspirators were given life sentences, 20 were given sentences of up to 30 years, and 29 others were acquitted of the charges.

Foreign Affairs. West Germany announced in April that it would grant almost $2 million for the training of Somalia's police force, while Communist China agreed in May to finance the construction of a 300-bed hospital in Mogadishu, the capital. The African Development Bank lent Somalia $1.5 million to finance an agricultural development scheme in Agfoi.

President Siad visited Libya in January and announced that stronger political, economic, and technical ties with Libya would be forthcoming. Siad also traveled to Morocco to attend the meeting of the heads of state of the Organization of African Unity (OAU). In July the presidents of Uganda, Sudan, and Somalia held a summit meeting in Somalia that, according to President Siad, opened the way to political, social, and cultural exchanges. In February, USSR Defense Minister Grechko visited Somalia, and further cooperation between the armed forces of the two countries was agreed upon. A high-level Ugandan military contingent visited Somalia in late summer.

In September, after terrorist attacks upon Israeli athletes in Munich, West Germany, and Israeli air attacks on terrorist bases in Syria and Lebanon, Somalia sponsored a United Nations Security Council resolution condemning the escalating violence in the Middle East. The resolution failed to pass.

PETER SCHWAB
State University of New York at Purchase

SOMALIA · Information Highlights

Official Name: Somalia.
Area: 246,200 square miles (637,657 sq km).
Population (1972 est.): 2,900,000. *Density,* 10 per square mile (4 per sq km). *Annual rate of increase,* 2.2%.
Chief City (1966 est.): Mogadishu, the capital, 200,000.
Government: *Head of state,* Gen. Mohammed Siad Barre, president of the Supreme Revolutionary Council (took office Oct. 21, 1969). *Head of government,* Gen. Mohammed Siad Barre. *Legislature*—Supreme Revolutionary Council, 24 members.
Languages: Somali, Arabic, English, Italian (all official).
Education: *Expenditure* (1969), 7.2% of total public expenditure. *School enrollment* (1969)—primary, 31,589; secondary, 23,434; technical/vocational, 906; higher, 548.
Monetary Unit: Somali shilling (6.925 S. shillings equal U. S. $1, July 1972).
Gross National Product (1970 est.): $181,000,000.
Manufacturing (major products): Refined sugar, meat, leather.
Major Agricultural Products: Bananas, sugarcane, sorghum.
Major Minerals: Salt, uranium.
Foreign Trade (1971): *Exports,* $34,000,000. *Imports,* $63,000,000. *Chief trading partners* (1969)—Southern Yemen (took 67% of exports, supplied 3% of imports); Italy (27%–31%); United States (2%–11%).
Communications: *Telephones* (1971), 4,740; *radios* (1970), 50,000; *newspapers* (1970), 2 (daily circulation, 5,000).

SOUTH AFRICA

Developments in South Africa in 1972 continued to be dominated by Prime Minister Balthazar J. Vorster and the ruling Nationalist party. If events seemed to suggest an abrupt reversal of the *verligte* (enlightened) policies of the Nationalist party's leadership in favor of the *verkrampte* (narrow-minded) opposition within the party, the appearances were probably more illusory than real. The violent reaction of the government to criticism, the toughness of the line taken with student demonstrators, the emotionally charged appeals to *volk* feeling in the parliamentary by-elections, and the complete antipathy to clerical opposition constituted nothing new in Nationalist policy. Nor were they accompanied by any clear concession to the *verkramptes* in those matters of fundamental importance to them, such as the "outward-looking" African policy.

South Africa continued to be concerned with its economic growth rate, its high cost of living, and the inherent difficulties in dealing with industrial expansion and labor shortages within the traditional framework of job reservation and other artificial barriers based on apartheid.

Politics. The opposition United party won significant victories in municipal elections in Johannesburg and several other cities in March, reducing Nationalist majorities on the city councils. But the Nationalist party scored an impressive victory on April 20 in a by-election in Oudtshoorn, following a campaign in which the antagonism between Afrikaans- and English-speaking South Africans became a major issue.

A new Democratic party was formed in March by a splinter group from the Nationalist party. The new party planned to work for improved economic conditions for the black population.

Domestic Affairs. The government took several important steps in 1972 toward its official policy of establishing "Bantu homelands." On June 1 it conferred "self-government" on Bophuthatswana, the Tswana "homeland," and on the Ciskei, the "homeland" of the Xhosa, in August. They became the second and third "homelands," after the Xhosa Transkei, to achieve that status.

In January, the Zulu government voted unanimously not to swear allegiance to the South African government because it could not accept many of its laws. The Zulu territory was granted a legislative assembly on April 1.

The year witnessed student concern on many campuses over aspects of apartheid. The normally uneasy relations between the government and white students at the English-language universities reached a new climax in June in violent street clashes with police, hundreds of arrests, and a temporary banning of meetings in Cape Town and Johannesburg. The confrontation arose from a protest against the inequality of black and white education and against the expulsion of a student leader at the black University of the North.

At the beginning of the year the government announced its intention to appoint a select committee of Parliament to investigate the affairs of four legal, multiracial organizations that oppose the policies of apartheid—the South African Institute of Race Relations, the National Union of South African Students, the Christian Institute, and the University Christian Movement. In July the University Christian Movement dissolved itself. Its one-time general

secretary, Basil Moore, was placed under a banning order for five years.

On April 14 the Supreme Court reversed the conviction on subversion charges of the Right Rev. Gonville ffrench-Beytagh, the Anglican dean of Johannesburg, and quashed his five-year sentence. A few hours later he left for London.

UN Relations. In 1972 the United Nations continued to demand that the South African government abandon its policies of apartheid and withdraw from South West Africa (Namibia) and recognize UN responsibility for the territory. UN Secretary General Kurt Waldheim made a five-day visit to South Africa and South West Africa in March. He met with both government officials and opponents of government policies. In July, Waldheim informed the Security Council that South Africa had agreed to the appointment of a special UN representative for matters involving South West Africa.

The Security Council condemned South Africa on September 29 for its persistent refusal to observe UN sanctions against Rhodesia. The Special Committee on Apartheid continued to press for the exclusion of South Africa from all international sports.

International Relations. The summit conference of the Organization of African Unity (OAU), meeting in Rabat, Morocco, in June, again condemned the policies of apartheid and called for sanctions against South Africa. The OAU Council of Ministers admitted for the first time representatives from several national liberation movements, including some from South Africa.

South Africa's relations with Malawi remained close. President Jacobus Johannes Fouche paid a

UPI

PROTESTING SOUTH AFRICA'S APARTHEID policy as well as a 1972 ban on open-air demonstrations, young people, many of them students, confront the police in Cape Town, South Africa's legislative capital, in June.

week-long visit to Malawi in March, the first visit by a South African head of state to an independent black African country. He was returning Malawi President Banda's visit to South Africa in 1971. Later in March it was announced that the two countries had signed an extradition agreement.

It was announced on May 4 that reciprocal consular representation had been arranged with Lesotho. But relations with that country were strained at the end of November when a South African political refugee was kidnapped from Lesotho by four South African policemen. After a protest by Lesotho, he was promptly released and returned.

Concern over the country's isolation from international sports continued to haunt South Africans and embarrass the government. Tennis and golf appeared to be the main exceptions to the country's isolation. It was readmitted to the Davis Cup tennis competition in January after having been barred for two years. The government continued to refuse to grant concessions to multiracial sports within South Africa. But exceptions have been made at specified "open international" events, such as the 1972 South African Open Tennis Championships.

The United States announced the appointment in 1972 of its first black diplomat on permanent assignment to South Africa.

Economy. The government announced in June that, as a result of Britain's devaluation of the pound, it would float the rand in order to maintain the currency link with its largest trading partner.

RONALD B. BALLINGER
Rhode Island College

SOUTH AFRICA • Information Highlights

Official Name: Republic of South Africa.
Area: 471,444 square miles (1,221,037 sq km).
Population (1972 est.): 21,100,000. *Density,* 41 per square mile (16 per sq km). *Annual rate of increase,* 2.4%.
Chief Cities (1960 census): Pretoria, the administrative capital, 303,684; Cape Town, the legislative capital, 508,341; Johannesburg, 594,290; Durban, 560,010.
Government: *Head of state,* Jacobus Johannes Fouche, president (took office April 1968). *Head of government,* Balthazar J. Vorster, prime minister (took office Sept. 1966). *Legislature*—Parliament: House of Assembly, 166 members; Senate, 54 members. *Major political parties*—Nationalist party; United party.
Languages: English, Afrikaans (both official), African languages.
Education: *Expenditure* (1961) 4% of gross national product. *School enrollment* (1963)—primary, 2,546,824; secondary, 532,299; technical/vocational, 76,724; university/higher, 67,363.
Monetary Unit: rand (0.8013 rand equals U. S.$1, July 1972).
Gross National Product (1971 est.): $17,500,000,000.
National Income per Person (1970): $728.
Economic Indexes: *Industrial production* (manufacturing, 1971), 163 (1963=100); *agricultural production* (1971), 185 (1952–56=100); *consumer price index* (1971), 133 (1963= 100).
Manufacturing (major products): Iron and steel, textiles, chemicals, fertilizers, assembled automobiles, metals, machinery and equipment.
Major Agricultural Products: Sugarcane, tobacco, corn, fruit, wheat, dairy products, wool.
Major Minerals: Gold (ranks 1st among world producers, 1970), antimony (world rank 1st, 1970), asbestos (world rank 3d, 1970), diamonds (world rank 2d, 1970), manganese (world rank 2d, 1970), coal, iron ore, chromium ore (world rank 2d, 1970), copper, uranium.
Foreign Trade (1971): *Exports,* $2,186,000,000 (chief exports —diamonds; wool). *Imports,* $4,039,000,000 (chief imports, 1969—nonelectrical machinery; transport equipment; chemicals; electrical machinery and appliances). *Chief trading partners* (1969)—United Kingdom (took 33% of exports, supplied 23% of imports); Japan (10%—9%); United States (7%—17%); West Germany (7%—14%).
Transportation: *Motor vehicles* (1970), 2,081,000 (automobiles, 1,653,000); *railroads* (1970), 13,732 miles (22,098 km); *merchant fleet* (1971), 538,000 gross registered tons; *major national airline,* South African Airways.
Communications: *Telephones* (1971), 1,553,825; *radios* (1970), 2,700,000; *newspapers* (1967), 23 (daily circulation, 783,-000).

SOUTH CAROLINA

South Carolina's economy improved significantly in 1972, reflected in a $36 million state surplus, gains in tax collections, $486 million gain in industrial expansion, an end to the textile slump, and increased employment. As expected, President Nixon received 71% of the votes in the election, and Sen. J. Strom Thurmond (R) was reelected by about 174,000 votes over his Democratic opponent, Eugene N. Zeigler.

Government and Politics. Election processes were confused during the year by court orders that delayed the June primary until August and ended the full-slate law whereby voters in a multiple-member district had to vote for a number equal to the seats to be elected.

U. S. Rep. John L. McMillan was defeated in the Democratic primary, and Republican Edward L. Young won his seat, giving the Republicans two of the six congressional positions.

The dean of the state Senate, Edgar A. Brown, retired after more than 50 years of legislative service, and two other senior state senators were defeated. As a result of resignations and defeats, many new chairmen will head legislative committees in 1973.

Democrats maintained control of the General Assembly, although the Republicans increased from 11 to 21 in the House and 2 to 3 in the Senate.

------- **SOUTH CAROLINA · Information Highlights** -------

Area: 31,055 square miles (80,432 sq km).
Population (1970 census): 2,590,516. *Density,* 87 per sq mi.
Chief Cities (1970 census): Columbia, the capital, 113,542; Charleston, 66,945; Greenville, 61,346.
Government (1972): *Chief Officers*—governor, John C. West (D); lt. gov., Earle E. Morris, Jr. (D); secy. of state, O. Frank Thornton (D); atty. gen., Daniel R. McLeod (D); treas., Grady L. Patterson, Jr. (D); supt., dept. of education, Cyril B. Busbee (D); chief justice, Joseph R. Moss. *General Assembly*—Senate, 46 members (44 Democrats, 2 Republicans); House of Representatives, 124 members (113 D, 11 R).
Education (1971–72): *Enrollment*—public elementary schools, 387,035 pupils, 15,950 teachers; public secondary, 242,-291 pupils, 12,050 teachers; nonpublic schools (1970–71), 31,011 pupils, 1,180 teachers; college and university, 62,-000 students. *Public school expenditures,* $414,050,000 ($700 per pupil). *Average teacher's salary,* $7,650.
State Finances (fiscal year 1970): *Revenues,* $926,335,000 (4% general sales tax and gross receipts taxes, $192,552,000; motor fuel tax, $87,238,000; federal funds, $193,273,000). *Expenditures,* $892,372,000 (education, $416,899,000; health, welfare, and safety, $98,528,000; highways, $114,-293,000). *State debt,* $350,452,000 (June 30, 1970).
Personal Income (1971): $8,306,000,000; per capita, $3,162.
Public Assistance (1971): $74,465,000. *Average monthly payments* (Dec. 1971)—old-age assistance, $48.95; aid to families with dependent children, $76.42.
Labor Force: *Nonagricultural wage and salary earners* (July 1972), 907,500. *Average annual employment* (1971)—manufacturing, 337,000; trade, 147,000; government, 157,000; services, 95,000. *Insured unemployed* (Aug. 1972)—11,300 (1.8%).
Manufacturing (1970): *Value added by manufacture,* $3,770,-600,000. Textile mill products, $1,384,300,000; chemicals and allied products, $549,600,000; apparel and other textile products, $281,800,000; paper and allied products, $275,800,000; nonelectrical machinery, $257,200,000.
Agriculture (1970): *Cash farm income,* $507,791,000 (livestock, $179,858,000; crops, $273,499,000; government payments, $54,434,000). *Chief crops* (in order of value, 1971)—Tobacco (ranks 3d among the states), soybeans, cotton lint, corn.
Mining (1971): *Production value,* $66,887,000 (ranks 42d among the states). *Chief minerals*—Cement, value not available; stone, $17,852,000; clays, $10,201,000.
Fisheries (1971): *Commercial catch,* 24,642,000 pounds ($8,-378,000). *Leading species by value:* Shrimp, $6,388,000; crabs, $616,000; oysters, $602,000; clams, $235,000.
Transportation: *Roads* (1971), 59,726 miles (96,117 km); *motor vehicles* (1971), 1,359,811; *railroads* (1971), 3,092 miles (4,-976 km); *public airports* (1972), 59.
Communications: *Telephones* (1972), 1,247,700; *television stations* (1971), 11; *radio stations* (1971), 141; *newspapers* (1972), 17 (daily circulation, 568,000).

Five women and four blacks will be in the House. The Republicans won control of a number of county councils and school boards.

The General Assembly had its longest session in history, spending much time drawing up a reapportionment plan for the state Senate finally approved by the federal courts. Important legislation was enacted, however, including provisions for salary increases for state employees and teachers, a health insurance plan for state employees, and improved workmen's compensation benefits; repeal of the lien law that applied to welfare recipients; and adoption of stricter safety standards for automobiles. The Assembly also passed a public disclosure law for state agencies and increased the gasoline tax by 1%.

The voters approved six revised articles to the constitution, including provisions affecting judicial reform and local government. If the General Assembly approves these amendments, 11 of the articles to the constitution will have been revised, leaving five for 1974. In addition, the sale of whiskey in minibottles was approved, repealing a longtime state constitutional restriction against the sale of whiskey by the drink.

The state reorganization commission continued to study the restructuring of the South Carolina state government, and sizable economies in governmental operations were achieved by applying the recommendations made by a group of businessmen who studied state government.

Education. The voters approved a constitutional amendment permitting public funds to be used indirectly for private and religious educational institutions. The state accepted Lander College as a part of the state system and approved coeducation for Winthrop College. The authority of the technical education system was expanded, paving the way for community colleges.

The state Department of Education reported significant gains in its five-year program to reduce dropouts and failures in the first grade. The number of students enrolled in adult courses and programs for the handicapped and of students in private schools increased significantly. The public schools operated peacefully in the fall, after experiencing racial conflicts in the spring.

ROBERT H. STOUDEMIRE
University of South Carolina

SOUTH DAKOTA

A variety of events made news in South Dakota in 1972. Democrats won most of the election contests, although South Dakotans cast their electoral votes for President Richard Nixon in preference to George McGovern, South Dakota's Democratic U. S. senator. A flood in the Rapid City area in June was the most devastating natural disaster in South Dakota's history. In March, militant young American Indians mobbed and looted the trading post at Wounded Knee.

Elections. Democratic candidates fared well. Gov. Richard Kneip was reelected, popular U. S. Rep. James Abourezk won the U. S. Senate seat vacated by Republican Sen. Karl Mundt, who has been incapacitated for several years, and U. S. Rep. Frank Denholm was reelected. Democrats also gained many seats in the state legislature.

Still recovering from defeat in 1970, the Republicans lacked unity and strong leadership. They

UPI

Rescue workers search for survivors of the flash flood that struck Rapid City, S. Dak., late on June 9.

------ **SOUTH DAKOTA · Information Highlights** ------

Area: 77,047 square miles (199,552 sq km).
Population (1970 census): 666,257. *Density,* 8.8 per sq mi.
Chief Cities (1970 census): Pierre, the capital, 9,699; Sioux Falls, 72,488; Rapid City, 43,836; Aberdeen, 26,476; Huron, 14,299; Brookings, 13,717; Mitchell, 13,425.
Government (1972): *Chief Officers*—governor, Richard Kneip (D); lt. gov., William Dougherty (D); secy. of state, Alma Larsen (R); atty. gen., Gordon Mydland (R); treas., Neal A. Strand (R); supt., dept. of public instruction, Donald P. Barnhart; presiding judge, Charles S. Hanson. *Legislature*—Senate, 35 members (24 Republicans, 11 Democrats); House of Representatives, 75 members (45 R, 30 D).
Education (1971–72): *Enrollment*—public elementary schools, 111,340 pupils, 5,335 teachers; public secondary, 52,117 pupils, 2,934 teachers; nonpublic schools (1970–71), 15,877 pupils, 650 teachers; college and university, 32,000 students. *Public school expenditures,* $121,914,000 ($781 per pupil). *Average teacher's salary,* $7,900.
State Finances (fiscal year 1970): *Revenues,* $254,075,000 (4% general sales tax and gross receipts taxes, $47,736,000; motor fuel tax, $24,012,000; federal funds, $86,480,000). *Expenditures,* $239,644,000 (education, $86,605,000; health, welfare, and safety, $31,093,000; highways, $65,755,000). *State debt,* $29,932,000 (June 30, 1970).
Personal Income (1971): $2,309,000,000; per capita, $3,446.
Public Assistance (1971): $30,619,000. *Average monthly payments* (Dec. 1971)—old-age assistance, $62.48; aid to families with dependent children, $160.25.
Labor Force: *Nonagricultural wage and salary earners* (July 1972), 182,700. *Average annual employment* (1971)—manufacturing, 16,000; trade, 46,000; government, 56,000; services, 33,000. *Insured unemployed* (Aug. 1972)—1,600 (1.5%).
Manufacturing (1970): *Value added by manufacture,* $229,800,000. Food and kindred products, $135,100,000; printing and publishing, $21,800,000; nonelectrical machinery, $14,700,000; stone, clay, and glass products, $12,000,000; lumber and wood products, $9,900,000; fabricated metal products, $9,900,000.
Agriculture (1970): *Cash farm income,* $1,143,529,000 (livestock, $796,886,000; crops, $254,945,000; government payments, $91,698,000). *Chief crops* (in order of value, 1971)—Corn, hay, wheat, oats (ranks 1st among the states).
Mining (1970): *Production value,* $53,290,000 (ranks 41st among the states). *Chief minerals*—Gold, $20,907,000; sand and gravel, $11,300,000; stone, $10,338,000; cement, $6,798,000.
Transportation: *Roads* (1971), 84,184 miles (135,477 km); *motor vehicles* (1971), 426,397; *railroads* (1971), 3,571 miles (5,747 km); *public airports* (1972), 70.
Communications: *Telephones* (1972), 350,500; *television stations* (1971), 10; *radio stations* (1971), 37; *newspapers* (1972), 13 (daily circulation, 175,000).

elected only one candidate to a major office—former Lt. Gov. James Abdnor to the congressional seat vacated by Abourezk. For the first time since the 1930's, the Republicans lost their firm control of the state legislature. The Democrats gained a 35–35 split in the 1973 Assembly and an 18–17 edge in the Senate.

Flood. Floodwater, which poured through Keystone and Rapid City when a dam broke during a heavy rainstorm on June 9, killed 239 persons. It washed out roads and tourist facilities and damaged businesses and homes at a multimillion dollar cost.

Legislature. The legislators turned down Governor Kneip's controversial income tax proposal—a $50 million plan designed to lower the taxes of property owners, yet raise more money for education. They passed measures less likely to hurt them in the elections, such as bills providing for control of water pollution and protection of wildlife.

Economy. Most South Dakotans experienced favorable economic conditions. Farmers and stockmen enjoyed adequate rainfall and good market conditions. Merchants prospered as attendance increased at most tourist sites. But there were 3,000 fewer jobs for the civilian work force than in 1971, and many industrial workers faced hardships.

Indian Affairs. Several hundred young Indians crossed the state line from Gordon, Nebr., on March 9 to investigate the alleged mistreatment of an Indian boy by the owner of a trading post at Wounded Knee, on the Pine Ridge reservation. They had assembled at Gordon to demand prosecution of persons charged on various counts in the death of a Pine Ridge resident, Raymond Yellow Thunder, at Gordon in February. Convinced that the allegation was true, they abused the trading post owner, seized Indian artifacts, and smashed merchandise—causing damages estimated at $50,000.

HERBERT T. HOOVER, *University of South Dakota*

605

SOUTH WEST AFRICA (Namibia)

South West Africa remained firmly under South African administration in 1972 in spite of repeated UN resolutions calling on South Africa to withdraw from the territory. The status of South West Africa has been the subject of a bitter dispute between the United Nations and South Africa since 1946, when South Africa refused to place the territory, which South Africa had governed as a League of Nations mandate, under the UN trusteeship system. South West Africa is called Namibia by the United Nations.

UN Relations. As a result of pressure from states desiring to substitute dialogue for confrontation, the Security Council in February 1972 authorized direct negotiations between Secretary General Kurt Waldheim and South Africa to achieve implementation of its resolutions. In response to an invitation from the South African government, Waldheim made a five-day visit to South Africa and South West Africa in March. Subsequently his representative, Albert Escher, carried on the conversations in the search for a formula that would imply South African recognition of UN responsibility for the territory of South West Africa and the right of the territory's people to self-government and independence.

South African Policy. The South African position has been that in applying the apartheid concept of "Bantu homelands" to the different peoples of the territory, it is fulfilling the "sacred trust" of the League mandate and the rights of the people to self-government and eventual independence.

The South African government has granted legislative councils to the "homelands" of three tribal groups—the Ovambo in 1968, the Kavango in 1970, and the East Caprivi in 1972. But such a position has satisfied neither the UN General Assembly nor the South West African political parties in exile.

Domestic Events. The most dramatic and perhaps the most important event of the year in domestic affairs was the first major strike by black workers in the territory. The strike, which had erupted among Ovambo migrant workers in December 1971 in protest against the contract labor system, temporarily paralyzed large sectors of the economy. As the strike spread to most of the mines, the government sent some 13,000 Ovambos to their "homeland." On January 20 the government signed an agreement to alter certain provisions of the system. Though the changes were minimal, leaving the migrant labor system largely intact, black workers had, for the first time, forced the territory's white employers to negotiate.

In February the administration ordered the Anglican bishop of Damaraland, the Rt. Rev. Colin Winter, and two of his Anglican co-workers to leave South West Africa by March 4. On June 6, eight Ovambo tribesmen, accused of leading the strike, were found guilty of incitement and given suspended prison terms.

RONALD B. BALLINGER
Rhode Island College

SOUTHERN YEMEN

In one of the most amazing developments in the Arab world in the past decade, Southern Yemen (People's Democratic Republic of Yemen) and

—— SOUTHERN YEMEN • Information Highlights ——

Official Name: People's Democratic Republic of Yemen.
Area: 111,075 square miles (287,683 sq km).
Population (1972 est.): 1,400,000. *Density,* 11 per square mile (4 per sq km). *Annual rate of increase,* 2.9%.
Chief Cities: Madinat al-Shaab, the capital, 29,897 (1966 est.); Aden, 225,000 (metropolitan area, 1964 est.).
Government: *Head of state,* Salim Rubai, chairman of Presidential Council (took office June 1969). *Head of government,* Ali Nasir Muhammad, prime minister (took office Aug. 1971). *Major political party*—National Liberation Front.
Languages: Arabic (official), English.
Education: *Expenditure* (1969), 3% of gross national product. *School enrollment* (1969)—primary, 104,708; secondary, 13,050; technical/vocational, 510.
Monetary Unit: Dinar (0.3744 dinar equals U. S.$1, June 1972).
Gross National Product (1970 est.): $140,000,000.
Manufacturing (major products): Petroleum products.
Major Agricultural Products: Cotton, gum arabic.
Foreign Trade (1971): *Exports,* $105,000,000. *Imports,* $160,000,000. *Chief trading partners* (1969)—United Kingdom (took 22% of exports, supplied 6% of imports); Japan (11%—13%).
Communications: *Telephones* (1971), 9,425; *television stations* (1971), 6; *television sets* (1971), 22,000; *radios* (1960), 60,000.

Yemen (Yemen Arab Republic) agreed in October to unify the two states within a year. The agreement followed several years of hostility between the two countries.

Relations with Yemen and Oman. Throughout 1972 there were border conflicts in the east with the new regime in Oman, and Southern Yemen gave aid and refuge to rebels in the Omani province of Dhofar. More disturbing and more serious were the continuing conflicts with Yemen. (See YEMEN.) To put an end to them, Southern Yemen suggested in April that talks take place, and that government presented seven points for discussion. In September, Yemen responded with its own counterproposals. Iraq, Syria, Kuwait, and finally Egypt urged the two Yemen governments to reach a settlement.

On Oct. 28, 1972, after a number of secret meetings in Syria, Algeria, and Egypt and a visit by a select committee of the Arab League to each country, the prime ministers of the two Yemens signed an agreement in Cairo to withdraw all troops from the borders and to halt all acts of sabotage and hostile activities.

This agreement was to be followed by a meeting of the presidents of the two countries, at which measures would be taken to unite the countries. It was agreed that the new country would have unified legislative, executive, and judicial bodies. A constitution would be submitted to the people by popular referendum in each country. The Arab League was to supervise the ceasefire.

Economic Decline. Ever since Southern Yemen had achieved its independence from Britain in 1967, its economy had rapidly deteriorated. The closing of the Suez Canal in that year reduced its economic importance, and ships using the great harbor of Aden dropped from 500 to 50 a year. Aden was left to depression and decay as all the services connected with this shipping activity declined. Even the large petroleum refinery there drastically cut back on production.

Finances in Aden reached a new low in the summer of 1972. Foreign travel was banned, and civil servants had their salaries reduced by 15% to 80%. On August 5 all privately owned buildings were nationalized. Libya suspended all aid to the government.

SYDNEY NETTLETON FISHER
The Ohio State University

SOVIET LITERATURE. See LITERATURE.

Apollo 17, last of its series, soars upward early on December 7. This first night launch of a manned U. S. craft drew thousands of spectators.

space exploration

A major chapter in space exploration was closed in 1972 with the final Apollo flight to the moon. Unmanned exploration of neighboring worlds continued as spacecraft returned data from Venus and Mars, and a probe was launched toward distant Jupiter. Important research satellites were orbited, including one equipped with a 32-inch telescope and another instrumented for surveying the earth's resources. Further advances were made in the applied fields of communications and meteorology.

MANNED SPACE FLIGHT

The U. S. manned space program in 1972 consisted of the successful missions of Apollo 16 and Apollo 17, the latter perhaps being the last manned flight that will be made to the moon for many years to come. The Soviet Union's Soyuz series of manned earth-orbital missions was not pursued during the year, perhaps because the last Soyuz mission, which took place in June 1971, ended in tragedy with the deaths of its three cosmonauts.

Apollo 16. The penultimate Apollo mission began its moonward journey on April 16 with a nearly perfect launch. The crew consisted of mission commander John W. Young, who had flown in previous Gemini and Apollo vehicles, and space rookies Thomas K. Mattingly and Charles Duke. Their task was to carry out the first exploration of a lunar highlands area. The landing site lay in the Cayley Plains of the Descartes Region, just below the moon's equator and slightly east of its prime meridian. The site stood 7,400 feet (2,255 meters) above the elevation of Tranquility Base, the first lunar exploration area, where Apollo 11 had touched down almost three years before.

There was some concern when silicone paint began to flake from the lunar module, *Orion,* shortly after launch, but it was soon decided that the situation was not serious. On April 19 the astronauts entered lunar orbit, and in the afternoon of the following day Young and Duke entered *Orion* to prepare for landing. However, a few minutes

before the descent began, a mission abort threatened when Mattingly found that it was not certain that the back-up control system of the command module, *Casper,* would work properly, if needed. Eventually the decision came to go ahead. *Orion* set down on the lunar surface after a six-hour delay, necessitating several changes in the astronauts' work schedule. Nevertheless Young and Duke spent a total of 71 hours and 14 minutes on the moon, of which 20 hours and 15 minutes were spent in three excursions outside the lunar module. They obtained about 213 pounds (97 kg) of rock and soil for analysis, as well as a great quantity of film.

On the first excursion the two men spent most of their time setting up a variety of scientific instruments, including an ultraviolet camera for photographing clouds of ionized hydrogen gas around the earth and other celestial objects. There was one unfortunate accident, when Young caught his foot in the output cable from a device for measuring heat flow from the lunar interior. The cable was ripped, destroying the important experiment. Otherwise the men carried out their extensive program successfully. They reported that the landing site lay on one of the rays extending from South Ray Crater, and that the densely cratered surface was covered with blocks up to one and a half feet (half a meter) in diameter. The boulders were apparently mostly breccias consisting of cemented chips, crystals, and lunar soil. The men also obtained a core sample nearly 9 feet (2.7 meters) deep and observed that the dark surface appeared to be underlain by a whiter soil. In the course of sample gathering they made use of their Lunar Rover, the same kind of four-wheel vehicle first employed in the Apollo 15 mission. Before their stay on the moon was over, the astronauts would drive more than 16.8 miles (27.1 km) in the dependable Rover.

The second excursion lasted nearly seven and a half hours and took Young and Duke halfway up the slopes of neighboring 1,600-foot (500-meter) Stone Mountain. There the men gathered more core and soil samples, and they tipped over one big boulder to collect material from the surface beneath, so that scientists could make a comparison of the effects of cosmic rays on exposed and protected soils. In addition, at a number of stops on their way back to *Orion,* they took careful measurements of the lunar magnetic field. Analysis of rocks previously returned from the moon had shown that the field was once surprisingly strong—possibly because the moon was once a molten body that spun much faster on its axis than it does today.

The third excursion, on April 23, lasted five hours and 40 minutes. Using the Rover, Young and Duke drove directly to North Ray Crater, which is about 3,000 feet (900 meters) in diameter. For television viewers this sojourn was the most rewarding, since it showed the astronauts inspecting a house-sized boulder and occasionally disappearing behind other rocks at the crater rim. The samples gathered at the site seemed to be primarily white breccias or dense, dark breccias, and the surface was less densely cratered. The men then returned to the landing site for lift-off later that afternoon. The launch of the upper stage of *Orion* was seen on television, and for the first time the camera managed to track the craft for about two minutes as *Orion* rose from Cayley Plains. The camera then swung back to look at the descent stage, left behind on the moon's surface.

Young and Duke took two hours to rejoin Mattingly in *Casper,* 69 miles (111 km) above the moon. After the docking they transferred their rocks and film packs to the command module. The following day *Casper* released an 85-pound (38.5-kg) satellite that would probably remain in lunar orbit for about one year, returning information on the moon's environment. When the men jettisoned *Orion,* however, failure to set a certain switch before leaving the craft the previous day caused it to tumble out of control. Therefore Houston decided not to command the lunar module's engine to fire and send it crashing back into the moon, as on other Apollo flights. The astronauts simply fired their own command module engine and entered a trajectory back to earth. The homeward trek was largely uneventful. Mattingly carried out the task of retrieving exposed film packs from the rear of the command module, and as part of his extravehicular activity he also stood in the hatch to expose a container of some 60 million microbes to solar radiation. On April 27 *Casper* entered the earth's atmosphere, and within a few minutes the spacecraft splashed down in the mid-Pacific Ocean, only a short distance from the waiting U. S. S. *Ticonderoga.*

While the full analysis of the vast amounts of material and data collected by Apollo 16 will take years, preliminary results are already very intriguing. An X-ray examination of the deep core drilled by the astronauts revealed a fairly large number of opaque objects that may be the first samples of metallic iron brought back from the moon—perhaps fragments of meteorites that impacted on the moon, or some primitive meteoritic material from the early days of the solar system. If it could be determined that the latter is the case, the evidence could substantiate the theory that the moon coalesced in orbit around the earth from a large cloud of dust and debris billions of years ago. The rock samples found by the astronauts were quite different from what scientists had thought might exist at the Cayley Plains site. That is, rather than being igneous or volcanic rock, the samples were primarily impact breccias with little evidence of any volcanic history. Some of the samples rich in aluminum may represent the "scum" that formed on the lunar surface long ago, when the moon first cooled.

Apollo 17. The sixth and last lunar landing mission in the Apollo program was scheduled to lift off from Cape Kennedy on December 6 a little more than two hours before midnight, the first manned U. S. launch to take place after dark. The unusual hour would permit the astronauts to reach their lunar landing site shortly after sunrise, a time that offered advantageous lighting conditions. The crew of Apollo 17 consisted of Eugene A. Cernan, who had previously flown in Gemini 9 and Apollo 10, and rookies Ronald E. Evans and Harrison H. Schmitt, the latter a civilian who had obtained a doctorate in geology from Harvard University.

Thirty seconds before lift-off, the computerized countdown sequencer brought the operation to a halt because of signal problems relating to pressurization of the liquid oxygen tank of the third-stage rocket. After an anxious hold of two hours and 40 minutes, the launch finally took place, dramatically lighting up the night sky for the thousands of onlookers at the Cape. The astronauts were on their way toward the Taurus-Littrow region on the southeastern rim of the moon's Sea of Serenity, an area that would offer both highlands and lowlands fea-

tures to the explorers—including, hopefully, some form of volcanic ash.

On December 10 the spacecraft entered lunar orbit. The following day Cernan and Schmitt landed their lunar module *Challenger* in the Taurus-Littrow valley, while Evans remained in the command module *America* conducting an intensive program of moon observations. The first comment that Cernan and his companion had to make about the site was that it appeared younger than expected, since both the lack of dust during landing and the large number of tiny craters—some mere pockmarks a fraction of an inch in diameter—indicated a relatively fresh and unspoiled surface. To the north rose a steep massif, while to the south lay an even higher mountain with boulder tracks cutting down its slopes. During the first excursion conducted later that day, the two men collected samples and set up an array of instruments that included probes for studying subsurface geological formations by means of shock waves and gravity measurements. The Lunar Rover was also equipped for such studies, using a gravity device and radio-wave soundings. Among the collected rocks was a pumice-like material never found on the moon by previous astronauts. Vesicular rocks containing pockets formed by gas were other clues that the area had once been a scene of volcanic activity. Early on the morning of December 12 the men reentered the *Challenger* to rest, after more than seven hours on the surface.

Cernan and Schmitt began their second exploration period that evening with a makeshift repair of a fender that had been torn off the Rover by accident the previous day. The improvised fender, consisting of four maps taped together and held on the Rover by clamps, served to keep the astronauts from being coated with dust as they bounced across the surface of the moon toward the boulders and

craters at the foot of the steep-walled mountain southwest of the landing site. There the men found two kinds of breccia rocks, one blue-gray and the other tan-gray. They also noticed blue-gray outcroppings on the mountain wall, perhaps representing some of the oldest rocks ever seen by man. Along the route Cernan and Schmitt collected samples of the thin, dark material that covered much of the valley floor, as well as some lighter material that ran out from the base of the mountain.

The most startling discovery of the mission was made by Schmitt as he stood at the rim of a deep crater called "Shorty," on the return leg of their drive. Mixed in the dark gray material constituting the rim he observed a layer of soil that was lighter in color and that appeared bright red to orange. Schmitt suggested that the orange soil might have come from a fumarole—that is, a vent in the crust, associated with volcanic activity. If this proved true, it would mark the first time that astronauts had inspected a site yielding conclusive evidence of past volcanism on the moon. When the men scooped up a sample of the unusual material, they found it to be so hard that it broke into jagged fragments. A core extracted from the formation was observed to have layers of black and orange—and such colored layering is also typical of materials around a fumarole on earth.

Besides these significant discoveries, the astronauts also made gravity measurements when the Rover was halted near the foot of the massif. The measurements were sufficiently below normal to indicate the presence of a deep mass of light rock such as the rock forming the massif itself, and it was deduced that the massif is a block that extends to a depth of a mile or more below the floor of the Taurus-Littrow valley. After perhaps the most productive exploration period of any of the six Apollo

LARGE BOULDER lying at the base of a mountain slope is examined by Apollo 17's geologist Harrison Schmitt during his third excursion on the surface.

NASA

APOLLO 16 CREWMEN, standing behind a globe of the moon that they visited in April, are (left to right) John W. Young, Thomas K. Mattingly, and Charles Duke, Jr.

landing missions, Cernan and Schmitt returned at last to the lunar module to rest from their stay of more than seven and a half hours on the surface, and to make preparations for the final outing they would make on the moon.

For this last period, the two astronauts once again boarded their electric car for a drive of more than eight miles (13 km), moving northward from the landing site. Exploring the base of a group of hills, they walked up slopes as steep as ski runs and chipped at house-sized boulders. However, they failed to find more evidence of the orange soil observed the previous day. Near the end of this final tour of Taurus-Littrow valley the men paused outside *Challenger*. Cernan addressed a few remarks to his television audience, stating his belief that the Apollo project had given mankind a challenge for the future: "The door is now cracked but the promise of the future lies in the young people, not just in America, but the young people all over the world learning to love and learning to work together."

On December 14 the lunar module blasted off from the lunar surface and rejoined *America* in lunar orbit for the long trip back to earth. The men had spent a total of 22 hours and 5 minutes in surface excursions, traveled 22 miles (35.4 km) in their moon buggy, and collected about 275 pounds (125 kg) of samples—including what may prove to be both the oldest and the youngest rocks yet returned from the moon, spanning a time scale of more than three billion years. The younger sample may include specimens of volcanic ash, if present reasoning about the moon's history is confirmed.

The uneventful return journey was marked, as usual, by a period of extravehicular activity on the part of the command module pilot. Evans collected three sets of film from the rear of the ship before resealing the hatch. On December 19 the Apollo 17 astronauts safely parachuted their spacecraft into the Pacific Ocean, a short distance from the waiting recovery ship. Three and a half years of manned exploration of the moon had come to an end. However, several years of scientific assessment of the results of the Apollo program still lay ahead. Nor

had the Apollo spacecraft itself seen the end of its working days, since a modified Apollo is to be used both in the Skylab project of 1973 and in the joint U. S.-Soviet docking effort that has been planned by the two countries for 1975.

EARTH SATELLITES AND SPACE PROBES

The National Aeronautics and Space Administration (NASA) achieved a perfect record for satellite launches in 1972, including the spacecraft that it orbited for Canada, West Germany, and others. The Soviet Union again carried out the greatest yearly number of launches, and Japan orbited its second satellite for scientific research.

Planetary Probes. On July 22, after 117 days of flight, the Soviet Union's Venera 8 reached the vicinity of the planet Venus and released a descent package that landed on the planet's surface in the thin crescent of the sunlit side—the first daylight landing on Venus. During the descent and for about 50 minutes after touching down, the instrumented package surveyed the atmosphere and the landing site. A photometer indicated that some sunlight did manage to penetrate the planet's dense cloud cover. Venera 8 also found that the soil of Venus contained 4% potassium and trace amounts of uranium and thorium, a composition like that of granite.

The U. S. Mariner 9 spacecraft continued its exploration of the planet Mars for nearly a year after it went into Martian orbit on Nov. 13, 1971. The probe transmitted more than 7,000 television pictures before its maneuvering rockets ran out of gas, and it obtained 100% coverage of the planet's surface, with a visual resolution of about 0.6 mile (1 km). The results of the mission have already shown Mars to be geologically and meteorologically active. The research programs conducted by the USSR's Mars 2 and Mars 3 spacecraft, placed in Martian orbit in late November and early December 1971, were also completed in 1972 after more than eight months of orbital flight. The Soviet probes investigated surface and atmospheric properties by analyzing the visible, infrared, and ultraviolet radiation from the planet and its atmosphere.

On March 3 the United States launched the Pioneer 10 spacecraft toward a planned encounter with the planet Jupiter on Dec. 3, 1973. All ten of the probe's active scientific instruments returned valid data on micrometeoroid density, solar wind, cosmic rays, and magnetic fields in interplanetary space as Pioneer 10 journeyed outward from the sun. After passing Jupiter, the probe may well continue to transmit data from as far away as the planet Uranus. It will then become the first manmade device to escape the solar system. On the extremely unlikely chance that it may someday be intercepted by another intelligent form of life, the probe bears a metal plate inscribed with basic data to convey the fact that the human race has existed.

Probes of the Moon. On February 14 the Soviet Union launched Luna 20. The probe entered lunar orbit and then, on February 21, landed on the moon in the area of the crater Apollonius. After collecting soil samples it lifted off from the surface on February 23 and reentered the earth's atmosphere two days later, making a soft landing in the USSR. The material that it brought back differed greatly from the samples returned from the Sea of Fertility by Luna 16. On Jan. 8, 1973, the Soviet Union launched the next entry in the series, Luna 21, toward the moon.

Astronomy from Space. On March 12 a European Space Research Organization (ESRO) satellite, TD-1A, was placed in orbit by a U. S. vehicle. The satellite carries ultraviolet, X-ray, gamma ray, and cosmic ray instrumentation provided by European universities, and it is designed to study radiations coming from the sun and the stars. On April 14 and June 29, respectively, the Soviet Union launched Prognoz 1 and Prognoz 2. The satellites will investigate the processes of solar activity and their influences on the interplanetary environment and the earth's magnetosphere. And on August 19 the Japanese launched their second scientific satellite, Denpa.

The major astronomical launch in 1972, however, was that of Copernicus, orbited by the United States on August 21. Copernicus is the most powerful observatory yet sent into space. It will study the heavens in the ultraviolet and X-ray regions of the electromagnetic spectrum, in order to help scientists to understand the evolutionary processes taking place in the universe. To accomplish this mission Copernicus carries a 32-inch (81.3-cm) Cassegrain telescope and a photoelectric spectrometer to gather high-resolution ultraviolet spectral data, along with three small telescopes and a collimated proportional counter to study X-ray sources at various wavelengths. Another U. S. astronomical satellite, Explorer 48, was launched into an equatorial orbit on November 15 from Italy's San Marco facility off the coast of Kenya. Explorer 48 is instrumented to measure gamma radiation, by which scientists hope to obtain important information on high-energy processes in stars and on matter and photon densities in interstellar space.

Survey of Earth Resources. On July 23 the United States launched its first Earth Resources Technology Satellite, ERTS-1. The revolutionary new package is designed to survey the earth's resources from space, mapping a daily average of about 2,320,000 square miles (6,000,000 sq km) of surface in spectral bands ranging from green to near infrared. The orbit of the satellite is plotted to pass over a given point on the earth every 18 days at approximately 9:30 A. M., local time. The experimental data are being analyzed to determine the usefulness of such information for a broad range of applications in earth resources management.

The following are some of the capabilities of the instruments aboard the craft: (1) For agriculture and forestry resources, data analysis can discriminate between different crop and forest species. (2) In the area of geology studies, ERTS-1 imagery can help to identify previously unmapped features even in regions that have been intensively studied and mapped. (3) For geographers, up-to-date regional land-use maps can be created quickly and accurately from ERTS-1 photographs. (4) In hydrology, ERTS-1 data have been used to detect underground sources of water, since the subterranean water has effects upon surface vegetation. In addition, snow surveys have been made to assist in decisions regarding discharge and retention of reservoir water. (5) Finally, in the area of ocean resources, images of the ocean obtained by ERTS-1 have shown the presence of high concentrations of chlorophyll, usually associated with the presence of fish.

Meteorological Satellites. On October 15 the United States launched its NOAA-2 operational weather satellite. The satellite carries three instruments that supply both daytime and nighttime views of the earth's cloud cover, in addition to vertical temperature readings of the atmosphere and readings of the ocean surface temperature.

On December 12 the United States also orbited the Nimbus 5 research satellite to take the first readings from space of temperatures through clouds. In addition Nimbus 5 is monitoring a mysteriously disappearing current off the west coast of South America and thermally mapping the earth's surface so that geologists can better understand what is happening below the crust. The sensors aboard the satellite, designed to improve man's knowledge of his environment, are making the most precise measurements yet obtained from space of the oceans, atmosphere, and earth's surface.

UNMANNED EARTH SATELLITES AND PROBES, 1972 HIGHLIGHTS

Name	Launch site and date[1]	Launch vehicle[2]	Spacecraft weight at lift-off (pounds)[3]	Initial apsides of orbit (miles)[4]	Initial period (minutes)	Initial inclination (degrees)	Remarks
Intelsat 4 F-4	K, 23 Jan	A–C	3,110	22,280/22,350	1,436.2	0.2	Communications satellite
Heos-A2	V, 31 Jan	Delta	257	247/15,150	7,473.0	89.95	ESRO research satellite
Luna 20	B, 14 Feb	N.A.[5]	N.A.	Trajectory to moon			Lunar sample and return
Pioneer 10	K, 3 Mar	A–C	570	Trajectory past Jupiter			Will leave solar system
TD-1A	V, 12 Mar	Delta	1,038	330/331	95.0	97.5	Astronomy satellite
Venera 8	B, 28 Mar	N.A.	2,600	Trajectory to Venus			Landed on Venus July 22
Meteor 11	P, 30 Mar	N.A.	N.A.	545/561	102.6	81.2	Meteorological satellite
Molniya 1 (20)	P, 4 April	N.A.	N.A.	297/24,400	705.0	65.6	Communications satellite
Intercosmos 6	B, 7 April	N.A.	4,000	126/159	89.0	51.8	Recovered April 11
Prognoz 1	B, 14 April	N.A.	1,859	1,590/124,000	5,820	65.0	Solar observatory
Molniya 2 (2)	P, 19 May	N.A.	N.A.	286/24,240	705	65.5	Communications satellite
Intelsat 4 F-5	K, 13 June	A–C	3,058	22,200/22,350	1,440.4	.4	Communications satellite
Prognoz 2	B, 29 June	N.A.	N.A.	341/124,000	5,820	65.0	Solar observatory
Intercosmos 7	KY, 30 June	N.A.	N.A.	166/351	92.6	48.4	Radiation monitor
Meteor 12	P, 30 June	N.A.	N.A.	555/570	103.0	81.2	Meteorological satellite
ERTS-1	V, 23 July	Delta	2,073	557/563	103.2	99.1	Earth resources surveyor
Explorer 46	W, 13 Aug	Sc	298	314/511	97.5	37.7	Meteoroid impact test
Denpa	U, 19 Aug	MU-4S	165	149/3,940	157.5	31.0	Japanese radio explorer
Copernicus	K, 21 Aug	A–C	4,900	455/461	99.6	35.0	Astronomy satellite
Explorer 47	K, 23 Sept	Delta	840	125,000/147,000	44,280	17.2	Particle and field studies
Molniya 2 (3)	P, 30 Sept	N.A.	N.A.	298/24,360	703	65.3	Communications satellite
Molniya 1 (21)	P, 15 Oct	N.A.	N.A.	298/24,420	705	65.3	Communications satellite
NOAA 2	V, 15 Oct	Delta	760	900/903	114.9	101.7	Meteorological satellite
Meteor 13	P, 27 Oct	N.A.	N.A.	555/562	102.6	81.2	Meteorological satellite
Telesat-A (Anik 1)	K, 10 Nov	Delta	1,238	22,233/22,239	1,436.0	0.1	Communications satellite
Explorer 48	SM, 15 Nov	Sc	205	276/393	95.4	1.89	Astronomy satellite
ESRO IV	V, 21 Nov	Sc	255	150/727	98.8	91.0	Polar ionosphere studies
Nimbus 5	V, 11 Dec	Delta	1,695	687/689	107.3	99.96	Meteorological satellite
Aeros	V, 16 Dec	Sc	277	135/538	95.47	96.95	Aeronomy satellite

[1] Launch sites: B, Baikonur, USSR; K, Cape Kennedy, Fla.; KY, Kapustin Yar, USSR; P, Plesetsk, USSR; SM, San Marco; U, Uchinoura Space Center, Japan; V, Vandenberg AFB, Calif; W, Wallops Island, Va. [2] Launch vehicles: A–C, Atlas-Centaur; Sc, Scout. [3] 1 pound equals 0.45 kg. [4] 1 mile equals 1.61 km. [5] Not available.

The Soviet Union launched three meteorological satellites during 1972. Meteors 11, 12, and 13 went up on March 30, June 30, and October 27, respectively.

Communications Satellites. Telesat Canada, a Canadian company, launched the first Canadian domestic communications satellite, Anik—an Eskimo word meaning "brother"—on November 10, using a U. S. vehicle and launch facilities. Anik completed its checkout and was ready for use by Jan. 1, 1973. Hundreds of small Canadian communities that had depended on short-wave radio for communication will be served by the satellite. Initially the satellite will rebroadcast three color television channels to the communities, one of them in French. Two more Aniks are planned.

On behalf of the International Telecommunications Satellite Consortium, the U. S. Communications Satellite Corporation launched two spacecraft in 1972: Intelsats 4 F-4 and F-5, on January 23 and June 13, respectively. The two satellites, which were placed in stationary orbits about 22,300 miles (35,900 km) above the earth, form part of a global communications network for the consortium. The satellites have a capacity for 3,000 to 9,000 circuits, depending on the mode of coverage, or for 12 television channels.

In the meantime the Soviet Union launched four communications satellites for its own domestic needs: the 20th Molniya 1, on April 4; the second and third Molniya 2, on April 19 and September 30, respectively; and the 21st Molniya, on October 15. The satellites form part of the Soviet Union's Orbita network for transmitting telephone, telegraph, radio, and television communications within the boundaries of the country.

Other Research Satellites. Two satellites that are instrumented to study the upper atmosphere were launched in 1972: ESRO IV, on November 21; and Aeros, on December 16. The European Space Research Organization satellite carries six experiments for measuring the ionosphere, thermosphere, exosphere, auroral zones, solar flares, and polar cap absorption. Aeros, a cooperative project of the Federal Republic of Germany and the United States, makes observations of the upper atmosphere and ionosphere. Related research into the solar-lunar-terrestrial relationship was continued with the launch of the ESRO Heos-2 satellite on January 31, with the mission of studying interplanetary physics and the high-altitude magnetosphere, and the U. S. Explorer 47 on September 23.

Two entries in a new generation of cosmic radiation research satellites, Intercosmos 6 and Intercosmos 7, were launched by the Soviet Union on April 7 and June 30, respectively. The experiments aboard the spacecraft are a joint venture of members of the Council for Mutual Economic Assistance (COMECON), the East European bloc of nations. The Soviet Union also launched France's SRET-1 engineering test satellite in tandem with its 20th Molniya 1 on April 4. The function of the satellite is to test solar cells and a new kind of lightweight battery. The United States also launched an engineering test satellite, Explorer 46, on August 13. The meteoroid technology satellite is evaluating the effectiveness of a typical, bumper-protected, multisheet spacecraft structure for protection against damage by meteoroid impacts.

PITT G. THOME
National Aeronautics and Space Administration

ADVANCES IN SPACE TECHNOLOGY

With the successful completion of the final Apollo flight in 1972, technologists for the U. S. manned space program turned their full attention to the forthcoming series of flights in the Skylab Orbital Workshop and to the longer-range task of developing an orbital shuttle. Research continued on several new fuel systems, but the Rover nuclear rocket project suffered a financial setback.

Apollo Countdown Sequencer. The last-minute drama of the Apollo 17 launch served as a vivid demonstration of the functions and operations of the program's remarkable countdown sequencer. This is an automated and computerized system that takes over from human operators the laborious and lengthy chore of checking each item and event in a launch sequence. All of the liquid or gas pressures in the various Apollo tanks are observed by sensors, and the information is fed into a computer that determines whether the pressures fall within established tolerance limits. When a given measurement has been made and checked, the sequencer gives the signal to go ahead automatically to the next programmed measurement. In this way all of the subtle and complicated electronic and guidance systems on the Apollo rocket and command module are ultimately checked out for functioning and reliability. The process is basically similar to the testing done by a television repairman who checks one part of a circuit board after another until he locates a problem, or to the final inspection of an automobile at the end of an assembly line.

During the Apollo 17 countdown on the night of December 6, this usually infallible programmer-sequencer malfunctioned. It "forgot" to pressurize the third stage of the launch vehicle with gas. When the launch control monitors—that is, the men in charge of the countdown—observed this failure, they overrode the sequencer and attempted to pressurize the third stage on their own command. However, by this time several other events that were closely dependent on the sequencer's cycling had shut themselves down, on the "presumption" that a malfunction had occurred. Thus only seconds before lift-off was to occur, the sequence went into an automatic hold.

The electronic device that was the source of the problem was soon determined, and technicians raced to find a way of working through the countdown along with the sequencer. After a most intense dry run at the Marshall Spaceflight Center at Huntsville, Ala., where a mockup of the Saturn is situated and where the results are linked by telephone to Cape Kennedy, the sequencer was backed off to an earlier stage in the countdown. All three stages of the Apollo rocket were depressurized and the entire portion of that sequence was begun over again. Thus, after a delay of two hours and 40 minutes, Apollo 17 made a flawless takeoff for the moon.

Current and Projected Manned Projects. One major activity of the National Aeronautics and Space Administration in 1972 was to prepare for the Skylab Orbital Workshop the following year. The Workshop consists of a habitation and laboratory based on Saturn rocket stages, and its crews arrive and leave in Apollo command modules. The laboratory is instrumented to conduct experiments in crystallography and astronomy, measure gravity, and scan the earth's surface for studies in the fields of agriculture, oceanography, and geology.

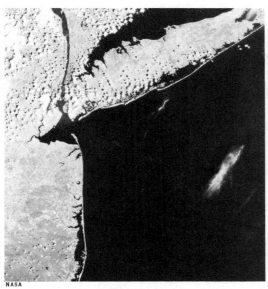

ERTS-1, shown in flight configuration (right) *prior to launch on July 23, provided a cloud-flecked view of area around New York City* (above) *from its polar orbit.*

Preparations also got under way for a program that will be conducted jointly by the United States and the Soviet Union in 1975. The principal technological innovation will be the docking unit that is to link the U. S. and Soviet craft when they rendezvous in space. Blueprints for this compatible unit have been drawn up and set into rigid specifications for construction by NASA contractors, after details were worked out with the Russians.

Another and longer-range task for NASA has been to plan an orbital shuttle system, scheduled for tests in the late 1970's. The present proposed shuttle consists of an unmanned, recoverable booster made up of two solid-propellant rockets, and a manned orbiter vehicle that is essentially a hybrid spacecraft and airplane. The delta-wing craft is about the size of a DC-9 and weighs approximately 70 tons (63 metric tons). In addition, under a $400,000 contract from NASA, a study was made of the concept of a shuttle "tug." The latter would be a liquid-propellant vehicle that could be deployed from the shuttle when the vehicle is in orbit, and it would act as a third stage for carrying payloads of up to a ton into synchronous, or "stationary," orbits. Long-range studies were also initiated for using the shuttle concept for the injection of payloads from orbit into deep space. An advanced scheme of this sort could conceivably permit manned flights to other planets within 20 years.

New Fuel Concepts. The Bell Aerospace Division of Textron, working on powder-propellant rocket engines, developed a "fluidized" powder fuel that offers several advantages over both liquid and solid propellants. Such powders flow like liquids, making rockets easier to start and stop than solid-fueled motors; they have the energy-storage capacity of solid fuels; and are not affected by the temperature extremes found in space.

The United Technology Center in California began an important series of test firings of a hybrid —that is, both liquid and solid—propellant system for the Department of Defense. The intent is to develop a High Altitude Supersonic Target Missile

(HAST). It is hoped that a maneuverable HAST will be produced for cruising at four times the speed of sound at altitudes of 35,000 to 100,000 feet (10,-000–30,000 meters).

Composites. NASA and the U. S. Air Force intensified their joint efforts for developing composite materials—sandwiches or segmented structures made of boron-epoxy fibers and laminates. It is expected that in the coming decade 20% to 40% of the critical areas of high-speed aircraft and of many rockets will be made of these light-weight and temperature-resistant materials, which are relatively inexpensive. The major drawbacks thus far include the high cost of development, difficulty in achieving tolerances, and poor stability. Once these problems are resolved, composites may take the place of such expensive structural materials as titanium or beryllium or high-strength aluminum alloys.

Nuclear Program. The joint Rover nuclear program of NASA and the Atomic Energy Commission was reduced in 1972 from its original annual funding of $110 million to a mere $30 million. The 15-year-old program also suffered a two-thirds reduction in personnel. Nevertheless, despite cutbacks, testing is still being carried out on the liquid-hydrogen nuclear engine, which has a thrust of 75,-000 pounds (34,000 kg). Personnel of Westinghouse and Aerojet Corporation, the prime contractors, hope that the small but efficient nuclear engine will have the opportunity to become operational within the next four years.

KURT R. STEHLING
U. S. Government Aerospace Consultant

FRANCO'S GRANDDAUGHTER, Maria, and Prince Alfonso, grandson of Spain's last king, were married on March 8 as Franco (left) looked on.

SPAIN

The year 1972 saw 79-year-old Generalissimo Francisco Franco with power and prestige apparently undiminished. However, he was obviously growing indifferent, through age, to increasing tensions between supporters of his conservative, dictatorial policies on the one hand and, on the other, reform-minded students and workers, liberal churchmen, and proponents of Spanish membership in NATO and the European Economic Community.

The Succession. Spain was obliged to think seriously of the post-Franco period because Franco reached 80 in December. He had previously named Prince Juan Carlos, grandson of Alfonso XIII, as future king of Spain, rather than Juan Carlos' liberal father, Prince Juan. The marriage (March 8) of Franco's granddaughter Maria del Carmen Martínez-Bordiu Franco to Alfonso de Borbón y Dampierre, another grandson of Alfonso XIII, caused Spaniards to wonder whether Franco might not be grooming an alternative choice to Juan Carlos in the event that the latter responded too strongly to the wishes of Spanish liberals.

Although Franco declared no change in his plan, it began to seem as if Juan Carlos, even if he became king, would have little power. The likelihood seemed to increase in July 1972, when Juan Carlos, standing at his father's side, seemed to approve a speech made by his father at Estoril, Portugal, pointedly criticizing the Franco government for freezing Spanish political evolution. Many Spaniards believed that Franco's real successor would be his assistant, the elderly but still vigorous Luis Carrero Blanco, a conservative charged with the task of preserving order and encouraging industrial growth in the nation.

Economy. The "Spanish Miracle"—the rapid development of Spanish industry—continued through 1972. Per capita income reached the equivalent of $1,000 a year. Spain rose to fourth place in world shipbuilding. Production of automobiles increased to the point that a capacity of 1,000,000 was foreseen by 1977. More than 11 million foreign visitors spent large sums of money in Spain, and a large flow of foreign investment continued.

There was, however, a darker side to the picture. One aspect of it was inflation, including living costs, which increased 5.6% from January to September. Although the government fixed some retail food prices, it was feared that inflation might damage the tourist trade. There was also a greater number of industrial strikes, often accompanied by violence. Business, though protected by tariffs, was traditionally fragmented into small units that had difficulty meeting foreign competition. In addition, rural conditions, especially in Castile, were depressed. Peasants continued to invest millions of pesetas in local savings banks, only to have that money drained off for developments elsewhere rather than being put into local agricultural improvement. Consequently, heavy migration to the cities continued, and thousands of seasonal workers left for other countries, notably West Germany.

The Church. At an unusually dramatic conference of Spanish bishops in March, Vicente Cardinal Tarancón, archbishop of Madrid and leader of the liberals in the Church, won a victory over the conservatives, led by José Guerra Campos, auxiliary archbishop of Madrid, and backed by Opus Dei, a theologically conservative lay group. Tarancón indirectly accused the conservatives of leaking to the press a Vatican report denouncing the liberal resolutions of a Spanish church congress held in 1971.

These resolutions reflected the liberals' desire to break the ties binding the church to the Franco administration and to involve the church in a struggle for social justice and increased liberty.

Then the papal nuncio, Msgr. Luigi Dadaglio, read a statement from the Vatican supporting, with some reservations, the liberal program. It asserted that the Catholic Church in Spain had the right and duty to be independent of the state and to criticize its actions. In the ensuing conference elections, liberals and moderates won nearly every important office. Tarancón gained the presidency, and another liberal replaced Guerra Compos as secretary.

Universities. In mid-January violence broke out between students and police at the University of Madrid after 4,000 medical students refused to end a seven-week strike in opposition to the government's lengthening the required course of study from six to seven years. The University of Barcelona and universities in many other cities shut down in sympathy, and thousands of students lost a year's credit by refusing to attend class or take examinations.

On July 29 the government suspended for two years the statutes under which the two universities in Madrid had been operating relatively autonomously for the previous two years and imposed rigid government controls. The government assumed the right to appoint rectors and close campuses or transfer centers of study elsewhere in case of trouble. Rectors could refuse admission to students for "bad conduct"—a warning to secondary school students. Similar measures were soon enforced in Barcelona and other cities, and there were rumors of lists of faculty slated for dismissal. As a reaction, many academic officials resigned, and the universities of Madrid and Barcelona did not open at the start of the academic year.

Military Affairs. In 1972, Spain began an extensive program of military modernization, which attracted arms salesmen from both Europe and the United States. Observers speculated that Spain would spend the equivalent of $500 million in 1972 and similar sums in the next four years.

European military attachés doubted whether such purchases would greatly strengthen Spain's forces. They admired the enlisted men but judged them lacking in the training necessary to maintain up-to-date, sophisticated equipment. Similarly they considered the younger officers enthusiastic but untrained in modern warfare. Believing that most senior officers were dominated by their outmoded experiences in the Spanish Civil War and World War II, these European observers recommended a change of military practice or the replacement of these officers. American military men stationed in Spain, who were better acquainted with the Spanish and who had to work with them, were more optimistic. They praised the skill of Spanish mechanics in maintaining ordinary equipment.

Foreign observers generally agreed that the West cannot hold a balance against growing Soviet strength in the western Mediterranean without a modernized Spanish navy and air force. The Americans wanted Spain in NATO, but Norway, Denmark, and the Netherlands opposed Spain's membership because of its authoritarian government.

Colonial Unrest. The little-known region of Spanish Africa began to be affected by general African unrest. In July and August a new movement, called Morhob (meaning "indigo robes"), was started by nationalists in the Spanish-owned cities of

---

SPAIN • Information Highlights

Official Name: Spanish State.
Area: 194,884 square miles (504,750 sq km).
Population (1972 est.): 33,900,000. *Density,* 171 per square mile (66 per sq km). *Annual rate of increase,* 1.0%.
Chief Cities (1969 est.): Madrid, the capital, 2,937,700; Barcelona, 1,749,700; Valencia, 634,100; Seville, 622,900.
Government: *Head of state,* Francisco Franco, president of the Council of Ministers (officially assumed power Aug. 1939). *Head of government,* Francisco Franco. *Legislature* —Las Cortes Españolas (unicameral), 570 members.
Language: Spanish (official).
Education: *Expenditure* (1969), 2.2% of gross national product. *School enrollment* (1968)—primary, 3,664,823; secondary, 1,602,232; technical/vocational, 338,266; university/higher, 178,255.
Monetary Unit: Peseta (63.56 pesetas equal U. S.$1, July 1972).
Gross National Product (1971 est.): $34,000,000,000.
National Income per Person (1970): $889.
Economic Indexes: *Industrial production* (1971), 216 (1963= 100); *agricultural production* (1971), 177 (1952–56=100); *consumer price index* (1971), 168 (1963=100).
Manufacturing (major products): Iron and steel, electrical machinery, automobiles, textiles, chemicals, ships, processed foods, leather goods, furniture.
Major Agricultural Products: Olives (ranks 2d among world producers, 1971), rye, barley, grapes, potatoes, vegetables, sheep, forest products, fish.
Major Minerals: Coal, iron ore, mercury, lead, magnesite.
Foreign Trade (1971): *Exports,* $2,938,000,000 (chief exports, 1969—fresh fruits and nuts, transport equipment, nonelectrical machinery, chemicals). *Imports,* $4,936,000,000 (chief imports, 1969—nonelectrical machinery, food, chemicals, crude petroleum). *Chief trading partners* (1969)— United States (took 15% of exports, supplied 17% of imports); West Germany (11%—13%); France (10%—10%); United Kingdom (9%—8%).
Tourism: *Receipts* (1970), $1,680,700,000.
Transportation: *Motor vehicles* (1970), 3,128,600 (automobiles, 2,377,700); *railroads* (1970), 8,496 miles (13,672 km); *merchant fleet* (1971), 3,934,000 gross registered tons; *major national airline,* IBERIA-Lineas Aereas de España.
Communications: *Telephones* (1971), 4,604,368; *television stations* (1971), 31; *television sets* (1971), 4,051,000; *radios* (1969), 7,042,000; *newspapers* (1970), 116 (daily circulation, 3,450,000).

Ceuta and Melilla in Morocco and in the Spanish Sahara. Their aim was that of "forcibly evicting Spain from her last colonial territories in Africa." Spanish Sahara has valuable phosphate deposits, which Spain expected to begin mining in 1973. Leaders of Morhob planned to train commandos in Morocco, to set up cells in the territories, and to conduct reprisals against Moroccan collaborators. The movement had support inside Morocco and claimed adherents in Algeria and Mauretania.

Foreign Relations. Spain's two most important foreign issues continued to be those relating to the ownership of Gibraltar and admission into the European Common Market. In the Gibraltar controversy, talks between British Foreign Secretary Sir Alec Douglas-Home and Spanish Foreign Minister Gregório Lopez Bravo in Madrid and London accomplished little. The British stressed the long-standing nature of the problem and said that it could not be solved quickly. Spain stated that it would not ease its blockade on Gibraltar, which prevented the entry of 5,000 commuting Spanish workers, until Britain conceded Spanish sovereignty over the crown colony.

Priorities were shifting, however. For the Spanish government, Gibraltar appeared to take second place to Spain's need to enter the European Economic Community (EEC). The Common Market countries had suggested that Spanish membership might be impossible while Franco held power. Britain, on the other hand, gave assurance that once it became a member, it would support a Spanish bid for entry.

CHARLES E. NOWELL, *University of Illinois*

SPANISH LITERATURE. See LITERATURE.
SPASSKY, Boris. See special feature on chess beginning on page 53.
SPITZ, Mark. See BIOGRAPHY.

Contract disputes and court litigation marked the year 1972 in professional sports. At Atlanta Stadium, pitcher Phil Niekro and manager Luman Harris await settlement of general strike, which cut ten days off the baseball season.

SPORTS

One of the salient features of sports in 1972 was the squabbling—among players and owners, owners and organizations, and organizations with each other. It became so involved at times that the athletic competition itself was overshadowed. Because of the many lawsuits, judges in higher courts were brought into play. Occasionally, their decisions were required before team lineups could be announced; sometimes these decisions were indirectly responsible for the shift in fortunes of some teams.

The year went out with the President of the United States handing the ball to the attorney general in a maneuver designed to force the National Football League to abandon its practice of blacking out the telecasts of local playoff games. The NFL commissioner bolstered his defense by calling on the federal court, and the President was stopped short of the goal at the time.

At year-end also baseball club owners were besieged again by player demands, despite a Supreme Court decision favorable to management. By a 5–3 vote in June, the court refused to overturn previous decisions exempting baseball from antitrust laws. The ruling came on a suit by Curt Flood challenging the reserve clause that bound a player to one club. The court, however, urged Congress to move to resolve the problem. The players looked for other means. The ruling came after the players had delayed the start of the season with a strike. They haggled over the owners' contribution to the pension fund.

By December the Major League Baseball Players' Association and the owners were bickering again over contract terms, and management was beginning to make concessions affecting the reserve clause. The players grew adamant in their push for "free agentry," or the right, after a certain period of time and under certain salary conditions, to change teams. The bickering was over the length of time and the salary. The portents were for another strike in 1973.

It was the reserve clause that President Nixon aimed at in his challenge to pro football, and it was primarily the reserve clause that had pro basketball at war with itself.

Basketball players had put up a strong front before congressional committees about their rights and how the possibilities of bargaining would be closed if Congress passed legislation that would allow a merger of the National Basketball Association and the American Basketball Association. The two leagues sought to join forces to end a bidding war for talent that was providing astronomical salaries and bonuses to players. It also was causing players to jump from one league to another, providing more action *in* court than *on* the court.

This was where the judges got into the game. Their rules varied. One said that Rick Barry had to go back to the Golden State Warriors (NBA) after starring for the New York Nets (ABA). Another said that Charley Scott, who abandoned the Virginia Squires (ABA) for the Phoenix Suns (NBA), could stay, but another unhappy Squire, Julius Erving, was ordered back to Virginia. He had caused an incredible ruckus by signing a five-year contract with Atlanta. Milwaukee reminded the Hawks, through the NBA commissioner, that it had draft rights to Erving in that league. When Erving was used in a game, the NBA fined the Hawks $2,500 and repeated the fine after the rookie played again. So the Hawks sued the NBA. Then the court ruled that

COACH DON SHULA *is carried off the field by Miami players following 14–7 victory over Washington in the 1973 Super Bowl. Dolphins' 17 straight wins tied mark of Chicago Bears.*

Erving would have to play for Virginia. Another judge ruled that Billy Cunningham would have to play for the Carolina Cougars (ABA), and the team he left, the Philadelphia 76ers (NBA), tied a league record in futility, losing 14 games in a row.

Meanwhile, the ABA sued the NBA as a monopoly, and the National Collegiate Athletic Association sued the NBA for allowing the signing of Jim McDaniel of Western Kentucky while he was still a student. The team had to forfeit its third-place finish in the annual college championship for using a pro.

The judges were also busy trying to keep hockey players properly, or legally, aligned. The World Hockey Association had come into being, and its 12 teams filled rosters by luring players from the National Hockey League with lots of money. However, a Chicago judge decided that Bobby Hull, the greatest WHA acquisition at $2.5 million for 10 years, could not play for the Winnipeg Jets. That kept many players out of the new league's lineups until a Philadelphia judge ruled that Hull did not have to go back to the Black Hawks. So the jumping players skated on, and the NHL kept the nonjumpers happy by providing salaries nearer to those of baseball, basketball, football, golf, and tennis stars.

The tennis players, however, were not completely satisfied. Most unhappy were the women. Led by Billie Jean King, who made over $100,000 again in 1972, the women demanded more of the purses at the big tournaments. They refused to allow their pro tour to play at Wimbledon and Forest Hills and the other big open tourneys scheduled for 1973, and were blacklisted by the amateur organizations that control such events. The men's tour had done the

same in 1971 but had come to terms and returned to the big tourneys in midseason 1972.

The struggle between the NCAA and the AAU continued, with the college group also declaring war against the U. S. Olympic Committee and withdrawing its support from that controlling group. The AAU said it would ask Congress to investigate the NCAA and its efforts to control amateur athletics. The Olympic heads were still battling over terms of amateurism, an issue that is likely to remain unsettled by the next games in Montreal in 1976. Some of the squabbles in pro sports may not be settled by that time either.

CONTENTS

EMERSON FITTIPALDI, with his wife, receives laurel wreath for winning Grand Prix auto race in England.

AUTO RACING

Two new drivers, George Follmer and Emerson Fittipaldi, whirled into the gallery of champions in 1972. But two of the chief pedestals were still occupied by the men who held them the year before. Joe Leonard repeated as the champion of the United States Auto Club big-car division, and Richard Petty won the title in the Grand National Division of the National Association for Stock Car Auto Racing for a record fourth time.

Follmer, a 38-year-old driver from Arcadia, Calif., won two championships in the Sports Car Club of America competitions, the first time for such a feat. His best achievement was winning the Canadian-American Challenge Cup, driving an L&M Porsche-Audi. His victory for the Roger Penske racing team broke the monopoly that the Denis Hulme-McLaren interests had held in the event. Follmer took five of the nine races and won a total of $123,350. Hulme and Milt Minter tied for second-place honors. Follmer's other title came in a Javelin in the Trans-American series.

Fittipaldi triumphed in the more glamorous Grand Prix competition, winning the world championship. The 28-year-old Brazilian finished first in five races and earned 61 points altogether. Jackie Stewart of Scotland, the 1971 champion, won the last two races, in Canada and the United States, and took second place with 45 points.

Leonard finished third in the Indianapolis 500 and won the Schaefer 500 at the Pocono track and two smaller races for most of his points. Billy Vukovich finished second in the point standing, but Bobby Unser led in victories with four. In the process of winning the pole for most of the races, Unser set a world closed-course record at the Ontario, Calif., track with a speed of 201.374 miles per hour.

The California 500, however, was won by Roger McCluskey, making him the first driver to win two USAC 500-mile events. He had taken the Pennsylvania 500, a stock-car race, at Pocono earlier.

The Indy 500 went to Mark Donohue in a Penske-prepared McLaren-Offy. He picked up a record purse of $218,768. Donohue missed most of the racing, however, because of a knee injury suffered in a sports-car race.

Auto Racing Highlights

World Championship Grand Prix Races

Argentina (Buenos Aires, Jan. 23)—Jackie Stewart, Scotland (driving a Tyrrell-Ford; distance 197¼ miles; time: 1 hour, 57 minutes, 58.62 seconds; average speed: 100.463 miles per hour)
South Africa (Johannesburg, March 4)—Denis Hulme, New Zealand (McLaren-Ford; 201.45 miles; 1:45:30; 114.23 mph)
Spain (Madrid, May 11)—Emerson Fittipaldi, Brazil (Lotus-Ford; 190 miles; 2:03:41.23; 92.35 mph)
Monaco (Monte Carlo, May 14)—Jean-Pierre Beltoise, France (BRM; 156 miles; 2:26:54.7; 63.84 mph)
Belgium (Nivelles, June 4)—Emerson Fittipaldi (196.7 miles; 1:44:06.7; 113.353 mph)
France (Clermont-Ferrand, July 2)—Jackie Stewart (189.73 miles; 1:52:21.5; 101.56 mph)
Britain (Brands Hatch, England, July 15)—Emerson Fittipaldi (201.4 miles; 1:47.50; 112.06 mph)
Germany (Neuerburgring, West Germany, July 30)—Jacky Ickx, Belgium (Ferrari; 198.65 miles; 1:42:12.3; 116.6 mph)
Austria (Zeltweig, Aug. 13)—Emerson Fittipaldi (200 miles; 1:29:58.4; 134.06 mph)
Italy (Monza, Sept. 10)—Emerson Fittipaldi (196.92 miles; 1:29:58.4; 131.333 mph)
Canada (Bowmanville, Ont., Sept. 24)—Jackie Stewart (196 miles; 1:43:16.9; 114.282 mph)
United States (Watkins Glen, N.Y., Oct. 8)—Jackie Stewart (248 miles; 1:41:45; 117.483 mph)

Nascar Events

Winston Western 500 (Riverside, Calif., Jan. 23)—Richard Petty, Randleman, S. C. (Plymouth; race cut to 390 miles because of rain, darkness; time: 3:45:11; average speed: 104.016 mph; winner's purse: $16,170)
Daytona 500 (Daytona Beach, Fla., Feb. 20)—A. J. Foyt, Houston, Texas (Mercury; 3:05:42; 161.550 mph; $44,600)
Miller 500 (Ontario, Calif., March 5)—A. J. Foyt (3:56:04; 127.082 mph; $25,595)
Carolina 500 (Rockingham, S. C., March 12)—Bobby Isaac, Catawba, N. C. (Dodge; 4:23:50; 113.895 mph; $15,250)
Atlanta 500 (Hampton, Ga., March 26)—Bobby Allison, Hueytown, Ala. (Chevrolet; 3:53:37; 128.214 mph; $19,605)
Rebel 400 (Darlington, S. C., April 16)—David Pearson; Spartanburg, S. C. (Mercury; 3:13; 124.406 mph; $15,100)
Winston 500 (Talladega, Ala., May 7)—David Pearson (3:43:15; 134.4 mph; $23,745)
World 600 (Charlotte, N. C., May 28)—Buddy Baker, Charlotte, N. C. (Dodge; 4:13:04; 142.255 mph; $22,075)
Lone Star 500 (Bryan, Texas, June 25)—Richard Petty (3:28:04; 44.185 mph; $13,245)
Dixie 500 (Hampton, Ga., July 23)—Bobby Allison (3:47:08; 131.295 mph; $15,955)
Talladega 500 (Talladega, Ala., Aug. 6)—James Hylton, Inman, S. C. (Mercury; 3:22:09; 148.728 mph; $24,865)
Firecracker 400 (Daytona Beach, Fla., July 4)—David Pearson (2:29:14; 160.281 mph; $15,650)
Yankee 400 (Irish Hills, Mich., Aug. 20)—David Pearson (2:58:31; 134.416 mph; $13,385)
Southern 500 (Darlington, S. C., Sept. 4)—Bobby Allison (3:54:46; 128.124 mph; $21,990)
Delaware 500 (Dover, Sept. 17)—David Pearson (4:08:57; 120.506 mph; $13,250)
National 500 (Charlotte, N. C., Oct. 8)—Bobby Allison (3:45:37; 133.234 mph; $19,450)
American 500 (Rockingham, N. C., Oct. 22)—Bobby Allison (4:13:49; 118.275 mph; $17,400)
Texas 500 (College Station, Nov. 12)—Buddy Baker (3:24; 147.059 mph; $12,920)

United States Auto Club Races

Indianapolis 500 (May 27)—Mark Donohue, Newtown Square, Pa. (McLaren-Offenhauser; 3 hours, 4 minutes, 5.54 seconds; average speed 162.962 mph; winner's purse: $218,716)
Schaefer 500 (Pocono International Speedway, Long Pond, Pa., July 29; postponed from July 2)—Joe Leonard, San Jose, Calif. (Parnelli-Offenhauser; 3:13:49.3; average speed 154.781; $84,780)
California 500 (Ontario, Calif., Sept. 3)—Roger McCluskey, Tucson, Ariz. (McLaren-Offenhauser; 3:21:20.978; 151.540 mph; $131,081)
Trenton 200 (Trenton, N. J., April 23)—Gary Bettenhausen, Tinley Park, Ill. (McLaren-Offenhauser; 1:22:49; 146 mph; $11,642)
Michigan 200 (Cambridge Hills, July 16)—Joe Leonard (1:26:08.1; 140.685 mph; $16,602)
Tony Bettenhausen 200 (Milwaukee, Aug. 13)—Joe Leonard (1:47:28.61; 111.652 mph; $14,734)
Trenton Times 300 (Sept. 24)—Bobby Unser, Albuquerque, N. Mex. (Eagle-Offenhauser; 2:05:06.24; 143.236 mph; $17,023)
Pennsylvania 500 (stock cars, at Long Pond, Pa., July 30)—Roger McCluskey (Plymouth; 3:56; 15.325; 127.035 mph; $19,150)

Other Major Race Winners

Daytona 6 Hours of Endurance (Daytona Beach, Fla., Feb. 6)—Mario Andretti, Nazareth, Pa., and Jacky Ickx, Belgium (Ferrari; 740.52 miles; 124.716 mph)
12 Hours of Sebring (Sebring, Fla., March 25)—Andretti and Ickx (Ferrari; 1,347 miles; 111.508 mph)

Auto Racing Highlights (continued)

Watkins Glen 6 Hours of Endurance (Watkins Glen, N.Y., July 23)—Andretti and Ickx (Ferrari; 658.515 miles; 109.39 mph)

Other Countries

BOAC 1,000 (Brands Hatch, England, April 16, 621.4 miles)—Mario Andretti, Nazareth, Pa., and Jacky Ickx, Belgium (Ferrari; 5:55:27.5; 105.12 mph)

Monza 1,000 (Monza, Italy, April 25)—Jacky Ickx and Clay Reggazoni, Switzerland (Ferrari; 5:52.00; 108.186 mph)

Spa 1,000 (Francorchamps, Belgium, May 7)—Brian Redman, England, and Arturo Merzario, Italy (Ferrari; 4:17:19; 145.89 mph)

Targa Florio (Cerda, Sicily, May 21, 491 miles)—Arturo Merzario and Sandro Munari, Italy (Ferrari, 6:27:48; 76 mph)

Neuerburgring 1,000 (Adenau, W. Germany, May 28)—Ronnie Peterson, Sweden, and Tim Schenken, Australia (Ferrari; 6:01:04.2; 104.2 mph)

24 Hours of LeMans (LeMans, France, June 10–11)—Graham Hill, England, and Henri Pescarolo, France (Matra-Simca; 2,915 miles; 121.46 mph)

Individual Champions

World Grand Prix—Emerson Fittipaldi, Brazil (61 pts)

U.S. Auto Club—*Championship Trail:* Joe Leonard, San Jose, Calif. (3,460 pts; $214,738); *stock car:* Butch Hartman, South Zanesville, Ohio (3,655 pts); *dirt track:* A.J. Foyt, Houston, Texas (550 pts); *sprint division:* Sam Sessions, Nashville, Mich. (881); *midgets:* Duane (Pancho) Carter, Jr., Long Beach, Calif. (711 pts)

Nascar—Grand National: Richard Petty, Randleman, N.C. (8,701.4 pts; $227,015); Grand National East: Neil Castles, Charlotte, N.C. (1,440.5; $9,730); Grand National West: Ray Elder, Caruthers, Calif. (2,782.25; $46,040); Late Model Sportsman: Jack Ingram, Asheville, N.C. (6,998 pts); Modified: Jerry Cook, Rome, N.Y. (4,004 pts); Grand American: Tiny Lund, Cross, S.C.

Sports Car Club of America Champions

Canadian–American Challenge Cup Series (9 races)—George Follmer, Arcadia, Calif. (Penske L&M Porsche-Audi; 130 pts; $123,350)

Continental 5,000 Series (8 races)—Graham McRae, New Zealand (STP McRae-Chevrolet; 87 pts; $73,750)

Trans-American Championship Series (7 races)—American Motors Javelin (48 pts); *leading driver:* George Follmer, Arcadia, Calif. (Roy Woods Racing Javelin; 95 pts; $26,800)

Two-Five Challenge Series (11 races)—Datsun (81 pts)

Formula Super Vee Championship Series (9 races)—Bill Scott, McLean, Va. (Scott Racing Royale)

Formula B Championship Series (8 races)—Chuck Sarich, Rockville, Md. (March; 80 pts)

Formula Ford—Jack Baldwin, Atlanta (Racing Titan)

Rally—*Class A* (equipped): Sam Jones and Clark Thorp, Huntsville, Ala.; *Class B* (unequipped): John Chidester, Uniontown, Pa., and R. Bruce Gezon, West Chester, Pa.; *manufacturers:* Datsun

American Road Race of Champions
(Road Atlanta, Gainesville, Ga., Nov. 23–26)

A Production—Jerry Hansen, Minneapolis (Corvette; 91.38 mph)

B Production—Allan Barker, Jeffersonville, Ind. (Corvette; 96.22 mph)

C Production—Bob Sharp, Wilton, Conn. (Datsun; 95.91 mph)

D Production—Robert McQueen, Smyrna, Ga. (Datsun; 91.28 mph)

E Production—Logan Blackburn, Indianapolis (MGB; 77.51 mph)

F Production—Jon Woodner, San Rafael, Calif. (MG Midget; 77.37 mph)

G Production—Rick Cline, Gainesville, Ga. (Triumph Spitfire; 83.48 mph)

H Production—Randy Canfield, Chevy Chase, Md. (Sprite; 81.97 mph)

A Sedan—Warren Agor, Rochester, N.Y. (Camaro; 95.61 mph)

B Sedan—Bob Sharp, Wilton, Conn. (Datsun; 91.75 mph)

C Sedan—William Fox, Studio City, Calif. (Austin-Cooper; 84.97 mph)

A Sports Racing—Jerry Hansen, Bloomington, Minn. (Lola; 84.49 mph)

B Sports Racing—Pete Harrison, Atlanta (Lola; 74.82 mph)

C Sports Racing—Bill Holbrook, Bethany, Conn. (Royale-Ford; 89.93 mph)

D Sports Racing—Harry Stephenson, Miami, Fla. (Maru-Honda; 86.17 mph)

Formula A—Jerry Hansen, Bloomington, Minn. (Lola; 77.01 mph)

Formula B—Chuck Sarich, Rockville, Md. (March; 74.63 mph)

Formula C—Harry Reynolds, Pottstown, Pa. (Brabham; 92.12 mph)

Formula Ford—Eddie Miller, Vail, Colo. (Hawke; 94.32 mph)

Formula Vee—Dave Weitzenhof, Akron, Ohio (Autodynamics; 73.25 mph)

Formula Super Vee—Bob Wheelock, Houston, Texas (Lola; 95.81 mph)

Petty, in a Plymouth, picked up the most points in the NASCAR races, but Bobby Allison, driving a Chevrolet, won the most money—$271,395 to Petty's $227,015. In points, Petty had 8,701 and Allison 8,573.

——————— BASEBALL ———————

A strike called in April put everyone out. This one was called by the players over the pension fund and was the first general strike in baseball history. The players' refusal to play until the issue was settled postponed the opening of the season for 10 days and cut 84 scheduled games from the season's competition. When it was settled with an additional $500,000 released from surplus funds for the pensions, neither side claimed a victory. The owners were out the proceeds from the canceled games, the players were out an average of nine days' wages for the games not played, and the fans were out of patience with the owners and the players.

When the season finally did get under way, the weather turned sour in many areas, and there was much trouble getting the games played. Spectator interest faded in many cities, especially in those with weak clubs. By midseason, attendance was lagging, interest seemed apathetic, and baseball detractors grew louder in downgrading the sport as too slow and dull to keep up with the present-day desire for action.

OAKLAND third baseman Sal Bando leaps to embrace star reliever Rollie Fingers and catcher Dave Duncan after win in seventh game clinched World Series title.

UPI

ROBERTO CLEMENTE (1934–1972)

WIDE WORLD

Persons associated with Roberto Clemente were impressed by his deep passions not only for playing baseball but also for aiding his less fortunate fellowmen. It was his concern for the victims of an earthquake in Nicaragua that led to his death in an airplane crash on December 31, 1972. He had headed a drive to collect supplies and money for relief and was en route to Managua to see that they were distributed properly. Fittingly, the governor of Puerto Rico proclaimed a 3-day mourning period for its most beloved athlete.

Roberto Walker Clemente was born in Carolina, a suburb of San Juan, Puerto Rico, on Aug. 18, 1934. He won attention while playing for Santurce in the Puerto Rican League, and at 20 he was signed by the Brooklyn Dodger organization and assigned to their Montreal farm club. After the 1954 season he was drafted by the Pittsburgh Pirates, for whom he played for 18 years.

Clemente won the National League batting championship four times (1961, 1964, 1965, 1967), had a lifetime average of .317, and clouted 240 homers. He was the 11th player in baseball history to amass 3,000 hits. A superb right fielder, with a great range and a rifle arm, he shared the major league mark for most years (five) leading in assists by an outfielder.

Clemente played in every All-Star game from 1960 to 1972, except for 1968, and was voted the most valuable player in the National League in 1966. Twice he helped Pittsburgh to win the World Series (1960 and 1971). For his hitting and fielding in the 1971 series he was named the most valuable player. His eventual selection to the Hall of Fame is assured.

So great was Clemente's popularity that Puerto Ricans in New York held a day for him at Shea Stadium in 1971. Unfulfilled at the time of his death was his dream of establishing a sports city, primarily for youngsters and underprivileged persons, in Puerto Rico.

BILL BRADDOCK

But the unseen hand that was directing the baseball production of 1972 came up with a series of finishes that fascinated even the detractors, and the season went out in an old-time blaze of glory. The rekindling began in the American League race for the division championships, burst into full flame in the playoffs in both leagues, and roared into a conflagration in the World Series.

In regular season play, there was close competition only in the Eastern Division of the American League by the time of the All-Star break in July. In the National League, Pittsburgh held a 5½-game edge over New York in the East, and Cincinnati was 6 games in front of Houston in the West. Oakland was rolling along 6½ games ahead of Chicago in the American League West, but in the East, Detroit was only one game ahead of Baltimore, the league champions. Boston was 5 games back and the New York Yankees, 7½.

The American League situation changed quickly, and by August 23, Oakland and Chicago were in a deadlock for first place in the Western Division. In the East, only 2½ games separated Detroit, the lead-

er, and fourth-place Boston. Actually Detroit, Baltimore, and the Yankees had all lost the same number of games—55—and Boston had lost one more. Detroit had won 63, the Orioles 62, New York 60, and Boston 59. They struggled on for three weeks, and on September 14 the four teams were only one game apart. But now Boston was in front with New York and Baltimore one-half game behind and the Tigers fourth, having played two more games than the Red Sox and lost them both. In the West, Oakland had moved two games in front of the White Sox, and they held on, widening the edge and leaving the only race in the majors in the Eastern Division.

The champion Orioles and the Yankees began to fade, but the Tigers and Red Sox stayed close. On October 1, Boston lost to Baltimore and Detroit beat Milwaukee, putting the Tigers one-half game behind the Red Sox. The two teams were to meet in a three-game series in Detroit, the final games of the season. On October 3, Detroit won the first game, 4–1, on a six-hitter by Mickey Lolich, taking over first place. The Tigers beat Boston again the next night, 3–1, clinching the Eastern Division title.

In the first game of the playoff series against Oakland for the American League pennant, the Tigers led off the 11th inning with a home run by Al Kaline only to have the Athletics come back with two runs for a 3–2 triumph. Oakland won the next game, 5–0, and seemed headed for a sweep, but the Tigers, back in their home park, evened the series with a 3–0 victory and an incredible 4–3 triumph. This one came with a three-run rally in the bottom of the 10th inning after the Athletics had tallied twice and crowned themselves the champions. The teams had to go back to Oakland, where the Athletics won 2–1, finally getting the trophy that had been delivered to their locker room the day before.

Meanwhile, the Pirates, the defending world champions, and Cincinnati were playing a similar tight series for the National League championship. Pittsburgh won the first game, 5–1, with three runs in the first inning. The Reds took the second, 5–3, getting four runs in the first inning. The Pirates went ahead again with a 3–2 victory but were walloped by the Reds, 7–1, in the fourth game. The deciding game at Cincinnati was as dramatic as any scriptwriter could dream up. The Reds went into the bottom of the ninth, trailing, 3 to 1. But Johnny Bench, their catcher, who later was chosen the league's most valuable player, hit a home run and tied the score, 3–3. Two singles followed, and Dave Giusti was replaced on the pitching mound by Bob Moose. He got the next batter to fly out, but it was deep enough for the runner on second to advance to third. The following batter popped up for the second out. Another extra-inning game seemed assured. But with the count 1 and 1, Moose's next pitch to Hal McRae hit the ground and bounced past the catcher. George Foster raced home from third, and the Reds were the champions—on a wild pitch and a 4–3 victory.

The World Series opened in Cincinnati, October 14, and Gene Tenace, the catcher for the mustachioed Athletics, hit two home runs as Oakland won, 3–1. Oakland took the second game, 2–1, behind the pitching of Catfish Hunter and a home run by Joe Rudi, who made a great catch in centerfield in the ninth that kept the tying run from scoring. But in Oakland, Jack Billingham and Clay Carroll held the Athletics to three hits, and the Reds won,

1–0. Oakland renewed its drive the next day, winning 3–2, with two runs in the ninth inning on four straight hits, three by pinch hitters. Tenace had hit his third homer of the series in the fifth. Now with the world championship almost in their hands, the Athletics allowed the Reds to score in the eighth and ninth and win the fifth game, 5–4. The teams went back to Cincinnati, and, after five games decided by one run, the Reds battered the Athletics for 10 hits and an 8–1 victory, taking the series to the seventh game. Oakland scored twice in the seventh inning for a 3–1 lead and held off a late threat for a 3–2 victory, winning the championship, 4 games to 3.

Lolich and Hunter were among six 20-game winners in the American League, and there were four in the National League. Steve Carlton of Philadelphia won 27 games, 15 of them in succession. He was voted the Cy Young Award, as was Gaylord Perry

of Cleveland, who was tied with Wilbur Wood of the Chicago White Sox for the lead in the American League with 24 victories. The other 20-game winners were Stan Bahnsen of Chicago and Jim Palmer of Baltimore in the American League, and Ferguson Jenkins of Chicago, Claude Osteen of Los Angeles, and Tom Seaver of New York in the National League.

Hank Aaron hit 34 home runs and passed Willie Mays for the runner-up role to Babe Ruth for career totals. Aaron has 673 and Mays, who went back to New York in a trade between the Giants and the Mets in midseason, has 654. Ruth's total was 714. Billy Williams of the Cubs won the National League batting title with a .333 average, and Rod Carew of the Twins led the American League with .318. Dick Allen of the Chicago White Sox was voted the most valuable player in the American League.

Baseball Highlights

Professional—Major Leagues

AMERICAN LEAGUE (Final Standings, 1972)

EASTERN DIVISION

	W	L	Pct.
Detroit	86	70	.551
Boston	85	70	.548
Baltimore	80	74	.519
New York	79	76	.510
Cleveland	72	84	.462
Milwaukee	65	91	.417

WESTERN DIVISION

	W	L	Pct.
Oakland	93	62	.600
Chicago	87	67	.565
Minnesota	77	77	.500
Kansas City	76	78	.494
California	75	80	.484
Texas	54	100	.351

NATIONAL LEAGUE (Final Standings, 1972)

EASTERN DIVISION

	W	L	Pct.
Pittsburgh	96	59	.619
Chicago	85	70	.548
New York	83	73	.532
St. Louis	75	81	.481
Montreal	70	86	.449
Philadelphia	59	97	.378

WESTERN DIVISION

	W	L	Pct.
Cincinnati	95	59	.617
Houston	84	69	.549
Los Angeles	85	70	.548
Atlanta	70	84	.455
San Francisco	69	86	.445
San Diego	58	95	.379

(Strike of players caused cancellation of games scheduled before April 15, and led to variance in number of games played by each club.)

Playoffs—American League: Oakland Athletics defeated Detroit Tigers, 3 games to 2; National League: Cincinnati Reds defeated Pittsburgh Pirates, 3 games to 2

World Series—Won by Oakland Athletics; paid attendance, 7 games, 363,149; total receipts: $3,954,543; total attendance for playoffs and series: 618,409; total receipts for playoffs and series: $5,184,476; players' share: $1,882,178, including full shares of $20,705 for each Oakland player and $15,080 for each Cincinnati player; Commissioner's office share: $593,181; each league's share: $544,736; each club's share: $554,736

Standing—Oakland (AL) won 4, lost 3, pct. .571; Cincinnati (NL) won 3, lost 4, pct. .429

First Game (Riverfront Stadium, Cinncinati, Oct. 14): Oakland 3, Cincinnati 2; second game (Cincinnati, Oct. 15): Oakland 2, Cincinnati 1; third game (Oakland-Alameda County Coliseum, Oakland, Oct. 18): Cincinnati 1, Oakland 0; fourth game (Oakland, Oct. 19): Oakland 3, Cincinnati 2; fifth game (Oakland, Oct. 20): Cincinnati 5, Oakland 4; sixth game (Cincinnati, Oct. 21): Cincinnati 8, Oakland 1; seventh game (Cincinnati, Oct. 22): Oakland 3, Cincinnati 2

All-Star Game (Atlanta, July 25)—National 4, American 3 (10 innings)

Most Valuable Players: American League: Dick Allen, Chicago first baseman; National League: Johnny Bench, Cincinnati catcher

Cy Young Memorial Awards (outstanding pitcher)—American League: Gaylord Perry, Cleveland; National League: Steve Carlton, Philadelphia

Rookies of the Year—American League: Carlton Fisk, Boston catcher; National League: Jon Matlack, New York pitcher

Leading Batters—Percentage: American: Rod Carew, Minnesota, .318; National: Billy Williams, Chicago, .333; Home Runs: American: Dick Allen, Chicago, 37; National: Johnny Bench, Cincinnati, 40; Runs Batted In: American: Dick Allen, Chicago, 113; National: Bench, 125

Leading Pitchers—Best Percentage (20 decisions or more): American: Jim Hunter, Oakland, .750 (21–7); National: Gary Nolan, Cincinnati, .750 (15–5); Victories: American: Gaylord Perry, Cleveland, and Wilbur

Wood, Chicago, 24; National: Steve Carlton, Philadelphia, 27; Earned Run Average: American: Luis Tiant, Boston, 1.91; National: Steve Carlton, Philadelphia, 1.98

No-Hit Games Pitched—Burt Hooton, Chicago (NL) vs. Philadelphia, 4–0; Milt Pappas, Chicago (NL) vs. San Diego, 8–0; Bill Stoneman, Montreal (NL) vs. New York, 7–0

Hall of Fame Inductees—Lawrence Peter (Yogi) Berra; Josh Gibson, Vernon L. (Lefty) Gomez; Will Harridge; Sanford (Sandy) Koufax; Walter F. (Buck) Leonard; Early Wynn, Ross (Pep) Youngs

Professional—Minor Leagues

(When two teams are named, the first team won the regular season championship and the second won the playoff; otherwise, the team named won both.)

American Association (AAA)—Evansville, Eastern Division and playoff; Wichita, Western Division

International League (AAA)—Louisville; Tidewater

Pacific Coast League (AAA)—Albuquerque, Eastern Division and playoff; Eugene, Western Division

Mexican League (AAA)—Cordoba, Southern Division and playoff; Saltillo, Northern Division

Eastern (AA)—West Haven, American Division and playoff; Three Rivers, National Division

Southern (AA)—Montgomery, Western Division and playoff; Asheville, Eastern Division

Texas (AA)—El Paso, Western Division and playoff; Alexandria, Eastern

California (A)—Bakersfield, first half; Modesto, second half and playoff

Carolina (A)—Burlington, first half; Salem, second half and playoff

Florida State (A)—Miami, Southern and playoff; Daytona Beach, Northern

Midwest (A)—Danville, Southern and playoff; Appleton, Northern

New York-Pennsylvania (A)—Niagara Falls; no playoff

Northwest (A)—Lewiston, Northern; Walla Walla, Southern

Western Carolina (A)—Spartanburg, first half and playoff; Greenville, second half

Appalachian (Rookie)—Bristol

Gulf Coast (Rookie)—Tie between Royals and Cubs

Pioneer (Rookie)—Dallas

Amateur Champions

World—Cuba
American Legion—Ballwin, Mo.
Babe Ruth World Series—Honolulu
Babe Ruth Senior—Seattle
Bronco League—St. Joseph, Mo.
Colt League—Riverside, Calif.
Connie Mack League—Compton, Calif. Mohawks
Dixie Youth—Huffman, Ala.
Mickey Mantle League—Sweeney Chevrolet, Cincinnati
National Baseball Congress—Fairbanks, Alaska, Goldpanners
Pee Wee Reese League—Dallas Drillers
Pony League—Monterrey, Mexico
Sandy Koufax League—Garden City, Mich.
Stan Musial League—Conetta Bren-Den, Stamford, Conn.

Intercollegiate Champions

NCAA—University Division: Southern California (defeated Arizona State, 1–0, in final); College Division: Florida Southern (defeated San Fernando State, 5–1, in final)

NAIA—La Verne (defeated David Lipscomb, 4–1, in final)

BASKETBALL

Professional

For a two-month span early in the season, the Los Angeles Lakers went undefeated in National Basketball Association competition. When they were finally stopped, by the Milwaukee Bucks on Jan. 9, 1972, the Lakers had run up a winning streak of 33 games, the longest by a modern professional team in any sport. They had played all through November and December of 1971 without a loss. The previous record in the NBA had been 20 consecutive victories, made by Milwaukee the preceding season.

The Lakers were paced by superstars Wilt Chamberlain and Jerry West, with Gail Goodrich, Happy Hairston, and Jim McMillian playing fine supporting roles. They were operating under a fast-break plan introduced by their new coach, Bill Sharman. The momentum of the streak carried the Lakers to a

WILT CHAMBERLAIN's power under the basket led the Lakers to NBA championship against the Knicks.

won-lost mark of 69–13, the best regular season record for the NBA.

Chamberlain's floor play and rebounding were outstanding in the playoffs. With West and Goodrich leading the scoring, the Lakers swept through the three series on their way to the championship. They beat the Chicago Bulls four straight; took the Bucks, the defending champions, 4 games to 2, and after a humiliating opening game loss to the New York Knicks, won four straight. Milwaukee, with Kareem Abdul-Jabbar, the league's most valuable player and leading scorer with a 34.8 average, could not cope with the all-round play of the Lakers.

In winning the American Basketball Association championship, the Indiana Pacers had to battle through 20 games in the playoffs. They got past the New York Nets, 4 games to 2, in the final, but to reach that bracket they were forced to seven games by the Denver Rockets and then by the Utah Stars, the 1971 league champions. The Nets, led by Rick Barry (who had defected from the NBA and then was sent back there by the courts after the season), were surprise winners in the East, defeating the Kentucky Colonels and the Virginia Squires.

College

The college basketball season rolled out as it had bounced in—with the fans still wondering who would stop the University of California at Los Angeles. UCLA won the National Collegiate Athletic Association championship for the sixth straight year with an undefeated season. It was the Bruins' eighth title in nine years. With a squad ably led by Bill Walton, a 6-foot 11-inch sophomore, they appeared to be the team to beat again in the 1972–73 season.

Actually, UCLA had its closest game of all in the finals against Florida State, 81–76, but there was no doubt of the Bruins' supremacy. With that triumph they ran their season string to 30 victories, their overall winning streak to 45, and their un-

Professional Basketball Highlights

National Basketball Association
(Final Standings, 1971–72)
Eastern Conference
Atlantic Division

	W	L	Pct.	Scoring Avg. For	Scoring Avg. Agst.
Boston Celtics	56	26	.683	115.6	110.8
New York Knickerbockers	48	34	.585	107.1	104.7
Philadelphia 76ers	30	52	.366	112.2	115.9
Buffalo Braves	22	60	.268	102.0	111.3

Central Division

	W	L	Pct.	For	Agst.
Baltimore Bullets	38	44	.463	107.1	108.3
Atlanta Hawks	36	46	.439	109.5	111.3
Cincinnati Royals	30	52	.366	107.8	111.8
Cleveland Cavaliers	23	59	.280	105.8	113.4

Western Conference
Midwest Division

	W	L	Pct.	For	Agst.
Milwaukee Bucks	63	19	.768	114.6	103.5
Chicago Bulls	57	25	.695	111.2	102.9
Phoenix Suns	49	33	.598	116.3	110.8
Detroit Pistons	26	56	.317	109.1	115.9

Pacific Division

	W	L	Pct.	For	Agst.
Los Angeles Lakers	69	13	.841	121.0	108.7
Golden State Warriors	51	31	.622	108.2	107.4
Seattle SuperSonics	47	35	.573	109.2	108.8
Houston Rockets	34	48	.415	109.7	111.2
Portland Trail Blazers	18	64	.220	106.8	116.5

Eastern Conference playoffs final: New York defeated Boston, 4 games to 1; *Western Conference playoffs final:* Los Angeles defeated Milwaukee, 4 games to 2; *NBA Championship:* Los Angeles defeated New York, 4 games to 1
Most Valuable Player—Kareem Abdul-Jabbar, Milwaukee
Rookie of the Year—Sidney Wicks, Portland
Leading Scorer—Abdul-Jabbar, 2,822 points; 34.8 average per game

American Basketball Association
(Final Standings, 1971–72)
Eastern Division

	W	L	Pct.	Scoring Avg. For	Scoring Avg. Agst.
Kentucky Colonels	68	16	.810	116.0	107.0
Virginia Squires	45	39	.536	118.9	118.0
New York Nets	44	40	.524	112.8	112.4
Floridians	36	48	.429	112.7	114.3
Carolina Cougars	35	49	.417	114.8	118.1
Pittsburgh Condors	25	59	.298	119.2	126.4

Western Division

	W	L	Pct.	For	Agst.
Utah Stars	60	24	.714	117.8	112.0
Indiana Pacers	47	37	.560	113.0	110.3
Dallas Chaparrals	42	42	.500	104.4	104.3
Denver Rockets	34	50	.405	112.0	113.1
Memphis Pros	26	58	.310	107.5	113.0

Eastern Division playoffs final: New York defeated Virginia, 4 games to 3; *Western Division playoffs final:* Indiana defeated Utah, 4 games to 3. *ABA Championship:* Indiana defeated New York, 4 games to 2
Most Valuable Player—Artis Gilmore, Kentucky
Rookie of the Year—Gilmore
Leading Scorer—Charlie Scott, Virginia, 2,524 points; 34.6 average per game

Amateur Basketball Highlights
Major Tournaments

NCAA (Los Angeles)—University of California at Los Angeles (defeated Florida State, 81–76, in final); College Division (Evansville, Ind.): Roanoke (defeated Akron, 84–72, in final)
National Intercollegiate (NAIA, at Kansas City)—Kentucky State (defeated Eau Claire, 71–62, in final)
National Invitation (New York)—Maryland (defeated Niagara, 100–69, in final)
Men's AAU—Armed Forces All-Stars (defeated Marathon Oil, Lexington, Ky., 92–80, in final)
Women's AAU—John F. Kennedy College, Nebraska (defeated Ouchita Baptist, 69–60, in final)

College Conference Champions

(Figures in parentheses represent victories and losses in conference games only.)
Atlantic Coast—North Carolina (9–3); won championship tourney
Big Eight—Kansas State (12–2)
Big Sky—Weber State (10–4)
Big Ten—Minnesota (11–3)
Central Intercollegiate—North: Norfolk State (15–2), won playoff; South: Winston-Salem (12–5)
Ivy League—Penn (13–1)
Mid-American—Tie between Ohio University and Toledo (7–3); Ohio won playoff for NCAA berth
Middle Atlantic—University Division: Eastern: Temple (6–0); won playoff; Western: Rider (8–2); College Division: Northern: Philadelphia Textile (9–0); Southern: Lebanon Valley (9–1); PMC (8-2), won playoff
Missouri Valley—Tie between Louisville and Memphis State (12–2); Louisville won playoff for NCAA berth
Ohio Valley—Tie among Eastern Kentucky, Morehead, and Western Kentucky (9–5); Eastern Kentucky won playoff for NCAA berth
Pacific-8—University of California at Los Angeles (14–0)
Southeastern—Tie between Kentucky and Tennessee (14–4); Kentucky won playoff for NCAA berth
Southern—East Carolina (7–5); won championship tournament
Southwest—Tie between Southern Methodist and Texas (10–4); Texas won playoff for NCAA berth
West Coast Athletic—San Francisco (13–1)
Pacific Coast Athletic—Long Beach State (10–2)
Western Athletic—Brigham Young (12–2)

Leading Major Independents

East—Syracuse (22–6); Providence (21–6); Duquesne (20–5); Villanova (20–8)
South—South Carolina (24–5); Florida State (27–6); Jacksonville (20–8)
Midwest—Marquette (24–2); Marshall (23–3); Detroit (18–6)
Southwest—Oral Roberts (26–2); Houston (20–7); Southwest Louisiana (Southland Conference, 25–4)
Far West—Hawaii (24–3)

---

beaten string in NCAA tourneys to 32 games.

To gain the final round, UCLA eliminated Louisville, 81–76, and Florida State ousted North Carolina, 79–75, in the semifinals. The Seminoles overcame Eastern Kentucky, Minnesota, and Kentucky in reaching that position. UCLA walloped Weber State and Long Beach in earlier rounds.

Led by Travis Grant, Kentucky State won the National Association of Intercollegiate Athletics championship for the third straight season. Grant broke all career records for College Division scoring with a total of 4,045 points in four years of play. Kentucky State defeated Eau Claire, 71–62, in the championship game. In the NCAA College Division title tournament, Roanoke defeated Akron, 84–72, in the final. Maryland defeated Niagara, 100–69, in the final of the National Invitation Tournament in New York.

——————— BOXING ———————

After Ernesto Marcel won the featherweight title, boxing aficionados in Panama were calling their country the pugilism capital of the world. Marcel became the fourth Panamanian to win a world championship in a period of five months. Alfonso Frazer was the first, gaining the junior welterweight crown on March 10. Then came Roberto Duran, lightweight, June 26; Enrique Pinder, bantamweight, July 29; and Marcel, August 19.

Frazer outpointed Nicolino Loche of Argentina; Duran stopped Ken Buchanan of Scotland in 13 rounds; Pinder won a decision over Rafael Herrera of Mexico; and Marcel defeated Antonio Gomez of Venezuela. The Duran bout at Madison Square Garden caused the biggest flurry, since Buchanan's handlers claimed he had been hit a low blow after the bell. Buchanan, in pain, was unable to continue, and the match was awarded to the Panamanian. The referee said that the blow was not low.

Duran was one of two lightweight champions. He held the World Boxing Association crown, but the World Boxing Council title belonged to Rodolfo Gonzalez of Long Beach, Calif. He won it on November 10 by stopping Chango Carmona of Mexico in the 13th round. Carmona had taken the title from Mando Ramos, Gonzalez' stablemate, two months earlier.

The busiest of the champions were Carlos Monzon of Argentina, the middleweight titleholder, and Bob Foster of Albuquerque, the light-heavyweight king.

Monzon defended his title successfully four times and Foster, three. In his first bout of the year, Foster, the WBA titleholder, knocked out Vicente Rondon, the WBC champion, in the second round. Foster then tried his prowess against Muhammad Ali in the heavyweight division in November and was put away in the fifth round.

Ali also defeated Mac Foster, George Chuvalo, Jerry Quarry, and Floyd Patterson, the former heavyweight champion, in bouts staged in New York, Tokyo, and rings in between.

However, Joe Frazier, the heavyweight champion, remained comparatively inactive, so much so that the boxing associations threatened to vacate his title if he did not fight a worthy foe. He had stopped Terry Daniels and Rod Stander, two unknowns, without difficulty. At year-end he was training to meet George Foreman in his first real test since beating Ali on March 8, 1971.

Boxing Highlights
World Professional Champions

Flyweight—Masao Ohba, Japan, World Boxing Association; Venice Borkorsor, Thailand, World Boxing Council
Bantamweight—Enrique Pinder, Panama
Featherweight—Ernesto Marcel, Panama, WBA; Jose Legra, Spain, WBC
Junior Lightweight—Ben Villaflor, Philippines, WBA; Ricardo Arrendondo, Mexico, WBC
Lightweight—Roberto Duran, Panama, WBA; Rodolfo Gonzalez, Long Beach, Calif., WBC
Junior Welterweight—Alfonso Frazer, Panama, WBA; Bruno Arcari, Italy, WBC
Welterweight—Jose Napoles, Mexico
Junior Middleweight—Koichi Wajima, Japan
Middleweight—Carlos Monzon, Argentina
Light Heavyweight—Bob Foster, Albuquerque
Heavyweight—Joe Frazier, Philadelphia

National AAU Championships
(Las Vegas, Nev., April 27–30)

106 Pounds—Davy Armstrong, Tacoma, Wash.
112 Pounds—Bobby Lee Hunter, Columbia, S. C.
119 Pounds—John David, Lake Charles, La. (U. S. Navy)
125 Pounds—Herman Artis, Philadelphia
132 Pounds—Norman Goins, St. Petersburg, Fla.
139 Pounds—Carlos Palomino, Westminster, Calif. (U. S. Army)
147 Pounds—Freddie Washington, Chicago Heights, Ill. (U. S. Army)
156 Pounds—Henry Johnson, Indianapolis (U. S. Army)
165 Pounds—Michael Colbert, Portland, Oreg.
178 Pounds—Hernando Molyneaux, New York
Heavyweight—Nick Wells, Fort Worth, Texas (USAF)
Team—United States Army

SUPER BOWL ACTION: Miami back Jim Kiick (21) starts power burst through Washington's goal-line defense for a touchdown in second period of game, won by Dolphins, 14–7.

FOOTBALL

Professional

The Miami Dolphins, who had won acclaim the year before by reaching—although losing—the Super Bowl, could not be stopped in 1972. The Dolphins, who were coached by Don Shula, set a record by winning all of their 14 regular season games and then tied the mark of 17 consecutive victories by triumphing in two playoff games and in the Super Bowl. The Chicago Bears had set the mark in the 1933–34 season and tied it in 1941–42.

In the Super Bowl, Jan. 14, 1973, for the National Football League championship, the Dolphins defeated the Washington Redskins, 14–7. The game, a rather dull, defensive battle, was unusual for a pro game in that records were set for the lack of passing and for passing inefficiency.

The Dolphins had an excellent passing game with Bob Griese doing the throwing in the Super Bowl and for the first five games of the regular season. But Griese was injured, and Earl Morrall directed the team to 11 of its victories. However, the Miami ground attack was the decisive factor. In the backfield were Larry Csonka, a powerful fullback, with Mercury Morris and Jim Kiick alternating at halfback. All were able blockers and capable receivers and they carried the Dolphins to a record of 2,951 yards in rushing in the 14 season games. Paul Warfield and Howard Twilley were outstanding as pass catchers, with Marv Fleming and Otto Stowe playing reliable roles. The defensive stars were Manny Fernandez, Nick Buoniconti, and Jake Scott. The placekicker was Garo Yepremian, whose attempt to become a passer after a blocked field goal try led to the Redskins' lone score in the Super Bowl.

The Redskins had Billy Kilmer at quarterback, but the star of their attack was Larry Brown, a hard-running halfback who won the NFC rushing title with 1,216 yards and was one of the leading receivers. Charley Taylor and Roy Jefferson were the other top receivers. The defensive line was made up of aging, experienced players gathered together by Coach George Allen and nicknamed the "Over the Hill Gang." In beating the Green Bay Packers, 16–3, and the Dallas Cowboys, 26–3, for the National Conference title, the opponents were kept from crossing the goal line. That final victory over the Cowboys was the Redskins' second and kept Dallas from repeating as NFL champion.

In the playoffs, the Dolphins defeated Cleveland, 20–14, and the Pittsburgh Steelers, 21–17, for the American Conference title. The Steelers had reached the playoffs for the first time in 40 years of play. They had beaten Oakland, 13–7, in a playoff game in the last five seconds on a pass that was deflected by a defender into the hands of Franco Harris, who raced 42 yards for a touchdown. The Pittsburgh defense had kept opponents from crossing the goal line in seven games.

The season was marked by the number of backs who exceeded 1,000 yards gained in rushing. They were O. J. Simpson of Buffalo with 1,251, the leader; Csonka; Morris; Brown; Harris; Ron Johnson, New York Giants; John Brockington, Green Bay; Marv Hubbard, Oakland; Calvin Hill, Dallas; and Mike Garrett, San Diego.

Don Maynard of the New York Jets took away Ray Berry's career record for total passes caught. In his 14th season, Maynard caught 29 passes for a career total of 632, one more than Berry, the former Colt star. Maynard increased his record total yardage to 11,816.

NATIONAL FOOTBALL LEAGUE
(Final Standings, 1972)

American Conference

Eastern Division

	Won	Lost	Tied	Pct.	Pts.	Opp.
Miami	14	0	0	1.000	385	171
N. Y. Jets	7	7	0	.500	367	324
Baltimore	5	9	0	.357	235	252
Buffalo	4	9	1	.321	257	377
New England	3	11	0	.214	192	446

Central Division

	Won	Lost	Tied	Pct.	Pts.	Opp.
Pittsburgh	11	3	0	.786	343	175
*Cleveland	10	4	0	.714	268	249
Cincinnati	8	6	0	.571	299	229
Houston	1	13	0	.071	164	380

Western Division

	Won	Lost	Tied	Pct.	Pts.	Opp.
Oakland	10	3	1	.750	365	248
Kansas City	8	6	0	.571	287	254
Denver	5	9	0	.357	325	350
San Diego	4	9	1	.321	264	344

* Fourth, or wild card, qualifier for playoffs

Playoffs—Miami defeated Cleveland, 20–14; Pittsburgh defeated Oakland, 13–7
Conference Championship—Miami (defeated Pittsburgh, 21–17, at Pittsburgh, Dec. 31)

National Conference

Eastern Division

	Won	Lost	Tied	Pct.	Pts.	Opp.
Washington	11	3	0	.786	336	218
*Dallas	10	4	0	.714	319	240
N. Y. Giants	8	6	0	.571	331	247
St. Louis	4	9	1	.321	193	303
Philadelphia	2	11	1	.179	145	352

Central Division

	Won	Lost	Tied	Pct.	Pts.	Opp.
Green Bay	10	4	0	.714	304	226
Detroit	8	5	1	.607	339	290
Minnesota	7	7	0	.500	301	252
Chicago	4	9	1	.321	225	275

Western Division

	Won	Lost	Tied	Pct.	Pts.	Opp.
San Francisco	8	5	1	.607	353	249
Atlanta	7	7	0	.500	269	274
Los Angeles	6	7	1	.464	291	286
New Orleans	2	11	1	.179	215	361

* Fourth, or wild card, qualifier for playoffs

Playoffs—Washington defeated Green Bay, 16–3; Dallas defeated San Francisco, 30–28
Conference Championship—Washington (defeated Dallas, 26–3, at Washington, Dec. 31)
League Champion (Super Bowl)—Miami (defeated Washington, 14–7, at Los Angeles, Jan. 14)
Pro Bowl—American Conference 33, National Conference 28, at Irving, Texas, Jan. 31, 1973

National Football League Leaders

American Conference

Scoring—Bobby Howfield, N.Y. Jets (27 field goals, 40 extra points, 121 points)
Scoring (nonkickers)—Emerson Boozer, N.Y. Jets (84 pts)
Passing—Earl Morrall, Miami (83 of 150 for 1,360 yards and 11 touchdowns; 55.3% completions)
Receiving—Fred Biletnikoff, Oakland (58 for 802 yds)
Interceptions—Mike Sensibaugh, Kansas City (8)
Rushing—O. J. Simpson, Buffalo (292 for 1,251 yds)
Punting—Jerrell Wilson, Kansas City (44.8 yds average)
Punt Returns—Chris Farasopoulos, N.Y. Jets (10.5 yds average)
Kickoff Returns—Bruce Laird, Baltimore (29.1 yds avg)

National Conference

Scoring—Chester Marcol, Green Bay (33 field goals, 29 extra points, 128 points)
Scoring (nonkickers)—Ron Johnson, N.Y. Giants (84 pts)
Passing—Billy Kilmer, Washington (120 of 225 for 1,648 yards and 19 touchdowns; 53.3% completions)
Receiving—Harold Jackson, Philadelphia (62 for 1,048 yds)
Interceptions—Bill Bradley, Philadelphia (9)
Rushing—Larry Brown, Washington (285 for 1,216 yds)
Punting—Dave Chapple, Los Angeles (44.2 yds average)
Punt Returns—Ken Ellis, Green Bay (15.4 yds average)
Kickoff Returns—Ronald Smith, Chicago (30.8 yds avg)

Canada

Grey Cup (Hamilton, Ont., Dec. 3)—Hamilton Tiger-Cats 13, Saskatchewan Roughriders, 10

College

Los Angeles, which had long been serving as the throne room for college basketball, took over the same role for football with a royal flourish. The University of Southern California, after completing the regular season unbeaten in 11 games, trounced Ohio State, 42–17, in the Rose Bowl on New Year's Day, 1973, squelching the last possible opposition to hailing USC as the unofficial king of college football.

USC received wonderful help from its bitter crosstown rival, the University of California at Los Angeles, in its bid for the national title. UCLA had upset Nebraska, which had reigned as king for two seasons, 20–17, on September 11. That defeat ended the Cornhuskers' winning streak at 23 games and their unbeaten string at 32. UCLA was guided by Mark Harmon, a son of Michigan's legendary Tom Harmon. The Trojans had Mike Rae at quarterback and an excellent running back in sophomore Anthony Davis. He scored six touchdowns as the Trojans routed Notre Dame, 45–23, in the season's final game. USC had started its season by upsetting Arkansas, 31–10, on the same day that UCLA knocked Nebraska off the top rung. When the two Los Angeles schools met, the Trojans triumphed, 24–7.

Ohio State reached the Rose Bowl as the Big Ten champion after a splendid victory over previously unbeaten Michigan, 14–11. The Wolverines were stopped twice at the goal line, once in each half. Two weeks earlier Ohio State had been upset by Michigan State, 19–12, with 12 of the Spartans' points coming on four field goals by Dirk Krijt, a Dutch placekicker playing his first game. The victory was most pleasant for Duffy Daugherty, the Spartan coach, who was to retire at season's end.

Nebraska's season turned more sour for Coach Bob Devaney, who was also retiring. The Cornhuskers were tied by Iowa State, 23–23, and then lost the Big Eight conference title to Oklahoma. The Sooners bottled up Johnny Rodgers, the flanker back, who was later named the Heisman Trophy winner as the outstanding college player, and won 17–14. Oklahoma had been knocked out of the unbeaten ranks by Colorado, 20–14, but retained second place in the final polls, as it had done in 1971.

Alabama had loomed near the end of the season as the second-ranking team to USC with an unbeaten record in 10 games. But in the final against Auburn, Bill Newton blocked two Alabama punts, and the Tigers won, 17–16. Alabama then was beaten by Texas, 17–13, in the Cotton Bowl. The Longhorns previously had lost only to Oklahoma, 27–0.

Oklahoma stopped Penn State, 14–0, in the Sugar Bowl for the Nittany Lions' second loss. They had fallen before Tennessee in their opening game, 28–21.

Delaware was adjudged the best of the College Division teams but turned down a postseason bid after winning its 10 games. Louisiana Tech won its 11 games and routed Tennessee Tech in the Grantland Rice Bowl for Mideast honors, 35–0. Tennessee State, Massachusetts, and North Dakota won the other NCAA small college bowls. In the NAIA, East Texas State won Division I honors by beating Carson Newman, 21–18, in the Champion Bowl. Missouri Southern took Division II honors by beating Doane and then Northwestern of Iowa in the final, 21–14.

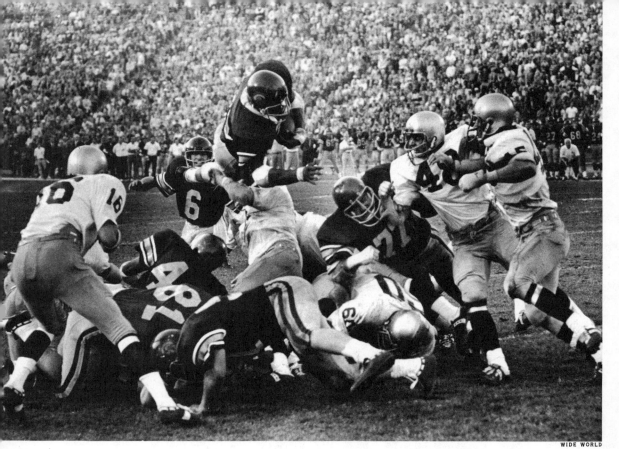

WIDE WORLD

FULLBACK SAM CUNNINGHAM dives for a touchdown as Southern California thumps Notre Dame, 45–23. Victory climaxed unbeaten season for Trojans, who went on to defeat Ohio State in Rose Bowl for honors as the nation's No. 1 team.

College Football Highlights

Intercollegiate and Conference Champions

National (AP and UPI polls)—University of Southern California
National Football Foundation Awards (MacArthur Bowl)—NCAA University Division: University of Southern California; NCAA College Division (John F. Kennedy Award): Delaware; Louisiana Tech
Dwight D. Eisenhower Award (NAIA)—East Texas State
Eastern (Lambert Trophy)—Penn State
Eastern Small College—Lambert Cup: Delaware; Lambert Bowl: Franklin and Marshall
Atlantic Coast—North Carolina (6–0)
Big Eight—Oklahoma (6–1)
Big Sky—Montana State (5–1)
Big Ten—Ohio State (7–1)
Ivy League—Dartmouth (5–1)
Mid-American—Kent State (4–1)
Missouri Valley—Tie among Louisville, Drake, and West Texas (4–1)
Ohio Valley—Tennessee Tech (7–0)
Pacific 8—University of Southern California (7–0)
Pacific Coast A.A.—San Diego (4–0)
Southeastern—Alabama (7–1)
Southern—East Carolina (6–0)
Southwest—Texas (7–0)
Western Athletic—Arizona State (5–1)
Yankee—Massachusetts (5–0)

Leading Independents

East—Penn State (10–1); West Virginia (8–3)
South—Tampa (9–2)
Midwest—Notre Dame (8–2)
Far West—Utah State (8–3)

NCAA Regional Bowls
(All games played Dec. 9)

Boardwalk (East at Atlantic City, N. J.)—Massachusetts 35, University of California at Davis 14
Grantland Rice (Mideast at Baton Rouge, La.)—Louisiana Tech 35, Tennessee Tech 0
Pioneer (Midwest at Wichita Falls, Texas)—Tennessee State 29, Drake 7
Camellia (West at Sacramento, Calif.)—North Dakota 38, California Poly at San Luis Obispo 21

NAIA Championship Bowls

Division I (Commerce, Texas, Dec. 9)—East Texas State 21, Carson-Newman 18
Division II (Joplin, Mo., Dec. 2)—Missouri Southern 21, Northwestern (Iowa) 14

Major Bowl and All-Star Games
(Nov.–Dec. 1972; Jan. 1973)

Alonzo Amos Stagg Bowl (Phenix City, Ala., Nov. 24)—Heidelberg College 28, Fort Valley State 16
Knute Rockne Bowl (Atlantic City, Nov. 24)—Bridgeport 27, Slippery Rock 22
College Club Championship (New York, Nov. 25)—Seton Hall 20, Marist College 18
Pelican Bowl (Durham, N. C., Dec. 2)—Grambling 56, North Carolina Central 6
Ohio Shrine Bowl (Columbus, Dec. 9)—East 20, West 7
Liberty Bowl (Memphis, Tenn., Dec. 18)—Georgia Tech 31, Iowa State 30
Fiesta Bowl (Tempe, Ariz., Dec. 23)—Arizona State 49, Missouri 35
North-South Shrine All-Stars (Miami, Dec. 25)—North 17, South 10
Blue-Gray All-Stars (Montgomery, Ala., Dec. 27)—Gray 27, Blue 15
Peach Bowl (Atlanta, Ga., Dec. 29)—North Carolina State 49, West Virginia 13
Tangerine Bowl (Orlando, Fla., Dec. 29)—Tampa 21, Kent State 18
Sun Bowl (El Paso, Texas, Dec. 30)—North Carolina 32, Texas Tech 28
Gator Bowl (Jacksonville, Fla., Dec. 30)—Auburn 24, Colorado 3
East-West Shrine Classic (San Francisco, Dec. 30)—East 9, West 3
Astro-Bluebonnet Bowl (Houston, Texas, Dec. 30)—Tennessee 24, Louisiana State 17
Sugar Bowl (New Orleans, Dec. 31)—Oklahoma 14, Penn State 0
Cotton Bowl (Dallas, Jan. 1)—Texas 17, Alabama 13
Orange Bowl (Miami, Jan. 1)—Nebraska 40, Notre Dame 6
Rose Bowl (Pasadena, Calif., Jan. 1)—Southern California 42, Ohio State 17
Senior Bowl (Mobile, Ala., Jan. 6)—South 33, North 30
Hula Bowl (Honolulu, Jan. 6)—South 17, North 3
American Bowl (Tampa, Fla., Jan. 7)—North 10, South 6

JACK NICKLAUS (left), after winning the U. S. Open at Pebble Beach, Calif., is escorted from green by former titleholder Lee Trevino.

GARY PLAYER won PGA title despite missing birdie putt in third round.

GOLF

Just before the start of the year, Jack Nicklaus set a goal for himself—that of winning the grand slam of professional golf. He failed after two of the tournaments, but he achieved so much else that he was named Golfer of the Year by the Professional Golfers' Association. Nicklaus won the Masters Tournament, the United States Open championship, and five other PGA tourneys. He broke his record for earnings in one season with a total of $320,542. He had set the previous mark in 1971 with $244,490.

Lee Trevino of El Paso, Texas, the 1971 Golfer of the Year, was the one who ended Nicklaus' hopes by winning the British Open for the second straight year. Trevino finished the year second to Nicklaus in earnings with $207,255.

Nicklaus began his campaign by leading each round of the Masters and winning it for the fourth time, by three strokes over Bruce Crampton of Australia. In the U. S. Open, Nicklaus shared the lead for two rounds, moved in front on the third day, and won again by three strokes over Crampton. He now had the British Open and the PGA championship to go. However, in Scotland, Trevino beat him by one stroke as Nicklaus carded a 66 on the final round, picking up five strokes on the Texan. In the PGA in August, Nicklaus had a bad second round and finished in a tie for 13th, six strokes behind the winner, Gary Player of South Africa.

Besides Nicklaus and Trevino, a number of golfers earned over $100,000 during the year: George Archer, Grier Jones, Jerry Heard, Tom Weiskopf, Gary Player, Bruce Devlin, Tommy Aaron, Lanny Wadkins (in his first year on the tour), Bobby Mitchell, Juan (Chi Chi) Rodriguez, Bruce Crampton, Hale Irwin, and Jim Jamieson.

Kathy Whitworth again set the pace in the Ladies Professional Golf Association tour. She won five tourneys and $65,062 in prize money. With a bonus of $7,500 as the Eve Challenge Cup winner, her total of $72,563 put her career earnings at a record of $415,306. However the two big tourneys were won by others. Mrs. Susie M. Berning took the U. S. Open championship, and Kathy Ahern, the runner-up to Mrs. Berning, captured the LPGA title.

In amateur competition, Vinney Giles 3d of Richmond, Va., took the men's national title after finishing second twice, and Mary Ann Budke of Dundee, Oreg., won the women's event. Bob Allard of Portland, Oreg., won the public links championship.

In international competition, the U. S. men's amateur team won the Eisenhower Cup by six strokes over Australia, and the American women took the Santo Espirito Trophy with a 4-stroke edge over France. Mrs. Jane B. Booth was low individual with a 290. A women's team had previously beaten Britain, 10–8, in the Curtis Cup matches.

The World Cup for professional teams, however, was captured by Taiwan, represented by Hsieh Minnan and Lu Liang-huan. Japan was second, two strokes back, South Africa third, and the U. S. tied for fourth with Australia.

Golf Highlights

Men's Individual Champions

U. S. Open—Jack Nicklaus, Lost Tree Village, Fla. (290)
British Open—Lee Trevino, El Paso, Texas (278)
Masters—Jack Nicklaus (286)
PGA Tourney—Gary Player, South Africa (281)
Canadian Open—Gay Brewer (275)
Western Open—Jim Jamieson (271)
U. S. Match Play—Jack Nicklaus (defeated Frank Baird in final)
U. S. Senior—Tommy Bolt (274)
USPGA Senior—Sam Snead (286)
Tournament of Champions—Bobby Mitchell (280)
Vardon Trophy—Lee Trevino
World Series of Golf—Gary Player (142)

PGA Tournament Winners

American Classic—Bert Yancey (276)
Atlanta Classic—Bob Lunn (275)
Byron Nelson—Chi Chi Rodriguez (273)
Cleveland Open—David Graham (278)
Colonial National—Jerry Heard (275)
Crosby Pro-Am—Jack Nicklaus (284)
Disney—Jack Nicklaus (267)
Doral-Eastern—Jack Nicklaus (276)
Florida Citrus—Jerry Heard (276)
Greensboro Open—George Archer (271)
Hartford Open—Lee Trevino (269)
Hawaiian Open—Grier Jones (274)
Heritage—John Miller (281)
Hope Desert Classic—Bob Rosburg (344)
Houston Open—Bruce Devlin (278)
Inverary Classic—Tom Weiskopf (278)
Jacksonville Open—Tony Jacklin (283)
Kaiser Open—George Knudson (271)
Kemper Open—Doug Sanders (275)
Los Angeles Open—George Archer (270)
Memphis Classic—Lee Trevino (281)
Milwaukee Open—Jim Colbert (271)
Monsanto Open—Dave Hill (271)
New Orleans Open—Gary Player (279)
Philadelphia Classic—J. C. Snead (282)
Phoenix Open—Homero Blancas (273)
Quad Cities Open—Deane Beman (279)
Robinson Open—Grier Jones (273)
Sahara Open—Lanny Wadkins (273)
St. Louis Open—Lee Trevino (269)
San Antonio Open—Mike Hill (223)
San Diego Open—Paul Harney (275)
Southern Open—DeWitt Weaver (276)
Tallahassee Open—Bob Shaw (273)
Tucson Open—Miller Barber (273)
USI Classic—Bruce Devlin (275)
Westchester Classic—Jack Nicklaus (270)

Pro Team

PGA—Babe Hiskey and Kermit Zarley (262)
World Cup—Taiwan (Nationalist China) (438); *individual low*: Hsieh Min-nan, Taiwan (217)

Men's Individual Amateur Champions

United States Amateur—Vinny Giles 3d, Richmond, Va. (285)
British Amateur—Trevor Homes, England
Canadian Amateur—Doug Roxburgh, British Columbia (276)
U. S. Public Links—Bob Allard, Portland, Oreg. (285)
U. S. Junior—Bob Byman, Boulder, Colo.
National Collegiate A. A. (NCAA)—*University:* tie between Ben Crenshaw, Texas, and Tom Kite, Texas (279); *College Division:* Tom Hilderbrand, Ashland (300)
National Intercollegiate (NAIA)—tie between Jim McAnnally, Angelo State, and Gaylord Burrows, Eastern Illinois (283)
U. S. Seniors G. A.—David Goldman, Dallas
USGA Seniors—Lew Dehmig, Chattanooga, Tenn.

Other Amateur Tournaments

Amputee—Dick Ferdinand, Las Vegas, Nev.
Blind—Jim Daniel, Summerville, Fla.
Eastern—Ben Crenshaw, Austin, Texas
French Open—Barry Jaeckel, Los Angeles
International Senior—Dick Storey, Scotland
Northeast—Wally Kuchar, Edgewood, Fla.
Pacific Coast—Mark Pfeil, San Diego
Porter Cup—Ben Crenshaw
Southern—Bill Rogers, Texarkana, Texas
Western—Gary Sanders, Anaheim, Calif.
World Junior—Jack Renner, San Diego
World Senior—Howard Everitt, Tequesta, Fla.

Team Championships

NCAA—*University:* Texas (1,146); *College:* Louisiana State at New Orleans (1,214)
NAIA—U. S. International College (1,176)
World (Eisenhower Cup)—United States (865); *individual low:* Anthony Gresham, Australia (285)

Women's Individual Pro Champions

U. S. Open—Mrs. Susie M. Berning, Incline Village, Nev. (299)
Vare Trophy—Kathy Whitworth
LPGA Tourney—Kathy Ahern, Denton, Texas (293)

Other LPGA Tour Winners

Alamo Open—Kathy Whitworth (209)
Bluegrass Invitation—Kathy Cornelius (211)
Birmingham Centennial—Betty Burfeindt (212)
Burdine's Invitation—Marlene Hagge (211)
Columbus Open—Marilynn Smith (210)
Corpus Christi Civitan—Jo Ann Prentice (210)
Dallas Civitan—Janie Blalock (211)
Dinah Shore-Colgate—Janie Blalock (213)
GAC-Tucson—Betsy Rawls (141)
George Washington Classic—Kathy Ahern (213)
Heritage Open—Judy Rankin (212)
Lady Carling—Carol Mann (210)
Lady Errol—Janie Blalock (214)
Lady Eve Open—Judy Rankin (210)
Lady Pepsi Open—Jan Ferraris (221)
Lincoln-Mercury Open—Sandra Haynie (215)
Knoxville Open—Kathy Whitworth (210)
National Jewish Hospital Open—Sandra Haynie (207)
Orange Blossom Classic—Carol Mann (213)
Portland Classic—Kathy Whitworth (212)
Raleigh Classic—Kathy Whitworth (212)
Sealy Classic—Betty Burfeindt (282)
Sears World Classic—Betsy Cullen
Susuki Internationale—Janie Blalock (208)
Titleholders—Sandra Palmer (283)
Southgate Open—Kathy Whitworth (216)
Waco Quality First—Sandra Haynie (206)

Women's Individual Amateur Champions

U. S. Amateur—Mary Ann Budke, Dundee, Oreg. (defeated Cynthia Hill, St. Petersburg, Fla., 5 and 4, in final)
Canadian Amateur—Mrs. Marlene Streit, Fonthill, Ont. (285)
USGA Senior—Mrs. Carolyn Cudone, Myrtle Beach, S. C.
USGA Junior Girls—Nancy Lopez, Roswell, N. Mex.
Collegiate—Ann Loughlin, Miami (Fla.)

Other Amateur Tournaments

British—Michelle Walker, England
French—Anne-Marie Palli, France
North and South—Mrs. Jane B. Booth, Palm Beach Gardens, Fla.
Pacific Northwest—Peggy Conley, Seattle
Southern—Beth Barry, Mobile, Ala.
Trans-Mississippi—Michelle Walker, England
Western—Debbie Massey, Bethlehem, Pa.

Team

Curtis Cup—United States 10, Britain 8
World (Espirito Santo Trophy)—United States (583); *individual low:* Mrs. Jan B. Booth (290)
Collegiate—Miami (Fla.)

Leading Money Winners in 1972

Men's PGA		Women's PGA	
Jack Nicklaus	$320,542	Kathy Whitworth	$65,064
Lee Trevino	214,805	Janie Blalock	57,323
George Archer	145,027	Judy Rankin	49,183
Grier Jones	140,177	Betty Burfeindt	47,529
Jerry Heard	137,198	Sandra Haynie	39,701
Tom Weiskopf	129,422	Kathy Ahern	38,072
Gary Player	120,719	Sandra Palmer	36,715
Bruce Devlin	119,768	Carol Mann	36,452
Tommy Aaron	118,924	Marilynn Smith	29,911
Lanny Wadkins	116,616	Jo Ann Prentice	27,583
Bobby Mitchell	113,719	Marlene Hagge	26,318
Chi Chi Rodriguez	113,503	Betsy Cullen	23,387
Hale Irwin	111,539	Clifford Ann Creed	22,738
Bruce Crampton	111,010	Gloria Ehret	19,763
Jim Jamieson	109,532	JoAnne Carner	18,901
Doug Sanders	102,252	Sharon Miller	18,870

Career Earnings		Career Earnings	
Jack Nicklaus	$1,703,706	Kathy Whitworth	$396,802
Arnold Palmer	1,544,194	Mickey Wright	291,601
Billy Casper	1,292,028	Betsy Rawls	273,780
Gary Player	935,472	Sandra Haynie	265,476
Julius Boros	883,865	Marilynn Smith	256,027
Lee Trevino	859,423	Carol Mann	253,119
Gene Littler	825,967	Marlene Hagge	248,766
Frank Beard	807,619	Louise Suggs	187,064
Bruce Crampton	791,443	Patty Berg	185,896
George Archer	728,348	Jo Ann Prentice	173,509
Doug Sanders	724,123	Judy Rankin	158,119
Bobby Nichols	650,066	Shirley Englehorn	150,933

Harness Racing Highlights
U. S. Trotting Association Champions
Trotters

2-Year-Old—Colonial Charm
3-Year-Old—Super Bowl
4-Year-Old—Speedy Crown
Aged—Fresh Yankee
Trotter of the Year—Super Bowl

Pacers

2-Year-Old—Ricci Reenie Time
3-Year-Old—Strike Out
4-Year-Old—Albatross
Aged—Isle of Wight
Pacer of the Year—Albatross

Harness Horse of the Year

Albatross (136 votes); Super Bowl (48); Strike Out (4); Speedy Crown (2); Romalie Hanover (1)

Major Stakes Winners
Trotting

American Championship (Roosevelt)—Speedy Crown
American Classic (Hollywood)—Dayan
American National Maturity (Sportsman's Park)—Savoir
Challenge Match Race (Roosevelt)—Speedy Crown
Colonial (Liberty Bell)—Super Bowl
Dexter Cup (Roosevelt)—Songcan
Hambletonian (DuQuoin, Ill.)—Super Bowl
Kentucky Futurity (Lexington)—Super Bowl
Maple Leaf (Toronto)—Speedy Crown
International (Roosevelt)—Speedy Crown
Prix d'Amerique (Paris)—Tidalium Pelo
Realization (Roosevelt)—Speedy Crown
Yonkers Futurity—Super Bowl
Westbury Futurity—Burning Speed

Pacing

Adios Stakes (The Meadows)—Dead heat between Jay Time and Strike Out
American Classic (Hollywood)—Albatross
American National (Sportsman's Park)—Albatross
Cane (Yonkers)—Hilarious Way
Fox (Indianapolis)—Ricci Reeni Time
Governor's Cup (Sportsman's Park)—Albatross
Little Brown Jug (Delaware, Ohio)—Strike Out
Messenger Stakes (Roosevelt)—Silent Majority
Prix d'Ete (Blue Bonnets)—Strike Out
Realization (Roosevelt)—Albatross

———— HARNESS RACING ————

Albatross, a 4-year-old pacer, had little difficulty in retaining the Harness Horse of the Year award. He received 136 of 191 votes for the honor, with his stablemate Super Bowl, a trotter, in second place with 48. On July 1, at Sportsman's Park, Cicero, Ill., Albatross posted the fastest time for a harness horse for a mile, with a clocking of 1:54⅗ on a ⅝-mile track. Ten weeks later at Delaware, Ohio, he set a record for a pacer on a half-mile track in 1:55⅗. In 1971 at Lexington, Ky., he had set the mark for the one-mile track of 1:54⅘. Albatross finished his racing career in December with a record for a pacer of $1,201,470. He had been syndicated for $2.5 million.

Super Bowl also was retired from racing with total earnings of $605,609 for two years. He won 18 straight races and took the three highest-rated trotting events—the Hambletonian, the Yonkers Futurity, and the Kentucky Futurity. In the Hambletonian, Super Bowl set a record for 3-year-old trotters on a mile track with a time of 1:56⅖. Super Bowl was trained and handled by Stanley Dancer, as was Albatross.

Speedy Crown, who was selected as the 4-year-old Trotter of the Year, won $417,505 in purses in one 4-week stretch at Roosevelt, defeating Une de Mai, the French champion, in one of them. Strike Out took the honors for 3-year-old pacers, winning the Little Brown Jug with a record of 1:56⅗ for a half-mile track at Delaware, Ohio. He also raced a rare dead heat with Jay Time in the Adios Stakes at The Meadows. Hilarious Way won the Cane Pace, and Silent Majority took the Messenger Stakes.

Hockey Highlights
NATIONAL HOCKEY LEAGUE
(Final Standings, 1972)
East Division

	Won	Lost	Tied	Goals For	Goals Against	Pts.
Boston	54	13	11	330	204	119
New York	48	17	13	317	192	109
Montreal	46	16	16	307	205	108
Toronto	33	31	14	209	208	80
Detroit	33	35	10	261	262	76
Buffalo	16	43	19	203	289	51

West Division

	Won	Lost	Tied	Goals For	Goals Against	Pts.
Chicago	46	17	15	256	166	105
Minnesota	37	29	12	212	191	86
St. Louis	28	39	11	208	247	67
*Pittsburgh	26	38	14	220	258	66
Philadelphia	26	38	14	200	236	66
California	21	39	18	216	288	60
Los Angeles	20	49	9	206	305	49

* Awarded fourth place on record in play against Philadelphia

Stanley Cup Playoffs

Preliminary Series—*East Division:* Boston defeated Toronto, 4 games to 1; New York defeated Montreal, 4 games to 2. *West Division:* Chicago defeated Pittsburgh, 4 games to 0; St. Louis defeated Minnesota, 4 games to 3
Semifinals—New York defeated Chicago, 4 games to 0; Boston defeated St. Louis, 4 games to 0
Final—Boston defeated New York, 4 games to 2

Individual National Hockey League Awards
(Trophy winners receive $1,500 each from league.)

Hart Trophy (most valuable player)—Bobby Orr, Boston
Ross Trophy (leading scorer)—Phil Esposito, Boston
Norris Trophy (leading defenseman)—Bobby Orr
Lady Byng Trophy (sportsmanship)—Jean Ratelle, New York
Vezina Trophy (goalies)—Tony Esposito and Gary Smith, Chicago
Calder Trophy (rookie)—Ken Dryden, Montreal
Conn Smythe Trophy (most valuable in playoffs)—Bobby Orr

NHL All-Star Teams

	First Team	Second Team
Goal	Tony Esposito, Chicago	Ken Dryden, Montreal
Defense	Bobby Orr, Boston	Bill White, Chicago
Defense	Brad Park, New York	Pat Stapleton, Chicago
Center	Phil Esposito, Boston	Jean Ratelle, New York
Right Wing	Rod Gilbert, New York	Yvan Cournoyer, Montreal
Left Wing	Bobby Hull, Chicago	Vic Hadfield, New York

All-Star Game (Bloomington, Minn., Jan. 23)—East 3, West 2

Other Professional Champions

American League—*Eastern Division:* Boston Braves (awarded first place for better record against Nova Scotia after tie in points); *Western Division:* Baltimore Clippers (awarded first for better record against Hershey Bears after tie in points)
Calder Cup Playoffs—Nova Scotia Voyageurs
Western League—*Regular season and playoffs:* Denver
Central League—*Regular season and playoffs:* Dallas

Amateur Champions

Eastern League—*Northern Division:* Syracuse Blazers; *Southern Division and playoffs:* Charlotte Checkers
International League—*Northern Division:* Muskegon Mohawks; *Southern Division:* Dayton Gems; *Playoffs:* Port Huron Wings
United States League—Green Bay
Memorial Cup (Canadian junior)—Cornwall (Ont.) Royals
Allan Cup (Canadian senior)—Spokane Jets
Amateur Hockey Association of the United States—*Pee Wee:* Amherst, N. Y.; *bantam:* Edina, Minn.; *midget:* Detroit; *juvenile:* Arlington, Mass.; *intermediate:* South St. Paul; *junior:* St. Paul-Minnesota North Stars

Intercollegiate

NCAA—Boston University (defeated Cornell, 4-0, in final)
NAIA—Lake Superior (defeated Gustavus Adolphus, 9-3, in final)
ECAC—*Division I:* Cornell; *playoffs:* Boston University; *Division II:* Bowdoin; *playoffs:* Massachusetts
WCHA—*Season:* Denver; *playoffs:* Wisconsin and Denver
Central Collegiate—Ohio State
Canadian—University of Toronto

International Series

Canada (National Hockey League stars) defeated USSR, 4 games to 3 with one tie. USSR won 2 and tied one of 4 games in Canada (Sept. 2-8); Canada won 3 of 4 games in Russia (Sept. 22-28). Total goals: Canada 32, USSR 31

UPI

NHL AWARD WINNERS with trophies for 1971–72 regular season play. From left are Tony Esposito, Chicago; Jean Ratelle, New York; Bobby Orr, Boston; and Ken Dryden, Montreal.

HOCKEY

Hockey reached its majority in 1972, moving up on a par with baseball, basketball, and football as a popular spectator sport. This marked the second big step after the first expansion of the National Hockey League in 1967. Not only did the NHL enlarge its sphere with penetration of the South to Atlanta and a second club in the New York metropolitan area, but also the World Hockey Association was formed, with franchises in 12 U. S. and Canadian cities. The game also received more exposure to more people through increased television coverage.

The new league did more to check the Boston Bruins than their opponents in the NHL had been able to do. In their search for top talent the new clubs raided the established teams, offering more money, and two of Boston's stalwarts, Derek Sanderson and John McKenzie, shifted to a new Philadelphia team, the Blazers. The WHA's finest acquisition, however, was Bobby Hull, who jumped from the Chicago Black Hawks to the Winnipeg Jets. He was lured by a $2 million long-term pact.

The Bruins had ended the 1971–72 season in possession of the league championship and the Stanley Cup. In the preceding season they had lost those prizes through overconfidence. Determined to prove they were the mightiest, they won the East Division with a 10-point edge over a strong New York Ranger team. They were again paced by center Phil Esposito and Bobby Orr. Esposito won the scoring championship with 133 points, and Orr was second with 117 besides being acclaimed, once again, the best defenseman. Jean Ratelle of the Rangers was giving Esposito a battle for the top-scorer role until he broke an ankle near the end of the season. He still took third place with 109 points, although he played 13 fewer games than the Boston stars.

Only the Rangers slowed the Bruins in the playoffs after each club had brushed aside their early opponents. Boston eliminated Toronto, 4 games to 1, and St. Louis, 4 games to 0. The Rangers, with apparently tougher teams, first disposed of Montreal, the defending champions, 4 games to 2, and then took four straight from Chicago, the champions of the West. In the final series, the Bruins took the first two games, but the Rangers came back and made a battle of it before Boston won out, 4 games to 2. Orr again won the Conn Smythe Trophy as the most valuable player in the playoffs. He had been chosen the most valuable player during the season for the second year in a row.

Before the start of the 1972–73 season, a select team of NHL stars played the Soviet Union national team, the perennial amateur champions. The Canadians were stunned after losing the first game and two others in Canada, but in Russia they won three and took the series, 4 games to 3, with one tie.

Horse Racing Highlights

Champions of the Year
Eclipse Awards

(Consolidation of polls of Thoroughbred Racing Association's Board of Selection, the *Daily Racing Form* staff, and the National Turf Writers Association)

Horse of the Year—Meadow Stable's (C. T. Chenery) Secretariat
2-Year-Old Filly—Jean-Louis Levesque's La Prevoyante
2-Year-Old Colt—Secretariat
3-Year-Old Filly—Fred W. Hooper's Susan's Girl
3-Year-Old Colt—Rokeby Stable's Key to the Mint
Older Filly or Mare—Westerly's Stud's Typecast
Older Colt—Mr. and Mrs. Sigmund Sommer's Autobiography
Steeplechase—Mrs. Marion Scott Soothsayer
Grass—Mary F. Jones' Cougar II

Major Stakes Winners
(Purses over $100,000)

American Derby (Arlington)—Dubassoff
Amory L. Haskell Handicap (Monmouth)—West Coast Scout
Arlington Handicap—Cloudy Dawn
Beldame (Belmont)—Susan's Girl
Belmont Stakes—Riva Ridge
Brooklyn Handicap (Aqueduct)—Key to the Mint
California Derby (Golden Gate)—Quack
California Juvenile—Kingly Dawn
Californian (Hollywood)—Cougar II
Campbell Handicap (Bowie)—*1st Division:* Favoricidian; *2d Division:* Boone the Great
Century Handicap (Hollywood)—Cougar II
Champagne Stakes (Belmont)—Stop the Music
Coaching Club American Oaks (Belmont)—Summer Guest
Delaware Handicap—Blessing Angelica
Flamingo (Hialeah)—Hold Your Peace
Florida Derby (Gulfstream)—Upper Case
Frizette (Belmont)—La Prevoyante
Futurity (Belmont)—Secretariat
Garden State Stakes—Secretariat
Gardenia—La Prevoyante
Gulfstream Park Handicap—Executioner
Hawthorne Gold Cup—Droll Role
Hialeah Turf Cup—Greaming
Hobson Handicap (Liberty Bell)—West Coast Scout
Hollywood Derby—Riva Ridge
Hollywood Gold Cup—Quack
Hollywood Juvenile—Bold Liz
Jersey Derby (Garden State)—Smiling Jack
Jockey Club Gold Cup—Autobiography
Kentucky Derby (Churchill Downs)—Riva Ridge
Laurel Futurity—Secretariat
Man o' War Handicap (Belmont)—Typecast
Matron (Belmont)—La Prevoyante
Metropolitan Handicap (Aqueduct)—Executioner
Michigan 1⅛-Mile (Detroit)—*1st Division:* King's Bishop; *2d Division:* Favoricidian
Monmouth Invitational—Freetex
Ohio Derby—Freetex
Pan-American Handicap (Gulfstream)—Unanime
Pontiac Grand Prix (Arlington)—King's Bishop
Preakness (Pimlico)—Bee Bee Bee
San Juan Capistrano (Santa Anita)—Practicante
Santa Anita Derby—Solar Salute
Santa Anita Handicap—Triple Bend
Santa Margarita (Santa Anita)—Turkish Trousers
Sapling (Monmouth)—Assagai Jr.
Selima (Laurel)—La Prevoyante
Suburban Handicap (Aqueduct)—Hitchcock
Travers (Saratoga)—Key to the Mint
United Nations Handicap (Atlantic City)—Acclimatization
Vanity (Hollywood)—Convenience
Washington, D. C. International (Laurel)—Droll Role
Widener (Hialeah)—Good Counsel
Wood Memorial (Aqueduct)—Upper Case
Woodward Stakes (Belmont)—Key to the Mint

Match Race
(Hollywood Park, June 17, 1⅛ miles)

Convenience defeated Typecast by a head

Quarter Horse
(Ruidoso, N. Mex., Sept. 4)

All-American Futurity (total purse $1 million)—Possumjet (Pete Herrera, jockey; time: 20.4 seconds; winner's purse: $337,000)

Other Races

Ascot Gold Cup (England)—Erima Hawk
Cambridgeshire (Newmarket, England)—Negus
Canadian International (Woodbine)—Droll Role
Epsom Derby (England)—Roberto
Epsom Oaks (England)—Ginevra
Grand National Steeplechase (England)—Well to Do
Grand Prix de Paris—Pleben
Irish Sweeps Derby—Steel Pulse
Irish Oaks—Regal Exception
King George VI and Queen Elizabeth (England)—Brigadier-Gerard
Melbourne Derby—Pipping Lane
1,000 Guineas (England)—Waterloo
2,000 Guineas—High Top
Prix de l'Arc de Triomphe (France)—San San
Queens Plate (Canada)—Victoria Song
St. Leger (England)—Boucher

THE NEW YORK TIMES

RIVA RIDGE, with jockey Ron Turcotte and owner Mrs. John Tweedy, after winning Belmont Stakes. Horse also won Kentucky Derby but failed in bid for Triple Crown.

HORSE RACING

After the running of the Belmont Stakes in June, Riva Ridge seemed headed for the Horse of the Year award even though he had failed to win the Triple Crown. A muddy track at Pimlico had kept the 3-year-old colt, owned by Christopher Chenery, out of the money in the Preakness, the second race of the Triple Crown series. But in winning the Belmont with a stronger performance than the one that took the Kentucky Derby, Riva Ridge was still the No. 1 horse.

The colt was sent to California and won the Hollywood Derby, defeating Bicker and Quack, two of the West's leading 3-year-olds. But back in the East he ran fourth in the Monmouth Handicap. The victor, Key to the Mint, was chipping away at Riva Ridge's prestige. The Paul Mellon-owned colt took the Brooklyn Handicap, the Whitney, and the Travers.

The horses faced each other in the Woodward, and Key to the Mint triumphed with Riva Ridge running third and losing more prestige. Then in the Jockey Cup Gold Cup they both lost to Autobiography, who was making a late bid for honors. Key to the Mint was second and Riva Ridge third.

Meanwhile, a Canadian-bred filly, La Prevoyante, was rolling up victories and drawing acclaim. The bay daughter of Buckpasser finished the season unbeaten in 12 races. She won $114,552 in her final race, raising her total to a record of $417,109 for her class.

Another 2-year-old, Secretariat, a stablemate of Riva Ridge, had little difficulty in being rated the best of his class. The colt, a son of Bold Ruler, took the $298,665 Garden State Stakes, America's richest thoroughbred race, in November, getting $179,199 of the purse. He won seven of nine races for a total of $456,404 in prize money.

A poll in December 1972 selected Secretariat as Horse of the Year, with La Prevoyante second.

OLYMPIC GAMES. See separate article.

MARK SPITZ, who won seven Olympic gold medals, shows world-record form in 200-meter butterfly trials at Chicago.

SWIMMING

In a meet that one coach called the greatest ever held, American swimmers broke world records 11 times and tied one in trying to land berths on the Olympic team. The performances were turned in at the United States Olympic trials at Portage Park, Chicago, that began on August 2. In the four-day meet, 433 men and women battled for trips to Munich, and the waves they made washed out lots of hope in Australia and Europe for Olympic success.

The American swimmers had trained for this meet and the Olympics fully aware of the strong challenges that would come from Germany, the USSR, Japan, and especially Australia. The year had begun with a continuation of freestyle record wrecking by Shane Gould, the 15-year-old Australian schoolgirl. By mid-January, she held the world marks for all standard events. Other Aussies had also posted world-record times.

But in Chicago the outlook changed. Shirley Babashoff, 15, of Huntington Beach, Calif., took away Miss Gould's 200-meter freestyle record with a time of 2:05.21, and another 15-year-old girl, Jo Harshbarger of Bellevue, Wash., deprived the Australian of the 800-meter mark, doing 8:53.83. Adding to the achievements of the 15-year-olds was Melissa Belote of Springfield, Va., who bettered the

Swimming Highlights

Men's National AAU Indoor Championships
(Dallas, Texas, April 5–8)

100-Yard Freestyle—Mark Spitz, Indiana (0:45.1)
200-Yard Freestyle—Steve Genter, Lakewood (Calif.) Swim Club (1:39.23)
500-Yard Freestyle—John Kinsella, Indiana (4:28.29)
1,650-Yard Freestyle—John Kinsella (15:31.3)
100-Yard Backstroke—Mike Stamm, Indiana (0:51.86)
200-Yard Backstroke—Mike Stamm (1:51.03)
100-Yard Breaststroke—Brian Job, Santa Clara (Calif.) Swim Club (0:57.5)
200-Yard Breaststroke—Brian Job (2:02.36; U.S. record)
100-Yard Butterfly—Mark Spitz (0:48.76)
200-Yard Butterfly—Mark Spitz (1:49.01)
200-Yard Medley—Gary Hall, Indiana (1:53.13)
400-Yard Medley—Gary Hall (3:58.09; U.S. record)
400-Yard Freestyle Relay—Southern California (Ed McCleskey, Kim Tutt, Mike Weston, Frank Heckl; 3:03.26)
800-Yard Freestyle Relay—Southern California (Frank Heckl, Kim Tutt, Ed McCleskey, Jim McConica; 6:42.16)
400-Yard Medley Relay—Indiana (Mike Stamm, Brock Ladewig, Mark Spitz, Gary Conelly; 3:24.40)
Team—University of Southern California (607 pts)

Diving
(Dallas, Texas, March 29–April 1)

1-Meter Springboard—Don Dunfield, Santa Clara S.C. (531.18 pts)
3-Meter—Phil Boggs, Air Force Academy (531 pts)
Platform—Dick Rydze, Pittsburgh (501 pts)

Women's National AAU Indoor Championships
(Dallas, Texas, April 5–8)

100-Yard Freestyle—Barbara Shaw, Riverside (Calif.) A.A. (0:52.0)
200-Yard Freestyle—Kim Peyton, David Douglas S.C., Phoenix (1:52.49)
500-Yard Freestyle—Keena Rothhammer, Santa Clara (Calif.) S.C. (4:57.87)
1,650-Yard Freestyle—Jo Harshbarger, Belleview, Wash. (16:59.33)
100-Yard Backstroke—Susie Atwood, Lakewood (Calif.) S.C. (0:58.75)
200-Yard Backstroke—Susie Atwood (2:04.01; U.S. record)
100-Yard Breaststroke—Lynn Vidali, Santa Clara (1:07)
200-Yard Breaststroke—Lynn Colella, Cascade (Wash.) S.C. (2:22.39)
100-Yard Butterfly—Deana Deardurff, Cincinnati Marlins (0:57.16)
200-Yard Butterfly—Karen Moe, Santa Clara (2:03.34; U.S. record)
200-Yard Medley—Jenny Bartz, Santa Clara (2:08.22)
400-Yard Medley—Susie Atwood (4:28.85; U.S. record)
400-Yard Freestyle Relay—Santa Clara S.C. (Mary Brunchurst, Jenny Bartz, Karen Moe, Keena Rothhammer; 3:35.11)
800-Yard Freestyle Relay—Santa Clara (Jenny Wylie, Sharon Berg, Jenny Bartz, Keena Rothhammer; 7:36.84; U.S. record)
400-Yard Medley Relay—Lakewood A.C. (Susie Atwood, Kim Brecht, Dana Schrader, Bonnie Adair; 3:57.43; U.S. record)
Team—Santa Clara (Calif.) S.C. (649 pts)

Diving
(Dallas, Texas, March 29–April 1)

3-Meter—Cynthia Potter, Houston (429.54 pts)
1-Meter—Capt. Micki King, Hermosa Beach, Calif. (436.78 pts)
Platform—Ulrika Knape, Sweden (370.56 pts)

Women's National AAU Outdoor Diving Championships
(Lincoln, Nebr., July 11–15)

1-Meter—Cynthia Potter, Houston (446.32 pts)
3-Meter—Cynthia Potter (427.33 pts)
Platform—Janet Ely, Ann Arbor, Mich. (389.55 pts)

Men's National AAU Outdoor Diving Championships
(The AAU outdoor, or long-course, swimming championships were not held in 1972.)
(Lincoln, Nebr., July 11–15)

1-Meter—Don Dunfield, San Jose, Calif. (524.61)
3-Meter—Mike Finneran, Columbus, Ohio (556.29)
Platform—Rick Early, Fresno, Calif. (490.77)

National Collegiate (NCAA) Championships
(West Point, N.Y., March 23–25)

50-Yard Freestyle—Dave Edgar, Tennessee (0:20.44)
100-Yard Freestyle—Dave Edgar (0:45)
200-Yard Freestyle—Jerry Heidenreich, Southern Methodist (1:38.36)
500-Yard Freestyle—John Kinsella, Indiana (4:24.50)
1,650-Yard Freestyle—John Kinsella (15:33.58)
100-Yard Backstroke—Paul Gilbert, Yale (0:51.29)
200-Yard Backstroke—Charlie Campbell, Princeton (1:50.55)
100-Yard Butterfly—Mark Spitz, Indiana (0:47.98)
200-Yard Butterfly—Mark Spitz (1:46.89)
100-Yard Breaststroke—Tom Bruce, UCLA (0:56.99) (Brian Job, Stanford, bettered American record in heat in 0:56.83)
200-Yard Breaststroke—Brian Job, Stanford (2:02.59)
200-Yard Medley—Gary Ball, Indiana (1:51.51)
400-Yard Medley—Gary Hall (3:58.71)
400-Yard Freestyle Relay—Tennessee (Ken Knox, Tom Lutz, Dave Edgar, John Trembley; 3:01.11)
400-Yard Medley Relay—Southern California (Bruce Kocsis, Dave Mayekawa, Frank Heckl, Mike Weston; 3:23.11)
800-Yard Freestyle Relay—Southern California (Ed McCleskey, Steve Tyrrell, Tom McBreen, Jim McConica; 6:38.63)
1-Meter Diving—Todd Smith, Ohio State (508.25 pts)
3-Meter Diving—Craig Lincoln, Minnesota (545.44 pts)
Team—University of Indiana (390 pts)

SHANE GOULD (above) flashes victory sign after setting world record for 100-meter freestyle in meet at Sydney, Australia, in January 1972. She went on to win three gold medals in Summer Olympics. Billie Jean King (right) holds trophy plate after winning singles tennis title in Wimbledon Open for fourth time.

world record in the 200-yard backstroke with 2:21.77. A fourth women's world mark was posted by Karen Moe of Santa Clara, Calif., in the 200-meter butterfly with 2:16.62. Three other American women's records were shattered.

The record-breaking in the men's division was led by Mark Spitz of Carmichael, Calif. He bettered the mark in the 100- and 200-meter butterfly events and the 100-meter freestyle. In the 200-meter fly on opening day, Spitz broke the record in the preliminaries with 2:01.78, then lowered the mark to 2:01.53 in the final. Two days later he repeated in the 100-meter event, bettering his record in the heats with 54.47 seconds in the final. On the next day, in the preliminaries, he hit 51.47 in the 100-meter freestyle for a record.

The other record-breakers were Gary Hall of Huntington Beach, Calif., in the 400-meter individual medley with 4:30.81; John Hencken of Cupertino, Calif., in the 200-meter breaststroke with 2:22.79; Rick DeMont of San Rafael, Calif., in the 1,500-meter freestyle with 15:52.91; and Kurt Krumpholz of Santa Clara, Calif., in the 400-meter freestyle with 4:00.11. Hall also tied the world mark of 2:09.30 in the 200-meter individual medley. Only Krumpholz' record and Hall's in the 400-meter medley lasted through the Olympics.

TENNIS

While the contract professionals continued to hassle over jurisdictional rights with the tennis associations, the fans waited rather impatiently for a match between their two new darlings—Chris Evert and Evonne Goolagong. They just missed meeting in Dallas in March, so the world turned its attention to the Wimbledon. Miss Evert, the 17-year-old star from Fort Lauderdale, who had drawn acclaim in 1971 for her play in the U. S. Open after a brilliant Wightman Cup series, moved into the semifinal round at Wimbledon. Pulling into the bracket opposite her was Miss Goolagong, the 20-year-old descendant of Australian aborigines, who held the Wimbledon title.

The young American moved in front quickly, taking the first set and gaining a 3–0 lead in the second. Miss Goolagong won the next seven games, taking the set 6–3, and getting the first game for the deciding set. But Chris came back and moved ahead, 3–2. They were even at 4–4 before experience came to the Aussie's aid, and she pulled through, 6–4. However, Miss Goolagong lost her title to Billie Jean King in the final, 6–3, 6–3.

Miss Evert evened her series with Miss Goolagong in the Bon Belle matches at Cleveland in July.

After beating Margaret Smith Court, 6–3, 6–3, she again had to play three sets with Miss Goolagong. This time the Australian faded, and Chris triumphed, 6–3, 4–6, 6–0. Then in a third meeting three weeks later, on courts more to her liking, Miss Evert swept past the Australian, 7–6, 6–1, after losing the first five games, in the match that gave her the clay courts title.

Chris wound up the year with a splendid victory in the Virginia Slims championship tourney in which she defeated Billie Jean King, 6–4, 6–2, in the semifinals for one of her most satisfying triumphs.

The United States retained the Davis Cup with a 3–2 victory over Rumania, with Stan Smith leading the way. Smith, who won the Wimbledon final by beating Ilie Nastase of Rumania in an excellent five-set match, defeated the Rumanian again in three sets in the opening match. He also defeated Ion Tiriac, and he and Erik Van Dillen won the doubles. Nastase had taken the U. S. Open crown at Forest Hills, N. Y., with a five-set triumph over Arthur Ashe.

Billie Jean King also won at Forest Hills as she showed her dominance in the women's field.

Tennis Highlights

Major Tournaments

Davis Cup—United States (defeated Rumania, 3–2, in final round at Bucharest, Oct. 13–15)
Wightman Cup (women)—United States (defeated Britain, 5–2, at Wimbledon, June 16–17)
Federation Cup (women)—South Africa (defeated Britain, 2–1, in final at Johannesburg, March 26)
Bon Belle Cup (women)—Australia (defeated United States, 5–2, at Cleveland, July 28–30)
Stevens Cup (seniors)—United States (defeated Mexico, 4–1, in final at New York, Sept. 11)
U. S. Open (Forest Hills, N. Y., Aug. 30–Sept. 10)—Men's singles: Ilie Nastase, Rumania; women's singles: Billie Jean King, Emeryville, Calif.; men's doubles: Cliff Drysdale, South Africa, and Roger Taylor, Britain; women's doubles: Françoise Durr, France, and Betty Stove, Netherlands; mixed doubles: Margaret Smith Court, Australia, and Marty Riessen, Evanston, Ill.; men's 35 singles: Mal Anderson, Australia; senior men's doubles: Straight Clark, Philadelphia, and Vic Seixas, Villanova, Pa.
U. S. Clay Court (Indianapolis, Aug. 8–13)—Men's singles: Bob Hewitt, South Africa; women's singles: Chris Evert, Fort Lauderdale, Fla.; men's doubles: Bob Hewitt and Frew McMillan, South Africa
U. S. Men's Amateur Grass Courts (Southampton, N. Y., Aug. 15–21)—Singles: Alex (Sandy) Mayer, Wayne, N. J.
U. S. Women's Amateur Grass Courts (Wilmington, Del., Aug. 15–21)—Singles: Marita Redondo, National City, Calif.; doubles: Pat Bostrom, Seattle, and Ann Lebedeff, San Diego
U. S. National Amateur Clay Courts (Atlanta, July 11–16)—Men's singles: Ross Walker, Britain; women's singles: Janice Metcalfe, Claremont, Calif.; men's doubles: Rez Reid, Greenville, S. C., and Fred McNair, Chevy Chase, Md.; women's doubles: Pat Bostrom, Seattle, and Ann Lebedeff, San Diego
U. S. National Senior Grass Court (Philadelphia, Aug. 28–Sept. 3)—Singles: Bobby Riggs, Newport Beach, Calif.; doubles: Tosten Johansson, Sweden, and Lari Legenstein; father and son: Fred McNair 3d and Fred McNair 4th, Chevy Chase, Md.
U. S. Women's Senior Grass Courts (Narragansett, R. I., Aug. 15–18)—Singles: Betty Pratt, Winter Park, Fla.; doubles: Betty Pratt and Nancy Neeld, Albuquerque, N. Mex.
U. S. Senior Clay Courts (Hot Springs, Va., Aug. 1–5)—Singles: Gus Palafox, Little Rock, Ark.; doubles: Gus Palafox and Jay Freeman, Little Rock, Ark.
U. S. National Public Parks (Glendale, Calif., Aug. 8–13)—Men's singles: Ken Stuart, Long Beach, Calif.; women's singles: Jan Hasse, Alhambra, Calif.; men's doubles: Dave Bohannon and Eddie Scott; women's doubles: Jan Hasse and Doreen Irish; mixed doubles: John Norgauer and Mickie Thomas
U. S. National Indoor Open (Salisbury, Md., Feb. 13–20)—Singles: Stan Smith, Pasadena, Calif.; doubles: Manuel Orantes and Andres Gimeno, Spain
U. S. National Indoor (Hampton, Va., Feb. 28–March 5)—Singles: Stan Smith, Pasadena, Calif.; doubles: Ilie Nastase and Ion Tiriac, Rumania
U. S. Nationals Indoor Amateur (Salt Lake City, Feb. 1)—Singles: F. D. Robbins, Salt Lake City; doubles: Stephen Mott and Brian Teacher, San Diego

Other U. S. Champions

National Collegiate (NCAA)—University Division: singles: Dick Stockton, Trinity College (Texas); doubles: Alex Mayer and Roscoe Tanner, Stanford; team: Trinity College (36 pts); College Division: singles: Charlie Owens, Samford; doubles: John Lowman and Mike Strickland, Rollins; team: tie between Rollins and University of California at Irvine (22 pts)
National Association of Intercollegiate Athletics (NAIA)—Singles: Harry Fritz, East Texas State; doubles: Harry Fritz and Bob Hochstadter, East Texas; team: East Texas State (37 pts)
Women's National Collegiate—Singles: Janice Metcalfe, Redlands, Calif.; doubles: Peggy Michel and Pam Richmond, Arizona State; team: Arizona State

American Tennis Association (Cambridge, Mass., Aug. 21–27)—Men's singles: Horace Reid, Atlanta; women's singles: Lorraine Bryant, Chicago; men's doubles: Arthur Carrington, Elizabeth, N. J., and Bill Morton; women's doubles: Elaine Busch and Brenda Johnson, Philadelphia; mixed doubles: Lee Stavins and Chris Scott; senior singles: Robert Miller
USLTA Juniors—Singles: Pat Dupre, Birmingham, Ala.; doubles: Stephen Mott and Brian Teacher, San Diego
USLTA Girls—Singles: Ann Kiyomura, San Mateo, Calif.; doubles: Marita Redondo, National City, Calif., and Laurie Tenney, Los Angeles
Interscholastic—Singles: Bill Matyastik, University School; doubles: David Dick and Buzz Willett, Baylor

Other Countries

Wimbledon Open (England, June 26–July 9)—Men's singles: Stan Smith, Pasadena, Calif.; women's singles: Billie Jean King, Emeryville, Calif.; men's doubles: Bob Hewitt and Frew McMillan, South Africa; women's doubles: Billie Jean King and Betty Stove, Netherlands; mixed doubles: Ilie Nastase, Rumania, and Rosemary Casals, San Francisco; senior doubles: Straight Clark, Philadelphia, and Vic Seixas, Villanova, Pa.
Australian Open (Melbourne, finals, Jan. 3)—Men's singles: Ken Rosewall, Australia; women's singles: Virginia Wade, England; men's doubles: Ken Rosewall and Owen Davidson, Australia; women's doubles: Helen Gourlay and Kerry Harris, Australia
French Open (Paris, May 24–June 4)—Men's singles: Andres Gimeno, Spain; women's singles: Billie Jean King, Emeryville, Calif.; men's doubles: Bob Hewitt and Frew McMillan, South Africa; women's doubles: Billie Jean King and Betty Stove, Netherlands; mixed doubles: Evonne Goolagong and Kim Warwick, Australia
Canadian Open (Toronto, Aug. 14–20)—Men's singles: Ilie Nastase, Rumania; women's singles: Evonne Goolagong, Australia; men's doubles: Ilie Nastase and Ion Tiriac, Rumania; women's doubles: Evonne Goolagong and Margaret Smith Court, Australia

LEADING MONEY WINNERS IN 1972

World Championship Tennis Tour
(Contract Professionals)

Ken Rosewall	$126,950	Marty Riessen	$74,436
Arthur Ashe	119,775	Cliff Drysdale	67,183
John Newcombe	110,600	Bob Lutz	62,225
Rod Laver	100,200	Mark Cox	50,750
Tom Okker	90,004	Roy Emerson	45,133

Virginia Slims Tour
(Contract Professionals)

Billie Jean King	$76,235	Françoise Durr	$33,275
Nancy Gunter	41,237	Margaret Smith	
Kerry Melville	41,037	Court	22,662
Chris Evert,		Wendy Overton	22,350
amateur	40,700*	Karen Krantzcke	16,312
Rosemary Casals	40,250	Valerie Ziegenfuss	15,625

* Ineligible as an amateur to receive prize money allotted for her finishes.

Commercial Union Grand Prix
Men

Ilie Nastase	$65,000	Andres Gimeno	$18,500
Stan Smith	45,000	Tom Gorman	16,000
Manuel Orantes	28,750	Bob Hewitt	15,500
Jan Kodes	23,750	Andrew Pattison	10,000
Jimmy Connors	19,500	Patrick Proisy	9,000

Masters Tourney (Barcelona)—Nastase defeated Smith in final, taking $15,000 first prize

Women

Billie Jean King	$22,500	Margaret Smith	
Evonne Goolagong	15,000	Court	$6,500
Rosemary Casals	11,250	Françoise Durr	5,500
Nancy Gunter	9,000	Chris Evert	....
Kerry Melville	7,500	Virginia Wade	4,500
		Lesley Hunt	4,000

TRACK AND FIELD

The United States regained the pole vault record in one of the most satisfactory achievements of the year. Bob Seagren of Monterey Park, Calif., who had held the record in 1968, brought it back with a leap of 18 feet 5¾ inches at Eugene, Oreg., on July 2. A few weeks before that he had gotten a share of the mark with Kjell Isaksson of Sweden, when they each cleared 18-4½ at El Paso. But Seagren's feat at the Olympic trials gave America its first pole vault record-holder since John Pennel in 1969.

The pole vault record has not been an American monopoly, but most of the development of the sport was American, and there were few occasions when a non-American held the world mark. From 1927 when Sabin Carr of Yale raised the record to 14 feet until 1970, only Pennti Nikula of Finland had been able to break the U. S. monopoly. Then Chris Papanicolaou of Greece, who learned most of his technique under American coaching, became the first to clear 18 feet, just after Wolfgang Nordwig of East Germany had broken through with a leap of 17-10½ that took the record away from Pennel by ¼ inch. Nordwig and Isaksson dominated the event during 1971, with the Swede becoming the world's foremost vaulter early in 1972, when he gained the outdoor record at 18-1 and 18-2¼. Nordwig failed to clear 18 feet until he won the Olympic championship in September.

Seagren was making a comeback. He had been inactive for about two years following a knee operation. But he was excited about defending his Olympic championship. He changed his style some and began using a lighter and smaller-diameter pole. He was eager to challenge Isaksson and was mentally prepared for the competition at El Paso on May 23. Since he had fewer misses than the Swedish athlete, he won the event as well as a share of the world record, clearing 18 feet in becoming the first American to do so. This put him in the right mood for the trials. After setting the mark, he said that 19 feet could be made, and he set his sights on that height.

Another notable feat at the trials was the victory of Dave Wottle of Canton, Ohio, in the 800-meter run. He equaled the world record of one minute, 44.3 seconds. He also finished second to Jim Ryun in the 1,500-meter event. Ryun had been trying for a year to get himself in shape to run in the Olympics again. Before going to Munich, he won a mile event in Toronto in 3:52.8. Not only was it the fastest mile of the year, but the third fastest ever run. Ryun had run the two faster races in 3:51.1 and 3:51.3 in 1967 and 1966. In the Olympics, he fell during a heat as his last bid failed. But he still held the world record for the half-mile and the 1,500-meter run along with the mile mark.

Immediately after the Olympics, European distance runners shattered records. Lasse Viren of Finland, the new Olympic champion, bettered the world mark in the 5,000-meter run at Helsinki, September 14, with 13:16.4, but six days later in Haysel, Belgium, Emiel Puttemans beat that time with 13:13.0. He also knocked out Ron Clarke's record for three miles with a 12:47.8 clocking. In the same meet, another Belgian, Willy Polleunis, broke the record for 10 miles with 46:04.2, and teammate Gaston Roelents bettered his own record for the one-hour run with a distance of 12 miles, 1,599 yards, and

for 20,000 meters with 57:44.4. Puttemans had taken over the world record for 3,000 meters, on September 14 at Aarhus, with a time of 7:37.6.

In October, Viktor Saneyev regained the triple-jump record from Pedro Perez of Cuba. Competing in his home town, Sukhami, USSR, Saneyev covered 57 feet 2¾ inches, which was 1¾ inches better than Perez.

Two Americans made the only inroads on sprint records. Eddie Hart of Pittsburg, Calif., and Reynaud Robinson of Lakewood, Fla., equaled the world mark for 100 meters in the final of the trials. Hart won the race with Robinson second. They were the two men who missed Olympic glory by arriving too late for the final.

Track and Field Highlights

National AAU Indoor Championships
(Madison Square Garden, N. Y., Feb. 25)

60 Yards—Delano Meriwether, Boston (0:06.2)
600 Yards—Lee Evans, Bay Area Striders, Oakland, Calif. (1:11.3)
1,000 Yards—Josef Plachy, Czechoslovakia (2:09.8)
Mile—Byron Dice, United A. A., New York (4:01.8)
3 Miles—Emiel Puttemans, Belgium (13:18.4)
60-Yard Hurdles—Rod Milburn, Southern Univ. (0:07.1)
Sprint Medley Relay—Adelphi (Al Salmon, Richard Hardware, William Johnson, Ray Lee; 2:05.5)
Mile Relay—BOHAA T. C., Brooklyn (LaMotte Hyman, Greg Dougherty, Larry James, Vincent Matthews; 3:14.7)
2-Mile Relay—Manhattan College (Cliff Bruce, John Lovett, Joe Savage, John Rothrock; 7:32.4)
Mile Walk—Dave Romansky, So. Jersey (6:13.4)
High Jump—Gene White, Penn A. C., Phila. (7 ft 2 in)
Pole Vault—Kjell Isaksson, Sweden (17 ft 10½ in)
Long Jump—Henry Hines, So. Calif. Univ. (25 ft 11¼ in)
Triple Jump—John Craft, Chicago Univ. T. C. (54 ft 4½ in)
*35-Pound Weight Throw—George Frenn, Los Angeles (72 ft 4 in)
*Shot Put—Fred DeBernardi, Texas-El Paso Univ. (66 ft 1½ in)

* Events held at West Point, N. Y.

National AAU Outdoor Championships
(Seattle, June 15-17)

100 Meters—Robert Taylor, Texas Southern (0:10.2)
200 Meters—Chuck Smith, So. California Striders (0:20)
400 Meters—Lee Evans, Bay State Striders, Oakland, Calif. (0:45.0)
800 Meters—Dave Wottle, Bowling Green Univ. (1:47.3)
1,500 Meters—Jerome Howe, Kansas State (3:38.2)
5,000 Meters—Mike Keogh, New York A. C. (13:51.8)
10,000 Meters—Greg Fredericks, Penn State (28:08)
3,000-Meter Steeplechase—James Dare, U. S. Navy (8:33.8)
5,000-Meter Walk—Larry Young, Mid-American T. C. (21:39.8)
110-Meter Hurdles—Rod Milburn, Southern Univ. (0:13.4)
400-Meter Hurdles—Dick Bruggeman, Ohio T. C., Columbus (0:50)
Long Jump—Arnie Robinson, U. S. Army (26 ft 5¾ in)
Triple Jump—John Craft, Chicago Univ. T. C. (54 ft 10 in)
High Jump—Barry Schur, Kansas (7 ft 2 in)
Pole Vault—Dave Roberts, Rice (18 ft ¼ in)
Shot Put—Randy Matson, Texas Striders (69 ft 6½ in)
Discus—Jay Silvester, Provo, Utah (213 ft)
Hammer Throw—Al Schoterman, New York A. C. (288 ft 1 in)
Javelin—Fred Luke, Husky T. C., Seattle (277 ft 5 in)

Women's AAU Indoor Championships
(Madison Square Garden, New York, Feb. 25)

60 Yards—Iris Davis, Tennessee State (0:06.9)
220 Yards—Esther Stroy, Sports International, Washington (0:24.6)
440 Yards—Kathy Hammond, Sacramento Roadrunners (0:54.9)
880 Yards—Cheryl Toussaint, Atoms T. C., Brooklyn (2:08.2)
Mile—Doris Brown, Falcon T. C., Seattle (4.44)
60-Yard Hurdles—Pat Johnson, Angels T. C., San Clemente, Calif. (0:07.5)
640-Yard Relay—Atoms T. C. Brooklyn (Linda Reynolds, Linda Cordy, Pat Hawkins, Carmen Brown; 1:10.4)
Sprint Medley Relay—Los Angeles Mercurettes (Jarvis Scott, Barbara Ferrell, Bobby Walker, Kathy Smallwood; 1:46.2)
Mile Relay—New York PAL (Francine Simuels, Denise Johnson, Valerie Carter, Marilyn Bastian; 3:51.6)

Track and Field Highlights (continued)

Long Jump—Martha Watson, Los Angeles T. C. (20 ft 11¾ in)
High Jump—Debbie Van Kiekebelt, Canada (5 ft 8 in)
Shot Put—Maren Seidler, Mayor Daley Y. F., Chicago (50 ft 11½ in)
Team—Atoms Track Club, Brooklyn, N. Y. (16 pts)

Women's AAU Outdoor Championships
(Canton, Ohio, July 1–2)

100 Meters—Alice Annum, Sports International, Washington (0:11.5)
200 Meters—Alice Annum (0:23.4)
400 Meters—Kathy Hammond, Sacramento Roadrunners (0:52.3)
800 Meters—Carol Hudson, Albuquerque, N. Mex. (2:06.7)
1,500 Meters—Francis Larrieu, San Jose (Calif.) Cinder Gals (4:18.4)
3,000 Meters—Tena Anex, Will's Spikettes, Sacramento, Calif. (9:42.6)
100-Meter Hurdles—Mamie Rallins, Tennessee State (0:13.5)
200-Meter Hurdles—Pat Hawkins, Atoms T. C. (0:26.3)
1,500-Meter Walk—Jeannie Socci, Wolverines, Detroit (6:59.1)
440-Yard Relay—Sports International (Alice Annum, Rose Allwood, Esther Stroy, Lacey O'Neal; 0:45.4)
880-Yard Medley Relay—Sports International (Alice Annum Rose Allwood, Esther Stroy, Lacey O'Neal; 1:40.6)
Mile Relay—Canton (Ohio) T. C. (Kathy Anderson, Bonnie Spring, Bonny Stewart, Nancy Shafer; 3:45.3)
2-Mile Relay—San Jose Cindergals (Cindy Poor, Valerie Cooper, Valerie Eberly, Francie Larrieu; 9:07.3)
High Jump—Audrey Reid, Texas Women's Univ. (6 ft ½ in)
Discus—Josephine Della Vina, Mayor Daley Y. F., Chicago (172 ft 9 in)
Shot Put—Maren Seidler, Chicago (52 ft 9 in)
Javelin—Sherry Calvert, Los Angeles (184 ft)
Long Jump—Willye White, Mayor Daley Y. F. (20 ft 6¼ in)
Team—Los Angeles Track Club (64 pts)

U. S. Track and Field Federation Indoor Championships
(Houston Astrodome, Feb. 12)
University Division

100 Yards—Cliff Branch, Colorado (0:09.3)
440 Yards—Edesel Garrison, So. California (0:45.7)
Mile—Dave Wottle, Bowling Green (4:03.7)
2 Miles—Bob Unger, Nebraska (8:41.4)
120-Yard Hurdles—Jerry Wilson, So. California (0:13.7)
Mile Relay—Nebraska (Priestley, Cimaro, Leonard, Case; 3:07.5)
2-Mile Relay—Illinois (Robert Mango, David Kaemerer, Lee LaBadie, Ron Phillips; 7:19.8)
Distance Medley Relay—Kansas State (Clardy Vinson, Fred Merrill, Rick Hitchcock, Jerome Howe; 9:33.8)

Open Division

2 Miles—George Young, unattached (8:32.9)
120-Yard Hurdles—Rod Milburn, Southern Univ. (0:13.4)
Pole Vault—Dave Roberts, Rice (17 ft)
Long Jump—Randy Williams, So. California (25 ft 8½ in)
High Jump—Chris Dunn, Colgate (7 ft 1 in)
Shot Put—Fred DeBernardi, Texas-El Paso (65 ft 8½ in)

U. S. Track and Field Federation Outdoor Championships
(Wichita, Kans., May 26–27)

100 Yards—Ben Vaughn, Georgia Tech T. C. (0:09.5)
220 Yards—Bob Vaughn (0:20.7)
440 Yards—Terry Musika, Pacific Coast Club (0:46)
880 Yards—Ken Sparks, Chicago Univ. T. C. (1:49.3)
Mile—Peter Kaal, Pacific Coast Club (3:59.9)
3 Miles—Jerome Howe, Kansas State (13:29.4)
6 Miles—David Antognoli, Edinboro State (28:24.7)
3,000-Meter Steeplechase—Randy Smith, Wichita State (8:43.4)
120-Yard Hurdles—Efren Gipson, Lamar T. C. (0:13.9)
440-Yard Hurdles—Efren Gipson (0:49.9)
440-Yard Relay—Southwestern Louisiana (0:40.5)
Mile Relay—Oklahoma (3:0818)
Long Jump—Preston Carrington, Wichita State (25 ft 8½ in)
High Jump—Gary Kafer, Baylor (6 ft 10 in)
Pole Vault—Jan Johnson, Alabama (17 ft)
Triple Jump—Lanier (50 ft 6½ in)
Javelin—Sam Colson, Kansas (272 ft 5 in)
Discus—Brian Oldfield, Chicago Univ. T. C. (193 ft 9 in)
Shot Put—George Woods, Pacific Coast Club (69 ft 9¼ in)
Hammer—Jim Neugent, Oklahoma Christian (182 ft 2 in)

National Collegiate (NCAA) Indoor Championships
(Detroit, March 10–11)

60 Yards—Herb Washington, Michigan State (0:06.1)
440 Yards—Larance Jones, Northeast Missouri (0:48.3)
600 Yards—Dale Gibson, Mississippi State (1:11.3)
880 Yards—Dave Wottle, Bowling Green (1:51.8)
1,000 Yards—Mike Mosser, West Virginia (2:08.9)
Mile—Ken Popejoy, Michigan State (4:02.9)
2 miles—Sid Sink, Bowling Green (8:36.6)
Invitation Mile—Tom Von Ruden, Pacific Coast Club, Long Beach, Calif. (4:04.3)

60-Yard Hurdles—Tom McMannon, Notre Dame (0:07.2)
Mile Relay—Adelphi (Ray Lee, Keith Davis, Dennis Walker, Clyde McPherson, 3:15.8)
2-Mile Relay—Illinois (Dave Kaemerer, Ron Phillips, Lee LaBadie, Rob Mango; 7:30)
Distance Medley Relay—Bowling Green (Craig MacDonald, Ted Farver, Sid Sink, David Wottle; 9:49.6)
Shot Put—Doug Lane, So. California (64 ft 3½ in)
35-Pound Weight Throw—Jacques Accambray, Kent State (71 ft 3¼ in)
Long Jump—Henry Hines, So. California (25 ft 10 in)
Triple Jump—Barry McClure, Middle Tennessee (52 ft 10½ in)
High Jump—Chris Dunn, Colgate (7 ft 2¾ in)
Pole Vault—Jan Johnson, Alabama (17 ft 1½ in)
Team—University of Southern California (19 pts)

National Collegiate (NCAA) Outdoor Championships
(Eugene, Oreg., June 1–3)

100 Meters—Warren Edmonson, UCLA (0:10.2)
200 Meters—Larry Burton, Purdue (0:20.5)
400 Meters—John Smith, UCLA (0:44.5)
800 Meters—Willie Thomas, Tennessee (1:47.1)
1,500 Meters—Dave Wottle, Bowling Green (3:39.7)
5,000 Meters—Steve Prefontaine, Oregon (13:31.4)
10,000 Meters—John Halberstadt, Oklahoma State (28:50.4)
3,000-Meter Steeplechase—Joe Lucas, Georgetown (8:30.2)
110-Meter Hurdles—Jerry Wilson, So. California (0:13.4)
400-Meter Hurdles—Bruce Collins, Pennsylvania (0:49.1)
440-Yard Relay—So. California (Randy Williams, Edesel Garrison, Leon Brown, Willie Deckard; 0:39.6)
Mile Relay—UCLA (Reggie Echols, Ron Gaddis, Benny Brown, John Smith; 3:05.3)
High Jump—Tom Woods, Oregon State (7 ft 3¼ in)
Long Jump—Randy Williams, So. California (26 ft. 8¼ in)
Triple Jump—James Butts, UCLA (52 ft 2¼ in)
Pole Vault—Dave Roberts, Rice (17 ft 3 in)
Shot Put—Fred DeBernardi, Texas-El Paso (66 ft 6½ in)
Discus—Fred DeBernardi (196 ft 5 in)
Hammer Throw—Al Schoterman, Kent State (231 ft 3 in)
Javelin—Rick Dowswell, Ohio University (265 ft 11 in)
Team—University of California at Los Angeles (82 pts)

Other AAU Events

440-Yard Relay—BOHAA T. C., Brooklyn, N. Y. (0:41.3)
880-Yard Relay—United A. A., Brooklyn (1:26.2)
2½-Mile Medley Relay—New York A. C. (9:58.2)
Mile Relay—United A. A. (3:16.5)
2-Mile Relay—New York A. C. (7:47)
4-Mile Relay—New York A. C. (17:28.4)
All-Around—Karl Harz, Rutherford, N. J. (7,976 pts)
56-Pound Weight Throw—Tom Miller, New York A. C. (41 ft 6¾ in)

Decathlon and Pentathlon Champions

AAU Decathlon—Jeff Bennett, U. S. Army (7,910 pts)
USTFF (national)—Bruce Jenner, Graceland College (7,670 pts)
USTFF Decathlon (meet)—Andrew Pettes, Oklahoma (7,447 pts)
NCAA Decathlon—Ron Evans, Connecticut (7,571 pts)
NAIA Decathlon—Gary Hill, Oklahoma Christian (7,538 pts)
AAU Women's Pentathlon—Jennifer Meldrum, Toronto (4,251 pts)
AAU Junior Pentathlon—Denoven Jones, unattached (3,279 pts)

Other Team Champions

NCAA College Division—Eastern Michigan (93 pts)
NAIA—North Carolina Central (68 pts)
IC4-A—Pennsylvania (53 pts)

Marathons

AAU—Edmund Norris, Brockton, Mass. (2:24:42.8)
Boston—Olavi Suomalainen, Finland (2:15.39)
USTFF (national)—Lucian Rosa, Wisconsin-Parkside (2:22.13)
USTFF (meet)—Terry Ziegler, Oklahoma (2:27.27)
NAIA—Wayne Franjello, Boston State (2:41:13.4)
Canada—Jerome Dayton, Toronto (2:23.13)

AAU Distance Runs

15 kilometers—Chuck Smead, Santa Barbara, Calif. (49:10.2)
20 kilometers—Tom Hoffman, Fort Atkinson, Wis. (1:05.04)
30 kilometers—Paul Talkington, Summit A. C. (1:35.17)

AAU Walks

10 kilometers—Larry Young, Sibley, Mo. (0:44.51)
15 kilometers—Larry Young (1:10:21.8)
20 kilometers—Larry Young (1:32:43.1)
25 kilometers—Larry Young (1:57.28)
30 kilometers—Larry Young (2:28:09)
40 kilometers—Larry Young (3:39:59.4)
One-Hour—Dave Romansky, Pennsville, N. J. (8 miles, 80 yards)

International Competition

At Richmond, Va. (March 17, indoors)—Men: United States 79, USSR 69; women: United States 53, USSR 43

MISCELLANEOUS SPORTS SUMMARIES

ARCHERY

World Championships
(Udine, Italy)

Men—Freestyle: John C. Williams, Cranesville, Pa. (1,068 pts); *bare bow:* L. Bergen, Sweden (952)
Women—Freestyle: Maureen Bechdolt, Cincinnati, Ohio (921); *bare bow:* I. Grandquist, Sweden (751)

National Field Archery Association Championships
(Ludlow, Mass., July 24–28)

Men—Open freestyle: C. Dean Pridgen, Kansas City, Mo. (2,774 pts); *amateur freestyle:* Gale Cavallin, George AFB, Calif. (2,779); *youth freestyle:* John Ashburn, Woodridge, Ill. (2,621); *over 55 freestyle:* Elmer Little, San Diego, Calif. (2,656); *open bare bow:* Dennis Cline, Geneva, Ill. (2,616); *amateur bare bow:* Mike Flier, Pekin, Ill. (2,535); *youth bare bow:* Allan Jobbes, Sunland, Calif. (2,259); *over 55 bare bow:* Martin Kenny, Carmel, N.Y. (2,186); *open bow hunter:* Cal Vogt, Van Nuys, Calif. (2,472)
Women—Open freestyle: Darlene Collier, Moab, Utah (2,715 pts); *amateur freestyle:* Lesley Truhel, Newcastle, Me. (2,394); *girls' freestyle:* Judith A. Rogers, Quincy, Ill. (1,858); *over 55 freestyle:* Sandy Elott, Atlanta, Ga. (2,253); *open bare bow:* Janis R. Beverly, Americus, Ga. (2,282); *amateur bare bow:* Sandy Clack, Dakota, Ill. (1,836)

National Archery Association Championships
(Oxford, Ohio, Aug. 8–11)

Men—Amateur: Kevin Erlandson, Sacramento, Calif. (2,842 pts); *professional:* Edward S. Brown, Ledyard, Conn. (2,699); *intermediate:* Darrell Pace, Cincinnati, Ohio (2,859); *junior:* Larry Murdock, West Chester, Pa. (2,840)
Women—Amateur: Ruth Rowe, Pittsburgh, Pa. (2,701 pts); *professional:* Nancy R. Brown, Ledyard, Conn. (2,319); *intermediate:* Louise Grondin, Hamilton, Miss. (2,636); *junior:* Jodi Crowl, York, Pa. (2,752)
Field Archery—Men: Freestyle: amateur: John C. Williams, Cranesville, Pa. (1,100 pts); *professional:* John Kleman, Latrobe, Pa. (1,058); *intermediate:* Douglas Brothers, Cincinnati (1,040); *bare bow:* Rodney L. Hoover, Myerstown, Pa. (993).—*Women: Freestyle: amateur:* Janet Craig, Aurora, Ind. (1,012); *intermediate:* Vicki Kimmich, Middletown, Pa. (536)

BADMINTON

United States Open Championships (Omaha, Nebr., April 3–5)—*Men's singles:* Sture Johnsson, Sweden; *women's singles:* Eva Twedberg, Sweden; *men's doubles:* Elliott Stuart and Derek Talbot, England; *women's doubles:* Anne Berglund and Pernille Kaagaard, Denmark; *mixed doubles:* Fleming Delfs and Pernille Kaagaard, Denmark; *senior men's singles:* Jim Poole, North Ridge, Calif; *senior men's doubles:* Jim McQuie, Kirkwood, Mo., and Ted Moehlmann, St. Louis; *senior women's doubles:* Ethel Marshall and Bea Massman, Buffalo, N.Y. *senior mixed doubles:* Jim Poole and Mary Ann Breckell, Los Angeles
United States Closed Championships (Omaha, Nebr., March 30–April 2)—*Men's singles:* Chris Kinard, Pasadena, Calif.; *women's singles:* Pam Stockton, Flint, Mich; *men's doubles:* Jim Poole, North Ridge, Calif., and Don Paup, East Lansing, Mich.; *women's doubles:* Polly Bretzke, Flint, Mich., and Pam Stockton; *mixed doubles:* Tom Carmichael, Clarkston, Mich., and Pam Stockton
United States Junior Championships (Eugene, Oreg., March 19–22)—*Boys' singles:* Charles Coakley, Costa Mesa, Calif.; *girls' singles:* Pam Stockton, Flint, Mich.; *boys' doubles:* Charles Coakley and Peter Steinbroner, Manhattan Beach, Calif.; *girls' doubles:* Pam Stockton and Sandy Muthig, Detroit; *mixed doubles:* Charles Coakley and Traci White, Manhattan Beach, Calif.
All-England Championships (Wembley, March 22–25)—*Men's singles:* Rudy Hartono, Indonesia; *women's singles:* Noriko Nakayama, Japan; *men's doubles:* Christian and Ade Chandra, Indonesia; *women's doubles:* Machiko Aizawa and Etsuko Takenaka, Japan; *mixed doubles:* Svend Pri and Ulla Strand, Denmark

BILLIARDS

Pocket

*World—*Irving Crane, Rochester, N.Y.
*United States Men's Open—*Steve Mizerak, Carteret, N.J.
*United States Women's Open—*Jean Balukas, Brooklyn, N.Y.
*Men's Intercollegiate—*Andy Tennant, Wisconsin
*Women's Intercollegiate—*Krista Hartmann, Santa Fe College, Fla.

3-Cushion

*World—*Raymont Ceulemans, Belgium

BOWLING

American Bowling Congress Tournament (Long Beach, Calif., Feb. 26–May 30)—*Regular Division: singles:* Bill Pointer, Pontiac, Mich. (739); *doubles:* Jerry Nutt and Bill Stanfield, Grand Rapids, Mich. (1,350); *all-events:* Mac Lowry, Seattle, Wash. (2,026); *team:* Hamm's Beer, Minneapolis (3,101).—*Classic Division: singles:* Teata Semiz, River Edge, N.J. (754); *doubles:* Carmen Salvino, Chicago, and Barry Asher,

Costa Mesa, Calif. (1,366); *all-events:* Teata Semiz (1,994); *team:* Basch Advertising, New York (3,099); score posted in 3-game roll-off among six highest teams).—*Booster Division: team:* North Avenue Furniture, Grand Junction, Colo. (2,824)
Women's International Bowling Congress (Kansas City, April 6–May 27)—*Open Division: singles:* D. D. Jacobson, Playa Del Rey, Calif. (737); *doubles:* Judy Roberts, Denver, and Betty Remmick, Lakewood, Colo. (1,247); *all-events:* Millie Martorella, Rochester, N.Y. (1,877); *team:* Angeltown Creations, Placentia, Calif. (2,838).—*Division I: singles:* Shirley Frank, New York (657); *doubles:* Evelyn Porter and Billie Caldwell, Chicago (1,215); *all-events:* Janice Denning, Wilmington, Del. (1,827); *team:* Donson Contractors, Alsip, Ill. (2,707).—*Division II: singles:* Elvadean Parrish, Edina, Mo. (587); *doubles:* Jerry Wise and Sue Minks, Higginsville, Mo. (1,109); *all-events:* Yvonne Wilcox, Shreveport, La. (1,647); *team:* Krolczyk's Plaza, Rosenberg, Texas (2,398).—*Queens Tournament: champion:* Dorothy Fothergill, North Attleboro, Mass. (defeated Maureen Harris, Madison, Wis., 890–841, in final, May 19)
Bowling Proprietors Association of America Open Championships—*Men* (New York, Jan. 3–8): Don Johnson, Akron, Ohio (defeated George Pappas, Charlotte, N.C., 233–224, in final); *women* (Denver, May 20–24): Lorrie Koch, Carpentersville, Ill. (defeated Mary Baker, Central Islip, N.Y., 222–193, in final)
National Duckpin Bowling Congress (Richmond, Va., March 18–May 17)—*Men: singles:* tie between Wally Adams, Cheshire, Conn., and Irvin Wagner, Mt. Airy, Md. (468); *doubles:* Charles Creamer and W. M. Jenkins, Richmond, Va. (915); *all-events:* James Garton, Hagerstown, Md. (1,292); *team:* Guida's Dairy, New Britain, Conn. (2,070).—*Women: singles:* Barbara Brown, Richmond, Va. (461); *doubles:* Terry Vaccaro and Dorothy Czjaka, Glastonbury, Conn. (798); *all-events:* Cathy Sanders, Baltimore (1,203); *team:* Ports Sports Shop, Baltimore (1,902); *mixed doubles:* Mary Orme and Bob Marchone, Washington (830)

BRIDGE, CONTRACT

World Team Olympiad (Miami Beach, Fla., June 9–24)—*Men:* Italy (Pietro Forquet, Benito Gorozzo, Georgio Belladonna, Walter Avarelli, Camillo Pabis Ticci, and Massimo D'Alelio) defeated United States in final by 65 points; *Women:* Italy; *Mixed Team:* Bob Goldman, Jim Jacoby, Robert Wolff, Dallas; Nancy Alpaugh, New Orleans, Mrs. Robert Wolff, Dallas, and Heidi Noland, Lake Charles, La.

American Contract Bridge Association Championships
Spring Nationals
(Cincinnati, March 18–27)

*Men's Pairs—*Steve Robinson and Kit Woolsey, Washington, D. C.
*Women's Pairs—*Kerri Davis and Rhoda Walsh, Los Angeles
*Men's Teams—*Jack Blair, Tulsa; Jim Jacoby, Dallas; John Simon, St. Louis; Paul Swanson, Morgantown, W. Va.; and Robert Wolff, Dallas
*Women's Teams—*Jane Farell, Los Angeles; Emma Jean Hawes, Fort Worth, Texas; Mrs. Dorothy Hayden Truscott, New York; and Sue Picus, Parsippany, N. J.
*Open Pairs—*Tie between team of Barry Crane, Los Angeles, and Dr. John Fisher, Dallas, and team of Merle Tom, New York, and Matt Granovetter, Jersey City, N. J.
*Vanderbilt Knockout Team—*Steve Altman, Gene Neiger, Alan Sontag, Joel Stuart, Peter Weichsel, all of New York, and Tom Smith, Greenwich, Conn.

Summer Nationals
(Denver, July 21–Aug. 2)

*Masters Mixed Teams—*Mike and Gail Moss, New York, and Bill and Marietta Passell, Ardsley, N. Y.
*Life Master Pairs—*Alvin Roth, New York, and Barbara Rappaport, East Orange, N. J.
*Spingold Knockout Teams—*B. Jay Becker, Michael Becker, Jeff Rubens, and Andy Bernstein, New York

Fall Nationals
(Lancaster, Pa., Nov. 10–21)

*Mixed Pairs—*John Nohan, Los Angeles, and Peggy Sutherlin, San Francisco
*Life Master Men's Pairs—*Marc Jacobus, Fair Lawn, N. J., and Les Bart, Englewood, N. J.
*Life Master Women's Pairs—*Amalya Kearse, New York, and Rhoda Walsh, Los Angeles
*Blue Ribbon Pairs—*Warren Kornfield, New York, and Richard Khautin, New York
*Reisinger Board-a-Match Teams—*Steve Goldberg, Marietta, Ga.; Steve Robinson, Washington, D. C.; Steve Parker, Alexandria, Va.; and Lou Bluhm, Atlanta

CANOEING

United States Championships
(Cambridge, Ohio, Aug. 12–13)

Men's Kayak

Singles, 500 Meters—John Van Cleave, Rusty Pelican O. A., Newport Beach, Calif. (1:56.9)
Singles, 1,000 Meters—Pete Weigand, Rusty Pelican (4:27)
Singles, 10,000 Meters—Joe Beczak, New York A. C. (44:40)
Tandem, 500 Meters—Gene and Henry Krawczyk, New York A. C. (1:47.6)

Tandem, 1,000 Meters—Pete Weigand and Bob Hoag, Rusty Pelican (3:49.1)
Tandem, 10,000 Meters—Clyde Britt and Joe Bilsky, Wanda C. C., N. J. (44:51.7)
Fours, 1,000 Meters—Rusty Pelican O. A. (Weigand, Van Cleave, Hoag, Bill Leach; 3:32.9)
Fours, 10,000 Meters—Rusty Pelican (Leach, John Glazier, Van Cleave, Greg Rose; 38:20.7)

Women's Kayak

Singles, 500 Meters—Marcia Smoke, Niles (Mich.) K. C. (2:08.7)
Singles, 5,000 Meters—Sperry Rademacher, Niles K. C. (26:19.6)
Tandem, 500 Meters—Marcia Smoke and Sperry Rademacher (2:04.3)
Tandem, 5,000 Meters—Marcia Smoke and Marian Flood, Niles K. C. (25:51.7)
Fours, 500 Meters—Niles K. C. (Marcia Smoke, Sperry Rademacher, Loli Flood, Marian Flood; 1:58)
Fours, 5,000 Meters—Lincoln Park B. C. (Carol Davis, Iva Sawtelle, Carol Triebold, Roxanne Triebold; 24:33.7)

Canoe

Singles, 500 Meters—Roland Muhlen, Rusty Pelican O. A. (2:05.4)
Singles, 1,000 Meters—Roland Muhlen (4:50.5)
Singles, 10,000 Meters—Ray Effinger, Inwood C. C., New York (49:19.5)
Tandem, 500 Meters—Roland Muhlen and Dave Landenwitch, Rusty Pelican (1:57.1)
Tandem, 1,000 Meters—Andy Weigand and Roland Muhlen (4:03.6)
Tandem, 10,000 Meters—Joe Brugger and Dean Ferrandini, Rusty Pelican (47:23.7)
Fours, 1,000 Meters—Rusty Pelican (Andy Weigand, Roland Muhlen, Pete Weigand, Dave Landenwitch; no time)

Wild Water Kayak Championships
(Buena Vista, Colo.)

Men—Eric Evans, Hanover, N. H. (25:32.5)
Women—Carol Fisher, Evanston, Ill. (29:08.3)
Junior—Bill Nutt, Etna, N. H. (27:03.8)

CHESS

World Championships

Men—Bobby Fischer, Los Angeles, defeated Boris Spassky, USSR, 12½–8½ at Reykjavik, Iceland, July 11–Sept. 1. (See special feature beginning on page 53)
Women—Nona Gaprindashvili, USSR, defeated Alla Kushnir, USSR, 8½–7½

National Championships

United States—Tie among Robert Byrne, Ossining, N. Y.; Lubomir Kavelek, Washington, D. C.; and Sam Reshevsky, Spring Valley, N. Y.
United States Open—Walter Browne, Australia
United States Women—Tie between Marilyn K. Braun, Milwaukee, and Eva Aronson, St. Petersburg, Fla.
United States Junior—Craig Chellstorp, Chicago

CROSS-COUNTRY

NCAA—*University Division* (Houston, Texas, Nov. 20, 6 miles): Neil Cusack, East Tennessee (28:23); *team:* Tennessee (134 pts). *College Division* (Wheaton, Ill. Nov. 11, 5 miles): Mike Slack, North Dakota State (24:36); *team:* North Dakota State (83)
NAIA (Liberty, Mo., Nov. 18, 5 miles)—Mike Nixon, Pittsburg State (24:29.4); *team:* Malone (92 pts)
AAU (Chicago, Nov. 25, 10,000 meters)—Frank Shorter, Florida Track Club, Gainesville (30:42); *team:* Florida Track Club (42 pts)
USTFF (Denton, Texas, Nov. 23, 6 miles)—John Halberstadt, Oklahoma State (29:01); *team:* Oklahoma State (30 pts)
IC4-A (New York, Nov. 13, 5 miles)—*University Division:* Mike Keogh, Manhattan (24:03.4); *team:* Manhattan (40). *College Division:* Daniel Moynihan, Tufts (24:34.9); *team:* Lehigh (50 pts)
Women's AAU (Long Beach, Calif., Nov. 25, 2½ miles)—Francie Larrieu, San Jose, Calif. (13:27); *team:* Falcon T. C., Seattle (29 pts)
Women's Pan-American (Victoria, Canada, Dec. 2; 2.2 miles)—Doris Brown, Seattle (11:38); *team:* Canada (14 pts)

CURLING

World (Garmisch-Partenkirchen, West Germany, March 21–25)—Canada (Orest Meleschuk, skip); defeated United States, 10–9, in final
United States—Grafton, N. Dak. (Robert LaBonte, skip)
Canada—Fort Rouge C. C., Winnipeg (Meleschuk, skip)
United States Women—Wilmette, Ill. (Mrs. Gerry Duguid, skip)

CYCLING

United States Championships
(Milwaukee, Aug. 1–6)

Road Events

Senior (120 miles)—John Howard, Springfield, Mo. (4:30:18)
Junior (48 miles)—Ted Waterbury, Columbus, Ohio (1:54:30)
Veterans (40 miles)—Andre Berclaz, East Islip, N. Y. (1:42:10)
Women (28 miles)—Debby Bradley, Iowa (1:19:10)
Intermediate Boys (12 miles)—Les Barcezewski, West Allis, Wis. (28:38)

Track Events
(Kenosha, Wis., Aug. 1–4)

Sprints—Gary Campbell, Paramount, Calif.
10 miles—Bob Phillips, Baltimore
1,000 Meters—Steve Woznick, Armed Forces (1:10.95)
4,000-Meter Pursuit—Jim Van der Velde, Glen Ellyn, Ill. (5:02.7)
4,000-Meter Team Pursuit—Southern California (Tom Sneddon, Butch Stinton, Ron Skarin, Cyril Johnson)
Women's Sprints—Sue Novarra, Detroit
3,000-Meter Pursuit—Clara Teyssier, San Diego, Calif.
Junior Overall—Nelson Saldana, New York, N. Y.
Intermediate Overall—Les Barcezewski, West Allis, Wis.

Other Events

Tour de France (2,380 miles)—Eddy Merckx, Belgium; fourth straight victory (riding time: 4 days, 12 hours, 27 minutes, 59 seconds)

DOG SHOWS

Westminster Kennel Club (New York, Feb. 14–15)—Group winners (3,093 dogs shown)—*sporting and best in show* (for second year in row): Dr. Milton E. Prickett's English springer spaniel, Ch. Chinoe's Adamant James, of Lexington, Ky.; *toy:* Mamie R. Gregory's Maltese, Ch. Joanne-Chen's Maya Dancer, of Fort Lauderdale, Fla.; *hound:* estate of Elaine S. Hoffman's basenji, Ch. Reveille Re-Up, of Washington, D. C.; *terrier:* Walter F. Goodman and Adele Goodman's Skye, Ch. Glamour Gang Buster, of Oyster Bay, N. Y.; *working:* Mr. and Mrs. Derek Rayne's Pembroke Welsh corgi, Ch. Nebriowa Miss Bobbi Sox, of Carmel, Calif.; *nonsporting:* Mr. and Mrs. Frank Dale's and Edward Jenner's miniature poodle, Ch. Tally Ho Tiffany, of Hidden Hills, Calif.
International Kennel Club (Chicago, April 1–2)—Group winners (3,690 dogs shown)—*toy and best in show:* Mrs. Mamie R. Gregory's Maltese, Ch. Joanne-Chen's Maya Dancer, of Fort Lauderdale, Fla.; *hound:* Krissy Kennedy's and Mrs. Janis Mackimm's bassett, Ch. Basil Rathbone II, of Palos Park, Ill.; *working:* Mr. and Mrs. J. W. Smith's Pembroke Welsh corgi, Ch. Kydor Cresta, of Gowanda, N. Y.; *terrier:* Mrs. B. G. Frame's West Highland white, Ch. Urston Pinmoney E. Pedlar, of Indianapolis; *nonsporting:* Edward Jenner's standard poodle, Ch. Acadia Xaari, of Richmond, Ill; *sporting:* Mrs. Peggy Westphal's ascob cocker Spaniel, Ch. Sagamore Toccoa, of Bedford, N. Y.

FENCING

United States Championships
(Waltham, Mass., July 1–8)

Individual—*Foil:* Bert Freeman, Quantico Marines; *épée:* James Melcher, New York Fencers Club; *saber:* Alex Orban, New York A. C.; *women's foil:* Ruth White, Baltimore.
Team—*Foil:* Salle Santelli, New York (Ed Ballinger, Uriah Jones, Bob Russell, Maurice Kamhi); *épée:* New York A. C. (George Masin, Paul Pesthy, Stephen Netburn, Vito Mannino); *saber:* New York A. C. (Jack Keane, Alex Orban, Al Morales, Scaba Gall); *women's foil:* Salle Santelli, New York (Denise O'Connor, Ann O'Donnell, Carol Chesney, Jay Reid)
Under 19 Division—*Foil:* Dave Littell, Champaign, Ill.; *épée:* Christopher Jennings, Peabody, Mass.; *saber:* Tom Losonczy, Passaic, N. J.; *women's foil:* Iza Farkas, New Brunswick, N. J.

National Collegiate (NCAA) Championships
(Chicago, March 23–25)

Individual—*Foil:* Tyrone Simmons, University of Detroit; *épée:* Ernesto Fernandez, University of Pennsylvania; *saber:* Bruce Soriano, Columbia
Team (3-weapon)—University of Detroit (73 pts)

Women's Intercollegiate F. A.
(University Park, Pa., April 7–8)

Individual—Ruth White, New York University
Team—Cornell (91 pts)

GYMNASTICS

National Collegiate (NCAA) Championships
(Ames, Iowa, April 6–8)

All-Around—Steve Hug, Stanford (107.75 pts)
Floor Exercises—Odess Lovin, Oklahoma (18.725)
Pommel Horse—Russ Hoffman, Iowa State (18.950)
Rings—Dave Seal, Indiana State (18.750)
Vault—Gary Morava, So. Illinois (18.40)
Parallel Bars—Dennis Mazur, Iowa State (18.45)
Horizontal Bar—Tom Lindner, So. Illinois (18.90)
Team—Southern Illinois (315.925)

HANDBALL

AAU Champions

One-Wall (New York)—*Singles:* Steve Sandler, New York; *doubles:* Marty Decatur and Marty Katzen, New York
4-Wall (Houston, Oct. 4–8)—*Singles:* Lou Russo, New York A. C.; *doubles:* Ray Neveau, Oshkosh, Wis., and Sammy Fein, Milwaukee; *masters singles:* Tom Schorendorf, Milwaukee; *masters doubles:* Alvis Grant, Dallas, and Cecil Lloyd, Shreveport, La.

U. S. Handball Association Champions

4-Wall (Seattle, April 15–23)—*Singles:* Fred Lewis, Miami Beach, Fla.; *doubles:* Kent Fusselman, Warren, Ohio, and Al Drews, Cleveland; *masters singles:* Rudy Stadleberger, San Francisco; *masters doubles:* Ken Schneider and Phil Elbert, Chicago; *golden masters doubles:* Bill Feivou and George Brotemarkle, Los Angeles
1-Wall (Brooklyn, N. Y.)—*Singles:* Wally Ulbrich, Brooklyn; *doubles:* Wally Ulbrich and Mark Levine, Brooklyn; *masters doubles:* Joe Danilczyk and Julie Rothman, New York; *junior singles:* Ken Ginty, New York A. C.

YMCA National Championships

4-Wall (Norfolk, Va., March 23–26)—*Singles:* Paul Haber, Chicago; *doubles:* Fred Lewis and Steve Lott, New York; *masters doubles:* Lloyd Wood, Norfolk, Va., and Al McCulloch, Springfield, Va.

Canadian Championships
(Edmonton, Alberta, March 16–18)

4-Wall—*Open: Singles:* Pat Kirby, Brooklyn, N. Y.; *doubles:* Simie Fein, Milwaukee, and Ray Neveau, Oshkosh, Wis.; *masters doubles:* Harold McClean and Norm Morehouse, Toronto.—*Closed: Singles:* Mel Brown, Vancouver, B. C.; *doubles:* Ron Billig and Jack Seed, Edmonton

HORSE SHOWS

American Horse Shows Association Champions

Green Conformation Hunter—Mr. and Mrs. John Leib's Automation
Regular Conformation Hunter—Mrs. Robert Fischer's Logically
Amateur-Owner Hunter—Jane Womble's Third of August
First-Year Green Working Hunter—Third of August
Second-Year Green Working Hunter—Dr. and Mrs. Harry Hemphill's Quiet Please
Regular Working Hunter—Jane Womble's Sign the Card
Junior Hunter—Nancy Baroody's War Dress
Small Pony Hunter—Mrs. J. Austin duPont's Liseter Gold Coin
Open 3-Gaited Saddle Horse—Julianne Schmutz' Forest Song
Amateur 3-Gaited Saddle Horse—Mrs. Alan Robson's Christmas Carol
Junior Exhibitor's 3-Gaited Saddle Horse—Nancy Clatworthy's Gala Affair
American Saddlebred 3-Gaited Pleasure Horse—Mr. and Mrs. Jone E. Huggins' Nom de Plume
Open 5-Gaited Saddle Horse—Julianne Schmutz' Reflections
Junior Exhibitor's 5-Gaited Saddle Horse—Mrs. Robert Wentz' Juarez
Amateur 5-Gaited Saddle Horse—Julianne Schmutz' Gold Treat
Open Fine Harness Horse—Mrs. Alan Robson's Serve Notice
Amateur Fine Harness Horse—Frank C. Gearhart's Strike Command
Roadster—Alpha-Sun Stables' Road Ranger
Hackney Pony—Mrs. Kenneth Wheeler's B & J's Mr. Orbit
Open Harness Pony—Mr. and Mrs. John Gridley's Tijuana Brass
Amateur Harness Pony—Mrs. Alan Robson's Debbie's Fashion
Shetland Harness Pony—Mrs. Virgil Cagle's Twinkles Challenger
Shetland Roadster Pony—River View Pony Farm's River View's Pistol Pete
Arabian—Lucille Betts' Burrtez
Half-Arabian—Phil Demery's Stormy Aka
Pleasure Morgan—Great Oaks Morgan Horses' Ashley De Boyd
Park Morgan—Edwin W. Schlehuber's San de Glenn R.
Stock Horse—Katherine H. Haley's Shirley Chex
Tennessee Walking Horse—Mr. and Mrs. Cebern L. Lee's Gala Go Boy
Trail Horse—Ashlyn Sansome's Sierra El Gallito
Welch Pleasure Pony—Donna Lynn Dickson's Broad Axe Jack Frost
Western Pleasure Horse—Gail Locke's Gringo's Tramp
Junior Exhibitor's Western Pleasure Horse—Norris R. Swindle's Sen Gee Bar

Special Awards

Horseman of the Year—Neal Shapiro, Glen Head, N. Y.
Horsewoman of the Year—Mrs. Max O. Bonham, Santa Barbara, Calif.
Devereux Trophy—Sullivan (Dave) Davis, Morristown, N. J.

Equestrian Championships

Saddle Seat—Judy Maccari, Fort Lauderdale, Fla.
Hunter Seat—Katie Monahan, Bloomington Hills, Mich.
Stock Seat—Cynthia Ostolaza, Washington, D. C.
Dressage—Mike Cabell, Denver

National Horse Show Awards

Saddle Seat (Good Hands) Trophy—Mary Lib DeNure, Albany, N. Y.
ASPCA Maclay Trophy—Leslie Burr, Long Valley, N. J.
International Jumping—*Team:* United States (Kathy Kusner, Frank Chapot, Bill Steinkraus, Neal Shapiro); *individual:* Frank Chapot

U. S. Equestrian Team Championships

Three-Day Championships—*Open Intermediate:* Johnny O, ridden by J. Michael Plumb, Chesapeake City, Md.; *Open Preliminary:* Clodomir, ridden by James C. Wofford, Milford, Kans.

ICE SKATING

Speed Skating
World Championships

Men (Oslo, Norway, Feb. 19–20)

All-Around—Ard Schenk, Netherlands (171.549 pts)
500 Meters—Tie between Ard Schenk and Roar Gronvold, Norway (0:40.14)
1,500 Meters—Ard Schenk (2:03.06)
5,000 Meters—Ard Schenk (7:22.84)
10,000 Meters—Ard Schenk (15:22.09)

Men, Sprints (Eskilstuna, Sweden, Feb. 26–27)

All-Around—Leo Linkovesi, Finland (160.925 pts)
500 Meters (first race)—Leo Linkovesi (0:38.97)
500 Meters (second race)—Leo Linkovesi (0:39)
1,000 Meters (first race)—Ard Schenk, Netherlands (1:20.02)
1,000 Meters (second race)—Ard Schenk (1:19.93)

Women (Heerenveen, Netherlands, March 4–5)

All-Around—Atje Keulen-Deelstra, Netherlands (185.341 pts)
500 Meters—Dianne Holum, Northbrook, Ill. (0:43.59)
1,000 Meters—Atje Keulen-Deelstra (1:30.49)
1,500 Meters—Atje Keulen-Deelstra (2:17.98)
3,000 Meters—Stien Baas-Kaiser, Netherlands (4:54.62)

ARD SCHENK of the Netherlands combined power and grace in winning four events and tying one in the World Speed Skating Championship at Oslo, Norway.

UPI

Women, Sprints (Eskilstuna, Sweden, Feb. 26–27)

All-Around—Monika Pflug, West Germany (183.085 pts)
500 Meters (first race)—Sheila Young, Detroit (0:44.20)
500 Meters (second race)—Sheila Young (0:44.76)
1,000 Meters (first race)—Dianne Holum, Northbrook, Ill. (1:31.88)
1,000 Meters (second race)—Dianne Holum (1:32.65)

United States Championships
National Outdoor
(St. Paul, Minn., Jan. 29)

Champion—Barth Levy, Colorado Springs (22 pts)
⅙-Mile—Mike Passarella, Chicago (0:23.7)
440 Yards—Bill Heinkel, West Allis, Wis. (0:35.5)
880 Yards—Barth Levy (1:19.3)
¾-Mile—Barth Levy (2:18.5)
Mile—Mike Crowe, St. Louis (3:00.3)
2 Miles—Barth Levy (5:57)
5 Miles—Mike Woods, West Allis, Wis. (14:05.6)

Women

All-Around—Tie between Ruth Moore, Newton, Mass., and Nancy Thorne, Madison, Wis. (15 pts)
⅙-Mile—Nancy Thorne (0:25.8)
440 Yards—Nancy Thorne (0:39)
880 Yards—Nancy Thorne (1:22.1)
¾-Mile—Ruth Moore (2:22.9)
Mile—Ruth Moore (3:17.6)

National Indoor
(St. Louis, March 11–12)

All-Around—Barth Levy, Colorado Springs (20 pts)
440 Yards—Barth Levy (0:38.2)
880 Yards—Barth Levy (1:19.4)
¾-Mile—Barth Levy (2:02.4)
Mile—Bill Noyes, DeMoria, Calif. (2:46)
2 Miles—Bill Noyes (5:52.8)

Women

All-Around—Michele Conroy, St. Paul (15 pts)
440 Yards—Jennie Walsh, Los Angeles (0:43.2)
880 Yards—Michele Conroy (1:26.7)
¾-Mile—Michele Conroy (2:16)
Mile—Michele Conroy (3:06)

North American Outdoor
(Alpena, Mich., Feb. 5–6)

All-Around—Barth Levy, Colorado Springs (33 pts)
Women's All-Around—Judy Spraggs, Berkeley, Mich. (20 pts)

North American Indoor
(Los Angeles, March 18–19)

All-Around—Bill Noyes, DeMoria, Calif. (18 pts)
Women's All-Around—Michele Conroy, St. Paul (15 pts)

Figure Skating

World Championships (Calgary, Alberta, Canada, March 7–11)—*Men:* Ondrej Nepela, Czechoslovakia; *Women:* Beatrix Schuba, Austria; *pairs:* Irina Rodnina and Alexsei Ulanov, USSR; *dance:* Ludmila Pakhomova and Aleksandr Gorshkov, USSR
United States Championships (Long Beach, Calif., Jan. 14–16)—*Men:* Ken Shelley, Downey, Calif.; *women:* Janet Lynn, Rockford, Ill.; *pairs:* Ken Shelley and Jo Jo Starbuck, Downey, Calif.; *dance:* James Sladky, Solvay, N.Y., and Judy Schwomeyer, Indianapolis
Canadian Championships (Toronto, Jan. 14–16)—*Men:* Toller Cranston, Toronto; *women:* Karen Magnussen, North Vancouver, B.C.; *pairs:* Val and Sandra Bezic, Toronto; *dance:* Louise and Barry Soper, West Vancouver, B.C.

JUDO

National AAU Championships
(Philadelphia, April 28–29)

139 Pounds—Brian T. Yakata, New York
154 Pounds—Patrick Burris, Anaheim, Calif.
176 Pounds—Irwin L. Cohen, Chicago
205 Pounds—Doug Graham, Pacific
Heavyweight—Doug Nelson, Reno, Nev.
Open—Johnny Watts, Sacramento, Calif.

Women's Kata

Nage-No-Kata—Joan Fielding, New England, and Louise Piche, New England
Ju-No-Kata—Elizabeth Lee, Southern Pacific, and Kazuko Swauger, Southern Pacific
Katame-No-Kata—Virginia Bellamy, Virginia, and Alice Burkett, Virginia

LACROSSE

National Collegiate A.A. Champion—Virginia (defeated Johns Hopkins, 13–12, in final at College Park, Md., June 3)
National Club—Carlings L.C., Baltimore
All-Star Collegiate Game—South 18, North 14
U.S. Intercollegiate Lacrosse Association Champion—Hobart (defeated Washington College, 15–12, in final at Hobart, N.Y., May 27)
College Division Champions—*Central Atlantic:* Franklin and Marshall; *Central New York:* Cortland; *Colonial:* tie between Boston State and Springfield; *Ivy League:* Cornell; *Metropolitan New York:* Adelphi; *Midwest:* tie between Denison and Kenyon; *New England:* Brown; *Northern California:* San Francisco University; *Northeast:* Massachusetts; *Northern New York:* tie between Ithaca, Albany, and Clarkson; *Rocky Mountain:* Air Force Academy; *South Atlantic:* Washington and Lee; *Southern California:* Palo Alto

BILL MUNCEY, *driving hydroplane for Atlas Van Lines, rounds turn ahead of field en route to victory in Gold Cup race at Detroit. First-place purse was worth $44,750.*

UPI

MOTORBOATING

Unlimited Hydroplane Trophy Winners

Champion Spark Plug Regatta (Miami, June 4)—Atlas Van Lines; Bill Muncey, driver; average speed 105.448 mph
Kentucky Governor's Cup (Owensboro, June 11)—Atlas Van Lines; Bill Muncey; 106.529 mph
Gold Cup (Detroit, June 25)—Atlas Van Lines; Bill Muncey; 103.547 mph
Indiana Governor's Cup (Madison, July 5)—Atlas Van Lines; Bill Muncey (based on performance in heats as floodwater debris forced cancellation of final)
President's Cup (Washington, July 9)—Pride of Pay 'N Pak; Bill Sterett, Jr.; 109.090 mph
Atomic Cup Regatta (Pasco, Wash., July 23)—Atlas Van Lines; Bill Muncey
Seattle Seafair Trophy (Aug. 6)—Atlas Van Lines; Bill Muncey; 113.876 mph (Pride of Pay 'N Pak, with Bill Sterett driving, set world qualifying record of 125.581 for 3 laps in trials)
National Champion—Atlas Van Lines (Lee Schoenith, Detroit, owner)
National Champion Driver—Bill Muncey

Distance Races

Bahamas 500 (Freeport, June 9, 542 miles)—Sandy Satullo, Copper Kettle; 73.7 mph
Griffith Memorial (Fort Lauderdale, Fla., May 5, 200 miles)—Sandy Satullo; 73.7 mph
Hennessy Grand Prix (Point Pleasant, N. J., July 19, 181.3 miles)—Sandy Satullo; 72 mph
Hennessy Hurricane Classic (St. Petersburg, Fla., Feb. 26, 182 miles)—Sandy Satullo; 73.78 mph
London-Monte Carlo (June 10–24, 2,700 miles)—Mike Bellamy, Eddie Chater, Jim Baker, Britain; average speed 27.75 mph
Long Beach (Calif.)–Ensenada, Mexico (April 15, 173.28 miles)—Bill Martin; 71.6 mph
Long Beach (Calif.)–Hennessy (Aug. 19, 181 miles)—Dante Tognole; Dante Inferno; 67 mph
World Outboard (Lake Havasu, Ariz., Nov. 25–26, 696 miles)—Johnnie Sanders, Denver; 87 mph

Champions

World Offshore—Bobby Rautbord, Miami Beach, Fla.
Sam Griffith Trophy (international outboard)—Bobby Rautbord
APBA Inboard High-Point Championship—Bob Magoon, Miami Beach, Fla.
APBA Outboard Offshore High-Point Championship—Steve Shere

Predicted Log Trophies

APBA National Champion—Thomas Chretien, Auburndale, Mass.
George Codrington Trophy—Thomas Chretien
James Craig Trophy—Robert Wilson, California Y. C.
Express Cruiser Trophy—Joseph Broccia, New Rochelle, N. Y.
George K. Mikkelsen Trophy—Thomas Chretien
Martini 7 Rossi Trophy—Thomas Chretien
Motor Yacht Trophy—Joseph Broccia
National Predicted Log Trophy—Thomas Chretien
Herbert L. Stone Trophy—Thomas Chretien
International Team Trophy—New York Yacht Club

PARACHUTING

United States Championships
(Tahlequah, Okla., June 21–25)

Men—Overall: Roy Johnson, Warren, Ohio; style: Roy Johnson; accuracy: Bill Hayes, St. Louis
Women—Overall: Susan Rademaekers, Oakland, Calif.; style: Joan Emmack, Taft, Ga.; accuracy: Susan Rademaekers

World Championships
(Tahlequah, Okla., Aug. 5–19)

Men—Overall: Clayton Schoelpple, Hartwood, Va. (3.923 pts); accuracy: Lubas Majer, Czechoslovakia (0.12); style: Jean-Claude Armaing, France (7.18); team overall: USSR (17.78); team accuracy: Switzerland (3.79)
Women—Overall: Barbara Karkoschka, East Germany (5.256); accuracy: Albina Dioujova, USSR (3:01); style: Marie Baulez, France (8.84); team overall: USSR (24.07); team accuracy: Bulgaria (8.79)

POLO

National Championships

Open (Oak Brook, Ill., Sept. 10)—Milwaukee Polo Club (Bill Ylvisaker, Tommy Wayman, Benny Gutierrez, Robin Uihlein) 9, Tulsa 5
20-Goal—Red Doors Farm (Barrington, Ill.) 10, Sun Ranch (Cameron, Mont.) 6
16-Goal—Meadow Brook 7, Midfield 6
14-Goal—Milwaukee 9, Fairfield-Myopia (Boston) 7
12-Goal—Ravens 9, Potomac 5
8-Goal—Tucson 8, New Mexico 7
Intercollegiate—Connecticut 17, Virginia 15
Interscholastic—Culver (Ind.) Military Academy
National Polo League—Milwaukee

Intracircuit Championships

12-Goal—Milwaukee 5, Bunntyco-Kraml 4
Pacific 12-Goal—Hollywood Park 9, Santa Rosa 7
Northeast 12-Goal—Myopia (Mass.) 11, Bethpage (N. Y.) 5

RODEO

Rodeo Cowboy Association Champions

All-Around—Phil Lyne, George West, Texas
Bareback Bronco—Joe Alexander, Cora, Wyo.
Saddle Bronco—Mel Hyland, Surrey, British Columbia
Bull Riding—John Quintana, Creswell, Oreg.
Steer Wrestling—Roy Duvall, Warner, Okla.
Calf Roping—Phil Lyne
Team Roping—Leo Camarillo, Donald, Oreg.
Barrel Racing—Gail Petska, Norman, Okla.

ROLLER SKATING

World Championships
(Bremen, West Germany, Sept. 28–Oct. 1)

Men's Singles—Michael Obrecht, West Germany
Women's Singles—Petra Hausler, West Germany
Pairs—Ron and Gail Robovitzky, Detroit
Dance—Bonnie Lambert and Tom Straker, Pontiac, Mich.

National Championships

Men—Singles: Michael Jacques, Norwood, Mass.; figures: Billy Boyd, Seabrook, Md.; figures, international style: Randy Dayney, East Meadow, N. Y.; speed: Pat Bergin, Irving, Texas
Women—Singles: April Allen, Houston, Texas; figures: Debra Ann Palm, East Meadow, N. Y.; figures, international style: April Allen; speed: Jan Irvin, Irving, Texas
Pairs—Ron and Gail Robovitzky, Detroit
Fours—Louis Stovall, Pat Hughes, Rick Weber, and Vicki Hughes, Long Beach, Calif.
Dance—American Style: Dana Marshall and Janis Ford, North Canton, Ohio; International Style: Bonnie Lambert and Tom Straker, Pontiac, Mich.
Men's Relays—Twos: Tom and Jim Roycroft, Hollywood, Fla.; fours: Tim and Tom Small, Tom and Jim Roycroft, Hollywood, Fla.
Women's Relays—Twos: Marcia Yager and Brenda Haggard, Cincinnati; fours: Mary Collins, Nancy Morris, Donna LaBriola, D'Andre Reed, Fullerton, Calif.

ROWING

United States Championships
(Philadelphia, July 15–16)

Elite Division

Single Sculls (500 meters)—John Van Blom, Long Beach (Calif.) R. A. (1:12)
Single Sculls—Jim Dietz, New York A. C. (8:08.7)
Double Sculls—John Van Blom and Tom McKibbon, Long Beach R. A. (6:45.39)
Pairs—Larry Haugh and Dick Lyon, Stanford (Calif.) R. A. (7:36.1)
Pairs with Coxswain—Mike Staines, Luther Jones, and Aaron Hermon, Coxswain, College B. C., Philadelphia (7:25.42)
Fours—Vesper B. C., Philadelphia (6:22.93)
Fours with Coxswain—College B. C. (7:22)
Quads—Undine Barge Club, Philadelphia (7:18.2)
Eights—Vesper B. C. (6:05.83)

150-Pound Division

Single Sculls (500 Meters)—Larry Klecatsky, New York A. C. (1:21.3)
Single Sculls—Larry Klecatsky (7:21.61)
Double Sculls—Fred Duling and Bill Belding, Undine B. C. (7:08.7)
Quads—Undine B. C. (7:25.3)
Fours with Coxswain—Potomac B. C., Washington (7:18.2)

Seniors

Single Sculls—Jody Trinsey, Malta B. C., Philadelphia (8:46)
Pairs—University of California at Irvine (7:34.38)
Fours with Coxswain—New Haven (7:02.6)
Eights—Potomac B. C. (6:45.1)

Intermediate Division

Single Sculls—Ed Good 3d, New York A. C. (8:04.6)
Fours—University of California at Irvine (7:51.9)
Eights—Undine B. C. (6:41.7)

Intercollegiate Team Champions

IRA Regatta (Lake Onondaga, Syracuse, N. Y., June 1–3)—Varsity: Pennsylvania (6:22.6); second varsity: Washington (6:18.8); freshmen: Wisconsin (6:19.8); varsity pairs: Dave Brown and Rick Ricci, Brown (8:10.9); varsity fours: University of California at Los Angeles (7:21.3); freshmen fours: Princeton (7:08.1); team (Jim Ten Eyck Trophy): Wisconsin (17 pts)
Dad Vail Trophy (Philadelphia, May 12–13)—Varsity: Coast Guard Academy (6:16); junior varsity: Marietta (6:48.5); freshmen: Marist College (6:45); lightweights: Coast Guard Academy (6:53.4); varsity fours: Drexel (7:46.2)
Eastern Sprints (Worcester, Mass., May 11–13)—Heavyweights: varsity: Northeastern (6:11.5); second varsity: Harvard (6:32); freshmen: Harvard (6:26); Rowe Cup: Harvard (37 pts).—Lightweights: varsity: Harvard (6:29); second varsity: Harvard (6:29.5); freshmen: Princeton (6:18.1); Jope Cup: Harvard (36 pts)
Mid-America Regatta (Marietta, Ohio, April 29)—Varsity: Marietta (4:54.6); junior varsity: Marietta (5:09.2); freshmen: Marietta (5:22); varsity lightweights: Marietta (5:24.5); varsity fours: Marietta (6:13)
Oxford-Cambridge (4½ miles)—Cambridge (18:36)

Western Sprints (Long Beach, Calif., May 20)—*Varsity:* Washington (5:58.5); *junior varsity:* Orange Coast (6:09.9); *freshmen:* Washington (6:17.5); *lightweights:* University of California at Los Angeles (6:19.4)

Yale-Harvard—Harvard (20:34.8)

Cups and Trophies—*Adams Cup:* Harvard (6:26); *Berger Cup:* Temple (6:23.5); *Bill Cup:* Rutgers (6:20.6); *Blackwell Cup:* Pennsylvania (5:54.2); *Callow Cup:* Coast Guard Academy (7:07); *Carnegie Cup:* Cornell (5:50.6); *Childs Cup:* Pennsylvania (6:21.1); *Cochrane Cup:* Massachusetts Institute of Technology (6:00.3); *Compton Cup:* Harvard (6:32.5); *Deering Cup:* Fordham (7:07.2); *Goes Cup:* Navy (6:42.5); *Grimaldi Cup:* Drexel (7:12); *Holding Cup:* Brown (7:19); *Logg Cup:* Princeton (6:50.4); *Mason-Downs Cup:* Marietta (6:11); *Madeira Cup:* Pennsylvania (5:49); *O'Hare Trophy:* Buffalo State (145 pts); *President's (Marist College) Cup:* St. Joseph's (5:30); *Reynolds Cup:* California (6:25.8); *Stein Cup:* Harvard (6:34)

British Henley
(Henley-on-Thames, June 28–July 1)

Diamond Sculls (singles)—Alexander Timoschinin, USSR (8:10)

Double Sculls—P. G. R. Delafield and T. J. Crooks, England (7:24)

Silver Goblets (pairs)—J. Broniec and A. Slusarski, Poland (7:59)

Wyfold Challenge Cup (fours)—Leander, England (7:25)

Stewards Challenge Cup (fours)—Sportak Moscow, USSR (won on disqualification of opponent)

Prince Philip Challenge Cup (fours with coxswain)—St. Catherines, Ontario, Canada (7:22)

Ladies Challenge Plate (eights)—DSR Laga, Netherlands (6:59)

Princess Elizabeth Cup (schoolboy eights)—Kent (Conn.) School (7:02)

Thames Challenge Cup (eights)—Harvard (6:55)

Grand Challenge Cup (eights)—WMF Moscow, USSR (6:33)

Canadian Henley
(St. Catherines, Ont., Aug. 4–8)

Single Sculls—Jim Dietz, New York A.C. (7:20.8)

Pairs—Dan Curphey and Greg Rokosh, Toronto Argonauts (7:19.6)

Single Sculls (500 meters)—Jim Dietz (1:37.4)

Double Sculls—Mike Graham and Doug Cox, University of British Columbia (7:01.4)

Senior Fours with Coxswain—St. Catherines R. C. (6:41)

Senior Eights—St. Catherines R. C. (6:06)

Senior 155-Pound Eights—St. Catherines R. C. (6:14.9)

Association Singles—Peter Barr, St. Catherines

Women's Singles (1,000 meters)—Karin Constant, Vesper B. C., Philadelphia (4:37.9)

Women's Fours with Coxswain (1,000 meters)—Vesper B. C. (4:57)

Women's Eights (1,000 meters)—Vesper B. C. (3:49.7)

Junior Eights—Ridley (Ont.) B. C. (6:44.2)

Junior Doubles—Kurt and Dwight Fox, Minnesota B. C., St. Paul (7:52.4)

Senior 155-Pound Singles—Larry Klecatsky, New York A. C. (8:03.4)

SHOOTING

Skeet Shooting
National Skeet Shooting Association Championships
(Rush, N. Y., July 29–Aug. 5)

All-Around—*Open:* Tony Rosetti, Biloxi, Miss. (548 x 550); *women:* Claudia Butler, Smoke Rise, N.J. (542 x 550); *seniors:* Chet Crites, Detroit (538 x 550); *veterans:* R. B. Ross, Brownsville, Texas (531 x 550); *junior:* Tito Killian, San Antonio, Texas (544 x 550); *junior women:* Marina Pakis, Hot Springs, Ark. (388 x 400); *industry:* Jimmy Prall, North Little Rock, Ark. (547 x 550)

Other Individual Champions—*12-gauge:* Tony Rosetti, Biloxi, Miss. (250 x 250); *women:* Jackie Ramsey, Dallas, Texas (250 x 250); *20-gauge:* Brad Rivenburgh, Durwood, Md. (100 x 100); *women:* Penny Norman, Fort Lauderdale, Fla. (99 x 100); *28-gauge:* Kenny Barnes, Bakersfield, Calif. (100 x 100); *women:* Diane Forbush, Hamburgh, N. Y. (100 x 100); *.410-gauge:* Tony Rosetti (100 x 100); *women:* Marina Pakis, Hot Springs, Ark. (98 x 100)

Trapshooting
Grand American Tournament
(Vandalia, Ohio, Aug. 21–26)

Grand American Handicap—*Men:* George Mushrush, Fairfield, Ohio (22 yds, 99, won shoot-off); *women:* Charlotte Wells, Middletown, Ohio (18 yds, 99); *junior:* Charvin Dixon, Harland, Ohio (23½ yds, 99, won shoot-off); *veterans:* W. G. Buckner, Zanesville, Ohio (21 yds, 95, won shoot-off); *industry:* Tom Garrigus, Beaverton, Oreg. (27 yds, 97); *past grand winner:* Pete Donal, Antwerp, Ohio (22½ yds, 94)

Overall—*Men:* Britt Robinson, Tahoka, Texas (976); *women:* Susan Nattrass, Edmonton, Alberta (946); *junior:* Robert Mieczkowski, Wintersville, Ohio (962); *veterans:* Marvin Driver, Council Bluffs, Iowa (934); *industry:* Tom Garrigus, Beaverton, Oreg. (963)

All-Around—*Men:* Britt Robinson, Tahoka, Texas (394, won coin-toss after tie with Larry Gravestock, Wichita Falls, Texas); *women:* Susan Nattrass, Edmonton, Alberta (389); *junior:* Jim Doyle, Rapid City, S. Dak. (391); *veterans:* Andrew Long, Shamokin, Pa. (375); *industry:* Tom Garrigus, Beaverton, Oreg. (389)

Clay Target—*Men:* Wallace Irwin, Spartanburg, S. C. (200, won shoot-off); *women:* Nadine Ljutic, Yakima, Wash. (200)

Champion of Champions—*Men:* Don Bonillas, San Jose, Calif. (100, won shoot-off); *women:* Nadine Ljutic, Yakima, Wash. (100)

SKIING

World Cup
Individual—*Men:* Gustavo Thoeni, Italy (154 pts); *leading American:* Mike Lafferty, Eugene, Oreg. (9th, 63).—*Women:* Annamarie Proell, Austria (269); *leading American:* tie between Barbara and Marilyn Cochran, Richmond, Vt. (12th, 67)

Team (Nations Cup)—*Men:* Switzerland (534 pts); *women:* France (771); *combined:* France (1,145)

United States Championships
Alpine (downhill at Aspen, Colo., Feb. 5; slaloms at Bend, Oreg., March 9–10)—*Men: Downhill:* Steve Lathrop, Waterville Valley, N. H. (1:54.6); *giant slalom:* Jim Hunter, Calgary, Alberta (2:46.41); *slalom:* Terry Palmer, Kearsarge, N. H. (1:32.69).—*Women: downhill:* Stephanie Forrest, Bellingham, Wash. (1:12.42); *giant slalom:* Sandy Poulsen, Olympic Valley, Calif. (1:21.03); *slalom:* Marilyn Cochran, Richmond, Vt. (1:31.44)

Nordic—*Jumping* (Berlin, N. H., March 5): *class A:* Greg Swor, Duluth, Minn. (205.7 pts); *veterans:* Jacques Charland, M. C. S. C. (142.4); *juniors:* Dave Toten, Eau Claire, Wis. (190.7).—*Cross-country* (Lydonville, Craftsbury Common, and Putney, Vt., Dec. 31, Jan. 2, 5, 7–9): *10 kilometers:* Mike Elliott, Durango, Colo. (29:44.88); *15 kilometers:* Elliott (49:38.76); *30 kilometers:* Elliott (1:46:52.84); *50 kilometers:* Bob Gray, Putney, Vt. (2:40:56.82).—*Combined: jumping* (Brattleboro, Vt.): Joe Lamb, Lake Placid, N. Y. (216.5); *15-kilometer race* (Putney, Vt.): Jim Miller, Mexico, Me. (46:34.66); *overall:* Mike Devecka, Government Camp, Oreg. (422.2 pts); *40-kilometer relay:* Rocky Mountain team (Ron Yeager, Mike Elliott, Clark Matis, Larry Martin; 2:11.57).—*Women: cross-country: 5 kilometers:* Martha Rockwell, Putney, Vt. (17:31.56); *10 kilometers:* Martha Rockwell (37:05.89); *15-kilometer relay:* Eastern Team (Ann McKinnon, Liz Chenard, Martha Rockwell; 57:37.03)

National Collegiate (NCAA) Championships
(Winter Park, Colo., March 16–18)

Downhill: Otto Tschudi, Denver (1:09.22); *team:* Colorado (98.19 pts); *slalom:* Mike Porcarelli, Colorado (1:25.71); *team:* Fort Lewis College (94.4); *Alpine combined:* Mike Porcarelli (139.6 pts); *cross-country:* Stale Engen, Wyoming (52:24); *team:* Wyoming (95.9); *jumping:* Odd Hammerness, Denver (224.5 pts); *team:* Denver (98.5); *Nordic combined:* Bruce Cunningham, New Hampshire (427.7 pts); *skimeister:* Kim Kendall, Nevada (336.1 pts.); *overall team champion:* Colorado (385.3 pts)

MARILYN COCHRAN, U. S. slalom champion in alpine skiing, is seen here soaring over downhill course in World Cup competition at Grindelwald, Switzerland.

UPI

Canadian-American Trophy Series

Overall—Men: Don Rowles, Sandy, Oreg. (154 pts); women: Cheryl Bechdoldt, Tahoe City, Calif. (170)
Event Leaders—Slalom: Steve Lathrop, Amherst, N. H. (70); giant slalom: Don Rowles (70); downhill: Rudd Pyles, Frisco, Colo. (75).—Women: slalom: Penny Lathrop, Ellicottville, N. Y. (75); giant slalom: Cheryl Bechdoldt (75); downhill: Stephanie Forrest, Bellingham, Wash. (48)

SOCCER

United States Championships

National Challenge Cup—Elizabeth, N. J.
Amateur—Busch, St. Louis
Junior—Seco, St. Louis
North American Soccer League—New York Cosmos
NCAA—St. Louis University (defeated UCLA, 4–2, at Orange Bowl, Miami, Dec. 29, in final. In semifinals, St. Louis defeated Howard, 2–1, and UCLA defeated Cornell, 1–0. College Division: Southern Illinois at Edwardsville defeated Oneonta State, 1–0, at Edwardsville, Dec. 9
NAIA—Westmont (defeated Davis and Elkins, 2–1, in second overtime period)

Other Countries

English Association Cup—Leeds
English League Cup—Stoke City
Scottish Association Cup—Glasgow Celtic
Scottish League Cup—Hibernian (defeated Glasgow Celtic, 2–1, in final)
English League, First Division—Derby
English League, Second Division—Norwich
English League, Third Division—Aston Villa
English League, Fourth Division—Grimsby
Scottish League, First Division—Glasgow Celtic
Scottish League, Second Division—Dumbarton
European Cup—Ajax of Amsterdam
European Cup Winners Cup—Glasgow Rangers
European Nations Cup—West Germany

SOFTBALL

World Championship

Men—Canada (defeated United States, 1–0, in 11 innings, in final at Manila, March 12)

American Softball Association Champions

Fast Pitch—Raybestos Cardinals, Stratford, Conn.
Women's Fast Pitch—Raybestos Brakettes, Stratford, Conn.
Slow Pitch—Jiffy Club, Louisville, Ky.
Women's Slow Pitch—Riverside Ford, Cincinnati
Industrial Slow Pitch—Pharr Yarn, McAdamville, N. C.
16-inch Slow Pitch—Carlucci Bobcats, Chicago
Class A—Vernhardt's Inn, Long Island, N. Y.

SQUASH RACQUETS

National Championships

Men

Singles—Victor Neiderhoffer, Berkeley, Calif.
Doubles—Larry Terrell and Jim Zug, Philadelphia
Senior Singles—Calvin MacCracken, Tenafly, N. J.
Veterans Singles—Charles Ufford, New York
Senior Doubles—Alden Johnson and Jackson Bowling, Buffalo
North American Open—Sharif Khan, Toronto
Team—New York
Intercollegiate Singles—A Division: Peter Briggs, Harvard; B Division: Andy Weigand, Harvard; C Division: Neil Vosters, Harvard
Intercollegiate Team—Harvard

Women

Singles—Mrs. Lee Moyer, Pennington, N. J.
Doubles—Mrs. Frances Vosters and Mrs. Halsey Spruance, Wilmington, Del.
Senior Singles—Mrs. W. Pepper Constable, Princeton, N. J.
Intercollegiate—Wendy Zaharko, Princeton
Mixed Doubles—Mrs. Nathan Stauffer, Haverford, Pa., and Tom Poor, Boston

SURFING

World Championships
(San Diego, Oct. 4–8)

Men—Jim Blears, Honolulu
Women—Sharon Weber, Honolulu

United States Championships
(Huntington Beach, Calif., Sept. 8–10)

Men—Dale Dobson, San Diego, Calif.
Women—Mary Setterholm, Corona del Mar, Calif.
Seniors—Les Williams, Dana Point, Calif.
Masters—Donald Takayama, Encinitas, Calif.
Juniors—Lennie Foster, Newport Beach, Calif.
Boys—Mike Cruickshank, Dana Point, Calif.
Kneeboarding—Dean Cleary, Huntington Beach, Calif.

TABLE TENNIS

United States Championships
(Hempstead, N. Y., March 17–19)

Singles—Dal Joon Lee, Cleveland
Women's Singles—Wendy Hicks, Santa Barbara, Calif.
Doubles—Dal Joon Lee and Peter Pradit, Miami Shores, Fla.

Women's Doubles—Vi Nesukaitis, Toronto, and Marianne Domonkos, Montreal
Mixed Doubles—Errol Caetano, Toronto, and Vi Nesukaitis
Seniors (over 40)—Derek Wall, Toronto
Seniors (over 50)—Max Marinko, Toronto
Seniors (over 60)—Laszlo Bellak, Miami Shores, Fla.
Senior Doubles—Bernie Bukiet, New York, and William Meszares, Barrington, Ill.
Junior Boys—Paul Klevinas, Mississagi, Ontario
Girls (under 17)—Judy Bochenski, Eugene, Oreg.
Junior Doubles—Ray Guillen and Erick Thom, Los Angeles
Junior Mixed Doubles—Ray Guillen and Judy Bochenski
Girls' Doubles (under 17)—Cindy Cooper, El Cajon, Calif., and Elsie Spinning, Coos Bay, Oreg.

VOLLEYBALL

United States Volleyball Association Champions

Open—Chart House, San Diego, Calif.
Women—South Texas, Houston
Senior—Balboa Bay V. C., Newport Beach, Calif.
College—Santa Monica

AAU Champions

Open—Santa Monica S and S
Women—Region 13 Seniors, Los Angeles
Senior—Balboa Bay, V. C., Newport Beach, Calif.

Intercollegiate

NCAA—UCLA (defeated San Diego State in final)
NAIA—Church College, Hawaii (defeated Graceland in final)

WATER SKIING

United States Championships
(Seattle, Aug. 17–20)

Men

Overall—Mike Suyderhoud, Petaluma, Calif. (2,847 pts)
Slalom—Kris LaPoint, Castro Valley, Calif. (51½ buoys)
Tricks—Robert Kempton, Tampa, Fla. (5,390 pts)
Jumping—Ricky McCormick, Independence, Mo. (157 ft)

Women

Overall—Liz Allan Shetter, Winter Park, Fla. (2,878 pts)
Slalom—Christy Weir, McQueeney, Texas (59 buoys)
Tricks—Liz Shetter (4,356 pts)
Jumping—Linda Leavengood, Miami, Fla. (99 ft)

Senior Men

Overall—J. D. Morgan, Key West, Fla. (2,659 pts)
Slalom—J. D. Morgan (51½ buoys)
Tricks—Bill Schouten, Flat Rock, Mich. (3,597 pts)
Jumping—Cecil Monnier, Rock Falls, Ill. (121 ft)

Senior Women

Overall—Barbara Cleveland, Hawthorne, Fla. (3,000 pts)
Slalom—Barbara Cleveland (47 buoys)
Tricks—Barbara Cleveland (4,433 pts)
Jumping—Barbara Cleveland (86 ft)

Masters Tournament
(Callaway Gardens, Ga., July 14–16)

Men

Overall—Wayne Grimditch, Hillsboro Beach, Fla. (2,801)
Slalom—Kris LaPoint, Castro Valley, Calif. (52 buoys)
Tricks—Rick McCormick, Independence, Mo. (4,990 pts)
Jumping—Wayne Grimditch (169 ft)

Women

Overall—Liz Allan Shetter, Winter Park, Fla. (2,898 pts)
Slalom—Lisa St. John, Fall River Mills, Calif. (51 buoys)
Tricks—Barbara Cleveland, Hawthorne, Fla. (3,850 pts)
Jumping—Linda Leavengood, Miami, Fla. (103 ft)

WEIGHT LIFTING

United States Championships
(Detroit, June 10–11)

Flyweight—John Yamauchi, Hawaii (595½ pounds, total)
Bantamweight—Sal Dominguez, York, Pa. (672½)
Featherweight—Philip Sanderson, Los Angeles (744)
Lightweight—Dan Cantore, San Francisco (931½)
Middleweight—Fred Lowe, York, Pa. (992)
Light Heavyweight—Michael Karchut, Chicago (1,043¾)
Middle Heavyweight—Rick Holbrook, York, Pa. (1,130)
Heavyweight—Frank Capsouras, York, Pa. (1,175½)
Super Heavyweight—Ken Patera, York, Pa. (1,329¼)

WRESTLING

National AAU Championships
(Cleveland, April 12–17)

Freestyle

105.5 Pounds—Dale Kestel, Michigan W. C.
114.5 Pounds—John Morley, New York A. C.
125.5 Pounds—John Miller, Multnomah A. C.
136.5 Pounds—Testu Ikeno, New York A. C.
149.5 Pounds—Mike Young, Boise, Idaho
163 Pounds—Wayne Wells, Oklahoma A. C.
180.5 Pounds—Jay Robinson, U. S. Army
198 Pounds—Wayne Baughman, U. S. Air Force
220 Pounds—Buck Deadrich, Olympic Club, San Francisco
Heavyweight—Greg Wojciechowski, Toledo, Ohio
Team—New York A. C.

SAILBOATS, *against backdrop of Chicago skyline, line up for start of Chicago-Mackinac yacht race, won by* Kahili.

Greco-Roman

105.5 Pounds—Karoly Kanscar, Nebraska Olympic Club
114.5 Pounds—Mike Thomson, U. S. Marine Corps
125.5 Pounds—Dave Hazewinkel, Minnesota W. C.
136.5 Pounds—Gary Alexander, Minnesota W. C.
149.5 Pounds—Phil Frey, Multnomah A. C.
163   Pounds—Larry Lyden, Minnesota W. C.
180.5 Pounds—Jay Robinson, U. S. Army
198   Pounds—Wayne Baughman, U. S. Air Force
220   Pounds—Henk Schenk, Multnomah A. C.
Unlimited—Greg Wojciechowski, Toledo, Ohio
Team—Minnesota W. C.

National Collegiate (NCAA) Championships
(College Park, Md., March 9–11)

118 Pounds—Greg Johnson, Michigan State
126 Pounds—Pat Milkovich, Michigan State
134 Pounds—Gary Barton, Clarion State
142 Pounds—Tom Milkovich, Michigan State
150 Pounds—Wade Schalles, Clarion State
158 Pounds—Carl Adams, Iowa State
167 Pounds—Andy Matter, Penn State
177 Pounds—Bill Murdock, Washington
190 Pounds—Ben Peterson, Iowa State
Heavyweight—Chris Taylor, Iowa State
Team—Iowa State (103 pts)

YACHTING

North American Yacht Racing Union Champions

Men (Mallory Cup)—Edwin Sherman, St. Petersburg, Fla.
Women (Adams Cup)—Sally Lindsay, Mass. Bay Dinghy Club
Junior (Sears)—Clark Thompson, Houston, Texas
Interclub (Prince of Wales Trophy)—Newport Harbor (Calif.) Y. C., Tim Hogan, skipper
O'Day—Craig Thomas, Seattle
National Sea Exploring—Paul LaBossiere, Wayne, N. J.

Ocean and Long Distance Racing

Around Hawaii (755 miles)—Nalu III; Herb Hodge, Waikiki Y. C.; 6 days, 8 hours, 5 minutes, 53 seconds
Bay View—Mackinac (188 miles)—Kahili; Frank Zurn, Erie, Pa.; 38:42:23 (corrected time)
Chicago–Mackinac (205 miles)—Kahili; 35.8571 (decimal hours)
Miami–Nassau (176 miles)—Charisma; Jesse Phillips, Chicago; 28.2464
St. Petersburg–Ft. Lauderdale (370 miles)—Celerity II; Bill Hough, St. Petersburg; 40.2298. *First to finish:* Equation; John Potter, Palm Beach, Fla.; 45:14:37 (record)

St. Petersburg–Isla Mujeres, Mexico (500 miles)—Heidi; George Hanzi, Corpus Christi, Texas
Newport–Bermuda (635 miles, 178 boats)—Noreyma, 48-foot, Class C sloop, owned by Ron Amey, England, and sailed by Ted Hicks; 3:02:34:58 (corrected time). *First to finish:* Robon, Class A, R. H. Grant; 3:08.18:55. *Other class winners:* Class B: Charisma, Jesse Philips; Class D: Dove, Stewart Green; Class E: Maverick, Rodney Hill; Class F: Aesop, Alexander R. Fowler
Trans-Atlantic (Bermuda–Spain; 2,700 miles, 48 boats)—Carina; Richard B. Nye, New York; 16 days, 7 hours, 52 minutes, 39 seconds. *First to finish:* Blackfin, Kenneth DeMeuse, San Francisco
Trans-Atlantic, Singlehanded (Plymouth, England–Newport, R. I.; 3,000 miles, 45 boats)—Pen Duick IV, Alain Colas, France; 20:13:15
Trans-Pacific (Los Angeles–Tahiti; 3,571 miles)—Pen Duick III; Eric Tabarly, France; 21:11:25:35. *First to finish:* Greybeard, L. H. Killiam, Vancouver, B. C.; 20:00:11:43
Trans-Pacific (Victoria, B. C.–Maui, Hawaii; 2,310 miles, 19 boats)—Cherokee, William M. Black, Seattle; 9:02:53:22 (corrected time). *First to finish:* Odusa, Eric H. Zahn, Seattle; 14:00:23:55 (record)
Trans-Pacific Multihull (Los Angeles–Honolulu; 2,225 miles)—Lani Kai, Dr. Robert Randle, Seal Beach (Calif.) Y. C.; 10:04:06:31

Major Trophy Winners

Canada's Cup—Dynamite, U. S. challenger (LLWYD Ecclestone, Skipper), defeated Mirage, Canadian defender (Gordon Fisher, skipper), in deciding race on Lake Ontario, Sept. 16.
Congressional Cup—Argyle Campbell, Newport Beach, Calif.
Little Americas Cup (at Melbourne, Australia)—Quest II, Australia, defeated Weathercock, U. S. challenger, in four straight races
Half-Ton Cup—Bes, Paul Elvstrom, Denmark
Cornelius Shields Trophy—Michigan, Bruce Nelson
Foster Trophy (collegiate singlehanded)—Gary Jobson, New York Maritime College
Kennedy Cup—U. S. Merchant Marine Academy, Jere White and Marc Donahue
Morss Trophy—University of California at Irvine
Women's Collegiate—Radcliffe, Janice Stroud and Barbi Grant
Interscholastic—Andover; Tony Leggett (skipper), Lawson Fisher, Peter Fernberger

SRI LANKA. See CEYLON.

Commemorative U. S. stamps issued in 1972 included those honoring stamp collecting, Tom Sawyer, and the Parent-Teachers Association. Five U. S. postal cards were issued in observance of "Tourism Year of the Americas '72," featuring, in addition to those pictured here, such tourist attractions as Mt. Rushmore, the Redwoods, and the Grand Canyon.

STAMP COLLECTING

Stamp enthusiasts in 1972 lined up at post office windows for a variety of special issues, presented with much fanfare. A noted American philatelist had a foreign stamp named in his honor; the astronauts smuggled covers aboard the Apollo 15; and Belgium held a major international competitive exhibit.

Postal Showmanship. Postmaster General E. T. Klassen, continuing the policies of his predecessor William M. Blount, promoted merchandising schemes to produce nonpostal profits. To increase public interest in collecting, marketing staffs opened boutiques in major city post offices for retail selling of stamp packets, mini-albums, a storybook stamp catalogue, and other items. They also offered souvenir covers for special events at 35¢ each, competing with private enterprise.

The U. S. government again exceeded the "15-commemoratives-per-year" rule, releasing nearly twice that many special issues (see accompanying table). Issues that were postally necessary comprised only a new $2 booklet of 8-cent stamps, new 7-cent and 14-cent stamps, and 6-cent postal cards.

More novel designs included the American Revolution Bicentennials and the Wildlife issues, printed as oversize four-in-one blocks, and a Cape Hatteras issue, with one picture divided into quarters, each worth 2 cents. A belated special stamp marking the 125th anniversary of the first U. S. Set, July 1847, was a tribute to the hobby of stamp collecting.

Steinway Honored. On September 7, Liechtenstein issued a 1.30-franc stamp honoring the late Theodore E. Steinway, piano maker, the first issue to recognize an American for philatelic achievement.

Other Events. A scandal of major proportions rocked stampdom when Apollo 15 astronauts David R. Scott, James B. Irwin, and Alfred M. Worden were found to have carried 400 envelopes to the moon (besides the one officially prepared for the Postal Service). Their aim was to provide an educational fund for their children, but it was announced they received no money. A German dealer bought 99 and offered them for sale at $1,500 each. NASA "reprimanded" the astronauts but refused to say what had happened to the other 301 envelopes.

In Belgium's major international show, the top prize went to Italian Count A. Gerli. Other important exhibits commemorated, in Lucerne, the first Swiss international air flight of 1922, and, in Rio de Janeiro, Brazil's 150th anniversary of independence.

ERNEST A. KEHR
Stamp News Bureau

U. S. COMMEMORATIVE STAMPS OF 1972

Subject	Denomination	Date of issue
Sidney Lanier, poet	8¢	Feb. 3
Peace Corps	8¢	Feb. 11
Yellowstone Park	8¢	March 1
Family Planning	8¢	March 18
Cape Hatteras (block of four)	4x2¢	April 5
Transport exhibit envelope	8¢	May 2
City of Refuge (Hawaii)	11¢	May 3
Wolf Trap Farm, Vienna, Va.	6¢	June 26
Revolution Bicentennial	4x8¢	July 4
Mt. McKinley	15¢	July 28
Olympics	6¢,8¢,11¢,15¢	Aug. 17
Parent-Teachers Assn.	8¢	Sept. 15
Wildlife Conservation block	4x8¢	Sept. 20
Mail Order centenary	8¢	Sept. 27
Tom Sawyer	8¢	Oct. 20
Christmas	2x8¢	Nov. 9
Pharmaceutical Assn.	8¢	Nov. 10
Stamp Collecting	8¢	Nov. 17

Attending the National Governors' Conference held in Houston on June 5–7, John C. West of South Carolina, Warren E. Hearnes of Missouri, and Jimmy Carter of Georgia (left to right) *confer on state and national political problems.*

state government

Passage of revenue sharing by the 92d Congress was the major event of 1972 for state and local governments. School finance, environmental protection, capital punishment, and reapportionment were among the chief state legislative concerns.

Revenue Sharing. The State and Local Fiscal Assistance Act of 1972, signed by President Nixon on October 20, marks a new beginning in U. S. federalism by returning fiscal power and responsibility to states and localities. It authorizes and appropriates $30.1 billion to state and local governments over a 5-year period. Two thirds of the funds go to local governments and one third to the states. No strings are placed on state expenditures. Localities must spend their share within seven broad categories: public safety, environmental protection, public transportation, health and recreation, social services, financial administration, and libraries. Passage of the act had been urged by major state organizations, including the National Governors' Conference and the National Legislative Conference.

By the time the first checks were being mailed in early December, many governors disclosed their proposals for allocation of the revenue sharing funds by the legislatures. Several governors suggested that the funds be used to expand existing state programs in education, health, law enforcement, and highways. But among the specific proposals, the most popular was the use of revenue sharing funds for property tax relief, directly or through increased state school aid. The governors of 11 states, including California, advocated this use, and on December 2 the California legislature passed a measure providing for increased school aid and property tax relief, funded by revenue sharing and increases in sales and business taxes.

Property Taxes and School Finance. Concern over property tax relief and increased state funding of local schools stems in part from court decisions in 1971 declaring school finance systems in California, Minnesota, and Texas to be unconstitutional because they make education a function of local wealth. The decisions did not rule out the use of property taxes for financing education but attacked the discrimination in spending between poor and wealthy school districts.

The Texas case is on appeal before the U. S. Supreme Court. Nationwide, localities support 52% of school costs, states support 41.1%, and the federal government, 6.9%. Most states have equalization-grant programs that allocate funds in inverse proportion to a district's taxing ability, but per pupil expenditures vary widely among poor and wealthy districts in each state.

Major tax revision proposals that would have limited property taxes and required new means of financing education were defeated in the November elections by voters in California, Colorado, Michigan, and Oregon. However, voters approved proposals to repeal the state property tax in Louisiana and to lower property tax ceilings in Washington.

Aid to Nonpublic Schools. Six states passed laws aiding nonpublic schools in 1972, despite court decisions that voided earlier efforts. The new plans are aimed at aiding parents through tax credits or grants covering such items as textbook costs. Court challenges are under way.

Taxes in General. In a reversal of the widespread tax rises of 1971, taxes were increased in 1972 by only 11 of the 42 state legislatures meeting in regular or special session. Corporation taxes were raised in California, Idaho, Nebraska, New Jersey, and Virginia. Connecticut retained its position as the state with the highest sales tax—and increased the tax from 6.5% to 7%. Cigarette taxes were raised in Idaho, Mississippi, and New Jersey and, by voter approval, in Oregon. Gasoline taxes were hiked in Idaho, Kentucky, Maryland, Mississippi, Missouri, New Jersey, and South Carolina. In November, tax proposals that would have substituted a graduated income tax for a flat rate were defeated in Massachusetts and Michigan. Repeal of Ohio's 1971 graduated income tax was rejected.

State and local tax collections for the period ending June 20, 1972, were a record $108.6 billion, according to the Commerce Clearing House. State tax yields increased to $59.9 billion, or 17.6% more than the previous year.

Environmental Protection. Environmental quality measures were enacted by 35 of the 42 legislatures in session. State aid to local sewer plant construction was approved in 10 states, strip mining was regulated in 6 states, and new environmental agencies were created in 6 states. Vermont joined Oregon in banning nonreturnable beverage containers.

Most environmental measures on the November ballot were approved. Coastline protection proposals limiting development along beaches won voter approval in California and Washington. Florida voters endorsed a $240 million bond issue to implement a comprehensive land and water management act. New York voters favored a $1.15 billion environmental bond issue. Environmental bonds totaling $265 million passed in Washington. Massachusetts and North Carolina voters approved constitutional proposals to protect the environment. Colorado voted to cut off state funding of the 1976 Winter Olympics.

Capital Punishment and Penal Codes. In June the U. S. Supreme Court ruled that capital punishment as imposed by most states is unconstitutional. At that time capital punishment was illegal in nine states and severely restricted in five others. No executions have occurred in the nation since 1967.

On December 1, the Florida legislature became the first state legislative body to enact a new death penalty law. It provides for separate determination of guilt and sentencing. In November, California voters restored the death penalty to their state constitution, following a February ruling by the California supreme court holding it unconstitutional. The Delaware supreme court in November upheld a state mandatory death penalty law for conviction of first-degree murder.

Laws affecting the criminal justice system were passed by most states in 1972. New penal codes were enacted in Delaware, Hawaii, Kansas, and Kentucky. Illinois passed a new corrections code. Maryland regulated handguns. Compensation was provided to innocent victims of violent crimes in Alaska and Rhode Island, bringing the number of states with such laws to eight. Four more states authorized prisoner work-study release programs, and four more established public defender programs.

Reapportionment. In 1972, the states continued their attempts to reapportion legislative and congressional districts to conform with one-man, one-vote requirements in light of the 1970 census. For the November elections, 43 state senates and 41 state houses of representatives had a valid legislative reapportionment based on the 1970 census. Reapportionment was accomplished by legislatures, courts, or special commissions. In the senate redistricting, single-member districts were utilized exclusively in 31 states. Some multimember districts were used in at least 23 house plans. Most of the court suits filed against plans in some 30 states were prompted by differences in population size among districts.

Modernization of Government. Legislatures in 12 states enacted governmental reorganization in 1972. Georgia consolidated 65 agencies into 25 departments. Maine implemented a 1971 law creating 11 executive departments. Executive agencies were established or merged in Arizona, Idaho, Iowa, Kentucky, Kansas, Maryland, Ohio, Rhode Island, Tennessee, and Virginia. Voters approved major executive branch reorganization in Idaho, Missouri, and South Dakota. A new executive article approved by Kansas voters allows the governor to initiate major executive reorganization, subject to legislative veto. Voters approved 4-year terms for elected state officers in Iowa, Kansas, South Dakota, and Texas, effective in 1974. Only four states (Arkansas, New Hampshire, Rhode Island, and Vermont) remain with 2-year terms for chief officers.

Voters in November were not so generous with legislative branch changes. Two-year legislative sessions, allowing carry-over of bills, were approved in California. Proposals for annual sessions won in Minnesota and Wyoming but failed in three other states. Legislative pay increases lost in five states.

Lower-level court systems were reorganized in Florida, Iowa, and Nebraska. Voters ratified new judicial articles providing for unified court systems in Kansas, South Carolina, and South Dakota. Juries of fewer than 12 persons were permitted in Arizona, Connecticut, New York, and Oregon.

Montana adopted a new constitution in 1972. A proposal for a new constitution was defeated in North Dakota. Louisiana elected delegates to a constitutional convention that opens in January 1973.

Other Developments. The proposed 27th Amendment to the U. S. Constitution, forbidding discrimination on account of sex, was passed by 22 states after its approval by Congress in March 1972. Sex discrimination was prohibited by law in 8 states, and voters approved measures forbidding such discrimination in 6 others.

Abortion remained a highly controversial issue. The California supreme court ruled vague restrictions on abortions in that state to be unconstitutional, thus opening the way to abortion on demand. Antiabortion laws were upheld by the state supreme courts of Missouri and South Dakota, and the governor of Pennsylvania vetoed a 1972 antiabortion bill. The U. S. Supreme Court stayed a federal court order that voided Connecticut's 1972 antiabortion law. The high court also was hearing abortion law cases from Georgia and Texas.

The number of states with some form of no-fault automobile insurance law was increased to 8, with legislative action in 1972 by Connecticut, Maryland, Michigan, and New Jersey. Many states continued to enact consumer protections laws, including cooling-off periods for door-to-door sales.

ELAINE S. KNAPP
Editor, "State Government News" and "State Headlines," Council of State Governments

WINNERS (seated) *in New Jersey lottery react to news that they are to receive $50,000 a year for 20 years. Governor Cahill is at center. In November the state became the first to operate a daily lottery.*

States Bet On Gambling

More and more states are betting on legalized gambling as a means of augmenting state revenues. By the end of 1972, government-run lotteries were in operation in seven states and Puerto Rico. Other common forms of legalized gambling are pari-mutuel betting and bingo.

History of U. S. Lotteries. Lotteries as a form of voluntary taxation were popular from early colonial times until the 1830's, when abuses led to a wave of abolition. By 1860, lotteries were operating in only two or three states, but there was soon to be a revival of lottery schemes, spurred in part by the cost of the Civil War. The best known was the Louisiana Lottery Company, established in 1865. It became so corrupt that the Louisiana legislature outlawed it in the early 1890's.

In 1895, Congress passed laws—which still remain—prohibiting lottery advertising, as well as ticket sale or redemption, in all forms of interstate commerce. By then most states had constitutional prohibitions or strong laws against lotteries.

Present-Day Lotteries. The state-operated lottery was revived by New Hampshire in 1963 (effective in 1964). New York followed in 1967, and New Jersey in 1970. In 1972, four states began the operation of lotteries—Connecticut in February, Massachusetts and Pennsylvania in March, and Michigan in November. In the November elections, Maryland voters approved a state lottery to go into effect in 1973, Washington voted for allowing a lottery if 60% of the legislature or electorate approves, and Iowa voted to lift a constitutional prohibition against lotteries, with the primary intent of allowing bingo. Lotteries would be allowed by new constitutions adopted by Virginia in 1970 and Montana in 1972. A privately run lottery is operating in South Dakota under a 1970 law allowing bingo and lotteries by nonprofit organizations.

The distribution formula used by most of the lotteries is 45% for prizes, 40% for state profits, and 15% for administration. Profits are earmarked for education in New Hampshire and New York, for cities and towns in Massachusetts, for senior-citizen property-tax relief in Pennsylvania, for education and state institutions in New Jersey, and for the "general fund" in Connecticut and Michigan.

New Hampshire began with several lotteries a year and $3 tickets. Initial response was good, but expectations were never met. As competition between states grew, drawings became more frequent, ticket prices were reduced, and the million-dollar lottery was introduced.

New Jersey was the first state to come up with a highly successful formula for a lottery—50-cent tickets, weekly drawings with numerous prizes, and multiple sales outlets. It grossed $210 million, with a net of $100 million, from January 1971 to June 30, 1972. Other states quickly copied the formula, and New Jersey revenues dropped from $29.3 million in the peak month of April 1971 to $15.3 million in September 1972. New York's switch from its monthly $1-a-ticket lottery to the weekly 50-cent formula contributed to sales of $70.5 million in fiscal 1970–71, compared with $47.2 million the previous year. Using the weekly formula, Pennsylvania grossed $53.6 million in its first 16 weeks of operation. Then New Jersey initiated the first state daily lottery on November 29, with prizes ranging from $2.50 to $2,500.

Other Legalized Gambling. Pari-mutuels were legalized at the racetracks in many states during the depression of the 1930's. By 1972, pari-mutuel betting—on horse or dog racing or both—was allowed in 30 states. It brought a total 1971 state income of $556,662,000. Off-track betting on pari-mutuel races is legal in Connecticut, Nevada, and New York. Profit from New York's off-track operation was $15 million in its first year.

Bingo and similar games of chance are legal in many states but are usually restricted to nonprofit organizations. Hawaii's new criminal code, effective in 1973, permits social gambling but prohibits gaming establishments. Nevada long has permitted most forms of gambling. The New York legislature has initially approved a constitutional amendment to permit the state to enter any form of gambling, but it must pass the legislature again and then be approved by popular vote.

ELAINE S. KNAPP

STEEL

The fortunes of the world's steel industry were on the rise in 1972 in contrast with the recession that was experienced in 1971.

The International Iron and Steel Institute estimated world raw steel production in 1972 at a record 692 million net tons. Only three times during the last 25 years—in 1954, 1958, and 1971—has world production failed to show an increase. The American Iron and Steel Institute estimated U. S. raw steel production in 1972 at 133 million net tons, a 10% increase over the previous year.

World Developments. The USSR continued as the world leader in raw steel production in 1972, a role it first assumed when it took the lead from the United States in 1971.

Steel production in the European Coal and Steel Community increased 8% and in the United Kingdom 4% during 1972. The recovery, though general, was stronger in some areas than in others. In West Germany high coal costs and heavy exports resulting from a currency revaluation in 1971 continued to cause problems, while in the United Kingdom the nationalized British Steel Corporation, formed in 1967, had still to show a profit.

Japanese steelmakers, guided by the Ministry of International Trade and Industry (MITI), have slowed down their ambitious expansion plans. According to MITI's statistics, steelmaking capacity was 137 million net tons a year while the output for 1972 was approximately 105 million net tons, a 7% increase over 1971. The increased production went into domestic consumption. The 1971 currency revaluation and the voluntary restraint of export agreements negotiated by the Japanese with the United States and Common Market countries resulted in a decreased export market.

U. S. Developments. The increase in steel mill shipments in 1972 reflected the growing strength of the economy. Shipment gains, however, were spread unevenly across the steel product mix, and all producers did not share equally in the increased profit. Steelmakers whose mix was heavily weighted towards flat-rolled products, especially sheets, benefited most from the economy's strength. Producers of structural steels and plates for construction did not fare as well.

The federal government negotiated a new voluntary restraint program under which steel producers in the European Economic Community, the United Kingdom, and Japan pledged to limit their shipments to the United States through 1974. Imports, which continued to hold a substantial share of the domestic steel market, accounted for about 16% of the nation's apparent steel supply in 1972. The decline in shipments resulting from the restraint agreements was somewhat offset by greater shipments from nations not having such agreements.

A newly developed submerged injection process may result in extending the life of the open-hearth steelmaking furnace, which has been giving way to the basic oxygen furnace. In the submerged injection process oxygen is injected into the open-hearth furnace below the surface of the bath.

National Steel Corporation announced the construction of a fully continuous cold-reduction rolling mill at its Weirton, W. Va., facility. This process —pioneered by Nippon Kokan of Japan—provides for improved utilization by continuously feeding coils of steel into the rolling mill.

GEORGE N. STOUMPAS
American Iron and Steel Institute

STEIN, Herbert. See BIOGRAPHY.

PRODUCTION OF IRON ORE, PIG IRON AND FERROALLOYS, AND RAW STEEL[1]

Country	1971 Iron ore, concentrates and agglomerates (long tons of 2,240 lb)	1971 Pig iron and ferroalloys (short tons of 2,000 lb)	1971 Raw steel[1] (short tons of 2,000 lb)	Country	1971 Iron ore, concentrates and agglomerates (long tons of 2,240 lb)	1971 Pig iron and ferroalloys (short tons of 2,000 lb)	1971 Raw steel[1] (short tons of 2,000 lb)
Algeria	2,707,000	...	...	Liberia	25,294,000	...	...
Angola	5,708,000	...	...	Luxembourg	4,468,000	5,057,000	...[3]
Argentina	246,000	970,000	2,108,000	Malaysia	1,083,000	...	...
Australia	56,690,000	6,757,000	7,496,000	Mauritania	8,710,000	...	...
Austria	4,035,000	3,140,000	4,420,000	Mexico	5,314,000	1,786,000	4,255,000
Belgium	89,000	11,604,000	19,493,000[2]	Morocco	640,000	...	...
Brazil	31,987,000	5,159,000	5,980,000	Netherlands	...	4,144,000	5,581,000
Bulgaria	2,716,000	1,488,000	2,116,000	New Caledonia	177,000	...	...
Burma	2,000	...	...	New Zealand	59,000	...	75,000
Canada	44,978,000	8,828,000	12,170,000	Norway	3,760,000	1,389,000	960,000
Chile	11,082,000	535,000	538,000	Pakistan	6,000	...	150,000
China, Mainland	43,305,000	20,944,000	19,975,000	Peru	9,350,000	99,000	300,000
China, Nationalist	...	88,000	325,000	Philippines	2,205,000	...	95,000
Colombia	591,000	254,000	341,000	Poland	2,559,000	8,058,000	12,784,000
Cuba	...	...	60,000	Portugal	103,000	364,000	425,000
Czechoslovakia	1,535,000	8,785,000	12,613,000	Rhodesia	541,000	276,000	165,000
Denmark	30,000	248,000	520,000	Rumania	3,307,000	4,773,000	7,430,000
Egypt	482,000	551,000	300,000	Sierra Leone	2,185,000	...	...
Finland	1,132,000	1,130,000	1,102,000	South Africa	10,531,000	4,376,000	5,401,000
France	55,588,000	20,201,000	25,204,000	Spain	6,968,000	5,401,000	8,488,000
Germany, East	394,000	2,216,000	5,758,000	Sudan	20,000	...	...
Germany, West	6,290,000	33,058,000	44,439,000	Swaziland	2,362,000	...	...
Greece	...	...	526,000	Sweden	32,812,000	2,846,000	5,798,000
Hong Kong	157,000	...	...	Switzerland	...	28,000	540,000
Hungary	650,000	2,194,000	3,527,000	Thailand	20,000	11,000	...
India	31,131,000	7,165,000	6,691,000	Tunisia	896,000	...	...
Iran	2,000	...	...	Turkey	2,953,000	970,000	1,102,000
Ireland	...	...	80,000	USSR	200,385,000	98,435,000	132,276,000
Israel	...	...	99,000	United Kingdom	10,482,000	17,262,000	26,648,000
Italy	1,014,000	9,429,000	19,167,000	United States	82,298,000	83,468,000	120,443,000[4]
Japan	1,398,000	79,640,000	97,614,000	Venezuela	22,145,000	551,000	1,020,000
Korea, North	8,366,000	2,535,000	2,039,000	Yugoslavia	3,730,000	1,620,000	2,690,000
Korea, South	463,000	6,000	536,000	Other countries	...	...	717,000
Lebanon	...	...	20,000	Total (estimate)[5]	758,131,000	467,839,000	632,600,000

[1] Steel in the first solid state after melting, suitable for further processing or sale. [2] Figure includes data from Luxembourg. [3] Included under Belgium. [4] United States data exclude 1,583,000 net tons of steel produced by foundries that reported their output to the Bureau of Census but did not report to American Iron and Steel Institute. [5] Detail does not necessarily add to total because figures are rounded. (Sources: Statistical Quarterly Report for Iron and Steel Industry, West Germany Iron and Steel Federation, Düsseldorf; American Iron and Steel Institute, New York.)

UPI

WALL STREETER celebrates as the Dow-Jones industrial average passed the 1,000 mark for the first time ever, November 14.

STOCKS AND BONDS

The stock market's path, though convoluted, took it to new highs in 1972. Stock prices entered the year on a buoyant note, extending the advance that began late in 1971. The list moved upward through mid-April. A consolidation period was aggravated by investor apprehension over President Nixon's decision in May to mine North Vietnamese waters. The list spent most of the summer in the doldrums, in response to uncertainties over the economy, the presidential election, and Vietnam. But in October, reports of progress in Vietnam peace negotiations touched off a dramatic rally.

The bond market traded in a narrow range in 1972. Prices followed a sawtooth pattern, starting strong in the forepart of the year, and then backing and filling through the balance.

STOCKS AND BONDS (Standard & Poor's Index)

	Date[1]	425 Industrials	20 Rails	55 Utilities	500 Stocks
1971 high	Apr. 28	115.84	48.32	64.81	104.77
1971 low	Nov. 23	99.36	35.03	54.48	90.16
1972 high	Dec. 11	132.95	48.31	61.20	119.12
1972 low	Jan. 3	112.19	40.40	52.95	101.67
1972 close	Dec. 29	131.87	44.26	61.05	118.05

[1] Dates are for industrials. Rail and Utility highs and lows in some instances occurred on other dates.

MOST ACTIVE STOCKS IN 1972— NEW YORK STOCK EXCHANGE

Stock	Sales	Close	Net Change
American Tel. & Tel.	38,574,700	52¾	+ 8
Gulf Oil	38,523,500	27	− 1⅞
Curtiss-Wright	26,228,000	32	+18½
Occidental Petroleum	25,069,400	11¾	− ⅛
American Motors	24,164,900	8¼	+ 1¼
Federal National Mortgage Assoc.	23,479,500	20	− 4¾
American Tel. & Tel. wts.	21,688,300	9⅛	+ ⅜
Texaco	21,655,400	37½	+ 3⅛
International Tel. & Tel.	20,608,400	60¼	+ 1⅞
Unionamerica	19,886,600	38	+ 6⅜
Pan American World Airways	18,861,900	9	− 6¼
Boise Cascade	17,741,000	11⅛	− 7⅝
Chrysler Corp.	17,723,300	41	+12⅜
General Motors	17,577,600	81⅛	+ ⅝
Levitz Furniture	16,291,900	26⅞	−12⅝

MOST ACTIVE STOCKS IN 1972— AMERICAN STOCK EXCHANGE

Stock	Sales	Close	Net Change
Champion Homes	12,742,100	14	+ 5½
Syntex Corp.	12,113,200	82⅜	− ⅝
Teleprompter	10,296,300	33¼	+ 4¼
Alcoa pfd. $3.75	8,315,800	52¾	− ¾
Banister Continental	8,285,900	35⅛	+19⅛
McCulloch Corp.	8,185,000	16	−12
O'Okiep Copper	7,615,000	54¾	− ½
American-Israeli	6,988,600	9⅝	+ 5¾
National General wts. (new)	6,688,600	6½	+ ⅛
Loew's Corp. wts.	6,464,100	18⅛	− 3⅞
Austral Oil	6,299,200	21¾	+ 4⅞
TWA wts.	6,194,200	25⅝	+ ⅝
Asamera Oil	6,157,100	13⅛	− 4⅝
Ozark Airlines	6,145,200	5¾	− 2⅝
Imperial Oil	6,085,100	49¼	+18

Stock Prices. The stock market began 1972 with a strong upward move. Subject to occasional periods of weakness, prices forged ahead through the middle of April. During the advance, the market surpassed the peak established in April 1971.

The November 1971–April 1972 surge was fueled by a number of factors, including favorable international currency developments stemming from the Smithsonian Agreement reached in late 1971. Other elements in the rise were improving business and economic prospects, as well as the Federal Reserve Board's stimulative monetary policies, which were reflected in low interest rates.

Although the initial leg of the rise encompassed most major groups, the later stage was spearheaded by a relatively small group of established growth stocks. Most securities registered gains nowhere near the select few that led the market. This disparity can be traced to the major participants in the investing arena at the time—the institutions. This market surge was not, by and large, fueled by money from the small investor. The investing public was still cautious, as the scars from the 1968–70 bear market were fairly new. However, the large institutional investors, anxious to recoup earlier losses, concentrated funds in established growth issues, and their prices skyrocketed.

The surge ran out of steam in the latter part of April, and prices trended downward, in slow trading, until August. Investors ignored many favorable developments, particularly in the economy. They

became increasingly concerned about inflation, the efficacy of economic controls, rising interest rates, and resurfacing imbalances in international monetary equilibrium. As the summer wore on, the allegedly antibusiness views of Sen. George McGovern, the Democratic presidential candidate, came into play. Also, there was the prospect of a huge federal budget deficit in fiscal 1973.

During the lackluster late spring and summer months, occasional bursts of activity came in response to the ebb and flow of peace hopes. Developments related to Vietnam became a major influence on the market's performance. The early August announcement that Henry Kissinger had met with North Vietnamese negotiators touched off a sharp two-week rally. However, stock prices eroded for the next few weeks.

The market came to life in late October on Dr. Kissinger's statement that a Vietnam settlement was at hand. That announcement, coupled with President Nixon's sweeping victory at the polls on November 7 and more favorable economic news, provided the impetus for a powerful rally. This surge enabled all major market averages to set new highs. On Nov. 14, 1972, all eyes were fastened on the Dow-Jones industrial average, which closed above 1,000 for the first time. The market continued its precedent-breaking ways through mid-December before selling off in response to a breakdown in the peace talks and the resumption of bombing over North Vietnam. However, a rally at the end of the year enabled the list to close only a shade below its earlier highs.

Mutual Funds. In 1972, the mutual funds continued to experience net redemptions; that is, investors cashed in a larger dollar amount of mutual fund shares than they bought. Except for January, the funds were in a net redemption position for all of 1972. Apparently many mutual fund shareholders were anxious to "get out even" after the 1968–70 bear market, and were disposing of their holdings as the market rose. "No-load" funds, which do not charge sales commissions, attracted a greater proportion of mutual fund investments.

Earnings and Dividends. A worthwhile earnings improvement occurred in 1972 for most companies. In terms of Standard & Poor's industrial stock price index, net income (partly estimated) rose to $6.74 a share, from 1971's $5.97.

Dividends also rose, and were the equivalent of $3.22 a share on Standard & Poor's 425-stock index, as against $3.18 for 1971. At year's end, S&P stocks sold at an average price of 19.6 times earnings with an average return of 2.4%, compared with a 1971 multiple of 18.9 and a yield of 2.8%.

Volume. Total trading on the New York Stock Exchange hit a new peak of 4.138 billion shares in 1972, up from the previous record of 3.891 billion shares in 1971. American Stock Exchange volume was 1.118 billion shares, as against 1971's total of 1.017 billion.

Bond Prices. The bond market in 1972 moved in a much narrower range than in 1971. Bond prices were at their best level of the year in the first week of January. Subsequently, they fluctuated throughout the spring and summer months. Yields began to rise and bond prices sagged in September, reflecting concern over rising short-term interest rates. But bond prices firmed somewhat as 1972 drew to a close. Yields on highest-grade industrials reached a low of 6.92% on January 6, and hit a high

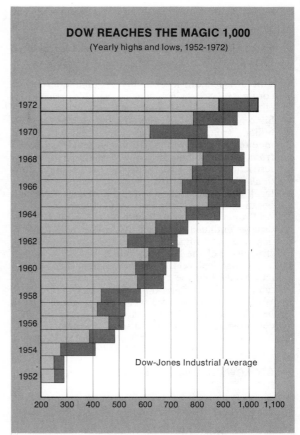

DOW REACHES THE MAGIC 1,000
(Yearly highs and lows, 1952-1972)

Dow-Jones Industrial Average

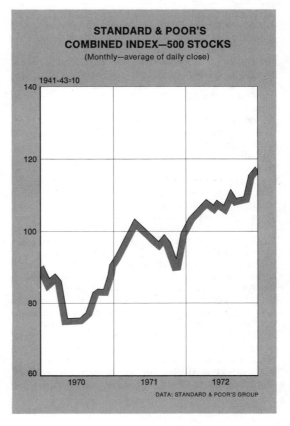

**STANDARD & POOR'S
COMBINED INDEX—500 STOCKS**
(Monthly—average of daily close)

1941-43=10

DATA: STANDARD & POOR'S GROUP

of 7.24% on September 28, before ending the year at 7.04%. Short-term government yields recorded a low for 1972 of 5.25% on January 13. The peak was 6.15% on September 14; at the end of the year they were 6.03%.

Both corporate and municipal bond offerings were at a reduced level in 1972. Public offerings of corporate bonds (including convertible issues) declined in 1972 to around $18.1 billion, from $24.8 billion in 1971. Municipal offerings slipped to $22.9 billion, from $24.4 billion. The reduced capital requirements from the corporate sector stemmed from increased liquidity, due partially to dividend restrictions under Phase 2 of the Nixon administration's economic controls program. Many state and local governments lessened their outside financing because of budget surpluses built up earlier.

Brokerage House Trends. The securities industry continued to debate its future in 1972. Perhaps the most important issue discussed was the restructuring of the business, that is, the move toward a new national central market system. Such a system would link the two New York exchanges with the regional exchanges throughout the United States. Wall Street also debated whether institutions should be allowed to hold seats on major exchanges. The commission structure was also of concern.

CAROLYN J. COLE
Standard & Poor's Corporation

STOKOWSKI, Leopold. See BIOGRAPHY.

SUDAN

In 1972 peace was restored to Sudan after almost 17 years of civil war between the Muslims of the north and the black tribesmen of the south. An agreement to end the conflict was reached in Addis Ababa, Ethiopia, on February 26 between the government of President Jaafar Mohammad al-Numeiry and the southern rebel movement, called the Anyana. The peace plan was part of an over-all policy on the part of Numeiry to bring about internal stability in a war-damaged country.

End of the Civil War. The peace agreement was signed in Addis Ababa by Sudanese Foreign Minister Manzur Khaled and Maj. Gen. Joseph Lagu, leader of the Anyana rebels. The pact brought an end to the southern secessionist movement, which had attempted to set up an independent state known as "Azania."

The agreement, which went into effect in March, called for an immediate cease-fire. The three rebel southern provinces—Equatoria, Upper Nile, and Bahr el-Ghazal—were to be united to form a single region known as South Sudan, with a popularly elected regional assembly. Under the terms of the agreement the region was to have an executive, appointed by the central government on the recommendation of the regional assembly, who would head a regional executive council. The council was to be responsible for all aspects of policy making and implementation except in the areas of defense, currency, and foreign affairs.

The agreement also provided for the southern guerrillas to be gradually incorporated into the Sudanese regular army. Southerners were always to make up at least 50% of the officers and enlisted men stationed in South Sudan. Arabic remained the country's official language, but English could be used for official business in the south.

─────── **SUDAN** • Information Highlights ───────

Official Name: Republic of The Sudan.
Area: 967,497 square miles (2,505,813 sq km).
Population (1972 est.): 16,800,000. *Density,* 16 per square mile (6 per sq km). *Annual rate of increase,* 3.1%.
Chief Cities (1965 est.): Khartoum, the capital, 194,000; Omdurman, 206,500.
Government: *Head of state,* Maj. Gen. Jaafar Mohammad al-Numeiry, president (took office Oct. 1971). *Head of government,* Maj. Gen. Jaafar Mohammad al-Numeiry. *Political party*—Sudanese Socialist Union.
Languages: Arabic (official), English, French, and African languages.
Education: *Expenditure* (1967), 20.3% of total public expenditure. *School enrollment* (1969)—primary, 610,798; secondary, 175,958; technical/vocational, 1,181; university/higher, 11,691.
Monetary Unit: Sudanese pound (0.3482 pound equals U. S.$1, Sept. 1972).
Gross National Product (1970 est.): $1,890,000,000.
National Income per Person (1968): $104.
Economic Indexes: *Agricultural production* (1971), 214 (1952–56 = 100); *consumer price index* (1971), 101 (1970 = 100).
Manufacturing (major products): Processed foods, vegetable oil, textiles.
Major Agricultural Products: Cotton, oilseeds, groundnuts.
Major Minerals: Iron ore, chromium ore, salt, gypsum.
Foreign Trade (1971): *Exports,* $328,000,000 (chief exports—cotton; gum arabic; groundnuts). *Imports,* $331,000,000 (chief imports, 1969—textile yarn and fabrics; food). *Chief trading partners* (1969)—India (took 12% of exports, supplied 10% of imports); West Germany (12%—6%); Italy (13%—5%); United Kingdom (7%—18%).
Transportation: *Motor vehicles* (1970), 43,900 (automobiles, 27,400); *major national airline,* Sudan Airways.
Communications: *Telephones* (1971), 46,371; *television stations* (1971), 2; *newspapers* (1970), 22.

Political Affairs. Elections were completed on October 4 for a new 207-member People's Assembly, which was to approve a permanent constitution. The cabinet resigned, and President Numeiry announced a new government on October 9 with himself as prime minister and defense minister.

As part of its policy of reconciliation with the south, the government granted amnesty to all rebels. One of the major problems facing the country was the need to resettle the 250,000 southerners who had fled to the bush during the long years of war and the nearly 180,000 southern refugees in neighboring Uganda, Ethiopia, and Zaïre.

Foreign Affairs. As part of its reconciliation with the south the government began to turn away from the Arab north and toward the black south of the African continent. Following a trip to Tanzania and Somalia, President Numeiry declared that Sudan might eventually join the East African Community, composed of Uganda, Tanzania, and Kenya, instead of Egypt, Libya, and Syria in the Federation of Arab Republics, as previously planned.

In a gesture heralding its new policy of peace both at home and abroad, the Sudanese government cooperated with the government of President Idi Amin of Uganda on May 11 in reopening the border between the two nations, which had been closed because of the civil war. Presidents Numeiry and Amin signed a mutual defense agreement on June 28.

Relations between Sudan and both Libya and Egypt were strained during the year. On September 20, Numeiry prevented five Libyan Air Force planes from carrying troops and arms to Uganda to support President Amin. In the same month Sudan withdrew the troops it had stationed at the Suez Canal since the 1967 Israeli-Arab War.

On July 25, Sudan reestablished diplomatic relations with the United States, broken since 1967.

JAMES D. L. BYRNES
Edinboro State College, Pennsylvania

SUHARTO. See BIOGRAPHY.
SUPREME COURT. See LAW.
SURGERY. See MEDICINE.

——— SWAZILAND • Information Highlights ———

Official Name: Kingdom of Swaziland.
Area: 6,704 square miles (17,363 sq km).
Population (1972 est.): 400,000. *Density,* 62 per square mile (24 per sq km). *Annual rate of increase,* 2.8%.
Chief City (1966 census): Mbabane, the capital, 13,803.
Government: *Head of state,* Sobhuza II, king (acceded in 1921). *Head of government,* Prince Makhosini Dlamini, prime minister (took office April 1967). *Legislature—* Parliament: Senate, 12 members; House of Assembly, 31 members.
Languages: English, siSwati (both official).
Education: *Expenditure* (1968), 17.7% of total public expenditure. *School enrollment* (1969)—primary, 64,955; secondary, 7,351; technical/vocational, 144; university/higher, 69.
Monetary Unit: South African rand (0.8013 rand equals U. S. $1, July 1972).
Gross National Product (1970): $90,000,000.
Manufacturing (major products): Processed agricultural products, processed foods.
Major Agricultural Products: Corn, cotton, tobacco, sugarcane, pineapples, rice, sorghum, forest products.
Major Minerals: Iron ore, asbestos.
Foreign Trade: *Chief exports*—Sugar; iron ore; wood pulp; citrus fruits. *Chief imports*—Machinery and transport equipment; beverages and tobacco; chemicals. *Chief trading partners*—United Kingdom; South Africa.
Communications: *Telephones* (1971), 5,095; *radios* (1970), 13,000.

SWAZILAND

The main events in Swaziland in 1972 were the first general election since independence in 1968 and talks on air service to link Swaziland more closely to other independent black African states.

General Election. King Sobhuza II dissolved Parliament on March 15 and called for a general election on May 16–17, the first since Swaziland gained its independence from Britain in 1968. Five parties contested for 24 Assembly seats previously held by the Imbokodvo National Movement, which had loyally supported the king. In winning three seats, the Ngwane National Liberatory Congress, Swaziland's main opposition party, though badly splintered, ended what had been one-party government by the Imbokodvo. The Congress party had charged that only the Swazi aristocracy get privileged government positions under Imbokodvo rule.

The king opened the second Parliament on June 2. The first legislative bill debated was one to restrict foreign land speculators and to confine land ownership to Swazi citizens and companies.

Air Service Talks. Officials moved closer to linking Swaziland by air to the independent black states of Botswana, Lesotho, Malagasy Republic, Zambia, Malawi, and Tanzania. Talks were held between representatives of Swaziland and the African Civil Aviation Commission. It was hoped that the air links might make Swaziland economically and ideologically more independent of its racially segregated and white-ruled neighbors, the Republic of South Africa and Portuguese Mozambique.

FRANKLIN PARKER
West Virginia University

SWEDEN

In 1972 economic problems, tax reforms, a free-trade agreement, and proposals for constitutional and church reforms were the subjects of much debate in Sweden.

Economic Developments. High unemployment and a depressed domestic economy caused considerable discussion in the Riksdag (parliament), party congresses, and mass media. The September unemployment figure of 121,000, about 3% of the working force, reached prewar totals. The lifting of price freezes in January and automatic increments in

farm and labor costs resulted in a 7% price rise by midyear, the highest of the past decade. Despite favorable tax benefits for business, government investments, and a loan fund of about 3 billion kronor, business failures occurred more frequently, and the state-owned enterprise enlarged its activities.

In its October report, the national federation of labor (Landsorganisation) predicted that the economy would not change measurably until late 1973. It asserted that Sweden was involved in a cycle of unsolved domestic fiscal, financial, and trade problems with stagnation as the most serious issue.

On the plus side were a foreign-trade surplus in balance of payments, with a 5% improvement over 1971, and good foreign reserves. Harvests were excellent, and there was a surplus of over a million tons of grain to be sold in the international market. A problem was that international prices were less than the Swedish fixed payments. In addition, the grain surplus could not lower costs of flour because of subsidies, and bakers asked for increases to meet advancing labor costs.

On July 22, Sweden signed a treaty with the European Economic Community, permitting entry of over half of Sweden's exports without duties or on a favorable schedule. Three days earlier, Sweden, Finland, and Norway signed an agreement with Britain for quotas on pulp and paper products that would preserve Nordic markets after Britain's entry into the EEC on Jan. 1, 1973.

Tax Reforms. Proposals for tax alterations by Finance Minister Gunnar Sträng were approved by the Riksdag in May. These changes eased taxes on lower-income groups, slightly augmented those on the top level, advanced the value-added tax to 20%, and raised excise duties on tobacco, liquor, and gasoline. The Riksdag approved encouragement of private investment through favorable tax policies on business enterprises, added to child welfare and

——— SWEDEN • Information Highlights ———

Official Name: Kingdom of Sweden.
Area: 173,649 square miles (449,750 sq km).
Population (1972 est.): 8,200,000. *Density,* 47 per square mile (18 per sq km). *Annual rate of increase,* 0.4%.
Chief Cities (1970 est.): Stockholm, the capital, 747,500; Göteborg, 446,900; Malmö, 258,300.
Government: *Head of state,* Gustav VI Adolf, king (acceded Oct. 1950). *Head of government,* Olof Palme, premier (took office Oct. 1969). *Legislature* (unicameral)—Riksdag, 350 members. *Major political parties*—Social Democratic party; Center party; Liberal party; Conservative party; Communist party.
Languages: Swedish (official), Lapp.
Education: *Expenditure* (1969), 30.2% of total public expenditure. *School enrollment* (1969)—primary, 606,220; secondary, 655,329; technical/vocational, 227,876; university/higher, 114,875.
Monetary Unit: Krona (4.750 kronor equal U. S.$1, Sept. 1972).
Gross National Product (1971 est.): $32,700,000,000.
National Income per Person (1970): $3,695.
Economic Indexes: *Industrial production* (1971), 161 (1963=100); *agricultural production* (1971), 113 (1952–56=100); *consumer price index* (1971), 145 (1963=100).
Manufacturing (major products): Pulp and paper, lumber, iron and steel, machinery and equipment, ships, automobiles.
Major Agricultural Products: Oats, sugar beets, potatoes, wheat, dairy products, livestock, forest products.
Major Minerals: Iron ore, lead, sulfur, tungsten, copper.
Foreign Trade (1971): *Exports,* $7,470,000,000 (chief exports—paper; wood pulp; wood; iron ore). *Imports,* $7,091,-000,000 (chief imports, 1969—nonelectrical machinery; food; chemicals; transport equipment). *Chief trading partners* (1969)—United Kingdom (took 13% of exports, supplied 14% of imports); West Germany (12%—19%); Denmark (10%—8%); Norway (10%—6%).
Tourism: Receipts (1970), $143,000,000.
Transportation: *Motor vehicles* (1970), 2,447,000 (automobiles, 2,289,000); *railroads* (1970), 7,583 miles (12,203 km); *merchant fleet* (1971), 4,978,000 gross registered tons; *major national airline,* SAS—Scandinavian Airlines System (with Denmark and Norway).
Communications: *Telephones* (1971), 4,505.802; *television stations* (1971), 173; *television sets* (1971), 3,200.000; *newspapers* (1970), 114 (daily circulation, 4,324,000).

pension payments, and allocated more funds to local governments. Unfortunately, because of economic conditions, tax income for 1972 will not bring anticipated revenue, and Sweden thus faces a budget deficit of about 4 billion kronor.

Constitutional Changes. A commission recommended the elimination of any role for the monarchy in Swedish government. Other recommendations were that cabinet formation be given over to speakers of the Riksdag, that cabinet officers be required to act as a unit, and that cabinet rank be opened to foreign-born citizens. The commission also suggested changing the number of Riksdag members and lowering the voting age to 18. It was felt that the Riksdag would approve these recommendations with little debate on the role of the monarchy.

Disestablishment of the Church. A government commission proposed ending state support for the church by 1983. This period allows for a transition to self-support and for the transfer of such duties as census compilation to government agencies. The church will keep its property, and salaries and pensions of current personnel will be paid out of general funds. At a meeting of bishops in Uppsala, committees were formed to plan for the transition.

Antipollution Laws. The Riksdag passed laws regulating sewerage and dumping in inland and coastal waters and bought land for recreational, environmental, and national purposes. In June, Sweden was host to the United Nations Conference on the Human Environment, which provided draft conventions and recommendations on significant environmental issues for international controls. (See ENVIRONMENT.)

Defense. The Riksdag approved a reduced defense budget that required rationalization within the forces. The defense system will confine itself to conventional arms, reduce research and development, especially in the air force, and lower the period of service for conscripts.

Abortions. A government report noted a drastic 33% increase in legal abortions in the past three years. The report stated that the number would have been larger had not lessened fears of the effects of the contraceptive pill caused its renewed use. Most abortions were among persons under 21. Increased instruction and services in sexual hygiene were also recommended because of a sizable rise in the incidence of venereal disease.

Anti-U. S. Sentiment. Antagonism to the United States and the war in Vietnam became more pronounced. Prime Minister Olof Palme's severe criticism of the United States role in Vietnam, voiced at the Environmental Conference in Stockholm in June, revealed Sweden's strong anti-American sentiments. News of impending peace in Vietnam was greeted with some skepticism.

RAYMOND E. LINDGREN
California State University, Long Beach

SWITZERLAND

Militant political groups, inflation, and a proposed ban on the export of arms and munitions were primary matters of Swiss concern in 1972.

Political Issues. Following the 1971 ratification of the vote for women in federal affairs, many cantons, previously opposed, altered their position in 1972. Sankt Gallen, Uri, Schwyz, and Nidwalden gave women the vote in both cantonal and municipal matters, while Grisons and Appenzell approved more limited forms, allowing a degree of local option.

Political unrest among youthful fringe elements emerged sporadically. After the defeat of a proposal to allow the Jura region in Bern canton to develop its own school system, 30 members of the Belier movement to win cantonal status for the Jura occupied the Swiss embassy in Paris on June 17. The destruction of a munitions depot at Glovelier, north of Bern, on July 16 was blamed on the movement.

Equally serious was the arrest on July 14 of 41 young members of an anarchist group. Two were convicted of stealing arms and threatening the existence of constitutional order. Although Swiss authorities confirmed that this group had ties with similar groups in West Germany and Berlin, they heatedly denied U. S. charges that a central coordinating agency for revolutionary groups from many areas, including Japan, Ireland, Uruguay, and Palestine, had been established in Switzerland.

To the great relief of the government, Swiss voters on September 24 narrowly defeated a constitutional amendment to ban exports of arms and munitions. However, a new law prohibited the sale of arms to any country that is at war or under extreme tension.

Economy. To combat inflation and restrict the influx of foreign currencies, the government imposed a new 8% tax on foreign deposits in Swiss banks effective July 3. It also initiated stiffer reserve requirements, forbade borrowing abroad by Swiss residents or companies without prior government consent, and prohibited nonresidents from buying property in Switzerland. It severely restricted the right of banks to change foreign into domestic currency.

Exports for the first half of 1972 rose 17.2% over the same period in 1971. Nevertheless, the unfavorable gap between exports and imports increased. It was therefore understandable that the government in September gave up plans for a multimillion dollar purchase of U. S. Corsair jet fighters.

SWITZERLAND · Information Highlights

Official Name: Swiss Confederation.
Area: 15,941 square miles (41,288 sq km).
Population (1972 est.): 6,400,000. *Density,* 394 per square mile (152 sq mi). *Annual rate of increase,* 1.0%.
Chief Cities (1970 census): Bern, the capital, 162,405; Zürich, 422,640; Basel, 212,857; Geneva, 173,618.
Government: *Head of state,* Nello Celio, president of the confederation (took office Jan. 1972). *Head of government,* Nello Celio, president of the Federal Council. *Legislature*—Federal Assembly; Council of States, 44 members; National Council, 200 members. *Major political parties*—Conservative Christian Social party; Social Democratic party; Radical Democratic party.
Languages: German, French, Italian, Rhaeto-Romanic (all official).
Education: *Expenditure* (1969), 19.2% of total public expenditure. *School enrollment* (1968)—primary, 487,583; secondary, 464,023; technical/vocational, 145,937; university/higher, 40,083.
Monetary Unit: Franc (3.801 francs equal U. S.$1, Sept. 1972).
Gross National Product (1971 est.): $21,400,000,000.
National Income per Person (1970): $2,859.
Economic Indexes: *Industrial production* (1971), 146 (1963=100); *agricultural production* (1971), 131 (1952–56=100); *consumer price index* (1971), 135 (1963=100).
Manufacturing (major products): Machinery, chemicals, textiles, watches.
Major Agricultural Products: Potatoes, sugar beets, wheat, dairy products.
Foreign Trade (1971): *Exports,* $5,726,000,000 (chief exports, 1969—chemicals; watches, clocks, and parts; electrical and nonelectrical machinery). *Imports,* $7,207,000,000 (chief imports, 1969—food; chemicals, nonelectrical machinery; transportation equipment). *Chief trading partners* (1969)—West Germany (took 15% of exports, supplied 29% of imports); United States (10%—8%); France (9%—12%); Italy (9%—10%).
Tourism: *Receipts* (1970), $733,000,000.
Transportation: *Motor vehicles* (1970), 1,521,300 (automobiles, 1,383,200); *railroads* (1970), 3,118 miles (5,018 km); *merchant fleet* (1971), 200,000 gross registered tons; *major national airline,* Swissair.
Communications: *Telephones* (1971), 3,025,779; *television stations* (1971), 83; *newspapers* (1970), 117.

Foreign Relations. In 1972, Switzerland joined with 20 other western European nations to form a central patent office. On July 22, Switzerland was one of 16 nations that agreed to create a western European free-trade area, effective Jan. 1, 1973. An August pact between East Germany and Switzerland established an exchange of trade missions, which were also to carry out limited consular functions.

Late in 1972, Swiss diplomats were go-betweens in U. S.-Cuban negotiations over air piracy.

PAUL C. HELMREICH
Wheaton College, Mass.

SYRIA

In 1972, Syria's President Hafez al-Assad continued the process begun in 1971 of democratizing Syria's governmental system by establishing the National Progressive Front. Syria's relations with its primary economic and military benefactor—the Soviet Union—and with its fellow members of the Federation of Arab Republics—Egypt and Libya—suffered through a midyear crisis sparked by Egyptian President Anwar el-Sadat's expulsion of Soviet military advisers in July. The apparently successful resolution of this crisis and the success of Assad's domestic political programs unfortunately had little or no effect on the Syrian economy, which, due to an inordinately high military allocation and the dubious wisdom of nationalizing the Iraq Petroleum Company's pipeline, remained in a hapless condition.

Domestic Politics. In March, a significant step was taken toward the liberalization of the Syrian political process. The National Progressive Front was established on March 7, 1972, thereby fulfilling President Assad's promise that the ruling Baath party would take steps to share its political power by unifying itself with the nation's progressive political forces.

The structure of the Front's central committee and the terms of its charter made it apparent that the Baath did not anticipate giving up its dominant position. The central committee, whose membership was announced on April 23, is made up of 18 members. The Baath holds ten positions, and two positions each are held by the Syrian Communists, the Syrian Arab Socialist Unionists, the Arab Socialist Movement, and the Socialist Unionists. The Baath's dominance was further ensured by the Front's charter, which gives only the Baath the authority to engage in political activity in the military and among students. In addition, the Front's policies were to be based on the resolutions of the Baath party's congresses.

Of further significance was the success on March 5, 1972, of conservative forces in nationwide local elections. Since Assad had been less than conciliatory with traditionalist forces in the past, observers pointed out that the conservative success could not have happened without the government's consent. The refusal of the Communists to merge with the Baath to form an Arab Socialist Union such as those in Egypt and Libya compromised the chances for forming a unified political base for the federation of Syria, Egypt, and Libya.

Foreign Affairs. Following the July 18, 1972, announcement by Egypt's President Anwar el-Sadat that the functions of Soviet military advisers in Egypt were terminated, Syria was caught between its Federation ties with Egypt and its reliance on Soviet economic and military aid. On April 20,

——————— **SYRIA** · **Information Highlights** ———————

Official Name: Syrian Arab Republic.
Area: 71,498 square miles (185,180 sq km).
Population (1972 est.): 6,600,000. Density, 85 per square mile (33 per sq km). *Annual rate of increase,* 3.3%.
Chief Cities (1970 census): Damascus, the capital, 835,000; Aleppo, 639,000; Homs, 216,000.
Government: *Head of state,* Lt. Gen. Hafez al-Assad, president (took office March 1971). *Chief Minister,* Gen. Abdel-Rahman Khlefawi, premier (took office May 1971). *Legislature*—People's Council, 173 members. *Major political parties*—Baath party; Syrian Arab Socialist Union; Socialist Union; Arab Socialist Movement; Syrian Communist party.
Language: Arabic (official).
Education: *Expenditure* (1969), 17.1% of total public expenditure. *School enrollment* (1969)—primary, 845,130; secondary, 295,717; technical/vocational, 10,445; university/higher, 37,540.
Monetary Unit: Pound (3.82 pounds equals U. S.$1, Sept. 1972).
Gross National Product (1970 est.): $1,590,000.000.
National Income per Person (1968): $244.
Economic Indexes: *Industrial production* (1968), 171 (1963=100); *agricultural production* (1971), 144 (1952–56=100); *consumer price index* (1971), 125 (1963=100).
Manufacturing (major products): Petroleum products, textiles, cement, glass, soap, processed food.
Major Agricultural Products: Wheat, barley, cotton, sheep and goats, wool.
Major Mineral: Petroleum.
Foreign Trade (1971): *Exports,* $195,000,000 (chief exports—cotton, barley, wool). *Imports,* $439,000,000 (chief imports, 1969—food and live animals, nonelectrical machinery, iron and steel, petroleum and petroleum products). *Chief trading partners* (1969)—USSR (took 17% of exports, supplied 9% of imports); Lebanon (14%—7%); Italy (12%—9%); France (3%—7%).
Transportation: *Motor vehicles* (1970), 48,000 (automobiles, 31,800); *railroads* (1970), 336 miles (541 km); *major national airline,* Syrian Arab Airlines.
Communications: *Telephones* (1971), 114,590; *television stations* (1971), 5; *television sets* (1971), 118,000; *radios* (1970), 1,367,000; *newspapers* (1970), 5.

President Assad had agreed to a Federation proposal to unify the foreign policies of the Federation's three members. Thus, many anticipated that Assad would follow the Egyptian example. However, the flare-up in the Middle East crisis following the guerrilla attacks at Tel Aviv airport and at the Munich Olympics necessitated the maintenance of close relations with the Soviet Union.

On September 3, Syria announced that it would not ask Soviet military personnel to leave. As a result of this announcement and an August 27 agreement with the Soviet Union that allowed the latter to move the main base for its Mediterranean fleet to the Syrian port of Latakia, Syria received massive arms shipments throughout September. These included sophisticated surface-to-air guided missile systems that aided the Syrian Army in retaliating against Israeli air strikes.

Syria's relations with the Federation's members was not overtly affected on other international questions. Assad combined with Sadat and Libya's Qaddafi to denounce strongly the peace plan proposed by Jordan's King Hussein.

Economy. In 1972, Syria went ahead with its efforts to liberalize its economy and attract foreign investments, although its perennial trade deficit, which rose 55.9% in 1971, worsened. The large military spending allocation was a heavy burden, partially offset by a one-year $30 million subsidy granted by Kuwait. However, Syria's economic situation deteriorated due to sagging cotton productivity, Syria's primary export commodity, and to the continuing difficulties it had in marketing its crude oil surpluses. In addition, Syria's nationalization of the Iraq Petroleum Company's petroleum pipeline resulted in a loss of approximately $25 million in royalties.

F. NICHOLAS WILLARD
Georgetown University

TANAKA, Kakuei. See BIOGRAPHY.

TANZANIA

The year 1972 in Tanzania was marred by political violence. Sheikh Abeid Karume, the country's first vice president, was assassinated in April. Later in the year, Ugandan guerrillas launched an invasion against neighboring Uganda from Tanzanian soil. Despite such turmoil, President Julius Nyerere kept the country on a course of innovative political and social reform.

Death of Karume. Sheikh Karume was assassinated on April 7 by an army lieutenant, Humud Mohammed Humud. In addition to being Tanzania's first vice president, Karume had served as chairman of the Zanzibar Revolutionary Council and president of the Afro-Shirazi party, which seized power on Zanzibar in a coup in 1964. President Nyerere appointed Aboud Jumbe, former minister of state in the first vice president's office, to replace Karume.

Ugandan Invasion. With former Ugandan President Milton Obote still in exile in the Tanzanian capital of Dar es Salaam, relations between Tanzania and the military regime in Uganda remained tense. Uganda and Tanzania are partners, together with Kenya, in the East African Community (EAC).

Relations between Tanzania and Uganda received a setback in September, when Ugandan guerrillas in exile in Tanzania crossed the Ugandan border in the hope of sparking a pro-Obote uprising. The invasion attempt was quickly repulsed. In early October, however, Tanzania's new foreign minister, John Malecela, met with representatives of Somalia, the Organization of African Unity, and Uganda at Mogadishu, Somalia, where a settlement of major differences between Tanzania and Uganda was announced. The settlement included agreements for a mutual pullback from the border and a cessation of hostile propaganda.

Decentralization of Government. A move to decentralize the organization of government was announced in January and implemented in July. Expenditures and planning, previously done on the national level, were now to be carried out on the regional level. A post of director of development was established for each region in Tanzania, and changes in spending priorities within regions were allowed without direct authorization from Dar es Salaam.

The program of decentralization was in keeping with the call of the Arusha Declaration of 1967 for self-reliance by individuals and by local areas. Decentralization was also expected to strengthen the ruling Tanganyika African National Union (TANU) party, since regional commissioners, area commissioners, and other district officials, all of whose roles were expanded under the new plan, were officials of TANU.

In February, in conjunction with the decentralization move, President Nyerere announced a reshuffling of his cabinet, including ministers, regional commissioners, and principal secretaries. Five ministers were sent to the various regions in Tanzania to upgrade government at the regional level.

At the same time, Rashidi Kawawa, formerly second vice president and a longtime lieutenant of Nyerere, assumed the new post of prime minister.

In other governmental changes, the National Assembly passed a bill allowing civil servants to become members of parliament. The action continued a trend toward merging the institutions of the ruling party with the organs of government. In another vote, however, the National Assembly rejected a constitutional amendment that would have permitted regional commissioners to be elected to parliament.

The merger of Tanzania's two leading English language newspapers, the *Nationalist* and the *Tanzanian Standard,* took place in April.

Economy. In 1972, Chinese technicians continued their work on the Tan-Zam railroad, which will eventually connect the port of Dar es Salaam with Lusaka, the capital of Zambia. Through its involvement in that project, China was replacing Britain as Tanzania's main supplier. According to the terms of the agreement, local costs of production must be offset by Zambian and Tanzanian purchases of Chinese products.

Economic assistance was also provided by the United States. American loans totalling $3.8 million were provided for the completion of the all-weather Tanzania-Zambia highway, a project in which U. S. aid was already playing a major role. In addition, Finland furnished $3.6 million of soft loans, and the International Development Association provided credits equivalent to $10.8 million.

JAY E. HAKES
Louisiana State University in New Orleans

─────── **TANZANIA • Information Highlights** ───────

Official Name: United Republic of Tanzania.
Area: 364,898 square miles (945,087 sq km).
Population (1972 est.): 14,000,000. *Density,* 36 per square mile (14 per sq km). *Annual rate of increase,* 2.6%.
Chief City (1967 census): Dar es Salaam, the capital, 272,821.
Government: *Head of state,* Julius K. Nyerere, president (took office April 1964). *Chief minister,* Rashidi Kawawa, prime minister (took office Feb. 1972). *Legislature* (unicameral) —National Assembly, 187 members. *Major political parties* —Tanganyika African National Union and its affiliate in Zanzibar, Afro-Shirazi party.
Languages: English, Swahili (both official).
Education: *School enrollment* (1968)—primary, 833,898; secondary, 38,288; technical/vocational, 1,064; university/ higher, 1,932.
Monetary Unit: Shilling (7.143 shillings equal U. S.$1, Sept. 1972).
Gross National Product (1970 est.): $1,332,000,000.
Manufacturing (major products): Textiles, cement, petroleum products, refined sugar, aluminum.
Major Agricultural Products: Cloves (ranks 1st among world producers, 1971), cotton, sisal, coffee, oilseeds, groundnuts, tea, tobacco, sugarcane.
Major Minerals: Diamonds, gold, gem stones.
Foreign Trade (1971): *Exports,* $251,000,000. *Imports,* $338,-000,000. *Chief trading partners* (1969)—United Kingdom (took 26% of exports, supplied 27% of imports); United States (8%—6%); Japan (5%—9%); India (8%—3%).
Communications: *Telephones* (1971), 36,051; *television stations* (1971), 1; *television sets* (1971), 3,000; *newspapers* (1969), 4 (daily circulation, 61,000).

TAXATION

Important U. S. federal tax changes enacted in the Revenue Act of 1971 went into effect at the beginning of 1972. They included a 7% investment tax credit, repeal of the automobile excise tax, and an increase in the personal income tax exemption for 1972. The investment tax credit was intended to increase corporate profits as a means of stimulating investment, and preliminary reports for 1972 indicated that this objective was accomplished. The repeal of the automobile excise tax was an important factor in the substantial increase in car sales during 1972. The personal income tax exemption of $750 for 1972, together with the low-income allowance of $1,300, eliminated the personal income tax on those below the poverty line. Unfortunately for many taxpayers this benefit was offset by an increase in social security taxes that went into effect in January 1972.

President Richard M. Nixon campaigned on a promise of no increase in federal tax rates and gen-

erally indicated his opposition to tax reform proposals. At the end of 1972, however, it appeared that it would be difficult to sustain the promise of no tax increases in the face of rapidly rising federal budget deficits.

Revenue Sharing. The most significant fiscal development in 1972 was the initiation of revenue sharing, signed into law in October. The legislation was the product of some eight years of debate over an important change in the structure of intergovernmental fiscal relations.

Traditionally, federal grants-in-aid were restricted to specific programs legislated by Congress. The great bulk of these federal grants went to the states, which then redirected certain funds to local governments. However, some federal grants went directly to local governments.

For the first time in history, revenue sharing provided generally unrestricted grants to both state and local governments. The State and Local Fiscal Assistance Act of 1972 provided for the distribution of $5.3 billion for calendar 1972. The amount to be distributed was to rise to about $5.7 billion in 1973 and to increase annually until it reached $6.6 billion in 1977. One third of the funds was to go to the states, while two thirds was to go to local governments.

States were given a choice of two formulas for determining their shares of the total revenue. One formula involves three factors: population, tax effort, and income level, with poor states receiving more than rich states. The second formula adds to these factors an income tax element and some weighting for the proportion of the state's population in urbanized areas. The states were generally unrestricted in the uses to which the funds may be put.

The legislation required that the two-thirds share for local governments be distributed to counties on the basis of population, tax effort, and income level. It also required that the counties redistribute a portion of their share to local governments on the basis of tax collections, except for taxes paid for education. Local governments were precluded from spending shared revenues for education and from using the shared revenues to match other federal grant programs.

Revenue sharing is intended to accomplish a number of objectives, including the transfer of control over public resources from federal to state and local governments, some equalization of the fiscal capacities of state and local governments, some reward to state and local governments that tax most heavily, and mild encouragement to states that have income taxes in their revenue structures.

The annual amounts involved in revenue sharing were relatively small. For example, recent annual increases in the total expenditures of state and local governments amounted to more than $5 billion, which is equivalent to the total amount for revenue sharing in 1972. Nevertheless, the Congress may appropriate additional funds in future years, thus giving state and local governments further access to the revenue of the federal government.

Social Security. In June legislation was approved for a 20% increase in social security benefits, with future benefits automatically linked to changes in the cost of living. In October, President Nixon signed a major congressional revision of the social security program. The legislation provided for an extension of medicare coverage to those already covered by disability insurance and increased

U. S. GOVERNMENT TAX REVENUES

Tax source	Fiscal year 1970	Fiscal year 1971	Fiscal year 1972
		(billions of dollars)	
Individual income......	$ 90.4	$ 86.2	$ 94.8
Corporation income.....	32.8	26.8	32.0
Social security.........	45.3	48.6	53.9
Excises...............	15.7	16.6	15.5
Estate and gift.........	3.6	3.7	5.4
Customs..............	2.4	2.6	3.3
Miscellaneous.........	3.4	3.9	3.6
Total...............	$193.7	$188.4	$208.6

monthly benefits for low-income wage earners. Supplementary federal payments were authorized for the aged, the blind, and the disabled. Income that might be earned by retirees without a reduction in their social security benefits was increased from $1,680 to $2,100.

To finance the provisions that were legislated in June and October, Congress raised payroll taxes for social security from 5.5% to 5.85% for both employers and employees and increased the annual taxable limit per employee to $10,800 in 1973 and $12,000 thereafter. In combination, the social security tax increase in 1972 and the investment tax credit reduced the overall progressivity of the federal tax system. (See also SOCIAL WELFARE—*Social Security.*)

State Tax Developments. In 1971 state legislatures adopted measures to increase tax collections by $5 billion, but in 1972 state measures for new or higher taxes amounted to only $875 million annually as estimated by the Tax Foundation Inc. In no state was there a major tax revision, although Idaho and New Jersey adopted fairly comprehensive tax increases. The personal income tax was increased in New York and Virginia and was modified in Idaho, Michigan, Missouri, and Vermont. Corporate income taxes were raised in Idaho, Nebraska, New Jersey, and Virginia, while sales tax rates were increased in Kentucky, Connecticut, Nebraska, and Tennessee. Connecticut and some parts of New York now are taxing sales at 7%, the highest rate in the nation. Excise taxes on motor fuels, alcoholic beverages, and cigarettes were increased in a large number of states. Missouri joined the list of states that moved toward making the state income tax base conform with the federal base. Property tax relief for the elderly and the disabled was growing as 11 states modified their revenue structures in this direction in 1972.

A number of state legislatures considered major proposals for shifting a part or all of the cost of public education from the local to the state level. In this important area of intergovernmental fiscal relations the states apparently will await the outcome of *San Antonio* vs. *Rodriguez,* which was argued before the U. S. Supreme Court in October. If a lower court ruling is sustained by the Supreme Court in 1973, the states will be required to equalize the taxable resources that are made available to all school districts within any state. This will require legislation, state by state, possibly in the form of uniform statewide property taxes for educational support.

State Referenda. In November, voters in California, Colorado, Michigan, and Oregon readily defeated proposed constitutional amendments to limit or kill the property tax as a source of funds for public education. In Washington an amendment to limit further use of the property tax for schools was approved.

U. S. Supreme Court Decisions. In *Coit* vs. *Green* the Supreme Court ruled that tax exemptions would not be permitted for private schools in Mississippi that practiced racial segregation, and that contributions to such schools would not be deductible for federal income tax purposes.

A significant estate tax decision was handed down in the case of *United States* vs. *Byrum*. The decedent had established an irrevocable trust consisting of nonvoting stock in three family-held corporations, while retaining control over the dividend policies of the corporations themselves. The Internal Revenue Service had ruled that the trusts must be included in the gross estate, but the court held that the trust must be excluded.

OTHER COUNTRIES

Austria completed legislation on a value-added tax to be introduced in 1973. It also reformed the income and wage tax to move toward taxation of individuals rather than family units.

Britain and *Ireland* completed legislation on a value-added tax in preparation for their entry into the Common Market in 1973.

Canada introduced the sweeping reforms legislated in 1971. These include the introduction of a capital gains tax and a reduction in corporate and individual income taxes.

Finland adopted a pattern of credits for individual and company taxes paid on the receipt of income from foreign sources. The credits apply to the income and net worth taxes.

Israel adopted a 10% value-added tax, accompanied by reductions in income and property tax rates.

Latin American countries, including Argentina, Brazil, Mexico, Paraguay, and El Salvador, initiated a series of tax concessions to encourage exports and domestic investment of foreign capital.

Pakistan announced increases in tax rates that affect sales, income, and wealth. The new rates were designed to obtain greater progressivity in the tax system.

Sweden reduced the first three lower bracket income tax rates by three percentage points. The starting rate became 7%, and the top rate was 54%.

International Tax Treaties. International tax treaties to avoid double taxation of income or capital or both were concluded in 1971–72 by France with Luxembourg and the United States and by Japan with Switzerland and the United States.

(See also STATE GOVERNMENT.)

JESSE BURKHEAD
Syracuse University

TELECOMMUNICATIONS

Two impressive anniversaries occurred in the telecommunications industry during 1972. The first was the 25th anniversary of the transistor, which has developed into a $2.5 billion industry. The second was the 10th anniversary of Telstar 1, the first communications satellite. Transistors and satellites have proven to be indispensable in telecommunications, which includes the transmission and reception of television, telephone, and computer data signals.

Telecommunications via Domestic Satellites. On June 16, 1972, the Federal Communications Commission (FCC) handed down a very important decision concerning the future of domestic satellites. In its decision, the FCC provided for "multiple entry" and "open skies" as they relate to domestic satellite communications. The multiple-entry and open-sky policies were intended to increase competition among companies in telecommunications.

By the decision, all qualified and authorized companies were to be given permission to operate domestic communications satellites. In further attempting to open competition, the FCC rejected a proposed joint effort by the American Telephone and Telegraph Company and Comsat (Communications Satellite Corp.). For a company to qualify, it must show that it is financially and technically competent and that its domestic satellite service would serve the public interest. Eight organizations, including Comsat and AT&T, have shown interest in providing their own domestic satellite service.

For a company to enter the domestic satellite communication business, it must pay the National Aeronautics Space Administration (NASA) about $26 million to launch a satellite into space. Although the initial cost of launching a satellite is high, there are some cost advantages once the satellite is up. For instance, as *Fortune* magazine pointed out, "it costs the same to transmit [by satellite] from New York to Honolulu as from New York to Newark, New Jersey." Another cost advantage of the satellite is that it can provide at least 12 television channels or 9,000 telephone circuits to all earth stations in or near the mainland of the United States. There is a very good chance that communication satellites will hasten economic growth in such areas as Puerto Rico, Hawaii, and Alaska. The reason for this is that a relatively inexpensive communication linkage to the mainland can be established and maintained.

Data Communications. Another rapidly growing area in the field of telecommunications is the transmission of computer data. This type of service, first introduced in 1958, probably was the fastest growing segment of the telecommunications industry in 1972. Early in the year the Bell System (part of AT&T) provided about 75 different types of Data-Phone (data communications) sets with some 20 speeds of operation to suit a user's particular needs. Its direct-dialed network handled digital computer data at a speed of 4,800 bits per second, while its private-line voice-grade channels could handle 10,-800 bits per second. The company said its data market accounted for more than $500 million in annual revenue.

As in the domestic communications satellite decision, the FCC has attempted to increase competition in data communications by opening the terminal equipment market and private-line services to small specialized companies. The opening up of such competition can be traced to the landmark Carterfone decision in 1968, which weakened the grip of giant AT&T and other big telecommunications companies.

After the Carterfone decision, competitors such as Microwave Communications, Inc., opened specialized communication lines between important centers such as Chicago and St. Louis. This type of new competition—about 1,800 applications for specialized communications have been filed with the FCC—has led to charge rate realignment by AT&T.

A new technique involving data transmission is called "Data Under Voice." In this technique the data signals occupy lower frequency bands than those used for telephone voice signals, and both the data and the voice signals are sent simultaneously over a radio relay system.

TELEPHONES IN MAJOR COUNTRIES

Country	Telephones Jan. 1, 1971	% increase over 1970	No. per 100 population
Argentina	1,746,015	4.7	7.17
Australia	3,913,167	8.7	31.18
Austria	1,427,333	7.0	19.29
Belgium	2,018,827	4.2	20.83
Brazil	2,000,720	12.0	2.17
Canada	9,752,537	4.9	45.23
Colombia	974,415	69.4	4.54
Czechoslovakia	2,003,421	5.7	13.82
Denmark	1,696,765	6.1	34.42
Finland	1,180,785	8.4	25.21
France	8,774,261	8.1	17.19
Germany, East	2,089,216	5.2	12.11
Germany, West	13,834,827	11.1	22.43
Greece	1,044,777	18.6	11.96
Hong Kong	583,222	16.1	14.76
Hungary	823,600	5.9	7.96
India	1,245,352	7.4	0.23
Israel	510,550	11.5	17.47
Italy	9,368,732	9.9	17.38
Japan	26,233,360	13.4	25.14
Korea, South	633,818	12.8	2.01
Mexico	1,507,363	13.5	2.97
Netherlands	3,409,842	9.3	26.00
New Zealand	1,262,427	5.0	44.14
Norway	1,144,795	5.0	29.41
Poland	1,867,086	6.3	5.67
Portugal	749,963	7.4	7.76
South Africa	1,553,825	4.8	7.06
Spain	4,604,368	11.6	13.56
Sweden	4,505,802	4.6	55.67
Switzerland	3,025,779	6.3	48.26
Turkey	576,943	12.3	1.62
USSR	11,000,000	..	4.51
United Kingdom	14,966,748	7.3	26.68
United States	120,218,000	4.3	58.35
Yugoslavia	736,045	18.2	3.57

THE AMERICAN TELEPHONE & TELEGRAPH COMPANY

THE AMERICAN TELEPHONE & TELEGRAPH COMPANY

REVERSAL of roles in the communications industry. Men in Wichita Falls, Texas (top), operate switchboard. In Yuba City, Calif. (bottom), one of several women employed as telephone linemen checks with her office.

Picturephone. Picturephone very likely will play an important role in the future of communications, even though this visual telephone service grew slowly in 1972. Picturephone was first introduced experimentally in 1964, and steady improvements have been made since then. In 1972, there were approximately 150 sets in operation in Chicago, which has become the largest Picturephone center. It was first introduced in Pittsburgh in 1970, but growth has slowed in that area.

So far Picturephone has been more successful in meeting the needs of special customers rather than those of the general customer. For instance, doctors can view medical specimens and X-ray photographs from distant points, businessmen can get visual information generated by computers, architects can examine blueprints, engineers can inspect machine parts, and bankers can compare signatures and check account balances.

Undersea Cable. The FCC approved an application for laying a $145 million undersea telephone and telegraph cable between the United States and Europe. The new cable, called TAT 6, will connect Green Hill, R. I., and St. Hilaire de Riez, France. Its traffic handling capacity will be four times greater than that of any existing undersea cable. TAT 6 will be shared by AT&T, ITT World Communications, RCA Global Communications, and Western Union International. The FCC also received a request to lay a new $121.6 million undersea cable between Hawaii and Okinawa via Guam.

Overseas Rate Changes. The cost of a three-minute station-to-station telephone call from the United States to the Soviet Union dropped from $12 to $9 on weekdays and from $9 to $6.75 on Sundays. The overtime cost per minute became $3 on weekdays and $2.25 on Sundays. About the same rates apply for U. S. calls to Okinawa.

In 1972, 18 countries were able to receive customer-dialed calls from the United States. The total international traffic in 1972 was about 33 million messages. This traffic is expected to rise to 200 million messages by 1980.

New Technology. A new "hands-free" coin telephone was being tried out in six cities in 1972. After the caller presses the button of a phone and dials the number, the other party's voice comes through a loudspeaker in the booth. More technical and complicated innovations were being tried out. For example, a new electronic switching system that will handle 350,000 calls an hour was being developed by Bell Telephone Laboratories. Also, the first commercial T2 transmission system was scheduled to go into service between Dallas and Longview, Texas. The system will use pulse-code modulation (PCM) in transmitting voice, data, and facsimile information. PCM is a digital transmission method and thus a very significant departure from the traditional analog method for transmitting telephone calls.

(See also TELEVISION AND RADIO—*Television and Radio Engineering*.)

PAUL WEINER, *University of Connecticut*

British-born Alistair Cooke examined the history and character of his adopted country in America: A Personal View, *shown in 13 episodes on NBC and produced by BBC and Time-Life Films.*

television and radio

The year 1972 was successful economically for both television and radio. But while radio stations had some of their rules eased, television was subjected to increasing government pressure. The Justice Department filed antitrust suits to restrict the role of the networks in the production of entertainment programs, and the White House drafted legislation that would hold individual TV stations accountable for the content of all network programs that they broadcast locally.

TELEVISION BROADCASTING

The year 1972, which must have seemed to the viewer a dull and routine year in television, was for the network and station operators a full 12 months of shocks and surprises. Attacks on TV drug advertising, on broadcasting freedom, on the ever-mounting use of reruns, along with still unresolved questions about cable television, prime-time access, the fairness doctrine, and the Justice Depart-

ment's suit against the networks—all of these sent shock waves coursing through the industry. On the bright side, however, 1972 was a banner year in terms of profits.

Economy. By the end of October it was clear that commercial television was headed for perhaps the best year in profits and revenues in its history. Projections were that the industry would hit a record peak of $3 billion, up 10% from 1971, and that earnings might be up 35%, to $590 million. Growth was greatest at ABC, Inc., which reported nine-month earnings up 154% over the previous year, and revenues up 161%. Only CBS, with a protracted technicians' strike, had much to worry about.

The strike against CBS by the International Brotherhood of Electrical Workers (IBEW), from November 3 to December 28, was called not over the usual issues of wages and fringe benefits, but over questions of automation. IBEW demanded full control over newly developed electronic equipment that requires no specialized technical knowledge or skill to operate. But CBS wanted the new devices available to be used by performers, especially newsmen, directors, and other non-IBEW personnel.

Earlier in the year CBS (the parent company) had found itself in the regrettable position of having to seek a new president. Charles Ireland, who had joined CBS in that post in October 1971, died on June 8, 1972, at the age of 51. The position went to 37-year-old Arthur R. Taylor, like Ireland a financial specialist rather than a broadcaster.

Government Actions. Surprise, shock, even disbelief were the industry's reaction to the Justice Department's announcement on April 10 that it planned to file civil antitrust suits against the TV networks, seeking to put them out of the business of program production. CBS stated that the purpose of the suits was to transfer control of network schedules "to advertising agencies and motion picture producers" and to prevent the networks from producing any TV entertainment programs or feature films. *Broadcasting* magazine pointed out that the suits seemed to be out of date, and were based on statistics and practices of no more recent vintage than 1967, which were no longer valid. As time went on, little more was heard of the issue, and it became clear that the suits would consume several years of court action before final resolution.

On December 18, Clay T. Whitehead, director of the White House Office of Telecommunications Policy announced that the White House had drafted legislation that would make local TV stations accountable for the content of all network programs that they broadcast, including news, entertainment, and advertisements. Condemning "ideological plugola" in network news, Whitehead said that individual stations would risk losing their licenses if they failed to "act to correct imbalance or consistent bias from the networks." The industry feared that the Nixon administration was seeking the means to censor news and documentary programming.

Television and Advertising. Criticism of television advertising was hardly new, but it took on fresh dimensions when the Federal Trade Commission (FTC) announced in April its intention of filing complaints against the three drug companies with the highest television advertising expenditures. The FTC was charging that some of the companies' claims for their products had not been validated. The three companies had been spending about $78 million annually in TV and radio advertising.

Broadcasting's immediate concern with these charges came from the FTC's request that 25% of all advertising time for a period of two years be given to correcting the questioned advertising. The Television Bureau of Advertising estimated that "counter-advertising" of this sort could turn broadcasting from a profitable enterprise into a multimillion-dollar loss operation.

Federal Communications Commission. Questions concerning prime-time access, public access to the air, and the fairness doctrine created ever stronger pressure on the FCC, partly because 1972 was an election year and many wished to be heard.

The networks remained unhappy with the FCC's limitation of their prime-time access to three hours a night. The FCC refused the request of ABC that it continue to be allowed an extra half-hour of prime time on Tuesdays. With the fall season, then, the three networks broadcast six nights from 8 to 11 P. M.; on Sundays CBS and NBC shifted to 7:30 to 10:30 P. M.

Requests for repeal of the prime-time rule came from many local stations, alleging financial loss and inability to program in the public interest in the extra half-hour (which had been the intention of the ruling). In July, Rep. Barry Goldwater, Jr. (R., Calif.) urged the FCC to abolish the prime-time access rule, claiming that it had failed in its purpose of creating diversity and had succeeded only in hurting broadcasters and TV and motion picture producers. A special report, instigated by the FCC, indicated that the rule in its first year had cost Hollywood producers $50 million worth of network program production.

On the question of public access to the air, the FCC has in the past permitted broadcasters to refuse time to public groups for the discussion of controversial matters, on the ground that the fairness doctrine requires broadcasters to inform the public of all sides of the issues. In July 1971 the U. S. Court of Appeals in Washington ruled that the public's First Amendment rights were being violated.

In February 1972 the Supreme Court ordered a stay of the Appeals Court decision and agreed to review the case in the fall. Fuel was added to the fire in the form of petitions from two groups of Congressmen—the Black Caucus and a group of 14—that had asked the networks to give or sell them time. Both of these groups had been refused time on the grounds that the networks had amply fulfilled their fairness doctrine requirements. At issue seemed to be the question of whether the fairness doctrine could legitimately be turned into a right-of-access doctrine.

The FCC got its first black commissioner with the nomination of Judge Benjamin L. Hooks of Memphis, Tenn., to succeed Robert T. Bartley, retiring after 20 years on the commission. Richard E. Wiley was confirmed for a full term after serving under a recess appointment.

Television News. In 1972 the public, in several polls, named television as its major source of news and, more importantly, affirmed television news as the most credible.

Several of the nation's courts, with the blessing of the Justice Department and, eventually, of the Supreme Court, refused any longer to allow TV or print journalists the traditional right to protect their sources of information. The Supreme Court decision, handed down at the end of June, specifically denied the right to newsmen testifying before grand juries. The decision had an immediate bearing on five cases involving four newspaper reporters and a TV cameraman. Both houses of Congress went back to work on legislation to protect newsmen's privilege, in the face of strongly expressed Justice Department opposition.

Television news had several events of major importance to cover, and handled them as adroitly as the public has come to expect. Coverage of the president's trip to China was sharply limited by the host country, but the trip to Moscow was freer and some 240 newsmen were on hand. Sportscasters became newsmen with the tragic events that oc-

MASTERPIECE THEATRE, *the highly praised British dramatic series shown on PBS, included the performances of Emmy winner Glenda Jackson as Queen Elizabeth I in* Elizabeth R (left), *and Margaret Tyzack in Balzac's* Cousin Bette (right).

curred in September at the Olympic Games in Munich. The conventions of the two national parties, election night returns, and the Apollo 17 mission were all handled smoothly.

Public Television. One of the basic issues in public broadcasting surfaced with President Nixon's veto in June of a two-year, $155 million funding bill for the Corporation for Public Broadcasting (CPB). In his veto message the President asked whether "an organization originally intended to serve only the local stations is becoming instead the center of control ... for the entire public broadcasting system." Even deeper than that question, however, was the question of whether an organization funded in large part by the government could be kept free of governmental control. Behind these questions lies the unresolved question of what is the proper function of public broadcasting.

The CPB received one-year funding of $45 million in August. There were three major changes in its composition. It had a new chairman, a new president, and, for the first time in its history, a Republican majority on its board. The new president was Henry W. Loomis, former deputy director of the United States Information Agency.

Cable Television. Although bound by FCC rules, the cable industry could take heart from the pronouncement made by the White House Office of Telecommunications Policy (OTP) that in the President's view cable should be allowed to develop as free of regulation as possible. In 1972 there were about 2,750 cable systems in operation in the United States, and another 1,950 approved but not built. Existing systems served about 18.5 million viewers in 6 million homes. Of note was the decision of Judge Constance Baker Motley of the U. S. Southern District Court in New York that, on the basis of existing law, cable had no copyright liability in the materials it picked up from on-air television.

Programming. It was not until 1972 was half gone that the question of reruns of prime-time programs came to the fore. It received full attention when the President instructed his Office of Telecommunications Policy to seek remedial action. The existing pattern calls for the making of about 22 new programs for each series annually, the remainder of the time being given to reruns and occasional specials. To limit reruns, as the Hollywood craft guilds urged, to 25% of prime-time would require the production of as many as 12 more programs in each series, an additional expenditure of about $120 million per year. According to CBS-TV president Robert D. Wood, such additional programs in 1971 would have resulted in a combined loss to the three networks of $65 million.

RADIO BROADCASTING

Radio's 50th anniversary (reckoned from 1922, the year in which radio stations jumped from 30 licenses to nearly 600) was celebrated with very little fanfare, consisting of an occasional feature story in a magazine or newspaper and some locally produced retrospective programs. Looking ahead, there were signs of significant changes.

Economics and Growth. Radio probably figured in the large economic upswing experienced in television in 1972, although the medium is known to lag behind TV in its response to economic change. Actual figures for group-owned stations are next to impossible to dig out of corporate reports, and require enormous spadework to amass for the independents. Still, industry spokesmen seemed to be

Peter Falk (left) *became a 1972 favorite as rumpled police detective Columbo on the* NBC Sunday Mystery Movie.

NBC-TV

content with the rate of growth, even predicting that radio could hit the $2 billion figure by 1976.

Even FM radio, for so long a stepchild, showed signs of taking its rightful place beside AM. More and more FM stations abandoned the traditional classical music format in favor of music of broader appeal (not always without listener opposition) and gave up their traditional identification with sister AM stations. For example, WOR(FM) New York, a progressive rock station, changed its call letters to WXLO. A record was set for an FM sale price when General Electric paid Kaiser Broadcasting $3.6 million for WJIB(FM), Boston.

Deregulation. The Federal Communications Commission took first steps toward easing some of the rules under which radio stations must operate. The National Association of Broadcasters had suggested such action more than two years earlier. But the fuse was really lit by Clay T. Whitehead, director of the Office of Telecommunications Policy, in a speech late in 1971, in which he suggested that radio should not be regarded as TV, and perhaps should be totally deregulated. In May 1972 the FCC amended its rules to allow third-class operators at small stations to assume some of the responsibilities of first-class license holders. In December it went a

UPI

ALL IN THE FAMILY *almost swept the 1972 Emmy awards in the comedy series division. Winning as best actor, actress, and supporting actress were* (from left) *Carroll O'Connor, Jean Stapleton, and Sally Struthers.*

NOTABLE U.S. TELEVISION PROGRAMS OF 1972

A CONVERSATION WITH PRESIDENT NIXON—A session conducted by Dan Rather. CBS, Jan. 2.

A MURROW RETROSPECTIVE—A week-long showing of several documentaries by the late Edward R. Murrow, originally done for CBS. PBS, Jan. 3–7.

AMERICA—Series of 13 programs examining American history, written and narrated by Alistair Cooke. NBC, alternate weeks beginning Nov. 14.

ANTIGONE (Playhouse New York)—Jean Anouilh's play based on Sophocles' tragedy, starring Genevieve Bujold, Fritz Weaver, and Stacy Keach. PBS, Oct. 1.

THE CAVE MEN OF MINDANAO (NBC Reports)—Documentary about the recently discovered Tasaday aborigines in a Philippine rain forest. NBC, Oct. 10.

CHINA LOST AND FOUND—A comprehensive report on relationships between China and the United States, narrated by John Chancellor. NBC, Feb. 15.

COUSIN BETTE (Masterpiece Theater)—A 5-part dramatization of Honoré de Balzac's brilliant story of jealousy and deadly revenge. PBS, weekly beginning Nov. 5.

ELIZABETH R (Masterpiece Theater)—The life story of Queen Elizabeth I, presented in six episodes and starring Glenda Jackson. PBS, weekly from Feb. 13.

ESSENE (Special of the Week)—Documentary by Fred Wiseman of a monastic brotherhood in the Midwest. PBS, Nov. 13.

GUILTY BY REASON OF RACE (NBC Reports)—An assessment of the detention of Japanese-Americans in camps in the United States during World War II, narrated by Robert Northshield. NBC, Sept. 19.

JACK LEMMON IN 'S WONDERFUL, 'S MARVELOUS, 'S GERSHWIN—A salute to the music and lyrics of George and Ira Gershwin, with Jack Lemmon, Fred Astaire, Leslie Uggams, Ethel Merman, Peter Nero, and others. NBC, Jan. 17.

LIFE, DEATH, AND THE AMERICAN WOMAN—Documentary examining diseases most likely to prove serious to the American woman and how to prevent them, narrated by Patricia Neal. ABC, April 27.

LIZA WITH A "Z"—Liza Minnelli. NBC, Oct. 10.

LOOK HOMEWARD, ANGEL (CBS Playhouse 90)—Adaptation of Ketti Frings' play based on Thomas Wolfe's novel, starring Geraldine Page, E. G. Marshall, and Timothy Bottoms. CBS, Feb. 25.

LORRAINE HANSBERRY: TO BE YOUNG, GIFTED, AND BLACK (NET Playhouse: Biographies)—Television adaptation of Off-Broadway play depicting the life and works of the black playwright, with Ruby Dee, Al Freeman, Jr., and Claudia McNeil. PBS, Jan. 20.

THE METROPOLITAN OPERA SALUTE TO RUDOLF BING—Highlights of the concert to honor the retiring general manager of the Met. CBS, April 30.

MISUNDERSTANDING CHINA—An exploration of a century of misconceptions that Americans have had about the Chinese, narrated by Charles Kuralt. CBS, Feb. 20.

ONCE UPON A MATTRESS—New production of the musical based on Hans Christian Andersen's fairy tale *The Princess and the Pea,* starring Carol Burnett and Ken Berry. CBS, Dec. 12.

THE ROADS TO FREEDOM—A 13-part dramatization of Jean-Paul Sartre's trilogy of novels—*The Age of Reason, The Reprieve,* and *The Troubled Sleep*—recreating the period leading to the fall of France in 1940, with Michael Bryant, Daniel Massey, Donald Burton, and Georgia Brown. PBS, weekly from Nov. 13.

THE SEARCH FOR THE NILE—A 6-part series narrated by James Mason examining the principal characters involved in the 19th century search for the source of the Nile. NBC, weekly from Jan. 25.

THE SHADOW OF A GUNMAN (Special of the Week)—Sean O'Casey's portrait of a poet in strife-torn Ireland in the 1920's, starring Jack MacGowran and Frank Converse. PBS, Dec. 4.

THE SLEEPING BEAUTY—Performed by the National Ballet of Canada and choreographed and danced by Rudolf Nureyev, and also starring Veronica Tennant. PBS, Dec. 17.

SUFFER THE LITTLE CHILDREN—News special showing the effects on children of the hatred and violence in Northern Ireland. NBC, Jan. 11.

SUMMER OLYMPIC GAMES—Opening, closing, and sporting events of the 1972 Olympics in Munich. ABC, Aug. 26–Sept. 11.

THE TROUBLE WITH PEOPLE—Five comedy sketches written for television by Neil Simon and starring George C. Scott, Alan Arkin, and others. NBC, Nov. 11.

THE UNDERSEA WORLD OF JACQUES COSTEAU: THE SMILE OF THE WALRUS—Special program with the French undersea explorer. ABC, Nov. 15.

UN DAY CONCERT 1972—Concert honoring the United Nations' 27th anniversary, featuring the New Jersey Symphony Orchestra, mezzo-soprano Marilyn Horne, and pianist Alicia de Larrocha. PBS, Oct. 23.

VD BLUES (Special of the Week)—Program launching a nationwide campaign to combat the venereal disease epidemic, hosted by Dick Cavett. PBS, Oct. 9.

WILL ROGERS, U.S.A.—James Whitmore in a one-man show as Will Rogers. CBS, March 9.

step further, easing technical requirements having to do with meter reading, logging, transmitter inspection, and rebroadcasts of programs. CBS suggested that a group of stations in a major market be allowed to test total deregulation for a time.

Radio at Its Finest. When tropical storm Agnes hit the northeast with floods in June, most local radio stations abandoned their usual programs and commercials to provide emergency services to the affected areas. A "flood information network" of 13 stations was quickly set up within the devastated areas, and stations on the periphery turned to the task of collecting and air-lifting goods and money for relief. Many stations operated on a 24-hour basis, often with temporary or make-shift equipment. It was a notable effort.

JOHN M. GUNN
State University of New York at Albany

TELEVISION AND RADIO ENGINEERING

The growth of commercial television broadcasting stations in the United States leveled off in 1972, apparently because most viewers were able to receive the signals of the three major commercial networks. Independent (nonnetwork) stations were flourishing in many of the larger cities, although competitive pressures and UHF reception problems caused the end of operations for some independent stations. The growth of educational (public) TV stations also lagged in 1972, due in part to a controversy over whether federal funds for public broadcasting should be concentrated at the national or local level.

TV Broadcasting. In the United States, there were 511 VHF and 190 UHF commercial stations on the air at the end of 1972, compared with 510 VHF and 189 UHF stations a year earlier. Also, there were 91 VHF and 130 UHF public stations on the air at the end of 1972, compared with 88 VHF and 117 UHF stations a year earlier.

Cable TV. Steady growth of cable TV (CATV) continued during 1972. CATV began to move significantly into the larger cities as a result of a February decision by the Federal Communications Commission (FCC) that permitted CATV systems in major markets to carry out-of-town programs on the local systems. The FCC also required larger CATV systems to originate their own programs after a June decision by the U. S. Supreme Court reversed a contrary holding by a U. S. court of appeals in 1971. The FCC also required that the larger systems provide "public-access" channels and be built for easy conversion to a cable system that carries messages out of the home as well as TV programs into it. However, actual use of two-way systems continued to be experimental in 1972.

TV via Satellites. The first North American domestic communications satellite, Anik 1, was launched from Cape Kennedy on November 9 for use by Telesat Canada. The Canadian satellite was to be used for radio, telephone, and television relaying throughout Canada, especially to remote northern regions that have had few or no communication links. In the United States, debate on the use of domestic satellites continued into its seventh year in 1972.

An experimental satellite for direct broadcasting was scheduled to be launched by the United States early in 1973. As a first step, it was planned to position the satellite so that it could be used for broadcasting educational television programs in the Rocky Mountain region for several months. Since the satellite signals cannot be picked up on ordinary home TV receivers, plans were being made to install a number of special receivers in schools and to carry the satellite programs on CATV systems in the Rocky Mountain area. Later, the satellite was to be repositioned for direct broadcasting to India.

International satellite relaying got a big boost in 1972 with two special events—the relaying of

---

SUMMARY OF WORLD TELEVISION
(As of March 1972)

Country	Stations	Number of TV sets	Country	Stations	Number of TV sets	Country	Stations	Number of TV sets
Albania	1	2,500	Haiti	1	10,500	Pakistan	5	150,000
Algeria	6	200,000	Honduras	5	45,000	Panama	11	171,500
Antigua	1	8,500	Hong Kong	3	633,000	Paraguay	1	45,000
Arab Republic of Egypt	23	550,000	Hungary	11	1,865,000	Peru	18	450,000
			Iceland	25	41,000	Philippines	28	426,000
Argentina	31	3,500,000	India	1	21,000	Poland	27	4,225,000
Australia	93	2,950,000	Indonesia	11	150,000	Portugal	11	390,000
Austria	128	1,627,000	Iran	12	250,000	Puerto Rico[1]		600,000
Barbados	1	20,000	Iraq	4	500,000	Qatar	1	25,000
Belgium	15	2,105,000	Ireland	22	522,000	Rhodesia	2	45,000
Bermuda	2	20,000	Israel	12	430,000	Rumania	17	1,485,000
Bolivia	1	12,000	Italy	74	11,800,000	Saudi Arabia	7	300,000
Brazil	53	6,580,000	Ivory Coast	4	70,000	Sierra Leone	1	3,500
Bulgaria	7	1,200,000	Jamaica	9	75,000	Singapore	2	169,000
Cambodia	2	30,000	Japan	195	23,100,000	Spain	32	4,372,000
Canada	401	8,260,000	Jordan	1	50,000	Sudan	2	65,000
Chile	3	500,000	Kenya	3	25,000	Surinam	1	30,000
China (Mainland)	30	300,000	Korea	10	650,000	Sweden	184	3,400,000
Colombia	15	700,000	Kuwait	3	120,000	Switzerland	108	1,355,000
Costa Rica	4	125,000	Lebanon	9	300,000	Syria	5	135,000
Cuba	25	555,000	Liberia	1	6,500	Taiwan	4	1,206,200
Cyprus	2	50,000	Libya	2	1,500	Thailand	5	225,000
Czechoslovakia	28	3,100,000	Luxembourg	1	78,000	Trinidad & Tobago	3	54,000
Denmark	30	1,527,000	Malaysia	18	180,000	Tunisia	9	72,000
Dominican Republic	6	150,000	Malta	1	65,000	Turkey	1	56,000
Ecuador	11	110,000	Martinique	1	9,500	Uganda	6	15,000
El Salvador	4	100,000	Mauritius	1	20,000	United Kingdom	247	16,600,000
Ethiopia	1	7,000	Mexico	80	4,000,000	United States[2]	914	98,600,000
Finland	68	1,111,000	Monaco	1	16,000	Upper Volta	1	4,000
France	130	12,400,000	Morocco	8	203,000	Uruguay	12	350,000
Gabon	2	2,400	Netherlands	16	3,575,000	USSR	167	40,000,000
Germany (East)	25	5,310,000	Netherlands Antilles	2	32,000	Venezuela	31	710,000
Germany (West)	176	17,300,000	New Zealand	24	697,000	Vietnam (South)	1	500,000
Ghana	4	18,000	Nicaragua	2	55,000	Virgin Islands[1]		17,000
Greece	4	450,000	Nigeria	8	75,000	Yemen	6	22,000
Guam[1]		35,000	Norway	69	900,000	Yugoslavia	35	1,799,000
Guatemala	2	109,400	Okinawa	2	230,000	Zambia	3	18,500

[1] Stations included in U. S. count.   [2] Preliminary estimate.   (Source: TV Factbook.)

the Olympic Games from West Germany, and the relaying of President Nixon's visit to the People's Republic of China.

TV Reception. Total sales of black and white and color TV receivers in the United States in 1972 soared to about 16,530,000, of which 8,400,000 were color sets. RCA introduced a new color picture tube to reduce the weight and cost of color sets.

Video Recording and Playback Systems. The realization of video recording and playback systems for home use continued to languish in 1972, although these systems were increasingly adopted for industrial and educational use. Several companies held successful experimental demonstrations of video playback systems that use plastic disks, while others worked on video recording and playback systems or playback-only systems that use magnetic tape loaded in a cartridge or a cassette. However, no system was ready for home use at the end of 1972.

AM and FM Radio. There was little growth in AM radio in the United States in 1972 as an FCC freeze continued to be in effect. At the end of 1972, 4,427 AM radio stations were on the air, up from 4,374 in 1971. There were 3,119 FM radio stations on the air at the end of 1972, compared with 2,275 a year earlier. The 3,119 total included 616 educational FM radio stations.

HOWARD T. HEAD
A. D. Ring & Associates

TENNESSEE

Passage of redistricting legislation for both Congress and the state legislature and the amendment of the state constitution to provide for classification of property for taxation were in the forefront of the Tennessee scene in 1972.

Legislation. The legislative session of March–April 1972 revised election and conflict-of-interest laws; created statewide systems of emergency medical services and alcoholic rehabilitation; brought the state into compliance with federal billboard control laws and occupational and safety standards for businesses; enacted strip mining legislation, including a severance tax on all coal mined in the state; and created new departments of transportation and economic development.

Politics. On November 7, Tennessee's electoral votes went to Nixon and Agnew by a wide margin. Seven of the nine Congressional representatives were reelected; one—Ray Blanton—found his district abolished under new redistricting laws and ran unsuccessfully against Howard H. Baker for U. S. senator, and Robin Beard (R) won against William Anderson, filling the eighth congressional post and giving the Republicans a 5–to–3 edge. The partisan division in the state Senate remained unchanged (19 Democrats, 13 Republicans, and 1 American party), but the Democrats gained a 52-to-47 margin over the Republicans in the House of Representatives.

Education and Culture. In all four major cities —Memphis, Nashville, Knoxville, and Chattanooga —racial integration in public schools, involving a considerable amount of busing of students under federal court orders, became effective despite delays and popular opposition. In higher education, a federal court ordered a "white presence" at predominantly black Tennessee State University, and a desegregation suit was filed regarding the Nashville center of the University of Tennessee. On July 1 the supervision of the institutions of higher educa-

tion in the state, other than the state university (controlled by its own board of trustees), was shifted from the state board of education to a new 11-member board of regents, of which Dr. Cecil C. Humphreys, former president of Memphis State University, was named chancellor.

The National Cancer Institute awarded a $117,-885 planning grant for cancer research in the Knoxville-Oak Ridge area, and in November the University of Tennessee announced the creation of a permanent Commission on Women to promote equal opportunities for women.

Economic Developments. The general economic outlook in the state improved during the year and outdistanced business conditions in the nation as a whole. The dollar income and outgo from the Tennessee Valley Authority (TVA) power program rose to new records during fiscal 1972. In January a federal court injunction halted work on the TVA's Tellico Dam across the Little Tennessee River because of possible environmental damage. The Cherokee Indians had also expressed opposition to the flooding of their burial grounds and to archaeological investigations in the area. The economy of Morgan county was seriously injured in July by the closing of Brushy Mountain State Prison at Petros because of a strike of prison guards.

Other News. Two notable Tennesseans died in 1972—former Gov. Buford Ellington and former Sen. Tom Stewart.

STANLEY J. FOLMSBEE
University of Tennessee, Knoxville

TEXAS

Conservative Democrats continued to dominate Texas state politics in 1972, but Republicans and liberal Democrats found cause for hope. The Republican presidential ticket carried Texas with an unprecedented 67% of the vote, and Republican Sen. John Tower was reelected with 53% of the vote, defeating Democratic nominee Barefoot Sanders. Aided both by the Nixon landslide and by recent redistricting, the Republicans won 4 of the state's 24 U. S. congressional seats, 3 of the 31 seats in the Texas Senate, and 17 of the 150 seats in the Texas House of Representatives—plus scattered local offices. Democrats, however, remained firmly in control of the legislature and managed to hold on to the governorship as well.

Politics and Elections. As usual, there was considerable conflict within the Democratic party. Although liberals were disappointed when former Sen. Ralph Yarborough was narrowly defeated for the senatorial nomination by Sanders, they took some consolation from the moderate stance of the nominees for the offices of attorney general and lieutenant governor, both of whom were elected.

But it was the gubernatorial election that provided the biggest surprises. Apparently because of an electoral backlash from the stock and banking scandals that surfaced in 1971, both incumbent Gov. Preston Smith and Lt. Gov. Ben Barnes fared poorly in the first Democratic gubernatorial primary. In the run-off primary, Dolph Briscoe, a moderately conservative banker-rancher from Uvalde, defeated Frances "Sissy" Farenthold of Corpus Christi, a leader of the reform group in the Texas House.

The Republican gubernatorial primary also was hotly contested, with the run-off victory going to the very conservative state senator from Houston, Henry Grover. Handicapped in the general election by a lack of campaign funds and of party support, Grover nevertheless was close to a stunning upset until late returns gave Briscoe the governorship.

Briscoe's narrow victory margin (48% to 45%) was due in part to the presence on the ballot of La Raza Unida, a new party organized by militant Chicanos. Capitalizing on widespread dissatisfaction with the nominees of both major parties, LRU's candidate, Ramsey Muñiz, polled 6% of the gubernatorial vote, most of it siphoned away from the Democratic ticket. In other state races, LRU fared poorly, though it won a few local offices in South Texas, where there is a high concentration of Mexican Americans.

Also on the ballot were 14 proposed constitutional amendments. Eleven of these were adopted, including four-year terms for state officials beginning after the 1974 elections and the convening of the state legislature as a constitutional convention in 1974.

Legislation and Legislators. Three special sessions of the Texas legislature were called during 1972: one in February to finance party primaries; one in May to appropriate funds for the second year of the budget cycle; and one in September to consider reform of state insurance laws.

It was not a tranquil year for Texas legislators. The speaker of the House, Gus Mutscher, and another House member were convicted on a charge of conspiracy to bribe, growing out of the 1971 scandals. Three other legislators were convicted on charges involving misappropriation of state funds and/or violation of the state nepotism law.

A three-judge federal court ordered single-member districts for the election of members of the Texas House from Dallas and Bexar (San Antonio) counties in place of the prevailing countywide multi-member district. A similar court invalidated the 1971 redistricting for the U. S. House of Representatives, but the U. S. Supreme Court stayed the order pending disposition of the state's appeal.

RESCUE WORKERS move through flood waters in Houston, Texas, on March 21, after heavy rains inundated the area.

UPI

──────── **TEXAS** • Information Highlights ────────

Area: 267,338 square miles (692,405 sq km).
Population (1970 census): 11,196,730. *Density:* 44 per sq mi.
Chief Cities (1970 census): Austin, the capital, 251,808; Houston, 1,232,802; Dallas, 844,401; San Antonio, 654,153.
Government (1972): *Chief Officers*—governor, Preston Smith (D); lt. gov., Ben Barnes (D); secy. of state, Robert D. Bullock (D); atty. gen., Crawford C. Martin (D); treas., Jesse James (D); commissioner of education, J. W. Edgar; chief justice, Robert W. Calvert. *Legislature*—Senate, 31 members (29 Democrats, 2 Republicans); House of Representatives, 150 members (140 D, 10 R).
Education (1971–72): *Enrollment*—public elementary schools, 2,000,299 pupils; 67,363 teachers; public secondary, 777,-893 pupils; 50,737 teachers; nonpublic schools (1970–71), 123,041 pupils; 5,490 teachers; college and university, 442,000 students. *Public school expenditures,* $1,761,901,-000 ($705 per pupil). *Average teacher's salary,* $8,650.
State Finances (fiscal year 1970): *Revenues,* $3,648,508,000 (4% general sales tax and gross receipts taxes, $552,-561,000); motor fuel tax, $312,349,000; federal funds, $927,-009,000). *Expenditures,* $3,344,948,000 (education, $514,-692,000; health, welfare, and safety, $519,079,000; highways, $689,853,000).
Personal Income (1971): $42,193,000,000; per capita, $3,682.
Public Assistance (1971): $631,059,000. *Average monthly payments* (Dec. 1971)—old-age assistance, $54.52; aid to families with dependent children, $116.11.
Labor Force: *Nonagricultural wage and salary earners* (July 1972), 3,785,400. *Average annual employment* (1971)—manufacturing, 713,000; trade, 896,000; government, 680,-000; services, 599,000. *Insured unemployed* (Aug. 1972)—34,900 (1.3%).
Manufacturing (1970): *Value added by manufacture,* $12,978,-500,000: Chemicals and allied products, $2,551,200,000; transportation equipment, $1,549,600,000; food and kindred products, $1,511,100,000; petroleum and coal products, $1,432,900,000; nonelectrical machinery, $1,048,600,000.
Agriculture (1970): *Cash farm income,* $3,760,782,000 (livestock, $1,956,233,000; crops, $1,261,393,000; government payments, $543,156,000). *Chief crops* (in order of value, 1971)—Cotton lint (ranks 1st among the states), sorghum grain (ranks 1st), hay, rice (ranks 1st).
Mining (1970): *Production value,* $6,341,761,000 (ranks 1st among the states). *Chief minerals*—Petroleum, $4,065,-270,000; natural gas, $1,242,311,000.
Transportation: *Roads* (1971), 245,532 miles (395,135 km); *motor vehicles* (1971), 6,693,280; *railroads* (1971), 13,616 miles (21,912 km); *public airports* (1972), 266.
Communications: *Telephones* (1972), 6,680,300; *television stations* (1971), 56; *radio stations* (1971), 412; *newspapers* (1972), 112 (daily circulation, 3,300,000).

Commerce and Industry. Several developments testified to the changing picture of energy and oil resources. The Texas Railroad Commission found it no longer necessary to limit crude oil production to market demand, and there was private and state movement toward the creation of a superport off the Texas Gulf Coast to handle the massive tankers needed to bring foreign crude oil to Texas refineries. Unusually cold weather in November and December forced curtailment of industrial and commercial uses of natural gas.

Issues and Actions. Contemporary social concerns loomed somewhat larger than usual in Texas during 1972, including questions of abortion policy, the reduction of penalties for the possession of marihuana, and women's liberation. Despite occasional flare-ups, racial and ethnic minorities continued to make slow progress in education, employment, and politics. The number of blacks in the Texas legislature increased from three to eight. Student activism, particularly in antiwar efforts, declined in intensity, in part because college students channeled more of their energies into politics.

State political and educational leaders continued to ponder the problem of financing the public schools while awaiting the decision of the U. S. Supreme Court on the 1971 ruling by a federal court in Texas that financing public education through property taxes denied children in poor districts equal protection of the law. The quest for additional tax revenues was at least temporarily eased by the advent of federal revenue-sharing.

CLIFTON MCCLESKEY
The University of Texas at Austin

TEXTILE INDUSTRY

In 1971 the per capita consumption of man-made, cotton, and wool fibers in the United States was 54.4 pounds, up sharply from 49.2 pounds in 1970. Man-made fiber consumption per capita rose dramatically; a moderate increase in cotton consumption was offset by a drop in wool consumption.

Fiber Consumption. Based on nine-month data the annual rate of total mill consumption of fibers in 1972 was 11.3 billion pounds, 8% more than the 10.5 billion pounds in 1971. The 1972 annual rate included an increase of 17% for man-made fibers, a decrease of 7% for raw cotton, and no change for wool and silk. Man-made fibers accounted for 66% of the total pounds consumed in 1972, compared with 60% in 1971. Cotton accounted for 32% in 1972, compared with 38% in 1971.

The total value of the four classes of fibers consumed domestically was estimated at $5,000 million in 1971. Man-made fiber consumption was valued at $3,850 million, raw cotton at $1,000 million, raw wool at $145 million, and silk at $5 million.

Fabric Output. Based on first-half data U. S. production of broad woven fabric in 1972 was expected to total some 11.6 billion linear yards, about 4% more than the 1971 output. On the same period basis, the projected cotton cloth output was about 2% less than in 1971, the output of man-made fiber cloths 11% more, and wool 6% lower.

Deliveries of man-made fibers for circular and warp knitting increased substantially, rising from 1,101 million pounds in 1971 to an estimated total of 1,400 million pounds in 1972.

Prices. The average price of 1-inch middling raw cotton for the first nine months of 1972 was 32.9 cents per pound, and the price of raw wool (clean basis, at Boston) was 101.4 cents. Quoted prices were 74 cents for 150-denier acetate yarn and 94.5 cents for 150-denier viscose yarn.

Employment and Earnings. Employment in the textile mill products industry, such as knitting and weaving mills, averaged some 870,000 employees in

SELECTED U. S. TEXTILE INDUSTRY DATA

Fiber	1969	1970	1971	First half 1972
	(Consumption, millions of pounds)			
Raw cotton	3,973	3,774	3,886	1,963
Raw wool, total[1]	355	273	219	132
Apparel class	261	197	144	90
Carpet class	94	76	75	42
Raw silk	2	1	..	..
Man-made fibers[2]	5,413	5,362	6,348	3,608
Rayon+acetate yarn	744	700	735	340
Rayon+acetate staple	871	714	755	404
Noncellulosic yarn[3]	1,649	1,804	2,335	1,374
Noncellulosic staple[4]	1,689	1,740	2,058	1,208
Textile glass fiber	460	404	465	282
Total fiber consumption	9,743	9,410	10,453	5,703
Tire cord and tire fabric[5]	(Output, millions of pounds)			
Total cotton	4	2	2	1
Total man-made	637	580	621	339
Tire cord and cord fabric	593	533	571	314
Rayon	119	92	113	54
Nylon	307	294	279	152
Polyester	167	147	179	108
Chafer and other	44	47	50	25
Total tire cord and fabric	641	582	623	340
Broad woven fabric[6]	(Output, millions of linear yards)			
Cotton	6,968	6,246	6,147	3,015
Man-made fiber	5,378	5,017	4,877	2,717
Woolen and worsted	223	178	113	53
Silk	12	8	6	3
Paper and other fabrics	4	3	3	1
Total broad woven goods	12,585	11,452	11,146	5,789

[1] Clean basis. [2] U.S. producers' domestic shipments plus imports for consumption. [3] Includes nylon, polyester, olefin, saran, spandex, vinyon, and TFE-fluorocarbon fiber. [4] Includes acrylic and modacrylic, nylon, olefin, polyester, and vinyon. [5] Exclusive of cotton chafer. [6] Except tire fabrics, carpets and rugs, and felts. (Source: Textile Economics Bureau, Inc.)

the first half of 1972, and the average weekly wage was $112.23. On the same period basis, employment in the apparel and related trades averaged 1,190,000 employees, and the average weekly wage was $95.43.

Imports and Exports. During 1971 imports of all textile fibers and products were valued at $2,945 million, and exports were valued at $1,606 million. Thus the U. S. textile import balance was a record $1,339 million, 17% more than the previous high of $1,142 million in 1970.

STANLEY B. HUNT
President, Textile Economics Bureau, Inc.

THAILAND

During 1972, Thailand's military regime confronted the usual Thai problems with only moderate success. There was continued uncertainty about the American presence in Thailand and, as the Indochina War moved toward a close, about the future role of Thailand in Southeast Asia.

Political Affairs. The military regime, which swept away a Thai civilian, constitutional government in a bloodless coup late in 1971, was headed by the aging Field Marshal Thanom Kittikachorn, with Gen. Praphas Charusathien as deputy. During 1972 it was generally in firm control, though not unopposed and frequently threatened by insurgency. Bangkok was put under military alert in March, and three prominent members of the former opposition party were jailed. Their arrests came after they had filed a criminal suit against Thanom for violating the constitution in mounting the coup the previous November. By mid-1972 at least 19 people had been executed in Bangkok—although not all for political crimes—and some Thais jocularly referred to the ruling National Executive Council as the "National Execution Council."

In mid-December the National Assembly was reinstituted under an interim constitution. Thanom, named premier, and Praphas, deputy premier, assumed major posts in the new 27-man cabinet.

Insurgency. It was estimated in March that the number of armed insurgents in Thailand had grown perhaps as much as 20% over the preceding 18 months. The most important areas of Communist-inspired insurgency lay in the extreme north and northeast, along the Laotian border, and in the extreme south, near the Malaysian border. Although Thai officials continued to discount the dangers of this insurgency, they expressed the belief that the next phase of Communist activity would be in the form of major guerrilla warfare. Assisted by U. S. military forces in training and staff support, the Thai Army was already utilizing regular units in trying to dislodge rebel bases. Thai efforts have proved expensive in both money and lives, yet have not been very effective.

The rebel and guerrilla forces did not hesitate to attack U. S. installations. In October the third attack of the year against a U. S. base was recorded at Udon, in northeast Thailand. The Thais claimed that most of the guerrillas who had attacked American bases had been North Vietnamese.

U. S. Presence. As the Indochina War wound down in Vietnam, U. S. forces were cut back in South Vietnam and shifted to Thailand. In the summer of 1972, U. S. troops in Thailand were numbered at a near-peak 49,000, mostly assigned to Air Force contingents used in the bombing of Vietnam. There were about 750 U. S. tactical aircraft at the Thai bases, including 80 B-52's. Information on the U. S. buildup in Thailand was not readily available because the bases were leased from the Thai government, which usually refused to divulge details.

Plane Crash. In late August a Thai police lieutenant was arrested for allegedly planting a bomb in a commercial plane that crashed in South Vietnam in June. Among the 81 persons killed in the crash were the 7-year-old daughter of the accused and his 20-year-old girl friend.

Foreign Affairs. Since the 1960's, Thai foreign policy has been closely geared to the U. S. presence in Southeast Asia. After Pakistan's withdrawal from the Southeast Asia Treaty Organization in July 1972, Thailand and the Philippines were the only remaining Asian members. Thailand seemed to be following the American lead in the reassessment of policy toward mainland China. Thanom expressed "great satisfaction" over President Nixon's reelection, calling him "a good friend of the Thai people."

The United States has been supporting the 10,-000-man Thai irregular army in Laos. In May, $100 million a year was pledged for this purpose.

In February the British monarch made a state visit to Thailand. Queen Elizabeth was accompanied by Prince Philip and Princess Anne.

Economy. The Thai economy remained dependent upon the American presence and U. S. subsidies, and the temporary reduction of U. S. forces in Thailand early in the year caused a mild economic slump. As in the past, inflation was characteristic of the Thai economy.

A new $100 million airport was being planned for Bangkok. Plans have been approved for a canal across the Isthmus of Kra between the Indian Ocean and the Gulf of Siam. Some 97 miles (156 km) long, it was expected to cost more than $400 million.

CARL LEIDEN
University of Texas at Austin

――――――― **THAILAND • Information Highlights** ―――――――

Official Name: Kingdom of Thailand.
Area: 198,456 square miles (514,000 sq km).
Population (1972 est.): 38,600,000. *Density,* 194 per square mile (75 per sq km). *Annual rate of increase,* 3.3%.
Chief Cities: Bangkok, the capital (1968 est.), 2,275,000; Thonburi (1967 est.), 606,300.
Government: *Head of state,* Bhumibol Adulyadej, king (acceded June 1946). *Head of government,* Thanom Kittikachorn (took office as premier Dec. 1963; seized power in military coup Nov. 1971). *Legislature*—National Assembly (suspended Nov. 17, 1971). *Major political parties*—United Thai People's party; Democratic party.
Language: Thai (official).
Education: *Expenditure* (1969), 16.3% of total public expenditure. *School enrollment* (1968)—primary, 5,122,728; secondary, 479,119; technical/vocational, 62,066; university/higher, 41,848.
Monetary Unit: Baht (21 bahts equal U. S.$1, Sept. 1972).
Gross National Product (1971 est.): $6,910,000,000.
National Income per Person (1969): $169.
Economic Indexes: *Agricultural production* (1971), 230 (1952–56=100); *consumer price index* (1971), 119 (1963=100).
Manufacturing (major products): Processed foods, textiles, clothing.
Major Agricultural Products: Natural rubber (ranks 3d among world producers, 1971), rice, tapioca, corn, tobacco, sugarcane, jute and kenaf, forest products.
Major Minerals: Tin (ranks 4th among world producers, 1970), tungsten, lignite, salt, manganese.
Foreign Trade (1971): *Exports,* $834,000,000 (chief exports—rice; corn; rubber; tin; tapioca products). *Imports,* $1,281,000,000 (chief imports, 1969—nonelectrical machinery; transport equipment; chemicals; electrical machinery, apparatus, appliances). *Chief trading partners*—Japan (took 22% of exports, supplied 36% of imports); United States (14%—18%); West Germany (8%—9%); United Kingdom (3%—8%).
Tourism: *Receipts* (1970), $104,300,000.
Transportation: *Motor vehicles* (1969), 284,700 (automobiles, 166,700); *railroads* (1970), 2,339 miles (3,764 km); *major national airline,* Thai Airways Company.
Communications: *Telephones* (1971), 152,959; *television stations* (1971), 5; *television sets* (1971), 225,000; *radios* (1970), 2,775,000; *newspapers* (1969), 24.

Moving with its five-man cast from Joseph Papp's Public Theater to open the new Broadway season, Jason Miller's That Championship Season *won the New York Drama Critics Circle Award as best American play in 1972.*

theater

In 1972, American theater was represented by a financially and artistically declining Broadway, a strong Off-Broadway season, and innovative Off Off-Broadway activity. The future of regional theater remained uncertain. The year was perhaps most memorable for a handful of productions originating in subsidized or experimental theaters.

Broadway's economic state remained perilous. The Schubert empire—today valued at between $60 million and $100 million, compared with a onetime peak of $400 million—was at its lowest ebb since the Depression. There was serious talk during the year of converting Lincoln Center's Beaumont Theater into a film-and-drama complex, a scheme finally thwarted by an ad hoc committee from New York's theatrical community.

At the end of 1972 nearly half of the Broadway theaters were dark, and concern was mounting over declining profits. Producer Alexander Cohen and others interested in improving the image of Broadway tried to put pressure on the City Council to rid the Times Square area of massage parlors and other fronts for prostitution that had given the area a bad name with theatergoers. In another attempt to spur flagging Broadway attendance, the League of New York Theaters developed plans to push back the evening curtain time to 8 P.M. on weekdays and to 8:30 P.M. on Sundays in exchange for a financial commitment from midtown restaurants, hotels, and garages to promote the theater.

In spite of the declining fortunes of the Times Square area, four new theaters were planned for mid-town and three have already been constructed. These include the American Place Theater, the Uris Theater, and the Circle in the Square-Joseph E. Levine Theater. Scheduled to open in 1973 is the 1,650-seat Minskoff Theater, erected on the site of the old Astor Hotel.

The opening of the new Uris Theater in November 1972 provided an ironic climax to an unfruitful year on Broadway. The Uris, a 1,896-seat house at the base of a new office building, is the home of Broadway's Hall of Fame. It opened with a production of the Galt MacDermot-Christopher Gore musical *Via Galactica,* a critical and financial disaster estimated to have lost $860,000 for its backers.

Broadway Plays. Most of the plays on Broadway in 1972 provided relatively uninteresting fare. There were happy exceptions, of course, although the majority of them did not originate on Broadway, moving there instead from abroad, from regional theater companies, or from Off-Broadway.

Few comedies and serious plays originating on Broadway in 1972 were successful. An outstanding exception was Neil Simon's new comedy *The Sunshine Boys,* starring Jack Albertson and Sam Levene. A moderately successful comedy was Bob Randall's *6 Rms Riv Vu,* with Jane Alexander and Jerry Orbach. Arthur Miller returned to the theater with a ponderous and unconvincing comedy, *The*

NEW SUCCESSES included the musical productions Grease *(top, left), an evocation of the 1950's and rock 'n' roll, and* Don't Bother Me, I Can't Cope *(top, right), a wry treatment of the black experience in America. Alan Bates (above) scored a personal triumph in the role of* Butley, *as he had previously in London, while Bob Randall's comedy* 6 Rms Riv Vu *(right) provided a diverting variation on the theme of an accidental affair.*

Creation of the World and Other Business, starring
Zoe Caldwell, Bob Dishy, and George Grizzard.
Among the dramas offered were Paul Foster's
leaden *Elizabeth I,* with Jeff Chandler and Penelope
Windust. From London's Royal Court Theater by
way of the Washington Arena Stage came a failing
but generally respected play, Michael Weller's
Moonchildren. English playwright, Simon Gray
offered Broadway two plays during 1972, the rather
unsuccessful *Wise Child,* and *Butley* a first-rate
tragicomedy about a London university professor,
with a brilliant performance by Alan Bates in the
title role. Robert Bolt's *Vivat! Vivat Regina!,* from
the Chichester Festival, enjoyed a modest run, as
did the Georges Feydeau farce *There's One in
Every Marriage,* contributed by the Stratford Festival, Canada.

From Off-Broadway came two award-winning
plays, both of which originated at Joseph Papp's
New York Shakespeare Festival Public Theater.
They were David Rabe's *Sticks and Bones* and Jason
Miller's *That Championship Season,* a comic but
bitter series of altercations among a group of aging
middle-American bigots.

Revivals on Broadway included the late Lorraine
Hansberry's *The Sign in Sidney Brustein's Window*
and Clifford Odets' *The Country Girl,* the latter in
an excellent production directed by John Houseman
and featuring George Grizzard, Roland Winters,
Jason Robards, and Maureen Stapleton. Eugene
O'Neill's *Mourning Becomes Electra,* with Colleen
Dewhurst, opened the new Circle in the Square–
Joseph E. Levine Theater.

Broadway Musicals. Original Broadway musicals included *Sugar,* adapted from the film *Some
Like It Hot* and featuring Robert Morse, Tony Roberts, and Cyril Ritchard, and the spectacular *Pippin,* about the son of Charlemagne, directed and
choreographed by Bob Fosse. Melvin Van Peebles,
whose disturbing musical *Ain't Supposed to Die a
Natural Death* opened in 1971, returned with *Don't
Play Us Cheap,* a lighthearted show about a Saturday night party.

Galt MacDermot, the composer of the highly
successful shows *Hair* and *Two Gentlemen of
Verona,* had an especially bad year. A few weeks
before his *Via Galactica* failed in November, the
MacDermot–Ragni musical *Dude* closed after 16
performances and a loss of $900,000. Less spec-
tacular but no less ominous were the year-end failures of two other musicals, Aristophanes' *Lysistrata,*
which starred Melina Mercouri, and *Ambassador,* a
musical adaptation of Henry James' novel *The Ambassadors,* with Howard Keel and Danielle Darrieux.

There were critically well-received revivals of
A Funny Thing Happened on the Way to the Forum
with Phil Silvers, and *Man of La Mancha* with
Richard Kiley. Well done but less well received
was a revival of the Kurt Weill–Maxwell Anderson
classic *Lost in the Stars,* based on Alan Paton's
novel *Cry, the Beloved Country.* Moving uptown
from Off-Broadway were *Grease,* the popular rock-
and-roll musical about growing up in the 1950's; the
long-running *Jacques Brel Is Alive and Well and
Living in Paris;* and the black revue *Don't Bother
Me, I Can't Cope,* written by Micki Grant and
staged by Vinette Carroll, which had begun life as
an Urban Arts Corps production. The Public
Theater's highly successful rock version of Shakespeare's *Much Ado About Nothing* also began a
Broadway engagement.

SHAKESPEARE REVAMPED by Joseph Papp began a Broadway engagement in a musical version
of *Much Ado About Nothing in Edwardian dress.*

Off-Broadway. In 1972, Off-Broadway continued
as a viable alternative theater and an important
feeder for the Broadway stage. One of the most
significant productions of the year was Fernando
Arrabal's angry and disturbing play about the
horror of Spanish prisons, *And They Put Handcuffs
on the Flowers.* Tennessee Williams returned to the
theater with a minor but often satisfying play, *Small
Craft Warnings,* and Tom Stoppard pleased Off-
Broadway audiences with his amusing double-bill,
The Real Inspector Hound and *After Magritte.*

Lincoln Center's Forum Theater offered several
controversial and interesting works. Among them
were *Suggs,* David Wiltse's ironic comedy about a
man destroyed by life in New York City; *The Ride
Across Lake Constance,* a complex work by German
playwright Peter Handke which left reviewers puzzled and, in some cases, positively annoyed; and
The Duplex, a play by Ed Bullins that aroused considerable controversy when the playwright publicly
disavowed the production as a "darkie minstrel
show." Ending the year was a four-play Samuel
Beckett festival, which included the world premiere of a new work, *Not I.* Following the Beckett
plays, the Forum announced that it was canceling
the remainder of its season due to shortage of funds
and that it would reopen in February 1973 with an

BROADWAY OPENINGS IN 1972

PLAYS

All the Girls Came Out to Play, by Richard T. Johnson and Daniel Hollywood; directed by John Gerstad; with Dennis Cole, Michael (M. P.) Murphy, and Bette Marshall; April 20–April 22.

Butley, by Simon Gray; directed by James Hammerstein; with Alan Bates and Hayward Morse; October 31–

Captain Brassbound's Conversion, by George Bernard Shaw; directed by Stephen Porter; with Pernell Roberts and Ingrid Bergman; April 17–April 29.

Children! Children! by Jack Horrigan; directed by Joseph Hardy; with Gwen Verdon and Dennis Patrick; March 7–March 9.

The Country Girl, by Clifford Odets; directed by John Houseman; with George Grizzard, Roland Winters, Jason Robards, and Maureen Stapleton; March 15–May 6.

The Creation of the World and Other Business, by Arthur Miller; directed by Gerald Freedman; with Bob Dishy, Stephen Elliott, Zoe Caldwell, and George Grizzard; November 30–December 16.

Don Juan, by Molière; directed and adapted by Stephen Porter; with Paul Hecht; December 11–January 21.

Elizabeth I, by Paul Foster; directed by John-Michael Tebelak; with Penelope Windust; April 5–April 8.

An Evening with Richard Nixon And ..., by Gore Vidal; directed by Edwin Sherin; with George S. Irving; April 30–May 13.

Fun City, by Lester Colodny, Joan Rivers, and Edgar Rosenberg; directed by Jerry Adler; with Joan Rivers, Gabriel Dell, and Rose Marie; January 2–January 8.

The Great God Brown, by Eugene O'Neill; directed by Harold Prince; with John McMartin and Clyde Burton; December 10–January 21.

The Last of Mrs. Lincoln, by James Prideaux; directed by George Schaefer; with Julie Harris; December 12–

The Lincoln Mask, by V. J. Longhi; directed by Gene Frankel; with Fred Gwynne and Eva Marie Saint; October 30–November 4.

The Little Black Book, by Jean-Claude Carriere; translated and adapted by Jerome Kilty; directed by Milos Forman; with Richard Benjamin and Delphine Seyrig; April 25–April 29.

The Love Suicide at Schofield Barracks, by Romulus Linney; directed by John Berry; with Mercedes McCambridge and William Redfield; February 9–February 12.

Moonchildren, by Michael Weller; directed by Alan Schneider; with James Woods, Kevin Conway, and Edward Herrmann; February 21–March 4.

Night Watch, by Lucille Fletcher; directed by Fred Coe; with Joan Hackett and Len Cariou; February 28–June 11.

Promenade, All! by David V. Robison; directed by Arthur Storch; with Richard Backus, Anne Jackson, Eli Wallach, and Hume Cronyn; April 16–May 27.

Ring Round the Bathtub, by Jane Trahey; directed by Harold Stone; with Elizabeth Ashley, Richard Mulligan, Carmen Mathews, and Eileen Kearney; April 29 for one performance.

The Secret Affairs of Mildred Wild, by Paul Zindel; directed by Jeff Bleckner; with Maureen Stapleton and Elizabeth Wilson; November 13–December 2.

The Sign in Sidney Brustein's Window, by Lorraine Hansberry; directed by Alan Schneider; with Hal Linden and Zohra Lampert; January 26–January 29.

6 Rms Riv Vu, by Bob Randall; directed by Edwin Sherin; with Jerry Orbach and Jane Alexander; October 17–

Sticks and Bones, by David Rabe; directed by Jeff Bleckner; with Tom Aldredge, Elizabeth Wilson, and Drew Snyder; March 1–October 1.

The Sunshine Boys, by Neil Simon; directed by Alan Arkin; with Sam Levene and Jack Albertson; December 20–

That Championship Season, by Jason Miller; directed by A. J. Antoon; with Charles Durning, Richard A. Dysart, Walter McGinn, Michael McGuire, and Paul Sorvino; May 2–

There's One in Every Marriage, by Georges Feydeau; adapted by Suzanne Grossmann and Paxton Whitehead; directed by Jean Gascon; with Roberta Maxwell, Richard Curnock, Peter Donat, Marilyn Gardner; January 3–January 15.

Tough to Get Help, by Steve Gordon; directed by Carl Reiner; with John Amos, Lillian Hayman, Billie Lou Watt, and Dick O'Neill; May 4 for one performance.

Vivat! Vivat Regina! by Robert Bolt; directed by Peter Dews; with Claire Bloom and Eileen Atkins; January 20–April 29.

Voices, by Richard Lortz; directed by Gilbert Cates; with Richard Kiley and Julie Harris; April 3–April 8.

Wise Child, by Simon Gray; directed by James Hammerstein; with Donald Pleasence, Bud Cort, George Rose, and Lauren Jones; January 27–January 29.

MUSICALS

Ambassador, based on novel *The Ambassadors* by Henry James; book by Don Ettlinger and Anna Marie Barlow; music by Don Gohman; lyrics by Hal Hackady; directed by Stone Widney; with Howard Keel and Danielle Darrieux; November 19–November 25.

The Contrast, by Royall Tyler, adapted by Anthony Stimac; music by Don Pippin; lyrics by Steve Brown; directed by Anthony Stimac; with Connie Danese, Elaine Kerr, and Gene Kelton; November 27–December 17.

Dear Oscar, book and lyrics by Caryl Gabrielle Young; music by Addy O. Fleger; directed by John Allen; with Richard Kneeland, Russ Thacker, Nancy Cushman, and Kimberly Vaughn; November 16–November 19.

Different Times, by Michael Brown; directed by Michael Brown; with Barbara Williams, Mary Bracken Phillips, and Sam Stoneburner; April 30–May 20.

Don't Bother Me, I Can't Cope, by Micki Grant; directed by Vinnette Carroll; with Micki Grant, Alex Bradford, and Bobby Hill; April 19–

Don't Play Us Cheap, by Melvin Van Peebles; directed by Melvin Van Peebles; with Esther Rolle; May 16–October 1.

Dude, book and lyrics by Gerome Ragni; music by Galt MacDermot; directed by Tom O'Horgan; with William Redfield, Rae Allen, Salome Bey, and Delores Hall; October 9–October 21.

A Funny Thing Happened on the Way to the Forum, book by Burt Shevelove and Larry Gelbart; music and lyrics by Stephen Sondheim; with Phil Silvers and Larry Blyden; March 30–August 12.

Grease, book, music, and lyrics by Jim Jacobs and Warren Casey; directed by Tom Moore; with Carole Demas and Barry Bostwick; February 14–

Hurry, Harry, book by Jeremiah Morris, Lee Kalcheim, and Susan Perkis; music by Bill Weeden; lyrics by David Finkle; directed by Jeremiah Morris; with Samuel D. Ratcliffe, Mary Bracken Phillips, and Phil Leeds; October 12–October 13.

Jacques Brel Is Alive and Well and Living in Paris, based on the works of Brel; conceived by Eric Blau and Mort Shuman; directed by Moni Yakim; with Elly Stone and Joe Masiell; September 15–October 28.

Lost in the Stars, based on *Cry, the Beloved Country* by Alan Paton; music by Kurt Weill; lyrics by Maxwell Anderson; directed by Gene Frankel; with Brock Peters, Gilbert Price, Margaret Cowie, Giancarlo Esposito, and Rod Perry; April 18–May 21.

Lysistrata, adapted from the play of Aristophanes by Michael Cacoyannis; music by Peter Link; directed by Michael Cacoyannis; with Melina Mercouri, Philip Bruns, Priscilla Lopez, and Richard Dmitri; November 13–November 18.

Man of La Mancha, book by Dale Wasserman; music by Mitch Leigh; lyrics by Joe Darion; directed by Albert Marre; with Richard Kiley, Joan Diener, Edmond Varrato, and Robert Rounseville; June 22–October 21.

Mother Earth, book by Toni Shearer and Ron Thronson; music by Toni Shearer; lyrics by Ron Thronson; directed by Ray Golden; with Kelly Garrett, Gail Boggs, John Bennett Perry, and Charlie J. Rodriguez; October 19–October 28.

Much Ado About Nothing, adapted from the play by Shakespeare; music by Peter Link; directed by A. J. Antoon; with Barnard Hughes, Sam Waterston, Douglass Watson, and Kathleen Widdoes; November 11–

Pippin, book by Roger O. Hirson; music and lyrics by Stephen Schwartz; directed by Bob Fosse; with John Rubinstein, Eric Berry, Jill Clayburgh, and Leland Palmer; October 23–

The Selling of the President, based on the book by Joe McGinniss; book by Jack O'Brien and Stuart Hample; music by Bob James; lyrics by Jack O'Brien; directed by Robert H. Livingston; with Pat Hingle, Karen Morrow, and Barbara Barrie; March 22–March 25.

Sugar, based on the film *Some Like It Hot;* book by Peter Stone; music by Jule Styne; lyrics by Bob Merrill; directed by Gower Champion; with Robert Morse, Tony Roberts, Cyril Ritchard, and Elaine Joyce, April 9–

That's Entertainment, revue with music and lyrics by Howard Dietz and Arthur Schwartz; directed by Paul Aaron; with David Chaney, Jared Holmes, and Michon Peacock; April 14–April 16.

Via Galactica, book by Christopher Gore and Judith Ross; music by Galt MacDermot; lyrics by Christopher Gore; directed by Peter Hall; with Raul Julia, Virginia Vestoff, Clebert Ford, and Keene Curtis, November 21–December 2.

STYLISH MUSICAL on historical character of Pippin won high praise
for Ben Vereen (above, chin in hand, behind John Rubinstein as Pippin).

opera repertory. Its future as a legitimate house, like that of the Beaumont, seemed to be in doubt.

A good revival of John Gay's famous *Beggar's Opera* opened at the Chelsea Theater Center of the Brooklyn Academy of Music. Also originating at the CTC was *Kaddish* by Allen Ginsberg, a powerful play reinforced by multiple projected images. Since its well-handled production of Jean Genet's *The Screens* in 1971, the CTC has established itself on a footing with Ellen Stewart's Cafe La Mama and Joseph Papp's Public Theater as a major contributor to the New York theater season. Among the foreign productions at the Brooklyn Academy in 1972 were García Lorca's *Yerma,* directed by the Argentine Victor Garcia.

The Negro Ensemble Company continued its generally first-rate work of recent years with Philip Hayes Dean's *The Sty of the Blind Pig* and *Frederick Douglas ... Through his Own Words,* by Arthur Burghardt and Michael Egan. Great interest was generated by a new group made up of recent Juilliard graduates, the City Center Acting Company, which demonstrated remarkable versatility in a six-play repertory season.

Off-Broadway musical productions included a reprise of Kurt Weill's songs, *Berlin to Broadway with Kurt Weill,* and a revival of the Gertrude Stein–Virgil Thompson opera about the life of Susan B. Anthony, *Mother of Us All. Oh Coward!,* a revue with words and music by Noel Coward, devised and directed by Roderick Cook, was well received. Also seen in 1972 was *Doctor Selavy's Magic Theater,* an intriguing revue with songs and mimes by Stanley Silverman and Richard Foreman.

Off Off-Broadway. The Off Off-Broadway theater is a collection of impoverished but often courageous and stimulating experimental groups, many of them in the SoHo area near Greenwich Village or on New York's Lower East Side. In 1972, 50 companies banded together to form the Off Off-Broadway Alliance. The Alliance was recognized by the Theater Development Fund, which announced that it will channel at least $50,000 annually in grants to Off Off-Broadway groups.

The Bread and Puppet Theater, which uses oversize puppets, presented several pieces in 1972, including *Stations of the Cross,* an Easter play, and a group of three short plays, two of them new, under the collective title *Coney Island Cycle.*

Charles Ludlam's Ridiculous Theatrical Company presented two productions, a mock Hollywood epic called *Eunuchs of the Forbidden City* and a very successful country Western spoof called *Corn.* Cafe La Mama, perhaps the most famous of the Off Off-Broadway producing organizations, offered several interesting productions. Playwright John Vacarro was represented by a mock-Oriental piece, *Persia, a Desert Cheapie.* The La Mama also offered an important production of *Medea,* conceived by Rumanian director Andrei Serban, a protégé of Peter Brook, and was host to Mark Long's impressive English company, *The People Show,* as well as to an excellent Belgian group, the *Théâtre Laboratoire Vicinal.* Also seen Off Off-Broadway was a revival of the Manhattan Project's well-known *Alice in Wonderland,* directed by Andre Gregory.

Important experimental productions were created by Richard Foreman, whose Ontological-Hysteric Theater presented first *Evidence* and, later in 1972, *Sophia.* Robert Wilson's new piece, *Overture for KA MOUNTAIN AND GUARDenia Terrace,* was part of a larger presentation by his Byrd Hoffman School of Byrds which was done outdoors later in the year at Shiraz, Iran.

Outside New York. In the spring of 1972, there were 34 regional professional theater companies operating in the United States. The mood among these companies was one of cautious optimism about the future of American regional theater. A gap between income from ticket sales and rising production costs was as apparent in many theaters outside New York as it was in the Broadway and Off-Broadway houses. In addition, a general decline in financial aid from foundations and private patrons helped to worsen the economic position of many important regional theaters. A case in point is Washington's long-established and prestigious Arena Stage, which faced a deficit of $428,000 in 1972 in spite of good productions, a favorable press, and strong audience support. Regional theaters such as the Arena, the Goodman Theater of Chicago, and the Long Wharf and Yale Repertory Theater of New Haven provided their cities with fine performances and, in some cases, offered outstanding works to New York as well. The question remains, however, whether resident professional theater will fulfill the promise it seemed to offer in the 1960's.

Among the year's outstanding productions by regional theaters were a dramatic version of John Steinbeck's *Of Mice and Men* at the Guthrie Theater in Minneapolis, Minn., and Shakespeare's *Hamlet* at the Long Wharf Theater in New Haven, Conn. The Steinbeck work was marked by the excellent performances of Richard McKenzie and Peter Michael Goetz. The Long Wharf's *Hamlet* introduced a powerful new interpreter of the title role in the person of Stacy Keach. Keach repeated his role later in the year for the New York Shakespeare Festival.

International Theater. A notable event in French theater was the move out of Paris of the famed Théâtre National Populaire. The company is relocating in an industrial suburb of Lyon. The Palais de Chaillot, former home of the TNP, was given to Jack Lang, founder of the Nancy festival, which in the last decade developed into a mecca of international avant-garde theater. In London at the end of 1972, some 35 West End theaters were open, compared with less than half that number in the Broadway area. In addition, theatergoers were able to choose from the offerings of the Royal Shakespeare Company and the National Theatre.

Although London does not possess the large number of peripheral attractions found in New York, it is clear that—except possibly for musicals—English audiences have a far better choice of major productions than Americans.

Awards. Offerings from Joseph Papp's organization dominated the 1972 theater awards. The New York Drama Critics Circle picked *That Championship Season* as the best play (with a special citation to *Sticks and Bones*), and *Two Gentlemen of Verona* as the best musical. The Antoinette Perry ("Tony") awards went to *Sticks and Bones* and *Two Gentlemen of Verona*. The Off-Broadway ("Obie") awards went to *The Mutation Show*, a collective work by the Open Theater, with a special citation to Jane Fonda's antiwar troupe for its *Free the Army* show. There was no Pulitzer Prize in drama for 1972.

BROOKS MCNAMARA
New York University
Contributing Editor, "The Drama Review"

THIEU, Nguyen Van. See BIOGRAPHY.

TOGO

Although President Étienne Eyadema had claimed that the army of Togo had "no political ambition," members of the military retained tight control during 1972.

Domestic Politics. A three-day congress of the ruling Rally of the Togolese People (RPT) rejected a recommendation for reinstating civilian rule on the grounds that the Togolese "consider the idea of constitutionalizing the regime inopportune and premature." A referendum held on January 9 bolstered Eyadema's claim to power. Of the 880,890 registered voters, 867,941 supported Eyadema, who was unopposed for president; only 878 voted against him. Eyadema hailed the results as the "first step in the return to normal institutions." However, he did not spell out other steps or a possible timetable.

Those imprisoned for participation in unsuccessful coups in 1969 and 1970 were released and pardoned, a further indication of Eyadema's security.

International Affairs. The annual summit conference of the Afro-Malagasy and Mauritius Joint Organization (OCAMM) was held in Lomé, April 25–26, with nine heads of state in attendance. Earlier the organization had been rocked by the resignation of OCAMM head François Tombalbaye, president of Chad, and by the withdrawal of the Zaïre Republic.

Relations between Togo and Nigeria became increasingly cordial. During the May visit of General Yakubu Gowon, the two states agreed to create a new economic grouping as the nucleus of a West African community. Gowon was mandated to call a summit conference on the proposal.

Economic Development. As a result of a $1.35 million loan from the African Development Bank, phosphate production was expanded from 1.8 to 2.4 million tons annually. France agreed to pay one-third of the cost of a new air terminal at Lomé, and it granted an additional $14.5 million for agricultural improvements. Shell Oil received prospecting rights on 3,170 square kilometers of land.

Education. The University of Benin was to be expanded, with more emphasis on practical courses. The cabinet approved plans for new colleges and institutes in administration, agriculture, business, education, industrial mechanics, and science.

CLAUDE E. WELCH, JR.
State University of New York at Buffalo

TOGO · Information Highlights

Official Name: Togolese Republic.
Area: 21,622 square miles (56,000 sq km).
Population (1972 est.): 2,000,000. *Density*, 85 per square mile (33 per sq km). *Annual rate of increase*, 2.5%.
Chief City (1970 census): Lomé, the capital, 148,443.
Government: Head of state, Étienne Eyadema, president (took office April 1967). Head of government, Étienne Eyadema. Major political party—Rally of the Togolese People.
Languages: French (official), Éwe, Twi, Hausa.
Education: Expenditure (1969), 20% of total public expenditure. School enrollment (1969)—primary, 206,283; secondary, 18,879; technical/vocational, 2,072; university/higher, 263.
Monetary Unit: CFA franc (255.79 CFA francs equal U. S.$1, Aug. 1972).
Gross National Product (1970 est.): $267,000,000.
Manufacturing (major products): Processed foods, textiles.
Major Agricultural Products: Coffee, cacao, sweet potatoes and yams, corn, cassava, palm kernels.
Major Mineral: Phosphate rock.
Foreign Trade (1971): Exports, $53,800,000. Imports, $76,100,000. Chief trading partners (1969)—France (took 34% of exports, supplied 32% of imports); Netherlands (24%—6%); West Germany (16%—7%); United Kingdom (3%—12%).
Communications: Telephones (1970), 4,567; radios (1970), 40,000; newspapers (1970), 3 (daily circulation, 13,000).

TORONTO'S 30-day garbage collectors' strike in April and May resulted in the city's parks and playgrounds being used as emergency dumping areas.

TONGA

The Kingdom of Tonga accelerated its economic development in 1972, emphasizing transportation.

Transportation. The interisland ferry *MV Olovaha,* which began service in 1971, proved to be a successful venture for the Tongan government. Both the number of passengers and the quantity of cargo exceeded prior expectations. One effect of the new service was that of increasing the movement of agricultural produce from Vavau in the north to the capital and principal settlement at Nukualofa. A tourist hotel on Vavau also benefits from the service. The Tongan Tourist and Development Co., which operates the hotel, has arranged for an Australian firm to provide a charter air service between Nukualofa and Vavau.

The Tonga Shipping Agency was disbanded on May 8 and replaced by a new organization, the Pacific Navigation Company. The prime minister, Prince Tuipelehake, became chairman of the board of directors, which also included other cabinet members.

Other Developments. Exploratory drilling for oil near Nukualofa was suspended late in 1971 after two dry holes had been sunk more than 5,000 feet (1,522 meters). Further exploration in Tongan waters was deferred until a detailed geological examination could be completed by a foreign consortium.

HOWARD J. CRITCHFIELD
Western Washington State College

TORONTO

Toronto, on Lake Ontario, is the capital of Ontario and Canada's second-largest city (1972 est. pop. 690,485). Major events in 1972 included a controversial proposal for a new airport, municipal elections, and a garbage strike.

Transportation. On March 2 the federal government announced plans for a second airport for Toronto to be built for $300 million in Pickering Township, 30 miles (48 km) northeast of the city. The citizens of Pickering, however, strongly opposed the plan on March 6. On April 10 a government document was made public, which said that a federal study group in 1970 had rejected Pickering and chosen another site. At Malton Airport, part of the new $35 million Terminal Two went into use.

Ontario tripled its subsidy for public transit in the Toronto area to $6 million. But Premier William Davis, who had vetoed the Spadina Expressway in 1971, rejected a proposal to revive it by paving a semifinished section. In November he announced plans for a $1.3 billion transit system for Ontario's major cities, using commuter trains. The province would pay 75% of the cost, and Toronto would have five or six new routes.

Government. In January the city council doubled the salaries and expense allowances of its members to allow aldermen $15,000. In the federal election in November, the 22 Toronto and suburban ridings

(districts) elected 19 Liberals, 3 Democrats, and no Conservatives.

David Crombie, a 36-year-old lecturer on urban affairs at Toronto's Ryerson College, was elected mayor in the December 4 municipal elections, succeeding the retiring William Dennison. Four of the five boroughs also elected new mayors. The turnover was part of a landslide for the reformers that will put 17 new faces on the Metro Council and a reform majority on the city council.

Urban Development. Plans for the controversial Eaton-Fairview Centre, a $200 million shopping complex, finally won the approval of the Toronto city council and historic Holy Trinity Church. The Bank of Montreal announced a new 70-story downtown office building, which will be the tallest in Canada. Work began on the $250 million Harbour Square development, planned to house 15,000 people.

Economy. In the spring a 30-day strike of garbage collectors led to an estimated accumulation of 116,000 tons of garbage in parks, sidewalks, and boulevards. The strike, which included other "outside" workers in the park, sewage, and water departments, was settled on May 8 by Provincial Labour Minister Fern Guindon with an 8% wage increase.

Education and Communications. In March the administration building of the University of Toronto was occupied by students for two hours after a disagreement over the use of the library stacks. In July, John Evans succeeded the retiring Claude Bissell as president. The heads of the Ontario College of Art and the Royal Ontario Museum were dismissed after disagreements with their directors.

Other Developments. The federal government promised $7 million toward a new Massey Hall for concerts. It also announced a five-year plan for a $30 million park that will occupy 86 acres (35 hectares) along the harbor. Toronto's morning newspaper, the *Sun,* increased its circulation to 80,000 in the first six months since its founding in 1971.

FREDERICK A. ARMSTRONG
University of Western Ontario

TOURISM

Turmoil in the travel industry continued unabated in 1972. Americans traveling abroad after the devaluation of the dollar suddenly found that everything cost about 12% more than before. Inflation and upward revaluation of some currencies, combined with the dollar devaluation, increased the cost of accommodations in several major cities by as much as 23% in a single year.

Air Travel. The use of sky marshals at first cut down on hijackings of aircraft but had less and less effect as the year wore on. Toward the end of 1972 there was hope of a U. S.–Cuban agreement that would stop the hijacking of planes to Cuba.

The struggle between scheduled and supplemental airlines over charter flights continued, while the underground organizers of illegal charters raked in money and stranded occasional planeloads of Americans in Europe. The U. S. Civil Aeronautics Board, after 20 months of investigation, announced in September a 3-2 decision permitting people to travel on charter flights without the "affinity" requirement that was often ignored. The relaxed rule faced strong legal opposition from scheduled air lines.

Very low winter transatlantic fares were set early in 1972 and reappeared late in the year. The European Travel Commission's Heinz Patzak produced a book listing 1,000 low-cost 8-day and 14- to 21-day trips—mostly group-inclusive tours—for the winter period, which was renamed the "Lively Months."

American Airlines stole a march on other airlines in domestic U. S. service with its "Great Airfare Sale," offering reductions of almost 50% on trips of over 1,000 miles (1,600 km) on Tuesdays, Wednesdays, and Thursdays from October 31 to December 7. Other lines followed suit, but American's strong promotion earned it significantly increased traffic.

U. S. Rail Travel. On the intercity rails, the National Railroad Passenger Corporation, known as Amtrak, made a valiant effort to woo back the train passengers long ago lost to airplanes and buses. But the trains were often less glamorous than the publicity. In its first complete financial year, fiscal 1972, Amtrak lost $153,470,000. A loss of $123 million was projected for fiscal 1973.

Amtrak's promotional moves in 1972 included reducing fares on many lines, accepting all major credit cards, cutting food prices, improving schedules and connections, striving for on-time performance, arranging for discount auto rental in the West, and providing a 25% discount for overseas visitors. Locomotives and cars began to receive long-deferred overhauls and refurbishments, and 40 new 3,000-hp diesel-electric locomotives were ordered.

The first comparative figures released by Amtrak showed that ridership for May–June 1972 was 13.7% above that for May–June 1971. Amtrak's major stumbling block appeared to be poor trackage, still controlled by individual rail lines and completely inadequate for the new high-speed trains.

Ship Travel. As ships were used less and less for intercontinental passenger traffic, ingenious owners devised many kinds of special-interest cruises. Home Lines engaged astronomer-lecturers and took a shipload of people to the mid-Atlantic to see the solar eclipse. Holland-America Cruises' *Statendam,* on a cruise from New York to St. Thomas and San Juan, stood off Cape Kennedy for the Apollo 17 launch, its passengers well prepared by briefings from an astronaut and several famous science writers. The *France* took 10 experts along on a "health and beauty" cruise from New York.

Some passenger ships were converted to educational use. World Campus Afloat had bought the *Queen Elizabeth* in 1970, changed its name to *Seawise University,* and begun refitting it for education and cruising; but the ship was destroyed by fire in Hong Kong in January 1972. The program continued, however, with the *Universe Campus,* which alternated between 37-day cruises and 4-month study trips. Purchase of another ship was under consideration.

Travel Aids and Curbs. In 1971 the U. S. Public Health Service had relaxed its requirement that U. S. citizens returning from abroad must show a valid certificate for vaccination against smallpox. Afterward only those returning from an area that had smallpox needed to be vaccinated. By the beginning of 1972, European countries had similarly relaxed the rule. Philadelphia imposed an airport departure tax of $2 or $3, depending on the distance to be flown, on all except military passengers. A dozen other cities and the state of New Hampshire followed suit. President Nixon vetoed a bill that would have banned such taxes and have increased federal airport subsidies, but the Air Transport Association began fighting the taxes in court.

ISLAND VENTURE, *a Norwegian cruise ship built in West Germany, arrives in New York after her 14-day shakedown voyage from the shipyard.*

Efforts to attract foreign visitors to the United States continued, spearheaded by the U. S. Travel Service (USTS). In late October, USTS brought a dozen British, French, and German journalists to Chattanooga, Tenn., for the Fall Color Cruise. The party cruised down the Tennessee River through the Grand Canyon of the Tennessee in a paddlewheel steamboat, the *Julia Belle Swain II,* then joined the crowd around a crude stage to admire a show that was mostly country music. The journalists responded with glowing reports of these "homey" activities. The tour was typical of many USTS trips for journalists and travel agents from abroad.

Bicentennial Plans. Preparations for celebrating the bicentennial of the American Revolution in 1976 proceeded slowly, in general, but the village of Pawtuxet, R. I., started things by celebrating the burning of the British revenue schooner *Gaspée* in 1972. Rhode Island proclaimed all of 1972 the Year of the *Gaspée,* and there were clambakes, parades, band concerts, musket-shooting, and tomahawk-throwing in several communities.

In support of the 1976 bicentennial, the Society of American Travel Writers announced that its annual convention in 1975 would be an around-the-world flight, with many stops. The idea was that the American writers could personally invite people from all over the world to visit the United States the following year.

Also in connection with the bicentennial, plans were advanced in 1972 for building a $16 million National Visitors' Center in Union Station, Washington, D. C. The center, to be operated by the National Park Service, was to have reception and orientation facilities, including a 500-seat theater and an elevated parking lot. Washington expected 35 million visitors in 1976.

Educational Travel. Study trips from the United States to other countries continued to proliferate in 1972. Some 20,000 young people went abroad on organized programs during the summer, typically for four weeks of campus study and two weeks of sightseeing. The minimum age for these trips was 10, but in 1973 it was expected to be 8. Courses were mainly in language, history, culture, and literature.

Black Travel. Trans World Airlines offered 50 departures in 1972 for its black-oriented vacation program, called "Sights, Sounds, and Soul of Europe." The 2- and 3-week packages included three to five western European capitals.

Exotic Trips. The Finnish National Tourist Office in late 1972 offered a 5-day "reindeer safari" in Finnish Lapland, with the traveler driving his own sleigh in the wilderness north of the Arctic Circle. Four safaris were scheduled for March 1973.

Pakistan International Airlines began operating "Tours to Mecca" for Muslim Americans. Sabena started tours to visit Masai warrior camps in Kenya. In the autumn, BOAC conducted a series of 29-day Himalayan wildlife tours, led by naturalists, in parks where tigers and rhinos live. Mike Banks, a former British commando, offered for March and April 1973 two 18-day expeditions by dog sled along the wild east coast of Greenland.

Pan American World Airways operated a weekly 747 "all-youth" flight to Amsterdam and Munich during the summer of 1972. Foods, films, publications, and music were all oriented to youth. Pan Am also offered 2- to 3-week Hotelbus tours of England, continental Europe, and Morocco. Passengers slept in a huge Hotelbus that met their touring bus in a different campsite each night.

Ireland. Tourism suffered in Eire—the Republic of Ireland—because of continued violence in Ulster —Northern Ireland—although there was no trouble in Eire. In addition, the U. S. Civil Aeronautics Board urged cancellation of Irish Aer Lingus' landing rights at New York unless U. S. carriers were permitted to land at Dublin. U. S. planes continued to land at Shannon, which has a large free-port store with prices in dollars. Overflying of Shannon would have meant ruin for western Ireland and might have toppled the Irish government. The U. S. State Department at the last moment deferred a decision until the end of 1972.

China. President Nixon's visit to Peking in February stirred much interest among prospective U. S. tourists. The restriction against visiting the People's Republic of China was removed from U. S. passports, but historian Barbara Tuchman, after a 40-day trip, reported that it would be a long time before ordinary U. S. tourists could go there. Meanwhile, all major airlines were seeking routes to mainland China, and many shipping lines planned cruises to Chinese ports in 1973.

U. S. Domestic Travel. By the early 1970's increasing interest in the preservation of America's wild places had greatly expanded participation in travel that results in direct contact with nature. Backpacking, hiking, mountain climbing, and simply walking in the wilderness are examples. The number of boaters was growing every year, and in 1972 the increase was especially noticeable in whitewater boating—canoeing and rafting on wild streams and rivers. Houseboating also increased markedly, especially in the TVA lakes in Tennessee—the "Great Lakes of the South." Downhill ski resorts were becoming so crowded, luxurious, and expensive that many skiers were forsaking the lifts for the quieter pleasures of walking through the woods on cross-country jaunts.

Interest in the national parks had brought more people and cars than the parks could accommodate. In 1972 the government was implementing long-range goals for the parks. These included doing away with parking lots, removing many of the roads, and placing tourist accommodations and services outside. In some cases, shuttle buses were being provided to carry people into the parks.

ROBERT SCOTT MILNE
Coauthor, "Around the World with the Experts"

Hotels and Motels

Income and occupancy in the U. S. lodging industry edged slightly higher in 1972 as compared with 1971, which was the worst year since 1932. Total sales rose to $7.4 billion in 1972 from $7.1 billion a year earlier. Average guest-room occupancy was 60%, up from 59% in 1971.

The number of U. S.-chain hotels and motels rose 6.4% and the number of guest rooms increased 6.8% over 1971 totals, according to the 1972 *Directory of Hotel & Motel Systems.* The number of chains remained at 193. The Directory also showed that the 25 largest hotel/motel chains accounted for 50.5% of the total increase in chain properties, which rose by 299. These larger chains accounted for 48.8% of the gain in number of chain rooms available (48,005).

Holiday Inns, Inc. maintained its position as the world's largest hotel/motel chain by opening 149 inns with a total of 27,237 rooms in 1972. This brings the number of Holiday Inns to 1,556 with a total of 233,413 rooms. Other major chains reported the following additions in 1972: Sheraton, 57 new hotels and motor inns with 12,551 rooms; and Hyatt, four new hotels with 2,680 rooms.

Budget-priced motels continued to grow in popularity, with Motel 6, Inc. reporting the opening of 35 new inns having 2,610 rooms.

Motion pictures on pay TV was the chief innovation in hotels and motels in 1972, with several computerized systems being introduced that permit guests to select what they want to see from a list of new films. Guests watch motion pictures or major sporting events on TV in their rooms and pay for them on their bills when checking out.

The Florida Board of Business Regulation adopted a new rule in 1972 that eventually may have a drastic impact on U. S. hotels and motels. As yet untested in the courts, the rule would require that people who have paid deposits in advance to a hotel or a travel or booking agent must receive a refund in full on demand from the property if it is unable to accommodate them.

New Hotels and Motels. The $26 million, 1,020-room Hyatt Regency Houston, Houston, Texas, was the largest hotel completed in the United States in 1972. Other major hotels opened during 1972 were the $20 million, 981-room O'Hare Towers, Des Plaines, Ill., the 956-room Marriott Motor Hotel in New Orleans; the $20 million, 700-room Hyatt on Union Square, San Francisco; and the 603-room Holiday Inn of Houston-Downtown, Houston.

Paris gained two big new hotels in 1972, the PLM Saint-Jacques, the first major new hotel to open in Paris since 1933, and the 1,000-room Meridien, the largest in the French capital. Buenos Aires, Argentina, got its first major new hotel in several decades, the $24 million, 800-room Buenos Aires-Sheraton Hotel, largest in South America.

Other large new hotels opened in 1972 in various parts of the world. They included the 1,466-room Four Seasons Sheraton, Toronto, Canada; the $40 million, 777-room Acapulco Princess, Acapulco, Mexico (which resembles an Aztec pyramid); the 750-room Holiday Inn of Toronto-Downtown, Toronto, Canada; the 650-room Sheraton Munich, Munich, Germany; and the 603-room Carlton Hotel, Johannesburg, Union of South Africa.

ALBERT E. KUDRLE
American Hotel & Motel Association

FORD MOTOR COMPANY

ROHR INDUSTRIES

THE BENDIX CORPORATION

"People Movers," a new idea in rapid urban transport, went on display at Transpo 72 at Dulles International Airport. The concept of pushbutton-control cars ranged from Rohr Industries' monorail (left), to the more complex, computerized Ford and Bendix systems (right, above and below).

transportation

News developments and technological advances in transportation during 1972 are reviewed in this article under the following headings: (1) General Survey; (2) Highways; (3) Motor Transport; (4) Railroads; and (5) Shipping.

Additional transportation news appears in separate entries for AIR TRANSPORTATION; AUTOMOBILES; BRIDGES; CANALS; TUNNELS.

General Survey

Growth in the financing and construction of urban mass transit facilities highlighted transportation developments in 1972. Virtually all modes of transportation continued to expand and improve their operations, although the U. S. merchant marine continued to decline.

Urban Mass Transit. The need for mass transit systems in urban areas was increasingly emphasized by urban planners and potential patrons in 1972. Both efficiency and economy were cited as compelling factors for developing mass transit. For instance, Federal Highway Administration figures showed that it costs the average motorist 13.55 cents per mile to drive his car, whereas the average bus fare costs only 3.81 cents per mile.

The final summary of Urban Mass Transit Administration (UMTA) grants for 1971 revealed that

269 new grants had been made and that 86 previous grants had been increased. The total federal commitment was $558.6 million, while the states provided an additional $298.1 million.

These awards continued on an accelerated basis in 1972. As an example of their use, an $84.2 million award to three transit authorities in the Chicago area was used to help finance 500 new buses, 100 rapid transit cars, 21 electric commuter cars, and 25 new two-level rail cars. In addition, award money was used to acquire the commuter railroad car fleet of Burlington Northern Inc., a major privately owned railroad.

The trend toward such public acquisition of privately owned transportation facilities has become well established. Other grants to public authorities for this purpose included $7.5 million to Atlanta, $6.3 million to San Francisco, and $5.9 million to Syracuse, N. Y. These grants also included funds for purchasing new equipment.

Many grants were primarily for the acquisition of new equipment. For instance, the Southeastern Pennsylvania Transit Authority was granted $8.3 million for the acquisition of 300 new diesel buses and the remodeling of 61 other buses, while the New Jersey Department of Transportation received $8.5 million for 70 new railroad cars.

Many of the grants merely helped to improve existing facilities. Grants of this type included $18 million to Minneapolis-St. Paul for five years of transit improvements, $11 million to the New Haven Transit Authority to help lay 173 miles of welded steel rail, and $9.6 million to the Massachusetts Bay Transit Authority to modernize seven rapid transit stations.

New or additional heavy-volume rapid-transit facilities in Atlanta, Baltimore, Chicago, Montreal, Toronto, and Washington, D. C., were in progress in 1972. In September, San Francisco opened the first 28-mile section of a planned 75-mile Bay Area Rapid Transit system. About 17,000 passengers used the section daily.

Personal Rapid Transit. The concept of a personal rapid transit (PRT) system moved closer to realization in 1972. The Dallas–Ft. Worth airport board received a grant of $7.6 million to develop a PRT system at the airport between the two cities. In addition, Denver was awarded $11 million to build a PRT system consisting of a one-mile guideway and five cars. This system was scheduled to be in operation sometime in 1975. If successful, the system might be extended to five miles of guideway and 200 cars.

A PRT system uses small vehicles that operate on a guideway. The vehicle responds to passenger pushbutton signals, much like automatic elevators. Generally, a PRT vehicle would carry relatively few persons—from as few as six to as many as 30. The main idea is that such a vehicle would lure automobile commuters from their cars more successfully than mass-transit vehicles. As a result, city traffic congestion and air pollution would be reduced.

Exclusive Lanes for Buses. Express bus operations on exclusive rights-of-way have been gaining in popularity because of their relatively high passenger capacity at relatively low cost. Buses using exclusive lanes began to carry 1,900 morning passengers into Washington, D. C., in 1969, and this service has grown to handle about 7,000 passengers. Also, an exclusive-lane bus operation on a four-mile approach to the Lincoln Tunnel has been carrying 35,000 commuters into Manhattan daily.

On the West Coast, a $54 million, 11-mile expressway only for buses into Los Angeles was under construction in 1972. In Seattle, a "Blue Streak" express bus operation proved a success. As a result, the people of Seattle approved a $96 million bond issue for developing an all-bus transit system, including highway lanes used exclusively by the buses. Milwaukee, St. Louis, and Minneapolis-St. Paul were considering such operations.

Railroads. The railroads generally had a very good year in 1972, although some of them experienced financial difficulties. In its first fiscal year, Amtrak reported losses totaling $153.5 million. Ridership at mid-1972 was up 13.7% as compared with the same period a year earlier, indicating possible better results in the future.

Burlington Northern applied to the Interstate Commerce Commission (ICC) to build a new 126-mile branch line in Wyoming to carry low-sulfur coal. When completed, the $32.5 million line will be the longest one built in the United States since 1931.

For the first time in history, the ICC permitted a railroad to own and operate a barge line. In getting this decision, the Southern Railway Company was supported by the Justice Department, which judged that the barge operation would increase competition. The railroad company will operate coal barges along the Ohio River and other areas.

Tracked Air-Cushion Vehicle. Early in 1972, the Department of Transportation awarded a contract to Rohr Industries, Inc., for the construction of a prototype of the nation's first passenger vehicle to run on a cushion of air. Called a tracked air-cushion vehicle, it is designed to glide along a concrete guideway on a thin cushion of air and be powered by a linear induction motor.

Merchant Marine Fleet. According to the U. S. Maritime Administration there were 1,179 vessels of 1,000 gross tons or more in the U. S. merchant fleet on Nov. 1, 1972, including 521 vessels in the National Defense Reserve Fleet.

On that date 80 ships were under construction or on order, and 6 other vessels were undergoing conversion. In addition, contracts were signed for six liquefied natural gas (LNG) tankers, which were scheduled to be delivered between 1975 and 1977. The six vessels were to cost $566 million. The $268.7 million agreement for building three of them was the largest peacetime shipbuilding contract ever signed in the United States.

In terms of registered tonnage, the U. S. merchant fleet in 1972 ranked seventh in the world according to Lloyd's Register of Shipping. The United States and the Netherlands were the only major maritime nations to have suffered declines in registered tonnage from the preceding year. About 62% of the world merchant fleet is less than 10 years old, whereas about 54% of the U. S. merchant fleet is more than 25 years old.

Inland and Coastal Waterway Carriers. In the first half of 1972, Class A and B carriers reported a decrease from the same period in 1971. In the period, traffic in ton-miles increased from 37.64 billion to 38.87 billion, revenue passengers decreased from 965,663 to 963,572, and passenger revenue increased from $3.1 million to $3.7 million.

Coastwise and Intercoastal Carriers. In 1970, 18 carriers reported revenues of $832.7 million for carrying 149 million tons of freight, up from $739 million for 17 carriers in 1969.

International Commerce. The U. S. Army Corps of Engineers estimated that U. S. imports and exports totaled 1.49 billion tons in 1971, down 2.6% from the high of 1.53 billion tons in 1970. Imports increased 5.2%, but exports decreased by 14.7%.

St. Lawrence Seaway. Record tonnage and revenue were realized by the St. Lawrence Seaway in 1971. Cargo increased 3.4% over 1970 to 52.9 million tons, producing $7.4 million in toll revenues, up 7.2% over 1970. Through Dec. 7, 1972, a total of 53.2 million tons of cargo already had cleared the canal, indicating another record year.

World's Largest Ship. Japan, the leading shipbuilding nation in the world, launched the world's largest ship in 1972. The *Globtik Tokyo,* a 477,000-deadweight-ton oil tanker, was scheduled to go into service early in 1973.

Airlines. The Civil Aeronautics Board (CAB) reported that trunk airlines had a 5.4% rate of return in fiscal year 1972, while local service carriers

TUNNEL-DIGGING deep beneath the Potomac River is part of a massive effort to help relieve Washington, D. C.'s perennial traffic problems. New link in subway system may be ready by 1975.

NEW INTERCHANGE built near Birmingham, England, links several major routes.
Known locally as "Spaghetti Junction," it is the most complex interchange in Europe.

had a rate of 5.0%. This compared favorably with fiscal 1971 when the rates were 1.2% and 1.7%, respectively.

For the first nine months of 1972, the nation's scheduled airlines increased their revenue passenger miles to 114.7 billion, up 13.1% over the corresponding period in 1971. With available seat miles up only 2.6%, the load factor increased from 48.9% to 54.5%.

The number of commuter air carriers serving 1,249 markets was down to 160 in 1971. However, the number of flights increased to 788,525, and the number of passengers increased to 4,925,000.

Subsidies to air carriers in fiscal year 1972 were expected to increase by $7.1 million over 1971. Local service carriers were to receive $62.8 million, while Alaskan carriers were to receive $4.4 million.

JAMES R. ROMAN, JR.
The George Washington University

Highways

Highway construction, highway expenditures, motor vehicle registration, highway speed, and bus operations increased in 1971, while the fatality rate dropped to its lowest figure in history. Preliminary data for 1972 showed much the same pattern.

Interstate Highway System. The Department of Transportation announced that as of Sept. 30, 1972, 27,383 miles of rural mileage and 6,413 miles of urban mileage of the Interstate Highway System were open to the public, making the system about 80% complete. This represents the completion of 1,404 miles since the previous year. Construction was under way on 3,742 miles, engineering and right-of-way acquisition were under way on 3,632 miles, and public hearings had been held for location approval on 506 more miles. Public hearings remained to be held on only 824 miles, or 2%, of the projected mileage.

The Federal Highway Administration reported to Congress that when completed the 42,500-mile Interstate Highway System will cost $76.3 billion, an increase of $6.4 billion over the estimate made in 1970. The federal government's share of this coast-to-coast network of controlled-access freeways is 90%, or $68.3 billion.

State Highway Finances. The Department of Transportation reported that the states spent $17.7 billion on highways in 1971, while receipts totaled $18.5 billion. The balance was placed in highway fund revenues. Income included $9.2 billion from state road-user taxes, $5.0 billion from federal road-user taxes, $2.6 billion from highway construction bonds, $0.9 billion from tolls, and $0.8 billion from other sources.

Capital expenditures were the most significant element of cost, including $4.2 billion on the Interstate Highway System, $4.5 billion on other federal-aid highways, and $1.2 billion on state highways. The states gave $2.5 billion to local governments as grants-in-aid for highway purposes, and they spent $2.4 billion on administration, safety, law enforce-

ment, and interest on highway bonds. Maintenance accounted for $2.1 billion, while highway bond retirements required $0.8 billion.

During the first six months of 1972, the Department of Transportation reported that state highway departments awarded 2,752 federal-aid highway contracts at a cost of about $2.5 billion. This was an increase of about 27% in both the number of contracts and the value of contracts as compared with the same period in 1971. It was estimated that for all of 1972, the states would have total receipts of $21.8 billion to use for highway projects, and 22.3 billion in 1973.

Motor Vehicle Registrations. The Federal Highway Administration reported that 92,752,515 automobiles, 19,772,212 trucks, and 397,627 buses were operating in the United States in 1971, a total of almost 113 million vehicles. States also registered 3,343,884 motorcycles, motor scooters, and motor bicycles. The states registered 10,167,720 trailers, even though many states exempt certain types of trailers from registration.

More than 1 million vehicles were registered in each of 34 states. The eight leading states were California, 12.3 million registrations; Texas, 7.0 million; New York, 6.9 million; Ohio, 6.0 million; Pennsylvania, 6.0 million; Illinois, 5.4 million; Michigan, 4.7 million; and Florida, 4.5 million.

The Federal Highway Administration projected a total registration of more than 117 million vehicles in 1972, or a 4.1% increase from 1971. Truck and bus registrations were expected to increase by 5% to over 21 million, while automobile registrations were expected to increase by 3.9% to more than 96 million vehicles. The ten leading states were expected to register 62.1 million vehicles in 1972, or 52.8% of the total registration.

Highway Speed. The Federal Highway Administration reported that the average vehicle speed on highways continued to climb in 1971, as it has since 1943. The average speed on the Interstate Highway System was 64.7 mph, including 66.3 mph for passenger cars, 64.5 mph for buses, and 59.4 mph for trucks. On main rural roads the average speed was 60.6 mph, including 62.0 mph for passenger cars, 60.2 mph for buses, and 56.1 mph for trucks. Nevada recorded the highest average speed, 66.0 mph, while West Virginia recorded the lowest average speed, 52.7 mph.

Traffic Fatalities. The National Safety Council reported that the highway fatality rate of 4.7 per 100 million vehicle miles in 1971 was the lowest rate in history. Nevertheless, 55,000 persons were killed in traffic accidents in 1971, second only to 1969 when 56,000 persons were killed. Motor carriers of property had a fatality rate of 11.1 per 100 million vehicle miles in 1971 according to the Bureau of Motor Carrier Safety. This was the second-lowest rate in five years.

Commercial Vehicle Defects. The Bureau of Motor Carrier Safety reported in 1972 that statistically reliable safety checks showed that 16.5% of all commercial vehicles were "mechanically too hazardous to be operated beyond the check point." Among tractor trailers, 27.8% were declared to be unsafe; among authorized carrier vehicles, 16.6% were unsafe; among private carriers, 15.1% were unsafe; and among exempt carriers, 19.8% were defective.

Bus Operations. The National Association of Motor Bus Owners reported that intercity bus travel totaled approximately 25.2 billion passenger miles in 1971, an increase of about 2 million passenger miles over 1970. This increased revenues about 6% to $765 million for the 70 Class I carriers that each gross over $1 million. Revenue from regular-route intercity travel was $543 million; from package express, $105 million; from charter and special service, $87 million; and from other sources, $30 million. Operating expenses climbed to $667 million in 1971, up from $638 million in 1970.

JAMES R. ROMAN, JR.
The George Washington University

Motor Transport

Truck transportation in the United States continued to grow in 1972 as the number of trucks, the ton-miles of freight, and the total operating revenues of the truck industry all showed gains over the preceding year. The trucking industry continued efforts to increase efficiency in its operations by making greater use of computers for processing billing, tariff, scheduling, and terminal operations data.

New and modified truck designs will continue to be required to meet changing government safety and air-pollution standards. Higher standards for accident-resistant fuel tanks are now effective, while new braking standards and improved lighting systems are anticipated.

Trucking. The U. S. motor-truck fleet increased by nearly 1 million vehicles during 1972. Registrations, excluding government-owned trucks, reached a record high of about 19.7 million vehicles, compared with 18.8 million in 1971. The industry carried approximately 455 billion ton-miles of freight in 1972, compared with about 430 ton-miles in 1971.

Total operating revenues for about 15,000 regulated for-hire truck lines engaged in U. S. interstate commerce in 1972 rose to more than $19 billion. This total is greater than the combined freight revenues of all other regulated modes of transportation—railroads, pipelines, inland water carriers, and air freight. Private and for-hire trucking operators not regulated by the Interstate Commerce Commission earned additional billions.

The trucking industry's impact on the economy was felt in several areas. It provided employment for about 9 million persons and had a payroll of about $72.5 billion. Record sales were set for all types of trucks, including diesels and truck-trailers, reflecting the greater transport flexibility required by shippers. Trucks used about 27.5 billion gallons of motor fuel in 1972 at a cost of almost $7 billion, exclusive of taxes. Also, motor-truck operators paid an estimated $5.9 billion in federal and state highway use taxes in 1972, including taxes levied for construction of the Interstate and Defense Highway System.

Containerization. Growth in the containerization of internationally shipped goods continued in 1972. In international trade, the use of containers permits land, sea, and air shipment of goods, with savings in repacking, loading, and unloading as a result of the great flexibility of transfer from one mode of transportation to another. Broad international standards for containers moved closer to final adoption in 1972, and lack of final agreement on standards did not significantly slow container development during the year.

WILLIAM A. BRESNAHAN
American Trucking Associations, Inc.

BART (Bay Area Rapid Transport), serving the San Francisco–Oakland area, began operating in 1972. It is hoped that the new system will reduce private car use.

Railroads

The 68 Class I railroads in the United States had a record-setting year in 1972. They established new peaks by hauling 26 million carloads of freight, producing 780 million ton-miles of service, and having $13.5 billion in gross operating revenues. But railway operating income of about $850 million represented a return on investment of only around 3%.

Prosperity continued for most Southern and Western railroads, but there was a crisis in the Northeast, where seven carriers were in bankruptcy.

Northeast Crisis. In mid-1972, the 3,000-mile Erie-Lackawanna Railroad came under the protection of a bankruptcy court. The railroad was a victim of record floods spawned by tropical storm Agnes, which inundated large portions of the East in mid-June. Earlier in the year, the 86-mile Lehigh & Hudson River Railroad filed for reorganization

under Section 77 of the Federal Bankruptcy Act. This section is designed to keep red-ink railroads in operation by relieving them of tax and debt payments during the period of reorganization. Railroads which were already in bankruptcy included the 20,000-mile Penn Central Transportation Co., the 1,140-mile Reading Co., the 920-mile Lehigh Valley Railroad, the 590-mile Central Railroad of New Jersey, and the 1,570-mile Boston & Maine Railroad. Thus, companies that have more than one eighth of the nation's 205,000 route miles of railroads were in bankruptcy at the end of 1972.

Increasing talk of government takeover of the entire industry led a number of railroad leaders to propose solutions short of nationalization. The most sweeping proposal was advanced by E. Spencer Miller, president of the marginally profitable Maine Central Railroad. He called for the merger of all U. S. railroads into a single system, the American Railroad Corporation. Miller's proposal generated considerable national publicity but little enthusiasm among railroad men. They were inclined to take more seriously the smaller consolidation plans advanced by the Lehigh Valley and the Reading.

Lehigh Valley trustees John F. Nash and Robert C. Halderman proposed a working consolidation of the Lehigh Valley, the Central of New Jersey, and the Reading, taking the best part of each for continued railroad operations and liquidating the remaining facilities for the benefit of creditors. Subsequently, Reading President Charles E. Bertrand called for the creation of a Northeast National Railway System that would piece together a single system from parts of the Reading, the Central of New Jersey, the Lehigh Valley, and the Lehigh & Hudson River. The debtor companies, retaining real estate and other assets not subject to the cyclical fortunes of railroading, would be free to reorganize as general business organizations.

Meanwhile, the Penn Central struggled to develop its own plan for reorganization, due in the spring of 1973. As of 1972, a major part of the Penn Central plan called for the abandonment of

about 5,000 miles of main line. By late autumn, Penn Central trustees had filed applications with the Interstate Commerce Commission for the abandonment of 2,780 miles of track but had been granted approval to abandon only 732 miles. Consequently, the trustees began considering other avenues of attack on the problem of unprofitable lines, such as contracting with local governments or shipper groups for the subsidization of deficit services.

The fundamental problem facing Eastern railroads was that too many lines were competing for a diminishing freight traffic. Forty years ago, 50% of the nation's manufactured products were produced in the Northeast, whereas in 1972 the figure was 25%. The mills that used to produce thousands of carloads of traffic have been replaced, according to Lehigh Valley's Nash, "by research or developing firms or by electronic companies whose entire production for a year can be transported in a couple of suitcases." At the same time, Nash observed, "there are locations in the Northeast where a golfer with a 6 iron can drop his golf ball on any of the main lines of four railroads:"

Amtrak. The National Railroad Passenger Corporation (Amtrak), which assumed responsibility for the operation of remaining intercity passenger trains on May 1, 1971, was running deep in the red in 1972. During its first fiscal year, which ended June 30, Amtrak took in $152.7 million and spent $306.1 million. Congress authorized $227 million in new federal assistance to Amtrak to meet operating deficits, buy new locomotives and rolling stock, and pay for new services linking New York City and Montreal, Canada; Seattle and Vancouver, Canada; and San Antonio, Texas, and Nuevo Laredo, Mexico. However, only $179 million was finally appropriated, so Amtrak had to postpone plans to acquire new high-speed turbine trains from France. At year's end, Amtrak was still hoping it could eventually buy new trains from France and Britain.

Amtrak commissioned a $200,000 public opinion survey by Louis Harris and Associates. It found that 82% of the persons surveyed think Americans should have the option of riding trains, but that only 4% of them had actually ridden a train in the preceding 12 months. The survey also found that 64% of the public favored continuing intercity service "even if it means federal subsidies."

Merger. The only important merger in 1972 brought the Illinois Central Railroad and the Gulf, Mobile & Ohio Railroad together in a 9,400-mile system, the Illinois Central Gulf. The merged railroad, with revenues of more than $450 million a year, is a wholly owned subsidiary of Illinois Central Industries.

Employee-Owned Railroad. The nation's first major employee-owned railroad came into being in 1972 when 1,000 executive, operating, and clerical personnel purchased the 10,700-mile Chicago and North Western Railway from the parent Northwest Industries.

Labor. A major advance in railroad labor relations came with the settlement of the fireman-manning case on Aug. 1, 1972. The dispute, which was rooted in the 1930's when the railroads agreed to keep firemen on diesel locomotives, had been a bitter controversy since 1959 when the railroads brought their antifeatherbedding fight into the open. Under the 1972 agreement, the 18,000 remaining firemen on diesel freight locomotives were to be phased out through normal attrition. The agreement also created a training program for firemen wishing to advance to engineer.

All of the remaining state laws on full crews were repealed in 1972, saving the railroads around $75 million a year. The repeals were voted in Ohio, Indiana, Wisconsin, and Arkansas.

Railroads in 1972 continued to pay for the 42%-in-42-months wage increases negotiated in 1970. A 5% wage increase amounting to $320 million a year went into effect April 1, and another 5% hike on October 5 added $325 million to payroll costs. Additional increases of 5% were to come due on Jan. 1 and April 1, 1973.

LUTHER S. MILLER
Editor, "Railway Age"

Shipping

A dramatic maritime development in 1972 was the growth of the Soviet merchant marine to the point where it surpassed in size that of the United States (see Table 1). The Soviets reached fifth place in the world, while the aging U. S. flag fleet slipped to seventh place. In another sense, however, the merchant fleet of the United States retains its supremacy, for about 40% of the ships flying the Liberian flag are American-owned and a great portion of them American-financed. If the U. S.-owned, U. S.-operated segments of the Liberian and other fleets are added to that under the U. S. flag, the U. S. merchant fleet becomes the largest in the world.

This is not to deny or belittle the importance of the Soviet merchant marine. During 1972, Russian ships in increasing numbers entered U. S. West Coast ports. In addition, the first Soviet merchant ship since World War II entered an East Coast port (Baltimore), bringing a hydrofoil craft as a gift to President Nixon from Communist party leader Leonid Brezhnev.

Forty U. S. ports were open to ships of the Soviet merchant marine by 1972. These included most of the major coastal and Great Lakes harbors. The ports still banned were those with U. S. Navy operating bases or shipyards, notably the Hampton Roads, Va., ports, on the East Coast, and San Diego, in the West. The ban was of great concern to the two Hampton Roads ports—Norfolk and Newport News—because both of them are major handlers of raw materials, including grain.

U. S.-Soviet Grain Transport Agreement. The 1972 agreement arranging for the Soviet purchase of at least $750 million worth of grain over a three-year period had important implications for shippers. The agreement called for one third of the wheat to be transported in Soviet ships, one third under the U. S. flag, and one third in ships of other nations. This arrangement, exacted by the politically powerful U. S. maritime unions, meant that for the first time, the United States had publically subscribed to flag discrimination. By favoring the vessels of one nation over those of others, it had reversed its former policy of freedom in ocean trade. The agreement thus became a matter of major concern to such maritime nations as Great Britain, Norway, and Greece, all of which were NATO partners of the United States.

The U. S. flag vessels engaged in the transport of American wheat to Russia would have to be subsidized by the American taxpayer because the Soviet Union refused to assume any of the cost difference involved in shipping the wheat in U. S. vessels as

Table 1. MAJOR MERCHANT FLEETS

Country	Gross registered tons[1] June 1, 1972	1 year gain or loss
Liberia	44,444,000	+5,892,000
Japan	34,929,000	+4,420,000
Britain	28,625,000	+1,290,000
Norway	23,507,000	+1,787,000
USSR	16,734,000	+ 540,000
Greece	15,329,000	+2,263,000
United States	15,024,000	−1,242,000
World total[2]	268,340,000	+21,137,000

Source: Lloyd's Register of Shipping, 1971.

Table 2. WORLD SHIPBUILDING, 1967–1972[3]

(In millions of gross registered tons)[1]

Country	On order July 1, 1972	Delivered July 1971– July 1972	Percentage built, 1967–72 Tonnage	Ships
Japan	34.50	12.89	50.20	36.78
Sweden	6.80	2.30	8.18	3.91
Spain	4.80	1.02	3.32	4.35
France	4.30	0.85	3.62	2.36
Britain	4.20	1.27	5.45	5.75
West Germany	4.30	1.60	6.93	10.12
Norway	3.50	0.95	3.62	3.62
Denmark	3.50	0.97	3.15	1.78
Netherlands	2.10	0.82	2.20	3.12
Yugoslavia	1.80	0.84	2.10	1.94
United States	1.80	0.54	1.55	1.63
Poland	1.30	0.62	1.20	2.94
World total[2]	80.60	26.63	100.00	100.00

Source: Lloyd's Register Shipbuilding Returns.
[1] Gross tonnage is volume capacity; deadweight tonnage (dwt) is lifting capacity. [2] Includes other countries in addition to those listed. [3] Not including USSR.

against foreign ships, the cost being about twice as great for U. S. ships. However, it was doubtful that, even with the help of subsidies, sufficient U. S. vessels would be available to fill the U. S. quota. The first ship of any nationality to set out for the USSR with U. S. wheat under the new agreement was a Japanese vessel sailing from Houston, Texas. The second was a British ship that sailed from Galveston. The first U. S.-flag ship to sail on this mission, also from Houston, was a grain-loaded tanker of World War II vintage.

The New Maritime America. The year 1972 saw the dismantling of the nuclear-powered merchant ship *Savannah,* completed in 1959, and the delivery and first voyage of the new Sea-Bee type ship, *Doctor Lykes,* carrying loaded barges, containers, and general cargo to Europe. These events emphasized the transition from the old to the new maritime America.

Public servants, the media, and people in general have tended to view maritime matters exclusively in terms of warships and merchant vessels. The oceans and their navigable waters, however, are now offering new possibilities, and Americans generally have been the first to exploit them. The United States is leading in the development of new sea concepts. Among these concepts are the use of large ships for the overseas transport of containers that are carried on land by trailer trucks, railroad cars, and river barges. This provides an integrated system of transport that links the internal systems of nations with overseas maritime systems. It also forms a separation of the prime mover from the carrier—a land transport concept as old as the horse and wagon but one seldom before applied to ocean shipping.

Also significant in the new maritime America is the development of barges for both inland-water and ocean transport. A shipper's dollar can move a ton of freight over 300 miles by barge, 66 miles by railroad, 15 miles by truck, and less than 5 miles by aircraft. Most of the freight moved today does not consist of processed goods but of the raw materials needed for industrial plants. Increasing numbers of plants, therefore, are being located on sites convenient to water transport facilities, as, for example, sites along the rivers of the Mississippi system, or along the Gulf Coast. This has been contributing to the movement of industrial complexes to these areas from inland northern cities.

The pressing needs of such states as Alaska and Hawaii and such nearby, water-surrounded countries as those of the Caribbean for low-cost bulk transport has helped promote the development of ocean barge transport. The barges now being built may be pushed as well as pulled (the more traditional method of ocean towing). Ocean barge building is centered in the Gulf of Mexico area, where such barges are most widely used. A second center is the Puget Sound area, which serves Alaska. The 5,000-deadweight-ton barge *Hawaii* was built in Galveston, Texas, to transport fertilizer to the state of Hawaii and carry pineapples and sugar on the return trip. Also built in Galveston was the recently launched chemical barge carrier *Ponciana,* which is 385 feet long and 56 feet wide, with a draft of 26 feet and a cargo capacity of 5,500 short tons.

The inland water and ocean barge transport industry is generally privately owned and employs nonunion labor.

JOHN D. HAYES
Rear Admiral, U. S. Navy (Retired)

STEWART J. CORT, *newest and largest ore carrier on the Great Lakes, is 1,000 feet (305 meters) long.*

TRINIDAD AND TOBAGO

Trinidad and Tobago celebrated its 10th anniversary as an independent nation on Aug. 31, 1972. The anniversary year was somewhat marred by an outbreak of poliomyelitis on the larger island.

Epidemic. The polio epidemic struck Trinidad in November 1971 and extended through February 1972. Over 176 persons became ill and 11 died, almost all of them children. Schools were closed, an immunization campaign undertaken, and a clean-up drive was carried out, but the spread of the illness had an adverse effect on the economy and the morale of the population. The epidemic occurred during the height of the tourist season. Many tourist ships bypassed the country. Tourism had replaced sugar as the second-largest source of government revenue in 1971, though not in 1972.

Economic Developments. Heavy rains during the cane-cutting season reduced Trinidad and Tobago's sugar production by 13,000 tons from 1971. The petroleum industry, which supplies about 30% of the country's revenue, was strengthened by a major gas find off the east coast of Tobago. The overall production of oil increased to 280,000 barrels daily in 1972, up from 133,000 in 1971.

The government took steps in 1972 to localize foreign banks operating in the islands. The first bank taken over was the Royal Bank of Canada.

Political Affairs. The political situation was less tense than in previous years, and the government lifted the state of emergency that had been in effect since October 1971. But the basic political problems continued. Parliament remained in the exclusive hands of the People's National Movement in spite of the constitutional requirement for the representation of minority parties. A commission to study the problem, appointed in 1971 by Prime Minister Eric Williams, completed its work in 1972, but no immediate action was taken on its report.

THOMAS G. MATHEWS, *University of Puerto Rico*

TRINIDAD AND TOBAGO · Information Highlights

Official Name: Trinidad and Tobago.
Area: 1,980 square miles (5,128 sq km).
Population (1972 est.): 1,100,000. *Density,* 477 per square mile (184 per sq km). *Annual rate of increase,* 1.1%.
Chief City (1960 census): Port-of-Spain, the capital, 93,954.
Government: *Head of state,* Elizabeth II, queen; represented by Sir Solomon Hochoy, governor general (took office Aug. 1962). *Head of government,* Eric Williams, prime minister (took office Nov. 1966). *Legislature*—Parliament: Senate, 24 members; House of Representatives, 36 members. *Major political parties*—People's National Movement; Democratic Labour party; Democratic Action Congress.
Languages: English (official), Hindi, French patois, Spanish.
Education: *Expenditure* (1969), 15.7% of total public expenditure. *School enrollment* (1968)—primary, 232,611; secondary, 51,848; technical/vocational, 4,679; university/higher, 1,267.
Monetary Unit: Trinidad and Tobago dollar (1.98 T. and T. dollar equal U.S.$1, Sept. 1972).
Gross National Product (1970 est.): $836,000,000.
National Income per Person (1968): $682.
Consumer Price Index (1971): 128 (1963=100).
Manufacturing (major products): Petroleum products, sugar products, fertilizers, plastics, textiles, cement.
Major Agricultural Products: Sugarcane, bananas, citrus fruits, coffee, cacao, coconuts.
Major Minerals: Petroleum, lignite, coal, gypsum.
Foreign Trade (1971): *Exports,* $518,000,000 (chief exports —petroleum products; sugar). *Imports,* $652,000,000 (chief imports, 1969—crude petroleum, food). *Chief trading partners* (1969)—United States (took 50% of exports, supplied 15% of imports); United Kingdom (10%—14%).
Tourism: *Receipts* (1970), $16,500,000.
Transportation: *Motor vehicles* (1970), 96,100; *major national airline,* British West Indian Airways.
Communications: *Telephones* (1971), 56,251; *television stations* (1971), 2; *newspapers* (1969), 3.

TRUDEAU, Pierre Elliott. See BIOGRAPHY.

WIDE WORLD

HARRY S. TRUMAN (1884–1972)
"He did what had to be done, when it had to be done, and because he did the world today is a better and safer place . . . ."
—*From a tribute by President Nixon.*

TRUMAN, Harry S.

Thirty-third President of the United States: b. Lamar, Mo., May 8, 1884; d. Kansas City, Mo., Dec. 26, 1972.

A dirt farmer and unsuccessful haberdasher who entered politics with the support of a corrupt political boss, Harry S. Truman attained the summit of power and public respect. As President of the United States from 1945 to 1953, he acted boldly to end the war with Japan and to avert a Communist take-over in South Korea, and he helped rebuild Europe to prevent an even bigger confrontation with the Soviet Union.

Truman, though identified with the notorious Pendergast machine of Kansas City, was a man of high personal integrity. As President he made major decisions with a speed and certainty that suggested impulsiveness and arrogance. Though he was often excoriated by the press and by political opponents for such rapid decisions, events often proved that he had acted correctly.

Truman's reputation has fluctuated widely. In 1962, 75 historians rated him a "near-great" President, but the morality of his decision to drop two atomic bombs on Japan in 1945 is still debated. Some critics of recent U.S. foreign policy have held Truman responsible for the onset of the Cold War with the Communist nations. Others agree with Winston Churchill that Truman "more than any other man . . . saved Western Civilization."

In appearance, Truman was not imposing. He was of less than average height, and the thick glasses that he wore gave him an owlish aspect. He spoke in the flat, nasal tone of the Midwesterner. Yet he exuded energy, and he enjoyed excellent health until his final illness at the age of 88.

RELISHING his upset victory over Thomas E. Dewey in the 1948 presidential race, President Truman holds aloft headline of the Chicago Daily Tribune proclaiming his defeat. Paper had rushed to press with an extra edition assuming that Dewey would win.

EARLY CAREER

Truman was the oldest of three children of John and Martha Truman. His father was a farmer. The family moved to Independence, Mo., where Harry entered school. A shy boy, he turned for recreation to reading rather than sports. After graduating from high school, he was rejected by West Point because of poor eyesight. For the next 15 years he worked at various jobs and on the family farm. After the United States entered World War I he obtained a commission and received artillery training. He was given command, with the rank of captain, of Battery D, 129th Field Artillery, and he won the respect and lifelong affection of his men.

Soon after returning to Missouri, Truman married Elizabeth (Bess) Wallace, his childhood sweetheart. A daughter, Margaret, was born in 1924. Truman entered the haberdashery business in 1919, but it failed during an economic slump in 1922.

Entry into Politics. The year 1922 marked the successful beginning of Truman's political career. A veteran, a Baptist, and a member of the American Legion and the Masons, the popular Truman seemed a likely candidate for office. Tom Pendergast persuaded Truman to run for judge of the Jackson County Court. Though defeated for reelection in 1924, Truman ran successfully for presiding judge of the county court in 1926. During the next eight years he supervised the spending of $60 million for highways and public buildings, a responsibility he discharged efficiently and honestly despite the corruption of Pendergast's Democratic machine. In 1934, Pendergast asked Truman to run for the U. S. Senate, and he was elected easily.

In the Senate. Truman settled happily into Senate routine, shunning the limelight and working diligently in his committees. He supported President Franklin Roosevelt's New Deal, voting for measures to regulate business and to aid workers and farmers. Meanwhile, Tom Pendergast was imprisoned for tax evasion, and even Roosevelt concluded that Truman should be replaced as Democratic candidate for the Senate in 1940. Running against two anti-Pendergast candidates, Truman was renominated by a small margin. He was then reelected narrowly over a Republican challenger.

The approach of World War II gave Truman his first chance to render significant public service. On a fact-finding trip around the country, he discovered evidence of waste and inefficiency by defense contractors. The Senate approved his resolution for a Senate Special Committee to Investigate the National Defense Program, and Truman was named chairman of the group.

Vice President. As the 1944 presidential election drew near, Truman was regarded as one of the men best informed about the conduct of the war effort. Roosevelt, seeking reelection, was under pressure to drop Vice President Henry Wallace, who was considered too liberal and had shown disdain toward some Democratic political leaders who feared that the ailing President might not survive another term. After considering other candidates, Roosevelt agreed to the replacement of Wallace with Truman. Truman was initially unwilling to run, and he received the nomination only after two tense ballots.

Roosevelt and Truman were elected, and the Missourian sank into the anonymity of the vice presidency. But he held the office for only 82 days, for on April 12, 1945, Franklin Roosevelt died.

THE PRESIDENCY

Truman thought himself ill-prepared to shoulder the burdens of the presidency, particularly during time of war. Never had a new president faced so many decisions so quickly. He met them squarely and in so doing gained self-confidence.

Foreign Affairs. In office for only two weeks, Truman presided over the charter conference of the United Nations in San Francisco. On May 8 he announced the surrender of Germany. In July he met with British and Russian leaders at Potsdam, Germany, where failure to resolve postwar boundaries for East European nations helped trigger the Cold War between the Soviet Union and the United States. With Truman's approval the first atomic bombs were dropped in August on Hiroshima and Nagasaki, killing some 100,000 persons. Japan surrendered, and Truman was convinced that he had saved the lives of millions of soldiers.

After the war, Truman accepted the challenge of international leadership thrust upon a nation that had long adhered to isolationism. In 1947 he advanced his European Recovery Program, or Marshall Plan, designed to achieve the restoration of Europe. Two years later he proposed his Point Four program for the economic development of nations emerging from colonialism. Congress funded these projects, both acclaimed as successes.

Reaction to Soviet political and economic pressures in Europe and the Middle East soon became

part of the complex of forces shaping American foreign policy. A U. S. airlift of food and medicine thwarted a Soviet attempt to swallow all of Berlin. Military aid to Greece and Turkey—the Truman Doctrine—was part of the overall policy of containing communism. The ratification by the Senate in 1949 of NATO committed the United States to the defense of western Europe.

War came not in Europe but in Asia, where Communists won an internal struggle in China in 1949. A year later the Communist regime in North Korea invaded South Korea. Truman rushed land, sea, and air forces to South Korea's defense, and won approval of the United Nations for his "police action." During the bloody struggle that followed, thousands of Chinese "volunteers" joined the fighting in behalf of North Korea. Gen. Douglas MacArthur, the UN commander in Korea, defied both the United Nations and his commander-in-chief by publicly advocating attacks on air bases in China. In perhaps his most courageous act, Truman relieved the popular MacArthur for insubordination.

Domestic Policies. At home, the President was guided by a sense of fair play and a sympathy for deprived people. In support of Negro Americans, Truman sought to establish a Fair Employment Practices Commission as well as legislation to end poll taxes, lynchings, and discrimination on public transportation. Congress approved federal aid to housing, but aid to education and a compulsory health insurance plan were among measures that were defeated. Many of Truman's domestic goals were realized during later administrations.

Controversy frequently visited the Truman White House. In 1947, Congress overrode a veto of the Taft-Hartley Act, which Truman said unfairly weakened the bargaining position of labor unions. Perceiving a threat from domestic communism, Congress overrode a veto of the Internal Security Act in 1950. In 1952 the U. S. Supreme Court negated Truman's seizure of the steel industry to prevent a strike and an increase in prices.

The 1948 Election. Without enthusiasm, the Democrats renominated Truman in 1948. Opinion polls fed an almost universal assumption that he would lose to the Republican nominee, Thomas E. Dewey. The country had shown a trend toward conservatism in the congressional election in 1946. The Democrats were hobbled by two splinter candidacies led by dissidents opposed respectively to Truman's firm stand against Russia and to his civil rights program. Truman conducted a vigorous campaign, rebuked the "do-nothing 80th Congress," and evoked cries of "Give 'em hell, Harry." He defeated Dewey by 2 million votes.

RETIREMENT

Truman's retirement in January 1953 was brightened by the marriage of his daughter to Clifton Daniel, a New York *Times* executive, and by the births of four grandsons. The ex-President published two volumes of *Memoirs* (1955–56) and oversaw the creation of the Truman Library in Independence, which houses his papers. On Dec. 5, 1972, he was taken to Research Hospital in Kansas City, where he died on the morning after Christmas. In a simple service, he was buried on the grounds of the Truman Library.

DONALD YOUNG
Author of "American Roulette: The History and Dilemma of the Vice Presidency"

TUNISIA

President Habib Bourguiba, whose term was to expire in 1973, tried to strengthen his position both at home and abroad in 1972 by tightening his control over the party machinery and by playing the role of peacemaker in the Arab world.

Party Affairs and Elections. President Bourguiba offered clemency to 46-year-old Ahmed Mestiri, leader of the liberal wing of the Destour Socialist Party. Bourguiba had suspended Mestiri from the party after Mestiri's faction at the party congress of October 1971 demanded more democracy within the party than Bourguiba wished to grant. Bourguiba's attempt at reconciliation with Mestiri was made in order to gain his support and to quiet the liberal wing of the party. On January 12, the president told Mestiri that if he would "return to his previous sound judgment," he would be accepted back into the party. Bourguiba had a statement of self-criticism prepared by the party's Discipline Commission for him to sign. Mestiri did not sign, and on January 21 the party expelled him.

The question of succession to the presidency was the subject of a constitutional reform on March 15. The new scheme required the premier, rather than the president of the National Assembly, to become temporary president in case of the president's incapacity or death. Presidential elections were to take place within the succeeding 40 days.

Elections were held in May for municipal offices. Candidates were elected by the local party units, and not appointed by party leaders. The party's rank and file were allowed to point the direction in these primaries, the first to be held.

Student Unrest and Educational Policies. On February 5, police entered the campus of Tunis University to put down student riots that had been brewing since the term's opening in October. When the riots continued and spread to the high schools, the government on February 9 closed down the university's faculties of letters and law. In commenting on the need to keep these schools closed until

——————— TUNISIA • Information Highlights ———————

Official Name: Republic of Tunisia.
Area: 63,378 square miles (164,150 sq km).
Population (1972 est.): 5,400,000. *Density,* 80 per square mile (31 per sq km). *Annual rate of increase,* 2.6%.
Chief City (1966 census): Tunis, the capital, 469,997.
Government: *Head of state,* Habib Bourguiba, president (took office July 1957). *Chief minister,* Hedi Nouira, premier (took office Nov. 1970; reappointed Oct. 1971). *Legislature* (unicameral)—National Assembly, 90 members. *Major political party*—Destour Socialist party.
Languages: Arabic (official), French.
Education: *School enrollment* (1968)—primary, 857,514; secondary, 149,414; technical/vocational, 50,587; university/ higher, 8,368.
Monetary Unit: Dinar (0.48 dinar equals U. S.$1, Sept. 1972).
Gross National Product (1971 est.): $1,320,000,000.
National Income per Person (1969): $215.
Economic Indexes: *Industrial production* (1971), 133 (1963= 100); *agricultural production* (1971), 150 (1952–56=100); *consumer price index* (1971), 135 (1963=100).
Manufacturing (major products): Processed foods, petroleum products, wine, pulp and wood products.
Major Agricultural Products: Wheat, olives, vegetables, grapes, citrus fruits, forest products.
Major Minerals: Phosphate rock, petroleum, iron ore, lead.
Foreign Trade (1971): *Exports,* $216,000,000 (chief exports— crude petroleum, olive oil, phosphates). *Imports,* $343,- 000,000 (chief imports, 1969—food and live animals, non-electrical machinery, chemicals, textile yarn and fabrics). *Chief trading partners* (1969)—France (took 27% of exports, supplied 33% of imports); Italy (14%—9%); West Germany (14%—8%); United States (1%—20%).
Tourism: *Receipts* (1970), $58,000,000.
Transportation: *Motor vehicles* (1970), 103,700 (automobiles, 66,400); *railroads* (1970), 1,429 miles (2,300 km); *major national airline,* Tunis Air.
Communications: *Telephones* (1971), 76,370; *television stations* (1971), 6; *newspapers* (1969), 4.

September, Premier Hedi Nouira told the National Assembly that pamphlets from neighboring Baathist states had stirred up the students against the government. Both Syra and Iraq had Baathist governments. The faculties reopened on April 18.

Such outbreaks of violence as these led government officials to reexamine the country's educational policy, which had been to provide education at least for all those of primary-school age. With too few jobs to absorb those leaving the schools and with a high drop-out rate due to poor training in the lower grades, an "intellectual proletariat" has sprung up with nowhere to go. Educational leaders had come to feel that the mistake in the past was to stress quantity rather than quality in education.

To remedy this, more attention was to be paid to better teaching within the grades and promotion from one grade to the next only when the grade's requirements were met. In this way it was hoped that there would be a lower drop-out rate as students reached higher levels of education. Furthermore, more attention was to be paid to manual training, especially in the lower grades, so that the young would be prepared for the jobs that exist in present-day Tunisia. The basic fact remains, however, that there are far too few jobs to go around, and unless the government vacillates less on how to stem the population growth rate, which averages about 3% per year, underemployment will continue to be chronic in this essentially agricultural country.

Foreign Affairs. After many years of sometimes hostile, sometimes fearful, reactions to Egypt's pan-Arab ambitions, President Bourguiba received Egypt's President Sadat in Tunis. For its part, Tunisia seemed impressed by Egypt's moderation in approving UN resolutions on Israel and accepting U. S. proposals, made by U. S. Secretary of State William Rogers, to improve Egyptian-Israeli relations. Egypt, in turn, welcomed Tunisia's greater interest in Arab affairs, especially as an agent for bringing peace.

In June 1972 the president paid a state visit to France. During this visit Bourguiba reasserted his belief that all the Mediterranean littoral states should make this inland sea a "lake of peace," which other nations must be prevented from dominating.

JAMES D. L. BYRNES
Edinboro State College, Pennsylvania

TUNNELS

More than 1,000 tunnel experts attended the first North American Rapid Excavation and Tunneling Conference in 1972 to discuss the state of the art of underground construction. At the meeting in Chicago, Commissioner Ellis L. Armstrong of the U. S. Bureau of Reclamation said that more rapid development of tunneling technology was critical in meeting urbanization problems and developing and conserving natural resources. Estimates indicate that more than 3,000 miles (4,828 km) of tunnels will be driven in the United States during the next 10 years.

The Bureau of Reclamation is planning to use a water tunnel project in Utah as a giant research and development laboratory. Some $5 million will be spent on research covering excavation techniques and equipment, support and lining systems, muck removal, geologic exploration, rock mechanics, testing methods, and environmental controls. The tunnel, called the Stillwater Tunnel, will be 8 miles (13 km) long and 10 feet (3 meters) in diameter. Its construction will cost about $25 million.

Washington Metro. The Metropolitan Area Transit Authority of Washington, D. C., continued work on its 98-mile (158-km) $3 billion subway system. It is expected that the first section, 4.5 miles (7.2 km) long, will be in operation within the District of Columbia in 1974. By 1979, the Metro will link Washington with Maryland and Virginia.

Hampton Roads Bridge-Tunnel. A 4-mile (6.4-km) long bridge-tunnel crossing of Hampton Roads is being built in Virginia. It will parallel an existing bridge-tunnel crossing of Hampton Roads between Norfolk and Hampton. The length of the $48 million tunnel portion is 1.3 miles (2 km). The underwater section consists of 21 steel tubes, each 300 feet (91 meters) long. Traffic congestion will be relieved when the new artery is completed in 1974.

Big Walker Mountain Tunnel. Big Walker Mountain Tunnel, on interstate 77 in southwest Virginia, was opened in 1972. It has two 26-foot (8-meter) roadways that are 4,229 feet (1,290 meters) long. The full length of the $26 million tunnel is in rock, about 800 feet (244 meters) below the top of the 3,650-foot (1,112-meter) mountain.

Queens-Manhattan Subway-Railroad Tunnel. In New York City, the 63d Street tunnel was holed through under the East River in 1972, connecting Queens and Manhattan. The double-deck tunnel will carry subway and railroad cars. The $69 million project will not be completed until 1976. The 3,140-foot (957-meter) tunnel consisting of four 375-foot (114-meter) concrete and steel tubes, 38 by 38 feet (12 by 12 meters), two end-to-end in the west channel of the river and two end-to-end in the east channel. They are joined by a tunnel 114 feet (35 meters) below Welfare Island.

BART. The first BART (Bay Area Rapid Transit) line opened in 1972 in the San Francisco-Oakland area. This California project is the first completely new transit system in the United States in over 50 years. The first line, 28 miles (45 km) long, is part of the 75-mile (121-km) BART system. The 3.6-mile (6-km) Transbay tube, under San Francisco Bay between Oakland and San Francisco, is scheduled to be completed by June 1973. The remainder of the system will be finished by 1974. The total cost of the completed BART will be around $1.5 billion.

Hong Kong Tunnel. Hong Kong completed its cross-harbor tunnel in 1972, providing the first road link between Kowloon on the mainland and Hong Kong Island. The 1-mile (1.6-km) tunnel was built under Hong Kong harbor in three years at a cost of $53 million. It consists of 15 twin-tube steel sections varying in length from 325 to 375 feet (99 to 114 meters). Each barrel, 34 feet (10 meters) in diameter, will carry two lanes of traffic. It is estimated that at least 35,000 vehicles will use the tunnel every day.

Frejus Tunnel. France and Italy will start work on the 7.9-mile (12.5-km) Frejus Tunnel through the Alps in 1973. The tunnel will connect the industrial regions of Lyon and Turin and will cost $160 million. It will be the second-longest highway tunnel in the world, topped only by the 10.2-mile (16-km) St. Gotthard Tunnel through the Alps. The two-lane Frejus Tunnel is scheduled for completion in 1978.

WILLIAM H. QUIRK
"Contractors & Engineers" Magazine

TURKEY

During 1972, Turkey continued to experience domestic unrest and disorder, as it had through much of the preceding year. In international affairs it sought to maintain good relations with both the United States and the Soviet Union.

Politics and Disorder. After a lull in late 1971, left-wing extremists once more perpetrated acts of terrorism and violence. The "above-party" government sought to meet the problem summarily without compromise. The martial law declared by Prime Minister Nihat Erim in 1971 was maintained. The request of 1,800 intellectuals in January to end the death penalty was ignored. In a trial of 227 left-wing extremists in February, the death penalty was asked for 15 leaders of the outlawed Dev-Genç party. In March the Army General Staff announced the dismissal and detention of 57 officers for subversive activities, including the supplying of arms to terrorists. On March 26 the extreme leftist, anti-American People's Liberation Army kidnapped three foreign radar technicians working for NATO. It held them as hostages for three terrorists condemned to death by the government for killing the Israeli consul general in 1971. The hostages were murdered before police surrounded and killed the terrorists. On May 4 the chief of the gendarmerie was wounded in an ambush in Ankara.

Erim's efforts to suppress violence by decree and to implement moderate reforms based on a memorandum by the generals in 1971 were blocked by a conservative, bickering legislature. He resigned on April 17 and was succeeded on May 15 by Defense Minister Ferit Melen, who also tried to lead an "above-party" government and to eliminate anarchy and implement the generals' reforms. Terrorism, including fall skyjacking incidents, continued, as did stern government measures to quell it. On May 24 the minister of the interior announced that 432 people had been arrested, bringing the total number of arrests since the declaration of martial law to 2,050. In October a martial-law court in Ankara sentenced 13 leaders of the outlawed Turkish Labor party, including Chairman Mrs. Behice Bovan, to 15 years in prison.

It was hoped that Melen's government might be able to calm the country so that general elections could be held in 1973. In November 1972, however, the Republican People's party (RPP), founded by Ataturk, which had turned markedly to the left, quit the government, a move that threatened the government's existence. Ismet Inonü, party leader for 33 years and former premier and president, resigned when he failed to win a vote of confidence.

Economy. Despite disorder, unemployment, and inflation, Turkey experienced considerable economic development. The first two five-year plans had called for a 7% increase in the gross national product, but the increase in 1971 was 9.4%. The most important item in the Turkish balance of accounts was the labor remittances of some 600,000 Turks employed in Europe, primarily in Germany. They totaled $273 million in 1970 and almost $500 million in 1971. Exports from January to September 1972 reached $584 million, a 47% increase over 1971, but imports totaled $1,117 million. The third five-year plan (1973–77), by which Turkey expected to achieve a substantial degree of economic independence, was approved by the National Assembly on October 28.

Foreign Affairs. There was no indication of any basic change in Turkey's international position. Both prime ministers Erim and Melen reaffirmed their fidelity to NATO and CENTO and maintained the primary importance of friendship with the United States within the larger alliances. But Melen also said that in addition to improving U. S. relations, he would seek to develop neighborly relations with the Soviet Union.

Turkey's close ties with the United States have existed since the post-World War II period. From the late 1940's to 1971 the United States had given $5,692,400,000 in aid to Turkey, about evenly divided between economic and military assistance. Toward the end of the period, however, problems had arisen due to the presence of U. S. military personnel in Turkey, the atmosphere of détente in Soviet-American relations, the development of new weaponry, and the Cyprus situation.

Another troublesome issue was Turkish cultivation of the opium poppy, an important cash crop for poor Turkish farmers and a major source of heroin in the United States. In 1971, under U. S. pressure, the raising of opium poppies was banned. To compensate for the resulting losses, the United States promised $35 million over three years.

In November 1972 the United States and Turkey signed a technical assistance agreement to aid in the production of wheat, sheep, cattle, and dairy products. The United States also agreed in August to sell Turkey 40 Phantom F-4 jets, costing $167 million, to enable it to maintain its military balance with Greece.

Turkey's relations with the Soviet Union have been colored by the USSR's concern over NATO bases in Turkey and by Turkey's worry about domestic violence caused by guerrillas backed by

--- **TURKEY • Information Highlights** ---

Official Name: Republic of Turkey.
Area: 301,381 square miles (780,576 sq km).
Population (1972 est.): 37,600,000. *Density,* 117 per square mile (45 per sq km). *Annual rate of increase,* 2.5%.
Chief Cities (1970 census): Ankara, the capital, 1,208,800; Istanbul, 2,247,600; Izmir, 520,700; Adana, 351,700.
Government: *Head of state,* Gen. Cevdet Sunay, president (took office Oct. 1967). *Head of government,* Ferit Melen, premier (took office May 1972). *Legislature*—Grand National Assembly: Senate, 183 members; National Assembly, 450 members. *Major political parties*—Justice; Republican People's; Democratic; Reliance.
Languages: Turkish (official), Kurdish, Arabic.
Education: *Expenditure* (1968) 20.2% of total public expenditure. *School enrollment* (1969)—primary, 4,905,107; secondary, 1,185,633; technical/vocational, 163,263; university/higher, 160,334.
Monetary Unit: Lira (14 liras equal U. S.$1, Sept. 1972).
Gross National Product (1971 est.): $9,870,000,000.
National Income per Person (1968): $362.
Economic Indexes: *Industrial production* (1966), 170 (1963=100); *agricultural production* (1971), 182 (1952–56=100); *consumer price index* (1971), 185 (1963=100).
Manufacturing (major products): Textiles, petroleum products, iron and steel, cement, fertilizers.
Major Agricultural Products: Wheat, cotton, rye, tobacco, barley, hazelnuts, raisins (ranks 1st among world producers, 1971), sheep and cattle.
Major Minerals: Chromium ore (ranks 4th among world producers, 1970), copper, iron ore, coal, lignite, mercury.
Foreign Trade (1971): *Exports,* $677,000,000 (chief exports—cotton, hazelnuts, tobacco, raisins, chromium ore). *Imports,* $1,088,000,000 (chief imports, 1969—chemicals; motor vehicles; electrical machinery, apparatus, and appliances; iron and steel). *Chief trading partners* (1969)—West Germany (took 21% of exports, supplied 19% of imports); United States (11%—17%); United Kingdom (6%—12%); Italy (8%—10%).
Tourism: *Receipts* (1970), $64,100,000.
Transportation: *Motor vehicles* (1970), 311,400 (automobiles, 147,000); *railroads* (1970), 4,976 miles (8,008 km); merchant fleet (1971), 714,000 gross registered tons; *major national airline,* Turk Hava Yollari.
Communications: *Telephones* (1971), 576,943; *television stations* (1971), 3; *television sets* (1971), 100,000; *radios* (1970), 3,072,000; *newspapers* (1969), 400 (daily circulation, 1,400,000).

Communist countries. Evidence of improved relations was provided by the April visit to Turkey of Soviet President N. V. Podgorny. Turkey also cultivated a more friendly attitude toward its Balkan neighbors and the Arab states. However, mindful of the vicissitudes of international politics, it did not weaken its strong ties with the West.

HARRY N. HOWARD, *The American University*

UGANDA

Erratic changes in policy and domestic and international turmoil marked Uganda's second year under the military regime of President Idi Amin.

Asian Exodus. Uganda attracted worldwide attention in 1972 by its expulsion of Asians. Acute pressure on the economically powerful Asian community began at the end of 1971 with a series of speeches by President Amin and culminated in an order by him on August 9 that all of the estimated 60,000 Asians with British or South Asian citizenship leave Uganda within 90 days. The order was later extended to include Asians of Kenyan, Tanzanian, and Zambian citizenship. Asians who were Ugandan citizens became subject to revocation of citizenship or relocation within Uganda.

By means of massive airlifts, more than half of which went to Britain, Amin's order was substantially implemented by the target date, November 8. The emigration required by Amin created obvious hardships on the Asian population of Uganda but also had economic repercussions for the country as a whole. The loss of a large part of the nation's business and professional class brought an increase in unemployment and a decrease in business activity.

The effects of the Asian exodus were only part of the internal disorder in 1972. In January, Amin released 3,000 detained members of the armed forces who had resisted his seizure of power in January 1971, but dissension in the armed forces was not eliminated. In addition, some of Uganda's

General Amin, president of Uganda.

GOKSIN SIPAHIOGLU—JOCELYNE BENZAKIN

UGANDA • Information Highlights ─────

Official Name: Republic of Uganda.
Area: 91,134 square miles (236,036 sq km).
Population (1972 est.): 9,100,000. *Density,* 106 per square mile (41 per sq km). *Annual rate of increase,* 2.6%.
Chief City (1969 est.): Kampala, the capital, 331,889.
Government: *Head of state,* Maj. Gen. Idi Amin, president (took office Feb. 1971). *Head of government,* Maj. Gen. Idi Amin. *Legislature*—National Assembly (dissolved Feb. 1971). *Major political parties*—(suspended).
Languages: English (official), Luganda.
Education: *Expenditure* (1968), 18.1% of total public expenditure. *School enrollment* (1968)—primary, 632,162; secondary, 39,456; technical/vocational, 4,292; university/higher, 2,494.
Monetary Unit: Shilling (7.143 shillings equal U. S.$1, Sept. 1972).
Gross National Product (1971 est.): $1,323,000,000.
National Income per Person (1963): $68.
Consumer Price Index (1971): 176 (1963=100).
Manufacturing (major products): Processed agricultural products.
Major Agricultural Products: Coffee, cotton, sisal, tobacco, groundnuts, tea, sweet potatoes and yams, cassava.
Major Minerals: Copper, tin, phosphate rock, salt.
Foreign Trade (1970): *Exports,* $246,000,000 (chief exports—coffee; cotton; copper; tea). *Imports,* $121,000,000 (chief imports, 1969—transport equipment; nonelectrical machinery; chemicals, electrical machinery, apparatus, appliances). *Chief trading partners* (1969)—Britain (took 23% of exports, supplied 34% of imports); United States (24%—4%); Japan (12%—14%); West Germany (3%—10%).
Transportation: *Motor vehicles* (1969), 38,300 (automobiles, 32,300); *railroads* (with Kenya and Tanzania, 1970), 3,676 miles (5,915 km); *major national airline,* East African Airways (with Kenya and Tanzania).
Communications: *Telephones* (1971), 30,186; *television stations* (1971), 6; *television sets* (1971), 12,000; *newspapers* (1970), 7 (daily circulation, 83,000).

---

leading citizens, including Chief Justice Benedicto Kiwanuka, mysteriously disappeared.

Shifts in Foreign Relations. Policy shifts during the year resulted in several sharp reversals in Uganda's relations with other states. Britain, one of the first nations to support the Amin regime in 1971, cut off its economic aid to Uganda after the expulsion of the Asians, and pressure on Britain to accept refugees entitled to British passports led to a breakdown in relations, culminating in the expulsion of the British high commissioner, Richard Slater, in October. In March, Amin ordered the closing of the embassy of Israel, another early ally of his regime. He later accused the Israelis of subversive activity in Uganda.

As relations with Israel were deteriorating, Uganda increased its cooperation with the Arab states, particularly Libya. During the year Libya agree to build two hospitals, furnish extensive economic aid, and train air force and other military personnel. On May 11, Uganda's border with Sudan was reopened.

Within East Africa, border incidents and disagreements over the treatment of Asians kept tensions high between Uganda and Tanzania. In September the two countries came close to war because of an abortive invasion of Uganda by Tanzania-based supporters of deposed President Milton Obote.

In early October representatives of Uganda, Tanzania, Somalia, and the Organization of African Unity met in Mogadishu, Somalia, where a settlement of outstanding differences between Uganda and Tanzania was announced.

Economic Development. Uganda's third five-year development plan was released in Kampala on January 26 after a delay of seven months. More modest than previous plans, the new document called for an overall annual growth rate of about 5%. Since the plan appeared before the expulsion of Uganda's Asian population, its targets would perhaps have to be revised downward.

JAY E. HAKES
Louisiana State University in New Orleans

(Above) *Communist party chief Leonid Brezhnev* (left) *of the USSR and U. S. President Richard Nixon conferred in Moscow on May 22.* (Right) *The U. S. and Russian flags flew side by side in Moscow during the Nixon visit.*

USSR

During 1972 the Soviet government achieved a great diplomatic success by negotiating a diplomatic déntente with the United States. President Richard M. Nixon's visit to the USSR in May resulted in a series of Soviet-American agreements mutually limiting armament, vastly expanding jointly scientific cooperation, and providing for a large increase in the previously small-scale Soviet-American trade. The Soviet press enthusiastically described this défente with United States. President Richard M. lasting cooperation beneficial to both countries.

Internally, the Soviet government was confronted by a disastrous harvest decline caused by the worst farming weather in 100 years. Industrial growth also slowed because hundreds of thousands of city workers were dispatched to rural areas to help salvage the poor crops. The five-year plan of 1971–75 was thrown off schedule by these unexpected economic difficulties, and had to be revised. To save the Soviet population from hunger, the USSR placed orders abroad for the import of 28 million tons of grain and corn, with U. S. firms contracting for most of these food deliveries.

The Kremlin in 1972 also encountered trouble with several restless non-Russian minorities within the USSR. In the Middle East, Soviet relations improved with Iraq, but deteriorated with Egypt, which in the past was one of the largest recipients of Soviet foreign aid.

FOREIGN AFFAIRS

United States. Intricate and difficult U. S.-Soviet negotiations culminated in 1972 in the signing of numerous treaties greatly improving relations between the two countries. On March 29 the United States, the USSR, Britain, and several other nations concluded a joint "Convention on International Liability for Damage Caused by Space Objects." The same three great powers and 40 other countries on April 10 signed a "Convention on the Prohibition of the Development, Production, and Stockpiling of Bacteriological and Toxin Weapons and on Their Destruction." Next day a U. S.-Soviet cultural exchange pact was concluded for 1972–73.

On May 22–30, President Nixon visited the USSR, where he was housed in the Kremlin and treated as an honored guest. During this visit the United States and the USSR signed a five-year agreement for cooperation in environmental protection (May 23), another five-year pact for cooperation in medical science and public health (May 23), a five-year treaty for cooperation in science and tech-

nology (May 24), a five-year pact for cooperation in the exploration and use of outer space, including joint docking of Soviet and American space vehicles in 1975 (May 24), and a three-year treaty for prevention of air and naval incidents on and over the open seas (May 25). All these agreements were overshadowed, however, by the two U. S.-Soviet treaties of May 26. The first perpetually limited each country to 200 antiballistic missiles apiece, with 100 to be placed around the national capital, and the second 100 to protect a cluster of intercontinental ballistic missiles (ICBM's). The second agreement was a five-year treaty limiting each country to its present number of ICBM's, submarine-based nuclear missiles, and nuclear-powered missile-firing submarines either in operation or being built. By these two historic pacts, the United States and the USSR were to maintain approximate parity in nuclear and missile armament, with the USSR leading in the number of ICBM's and the United States superior in the quantity of missile warheads. Neither treaty provided for on-the-ground inspection, but both sides presumed that spy satellites would reveal any treaty violations.

After the President's return to the United States, more Soviet-U. S. agreements were concluded to implement the Moscow pacts. Thus in July agreements were signed defining the precise areas of cooperation in scientific research; a pact in September listed 30 joint projects in environmental improvement; and a November agreement between the U. S. and the Soviet academies of science increased by 50% the previous exchange of visiting scientists.

Meanwhile, on October 18, the United States and the Soviet Union concluded their first trade treaty since 1951, with the United States granting most-favored-nation status to the USSR in trade, and promising U. S. Export-Import Bank credits for Soviet purchases of U. S. goods. An accompanying agreement obliged the USSR to pay $722 million to the United States over a period of 30 years to settle the Soviet debt to the United States for Lend-Lease aid during World War II. Four days earlier, on October 14, the two countries had signed a maritime treaty opening 40 ports on each side to each other's ships, setting rates for shipment of U. S. grain to the USSR, and providing that one third of Soviet-American marine trade would be carried in U. S. ships and one third in Soviet ships.

In July, before the Soviet government realized the full extent of its harvest failure, it purchased 12 million metric tons of U. S. grain worth $750 million, to be delivered over a period of three years. During the autumn, when the crop slump became apparent, the USSR increased its orders to 17.4 million tons of U. S. corn and other grain (worth $1 billion), to be delivered during the following 12 months. These purchases greatly expanded the total amount of U. S. exports to the USSR in 1972, which in 1971 had consisted of goods of approximately $125 million in value.

The USSR during 1972 also concluded several contracts to purchase industrial wares from U. S. firms. Thus the International Harvester Company agreed to sell $40 million worth of machinery to the Soviet Union, and the Pepsi-Cola Company obtained a franchise to produce and market its soft drink within the USSR.

Despite all these diplomatic, scientific, and commercial agreements, a number of incidents disturbed Soviet-American relations during 1972. In January, U. S. Congressman James H. Scheuer, a Democrat from the Bronx, was expelled from the USSR apparently because he befriended Soviet Jews desiring to emigrate from the Soviet Union. During February, Valeri Ivanovich Markelov, a Soviet citizen

working for the UN Secretariat as a translator, was arrested by U. S. authorities as an alleged spy.

Throughout the year many U. S. Jews protested against the mistreatment of Jews in the USSR. Some harassed performances of Soviet concert artists in the United States. At one point animal blood was poured over the head of a Soviet diplomat. The most serious incident occurred in May, when incendiary bombs started a fire in the Washington office of TASS, the Soviet official news agency. The Soviet government officially demanded better police protection for Soviet citizens in the United States.

In April the Soviet government condemned the increased U. S. bombing of North Vietnam, and made a sharp protest to the U. S. government about

EMBARRASSED Premier Kosygin and President Podgorny (opposite page, 3d and 2d from right), at Moscow airport May 29, listen as pilot of Soviet plane carrying the Nixons explains engine trouble. (Below) The Nixons change aircraft.

UPI

U. S. bomb damage to four Soviet freighters anchored in Haiphong harbor. The USSR also declared that Soviet ships would continue to visit North Vietnamese ports despite the U. S. naval blockade of North Vietnam's coast, but this declaration was not fulfilled in practice.

Europe. During 1972 the USSR tried to improved its relations with various West European countries. The Russians concluded economic cooperation treaties in March with Norway and in July with the Netherlands, a long-term trade agreement with West Germany also in July, and a pact with Italy in October calling for mutual consultation on matters of common interest. On June 3 two agreements came into force: the previously concluded West German-Soviet nonaggression pact and the U. S.-British-French-Soviet treaty easing traffic and travel in and out of West Berlin. The USSR on September 15 signed a trade treaty with Spain, which, however, did not entail Soviet recognition of Spain. This pact was the first major Spanish-Soviet treaty since Franco became Spain's dictator.

Early in 1972 the USSR protested to the Greek government against the establishment of a U. S. naval base in Greece. Later, in November, Soviet-Greek relations improved with a Soviet grant of $89 million worth of technical aid for construction of an electric power station in northern Greece.

Also in November, for the first time since 1948, the USSR resumed technical aid to Yugoslavia by granting a large credit, equal to $500 million, which Yugoslavia was to use for importing Soviet machinery over a period of several years.

Asia. As before, relations between the USSR and mainland China remained poor in 1972, although in June the two countries concluded an annual barter pact increasing their small-scale trade. Sino-Soviet negotiations continued throughout the year to determine the exact Sino-Soviet border, but with no concrete results.

Of all non-Communist countries in the world, Japan in 1972 was the USSR's largest trading partner. Soviet-Japanese agreements were concluded in January for cultural exchange, and in June for regulating the use of common fishing waters. Negotiations in October for the long-delayed Soviet-Japanese peace treaty nevertheless were at least temporarily halted because the USSR balked at returning to Japan several small Kuril islands that the Soviet Union seized at the close of World War II.

The newly independent country of Bangladesh was recognized in January by the USSR. In March, Soviet-Bangladesh pacts were concluded for trade, technical aid, and emergency assistance. Agreements concluded on December 9 continued Soviet military and economic aid to North Vietnam, and called for joint planning of North Vietnamese postwar reconstruction. In October, the USSR signed technical aid and cultural exchange treaties with Malaysia.

In the Middle East the USSR signed new technical aid pacts with Syria and Iraq, a five-year cultural exchange agreement with Iran, and a Soviet-Iranian 15-year treaty of economic cooperation. Syria was promised additional shipments of Soviet armament. More important was a Soviet-Iraq 15-year treaty of friendship and cooperation, concluded on April 9, which provided for cultural exchange, technical aid, armament shipments, a joint struggle against "Zionism," and mutual consultation on threats to peace.

PRESIDENTS Podgorny of the Soviet Union and Nixon of the United States review the honor guard at the Moscow airport, May 29.

During the year the Soviet government repeatedly condemned alleged Israeli aggression against Lebanon and Syria. Soviet sport organizations, however, publicly denounced the Arab assassination of several Israeli athletes at the 1972 Olympic Games.

Africa. Trying to expand its influence in Africa, the USSR established diplomatic relations with Niger in February, Liberia in June, and Malagasy in September. Soviet cultural exchange pacts during the year were concluded with Chad, Uganda, and the Central African Republic. On March 4 a Soviet-Libyan treaty provided for Soviet aid in operating oil fields that Libya had expropriated from the British Petroleum Company in December 1971.

The USSR and Egypt signed a long-term trade agreement in January 1972, and their relations appeared excellent. But on July 18, the Egyptian government requested the departure of most Soviet military personnel stationed in Egypt. The USSR hastily withdrew from Egypt approximately 20,000 Soviet troops, including all air and rocket units. Thereafter Soviet-Egyptian relations cooled.

Latin America. Soviet policy toward Latin America consisted largely of efforts to befriend legal governments and increase mutual trade. Though normally exporting sugar, the USSR helped Brazil's economy by buying 200,000 tons of Brazilian sugar. Peru and the USSR concluded a technical aid pact in June, and Chile received much Soviet economic aid throughout the year. In March, Bolivia abruptly expelled 40 Soviet diplomats for allegedly assisting Bolivian leftist anti-government rebels.

Canada. Soviet-Canadian relations remained good during 1972. As part of its emergency grain imports, the USSR purchased 5.2 million tons of Canadian grain for delivery during 1972–73.

ECONOMY

Harvest Decline. A severe winter with little snow ruined one third of the winter grain crop, which is planted each fall for harvest in the following year. The 1972 spring was cold with unseasonable snow, which delayed spring sowing. During the summer most of European USSR suffered the worst drought in 100 years, following in the autumn by heavy rains that hampered fall harvesting of the already meager crops. As a result the sugar beet and potato harvests were poor, and the grain crop declined from 181 million metric tons in 1971 to 168 million in 1972. To save both its population and livestock herds from hunger, the USSR placed orders for the import of 28 million tons of grain and corn during 1972–73, mostly from the United States, Canada, France, and Australia.

The collective and state farms were hampered by shortages of agricultural machinery, spare parts for machines on hand, farm machine operators, truck drivers, and veterinarians. In March wages were raised by 12% to 25% for shepherds in desert, semi-desert, and mountainous areas.

Industry. To help peasants gather the 1972 crops, hundreds of thousands of urban workers left their city jobs during the autumn for work in rural areas. As a result Soviet industrial growth in 1972 was only 6.7%, compared with 7.8% during 1971.

Early in 1972 more data were published about the 1971–75 five-year plan, revealing that heavy industry would receive 40% of all capital investments, agriculture 22%, housing 15%, transport and communications 10%, light consumer-goods industry 5%, and consumer services less than 1%. By the fall of 1972, however, the harvest slump had required revision of this five-year plan, with a higher percentage of capital investments being assigned to agriculture. This reduced industrial investment and, consequently, the rate of future planned industrial expansion, especially in light industry.

In Janaury the first Soviet "breeder" atomic power station of commercial size began operation at Shevchenko, an oil mining town on the northeast Caspian seacoast.

Foreign Trade. In 1971, 65% of Soviet foreign commerce was with other Communist nations (mostly Eastern Europe), 13% with developing

countries (mostly in Asia), and 22% with developed capitalist countries (including Japan). This trade pattern, which had been almost the same for several years, changed in 1972 when the huge Soviet grain imports increased USSR trade with the developed nations, which supplied most of the grain. (Eastern Europe also had a harvest slump, and the developing countries had no food to spare.) To pay for the grain imports, the USSR had to reduce its imports of machinery for fast industrial growth. Some of the grain was bought on credit, increasing the Soviet foreign debt that already had totaled $2.2 billion (owed mainly to Western Europe).

Statistics released in 1972 by the U. S. State Department estimated that the USSR had exported $8 billion worth of arms during 1955–71, with these billions divided roughly as follows: 2.5 to Egypt, 1.1 to India, 1.1 to Indonesia (in the Sukarno period), 1.0 to Iraq, 1.0 to North Vietnam, and 0.7 to various African countries.

India continued to be the largest non-Communist recipient of Soviet economic aid in 1972, accounting for about one fifth of the total. Most of the remaining aid went to South Asia and the Middle East. Technical aid commitments to Africa increased by about 50% during 1971–72.

Transport. In 1972, as before, the railways continued to haul about four fifths of the internal freight. Oil pipelines were becoming increasingly important, and in March a new 500-mile (800-km) pipeline was completed from the West Siberian oil fields south to the Trans-Siberian railway.

In January, after 10 years of construction work, a 300-mile (480-km) canal was opened in northeast Central Asia, supplying water from the Irtysh River to the industrial city of Karaganda, which is located in a semi-desert area.

Aeroflot, the Soviet airline company, began regular passenger flights to Bangladesh and to Chile in 1972. On October 13 an Aeroflot passenger plane flying from Paris to Moscow via Leningrad crashed in the rain near Moscow, reportedly killing all 176 people on board. This was the worst civil-aviation disaster in both Soviet and world history.

Standard of Living. The 98 million state workers and employees in 1972 received an average monthly salary of 128.5 rubles ($156.77), with farm wages much lower. Few Soviet citizens could afford to buy an automobile, since the cheapest passenger car cost 3,500 rubles ($4,270). Most able-bodied married women worked to supplement their husbands' income. In 1972, 72% of all doctors and 71% of all teachers were female. On September 1, teachers' average salaries were raised by 21%, and those of doctors by 23% in an effort to improve their performance.

Though the USSR is a socialist state with extensive public housing, in 1972 some 20% of the urban population and 75% of the rural inhabitants still lived in privately owned houses.

The Soviet press admitted that there were shortages in the stores of clothing, medicines, milk, meat, eggs, vegetables, and fruit. Late in the year the poor harvest even created some scarcity of potatoes and rye bread, which are normally abundant.

DEFENSE AND SPACE

Armed Forces. The Soviet armed forces in 1972 totaled about 3.3 million men, whose equipment included some 40,000 tanks, 140 intercontinental bombers, 1,500 helicopters, 1,700 military transport planes, 313 conventional submarines, 95 nuclear submarines, 27 cruisers, 2 helicopter carriers, 101 destroyers, 710 submarine-based nuclear missiles, 67 antiballistic missiles (ABM's, which were all located around Moscow), and 1,618 intercontinental ballistic missiles (ICBM's). The USSR thus led the United States in number of tanks, submarines, ABM's, and ICBM's.

Though the majority of Soviet army divisions continued to be stationed in European USSR and East Europe, three divisions were moved eastward during 1972 to strengthen the troops guarding the Sino-Soviet frontier. During the year, five new Soviet storage depots for tactical nuclear weapons were built close to the Chinese border.

Displaying their ability to operate far from home waters, Soviet naval flotillas in 1972 paid official visits to Sweden, Yugoslavia, Iran, Iraq, Senegal, Mauritius, and Morocco. Throughout the year the USSR stationed about 30 warships in the Mediterranean and 5 in the Indian Ocean.

Space Program. Among the many achievements of the Soviet space program in 1972 were the launching of eight earth satellites from one rocket in July and again in November, the soft landing in July of a capsule on the planet Venus from an unmanned spacecraft launched in March, and the moon landing and return to earth of an unmanned spacecraft in February. Soviet intercontinental rockets were test-fired in October from Central Asian bases into the south Pacific Ocean.

MRS. NIXON tried the Moscow subway on May 23. She told the Soviet metro administrator it was the world's "loveliest" subway.

UPI

──────── USSR • Information Highlights ────────

Official Name: Union of Soviet Socialist Republics.
Area: 8,647,489 square miles (22,402,200 sq km).
Population (1972): 246,300,000. *Density,* 29 per square mile (11 per sq km). *Annual rate of increase,* 1.1%.
Chief Cities (1970): Moscow, the capital, 7,061,000; Leningrad, 3,950,000; Kiev, 1,632,000; Tashkent, 1,385,000.
Government: *Head of state,* Nikolai V. Podgorny, president (took office 1965). *Head of government,* Aleksei N. Kosygin, premier (took office 1964). *Legislature*—Supreme Soviet: Soviet of the Union, 767 members; Soviet of Nationalities, 750 members. *Major political parties*—Communist (sole legal party).
Languages: Russian (official), also 80 minority languages.
Education: *Expenditure* (1971), 10% of total public expenditure. *School enrollment* (1972)—primary and secondary, 49,000,000; technical/vocational, 4,400,000; university/higher, 4,600,000.
Monetary Unit: ruble (0.829 ruble equals U. S.$1, 1972).
Gross National Product (1970): $292,930,000,000.
National Income per Person (1970): $1,200.
Economic Indexes: *Industrial production* (1971), 300 (1958=100); *agricultural production* (1971), 143 (1958=100).
Manufacturing (major products): 1971—Steel, 121,000,000 metric tons, cement, 100,300,000 metric tons, chemical fertilizer, 61,400,000 metric tons.
Major Agricultural Products: 1971—Grain (ranks 3d among world producers), 181,000,000 metric tons, potatoes (1st), 92,300,000 metric tons, sugar beets (1st), 72,100,000 metric tons.
Major Minerals: 1971—Coal (ranks 1st among world producers), 641,000,000 metric tons, crude petroleum (2d), 372,000,000 metric tons, iron ore (1st), 203,000,000 metric tons.
Foreign Trade (1971): *Exports,* $14,880,000,000 (chief exports —machinery and equipment, $3,243,840,000; ores and metals, $2,782,560,000; electricity and fuels, $2,678,400,-000). *Imports,* $13,440,000,000 (chief imports—machinery and equipment, $4,569,600,000; consumer goods, $2,701,-440,000; foodstuffs, $2,042,880,000). *Chief trading partners* (1971)—East Germany (took 14% of exports, supplied 15% of imports); Poland (10%—11%); Czechoslovakia (10%—11%).
Transportation: *Motor vehicles* (1972), 6,000,000 (automobiles, 1,800,000); *railroads* (1971), 84,000 miles (135,060 km); *merchant fleet* (1971), 16,194,000 gross registered tons; *major national airline,* Aeroflot.
Communications: *Telephones* (1969), 12,000,000; *television stations* (1971), 167; *television sets* (1971), 30,800,000; *radios* (1969), 46,700,000; *newspapers* (1972), 6,878.

GOVERNMENT AND POLITICS

Personnel Changes. The highest level demotion during 1972 was that of Politburo member Pyotr Y. Shelest, who on May 20 was removed from his position as first Communist party secretary of the Ukrainian Soviet Republic and given the lesser post of a USSR vice premier. Reportedly he had opposed the Soviet-U. S. détente and was demoted on the eve of President Nixon's visit to Moscow.

Shelest's demotion resulted in a shuffle of other Ukrainian top officials. Politburo member Vladimir V. Shcherbitsky changed jobs from premier of the Ukraine to Ukrainian first party secretary, Aleksandr P. Lyashko from Ukrainian president to Ukrainian premier, and Ivan S. Grushetsky from chief of the Ukrainian party courts to Ukrainian president. In the autumn Shcherbitsky also replaced Shelest as a member of the USSR Supreme Soviet Presidium.

On May 19, Soviet party Secretary Boris Ponomarev was given the additional rank of Politburo candidate member. Also in May, Gen. Vladimir Fyodorovich Tolubko was promoted from being chief of the Far Eastern military district to commander of the USSR strategic missile forces. The change was effected to replace Marshal Nikolai Krylov, who died on February 9 at the age of 68.

Ecology. In 1972, for the first time in Soviet history, the government displayed serious interest in environmental protection. A governmental decree issued in March ordered 15 cities and 421 industrial enterprises to install by 1975 purification facilities for the waste and sewage they dump into the streams of the Volga and Ural river basins. Another law in September instructed the USSR Council of Ministers (cabinet) to include environmental protection in all future annual and five-year economic planning.

In March a large-scale earthquake created much damage in the northern area of the Central Asian republic of Tadzhikistan. A combination of drought and human carelessness caused forest fires north, east, and west of Moscow during August, as well as an 8,000-acre (3,200-hectare) fire in peat bogs 50 miles (80 km) east of the city. Army troops helped to extinguish these fires, the smoke of which enveloped Moscow for days.

For improvement of human health the USSR Communist party on June 13 ordered all party organizations to mount campaigns against heavy drinking and alcoholism. On June 16, a government law decreased the production of hard liquor and the number of stores selling it.

Minority Problems. During 1972 the Soviet government had some problems with non-Russian minorities in the USSR. Early in the year about 20 Ukrainian intellectuals were imprisoned for participating in an allegedly "pro-Chinese Ukrainian group." In August the Soviet fishing trawler *Vishera* sailed from the Black Sea to Greece, where most of the crew defected and received asylum. Most of them were of Ukrainian or Lithuanian nationality.

Meanwhile, on May 14, Roman Kalanta, a 20-year-old Lithuanian youth, committed suicide in the Lithuanian city of Kaunas by burning himself to death in public to protest Russian rule. His funeral on May 18–19 inspired mass Lithuanian riots, which were finally quelled by Soviet troops, who arrested hundreds of the rioters. According to the Soviet press, these Kaunas riots were caused by a small group of nonpolitical hooligans, eight of whom were punished by prison terms of up to three years.

During the spring a Georgian Communist party decree reprimanded an author, 10 editors, publishers, censors, and critics for the publication of a history book praising Georgia's declaration of independence from Lenin's Russia in the early Soviet period. Later the Soviet government indicated its disapproval of the widespread profiteering in both the government and state industry of Georgia. Several high Georgian officials were removed from office. During the autumn Politburo candidate member Vasili P. Mzhavanadze was retired at the age of 70 from his post of Georgian first party secretary and was replaced by 44-year-old Eduard A. Shevardnadze, a former Georgian minister of police, who immediately began a strong campaign against corruption and local nationalism. Mzhavanadze lost his Politburo post on December 18.

With little publicity, a few thousand Soviet Germans were allowed during 1972 to emigrate to West Germany, in an apparent attempt to please the Bonn government. They were descendants of Germans invited to settle in czarist Russia by Empress Catherine the Great.

CULTURE AND SOCIETY

Religion. During 1972 many Soviet Jews continued to petition the Soviet government for permission to emigrate to Israel. At first the government eased its emigration policy, permitting the departure of approximately 30,000 Jews—twice as many as in 1971 and more than the total Jewish emigration of 1946–71. Then on August 3 a new Soviet law established emigration fees ranging from the ruble equivalent of $4,400 to $30,600 for each person holding

a college or graduate-school degree. Though not specifically directed against Jews, this law slowed Jewish emigration since most Soviet Jews fell in these categories. Yet in the fall, possibly to please the United States, the Soviet government waived this education tax for more than 100 emigrating Jewish families.

During the spring, Moscow police dispersed a crowd of 2,000 Jews celebrating Passover outside the city's chief synagogue. In the fall the Soviet magazine *October* published the first installment of Yuri Kolesnikov's new novel, *Inhabited Land,* which alleged that European Zionists had allied themselves with both Mussolini and Hitler.

In January, 17,000 Lithuanian Catholics signed a petition to Soviet leader Brezhnev protesting the arrest of Lithuanian clergymen and the closing of Catholic churches. When the petition remained unanswered, it was forwarded to the United Nations.

Pimen, the new patriarch of the Russian Orthodox Church, in 1972 made good-will visits to Orthodox congregations in various European and Near Eastern countries, including Lebanon, Yugoslavia, Rumania, and Greece.

Intellectual Unrest. During 1972 the Soviet police made a strong but unsuccessful effort to suppress the illegal underground literature called *samizdat,* which publishes the reformist views of civil rights advocates, Christian socialists, humanitarian Marxists, and isolationist Slavophiles. As part of this repression, the writer Vladimir K. Bukovsky, the physicist Yuri Melnik, historian Pyotr I. Yakir, and biologist Ilya Glezer were all imprisoned under the charge of disseminating anti-Soviet propaganda. The usual sentence was three years of prison or forced labor, but Bukovsky received 12 years of imprisonment and banishment from Moscow.

On November 4, the 33-year-old rebel poet Yuri Galanskov died in prison camp after an operation to alleviate his stomach ulcers.

A few leading dissidents were allowed to leave the USSR during 1972. The mathematician Aleksandr Yesenin-Volpin, who had been punished five times by confinement in insane asylums, was permitted to emigrate permanently. Joseph Brodsky departed to become poet-in-residence at the University of Michigan. The physicist Valeri N. Chalidze, a founding member of the Moscow Human Rights Committee, could not return home after lecturing in the United States.

In January the Soviet minister of culture stated that the novelist Aleksandr I. Solzhenitsyn would not be permitted to return to the USSR if he went to Sweden to receive his Nobel prize for literature. Later the Soviet press condemned Solzhenitsyn's new historical novel, *August 14,* which appeared in the West but was banned in the USSR.

Among the boldest *samizdat* documents during 1972 were the March and July letters from physicist Andrei D. Sakharov to Brezhnev appealing for democratic freedoms, more private enterprise, and a milder foreign policy. Brezhnev did not reply. In June, anonymous *samizdat* leaflets were circulated in Moscow urging workers to strike against the housing shortage, high food prices, food exports, and excessive material aid to Cuba, Arab countries, and North Vietnam.

Aleksandr E. Korneichuk, a party-line writer and playwright, died in the USSR on May 14 at the age of 67. The Soviet government published an obituary giving him high praise.

UPI

RUSSIAN SCHOOLCHILDREN, sightseeing in Moscow, head for the Kremlin, where President Nixon and Soviet leaders were discussing issues affecting their future.

Athletics. The USSR won 207 medals at the 1972 Olympic Games in Munich, West Germany, more than any other country. These included 110 gold medals, 46 silver, and 51 bronze. One fourth of the Soviet Olympic athletes were military men from sport clubs of the USSR armed forces.

Education. The 1972 Soviet press revealed that one fifth of USSR grade school graduates do not enter high school, and four fifths of high school graduates do not go to college.

On September 1, the monthly stipends (cost-of-living allowances) were raised 25% for students in colleges and technical schools. Thereafter college student stipends were to range between 40 to 60 rubles per month ($48.80 to $73.20), and those for technical school students between 35 and 45 rubles ($42.70 to $54.90). The Soviet press stated, however, that most students received money from home to supplement their stipends.

In the autumn, Soviet technical high schools changed their compulsory course in civil defense to one of elementary infantry training.

A new Soviet law in August provided that college and graduate-school degrees could be rescinded if the degree holder was later found guilty of "immoral or unpatriotic activities."

ELLSWORTH RAYMOND
New York University

UNITED ARAB EMIRATES. See PERSIAN GULF STATES.

UNITED ARAB REPUBLIC. See EGYPT.

UNITED KINGDOM. See GREAT BRITAIN.

Bringing down the gavel, Jeanne Martin Cisse of Guinea becomes the first woman to preside over the UN Security Council. The November 15 session took up the problem of Portuguese territories.

UNITED NATIONS

Interest at the United Nations in 1972 centered to a large extent on what influence the seating of mainland China, especially as a permanent member of the Security Council, would have on the organizations effectiveness. China followed a policy dictated by its own interests, particularly when questions concerning Asia and what China regarded as its own spheres of influence were under consideration. Thus there were times when China voted with the Communist bloc, and others when the delegation found itself in complete opposition to that bloc, most noticeably when its differences with the USSR came to the surface. Fears that China's membership would contribute further to the ineffectiveness of the United Nations proved for the most part groundless. But it was apparent throughout the year's deliberations that a new, strong voice had been added to the world's councils.

A new departure for the Security Council was the holding of a meeting in Africa, from January 28 to February 4, at which only African problems were discussed. Addis Ababa, Ethiopia, the seat of the Economic Commission for Africa, was chosen as the meeting site because of the facilities available. The idea of a meeting in Africa had been supported by China, the USSR, and the African members of the Council. It was opposed by the Western powers, both on the grounds of expense (the meeting cost $140,000), and because the Council would have been hampered by being away from its base if any real crisis had developed. But the decision to hold the meeting in Addis Ababa was taken without any formal objections being registered. On balance, it was felt that the meeting served a useful purpose both by drawing attention to African problems and by making the United Nations better known through the wide publicity that the meeting attracted in Africa.

The assumption by Kurt Waldheim of the office of secretary general on January 1 brought a new personality on to the scene. His methods of operation proved to be different from those of any of his predecessors, and have not been without criticism among the delegations. Seldom did the new secretary general fail to speak out or take action when he felt it was necessary, and he traveled much more than did his predecessors.

One of Waldheim's first actions on taking office was to initiate an economy campaign—largely in terms of reductions in staff costs, office supplies, and documentation—which had saved $6 million by September. The United Nations remained plagued by financial troubles in 1972, but there was no deficit in the year's working budget, largely because of Waldheim's efforts.

The secretary general was unable to solve the problem of withheld contributions on the part of some defaulters. However, he persuaded a number of countries to advance the date of payment of their annual contributions, thus providing the secretariat with funds to meet its current bills. As a result of Waldheim's visit to Paris in April, France, for the first time, included its share of the interest on the UN bond issue with its advance payment. The results of the U.S. effort to reduce its contribution to 25% of the total budget may, however, nullify much of the progress made. But it is expected that the admission in the near future of new members, such as East and West Germany, would counterbalance the reduced U.S. payment.

The principal activities of the United Nations in its 27th year are summarized below under the headings: (1) General Assembly; (2) Security Council; (3) Economic and Social Council; (4) Trusteeship Council; and (5) International Court of Justice.

GENERAL ASSEMBLY

The 27th annual session of the General Assembly met in New York on Sept. 19–Dec. 19, 1972. Its president, Stanislaw Trepczynski of Poland, departed from the tradition that an Assembly president avoids controversy in his inaugural address, and spoke out vigorously on a wide range of world issues. The opening of the Assembly was notable also for the stringent security precautions made necessary by a stream of bomb threats received both at UN headquarters and at a number of individual foreign missions.

Acting on the recommendations of its General Committee, the Assembly adopted an agenda of 92 items on September 23. The agenda included a number of controversial subjects, including terrorism, the admission of Bangladesh, the Middle East, Rhodesia, and disarmament.

Terrorism. The inscription of an agenda item

on terrorism was first proposed by Secretary General Waldheim following the killing of 11 Israeli coaches and athletes at the Olympic Games in Munich on September 5. The General Committee, on September 22, recommended the inclusion of terrorism in the Assembly's agenda, and the Assembly adopted an amended version of the original item the next day.

The amended version called for "measures to prevent international terrorism, which endangers or takes innocent human lives or jeopardizes fundamental freedoms, and study of the underlying causes of those forms of terrorism and acts of violence which lie in misery, frustration, grievance, and despair and which cause some people to sacrifice human lives, including their own, in an attempt to effect radical change." The original version had made no mention of a study of the causes of terrorism. But despite the change, the item was still opposed by China, Cuba, and most of the Arab bloc.

On December 11 the Assembly's Legal Committee, by a vote of 76 to 34 with 16 abstentions, approved a resolution concerned primarily with exploring the causes of acts of terrorism. It was a defeat for those nations favoring strong international legal action against terrorism.

Bangladesh. The question of the admission of Bangladesh to the United Nations did not appear as such on the agenda. On September 23, the Assembly approved without a vote the inclusion of an item on the admission of new members on its agenda. But not only was the application for membership from Bangladesh the only such application that had been received, it also became clear from the statements made by a number of delegations that Bangladesh was uppermost in their minds.

China argued against Bangladesh's admission, and Pakistan, which has not recognized Bangladesh, wanted discussion of the issue deferred. Belgium felt the matter fell within the competence of the Security Council, and that the Assembly should not bypass the provisions of the UN Charter. The USSR was in favor of Bangladesh's admission, but Yugoslavia's delegate best expressed the general feeling when he said that the item should come before the Assembly. When the question of Bangladesh's admission was placed before the Assembly on November 29, two resolutions were adopted without vote or debate, one urging UN membership for Bangladesh, and the other calling for the release of Pakistani prisoners captured in Bangladesh.

Arms Control. After a four-week debate that ended on November 25 the Political Committee adopted a resolution, later adopted by the Assembly as a whole, favoring examination of prospects for a world disarmament conference and providing for a committee to examine the opinions of governments and report the result. The United States, contending that a world conference would be unwieldy and costly, and likely to end up as a propaganda exercise, abstained on the vote. The Chinese delegation, immediately after voting for the resolution, declared that China would not take part in the work of the committee, but would exchange views with it. China, in fact, opposed the actual holding of the conference unless its conditions, including the dismantling of all foreign military bases and the withdrawal of all foreign troops were met in advance. While the USSR strongly supported the idea of such a conference, the United Kingdom only agreed to take part if the other nuclear powers did so, and

France, which has consistently boycotted the 25-member Geneva disarmament conference, promised to cooperate with the committee.

The Political Committee also adopted a number of resolutions on various aspects of arms control, including one deploring the use of napalm and other incendiaries in warfare. Other resolutions urged that the 1963 test-ban treaty prohibiting nuclear tests under water, in space, or in the atmosphere be extended to ban underground explosions as well, and called for an end to atmospheric tests in the Pacific.

Middle East. The annual debate on the Middle East opened in the Assembly on November 27, with the situation no nearer a solution than it had been a year previously. The fundamental differences in approach of Israel and Egypt were shown once again in the speeches of their delegates, Israel favoring direct negotiation and Egypt looking to a settlement through the United Nations. Finally, on December 8, after ten days of fruitless debate, yet another resolution calling for Israel's withdrawal from the territories it occupied was passed by a vote of 86 to 7, with 31 abstentions (including the United States). Its only new feature was a request to all states to avoid giving Israel any assistance that could help it in consolidating control over the Arab territory it held.

Korea. An attempt to place two items on Korea on the Assembly's agenda was made by China, with the aid of the Soviet bloc, in the General Committee on September 20. The Chinese delegate, Huang Hua, argued that a serious obstacle to Korea's independent and peaceful reunification was the continuous interference carried out in the name of the United Nations. The USSR, Rumania, and Czechoslovakia supported the Chinese point of view. Opponents, led by the United Kingdom, felt that no useful purpose would be served by a debate, particularly in view of the direct contact established during the year between North and South Korea with the express purpose of unification of the country. The British proposal to defer the matter to the next session of the Assembly was approved by the committee by a vote of 16 to 7. This decision was confirmed by the Assembly on September 23.

Other Political Questions. In his speech to the General Assembly on September 27, British Foreign Secretary Sir Alec Douglas-Home asked that an item concerning the expulsion of Asians from Uganda be put on the agenda.

Portugal was condemned by the General Assembly on November 14 by a vote of 98 to 6, with 8 abstentions, for conducting "colonial wars" in its African territories.

Administrative and Budgetary Questions. Secretary General Waldheim appeared before the Administrative and Budgetary Committee on September 29 to present his 1973 budget proposals. Appropriations for 1973, estimated at $224,150,100, exceeded by $11 million, or 5.17%, the amount approved for 1972, the lowest percentage increase for many years. All but $728,000 of the increase was due to factors beyond the secretariat's control, the result of such expenses as currency realignments, increased construction costs, and higher salary and contractual costs.

A U.S. move to cut its contribution from the 31.5% of the budget total required by the assessment formula to 25% started with a vote in favor of such a reduction in the U.S. House of Representatives on May 18. It was approved for inclusion on

TABLE TENNIS team from China entertained UN members in the Trusteeship Council chamber in April as part of its tour of North America. The exhibition was a benefit performance for the UN International School.

the Assembly's agenda by the Finance Committee on December 1. On December 13 the Assembly, by a vote of 81 to 27, with 22 abstentions, approved the reduction of the U. S. contribution. The move was based on the principle that it was unhealthy for a single country to pay more than a quarter of the organization's cost.

SECURITY COUNCIL

The Security Council experienced a comparatively uneventful year in 1972. Its most notable departure from routine was its first meeting, held in Addis Ababa, Ethiopia, from January 28 to February 4. It was the Council's first meeting away from New York since 1952, when it met in Paris. During the year the Council passed several resolutions on various aspects of the Middle East situation, Rhodesia, apartheid, Namibia (South West Africa), and Portuguese Guinea, but it failed to make any recommendation on Bangladesh.

Apartheid. A resolution on apartheid was among the four resolutions on African problems passed on February 4 at the Council meeting in Addis Ababa. Sponsored by Guinea, India, Somalia, Sudan, and Yugoslavia, it was adopted by a vote of 14 to 0, with France abstaining. The resolution condemned the South African government for continuing its policies of apartheid, called on all states to observe strictly the arms embargo, and decided as a matter of urgency to examine methods of resolving the present situation arising out of policies of apartheid.

Portuguese Guinea. Also among the resolutions passed at the Addis Ababa meeting on February 4 was one on Portuguese Guinea, or Guinea (Bissau), which was adopted by a vote of 9 to 0, with 6 abstentions. The resolution reaffirmed the inalienable rights of the people of Angola, Mozambique, and Guinea (Bissau) to self-determination and independence, and recognized the legitimacy of their struggle to achieve that right. It affirmed that the situation resulting from the policies of Portugal "seriously disturbed international peace and security in the African continent," called for the cessation of Portuguese acts of repression, and called on Portugal to refrain from violations of the sovereignty and territorial integrity of African states. The Council called on all states to refrain from offering the Portuguese government any assistance to enable it to continue repression and to take all necessary measures to prevent the sale and supply of arms and military equipment to the Portuguese government for that purpose.

Namibia (South West Africa). Two resolutions concerning Namibia were adopted by the Council on February 4. The first was passed by a vote of 14 to 0, with China not participating. It invited the secretary general, in consultation with a group of Security Council members, to initiate contacts with all the parties concerned with a view to establishing conditions to enable the people of Namibia to exercise their right to self-determination and independence. It also called on the government of South Africa to cooperate with the secretary general in the implementation of the resolution. The second resolution was adopted by a vote of 13 to 0, with France and the United Kingdom abstaining. It condemned the repressive measures employed against African laborers in Namibia, and called for the withdrawal of South African police and military forces as well as civilian personnel.

A further resolution, which was adopted by the Council on August 1, followed up the first of the two Addis Ababa resolutions. It invited the secretary general to continue contacts with all parties concerned with a view to establishing the necessary conditions for self-determination and independence, and it empowered him to appoint a representative to assist him.

Rhodesia. A resolution condemning the terms of the independence settlement worked out between the United Kingdom and Rhodesia at the end of 1971 was vetoed by the United Kingdom at the Addis Ababa meeting on February 4, with Belgium, France, Italy, Japan, and the United States abstaining. A further Council meeting later in the month was concerned with legislation passed by the U. S. Congress permitting the import of chrome into the United States from Rhodesia after Jan. 1, 1972. On February 28 the Council urged all states to implement fully every Security Council resolution

ORGANIZATION OF THE UNITED NATIONS

THE SECRETARIAT

Secretary General: Kurt Waldheim (until Dec. 31, 1976)

THE GENERAL ASSEMBLY (1972)

President: Stanislaw Trepczynski (Poland). The 132 member-nations were as follows:

Afghanistan	Gambia	Nigeria
Albania	Ghana	Norway
Algeria	Greece	Oman
Argentina	Guatemala	Pakistan
Australia	Guinea	Panama
Austria	Guyana	Paraguay
Bahrain	Haiti	Peru
Barbados	Honduras	Philippines
Belgium	Hungary	Poland
Belorussia	Iceland	Portugal
Bhutan	India	Qatar
Bolivia	Indonesia	Rumania
Botswana	Iran	Rwanda
Brazil	Iraq	Saudi Arabia
Bulgaria	Ireland	Senegal
Burma	Israel	Sierra Leone
Burundi	Italy	Singapore
Cambodia	Ivory Coast	Somalia
(Khmer Republic)	Jamaica	South Africa
Cameroon	Japan	Southern Yemen
Canada	Jordan	Spain
Central African	Kenya	Sudan
Republic	Kuwait	Swaziland
Ceylon (Sri Lanka)	Laos	Sweden
Chad	Lebanon	Syria
Chile	Lesotho	Tanzania
China	Liberia	Thailand
Colombia	Libya	Togo
Congo	Luxembourg	Trinidad and
Costa Rica	Malagasy	Tobago
Cuba	Republic	Tunisia
Cyprus	Malawi	Turkey
Czechoslovakia	Malaysia	Uganda
Dahomey	Maldives	Ukraine
Denmark	Mali	USSR
Dominican	Malta	United Arab
Republic	Mauritania	Emirates
Ecuador	Mauritius	United Kingdom
Egypt	Mexico	United States
El Salvador	Mongolia	Upper Volta
Equatorial Guinea	Morocco	Uruguay
Ethiopia	Nepal	Venezuela
Fiji	Netherlands	Yemen
Finland	New Zealand	Yugoslavia
France	Nicaragua	Zaïre
Gabon	Niger	Zambia

COMMITTEES

General: Composed of 25 members as follows: The General Assembly president; the 17 General Assembly vice presidents (heads of delegations or their deputies of China, Colombia, Cyprus, Ethiopia, France, Haiti, Iceland, Libya, Mauritania, New Zealand, Paraguay, Philippines, Rwanda, Syria, USSR, United Kingdom, and United States), and the chairmen of the following 7 main committees, which are composed of all 132 member countries:

First (Political and Security): Radha Krishna Ramphul (Mauritius)

Special Political: Hady Touré (Guinea)

Second (Economic and Financial): Bruce Rankin (Canada)

Third (Social, Humanitarian, and Cultural): Carlos Giambruno (Uruguay)

Fourth (Trust and Non-self-governing territories): Zdenek Cernik (Czechoslovakia)

Fifth (Administrative and Budgetary): Motoo Ogiso (Japan)

Sixth (Legal): Erik Suy (Belgium)

THE SECURITY COUNCIL (1973)

(Membership ends on December 31 of the year noted; asterisks indicate permanent membership)

Australia (1974)	India (1973)	Sudan (1973)
Austria (1974)	Indonesia (1974)	USSR*
China*	Kenya (1974)	United Kingdom*
France*	Panama (1973)	United States*
Guinea (1973)	Peru (1974)	Yugoslavia (1973)

Military Staff Committee: Representatives of chiefs of staffs of China, France, USSR, United Kingdom, and United States.

Disarmament Commission: Representatives of all 132 members.

THE ECONOMIC AND SOCIAL COUNCIL (1973)

President: Karoly Szarka (Hungary), 52d and 53d sessions (1972). (Membership ends on December 31 of the year noted.)

Algeria (1975)	Japan (1974)	Poland (1974)
Bolivia (1974)	Lebanon (1973)	Spain (1975)
Brazil (1975)	Malagasy Republic	Trinidad and Tobago
Burundi (1974)	(1973)	(1975)
Chile (1974)	Malaysia (1973)	Uganda (1975)
China (1974)	Mali (1975)	USSR (1974)
Finland (1974)	Mongolia (1975)	United Kingdom
France (1975)	Netherlands (1975)	(1974)
Haiti (1973)	New Zealand (1973)	United States (1973)
Hungary (1973)	Niger (1973)	Zaïre (1973)

THE TRUSTEESHIP COUNCIL (1972–73)

President: W. Tapley Bennett, Jr. (United States) 39th session (1972)

Australia[1]	France[2]	United Kingdom[2]
China[2]	USSR[2]	United States[2]

[1] Administers trust territory. [2] Permanent member of Security Council not administering trust territory.

THE INTERNATIONAL COURT OF JUSTICE

President: Sir Muhammad Zafrullah Khan (Pakistan)
Vice President: Fouad Ammoun (Lebanon)

(Judges listed in order of precedence)

Cesar Bengzon (Philippines)	Eduardo Jiminez de Aréchaga
Manfred Lachs (Poland)	(Uruguay)
Charles D. Onyeama (Nigeria)	Platon D. Morozov (USSR)
Sture Petrén (Sweden)	Isaac Forster (Senegal)
Federico de Castro (Spain)	André Gros (France)
Hardy Cross Dillard	José Maria Ruda (Argentina)
(United States)	Nagendra Singh (India)
Louis Ignacio-Pinto	Sir Humphrey Waldock
(Dahomey)	(United Kingdom)

SPECIALIZED AGENCIES

Food and Agriculture Organization (FAO); Intergovernmental Maritime Consultative Organization (IMCO); International Atomic Energy Agency (IAEA); International Bank for Reconstruction and Development (World Bank; IBRD); International Civil Aviation Organization (ICAO); International Development Association (IDA); International Finance Corporation (IFC); International Labor Organization (ILO); International Monetary Fund (IMF); International Telecommunication Union (ITU); United Nations Educational, Scientific and Cultural Organization (UNESCO); Universal Postal Union (UPU); World Health Organization (WHO); World Meteorological Organization (WMO).

---

establishing sanctions against Rhodesia, and deplored the attitude of those states that had persisted in giving moral, political, and economic assistance to the illegal regime. Both the United Kingdom and the United States abstained on the vote.

A further resolution was passed by a vote of 14 to 0 on July 28, with the United States again abstaining. This resolution called on all states continuing to have economic and other relations with Rhodesia to end them immediately. The Council approved another resolution on September 29 that, in essence, reaffirmed economic sanctions against Rhodesia. Both the United Kingdom and the United States abstained. A second resolution on the same day, in effect seeking to direct a settlement of the political question, was vetoed by the United Kingdom, with Belgium, France, Italy, and the United States abstaining.

Bangladesh. According to Article 4 of the UN Charter, admission of any state to membership is "effected by a decision of the General Assembly upon the recommendation of the Security Council." Thus, following Bangladesh's August 8 application for membership, the Council met to consider it on August 10, 24, and 25. China opposed admission, while Guinea, Somalia, and Sudan were inclined to delay. A Chinese resolution postponing consideration of the question, however, failed to pass.

A draft resolution recommending Bangladesh's admission, sponsored by India, the USSR, the United

Kingdom, and Yugoslavia, was vetoed by China on August 25. The first use of the veto by China, it was cast on the grounds that Bangladesh was still in violation of General Assembly and Security Council resolutions calling for the return of all prisoners of war taken in the 1971 fighting between India and Pakistan and for the removal of all foreign troops still on Bangladesh soil. An amended resolution also failed to pass, and the Council adjourned without taking any action.

Middle East. The Council met periodically during the year to consider complaints from both Israel and the Arab states, and passed a number of resolutions, most of which were ineffective. On February 28 and June 26, the Council called on Israel to refrain from military action against Lebanon, the latter resolution also calling on Israel to return all Syrian and Lebanese military and security personnel abducted by Israeli armed forces. A further resolution on July 21 again called on Israel to return Syrian and Lebanese personnel "without delay." The United States abstained on both the June 26 and July 21 resolutions, and finally, on September 10, exercised its veto, for only the second time in the history of the United Nations. The September 10 resolution called for an immediate halt to military operations in the Middle East, but made no mention of the terrorist acts that had led to Israeli air strikes against Syria and Lebanon, thereby provoking the U. S. veto. All attempts failed to work out a resolution that would not only have called for a cessation of military action, but also have condemned terrorism.

Cyprus. Acting on the recommendation of the secretary general, the Security Council on June 15 adopted, by a vote of 14 to 0 with China abstaining, a resolution to extend the stationing of the UN peace-keeping force in Cyprus for a further 6-month period, "in the expectation" that by that date "sufficient progress toward a final solution will make possible a withdrawal or substantial reduction of the force."

Hijacking. A resolution passed by consensus on June 20 condemned aerial hijacking, and called on all states "to take all appropriate measures within their jurisdiction to deter and prevent such acts and to take effective measures to deal with those who commit such acts."

ECONOMIC AND SOCIAL COUNCIL

The 52d session of the Economic and Social Council (ECOSOC) met in New York from Jan. 5 to 7, 1972, and from May 15 to June 2. Acting under the provisions of a General Assembly resolution of Dec. 20, 1971, which urged member states to ratify an amendment to the UN Charter doubling the size of the Council (from 27 to 54 members) and recommending a similar increase in the size of its committees, the Council elected an additional 27 members to its sessional committees on January 7.

In the economic field, it adopted a resolution establishing guidelines for action in the development of natural resources and three resolutions on housing, building, and planning. It urged that high priority be given to preparations for the World Population Year and the World Population Conference scheduled for 1974, and recommended that the United Nations sponsor the Protein Advisory Group. In the social area, the Council adopted 22 resolutions on human rights, the advancement of the status of women, and the elimination of the

slavery-like practices of apartheid and colonialism, and acted on other recommendations of the Commission of Human Rights. A number of resolutions were also approved on social development, the use of drugs, and capital punishment.

At its 53d session in Geneva from July 3 to 28, the Council requested a study on the impact of multinational corporations on the development process and international relations, and adopted a resolution on international relations and multinational trade negotiations. It also made recommendations on land reform, approved measures to eliminate mass poverty and unemployment in developing countries, and called for action to stop the clandestine trafficking in labor from Africa to Europe.

The session was resumed on September 12 to 15, October 16 to 20, and November 13. On September 15 the Council recommended that the General Assembly establish an international university. The proposal was taken a step further on November 30, when the Assembly's Economic Committee approved it by a vote of 86 to 8, with 3 abstentions, the Soviet bloc voting against it.

TRUSTEESHIP COUNCIL

The 39th session of the Trusteeship Council met in New York from May 23 to June 16, 1972. China was unable to take part because of staffing problems. The Council considered the annual reports of the administering authorities of the two remaining trust territories—the Pacific Islands (administered by the United States) and Papua-New Guinea (administered by Australia)—and the report of the UN visiting mission to observe the 1972 elections for the Papua-New Guinea House of Assembly. It adopted resolutions on the political, economic, social, and educational advancement of the territories, and decided that a visiting mission—composed of Australia, France, the USSR, and the United Kingdom—would go to the Pacific Islands for a period of six weeks early in 1973.

INTERNATIONAL COURT OF JUSTICE

The International Court of Justice opened hearings on India's case against Pakistan on June 19. The case involved India's questioning of the jurisdiction of the Council of the International Civil Aviation Organization (ICAO) in connection with the Pakistani complaint against India's decision in February 1971 to no longer permit overflights of its territory by Pakistani aircraft. Sir Muhammad Zafrullah Khan, a Pakistani citizen, relinquished the presidency of the court for the duration of the case to Fouad Ammoun, the vice president.

The court's judgment was published on August 18. By a vote of 14 to 2 it found that the Council of ICAO was competent to entertain Pakistan's complaint. At the same time, the court, by a vote of 13 to 3, rejected Pakistan's objections on the questions of the court's competence, and found that it had jurisdiction to entertain India's appeal.

On April 14, the government of the United Kingdom instituted proceedings against Iceland, arising from the Icelandic government's decision to extend, as of Sept. 1, 1972, its exclusive fishery limits to 50 nautical miles (80 km) from its coastlines. West Germany instituted a similar case on June 5. (See also LAW—*International Law*.)

RICHARD E. WEBB
*Former Director, Reference and Library Division
British Information Services, New York*

Presidential adviser Henry Kissinger waves before boarding a helicopter at Camp David, Md., on November 17 after consulting President Nixon on Vietnam peace talks.

UNITED STATES

The highlights of the election year 1972 were the sweeping victory of President Richard M. Nixon in November and the retention of control of the Senate and the House by the Democrats. In foreign affairs, the President also scored by his unprecedented visits to Peking and Moscow.

During the year the war in Vietnam remained a paramount issue in both domestic and foreign affairs. Although hopes for peace were raised in late October, the longest war in American history continued to drag on as the year ended.

DOMESTIC AFFAIRS

In an election-eve interview with the Washington *Star-News,* President Nixon said, "The liberal establishment during the four years I have been in office thought that I was out of touch with the country. That is not true. What this election will demonstrate is that out across the country . . . you will find that a solid majority of American people do not want to go to the far left."

In the face of the election returns in November 1972, no one could quarrel with the President's analysis, as far as it went. While the country did not seem to want to shift far to the left, it was by no means clear which way the country did want to go. Although America had settled down after the upheavals of the 1960's, it had yet to chart a firm course for the future. Indeed, the year 1972 was a period of crosscurrents and contradictions, unexpected setbacks and uncertain triumphs.

On the political front, despite President Nixon's immense personal success in November, his party failed to win control of Congress and in fact lost ground in the Senate. Many observers read Nixon's victory as an endorsement of the traditional values and institutions that he championed. Nevertheless, 54% of the Americans surveyed in a special Gallup Poll favored "basic change" in the way "our governmental system is now set up." The social scientists who sponsored the poll concluded that Americans are "searching for a new political, social, and economic philosophy," one that will infuse them with new purpose."

On social issues, Nixon's steadfast opposition to "permissiveness" apparently reflected the views of his "solid majority." Yet books and movies with explicit sexual material proliferated, 64% of the

Americans surveyed by Gallup favored liberalization of abortion laws, and a prestigious national commission recommended the elimination of all criminal penalties for private use of marihuana.

Economic indicators were mixed, too. The major signposts suggested that the economy had at last turned the corner, but at the same time unemployment was disturbingly high. Another paradox was that the climb in the overall cost of living was slowed while food prices rose at a vexing rate.

The anomalies that marked the year extended into the literary field. The most talked-about book of the year—a supposedly authorized biography of financier Howard Hughes—was never published. Hughes repudiated the book, and its author, Clifford Irving, went to prison after admitting he had tried to swindle the McGraw-Hill publishing company out of $750,000.

Perhaps the most tragic irony of the year had to do with the war in Vietnam. In late October, presidential adviser Henry Kissinger announced that "peace is at hand." By mid-December that promise had crumbled, and the bombing of North Vietnam was resumed on a larger scale than ever before.

Politics. The presidential election dominated the year 1972, shaping other events. On the Republican side, President Nixon had little opposition for renomination. The only suspense about the GOP ticket was over the selection of his running mate, and Nixon answered that question in July when he announced his preference for Vice President Spiro T. Agnew. Nixon and Agnew each swept to renomination on the first ballot at the party's convention in Miami Beach.

Among the Democrats, the competition was much more intense. Sen. Edmund Muskie of Maine, a heavy favorite when the year began, faded in the primaries. Sen. George McGovern of South Dakota, who had been given little chance by political experts, was aided by an aggressive campaign organization that took advantage of reforms in the Democratic party machinery. As a result, he built up a commanding lead in delegates before the convention.

Alabama Gov. George Wallace, who had run for President on a third-party ticket in 1968, sought the Democratic nomination in 1972, and he ran surprisingly well in the early primaries. His campaign was moving strongly when he was cut down in an assassination attempt at a Maryland rally in mid-

May. The would-be assassin, Arthur Bremer, an emotionally disturbed drifter who had previously plotted to kill President Nixon, was sentenced to 63 years in prison. Although Wallace survived the shooting, his wounds left him paralyzed from the waist down and eliminated him from any active role in the campaign, either as a Democrat or as a third-party candidate. The removal of Wallace from the race damaged the McGovern candidacy since most of the governor's 1968 supporters cast their votes for Nixon in November.

McGovern had other problems, too. His nomination disturbed union leaders and other traditional Democratic supporters who regarded the candidate's views as too radical. Then it was disclosed that Sen. Thomas Eagleton of Missouri, whom McGovern had chosen as his running mate, had received electroshock therapy for depression earlier in his career. Senator Eagleton was forced off the ticket and replaced by R. Sargent Shriver, former head of the Peace Corps and the Poverty Program. The episode set off widespread criticism that McGovern lacked judgment and decisiveness.

Developments stemming from a mysterious raid on the headquarters of the Democratic National Committee on June 17 seemed to offer potential political dividends for the Democrats. On that date, the Washington police arrested five men inside the Democratic party's offices in the Watergate Hotel. The five men were James W. McCord, security coordinator for the Committee for the Reelection of the President; Bernard Barker, president of a Miami real estate firm and a refugee from Castro's Cuba; and three associates of Barker. An FBI investigation led to two other men, G. Gordon Liddy and E. Howard Hunt, Jr., both former White House aides. In September, all seven were indicted on charges of conspiring to obtain information illegally from the headquarters as well as charges of breaking and entering, stealing and photographing documents, and planting telephone taps and electronic bugging devices.

The bizarre incident led to charges from Democrats that the Republicans had engaged in a broad espionage and sabotage campaign directed by men close to the President. McGovern sought to exploit these suspicions by charging that the Nixon administration was "the most corrupt" in history. For its part, the White House denied any role in political espionage, and the Democrats lacked firm evidence to the contrary. At year-end, further light on the affair awaited the trial of the Watergate Seven.

The Watergate affair seemed to have little impact on voter opinion. On November 7, President Nixon won 49 states, losing only Massachusetts and the District of Columbia. This gave him 521 electoral votes, second only to Franklin D. Roosevelt's total of 523 in 1936.

Nonetheless, the Republicans gained only 13 seats in the House of Representatives, leaving them with 192 out of 435, far short of a majority. In the Senate, the Democrats made a net gain of two seats, giving them a 57 to 43 advantage in the new Congress as incumbent Republican Senators Margaret Chase Smith of Maine, Gordon Allott of Colorado, Caleb Boggs of Delaware, and Jack Miller of Iowa were upset. The Democrats emerged from the election controlling 31 out of the 50 state governorships, a net increase of one, by defeating Republican incumbents Richard Ogilvie in Illinois and Russell W. Peterson in Delaware.

Just before the election, consumer advocate Ralph Nader published detailed profiles of 92 senators and 392 representatives in an effort to help voters judge congressmen more knowledgeably. All 435 House seats and 33 of 100 Senate seats were contested in the election.

Nixon Administration. With its energies diverted by the political campaign and by ambitious ventures in diplomacy, the administration's domestic programs and accomplishments in 1972 were on a relatively modest scale. In his State of the Union message in January, President Nixon called for "high statesmanship" from Congress. He offered few new proposals, instead urging the lawmakers to act on measures previously presented, including the mainstays of "a new American Revolution" he had proclaimed in his State of the Union message in 1971. In that message he had called for revenue sharing, cabinet reorganization, welfare system reform, environmental cleanups, and improved health care.

During the year the administration was discomfited by public controversies arising from its handling of various aspects of public affairs. Its antitrust policies came under fire as a result of allegations that the Justice Department's settlement of litigation with the International Telephone and Telegraph Corp. (ITT), the nation's largest conglomerate, had been influenced by political considerations. According to a memorandum allegedly written by ITT Washington lobbyist Dita Beard, the pledge of a substantial ITT contribution to support the GOP national convention, then planned for San Diego, had helped the corporation to win relatively favorable terms from the Justice Department.

Administration officials denied any connection between the convention pledge and the antitrust settlement. Nevertheless, columnist Jack Anderson's publication of the so-called Beard memo on February 29 led to a prolonged Senate battle over the nomination of Richard Kleindienst as attorney general. In his position as deputy attorney general, Kleindienst had been responsible for review and approval of the suits against ITT. Ultimately Kleindienst was confirmed, and the convention site was moved from San Diego on grounds that the party could cut costs by meeting in Miami Beach instead.

In late August, conflict of interest charges were raised against two U. S. Department of Agriculture (USDA) officials following an agreement whereby U. S. grain dealers were to sell about $1 billion worth of grain to the Soviet Union. Consumers Union complained that the two USDA officials, Clarence D. Palmby and Clifford G. Pulvermacher, had taken part in negotiating the sale and had then left the government to work for exporting firms involved in the grain shipments. Broadening the charge on September 8, George McGovern accused the administration of engaging in "a conspiracy of silence" with large grain exporters at the expense of grain farmers. Vice President Agnew replied that the Democrats were confusing the issue with unfounded innuendo. Nevertheless, the administration ordered an investigation by the Federal Bureau of Investigation (FBI). The FBI was ordered to determine whether some exporters had made illegal excess profits from the deal, and several congressional committees launched inquiries of their own.

Questions also were raised about the Depart-

AN AMERICAN B-52 bomber takes off from air base on Guam for raid over North Vietnam as the United States renewed heavy bombing of Hanoi area in December.

DEMOCRATIC presidential candidate Sen. George McGovern of South Dakota greets an airport crowd as his campaign shifts into high gear in September.

REPUBLICAN candidate President Richard Nixon chats with a group of excited band members as he campaigns in Cleveland, Ohio, in October.

ment of Defense because of its disclosure in May that Gen. John D. Lavelle had been relieved of his post as commander of the U. S. 7th Air Force in Vietnam in March after ordering unauthorized bombing raids on North Vietnam. In September the Senate Armed Services Committee began an inquiry to determine whether the responsibility for the raids was shared by others in command, particularly Gen. Creighton Abrams, U. S. military chief in Vietnam, who had been chosen by Nixon on June 20 to be Army chief of staff. Eventually the committee concluded that the blame lay solely with Lavelle, and Abrams was confirmed as chief of staff by the Senate on October 12. Faced with growing congressional concern about the unauthorized bombings, Defense Secretary Melvin Laird on October 19 announced changes in procedure aimed at strengthening civilian control over the military in Vietnam.

Although the Nixon administration weathered these and other storms, no sooner were the election returns posted than the President ordered a high-level shakeup of the government. Striving to avoid what he called the traditional "downhill" syndrome afflicting second-term administrations, Nixon changed five of the 11 members of his cabinet. The new faces were New York union leader Peter J. Brennan, nominated as secretary of labor; James T. Lynn, commerce undersecretary, as secretary of housing and urban development; Caspar W. Weinberger, director of the Office of Management and Budget (OMB), as secretary of health, education, and welfare (HEW); Claude S. Brinegar, oil company official, as secretary of transportation; and Frederick B. Dent, South Carolina businessman, as secretary of commerce. In addition, the President nominated HEW Secretary Elliot Richardson as secretary of defense. George P. Shultz, who remained on as treasury secretary, was given additional responsibility as a head of a new cabinet-level council on economic policy. Litton Industries President Roy Ash was appointed to Weinberger's old post at OMB.

Congress. The Democratic-controlled 92d Congress and the Republican administration did not often see eye to eye in the 1972 election year. The lawmakers were most responsive to the President in foreign affairs and national defense, areas traditionally considered the prerogative of the executive branch. The Congress approved a joint resolution endorsing the five-year U. S.-Soviet agreement limiting the deployment of offensive nuclear weapons. The Senate ratified a companion treaty limiting each country to two antiballistic missile sites, after tacking on an amendment that any future treaty must provide approximate numerical equality in intercontinental strategic weapons. The Senate tried once again to end U. S. involvement in the Indochina War by amending defense spending bills to cut off funding for military operations in that area. But the House, as in the past, rejected all such end-the-war legislation.

On the domestic side, revenue sharing was probably the most significant administration proposal to win approval. Under the five-year program enacted, the federal government will share $30.2 billion in revenues with state and local governments, starting with $5.3 billion in 1972.

Other spending proposals produced sharp disagreement, with the administration generally stressing national defense and foreign aid while Congress usually emphasized public works, health, welfare,

and the like. The showdown came in the closing days of the session in October when Congress rejected a proposal setting a $250 billion ceiling on federal spending in the fiscal year 1973 and granting the President authority to eliminate appropriations for any program in order to keep under that limit. President Nixon retaliated for that rebuff after Congress had adjourned by pocket-vetoing 11 bills, most of them public works or social service measures that authorized or appropriated more funds than he had requested. He was determined, the President explained, to keep his promise to the American people not to raise taxes in 1973.

Despite such friction with the White House, the Congress in 1972 passed a wide range of proposals that the lawmakers themselves had initiated. A constitutional amendment guaranteeing equal rights for women was approved and sent to the states for ratification. The Equal Employment Opportunity Commission was vested with power to start lawsuits to enforce federal laws against job discrimination. The ill-defined, oft-evaded rules for campaign spending were overhauled, and requirements for reporting campaign contributions and costs were strengthened. Colleges, universities, and other post-

(Continued on page 713)

—— UNITED STATES • Information Highlights ——

Official Name: United States of America.
Area: 3,615,123 square miles (9,363,169 sq km).
Population (Nov. 1972 est.): 210,000,000. *Density,* 57 per square mile (22 per sq km). *Annual rate of increase,* 1.0%.
Chief Cities (1970 census): Washington, D. C., the capital, 756,510; New York, 7,895,563; Chicago, 3,-369,359; Los Angeles, 2,809,596; Philadelphia, 1,-950,098.
Government: *Head of state,* Richard M. Nixon, president (took office Jan. 20, 1969). *Head of government,* Richard M. Nixon. *Legislature*—Congress; Senate, 100 members; House of Representatives, 435 members. *Major political parties*—Democratic party; Republican party.
Language: English (official).
Education: *Expenditure* (1971), 7.7% of gross national product. *Public school enrollment* (1971–72)—primary, 28,069,411; secondary, 18,099,129; university/higher, 8,387,000.
Gross National Product (Nov. 1972 est.): $1,162,000,000,-000.
National Income per Person (1971): $4,138.
Economic Indexes: *Industrial production* (May 1972), 146 (1963=100); *agricultural production* (1971), 135 (1952–56=100); *consumer price index* (1971), 132 (1963=100).
Manufacturing (major products): Automobiles, aircraft, railroad equipment, industrial machinery, processed foods, chemicals, electrical equipment and supplies, fabricated metals, textiles, clothing, paper and paper products.
Major Agricultural Products: Corn (ranks 1st among world producers, 1971), soybeans (world rank 1st, 1971), wheat (world rank 2d, 1971), tobacco (world rank 1st, 1971), cotton (world rank 1st, 1971), sorghum grain, peanuts, potatoes, citrus fruits, vegetables, dairy products, cattle.
Major Minerals: Petroleum (ranks 1st among world producers, 1970), iron ore (world rank 2d, 1970), coal (world rank 2d, 1970), silver (world rank 1st, 1970), zinc (world rank 1st, 1970), copper (world rank 1st, 1970), nickel, natural gas, lead (world rank 1st, 1970), sulfur, uranium, phosphate rock (world rank 1st, 1970).
Foreign Trade (1971): *Exports,* $43,497,000,000 (chief exports, 1969—nonelectrical machinery; motor vehicles; food; chemicals). *Imports,* $45,546,000,000 (chief imports, 1969—motor vehicles and parts; food; petroleum and petroleum products; nonelectrical machinery). *Chief trading partners* (1971)—Canada (took 23% of exports, supplied 28% of imports); Japan (9%—16%); West Germany (6%—8%); United Kingdom (5%—5%).
Tourism: Receipts (1970). $2,319,000,000.
Transportation: *Motor vehicles* (1971). 108,407,300 (automobiles, 89,279,900); *railroads* (1971), 206,265 miles (331,942 km); *merchant fleet* (1971), 16,266,000 gross registered tons.
Communications: *Telephones* (1971), 120,218,000; *television stations* (1971), 930; *television sets* (1971), 93,347,000; *radios* (1970), 290,000,000; *newspapers* (1971), 1,749 (daily circulation, 62,231,000).

UPI

93d CONGRESS OF THE U.S.

SENATE

OFFICERS

President of the Senate: Spiro T. Agnew
President Pro Tempore: James O. Eastland (D-Miss.)
Majority Leader: Mike Mansfield (D-Mont.)
Majority Whip: Robert C. Byrd (D-W. Va.)
Minority Leader: Hugh Scott (R-Pa.)
Minority Whip: Robert P. Griffin (R-Mich.)

COMMITTEE CHAIRMEN

Aeronautical and Space Sciences: Frank E. Moss (D-Utah)
Agriculture and Forestry: Herman E. Talmadge (D-Ga.)
Appropriations: John L. McClellan (D-Ark.)
Armed Services: John C. Stennis (D-Miss.)
Banking, Housing, and Urban Affairs: John J. Sparkman (D-Ala.)
Commerce: Warren G. Magnuson (D-Wash.)
District of Columbia: Thomas F. Eagleton (D-Mo.)
Finance: Russell B. Long (D-La.)
Foreign Relations: J. William Fulbright (D-Ark.)
Government Operations: Sam J. Ervin, Jr. (D-N. C.)
Interior and Insular Affairs: Henry M. Jackson (D-Wash.)
Judiciary: James O. Eastland (D-Miss.)
Labor and Public Welfare: Harrison Williams (D-N. J.)
Post Office and Civil Service: Gale W. McGee (D-Wyo.)
Public Works: Jennings Randolph (D-W. Va.)
Rules and Administration: Howard W. Cannon (D-Nev.)
Veterans' Affairs: Vance Hartke (D-Ind.)

HOUSE

OFFICERS

Speaker of the House: Carl Albert (D-Okla.)
Majority Leader: Thomas P. O'Neill, Jr. (D-Mass.)
Majority Whip: John J. McFall (D-Calif.)
Minority Leader: Gerald R. Ford (R-Mich.)
Minority Whip: Leslie C. Arends (R-Ill.)

COMMITTEE CHAIRMEN

Agriculture: W. R. Poage (D-Texas)
Appropriations: George H. Mahon (D-Texas)
Armed Services: F. Edward Hébert (D-La.)
Banking and Currency: Wright Patman (D-Texas)
District of Columbia: Charles C. Diggs, Jr. (D-Mich.)
Education and Labor: Carl D. Perkins (D-Ky.)
Foreign Affairs: Thomas E. Morgan (D-Pa.)
Government Operations: Chet Holifield (D-Calif.)
House Administration: Wayne L. Hays (D-Ohio)
Interior and Insular Affairs: James A. Haley (D-Fla.)
Internal Security: Richard H. Ichord (D-Mo.)
Interstate and Foreign Commerce: Harley O. Staggers (D-W. Va.)
Judiciary: Peter W. Rodino, Jr. (D-N. J.)
Merchant Marine and Fisheries: Leonor K. Sullivan (D-Mo.)
Post Office and Civil Service: Thaddeus J. Dulski (D-N. Y.)
Public Works: John A. Blatnik (D-Minn.)
Rules: Ray J. Madden (D-Ind.)
Science and Astronautics: Olin E. Teague (D-Texas)
Standards of Official Conduct: Melvin Price (D-Ill.)
Veterans' Affairs: William J. B. Dorn (D-S. C.)
Ways and Means: Wilbur D. Mills (D-Ark.)

SENATE MEMBERSHIP

(As of January 1973: 57 Democrats, 43 Republicans)

Letters after senators' names refer to party affiliation—D for Democrat, R for Republican. Single asterisk (*) denotes term expiring in January 1975; double asterisk (**), term expiring in January 1977; triple asterisk (***), term expiring in January 1979.

ALABAMA
***J. Sparkman, D
*J. B. Allen, D

ALASKA
*M. Gravel, D
***T. Stevens, R

ARIZONA
*B. Goldwater, R
**P. J. Fannin, R

ARKANSAS
***J. L. McClellan, D
*J. W. Fulbright, D

CALIFORNIA
*A. Cranston, D
**J. V. Tunney, D

COLORADO
***F. K. Haskell, D
*P. H. Dominick, R

CONNECTICUT
*A. A. Ribicoff, D
**L. P. Weicker, Jr., R

DELAWARE
***J. R. Biden, Jr., D
**W. V. Roth, Jr., R

FLORIDA
*E. J. Gurney, R
**L. Chiles, D

GEORGIA
***S. Nunn, D
*H. E. Talmadge, D

HAWAII
*D. K. Inouye, D
**H. L. Fong, R

IDAHO
***J. A. McClure, R
*F. Church, D

ILLINOIS
***C. H. Percy, R
*A. E. Stevenson III, D

INDIANA
*B. Bayh, D
**V. Hartke, D

IOWA
***R. Clark, D
*H. E. Hughes, D

KANSAS
***J. B. Pearson, R
*R. Dole, R

KENTUCKY
***W. Huddleston, D
*M. W. Cook, R

LOUISIANA
***J. B. Johnston, Jr., D
*R. B. Long, D

MAINE
***W. D. Hathaway, D
**E. S. Muskie, D

MARYLAND
*C. McC. Mathias, Jr., R
**J. G. Beall, Jr., R

MASSACHUSETTS
***E. W. Brooke, R
**E. M. Kennedy, D

MICHIGAN
***R. P. Griffin, R
**P. A. Hart, D

MINNESOTA
***W. F. Mondale, D
**H. H. Humphrey, D

MISSISSIPPI
***J. O. Eastland, D
**J. C. Stennis, D

MISSOURI
*T. F. Eagleton, D
**S. Symington, D

MONTANA
***L. Metcalf, D
**M. Mansfield, D

NEBRASKA
***C. T. Curtis, R
**R. L. Hruska, R

NEVADA
*A. Bible, D
**H. W. Cannon, D

NEW HAMPSHIRE
***T. J. McIntyre, D
*N. Cotton, R

NEW JERSEY
***C. P. Case, R
**H. A. Williams, Jr., D

NEW MEXICO
***P. V. Domenici, R
**J. M. Montoya, D

NEW YORK
*J. K. Javits, R
**J. L. Buckley, R[1]

NORTH CAROLINA
***J. A. Helms, R
*S. J. Ervin, Jr., D

NORTH DAKOTA
*M. R. Young, R
**Q. N. Burdick, D

OHIO
*W. B. Saxbe, R
**R. Taft, Jr., R

OKLAHOMA
***D. F. Bartlett, R
*H. Bellmon, R

OREGON
***M. Hatfield, R
*B. Packwood, R

PENNSYLVANIA
*R. S. Schweiker, R
**H. Scott, R

RHODE ISLAND
***C. Pell, D
**J. O. Pastore, D

SOUTH CAROLINA
***S. Thurmond, R
*E. F. Hollings, D

SOUTH DAKOTA
***J. Abourezk, D
*G. McGovern, D

TENNESSEE
***H. H. Baker, Jr., R
*W. E. Brock 3d, R

TEXAS
***J. G. Tower, R
**L. M. Bentsen, Jr., D

UTAH
*W. F. Bennett, R
**F. E. Moss, D

VERMONT
*G. D. Aiken, R
**R. T. Stafford, R

VIRGINIA
***W. L. Scott, R
**H. F. Byrd, Jr., D[2]

WASHINGTON
*W. G. Magnuson, D
**H. M. Jackson, D

WEST VIRGINIA
***J. Randolph, D
**R. C. Byrd, D

WISCONSIN
*G. Nelson, D
**W. Proxmire, D

WYOMING
***C. P. Hansen, R
**G. W. McGee, D

[1] Ran as a Conservative.   [2] Ran as an independent.

HOUSE MEMBERSHIP

(As of January 1973: 240 Democrats, 192 Republicans, 3 vacancies)

Letters after representatives' names refer to party affiliation—D for Democrat, R for Republican. The abbreviation "At-L." in place of congressional district number means "representative at large." Asterisk (*) before member's name indicates incumbent reelected in 1972 (served in 92d Congress); double asterisk (**) before name indicates nonincumbent elected in 1972.

ALABAMA
1. *J. Edwards, R
2. *W. L. Dickinson, R
3. *B. Nichols, D
4. *T. Bevill, D
5. *R. E. Jones, D
6. *J. Buchanan, R
7. *W. Flowers, D

ALASKA
At-L. Vacancy

ARIZONA
1. *J. J. Rhodes, R
2. *M. K. Udall, D
3. *S. Steiger, R
4. **J. B. Conlan, R

ARKANSAS
1. *B. Alexander, D
2. *W. D. Mills, D
3. *J. P. Hammerschmidt, R
4. **R. Thornton, D

CALIFORNIA
1. *D. H. Clausen, R
2. *H. T. Johnson, D
3. *J. E. Moss, D
4. *R. L. Leggett, D
5. *P. Burton, D
6. *W. S. Mailliard, R
7. *R. V. Dellums, D
8. **F. H. Stark, D

9. *D. Edwards, D
10. *C. S. Gubser, R
11. **L. J. Ryan, D
12. *B. L. Talcott, R
13. *C. M. Teague, R
14. *J. R. Waldie, D
15. *J. J. McFall, D
16. *B. F. Sisk, D
17. *P. N. McCloskey, Jr., R
18. *R. B. Mathias, R
19. *C. Holifield, D
20. **C. J. Moorhead, R
21. *A. F. Hawkins, D
22. *J. C. Corman, D
23. *D. Clawson, R
24. *J. H. Rousselot, R
25. *C. E. Wiggins, R
26. *T. M. Rees, D
27. *B. M. Goldwater, Jr., R
28. *A. Bell, R
29. *G. E. Danielson, D
30. *E. R. Roybal, D
31. *C. H. Wilson, D
32. *C. Hosmer, R
33. *J. L. Pettis, R
34. *R. T. Hanna, D
35. *G. M. Anderson, D
36. **W. M. Ketchum, R
37. *Y. B. Burke, D
38. **G. E. Brown, Jr., D
39. **A. J. Hinshaw, R

40. *B. Wilson, R
41. *L. Van Deerlin, D
42. **C. W. Burgener, R
43. *V. V. Veysey, R

COLORADO
1. **P. Schroeder, D
2. *D. G. Brotzman, R
3. *F. E. Evans, D
4. **J. Johnson, R
5. **W. L. Armstrong, R

CONNECTICUT
1. *W. R. Cotter, D
2. *R. H. Steele, R
3. *R. N. Giaimo, D
4. *S. B. McKinney, R
5. **R. A. Sarasin, R
6. *E. T. Grasso, D

DELAWARE
At-L. *P. S. du Pont 4th, R

FLORIDA
1. *R. L. F. Sikes, D
2. *D. Fuqua, D
3. *C. E. Bennett, D
4. *B. Chappell, Jr., D
5. **W. D. Gunter, Jr., D
6. *C. W. Young, R
7. *S. Gibbons, D
8. *J. A. Haley, D

9. *L. Frey, Jr., R
10. **L. A. Bafalis, R
11. *P. G. Rogers, D
12. *J. H. Burke, R
13. **W. Lehman, D
14. *C. Pepper, D
15. *D. B. Fascell, D

GEORGIA
1. **R. B. Ginn, D
2. *M. D. Mathis, D
3. *J. T. Brinkley, D
4. *B. B. Blackburn, R
5. **A. Young, D
6. *J. J. Flynt, Jr., D
7. *J. W. Davis, D
8. *W. S. Stuckey, Jr., D
9. *P. M. Landrum, D
10. *R. G. Stephens, Jr., D

HAWAII
1. *S. M. Matsunaga, D
2. *P. T. Mink, D

IDAHO
1. **S. D. Symms, R
2. *O. Hansen, R

ILLINOIS
1. *R. H. Metcalfe, D
2. *M. F. Murphy, D
3. **R. P. Hanrahan, R

4. *E. J. Derwinski, R
5. *J. C. Kluczynski, D
6. *H. R. Collier, R
7. Vacancy
8. *D. Rostenkowski, D
9. *S. R. Yates, D
10. **S. H. Young, R
11. *F. Annunzio, D
12. *P. M. Crane, R
13. *R. McClory, R
14. *J. N. Erlenborn, R
15. *L. C. Arends, R
16. *J. B. Anderson, R
17. **G. M. O'Brien, R
18. *R. H. Michel, R
19. *T. Railsback, R
20. *P. Findley, R
21. **E. R. Madigan, R
22. *G. E. Shipley, D
23. *M. Price, D
24. *K. J. Gray, D

INDIANA
1. *R. J. Madden, D
2. *E. F. Landgrebe, R
3. *J. Brademas, D
4. *J. E. Roush, D
5. *E. Hillis, R
6. *W. G. Bray, R
7. *J. T. Myers, R
8. *R. H. Zion, R
9. *L. H. Hamilton, D
10. *D. W. Dennis, R
11. **W. H. Hudnut III, R

IOWA
1. **E. Mezvinsky, D
2. *J. C. Culver, D
3. *H. R. Gross, R
4. *N. Smith, D
5. *W. J. Scherle, R
6. *W. Mayne, R

KANSAS
1. *K. G. Sebelius, R
2. *W. R. Roy, D
3. *L. Winn, Jr., R
4. *G. E. Shriver, R
5. *J. Skubitz, R

KENTUCKY
1. *F. A. Stubblefield, D
2. *W. H. Natcher, D
3. *R. L. Mazzoli, D
4. *M. G. Snyder, R
5. *T. L. Carter, R
6. **J. B. Breckinridge, D
7. *C. D. Perkins, D

LOUISIANA
1. *F. E. Hébert, D
2. Vacancy
3. **D. C. Treen, R
4. *J. D. Waggonner, Jr., D
5. *O. E. Passman, D
6. *J. R. Rarick, D
7. *J. B. Breaux, D
8. **G. W. Long, D

MAINE
1. *P. N. Kyros, D
2. **W. S. Cohen, R

MARYLAND
1. *W. O. Mills, R
2. *C. D. Long, D
3. *P. S. Sarbanes, D
4. **M. S. Holt, R
5. *L. J. Hogan, R
6. *G. E. Byron, D
7. *P. J. Mitchell, D
8. *G. Gude, R

MASSACHUSETTS
1. *S. O. Conte, R
2. *E. P. Boland, D
3. *H. D. Donohue, D
4. *R. F. Drinin, D
5. **P. W. Cronin, R
6. *M. J. Harrington, D
7. *T. H. Macdonald, D
8. *T. P. O'Neill, Jr., D
9. **J. J. Moakley, D[1]
10. *M. M. Heckler, R
11. *J. A. Burke, D
12. **G. E. Studds, D

MICHIGAN
1. *J. Conyers, Jr., D
2. *M. L. Esch, R
3. *G. Brown, D
4. *E. Hutchinson, R
5. *G. R. Ford, R
6. *C. E. Chamberlain, R
7. *D. W. Riegle, Jr., R

8. *J. Harvey, R
9. *G. A. Vander Jagt, R
10. *E. A. Cederberg, R
11. *P. E. Ruppe, R
12. *J. G. O'Hara, D
13. *C. C. Diggs, Jr., D
14. *L. N. Nedzi, D
15. *W. D. Ford, D
16. *J. D. Dingell, D
17. *M. W. Griffiths, D
18. **R. J. Huber, R
19. *W. S. Broomfield, R

MINNESOTA
1. *A. H. Quie, R
2. *A. Nelsen, R
3. *B. Frenzel, R
4. *J. E. Karth, D
5. *D. M. Fraser, D
6. *J. M. Zwach, R
7. *B. Bergland, D
8. *J. A. Blatnik, D

MISSISSIPPI
1. *J. L. Whitten, D
2. **D. R. Bowen, D
3. *G. V. Montgomery, D
4. **T. Cochran, R
5. **T. Lott, R

MISSOURI
1. *W. L. Clay, D
2. *J. W. Symington, D
3. *L. K. Sullivan, D
4. *W. J. Randall, D
5. *R. Bolling, D
6. **J. Litton, D
7. **G. Taylor, D
8. *R. H. Ichord, D
9. *W. L. Hungate, D
10. *B. D. Burlison, D

MONTANA
1. *R. G. Shoup, R
2. *J. Melcher, D

NEBRASKA
1. *C. Thone, R
2. *J. Y. McCollister, R
3. *D. T. Martin, R

NEVADA
At-L. **D. Towell, R

NEW HAMPSHIRE
1. *L. C. Wyman, R
2. *J. C. Cleveland, R

NEW JERSEY
1. *J. E. Hunt, R
2. *C. W. Sandman, Jr., R
3. *J. J. Howard, D
4. *F. Thompson, Jr., D
5. *P. H. B. Frelinghuysen, R
6. *E. B. Forsythe, R
7. *W. B. Widnall, R
8. *R. A. Roe, D
9. *H. Helstoski, D
10. *P. W. Rodino, Jr., D
11. *J. G. Minish, D
12. **M. J. Rinaldo, R
13. **J. J. Maraziti, R
14. *D. V. Daniels, D
15. *E. J. Patten, D

NEW MEXICO
1. *M. Lujan, Jr., R
2. *H. L. Runnels, D

NEW YORK
1. *O. G. Pike, D
2. *J. R. Grover, Jr., R
3. *A. D. Roncallo, R
4. *N. F. Lent, R
5. *J. W. Wydler, R
6. *L. L. Wolff, D
7. *J. P. Addabbo, D
8. *B. S. Rosenthal, D
9. *J. J. Delaney, D
10. *M. Biaggi, D
11. *F. J. Brasco, D
12. *S. Chisholm, D
13. *B. L. Podell, D
14. *J. J. Rooney, D
15. *H. L. Carey, D
16. **E. Holtzman, D
17. *J. M. Murphy, D
18. *E. I. Koch, D
19. *C. B. Rangel, D
20. *B. S. Abzug, D
21. *H. Badillo, D
22. *J. B. Bingham. D
23. *P. A. Peyser, R
24. *O. R. Reid, D

25. *H. Fish, Jr., R
26. **B. A. Gilman, R
27. *H. W. Robison, R
28. *S. S. Stratton, D
29. *C. J. King, R
30. *R. C. McEwen, R
31. **D. J. Mitchell, R
32. *J. M. Hanley, D
33. **W. F. Walsh, R
34. *F. Horton, R
35. *B. B. Conable, Jr., R
36. *H. P. Smith III, R
37. *T. J. Dulski, D
38. *J. F. Kemp, R
39. *J. F. Hastings, R

NORTH CAROLINA
1. *W. B. Jones, D
2. *L. H. Fountain, D
3. *D. N. Henderson, D
4. **I. F. Andrews, D
5. *W. Mizell, R
6. *R. Preyer, D
7. **C. G. Rose III, D
8. *E. B. Ruth, R
9. **J. G. Martin, R
10. *J. T. Broyhill, R
11. *R. A. Taylor, D

NORTH DAKOTA
At-L. *M. Andrews, R

OHIO
1. *W. J. Keating, R
2. *D. D. Clancy, R
3. *C. W. Whalen, Jr., R
4. **T. Guyer, R
5. *D. L. Latta, R
6. *W. H. Harsha, R
7. *C. J. Brown, R
8. *W. E. Powell, R
9. *T. L. Ashley, D
10. *C. E. Miller, R
11. *J. W. Stanton, R
12. *S. L. Devine, R
13. *C. A. Mosher, R
14. *J. F. Seiberling, D
15. *C. P. Wylie, R
16. **R. S. Regula, R
17. *J. M. Ashbrook, R
18. *W. L. Hays, D
19. *C. J. Carney, D
20. *J. V. Stanton, D
21. *L. Stokes, D
22. *C. A. Vanik, D
23. *W. E. Minshall, R

OKLAHOMA
1. **J. R. Jones, D
2. **C. R. McSpadden, D
3. *C. Albert, D
4. *T. Steed, D
5. *J. Jarman, D
6. *J. N. Camp, R

OREGON
1. *W. Wyatt, R
2. *A. Ullman, D
3. *E. Green, D
4. *J. Dellenback, R

PENNSYLVANIA
1. *W. A. Barrett, D
2. *R. N. C. Nix, D
3. *W. J. Green, D
4. *J. Eilberg, D
5. *J. Ware, R
6. *G. Yatron, D
7. *L. G. Williams, R
8. *E. G. Biester, Jr., R
9. **E. G. Shuster, R
10. *J. M. McDade, R
11. *D. J. Flood, D
12. *J. P. Saylor, R
13. *R. L. Coughlin, R
14. *W. S. Moorhead, D
15. *F. B. Rooney, D
16. *E. D. Eshleman, R
17. *H. T. Schneebeli, R
18. *H. J. Heinz III, R
19. *G. A. Goodling, R
20. *J. M. Gaydos, D
21. *J. H. Dent, D
22. *T. E. Morgan, D
23. *A. W. Johnson, R
24. *J. P. Vigorito, D
25. *F. M. Clark, D

RHODE ISLAND
1. *F. J. St. Germain, D
2. *R. O. Tiernan, D

SOUTH CAROLINA
1. *M. J. Davis, D
2. *F. Spence, R
3. *W. J. B. Dorn, D
4. *J. R. Mann, D
5. *T. S. Gettys, D
6. **E. L. Young, R

SOUTH DAKOTA
1. *F. E. Denholm, D
2. **J. Abdnor, R

TENNESSEE
1. *J. H. Quillen, R
2. *J. J. Duncan, R
3. *L. Baker, R
4. *J. L. Evins, D
5. *R. H. Fulton, D
6. **R. L. Beard, Jr., R
7. *E. Jones, D
8. *D. Kuykendall, R

TEXAS
1. *W. Patman, D
2. **C. Wilson, D
3. *J. M. Collins, R
4. *R. Roberts, D
5. **A. Steelman, R
6. *O. E. Teague, D
7. *B. Archer, R
8. *B. Eckhardt, D
9. *J. Brooks, D
10. *J. J. Pickle, D
11. *W. R. Poage, D
12. *J. Wright, D
13. *R. Price, R
14. *J. Young, D
15. *E. de la Garza, D
16. *R. C. White, D
17. *O. Burleson, D
18. **B. C. Jordan, D
19. *G. H. Mahon, D
20. *H. B. Gonzalez, D
21. *O. C. Fisher, D
22. *B. Casey, D
23. *A. Kazen, Jr., D
24. **D. Milford, D

UTAH
1. *K. G. McKay, D
2. **W. Owens, D

VERMONT
At-L. *R. W. Mallary, R

VIRGINIA
1. *T. N. Downing, D
2. *G. W. Whitehurst, R
3. *D. E. Satterfield III, D
4. **R. W. Daniel, Jr., R
5. *W. C. Daniel, D
6. **M. C. Butler, R
7. *J. K. Robinson, R
8. **S. E. Parris, R
9. *W. C. Wampler, R
10. *J. T. Broyhill, R

WASHINGTON
1. **J. Pritchard, R
2. *L. Meeds, D
3. *J. B. Hansen, D
4. *M. McCormack, D
5. *T. S. Foley, D
6. *F. V. Hicks, D
7. *B. Adams, D

WEST VIRGINIA
1. *R. H. Mollohan, D
2. *H. O. Staggers, D
3. *J. M. Slack, D
4. *K. Hechler, D

WISCONSIN
1. *L. Aspin, D
2. *R. W. Kastenmeier, D
3. *V. W. Thomson, R
4. *C. J. Zablocki, D
5. *H. S. Reuss, D
6. *W. A. Steiger, R
7. *D. R. Obey, D
8. **H. V. Froehlich, R
9. *G. R. Davis, D

WYOMING
At-L. *T. Roncalio, D

PUERTO RICO
Resident Commissioner
**Jamie Benitez

DISTRICT OF COLUMBIA
Delegate
*W. E. Fauntroy, D

---

[1] Ran as an independent.

(Continued from page 709)
secondary schools were authorized $19 billion in federal aid through fiscal year 1975, and another $2 billion in emergency help was promised to desegregating school districts. A 13-year program to clean up the nation's waterways, launched over a presidential veto, authorized $24.7 billion in federal help over the next three years. Social security benefits were raised 20% across the board, and additional improvements were made in benefits for specific categories of recipients. To finance the increases, contributions by employers and employees were raised to $632 on the first $10,800 in wages earned in 1973 and to $702 on the first $12,000 in 1974. (See also SOCIAL WELFARE.)

The Economy. Phase II of the administration's new economic policy, the system of wage and price controls established in late 1971, went through its first full year in 1972, and most economic analysts agreed that the program was at least a qualified success. The administration could muster abundant evidence to show that it had curbed the trend toward recession or runaway inflation. In the third quarter of the year the gross national product—the total output of goods and services—was growing at

FORMER PRESIDENT Harry S. Truman, who died December 26, lies in state in the Truman Library in Independence, Mo. (below). *His widow, Mrs. Bess Truman, receives the flag from the casket (left) as her daughter and son-in-law, Mr. and Mrs. Clifton Daniel, look on.*

UPI
WIDE WORLD

ARTHUR BREMER, who was convicted of shooting George Wallace and three others at a May 15 political rally in Laurel, Md. This picture was snapped at a Wallace rally in Wheaton, Md., held earlier the same day.

an annual rate of 6.3%, discounting the effects of inflation, compared with a growth rate of only 2.7% in 1971. Corporate profits were running at an annual rate of $53.7 billion, 6% above the record established in 1966. Personal income was growing at an annual rate of 8%, and in October the average worker's real income was up 4.5% from the previous year. That same month the number of persons employed totaled 82.5 million, an increase of 2.3 million over October 1971.

The Pay Board continued to maintain the 5.5% maximum guideline for most wage increases. Its policies were credited with helping to reduce the rise in the cost of living from over 4% before controls were instituted to about 3.5% after controls. But this figure was still above the 2% to 3% range, which was the goal the administration had set for itself. A major reason for this lack of success was the price of food, which farmers were able to sell free of controls. Food prices rose more than 4% during 1972 and in November climbed 5.4% above the levels of November 1971.

Unemployment dropped from over 6% in 1971 to an average rate of about 5.5% in 1972, but labor leaders and other critics argued that this was still too high. The Joint Economic Committee of Congress contended that unemployment should be reduced to 4% and complained that the administration was "unduly influenced by a fear of inflation and by a stubbornly held, but erroneous belief that the way to control inflation is to restrict the growth of output and employment." (See also ECONOMY OF THE U. S.; LABOR.)

Busing. The long legal struggle against segregated education ran into major opposition over the issue of busing. The issue was brought to a head not only by a series of court rulings ordering busing to eliminate segregation but also by the onset of the political campaign. One of the most controversial decisions, handed down in January, merged the predominately black public schools of Richmond,

Va., with the nearly all-white schools of two adjoining suburban counties. Implementation of the order would mean that many of the 104,000 pupils in the newly merged district would have to travel by bus to school. A chorus of protest arose, and it was swelled by concerned white parents in other cities where similar orders had been issued or were pending.

In the Florida Democratic primary held on March 14, 74% of the voters registered their support for an amendment to the U. S. Constitution that would prohibit busing and guarantee the right of a student to attend the school nearest his home. Two days later, in a televised address to the nation, President Nixon charged that some lower federal courts had overreached themselves in ordering busing, and were therefore responsible for creating "anger, fear, and turmoil in local communities." The next day the President proposed to Congress that it declare a moratorium on all new busing orders and establish national standards for desegregation, which would be achieved mainly by improvements of neighborhood schools rather than by busing.

Liberals charged that the President's proposals would mean losing much of the ground gained since the Supreme Court's 1954 ruling striking down segregation. Foes of busing claimed that only a constitutional amendment would put an end to it. Congress passed compromise legislation that not only sought to delay all new busing orders until appeals had been exhausted, or until 1974, but also restricted the use of federal funds to support busing. A stronger proposal, which would have banned all busing except to nearby schools and allowed reopening of previous court desegregation orders, was killed by a filibuster in the Senate. (See also EDUCATION.)

Dissent. With the reduced American involvement in the Indochina conflict, the tide of protest against the war receded. Nevertheless the aftermath of the peace movement and other dissent still occupied the courts. In April, the trial of the Rev. Philip Berrigan and six others on charges of conspiring to kidnap presidential aide Henry Kissinger ended in a hung jury. Berrigan was convicted only of smuggling letters out of the federal penitentiary where he was serving a sentence for draft board raids. The government decided not to retry Father Berrigan, and he was paroled shortly before Christmas.

Angela Davis, a black militant leader, who was charged with conspiracy, murder, and kidnaping in connection with a shootout in a California courthouse in 1970, was acquitted by an all-white jury on June 4, 1972. Tass, the Soviet news agency, hailed the verdict as "a victory for the progressive American and world community."

Five antiwar activists convicted of inciting a riot at the 1968 Chicago Democratic convention won a reversal in a federal appeals court on Nov. 21, 1972. The main reasons given for overturning the verdict against Abbie Hoffman, Jerry C. Rubin, Thomas E. Hayden, David T. Dellinger, and Rennard C. Davis were the "deprecatory and antagonistic" behavior of the presiding judge, Julius Hoffman, and the remarks of the government's chief prosecutor, Thomas A. Foran.

ROBERT SHOGAN
Washington Bureau
"Newsweek" Magazine

FOREIGN AFFAIRS

When Air Force One touched down in Peking on Feb. 21, 1972, President Richard M. Nixon became the first American president to visit China while in office. What was unclear after his visit was whether it constituted a postlude to the Cold War or a prelude to a new foreign policy outlook. Those who took the former view pointed to the continuing war in Vietnam, which smouldered during the year and finally flared up again in mid-December when peace negotiations reached a new impasse. Those who argued that the visit to China was a prelude to a new foreign policy could point to several developments: the signing of a Strategic Arms Limitation Talks (SALT) agreement with the Soviet Union, new contacts throughout Eastern Europe, the reduction of Soviet-American tensions in the Middle East, and the remarkable trade agreements signed with both the Soviet Union and the People's Republic of China. There were even signs, albeit highly tentative ones, that the frozen state of Cuban-American relations might be thawing a tiny bit.

Chinese-American Relations. Television coverage of the President's visit to China revealed to the world an amazing degree of cordiality between men who had only recently expressed a bitter dislike for one another's foreign policies and social systems. From atop the Great Wall of China, however, even the Cold War seemed to be an historical event rather than a permanent state of affairs.

The formal talks with Chinese leaders produced an agreement to proceed with the "normalization" of relations between the two powers, but there was no announcement of a resumption of formal diplomatic contacts through an exchange of ambassadors. Also, "the progressive development of trade between their two countries" was listed high on the agenda for future discussions.

In the talks, the Chinese leaders declared that the status of Taiwan, still held by Chiang Kai-shek as the last bastion of the Kuomintang Republic of China, was the "crucial question" in any listing of Sino-American problems. American spokesmen affirmed that their "ultimate objective" was a complete withdrawal of all U. S. forces and military installations from the island. Both parties agreed that the Taiwan issue should be settled between the mainland and nationalist Chinese without any outside interference.

A central purpose of his China policy, Nixon told Congress, was to encourage the People's Republic of China to "play its appropriate role in shaping international arrangements that affect its concerns. Only then will that great nation have a stake in such arrangements; only then will they endure."

The visit to China had several immediate advantages for the President's foreign policy goals. For example, he was now able to take greater advantage of the Sino-Soviet split.

Soviet-American Relations. Soviet concern about the apparent Sino-American understandings no doubt played a role in the successful conclusion of the initial SALT agreement in late May when President Nixon made a visit to Moscow, the first by an American president. The pact was signed in the Soviet capital by the President and Communist party

SIGNING the Seabed Arms Control Treaty in Washington, D. C., May 18, are (left to right) British Ambassador to the United States the earl of Cromer, U. S. Secretary of State Rogers, and Soviet Ambassador to the United States Dobrynin.

UPI

U.S.A.

leader Leonid I. Brezhnev. It allowed the Soviet Union a quantitative offensive edge in intercontinental ballistic missiles (ICBMs) and submarine-launched missiles. The pact also limited the defense of each nation to a total of two antiballistic missile (ABM) sites and 200 antiballistic missiles.

When President Nixon presented the two agreements to Congress, he received a loud ovation from the legislators. However, that did not prevent a few critics from pressing arguments against the SALT treaty as unwise and a bad precedent for the future. Administration spokesmen countered these objections by asserting that the limits established on the Soviet ABM systems ensured that this nation's qualitative offensive edge more than balanced the Soviet edge in the numbers of long-range missiles. Moreover, the administration welcomed congressional support for its plan to go ahead with the expansion of weapons systems not covered under the SALT agreement. (See also DISARMAMENT.)

It was difficult to argue in the wake of this successful negotiation that the President has been wrong in contending that the only way to obtain agreements was to continue to build situations of strength. On the other hand, the continued improvement in Soviet-American relations suggested that attitudes were more important than armaments.

The best example of changed attitudes came in the settlement of the USSR's old World War II Lend-Lease debt. Throughout the Cold War, American policy-makers had cited the Soviet Union's refusal to meet the U. S. request for a $1.3 billion payment (later reduced to $800 million) toward a $2.6 billion debt from nonwritten-off Lend-Lease aid as additional proof that Moscow ignored its legal and moral obligations to other nations. On Oct. 18, 1972, the administration accepted a Russian offer to pay $722 million, including interest, as a final settlement of the debt.

Along with this announcement came Secretary of Commerce Peter Peterson's explanation of the economic benefits of a new Soviet-American trade agreement. This new agreement provided for a tripling of current trade levels over a three-year period—from $0.5 billion in 1969–71 to $1.5 billion during 1973–75. This trade was in addition to the previously announced $1 billion worth of grain sales to the Soviets in 1973, which would make the USSR the second-largest importer of American grains.

"The goods that we are likely to export to the Soviet Union," said Peterson, "are products like machine tools, earthmoving equipment of various kinds, consumer goods, grain products, which are characterized by what the economists call high-labor intensive products. In plainer language, jobs."

U. S. Trade Policy. An interesting sidelight to Peterson's description of the new agreement was that it seemed to cover products and manufactures once considered "strategic" at the height of the Cold War. It also covered goods that America's competitors within the "Free World" had been willing to sell to the Communists. "The rest of the world," said White House adviser Pierre Rinfret, "has had a monopoly on trade with China and Russia for a little too long." "We have, in my judgment," concluded Rinfret, "dealt ourselves a new hand in world trade and done it with a trump card."

Prospects for increased trade with the People's Republic of China and with the Communist nations of Eastern Europe also seemed good. New U. S. consular offices were being opened in Eastern Europe, and China announced the purchase of 10 large passenger aircraft from the United States for a total of more than $150 million.

Cuban-American Relations. During most of 1972 there seemed to be no indication of a change for the better in diplomatic relations between the United States and Cuba. Then, in November, Havana announced that it was willing to discuss an agreement with Washington concerning the troublesome problems of aerial hijacking and the hijacking of Cuban ships. Cuban officials insisted that their interest pertained only to the need to find a way to deal with the specifics of those issues, but it was speculated that Premier Fidel Castro was testing the atmosphere for reestablishing diplomatic contacts with the United States. The State Department, meanwhile, said it welcomed the opportunity to talk over what had become more than a minor irritant for airlines officials and the public. At year-end, what might come out of these talks was a matter of conjecture.

Chilean-American Relations. U. S. relations with Chile, which has the other Marxist government in the Western Hemisphere, continued to worsen during 1972. In the fall, President Salvador Allende Gossens wound up a hemisphere tour with a denunciatory speech at the United Nations in which he declared that U. S.-controlled companies in Chile "had driven their tentacles deep into my country, and even proposed to manage our political life." He said that was why his government had expropriated their properties and assets. George Bush, the U. S. representative to the UN, replied that "there is nothing in our system designed to exploit anyone."

Indochina War. After a North Vietnamese offensive beginning March 31 had threatened to divide South Vietnam in two along a line south of Hue, President Nixon responded on May 8 by ordering new bombing raids on the Hanoi area as well as the mining of Haiphong harbor and other North Vietnamese ports. American military leaders had wanted to take these steps, especially the mine blockade of North Vietnam's only major port, since at least 1967. It had always been rejected by civilian policy-makers as too risky because such a move might drive the Chinese and Russians together and thus lead to a much wider and longer war.

Nixon gambled that he could get away with the mining of Haiphong harbor, and won. His estimate of the Chinese reaction was more accurate than that of his critics, who had predicted that the military escalation would endanger the new China policy and ruin chances for the SALT agreement. The President's aides had argued that he could never sign an arms agreement if North Vietnamese forces were swarming into Hue at the very moment. The Soviet response to the mine blockade was far milder than what many had expected. Possibly the Sino-American talks were the reason, but whatever it was, the Soviet leadership behaved as if nothing unusual had happened in Vietnam when President Nixon arrived in Moscow on May 21.

The North Vietnamese offensive continued into the summer and then stalled around Quangtri City north of Hue. Quangtri fell but was later retaken after a lengthy seige by Saigon's ground units aided by American air power. Meanwhile, the United States continued to withdraw its own ground forces. By year-end there were less than 25,000 American soldiers remaining in Vietnam, the lowest number since 1965 when the big buildup began.

CELEBRATING the arms limitation pact with the USSR, President Nixon clinks glasses with foreign affairs adviser Henry Kissinger in Moscow, May 26. Secretary Rogers and party chairman Brezhnev smile approval.

On the diplomatic front nothing moved until mid-October, when, just before the American presidential election, the North Vietnamese presented a new proposal. As a result, Henry Kissinger, President Nixon's adviser on national security, rushed off to Paris to meet with Hanoi's special negotiator, Le Duc Tho. The essence of the North Vietnamese offer was that Hanoi no longer insisted on a simultaneous military and political settlement. The North Vietnamese also gave full assurances in this new document that American prisoners of war would be returned as American military forces were being withdrawn.

When the North Vietnamese then announced these terms to the world, Kissinger held his own press conference on October 26 and stated that "peace is at hand." According to Kissinger, there remained only a few minor details to be worked out in one or two more negotiating sessions.

It soon became apparent that these details involved central issues that had been in dispute since the beginning of the war. According to the terms of the proposal, for example, North Vietnamese troops, more than 100,000 of them, would be permitted to remain in place after a military cease-fire throughout South Vietnam.

If previous experience was a reliable guide, the military force that controlled a region in Vietnam also controlled the outcome of elections. On this basis, a new election would mean that President Nguyen Van Thieu would be defeated at least in areas controlled by North Vietnam and the Vietcong. By mid-December the renewed talks in Paris had bogged down on that issue. Kissinger told a press conference that the sticking point was the size and duties of an international truce commission, but he admitted that the matter of Saigon's "sovereignty"

in areas where North Vietnamese forces were located had not been settled satisfactorily.

On December 16, Kissinger reported to the nation that the United States and North Vietnam had not yet reached "a just and fair agreement." Two days later, Secretary of Defense Melvin Laird announced that restrictions on bombing above the 20th Parallel, which had been in force since the October 21–22 weekend, had been removed.

The long-awaited announcement that an agreement had been reached to end the war came on Jan. 23, 1973. The accord was formally signed by the four parties in the conflict, in Paris on January 27, and a cease-fire went into effect the same day.

(See also INDOCHINA WAR.)

LLOYD C. GARDNER
Rutgers University

UNIVERSITIES AND COLLEGES

A selected list of accredited junior colleges, senior colleges, and universities in the United States and Canada appears on the following pages.

The information given for each school comprises the following data: its degree-granting status (if it is a senior college or university); the composition of its student body (by sex); the legal controlling agency; and the total enrollment of students of college grade as reported by the registrar (U. S. figures are for 1971–72; Canadian figures are for 1970–71).

All the U. S. institutions listed are recognized by *Accredited Institutions of Higher Education*, published by the American Council on Education. The Canadian institutions listed are accredited by the provinces in which they are located.

See also EDUCATION.

MAJOR UNIVERSITIES AND COLLEGES, U.S. AND CANADA

Note: Symbols and abbreviations that follow the name of each school listed are as follows: *Level of Instruction*— (1) 2-year junior college; (2) senior college granting bachelor's and/or first professional degree; (3) senior college granting master's and/or second professional degree; (4) college or university offering a doctoral program. *Student Body*—(M) men only; (W) women only; (Coed) coeducational; (Coord) separate colleges for men and women. *Control*—(Public) district, municipal, state, or federal; (Private) proprietary, corporation, or church. *Enrollment*—For the United States, all students of college grade for the academic year 1971–72 excepting correspondence course students. Canadian figures are for 1970–71.

Name and Location	Level of Instruction	Student Body	Control	Enrollment
Abilene Christian College, Abilene, Texas	3	Coed	Pvt-Church of Christ	3,290
Abraham Baldwin Agricultural College, Tifton, Ga.	1	Coed	Public	2,153
Acadia University, Wolfville, Nova Scotia	3	Coed	Pvt-Baptist	2,350
Adams State College, Alamosa, Colo.	3	Coed	Public	2,936
Adelphi University, Garden City, N.Y.	4	Coed	Private	7,858
Adirondack Community College, Glens Falls, N.Y.	1	Coed	Public	1,412
Adrian College, Adrian, Mich.	2	Coed	Pvt-Methodist	1,447
Aeronautics, Academy of, Flushing, N.Y.	1	Coed	Private	1,205
Akron, University of, Akron, Ohio	4	Coed	Public	19,674
Alabama, University of, in Birmingham, Ala.	4	Coed	Public	7,439
Alabama, University of, in Huntsville, Ala.	3	Coed	Public	2,603
Alabama, University of, in Tuscaloosa, Ala.	4	Coed	Public	13,564
Alabama Agricultural and Mechanical College, Normal, Ala.	3	Coed	Public	2,129
Alabama State University, Montgomery, Ala.	3	Coed	Public	2,704
Alaska, University of, College, Alaska (incl. community colleges at Anchorage, Juneau, Kenai, Ketchikan, Kodiak, Palmer, Sitka)	4	Coed	Public	2,958
Alaska Methodist University, Anchorage, Alaska	3	Coed	Pvt-Methodist	814
Albany Junior College, Albany, Ga.	1	Coed	Public	1,410
Albany State College, Albany, Ga.	2	Coed	Public	1,926
Albemarle, College of the, Elizabeth City, N.C.	1	Coed	Public	946
Alberta, University of, Edmonton, Alberta	4	Coed	Public	18,742
Albion College, Albion, Mich.	2	Coed	Pvt-Methodist	1,782
Albright College, Reading, Pa.	2	Coed	Pvt-Methodist	1,593
Albuquerque, University of, Albuquerque, N. Mex.	2	Coed	Pvt-Roman Catholic	2,919
Alcorn Agricultural & Mechanical College, Lorman, Miss.	2	Coed	Public	2,677
Alderson-Broaddus College, Philippi, W.Va.	2	Coed	Pvt-Baptist	1,067
Alexander City State Junior College, Alexander City, Ala.	1	Coed	Public	1,134
Alfred University, Alfred, N.Y.	4	Coed	Private	2,364
Allan Hancock College, Santa Maria, Calif.	1	Coed	Public	6,568
Allegany Community College, Cumberland, Md.	1	Coed	Public	1,226
Allegheny College, Meadville, Pa.	2	Coed	Pvt-Methodist	1,792
Alma College, Alma, Mich.	2	Coed	Pvt-Presbyterian	1,328
Alpena Community College, Alpena, Mich.	1	Coed	Public	1,044
Alverno College, Milwaukee, Wis.	2	Coed	Pvt-Roman Catholic	1,101
Alvin Junior College, Alvin, Texas	1	Coed	Public	1,802
Amarillo College, Amarillo, Texas	1	Coed	Public	3,472
American International College, Springfield, Mass.	3	Coed	Private	2,761
American River College, Sacramento, Calif.	1	Coed	Public	14,710
American University, Washington, D.C.	4	Coed	Private	14,508
Amherst College, Amherst, Mass.	2	Coed	Private	1,227
Anchorage Community College, Anchorage, Alaska	1	Coed	Public	4,546
Anderson College, Anderson, Ind.	2	Coed	Pvt-Church of God	1,754
Anderson College, Anderson, S.C.	1	Coed	Pvt-Baptist	952
Andrews University, Berrien Springs, Mich.	4	Coed	Pvt-Seventh-day Adventist	2,142
Angelina College, Lufkin, Texas	1	Coed	Public	1,018
Angelo State College, San Angelo, Texas	3	Coed	Public	3,892
Anne Arundel Community College, Arnold, Md.	1	Coed	Public	3,784
Antelope Valley College, Lancaster, Calif.	1	Coed	Public	3,973
Antioch College, Yellow Springs, Ohio	3	Coed	Private	2,275
Appalachian State University, Boone, N.C.	3	Coed	Public	8,229
Aquinas College, Grand Rapids, Mich.	3	Coed	Pvt-Roman Catholic	1,422
Arapahoe Community College, Littleton, Colo.	1	Coed	Public	2,366
Arizona, University of, Tucson, Ariz.	4	Coed	Public	26,910
Arizona State University, Tempe, Ariz.	4	Coed	Public	30,319
Arizona Western College, Yuma, Ariz.	1	Coed	Public	3,014
Arkansas, State College of, Conway, Ark.	4	Coed	Public	4,499
Arkansas, University of, Fayetteville, Ark.	4	Coed	Public	12,131
Arkansas Polytechnic College, Russellville, Ark.	2	Coed	Public	2,656
Arkansas State University, State University, Ark.	3	Coed	Public	2,525
Armstrong State College, Savannah, Ga.	3	Coed	Public	7,092
Art Center College of Design, Los Angeles, Calif.	3	Coed	Private	2,712
Art Institute of Chicago, Schools of the, Chicago, Ill.	3	Coed	Private	1,062
Asbury College, Wilmore, Ky.	2	Coed	Private	1,464
Asheville-Buncombe Technical Institute, Asheville, N.C.	1	Coed	Private	1,091
Ashland College, Ashland, Ohio	3	Coed	Pvt-Brethren	1,187
Assumption College, Worcester, Mass.	3	Coed	Pvt-Roman Catholic	2,686
Athens College, Athens, Ala.	2	Coed	Pvt-Methodist	1,054
Atlanta University, Atlanta, Ga.	4	Coed	Private	906
Atlantic Christian College, Wilson, N.C.	2	Coed	Pvt-Disciples of Christ	1,048
Atlantic Community College, Mays Landing, N.J.	1	Coed	Public	1,794
Auburn Community College, Auburn, N.Y.	1	Coed	Public	2,771
Auburn University, Auburn, Ala.	4	Coed	Public	3,031
Auburn University at Montgomery, Ala.	3	Coed	Public	16,046
Augsburg College, Minneapolis, Minn.	2	Coed	Pvt-Lutheran	992
Augustana College, Rock Island, Ill.	2	Coed	Pvt-Lutheran	1,616
Augustana College, Sioux Falls, S.Dak.	3	Coed	Pvt-Lutheran	2,973
Aurora College, Aurora, Ill.	3	Coed	Pvt-Advent Christian	2,261
Austin College, Sherman, Texas	3	Coed	Pvt-Presbyterian	2,078
Austin Peay State University, Clarksville, Tenn.	3	Coed	Public	1,094
Austin State Junior College, Austin, Minn.	1	Coed	Public	1,145
Averett College, Danville, Va.	2	Coed	Pvt-Baptist	3,822
Avila College, Kansas City, Mo.	2	Coed	Pvt-Roman Catholic	1,058
Azusa Pacific College, Azusa, Calif.	3	Coed	Private	816
Babson College, Babson Park, Mass.	3	Coed	Private	754
Baker University, Baldwin City, Kans.	2	Coed	Pvt-Methodist	1,039
Bakersfield College, Bakersfield, Calif.	1	Coed	Public	1,599
Baldwin-Wallace College, Berea, Ohio	2	Coed	Pvt-Methodist	868
Ball State University, Muncie, Ind.	4	Coed	Public	11,277
Baltimore, University of, Baltimore, Md.	2	Coed	Private	2,982
Bank Street College of Education, New York, N.Y.	3	Coed	Private	19,403
Baptist College at Charleston, S.C.	2	Coed	Pvt-Baptist	4,855
Bard College, Annandale-on-Hudson, N.Y.	2	Coed	Private	926
Barry College, Miami, Fla.	3	Coed	Pvt-Roman Catholic	1,839
Barstow College, Barstow, Calif.	1	Coed	Public	772
Bates College, Lewiston, Me.	2	Coed	Private	1,248
Baylor University, Waco, Texas	4	Coed	Pvt-Baptist	1,202
Beaver College, Glenside, Pa.	2	W	Pvt-Presbyterian	1,237
Bee County College, Beeville, Texas	1	Coed	Public	7,051

Name and Location	Level of Instruction	Student Body	Control	Enrollment
Bellarmine-Ursuline College, Louisville, Ky.	2	Coed	Pvt-Roman Catholic	1,655
Belleville Area College, Belleville, Ill.	1	Coed	Public	4,913
Bellevue Community College, Bellevue, Wash.	1	Coed	Public	3,563
Belmont College, Nashville, Tenn.	2	Coed	Pvt-Baptist	882
Beloit College, Beloit, Wis.	3	Coed	Private	1,783
Bemidji State College, Bemidji, Minn.	3	Coed	Public	4,839
Benedict College, Columbia, S.C.	2	Coed	Pvt-Baptist	1,405
Benedictine College, The, Atchison, Kans.	2	Coed	Pvt-Roman Catholic	1,288
Bentley College, Waltham, Mass.	2	Coed	Private	3,437
Berea College, Berea, Ky.	2	Coed	Private	1,448
Bergen Community College, Paramus, N.J.	1	Coed	Public	4,470
Berkeley-Charleston-Dorchester Technical Education Center, North Charleston, S.C.	1	Coed	Public	2,290
Berkshire Community College, Pittsfield, Mass.	1	Coed	Public	1,262
Berry College, Mount Berry, Ga.	2	Coed	Private	973
Bethany College, Bethany, W.Va.	2	Coed	Pvt-Disciples of Christ	1,138
Bethany Nazarene College, Bethany, Okla.	3	Coed	Pvt-Nazarene	1,044
Bethel College, St. Paul, Minn.	2	Coed	Pvt-Baptist	1,219
Bethune-Cookman College, Daytona Beach, Fla.	2	Coed	Pvt-Methodist	798
Big Bend Community College, Moses Lake, Wash.	1	Coed	Public	1,628
Biola College, La Mirada, Calif.	3	Coed	Private	1,031
Birmingham-Southern College, Birmingham, Ala.	3	Coed	Pvt-Methodist	1,561
Bishop College, Dallas, Texas.	2	Coed	Pvt-Baptist	1,159
Bishop's University, Lennoxville, Quebec.	3	Coed	Pvt-Anglican	1,632
Bismarck Junior College, Bismarck, N.Dak.	1	Coed	Public	
Black Hawk College, Moline, Ill.	1	Coed	Public	3,685
Black Hills State College, Spearfish, S.Dak.	3	Coed	Public	3,969
Blinn College, Brenham, Texas.	1	Coed	Public	1,661
Bloomfield College, Bloomfield, N.J.	3	Coed	Pvt-Presbyterian	1,698
Bloomsburg State College, Bloomsburg, Pa.	3	Coed	Public	4,949
Blue Mountain Community College, Pendleton, Oreg.	1	Coed	Public	1,099
Blue Ridge Community College, Weyers Cave, Va.	1	Coed	Public	1,263
Bluefield State College, Bluefield, W.Va.	2	Coed	Public	1,316
Boise State College, Boise, Idaho.	2	Coed	Public	8,300
Boston College, Chestnut Hill, Mass.	4	Coed	Pvt-Roman Catholic	11,111
Boston State College, Boston, Mass.	3	Coed	Public	8,290
Boston University, Boston, Mass.	4	Coed	Private	24,568
Bowdoin College, Brunswick, Me.	3	Coed	Private	1,034
Bowie State College, Bowie, Md.	3	Coed	Public	2,353
Bowling Green State University, Bowling Green, Ohio.	4	Coed	Public	18,874
Bradley University, Peoria, Ill.	3	Coed	Private	5,703
Brandeis University, Waltham, Mass.	4	Coed	Private	2,247
Brandon University, Brandon, Manitoba.	3	Coed	Public	1,150
Brandywine College, Wilmington, Del.	1	Coed	Private	1,709
Brazosport College, Lake Jackson, Texas.	1	Coed	Public	1,601
Brescia College, Owensboro, Ky.	2	Coed	Pvt-Roman Catholic	957
Brevard Community College, Cocoa, Fla.	1	Coed	Public	6,625
Briar Cliff College, Sioux City, Iowa.	2	Coed	Pvt-Roman Catholic	1,096
Bridgeport, University of, Bridgeport, Conn.	3	Coed	Private	8,318
Bridgewater College, Bridgewater, Va.	2	Coed	Pvt-Brethren	876
Bridgewater State College, Bridgewater, Mass.	3	Coed	Public	6,792
Brigham Young University, Provo, Utah.	4	Coed	Pvt-Latter-day Saints	26,616
Bristol Community College, Fall River, Mass.	1	Coed	Public	1,524
British Columbia, University of, Vancouver, B.C.	4	Coed	Public	20,157
Brock University, St. Catharines, Ontario.	3	Coed	Public	2,163
Brookdale Community College, Lincroft, N.J.	1	Coed	Public	5,426
Brooklyn, Polytechnic Institute of, Brooklyn, N.Y.	4	Coed	Private	3,852
Brooks Institute, Santa Barbara, Calif.	2	Coed	Private	733
Broome Community College, Binghamton, N.Y.	1	Coed	Public	4,384
Broward Community College, Fort Lauderdale, Fla.	1	Coed	Public	7,923
Brown University, Providence, R.I.	4	Coed	Private	6,206
Brunswick College, Brunswick, Ga.	1	Coed	Public	1,013
Bryant College, Providence, R.I.	3	Coed	Private	3,767
Bryn Mawr College, Bryn Mawr, Pa.	4	Coed	Private	1,421
Bucknell University, Lewisburg, Pa.	3	Coed	Private	2,962
Bucks County Community College, Newtown, Pa.	1	Coed	Public	5,145
Buena Vista College, Storm Lake, Iowa.	2	Coed	Pvt-Presbyterian	884
Burlington County College, Pemberton, N.J.	1	Coed	Public	2,477
Butler County Community College, Butler, Pa.	1	Coed	Public	1,030
Butler County Community Junior College, El Dorado, Kans.	1	Coed	Public	1,724
Butler University, Indianapolis, Ind.	3	Coed	Private	4,363
Cabrillo College, Aptos, Calif.	1	Coed	Public	6,118
Caldwell College, Caldwell, N.J.	2	Coed	Pvt-Roman Catholic	829
Caldwell Community College & Technical Institute, Lenoir, N.C.	1	Coed	Public	817
Calgary, University of, Calgary, Alberta.	4	Coed	Public	9,256
California, University of:			Public	108,440
Berkeley.	4	Coed	Public	27,712
Davis.	4	Coed	Public	13,981
Irvine (includes California College of Medicine, Los Angeles).	4	Coed	Public	6,523
Los Angeles.	4	Coed	Public	27,891
Riverside.	4	Coed	Public	6,168
San Diego.	4	Coed	Public	6,178
Santa Barbara.	4	Coed	Public	12,916
Santa Cruz.	4	Coed	Public	4,396
California College of Arts & Crafts, Oakland, Calif.	3	Coed	Private	1,529
California Institute of Technology, Pasadena, Calif.	4	Coed	Private	1,504
California Institute of the Arts, Burbank, Calif.	3	Coed	Private	818
California Lutheran College, Thousand Oaks, Calif.	3	Coed	Pvt-Lutheran	1,286
California Polytechnic State University, San Luis Obispo, Calif.	3	Coed	Public	12,343
California State College, California, Pa.	3	Coed	Public	2,703
California State College, Bakersfield, Calif.	3	Coed	Public	2,599
California State College, Dominguez Hills, Calif.	3	Coed	Public	3,628
California State College, San Bernardino, Calif.	3	Coed	Public	3,656
California State College, Sonoma, Calif.	3	Coed	Public	6,971
California State College, Stanislaus, Calif.	3	Coed	Public	4,036
California State Polytechnic College, Pomona, Calif.	3	Coed	Public	10,368
California State University, Chico, Calif.	4	Coed	Public	12,935
California State University, Fresno, Calif.	4	Coed	Public	18,573
California State University, Fullerton, Calif.	4	Coed	Public	16,100
California State University, Hayward, Calif.	3	Coed	Public	15,750
California State University, Humboldt, Calif.	3	Coed	Public	6,360
California State University, Long Beach, Calif.	4	Coed	Public	28,667
California State University, Los Angeles, Calif.	4	Coed	Public	25,134
California State University, Northridge, Calif.	4	Coed	Public	25,918
California State University, Sacramento, Calif.	4	Coed	Public	20,045
California State University, San Diego, Calif.	4	Coed	Public	32,493
California State University, San Francisco, Calif.	4	Coed	Public	22,450
California State University, San Jose, Calif.	4	Coed	Public	30,608
Calvin College, Grand Rapids, Mich.	3	Coed	Pvt-Christian Reformed	3,306
Camden County College, Blackwood, N.J.	1	Coed	Public	4,240
Campbell College, Buies Creek, N.C.	2	Coed	Pvt-Baptist	2,401
Campbellsville College, Campbellsville, Ky.	2	Coed	Pvt-Baptist	856
Cañada College, Redwood City, Calif.	1	Coed	Public	6,211
Canal Zone College, Balboa, C.Z.	1	Coed	Public	1,310
Canisius College, Buffalo, N.Y.	3	Coed	Pvt-Roman Catholic	4,162
Canyons, College of the, Valencia, Calif.	1	Coed	Public	1,586
Cape Cod Community College, West Barnstable, Mass.	1	Coed	Public	2,506
Capital University, Columbus, Ohio.	3	Coed	Pvt-Lutheran	2,276
Cardinal Stritch College, Milwaukee, Wis.	2	Coed	Pvt-Roman Catholic	869
Carleton College, Northfield, Minn.	3	Coed	Private	1,600
Carleton University, Ottawa, Ontario.	4	Coed	Public	8,270
Carlow College, Pittsburgh, Pa.	2	Coed	Pvt-Roman Catholic	1,045
Carnegie-Mellon University, Pittsburgh, Pa.	4	Coed	Private	4,340
Carroll College, Helena, Mont.	2	Coed	Pvt-Roman Catholic	1,079
Carroll College, Waukesha, Wis.	2	Coed	Pvt-Presbyterian	1,259

Name and Location	Level of Instruction	Student Body	Control	Enrollment
Carson-Newman College, Jefferson City, Tenn	2	Coed	Pvt-Baptist	1,726
Carthage College, Kenosha, Wis	2	Coed	Pvt-Lutheran	1,807
Case Western Reserve University, Cleveland, Ohio	4	Coed	Private	9,172
Casper College, Casper, Wyo	1	Coed	Public	3,001
Castleton State College, Castleton, Vt	2	Coed	Public	1,534
Catawba College, Salisbury, N.C	2	Coed	Pvt-United Church of Christ	1,133
Catawba Valley Technical Institute, Hickory, N.C	1	Coed	Public	1,078
Catholic University of America, Washington, D.C	4	Coed	Pvt-Roman Catholic	6,486
Catholic University of Puerto Rico, Ponce, P.R	4	Coed	Pvt-Roman Catholic	6,697
Catonsville Community College, Catonsville, Md	1	Coed	Public	6,122
Cedar Crest College, Allentown, Pa	2	W	Pvt-Church of Christ	773
Centenary College, Shreveport, La	2	Coed	Pvt-Methodist	924
Central College, Pella, Iowa	2	Coed	Pvt-Episcopal	1,253
Central Connecticut State College, New Britain, Conn	3	Coed	Public	12,318
Central Florida Community College, Ocala, Fla	1	Coed	Public	1,444
Central Methodist College, Fayette, Mo	2	Coed	Pvt-Methodist	806
Central Michigan University, Mt. Pleasant, Mich	3	Coed	Public	16,931
Central Missouri State College, Warrensburg, Mo	3	Coed	Public	12,957
Central Oregon Community College, Bend, Oreg	1	Coed	Public	1,600
Central Piedmont Community College, Charlotte, N.C	1	Coed	Public	13,514
Central State University, Wilberforce, Ohio	2	Coed	Public	2,421
Central State University, Edmond, Okla	4	Coed	Public	10,678
Central Texas College, Killeen, Texas	1	Coed	Public	4,011
Central Virginia Community College, Lynchburg, Va	1	Coed	Public	1,671
Central Washington State College, Ellensburg, Wash	3	Coed	Public	7,425
Central Y.M.C.A. Community College, Chicago, Ill	1	Coed	Private	4,288
Centralia College, Centralia, Wash	1	Coed	Public	2,449
Cerritos College, Norwalk, Calif	1	Coed	Public	17,117
Chabot College, Hayward, Calif	1	Coed	Public	13,280
Chadron State College, Chadron, Nebr	3	Coed	Public	2,428
Chaffey College, Alta Loma, Calif	1	Coed	Public	7,865
Chaminade College of Honolulu, Hawaii	2	Coed	Pvt-Roman Catholic	1,574
Chapman College, Orange, Calif	2	Coed	Private	4,935
Charles County Community College, La Plata, Md	1	Coed	Public	1,188
Charleston, College of, Charleston, S.C	2	Coed	Pvt-Disciples of Christ	878
Chattanooga State Technical Institute, Chattanooga, Tenn	1	Coed	Public	1,204
Chesapeake College, Wye Mills, Md	1	Coed	Public	781
Chestnut Hill College, Philadelphia, Pa	2	W	Pvt-Roman Catholic	1,118
Cheyney State College, Cheyney, Pa	2	Coed	Public	2,162
Chicago, City Colleges of, Chicago, Ill.:			Public	39,472
Kennedy-King College, Chicago	1	Coed	Public	4,803
Loop College, Chicago	1	Coed	Public	10,142
Malcolm X College, Chicago	1	Coed	Public	8,150
Mayfair College, Chicago	1	Coed	Public	3,752
Olive-Harvey College, Chicago	1	Coed	Public	5,172
Southwest College, Chicago	1	Coed	Public	5,359
Wright College, Chicago	1	Coed	Public	8,165
Chicago, University of, Chicago, Ill	4	Coed	Private	8,497
Chicago State University, Chicago, Ill	3	Coed	Public	5,806
Chipola Junior College, Marianna, Fla	1	Coed	Public	1,267
Chowan College, Murfreesboro, N.C	2	Coed	Pvt-Baptist	1,545
Christian Brothers College, Memphis, Tenn	2	Coed	Pvt-Roman Catholic	864
Christopher Newport College, Newport News, Va	2	Coed	Public	1,768
Cincinnati, University of, Cincinnati, Ohio	4	Coed	Public	34,552
Raymond Walters General & Technical College, Cincinnati	1	Coed	Public	1,891
Cisco Junior College, Cisco, Texas	1	Coed	Public	951
Citadel, The, Charleston, S.C	3	Coed	Public	2,768
Citrus College, Azusa, Calif	1	Coed	Public	7,859
Clackamas Community College, Oregon City, Oreg	1	Coed	Public	3,562
Claflin College, Orangeburg, S.C	2	Coed	Pvt-Methodist	795
Claremont Graduate School, Claremont, Calif	4	Coed	Private	1,212
Claremont Men's College, Claremont, Calif	2	M	Private	804
Claremore Junior College, Claremore, Okla	1	Coed	Public	950
Clarion State College, Clarion, Pa	3	Coed	Public	4,371
Clark College, Atlanta, Ga	2	Coed	Pvt-Methodist	1,182
Clark College, Vancouver, Wash	1	Coed	Public	4,095
Clark University, Worcester, Mass	4	Coed	Private	3,228
Clarke College, Dubuque, Iowa	3	W	Pvt-Roman Catholic	733
Clarkson College of Technology, Potsdam, N.Y	4	Coed	Private	2,608
Clatsop Community College, Astoria, Oreg	1	Coed	Public	1,622
Clayton Junior College, Morrow, Ga	1	Coed	Public	2,250
Clemson University, Clemson, S.C	4	Coed	Public	2,190
Cleveland State Community College, Cleveland, Tenn	1	Coed	Public	15,201
Cleveland State University, Cleveland, Ohio	3	Coed	Public	2,158
Cochise College, Douglas, Ariz	1	Coed	Public	1,164
Coe College, Cedar Rapids, Iowa	2	Coed	Pvt-Presbyterian	802
Coffeyville Community Junior College, Coffeyville, Kans	1	Coed	Public	1,572
Colby College, Waterville, Me	3	Coed	Private	935
Colby Community College, Colby, Kans	1	Coed	Public	2,329
Colgate University, Hamilton, N.Y	3	Coed	Private	2,312
Colorado, University of, Boulder, Colo	4	Coed	Public	31,712
Colorado Springs		Coed	Public	2,312
Denver		Coed	Public	6,987
Colorado College, Colorado Springs, Colo	3	Coed	Private	1,820
Colorado School of Mines, Golden, Colo	4	Coed	Public	1,699
Colorado State University, Fort Collins, Colo	4	Coed	Public	17,608
Columbia Basin College, Pasco, Wash	1	Coed	Public	3,680
Columbia College, Columbia, Mo	2	Coed	Pvt-Disciples of Christ	756
Columbia College, Columbia, S.C	2	Coed	Pvt-Methodist	892
Columbia Junior College, Columbia, Calif	1	Coed	Public	1,953
Columbia State Community College, Columbia, Tenn	1	Coed	Public	1,526
Columbia Union College, Takoma Park, Md	2	Coed	Pvt-Seventh-day Adventist	1,003
Columbia University, New York, N.Y	4	Coed	Private	15,124
Barnard College, New York	2	Coed	Private	1,930
Teachers College, New York	4	Coed	Private	5,280
Columbus College, Columbus, Ga	2	Coed	Public	3,814
Community College of Allegheny County, Pittsburgh, Pa.:				
Allegheny Campus	1	Coed	Public	3,651
Boyce Campus	1	Coed	Public	3,351
Community College of Baltimore, Md	1	Coed	Public	7,156
Community College of Beaver County, Monaca, Pa	1	Coed	Public	1,400
Community College of Philadelphia, Pa	1	Coed	Public	5,830
Compton College, Compton, Calif	1	Coed	Public	6,715
Concord College, Athens, W. Va	2	Coed	Public	2,019
Concordia College, Moorhead, Minn	2	Coed	Pvt-Lutheran	2,402
Concordia Teachers College, River Forest, Ill	3	Coed	Pvt-Lutheran	1,666
Concordia Teachers College, Seward, Nebr	2	Coed	Pvt-Lutheran	1,737
Connecticut, University of, Storrs, Conn	4	Coed	Public	21,253
Connecticut College, New London, Conn	3	Coed	Private	1,767
Connors State College, Warner, Okla	1	Coed	Public	919
Contra Costa College, San Pablo, Calif	1	Coed	Public	7,378
Converse College, Spartanburg, S.C	3	Coed	Private	871
Cooke County Junior College, Gainesville, Texas	1	Coed	Public	1,916
Cooper Union, New York, N.Y	4	Coed	Private	1,011
Copiah-Lincoln Junior College, Wesson, Miss	1	Coed	Public	969
Coppin State College, Baltimore, Md	2	Coed	Public	2,488
Cornell College, Mount Vernon, Iowa	2	Coed	Pvt-Methodist	988
Cornell University, Ithaca, N.Y	4	Coed	Private	16,144
Corning Community College, Corning, N.Y	1	Coed	Public	2,777
Cosumnes River College, Sacramento, Calif	1	Coed	Public	2,146
Creighton University, Omaha, Nebr	4	Coed	Pvt-Roman Catholic	4,271
Cuesta College, San Luis Obispo, Calif	1	Coed	Public	1,807
Cumberland College, Williamsburg, Ky	2	Coed	Pvt-Baptist	1,517
Cumberland County College, Vineland, N.J	1	Coed	Public	931
Curry College, Milton, Mass	2	Coed	Private	
Cuyahoga Community College–Metropolitan Campus, Cleveland, Ohio	1	Coed	Public	10,719

Name and Location	Level of Instruction	Student Body	Control	Enrollment
Cuyahoga Community College—Western Campus, Parma, Ohio	1	Coed	Public	6,356
Cypress College, Cypress, Calif.	1	Coed	Public	7,791
Dakota State College, Madison, S.Dak.	2	Coed	Public	1,208
Dalhousie University, Halifax, Nova Scotia	4	Coed	Private	5,545
Dallas, University of, Dallas, Texas	4	Coed	Pvt-Roman Catholic	1,403
Dallas Baptist College, Dallas, Texas	4	Coed	Pvt-Baptist	1,451
Dalton Junior College, Dalton, Ga.	1	Coed	Public	1,089
Dana College, Blair, Nebr.	2	Coed	Pvt-Lutheran	848
Danville Community College, Danville, Va.	1	Coed	Public	1,835
Danville Junior College, Danville, Ill.	4	Coed	Public	1,874
Dartmouth College, Hanover, N.H.	2	Coed	Private	3,279
David Lipscomb College, Nashville, Tenn.	2	M	Pvt-Church of Christ	2,196
Davidson College, Davidson, N.C.	1	Coed	Pvt-Presbyterian	1,089
Davidson County Community College, Lexington, N.C.	1	Coed	Public	1,340
Davis and Elkins College, Elkins, W.Va.	4	Coed	Pvt-Presbyterian	815
Dayton, University of, Dayton, Ohio	4	Coed	Pvt-Roman Catholic	8,713
Daytona Beach Community College, Daytona Beach, Fla.	2	Coed	Public	2,708
Dean Junior College, Franklin, Mass.	1	Coed	Private	1,037
De Anza College, Cupertino, Calif.	2	Coed	Public	6,050
Defiance College, Defiance, Ohio	1	Coed	Pvt-Church of Christ	1,036
DeKalb College, Clarkston, Ga.	4	Coed	Public	6,645
Del Mar College, Corpus Christi, Texas	1	Coed	Public	5,862
Delaware, University of, Newark, Del.	4	Coed	Public	16,784
Delaware County Community College, Media, Pa.	1	Coed	Public	800
Delaware State College, Dover, Del.	2	Coed	Public	2,606
Delaware Technical and Community College, Northern Branch, Wilmington, Del.	1	Coed	Public	2,867
Southern Branch, Georgetown, Del.	1	Coed	Public	1,921
Delaware Valley College of Science & Agriculture, Doylestown, Pa.	2	Coed	Private	1,278
Delgado Vocational-Technical Junior College, New Orleans, La.	1	Coed	Public	4,724
Delta College, University Center, Mich.	1	Coed	Public	6,401
Delta State College, Cleveland, Miss.	3	Coed	Public	3,211
Denison University, Granville, Ohio	2	Coed	Pvt-Baptist	2,132
Denver, University of, Denver, Colo.	4	Coed	Pvt-Methodist	9,404
DePaul University, Chicago, Ill.	4	Coed	Pvt-Roman Catholic	9,119
DePauw University, Greencastle, Ind.	3	Coed	Pvt-Methodist	2,274
Desert, College of the, Palm Desert, Calif.	1	Coed	Public	5,559
Detroit, University of, Detroit, Mich.	4	Coed	Pvt-Roman Catholic	9,597
Detroit Institute of Technology, Detroit, Mich.	2	Coed	Private	1,086
Diablo Valley College, Pleasant Hill, Calif.	1	Coed	Public	14,057
Dickinson College, Carlisle, Pa.	2	Coed	Pvt-Methodist	1,621
Dickinson State College, Dickinson, N.Dak.	2	Coed	Public	1,412
Dillard University, New Orleans, La.	2	Coed	Private	977
District of Columbia Teachers College, Washington, D.C.	2	Coed	Public	2,782
Dixie College, St. George, Utah	1	Coed	Public	1,145
Dodge City Community Junior College, Dodge City, Kans.	1	Coed	Public	834
Dominican College, Racine, Wis.	3	Coed	Private	795
Dominican College of San Rafael, San Rafael, Calif.	3	Coed	Pvt-Roman Catholic	953
Dordt College, Sioux Center, Iowa	2	Coed	Pvt-Christian Reformed	970
Dowling College, Oakdale, N.Y.	4	Coed	Private	1,800
Drake University, Des Moines, Iowa	4	Coed	Private	7,749
Drew University, Madison, N.J.	4	Coed	Pvt-Methodist	1,691
Drexel University, Philadelphia, Pa.	4	Coed	Private	8,622
Drury College, Springfield, Mo.	3	Coed	Pvt-Church of Christ	2,469
Dubuque, University of, Dubuque, Iowa	2	Coed	Pvt-Presbyterian	992
Duke University, Durham, N.C. (incl. Trinity College & Woman's College)	4	Coord	Pvt-Methodist	8,338
DuPage, College of, Glen Ellyn, Ill.	1	Coed	Public	8,705
Duquesne University, Pittsburgh, Pa.	4	Coed	Pvt-Roman Catholic	8,427
Durham Technical Institute, Durham, N.C.	1	Coed	Public	1,038
Dutchess Community College, Poughkeepsie, N.Y.	1	Coed	Public	4,200
Dyersburg State Community College, Dyersburg, Tenn.	1	Coed	Public	808
D'Youville College, Buffalo, N.Y.	2	Coed	Pvt-Roman Catholic	1,205
Earlham College, Richmond, Ind.		Coed	Pvt-Friends	1,155
East Carolina University, Greenville, N.C.	3	Coed	Public	10,106
East Central State College, Ada, Okla.	3	Coed	Public	3,092
East Los Angeles College, Los Angeles, Calif.		Coed	Public	14,042
East Stroudsburg State College, East Stroudsburg, Pa.	3	Coed	Public	3,400
East Tennessee State University, Johnson City, Tenn.		Coed	Public	9,545
East Texas Baptist College, Marshall, Texas	2	Coed	Pvt-Baptist	730
East Texas State University, Commerce, Texas	4	Coed	Public	9,759
Eastern Arizona College, Thatcher, Ariz.		Coed	Public	1,792
Eastern Connecticut State College, Willimantic, Conn.	3	Coed	Public	2,791
Eastern Illinois University, Charleston, Ill.	3	Coed	Public	8,893
Eastern Kentucky University, Richmond, Ky.	3	Coed	Public	10,170
Eastern Mennonite College, Harrisonburg, Va.	3	Coed	Pvt-Mennonite	959
Eastern Michigan University, Ypsilanti, Mich.	3	Coed	Public	21,217
Eastern Montana College, Billings, Mont.	3	Coed	Public	3,480
Eastern Nazarene College, Quincy, Mass.		Coed	Pvt-Nazarene	902
Eastern New Mexico University, Portales, N.Mex.	4	Coed	Public	4,298
Eastern Oklahoma State College, Wilburton, Okla.		Coed	Public	1,536
Eastern Oregon College, La Grande, Oreg.	3	Coed	Public	1,628
Eastern Utah, College of, Price, Utah		Coed	Public	800
Eastern Washington State College, Cheney, Wash.	3	Coed	Public	6,618
Eckerd College, St. Petersburg, Fla.		Coed	Pvt-Presbyterian	1,112
Edgecliff College, Edgecliff, Ohio	2	Coed	Pvt-Roman Catholic	800
Edinboro State College, Edinboro, Pa.		Coed	Public	7,155
Edison Junior College, Fort Myers, Fla.	1	Coed	Public	1,779
El Camino College, Torrance, Calif.		Coed	Public	22,068
El Centro College, Dallas, Texas		Coed	Public	6,653
Elgin Community College, Elgin, Ill.		Coed	Public	2,830
Elizabeth City State University, Elizabeth City, N.C.	2	Coed	Public	1,104
Elizabethtown College, Elizabethtown, Pa.		Coed	Pvt-Brethren	1,751
Ellsworth Community College, Iowa Falls, Iowa		Coed	Public	1,062
Elmhurst College, Elmhurst, Ill.	2	Coed	Pvt-Church of Christ	2,891
Elmira College, Elmira, N.Y.		Coed	Private	3,266
Elon College, Elon College, N.C.	2	Coed	Pvt-Church of Christ	1,862
Embry-Riddle Aeronautical Institute, Daytona Beach, Fla.		Coed	Private	1,755
Emerson College, Boston, Mass.		Coed	Private	1,879
Emmanuel College, Boston, Mass.	3	Coed	Pvt-Roman Catholic	1,333
Emory and Henry College, Emory, Va.		Coed	Pvt-Methodist	799
Emory University, Atlanta, Ga.	4	Coed	Pvt-Methodist	5,897
Endicott Junior College, Beverly, Mass.		W	Private	805
Enterprise State Junior College, Enterprise, Ala.		Coed	Public	1,619
Erie Community College, Buffalo, N.Y.		Coed	Public	7,425
Essex Community College, Baltimore, Md.		Coed	Public	4,604
Evangel College, Springfield, Mo.	2	Coed	Pvt-Assemblies of God	1,228
Evansville, University of, Evansville, Ind.	2	Coed	Pvt-Methodist	5,393
Everett Community College, Everett, Wash.	1	Coed	Public	5,418
Fairfield University, Fairfield, Conn.	3	Coed	Pvt-Roman Catholic	2,284
Fairleigh Dickinson University, Rutherford, Teaneck, Madison, N.J.	4	Coed	Private	20,130
Fairmont State College, Fairmont, W.Va.	2	Coed	Public	3,680
Fashion Institute of Technology, New York, N.Y.		Coed	Public	5,020
Fayetteville State University, Fayetteville, N.C.	3	Coed	Public	1,482
Fayetteville Technical Institute, Fayetteville, N.C.		Coed	Public	1,118
Ferris State College, Big Rapids, Mich.	2	Coed	Public	9,161
Ferrum College, Ferrum, Va.	1	Coed	Pvt-Methodist	1,175
Findlay College, Findlay, Ohio	2	Coed	Pvt-Church of God	1,175
Fisk University, Nashville, Tenn.	3	Coed	Private	1,413
Fitchburg State College, Fitchburg, Mass.	3	Coed	Public	3,167
Flathead Valley Community College, Kalispell, Mont.	1	Coed	Public	1,220
Florence State University, Florence, Ala.	3	Coed	Public	3,425

Name and Location	Level of Instruction	Student Body	Control	Enrollment
Florence-Darlington Technical Education Center, Florence, S.C.	1	Coed	Public	720
Florida, University of, Gainesville, Fla.	4	Coed	Public	23,672
Florida Agricultural & Mechanical University, Tallahassee, Fla.	3	Coed	Public	4,944
Florida Atlantic University, Boca Raton, Fla.	3	Coed	Public	5,732
Florida Institute of Technology, Melbourne, Fla.	3	Coed	Private	2,119
Florida Junior College at Jacksonville, Fla.	1	Coed	Public	8,303
Florida Keys Community College, Key West, Fla.	1	Coed	Public	1,098
Florida Memorial College, Miami, Fla.	2	Coed	Pvt-Baptist	777
Florida Southern College, Lakeland, Fla.	2	Coed	Pvt-Methodist	1,480
Florida State University, Tallahassee, Fla.	4	Coed	Public	18,367
Florida Technological University, Orlando, Fla.	3	Coed	Public	4,906
Fontbonne College, St. Louis, Mo.	2	Coed	Pvt-Roman Catholic	738
Foothill College, Los Altos Hills, Calif.	1	Coed	Public	9,380
Fordham University, Bronx, N.Y.	4	Coed	Pvt-Roman Catholic	13,841
Forsyth Technical Institute, Winston-Salem, N.C.	1	Coed	Public	1,051
Fort Hays Kansas State College, Hays, Kans.	3	Coed	Public	6,144
Fort Lewis College, Durango, Colo.	2	Coed	Public	2,315
Fort Valley State College, Fort Valley, Ga.	3	Coed	Public	2,373
Framingham State College, Framingham, Mass.	3	Coed	Public	4,452
Franklin & Marshall College, Lancaster, Pa.	3	Coed	Pvt-Church of Christ	2,608
Franklin College of Indiana, Franklin, Ind.	2	Coed	Pvt-Baptist	743
Franklin Institute of Boston, Boston, Mass.	1	Coed	Private	1,110
Franklin Pierce College, Rindge, N.H.	2	Coed	Private	1,077
Frederick Community College, Frederick, Md.	1	Coed	Public	1,208
Freed-Hardeman College, Henderson, Tenn.	2	Coed	Pvt-Church of Christ	851
Fresno City College, Fresno, Calif.	1	Coed	Public	12,999
Friends University, Wichita, Kans.	2	Coed	Pvt-Friends	922
Frostburg State College, Frostburg, Md.	3	Coed	Public	2,736
Fullerton Junior College, Fullerton, Calif.	1	Coed	Public	15,397
Fulton-Montgomery Community College, Johnstown, N.Y.	1	Coed	Public	1,295
Furman University, Greenville, S.C.	3	Coed	Pvt-Baptist	2,246
Gadsden State Junior College, Gadsden, Ala.	1	Coed	Public	3,189
Gainesville Junior College, Gainesville, Ga.	1	Coed	Public	1,162
Gallaudet College, Washington, D.C.	3	Coed	Private	1,019
Galveston College, Galveston, Texas	1	Coed	Public	1,306
Gannon College, Erie, Pa.	3	Coed	Pvt-Roman Catholic	3,568
Gardner-Webb College, Boiling Springs, N.C.	2	Coed	Pvt-Baptist	1,528
Gaston College, Dallas, N.C.	1	Coed	Public	2,075
Gavilan College, Gilroy, Calif.	1	Coed	Public	1,645
General Motors Institute, Flint, Mich.	3	Coed	Private	3,075
Genesee Community College, Flint, Mich.	1	Coed	Public	10,983
Genesee Community College, Batavia, N.Y.	1	Coed	Public	1,753
Geneva College, Beaver Falls, Pa.	3	Coed	Pvt-Presbyterian	1,605
George C. Wallace State Technical Junior College, Dothan, Ala.	1	Coed	Public	1,889
George Mason University, Fairfax, Va.	2	Coed	Public	3,140
George Peabody College for Teachers, Nashville, Tenn.	4	Coed	Private	1,993
George Washington University, Washington, D.C.	4	Coed	Private	20,969
George Williams College, Downers Grove, Ill.	3	Coed	Private	932
Georgetown College, Georgetown, Ky.	2	Coed	Pvt-Baptist	1,300
Georgetown University, Washington, D.C.	4	Coed	Pvt-Roman Catholic	4,387
Georgia, University of, Athens, Ga.	4	Coed	Public	21,298
Georgia College, Milledgeville, Ga.	3	Coed	Public	2,330
Georgia Institute of Technology, Atlanta, Ga.	4	Coed	Public	8,125
Southern Technical Institute, Marietta, Ga.	2	Coed	Public	1,627
Georgia Southern College, Statesboro, Ga.	3	Coed	Public	6,156
Georgia Southwestern College, Americus, Ga.	2	Coed	Public	2,383
Georgia State University, Atlanta, Ga.	4	Coed	Public	16,044
Georgian Court College, Lakewood, N.J.	2	W	Pvt-Roman Catholic	731
Gettysburg College, Gettysburg, Pa.	3	Coed	Pvt-Lutheran	1,887
Glassboro State College, Glassboro, N.J.	3	Coed	Public	11,335
Glendale College, Glendale, Calif.	1	Coed	Public	6,163
Glendale Community College, Glendale, Ariz.	1	Coed	Public	6,589
Glenville State College, Glenville, W.Va.	2	Coed	Public	1,617
Goddard College, Plainfield, Vt.	3	Coed	Private	1,599
Golden Gate College, San Francisco, Calif.	3	Coed	Private	4,499
Golden West College, Huntington Beach, Calif.	1	Coed	Public	11,321
Gonzaga University, Spokane, Wash.	3	Coed	Pvt-Roman Catholic	2,873
Gordon College, Wenham, Mass.	2	Coed	Private	813
Goshen College, Goshen, Ind.	3	Coed	Pvt-Mennonite	1,258
Goucher College, Baltimore, Md.	3	W	Private	1,050
Graceland College, Lamoni, Iowa	2	Coed	Private[1]	1,349
Grambling College, Grambling, La.	2	Coed	Public	3,913
Grand Canyon College, Phoenix, Ariz.	2	Coed	Pvt-Baptist	796
Grand Rapids Junior College, Grand Rapids, Mich.	1	Coed	Public	5,568
Grand Valley State College, Allendale, Mich.	2	Coed	Public	4,174
Grand View College, Des Moines, Iowa	1	Coed	Pvt-Lutheran	1,214
Grays Harbor College, Aberdeen, Wash.	1	Coed	Public	1,046
Grayson County College, Denison, Texas	1	Coed	Public	1,031
Great Falls, College of, Great Falls, Mont.	2	Coed	Pvt-Roman Catholic	2,798
Green River Community College, Auburn, Wash.	1	Coed	Public	4,512
Greenfield Community College, Greenfield, Mass.	1	Coed	Public	1,263
Greenville College, Greenville, Ill.	2	Coed	Pvt-Methodist	838
Greenville Technical Education Center, Greenville, S.C.	1	Coed	Public	6,380
Grinnell College, Grinnell, Iowa	3	Coed	Private	1,304
Grossmont College, El Cajon, Calif.	1	Coed	Public	11,270
Grove City College, Grove City, Pa.	2	Coed	Pvt-Presbyterian	2,114
Guam, University of, Agana, Guam	3	Coed	Public	2,349
Guelph, University of, Guelph, Ont.	4	Coed	Public	6,217
Guilford College, Greensboro, N.C.	3	Coed	Pvt-Friends	1,740
Guilford Technical Institute, Jamestown, N.C.	1	Coed	Public	1,375
Gulf Coast Junior College, Panama City, Fla.	1	Coed	Public	2,065
Gustavus Adolphus College, St. Peter, Minn.	3	Coed	Pvt-Lutheran	1,918
Gwynedd-Mercy College, Gwynedd Valley, Pa.	2	Coed	Pvt-Roman Catholic	1,100
Hagerstown Junior College, Hagerstown, Md.	1	Coed	Public	2,508
Hamilton College, Clinton, N.Y.	3	M	Private	937
Hamline University, St. Paul, Minn.	3	Coed	Pvt-Methodist	1,283
Hampden-Sydney College, Hampden-Sydney, Va.	3	M	Pvt-Presbyterian	689
Hampton Institute, Hampton, Va.	3	Coed	Private	2,313
Hanover College, Hanover, Ind.	3	Coed	Pvt-Presbyterian	1,031
Harcum Junior College, Bryn Mawr, Pa.	1	W	Private	616
Hardin-Simmons University, Abilene, Texas	3	Coed	Pvt-Baptist	1,610
Harding College, Searcy, Ark.	3	Coed	Pvt-Church of Christ	2,060
Harford Community College, Bel Air, Md.	1	Coed	Public	1,830
Harris Teachers College, St. Louis, Mo.	3	Coed	Public	1,156
Harrisburg Area Community College, Harrisburg, Pa.	1	Coed	Public	4,232
Hartford State Technical College, Hartford, Conn.	1	Coed	Public	8,902
Hartnell College, Salinas, Calif.	1	Coed	Public	1,439
Hartwick College, Oneonta, N.Y.	3	Coed	Private	2,759
Harvard University, Cambridge, Mass.	4	Coed	Private	1,687
Hastings College, Hastings, Nebr.	2	Coed	Pvt-Presbyterian	826
Hawaii, Church College of, Oahu, Hawaii	3	Coed	Pvt-Latter-day Saints	1,299
Hawaii, University of, Honolulu, Hawaii	4	Coed	Public	22,118
Heidelberg College, Tiffin, Ohio	2	Coed	Pvt-Church of Christ	1,240
Henderson County Junior College, Athens, Texas	1	Coed	Public	1,238
Henderson State College, Arkadelphia, Ark.	3	Coed	Public	3,300
Hendrix College, Conway, Ark.	2	Coed	Pvt-Methodist	997
Henry Ford Community College, Dearborn, Mich.	1	Coed	Public	10,497
Herkimer County Community College, Herkimer, N.Y.	1	Coed	Public	1,092
Hibbing State Junior College, Hibbing, Minn.	1	Coed	Public	772
High Point College, High Point, N.C.	2	Coed	Pvt-Methodist	1,060
Highland Park Community College, Highland Park, Mich.	1	Coed	Public	3,597
Highline Community College, Midway, Wash.	1	Coed	Public	6,279
Hill Junior College, Hillsboro, Texas	1	Coed	Public	700

[1] Reorganized Church of Jesus Christ of Latter Day Saints.

Name and Location	Level of Instruction	Student Body	Control	Enrollment
Hillsborough Community College, Tampa, Fla.	1	Coed	Public	5,559
Hillsdale College, Hillsdale, Mich.	2	Coed	Private	1,085
Hinds Junior College, Raymond, Miss.	1	Coed	Public	4,379
Hiram College, Hiram, Ohio.	2	Coed	Pvt-Disciples of Christ	1,284
Hobart & William Smith Colleges, Geneva, N.Y.	2	Coord	Private	1,695
Hofstra University, Hempstead, L.I., N.Y.	4	Coed	Private	12,616
Hollins College, Hollins, Va.	3	Coed	Private	1,133
Holmes Junior College, Goodman, Miss.	1	Coed	Public	940
Holy Cross, College of the, Worcester, Mass.	3	Coed	Pvt-Roman Catholic	2,492
Holy Family College, Philadelphia, Pa.	3	W	Pvt-Roman Catholic	752
Holy Names College, Oakland, Calif.	3	Coed	Pvt-Roman Catholic	813
Holyoke Community College, Holyoke, Mass.	1	Coed	Public	2,464
Honolulu Community College, Honolulu, Hawaii	1	Coed	Public	2,377
Hope College, Holland, Mich.	2	Coed	Pvt-Reformed	2,101
Houghton College, Houghton, N.Y.	2	Coed	Pvt-Methodist	1,210
Houston, University of, Houston, Texas.	4	Coed	Public	26,475
Houston Baptist College, Houston, Texas.	2	Coed	Pvt-Baptist	1,126
Howard County Junior College, Big Spring, Texas.	1	Coed	Public	1,070
Howard Payne College, Brownwood, Texas.	3	Coed	Pvt-Baptist	1,407
Howard University, Washington, D.C.	4	Coed	Public-Private	10,090
Hudson Valley Community College, Troy, N.Y.	1	Coed	Public	6,062
Huron College, Huron, S.Dak.	2	Coed	Pvt-Presbyterian	730
Hutchinson Community Junior College, Hutchinson, Kans.	1	Coed	Public	2,210
Idaho, College of, Caldwell, Idaho.	3	Coed	Pvt-Presbyterian	1,024
Idaho, University of, Moscow, Idaho.	4	Coed	Public	7,935
Idaho State University, Pocatello, Idaho.	3	Coed	Public	6,862
Illinois, University of, Urbana & Chicago, Ill.	4	Coed	Public	57,084
Illinois Benedictine College, Lisle, Ill.	2	Coed	Pvt-Roman Catholic	1,022
Illinois Central College, East Peoria, Ill.	1	Coed	Public	8,907
Illinois College, Jacksonville, Ill.	2	Coed	Pvt-Presbyterian and Church of Christ	876
Illinois Institute of Technology, Chicago, Ill.	4	Coed	Private	7,067
Illinois State University, Normal, Ill.	4	Coed	Public	17,930
Illinois Valley Community College, Oglesby, Ill.	1	Coed	Public	2,811
Illinois Wesleyan University, Bloomington, Ill.	3	Coed	Pvt-Methodist	1,727
Immaculata College, Immaculata, Pa.	3	Coed	Pvt-Roman Catholic	1,473
Immaculate Heart College, Los Angeles, Calif.	3	Coed	Pvt-Roman Catholic	624
Imperial Valley College, Imperial, Calif.	1	Coed	Public	2,951
Incarnate Word College, San Antonio, Texas.	3	Coed	Pvt-Roman Catholic	1,835
Indian River Community College, Fort Pierce, Fla.	1	Coed	Public	2,469
Indiana Central College, Indianapolis, Ind.	3	Coed	Pvt-Methodist	
Indiana State University, Terre Haute, Ind.	4	Coed	Public	16,274
Indiana University, Bloomington, Ind.	4	Coed	Public	67,448
Indiana University Regional Campuses				
East at Richmond.	1	Coed	Public	829
Fort Wayne.	2	Coed	Public	3,990
Kokomo.	2	Coed	Public	1,715
Northwest at Gary.	2	Coed	Public	4,516
Purdue at Indianapolis.	2	Coed	Public	14,605
South Bend.	2	Coed	Public	4,803
Indiana University of Pennsylvania, Indiana, Pa.	4	Coed	Public	10,206
Insurance, College of, New York, N.Y.	3	Coed	Private	1,572
Inter American University of Puerto Rico, San Germán, P.R.	3	Coed	Private-Presbyterian	8,718
Iona College, New Rochelle, N.Y.	4	Coed	Pvt-Roman Catholic	4,140
Iowa State University, Ames, Iowa.	4	Coed	Public	19,642
Iowa, University of, Iowa City, Iowa.	4	Coed	Public	20,981
Iowa Wesleyan College, Mt. Pleasant, Iowa.	2	Coed	Pvt-Methodist	873
Itawamba Junior College, Fulton, Miss.	1	Coed	Public	1,339
Ithaca College, Ithaca, N.Y.	3	Coed	Private	4,038
Jackson Community College, Jackson, Mich.	1	Coed	Public	3,515
Jackson State College, Jackson, Miss.	3	Coed	Public	5,058
Jackson State Community College, Jackson, Tenn.	1	Coed	Public	1,351
Jacksonville State University, Jacksonville, Ala.	3	Coed	Public	5,749
Jacksonville University, Jacksonville, Fla.	3	Coed	Private	3,016
James H. Faulkner State Junior College, Bay Minette, Ala.	1	Coed	Public	1,011
Jamestown Community College, Jamestown, N.Y.	1	Coed	Public	2,554
Jefferson College, Hillsboro, Mo.	1	Coed	Public	1,069
Jefferson Community College, Watertown, N.Y.	1	Coed	Public	1,538
Jefferson State Junior College, Birmingham, Ala.	1	Coed	Public	5,631
Jersey City State College, Jersey City, N.J.	3	Coed	Public	9,157
John A. Logan College, Carterville, Ill.	1	Coed	Public	1,326
John C. Calhoun State Technical Junior College, Decatur, Ala.	1	Coed	Public	2,215
John Carroll University, Cleveland, Ohio.	3	Coed	Pvt-Roman Catholic	3,964
John Tyler Community College, Chester, Va.	1	Coed	Public	2,015
Johns Hopkins University, Baltimore, Md.	4	Coed	Private	9,632
Johnson C. Smith University, Charlotte, N.C.	2	Coed	Pvt-Presbyterian	1,036
Johnson State College, Johnson, Vt.	2	Coed	Public	1,123
Joliet Junior College, Joliet, Ill.	1	Coed	Public	4,769
Jones County Junior College, Ellisville, Miss.	1	Coed	Public	2,033
Juilliard School, The, New York, N.Y.	4	Coed	Private	1,121
Juniata College, Huntingdon, Pa.	2	Coed	Private	1,222
Kalamazoo College, Kalamazoo, Mich.	3	Coed	Pvt-Baptist	1,360
Kalamazoo Valley Community College, Kalamazoo, Mich.	1	Coed	Public	3,448
Kansas, University of, Lawrence, Kans.	4	Coed	Public	20,043
Kansas City Kansas Community Junior College, Kansas City, Kans.	1	Coed	Public	1,892
Kansas State College of Pittsburg, Kans.	3	Coed	Public	5,894
Kansas State Teachers College, Emporia, Kans.	3	Coed	Public	7,112
Kansas State University, Manhattan, Kans.	4	Coed	Public	14,789
Kapiolani Community College, Honolulu, Hawaii.	1	Coed	Public	2,760
Kaskaskia College, Centralia, Ill.	1	Coed	Public	1,491
Kauai Community College, Kauai, Hawaii.	1	Coed	Public	839
Kearney State College, Kearney, Nebr.	3	Coed	Public	5,783
Keene State College, Keene, N.H.	3	Coed	Public	2,706
Kellogg Community College, Battle Creek, Mich.	1	Coed	Public	3,315
Kennesaw Junior College, Marietta, Ga.	1	Coed	Public	1,773
Kenosha Technical Institute, Kenosha, Wis.	1	Coed	Public	4,612
Kent State University, Kent, Ohio.	4	Coed	Public	20,794
Kentucky, University of, Lexington, Ky.	4	Coed	Public	20,455
Kentucky State University, Frankfort, Ky.	3	Coed	Public	1,970
Kentucky Wesleyan College, Owensboro, Ky.	2	Coed	Pvt-Methodist	854
Kenyon College, Gambier, Ohio.	3	Coed	Pvt-Episcopal	1,300
Keuka College, Keuka Park, N.Y.	2	Coed	Private	798
Keystone Junior College, La Plume, Pa.	1	Coed	Private	1,153
Kilgore College, Kilgore, Texas.	1	Coed	Public	2,664
King's College, The, Briarcliff Manor, N.Y.	2	Coed	Private	746
King's College, Wilkes-Barre, Pa.	3	Coed	Pvt-Roman Catholic	2,669
Kirkwood Community College, Cedar Rapids, Iowa.	1	Coed	Public	2,861
Knox College, Galesburg, Ill.	3	Coed	Private	1,439
Knoxville College, Knoxville, Tenn.	2	Coed	Pvt-Presbyterian	1,039
Kutztown State College, Kutztown, Pa.	3	Coed	Public	4,928
Lafayette College, Easton, Pa.	2	Coed	Pvt-Presbyterian	2,212
Lake City Community College, Lake City, Fla.	1	Coed	Public	749
Lake Erie College, Painesville, Ohio.	3	Coed	Private	1,462
Lake Forest College, Lake Forest, Ill.	3	Coed	Pvt-Presbyterian	1,223
Lake Michigan College, Benton Harbor, Mich.	1	Coed	Public	3,160
Lake-Sumter Community College, Leesburg, Fla.	2	Coed	Public	1,210
Lake Superior State College, Marie, Mich.	3	Coed	Public	1,712
Lakehead University, Port Arthur, Ontario.	4	Coed	Private	2,931
Lamar University, Beaumont, Texas.	3	Coed	Public	8,942
Lambuth College, Jackson, Tenn.	3	Coed	Pvt-Methodist	787
Lander College, Greenwood, S.C.	2	Coed	Public	986
Lane College, Jackson, Tenn.	2	Coed	Pvt-Methodist Episcopal	921
Lane Community College, Eugene, Oreg.	1	Coed	Public	5,511
Laney College, Oakland, Calif.	1	Coed	Public	11,975

Name and Location	Level of Instruction	Student Body	Control	Enrollment
Langston University, Langston, Okla.	2	Coed	Public	1,236
Lansing Community College, Lansing, Mich.	1	Coed	Public	7,951
Laredo Junior College, Laredo, Texas	1	Coed	Public	2,194
La Salle College, Philadelphia, Pa.	3	Coed	Pvt-Roman Catholic	6,565
Lasell Junior College, Auburndale, Mass.	1	W	Private	789
Lassen College, Susanville, Calif.	1	Coed	Public	1,626
Laurentian University of Sudbury, Sudbury, Ontario	2	Coed	Public	2,108
Laval University, Quebec, Quebec	4	Coed	Pvt-Roman Catholic	10,328
La Verne College, La Verne, Calif.	2	Coed	Pvt-Brethren	850
Lawrence Institute of Technology, Southfield, Mich.	3	Coed	Private	4,107
Lawrence University, Appleton, Wis.	3	Coed	Private	1,456
Lebanon Valley College, Annville, Pa.	2	Coed	Pvt-Methodist	1,307
Lee College, Cleveland, Tenn.	1	Coed	Pvt-Church of God	1,093
Lee College, Baytown, Texas	1	Coed	Public	2,452
Leeward Community College, Oahu, Hawaii	1	Coed	Public	2,347
Lehigh County Community College, Schnecksville, Pa.	1	Coed	Public	5,200
Lehigh University, Bethlehem, Pa.	4	Coed	Private	5,475
Le Moyne College, Syracuse, N.Y.	2	Coed	Pvt-Roman Catholic	1,713
Lenoir Community College, Kinston, N.C.	1	Coed	Public	1,537
Lenoir Rhyne College, Hickory, N.C.	2	Coed	Pvt-Lutheran	1,395
Lesley College, Cambridge, Mass.	2	W	Private	914
Lethbridge, University of, Lethbridge, Alberta	3	Coed	Public	1,409
Le Tourneau College, Longview, Texas	2	Coed	Private	762
Lewis & Clark College, Portland, Oreg.	3	Coed	Pvt-Presbyterian	2,443
Lewis and Clark Community College, Godfrey, Ill.	1	Coed	Public	1,821
Lewis-Clark State School, Lewiston, Idaho	2	Coed	Public	1,282
Lewis College, Lockport, Ill.	3	Coed	Pvt-Roman Catholic	2,536
Lincoln University, Jefferson City, Mo.	3	Coed	Public	2,620
Lincoln University, Lincoln University, Pa.	3	Coed	Private	1,078
Linfield College, McMinnville, Oreg.	3	Coed	Pvt-Baptist	1,085
Livingston University, Livingston, Ala.	3	Coed	Public	1,638
Livingstone College, Salisbury, N.C.	2	Coed	Pvt-Methodist Episcopal	754
Lock Haven State College, Lock Haven, Pa.	2	Coed	Public	2,387
Loma Linda University, Loma Linda, Calif.	4	Coed	Pvt-Seventh-day Adventist	3,574
Long Beach City College, Long Beach, Calif.	1	Coed	Public	26,497
Long Island University, Greenvale, N.Y. (incl. Bklyn. Center; Bklyn. College of Pharmacy; C.W. Post & Southampton campuses, Long Island, N.Y.)	4	Coed	Private	23,879
Longwood College, Farmville, Va.	3	Coed	Public	2,363
Lorain County Community College, Elyria, Ohio	1	Coed	Public	3,566
Loras College, Dubuque, Iowa	2	Coed	Pvt-Roman Catholic	1,538
Loretto Heights College, Denver, Colo.	2	Coed	Pvt-Roman Catholic	846
Los Angeles City College, Los Angeles, Calif.	1	Coed	Public	17,802
Los Angeles Harbor College, Wilmington, Calif.	1	Coed	Public	9,130
Los Angeles Pierce College, Woodland Hills, Calif.	1	Coed	Public	16,317
Los Angeles Southwest College, Los Angeles, Calif.	1	Coed	Public	3,858
Los Angeles Trade-Technical College, Los Angeles, Calif.	1	Coed	Public	15,645
Los Angeles Valley College, Van Nuys, Calif.	1	Coed	Public	19,066
Louisburg College, Louisburg, N.C.	1	Coed	Pvt-Methodist	777
Louisiana College, Pineville, La.	2	Coed	Pvt-Baptist	949
Louisiana State University & Agricultural & Mechanical College System, Baton Rouge and New Orleans, La.	4	Coed	Public	38,731
Louisiana Tech University, Ruston, La.	4	Coed	Public	8,135
Louisville, University of, Louisville, Ky.	4	Coed	Public	10,468
Lowell State College, Lowell, Mass.	3	Coed	Public	1,894
Lowell Technological Institute, Lowell, Mass.	4	Coed	Public	6,891
Lower Columbia College, Longview, Wash.	1	Coed	Public	2,250
Loyola College, Baltimore, Md.	3	Coord	Pvt-Roman Catholic	1,270
Loyola University, Chicago, Ill.	4	Coed	Pvt-Roman Catholic	14,752
Loyola University, New Orleans, La.	4	Coed	Pvt-Roman Catholic	4,981
Loyola University of Los Angeles, Los Angeles, Calif.	3	Coed	Pvt-Roman Catholic	3,822
Lubbock Christian College, Lubbock, Texas	2	Coed	Pvt-Church of Christ	957
Luther College, Decorah, Iowa	2	Coed	Pvt-Lutheran	2,041
Lycoming College, Williamsport, Pa.	2	Coed	Pvt-Methodist	1,635
Lynchburg College, Lynchburg, Va.	3	Coed	Pvt-Disciples of Christ	2,044
Lyndon State College, Lyndonville, Vt.	2	Coed	Public	768
Macalester College, St. Paul, Minn.	3	Coed	Pvt-Presbyterian	2,097
Macomb County Community College, Warren, Mich. Center Campus; South Campus	1	Coed	Public	3,332
Macon Junior College, Macon, Ga.	1	Coed	Public	14,399
Madonna College, Livonia, Mich.	2	Coed	Pvt-Roman Catholic	1,810
McGill University, Montreal, Quebec.	4	Coed	Private	727
McLennan Community College, Waco, Texas.	1	Coed	Public	15,171
McMaster University, Hamilton, Ontario.	4	Coed	Private	2,448
MacMurray College, Jacksonville, Ill.	2	Coed	Pvt-Methodist	7,928
McMurry College, Abilene, Texas.	2	Coed	Pvt-Methodist	980
McNeese State University, Lake Charles, La.	3	Coed	Public	1,600
Madison Area Technical College, Madison, Wis.	1	Coed	Public	6,025
Madison College, Harrisonburg, Va.	3	Coed	Public	4,432
Maine, University of at Farmington.	2	Coed	Public	4,579
Maine, University of at Orono.	4	Coed	Public	1,624
Maine, University of at Portland-Gorham.	4	Coed	Public	9,486
Maine, University of at Presque Isle.	1	Coed	Public	6,107
Mainland, College of the, Texas City, Texas.	1	Coed	Public	1,170
Malone College, Canton, Ohio.	2	Coed	Pvt-Friends	1,335
Manatee Junior College, Bradenton, Fla.	1	Coed	Public	836
Manchester College, North Manchester, Ind.	2	Coed	Pvt-Brethren	2,958
Manchester Community College, Manchester, Conn.	1	Coed	Public	1,410
Manhattan College, Bronx, N.Y.	3	Coed	Pvt-Roman Catholic	3,371
Manhattan School of Music, New York, N.Y.	3	Coed	Private	4,572
Manhattanville College, Purchase, N.Y.	3	Coed	Pvt-Roman Catholic	987
Manitoba, University of, Winnipeg, Man.	4	Coed	Public	1,518
Mankato State College, Mankato, Minn.	3	Coed	Public	12,892
Mansfield State College, Mansfield, Pa.	3	Coed	Public	13,232
Marian College, Indianapolis, Ind.	3	Coed	Pvt-Roman Catholic	3,097
Maricopa Technical College, Phoenix, Ariz.	1	Coed	Public	9,323
Marietta College, Marietta, Ohio.	3	Coed	Private	5,683
Marin, College of, Kentfield, Calif.	1	Coed	Public	1,913
Marion College, Marion, Ind.	2	Coed	Pvt-Methodist	6,069
Marist College, Poughkeepsie, N.Y.	2	Coed	Pvt-Roman Catholic	829
Marquette University, Milwaukee, Wis.	4	Coed	Pvt-Roman Catholic	1,796
Mars Hill College, Mars Hill, N.C.	3	Coed	Pvt-Baptist	10,295
Marshall University, Huntington, W.Va.	3	Coed	Public	1,467
Marshalltown Community College, Marshalltown, Iowa.	1	Coed	Public	9,476
Mary Baldwin College, Staunton, Va.	2	W	Pvt-Presbyterian	951
Mary Hardin-Baylor College, Belton, Texas.	3	Coed	Pvt-Baptist	764
Marycrest College, Davenport, Iowa.	3	Coed	Pvt-Roman Catholic	947
Marygrove College, Detroit, Mich.	3	Coed	Pvt-Roman Catholic	1,027
Maryland, University of, College Park & Baltimore, Md.	4	Coed	Public	1,102
Maryland Institute, College of Art, Baltimore, Md.	3	Coed	Private	36,028
Marymount College, Tarrytown, N.Y.	2	Coed	Pvt-Roman Catholic	1,051
Marymount College at Loyola University, Los Angeles, Calif.	2	W	Pvt-Roman Catholic	1,007
Marymount Manhattan College, New York, N.Y.	2	Coed	Pvt-Roman Catholic	1,161
Maryville College, Maryville, Tenn.	2	Coed	Pvt-Roman Catholic	865
Marywood College, Scranton, Pa.	3	Coed	Pvt-Presbyterian	833
Massachusetts, University of, Amherst, Mass.	4	Coed	Public	2,214
Massachusetts, University of, Boston, Mass.	3	Coed	Public	22,505
Massachusetts Bay Community College, Watertown, Mass.		Coed		4,853
Massachusetts College of Art, Boston, Mass.	2	Coed	Public	1,441
Massachusetts Institute of Technology, Cambridge, Mass.	4	Coed	Public	1,212
Massasoit Community College, Brockton, Mass.	3	Coed	Private	7,717
Maui Community College, Kahului, Hawaii.	2	Coed	Public	1,625
Memorial University of Newfoundland, St. John's, Nfld.	1	Coed	Public	1,187
Memphis State University, Memphis, Tenn.	4	Coed	Public	6,378
Merced College, Merced, Calif.	1	Coed	Public	19,701
				5,450

Name and Location	Level of Instruction	Student Body	Control	Enrollment
Mercer County Community College, Trenton, NJ	1	Coed	Public	5,288
Mercer University, Macon, Ga.	3	Coed	Pvt-Baptist	1,903
Mercy College, Dobbs Ferry, N.Y.	2	Coed	Pvt-Roman Catholic	1,583
Mercy College of Detroit, Detroit, Mich.	2	Coed	Pvt-Roman Catholic	1,620
Mercyhurst College, Erie, Pa.	2	Coed	Pvt-Roman Catholic	954
Meredith College, Raleigh, N.C.	2	W	Pvt-Baptist	1,711
Meridian Junior College, Meridian, Miss.	1	Coed	Public	1,206
Merrimack College, North Andover, Mass.	2	Coed	Pvt-Roman Catholic	2,846
Merritt College, Oakland, Calif.	1	Coed	Public	7,634
Mesa Community College, Mesa, Ariz.	1	Coed	Public	6,723
Mesa College, Grand Junction, Colo.	2	Coed	Public	3,210
Mesabi State Junior College, Virginia, Minn.	1	Coed	Public	771
Messiah College, Grantham, Pa.	2	Coed	Pvt-Brethren	800
Methodist College, Fayetteville, N.C.	2	Coed	Pvt-Methodist	756
Metropolitan Junior College District, Kansas City, Mo.	1	Coed	Public	7,778
Longview Community College, Lee's Summit, Mo.		Coed	Public	2,757
Maple Woods Community College, Kansas City		Coed	Public	1,745
Penn Valley Community College, Kansas City		Coed	Public	4,674
Metropolitan State College, Denver, Colo.	2	Coed	Public	6,853
Miami, University of, Coral Gables, Fla.	4	Coed	Private	15,754
Miami University, Oxford, Ohio.	4	Coed	Public	17,724
Hamilton Campus	2	Coed	Public	1,724
Middletown Campus	2	Coed	Public	2,242
Miami-Dade Junior College, Miami, Fla.	1	Coed	Public	30,853
Michigan, University of, Ann Arbor, Mich.	4	Coed	Public	39,986
Dearborn Campus	2	Coed	Public	875
Flint.	2	Coed	Public	1,819
Michigan State University, East Lansing, Mich.	4	Coed	Public	43,888
Michigan Technological University, Houghton, Mich.	4	Coed	Public	5,002
Middle Georgia College, Cochran, Ga.	1	Coed	Public	2,075
Middle Tennessee State University, Murfreesboro, Tenn.	3	Coed	Public	8,646
Middlebury College, Middlebury, Vt.	3	Coed	Private	1,892
Middlesex County College, Edison, N.J.	1	Coed	Public	7,134
Midland Lutheran College, Fremont, Nebr.	2	Coed	Pvt-Lutheran	867
Midlands Technical Education Center, Columbia, S.C.	1	Coed	Public	1,474
Midwestern University, Wichita Falls, Texas.	3	Coed	Public	4,100
Miles College, Birmingham, Ala.	2	Coed	Pvt-Methodist	1,280
Millersville State College, Millersville, Pa.	2	Coed	Public	4,729
Milligan College, Milligan College, Tenn.	2	Coed	Private	785
Millikin University, Decatur, Ill.	2	Coed	Pvt-Presbyterian	1,755
Mills College, Oakland, Calif.	3	W	Private	1,040
Millsaps College, Jackson, Miss.	2	Coed	Pvt-Methodist	996
Milton College, Milton, Wis.	2	Coed	Private	830
Milwaukee Area Technical College, Milwaukee, Wis.	1	Coed	Public	14,273
Milwaukee School of Engineering, Milwaukee, Wis.	3	Coed	Private	2,431
Mineral Area College, Flat River, Mo.	1	Coed	Public	1,052
Minnesota, University of, Minneapolis, Minn.	4	Coed	Public	68,336
Duluth	3	Coed	Public	5,712
Morris.	2	Coed	Public	1,719
Minot State College, Minot, N.Dak.	3	Coed	Public	3,138
MiraCosta College, Oceanside, Calif.	1	Coed	Public	1,390
Misericordia, College, Dallas, Pa.	2	Coed	Pvt-Roman Catholic	919
Mississippi, University of, University, Miss.	4	Coed	Public	7,823
Mississippi College, Clinton, Miss.	2	Coed	Pvt-Baptist	2,415
Mississippi Delta Junior College, Moorhead, Miss.	1	Coed	Public	1,137
Mississippi Gulf Coast Junior College, Perkinston, Miss.	1	Coed	Public	2,899
Mississippi State College for Women, Columbus, Miss.	3	W	Public	2,591
Mississippi State University, State College, Miss.	4	Coed	Public	10,068
Mississippi Valley State College, Itta Bena, Miss.	2	Coed	Public	2,410
Missouri, University of:				
Columbia.	4	Coed	Public	48,152
Kansas City.	4	Coed	Public	21,942
Rolla.	4	Coed	Public	9,894
St. Louis.	4	Coed	Public	5,829
Missouri Southern State College, Joplin, Mo.	2	Coed	Public	10,487
	2	Coed	Public	3,185
Missouri Valley College, Marshall, Mo.	2	Coed	Pvt-Presbyterian	846
Missouri Western College, St. Joseph, Mo.	2	Coed	Public	2,884
Mitchell College, New London, Conn.	1	Coed	Private	1,153
Mobile State Junior College, Mobile, Ala.	1	Coed	Public	915
Modesto Junior College, Modesto, Calif.	1	Coed	Public	9,048
Mohawk Valley Community College, Utica, N.Y.	1	Coed	Public	5,046
Molloy College, Rockville Center, N.Y.	2	Coed	Pvt-Roman Catholic	1,161
Moncton, University of, Moncton, New Brunswick.	3	Coed	Pvt-Roman Catholic	3,149
Monmouth College, Monmouth, Ill.	2	Coed	Pvt-Presbyterian	1,178
Monmouth College, West Long Branch, N.J.	3	Coed	Private	5,020
Monroe Community College, Rochester, N.Y.	1	Coed	Public	8,280
Monroe County Community College, Monroe, Mich.	1	Coed	Public	1,741
Montana, University of, Missoula, Mont.	4	Coed	Public	8,800
Montana College of Mineral Science and Technology, Butte, Mont.	3	Coed	Public	899
Montana State University, Bozeman, Mont.	4	Coed	Public	8,113
Montclair State College, Montclair, N.J.	3	Coed	Public	10,453
Monterey Peninsula College, Monterey, Calif.	1	Coed	Public	5,809
Montevallo, University of, Montevallo, Ala.	3	Coed	Public	2,564
Montgomery College, Rockville, Md.	1	Coed	Public	9,535
Montgomery County Community College, Blue Bell, Pa.	1	Coed	Public	3,301
Montreal, University of, Montreal, Quebec.	4	Coed	Pvt-Roman Catholic	13,132
Loyola College, Montreal, Quebec.	2	Coed	Pvt-Roman Catholic	3,865
Moorhead State College, Moorhead, Minn.	3	Coed	Public	5,160
Moorpark College, Moorpark, Calif.	1	Coed	Public	6,153
Moravian College, Bethlehem, Pa.	2	Coed	Pvt-Moravian	1,709
Morehead State University, Morehead, Ky.	3	Coed	Public	6,255
Morehouse College, Atlanta, Ga.	2	M	Private	1,227
Morgan State College, Baltimore, Md.	3	Coed	Public	4,889
Morningside College, Sioux City, Iowa	2	Coed	Pvt-Methodist	1,643
Morris, County College of, Dover, N.J.	1	Coed	Public	4,295
Morris Brown College, Atlanta, Ga.	2	Coed	Pvt-Methodist Episcopal	1,527
Morris Harvey College, Charleston, W.Va.	2	Coed	Private	3,095
Morton College, Cicero, Ill.	1	Coed	Public	2,490
Motlow State Community College, Tullahoma, Tenn.	1	Coed	Public	851
Mount Allison University, Sackville, New Brunswick.	3	Coed	Pvt-United Church	1,347
Mount Holyoke College, South Hadley, Mass.	3	W	Private	1,919
Mount Mary College, Milwaukee, Wis.	2	W	Pvt-Roman Catholic	780
Mount St. Joseph-on-the-Ohio, College of, Mt. St. Joseph, Ohio.	2	Coed	Pvt-Roman Catholic	793
Mount St. Mary College, Newburgh, N.Y.	2	Coed	Pvt-Roman Catholic	696
Mount St. Mary's College, Los Angeles, Calif.	3	W	Pvt-Roman Catholic	1,201
Mount St. Mary's College, Emmitsburg, Md.	3	M	Pvt-Roman Catholic	1,149
Mount St. Vincent, College of, Riverdale, N.Y.	2	W	Pvt-Roman Catholic	1,061
Mount St. Vincent University, Halifax, Nova Scotia.	3	Coed	Pvt-Roman Catholic	944
Mount San Antonio College, Walnut, Calif.	1	Coed	Public	15,371
Mount San Jacinto College, Gilman Hot Springs, Calif.	1	Coed	Public	1,622
Mount Wachusett Community College, Gardner, Mass.	1	Coed	Public	1,325
Mount Union College, Alliance, Ohio.	2	Coed	Pvt-Methodist	1,206
Muhlenberg College, Allentown, Pa.	2	Coed	Pvt-Lutheran	1,785
Mundelein College, Chicago, Ill.	3	Coed	Pvt-Roman Catholic	1,362
Murray State College, Tishomingo, Okla.	1	Coed	Public	869
Murray State University, Murray, Ky.	4	Coed	Public	7,331
Muskegon Community College, Muskegon, Mich.	1	Coed	Public	3,889
Muskingum College, New Concord, Ohio.	2	Coed	Pvt-Presbyterian	1,358
Napa College, Napa, Calif.	1	Coed	Public	3,408
Nassau Community College, Garden City, N.Y.	1	Coed	Public	18,092
Nasson College, Springvale, Me.	2	Coed	Private	878
Nathaniel Hawthorne College, Antrim, N.H.	2	Coed	Private	843
National College of Education, Evanston, Ill.	4	Coed	Private	3,088
Naval Postgraduate School, Monterey, Calif.	4	Coed	Public	1,766
Navarro Junior College, Corsicana, Texas.	1	Coed	Public	1,122
Nazareth College of Rochester, N.Y.	2	Coed	Pvt-Roman Catholic	1,348
Nebraska, University of, Lincoln and Omaha, Nebr.	4	Coed	Public	21,541

Name and Location	Level of Instruction	Student Body	Control	Enrollment
Nebraska Wesleyan University, Lincoln, Nebr.	2	Coed	Pvt-Methodist	1,177
Nevada, University of, Reno and Las Vegas, Nev.	4	Coed	Public	11,938
New Brunswick, University of, Fredericton, New Brunswick.	4	Coed	Public	5,102
New England College, Henniker, N.H.	2	Coed	Private	1,190
New Hampshire, University of, Durham, N.H.	4	Coed	Public	10,517
New Haven, University of, West Haven, Conn.	3	Coed	Private	5,120
New Mexico, University of, Albuquerque, N.Mex.	4	Coed	Public	19,451
New Mexico Highlands University, Las Vegas, N.Mex.	3	Coed	Public	2,655
New Mexico Institute of Mining & Technology, Socorro, N.Mex.	4	Coed	Public	1,004
New Mexico Junior College, Hobbs, N.Mex.	1	Coed	Public	1,079
New Mexico State University, Las Cruces, N.Mex.	4	Coed	Public	9,075
New Rochelle, College of New Rochelle, N.Y.	3	Coed	Pvt-Roman Catholic	1,400
New School for Social Research, New York, N.Y.	4	Coed	Private	3,286
New York, City University of, New York, N.Y.:		Coed	Public	
Bernard M. Baruch College, New York.	3	Coed	Public	12,053
Borough of Manhattan Community College, New York.	1	Coed	Public	8,981
Bronx Community College, Bronx.	1	Coed	Public	11,756
Brooklyn College, Brooklyn.	3	Coed	Public	29,509
City College, New York.	4	Coed	Public	21,181
Graduate School and University Center, New York.	4	Coed	Public	2,325
Herbert H. Lehman College, Bronx.	3	Coed	Public	13,078
Hunter College, New York.	3	Coed	Public	23,465
John Jay College of Criminal Justice, New York.	3	Coed	Public	5,554
Kingsborough Community College, Brooklyn.	1	Coed	Public	7,058
New York City Community College, Brooklyn.	1	Coed	Public	13,750
Queens College, Flushing.	3	Coed	Public	27,075
Queensborough Community College, Bayside.	1	Coed	Public	13,151
Richmond College, Staten Island.	3	Coed	Public	3,133
Staten Island Community College, Staten Island.	1	Coed	Public	8,559
York College, Flushing.	3	Coed	Public	2,707
New York, State University of, Albany, N.Y.:	4	Coed	Public	348,686
Agricultural & Technical College at Alfred.	1	Coed	Public	3,899
Agricultural & Technical College at Canton.	1	Coed	Public	2,077
Agricultural & Technical College at Cobleskill.	1	Coed	Public	2,164
Agricultural & Technical College at Delhi.	1	Coed	Public	2,542
Agricultural & Technical College at Farmingdale.	1	Coed	Public	11,765
Agricultural & Technical College at Morrisville.	1	Coed	Public	2,767
College of Environmental Science and Forestry, Syracuse.	4	Coed	Public	1,768
Downstate Medical Center, Brooklyn.	4	Coed	Public	1,142
Maritime College, Bronx.	4	Coed	Public	747
State University College at Brockport.	3	Coed	Public	8,302
State University College at Buffalo.	3	Coed	Public	10,182
State University College at Cortland.	3	Coed	Public	5,130
State University College at Fredonia.	3	Coed	Public	4,768
State University College at Geneseo.	3	Coed	Public	5,278
State University College at New Paltz.	3	Coed	Public	8,027
State University College at Oneonta.	3	Coed	Public	5,435
State University College at Oswego.	3	Coed	Public	8,044
State University College at Plattsburgh.	3	Coed	Public	5,220
State University College at Potsdam.	3	Coed	Public	4,568
State University at Albany.	4	Coed	Public	13,288
State University at Binghamton.	4	Coed	Public	7,182
State University at Buffalo.	4	Coed	Public	23,723
State University at Stony Brook.	4	Coed	Public	10,697
Upstate Medical Center, Syracuse.	4	Coed	Public	742
New York Institute of Technology, Old Westbury, L.I., N.Y.	2	Coed	Private	5,207
New York University, New York, N.Y.	4	Coed	Private	30,540
Newark College of Engineering, Newark, N.J.	3	Coed	Public	4,527
Newark State College, Union, N.J.	3	Coed	Public	12,059
Newberry College, Newberry, S.C.	2	Coed	Pvt-Lutheran	804
Newton College of the Sacred Heart, Newton, Mass.	2	W	Pvt-Roman Catholic	1,007

Name and Location	Level of Instruction	Student Body	Control	Enrollment
Niagara County Community College, Niagara Falls, N.Y.	1	Coed	Public	3,209
Niagara University, Niagara University, N.Y.	3	Coed	Pvt-Roman Catholic	3,336
Nicholls State University, Thibodaux, La.	3	Coed	Public	5,411
Nichols College, Dudley, Mass.	2	M	Private	710
Norfolk State College, Norfolk, Va.	3	Coed	Public	5,678
North Adams State College, North Adams, Mass.	3	Coed	Public	2,450
North Carolina, University of, Chapel Hill, N.C.:		Coed	Public	47,452
Asheville	2	Coed	Public	1,107
Chapel Hill	4	Coed	Public	19,160
Charlotte	4	Coed	Public	4,676
Greensboro	4	Coed	Public	6,983
Wilmington	2	Coed	Public	2,043
North Carolina State University at Raleigh	4	Coed	Public	13,483
North Carolina Agricultural and Technical State University, Greensboro, N.C.	4	Coed	Public	4,445
North Carolina Central University, Durham, N.C.	3	Coed	Public	3,723
North Central College, Naperville, Ill.	2	Coed	Pvt-Methodist	932
North Central Michigan College, Petoskey, Mich.	1	Coed	Public	764
North Central Technical Institute, Wausau, Wis.	1	Coed	Public	1,432
North Dakota, University of, Grand Forks, N.Dak.	4	Coed	Public	8,823
North Dakota State School of Science, Wahpeton, N.Dak.	1	Coed	Public	3,047
North Dakota State University, Fargo, N.Dak.	4	Coed	Public	7,118
North Florida Junior College, Madison, Fla.	1	Coed	Public	1,150
North Georgia College, Dahlonega, Ga.	2	Coed	Public	1,336
North Hennepin State Junior College, Minneapolis, Minn.	1	Coed	Public	2,380
North Idaho College, Coeur d'Alene, Idaho.	1	Coed	Public	1,206
North Iowa Area Community College, Mason City, Iowa.	1	Coed	Public	1,562
North Park College, Chicago, Ill.	2	Coed	Pvt-Evangelical Covenant	1,294
North Shore Community College, Beverly, Mass.	1	Coed	Public	5,102
North Texas State University, Denton, Texas.	4	Coed	Public	15,579
Northampton County Area Community College, Bethlehem, Pa.	1	Coed	Public	2,875
Northeast Alabama State Junior College, Rainsville, Ala.	1	Coed	Public	783
Northeast Louisiana University, Monroe, La.	4	Coed	Public	8,810
Northeast Mississippi Junior College, Booneville, Miss.	1	Coed	Public	1,401
Northeast Missouri State College, Kirksville, Mo.	3	Coed	Public	6,819
Northeastern Illinois University, Chicago, Ill.	3	Coed	Public	7,764
Northeastern Junior College, Sterling, Colo.	1	Coed	Public	1,233
Northeastern Oklahoma Agricultural & Mechanical College, Miami, Okla.	1	Coed	Public	2,316
Northeastern State College, Tahlequah, Okla.	3	Coed	Public	5,520
Northeastern University, Boston, Mass.	4	Coed	Private	34,150
Northern Arizona University, Flagstaff, Ariz.	4	Coed	Public	9,869
Northern Colorado, University of, Greeley, Colo.	4	Coed	Public	10,756
Northern Essex Community College, Haverhill, Mass.	1	Coed	Public	3,563
Northern Illinois University, De Kalb, Ill.	4	Coed	Public	24,667
Northern Iowa, University of, Cedar Falls, Iowa.	3	Coed	Public	10,234
Northern Michigan University, Marquette, Mich.	3	Coed	Public	12,906
Northern Montana College, Havre, Mont.	2	Coed	Public	1,330
Northern Oklahoma College, Tonkawa, Okla.	1	Coed	Public	1,453
Northern State College, Aberdeen, S.Dak.	3	Coed	Public	3,083
Northern Virginia Community College, Annandale, Va.	1	Coed	Public	12,047
Northrop Institute of Technology, Inglewood, Calif.	3	Coed	Private	932
Northwest Alabama State Junior College, Phil Campbell, Ala.	1	Coed	Public	728
Northwest Community College, Powell, Wyo.	1	Coed	Public	946
Northwest Mississippi Junior College, Senatobia, Miss.	1	Coed	Public	1,694
Northwest Missouri State College, Maryville, Mo.	3	Coed	Public	5,632
Northwest Nazarene College, Nampa, Idaho.	2	Coed	Pvt-Nazarene	1,114
Northwestern Connecticut Community College, Winsted, Conn.	1	Coed	Public	1,492
Northwestern Michigan College, Traverse City, Mich.	1	Coed	Public	1,964
Northwestern State College, Alva, Okla.	3	Coed	Public	2,258

Name and Location	Level of Instruction	Student Body	Control	Enrollment
Northwestern State University of Louisiana, Natchitoches, La.	4	Coed	Public	6,268
Northwestern University, Evanston, Ill.	4	Coed	Private	15,006
Norwalk State Technical College, Norwalk, Conn.	1	Coed	Public	1,723
Norwich University, Northfield, Vt.	4	Coed	Private	1,042
Notre Dame, College of, Belmont, Calif.	3	Coed	Pvt-Roman Catholic	1,152
Notre Dame, University of, Notre Dame, Ind.	4	Coed	Pvt-Roman Catholic	8,237
Notre Dame of Maryland, College of, Baltimore, Md.	2	Coed	Pvt-Roman Catholic	970
Oakland Community College, Bloomfield Hills, Mich.				
Auburn Hills Campus	1	Coed	Public	4,344
Highland Lakes Campus	1	Coed	Public	2,200
Orchard Ridge Campus	1	Coed	Public	6,247
Oakland University, Rochester, Mich.	4	Coed	Public	7,069
Oberlin College, Oberlin, Ohio	3	Coed	Private	2,710
Ocean County College, Toms River, N.J.	1	Coed	Public	3,117
Occidental College, Los Angeles, Calif.	3	Coed	Pvt-United Presbyterian	1,879
Odessa College, Odessa, Texas	1	Coed	Public	2,769
Oglethorpe College, Atlanta, Ga.	2	Coed	Private	1,051
Ohio Dominican College, Columbus, Ohio	2	Coed	Pvt-Roman Catholic	965
Ohio Northern University, Ada, Ohio	2	Coed	Pvt-Methodist	2,450
Ohio State University, Columbus, Ohio	4	Coed	Public	50,804
Ohio University, Athens, Ohio	4	Coed	Public	23,918
Ohio Wesleyan University, Delaware, Ohio	3	Coed	Pvt-Methodist	2,543
Ohlone College, Fremont, Calif.	1	Coed	Public	3,956
Okaloosa-Walton Junior College, Niceville, Fla.	1	Coed	Public	2,270
Oklahoma Baptist University, Shawnee, Okla.	2	Coed	Pvt-Baptist	1,588
Oklahoma Christian College, Oklahoma City, Okla.	2	Coed	Pvt-Church of Christ	1,140
Oklahoma City University, Oklahoma City, Okla.	3	Coed	Pvt-Methodist	2,471
Oklahoma College of Liberal Arts, Chickasha, Okla.	2	Coed	Public	1,015
Oklahoma Panhandle State College, Goodwell, Okla.	2	Coed	Public	1,268
Oklahoma State University, Stillwater, Okla.	4	Coed	Public	21,297
Old Dominion College, Norfolk, Va.	3	Coed	Public	9,666
Olivet College, Olivet, Mich.	2	Coed	Private	832
Olivet Nazarene College, Kankakee, Ill.	3	Coed	Pvt-Nazarene	1,805
Olympic College, Bremerton, Wash.	1	Coed	Public	3,200
Onondaga Community College, Syracuse, N.Y.	1	Coed	Public	4,697
Oral Roberts University, Tulsa, Okla.	2	Coed	Private	1,334
Orange Coast College, Costa Mesa, Calif.	1	Coed	Public	19,262
Orange County Community College, Middletown, N.Y.	1	Coed	Public	3,595
Orangeburg-Calhoun Technical Education Center, Orangeburg, S.C.	1	Coed	Public	822
Oregon, University of, Eugene, Oreg.	4	Coed	Public	15,249
Oregon College of Education, Monmouth, Oreg.	3	Coed	Public	3,975
Oregon State University, Corvallis, Oreg.	4	Coed	Public	15,483
Oregon Technical Institute, Klamath Falls, Oreg.	2	Coed	Public	1,038
Otero Junior College, La Junta, Colo.	1	Coed	Public	760
Ottawa, University of, Ottawa, Ontario	4	Coed	Pvt-Roman Catholic	8,243
Ottawa University, Ottawa, Kans.	2	Coed	Pvt-Baptist	758
Otterbein College, Westerville, Ohio	2	Coed	Pvt-Methodist	1,356
Ouachita Baptist University, Arkadelphia, Ark.	2	Coed	Pvt-Baptist	1,377
Our Lady of the Lake College, San Antonio, Texas	3	Coed	Pvt-Roman Catholic	2,018
Ozarks, School of the, Point Lookout, Mo.	2	Coed	Pvt-Presbyterian	1,115
Pace College, New York, N.Y.	3	Coed	Private	7,621
Pacific, University of the, Stockton, Calif.	4	Coed	Private	4,444
Pacific Lutheran University, Tacoma, Wash.	3	Coed	Pvt-Lutheran	3,038
Pacific Union College, Angwin, Calif.	3	Coed	Pvt-Seventh-day Adventist	1,235
Pacific University, Forest Grove, Oreg.	3	Coed	Pvt-Church of Christ	
Paine College, Augusta, Ga.	2	Coed	Pvt-Methodist Episcopal & Methodist	736
Palm Beach Junior College, Lake Worth, Fla.	1	Coed	Public	5,985
Palomar College, San Marcos, Calif.	1	Coed	Public	7,528
Pan American University, Edinburg, Texas	2	Coed	Public	6,217
Panola College, Carthage, Texas	1	Coed	Public	743
Paris Junior College, Paris, Texas	1	Coed	Public	1,140
Parkersburg Community College, Parkersburg, W.Va.	1	Coed	Public	2,256
Parkland College, Champaign, Ill.	1	Coed	Public	4,007
Parks College of Aeronautical Technology, Cahokia, Ill.	2	Coed	Pvt-Roman Catholic	742
Parsons College, Fairfield, Iowa		Coed	Private	1,270
Pasadena City College, Pasadena, Calif.	1	Coed	Public	14,658
Pasadena College, Pasadena, Calif.	3	Coed	Pvt-Nazarene	1,329
Pearl River College, Poplarville, Miss.	1	Coed	Public	1,211
Peirce Junior College, Philadelphia, Pa.		Coed	Private	1,742
Pembroke State University, Pembroke, N.C.	2	Coed	Public	2,077
Peninsula College, Port Angeles, Wash.		Coed	Public	1,200
Pennsylvania, University of, Philadelphia, Pa.	4	Coed	Private	19,548
Pennsylvania State University, University Park, Abington, Allentown, Altoona, Chester, Dubois, Erie, Hazleton, Hershey, McKeesport, Middletown, Monaca, Mont Alto, New Kensington, Schuylkill Haven, Scranton, Sharon, Uniontown, Wilkes-Barre, Wyomissing and York, Pa.	4	Coed	Public	59,598
Pensacola Junior College, Pensacola, Fla.	1	Coed	Public	5,707
Pepperdine College, Los Angeles, Calif.	3	Coed	Pvt-Church of Christ	2,802
Peru State College, Peru, Nebr.	2	Coed	Public	1,001
Pfeiffer College, Misenheimer, N.C.	2	Coed	Pvt-Methodist	1,088
Philadelphia College of Art, Philadelphia, Pa.	3	Coed	Private	1,088
Philadelphia College of Pharmacy & Science, Philadelphia, Pa.	4	Coed	Private	975
Philadelphia College of Textiles & Science, Philadelphia, Pa.	2	Coed	Private	2,130
Phillips County Community College, Helena, Ark.	1	Coed	Public	794
Phillips University, Enid, Okla.	3	Coed	Pvt-Disciples of Christ	1,361
Phoenix College, Phoenix, Ariz.	1	Coed	Public	5,473
Pikeville College, Pikeville, Ky.	2	Coed	Pvt-Presbyterian	785
Pitt Technical Institute, Greenville, N.C.	1	Coed	Public	672
Pittsburgh, University of, Pittsburgh, Bradford, Greensburg, Johnstown, and Titusville, Pa.	4	Coed	Private	30,587
Pitzer College, Claremont, Calif.	3	Coed	Private	792
Plymouth State College, Plymouth, N.H.	3	Coed	Public	2,637
PMC Colleges, Chester, Pa.	3	Coed	Private	3,061
Point Park College, Pittsburgh, Pa.	2	Coed	Private	2,584
Polk Community College, Winter Haven, Fla.	1	Coed	Public	3,945
Pomona College, Claremont, Calif.	2	Coed	Private	1,383
Porterville College, Porterville, Calif.	1	Coed	Private	1,552
Portland, University of, Portland, Oreg.	4	Coed	Private	1,945
Portland Community College, Portland, Oreg.	1	Coed	Public	20,000
Portland State University, Portland, Oreg.	4	Coed	Public	14,497
Potomac State College of West Virginia University, Keyser, W.Va.	1	Coed	Public	766
Prairie State College, Chicago Heights, Ill.	1	Coed	Public	3,817
Prairie View Agricultural & Mechanical College, Prairie View, Texas	3	Coed	Public	4,001
Pratt Institute, Brooklyn, N.Y.	3	Coed	Private	4,530
Presbyterian College, Clinton, S.C.	2	Coed	Pvt-Presbyterian	857
Prince Edward Island, University of, Charlottetown, P.E.I.	2	Coed	Public	1,755
Prince George's Community College, Largo, Md.	1	Coed	Public	7,765
Princeton University, Princeton, N.J.	4	Coed	Private	5,400
Principia College, Elsah, Ill.	2	Coed	Pvt-Christian Science	808
Providence College, Providence, R.I.	2	Coed	Pvt-Roman Catholic	3,507
Puerto Rico, University of, Rio Piedras, P.R.	4	Coed	Public	42,516
Puerto Rico Junior College, Rio Piedras, P.R.	1	Coed	Private	4,764
Puget Sound, University of, Tacoma, Wash.	3	Coed	Pvt-Methodist	3,652
Purdue University, Lafayette, Ind.	4	Coed	Public	35,372
Purdue University Regional Campuses:				
Calumet at Hammond	2	Coed	Public	4,640
Fort Wayne	2	Coed	Public	2,441

Name and Location	Level of Instruction	Student Body	Control	Enrollment
Quebec, University of, Quebec, Que.	2	Coed	Public	6,873
Queen's University at Kingston, Ontario	4	Coed	Private	8,087
Quincy College, Quincy, Ill.	2	Coed	Pvt-Roman Catholic	2,164
Quinnipiac College, Hamden, Conn.	3	Coed	Private	2,975
Quinsigamond Community College, Worcester, Mass.	1	Coed	Public	1,662
Radford College, Radford, Va.	3	Coed	Public	3,860
Randolph-Macon College, Ashland, Va.	2	Coed	Pvt-Methodist	784
Randolph-Macon Woman's College, Lynchburg, Va.	3	W	Pvt-Methodist	794
Redlands, University of, Redlands, Calif.	3	Coed	Pvt-Baptist	2,005
Redwoods, College of the, Eureka, Calif.	1	Coed	Public	4,564
Reed College, Portland, Oreg.	3	Coed	Private	1,318
Reedley College, Reedley, Calif.	1	Coed	Public	2,469
Regis College, Denver, Colo.	2	Coed	Pvt-Roman Catholic	1,414
Regis College, Weston, Mass.	2	W	Pvt-Roman Catholic	849
Rend Lake College, Ina, Ill.	1	Coed	Public	1,101
Rensselaer Polytechnic Institute, Troy, N.Y.	4	Coed	Private	4,737
Rhode Island, University of, Kingston, R.I.	4	Coed	Public	15,450
Rhode Island College, Providence, R.I.	4	Coed	Public	7,534
Rhode Island Junior College, Providence, R.I.	1	Coed	Public	4,043
Rhode Island School of Design, Providence, R.I.	3	Coed	Private	1,276
Rice University, Houston, Texas	4	Coed	Private	3,218
Richmond, University of, Richmond, Va.	4	Coord	Pvt-Baptist	4,992
Ricks College, Rexburg, Idaho	1	Coed	Pvt-Latter-day Saints	5,123
Rider College, Trenton, N.J.	3	Coed	Private	5,920
Rio Grande College, Rio Grande, Ohio	2	Coed	Private	750
Rio Hondo College, Whittier, Calif.	1	Coed	Public	10,570
Ripon College, Ripon, Wis.	3	Coed	Private	1,024
Riverside City College, Riverside, Calif.	1	Coed	Public	10,123
Roanoke College, Salem, Va.	2	Coed	Pvt-Lutheran	1,355
Robert Morris College, Coraopolis, Pa.	2	Coed	Private	4,349
Rochester, University of, Rochester, N.Y.	4	Coed	Private	8,461
Rochester Institute of Technology, Rochester, N.Y.	3	Coed	Private	10,436
Rochester State Junior College, Rochester, Minn.	1	Coed	Public	2,302
Rock Valley College, Rockford, Ill.	1	Coed	Public	3,916
Rockford College, Rockford, Ill.	3	Coed	Private	1,433
Rockhurst College, Kansas City, Mo.	2	Coed	Pvt-Roman Catholic	2,415
Rockingham Community College, Wentworth, N.C.	1	Coed	Public	1,244
Rockland Community College, Suffern, N.Y.	1	Coed	Public	5,495
Roger Williams College, Bristol, R.I.	2	Coed	Private	1,539
Rollins College, Winter Park, Fla.	3	Coed	Private	3,547
Roosevelt University, Chicago, Ill.	3	Coed	Private	7,049
Rosary College, River Forest, Ill.	3	W	Pvt-Roman Catholic	1,300
Rosary Hill College, Buffalo, N.Y.	2	W	Pvt-Roman Catholic	1,249
Rose-Hulman Institute of Technology, Terre Haute, Ind.	3	M	Private	1,138
Rowan Technical Institute, Salisbury, N.C.	1	Coed	Public	758
Russell Sage College, Troy, N.Y.	3	W	Private	3,404
Rust College, Holly Springs, Miss.	2	Coed	Pvt-Methodist	747
Rutgers University, New Brunswick, N.J.	4	Coord	Public	36,869
Sacramento City College, Sacramento, Calif.	1	Coed	Public	11,694
Sacramento State College, Sacramento, Calif.	3	Coed	Public	19,750
Sacred Heart, College of the, Santurce, P.R.	3	W	Pvt-Roman Catholic	797
Sacred Heart University, Bridgeport, Conn.	2	Coed	Pvt-Roman Catholic	2,042
Saddleback College, Mission Viejo, Calif.	1	Coed	Public	3,518
Saginaw Valley College, University Center, Mich.	2	Coed	Public	2,124
St. Ambrose College, Davenport, Iowa	3	Coed	Pvt-Roman Catholic	1,336
St. Andrews Presbyterian College, Laurinburg, N.C.	2	Coed	Pvt-Presbyterian	892
St. Anselm's College, Manchester, N.H.	2	Coed	Pvt-Roman Catholic	1,674
St. Augustine's College, Raleigh, N.C.	2	Coed	Pvt-Episcopal	1,118
St. Benedict, College of, St. Joseph, Minn.	2	W	Pvt-Roman Catholic	927
St. Bernard College, St. Bernard, Ala.	2	Coed	Pvt-Roman Catholic	632
St. Bonaventure University, St. Bonaventure, N.Y.	4	Coed	Pvt-Roman Catholic	2,637
St. Catherine, College of, St. Paul, Minn.	2	W	Pvt-Roman Catholic	1,367
St. Clair County Community College, Port Huron, Mich.	1	Coed	Public	3,129
St. Cloud State College, St. Cloud, Minn.	3	Coed	Public	9,965
St. Edward's University, Austin, Texas	3	Coed	Pvt-Roman Catholic	1,236
St. Elizabeth, College of, Convent Station, N.J.	2	W	Pvt-Roman Catholic	686
St. Francis, College of, Joliet, Ill.	2	Coed	Pvt-Roman Catholic	840
St. Francis College, Fort Wayne, Ind.	3	Coed	Pvt-Roman Catholic	2,226
St. Francis College, Brooklyn, N.Y.	2	Coed	Pvt-Roman Catholic	2,624
St. Francis College, Loretto, Pa.	3	Coed	Pvt-Roman Catholic	1,554
St. Francis Xavier University, Antigonish, Nova Scotia	3	Coed	Pvt-Roman Catholic	3,087
St. John Fisher College, Rochester, N.Y.	2	Coed	Pvt-Roman Catholic	849
St. John College of Cleveland, Ohio	2	Coed	Pvt-Roman Catholic	1,356
St. Johns River Community College, Palatka, Fla.	1	Coed	Public	1,299
St. John's University, Collegeville, Minn.	3	M	Pvt-Roman Catholic	1,604
St. John's University, Jamaica, N.Y.	4	Coed	Pvt-Roman Catholic	13,735
St. Joseph College, West Hartford, Conn.	3	W	Pvt-Roman Catholic	934
St. Joseph's College, Rensselaer, Ind.	2	Coed	Pvt-Roman Catholic	1,197
St. Joseph's College, Calumet Campus, East Chicago, Ind.	2	Coed	Pvt-Roman Catholic	1,605
St. Joseph's College, Philadelphia, Pa.	2	Coed	Pvt-Roman Catholic	6,897
St. Lawrence University, Canton, N.Y.	3	Coed	Private	2,508
St. Leo College, St. Leo, Fla.	2	Coed	Pvt-Roman Catholic	1,153
St. Louis, Junior College District of, St. Louis, Mo.	1	Coed	Public	
Florissant Valley Community College, St. Louis, Mo.	1	Coed	Public	6,415
Forest Park Community College, St. Louis, Mo.	1	Coed	Public	6,831
Meramec Community College, Kirkwood, Mo.	1	Coed	Public	7,273
St. Louis University, St. Louis, Mo.	4	Coed	Pvt-Roman Catholic	9,398
St. Mary's College, St. Mary's College, Calif.	3	M	Pvt-Roman Catholic	1,265
St. Mary's College, Notre Dame, Ind.	3	W	Pvt-Roman Catholic	1,789
St. Mary's College, Winona, Minn.	2	Coed	Pvt-Roman Catholic	995
St. Mary's College of Maryland, St. Mary's City, Md.	1	Coed	Public	941
St. Mary's Dominican College, New Orleans, La.	2	W	Pvt-Roman Catholic	859
St. Mary's Junior College, Minneapolis, Minn.	1	Coed	Pvt-Roman Catholic	737
St. Mary's University, Halifax, N.S.	3	Coed	Pvt-Roman Catholic	2,296
St. Mary's University, San Antonio, Texas	3	Coed	Pvt-Roman Catholic	3,977
St. Michael's College, Winooski Park, Vt.	3	Coed	Pvt-Roman Catholic	1,281
St. Norbert College, West De Pere, Wis.	2	Coed	Pvt-Roman Catholic	1,647
St. Olaf College, Northfield, Minn.	3	Coed	Pvt-Lutheran	2,650
St. Peter's College, Jersey City, N.J.	2	Coed	Pvt-Roman Catholic	4,561
St. Petersburg Junior College, St. Petersburg, Fla.	1	Coed	Public	9,979
St. Philip's College, San Antonio, Texas	1	Coed	Public	3,033
St. Rose, College of, Albany, N.Y.	3	Coed	Private	958
St. Scholastica, College of, Duluth, Minn.	3	Coed	Pvt-Roman Catholic	915
St. Teresa, College of, Winona, Minn.	2	Coed	Pvt-Roman Catholic	987
St. Thomas, College of, St. Paul, Minn.	3	Coed	Pvt-Roman Catholic	2,488
St. Thomas, University of, Houston, Texas	3	Coed	Pvt-Roman Catholic	1,510
St. Vincent College, Latrobe, Pa.	2	Coed	Pvt-Roman Catholic	1,027
St. Xavier College, Chicago, Ill.	2	Coed	Pvt-Roman Catholic	1,103
Salem College, Salem, W.Va.	3	Coed	Private	1,452
Salem State College, Salem, Mass.	3	Coed	Public	7,304
Salisbury State College, Salisbury, Md.	3	Coed	Public	1,984
Salve Regina College, Newport, R.I.	3	Coed	Pvt-Roman Catholic	817
Sam Houston State University, Huntsville, Texas	3	Coed	Public	11,844
Samford University, Birmingham, Ala.	3	Coed	Pvt-Baptist	2,973
San Antonio College, San Antonio, Texas	1	Coed	Public	16,059
San Bernardino Valley College, San Bernardino, Calif.	1	Coed	Public	13,808
San Diego, University of, College for Men, San Diego, Calif.	3	Coed	Pvt-Roman Catholic	1,501
San Diego City College, San Diego, Calif.	1	Coed	Public	4,894
San Diego Evening College, San Diego, Calif.	1	Coed	Public	12,479
San Diego Mesa College, San Diego, Calif.	1	Coed	Public	6,922
San Francisco, City College of, San Francisco, Calif.	1	Coed	Public	14,703
San Francisco, University of, San Francisco, Calif.	3	Coed	Pvt-Roman Catholic	6,311
San Francisco Art Institute, San Francisco, Calif.	3	Coed	Private	1,046
San Jacinto College, Pasadena, Texas	1	Coed	Public	6,995
San Joaquin Delta College, Stockton, Calif.	1	Coed	Public	12,099

Name and Location	Level of Instruction	Student Body	Control	Enrollment
San Jose City College, San Jose, Calif.	1	Coed	Public	14,814
San Mateo, College of, San Mateo, Calif.	1	Coed	Public	13,190
Sandhills Community College, Southern Pines, N.C.	1	Coed	Public	1,393
Santa Ana College, Santa Ana, Calif.	1	Coed	Public	9,352
Santa Barbara City College, Santa Barbara, Calif.	1	Coed	Public	6,453
Santa Clara, University of, Santa Clara, Calif.	4	Coed	Pvt-Roman Catholic	6,085
Santa Fe, College of, Santa Fe, N.Mex.	2	Coed	Pvt-Roman Catholic	1,264
Santa Fe Junior College, Gainesville, Fla.	1	Coed	Public	4,054
Santa Monica College, Santa Monica, Calif.	1	Coed	Public	12,254
Santa Rosa Junior College, Santa Rosa, Calif.	1	Coed	Public	10,659
Sarah Lawrence College, Bronxville, N.Y.	3	Coed	Private	841
Saskatchewan, University of, Saskatoon and Regina, Sask.	4	Coed	Public	13,257
Sauk Valley College, Dixon, Ill.	1	Coed	Public	1,614
Savannah State College, Savannah, Ga.	2	Coed	Public	2,444
Schoolcraft College, Livonia, Mich.	1	Coed	Public	6,017
Scranton, University of, Scranton, Pa.	3	Coed	Pvt-Roman Catholic	3,258
Seattle Central Community College, Seattle, Wash.	1	Coed	Public	7,200
Seattle Pacific College, Seattle, Wash.	3	Coed	Pvt-Methodist	1,984
Seattle University, Seattle, Wash.	3	Coed	Pvt-Roman Catholic	3,170
Seminole Junior College, Sanford, Fla.	1	Coed	Public	2,512
Sequoias, College of the, Visalia, Calif.	1	Coed	Public	5,896
Seton Hall University, South Orange, N.J.	4	Coed	Pvt-Roman Catholic	9,609
Seton Hill College, Greensburg, Pa.	2	Coed	Pvt-Roman Catholic	786
Shasta College, Redding, Calif.	1	Coed	Public	7,725
Shaw University, Raleigh, N.C.	2	Coed	Pvt-Baptist	1,060
Shepherd College, Shepherdstown, W.Va.	2	Coed	Public	2,054
Sherbrooke, University of, Sherbrooke, Quebec.	3	Coed	Pvt-Roman Catholic	4,165
Shippensburg State College, Shippensburg, Pa.	3	Coed	Public	4,059
Shoreline Community College, Seattle, Wash.	2	Coed	Public	6,883
Siena College, Loudonville, N.Y.	2	Coed	Pvt-Roman Catholic	1,821
Sierra College, Rocklin, Calif.	3	Coed	Public	3,081
Simmons College, Boston, Mass.	3	Coed	Private	2,585
Simon Fraser University, Burnaby, B.C.	4	Coed	Public	4,377
Simpson College, Indianola, Iowa.	1	Coed	Pvt-Methodist	957
Sinclair Community College, Dayton, Ohio.	1	Coed	Public	4,746
Sioux Falls College, Sioux Falls, S.Dak.	1	Coed	Pvt-Baptist	955
Sir George Williams University, Montreal, Quebec.	4	Coed	Pvt-YMCA	5,766
Siskiyous, College of the, Weed, Calif.	1	Coed	Public	1,333
Skagit Valley College, Mount Vernon, Wash.	2	Coed	Public	3,432
Skidmore College, Saratoga Springs, N.Y.	2	Coed	Private	1,868
Skyline College, San Bruno, Calif.	1	Coed	Public	4,742
Slippery Rock State College, Slippery Rock, Pa.	3	Coed	Public	6,020
Smith College, Northampton, Mass.	4	Coord	Private	2,794
Snead State Junior College, Boaz, Ala.	1	Coed	Public	1,175
Snow College, Ephraim, Utah.	1	Coed	Public	821
Solano Community College, Suisun City, Calif.	1	Coed	Public	6,139
Somerset County College, Somerville, N.J.	1	Coed	Public	1,343
South, University of the, Sewanee, Tenn.	3	Coed	Pvt-Episcopal	938
South Alabama, University of, Mobile, Ala.	3	Coed	Public	5,440
South Carolina, Medical University of, Charleston, S.C.	4	Coed	Public	1,185
South Carolina, University of, Columbia, S.C.	4	Coed	Public	16,615
South Carolina State College, Orangeburg, S.C.	3	Coed	Public	2,148
South Dakota, University of, Vermillion, S.Dak.	4	Coed	Public	6,854
South Dakota School of Mines & Technology, Rapid City, S.Dak.	4	Coed	Public	1,625
South Dakota State University, Brookings, S.Dak.	4	Coed	Public	7,057
South Florida, University of, Tampa, Fla.	3	Coed	Public	17,428
South Georgia College, Douglas, Ga.	1	Coed	Public	1,270
South Plains College, Levelland, Texas.	1	Coed	Public	1,739
Southeast Missouri State College, Cape Girardeau, Mo.	3	Coed	Public	7,554
Southeastern Community College, Whiteville, N.C.	1	Coed	Public	1,299
Southeastern Louisiana University, Hammond, La.	3	Coed	Public	5,790
Southeastern Massachusetts University, North Dartmouth, Mass.	3	Coed	Public	4,857
Southeastern State College, Durant, Okla.	3	Coed	Public	3,793
Southern Baptist College, Walnut Ridge, Ark.	1	Coed	Pvt-Baptist	722
Southern Baptist Theological Seminary, Louisville, Ky.	4	Coed	Pvt-Baptist	1,083
Southern California, University of, Los Angeles, Calif.	4	Coed	Private	18,884
Southern Colorado State College, Pueblo, Colo.	3	Coed	Public	6,344
Southern Connecticut State College, New Haven, Conn.	3	Coed	Public	12,727
Southern Idaho, College of, Twin Falls, Idaho.	1	Coed	Public	2,962
Southern Illinois University, Carbondale, Ill.:	4	Coed	Public	36,335
Southern Illinois University, Carbondale.	4	Coed	Public	24,543
Southern Illinois University, Edwardsville.	3	Coed	Public	14,266
Southern Methodist University, Dallas, Texas.	4	Coed	Pvt-Methodist	10,016
Southern Missionary College, Collegedale, Tenn.	4	Coed	Pvt-Seventh-day Adventist	1,414
Southern Mississippi, University of, Hattiesburg, Miss.	4	Coed	Public	10,868
Southern Oregon College, Ashland, Oreg.	2	Coed	Public	4,766
Southern State College, Magnolia, Ark.	3	Coed	Public	2,050
Southern Union State Junior College, Wadley, Ala.	1	Coed	Public	794
Southern University and Agricultural and Mechanical College, Baton Rouge, La.	3	Coed	Public	8,315
Southern Utah State College, Cedar City, Utah.	2	Coed	Public	1,947
Southwest Baptist College, Bolivar, Mo.	2	Coed	Pvt-Baptist	1,160
Southwest Minnesota State College, Marshall, Minn.	2	Coed	Public	3,136
Southwest Mississippi Junior College, Summit, Miss.	1	Coed	Public	852
Southwest Missouri State University, Springfield, Mo.	3	Coed	Public	9,478
Southwest Texas Junior College, Uvalde, Texas.	1	Coed	Public	1,274
Southwest Texas State University, San Marcos, Texas.	3	Coed	Public	11,280
Southwest Virginia Community College, Richlands, Va.	2	Coed	Public	1,012
Southwestern at Memphis, Tenn.	2	Coed	Pvt-Presbyterian	1,051
Southwestern Baptist Theological Seminary, Fort Worth, Texas.	4	Coed	Pvt-Baptist	1,920
Southwestern College, Chula Vista, Calif.	1	Coed	Public	8,008
Southwestern Junior College of the Assemblies of God, Waxahachie, Texas.	1	Coed	Pvt-Assemblies of God	635
Southwestern Louisiana, University of, Lafayette, La.	4	Coed	Public	10,654
Southwestern Michigan College, Dowagiac, Mich.	1	Coed	Public	1,140
Southwestern Oregon Community College, Coos Bay, Oreg.	1	Coed	Public	2,200
Southwestern University, Georgetown, Texas.	3	Coed	Pvt-Methodist	5,482
Spalding College, Louisville, Ky.	3	Coed	Pvt-Roman Catholic	862
Spartanburg County Technical Education Center, Spartanburg, S.C.	1	Coed	Public	1,067
Spartanburg Junior College, Spartanburg, S.C.	1	W	Pvt-Methodist	875
Spelman College, Atlanta, Ga.	2	Coed	Private	1,119
Spokane Community College, Spokane, Wash.	2	Coed	Public	5,805
Spring Arbor College, Spring Arbor, Mich.	2	Coed	Pvt-Methodist	721
Spring Hill College, Mobile, Ala.	3	Coed	Pvt-Roman Catholic	930
Springfield College, Springfield, Mass.	4	Coed	Private	2,692
Springfield Technical Community College, Springfield, Mass.	1	Coed	Public	2,643
Stanford University, Stanford, Calif.	4	Coed	Private	12,479
State Technical Institute at Memphis, Tenn.	1	Coed	Public	1,571
Stephen F. Austin State University, Nacogdoches, Texas.	3	Coed	Public	9,976
Stephens College, Columbia, Mo.	2	Coed	Private	2,052
Stetson University, De Land, Fla.	3	Coed	Private	3,034
Steubenville, College of, Steubenville, Ohio.	3	Coed	Pvt-Roman Catholic	1,304
Stevens Institute of Technology, Hoboken, N.J.	4	Coed	Private	2,340
Stonehill College, North Easton, Mass.	2	Coed	Pvt-Roman Catholic	1,905
Suffolk County Community College, Selden, N.Y.	1	Coed	Public	10,818
Suffolk University, Boston, Mass.	4	Coed	Private	2,537
Sul Ross State College, Alpine, Texas.	3	Coed	Public	1,238
Sullivan County Community College, South Fallsburg, N.Y.	1	Coed	Public	1,350
Sumter Area Technical Education Center, Sumter, S.C.	1	Coed	Public	963
Surry Community College, Dobson, N.C.	1	Coed	Public	1,501
Susquehanna University, Selinsgrove, Pa.	2	Coed	Pvt-Lutheran	1,501

Name and Location	Level of Instruction	Student Body	Control	Enrollment
Swarthmore College, Swarthmore, Pa.	3	Coed	Private	1,170
Sweet Briar College, Sweet Briar, Va.	2	W	Private	733
Syracuse University, Syracuse, N.Y.	4	Coed	Private	18,727
Tacoma Community College, Tacoma, Wash.	1	Coed	Public	4,066
Taft College, Taft, Calif.	1	Coed	Public	940
Talladega College, Talladega, Ala.	2	Coed	Pvt-Church of Christ	520
Tallahasse Community College, Tallahasse, Fla.	1	Coed	Public	2,556
Tampa, University of, Tampa, Fla.	2	Coed	Private	2,449
Tarleton State College, Stephenville, Texas	2	Coed	Public	3,181
Tarrant County Junior College, Fort Worth, Texas	1	Coed	Public	6,988
Taylor University, Upland, Ind.	2	Coed	Private	1,418
Technical Institute of Alamance, Burlington, N.C.	1	Coed	Public	932
Temple Buell College, Denver, Colo.	2	W	Public	896
Temple Junior College, Temple, Texas	1	Coed	Public	1,170
Temple University, Philadelphia, Pa.	4	Coed	Private	28,902
Tennessee, University of, System:				
Chattanooga	3	Coed	Public	4,873
Knoxville	4	Coed	Public	26,620
Martin	3	Coed	Public	4,907
Medical Units, Memphis	4	Coed	Public	1,784
Nashville	3	Coed	Public	2,945
Tennessee State University, Nashville, Tenn.	3	Coed	Public	4,404
Tennessee Technological University, Cookeville, Tenn.	3	Coed	Public	6,312
Texarkana College, Texarkana, Texas	1	Coed	Public	1,952
Texas, University of, System, Austin, Texas	4	Coed	Public	72,665
Arlington	4	Coed	Public	14,115
Austin	4	Coed	Public	45,442
El Paso	3	Coed	Public	11,484
Texas Agricultural & Mechanical University, College Station, Texas	4	Coed	Public	14,775
Texas Arts and Industries University, Kingsville, Texas	3	Coed	Public	8,096
Texas Christian University, Fort Worth, Texas	4	Coed	Pvt-Disciples of Christ	6,537
Texas Lutheran College, Seguin, Texas	2	Coed	Pvt-Lutheran	1,071
Texas Southern University, Houston, Texas	3	Coed	Public	6,174
Texas Southmost College, Brownsville, Texas	1	Coed	Public	1,583
Texas State Technical Institute, Waco, Texas	1	Coed	Public	1,558
Texas Tech University, Lubbock, Texas	4	Coed	Public	21,313
Texas Wesleyan College, Fort Worth, Texas	2	Coed	Pvt-Methodist	1,874
Texas Woman's University, Denton, Texas	4	W	Public	5,810
Thames Valley State Technical College, Norwich, Conn.	1	Coed	Public	1,018
Theodore Alfred Lawson State Junior College, Birmingham, Ala.	1	Coed	Public	1,127
Thiel College, Greenville, Pa.	3	Coed	Pvt-Lutheran	1,354
Thomas More College, Fort Mitchell, Ky.	2	Coed	Pvt-Roman Catholic	1,812
Thomas Nelson Community College, Hampton, Va.	1	Coed	Public	2,305
Thornton Community College, South Holland, Ill.	1	Coed	Public	6,797
Tidewater Community College, Portsmouth, Va.	1	Coed	Public	1,725
Toledo, University of, Toledo, Ohio	4	Coed	Public	14,887
Toronto, University of, Toronto, Ontario	4	Coed	Public	26,568
St. Michael's College, University of, Toronto	4	Coed	Pvt-Roman Catholic	
Trinity College, University of Toronto	4	Coed	Private	
Victoria College, University of Toronto	4	Coed	Private	
Tougaloo College, Tougaloo, Miss.	2	Coed	Private	752
Towson State College, Towson, Md.	3	Coed	Public	8,174
Transylvania College, Lexington, Ky.	2	Coed	Pvt-Disciples of Christ	971
Treasure Valley Community College, Ontario, Oreg.	1	Coed	Public	1,653
Trent University, Peterborough, Ontario	3	Coed	Private	2,725
Trenton State College, Trenton, N.J.	3	Coed	Public	10,929
Trevecca Nazarene College, Nashville, Tenn.	2	Coed	Pvt-Church of Nazarene	760
Trinidad State Junior College, Trinidad, Colo.	1	Coed	Public	1,398
Trinity College, Hartford, Conn.	3	Coed	Private	1,995
Trinity College, Washington, D.C.	2	W	Pvt-Roman Catholic	2,550
Trinity College, Deerfield, Ill.	3	Coed	Pvt-Evangelical	737
Trinity University, San Antonio, Texas	3	Coed	Pvt-Presbyterian	3,106
Tri-State College, Angola, Ind.	2	Coed	Private	1,605
Triton College, River Grove, Ill.	1	Coed	Public	12,222
Troy State University, Troy, Ala.	3	Coed	Public	6,082
Tufts University, Medford, Mass.	4	Coed	Private	5,560
Tulane University, New Orleans, La.	4	Coord	Private	8,732
Tulsa, University of, Tulsa, Okla.	4	Coed	Pvt-Presbyterian	6,194
Tuskegee Institute, Tuskegee Institute, Ala.	3	Coed	Private	3,073
Tyler Junior College, Tyler, Texas.	1	Coed	Public	3,882
Ulster County Community College, Stone Ridge, N.Y.	1	Coed	Public	2,129
Umpqua Community College, Roseburg, Oreg.	1	Coed	Public	1,049
Union College, Barbourville, Ky.	3	Coed	Pvt-Methodist	902
Union College, Lincoln, Nebr.	2	Coed	Pvt-Seventh-day Adventist	808
Union College, Cranford, N.J.	1	Coed	Private	3,624
Union College and University, Schenectady, N.Y.	3	Coed	Private	4,656
Union University, Jackson, Tenn.	2	Coed	Pvt-Baptist	862
United States Air Force Academy, Colorado Springs, Colo.	2	M	Public	4,201
United States Coast Guard Academy, New London, Conn.	2	M	Public	1,000
United States International University (including California Western Campus, Elliott Campus, and School of Performing Arts), San Diego, Calif.	4	Coed	Private	4,108
United States Merchant Marine Academy, Kings Point, N.Y.	2	M	Public	969
United States Military Academy, West Point, N.Y.	2	M	Public	4,000
United States Naval Academy, Annapolis, Md.	2	M	Public	4,310
Upper Iowa University, Fayette, Iowa	2	Coed	Private	988
Upsala College, East Orange, N.J.	2	Coed	Pvt-Lutheran	1,954
Ursinus College, Collegeville, Pa.	2	Coed	Pvt-Church of Christ	1,869
Utah, University of, Salt Lake City, Utah	4	Coed	Public	21,668
Utah State University, Logan, Utah	4	Coed	Public	8,842
Utah Technical College at Provo, Utah	1	Coed	Public	2,563
Utah Technical College at Salt Lake, Utah	1	Coed	Public	3,976
Valdosta State College, Valdosta, Ga.	3	Coed	Public	3,232
Valencia Junior College, Orlando, Fla.	1	Coed	Public	3,774
Valley City State College, Valley City, N.Dak.	2	Coed	Public	1,200
Valparaiso University, Valparaiso, Ind.	4	Coed	Pvt-Lutheran	4,703
Vanderbilt University, Nashville, Tenn.	4	Coed	Private	6,756
Vassar College, Poughkeepsie, N.Y.	3	Coed	Private	2,130
Ventura College, Ventura, Calif.	1	Coed	Public	4,808
Vermont, University of, Burlington, Vt.	4	Coed	Public	9,064
Victor Valley College, Victorville, Calif.	1	Coed	Public	1,967
Victoria, University of, Victoria, B.C.	4	Coed	Public	5,119
Victoria College, Victoria, Texas.	1	Coed	Public	1,711
Villanova University, Villanova, Pa.	4	Coed	Pvt-Roman Catholic	9,993
Vincennes University, Vincennes, Ind.	1	Coed	Public	3,900
Virgin Islands, College of the, St. Thomas, V.I.	2	Coed	Public	1,446
Virginia, University of, Charlottesville, Va.	4	Coord	Public	12,351
Mary Washington College, Fredericksburg, Va.	2	W	Public	2,111
Virginia Commonwealth University, Richmond, Va.	4	Coed	Public	14,892
Virginia Military Institute, Lexington, Va.	2	M	Public	1,154
Virginia Polytechnic Institute, Blacksburg, Va.	4	Coed	Public	14,492
Virginia State College, Petersburg, Va.	3	Coed	Public	3,684
Virginia Union University, Richmond, Va.	3	Coed	Pvt-Baptist	1,313
Virginia Western Community College, Roanoke, Va.	1	Coed	Public	3,174
Voorhees College, Denmark, S.C.	2	Coed	Pvt-Episcopal	735
W. W. Holding Technical Institute, Raleigh, N.C.	1	Coed	Public	861
Wabash College, Crawfordsville, Ind.	3	M	Private	790
Wagner College, Staten Island, N.Y.	3	Coed	Pvt-Lutheran	3,298
Wake Forest University, Winston-Salem, N.C.	4	Coed	Pvt-Baptist	3,738
Walker College, Jasper, Ala.	1	Coed	Private	723
Walla Walla College, College Place, Wash.	3	Coed	Pvt-Seventh-day Adventist	1,820
Walla Walla Community College, Walla Walla, Wash.	1	Coed	Public	2,319

Name and Location	Level of Instruction	Student Body	Control	Enrollment
Walsh College, Canton, Ohio	2	Coed	Pvt-Roman Catholic	899
Wartburg College, Waverly, Iowa	2	Coed	Pvt-Lutheran	1,361
Washburn University of Topeka, Kans.	3	Coed	Public	5,196
Washington, University of, Seattle, Wash.	4	Coed	Public	33,478
Washington and Jefferson College, Washington, Pa.	2	M	Private	1,094
Washington and Lee University, Lexington, Va.	3	M	Private	1,612
Washington College, Chesterton, Md.	2	Coed	Private	879
Washington State University, Pullman, Wash.	4	Coed	Public	14,539
Washington Technical Institute, Washington, D.C.	1	Coed	Public	3,042
Washington University, St. Louis, Mo.	4	Coed	Private	11,197
Waterbury State Technical College, Waterbury, Conn.	1	Coed	Public	1,365
Waterloo, University of, Waterloo, Ont.	4	Coed	Public	11,716
Waterloo Lutheran University, Waterloo, Ontario	3	Coed	Pvt-Lutheran	2,826
Waubonsee Community College, Sugar Grove, Ill.	1	Coed	Public	3,564
Wayland Baptist College, Plainview, Texas	2	Coed	Pvt-Baptist	746
Wayne Community College, Goldsboro, N.C.	1	Coed	Public	1,680
Wayne State College, Wayne, Nebr.	3	Coed	Public	2,668
Wayne State University, Detroit, Mich.	4	Coed	Public	36,765
Waynesburg College, Waynesburg, Pa.	2	Coed	Pvt-Presbyterian	1,081
Weatherford College, Weatherford, Texas	1	Coed	Public	1,105
Weber State College, Ogden, Utah	3	Coed	Public	9,818
Webster College, St. Louis, Mo.	3	Coed	Private	1,665
Wellesley College, Wellesley, Mass.	2	W	Private	1,872
Wells College, Aurora, N.Y.	2	W	Private	617
Wenatchee Valley College, Wenatchee, Wash.	1	Coed	Public	1,637
Wentworth Institute, Boston, Mass.	1	M	Private	1,661
Wesley College, Dover, Del.	1	Coed	Pvt-Methodist	990
Wesleyan University, Middletown, Conn.	4	Coed	Private	1,881
West Chester State College, West Chester, Pa.	3	Coed	Public	8,151
West Coast University, Los Angeles, Calif.	3	Coed	Private	1,029
West Florida, University of, Pensacola, Fla.	3	Coed	Public	3,843
West Georgia College, Carrollton, Ga.	3	Coed	Public	6,114
West Hills College, Coalinga, Calif.	1	Coed	Public	745
West Liberty State College, West Liberty, W.Va.	2	Coed	Public	3,953
West Los Angeles College, Culver City, Calif.	1	Coed	Public	4,832
West Texas State University, Canyon, Texas	3	Coed	Public	7,351
West Valley College, Campbell, Calif.	1	Coed	Public	12,293
West Virginia College of Graduate Studies, Institute, W.Va.	3	Coed	Public	1,116
West Virginia Inst. of Technology, Montgomery, W.Va.	2	Coed	Public	2,411
West Virginia State College, Institute, W.Va.	3	Coed	Public	3,590
West Virginia University, Morgantown, W.Va.	4	Coed	Public	17,941
West Virginia Wesleyan College, Buckhannon, W.Va.	1	Coed	Pvt-Methodist	1,675
Westchester Community College, Valhalla, N.Y.	1	Coed	Public	5,749
Western Carolina College, Cullowhee, N.C.	3	Coed	Public	5,517
Western Connecticut State College, Danbury, Conn.	3	Coed	Public	4,372
Western Illinois University, Macomb, Ill.	3	Coed	Public	13,711
Western Kentucky University, Bowling Green, Ky.	3	Coed	Public	11,922
Western Maryland College, Westminster, Md.	2	Coed	Private	2,325
Western Michigan University, Kalamazoo, Mich.	4	Coed	Public	21,846
Western Montana College, Dillon, Mont.	3	Coed	Public	1,008
Western New England College, Springfield, Mass.	3	Coed	Private	3,586
Western New Mexico University, Silver City, N.Mex.	3	Coed	Public	1,505
Western Ontario, University of, London, Ontario	4	Coed	Public	12,219
Western Piedmont Community College, Morganton, N.C.	1	Coed	Public	1,076
Western State College of Colorado, Gunnison, Colo.	3	Coed	Public	3,194
Western Washington State College, Bellingham, Wash.	3	Coed	Public	10,868
Western Wisconsin Technical Institute, La Crosse, Wis.	1	Coed	Public	1,975
Westfield State College, Westfield, Mass.	3	Coed	Public	2,667
Westmar College, Le Mars, Iowa	2	Coed	Pvt-Methodist	979
Westminster College, New Wilmington, Pa	2	Coed	Pvt-Presbyterian	2,011
Westminster College, Salt Lake City, Utah	2	Coed	Pvt-Methodist	813
Westmont College, Santa Barbara, Calif.	2	Coed	Private	894
Wharton County Junior College, Wharton, Texas	1	Coed	Public	2,017
Wheaton College, Wheaton, Ill.	3	Coed	Private	2,079
Wheaton College, Norton, Mass.	2	Coed	Private	1,217
Wheelock College, Boston, Mass.	3	Coed	Private	914
Whitman College, Walla Walla, Wash.	2	Coed	Private	1,062
Whittier College, Whittier, Calif.	3	Coed	Private	2,363
Whitworth College, Spokane, Wash.	3	Coed	Pvt-Presbyterian	1,654
Wichita State University, Wichita, Kans.	4	Coed	Public	13,034
Widener College, Chester, Pa.	3	Coed	Private	1,574
Wilberforce University, Wilberforce, Ohio.	3	Coed	Pvt-Methodist Episcopal	1,291
Wilkes College, Wilkes-Barre, Pa.	3	Coed	Private	3,436
Wilkes Community College, Wilkesboro, N.C.	1	Coed	Public	992
Willamette University, Salem, Oreg.	3	Coed	Pvt-Methodist	1,713
William and Mary, College of, Williamsburg, Va	4	Coed	Public	7,211
William Carey College, Hattiesburg, Miss.	2	Coed	Pvt-Baptist	797
William Jewell College, Liberty, Mo.	2	Coed	Pvt-Baptist	1,089
William Paterson College of New Jersey, Wayne, N.J.	3	Coed	Public	7,139
William Penn College, Oskaloosa, Iowa	2	Coed	Pvt-Friends	822
William Rainey Harper College, Palatine, Ill	1	Coed	Public	8,917
William Woods College, Fulton, Mo.	2	W	Pvt-Disciples of Christ	1,200
Williams College, Williamstown, Mass	3	Coed	Private	1,592
Williamsport Area Community College, Williamsport, Pa.	1	Coed	Public	4,009
Willmar State Junior College, Willmar, Minn.	1	Coed	Public	788
Wilmington College, Wilmington, Ohio.	2	Coed	Pvt-Friends	996
Windham College, Putney, Vt.	2	Coed	Private	876
Windsor, University of, Windsor, Ont.	4	Coed	Private	5,940
Wingate College, Wingate, N.C.	1	Coed	Pvt-Baptist	1,667
Winnipeg, University of, Winnipeg, Manitoba	3	Coed	Pvt-United Church	2,408
Winona State College, Winona, Minn.	3	Coed	Public	4,261
Winston-Salem State University, Winston-Salem, N.C.	2	Coed	Public	1,623
Winthrop College, Rock Hill, S.C.	3	Coed	Public	3,879
Wisconsin, University of:				
Eau Claire, Wis.	3	Coed	Public	8,679
Green Bay, Wis.	3	Coed	Public	4,579
La Crosse, Wis.	3	Coed	Public	7,009
Madison, Wis.	4	Coed	Public	33,943
Milwaukee, Wis.	4	Coed	Public	22,277
Oshkosh, Wis.	3	Coed	Public	11,811
Parkside, Wis.	2	Coed	Public	1,710
Platteville, Wis.	3	Coed	Public	4,708
River Falls, Wis.	3	Coed	Public	4,255
Stevens Point, Wis.	3	Coed	Public	9,154
Stout, Wis.	3	Coed	Public	5,231
Superior, Wis.	3	Coed	Public	3,004
Whitewater, Wis.	3	Coed	Public	8,867
Wisconsin, University of, Center System, Madison, Wis.	1	Coed	Public	5,841
Wittenberg University, Springfield, Ohio	2	Coed	Pvt-Lutheran	3,121
Wofford College, Spartanburg, S.C.	2	M	Pvt-Methodist	1,030
Woodbury College, Los Angeles, Calif.	2	Coed	Private	2,236
Wooster, College of, Wooster, Ohio.	3	Coed	Pvt-Presbyterian	1,881
Worcester Junior College, Worcester, Mass.	1	Coed	Private	1,725
Worcester Polytechnic Institute, Worcester, Mass.	4	Coed	Private	2,476
Worcester State College, Worcester, Mass.	3	Coed	Public	3,919
Wright State University, Dayton, Ohio.	3	Coed	Public	12,199
Wyoming, University of, Laramie, Wyo.	4	Coed	Public	8,546
Wytheville Community College, Wytheville, Va.	1	Coed	Public	1,014
Xavier University, Cincinnati, Ohio.	3	Coed	Pvt-Roman Catholic	5,964
Xavier University of Louisiana, New Orleans, La	3	Coed	Pvt-Roman Catholic	1,554
Yakima Valley College, Yakima, Wash	1	Coed	Public	3,602
Yale University, New Haven, Conn	4	Coed	Private	9,245
Yeshiva University, New York, N.Y.	4	Coord	Pvt-Jewish	3,891
York College of Pennsylvania, York, Pa.	2	Coed	Private	2,321
York County Technical Education Center, Rock Hill, S.C.	1	Coed	Public	946
York University, Toronto, Ont.	4	Coed	Public	9,787
Youngstown State University, Youngstown, Ohio	3	Coed	Public	14,588
Yuba College, Marysville, Calif.	1	Coed	Public	5,392

─────── UPPER VOLTA • Information Highlights ───────

Official Name: Republic of Upper Volta.
Area: 105,869 square miles (274,200 sq km).
Population (1972 est.): 5,600,000. *Density,* 52 per square mile (20 per sq km). *Annual rate of increase,* 2.0%.
Chief Cities (1966 est.): Ouagadougou, the capital, 77,500; Bobo Dioulassa, 72,500.
Government: *Head of state,* Gen. Sangoulé Lamizana, president (took office Jan. 1966). *Chief minister,* Gérard Kango Ouédraogo, prime minister (took office Feb. 1971). *Legislature* (unicameral)—National Assembly, 57 members. *Major political parties*—Voltaic Democratic Union; Party of African Regroupment; National Liberation Movement.
Languages: French (official), Mossi.
Education: *School enrollment* (1968)—primary, 99,827; general secondary, 8,117; technical/vocational, 1,298; university/higher, 122.
Monetary Unit: CFA franc (255.79 CFA francs equal U. S.$1, Aug. 1972).
Gross National Product (1970 est.): $305,000,000.
Manufacturing (major products): Processed agricultural products.
Major Agricultural Products: Groundnuts, sesame, cotton, millet and sorghum, corn, livestock.
Major Minerals: Limestone, manganese.
Foreign Trade (1971): *Exports,* $16,000,000. *Imports,* $50,-000,000. *Chief trading partners* (1969)—Ivory Coast (took 40% of exports, supplied 14% of imports); France (13%—49%); Ghana (11%—4%).
Communications: *Telephones* (1970), 4,000; *television stations* (1971), 1; *television sets* (1971), 3,000; *radios,* 87,000.

UPPER VOLTA

During 1972, Upper Volta continued to be ruled by the combined military-civilian government that had been instituted in 1971.

Domestic Affairs. The Voltaic Democratic Union (UDV), led by Prime Minister Gérard Kango Ouédraogo, maintained its control over the National Assembly. The only significant opposition came from the National Liberation Movement (MLN), headed by Joseph Ki-Zerbo. The army seemed content to leave the running of the state mainly in civilian hands, perhaps because the presidency was held by a member of the military, Gen. Sangoulé Lamizana, who was to remain in power at least until 1975.

Despite some signs of friction, notably over the details of the budget presented in January, Upper Volta's unusual dual-control governmental system worked well throughout the year. It provided the country with one of the freest and least authoritarian regimes in West Africa.

Foreign Affairs. President Lamizana made a state visit to Egypt and Libya in February. The main result of his mission was the negotiation of two agreements between Upper Volta and Egypt, one cultural and the other for technical cooperation. The parties agreed to exchange students, teachers, and the results of scientific research, and Egypt contracted to supply teachers of Arabic for schools in Upper Volta.

Economy. Inadequate rainfall during 1971 led to conditions of near famine in some parts of Upper Volta. In January 1972 the United Nations Food and Agriculture Organization granted $488,000 to aid victims of drought.

With scant natural resources of its own, Upper Volta sought solutions to its economic development problems in two main ways in 1972: by encouraging aid from outside Africa, and by cooperating with its neighbors. On January 13 an important treaty was signed with France. By the terms of this agreement the French government placed a total of 111,950,000 CFA francs at the disposal of Upper Volta. These funds, intended to cover 1973 as well as 1972, were to assist in providing social services and to finance research projects in agriculture and livestock raising.

Upper Volta is a signatory to the treaty that set up the West African Economic Community (CEAO) in June 1972. It is also, with Mali and Niger, a member of the Liptako-Gourma authority, which held a meeting at the head-of-state level in August at Ouagadougou. The authority is responsible for formulating plans that deal with international highways, the flow of the Niger River, dam construction and irrigation, crop management, and education within the three-state area.

GRAHAM W. IRWIN, *Columbia University*

URUGUAY

Juan M. Bordaberry, a Colorado party leader, became president of Uruguay for a five-year term on March 1, 1972. By late 1972, as the armed forces moved into active politics and the economy faltered, there was serious doubt that he could maintain the constitutional, civilian-controlled system in effect since 1897.

Political Developments. By 1971 the extremist Tupamaros, once considered roguish and romantic, had become openly terrorist. Former President Jorge Pacheco was forced to obtain army support, and by the end of his term some senior officers were advocating a coup d'etat.

Bordaberry at first enjoyed some success against the Tupamaros, although the quasi-truce practiced during the election was broken by terrorist attacks before he took office, and sporadic terrorism continued throughout 1972. Sen. Wilson Ferreira Aldunate, leader of the opposition Nacional party, collaborated on security measures, but refused to support the president in a parliamentary coalition until there was government acceptance of fundamental economic reforms regarding land ownership and tax policy. Bordaberry, a rightist conservative and the country's largest landowner, rejected this position and decreed austerity measures bearing heavily on urban workers and the middle class.

Hard-line army leaders moved against the Tupamaros with generous use of massive arrests and torture. By mid-1972 the military also was openly defying Bordaberry. In October, Jorge Batlle, a minority faction Colorado leader, was arrested and tried by the military for "insults" to its honor. Three ministers resigned in protest, and the president was forced to name a new cabinet. Severely

─────── URUGUAY • Information Highlights ───────

Official Name: Eastern Republic of Uruguay.
Area: 68,536 square miles (177,508 sq km).
Population (1972 est.): 3,000,000. *Density,* 41 per square mile (17 per sq km). *Annual rate of increase,* 1.2%.
Chief City (1970 est.): Montevideo, the capital, 1,400,000.
Government: *Head of state,* Juan M. Bordaberry, president (took office March 1972). *Head of government,* Juan M. Bordaberry. *Legislature*—National Assembly: Senate, 31 members; Chamber of Deputies, 99 members. *Major political parties*—Colorado party; Blanco (Nacional) party.
Language: Spanish (official).
Education: *Expenditure* (1967), 2% of gross national product. *School enrollment* (1968)—primary, 369,816; secondary, 160,693; technical/vocational, 35,648; university/higher, 18,650.
Monetary Unit: Peso (647 pesos equal U. S.$1, Sept. 1972).
Gross National Product (1971 est.): $2,435,000,000.
Manufacturing (major products): Meat products, textiles, construction and building materials, beverages, chemicals.
Major Agricultural Products: Wheat, corn, rice, livestock, wool.
Major Minerals: Marble, building stone, gravel.
Foreign Trade (1971): *Exports,* $206,000,000. *Imports,* $227,-000,000. *Chief trading partners* (1969)—West Germany (took 10% of exports, supplied 11% of imports); United Kingdom (13%—6%); United States (7%—14%); Brazil (5%—14%).
Communications: *Telephones* (1971), 215,299; *television stations* (1971), 12; *television sets* (1971), 225,000; *radios* (1970), 1,081,000; *newspapers* (1969), 31.

challenged by the military and the terrorists, and beset by a ravaged economy, Bordaberry appeared unable to stem collapse.

Economic Affairs. With outgoing President Pacheco rejecting even minimal change in economic policy, Uruguay approached bankruptcy in 1971. Money in circulation rose 33.5% to pay budget deficits in 1971 alone and finance inflation. Bordaberry's first week in office saw a 100% devaluation of the peso. Six "mini-devaluations" cut the official value another 25% by September. Gross domestic product fell 1% in 1971 and was expected to drop further in 1972.

In the first eight months of 1972 living costs rose 54%. Despite labor union pressure, Bordaberry permitted only 40% increases in wages, in two stages. Even this brought severe criticism from the International Monetary Fund.

Combined public and private foreign debt reached about $750 million, much of it short term. Scheduled amortization and interest payments in 1972 were $300 million, and on January 1 the foreign exchange holdings of the Central Bank were under $1 million. The expected 1972 budget deficit was about $40 million. Some foreign refinancing was obtained, but export capability fell sharply as severe weather had destroyed grain crops and live cattle had been smuggled into Brazil in response to Pacheco's unrealistic controls over meat pricing.

International Relations. During the 1971 elections, many Uruguayans were upset by leftist claims that Brazil was about to attack Uruguay on grounds that Tupamaro activity was posing a security threat across the border. Seeking to reassure Uruguay, Brazil gave both trading concessions and financial help to the hard-pressed country, but private Brazilian speculative purchases of Uruguayan ranchland created alarm. Argentine relations generally were good, but Uruguay's financial straits forced suspension of major joint public-works projects.

PHILIP B. TAYLOR, JR., *University of Houston*

UTAH

In 1972, news in Utah was made by the death of a church leader and by the elections.

Religion. President Joseph Fielding Smith, the tenth president of the Church of Jesus Christ of Latter-day Saints, died on July 2, 1972. He would have been 96 years old on July 19. President Smith was sustained by more than 3 million members of his church as a Prophet of God in January 1970. He served as church president for almost two and a half years and had been a general authority for more than 62 years. Smith had long been acknowledged as the leading authority on his church's history and doctrine, continuity and mission. President Harold B. Lee, who has been first counselor to President Smith, was later named and sustained as the 11th president and Prophet of the Church of Jesus Christ of Latter-day Saints.

Politics. Utah's voters overwhelmingly gave President Nixon the state's four electoral votes, while electing Democrat Calvin L. Rampton to an unprecedented third gubernatorial term by a crushing margin over his opponent, Nicholas L. Strike, a Salt Lake City businessman. The voter turnout in Utah far exceeded the estimated national turnout of 56%. A political survey shows that, starting with 1920, Utah has always been among the top six states in voter turnout.

Ticket-splitting was prevalent. For example, Democratic freshman Congressman K. Gunn McKay was reelected over a Republican challenger in Utah's 1st congressional district, and the voters retired Republican Congressman Sherman Lloyd, who had served four terms, in favor of a newcomer to Utah politics, Democrat Wayne Owens, in the state's 2d congressional district.

Owens waged a unique campaign against the incumbent by "walking the length and breadth of the state." Aware of his lack of identity with the voters, Owens set out to become known by literally walking through every county in the state and concentrating finally on the 11 counties in the 2d congressional district. According to his account, he logged over 1,200 miles on foot and, as is now apparent, was successful.

Utahans also approved by wide margins four major propositions to amend the state constitution. These amendments were drafted by the Utah Constitutional Revision Committee and were passed by the Legislature before being submitted to the electorate. The propositions were designed (1) to streamline the legislative process; (2) to deny bail to anyone on parole or probation on a previous felony conviction or to anyone already free on bail on a felony arrest if the magistrate feels there is a strong case against the suspect; (3) to remove the mandatory requirements for separate school districts between counties and cities of first- or second-class status (60,000 or more); and (4) to give counties the opportunity to select their own forms of government, subject to referendum.

LORENZO K. KIMBALL
University of Utah

──────── **UTAH • Information Highlights** ────────

Area: 84,916 square miles (219,932 sq km).
Population (1970 census): 1,059,273. *Density,* 13 per sq mi.
Chief Cities (1970 census): Salt Lake City, the capital, 175,-885; Ogden, 69,478; Provo, 53,131; Bountiful, 27,956.
Government (1972): *Chief Officers*—governor, Calvin L. Rampton (D); secy. of state, Clyde L. Miller (D); atty. gen., Vernon B. Romney (R); treas., Golden L. Allen (R); supt. of public instruction, Walter D. Talbot; chief justice, E. Richard Callister, Jr. *Legislature*—Senate, 28 members (16 Republicans, 12 Democrats); House of Representatives, 69 members (31 R, 38 D).
Education (1971–72): *Enrollment*—public elementary schools, 164,363 pupils, 5,828 teachers; public secondary, 141,383 pupils, 5,570 teachers; nonpublic schools (1970–71), 4,729 pupils, 190 teachers; college and university, 79,000 students. *Public school expenditures,* $200,343,000 ($696 per pupil). *Average teacher's salary,* $8,981.
State Finances (fiscal year 1970): *Revenues,* $552,785,000 (4% general sales tax and gross receipts taxes, $90,-976,000; motor fuel tax, $37,805,000; federal funds, $161,-883,000). *Expenditures,* $527,938,000 (education, $253,-904,000; health, welfare, and safety, $59,050,000; highways, $108,118,000). *State debt,* $103,089,000 (June 30, 1970).
Personal Income (1971): $3,731,000,000; per capita, $3,395.
Public Assistance (1971): $53,980,000. *Average monthly payments* (Dec. 1971)—old-age assistance, $62.66; aid to families with dependent children, $185.93.
Labor Force: Nonagricultural wage and salary earners (July 1972), 387,400. *Average annual employment* (1971)—manufacturing, 55,000; trade, 83,000; government, 102,000; services, 61,000. *Insured unemployed* (Aug. 1972)—7,000 (2.9%).
Manufacturing (1969): *Value added by manufacture,* $1,054,-600,000. Food and kindred products, $98,400,000; transportation equipment, $86,700,000; nonelectrical equipment, $69,000,000; petroleum and coal products, $47,700,-000; printing and publishing, $45,400,000.
Agriculture (1970): *Cash farm income,* $237,161,000 (livestock, $181,299,000; crops, $44,718,000; government payments, $11,144,000). *Chief crops* (in order of value, 1971)—Hay, wheat, barley, sugar beets.
Mining (1970): *Production value,* $629,587,000 (ranks 15th among the states). *Chief minerals*—Copper, $358,826,000; petroleum, $66,975,000; coal, $37,900,000; molybdenum.
Transportation: *Roads* (1971), 40,440 miles (65,080 km); *motor vehicles* (1971), 825,870; *railroads* (1971), 1,760 miles (2,832 km); *public airports* (1972), 54.
Communications: *Telephones* (1972), 635,200; *television stations* (1971), 3; *radio stations* (1971), 42; *newspapers* (1972), 5 (daily circulation, 259,000).

PREMIER-ELECT David Barrett talks to newsmen after New Democratic party victory in British Columbia.

VANCOUVER

Vancouver, the largest city of British Columbia, received in 1972 the prospect of policies to restrict development—in line with popular arguments against the "Manhattanization" of the city. The election in December 1972 of a younger city council was preceded by the election in August 1972 of a provincial government formed by the socialist New Democratic party, which promised new directions in dealing with Vancouver. The population of the city, according to the 1971 census, was 426,256, and of the metropolitan area, 1,082,352.

Municipal Government. The conservative wing of the Vancouver city council, headed by Tom Campbell, who retired was defeated in the December civic election. Campbell was replaced as mayor by Art Phillips, who said: "We don't want to halt all development, but we don't want Vancouver to become another Manhattan." Steps to ease Manhattanization were also taken by the new provincial government. Among other things, it promised to reduce the height—55 stories—of a proposed downtown government building. It killed plans for a road tunnel under Burrard Inlet, linking Vancouver and the North Shore, and promised to push a rapid transit program instead. In October, consultants proposed a carnival park, along the lines of Copenhagen's Tivoli Gardens, for Vancouver's Granville Island. It would tie in with plans to redevelop the False Creek industrial slum area.

In May the council extended to tenants the right to vote on money bylaws. Previously this right was restricted to property owners. A strike by Vancouver civic employees at the end of April spread to four metropolitan municipalities before settlement in mid-June.

Education. The fall 1972 enrollment at the University of British Columbia slipped to 19,259 from 20,183 in 1971. At Simon Fraser University, there was an increase—from 5,048 in 1971 to 5,491 in 1972. The number of persons, some 10,000, taking courses at Vancouver City College remained about the same as in 1971.

Commerce. The port of Vancouver, the largest cargo port on the Pacific, handled an estimated 35 million tons of cargo in 1972, matching the 1971 record despite the closing of the port from August 7 to September 5 by a longshoremen's labor dispute. Bids for construction of a new container cargo terminal were asked in November, and construction of a general cargo terminal on the North Shore was approved.

Hughes Visit. Billionaire industrialist-recluse Howard Hughes made Vancouver his home from March through August. He arrived secretly from the Bahamas, lived in tight security in a $1,000-a-day suite atop the Bayshore Inn, and left secretly for Nicaragua.

Don MacLachlan, *"The Province," Vancouver*

VENEZUELA

Politics were much in evidence in Venezuela in 1972, a nonelection year. Student unrest continued, but economic development was sustained.

Political Affairs. Although presidential elections were scheduled for December 1973, political parties chose their candidates during the summer of 1972. President Rafaél Caldera was constitutionally unable to succeed himself, and his Social Christian party (COPEI) named Lorenzo Fernández, a former interior minister. Democratic Action, the country's largest party, nominated Carlos Andrez Pérez, the party secretary, after former president Romulo Betancourt declined to run. Other nominees were José Angel Paz Galarraga, candidate of the Democratic Republican Union, the Communist party and several smaller groups; José V. Rangel, representing dissident Communists; and, possibly, former dictator Marcos Pérez Jiménez. The latter, who has been

─────── VENEZUELA • Information Highlights ───────

Official Name: Republic of Venezuela.
Area: 352,143 square miles (912,050 sq km).
Population (1972 est.): 11,500,000. *Density*, 32.7 per square mile (12.6 per sq km). *Annual rate of increase*, 3.4%.
Chief Cities (1969 est.): Caracas, the capital, 1,600,000; Maracaibo, 625,100; Barquisimeto, 280,100.
Government: *Head of state*, Rafaél Caldera, president (took office March 1969). *Head of government*, Rafaél Caldera. *Legislature*—National Congress: Senate, 52 members; Chamber of Deputies, 214 members. *Major political parties*—Democratic Action party (AD); Social Christian party (COPEI); People's Electoral Movement (MEP).
Language: Spanish (official).
Education: *Expenditure* (1969), 20.9% of total public expenditure. *School enrollment* (1969)—primary, 1,681,947; secondary, 448,214; technical/vocational, 146,421; university/higher, 70,185.
Monetary Unit: Bolivar (4.40 bolivares equal U. S.$1, Sept. 1972).
Gross National Product (1971 est.): $10,020,000,000.
National Income per Person (1970): $837.
Economic Indexes: *Industrial production* (1970), 127 (1963 = 100); *agricultural production* (1971), 241 (1952–56 = 100); *consumer price index* (1971), 115 (1963 = 100).
Manufacturing (major products): Petroleum products, processed foods, paper and paperboard, chemicals, beverages, metal products, furniture, clothing.
Major Agricultural Products: Coffee, cacao, bananas, sugarcane, cotton, rice, corn, dairy products.
Major Minerals: Petroleum (ranks 5th among world producers, 1970), natural gas, iron ore, gold, nickel, diamonds.
Foreign Trade (1971): *Exports*, $3,098,000,000 (chief exports—petroleum; iron ore). *Imports*, $1,931,000,000 (chief imports, 1969—nonelectrical machinery; motor vehicles; chemicals; electric machinery and appliances). *Chief trading partners* (1969)—United States (took 34% of exports, supplied 50% of imports); Netherlands Antilles (20%—1%); Canada (12%—5%).
Tourism: *Receipts* (1970), $50,000,000.
Transportation: *Motor vehicles* (1969), 752,000 (automobiles, 552,000); *railroads* (1970), 109 miles (175 km); *merchant fleet* (1971), 412,000 gross registered tons; *major national airline*, VIASA (Venezolana Internacional de Aviacion).
Communications: *Telephones* (1971), 405,613; *television stations* (1971), 29; *television sets* (1971), 700,000; *radios* (1970), 1,700,000; *newspapers* (1969), 38 (daily circulation, 709,000).

living in exile in Spain, received a warm greeting from his followers during a brief visit to Caracas in the spring, but efforts were under way to legally bar him from seeking office because of a past conviction for misusing public funds. Pérez Jiménez also was threatened with a murder charge.

President Caldera reorganized his cabinet in April and added a Ministry of Youth. He also appointed a number of new state governors. At the beginning of the year his government announced it would take strong measures against subversion. An upsurge of guerrilla activities, including detected kidnap plots against a number of prominent Venezuelans, was attributed to the Cubans and to the Uruguayan-based urban guerrillas known as Tupamaros. Several students were shot during the year in confrontations with the police, and all schools in Caracas were closed for several weeks in April and May because of student unrest. Central University was re-opened after a two-year suspension under stringent new rules, which gave the government greater control over the university.

Economic Affairs. The 1972–73 budget of $2.9 billion was twice that of 1965. Major expenditures were to be in education, public works, defense, and health. The gross national product continued to grow at the rate of 5% a year. The first pension checks payable to citizens under the terms of the 1967 revised Social Security Act were mailed to 20,000 recipients. More than 180,000 persons benefited from the completion of 30,000 new low-cost housing units, and the government was hoping to construct another 150,000 in the next three years.

The Petrochemical Institute was spending $4 million to build four new plants, and the Electrical Development Administration, $66.2 million to expand some of its facilities. The government planned to invest $4 million in improving communication facilities in western Venezuela. The InterAmerican Development Bank (IDB) granted Venezuela a loan of $75 million for hoof and mouth disease control and $30 million for the construction of 12 miles (19 km) of freeway around Caracas. A bill pending in Congress would enable the government's Venezuelan Petroleum Corporation (CVP) to take over the marketing of gas and oil derivatives by 1975. The three largest oil companies have signed 23-year service contracts with CVP.

International Affairs. The relationship of Venezuela to the Andean Pact Common Market remained undecided in 1972 despite prolonged discussions. On June 30, Venezuela terminated its reciprocal trade agreement with the United States, which had been in force since 1939. Caldera had rejected arbitration in the standing dispute with Colombia over ownership of the continental shelf of the Gulf of Venezuela, but bilateral discussions continued.

In July, Venezuela purchased $60 million in arms from France, the largest single purchase of ground weapons in Latin America since World War II. The United States agreed to deliver 100 air-to-air missiles to Venezuela, the first such concession to a Latin American country. Venezuela also bought 10,000 voting machines from the United States.

Brazil, Venezuela, and Colombia were studying the feasibility of transportation links between the Amazon and Plate river system.

Death of Leoni. Raúl Leoni, president of Venezuela from 1964 to 1969, died in July in New York, where he had gone for medical treatment.

LEO B. LOTT, *University of Montana*

VERMONT • Information Highlights

Area: 9,609 square miles (24,887 sq km).
Population (1970 census): 444,732. *Density,* 49 per sq mi.
Chief Cities (1970 census): Montpelier, the capital, 8,609; Burlington, 38,633; Rutland, 19,293; Bennington, 14,586; Brattleboro, 12,239; Essex, 10,951; Barre, 10,209.
Government (1972): *Chief Officers*—governor, Deane C. Davis (R); lt. gov., John S. Burgess (R); secy. of state, Richard C. Thomas (R); atty. gen., James M. Jeffords (R); treas., Frank H. Davis (R); commissioner, dept. of education, James Oakey; chief justice, P. L. Shangraw. *General Assembly*—Senate, 30 members (22 Republicans, 8 Democrats); House of Representatives, 150 members (95 R, 52 D, 3 neither party).
Education (1971–72): *Enrollment*—public elementary schools, 67,236 pupils, 3,186 teachers; public secondary, 48,784 pupils, 3,118 teachers; nonpublic schools (1970–71), 12,143 pupils, 890 teachers; college and university, 22,000 students. *Public school expenditures,* $124,637,000 ($1,208 per pupil). *Average teacher's salary,* $8,978.
State Finances (fiscal year 1970): *Revenues,* $274,624,000 (3% general sales tax and gross receipts taxes, $17,065,000; motor fuel tax, $16,094,000; federal funds, $71,029,000). *Expenditures,* $288,767,000 (education, $98,910,000; health, welfare, and safety, $44,187,000; highways, $73,076,000). *State debt,* $220,603,000 (June 30, 1970).
Personal Income (1971): $1,654,000,000; per capita, $3,610.
Public Assistance (1971): $39,795,000. *Average monthly payments* (Dec. 1971)—old-age assistance, $75.07; aid to families with dependent children, $231.69.
Labor Force: *Nonagricultural wage and salary earners* (July 1972), 155,100. *Average annual employment* (1971)—manufacturing, 38,000; trade, 29,000; government, 28,000; services, 29,000. *Insured unemployed* (Aug. 1972)—4,300 (4.2%).
Manufacturing (1970): *Value added by manufacture,* $556,300,000. Nonelectrical machinery, $105,000,000; stone, clay, and glass products, $50,300,000; printing and publishing, $48,600,000; food and kindred products, $36,500,000.
Agriculture (1970): *Cash farm income,* $165,063,000 (livestock, $148,706,000; crops, $14,977,000; government payments, $1,380,000). *Chief crops* (in order of value, 1971)—Hay, apples, maple syrup, potatoes.
Mining (1971): *Production value,* $36,284,000 (ranks 46th among the states). *Chief minerals*—Stone, $28,135,000; sand and gravel, $3,518,000; asbestos, value not available; talc, value not available.
Transportation (1971): *Roads,* 14,464 miles (23,277 km); *motor vehicles,* 228,796; *railroads,* 769 miles (1,238 km); *public airports* (1972), 13.
Communications: *Telephones* (1972), 249,800; *television stations* (1971), 2; *radio stations* (1971), 22; *newspapers* (1972), 9 (daily circulation, 117,000).

VERMONT

Elections, beginning in January and extending to November, tended to dominate events in Vermont in 1972. In a major political upset, Thomas Salmon, a Democrat, was elected governor to succeed outgoing Republican Gov. Deane C. Davis.

Elections. A special election was held on January 7 to fill the unexpired term of Republican U. S. Sen. Winston L. Prouty, who died in September 1971. The Republican interim appointee, former U. S. Rep. Robert T. Stafford, won easily. Richard W. Mallary, a Republican and a former speaker of the state House of Representatives, was elected to Vermont's single seat in the U. S. House of Representatives, vacated by Stafford.

The Republican gubernatorial campaign began early in the spring, and in the September primary election, Luther Hackett, the candidate favored by the party organization and most businessmen, won the nomination over state Attorney General James Jeffords, a liberal and an environmentalist. The Democratic gubernatorial candidate, Thomas Salmon, was unopposed in that party's primary.

In the November general election, the Republican presidential candidate, President Richard Nixon, won 63% of Vermont's popular vote. Republicans also triumphed in the contests for seats in the state legislature. Although there was considerable turnover, the political balance of the legislature remained unchanged. In the gubernatorial race, Hackett was the favorite from the first and was expected to win by a large margin, but because of some

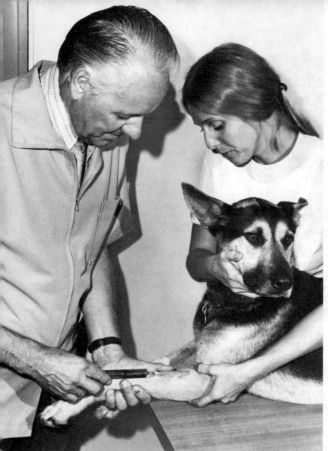

THE NEW YORK TIMES

VETERINARIAN in St. Augustine, Fla., inoculates a dog against heartworms, a life-threatening infection that is spreading in the South.

costly mistakes and the vigorous campaign waged by Salmon, he received only 43% of the popular vote to 56% for Salmon.

Reapportionment and Other Legislative Action. The 1972 legislature reapportioned the state Senate, only to have the plan declared unconstitutional by the Vermont supreme court, which ordered the Legislative Apportionment Board to bring in a new plan in two weeks. The court also rejected this plan and directed that the fall elections be held under the existing apportionment, while the board and the legislature were to prepare and enact a new and acceptable plan by June 1973. A suit was filed in federal district court, asking that elections be held in mid-1973, once a new plan has been accepted.

Protection of the environment loomed large as a subject of debate and legislation. Stringent laws were enacted to regulate such sources of pollution or environmental damage as nonreturnable containers and snowmobiles.

ANDREW E. NUQUIST, *University of Vermont*

VETERINARY MEDICINE

The U. S. poultry industry was threatened by an exotic bird disease in 1972, and a flare-up of hog cholera occurred in several states. The use of a growth stimulant called diethylstilbestrol was banned in animal feeds.

Poultry Hazard. Exotic Newcastle disease, a viral disease introduced into the United States in a shipment of exotic birds and distinguished from domestic Newcastle disease, reached serious proportions in southern California early in 1972. Because it is highly contagious, and usually fatal, it posed a threat to the entire U. S. poultry industry. In March, Secretary of Agriculture Butz declared a national emergency so that funds could be allocated to fight the disease. More than 1,200 departmental and state veterinarians and other personnel, assisted by more than 130 Air Force and Army veterinarians and 295 other military personnel assigned on a temporary basis, took part in the program.

First, a massive vaccination program was launched that eventually handled many millions of birds. By July these efforts were beginning to take effect, and the spread of the disease was slowed. The vaccine is considered to be 80% effective, but unfortunately the virus persists in a flock once birds are infected. Birds protected by the vaccine can carry the virus and shed it intermittently. One method of detecting such carriers is to place "sentinel" birds in flocks—that is, birds raised in a disease-free environment and therefore highly susceptible to the disease. Second, inspection stations were set up along major highways to make certain that vehicles transporting poultry and poultry products were complying with quarantine regulations. Pet birds were allowed into but not out of quarantine areas. In August, commercial imports of all live pet and exotic birds were banned, including finches, parakeets, canaries, parrots, and mynahs. Owners were allowed to bring caged birds into the country, but only under certain conditions. Third, infected and exposed flocks were destroyed and indemnities paid to owners. By August, 4.3 million birds had been destroyed. Toward the end of the year the disease was being controlled.

Hog Cholera. The 10-year-old program of hog cholera eradication received a serious setback when outbreaks flared up in states thought free of the disease: Indiana, Kentucky, Nebraska, Ohio, and Tennessee. Over 100 cases were reported in July–October 1972, compared with 76 for the previous 12-month period. To counter the threat to the $4.5 billion U. S. pork industry, the Department of Agriculture took emergency action to increase indemnities to producers whose hogs had to be destroyed. Quarantines were extended to include all or parts of 43 counties in nine states, and specially trained veterinarians were assigned to investigate suspected cases and to inspect hog markets.

Ban of DES in Feeds. With the release of new data showing that residues of diethylstilbestrol (DES) persist in animal tissues for as long as 30 days, the Food and Drug Administration banned use of the chemical as a growth stimulant in animal feeds, beginning Jan. 1, 1973. The delay was permitted because FDA Commissioner Charles Edwards said DES, which has produced cancer in experimental animals, does not represent an imminent health hazard. The ban also does not apply to the use of DES in implants, since residues of the chemical have not been found in tissues when implantation was employed. Livestock men find DES valuable because the estimated weight gains brought about by its use save them about $90 million annually in grain and feedlot costs. The rising number of DES-positive tissue specimens was attributed to improper use of the chemical.

ARTHUR FREEMAN, D. V. M.
*Editor of the Journal of the American
Veterinary Medical Association*

Survivors of the siege of An Loc, a town just north of Saigon, search through the rubble of the chief market for food or other items of value.

VIETNAM

North Vietnam's military offensive that began Easter weekend in April 1972 and the high-level peace talks between Washington and Hanoi late in the year had political and economic effects on both Vietnams.

SOUTH VIETNAM

The Communist military thrust in the spring further battered South Vietnam's economy. Worse, it also had a visibly adverse effect on national morale. Peace talks between the U. S. and North Vietnamese negotiators, Henry Kissinger and Le Duc Tho, later in the year caused South Vietnam's President Nguyen Van Thieu to seek to consolidate his political position at home.

End of an Era. The United States, a dominant political and economic—as well as military—force in the country for many years, cut back its presence in 1972. It was the end of an era, and Thieu, as a result, variously expressed his independence of Washington. U. S. pressure for Saigon's acquiescence in the results of the Kissinger negotiations threw Thieu off balance. His opposition to a settlement on terms prejudicial to the survival of his government strained relations with the United States.

As the United States disengaged, Thieu felt under less pressure to govern as the Americans wished him to do. Critical of "disorderly democracy," he jailed many civilians for political reasons, reduced the influence of the legislature, and further restricted the press.

Politics. President Thieu resorted to a midnight vote in June—when most senators were honoring the government's curfew—to gain the right to rule by decree on matters of defense and economy for six months. In August he abolished elections for the country's 10,795 hamlets. Appointed province chiefs, mostly soldiers, henceforth were to name both village and hamlet officials. Having announced, in February, that he would launch a new political party, Thieu indicated in November that plans were underway to complete a new mass party and that four or five existing parties would join the organization.

The South Vietnamese leader's political efforts were designed to solidify his hold on the country as a cease-fire approached. The signs pointed to military domination at all levels of Vietnamese political life.

Communist Thrust. The North Vietnamese Easter offensive took its toll in the South Vietnamese countryside, adding one million persons to the refugee rolls. Although the percentage of South Vietnam's population under Communist rule doubled as a result of the strong Communist thrust into the south, it stood at only 2% at year-end, with another 8% living in contested areas. One positive result of

> *Coverage of the war will be found under INDO-CHINA WAR. See also separate articles on ASIA and on countries involved in the conflict.*

SOUTH VIETNAMESE airman paints his country's flag insignia on the tail of one of the dozens of aircraft the United States turned over to South Vietnam.

the offensive was the disillusionment with Communist rule of those South Vietnamese who lived under it temporarily until liberated by the army.

Economy. Economically, 1972 was a bad year for South Vietnam. The Easter invasion cut the annual rice harvest by 500,000 tons, necessitating the import of 200,000 tons from the United States. Meanwhile, the economic effect of the U. S. military pullout, was to cut annual dollar earnings in half, to $200 million. Many small businesses closed because of insufficient American patronage.

The badly damaged rubber industry was hurt further by the fierce fighting around the rubber towns of Loc Ninh, An Loc, and Dau Tang. The

---

SOUTH VIETNAM • Information Highlights

Official Name: Republic of Vietnam.
Area: 67,108 square miles (173,809 sq km).
Population (1972 est.): 18,700,000. *Density,* 279 per square mile (107 per sq km). *Annual rate of increase,* 2.6%.
Chief Cities (1968 est.): Saigon, the capital, 1,681,900; Da Nang, 334,200; Hue, 156,500.
Government: *Head of state,* Nguyen Van Thieu, president (re-elected Oct. 1971). *Head of government,* Nguyen Van Thieu. *Legislature*—National Assembly: Senate, 60 members; House of Representatives, 159 members.
Languages: Vietnamese (official), French, English.
Education: *Expenditure* (1969), 4.2% of total public expenditure. *School enrollment* (1969)—primary, 2,375,982; secondary, 655,413; technical/vocational, 14,569; university/higher, 47,296.
Monetary Unit: Piaster (435 piasters equal U. S.$1, Sept. 1972).
Gross National Product (1970 est.): $3,200,000,000.
Manufacturing (major products): Processed foods, textiles.
Major Agricultural Products: Rice, natural rubber, poultry, fish.
Foreign Trade (1970): *Exports,* $7,000,000. *Imports,* $325,-000,000. *Chief trading partners* (1969)—France (took 48% of exports, supplied 5% of imports); Japan (17%—25%); United States (2%—39%).
Communications: *Telephones* (1971), 34,889; *television stations* (1971), 1; *television sets* (1971), 14,000; *radios* (1969), 1,300,000; *newspapers* (1970), 56 (daily circulation, 1,221,000).

---

textile industry also was hurt by the temporary escalation of the war. Vietnamese consumers held off purchases because of general uncertainty, and some manufacturers were forced to shut down.

The dreary state of the economy was reflected in the budget for 1973, with expenditures up 18.5% over 1972. The largest single source of revenue was to be the printing of more piasters—this despite the chronic 20% rate of inflation.

Foreign Relations. President Thieu's fears respecting the intentions of his key ally, the United States, increased during the year. Thieu, unhappy over the fact of President Nixon's February trip to Peking, was visibly upset by the resulting Shanghai communiqué, which emphasized U. S. military disengagement from Asia. The Saigon leader also feared that Nixon's May visit to Moscow was part of a big power strategy to end the Indochina War on terms prejudicial to South Vietnam.

The apparent progress in the Paris talks late in 1972 seemed to Thieu to confirm his fears. Finding the peace proposals "objectionable," he strongly pressed the Americans not to allow North Vietnamese forces to remain in his country. Accelerated U. S. military shipments to Saigon late in the year were designed to placate Thieu.

NORTH VIETNAM

North Vietnam's Easter offensive probably was intended as a last push to enlarge the South Vietnamese territory under Hanoi's control prior to the seemingly imminent political settlement. But it was a costly move, resulting in stepped-up U. S. bombing raids.

Preparing for "Peace." Besides the April offensive, the Communists made a last-ditch effort to gain new territory on the eve of an expected agreement, while peace negotiations were underway in October. The Vietcong reappeared in strength in

PRESIDENT THIEU of South Vietnam, shown at Saigon rally, balked at terms of proposed peace pact.

provinces surrounding Saigon, from which they previously had been driven out. They also engaged in new acts of terrorism, assassination, and all manner of psychological guerrilla warfare. These were expected to continue—and possibly to accelerate—after a U. S. withdrawal.

This resumption of harassment was related to the anticipated "peace." The Communists would be represented on the National Council for Reconciliation and Concord, which was expected to be set up as part of a settlement, and to play a part in the establishment of a new government structure. Their military strategy was calculated to ensure maximum attainment of their political objectives.

Politics. There were reports of political struggles in 1972 within both the Hanoi ruling elite and the allied pro-Communist provisional revolutionary government in the south, as well as between these two political partners. Pham Van Dong, North Vietnam's 64-year-old premier, reportedly was seriously ill, and there was speculation as to what effect his health and possible demise might have on the collegium that has ruled North Vietnam since Ho Chi Minh's death in 1969. Claims that the moderates had gained the upper hand in Hanoi were supported by the apparent progress in the peace talks. Yet some observers found no significant differences in Hanoi's negotiating position.

Within the Vietcong a power struggle was developing over who would represent the movement in key roles in post-settlement South Vietnamese politics. Some Vietcong leaders also resented their non-participation in the shaping of a settlement.

Economy. North Vietnam was hurt even more than the south by the war during 1972. Its economy already shattered by years of bombing, the north suffered greater destruction of its physical facilities and a further loss of lives as a result of U. S. retaliatory bombing after the Eastern offensive.

Industries, power plants, and communications centers were the chief casualties of the accelerated air raids. Decentralization of industry, however, allowed the north to continue its output of farm tools, cement, and other light manufactures.

A major food crisis was experienced during the year—more as a consequence of weather conditions, however, than the war. Rice and other foodstuffs were sent by China, and famine was averted.

Relations with China and the USSR. Despite such help from China, Hanoi's relations with Peking —and with Moscow—were ruffled in 1972. The Hanoi leadership was upset when the Chinese hosted President Nixon in February, and, while the event was never reported in the North Vietnamese press, there was strong, if veiled, criticism of Peking for placing its relations with Washington above those with an ally. China's Premier Chou En-lai made a hasty visit to placate Hanoi.

Hanoi similarly was displeased with Moscow's hosting of the U. S. President in May. Its subsequent reception of Soviet President Podgorny was cooler than on the latter's visit six months earlier.

Like Saigon, Hanoi feared that the big powers were trying to force a settlement. Both Peking and Moscow apparently did put pressure on North Vietnam to reach an early agreement with the United States. Yet Hanoi, itself, in November and December sought Soviet and Chinese help to ensure that the Americans would not abandon the peace talks.

RICHARD BUTWELL
State University of New York at Brockport

VIETNAM WAR. See INDOCHINA WAR.

VIRGIN ISLANDS

Early in 1972 the U. S. Congress and President Nixon approved a law providing for a resident commissioner from the Virgin Islands to participate with voice but no vote in the deliberations of the House of Representatives. In the November election Ron de Lugo, a native of St. Thomas who for two years had been the unofficial representative of the Virgin Islands in Washington, was elected for a two-year term as a nonvoting congressman.

In 1972 a 33-member constitutional convention met several times in the Virgin Islands to draw up the territory's first constitution. The unique document provided for a unicameral legislature of 15 members, who will serve for two years. The executive branch will continue to be directed by a governor, who is to be chosen every four years. The proposed constitution surprisingly received lukewarm support in a referendum, thus putting in doubt the necessary approval by Congress and the President before becoming the law of the islands.

A resolution adopted by the convention asserted that the Virgin Islands wished to remain an unincorporated territory under the United States. This resolution was to be sent to the United Nations as well as to Congress.

Increased returns from tourism and from tax receipts on products sold in the United States bolstered a booming economy in the islands. Relief from continual water shortages was expected with the construction of two new desalination plants, which were scheduled for completion by mid-1974.

THOMAS G. MATHEWS
University of Puerto Rico

NORTH VIETNAM • Information Highlights

Official Name: Democratic Republic of Vietnam.
Area: 61,294 square miles (158,750 sq km).
Population (1972 est.): 22,000,000. *Density,* 359 per square mile (139 per sq km). *Annual rate of increase,* 2.4%.
Chief City (1960 census): Hanoi, the capital, 414,620.
Government: *Head of state,* Ton Duc Thang, president (took office Sept. 1969). *Head of government,* Pham Van Dong, premier (took office July 1954). *First Secretary of Communist party,* Le Duan. *Legislature*—National Assembly, 420 members.
Language: Vietnamese (official).
Monetary Unit: Dong (2.71 dongs equal U. S.$1, June 1972).
Gross National Product (1970 est.): $1,600,000,000.
Manufacturing (major products): Processed foods, cement.
Major Agricultural Products: Rice, sweet potatoes, and yams.
Major Minerals: Coal, iron ore, apatite, chromium ore.
Foreign Trade: *Chief export*—Coal. *Chief imports*—Food; petroleum products; motor vehicles, machinery; textiles.

VIRGIN ISLANDS • Information Highlights

Area: 133 square miles (344 sq km).
Population (1970 census): 62,468.
Chief Cities (1970 census): Charlotte Amalie (St. Thomas), the capital, 12,220; Christiansted (St. Croix), 3,020; Frederiksted (St. Croix), 1,531.
Government (1972): *Chief Officers*—governor, Melvin H. Evans (took office Jan. 4, 1971); lt. gov., David Maas; atty. gen., Ronald Tonkin. *Legislature*—Territorial Legislature, 15 members.
Education (1970–71): *Enrollment*—public schools, 17,362 pupils; nonpublic schools, 5,705 pupils; college and university (fall 1971), 1,500 students. *Average teacher's salary,* $8,500.
Per Capita Personal Income (1971): $3,000.
Mining (1971): *Production value,* $1,700,000. *Chief mineral* —Stone, $1,700,000.
Trade with the United States (1970): *Exports,* $240,300,000; *imports,* $168,500,000.
Transportation: *Roads* (1972), 420 miles (676 km); *motor vehicles* (1971), 26,485.
Communications: *Telephones* (1971), 24,644; *television stations* (1971), 2; *radio stations* (1971), 5; *newspapers* (1971), 4 (daily circulation, about 7,000).

────── **VIRGINIA · Information Highlights** ──────

Area: 40,817 square miles (105,716 sq km).
Population (1970 census): 4,648,494. *Density:* 118 per sq mi.
Chief Cities (1970 census): Richmond, the capital, 249,430; Norfolk, 307,951; Virginia Beach, 172,106; Newport News, 138,177; Hampton, 120,779.
Government (1972): *Chief Officers*—governor, Linwood Holton (R); lt. gov., Henry E. Howell, Jr. (independent); secy. of state, Mrs. Cynthia Newman (R); atty. gen., Andrew P. Miller (D); treas., Walter W. Craigie, Jr. (R); supt. of public instruction, Woodrow W. Wilkerson; chief justice, Harold F. Snead. *General Assembly*—Senate, 40 members (33 Democrats, 7 Republicans); House of Delegates, 100 members (74 D, 23 R, 3 independents).
Education (1971–72): *Enrollment*—public elementary schools, 672,257 pupils; 29,450 teachers; public secondary, 401,816 pupils, 21,950 teachers; nonpublic schools (1970–71), 65,939 pupils; 3,210 teachers; college and university, 146,000 students. *Public school expenditures,* $880,450,000 ($875 per pupil). *Average teacher's salary,* $9,400.
State Finances (fiscal year 1970): *Revenues,* $1,768,415,000 (3% general sales tax and gross receipts taxes, $210,045,000; motor fuel tax, $146,477,000; federal funds $327,927,000). *Expenditures,* $1,681,245,000 (education, $673,781,000; health, welfare, and safety, $102,370,000; highways, $427,094,000). *State debt,* $323,194,000 (June 30, 1970).
Personal Income (1971): $18,225,000,000; per capita, $3,866.
Public Assistance (1971): $181,760,000. *Average monthly payments* (Dec. 1971)—old-age assistance, $69.86; aid to families with dependent children, $174.72.
Labor Force: *Nonagricultural wage and salary earners* (July 1972), 1,557,800. *Average annual employment* (1971)—manufacturing, 362,000; trade, 312,000; government, 315,000; services, 227,000. *Insured unemployed* (Aug. 1972) —9,600 (0.9%).
Manufacturing (1970): *Value added by manufacture,* $4,867,500,000. Chemicals and allied products, $807,500,000; tobacco manufactures, $569,500,000; food and kindred products, $480,600,000; electrical equipment and supplies, $388,800,000; transportation equipment, $382,300,000; textile mill products, $342,600,000.
Agriculture (1970): *Cash farm income,* $622,363,000 (livestock, $344,014,000; crops, $258,338,000; government payments, $20,011,000). *Chief crops* (in order of value, 1971)—Tobacco (ranks 4th among the states), hay, corn.
Mining (1971): *Production value,* $385,161,000 (ranks 19th among the states). *Chief minerals*—Coal, $254,870,000; stone, cement, sand and gravel.
Fisheries (1971): *Commercial catch,* 488,981,000 pounds ($21,937,000). *Leading species by value:* Lobsters, $5,341,000; crabs, $4,008,000; clams, $1,925,000; squid, $802,000.
Transportation: *Roads* (1971), 61,136 miles (98,386 km); *motor vehicles* (1971), 2,262,721; *railroads* (1971), 3,880 miles (6,244 km); *public airports* (1972), 52.
Communications: *Telephones* (1972), 2,652,300; *television stations* (1971), 12; *radio stations* (1971), 182; *newspapers* (1972), 32 (daily circulation, 1,009,000).

VIRGINIA

Republicans fared well in Virginia politics during 1972. President Richard M. Nixon carried the state easily over Democratic candidate Sen. George McGovern.

Democratic and Republican Reorganizations. At the state convention of the Democratic party, liberals ousted moderates, by narrow margins, from positions as national committeeman and state chairman and, by larger margins, elected a largely McGovern delegation to the national convention. When McGovern was later nominated, many conservative Democrats joined former Gov. Mills Godwin in campaigning actively for Nixon's reelection.

At the Republican state convention, conservatives elected one of their own as party chairman, defeating the reelection bid of a moderate associated with the faction headed by Gov. Linwood Holton. The Senate nomination went by default to conservative Congressman William Scott.

Fall Campaign. In his campaign against Democratic incumbent William Spong, Scott portrayed himself as a conservative in Nixon's image, while he also attempted to identify Spong as a liberal in McGovern's mold. But Spong declined to endorse McGovern, and he accused Scott of attempting to ride the coattails of President Nixon. Vice President Agnew made two trips to Virginia on behalf of Scott and Nixon. Unlike the divided Democrats, the Republicans united in support of the national ticket.

Election Results and Consequences. In the November election Nixon trounced McGovern by a 69% to 30% margin. Scott defeated Spong by a surprisingly safe margin of about 80,000 votes. In the House races in the 10 realigned districts, Republicans retained their six seats and added a seventh vacated by retiring conservative Democrat Watkins Abbitt. Two of the three remaining Democratic congressmen were unopposed Byrd-style conservatives.

The apparent conservative take-over of the Republican party, together with ex-Governor Godwin's support of Nixon, led to speculation that Godwin would run for the governorship in 1973 as a Republican or as an independent without Republican opposition. Meanwhile, the liberal Lt. Gov. Henry Howell, elected as an independent, added to the confusion by announcing his candidacy for the governorship but declining to indicate whether he would run as a Democrat or an independent.

Legislation. The reapportioned General Assembly met in regular session early in the year. Fifty of the 140 members were new. The Assembly continued its basically progressive course.

In brief, the legislature (1) raised the income tax from 5% to 5.75% on incomes exceeding $12,000 and increased corporate and gasoline taxes; (2) established a cabinet-type structure under the governor, consisting of six secretaries (finance, education, human affairs, commerce and resources, transportation and public safety, and administration); (3) passed legislation to help finance low-cost housing; (4) increased the general fund appropriations for higher education by 37%; (5) passed various bills designed to protect the environment, including a rather weak measure aimed at strip mining; (6) passed a bill authorizing loans to state students attending private colleges in Virginia; (7) stiffened the laws against drunk driving; (8) established day-care centers for children of mothers on welfare; (9) eliminated the ban on cocktail lounges at public places; (10) extended majority rights to 18-year-olds except for jury duty and liquor purchases; and (11) lowered the penalties for marihuana possession.

The establishment of a governor's cabinet was considered a victory for Republican Governor Holton. But the Democratic Assembly balked at his budget recommendations, trimming 5%, for example, from his proposed budget for education.

School Integration. On January 10 federal Judge Robert Merhige, Jr., rendered a school decision that attracted nationwide attention. He ordered the merger of three school districts (Richmond city and the surrounding counties of Henrico and Chesterfield). This was the first time any judge had ordered mergers of separate school districts to achieve racial balance. Later, however, the Fourth District Court of Appeals overturned Merhige's decision, and an appeal was made to the U. S. Supreme Court.

Poff's Appointment. Governor Holton appointed Congressman Richard Poff to the Virginia Supreme Court. In 1971 Poff had declined to accept President Nixon's nomination to the U. S. Supreme Court. He became the first Republican in the 20th century to occupy a seat on the Virginia bench.

WILLIAM LARSEN, *Radford College*

VITAL STATISTICS. See POPULATION.
WALDHEIM, Kurt. See BIOGRAPHY.
WALLACE, George C. See BIOGRAPHY.
WANKEL, Felix. See BIOGRAPHY.

UPI

WASHINGTON

In the 1972 elections in Washington, which were highlighted by the longest ballot in the state's history, Gov. Daniel J. Evans, a Republican, won an unprecedented third consecutive four-year term over Albert D. Rosellini, a Democrat and two-term former governor. However, the Legislature, previously divided, went to the Democrats. All six incumbent Democratic representatives were returned to Congress. The seat of Rep. Thomas Pelly, a Republican, who did not seek reelection, was won by another Republican, former state Sen. Joel Pritchard, in a contest decided by absentee ballots.

Election Issues. Much of the election interest centered on six job-creating bond issues of Governor Evans' "Washington Future" program. The voters approved five bond issues totaling $415 million—for waste disposal, water quality, outdoor recreation, community health facilities, and expansion of the community college system. They rejected only a bond issue for public transportation.

A special session of the Legislature, called early in the year to consider means of achieving economic recovery, contributed to the long ballot in the general election. The special session added one proposal for a constitutional amendment and eight referendum measures to the seven other proposals for constitutional amendment, which had been advanced by the regular legislative session. In addition, there were several voter-sponsored initiatives, including one to legalize dog racing and another to remove the state liquor monopoly and allow retail sales; both of these were defeated.

The proposals for constitutional amendment that generated the most discussion were those to legalize gambling, to limit property taxes to 1% of true and fair value, and to guarantee "equality of rights and responsibilities" for every person regardless of sex. The voters adopted all three amendments. However, the equal rights amendment owed its passage to absentee ballots.

GRADE SCHOOL was one of several buildings in Vancouver, Wash., that were leveled by a freak tornado in April. Six persons were killed.

─────── **WASHINGTON • Information Highlights** ───────

Area: 68,192 square miles (176,617 sq km).
Population (1970 census): 3,409,169. *Density,* 50 per sq mi.
Chief Cities (1970 census): Olympia, the capital, 23,111; Seattle, 530,831; Spokane, 170,516; Tacoma, 154,581.
Government (1972): *Chief Officers*—governor, Daniel J. Evans (R); lt. gov., John A. Cherberg (D); secy. of state, A. Ludlow Kramer (R); atty. gen., Slade Gorton (R); treas., Robert S. O'Brien (D); supt. of public instruction, Louis Bruno; chief justice, Orris L. Hamilton. *Legislature*—Senate, 49 members (29 Democrats, 20 Republicans); House of Representatives, 99 members (51 R, 48 D).
Education (1971–72): *Enrollment*—public elementary schools, 427,401 pupils, 17,249 teachers; public secondary, 377,648 pupils, 16,231 teachers; nonpublic schools (1970–71), 46,228 pupils, 2,230 teachers; college and university, 168,-000 students. *Public school expenditures,* $650,000,000 ($866 per pupil). *Average teacher's salary,* $10,705.
State Finances (fiscal year 1970): *Revenues,* $1,956,640,000 (4.5% general sales tax and gross receipts taxes, $546,-236,000; motor fuel tax, $140,878,000; federal funds, $357,930,000). *Expenditures,* $1,972,584,000 (education, $788,420,000; health, welfare, and safety, $260,802,000; highways, $272,582,000). *State debt,* $719,724,000 (June 30, 1970).
Personal Income (1971): $14,260,000,000; per capita, $4,135.
Public Assistance (1971): $258,662,000. *Average monthly payments* (Dec. 1971)—old-age assistance, $61.74; aid to families with dependent children, $196.79.
Labor Force: *Nonagricultural wage and salary earners* (July 1972), 1,079,400. *Average annual employment* (1971)—manufacturing, 213,000; trade, 236,000; government, 252,-000; services, 171,000. *Insured unemployed* (Aug. 1972)—47,600 (5.9%).
Manufacturing (1970): *Value added by manufacture,* $3,637,-800,000. Transportation equipment, $631,800,000; lumber and wood products, $529,300,000; food and kindred products, $502,500,000; paper and allied products, $433,200,-000; primary metal industries, $358,300,000; chemicals and allied products, $173,900,000.
Agriculture (1970): *Cash farm income,* $860,385,000 (livestock, $290,290,000; crops, $512,207,000; government payments, $57,888,000). *Chief crops* (in order of value, 1971)—Wheat (ranks 3d among the states), apples (ranks 1st), hay, potatoes (ranks 3d).
Mining (1971): *Production value,* $94,687,000 (ranks 35th among the states). *Chief minerals*—Sand and gravel, $26,-744,000; cement, $23,880,000; stone, $20,489,000; uranium.
Fisheries (1971): *Commercial catch,* 130,449,000 pounds ($30,-238,000).
Transportation: *Roads* (1971), 75,098 miles (120,855 km); *motor vehicles* (1971), 2,101,961; *railroads* (1971), 4,931 miles (7,935 km); *public airports* (1972), 105.
Communications: *Telephones* (1972), 2,048,000; *television stations* (1971), 15; *radio stations* (1971), 139; *newspapers* (1972), 23 (daily circulation, 1,012,000).

Legal Action. On July 27, 1971, after several months of secret testimony, a King county (Seattle) grand jury had indicted 19 incumbent and former city and county officials for conspiring to perpetuate a tolerance policy toward bribery, gambling, prostitution, extortion, blackmail, and violation of liquor laws. The indictments were later dismissed on a technicality, and the King county prosecutor pressed for a state supreme court review. On Aug. 3, 1972, the court ordered the indictments reinstated. Before any action was resumed against those indicted, the prosecutor, on November 20, added the names of 180 present and former police officers, public officials, and businessmen to the original indictment as co-conspirators.

San Francisco Mayor Joseph Alioto, former Washington state Attorney General John J. O'Connell, and Assistant Attorney General George K. Faler had all criminal bribery, conspiracy, and mail fraud charges against them dismissed by a U. S. district judge on June 19. Earlier, a Vancouver, Wash., jury had acquitted them in a civil suit alleging a conspiracy to raise and share legal fees. Alioto had been engaged by O'Connell in the mid-1960's to represent 15 Washington public utility districts and municipalities in an antitrust action against 29 electrical equipment manufacturers. Subsequently, the state charged that Alioto and the two state officials had conspired to remove the $1 million legal fee limit and share a $2.3 million fee.

Economic Recovery. Aided principally by a record year in the agricultural sector and an increase in airplane orders for the Boeing Company, the state began to recover from the severe economic slump of 1970–71. Though much improved, the unemployment rate was approximately 9% in 1972, well above the national average.

WARREN W. ETCHESON
University of Washington

WASHINGTON, D. C.

On Nov. 7, 1972, District of Columbia voters gave Sen. George S. McGovern 78% of their votes in his race for the presidency and reelected Walter E. Fauntroy, a Democrat, as a nonvoting delegate to Congress. Fauntroy's closest opponent was William Chin-Lee, a Republican.

Home Rule. Controversy and repeated lack of a quorum in the House District Committee stalled all efforts to pass a home-rule bill for the city in 1972.

City Government. In April, Mayor Walter E. Washington consolidated almost all of the city's financial operations under Comer S. Coppie, the city's chief budget officer and one of the mayor's closest advisers. Coppie was made responsible not only for preparing the city's annual budget but also for accounting for all city expenditures throughout the year. This move was prompted largely by a report of the federal General Accounting Office that the city had overspent, in 18 separate instances, its fiscal 1971 budget by a total of $5 million.

Also in April, President Richard M. Nixon appointed John A. Nevius to the post of D. C. City Council chairman, to replace Gilbert Hahn, Jr. Nevius, a former Council member, became the third chairman of the Council since its creation in 1967. The President also reappointed Sterling Tucker to a second term as vice chairman and named Marjorie Parker, Rockwood H. Foster, and the Rev. Jerry A. Moore to Council vacancies.

Transportation. In October, House-Senate conferees killed a proposal to prohibit court interference in the construction of the controversial Three Sisters Bridge, part of the city's interstate highway program. Differences over whether the bill should also allow urban areas to use federal highway trust funds for bus and rail rapid transit led to the break-up of the conference.

After denying a stopgap subsidy of $3 million to the privately owned D. C. Transit Corporation, Congress in October approved the purchase of that system and of three suburban bus companies, all to be administered by Metro, which will run the city's subway system. In June, Congress approved a federal guarantee for bonds to complete the entire 98-mile Metro system, ending a major funding crisis that had threatened further delay in construction already delayed by labor strikes. The Metro system is to be fully operating by 1976.

Other Legislation. In October the President signed six major bills for the national capital area, including one that authorized construction of the Dwight D. Eisenhower Memorial Bicentennial Civic Center and a second that created the Pennsylvania Avenue Development Corp., which will plan and develop land along the city's most historic avenue. Along with bills for transportation and teachers' salaries, the President also signed the Implied Consent Act, dealing with drinking drivers; and the Equal Rights for the Blind and Physically Disabled Act, which, in part, requires equal educational opportunities for the blind and disabled in the city.

Education. In September, Congress approved a 7% across-the-board teachers' pay increase and boosted three city taxes to finance it. The pay bill was passed in response to a teachers' strike in the opening weeks of the fall term. The teachers had demanded a 17% increase equal to that granted to city police and firemen earlier in the year.

Public education in the city remained in a state of intense controversy. It was reported that two years after the adoption of the highly publicized Clark Plan, devised by psychologist Kenneth B. Clark to bring city reading and mathematics levels up to national standards, there had been no appreciable overall improvement in pupil test scores. In addition to efforts to raise student achievement levels, the school system faced additional pressures from a 1971 federal court ruling that all spending on teachers' salaries be equalized throughout the city's elementary schools. In April 1972, Julius W. Hobson, who initiated the 1971 suit, threatened further court action, charging the city with noncompliance with the 1971 order.

Crime. In October, serious crime fell in the city to the lowest level for that month since 1966. While such crimes totaled 3,073, this was far below the 4,317 reported in October 1971. However, crime reporting for the city came under strong attack in 1972, with charges that the city had been deliberately underreporting since 1969. Police Chief Jerry V. Wilson, denied any such effort, citing extra federal funding and anticrime programs as the reason for the falling crime rate.

JEAN E. SPENCER
University of Maryland

WEATHER. See METEOROLOGY.
WELFARE. See SOCIAL WELFARE.
WEST INDIES. See CARIBBEAN and articles on Caribbean countries.

WEST VIRGINIA

Significant events in West Virginia in 1972 included Republican gains, some major legislative achievements, and a mining disaster.

Politics and Legislation. More Republicans were named to high office in West Virginia than in any election since 1928, with Gov. Arch Moore becoming the first chief executive in the state's history to succeed himself. His reelection was made possible by an amendment to the state constitution in 1970. Moore defeated Secretary of State John D. (Jay) Rockefeller IV by more than 70,000 votes. Republicans also won two of five Board of Public Works positions. Edgar Heiskell, Jr. was named secretary of state, and John Gates was elected auditor following the death less than 10 days before the balloting of the popular 12-year Democratic veteran in that office, Denzil Gainer. Reelected Democrats included Attorney General Chauncey Browning, Jr., Treasurer John H. Kelly, and Secretary of Agriculture Gus Douglass.

Democrats maintained their 40-year control of both houses of the state legislature and returned Sen. Jennings Randolph to Washington, along with incumbent Representatives Harley Staggers, John Slack, Robert Mollohan, and Ken Hechler.

Voters also approved four amendments to the state constitution, including one establishing a Public School Building Authority and another abandoning personal property taxes. The Legislature had placed all four on the ballot in the regular session, which was dominated by arguments over the control of strip mining. Additional mental health reform also came out of the two-month session.

Governor Moore called a special session in April, primarily to force further consideration of a public employee insurance program, more road-building authority, reapportionment proposals af-

Flash flood killed 118 persons in West Virginia's Buffalo Creek Valley when a dam gave way on February 26.

UPI

fecting both houses of the Legislature, and more support for the state's new public kindergartens. The lawmakers approved the insurance package and granted an additional $100 million in bonding power to continue a road-building program that had placed West Virginia among the nation's leaders in completed mileage during the past three years. They then went into recess until June, when they passed reapportionment and kindergarten legislation.

Mining Disaster. Public controversy over several aspects of mining, easily West Virginia's most inflammatory subject during the election year, exploded on February 26 when an earthen dam in the southern coal fields collapsed after days of heavy rain, sending an estimated 20 million cubic feet of water down the narrow, twisting 17-mile valley of Buffalo Creek. The final toll was 118 dead, 7 missing, and more than 4,000 homeless, with 16 coal company camps and small towns obliterated and buried under tons of mud and mine refuse. A special investigating committee and grand jury failed to fix any criminal responsibility for the tragedy but urged stricter enforcement and inspection procedures. Mine disasters also claimed nine lives in July near Morgantown and five more in December not far from Buffalo Creek. The worst industrial accident of the year occurred on December 15 at Weirton, where a new coking plant was under construction. A gas leak triggered an explosion that claimed 19 lives.

DONOVAN H. BOND, *West Virginia University*

WESTERN SAMOA

Increased economic development and a decision to establish diplomatic relations with New Zealand were the highlights of 1972 in Western Samoa.

Foreign Relations. The government of Western Samoa revealed its intention of establishing formal diplomatic links with New Zealand by announcing that it would appoint a high commissioner to reside in Wellington. Western Samoa was a United Nations Trusteeship under the administration of New Zealand prior to independence in 1962.

Economy. Western Samoa's economy continued in 1972 an upward trend that had begun in the preceding year. Value of exports in 1971 had increased by 33% over 1970, and imports had decreased by 2%. Copra exports reached their highest level in 20 years despite declining prices.

The government initiated planning for a major hydroelectric plant at Afulilo about 25 miles (40 km) east of the capital city of Apia. The project includes a dam and a sea-level power station.

------ **WESTERN SAMOA • Information Highlights** ------

Official Name: Independent State of Western Samoa.
Area: 1,097 square miles (2,842 sq km).
Population (1971 est.): 146,000. *Density,* 129 per square mile (50 per sq km). *Annual rate of increase,* 2.5%.
Chief City (1966 census): Apia, the capital, 25,480.
Government: *Head of state,* Malietoa Tanumafili II, King (acceded Jan. 1962). *Head of government,* Tapua Tamasese Lealofi IV, prime minister (took office Feb. 1970). *Legislature* (unicameral)—Legislative Assembly, 47 members.
Languages: Samoan (official), English.
Education: *School enrollment* (1969)—primary, 27,596; secondary, 9,877; technical/vocational, 84.
Monetary Unit: Tala (0.8367 tala equals U.S.$1, July 1972).
Major Agricultural Products: Bananas, cacao, copra, taro, yams, breadfruit.
Foreign Trade (1971): *Exports,* $6,000,000. *Imports,* $13,000,-000. *Chief trading partners* (1969)—New Zealand (took 31% of exports, supplied 28% of imports); Australia (0.5%—20%); United States (4%—10%).
Communications: *Telephones* (1971), 1,960.

Transportation. Western Samoa announced early in 1972 that it would assume control of Polynesian Airlines, a private company that had already been designated as the national flag carrier. A ferry service between the main islands of Upolu and Savaii was to be established early in 1973.

HOWARD J. CRITCHFIELD
Western Washington State College

WHITELAW, William. See BIOGRAPHY.
WHITLAM, Gough. See BIOGRAPHY.
WHITMAN, Marina von Neumann. See BIOGRAPHY.
WHOLESALE SALES. See ECONOMY OF THE U. S.

WILSON, Edmund

American critic: b. Red Bank, N.J., May 8, 1895; d. Talcottville, N.Y., June 12, 1972.

When challenged by his father about the apparent lack of direction in his intellectual interests and enthusiasms, the young Edmund Wilson responded, "Father, what I want to do is try to get to know something about all the main departments of human thought." Wilson lived to fulfill that goal with verve and authority as novelist, student of foreign languages, literary critic, travel writer, poet, historian, dramatist, and urbane commentator on the forces of contemporary history. While his political and social attitudes underwent dramatic alterations, the moral rigor of his thought remained consistent, and his authoritarian tone caused him to be accused more than once of "old-fogyism." Nonetheless, in an astonishingly prolific career, he established himself as one of the most versatile and accomplished men of letters of the modern period.

EDMUND WILSON (1895–1972)

"... the quintessential man of letters"

JAMES A. SUGAR

Life and Works. Edmund Wilson often reflected that he was a true child of the 19th century, and nostalgically recalled his gentle, comfortable childhood with its abundant signs of genteel order and stability. But even as a child he seemed to sense that this order was threatened from without by 20th century realities, and from within by emotional strife. Wilson's father was a prosperous lawyer known for his dedicated social consciousness, but he was also a hypochondriac whose mental "eclipses" badly strained the fabric of family life. Edmund, Jr., the only child, was doted on by his mother, who went mysteriously deaf after her husband's final collapse.

Wilson's interest in literature manifested itself strongly during his prep school years, and became his clear vocation shortly after he entered Princeton University in 1912—a determination reinforced by his involvement with the *Nassau Literary Magazine* and his friendship with such fellow contributors as F. Scott Fitzgerald and John Peale Bishop. Between his junior and senior years Wilson attended summer school at Columbia University, where he studied sociology and labor problems. For the remainder of his life he was to be committed to both the literary arts and the causes of social reform.

Wilson's first job was as a reporter for the New York *Evening Sun,* but his journalistic career was interrupted by the two years he served in the Army in France. In 1920 he became managing editor of *Vanity Fair* and began contributing articles to numerous journals. Later, as a critic for the *New Republic,* he published pioneering appreciations of F. Scott Fitzgerald and Ernest Hemingway. With his friend John Peale Bishop he wrote a series of satirical poems and stories under the title *The Undertaker's Garland* (1922), which suggested his alarm over the economic and social abuses that abounded during the 1920's.

The scope of Wilson's interest in literature was prominently demonstrated in his study of European symbolist writers, *Axel's Castle* (1931), which has been widely acclaimed as a major work of "contextual" criticism. It established a role that Wilson was to play frequently—that of urbane intermediary between a general audience and the complexities of modern literature. The following year Wilson published *The American Jitters* (1932), an account of his personal investigations into poverty, racism, and labor difficulties in America.

Wilson's social conscience and his growing sense of unease about his own country led him, like many of the writers of his time, to explore communism as an alternative. The culmination of this interest was *To the Finland Station* (1940), in which he expressed his admiration for the principles of communism but repudiated Marxist dogma and, in particular, the tyrannies of Stalin. The breathtaking scope of this important work includes all the major scenes and characters in the history of modern radical thought. The book has been described as "the last great 19th century novel" and a legitimate child of *War and Peace.*

More and more, Wilson came to think of himself as an "independent radical." His quarrels with prejudice, bureaucracy, and federal spending continued to manifest themselves in articles and reviews, and in such books as *Patriotic Gore* (1962), *The Cold War and the Income Tax* (1963), and *O Canada* (1965).

The lure of fiction, however, was always strong. In *I Thought of Daisy* (1929) he created a slight but memorably lyric portrait of Edna St. Vincent Millay, and *Memoirs of Hecate County* (1946) was a powerful collection of interlocked studies in diabolism, as well as something of a *cause célèbre* in its own day as a result of the obscenity charges brought against it. Wilson also published several volumes of poetry, wrote for the theater, and frequently composed ruthlessly honest self-criticism— of his youthful infatuation with communism, his four marriages (one of them to novelist-critic Mary McCarthy), his mental breakdown, and his battles with the Internal Revenue Service. From 1944 to 1948 Wilson was book reviewer for *The New Yorker* magazine, and in 1945 he edited *The Crack-Up,* a volume of essays and letters by F. Scott Fitzgerald.

Significance. Whether he was quarreling with Vladimir Nabokov over the niceties of the Russian language, puzzling over the meaning of *The Scrolls from the Dead Sea* (1955), or expounding on the plight of the Indians in *Apologies to the Iroquois* (1959), Wilson's voice was always characterized by the tone of dissent. Many of his contemporaries found him "cranky," but few denied his "belief in human progress, the conviction that the world won't fall apart, the faith in the value of reform." Wilson was the quintessential man of letters, who brought a rare gift for thoughtful observation to many literary forms, and he was always concerned to determine what literature could do for life.

DAVID D. GALLOWAY
Ruhr University, West Germany

WINDSOR, DUKE OF

The former Edward VIII, king of the United Kingdom of Great Britain and Northern Ireland: b. Richmond Park, Surrey, England, June 23, 1894; d. Paris, France, May 28, 1972.

Prince Edward Albert Christian George Andrew Patrick David became Britain's king in January 1936. In December of that year he abdicated to marry Wallis Simpson, a twice-divorced American woman. This act caused a furor among the many who believed that it endangered the institution of the monarchy in Britain. That the monarchy was not seriously damaged by this crisis owed much to the sense of responsibility of Edward himself. He carefully avoided doing or saying anything that might discredit British institutions. As the duke and duchess of Windsor, Edward and his wife lived quiet, but useful lives and comported themselves with dignity to the time of his death.

As Price of Wales and during his brief time as king, Edward had been immensely popular with the people. When he died, tens of thousands visited Windsor Castle, where he lay in state. This was only one of many indications of the affection in which he was still held.

The Prince of Wales. Prince Edward was the first child of George, duke of York, and Princess Mary. His childhood was spent with his affectionate but firm parents, and in 1907 he followed his father's example in entering naval college. In 1910 his father ascended the throne as King George V, and Edward became the Prince of Wales. His new duties involved his leaving naval college, although he spent a year at Oxford in 1912.

In 1914, on the outbreak of World War I, Prince Edward joined the Grenadier Guards and, despite the reluctance of the high command, served in France and Italy. After the war he visited the United States and between 1919 and 1925 went to nearly every major area in the British Empire. The public enthusiasm in the places he visited was a testament to the success of his efforts to cement imperial and Anglo-American friendship.

In the late 1920's, Prince Edward placed a special emphasis on visits to the areas of greatest deprivation within the United Kingdom. In this way he developed a long-standing concern with the problems of the unemployed. He spoke frequently on the importance of voluntary aid in the alleviation of poverty, and in 1932 he began a campaign to sponsor occupational clubs in distressed districts.

In 1930, Prince Edward became the friend of Mr. and Mrs. Ernest Simpson, an American couple who became his frequent companions. Edward's relationship with Mrs. Simpson, who had divorced her first husband in 1927, became increasingly close. By 1934 he was aware of the depth of his feelings for her.

King Edward VIII. On Jan. 20, 1936, George V died, and Edward became king. In keeping with his earlier activities, he evinced an immediate interest in the modernization and simplification of many of the outward forms of the monarchy with a view to maintaining its reputation as a popular, responsive institution.

In August 1936, Mrs. Simpson accompanied King Edward on a Mediterranian cruise, and the European and American press increased their already voluminous speculations on the implications of their relationship. In October 1936, Mrs. Simpson was divorced from her husband Ernest, and in November the king informed his prime minister, Stanley Baldwin, of his desire to marry her, even at the cost of relinquishing the throne. Baldwin, fearful for the reputation of the monarchy, advised that even a morganatic marriage—one in which the wife and children receive no royal titles or privileges—would fail to command public support. The ending in early December of British press silence on the subject made a speedy settlement imperative. Faced with the choice between his throne and marriage to Mrs. Simpson, the king decided to abdicate, becoming the first British monarch to do so voluntarily. On December 11, Edward announced his abdication in a radio broadcast, explaining that he felt it impossible to discharge his duties as he would like "without the help and support of the woman I love." The marriage took place in France in June 1937. Edward's brother, the duke of York, succeeded him as King George VI, and immediately granted Edward the new title of duke of Windsor.

The Duke of Windsor. After his abdication, Edward, duke of Windsor, served as liaison officer at the French general headquarters from the outbreak of World War II until the fall of France, when, at the request of Prime Minister Winston Churchill, he became governor of the Bahamas (1940–45).

After the war, the duke and his wife traveled between their homes in France and the United States. In 1951 the duke published his autobiography, *A King's Story.* He occasionally visited Britain in a private capacity, though he never attended high official functions. Shortly before his death he was visited by his niece Queen Elizabeth II.

A. J. BEATTIE, *London School of Economics*

THE DUKE OF WINDSOR (1894–1972)

"...I have found it impossible...to discharge my duties as King as I would wish to do without the help and support of the woman I love."

—*From his farewell broadcast, Dec. 11, 1936*

WISCONSIN

New consumer legislation, a controversial prison reform proposal, and national and state elections highlighted the year 1972 in Wisconsin.

Legislature. In an eight-week session designed to dispose of issues left over from the 1971 session, the Legislature passed a number of important bills. A major measure was a sweeping consumer credit bill whose 60 protective provisions include limits on the techniques that may be employed by debt collectors and disclosure requirements for lending contracts. Other legislation included measures to regulate billboards and the use of snowmobiles; a measure to establish a state housing finance authority to stimulate construction of low- and moderate-cost housing; and a bill to create a state Department of Business Development.

The Legislature failed to act on one of its most controversial issues—providing tax credits to parents of children in private and parochial schools. Efforts to allow the sale of contraceptives to unmarried persons were again rejected.

Task Forces. Proposals for the 1973–75 session were made ready during the year by the numerous citizens' task forces appointed by Gov. Patrick J. Lucey. A task force studying the state's prison system aroused considerable opposition when it recommended closing the institutions by June 30, 1975, and sending all but the most hardened criminals back to their local communities for treatment. The task force said that the present system had

————— **WISCONSIN • Information Highlights** —————

Area: 56,154 square miles (145,439 sq km).
Population (1970 census): 4,417,933. *Density, 82 per sq mi.*
Chief Cities (1970 census): Madison, the capital, 172,007; Milwaukee, 717,372; Racine, 95,162; Green Bay, 87,809; Kenosha, 78,805; West Allis, 71,649; Wauwatosa, 58,676.
Government (1972): *Chief Officers*—governor, Patrick J. Lucey (D); lt. gov., Martin J. Schreiber (D); secy. of state, Robert C. Zimmerman (R); atty. gen., Robert W. Warren (R); treas., Charles P. Smith (D); supt. of public instruction, William C. Kahl; chief justice, E. Harold Hallows. *Legislature*—Senate, 33 members (20 Republicans, 13 Democrats); Assembly, 100 members (34 R, 66 D).
Education (1971–72): *Enrollment*—public elementary schools, 580,296 pupils, 26,806 teachers; public secondary, 419,625 pupils, 23,727 teachers; nonpublic schools (1970–71), 191,867 pupils, 9,170 teachers; college and university, 185,000 students. *Public school expenditures*, $956,250,000 ($1,069 per pupil). *Average teacher's salary,* $10,780.
State Finances (fiscal year 1970): *Revenues,* $2,132,166,000 (4% general sales tax and gross receipts taxes, $272,614,000; motor fuel tax, $130,512,000; federal funds, $344,009,000). *Expenditures,* $2,018,701,000 (education, $725,792,000; health, welfare, and safety, $172,335,000; highways, $176,131,000). *State debt,* $536,220,000 (June 30, 1970).
Personal Income (1971): $17,366,000,000; per capita, $3,880.
Public Assistance (1971): $303,761,000. *Average monthly payments* (Dec. 1971)—old-age assistance, $131.78; aid to families with dependent children, $244.73.
Labor Force: *Nonagricultural wage and salary earners* (July 1972), 1,570,800. *Average annual employment* (1971)—manufacturing, 478,000; trade, 334,000; government, 270,000; services, 237,000. *Insured unemployed* (Aug. 1972)—26,300 (2.3%).
Manufacturing (1970): *Value added by manufacture,* $7,815,100,000. Nonelectrical machinery, $1,763,800,000; food and kindred products, $1,118,600,000; paper and allied products, $744,700,000; electrical equipment and supplies, $728,400,000; fabricated metal products, $663,000,000; transportation equipment, $505,500,000.
Agriculture (1970): *Cash farm income,* $1,653,071,000 (livestock, $1,381,527,000; crops, $219,888,000; government payments, $51,656,000). *Chief crops* (in order of value, 1971)—Corn, hay (ranks 1st among the states), oats (ranks 4th), potatoes.
Mining (1971): *Production value,* $84,294,000 (ranks 38th among the states). *Chief minerals*—Sand and gravel, $32,676,000; stone, $25,105,000; iron ore, value not available; lime, $4,570,000.
Fisheries (1971): *Commercial catch,* 42,875,000 pounds ($2,352,000). *Leading species by value:* Chub, $759,000; whitefish, $376,000; alewives, $267,000.
Transportation: *Roads* (1971), 103,232 miles (166,131 km); *motor vehicles* (1971), 2,188,463; *railroads* (1971), 5,955 miles (9,583 km); *public airports* (1972), 100.
Communications: *Telephones* (1972), 2,479,000; *television stations* (1971), 18; *radio stations* (1971), 174; *newspapers* (1972), 37 (daily circulation, 1,212,000).

failed to rehabilitate inmates. Its other recommendations included one that said inmates and staff members should jointly determine the operation of the prisons until they are closed.

Meanwhile, a task force studying the judicial system recommended that instead of electing its judges, Wisconsin should adopt an appointive plan based on merit. The group also recommended the legalization of marihuana and of practices now considered crimes against sexual morality. Another task force urged emergency state aid to keep urban bus systems alive. A task force studying new ways to finance education recommended that wealthy school districts return some money to the state to help poorer districts.

Elections. Although President Nixon carried Wisconsin, receiving 53.4% of the vote compared to Sen. George McGovern's 43.7%, there was little evidence of a coattail effect. Because of the 1970 census the state's congressional districts were reduced from ten to nine, and the elections put five Democrats and four Republicans in the House, compared to the previous session's even split. Incumbents David Obey, a Democrat, and Alvin O'Konski, a Republican, were put together in a new district, and Obey defeated the 15-term veteran. Rep. John W. Byrnes retired after 14 terms in the House, and fellow Republican Harold Froehlich, a leader in the state Assembly, was elected to succeed him. Other incumbents were reelected.

In legislative elections, Democrats held control of the Assembly, 62 to 37, while Republicans kept a majority in the Senate, 18 to 15. The fledgling American party put up 42 candidates for legislative positions, the largest number of third-party candidates since the Progressive party's efforts three decades ago, but none was elected.

Economy. Economic conditions showed improvement in the state during 1972, although the change from earlier recession levels was not dramatic. Employment increased slightly, but so did unemployment. Prices went up for many farm commodities, especially milk. Unusual weather hurt farmers in several areas. Construction of new factories and expansion of existing ones exceeded the 1971 pace.

PAUL SALSINI, *The Milwaukee "Journal"*

WOMEN'S LIBERATION MOVEMENT

In 1972 American women achieved important political and economic gains. The 49-year-old Equal Rights Amendment, providing that "equality of rights under the law shall not be denied or abridged by the United States or by any State on account of sex," was passed by Congress, under pressure from many women's rights organizations.

Other legislation also extended protection of the Equal Pay Act, requiring the same pay for men and women doing "substantially equal work," to 15 million executive, administrative, and professional employees and outside salespeople. A revised order by the U. S. Labor Department's Office of Federal Contract Compliance required federal contractors (except in construction) with 50 employees and $50,000 in contracts to file action programs scheduling the hiring and promotion of women as well as minorities. New York City issued similar regulations, providing that contractors must develop goals and timetables for hiring and upgrading women, and that maternity leave be granted without fixed dates and with guaranteed reinstatement.

Many companies for the first time added women directors. Miss Catherine B. Cleary of Milwaukee, president of the First Wisconsin Trust Co., was elected a director by both General Motors Corp. and the American Telephone and Telegraph Co.

Equal Rights Amendment. Democratic Sen. Birch Bayh of Indiana and Republican Sen. Marlow Cook of Kentucky won approval (84 to 8) of the Equal Rights Amendment by the Senate on March 22, after defeating crippling modifications. The amendment had been approved unanimously in October 1971 by the House, where Martha W. Griffiths of Michigan freed it from the Judiciary Committee by a rarely invoked discharge petition.

Acting 32 minutes after the vote, Hawaii became the first state to ratify ERA. New Hampshire and Nebraska followed, then came Iowa, Idaho, Delaware, Kansas, Texas, Maryland, Tennessee, Alaska, Rhode Island, and New Jersey; and finally New York, Colorado, Kentucky, Michigan, West Virginia, Wisconsin, and Massachusetts. In September, Pennsylvania became the 21st state to ratify.

Gains by EEOC. The Equal Employment Opportunity Commission was empowered to use federal courts to enforce its decisions. The new law extended coverage as of March 1973 to firms and unions with 15 or more employees, rather than 25, and March 1972 to 12 million previously exempt teachers and state and local government employees.

WOMEN DELEGATES to the Democratic convention in July represented 38% of the total, compared with only 13% in 1968, and women played leading roles at the gathering. Democrats adopted a strong women's rights plank in their party platform.

THE NEW YORK TIMES

Hundreds of suits charging sex discrimination have been filed in court by the Department of Labor, and by individuals or organizations, often as "class actions." For example, the U. S. Court of Appeals required the Wheaton Glass Co., Millville, N. J., to pay $901,062 in wages and interest to 400 women who inspected and packed bottles at $2.14 an hour while men received $2.35.

The Movement. The National Organization for Women (NOW), headed by Wilma Scott Heide, doubled its chapters to 400 and increased members by 50% to 15,000. Women's Equity Action League (WEAL) had divisions in 16 states. Hundreds of state and local caucuses, committees, and task forces fought for women in special fields. Emphasis was on salary inequities and deeply felt issues such as the right to abortion. NOW induced the Federal Communications Commission (FCC) to require broadcasting stations not to discriminate against women in hiring and programming. The 65-year-old *American Men of Science* volumes became *American Men and Women of Science.*

Politics. In a Democratic primary Elizabeth Holtzman, a 30-year-old Brooklyn lawyer, defeated the 88-year-old Rep. Emanuel Celler who, as chairman of the House Judiciary Committee, long had blocked the Equal Rights Amendment. Rep. Shirley Chisholm, the nation's first black congresswoman, sought the Democratic presidential nomination and won 151 votes at the national convention. Frances (Sissy) Farenthold of Texas received 408 votes for the vice presidential nomination.

Thanks to the National Women's Political Caucus, more women were delegates or alternatives to the two national conventions than ever before— almost 40% at the Democratic and 35% at the Republican conventions. Their presence led to the inclusion of recommendations for day-care center programs and other movement goals in platforms.

The Democratic National Committee chose Mrs. Jean Westwood of Utah as chairperson, the first time a woman had gained such a post. Mrs. Anne Armstrong of Texas was co-chairwoman of the Republican National Committee and the first woman keynote speaker. In 1972, the mayors of Oklahoma City and 10 other cities of more than 30,000 were women.

Pioneers. Alene Bertha Duerk, head of the Navy Nurse Corps, became the Navy's first woman admiral, sharing flag rank with two Air Force and four Army woman generals. The Navy authorized sending women to sea. The Army and Air Force opened Reserve Officer Training to women. Service women are now allowed to marry and have custody of minor children.

Dr. Marina von Neumann Whitman became the first woman member of the President's Council of Economic Advisers, and Mrs. Mary Hamilton, another economist, replaced her on the Price Commission. Dr. Dixy Lee Ray became the second woman on the Atomic Energy Commission, and the first in a five-year term.

In proclaiming August 26 as Women's Rights Day, President Nixon boasted of naming 118 women to responsible government jobs paying $28,-000 or more. But 96% of federal jobs in grades GS-13 or higher were still held by men. Joanne E. Pierce and Susan Lynn Roley became the first female FBI agents.

At Bennington College, Dr. Gail T. Parker, as president, and her husband, Thomas, as vice president, became the first wife and husband to head a major college. Sally J. Priesand, 25, a graduate of Cincinnati's Hebrew Union College, became the world's first practicing woman rabbi.

International Developments. Women continued as prime ministers in Israel, India, and Ceylon, and fought as paratroopers in the Cambodian army. The Status of Women Commission of the United Nations asked the world body to designate 1975 "International Women's Year." Jeanne M. Cisse of Guinea became the first woman president of the UN Security Council.

In Britain, women asked for more seats on boards running nationalized industries and became members, as of March 1973, of the London Stock Exchange. Professor Margaret Burbidge became the first woman director of the Royal Greenwich Observatory. In France, a "Crimes Against Women" trial was staged. In Italy, women campaigned for free abortions. Women for the first time had seats in the Swiss Parlament, and the Mexican Senate had its first woman president.

CAROLINE BIRD, *Author of "Born Female"*

——————— WYOMING · Information Highlights ———————

Area: 97,914 square miles (253,597 sq km).
Population (1970 census): 332,416. *Density,* 3.5 per sq mi.
Chief Cities (1970 census): Cheyenne, the capital, 40,914; Casper, 39,361; Laramie, 23,143; Rock Springs, 11,657; Sheridan, 10,856.
Government (1972): *Chief Officers*—governor, Stanley K. Hathaway (R); secy. of state, Mrs. Myra Thomson (R); atty. gen., Clarence A. Brimmer (R); treas., James Griffith (R); supt., dept. of public instruction, Robert G. Schrader (R); chief justice, John J. McIntyre. *Legislature*—Senate, 30 members (19 Republicans, 11 Democrats); House of Representatives, 61 members (40 R, 20 D, 1 independent).
Education (1971–72): *Enrollment*—public elementary schools, 45,855 pupils, 2,312 teachers; public secondary, 40,575 pupils, 2,316 teachers; nonpublic schools (1970–71), 2,265 pupils, 140 teachers; college and university, 15,000 students. *Public school expenditures,* $77,469,000 ($940 per pupil). *Average teacher's salary,* $9,611.
State Finances (fiscal year 1970): *Revenues,* $228,062,000 (3% general sales tax and gross receipts taxes, $30,967,000; motor fuel tax, $16,370,000; federal funds, $81,886,000). *Expenditures,* $214,420,000 (education, $70,701,000; health, welfare, and safety, $7,303,000; highways, $62,195,000). *State debt,* $51,091,000 (June 30, 1970).
Personal Income (1971): $1,276,000,000; per capita, $3,753.
Public Assistance (1971): $9,569,000. *Average monthly payments* (Dec. 1971)—old-age assistance, $56.48; aid to families with dependent children, $146.85.
Labor Force: *Nonagricultural wage and salary earners* (July 1972), 125,000. *Average annual employment* (1971)—manufacturing, 7,000; trade, 24,000; government, 30,000; services, 17,000. *Insured unemployed* (Aug. 1972)—600 (0.8%).
Manufacturing (1969): *Value added by manufacture,* $98,700,000. Petroleum and coal products, $39,600,000; food and kindred products, $13,700,000; stone, clay, and glass products, $11,100,000; printing and publishing, $8,300,000.
Agriculture (1970): *Cash farm income,* $247,017,000 (livestock, $194,182,000; crops, $37,650,000; government payments, $15,185,000). *Chief crops* (in order of value, 1971)—Hay, sugar beets, wheat, barley.
Mining (1970): *Production value,* $683,324,000 (ranks 11th among the states). *Chief minerals*—Petroleum, $456,370,000; natural gas, $48,731,000; uranium, $35,747,000.
Transportation: *Roads* (1971), 40,636 miles (65,396 km); *motor vehicles* (1971), 246,661; *railroads* (1971), 1,812 miles (2,916 km); *public airports* (1972), 41.
Communications: *Telephones* (1972), 205,800; *television stations* (1971), 3; *radio stations* (1971), 30; *newspapers* (1972), 9 (daily circulation, 77,000).

WYOMING

Elections, the economy, and environmental problems dominated Wyoming news in 1972.

Elections. More than 146,000 voters went to the polls on November 7, a record turnout accounted for by the 18-year-old voters and the change from a one-year to a 30-day residence requirement. A record high plurality of 60,000 was registered when U. S. Sen. Clifford Hansen (R), seeking a second term, defeated Michael Vinich (D) 101,314 to 40,753. President Richard Nixon's plurality over Sen. George McGovern was 56,000. Teno Roncalio (D) won reelection to the state's only seat in the U. S. House of Representatives with a margin of almost 5,000 over William Kidd (R).

The Republican party as usual won control of the state legislature, 17–13 in the Senate and 44–18 in the House. The electorate adopted three constitutional amendments that granted more home rule to cities and towns, allowed annual sessions of the legislature, and substituted appointment for election of district and supreme court judges.

The Economy. The economy had a better than average year. Higher cattle prices, adequate irrigation water, and favorable weather aided agriculture. Major construction projects included the Jim Bridger steam power plant northeast of Rock Springs; addition of a fourth unit to the Dave Johnston power plant at Glenrock; expansion at three trona processing plants in Sweetwater county; a state office building at Cheyenne; and a fine arts building, a hospital, and a student union expansion at Laramie.

As usual, minerals production constituted the largest segment of the economy. Petroleum output declined slightly to 130 million barrels, while sales of natural gas increased. Of the more than 800 new oil and gas wells most excitement attached to the Brady Unit Nugget (Jurassic) oil and gas well, which was completed in Sweetwater county in October.

Strip-mining of low-sulfur coal increased substantially in several areas to meet orders from steam power plants in Wyoming and several other states. The Burlington-Northern Railroad Company announced plans to build a 126-mile rail line from Gillette to Douglas to facilitate marketing of vast reserves of Powder River Basin coal.

The Environment. Strip-mining and various forms of air and water pollution came under attack, as citizens demanded stricter laws and better enforcement. The Pacific Power and Light Company in November announced plans to spend more than $30 million for wet scrubbers and cooling towers at its Dave Johnston plant.

In a referendum, citizens of Sublette county, fearing damage to the environment, opposed by a 3-to-1 vote the Wagon Wheel Project, which had been undertaken by the Atomic Energy Commission and the El Paso Natural Gas Company. This project called for sequential detonation of five underground nuclear explosions to release trapped natural gas.

T. A. LARSON, *University of Wyoming*

YEMEN

The year 1972 opened with conflict between Yemen and Southern Yemen and closed with moves toward the unification of the two countries.

Relations with Southern Yemen. Neither Yemen nor Southern Yemen was eager for war. But the presence in Yemen of many dissidents from Southern Yemen, anxious to overthrow Southern Yemen's Marxist regime, strained relations between the two countries. In February, 65 Yemenis were killed in Southern Yemen. Yemen claimed they had been invited there for peace talks. Yemen accused Southern Yemen of bombing and shelling Yemeni villages. In one week in March, 188 Yemenis were killed in border incidents, and Yemen massed troops along the boundary. In August, Yemen asked the Soviet Union to remove its strategic bases and military experts, reported to number 100.

Both Kuwait and Iraq sent high-level statesmen to try to settle the dispute, and in October a committee of the Arab League visited the two Yemens. As a result of these and other efforts at reconcilia-

——————— YEMEN · Information Highlights ———————

Official Name: Yemen Arab Republic.
Area: 75,290 square miles (195,000 sq km).
Population (1972 est.): 6,100,000. *Density,* 80 per square mile (29 per sq km). *Annual rate of increase,* 2.8%.
Chief Cities: Sana, the capital, 100,000 (1964 est.); Taiz, 80,000 (1963 est.); Hodeida, 50,000 (1969 est.).
Government: *Head of state,* Abd al-Rahman al-Iryani, chairman of the Presidential Council (took office April 1971). *Head of government,* Muhsin al-Ayni, prime minister (took office Sept. 1971). *Legislature*—Majlis al-Shura (Consultative Assembly), 159 members.
Language: Arabic (official).
Education: *Expenditure* (1967), 6.8% of total public expenditure. *School enrollment* (1970)—primary (1969), 72,107; general secondary, 4,934; technical/vocational, 640.
Monetary Unit: Rial (4.690 rials equal U. S.$1, July 1972).
Gross National Product (1970 est.): $460,000,000.
Major Agricultural Products: Wheat, coffee, cotton, kat (a narcotic drug), barley, vegetables.
Major Mineral: Salt.
Foreign Trade: *Chief exports*—coffee, hides and skin, salt, kat. *Chief imports*—textiles, sugar, machinery.
Communications: *Telephones* (1971), 3,550.

tion, on October 28 the prime ministers of the two Yemens signed an agreement in Cairo providing for the cessation of hostilities and provocative acts and for the unification of the two countries in the near future. (See also SOUTHERN YEMEN.)

Economic Developments. To stimulate the sluggish economy, a law of February 27 offered incentives to foreign and domestic investors. In July, U. S. Secretary of State Rogers visited Yemen and indicated that full diplomatic relations would soon be reestablished and the former aid programs would be renewed. Yemen's president stated on July 4 that this would not change Yemen's relations with other Arab socialist states.

SYDNEY NETTLETON FISHER
The Ohio State University

YEMEN, People's Democratic Republic of. See SOUTHERN YEMEN.

YUGOSLAVIA

In 1972 there was persistent turmoil both within and outside the ruling League of Communists of Yugoslavia (LCY), and President Tito moved forcefully to strengthen and unify his party. Although there were some hopeful signs in the economy, inflation continued to be the country's chief economic problem. In foreign affairs, there was a significant improvement in Yugoslav-Soviet relations.

Political Conflicts and Purges. The disturbances that erupted in Croatia late in 1971 continued unabated into 1972. Prominent intellectual and student leaders, accused of national separatism and other subversive or oppositional political acts, were arrested and tried. There were also displacements and purges in the state and LCY hierarchy, and numerous publications were banned. In early July, a group of young Croatian nationalists, hoping to capitalize on the troubled situation, entered the country illegally, but they were wiped out by the Yugoslav army in Western Bosnia.

These disturbances in the country and the party prompted Tito to rebuild the LCY and tighten its discipline. In a stern letter, issued in September, Tito and the executive bureau of the LCY presidium announced forthcoming reprisals against all who failed to implement LCY policy. He also denounced wealthy Yugoslavs who acquire revenue, without work, from their accumulated funds, threatening to remove the sources of their enrichment. Early in October, Tito assailed the 1952 LCY Congress, which had played down the authoritarian role of government in favor of a policy of "education and persuasion," for having brought about the weakening of the party. He argued for a new "avant-garde" communism that would achieve unity of thought and action, reassert democratic centralism, and make the LCY "the monolith of our socialist society."

Late in 1972, a political crisis erupted in the Serbian League of Communists. Throughout the year, Serbia had witnessed dissatisfaction with the policies of the regime, leading to arrests, the sentencing of intellectuals and students, and the banning of certain publications. In mid-October, Tito described the situation within the Serbian LC as "unhealthy" and criticized its leadership for factionalism, liberalism toward class enemies, preoccupation with local interests, and failure to implement the LCY's basic policies. Consequently, in late October, Serbian party chairman Marko Nikezić

and Serbian party secretary Latinka Perović resigned. Their resignations were followed, early in November, by those of Mirko Tepavac, Yugoslavia's foreign minister, and of Koča Popović, member of the collective Federal Presidency and the most prominent Serbian politician.

Economy. The 1971–75 development plan, the aim of which is to stabilize and restructure the Yugoslav economy, was belatedly adopted by the Federal Assembly in June. The economy in 1972 showed some improvement but also reflected persistent shortcomings. In a comparison of the first six months of 1972 with the comparable period in 1971, the trade deficit declined 59%, with exports rising 24% and imports dropping 16%. Invisible earnings, including tourism and the remittances of permanent emigrants and workers temporarily employed abroad, increased 28%. Industrial production rose 9%, but agricultural output decreased.

Yugoslavia's inflation rate, one of the highest of all countries in the Organization for Economic Cooperation and Development (OECD), remained the major economic problem. In the first half of 1972, wholesale and retail prices of industrial goods increased. The cost of living in May 1972 was almost 10% higher than that of May 1971.

Foreign investments in Yugoslavia grew in 1972 as a result of new joint-venture agreements with Western companies. Fresh loans were also contracted from various banks, including the First National Bank of Chicago, the Export-Import Bank of Japan, and the East German Bank for Foreign Trade. Closer economic ties were sought and some established with EEC and Comecon countries.

Foreign Relations. The most important political event in Yugoslav foreign affairs in 1972 was Tito's official visit to the Soviet Union on June 5–10.

--------- **YUGOSLAVIA · Information Highlights** ---------

Official Name: Socialist Federal Republic of Yugoslavia.
Area: 98,766 square miles (255,804 sq km).
Population (1972 est.): 21,000,000. *Density*, 207 per square mile (80 per sq km). *Annual rate of increase*, 0.9%.
Chief Cities (1971 census): Belgrade, the capital, 800,000; Zagreb, 565,000; Skopje, 250,000.
Government: *Head of state*, Tito (Josip Broz), president (first elected Jan. 1953). *Prime minister*, Džemal Bijedić (took office July 1971). *Legislature*—Federal Assembly (5 chambers), 670 members. *Major political party*—League of Communists of Yugoslavia (LCY).
Languages: Serbo-Croatian, Slovenian, Macedonian (all official).
Education: *Expenditure* (1969), 5.1% of gross material product. *School enrollment* (1969)—primary, 2,857,291; secondary, 705,746; technical/vocational, 500,484; university/higher, 239,701.
Monetary Unit: Dinar (17 dinars equal U. S.$1, Sept. 1972).
Gross National Product (1970 est.): $18,000,000,000.
Per Capita Gross National Product (1970): $885.
Economic Indexes: *Industrial production* (1971), 186 (1963=100); *agricultural production* (1970), 124 (1957–59=100); *consumer price index* (1971), 292 (1963=100).
Manufacturing (major products): Steel and iron, chemicals, textiles, processed foods, wood products.
Major Agricultural Products: Corn, wheat, sugar beets, fruits, potatoes, forest products, fish, livestock.
Major Minerals: Coal, iron ore, petroleum, bauxite, copper, lead, zinc.
Foreign Trade (1971): *Exports*, $1,837,000,000 (chief exports, 1969—food and live animals; nonferrous metals; transport equipment; electrical machinery, apparatus, appliances). *Imports*, $3,298,000,000 (chief imports, 1969—nonelectrical machinery; chemicals; transport equipment; iron and steel). *Chief trading partners* (1969)—Italy (took 15% of exports, supplied 15% of imports); USSR (14%–8%); West Germany (11%–18%); United Kingdom (6%–6%).
Tourism: *Receipts* (1970), $274,600,000.
Transportation: *Motor vehicles* (1970), 843,100 (automobiles, 720,900); *railroads* (1970), 6,394 miles (10,289 km); *merchant fleet* (1971), 1,543,000 gross registered tons; *major national airline*, JAT (Jugoslovenski Aero Transport).
Communications: *Telephones* (1971), 736,045; *television stations* (1971), 35; *television sets* (1971), 1,767,000; *radios* (1970), 3,372,000; *newspapers* (1970), 24 (daily circulation, 1,738,000).

Tito was awarded the highest Soviet decoration, the Order of Lenin, by Soviet President Nikolai V. Podgorny. Podgorny hailed Tito as "a prominent leader of the international Communist and working class movement, and an outstanding leader of the working people of socialist Yugoslavia, friendly to the Soviet Union." The communiqué issued at the end of the visit outlined wide areas of agreement between the two countries and parties in the realm of international affairs, with the Soviet Union upholding the role of nonaligned countries in international affairs and approving their anti-imperialist policy orientation. The communiqué also stressed the "substantive expansion" of economic and commercial relations between Yugoslavia and the USSR.

Yugoslavia's links with eastern Europe were strengthened in 1972. Tito visited Poland at the end of June. In July, Premier Džemal Bijedić attended the Moscow meeting of the Comecon Council.

There were several top-level diplomatic contacts with the West in 1972. Queen Juliana of the Netherlands visited in September, and Queen Elizabeth II of Britain was in Yugoslavia in October. U. S. Secretary of State William Rogers visited Tito on July 9. The joint communiqué following their meeting hinted that additional U. S. economic assistance to Yugoslavia would be negotiated.

Anwar el-Sadat, president of the Arab Republic of Egypt, visited Yugoslavia on February 4–5, and Haile Selassie, the Emperor of Ethiopia, arrived in Belgrade at the end of June.

MILORAD M. DRACHKOVITCH
Stanford University

SMALLPOX VACCINATION was ordered in March for all residents of Belgrade, Yugoslavia, after several cases of the disease were reported in one of the outlying regions.

UPI

YUKON TERRITORY

The Yukon Territory continued to enjoy increasing economic prosperity in 1972. In response to the growth of the economy, work on highway improvement proceeded at a brisk pace. The heat generated by the excitement of the Arctic Winter Games seemed to dispel the bitter winter cold.

Economy. Throughout 1972 the economy continued to increase at a rate that was only slightly below that of the preceding five or six years. Mining remained the largest single contributor to the economy, even though its production leveled off during the year. Commercial and residential construction continued to increase, especially in Whitehorse, the territorial capital.

The leveling off of mining was counteracted in part by the accelerated rise in tourism, the Yukon's second largest industry. About 220,000 persons visited the territory in 1972, an increase of 20% over the preceding year. The estimated value of the tourist trade for the year was $15 million. According to the Yukon Department of Travel and Information, visitors from the United States far outnumbered those from the rest of Canada or from any other country. The largest number came from California, the second-largest from Alaska.

Winter Games. Many of the visitors to the Yukon were attracted by the Arctic Winter Games, held March 6–11 in Whitehorse, where the temperature approached $-30°$ F. The games, which are staged every two years in communities north of the 60th parallel, were the largest ever held in the Yukon. More than 1,000 athletes participated, some coming from as far away as Arctic Quebec on the other side of the continent. The Yukon won the competition with 38 points against 37½ for Alaska, although Alaskan athletes won the most medals.

Transportation. Road paving in the Whitehorse area and the upgrading of existing territorial roads helped ease the Yukon's chronic transportation problems. Construction also continued on the Dempster Highway. When completed in 1974, this highway will extend from Dawson, on the Yukon River, to Inuvik, near the east channel of the Mackenzie River in the Northwest Territories, and probably to Tuktoyaktuk on the Beaufort Sea. As expected, the portion of the Alaska Highway that passes through the Yukon was turned over to the territory in 1972 by the federal government.

DON SAWATSKY
Yukon Department of Travel and Information

—— YUKON TERRITORY · Information Highlights ——

Area: 207,076 sq miles (536,327 sq km).
Population: 18,388 (June 1, 1972 est.).
Chief City (1972 est.): Whitehorse, the capital (11,600).
Government (1972): *Chief Officers*—Commissioner James Smith; Executive Committee Members: Keith Fleming (appointed); Mrs. H. Watson (elected); N. S. Chamberlist (elected). Territorial Council—Elected Members: speaker Ron Rivet; Ken McKinnon, Don Taylor, Mrs. H. Watson, N. S. Chamberlist, Clive Tanner, Mike Stutter.
Education: School enrollment (Sept. 1972)—*Elementary and secondary,* 4,578 pupils; *vocational training center,* 430 pupils (20 full-time teachers).
Public Finance: (fiscal year 1972 est.)—*Revenues,* $24,696,729 (liquor profits $1.5 million; motor vehicle licenses and fuel tax, $2,248,319; property and school tax, $1,000,000; federal funds, $9,312,576). *Expenditures,* $25,683,434 (education, $5,948,800; health and social welfare, $4,024,507; highways and public works, $4,143,474).
Mining: (1972 est.)—$100,000,000. *Chief minerals* (tons): Zinc, 114,651; asbestos, 99,000; lead, 108,092; silver, 5,852,000 troy ounces; gold, 17,000 troy ounces.
Transportation: *Roads* (1972 est.), 2,500 miles; *motor vehicles,* 14,054; *railroads,* 58 track miles; *licensed airports,* 9.
(All monetary figures given in Canadian dollars.)

ZAÏRE

Major developments in Zaïre in 1972 were related to the government's well-publicized campaign in favor of "national authenticity." The campaign had begun in October 1971 with the decision to change the country's name from Democratic Republic of Congo to Republic of Zaïre. This small-scale cultural revolution remained the center of public attention throughout most of 1972, obscuring to some extent the economy's temporary slowdown.

Authenticity Campaign. A further wave of name changes was initiated in January. All European names still attached to geographical features were Africanized, including Lake Albert, which was rebaptized Lake Mobutu in October. Even the purely local name of Katanga was changed to Shaba (Swahili for "copper"), perhaps in the hope of erasing the memory of that region's turbulent past.

Zaïrese citizens with European family names were ordered to relinquish them in favor of African surnames. Though not legally banned at first, Christian names were equally frowned on, especially after the president changed his own name from Joseph Désiré Mobutu to Mobutu Sese Seko. The Christian clergy was forbidden to refuse to baptize children under African names.

Conflict With the Catholic Church. In February the Catholic weekly *Afrique Chrétienne* published an article that was critical of the name-changing policy. The article, allegedly inspired by Joseph Cardinal Malula, the archbishop of Kinshasa, prompted a vigorous reaction by Mobutu against the Catholic clergy in general and against Malula in particular. Malula left for the Vatican, and his official residence was taken over by members of the youth wing of the ruling Mouvement Populaire de la Révolution (MPR).

Hoping to ease tensions, Pope Paul issued a conciliatory ruling approving the use of African names for Christian baptism. But an appeal by the national bishops' conference on behalf of Malula led only to a stiffening of the government's position. Several Belgian missionaries were expelled from Zaïre, and official attendance at religious functions was forbidden. The government also ordered all Catholic seminaries to set up party youth committees among their students or be closed down. When the bishops bowed to this demand the way was paved for an official reconciliation. Mobutu authorized the return of Cardinal Malula on May 15.

Political Affairs. The MPR held a congress in Kinshasa in May and offered to make Mobutu president for life. But Mobutu's power was so secure he could afford to decline the life presidency. The Catholic Church, long a "state within the state," had been humbled. Student opposition was muted, and all major civilian political figures had been eliminated from the public scene. Mobutu further consolidated his power by merging the cabinet and the executive of the MPR into a single agency called the National Executive Council.

With the exception of a minor plot involving a former colonel in December 1971, the army has remained a mainstay of the regime. In July, to make room at the top for ambitious younger officers, Mobutu retired 10 aging generals, including his uncle, General Bobozo.

Economic Development. The economic situation in Zaïre continued to be marred by the weakness of world copper prices, which had caused a 13% drop of export earnings and an $82 million balance-of-payments deficit in 1971. But copper production continued to increase regularly, and the Zaïre-Japanese consortium, Sodimiza, went into production in October. The world's largest hydroelectric complex, being developed at Inga, will power an aluminum smelter and a steel plant.

Although the country's long-term future was not in doubt, short-term prospects remained somewhat uncertain. The government hoped to reduce the 1971 budgetary deficit of $120 million by half in 1972, but its determination to proceed with development plans led to outside borrowing of about $50 to $60 million a year.

Foreign Affairs. Zaïre's unique position between East and West Africa and between former French and former British territories has often proved to be a drawback as well as an asset. The nation withdrew from the Afro-Malagasy and Mauritius Joint Organization (OCAMM) in April, implicitly acknowledging that it could never hope to lead what is essentially a "family" of former French territories.

By virtue of its size, wealth, and location, Zaïre was eminently qualified to play a continent-wide role, especially since, for the first time since becoming independent, it had no conflict with any of its neighbors. During the year Zaïre gradually became reconciled with neighboring Congo, after Congo's President Marien Ngouabi had begun to curb left-wing radicals. In June both governments agreed to urge a rapprochement between the two competing Angolan nationalist movements, which were based respectively in Zaïre and Congo and whose running feud had been a constant source of friction between the two countries.

The decision of West African members of OCAMM (along with Mali) to organize a West African Economic Community left the central African members of that organization in an awkward position that Zaïre might be tempted to exploit in order to revive the idea of an Equatorial union. Some

---
ZAÏRE · Information Highlights

Official Name: Republic of Zaïre.
Area: 905,565 square miles (2,345,409 sq km).
Population (1972 est.): 18,300,000. *Density*, 18 per square mile (7 per sq km). *Annual rate of increase*, 2.1%.
Chief Cities (1967 est.): Kinshasa, the capital, 901,520; Lubumbashi, 233,100.
Government: *Head of state*, Mobutu Sese Seko, president (took office Nov. 1965). *Head of government*, Mobutu Sese Seko. *Legislature* (unicameral)—National Assembly. *Major political party*—Popular Movement of the Revolution.
Languages: French (official), Kikongo and other Bantu languages.
Education: *Expenditure* (1969), 18.7% of total public expenditure. *School enrollment* (1969)—primary, 2,822,908; secondary, 243,998; technical/vocational, 33,985; university/higher, 10,165.
Monetary Unit: Zaïre (0.50 zaïre equals U.S.$1, as of Aug. 1972).
Gross National Product (1971 est.): $2,040,000,000.
National Income per Person (1968): $65.
Consumer Price Index (1971): 399 (1963 = 100).
Manufacturing (major products): Processed foods, clothing, textiles, soap.
Major Agricultural Products: Palm kernels (ranks 2d among world producers, 1971), coffee, natural rubber, tea, cacao, bananas, groundnuts.
Major Minerals: Diamonds (ranks 1st among world producers, 1970), copper, manganese, gold, tin, cobalt.
Foreign Trade (1970): *Exports*, $735,000,000 (chief exports—copper; diamonds; coffee; palm oil; tin and cassiterite). *Imports*, $503,000,000 (chief imports, 1968—nonelectrical machinery; cereals and preparations; cotton fabrics; petroleum products). *Chief trading partners* (1969)—Belgium-Luxembourg (took 43% of exports, supplied 24% of imports); United Kingdom (9%—6%); France (7%—8%); United States (2%—13%).
Transportation: *Motor vehicles* (1969), 98,900 (automobiles, 55,800); *railroads* (1970), 3,144 miles (5,060 km); *major national airline*, Air Zaïre.
Communications: *Telephones* (1971), 22,344; *radios* (1970), 63,000; *newspapers* (1969), 7.

French observers interpreted this trend as part of a U. S.-inspired plan to weaken French positions in Subsaharan Africa. U. S. influence was strong in Kinshasa and, by contrast, Belgian influence had visibly declined. President Mobutu's threat to reduce Belgium's share of Zaïre's total imports to a maximum of 15% was only one of many pinpricks aimed at the former colonial power.

The government announced on May 3 that it was sending troops to help Burundi suppress an attempted coup. The only notable setback for Mobutu's foreign policy in Africa during 1972 was his failure in October to persuade Uganda's President Idi Amin to modify his stand on the expulsion of Asians from that country.

EDOUARD BUSTIN
Boston University

ZAMBIA

The year 1972 in Zambia was marked by a continued economic slump caused by lower copper prices, the banning of a new opposition political party, and plans to create a one-party state.

Economic Decline. A 40% drop in income from copper was responsible for Zambia's troubled economy, which was reflected in the devaluation of the kwacha on Dec. 3, 1971. The country was also still suffering from the effects of the September 1970 Mufulira copper mine cave-in, which had cut production by one fifth.

President Kenneth Kaunda launched the second 5-year development plan on January 12, and gave top priority to agricultural development. (In 1971, Zambia had been embarrassed by having to buy maize from white-ruled Rhodesia.) Finance Minister John Mwanakatwe said on January 31 that landlocked Zambia would import more goods from white-ruled South Africa because they were cheaper than

------------ **ZAMBIA · Information Highlights** ------------

Official Name: Republic of Zambia.
Area: 290,585 square miles (752,614 sq km).
Population (1972 est.): 18,300,000. *Density*, 15 per square mile (6 per sq km). *Annual rate of increase*, 2.1%.
Chief Cities (1969 census): Lusaka, the capital, 238,200; Kitwe, 179,300; Ndola, 150,800.
Government: *Head of state*, Kenneth David Kaunda, president (reelected Dec. 1968). *Head of government*, Kenneth David Kaunda. *Legislature* (unicameral)—National Assembly, 105 elected members. *Major political parties*—United National Independence party, African National Congress; United Progressive party.
Languages: English (official), Bemba, Lozi, Luvale, Tonga, Nyanja.
Education: *Expenditure* (1966), 6.2% of gross national product. *School enrollment* (1970)—primary, 694,670; secondary, 55,566; technical/vocational, 948; university/higher, 1,466.
Monetary Unit: Kwacha (0.7143 kwacha equals U. S.$1, Aug. 1972).
Gross National Product (1970 est.): $1,682,000,000.
National Income per Person (1969): $375.
Economic Indexes: *Industrial production* (1970), 129 (1963= 100); *consumer price index* (1971), 109 (1969=100).
Manufacturing (major products): Processed foods, metals and metal products, beverages.
Major Agricultural Products: Tobacco, corn, groundnuts, cotton.
Major Minerals: Copper (ranks 3d among world producers, 1970), zinc, cobalt, lead.
Foreign Trade (1971): *Exports*, $679,000,000 (chief export—copper). *Imports*, $555,000,000 (chief imports, 1969—nonelectrical machinery; transport equipment; mineral fuels, lubricants, electric energy; food). *Chief trading partners* (1969)—United Kingdom (took 26% of exports, supplied 23% of imports); Japan (24%—7%); West Germany (13%—4%).
Transportation: *Motor vehicles* (1968), 74,100 (automobiles, 48,200); *railroads* (1970), 649 miles (1,045 km); *major national airline*, Zambia Airways.
Communications: *Telephones* (1971), 55,754; *television stations* (1971), 3; *television sets* (1971), 18,500; *radios* (1970), 75,000; *newspapers* (1970), 1 (daily circulation, 57,000).

goods requiring road or air freight charges from Tanzania's port of Dar es Salaam. This change was another embarrassing turnabout for Zambia.

Opposition Party Banned. President Kaunda banned the new opposition United Progressive party (UPP) on February 4, charging it with subversion. Some 130 members of the UPP were arrested, including its founder, Simon Kapwepwe. A former vice president of Zambia, Kapwepwe had broken with the ruling United National Independence party (UNIP) to found the UPP in August 1971, and had won the party's only parliamentary seat in an election in December 1971. Observers attributed the ban and arrests partly to economic troubles, but also noted that Kapwepwe was a likely political alternative to Kaunda. It was also suggested that Kaunda was concerned that the UPP's challenge was exciting tribal feelings; Kapwepwe is a member of the Bemba, the largest tribal group in Zambia.

No action was taken against the older opposition African National Congress (ANC). But Kapwepwe's slight UPP success coincided with talk about the creation of a one-party state, which Kaunda said was demanded by the public.

One-Party State. On February 25, Kaunda announced that Zambia would become a one-party state, and named a 21-member commission to recommend constitutional means of making the dominant UNIP Zambia's only political party. Chaired by Vice President Mainza Chona, the commission will examine the likely effects of a one-party state on the country's institutions, cabinet, and parliament.

ANC leader Harry Nkumbula objected to the one-party plan on February 28, announcing that he had refused the two seats on the commission offered to the ANC. On October 1, Kaunda's opponents announced the formation of a new opposition political party, the United People's party, to fight the government's plan for a one-party state. Most of its officers were opposition politicians who had been released from detention.

Foreign Relations. The new U. S. ambassador to Zambia, Jean M. Wilkowski, appointed in June, became the first U. S. woman ambassador in Africa.

Rumanian President Nicolae Ceauşescu visited Zambia during an African tour in March. He agreed to extend the country about $50 million in development funds.

FRANKLIN PARKER
West Virginia University

ZOOLOGY

Zoologists continued their investigations into the possibility of gene manipulation in 1972. Much effort was devoted to problems in applied zoology, such as insect control and pollution control, an emphasis that reflected concern about the continuing effects of man's activities on the animal world. Also, data supporting a century-old theory of mimicry were supplied by a 1972 field experiment.

Genetics. Speculations about the possible manipulation of human genetic traits appeared again and again in the popular press. A summary of current actual knowledge in this field that appeared in March raised the question of possible gene therapy for genetic diseases, since at least 1,500 human diseases are reported to be caused by genetic defects. Some of these diseases occur as frequently as once every 2,500 births, whereas others are rare, but the total can be considered a significant medical

problem. Some of the diseases can be treated by diet supplements and others by various drugs, while a few respond to the replacement of substances produced by the defective genes.

Efforts aimed at the chemical synthesis of single genes and their incorporation into the DNA material of host cells currently involve the utilization of viruses as transporting agents. However, the techniques thus far are applicable only to cell cultures in the laboratory and not to human beings. In fact, geneticists Maurice S. Fox of the Massachusetts Institute of Technology and John W. Littlefield of Harvard Medical School stated that very few of the known human genetic defects could be helped by current techniques, even in theory, and that various probable side effects would be much worse than the original disease. They held that scientists are still primarily at a descriptive phase in their understanding of human genetics, with little, if any, idea of how to intervene safely in genetic activities at any level. (See also GENETICS.)

Insect Control Techniques. The immediate applicability of chromosomal rearrangement techniques seems much more likely in the area of the control of insect pests. Another method of control involves the use of pheromones, the chemical messengers secreted into the external environment by animals. Many zoologists conducted research into the isolation and synthesis of such pheromones in 1972.

For example, D. A. Carlson and his co-workers at the U. S. Department of Agriculture's research service in Gainesville, Fla., synthesized and tested the sex-attractant pheromone of the house fly. They reported that the chemical should be inexpensive to manufacture and useful in reducing the amounts of insecticide needed to control this common pest. Other workers have reported similar results with

FIRST GORILLA born in the New York area is shown off by her mother, Lulu. It was born in the Central Park Zoo.

THE NEW YORK TIMES

the sex-attractant pheromones of the gypsy moth, originally introduced into Massachusetts in 1869 as a possible commercial source of silk; the codling moth, a serious pest in fruit orchards around the world; and the tortix moth, an orchard pest in Europe. The sex-attractant pheromones of these various insects are used to lure the males into traps, thus reducing the numbers of fertile eggs laid by the females.

Pollution and Environmental Problems. The physiological effects of various environmental contaminants continued to be studied by many zoologists in 1972. For example, fish are known to be the most sensitive of all vertebrates to DDT and other organochloride compounds. William B. Kinter of Upstate Medical Center in Syracuse, N. Y., and R. H. Janicki of Mount Desert Island Biological Laboratory, Maine, reported that such compounds in eels disrupt osmotic regulatory activity in the intestines—that is, the movement of liquids through membranes—resulting in the insufficient movement of water from the intestines into the body of the eel. Gilbert S. Stoewsand and associates at Cornell University found that one to eight parts per million of mercuric chloride, when fed to quail, resulted in thinner shells in the eggs laid by the birds.

On the other hand, the concern created some months ago by the percentages of mercury found in tuna and other canned fish was complicated somewhat by recent studies. George E. Miller and associates at the University of California in Irvine determined the mercury levels in museum specimens of tuna taken 62 to 93 years ago and compared their findings with mercury levels in freshly taken and recently canned tuna. The surprising result was that no significant differences in mercury level were found.

Tropical storm Agnes, which swept the Eastern seaboard in late June, not only did great property damage but also disrupted much of the natural environment. For example, record-breaking floods in the Chesapeake Bay area did serious damage to the mussels, clams, and oysters in the bay. Contamination of the bay by untreated sewage carried in by the floods forced clam harvesting to cease at the height of the season. More seriously, many shellfish beds were covered by silt, and the salt water was diluted to levels lethal to most shellfish. These disasters occurred at the height of the spawning season of the bay oyster, a most critical point in its life cycle. While no biologists think that the results will be permanent, most think that some years will be needed for the bay to recover.

Ecological Studies. By means of scuba equipment, R. W. Gilmer of the University of California at Davis was able to determine that certain fragile, free-swimming, planktonic gastropods less than one inch (2.5 cm) long, which were thought to be rare and of no great importance in marine habitats, were actually quite common and an important part of the marine ecosystem. He also clearly demonstrated how the animals use free-floating mucus webs as "seines" to entrap the food they need from the waters of the open ocean.

Various zoologists in the 19th century had proposed theories which stated that mimicry of one species by another can have survival advantages to the mimicking animal, if the original is not palatable as food to potential predators. In succeeding years such theories have been widely accepted, but this acceptance has been based primarily on empirical evidence rather than on laboratory or field tests. In

Animals Play
International Role

In an exchange of gifts following President Nixon's visit to Communist China, the Chinese sent the American people a pair of giant pandas, and the United States sent the Chinese people a pair of musk oxen. At the San Francisco Zoo (*top*), Milton, one of the musk oxen, is coaxed into the shipping crate that will take him to China. In the National Zoo in Washington, D. C. (*bottom*), Ling Ling, the female panda, sits up and licks her paw.

1972, a field experiment by W. W. Benson of the University of Washington has provided quantitative data supporting these theories. Benson selected for his experiment a Costa Rican butterfly that has bright "warning" markings mimicking the colorations of bad-tasting species of butterflies. He dyed the bright patches black on a number of his specimens and then released them. The altered butterflies were soon injured or killed by birds that feed on the insects, whereas the brightly colored control specimens of his group were not attacked.

E. Lendell Cockrum
University of Arizona

contributors

Following is a list of the distinguished authorities who contributed articles to this edition of THE AMERICANA ANNUAL. Their professional affiliations are shown, together with the titles of their articles.

ABEL-SMITH, BRIAN, Professor of Social Administration, The London School of Economics and Political Science: NATIONAL HEALTH INSURANCE (in part)

ADAMS, GEORGE, Legislative Reference Librarian, Connecticut State Library: CONNECTICUT

ADRIAN, CHARLES R., Professor of Political Science, University of California, Riverside: CALIFORNIA; LOS ANGELES

ALEXANDER, ROBERT J., Professor of Economics and Political Science, Rutgers University: DOMINICAN REPUBLIC; GUYANA; JAMAICA

ALLER, LAWRENCE H., Professor of Astronomy, University of California, Los Angeles: ASTRONOMY

ALVEY, EDWARD, JR., Professor Emeritus of Education, Mary Washington College: EDUCATION

AMBRE, AGO, Current Business Analysis Division, Bureau of Economic Analysis, U. S. Department of Commerce: ECONOMY OF THE U. S.—*Industrial Production*

AMELIA, WILLIAM F., Public Relations Consultant, The Equitable Trust Co., Baltimore: BALTIMORE

ANDERSON, JEANNE F., Editor, *Washington Drug & Device Letter:* MEDICINE—*Pharmacology*

ANDERSON, SAMUEL K., Professor of History, Oregon College of Education: EDUCATION

ARMSTRONG, FREDERICK H., Associate Professor of History, Talbot College, University of Western Ontario: TORONTO

BAKER, RICHARD T., Professor of Journalism, Columbia University: PUBLISHING—*Newspapers*

BALL, ROBERT M., Commissioner, Social Security Administration: SOCIAL WELFARE—*Social Security*

BALLINGER, RONALD B., Professor and Chairman, Department of History, Rhode Island College: SOUTH AFRICA; SOUTH WEST AFRICA

BANKS, RONALD F., Assistant to the President, University of Maine: MAINE

BARNES, DANIEL R., Assistant Professor of English, The Ohio State University: AMERICAN LITERATURE; POUND, EZRA

BEATTIE, A. J., Senior Lecturer in Political Science, London School of Economics and Political Science: GREAT BRITAIN; HEATH, EDWARD; WINDSOR, DUKE OF

BENDER, CHESTER R., Admiral, USCG; Commandant, U. S. Coast Guard: COAST GUARD

BENEDICT, BURTON, Professor of Anthropology, University of California, Berkeley: MAURITIUS

BERGEN, DANIEL P., Associate Professor, Graduate Library School, University of Rhode Island: LIBRARIES

BERGER, WOLFGANG H., Assistant Professor of Oceanography, Scripps Institution of Oceanography, University of California, San Diego: OCEANOGRAPHY

BEST, JOHN, Foreign Affairs Editor, The Canadian Press, Ottawa: NEW BRUNSWICK

BIRD, CAROLINE, Author, *The Invisible Scar* and *Born Female;* Consulting Editor, *New Woman:* WOMEN'S LIBERATION MOVEMENT

BLACK, KENNETH, JR., Regents Professor of Insurance, Georgia State University; Coauthor, *Life Insurance* and *Cases in Life Insurance:* INSURANCE

BLOUNT, JOSEPH H., Chief, Evaluation and Statistical Services Unit, Venereal Disease Branch, Public Health Service: MEDICINE—*Venereal Disease*

BOGARDUS, EMORY S., Professor Emeritus of Sociology, University of Southern California; Editor Emeritus, *Sociology and Social Research:* SOCIOLOGY

BOND, DONOVAN H., Executive Director of Development and Professor of Journalism, West Virginia University: WEST VIRGINIA

BOND, JOHN G., Senior Geologist, Idaho Bureau of Mines and Geology: MINING—*U. S. Mining Technology*

BOULAY, HARVEY, Assistant Professor of Political Science, Boston University: BOSTON; MASSACHUSETTS

BOVEY, JOHN A., Provincial Archivist of Manitoba: MANITOBA

BOWERS, Q. DAVID, Columnist, *Coin World;* Author, *Coins and Collectors:* COIN COLLECTING

BOYLAN, JAMES R., Graduate School of Journalism, Columbia University: PUBLISHING—*Magazines*

BRADDOCK, BILL, Sports Department, *The New York Times:* OLYMPIC GAMES; ROBINSON, JACKIE; SPORTS; other sports biographies

BRADLEY, C. PAUL, Professor of Political Science, University of Michigan—Flint: MALAYSIA; SINGAPORE

BRAMMER, DANA B., Assistant Director, Bureau of Governmental Research, University of Mississippi: MISSISSIPPI

BRAZDA, JEROME F., Editor, *Washington Report on Medicine & Health:* MEDICINE—*Hospitals;* NATIONAL HEALTH INSURANCE (in part)

BRESNAHAN, WILLIAM A., Managing Director, American Trucking Associations, Inc.: TRANSPORTATION—*Motor Transport*

BRIDGE, LAWRENCE, Assistant Director for Statistics, Bureau of Economic Analysis, U. S. Department of Commerce: ECONOMY OF THE U. S.—*Retail Sales; Wholesale Sales*

BRODIN, PIERRE, Director of Studies, Lycée Français de New York: FRENCH LITERATURE

BROWN, BERTRAM S., Director, National Institute of Mental Health: MEDICINE—*Mental Health*

BROWN, FREDERICK W., JR., Reporter (Politics), The Denver *Post:* COLORADO

BURDETTE, FRANKLIN L., Professor and Director, Bureau of Governmental Research, University of Maryland: ELECTIONS; POLITICAL PARTIES

BURKHEAD, JESSE, Professor of Economics, Syracuse University: TAXATION

BURKS, ARDATH W., Professor of Political Science and Director of International Programs, Rutgers University: JAPAN; TANAKA, KAKUEI

BURLINGAME, MERRILL G., Professor of History, Montana State University: MONTANA

BUSH, GRAHAM, Senior Lecturer in Political Studies, The University of Auckland: NEW ZEALAND

BUSTIN, EDOUARD, Professor of Political Science, Boston University: BURUNDI; CONGO; GABON; RWANDA; ZAIRE

BUTWELL, RICHARD, Chairman, Department of Political Science, State University of New York at Brockport; Author, *Southeast Asia Today—and Tomorrow:* BURMA; CAMBODIA; INDOCHINA WAR; LAOS; VIETNAM

BYRNES, JAMES D. L., Visiting Scholar, Hoover Institution, Stanford University; Associate Professor of Political Science, Bureau of Government Service, Edinboro State College, Pa.: LIBYA; SUDAN; TUNISIA

CAIRNS, JOHN C., Professor of History, University of Toronto: FRANCE; POMPIDOU, GEORGES

CALDWELL, SALLY, Department of Sociology, North Texas State University: DALLAS

CANFIELD, ROBERT L., Associate Professor of Anthropology, Washington University, St. Louis: ETHNIC GROUPS

CANN, STAN, State Editor, *The Forum,* Fargo, N. Dak.: NORTH DAKOTA

CARMONY, DONALD F., Professor of History, Indiana University; Editor, *Indiana Magazine of History:* INDIANA

CHAFETZ, MORRIS E., M. D., Director, National Institute on Alcohol Abuse and Alcoholism: MEDICINE—*Alcoholism*

CHALMERS, J. W., Faculty of Education, University of Alberta: ALBERTA

CHINN, RONALD E., Associate Professor and Head, Department of Political Science, University of Alaska: ALASKA

CHRIEN, ROBERT E., Physicist, Brookhaven National Laboratory: ENERGY—*Nuclear Energy*

CLARK, C. B., Doctoral Candidate in History, University of Oklahoma: OKLAHOMA

CLARK, ROBERT S., Contributing Editor, *Stereo Review:* MUSIC

COCKRUM, E. LENDELL, Professor of Biological Sciences, University of Arizona: ZOOLOGY

COHEN, SIDNEY, Executive Director, Council on Drug and Alcohol Abuse, University of California, Los Angeles: DRUG ADDICTION AND ABUSE

COLE, CAROLYN J., Editor, *Facts and Forecasts,* Standard & Poor's Corp.: STOCKS AND BONDS

COMEAU, ROBERT, Professeur d'histoire, Université du Québec à Montréal: MONTREAL; QUEBEC

CONDAX, PHILIP L., Equipment Archives Curator, International Museum of Photography, George Eastman House: PHOTOGRAPHY

COPPAGE, NOEL, Contributing Editor, *Stereo Review:* RECORDINGS—*Popular Records*

CORNWELL, ELMER E., JR., Professor of Political Science, Brown University: RHODE ISLAND

CRAIG, ROBERT E., Assistant Professor of Political Science, University of New Hampshire: NEW HAMPSHIRE

CRITCHFIELD, HOWARD J., Professor and Chairman, Department of Geography, Western Washington State College: FIJI; NAURU; PACIFIC ISLANDS; TONGA; WESTERN SAMOA

CURTIS, L. PERRY, JR., Professor of History, University of California, Berkeley: GREAT BRITAIN—*Northern Ireland;* IRELAND

DAVIS, BENJAMIN, O., JR., Lieutenant General; Assistant Secretary for Safety and Consumer Affairs, U. S. Department of Transportation: SKYJACKING (in part)

DAVIS, PETER G., Music Editor, *High Fidelity* Magazine: RECORDINGS—*Classical Records*

DELZELL, CHARLES F., Professor and Chairman, Department of History, Vanderbilt University: ITALY

DOBLER, CLIFFORD, Professor of Business Law, University of Idaho: IDAHO

DOLAN, PAUL, Professor of Political Science, University of Delaware: DELAWARE

DORPALEN, ANDREAS, Professor of History, The Ohio State University: BRANDT, WILLY; GERMANY

DORSEN, NORMAN, Professor of Law, New York University: CIVIL LIBERTIES AND CIVIL RIGHTS

DRACHKOVITCH, MILORAD M., Senior Fellow, The Hoover Institution, Stanford University: YUGOSLAVIA

DRIGGS, DON W., Chairman, Department of Political Science, University of Nevada, Reno: NEVADA

DuBOIS, RUTH MARY (PACKARD), Freelance Fashion Writer, Lecturer, and Columnist: FASHION; BALENCIAGA; NORELL, NORMAN

DUCHON, M. L., Consultant in Ophthalmology: MEDICINE—*Eye Diseases*

DUFF, ERNEST A., Professor of Political Science, Randolph-Macon Woman's College: COLOMBIA

DULANEY, WILLIAM L., Associate Professor of Journalism, The Pennsylvania State University: PENNSYLVANIA; PHILADELPHIA

DUPREE, LOUIS, American Universities Field Staff: AFGHANISTAN

DUPREE, NANCY HATCH, American Universities Field Staff: AFGHANISTAN

DURRENCE, J. LARRY, Department of History, Florida Southern College: FLORIDA

EDE, DAVID, Assistant Professor of Religion, Western Michigan University: RELIGION—*Islam*

EMANUEL, VICTOR L., Lecturer in Political Science, Rice University: HOUSTON

ENQUIST, IRVING F., M. D., Director of Surgery, Methodist Hospital of Brooklyn: MEDICINE—*Surgery*

ETCHESON, WARREN W., Professor of Business Administration, University of Washington: WASHINGTON

EVANS, LARRY, International Chess Grandmaster; Syndicated Chess Columnist: CHESS

FAIRBROTHERS, DAVID E., Professor of Botany, Rutgers University: BOTANY

FARRELL, RAYMOND F., Commissioner of Immigration and Naturalization, U. S. Department of Justice: IMMIGRATION

FISHER, PAUL, Director, Freedom of Information Center, University of Missouri: CENSORSHIP

FISHER, ROBERT W., Economist, Bureau of Labor Statistics, U. S. Department of Labor: LABOR

FISHER, SIDNEY NETTLETON, Emeritus Professor of History, The Ohio State University; KUWAIT; OMAN; PERSIAN GULF STATES; SAUDI ARABIA; SOUTHERN YEMEN; YEMEN

FOLMSBEE, STANLEY J., Professor Emeritus of History, University of Tennessee: TENNESSEE

FOWLER, JOHN, Architect: ARCHITECTURE

FREEMAN, ARTHUR, Editor, Journal of the American Veterinary Medical Association: VETERINARY MEDICINE

FRIEDMAN, HARVEY L., Assistant Professor of Political Science, and Director, Labor Relations and Research Center, University of Massachusetts: POSTAL SERVICE

GAIGE, FREDERICK H., Director, South Asia Studies Program, Davidson College: BHUTAN; NEPAL

GAILEY, HARRY A., Professor of History, California State University, San Jose: GAMBIA; GUINEA; NIGERIA; SENEGAL

GALLOWAY, DAVID D., Professor of English, Ruhr University, Bochum, Germany: WILSON, EDMUND

GARDNER, LLOYD C., Professor of History, Rutgers University: UNITED STATES—*Foreign Affairs*

GEIS, GILBERT, Visiting Professor, Program in Social Ecology, University of California, Irvine; Author, *Man, Crime, and Society:* CRIME; POLICE

GIBBONS, CHARLES A., Statistician, Foreign Regional Analysis Division, Economic Research Service, U. S. Department of Agriculture: FOOD—*World Food Supply*

GJESTER, THOR, City Editor, *Norwegian Journal of Commerce and Shipping,* Oslo: NORWAY

GORDON, MAYNARD M., Editor, *Motor News Analysis* and *The Imported Car Reports:* AUTOMOBILES

GORMAN, JOHN A., Associate Chief, National Income and Wealth Division, Bureau of Economic Analysis, U. S. Department of Commerce: ECONOMY OF THE U. S.—*National Income and Product*

GRANNIS, CHANDLER B., Editor-at-Large, Publishers' Weekly: PUBLISHING—*Books*

GRAVER, LAWRENCE, Professor of English, Williams College: ENGLISH LITERATURE

GRIGG, AUSTIN E., Dean, Richmond College, University of Richmond, Va.: PSYCHOLOGY

GROSS, NELSON G., Assistant Secretary of State, Senior Adviser and Coordinator for International Narcotics Matters, U. S. Department of State: NARCOTICS TRAFFIC (in part)

GROTH, ALEXANDER J., Professor of Political Science, University of California, Davis: POLAND

GULICK, LEWIS, Diplomatic Affairs Reporter, The Associated Press: FOREIGN AID

GUNN, JOHN M., Professor of Radio-TV-Film, State University of New York at Albany: TELEVISION AND RADIO—*Television Broadcasting; Radio Broadcasting*

GWERTZMAN, BERNARD M., Diplomatic Correspondent, Washington Bureau, "The New York Times": NARCOTICS TRAFFIC (in part)

HAKES, JAY E., Assistant Professor of Political Science, Louisiana State University in New Orleans: KENYA; TANZANIA; UGANDA

HALE, JOE, Director of Cooperative Evangelism, Board of Evangelism of the United Methodist Church; Executive Committee, Key 73: RELIGION FEATURE (in part)

HALL, FRANCES L., Director, International Trade Analysis Division, Bureau of International Commerce, U. S. Department of Commerce: INTERNATIONAL TRADE

HANSON, EARL PARKER, Geographer; Former Consultant to the Puerto Rico Department of State: PUERTO RICO

HARGREAVES, J. D., Professor of History, University of Aberdeen: GHANA; SIERRA LEONE

HARVEY, ANDREW S., Research Associate, Institute of Public Affairs, Dalhousie University: NOVA SCOTIA

HAYES, JOHN D., Rear Admiral, USN (Ret.); U. S. Naval Academy Alumni Association: TRANSPORTATION—*Shipping*

HAYES, KIRBY M., Professor of Food Science, University of Massachusetts: FOOD—*U. S. Food Industry;* NUTRITION

HEAD, HOWARD T., Partner, A. D. Ring & Associates, Consulting Radio Engineers: TELEVISION AND RADIO—*Television and Radio Engineering*

HELMREICH, E. C., Thomas B. Reed Professor of History and Political Science, Bowdoin College: AUSTRIA

HELMREICH, PAUL C., Associate Professor and Chairman, Department of History, Wheaton College, Norton, Mass.: SWITZERLAND

HENDERSHOT, LELAND C., Editor-in-Chief, American Dental Association: MEDICINE—*Dentistry*

HERSHKOWITZ, LEO, Professor of History, Queens College, City University of New York: NEW YORK CITY; NEW YORK STATE

HODGES, RALPH W., Associate Technical Editor, *Stereo Review:* RECORDINGS—*Audio Equipment and Techniques*

HOFFMAN, CHARLES A., M. D., President, American Medical Association: NATIONAL HEALTH INSURANCE (in part)

HOOVER, HERBERT T., Associate Professor of History, The University of South Dakota: SOUTH DAKOTA

HOPKINS, JAMES F., Professor of History, University of Kentucky: KENTUCKY

HOPKO, THOMAS, St. Vladimir's Orthodox Theological Seminary: ATHENAGORAS I; RELIGION—Orthodox Eastern Church

HOWARD, HARRY N., Adjunct Professor of Middle East Studies, School of International Service, The American University: TURKEY

HUCKSHORN, ROBERT J., Professor and Chairman, Department of Political Science, Florida Atlantic University: NIXON, RICHARD M.

HUNKINS, KENNETH L., Senior Research Associate, Lamont–Doherty Geological Observatory of Columbia University: ARCTIC REGIONS

HUNT, STANLEY B., President, Textile Economics Bureau, Inc.: TEXTILE INDUSTRY

HUTH, JOHN F., JR., Reporter-Columnist, The Plain Dealer, Cleveland, Ohio: CLEVELAND

IRWIN, GRAHAM W., Professor of History, Columbia University: CAMEROON; CENTRAL AFRICAN REPUBLIC; CHAD; LIBERIA; UPPER VOLTA

JACOBS, WALTER DARNELL, Professor of Government and Politics, University of Maryland: CONNALLY, JOHN B.; KISSINGER, HENRY A.; LAIRD, MELVIN R.; McGOVERN, GEORGE S.; ROGERS, WILLIAM P.; WALLACE, GEORGE C.

JAFFE, HERMAN, Department of Anthropology, Brooklyn College, City University of New York: ANTHROPOLOGY

JENSEN, J. GRANVILLE, Professor of Geography, Oregon State University: CONSERVATION

JONES, ISABELLA J., Executive Vice President, National Association of Consultants for Children and Youth: SOCIAL WELFARE—Child Welfare

KAMINS, ROBERT M., Professor of Economics, University of Hawaii: HAWAII

KANTOR, HARRY, Professor of Political Science, Marquette University: CHILE; COSTA RICA; PERU

KAPLAN, ALAN R., Editor, Modern Data Magazine: COMPUTERS

KARSKI, JAN, Department of Government, Georgetown University: BULGARIA; HUNGARY

KEHR, ERNEST A., Director, Stamp News Bureau; Executive Chairman, Philatelic Press Club; Stamp News Editor, The Chicago Daily News: STAMP COLLECTING

KELLER, EUGENIA, Managing Editor, Chemistry: CHEMISTRY

KENNEDY, EDWARD M., U. S. Senator from Massachusetts: NATIONAL HEALTH INSURANCE (in part)

KIMBALL, LORENZO K., Associate Professor of Political Science, University of Utah: UTAH

KING, PETER J., Associate Professor of History, Carleton University: ONTARIO; OTTAWA

KLAUSLER, ALFRED P., Executive Director, Associated Church Press; Religion Editor, Westinghouse Broadcasting Co.: RELIGION—Protestantism

KNAPP, ELAINE S., Editor, State Government News, State Headlines, Council of State Governments: STATE GOVERNMENT

KOLEHMAINEN, JOHN I., Chairman, Department of Political Science, Heidelberg College, Tiffin, Ohio: FINLAND

KOMINUS, NICHOLAS, Kominus Agri-Info Associates: AGRICULTURE—Fruits; Grains; Vegetables

KRAFT, BETSY, Education Division, National Coal Association: ENERGY—Coal

KREITZMAN, STEPHEN N., Professor of Biochemistry, Emory University School of Dentistry: BIOCHEMISTRY

KREPS, CLIFTON H., JR., Wachovia Professor of Banking, University of North Carolina: BANKING

KUDRLE, ALBERT E., Director of Public Relations, American Hotel & Motel Association: TOURISM—Hotels and Motels

LAI, DAVID CHUEN-YAN, Assistant Professor of Geography, University of Victoria, B. C.: HONG KONG

LANDSBERG, H. E., Research Professor, Institute for Fluid Dynamics and Applied Mathematics, University of Maryland: METEOROLOGY

LARSEN, WILLIAM, Professor of History, Radford College: VIRGINIA

LARSON, T. A., Professor of History, University of Wyoming; Author, History of Wyoming: WYOMING

LAWRENCE, ROBERT M., Department of Political Science, Colorado State University: DEFENSE FORCES (part)

LEE, STEWART M., Professor and Chairman, Department of Economics and Business Administration, Geneva College: CONSUMERISM

LEFEVER, ERNEST W., Senior Fellow, Foreign Policy Studies Program, The Brookings Institution: DISARMAMENT AND ARMS CONTROL

LEIDEN, CARL, Professor of Government, University of Texas at Austin: BANGLADESH; EGYPT; PAKISTAN; SADAT, ANWAR EL-; THAILAND

LEONARD, OLEN E., Department of Sociology, University of Arizona: BOLIVIA

LEVY, JAMES R., Assistant Professor of History, Pomona College: ARGENTINA

LEWIS, OSCAR, Author, San Francisco: Mission to Metropolis, The Big Four, and other books: SAN FRANCISCO

LINDGREN, RAYMOND E., Professor of History, California State University, Long Beach: DENMARK; ICELAND; SWEDEN

LINDSEY, ROBERT H., Aviation Reporter, The New York Times: AEROSPACE INDUSTRY; AIR TRANSPORTATION; SKYJACKING (in part)

LINEBACK, RICHARD H., Professor of Philosophy, Bowling Green State University, Ohio: PHILOSOPHY

LINGARD, C. CECIL, Former Editor, The Canada Year Book: NORTHWEST TERRITORIES

LIVINGSTONE, WILLIAM, Reviewer, Ballet Review; Managing Editor, Stereo Review: DANCE

LOHMANN, LAWRENCE C., City Hall Reporter, The Milwaukee Journal: MILWAUKEE

LOTT, LEO B., Professor and Chairman, Department of Political Science, University of Montana: PARAGUAY; VENEZUELA

LYNCH, J. JOSEPH, S. J., Director, Fordham Seismic Observatory: EARTHQUAKES

MABRY, DONALD J., Assistant Professor of History, Mississippi State University: MEXICO

MACAULAY, NEILL, Associate Professor of History, University of Florida; Author, A Rebel in Cuba: CUBA; LATIN AMERICA

McCLESKEY, CLIFTON, Professor of Government, University of Texas at Austin: TEXAS

McCONNELL, WILLIAM J., Assistant Professor of Political Science, Colorado State University; Colonel, USA (Ret.): DEFENSE FORCES—U. S. Army; U. S. Marine Corps; National Guard

McCORQUODALE, SUSAN, Assistant Professor of Political Science, Memorial University of Newfoundland: NEWFOUNDLAND

McKAY, HELEN A., Head of Adult Services, Regina Public Library, Sask.: SASKATCHEWAN

McKAY, W. A., Scarborough College, University of Toronto: CANADA; TRUDEAU, PIERRE E.

MacLACHLAN, DONALD, Assistant City Editor, The Province, Vancouver: VANCOUVER

McNAMARA, BROOKS, Professor of Drama, New York University; Contributing Editor, The Drama Review: THEATER

MAJOR ANDRÉ, Literary Critic, Montreal: FRENCH CANADIAN LITERATURE

MARCOPOULOS, GEORGE J., Associate Professor of History, Tufts University: CYPRUS; GREECE

MARKE, JULIUS J., Law Librarian and Professor of Law, New York University: LAW—U. S. Legislation and Case Law

MARTIN, J. A., JR., Professor of Religion, Columbia University: RELIGION—General Survey

MARTY, MARTIN E., Professor of Modern Church History, University of Chicago; Author, Righteous Empire: The Protestant Experience in America: RELIGION FEATURE (in part)

MARWICK, CHARLES S., Senior Writer, Medical World News: MEDICINE—General Survey

MATHEWS, THOMAS G., Research Professor, Institute of Caribbean Studies, University of Puerto Rico: BARBADOS; CARIBBEAN; TRINIDAD AND TOBAGO; VIRGIN ISLANDS

MECHAM, J. LLOYD, Professor Emeritus of Government, University of Texas at Austin: BRAZIL

MEREDITH, J. R., Director, Bureau of Economics and Statistics, British Columbia: BRITISH COLUMBIA

MEYER, EDWARD H., President, Chairman of the Board, and Chief Executive Officer, Grey Advertising Inc.: ADVERTISING

MEYER, RALPH C., Assistant Professor of Political Science, Fordham University at Lincoln Center: ASIA

MIESEL, VICTOR H., Professor of the History of Art, University of Michigan; Author, Voices of German Expressionism: ART

MILLER, LUTHER S., Editor, Railway Age: TRANSPORTATION—Railroads

MILLER, NYLE H., Executive Director, Kansas State Historical Society; Coauthor, Kansas: A Pictorial History: KANSAS

MILNE, ROBERT SCOTT, Society of American Travel Writers; coauthor, Around the World with the Experts: TOURISM

MITCHELL, GARY, Associate Professor of Physics, North Carolina State University at Raleigh: PHYSICS

MORGAN, CHARLES S., General Manager, National Fire Protection Association: FIRES

MUSTO, DAVID F., M. D., Assistant Professor of History and Psychiatry, Yale University: NARCOTICS TRAFFIC (in part)

NEILL, R. F., Associate Professor of Economics, St. Patrick's College, Carleton University: PRINCE EDWARD ISLAND

NELSON, RALPH L., Professor of Economics, Queens College, City University of New York; Author, *Economic Factors in the Growth of Corporation Giving:* PHILANTHROPY

NEWSOM, DONALD W., Professor and Head, Department of Horticulture, Louisiana State University: GARDENING AND HORTICULTURE

NOLAN, WILLIAM C., Associate Professor of Political Science, Southern State College: ARKANSAS

NOSS, JOHN B., Emeritus Professor of Philosophy, Franklin and Marshall College; Author, *Man's Religions:* RELIGION—*Oriental Religions*

NOWELL, CHARLES E., Professor of History, Emeritus, University of Illinois: PORTUGAL; SPAIN

NUQUIST, ANDREW E., Professor Emeritus of Political Science, University of Vermont: VERMONT

NYSTROM, J. WARREN, Executive Director, Association of American Geographers: GEOGRAPHY

O'DONNELL, JOHN J., President, Air Line Pilots Association: SKYJACKING (in part)

O'HARE, JOSEPH A., S. J., Associate Editor, *America:* PAUL VI, POPE; RELIGION—*Roman Catholicism*

PALMER, NORMAN D., Professor of Political Science and South Asian Studies, University of Pennsylvania: CEYLON; GANDHI, INDIRA; INDIA

PANO, NICHOLAS C., Assistant Professor of History, Western Illinois University: ALBANIA

PARKER, FRANKLIN, Benedum Professor of Education and Research Associate, Human Resources Institute, West Virginia University: BOTSWANA; EQUATORIAL GUINEA; LESOTHO; MALAGASY REPUBLIC; MALAWI; RHODESIA; SWAZILAND; ZAMBIA

PARTAN, DANIEL G., Professor of Law, Boston University: LAW—*International Law*

PATAI, RAPHAEL, Professor of Anthropology, Fairleigh Dickinson University: RELIGION—*Judaism*

PEARCE, JOHN B., Acting Laboratory Director, Ecosystems Investigations, Sandy Hook Laboratory, N. J.: MARINE BIOLOGY

PETERSEN, WILLIAM, Robert Lazarus Professor of Social Demography, The Ohio State University; Author, *Population (2d ed.):* POPULATION

PETERSON, ROBERT L., Associate Professor of Political Science, University of Texas at El Paso: EL SALVADOR; NICARAGUA

PHEBUS, GEORGE E., JR., Supervisor, Processing Laboratory, Department of Anthropology, National Museum of Natural History, Smithsonian Institution; ARCHAEOLOGY—*Western Hemisphere*

PHILLIPS, JACKSON, Vice President, Moody's Investors Service: ECONOMY OF THE U. S.—*Economic Review*

PIPPIN, LARRY L., Professor of Political Science, Elbert Covell College, University of the Pacific: GUATEMALA; HONDURAS; PANAMA

PLATT, HERMANN K., Associate Professor of History, St. Peter's College, Jersey City: NEW JERSEY

POLK, IRWIN J., Director of Children's Allergy Service, St. Luke's Hospital, New York City: MEDICINE—*Allergies*

PORTER, J. R., Professor and Chairman, Department of Microbiology, College of Medicine, University of Iowa: MICROBIOLOGY

PORTNOY, BERNARD, Professor of Community Medicine, Public Health, and Pediatrics, University of Southern California: MEDICINE—*Respiratory Diseases*

POWELL, WILLIAM S., Curator, North Carolina Collection, University of North Carolina: NORTH CAROLINA

PRICE, EDWIN W., JR., Managing Editor, *The Morning Advocate,* Baton Rouge, La.: LOUISIANA

PRITCHETT, C. HERMAN, Professor of Political Science, University of California, Santa Barbara: LAW—*Supreme Court*

PRITIKIN, ROLAND I., Eye Surgeon and Consulting Ophthalmologist; Author, *Essentials of Ophthalmology:* MEDICINE—*Eye Diseases*

PUMPHREY, RALPH E., Professor of Social Work, Washington University, St. Louis: SOCIAL WELFARE

PYLE, HOWARD, President, National Safety Council: ACCIDENTS AND DISASTERS

QUIRK, WILLIAM H., Editorial Director, *Contractors & Engineers* Magazine: BRIDGES; CANALS; DAMS; TUNNELS

RAKOVE, MILTON, Professor of Political Science, University of Illinois at Chicago Circle: CHICAGO; ILLINOIS

RANDALL, CHARLES E., Staff, *Journal of Forestry:* FORESTRY AND LUMBERING

RANDAZZO, VINCENT P., JR., City Editor, *The Times-Picayune,* New Orleans, La.: NEW ORLEANS

RATHBONE, ROBERT B., Director, Information Division, Agricultural Research Service: AGRICULTURE—*U. S. Agricultural Research*

RAYMOND, ELLSWORTH, Associate Professor of Politics, New York University; Author, *The Soviet State* and *A Picture History of Eastern Europe:* BREZHNEV, LEONID; COMMUNISM; KOSYGIN, ALEKSEI; MONGOLIA; UNION OF SOVIET SOCIALIST REPUBLICS

RAYMOND, JACK, President and Chief Executive Officer, International Institute for Environmental Affairs; Author, *Power at the Pentagon:* ENVIRONMENT

RODRIGUEZ, ALFRED, Professor of Languages, University of New Mexico: SPANISH LITERATURE

ROMAN, JAMES R., JR., Associate Professor of Business Administration, The George Washington University: TRANSPORTATION—*General Survey; Highways*

RONNE, EDITH M., Antarctic Specialist: ANTARCTICA

ROSE, ERNST, Author, *A History of German Literature:* GERMAN LITERATURE

ROSS, RUSSELL M., Professor and Chairman, Department of Political Science, University of Iowa: IOWA

ROTHMAN, FRANK G., Professor of Biology, Brown University: GENETICS

ROWLETT, RALPH M., Associate Professor of Anthropology, University of Missouri: ARCHAEOLOGY—*Eastern Hemisphere*

SALGADO, MARIA A., Associate Professor of Spanish, University of North Carolina at Chapel Hill: LATIN AMERICAN LITERATURE

SALMANS, SANDRA, Associate Editor (Business and Finance), *Newsweek* Magazine: ENERGY—*General Survey; Electricity; Gas*

SALSINI, PAUL, State Editor, The Milwaukee *Journal:* WISCONSIN

SARRATT, WILLIAM A., Editor, *The Fish Boat,* New Orleans: FISHERIES

SARRIS, ANDREW, Associate Professor of Cinema, Columbia University: MOTION PICTURES

SAVAGE, DAVID, Instructor, Department of English, Simon Fraser University: CANADIAN LITERATURE

SAWATSKY, DON, Information Officer, Yukon Department of Travel and Information: YUKON TERRITORY

SCHMITT, KARL M., Associate Director, Institute of Latin American Studies; Professor of Government, University of Texas at Austin: HAITI

SCHNEIDERMAN, RONALD A., Senior Editor—Government Electronics and Features, *Electronic News:* ELECTRONICS

SCHRATZ, PAUL R., Director, Office of International Studies, University of Missouri; Captain, USN (Ret.): DEFENSE FORCES—*U. S. Navy*

SCHWAB, PETER, Assistant Professor of Political Science, State University of New York at Purchase: ETHIOPIA; SOMALIA

SCOTT, RALPH C., Professor of Medicine, Cardiac Laboratory, University of Cincinnati Medical Center: MEDICINE—*Heart and Vascular Disease*

SEGAR, WILLIAM E., Professor of Pediatrics, University of Wisconsin: MEDICINE—*Pediatrics*

SHEATSLEY, PAUL B., Director, Survey Research Service, National Opinion Research Center, University of Chicago: PUBLIC OPINION RESEARCH

SHOGAN, ROBERT, Washington Bureau, *Newsweek:* UNITED STATES—*Domestic Affairs*

SIMMONS, MARC, Farrier; Author, *Spanish Government in New Mexico* and *The Little Lion of the Southwest:* NEW MEXICO

SINNEN, JEANNE, Senior Editor, University of Minnesota Press: MINNESOTA

SKELDING, FRANK H., Director of Corporate Planning, Fluor Utah (Engineers & Constructors), Inc.: MINING—*World Mineral Production*

SKURNIK, W. A. E., Associate Professor of Political Science, University of Colorado: MALI; MAURITANIA

SLOAN, HENRY S., Associate Editor, *Current Biography:* BIOGRAPHY (in part); NECROLOGY (in part)

SLONIM, MARC, Director, Sarah Lawrence College Foreign Studies: ITALIAN LITERATURE; SOVIET LITERATURE

SMYLIE, JAMES H., Professor of American Church History, Union Theological Seminary, Richmond, Va.: RELIGION FEATURE (in part)

SPECTOR, SHERMAN D., Professor of History, Russell Sage College; Author, *A History of the Balkan Peoples:* RUMANIA

SPENCER, JEAN E., Assistant Professor of Government, University of Maryland: MARYLAND; WASHINGTON, D. C.

STEHLING, KURT R., Aerospace Consultant, U. S. Government: SPACE EXPLORATION—*Advances in Space Technology*

STEPHENS, GENE, Urban Life Center, Georgia State University: ATLANTA; GEORGIA

STOKES, W. LEE, Professor of Geology, University of Utah: GEOLOGY

STOUDEMIRE, ROBERT H., Associate Director, Bureau of Governmental Research and Associate Professor of Political Science, University of South Carolina: SOUTH CAROLINA

STOUMPAS, GEORGE N., Metallurgical Engineer, American Iron and Steel Institute: STEEL

SWANSON, CURTIS E., Manager, Public Relations Division, American Library Association: LIBRARIES—*American Library Association*

SWINTON, WILLIAM E., Professor and Fellow of Massey College, University of Toronto: PALEONTOLOGY

SYNAN, VINSON, Chairman of Social Science Division, Emmanuel College, Ga.: RELIGION FEATURE (in part)

TABORSKY, EDWARD, Professor of Government, University of Texas at Austin: CZECHOSLOVAKIA

TAKUWA, SHINJI, Professor of English and American Studies, Kyushu University: JAPANESE LITERATURE

TAN, CHESTER C., Professor of History, New York University; Author, *The Boxer Catastrophe* and *Chinese Political Thought in the Twentieth Century*: CHINA; CHOU EN-LAI

TAYLOR, PHILIP B., JR., Professor of Political Science; Director of Latin American Studies, University of Houston: ECUADOR; URUGUAY

TAYLOR, ZACK, Boating Editor, *Sports Afield*; Regional Editor, *Waterway Guide*: BOATING

THEISEN, CHARLES W., Assistant City Editor, The Detroit News: DETROIT; MICHIGAN

THOMAS, JAMES D., Professor of Political Science, University of Alabama: ALABAMA

THOME, PITT G., Deputy Director for Earth Observations Flight Program, National Aeronautics and Space Administration: SPACE EXPLORATION—*Manned Space Flight; Earth Satellites and Space Probes*

THOMPSON, RICHARD E., President, Revenue Sharing Advisory Service, Inc.: CITIES AND URBAN AFFAIRS

THORNTON, ALLAN F., Director, Economic and Market Analysis Division, Federal Housing Administration: HOUSING

TIBBITTS, CLARK, Director, Division of Manpower Development, Administration on Aging, Department of Health, Education, and Welfare: OLDER POPULATION

TINKLEPAUGH, JAMES R., Associate Professor and Director of Technical Services, College of Ceramics at Alfred University, State University of New York: MATERIALS

TRUMAN, EDWIN M., Associate Professor of Economics, Yale University: INTERNATIONAL FINANCE

TURNER, ARTHUR C., Professor of Political Science, University of California, Riverside: AFRICA; IRAN; IRAQ; ISRAEL; MIDDLE EAST

UHL, WILLIAM, Editorial Director, *World Petroleum*: ENERGY —*Petroleum*

VANDENBOSCH, AMRY, Professor Emeritus of Political Science, University of Kentucky: BELGIUM; INDONESIA; LUXEMBOURG; NETHERLANDS; SUHARTO

WAMSLEY, GARY L., Assistant Professor of Political Science, Vanderbilt University: SELECTIVE SERVICE

WARD, DAVID A., Professor of Sociology and Chairman, Criminal Justice Studies, University of Minnesota: PRISONS

WARNER, ANNE R., Director, Public Relations Department, American Nurses' Association, Inc.: MEDICINE—*Nursing*

WARNER, DAVID Y., News Correspondent, Pittsburgh: PITTSBURGH

WASHBURN, WILCOMB E., Director, Office of American Studies, Smithsonian Institution; Adjunct Professor, The American University: INDIANS, AMERICAN

WEBB, RICHARD E., Former Director, Reference and Library Division, British Information Services: BERMUDA; COMMONWEALTH OF NATIONS; MALTA; UNITED NATIONS; WALDHEIM, KURT

WEEKS, JEANNE, Contributing Editor and Associate, Kirk-Brummel Associates Inc.; Associate, Association of Interior Designers: INTERIOR DESIGN

WEINER, PAUL, Professor of Economics, University of Connecticut: TELECOMMUNICATIONS

WEISENBURGER, FRANCIS P., Professor of History, The Ohio State University: OHIO

WELCH, CLAUDE E., JR., Professor of Political Science, State University of New York at Buffalo: DAHOMEY; IVORY COAST; NIGER; TOGO

WENTZ, RICHARD E., Associate Professor of Humanities and Coordinator of Religious Studies, Arizona State University: RELIGION FEATURE (in part)

WESTERN, JOE, Kominus Agri-Info Associates: AGRICULTURE—*World Agriculture; U. S. Agriculture; Dairy Products; Livestock and Poultry*

WHITE, JOHN P., Professor of Political Science, Arizona State University: ARIZONA

WILLARD, F. NICHOLAS, Department of History, Georgetown University: JORDAN; LEBANON; SYRIA

WILLIS, F. ROY, Professor of History, University of California, Davis: EUROPE

WILLNOW, RONALD D., City Editor, The St. Louis *Post-Dispatch*: MISSOURI; SAINT LOUIS

WILSON, JOHN S., Reviewer of Jazz Records, *The New York Times* and *High Fidelity* Magazine; Author, *Jazz: The Transition Years—1940–1960*: RECORDINGS—*Jazz Records*

WILSON, R. NORRIS, Executive Vice President, United States Committee for Refugees: REFUGEES

WILSON, VERNON E., Administrator, Health Services and Mental Health Administration, U. S. Public Health Service: MEDICINE—*Public Health*

WOODS, GEORGE A., Children's Books Editor, *The New York Times*: CHILDREN'S LITERATURE

YOUNG, CHARLES W., Sloan-Kettering Institute for Cancer Research: MEDICINE—*Cancer*

YOUNGER, R. M., Author, *The Changing World of Australia; Australia and the Australians*: AUSTRALIA

ZABEL, ORVILLE H., Professor of History, Creighton University: EAGLETON, THOMAS F.; NEBRASKA; SHRIVER, R. SARGENT

ZAFRA, NICOLAS, Professor Emeritus of History, University of the Philippines: PHILIPPINES

necrology · 1972

The following is a selected list of over 300 prominent persons who died during 1972. Separate articles on those persons whose names are preceded by an asterisk (*) may be found in the text under their own heading. Cross references in this list are to articles in the text where biographical sketches of the subject will be found.

Alinsky, Saul (David) (63), U. S. social organizer: b. Chicago, Ill., Jan. 30, 1909; d. Carmel, Calif., June 12, 1972. A self-styled professional radical, he worked for more than three decades organizing impoverished communities and deprived minorities at a grass-roots level to enable them to press their demands for better housing, schools, and job opportunities. In 1938 he organized the Back-of-the-Yards Council, an effective community organization of Irish-American Chicago slum dwellers. The following year he founded the Industrial Areas Foundation, which sponsored community organizations in cities from coast to coast, and he served as its executive director until his death. In the 1960's he worked extensively with black ghetto dwellers, and during the last years of his life he organized members of white middle-class communities as social activists. His published works include *Reveille for Radicals* (1946) and *Rules for Radicals* (1971).

Anderson, Thomas V. (91), Canadian general; major general, was Canadian chief of staff (1938–40); saw action in World War I and was quartermaster general (1935–38): d. Toronto, Canada, Nov. 8.

Andrews, Tod (51), U. S. actor; played on Broadway in *Mister Roberts* and *Summer and Smoke;* his TV appearances included *Ironsides, The F. B. I.,* and *The Bold Ones:* d. Beverly Hills, Calif., Nov. 4.

Austin, Gene (71), U. S. singer; crooner of the 1920's and 30's; famous for his recordings of *My Blue Heaven, Ramona,* and *Girl of My Dreams;* his recordings sold more than 86 million copies: d. Palm Springs, Calif., Jan. 24.

Bach-Zelewsky, Erich von dem (78), German Nazi general; as S. S. chief of Warsaw in 1944, he led the suppression of the Warsaw uprising; he was sentenced to life in prison for war crimes in 1964: d. Munich, Germany, March 8.

Balenciaga, Cristobal (77), Spanish fashion designer: d. Valencia, Spain, March 24. (See FASHION.)

Barlow, Howard (79), U. S. conductor; led the Firestone orchestra on the Voice of Firestone program on radio and then on radio and television from 1943 to 1963: d. Bethel, Conn., Jan. 31.

Bastico, Ettore (96), Italian field marshal; commander of Axis forces in North Africa (1941–43): d. Rome, Italy, Dec. 1.

Bates, Sanford (88), U. S. penologist; director of the federal prison system (1930–37); as parole commissioner of New York (1940–45) and commissioner of institutions and agencies of New Jersey (1945–54), he created model parole systems and made numerous innovations: d. Trenton, N. J., Sept. 8.

Bates, Ted (Theodore Lewis) (70), U. S. advertising executive: b. New Haven, Conn., Sept. 11, 1901; d. New York, N. Y., May 30, 1972. Through Ted Bates & Co., which he founded in 1940 and built into one of the world's five leading advertising agencies, he pioneered in the use of television as an advertising medium. He worked for the Chase National Bank, and for the advertising firms of Batten, Barton, Durstine & Osborne and Benton & Bowles before establishing his own agency. Serving successively as president, chairman of the board, and honorary chairman of Ted Bates & Co., he launched "hard sell" television advertising campaigns for such clients as the Colgate-Palmolive Co. and Wonder Bread, and he directed the firm's overseas expansion.

Battle, John Stewart, Sr. (81), U. S. public official; Democratic governor of Virginia (1950–54); successfully led fight against a party loyalty oath at the Democratic national convention in 1952: d. Albermarle County, Va., April 8.

Bedacht, Max (89), German-born U. S. Communist; cofounder of the Communist party in the U. S. in 1919; expelled in 1948 after being accused of opposing the party leadership; he was reportedly reinstated later on: d. Jamaica, N. Y., July 2.

Begich, Nick (40), U. S. public official; Democratic congressman from Alaska from 1970: d. in airplane crash on flight from Anchorage to Juneau, Alaska, Oct. 16.

Benson, Sally (71), U. S. author; wrote *Meet Me in St. Louis* (1942), which was later made into a movie; contributed numerous short stories to *The New Yorker* magazine and wrote a number of screen plays: d. Woodland Hills, Calif., July 19.

Bentley, Doug (56), Canadian hockey player; forward for the Chicago Black Hawks (1939–52) and the New York Rangers (1953–54); best season was 1943–44 with 38 goals; made 219 goals in regular season play: d. Saskatoon, Saskatchewan, Canada, Nov. 24.

Berg, Morris (Moe) (70), U. S. major league baseball player; during career (1924–39) was catcher for Brooklyn Dodgers, Chicago White Sox, Boston Red Sox; expert linguist and scholar: d. Belleville, N. J., May 29.

Berman, Eugene (73), Russian-born U. S. artist; neoromantic painter and set designer for opera and ballet; designed sets for *Don Giovanni* (1957) and *Othello* (1962) for the Metropolitan Opera: d. Rome, Italy, Dec. 14.

Berry, Charley (69), U. S. baseball umpire; American League umpire (1942–62); catcher for the Philadelphia Athletics, Boston Red Sox, and Chicago White Sox (1925–38): d. Evanston, Ill., Sept. 6.

Berryman, John (57), U. S. poet and educator: b. McAlester, Okla., Oct. 25, 1914; d. (suicide) Minneapolis, Minn., Jan. 7, 1972. Was regents professor at University of Minnesota; first notable work was *Homage to Mistress Bradstreet* (1950). He expressed his thoughts through his characters, preferring to write long poems which used language and themes drawn from the American experience. He won a Pulitzer Prize in 1965 for *77 Dream Songs* (1964) and the National Book Award in 1969 for *History, His Dream, His Rest* (1968).

Bickel, Karl A. (90), U. S. newspaperman; president of United Press news service (1923–35); introduced feature syndication and service for radio news broadcasts: d. Sarasota, Fla., Dec. 11.

Blank, Theodor (66), German public official; as the first post-World War II defense minister (1955–56) of West Germany, he reorganized the German army along defensive lines; minister of labor and social affairs (1957–65): d. Bonn, Germany, May 14.

Blocker, Dan (43), U. S. actor; played "Hoss Cartwright" on the *Bonanza* television series since 1958: d. Englewood, Calif., May 13.

Blythe, Betty (72), U. S. movie actress; starred in silent films and more than 50 talkies; among her pictures were *Queen of Sheba, The Scarlet Letter,* and *My Fair Lady:* d. Woodland Hills, Calif., April 7.

Boeschenstein, Harold (76), U. S. industrialist; founder and first president of the Owens-Corning Fiberglas Corp. (1938–63); chairman of the board of Owens-Corning (1963–67): d. New York, N. Y., Oct. 23.

Boggs, Hale (68), U. S. public official; Democratic congressman from Louisiana (1940–42; 1946–72); House majority leader since 1970; as majority whip, he helped steer Medicare and school aid programs through Congress: d. in airplane crash on flight from Anchorage to Juneau, Alaska, Oct. 16.

Bond, Horace M. (68), U. S. educator; director of Bureau of Education and Social Research of Atlanta University (1966–71); president of Lincoln University (1939–45) and of Fort Valley State College (1945?57); dean of School of Education, Atlanta University (1957–66): d. Atlanta, Ga., Dec. 21.

Bonfils, Helen G. (82), U. S. newspaper publisher and patron of the theater; chairman of the board of *The Denver Post:* d. Denver, Colo., June 6.

Bow, Frank T. (71), U. S. public official; Republican congressman from Ohio (1950–72); led budget-cutting efforts as senior minority member of the House Appropriations Committee: d. Washington, D. C., Nov. 13.

Boyd, Louise Arner (84), U. S. explorer; organized several Arctic expeditions from 1926 to 1938 to study areas around Spitsbergen, Greenland, and eastern Canada; in June 1955 she became the first woman to make a successful flight over the North Pole: d. San Francisco, Calif., Sept. 14.

Boyd, William (74), U. S. actor: b. Hendrysburg, Ohio, June 8, 1898; d. South Laguna Beach, Calif., Sept. 12, 1972. As the star of over 100 films and television shows in the role of Hopalong Cassidy, the gentlemanly cowboy who abstained from smoking, drinking, and swearing, Boyd served as an inspiration to millions of youngsters. The son of a farm laborer, he left school after the sixth grade and eventually went to Hollywood. In the 1920's he was a romantic idol, appearing in such films as *The Volga Boatmen* and *Two Arabian Nights*. In 1935, after a period of eclipse, he accepted the starring role in a series of cowboy films by Paramount. He took the character of Hopalong Cassidy, created by the writer Clarence Mulford, and made it his own. From 1948, when the Hopalong Cassidy show made its television debut, until his retirement in 1953, Boyd enjoyed great popularity. Over the years, he contributed generously to philanthropic activities benefiting youth.

Boyden, Frank L. (92), U. S. educator; headmaster of Deerfield Academy (1902–68), which under him became a leading private prep school in the U. S.: d. Deerfield, Mass., April 25.

Bozell, Harold V. (86), U. S. corporate executive; president (1940–51) of General Telephone; vice president of Telephone Utility Co. (1932): d. New Rochelle, N. Y., Nov. 28.

Braun, J. Werner (58), German-born U. S. scientist; microbial geneticist was professor of microbiology at Rutgers University; best known for studies of cellular activity and the immunological defense systems in man and animals: d. Bethesda, Md., Nov. 19.

Brockway, Wallace (67), U. S. editor and author; expert on music; co-authored *The World of Music* (1939); *Opera, A History of Its Creation and Performance* (1942); and *The World of Opera* (1962): d. New York, N. Y., Nov. 5.

Broda, Turk (58), Canadian hockey player; goalie for the Toronto Maple Leafs (1938–52); won the Vezina Trophy for allowing the fewest goals in 1941 and 1948: d. Toronto, Canada, Oct. 17.

Budenz, Louis (80), U. S. newspaper editor, author, and ex-Communist; star witness before Sen. Joseph McCarthy's congressional hearings in 1950 and at numerous other government hearings; editor of the *Daily Worker* (1935–45); renounced communism in 1945; author of *This Is My Story* (1947), *Men Without Faces* (1950), and *The Techniques of Communism* (1951): d. Newport, R. I., April 27.

Burke, Billy (69), U. S. professional golfer; won the U. S. Open title in 1931: d. Clearwater, Fla., April 19.

Burkholder, Paul R. (69), U. S. scientist; isolated an early drug, Azaserine, used in the treatment of leukemia; developed a method of taking vitamin B-12 orally; taught at Wisconsin, Yale, and Cornell universities: d. Madison, Wis., Aug. 11.

Bush, Prescott (77), U. S. public official; Republican senator from Connecticut (1952–63); expert on government finance and national economy; partner in Brown Brothers Harriman & Co., investment firm: d. New York, N. Y., Oct. 8.

Byrnes, James F(rancis) (92), U. S. statesman and jurist: b. Charleston, S. C., May 2, 1879; d. Columbia, S. C., April 9, 1972. During a career that spanned nearly five decades, he served in top-level posts in virtually every area of the U. S. government. He was successively a lawyer, newspaper publisher, and county prosecutor before serving in the U. S. House of Representatives from 1911 to 1925. Elected to the U. S. Senate in 1930, Byrnes, although essentially a conservative, became one of the strongest supporters of the New Deal legislation and foreign policies of President Roosevelt, who appointed him an associate justice of the U. S. Supreme Court in 1941. At the President's request he resigned from the court in 1942 to become director of economic stabilization. From 1943 to 1945, as director of war mobilization, he had virtually complete authority over domestic policy. As secretary of state under the Truman administration he attended the Potsdam, London, and Moscow international conferences and served as a UN delegate. He resigned in 1947 because of policy differences with the President. His administration as governor of South Carolina, from 1951 to 1955, was marked by stringent economy measures and opposition to racial integration of public schools.

Cabot, Bruce (67), U. S. film actor; played a leading role in *King Kong;* among his other films were *Dodge City, The Bad Man of Brimstone*, and *The Green Berets:* d. Woodland Hills, Calif., May 13.

Carroll, Leo G. (80), British-born actor; best known for his television roles as Cosmo Topper on the *Topper* series and Mr. Waverly on *The Man From U.N.C.L.E.;* his Broadway credits included *Angel Street* and *The Late George Apley;* among his movies were *Wuthering Heights, Father of the Bride*, and *North by Northwest:* d. New York, N. Y., Oct. 16.

Casadesus, Robert Marcel (73), French pianist and composer: b. Paris, France, April 7, 1899; d. Paris, Sept. 19, 1972. A leading piano virtuoso, Casadesus was noted for his elegance of style and clarity of expression. He gave over 3,000 concerts during a career that spanned 55 years. The son of an actor, he studied at the Paris Conservatoire, and after his Paris debut in 1917 he made many international tours. He made his American debut in 1935 with the New York Philharmonic Orchestra. After the outbreak of World War II, he settled in the United States with his wife and children. Casadesus was also noted as a teacher until 1952, when he began to concentrate more on composing. His compositions, many of them in neoclassic style, but also reflecting the influence of impressionism, include symphonies, chamber music, songs, and works for instrumental soloists.

Casadesus, Jean (44), French-born concert pianist; studied at the Paris Conservatory and made his debut with the Philadelphia Orchestra under Eugene Ormandy in 1946; artist in residence at N. Y. State University at Binghampton: d. (auto accident) near Renfrew, Ont., Canada, Jan. 20.

Ceram, C. W. (57), German-born author; C. W. Ceram was the pen name of Kurt W. Marek; wrote best seller on archaeology, *Gods, Graves, and Scholars* (1949), which sold more than 4 million copies; also wrote *The Secret of the Hittites* (1956): d. Hamburg, Germany, April 12.

Chandos, Lord (78), British financier; managing director of the British Metal Corporation; during World War II was president of the Board of Trade and served as minister of production (1942–45); secretary of state for the colonies (1951–54); member of Parliament (1940–54): d. London, England, Jan. 21.

Chapin, Cornelia Van Auken (80), U. S. sculptress; worked in stone and wood; among her more famous works are *Christ the King* in the Cathedral of St. John the Divine, New York City, and the *Giant Turtle* in Rittenhouse Square, Philadelphia: d. Lakeville, Conn., Dec. 4.

Chapman, John (71), U. S. drama critic; reviewed theater for the New York *Daily News* (1946–71): d. Wesport, Conn., Jan. 19.

Chen Yi (70), Chinese army officer and government official: b. Pengan, Szechwan, China, 1901; d. Peking, China, Jan. 6, 1972. One of the top military commanders of Communist forces in their struggle to gain control of China, he served for some 10 years as foreign minister of the Chinese People's Republic. He became involved in Communist activities as a student in Paris in 1919. After the outbreak of war with Japan in 1937 he became a commander, and then acting commander in chief, of the Communist Fourth Army. In 1947 he took command of the People's Liberation Army. A member of the Communist party's central committee since 1945, he served as mayor of Shanghai from 1949 to 1958 and was named a marshal in 1954. In 1958 he was appointed foreign minister and deputy premier. Denounced by Red Guards during the Cultural Revolution, he ceased to function as foreign minister in 1968 and was removed from the politburo in 1969. At the time of his death, however, he appeared to have been restored to honor.

Chevalier, Maurice (83), French actor and singer: b. Paris, France, Sept. 12, 1888; d. there, Jan. 1, 1972. As France's most popular show business personality of the 20th century, he epitomized the gayety and elegance popularly attributed to Paris, and he won international acclaim as an actor, comedian, dancer, and singer of such popular hits as *Mimi* and *Ma Louise*. He made his Folies-Bergère debut in 1909 with the famed Mistinguett. During the late 1920's and early 1930's he starred in a series of Hollywood films, including *Love Parade* and *The Merry Widow*. In the 1950's he began to appear as a character actor in several American films, including *Love in the Afternoon, Can-Can*, and *Fanny*, and he was acclaimed for his performance as the aging ladies' man and his rendition of *Thank Heaven for Little Girls* in *Gigi* (1958). He retired after a final world tour in his one-man show in 1968.

Chichester, Sir Francis (70), British yachtsman and aviator: b. North Devon, England, Sept. 17, 1901; d. Plymouth, England, Aug. 26, 1972. Chichester, who took up sailing in his fifties, won international acclaim for his record-breaking nine-month, 28,500-mile solo voyage in the 53-foot ketch *Gipsy Moth IV* in 1966–67. The son of a clergyman, he briefly attended Marlborough College before moving to New Zealand, where he became successful in real estate. In 1929 he returned to England and took up flying. In the next few years he made several long-distance solo flights, including one from Sydney to Lon-

don via Peking. After he began sailing in about 1953, he participated in many yacht races and made several solo crossings of the Atlantic. On his world-circling voyage, which followed the routes of the old clipper ships, he saw land at only four places and covered more distance in less time than anyone before him in nautical history. In 1967 he was knighted by Queen Elizabeth II. His books include *Gipsy Moth Circles the World* (1968).

Christofilos, Nicholas C. (56), U. S. nuclear scientist; head of the Aston Project of the University of California's Radiation Laboratory, an attempt to use thermonuclear power to produce electricity: d. Harvard, Calif., Sept. 25.

Chubb, Thomas C. (72), U. S. author and book reviewer; an Italian Renaissance expert, he wrote biographies including *The Life of Giovanni Boccaccio* (1930) and *Dante and His World:* d. Thomasville, Ga., March 20.

Church, Richard (78), British poet and author; his autobiographical *Over the Bridge* (1955) became a best seller; other works included a collection of poems, *Flood of Life* (1917), and a novel, *The Porch* (1937): d. Sissinghurst Castle, Kent, England, March 4.

Churchill, Edward D. (76), U. S. physician; noted surgeon, expert in thoracic and cardiac surgery; one-time head of surgical services at Massachusetts General Hospital and professor of surgery at Harvard University: d. Strafford, Vt., Sept. 2.

Churchill, Peter (63), British war hero and author; during a mission to the French Resistance in 1942 he was captured by the Nazis but escaped execution because the Germans thought he might be related to Winston Churchill, which he was not; wrote *Of Their Own Choice* (1952) and *Duel of Wits* (1953): d. Cannes, France, May 1.

Clapp, Verner W. (71), U. S. librarian; chief assistant librarian of the Library of Congress (1947–56) and president of the Council on Library Resources (1956–65) of the Ford Foundation: d. Alexandria, Va., June 15.

Clavier, Andre G. (77), French-born U. S. radio pioneer; directed the first microwave radio broadcast across the English Channel in 1931; a vice president of IT&T in charge of research (1956–59): d. Hollywood, Fla., Jan. 9.

Clemente, Roberto (38), U. S. baseball player: d. in an airplane crash off San Juan, Puerto Rico, Dec. 31, 1972. (See SPORTS—*Baseball*.)

Clyde, George D. (73), U. S. public official; Republican governor of Utah (1956–1965); feuded with the state's teachers over funds for education: d. Salt Lake City, Utah, April 2.

Coanda, Henri-Marie (86), Hungarian scientist; pioneer in aerodynamics; discovered the "Coanda effect," that air forced over curved surfaces tends to cling to them forming vacuums above an object and that the normal atmosphere below would cause object to rise; the theory forms the basis of vertical lift planes: d. Bucharest, Hungary, Nov. 25.

Collins, George W. (47), U. S. public official; Democratic congressman from Chicago since 1970; alderman of Chicago (1964–70): d. in an airplane crash, Chicago, Ill., Dec. 8.

Colum, Padraic (90), Irish poet and author: b. Longford, Ireland, Dec. 8, 1881; d. Enfield, Conn., Jan. 11, 1971. A representative of the Irish Renaissance, he was noted in particular for his gentle lyric verse about nature. Over the years he produced some 50 volumes, including poetry, plays, novels, history, folklore, biography, critical essays, travel descriptions, and children's tales. His early published verse came to the attention of W. B. Yeats, J. M. Synge, and Lady Gregory. He became a member of their circle and was one of the founders of Dublin's Abbey Theatre. In 1914 he settled in the United States. His works include *Dramatic Legends* (1922), *Collected Poems* (1932), *Treasury of Irish Folklore* (1954), *Poet's Circuit* (1960), and *Images of Departure* (1968). With his wife, Mary Gunning Maguire Colum, he wrote *Our Friend James Joyce* (1958).

Cornell, Joseph (69), U. S. sculptor; famed for his collages and constructions of small boxes which juxtaposed objects with poetic imagery; his works were exhibited at the Metropolitan Museum, the Whitney, and the Museum of Modern Art: d. Flushing, N. Y., Dec. 29.

Correll, Charles J. (82), U. S. actor; played "Andy" on the *Amos 'n' Andy* radio comedy show from 1928 to the 1950's: d. Chicago, Ill., Sept. 26.

Coudenhove-Kalergi, Count Richard (77), Austrian advocate of European unity; founded the Pan-Europe Union in 1923 and was general secretary of the European Parliamentary Union in 1947; author of *Pan-Europe* (1923) and *An Idea Conquers the World* (1954): d. Schruns, Austria, July 27.

UPI   PHOTOREPORTERS
William Boyd   **Maurice Chevalier**

Courant, Richard (84), German-born mathematician; helped to provide the mathematical formulas necessary for the use of computers in the solution of scientific problems; created the Mathematics Institute at the University of Göttingen and what is now known as the Courant Institute of Mathematical Sciences at New York University: d. New Rochelle, N. Y., Jan. 27.

Creasy, Sir George (77), British admiral; commander-in-chief of the British Home Fleet (1952–55); as chief of staff of Allied Naval Forces in World War II, he planned D-Day naval operations: d. London, England, Nov. 1.

Crooks, Richard (72), U. S. tenor: b. Trenton, N. J., June 16, 1900; d. Portola Valley, Calif., Oct. 1, 1972. One of the most popular stars of the Metropolitan Opera during the 1930's and 1940's, Crooks was noted for his sweet and mellow voice and his smooth, effortless delivery. He made his debut in 1922, singing with the New York Symphony Orchestra under Walter Damrosch. In 1925 he went on a European concert tour and two years later he was heard in the opera houses of Hamburg and Berlin. He made his debut with the Metropolitan Opera in 1933 as Des Grieux in *Manon*. For the next 10 years or so he sang regularly at the Met in such operas as *La Traviata, Don Giovanni,* and *Faust*. For about 14 years he was the featured performer on radio's *Voice of Firestone*. Crooks retired in the early 1950's.

Crowder, Alvin (73), U. S. baseball player; pitcher (1926–36) for the Washington Senators, Detroit Tigers, and St. Louis Browns; posted career record of 167 victories and 115 losses: d. Winston-Salem, N. C., April 3.

Cullman, Howard S. (80), U. S. executive; commissioner of the Port of New York Authority (1927–69); well-known philanthropist and backer of Broadway shows, including *South Pacific:* d. New York, N. Y., June 30.

Day-Lewis, Cecil (68), British poet and author: b. Ballintogher, Ireland, April 27, 1904; d. High Barnet, England, May 22, 1972. A versatile man of letters, known for his novels and works of literary criticism as well as for his poetry, he was named poet laureate of England by Queen Elizabeth II in 1968. During the 1930's, as a member of the Communist party, he wrote fervent revolutionary poetry and prose, but after his break with communism, about 1939, he became more meditative and subjective. His anthologies of poetry include *Collected Poems 1929–1933* (1935), *Short Is the Time: Poems 1936–1943* (1945), *An Italian Visit* (1954), *Pegasus* (1958), *The Gate* (1962), and *The Whispering Roots* (1970). His 20 detective novels, written under the pseudonym "Nicholas Blake," attained great popularity.

Dean, Vera Micheles (69), Russian-born U. S. author and lecturer; expert on foreign affairs; was editor and research director of the Foreign Policy Association (1931–61); professor of international development at New York University (1962–71); among her books are *Foreign Policy Without Fear* (1953) and *The UN Today* (1965): d. New York, N. Y., Oct. 11.

Deeter, Jasper (77), U. S. producer, director, and actor; founder and director (1923–56) of the Hedgerow Theater, Moylan-Rose Valley, Pa., an early repertory theater in U. S.: d. Media, Pa., May 30.

Delderfield, R(onald) F. (60), English author; wrote best-selling saga of an English family *God Is an Englishman* (1970) and a sequel, *Theirs Was the Kingdom* (1971): d. Sidmouth, England, June 24.

Dell'Acqua, Angelo (68), Italian Roman Catholic cardinal; vicar general of Rome since 1967; advisor to Popes Pius XII, John XXIII, and Paul VI: d. Lourdes, France, Aug. 27.

Denfield, Louis E. (80), U.S. admiral; chief of naval operations (1947–49); was relieved of his post after a long dispute over the role of the Navy in U.S. defense strategy: d. Westboro, Mass., March 28.

Deval, Jacques (82), French playwright; the most famous of his plays is *Tovarich* (1933), later made into a movie; his other plays include *Soubrette* (1939) and *Bathsheba* (1947): d. Paris, France, Dec. 19.

De Wilde, Brandon (30), U.S. actor; famous child actor who appeared on Broadway and in films; his credits included *Member of the Wedding* on Broadway and the films *Shane* and *Hud:* d. (auto accident) Katewood, Calif., July 6.

Dickson, Donald (61), U.S. singer; sang baritone at the Metropolitan Opera and on radio in the Chase & Sanborn Hour in the 1930's: d. New York, N.Y., Sept. 21.

Dickson, Fred (43), U.S. sunken treasure hunter; spent the last five years in search of the wreck of Columbus' *Santa Maria* off Haiti: d. while diving off the coast of Haiti, Nov. 16.

Dies, Martin (71), U.S. public official: b. Colorado, Texas, Nov. 5, 1901; d. Lufkin, Texas, Nov. 14, 1972. A Democratic congressman from Texas (1930–45; 1952–58), he was the first chairman of the House Un-American Activities Committee (1938–45). His investigations were often colorful, noisy, and controversial. He accused numerous government employees of being Communist sympathizers and also attacked the CIO Political Action Committee as following the Communist line. His activities were hailed by some patriotic groups, derided by others. President Roosevelt was among his critics. His committee won numerous extensions of its life and was made permanent in 1945 after he decided not to run again. He failed in two bids for a U.S. Senate seat in 1941 and 1956, but was reelected to the House with bipartisan backing in 1952, serving until 1958.

Dieterle, William (79), German-born U.S. film director; the most notable of his films was *The Life of Emile Zola;* among his other credits were *Pasteur, Juarez, The Hunchback of Notre Dame,* and *All That Money Can Buy:* d. Ottobrünn, West Germany, Dec. 9.

Dolan, Robert E. (64), U.S. composer; wrote scores and conducted orchestras for numerous Broadway shows, including *Strike Me Pink* and *Coco;* as musical director for Paramount Pictures he did the scores for *Going My Way* and *The Bells of St. Mary's:* d. Westwood, Calif., Sept. 27.

Donlevy, Brian (71), U.S. actor: b. Cortadown, County Armagh, Ireland, Feb. 9, 1901; d. Hollywood, Calif., April 5, 1972. He was well known to movie fans for his portrayals of hard-boiled characters in scores of Hollywood Westerns, war dramas, detective thrillers, and adventure films. In 1939 he was nominated for an Academy Award as best supporting actor for his performance as the sadistic sergeant in the Foreign Legion drama *Beau Geste.* He decided upon an acting career after service in World War I. He appeared in *What Price Glory* and several other Broadway plays with some success. He had his first major film role in *The Milky Way,* in which he portrayed a boxer. Among his other films are *Barbary Coast, Jesse James, Wake Island, Destry Rides Again,* and *Two Years Before the Mast.* In the 1950's he starred in the television adventure series *Dangerous Assignment.*

Dreyfus, Henry (68), U.S. industrial designer; his designs included clocks, the interiors of the 20th Century Limited and American Airlines 707, farm equipment, and appliances; author of *The Measure of Man* (1955) and *Symbols Sourcebook* (1970): d. South Pasadena, Calif., Oct. 5.

Drinker, Philip (77), U.S. educator and engineer; co-inventor in 1928 of the iron lung, used to assist those with respiratory problems, particularly from polio; professor of industrial hygiene at Harvard's School of Public Health (1936–60): d. Fitzwilliam, N.H., Oct. 19.

Duckworth, George E. (69), U.S. classical scholar; Giger professor emeritus of classics at Princeton University, where he taught from 1926 to 1971; his *Structural Patterns and Proportions in Vergil's Aeneid* (1962) gave new insight into the poetical structure of Virgil's poetry: d. Merwick, N.J., April 5.

Duffy, Bernard C. (70), U.S. advertising executive; president of Batten, Barton, Durstine & Osborne, Inc., one of the world's largest advertising agencies (1946–56): d. White Plains, N.Y., Sept. 1.

Durnan, Bill (57), Canadian hockey player; goalie for the Montreal Canadiens (1943–50); posted 34 shutouts and allowed an average 2.35 goals in 383 games; won six Vezina trophies: d. Toronto, Canada, Oct. 31.

Eboli, Thomas (61), reputed U.S. gangland leader; also known as Tommy Ryan, he was reportedly involved in organized crime in New Jersey: d. (murdered) New York, N.Y., July 16.

Ellender, Allen J. (81), U.S. senator: b. Montegut, La., Sept. 24, 1890; d. Bethesda, Md., July 27, 1972. A member of the U.S. Senate for 35 years, he was its senior member and, from 1971, its president pro tem. After obtaining his law degree from Tulane University in 1913, he served as an attorney and was elected in 1924 to the Louisiana House of Representatives, where he was closely associated with the political machine of Huey P. Long. After Long's assassination in 1935, Ellender was elected to succeed him in the U.S. Senate in 1936. There he supported liberal New Deal legislation but staunchly adhered to the Southern conservative position regarding civil rights. In his foreign policy views, Ellender, who made many trips abroad, criticized foreign aid and favored South African apartheid but advocated a conciliatory attitude toward the Soviet Union. At the time of his death he headed the powerful Senate appropriations committee.

Eriksen, Erik (70), Danish public official; premier of Denmark (1950–53) who signed new constitution (1953) incorporating Greenland into Denmark and abolishing the upper house of parliament: d. Copenhagen, Denmark, Oct. 7.

Fainsod, Merle (64), U.S.-Soviet scholar; director of Harvard University Library since 1964; director of the Russian Research Center at Harvard (1959–64); author of *How Russia Is Ruled* (1952): d. Cambridge, Mass., Feb. 10.

Fairbairn, Ann (70), U.S. novelist (born Dorothy Tait); wrote best seller *Five Smooth Stones* (1966): d. Monterey, Calif., Feb. 8.

Feis, Herbert (78), U.S. historian and economist; won the Pulitzer Prize in 1961 for his account of the Potsdam Conference, *Between War and Peace;* served as an adviser in the U.S. Departments of State (1931–43) and War (1943–47); also wrote *From Rust to Terror* (1970), an account of the origins of the Cold War: d. Winter Park, Fla., March 2.

Fischer, Ernst (73), Austrian writer and Communist leader; independent minded Communist, he was a frequent critic of the Soviet Union; wrote *Ideology and Coexistence* (1950) and *The Necessity of Art: A Marxist Approach* (1961): d. Deutsch Feistritz, Austria, Aug. 1.

Fisher, Geoffrey Francis (85), archbishop of Canterbury: b. Nuneaton, Warwickshire, England, May 5, 1887; d. Sherborne, Dorset, England, Sept. 14, 1972. As head of the Church of England from 1945 to 1961, he was the spiritual leader of Anglicans throughout the world. He attended Marlborough College and Oxford University and was ordained in 1913. He became headmaster of Repton School in 1914, bishop of Chester in 1930, and bishop of London in 1939. Succeeding to the see of Canterbury in 1945, he presided over the coronation of Elizabeth II in 1952 and was president of the World Council of Churches from 1946 to 1954. He was a leader of the ecumenical movement, and in 1960 he made a historic visit to Pope John XXIII. On his retirement in 1961, the queen elevated him to life peer as Lord Fisher of Lambeth.

Fleischer, Nat(haniel) S. (84), U.S. boxing expert; founder and editor of *The Ring,* a monthly boxing magazine: d. New York, N.Y., June 25.

Flick, Friedrich (89), German industrialist; major industrial backer of the Hitler regime; imprisoned for war crimes (1947–50); rebuilt his fortune in coal, steel, and other industries, becoming one of Germany's richest men: d. Düsseldorf, Germany, July 20.

Forand, Aime J. (76), U.S. public official; Democratic congressman from Rhode Island; served in the House of Representatives (1936–38 and 1940–60); introduced Medicare legislation in 1957; such a bill was passed in 1965: d. Boca Raton, Fla., Jan. 19.

Forster, J. Frank (64), U.S. corporate executive; chief executive officer (since 1965) and chairman of the board (since 1967) of the Sperry Rand Corp.; joined Sperry Gyroscope as a manager in 1938: d. New York, N.Y., July 3.

Fosdick, Raymond B. (89), U.S. foundation executive; president of the Rockefeller Foundation (1920–36); U.S. representative to the League of Nations before the Senate refused to ratify U.S. participation in 1919: d. Newtown, Conn., July 18.

Franklin, Sidney (79), U.S. film producer; his film *Mrs. Miniver* won an Oscar for best picture in 1942; among his other movies were *The Barretts of Wimpole Street, Madame Curie,* and *The Yearling:* d. Santa Monica, Calif., May 18.

Franklin, Walter (88), U. S. railroad executive; president of the Pennsylvania Railroad (1949–54): d. Northeast Harbor, Maine, Aug. 17.

Frederik IX (72), king of Denmark: b. Copenhagen, Denmark, March 11, 1899; d. there, Jan. 14, 1972. Denmark's "citizen-king," whose easy informality made him highly popular among his countrymen, he ascended the throne on April 20, 1947, following the death of his father, King Christian X. He was noted for his patronage of the arts, in particular, music. In 1953 he signed a new constitution, approved by popular referendum, establishing the right of female succession to the throne, thus enabling his eldest daughter, Margrethe, to succeed him.

Friml, Rudolf (92), Bohemian-born U. S. composer: b. Prague, Bohemia (modern Czechoslovakia), Dec. 7, 1879; d. Hollywood, Calif., Nov. 12, 1972. He composed a number of famous operettas including *The Vagabond King* (1925), *Rose-Marie* (1923), and *The Three Musketeers* (1928). He first went to the United States as an accompanist to Jan Kubelik, a concert violinist, and returned to stay in 1906. His first operetta was *Firefly* (1912), which was followed by a number of less famous works, including *The Peasant Girl* (1914), *Gloriana* (1918), and the Ziegfeld Follies of 1921 and 1923–25. Among his more popular songs were *Indian Love Call, Rose-Marie,* and *The Donkey Serenade.* Although he also wrote for the movies, none of his later works attained the vogue of his operettas.

Frohman, Philip H. (84), U. S. architect; specialized in church architecture; among his designs are the Washington Cathedral (Episcopal cathedral church of Sts. Peter and Paul), the Roman Catholic Cathedral of Los Angeles, and Trinity Chapel at Harvard: d. Washington, D. C., Oct. 30.

Fu-chih, Hsieh (74), Chinese political leader; minister of public security (1959–65) and member of the Politburo; leader of the Revolutionary Committee of Peking since 1965: d. Peking, China, announced March 29.

Garrigue, Jean (59), U. S. poet; taught at several colleges and was poet in residence at the University of California at Riverside and at Rhode Island College; among her collections of poems are *The Monument Rose* (1943), *Country Without Maps* (1964), and *New and Selected Works* (1968): d. Boston, Mass., Dec. 27.

Gentele, Goeran (54), Swedish and American opera director: b. Stockholm, Sweden, Sept. 20, 1917; d. (auto accident) Sardinia, Italy, July 18, 1972. Noted for his abilities as an administrator as well as for his talents as an artistic innovator, he was named in 1970 to succeed Sir Rudolph Bing as general manager of the Metropolitan Opera in New York, a position that he assumed only 18 days before his death in an automobile crash. The son of a Swedish army officer, he studied at the Sorbonne and the University of Stockholm before entering the school of Sweden's Royal Dramatic Theatre to prepare for a theatrical career. After some success as a director of plays and motion pictures, he was named staff director of the Royal Opera House in Stockholm in 1952 and became its general manager in 1963. During his next eight years with the Royal Opera he modernized its administration and overhauled its repertoire, adding new and experimental works. In line with his view of opera as a "folk art," he took steps to attract a wider audience, particularly young people, to it.

Giobbe, Paolo (92), Italian Roman Catholic churchman; made a cardinal in 1958; had served as nuncio to Colombia and internuncio to the Netherlands; headed the Apostolic Datary (1959–67): d. Rome, Italy, Aug. 14.

Glarner, Fritz (73), Swiss artist; painted the murals in UN headquarters in New York: d. Locarno, Switzerland, Sept. 18.

Gold, Harry (72), Russian-born U. S. physician; heart specialist and pharmacologist who helped develop modern forms of digitalis; professor of clinical pharmacology at Cornell University Medical College (1947–65): d. New York, N. Y., April 21.

Goodman, Al (81), Russian-born U. S. orchestra leader; he conducted numerous Broadway show orchestras; led the orchestras on radio's *Hit Parade* and the Fred Allen show: d. New York, N. Y., Jan. 10.

Goodman, Paul (60), U. S. author and social philosopher: b. New York, N. Y., Sept. 9, 1911; d. North Stratford, N. H., Aug. 2, 1972. Regarded by some as the father figure of the New Left, Goodman espoused a humanist anarchism which held that man's natural tendencies as a creative, loving being are suppressed by the social institutions in which he is imprisoned. He graduated from the City College of New York in 1931 and then led a precarious existence for a number of years as part-time student, teacher, writer, lecturer, and lay psychotherapist. His *Growing Up Absurd* (1960), an attack on the dehumanizing materialism of American society and a defense of alienated youth who drop out of it, was a best seller. In *Compulsory Mis-Education* (1964), he urged abandonment of standardized schooling for a more flexible and personalized educational system. He also published poems, plays, and novels, and collaborated with others on books dealing with psychology and city planning. His last book, *Defense of Poetry,* was published in 1972.

Gorbach, Alfons (73), Austrian public official; chancellor of Austria (1961–64); a leader of the conservative People's Party: d. Graz, Austria, July 31.

Gove, Philip B. (70), U. S. dictionary editor; editor of *Webster's Third New International Dictionary* (1961); his criteria for inclusion was usage rather than correctness, which raised some controversy: d. Warren, Mass., Nov. 15.

Grace, John (70), U. S. religious leader; lieutenant commissioner of the Salvation Army; served as national chief secretary (1961–70): d. Philadelphia, Pa., July 23.

Graham, Frank P. (85), U. S. educator and civil rights advocate; first president of the consolidated University of North Carolina (1930–49); appointed to fill an unexpired U. S. Senate term in 1949; UN representative mediating the Kashmir dispute between India and Pakistan (1951–67): d. Chapel Hill, N. C., Feb. 16.

Grant, William T. (96), U. S. retail store executive: b. Stevensville, Pa., June 27, 1876; d. Greenwich, Conn., Aug. 6, 1972. He was the founder of the W. T. Grant Company, which grew from a single store in 1906 into one of the largest retail store chains in the United States. In 1972 there were 1,176 stores in over 40 states, with over 60,000 employees. Grant, who grew up in New England, left high school in his second year. In 1906 he joined with three partners and opened the first W. T. Grant store in Lynn, Mass., with 15 employees and a 25-cent maximum price on merchandise. Operating on the principles of strict economy, rapid merchandise turnover, and good public relations, Grant built the chain into a flourishing enterprise. He served as president of the company until 1924 and as chairman of the board from 1924 until his retirement in 1966.

Gray, Harold (66), U. S. airline executive; president and chief executive officer of Pan American World Airways (1964–68); chairman of the board (1968–70); joined the company as pilot in 1929: d. New York, N. Y., Dec. 23.

Grier, Harry D. M. (58), U. S. museum official; director of the Frick Collection (1964–72) New York City: d. New York, N. Y., May 30.

Grierson, John (73), U. S. film maker; coined the word "documentary" for the film form he helped to develop; his movies included *Drifters, Song of Ceylon,* and *Night Mail:* d. Bath, England, Feb. 19.

Grimes, William H. (79), U. S. journalist; editor of *The Wall Street Journal* (1941–58); won the Pulitzer Prize in 1946 for editorial writing: d. Delray Beach, Fla., Jan. 14.

Grossinger, Jennie (80), U. S. resort owner; with other members of the Grossinger family built a family guest farm into a famous 1,300-acre, 600-room resort, Grossinger's, in the Catskill Mountains of New York: d. Grossinger's, N. Y., Nov. 20.

Gulbenkian, Nubar S. (75), Turkish oil millionaire; his fortune was built upon extensive oil interests, which he developed with his father; flamboyant in the enjoyment of his wealth, he was a noted gourmet and bon vivant: d. Cannes, France, Jan. 10.

Hall, Cliff (78), U. S. entertainer; comedian played Sharlie, the straight man in Jack Pearl's radio series in 1930's and 1940's; among his Broadway credits were *Miracle on 34th Street, The Music Man,* and *No Time for Sergeants:* d. Englewood, N. J., Oct. 6.

Halpern, Julius (60), U. S. nuclear physicist; professor of physics at the University of Pennsylvania since 1947; helped to develop radar during World War II; headed a project in 1970 which attempted to prove existence of the ultimate theoretical particle, the quark: d. Philadelphia, Pa., May 13.

Hartnett, Gabby (72), U. S. baseball player: b. Woonsocket, R. I., Dec. 20, 1900; d. Park Ridge, Ill., Dec. 20, 1972. A star catcher renowned for his ability to handle pitchers, Charles Leo Hartnett played for the Chicago Cubs from 1922 to 1940 and was a member of the Baseball Hall of Fame. He held the career record for home runs for a catcher (236) until it was broken by Yogi Berra, who was to hit 358. Taking over as manager of the Cubs in mid-season of 1938, while still catching, Hartnett brought the team to a pennant. The Cubs did badly in the next two years, and in 1940 he moved to the Giants, for whom he played for one year. He

managed minor league teams for several years and returned to the majors as a coach for the Kansas City A's in 1965–67.

Hayden, Carl T. (94), U. S. public official; senator from Arizona from 1926 to 1970, serving longer than any other senator in U. S. history; member of the House of Representatives (1912–26): d. Mesa, Ariz., Jan. 25.

Hearst, George R. (67), U. S. newspaper publisher; vice president of the Hearst Corp., which controls the Hearst newspapers; he was also a well-known aviator and pioneer in cross-country flight: d. Los Angeles, Calif., Jan. 26.

Heatter, Gabriel (82), U. S. news commentator and journalist: b. New York, N. Y., 1890; d. Miami Beach, Fla., March 30, 1972. One of the most popular radio personalities of the Depression, World War II, and Cold War eras, he was known for his emotional, dramatic, and often optimistic commentaries in which he made world events come alive in the homes of millions of Americans. After a number of years as a newspaper reporter and magazine writer he was hired in 1932 as a radio commentator. For nearly 20 years he was a regular commentator on station WOR of the Mutual Broadcasting System. In 1951 he moved to Miami Beach, where he appeared on radio and television news programs until 1965 and wrote a column for the Miami Beach *Sun* until 1968.

Heiser, Victor G. (99), U. S. physician and author; toured the world for the Rockefeller Foundation helping to set up programs to deal with typhus, yellow fever, cholera, and dysentery (1914–34); author of a best-selling autobiography, *American Doctor's Odyssey* (1936): d. New York, N. Y., Feb. 27.

Heiskell, John N. (100), U. S. journalist; editor of *The Arkansas Gazette* since 1902, he was the oldest working newsman in the U. S.; opposition to state segregation policy in Arkansas won a Pulitzer Prize for his paper in 1958: d. Little Rock, Ark., Dec. 28.

Hemsley, Rollie (65), U. S. baseball player; catcher who played for several teams (1938–47) including the Pittsburgh Pirates, Chicago Cubs, and Cincinnati Reds: d. Washington, D. C., Aug. 14.

Herreshoff, L. Francis (82), U. S. yacht designer; called the "dean" of American yacht designers; among his designs were yachts and ocean ketches *Araminta, Nereia,* and *Ticonderoga;* wrote *Introduction to Yachting* and *The Compleat Cruiser:* d. Boston, Mass., Dec. 3.

Heschel, Abraham Joshua (65), Polish-born U. S. rabbi and religious leader; was professor at Jewish Theological Seminary of America (NYC), where he taught since 1945; among his books were *God in Search of Man, A Philosophy of Judaism* (1955), and *Theology of Ancient Judaism,* 2 vols. (1962, 1965): d. New York, N. Y., Dec. 27.

Hodges, Gil(bert Ray) (47), U. S. baseball player and manager: b. Princeton, Ind., April 4, 1924; d. West Palm Beach, Fla., April 2, 1972. One of the most popular figures of professional baseball, he distinguished himself as a first baseman during 15 seasons with the Dodgers, in Brooklyn and Los Angeles, and as manager of the New York Mets. First signed by the Dodgers in 1943, he became a regular member of the team in 1947 and soon established himself as one of the most skilled fielders in baseball history. In 1962 he played first base for the newly organized New York Mets. He became manager of the Washington Senators in 1963, and during five seasons he guided them from last to sixth place in the American League. Taking charge of the Mets in 1968, he presided over their World Series victory against the Baltimore Orioles the following year. Hodges' lifetime

record included 1,274 runs batted in and a batting average of .273. His 370 home runs made him one of the leading career home run hitters.

Homer, Arthur B. (76), U. S. corporate executive; president of Bethlehem Steel Corp. (1945–60), and chief executive officer (1960–64): d. Hartford, Conn., June 18.

Hoo, Victor Chi-tsai (78), Nationalist Chinese diplomat and UN official; UN commissioner for technical cooperation (1962–72) and assistant secretary general in charge of the trusteeship department (1946–62): d. Yonkers, N. Y., June 9.

*Hoover, J. Edgar (77), U. S. law-enforcement executive: d. Washington, D. C., May 2.

Hopkins, Miriam (69), U. S. actress; starred in movies and on Broadway; her movies include *Becky Sharp, Design for Living,* and *The Chase;* on Broadway she appeared in *Jezebel* and *Look Homeward Angel:* d. New York, N. Y., Oct. 9.

Howkins, Elizabeth P. (71), British-born journalist; as women's news editor of *The New York Times* (1955–65), she transformed newspaper presentation of women's news with imaginative use of photography and a literary style; editor of *Glamour* magazine (1941–54): d. New York, N. Y., Jan. 10.

Huebner, Clarence R. (83), U. S. general; a lieutenant general, he led the First Division in World War II in Sicily, France, and Germany; retired in 1949 as chief of the European Command: d. Washington, D. C., Sept. 23.

Hurley, Jack (74), U. S. fight promoter and manager; managed lightweight Billy Petrolle in the 1920's and Harry (Kid) Matthews, a heavyweight, in the 1940's; promoted match between Tony Zale and Rocky Graziano (1947) which set a gate record for an indoor fight: d. Seattle, Wash., Nov. 16.

Jackson, Mahalia (70), U. S. entertainer: b. New Orleans, La., Oct. 26, 1901; d. Evergreen Park, Ill., Jan. 27, 1972. She began to sing in church choirs and gradually won acceptance for her gospel singing in middle-class black and white communities. She made her Carnegie Hall debut in 1950. She was closely associated with the civil rights activities of Dr. Martin Luther King, Jr., and sang at the Lincoln Memorial during the 1963 March on Washington. Her best-known renditions included *He's Got the Whole World in His Hands* and *Move On Up a Little Higher.*

Johnson, Howard (75), U. S. restaurateur; founder and director of the nationwide Howard Johnson restaurant chain until his retirement in 1959: d. New York, N. Y., June 20.

Kallet, Arthur (69), U. S. consumer expert; a founder of Consumer's Union (1936), which tests consumer goods and publishes *Consumer's Reports;* executive director of *The Medical Letters* since 1957: d. New Rochelle, N. Y., Feb. 24.

Kawabata, Yasunari (72), Japanese author: b. Osaka, Japan, June 11, 1899; d. Zushi, Japan, April 16, 1972. A novelist and short-story writer highly esteemed by his countrymen, he became, in 1968, the first Japanese to win a Nobel Prize for literature. While assimilating elements of Western literature, his writings are essentially in the Japanese tradition. In *Snow Country* (1957) and *A Thousand Cranes* (1959), the novels for which he is best known in the West, he evokes the beauty of the natural landscape, the harmony and simplicity of the traditional Japanese tea ceremony, and the nuances of human emotions, particularly in his female characters.

Kedrov, Mikhail (78), Russian actor and director; chief director of the Moscow Art Theater (1946–55); he was a protégé of Konstantin Stanislavski, whose method he taught: d. Moscow, USSR, March 22.

Keefer, Chester (74), U. S. physician; Wade professor emeritus of Boston University; dean of Boston University School of Medicine (1955–62); special medical adviser to the Department of Health, Education and Welfare in the 1950's: d. Brookline, Mass., Feb. 3.

Kelly, Sir Gerald (92), British artist; portrait painter whose subjects included King George VI; president of the Royal Academy (1950–54): d. London, England, Jan. 4.

Kendall, Edward C. (86), U. S. research chemist; shared the Nobel Prize in medicine and physiology in 1950 for his work in the development of cortisone; visiting professor of chemistry at Princeton University since 1951: d. Rahway, N. J., May 4.

Kenyon, Dorothy (83), U. S. women's rights leader and former judge; municipal court judge in New York City (1939–40); lawyer and member of the UN Commission on the Status of Women (1946–50): d. New York, N. Y., Feb. 12.

Gil Hodges　　　　**Oscar Levant**

Kinkaid, Thomas C. (84), U. S. admiral: b. Hanover, N. H., April 3, 1888; d. Washington, D. C., Nov. 17, 1972. He was commander of U. S. naval forces in the Pacific in World War II during the battles of the Coral Sea, the South Solomon Islands, and the landings at Guadalcanal in 1942. Cool and unruffled under pressure, he commanded the carrier *Enterprise* in the first major attacks on Japanese forces after Pearl Harbor. He was commander of the Seventh Fleet and of Allied forces in the Pacific (1943–45), and accepted the surrender of Japanese forces in Korea in 1945. The son of an admiral, he served as naval attaché in Rome (1938–41). He was promoted to admiral a few weeks before Pearl Harbor. At his retirement in 1950, he was commander of the Eastern Sea Frontier and of Atlantic Reserve Forces.

Klein, Abraham M. (63), Canadian poet and lawyer, whose poetry reflects his Jewish heritage; among his volumes of poetry are *Hath Not a Jew* (1940) and *The Hitleriad* (1944): d. Montreal, Canada, Aug. 21.

Kolb, Lawrence (91), U. S. psychiatrist; early expert on the treatment of narcotics addiction; director of the division of mental hygiene of the Public Health Service (1938–44): d. Washington, D. C., Nov. 17.

Kolder, Drahomir (46), Czechoslovak Communist leader; a member of the Troika that took control of the government after the fall of the liberalizing regime of Alexander Dubček in 1968; he fell out of favor for a time in 1969: d. Prague, Czechoslovakia, Aug. 19.

Kormendi, Ferenc (72), Hungarian-born novelist; wrote novels with Hungarian settings; among his best-known books are *The Happy Generation* (1949) and *Escape to Life* (1932): d. Bethesda, Md., July 20.

Korniechuk, Aleksandr Y. (66), Soviet playwright; wrote *The Wreck of the Squadron* (1933), a revolutionary drama; winner of five Stalin Prizes; first deputy premier of the Ukraine (1953–55): d. Kiev, USSR, May 14.

Krylov, Marshal Nikolai I. (69), Soviet military leader; commander of the Soviet Union's strategic missile forces since 1963; during World War II, led troops at battles of Leningrad and the sieges of Odessa and Sevastapol; member of the Central Committee of the Communist party since 1961: d. Moscow, USSR, Feb. 9.

Küntscher, Gerhard (72), German physician and surgeon; in the 1930's he developed osteosynthesis, a method of inserting metal rods inside fractured bones to promote proper knitting: d. Glucksburg, West Germany, Dec. 17.

Kuo-hua, Chang (58), Chinese leader; commander of the Chinese army that conquered Tibet in the early 1950's; he became head of the Communist Party Committee in 1965: d. Chengtu, Szechwan, China, Feb. 21.

Landis, Jessie Royce (67), U. S. actress; starred on Broadway and London stage and in films; played in *Larger Than Life* and *Kiss and Tell* and the movies *North By Northwest* and *Critic's Choice*: d. Danbury, Conn., Feb. 2.

Lang, Walter (73), U. S. film director; best known for his musicals and comedies; among his films were *Call Me Madame, Can Can,* and *The King and I*: d. Palm Springs, Calif., Feb. 8.

Lazareff, Pierre (65), French newspaper publisher; publisher of *France-Soir,* daily newspaper with the largest circulation in France, since 1945; also published *Elle,* a woman's magazine, and a Sunday newspaper, *Journal du Dimanche*: d. Paris, France, April 21.

Leakey, Louis S. B. (69), British archaeologist: d. London, England, Oct. 1. (See ARCHAEOLOGY.)

Leduc, Vilette (65), French novelist; existentialist author whose autobiographical *La Bâtarde* (1964; The Bastard), detailed her early life and lesbian love affairs and became a best seller; also wrote *La Folie en Tête* (1970; Mad in Pursuit): d. Faucon, France, May 28.

Lefschetz, Solomon (88), Russian-born U. S. mathematician; taught mathematics (1924–53) and was chairman of the department (1945–53) at Princeton University; pioneered in research in the development of topology: d. Princeton, N. J., Oct. 5.

Leibold, Paul F. (57), U. S. Roman Catholic clergyman; Archbishop of Cincinnati, Ohio; bishop of the diocese of Evanston, Ind. (1966–69): d. Cincinnati, Ohio, June 1.

Leisen, Mitchell (74), U. S. film director; directed such films as *Death Takes a Holiday, To Each His Own,* and *Hold Back the Dawn*: d. Woodland Hills, Calif., Oct. 30.

Leoni, Raul (67), Venezuelan public official; president of Venezuela (1964–69); prior to his election he was in exile repeatedly from 1936 to 1958; helped stabilize a democratic form of government and supervised an orderly transfer of power to the newly elected opposition party: d. New York, N. Y., July 5.

Leskinen, Väinö O. (55), Finnish public official; foreign minister (1970–71); as Social Democratic party leader, he modified the party's rigid anti-Communist stance: d. Helsinki, Finland, March 8.

Levant, Oscar (65), U. S. pianist, composer, and wit: b. Pittsburgh, Pa., Dec. 27, 1906; d. Beverly Hills, Calif., Aug. 14, 1972. A gifted concert pianist and composer, Levant was perhaps even better known for the eccentric behavior and barbed wit that was his trademark as a personality of radio and television. The son of a watch repairman, he went to New York at 16 to study music. In the late 1920's he worked in Hollywood, where he composed motion picture soundtracks and popular songs. A close friend of George Gershwin and a leading interpreter of his music, Levant played himself in the film on Gershwin's life, *Rhapsody in Blue*. Other films in which he appeared include *Humoresque* and *An American in Paris*. He also gave many concerts in the 1940's and, over the years, made over 100 recordings. From 1938 to 1944 he was a member of the panel of the radio quiz show *Information Please*. Later he became a familiar figure on radio and television talk shows. Among his books are *A Smattering of Ignorance* (1940).

Lichine, David (62), Russian-born American choreographer and ballet dancer; danced with the Ballets Russes de Monte Carlo (1932–41); choreographed *The Prodigal Son* and *Helen of Troy*: d. Los Angeles, Calif., June 26.

Limón, José (64), Mexican-born U. S. dancer, choreographer, and teacher: b. Culiacán, Sinaloa, Mexico, Jan. 12, 1908; d. Flemington, N. J., Dec. 2, 1972. One of the leading creators of modern dance, Limón went to the United States in 1915. He turned from painting to the dance in 1928, working with the pioneer choreographer Doris Humphrey. He began choreographing his own dances and eventually created his own troupe in the late 1940's, with Miss Humphrey as artistic director. She composed many works for him, including the Hispanic *Lament for Ignacio Sanchez Mejías* (1947). Capitalizing on his exotic appearance, his Indian and Catholic background, and his love of classical music, he produced works of great human sensitivity and lofty artistic tone. Among his best-known works are *The Moor's Pavane* (1949), *Missa Brevis* (1958), and *The Unsung* (1970).

Litel, John (77), U. S. actor; acted on the stage, screen, and television; his credits included the Broadway play *Irene,* the movies *Cass Timberlane* and *Double Jeopardy,* and many TV roles: d. Woodland Hills, Calif., Feb. 3.

Litton, Charles (69), U. S. industrialist; founder of Litton Industries in 1932; developed and manufactured electrical components; the modern conglomerate, Litton Industries, grew out of his original firm, which he sold in 1953: d. Carson City, Nev., Nov. 14.

Lloyd, Woodrow S. (58), Canadian public official; premier of the province of Saskatchewan (1961–64); minister of education for Saskatchewan (1944–59): d. Korea, April 8.

Long, Edward V. (64), U. S. public official; Democratic senator from Missouri (1960–69), who generally supported liberal legislation; served in the Missouri legislature (1946–56) and was lieutenant governor when appointed to fill a Senate vacancy: d. Eolla, Mo., Nov. 6.

Loomis, Stanley (49), U. S. writer; expert on French literature and history; author of *DuBarry* (1959) and *Paris in Terror* (1964): d. Paris, France, Dec. 18.

Loper, Don (65), U. S. fashion designer; one-time dancer and choreographer, he designed clothes for such stars as Marlene Dietrich, Joan Crawford, and Lana Turner: d. Santa Monica, Calif., Nov. 21.

Lübke, Heinrich (77), West German public official; president of the Federal Republic of Germany (1959–69); minister of agriculture (1953–59); he ran for the largely ceremonial presidency at the behest of Chancellor Adenauer: d. Bonn, Germany, April 6.

McBride, Arthur (85), U. S. businessman and football club owner; founded the Cleveland Browns football team (1946), which became one of the most successful clubs in the U. S.: d. Cleveland, Ohio, Nov. 10.

McElroy, Neil H. (68), U. S. public official; secretary of defense in the Eisenhower administration (1957–59); reported the so-called missile gap between the U. S. and the Soviet Union in 1959; president of Proctor & Gamble (1948–57) and chairman of the board (1961–71): d. Cincinnati, Ohio, Nov. 30.

Machen, Eddie (40), U. S. boxer; heavyweight contender in the 1950's and 1960's; won 50 fights and lost 11; fought Sonny Liston and Floyd Patterson: d. San Francisco, Calif., Aug. 7.

McKenney, Ruth (60), U. S. novelist; author of *My Sister Eileen* (1938), which was made into a play and a movie and finally a musical, *Wonderful Town*: d. New York, N. Y., July 25.

Mackenzie, Sir Compton (89), British author; wrote over 100 novels and biographies, including *Whisky Galore* (1947), which was made into the movie *Tight Little Island;* among his other works were a series of novels *The Four Winds of Love* (1937–41) and *Adventures of*

Sylvia Scarlet (1950) and the biographies *Mr. Roosevelt* (1943) and *Prince Charlie and His Ladies* (1934): d. Edinburgh, Scotland, Nov. 30.

McLaughlin, R. Samuel (100), Canadian industrialist; chairman of the board of General Motors of Canada; developed McLaughlin Carriage Co. into the largest automobile manufacturer in Canada: d. Oshawa, Ont., Canada, Jan. 6.

MacVeagh, Lincoln (81), U. S. diplomat and publisher; from 1933 to 1953, he served successively as ambassador to Greece, Iceland, South Africa, Greece, Portugal, and Spain; founded Dial Press: d. Adelphi, Md., Jan. 15.

Madden, J. Warren (82), U. S. judge; judge on the U. S. Court of Claims (1940–61); first chairman of the National Labor Relations Board (1935–40): d. San Francisco, Calif., Feb. 17.

Madeira, Jean (53), U. S. opera singer; a contralto, she sang with the Metropolitan Opera (1956–71); had roles in *Aïda, Elektra,* and *Il Travatore:* d. Providence, R. I., July 10.

Mahendra (51), Nepalese ruler; became king on May 2, 1956; he kept Nepal a nonaligned nation: d. Katmandu, Nepal, Jan. 31.

Marlborough, Duke of (74), British peer who in 1950 opened portions of Blenheim Palace to the public to defray the costs of upkeep; John Albert Spencer-Churchill inherited the title in 1934: d. London, England, March 11.

Marzotto, Count Gaetano (77), Italian textile manufacturer; modernized his family's mills and increased foreign markets; founded a model farm at Valdagno where research is carried on: d. Valdagno, Italy, Aug. 11.

Mathewson, Champion H. (90), U. S. educator; emeritus professor of metallurgy and metallography at Yale University, where he taught from 1910 to 1950; noted for his work on the constitution of alloys, crystallography, and recrystallization of metals: d. New Haven, Conn., July 4.

Maxwell, Marilyn (49), U. S. actress; played in movies in the 1940's and later on television; among her picture credits are *Stand by for Action* and *Key City:* d. Beverly Hills, Calif., March 20.

Mayer, Maria Goeppert (65), German-born physicist; professor of physics at the University of California at San Diego since 1960; shared a Nobel Prize with two others in 1963 for describing the interaction of protons and neutrons that compose the nuclei of atoms: d. San Diego, Calif., Feb. 20.

Mayer, René (77), French public official; premier of France in 1953; served in several post-World War II cabinets in various posts, including minister of public works, finance, and defense and justice; he had extensive business interests in railroads and was a founder of Air France: d. Paris, France, Dec. 13.

Meehan, Chick (79), U. S. college football coach; coached Syracuse University team to 35 victories (1920–24); also coached at New York University (1924–32) and Manhattan College (1932–37): d. Syracuse, N. Y., Nov. 9.

Meyer, Frank R. (62), U. S. author and editor; senior editor of the *National Review,* which he joined in 1955; member of the Communist party until 1945, he became vice chairman of the Conservative Party in New York; among his books were *The Conservative Mainstream* (1969): d. Woodstock, N. Y., April 1.

Mezzrow, Mezz (73), U. S. musician; jazz clarinetist who played with Louis Armstrong, Django Reinhardt, and Jack Teagarden; wrote autobiography, *Really the Blues* (1946), with Bernard Wolfe: d. Paris, France, Aug. 5.

Miers, Earl Schenck (62), U. S. author; founder and first director (1944–49) of the Rutgers University Press; best known for his works on the Civil War and Abraham Lincoln; among his books are *The Great Rebellion: The Emergence of the American Conscience* (1958) and *Gettysburg* (1948); co-editor of *The Living Lincoln* (1955): d. Edison, N. J., Nov. 17.

Milch, Erhard (79), German Nazi general; a protégé of Hermann Goering, he served as Luftwaffe chief of staff (1933–45) and directed the creation of the German air force; served a sentence for war crimes (1947–54): d. Luneburg, Germany, Jan. 25.

Montherlant, Henri Millon de (76), French novelist and playwright; pessimistic author whose major novels include the tetralogy *Les Jeunes Filles* (1936–39) and *Les Célibatières* (1934), which won the Grand Prix; his plays include *La Reine morte* (1942) and *La Ville dont est un enfant* (1951); he was a member of the French Academy: d. (suicide) Paris, France, Sept. 21.

Moore, Marianne C. (84), U. S. poet: d. New York, N. Y., Feb. 5. (See LITERATURE—*American.*)

Mosley, Philip E. (66), U. S. expert on Russia; Adlai E. Stevenson Professor of International Relations at Columbia University; founder (1946) and director (1951–55)

of the Russian Institute at Columbia University; director of studies for the Council on Foreign Relations (1955–63): d. New York, N. Y., Jan. 13.

Neal, Tom (59), U. S. actor; played in over 175 movies, usually in "he-man" roles; credits included *The Flying Tigers* and *First Yank Over Tokyo;* imprisoned for 7 years for manslaughter in the death of his wife in 1965: d. Hollywood, Calif., Aug. 7.

Ngala, Ronald G. (49), Kenyan public official; minister for power and communication since 1969 and founder and president of the Kenya African Democratic Union, which represented tribal minorities in Kenyan independence movement; led opposition to Jomo Kenyatta's ruling Kenya African National Union at independence but joined forces with him in 1964, holding various ministries: d. Nairobi, Kenya, Dec. 25.

Nkrumah, Kwame (62), Ghanaian statesman: b. Nkroful, British West Africa, Sept. 21, 1909; d. Bucharest, Rumania (?), April 27, 1972. Once known to the people of Ghana as Osagyefo (Redeemer), he was the first statesman to guide an African colony to sovereignty after World War II. After studying in the United States and England, he returned to his native Gold Coast in 1947. He formed the independence-oriented Convention People's party in 1949. When the Gold Coast gained internal self-government in 1954, Nkrumah became prime minister, a post he retained after the colony became the independent nation of Ghana in 1957. In 1960 he became president of the newly proclaimed Republic of Ghana, and in 1961 he took absolute control of its government. Domestic discontent, engendered by his despotism, corrupt practices, and extravagant economic policies, culminated in a coup by army dissidents in 1966. Fleeing to neighboring Guinea, he was granted asylum by its president, Sekou Touré, who named him nominal co-president.

Nolde, O. Frederick (72), U. S. Lutheran clergyman; associate secretary of the World Council of Churches, responsible for international affairs; dean of the Graduate School of the Lutheran Theological Seminary in Philadelphia (1943–62): d. Philadelphia, Pa., June 17.

Norell, Norman (72), U. S. fashion designer: d. New York, N. Y., Oct. 25. (See FASHION.)

O'Connor, Basil (80), U. S. lawyer and foundation director: b. Taunton, Mass., Jan. 8, 1892; d. Phoenix, Ariz., March 9, 1972. As co-founder and president of the National Foundation—March of Dimes, he raised hundreds of millions of dollars for poliomyelitis research that led to the development of successful vaccines against the disease. In 1927, O'Connor, Franklin D. Roosevelt, and others established the Georgia Warm Springs Foundation as a polio therapy center. It was reconstituted as the National Foundation for Infantile Paralysis, or March of Dimes, in 1938, and O'Connor served as its president until his death. Through his efforts, funds were made available for development of Dr. Jonas E. Salk's polio vaccine in the early 1950's and of Dr. Albert B. Sabin's oral vaccine in 1960–61.

Overton, Hall (52), U. S. composer; taught at Juilliard School of Music from 1960; jazz pianist and symphonic composer; wrote opera *Huckleberry Finn,* orchestral work *Sonorities,* and ballet score *Nonage:* d. New York, N. Y., Nov. 22.

Owen, Reginald (85), English-born actor; stage and screen actor best known for stiff comedy roles which he played with sardonic humor; his plays included numerous Shakespearean roles; his movie credits included *Mrs. Miniver, Green Dolphin Street,* and *The Valley of Decision:* d. Boise, Idaho, Nov. 5.

Parenti, Tony (71), U. S. musician; jazz clarinetist known for his mellow tone; also played classical music; began his career in New Orleans: d. New York, N. Y., April 17.

Parker, Lord Hubert L. (72), English jurist; lord chief justice of England (1959–71); a one-time advocate of harsh sentences, he was in favor of the abolition of capital punishment; instituted a number of judicial reforms: d. near Shaftesbury, Dorsetshire, England, Sept. 15.

Parker, Lew (64), U. S. entertainer; comedian played on Broadway, in movies, and on radio and television; best known for his role as the father on television series *That Girl:* d. New York, N. Y., Oct. 27.

Parsons, Louella O., U. S. journalist: b. Freeport, Ill.; d. Santa Monica, Calif., Dec. 9, 1972. The queen of the Hollywood gossip columnists, she reported on life in the movie capital for over 40 years for 20 million readers of her syndicated column. In her breathless style she covered the marriages, divorces, romances, careers, and peccadillos of movie stars, gleaning her information from tips from press agents and from an endless round of

parties, dinners, and openings. Not always accurate and sometimes spiteful, she became an all-powerful figure. Her radio program, *Hollywood Hotel* (1934–38), added to her influence. Born Louella Oettinger, she never revealed the exact date of her birth, given variously as 1880 and 1893. In 1914, after the death of her husband, she began to write a movie column for *The Chicago Herald*. In 1922 she began her association with the Hearst papers, writing for the New York *American*. Going to California in 1925 to recuperate from tuberculosis, she stayed there to report on the movie world until her retirement in 1965.

Paul-Boncour, Joseph (98), French public official; minister of war (1932); foreign minister (1933–34); minister of state (1936); became a member of the French Chamber of Deputies in 1905; councilor of the Republic (1946–48): d. Paris, France, March 28.

Peale, Mundy I. (66), U. S. industrialist; president of Republic Aircraft (1947–64); directed development of the F-84 fighter jet: d. Laramie, Wyo., Nov. 1.

Pearson, Lester B. (75), Canadian public official: d. Rockcliffe, Ont., Canada, Dec. 27, 1972. (See CANADA.)

Perini, Lou (68), U. S. baseball club owner and builder; former owner of the Boston Braves, he moved the team to Milwaukee in 1953; sold interest in the club in 1962: d. West Palm Beach, Fla., April 16.

Philbin, Philip J. (74), U. S. politician; Democratic member of the U. S. House of Representatives from Massachusetts (1942–70): d. Bolton, Mass., June 14.

Phillips, Harold (Lefty) (53), U. S. baseball manager; manager of the California Angels (1969–71): d. Orange, Calif., June 12.

*Pound, Ezra (88), U. S. poet: d. Venice, Italy, Nov. 1.

Powell, Adam Clayton, Jr. (63), U. S. congressman and clergyman: b. New Haven, Conn., Nov. 29, 1908; d. Miami, Fla., April 4, 1972. Once the most powerful and influential black political leaders in the United States, he was a Democratic member of the U. S. House of Representatives for over 25 years. He was noted for his flamboyant life style as well as for his struggles for social justice. After succeeding his father as pastor of Harlem's Abyssinian Baptist Church in 1936, he directed a crusade from its pulpit to uplift the economic and social status of his community. In 1941 he won election to the New York city council, and in 1945 he entered the U. S. Congress. As chairman of the powerful House Education and Labor Committee from 1960 to 1967, he had a major role in the adoption of some 50 important pieces of social legislation. In March 1967 the House voted to expel him, charging, among other things, misuse of public funds. Reelected two months later, the U. S. Supreme Court ruled in his behalf in 1969. His political career ended in 1970, when he was defeated in a primary election.

Pully, B. S. (61), U. S. comedian; born Murray Lerman; famed for his role in the Broadway play *Guys and Dolls* and its movie version: d. Philadelphia, Pa., Jan. 6.

Purdy, Ken W. (59), U. S. author, expert on classic cars and auto racing; contributing editor of *Playboy* magazine; among his books are *Bright Wheels Rolling* (1954): d. Wilton, Conn., June 7.

Rabin, Michael (35), U. S. concert violinist; made his debut in Carnegie Hall in 1950; traveled over 700,000 miles in his concert tours: d. New York, N. Y., Jan. 19.

Rado, Sandor (82), Hungarian-born psychoanalyst; leader of the American school of Freudian psychoanalysis; studied under Freud and went to the U. S. in the 1930's; director of the Psychoanalytic Clinic of Columbia University (1944–55): d. New York, N. Y., May 13.

Rajagopalachrai, Chakravati (94), Indian statesman: b. Thorapalli, Madras, India, Dec. 8, 1878; d. Madras, India, Dec. 25, 1972. A leader in India's independence movement, he joined Gandhi's passive resistance movement in 1919 and was jailed five times. Rajagopalachrai, popularly known as Rajaji, was named governor general of the Dominion of India in 1950, the only Indian ever to hold the position. In that office he presided over the independence of India in 1950, becoming minister of home affairs in the new government. He was chief minister of Madras in 1952–54. An ascetic intellectual, he was a vigorous opponent of communism and also split several times with his old friend Jawaharlal Nehru and the ruling All-India Congress party. Eventually he founded his own ultra-conservative Swatantra party, which as part of a coalition movement failed to unseat Prime Minister Gandhi's party in the 1971 elections.

Rank, Lord (83), British film tycoon; founder of the Rank Organisation, major producer of British films and owner of numerous theaters; reputed to be one of England's wealthiest men, with a fortune estimated at $250 million: d. Winchester, England, March 29.

Ravdin, Isidore S. (77), U. S. physician; internationally known surgeon and cancer authority; professor of research surgery at the University of Pennsylvania: d. Wallingford, Pa., Aug. 27.

Richmond, Harry (77), U. S. entertainer; Broadway song and dance man of the 1930's, he appeared in a number of revues and on radio; among the songs with which he was associated were *Puttin' on the Ritz, On the Sunny Side of the Street,* and *Linger A While:* d. Los Angeles, Calif., Nov. 3.

Richter, Gisela M. (90), English-born U. S. museum curator; expert on Greco-Roman works, she was curator of Greek and Roman Art at the Metropolitan Museum of Art (1925–48); among her books are *Sculpture and Sculptors of the Greeks* (1950) and *A Handbook of Greek Art* (1959): d. Rome, Italy, Dec. 25.

Rieu, Emil V. (85), British editor; editor (1944–64) of Penguin Classics, a paperback series, which included his own best-selling translation of the *Odyssey* (1946): d. London, England, May 12.

*Robinson, Jackie (53), U. S. baseball player: d. Stamford, Conn., Oct. 24.

Robinson, Samuel M. (90), U. S. admiral; founder and first director of the U. S. Navy Bureau of Ships (1940); directed design and shipbuilding operations during World War II; he was the first engineering officer to reach four-star rank: d. Houston, Texas, Nov. 11.

Rolz-Bennett, José (54), Guatemalan diplomat; served in a number of high-level posts at the UN (1958–71); supervised transfer of New Guinea from Dutch to Indonesian control (1962–63); successively deputy chief of cabinet under U Thant and undersecretary for political affairs: d. Guatemala City, Guatemala, Dec. 18.

Romain, Jules (86), French author: d. Paris, France, Aug. 14. (See LITERATURE—*French*.)

Ruggles, Wesley (84), U. S. film director; his film *Cimarron* won the Academy Award for best picture in 1931; among his other pictures were *I'm No Angel* and *Condemned:* d. Santa Monica, Calif., Jan. 8.

Rushing, Jimmy (68), U. S. entertainer; blues singer with Count Basie's orchestra from the early 1930's until 1950; famous for his renditions of *Harvard Blues* and *Good Morning Blues,* among others: d. New York, N. Y., June 8.

Rutherford, Margaret (80), British actress and comedienne: b. London, England, May 11, 1892; d. Chalfont St. Peter, Buckinghamshire, England, May 22, 1972. Internationally acclaimed for her comic portrayals of eccentric, and typically British, elderly ladies, she won an Academy Award as best supporting actress in 1964 for her performance as the Duchess of Brighton in the *V. I. P's*. She embarked on a theatrical career as a drama student at the Old Vic in 1925 but did not achieve stardom until 1938, when she appeared in *Spring Meeting* on London's West End. She was best known for her performances in such films as *Blithe Spirit* (1945), *The Importance of Being Earnest* (1952), *The Mouse on the Moon* (1963), and four Agatha Christie mystery thrillers, in which she portrayed the bumbling amateur detective Miss Jane Marple. Queen Elizabeth II created her a Dame of the British Empire in 1967.

Ryan, William Fitts (50), U. S. public official; Democratic congressman from New York City (1960–1972); a liberal Democratic leader, he was an early opponent of the Vietnam War: d. New York, N. Y., Sept. 17.

Saarinen, Aline (58), U. S. art critic and television personality; gave art criticism and commentary on the TV shows *Today* and *For Women Only;* became chief of NBC's Paris news bureau in 1971: d. New York, N. Y., July 13.

Salisbury, 5th Marquess of (78), British public official; Conservative member of Parliament (1929–40); Lord Privy Seal (1942–43 and 1951–52); Conservative leader in the House of Lords (1942–45 and 1951–57): d. Hatfield, Hertfordshire, England, Feb. 23.

Sanders, George (65), British film actor; won an Academy Award in 1950 for his role in *All About Eve;* played roles as cynical villain; among his other films were *Rebecca, The Picture of Dorian Gray,* and *The Quiller Memorandum:* d. (suicide) Castelldefels, Spain, April 25.

Sanjivayya, Damodaram (60), Indian public official; president of India's ruling National Congress Party (1962–64); born an "untouchable" in the Hindu caste system, he worked to abolish the distinction; from 1964, he served successively as minister of labor and unemployment, minister of industry, and minister of labor and rehabilitation: d. New Delhi, India, May 7.

Sayre, Francis B. (86), U. S. diplomat; high commissioner of the Philippines (1939–42); U. S. representative on the UN Trusteeship Council (1947–52): d. Washington, D. C., March 29.

Schmitt, Gladys (63), U.S. novelist; author of the best seller *David the King* (1946); Theodor S. Baker Professor of Literature at Carnegie-Mellon University since 1970; among her other books are *The God Forgotten* (1971) and *Rembrandt* (1961): d. Pittsburgh, Pa., Oct. 3.

Schuster, George (99), U.S. auto driver; drove a Thomas-Flyer on part of a 13,341-mile race across the U.S. and Russia to Paris in 1908; wrote *The Longest Auto Race* (1966) with Tom Mahoney: d. Springville, N.Y., July 4.

Scoccimarro, Mario (76), Italian public official; a founder of the Italian Communist party; senator since 1948; finance minister (1945–47): d. Rome, Italy, Jan. 1.

Segni, Antonio (81), Italian public official: b. Sassari, Sardinia, Feb. 2, 1891; d. Rome, Italy, Dec. 1, 1972. A Christian Democratic party leader, he served as premier of Italy from 1955 to 1957 and again from 1959 to 1960. He was elected president (a largely ceremonial post) by the Italian parliament in 1962, resigning in 1964 because of a stroke. A professor of law from 1920, Segni kept up his academic career while serving in various ministerial roles. While minister of agriculture and forestry (1946–51), he inaugurated an extensive and controversial land reform program. He was minister of education before becoming premier for the first time in 1955. He also served as deputy premier and defense minister (1958–59) and as minister of foreign affairs (1960).

Shapley, Harlow (86), U.S. astronomer: b. Nashville, Mo., Nov. 2, 1885; d. Boulder, Colo., Oct. 20, 1972. One of the world's most distinguished astronomers, he was noted for discovering a distance scale for the universe and for establishing the location of the solar system within our galaxy, the Milky Way. He also was noted for his activities in behalf of peaceful coexistence during the Cold War era. The son of a farmer and schoolteacher, he worked his way through the University of Missouri and obtained his Ph. D. from Princeton in 1913. While working at Mount Wilson Observatory, he found a new means of measuring astronomical distances; his yardstick was the brightness and period of certain variable stars called Cepheids. From this work, he concluded that the diameter of the Milky Way was 150,000 light-years, very much larger than had been believed previously. He also concluded that the solar system was 30,000 to 40,000 light-years away from the center of the Milky Way, rather than at its center, as had been taught. He became the director of the Harvard College Observatory in 1921 and remained at Harvard until his retirement in 1956.

Shaw, Ralph (65), U.S. librarian; dean of the school of Library Service at the University of Hawaii (1964–68); invented a photocharging machine for checking out books in wide use and adapted other machines for library use; professor at Rutger's University Graduate School of Library Service (1954–64): d. Honolulu, Hawaii, Oct. 14.

Shawn, Ted (Edwin Myers) (80), U.S. dancer, choreographer, and educator: b. Kansas City, Mo., Oct. 21, 1891; d. Orlando, Fla., Jan. 9, 1972. Known as the "father of the modern dance," he inaugurated the "Denishawn era" of American dancing with his wife, the late Ruth St. Denis. In 1914 he married Miss St. Denis, whose unorthodox dance style, based in part on Oriental forms, helped inspire the modern dance. Together they founded the Denishawn Company, with which they toured the U.S. and Europe for a number of years. In 1915, at Los Angeles, they established their first Denishawn school, which trained Martha Graham, Doris Humphrey, and other leading representatives of the modern dance. In 1932, following their separation, Shawn founded and became director of a dance center at Jacob's Pillow, near Lee, Mass., that became a major force in the teaching and performance of modern dancing and the site of a world-famous dance festival.

Sibylla, Princess (64), member of the Swedish Royal family; mother of Crown Prince Carl Gustaf, grandson of King Gustaf VI; daughter of Duke Carl Eduard of Saxony, she married the eldest son of the present king: d. Stockholm, Sweden, Nov. 28.

Sikorsky, Igor I(van) (83), Russian-born U.S. aeronautical engineer: b. Kiev, Ukraine, May 25, 1889; d. Easton, Conn., Oct. 26, 1972. He revolutionized aviation by developing the world's first practical helicopter, the VS-300, which made its first flight in 1939. The son of a physician and psychiatrist, he developed the idea of a helicopter as a boy, after reading the science fiction novels of Jules Verne. He attended the Naval Academy in St. Petersburg, studied engineering and aeronautics in Germany and France, and then returned to Russia. In 1913 he designed the first multiple-engine airplane, which was used as a Russian bomber in World War I. After the Communist Revolution he settled in the United States, where he founded the Sikorsky Aero Engineering Corporation in

1923. The company, later a division of United Aircraft, designed several successful passenger planes, including the S-40 four-engine, single-wing flying boat, built in 1931.

Singer, Charles H. (69), U.S. radio pioneer; designed and built some of the first radio stations in New York; designed and directed the installation of communication systems for NATO and other radio defense systems: d. Washington, D.C., March 26.

Singh, Sant Fateh (61), Indian religious and political figure; Sikh leader who dominated politics in Punjab since 1962; successfully advocated the establishment of a separate state of Punjab (1966): d. Amritsar, India, Oct. 30.

Smallens, Alexander (83), Russian-born conductor; associated with the Philadelphia Orchestra (1930–48); conducted symphony and opera orchestras, including the Chicago Opera Company and the New York Philharmonic; also conducted for original Broadway production of *Porgy and Bess* in 1935: d. Tuscon, Ariz., Nov. 24.

Smith, Betty (75), U.S. novelist; wrote the best seller *A Tree Grows in Brooklyn* (1943), the story of a girl and tenement life in the early 20th century: d. Shelton, Conn., Jan. 17.

Smith, Joseph Fielding, Jr. (95), U.S. religious leader: b. Salt Lake City, Utah, July 19, 1876; d. Salt Lake City, July 2, 1972. As the 10th president of the Church of Jesus Christ of Latter-day Saints, he was the spiritual leader of some 3 million Mormons throughout the world and was known as their "prophet, seer and revelator." A grand-nephew of Joseph Smith, the founder of the Mormon Church, he served for two years as a missionary in Britain before being named church historian in 1906. He became one of the 12 apostles in 1910 and was designated president of the Council of Apostles in 1951. On the death of David O. McKay in early 1970, Smith was elected to succeed him as president. A fundamentalist, he supported the Mormon Church's controversial practice of excluding Negroes from the priesthood.

Smith, Warren L. (58), U.S. economist; professor of economics at the University of Michigan (since 1957); as a member of President Johnson's Council of Economic Advisers (1968–69), he suggested tighter government spending coupled with easier monetary policy: d. Ann Arbor, Mich., April 23.

Snow, Edgar (Parks) (66), U.S. author and journalist: b. Kansas City, Mo., July 19, 1905; d. Eysins, Switzerland, Feb. 15, 1972. One of the few Westerners with regular access to the Chinese Communist leaders, he chronicled their early struggles and rise to power in his best-selling books *Red Star Over China* (1937) and *The Other Side of the River: Red China Today* (1962). He first went to China as a free-lance writer in 1928 and remained for 12 years as a foreign correspondent and lecturer. In 1936 he sought out Mao Tse-tung, Chou En-lai, and other Communist leaders in their hideout in Yenan and won their confidence. In his sympathetic, nonideological accounts of those meetings, he predicted the ultimate triumph of communism in China. Over the years he continued to make regular visits to China; his last was in 1970.

Sontag, Raymond J. (75), U.S. historian; edited captured German documents after World War II published as *Nazi-Soviet Relations* (1948) and *Documents of German Foreign Policy* (1949); professor of history at the University of California at Berkeley (1941–65); chairman of the department of history at Princeton (1939–41): d. Berkeley, Calif., Oct. 27.

Southworth, George (81), U.S. scientist; research scientist at Bell Telephone Laboratories; helped develop guided-wave radio; made practical application of microwave radiation and wave-guide transmission to radar and audio and visual signals: d. Summit, N.J., July 6.

Spaak, Paul-Henri (73), Belgian statesman: b. Schaerbeck, Belgium, Jan. 25, 1899; d. Brussels, Belgium, July 31, 1972. A lifelong socialist who served three times as Belgium's premier, he earned the title "Mr. Europe" for his post-World War II role in promoting Western European unity, particularly as an architect of the North Atlantic Treaty Organization and the European Common Market. Spaak studied law in the 1920's and was elected to the Belgian parliament in 1932. After serving in several cabinet posts, he became the youngest premier in Belgian history in 1938. During World War II he and others set up a Belgian government in exile in London. He helped draft the UN charter and was the first president of the UN General Assembly in 1946. Spaak again served as Belgian premier in 1946 and from 1947 to 1950. Convinced of the need for Western European solidarity in cooperation with the United States, he helped form NATO and was its secretary-general from 1957 to 1961. He was also one of the signatories of the Treaties of Rome that created the European Economic Community in 1957.

Earlier, he had been president of the European Coal and Steel Community, the Council of Europe, and the Organization for European Cooperation.

Spofford, William B. (80), U. S. clergyman and editor; edited *Witness*, a national Episcopalian weekly (1919–1970's); associated with liberal labor causes; onetime trustee of the American Civil Liberties Union: d. Tunkhannock, Pa., Oct. 9.

Stark, Admiral Harold Raynsford (91), U. S. Navy officer: b. Wilkes-Barre, Pa., Nov. 12, 1880: d. Washington, D. C., Aug. 20, 1972. As chief of naval operations, he was the top-ranking U. S. Navy officer at the time of the Japanese attack on Pearl Harbor in 1941. After Pearl Harbor he was succeeded by Adm. Ernest J. King and given command of U. S. naval forces in Europe, a largely administrative post that he held until 1945. A Navy court in 1945 criticized him for failure to transmit intelligence reports in 1941 that might have warned Adm. Husband E. Kimmel, Pacific Fleet commander, of the Japanese threat. Although Stark retired under a cloud in 1946, later reviews of the Pearl Harbor events tempered the Navy's judgment of him.

Stokes, Joseph (74), U. S. pediatrician; he helped develop vaccines against German measles, mumps, and influenza; physician-in-chief of Children's Hospital, Philadelphia (1939–64): d. Philadelphia, Pa., March 9.

Stump, Felix (77), U. S. admiral; commander of the Pacific Fleet (1953–58); commander of the U. S. S. *Lexington*, he led a carrier task force that defeated the Japanese in the battle of Leyte Gulf in World War II: d. Bethesda, Md., June 13.

Summerfield, Arthur E. (73), U. S. public official; served as postmaster general of the U. S. (1953–61); chairman of the Republican National Committee (1952–53); managed the Eisenhower presidential campaigns in 1952 and 1956: d. West Palm Beach, Fla., April 26.

Swados, Harvey (52), U. S. novelist and social critic: b. Buffalo, N. Y., Oct. 28, 1920; d. Holyoke, Mass., Dec. 11, 1972. His novels and other writings dealt with the ideals and frustrations of the American social scene. While his writing was frequently criticized for faulty technique, few found it unmoving. In *Standing Fast* (1970) he followed the hopes and disappointments of a group of radicals in America from 1939 to the assassination of President Kennedy. In *On the Line* (1957), a novel, and in his collection of essays, *A Radical's America* (1962), he dealt with the boredom and tedium of the laboring man's life. Swados taught creative writing at a number of colleges and was a professor at the University of Massachusetts from 1970.

Talal (73), king of Jordan; reigned in 1951–52 before he was removed because of mental illness; succeeded by his brother, King Hussein: d. Istanbul, Turkey, July 8.

Tamiroff, Akim (72), Russian-born actor; played strong character roles and comedy parts in movies; his credits included *For Whom the Bell Tolls, You Can't Take It With You, Anastasia,* and *Funeral in Berlin:* d. Palm Springs, Calif., Sept. 17.

Tashlin, Frank (59), U. S. film director; best known for his slapstick comedies; among his pictures were *Will Success Spoil Rock Hunter?* and *The Lieutenant Wore Skirts:* d. Beverly Hills, Calif., May 5.

Taylor, George W. (71), U. S. labor arbitrator and educator; professor at Wharton School of the University of Pennsylvania (1937–70); chairman of the National War Labor Board during World War II and of the Wage Stabilization Board during the Korean War; member of the Hoover Commission on government reorganization (1948–49): d. Philadelphia, Pa., Dec. 15.

Tazewell, Charles (73), U. S. author; wrote *The Littlest Angel* (1945), a Christmas story for children: d. Chesterfield, N. H., June 26.

Theiler, Max (73), South African-born U. S. physician; developed a vaccine against yellow fever for which he received a Nobel Prize in 1951; director of the virus laboratories of Rockefeller Institute until 1961 when he became a professor at Yale University (1964–67): d. New Haven, Conn., Aug. 11.

Thompson, Llewellyn E., Jr. (67), U. S. diplomat: b. Las Animas, Colo., Aug. 24, 1904; d. Bethesda, Md., Feb. 6, 1972. A leading expert on Soviet affairs and a practitioner of the art of "quiet diplomacy," he served as U. S. ambassador to Moscow during the crucial Cold War years, from 1957 to 1962, and again from 1967 to 1969. The son of a rancher, he graduated from the University of Colorado in 1928 and joined the U. S. Foreign Service in 1929. He served in consular posts in Moscow and London during World War II. Assigned to Vienna in 1952, he helped negotiate the Trieste settlement (1954)

HARVARD UNIV. NEWS OFFICE   PICTORIAL PARADE
Harlow Shapley   **Walter Winchell**

and the Austrian State Treaty (1955). As ambassador to the USSR, he helped set up the Camp David meeting between Soviet Premier Khrushchev and President Eisenhower in 1959 and the Vienna summit between Khrushchev and President Kennedy in 1961, and he was instrumental in arranging the cultural exchange agreement and the nuclear test ban treaty with the Soviet Union. He last served as a delegate to the strategic arms limitation talks (SALT) with the USSR.

Tisserant, Eugène Cardinal (87), Roman Catholic prelate: b. Nancy, France, March 24, 1884; d. Albano, Italy, Feb. 21, 1972. He served the Roman Catholic Church for more than 60 years as priest, scholar, and administrator and was a leading figure in the ecumenical movement. From 1951 until his death he was dean of the church's Sacred College of Cardinals. Named a cardinal in 1936, he served until 1959 as secretary of the Sacred Congregations for the Oriental Church, which supervises the affairs of Eastern Rite Roman Catholics. As an administrator of the Vatican Library in the 1920's and 1930's, and as its librarian and archivist from 1959 until his retirement in 1971, he modernized and reorganized its operations.

Traubel, Helen, U. S. singer: b. St. Louis, Mo.; d. Santa Monica, Calif., July 28, 1972. The Metropolitan Opera's leading Wagnerian soprano in the 1940's, Miss Traubel was equally at home in the world of radio, television, nightclubs, and motion pictures. Her date of birth has been variously given as June 1899 and June 1903. She began to sing at 12 in a St. Louis choir and dropped out of school at 13 to devote herself to voice study. She made her debut with the St. Louis Symphony Orchestra in 1925 and her Metropolitan Opera debut in 1937 in Walter Damrosch's opera *The Man Without a Country.* Specializing in Wagnerian roles, she became the Met's leading singer of German opera after Kirsten Flagstad's departure in 1941. After Met general manager Rudolph Bing objected to her appearances in nightclubs and other entertainment media, she chose to end her association with the company in 1953. In the 1950's, she appeared in the Broadway musical *Pipe Dream* and in several films.

Traynor, Harold (Joseph) "Pie" (72), U. S. baseball player: b. Framingham, Mass., Nov. 11, 1899; d. Pittsburgh, Pa., March 16, 1972. One of the star players on the Pittsburgh Pirates team in the 1920's and 1930's, he was elected to baseball's Hall of Fame in 1948 and was named by sportswriters in 1969 as the greatest third baseman in the game's history. He joined the Pirates in 1920 and played with them for 17 seasons. From 1934 to 1939 he also served as the team's manager. He had a lifetime batting average of .320 and drove in 1,273 runs, more than any other Pirate in the team's history.

Trout, Paul Howard (Dizzy) (56), U. S. baseball player; pitcher for the Detroit Tigers (1939–1952) with a lifetime record of 170 victories and 161 defeats; since 1958 he was a member of the Chicago White Sox organization: d. Chicago, Ill., Feb. 28.

*****Truman, Harry S.** (88), U. S. President: d. Independence, Mo., Dec. 26, 1972.

Tupolev, Andrei N. (84), Soviet aircraft designer: b. Tver Province, Russia, Nov. 10, 1888; d. Moscow, USSR, Dec. 23, 1972. The dean of Russian aircraft designers and a pioneer in all-metal planes, Tupolev was associated with most major Soviet military and civilian aircraft since the 1920's. The latest craft to come from him and his staff was the delta-winged supersonic jet, the Tu-144, which was expected to be in service by 1975. His first major successes were his ANT series (from the initials of his name) in the 1920's and 1930's. In 1937 his ANT-25 was flown nonstop from Russia to the United States across the

North Pole. He was arrested in 1938, apparently for his dissent from Communist ideology, and imprisoned until 1941. During World War II he adapted the design of some commandeered B-29's and supervised the building of some 2,000 Tu-4's, which were copies of the American bombers. He received three Stalin prizes and one Lenin Prize for his designs.

Van Doren, Mark (78), U. S. educator and author: d. Torrington, Conn., Dec. 10, 1972. (See LITERATURE—*American Literature*.)

Vann, John Paul (47), U. S. government official: b. Roanoke, Va., July 2, 1924; d. (helicopter crash) near Kontum, South Vietnam, June 9, 1972. As senior U. S. adviser in South Vietnam's central highlands, he was one of the most esteemed American officials in Indochina. An expert on guerrilla warfare and counterinsurgency, and an early advocate of "Vietnamization," he was unstinting in his criticism of the waste and corruption he saw in the conduct of the Indochina War. In 1962, as a lieutenant colonel in the U. S. Army, he volunteered to go to Vietnam. He resigned from the Army in 1963, after his recommendations were disregarded by the Pentagon. He returned to Vietnam in 1965 as a civilian employee of the Agency for International Development. In 1971 he was named director of the Second Regional Assistance Group in South Vietnam's central highlands.

Wallington, Jimmy (65), U. S. radio announcer; worked for the National Broadcasting Co. in the 1930's and 1940's, notably on the Eddie Cantor and Fred Allen shows: d. Arlington, Va., Dec. 22.

Wangchuk, Jigme Dorji (45), king of Bhutan; ruled the tiny Himalayan kingdom for 20 years; carried out an extensive modernization program for schools, hospitals, and roads: d. Nairobi, Kenya, July 21.

Watkins, Franklin C. (77), U. S. artist; expressionist painter noted for his portraits; won the Carnegie International Award in 1931 and held shows in the Museum of Modern Art in New York (1950) and a retrospective at the Philadelphia Museum (1964): d. Bologna, Italy, Dec. 4.

Watson, Morris (71), U. S. journalist and union leader; early leader of the American Newspaper Guild; won a case against the Associated Press in 1937 which established the constitutionality of the National Labor Relations Act: d. San Francisco, Calif., Feb. 12.

Webster, Margaret (67), British actress and director: b. New York, N. Y., March 15, 1905; d. London, England, Nov. 13, 1972. The last of a distinguished English theatrical family, she played in numerous Shakespearean and other roles on the London and New York stages and in repertory. Her first professional appearance was with Sybil Thorndike in *The Trojan Women* in 1924. She began directing between acting assignments with the Old Vic Company in London and in 1937 staged *Richard II* on Broadway to great critical acclaim. This was followed by *Hamlet* in 1938, *Henry IV (Part I)* in 1939, and *Twelfth Night*, with Helen Hayes, in 1940. She created a repertory company in 1945 with Eva Le Galliene, but the effort was discontinued in 1949 because of financial difficulties. Invited to help with the theatrical staging of New York Metropolitan Opera performances in 1952, she staged *Aïda* and *Don Carlos*. Her autobiography, *The Same Only Different*, appeared in 1969.

Weede, Robert (69), U. S. singer; a baritone, he sang with the Metropolitan and San Francisco Operas and on Broadway; appeared in the musicals *The Most Happy Fella, Milk and Honey,* and *Cry for Us All:* d. Walnut Creek, Calif., July 7.

Weeks, Sinclair (78), U. S. public official; secretary of commerce (1953–58) and Republican party leader; appointed to fill a vacant Senate seat from Massachusetts (1944): d. Lancaster, N. H., Feb. 7.

Weiss, George (78), U. S. baseball manager; general manager of the New York Yankees (1947–60) during the time they won 10 pennants and 7 World Series; first president of the New York Mets (1961–65); voted into the Baseball Hall of Fame: d. Greenwich, Conn., Aug. 13.

Weissman, Philip (61), U. S. psychiatrist; best known for his studies of creative imagination in the theater; author of *Creativity in the Theater:* d. New York, Feb. 27.

Wellington, 7th Duke of (86), British peer and architect; practicing architect specializing in restorations; served as diplomatic secretary (1909–1919) in Russia, Turkey, and Italy: d. near Reading, Berkshire, England, Jan. 13.

Wild, John D. (70), U. S. educator; professor of philosophy at Yale (1963–69); best known for his work on existentialism; among his books are *Challenge of Existentialism* (1955) and *Existence and the Worlds of Freedom* (1963); president of the American Philosophical Society (1959–60): d. New Haven, Conn., Oct. 23.

William, Prince of Gloucester (30), member of the British royal family; a cousin of Queen Elizabeth, he held various posts in the British diplomatic service (1965–70): d. (in an airplane crash) near Wolverhampton, England, Aug. 28.

Williams, Billy (62), U. S. singer and composer; blues singer wrote and recorded in the 1950's the million-record seller *I'm Going to Sit Right Down and Write Myself a Letter;* as leader of the Charioteers and the Billy Williams Quartet, was the first black to appear regularly on television: d. Chicago, Ill., Oct. 12.

Willoughby, Charles A. (80), German-born U. S. major general; assistant chief of staff for Army intelligence in the Pacific (1941–51); served as intelligence aide to General MacArthur; author with John R. Chamberlain of *MacArthur—1941–1951* (1954) and of *Shanghai Conspiracy* (1965): d. Naples, Fla., Oct. 25.

Wilson, Charles E. (85), U. S. corporate executive; president of the General Electric Co. (1939–42 and 1944–50); executive vice chairman (1942–44) of the War Production Board; director of the Office of Defense Mobilization (1950–52): d. Bronxville, N. Y., Jan. 3.

*****Wilson, Edmund** (77), U. S. man of letters: d. Talcottville, N. Y., June 12.

Wilson, Edwin C. (79), U. S. diplomat; ambassador to Turkey (1945–48) who supervised $100 million aid program there; joined the U. S. Foreign Service in 1920: d. Washington, D. C., Sept. 10.

Wilson, Sir Horace (89), British public official; as adviser to Prime Minister Neville Chamberlain, he favored an appeasement policy toward Hitler; served as head of the British Civil Service until 1942: d. London, England, May 19.

Wilson, Marie (56), U. S. actress; played buxom "dumb blonde" star of radio and TV series *My Friend Irma* (1947–54); her film credits include *Satan Met a Lady, Boy Meets Girl,* and *Marry Me Again:* d. Hollywood, Calif., Nov. 23.

Wilson, Orlando (72), U. S. public official; superintendent of police in Chicago (1960–67) who reorganized the department after a police corruption scandal: d. Poway, Calif., Oct. 18.

Winchell, Walter (74), U. S. journalist and radio commentator: b. New York, N. Y., April 7, 1897; d. Los Angeles, Calif., Feb. 20, 1972. The originator of the modern gossip column, he was one of the most colorful and controversial personalities in the world of Broadway show business, over which he exercised considerable power during his heyday in the 1930's and 1940's. He began his career in journalism as a columnist with the *Vaudeville News* in 1922. His column "On Broadway," featuring gossip on show business people, society figures, and politicians, was published in the New York *Daily Mirror* from 1929 to 1963, and at the height of his career it was syndicated to some 800 newspapers. For about 30 years, beginning in 1933, he also had a highly popular weekly radio broadcast, addressed to "Mr. and Mrs. America and all the ships at sea." Like his column, it was delivered in a breathless staccato style and in a jargon that included such coined words as "Chicagorilla" and "presstitute." During the 1960's his popularity waned, and he gradually withdrew from public life.

*****Windsor, Duke of** (77), former British king: d. Paris, France, May 28.

Wolpe, Stefan (69), German-born composer; composer of avant-garde music; taught composition at C. W. Post College (1958–70); best known for his chamber music which employed unusual combinations of instruments: d. New York, N. Y., April 4.

Youlou, Fulbert (55), Congolese public official; first president of the Republic of Congo (1960–63): d. Madrid, Spain, May 5.

Young, Kenneth T. (56), U. S. diplomat; served as ambassador to Thailand (1961–63); joined U. S. State Department in 1946 and was director of the Office of Southeast Asia Affairs (1956–58): d. Washington, D. C., Aug. 29.

Youtz, Philip N. (78), U. S. inventor and educator; invented the lift slab construction method, using pre-poured reinforced concrete sections which were then raised into position; dean of the College of Architecture and Design of the University of Michigan (1957–65): d. Walnut Creek, Calif., Jan. 12.

Zerbe, Karl L. (69), German-born artist; expressionist painter best known for symbolic still lifes, city landscapes, and studies of circus figures; taught at Florida State University since 1954: d. Tallahassee, Fla., Nov. 28.

Zuyevsky, Viktor A. (53), Russian nuclear expert; chief designer of Soviet nuclear warheads; worked on the staff of the Scientific Design Institute, which produces missiles: d. Moscow, USSR, July 5.

A

Main article headings appear in this Index as bold-faced capitals; subjects within articles appear as lower-case entries. Main article page numbers and general references are listed first under each entry; the sub-entries which follow them on separate lines direct the reader to related topics appearing elsewhere. Both the general references and the subentries should be consulted for maximum usefulness of this Index. Illustrations are indexed herein. Cross references are to the entries in this Index.

D